P9-DYZ-959

International Directory of
COMPANY
HISTORIES

INTERNATIONAL DIRECTORY OF COMPANY HISTORIES

International Directory of

COMPANY HISTORIES

VOLUME IV

Editor
Adele Hast

Associate Editors
Diane B. Pascal (Chicago)
Philippe A. Barbour (London)
Jessica Griffin (London)

Consulting Editor
Kate Berney

St James Press

Chicago and London

Belmont College Library

© 1991 by St. James Press
For further information, write:

ST. JAMES PRESS
233 East Ontario Street
Chicago, Illinois 60611
U.S.A.

or

2-6 Boundary Row
London SE1 8HP
England

All rights reserved.

Library of Congress Catalog Number: 89-190943

British Library Cataloguing in Publication Data

International directory of company histories. Vol. 4
I. Hast, Adele
338.7409

ISBN 1-55862-060-5

First published in the U.S.A. and U.K. 1991
Typeset by BookMasters, Inc., Ashland, Ohio, U.S.A.

Cover photograph of the Tokyo Stock Exchange courtesy of
the Tokyo Stock Exchange London Research Office

149786

Belmont College Library

Ref
HD
2721
.D36
v.4

INDUSTRIES COVERED IN THE DIRECTORY ___

CONTENTS

EDITOR'S NOTE

The *International Directory of Company Histories* provides accurate and detailed information on the development of the world's largest and most influential companies. When completed, the *Directory's* five volumes will cover approximately 1,200 companies.

Most companies chosen for inclusion in the *Directory* have achieved a minimum of two billion U.S. dollars in annual sales. Some smaller companies are included if they are leading influences in their respective industries or geographical locations. State-owned companies that are important in their industries and that may operate much like public or private companies also are included. Wholly owned subsidiaries of other companies are entries if they meet the requirements for inclusion, provided they were independent within the past five years or are still highly visible and important in their respective industries. Sales for real estate companies, included in Volume IV, may cover not only outright sales but also other measures such as managerial income and rentals

Each entry begins with a company's legal name, the address of its headquarters, its telephone number and fax number, and a statement of public, private, or state ownership. A company with a legal name in both English and the language of its headquarters country is listed by the English name, with the native-language name in parentheses.

Also provided are the company's earliest incorporation date, the number of employees, and the most recent sales or assets figures available, for fiscal year 1990 unless otherwise noted. Sales figures are given in local currencies with equivalents in U.S. dollars at the exchange rate on December 31, 1990, the last trading day of the year. For some private companies, sales figures are estimates. Finally, the entry lists the cities where a company's stock is traded. Throughout the *Directory* spelling is according to American style, and the word "billion" is used in its American sense of a thousand million.

The histories were compiled from publicly accessible sources such as magazines, general and academic periodicals, books, and annual reports, as well as from material supplied by the companies themselves. The *Directory* is intended for reference use and research, for students, business people, librarians, historians, economists, investors, job candidates, and others who want to learn more about the historical development of the world's most important companies.

St. James Press does not endorse any of the companies or products mentioned in this book. Companies that appear in the *Directory* were selected without reference to their wishes and have in no way endorsed their entries. The companies were given the opportunity to read their entries for factual inaccuracies, and we are indebted to many of them for their comments and corrections. We thank them for allowing the use of their logos for identification purposes.

St. James Press would like to thank the staffs of the following institutions for their courteous assistance and invaluable guidance: in Chicago, The Chicago Public Library, the University of Chicago Library, the Paul V. Galvin Library at the Illinois Institute of Technology, The Newberry Library, the Japan Information Service, and the Japan External Trade Organization; Northwestern University Library in Evanston, Illinois; and in London, The British Library, Business Archives Council, The City Business Library, The Financial Times Editorial Library, The London School of Economics and Political Science Business History Unit, and Westminster Reference Library.

The editors wish to thank the advisers, whose counsel assisted us in the organization of industries and the selection of companies. In addition, we thank Trudy Ring and Naomi S. Suloway for their editorial assistance and meticulous attention to content and style.

Adele Hast

ADVISERS

T.C. Barker
Beate Brüninghaus

Alfred D. Chandler, Jr.
Stephanie Zarach

CONTRIBUTORS

Sarah Ahmad Khan
William Ashworth
Claire Badaracco
William Baranès
Philippe A. Barbour
John Barham
Dirk Bavendamm
Hannelore Becker-Hess
Elaine Belsito
Nills G. Björklund
Joachim F.E. Bläsing
Bernard A. Block
Jim Bowman
Andrew Burchill
John Burton
Ron Chepesiuk
Alison Classe
Olive Classe
Lisa Collins
Paul Conrad
T.A.B. Corley
Joanne E. Cross
Michael Doorley
Sina Dubovoj
Karl-Peter Ellerbrock
Tom C.B. Elliott
Graham Field
Philip Gawith
Jessica Griffin
Daniel Gross
William R. Grossman
Anastasia N. Hackett
Leslie C. Halpern
Joan Harpham
Charles Edward Harvey
Richard Hawkins
Carole Healy

Patrick Heenan
Gerd Henniger
Hubert Hoskins
Kris E. Inwood
David Isaacson
Robert R. Jacobson
Debra Johnson
Geoffrey Jones
Lynn M. Kalanik
Simon Katzenellenbogen
Carol I. Keeley
Renate Köhne-Lindenlaub
Sonia Kronlund
Gwen M. LaCosse
Monique Lamontagne
Ellen NicKenzie Lawson
Laura Le Cornu
Patricia Leichenko
Scott M. Lewis
Wilson B. Lindauer
Andreas Loizou
Brian S. McBeth
Susan Mackervoy
Kim M. Magon
Jonathan Martin
Julia Meehan
Diane C. Mermigas
Peter W. Miller
Amy Mittelman
Betty T. Moore
Dieter Müller
Henk Muntjewerff
David Myers
Frances E. Norton
D.H. O'Leary
John Orbell
Beatrice Rodriguez Owsley

J.G. Parker
William Pitt
Manfred Pohl
Nancy L. Post
Cliff Pratten
Janie Pritchett
Heiner Radzio
Trudy Ring
Richard Roberts
Juliette Rossant
Roger W. Rouland
Elizabeth Rourke
Maya Sahafi
Sandy Shusteff
Mary Scott
Peter Scott
Adam H. Seymour
Timothy J. Shannon
Nina Shapiro
Clark Siewert
Donald R. Stabile
Douglas Sun
John Swan
Gerardo G. Tango
Justine Taylor
Mark Uri Toch
Thomas M. Tucker
Rosanne Ullman
Reijo Virta
Etan Vlessing
Ray Walsh
Jordan Wankoff
Susanna Wilson
Gillian Wolf
Mechthild Wolf
Angela Woodward
Kenichi Yasumuro

ABBREVIATIONS FOR FORMS OF COMPANY INCORPORATION

A.B.	Aktiebolaget (Sweden)
A.G.	Aktiengesellschaft (Germany, Switzerland)
A.S.	Atieselskab (Denmark)
A.S.	Aksjeselskap (Denmark, Norway)
A.Ş.	Anonim Şirket (Turkey)
B.V.	Besloten Vennootschap met beperkte, Aansprakelijkheid (The Netherlands)
Co.	Company (United Kingdom, United States)
Corp.	Corporation (United States)
G.I.E.	Groupement d'Intérêt Economique (France)
GmbH	Gesellschaft mit beschränkter Haftung (Germany)
H.B.	Handelsbolaget (Sweden)
Inc.	Incorporated (United States)
KGaA	Kommanditgesellschaft auf Aktien (Germany)
K.K.	Kabushiki Kaisha (Japan)
LLC	Limited Liability Company (Middle East)
Ltd.	Limited (Canada, Japan, United Kingdom, United States)
N.V.	Naamloze Vennootschap (The Netherlands)
OY	Osakeyhtiöt (Finland)
PLC	Public Limited Company (United Kingdom)
PTY.	Proprietary (Australia, Hong Kong, South Africa)
S.A.	Société Anonyme (Belgium, France, Switzerland)
SpA	Società per Azioni (Italy)

ABBREVIATIONS FOR CURRENCY

DA	Algerian dinar	LuxFr	Luxembourgian franc
A$	Australian dollar	M$	Malaysian ringgit
Sch	Austrian shilling	Dfl	Netherlands florin
BFr	Belgian franc	NZ$	New Zealand dollar
Cr	Brazilian cruzado	N	Nigerian naira
C$	Canadian dollar	NKr	Norwegian krone
DKr	Danish krone	RO	Omani rial
E£	Egyptian pound	Esc	Portuguese escudo
Fmk	Finnish markka	R	South African rand
FFr	French franc	Pta	Spanish peseta
DM	German mark	SKr	Swedish krona
HK$	Hong Kong dollar	SFr	Swiss franc
Rs	Indian rupee	NT$	Taiwanese dollar
IR£	Irish pound	TL	Turkish lira
L	Italian lira	£	United Kingdom pound
¥	Japanese yen	$	United States dollar
W	Korean won	B	Venezuelan bolivar
KD	Kuwaiti dinar	K	Zambian kwacha

International Directory of

COMPANY
HISTORIES

MINING & METALS

Alcan Aluminium Limited
Aluminum Company of America
AMAX Inc.
Anglo American Corporation of
    South Africa Limited
ARBED S.A.
Armco Inc.
ASARCO Incorporated
Bethlehem Steel Corporation
British Coal Corporation
British Steel plc
Broken Hill Proprietary Company Ltd.
Coal India Limited
Cockerill Sambre Group
Companhia Valc do Rio Ducc
CRA Limited
Daido Steel Co., Ltd.
De Beers Consolidated Mines Limited/
    De Beers Centenary AG
Degussa Group
Dofasco Inc.
Echo Bay Mines Ltd.
Engelhard Corporation
Freeport-McMoRan Inc.
Fried. Krupp GmbH
Gencor Ltd.
Gold Fields of South Africa Ltd.
Heraeus Holding GmbH
Hitachi Metals, Ltd.
Hoesch AG
Imetal S.A.
Inco Limited
Inland Steel Industries, Inc.
Johnson Matthey PLC
Kaiser Aluminum & Chemical Corporation
Kawasaki Steel Corporation
Klöckner-Werke AG
Kobe Steel, Ltd.
Koninklijke Nederlandsche Hoogovens en
    Staalfabrieken NV
The Marmon Group
Metallgesellschaft AG
Minerals and Metals Trading Corporation
    of India Ltd.
Mitsui Mining & Smelting Co., Ltd.

Mitsui Mining Company, Limited
Nichimen Corporation
Nippon Light Metal Company, Ltd.
Nippon Steel Corporation
Nisshin Steel Co., Ltd.
NKK Corporation
Noranda Inc.
Okura & Co., Ltd.
Peabody Holding Company, Inc.
Pechiney
Phelps Dodge Corporation
The Pittston Company
Pohang Iron and Steel Company Ltd.
Reynolds Metals Company
The RTZ Corporation PLC
Ruhrkohle AG
Saarberg-Konzern
Salzgitter AG
Sandvik AB
Steel Authority of India Ltd.
Stelco Inc.
Sumitomo Metal Industries, Ltd.
Sumitomo Metal Mining Co., Ltd.
Tata Iron and Steel Company Ltd.
Thyssen AG
Tomen Corporation
Usinor Sacilor
VIAG Aktiengesellschaft
Voest-Alpine Stahl AG
Weirton Steel Corporation
Zambia Industrial and Mining
    Corporation Ltd.

PAPER & FORESTRY

Abitibi-Price Inc.
Amcor Limited
Avery Dennison Corporation
Boise Cascade Corporation
Bowater PLC
Bunzl plc
Champion International Corporation
Daio Paper Corporation
Daishowa Paper Manufacturing Co., Ltd.
Domtar Inc.
Enso-Gutzeit Oy
Fletcher Challenge Ltd.

Georgia-Pacific Corporation
Honshu Paper Co., Ltd.
International Paper Company
James River Corporation of Virginia
Japan Pulp and Paper Company Limited
Jefferson Smurfit Group plc
Jujo Paper Co., Ltd.
Kymmene Corporation
Louisiana-Pacific Corporation
MacMillan Bloedel Limited
The Mead Corporation
Metsä-Serla Oy
Mo och Domsjö AB
Oji Paper Co., Ltd.
PWA Group
Rengo Co., Ltd.
Sanyo-Kokusaku Pulp Co., Ltd.
Scott Paper Company
Stone Container Corporation
Stora Kopparbergs Bergslags AB
Svenska Cellulosa Aktiebolaget
Temple-Inland Inc.
Union Camp Corporation
United Paper Mills Ltd. (Yhtyneet
    Paperitehtaat Oy)
Westvaco Corporation
Weyerhaeuser Company
Willamette Industries, Inc.

PETROLEUM

Abu Dhabi National Oil Company
Amerada Hess Corporation
Amoco Corporation
Ashland Oil, Inc.
Atlantic Richfield Company
British Petroleum Company plc
Burmah Castrol plc
Chevron Corporation
Chinese Petroleum Corporation
CITGO Petroleum Corporation
The Coastal Corporation
Compañia Española de Petróleos S.A.
Conoco Inc.
Cosmo Oil Co., Ltd.
Den Norske Stats Oljeselskap AS
Diamond Shamrock, Inc.

Egyptian General Petroluem Corporation
Empresa Colombiana de Petróleos
Ente Nazionale Idrocarburi
Entreprise Nationale Sonatrach
Exxon Corporation
General Sekiyu K.K.
Idemitsu Kosan K.K.
Imperial Oil Limited
Indian Oil Corporation Ltd.
Kanematsu Corporation
Kerr-McGee Corporation
Koch Industries, Inc.
Kuwait Petroleum Corporation
Libyan National Oil Corporation
Lyondell Petrochemical Company
MAPCO Inc.
Mitsubishi Oil Co., Ltd.
Mobil Corporation
National Iranian Oil Company
Neste Oy
Nigerian National Petroleum Corporation
Nippon Mining Co., Ltd.
Nippon Oil Company, Limited
Occidental Petroleum Corporation
Oil and Natural Gas Commission
ÖMV Aktiengesellschaft
Pennzoil Company
PERTAMINA
Petro-Canada Limited
Petrofina
Petróleo Brasileiro S.A.
Petróleos de Portugal S.A.
Petróleos de Venezuela S.A.
Petróleos del Ecuador
Petróleos Mexicanos
Petroleum Development Oman LLC
Petronas
Phillips Petroleum Company
Qatar General Petroleum Corporation
Repsol SA
Royal Dutch Petroleum Company/
    The "Shell" Transport and Trading
    Company p.l.c.
Sasol Limited
Saudi Arabian Oil Company
Shell Oil Company
Showa Shell Sekiyu K.K.

MINING & METALS

ALCAN ALUMINIUM LIMITED
ALUMINUM COMPANY OF AMERICA
AMAX INC.
ANGLO AMERICAN CORPORATION OF
    SOUTH AFRICA LIMITED
ARBED S.A.
ARMCO INC.
ASARCO INCORPORATED
BETHLEHEM STEEL CORPORATION
BRITISH COAL CORPORATION
BRITISH STEEL PLC
BROKEN HILL PROPRIETARY COMPANY LTD.
COAL INDIA LIMITED
COCKERILL SAMBRE GROUP
COMPANHIA VALE DO RIO DUCE
CRA LIMITED
DAIDO STEEL CO., LTD.
DE BEERS CONSOLIDATED MINES LIMITED/
    DE BEERS CENTENARY AG
DEGUSSA GROUP
DOFASCO INC.
ECHO BAY MINES LTD.
ENGELHARD CORPORATION
FREEPORT-MCMORAN INC.
FRIED. KRUPP GMBH
GENCOR LTD.
GOLD FIELDS OF SOUTH AFRICA LTD.
HERAEUS HOLDING GMBH
HITACHI METALS, LTD.
HOESCH AG
IMETAL S.A.
INCO LIMITED
INLAND STEEL INDUSTRIES, INC.
JOHNSON MATTHEY PLC
KAISER ALUMINUM & CHEMICAL
    CORPORATION
KAWASAKI STEEL CORPORATION
KLÖCKNER-WERKE AG
KOBE STEEL, LTD.

KONINKLIJKE NEDERLANDSCHE
    HOOGOVENS EN STAALFABRIEKEN NV
THE MARMON GROUP
METALLGESELLSCHAFT AG
MINERALS AND METALS TRADING
    CORPORATION OF INDIA LTD.
MITSUI MINING & SMELTING CO., LTD.
MITSUI MINING COMPANY, LIMITED
NICHIMEN CORPORATION
NIPPON LIGHT METAL COMPANY, LTD.
NIPPON STEEL CORPORATION
NISSHIN STEEL CO., LTD.
NKK CORPORATION
NORANDA INC.
OKURA & CO., LTD.
PEABODY HOLDING COMPANY, INC.
PECHINEY
PHELPS DODGE CORPORATION
THE PITTSTON COMPANY
POHANG IRON AND STEEL COMPANY LTD.
REYNOLDS METALS COMPANY
THE RTZ CORPORATION PLC
RUHRKOHLE AG
SAARBERG-KONZERN
SALZGITTER AG
SANDVIK AB
STEEL AUTHORITY OF INDIA LTD.
STELCO INC.
SUMITOMO METAL INDUSTRIES, LTD.
SUMITOMO METAL MINING CO., LTD.
TATA IRON AND STEEL COMPANY LTD.
THYSSEN AG
TOMEN CORPORATION
USINOR SACILOR
VIAG AKTIENGESELLSCHAFT
VOEST-ALPINE STAHL AG
WEIRTON STEEL CORPORATION
ZAMBIA INDUSTRIAL AND MINING
    CORPORATION LTD.

ALCAN ALUMINIUM LIMITED

1188 Sherbrooke Street West
Montreal, Quebec H3A 3G2
Canada
(514) 848-8000
Fax: (514) 848-8115

Public Company
Incorporated: 1902 as Northern Aluminum Company Limited
Employees: 57,000
Sales: US$8.76 billion
Stock Exchanges: New York Toronto Montreal Vancouver Midwest Pacific London Paris Brussels Amsterdam Frankfurt Basel Geneva Zürich Tokyo

Alcan Aluminium Limited is a primary force in the aluminum industry worldwide, competing with Aluminum Company of America (Alcoa) for the number-one ranking. The company has performed extraordinarily well, and is one of Canada's highest profit-making companies, although profits dipped somewhat to US$835 million in 1989, and further to US$543 million in 1990, reflecting weak business conditions and lower prices. The company is a fully integrated aluminum producer, handling the light-weight metal at all stages of development, from bauxite mining to high-tech component fabrication.

Alcan is a multinational corporation. Operations are vertically integrated across ten operating areas worldwide. Bauxite is mined in seven countries and refined to alumina in nine. Primary aluminum smelters operate in seven countries, and a wide variety of aluminum goods are fabricated to differing degrees in plants in nineteen different nations. Alcan sells primary and fabricated aluminum in more than 100 countries around the world. Historically the company has followed a decentralized corporate model; overseas subsidiaries are left to manage their own affairs, even to the extent of financing expansion on their own.

Alcan's international orientation dates back to its origins. In June 1928 the Aluminum Company of America, then the world's undisputed leader in aluminum, spun off its foreign operations, forming a Canadian holding company called Aluminium Limited. Shareholders received one share of the new company for every three shares of Alcoa stock. For more than 20 years the two companies were controlled by the same individuals. Aluminium Limited penetrated foreign markets, and participated in international cartels away from the scrutiny of

the United States Justice Department. Alcoa, meanwhile, dominated the U.S. market.

Alcan's history, however, began long before the 1928 spin-off. In 1899 The Pittsburgh Reduction Company—later Alcoa—began construction of a power plant and the first Canadian reduction works at Shawinigan Falls, Quebec. Aluminium production began two years later. This first Canadian subsidiary became known in 1902 as Northern Aluminum Company Limited.

Northern Aluminum became an important player in the global aluminium markets. Aluminum was still a new metal. A commercially feasible refinement process had been discovered in 1886, but industrial applications were somewhat slow in developing. Skepticism among manufacturers forced producers toward vertical integration. Pittsburgh Reduction, and its Canadian subsidiary Northern, were tireless in trying to develop aluminum markets, but eventually turned to fabricating products such as cooking pots to promote the metal and broaden sales.

Several countries, in addition to the United States and Canada, each had one or two aluminum producers. European businesses often organized distribution in industries where demand was limited, and after the turn of the century, cartels were formed to set the prices and quotas for individual aluminum companies. The first of these cartels began in 1901, and was known as the Aluminium Association. The cartel, which was made up of the leading Swiss company, the leading British company, and a pair of French companies, in addition to the Canadian concern, divided the world into reserved markets and free markets. Each company was allotted a reserved market and given a quota on a percentage basis for the free markets. The Swiss company was the distributor for all participants. This cartel operated until 1908, and then broke up over disagreements on price-setting. In 1912 a new cartel was created, this time allowing any member to sell its quota directly to customers in any market without restriction. This second cartel broke up in 1915, disrupted by World War I.

While technically Alcoa was not a member of the cartels, it did effectively participate through its wholly owned Canadian subsidiary. This association would later fuel antitrust actions against Alcoa and eventually contributed to the divestiture of Northern Aluminum and Alcoa's other foreign operations in 1928.

Demand for aluminum grew in the early years of the 20th century. Applications for the metal were found in the electrical and automotive industries. By 1914 80% of U.S.-made cars had aluminum crank and gear cases. Aviation, at that time a new industry, called for light-weight metals. Orville and Wilbur Wright had used aluminum in their first plane at Kitty Hawk, North Carolina.

World War I provided new applications for aluminum. Massive quantities of the metal were employed in explosives, ammunition, and machine guns; and the Liberty V-12 engine, which powered Allied planes, was one-third aluminum. Military usage absorbed 90% of the aluminum produced during the war years. The widespread use during the war translated into widespread acceptance by consumers after the war. Furthermore, the interruption of European aluminum shipments to North America served as a boon to Northern Aluminum after the war. In 1919 Northern alone exported 5,643 tons of Canadian aluminum to the United States compared to 2,360 for all European producers combined.

The 1920s saw fantastic growth for Northern Aluminum. In the early years of the decade, Arthur Vining Davis, head of Alcoa, became interested in two or three hydroelectric plants being proposed by U.S. tobacco magnate James B. Duke on Quebec's Saguenay River because the refinement of aluminum requires vast amounts of electricity.

Davis called upon A.W. Mellon, renowned financier and major stockholder in Alcoa, to help negotiate a deal with Duke. In 1925 a deal was struck. The aluminum company acquired the hydroelectric site at the so-called Lower Development, as well as water rights to the Upper Development. Duke took $16 million in preferred stock and 15% of the common stock of Alcoa. When Duke died three months after the deal was signed, Alcoa was given the opportunity to purchase a controlling interest in the Upper Development. Also in 1925, Northern Aluminum Company changed its name to Aluminum Company of Canada Limited.

These events secured the Saguenay River hydroelectric facilities, the foundation for today's Alcan operations. Growth on the site was feverish; by 1927, the power plant on the Upper Development supplied a new 27,000-ton smelter, and the refinery neared completion. The company town of Arvida, named after Arthur Vining Davis, sprang up, and the development became the world's largest aluminum production site during World War II.

In 1928 when Alcoa divested its overseas operations, the Aluminum Company of Canada, Limited became the chief operating subsidiary of Aluminium Limited. Aluminium Limited also took over all of Alcoa's other non-U.S. holdings including Norwegian, Italian, French, and Spanish manufacturing and power concerns. Alcoa retained ownership of the power plants on the Saguenay until 1938, when Aluminium Limited purchased them for $35 million. Also at this time, the company moved its headquarters to Montreal from New York, although some senior executives continued to work in New York.

There were several reasons for the spin-off of Aluminium Limited (AL) from Alcoa. Davis felt that Alcoa's sales force neglected overseas markets in favor of the domestic market. He believed a Canadian company, with its own directors and own staff, would be in a better position to exploit international markets throughout the British Empire and elsewhere. Also, Alcoa's domination of the aluminum industry made it a frequent target of U.S. antitrust accusations. By divesting its foreign subsidiaries, Alcoa at least created the impression that it was not excluding competition from abroad. Meanwhile, the new company was free to participate in international cartels as it pleased.

Finally, Davis was nearing retirement, and would soon be faced with choosing a successor. The choice was between his brother Edward K. Davis, and his long-time close friend and colleague, Roy Hunt. Hunt was the son of Alcoa's co-founder, Captain Alfred E. Hunt. Davis solved his problem by sending Edward Davis north to head the new international corporation.

Edward Davis, as AL's first chief faced some difficult challenges in the company's early years. Although not truly an infant company, AL had to redefine its approach. Formerly, the company had been a part of a vertically integrated whole. Now it was expected to compete worldwide, but it lacked the aluminum-fabrication capability to make finished products that Alcoa and the European producers had.

The Depression struck the company hard, and it was forced to borrow heavily to survive. Technical support and operating agreements with a benevolent Alcoa helped the company stay afloat. For the most part, AL did not compete with Alcoa in the U.S. market, due to a substantial U.S. tariff on imports and to the influence of Alcoa's and AL's common shareholders. As a result, AL pursued instead Asian and European markets.

Realizing it could not survive unless it integrated its operations, AL built fabricating plants in a number of countries worldwide. The growth of the automotive and aviation industries improved the position of AL. By 1937 the company was out of debt and operated profitably. Production capacity at the Arvida plant had doubled and the number of employees worldwide since 1928 had tripled. In 1937 the U.S. Justice Department filed an antitrust suit against Alcoa, Aluminium Limited, and 61 related subsidiaries and individuals. The suit called for the break-up of Alcoa, and its divorce from AL. The suit alleged Alcoa and its confederates had conspired to restrain imports and to preserve its U.S. monopoly. In 1942 Alcoa and Aluminium Limited were cleared of the charges. The 1942 decision was appealed and was upheld on all counts except one. The appeals court opined that at the time of the original decision, Alcoa monopolized the U.S. ingot market, but that since that time new competition seemed to have evolved. The court therefore delayed further action until an assessment of the postwar industry could be made.

In 1950 the court calculated that the same nine stockholders controlled 44.65% of AL's stock and 46.43% of Alcoa's stock. While the court said that the relationship between the two companies had been lawful in the past, it ordered the investors to divest the shares of one company or the other. It was the first time in history that U.S. investors had been ordered by their government to give up control of a foreign company. All of the investors except Edward Davis, who sold his Alcoa stock, sold their shares in the Canadian company. The suit remained open until 1957, when a Justice Department request for extended court supervision was denied. In the 20 years this case was open, the aluminum industry had undergone tremendous change, and AL had grown into a giant.

The late 1930s had seen demand for aluminum explode, fueled by war preparations. AL was the largest supplier within the British Empire, and Britain's demand for airplanes and other military hardware was great. During the war, the Canadian company received US$78 million in low-interest loans from the British government to expand its power and reduction facilities. In return, the additional output was earmarked for the British market. The U.S. government also offered assistance to AL; the Defense Plant Corporation, the branch of the Reconstruction Finance Corporation charged with fostering war-industries production, paid US$68 million in advance for 1.3 million pounds of aluminum. AL reportedly used the cash flow to construct another dam on the Saguenay, the Shipsaw Power Plant Number 2. The purchase agreement annoyed U.S. producers, who saw it as a boost to a potential competitor after the war. AL's contribution to the war effort was, however, paramount.

The Aluminium Limited subsidiary Aluminum Company of Canada (Alcan) ended the war five times larger than it was in 1937. This expansion posed the threat of idle facilities after the war. The company's researchers worked on expanding aluminum applications in the automotive and rail transport industries.

World War II boosted other companies as well. In the United States, two new integrated concerns, Reynolds Metals Company and Kaiser Aluminum & Chemical Corporation, were born from favorable sales of government-owned aluminum plants built during the war. This new competition was not immediately threatening to Alcan, whose chief production at that time was in ingot rather than fabricated or semi-fabricated products. In addition, Alcan's Shipsaw Power plant in Quebec had indeed made Alcan's electricity costs the lowest in the world.

In 1946 Alcan announced a reduction in the ingot aluminum price to C13.25¢, or US12.04¢ per pound. This was well below most international producer's prices, and kept Alcan's price on a par with the price of US15¢. The signal was that Alcan intended to be the dominant primary—ingot—aluminum supplier worldwide.

In 1947, Nathanael V. Davis took over as CEO of Aluminium Limited from his father, Edward Davis. After a brief dip in aluminum consumption right after the war, consumer goods began to use the metal in quantities as never before. By 1950 the Korean War demanded a steady flow of aluminum for the military, and a shortage developed in the United States. U.S. producers increased their output, and several new competitors joined the field.

During the 1950s the United States imported 10% to 20% of its primary aluminum. Alcan controlled 90% of that import business. In 1951 Alcan began a $350 million expansion program, which included additions to the Quebec plants and a new hydroelectric and reduction site in British Columbia, which began operations in 1954.

In 1950, when the strong ownership ties between Alcoa and Alcan were severed, the Canadian company began to make more aggressive forays into the U.S. market. Occasionally, Alcan broke with tradition and set prices at rates lower than Alcoa. Alcoa's price leadership was followed loyally by other U.S. producers. Alcan focused on aluminum in primary-ingot form, while Alcoa, Reynolds, and Kaiser dove into the semi-fabricated and fabricated products. Alcan's U.S. customers, were independent fabricators, as well as Alcoa, Reynolds, and Kaiser themselves. The independents were Alcan's political allies, lobbying for low tariffs on primary aluminum.

While Alcan's exports to the United States grew in the early 1950s, market shares in other areas began to shrink. Norway and France doubled their domestic aluminum capacity, while historic importers like Germany and Japan began to develop their own industries. Although overall output increased, Alcan's percentage of world production declined from 21% in 1954 to 19% by 1960. By 1969 it had slid to 13%.

In 1957 Alcan's first domestic competitor, Canadian British Aluminum (CBA), was started. During the summer of 1957 a strike at Alcan's Arvida plant idled 45% of production capacity for four months, resulting in a loss of about 1,000 tons of aluminum production per day. Later in the year, recessionary conditions caused a global oversupply of aluminum, and Aluminium Limited's profits dipped for 1958. Sales of primary aluminum to U.S. and U.K. producers declined.

Alcan decided to bolster its fabrication efforts. In 1958 Alcan expanded fabricating operations in plants in 11 countries. The global oversupply lasted into the early 1960s, however, and as it worsened, U.S. producers slashed prices to near cost to keep plants running. Alcan slowly was being squeezed out of the U.S. market. In response, Alcan decided to build semi-fabricating plants of its own in the United States to establish stable outlets for its ingot.

In 1963 AL acquired a small U.S. metal-powders firm and an aluminum-wire and -cable firm. Alcan and three of its biggest U.S. independent customers, Cerro Corporation, Scovill Manufacturing, and National Distillers & Chemical Corporation, began construction of a US$45 million hot mill in Oswego, New York, that would produce coils and aluminum plate. Alcan bought out its partners in 1965, and also acquired other sheet-fabricating plants owned by Cerro and National Distillers. A U.S. subsidiary, Alcan Aluminum Corporation, was founded in Cleveland, Ohio, in 1965 to manage AL's U.S. fabrication concerns. The unit lost US$10.4 million in its first year, but persevered. By 1967 Alcan operated 12 plants in 8 U.S. states. In 1966 Aluminium Limited was renamed Alcan Aluminium Limited.

In 1968 Alcan reorganized its corporate structure. Rapid expansion taxed the company's decentralized system; 33 managing directors reported directly to presidental CEO Davis. Subsequently, management was divided into three groups: raw materials, smelting, and fabricating and sales.

In the late 1960s another fundamental shift occurred in Alcan Aluminium's business. Higher transportation and labor costs eroded the advantage of refining aluminum in Canada, as did the availability of cheaper power in the United States. Political developments around the globe made it advantageous for Alcan Aluminium to build primary smelters in Australia, Britain, India, Norway, and Japan. By 1972, Alcan Aluminium's foreign smelting capacity equaled that of its Canadian facilities. Alcan Aluminium had begun to develop integrated units within each country of operations.

Alcan Aluminium's shift toward finished products continued. In 1971 Alcan Aluminium shipped more fabricated and semi-fabricated tonnage than ingot for the first time. In 1972 Paul H. Leman took over as president of Alcan Aluminium Limited. Davis remained CEO and took on the new post of chairman. The French-Canadian Leman was Alcan's first president outside the Davis family. He had joined Alcan in 1938. In 1975 global recession brought on by the oil crisis, caused a decline in Alcan Aluminium's aluminum shipments by 16% worldwide. Profits took a dive as demand fell in all markets except Latin America. Alcan Aluminium continued to build plants overseas, however, adding an alumina refinery in Ireland, and participating in the development of new bauxite mines in Brazil in the mid-to late-1970s.

Labor troubles caused the shutdown of four of the company's five Canadian smelters in 1976. Damage to one plant, caused by molten aluminum hardening in the potlines when workers cut the power, cost an estimated US$25 million. Another strike three years later had a similar effect on Alcan Aluminium's production levels. During both of these strikes other producers took advantage of the banner growth years for aluminum.

In the mid-1970s, plans to expand smelting capacity in Canada were mapped out. Uncertainty about the future of energy costs encouraged Alcan Aluminium and its Alcan subsidiary to take advantage of its own Canadian hydroelectric plants. In 1977 David Culver replaced Leman as president. The executive observed that Alcan Aluminium was the only aluminum producer in the world with the ability to expand by 30% without increasing its power costs. By 1978 construction on a new primary smelter in Quebec was well under way.

In July 1979 Davis stepped down as Alcan Aluminium's CEO, and was replaced by Culver but continued as chairman until 1986. Culver had joined Alcan Aluminium in 1949, and had worked his way up the sales side. He set out to bolster Alcan Aluminium's marketing efforts and strengthen the emphasis on fabricated products, eventually limiting ingot sales to 25% of the total. Culver initiated a new research-and-development push in 1980. Alcan Aluminium lagged in high-margin aerospace, automotive, and beverage-container markets due to dated technology.

In the early 1980s Alcan Aluminium opened new smelters in Australia and Brazil, and expanded facilities in West Germany, Britain, and Spain. The company was in a very strong financial position to face the next decade. Annual revenues had doubled since 1975 and earnings had increased eightfold. Debt was low.

Alcan Aluminium's financial strength proved a blessing when the recession of 1980 to 1982 reached the aluminum industry. Demand fell sharply. In 1982 Alcan Aluminium lost US$58 million, its first loss in 50 years. Several long-term factors came to a head in the 1980s. Increased use of scrap resulted in lower aluminum prices. New Third World producers entered the market in force. In 1960, six producers—Alcan Aluminium, Alcoa, Reynolds, Kaiser, France's Pechiney, and Switzerland's Alusuisse, controlled 70% to 80% of the free world's aluminum market. By 1981 their share was 40% to 50%. More than 80 companies, double the 1960 number, produced aluminum goods worldwide, and about 30% of Third World producers were owned at least in part by their governments, whose interest was oriented toward full employment and acquiring hard currency rather than toward maximizing profits or maintaining supply-and-demand equilibrium. Another factor was increased price volatility after aluminum was listed on the London Metals Exchange in 1978. Private deals between producers and buyers became obsolete, and buyers gained tremendous advantage when the exchange price was publicized daily.

The industry would adjust to these developments, but not until the latter half of the 1980s. Meanwhile, Alcan Aluminium overproduced, partly to exploit its hydroelectric power advantage while high oil prices greatly affected other producers, and partly to placate labor. Profits returned in 1983 and 1984.

In 1985 Alcan Aluminium trimmed 1,100 management jobs, cutting an estimated C$40 million in costs annually. Alcan Aluminium went forward with plans to modernize its plants in Quebec, and when aluminum prices rebounded in 1985, Alcan Aluminium was better prepared to take advantage of it than any of its competitors.

In 1986 Alcan Aluminium's top managers devised a new long-term strategy to improve Alcan Aluminium's return on equity. The plan focused on technological applications of aluminum and related metals particularly in aerospace, electronics, and ceramics. Aluminum-lithium alloys were tested in Canadian and British aircraft. Composite aluminum materials also found applications in rail-car and automotive assembly. Alcan Aluminium bought a gallium-purification subsidiary of Alusuisse in 1985, and planned to manufacture gallium arsenide semiconducting wafers. The company also reaffirmed its commitment to existing aluminum operations, including ingot production.

In 1987 Alcan Aluminium underwent a reorganization. Alcan Aluminium Limited, the parent company, was merged with its chief operating unit, Aluminum Company of Canada. All of the former parent's subsidiary units worldwide were transferred to the former Canadian operating unit, and the reorganized company took the name Alcan Aluminium Limited (Alcan). The arrangement shed layers of management. Alcan's leaner structure and clear direction helped the company earn record profits in 1988. Alcan's net of US$931 million was more than any Canadian company had ever earned.

In July 1989 David Culver retired. Alcan's new chairman and CEO was David Morton, who had joined the company's British subsidiary in 1954. As Morton took over as CEO of Alcan, the world was headed for another recession.

Alcan's future looks sound. Diversification into related fields and emphasis on high-tech fabrication should help the company meet the challenges of the 1990s. Alcan planned to replace its outdated smelters in Quebec, hoping to spend US$1 billion by 1994 if aluminum prices were favorable. A free trade agreement with the United States gives Alcan extra punch in the world's single largest aluminum market. As business trends continue to emphasize global markets, Alcan's long history of successfully developing foreign markets and industries is likely to give it still another advantage in the aluminum industry of the future.

Principal Subsidiaries: Alcan Aluminio del Uruguay S.A. (89.2%); Alcan Aluminio do Brasil S.A. (Brazil); Alcan Aluminum Corporation (U.S.A.); Alcan Asia Limited (Hong Kong); Alcan Australia Limited (73.3%); Alcan Alluminio S.p.A. (Italy); Alcan Deutschland GmbH (Germany); Alcan International Limited; Alcan Jamaica Limited; Alcan New Zealand Limited; Alcan Nikkei Korea Limited (Hong Kong, 51%); Alcan Pacific Limited (Japan); Alcan Rorschach AG (Switzerland); Alcan Siam Limited (Thailand, 70%); Alcan Smelters and Chemicals Limited; Aluminium Company of Malaysia Berhad (63.9%); Aughinish Alumina Limited (Ireland, 65%); Alcan Rolled Products Company; British Alcan Aluminium plc (U.K.); CAMEA S.A. (Argentina, 99.6%); Compagnie des Bauzites de Guinee (Guinea, 13.8%); Ghana Bauxite Company Limited (Ghana, 45%); Indian Aluminium Company Limited (India, 39.6%); Johore Mining and Stevedoring Company Sdn. (Malaysia, 70%); Mineracao Rio do Norte S.A. (Brazil, 24%); Nippon Light Metal Company, Ltd. (Japan, 45%); Nonfemet International Aluminium Company Limited (China, 33%); Petrocoque S.A.—Industria & Comfcio (Brazil, 25%); Queensland Alumina Limited (Australia, 21.4%); Roberval and Saguenay Railway Company; Technal S.A. (France); Toyo Aluminium K.K. (Japan, 49%); Tubopack S.A. (Chile, 45%).

Further Reading: Hight, Jack, "Kingdom of the Saguenay: Canada's Sprawling Aluminium Giant," *The Iron Age,* April 5, 1945; Farin, Philip, and Gary G. Reibsamen, *Aluminium: Profile of an Industry,* New York, Metals Week, 1969; "Why Alcan spends so much," *Business Week,* July 10, 1971; Levy, Yvonne, *Aluminium: Past and Future,* San Francisco, Federal

Reserve Bank of San Francisco, 1971; "Alcan's Latest Cliff-Hanger," *Forbes*, November 1, 1977; Smith, George David, Campbell, Duncan C., *Global Mission: The Story of Alcan*, 3 Vols., Montreal, Alcan Aluminium Limited, 1985-1990; *From Monopoly to Competition; The Transformation of Alcoa, 1888–1986,* Cambridge, Cambridge University Press, 1988; Ross, Alexander, "The Alcan Succession," *Canadian Business*, June 1989.

—Thomas M. Tucker

ALUMINUM COMPANY OF AMERICA

1501 Alcoa Building
Pittsburgh, Pennsylvania 15219
U.S.A.
(412) 553-4545
Fax: (412) 553-4498

Public Company
Incorporated: 1888 as The Pittsburgh Reduction Company
Employees: 63,500
Sales: $10.71 billion
Stock Exchanges: New York Basel Brussels Frankfurt Geneva
　Lausanne London Zürich

Aluminum Company of America (Alcoa) has had two incarnations. In the first, it was the only aluminum producer of consequence in the United States and had a monopoly in the U.S. market. In the second, which was spawned by judicial decree, it has been forced to diversify to cope with the competitive demands of its new condition, although it has refocused on its core aluminum business. Alcoa is still the world's largest aluminum producer, and has subsidiaries involved in aerospace and industrial products, packaging, and materials science.

Alcoa was founded in 1888 in Pittsburgh, Pennsylvania, under the name The Pittsburgh Reduction Company. Its founders were a coalition of entrepreneurs headed by Alfred Hunt, a metallurgist who had been working in the steel industry, and a young chemist named Charles Martin Hall. Pittsburgh Reduction's sole property was a patented process for extracting aluminum from bauxite ore by electrolysis, which Hall had invented in the woodshed of his family house in 1886, just one year after his graduation from Oberlin College. Hall's discovery had promised to make aluminum economical to produce for the first time in history. Later in 1886, Hall had taken his process to a smelting company in Cleveland, Ohio, but left in 1888 after it showed little interest. One of his associates there, who had also worked with Hunt at another company, introduced the two men, and Pittsburgh Reduction was started as a result of their meeting.

Despite its relative abundance, few practical uses existed for aluminum because it was so expensive to extract. By 1893, however, Hall's process allowed Pittsburgh Reduction to undercut its competitors with aluminum that had been produced at a lower price. The company then faced two challenges: to generate a larger market for aluminum by promoting new uses

for the metal and to increase production so that it could cut costs even further through economies of scale. Efforts in the former area proved most successful in the manufacturing of cooking utensils, so much so that the company formed its own cookware subsidiary, Aluminum Cooking Utensil Company, in 1901. Aluminum Cooking Utensil adopted the Wear-Ever brand name.

Pittsburgh Reduction also began the process of vertical integration, insuring itself against the day when Hall's patent would expire and it would no longer have a monopoly on his process. In the mid-1890s, it began acquiring its own bauxite mines and power-generating facilities. This process continued after the death of Alfred Hunt, who had served as president since founding the company. In 1899 Hunt, an artillery captain in the Pennsylvania militia, was sent to Puerto Rico with his battery during the Spanish-American War and succumbed to malaria there. He was succeeded by R.B. Mellon of the Mellon banking family, which had loaned the company much of its start-up capital and controlled a substantial minority stake. The Mellons, however, had been content to let the engineers run the company. Arthur Vining Davis, a partner who had joined Pittsburgh Reduction only months after its founding, acted as president during this time, and the Mellons formally ceded power to him in 1910. In 1907 The Pittsburgh Reduction Company changed its name to Aluminum Company of America. In 1914 Davis became the company's last surviving link to its early days when Charles Martin Hall died, leaving an estate with an estimated worth of $45 million.

Alcoa had virtually created the market for aluminum, and its only competition came from foreign producers, who were hindered by high tariffs. Alcoa also benefited from rising demand from the automobile industry; by 1915, 65% of all new aluminum went into automotive parts. The outbreak of World War I ended the threat from foreign producers, and Alcoa even became an exporter. Annual production rose from 109 million pounds to 152 million pounds between 1915 and 1918, with much of it going to Great Britain, France, and Italy. At home, the vast majority of Alcoa's output was used for military applications.

The export boom that the war had fostered made it seem natural that Alcoa should expand its overseas operations once hostilities ended. Throughout the 1920s, the company acquired factories, mines, and power-generating facilities in Western Europe, Scandinavia, and, most prominently, in Canada. Late in the decade, however, the difficulty of managing far-flung operations, combined with a rising tide of economic nationalism abroad, made Alcoa's position overseas increasingly untenable. In 1928 it divested all of its foreign operations except its Dutch Guiana bauxite mines, spinning them off as Aluminium Limited, based in Montreal and headed by Edward Davis, A.V. Davis's brother. Aluminium Limited was renamed Alcan Aluminium Limited in 1966. In 1929 Arthur Vining Davis retired as president and became chairman. He was succeeded by Roy Hunt, the son of Alfred Hunt.

At home, the general economic boom carried Alcoa with it, but between 1929 and 1932, during the early years of the Great Depression, sales fell from $34.4 million to $11.1 million. Alcoa laid off half of its work force in this time, slashed wages for those who remained, and cut back its research-and-development budget. Demand for aluminum did not recover until 1936. Even so, Alcoa's market share remained unchallenged, as it was still the only aluminum smelter in the United States thanks to its technological lead and economies of scale—a position that had not gone unnoticed.

Aluminum Company of America had been having antitrust run-ins with the Justice Department since 1911, but all of the blows had glanced off of it until U.S. Attorney General Homer Cummings filed suit in 1937, charging monopolization and restraint of trade on Alcoa's part. The trial lasted from 1938 to 1940 and was the largest proceeding in the history of U.S. law to that time. A district court ruling in 1942 found in favor of Alcoa, but the government appealed. In 1945 an appeals court sustained that appeal. In his decision, Judge Learned Hand ruled that although Alcoa had not intended to create its monopoly, the fact remained that it had a monopoly on the domestic aluminum market in violation of antitrust law and it would be in the nation's best interest to break it up. Hand's decision became a landmark in the history of judicial activism, although it did leave open the question of how Alcoa's grip on aluminum was to be broken.

Meanwhile, of course, the United States had entered World War II. Demand for aluminum skyrocketed. Alcoa, however, proved to be unable to keep up with the increases in demand, disappointing the War Department. During the war the government financed new plants that were built and run by Alcoa, but also encouraged the development of other aluminum producers. As the tide of the war shifted in favor of the Allies in 1944, the U.S. government began deliberations on how to dispose of these plants, which would soon become surplus capacity. As a result, a solution to the problem of how to carry out Hand's ruling became apparent. The Alcoa plants that the government had financed would be sold off to two new rivals: Reynolds Metals Company and Permanente Metals Corporation, owned by industrialist Henry Kaiser. Reynolds and Permanente were to buy the plants at cut-rate prices. In effect, this divestiture created an oligarchy where there had formerly been a monopoly. In 1950 a district court decree carved up the U.S. aluminum market between the three: Alcoa would get 50.9% of production capacity, Reynolds 30.9%, and Kaiser Aluminum & Chemical Corporation, as Permanente Metals was renamed, 18.2%.

Roy Hunt retired in 1951 and was succeeded by Irving Wilson. During the 1950s, Alcoa's share of U.S. production capacity declined as it expanded more slowly than Reynolds and Kaiser. Faced with increased competition, Alcoa also found itself without any brand-name recognition on which to capitalize in the consumer products arena; Reynolds, by comparison, had established a name for itself quickly with its Reynolds Wrap aluminum foil. Nevertheless, booming demand for aluminum, the result of successful wartime experiments in using the metal to build military aircraft, helped compensate for decreased market share. Despite increased competition, Alcoa remained the industry's largest member and its acknowledged price leader.

Davis retired in 1957, ending his 69 years of service with Alcoa. He was succeeded by Wilson, and Frank Magee became president and CEO. Alcoa came out of the brief recession of 1957–1958 by realizing that it would have to internationalize and diversify in order to ensure its future. In 1958 Alcoa joined with Lockheed and Japanese manufacturer Furukawa Electric Company to form Furalco, which would produce aluminum aircraft parts for Lockheed. Also that year,

Alcoa became a player in what was then the largest takeover battle in British corporate history when it negotiated a friendly acquisition of a stake in struggling British Aluminium, Ltd. The acquisition was aborted, however. Alcoa had been approached by British Aluminium chairman Lord Portal, Viscount of Hungerford, who had neglected to consult his major stockholders before closing the deal. Thus, when Reynolds and British manufacturer Tube Investments made a substantially sweeter bid, a bitter struggle ensued. Institutional investors sold their shares to the Reynolds and Tube venture and Alcoa lost out. The fight over British Aluminium became a sensation in Britain not only because of the sheer spectacle of foreign interests vying for control of a major domestic corporation, but also because hostile takeovers were considered a breach of etiquette in British finance. What came to be known as The Great Aluminium War split British investment banks between the old-line, established houses that backed Alcoa and Portal, and the upstart firms that supported Reynolds and Tube.

Undeterred by this setback, Alcoa went on to spread its mining operations into other parts of the world, re-establishing an international presence it had not had since it spun off Alcan. Back home, the company moved aggressively into producing finished aluminum products. In 1959 it acquired Rome Cable and Wire Company. The next year, it purchased Rea Magnet Wire Company and Cupples Products Company, a manufacturer of aluminum curtain walls and doors. Both Rome and Cupples eventually had to be divested, however, because of antitrust objections.

When John Harper became president and CEO in 1963, Alcoa found its profit margins squeezed by increased competition, high overhead, and a generally low market price for aluminum. One of Harper's solutions was to move more aggressively into manufacturing finished products, which provided higher returns than smelting. On his initiative, Alcoa began producing sheet metal for aluminum cans, which became more popular among beverage consumers in the 1960s after the invention of the pop top, and aerospace parts. In 1966 the company posted a record profit, finally exceeding a mark it had set ten years before.

High labor costs, dramatically high energy prices, unpredictable bauxite prices, a slower national economy, and new competitors trying to break up the aluminum oligarchy all conspired against Alcoa in the 1970s. Sales and other operating revenues grew from $1.8 billion to $4.6 billion between 1972 and 1982, but profits as a percentage of gross income remained below historical levels. High interest rates forced Alcoa to slow its expansion and concentrate on paying down existing debt. In 1972 the company also decided to sell its technology to other manufacturers on a large scale, something it had been loath to do in the past.

W.H. Krome George succeeded John Harper as chairman and CEO in 1975, and Aluminum Company of America began to show new signs of life. In the late 1970s it seized upon recycling as an alternative to the high cost of smelting, although somewhat later than rival Reynolds. By 1979 Alcoa was reprocessing 110 million pounds of scrap aluminum. By 1985 that figure would rise to over 500 million pounds and recycling would account for 19% of the company's aluminum ingot capacity. George, who was more scientifically oriented than his predecessors, also led Alcoa into expansive research into high-tech applications of aluminum. By the time George retired in 1983, he had started the company on the path once again to developing new high-strength alloys for use in the aerospace business. Other areas of research and development, often pursued as joint ventures with other companies, included alumina chemicals, satellite antennae, and computer memory discs.

George's successor, Charles Parry, took over in 1983, and was even more committed to diversifying Alcoa. His goal, he said, was that half of the company's revenue should come from non-aluminum sources by 1995. Immediately, Alcoa began scouting around for companies to acquire, particularly in high-tech fields. At the same time, however, Parry's vigor in attempting to reshape the company was not well received in all quarters. He was attempting to radically change corporate thinking in a short period of time even as he continued the layoffs and plant closures that George had begun in an effort to cut costs, and employee morale suffered. Many did not see how he could create new business worth between $7 billion and $9 billion from scratch in less than ten years. Although Alcoa made only minor acquisitions during Parry's tenure, which ended in 1987, the directors became concerned that the deals that Parry proposed to make would not fit in well. Some worried that the risks involved were more appropriate to a young company just starting up, not a major corporation nearing its centennial.

Even George became uncomfortable with his successor, and in 1986 he led the search for Parry's replacement. Aware of his board's discontent, Parry took an early retirement in 1987. He was replaced by Paul O'Neill, former president of International Paper Company and deputy director of the Office of Management and Budget during the administration of President Gerald R. Ford. O'Neill's appointment was largely George's doing; the two had met because of the latter's directorship at International Paper.

Under O'Neill, the first outsider ever to run Alcoa, the company had slowed its diversification and refocused on its core aluminum business. In 1990 it formed a joint venture with Japanese manufacturer Kobe Steel, Ltd. to make sheet metal for aluminum cans for the Asian market. O'Neill had also sought to revitalize employee morale and ensure product quality by emphasizing safety as a primary concern, and by instituting a profit-sharing plan.

The results of O'Neill's tenure have been promising. Alcoa's combined profits for 1988 and 1989 more than doubled its total for the first eight years of the decade. Alcoa has been and remains a leader of the aluminum industry.

Principal Subsidiaries: Alcoa Brazil Holdings Co. (79%); Alcoa Aluminio S.A. (Brazil, 74.8%); Alcoa-Deutschland GmbH (Germany); Alcoa Generating Corp.; Alcoa International Holdings Co.; Alcoa Manufacturing (G.B.) Ltd. (U.K.); Alcoa Minerals of Jamaica, Inc.; Alcoa Nederland Finance B.V. (Netherlands); Alcoa Properties, Inc.; Alcoa Recycling Company, Inc.; Alcoa Securities Corp.; ALCOA/TRE, Inc.; Capsulas Metalics, S.A. (Spain, 80%); Grupo Aluminio, S.A. de C.V. (Mexico, 44%); Halco Inc. (27%); H.C. Industries, Inc.; H-C Industries, Inc. of Mississippi; Inversiones Alcoa, S.A. (Venezuela, 42%); Moralco Limited (Japan, 75%); Shibazaki Seisakusho Limited (Japan, 51%); The Stolle Corp.; Suriname Aluminum Co.; Tapoco, Inc; Texas Engineered Products Co., Inc.; Yadkin, Inc.

Further Reading: Schroeder, Michael, "The Quiet Coup at Alcoa," *Business Week,* June 27, 1988; Smith, George David, *From Monopoly to Competition: The Transformation of Alcoa, 1888–1986,* Cambridge, Cambridge University Press, 1988; Stewart, Thomas A., "A New Way to Wake Up a Giant," *Fortune,* October 22, 1990.

—Douglas Sun

AMAX INC.

200 Park Avenue
New York, New York 10166
U.S.A.
(212) 856-4200
Fax: (212) 856-5986

Public Company
Incorporated: 1887 as American Metal Co. Limited
Employees: 20,200
Sales: $3.79 billion
Stock Exchanges: New York Midwest Pacific Amsterdam
    Brussels Frankfurt London Paris Basel Geneva Zürich
    Toronto Vienna

AMAX is a mining, metals, and energy concern based in the United States with international operations and experience. Decades of diversification have made AMAX a leading natural resource company, although too much of that same diversification nearly brought the company to its knees. AMAX now concentrates on consolidation while working to maintain the spirit of acquisitional adventure, at home and abroad, that allowed it to supply products for two world wars, create new markets for its new discoveries, and stay at the cutting edge of foreign investment. AMAX was formed in 1957 with the merger of American Metal Co. Limited and its longtime associate, Climax Molybdenum Company.

AMAX evolved out of a combination of German bankers, New York traders, and Rocky Mountain miners. The company's earliest predecessor was incorporated as the American Metal Co. Limited (Amco) in 1887 when it was spun off from the Frankfurt-based Metallgesellschaft, a metals trading concern. In 1884 Metallgesellschaft sent Berthold Hochschild to New York to initiate a metal-trading business. There Hochschild quickly built Metallgesellschaft's U.S. metals business, due in great part to startlingly productive U.S. copper mines. Amco exported nickel and opened treatment plants for lead and copper. The fledgling company benefited from its German connections during this period, as Germany consumed one-third of U.S. copper exports. Following U.S. entry into World War I in 1917 the 49% German stake in Amco was seized by the U.S. Alien Property Custodian and resold, and all trade with Germany was halted. The huge profits generated by Allied military needs, however, more than compensated for the loss of Amco's German business. Use of the metal molybdenum also increased during the war. Molybdenum's special

properties as an alloying metal in steel were first recognized during the late 19th century. By 1916 demand for its properties, battle-tough hardness and elasticity, was great. Max Schott, head of Amco's Denver, Colorado, office, promptly enlisted the aid of Amco's leadership to buy a mine in Climax, Colorado, that would eventually produce 75% to 85% of the world's molybdenum. The Climax Molybdenum Company was formed in 1917 by a syndicate that included American Metal Co. Amco's share of Climax was 10%. Amco president, Manhattan banker Carl M. Loeb, became president of the new corporation.

By 1924 it was recognized that molybdenum, or "moly," was more than a wartime wonder. Its use as wire for vacuum tubes and incandescent lamps; in steel for machines, railroad and construction equipment, and automobiles; and its compounds in dyes and pharmaceuticals, caused *Scientific American* in March 1924 to label the nascent industry "one of the most important branches of American metallurgy."

During the interwar years Amco diversified into copper- and zinc-smelting plants. Also after the end of the war, Amco's German connection re-emerged. The Germans who formerly had owned 49% of Amco's stock were alleged to have paid a $441,000 bribe to the Alien Property Custodian, Thomas W. Miller, in a convoluted attempt to gain control of the $7 million that had resulted from the sale of the Germans's Amco stock in 1917. Miller turned the $7 million over to the German contingent and was subsequently indicted for his actions.

Meanwhile, Climax's sales of molybdenum soon took off. Climax's stock rose 116,900% from 1926 to 1936 and as a major Climax Molybdenum Company stockholder, Amco, too, enjoyed huge profits.

Copper once again came to the forefront of American Metal Co.'s concerns in the 1930s, with the overseas development of the Roan Antelope and Mufulira mines on the Rhodesia-Congo border. The Roan Antelope mines were one-third owned by Amco, and the Mufulira mines were two-thirds owned by Amco, through its majority ownership of Rhodesian Selection Trust, Ltd. African investment would prove to be among American Metal Co.'s most volatile, and profitable, ventures. In 1952 Amco's stake in these mines brought the company about $4 million.

In 1938, during the Soviet Union's war with Finland, Climax participated in a U.S. embargo of trade with Russia. World War II led to a shift in who mined moly and where it went. In 1939 Climax had halted all exports to the Axis powers. When the United States joined the war, in 1941, moly was mined for use in military products. The end of the war again meant a decrease in the need for molybdenum. Climax responded by advertising new uses for moly including its application as a greaseless multipurpose lubricant in powder form, and in the manufacture of aircraft engines. Climax also diversified into uranium. The company was thus able to keep profits on the rise.

American Metal Co. expanded its African holdings in 1946 by buying, with the Newmont Mining Corporation and Rhodesian Selection Trust, Ltd., the Tsumeb mine in South West Africa, now Namibia. The South African government that controlled South West Africa had seized the copper, lead, and zinc mine from its German owners during World War II. Thanks to modern mining techniques, hospitable South African tax breaks, and low wages, the Tsumeb Corporation, which owned the Tsumeb mine, managed to improve greatly on the production and profits of the previous German ownership.

In 1954 and 1955 racial problems at the Roan Antelope and Mufulira mines came to a head. Black African workers were struggling for the right to work in skilled positions alongside white workers. The white European labor union, making up only 12% of the work force at some mines, opposed a policy of racial equality. The union had successfully enforced a color bar during World War II, when the Allied need for copper was so great that the copper companies could not afford a strike. After the war, however, American Metal Co. and others recognized the benefits of a skilled indigenous work force, and, much to the displeasure of the white union and the powerful South African government, campaigned against the color bar. In early 1955, 18,000 of the 48,000 black Africans at work in the Rhodesian copper mines went on strike. By the end of the year, an agreement between the white union and the Rhodesian Selection Trust, in which Amco participated, brought down the color bar, but did not guarantee blacks equal pay for equal work.

Amco had been consistently augmenting its holdings in North America, as well. Southwest Potash Corporation—later AMAX Chemical Corporation and by 1991 AMAX Potash Corporation—and Heath Steele Mines Ltd., both wholly owned subsidiaries, were formed in 1948 and 1954, respectively. Heath was sold in 1979. AMAX Potash was slated to be sold in 1991. Amco also began developing oil properties in concert with Climax Molybdenum in 1950. In 1957, the two companies, via a stock swap, merged. Climax had been modernizing its facilities, and production of molybdenum had doubled from 1951 to 1955. Climax also had begun mining tungsten and vanadium, as well as developing its uranium interests. Climax president Arthur H. Bunker became chairman of the newly named American Metal Climax, Inc. (AMAX).

During the 1960s, AMAX's Southwest Potash company purchased a nitrate of potash and chlorine plant. AMAX itself delved further into tungsten with the 1961 acquisition of an interest in Canada Tungsten Mining Corporation, Ltd.; pursued lead in a joint lead-mine-smelter venture with the Homestake Mining Company that went on-line in 1969; and formed AMAX Petroleum Corporation in 1962, which the following year acquired the oil and gas properties of four separate petroleum companies.

Also in 1962, AMAX began work in aluminum by buying the Michigan-based Kawneer Company and Chicago's Apex Smelting Company. Further diversification into aluminum followed: a factory in West Germany was procured and Kawneer G.m.b.H.—now Kawneer Aluminum GmbH—was established to manufacture aluminum building materials for the European market. In California, Hunter Engineering Company was acquired in 1963, and added the production of aluminum sheet. In 1963 Bellingham, Washington, was the site of a 50%-owned plant to produce primary aluminum. Johnston Foil Company of St. Louis, Missouri, was acquired in 1966 and produced aluminum, tin, and lead foils.

In 1965 a new AMAX subsidiary was formed to hold the aluminum subsidiaries: the AMAX Aluminum Group. By 1990, it would be the third-largest U.S. aluminum company.

Of intrinsic importance to the company's future was its entrance into the coal market in 1969. Ayshire Collieries of Indi-

ana was purchased and would soon become a new subsidiary: AMAX Coal Company. Four years later, it was the fifth-largest U.S. coal producer. By 1980, it was number three.

The Climax mine continued to be AMAX's bread-and-butter property, still contributing half of the company's earnings at the end of the decade. A small molybdenum mine in Clear Creek County, Colorado, added to the profits, and, in 1965, company geologists discovered what many other prospectors had searched for, a moly reserve that rivaled Climax. The Henderson mine, as it became known, was about 40 miles northeast of Climax.

In 1969 Ian K. MacGregor, a former head of AMAX Aluminum Group, became chairman of American Metal Climax, Inc. MacGregor, noted for a managerial style based on consensus, launched a $2 billion expansion program in 1971.

AMAX continued to advance its international status with new holdings in Australia, the Netherlands, and the United Kingdom. The African holdings were affected by local governmental policy. Northern Rhodesia, the site of the Roan Antelope and Mufulira mines, was now independent Zambia; Rhodesian Selection Trust, of which AMAX had 42% ownership, was renamed Roan Selection Trust (RST); and the government of the British Empire had been replaced by nationalist leader Kenneth Kaunda. As early as 1962 Kaunda had stated that he opposed nationalization of the copper industry. As late as the spring of 1969, he was making the same assurances. A year later, however, under pressure from tribal militants, Kaunda took over 51% of RST. AMAX negotiated control of RST's remaining 49% in the mines, while Zambia would reimburse AMAX in bonds for the 51%. AMAX also negotiated a management contract that would allow it to continue to supervise day-to-day mine operations for 25 years. In 1991 AMAX owned 29.8% of RST.

In bordering Namibia, formerly South West Africa, however, AMAX was being accused of handling itself with less sensitivity. The Tsumeb mine was still a profitable source of copper, and the country was still conflict-ridden. The United Nations (U.N.) had, in 1966, repudiated South Africa's control of the country. South Africa ignored the U.N. resolution, as did AMAX, which continued paying taxes to South Africa instead of to the United Nation's Council for Namibia. AMAX forced opposition within Namibia, where workers went on strike in 1971, and at home, where descendants of Max Schott initiated a suit on behalf of AMAX stockholders that charged the company with paying taxes that were illegal in the eyes of the world.

Another big challenge for MacGregor was financing the multitude of businesses into which AMAX was buying. The company's long-term debt, $15 million in 1960, reached $500 million by 1973. Joint ventures were one solution. In hopes of getting debt-stalled projects off the ground, AMAX sold half its AMAX Aluminum Group to the Japanese Mitsui & Co. in 1973. AMAX Aluminum was subsequently renamed Alumax, Inc. MacGregor's active interest in U.S.-Japanese trade put AMAX once again on the cutting edge of international investment. The joint venture with Mitsui marked the biggest U.S.-Japanese venture to that point. An even larger infusion of cash came with the sale of 20% of AMAX to Standard Oil Company of California (Socal) in April 1975.

In 1974 American Metal Climax, Inc. officially adopted its nickname and became AMAX Inc. In 1977 MacGregor named

Pierre Gousseland AMAX's new CEO. MacGregor remained chairman of Alumax briefly, still pursuing heavy-spending policies. While the rest of the aluminum industry was cutting back production, Alumax raised some eyebrows by putting upward of $500 million into expansion. At the end of the 1970s Alumax was the fastest-growing aluminum company in the United States.

Standing in the way of AMAX's continued growth were numerous delays consequent to increasingly stringent environmental regulations. AMAX, however, displayed less reluctance to bow to environmental concerns than many of its competitors. The restoration of one AMAX mine site won a national environmental industry award. The Henderson mine featured nearly ten miles of underground railroad to preserve the integrity of the surface landscape. The contradictions between massive mining projects and the environment came to a head in the highly publicized battle over Crested Butte, Colorado. In 1978, after four years of exploratory drilling, AMAX announced it had found more moly in the tiny, low-key Rocky Mountain resort town of Crested Butte. Townspeople and environmental groups, led by the town's mayor, W. Mitchell, vociferously campaigned against the planned mine. The company lobbied with equal fervor to win the support of the town, even bringing in psychologists to study the social effects of the proposed mine. The battle remained a stalemate until a metals recession in 1982 led to a slump in moly prices that made AMAX postpone the project indefinitely.

Crested Butte's orebody was not the only moly that went unmined in the wake of the slump. In February 1981 AMAX had agreed to initiate a joint venture with Washington's Colville Confederated Tribes to mine a 900–million–ton moly reserve found on the tribe's reservation. The price of molybdenum oxide, however, dropped from $25.50 per pound to $4.25 per pound in just two years. The project was halted. AMAX, which had enjoyed sales increases of 43% in 1979 and a ninefold earnings increase over a ten-year period, found most of its businesses bottoming out. During the first nine months of 1981 profits were down 43%; the company's long-term debt was $1.2 billion; the following year would find it up to $1.7 billion.

The same spending spree that had made AMAX profits soar in the 1970s made them crash when the market dipped. Some stockholders blamed Gousseland; others felt he was the victim of MacGregor's debts. Even Gousseland's backers, however, had difficulty defending his rejection of Socal's 1981 merger offer. After failing in 1978 to acquire the 80% of AMAX it did not already own, Socal tried again three years later. It raised its offer from $57 to $78.50 a share, double the market value of AMAX's stock. Gousseland decided to remain independent. AMAX's stock plummeted from $68 at the height of merger speculation to $26.25 a year later.

Gousseland, however, kept buying, depending on silver and coal sales to lift AMAX's profits. Finally, in 1985, Gousseland started divesting, but following the 1985 shareholders meeting, amid shareholder accusations of mismanagement and unethical behavior, the board of directors stripped Gousseland of the titles of president and chief operating officer. These responsibilities were conferred on Allen Born, head of Placer

Development Ltd. and a former AMAX executive. A year later Born was also CEO.

Born settled on a five-pronged approach, emphasizing molybdenum, aluminum, coal, oil and gas, and gold. He bought back Mitsui's half of Alumax, developed the Sleeper Gold Mine in Nevada, and sold many other parts of the business. Sleeper turned out to be one of the lowest-cost gold producers in North America, and aluminum prices jumped in the year following the Alumax purchase. Born cut 4,300 people from the payroll and, as part of a general downsizing of moly operations, mothballed the Climax mine. Results were swift: the company, after years of losses, made $14 million in 1986, $146 million in 1987, and $740.9 million in 1988. Lower sales and a decrease in the price of aluminum reduced profits by almost 51% the following year.

The year 1990 found AMAX increasing holdings and enjoying the ensuing profits in gold; increasing profits in coal, although a May bid for Peabody Holding Company, the largest U.S. coal producer, fell through; increasing ventures and earnings in oil and natural gas exploration; continuing to downsize molybdenum production; and consolidating corporate structure—AMAX cut 40% of its corporate work force in June 1990. Aluminum prices continued low, but Alumax seemed to be riding out the storm and planned to double its aluminum capacity with a new aluminum smelter in Quebec.

Environmental problems continued to challenge AMAX as it entered the 1990s. Allen Born favored "regulation that legitimately protects public health and the environment without restricting our free-enterprise system. . . . And the costs of such controls should be weighed in terms of the benefits achieved not only in environmental improvement but also on the international competitiveness of United States industry," as reported by *American Metal Market,* September 29, 1988. This mixed view of environmental policy had mixed results: while AMAX's Belle Ayr mine was named the safest in the United States by the Mine Safety and Health Administration in 1987, Citizen Action, a private group based in Washington, rated AMAX among the top-ten offenders in the release of toxic industrial waste in 1988.

AMAX retains important elements of the two companies from which it sprang. Like Climax Molybdenum, AMAX is a mining company that owes most of its profits to one metal, but aluminum has replaced molybdenum in this regard. AMAX concentrates on downstream operations, creating aluminum products that will create markets. Like its predecessor American Metal Co. in Africa, AMAX is willing to explore potentially profitable operations in other countries.

Principal Subsidiaries: Alumax Inc.; Amax Coal Industries, Inc.; Amax Gold Inc. (87%); Amax Oil & Gas Inc.; Climax Metals Company.

Further Reading: "Element Number Forty-Two," *Fortune,* October 1936; "Can Coal Save Pierre Gousseland?," *Business Week,* October 18, 1982; Wilson, Arthur J., *The AMAX Century,* Greenwich, Connecticut, AMAX, 1987.

—David Isaacson

Anglo American Corporation of South Africa Limited

ANGLO AMERICAN CORPORATION OF SOUTH AFRICA LIMITED

44 Main Street
Johannesburg 2001
Republic of South Africa
(11) 638 9111
Fax: (11) 638 3221

Public Company
Incorporated: 1917
Employees: 280,000
Sales: R1.75 billion (US$682.93 million)
Stock Exchanges: Johannesburg London Paris Brussels Antwerp Frankfurt Zürich

Formed in 1917 as South Africa's first home-based public limited company, the Anglo American Corporation of South Africa (Anglo) has become a unique multinational group. It is the world's largest gold mining organization and, through its 34% share in De Beers Consolidated, has a major interest in the distribution of some 80% of the world's rough-diamond production. At the same time, it dominates South Africa's domestic economy, with interests in an estimated 1,300 South African companies. Its founding family, the Oppenheimers, has remained closely involved in the daily running of the group, although direct family control has become somewhat weakened. The group's corporate structure is based only in part on majority share ownership of subsidiary, associate, and other companies. Much of its control and influence lies in a complex web of connections based on family ties, friendships, and mutual business interests, although that interest is not infrequently accompanied by various forms of financial or commercial pressure.

The complexity of the connections is such that it is often difficult to distinguish between Anglo itself and the Anglo–De Beers group of companies or what might be referred to as the "Oppenheimer empire." The corporation has become in many respects a holding company, with various interests, such as gold mining, being the formal responsibility of a group of associate companies.

Politically, Anglo occupies a prominent position in southern Africa, not simply because of the extent of its economic involvement, but also because the Oppenheimers and the group itself have over the years criticized various aspects of the apartheid system. Many of apartheid's opponents have, however, attacked Anglo on the grounds that it has, in fact, profited greatly from the system, and in practice has done very little to change, or to mitigate, its effects.

The roots of Anglo's history can be traced back to 1902, when Ernest Oppenheimer arrived in Kimberley representing diamond merchants A. Dunkelsbuhler & Co., a member of the Diamond Syndicate, the cartel which attempted to maintain prices for South African diamonds by regulating production. Working for Dunkelsbuhler and on his own account, Oppenheimer also became interested in gold and coal mining, and in 1905 acquired the Consolidated Mines Selection Company (CMS), originally formed in 1887, with properties on the Far East Rand gold field. By 1916, when that field's true value was more widely appreciated, Oppenheimer/CMS was in a stronger position there than any of the other Transvaal mining-finance groups.

CMS had a large number of German shareholders and directors, causing it to be rather unpopular during World War I. Oppenheimer was a naturalized British subject who identified strongly throughout his life with South Africa's British, against its Afrikaner—Dutch origin—white community. Oppenheimer was nevertheless attacked because of his German origins. These points, coupled with the war-imposed restrictions on British capital exports, led him to seek U.S. financing to develop the field. An American connection in CMS introduced him to Herbert Hoover, through whom Newmont Mining Corporation, J.P. Morgan & Co., and Guaranty Trust became involved. With their support, Anglo was formed on December 25, 1917, with £2 million of authorized capital, half of which was issued. Various political reasons have been advanced for the decision to locate the company in South Africa rather than Britain, but the primary reason was to avoid the possibility of double taxation problems.

Anglo joined the ranks of the mining-finance groups characteristic of South African mining. Cecil Rhodes and other early financiers concentrated ownership of individual mines in the hands of a few holding companies that provided basic financial, administrative, and technical services for the mines they owned. This process of concentration had begun with the diamond mines, initially because some claimholders had insufficient capital to continue exploitation as workings went deeper, and ultimately because ownership concentration meant more efficient production control. Gold mining did not face oversupply problems, but given gold's fixed price and the highly speculative nature of mining investment, concentration of ownership meant more efficient use of technical and administrative resources. It also focused wealth and power in the hands of the relative few who sought it and were able to command the necessary capital. A system of interlocking directorships developed, creating a close, interdependent network. A relative latecomer to the field, Oppenheimer soon showed that he was more than a match for his predecessors, going on to absorb much of what they had built, and taking the concept of group control very much further.

With a strong base in gold and access to U.S. capital, Oppenheimer was able to challenge the Diamond Syndicate and De Beers, the dominant producer. He was helped by influential British and German connections, and by contacts between Anglo director H.C. Hull, former finance minister of the

Union of South Africa, and his former political colleague, Prime Minister Jan Smuts. Oppenheimer acquired most of the diamond mines in Namibia—then known as South West Africa—when the German companies operating them were encouraged to sell out to British interests. By the time De Beers and others learned of the negotiations, it was too late to prevent the sale to Anglo, and they initially welcomed the stability these acquisitions implied.

Anglo's Namibian mines were quickly brought under centralized control in Consolidated Diamond Mines of South West Africa (CDM). Initially CDM cooperated with the Diamond Syndicate, but in 1922 Anglo and Barnato Bros. reached a separate agreement for the purchase of the Belgian Congo's diamond output. In 1923 they acquired major interests in the Companhia de Diamantes de Angola, diamond mines in west Africa, and a share in British Guiana's diamond production. CDM subsequently became part of the De Beers group in 1930. More recently, CDM and Anglo have been cooperating with the Namibian government in developing the country's gold resources.

In 1924, Anglo was given an 8% share in the Diamond Syndicate. The purchasing agreements Anglo had with non–South African producers, including the right to take up all of CDM's production, gave Anglo apparent control over such producers. This control was more apparent than real, but led smaller South African producers to look to Anglo as an alternative to the syndicate, with whom they were increasingly dissatisfied, owing to the prices they were offered. The principle of selling all of South Africa's diamonds through a single channel was seriously weakened. Anglo was asked to leave the syndicate, and established a rival organization joined by Dunkelsbuhler; Barnato Bros.; and Johannesburg Consolidated Investments Ltd. (JCI), a group originally established by Barnato, and subsequently absorbed into Anglo's ambit.

The South African government was concerned about the implications for revenue of limited diamond production and a potentially disastrous price-cutting war between the two syndicates. The Diamond Control Act of 1925 gave the government sweeping powers to take over diamond production and distribution, and to prevent extreme behavior, namely price-cutting. As a member of Parliament, Oppenheimer had been able to introduce an amendment which required the government, if it enforced any provisions of the law, to give preference to South African–registered diamond purchasers; Anglo was the only one, while all the others were registered in London.

With Anglo continuing to grow financially stronger in the face of declining world diamond demand, the new syndicate was able to outbid the old in an offer to South African producers. On July 30, 1925, the new syndicate's offer was accepted and the old syndicate collapsed. Having gained effective control of distribution, Oppenheimer moved to control production as well. He became a De Beers director, while Anglo further strengthened its position by buying properties in two new South African fields and by consolidating and expanding its links with outside producers. Resistance was strong. Oppenheimer's bid, first made in May 1927, to take control of De Beers, only succeeded in December 1929 with the support of the Rothschilds, introduced through Morgan Grenfell. Oppenheimer became chairman of De Beers, clearing the way for the consolidation of production and distribution functions in one organization, the Diamond Corporation,

formed in February 1930 under De Beers's and Oppenheimer's effective control.

Negotiations with Sir Chester Beatty and Sir Edmund Davis, which had led to agreements for purchasing west African, Angolan, and Congolese diamonds, also led Oppenheimer to participate in the development of the Northern Rhodesian—now Zambian—copperbelt and that country's lead and zinc mines. Although these rich deposits had been known to exist for several decades at least, technological difficulties had prevented exploitation. Progress in the use of flotation techniques opened up new possibilities after World War I. Anglo acted as consulting engineers to several companies formed to exploit these deposits, bringing some of them together in Rhodesian Anglo American Limited (Rhoanglo), formed in December 1928. American capital was also involved in this venture, as it was in the other group operating on the copperbelt, Beatty's Rhodesian Selection Trust.

Oppenheimer wanted to combine Morgan Grenfell, Beatty, and others in a syndicate to develop the Mount Isa lead mine in northwest Queensland, Australia. Initial surveys were not promising, and Anglo withdrew. Anglo subsequently became involved in various Australian undertakings, ultimately establishing an Australian subsidiary. Overall, however, the group's direct involvement in Australia has been rather limited.

The 1930s saw further expansion of Anglo's holdings in the Far East Rand, in some cases in conjunction with New Consolidated Gold Fields. Anglo also began to move into the Orange Free State gold fields. The areas it acquired initially were generally unpromising. It was only by purchasing a stake in European and African Investments Ltd. in 1943, and subsequently acquiring full ownership by acquiring most of the shares of its parent company Lewis and Marks in 1945, that Anglo laid the foundation for its subsequent domination of Free State gold mining.

The 1930s and 1940s also saw the establishment of several subsidiary holding companies and the extension of the administration decentralization which characterizes Anglo. The precise extent to which effective Oppenheimer family control was maintained through E. Oppenheimer Sons, which absorbed A. Dunkelsbuhler & Co. in 1935, is unclear, but it is clear that personal influence remained strong. Anglo American Investment Trust (ANAMINT) took over Anglo's diamond interests in 1936, while West Rand Investment Trust (WRITS) took responsibility for gold mines in the Far West Rand field then opening up.

The decentralized structure was intended to allow, indeed to stimulate, on-the-spot decision making, and to enable ideas to filter up from the people most directly involved in day-to-day operations. It also makes it extremely difficult to trace the details of financial connections within the group as the constituent companies remain separately incorporated. Effective control, or at least coordination by central management, has not been sacrificed; information is constantly exchanged, both formally and informally. Interlocking directorships, and the power to appoint directors, were augmented by personal contacts based on friendship and, more importantly, by family connections. Members of the Oppenheimer family held important positions in many of the companies. On another level, Anglo recruits people considered potentially high-powered, including a substantial number of former Rhodes scholars.

As the group developed, acquiring or establishing companies in various fields, the decentralized structure remained.

Société Nationale Elf Aquitaine
Sun Company, Inc.
Texaco Inc.
Tonen Corporation
Total Compagnie Française des Pétroles S.A.
Türkiye Petrolleri Anonim Ortakliği
Ultramar PLC
Unocal Corporation
USX Corporation
The Williams Companies, Inc.
YPF Sociedad Anónima

PUBLISHING & PRINTING

Advance Publications Inc.
Arnoldo Mondadori Editor S.p.A.
Axel Springer Verlag AG
Bertelsmann AG
Cox Enterprises, Inc.
Dai Nippon Printing Co., Ltd.
Dow Jones & Company, Inc.
The Dun & Bradstreet Corporation
The E.W. Scripps Company
Elsevier NV
Gannett Co., Inc.
Groupe de la Cité
Hachette
Hallmark Cards, Inc.
Harcourt Brace Jovanovich, Inc.
The Hearst Corporation
Knight-Ridder, Inc.
Kodansha Ltd.
McGraw-Hill, Inc.
Maclean Hunter Limited
Maxwell Communication Corporation plc

Moore Corporation Limited
The New York Times Company
News Corporation Limited
Nihon Keizai Shimbun, Inc.
Pearson plc
R.R. Donnelley & Sons Company
The Reader's Digest Association, Inc.
Reed International P.L.C.
Reuters Holdings PLC
Simon & Schuster Inc.
Time Warner Inc.
The Times Mirror Company
Toppan Printing Co., Ltd.
Tribune Company
United Newspapers plc
The Washington Post Company

REAL ESTATE

Cheung Kong (Holdings) Limited
The Hammerson Property Investment and
    Development Corporation plc
Hongkong Land Holdings Limited
JMB Realty Corporation
Land Securities PLC
Lend Lease Corporation Limited
MEPC plc
Mitsubishi Estate Company, Limited
Mitsui Real Estate Development Co., Ltd.
New World Development Company Ltd.
Olympia & York Developments Ltd.
Slough Estates plc
Sumitomo Realty & Development Co., Ltd.
Tokyu Land Corporation

Some companies became subsidiaries, with at least 50% of their shares held by Anglo. In other cases control mechanisms were more flexible, but just as effective. These included holding a greater number of shares than anyone else; the control of essential supplies, markets, or technology; and various financial links.

Between 1945 and 1960, Anglo became the world's largest gold mining group, owing to expansion in the Orange Free State as well as the richer mines in the Far West Rand and Klerksdorp fields. Capital requirements were high, in part because the Free State gold deposits lay at considerably deeper levels than the Rand's. The 1946 African miners' strike, although rapidly repressed, was evidence of considerable upward pressure on African wages. Anglo decided to base Free State development on more capital-intensive techniques.

Building on its original financial concept, Anglo went further afield in its search for capital, securing about 27% of the £370 million raised from British sources, 23% from Switzerland, Germany, elsewhere in Europe, and the United States; and 43% from within the Anglo group itself. Most innovative, and significant in the longer term, was Anglo's drawing on surplus capital and non-mining savings generated within South Africa itself for 7%. The greater availability of domestic capital was a particularly important development after World War II, forming the basis for a measure of domestic financing of development which was associated in part with the expansion of Afrikaner, as opposed to British, capitalism. As internal savings increased over the following decades, they also laid the foundation for South Africa's ability to absorb a substantial portion of shares disposed of through disinvestment by foreign firms, although heavy reliance on foreign investment remained.

By 1960, Anglo had taken over the leadership of the gold mining industry. It was also making heavy inroads into the country's industrial and service sectors. The difficulties of importing manufactured goods from Europe during World War I had stimulated interest in domestic industrialization. Increasingly powerful Afrikaner politicians were wary of mining interests prepared to finance industrial development, partly because of an underlying antipathy to capitalists, and partly because of their foreign, particularly British, identity. This led in 1928 to the formation of the Iron and Steel Corporation (ISCOR) as a nationalized basis for the country's iron and steel industry. As post-World War II mining developments generated more capital, pressure to create domestic investment opportunities led to increased, though often reluctant, cooperation between the government and the private sector which was increasingly dominated by Anglo.

Social and political considerations also became important, particularly after 1948 when the rationale for the apartheid system included the expectation that industries would be established along the borders of homeland territories, providing employment for the Africans increasingly forced to inhabit them. While that hope was never fulfilled, antagonism between British and Afrikaners began to diminish in the face of a perceived common threat from black Africans, and by the growth of Afrikaner involvement in business. The importance of Oppenheimer's and Anglo's financial strength also diminished some of the specific antagonism toward them. Despite the fact that Harry Oppenheimer, who succeeded his father as head of the group after World War II, often criticized the apartheid regime, it was widely accepted that he did not intend

to attempt to destroy it, was prepared to work within it, and was pressing for changes that would improve the position of Africans primarily because it made good business sense.

In 1942 the government established the Industrial Development Corporation to promote and finance—through war taxes imposed on the mining industry—the expansion of ISCOR and a range of private industrial concerns. This was in some measure an attempt to create a counterweight to Anglo. Anglo's ability to draw on foreign capital sources, as well as foreign technology and other expertise, meant that the counterweight soon fell.

Initially, most of Anglo's industrial activity was directly related to mining. It had acquired African Explosive and Chemical Industries through its earlier investments in diamond interests. Its acquisition of Lewis and Marks brought it Union Steel and Vereeniging Refractories. In 1936 Anglo established Boart and Hard Metals, concerned with the use of industrial diamonds in mining and other drilling applications. In 1961 it created the Highveld Steel and Vanadium Corporation which, along with Steel Ceilings and Aluminum Works (SCAW), acquired in 1964, formed the basis of Anglo's control of South African specialized steel production, as well as creating a strong foundation for heavy engineering. The merging of three construction companies—Lewis Construction, James Thompson, and Anglo American Construction—into LTA Ltd. created a construction giant.

Diversification has also led Anglo into paper manufacturing—Mondi Paper Co., formed in 1967—and, through its 1960 takeover of Johannesburg Consolidated Investments, newspaper publishing—the Argus group and Times Media Limited. Building on motor vehicle distribution in the McCarthy group, it has moved—by combining with Chrysler and then Ford—into automobile production as well. In freight services, in conjunction with Safmarine, it led the growth of containerized shipping in the country. Retail stores and large property holdings have also been acquired.

An important merger involving Anglo in the 1970s was between Rand Mines and Thomas Barlow. Rand Mines was a mining group which had not acquired interests in the Far West Rand and Orange Free State as its older Witwatersrand mines reached depletion. Seriously ailing, it came under Anglo control in the 1960s, but Anglo did little to revive it. Thomas Barlow had been a small engineering supply importer, which by 1970 controlled more than 70 companies manufacturing a wide variety of products. Barlow acquired all Rand Mines's issued shares in 1971. Anglo held 10% of Barlow Rand's shares directly. By 1972, after reorganization and expansion, the merged group controlled 131 subsidiaries and associates in nine countries. Although executive control remains in Barlow family hands, Anglo is not without influence in the firm.

Anglo has created a vertically integrated organization whose power within the South African economy is widespread and probably comparable to that of other corporate giants in other smaller economies. It operates on a multinational level, but the greater part of its interests remain in South Africa. Considerable importance has been attached to coming to terms with the changes taking place there, in an effort to ensure the company's future under black majority rule.

At least as important as its industrial links is Anglo's involvement in the financial sector. In 1949, the South African government set up the National Finance Corporation (NFC) to receive large deposits—minimum £50,000—to be used for investment. Much of the NFC's funds came from and went back into mining. Anglo, for its part, formed a private merchant bank, Union Acceptances Ltd. (UAL) in 1955, supported by Lazard Freres and Barclays Bank. Offshoots and mergers followed, the most important mergers being those in the 1970s which brought UAL, Syfrets Trust Co., Old Mutual, and Nedbank together as Nedsual, providing commercial banking, insurance, and other financial services. Anglo went on to increase its holdings in insurance, and other financial-service institutions. Although Anglo disposed of its Nedbank holdings by the late 1970s, the merger with Nedbank was only one of the moves made by Anglo which contributed strongly to the destruction of the barrier between British and Afrikaner capital.

Anglo did not merely compete with Barclays. The 1970s expansion saw Anglo's holdings in Barclays National Bank reach 17.5% of the total shares issued. In 1986, when Barclays International was forced by public pressure to complete its disinvestment in South Africa, Anglo acquired the greater part of the shares divested.

On the international scene, using many of the channels it had opened to bring capital into South Africa, Anglo also expanded its own holdings, primarily in mining, throughout the world. In London, Charter Consolidated, a 1965 merger of the British South Africa Company, Central Mining, and CMS, gave Anglo considerable investment opportunities in Africa, Europe, and Australasia.

Although diamonds replaced gold as Anglo's single most important source of profit in the 1980s, and despite wide-ranging diversification, gold has remained at the heart of the group's activities. A substantial holding in the U.S. precious metals refiners Engelhard Corporation, along with a stake in the U.K.'s Johnson Matthey, has given Anglo access to important sources of highly profitable information about the world's gold trade.

Anglo's share in Engelhard is held by its subsidiary Minerals and Resources Corporation (Minorco), officially renamed Minorco in 1974. Minorco grew out of Rhoanglo. It was through Minorco that Anglo attempted to take over Consolidated Gold Fields (Consgold) in 1988. Anglo and Consgold had been closely associated—directly and indirectly—in many enterprises over the years, but relations between them were based at least as much on rivalry as on common interest, and the attempted takeover came as no surprise. Anglo acquired about 25% of Consgold. This attempt came up against U.S. antitrust legislation and Consgold was bought by Hanson Trust instead.

Anglo is at the center of political controversy in South Africa, not merely because of its economic strength, but because the Oppenheimers and the group itself have taken a public stand on the apartheid question. Politically active Ernest Oppenheimer and his son Harry, were not in favor of black majority rule, but they did press for relaxation of certain aspects of the apartheid regime. Not surprisingly, they were particularly interested in decreasing dependence on migrant labor. A more settled, stable labor force was considered more productive and efficient. Although some stabilization of labor did occur, relatively little could be done in the face of government opposition. In 1987, along with some other mining groups, Anglo began to replace migrant workers' hostels with low-cost family accommodation. Like many other changes, this was seen by many as too little too late, and by others as merely a new method of social control. Anglo was not prepared to raise African wages sufficiently to allow workers effective freedom of housing choice.

In 1985, Anglo's chairman, Gavin Relly, and other senior Anglo personnel met representatives of the African National Congress (ANC) in exile. In April 1990 Anglo's Scenario Planning Team published proposals for South Africa's constitutional development. These placed great emphasis on federalism and devolution of power. More dispersed state power, Anglo argues, will facilitate accommodation of divergent interest groups. This, along with a massive image-building campaign in the U.K. press is part of Anglo's campaign to remain a major economic force in the country as its political structure changes inexorably.

Anglo's critics, while acknowledging that Anglo has been more consistently liberal than other mining groups, maintain that Anglo is merely bowing to the strongest wind of the moment. Black workers who have always been given wage increases substantially lower than demanded, and whose living standards are much lower than those of their white co-workers, are skeptical of what their future with Anglo holds.

Anglo is clearly facing a difficult time. Fluctuating gold prices and increased production costs are only the beginning. De Beers Consolidated has moved its foreign assets to Switzerland, but most of the rest of the greater Anglo group cannot do so, and must attempt to secure its future in South Africa, under whatever system the black majority ultimately creates.

Principal Subsidiaries: Abalyn Investment Holdings; African and European Investment Company; Calince Investment Holdings; Centesis Investment Holdings; Dalaunay; Dalaunay Two; Ixion Investment Holdings; Lagen Investment Holdings; Lodestone Holdings; Namitor Investment Holdings; New Era Consolidated; Rand American Investments; Rand Selection Corporation; Randsel Investments; Runcorn Holdings; South African Mines Selection; South African Township, Mining and Finance Corporation; Ammereosa Land and Estates; Anglo American Property Services.

Further Reading: Gregory, Theodore, *Ernest Oppenheimer and the Economic Development of Southern Africa,* Cape Town, Oxford University Press, 1962; Jessop, Edward, *Ernest Oppenheimer: A Study in Power,* London, Rex Collings, 1979; Innes, Duncan, *Anglo American and the Rise of Modern South Africa,* London, Heinemann Educational Books, 1984; Pallister, David, Sarah Stewart, and Ian Lepper, *South Africa Inc.— The Oppenheimer Empire,* London, Simon & Schuster, 1987.

—Simon Katzenellenbogen

ARBED S.A.

Avenue de la Liberté 19
L-2930
Luxembourg
(352) 47 92-1
Fax: (352) 47 92-26 75

Public Company
Incorporated: 1882 as Société Anonyme des Hauts Fourneaux
et Forges de Dudelange
Employees: 54,000
Sales: LuxFr209.00 billion (US$6.77 billion)
Stock Exchanges: Luxembourg Brussels Paris Frankfurt
Amsterdam London

ARBED S.A., based in the Grand Duchy of Luxembourg, heads an international group of 430 companies engaged in the integrated production of iron and steel from the mining process to the production of highly sophisticated finished goods. It can be seen as both product and agent of the economic revolution that in approximately the last 100 years has transformed the small agricultural Luxembourg into a major industrial power with its activities centered on the great iron- and steel-producing complexes in the southwest of the country. Three-quarters of the group's turnover is accounted for by steel production and related activities. ARBED is the Grand Duchy's largest exporter and industrial employer, and the fifth largest iron- and steel-producing group in Europe, with an annual output of 7–7.5 million tons. It counts among the 13 leading producers in the world's market-economy countries.

Iron has a long history in the area that now constitutes the Grand Duchy of Luxembourg. It was mined by the Celts, then later by the Romans, not only from alluvial deposits in the valleys of the rivers Eisch and Alzette but also from oolitic ore, found in the southwest of the region—*minette,* low in iron content and high in phosphorus, whose rediscovery in the mid–19th century gave an impetus to the modern industry and decided its location. Traces have been found in the canton of Esch of underground mining by the Romans, who made charcoal from the wood of local forests to smelt the ore in primitive furnaces, obtaining the metal they then fashioned into arms and armor. After the Germanic invasions the recovery of *minette,* for which underground mining skills were needed, died out. Iron production based on alluvial ore persisted in the region as a domestic craft, providing household and farm implements during the succeeding centuries as the region slowly

and intermittently evolved, despite periods of anarchy, civil war, plague, misrule, and invasion, toward a sense of identity. Smelting plants and forges were set up near sources of charcoal and water power, the first very small-scale blast furnace making its appearance in the region in 1564.

Iron- and steel-making emerged on an industrial scale in the middle of the 19th century, in the region that had been the Grand Duchy since 1815. It is there that the origins of ARBED lie, although the company itself did not come into being until 1911. When the years of adversity came to an end, there were Luxembourgers ready to seize the country's chance at prosperity—business men with the drive and confidence to adapt Luxembourg's natural, human, and technological resources to the huge but inconstant market for iron and steel opening up at home and especially abroad, as industrialization gathered pace.

Several circumstances converged to favor an upswing in iron and, increasingly, in steel production: the expanding use of the steam engine which allowed greater freedom in siting and a larger scale of operations; the rediscovery in south Luxembourg of *minette* deposits that would not be exhausted until 1981; the construction of railway lines linking Luxembourg with the European systems; Luxembourg's entry in 1842 into the German customs union, the *Zollverein;* and the invention in 1878 by S.G. Thomas and P. Gilchrist of the Thomas-Gilchrist—or Thomas, or basic Bessemer—process, an improvement of the Bessemer converter, permitting elimination of the phosphorus that had hitherto presented problems in the smelting of the phosphoric *minette* ores of Luxembourg and Lorraine. When, following lengthy initiatives by Emile Mayrisch and Gaston Barbanson, Aciéries Réunies de Burbach-Eich-Dudelange was formed in 1911, it was on foundations laid earlier by a number of iron and steel manufacturers. The latter were mainly Luxembourgers, linked by several family connections as well as by business interests. They had built up three companies, whose resources were now to be combined and directed to modern large-scale production of steel and steel products centered on Esch-Schifflange.

The first of the three companies, already operating and cooperating in close proximity to each other in the southwest of the Grand Duchy and in nearby Germany and Lorraine, was the Forges d'Eich—Le Gallais, Metz et Cie, founded in 1838. It had originated in 1838 when three brothers, Charles, Norbert, and Auguste Metz, who played major roles in Luxembourg industry, politics, and journalism, set up a limited partnership, Auguste Metz et Cie, known since 1865 as the Société des Forges d'Eich—Metz et Cie. In 1879 this company had acquired a license to use the Thomas-Gilchrist dephosphorization process. Its main works were at Dommeldange and Esch-Schifflange, the latter a joint venture started in 1871 by Norbert Metz and Victor Tesch, his cousin by marriage.

The second company, Société Anonyme des Mines du Luxembourg et des Forges de Sarrebruck, had been created in 1856 by Victor Tesch and other Belgians of Luxembourg origin. Its coke ovens and blast furnaces were at Burbach in Germany, northeast of Saarbrücken. The third company, the Société Anonyme des Hauts Fourneaux et Forges de Dudelange, had been established in 1882 by the first two companies in order to exploit the Thomas-Gilchrist process in a steel plant at Dudelange, where the first charge of Thomas steel was blown in 1886. In 1911 the first two companies were dissolved and their assets transferred to the third, whose title was changed to Aciéries Réunies de Burbach-Eich-Dudelange S.A. (ARBED).

By 1911 the first company's original Eich works were of minor importance. At Esch-Schifflange it had four blast furnaces, two of them belonging to the Société des Mines du Luxembourg et de Sarrebruck, and its works at Dommeldange had three blast furnaces and four electric furnaces. The second company's Burbach plant had eight blast furnaces, a steel works, and rolling mills. The third company's property at Dudelange comprised six blast furnaces, a steel works, and rolling mills. All three constituent companies also brought with them the iron ore mining concessions they held in Luxembourg and Lorraine. Between them the companies produced cast iron and Thomas steel; laminated items—semi-finished goods; and sections, girders, rails and flat bars. With Emile Mayrisch, managing director from 1897 of the Société des Mines du Luxembourg et des Forges de Sarrebruck, as overall technical director of ARBED, the new company proceeded rapidly with its plans for modernization, vertical integration, and expansion.

In 1912 ARBED's annual output of crude steel was 824.5 thousand tons. Old furnaces, blowers, and other installations were being refurbished or replaced, and new, more efficient equipment was being brought in, notably equipment which utilized waste gases from smelting to power other processes further down the line. In 1913 new installations, including three blast furnaces, started up at the company's Esch-Schifflange and Esch-Belval works.

In April of the same year ARBED protected its coke supplies by forming a contractual association with the Eschweiler collieries—Eschweiler Bergwerks-Verein AG (EBV)—near Aachen, Germany. This move was in keeping with a policy of cooperation with other European firms, designed to ensure ARBED's supplies of raw materials—ore, coal, and coke—as well as to find customers for its crude, semi-finished, and finished products and to extend its product range. In 1913 ARBED joined with a Belgian cement-making firm to start a new company, later to become the Société Anonyme des Ciments Luxembourgeois, for their mutual advantage; in exchange for a site near the Esch-Schifflange works, together with a supply of slag and electric current, ARBED would receive cement for its own use at a reduced price.

In 1919, together with the French company Schneider et Cie, ARBED took over all the Luxembourgian and Lorraine iron mines, iron and steel works, including Belval, and wire-drawing works that had belonged before the war to the German company Rhein-Elbe Gelsenkirchener Bergwerks A.G., and set up two linked companies, the Société Métallurgique and the Société Minière des Terres Rouges, of which the first, the Société Métallurgique des Terres Rouges—at Esch-Belval—was to be absorbed in 1937 by ARBED, who acquired a majority holding in the second, the Société Minière des Terres Rouges, in 1954.

ARBED was recovering from the setback to its ambitions suffered during World War I. As so often over the centuries, Luxembourg's geographical location had placed it between the hammer and the anvil of contending foreign powers. In spite of its neutral status, guaranteed since 1867, it was invaded by German troops as soon as war broke out, and occupied for the duration. The Grand Duchy has historic, linguistic, and com-

mercial affinities with Belgium and France and with Germany, but the German invasion settled the question of where loyalties should lie in 1914. ARBED's situation was made particularly painful by its ownership of works—Burbach and Hostenbach—in enemy territory. Company policy was to lend as little comfort as possible to the occupying power, while safeguarding as far as possible the survival and future prospects of ARBED and its employees. In the Grand Duchy, after a brief initial shutdown, which the company had offered to prolong if the Luxembourgian government wished, production was resumed by the blast furnaces—four at Dudelange, one at Esch-Schifflange, and one at Dommeldange. Production followed in the steelworks and rolling mills of Dudelange and Esch-Schifflange and in the electric steelworks at Dommeldange. There were shortages of raw materials—fuel, manganese, and lubricants—and of staff, as well as of food. At one point, in 1917, the Germans occupied the factories in an effort to put down a protest strike by hungry workers. The Saar works, Burbach and Hostenbach, were also kept in operation while hostilities lasted, in spite of reduced supplies and the progressive call-up of staff to the German army. Over the war period, in spite of the new installations, ARBED's total monthly steel output dropped from nearly 87,000 tons in July 1914 to just under 50,000 tons in October 1918.

Undercapacity persisted after the war, with continuing fuel and transport problems, plus commercial difficulties arising from Luxembourg's economic isolation, which ended in 1922 with the treaty of economic union with Belgium. Long-term plans proceeded, including the linkage of all the plants located at Esch-sur-Alzette into one huge complex served by its own railway, completed in 1927; by gas-pipes; and by electric cables.

In 1920 ARBED set up a company, the Comptoir Métallurgique Luxembourgeois (COLUMETA), to deal with the sales of its wide range of products. This branch of the group's activities was to flourish and multiply worldwide, with most of the company's sales directed abroad. In 1976 the name COLUMETA was changed to TradeARBED; this company has foreign subsidiaries in 50 foreign countries and in every continent.

Also in 1920, ARBED acquired holdings in the German firm of Felten & Guilleaume, makers of wires, cables, and electrical apparatus; TAMET (Argentina), which produced metal tubes, frames, and bolts; Paul Wurth (Luxembourg) metal constructions; and the Helchteren-Zolder collieries in Belgium. In 1922 it bought a holding in the Belgian nail-making and wire-drawing Clouterie et Tréfilerie des Flandres.

After the death in a motor accident of Emile Mayrisch in 1928, the inter-war technical development of the group's mines and factories was led by Aloyse Meyer. The iron mines in Luxembourg and Lorraine were mechanized and modernized. At the steel works, major additions and improvements were made to installations and processes, with constant adjustments to methods of reducing impurities that were present in the ores or were introduced at the manufacturing stage. Production rose steeply, with peaks in 1929 and 1937. Meanwhile the company continued to provide for the welfare of its employees as it had from the beginning, through its own social services—including training, insurance, pensions, bonuses, and help with housing. Responsibility for some of these services has, of course, been taken over gradually by the state, pensions, for example, in 1931, and family allowances in 1947.

In World War II, the Grand Duchy was occupied again, first by German troops, then from August 1940 to September 1944 by Nazi officials. Based on its World War I experience, ARBED had earlier moved out key officials and documents to places of safety, and had obtained legal powers to arrange for its operations to be directed from abroad. Once more production was prudently maintained, at a reduced level, by those who had to stay, working in the face of prolonged hardships and shortages. Output, diminished drastically during the war, ceased entirely for 11 months after the occupation and recovered only slowly from the fuel shortage and transport difficulties that were part of the aftermath of conflict. It was not until 1951 that ARBED reached full capacity once more and achieved production figures—nearly two million tons—that were higher that those of the previous peak years 1929 and 1937.

In the 1950s and 1960s ARBED continued its policy of development and integration within the group. The group expanded through acquisitions and participations at home and abroad—in Europe and South America—aimed at securing its supplies and diversifying its steel production. It continued moving downstream in advance of some of its larger and better-known European competitors.

In 1953 it absorbed the Clouterie et Tréfilerie des Flandres and in the following year acquired a majority holding in the Société Minière des Terres Rouges. In 1962 it was a major participant in the setting-up of the Sidérurgie Maritime company (SIDMAR) to construct an important complex, with integrated steelworks and marine terminal, on the Belgian coast.

In 1965 ARBED acquired a major holding in the Société Anonyme des Hauts Fourneaux et Aciéries de Differdange-St. Ingbert-Rumelange (HADIR), a consortium of Luxembourgian, French, and Belgian companies that had been developing since 1896. The consortium was absorbed completely by ARBED in 1967. HADIR's Differdange works augmented ARBED's Esch complex. In 1911 Differdange had begun to roll Grey beams. In 1959 ARBED's Dudelange works had started producing steel using the LD-AC (Linz-Donavitz-ARBED-Centre) process. ARBED's wire-works were grouped in 1968 to form a new company, ARBED-Felten & Guilleaume Tréfileries Réunies, which, with other later wire-making acquisitions, was to become TrefilARBED in 1974. The 1970s saw the extension of ARBED's activities in several other directions: refractory products; reinforcing wires for car tires; mining operations in Brazil, the United States, and Korea; and mechanical engineering and steel construction. At the end of the 1970s ARBED accounted for a quarter of the Grand Duchy's gross national product. Two important structural measures taken in advance of the world steel crisis of the mid-1970s and 1980s were the establishment of the ARBED Research Centre in 1971 and of ARBED Finance S.A. in 1972, a holding company designed to provide finance for the group. The acronym ARBED S.A. was adopted in 1978 as the company's official name.

In 1975 the Luxembourgian economy went into a long recession caused by many factors: the continuing effects of the 1973 world oil crisis; strengthening foreign competition; inflation; rising wages; fluctuating foreign currencies; and depletion of the country's iron ore. ARBED's crisis lasted until 1984, and ever since then ARBED, like all other European steelmakers, has had to take account of falling demand for steel, increasing use of plastics, growing competition from the developing world, uncertainties about the new eastern European markets, and currency fluctuations.

In the 1970s and 1980s overcapacity and financial losses called for vigorous adaptation—organizational, financial, and technological. Competitiveness had to be improved. Over the crisis period ARBED economized by reducing its debts, increasing its share capital, and shedding, without sackings, more than half of its work force, some being redeployed in new industries, others taking the early retirement, at 57 years of age, imposed on steelworkers by the government in 1980.

The company pursued a policy of rationalization. In 1984 the blast furnaces, the steelmaking facilities, and the hot rolling mill at Dudelange closed down. At the same time ARBED needed to invest in new equipment and implement the results of technological research. In 1980 the first continuous caster was commissioned at Esch-Schifflange, and in 1981 the first continuous annealing line went into service at SIDMAR's plant in Ghent.

For a time ARBED was helped by the European Economic Community steel quota system. The Luxembourg government provided some financial support on the restricted scale possible for a small country. When by 1983 ARBED could see the tide beginning to turn again, it was largely the result of the group's own efforts under the chairmanship of Emmanuel Tesch—a descendant of Victor Tesch, one of ARBED's founders. By the end of its boom year, 1989, helped by the peak in the post-crisis upturn of the European steel market, ARBED was able to pay its shareholders their first dividend since 1975.

In the first years of the 1980s the Luxembourgian steel industry had moved back to closer cooperation with Belgium. In 1987 ARBED acquired a 3% share in the Société Générale de Belgique. This holding company holds 25% of ARBED's shares while the government of Luxembourg holds 32%.

In 1983 ARBED began to detach itself from its group holdings in German steel companies. In 1988 it ended a 75-year association with its traditional supplier of metallurgical coke when Eschweiler Bergwerks-Verein (EBV) joined Ruhrkohle AG. Ruhrkohle, however, is contracted to provide the same service until the beginning of the next century.

In the boom year 1989, ARBED decided to double the capacities of the steel processing works at Galvalange, which produces goods for the construction industry—roofing, flashing, fencing—and for the car and goods vehicle industry—exhaust parts, cabs and trailers—as well as garden tools and parts for domestic appliances such as microwave ovens, refrigerators, and air-conditioners. In 1990, acting with the Japanese firm Furukawa Electric, ARBED acquired Yates Circuit Foil (USA), which specializes in copper foil and electronic circuits.

Negotiations began in the summer of 1990 between ARBED and the large Belgian steel producer, Cockerill Sambre, for a partial merger that would pool most of the flat steel–making capacity of Cockerill Sambre's two plants in Wallonia and of ARBED's Sidmar subsidiary in Flanders. The plan fell through at the end of the year, partly because of regional differences between Flanders and Wallonia over possible closures. However, other cooperative plans aimed at economies of scale and reduction of market overlap are under consideration.

The parent company ARBED S.A.'s main divisions are the works at Esch-Belval, Esch-Schifflange, Differdange, and Dudelange, all in the southwest of the Grand Duchy, not far from ARBED's head offices in Luxembourg city and served by the ARBED Research Centre at Esch-sur-Alzette. Esch-Belval, employing 3,800 people, is the sole ironmaking center for Luxembourg's steel industry, and its two blast furnaces supply the hot-metal requirements of ARBED S.A.'s three steelworks, Esch-Schifflange, Esch-Belval, and Differdange. Since 1981, when the grand duchy's own *minette* mines became exhausted, Esch-Belval's siliceous and calcareous *minette* ores have come from ARBED's French mines division. In addition to its blast furnaces, producing 8,000 tons of iron and 4,000 tons of slag daily, Esch-Belval has a power station, steelworks, and rolling mills that include two blooming mills, a billet mill, and four finishing trains.

Esch-Schifflange, with 1,600 employees, and with steel works whose two 95 ton converters use the LBE top-blowing oxygen process, continuous casting machines, and rolling mills, specializes in high-quality wire rod and merchant bars. Differdange, with 2,400 employees, and with LDAC/LBE steelworks, rolling mills, a Grey mill, and a tube mill, specializes in producing large and tailor-made Grey beams as well as sheet piles and tubes. At Dudelange, with a work force of 700, the installations comprise a new CVC cold-rolling mill that processes coils supplied by the Belgian group Cockerill Sambre and by Sidmar, plus a slitting unit, a galvanizing unit, and a foundry producing ingot moulds.

Principal Subsidiaries: Métallurgique et Minière de Rodange-Athus S.A. (MMRA) (45%); SIDMAR S.A. (Belgium, 51%); ALZ N.V. (Belgium, 75%); Companhia Siderúrgica Belgo-Mineira S.A. (Brazil, 20.2%); TradeARBED Luxembourg S.A.; TradeARBED Participations S.à r.l.; Trefil-ARBED S.A.; Hein, Lehmann AG (Germany); Paul Wurth S.A. (47.87%); MecanARBED Dommeldange, S.à r.l.; Galvalange S.à r.l. (50%); ESP (Belgium, 99.99%); COGIFER A.A. (France, 35.27%); Ciments Luxembourgeois S.A. (50.49%).

Further Reading: Chomé, Félix, ed., *Un Demi-Siècle d'Histoire industrielle 1911–1964,* Luxembourg, ARBED Archives [n.d.]; Newcomer, James, *The Grand Duchy of Luxembourg,* Lanham, Maryland, University Press of America, 1984.

—Olive Classe

ARMCO INC.

300 Interpace Parkway
Parsippany, New Jersey 07054
U.S.A.
(201) 316-5200

Public Company
Incorporated: 1917 as The American Rolling Mill Company
Employees: 9,800
Sales: $1.73 billion
Stock Exchange: New York

Armco Inc. is a worldwide producer of stainless, electrical, and carbon steel products. Through several joint ventures in the United States and abroad, Armco produces oil-field machinery and coated, high-strength, porcelain-enameled steel and low-carbon flat rolled steel. In 1991 the company was in the process of selling Armco Financial Services Group (AFSG), its financial-services division, which specializes in providing insurance services.

Armco was founded in 1900 by George M. Verity as the American Rolling Mill Company. Verity was at the time in the roofing business in Cincinnati, Ohio. The chaotic conditions existing in the emerging U.S. steel industry created a supply problem for Verity's small roofing enterprise, and Armco originally was conceived as an attempt to solve Verity's own sheet-metal supply problems. American Rolling Mill's first plant was opened in Middletown, Ohio, in 1900 and was the first steel plant to consolidate all the steps necessary to produce, roll, galvanize, corrugate, and fabricate metal sheets into specific finished products. The nation's first integrated steel-production plant started with 35 stockholders and a total of 325 employees.

The growth of the rolled steel industry was fueled by pressure from the automobile business. The need for long, wide sheets of metal to finally construct an all-steel car provided incentive to improve the milling processes used at the time. In the years following the turn of the century there was an ample supply of rolled metal sheets. Their size and quality, however, were not acceptable to automobile makers. There was a lack of uniformity in sheet thickness, and the steel had unacceptable surface defects. The deficiencies were the result of hand-sheet mills. As late as 1926 there were approximately 1,200 such mills in the United States, each producing a small amount of product of variable quality. The need for a better rolling process was apparent.

In 1904 John Butler Tytus was hired as a "spare hand" by Armco's superintendent, Charles Hook. Tytus, son of a well-to-do Middletown family and a Yale University graduate was fascinated with the archaic milling process as it existed. Within two-and-a-half years, Tytus rose through the ranks of the company and became superintendent of American Rolling Mill's Zanesville, Ohio, plant. Tytus believed that the same rolling process that was used in the manufacture of paper stock—his family was in the paper-milling business—could be modified and the same milling principles applied to the production of rolled metal sheets.

World War I afforded Tytus the opportunity to test his theories. During the war American Rolling Mill, like most steel operations in the United States, was concentrating on heavy-steel manufacturing that employed forging processes. The nation's sheet mills were mostly standing idle. During the war years Tytus was given permission to use one of the rolling mills as a laboratory. In 1921 American Rolling Mill purchased the closed plant owned by the Ashland Iron and Mining Company of Ashland, Kentucky. Under a cloak of secrecy, Tytus, his blue prints, and about 100 of the company's most skilled workers converged on the newly purchased plant and began to construct an experimental facility. After three years of trial and error, a completed wide-sheet mill was finally operational. The mill was capable of producing milled sheets up to 36 inches in width and as thin as 0.065 inch.

The process was far from perfect. The Tytus mill had some problems. The metal sheets slipped from side to side as they went through the milling process, and there were difficulties in maintaining the proper pressure between the rollers. The Columbia Steel Company solved these problems in 1926 with the development of a mill similar to the Tytus design. Named the Butler mill, it became the prototype of the modern continuous wide hot strip mill. American Rolling Mill and Columbia Steel soon were confronted with the problem of conflicting patents which was resolved with American Rolling Mill Company's purchase of Columbia Steel in 1930. The acquisition left American Rolling Mill with complete control of all basic patents on the continuous wide hot strip mill. The company opted to share the process with the rest of the steel industry by licensing the use of its patents, and over the following ten years, an estimated $500 million was invested in the construction of more than 25 continuous wide strip mills.

In 1940 Charles Hook who was then president, took American Rolling Mill one step further with the development of the cold reduction mill. This process produced a smooth, polished surface on the steel with just a slight reduction in its thickness. The development of the new milling systems not only gave a superior product but increased production and lowered operating costs for the producers. As a result, American Rolling Mill was able to lower its price for iron and steel sheets from $110.15 per ton in 1923 to $57.31 per ton in 1939. Lower steel costs helped fuel the industrialized world's economies as well as American Rolling Mill's growth during those years. The company changed its name to Armco Steel Corporation in 1948. Between 1925 and 1950, more than 500 million tons of thin flat steel was absorbed by the U.S. economy. The development of modern conveniences such as automatic washing machines, and steam irons were manufactured by machines that were supplied with the unending flow of sheet metal produced by U.S. steel manufacturers. During the 1950s, 1960s, and

1970s, many other steel-fabricating and industrial products were added to the company's steel-based business.

Armco Steel entered into the coal business with the acquisition of Princess Dorothy Coal Company of West Virginia in 1954. Several other coal companies were purchased following Princess Dorothy. In 1958 Armco acquired National Supply Company, the world's largest producer of oil- and gas-well drilling machinery and equipment. Overall, Armco acquired or bought considerable interest in more than 24 heavy-industry companies by the end of 1979. The company expanded overseas by moving its corrugated pipe, tubing, and steel fabricating technologies to developing countries such as Spain and Brazil.

In 1965 C. William Verity Jr., grandson of Armco Steel's founder, became the company's president and CEO. He assumed leadership of the company at a time when the steel industry was facing increased foreign competition, slower growth, and a decline in profits. The company's new president chose to remain competitive in the steel business while diversifying into enterprises that he felt would continue to prosper even during the potential cyclical downturns that were being projected for the steel business.

Armco expanded aggressively into oil-well equipment and oil exploration, building products, strategic metals, and financial services. At first the moves into these new business areas seemed to pay off. Between 1976 and 1981, the company prospered through two recessions and boosted its net income by more than 135% to $295 million based on almost $7 billion in sales. During these years, Verity won high praise by leading Armco into trade with both the Soviet Union and China. In 1978 Armco Steel Corporation again changed its name, to Armco Inc.

The accelerated growth of the company into new areas of business was not without its problems. Armco's upper management was composed of steel people, who, isolated in the Middletown, Ohio, steel community often came into conflict with lower divisional managers. Verity's proposed solution to this problem was to decentralize, moving the decision-making process to 15 separate business units.

During 1982 and the first nine months of 1983, Armco showed losses totaling over $970 million. Corporate restructuring included the closing of steel mills in Kansas City, Missouri; Ashland, Kentucky; and Middletown, Ohio. The company was forced to sell coal properties and an oil- and gas-producing property, Strata Energy, Inc. Circumstances did not improve much in 1984. Armco reported a loss of $295 million on $4.5 billion in sales. The company was forced to eliminate 250 corporate staff positions. During the period from 1981 to 1988, Armco sold or divested enterprises both in the United States and abroad.

The company began a slow process of greatly reducing its size. The closing of several of its steel mills, and the sale of coal and oil properties—difficult to sell because of the lower energy costs and depressed circumstances in the U.S. energy exploration business—was followed by an attempt to sell off the company's extensive finance, leasing, and insurance businesses.

Many observers felt that Armco's expansion into insurance and finance accounted for most of the company's financial woes. Until 1977 its involvements in financial services had been limited to ownership of the Bellefonte Insurance Company and a leasing and finance operation, Armco-Boothe Cor-

poration. With the formation of Armco Financial Services Corporation in 1977, the company became heavily involved in the acquisition of insurance, reinsurance, and finance businesses. Verity believed that there was great potential for Armco in insurance. Bellefonte had been a pioneer in the self-insurance field and had established a profitable record by providing customers outside of Armco with coverage.

Between 1977 and 1981, Armco acquired seven insurance organizations in the United States and abroad. Spearheaded by Bellefonte, which specialized in self-insurance, high-risk policies were sold at low premiums to insurers seeking to spread the risk of their own existing policies. Armco went so far as to help insure the Libyan navy. Many of the policies written had exposure lasting up to 20 years for Armco. Eagerness to grow in the insurance field resulted in AFSG taking on many inordinately risky policies, reportedly due to the naivete of its executives. In the steel business it is easy to track production costs and adjust prices to guarantee profits. An insurance company's profitability cannot be estimated until all claims against the company come due. Armco's aggressive entrance into the insurance business initially showed high profits. This picture did not last long. As early as 1979 claims against Armco-held policies began pouring in.

C. William Verity Jr. retired in 1979. He named as his successor Harry Holiday, a 30-year veteran of the steel business. A steel man, Holiday often was more concerned with how the blast furnaces at the Middletown mill were working than what was happening to Armco's far-flung enterprises. Holiday began to hire non-steel executives in an attempt to round out the corporation's management team. Still committed to the plans of Armco's recently retired CEO, the company acquired Northwestern National Insurance Company in 1980 at a cost of $393 million. Holiday hired more insurance management to help run the newly acquired company.

The recession in 1982 forced Holiday to curtail his plans for further expansion and forced the company to reduce the size of its work force and close some aging steel mills. With a loss of $1.5 billion during the period between 1982 and 1984, mostly from steel, oil, and insurance, the company continued to sell many of its holdings in an attempt to raise needed cash and reduce its size.

In April of 1985, Standard & Poor's Corporation placed Armco on its Credit-Watch list and downgraded the company's rating. That same year, in an attempt to upgrade its image, the company moved its headquarters from Middletown, to Morristown, New Jersey. The move allowed Armco to decentralize its structure and separate its corporate staff from the steel industry. At the same time, the company was able to eliminate over $535 million of its debt with the sale of Armco Financial Corporation to Glendale Federal Savings; its Australian and European financial leasing subsidiaries had been sold the previous month. The April sale to Glendale ended Armco's involvement in financial leasing.

In 1984 Holiday was forced by his health to retire. During the following 12 months, insurance officials in several states demanded large additions of capital for several of Armco's floundering insurance subsidiaries. Faced with a payment of more than $600 million in corporate debt, the company's next president, Robert E. Boni, negotiated recovery plans with insurance regulators and won new credit from a group of nervous bankers. The agreements were reached with Boni's promise to reverse Armco's diversification and return the company to its roots in the steel business.

In the five years following Boni's agreement in 1985, the company sold 12 of its subsidiaries, some located in Spain, Canada, Australia, and England. Between 1980 and 1990, Armco's employee base shrank from 47,000 to less than 11,000. In 1989 the company's profits were beginning to increase as the consolidation of Armco's business centers continued. Although the company's sales dropped form $2.9 billion in 1987 to $2.4 billion in 1989, the company's operating profit rose over $100 million in the same period of time.

Operating from Armco's headquarters in Parsippany, New Jersey, Boni kept his word to his bankers. The company reduced its debt significantly after 1987, bringing it down to 30% of total capitalization in 1989. Insurance operations, which in 1990 were still in the process of being liquidated, showed profits from 1986 onward. The run-off business, claims being paid by subsidiaries that are no longer writing new policies, was still a problem for Armco in 1991, but appeared to be manageable.

A joint venture with Kawasaki Steel Corporation involving the company's eastern U.S. division won approval by Armco stockholders in May 1989. A cash infusion of $350 million as a result of the deal was earmarked primarily to overhaul and modernize the company's mills. The eastern steel division is a flat roll producer that accounts for about 60% of Armco's business, serving mainly appliance, construction, and automotive markets.

As the company moved into the 1990s, the need for cash was still pressing. Cash conservation programs were in effect.

Modernization of the production plants along with more corporate restructuring was expected to further reduce operating costs. Laser welding techniques used to recycle steel were being researched, along with lighter-weight steel products for the automobile industry. Nevertheless, Armco lost $89.5 million in 1990, and chairman Robert L. Purdum, elected in 1990, foresaw additional trouble in 1991. Despite Armco's cash difficulties, in 1991 the company's new aluminized stainless steel products were well received, and Armco had plans to introduce many more new products and technologies.

Principal Subsidiaries: Armco Argentina, S.A. Industrial y Comercial; Armco Chile S.A. Metalurgica Industrial; Armco Financial Services Corporation; Armco Insurance Group, Inc.; Armco Management Corp.; Armco G.M.B.H. (Germany); Armco Perunan, S.A. (Peru); C.A. Armco Venezolana (Venezuela); Productos Metalicos (Ecuador); Armco Colombiana (Columbia); Prolansa (Peru); Adesur (Peru); Armco Uruguaya S.A. (Uruguay); Armco Molycop S.p.A. (Italy); Southwestern Ohio Steel, Inc.; Southwestern Ohio Steel Leveling Co. Inc.

Further Reading: Fisher, Douglas Alan, *The Epic of Steel*, New York, Harper & Row, 1963; "Armco Inc.: A Brief History," Armco corporate typescript, 1987.

—William R. Grossman

ASARCO INCORPORATED

180 Maiden Lane
New York, New York 10038
U.S.A.
(212) 510-2000
Fax: (212) 510-1835

Public Company
Incorporated: 1899 as American Smelting and Refining
Company
Employees: 9,300
Sales: $2.21 billion
Stock Exchange: New York

ASARCO Incorporated is a world leader in the production of nonferrous metals, including copper, lead, zinc, silver, and gold. Among the mines operated by ASARCO or its associated companies are the Mission and Ray open-pit copper mines in Arizona; the Silver Bell Mine in Arizona; the Continental Mine in Montana; four zinc mines near Knoxville, Tennessee; the West Fork and Sweetwater lead mines in Missouri; the zinc, lead, silver, and gold mine at Leadville in Colorado; the Troy silver-copper mine in Montana; and two silver mines in Idaho, at Galena and Coeur. Processing facilities operated by ASARCO include copper smelters in Hayden, Arizona, and El Paso, Texas; a copper refinery in Amarillo, Texas; a lead smelter in East Helena, Montana; and a lead refinery in Omaha, Nebraska.

In 1990 ASARCO and its associated companies in Australia, Mexico, and Peru accounted for 12% of free-world mine production of copper, 14% of silver, 14% of lead, and 9% of zinc. Through its subsidiaries, ASARCO is heavily involved in the manufacture of specialty chemicals for electroplating, metal finishing, and electronics applications. In addition to processing the products of its own mines, ASARCO acquires ore from other companies, either to process for a fee or to process and then sell on the open market. Consumers encounter these refined metals in many forms, including zinc in the form of flashlight batteries, copper in the form of car radiators, lead in the form of automotive batteries, and silver in the form of coatings on photographic film. ASARCO has entered into hazardous-waste recycling as well.

Founded in 1899 as American Smelting and Refining Company—known informally as ASARCO—the company was a giant from the start. Henry H. Rogers was a 19th-century financial baron who had collaborated with John D. Rockefeller

in constructing the huge Standard Oil Trust. ASARCO was his attempt to similarly dominate the nonferrous metals industry. In that era of corporate consolidation and combination, the smelting and refining business seemed to be a perfect candidate for monopolization. Rogers—along with William Rockefeller and the copper-rich Lewisohn brothers, Adolph and Leonard—had formed the United Metals Selling Company in the 1890s. This trust was so successful that they launched the even larger American Smelting and Refining Company in 1899. At its creation ASARCO consisted of 23 different smelting companies. Conspicuously absent from the ASARCO roster were concerns controlled by the Guggenheim family. In 1899, Rogers invited the Guggenheims to become part of ASARCO. They turned down his offer. The Guggenheims were not interested in being part of an organization that was not under their family control. Over the next couple of years, the Guggenheims took the matter into their own hands and gained control of ASARCO through aggressive business tactics.

Meyer Guggenheim, the patriarch of the family, had emmigrated from Switzerland in 1848. He amassed his fortune through an extremely diverse variety of business ventures, from manufacturing and peddling stove polish, to wholesale spice sales, to importing fine laces and embroideries. By 1879, at the age of 51, Meyer Guggenheim was nearly a millionaire. His entrance into the metals industry came in 1881, when he bought a one-third interest in the A.Y. and the Minnie lead and silver mines in Leadville, Colorado. By 1888 these two mines were making about $750,000 a year, and the Guggenheim metal empire had been born.

Meyer Guggenheim soon determined that more profits were being taken in by the middlemen of the industry—the smelters—than by the miners. He bought a controlling interest in the Holden Smelter in Denver, Colorado, where his ore was refined, started the Philadelphia Smelting and Refining Company, and began building a new smelter at Pueblo, Colorado. Next he consolidated the various businesses, including his share of Philadelphia Smelting, under the firm M. Guggenheim's Sons, which until then was just a lace importing firm. He delegated various duties among his seven sons. The Pueblo smelter at first was a financial disaster. The Guggenheims's inexperience in the industry and the mine workers' strikes against the 12-hour day brought the company to the brink of ruin. It was saved, in part, by the Sherman Silver Purchase Act, passed by Congress in 1890, as a consequence of which the U.S. Treasury Department agreed to buy four million ounces of silver every month, producing a sharp rise in silver prices.

By 1890 the Guggenheims had for some time imported lead and silver ores from Mexico for their Pueblo smelter. The McKinley Tariff Act of 1890, would have made this a more expensive activity. The Guggenheims, however, built two smelters in Mexico, thereby taking advantage of cheap Mexican labor and avoiding the tariff. By 1895, the Guggenheims were reaping over $1 million a year from their smelters at Pueblo, Monterrey, and Aguascalientes, and were one of Mexico's greatest industrial powers. This was the healthy state of the Guggenheim enterprise at the time Rogers was assembling American Smelting and Refining Company.

In 1900 ASARCO was hit with two months of worker strikes and Daniel Guggenheim increased production at his family's operations, flooding the market with cheap lead and silver and driving prices downward. He also lured mine owners throughout the West into selling their ore to the more stable Guggenheims. As ASARCO stock fell in price, Daniel Guggenheim bought it up. ASARCO officials, now worried, tried again to buy out the Guggenheims. A deal was negotiated: Guggenheim properties and working capital in exchange for $45.2 million in ASARCO stock, a controlling interest, and board positions for the Guggenheim brothers. In April 1901, the merger was completed. Daniel Guggenheim became chairman of the board and president of ASARCO; Solomon Guggenheim became treasurer; Isaac, Murry, and Simon Guggenheim, members of the board. ASARCO would be headed by a member of the Guggenheim family until 1957, when Roger Straus, son-in-law of Daniel Guggenheim, retired.

The first decade of the 20th century was a time of great growth and diversification for ASARCO under Daniel Guggenheim's leadership. By 1903 ASARCO had acquired stock control of the United States Zinc Company, contracted with the National Lead Company for the sale of its lead requirements, and purchased rights from the Federal Mining and Smelting Company to all silver-lead ores mined from its Coeur d'Alene, Idaho, properties.

In 1905 the American Smelters Securities Company (ASSC) was organized. ASSC was a public company but was controlled by the officers and directors of American Smelting and Refining Company. Since expansion further into mining would cost much more than ASARCO possessed in cash resources, ASSC offered securities guaranteed by ASARCO in order to finance new and expensive projects. The officers were essentially the same as those of ASARCO, and the floating of these securities made several purchases possible, including a Tacoma, Washington, lead and copper smelter; the Selby lead smelter and refinery at San Francisco, California; and a Baltimore, Maryland, copper refinery. The securities also paid for construction of a new copper refinery at Tacoma and a huge copper smelter at Garfield, Utah. Five mines in Mexico were purchased as well, plus the Flat River mines of the Federal Lead Company.

Expansion and acquisition continued during the years prior to World War I. The building of the Amarillo, Texas, smelter in 1915 marked the company's plunge into zinc refining. In 1916, ASARCO began operating in Chile, with the purchase of the Caldera Smelter. This era of continued growth progressed in spite of obstacles. Mine owners in Colorado, believing that smelters were charging excessive rates for processing ores, attempted to pass a bill through the state legislature making smelters public utilities under control of the state. This action failed. Farmers in California and Utah filed lawsuits against ASARCO charging crop damage from sulfur dioxide, a chemical released when zinc, lead, and copper ores are processed. This issue was neutralized somewhat by the creation of an ASARCO research division to address environmental concerns.

The outbreak of World War I created a huge need for metals, including copper, zinc, and lead. ASARCO benefited even before the United States entered the war, since Europe was largely dependent on the United States for its copper supply. Between 1914 and the U.S. entry into the war in 1917, U.S. copper production had nearly doubled, and copper prices had nearly tripled before government price limits were initiated.

Once the war ended, there was a backlash. Mines were urged to continue producing in order to avoid unemployment and recession. Demand for copper products was down, yet American Smelting and Refining Company was still under contract to buy huge amounts of copper. Mining and smelting companies found it necessary to borrow millions of dollars to cover their growing inventories, and in 1920 ASARCO found itself $12 million in debt to various banks.

In 1919 Daniel Guggenheim resigned as president of American Smelting and Refining Company, and Murry and Solomon Guggenheim gave up their board positions. Simon Guggenheim assumed the leadership of the company. This was a period of some turmoil at ASARCO. Karl Eilers, son of Anton Eilers, a member of Henry Rogers's original ASARCO combination, attacked the way ASARCO was being managed, and sought Simon Guggenheim's resignation as president. At the annual stockholders meeting of 1921, Eilers unsuccessfully attempted to have a slate of directors elected that was outside of the Guggenheim influence. Allegations were made that the Guggenheims were diverting ASARCO funds for their non-ASARCO family business interests. These suspicions were fueled in part by the existence of a secret stairway used by Daniel Guggenheim that connected his ASARCO office with his Guggenheim Brothers office a floor below in the same building. Although a committee of stockholders officially cleared the family of any wrongdoing, 1922 marked the end of the Guggenheims's overpowering control of ASARCO, although they were still well represented.

During the 1920s, the direction of ASARCO's growth was toward fabrication of products made of the metals it produced. In 1923 a rod and wire plant was built at the company's Baltimore refinery. The rod and wire business was soon combined with several other wire and cable companies to form the General Cable Company, which began operating in 1927, with ASARCO holding about an 11% interest. ASARCO would later increase its share considerably. In 1928, ASARCO entered a similar arrangement with its Baltimore copper and brass rolling mill. In that year, Revere Copper and Brass Company was formed, with ASARCO holding a 19% share, a percentage also destined to grow.

By 1929 American Smelting and Refining Company was the largest refiner of nonferrous metals in the world, but it was not unharmed by the Great Depression. After earning a net income of nearly $22 million in 1929, ASARCO's business declined, resulting in a $4.5 million deficit in 1932. In spite of the hard times, ASARCO continued to expand, purchasing the Federated Metals Corporation, a huge source of scrap metal, in 1932. The company's recovery was aided by President Franklin D. Roosevelt's silver-purchase plan and his devaluation of the dollar, which caused the prices of precious metals to rise.

During the 1930s ASARCO introduced two innovative methods of inventory accounting, the "last in, first out" system in 1935, and the "normal" system in 1939. These systems addressed the question of whether money was actually being made from smelting and selling or on mere speculation of future metal prices. Both of these systems tended to reduce the effects of profits resulting from price fluctuations by setting the value of excess metal stock lower than the price was expected ever to drop.

ASARCO's involvement with the mine at Mount Isa in Australia began in the 1930s. Mount Isa began as a lead and silver mining effort by an English group, the Mining Trust Ltd. In 1930 the trust needed money, and ASARCO invested a small sum. After numerous mining catastrophes, money shortages, and subsequent bailouts by ASARCO, by 1934 the investment amounted to more than $8 million. Mount Isa made its first profit in 1937. Shortly after that, copper was discovered there, boding well for Australia's soon-to-come war needs. During World War II the mine was used to supply copper, but it was not until 20 years later that it was known to be a phenomenal copper strike.

The effects of World War II on ASARCO were not as great as those of World War I. Because mines in Canada, South America, and South Africa had been developed, Europe's reliance on U.S. copper was not as great. The price of copper did not rise, therefore, until 1941, when the United States entered the war and needed its own supply. Then the government put ceilings on prices at the levels that existed. These ceilings lasted until 1946. The government also adopted a premium price plan, under which each mine that produced copper, lead, or zinc was paid enough to earn it a fixed profit. This way, the necessary amounts of metal were produced, and mines were not stuck with huge excesses when the war ended.

Simon Guggenheim died in 1941. After his death, American Smelting and Refining Company's by-laws changed so that the chairman of the board, rather than the president, was the chief executive officer. Francis H. Brownell, already chairman, was thus in charge until 1947, when Roger Straus, son-in-law of Daniel Guggenheim, took over.

After World War II, secondary products became increasingly important for ASARCO. Often eight or nine different metals are found in tiny amounts from a single charge of ore, and ASARCO took advantage of this diversity as much as possible. The company became a market leader in selenium, used in electronic parts; a leading supplier of cadmium, used for metal plating; and a supplier of germanium, used in transistors. Its Garfield, Utah, copper smelter began to produce more sulfuric acid than copper. ASARCO recovered bismuth and antimony from lead refining, indium from zinc smelting, and arsenic and tellurium from copper processing.

By the 1950s it became clear that ASARCO's future expansion needed to focus on mining. As large mining companies began to do their own smelting, ASARCO adjusted by seeking to become its own best customer, assuring a steady source of raw ores. ASARCO had obtained full rights to the rich copper property of Toquepala in southern Peru in 1948. By the mid-1950s the company had teamed with Phelps Dodge, Cerro de Pasco Corporation, and Newmont Mining to form the Southern Peru Copper Corporation, with ASARCO controlling a 57% share. Southern Peru borrowed $120 million from the Export-Import Bank to develop an open-pit mine at Toquepala, and the mine was still productive in 1990.

In 1952, ASARCO further diversified by entering the asbestos field at Black Lake in Quebec. The 1950s were not particularly profitable for ASARCO. Income from the Mexican properties, which were crucial to the company's survival through the Depression, was cut into by an increase in the export duty and devaluation of the peso in 1954. Lead and zinc prices declined around this time as well. Kenneth Brownell, chairman since Roger Straus's retirement a year earlier, died in

1958, and John D. MacKenzie took over as chief executive. The same year, the Kennecott Copper Corporation, a huge source of copper for ASARCO's smelters for over 50 years, ended its contract, and finally bought ASARCO's Garfield smelter in 1959. The year 1959 also brought the longest copper strike in history, which kept ASARCO's 13 U.S. smelters and refineries shut down for 113 production days.

American Smelting and Refining Company entered the 1960s still the world's leading custom smelter. As lead and zinc prices continued to decline, the company's emphasis was turned toward copper mining. With the Mount Isa and Toquepala properties beginning to pay off well and the addition of the Mission copper mine in Arizona, ASARCO was the fourth-largest copper producer by 1963, behind Kennecott, Anaconda, and Phelps Dodge. Under MacKenzie, efforts were made to cut costs, including a 20% decrease in payroll, and more importantly, the use of inexpensive strip mining techniques at the Peru mines. At the time Edward Tittman assumed the chairmanship in 1963, ASARCO was continuing to integrate downward into mining while many of its major customers integrated upward into ore processing. Secondary metals remained important, with the construction of a plant to process molybdenum, a copper by-product, at the Mission site in 1964. In 1965, with profits from the Mexican operations drying up, the Mexican mines and plants were reorganized as ASARCO Mexicana, S.A., and a majority interest was sold to Mexican investors. The San Xavier North mine adjacent to Mission began operating in 1967.

By the early 1970s copper was accounting for nearly two-thirds of ASARCO's earnings. The company remained active in other areas as well, purchasing the American Limestone Company and four zinc mines in Tennessee in 1971. ASARCO continued to expand in copper production under chairman Charles Barber, opening the Sacaton copper mine in Arizona in 1974. In 1975 American Smelting and Refining Company officially changed its name to ASARCO, and the obsolete copper-refining plants in Baltimore and Perth Amboy, New Jersey, were replaced by the new facility in Amarillo, Texas.

During the period from 1974 to 1978, ASARCO's growth was impeded by labor problems and market fluctuations. Wall Street observers voiced concern that the Peruvian government might expropriate ASARCO's properties there, expropriation having been a problem for Anaconda and Kennecott in Chile. Between 1977 and 1978 ASARCO borrowed more than $200 million from nine banks, including Chase Manhattan, where Charles Barber was a director.

Throughout the 1970s antipollution regulations caused problems for ASARCO. The copper smelter in Tacoma was a long-standing source of controversy over its arsenic emissions. Compliance with Environmental Protection Agency regulations was difficult both because of the plant's age and the fact that ASARCO was producing arsenic there as a commercial by-product. The Tacoma smelter was finally closed in 1985, after many variances from compliance, because adapting the smelter to meet emissions standards was considered too costly.

ASARCO recovered somewhat in 1979. Construction began on the Troy silver mine in Montana that year. The Eisenhower Mining Company, a partnership of ASARCO and the Anamax Mining Company, began to gain benefits from the Palo Verde copper deposit near the Mission mine.

The early 1980s were not good years for the mining industry. The price of copper was dropping although demand was up, caused in part by the flooding of the copper market by state-owned companies, particularly in Chile. In 1984 ASARCO lost $306 million. Chairman Ralph Hennebech's only recourse was to cut costs. In 1985, with ASARCO losing $20 million a quarter, Hennebach retired. Richard de J. Osborne, then chief financial officer, became CEO and chairman of the board. Osborne laid off several layers of managers, renegotiated wages and transportation contracts, and cut pension costs. Between 1981 and 1985 annual expenses were cut by more than $200 million. While other companies were selling off assets, ASARCO used its newly replenished cash flow to buy new mines and reserves, such as Kennecott's Ray copper mine, to assure business for its smelters. By the end of 1987 ASARCO was making money again.

Through the late 1980s ASARCO continued to diversify. The company's acquisition of OMI International Corporation in 1988 and the Imasa Group in 1989 helped establish it as a major force in specialty chemicals, metal finishing, and electronics. By 1989 ASARCO was on track toward its goal of becoming a fully integrated, self-sufficient producer of copper and lead. With the 1989 purchase of 49.9% of the Montana copper mining business of Montana Resources, Inc. and the expansion of capacity at the Mission and Ray mines, it was estimated that ASARCO would be able to supply the entire capacity of its own copper-smelting facilities by 1992.

Since its creation just before the turn of the century, ASARCO has survived by adapting. In an industry at the mercy of both historical and geological forces, the company has managed to adjust during every cycle, often by going against the tide of the rest of the industry. If it is able to adapt to the greater environmental and higher technological needs of the metal industry's future, ASARCO's prospects remain good.

Principal Subsidiaries: Enthone-OMI, Inc.; Imasa Group; Southern Peru Copper Corporation (52%); Mexico Desarrollo Industrial Minero, S.A. de C.V. (34%); M.I.M. Holdings Limited (Australia, 19%); Asarco Australia Ltd. (60%).

Further Reading: Marcosson, Isaac, *Metal Magic*, New York, Farrar, Straus and Company, 1949; "Asarco Bids to be a Giant in Mining," *Business Week*, November 24, 1956; McDonald, John, "The Big New Kicker at Asarco," *Fortune,* January 1963; Davis, John, *The Guggenheims*, New York, William Morrow and Company, 1978; *Asarco: The Metal Maker*, New York, ASARCO Incorporated, 1981.

—Robert R. Jacobson

BETHLEHEM STEEL CORPORATION

Bethlehem, Pennsylvania 18016
U.S.A.
(215) 694-2424
Fax: (215) 694-5743

Public Company
Incorporated: 1904
Employees: 29,600
Sales: $4.90 billion
Stock Exchanges: New York Midwest

Bethlehem Steel Corporation is the second-largest integrated steel producer in the United States, with control of supply sources, production, and distribution, from raw materials to products. The company manufactures and sells a wide variety of steel-mill products. The company also mines and sells coal and other raw materials. Bethlehem also is involved in the repair of ships and offshore-drilling-platform businesses, and in the manufacture of forgings, castings, railroad cars, and trackwork.

The company had its origin in 1857 as the Saucona Iron Company in South Bethlehem, Pennsylvania. Its primary business was the rolling of iron railroad rails. In 1899, after broadening the product line to include heavy forging for electric generators, tool steels for metal cutting, and armor plate for U.S. Navy ships, the company's name was changed to the Bethlehem Steel Company.

Bethlehem Steel Corporation was incorporated in December 1904 by Charles M. Schwab, a former Andrew Carnegie disciple and first president of United States Steel Corporation (U.S. Steel). Schwab left U.S. Steel over difficulties that he felt inhibited his freedom to run the company properly. At its incorporation the company included Bethlehem Steel, a Cuban iron ore mine, and several shipbuilding concerns in California and Delaware. Schwab became president and chairman of the board.

Soon after the formation of the company, Schwab hired an electrical engineer, Eugene G. Grace, whose management skills allowed the more entrepreneurial Schwab the freedom he needed to plan the growth of the company. Together, the two men became the team that built Bethlehem from a small producer with an ingot capacity of less that 1% of the national total in 1905 to the world's second-largest producer in fewer than 35 years.

In 1908 the two men staked the company's future on a new type of mill invented by Henry Grey. It was capable of rolling a wide flange structural steel section that was stronger, lighter, and less expensive than the fabricated steel sections that were being used at the time. The gamble paid off for Bethlehem. The wide-flange section made it possible to build skyscrapers and modern cities.

In the years preceding World War I, the company acquired an interest in a Chilean iron ore mine with ore of a higher quality than available from the U.S. upper–Great Lakes region. As a result of the acquisition, the company built a fleet of ore carriers and entered the ocean transportation business. With the outbreak of the war, Bethlehem became a business of international scope, building warships for Great Britain at the company's shipyards. Bethlehem also filled orders for guns and munitions, armor, and ordnance placed by the British, French, and Soviets. In the process of contributing to the Allied cause in Europe, Bethlehem created a financial base that would help in expanding the company's steelmaking facilities.

Eugene Grace was named president of the company in 1916, with Schwab staying on as chairman of the board. In that same year, bolstered by wartime profits, Bethlehem acquired American Iron and Steel Manufacturing Company, Pennsylvania Steel Company, and Maryland Steel Company. In the years following World War I, the company continued its growth with the acquisition of Lackawanna Steel & Ordnance Company in 1922 and Midvale Steel and Ordnance Company, and Cambria Steel Company one year later. In the years preceding the Great Depression, the company boosted its steelmaking capacity to 8.5 million tons and employed over 60,000 people.

Bethlehem's growth was tied to an incentive program from which its upper management profited handsomely. In 1929, Grace received a bonus in excess of $1.6 million; about 3.3% of earnings. The policy of paying out such large awards to its executives eventually caused problems. In early 1931, a group of stockholders filed suit against Schwab and 12 other officers of the company, charging that the bonus program constituted a misuse of company funds. The suit asked that a total of $36 million in bonuses distributed since 1911 be returned to the company's coffers. The action resulted in the formation of the Protective Committee for Stockholders of Bethlehem Steel Corporation, a watchdog group that sought the elimination of the bonus program in its existing form. Though no funds were returned to the company, the suit was settled in July 1931, about six months after it was filed. The settlement resulted in a new policy that included the publication of executive bonuses in the company's annual reports and a revised executive salary and bonus package. In subsequent years labor unions used the bonus issue in their demands for higher compensation and benefits for the rank-and-file steelworkers.

The 1920s were years of growth for Bethlehem. In the early years of the Great Depression, the company weathered the economic storm and continued to improve its production plants and introduce new products. The Depression caught up with Bethlehem in September 1931 when the company posted a quarterly loss for the first time since 1909. In the face of a stagnant economy and an eroding demand for steel products, the company had overexpanded and was forced to shut down many of its facilities, including a newly constructed jumbo-size open hearth at the Sparrows Point, Maryland, plant. Bethlehem, along with other major steel producers, struggled through the Depression. Help arrived with President Franklin D. Roosevelt's New Deal and the National Industrial Recovery Act of 1933. The government suspended antitrust laws, and the steel industry established codes approved by the National Recovery Administration providing for labor reform, workers rights to organize, minimum wages, and maximum work hours. In December 1933, Bethlehem reported a modest net profit in excess of $600,000 after nine quarters totaling more than $30 million in losses.

During the 1930s, Bethlehem acquired steelmaking plants in Los Angeles and San Francisco, California, and Seattle, Washington. McClintic-Marshall, a large fabricator and builder of bridges, was also purchased, enabling Bethlehem to participate in the construction San Francisco's Golden Gate Bridge. Through this subsidiary, Bethlehem was also involved in the construction of other large bridges and notable buildings, including Rockefeller Plaza; and the Waldorf Astoria Hotel in New York City; the Chicago Merchandise Mart; and the U.S. Supreme Court Building in Washington, D.C.

During the mid-1930s, Bethlehem went through an expensive retooling. With the largest capital expenditure since before the Depression, in 1937 and 1938 the company spent approximately $20 million on the construction of a continuous strip and tin-plate mill at Sparrows Point. A primary reason for the new project was beer. After six years of research and development, the American Can Company had produced a coated tin can suitable for packaging beer and the tin-plate market exploded.

Charles M. Schwab died in September 1939, leaving Bethlehem under the tight controls of Eugene Grace. With U.S. involvement in World War II imminent, Grace geared the company's entire capacity toward war production. Furnaces, shops, and mills worked around the clock producing armor plate for ships, structural steel for defense plants, munitions, and aircraft engines. Between 1941 and 1944, Grace pushed production at Bethlehem to 101% of usual capacity. During the war, the company's 15 shipyards produced over 1,100 ships, including aircraft carriers, destroyers, heavy cruisers, and cargo ships. In 1943 alone, the company built 380 vessels.

During World War II, from 1940 to 1945, Bethlehem produced over 73 million tons of steel. This total represented almost one-third of the armor plate and gun forgings used by the United States in the war. Prior to U.S. entrance into the war, the company's gross sales were $135 million. In 1945, sales topped $1.33 billion, with more than 300,000 employees. Bethlehem became a global giant in the steel industry.

In December 1945, six years after the death of Charles Schwab, Grace was elected the company's chairman. Arthur B. Homer, director of the Bethlehem's wartime shipbuilding program, became president.

With war's end, the global demand for steel was even greater than during the conflict. Consumer demands for new cars and household goods, along with the massive amounts of structural steel needed to rebuild war-torn economies, resulted in further expansion. Bethlehem built new furnaces and mills at many of its plants, and by 1950 was producing 23 million tons annually. The nature of the company's shipbuilding business began to change as Bethlehem produced larger, longer cargo ships. Forerunners to today's supertankers, the new line of ships produced by Bethlehem cost less per unit, carried more tonnage, and were able to cruise at speeds 30% faster than their prewar predecessors. More iron ore was delivered in less time. In 1957, Bethlehem's peak postwar production year, the company made more than 19 million tons of steel, and earned $190 million on sales of $2.6 billion. At the close of the decade, Bethlehem's full-time postwar employee roster stood at 165,000.

In 1960, the United States imported more steel than it exported for the first time in the American steel industry's history. This situation was a harbinger. The deterioration of Bethlehem's enterprises, as well as those of other U.S. steel manufacturers, can be traced to several major factors. High wages, foreign competition, and the enormous costs of environmental clean-up of the lands and waters around the company's many production plants cut deeply into the company's profits and cash reserves. In addition, decades of unlimited growth, expansion, and profits had made Bethlehem's leadership complacent. Antitrust and price fixing suits against several U.S. steel giants including Bethlehem followed. Throughout the 1960s and 1970s company leaders believed that procedures could continue as they had been for over a half century without change in processes or structure.

Bethlehem's leaders did not engage in product research, innovation, or reorganization. The company, like its competitors, relied on continual price increases to protect profits. These policies allowed opportunities for entrance into the U.S. market by Japanese and other foreign steelmakers, who rebuilt their steel industries after World War II and captured the competitive edge worldwide. This new competition, a shrinking domestic market, and the expansion of steel substitutes such as aluminum and plastics, created a still-existent threat to Bethlehem's future.

Following Grace's death in 1960, Arthur B. Homer, the company's new chairman, committed the company to a $3 billion modernization and expansion program. The old mentality still prevailed as the company pushed to produce more tonnage. Bigger still seemed to be better.

Two important factors permitted Bethlehem to sustain its business and expansion through the early 1970s. First, pressure was brought to bear on the U.S. government to limit the amount of foreign steel allowed into the country. Early in 1969, the State Department persuaded Japanese and European steel producers voluntarily to cut their imports to the United States by 25%. The second factor that helped sustain Bethlehem during the 1970s was the Vietnam War, which stimulated production in all sectors of the U.S. economy. Bethlehem again pushed for more production and higher steel prices. After the price of steel rose steeply in 1969, the administration of President Richard Nixon instituted price controls on steel in August 1971.

The company faced growing competition from mini-mills. These small operations challenged the premise that the steel business had to be huge and integrated to survive. Using scrap metal melted down in electric furnaces, the small operations were capable of producing simple iron and steel products at a much lower cost than the large steelmakers. In light of increased competition, the company chose to grow with the construction of a huge blast furnace at Sparrows Point. Named Big L, it was built at a cost of $275 million. The furnace began operations three years after the end of the early-1970s boom years and one year after the company had shown a net operating loss of over $448 million. Bethlehem Steel was in trouble.

Drastic action was needed to save the company. In 1980, Donald Trautlein, Bethlehem's controller, was named chairman. Trautlein began to cut away at the company's cost of doing business. The company possessed outmoded production plants, steep labor costs, rising foreign and domestic competition, and eroding profits at a time when the steel industry was experiencing the worst downturn in over 50 years. Trautlein had other problems as well. He knew little about the business of steelmaking; he felt that most of Bethlehem's problems were due to external forces beyond the company's control. Trautlein chose first to diversify, then to remain exclusively in the steel business, and then began a diversification that was not completed.

The company's new chairman began cutting costs at the top. Salaries were cut by 20% over a four-year period. Lump-sum retirement packages were offered to employees over the age of 55; vacations were cut back; and by the fall of 1982, 13 upper-echelon executives had taken early retirement. These measures were accompanied by mass firings and layoffs. Further cutbacks eliminated such perquisites as company limousines and drivers, security forces for executives' homes, and a fleet of jet airplanes. By 1984, the number of Bethlehem employees had shrunk almost 50%. Trautlein replaced some of the executive-level positions made vacant with professional managers who had little or no experience in the steel business; many positions were left unfilled.

The company also began the liquidation of some subsidiaries. During the 1980s, 11 of the company's operations were sold. In that same period, Bethlehem began to consolidate many of its steelmaking operations by closing marginal facilities and modernizing aging plants. The company closed its west-coast steel plants, scaled back shipbuilding operations, and in 1983, steelmaking was discontinued at the Lackawanna plant.

Between 1982 and 1985, the company posted losses of $1.9 billion. Under pressure and criticism, Donald Trautlein resigned in 1986. He was replaced by the company's president, Walter F. Williams, who had more than 30 years of experience in the business. Williams was faced with a downward momentum that was not going to be easy to reverse. The company's stock hovered around to an all-time low of $4 per share.

Williams instituted a campaign to improve and revitalize Bethlehem's basic steel business. He began by selling off the assets that were not related to steel. He smoothed relations with both customers and suppliers and persuaded bankers to stay with the company. Slowly, Williams's program began to make a difference. For the year ending December 31, 1987, the company reported over $174 million in profits compared to a net loss of over $150 million the previous year. In 1988, the company increased its sales volume another 18% over 1987 sales figures, and reported record earnings of over $400 million. Two important problems were solved in 1989. First, a 50-month labor contract that included cost-of-living increases and profit sharing was signed with the United Steelworkers. Second, the U.S. government's steel-trade-liberalization program with other countries extended voluntary restraint arrangements previously negotiated with other countries by the Reagan Administration.

In 1990 and 1991 Bethlehem worked at increasing its market share in products that produced higher profit margins. Further, the company focused on modernization, development of high-technology production methods, and increased research and development into new products and processes.

Principal Subsidiaries: Bethlehem Hibbing Corp.; Bethlehem Mines Corp.; Bethlehem Steel International Corp.

Further Reading: Fisher, Douglas Alan, The Epic of Steel, New York, Harper & Row, 1963; Strohmeyer, John, *Crisis in Bethlehem: Big Steel's Struggle to Survive*, Bethesda, Maryland, Adler & Adler, 1986; Reutter, Mark, *Sparrows Point: Making Steel—the Rise and Ruin of American Industrial Might*, New York, Summit Books, 1988; Hessen, Robert, *Steel Titan: The Life of Charles M. Schwab*, Pittsburgh, University of Pittsburgh Press, 1990; *A Brief History of Bethlehem Steel*, Bethlehem, Pennsylvania, Bethlehem Steel Corporation, 1990.

—William R. Grossman

BRITISH COAL CORPORATION

Hobart House
Grosvenor Place
London SW1X 7AE
United Kingdom
(071) 235-2020
Fax: (071) 2020 extension 34682

State-Owned Company
Incorporated: 1946 as National Coal Board
Employees: 105,000
Sales: £4.30 billion (US$8.30 billion)

The British Coal Corporation (BCC) is a state-owned under-taking, which has had a virtual monopoly in the output of coal in the United Kingdom since just after World War II. Though still among the largest coal producers in Western Europe, it has for many years been shrinking in size, and the range of its markets has narrowed. About 80% of its output is sold to the power stations, also state-owned, although in 1990, the Conservative government under Margaret Thatcher was actively proposing the privatization of the entire electricity industry. More than two-thirds of the United Kingdom's electricity is generated by coal-fired stations, a proportion which has generally been higher until some of the newer nuclear power stations have come nearer to full output. Proposals in 1990, to use more imported coal at power stations and to use natural gas for some future additions to generating capacity, indicate that BCC's sales and size may contract further. BCC's prospects have also been influenced by the Thatcher government's announcement of intent to privatize the company, an intention not shared by the parliamentary opposition.

The Coal Industry Nationalisation Act of 1946 set up the National Coal Board (NCB) to own and operate the coal industry from a date subsequently fixed as January 1, 1947. This measure was an early part of the incoming Labour government's program to nationalize a large part of the country's basic industries and utilities. It was also a reaction to the parlous condition of the coal industry under private ownership. Output and stocks had been falling and it had been impossible to recruit adequate numbers of mineworkers. In 1945 an official committee chaired by Sir Charles Reid, a leading Scottish coal owner and mining engineer, had produced a report that exposed the technological and organizational weaknesses of the industry and pointed to the need for complete restructuring.

Immediately before nationalization there were about 1,470 operating collieries, owned by over 800 firms. The NCB did not take over any of these firms but acquired their physical assets for the production of coal, coke, manufactured fuel, some of the primary by-products of carbonization, and bricks. The NCB also owned the entire national reserves of unworked coal. Only in coal did it have a virtual monopoly, but the NCB, the gas works, and the steel works produced nearly all the nation's coke, and the NCB was one of the larger brick-making undertakings, responsible for about 12% of national output at its peak in the 1950s. The coal industry assets were given a lump sum valuation by a special tribunal. Other assets had to be separately valued, and this process took nearly ten years. The NCB eventually paid £394 million for its assets, of which £81 million were for the mineral reserves and the rest for operational assets.

The NCB licensed the smallest mines for private operation but operated everything else directly. No exact total of the original number of employees is available but it was probably 770,000 to 780,000. In terms of employment, the NCB at its inception was believed to be the largest business unit in the non-communist world. It was controlled by a board of nine members of whom the chairman, Lord Hyndley, was a former managing director of the largest colliery firm, Powell Duffryn, and the deputy chairman, Sir Arthur Street, had been a senior civil servant.

Because the undertaking was so large and had so many and such dispersed production units, it needed a carefully integrated structure of staff departments and subordinate levels. This was devised mainly by Street and proved remarkably enduring. The main business centers were 48 areas—later increased to 51 and then gradually decreased—each controlling up to about 20 collieries through an intermediate tier of Groups. Between the areas and the NCB was another layer of management consisting of eight geographically based divisions, soon increased to nine, each with a board which was a simplified replica of the NCB. This was a highly devolved structure and the NCB received many parliamentary and journalistic accusations of over-centralization. The second chairman, Sir Hubert Houldsworth, in office from 1951–1956, greatly relaxed the authority of headquarters and the accountability of the lower levels, and this relaxation was severely criticized in 1955 by an outside committee under Sir Alexander Fleck, chairman of Imperial Chemical Industries, which the NCB had appointed. Subsequently the lines of authority and accountability were more clearly defined and enforced.

The NCB was financed by loans from the government, on which interest always had to be paid. In the absence of any equity, the cost of servicing capital could not be adjusted to the current prosperity of the business. The NCB was by statute not required to make profits and until the 1960s was discouraged by the government from doing so, but it was required at least to break even on revenue account over a period of years. All proposals for price rises were submitted to the government, which usually delayed approval. These conditions made it difficult to achieve good commercial results.

This situation was made still more difficult by the constant pressure put on NCB by the government to provide the maximum output of coal, which could not be done without keeping large numbers of lossmaking collieries in operation and without repeatedly striving to recruit more miners. Such recruitment, in a strongly unionized industry involved granting substantial concessions on wages and hours. A further problem was that in some years the government expected the NCB, as a precaution, to augment supplies by imports. These had to be sold at home prices, although imports were much more expensive than home production. As a result the NCB had to carry in its accounts a financial loss from this source, which eventually amounted to £74 million.

Nevertheless, for ten years the NCB kept fairly well in line with government expectations. From 1950 it embarked on a long-term plan for reconstructing the collieries with the best prospects, sinking some new ones and closing the worst, but this plan took a long time to complete. From 1952 it took over the small, lossmaking opencast mining previously conducted by the Ministry of Fuel and Power and began to develop it into a consistently profitable business. In piecemeal ways it significantly improved labor productivity and began to play a major part in a fundamental revolution of mining techniques. In particular within the NCB organization James Anderton, general manager of the St. Helen's area in Lancashire, invented the shearer-loader, which was later developed to become the most important cutting and loading machine throughout the world. Despite the need to retain capacity, at great expense, which meant that six of the NCB's nine divisions were usually lossmaking, excellent profits were made in the east Midlands, Nottinghamshire, Derbyshire, and Leicestershire; and Yorkshire, while the west Midlands broke even. There were also profits from non-mining products, notably coke and some manufactured fuels. From 1948 to 1956 inclusive the NCB maintained the required break-even financial result and coal output was raised from 200 million in 1947 to a plateau of 227 to 228 million tons in the mid-1950s.

From the late 1950s the market for coal changed permanently. For technical reasons the railways rapidly began to abandon steam traction and the gas industry first turned to using oil as a feedstock and then to the natural gas that was found in abundance beneath the continental shelf. Above all, oil became abundantly available at reduced real cost and only the most cheaply produced coal could compete with it.

U.K. coal consumption peaked in 1956 and after 1957 there was a marked downturn, with a rapid rise in unsold stocks that had to be financed. Though the decline in demand was checked for a few years in the early 1960s, it soon resumed. For the NCB the difficulties were increased by two factors. Firstly, the program of colliery reconstruction and new sinkings, which had been undertaken in response to governmental pressure for more output, came to full fruition after demand had turned down and exacerbated the new problem of surplus capacity. Secondly, the government began to seek more profitability from the nationalized industries from 1961 onwards. If the NCB had charged international prices in its first ten years, it might have made annual surpluses of around £200 million, but in the 1960s it was hard to make any profit and the government appeared to regard coal as a declining industry. When a new official energy policy was announced in 1967, it was based on a four-fuel economy with coal in the last place.

The NCB had to make a drastic response to these conditions. From 1956 to 1961 it was chaired by Sir James Bowman, a former mining trade unionist with an excellent grasp of labor relations, and then between 1961 and 1971 by Lord Robens, an ex-cabinet minister who fought a public battle in the political arena on behalf of coal. The great tasks were to make coal more attractive to consumers in terms of quality and price, and to reduce capacity to match reduced demand. Cost control was aided by the progress of the great technical revolution in mechanized mining. Every effort was made to continue installing the new equipment, although there was little money to invest in other improvements. The falling number of jobs made it possible to keep a tight hold on the level of wages and seemed to have stimulated a better response from workers as shown by a great reduction in the number of unofficial strikes. Reductions of capacity continued apace. The number of collieries and of workers was reduced by more than half and the output of coal by more than a quarter in ten years. From 1961 to 1969 prices in real terms generally held firm, but declined in the lowest cost coalfield of the east Midlands, and Yorkshire.

Other economies were made by adjusting the administrative structure to suit the reduced size of the undertaking. A three-tier hierarchy replaced the original five tiers through the abolition of divisions and groups in 1967, and the number of Areas was gradually reduced. Finances also had to be adjusted. A reconstruction was statutorily approved in 1966 and applied retrospectively to 1965. Of the £960 million of loan capital, £415 million were effectively cancelled by using the sum to write off the book value of colliery and coke oven assets that had been closed down or reduced to unremunerative levels, and the interest on the remaining £545 million was reduced.

Efforts were made to gain additional revenue through modest diversification, mainly by way of joint ventures with private sector companies. These included retail and wholesale distribution of coal and heating appliances, chemical manufacture from the by-products of the coke ovens, and above all entry, in association with Continental Oil Company and others, into exploration and exploitation of the natural gas—and later oil—beneath the North Sea. This last was a very successful venture, as it brought a 50% share in one of the major gas fields.

Despite all these efforts, deficits were kept to low levels only in some years, although in others the NCB broke even or even did very slightly better. In 1970–1971 there was a minute surplus but by then costs were rising steeply, mainly because of inflation in the price of inputs. Productivity was ceasing to rise enough to absorb other increases in costs. Capacity had been so far reduced that output at 133 million long tons was less than could have been sold remuneratively. The miners were becoming restive about the relative decline of their pay in comparison with that in other industries. There were extended national strikes in 1972 and 1974, from which the miners extracted large increases in pay without doing much more than restoring their old relative position. The strikes did, however, encourage further switching to other fuels and led to heavy losses at the NCB. The two strikes caused the government to pay grants totalling £231 million to keep the NCB's deficit within statutory limits. Another financial reconstruction in 1973 cleared accumulated deficits and wrote off other capital, reducing the NCB's liabilities by £450 million altogether. The possibility of the NCB requiring regular subsidiaries was also considered.

Yet the NCB's prospects were improving. In 1973 the United Kingdom entered the European Coal and Steel Community, giving the NCB freedom to fix its own prices. It was able to use this freedom because the huge rise in oil prices in

1973–1974 transformed the energy market. Coal prices were raised to cover the recent large increases in production costs, yet coal retained a cost advantage over oil, very notably in electricity generation. The NCB, which for the first time was headed by a man who had spent his career within the organization, Sir Derek Ezra, chairman from 1971–1982, produced a Plan for Coal that was endorsed by the government. This plan involved replacing obsolescent by new capacity to stave off a prospective decline in output, in the hope—which proved vain—of proceeding to renewed expansion ten years later.

The revival of the NCB was less dramatic than had been hoped. Higher coal prices made opencast mining very profitable, but the cost of inputs continued to increase for deep mining. Labor productivity stagnated, and there was both employee and political resistance to the closure of badly lossmaking collieries. The troubles of the steel industry caused the shrinkage of an important market, and after 1979 the general industrial depression and permanent decline in some heavy industries were further blows. There was competition from cheaper foreign coal, and coal and other solid fuels were at a marked disadvantage in competition with gas for domestic heating. Sales and output of coal made a small recovery for a couple of years after the further huge rise in oil prices in 1979, but the long term trend was slightly downwards. Some of the non-mining businesses, which had been regrouped in two subsidiary holding companies in 1973, contributed valuable profits, but coke ovens fared badly as their markets shrank, and other holdings were not popular with governments. Nearly all the brickworks were sold in 1973. The North Sea gas and oil holdings were compulsorily transferred to the British National Oil Corporation in 1976, with no compensation for loss of expected profits. On the other side of the account, all the reconstruction under the Plan for Coal had to be financed by loans at high rates of interest. For seven years from 1974 onwards, the NCB generally made operating profits in excess of any operating grants received from the government. However, in all but two of the years, this profit became an overall deficit, mainly due to high and rising interest charges.

The 1980s were a traumatic time for the NCB. The problems of market stagnation or contraction, the high costs of some collieries, and high interest charges continued and were reinforced by extreme pressure from the Thatcher government to get rid of financial deficits. Proposals to meet this situation by accelerating colliery closures almost precipitated a strike in 1981. The strike was averted by the provision of government money, though it left a legacy of suspicion. Nevertheless the NCB made much more progress in matching capacity to needs during the brief chairmanship of Sir Norman Siddell in 1982 and 1983. He was both firmer and more persuasive in the pursuit of individual closures. After his retirement, his replacement, Ian MacGregor, who as chairman of British Steel had withstood a national strike in the steel industry, re-aroused the old suspicions and helped the miners' leader, Arthur Scargill, to bring his union into confrontation with the NCB and the government. After an overtime ban from October 1983 there was a bitter year-long strike from March 1984, which the miners lost.

These events created both an urgent need and a better opportunity for a restructuring of the NCB and its business. Its fi-

nances were in ruins and needed a large injection of government money to restore them: losses were £875 million in 1983–1984 and £2,225 million in 1984–1985. Confidence in the ability to maintain a regular supply of fuel had been shaken and although the market was buoyant in 1985–1986 because of the need to restock after the strike, sales subsequently fell to a lower level than before. However, the right of management to manage had been thoroughly restored.

Sir Ian MacGregor's function appeared to have been to defeat the strike; he had little lasting effect on the structure of the NCB. The main changes were carried out under Sir Robert Haslam, a mining engineer whose business career had been mainly outside the coal industry and who was chairman from 1986. He concentrated on improving efficiency, cutting out sources of loss, and matching the size of the business to the size of the market. In four years after the strike, the number of collieries was reduced from 169 to 86, and the number of employees from 221,000 to 105,000. The remaining collieries were given more productive equipment with an insistence on its more intensive use. Productivity rose by 90% and colliery costs fell by one-third. A higher level of total output was obtained by the extremely profitable opencast method. The organization was simplified, with only four areas—in Yorkshire and the Midlands, where costs had long been lowest—and the remaining collieries elsewhere forming groups which reported directly to national headquarters. Many of the non-mining businesses were disposed of, partly in response to government pressure, and steps were taken to reduce capacity and improve the organization of the lossmaking coke division. A new image was sought by changing the NCB's name to British Coal Corporation in 1987.

These changes gave rise to heavy restructuring costs and the burden of interest charges remained severe. As a result, deficits continued and amounted in four years to over £1,000 million. However, operating profits recovered in 1985–1986 and were much higher in relation to both capital and turnover than for many years before the strike. It appeared that although the market remained precarious, the BCC had been sufficiently reshaped to have a better chance of coping with its difficulties.

Principal Subsidiaries: Coal Products Ltd.; National Fuel Distributors Ltd.; British Coal Enterprise Ltd.

Further Reading: Colliery Guardian, *National Coal Board: the first ten years,* London, The Colliery Guardian Company Ltd., 1957; Robens, Lord, *Ten Year Stint,* London, Cassell, 1972; Reid, G.L., Keven Allen, and D.J. Harris, *The Nationalized Fuel Industries,* London, Heinemann Educational Books, 1973; "Structure of the National Coal Board," *The Colliery Guardian,* October 1975 to June 1978; Monopolies and Mergers Commission, *National Coal Board,* 2 Vols., London, HMSO, 1983; Ashworth, William, *History of the British Coal Industry,* Vol. 5, *1946–1982 The Nationalized Industry,* Oxford, Clarendon Press, 1986; Adeney, Martin, and John Lloyd, *The Miners' Strike 1984–5: Loss Without Limit,* London, Routledge & Kegan Paul, 1986.

—William Ashworth

BRITISH STEEL PLC

9 Albert Embankment
London SE1 7SN
United Kingdom
(071) 735-7654
Fax: (071) 587-1142

Public Company
Incorporated: 1967 as the British Steel Corporation
Employees: 53,300
Sales: £5.11 billion (US$9.86 billion)
Stock Exchanges: London New York Toronto

British Steel plc is the fourth-largest steel producer in the world. Its five integrated plants, at Port Talbot and Llanwern, Wales; Ravenscraig, Scotland; and Scunthorpe and Teesside, England, account for 75% of the liquid steel produced in the United Kingdom. The company also produces stainless steels, tubes, and pipes. Two-thirds of its sales are to customers in the United Kingdom; it supplies over 60% of the U.K. market for steel, while nearly one-fifth of its output goes to the rest of the European Community. The company is the sixth-largest non-oil exporter in Britain.

The company is the successor, by way of the state-owned British Steel Corporation (BSC), to the leading private steel companies that had survived the Depression of the 1920s and 1930s and World War II. Under the Labour government of 1945–1951 these companies first profited from the large compensation payments they received for giving up their coal-mining interests to the state and then were nationalized themselves, on the grounds that they formed an oligopoly with the power to restrict output, raise prices, and prevent technical progress. The Iron and Steel Corporation of Great Britain was established in 1950 as a state holding company for their shares, but the steelmasters retained the initiative, mainly through a boycott organized by the British Iron and Steel Federation (BISF), the industry's trade association, which they controlled.

In autumn 1951 a new Conservative government suspended the corporation's activities after eight months of largely ineffective existence. Between 1953 and 1963 an Iron and Steel Holding and Realisation Agency sold off 16 of the 17 nationalized firms, mostly to the former shareholders. At the same time an Iron Steel Board was given the negative powers of fixing maximum prices for products sold in the United Kingdom and approving or rejecting any investment of over

£100,000. Price control was nothing new, having begun on a more modest scale in 1932, with the result by the 1950s that losses during low points of the economic cycle could not be offset by higher profits in more prosperous times. The companies' reluctance to invest intensified, and the Iron and Steel Board—or rather the taxpayers who financed it—became the major source of new investment funds.

During the 1950s and 1960s the British steel industry lost its historic advantages of cheap coal and plentiful iron ore, the industry's basic raw materials. Coal prices rose by 134% between 1950 and 1967, and the domestic iron ore industry was neglected in favor of ore from new fields overseas. Rearmament, from 1950 onwards, caused the company to retain old plant, instead of investing in costly new plant, the attempt to keep up with demand. Between 1945 and 1960 total crude steel production in the United Kingdom doubled in volume, an increase largely attributable to such technical innovations as oxygen-based production and continuous casting. The claim that the industry had now been taken out of politics was belied by the events of 1958–1959, when the Conservative prime minister, Harold Macmillan, sanctioned not the single extra strip mill the industry wanted, but two, one at Llanwern in Wales and another at Ravenscraig in Scotland, both subsidized from public funds and neither able to operate at full capacity.

However, the British steel industry's problems were not all due to the government or the companies. It faced new rivals, especially in Japan, as well as old ones, in France, West Germany, Belgium, and Luxembourg, which were now protected by the European Coal and Steel Community and some of which were blessed with deep-water harbors taking in high-grade ores. In addition there was a general fall in the rate of growth of world demand for steel from around 1960, leading to declining prices and profits for the steel industry worldwide, a scramble to dispose of surplus output at the lowest sustainable prices, and a worldwide steel glut which lasted until 1969. The British industry in particular continued to be marked by a cautious attitude learned in the 1920s and never shaken off, and by the refusal of the individual firms to cooperate with one another in anything that might threaten their own identities. The steel industry faced the 1960s with a fragmented structure based on investment decisions which, apart from the establishment of the Ravenscraig mill, had been taken in the 1930s.

In 1964 the Labour Party returned to office with a commitment to renationalize steel. The BISF's response was the Benson report, which concluded that the industry needed to go over entirely to the basic oxygen process, to build extra capacity in much larger plants, to site them near the coasts (for raw materials supplies), and to shed 65% of existing plant and 100,000 workers. These proposals gave the government new ammunition, since in spite of the companies' claims that they could provide most of the necessary capital from their falling profits, it was clear that the industry alone could not hope to finance these developments. The nationalized British Steel Corporation (BSC) began operations on July 28, 1967, just when new orders were at their lowest level in five years, and in a period of mergers among companies in France, Germany, and Japan. At its inception BSC was the second largest steel company in the noncommunist world, endowed with the assets of the 14 crude steel companies, whose output exceeded 475,000 tons. They employed 268,500 people, and included

Richard Thomas & Baldwins, a company that had remained in state ownership since 1951.

BSC faced some formidable problems. Firstly, since compensation to the former owners was based on stock market values, and not—as in private mergers and acquisitions—on net assets or future profitability, the shareholders received about £350 million more than the assets were worth. A later Conservative government recognized the loss to BSC and wrote off that amount of its debt in 1972. Secondly, the 14 companies' return on capital had fallen from 15% in 1956 to 3.7%, making them unable to carry out the Benson plan they had commissioned, and the sorry state of their assets was bound to damage BSC's profitability for some time to come. Thirdly, 10% of crude steel production and about 30% of finished steel production remained in the private sector, leaving BSC with the generally less profitable bulk steel and lower-quality finished steel business. As the private firms were effectively subsidized through the controls on BSC's pricing of crude steel sold to them, they could concentrate resources on technical advances which allowed higher productivity, giving them about a third of the market for finished steel, with only a quarter of total capacity, by the late 1970s. In this respect BSC was unlike its major rivals abroad, which were diversified within steel and across other sectors. Fourthly, BSC's capital consisted of £834 million, to be repaid to the Treasury at a fixed rate of interest, regardless of its profit cycle. Between 1967 and 1980 BSC's interest payments were equivalent to 73% of its losses. A private-sector company in the same situation would not have been burdened with interest payments.

Unlike other public corporations BSC had been given the freedom to decide organizational questions for itself. Its structure was regionally based until 1970, divided into six product divisions until 1976, put onto a different geographical basis until 1980, and then re-divided into different product divisions, with numerous profit centers within them, linked to a new system of mostly self-financing local bonus schemes for the workers.

One unique aspect of BSC's organization was the presence of worker-directors, first on the boards of the regional groups, then on the boards of the product divisions, and lastly, after 1976, on the main board. The steel industry had long enjoyed a relatively good record in industrial relations. The relatively few strikes in the industry's history had usually been over demarcation among the trade unions, of which there were 17 in the industry in 1967, and among which the Iron and Steel Trades Confederation was dominant, containing half of the 80% of the work force which belonged to unions. It was the ISTC that felt most threatened by change, since it would tend to cut into the union's base among the less skilled blue collar workers. The part-time worker-directors were appointed after consultations with these unions and with the Trades Union Congress, the national labor federation. Since the management retained its monopoly of information and authority, the influence of these unelected representatives was minimal, ceasing altogether with their abolition in 1983, three years after the defeat of the national steelworkers' strike had signaled the end of the trade unions' influence in the company. In 1970-1971 the new Conservative government at first considered various ways of breaking up or partially privatizing BSC, then decided to continue with the status quo while raising the corporation's borrowing limits and giving some flexibility on pricing. BSC

later announced that with British steel prices held below European Community levels from 1967 to 1975 the losses amounted to about £780 million, representing another indirect subsidy to the private sector, in this case to steel consumers.

The corporation initiated its "heritage program" in 1971-1972 to develop the strengths and overcome the weaknesses of the assets inherited from the private companies, in particular the low productivity of blast furnaces, which was due to inefficient cooling and the use of low-grade material such as coking coal with a high sulfur content. By 1973 BSC had invested £764 million in this program and in new projects such as Anchor III, the construction of a new plant at the Appleby-Frodingham complex in Scunthorpe, Lincolnshire, on the site of abandoned ironstone workings. At the nearby port of Immingham, a terminal was built where 100,000-ton vessels could bring foreign ore for the furnaces. The opening of the plant only three years after the scheme was authorized seemed to bode well for BSC's increased efficiency, and helped accelerate the trend whereby imported ores rose from 55% of the total used in the United Kingdom in 1967 to 85% in 1974.

By 1973 British steel consumption had exceeded 18 million tons a year. The ten-year development strategy started in 1973 envisaged concentration of resources on five inherited sites, and on a new sixth complex on Teesside. Some £3 billion—half from BSC, half from the taxpayers—were to be spent on raising capacity and on shutting down older plants, with the loss of at least 50,000 jobs—in other words, a slightly revised version of the BISF's Benson report. BSC also did something that the steelmasters had never done; it created a subsidiary, BSC (Industry) Ltd. in 1975, to invest in new non-steel ventures in areas where its closure program would hit hardest.

The development strategy committed the government, BSC, and the country to the largest capital investment program in British history. Also in 1973, the United Kingdom joined the European Community, where excess capacity in steel was already at the highest level in the world and where BSC could no longer rely on an 8% tariff to keep European imports out. Then came a worldwide slump, caused by the oil crisis. The collapse of demand for steel during 1975 caused BSC to accelerate its closure program, after a public fight over the issue with the Labour government and, in 1977, to give up the ten-year strategy in favor of aiming for 30 million tons by 1982.

The Conservative government elected in 1979 at first announced that no more money would be available for BSC. Then in 1980, when BSC's losses rose to £545 million, the government increased its borrowing limit once again, while the board announced that 60,000 jobs would be cut within 12 months. The 13-week national strike which followed, the first in the steel industry since 1926, cut deeper into BSC's profits as imports rose to fill the gap it caused.

In 1980-1981 the Conservative government abolished the BSC's statutory duties to promote the supply of iron and steel and to further the public interest, took new powers to direct BSC's use of its assets, and wrote off a total of £5 billion of debts. In the next few years BSC regained some lost ground, and beat European records for closing plants and making cuts in the work force, but by 1982 British customers' demand for steel was down to just over 12 million tons and BSC's share of this market went below 50% for the first time. The majority of the private steelmakers also sought state aid, and received about £50 million in 1982 and more in later years. They also benefited from the "Phoenix" series of joint ventures with BSC, starting in 1981, since they were financed mainly out of public funds.

Having failed to persuade the government to allow the closure of the integrated plant at Ravenscraig, Ian MacGregor left BSC in 1983 to run the coal industry. BSC had made 105,000 workers redundant during his three years there, compared with 82,500 between 1967 and 1979 and 28,000 between 1983 and 1990. The mineworkers' strike of 1984–1985 which MacGregor then helped to precipitate and to defeat, dealt BSC another unexpected blow, causing £180 million of losses in that financial year and helping to turn an operating profit of £40 million into a loss of £409 million.

In 1986 the chairmanship of BSC passed to Robert Scholey, who had spent his entire career in the industry, and whose father was a director of one of the pre-1967 private steel firms. In 1987, with Scholey's full support, the government announced its intention to privatize BSC, and the company became British Steel plc in 1988, just before demand for steel began to fall. The new company undertook to keep all five of its main plants open until the end of 1994, subject to market conditions.

British Steel plc's first 18 months were certainly eventful. The company carried out the fourth overhaul of its production structure since 1967, ending up with five divisions—general steels, strip products, stainless steels, distribution, and diversified activities. The company then won the contract to supply rails for the Channel Tunnel, was fined by the European Commission—along with five other steel companies—for participating in an illegal cartel to fix stainless steel prices, acquired the Mannstädt division of the German steel firm Klöckner-Werke, and announced that the hot strip mill at Ravenscraig would be shut down in 1991. It replaced national pay bargaining with divisional and local talks to reinforce the emphasis on productivity and increased total payments to the directors of the company by 78%.

It is important not to allow the issue of state versus private ownership in the United Kingdom to obscure crucial facts. The state sector has not been a drain on the private sector's resources. On the contrary, many private firms have benefited from the artificially low prices of BSC's and other public corporations' products, or from subsidies and other assistance given by successive governments, including those committed to the free market. The public corporations have been run by the same kinds of executives as in the private sector.

The act of nationalizing the company made little difference to its operations. Even BSC's huge investment program might have been carried out by a public board aiding private firms, as in the 1960s, although BSC's second chairman, Sir Monty Finniston, told the House of Commons Select Committee on Nationalised Industries, in 1977 that "we would have done nothing if we were in the private sector, absolutely nothing." At the same time the company's history shows that the act of privatizing a company does not automatically improve its efficiency or contribute to economic growth.

It is misleading to treat the British steel industry as a special case within the world steel industry, as both supporters and opponents of state ownership have done. Steel production is deeply affected by changes beyond the steelmakers' control. Supplies of coal and iron ore are subject to enormous fluctuations in price and volume. The industry has fixed capital costs. Steel is a raw material, with construction accounting for 18.5% of British Steel's sales in 1989–1990; the motor industry accounting for 14.6% of sales; and other manufacturers providing further sales. Fluctuations in the steel industry's economic conditions depend on the demand for its customers' products, not for steel itself. Government intervention, to control prices, protect jobs, promote regional development, and secure self-sufficiency, has been pervasive but inconsistent. Steel production has displayed long-term tendencies toward alternating crises of under-and over-production, in what has generally been a four-yearly cycle. The postwar history of the British steel industry has displayed all of these features, and would have done so whoever had owned most of its assets.

The company's improved results in the late 1980s, both in and out of state ownership, were due—at least in part—to the growth of the British economy, to the global fall in the prices of raw materials—often creating a benefit to the British steel industry at the cost of Third World producers—and to favorable movements on the foreign exchange markets since 1985. Post-tax profit, declared in June 1990 after BSC's first full year in the private sector, was £565 million.

It is open to question whether the company's profits can continue at a high level in the 1990s. In the year up to November 1990 iron ore and coal prices moved upwards again, while sales of steel in the United Kingdom fell by 10%, and the company's own pre-tax profits fell by 27%. The company decided to shut down the Clydesdale seamless tube works, and the chairman stated that running five big integrated plants put the company at a competitive disadvantage.

After passing into and out of the public sector, twice over in 40 years, the company's chances of success or failure still depend not on its changing ownership but on the enduring features indicated by its name. British Steel plc is very much part of the British economy, and it is part of the world steel industry.

Principal Subsidiaries: Bore Steel Group Ltd.; British Steel Service Centres Ltd.; British Tubes Stockholding Ltd.; Cold Drawn Tubes Ltd.; H.E. Samson Ltd.; Seamless Tubes Ltd.; Whitehead (Narrow Strip) Ltd.; British Steel Exports Ltd.; British Steel Tubes Exports Ltd.; British Steel (Industry) Ltd; C. Walker & Sons (Holdings) Ltd.; British Steel Consultants Ltd.

Further Reading: Heal, David W., *The Steel Industry in Post War Britain,* London, David & Charles, 1974; Vaizey, John, *The History of British Steel,* London, Weidenfeld & Nicolson, 1974; Ovenden, Keith, *The Politics of Steel,* London, Macmillan, 1978; Bryer, R.A., et al., *Accounting for British Steel,* Aldershot, Gower Publishing, 1982; Abromeit, Heidrun, *British Steel,* Leamington Spa, Berg Publishers, 1986.

—Patrick Heenan

BROKEN HILL PROPRIETARY COMPANY LTD.

BHP House
140 William Street
Melbourne, Victoria 3000
Australia
(03) 609-3333
Fax: (03) 609-3015

Public Company
Incorporated: 1885
Employees: 50,887
Sales: A$10.00 million (US$7.72 million)
Stock Exchanges: Australia London Frankfurt Tokyo
 New Zealand Basel Geneva Zürich New York

Broken Hill Proprietary Company (BHP) is Australia's largest commercial organization and by world standards a significant multinational operation. Its size and influence have led some to refer to it as Australia's eighth state. Currently BHP's business is based on three core activities: steel making, mineral exploration, and mineral production—principally iron ore, coal, copper, and manganese—and petroleum exploration and refining.

BHP owes its foundation to Charles Rasp, a boundary rider working in the early 1880s on the Mt. Gipps station near Silverton in New South Wales. As a boundary rider, Rasp patrolled the property, repairing fences and generally checking the property. The station was managed by George McCulloch. Rasp believed that a low broken-backed ridge on the property—the Broken Hill—contained argentiferous ores. He persuaded McCulloch and five others to form a syndicate for the purpose of testing the ridge. The first shaft sunk proved disappointing and some of the original syndicate members sold their shares, but the core members decided to raise the capital necessary for further investigation by floating a public company; they issued a prospectus in 1885 in the name of the Broken Hill Proprietary Company. Almost simultaneously, news arrived of a significant silver strike. BHP shares rose sharply in value once it was announced that the company's first consignment of 48 tons of ore had realized 35,605 ounces of silver, worth nearly £7,500.

None of the directors of the new company had been trained as mining engineers. BHP therefore imported the talents of two U.S. engineers, William Patton and Hermann Schlapp, whose technical work rescued the company's collapsing Big Mine at Broken Hill.

Easily accessible high grade ores, low labor and equipment costs, and high silver and lead prices made the 15-year period to the end of the 19th century extremely profitable for BHP. The establishment of a head office in Melbourne and a lead refinery at Port Pirie were evidence of the company's increasing contribution to and investment in the states of Victoria and South Australia but in New South Wales (NSW), around Broken Hill itself, the *laissez-faire* attitude of both BHP and the state government led to the growth of a primitive shanty town. The dangerous conditions in which the miners themselves had to work and the squalid circumstances in which their families had to live brought the Amalgamated Miners' Association (AMA) and other unions into conflict with BHP in 1889 and 1890. As a result of the 1892 slump in world silver and lead prices, BHP decided to scrap a work-practice agreement with the AMA and to prompt a showdown with a union movement it openly regarded with contempt. BHP led the other mining companies established at Broken Hill in the bitter and violent strike which ensued, declaring its intention of breaking free from union-imposed wage agreements by offering freedom of contract instead as the basis for future employment. After four months, with their leaders imprisoned, the unions capitulated and the work force returned to the mines, with the exception of known strike leaders whom BHP refused to re-employ. A legacy of bitterness had been created between labor and management, which was to surface repeatedly to poison BHP's relations both with its own employees and with the Australian labor movement in general. The ambivalent attitude towards their country's largest company that many Australians still retain arose from the 1892 strike and the many others which succeeded it.

In the first decade of the 20th century, BHP faced a decline in silver prices coupled with the mining-out of the accessible top-side ores which had been cheap to mine. Henceforth it had to work the deeper-lying sulfide ores, a more costly operation compounded by the greater difficulty of extracting silver from this type of ore.

Guillaume Delprat, a Dutch engineer and chemist whom BHP had brought to Australia from Europe, provided the solution to the problem of treating sulfide ores with his invention in 1902 of the flotation process. This method and later variants enabled BHP and other Broken Hill companies to extract silver, lead, and especially zinc from sulfide tailings, which had until then been deemed almost worthless. Delprat had become BHP's general manager in 1899 and under his careful but imaginative stewardship BHP's productivity rose steadily.

Delprat and BHP's directors insisted that an important factor in the company's success was the flexibility that the free contract system of employment allowed amid fluctuating and uncertain world metals markets. They were staunch believers in loyalty to the company, hard work, and self-help, and held that these virtues rather than socialism or unionism were the real allies of the Australian worker. The union movement disagreed with this analysis and in 1905 militants urged the NSW government not to renew BHP's leases at the Big Mine. Two years later BHP announced that it could no longer honor the remainder of its existing wage agreements on the grounds that plunging metals prices made these unworkable.

Early in 1909 the AMA launched a new strike. This time BHP stood alone, its intransigence and stubborn refusal to deal with the union having alienated it from the other Broken Hill companies. The strike was marked throughout by exceptional violence and intimidation of scab labor brought in by BHP to work the mine. When Australia's Arbitration Court ruled against the company, the latter appealed to the High Court, unsuccessfully. BHP's response was to delay the opening of the mine and then reduce the number of workers employed.

Delprat and his fellow directors had already perceived that the Big Mine's days of economic productivity were numbered. Rather than buying new leases and opening new mines they decided that BHP's future lay in steel manufacture. At that time Australia possessed no steel industry and there was considerable skepticism both in Australia and abroad as to whether such an industry could be established successfully in a country far removed from the world's traditional steel markets and with no appreciable industrial base.

Delprat, however, was certain that a local steel producer could quickly capture a growing local market still dependent on costly imports from the United Kingdom and pointed to the advantages which Australia and BHP possessed—cheap energy in the form of large and accessible coal fields in NSW, and the company's own sizeable and high quality iron ore deposits at Iron Knob in South Australia. On the advice of a U.S. steel expert, David Baker, BHP chose Newcastle on the NSW coast as the site of its first steel works due to the proximity of the coalfields and the presence of both labor and manufacturing industry in the area. Newcastle was also connected by rail to Sydney, Australia's largest city and manufacturing center.

BHP acted swiftly to forestall the setting up of a proposed state-owned steel works. Baker designed the new plant along the latest U.S. lines, the whole project being financed out of an increase in share capital, two debenture issues, and the sale in 1915 of BHP's Port Pirie lead smelter to the Broken Hill Associated Smelters Company for £300,000. Steel production commenced in April 1915.

Wartime demand for armaments and sheet steel ensured production at full capacity and guaranteed the steel mill's early years. At Broken Hill, however, inflation during World War I worsened conditions, producing strikes in 1915, 1917, and 1919, the last of which was settled in the unions' favor, resulting in a new 35-hour work week and a rise in wage rates. By this time, however, BHP's energies were focused on its expanding steel business and the Big Mine played a progressively smaller role in the company's calculations, closing altogether in 1939 and thereby ending BHP's association with Broken Hill.

In 1921 Delprat was succeeded by Essington Lewis, a mining engineer who had joined BHP in the first decade of the century and risen swiftly in the corporate hierarchy. Lewis continued the policy of supporting the establishment of secondary manufacturers who would use BHP steel in their products, thus creating new customers for the company and new industries for Australia.

The short-lived postwar steel boom was followed by a scramble for shrinking world markets. BHP suffered several handicaps in the race. The most serious of these was its having to serve a small home market with a diverse range of products, thereby failing to obtain the economies of scale achieved by its foreign competitors. In addition freight costs for export had soared due to the postwar shortage of shipping, and rises in the price of coal were reducing BHP's margins.

Lewis campaigned for protection, and the William M. Hughes government eventually imposed import duties on imported steel. The 1920 seamen's strike convinced BHP that it had to control its own shipping. This belief led to the foundation of BHP's fleet of dedicated ore carriers.

Despite import duties, foreign steel was still managing to undersell the local product. BHP announced it would have to shut down capacity unless the steel unions—chiefly the Federated Ironworkers Association (FIA)—were willing to accept wage reductions. This acceptance was not forthcoming and in May 1922 temporary closure of the Newcastle mill for a month was followed by a total shutdown lasting nine months until a ruling of the Arbitration Court compelled BHP to reopen it. Terrible hardship had been caused in the Newcastle area, and union leaders and elements in the Labour Party began to call for BHP's nationalization.

After this difficult start Lewis launched a program concentrating on improving the efficiency, safety, and cleanliness of the steel plant, all concepts closely linked in Lewis's mind and to which he attached the greatest importance. He placed particular emphasis on the replacement of old machinery, with the result that by the end of the 1920s BHP was operating one of the cleanest, safest, and most cost-effective steel plants in the world. Thus the Depression which began in 1929 and so devastated other Australian industries left the steel industry comparatively unscathed.

Just as control of shipping was essential to reduce freight costs, so Lewis reasoned that ownership of coal would make BHP independent of the demands of the mine owners. BHP therefore began to buy up coal mines, a foretaste of the great expansion of its coal interests in the 1970s and 1980s.

Although BHP entered the Depression with an unusually small debt burden—Lewis disliked paying for new machinery with borrowed money—and an efficient steel operation, it was not immune from the effects. A collapse of world prices in steel, silver, and lead forced BHP to reduce production levels and lay off large numbers of mill workers. The Big Mine was shut down until a rise in metals prices made reopening worthwhile, and from 1930 until 1932 BHP did not pay dividends to its shareholders. The company viewed with distrust the economic policies of Scullin's Labour government, which it regarded as populist and short-sighted. This attitude was mollified when the government sought to stimulate local industry by imposing a new round of duties on imports, and devalued the Australian currency to encourage Australian exporters. These measures, in tandem with BHP's underlying financial strength and Lewis's policy of low-cost selling, ensured the company's survival.

In 1935 BHP's only competitor in Australia, the struggling Australian Iron & Steel Company (AIS), sought a merger with its larger rival. BHP was quick to agree and at a stroke acquired AIS's valuable steelworks at Port Kembla, NSW, and its iron ore deposits at Yampi Sound in Western Australia. BHP's opponents attacked the merger as monopolistic and called for an official enquiry. The issue became intensely political with two future Australian prime ministers, John Curtin and Robert Menzies, respectively attacking and defending the merger.

Two years later the South Australian government asked BHP to construct a steel plant in the state. BHP, anxious to see its leases at Iron Knob extended, agreed to build a furnace and port at Whyalla on the Spencer Gulf. This and other investments in the years immediately prior to World War II were paid for by four major restructurings in the company's capital base.

In 1938 BHP became embroiled in another political battle when union labor refused to handle cargoes of iron ore destined for Japan, at that time engaged in a brutal and aggressive war in China. BHP's insistence on carrying through its contractual obligations aroused strong emotions in Australia and Attorney General Robert Menzies's defense of BHP's action earned him the unflattering sobriquet of 'pig-iron Bob'.

In 1940 Menzies appointed Lewis Director General of Munitions with the responsibility of harnessing the nations' entire manufacturing industry to the war effort. Lewis applied to this demanding job all the energy and concentration which enabled BHP to achieve the new targets set by his wartime planning. New blast and open-hearth furnaces were built at Port Kembla and a shipyard established at Whyalla. Comparatively far removed from the area of battle, BHP's mills suffered no physical damage during the war, but were subjected to brief and ineffectual shelling of Newcastle by a Japanese submarine. However, the company lost two of its ore carriers to enemy torpedoes. Japan's frighteningly rapid advance into Southeast Asia up to Australia's not-so-distant neighbor, New Guinea, in 1942, served to quell union antagonism towards BHP. As this threat receded, the unions renewed their attacks, culminating in a protracted strike in late 1945, which began at Port Kembla and then drew in coal miners and seamen, rapidly assuming the proportions of a national crisis. Although the militant far Left in the unions failed to achieve its objective of BHP's nationalization and lost its influence during the strike, this episode had the effect of dampening BHP's plans for renewed investment in its steel business. Not until the end of the 1940s did this situation change, when a rising demand for steel encouraged increased production and investment.

In 1950 Lewis became chairman of BHP. Two years later he relinquished his position to Colin Syme, a lawyer who had joined BHP's Board in 1937.

During the early 1950s Japan's resuscitated steel industry began to demonstrate its capacity for large scale low-cost production, which in the 1960s helped underwrite Japan's extraordinary economic growth. Once again the Japanese renewed their search abroad for low-cost iron ore reserves. The Australian government's lifting in 1960 of its pre-war restrictions on the export of iron ore encouraged BHP to enter the field once again as a prospector. This entry led to the identification of large iron ore deposits, notably at Koolanyobbing, Western Australia, and Koolan Island, Western Australia. Quarries were commissioned at these two sites, but the centerpiece of BHP's iron ore business became the Mt. Newman ore body in the Pilbara region of Western Australia. In association with AMAX (American Metal Climax, Inc.) and CSR, the company established a joint venture operation to develop and operate the world's largest open-pit iron ore mine. BHP initially held a 30% interest but in 1985 bought out the remaining AMAX and CSR shareholdings.

During the early 1960s BHP transformed the nature of its business by deciding to enter the oil exploration and production industry. Australia's geology had tended to discourage oil prospecting but in 1960, true to its tradition of seeking expertise outside Australia, BHP asked the U.S. petroleum expert L.G. Weekes to examine some of its leases. Weekes advised BHP to drill offshore in the Bass Strait area. Despite the con-

siderable technical difficulties involved, but encouraged by the subsidies of an Australian government keen to see the country's costly dependence on imported oil reduced, BHP went into a 50/50 partnership with Standard Oil's Australian subsidiary, Esso Standard. In 1964 the first well was commissioned in the Gippsland Basin area off the coast of Victoria. The extensive gas fields found as a corollary were developed for domestic use and export to Japan.

At about the same time, BHP began the development of a manganese mine at Groote Eylandte in the Gulf of Carpentaria. As at Mt. Newman this enterprise comprised not only the commissioning of the mine itself but also the building of a whole township, transport links, and a port area.

A booming minerals and steel market enabled BHP to double its net profit between 1960 and 1970. Such rapid growth began to out-distance a management structure that had remained essentially unaltered since Essington Lewis's day. On the advice of a firm of U.S. management consultants, BHP adopted the concept of independent profit centers, each responsible for its own performance.

Such moves did not prevent BHP's critics from claiming that the company was still too large, too secretive, and above all too unaccountable to the Australian public for its decisions. Antimonopolists held that BHP's stranglehold on sales outlets prevented any rival steelmaker from setting up operations in Australia, while environmentalists questioned the company's record on industrial pollution. The unions attacked it for its strict adherence to the "minimum wage policy" laid down by the Arbitration Court, justified by BHP as a necessary measure in the light of competition from producers with lower labor costs, such as Japan and Taiwan.

The Labour Government elected in 1972 took several actions against BHP. Rex Connor, Minister for Minerals and Energy, attacked BHP for profiteering and proceeded to remove the subsidies BHP had been given for its oil exploration work. Tax concessions were cancelled. Particularly irritating for the company were the decisions and comments of the Government's Prices Justification Tribunal before which BHP was required to defend its pricing policies.

In the middle of the decade BHP announced its decision to enter into a partnership with Shell to exploit the natural gas deposits found off the northern coast of Western Australia. Known as the North West Shelf Natural Gas Project, the justification for the huge investment needed lay in the interest shown by foreign energy consumers, especially the Japanese. Construction work began in 1981 and by 1984 the domestic gas phase of the project had been commissioned, followed by the launch of the export phase in 1989. Further offshore oil discoveries in the Timor Sea at Jabiru in the early 1980s launched another production program.

In the core business of steel production, however, the 1970s and 1980s were marked by rising production costs and falling world steel prices as overcapacity in world production drove down the world market. In 1976 BHP Steel announced losses of some A$50 million, and in 1979 it had to abandon plans for a steel mill in western Australia. The collapse in steel prices in 1983 forced BHP to rationalize its business, and in that year nearly a third of the Steel Division's employees were made redundant. In an effort to safeguard the steel industry's future, the Labour Government of the day announced a five-year Steel Industry Plan under which the steel unions promised to refrain from industrial action in return for guarantees from BHP relating to security of employment for their members. Under the new dispensation BHP managed to boost its productivity from only 150 tons per worker per annum in 1982 to some 250 tons in 1984. The five-year plan was widely regarded as a milestone in Australian industrial relations. With A$2 billion worth of new plant commissioned since the mid-1980s, BHP Steel has substantially restructured its business to achieve international competitiveness. Its three integrated steelworks in Australia have a steelmaking capacity of almost seven million tons per year. It also operates a range of downstream processing facilities in Australia, and steel forming and building products facilities in Asia and the west coast of the United States. The steel group aims to maintain exports at about 25% of production on a continuing basis and increase the amount of value-added steel in the export product mix.

Besides Australia's vast iron ore deposits, foreign industries looked towards the country's coal fields as a source of energy not subject to the vagaries of Middle Eastern power politics and price instability. The sharp rises in oil prices in 1973 and 1979 began to renew BHP's interest in coal and coal mining for export purposes. In 1976–1977, BHP acquired Peabody Coal's Australian assets, thereby gaining a 60% interest in the Moura and Kianga coal mines in Queensland. In 1979 the huge Gregory mine was opened, followed a year later by the Saxonvale mine in NSW. In 1985 BHP increased its holding in Thiess Dampier Mitsui, operator of the Moura and Kianga mines, to more than 80%.

The largest and the most important acquisition BHP has ever made occurred a year earlier when it bought the U.S. mining and construction company Utah Mines Ltd. from General Electric. This move extended BHP's interests abroad into the United States, Canada, and South America and greatly enlarged BHP's interests in coal, iron ore, and copper mining. The Escondida copper mine in Chile, which commenced production in December 1990, is the third largest in the world. BHP manages the mine and has a 57.5% interest. This mine's low production costs and large reserves base mean it is competitively positioned. Another significant acquisition for BHP was a 30% interest in the OK Tedi gold and copper mine in Papua New Guinea, which began producing in 1984. In Australia during the 1980s BHP commissioned gold mines at Ora Banda and Boddington and a new lead and zinc mine at Cadjebut. BHP added to its iron ore interests in the Pilbara region of Australia through the purchase in 1990 of the remaining 70% of Mt. Goldsworthy Mining Associates it did not already own. It has since sold a minority interest in Mt. Goldsworthy and a new iron ore mine named Yandi to its Japanese partners in the Mt. Newman joint venture. BHP Gold Mines Ltd. merged with Newmont Australia Ltd. in 1990. The merger created a major Australian gold company renamed Newcrest Mining Ltd. in which BHP has the largest single shareholding, 23%. The major acquisitions of Hamilton Oil in 1987 and of Pacific Resources Inc. in 1989 further increased BHP's strength in the fields of oil exploration and refining in the North Sea and Pacific Ocean. BHP was in the early 1990s in the process of acquiring full ownership of Hamilton Oil Corporation.

In 1987 BHP reorganized into three core business groups, steel, petroleum, and minerals, which operate worldwide. BHP is also engaged in transport, engineering, and research activities to support its main businesses and invests in promising new industries that build on its skills and competitive position.

BHP shows little likelihood of relinquishing its position as Australia's industrial and resources flagship in the near future. Twice in its history BHP's management has shown remarkable vision and courage in moving the company into entirely new fields of enterprise at the right moment and in the right manner. It is this unusual flexibility as much as its size that has for long made its shares valuable property both in Australia and abroad and provided Australia with its steel and oil industries, two cornerstones of its economy. In whatever industries BHP chooses to make its investment in the future, the impact on Australia and increasingly in other parts of the world will be considerable.

Principal Subsidiaries: Australian Iron & Steel Pty Ltd.; AWI Holdings Pty Ltd.; BHP Finance Ltd.; BHP Gold Mines Ltd. (55.7%); BHP Investment Holdings Ltd. (U.K.); BHP Minerals Holdings Pty Ltd.; BHP Minerals Ltd.; Mt. Newman Iron Ore Company Ltd. (85%); Pilbara Iron Ltd.; BHP Petroleum International; BHP Petroleum (North West Shelf) Pty Ltd.; BHP Petroleum (Americas) Inc. (U.S.A.); BHP-Utah International Inc. (U.S.A.); Hamilton Oil Corporation (U.S.A., 50.6%); BHP Transport Ltd.; Groote Eylandt Mining Company Pty Ltd.; BHP-Utah Coal Ltd.; John Lysaght (Australia) Ltd.

Further Reading: Raggatt, H.G., *Mountains of Ore*, Melbourne, Lansdowne Press, 1968; Trengrove, A., *What's Good for Australia—A History of BHP*, London, Cassell, 1975; BHP, *Australians in Company*, Melbourne, BHP, 1985.

—D.H. O'Leary

COAL INDIA LIMITED

Coal Bhawan
10 Netaji Subhase Road
Calcutta
700001
India
(33) 20 21 03
Fax: (33) 03 28 373

State-Owned Company
Incorporated: 1975
Employees: 700,000 (1989)
Sales: Rs8.30 billion (US$457.30 million) (1988)

Coal India Limited (CIL), a holding company, is a state-owned mining corporation and the largest coal producer in India. In 1990, production was 179 million tons of hard coal, up from 172 million tons the previous year. This comprised almost 88% of the coal output in India. However, like many state-owned concerns, CIL's financial performance has been generally poor, and it has made profits in only two years since its creation in 1975. During the financial year 1989-1990 CIL made a loss of Rs230 million. Although this loss was less severe than those made in the period immediately after nationalization, it marked a decline from the previous financial year when it made a profit of Rs82 million. Coal provides more than 50% of India's energy requirements. However, India's per capita energy consumption is among the lowest in the world. India has vast coal reserves, and these can be mined cheaply, although the coal is generally of poor quality and has a high ash content. In 1991, India's total coal reserves were estimated at 176 billion tons, of which over 30 billion tons are proven reserves, within 200 meters of the coal pit or the workings. Of the total, coking coal—coal from which the volatile elements have been removed, making it suitable as a fuel, and for metallurgical purposes—comprises 24 billion tons (11 billion tons proven). The bulk of India's coal reserves are in the Bengal-Bihar coalfields in the west of the country. Due to the structure of the coal mining industry in India, CIL's role is a major one, and its performance and operations very much reflect the policies and priorities of the government of India.

The Indian coal industry has its origins in the early 19th century, when mining activity became commercial in conjunction with the expansion of the railway network, particularly in the west of the country. The monopoly interests of the British East India Company were revoked in 1813. Initially, the coal fields were operated by a large number of Indian private companies which possessed captive—or company-owned—coalfields to support their iron and steel works. By 1900 there were 34 companies producing 7 million tons of coal from 286 mines. Production continued to grow in the first half of the 20th century, especially during World War I. Demand continued to grow during World War II, and production reached 29 million tons by 1945. By then, the number of companies had increased to 307, and the number of mines to 673. The trend continued for almost a decade after India's independence in 1947. However, India's ambitious economic development plans led to a tremendous demand for energy, and in the absence of alternative sources, coal was targeted as the major source of power for industrialization. Under the government's Second Five Year Economic Development Plan 1957–1961, a target of 60 million tons was set for the end of the plan period. However, government economic planners were convinced that the private sector would be unable to meet this target. Hence, the National Coal Development Corporation (NCDC) was formed, which took the old railway collieries as its nucleus and opened new mines as well. Production of coal increased from 38 million tons in 1956 to 56 million tons in 1961.

During the 1960s, most of India's collieries continued to be operated by the private sector, with the exception of NCDC and the Singareni Collieries, both in the public sector. At the national level, three factors emerged to force the government to consider the nationalization of the coal industry. First, there was a fear that contemporary mining methods were leading to great wastage. Second, the government predicted that future demand for coal would be particularly heavy in view of its industrial development priorities. Finally, during the Third Five Year Plan 1962–1966, as well as the period 1966–1969, despite the increase in production, there was a shortfall in private capital investment in the industry.

During the period 1971–1973, the government carried out a series of nationalizations of the privately owned coal companies in a major effort to increase production and overcome the shortage of coal. At the time of the nationalizations, total coal production in the country was 72 million tons, and the industry had been passing through cycles of shortages and surpluses which prevented effective planning for expansion and modernization. There were over 900 mines in operation, some of which were producing only a few thousand tons of coal a month, and methods of mining were obsolete.

Coking coal mines, with the exception of the Tata Iron and Steel Company, were nationalized in May 1972, and a new public sector company, Bharat Coking Coal Limited (BCCL), was floated to manage them. In May 1973, the non-coking coal mines were also nationalized and brought under the control of the Coal Mines Authority (CMA). The Department of Coal was set up in the Ministry of Energy to oversee the public sector companies. Further reorganization of the industry led to the formation of Coal India Limited (CIL), which also absorbed NCDC, in November 1975. The reorganization involved placing the majority of the public sector coal companies under CIL. CIL has six subsidiaries. Five of these are involved in production: BCCL, located at Dhanbad; Central Coalfields Limited at Ranchi; Western Coalfields Limited (WCL) at Nagpur; Eastern Coalfields Limited (ECL) at Sanctoria; and North Eastern Coalfields Limited (NECL) at Margherita; the sixth is the Central Planning & Design Institute at

Ranchi. Together with the Neyveli Lignite Corporation (NLC), CIL is operated directly by the Indian government through the Department of Coal in the Ministry of Energy. All the subsidiaries of CIL have the status of independent companies, but the authority for framing broad policies and taking administrative decisions rests with CIL.

The present structure of the Indian coal industry is a reflection of the priorities placed by the government on coal as a source of fuel and energy in economic development. Most of the production is the responsibility of the five subsidiaries of CIL, but there are four other coal producers in the public sector: the Singareni Collieries Limited, the government of Jammu and Kashmir collieries, the Damodar Valley Corporation, and the Indian Iron & Steel Co. Ltd. These last four concerns are responsible for about 10% of the output. Some 2% of the total output of coal is provided by the captive mines—company-owned mines which ensure coal supplies—of the Tata Iron and Steel Company, the only coal producer in the private sector.

Financially, the subsidiaries of CIL have an average authorized capital of Rs1.5 billion each. Each employs between 100,000 and 180,000 people, and has an annual turnover of between Rs1.1 and Rs1.7 billion. Their shares in the total production of coal vary from 25% for the Central and Western Coalfields, and about 20% for Bharat Coking Coal and Eastern Coalfields. The financial performance of the subsidiaries varies. BCCL made cumulative losses of Rs4.5 billon over the five year period 1981–1986. Similarly, Eastern Coalfields made cumulative losses of Rs3.6 billion over the same five year period. In 1988, BCCL made a loss of Rs900 million on a turnover of Rs5.3 billion. However, in the same year the Neyveli Lignite Corporation Limited made a profit of Rs570 million on a turnover of Rs1.9 billion.

As a result of the nationalizations, some rationalization took place in the sector. The mines were regrouped and reduced to 350 individual mines. New technology was introduced, and there was a shift from pick mining to blast mining, which resulted in considerable increases in production. The latter totaled 87 million tons in 1975, and 99 million tons in 1976. CIL's share of total production was about 88%. Nationalization was intended to provide the basis for modernizing the coal industry, but after the initial increase in production, output stagnated in the period 1976–1980. This was the result of shortages of power and explosives, labor unrest, and absenteeism, excessive employment, technical inefficiencies, and problems of flooding in the western coal fields, as well as fires in the vast Jharia coalfield. The latter possesses the largest known coking coal reserves in the country and it has been estimated that ongoing fires since around 1931 have accounted for the loss of some 40 billion tons of coking coal. Consequently, CIL'S financial performance was poor during this period. It suffered losses throughout the 1976–1981 period. These losses peaked at Rs2.4 billion in 1978–1979, but came down to Rs882 million the following year, and came down even further to Rs337 million the year after. Total losses for the five year period were almost Rs6 billion.

Production picked up in 1980 when it finally exceeded 100 million tons, and increased to 115 miilion tons by 1983. However, the problems suffered by CIL in particular and the coal industry in general had led to considerable shortages, especially for industrial users. This shortage was compounded by the poor quality of India's coking coal, which has difficult washing characteristics and requires the coal preparation plants to run extremely complex processes. The result was that the country had to import coal from abroad, a trend that still persists. The bulk of the imported coal came from the United States, Australia, and Canada, and was significantly more expensive than locally produced coal. This situation had two implications. First, it became feasible for CIL to adopt more expensive mining methods, since they were still cheaper than the imported coal. Second, a need was perceived to improve the coal handling facilities at India's major ports. This need was reflected in the Sixth Five Year Plan, when it was projected that the ports would have to handle at least 4.4 million tons of imported coal by the mid-1980s.

During the Sixth Five Year Plan, coal production grew at 6.2% per year, especially in the open-cast mines. Targeted production for the end of the plan period—1984–1985—was for 165 million tons per annum, although actual production fell short at 148 million tons. During the first two years of the plan, CIL made a profit for the only time in its history. This was largely due to the Indian government's increasing the price of coal in both February 1981 and May 1982. The issue of pricing has always been a serious problem for the Indian coal industry and for CIL. Coal prices have been administered by the government since 1941, with the exception of a period of seven years, 1967–1974. The pricing formula is based on an Indian industry-wide average with differentials for different grades, but in practice the price is usually set below the industry's average cost. This practice may explain in part CIL's poor overall financial performance.

Coal production in the year 1981–1982 was 125 million tons, above the targeted figure. Total production of coal and lignite was 146 million metric tons in 1983–1984, and 155 million tons in 1984–1985, 162 million tons in 1985–1986, 175 million tons in 1986–1987, 191 million tons in 1987–1988, and 207 million tons in 1988–1989. Despite the increase in production, problems related to operations, such as cost-overruns, poor quality, and low productivity, meant that targeted output was frequently revised downwards. Part of the problem was the high cost of new equipment necessitating new investment, since targeted budgets were overrun. Furthermore, the number of mines, which had been reduced immediately following nationalization, had again increased, to 684 by 1982, thereby negating some of the initial cost reduction benefits of reorganization.

Since coal was meeting over 70% of the energy requirements of Indian industry, CIL believed the output needed to increase by 25 million tons a year during the 1980s in order to keep up with demand. Demand for coal was projected to reach 165 million tons by 1985, 230 million tons by 1990, and over 400 million tons by the year 2000. The structure of demand for coal had changed. The railways were no longer the primary source of demand for coal. Rather, demand now lay primarily with the steel plants, other industrial units, and thermal power stations. The reliance on coal-fired thermal power plants for power generation led to a steady increase in the demand for coal throughout this period. To satisfy this demand, CIL relied primarily on the expansion of open-pit mines. Mining coal from shallow seams was financially sound, but it resulted in a steady deterioration of coal quality over time. The Seventh Five Year Plan of 1985 included some important changes introduced by CIL in the structure of its production.

The plan had set a production target of 226 million tons for coal, and by 1988–1989, output for coal alone, excluding lignite, had reached 195 million tons. As a result of the greater need for coal, new opportunities were created for international partnerships in the coal sector throughout the 1980s. CIL signed agreements with the Soviet Union, United Kingdom, Poland, and France, for the construction and development of new mines, and the introduction of new technology. The agreement with the Soviet Union called for investment in the Jayant open cast project with a production capacity of ten million tons a year, as well as a number of other projects.

The output from both surface and underground mining was to be increased through additional investment. Open cast—surface—mining was to provide an increased share of total production, from about 30% in 1980, to 56% in 1990. One of the major factors in increasing underground production was the introduction of additional longwall faces. Longwall mining differs from the traditional board and pillar method of underground mining in that the seams are at a greater depth and the capital costs are higher because of the complexity and greater powered support in the mining. During the 1990s, a series of new developments occurred in an attempt to increase production of the Indian coal mining industry. In February 1990, CIL decided to invest US$250 million in longwall mining over the period 1990–1995. This development would increase the powered support longwall faces from 14 in 1990 to 28 in 1995, and 47 in the year 2000. Longwall coal production, allowing deeper seams to be worked, would increase to nine million metric tons by 1995. In April 1990, CIL also approved five additional projects worth some US$712 million, as part of its program to increase output to meet the needs of industry into the 21st century. Total investment for the Seventh Five Year Plan was about US$8 billion dollars.

Despite increases in output of almost 9% per annum during the duration of the Seventh Five Year Plan, serious coal shortages still exist due to CIL'S inability to meet specific needs such as the provision of high-quality coking and non-coking coal. CIL'S distribution system remains poor, and the Indian Railway system is already heavily overloaded. Consequently there are cost overruns and a buildup of coal reserves at the pit heads. Furthermore, many of the targeted output figures are based on projects sanctioned but not completed by CIL, thus adding to infrastructural and distribution problems. This problem was compounded by poor coal quality, the system of pricing, and it both added to and was affected by CIL's financial position. If coal is to be a major source of energy and fuel in the future, CIL must be able to generate sufficient resources internally to meet its investment requirements. In this context, the government continues to show concern about the financial performance of CIL. About 100 of the 248 corporations owned by the Indian government are heavy loss-makers, and CIL is no exception. It is thus being seriously considered as a candidate for public flotation.

Principal Subsidiaries: Bharat Coking Coal Limited; Central Coalfields Limited; Eastern Coalfields Limited; Western Coalfields Limited.

Further Reading: Varma, S.C., "Coal: Its Extraction and Utilization in India," *World Coal,* July 1979; Shafer, Frank E., "A Review of India's Coal Mining Industry," *World Coal,* July 1979; Khosla, R.P., "India's Coal Development Plans," *Coal and Energy Quarterly,* Summer 1981; Murty, B.S., and S.P. Panda, *Indian Coal Industry and the Coal Mines,* Delhi, Discovery Publishing House, 1988.

—Sarah Ahmad Khan

COCKERILL SAMBRE GROUP

Chaussée de la Hulpe 187
B-1170 Brussels
Belgium
(2) 674 02 11
Fax: (2) 660 36 40

Public Company
Incorporated: 1981 as Cockerill Sambre S.A.
Employees: 31,000
Sales: BFr200.00 billion (US$6.48 billion)
Stock Exchanges: Brussels Paris Luxembourg

The Cockerill Sambre Group is the sixth-largest industrial group in Belgium. The primary activity of the group is the production of integrated steel and thin flat-steel products. Its specialties include metal and organic coating of steel sheets, with paint or plastic, and the manufacturing of products derived from these for the automobile and construction industries. The group also has its own large distribution network, operating primarily in France and the Netherlands in addition to Belgium. There is also a mechanical engineering division, producing steelmaking equipment and coating lines, diesel engines, and traction locomotives, transmission systems, boilers, and armaments—activities which date back to the start of the Cockerill company in 1817.

The Cockerill Sambre Group as it exists today results from the 1981 merger of the two major iron and steel groupings of the Walloon region of Belgium. From its beginnings, the Cockerill Group had been based at Seraing on the River Meuse a few miles upstream from Liège, while the company Hainaut-Sambre was based at the town of Charleroi, some 65 miles east of Liège on the banks of the River Sambre. The Sambre flows into the Meuse and provides a geographical link between these two regions, formerly rich in coal. In both areas, iron and steel production dates back before the 18th century, based on the coal mines of the areas, but the majority of the companies which have been absorbed gradually into the group were originally founded between 1800 and 1838.

The key figure of the Liège region was an Englishman, John Cockerill, whose name the group still bears to this day. His father William was an English engineer who had emigrated and established a successful textile machinery manufacturing firm at Verviers, 15 miles from Liège. In 1814 John Cockerill acquired from King William of Orange the old chateau at Seraing, formerly the summer residence of the prince-bishops of Liège. This has remained the registered office of Cockerill Sambre, and still houses the mechanical engineering division. The new factory opened in 1817, at first producing steam engines for spinning mills and winding and pumping engines for collieries. As coal was available on site, the company decided to produce the metal it required as well. The company was the first in Europe to erect a coke-fired blast furnace, which began production in 1826. By 1847 there were six blast furnaces in use. The state of Belgium was not created until 1830, following a revolutionary episode which necessitated the closure of the works at Seraing for a time. When production resumed, the company produced some of the first locomotives for the Belgian State Railways.

When John Cockerill died in 1840, the financial crisis which followed resulted in the winding up of the company. However, it was soon reconstituted as a limited company in 1842, and production began to revive in earnest the following year. By 1845, good progress was being made, and Cockerill engines obtained a Grand Medal at the 1851 Great Exhibition in London. All kinds of heavy machinery were produced during this period: ships, including ironclad gunboats for Russia and cross-channel mailboats for the Dover-Ostend route; tunnelling machines; bridges; and various plant for steel works. In 1866 a new director-general, Eugene Sadoine, initiated the development of adjacent coal mines at Colard, and acquired two-fifths of the neighboring Esperance coal mines as well as iron mines in Spain. A new steel works was opened in 1883, accompanied by much modernization of the existing works. The social requirements of the workers were not neglected, there being workmen's houses, refectories, schools for both adults and children, a 250-bed hospital, a dispensary, and an orphanage with more than 100 places. During the International Exhibition held in Liège in 1905, the (British) Institution of Mechanical Engineers held its annual convention in the town, during which various visits were arranged for the members, including one to the Cockerill works. They were to see "large gas engines, steam turbines, blast-furnaces, steel works, collieries, etc." The party of British engineers also visited the Société d'Ougrée-Marihaye, to see another steel works which exactly 50 years later, in 1955, was to become part of the Cockerill company. The origins of the company Ougrée-Marihaye, which was founded in 1835, lie in an iron foundry established at the beginning of the 19th century in the commune of Ougrée, between Seraing and the town of Liège itself, and the coal mines of Marihaye which had existed since 1778. This company occupied an important place in the Belgian iron and steel industry right up until the 1955 merger.

The other key company from the Liège area was Esperance-Longdoz. Its origins can be traced back to the Dothée family, which was already trading in ironmongery, copper ware, zinc objects and utensils, sheet metal, and hardware during the early 18th century. Esperance-Longdoz was formed in 1836, based on coal mines at Esperance, near Seraing, and with the involvement of John Cockerill. The first blast furnace opened here in 1838, followed in 1846 by a tin-plate works in the Longdoz district of Liège. The company was involved in joint ventures with Cockerill to exploit mineral rights, and became a major coke producer of this period. Esperance-Longdoz proved to be one of the most dynamic companies in the history of the group, surviving as a separate entity for 135 years until one of the penultimate mergers in 1970; as late as 1963 a brand new steelworks was built by Esperance-Longdoz on a greenfield site at Chertal, to the north of Liège.

However, the 18th-century companies of the Liège region are only half of the story, and it is necessary to follow the rivers Meuse and Sambre upstream to Charleroi and examine the group's industrial antecedents there. Most of the local companies here remained part of the Hainaut-Sambre side of the group until the formation of Cockerill Sambre in 1981, with the interesting exception of the Forges de la Providence. This company was founded in 1838 with the help of another Englishman, Thomas Bonehill, who had also been introducing industrial innovations to the Europeans. His successor, Alphonse Halbou, rose to fame by patenting the rolled I-section girder—often known today as the RSJ—in 1849, which accelerated the construction of high-rise buildings, undertaken first in Paris and eventually throughout Europe. Forges de la Providence remained separate until 1966, when it was merged with Cockerill-Ougrée in Liège, forming Cockerill-Ougrée-Providence. At this time, Forges de la Providence was a major steel producer based at Marchienne-au-Pont in Charleroi, but also owned two factories in France along with six other important French subsidiaries. By a twist of fate, rationalizations during the late 1970s led to the disposal of the Providence works to the Charleroi-based Thy-Marcinelle et Monceau (TMM) group. This could be said to have restored the geographic balance, but too late, as TMM itself—which first became Thy-Marcinelle et Providence—was to become part of Hainaut-Sambre in 1980, and so by 1981 found itself back with its old parent Cockerill, following the final merger which created Cockerill Sambre. As for the other Charleroi companies, TMM had been formed in 1966 from the merger of Thy-Marcinelle and Acieries et Minières de la Sambre. The origins of TMM include the forge of Thy-le-Chateau, which had existed as early as 1763, and Marcinelle, on the south bank at Charleroi. During the 17th and 18th centuries the whole region between the Sambre and the Meuse was known for its ironmasters, and it was one of these, Ferdinand Puissant, who had enlisted the services of Thomas Bonehill at Forges de la Providence. A Frenchman, Albert Goffart, had established his blast furnace in the nearby town of Monceau-sur-Sambre in 1836.

The other main grouping of firms in the surrounding area became the Hainaut-Sambre company in 1955, Hainaut being the name of the province in which Charleroi is situated. The two companies involved in the first merger were the Usines Métallurgiques de Hainaut, founded in 1829, and Sambre-et-Moselle, founded in 1835. The merger between Hainaut-Sambre and Thy-Marcinelle et Providence took place in 1979, not long after the transfer of Providence to TMM by Cockerill.

A chronological perspective provides a clearer overview of the complexities of all these mergers and regroupings. Beginning with the rise of the 19th-century companies, there were, to start with, four principal companies in each of the two regions of Liège and Charleroi. The first significant mergers did not take place until 1955, following reorganization plans initiated after the formation of the European Commission for Coal and Steel in 1952. These resulted in the formation of Hainaut-Sambre in the Charleroi region, and Cockerill-Ougrée at Liège. Another ten years passed before the mid-1960s witnessed two further rationalizations: the incorporation of Providence to form Cockerill-Ougrée-Providence at Liège, and the coming-together of some of the earliest Charleroi-based companies to form Thy-Marcinelle et Monceau.

During this period the other important Liège steelmaker, Esperance-Longdoz, had constructed a modern steel complex at Chertal to the north of the town, opened in 1963 to replace its works on sites nearer the town. These had become surrounded by other developments and were consequently suffering from a shortage of space in which to expand and introduce the wider strip mills which had become necessary in order to remain competitive in the market. At the end of the 1960s, a government committee which had been formed to study the problems of the Belgian metallurgical industries decided that further concentration was necessary in this region in order to maintain the competitiveness of the industry nationally, reduce overproduction, improve efficiency, and target investment and subsidies. Problems were also due to the rises in the price of oil at this time, as the industry had become increasingly reliant on this form of energy following the decline in coal production. The two companies therefore decided to effect a complete merger, following a one-year period of joint management beginning in July 1979. This led to the formation in June 1970 of Cockerill-Ougrée-Providence et Esperance-Longdoz. It was logical at that time for the new group to dispose of the Providence works—which were in Charleroi, not Liège—to the TMM company at Charleroi. For the next ten years, the company was known simply as Cockerill, appearing to renew the link with the years 1817 to 1955.

The early 1970s saw increasing steel production in Belgium, peaking in 1974, when there were nine major steelworks in operation. This resulted in overproduction, as the market was becoming saturated, and meant that drastic measures had to be taken. By 1979 both production and the number of plants had been halved, with reductions in the work force continuing up until 1985, by which time employment in the industry had fallen to half its 1975 level. The Charleroi region, which had not benefited from the concentration effected in Liège ten years earlier, was now obliged to undergo its own rationalization, with the absorption of Thy-Marcinelle et Providence—formerly TMM—by Hainaut-Sambre in 1980. However, this step was not enough to stabilize the industry, and the government, which had already taken a 50% stake in the industry in 1978, now decided that complete integration of the metallurgical industries of the two regions under one management was necessary. There were also the wider problems of Belgian industry connected with the difficulties between the French-speaking Wallonia region, which includes Charleroi and Liège, and the Flemish-speaking northern regions. The two complexes were united with 80% state ownership, on June 26, 1981.

The union took place in the depths of an economic recession, and the newly organized group of Cockerill Sambre began by making massive losses. The European Economic Community was insisting that large government subsidies to the industry were unfair and had to be reduced substantially. A new center-right government introduced economic austerity measures and commissioned a report on the steel industry. This proposed further reductions in capacity, including plant closures at Cockerill Sambre—one at Charleroi and one at Liège—and more job losses. Each region was to be allotted a specialty. The restructuring plan, known as the "Gandois report," after the present chairman of Cockerill Sambre, was implemented in 1984. Production of steel was stabilized at around 1975 levels, concentrated on only three plants, and the work force was reduced to 15,000, with the hope of even more reductions. It was also agreed that ARBED, the Luxembourg state steel producer, would reduce its rolled steel capacity in exchange for the securing of orders from Cockerill.

The number of blast furnaces operating in Wallonia declined from their peak of 30 during the postwar period up to 1963: only a third of these were in use by the late 1970s, and by 1988 only 4 remained at Cockerill Sambre.

Within a few years of the implementation of the Gandois plan, the success of the measures had become evident, with the company being given a new lease of life, and diversification into other steel-based products taking place. The mid-1980s were a relatively stable period, culminating in further internal rationalizations, such as the decision to specialize in thin flat products on the steel production side; the development of new products such as coated steel roof tiles by the French-based construction products division; and concentration on heavy engineering in the mechanical engineering division. A recent development was the acquisition in 1990 of a majority holding in YMOS A.G., a major German manufacturer of metal and plastic parts for automobiles. Other recent diversification activities include ventures into financial and data processing services.

In the main, however, Cockerill Sambre seems to have survived by concentrating on what it did best—first making machines, and then producing the materials needed for them, and returning to consolidate its base of expertise after traversing the difficult periods of retrenchment which the metallurgical industries underwent during the second half of the 20th century. It seems more than coincidence that after the positive flood of mergers which took place, the two names surviving in the company today are those of an Englishman who began work in an old castle by the river in Liège, and of the other river, which provides the link with the group's other center further upstream in Charleroi. The latest building is a new research and development center for the group, built on the campus of the University of Liège and opened in April 1990.

Principal Subsidiaries: S.A. Société Carolorégienne de Laminage (CARLAM) (75%); S.A. Laminoirs du Ruau (78%); S.A. Société Carolorégienne de Cokéfaction (CAR-COKE) (78%); S.C. L'Oxygène Métallurgique; S.A. Steelinter; S.A. Disteel (70%); S.A. Produits d'Usines Métallurgiques (PUM); B.V. Cockerill Nederland Holding (Netherlands); S.A. Société Européenne pour le Commerce International (Eurinter); S.A. Tôleries Delloye-Matthieu (TDM) (91%); S.A. Société des Forges d'Haironville (France) (93%); S.A. Cockerill Mechanical Industries (CMI); S.A. Vulcain Financier; S.A. Cockerill Sambre Finances et Services; Société de Service et de Conseil en Informatique, Bureautique et Télématique (S.A. "IBT"); YMOS A.G.

Further Reading: Willem, Leon, *450 Ans D'Espérance: La S.A. Métallurgique D'Esperance-Longdoz de 1519 a 1969,* Alleur Editions du Perron, 1990.

—Peter W. Miller

Companhia Vale do Rio Doce

COMPANHIA VALE DO RIO DOCE

Avenida Graça Aranha
26-20 Andar
Post Office Box 2414
20005 Rio de Janeiro
Brazil
(21) 272 4477

State-Owned Company
Incorporated: 1942
Employees: 21,755
Sales: US$2.33 billion

Companhia Vale do Rio Doce (CVRD) is one of the world's most important producers of iron ore, iron pellets, and other minerals. Owned primarily by the Brazilian government, it has taken a leading role in developing the mineral resources of the Amazonia region. Much of the company's success is based on its ability to draw on foreign expertise and capital while at the same time retaining effective control in Brazilian hands.

Companhia Vale do Rio Doce was formed in 1942, receiving the assets of the Itabira Iron Ore Company, including the "iron mountain" of Caué Peak in the Itabira region of Minais Gerais state. The Brazilian government held 80% of the shares in the company, reduced to the present level of 53%. Initially hampered by poor management and inadequate transport facilities, it was only in the early 1950s that the company started on its path to becoming one of the world's most important exporters of iron ore.

With its success closely linked to improvements in transport which it helped to finance, CVRD also expanded into the production of other minerals, the provision of shipping services, and iron pelleting. It also helped finance and organize a wide range of other industrial and service enterprises. When the huge iron ore reserves of the Amazon region were discovered in the 1960s, it was natural that CVRD be given responsibility for spearheading their exploitation. It was equally natural that CVRD become a specific target of international opposition to mining activities in the region, which were considered to threaten the traditional lifestyles of inhabitants.

Funds for expansion came not only from government grants and the company's reinvested profits, but also from foreign investment in the form of loans and joint financing of new ventures involving Brazilian and various foreign banks and companies. By 1990, CVRD ranked 294 in *Fortune*'s list of the 500 largest companies in the world. In the mining and crude oil production sector, it ranked fifth in terms of sales value, but first in terms of profits; at some US$2.944 billion, these represented 65.1% of sales and a 45.5% return on assets, figures which no other firm on the *Fortune* list approaches.

Brazil is one of the world's major sources of iron ore with reserves estimated at about 50 billion tons, second only to the Soviet Union. Some of the more easily accessible deposits were worked in the early days of Portuguese rule, but were developed more significantly in the wake of the 18th-century gold and rubber booms. Even these were very small-scale operations, and it was only in the late 19th and early 20th centuries that serious efforts to promote iron mining and exports, along with steel manufacturing, began. Not until after World War II did Brazil's iron ore exports begin to acquire worldwide significance, with CVRD in the vanguard.

The company's roots are in the formation of the Itabira Iron Ore Company Ltd. by Sir Ernest Cassel on March 31, 1911. The company acquired Caué Peak and 18,000 acres of land around it, along with a 52% interest in the then-uncompleted Vitória-Minas railway line. Caué Peak, largely made up of hematite, containing 69% exceptionally pure iron, was expected to be the foundation of an enterprise integrating iron mining, steelmaking, and shipping. Ore was to be sent to and exported from a port that the company was to build about 52 kilometers north of Vitória, the ships returning with coke for the company's steel mill, replacing the charcoal that was and has continued to be used for Brazilian iron smelting.

In 1918, Cassel sold out to a group of British financiers and steel manufacturers, who sought the support of Percival Farquhar, an American entrepreneur of varying fortunes, who took the lead in subsequent negotiations. He too was unsuccessful in securing government approval for Itabira's scheme. Brazilian firms and various individuals objected to the grant of such extensive rights to foreigners. In 1923, agreement seemed likely, but was not achieved, at least in part because of Farquhar's insensitive treatment of members of the Brazilian government, but also because of continuing and growing feelings of economic nationalism. Brazilians increasingly wanted to limit the extent of foreign control of their economic resources in order to ensure that they secured a substantial share of the profits generated, and that the exploitation of the resources would be managed to Brazil's own advantage.

Some of the objections were recognized in 1940 when the Companhia Brasileira de Mineração e Siderurgica was created as an all-Brazilian company, acquiring Itabira's assets without the proposed steel mill. That year Itabira shipped out its first cargo of 6,000 tons of ore, and over the next two years exported a further total of 100,000 tons. Hardly a successful company, Itabira's fate was sealed in 1942 when the British government, apparently at the behest of the United States, using special war powers, expropriated the Brazilian holdings of the company's British investors. These assets were handed over to the Brazilian government, which in turn took over most of the original company's Brazilian assets which became the base of CVRD. The Itabira company was dissolved in 1945.

Although it did not reach any significant agreement with Farquhar, the Brazilian government was very eager to promote the development of the region's mineral potential, an aim which coincided with Allied interests during World War II.

The agreement whereby the Brazilian government acquired Itabira also included provision for U.S. assistance for the extension of the Vitória-Minas railway, which had been completed in 1936, and of ore-loading facilities at Vitória, as well as the development of the mines themselves. Also of strategic importance to the Allies was the formation, in the previous year, of the Companhia Brasileira de Aluminio to develop the bauxite deposits at Pocos de Caldas.

To finance CVRD, a grant of US$14 million was made by the Office of Lend Lease Administration, the U.S. agency which administered the post–World War II lend lease scheme for helping the Allies recover from the effects of the war. An equal amount was put up by the Brazilian government. A part of the loan made by the United States Export-Import Bank for the development of the important Volta Redonda steelworks was also available for developing the Itabira deposits. Even with this financial injection, CVRD's early years were marked by inefficient management, political interference, and a serious bottleneck created by limitations on the railway's carrying capacity. Against an annual export target of 1.5 million tons, in 1947 only one-sixth of that amount was being shipped. In the late 1940s Morrison-Knudson, a U.S. company, was brought in to upgrade the railway, but local political machinations were such that improvements could only be made in 1951–1952 when a new administrator was appointed by Brazilian President Getúlio Vargas after his return to power. By 1953, CVRD reached its initial export target, and by 1963 the company was exporting 7 million tons annually through the port of Vitória, out of a total Brazilian production of 10 million tons. Of the difference, 1.5 million tons was consumed domestically, the remainder being exported via Rio de Janeiro.

By this time, the railway and port once again created a bottleneck, but improvements were hampered by political unrest which sapped the confidence of foreign investors. That confidence returned in 1964 following the military takeover which brought down the government of President João Goulart who, among other things, was considered by U.S. investors to be too close to the Brazilian communists. In 1965 the Inter-American Development Bank provided the funds for CVRD to improve its mining equipment; construct a new port at Tuberao, some ten kilometers south of Vitória; and expand the Minas railway's capacity. The ore terminal at Tuberao was completed in 1966 with an annual capacity of 15 million tons, doubled in 1969 to meet the increased demands associated with the start up of CVRD's pelletizing plant.

The export of iron pellets, in addition to iron ore, became an important part of CVRD's activities, and of several associated companies. By 1989, CVRD itself produced 5.3 million tons of pellets, while three associated companies devoted to pelletizing, NIBRASCO, HISPANOBRAS, and ITABRASCO, produced a further 12.9 million tons. The pelletizing work is actually done by CVRD, but these associate companies are examples of one of the important ways in which CVRD has secured foreign finance for expansion as well as assured markets. The production of each of these companies is destined exclusively for the participating country's steel industry which, along with banks in that country, helped finance the building of the plant. In addition to the immediate financial and commercial advantages this provides, such arrangements help protect CVRD from the vagaries of decision-making by foreign companies which might otherwise be inclined to give a lower priority to CVRD's or Brazil's interests.

Another important technique used to finance expansion and diversification has been the negotiation of long-term supply contracts linked to or separate from joint ventures. Expansion in the 1960s was partly a response to an agreement reached in 1962 with a consortium of Japanese steel producers for the supply of 50 million tons of iron ore over 15 years from 1966. Similar contracts have enabled CVRD to bring in important foreign investment to supplement grants from the Brazilian government and the company's own reinvestment of profits. Such cooperation also has facilitated the importing of modern technology on terms which, unlike the situation often found in connection with technology transfers to Third World countries, have been favorable to Brazil and CVRD.

During the 1970s CVRD embarked on major expansion and diversification. This went further than its investment in infrastructure—ports, roads, shipping, and railways—which serve CVRD, the region, and the country in general, as well as a number of companies which actually compete with CVRD. On the basis of substantial profits derived from iron ore exports, CVRD helped finance a range of companies involved in mining a variety of nonferrous metals including gold; mineral surveying; reforestation; and pulp and paper production. The joint pelletizing ventures, like CVRD's involvement in shipping, were also important for diversification and had the additional advantage of enabling CVRD to process and transport ores produced by other companies, thereby gaining a share in overall profits.

The massive rise in oil prices in 1973–1974, followed by a prolonged worldwide slump in steel production, led to problems for CVRD's investment plans. When iron ore prices fell drastically in 1977, cutbacks in what critics referred to as CVRD's "empire building" and "irresponsible diversification" were necessary. Some subsidiary activities were sold off to the private sector and a substantially higher proportion of supplies were acquired from domestic rather than foreign producers—some 60% in 1976 compared with less than 20% earlier in the decade.

Support from the Brazilian government was clearly an important factor in CVRD's success. In contrast to its early days, the quality of its management has also played a significant part, but of prime importance has undoubtedly been the purely fortuitous circumstances of declining iron ore production in the United States and the Soviet Union coupled with the development and expansion of steel production in Japan, South Korea, and other countries with limited or no domestic sources of iron, to an extent, Brazil itself. For whatever combination of reasons, by the late 1970s CVRD had become the most important single company in the world's oceanborne iron ore trade—accounting for some 18.3% of world trade in 1978—and was well placed to play a major role in the opening and exploitation of mineral resources in the Amazon area, more specifically the greater Carajás region.

This part of Brazil is immensely rich in a wide variety of nonferrous metals, manganese, copper, bauxite, cassiterite, nickel, and gold, as well a containing massive iron ore reserves. These last were discovered accidentally in 1967 when a geologist, prospecting for manganese for U.S. Steel's Brazilian subsidiary landed his helicopter to refuel on a hill which subsequently proved to be composed of some 18 billion long tons of hematite, average grade 66% iron. U.S. Steel sought exploration rights over 160,000 hectares in the region, but because of Brazilian reluctance to allow a foreign company to have such extensive rights, it was only able to secure a 49% share in a joint undertaking—Amazôna Mineraçao SA—formed in 1970, with CVRD holding a 51% stake. U.S. Steel sold its share to U.S. CVRD in 1977 for US$50 million.

U.S. Steel and other multinational companies have reason to be cautious about involvement in the region's development due to its remoteness, requiring the construction of extensive infrastructure—railways, roads, and hydroelectric capacity. By late 1981, these development costs were estimated to be some US$3.62 billion, excluding financing charges. Private investors preferred to leave this to the Brazilian government, and waited until the region was opened up to bid for its nonferrous ores.

In elaborating Brazil's Grand Carajás Program (PGC), which was formally announced in November 1980, CVRD was to play a major role in the agricultural, industrial, ranching, and forestry project, as well as in the development of mineral resources. Both CVRD and the Brazilian government relied heavily during the 1970s on advice and subsequently investment from Japan. The Japan International Co-operation Agency (JICA), part of the Ministry of Foreign Affairs, continued to play an influential role until the mid-1980s, and aroused considerable opposition in various quarters, Brazilian and foreign.

CVRD began to develop the Carajás iron ores in 1978, the failure to attract foreign capital forcing it to scale down the project from its original size. Neither this nor most other parts of the PGC were viable without the construction of a railway, the Estrada de Ferro de Carajás, to the coast at a port in Sao Luis. This impressive engineering feat was completed 18 months earlier than planned and—at a cost of US$1.5 billion—some US$600 million under budget, in February 1985.

Also vital to the success of the PGC was the Tucurui hydroelectric project, which was particularly important for the development of aluminum processing. As early as 1976, a tied loan from France of US$230 million was destined for this scheme. The uncertainties of the 1970s, exacerbated by the 1979 oil-price rise, meant that serious work only began in 1981, and the scheme was inaugurated in 1984. Aluminum production has, over the years, involved various foreign companies such as Aluminum Company of America and Billiton Metals, and has been subject to considerable reorganizaton; for CVRD, aluminum has not always been particularly profitable.

The need for Japanese cooperation and cheap loans meant that the Brazilian government had not only to provide necessary basic infrastructure, but also to agree to subsidize electricity prices very heavily. Throughout Carajás, subsidized electricity has indeed proved essential for industrial and commercial success, at considerable cost to the Brazilian government—a cost, however, considered acceptable because of the perceived advantages of development.

For the iron ore project itself, CVRD raised about US$200 million of the US$3.3 billion investment by issuing debentures. This resulted in the gradual reduction of the state shareholding in the company from 70% to 56% by 1985. In contrast to earlier government reluctance, a further US$700 million came from the National Development Bank. In 1981, Brazil's planning minister traveled the world to seek finance, arranging

loans of US$1.7 billion for PGC, most of which was destined for the iron mine. This total included US$600 million from the European Economic Community, US$500 million from Japan, and US$305 million from the World Bank. The European and Japanese loans were tied to contract to supply ore to particular European or Japanese steel companies at world market prices, which were soon to fall. Further loans were later arranged: US$250 million from United States commercial banks, and US$60 million from the USSR. In 1986, CVRD and the USSR signed contracts for the supply of ferro manganese. CVRD needed the finance, but with repayment terms of 10% interest over 15 years, the terms were not favorable.

Having in essence drawn up the PGC in the first place, CVRD continued to play a major administrative as well as financial role in it, in the opening up of mineral resources, the creation of infrastructure, agriculture, and the provision of housing and other amenities. As the government's mining company, it was inevitable that CVRD should be seen as an enemy by those opposed to the destruction of the Amazonian rain forest and the disruption of the lifestyle of the people living in it. This opposition has been repressed by CVRD. In 1982 the company signed an agreement with the National Indian Foundation (FUNAI) in support of FUNAI's projects designed to support and protect the 14 indigenous groups living in the Carajás iron ore area. While this shows a greater degree of interest than might be expected, there is justification for considering this a token gesture.

In one activity, the mining of Amazonian gold, CVRD finds itself in conflict not only with people living in the region, but also with the Brazilian government. This centers on the prevalence of *garimpeiros*, or freelance miners who, organized to a greater or lesser degree in groups, work open-pit or alluvial gold deposits, often as a way of paying off creditors, sometimes simply to earn a living in circumstances of poverty, both rural and urban. These workers, some of them children, labor in inadequately supported but ever-deepening pits. Another problem is the uncontrolled use of mercury to separate gold from its ores. Nonetheless, with little or no alternative for many people, there is strong local pressure for it to continue.

In attempting to stamp out *garimpeiro* production, CVRD has not always had government support, as it has generally been in the government's interest to have access to unofficial supplies of gold. In 1983, for example, arrangements with creditors required Brazil to sell gold worth US$500 million, approximately 40 tons. A high proportion of the total 54 tons acquired by the Brazilian Central Bank that year was *garimpeiro*-produced, bought at the going black market rate with no questions asked regarding taxes. A further political argument was that *garimpeiro* gold working provided a safety valve for urban tensions, leading the government in 1984 to extent *garimpeiro* rights for a further five years.

CVRD for its part has argued that *garimpeiro* working is wasteful, leaving large amounts of gold untouched, depriving the company and its subsidiaries of profits and the government of revenue, and making it more difficult and costly ultimately to work the deposits when the *garimpeiros* have abandoned them. Throughout the 1980s the company was attempting to expand and improve production, opening new mines and reopening old ones. Once again there was foreign financial support from companies such as Rio Tinto-Zinc, Anglo American Corporation of South Africa, and BP Minerals, as well as technical services in prospecting and treatment. In 1987, CVRD sold 460,575 grams of gold; in 1988, 834,676 grams. In 1989, it sold no gold, but produced 2.79 million grams, 79% from the Fazenda Brasileiro mine, the remainder from Itabira.

With the Brazilian government's financial support and building on its generally profitable arrangements with foreign markets and investors, CVRD has been a profitable company, bringing in a substantial portion of the country's foreign-exchange earnings. In 1987 the company recorded losses totaling some US$179 million because of circumstances outside its control. The worldwide fall in iron prices and the weakening of the dollar against European currencies and the Japanese yen had serious consequences, while the need to protect the company's foreign debt, which was calculated in dollars, against further devaluation placed further strains on finance. The company returned to profit in 1988, and by the end of 1989, with the help of the Brazilian government, was able to reduce its corporate debt—US$3 billion at the end of 1987—by half. Overall, the success of CVRD demonstrates that state ownership is by no means incompatible with financial and commercial success.

Principal Subsidiaries: Vale do Rio Doce Navegaçao S.A. (96.8%); Vale do Rio Doce Aluminio S.A.; Florestas Rio Doce S.A. (99.7%); Rio Doce Finance Ltd. (U.K., Cayman Islands, 99.8%); Itabira International Co. Ltd. (U.K., 99.9%); Rio Doce International S.A. (99.9%); Rio Doce Geologia e Mineraçao (99.9%).

Further Reading: Hunnicutt, Benjamin H., *Brazil, World Frontier,* New York, Van Nostrand, 1949; Gauld, Charles A., *The Last Titan: Percival Farquhar, American Entrepreneur in Latin America,* Stanford, Institute of Hispanic American and Luso-Brazilian Studies, 1964; Henshall, Janet D., and R.P. Momsen, *A Geography of Brazilian Development,* London, G. Bell & Sons, 1974; Trebat, Thomas J., *Brazil's State-Owned Enterprises: A Case Study of the State as Entrepreneur,* Cambridge, Cambridge University Press, 1983; Hall, Anthony L., *Developing Amazonia: Deforestation and Social Conflict in Brazil's Carajás Programme,* Manchester, Manchester University Press, 1989.

—Simon Katzenellenbogen

CRA LIMITED

55 Collins Street
Melbourne
Victoria 3001
Australia
(03) 658-3333
Fax: (03) 658-3707

Public Company
Incorporated: 1959
Employees: 19,000
Sales: A$4.59 billion (US$3.55 billion)
Stock Exchanges: Australia New Zealand

CRA Limited is an Australian grouping of predominantly resource-based companies. Its principal activities are the mining of iron ore, bauxite, diamonds, coal, and a variety of minerals and precious metals. The diversity, size, and international spread of CRA's activities are such that it rivals Broken Hill Proprietary in its influence on Australia's political and economic affairs. CRA (Conzinc Riotinto of Australia) was formed in July 1962 through the merging of the Australian interests of two U.K. companies, the Consolidated Zinc Corporation (CZC) and Rio Tinto. At the same time the Rio Tinto-Zinc Corporation of the United Kingdom came into being. This company took a majority interest in CRA which lasted for nearly 25 years. CZC was itself the product of the 1949 merger of two U.K. firms, the Imperial Smelting Corporation and The Zinc Corporation (ZC), the latter of whose interests were largely centered in Australia.

ZC was founded in 1905 for the purpose of recovering the huge amounts of zinc locked in the tailings—or waste material—dumps, which had grown up around the silver-lead mines at Broken Hill, New South Wales, since the start of mining there in the 1880s. Recovery of the zinc—a valuable commodity since the discovery of its suitability for such industrial applications as galvanization—would, it was hoped, offset the declining price of lead in the early 1900s and help keep the Broken Hill mines open.

Extraction of zinc from the tailings depended on the froth flotation process jointly patented by Delprat and Potts in 1907 and on later, more efficient variants such as selective and differential flotation. ZC's first years were beset with financial and technical difficulties and several different plants were built before a fully satisfactory extraction process was developed in 1912.

In the previous year ZC had extended its operations into mining proper with its acquisition of the Broken Hill South Blocks Co., which at that time held the southernmost leases of the Broken Hill mining area. The low sale price was the result of a widespread belief that the ore in the South Blocks leases lay at too great a depth to be mined economically. Fortunately for ZC this conviction proved mistaken. The southern end of the field soon began to produce more easily accessible ore, and in larger quantities, than the preferred northern leases.

Treatment of the tailings at Broken Hill continued during World War I and into the early 1920s when the supply of tailings ran out. During the war itself, ZC and the other Broken Hill mining companies found themselves deprived of their two main customers, Belgium and Germany. The Australian government took advantage of this situation by informing the Broken Hill companies that henceforth concentrates would have to be refined in Australia rather than abroad. As a result of this restriction, in 1915 ZC and two other companies set up the Broken Hill Associated Smelters Proprietary Company (BHAS) to take a controlling interest in the Broken Hill Proprietary's lead-zinc smelting plant at Port Pirie in South Australia. ZC thus took its first steps into secondary production.

During the 1920s the Australian mining industry experienced a decline due to falling world metals prices, the working out of the more accessible ore deposits and rising mining, transport, and labor costs. The onset of the Depression in 1929 forced metals prices even lower so that by 1931 the value of Australian metals production reached a new low point. Thereafter metals prices began to rise, albeit slowly at first, and in turn stimulated recovery in the Australian mining industry. By 1936 ZC had re-established a sufficient capital base to embark on an extensive rebuilding of its mine and concentration plant at Broken Hill. By 1939 a new all-flotation zinc extraction circuit had been constructed.

New Broken Hill Consolidated (NBHC), which was intended to seek southern extensions of the Broken Hill line of lode, was formed in 1936. ZC and NBHC remained closely associated, and 30 years later CRA and NBHC jointly discovered the large copper deposits at Panguna on Bougainville Island, Papua New Guinea.

World War II forced Australia to develop its steel and chemical industries at the expense of its mining operations. Although the contribution of the Broken Hill mines to the war effort was considerable, J.B. Chifley's post-war government recognized the low state of the industry and accordingly instituted tax reforms and bounties to encourage renewed prospecting. Simultaneously the first systematic surveys of Australia's mineral reserves were undertaken.

ZC made an important acquisition in its 1948 purchase of the Sulphide Corporation and its Cockle Creek lead smelting plant. The merger in the following year of ZC and the Imperial Smelting Corporation enabled the Sulphide Corporation to take advantage of Imperial's advanced process for the simultaneous production of lead and zinc from lead/zinc sinter. By 1961 a new plant using the Imperial process had been installed.

The 1949 merger of the U.K. interests of ZC and Imperial led to the establishment of CZC and its Australian subsidiary, Consolidated Zinc Proprietary (CZP). It rapidly became apparent that efficient management of the Australian operations of ZC and NBHC from London was proving difficult. In 1951, management control was transferred to Melbourne, and CZP was appointed manager for ZC, NBHC, and other interests. Toward the end of World War II the search began in Australia for uranium, a mineral which had become extremely valuable once its use in prewar experiments in nuclear fission had been demonstrated. The Australian government offered tax-free rewards to prospectors, one of whom, Jack White, found a large deposit in 1952 at Rum Jungle in the Northern Territory south of Darwin. After initial investigation the Australian Atomic Energy Commission handed over development of the site to CZP's specially formed Territory Enterprises Ltd. Rum Jungle supplied some 3,530 tons of yellowcake—the form in which uranium is produced—between 1954 and 1971. Until 1964, this was in the main supplied to the United Kingdom's military authorities.

An even larger uranium deposit, named Mary Kathleen, was found 40 miles east of the Mount Isa copper mine in Queensland. CZP bought an initial 51% holding in the development company, Mary Kathleen Uranium (MKU), set up to operate the mine. Production commenced in June 1958 and until its temporary closure in 1963 the mine produced over 4,000 tons of yellowcake. The closure was prompted by a sharp drop in uranium prices and it was not until MKU's partners had judged these to have recovered sufficiently to justify reopening the mine that production was restarted in 1976.

The rise in uranium prices had not been foreseen by the U.S. company Westinghouse, which found itself without sufficient uranium reserves to honor its commitments as a supplier to its U.S. customers. Westinghouse brought a legal action against CRA, accusing it, through its link with Rio Tinto-Zinc, of participating in a uranium producers' cartel designed to control the price of uranium. A U.S. court ordered CRA's directors to give evidence before it, whereupon the directors appealed to Canberra for protection. The Australian government took the unusual step of passing legislation forbidding CRA to obey the court's injunction. As a result the allegation of price-fixing remained unresolved.

Soon after the Mary Kathleen discovery came news of vast bauxite ore deposits at Weipa on the Cape York peninsula in northern Queensland. These had been discovered by Harry Evans, chief geologist of the Frome Broken Hill Company, an enterprise in which CZP held a one-third interest. CZP immediately undertook operations to establish the size of this orebody—over three billion tons, forming nearly two-thirds of total known Australian reserves and just over one-third of total proved world reserves.

In setting out to exploit these vast bauxite ore deposits—the base material for the production of alumina and thence aluminum—CZP needed access to the huge amount of capital—foreign, as the required funds had to be found outside Australia at that time—necessary for development of a mine and its related facilities. It also required an alliance with a partner already experienced in such projects, which was also a member of the group of five companies that then controlled the world's aluminum industry. These were Alcoa, Reynolds, and Kaiser Aluminum of the United States, Alcan of Canada, and the French company Pechiney. CZP came to an agreement with Kaiser, and a new company called the Commonwealth Aluminium Corporation (Comalco) was formed in 1956 to develop the mine, with CZP and Kaiser initially holding 50% of the equity each.

The Weipa mine was CZP's largest project to date, involving the construction not only of the mine itself but of new deep-water port facilities and an entire township for Comalco's employees. The bulk of production was destined for immediate shipment to Europe and Japan, but the Queensland government, anxious like most Australians to see its country increase the volume of its value-added exports, had stipulated in its agreement with Comalco that at least part of the mined bauxite ore had to be refined in the state. Consequently, in 1963, CZP's successor CRA became a partner with Kaiser and Pechiney in the establishment of Queensland Alumina (QAL). The task of QAL was to process Comalco's Weipa bauxite ores at a new refinery which was built at Gladstone on the east coast of Queensland near Rockhampton. In turn, the Gladstone plant supplied alumina to the Bell Bay aluminum smelter in Tasmania in which Comalco had bought the Australian government's two-thirds interest in 1960.

In 1968, flushed with the success of the Gladstone refinery, Comalco and a group of German, Swiss, and Italian aluminum companies had formed the Euralumina consortium to build an alumina refinery in Sardinia. This was Comalco's first venture into Europe.

Since aluminum smelters are intensive users of energy, reliable sources of low-cost power are an important factor in their siting and operation. In 1968 Comalco announced the setting up of New Zealand Aluminum Smelters in a partnership with two Japanese aluminum concerns. A sizable smelter was built at Bluff on the southern tip of the South Island of New Zealand. The Bluff smelter linked Australia's bauxite with the South Island's abundant hydroelectric power and thus provided another outlet for Gladstone's alumina. Production began in 1971.

Another kind of ore brought CRA to the attention of the industrial world in the early 1960s. From 1938 until 1960 the Australian government had restricted the export of iron ore on the grounds that Australia's known reserves were barely adequate for its own industrial purposes. The lifting of these restrictions caused a rush of discoveries, chief among which were those in the Pilbara region in the northwest of Western Australia. Amongst the largest of these were the ore deposits found in the Hamersley Ranges by a grazier and prospector named Lang Hancock.

Hancock and his partner Wright approached the Rio Tinto Mining Company of Australia (RTMA) in 1962 and this company (soon to merge with CZP) estimated iron ore reserves at some 5 billion tons, including at least 500 million tons of high grade hematite ore. In the Hamersley Iron Province, as the area soon became known, Australia now possessed iron ore fields of extraordinary quality and size.

The remoteness and harsh conditions of the Pilbara necessitated a massive scale of operation to justify the huge investment required to mine the iron ore under such conditions and transport it to the coast for shipment. As at Weipa, only the largest international mining companies were capable of amassing the necessary financing and technological expertise. CRA approached Kaiser Steel, and the two formed Hamersley Holdings in 1962 to initiate a four-year process of mine, railway, port, and township construction. This was completed ahead of schedule by its operating subsidiary Hamersley Iron.

The justification for this investment lay in the tremendous expansion of the Japanese steel industry in the 1960s and the development in that decade of a generation of large ore-carriers which made the supplying of iron ore from a distant country like Australia economically feasible for the first time.

Crucial also for Hamersley were the long-term supply contracts offered by the Japanese steel mills. Although the Japanese were to prove less reliable customers in the early 1980s, without the security offered by such agreements CRA and other Australian mining houses would not have been so eager to mine the Pilbara ore deposits. In 1969 Hamersley Iron announced plans for a second mine at nearby Paraburdoo, which came into operation in 1972.

Hamersley's first shipment of ore took place in August 1966. Within two years the company had opened a two million ton-a-year oxide pellet plant on the coast at Dampier. Some Australians chose to see this expansion as part of CRA's strategy to head off growing public criticism of the way in which large and often foreign-owned mining companies appeared to be making huge profits out of Australia's finite resources. CRA was singled out as an example of this phenomenon, because the United Kingdom's Rio Tinto-Zinc had held a majority interest in the company since its inception in 1962. CRA argued that the Australian public would not choose to help underwrite the huge costs associated with the risky business of mine development and that it was therefore pointless to offer the public an increased shareholding in the company. A number of Australian politicians disagreed, claiming that the real reason was Rio Tinto's unwillingness to lose control of CRA and its interests in Comalco and Hamersley.

Nowhere was this controversy more acrimonious than in regard to Australia's uranium mines where an added moral dimension—the end use of the product—fueled years of controversy. MKU ceased operations in 1982. Since then the Australian government has confined uranium mining to three mines in the Northern Territory and South Australia. In the mid 1980s CRA located a significant uranium deposit at Kintyre in Western Australia but the federal government has refused to revoke its three-mine policy.

Copper was another metal in which CRA took a major interest in the 1960s. CRA/NBHC teams identified large copper ore deposits on Bougainville Island, Papua New Guinea, estimated at some 230 million tons. Once again a huge mining operation was set in motion and Bougainville Copper Pty. (BCL) emerged in 1967 to operate the venture.

CRA's 1968 purchase of a major interest in the Blair Athol coal field of central Queensland provided it with valuable export potential. CRA expanded its coal mining capacity substantially in the late 1980s.

In the 1970s public and political pressure built up strongly in favor of the naturalization of foreign-owned companies operating in Australia. CRA's failure in its 1978 bid for Australian industrial group AAR due to the size of foreign shareholding may have been instrumental in convincing CRA's board that the company had to begin the process of transforming itself into an Australian company. In that same year, CRA was granted the status of a naturalizing company—a company becoming properly Australian rather than merely a foreign company operating in Australia—in line with the government's foreign investment guidelines. By the end of the decade Rio Tinto-Zinc's shareholding in CRA had fallen to just over 70% with a concomitant rise in public ownership.

In association with Ashton Mining, CRA discovered diamonds in the far north of Western Australia in 1972 near Lake Argyle. A large deposit was found at Ellendale and an even greater one at Smoke Creek, south of the lake. In partnership with Ashton, CRA set up the Ashton Joint Venture (AJV) to exploit this important series of discoveries, CRA holding nearly 60% of the equity of the new company. Ironically enough, the giant South African mining concern De Beers had surveyed the Lake Argyle area in the 1960s and had pronounced it lacking in diamondiferous deposits. AJV's estimate of a yearly production of 20 million to 25 million carats, about half total world production, caused De Beers to fear it might lose its domination of the world diamond market.

De Beers entered into negotiations with AJV in 1981, inviting it to market its diamond production through De Beers's Central Selling Organisation (CSO), which handled about 80% of the world's diamonds. The attraction for AJV was that the CSO guaranteed to buy the mine's production whatever the state of the world diamond market, an important consideration during the expensive and risky early years of the mine's life. In 1982 the CSO was contracted to market the bulk of AJV's production until the end of the decade.

In 1984, CRA and its partners opened a new five million ton-a-year mine at Blair Athol. It was Australia's largest thermal coal development. At the time of its opening, the Japanese sought a short-term reduction of 25% in contract tonnage, but within two years sales to Japan were at original contract levels. This episode highlighted a contraction in the late 1970s and early 1980s of the volume of coal and iron ore moving to Japan as the rate of growth in that country's heavy industries slowed.

This dispute graphically illustrated the danger of overdependence on one customer. The low metals prices at the start of the 1980s demonstrated the equal danger of dependence on fluctuating commodities markets. The depressed metals prices, combined with labor unrest, rising production costs, and an unfavorable rate of exchange, caused CRA's earnings to fall 84% in the financial year 1981.

The recession in metals prices had a particularly severe impact on CRA's profits because it occurred at a time when the company's expenditure on several large projects—for example the Argyle mine development, Comalco's A$600 million Boyne Island smelter, and CRA's 1982 purchase of a further 22% holding in Comalco—was at a particularly high level.

The lesson was clear: CRA would have to move much further into secondary or downstream production, using its own dedicated supplies of ores to make steel and aluminum rather than simply selling those ores to foreign producers at whatever price a volatile market might dictate.

CRA had to seek its downstream opportunities abroad because Australia itself could offer nothing suitable. Initially there were setbacks. CRA's 1984 bid for Kaiser's Fontana steelworks in California fell through, as did its attempt to take a 35% interest in a new steel group formed from the intended merging of the two West German steel giants Krupp and Klöckner-Werke. CRA was to have supplied iron ore to a single rationalized company but political opposition to the prospective Krupp-Klöckner merger put paid to the deal. Comalco, however, succeeded in acquiring most of the aluminum interests of the Martin Marietta Corporation, a U.S. aviation and aerospace manufacturer. The deal cost US$400 million in 1985, but CRA's disposal in that year of a number of assets not central to its core activities helped improve the year's financial result.

The mid-1980s were again a time of depressed base metals prices. Some industry analysts felt that it was the devaluation of the Australian dollar rather than reduced production costs and/or increased productivity that was maintaining CRA's profit levels. CRA undertook a restructuring of its management and work practise with the aim of decentralizing operations and promoting increased efficiency. This proved unacceptable to some of the mining unions, and a series of strikes and disputes at the company's mines at Broken Hill seriously affected the company's 1986 results and dragged on until 1987.

The naturalizing process, begun in 1978, ended in 1986 when Rio Tinto-Zinc sold nearly 16.4 million shares to the Australian Mutual Provident Society, reducing its holding in CRA below the critical 50% level to 49% and transforming CRA into a majority Australian publicly owned company. The change of ownership occurred at a time when two major coal projects—Blair Athol and Tarong in Queensland—and the Argyle diamond venture came to fruition. In the same year, however, Comalco withdrew from a troubled four-year joint venture with Japan's Showa Denko, representing the failure of another attempt to move production downstream.

Better news came with Hamersley's announcement of a joint development project with the Chinese Metallurgical Import and Export Corporation to exploit the Channar iron ore deposit in Western Australia. CRA's search for new Asian customers had borne fruit.

In 1988 CRA continued its tradition of adding to Australia's mineral wealth by revealing its discovery of a 5,000 million ton heavy minerals field near Horsham, Victoria. As with bauxite and iron ore CRA's discovery overnight transformed Australia's reserves figures, and commentators noted that the find would enable CRA virtually to set the market in titanium and zircon well into the 21st century, provided metallurgical problems can be overcome. A 120–ton-per-day pilot plant was commissioned on the Horsham site.

CRA and NBHC had merged their lead, zinc, and silver interests in 1971, and in 1986 the ZC and NBHC mines were combined and renamed Z.C. Mines. In June 1988 the situation changed again when CRA reached an agreement with another Broken Hill mining company, North Broken Hill Peko, on the merging of their lead and zinc interests in a new joint venture called Pasminco. The move was widely seen as a response to a series of mergers and associations among other base metals producers resulting in the formation of fewer and larger groupings in the industry. Agglomeration along these lines was designed to cut costs and strengthen marketing positions at a time of oversupply and consequent low prices in the world's base metals markets.

The proposed merger attracted the attention of the Australian Trade Practices Commission, which feared it would unite the country's only producers of zinc metal and refined lead. CRA and its partner successfully argued that since a new en-

tity known as Enterprise Metals had been formed to handle domestic sales and since this entity could buy from either partner, no monopoly would be created. In March 1989 Pasminco became a publicly listed company.

After years of profitable activity since the start of its operations in 1972, Bougainville Copper was forced to close down its Panguna mine in May 1989 because of attacks on BCL employees and equipment by native activists bent on Bougainville's secession from Papua New Guinea. The mine is unlikely to reopen until the PNG government has convinced CRA that it has brought the situation on the island under control.

A few months after this closure, British Petroleum announced the sale of its Australian coal assets to CRA for $275 million, the outcome of negotiations between BP and Rio Tinto-Zinc which had begun a year earlier. For BP this sale represented a step in its divestment of its worldwide coal interests, and for CRA a new contribution to its existing coal assets at Blair Athol and Tarong.

CRA is rightly regarded as one of a small body of elite Australian mining and resource companies, which includes, for example, Broken Hill Proprietary, the Western Mining Corporation, and Mount Isa Mines. In the 85 years since its birth amid the Broken Hill tailings dumps, CRA has grown into a large multinational mining enterprise with extensive downstream interests. Despite continuing uncertainty about the future of Bougainville Copper, CRA possesses a powerful base for the necessary move towards increased secondary production and manufacture.

Principal Subsidiaries: Argyle Diamond Mines Pty Ltd; Australian Mining & Smelting Limited; Bougainville Copper Limited; Comalco Limited; Conzic Asia Pty Limited; CRA Exploration Pty Limited; Dampier Salt Limited; Enterprise Metals Pty Limited; Hamersley Holdings Limited; Kembla Coal & Coke Pty Limited; Minenco Pty Limited; Novacoal Australia Pty Limited; Pacific Coal Pty Limited; Pacific Oil and Gas Pty Limited; Wimmera Industrial Minerals Pty Limited.

Further Reading: Hughues, H., *The Australian Iron and Steel Industry,* Victoria, Melbourne University Press, 1964; Raggatt, H.G., *Mountains of Ore,* Melbourne, Lansdowne, 1968; Coghill, I., *Australia's Mineral Wealth,* Melbourne, Sorrett Publishing, 1971; Elliott, Mary, (ed.), *Ground for Concern,* London, Penguin, 1977; Bambrick, S., *Australian Minerals and Energy,* Canberra, Australia National University Press, 1979.

—D.H. O'Leary

DAIDO STEEL CO., LTD.

DAIDO STEEL CO., LTD.

11-18, Nishiki 1-chome
Naka-ku, Nagoya, Aichi 460
Japan
(052) 201-5111
Fax: (052) 201-5754

Public Company
Incorporated: 1916 as Denki Seikosho
Employees: 7,561
Sales: ¥302.55 billion (US$2.23 billion)
Stock Exchanges: Tokyo Osaka Nagoya

Daido Steel Co., Ltd. is the world's largest maker of specialty steel. In addition to its wide variety of alloyed and treated steels, Daido makes semifinished and finished products for the automotive and construction fields and is one of Japan's leading suppliers of heavy equipment for the metallurgical industry. Daido has not suffered as badly as some of Japan's steelmakers from the industry's prolonged recession, dating back to the oil crisis of 1973, because its specialty products are less easily duplicated elsewhere by cheaper competitors. Daido has nevertheless felt the impact of the shrinking steel market and hopes to shift an ever greater proportion of its production to high-tech steels, the so-called new materials area, and industrial machinery.

Daido Steel has its origin in Japan's electric-light industry. Like most other technological innovations, the electric light came late to Japan, and it was not until the early part of the 20th century that any substantial portion of the country had electricity. In the city of Nagoya, on the east coast of Honshu, electric illumination was pioneered by Nagoya Electric Light Co. Nagoya Electric Light soon was involved deeply in the manufacture and finishing of steel rods for use in wires and various electrical applications. In 1916 Nagoya Electric Light spun off its steel-production division as a freestanding corporation, named Denki Seikosho. Encouraged by the booming World War I economy, Denki Seikosho quickly expanded its production to include not only wire rod but a variety of alloy and tool steels.

In 1921, a similar divestment was undertaken by a local supplier of electric power, Daido Electric Power Co., Ltd. Daido Electric Power's steel division was made independent and renamed Daido Steel Co., Ltd., with its main plant at Tsukiji near Nagoya. Daido Steel and Denki Seikosho briefly competed for the limited available business in wire rod and specialty steel, but in 1922 they agreed to merge as Daido Electric Steel Co., Ltd. As a maker of specialty steel products, Daido Electric Steel's growth would necessarily be limited for some time by the rather primitive state of Japan's industrial economy, which was then still far behind the leading Western nations. In particular, Japan remained in the 1920s a net importer of iron and steel, which meant that its automotive, construction, and shipping industries were relatively undeveloped, a condition that in turn tended to limit the range of applications for specialty steels.

The Japanese industrial base, however, soon was given a tremendous stimulus by the country's increasing preparations for war in China. During the Great Depression Japanese ultranationalists mapped out a plan for Asian domination that called for greatly increased production of all heavy-industrial products, especially weaponry and the various modes of transport. Daido Electric Steel's specialty steels played an important role in such products, which typically demand greater strength, corrosion resistance, and temperature stability than more common steel applications. Daido Electric Steel's fortunes thus improved with Japan's increasing militarism; a steady stream of orders for crankshafts, hardened steel, fuel nozzles, shell casings, and other special steels drove up company revenue and eventually forced the construction of a major new plant at nearby Hoshizaki. The new facility was completed in 1937, the year in which Japan initiated full-scale hostilities with China. In 1938 the company dropped "Electric" from its name to become Daido Steel Co., Ltd.

With the country's rapid descent into World War II, Daido Steel, like other important industrial organizations in Japan, was placed under the command of the armed forces, its production schedule largely set by the needs of the war administration. Capacity was stretched by the endless demand for weaponry, a situation made all the more difficult by the scarcity of workers and chronic shortages of scrap iron and petroleum. Scrap iron is the single most important raw material used in the production of specialty steels, and prewar Japan had been heavily dependent on foreign sources of scrap, buying much from the United States. With the coming of war, this supply was no longer available, and Daido Steel was often faced with critical shortages of its primary base material. Company sales nevertheless reached all-time highs in the war years.

After the war, Allied occupation forces were anxious to break Japan's industrial might, and ordered the dissolution of the *zaibatsu,* or conglomerates, and of many of the leading independent corporations. Among the latter was Daido Steel, which in 1950 was whittled down in size and given the name of New Daido Steel Co., Ltd. New Daido Steel comprised six of the former company's eleven plants, two of the others having become independent corporations and the remaining three closed altogether. Like most other Japanese companies, New Daido Steel began the postwar period with severely damaged assets, uncertain raw material supplies, worker shortages, and depleted capital funds; but, also in common with the bulk of Japanese industry, New Daido Steel managed not only to survive the postwar chaos but also to lay the foundation of its growth in the following decades.

With government assistance and coordination, Japan's steel industry rebuilt its shattered plants and embarked on a new era of peacetime productivity, centered around the automobile and shipbuilding industries. In a sense, Japan's defeat in World War II proved to be a boon to its economic future, giving the country's engineers and planners a chance to redesign its industrial base from the ground up, incorporating the latest in Western technology and production methods. In addition, Japanese steelmakers could rely on the domestic market for unlimited sales, as Japan leaped from a state of semifeudalism to a modern economy. Buildings, bridges, subways, ships and automobiles, radios, and computers were to be built. Most of these products require steel, and much of the steel would be special steel. New Daido Steel was well positioned to take advantage of Japan's economic advance, and the company grew at a prodigious pace.

To keep up with increasing demand, Daido Steel—the name was again changed in 1953—participated in a number of mergers in the 1950s. In 1952 Daido Steel Co., Ltd. added a new plant in Takakura. In 1955 it merged with Shinriken Kogyo, which had plants at Hirai and Oji, and in 1957 Daido Steel acquired Tokyo Steel Works Co, Ltd., a division of Nissan Motors. The latter move was indicative of Daido's increasing business with the Japanese automobile industry, then beginning its own rise to world leadership. Automakers use special steel in a number of ways, not only for many engine and frame parts but also indirectly, as the source to the tool and die works needed for basic fabrication. For years, Daido Steel has itself manufactured a variety of auto parts as well as supplying the super-hard steels needed for cutting and shaping such parts.

In the 1960s Japan's economy entered its period of most spectacular growth, averaging 10% yearly gains in its gross national product. Japanese steel did considerably better, however, expanding at the rate of 25% annually. In 1962, Daido Steel opened yet another new plant, this one a steel strip facility at the Nagoya headquarters; and in the following year it made allowance for the increasing use of stainless steel by absorbing Shimura Kako's stainless steel division. In 1964 Daido Steel merged again, combining with Kanto Steel Co., Ltd. to form the largest supplies of specialty steel in Japan. It was a period of rapid innovation in metallurgy, and Daido Steel's technical sophistication made the company a natural supplier to the latest developments in the space, auto, and electronic steel markets. Its technical orientation would prove invaluable for Daido Steel in the coming era of decline and fragmentation in the Japanese steel industry.

The collapse of the Japanese steel industry, beginning in 1974, had several causes. Most fundamental was the maturing of Japan's own economy, which no longer needed the tremendous capacity built up by the nations's steelmakers. Mature economies do not use as much steel as those still adding basic infrastructure. Fresh competition appeared in the form of Third World countries such as South Korea and Brazil. The last, and most spectacular reason was the worldwide decline in industrial production following the 1973 oil crisis. The latter was especially hard on Japan's shipping industry, built largely around the need for huge oil tankers, and the collapse of shipbuilding intensified the weakness in steel, which in turn hurt the prospects of Daido Steel and the specialty steel market.

Daido Steel, however, suffered less severely than the big manufacturers of commodity steel. Daido Steel's precision crafting of special steels was less vulnerable to competitors such as South Korea, and while the other Japanese steelmakers hurried to develop value-added products, Daido Steel was already firmly established in that niche. The post-1973 slump was nevertheless painful for Daido Steel, and in 1976 the company took a major step toward shoring up its market position when it acquired two of the other largest specialty steelmakers in Japan, Tokushu Seiko, Ltd. and Japan Special Steel Co., Ltd. The new company controlled about 30% of the Japanese market and would be less vulnerable to the price wars then racking the industry. Although the merger was subjected to some scrutiny by the Japanese Fair Trade Commission, Daido Steel was permitted to carry out its amalgamation.

Since the 1976 merger, Daido Steel has pared considerably its employee ranks, shedding more than one-third of its workers between 1986 and 1990 alone. If the general trend among Japanese industrial concerns is toward higher value-added products, Daido Steel might be said to have reached the ultra-value market with such developments as its 1977 nonmagnetic support beams for the latest super trains, or its current crop of high-alloy electronic components and stainless steel powder products. While the bulk of Daido's sales are still shipped in the form of standard rollings—bars and wire rod—it has made clear its intention to steer toward the more demanding and profitable area of new materials, and has also developed a strong machine-fabricating division. Although not yet a force in the export markets, in 1988 Daido announced a joint venture in Ohio with CSC Industries, Inc., and has since bought one-third of the latter's stock. Finally, Daido enjoys the indirect but very powerful support of Nippon Steel Company the world's largest steel manufacturer and for many years a close collaborator with Daido. In 1991 Nippon Steel owned over 10% of Daido's stock, and the two companies are frequent joint-venture partners.

Principal Subsidiaries: Daido Kogyo, Ltd. (67.5%); Fuji Valve Company, Ltd. (55%); Daido Life Service Company, Ltd.; Daido Machinery, Ltd. (93.9%); Daido Stainless Steel Company, Ltd.; Shin Mitsuboshi Shoko Company, Ltd.; Tokushu Spring Industry Company, Ltd.; Daido Service Center Company, Ltd.; Shimomura Tokushu Seiko Company, Ltd. (59.5%); Daido Shizai Service Company, Ltd.; Daido Genryo Service Company, Ltd.; Maruta Industry Company, Ltd. (55%).

Further Reading: This is Daido Steel, Nagoya, Daido Steel Co, Ltd. [n.d.].

—Jonathan Martin

DE BEERS CONSOLIDATED MINES LIMITED

DE BEERS CENTENARY AG

36 Stockdale Street
Kimberley 8301
Republic of South Africa
(531) 22171
Fax: (531) 24611

Langensandstrasse 27
CH-6000 Lucerne 14
Switzerland
(41) 403 540
Fax: (41) 444 468

Public Company
Incorporated: 1888 and 1990
Employees: 27,000
Sales: US$4.17 billion
Stock Exchanges: Johannesburg London Paris Brussels
　Frankfurt Zürich Geneva Basel

The De Beers Group dominates the world market in rough diamonds. In 1990 it was split into two basic parts, De Beers Consolidated Mines Limited (De Beers Consolidated) and De Beers Centenary AG (Centenary). The first is a South African holding company controlling the group's South African assets. The second is a Swiss-registered holding company, created to direct all the De Beers interests outside South Africa, accounting for 81% of attributable earnings and 62% of equity-accounted earnings of combined results in 1990. The two share identical boards of directors and their stock is traded as a linked unit. De Beers Consolidated has a 9.5% interest in Centenary.

The combined group's main activities include prospecting for and mining diamonds; the tightly controlled global marketing of its own rough—that is, uncut and unpolished—diamond production and that of cooperating producers via the Central Selling Organisation (CSO), the De Beers marketing arm; and exceptionally, given that it does not retail the finished product, the worldwide advertising and promotion of diamond jewelry. It also manufactures synthetic diamond and abrasive products. In 1990 De Beers produced nearly 50% of the world's rough gem diamonds, and through the CSO, based in London, was marketing approximately 80% of the world diamond produc-

tion. The group has a considerable investment portfolio, affording it the financial strength to keep stocks of rough diamonds, particularly important at times when the market cannot absorb them. Stocks in 1990 were valued at $2.684 billion.

Formed by Cecil Rhodes and others, De Beers is a close associate of the Anglo American Corporation of South Africa (Anglo), founded by Ernest Oppenheimer in 1917. Together they are often referred to as the Oppenheimer empire or "greater group," forged by Ernest Oppenheimer. Since 1929 they have almost always shared the same chairman. De Beers Consolidated holds 39% in Anglo, and Anglo has a 33% holding in De Beers Consolidated and 29% in Centenary. The greater group wields significant influence within the South African economy.

The vision and dogged determination of three chairmen, Cecil Rhodes, Ernest Oppenheimer and the latter's son, Harry Oppenheimer, have dictated the path taken by De Beers and the modern diamond trade over most of its existence.

The first authenticated diamond discovery in South Africa occurred in 1866, setting the modern diamond industry in motion. Prospectors came by the thousands to stake claims along the Orange and Vaal rivers. Between 1869 and 1871, six major diamond pipes or veins were discovered: Bultfontein, Koffiefontein, Jagersfontein, Dutoitspan, De Beers and Kimberley, or the "Big Hole," as it became known.

Cecil Rhodes arrived at the New Rush settlement, renamed Kimberley in 1873. From starting by supplying drinking water and ice to the community and contracting to pump water from the De Beers and Dutoit-Span Mines with a friend, Charles Rudd, and their buying a claim apiece, he was to build his business empire.

De Beers Mining Company Ltd. was founded on April 28, 1880, by Rhodes and Rudd, with other partners. The company arose once the restrictions on the number of claims individuals could hold were lifted. Barney Barnato, Rhodes's main rival in acquiring dominant control of South African diamond production, meanwhile purchased claims in the center of the Kimberley mine and in 1885 merged with the Kimberley Central Mining Company. Rhodes, however, raised a £1 million loan from the London merchant bank N.M. Rothschild & Sons to outbid Barnato in 1887 to acquire the important Compagnie Française des Mines de Diamants du Cap claims adjacent to those of Kimberley Central. Rhodes and Barnato drained each other's profits by their rivalry through the mid-1880s. Barnato, however, eventually gave way to Rhodes's vision of a single controlling company and agreed to exchange his shares in the Kimberley Central mine for shares in De Beers.

De Beers Consolidated Mines was established on March 12, 1888, controlling around 90% of contemporary world diamond production. It owned the De Beers mine, three-quarters of the Kimberley mine and held controlling interests in the Dutoitspan and Bultfontein mines. The merger of the De Beers and Kimberley Central mines was contested in court by unhappy Kimberley Central shareholders. Rhodes and Barnato overcame this obstacle by liquidating Kimberley Central. De Beers paid the liquidators £5.34 million for Kimberley Central.

The move towards the consolidation of South African production was followed by a centralization in the control of sales of South African diamonds. Prior to De Beers Consolidated's creation, individual mines sold their production through different London dealers. In February 1890 De Beers concluded a sales contract with a new dealers' and brokers' syndicate, the London Diamond Syndicate. Ties between production and sales control were thus strengthened, several of the dealing firms having significant shareholdings in De Beers.

Fluctuation in demand, however, led to great ups and downs in these early days. In 1890, for instance, the company closed down operations at Dutoitspan, which was proving uneconomical. A new pipe, Wesselton in Kimberley, was discovered the same year. De Beers purchased it in 1891, determinedly continuing its policy of acquisition. De Beers, though, was deprived of the excitement of the discovery in 1893 of the Excelsior diamond at Jagersfontein, the second-largest rough diamond ever found. The Jagersfontein mine would finally be acquired by De Beers in 1930.

The end of the century was marked in South Africa by political upheaval and the Boer War. Kimberley lay under siege by the Afrikaners between October 1899 and February 1900. Once the war was over, the great threat at the start of the new century came from the Premier (Transvaal) Diamond Mining Company, founded in 1902 following the discovery of diamonds near Pretoria. Its chairman was Thomas Cullinan, after whom the world's largest rough diamond, 3,106 carats, found at Premier in 1905, was named. The rich finds at the Premier mine opened a new period of bruising competition.

The American financial crisis of 1907 to 1908 severely affected the demand for diamonds, and coupled with Premier's bid for independence of sales, when it abandoned selling via the syndicate in 1906, had a crippling effect on trade. Premier soon recommenced selling via the syndicate, after the price it was receiving per carat had almost halved in a year, and the two companies agreed to limit sales, but De Beers had already had to reduce its mining activities considerably.

Still more significantly, diamonds were discovered in 1908 along the coast of the then German South West Africa. Exclusive prospecting and mining rights were given to German companies. The Germans set up the Diamond Regie to regulate their production and marketing. For a brief period De Beers, with the London Diamond Syndicate, had an agreement to purchase diamonds from the Regie. But the latter moved to selling first to an Antwerp syndicate, then onto the open market by tender.

The discovery of diamonds in South West Africa heralded a great expansion in the areas of diamond production, further threatening De Beers's control. Alluvial diamond gravels were discovered in the Belgian Congo (now Zaire) in 1912. The Belgian Société Internationale Forestière et Minière (La Forminière) began production in 1913. The year 1912 also saw the discovery of diamonds in Angola. The Companhia de Pesquisas Mineras de Angola (Pema) was created to exploit these finds.

The outbreak of World War I brought De Beers to a standstill. Mining was suspended in 1914 and the Diamond Syndicate stopped its contract. Only an essential core of workers remained, many others leaving to join the forces. In 1915 South Africa invaded South West Africa, defeating the German forces there and paving the way for the takeover of German diamond interests in the region.

Ernest Oppenheimer, who had arrived in South Africa in 1902—the year of Rhodes's death—to work as an agent for the diamond brokers A. Dunkelsbuhler & Co., founded Anglo in 1917. One of this company's primary aims was to mine gold on the eastern Witswatersrand. In 1919 it set about acquiring diamond interests in South West Africa previously belonging to the members of the German Diamond Regie, beating De Beers in securing them. These interests were transferred to the specially incorporated Consolidated Diamond Mines of South West Africa Ltd. (CDM) in 1920—the year in which the League of Nations mandated South West Africa to South African administration.

De Beers had secured a controlling share of its previous rival, the Premier mine, in 1917. At the time the purchase seemed important for maintaining its control of diamond production. Under Francis Oats, chairman of De Beers from 1908 to 1918, it was slow to respond to its encirclement by Ernest Oppenheimer, who continued busily acquiring diamond interests outside South Africa. Added to this, in 1918 the world's largest contemporary diamond deposits were found by a Belgian rail company in the Bakwanga region of the Belgian Congo.

While De Beers faced another depression in world markets at the beginning of the 1920s, exacerbated by the sale by the new government of the Soviet Union of diamonds and jewellery confiscated during the Russian Revolution, Anglo continued buying into various areas of the southern African diamond industry. In 1923 it purchased a 16% share in Diamang, the new name given to Pema in 1917. Then in 1924 it was granted membership of the London Diamond Syndicate . . . only to rock the boat. Anglo and Dunkelsbuhler were asked to retire from the syndicate, having attempted to bid for the entire South African output.

The new Diamond Syndicate created in 1925 by Sir Ernest—knighted in 1921—quickly caused the London Diamond Syndicate's dissolution by offering better terms and bought out its assets. Oppenheimer had been steadily building up his shareholding in De Beers and cementing a friendship with De Beers's largest shareholder, Solly Joel and his firm, Barnato Brothers. In 1926 Oppenheimer was elected to the De Beers board.

Spectacular new diamond discoveries were made in South Africa in 1926 and 1927, first in Lichtenburg, where hundreds of prospectors were allowed to rush off from a starting line to stake their claims, and then in Alexander Bay. By January 1927 Oppenheimer had secured a controlling interest in the Lichtenburg region and by 1929 he had bought out the remaining interests belonging to Dr. Merensky, the discoverer of the Alexander Bay deposits, for just over £1 million. The markets were flooded, however, by these massive discoveries, De Beers suffering considerably.

Through Oppenheimer's dynamic policies, his ever-expanding acquisitions of diamondiferous areas, and his control of the syndicate, he was elected chairman of De Beers in December 1929. He took the helm as the Great Depression began. Sales throughout the 1930s were poor to non-existent. In 1932, mining came to a complete halt.

However, important structural changes for De Beers and the diamond sales pipeline were put in place in the decade. Oppenheimer felt the original purpose of a diamond syndicate to sell South African production was becoming too restricted. He envisaged a single organization for the producers and sellers of rough that would become, as far as possible, the exclusive marketing channel for world rough diamond production. The Diamond Corporation Ltd. was founded in 1930. De Beers, CDM, Premier and other leading producers took a 50% holding, the Diamond Syndicate the other 50%. Sir Ernest became chairman. Anglo gave up its CDM holding for De Beers shares in the same year. This arrangement radically diminished the divergence of interests between the diamond producers and the sellers of rough and effectively saw the start of a single central selling organization. The Diamond Corporation also established important financial resources to enable it to acquire further outside production. The Diamond Trading Company (DTC) was further formed as a subsidiary of the Diamond Corporation in 1934 to sell at "sights"—when the boxes of rough gems prepared by the DTC, which painstakingly grades the individual diamonds and selects a percentage of the graded categories, are offered to the individual clients or "sightholders," diamond manufacturers and dealers it has carefully chosen from the world's cutting centers. The combined structures have become known as the CSO.

The concept behind the Diamond Corporation was expanded with the creation in 1934 of the Diamond Producers' Association (DPA), encompassing the members of the Diamond Corporation and representatives of the South African government and the administration of South West Africa. The DPA arose to create a pooling arrangement to enable the large producers to protect the market together.

On the industrial diamond side, the Diamond Development Company Ltd. was created in 1934 to explore new uses for industrial diamonds. By 1936, the British company, Sierra Leone Selection Trust, entered into an initial marketing agreement with the Diamond Corporation.

World War II brought production to a halt. But just prior to the outbreak of war, De Beers embarked on a significant new policy, advocated by Harry Oppenheimer—its first advertising campaign, launched in the United States. Thus De Beers, selling the rough product, built a bridge of promotional support and solidarity with the jewelers, retailers of the final product. The De Beers campaigns, and in particular such catchphrases as "A Diamond is Forever" and "Diamonds are a Girl's Best Friend," have become something of a legend, promoting the romantic image of gem diamonds.

During World War II the company's production of industrial diamonds acquired greater importance. Sales of these rose to £4.3 million in 1942, representing nearly 40% of the total trade in diamonds. Surprisingly, the diamond market recorded record sales in 1943 (£20.5 million) and 1945 (£24.5 million). However, conflict arose with the U.S. government. The latter accused De Beers of being unwilling to loosen control of its diamond stockpile to help the war effort; it was further concerned about the shortage of industrial diamonds, and that Britain would fall under enemy control. Sir Ernest denied the accusation and the shortage, and proposed the compromise of stockpiling in Canada. Industrial diamond sales were in fact supervised by the British government and prices were frozen. But Sir Ernest had angered the U.S. government, which pursued De Beers as an anti-competitive cartel. The U.S. Justice Department filed antitrust actions against De Beers in 1945, 1957 and 1974. De Beers did not take up the challenge of the U.S. courts and does not operate in the United States.

A further important discovery of diamonds had been made in Tanganyika (now Tanzania) at the beginning of the 1940s by

a Canadian, Dr. John Williamson. Williamson first agreed to join the Producers' Association in 1947, but then changed his mind. He stockpiled his production and threatened to damage the CSO's position. Harry Oppenheimer eventually managed to negotiate a settlement. On Williamson's death, he negotiated with the heirs and secured a 50% share in the Williamson mine in 1958, the government taking the other 50%.

In 1952 De Beers was to benefit from a windfall profit of £40 million thanks to the sale of a stockpile of diamonds held since the Depression, helping to strengthen substantially its financial base. The unknown quantity for De Beers in the 1950s came from the production of synthetic diamonds by foreign companies. The Swedish Allmänna Svenska Elektriska Aktiebolaget was the first successfully to create synthetic diamonds. But it failed to secure the patent rights, taken up exclusively by the U.S. General Electric Company (GEC) in 1955. In response De Beers set up its Adamant Research Laboratory in Johannesburg. By 1960 De Beers founded Ultra High Pressure Units Limited for the commercial manufacturing of synthetic diamonds. Only in 1966 would a lengthy and costly dispute with GEC over the patent rights be resolved. De Beers Industrial Diamond Division continues, with GEC, to be one of the main market leaders in synthetic industrial diamond production.

In 1955 De Beers began prospecting in the Bechuanaland Protectorate (now Botswana) and 1956 saw its founding of the Diamond Corporation Sierra Leone Limited (Dicosil). The Sierra Leone government granted it sole exclusive exporting rights. Outside De Beers control, Russia had been finding diamonds in the Urals and Siberia. In 1959 the first shortlived marketing deal was signed between the Diamond Corporation and the Soviet government for sales via the CSO.

Diamond buying offices were established by the CSO across West Africa with the incorporation in 1961 of the Diamond Corporation West Africa Ltd. (Dicorwaf). These purchased diamonds from the independent individual alluvial diggers, helping to maintain market price stability.

That year independent prospectors discovered rich diamond deposits—Sammy Collins on the coast off CDM's concessions, Allister Fincham and William Schwabel (forming the Finsch mine) in South Africa, northwest of Kimberley. By 1962, De Beers had secured a contract to prospect the latter; in 1963 it bought the rights to the Finsch pipe for £2.3 million, leasing the 70% state share. By 1965, it had taken a controlling stake in Sammy Collins's Marine Diamond Corporation by buying 53% of his Sea Diamonds Limited. De Beers's pursuit of rights may have been relentless. But certain smaller interests remained outside its control, for example in Ghana, the Central African Republic, Guinea and South America.

The dramatic discovery of the 1960s, the Orapa pipe on the edge of the Kalahari desert in Botswana, was made in 1967 by De Beers geologists. De Beers Botswana Mining Company Limited (Debswana) was incorporated in 1969 as a joint venture between De Beers and the Botswana government. Diamonds are now responsible for about 45% of Botswana's Gross Domestic Product and more than half of government revenue. Further discoveries ensued at Letlhakane and Jwaneng, the latter, buried some 150 feet in the sand, hailed as a particular technological triumph. Debswana became a 5.27% shareholder in De Beers in 1987 in exchange for De Beers's acquisition of the diamond stocks built up by Debswana from 1982 to 1985.

Business cooperation did not always go so smoothly with the other African diamond-producing countries through the 1960s, 1970s and 1980s. New-found independence, political upheaval, vacillating policies and illegal mining led to certain unstable relationships for De Beers. Sierra Leone declared an open market in 1974. Dicorwaf, which had superseded Dicosil, lost its sole exclusive exporting rights. Its supposed monopoly had been undermined by theft from and illegal mining on Selection Trust's concessions.

For some 50 years, until the early 1970s, sales of Angolan diamonds by Diamang via the CSO went smoothly. The Portuguese withdrawal before the country's independence in 1975 and the civil war that raged afterwards saw this position collapse. Diamang's operations disintegrated, leaving a great deal of production to be smuggled out to Lisbon in Portuguese luggage and to Antwerp. The volume of this trade was so important that the CSO was forced to buy quantities of these diamonds, when they came onto the open market in Belgium, to maintain price stability. In 1977, the government took a majority interest in Diamang—later to become Endiama—De Beers being left with a nominal shareholding. The government could not be seen to be dealing with a South African company, being officially at war with her neighbor. Thirty Cornish tin miners were recruited in London by Mining and Technical Services, a Liberian-registered company with several members of De Beers as directors, to go to Angola to advise and assist the state company. Endiama sold what diamond production there was by tender to Antwerp dealers. However, following growth in production, Endiama signed an agreement with the CSO in 1991 for the marketing of all the diamonds from the important Cuango River region and for help in extending production.

After independence, the Tanzanian government fully nationalized the Mwadui (formerly Williamson) mine and set up its own sorting and valuing office. Production has been run down and investment lacking, but the diamonds continue to be sold via the CSO.

In Zaire, the CSO had set up a buying company, British Zaire Diamond Distributors Limited (Zaïrebrit, later Britmond) on the former La Forminière site and from 1972 embarked on exploration. De Beers's involvement in Zaire underwent a serious crisis when the Zaire government broke off its contract, in operation since 1967, for the exclusive marketing of the Société Minière de Bakwanga (MIBA) diamonds by the CSO. Unhappy at being offered equal sales rights as one of four, the CSO withdrew from the country. The situation was resolved in 1983, first when the government allowed the CSO amongst others to buy the open-market production, and then when a new agreement was signed for the exclusive marketing of MIBA's production via the CSO. Illicit mining and black market buying have been even more rife here than in Sierra Leone.

In Namibia, De Beers's CDM has enjoyed a remarkably stable position since the 1920s, only briefly troubled by Sammy Collins. To exploit the foreshore alluvial reserves of very high-quality gems, it has developed sophisticated techniques, basically shifting sand dunes seawards, pushing the sea back by up to a quarter of a mile along ten miles. The area is said to have the most concentrated fleet of earth-moving equipment in the world. Security is high, although diamond theft is a problem. In the late 1960s and early 1970s, CDM produc-

tion accounted for up to 40% of De Beers's total taxed profits. Since 1974, no separate accounts have been published. South Africa ignored the United Nations' lifting in 1966 of its Namibia mandate and the International Court of Justice's 1971 ruling that the territory be surrendered. Namibia finally achieved independence in 1989. De Beers was accused in the early 1980s by an ex-employee of deliberately overmining its Namibian territory before it might lose out with independence, and of transfer pricing. The Thirion commission supported allegations of overmining and tax evasion, but a government white paper later exonerated CDM on both counts. At present CDM remains 100% De Beers–owned and holds the lease on the area until 2010.

The largest diamond discoveries of the past two decades have been in Australia, now the world's largest diamond producer in carats. The mainly Australian Kalumburu Joint Venture began prospecting in Kimberley, Northwest Australia, in 1972. Conzinc Riotinto of Australia Ltd. (CRA) joined the consortium in 1976, building up a 35% stake, increased to almost 70% some years later. In 1977, it took over the management of the joint venture, now named Ashton Joint Venture (AJV). Ironically, De Beers had surveyed and dismissed the region in the 1960s. In 1982 CRA and Ashton Mining Ltd., holding 95% of the Australian production sales rights, approved a sales contract with the CSO until the end of the decade, the CSO guaranteeing its purchase of the entire production regardless of the state of the markets. This important contract was renewed in 1991.

In the late 1970s, speculation by diamond traders, who had purchased and stockpiled large quantities of rough diamonds as a hedge against inflation, resulted in large numbers of diamonds in excess to jewelry demand later being released on the markets. Consequently, the early 1980s were adversely marked for De Beers. It had to limit its sales substantially so that the stocks that had built up in the cutting centers could be absorbed into the retail markets. Owing to De Beers's strict control over supply and thanks to the strength of its investments outside diamonds, it managed to ride out the severe recession.

The Soviet Union, now one of the world's largest diamond producers, had abandoned official dealings with the CSO in 1963 because of De Beers's South African status, although it was revealed in the media that the Soviets were involved in covert dealing via a third party. Having developed their own cutting industry, though, the Soviets were able to sell certain stocks onto the open market independently. Occasionally they did dump large amounts onto the international market, for example in 1984. Once again, the CSO weathered the storm. In 1990 dealing between the two parties came back into the open and Centenary concluded an extraordinary US$5 billion sales agreement with Glavalmazzoloto, the main precious metals and diamonds administrative body in the USSR, under which the CSO will market the USSR's rough diamond production for five years.

The acrimonious takeover bid by Minorco—an international mining investment house of the greater Anglo-De Beers empire in which Centenary now holds 21%—for Consolidated Gold Fields (Consgold) brought De Beers unwanted publicity. Rudolph Agnew, chairman of Consgold, argued the undesirability of a South African group wielding such power over the gold industry, and attempted to discredit De Beers by asking the British Office of Fair Trading (OFT) to investigate the CSO as a "negative monopoly." In May 1989 Minorco's bid fell through due to legal obstacles, but in August 1989 the OFT announced that it would not mount an investigation into the CSO.

It is not without controversy that De Beers exercises its formidable power over the diamond industry. It has frequently been attacked as an anti-competitive, secretive cartel. De Beers likes to refer to the system as a "producers' cooperative." De Beers is also attacked for profiting initially from exploitation through colonialism and then from the system of apartheid. Within South Africa, De Beers and Anglo are considered liberal. The greater group has consistently opposed the government on its racial policy. Harry Oppenheimer served for many years as a member of parliament for the anti-apartheid opposition, but progress in conditions for black workers has been slow.

A fully integrated wage scale was established for all employees, regardless of race, in 1978. In 1981, for the first time in South African mining history, a recognition agreement with an established black trade union was signed, allowing for the representation of black employees in wage and other negotiations. At the end of the 1980s, most of the black workers still migrated to the mines from neighboring states or South Africa's so-called homelands and lived in single-sex hostels away from their families. In 1988 the law was changed giving blacks the right to acquire blasting certificates, opening the way for them to fill more skilled posts. Black workers' pay at the end of the 1980s was, on average, one-sixth of that of white workers, who were generally skilled workers. De Beers, with Anglo, makes major investments in social programs, calculated on a percentage of Anglo–De Beers dividend payments, via the joint Chairman's Fund. It embarked in 1987 on an employee share-ownership scheme to which 9,000 have subscribed, and on a small-scale home-ownership scheme. It is encouraging small black business enterprises by contracting out work to them and is a major contributor to the Urban Foundation for black housing. The greater group is recognized to have led the way in South Africa in such initiatives, and for its business in the future, as well as for social reasons, sees its interest in encouraging the creation of a prosperous, capitalist black middle class. However, partly due to the cyclical nature of such a luxury-goods market, its shares trade at a discount to the asset worth of the company.

New exploration and operations are continuing all the time, with particularly important new developments for the 1990s at the Venetia mine in South Africa and at Elizabeth Bay and Auchas in Namibia. Harry Oppenheimer stepped down as chairman in 1984 to be replaced by Julian Ogilvie Thompson, now also chairman of Anglo and of Minorco, and Harry Oppenheimer's son Nicky became deputy chairman of De Beers and chairman of the CSO.

At the end of the 1980s, sales soared to new heights, reaching a record $4.17 billion in 1988, almost four times what they stood at in the early 1980s. The massive De Beers advertising budget of around $140 million was spent on major campaigns

in 29 countries. Twenty years ago, the tradition of the diamond engagement ring hardly existed in Japan; now 77% of Japanese brides receive one. In 1990 De Beers Marine recovered some 29,000 carats from CDM's off-shore areas, and is developing the technology for sea-floor mining.

The great aim of De Beers through its history has been to maintain the long-term stability of diamond prices for the prosperity of the diamond industry. De Beers prides itself on the fact that the price of diamonds has shown a steady growth more consistent than any other commodity since World War II and that market fluctuations and volatility have been avoided. *Fortune* ranked De Beers second in the world in 1989 among the companies with the highest returns on sales and tenth among those with the highest returns on assets.

All the major diamond producers now sell through De Beers. Only some small producers do not. De Beers keeps a very tight grip on the diamond industry. Despite the uncertainty of South Africa's political future, with its expertise in technology and marketing and its sound financial footing, De Beers seems set to maintain the industry's stability and its preeminent position.

Principal Subsidiaries: CDM Properties (Pty) Ltd.; CDM Prospecting (Pty) Ltd.; De Beers Consolidated Investments (Pty) Ltd.; De Beers Diamantes Industriais do Brasil Ltda; De Beers Holdings (Pty) Ltd.; De Beers Industrial Diamond Division (Ireland) Ltd.; De Beers Industrial Diamonds (Ireland) Ltd.; De Beers Industrial Diamond Division (Pty) Ltd.; De Beers Industrial Diamonds (South Africa) (Pty) Ltd.; De Beers Marine (Pty) Ltd.; De Beers Prospecting Botswana (Pty) Ltd.; Diamond Corp (Pty) Ltd.; Eronia Investments Ltd.; Exclusive Properties (Pty) Ltd.; Marine Diamond Corp (Pty) Ltd.; Marine Group Investments (Pty) Ltd.; Olivia Properties (Pty) Ltd.; Orama Holdings (Pty) Ltd.; Premier (Transvaal) Diamond Mining Co. (Pty) Ltd.; Sea Diamond Corp (Pty) Ltd.; Finsch Diamonds (Pty) Ltd.; (80.78%); Griqualand West Diamond Mining Co. Dutoitspan Mine Ltd. (72.87%); Consolidated Co Bultfontein Mine Ltd. (67.47%); International Diamond Products Ltd. (50%); Ultra High Pressure Units (Pty) Ltd.; Ultra High Pressure Units (Ireland) Ltd. (50%).

Further Reading: Chilvers, Hedley A., *The Story of De Beers,* London, Cassell and Company, Ltd., 1939; Gregory, Sir Theodore, *Ernest Oppenheimer and the Economic Development of Southern Africa,* Cape Town, Oxford University Press, 1962; Hocking, Anthony, *Oppenheimer and Son,* Johannesburg, McGraw-Hill Book Company, 1973; Jessup, Edward, *Ernest Oppenheimer A Study in Power,* London, Rex Collins, 1979; Green, Timothy, *The World of Diamonds,* London, Weidenfeld & Nicolson, 1981; Newbury, Colin, *The Diamond Ring Business, Politics and Precious Stones in South Africa 1867–1947,* Oxford, Clarendon Press, 1989; Jamieson, Bill, *Goldstrike: The Oppenheimer Empire in Crisis,* London, Hutchinson Business Books, 1990.

—Philippe A. Barbour

Degussa ◆

DEGUSSA GROUP

Postfach Box 11 05 33
Weissfrauenstrasse 9
D-6000 Frankfurt am Main 11
Federal Republic of Germany
(069) 218-01
Fax: (069) 218-3218

Public Company
Incorporated: 1873 as Deutsche Gold-und Silber-Scheideanstalt
 vormals Roessler
Employees: 35,000
Sales: DM14.40 billion (US$9.64 billion)
Stock Exchanges: Frankfurt Düsseldorf Hamburg Munich
 Zürich Basel Geneva

Degussa is the only company in the world operating simultaneously in the three fields of metals, chemicals, and pharmaceuticals. It has production sites in more than 25 countries and has expert representatives of its own throughout the world.

Degussa's story begins in Frankfurt am Main in the first half of the 19th century. The Free City of Frankfurt, as it was known in those days, built its new mint in 1840 in the immediate vicinity of Degussa's present head office, following a commitment it had accepted in 1837 at the Mint Conference in Munich. Here, the South German states and the Free City of Frankfurt, which together made up the states forming the German Customs Union of the day, had agreed for the first time on a common monetary unit, the florin, and had undertaken to coin certain amounts of the new currency. The director of the mint, Friedrich Ernst Roessler, son of the mint counsellor of the grand duchy of Hesse and living in the neighboring town of Darmstadt, at the same time established a precious-metals refinery within the mint at the behest of the city. He took a lease on the refinery and in January 1843 started operations at his own expense. Roessler thus laid the foundation for what was to become Degussa AG.

In addition, Friedrich Ernst Roessler established a chemical engineering laboratory not far from the Frankfurt Mint on the site now occupied by Degussa's head office. By-products of the sulfuric acid refinement process, in those days the standard method, were processed there and silver nitrate for photography and cyanide compounds were produced.

As a consequence of the Austro-Prussian War of 1866, in which Frankfurt lost its political independence, Friedrich Ernst Roessler became a Prussian civil servant and had to discontinue his private refinery business. He was nevertheless able to acquire the now private refinery for his two eldest sons Hector and Heinrich, both of whom had studied chemistry. They transferred refinery operations to the chemical engineering laboratory, located in a new factory built for the purpose, and continued to run both lines of business under the name Friedrich Roessler Söhne (Friedrich Roessler Sons) as a private company.

By developing an economical form of sulfuric acid refinement, a process which was still common—the electrolytic process was introduced in 1892 and 1895—Friedrich Roessler Söhne was technically well-equipped to take advantage of the creation of the new German Empire in 1871, when the coins of the former independent German states were replaced by the newly introduced mark currency, thus providing a favorable opportunity for extensive minting and refining activities. However, since the securities required by the empire on refinement orders could not be met, the precious-metals refinery Friedrich Roessler Söhne was converted into a joint-stock company, or *Aktiengesellschaft,* in January 1873 in order to enlarge its capital resources. Several banking institutions were behind the founding of the present Degussa, which from then on operated under the name of Deutsche Gold-und Silber-Scheideanstalt vormals Roessler (German Gold and Silver Refinery, formally Roessler) for more than a century. Only in 1980 was the acronym and telegram address Degussa, in common use since the 1930s, entered into the trade register with the addition of the term *Aktiengesellschaft* identifying it as a share-issuing company.

Its initial capital amounted to 1.2 million gold marks. Of the 2,000 shares issued, 525 were held by the Roessler family, representing 26% of the stock capital. The company's identity as a family business was preserved nevertheless, owing to the appointment of the brothers Hector and Heinrich Roessler to Degussa's first board of directors.

Degussa's first great commercial success came about as a result of its newly developed method of producing bright gold for the fire-resistant embellishment of china ware and glass, following the completion in 1879 of the large-scale minting contracts for the German Empire. Other ceramic colors were later added to the list of products.

Shortly afterward in 1882, Degussa began to produce bright gold in the United States. This led to the foundation of the Roessler & Hasslacher Chemical Company of New York in 1889, with affiliated companies and a plant in Niagara Falls, New York, which gradually took on the entire Degussa production program. As a consequence of World War I, these companies were lost to Degussa after their confiscation as German property. They were acquired in 1930 by E.I. du Pont de Nemours & Company, with which they merged two years later.

After the end of the 19th century Degussa's trade business expanded particularly rapidly. The company acted as sales agent for individual products and product groups manufactured by other chemicals companies, and conventions regulating production and sales were set up in both Germany and Europe. In order to obtain access to new products, the company often participated, even in a minor role, in their production. This business policy enabled Degussa to make considerable profits, with a relatively restricted capital participation, over a considerable number of years.

In 1898, together with the Aluminium Company of London, Degussa founded the Electro-Chemische Fabrik Natrium

GmbH in Frankfurt. At Rheinfelden, on the Upper Rhine not far from the Swiss border, the company established a plant to produce sodium using the Castner process. This substance was needed by Degussa for manufacturing cyanide salts. Over the years the Rheinfelden plant, owned exclusively by Degussa from 1918, has been the site of many production developments, in particular of active oxygen compounds—peroxocompounds—and the fumed silica Aerosil. At present, catalytic converters for the purification of automobile exhaust emissions are also made in Rheinfelden.

In 1905 the Degussa chemist, Otto Liebknecht, developed a process for the production of sodium perborate from a sodium peroxide base. Sodium perborate had already become a highly successful product in a matter of months, with the introduction onto the market of the Henkel company product Persil, the first active detergent, in 1907. Persil at that time consisted of 15% sodium perborate produced by Degussa and 85% bleaching soda manufactured by Henkel. Degussa's participation in the world's first electrolytic hydrogen peroxide factory at Weissenstein, Carinthia, in Austria, also dates back to this time.

As early as 1905 Degussa had already been involved in the establishment of the Chemische Fabrik Wesseling AG in Wesseling, near Cologne. It thus consolidated its position in cyanide chemistry, now one of its longest-established fields of activity.

Expansion continued in the metals division as well. By taking a holding in the G. Siebert platinum smelting works in Hanau, today a Degussa subsidiary, Degussa became active in the production of semi-finished precious metal goods.

Because a policy of international expansion was no longer possible during and immediately after World War I, Degussa strove to acquire domestic production sites. As early as 1919, it accepted an offer from the precious metal refinery, Dr. Richter & Co., in Pforzheim, southwest Germany, to take over this company. Today, Pforzheim is the main production plant for Degussa's dental products, which form part of the pharmaceuticals division. Gold alloys for jewelry and dentistry, solders, silver amalgams, and dental equipment are produced here.

An important new field of activity, organic chemistry, was entered into by Degussa in 1930–1931 following many years of negotiations concerning the acquisition of the two large German charcoal production companies, the Holzverkohlungs-Industrie AG in the town of Constance and the Verein für Chemische Industrie in Frankfurt, with its numerous plants. Degussa now had access to a wide variety of organic chemical products. The Holzverkohlungs-Industrie AG had already succeeded in modernizing its processes and changing over to new products such as adhesives—Atlas Ago—during the merger negotiations. The company expanded its product range on an even more intensive scale after the merger, moving from methanol to formaldehyde, and from formaldehyde to pentaerythritol and acrolein—which gained great significance in methionine synthesis after World War II, when the amino acid acid methionine was used to treat widespread malnutrition—and ultimately to the plastic polyoxymethylene, developed jointly with BASF AG.

The company also began acetone production, based on the low-cost raw material alcohol. British Industrial Solvents Ltd. was founded as a joint venture with a partner company, Distillers Co. Ltd., of Edinburgh, in 1928. Based on methods of developed by the Holzverkohlungs-Industrie AG, a large-scale plant in Hull was built for the production of acetone, acetaldehyde, acetic acid, and butanol. A process for the manufacture of water-free alcohol, which met with considerable demand as an admixture for fuel, proved a commercial success. Soon many domestic and foreign licenses were using the method at a total of 68 plants, together producing over 5 million hectoliters of absolute alcohol per year. Acetone paved the way for the production of acetone cyanohydrin, and acetone cyanohydrin led to methylmethacrylate (MMA) and polymeric methylmethacrylate (PMMA).

In 1932, Degussa acquired a small flame soot factory in Kalscheuren, near Cologne, which had run into financial difficulties. Degussa's involvement with carbon black can be traced to this date. By 1934 it had already succeeded in producing active gas black CK3 at Kalscheuren. Gas black produced in America had been for many years an indispensable product in the tire industry, which uses carbon black as a strengthening filler. In the late summer of 1933, the German Ministry for the Economy had approached Degussa with the demand that Degussa produce active gas black, based on domestic raw materials, at Kalscheuren. In 1935, Degussa researchers succeeded in developing the so-called gas black production process. This breakthrough yielded a product which could finally compete in the market against so-called channel blacks, which had been dominated by U.S. manufacturers until then. Together with the German tire manufacturers, Degussa founded the Russwerke Dortmund GmbH in 1936 for the production of carbon black using the Degussa CK3 process. Furnace black is used nowadays as a strengthening agent by the tire manufacturing industry.

In addition to metals and chemicals, Degussa has a pharmaceuticals division. This division's beginnings date back to 1933 when Degussa purchased the Chemisch-Pharmazeutische AG Bad Homburg in Frankfurt am Main from its Jewish owners. It was difficult for Jewish-owned companies to operate under Nazi economic restrictions, so the owners offered to sell to Degussa. Shortly before the outbreak of World War II Degussa had developed into a significant group of companies. During World War II, all of Degussa's links with Allied countries were severed. However, Degussa continued its traditional activities within the framework imposed on the German economy by the government's war policies. Its broad production base provided Degussa with a large number of starting points in the initial period of reconstruction after World War II, during which destruction was considerable. In addition to war damage, the dismantling of the hydrogen peroxide plant—virtually the only production site left intact—in Rheinfelden on the Swiss border, the loss of all foreign assets, and of all plants and holdings located in the Soviet-occupied sector of Germany, Degussa also lost a large part of its precious metal stocks. The progress of reconstruction before the 1948 German currency reform was further hindered by forced decartelization measures introduced against Degussa, the investigation of its technical and trade secrets by the Special Services of the occupying powers, and the forced sequestration of Degussa plants located in the French Zone of occupation, including the factories in Constance and Rheinfelden.

The June 1948 German currency reform created the foundation for a new economic beginning. In the same year, Degussa began to rebuild its head office on the original site in Frankfurt.

An additional administrative building was erected in Frankfurt in 1953.

A new hydrogen peroxide plant in Rheinfelden, a replacement for the one dismantled, was one of the first construction projects realized in Germany in the early 1950s. Plants for production based on the anthraquinone method were built in the 1960s and 1980s. Production of the fumed silica Aerosil also commenced in Rheinfelden. It had first been produced successfully in 1942 in the course of efforts to manufacture a cheap substitute for carbon black from readily available raw materials such as sand or silicates.

In 1952, Degussa began to build its own hydrogen cyanide factory in the newly established plant at Wesseling, near Cologne, very close to the Chemische Fabrik Wesseling branch; both are referred to jointly as the Wesseling plant. Production was later switched to Degussa's own process based on methane and ammonia. New markets for hydrogen cyanide, produced in Wesseling, emerged along with the discovery of the amino acid methionine and cyanuric chloride. Methionine met with considerable demand as an animal feed additive, improving the quality of protein. Cyanuric chloride is a primary product for herbicides, optical brighteners in textiles and paper, and reactive dyes.

The first plans for an overseas production site after World War II dated back to the early 1950s. Degussa founded the company Bragussa in Brazil and built a plant for production of ceramic colors on a site not far from Sao Paulo. Production began in 1955. The company was later merged with other Brazilian subsidiaries to constitute Degussa s.a., operating in all three Degussa sectors: metals, chemicals, and pharmaceuticals.

As well as building up a worldwide sales network, Degussa focused its attention on research activities that had to be postponed immediately after the war in favor of reconstruction of production facilities. Prior to World War II, Degussa's research center was housed at the head office in Frankfurt, but had to be evacuated to various sites during the war years and could not be reestablished on its former site owing to insufficient space. Consequently, at the start of the 1960s, a chemicals research center with laboratories and workshops was built on the site of Degussa's subsidiary at Wolfgang, near Hanau. The chemicals research and applications technology facilities, which were also moved to Wolfgang, are constantly being expanded.

Metals research operations were also grouped together directly next to the chemicals research center, and the precious metals refining and metallurgy operations were moved away from the center of Frankfurt in 1972 to take up residence in a new metals plant in Wolfgang.

As Degussa's production capacities in the Federal Republic of Germany were no longer sufficient, a large-scale chemical plant was built in Antwerp, Belgium, around 1970. The first production plants for sodium perborate, Aerosil, hydrogen cyanide acid, and cyanuric chloride started operations in 1970. A few years later, in 1974, the company took the first steps towards the construction of another large-scale chemical plant, this time in the United States, more than 90 years after the establishment of Degussa's first U.S. production plant. The Degussa Corporation U.S. produces silicon tetrachloride, Aerosil, methionine, cyanuric chloride, the herbicide Bladex, hydrogen peroxide, formaldehyde, and hydrogen cyanide at its plant in Mobile, Alabama. Polyoxymethylene is produced jointly with the BASF Corporation.

The United States contains the largest proportion of Degussa's foreign investments. These belong to the chemical division, which includes such products as catalytic converters for automobile exhaust emissions and chemicals, precipitated silicas, the vitamin B nicotinamide and, since 1988, three large-scale carbon black plants. Degussa's activities in the United States also include metals.

Carbon black activities in the 1980s were not only restricted to the United States, where Degussa acquired the carbon black plants of Ashland Oil in Ashland, Kentucky, and grouped them together into a separate company, the Degussa Carbon Black Corporation, a fully owned subsidiary of the Degussa Corporation. Degussa also purchased the European carbon black plants of the Phillips Petroleum Company of Bartlesville, Oklahoma. The carbon black plants in Ambes, France; Botlek in the Netherlands; and Malmö in Sweden became Degussa's property entirely, while Degussa also acquired a 50% holding in a carbon black plant in Ravenna, Italy. The company also acquired a 50% stake in a carbon black plant in South Africa.

Degussa's pharmaceuticals division, which dates back to the 1930s, also underwent a major expansion. A majority holding in the Bielefeld-based Asta Werke AG, which produces anti-cancer drugs, had been acquired by the end of the 1970s. In 1983, the company became a fully owned Degussa subsidiary. A few years later, in 1987, the entire domestic and foreign pharmaceuticals activities—the Chemiewerk Homburg Branch, Asta Werke AG, and various holdings in Brazil, Italy, Austria, Switzerland, and India—were amalgamated to form Asta Pharma AG, whose headquarters are in Frankfurt. A further important acquisition by the pharmaceuticals division in the same year was the French pharmaceuticals group Sarget S.A. in Mérignac, near Bordeaux, together with several European subsidiaries. The Sarget group's principal products are analgesics, cardio-circulatory compounds, antiseptics, vitamins, and amino acid preparations.

The increasing influence of Japan and the steadily growing economic impact of Southeast Asia prompted Degussa to establish, in addition to its organizational network, its own production sites, and technical application centers in the Pacific Basin region.

In the course of the company's worldwide expansion, Degussa's organization has been streamlined. In addition to disincorporating the pharmaceuticals division and converting it to the Asta Pharma AG, Degussa's oldest area of activities, the metals division, has been the target of extensive restructuring measures, including the complete takeover of the high-tech company Leybold AG and the resumption of primary recovery activities after an interlude of almost 100 years.

Principal Subsidiaries: Asta Pharma AG; Degussa Bank GmbH; Degussa Elektronik GmbH; Leybold AG; Degussa Antwerpen N.V. (Belgium); Degussa Corporation (U.S.A.); Degussa s.a. (Brazil); Leukon AG (Switzerland); Nippon Aerosil Co., Ltd. (Japan, 50%).

Further Reading: Deutsche Gold- und Silber Scheideanstalt vormals Roessler 1873–1923, Frankfurt am Main, Degussa, 1923; Pinnov, Hermann, *Degussa 1873–1948*, Frankfurt am Main, Degussa, 1948; Mayer-Wegelin, Heinz, *Aller Anfang ist schwer: Bilder zur hundertjährigen Geschichte der Degussa,*

Frankfurt am Main, Degussa, 1973; Dittrich, Gunther, H. Offermanns, & H. Schlosser, "Von der Münzscheiderei zum L-Methionin," *Chet,* June 1977; Wolf, Mechthild, "Porträt Heinrich Roessler 1845–1925," *Chemie in unserer Zeit,* June 3, 1986; Wolf, Mechthild, *Von Frankfurt in die Welt,* Frankfurt am Main, Degussa, 1988; Wolf, Mechthild, *It all began in Frankfurt: Landmarks in the history of Degussa AG,* Frankfurt am Main, Degussa, 1989.

—Mechthild Wolf

DOFASCO

DOFASCO INC.

Post Office Box 2460
Hamilton, Ontario L8N 3J5
Canada
(416) 544-3761
Fax: (416) 548-4265

Public Company
Incorporated: 1912 as Dominion Steel Castings Company, Ltd.
Employees: 19,200
Sales: C$3.25 billion (US$2.80 billion)
Stock Exchange: Toronto

Dofasco Inc. is Canada's largest steelmaker, accounting for 42% of the country's total raw steel production. Dofasco and its subsidiaries manufacture hot and cold rolled steel; carbon and low–alloy steel castings; galvanized steel; prepainted steel; tinplate; chromium coated and electrical steels in coils, cut lengths, and strip; seamless and welded pipe; structural shapes; and rails. The company also runs a limestone quarry, and is Canada's largest railroad car manufacturer.

Clifton W. Sherman, built the foundry that served as the cornerstone for Dofasco in Hamilton, Ontario, in 1912. Then known as the Dominion Steel Castings Company, the foundry initially made steel castings for Canada's expanding railway system. The original plant covered five acres. In 1913 Dominion merged with Hamilton Malleable Iron Company, and took a new name, Dominion Steel Foundry Company (Dominion).

In 1914 Frank A. Sherman, brother of the founder, joined the firm. Production for war goods began to roll. As World War I progressed, orders for stirrups, bridles, and clevises were replaced with orders for munitions, marine forgings, and steel plate, reflecting changes in the nature of warfare. In 1917 a plate mill was purchased, and a new forging plant began churning out shell forgings. The company's name changed again that year, to Dominion Foundries and Steel, Limited, even then known as Dofasco. When the war drew to a close in 1918, Dofasco had 11 open hearth furnaces producing about 750 tons of steel per day. The plant had sprawled to 26 acres, and about 2,280 workers were on the payroll, nearly ten times the number just four years prior.

The 1920s were a difficult decade for the Canadian steelmaker. Following the end of the war, demand for steel dropped off drastically. To make matters worse, low tariffs allowed U.S. steel producers to control a sizable chunk of the Cana-

dian steel market. Dofasco operated Canada's only heavy plate mill capable of producing 6- to 42-inch universal steel plate. It was completed in 1921, but tough foreign competition kept the mill working below capacity for most of the decade. The foundry, however, picked up the slack for the mill during the 1920s, and the company's expertise in steel castings improved accordingly. By 1928, the market for Canadian steel plate improved, and in 1929 a second shift was operating at the universal plate mill.

In 1930 Dofasco's foundry poured a 95,000 pound casting for a hydroelectric development in Quebec. It was the largest such casting ever produced in Canada. During the Great Depression demand for steel was up and down. Canada's rail system continued to expand, and provided sporadic orders for Dofasco. Sometimes the foundry was overbooked; at others it was virtually idle.

The second half of the decade saw many improvements at Dofasco. In 1935 a 20-inch cold reducing mill was brought on line, and the company began producing the first Canadian tin plate. Dofascolite, the name under which the company's tin plate was marketed, was a tremendously successful product. In 1937, a 42-inch cold mill was built, enabling the company to produce 100 tons of cold-rolled steel per day.

By the late 1930s the menace of war once again loomed on the horizon. Dominion Foundries and Steel geared up to meet Canada's war demands. Between 1935 and 1940, the company spent $5.8 million on new facilities. Three-quarters of all steel and one-third of all tin produced in Canada came from Dofasco. In 1941 the company became Canada's only domestic producer of armor plate, supplying the Canadian armed forces until the end of World War II.

After the war the company continued to produce at record levels. In August 1951, Dofasco ignited its first blast furnace. Three years later, it became the first North American company to produce basic oxygen steel. This new process resulted in higher quality steel at reduced costs. Also in 1954, Dominion Foundries and Steel acquired the galvanized sheet division of Lysaght's Canada, Limited.

In 1955, the company began operating a 56-inch cold mill with a continuous galvanizing line. In 1956 a second blast furnace began operations. Substantial replacement of facilities was made during the next five years. Between 1950 and 1959, Dofasco had invested $120 million in new plant facilities.

Dofasco's postwar growth continued into the next decade. In 1960 a second galvanizing line was installed. Steel production potential was up to one million tons per year. Dofasco next branched out through acquisition. In 1961 a joint venture to run the Wabush Iron Company was initiated. In 1962 National Steel Car Corporation, a leading manufacturer of railroad cars, was purchased. Another purchase was the Temagami property, destined to become the Sherman mine. The Sherman mine delivered its first iron ore pellets to the Hamilton plant in 1968. In 1970 the company expanded its iron ore capacity when it bought the Adams mine in northern Ontario.

Capital investments continued throughout the 1960s. When industrial impact on the environment became a growing concern in the late 1960s, Dominion Foundries and Steel reacted. In 1968 the company installed pollution-control equipment in order to improve the quality of water returned to Lake Ontario from the plant.

Steady demand for steel kept the facilities at Dofasco humming through the late 1960s and early 1970s. In March 1973

Dofasco bought the BeachviLime Ltd. quarry, insuring a steady supply of lime. A month later, a pipe manufacturer, Prudential Steel, was acquired.

In the mid-1970s massive construction was underway to double steel output within 20 years. A second five-stand cold mill was built in 1974. While the world economy was in recession, Dofasco spent several million dollars on environmental controls and renovated its foundry. By 1976 sales rebounded from the recessionary trough, reaching record levels in some areas.

In 1978 the company launched what was at that time its largest single construction project, a second melt shop. It also purchased Guelph Dolime that year, a lime quarry to be operated as a part of the BeachviLime unit. As the 1970s drew to a close, Dofasco announced its plans to built a fourth galvanizing line and a second hot strip mill.

In October 1980 Dominion Foundries and Steel, Limited, officially changed its name to Dofasco Inc. A severe recession struck Canada in the second half of 1980, causing a plant shutdown for part of July. The steel industry was hard hit, but Dofasco continued with new plant construction on schedule. As the recession deepened, however, Dofasco had to take cost-cutting measures. Demand for steel was low. In November 1982 the company laid off 2,100 employees. Net income in 1982 dropped to $63.8 million from $169.3 million the previous year.

In 1983 production levels improved, and laid-off employees were called back. Demand for higher-quality steel prompted Dofasco's conversion in 1984 of its number-one galvanizing line to production of a new corrosion-resistant steel, Galvalume. In 1985 a $750 million cast slab expansion, Dofasco's most expensive project ever, was begun. The new facilities enabled Dofasco to produce new and higher-quality steel products.

Several major acquisitions helped Dofasco's sales jump from $1.9 billion in 1985 to $3.9 billion in 1989. In December 1986 Dofasco acquired the Whittar Steel Strip Company of Detroit. Whittar specializes in strip products used in the automotive industry. In August 1988 Dofasco purchased the Algoma Steel Corporation of Sault Sainte Marie, Ontario. Algoma, a fully integrated steel manufacturer, was written off in 1991.

Demand for durable consumer goods was weak during the early 1990s, and as a result Dofasco's major customers—the automotive, appliance, and construction industries—cut orders. To combat overcapacity problems, Dofasco's new construction turned toward joint ventures. In 1990 the company announced plans to build a hot-dip coated steel plant with NKK Corporation of Japan and National Steel Corporation of the United States. The venture is the first steel industry joint venture involving companies from three countries. The plant was to be completed in 1993, and each company was to share in the profits of the specialized product, without each having to built a plant of its own, keeping the overall supply within acceptable limits.

Dofasco's success has been due in large part to the company's ability to react quickly to changes in the steel market. Specialized products, particularly non-corrosive steels, were and are in demand, and Dofasco has stayed on top of new technology. As a demand for lighter alloys increases, the company will surely respond.

Principal Subsidiaries: The Algoma Steel Corporation, Limited; BeachviLime Limited; National Steel Car Limited; Prudential Steel Limited; Whittar Steel Strip (U.S.A.); Quebec Cartier Mining Co. (50%); Wabush Mines (16.4%); Baycoat Limited (50%); Sorevco Inc. (50%); DNN Galvanizing (50%); Ventra Group Inc. (8.5%).

Further Reading: Dofasco 75: 1912–1987, Hamilton, Ontario, Dofasco Inc., 1987.

—Thomas M. Tucker

ECHO BAY MINES

ECHO BAY MINES LTD.

10180 101st Street
Edmonton, Alberta T5J 3S4
Canada
(403) 429-5811
Fax: (403) 429-5899

Public Company
Incorporated: 1964
Employees: 2,040
Sales: US$338.90 million
Stock Exchanges: Toronto American Montreal Alberta Paris
    Brussels Zürich Geneva Basel Frankfurt Düsseldorf Berlin

Echo Bay Mines is one of North America's largest and most successful gold mining concerns. Founded in 1964 as a high-risk silver mining outfit, Echo Bay has grown into one of the most successful precious-metal miners in the world. Echo Bay is respected for its excellence in mining in remote and hostile regions. The company's mining expertise has made it a sought-after partner for joint ventures. Echo Bay has a history of turning a profit on risky enterprises that other mining groups declined.

In the early 1960s a group of Edmonton entrepreneurs operating under the name Northwest Explorers saw an opportunity in Canada's northwest. A forgotten silver claim, a dormant mill, and a new railroad were the ingredients N.S. Edgar, E.R. Mead, and A.J. McBeth saw as the recipe for a fortune. The Edmonton businessmen devised a plan to finance and operate a silver mine near Canada's frigid Great Bear Lake. The venture centered around a silver deposit first discovered in 1935 by the Consolidated Mining and Smelting Company, later known as Cominco. Cominco had drilled two adits—gradually declining tunnels—in the mid-1930s, to check the ore grade and extent of the vein, and concluding that the Echo Bay claim would not be profitable, Cominco tabled the idea indefinitely.

The Northwest Explorers group, remembering the old Echo Bay claims, observed developments in the early 1960s that changed the picture. In 1960 the Eldorado mining operation, located five miles west of the Echo Bay site, shut down. Its facilities seemed destined to rust in the Arctic cold. Meanwhile, the decision to build the Pine Point Railway reduced the transportation problems associated with operating a mine so far north. Armed with this knowledge, and certain optimism, the Northwest Explorers raised the capital, optioned the prop-

erty, and leased the Eldorado mill. In 1963 new surveys indicated that the mine could turn a profit, and, by October 1964, the Echo Bay mine at Port Radium was fully operative, milling 80 tons of silver ore per day. In 1965 Echo Bay averaged 52.6 ounces of silver per ton of ore, making it the richest silver mine in Canada. By 1966 new drilling indicated that the deposits were much more extensive than anyone had dreamed. Echo Bay bought the Eldorado mill and plant outright, and stepped up production.

Most silver producers mine the metal secondarily to another metal such as gold, copper, lead, or zinc. Echo Bay, however, is one of a handful of mines whose principal product is silver. Industrial usage of silver as a conductor of electricity and in photographic films helped keep the metal in short supply and thus priced high. North American consumption was actually twice production. As a result at that time, in the mid-1960s, Echo Bay was extremely profitable.

In 1967 International Utilities Corporation, a Philadelphia, Pennsylvania–based conglomerate, purchased a majority of Echo Bay stock, eventually holding three-fouths of the company's shares. International Utilities operated the company as a subsidiary, focusing on silver production at the Echo Bay mine.

In 1969 Echo Bay experienced a decrease in profits as silver prices dropped and the favorable tax conditions for new mines ran out. Echo Bay's earnings were tied more closely to the price of silver than were the earnings of other companies that mined silver primarily as a by-product of copper or of other metals. As a result Echo Bay stockpiled silver when prices were low, as in 1971, and mined lower grade ores when prices were high. This strategy, along with cost efficiency efforts, insured a long life for the mine.

Throughout the 1970s Echo Bay remained a medium-sized silver-mining concern excavating the rich veins beneath the frozen earth at Port Radium. In 1975, however, an event occurred that changed drastically the company's make-up. The long standing U.S. ban on private ownership of gold bouillon was lifted, and the metal's price rocketed from the US$35-an-ounce range. The soaring price of gold, which eventually reached US$600 an ounce in 1981, sparked the interest of Echo Bay. In 1979 the company optioned rights to develop the Lupin gold claim from another Canadian mining company, Inco Limited.

The Lupin site was 56 miles south of the Arctic circle, making it a high-cost operation; but Echo Bay's expertise in mining frozen wastelands had been sharpened through its years of experience at its Port Radium operation, and the company was optimistic it could turn a profit. Lupin's probable and possible reserves were about 2.7 million tons of ore, with a grade of 0.38 troy ounces per ton, giving the mine about a seven-year life expectancy. Financing was raised through a preferred stock and warrant issue, and preliminary planning anticipated active production by 1982. The cost of developing the mine was expected to be C$108 million. Mining leases and permits were purchased in 1980, and the free world's northernmost gold mine began operations on schedule in 1982.

The Lupin mine proved to be a good investment indeed. The mine averaged 156,000 troy ounces of gold during its first two years, making it Canada's third-largest gold mine. Production gradually increased during the 1980s, averaging about 195,880 ounces per year in the latter half of the decade. New reserves were found, extending the mine's life. By 1990, the main shaft was deepened to about 4,000 feet, and Echo Bay anticipated production of about 190,000 ounces annually for the foreseeable future.

Operating a mine so far north has unique problems, transportation being the most severe. When the Lupin mine was constructed in the early 1980s, all the materials had to be shipped in by airplane, at great cost. Each winter since, Echo Bay has spent about US$3 million to build and maintain a 360-mile ice road, 340 miles of which is over frozen lakes. Between January and April, trucks deliver much of Lupin's supplies for the year, including some 5 million gallons of diesel fuel and 15 million pounds of chemicals, explosives, and other bulk materials. Some 700 to 900 round trips are made every winter between Lupin and Yellowknife, taking 24 hours each way. The ice road allows Echo Bay to avoid the even higher cost of air freight. Although the cost of operating a mine so far north results in an "Arctic premium" of about 35%, the high grade of the z-shaped ore deposit at Lupin allows the mine to operate profitably.

The opening of the Lupin mine in 1982 coincided with the closing of Echo Bay's flagship silver mine near Port Radium. After 19 years, the original Echo Bay silver operation was tapped out. Echo Bay Mines had been transformed from a silver miner to a gold miner, and with the transition came new anxieties. Gold mines generally trade at a much higher price-to-earnings ratio than silver mines or conglomerates; and Echo Bay's parent, International Utilities Corporation, feared a corporate raid. In 1983 International Utilities spun off Echo Bay's shares directly to its own shareholders, who benefited from the higher stock values of a publicly owned gold mine. The parent company, meanwhile, decreased the risk of a hostile takeover.

Echo Bay Mines's success with the Lupin operation inspired the company to expand further into the gold-mining industry. In 1984 Echo Bay acquired the Copper Range Company from Louisiana Land and Exploration, for US$55 million. Echo Bay was interested by the Round Mountain gold mine in Nevada, which was 50%-owned by Copper Range. Two other gold miners—Homestake Mining Company and Case, Pomeroy & Company, Inc.—each owned a quarter of the mine. The Round Mountain mine used heap leaching, a process that allows cheap mineral recovery from low-grade ores. With this method, deposits previously disregarded can be mined profitably. Echo Bay Chairman Robert F. Calman told *The Wall Street Journal*, December 11, 1984, that in buying Cooper Range Company, "We've bought the expertise as well as the company."

Heap-leaching technology would prove invaluable to Echo Bay in future ventures. Simplified, the process begins with recovery of ore from the traditional open pit. The ore is then crushed into pebbles smaller than an inch in diameter, and placed on massive impermeable pads that extend for acres. The three-story-high heaped ore is then sprinkled with sodium cyanide for 100 days. The solution penetrates the ore, bonding with the gold and silver and runs off to a collection drain. The precious-metal—pregnant solution is then pumped into tanks where it is concentrated by a carbon absorption and desorption process. Gold and silver are then removed from the concentrated solution by electrolysis, and refined into doré bars—part silver, part gold with some impurities. The doré is then sent to a separate refinery for processing into pure bouillon bars.

With its expertise in Artic mining and heap-leach processing, Echo Bay set out on a program of exploration and acquisi-

tion. In late 1985 the company agreed to buy the Sunnyside gold and silver mine in Colorado from Standard Metals Corporation for US$20 million plus royalties. In 1986 Echo Bay bought several properties from Tenneco, including three gold mines in Nevada—Borealis, Manhattan, and McCoy—for US$130 million and royalties.

The McCoy mine turned out to be a jewel. Several months after it took over the operation, Echo Bay discovered a massive gold deposit one mile from the McCoy mine. Known as the Cove deposit, the discovery contained an estimated 1.2 million ounces of gold and 53 million ounces of silver. Later estimates assessed Cove's riches at 4 million ounces of gold and 250 million ounces of silver. Plans for a new mill, to be ready by 1989, were developed. Heap leaching began in 1988.

The combined McCoy and Cove mining complex covers 110 square miles, and in 1989 produced 246,800 gold equivalent ounces, which includes silver value converted to gold ounces at the average market price ratio, twice the 1988 level. Both mines operate with open pits and underground ramps; they share milling and leaching facilities. By the end of 1989 Echo Bay had invested US$383 million in the acquisition and development of McCoy and Cove. The company expected to mine 350,000 gold equivalent ounces from the operation in 1990, at a cost of about US$240 per ounce.

In 1988 Echo Bay entered a joint venture with Silver King Mines and Pacific Silver Corporation. Echo Bay's Sunnyside mine in Colorado, Illipah mine in Nevada, Easy Junior and Pan development properties in Nevada, and Pacific Silver's Robinson and Golden Butte mines in Nevada would be operated by Silver King. The deal promised to improve Echo Bay's overall gold output in the long run while allowing the company to concentrate its own efforts on other projects. Subsequently, the operating partner became known as the Alta Gold Company.

In 1987 Echo Bay decided to expand the Round Mountain mine. The mill at the Manhattan mine, located 18 miles from Round Mountain began processing Round Mountain's high-grade ores. Milling is preferred to heap leaching where an ore grade measures a certain richness because more gold can be milled out of the high grade ore than can be recovered by leaching. The complex, including the Manhattan operation was expected to produce 440,000 ounces of gold in 1990. New reserves placed the mine's active life at 15 years at that rate.

In April 1988 Echo Bay Mines acquired significant interests in the Muscocho mining group of companies—consisting of Muscocho Explorations Ltd., Flanagan McAdam Resources Inc., and McNellan Resources Inc. The deal included the purchase by Echo Bay of C$26.5 million worth of newly issued common shares and C$23.5 million in convertible bonds. Echo Bay agreed not to increase its interests in the group to more than 33% for six years. Muscocho group's Magino and Magnacon properties in Ontario, and the Montauban mine in Quebec, represented Echo Bay's first participation in eastern Canadian mines.

The acquisition proved a major disappointment for Echo Bay, however. By mid-1989, Muscocho's Magino and Magnacon mines were far behind schedule. Echo Bay traded its one-third equity in Muscocho plus some cash and loans for 36% direct ownership of Magnacon and 50% of Magino; and Echo Bay also became the mines' operator. Although the Muscocho investment was a costly write-down for Echo Bay, the future of the two mines it retained from the deal was bright.

In February 1990 Echo Bay began operating its 70%-owned Kettle River gold mine in Washington state. The mine was expected to produce 110,000 ounces of gold annually, and the possibility of discovering additional reserves seemed excellent. Other promising ventures for Echo Bay's future include two major mine development properties in Alaska. The Alaska-Juneau mine was at one time the largest gold mine in North America. It was shut down during World War II. Echo Bay owns 85% of the mine and was preparing in 1990 to start large-scale production, expected to be about 365,000 ounces annually in 1993 or 1994. Echo Bay also owns 50% of the Kensington mine located 45 miles north of the Alaska-Juneau property, and is studying the feasibility of starting operations there. The ore body there is especially rich, three times the grade at Alaska-Juneau. The company hoped to mine 200,000 ounces of gold per year at a cost somewhat lower than its other operations.

Echo Bay Mines is regarded as one of the best-run gold mining companies in the world. By keeping operation costs well below the market price of gold, the company will be able to continue to tally high margins.

Principal Subsidiaries: Can Am Gold Corporation; Can Am Minerals Company; Echo Bay, Inc.; C.R. Exploration Company; Round Mountain Gold Corp. (U.S.A., 50%); Sunnyside Gold Corp (U.S.A., 26.8%); Echo Bay Exploration.

Further Reading: "Daring Pays Off for Company: Great Bear Lake Prospect Achieves," *Northern Miner,* November 24, 1966; Martin, Neil A., "Quest for Silver," *Barron's,* April 17, 1972; Rudnitsky, Howard, "Men who moil for gold," *Forbes,* October 5, 1987; Henriques, Diana, "More Brass Than Gold?" *Barron's,* February 15, 1988; McCartney, Laton, "Time For Gold?" *Town & Country,* March 1990.

—Thomas M. Tucker

ENGELHARD CORPORATION

101 Wood Avenue
Iselin, New Jersey 08830
U.S.A.
(908) 205-5000
Fax: (908) 321-1161

Public Company
Incorporated: 1981
Employees: 7,000
Sales: $2.94 billion
Stock Exchanges: New York   London   Zürich   Basel   Geneva

Engelhard Corporation is a leading supplier of catalysts used in the petroleum, chemical, and food industries. An unusually diversified company, Engelhard also produces a variety of industrial products such as paper coating agents, color pigments, temperature sensing devices, and precious-metal-coated anodes, and offers a precious-metals management service for its customers. From the company's present configuration it is not apparent that the unifying thread of its many activities has been the refining and fabricating of precious metals for industrial as well as decorative uses. Engelhard Corporation took on its present corporate form only in 1981, but for most of the 20th century the name Engelhard had been associated with the glamorous, and sometimes notorious, world of precious metals: gold, silver, and those metals in the platinum group.

The company's roots in the precious-metals industry extend back to 1891, the year in which Charles Engelhard immigrated to the United states from his native Germany to work as a foreign sales agent for his employer, a marketer of platinum. Engelhard decided to remain in the United States and soon was able to secure equity positions in a number of precious metals companies, chief among them Baker & Co., platinum; Irvington Smelting, which dealt with gold and silver; Hanovia Company; and American Platinum Works. Engelhard, who in *Forbes*, August 1, 1965, was described by his son as a "tough businessman" and "very Germanic," united the companies into a comprehensive precious-metals fabricator under the name of Engelhard Industries. The Engelhard interests bought, refined, and sold the full range of precious metals, but, with Baker & Co. taking the lead, soon developed a special expertise in platinum.

Platinum is valuable not only for its beauty but because it exhibits a number of unusual and useful physical properties, among them the virtually complete resistance to corrosion by chemicals or heat, and a molecular formation well suited to various types of catalysis. By the early 1900s Engelhard had begun to exploit the metal's industrial value as well as its importance to the jewelry and dental trades, helping develop its use as a heat resistant liner for chemical vessels and as filaments in electric light bulbs. As platinum was scarce, however, the metals industry did not much pursue its industrial applications. Engelhard Industries remained a supplier of precious metals primarily for ornamentation and dentistry. It was not until the 1920s that a secure supply of platinum encouraged further study of the metal's engineering value. A Canadian mining concern, Inco, formerly called International Nickel Company, demonstrated that platinum could be produced as a by-product of nickel, thus temporarily stabilizing the supply of platinum and prompting intensive research into its properties. Charles Engelhard became Inco's exclusive dealer of platinum in the United States, and in the early 1930s created a research-and-development department of his own to pioneer new uses for the metal. In conjunction with Du Pont, Engelhard's Baker & Co. came up with a revolutionary process for the manufacture of nitric acid, that employed a platinum and rhodium catalyst. The process was soon adopted throughout the chemicals industry. Engelhard Industries began a long evolution that would first transform the company into the world leader in precious-metals fabricating and later encourage its present focus on catalysis in many of its forms.

The 1930s saw the development of the platinum spinnerette, a platinum nozzle perforated by thousands of microscopic holes designed to spin out synthetic fibers for the manufacture of textiles. World War II fostered other uses of platinum, such as the platinum-tipped sparkplug for aircraft engines, able to withstand high temperatures for long periods without corroding. In the early 1950s platinum began to be used in the petroleum industry for the catalysis of high-octane gasoline and to refine heavy crude oils. Engelhard Industries continued to derive the large majority of its sales from nonindustrial markets such as jewelry, but in the 1940s Charles Engelhard added to his growing assortment of companies with the purchase of D.E. Makepeace Company of Massachusetts, makers of gold and silver sheet, tube, and wire; Amersil Company, industrial appliers of fused quartz; and National Electric Instruments Company, a manufacturer of medical instruments. With these and other industrial acquisitions, Engelhard laid the groundwork for the later expansion of his business carried out by his son, Charles Engelhard Jr. Engelhard Jr., born in 1917, served as a pilot in World War II and afterward joined his father in the metals business. Anxious to make his own mark, young Engelhard soon moved to South Africa and began exploring opportunities in that mineral-rich country, source of much of the world's gold, platinum, and diamonds.

Until 1971 the history of Engelhard Corporation was largely the story of Charles Engelhard Jr. The founder's son had the unusual good fortune to succeed in both of the roles available to a wealthy scion. He became an international socialite and built his father's company into a far greater success. Upon settling in South Africa, Engelhard started a gold-exporting business to supply his father's companies with raw material, as well as to turn a profit. At the time, gold could not be traded except in the form of art objects, so Engelhard shipped his gold in the shape of dishes, jewelry, and even solid gold pulpit tops, much of which was later melted down by the customer. Engelhard incorporated his firm, Precious Metals Development, in London in 1949, using the services of Robert Fleming & Co. At Fleming & Co. Engelhard met Ian Fleming, the creator of James Bond, who is believed to have used the portly, gold-toting Engelhard as the model for his famous villain, Auric Goldfinger. When his father died in 1950, the younger Engelhard assumed control of a complex, heterogenous mix of companies headquartered in Newark, New Jersey. He once again made the United States his home, bringing with him connections with many of the leading figures in South African mining.

Engelhard found that his autocratic father had run his various metals businesses virtually without administrative help, and set about centralizing authority while also delegating its daily implementation. In 1953 he brought in Gordon Richdale as president of Engelhard Industries, the main operating company for the family interests. Richdale had experience in mining in the Transvaal region of South Africa, and was a good friend of Sir Ernest Oppenheimer, the chairman of that country's dominant mining company, Anglo American Corporation of South Africa. Engelhard had become friends with Oppenheimer's son Harry as well, so when the Oppenheimers needed a partner for a 1957 bailout of Central Mining and Investment Corporation they turned to Engelhard. Central Mining was a large, London-based oil and mining company with extensive South African holdings, in danger of a hostile takeover, which it hoped to prevent with Engelhard's help. For a relatively small amount of cash, $3.5 million, Engelhard was able to gain a 30% share of Rand American Investments Limited, an Oppenheimer creation that then won the proxy fight at Central Mining and took control of its 12 gold mines, timber holdings, lime quarries, and 13 newspapers, with a total estimated value of $500 million. Charles Engelhard Jr. was named chairman of Rand American, having parlayed a youthful lark in South Africa into an intimate partnership with one of the most powerful families in international business.

The South African venture was kept separate from Engelhard's stable of U.S. companies, which in 1957 had sales of $173 million, more than one-third of them derived from platinum fabricating. Engelhard Industries also did about $32 million in gold fabricating, and $55 million in silver, making it a world leader in all three of the major precious-metals markets. Industrial applications of precious metals were on the rise, and Engelhard Industries was well positioned to profit from their growing importance. Charles Engelhard Jr. also continued to pursue his valuable South African connections. As part of the 1957 takeover of Central Mining, Engelhard and Harry Oppenheimer had agreed to a stock swap, each of them taking 10% of the other's family holding company. Engelhard thus gained a very valuable piece of Ernest Oppenheimer and Sons, the force behind Anglo American Corporation and the De Beers diamond mines; while Harry Oppenheimer took a similar chunk of Engelhard Hanovia, the family-owned corporation that, in turn, controlled 72% of Engelhard Industries. The trade would appear to have been one-sided, as Anglo American was a much larger concern than the Engelhard interests. Over the next two decades, however, Harry Oppenheimer continued to buy stock in Engelhard Hanovia and by 1970 came to own 70%, at which time his investment proved to have been very wise indeed.

In the meantime, Engelhard upped his investments in South Africa. In 1958 he set up the American-South African Investment Company Limited, with $34 million in assets. American-South African was an investment trust trading in South African gold stocks and was the first South African company listed on the New York Stock Exchange. As chairman of Rand Mines, one of the former Central Mining companies, Engelhard greatly expanded the firm's holding into uranium, coal, and copper refining; and in 1961 he paid $17 million for two gold mines owned by Kennecott Copper, rolling all of his South African holdings into a new joint investment company with the Oppenheimers called Rand Selection Corporation Limited. Engelhard had by that time become a figure of recognized importance in South African affairs, an honor that brings with it involvement in all of the moral and political difficulties besetting that country. After the Sharpeville massacre of 1960, Engelhard became more open in his criticisms of apartheid and somewhat curtailed his active investment in the country. Engelhard did not seem to bother himself with apologies or explanations of the relation between his fortune and apartheid. As a businessman and as a strong supporter and confidante of Democratic politicians, he appears to have viewed apartheid as inefficient and doomed but did not further concern himself with its injustices.

In 1963 Engelhard put together the deal that would determine the future of his company. At the urging of Andre Meyer of Lazard Freres, the investment-banking house, Engelhard took a 20% interest in Minerals & Chemicals Philipp (MCP), a recently formed partnership between a rather small producer of nonmetallic minerals like kaolin and fuller's earth, and Philipp Brothers, a powerful trading firm specializing in the buying and selling of ores on the international market. Again Engelhard made a stock swap an important part of the deal, giving up 8% of Engelhard Hanovia as partial payment for his 20% interest in MCP, which in 1964 had sales of $447 million, the bulk of it generated by Philipp Brothers's fast-growing ore trading. In fact, Engelhard's purchase of MCP stock soon proved prescient, as worldwide demand for precious and industrial metals began to take off, and Philipp's sales skyrocketed, gaining as much as 45% in a single year.

By 1966 MCP sales had reached $709 million, while Engelhard Industries did only about 40% of that figure. Engelhard nevertheless worked out a merger of the two companies, in September of 1967, creating Engelhard Minerals & Chemicals Corporation (EMCC), with the Engelhard family controlling about 40% of the new giant's stock. Given the relative size of the partners in this transaction, and Harry Oppenheimer's increasing role in the Engelhard family interests, it is probable that the merger was made possible by the financial power of Oppenheimer's Anglo American Corporation. EMCC was already a large corporation, but its potential was not yet apparent to many observers. Nearly one-half of the company's 1967 net income of $28 million was generated by the Philipp trading division, with the Engelhard metal processing contributing 34%, and minerals and chemicals about 19%. Philipp's trading worked on a small profit margin but was soon to enjoy phenomenal growth, as the world turned increasingly to spot traders to move scarce natural resources around the globe quickly and efficiently. By 1972 EMCC's sales hit $2 billion, about 80% of it supplied by Philipp, and in 1974 revenue reached the astonishing figure of $5 billion and continued to climb.

Charles Engelhard Jr. did not live to see the success of his combination, however. When the "platinum king," as he was called, died in early 1971, his family's Engelhard Hanovia owned 43% of the increasingly profitable EMCC; but by that time 70% of Hanovia was controlled by Anglo American, which promptly exchanged its Hanovia shares for 30% of EMCC, leaving the Engelhard family with 10% of EMCC and all of its other interests. The friendship of Engelhard and Oppenheimer thus ended with a rough parity of gain—with the help of Oppenheimer, Engelhard had built an enormous metals combination, but when the dust settled it was Oppenheimer who would reap the long-term benefits.

In the absence of an Engelhard heir interested in business, Milton Rosenthal was appointed chairman of EMCC. Rosenthal had been president of EMCC since the 1967 merger, and after Engelhard's death inaugurated a tightening of controls and general overhaul of the company. In part, this was an inevitable concomitant of the executive change, which saw Engelhard's largely blue-blood management give way to a team dominated by Philipp Brothers's trading veterans, chief among them Ludwig Jesselson. Neither side of the merger particularly enjoyed working with the other, and when the MCP men gained control of the company many of the Engelhard people left or were fired, and an air of hardworking sobriety settled over the firm. Rosenthal and his advisors cut back on luxuries but expanded mightily their trading business, which, soon after the 1973 oil crisis, began handling oil on the spot market. Commodities traded on the spot market, as opposed to the futures market, are for immediate delivery. From modest beginnings, the oil spot market quickly reached critical importance during the 1970s, a decade in which all natural resources seemed in short supply, and by 1978 Philipp was trading $4.5 billion in oil alone. Its $9 billion in total sales dwarfed the minerals-and-chemicals and precious-metals business of its partners, even as the latter became increasingly successful in the development of fluid catalytic cracking materials and exhaust emission control converters.

Philipp Brothers owed its success primarily to the scarcity of its commodities and the skill of its traders. By keeping tabs on the needs of both producers and consumers of over 100 kinds of raw materials, Philipp was able to buy and sell large quantities of goods for small but almost instant profits, and even offered its clients the use of a company bank in Switzerland to help finance the construction of new plants or to make unusually large purchases. As the markets for raw materials became increasingly widespread, Philipp's business continued to grow at a fantastic rate, and from 1978 to 1980 EMCC's sales jumped from $10 billion to $26.5 billion, about 90% of which was due to Philipp. So great a disparity between former partners naturally strained corporate relations, as minerals-and-chemicals people along with those in precious metals felt overshadowed by their trading counterparts and had trouble justifying time spent managing assets that grew at so comparatively slow a rate. In the spring of 1981, therefore, metals-and-minerals and precious-metals division of EMCC were spun off as a new, publicly traded entity to be called Engelhard Corporation, while Philipp Brothers went its way as Phibro toward an eventual merger with Salomon Inc. Harry Oppenheimer's Anglo American Corporation maintained a 30% stake in both companies, a double wild card waiting to be played at any time.

The new Engelhard Corporation set about revising its mix of sales. In 1983, for example, when the company did about $2 billion in sales, 85% of the sales were generated by the precious-metals business, but the much smaller minerals-and-chemicals-division produced 60% of Engelhard's net income. As a result, in that year the company began referring to itself as a specialty chemicals firm, and two years later regrouped its businesses according to function rather than the raw material involved. Thus, all catalytic businesses became part of the specialty-chemicals division, regardless of whether they made use of kaolin or platinum for their catalysis; while the specialty-metals division worked strictly with metals technology and metals management services. This gradual redefinition and housecleaning continued up to the 1990s, with Engelhard announcing that it would sell off some of its remaining gold and silver businesses and begin deep cuts in its salaried staff, in anticipation of which the company took a special charge of $160 million in 1989.

At the end of the 1980s Engelhard Corporation derived the lion's share of its sales from the remaining portion of its precious-metals fabrication business, $1.6 billion, but far more profitable was the catalysts-and-chemicals division, which earned $43 million on sales of $450 million in 1989. Much of that was generated by fluid catalytic cracking materials made for the petroleum industry. Even more promising was the performance of the company's third product grouping, now known as pigments and additives. This group, a descendent of the EMCC merger partner that produces paper coatings and pigments for the plastic and paint industries, along with several businesses purchased in 1988 from the Harshaw/Filtrol Partnership, netted $53 million on only $360 million in sales. It was no surprise, therefore, that despite its heritage as one of the world's premier users of precious metals, Engelhard is steadily moving toward the more lucrative fields of catalysis and specialty chemicals.

Principal Subsidiaries: Engelhard-Kalichemie (Germany, 50%); Hankuk-Engelhard (Republic of Korea, 50%); N.E. Chemcat (Japan, 38.8%).

Further Reading: "The Engelhard Touch," *Forbes,* August 1, 1965.

—Jonathan Martin

FREEPORT-MCMORAN INC.

1615 Poydras Street
New Orleans, Louisiana 70112
U.S.A.
(504) 582-4000

Public Company
Incorporated: 1981
Employees: 7,656
Sales: $1.58 billion
Stock Exchange: New York

Freeport-McMoRan Inc. (FMI) is engaged in exploring, mining, producing, processing, and marketing natural resources. Commodities include phosphate rock, phosphate fertilizers, sulfur, oil, natural gas, copper, gold, and other natural resources. It ranks as the largest U.S. producer of phosphate fertilizer and one of the largest independent companies involved in oil and natural gas production. FMI also is recognized as a cost-effective producer of copper. FMI was incorporated in 1981 through a merger of Freeport Minerals Company and McMoRan Oil & Gas Company. Each company became a wholly owned subsidiary of Freeport-McMoRan Inc.

Freeport Minerals Company (FMC) was incorporated in 1912 under the name of Freeport Sulphur Company. It pioneered the use of the Frasch invention in the United States as an engineering method to mine sulfur.

Prior to the Frasch invention, Italy monopolized the sulfur market because of its cheap labor. However, Herman Frasch's invention, using machinery rather than manual labor, allowed U.S. companies to produce the element at competitive world prices. The process involves flushing large quantities of hot water into pipelines that have been sunk inward toward the sulfur find. As the ore melts, it is pumped to the surface in liquid form. The process initially had been engineered on a find near Lake Charles, Louisiana, in 1894. Frasch, along with a group of financiers, had established the Union Sulphur Company in 1896 and acquired title to the Lake Charles site, as well as mineral rights and control over the Frasch patents.

Subsequently, sulfur was discovered at the Bryanmound site on the gulf coast of Texas near the Brazos River. Francis R. Pemberton, an entrepreneur, together with other investors, took an option on leases covering the Bryanmound property. Because the expiration of the patent that covered the major components of the Frasch process was imminent, Pemberton brought the find to the attention of several investors. Eric P.

Swenson, vice president of National City Bank in New York and a native Texan who retained strong financial ties throughout Texas, showed interest and visited the find in 1911. When Swenson saw the site, he realized that he could also develop a duty-free port nearby. Upon returning to New York, he formed the Vanderlip-Swenson-Tilghman Syndicate, and with a pooled capital of $700,000 to finance the project, purchased Bryanmound and the surrounding area.

Frasch's Union Sulphur Company sued to bar the syndicate from using the Frasch engineering method at Bryanmound on the grounds that supplementary unexpired patents were crucial to the process. After lengthy litigation, a U.S. circuit court of appeals ruled that the remaining unexpired patents did not provide needed insight to the invention. As a consequence, the syndicate founded Freeport Sulphur Company in 1912, along with Freeport Townsite Company to develop a city on the west bank of the Brazos River and Freeport Terminal Company to maintain train facilities to the port. In 1913, Freeport Texas Company was chartered as a holding company for Freeport Sulphur Company; Freeport Townsite Company; Freeport Asphalt Company; Freeport Sulphur Transportation Company; Freeport Terminal Company; South Texas Stevedore Company; and La Espuela Oil Company, Ltd. Headquarters for the holding company were located in New York City and Eric Swenson became the company's first president, remaining in that office until 1930.

New mining methods were introduced at Bryanmound during its early years of operation. Elevated pipes carrying the molten sulfur from the well to the storage vats were replaced with three-inch-wide sulfur lines encased in six-inch-thick pipes through which steam could circulate to protect the lines from inclement weather and to reduce clogging. During World War I demand for sulfur rose sharply. Approximately 1,500 tons were generated daily at Bryanmound to cover shipments sent to U.S. factories producing combat weapons. Before its closure in 1935, the find yielded more than five million long tons of sulfur.

The company began exploration on a second mine in 1922 when it acquired sulfur rights to Hoskins Mound, 15 miles from Bryanmound. Unfavorable geological formations in the mound prompted innovative drilling methods that later were used at other sites. Company engineers checked the escape of hot water into sedimentary deposits of sand by pumping large quantities of mud into the formation, thus making the find a successful venture. They also developed a process to heat water with water boiler gases. The plant at Hoskins Mound closed in 1955 after producing more than ten million long tons of sulfur.

A growing opposition to Eric Swenson's attitude as president of FMC led to his deposal by stockholders, who felt Swenson was insensitive to their concerns. In 1930 Eugene Norton became president and under his leadership the company became the first sulfur-producing firm in the United States to diversify its interests. In 1931 FMC purchased controlling interest in Cuban-American Manganese Corporation, and through its Cuban subsidiary in Oriente Province, gained access to rich deposits of low-grade manganese oxide ores. FMC's research department developed a process to refine manganese from low-grade ore for use in the manufacture of steel. As a result, between 1932 and 1946, when the find was exhausted, the company produced more than one million tons of manganese oxide. In 1936, the corporate name was changed from Freeport Texas Company to Freeport Sulphur Company.

Langbourne M. Williams was associated with FMC for many years. He was elected president of the company in 1933 and chairman in 1957, staying on the board until 1977. When he became president in 1933, company operations began at Grand Ecaille, a sulfur dome in the Mississippi delta region, 45 miles south of New Orleans, Louisiana. Because the dome was located beneath marshland, engineers drove thousands of wooden pilings into the land and built reinforced concrete mats over them to provide transportation to and from the mine. Company workers also dug a ten-mile canal between the plant and a site near the Mississippi River where they shipped the product to market. The site was later named Port Sulphur. Grand Ecaille served as a model in developing engineering solutions that would be applied in the future. When the plant at Grand Ecaille closed in 1978, more than 40 million tons of sulfur had been produced. During World War II company plants at Hoskins Mound and Grand Ecaille received army and navy "E" awards from the U.S. government for outstanding wartime production. Another FMC subsidiary, Nicaro Nickel company, chartered in 1942, was under contract to the U.S. government and contributed more than 63 million pounds of nickel to the war effort. The plant closed in 1947 when it became unworkable to cover production costs and sell the ore at competitive peacetime prices.

Charles Wight became a director of FMC in 1948 and president in 1958. During the 1950s new mining discoveries allowed for continued product diversification. Discoveries of substantial finds of potash in New Mexico and Canada prompted FMC to establish the National Potash Company in 1955, in partnership with Consolidated Coal Company. Production began in 1957, and in 1966 FMC acquired full ownership of the successful operation.

At the same time, FMC's research center developed several technological advances, some resulting in lower mining production costs. In 1952 the company pioneered a process substituting seawater for fresh water in sulfur mining. This process eliminated the need to transport fresh water to sites located near sources of seawater. Another process developed at FMC's research center produced pure nickel and cobalt from nickel ore, and rekindled company interest in mining Cuban ores. In 1955 FMC chartered the Cuban American Nickel Company and a subsidiary, the Moa Bay Mining Company. The company invested $119 million in constructing plant facilities and a town at Moa Bay, Cuba, as well as a refinery at Port Nickel, Louisiana.

In 1960, however the government of Fidel Castro confiscated the Cuban facility. In all, FMC produced more than 3 million pounds of nickel, 310,000 pounds of cobalt, and more than 7,000 tons of the by-product ammonium sulfur before the plant closed. Later, FMC listed the Cuban facility as a tax loss.

Although FMC began oil exploration in 1913 when it chartered La Espuela Oil Company, Ltd. to handle fuel requirements for its operation at Bryanmound, it was not until 1948 that the company began a sustained program of oil and gas exploration. In 1956 it formed Freeport Oil Company to handle ventures in Louisiana, Kansas, Texas, and New Mexico. In association with two other interests, it discovered oil and gas reserves at Lake Washington, Louisiana, and set a record, at the time, by producing oil from the world's deepest well, lo-

cated 22,570 feet below the ground. In 1958 Freeport Oil Company sold its interest at Lake Washington for approximately $100 million to Magnolia Petroleum Company. Throughout the 1960s and 1970s the company participated in various joint oil and gas discoveries throughout the United States.

Robert C. Hills became president of FMC in 1961 and remained in office for six years. During his administration FMC produced a record two million tons of sulfur and became the world's largest sulfur producer for 1963. At the same time, FMC launched several new subsidiaries to meet company needs. It formed Freeport Kaolin Company in 1963 after purchasing the main assets of Southern Clays Inc. Included in the sale were white clay reserves used as filler and coating materials in the manufacture of paper. From 1964 through 1981 Freeport Kaolin Company underwent a major expansion program designed to increase mining and processing capacity and to upgrade its products.

In addition, FMC organized Freeport of Australia in 1964, to oversee its mineral exploration, development, and production activities in Australia as well as in the surrounding Pacific Ocean region. In 1967 Freeport of Australia, in a joint venture with Metals Exploration, located large Australian nickel deposits near Greenvale, Queensland.

In 1966 FMC established Freeport Chemical Company to embark on a phosphate chemical project, and constructed a plant at Uncle Sam, Louisiana. The plant produced its first shipments of phosphoric acid and sulfur acid in 1968. In the 1970s plant facilities were expanded at Uncle Sam and a plant to produce sulfuric acid was added in Port Sulphur, Louisiana. A research project undertaken at FMC led to the recovery in 1988 of uranium oxide, commonly referred to as yellowcake, from phosphoric acid. Subsequently two uranium-recovery plants were opened: one at Uncle Sam and the second one at Agrico Chemical Company's phosphoric acid facility in Donaldsonville, Louisiana.

In 1966 FMC founded Freeport Indonesia, Inc., to mine copper in the province of Irian Jaya. Because the find, known as Grasberg Prospect, was located in a remote, mountainous region, open-pit mining operations did not begin until late 1972. The first copper shipment was made the following year, however, and was valued at $2 million. Gold and sliver also were mined at the find.

During the 1970s through 1982, significant changes occurred in the company. In 1971 the company name changed from Freeport Sulphur Company to Freeport Minerals Company to reflect its role as a diversified mineral producer. Paul W. Douglas became president in 1975. FMC continued a policy of diversification in 1981 when it formed Freeport Gold Company to operate a gold find located in Jerrit Canyon, Nevada.

In 1980 FMC reported a record of $147.4 million in company earnings. Over the years FMC had worked in joint mining ventures with McMoRan Oil & Gas Company and owned three million shares of its convertible preferred stock. In 1982, when the companies merged, it became one of the leading natural-resources companies in the country.

W.K. McWilliams Jr. and James R. (Jim Bob) Moffett, both geologists, started a privately owned company, McMoCo, during the mid-1960s. McMoCo became the forerunner of McMoRan Oil & Gas Company. It began as a consultant for oil and gas exploration programs, but soon added personnel to enable it to handle entire projects from locating finds, to drilling and producing the product. Because it had limited funds, outside sources provided risk capital. In return for its work, McMoCo received 25% interest in each find. B.M. Rankin Jr., a specialist in land-leasing and sales operations, joined as an associate about 1967. With his arrival, McMoCo was liquidated and the three owners formed McMoRan, a company whose name combined portions of their surnames. In order to secure necessary funding for its many drilling programs, the company decided to become a public company. In 1969 it merged with Horn Silver Mines Company, a public firm incorporated in 1932 and controlled by television personality Art Linkletter and several associates, that was listed on the Salt Lake City Stock Exchange. As a consequence, a new public firm, named McMoRan Exploration Company, emerged with Linkletter as a board member. One of the firm's earliest oil explorations was on the gulf coast of Louisiana in LaFourche Parish; McMoRan owned 50% of the successful find.

During the 1970s, the company acquired a reputation as an aggressive petroleum explorer with cost-efficient drilling programs. It formed drilling partnerships with several organizations. In 1972 it signed an agreement with Geodynamics Oil & Gas Inc. and Comprehensive Resources Corporation and bought working interests in several oil- and gas-producing properties in Texas and Louisiana. In 1973 it formed a joint petroleum-exploration program with Dow Chemical Company. In this venture, Dow Chemical Company received 50% interest in all exploration finds, while McMoRan Exploration Company's interest varied from 25% to 38% per find. In 1975 the company began a $36 million onshore oil and gas exploration and development program with Transco Exploration Company. During its first year of operation, McMoRan Exploration Company successfully completed 5 of the 17 wells drilled. As a result, budgets for the second and third year of operation were expanded from $8 million to $14 million.

While many exploration programs were in progress, administrative and operational changes took place within the organization. In 1970 stockholders voted to de-list the company from the Salt Lake City Stock Exchange. In 1977 a four-member operating committee headed by Moffett was named to assume the duties of McWilliams and Rankin, who stepped down as co-chairmen. Moffett became president and chief executive officer, while McWilliams and Rankin remained as consultants, directors, and stockholders. In 1978 the company was reincorporated in Delaware and was listed on the New York Stock Exchange. In 1979 the name was changed from McMoRan Exploration Company to McMoRan Oil & Gas Company.

Other operational changes included the creation of subsidiaries to separate distinct operations within the organization and provide the company with additional exploration exposure. In 1977 McMoRan Offshore Exploration Company (MOXY) began operation to manage and expand oil and gas explorations in federal waters off the Gulf of Mexico. Interests in federal offshore lease blocks were acquired through sublease arrangements. In 1980 MOXY entered a three-year program with several organizations, including Transco Exploration Company and Freeport Minerals Company. Under the agreement, MOXY provided 25% of exploratory expenses in exchange for 35% working interest in the finds.

Another subsidiary, McMoRan Exploration Company (MEC), was formed in 1979 to handle exploration and production of oil and gas properties located primarily along the gulf area of Texas and Louisiana, both onshore and in waters owned by these states. In 1980, MEC began an exploration and development program for oil and gas operations in the gulf region with several organizations. MEC provided 25% of total exploration funds in return for a 37.5% working interest in the finds.

In 1981 McMoRan Oil & Gas Company merged with Freeport Minerals Company. The new company, Freeport-McMoRan Inc. elected Paul Douglas as president and Benno C. Schmidt as chairman of the board. James R. Moffett became vice chairman but remained president of McMoRan Oil & Gas Company, directing all combined oil and gas activities. FMI's policy put greater emphasis on domestic oil and gas exploration programs yet sustained interest in growth programs in minerals and chemical products.

In 1982 Freeport Gold Company completed its first full year of operation. It held the record as the largest gold producer for the year, reporting an output of 196,000 ounces of gold. In 1983 FMI created Freeport-McMoRan Oil and Gas Royalty Trust to afford shareholders direct participation in the income from selected U.S. offshore oil and gas properties held by McMoRan Oil & Gas Company. Although the company was unable to put a value on these properties, its annual report for 1982 listed entire oil and gas assets at $1.06 billion.

FMC in 1983 purchased Stone Exploration Corporation, a company engaged in gas exploration, development, and production, primarily in south Louisiana. At the time, Stone Exploration had estimated proven reserves of 57 billion cubic feet of gas and gas equivalents. In 1983 Paul W. Douglas resigned as president and chief executive officer. Schmidt, chairman of the company, assumed the additional position of chief executive officer but the position of president remained vacant. In 1984 James R. Moffett succeeded Schmidt as chairman and chief executive officer. Schmidt became executive committee chairman and a director. Richard B. Stephens replaced Moffett as president of McMoRan Oil & Gas Company. Milton H. Ward assumed the duties of president and chief operating officer of FMI. At the time, FMI's asset base was valued at $1.4 billion.

In 1984 FMI enjoyed a 133% increase in its oil and gas reserves when it purchased a 50% working interest in Voyager Petroleum Ltd. of Canada and Midlands Energy Company, operating in the midwestern and western United States. Freeport-McMoRan Oil & Gas Company, a fully owned subsidiary of FMI, also became managing general partner of Freeport McMoRan Energy Partners, Ltd., which it incorporated in 1984.

In 1985 FMI sold certain assets to reduce its long-term debt. It sold Freeport Kaolin Company for more than $95 million to Engelhard Corporation, a manufacturer of specialty chemical and metallurgical products and a trader in precious metals. In June 1985 it sold a 25% interest in Midlands Energy Company to Bristol PLC, a British energy company, for $73 million. The 25% interest included natural gas and oil reserves, exploration land, and a stake in three processing plants. It sold 14% of its domestic oil and gas business for more than $125 million on the New York Stock Exchange in the form of depository receipts representing limited partnership units in its Freeport-McMoRan Energy Partners, Ltd. (FMP) Additionally, it sold approximately 11% of its common shares in Freeport-McMoRan

Gold Company, formerly known as Freeport Gold Company, to the public for more than $39 million.

Also in 1985, FMI acquired two new companies and announced a program to repurchase up to ten million common shares of its stock depending on market conditions. It bought Geysers Geothermal Company (GGC), a producer of steam for electric power generation, for $216.7 million. The purchase allowed FMI to extend the use of the hot-water technology it had developed while operating its sulfur reserves. It also bought most of the assets of Pel-Tex Oil Company for $74 million, thereby acquiring its oil and gas properties located in the gulf area of Louisiana and Texas.

Operational costs of the organization were significantly reduced beginning in 1985 when corporate headquarters in New York City were moved to New Orleans, Louisiana, and combined with FMI's office there. Oil and gas and certain mineral functions were also moved to the new Freeport-McMoRan Building built to serve as headquarters for the organization.

In 1986 FMI formed Freeport-McMoRan Resource Partners (FRP), whose operations included the production of phosphate, nitrogen fertilizer products, sulfur, and geothermal resources, and the recovery of uranium oxide from phosphoric acid. FRP stock was placed on the New York Stock Exchange. The same year, in partnership with Kidder, Peabody & Company, FMI reached an agreement to buy Petro-Lewis Corporation and an affiliate, American Royalty Trust Company, for $440 million. The acquisition increased FMI's domestic oil and gas production.

In 1987 FRP acquired a chemical-fertilizer plant located in Taft, Louisiana, from Beker Industries for $22.5 million. It also bought Agrico Chemical Company from The Williams Companies for more than $250 million. Agrico assets included phosphate rock mines, production facilities for phosphate and nitrogen fertilizers, and a large sales and distribution network.

During the year FMI changed its interests in Australia. It sold most of its holdings in Greenvale Nickel project in Queensland in two transactions totaling $26 million in cash and a deferred payment of $11 million. It set up Freeport McMoRan Australia Ltd. in 1987 to handle its gold and diamond projects in that country. Late in 1988 the new subsidiary merged with Poseidon Ltd., and Australian mining concern and a new company emerged called Poseidon Exploration Ltd.

In November 1989 Moffett, the chairman and chief executive officer of FMI, outlined a plan to sell between $1.2 billion to $1.5 billion in assets to reduce long-standing debts. Future company focus would be concentrated on developing two mammoth mining discoveries: the sulfur find in the Gulf of

Mexico off Louisiana, Main Pass project, and the copper and gold finds in Indonesia, the Grasberg and Ertsberg projects. Plans outlined at this time included the sale of Freeport-McMoRan Gold Company and about $85 million of its oil and gas properties. In line with this program, Voyager Energy was sold to Trical Resources for $212 million in cash and notes. Geothermal energy assets were sold to a joint venture group led by Calpine Corporation for about $254 million. It sold its interest in an Australian mining company for $60 million.

In 1990, the company sold its nitrogen fertilizer business to Agricultural Minerals Corporation for $275 million. Also, it sold Freeport-McMoRan Gold Company to Minorco South Africa for about $705 million. At the end of 1990, FMI stated that it planned to auction an additional $750 million of its assets, again as part of its debt-reduction goal.

In 1991 FMI reported stronger earnings in the first quarter of the year, benefiting from higher fertilizer prices and sales and lower sulfur production costs. Moffett announced in mid-1991 that a preliminary agreement had been signed to market sulfur produced in the Soviet Union, including operation of a terminal with a capacity to handle 1.5 million tons of sulfur per year. In 1991 capital expenditures were expected to total $700 million, with most of the money to be spent on the Indonesian and Gulf of Mexico capital projects. Both projects have exceeded original find predictions.

Principal Subsidiaries: Freeport-McMoRan Resource Partners, Limited Partnership (62%); Freeport-McMoRan Energy Partners, Ltd. (80%); Freeport-McMoRan Copper Company, Incorporated (77%).

Further Reading: Haynes, Williams, *The Stone That Burns; The Story of the American Sulphur Industry*, Princeton, New Jersey, Van Nostrand, 1942; Haynes, Williams, *Brimstone; The Stone That Burns, The Story of the Frasch Sulphur Industry,* Princeton, New Jersey, 1959; *First in Sulphur, First in Service: Freeport Sulphur Company*, New York, Freeport Sulphur Company, [1961]; "Freeport says it with sulfur," *Business Week*, November 4, 1967; "A Freeport First?" *Forbes*, May 1, 1970; *Freeport-McMoRan*, New Orleans, Freeport-McMoRan Inc., [1980]; Mullener, Elizabeth, "Jim Bob Moffett: The style of a hot shot, the heart of a wildcatter and the soul of an entrepreneur," *Dixie*, April 13, 1986; "Highlights of the Freeport Story," Freeport-McMoRan Inc. corporate typescript, 1986.

—Beatrice Rodriguez Owsley

KRUPP

FRIED. KRUPP GMBH

Postfach 10 22 52
Altendorfer Strasse 103
4300 Essen 1
Federal Republic of Germany
(201) 188-1
Fax: (201) 188-4100

Private Company
Incorporated: 1861 as Friedrich Krupp in Essen
Employees: 59,044
Sales: DM15.60 billion (US$10.44 billion)

Krupp is active worldwide as a manufacturer and supplier of capital goods. The group's business divisions are: mechanical engineering, plantmaking, electronics, steel, and trading.

The firm was established on November 20, 1811 by Friedrich Krupp, member of a family of merchants whose roots in Essen can be traced back to 1587, and his two partners, brothers Georg Carl Gottfried von Kechel and Wilhelm Georg Ludwig von Kechel. They set up a factory for making English cast steel and products manufactured from it. There was a ready market for these products due to Napoleon's Continental Blockade, which prevented imports of cast steel from England. The two partners contributed the metallurgical knowledge, while Friedrich Krupp handled the commercial side and provided the necessary capital. When the steelmaking experiments of the two partners—and later of a third, Friedrich Nicolai,—proved unsuccessful, Friedrich Krupp ran the factory on his own from 1816 onwards and developed a process for making high-quality cast steel on a factory scale. His products included cast steel bars, tanner's tools, coining dies, and unfinished rolls. In the years that followed, however, Friedrich Krupp failed to operate the factory at a profit. Competition was severe—particularly from Britain—and while Krupp's prices were too low, his production costs were too high. In addition, product quality varied because, owing to a lack of funds, Krupp occasionally had to use inferior raw materials. Only the family's considerable assets, which in the end were totally consumed, prevented the firm from going bankrupt. When Friedrich Krupp died in 1826, production had almost come to a standstill.

Therese Krupp, his widow, kept the firm going, supported by her relatives and her 14-year-old eldest son, Alfred. With only a few workers at first, the manufacture of cast steel continued. When in 1830 Alfred Krupp started to manufacture finished products, he was able to endorse these with his personal guarantee of quality. Output, however, remained at a low level.

Only after 1834 did the firm experience vigorous expansion. The lifting of customs barriers by the German Customs Union—an agreement between the German states, before their unification, to remove trade barriers between them and create a single economic entity—in 1834 boosted sales, and the purchase of a steam engine, financed by a new partner, helped to make production more cost-efficient. Alfred Krupp endeavored above all to perfect the manufacture of high-precision rolls, which he later supplied additionally in rolling machines and rolling mills. Together with his two brothers he developed in the early 1840s a mill for stamping, rolling, and embossing spoons and forks in one operation. Krupp took numerous journeys to find customers abroad, particularly in France, Austria, and Russia. A long sojourn in England enabled him to widen his knowledge of steelmaking and factory organization.

The firm's expansion did not follow a steady course, mainly because the market for rolls and rolling mills was limited. Further, there was no replacement market, since Krupp's rolls were virtually indestructible. The attempt to establish cutlery factories succeeded only in Austria, where in 1843 Krupp—together with Alexander Schoeller—founded the works at Berndorf near Vienna, which from 1849 onwards was managed by his brother Hermann. The search for new applications for his high—quality but expensive cast steel was unsuccessful at first. The general economic malaise which set in around 1846–1847 hit the cast steel works badly. In April 1848 Alfred Krupp, now sole owner, could only save it from ruin by selling off personal assets and then by winning a major order from Russia for cutlery machinery.

Around 1850 business started to pick up again. The burgeoning of the railways opened up a virtually unlimited market for Krupp's hard-wearing cast steel. Along with axles and springs, the firm's most important product in this field was the forged and rolled seamless railway tire. Invented by Alfred Krupp in 1852–1853, this proved able to withstand the increasing track speeds without fracturing. In 1859 the breakthrough into cannon-making was achieved with an order from Prussia for 300 cast-steel cannon-barrel ingots.

To secure sales, Alfred Krupp sought new markets on other continents. He journeyed abroad, established agencies, and participated in international exhibitions. At the Crystal Palace Exhibition held in London in 1851, Krupp displayed a cast-steel cannon barrel which attracted great interest; for a cast-steel ingot weighing approximately 40 hundredweight he received the highest accolade, the Council Medal.

At an early stage Krupp introduced new, economic steel-making processes, for instance the Bessemer process in 1862 as well as the open-hearth process in 1869. For products that had to be particularly tough, crucible steel remained his most important starting material. It was around this time that Krupp adopted a policy of acquiring ore deposits, coal mines, and iron works to secure the company's rapidly growing requirement of raw materials. With the rapid expansion of the company—in 1865 the work force totaled 8,248 and sales 15.7 million marks—it became necessary to delegate managerial tasks. In 1862 Alfred Krupp established a corporate body of management bearing joint responsibility for the affairs of the firm. His general directive of 1872 laid down the principles to be applied in running his enterprise as well as the social welfare policy to be pursued.

From the outset Alfred Krupp strove to create and maintain a loyal set of highly skilled employees. Only thus could he guarantee the high quality of his products. To alleviate the social problems caused by industrialization he introduced employee welfare schemes, at the same time enjoining his workers not to become involved in trade-union or social-democratic activity. As early as 1836 he set up a voluntary sickness and burial fund, which became a compulsory sickness and death benefit insurance scheme in 1853. In 1855 Alfred Krupp established a pension scheme and in 1858 a company-owned bakery that evolved into the employees' retail store. In 1856 the first hostels were built offering board and lodging to bachelor workers. 1861 saw the construction of the first company dwellings for foremen. Worker's housing estates, incorporating schools and branches of a retail store, followed in 1863, and from the early 1870s grew apace. In 1870 a company hospital was established.

In the years up to 1873 the firm continued to expand strongly. However, in the economic slump of 1874 it almost suffered financial collapse because Krupp had raised large bank loans without arranging adequate security. Thereafter the company entered a phase of steady development. The gunnery division was engaged in efforts to develop better field, siege, and naval guns. The divisions producing machinery components, shipbuilding material, and railway equipment were expanded. When Alfred Krupp died in 1887, the firm's employees numbered 20,200 and sales for 1887–1888 amounted to 47.5 million marks.

Even during his lifetime Alfred Krupp was known as the Cannon King, mainly because during the Franco-Prussian War of 1870–1871 Krupp's cast-steel guns had proved superior to the French bronze cannon. The way the firm presented itself to the public reflected the spirit of the times and for decades the manufacture of guns was given a prominence beyond its actual share of production. In fact, up to 1905 armaments generally accounted for less—and in some cases considerably less—than 50% of output; in the years leading up to World War I the proportion was between 50% and 60%.

Alfred's only son and heir, Friedrich Alfred Krupp, continued the expansion of the enterprise into a horizontally and vertically integrated concern. Entry into the production of armor plate at the behest of the Imperial Navy led in 1892–1893 to the acquisition of the strongest competitor in this field, the Gruson works in Magdeburg. Production of armor plate was then concentrated in Essen while work in Magdeburg focused on the design and construction of plant and machinery.

At the urgings of his directors, as well as of Emperor Wilhelm II and the Imperial Navy, Krupp decided in 1896 to take over the Germania shipyard in Kiel. The plant was leased that year, and acquired in 1902. At this time Admiral Tirpitz, secretary of state for the Imperial Navy, introduced the program for the expansion of the German fleet under the Fleet Acts. The resultant boost to the German shipbuilding industry also benefited the Germania yard where, in addition to merchant vessels, warships clad in Krupp armor plating were now built. 1902 saw the building of the experimental submarine *Forelle*, forerunner of the U-boat. At the same time the company began producing diesel engines at the Germania yard, following the development of the first working diesel engine in 1897 by Rudolf Diesel in collaboration with Krupp and Maschinenfabrik Augsburg.

The construction in 1897 of a large integrated iron and steel works at Rheinhausen strengthened the company's solid footing in iron and steel. A few years later the Thomas process was adopted there for the mass production of steel. Further ore and coal mines were acquired to cover the increasing raw materials requirements. Friedrich Alfred Krupp was particularly interested in the technology of steelmaking. He introduced scientific research into steel at Krupp and thus created the springboard for the successful development of special-steel production.

Friedrich Alfred Krupp expanded the employee welfare and benefit schemes, not only at Essen but also at the outlying works. He widened the scope of the health funds, built new housing estates, and created the Altenhof estate for retired and disabled workmen. He established educational and leisure amenities for his employees, in particular a lending library with numerous branches and an educational society.

During his lifetime Friedrich Alfred Krupp was caught in the crossfire of public debate. While to many he was a successful industrialist with a sense of national responsibility, his critics saw him as a capitalist entrepreneur who, through his links with the Imperial House and his support of the German Navy League, a non-government association formed to promote the strengthening of the German fleet, exerted influence on the country's naval policy in order to gain lucrative contracts for his company. The spectacular acquisitions of the Gruson works and the Germania yard readily lent themselves to such an interpretation.

In later literature too, Friedrich Alfred Krupp has been presented in controversial terms. New research has proved, however, that it was not he who initiated the program of naval expansion started in 1897–1898. The main impetus came from Admiral Tirpitz and the circle of people close to Emperor Wilhelm II. Friedrich Alfred Krupp only acted in response to this policy.

When Friedrich Alfred Krupp died suddenly at the age of 48 in 1902, Bertha Krupp, the elder of his two daughters, inherited the company, which—as recommended in the will of the later owner—was converted into a stock corporation in 1903, when it became known as Fried. Krupp AG. Almost all the shares remained in the ownership of Bertha Krupp. When in 1906 she married Gustav von Bohlen und Halbach, counsellor to the Royal Prussian Legation at the Vatican, Wilhelm II as king of Prussia accorded Gustav the right to bear the name Krupp von Bohlen und Halbach and to pass on this name to his successors as owners of the company. After the wedding Gustav Krupp von Bohlen und Halbach was appointed to the supervisory board of Fried. Krupp AG, which he chaired from 1909 until the end of 1943.

In the years leading up to World War I, order books were healthy and the company continued to expand. By 1903 the workforce had increased to 42,000 and by 1913 to 77,000, with sales rising from 91.4 million marks in 1902–1903 to 430.7 million marks in 1912–1913. The increase in productivity mainly reflected the expansion of the Rheinhausen iron and steel works and the resultent fundamental reorganization of production in Essen.

In 1908 electric steelmaking was introduced at the Essen works. After a few years the company was making electric steels of such quality that they were able to partly replace high-grade crucible steel. Intensive research into alloying came to fruition in 1912 with the development of stainless chromium-nickel steels which, besides being resistant to corrosion, were also able to withstand the effects of acid and heat and were thus suitable for a wide range of applications.

The continuation and expansion of employee benefits and welfare remained key elements of corporate policy. Margarethe Krupp, the widow of Friedrich Alfred Krupp, established a domestic nursing service and provided the financial base for the Margarethenhöhe garden suburb. The company continued to build housing estates for its workers, these efforts being increasingly supplemented by independent housing associations closely linked to Krupp. Convalescent homes and a dental clinic were built, and the Arnoldhaus lying-in hospital was founded.

World War I brought an increase in armaments production and a further expansion of the company. In order to fulfill government contracts, munitions output was doubled in the first year of the war and by the third year it had reached more than five times its pre-1914 level. This output was achieved, particularly after 1916, by building huge new factories and increasing the work force substantially. In November 1918 Krupp's employees totaled 168,000. Well known products in these years were the 16.5-inch Big Bertha gun, 27 of which went into action in 1914; the merchant submarines *Deutschland* and *Bremen*, built at the Germania yard in 1915–1916; and the long-barreled "Paris gun" with a range of 85 miles, of which seven were built.

Both at the time and in some of the subsequent literature the firm and the Krupp family were accused of having been the main beneficiaries of the war. More recent researches have demonstrated how inaccurate a picture this was: compared with other companies only a relatively small portion of the profits initially earned were distributed to the shareholders, whereas the main part was invested in the new factory buildings which later were of little use. High personnel and welfare costs during but most especially immediately after the war and the cost of converting to peacetime manufacture exhausted the company's substantial reserves. With the ending of hostilities the demand for armaments ceased. Under the Treaty of Versailles the company was prohibited from making ammunition, and cannon manufacture was allowed only to a limited extent. Krupp changes its production and embarked on the manufacture of locomotives, motor trucks, agricultural machinery, and excavators. The cost of reorganization, the wages for workers actually no longer needed, and the losses incurred through dismantling, inflation, and the dispute over the Ruhr River, when the government implemented a strategy of passive resistance to the occupation of the region by French and Belgian troops, plunged the company into a crisis in 1924–1925 that threatened its very existence. Gustav Krupp von Bohlen und Halbach had no choice but to implement drastic cutbacks. Having initially refused for social reasons, he reduced the work force within two years from 71,000 to 46,000. Unviable operations were closed down, production was streamlined, and newly launched but unprofitable mechanical engineering activities were discontinued. Even then the company would not have overcome the crisis had it not been for the financial support it received from a combination of government agencies and banks.

Gustav Krupp von Bohlen und Halbach rejected the proposal of his directors that the Krupp works be closed down or incorporated in Vereinigte Stahlwerke, a combination of German steel companies, which was about to be established. He did, however, finally accept the suggestion made by Krupp director Otto Wiedfeld, who from 1922 until early 1925 was German ambassador to the United States, that the company be rehabilitated by selling a 50% shareholding to the British government. This plan had to be quickly abandoned, however, because the German government felt its policy of rapprochement with France might be jeopardized.

In the years that followed, the company gained a more stable footing, mainly by streamlining the fabricating operations and expanding the production of special steels. Between 1927 and 1929 a blast-furnace plant was added to the melting shops and rolling mills in the Borbeck district of Essen to form an integrated iron and steel works. One of the most modern in Europe, it enabled the production of special steel to be increased further. In 1926 Krupp introduced WIDIA sintered carbide, a product which, by virtue of exceptional hardness and wear resistance, brought a major breakthrough in tool engineering.

The Depression, which first hit the world economy in 1929, brought this revival to an abrupt halt. The work force, which by 1928 had risen to 92,300, fell back to 46,100 by 1932. Sales dropped from 577.5 million reichsmarks in 1928–1929 to 240 million in 1931–1932. After 1933 Germany experienced an economic upturn during which corporate policy at Krupp became closely entwined with the economic policy of the National Socialists. Governmental efforts to achieve self-sufficiency included the development of the country's iron ore deposits. The Renn process introduced by Krupp in 1929 permitted these inferior ores to be reduced economically. A coal conversion plant was built for producing petrol from coal. Increasing demand for rolled-steel products, especially for building the new autobahns, spawned the expansion of Krupp's structural engineering shops in Rheinhausen. Under the Four-Year Plan the state took increasing control of industry and at Krupp the production of locomotives, motor trucks, and ships was stepped up against the will of the company's directors. They wanted to give priority to the successful production of special steels and their fabrication for use in chemical process plant and other applications. In 1938, following the death of proprietor Arthur Krupp, son of Hermann Krupp, the Berndorf works near Vienna was incorporated in the concern. Krupp also expanded its shipbuilding activities by acquiring a majority shareholding in Deutsche Schiff-und Maschinenbau Aktiengesellschaft "Deschimag" in 1940–1941. Sales rose from 809.6 million reichsmarks in 1937–1938 to 1.1 billion in 1942–1943; in the same period the number of employees rose from 123,400 to 235,000.

In the 1920s Krupp had, at the behest and later with the financial support of the German Reichswehr Office, undertaken design work of a military nature going beyond the tight restrictions imposed by the Treaty of Versailles. The resultant vehicles and equipment were manufactured in collaboration with other firms. In the 1930s work on the design and manufacture of armaments was stepped up, and during the war these activities were greatly intensified, controlled as they were by the state's grip on the economy. Weapons made up a much smaller proportion of total output than during World War I, however, because the manufacture of motor trucks, locomotives, bridges, ships, and especially submarines, continued at a high level.

Research has shown that in spite of claims to the contrary, Gustav Krupp von Bohlen und Halbach, president of the federation of Germany industry from 1931 to 1934, did not support Hitler or the Nazi party before they came to power. In keeping with his sense of national loyalty, however, he expressed his support for the state after Hitler's appointment as Reichskanzler.

At the end of 1943 the firm was reconverted into a sole proprietorship and transferred to Gustav's eldest son Alfried. The armaments authorities and semi-official control committees were intervening more and more in industrial activity. Out of loyalty to his war-torn country Alfried endeavored to meet the demands imposed, although the lack of skilled workers, air raids, and the relocation of operations made this increasingly difficult. Like most of the armament factories in Germany during the war, Krupp used forced labor, as most of its workers had been called up for military service.

At the end of the war large areas of the works lay in ruins and much of what remained, like the iron and steel works in Essen-Borbeck, was compulsorily dismantled. The Gruson works and Berndorfer Metallwarenfabrik were expropriated by order of the Allies, and the Germania shipyard, also severely damaged by bombing, was dismantled and liquidated.

Gustav Krupp von Bohlen und Halbach was indicted for war crimes by the International Military Tribunal in Nuremberg but was found to be physically and mentally unable to stand trial. The suggestion made by the American, Russian, and French prosecuting counsels that his son Alfried be indicted in his place was rejected by the British prosecutor on the grounds that they were not conducting a game in which one player could be replaced by another. Nevertheless, Alfried Krupp von Bohlen und Halbach was put under arrest by the American occupying troops in Essen on April 11, 1945. His property was confiscated, and he was kept in prison until he was accused before an American military court in 1947 together with members of the firm's senior staff. This was one of three trials against industrialists. Alfried Krupp von Bohlen und Halbach and his leading staff were accused of having planned a war of aggression and participated in it, but were declared not guilty of these charges. Of the other charges of the indictment, criminal spoliation in occupied countries and promotion of slave labor, they were found guilty on July 31, 1948. In 1951 their prison terms were cut short and they were released. Two years later Alfried Krupp von Bohlen und Halbach resumed the management of his firm, which since 1945 had been under the control of the British military government.

The company's situation was parlous. On top of the losses already mentioned came the Allied divestment order under which Krupp was compelled to sever and sell its mining and steelmaking operations. The firm thus faced the loss of its raw materials base, in particular its vital steel interests. In 1951 Alfried Krupp von Bohlen und Halbach had declared that he would never again produce weapons. The object, therefore, was to shape a newly structured concern from the remaining manufacturing and engineering activities, comprising the locomotive and motor truck works, the Widia hard-metal plant, the forging and foundry shops, and the structural engineering operation in Rheinhausen. This restructuring was achieved in the years that followed. New markets were opened up in the devel-

oping countries for the engineering and construction of industrial plant. Together with Berthold Beitz, whom he had appointed as his chief executive at the end of 1953, Krupp contributed personally to this effort by making numerous order-winning trips abroad. The range of manufacturing and engineering activities was made as varied as possible in order to assure continuity of employment in the face of changing markets. In 1958 sales, including the coal and steel operations still subject to the divestment order, amounted to DM3.3 billion, generated by a work force of 105,200. Krupp had become the highest-revenue German company.

The Allied divestment order could only be complied with to a minor extent for lack of purchase offers. In 1960 Krupp therefore combined its remaining coal and steel operations and strengthened this base in 1965 through a merger with Bochumer Verein für Gusstahlfabrikation, a steel company in Bochum in which a majority shareholding had been acquired at the end of the 1950s. Krupp thus regained a position in the production of special steels, which it had lost with the dismantling of the Borbeck steel plant. In 1961 the company opened a plant in Brazil to make drop forgings for internal combustion engines and vehicles. In 1964 Krupp acquired a majority shareholding in Atlas-Werke AG, Bremen, including MaK Maschinenbau GmbH, Kiel.

In line with the general economic situation, the company followed a positive course into the mid-1060s, apart from a brief downturn in 1962–1963. However, until withdrawn in 1968, the divestment order prevented the company from developing a comprehensive long-term policy of corporate restructuring and investment. The financial crisis into which the company plunged in 1967 was largely triggered by the high level of supplier credits that had to be granted in the strongly expanding export business. As security for the banks, the federal and state governments provided guarantees, which, however, did not need to be taken up. The guarantees were subject to the condition that the sole proprietorship Fried. Krupp be converted into a stock corporation. This requirement dovetailed with the decision already taken by the owner to adapt the enterprise to the requirements of modern business and secure its future by changing its legal structure. In the terms of his will, Alfried Krupp von Bohlen und Halbach provided for the establishment of a nonprofit foundation. Since his son Arndt had renounced his inheritance before his father's death, leaving the way clear for the firm to be converted into a corporation, ownership of the late owner's private assets and the corporate property combined in the firm of Fried. Krupp was vested in the foundation. Alfried Krupp thus continued in modern form the idea formulated by his great-grandfather that ownership incurs social responsibility: the company would be run as a private-sector enterprise but its earnings used to serve the community at large.

Alfried Krupp von Bohlen und Halbach died in July 1967. In 1968 the firm was entered in the Commercial Register as a limited-liability company, Fried. Krupp GmbH, with a capital stock of DM500 million. Managerial responsibility was assigned to an executive board having the same powers as the management board of a stock corporation under German law. It funds projects in Germany and abroad in the fields of science and research, education and training, public health, sport, literature, and fine art. Between 1968 and 1990 the foundation awarded grants totaling around DM360 million.

All shares in Fried. Krupp GmbH were placed in the ownership of the Alfried Krupp von Bohlen und Halbach Foundation, whose object was—and remains—to preserve the company's coherence and to serve the public benefit. Berthold Beitz is chairman of the foundation's board of trustees. From 1970 to 1989 he was chairman of the supervisory board of Fried. Krupp GmbH is now its honorary chairman.

In 1969 the coal mining assets were served from the group and transferred to Ruhrkohle AG. Over the subsequent years activities in the engineering and construction of industrial plant were expanded, especially with the acquisition of Polysius AG and Heinrich Koppers GmbH. The steelmaking arm further strengthened its special-steel operations by acquiring Stahlwerke Südwestfalen AG.

In 1974 the state of Iran acquired a 25.04% interest in the stock capital of the steel subsidiary, Fried. Krupp Hüttenwerke AG, strengthening the equity base. In 1976 Iran also acquired a 25.01% stake in Fried. Krupp GmbH, whose capital stock was increased to DM700 million by the summer of 1978. Today these ownership interests are held by the Islamic Republic of Iran.

The 1980s saw the implementation of various restructuring schemes. Krupp sold off its interests in shipbuilding, an area of heavy losses. The steelmaking sector reduced its output of tonnage steel and in 1987–1988 the plan to close the iron and steel works in Rheinhausen was met by a campaign of protest from the work force. The works have been kept in operation to a limited extent. At the same time Krupp has further strengthened its activities in special steel—for example, by acquiring VDM Nickel-Technologie AG in 1989—as well as in mechanical engineering and electronics. In 1991, the parent company Fried. Krupp GmbH largely provided strategic guidance for the free-standing member companies in the business divisions of mechanical engineering, plant-making, electronics, steel, and trading.

Principal Subsidiaries: Krupp Maschinentechnik GmbH; Krupp MaK Maschinenbau GmbH; Werner & Pfleiderer GmbH (50.1%); Krupp Widia GmbH; Krupp Industrietechnik GmbH; Krupp Koppers GmbH; Krupp Polysius AG (82.5%); Krupp Atlas Elektronik GmbH; Krupp Stahl AG (70.4%); Krupp Lonrho GmbH (50.0%); Krupp Metalúrgica Campo Limpo Ltda. (Brazil, 59.8%).

Further Reading: Krupp: A Century's History of the Krupp Works 1812–1912. Essen, Krupp Works, 1912; Klass, Gert von, *Krupps: The Story of an Industrial Empire,* translated by James Cleugh, London, Sidgwick and Jackson, 1954; Muhlen, Norbert, *The Incredible Krupps: The Rise, Fall and Comeback of Germany's Industrial Family,* New York, Henry Holt and Company, 1959; Manchester, William, *The Arms of Krupp 1587–1968,* Boston, Little, Brown and Cie., 1968; Köhne-Lindenlaub, Renate, "Krupp," in *Neue Deutsche Biographie Bd.13,* Berlin, Duncker Humblot, 1982; Schröder, Ernst, *Krupp: Geschichte einer Unternehmerfamilie,* Göttingen, Muster-Schmidt Verlag, 1984; Burchardt, Lothar, "Zwischen Kriegsgewinnen und Kriegskosten: Krupp im Ersten Weltkrieg," *Zeitschrift für Unternehmensgeschichte,* Wiesbaden, 32, 1987; Lindenlaub, Jürgen and Renate Köhne-Lindenlaub, "Unternehmensfinanzierung bei Krupp 1811–1848: Ein Beitrag zur Kapital-und Vermögensentwicklung." *Beiträge zur Geschichte von Stadt und Stift Essen,* Neustadt a.d.Aisch, 102, 1988; Epkenhans, Michael, "Zwischen Patriotismus und Geschäftsinteresse: F.A.Krupp und die Anfänge des deutschen Schlachtflottenbaus 1897–1902," *Geschichte und Gesellschaft,* Göttingen, 15, 1989.

—Renate Köhne-Lindenlaub

GENCOR LTD.

6 Hollard Street
Johannesburg, 2001
Republic of South Africa
(11) 3769111

Public Company
Incorporated: 1895 as General Mining and Finance
   Corporation Ltd.
Employees: 233,000
Sales: R22.20 billion (US$8.66 billion)
Stock Exchanges: Johannesburg London Paris Munich Geneva
   Basel Frankfurt

Gencor Ltd., formerly General Mining Union Corporation Ltd., is the second-largest mining house in South Africa. Although approximately half its income comes from mining sources, it has, like many of the country's other major mining houses, used cash flows from its mining activities to diversify. It has a wide range of industrial interests and major investments in the energy and paper industries.

Gencor is the product of a 1980 merger between General Mining and Finance Corporation and Union Corporation, both of which were founded in the 19th century. General Mining was founded on December 30, 1895, by two Germans, George and Leopold Albu, who controlled a number of gold mines. In the same year they changed the name of their firm from G&L Albu to General Mining and Finance Corporation.

In its early years the company's activities were focused primarily on gold; developing new mines and managing existing ones. In 1910, the company had seven mines under its management, including such well-known names as Meyer and Charlton, Van Ryn Gold Mines Estate, and West Rand Consolidated Mines, and was developing another two.

World War I was a difficult time for the industry; a flat gold price was accompanied by flagging productivity and rising costs on all fronts. The shortage of unskilled labor was a major issue, and its costs increased as contractors, who had to recruit and deliver the workers to the mines, became involved. The mines also had problems during this period with labor unrest, principally among white miners. The best-known example was the 1922 General Strike, during which two months of production were lost. In 1919, activities were diversified with the formation of Transvaal Silver and Base Metals to mine the lode outcrops and lead-bearing ore which the company owned. After six years, this venture was closed owing to

its poor prospects. More successful was General Mining's acquisition of a large stake, during the 1920s, in Phoenix Oil and Transport Company, which had major interests in Romanian oil companies.

The mining houses were equally hard hit by World War II, which resulted in shortages of all forms of labor, lack of machinery, and delays in plant and machinery delivery. Good news came soon after, however, with the discovery of the Free State gold fields, which General Mining, together with other mining houses, had the right to develop. It also participated in the opening-up of gold mines on the Far West Rand. General Mining achieved some notable firsts: it was the first mining house to use the cyanide process for the extraction of gold; and, through West Rand Cons, it was the first mining house in the country to produce uranium.

During the 1950s the company's activities were boosted when it gained control of the Consolidated Rand-Transvaal Mining Group. This control brought with it a substantial interest in the gold mine Geduld; platinum, through Lydenburg; pipe fabrication; and sugar.

In 1964 the company merged with Strathmore Consolidated Investments and came to control two mines on Klerksdorp gold field; Stilfontein, and Buffelsfontein. A major change took place during the 1960s when the Afrikaner-dominated mining house Federale Mynbou took control of General Mining. This was effected with the assistance of Anglo American, and its chairman Harry Oppenheimer in particular, who wished to assist the Afrikaans business community to get a better foothold in the mining industry. This aim had a political purpose: to counteract government policies which sought to separate Afrikaner from English, whites from black, by showing that these groups could cooperate in the same spheres of interest.

The outcome was that Federale made the takeover while Anglo took a substantial minority interest. Later, in 1965, it was decided to merge Federale and General Mining with Federale gaining effective control.

The merger resulted in the creation of the Federale Mynbou/General Mining group, the country's largest producer of uranium, accounting for more than a third of output, and also producing approximately 7.25% of the country's gold. "Federale Mynbou" was dropped from the group's name in 1965. The group's ten collieries produced 10% of the country's output and it had further mineral interests—asbestos fiber production, platinum, and copper. It was also involved in oil production, exploration, and marketing and managed the petroleum company Trek.

The late 1960s saw a program of diversification. It was the era of conglomerates and the prospects for gold were not exciting. However, many new projects pursued, particularly in the industrial field, were not compatible with the company's expertise, and failed. The turnaround came in 1970 with the arrival of Dr. Wim De Villiers as chief executive. He instituted a rationalization of activities which led to improved profitability. The major changes he implemented concerned decentralized management, strategic planning, and better utilization of labor. On the industrial side, De Villiers sold off the consumer interests of General Mining.

The other company involved in the eventual 1980 merger, Union Corporation, was of a similar age to General Mining. It was founded in 1897 by a German, Adolf Goertz, the local representative of Deutsche Bank, and was initially known as A. Goertz and Co. Goertz became involved in the gold rush and staked 326 claims on the Modderfontein farm on the East Rand, from which emerged the Modder Deep Levels mine, "the jewelbox of the Reef," in Goertz's words.

In 1902 Goertz and Co., with the assistance of U.K. and French investors, who took up shares, became the first Transvaal finance house to obtain a London listing. During World War I the company changed its name to Union Corporation.

There was much uncertainty in the early days, with financing for the Modderfontein mine being obtained literally hours before war broke out. After the declaration of war, all transactions with Germany were frozen.

From 1908, Union Corporation pioneered the Far East Rand, and in 1938 it discovered the Orange Free State gold fields. The first shaft was sunk at St. Helena in 1947, which became the first mine to produce gold in the Orange Free State. 1951 saw the discovery of the Evander gold field, over which Union Corporation had sole control. It established four mines there: Bracken, Kinross, Leslie, and Winkelhaak.

Later mining ventures included involvement in Impala Platinum, where mining began in 1969. Impala was the first platinum concern in the world to provide an integrated operation from the mining of the ore to the marketing of high purity platinum group metals. The gold mine Unisel was developed in 1974, and in 1978 Beisa, the first mine in the country to be established as a primary uranium producer, was opened.

Union Corporation also owned the original interest in Richards Bay and helped put together Richards Bay Minerals, which mines heavy mineral deposits from sand dunes north of the harbor, recovering ilmenite, rutile, zircon, and titanium. General Mining's rights in Richards Bay were later merged with these.

Union Corporation's diversification into the manufacturing industry started in earnest in 1936–1937, with the formation of the paper company Sappi in the East Rand town of Springs. It was a long term grassroots project which only really became profitable in the 1970s. It is now one of Gencor's major investments.

During the 1960s, investments were acquired in the packaging company Kohler Brothers; African Coasters, forerunner of Unicorn Shipping Lines; and engineering companies Darling and Hodgson and Evelyn Haddon. At the time of the 1980 merger, Union Corporation had a 58% stake in Sappi, 74% of Kohler Brothers, 55% of Darling and Hodgson, 17% of Haggie—a wire rope manufacturer—and 27% of Kanhym. It also held a stake in Capital and Counties, the U.K. property concern which later became the major investment of First International Trust, the overseas arm of the Liberty Life group, a major player in the South African insurance field.

In 1978, 56% of Union Corporation's assets were in minerals, including 33% in gold. It was operating seven gold mines—Marievale, Bracken, Kinross, St. Helena, Winkelhaak, Leslie, and Grootvlei—in addition to developing the Unisel gold mine. Approximately 50% of net income came from industrial interests in the fiscal year 1977/1978.

Although the General Mining/Union Corporation merger was only consummated in 1980, the courtship had begun in 1974 when General Mining acquired a 29.9% stake in Union Corporation after a tremendous battle with Gold Fields of South Africa. A further step was taken in 1976 when Union Corporation became a subsidiary of General Mining and the takeover, still spoken of as the country's most bitterly contested hostile bid, was completed four years later.

The decade under De Villiers had been a golden one for General Mining, whose earnings per share increased at an average rate of 26.2% per annum over the period. Prior to De Villiers's arrival, the company had paid a maintained dividend—unchanged for the ten years up to 1968, with the dividend only marginally higher in 1969. At the time of the merger, Union Corporation and General Mining were the fourth- and fifth-largest mining houses in South Africa, ranked by equity capitalization. More than a third of each company's income derived from manufacturing.

The major reason for the merger was General Mining's need to create an improved capital base from which to undertake new investments, such as the first phase of Sappi's Ngodwana mill, the Beatrix mine, which was initially funded from within, and the Beisa uranium mine. There were also the additional benefits of manpower rationalization and, with the exception of gold, the two groups' activities supplemented each other rather than overlapping. It was also felt that Union Corporation's growth prospects would be improved through closer links with the ruling Afrikaner power bloc.

Given the hostile nature of the bid, it was inevitable that merging the two corporations would take time. Initially they remained separate operating entities, merging their corresponding product divisions whenever conditions were favorable. The process seems to have proved more difficult than anyone imagined, and the period 1980–1986 was to prove difficult for the group. In 1982 the two major stakeholders, Sanlam and Rembrandt, clashed over Gencor. Sanlam, the second-largest South African life insurer, had been a major shareholder in the two companies which joined to form Federale Mynbou, and thus become involved in General Mining, and subsequently Gencor. The result of the clash was the replacement of De Villiers—later a member of the cabinet—as chief executive by former Union Corporation managing director Ted Pavitt, after a clash between De Villiers and Dr. Andries Wassenaar, head of Sanlam, about the management of Gencor.

In the early 1980s, Gencor started to expand its interests, particularly in manufacturing, thinking that the outlook for metals, especially base metals, was poor. However, the group was caught by recession, high inflation, and high interest rates, which pushed up costs of new investments and led to a R410 million rights issue in 1984 to reduce leverage.

The biggest project was a R1.6 billion expansion at Sappi, which was plagued by technical difficulties and cost overruns. Problems were also experienced at Tedelex and Kanhym, which likewise needed to resort to rights issues. Foreign exchange losses of R200 million in 1984, with Impala and Tedelex worst hit, were followed, in 1985, by appalling performances by the manufacturing interests: Sappi, Kohler, Tedelex, and Kanhym.

The group's industrial relations image within the industry also took a battering at this time following troubles at Impala and Marievale and, later, mining disasters involving multiple fatalities at Kinross and St. Helena. The Beisa uranium mine which opened in 1981 was closed in 1984, having constantly failed to produce profits. This was primarily the result of a soft world uranium market.

The perception that all was not well within the group was compounded in 1983 by the group's failure to find a new chief executive to succeed De Villiers. It settled instead for management by its five most senior executives: Johan Fritz, George Clark, Basil Landau, Tom de Beer, and Hugh Smith. Pavitt had relinquished executive responsibilities in August 1984.

In 1984 manufacturing interests were underperforming; there was massive foreign loan exposure, and Gencor appeared to be something of a rudderless ship. The executive committee was thought to be concerning itself too much with operational issues and not enough with strategy and planning. Investor confidence waned. To some extent, such perception was unfair. Steps were being taken to address problems, such as the 1984 reorganization of mining and industrial interests in line with a policy of greater divisional autonomy.

Major developments were also underway, including that of the Beatrix mine, perhaps the most successful new gold mine of the 1980s; the development by Sappi of the massive mill at Ngodwana; and the gaining of control of Samancor. Gencor raised its stake in Semancor from around 30% to 50% by swapping various interests with Iscor, the state steel producer which was the controlling shareholder in Samancor. Next to these, the problems at Tedelex and Kanhym were relatively minor. Still, they were symptoms of malaise.

The interest in Samancor dated back to the 1970s when General Mining took steps to become more involved in the production of ferrochrome. At the time, General Mining held 15% of Montrose Chrome. After building up a controlling stake in Montrose, it went on to buy Union Corporation's operations, but the quantum leap in the formation of what is today Samancor came with the Tubatse ferrochrome project, a 50-50 joint venture with Union Carbide, which was bought out in the 1980s.

Gencor had battled with Anglo American for control of Samancor. The government had stepped in at one stage to prevent a successful Anglo bid, on monopoly grounds. At that time, Samancor was not a chrome company but a manganese company controlled by Iscor. Anglo later put its manganese interests into Iscor and took a 25% stake in Samancor, which it still retains.

Another important event was the creation in November 1983 of Genbel, through the merger of Gencor's investment holding companies UCI and Sentrust. UCI, on the Union Corporation side, was formed in 1946 to explore the Evander gold field. It was listed in the 1960s as part of a pyramid exercise to raise funds for the development of Kinross. Through a pyramid exercise, a holding company can control a large number of companies with a combined capital very much greater than its own, since it needs to hold only half or even less of the shares of its subsidiaries.

General Mining had no less than seven similar companies, whose most valuable assets were interests in the Free State and Klerksdorp gold fields. They were combined in 1968 to form Sentrust, which eventually constituted about a third of the merged Genbel as against UCI's two-thirds.

Historically, Genbel grew by exploring mineral rights and then putting these into new mines in exchange for shares, thus becoming an investment company by default. It continued to grow from opportunities offered by the Gencor group, as well as through developing its own mineral rights.

While the 1984-1985 period was a difficult one for the South African economy, Gencor's particular difficulties were compounded by an identity crisis. Staff had not outgrown their previous allegiances and still tended to see themselves as Union Corporation or General Mining employees. The two corporate cultures were very different. Union Corporation had a reputation for good engineering and exploration, and General Mining for financial engineering.

Gencor's failings were analyzed in 1986 in a report commissioned by Federale, at that time controlling company of Gencor, and produced by Arthur D. Little, the U.S.-based management consultants. The report contained some strong criticisms, accusing the group of lack of focus and direction, weak leadership, and a lack of corporate loyalty amongst employees. The report served as a spur to change but the man to whom it fell to implement this, Derek Keys, appointed executive chairman in April 1986, had no background in mining, having come from the industrial group Malbak. The appointment was not universally popular, and caused Johan Fritz to resign and Basil Landau to take early retirement.

Keys made a number of important moves, one of which was to separate the manufacturing interests. He brought Malbak into the group and then sold into it all the manufacturing interests—bar Sappi, which was much too large, and Trek, which later found a home in Engen. Thus at one stroke the manufacturing interests were separated from the mining interests, and Malbak was given the task of managing them. Previously, the manufacturing interests had been managed in true mining house style—from the center. Keys and Grant Thomas, managing director at Malbak, introduced a new decentralized structure.

This was part of Keys's strategy of increasing the powers of divisional managers within the group. Head office staff was cut from 1,700 to 54 in the three years to 1989. In many ways, Keys was responsible for putting into practice the decentralized management philosophy first articulated 15 years earlier by De Villiers.

The period from Keys's arrival was one of considerable expansion and growth, both organic and through acquisitions. On the mining side, the Oryx gold mine was developed as well as the smaller Weltevreden mine near Klerksdorp, and Impala Platinum developed the Karee mine. In 1989, Gencor bought a 30.7% controlling interest in Alusaf, the Richards Bay aluminum smelter, from the Industrial Development Corporation for R270 million. A R1.47 billion rights issue in 1989 helped fund these developments and acquisitions. Other acquisitions included Sappi's purchase of Saiccor, which specializes in the productions of chemical cellulose pulp, and of a 49% interest in the Usuthu pulp mill in Swaziland. In mid-1990 Sappi also bought five paper mills in the U.K. subsidiary, Malbak, while Abercom Holdings bid £42million for the U.K.-quoted packaging group MY Holdings.

Another important event was the publication in 1988 of the Gencor mission, a brief statement of the group's fundamental corporate goals, which went a long way toward clarifying to the public and to its employees what Gencor stood for. In Keys's words, "Now they know that Gencor has only two businesses—to start or to acquire major businesses and to accelerate the development of those businesses which it already has."

Two major developments took place within Gencor in 1989. The first was the formation of General Mining Metals and Minerals Limited (Genmin) in March 1989. Genmin was made responsible for managing the group's mining, metals, and minerals interests, which comprise some 60 operations. These include 14 gold mines, the base metals group Samancor, the platinum producer Impala, the coal group Trans-Natal, and the minerals division.

The second major development was the formation of Engen, the company responsible for the group's energy interests, which include exploration and refining of crude oil and marketing of the final products. General Mining had first become involved in the petroleum sector back in 1968 when it participated in a joint venture launching the country's first petrol marketing company, Trek Beleggings (Trek Investment). The key event in the formation of Engen took place in July 1989 with Gencor's purchase, for US$150 million, of Mobil Southern Africa from its disinvesting parent company. Its major assets were a refinery in Durban, the Mobil management team, and a country-wide network of approximately 1,150 service station sites.

Engen's other major interests include: the Trek network of petroleum outlets; 20% interest in the oil and gas exploration outfit, Soekor; and a 30% stake in, as well as the management contract for, Mossgas, a synthetic fuels venture.

In 1991 Gencor was an investment holding company with a mining house as its major interest. It has been left, in Keys's words, as "a pool of risk capital with connected businesses that are in our sphere of control but which in no sense can be regarded as one large business."

Control rested with the Sanlam insurance group, still a major shareholder in Federale Mynbou. The other major shareholder, Rembrandt is the tobacco and luxury goods empire built up by South African entrepreneur Anton Rupert, which controls such companies as Rothmans, Dunhill, and Cartier Monde. Rembrandt has been willing to put up money for Gencor acquisitions. Probably half the major assets which have come into play in the country in the late 1980s have been bought by Gencor.

The ten years since Gencor was formed have been a time of upheaval for the group. In the first half of the 1980s there was a lack of direction at Gencor but this changed with the advent of Derek Keys. The group has since performed well, and is highly regarded by the investment community. The wide spread of mineral interests, Sappi, and Malbak can all be expected to continue generating solid earnings while Engen enjoys considerable growth prospects.

Principal Subsidiaries: Samancor Ltd. (43.6%); Trans-Natal Coal Corporation (41.6%); Impala Platinum Holdings (42%); Sappi Ltd. (49.9%); Malbak Ltd. (58%); Genbel Investments Ltd. (50%); Engen (97%); Beatrix (64%); Unisel (40%).

Further Reading: "Mining Survey," Supplement to *Financial Mail,* July 28, 1978; Mcnulty, Andrew, "Man of the Year—Gencor's Derek Keys," *Financial Mail,* December 25, 1987; Kilalea, Des, "Gencor Looks Ahead," *Finance Week,* April 27–May 3, 1989; "Meet Genmin," Johannesburg, Gencor, March 1990; Freimond, Chris, "Rob Angel—Driving Engen," *The Executive,* May 1990.

—Philip Gawith

GOLD FIELDS OF SOUTH AFRICA LTD.

75 Fox Street
Johannesburg 2001
Republic of South Africa
(11) 639-9111
Fax: (11) 639-2101

Public Company
Incorporated: 1887
Employees: 98,580
Sales: R5.65 billion (US$2.20 billion)
Stock Exchanges: Johannesburg London Paris Zürich Basel
    Geneva

Gold Fields of South Africa was formed in 1887 by Cecil
Rhodes and Charles Rudd to hold properties they had acquired
on the Transvaal's Witwatersrand gold fields. The first of the
financial groups that were to characterize the South African
mining industry's organization, it generally remained heavily
dependent on one or two profitable South African mines,
while going on to become a major international mining finance
house. The present company was formed to take over the African assets of Consolidated Gold Fields, and was not included
in that group's acquisition by Hanson PLC in 1989. The company has diversified into the production of other minerals, notably platinum, but unlike Anglo American Corporation and
some other mining houses, it has not made any significant
impact outside the mining sector.

Reorganized as Consolidated Gold Fields of South Africa
(Consgold) in 1892, it was plagued by uncertainties, and found
itself on a really firm footing only in the 1930s when it took
the lead in opening up the Western Rand—often referred to as
the West Wits Line—in conjunction with, among others, the
Anglo American Corporation. West Witwatersrand Areas Ltd.
was formed in 1932 to work the new field. In 1959, as part of
a major restructuring exercise, the name "Gold Fields of
South Africa" was revived for a South African rather than a
British domiciled company, a wholly owned subsidiary to take
over the management of the parent company's southern African assets. In 1971, West Wits took over all of Gold Fields of
South Africa's assets as well as its name.

In 1886, when gold was discovered on the Witwatersrand,
Cecil Rhodes was sceptical because of earlier disappointments
in the eastern Transvaal, and was still very much preoccupied
with De Beers Consolidated. Most of the properties acquired

by Rhodes and his partner Charles Rudd when they finally
joined the Rand rush were valueless, at least for the time being, due both to chance and to Rhodes's lack of firm commitment. He and Rudd formed Gold Fields of South Africa Ltd.
on February 9, 1887, to hold their Transvaal interests, but
quickly turned their attention to the area further north, later
known as Rhodesia, where they hoped to recoup some of their
Transvaal losses and to further Rhodes's political and imperial
ambitions. In 1889, the British South Africa Company
(BSAC) was formed with a charter from the British government to administer the territory and with the right to a share in
all mining operations that took place there. Rhodes, as joint
managing director of Gold Fields, with wide personal power
and freedom, was able to use that company to finance the
BSAC through its early days, which were even less profitable
than those of Gold Fields.

Although some of Rhodes's decisions had led to disastrous
consequences for Gold Fields, it, like all other groups on the
Rand, had to face difficulties caused by the fact that the Witwatersrand's gold bearing reefs tilted sharply, outcrops tending
to be depleted at relatively shallow levels. Sinking shafts necessary to work the reef at greater depths required capital that
investors were reluctant to provide. In 1892 Alfred Beit,
Rhodes's close colleague in De Beers and other ventures, supported by Rudd, persuaded Rhodes to involve Gold Fields in a
company that would work deep levels, Rand Mines Ltd. To
finance the venture, Gold Fields brought several Rand companies together in 1892 to form Consolidated Gold Fields
of South Africa. Deep levels produced more gold and new
problems.

The weathered, oxidized outcropping ores could be treated
relatively easily and cheaply by crushing and amalgamation,
essentially the same technique used by the Spanish in Mexico
in the 16th century. Ores found below about 100 feet were
pyritic—containing sulphides—and therefore required more
complex, expensive treatment. The 50% recovery rate of the
chlorination process which was first used was too low for
profit. The MacArthur-Forrest cyanide process, introduced
into the Transvaal in 1889, solved the problem, ultimately
convincing even the most pessimistic of the Rand gold fields'
longterm viability.

Gold Fields acquired several new properties and began to
change its management structure and style in the aftermath of
the 1895 Jameson Raid, reducing Rhodes's unrestricted personal power. Substantial dividends were declared in 1895 and
1896, on profits derived from dividends paid on the company's
holdings in De Beers Consolidated rather than from its own
operational profits. Subsequent dividends were low or nonexistent. Despite shareholder protests, this situation enabled
the company to survive depression and accumulate £2 million
reserves.

In 1908, using these reserves, Gold Fields began expanding
investment outside Rhodesia and South Africa. Gold mines in
Ghana—the Gold Coast—were not profitable; Nigeria's Ropp
tin mines were. The gold of Siberia's Lena River basin also
held considerable promise. When the Russian company operating there sought more advanced U.S. and British technology,
Gold Fields became the largest single shareholder in Lena
Goldfields Ltd., formed in 1908.

By 1911 Gold Fields had quietly disposed of its Lena share,
using the £360,000 profit on the sale to help replenish the

reserves depleted by purchases in the Americas and elsewhere. Encouraged by its consulting engineer, John Hays Hammond, Gold Fields bought shares in U.S. gold and other mines, U.S. power companies, Mexican and Trinidadian oil, and American Telephone & Telegraph (AT&T), among others. In 1911, a new company, Gold Fields American Development Company (GFADC), was formed to administer holdings in the United States. These and other expansionist moves made at about the same time did not live up to expectations, in part perhaps because of American hostility to foreign investors who took an interest in mining enterprises, but did not control them. However, not all of Gold Fields's investments were total failures. Investments outside mining, such as AT&T and Trinidad Oil, in activities in which they had no prior experience or expertise, tended to be more profitable than those in mining.

Throughout most of its history, Gold Fields was sustained by one or two particularly successful operations. During the period 1904–1920, for example, these operations were two Transvaal mines, the Robinson Deep and the Simmer and Jack, whose profitable working protected the company from the burdens of developing and working less profitable mines, old and new. Nonetheless, by 1918 the £2 million reserves and the Lena profits had disappeared, and the company faced hard times. Temporary relief was obtained in 1919 when all South African mining companies were allowed to sell their output on the free market, earning a premium of about 16 shillings per ounce. Reliance on gold mines—a wasting asset in any case as they were finite and would eventually be exhausted—was now seen as a fundamental weakness, and diversification as essential for salvation.

Since Gold Fields's Articles of Association limited the company's activities to mining and kindred ventures, New Consolidated Gold Fields was created, a wholly owned subsidiary with the same directors, in effect the same company, but with greater freedom than its parent. The new company acquired a range of interests including property, cement, and carpets, but the benefits of diversification were elusive.

The company hit its lowest depths in 1922, as even Robinson Deep and Simmer and Jack profits declined, and the entire industry was affected by the major white miners' strike, the Rand Rebellion. The Rebellion was quelled by Prime Minister Smuts's politically disastrous use of the army, while financial rescue came from the Sub Nigel mine in the East Rand. Gold Fields had bought property in the Nigel district before the Boer War, but work there only began in 1909, reaching the commercial production stage in the early 1920s, and continuing to produce gold into the 1990s, as did the Simmer and Jack and Robinson Deep, albeit at rather lower yields.

In Western Australia, Gold Fields moved from a profitable share in the Wiluna mine in 1926 into the rich Kalgoorlie field, and secured a controlling interest in Gold Mines of Australia, formed by the Australian financier, W.S. Robinson, in 1930. Gold Fields also participated in Bulolo Gold Dredging, formed in 1930 to work alluvial gold in Papua New Guinea. This company produced about US$60 million worth of gold by the time it stopped dredging in 1965, while New Guinea Goldfields, which had a less promising start in 1929, benefited from the late 1970s rise in gold prices. Gold Fields's Australasian interests were brought under the administration of a holding company, Gold Fields Australian Development Company, in 1932.

A relatively little-known and not particularly successful Australian venture was the Gold Exploration and Finance Company of Australia (GEFCA), established in 1934. In this venture, Gold Fields joined with two South African mining groups, Central Mining and Investment Corporation and Union Corporation, and an Australian consortium led by Robinson. Initially GEFCA operated primarily in eastern Australia, with mixed success. There was considerable friction between the main London board and the Australian committee, in part because the Australians seemed to regard Gold Fields's finances as unlimited, and in part because Gold Fields was reluctant to allow GEFCA to move into Western Australia. In 1949 GEFCA was transferred to Australia and absorbed by the Western Mining Corporation, previously a GEFCA subsidiary.

American, Australian, and other expansion was financed largely by the recovered Robinson Deep, the Simmer and Jack, and the Sub Nigel. Help also came from the sale of the American Potash and Chemical Corporation, originally the Trona Corporation, which extracted salt from Searles Lake in California's Mojave Desert. GFADC had helped rescue the undertaking as part of its early United States acquisitions. By 1929, it was profitable and sufficiently attractive for a European group to offer to buy up all the issued shares. Gold Fields and GFADC made a total profit of £1.09 million. GFADC retained managerial control, but lost it in 1942 for violating the Sherman Antitrust Act by the sale, including allegations of a secret sale to Germans.

As Gold Fields fell prey to the world Depression, it was once again Witwatersrand gold which provided a foundation for recovery. In December 1930, Gold Fields financed a magnetometer survey of the West Rand, which was separated from the central fields by a major fault that had taken the gold bearing reefs to substantially greater depths. The Rand strata were known to be very regular, however, and a layer of iron-bearing shales lay about 400 feet below the gold reef. The magnetometer survey, confirmed by subsequent boreholes, traced the reefs very accurately.

Earlier attempts to work these deposits had been defeated by uncontrollable flooding. An effective cementation or grouting process developed subsequently by a Belgian, Albert François, initially in connection with coal mining, solved the problem. In November 1932, Gold Fields formed West Witwatersrand Areas Ltd. (West Wits) to begin developing the West Rand. Several of the Rand mining groups were unable or unwilling to participate in financing the new company. The Anglo American Corporation of South Africa and the General Mining and Finance Corporation were among those who agreed to take part. Gold Fields had to retain 30% of the shares, unhappily at first, but ultimately to its great advantage. By October 1939, when the first West Rand ores were being milled, Gold Fields was once again on a sound financial footing. In the 1950s, when further development was going on in the West Rand fields, Gold Fields was unable to participate as fully as it would have liked because of heavy financial commitments elsewhere. Anglo American took the lead here as it had already done in the Orange Free State.

Gold Fields and Anglo American worked together in other ventures as well, some of them in America and elsewhere, some in South Africa, notably in the Far East Rand. The most important area in which the two companies did not work together was in the Orange Free State gold fields. Geologically very different from the Rand, the Free State gold deposits lay at considerable depth, and were not susceptible to magnetometer investigation. Prospecting there was very costly, with boreholes frequently proving the absence of gold rather than confirmation as they had done in the West Rand.

In a manner reminiscent of the company's 19th-century Witwatersrand acquisitions, Gold Fields came late to the Orange Free State, although this time for financial reasons rather than lack of interest. When it did begin to acquire claims, most proved worthless. The Saaiplaas mine seemed a good proposition in 1955, but failed to live up to its promise. Earlier, Gold Fields had attempted to participate in the areas which ultimately proved to include the most profitable Free State mines, but were rebuffed by the claimholders, African and European Investment, whose major shareholder was the Lewis and Marks group. Anglo American bought up enough African and European shares to take control of it, using it as the basis of its subsequent dominance of Free State gold mining. Gold Fields did have a share in the Harmony mine, but its involvement in the field was very limited. In 1990, the company anticipated that the next gold mine it opened would be in the southern Free State.

Although West Wits only paid its first dividends in 1954, its success helped strengthen Gold Fields generally. Further support came from Rustenberg Platinum, the result of a series of mergers in the 1920s and 1930s, which began paying dividends in 1942. Gold Fields itself was able to pay dividends throughout the war.

The postwar period saw new mines coming into production, with profits flowing in from Venezuelan oil and the sale of the Trinidad Oil company. By the mid-1950s Gold Fields had again built up substantial reserves and again began diversifying. In order to decrease dependence on gold, mining, and Africa—which by then appeared to be becoming less stable—it began investing in a variety of industries, concentrating more on the United States, Canada, Australia, and New Zealand.

In 1956, New Consolidated Canadian Exploration Company was established in Toronto and New Consolidated Gold Fields (Australasia) in Sydney. The same year, Gold Fields and Central Mining and Investment Corporation discussed, but did not complete a merger. Gold Fields continued its own takeover and diversification program however, acquiring some other African mining companies, and some British manufacturers as well. One takeover included a wine firm.

In 1959, a major restructuring led to the re-emergence of the name Gold Fields of South Africa, reorganized as a Johannesburg-based company which controlled all the company's African assets. Apart from any financial and administrative advantages that might have accrued from this restructuring, it also met the South African desire to have domestic companies, rather than London-based ones, exploiting the country's natural resources.

It is not likely that the decision to set up a separate South African company was specifically motivated, at the time, by political considerations. That separation did give Consolidated Gold Fields an excuse—not necessarily accepted—to distance itself from its South African "associate" when the mining industry in general, and Gold Fields of South Africa in particular, began to come under fire as opposition to apartheid, domestic and international, strengthened after 1960. In addition to widespread general enthusiasm for the independence of

Black African colonies at the time, there was a tremendous wave of revulsion against the South African regime because of the Sharpeville Massacre that year.

Before the growth of that opposition began to impinge seriously on Gold Fields, the company continued to work its mines in different parts of the Rand. These remained generally profitable, but the fact that Gold Fields was not participating in the Orange Free State field limited the extent to which it could expand. The older Rand mines were moving towards depletion, requiring working at greater depth and consequently greater cost. Only by keeping labor costs very low was it possible to maintain profitability.

Working through its subsidiary, Gold Fields Mining and Development Corporation, Gold Fields also attempted to widen its asset base. Though not entirely failing in this endeavor, it was unable to compete successfully either with the Anglo American group, which came to have a substantial role, direct or indirect, in virtually every sector of the South African economy, or with that country's other major mining/industrial/financial conglomerate, Barlow Rand. Gold Fields did move into other minerals in South Africa, but even as late as 1990, stated company policy was to concentrate on minerals in southern Africa. Newspapers reported that the group was about to embark on a foreign investment program, but the company was officially only willing to move cautiously, and to focus on the opening-up of new mineral fields rather than portfolio investment in existing operations.

Throughout the 1970s and 1980s, Gold Fields did indeed invest in a variety of other minerals, including zinc, lead, silver, tungsten, and others. The most important of these was platinum which, with gold, accounted for 55% of the group's income in 1990, but constituted 74% of assets. In contrast, other minerals were responsible for 17% of group income against only 7% of its assets. However, these figures do not take account of the Northam platinum mine, which was expected to begin producing in 1991. The major producers of gold continued to be sufficiently successful to enable Gold Fields to rank as South Africa's second most important gold producer. There was also some involvement in engineering, generally related to mining; in mineral treatment; and, in a fairly small way, in property. Limited diversification did not alter the company's basic orientation.

During the 1980s, Gold Fields—and Consgold—came under particularly strong pressure from anti-apartheid groups and from supporters of the black trade union movement in South Africa. The group was criticized on the grounds of its safety record; accident and death rates, it was argued, were worse than in the industry as a whole. Gold Fields was also attacked because of its reluctance to recognize trade unions, and because of its relatively lower rates of pay. There was some justification in these claims. Gold Fields argued that its continued profitability—and therefore its ability to employ people—required it to remain a low-cost producer. Many of its mines were older and were worked at greater depth, and therefore higher cost, than those of other groups. Gold Fields also maintained that most of its workers were happy with their pay and conditions and appreciated the company's policy of training unskilled workers and employing the children of people it had employed previously. Unrest among the workers, the company argued, had been stirred up by a small number of militants.

Whether or not workers did in fact appreciate some aspects of the group's employment policies, the first and last of these arguments cannot be sustained. Strikes of varying duration continued to affect Gold Fields's operations. The group followed rather than led as the South African gold mining industry moved towards the full recognition of the National Union of Mine Workers, the elimination of the color bar in job allocation and training, and in general improvement of housing and health provision for black workers. These changes took place against a background of political and social unrest, a declining real gold price, and retrenchment throughout the mining industry.

In 1989, Consolidated Gold Fields was taken over by Hanson PLC after Minorco, an arm of Anglo American, had attempted a strongly opposed takeover bid. Consgold's remaining 38% stake in Gold Fields was sold. In August 1989, 30% was acquired by Gold Fields of South Africa Holdings, in which the Rembrandt Group held a 40% interest as did Asteroid, a company owned equally by Remgro and Gold Fields, with the insurance company Liberty Life holding the remaining 20%. Before the end of the year, Hanson had also disposed of the remaining 8%. Gold Fields was more than ever a South African company, firmly rooted in the Witwatersrand but still looking for other opportunities, expecting the next gold mine it opened to be in the southern Orange Free State.

Principal Subsidiaries: Gold Fields Mining and Development Corporation Ltd. (South Africa); Northam Platinum Ltd. (South Africa); Gold Fields Coal Ltd. (South Africa); Black Mountain Mineral Development Company (Proprietary) Ltd. (South Africa); Gold Fields Namibia Ltd. (Namibia); Witwatersrand Deep Ltd. (South Africa).

Further Reading: Cartwright, A.P., *Gold Paved the Way: The Story of the Gold Fields Group of Companies,* London, Macmillan, 1967; Counter Information Services, *Consolidated Gold Fields,* London, Counter Information Services, 1973; *Consolidated Gold Fields PLC: Partner in Apartheid,* London, Counter Information Services, 1986; Johnson, Paul, *Consolidated Gold Fields: A Centenary Portrait,* London, Weidenfeld & Nicolson, 1987; Flint, John, *Cecil Rhodes,* London, [n.p.], [n.d.].

—Simon Katzenellenbogen

Heraeus
HOLDING

HERAEUS HOLDING GMBH

Heraeusstrasse 12-14
Postfach 15 61
6450 Hanau 1
Federal Republic of Germany
(6181) 35 1
Fax: (6181) 3 35 91

Private Company
Incorporated: 1985
Employees: 9,534
Sales: DM4.98 billion (US$3.33 billion)

Heraeus is a family-owned company whose principal activities are the processing of specialty metals, particularly platinum and associated metals; the production of industrial and scientific equipment; and the development of related technologies. About 30% of Heraeus's employees work in subsidiaries outside Germany, and 64% of sales are made abroad. The five operating divisions of Heraeus encompass a wide range of products and technologies, all of which have evolved from, and can ultimately be traced back to, the business with which the company began in the mid–19th century: the melting and processing of platinum.

The company's origins go back to the Einhorn-Apotheke (the Unicorn Pharmacy) at Hanau near Frankfurt, owned by the Heraeus family since 1660. The family had produced a series of chemists, pharmacists, and doctors, going back to Johannes Heraeus, a pharmacist who studied at Giessen and died in 1650. The pharmacy itself had passed from father to son for eight generations, when it was taken over by Wilhelm Carl Heraeus in 1851. At this time Germany's development into a major industrial nation had hardly begun; communications were improving and trade barriers between the separate German states were gradually being dismantled.

Wilhelm Carl Heraeus had studied pharmacy and chemistry in Göttingen. When he took over the business in Hanau, he continued with chemical experiments in the laboratory he had installed in the pharmacy, processing chemical products, especially iron preparations for medical purposes. However, the town of Hanau had traditionally been a center for master goldsmiths and the jewelry industry, and this situation brought about a change of direction in the Heraeus family business.

The jewelers of Hanau at this time were using significant, and increasing, amounts of platinum. Waste material containing platinum from jewelry production was sent to the Heraeus

laboratory, where the platinum was separated out. However, no commercial melting process for platinum existed at the time. The metal has a very high melting point, around 2,000 degrees centigrade. Before the platinum waste could be re-used, it had to be sent to London or Paris to be forged at white heat, an expensive and inconvenient process for the Hanau jewelers. Heraeus, who had worked with precious metals during his studies at Göttingen, knew that two French scientists had discovered a process by which platinum could be melted in an oxyhydrogen compressor. He applied himself to developing this process for industrial purposes. In 1856, he succeeded in melting two kilograms (kg) of platinum by this method.

Production at Heraeus was initially on a small scale. The bars of melted platinum, weighing around two kg, were sent to a master metalworker, who forged them into rods at the anvil. Some of the platinum was sold in this form, while some was processed into sheet metal in the pharmacy. Several people, including Heraeus himself, took part in the exhausting rolling process. The sheet platinum was then passed to the Hanau copper and goldsmiths for processing into tubes, dishes, and crucibles. At this stage the Heraeus pharmacy employed two pharmaceutical assistants and three or four other workers.

Sales grew rapidly and in 1857 the company completed its first significant export order with the dispatch to New York of bars, sheet metal, and wire weighing 30 kg. A total of 59 kg of platinum was sold in 1859; 20 years later the total had risen to 400 kg, and by 1888 it had reached 1,000 kg. Russia was the almost exclusive source of platinum ore, supplying between a quarter and a third of its total yearly production to Hanau in the years before World War I. The customers of the platinum melting works were pharmacies and dentists, the jewelry industry, the chemicals industry, and later also the electrotechnical industry, which used large quantities of platinum wire for electric light bulb production.

Wilhelm Carl Heraeus continued with his chemical experiments outside the platinum field, producing rare metals such as ruthenium as well as other chemical products. On January 1, 1889, he retired, handing over the management of the business—at this stage numbering eight employees—to his sons Wilhelm and Heinrich. The new managers faced problems of platinum supply. Russian platinum production could not keep pace with world demand, and the metal soon became an investment commodity, subject to large and unpredictable price fluctuations. Platinum was not always to be had in the necessary quantities, forcing the company to devote research efforts to platinum-saving processes, substitute materials, and alloys.

After 1891 the company began to extend its sphere of activity beyond the manufacture of unfinished platinum products, taking up the production of the articles required by its customers. During the next five years, new workshops for the processing of platinum were built on the edges of Hanau; the workshops went into operation in 1896 with about 40 employees.

At the beginning of this century, Heraeus's competitors in France and England derived much of their business from manufacturing large vessels for the chemicals industry, for the concentration of sulfuric acid. Initially Heraeus only carried out repairs on these vessels, but soon the company was able to patent its own version of the product, using a more highly resistant mixture of gold and platinum, which ousted the opposition and eventually dominated the market. Yet this product itself became obsolete with the development of a new process for manufacturing concentrated sulfuric acid. The quantities of used platinum which Heraeus acquired as a result formed a valuable reserve in the face of world platinum shortage. Changes in the application of platinum have been frequent over the years. As other, cheaper materials or technologies have been found to replace it, Heraeus has repeatedly had to respond by finding new uses for its product.

By 1894 the turnover of Heraeus was equal to that of the melting works in London and in Paris. By the time of its 50th anniversary in 1901, the company had 64 employees, and before the outbreak of World War I Heraeus had become the largest platinum melting business in the world, with sales surpassing the combined total of its competitors in England and in France. Sales to the United States were growing fast; in 1891, the brother-in-law of Wilhelm Heraeus, Charles Engelhard, had been appointed the company's representative in the United States and soon, cooperating with the works at Hanau, he had become the leading figure in the U.S. platinum industry.

During the years before World War I, the company developed a number of new activities drawing on its expertise in platinum manufacture and alloying. These included aluminum welding; in the Paris Exhibition of 1900, Heraeus exhibited aluminum equipment for the chemicals industry produced by the hammer welding method. Gold color, used in the ceramics industry for decorative purposes and manufactured using the by-products of platinum ore, was an important new product, developed in the 1890s. A ceramics division was established, developing heat-resistant gold, silver, platinum, matte gold, and luster colors. Platinum alloys also served as heat conductors in electrically-heated equipment; in 1910 Heraeus produced its first resistance-heated furnaces. As cheaper alloys were developed, electrical furnaces and drying ovens could be produced in larger quantities to satisfy industrial demand.

The new ovens brought with them the requirement for exact temperature measurement, and improvements in the purity of the platinum produced by the company, as well as the development of quartz glass, paved the way for the resistance thermometer in 1906. This thermometer, invented in 1906 by Dr. Ernst Haagn, the manager of Heraeus's electrical heating division, consisted of a thin layer of platinum foil encased in quartz glass, and was able to measure temperatures between $-200°$ and $+700°$. From this time onwards the development of electrical heating technology and temperature measurement equipment have progressed hand in hand.

The use of high temperatures linked quartz glass, another of the company's major products developed during this period, with platinum production techniques. In 1899 Dr. Richard Küch had succeeded in melting large quantities of rock crystal in the oxyhydrogen compressor, forming quartz glass. A number of qualities make quartz suited to all kinds of laboratory equipment: it lets through ultraviolet rays, has a high temperature resistance, and can withstand sudden temperature changes, as well as being resistant to most acids. The company's quartz division was founded in 1901.

In 1904 the sunray lamp, made of mercury and quartz glass, was invented. It was initially used for lighting large spaces, such as streets and halls, until it was replaced by the more powerful metal-wire lamps. Küch had noticed that close proximity to the lamp caused burns to appear on his face and hands an effect attributable to the ultraviolet light which penetrated the quartz glass. The healing effects of the lamp made it one of the company's most famous products.

A new use for platinum was created by the manufacture of artificial silks. Artificial silks and rayons were produced using platinum spinnerets, which Heraeus had supplied for experimental purposes in the first years of the century. The spinnerets were manufactured in significant numbers after 1910. Initially the holes in the spinnerets had to be bored outside the company; with the foundation of a new workshop in 1922, the company also carried out this part of the production process, establishing the manufacture of spinnerets on a large scale, and becoming a major supplier to the fast-growing artificial fiber industry.

During World War I, a shortage of Chile saltpeter threatened to bring the manufacture of gunpowder and explosives to a halt. This crisis was resolved through the adoption of the Haber-Bosch process of nitrogen production, which used fine-meshed platinum catalyst gauzes. Heraeus supplied the wire for these gauzes, which were woven outside the company. Around this time Heraeus also developed the manufacture of osmium alloys for use in fountain pen nibs—a product that led the market at home and abroad in the 1920s.

Up to this point the company had enjoyed steady, uninterrupted growth. World War I and the years that followed brought a renewed crisis in platinum supply, however. Stocks had been used up, the Russian Revolution had stopped supplies from the Ural, and any available platinum was prohibitively expensive. This crisis dominated the company's situation, as the third generation of the Heraeus family took over the management of the business. The new directors were able to overcome these problems, however, and soon the path of expansion and product diversification was resumed. The work force, which had numbered 400 at the outbreak of World War I, had grown to 650 by 1926.

Spinnerets continued to be an important product. Now they were produced in larger quantities, and to higher specifications, in gold-platinum and gold-palladium alloys. Tantalum, a hard, light-colored metal newly developed by the company, was also used for rayon spinnerets. The catalyst gauzes supplied for nitrogen production during the war had been woven outside the company; a weaving facility was established within the company, with improved looms allowing for the production of larger, seamless gauzes. The ortho-dental sector grew significantly and a separate subsidiary, Heraeus Edelmetalle GmbH, was established for this part of the business. The quartz glass division had initially been devoted almost entirely to the production of parts for sunray lamps; now the development of high-quality quartz glass, free from imperfections, opened up possibilities for its use in optical technology as well as for the production of laboratory equipment.

The refractory metals titanium, tantalum, niobium, and zirconium, like platinum, have high melting temperatures. During the 1930s, Heraeus developed the high-vacuum techniques necessary to melt these metals. High vacuum vapor techniques were also devised by the company, allowing for thin-layer surface metal coatings. This technology enabled the company to produce mirrors with greater surface resistance and higher reflective potential than had hitherto been possible. Heraeus Vakuumschmelze, the division of the company responsible for high-vacuum melting technology, was founded in 1923. After the almost complete destruction of its works during World War

Belmont College Library

II, Heraeus recovered rapidly, continuing to grow and expand its product range in the 1950s and beyond. At the time of its centenary in 1951 the company's work force had reached nearly 1,000; by 1957 this number had increased to 3,000. Expansion continued throughout the 1960s and 1970s, and in 1980 Heraeus had a total of 6,300 employees in Germany and abroad. Sales levels show a similar pattern of strong growth during this period: from around DM100 million in 1960, turnover had passed the DM500 million mark by 1970 and had reached DM2.4 billion by 1980.

In 1958 the company began to expand abroad, with the establishment of subsidiaries in France and Italy. By 1964 further foreign subsidiaries had been added in Switzerland and the Netherlands, and in 1969 the group acquired a number of laboratory equipment manufacturers. Product and technological development continued in the fields of medical and industrial lamps, catalysts, dental equipment, laboratory equipment, and temperature measurement technology. Arc and electron-beam furnaces were developed after 1950, and 1978 saw the introduction of novelle incubator technology.

The long tradition of steady growth at Heraeus continued in the 1980s, with an important shift of emphasis. In order to establish the group's access to all important world markets and thus ensure its long-term competitiveness, Heraeus concentrated increasingly on the internationalization of its activities. Between 1980 and 1989 the work force grew from 6,300 to 9,300, and the proportion of employees based outside Germany rose from 11% to 28%. At the same time turnover nearly doubled, rising from DM2.4 billion to DM4.6 billion, with an increase in the share of overseas sales from 53% to 63%.

The gradual change in the company's profile was brought about both by organic growth and by acquisition. In 1980, Heraeus acquired Cermalloy, a U.S.-based producer of thick film and polymer pastes, from Plessey, and in 1982 the company acquired Pacific Platers Ltd., now Heraeus Ltd., in Hong Kong. In 1983, work was begun on new plants at Kleinostheim in Germany, and in 1985 new quartz glass factories were built in Japan and the United States. Two major acquisitions were made in 1988. The group acquired Electro-Nite International N.V. of Belgium, a manufacturer of measurement systems for metal melts, with 1,000 employees worldwide and manufacturing subsidiaries in Belgium, France, Britain, the United States, Brazil, South Africa, and Japan. The same year saw the acquisition of the surgical lasers division of Cooper Laser-Sonics Inc. in the United States, one of the world's largest suppliers in its field. In 1988 to 1989, joint ventures were established in Sweden, producing catalytic converters for the automotive industry; in Singapore, manufacturing lead frames for integrated circuits; and in Japan, distributing dental products.

Important changes in group organization were made in the early 1990s. Heraeus Holding GmbH, a holding company providing strategic leadership for the different divisions of the company, was founded at the end of 1985. With effect from January 1, 1990, the group was restructured: five operating units were formed, to function independently under the general umbrella of Heraeus Holding. Heraeus Instruments GmbH is responsible for the equipment division, whose principal products are laboratory equipment, medical equipment, and equipment for climate simulation. This division accounted for 30% of the company's sales in 1989. The metals and chemicals division, headed by W.C. Heraeus GmbH, focuses on the industrial uses of precious metals, with subsidiaries encompassing the refining of pure metals from ore and recycled sources, the manufacture of electronic components and other metal products, and the production of ceramic colors and precious metal preparations. This division accounted for 22% of 1989 sales. Group activities in the field of sensors were brought together in the Heraeus Electro-Nite division, consisting principally of the Electro-Nite group acquired in 1988. Products of the division accounting for 21% of company turnover in 1989 include temperature measurement and thermal analysis systems, especially for the steel industry. Heraeus Quarzglas GmbH is responsible for subsidiaries concerned with the various applications of quartz glass, in the fields of semiconductor technology and fiber optics, as well as for optical components. This division represented 17% of the company's sales in 1989. Finally, the company's traditional activity of supplying precious metals and alloys for dental uses, as well as semi-finished products for the jewelry industry, was continued under the leadership of Heraeus Kulzer GmbH, representing 10% of 1989 turnover.

The restructuring of the group seems to have paid off in terms of profitability: pretax profits rose to DM55.9 million in 1989, an increase of 23% over the previous year, and an increase of 51% over 1987. Of the sales made abroad, Europe was the group's most important market, accounting for 42% of foreign sales, followed by the United States (31%), and Asia (24%). The company is still entirely owned by members of the Heraeus family, a tradition that is not likely to be broken in the foreseeable future, in order to avoid the influence of foreign owners, and to keep its entrepreneurial freedom. Jürgen Heraeus is the chairman of the management board.

Principal Subsidiaries: W.C. Heraeus GmbH; Heraeus Kulzer GmbH; Heraeus Quarzglas GmbH; Heraeus Electro-Nite (Belgium); Heraeus Instruments GmbH.

Further Reading: Küch, Otto, and Fritz Küch, *Heraeus, Der Ursprung der deutschen Platinindustrie und die Entwicklung der Platinschmelze W.C. Heraeus GmbH 1851–1951*, Hanau, [n.p.], 1951; Ruthardt, K., ed., *100 Jahre Heraeus, eine wissenschaftlich-technische Festschrift aus Anlass des 100 jährigen Jubiläums der Firma W.C. Heraeus GmbH*, Hanau, [n.p.], 1951.

—Susan Mackervoy

Hitachi Metals, Ltd.

HITACHI METALS, LTD.

Chiyoda Building
1-2, Marunouchi 2-chome
Chiyoda-ku, Tokyo 100
Japan
(03) 3284-4511
Fax: (03) 3287-1793

Public Company
Incorporated: 1956 as Hitachi Metals Industries Ltd.
Employees: 8,288
Sales: ¥419.76 billion (US$3.09 billion)
Stock Exchanges: Tokyo Osaka

Established in 1956, Hitachi Metals, Ltd. (HML) is a leading manufacturer of high-grade specialty steels. While HML's steel division is its largest, other products include magnetic materials, pipe components, steel-rolling-mill rolls, and malleable iron castings. Starting in the late 1980s, HML turned its research-and-development attention to electronic materials.

Hitachi Metals, Ltd., is an outgrowth of Hitachi, Ltd. (HL), which is a leading manufacturer of industrial machinery. HL has its roots in the desire of its founder, Namihei Odaira, to reduce Japan's dependency on imported technology and equipment during the early years of the 20th century. Odaira had opened a motor-repair shop north of Tokyo, in Hitachi, to service a copper mine there. He saw that all of the mine's equipment was imported. This was not uncommon in 1910 because of a domestic mistrust of Japanese equipment. Odaira saw the need for dependable domestically produced engines, and in 1910 began to produce his own five-horsepower engines. Odaira leased his engines to the local copper mine. It took many years and much perseverance—and the intercession of two world wars—for Odaira's vision and Hitachi's products to succeed in overcoming this mistrust.

In 1920 Hitachi Ltd. was incorporated. In 1924 HL built Japan's first electric locomotive. By 1926 the company was exporting electric fans to the United States. It was not, however, until the 1950s that Hitachi sought, under new president Chikara Kurata, to pursue market expansion. It saw its future in electronic engineering, especially computer equipment and consumer goods, such as household appliances and televisions and later video cassette recorders. These would later become HL's strength.

In 1956 the iron and steel division of HL was spun off to become an independent company. Under the name Hitachi

Metals Industries Ltd., the new company started operations that same year with five works, located in Tobata, Fukagawa, Kuwana, Wakamatsu, and Yasugi.

Hitachi Metals was listed on the Tokyo Stock Exchange in 1961, the same year it completed construction of its Kumayaga works. In 1965 Hitachi Metals America, Ltd. (HMA) was founded in New York City. Beginning as a four-man office with $50,000 capital, HMA's purpose was to sell Hitachi Metals Industries's specialty steel products, in particular, its razor blade steel. In 1967 Hitachi Metals Industries Ltd. changed its name to Hitachi Metals, Ltd. A larger U.S. division, Hitachi Metals International (U.S.A.), Ltd., was founded in 1976. This subsidiary administers investments, loans, and finances for subsidiaries and divisions in North America.

The company continued its overseas expansion with the founding of Hitachi Metals Europe GmbH in Düsseldorf, in 1970 and a subsidiary in Singapore in 1979. In the early 1970s HML began exploring other metal-product possibilities, especially in the growing field of electronics. In 1971 the company established its magnetic- and electronic-materials research laboratory. Research from this laboratory led to the 1973 founding of the Hitachi Magnetics Corporation in Michigan and the Systems Magnetic Company, founded in California in 1984. Systems Magnetic is a manufacturer of computer components. In the early 1990s HML still devoted a high level of investment to research and development.

Magnetic materials in 1990 comprised HML's second-largest division and about 19% of net sales in that year. This division produces alnico, ceramic, and rare-earth magnets; parts such as magnet rolls for copy machines and printers; voice coil motors for hard-disc drives; and magnetic head parts used in computers, video cassette recorders, and terminals. In the late 1980s demand for copy machine parts and office automation equipment declined, but the sale of ceramic magnets for automobiles had grown. In 1989 Hitachi Metals North Carolina, Ltd. was formed to manufacture ceramic magnets.

HML founded a subsidiary in Australia in 1984, for sales of its metal products there. Two more laboratories were established in the 1980s, reflecting new product areas; the equipment-design-development research laboratory was opened in 1985 and the advanced-materials research laboratory was established in 1988. The company's plant and equipment division in 1990 represented 7% of HML's net sales. The division's main products are treatment equipment for sewage, water, and garbage; incinerators for industrial waste; factory-automation-related equipment; feed-production plants; silo equipment; and chains.

In 1986 and 1987 HML suffered some setbacks, the result of a reduced profit margin on exports. It responded by integrating factories and reducing its work force. The company also concentrated on growth-promising products, such as electronics-related products and magnetic-head materials. Although automotive parts exports had declined, sales of HML's iron castings for domestic automobile use had increased enough to represent significant growth in the automotive-components division. Aluminum castings for motor vehicles also increased. The automotive-components accounted for 22% of HML's net sales in 1990.

In addition to the ceramic magnets company begun in North Carolina in 1989, HML founded Ward Manufacturing Inc. in Pennsylvania to manufacture malleable cast iron pipe fittings.

Pipe-fitting sales had fallen for the company in the late 1980s, but new products, such as corrugated stainless steel gas tubes and corrosion-resistant water-pipe fittings, had made up for the loss.

In 1989 HML founded HMT Technology Corporation. This California-based subsidiary manufactures thin-film magnetic discs. Hitachi Metals, Ltd.'s goal is to build a flexible, broad-ranging corporate base with a strong international presence to help maintain the company's stability.

Principal Subsidiaries: Hitachi Kinzoku Shoji, Ltd.; Hitachi Metals Techno, Ltd.; Hitachi Tool Engineering, Ltd.; Hitachi Ferrite, Ltd.; Hitachi Metals Precision, Ltd.; Tokyo Seitan, Inc.; Hitachi Valve, Ltd.; Hitachi Metals Estate Ltd.; Hitachi Metals America, Ltd.; Hitachi Magnetics Corp. (U.S.A.); Systems Magnetic Company, Inc. (U.S.A.); Hitachi Metals Europe GmbH (Germany); Singapore Foundry & Machinery Co. Pte. Ltd.; Hitachi Metals Singapore Pte. Ltd.; Hitachi Metals Australia Pty., Ltd.; Hitachi Metals Hong Kong Ltd.; AAP St. Marys Corp. (U.S.A.); Hitachi Metals Electronics (Malaysia) Sdn. Bhd.; HMT Technology Corp. (U.S.A.); Ward Manufacturing Inc. (U.S.A.); Hitachi Metals North Carolina, Ltd. (U.S.A.).

—Carol I. Keeley

HOESCH

HOESCH AG

Eberhardstrasse 12
D-4600 Dortmund 1
Federal Republic of Germany
(231) 8410
Fax: (231) 2345

Public Company
Incorporated: 1871 as Eisen-und Stahlwerk Hoesch
Employees: 50,000
Sales: DM14.00 billion (US$9.37 billion)
Stock Exchanges: Frankfurt Munich Berlin Düsseldorf Hamburg Stuttgart Hanover Bremen Zürich Basel Geneva

Hoesch is one of the oldest companies in the Ruhr area of Germany. Over its long history, the profile of the company has undergone substantial changes: from an iron works, it evolved into a mass steel manufacturer; from this to a provider of specialty sheet steels; and from a pure steel company, it has become a diversified producer of industrial materials. The modern Hoesch is a group of companies operating globally, with subsidiaries and associates at home and abroad, offering a broad range of products and services.

Hoesch's activities include the mining of raw materials, the production and refining of materials, the manufacture of components and building sections, the construction of complete installations and systems, trade in metals and the recycling of waste materials, the development of software, components, and system solutions for industrial automation, measurement and navigation technology, and communications technology.

At the beginning of the 19th century, according to the *Westfälisches Magazin* of 1798, Dortmund was still "a large village with walls, an hour's walk in circumference, its citizens all farming people." The town owed its later industrial advancement to mining and to the iron and steel industry. The engines of this advancement were the Hermannshütte company, founded by Hermann Diedrich Piepenstock in 1841; the Dortmunder Union of 1854; and the Eisen-und Stahlwerk Hoesch (Hoesch Iron and Steel Works), established in 1871. These originally independent companies have all belonged to Hoesch since 1966, and form the core of Hoesch Stahl AG, the 100%-owned subsidiary of Hoesch AG. Technical achievements such as the exclusive patent for the Thomas process, which used phosphorus-rich pig iron in the blasting process, acquired in 1879—the process had been developed to operational standard in Hörde, now part of Dortmund, in the same

year—illustrate the innovatory strength of Dortmund as a steel-producing town. Hoesch has remained exemplary for its innovation. Feinblech-Contiglühe, for example, established in 1985 for the production of new high-quality thin sheet metals, is one of the most modern plants in the world.

The company's origins can be traced to the 1820s, when Eberhard Hoesch acquired the Lendersdorfer Hütte (Lendersdorf Rolling Mill) near Düren in the Eifel region. Within a few years, he developed Lendersdorf, following English models, into one of the most modern puddling and rolling works of its time. Its major product was tracks for the expanding railway construction industry. After the ore resources of the Eifel area had been exhausted and the traditional energy supplies of water power and charcoal had been superceded by coal and steam power, the descendents of Eberhard Hoesch decided to move to the Ruhr. They chose Dortmund, with its large coal resources and good communications, as their location.

On September 1, 1871, Leopold, Eberhard, Viktor, Albert, and Wilhelm Hoesch founded the Eisen-und Stahlwerk Hoesch as an ordinary trading partnership with a capital of 2.4 million marks. Initially the company was purely a Bessemer steelworks with added rolling mills. Two-thirds of the pig iron used in the Bessemer process was imported from England. There was as yet no processing of the rolled steel.

In September 1873, six months after the Vienna stock market crash, Hoesch took the bold step of becoming an *Aktiengesellschaft,* with capital of 3.6 million marks. This was only possible because of considerable investment by the Hoesch family. Hoesch shares were not listed on the stock exchange until 1895–1896, when the company's expansion caused its capital to rise initially to 6 million marks and then, in 1914, to 28 million marks.

The economic crisis of the 1870s, which followed the boom of the *Gründerjahre,* a period of intensive industrial growth in Germany, had a contradictory effect on the new company; although profits collapsed, production rose steadily. After 1878 Hoesch again began to make profits. In 1881 a first dividend of 5% was paid. After this, the company's profitability rose sharply; dividends did not fall below 10% in the years leading up to World War I, reaching a peak of 24% in 1914.

Hoesch developed into a highly integrated group at an early stage, encompassing all the production stages from ore and coal mining, to pig iron and steel production, through to mechanical engineering. In 1896 the first blast furnaces, of the latest design, were set in operation; in 1899 the Kaiserstuhl mines I and II were purchased; and in 1907 the Limburger Fabrik und Hüttenverein, now Hoesch Hohenlimburg AG, became part of the group. Further acquisitions followed; for example, in 1911 the Maschinenfabrik Deutschland, founded in 1872, and in the following year the hammer mill Von der Becke. The group's coal base was extended in 1920–1921 by a cooperation agreement with the Köln Neuessener Bergwerksverein mining union.

The company's products spanned the whole range of contemporary iron and steel applications, encompassing rails and finished railway carriages; special sections for machine construction; steel girders; castings, such as ship's propellors or crankshafts; and bulkheads for canal and harbor construction. The products were supplied throughout the world. A separate section of the business was responsible for bridge construction alone. Dortmund steel was used to build many of the structures that appeared in significant numbers in Europe and the United States from the end of the 19th century onwards, including the Wuppertal suspension railway, the platform hall at Cologne Central Railway Station, and the Limmat Bridge in Zürich. Railway bridges were built in Russia, the Balkans, the Near East, and India, and dock and port installations in Hamburg; Lisbon; and Canton, China, using Dortmund steel. The expansion of the group required capital resources stretching far beyond the limits of the founding capital. The group's share capital reached almost 150 million reichsmarks by 1931. Although Hoesch had grown beyond being purely a family business, the company's capital structure revealed the continuing dominance of the family's share-holding.

Bank shareholdings in Hoesch before World War II amounted to less than 30%, which meant that the banks did not have a significant presence on Hoesch's supervisory board. Demands for such a presence in the 1920s had been categorically opposed by Hoesch director Friedrich Springorum, who had even threatened to terminate business relations. So Hermann Fischer, a board member since 1921 in his capacity as director of the Abraham Schaaffhausenscher Bankverein, remained the sole representative of the banks until the merger with Köln-Neuessener Bergwerksverein in 1930.

The continuing development of the group was overseen by Albert Hoesch and his successors Friedrich Springorum and the latter's son Fritz Springorum, the directors of the company until the outbreak of World War II. They steered the company through a time of deep economical, political, and social changes and preserved Hoesch's commercial independence. In July 1925, Friedrich Springorum declared that Hoesch would not join the Vereinigte Stahlwerke (Union of Steelworks). Thus Hoesch, like Krupp in Essen and the Gutehoffnungshütte Aktienverein in Oberhausen, remained outside the gigantic mining group formed by the merger of 21 German companies. The Vereinigte Stahlwerke had a share capital of 800 million marks and the work force amounted to 200,000 employees. Its pig iron capacity was ten million tons.

World War I and subsequent interventions by French occupation forces, culminating in the *Ruhrkampf* of the early 1920s when miners and foundry workers staged a passive resistance directed at the French troops occupying the Ruhr, submitted the iron and steel industry of the Ruhr to the mechanisms of state management. Production levels fell to a low point. As a result of the Versailles Treaty, Alsace-Lorraine, the Saarland, and parts of Upper Silesia had to be conceded. Compared with pre-war capacities, this meant a loss of nearly 80% of ore production, 43.5% of pig iron production, and 35.8% of raw steel production. By 1926, however, Germany had already reattained prewar production levels. The Ruhr, doubling its share of production to around 80%, played a decisive part in this.

At Hoesch, pig iron production after World War I had fallen back to the level of the year 1900. Yet production overtook prewar levels as early as 1925, rising to an all-time high of 800,000 tons in 1929. However, after the collapse of the New York stock market on "Black Friday" in October 1929, the flight of capital and falling prices in Germany led to a slump in production and to mass unemployment. The economic stabilization that had begun to take shape came to an abrupt halt, at

Hoesch as elsewhere. The severity with which this economic collapse affected the Ruhr mining industry as a whole was already a clear indication of a structural crisis, the real extent of which would not be fully recognized until after the steel crisis of the 1970s.

Up to 1928, successful efforts at rationalization—which resulted in a 20% rise in employee productivity—were still able to offset the risks inherent in creating overcapacity. In 1928–1929 Hoesch had just established a new Thomas-process steelworks, with the largest converter in the world at that time. As production fell back to the levels of the postwar period, Hoesch began to take losses, a trend that was not reversed until 1933–1934. The rationalization measures that had been adopted only brought positive results in a favorable economic climate; the high fixed costs meant a lack of flexibility in times of crisis. Reductions in the work force became necessary for Hoesch as for other companies. Between 1929 and 1932 the total number of employees—workers and administrative staff—in the Hoesch group fell from 31,405 to 18,960. The crisis moved towards its climax, not only in the Ruhr, in 1932, the year of hunger marches and street riots. The merger with the Köln-Neuessener Bergwerksverein and the reserves maintained by managing director Fritz Winkhaus enabled Hoesch to survive these years of heavy losses and to keep its debt to a manageable level.

After Hitler came to power, Germany's economic development was characterized by a program of job creation and armament. The National Socialists's policy of autarchy and the pressing scarcity of foreign currency forced the iron and steel industry to smelt increasing quantities of inferior native ore. By the time Hitler ordered the German economy to prepare itself for war, the associations of iron and steel producers had long been brought into line. The dictatorial steel policy no longer allowed any scope for entrepreneurial planning of production and investment. After 1934 foreign trade in raw materials and semi-finished products was strictly controlled; from 1937, raw materials and production were subject to quotas.

The effects of World War II and the economic controls on Hoesch were disastrous; the work force had shrunk to less than 7,000, and production had fallen to a low point of less than 2,000 tons of raw steel. After November 11, 1944, production stopped completely. After a total of 22 bomb attacks, Hoesch was one of the worst-hit of the businesses on the coalfield. According to the investigation undertaken by the Allied Control Commission (Combined Steel Group), the costs of the war damage amounted to considerably more than 200 million marks. A total of 3,000 employees were numbered among the victims of World War II. On New Year's Day in 1945, operation of blast furnaces I and II was resumed. In 1946, its 75th year of existence, Hoesch's production was nearly one-fifth of prewar levels.

In the Potsdam Treaty of 1945, it was decided to decentralize Germany's economy. The 10 conglomerates in the Ruhr area with their 385 subsidiaries were broken up into 24 independent companies with a restricted share capital of 100,000 Reichsmarks each. In 1950, Hoesch AG also went into liquidation. The traditional alliance of ore, coal, and steel had been torn apart.

With the establishment of Hoesch Werke AG in July 1952, the managing director Friedrich Wilhelm Engel was able to rejoin some of the old coal mining and processing businesses to the steel production business.

In 1955 Hoesch emerged as one of the first groups in the coalfield to have regained ownership of all its former companies. Between 1952 and 1960, a total of DM1.4 billion was invested in reconstruction. The construction of new steel production plants, the blast furnace VI in 1953, the new continuous semi-finished production train, the new Siemens-Martin-Works III, the fully continuous fine-iron train with 234 trusses, and the semi-continuous wide strip train, ensured the highest technological standards. In 1951 raw iron production reached the levels attained before the global economic crisis and by 1960 had doubled to over 1.6 million tons. During the same period, raw steel production also increased, to over 2.3 million tons. In the financial year 1959–1960, the turnover of the Hoesch group was DM2.5 billion.

These developments were overshadowed by the coal crisis, which had broken out in 1957–1958. The crisis was a result of increased competition from U.S. coal in the German market—its share of the market almost doubled—and from a new source of energy, oil. Political and institutional conditions were also responsible in part for the crisis. The *Investitionshilfegesetz* (Investment Assistance Law) of 1952 had allowed investments in coal mining in the Ruhr, which had amounted to DM345 million in 1950, to rise to DM900 million in 1957. Production capacity reached a record level of nearly 130 million tons, which now could barely be utilized. By 1968 total production levels had fallen by 30%. The policy of coal price subsidies also prevented the Ruhr mining industry from competing properly with other suppliers on the basis of real market prices.

The answers to the coal crisis lay above all in intensive rationalization and mechanization, involving the concentration of businesses and work force reductions. In the Hoesch mining businesses, for example, the average productivity per miner between 1950 and 1957 changed only marginally from 367 to 400 tons per year, but by 1968 it had increased to over 800 tons per year. In 1956 production at Hoesch reached its highest level at 6.8 million tons; after this it was cut to a level of 4.8 million tons in 1968. On June 30, 1966, the Kaiserstuhl mine, Hoesch's oldest mine, dating from 1899, was closed. The *Kohleanpassungsgesetz* (Coal Adjustment Law) of June 14, 1968, sought to bring about a fundamental reorganization and rehabilitation of coal mining in the Ruhr and smoothed the path towards the foundation of Ruhrkohle AG, in which 52 pits, 29 coking plants, and power stations with a combined production of 950 megawatts were merged. Hoesch too exchanged its pits for an 8% share in the new company, and so bid farewell to 10,500 mine workers, who had been part of the company's history for over seven decades.

In 1966 Hoesch was merged with the Dortmund-Hörder Hüttenunion, which had been founded in 1951 through the merger of the Hermannshütte at Hörde, established in 1841, and the Dortmunder Union, established in 1854. Both the Hermannshütte and the Dortmunder Union had joined the Vereinigte Stahlwerke in 1926, through their respective membership of the large groups Phoenix (from 1906) and Deutsch-Luxembergische Bergwerks und Hütten AG (from 1910).

After the Vereinigte Stahlwerke had been broken up by the Allies, the companies had remained independent until their merger. With raw steel production of nearly two million tons, making up 12% of total German steel production, the new company became one of the largest iron and steel companies in Germany.

With the Hüttenunion's integration into the Hoesch group, the 43% stake in the Hüttenunion owned by Koninklijke Nederlandsche Hoogovens en Staalfabrieken NV of IJmuiden, Netherlands—a stake that went back to the days of the company's participation in the Vereinigte Stahlwerke—was converted into a 14% stake in Hoesch AG. At the same time, an outline agreement was reached between Hoesch and Hoogovens that paved the way for close cooperation between the companies and set the course for Hoesch's first international commercial alliance. Through a founding agreement, signed on July 17, 1972, Estel N. V. was established as a joint venture, the central company of the new multinational business. With raw steel production of 11 million tons and nearly 80,000 employees, Estel ranked third in Europe and seventh in the world.

As a result of the steel crisis, which caused Estel to take losses after 1975, Hoesch broke away from Hoogovens, through the resolution of an extraordinary shareholders' meeting on November 16, 1982. The successful turnaround of Hoesch under the leadership of the new chairman of the board of management, Detlev Rohwedder, was the result of a comprehensive program of restructuring in the steel sector and of a strategy of opening up and developing new spheres of activity. This reduced the company's dependence on the steel market and set the profits of the business on a broader base. Between 1983 and 1987, only DM1.5 million was invested in modernization in the steel sector, which moved towards specialization in new and improved fine metals, and in uncoated and refined-surface sheet steel products. The Hoesch group in the early 1990s consisted of the steel and steel refining division, the processing and industrial technology division, the trade and services division, and the automation and systems technology division. The steel division accounted for less than 30% of the total turnover, while the processing and industrial technology division and the automation and systems technology division with a combined share of over 50%, are becoming increasingly important. The company is an outstanding example, applicable outside as well as within the Ruhr area, of well-managed structural evolution.

Principal Subsidiaries: Hoesch Stahl AG; Hoesch Hohenlimburg AG; August Bilstein GmbH & Co., AG; Hoesch Verpackungssysteme GmbH; Hoesch Rothe Erde-Schmiedag AG; Nippon Roballo Company Ltd. (Japan); Hoesch Maschinenfabrik Deutschland AG; Camford Engineering PLC (U.K.); Hoesch Bausysteme GmbH; Isselwerk GmbH & Co. KG; Eisen und Metall AG; Hoesch Rohstoff GmbH; Herzog Coilex GmbH; Hoesch Export AG; mbp Software & Systems GmbH; RAFI GmbH; Schroff GmbH; Hans Kolbe & Co. (37%).

Further Reading: Mönnich, Horst, *Aufbruch ins Revier, Aufbruch nach Europa. Hoesch 1871–1971*, Munich, [n.p.], 1971;

Dascher, Ottfried, *Kammer und Region. 125 Jahre Industrie- und Handelskammer zu Dortmund (1863–1988)*, Dortmund, [n.p.], 1988; Ellerbrock, Karl-Peter, *Eberhard Hoesch (1790–1852) Lebenserinnerungen eines Industriepioniers*, Dortmund, [n.p.], 1989; Ellerbrock, Karl-Peter, *Von Piepenstock zum "Phoenix." Geschichte der Hermannshutte (1841–1906)*, Dortmund, [n.p.] 1990; Ellerbrock, Karl-Peter, *650 Jahre Stadtrechte Hörde (1340–1990)*, Dortmund, Hoesch, 1990.

—Karl-Peter Ellerbrock
Translated from the German by Susan Mackervoy

IMETAL S.A.

Tour Maine-Montparnasse
33, avenue du Maine
75755 Paris Cedex 15
France
(1) 45 38 48 48
Fax: (1) 45 38 74 78

Public Company
Incorporated: 1880 as Société Le Nickel
Employees: 6,000
Sales: FFr20.00 billion (US$3.93 billion)
Stock Exchange: Paris

Imetal, a French holding company, was founded in 1974 to control three major companies: Société Le Nickel, Peñarroya, and Compagnie de Mokta. Although it was then a major participant in the nonferrous sector, Imetal gradually moved away from this field of activity in order to concentrate on construction materials, now the company's largest profit-earner.

Established in 29 countries, the industrial group has four main divisions: construction materials, industrial minerals, international trading, and metal processing. Although it has redefined and modified its targets since 1986, Imetal's history dates back to the 19th century and is associated with one of the most famous dynasties of French bankers and industrialists, the Rothschild family. Guy de Rothschild, Imetal's chairman for almost 20 years, was responsible for the company's direction and reputation before the present chairman, Bernard de Villeméjane, oversaw the company's next incarnation.

Imetal's history began in 1863 in the French colony of New Caledonia, when Jules Garnier, an engineer, discovered important nickel deposits. Some ten years later, together with Henri Marbeau, he founded La Société de Traitement des Minerais de Nickel, Cobalt et Autres. Four years later, in 1880, Garnier and Marbeau's company merged with Higginson et Hanckar to form Imetal's direct predecessor, Société Le Nickel (SLN). Although its headquarters were located in Paris, the SLN built small factories near Marseilles and a blast furnace at Nouméa, New Caledonia. Its early progress was encouraging. However, the first nickel crisis in 1884 slowed down its activities, and after the closing of the main factory at Chaleix, Garnier and Marbeau were forced to relocate production to France, Britain, and Germany.

This was the era of tall sailing ships of 3,000 to 5,000 tons, that were able to cross in 100 days and to transport around 60,000 tons of minerals annually. These transported nickel from New Caledonia to Europe until World War I interrupted the company's expansion. By the end of the war, only the Le Havre factory had escaped damage. The SLN took nearly 15 years to recover from the disaster. In 1931 it entered into partnership with the Société Calédonia and created Calédonickel, a company that managed the large factory of Doniambo, near Nouméa. Six years later, having absorbed Calédonickel, the SLN was the only company exploiting nickel in New Caledonia and was already producing 10% of the world's nickel consumption. Calédonickel and, more generally, the SLN were not only responsible for considerable improvements in the Caledonian economy but also played a leading role in the urbanization and social development of the island. They took on workers from abroad, but also trained and employed natives. During World War II, the Doniambo factory's output reached the United States, since a great part of it was sent to help in the construction of U.S. weapons. Although these transactions increased SLN's international status, the war left the company in a precarious state. The need was felt to concentrate and modernize its structure and equipment. This process took SLN about ten years, but in 1950 the company's nickel production (6,900 tons) finally exceeded that of 1939 (6,700 tons). In spite of several other crises, the next 20 years saw the continuation of SLN's development from the level of a cottage industry to that of an advanced technology company.

Peñarroya, which was to merge with SLN in 1967, had grown rapidly in parallel with SLN. Although both companies were partly owned by the Rothschild empire, which had been one of the founders of Peñarroya, they had separate identities, management, and operations. Created in 1881 by Charles Leroux in order to exploit the coal and lead mines of the Andalusian village that gave its name to the company, Peñarroya, after a very difficult start, made great progress at the beginning of the 20th century. For his efforts, Charles Leroux received a medal at the Paris Universal Exhibition (Exposition Universelle) of 1900. In 1910, Peñarroya's new chairman, Fréderic Ledoux, decided to extend the company's activities beyond Spain. World War I had little effect on Peñarroya, since Spain was not at war with Germany, and the company rapidly turned to the exploitation of nonferrous metals in the Mediterranean basin. It prospected for zinc in North Africa and its French colonies, in Greece, and in Italy. After the shock of World War II, Peñarroya expanded as far as South America and Mauritania, under the influence of the new chairman René Fillon, who used to work for the Banque Rothschild and whose tenure would last until 1961. Peñarroya then became a world leader in zinc but also produced silver, cadmium, germanium, and later—in association with Mokta—uranium and aluminum. In 1961 the company's structure was redefined and Peñarroya found itself in need of a new chairman to replace René Fillon. The Rothschild group proposed Georges Pompidou, who was, however, unable to accept the offer as he was shortly to become prime minister of France. It was therefore Guy de Rothschild himself who became chairman, this being the first time that a Rothschild had personally participated in the management of one of the family's businesses. He also recruited Bernard de Villeméjane, the present chairman of Imetal.

On his arrival at Peñarroya, Guy de Rothschild found that there were numerous problems to solve. To modernize the company's plant, he introduced a new zinc furnace. The commercial problems were more serious, as Peñarroya was not able to sell its own products. Rothschild established and bought small businesses to counterbalance Peñarroya's losses and entered into partnership with several other companies, which included Pechiney, the iron and steel leader. Throughout this period, Rothschild actively sought new sources of financing and revenue. After the metal crisis of 1967, when metal prices plunged, this search gave birth to Imetal.

The year 1967 was important for both SLN and Peñarroya. Through COFIRED, a company owned by the Compagnie du Nord, itself belonging to the Rothschilds, which bought 50% of Peñarroya's capital and gave it back to SLN, SLN became the majority shareholder in Peñarroya and therefore controlled it. Yet until 1970, although the two companies were run along the same lines, they retained separate management and headquarters. In 1970, just before the takeover of Mokta, the companies eventually merged and become a single group, SLN-Peñarroya. The nomination of Bernard de Villeméjane as president of the group coincided in 1971 with Mokta's entry into the group, through a public offer of exchange which was accepted by 92% of Mokta's shareholders. Created in 1865 to exploit magnetic iron ore deposits in Mokta-el-Hadid, Algeria, Mokta had developed slowly under the control of the Suez Bank. It diversified primarily into manganese and uranium and later became a holding company. With iron interests in Spain, manganese in Gabon and Morocco, and—most importantly—uranium in France, Nigeria, Gabon, and Canada, Mokta was only fully absorbed by Imetal in 1980.

The three Rothschild companies were now faced with the merger of Pechiney and Ugine-Kuhlmann, their direct competitors, in 1971. Three years later, in 1974, the Rothschild group became an industrial holding company. A new name, Imetal, was chosen for its modern connotations although it had no actual meaning. It was a public limited company with headquarters in the 15th *arrondissement* of Paris and moved in 1977 into the 51st floor of the famous Tour Montparnasse. This concentration and merging was, of course, part of the logical continuation of SLN's growth policy, but was also prompted by the international oil crisis of 1973 that affected the nickel industry more directly in 1975. Although Mokta and its uranium survived the energy crisis quite well, the 30% decrease in construction as well as the fall in prices and of the dollar deeply affected the group. Imetal did not recover fully from the crisis until the end of the 1980s.

However, one year after its formation Imetal was to receive international attention through the highly publicized Copperweld case. Imetal was trying to expand into the United States and made a takeover bid for Copperweld, a company created in 1915 that manufactured specialty tubing, bimetallic wire, and alloy steel. Copperweld's employees and management opposed the bid and took the case to court. The court decision in favor of Imetal provoked protests by U.S. workers in the streets of Washington, D.C. and New York. The anti-French movement reached its climax and was fueled by antisemitic slogans directed against Baron Guy de Rothschild. The latter eventually came to Pittsburgh to defend his company and succeeded in turning opinion in his favor. He ended by acquiring 67% of Copperweld, and now owns the company entirely.

Rothschild did not stop there, and on his way toward internationalization he bought 25% of the Lead Industries Group, formed in 1930 as the result of the amalgamation of a number

of U.K. lead manufacturers in the 1920s. Then through Mokta, Imetal managed to take over the largest private uranium-ore company in France, la Compagnie Française des Minerais d'Uranium. The latter is now a major subsidiary of Mokta.

These events were followed in 1976 by the creation of Minemet, which combined in a single entity all of the marketing companies of the Imetal group, together with Minemet Recherche, a subsidiary conducting the major part of its operations at the Trappes Research Center, near Paris, which was opened in 1972. In 1979, Guy de Rothschild, who had passed the retirement age laid down by the company, was obliged to resign, and, Bernard de Villeméjane became chairman of Imetal. In 1980, when SLN celebrated its 100th anniversary, Imetal's consolidated profits totalled FFr200 million, to which Copperweld had made a major contribution. However, Bernard de Villeméjane had to face another crisis, mainly affecting nickel production and caused by recession in the minerals market. The industry was, if not depressed, certainly in stagnation. Change was urgently needed and the possibility of a change of product line gradually became apparent.

At the beginning of the 1980s, Bernard de Villeméjane took a series of measures to reduce the importance of uranium and minerals in Imetal's activities. In his opinion, they were no longer profitable. First, in 1983, he conceded the majority of SLN's shares to Eramet and the latter became Eramet-SLN, of which Imetal now controls only 15%. In 1986 the situation had deteriorated still further and Imetal's losses amounted to FFr586 million. Mokta, which was partly responsible for this, was sold to Cogéma in 1986. In 1987 it was Peñarroya's turn; Imetal's share in the company was reduced from 59% to 34.1% and later to 15%. Peñarroya in the early 1990s was owned by Metaleurop. As Bernard de Villeméjane explained to *Le Nouvel Economiste,* on August 21, 1987, "Ten years ago, uranium and mining represented 80% of our activity. Today, it is less than one fifth."

As it was moving away from its old activities, Imetal was buying new companies and specializing in construction materials. It obtained 100% control of Huguenot Fenal, a company constructing roof shingles and with many affiliates. Imetal then bought the Industrie Regionale du Bâtiment (IRB), which included ten companies. Imetal's move into the construction materials sector and its subsequent financial recovery were spectacular. From losses of FFr586 million in 1986, the group had moved to profits of FFr550 million in 1988. After this success, Bernard de Villeméjane decided to diversify into baked clay, tiling, ceramics, and brick. These seem incongruous activities for a mining group but as its chairman stated in *Entreprises,* December 12, 1988, "it appears to be different from what we used to do, but in reality it does correspond to our company culture." Indeed, the manufacturing technique employed in construction materials is not far removed from that used in nonferrous metals; both rely on the use of kilns. The success of Imetal in this sector can also be explained by the company's considerable experience in energy conservation and the way in which Imetal used this experience to adapt itself to an increasingly competitive sector such as construction.

After the purchase of la Société Gélis-Poudenx-Sans—shingles and bricks—and the Groupe de la Financière d'Angers—slate—in 1989, Imetal became the world leader in shingles and the foremost brick producer in France. Yet

Imetal's outlook remained if not regional, at the most national. Naturally, the next step will be internationalization in its new sector. "We are on the threshold of a European development phase" said Imetal's chairman, in *La Cote Desfossée,* April 4, 1989. Its first two partners were Italy and Germany, through Metaleurop, created in association with Preussag. Then came the United Kingdom, in the form of Steely, a company with which Imetal entered into partnership in September 1990, for the distribution of its products in the United Kingdom. Imetal also maintains good relations with the United States and, having bought all the remaining shares in Copperweld, Imetal acquired CE-Minerals, a subsidiary of Asea Brown Boveri and an important producer of clay.

"Imetal" is becoming more and more of a misnomer. The company has definitely passed from the nonferrous metal industry to that of construction materials, although its dramatic success in the sector has not kept it from maintaining its former and traditional activities. Although the company tried very hard to justify these changes and to make them seem consistent, there was a paradox in the fact that this company, which once had an enormous network of international branches, was—in 1989—"on the threshold of a European development phase." In spite of its brilliant successes in its new field, Imetal has entered a sector far less prestigious and far more competitive, especially on a European scale, than its former field. As Bernard de Villeméjane stated in *l'Usine Nouvelle,* on November 11, 1989, "Making money in sectors that one may find less glamorous, is preferable to losing money in other, more prestigious sectors." Imetal is, after more than a century's existence, actually building itself a new future.

Principal Subsidiaries: Huguenot Fenal; Industrie Régionale du Bâtiment; Gélis-Poudenx-Sans; Financière d'Anger (98%); Mircal; Copperweld (USA).

Further Reading: Black, Ralph, "Les Grandes Options de la Stratégie de Peñarroya-Le Nickel," *Les Echos,* January 25, 1971; *Le Nickel-SLN, 1880–1980, 100 ans d'une entreprise et d'une industrie,* SLN, Paris, 1980; *Peñarroya, 1881–1981, histoire d'une société,* Paris, Peñarroya, 1981; de Rothschild, Guy, *Si j'ai Bonne Mémoire,* Paris, Belfond, 1983; Bouvier, Jean, *Les Rothschild,* Edition Complexe, Paris, 1983; Gout, Didier, "Imetal se Construit un Nouvel Avenir," *l'Usine Nouvelle,* November 16, 1989; Baron, Benoit and Chantal Colomer, "Les Fers au Feu Internationaux d'Imetal," *La Cote Desfossées,* April 6, 1990.

—Sonia Kronlund

INCO LIMITED

Royal Trust Tower
Toronto-Dominion Centre
Toronto, Ontario M5K 1N4
Canada
(416) 361-7511
Fax: (416) 361-7781

Public Company
Incorporated: 1916 as International Nickel Co. of Canada, Ltd.
Employees: 19,387
Sales: US$3.11 billion
Stock Exchanges: Toronto Montreal New York London Paris Amsterdam Brussels Zürich Berne Basel Geneva Lausanne

Inco Limited has been the world's leading producer of nickel since it was founded in 1902. Though it no longer has the monopoly it once had, Inco still supplies 35% of the free world's nickel, and after weathering the commodities recession of the early and mid-1980s its earnings have soared to record heights in the recent past. Inco has developed a substantial business in precious metals and produces a number of highly-engineered parts for the aerospace industry, but the bulk of its sales still originate in the vast nickel and copper reserves of its Canadian mines.

Nickel was first isolated as an element in the middle of the 18th century, but it was not until the following century that it came into demand as a coin metal. Up to around 1890, coining remained the metal's only use, and most of the world's nickel was mined by Le Nickel, a Rothschild company on the island of New Caledonia. At that time, however, it was determined that steel made from an iron-nickel alloy could be rolled into exceptionally hard plates, called armorplate, for warships, tanks, and other military vehicles, and the resulting surge in demand spurred a worldwide search for nickel deposits. The world's largest nickel deposit was in Ontario's Sudbury Basin, and it was not long before one of the area's big copper mining companies, Canadian Copper, began shipping quantities of nickel to a U.S. refinery in Bayonne, New Jersey, the Orford Copper Company. Orford had devised the most economical process for the refining of nickel, and its alliance with Canadian Copper proved an unbeatable combination. Orford dominated the U.S. nickel business, supplying much of the metal needed by the growing steel industry, and managed to make inroads into the European market as well.

The U.S. steel industry did not feel comfortable having to rely on a single Canadian source for one of its essential materials, and in 1902 Charles Schwab of U.S. Steel and a group of other steelmen used the financial backing of J.P. Morgan to take control of and merge Orford and Canadian Copper. The new company was called International Nickel, nicknamed Inco, and was based in New York. From the first, Inco was able to control a majority of the U.S. nickel market, and by 1913 had increased its share to 70%. Its large-scale operations in the Sudbury Basin allowed Inco to eliminate competition by means of price wars and sheer staying power. According to *Fortune*, May 1957, Inco was able to maintain without interruption its control of the U.S. market for about 40 years. Despite U.S. antitrust laws, the steel industry thus achieved its aim of a guaranteed supply of reasonably priced nickel.

As the world's leading nickel producer, Inco enjoyed an enormous increase in business during World War I, when the need for armor plate drove up steel sales. This good fortune soon changed, when the 1921 world disarmament agreements killed the munitions market and Inco was left with a huge backlog of nickel. Its record 1921 profit of US$2 million slipped to a US$1.2 million loss the following year, and the Sudbury mines were shut down for over six months. The shock of this setback stayed with the company for many years in the form of a conservative management policy and a determination to avoid large inventories. In 1922 Robert Crooks Stanley began a 30-year tenure as president—and later chairman—of Inco, intent upon building new markets in fields other than munitions. Stanley created a vigorous research and development department whose task it was to find new peacetime uses for nickel. So effective were the Inco engineers that many of the innovations in nickel metallurgy over the next 50 years can be traced to their efforts. In effect, Inco became the research department for the entire nickel industry, sharing its findings with customer and competitor alike. Of course, for many years Inco had few of the latter.

By the late 1920s, Stanley brought Inco sales back up to their wartime peak, much of the peacetime addition coming from the auto industry. Inco's first major postwar investment was a US$3 million rolling mill in Huntington, West Virginia, designed to produce Monel metal, a widely used copper-nickel alloy. At the same time, Stanley effectively blocked the growth of competition from such newcomers as British America Nickel, which in 1923 made a serious bid for the U.S. market. Inco promptly lowered its price from US34¢ per pound to US25¢ per pound, driving British America to bankruptcy a year later. No one volunteered to purchase the company's assets until a little-known firm, Anglo-Canadian Mining & Refining bought them very cheaply. Anglo-Canadian was a dummy corporation owned by Inco, which simply took what it could use of British America's refinery and sold the rest for scrap.

A more serious competitor was handled in a different manner. Mond Nickel Company had been operating in the Sudbury Basin since just after the turn of the century, shipping its nickel to Europe to compete with France's Le Nickel and Inco's European offices. Mond, the creation of Ludwig Mond, the British chemist who founded the great Imperial Chemical Industries (ICI), owned half of the best nickel deposits in Sudbury, in an area known as the Frood. The other owner of those deposits was Inco. In 1928 Inco decided that rather than fight over the world's largest nickel mine, it would be wiser to join forces. Mond and Inco were therefore merged at the end of that year to form International Nickel Co. of Canada, Ltd., still nicknamed Inco. Mond remained as a U.K. subsidiary of Inco, handling both European and Asian customers. By moving its incorporation to a foreign country, Inco was better able to deflect inevitable and periodic attempts by the U.S. Department of Justice to prosecute it for antitrust violations. The 1929 appearance of a small competitor called Falconbridge Nickel Mines Limited, another European supplier, was tolerated by Inco to avoid the impression of absolute monopoly.

The Great Depression caused Inco temporary losses for the second time in its history, but the growing number of industrial uses for nickel soon pulled sales back up to healthy levels. By this time, Inco had become a major producer of copper and platinum as well as nickel, the Sudbury Basin providing a rich supply of many minerals. The company was the sixth-largest copper producer in the world and the largest supplier of platinum, a metal whose unusual properties had found many industrial applications; but it was in nickel that Inco held unchallenged power. As the supplier of 90% of the non-communist world's nickel, Inco was in a position of importance. Its metal was needed by all of the world's arms makers in the production of super-hard steel for dozens of uses, from armor plate to exhaust valves on aircraft engines to gun recoil systems. Inco became the supplier of nickel to both sides of the approaching World War II, signing a long-term contract with Germany's I.G. Farben in the mid-1930s. Ten years later, the Department of Justice charged, in antitrust action, that Inco's agreement with Farben was part of its effort to form a worldwide nickel cartel, and that it had in the process supplied Germany with a stockpile of nickel critical to its imminent war plans. The antitrust action was settled in 1948 when Inco signed a consent decree, agreeing only that it would sell nickel in the United States at fair prices; its worldwide monopoly, however, was beyond the reach of the Department of Justice.

World War II taxed Inco's capacity and strained its relationship with the U.S. armed forces. Still mindful of its near collapse after World War I, Inco refused to stockpile an inventory as large as that which the armed forces desired, but the company provided timely delivery of its critical metal. As an insurance policy, the U.S. government in 1942 financed the creation of Nicaro Nickel Company, a Cuban venture under the direction of the Freeport Sulphur Company. Although Nicaro managed to produce some nickel, it never really got off the ground and was mothballed soon after the war. Its decline may have been hastened by Inco's price cutting on nickel oxides, Nicaro's specialty. The extent of Inco's monopoly on nickel is further suggested by the fact that, aside from the case of nickel oxide, its nickel price never varied between 1928 and 1946—an indication of complete freedom from the normal pressures of competition. At the war's end, Inco's assets were valued at about US$135 million, sales stood at US$148 million, and the company showed a very healthy net income of about US$30 million.

Inco's hesitation to expand its production of nickel helped it to avoid a serious postwar slump, but it also left the company unprepared for what soon followed. In the booming economy of the 1950s, nickel assumed new importance, finding applications in stainless steel, home appliances, its use with chrome for automobiles, jet engines, and atomic power plants. When

the Korean War of 1950–1953 added the usual backlog of orders for armor plate, Inco and the western world faced a severe and growing nickel shortage. The U.S. government made the situation more difficult by adding nickel to its list of stockpiled metals critical to national defense, a contract that Inco was naturally called upon to fulfill. Indeed, Inco and the U.S. Department of Commerce together allocated nickel to customers across the country. This shortage of nickel had two long-term consequences for Inco. First, it made inevitable a rise in price, which increased by 60% between 1946 and 1950 alone. Second, a host of new competitors entered the nickel market, encouraged by the acute shortage, rising prices, and by the U.S. government's willingness to finance alternative suppliers of the important metal. Inco's share of the free-world market, which was estimated at 85% as late as 1950, soon began a decline to its early 1990s level of 34%.

Once assured that the boom in nickel was permanent, Inco increased production and began to search for new deposits. After several years of exploration it made a major find in 1956 in northern Manitoba, a field it christened "Thompson" after company chairman John F. Thompson, successor to Robert Stanley. Thompson was the most significant new deposit of nickel found since the discovery of Sudbury in the 1880s. After Inco had spent about US$175 million building mines, smelters, refineries, a town to house its employees, and a railroad to reach the town, the site added about 30% to the company's 1956 sales of US$445 million. Inco remained an extremely profitable company despite its new competitors, and still carried no long-term debt. In the recession of 1958, sales dropped to US$322 million but a strike by the Mill, Mine and Smelter Workers Union kept inventories low and prevented a loss for the year.

After the 1958 recession, sales of nickel took off once again. Inco's research engineers continued to provide a new generation of customers with ingenious uses for nickel, as in the rapidly growing electronics and aerospace industries, the use of stainless steel—then as now the most important nickel alloy—was just beginning to mushroom. Under the leadership of new chairman Harry S. Wingate, Inco's sales hit US$572 million in 1965, and its net income remained a remarkably high US$136 million. The Thompson field had grown into a thriving town and its deposits were proving to be every bit as rich as had been hoped. Nickel sales were given yet another boost by the Vietnam War, in which the United States employed a vast array of sophisticated weaponry, the bulk of it requiring nickel-hardened steel. Responding to the bull market, Inco launched a comprehensive program of refurbishment and expansion of its facilities that would eventually cost more than US$1 billion. For the first time in its history, Inco borrowed money to finance its big expansion, and it chose to continue to concentrate on the mining of high-grade, relatively expensive nickel at a time when many competitors had come up with useable nickel oxides and ferro-nickels that were readily available and inexpensive.

The impact of these decisions was felt in the period 1969–1971, when a devastating strike by 17,000 workers at Sudbury was followed by the sharp recession of 1971; nickel sales dropped by 25%, and Inco's stock fell by 50% in a matter of months. The company did not show a loss for the year, but it was thoroughly shaken by the loss of sales and mounting debt burden. Wingate retired and his successor, L. Edward Grubb, moved to curtail the expansion program then just coming on-stream. Grubb cut production back to 80% of capacity and reduced labor where possible. To protect Inco against the further erosion of sales by ferro-nickel competitors, he spent another US$750 million to exploit the company's own ferro-nickel sources in Guatemala and Indonesia, where nickel can be extracted from laterite ore by means of a refining process using petroleum. In 1974 Inco made its first and only major acquisition, paying US$224 million for ESB Inc., a leading manufacturer of large storage batteries using nickel. Inco's thinking was that ESB sales would help balance cyclical downturns in nickel, and that batteries would be increasingly in demand in a world growing short of oil.

Inco's share of the free world's nickel sales had slipped below 50% by this time. Except in 1974, a boom year for commodities, the nickel market remained generally soft for the rest of the decade. More worrisome, the soaring price of oil made Inco's huge investments in laterite nickel practically a dead loss, as the cost of refining the ore with petroleum rendered the product too expensive to sell. In 1976 International Nickel Co. of Canada, Ltd. officially changed its name to Inco Limited. An additional problem was Inco's US$850 million debt burden, which grew less manageable as interest rates reached a peak in the early 1980s. Finally, Inco seems to have been unable to run its new battery subsidiary, which was floundering. In the severe recession of 1981, Inco found itself in deep trouble. It was forced to write off its Guatemalan investment. Sales began a steep slide, and the company reported a disastrous year-end loss of US$470 million, its first loss since 1932. In the following three years, Inco's sales fell another US$500 million, as the recession and corporate debt proved to be an almost fatal combination.

Inco had one asset that remained invulnerable, however. It still owned the world's richest nickel fields. Under chief operating officer Donald J. Phillips, Inco wrote off its ill-fated battery venture, almost halved its work force, closed all excess production facilities, and sat tight, waiting for the severely depressed price of nickel to recover. New techniques allowed the extraction of ore in far bigger chunks than was previously possible, and the reduced staff performed the smelting and refining tasks with improved methods. A rebound in the nickel market in 1987 brought the boost that Inco needed. Its profit of US$125 million was encouraging, and would soon be surpassed as the price of nickel reached all-time highs, and Inco achieved a US$735 million profit in 1988 and US$753 in the following year.

As a reward for his efforts in raising productivity, Donald J. Phillips was made chairman and chief executive officer of Inco. His first task was to decide what to do with US$1.5 billion in retained earnings. Mindful of the poor results of past efforts at diversification, Phillips reinvested some of the money in further production refinements and gave the rest of it to Inco's stockholders in the form of a special dividend. Inco seems ideally prepared to reach its centennial year, 2002, in good shape. It had cut back its debt, pruned its production methods, and avoided rash investments. Better yet, in the early 1990s Inco still owned the world's largest known hoard of high-grade nickel.

Principal Subsidiaries: Inco Alloys International, Inc. (U.S.A.); Inco Engineered Products Limited (U.K.); Inco Europe Limited (U.K.); P.T. International Nickel Indonesia; Wiggen Steel & Alloys Limited (U.K.); International Nickel Oceanie S.A. New Caledonia; International Nickel Oceanie S.A. (France); Inco Gold Inc.; Inco Alloys Limited (U.K.).

Further Reading: "The Squeeze on Nickel," *Fortune,* November 1950; "Inco," *Fortune,* May 1957; Lamont, Lansing, "Inco: A Giant Learns How to Compete," *Fortune,* January 1975.

—Jonathan Martin

 **Inland Steel Industries**

INLAND STEEL INDUSTRIES, INC.

30 West Monroe Street
Chicago, Illinois 60603
U.S.A.
(312) 346-0300
Fax: (312) 899-3323

Public Company
Incorporated; 1893 as Inland Steel Company
Employees: 20,200
Sales: $3.87 billion
Stock Exchanges: New York Midwest

Inland Steel Industries has long been one of the most innovative and technologically advanced major U.S. steel companies. Inland is a holding company with two main divisions, integrated steel operations and steel service centers. The integrated steel segment is engaged in the production and sale of bar and flat-rolled steel, while the steel service centers are involved in the sale and production of custom cut, formed, ground, welded, and otherwise processed steel, as well as other metals and industrial plastics. One of the most successful of the major independents in the steel industry, Inland has a reputation as a top performer in both prosperous and lean periods for steel producers. Inland remained one of the industry's top performers through the 1970s, but in the early 1980s a poor economy coupled with the rising tide of imports and a depressed international steel market took its toll on the whole of the industry. Inland, however, remained a leader in modernization and in utilizing technology during the troubled 1980s, and, by relying on continued new developments in steel production, Inland expects to once again become a front-runner in profitability.

Inland had its beginnings in the depression of 1893. It was in that year that the Chicago Steel Works, a manufacturer of farm equipment, along with many other companies went out of business. A group that included a foreman from the defunct company made an attempt to form a new company to begin producing steel on a site that Chicago Steel Works had acquired, in the village of Chicago Heights, Illinois. The necessary capital to finance the venture, however, could not be found, until the group enlisted Joseph Block, a Cincinnati, Ohio, iron merchant who was in Chicago to visit the World's Fair. He brought his son Phillip D. Block into the venture.

After incorporating as Inland Steel Company in October 1893, and purchasing the idle machinery of Chicago Steel Works, Inland was ready to begin production in early 1894. By the end of the year, another of Joseph Block's sons, L.E. Block, had joined the company. In the next few years, the business grew steadily, with production centered on agricultural implements. Sales were boosted by a new product, the side rails for bed frames.

In 1897 sales topped $350,000, and the company, which had been sinking much of its profits into improving machinery at the mill, purchased the East Chicago Iron and Forge Company and renamed it Inland Iron and Forge. The new addition was operated by L.E. Block and produced equipment for the railroad industry. The plant was sold in 1901 for ten times its original purchase price of $50,000.

By the end of the 19th century Inland was doing well, and sales were growing steadily. In 1901 it thus found itself in a position to raise enough money to accept an offer by a real estate developer promising 50 acres of to any firm that would spend at least $1 million to build a steel plant on the site. The patch of land was on Lake Michigan, which could provide water needed for operating a mill and a waterway for transporting material. The land also was near several major railroad lines. In 1902, when the first phase of construction of the new Indiana Harbor, Indiana, plant was completed, Inland had a steel ingot capacity of 60,000 tons. Due to a general recession, Inland lost $127,000 in 1903–1904. Due to debt and the recession, from 1901 until 1906 the company did not pay dividends. By 1905 the plant got its first big order, for 30,000 tons of steel channels and plates.

In 1906, to meet the growing demand for steel, Inland added its fifth open hearth furnace and constructed the first blast furnace in northern Indiana. By purchasing the lease on an iron mine in Minnesota, Inland ensured itself of a source of iron ore to feed its furnaces that allowed it to reduce costs and significantly increase steel production. Production was increased further as Inland added more open hearth furnaces and sheet mills.

In 1911 the Inland Steamship Company was formed to transport ore from Inland's growing mining concerns in Minnesota to the Indiana Harbor mill. A year later, Inland was manufacturing spikes and rivets for the railroad industry.

By 1914 when Joseph Block died, Inland had a steel ingot capacity of 600,000 tons. Capacity reached one million tons by 1917, and to accommodate the world market's growing demand for steel, Inland completed construction of a second plant at Indiana Harbor that year. Demand for steel increased during World War I, and following the war, between 1923 and 1926, all of the mills and machinery at the new plant were completely electrified, which provided the efficient production.

When the war ended, the railroad industry became Inland's top customer, replacing agriculture. When Phillip D. Block became president of Inland in 1919, Inland started to improve working conditions and to provide benefits for its employees. It was one of the first companies in the steel industry to introduce an eight-hour workday. The measure was soon abandoned, however, when the rest of the industry did not follow suit. In 1920 Inland was the first steel company to adopt a pension plan for its employees.

In the early 1920s Inland began to make steel rails in its 32-inch roughing and 28-inch finishing mills that previously had been used only for rolling structural shapes. This was an innovation in the steel industry, and within a short time rolling and finishing rails was Inland's most successful operation in terms of both sales and earnings. At the same time, the company spent $1 million to build a structural steel finishing mill. During this period, Inland continued to modernize and expand. Millions of dollars were spent to improve quality and efficiency as demand for steel rose and sales skyrocketed.

The early 1920s were not only a time of great prosperity for the steel industry, they were also a period of upheaval. The second great wave of mergers and attempted mergers in the steel industry since the turn of the century began in 1921. As it had been in the early 1900s, Inland was again the object of schemes designed to merge smaller independent companies into one huge corporation. A plan initiated in 1921 envisioned the consolidation of seven large steel companies—Inland, Republic Steel Corporation, Brier Hill, Lackawanna, Midvale Steel and Ordnance, Youngstown, and Steel and Tube Company of America. Rumors of the proposed plan circulated in the press in late 1921 and early 1922, but in May 1922 Lackawanna withdrew from the plan. Negotiations continued between Republic, Inland, and Midvale. After the Federal Trade Commission (FTC) issued a complaint in August 1922, however, executives of the three companies announced that financing would be difficult while the legal issues raised by the FTC complaint were being resolved. The plan was dropped.

Sales at Inland increased, and while the company continued to spend on expansion, it became the number-one U.S. steel company in rate of return on fixed assets in the period from 1926 to 1930. In 1928 Inland was able to acquire a limestone quarry on the upper peninsula of Michigan, and formed Inland Lime and Stone Company. Inland acquired another source of raw materials by purchasing 15 acres of land in Kentucky holding high-grade coking coal.

Inland's expansion continued through the late 1920s and did not stop even when the Great Depression hit in 1929. Between 1929 and 1932 Inland spent $30 million on expansion. In 1932, the only Depression year in which Inland was not in the black, the company unveiled the widest continuous hot-strip mill in the United States. At a cost of $15 million, the mill was 76 inches wide and would later be used to roll sheet for the auto industry and for the navy during World War II. While 1932 was a financially dismal year for Inland, operating at only 25% of capacity, that figure was one-third higher than that for the balance of the industry. During the period from 1931 to 1935, Inland's operating profit in terms of fixed assets was 6.1%, the highest in the industry.

At the time that Inland built the new mill, competition in the steel industry was intense, and Inland was forced to compete with companies like United States Steel, among others, that had their own warehouse operations through which to market its products. To remain competitive with its rivals, Inland chose to go into the steel warehouse business and in 1935 acquired Joseph T. Ryerson and Son Inc., a steel-warehousing and -fabricating chain. Ryerson provided an outlet through which Inland's customers could buy steel and have it custom processed. In 1936 Inland acquired Milcor Steel Company of Milwaukee, Wisconsin, which made a wide variety of steel products and had plants and warehouses in seven cities. Milcor provided Inland with a market for the products of its sheet-rolling mills.

When World War II began, Inland, still under the direction of Chairman Phillip D. Block, immediately began a program of expansion to provide added capacity, by building new blast furnaces and coke ovens to provide steel for bombs, shells, tanks, ships, and planes. By 1944 Inland had become completely integrated. The company controlled its own sources of raw materials including coal, ore, and limestone. With a total ingot capacity of 3.4 million tons by 1944, Inland's sales in the years between 1940 and 1950 ranged from $200 million to $400 million per year.

In the 1940s prosperity was tempered somewhat by a series of labor disputes in which the United Steel Workers of America (USWA) sought higher wages and certain benefits for its members. Although labor and industry had agreed to a no-strike, no-lockout pledge during the early 1940s, steel workers across the country went on strike to demand a $1 a day wage increase in March 1942. The effects of the strike on war production were not significant, and Inland and the USWA signed a contract covering working conditions for the company's 14,000 employees at both Indiana Harbor and Chicago Heights.

A much more serious strike, involving 750,000 steel workers, took place in 1946 and virtually crippled the steel industry as production fell to its lowest level in half a century. The strike lasted 26 days and affected 11,000 employees at Inland's Indiana Harbor and Chicago Heights plants. Only after Inland and the other companies involved agreed to a wage rise of 18.5¢ per hour, did the strike end. Inland was then able to continue to produce the steel required by the huge postwar demand for consumer products. The steel Inland produced then went primarily to the automobile and home-appliance industries. After the war, Inland continued to expand its facilities for sheet and strip and also acquired more property from which to mine raw materials, in Minnesota, Michigan, and Kentucky. In 1945 Phillip D. Block resigned as chairman after serving for more than 22 years. He was replaced by his brother, L.E. Block, who served until 1951.

During the early 1950s expansion slowed at Inland. From 1952 to 1955 steel production capacity increased by 700,000 tons. This was half the amount needed to close the gap between Chicago area demand and capacity. In the years between 1947 and 1958 Inland's capital expenditures of $121 million were the most modest among the major steel companies. Expansion, however, picked up during the steel boom of 1956, when Inland began a new program in which the company spent $360 million to modernize its plants, to acquire new mining properties, and to build a steel building to serve as its new headquarters in downtown Chicago. The stainless steel for the curtain walls of the 19-story building had to be purchased from another steel company because Inland was still producing carbon steel almost exclusively.

Although the early 1950s were relatively unremarkable for Inland in terms of production and growth, they marked the beginning of a decade that was to include two bitter and costly disputes between the steel workers and the industry. The first conflict began in November 1951 when the USWA notified the industry that it wanted to bargain for a wage increase. In December, after no agreement was reached, union president Phillip Murray called for a strike. Almost immediately, President Harry S Truman referred the case to the Wage Stabilization Board. The board held hearings and made a recommendation that the union accepted but that was rejected by the industry. In April 1952 the board tried unsuccessfully to avert a strike. A few days later, on the eve of a strike, President Truman issued an order for the nation's steel mills to be seized by the government to keep them open and avert a strike. The industry was outraged by the president's order and Inland's president, Clarence B. Randall, was chosen to give the industry's viewpoint in an address that was broadcast on nationwide radio and television. Randall called the president's order an "evil deed" that he had no legal right to issue. The U.S. Supreme Court agreed, and in June 1952 ordered that the mills be returned to their owners. Within a few hours, 600,000 workers walked off their jobs to begin a strike that would affect 95% of the nation's steel mills and last for 55 days.

Randall became chairman of Inland in 1953. After a few years of calm, the industry and the USWA became involved in another dispute that was to prove the longest and most costly in the industry's history. The dispute began in May 1959 when the industry called for a wage freeze. When negotiations stalled in July 500,000 steel workers went on strike. In October, President Dwight D. Eisenhower applied for an 80-day injunction under the Taft-Hartley Act, ordering the workers back to the plants while negotiations continued. The Supreme Court upheld the injunction, and the plants reopened in November. In January 1960 the USWA won an agreement that gave it a substantial wage increase. The agreement brought to an end the 116-day strike that had shut down the steel industry and forced the closing of automobile plants because of a shortage of steel.

As the 1960s began, the steel industry planned record production to fill consumer orders and replenish inventories left depleted by the strike. Inland's steel shipments in the years 1961 to 1965 averaged 4.1 million tons per year, compared to 3.6 million tons per year in the previous five years. To keep up with new production demands, Inland embarked on a new expansion program in 1962. The plan included a new 80-inch continuous hot strip mill as well as Inland's first oxygen steelmaking shop. The new shop meant a shift away from the open hearth steelmaking process. It had a capacity to produce more than two million tons per year and enabled Inland to close down its oldest open hearth furnace plant, which had been operating for 60 years, since 1902.

The expansion plan was completed in 1966 and had helped Inland to lower costs, improve product quality, and increase capacity. An important milestone for Inland was the completion in 1967 of its new research facilities in East Chicago, Indiana, where company scientists could investigate new processes in steel metallurgy and production. The large amount of capital that Inland invested in expansion in the mid-1960s, along with stronger competition, had the effect of lowering earnings by 25% in the period from 1964 to 1967. Joseph L. Block, who succeeded Randall as chairman in 1959, believed that the expansion was important for the future, as Inland faced stiff competition for its midwestern market.

When Joseph L. Block retired in 1967, he had earned a reputation as a maverick in the steel industry. In 1962, when the steel industry had clashed with President John F. Kennedy over a proposed rise in steel prices, Block broke with industry ranks and insisted that the time was not right for a steel price hike. In 1966, however, Block took the lead in raising prices with the largest increase since 1963. Block was well known, as

Time, November 3, 1967, reported, for strengthening "Inland's reputation as a civic-minded company" by, among other things, supporting a fair-employment law in Illinois as well as a redevelopment project for East Chicago.

Block was replaced as chairman by his cousin Phillip D. Block Jr. Under the new chairman, Inland was able to maintain its share of the midwestern market and also achieved the highest profit-to-sales ratio among the big-eight steel makers. In the late 1960s, as competition increased from foreign imports and markets eroded, Inland began a diversification program. The first step was into the housing market with the acquisition of Scholz Homes Inc. and later the formation of Inland Steel Urban Development Corporation. By 1974 diversification had led Inland into areas such as steel building products, powdered metals, and reinforced plastics.

The steel business started off slowly in the 1970s for the whole industry. Profits were down, and Inland's net profit declined from $81.7 million in 1968 to $46.7 million in 1970. By 1974, however, things had turned around, and the steel industry experienced one of the biggest booms in its history. After a tight period in the previous two years, demand for steel increased dramatically in 1974, and Inland's sales climbed to $2.5 billion. With demand showing no evidence of slowing, Inland, under Chairman Frederick G. Jaicks, who had replaced Phillip D. Block Jr. in 1971, made plans for a $2 billion expansion, which it planned to finance from strong earnings and outside financing. Inland, however, along with the rest of the industry was hurt by the recession of 1975, and by 1977 the industry, plagued by over-capacity, faced another downturn, as imports flooded the market at prices domestic companies were unable to match. Inland's earnings slumped as costs went up and demand dropped, forcing the company to hold up the first phase of its expansion plan.

Business turned around for Inland in 1978, a record year for the company, in which it was able to capture 6.5% of the domestic steel market. The company produced 8.6 million tons of steel and generated profits of $158.3 million on $3.25 billion in sales. By the early 1980s, however, the steel industry was in trouble again. A combination of factors including the high level of imports, decreased demand, and an oversupply of steel drove down prices at the same time that costs such as labor and energy were on their way up. These factors, combined with high investment expenses as well as depressed midwestern industries—autos, farming, construction, and appliances—caused Inland's profits to drop 64% from their 1978 peak to $57.3 million in 1981.

Inland suffered four straight years of losses totaling $456 million in 1982 through 1985. The company was forced to shut down some of its steel mills and to lay off some workers. Yet Inland continued to develop new products and improve production efficiency. The company had success with lightweight, high-strength, and corrosion-resistant steel for the auto, farm, and construction industries; and in 1981 it was able to push its market share to a record 6.7%.

In order to survive in a depressed industry, Inland—under Chairman Frank Luerssen, who took over in 1983—cut costs by shutting down unprofitable operations and divesting itself of certain assets. Inland began to sell various subsidiaries, including companies that had supplied it with raw materials. In addition, seven major operations at the Indiana Harbor works were shut down. Steel making capacity was reduced by 30%.

While producing less steel, Inland began to shift its efforts into more profitable areas such as its highly successful steel-distribution operations which it sought to expand by acquiring J.M. Tull Metals Company, a large metal-products maker, processor, and distributor, in 1986.

In May 1986 Inland made a move to separate its waning steel-manufacturing operations from its profitable steel-distribution sector by reorganizing as Inland Steel Industries, Inc., a holding company for Inland Steel Company, and Inland Steel Services, Inland's service-center operations. Inland executives hoped that the reorganization would facilitate diversification and joint ventures.

Shortly thereafter, Inland formed a partnership with a Japanese firm, Nippon Steel Corporation. The partnership, known as I/N Tek, was created to construct a continuous cold rolling facility near New Carlisle, Indiana. The I/N Tek facility was the only U.S. continuous cold rolling mill. By combining five basic operations that are usually done separately, the facility is able to complete in less than an hour a process that had taken 12 days. The cold rolled steel produced by the plant is used for, among other applications, autos and appliances. Another joint venture with Nippon Steel, I/N Kote, was started in 1989 to construct and operate two steel-galvanizing lines adjacent to the I/N Tek facility. The project was to be used in combination with I/N Tek to galvanize the cold rolled steel.

With profits having declined 54% in 1989 and losses of $21 million for 1990, Inland expected its continued expansion and modernization through projects such an I/N Tek and I/N Kote to result eventually in profits nearly double the-then record $262 million earned in 1988. This predicted turnaround would ensure that Inland will remain an industry leader in growth and technology, while once again becoming a top industry performer.

Principal Subsidiaries: Inland Steel Company; Joseph T. Ryerson & Son, Inc.; J.M. Tull Metals Company, Inc.

Further Reading: Solow, Herbert, "Inland Does it Again," *Fortune,* July 1958; Gilbert, R., and W. Korda, *The Story of Inland Steel,* Chicago, Inland Steel Company, 1974.

—Patricia Leichenko

JOHNSON MATTHEY PLC

2-4 Cockspur Street
Trafalgar Square
London SW1Y 5BQ
United Kingdom
(071) 269-8400
Fax: (071) 269-8433

Public Company
Incorporated: 1891 as Johnson, Matthey & Co., Limited
Employees: 7,045
Sales: £1.73 billion (US$3.34 billion)
Stock Exchange: London

Johnson Matthey PLC has been involved in the processing and marketing of precious metals since its founding in 1817. It is most widely known for its activities in platinum, as a world leader in the refining, marketing, and technological development of the metal. Johnson Matthey is the leading manufacturer of auto-catalysts, which help break down noxious fumes from motor vehicle exhaust systems. The group also has diverse interests in the industrial and commercial use of other precious and rare-earth metals, with a significant presence in colors, dyes, and ceramics.

The founder of Johnson Matthey was Percival Johnson, who in 1817 set himself up at 79 Hatton Garden in Holborn, London, as an "Assayer and Practical Mineralogist." As such, he valued gold by applying chemical and physical tests to determine the exact quantity of gold in a bar. Johnson's business rapidly gained distinction when be began to offer to buy back the bars of gold that he assayed, thereby becoming the first London assayer to offer a guarantee of quality. In the early 1830s a small gold refinery was built at the Hatton Garden premises for the refining and assaying of gold bars which were then coming into London from Brazil. These were complex gold bars, containing impurities which were not easy to remove. Having successfully extracted platinum group metals from the bars, Johnson's technical prowess established the firm at the forefront of the London bullion market. The firm took full advantage of the gold rushes of California, from 1848, and of Australia, from 1851, while supplies of silver arrived throughout the 1850s and 1860s in the form of demonetized silver coinage—coinage which had gone out of circulation—from European states. A large-scale silver refinery was built at adjacent premises in Hatton Garden.

Johnson's interest in metallurgy had already brought him into contact with platinum, which had been the subject of considerable scientific interest throughout the early 19th century on account of its strength and resistance to corrosive acids. He set up a small-scale refinery for the metal at Hatton Garden, with limited supplies coming from Colombia.

In 1838 George Matthey joined the company as an apprentice. Matthey's scientific talents, coupled with a shrewd business sense, was the driving force behind the company's development in the platinum industry during the second half of the 19th century. When the Great Exhibition was first proposed, Matthey persuaded Johnson to exhibit a number of platinum articles, together with specimens of other platinum-group metals: palladium, iridium, and rhodium. The display was a success, and Matthey became determined to make the company pre-eminent in the platinum business. He succeeded in gaining a more assured supply of the metal through direct arrangements with owners of a mine in the Ural mountains in Russia, then a newly discovered source. In the 1867 International Exhibition in Paris, the company exhibited a wide variety of platinum-manufactured goods on a scale never seen before. The exhibit was awarded a gold medal "for perfection and improvement in the working of platinum." Under Matthey's direction, platinum refining and fabricating grew from about 15,000 ounces in 1860 to about 75,000 ounces a year in the 1880s. The manufacturing of sulfuric acid boilers was the largest single use of platinum until the early 1900s. The diversity of the company was established from the beginning by Percival Johnson. From the chemical refining of gold, Johnson produced a range of vitreous colors for the glass and pottery industries. He became the first refiner of nickel in Britain, with "nickel silver," popular as a silver plate. In 1833 production of silver nitrate began, its use being primarily for medical purposes in the form of lunar caustic. Over the following decades the development of photography generated considerable demand for silver nitrate.

By 1860 the year of Johnson's retirement, the company's present-day activities had been established: assaying and refining of bullion, platinum refining and marketing, the production of vitreous colors for glass and pottery manufacturers, and a constant experimentation and development of niche markets for other rare and precious metals. Hatton Garden remained the rather compact home of the refining, assaying, and experimental work so vital to the firm's future. There was, in addition, a small workshop in Clerkenwell, used for the manufacture of platinum dishes, crucibles, and other laboratory instruments. Twenty-five people were employed in 1860, with a trio of partners who dominated the firm's development over the next four decades: George Matthey, his younger brother Edward Matthey, and John Sellon—Percival Johnson's nephew. It was this trio, and their descendants, who were to dominate the company's development until the mid-20th century.

Over the next 50 years, technological and marketing progress coincided with a securing of supplies. Gold refining facilities were improved and expanded at Hatton Garden in response to the arrival of African gold, and the silver refinery received constant supplies of de-monetized coin from across Europe. The reputation of the assaying and chemical laboratories grew, and in the mid-1880s Johnson Matthey succeeded in establishing itself as the ultimate referee of assayers, and as a certifier of ore quality, of South African Rand gold. Platinum supplies were secured from Russia through the co-operation of the metals houses of Quennessen of France and Heraeus of Germany; together the three European companies dominated the world platinum trade through control of this source, and ignored demands from the tzar for a refinery to be built within Russia. In 1894 the cartel was formalized through the creation of an association named The Allied Houses. In 1911 Johnson Matthey signed an agreement with the Nicolai Pavdinsky Company in the Urals, which gave Johnson Matthey the rights to mine a substantial body of platinum-bearing ore in return for Johnson Matthey building a local refinery. Despite World War I, and the chaos caused by the overthrow of the tzar, the plant was in full operation by 1918. However, no platinum ever reached London. During this period Johnson Matthey promoted the use of platinum as a corrosive-resistant electric conductor, and when platinum prices rose above gold for the first time in the 1900s the company encouraged the interest of jewelers. When the market for sulfuric acid boilers died at the turn of the century, fresh demand had been built up in other sectors.

In 1898 the company expanded its service to jewelers by purchasing new rolling mills in nearby Hop Gardens; here silver and gold alloys were formed into sheet, wire, and tube semi-manufactured goods. The company's interest in colors had been boosted in the late 1870s when it gained the British and Empire marketing rights to a variety of industrial glazes, stains, and enamels, including so-called rolled gold, from the Roessler company of Frankfurt. Roessler was shortly renamed Degussa; the two companies have a history of close association that goes back to the 1860s. After initial skepticism, the Staffordshire potters took to the advanced colors and Johnson Matthey became an established supplier in that area. Meanwhile the company's interest in the rare and often novel metals was given a strong commercial footing with the 1870 acquisition of the Manchester-based Magnesium Metal Company. During the 40 years that followed, the Magnesium Metal Company's plant at Patricroft produced magnesium for flash photography and laboratory work, antimony for hardening bullet heads, vanadium for black dye and ink, and electrolytically-produced aluminum. It is thought that the statue of Eros in London's Piccadilly Circus—dedicated to the philanthropist seventh Earl of Shaftesbury—is of aluminum made at the Patricroft works.

In 1891 the company became Johnson, Matthey & Co. Limited, a private limited company, and during the 1890s and 1910s an increasing amount of departmentalism took place as the sons and nephews of the ruling trio took over the responsibilities, and increasingly delegated power to trusted clerks and technical experts. It was at this point that a corporate policy was adopted that remains at the heart of the company still: only to take part in activities in which the company could dominate. When a product's development fell out of the control of the company, Johnson Matthey's interests in it would be sold off.

During World War I Johnson Matthey established itself as an innovative developer of strategic materials, despite significant supply disruptions affecting most of the metals that the company dealt with. The company was able to satisfy the Allied demand for products such as platinum catalysts, with which to make sulfuric acid for explosives manufacturing, and magnesium powder, to make incendiary bombs for dropping on German airships. In 1916 the company was brought under the direct control of the government, and platinum catalysts and electrical and magneto contacts for cars, airplanes, and tanks were manufactured in a modernized platinum workshop. The company expanded its production of silver nitrate to meet the demands of the photographic industry, and in 1916 began manufacturing its own liquid gold. In 1918 the colors division was given a firm production base through acquisition of the Sneyd color works at Burslem. A Birmingham branch of Johnson Matthey was established in the same year to supply the city's jewelry trade, and the Sheffield silversmith E.W. Oakes & Co. Ltd. was purchased. Despite difficulties in obtaining supplies, demands of industry were met and at the end of the war the air ministry gave an official message of thanks to the company for its supplies of high precision equipment.

In 1918 John Sellon died. In order to secure a closer working relationship with the two South African mining houses that were of most significance to the company's gold activities, his shares in the company were offered in equal parts to Consolidated Gold Fields of South Africa Ltd. and to the Johannesburg Consolidated Investment Company. This is the origin of the controlling stake held by the Anglo American Corporation today.

During the early 1920s the company faced considerable problems due to continued disruptions in the supply of precious metals. From 1922 the South Africans refined their own gold, while regular supplies of platinum from the Urals had failed to resume after the war despite the ingenious attempts of Arthur Coussmaker. Coussmaker was a platinum expert with Johnson Matthey, whose attempts to gain a secure supply of Russian platinum had involved deals with White Russian military forces and introducing himself at unexpected moments to Soviet officials in Western European cities. The difficulties of supply led to the early 1920s being a low point in the fortunes of Johnson Matthey. In 1924, however, Dr. Hans Merensky discovered the huge platinum-bearing reef in the South African Transvaal that bears his name today. Coussmaker, by then a board member, made an immediate trip to the Transvaal where he identified the Rustenburg area as the most promising part of the reef. Consolidated Goldfields of South Africa and Johannesburg Consolidated Investments had mines in the Rustenburg district, and after an initial platinum mine boom in the mid-1920s those were the only mines operating in the slump that followed. Coussmaker persuaded the two mining houses to merge their platinum interests, and in 1931 the Rustenburg Platinum Company was formed. Johnson Matthey became a refiner and distributor for what was, and remains, the world's largest platinum mine. A smelting works and a electrolytic refinery were built at Brimsdown, in Essex, to extract the platinum metals according to a refining method established by Ernest Deering and Alan Powell of the Hatton Garden staff.

In 1919 Johnson Matthey joined N.M. Rothschild's bank and four other leading bullion brokers to form the London Gold Market, where a daily price-fixing still sets the price of gold. When gold supplies from South Africa ended, the sulfuric acid refinery at Hatton Garden was kept in operation through a constant stream of de-monetized silver from Central and Eastern Europe. Much of this came via the Silberfeld brothers, initially based in Riga, who throughout the inter-war period supplied Johnson Matthey with Russian Imperial coins and gold rubles, and with silver Maria Theresa coins from an office in Vienna. The company established branches in Warsaw and Prague, and came to own 75% of the Bank Powszechny Depozytowy in Poland.

Johnson Matthey's manufacturing capacity in this period was boosted by the acquisition in the early 1920s of the metal fabricating firm of R. Buckland & Son Ltd., and manufacturer of semi-manufactured products. In 1925 Johnson and Sons Smelting Works Ltd. of Brimsdown, Middlesex, was acquired. This was a sweeps, scrap and residue, refinery business that had been set up originally in the mid-19th century by a brother of Percival Johnson. During the 1930s the bullion refining and smelting operations were rationalized, the colors section was strengthened by a full-time research department, and a team of enterprising salesmen crossed Europe in motor cars.

At the outbreak of World War II Johnson Matthey was appointed government agent for the control and handling of platinum stocks, and manufactured items of the material grew in response to the rising demand. Products included electrical fine wires, electrodes, aircraft spark plugs, laboratory crucibles, and wire gauze catalysts for the preparation of nitric acid. Demand for platinum with a high iridium content led to Coussmaker's establishment of a refinery in Pennsylvania, where concentrates from Alaskan deposits were turned into contact tips for auto-magnets.

While bullion trade was severely limited by Bank of England supervision, and jewelry sales were almost forbidden, industrial demand—especially from photographic related industries—was strong for silver-based products. Some special uses of silver compounds included the manufacture of silver ball bearings for airplane engines, and desalination packs that enabled ditched airmen, or shipwrecked sailors, to survive on sea water. Bomb damage during the blitz of autumn 1940 resulted in the Brimsdown smelting works being put out of action temporarily, and the entire contents of the company museum and archive collection were destroyed.

With the end of the war came a period of rapid overseas growth for the company, much of it having been prepared from the early 1940s in expectation of a postwar boom. Representatives were sent around the world to study competitors, examine suppliers, and to establish new markets. Operations in North America, South Africa, Australia, and India were expanded as a result, with growth in Europe taking place later with the establishment of subsidiaries in France and the Netherlands in 1956, Italy in 1959, Sweden in 1960, Belgium in 1961, and Austria in 1962. Developments at home moved at an equally rapid pace: two colors factories in Staffordshire were opened immediately after the war, and in 1951 the colors section acquired Universal Transfers Co. Ltd. Johnson Matthey was now a market leader in the manufacture of color pigments and screen-printed transfers for the pottery and glass industries. In 1953 the Harlow Metal Co. Ltd. was formed to merge the company's mechanical production interests, and in 1957 a new platinum refinery was built at Royston which brought together the company's refining operations. In 1954 Universal Matthey Products Ltd. was formed, to produce platinum catalysts for U.S. manufacturers of high-octane petrol. Enthusiasm by the North American auto industry for catalytic converters encouraged Johnson Matthey to conduct extensive research on the auto catalyst during the late 1950s and early 1960s. In 1962 L.B. Hunt was appointed director of research at new purpose-built laboratories at Wembley.

In 1963 Blythe Colours, based in Stoke-on-Trent, was acquired. This brought to Johnson Matthey an extended range of industrial colors, a worldwide network of agents, and a strong North European section based in the Netherlands. A consolidation of bullion activity took place during the 1950s and 1960s, culminating in the formation of Johnson Matthey Bankers Ltd. (JMB). Representing Johnson Matthey on the London gold market, JMB traded in the gold, silver, and precious metals produced by Johnson Matthey subsidiaries around the world.

A major reorganization of the company took place in 1966 and 1967, with the establishment of four divisions within which all the company's activities and subsidiaries were placed. These were the jewelry and allied traders division (J.A.T.); the chemical division; the industrial division; and the ceramic division. A mechanical production unit was established to cater to the production needs of the four divisions. In 1969 expansion into Asia culminated with the establishment of Tanaka Matthey KK, a joint venture company with Tanaka Kikinzoku Kogyo KK of Japan. Japan is a major consumer of platinum jewelry, and the joint venture has enabled Johnson Matthey to dominate the market there.

The 1970s were a decade of organic growth, with few acquisitions taking place. In 1980, however, a significant move into the U.S. jewelry trade—a business that was unfamiliar to the company—led to losses estimated at over £60 million and in 1981 the board looked to JMB to help make up the loss. JMB had done well from the spectacular rise in bullion activity that had accompanied the Soviet invasion of Afghanistan in 1980, and pressure was placed on the subsidiary to expand out of bullion-related loans and into high-risk lending in areas with which it was unfamiliar. The bank's loan book expanded, from £50 million at the end of 1981 to some £500 million by March 1984, with its contribution to group profits going from just under 25% in 1981 to over 60% in 1983. However, by late 1983 the Bank of England had begun to suspect the quality of some of the loans. In the summer of 1984 their suspicions extended to cover the accounting practices of Arthur Young. In September 1984 the full extent of the bad loans taken on by JMB became apparent, and the Bank of England organized a bailout by JMB's creditors, shareholders, and U.K. clearing and merchant banks. The Bank of England purchased JMB for a token £1. The collapse of JMB was a disaster: in the words of *The Economist*, October 6, 1984, "The Johnson Matthey Parent Company lost its shirt, [and] its shareholders a lot of money." In 1981 Johnson, Matthey & Co. Ltd. officially changed its name to Johnson Matthey PLC.

Charter Consolidated, effectively the holding company for Anglo American's interests in Johnson Matthey, found itself with a 38% stake in the group as a result of its assistance in the bailout of JMB, and sent in its own man, Neil Clarke, to become Johnson Matthey's chairman. In June 1985 Clarke appointed Gene Anderson as chief executive. Over the next five years the company was transformed, with £70 million of disposals made over the next two years, including an interest acquired in Wembley Stadium. The work force was cut significantly while profits doubled to £64 million between 1986 and 1989. Seventy-four semi-autonomous companies, loosely grouped into divisions, but many legally distinct and with their own boards, were reorganized into four operating divisions. These are the catalytic systems division, which includes automotive exhaust and industrial air pollution control systems; the materials technology division, which combines the group's rare-earth, pharmaceutical, and special materials interests; the precious metals division, which acts as the sole marketing agency for Rustenburg Platinum and that controls the group's gold and silver marketing and refining businesses; and the color and print division that ties together the group's industrial colors and printing businesses. Investment in new plant and research was expanded, and in 1990 a new autocatalyst production plant was opened in Belgium to meet anticipated European demand. Research into the medical possibilities of platinum-based drugs was boosted, with cancer and HIV-fighting drugs developed.

In December 1989 Anderson resigned after failing to persuade the board to expand into nonplatinum areas. The proposed move would have diluted Anglo American's shareholding in Johnson Matthey through a share issue, and moved Johnson Matthey away from an increasing reliance on the Rustenburg mine. In testing the resolve of the South Africans, Anderson confirmed their control over the group. Almost immediately after Anderson resigned, Clarke also resigned. David Davies, Charter's deputy chairman, was transferred to become Johnson Matthey's chairman.

Johnson Matthey established itself in its principal activity of trading and marketing precious metals in the lifetime of its founder, Percival Johnson. The company has grown from being a bullion and precious metals assayer and refiner, to becoming a major producer of precious metal industrial materials. Together, George Matthey and Arthur Coussmaker dominate the history of the platinum business of the company, which today dominates the company's activities.

The broad range of its activities has traditionally been the key to the company's success. When supplies of, or demand for, a particular metal dried up, there was usually an alternative activity ready for expansion. Such opportunity sometimes led to an unjustified expansion into business the company knew little about—witness JMB—but technological and marketing skills have in the past allowed the company to be a leading player in several activities at any one time, allowing mistakes to be rectified quickly. However, the reliance on platinum-based business for three-quarters of its sales runs contrary to the tradition of diversity. While the medium-term outlook for platinum-based products is good, the company risks becoming a mere downstream unit of the Rustenburg Platinum Mine, if it fails to expand its other activities in line with platinum.

Principal Subsidiaries: Johnson Matthey Limited (Australia); SA Johnson Matthey NV (Belgium); Johnson Matthey Limited (Canada); Matthey Beyrand & Cie SA (France, 80%); Blythe Colours BV (Netherlands); Metalli Preziosi SpA (Italy); Johnson Matthey Inc. (U.S.A.)

Further Reading: McDonald, Donald, "The Rise of Johnson, Matthey & Co. Ltd.," in *A History of Platinum,* London, Johnson Matthey, 1961; Hunt, L.B., "George Matthey and the Building of the Platinum Industry," *Platinum Metals Review,* April 1979; "How Johnson Matthey kept bankers up from dusk to dawn," *The Economist,* October 6, 1984.

—Tom C.B. Elliott

KAISER ALUMINUM & CHEMICAL CORPORATION

KAISER ALUMINUM & CHEMICAL CORPORATION

Kaiser Center
300 Lakeside Drive
Oakland, California 94643
U.S.A.
(415) 271-3300
Fax: (415) 271-8930

Wholly Owned Subsidiary of MAXXAM Inc. through Kaiser Aluminum Corporation and MAXXAM Group Inc.
Incorporated: 1940 as Todd Shipbuilding Corporation
Employees: 10,661
Sales: $2.09 billion

Kaiser Aluminum & Chemical Corporation (KACC) was incorporated in December 1940 as Todd Shipbuilding Corporation. The firm changed its name to Permanente Metals Corporation in November 1941 and adopted its present name in November 1949. KACC mines bauxite, refines it into alumina, smelts alumina into aluminum, and manufactures a wide range of fabricated products that are sold primarily to the transportation, aerospace, and construction industries. The company's link with the latter two markets is not accidental. Henry J. Kaiser, the company founder, worked his way up through numerous business ventures, eventually establishing strong ties with both the construction and aerospace industries.

In 1895 Kaiser left school at age 13 to work in a dry-goods store. Three years later Kaiser marched into a Sprout Brook, New York, photography studio and told the owner he would triple the store's profits in two months. Offering one-day photo service, the young Kaiser fulfilled his promise to the proprietor and became a partner by his third month on the job. Kaiser later bought out the original owner and eventually operated three photographic studio and supply stores on the East Coast.

Kaiser moved west in 1906, working in the hardware business until 1914 when he formed his own road-construction company. By 1923 Kaiser had ventured into the sand and gravel business. Kaiser established headquarters in the late 1920s in Oakland, California, site of KACC's present corporate office.

During the 1930s Kaiser helped found Six Companies, Inc., a loose grouping of builders and earth movers that between 1931 and 1936 built Grand Coulee and Bonnneville dams on the Columbia River, and piers for the Bay Bridge between San Francisco and Oakland, California. Later the group started work on Boulder and Hoover dams. The unprecedented speed of the Hoover Dam construction—a project completed two years ahead of schedule—was Kaiser's doing. His hurry led him into a tangle with U.S. Secretary of the Interior Harold Ickes. Six Companies was charged with violations of the eight-hour work-day law; the fines reached $350,000. In a public-relations blitz, Kaiser sent documents dramatizing the company's effort to complete the project to high government officials and congressmen. Not only did Kaiser's tactic lead to a reduction of the fine to $100,000; more importantly, Kaiser became known to the government and public at large as a force to be reckoned with.

World War II prompted Six Companies to move into the shipbuilding, aircraft, steel, and magnesium industries. The Kaiser-led operation turned out 1,440 cargo ships and more than 50 aircraft carriers. The most significant of these ventures, which eventually led Kaiser into the aluminum business, was the 1940 formation of Todd Shipbuilding Corporation in northern California.

As early as year-end 1940, Kaiser and a colleague, Chad Calhoun, had barraged government officials in Washington, D.C., with proposals for an aluminum plant in the Northwest. From their experience in dam construction, the men knew that water was an inexpensive and abundant energy source available to power the plant. In May 1941 the U.S. government had granted an extensive contract involving more than 30 plants to the leading industry producer, the competitor Aluminum Company of America (Alcoa). Undaunted, Kaiser's Permanente subsidiary stepped up magnesium production, to meet heavy war time demand. After the war, with an eye on rebuilding U.S. industry, Kaiser was convinced that private capital should take the place of government funds. Practicing what he preached, Kaiser announced his intentions to enter the aluminum industry. With a government surplus of 36 aluminum plants and Alcoa out of the running because of an antitrust injunction, the stage was set for Kaiser.

Another force that indirectly propelled Kaiser into aluminum was Kaiser-Frazer Corporation, an automobile-producing business that he formed with Joseph Frazer, in 1945. As a new firm, Kaiser-Frazer was nearly last in line for steel allotment. This situation prompted Kaiser to consider manufacturing aluminum automobiles. The idea was too advanced at the time, however, to be considered.

In 1946 Kaiser-Frazer and Kaiser Cargo, Inc., another Kaiser-controlled company, leased two government-owned aluminum plants in the state of Washington. The metals market had fallen off following the war, surplus aluminum abounded, and bauxite, the chief raw material needed to produce aluminum, was hard to find. Kaiser had advantages in his favor. Because of the postwar drop in production, Alcoa had discharged knowledgeable employees. Kaiser snapped up the available talent, as well as an idle Baton Rouge, Louisiana, aluminum smelter. Consumer demand for aluminum pots and pans and the international need for building materials gave the fledgling company a market to supply.

To be an autonomous aluminum producer Kaiser needed to obtain a steady source of bauxite. With Calhoun, Kaiser approached Alcoa. One short meeting later, a five-year contract was worked out. By late 1946 Permanente bought an empty aluminum plant in Tacoma, Washington. To ensure the capital necessary for expansion, Permanente went public in July 1948. Within a year the company acquired a German aluminum foil mill, which it moved piece by piece from Germany and rebuilt at the Permanente site; and a Newark, Ohio, wire, bar, and cable mill. With the latter purchase, Permanente was in the electrical-conductor business.

In November 1949 Permanente Metals became Kaiser Aluminum & Chemical Corporation, already the nation's third-largest aluminum producer. Anticipating continued growth, KACC officials began scouting for additional bauxite deposits, which they located in Jamaica. The Kaiser Bauxite Company, a Bermuda mining operation, was organized in 1950 as a wholly owned subsidiary.

KACC had barely adjusted to a peacetime economy when the United States entered the Korean War. In response to the Federal Munitions Board order to increase aluminum production, KACC acquired a $115 million loan from the War Assets Administration and expanded operations. Chalmette, Louisiana, was chosen as the site for construction of the nation's largest aluminum plant; it was the first ever to use gas as a power source. To integrate its aluminum manufacturing with aircraft production, KACC leased several war-surplus operations: an extrusion plant in Halethorpe, Maryland, in 1951; and a forgings plant in Erie, Pennsylvania, in 1954. The company bought the Erie plant outright within two years. Although the Korean War ended in 1952, the company's contacts with the government remained in place.

In March 1952, KACC signed a contract with the U.S. Air Force to design, build, and operate an aircraft-parts plant near the existing Halethorpe operation. Although the company ran into some snags at the Chalmette construction site, KACC did not slow down. By August 1954 the company announced plans to build a foil and sheet mill in Ravenswood, West Virginia. With the Ravenswood plant, Kaiser would not only be closer to the East Coast market; it would cut freight costs by two-thirds. The company was currently shipping bauxite from Louisiana to Washington state and from Washington to California to complete the production into aluminum. Kaiser's product was traveling close to 8,000 miles before it ever reached a customer. When completed in the late 1950s, Kaiser's Ravenswood plant would house one of the world's largest aluminum smelters and mills.

By the mid-1950s the foil and automobile-parts markets opened up. KACC was the third-largest U.S. aluminum producer, right on the heels of Alcoa and Reynolds Aluminum. In the basic metals market, aluminum was second only to steel. In stride with expanded business options, in 1955 Henry J. Kaiser broke ground for the Kaiser Center, in Oakland, California. From Oakland's largest new office complex, Kaiser was controlling a $1 billion industrial complex, employing 41,000 people in 96 plants.

KACC research during the 1950s was fruitful, pushing the company into new ventures. At the Halethorpe plant, KACC engineers invented a device known as a plate-stretcher, designed to keep hot sheet-aluminum from buckling. Based on the Newark plant's production of an all-aluminum electrical-conductor alloy, Kaiser moved into the electrical-power industry. In 1957 the company acquired a wire and cable plant in Bristol, Rhode Island, which produced a greater variety of conductors than any other plant in the United States. The same year a Kaiser chemist devised a method of manufacturing cry-

olite, a compound necessary to the aluminum-reduction process. Naturally occurring cryolite was found only in Greenland, and the synthetic product had been available only from European suppliers. After pilot projects, Kaiser built a successful cryolite-manufacturing plant in Mulberry, Florida, thus freeing itself from dependence on foreign suppliers. At a newly constructed alumina plant in Gramercy, Louisiana, Kaiser chemists produced chlorine in the aluminum reduction process. The company, therefore, moved into chlorine sales.

Other significant aluminum product developments were the production of an alloy used to manufacture automobile bumpers, and a malleable corrugated roofing material, both popular sellers. More importantly, Kaiser designed a two-piece aluminum can, an industry first, and copyrighted Kalcolor, an aluminum-coloring technique imparted by an electrochemical process during the production of the metal.

By 1955 after barely 15 years in business, KACC was budgeting more than $3 million for research in metallurgy, chemical products, and electrical products. The corporation was growing too quickly for Henry J. Kaiser to hand-pick candidates and promote them. On the advice of KACC president Donald Rhoades, KACC took on several development specialists to implement an internal promotion plan.

After the boom of the 1950s, Kaiser reorganized, decentralizing into five major divisions: products, metals, industrial, electric conductor, and international. Separate sales teams worked to keep the growing supply of aluminum and related products moving.

With increased competition causing a drop in aluminum prices, overseas expansion seemed the next logical step. The Kaiser International division was organized to investigate aluminum opportunities worldwide; by 1959 it had launched offices in Zürich, London, and Buenos Aires. By year-end 1960 KACC announced completed negotiations for the purchase and construction of plants in London, South America, Central America, and Spain. In all of these international acquisitions, KACC maintained partnership relations.

Two significant partnerships were established at this time. In 1960 Kaiser teamed up with Consolidated Zinc to form Commonwealth Aluminium Corporation, Ltd. Commonwealth Aluminium began construction on fully integrated aluminum production facilities in New Zealand and Australia, site of the world's largest bauxite deposits. Kaiser also headed, with a 90% interest, the Volta Aluminium Company, Ltd., of Ghana. The massive project, which was first discussed in 1958, included construction of a port, a dam, a bauxite mine, an aluminum smelter, as well as transportation and housing facilities. By 1967, Volta's operations were in full swing and Kaiser had expanded, establishing aluminum fabricating plants in Canada; Europe, including Germany, France, Belgium, Switzerland, Norway, Turkey, and Sweden; and Thailand.

Thomas J. Ready, with KACC since 1946, was named president in 1963. On the domestic front, in 1965 Kaiser built a plant in Norco, Louisiana, to supply material for the aluminum reduction process, and a forgings plant in Oxnard, California. Through a separate division managing the manufacture and sales of highway products, KACC operated plants in Indiana, Florida, Washington, New York, California, and Utah. To manufacture its all-aluminum can, in 1968, KACC opened a plant in Union City, California. Immediate sales prompted construction of similar plants in Florida, New Jersey, and Texas.

To insulate Kaiser against the dramatic ups and downs of the aluminum market, Ready pushed to diversify. Kaiser's chemical division expanded into fluorocarbons, used to manufacture aerosol products, and urethane foamed plastics. By 1966 the company had secured the nation's largest aerosol account. Related acquisitions included the Standard Magnesium & Chemical Company of Oklahoma and Southern Nitrogen Company of Georgia. Through the Southern Nitrogen purchase, Kaiser moved into production and sales of agricultural chemicals such as fertilizer, pesticides, and cattle feed. KACC's 1967 purchase of Texada Mines, Ltd. further extended the company's holdings of phosphate deposits, iron, and other raw materials needed to keep Southern Nitrogen at the forefront in industrial chemicals.

When Henry J. Kaiser died in 1967, he left his son Edgar F. Kaiser as chairman of the board. At that time KACC controlled 196 plants in 34 states and 50 foreign countries. Employees numbered 90,000 while sales exceeded $2 billion.

With the formation of Kaiser Trading Company, in 1964, a wholly owned subsidiary, the firm entered the commodities business. Through a partnership with Aetna Life and Casualty Company KACC bought real estate in the United States, Australia, and Guam. Both ventures realized profits by 1970. Other new markets entered under Ready were in the nickel, shipping, and refractories industries.

Cornell C. Maier, an electrical engineer with KACC since 1949, succeeded Ready in 1972. Maier tackled pricing, always a thorn in the aluminum industry's side. As reported in *Business Week,* February 5, 1972, Maier set forth a price escalation policy "designed to prevent further erosion of profits due to increasing costs." Before Maier's system, aluminum producers booked all orders for a given year at a fixed rate, regardless of price increases during that year.

Ready's decision to diversify into agricultural and industrial chemicals panned out in 1974; non-aluminum sales accounted for nearly half the company's pretax profits. The combination of a drop in aluminum prices and a recession, however, caused Kaiser profits to dwindle quickly. Maier acted fast, unloading the nickel, shipping, and some chemical holdings, as well as some real estate.

With energy costs high and opportunities low in the United States, Kaiser once again looked to Europe for possibilities. Several partnerships, initiated in the early 1970s, resulted in the 1979 formation of Kaiser Aluminium Europe, a wholly owned subsidiary, and the construction of a new fabricating plant in Wales. Kaiser announced plans to build a new smelter in Queensland, Australia.

By the early 1980s aluminum industry prices hit record lows; soaring energy bills nearly doubled production costs. To combat the energy crunch, Kaiser invested in energy-saving heat-recovery equipment in its Louisiana plants, and modernized its Newark, Ohio, bar and cable plant. New projects were energy related. Kaiser invested $40 million in an oil exploration subsidiary, Kaiser Energy, Incorporated, and bought an aluminum-scraps reclamation plant in Indiana. Kaiser's industrial-chemicals division bought Filtrol Corporation, a petroleum refining business, in the effort to move into specialized alumina.

During the early 1980s aluminum prices fell yet again. With a backlog of supply and no expected increase in the automobile-consuming public, no increase in the demand for aluminum could be expected. In 1982 A. Steven Hutchcraft Jr. was elected president, and Maier, then chairman of the board, wasted no time in responding to this downturn. KACC cut labor and production by 50% at the Mead, Washington, and Ravenswood, West Virginia, plants, and idled one-third of aluminum production in Louisiana.

By the mid-1980s KACC divested at every level: the company sold a 45% stake in Commonwealth; the refractories and fertilizer businesses; and Kaiser International, its trading firm. Blocking an attempted takeover, in first quarter 1987 KACC was reorganized as a subsidiary of KaiserTech Limited, a holding company. KaiserTech divestitures included Kaiser Aluminium Europe to Hoogovens, and Kaiser Energy to Presidio Oil. In October 1988 KaiserTech was acquired by MAXXAM Group Inc., a subsidiary of MAXXAM Inc. MAXXAM was considerably smaller than KaiserTech, and following the acquisition MAXXAM's sales shot up. In 1987 MAXXAM's sales had been $34.6 million, primarily on sales of lumber and related products and real estate development. In 1988 sales jumped to $519.2 million, and in 1989, with KaiserTech fully acquired, sales were $2.4 billion. Kaiser Aluminum & Chemical remained a subsidiary of KaiserTech Limited, the holding company. In 1990 KaiserTech Limited was renamed Kaiser Aluminum Corporation. In 1989 KACC acquired a controlling interest in Alumina Partners of Jamaica, while selling Filtrol Corporation.

Kaiser Aluminum & Chemical Corporation enters the 1990s a smaller and more tightly run operation. Concentrating its energies on what it knows best, KACC remains a fully integrated aluminum producer, operating 20 plants in 10 states and 5 foreign countries.

Principal Subsidiaries: Alpart Farms (Jamaica), Ltd.; Alpart Jamaica Inc.; Alumina Partners of Jamaica (50%); Anglesey Aluminium Limited (U.K.); Kaiser Alumina Australia Corporation; Kaiser Aluminium Europe (U.K.) Limited; Kaiser Aluminium International, Inc.; Kaiser Aluminum & Chemical International N.V. (Netherlands Antilles); Kaiser Aluminum & Chemical of Canada Limited; Kaiser Aluminum Properties, Inc.; Kaiser Aluminum Technical Services, Inc.; Kaiser Bauxite Company; Kaiser Center, Inc.; Kaiser Center Properties (50%); Kaiser Finance Corporation; Kaiser Jamaica Bauxite Company; Kaiser Jamaica Corporation (50%); Oxnard Forge Die Company Inc.; Queensland Alumina Limited (Australia); Strombus International Insurance Company, Ltd. (Bermuda); Trochus Insurance Company Limited (Bermuda); Volta Aluminum Company Limited (Ghana).

Further Reading: Lyons, Leonard, "Unforgettable Henry J. Kaiser," *The Reader's Digest,* April 1968; Stein, Mimi, *A Special Difference,* Oakland, California, Kaiser Aluminum & Chemical Corporation, 1980.

—Frances E. Norton

KAWASAKI STEEL CORPORATION

Hibiya Kokusai Building
2-3, Uchisaiwaicho 2-chome
Chiyoda-ku, Tokyo 100
Japan
(03) 3597-3111
Fax: (03) 3597-4868

Public Company
Incorporated: 1950
Employees: 18,128
Sales: ¥1.11 trillion (US$8.17 billion)
Stock Exchanges: Tokyo Osaka Nagoya Sapporo Niigata Kyoto
  Hiroshima Fukuoka Frankfurt

Among the world's top steel producers is Kawasaki Steel Corporation, ranked third among Japan's producers of raw steel. Kawasaki Steel had begun to diversify and in 1991 intended to raise nonsteel production to almost half its total output by the turn of the century. The company does not plan to stray far from products that have some connection with the core industry that has seen it grow to gigantic proportions in the post-World War II period. The magnitude of Kawasaki's expectations for the continuing strength of its steel business can be gauged by references to steel as its primary money-maker furnishing the wherewithal for development and sustenance of its add-on businesses. Steel provided approximately 80% of the company's income at the time Kawasaki announced its intent to build nonsteel activity; engineering and construction services and chemical products supplied the other 20%. The company's plans anticipate that by 2000, nonsteel enterprises, which were intended to include electronics, information and communications services, materials, and realty development enterprises, will amount to about 40% of business. The bulk of Kawasaki's research-and-development activities and new products continue to focus on steel production and improved manufacturing techniques and facilities. Raw steel, as well as steel plates and sheets, the company's most prominent products, continue to fill a strong market demand.

Kawasaki's technological leadership, sensitivity to market dynamics, and willingness to look abroad for the solutions to productivity problems are some of the aspects of the long-term corporate philosophy underlying the company's rapid and fairly consistent growth. Those characteristics have provided staying power for the company through difficult periods of supply shortages, stock market repercussions, and monetary fluctuations.

The Kawasaki name and business leadership date back many decades beyond Kawasaki Steel Corporation's date of incorporation in 1950—more than 70 years. With the restoration of the Japanese empire under the Meiji dynasty in 1868, Japan had begun to wrest itself from the centuries of economic and cultural isolation that had been imposed by the Tokugawa shogunate's long-term regime. Despite some opposition to adopting the new notions that Western nations were communicating to Japan, the new emperor and the nobles in his court were not only receptive but eager to learn and adopt those they considered promising.

Among the sweeping changes the new regime made in the business sector was the transfer of companies owned by the government to ownership by individuals. In April 1878, ten years into the Meiji regime, Shozo Kawasaki was able to acquire the proprietorship of a government-established shipbuilding business. The site, Tokyo Bay, was propitious. Tokyo business had begun a new era of prosperity since the Meiji emperor had selected Tokyo as Japan's capital.

War broke out with China in 1894, making shipbuilding an essential industry. In October 1896 the company was reorganized as the Kawasaki Dockyard Co., Ltd. Within eight years the Japanese fleet had become so strong that when war with Russia was declared in 1904, the fleet challenged the Russian fleet and the following year, destroyed it in the Battle of Tsushima Strait.

As the company grew, new facilities were added. The Hanshin works began to manufacture flat rolled steel. In May 1906 the Hyogo works began to manufacture steel castings. Eleven years later, the Fukuai works opened to produce ship plates. Shipbuilding and steel production again became essential industries, and Japan took an active role in World War I. Emerging on the victorious side, Japan began a domestic public works program that created a new market for steel and steel products. The aftermath of the Great Kantu Earthquake of 1923 eventually diverted some of these materials to a long-term rebuilding effort. In 1924 the Hanshin works produced Japan's first batch of thin-gauge sheet steel.

Kawasaki Dockyard grew to gigantic proportions during the 1930s, as the country again geared for war and became actively engaged, first in Manchuria, and in 1941 in World War II. Like other Japanese industries, the company was devastated when the nation was defeated, and had to begin a rebuilding process with the help of the Allied occupational forces. Under the new constitution that Japan adopted in 1949, the company could no longer resume its prewar status as a member of a *zaibatsu,* or conglomerate. Instead, two new entities were created: Kawasaki Heavy Industries, Ltd. and Kawasaki Steel Corporation.

On August 7, 1950, Kawasaki Steel Corporation began to function, on a much smaller scale and without the benefit of the advanced technology that had created a reputation for quality in production. Starting the business without a single blast furnace, Yataro Nishiyama, the company's first president, had to negotiate with competing companies to obtain pig iron. The pig iron was melted in Kawasaki's open hearth furnaces and rolled into ingot steel on outmoded equipment, but the new enterprise managed to remain competitive despite these early difficulties. Within a year, Kawasaki Steel was able to start constructing a new blast furnace on a landfill at its Chiba works. The blast furnace, put into operation in June 1953, brought an increase in the momentum of productivity that continued throughout the ensuing decades.

To keep its competitive edge, based on early use of new technology, Kawasaki Steel devoted considerable effort to modernizing its plants and increasing its production capacity. In 1966 Ichiro Fujimoto succeeded Nishiyama as president. In April 1967 a new blast furnace at the company's Mizushima works created an upsurge in the company's productivity. Expansion continued at Mizushima works through April 1973, greatly increasing the capacity of the Mizushima works.

The prospect of worldwide shortages of energy and raw materials in the early 1970s motivated Kawasaki Steel to look for new resources overseas. In March 1974 the company entered into a joint venture with Finsider, of Italy, and Siderbrás, of Brazil, to form a Brazilian slab production company, Companhia Siderurgica de Tubarao. As new Kawasaki Steel president Eiro Iwamura took office in 1977, the company was in the process of acquiring Philippine Sinter Corporation on the island of Mindanao.

Five years later, Yasuhiro Yagi was installed as Kawasaki Steel's president; in 1990 he became chairman of the board, and Shinobu Tosaki was named president. Modernization of the company's two main plants had become an ongoing process in the 1980s, as the company's growth reflected the efficacy of using advanced technology. Three years after the Chiba works underwent a complete renovation, that plant's production of raw steel passed the cumulative ten-million-ton mark.

Kawasaki Steel continued to acquire subsidiaries and enter into joint ventures around the globe in the early 1980s, acquiring, for example, a sizable interest in California Steel Industries, which began to absorb some of the slab production of Companhia Siderurgica de Tubarao. This time the motivation for acquiring new interests was to gain a share of some of the better markets for steel products.

In the mid-1980s, a worldwide slump in the steel markets coupled with rising costs of labor and production caused Kawasaki Steel to enter into a major retrenchment program, cutting back on production, on operating facilities, and on personnel during a two-year period. In fiscal year 1987 Kawasaki Steel lost money. In fiscal year 1988, the company's books were again showing a profit.

At the same time Kawasaki introduced the cutbacks in steel production and plant operation, the company entered into an ambitious diversification plan. An agreement with Armco Inc. culminated in joint operation and ownership of a carbon steel company. In the late 1980s and early 1990s, Kawasaki Steel rapidly entered a variety of other businesses, manufacturing permanent magnets, semiconductors, silicon wafers, and fiber-reinforced plastic sheets. After forming Clef, a biotech-nology company, plans were announced to enter the cable television business.

By 1990 the company's research-and-development facilities had grown in size and complexity to accommodate research in a wide number of fields. New products introduced by Kawasaki Steel included a laser-beam fingerprint detector and a catalytic converter made of stainless steel foil. The possibilities of manufacturing large-scale integrated circuits, magnetic materials, and injection-molded powder-metallurgy parts were being explored, and the research center staff worked closely with the engineering and marketing staff.

As Shinobu Tosaki assumed the company's presidency in mid-1990, Kawasaki Steel's steel operations were generating unprecedented cash flow, its engineering business was flourishing, the new businesses were reportedly getting "on their feet," and capital spending was again on the rise, indicating optimism about the company's plans for future development.

Principal Subsidiaries: Kawasho Corporation; Kawasaki Refractories Co., Ltd.; Kawatetsu Mining Co., Ltd.; Mizushima Ferro-Alloy Co., Ltd.; Mizushima Joint Thermal Power Co., Ltd.; Philippine Sinter Corporation; Chita Pipe Fitting Co., Ltd.; Daiwa Steel Corporation; Hanshin Metal Machining Co., Ltd.; Kawaden Co., Ltd.; Kawasaki Thermal Systems Inc.; Kawatetsu Container Co., Ltd.; Kawatetsu Electrical Steel Co., Ltd.; Kawatetsu Galvanizing Co., Ltd.; Kawatetsu Instruments Co., Ltd.; Kawatetsu Kizai Kogyo Co., Ltd.; Kawatetsu Kozai Kogyo Kaisha, Ltd.; Kawatetsu Metal Industry Co., Ltd.; Kawatetsu Steel Product Corporation; Kawatetsu Steel Tube Co., Ltd.; Kawatetsu Wire Products Co., Ltd.; Kohnan Steel Center Co., Ltd.; River Building Materials Co., Ltd.; River Steel Co., Ltd.; Shikoku Iron Works Co., Ltd.; Tohoku Steel Corporation; Toyohira Seiko Co., Ltd.; California Steel Industries, Inc. (U.S.A.); Chiba Riverment and Cement Corporation; Kawasaki Enterprises Inc.; Kawasaki Steel Systems R&D Corporation; Kawasaki Steel Techno-research Corporation; Kawatetsu Civil Engineering Co., Ltd.; Kawatetsu Electric Engineering Co., Ltd.; Kawatetsu Engineering, Ltd.; Kawatetsu Real Estate Co., Ltd.; Kawatetsu Systems Development Corporation; Kawatetsu Transportation Co., Ltd.; Kawatetsu Warehouse Co., Ltd.; K&D Fine Chemical Co., Ltd.; KX Corporation; Kobe Catering Co., Ltd.; Mizushima Riverment Corp.; NBK Corporation; Nihon Semiconductor Inc.; Nihon UGIMAG Corporation; Nihon Yupro Co., Ltd.; Rifine Co., Ltd.; Saikai Industry Co., Ltd.

Further Reading: Kawasaki Steel Corporation: Ushering in radical innovations in diverse areas, Tokyo, Kawasaki Steel Corporation, 1989.

—Betty T. Moore

KLÖCKNER
WERKE AG

KLÖCKNER-WERKE AG

Klöcknerstrasse 29
Postfach 10 08 53
D-4100 Duisburg
Federal Republic of Germany
(203) 39 61
Fax: (203) 396 35 35

Public Company
Incorporated: 1897 as Lothringer Hütten– und
    Bergwerksverein
Employees: 34,793
Sales: DM8.04 billion (US$5.38 billion)
Stock Exchanges: Berlin Bremen Düsseldorf Frankfurt
    Hamburg Hanover Munich Stuttgart

Klöckner-Werke AG of Duisburg is a leader in three industrial fields: steel, machinery, and plastics. In 1989 the company was the ninth-largest iron and steel concern in West Germany and ranked 23rd-largest in the European Economic Community. Besides the production and processing of iron and steel, Klöckner-Werke AG also specializes in the construction of machinery for mining and for the food and drink industries, electric power production, and the manufacture of plastics for packaging and automobile parts.

Its history has been closely linked with that of the international trading and industrial services company of Klöckner & Co. established in 1906 and since 1988 known as Klöckner & Co. AG, also based in Duisburg and with its head offices in the Klöcknerhaus there. Klöckner & Co., created with the intention of providing a link between producers and users of coal, iron, and steel, has acted almost throughout as a holding company for Klöckner-Werke AG. The founder of both companies was Peter Klöckner, members of whose family have played major parts in the development of the two organizations.

Klöckner-Werke AG's story begins in 1897. By that time Peter Klöckner, one of the outstanding personalities of German industry and commerce in the first half of the 20th century, had already taken preliminary steps towards the fulfillment of his ambition: to build his own self-contained trading organization integrating the three basic industries of coal mining, iron and steel production, and steel-processing. After 20 years spent as an employee, learning the commercial aspects of the iron and steel business, Klöckner had set about rescuing ailing industrial companies, in the role of shareholder

and board member. One such firm was the Eisen-und Stahlwerk Haspe AG, of which he became a director in 1894 and chairman in 1899. Its history was to be intertwined with that of Klöckner-Werke AG.

The forerunner of Klöckner-Werke AG was another iron and steel company that Klöckner found in need of rehabilitation, the Lothringer Bergwerks- und Hüttenverein Aumetz-Friede AG, founded in 1897. This company owned coal mines and a blast furnace at Kneuttingen, in Alsace-Lorraine, at that time German territory. In 1903 Peter Klöckner joined the board of the Lothringer Bergwerks- und Hüttenverein Aumetz-Friede AG, becoming chairman in 1913. He reorganized and expanded the firm, making it one of the largest and most modern production complexes in Europe at the time. In 1911 he ensured its energy base by adding to it the Victor and Ickern coal mines at Castrop-Rauxel. The years leading up to World War I saw Germany in a phase of rapid industrialization and, with the pig-iron, rolled steel, and wire products of the Haspe and Kneuttingen works, the trading house Klöckner & Co. was able to take the opportunities presented by a strong domestic demand.

At the end of World War I the Kneuttingen works in Lorraine were lost to the Lothringer Bergwerks- und Hüttenverein Aumetz-Friede company, when the region was returned to France. Undaunted by this setback, Peter Klöckner started at once on a reconstruction process that was to lead to the founding of Klöckner-Werke AG in 1923. In 1920 Eisen-und Stahlwerk Haspe AG, Peter Klöckner's first protégé, signed an operating agreement with the Lothringer Bergwerks- und Hüttenverein, and in 1923 it merged with that company's legal successor, Klöckner-Werke AG, of which it became a subsidiary.

With Klöckner-Werke AG Peter Klöckner had now achieved the construction of his own new industrial group. It possessed coal mines at Castrop-Rauxel, Königsborn, and Werne, and iron and steel works and processing factories at Hagen-Haspe, Georgsmarienhütte, Osnabrück, Troisdorf, Düsseldorf, and Quint, all supplying goods for the trading activities of Klöckner & Co. Later he added to Klöckner-Werke AG a large automobile and engineering organization, Humboldt-Deutz-Motoren AG, that had been produced by the merging of the engine factory of Deutz with the Humboldt engineering works and the Oberursel car factory. Humboldt-Deutz-Motoren AG merged in turn in 1936 with Magirus of Ulm, which made lorries and firefighting equipment, to become in 1938 Klöckner-Humboldt-Deutz AG (KHD), of Cologne, an almost fully-owned subsidiary of Klöckner-Werke AG. This subsidiary was to be split off from Klöckner-Werke AG after World War II as a result of the Allied decartelization policy, going to Klöckner & Co., which in 1953 became its main shareholder. KHD has been independent of Klöckner & Co. AG for several years.

During the 1920s, in the face of limitations imposed on German industry by the aftermath of war and the lasting effects of the Treaty of Versailles, Klöckner-Werke AG continued under its founder to expand its coal and iron and steel activities. It also diversified, embarking on the manufacture of coal byproducts and buying a 50% interest in a factory producing synthetic fertilizers.

Political and economic instability at home, as well as the world Depression, set limits to the growth of German industries in the 1930s. National defense requirements afforded the steel industry some protection from the worst effects of the economic crisis, but at one point Klöckner-Werke AG's Georgsmarienhütte and its steelworks at Haspe were working only a month at a time, each in turn, in order to avoid complete closure.

In 1937 Peter Klöckner's son-in-law, Günter Henle, joined the board of directors of Klöckner-Werke AG and took up a post first at the Osnabrück works and then at the Duisburg headquarters. He inherited the leadership of the Klöckner groups when his father-in-law died in 1940, but about a year later he was removed from his offices and duties, apart from those of Klöckner & Co. in Duisburg, by the Nazi authorities. He did not return to the Klöcknerhaus until January 1947, having been imprisoned for nine months by the British, who took over the running of the group's business when they occupied Duisburg, in succession to the U.S. forces after the end of the war.

In the meantime, although the steelworks at Haspe had remained more or less intact, much of the rest of Klöckner-Werke AG's property, including the mines at Castrop-Rauxel and Troisdorf, had been badly damaged by Allied air raids. KHD's Oberursel automobile factory had been dismantled and its premises used as a repair-shop for Allied vehicles. Large numbers of Klöckner-Werke AG's staff housing units had been destroyed or damaged.

Restarting the shattered production systems was a huge task, and conditions were inauspicious. Much plant was damaged beyond repair and raw materials were in short supply. In addition the company, like the rest of the German coal-and-steel firms during the Allied occupation, had to cope with the organizational problems posed by Allied Control Commission restrictions. These were based on an overall policy of deconcentration or *Entflechtung,* aimed at reversing the trend that had produced such large self-contained organizations as the Klöckner combination.

The management of mines was taken from their owners, separated from that of factories, and in Klöckner-Werke AG's operating area put under the control of the British-run North German Coal Control. In the iron and steel divisions of firms, owners' rights were also suspended and assigned to the North German Iron and Steel Control, which in a trust management system introduced in 1947 obliged iron and steel firms to break up into single companies with a capital of no more than 100,000 reichsmarks. Klöckner-Werke AG's management board in Duisburg was removed from office and not allowed contact with the works. The Haspe, Osnabrück, and Georgsmarienhütte steel works were broken up into small companies as prescribed. The new parent holding company for these new independent individual works—the mines, three steelworks, and four finishing factories—had to drop the respected name of Klöckner-Werke AG for the simple Klöckner.

Klöckner-Werke AG and KHD were required to sever their connections with each other. Therefore in 1953, Klöckner-Werke AG ceased to be a holding company for KHD and handed over this role to Klöckner & Co. Klöckner & Co., for its part, had to divest itself of its shareholding in Klöckner-Werke AG, which it had previously controlled jointly with Peter Klöckner's Dutch holding company Handelsmaatschappij Montan N.V. of the Hague. The Dutch firm then became the main shareholder of Klöckner-Werke AG's fragmented successor, Klöckner.

In the course of the 1950s the Klöckner companies' fortunes revived. Postwar economic reconstruction and the rapid growth of the market for consumer durables created a strong demand for steel. The regulations that had been imposed by the Allied Control Commission were gradually being relaxed. The various independent companies into which the *Entflechtung* policy had split Klöckner-Werke AG were gathered back into one unit, with their assets returning to the parent company, which in 1954 had resumed its old name Klöckner-Werke AG. From being temporarily a mere holding company it reverted to being a self-contained production company.

In 1957 Günter Henle resumed his chairmanship of Klöckner-Werke AG. In the same year the new Klöckner-Werke AG steel works in Bremen, planned since 1952 and costing DM1 billion, was ready to come onstream with an annual capacity of seven million tons of raw steel. It was the first steelworks in the country to be built on a coastal site, and it had three Siemens-Martin furnaces and a rolling mill. In 1958 a hot strip mill was added, followed in 1959 by the first blast furnace and three more Siemens-Martin furnaces. When in 1966 a larger furnace was blown in, or set in action for the first time, the works became one of the most modern steel installations in Europe.

Even during the boom of the late 1950s and the first half of the 1960s there were already signs of overcapacity in the European steel market, indicating a need for steelmakers to develop other activities. Klöckner-Werke AG, conscious of the fact that in 1953 it had lost, with KHD, the largest and most important of the finishing works it owned, was making efforts to broaden further its original range of coal, steel, and steel processing products. In the 1950s Klöckner-Werke AG built an electric power station at Rauxel, which used coal from the company's mines to supply power to those mines and to the United Westphalia Electricity Company network. In 1955 it created Klöckner-Ferromatik GmbH at Castrop-Rauxel, which was to win a world reputation with its mine construction equipment, and at Osnabrück and in other factories it was producing fiberglass and other plastics. At the end of 1967 Klöckner-Werke AG was deriving 10% of its income from products other than coal and steel.

In 1965 Klöckner-Werke AG's coalmines were united into a mining subsidiary. There had been by then a ten-year period of growth, following the easing of postwar restrictions. While in the last full year of peace, 1938–1939, Klöckner-Werke AG's sales had totaled 245 million reichsmarks, by the business year 1964–1965 they had nearly quadrupled to a value of DM2 billion.

However, 1965 saw a downturn in West German industry and in Klöckner-Werke AG's sales. Competition was growing at home and abroad. Investment costs were rising. The then widespread implementation of new technologies such as basic oxygen steelmaking, continuous casting, and computerized control systems, had increased efficiency and quality and reduced unit production costs. The general drive was towards maximizing output, just when demand was about to fall. The year 1966 saw the collapse of the German capital markets and the failure of official economic policy. By 1973 the year of the first oil price shock, the postwar boom in steel had given way to recession, and much of the high capacity of new installations was superfluous.

The West German state tried to help combat the problems posed for the economy and the labor market by this overcapacity, offering financial inducements for mergers or cooperation deals between various big steelmakers. Klöckner-Werke AG was involved in two of these proposals, one in 1983 for a Ruhr group incorporating Hoesch, Klöckner, and Salzgitter, and another in 1984 for a merger between Klöckner and Krupp, but like the rest these proved impracticable.

The year 1974 had ushered in a decade and a half during which the Klöckner-Werke AG's shareholders would receive no dividends. Also in that year Herbert Gienow, a director since 1962, became chairman of the board of directors. During the worst years of the steel crisis of 1974–1984 and until his retirement in April 1991, Gienow oversaw the transformation of an unprofitable conglomerate still largely based on steel production and processing into an efficient and profitable manufacturing and processing triad with a reorganized steel section and a new emphasis on machinery and plastics. In the business year 1989–1990, with an operating profit of DM290 million, the company at last found itself able to pay its shareholders a dividend of DM5 per DM50 share, and with good prospects of keeping up the performance.

The background to this achievement had been unfavorable. Between 1974 and 1983 West Germany's annual raw steel production had dropped from 53 million tons to 36 million. The steel crisis was felt most strongly in the Ruhr after 1980. In 1980 Klöckner-Werke AG's finances were still in balance. Early in that year the company had raised its capital, and Klöckner & Co. acquired a 10% holding. By 1981 the company was experiencing its worst results for 30 years, and by the autumn of 1982 the Bremen factory was working at 48% capacity. Thanks to an energetic policy of cost-cutting, shift of emphasis, and development abroad, Klöckner-Werke AG, led by Gienow, was able to make a recovery.

During the 15 years of Gienow's stewardship the company, in addition to diversifying its product lines, went international. About the time he took over, it employed 35,000 people, all in Germany, and almost all producing steel in one form or another for four types of domestic customer: the automotive, engineering, mining, and construction industries. By 1991 the same number of people was deployed at 90 production points, more than half of which are outside Germany. Nearly a third of the work force is located abroad. Steel's share of sales for 1989 and 1990 was 37.5%, with engineering at 37.5%, and plastics at 25%. Of the year's total turnover of DM8.035 billion, 60% came from West Germany, 30% from other European countries, and 10% from overseas.

In the first year of the 1990s, the move towards greater reliance on engineering and plastics continued. Steel still played a major role. In the steel sector, in 1987–1988, Klöckner-Werke AG acquired 11% of NMH Stahlwerke GmbH, and in 1988–1989 it embarked on a joint venture with the Belgian firm of SIDMAR NV to build a steelworks, SIKEL NV, in Limburg, in the Netherlands; though in August 1990 it sold its Mannstaedt division at Troisdorf, making hot rolled special sections and hollow and cold formed sections, to British Steel for DM300 million. In 1988–1989, in the engineering and plastics processing sector, Klöckner-Werke AG acquired 59% of Kautex Werke Reinold Hagen AG, 60% of Kautex-Bayern GmbH, 100% of Kautex-Ostfriedland GmbH, and 98% of the

Eurotec group, the largest supplier in Europe of plastic components for the automobile industry. Also in 1988–1989, Klöckner-Werke AG increased its holding in SEN AG of West Germany, one of the world's largest manufacturers of drink vending machines.

Klöckner-Werke AG is targeting products from all its divisions at the newly liberalized East German market, with projects such as a planned takeover of the Muldenstein tube factory which, if the deal went through, would buy its raw materials from the Bremen works instead of from the Soviet Union as hitherto.

In 1989–1990 Klöckner-Werke AG increased its share capital again, by a rights issue, from DM250 million to DM458 million, and its own holding from 10% to 20%; another 25% is in the friendly hands of the Dutch firm Internationale Industriële Beleggung Maatschappij Amsterdam BV, belonging to descendants of Peter Klöckner and Günter Henle. The latter's son, Jörg A. Henle, is the present chairman of Klöckner-Werke AG's supervisory board.

DM300 million was invested in 1989–1990 in quality control assurance and in further rationalization. The group continues to aim at reducing its energy consumption and improving pollution control.

In nearly a century of existence Klöckner-Werke AG has shown an enduring ability to adapt to changing circumstances. From the coal, iron, and steel profile of its earliest days it has moved on to another triple pattern; in the 1990s the name Klöckner-Werke AG stands for "Steel—Machinery—Plastics." Under Herbert Gienow's successor as chairman of the board of directors, Hans Christoph von Rohr, who began a career spent in different Klöckner enterprises at Klöckner-Werke AG's Bremen works, the company is well prepared to find its way in the rapidly changing world landscape of industry.

Principal Subsidiaries: Klöckner-Werke Stahl OHG; Klöckner Stahl GmbH; Holstein und Kappert AG; Klöckner Ferromatic Desma GmbH; Klöckner Durilit GmbH; Klöckner Ionon GmbH; Weserport Umschlaggesellschaft mbH (99%); Klöckner Datentechnik GmbH; Klöckner-Wilhelmsburger GmbH; Klöckner Planungs-und Neubau GmbH; Klöckner Mercator Maschinenbau GmbH; SEITZ ENZIGER NOLL Maschinenbau AG (92%); H&K S.A.R.L. (France); H&K (Far East) Corporation (Japan, 75%); ALZ NV (Belgium, 15.5%): Sikel NV (Belgium, 33.3%); Kautex of Canada Inc. (Canada); Klöckner Technologie und Entwicklung GmbH; Klöckner Capital Corporation (U.S.A.)

Further Reading: Henle, Günter, *Weggenosse des Jahrhunderts,* Stuttgart, Deutsche Verlags-Anstalt, 1968; *75 Jahre Klöckner & Co 1906–1981,* Klöckner & Co, Duisburg, 1981, reprinted 1991; Hudson, Ray, and David Sadler, *The International Steel Industry,* London, Routledge, 1989; Mény, Yves and Vincent Wright, et al., *La Crise de la Sidérurgie Européenne 1974–1984,* Paris, Presses Universitaires de France, 1985.

—Olive Classe

KOBE STEEL, LTD.

KOBE STEEL, LTD.

Tekko Building
8-2, Marunouchi 1-chome
Chiyoda-ku, Tokyo 100
Japan
(03) 3218-7111
Fax: (03) 3218-6330

Public Company
Incorporated: 1911 as Kobe Steel Works, Ltd.
Employees: 21,303
Sales: ¥1.22 trillion (US$8.98 billion)
Stock Exchange: Tokyo

Kobe Steel, Ltd., is Japan's 5th-largest steelmaker, and the 15th-largest worldwide. The company markets a wide variety of iron and steel products. It is also the Japanese leader in welding rods and titanium products, and a strong competitor in rolled aluminum and copper. Kobe Steel has consistently shown a progressive edge. The company entered specialty steel markets early in its development, and was one of the first steelmakers to diversify into related markets such as machinery and plant-engineering. Kobe has also shown a keen interest in developing foreign markets; the company established offices in New York and Düsseldorf as early as 1960.

Kobe has focused on higher value-added steel products, and has expanded into high-technology industries such as computer components and bio-engineering. Kobe leads its Japanese competitors in establishing U.S. subsidiaries and joint ventures. In 1989, the company incorporated Kobe Steel Co. to administer more efficiently its growing number of U.S. enterprises. Lower demand for steel products in recent years, as well as cheaper production costs from competitors in developing countries like Brazil and Korea, have threatened steelmakers in Japan. Kobe seeks to diversify further into related fields where the company's existing expertise can be applied.

Kobe Steel was established as the Kobe Steel Works (Kobe Seikosho) in 1905 by the Japanese trading firm Suzuki and Company. In 1911 the company was incorporated as Kobe Steel Works, Ltd., with capital of ¥1.4 million. Kobe Steel Works grew over the next 15 years, as Japan's main industry, textiles, was replaced by heavier manufacturing. Although Kobe was relatively small among Japanese steelmakers, the company successfully carved a niche in the growing markets. Four new plants were added between 1917 and 1921. Capital had increased to ¥20 million.

The Great Depression that would eventually engulf the world struck Japan as early as the late 1920s. Kobe Steel Works experienced some difficult times. In 1928, ¥10 million was written off against accumulated losses, and then another ¥10 million in capital was raised to reduce debt. These measures helped the company survive the crisis. A year later, Kobe established a shipbuilding subsidiary, Harima Zosenjo, Limited.

The 1930s brought substantial changes to Japan's government and industry. A militant group of nationalists dominated Japanese politics, and the country geared up for war. In 1931 Japan entered the first of its military adventures, in Manchuria. By 1937 the country was embroiled in all-out war with China. The Japanese government encouraged rapid development of heavy industry and began to coordinate distribution of raw materials. Kobe Steel Works's production capabilities expanded over the next few years. Eight new plants opened, and two were acquired from other companies between 1937 and the end of the war in 1945. Although World War II had stimulated Japanese heavy industrial development, it also left the nation considerably weakened.

After the war, Allied forces wrote a new constitution for Japan. The old family-run *zaibatsu*, or trusts, were broken up and Japanese industry began to rebuild. In 1949, Kobe Steel Works was restructured. Its Moji and Chofu plants were spun off into a separate company, Shinko Kinzoku Kogyo Ltd., while its Toba, Yamada, Matsuzaka, and Tokyo plants formed yet another company, Shinko Electric Company, Ltd. The remaining nine plants continued to operate as Kobe Steel Works, Ltd.

During the 1950s, Japanese industry pursued rebuilding at a furious pace. The Japanese government instituted two five-year plans aimed at boosting steel production levels. Like other Japanese steelmakers, Kobe Steel Works embarked on a program of expanded production. Kobe supplied Japan's peacetime industries that produced television sets, refrigerators, and washing machines for eager consumers. A new plant was brought on line in 1951, while another was acquired from the Japanese Ministry of Finance in 1953. Several of Kobe's divisions were turned into subsidiaries to foster their own growth. In 1954 the Amagasaki plant became the Shinko Wire Company, Ltd., and the enameled products department became the Shinko Pfaudler Company, Ltd., then called Shinko Pantec Company Limited. In 1957 the construction department became Shinko Koji K.K. In 1959 the steel works in the Nadahama area in the city of Kobe was upgraded and named the Kobe works, making the company a fully integrated steel manufacturer. By that year Kobe Steel Works had capital of ¥12 billion.

The high cost of raw materials, which to a great degree had to be imported to Japan, forced Kobe—along with other Japanese steel producers—to find new ways to streamline production costs. Japanese steelmakers developed techniques to reduce the amount of coke used in production, thereby diminishing the impact of high priced imported coal. Emphasis was also placed on exporting steel to balance the cost of importing raw materials. Relatively low labor costs, new plants, and the technological superiority dictated by necessity catapulted Japan's steel industry to the top of the world steel manufacturing league. By 1960 Japan had pushed past the United Kingdom and France to become the fourth-largest producer of steel in the world, behind the United States, the Soviet Union, and West Germany. In 1964 Japanese steel production surpassed that of West Germany.

Kobe Steel Works, found a unique position among Japanese steelmakers. In 1961 it was the sixth-largest steel manufacturer in Japan. Yet Kobe was the only one of the leading eight manufacturers that did not supply steel in sheets or plate, instead focusing on steel pipes and tubing, wire rods, and specialty steels. In addition, Kobe's steel bars gained an uncommon reputation for quality over the years.

Kobe Steel Works's engineering division, first licensed in 1950, was thriving. Kobe received its first order to build a complete plant in 1958. The ¥19 billion fertilizer plant in Bangladesh was the first of dozens of plants that the engineering division would build. Kobe's machinery operations also expanded in the 1950s and 1960s. Machinery production began in the late 1930s when a demand for cutting tools and welding supplies combined with Kobe's steel stockpile to create a natural diversification.

In 1960 Kobe Steel Works, Ltd. opened liaison offices in New York and Düsseldorf to help coordinate the company's sales efforts overseas. Japanese steelmakers had the most up-to-date manufacturing facilities, low labor costs, and a desire to increase exports. China and Australia proved to be good markets for Japanese steel, but the United States became the biggest importer of steel from Japan, actually accounting for one-third of the country's steel exports. By the mid-1960s U.S. steel manufacturers began to charge Japanese exporters with dumping—selling below cost to gain market share. These charges persisted for years, but no anti-dumping legislation was introduced because evidence that Japanese domestic prices were higher, and that U.S. producers were injured by the low-priced imports, was difficult to substantiate. U.S. construction contractors and other manufacturers, meanwhile, enjoyed high quality Japanese steel at relatively low prices.

Three new plants were opened between 1961 and 1962 and an older plant was closed. In 1965 Kobe Steel Works, Ltd. merged with the Amagasaki Steel Company, Ltd., bringing three more plants into the Kobe family. One of these, the Sakai plant, was sold to Nisshin Steel a year later. Between 1966 and 1970, five more plants, including a steel-plate facility, were brought on line. By the 1970s Kobe Steel operated some of the most efficient steelmaking factories in the world.

In 1968 the two largest Japanese steelmakers, Yawata Iron & Steel and Fuji Iron & Steel, combined to form Nippon Steel, which is still the largest Japanese steel manufacturer. Kobe Steel Works was then the fifth-largest producer in the country, and competition for Japanese automobile and appliance makers' accounts remained fierce, keeping the price of domestic steel low in Japan.

The oil crisis of 1973 caused a worldwide recession that severely affected heavy manufacturing. Kobe Steel streamlined its iron and steel division and expanded its machinery division. The engineering division received two large orders for plants in 1974, cushioning the impact of the recession. Kobe's engineering division played a crucial role throughout the later 1970s, and the 1980s. Basic steel production was not ignored, however; in 1975, the new Fukuchiyama plant was opened.

Kobe Steel continued to fare well with exports. Liaison offices were opened in Singapore and Los Angeles in 1976, in Sharjah in 1977, and in London in 1978. The company's success in the United States continued to disturb U.S. manufacturers. Charges of unfair trade practices increased. In October 1977 Kobe Steel Works and the four other top Japanese steel manufacturers were accused of dumping carbon steel plate at a loss of up to US$50 per ton—32% below fair value. The Treasury Department investigated and found dumping margins of 5.4% to 18.5%. In January 1978, it was established that Kobe was selling steel at about 13.9% below fair value. The worst offender, Sumitomo Metal Industries, was found to be dumping carbon steel at 18.5% below fair value. At these percentages, actual damage to U.S. producers was not clearly evident.

Continued protests from U.S. manufacturers led to the institution of a trigger price system for steel imports. If a foreign company attempted to sell below a stipulated trigger price, an investigation could begin automatically, without the formality of a suit being filed by a U.S. company. Companies caught dumping would have to pay penalties. The system resulted in the voluntary reduction of exports of certain steel products by Japanese companies.

By the late 1970s, it was clear that global production capacity for steel was much greater than anticipated demand; the steel industry was maturing. At the same time, developing countries like Korea were producing more and more steel with the most modern plants and lower labor costs than in Japan, pressuring Japanese steel manufacturers, much as U.S. and European manufacturers had been pressured by the Japanese 15 years earlier. Kobe Steel Works reduced its emphasis on basic steel products, and began to focus on higher value-added steel products, while maintaining its efforts in machinery and engineering.

Kobe began to streamline its facilities and increase spending on energy-saving equipment in 1980. The appreciation of the yen against the dollar in the mid-1980s had a serious effect on revenues. Kobe Steel showed a net loss of US$36.7 million in 1984. Five steel plants were closed between 1984 and 1987. In December 1986 Kobe announced plans to reduce its labor force by 6,000 workers—21% of its entire staff—over a three year period. The measures were considered drastic in a country that traditionally guaranteed workers employment until retirement.

At the same time that Kobe Steel was encountering flattening demand for basic steel products, it was preparing for the future by expanding into new but related fields. In 1981 the company became the largest shareholder in a Wisconsin-based construction equipment manufacturer, the Harnischfeger Corporation. In 1983 Kobe took over the U.S. engineering company, Midrex Corporation, and its Japanese affiliate, Yutani Heavy Industries, Ltd. In 1987 Kobe began construction on a metal powders plant in the United States. Steel powders had growing use in the automotive industry. In 1988, Kobe Precision Incorporated began producing aluminum substrates for magnetic computer discs. Kobe Copper Products, a U.S. subsidiary, made copper tubing for cooling systems, and in 1989, Stewart Bolling Company, a U.S. rubber and plastic firm, was acquired.

In the late 1980s Kobe Steel entered a number of joint ventures with U.S. firms. In 1989 USX, the largest U.S. steelmaker, formed a 50–50 partnership with Kobe to produce steel bars for Japanese automakers, who were now locating their plants inside the United States. In 1990 a major joint venture with Texas Instruments was undertaken to produce application-specific integrated circuits. Plant construction began in the western Kansai region of Japan and was set for completion in 1992. Later in 1990 the Aluminum Company of America entered a 50–50 joint venture with Kobe to produce aluminum can stock in Japan. The new venture was scheduled to open in 1993.

In spite of difficult times in basic products during the mid-1980s research and development in new areas remained a priority. In 1985 Kobe opened a Biotechnology Research Laboratory in the city of Kobe. In 1987 the first phase of another major research facility, the Seishin Laboratories in Kobe, was completed. In 1988 the Kobe Steel Europe Research Laboratory in Surrey, U.K., was opened. In 1989 the Kobe Steel Research Laboratories USA–Electronics Materials Center was opened in Research Triangle Park, North Carolina, and an Applied Electronics Center was opened in 1990 in Palo Alto, California. The Palo Alto facility was soon expanded to include artificial intelligence research.

Kobe's overseas expansion had reached fever pitch in the 1980s. A new office was opened in Mexico City in 1981, and the New York City and Los Angeles offices were incorporated as Kobe Steel America Inc., later combined to form Kobe Steel USA. An office was opened in Melbourne in 1983. In 1984 the London office became the subsidiary, Kobe Steel Europe, Ltd., and the Sharjah office was moved to Bahrain and incorporated as Gulf Engineering Company Ltd., later renamed Kobelco Middle East.

In 1988 Kobe Steel America was reorganized into a holding company, Kobe Steel USA Inc., to manage Kobe's growing number of diversified U.S. holdings, which now numbered 15 companies. By placing the company's U.S. subsidiaries under one corporate roof, a quicker response to changing market conditions was made possible. Kobe was the first Japanese steelmaker to reorganize itself in this way.

Kobe entered markets previously considered impenetrable; in 1986 a liaison office was established in Beijing, and in 1989 in Moscow. In 1990 the Singapore office was incorporated as Kobe Steel Asia Pte Ltd. Also in 1990, Kobe Steel Australia Pty. Ltd., based in Sydney, absorbed the Melbourne office. By the early 1990s under President Sokichi Kametaka, Kobe Steel was well diversified both geographically and by industry and ready for growth in new areas.

Principal Subsidiaries: Ark System Co., Ltd. (60%); Cybernet Systems Co., Ltd.; Genesis Technology Inc. (32.5%); Japan Magnet Technology Inc. (60%); Kansai Coke and Chemicals Co., Ltd. (39%); Kobe Kennametal Co., Ltd. (51%); Kobelco Construction Machinery Co., Ltd.; Kobelco Research Institute Inc.; Kobelco Systems Corporation; Kobelco Telecommunications Technology Co., Ltd.; LED Corporation (80%); Nippon Air Brake Co., Ltd. (31.5%); Osaka Chain and Machinery, Ltd. (46.3%); Sakai Steel Sheet Works, Ltd. (62.5%); Sensor Technology Co., Ltd. (32%); Shinko Acteq Co., Ltd.; Shinko Airtech, Ltd.; Shinko Electric Co., Ltd. (39.6%); Shinko Engineering Co., Ltd. (48.7%); Shinko Industrial Co., Ltd. (83%); Shinko Kaiun Co., Ltd. (53.5%); Shinko Kenzai, Ltd., (84.2%); Shinko Kosan, Ltd. (44.7%); Shinko Lease Co., Ltd.; (60%); Shinko Medical Consultation Co., Ltd.; Shinko-North Co., Ltd. (95%); Shinko Pantec Co., Ltd. (91.7%); Shinko Plant Construction Co., Ltd.; Shinko Pyropower, Ltd. (60%); Shinko Wire Co., Ltd. (49.2%); Shinsho Corporation (46.2%); Sun Aluminum Industries, Ltd. (65.4%); Twin Foods Co., Ltd. (55%); Yutani Heavy Industries, Ltd. (99.1%); Durakut International Corporation (U.S.A., 66.7%); Glastic Corporation (U.S.A., 85%); Kobe Copper Products, Inc. (U.S.A., 55%); Kobe Development Corporation (U.S.A.); Kobe Precision, Inc. (U.S.A.); Kobe Steel International Inc. (U.S.A.); Kobe Steel USA Holdings Inc.; Kobe Steel USA Inc.; Kobelco America Inc. (U.S.A., 58.8%); Kobelco Compressors (America) Inc. (U.S.A., 90%); Kobelco Construction Machinery, Inc. (U.S.A.); Kobelco Metal Powder of America, Inc. (U.S.A., 70%); Kobelco Stewart Bolling, Inc. (U.S.A.); Kobelco Welding of America Inc. (U.S.A.); Komag Material Technology, Inc. (U.S.A., 45%); Midrex Corporation (U.S.A.); Operaciones al Sur del Orinoco, C.A.; QC Optics Inc.; (84%); RACET Computes, Inc. (U.S.A., 51%); Titan Steel & Wire Co., Ltd. (Canada, 28.9%); USS/Kobe Steel Company (U.S.A., 50%); Bimarco A.G. (51%); Kobe Steel Europe, Ltd. (U.K.); Kobelco Middle East (Bahrain); Midrex International B.V.; Chiaphua-Shinko Copper Alloy Co., Ltd. (Hong Kong, 30%); Earth Development Pte. Ltd. (Singapore); Kobe Copper Sdn. Bhd. (Malaysia, 70%); Kobe International Co., Pte. Ltd. (Singapore); Kobe Leadframe Singapore Pte. Ltd.; Kobe MIG Wire (Thailand) Co., Ltd. (51%); Kobe Precision Parts (Malaysia) Sdn. Bhd.; Kobe Steel Asia Pte Ltd. (Singapore); Kobe Steel Australia Pty. Ltd.; Kobe Welding (Singapore) Pte. Ltd. (62%); Singapore Kobe Pte. Ltd. (70%); Taiwan Shinko Tool Co., Ltd. (54%); Thai-Kobe Welding Co., Ltd. (Thailand, 36.7%).

Further Reading: "Little Industry, Big War," *Fortune,* April 1944; "Anatomy of an Oriental Giant," *Steel,* December 24, 1962; Yoder, Stephen Kreider, "Japan's Smokestack Industries Pin Hope on Research," *The Wall Street Journal,* March 25, 1987; "Kobe Steel Controls 15 U.S. Firms," *Purchasing,* December 15, 1988.

—Thomas M. Tucker

Hoogovens Groep

KONINKLIJKE NEDERLANDSCHE HOOGOVENS EN STAALFABRIEKEN NV

Post Office Box 10000
1970 CA IJmuiden
The Netherlands
(2550) 02514-96644
Fax: 2514 70000

Public Company
Incorporated: 1918
Employees: 27,000
Sales: Dfl 18.17 billion (US$10.78 billion)
Stock Exchange: Amsterdam

Koninklijke Nederlandsche Hoogovens en Staalfabrieken NV (Hoogovens) first came into existence just after World War I and has gradually developed into a business specializing in steel and aluminum raw materials and products. As part of the trend in the Netherlands towards self-sufficiency in vitally important products, the idea proposed by a group of prominent manufacturers, led by H.J.E. Wenckebach from 1918 to 1924, took increasingly firm hold. They set out to establish a fully integrated national iron and steel industry capable of converting pig-iron into steel products and semi-finished products. It was Wenckebach's vision, reinforced by his wide business experience, that sustained the project.

With the support of major industrialists such as the brothers, Stork, owners of a machine factory; J. Muysken, transport; H. Colijn, Royal Dutch/Shell; F.H. Fentener van Vlissingen, Steenkolen Handelsvereniging (SHV); and A.F. Philips, in the incandescent lamps industry, a large part of the capital needed was acquired by subscription. The national interest and considerations of business prestige marked the nexus of personal relations between government officials and financiers. Without the contribution of Dfl 7.5 million from the Dutch state and of Dfl 5 million from the municipality of Amsterdam, the Dfl 30 million required could not have been raised. Participation by the state proved to be of crucial importance in enabling the company to stand up to the powerful competition in Europe. The execution of the major project, a blast furnace, steel, and rolling-mill works, was spread over a lengthy period because of the rapidly rising costs. Not until 1953 was it put into full effect.

Besides financing, finding a suitable location was a significant strategic problem. The choice fell on the city of IJmuiden, owing to its favorable seaboard location, symbolized in the emblem of the enterprise, the starfish. In the Netherlands, poor in raw materials, a ready supply of imported iron ore and pit-coal was of vital importance, as was the possibility of easy export. Other locations—near Rotterdam and Moerdijk—were ruled out because of the poor structure of the local soil. However, the construction of the first blast furnaces still had to wait.

The first step was taken in 1918 in collaboration with the steel manufacturing firm of Demka at Utrecht. In 1920 a contract was concluded with the German steel business of Phoenix in Dortmund, enabling Hoogovens to convert its own pig iron into steel products at another factory. At this stage, Hoogovens was to confine itself to building two blast furnaces. A minority interest in Phoenix ensured a permanent place for Hoogovens within the European steel industry. This interest ran counter to the original plan for an independent basic industry, a conflict mitigated, however, by the resulting transfer of expertise. This dichotomy was to be Hoogovens's persisting paradox.

The production of pig iron in the first furnace began on January 24, 1924, under the control of the technical manager, A.H. Ingen Housz. The director from 1920 to 1945, G.A. Kessler, was faced with the task of placing the business on a sound economic footing. Hoogovens secured a foothold in the pig-iron export market by maintaining direct contact with its customers. It could deliver a high-quality product at a low price. On the domestic market, growth in turnover was explosive. The volume of business rose from a quarter of the domestic pig iron market in the first year of production to three-quarters in 1934.

Production costs were kept under control by the utilization of various by-products. In 1928, the fertilizer factory, Mekog, was launched, in conjunction with Royal Dutch/Shell, for the consumption of coking-oven gas. In 1930 the cement factory, Cemij, a subsidiary enterprise, was formed in collaboration with ENCI, to produce blast furnace sealants. By this means a competitive war between the Dutch cement producers Hoogovens and ENCI was prevented, and independence from foreign competition achieved. Compared with pig iron turnover, sales of by-products were stable, and were sufficient to cover Hoogovens's fixed expenses.

To strengthen Hoogovens's position on the domestic market, a steel study center was set up, in cooperation with the Dutch authorities, which resulted in a steel plan. The steel plan had become necessary in view of the recession affecting—in the first instance—participation in the Vereinigte Stahlwerke (German Consolidated Steelworks). Demand for pig iron declined. Meanwhile, from 1936 onward, demand for raw steel and steel semi-finished products was very much on the increase, making it feasible to start building a steel factory. In 1939 steel production began at the Siemens-Martin factory. The age of iron was over. Consequently, the twin-headed directorate was expanded to include a doctor of economics, M.W. Holtrop, later to become director of De Nederlandse Bank. In 1940 the turnover of pig iron amounted to Dfl 10.2 million, of by-products Dfl 3.1 million, of steel Dfl 7.1 million, and of tubing Dfl 1 million.

A dividend was paid to shareholders for the first time in 1939. The large scale of investments, along with the devaluation of the monetary value of the part-holding in Vereinigte Stahlwerke necessitated a strict internal policy regarding costs. Thanks to considerable credits from the Nederlandse Handel

Maatschappij (Dutch Trading Company) and Royal Dutch/ Shell, the crisis of the 1930s was surmounted. Yet up to 1940 Hoogovens was still no more than a moderate-sized enterprise compared to the steel giants of Europe.

During World War II, more than 50% of Hoogovens's shares were assigned to an Office of Administration in order to enable Hoogovens as a group of interested parties to resist excessive German infiltration. It worked. During the war, Hoogovens took over B. Van Leer's roller business. Until then Hoogovens had had its semi-finished products made in the rolling-mills of Demka and Van Leer.

Social responsibilities were a primary concern for Hoogovens's board, and a social department was established. After a difficult start, accompanied by strikes, good labor relations were important to the employers' association. There was no strict hierarchy. The cooperation of a flexible, informed, and dedicated work force determined the free and easy organizational structure. Team spirit was reinforced by the technical character of the business and the hard physical work. Staff associations were encouraged and training, both general and technical, was carried out within the factory. In 1926 a social fund, the Wenckebach Fund, was created for the benefit of the staff. Pension funds followed, in 1929 for executives, and in 1938 for the work force.

Foremost during the early postwar years was the Breedband project, which included the construction of a hot strip mill, cold band, and tinning installations. The tinplate surface inspectors in the tinning mills were the first women production assistants in a traditionally men's occupation. The Breedband rolling-mills were financed by a contribution of Dfl 150 million from the state, within the framework of its industrial policy, Dfl 23.5 million of which came from Marshall Plan aid. The subsidiary, set up in 1950 as Breedband NV, in which Hoogovens itself invested Dfl 60 million, was fully incorporated in the blast furnace business in 1964 when Hoogovens purchased the state's shares. To put into effect the integration of furnaces, steel factory, and rolling-mills, management was from the outset in the hands of Hoogovens. During this period engineer Ingen Housz was in charge.

Hoogovens's share of output in the European Coal and Steel Community rose from 1.1% in 1952 to 3.4% in 1967. New production methods followed in rapid succession. In 1958 the oxysteel factory went into production. The process entailed blowing oxygen into liquid pig iron, by which process the carbon was burned off and steel obtained. From the beginning in 1924 it had been necessary to operate, whatever the state of the market, in a factory in a constant state of reconstruction; technical innovation was of crucial importance. In 1980 the continuous casting machine was introduced, realizing a continuous output of steel for slabs.

Hoogovens has been managed since 1961 by a five-member directorate. The directorate, known since 1965 as the board of directors, had proceeded on the policy of previous directors. Company programs included profit-sharing for personnel, 1949, the introduction of an industrial council, 1957, uniform conditions of labor for workers and salaried staff, 1966, and a comprehensive program of training, accommodation, and recreation. As a rule, half the personnel had been involved in in-house training schemes. Without well-trained steel workers, Hoogovens could not have kept pace with technological developments.

By 1971 Hoogovens's activities were no longer restricted to steel production. The Hoogovens concern had established its present structure with the acquisition of subsidiaries in the aluminum, oil and gas, and coal sectors. In 1966 the board voted in favor of collaborating with the German steel firm of Hoesch in Dortmund, in the belief that this cooperation would take the companies into joint position among the top ten steel enterprises in Europe. Hoogovens had a 15% share in Hoesch. According to the chairman of the board of directors, P.L. Justman Jacob, this collaboration was a good thing for Hoogovens. All the same, mergers across the frontiers struck him, in 1968, as "damned difficult." In 1972 Hoogovens IJmuiden and Hoesch Dortmund, the main industrial plants of the respective companies, amalgamated to form the steel firm of Estel, taking them to fourth place in Europe. Yet only 25% of turnover was achieved on the domestic market. The shipment of raw materials and products to and from its own port, the largest in the Netherlands after Rotterdam and Amsterdam, made Hoogovens a desirable partner in a merger.

After the worldwide economic crisis of 1973 came the 1975 European steel crisis. Schemes for curbing the overproduction of steel in Europe made it essential that Hoogovens keep abreast of technology. Only modern businesses that could provide a high quality product at a low price would survive. The much criticized Maasvlakte project—involving the establishment of a second blast furnace concern in Rotterdam—was then abandoned. By May 25, 1983, Hoogovens had produced 100 million tons of steel since 1939. The one million frontier had been crossed in 1958.

After seven years of crisis in the steel industry and handicapped by governmental financial support given to its European competitors, Estel was no longer strong enough financially to carry out independently a restructuring of—in particular—the steel business in Dortmund. Among the last steel enterprises in the European Economic Community (EEC) to ask for assistance from a government, Estel requested help from the German and Dutch authorities. The conditions laid down by the German authorities meant that the merger between Hoesch Dortmund and Hoogovens would have to be terminated. What Justman Jacob had anticipated in 1968 came to pass. The crisis in steel and the government subsidies of other European steelworks, as well as differences in national industrial policies, made a binational undertaking unworkable.

In 1981 the European Commission ruled that any offer of support must be dependent on a commitment to reduction in capacity and a program of restructuring. This would result in a recovery of earning power. Production and pricing agreements, imposed by Brussels, have controlled the European steel industry since 1980. Through the closure of Demka and curtailment of hot strip mill production, Hoogovens contributed more than its share towards putting the EEC steel industry on a sound footing. As a result, in 1982 Hoogovens developed a strategy for the years 1982 to 1985.

The strategy was then focused on diversifying activities in steel manufacture, maintaining low price levels, and raising productivity. An extensive investment program, centered on the steel business, was intended to be one-third financed by the Dutch government. The viability of the Hoogovens business was evident from the fact that other European steel concerns received considerably greater government support. Again, the company had no trouble obtaining money from the capital market, owing to the soundness of its planning and support from the Dutch government.

Over the period 1974 to 1985, as one of the few large integrated steel businesses in the EEC, Hoogovens was able to limit cuts in staffing to 22%. This took place without forced dismissals, through natural attrition and retraining. The industrial council had from the start opposed any loss of jobs. The management made it a point of policy. Hoogovens's commitment to reducing job cuts, as far as possible, corresponded to the government's wishes. The state with 14% and the city of Amsterdam with 6% had initially owned a fifth of Hoogovens's shares.

After 1984 the state of the steel market improved, enabling Hoogovens as one of the primary European steel concerns to become profitable again. Hoogovens diversified in an attempt to become less dependent on the cyclical movement in steel. The aluminum division was expanded substantially in 1987 by the takeover of several German firms. All the same, Hoogovens remained a medium-sized business in which 4.5% of EEC steel production was concentrated. Liberalizing of the steel market could lead to a rise in production for export-oriented business.

In the early 1990s Hoogovens's aim had been to concentrate on its core activities, steel and aluminum, at expense of secondary activities. In 1988 the Noordwinning Group, in natural gas, and in 1989 the cement factory and the cable factory were sold off. As a result, Hoogovens became a two-metal concern, with the aluminum sector accounting for 30% of the turnover. Growing environmental and technical requirements had resulted in Hoogovens's developing into a supplier of flue-gas desulfurizing installations. On his retirement in 1988 the departing director, J.D. Hooglandt, summed up the current strategy: "not more steel, but doing more with it."

Principal Subsidiaries: Hoogovens Groep BV; Hoogovens IJmuiden; Hoogovens IJmuiden Verkoopkantoor BV; NVW (U.S.A.) Inc.; Huizenbezit "Breesaap" BV; NEBAM Nederlandse Bevrachting en Agentuur Maatschappij BV; Cindu Chemicals BV (50%); Hoogovens Court Chrome vof (50%); Hoogovens Delfstoffen BV; SA Carrières de Namêche (Belgium, 50%); SA Dolomeuse (Belgium, 50%); Oremco Inc. (U.S.A., 60%); Hoogovens (UK) Ltd.; Hille & Müller Group (Germany, 50%); Holco Corporation (U.S.A.); SAB Profiel BV; Hoogovens Aluminium BV; Hoogovens Aluminium GmbH (Germany); Aluminium Delfzijl BV; Hoogovens Aluminium Hüttenwerk GmbH (Germany 99.5%); Sidal NV (Belgium); Geisler Lignian Distributie NV (Belgium, 77.8%); Sidal Aluminium Service Center NV (Belgium); Sidal Alluminio SpA (Italy); Sidal Aluminio SA (Spain); Sidal Aluminium A/S (Denmark); Sidal Aluminium Sàrl (France); Sidal Aluminum Corporation (U.S.A.); Sidal Aluminium Ltd. (U.K.); Sidal (Portugal) Lda.; Simec NV (Belgium); Sidalmetaal BV; Sidalmetall GmbH (Germany); Werk Koblenz (Germany); BUG-Alutechnik GmbH (Germany); Vaassen Aluminium BV; Nyffeler Corti AG (Switzerland); Phénix Aluminium S.A. (Belgium); Hoogovens Technische Dienstverlening BV; ESTS BV; Hoogovens Technical Services (U.S.A.) Inc.; Bailey-Hoogovens U.S.A., Inc.; Esmil Water Systems BV; CIM Engineering CV (Eindhoven, 50%); Nucon Engineering and Contracting BV (50%); TAC-Groep BV; "GEN.CHART" vof (50%); Cobam NV (Belgium, 50%); CV Assurantiebedrijf Gebroeders Scheuer (66.7%); Scheuer Holding BV (50%); Esmil BV; Esmil International BV; Hoogovens Industriële Toeleveringsbedrijven BV; Alu Vaassen BV/Premetaal BV; Gieterij Nunspeet BV; Nederlandse Draadindustrie NDI BV/Thibo Draad BV; Staalcenter Roermond BV; Van Schothorst BV; Rigida SA (France); Cirex BV; De Globe BV (50%); Hoogovens Handel BV; Hoogovens Handel Wapeningsstaal BV; Hoogovens Handel Constructiestaal BV; Hoogovens Handel Metals BV; NV Charles Sternotte (Belgium, 99.9%); VBF Buizen BV.

Further Reading: de Vries, Joh., *Hoogovens IJmuiden, 1918–1968. Ontstaan en groei van een basisindustrie,* Amsterdam, KNHS, 1968; Heerding, A., *Cement in Nederland,* Amsterdam, CEMIJ, 1971; de Vries, Joh., "From Keystone to Cornerstone. Hoogovens IJmuiden 1918–1968. The birth and development of a basic industry in the Netherlands," in *Acta Historiae Neerlandicae,* The Hague, 1973; van Elteren, Mel C.M., *Staal en Arbeid. Een sociaal-historische studie naar industriële accomodatieprocessen onder arbeiders en het desbetreffende bedrijfsbeleid bij Hoogovens 1924–1966,* Leiden, Brill, 1986.

—Henk Muntjewerff and Joachim F.E. Bläsing
Translated from the Dutch by Hubert Hoskins

THE MARMON GROUP

225 West Washington Street
Chicago, Illinois 60606
U.S.A.
(312) 372-9500
Fax: (312) 845-5305

Private Companies
Incorporated: 1953 as Colson Company
Employees: 25,074
Sales: $3.90 billion

The Marmon Group, one of the United States's largest privately owned industrial organizations, is a diverse industrial complex composed of more that 60 individually operated companies. A small central office in Chicago manages and invests the financial resources of member companies, and aids and advises them on accounting, legal, tax, finance, personnel, and other matters. Owned by entities which are owned indirectly by the Pritzker family of Chicago, Marmon companies consistently achieve high returns from low-technology, low-glamour industries. Marmon has repeatedly bought and turned around troubled "smokestack" companies. Its diversified products and services include mining, metals, and mining equipment. In recent years Marmon has added large-scale industrial and commercial services to its activities and has moved into production of headware and gloves and of electronic products and systems.

Marmon's history as a corporate entity dates from 1953, but the Pritzker family, who built and control the massive conglomerate, has been active significantly longer. In the late 19th century, the Pritzkers immigrated to the United States from the Ukraine. Patriarch Nicholas Pritzker led them to Chicago, and in 1902 he founded Pritzker & Pritzker, the law firm that was to evolve into a management company and the center of the Pritzkers's many and varied investments.

Pritzker & Pritzker grew, and by the late 1920s it had become a respected local firm. At that time, the Pritzkers's best client was Goldblatt Brothers, the low-priced Chicago department store chain. Through the Goldblatts, Abram (A.N.) Pritzker, Nicholas Pritzker's son, met Walter M. Heymann, then a leading Chicago commercial banker and an officer at the First National Bank of Chicago. In succeeding years A.N. Pritzker and Walter Heymann became business associates, and the powerful First National Bank of Chicago became the financial cornerstone of the Pritzker family empire.

Using a line of credit from the First National Bank, A.N. Pritzker began acquiring real estate, something he already knew about from Pritzker & Pritzker's concentration on real estate reorganization. As his and the family's investments grew, the law practice shrank, and in 1940 Pritzker & Pritzker stopped accepting outside clients, concentrating solely on Pritzker family investments. At the same time A.N. Pritzker began the family practice of sheltering his holdings within a dizzying array of interrelated family trusts.

The story of Marmon, however, begins with the generation of Pritzkers following A.N.'s. By the early 1950s, Pritzker's oldest son, Jay, had become active in the family business. Something of a prodigy, Jay Pritzker had graduated high school at 14. He finished college soon thereafter and then took a law degree from Northwestern University. During World War II he worked first as a flight instructor and later for the U.S. government agency that managed German-owned companies. In that position, he sat on corporate boards with men many years his senior. An accomplished deal-maker even in his earliest years, Jay would later become well known for his quickness at sizing up balance sheets and offering deals.

While Pritzker was beginning his career as a deal-maker, his younger brother Robert Pritzker was finishing advanced training in industrial engineering at the Illinois Institute of Technology in Chicago. Robert Pritzker, A.N.'s second son, was the family's only engineer. During the 1950s and later, his interest in industrial processes, both theoretical and practical, led the family into manufacturing and later enabled him to turn around a staggering array of troubled companies.

The relationship between Jay Pritzker, the lawyer-deal-maker, and Robert Pritzker, the engineer-manager, became the basis for the continuing operations of The Marmon Group. Their youngest brother, Donald Pritzker, would later become the force behind Hyatt Hotels before dying suddenly at the age of 39 in 1972. Jay would buy troubled companies, usually for less than 80% of their book value. Then Robert would nurse the companies back to health, finding their real profit-making potentials and with Jay's help exploiting any tax advantages a company's previous losses might produce.

Their first venture was the acquisition of Colson Company in 1953. Colson, a money-loser, was a small, $8 million in sales, manufacturer of casters, bicycles, navy rockets, and wheelchairs. In Colson, Jay Pritzker saw a company that had some profit-making potential but whose assets could nevertheless be liquidated at a price higher than what the family had paid for it.

After Jay completed the deal, Robert Pritzker, went to Ohio and took over the running of Colson. He began by eliminating unprofitable lines. Bicycles went first. He knew he could not compete with cheaper European bikes, so he dropped them. To improve production of U.S. Navy rockets, Pritzker instituted modern statistical quality controls. Cost-cutting steps paid for most of Colson. When the program ended, he discontinued military production. This left him with casters and wheelchairs, products he was able to promote and sell successfully.

Over the next several years, the Pritzkers acquired several more manufactures of small metal products. Chief among these was the L.A. Darling Company of Bronson, Michigan, a maker of merchandising display equipment and retail fixtures; it also operated a plastics division and a foundry division. To achieve economies of scale, the Pritzkers combined and affiliated their new companies with Colson and, in a typically adept financial move, made Colson a subsidiary of L.A. Darling.

It was not until ten years after acquiring Colson that the Pritzker brothers made their next major acquisition. In 1963 the Pritzkers acquired the Marmon-Herrington Company, successor to the Marmon Motor Car Company. The way Jay Pritzker structured the deal, the L.A. Darling Company, which was headed by Robert Pritzker, paid approximately $2.7 million for 260,000 shares of Marmon-Herrington's 580,000 outstanding shares of stock. This acquisition gave the Pritzkers's industrial holdings their permanent name, The Marmon Group. Marmon discontinued the company's production of heavy-duty tractors, transit vehicles, and bus chassis. The most significant addition to the Pritzker holdings was the Long-Airdox Company, a division of Marmon-Herrington that added a broad range of coal mining equipment to Darling's display equipment and fixtures, and its foundry operations; and to Colson's casters, institutional housekeeping trucks, and hospital equipment. The acquisition was also indicative of the complex, interlocking ways that the Pritzkers owned their companies. Sales grew quickly, and in 1965 Marmon topped $51.8 million in total revenues.

In 1966 Marmon merged with publicly held Fenestra Incorporated, a maker of architectural steel doors and leaf springs for trucks. As the deal was structured as a stock swap, Marmon itself became a public company, The Marmon Group, Inc., and for the first time, the Pritzkers' industrial empire was exposed to the scrutiny of shareholders.

Shy of the public eye and jealous of their controlling interest, the Pritzkers soon moved to take greater control of The Marmon Group. In a complicated stock transaction of October 1967, Jay Pritzker had Fenestra, which was technically controlled by a subsidiary of The Marmon Group, Inc., acquire both The Marmon Group, Inc., and Boykin Enterprises, another newly acquired Pritzker company, that produced and exported agricultural equipment. At the end of the deal the Pritzkers owned more than 84.3% of voting stock of Fenestra and had changed Fenestra's name to The Marmon Group, Inc.

In 1968 Marmon acquired Triangle Auto Springs Company, a manufacturer of flat-leaf truck springs for the replacement market. Triangle's line of springs fit in well with the products Marmon was already making at Fenestra's Detroit Steel Products subsidiary.

In 1969 Marmon further consolidated its role in the parts replacement business by buying Lowell Bearing Company, a distributor of replacement parts to truck, bus, and trolley fleets in the United States and around the world. The same year, the L.A. Darling plant was moved from Michigan to Paragould, Arkansas. In 1969, also, the company acquired the rights to the Universal Track Machine, a machine, which Marmon had previously manufactured under contract. It performed mechanized maintenance on the nations railroad tracks and railroad rights-of-way. Rising labor costs had made this robotic maintenance device a highly desirable product.

By the end of 1969, Marmon had become a diversified industrial company supplying low-tech goods in noncompetitive fields not vulnerable to changes in consumer tastes. About 39% of sales came from automotive replacement parts; 30% came from building materials, hardware, and retail fixtures, much of which was sold by the L.A. Darling Fixture division. Mining equipment supplied by Long-Airdox and Pickrose &

Co., of England, accounted for 25% of sales; and agricultural, irrigation, and animal husbandry equipment by Jamesway Company Limited, now Jamesway Incubator Corporation, of Canada, and the AMISA export arm accounted for the remaining portion of sales.

The year 1970 was a time of internal investment and growth. Sales climbed from $77 million to $87 million. Triangle Auto Springs and Jamesway each made additions to its physical plant. The Darling Store Fixtures division was in the process of building a new plant in Corning, Arkansas. New plant equipment was bought for Fenestra, Detroit Steel Products, and Darling. Finally, in December of 1970, Marmon paid $6 million for Keystone Pipe and Supply Company, a nationwide supplier of pipes and tubes based in Butler, Pennsylvania. In succeeding years, Great Lakes Corporation, which was owned by Marmon Holdings, which was itself owned by the Pritzkers, bought up outstanding shares and converted preferred stock to voting stock. In 1970 sales topped $100 million, and by 1971 The Marmon Group was again private.

Marmon's largest and most successful acquisition of the 1970s was Cerro Corporation, with $800 million in sales, a company that the Pritzkers gradually acquired between 1973 and 1976. Cerro's operations included mining, manufacturing, trucking, and real estate. Like many Marmon acquisitions, the Cerro deal was financed through the First National Bank of Chicago. The relationship between the Pritzkers and First Chicago had remained strong since their initial contacts in the late 1920s.

Cerro was a typical, if much larger than previous, Marmon acquisition. It was rich in assets and selling at far below book value. In fact, Cerro was atypical only in that it was publicly held and that the Pritzkers ousted the current management and installed Jay Pritzker as chief executive officer and Robert Pritzker as president.

Soon after taking a controlling interest in Cerro, Robert Pritzker began commuting to Cerro's New York headquarters, where he oversaw its industrial processes and worked at freeing up the somewhat tense corporate culture. Robert Pritzker told *The Wall Street Journal*, of March 27, 1975, that "Cerro is one of those typical, highly structured big companies. . . . We think that loosening it up will make people there feel better and perform better, too." By 1977, Marmon had the Cerro acquisition under control. It sold Cerro's trucking subsidiary, ICX, for $22.6 million, and it was also dealing with Cerro's troubled Florida real estate venture, Leadership Housing Incorporated.

During the same period in which Marmon was acquiring Cerro, it bought the Hammond Corporation. Completed in 1977, the acquisition of the organ manufacturer was neither as successful nor as canny as the Cerro acquisition had been. The Pritzkers bought Hammond just as a recession struck and the decline in the economy caused a slump in organ sales. The one bright spot of the deal was Hammond's work gloves subsidiary, Wells Lamont. Using these facilities as a basis, Marmon has gone on to become a leading manufacturer of gloves and other apparel items.

In 1978 Marmon paid $27.3 million for American Safety Equipment Corporation, a maker of seat-belt systems for cars and aircraft, with $48.1 million in sales and owner of Kangol Limited, a British headwear manufacturer. Marmon also in 1978 divested itself of Leadership Housing, by distributing as dividends its investments in the company.

Between 1970 and 1980 Marmon's sales grew from $103 million to $1.9 billion, and during the same period profits rocketed from $5 million to $79 million. Marmon had expanded from five basic product groups to a much larger cluster of companies making pipe and tubing, wire and cable, automotive products, other metal products, apparel accessories, mining and agricultural equipment, and musical instruments. Services such as metals trading and coal mining were becoming increasingly important elements of the business.

Some of The Marmon Group's successes of the 1970s can be attributed to the advantages of a privately owned company whose owners get on well. In a March 27, 1975, interview with *The Wall Street Journal* J. Ira Harris, then a Chicago-based partner of Salomon Brothers, said that the Pritzkers's ability to work together ". . . gives them the kind of flexibility that doesn't exist elsewhere at their level of operations. They've closed a lot of important deals because they were able to move faster than the competition."

The ability to move fast also helped Robert Pritzker deal effectively with Marmon's divisions. Normally a manager who allows Marmon's component companies substantial autonomy, he was able to make necessary decisions on a person-to-person basis without expensive and time consuming studies. The Marmon Group's board of directors, which is headed by Jay Pritzker, rarely meets, and the corporate office is sparsely staffed. The divisions themselves spend little on advertising and less on their offices.

While Robert Pritzker cedes authority to managers, he keeps the accounting tight. Divisional controllers report not only to their general managers, they also report to a corporate controller in Chicago. Robert Pritzker often leaves final decisions to local managers. Marmon's commitment to capital investment and drive to be the low-cost producer allows local managers to make the large investments that stand-alone companies could never make. After buying Midwest Foundry Company in 1960, for example, Marmon's capital commitment led the company to expand tenfold in 20 years. During the same period, 40% of all gray-iron foundries in the United States shut down. In the early years of the 1980s, Midwest Foundry was returning 40% on Marmon's investment.

In September 1980, Marmon announced the proposed acquisition of Illinois-based Trans Union Corporation for $688 million. Trans Union was a $1.1 billion conglomerate whose businesses included rail car and general-equipment leasing by its Union Tank Car Company subsidiary; credit information services; international trading by the subsidiary Getz Corporation; and the manufacture of waste and water treatment equipment.

Completed in 1981, the Trans Union acquisition was unusual in that it was both huge and expensive. Jay Pritzker had been attracted by Trans Union's large accumulation of investment tax credits and federal tax deferrals, which Marmon could use to offset taxable income. Further, once bought, Robert Pritzker found a series of unexpectedly profitable components within the larger Trans Union. A case in point is the Getz Corporation, a San Francisco–based Pacific trading company that grossed over $600 million in 1989. When Marmon acquired Trans Union, Getz was failing. Within a few years, Robert Pritzker had solidified Getz's management and was exploiting Getz's untapped potential as a travel agency and its experience as a player in the expanding market of the Pacific Rim. Getz deals in a wide array of automotive, industrial, and food products—from farm tractors in Thailand to powdered milk in Taiwan.

In January 1984 Marmon purchased Altamil Corporation and thereby acquired the Fontaine Trucking Company, manufacturer of truck and trailer couplers, trailers and special purpose truck bodies; Aluminum Forge Company, a producer of precision aluminum forging for aerospace industries; and American Box Company, producer of wirebound boxes and crates, which later was sold.

During the late 1980s Marmon grew to such an extent that some questioned the ability of its corporate structure to handle its holdings, which are increasingly technically and geographically diverse. Much of the expansion came through member companies themselves making acquisitions. For example, the Microware Surgical Instruments Corporation acquired the medical-products division of the National Standard Corporation in early 1990.

Like other smokestack industries, Marmon may face the necessities in the future of pollution control. Robert Pritzker demonstrated his basic commitment to the environment in 1970, when he gave $1.4 million to launch a center for environmental studies as the Illinois Institute of Technology, his alma mater. At least two Marmon companies are involved in the growing environmental-protection industry. EcoWater Systems makes commercial water treatment systems, and the Avendt Group provides environmental management consulting services for regulatory compliance and the correction and avoidance of environmental liabilities.

For the early 1990s Marmon's outlook is excellent. Between 1980 and 1989 revenues jumped from $1.9 billion to $3.9 billion. During the same time earnings swelled from $84 million to $205 million. At the start of the decade, Marmon's average return on equity, profits as a percentage of the company's total worth, ran 19.1%, a full five points higher than the median of the *Fortune* 500, and in 1989 that proportion reached 26.3%, more than ten points higher than the median of the *Fortune* 500.

From a small company making casters and wheelchairs, The Marmon Group has grown through acquisition and internal reinvestment into a diversified industrial conglomerate the chief products and services of which include industrial materials and components; metals trading; mining; automotive, building, medical, and consumer products; electronic monitoring instruments; water and industrial-fluids treatment systems; the manufacture, sales, and leasing of systems equipment for mining, agriculture, offices, and institutions; the manufacture, sales and leasing of rail transportation equipment; credit information services; and the international marketing of consumer and industrial products. With an aging yet stable management team in place, and a new generation of Pritzkers entering the business, Marmon's future looks bright.

Principal Companies: Accutronics, Inc.; Albion Industries, Inc.; Aluminum Forge Company; Amarillo Gear Company; Am-Safe, Inc.; Anderson Copper and Brass Company; Arzco Medical Electronic, Inc.; Atlas Bolt & Screw Company; The Avendt Group, Inc.; Bonanza Aluminum Corp.; Cerro Copper Products Co.; Cerro Metal Products Company; Cerro Sales Corporation; Cerro Wire & Cable Company, Inc.; Colson

Caster Corporation; Colson Equipment, Inc.; Croydon Furniture Systems, Inc. (Canada); L.A. Darling Company; Data Preference Inc.; Detroit Steel Products Co., Inc.; Eagle-Gypsum Products; Ecodyne MRM, Inc.; EcoWater Systems, Inc.; Fenestra Corporation; Fontaine International, Inc.; Getz Bros. & Co.; The Graver Company; Huron Steel Company, Inc.; Jamesway Incubator Corp. (Canada); Kangol Limited (U.K.); Leasametric, Inc.; Long-Airdox Co.; MTN Services, Inc.; MarCap Corporation; Marlok Co.; Marmon/Keystone Corporation; Meyer Material Co.; Micro-Aire Surgical Instruments, Inc.; Miles Metal Company; National Energy Systems, Inc.; New Century Freight Traffic Association, Inc.; Penn Aluminum International, Inc.; Perfection Hy-Test Co.; Pikrose and Company Limited (U.K.); Polymer Technologies Inc. (Canada); Procor Engineering Limited (U.K.); Procor Limited (Canada); Procor LPG Storage Inc. (Canada); Robertson Whitehouse Inc. (Canada); Rochester Instrument Systems, Inc.; The Rockbestos Co.; Solidstate Controls, Inc.; Southern Peru Copper Corp.; Trackmobile, Inc.; Trans Union Corp.; Triangle Auto Spring Co.; Union Tank Car Co.; Webb Wheel Products; Wells Lamont; WCTU Railway Co.

Further Reading: Klein, Frederic C., "Family Business: The Pritzkers are an Acquisitive Bunch Which Pays Off Well," *The Wall Street Journal,* March 27, 1975; "The Hustling Pritzkers," *Business Week,* May 5, 1975; Worthy, Ford S., "The Pritzkers; Unveiling A Private Family," *Fortune,* April 25, 1988.

—Jordan Wankoff

METALLGESELLSCHAFT AG

Reuterweg 14
6000 Frankfurt am Main 1
Federal Republic of Germany
(69) 159-0
Fax: (69) 159-2125

Public Company
Incorporated: 1881
Employees: 52,000
Sales: DM19.83 billion (US$13.27 billion)
Stock Exchanges: Berlin Düsseldorf Frankfurt Munich
  Hamburg Stuttgart

Metallgesellschaft (MG), based in the heart of Frankfurt since its foundation, is an international group providing raw materials and technological services. It is divided into three branches of services—trade, finance and engineering—and into eight industrial business units, in which it has substantial shareholdings.

"The trade in and manufacturing of metals and metal oxides" were the business aims of the firm according to its articles of association. The company was founded on May 17, 1881, by the Anglo-German merchant Wilhelm Merton and his two partners, Leo Ellinger and Zachary Hochschild, with a share capital of 2 million marks. It had its roots in the firm of Philipp Abm. Cohen, already established some 150 years previously, with its headquarters in Hanover. Initially this company was involved in banking, then increasingly in metal trading, and was incorporated in Frankfurt in 1821. In 1856, Philipp Abm. Cohen entrusted his business interests to his son-in-law Ralph Merton, who had emigrated from London to Frankfurt. One of Ralph Merton's sons, William, born in 1848 and later to change his name to Wilhelm, became an associate partner in 1876, having worked for many years both in London and in Frankfurt. Close business as well as personal ties were formed with the firm of Henry R. Merton (HRM), the metals trading firm of the English branch of the family, named after another of Ralph's sons.

MG, with 40 employees and one telephone—the first telephones were installed in Frankfurt in 1881—at the outset traded in copper, lead, and zinc, later diversifying into nickel and aluminum. The firm Philipp Abm. Cohen had also been involved in silver trading, but abandoned this line in 1872, leaving the way open for the founding of the Deutsche Gold-und Silber-Scheideanstalt (Degussa).

Since the domestic mines could not satisfy the country's metal requirements, the company rapidly developed extensive relations abroad and within a short time MG was represented in such cities as Basel, Amsterdam, Milan, Brussels, Stockholm, St. Petersburg, Moscow, Vienna, and Paris. Within a few years, therefore, a network of subsidiaries spanned the globe. In 1887, the American Metal Company was founded in New York; in 1889, the Companhia de Minerales y Metales in Mexico; and in 1889 the Australian Metal Co. The last was the result of an expedition the company organized together with HRM and Degussa into the ore-rich Broken Hill district, where lead and lead concentrates were produced in vast quantities. This constituted the start of MG's trading in ore, which would assume greater and greater importance in the future.

From 1889, these ores were analyzed and tested by the specially created technical department. This technical department was to be the seed from which grew the largest enterprise that MG has ever created; from it arose in 1897 the Metallurgische Gesellschaft Aktiengesellschaft, a fully owned MG subsidiary, to look after MG's industrial and technical interests. Under the abbreviation it uses for telegrams, LURGI, this enterprise has become known as a leading worldwide engineering business. The appointment of the scientists Clemens Winkler and Curt Netto to the supervisory board is clear evidence of the importance technological skills had acquired for MG.

MG developed and flourished in the generally favorable climate of the late period of the *Gründerjahre*—the period, beginning in 1871, of rapid industrial expansion in Germany. In the company's first ten years, its capital was raised to 6 million marks and the dividend payments were between 7% and 33%. From the outset MG had proved exemplary in its social provisions. For example, a pension fund was established for employees long before this became a legal obligation. The founder of MG's social policy was legendary. He founded numerous institutions, using the anonymity of the holding company, the Institut für Gemeinwohl, which were concerned with research into social questions and with providing practical assistance. The feeling that those involved in the business world generally lacked grounding in academic background knowledge in commerce, economics, and social sciences led him to found the Akademie für Sozial-und Handelswissenschaften. The University of Frankfurt would emerge from this academy, once again backed by Wilhelm Merton's strong personal and financial involvement.

By 1906, the year of its 25th anniversary, MG was a steadily growing, prosperous concern, involved in many sectors, and active internationally in trading and engineering technology, in the fields of mining and metallurgy. In the same year, Wilhelm Merton brought about the long-envisaged creation of a separate finance company and a broader financial base for the group through the founding of the Berg- und Metallbank. This was merged with the Metallurgische Gesellschaft in 1910, after it was realized that a precise division between the industrial business and its financing was creating unnecessary duplication of work and was not economically favorable to the group.

Although Wilhelm Merton is recorded in autobiographical notes as saying of MG that: "Our trading company will not be involved in any kind of advertising" and is credited with the remark that it would be far more pleasant "to be able to pursue one's business without the need of the stock exchange, the public or the press," he broke fundamentally with his principles in one important way—the publication *Metallstatistik,* which had appeared annually since 1892, giving an overview of metal production, consumption and prices worldwide, made MG's name, to quote Wilhelm Merton again, "known, and I might add, respected." In general, however, Wilhelm Merton strongly objected to any interest in the firm which he considered to be excessive.

World War I hit MG hard. The good relations established abroad were broken off, imports of raw material dried up, the sister company HRM fell under the British Non Ferrous Metals Industry Bill of November 1917, designed to eliminate enemy influence and control over the British ore and metal trade, and the deliveries of Australian ore failed to appear. This meant MG had to obtain its metal supplies from neutral countries for as long as possible and eventually to use up domestic sources or intensify their exploitation. Three aluminum works were built, in conjunction with the firm Griesheim Elektron: in Horrem, close to Cologne; in Berlin-Rummelsburg; and in Bitterfeld near Halle.

In the middle of World War I, on December 15, 1916, Wilhelm Merton died suddenly on a business trip to Berlin. His partner Hochshild had died in 1912 and Ellinger had died in the summer of 1916. This meant none of the founders were left. Wilhelm had prepared his sons to continue the businesses and Richard and Alfred took on the top management positions in MG and in Metallbank.

After the war, they were faced with three main tasks: overcoming the consequences of inflation; re-establishing ties abroad; and adjusting MG's organization to the altered circumstances. Representation abroad was cautiously and gradually re-established, and a cooperation agreement was signed and shares exchanged with the successor to HRM, which had gone into liquidation during the war.

MG was reorganized into four and later five constituent parts between 1919 and 1922, reflecting its different areas of activity. Through the acquisition of water transport companies—Schleppschiffahrtsgesellschaft Unterweser in 1919 and Lehnkering AG in 1926, a land transport company—Kommanditgesellschaft S. Elkan & Co., Hamburg—in 1922, and the founding of its own land transport company, Montan Transport GmbH, MG created its own transport services. In 1928, MG and the group Berg -und Metallbank and Metallurgische Gesellschaft which had merged in 1910 were brought together with the aim of operating more efficiently.

In the field of metal working, the Vereinigte Deutsche Metallwerke AG (VDM) was founded in 1930 through mergers and partnerships. MG had the majority shareholding.

In the 1920s, the company's constant efforts to reestablish contacts abroad, especially through Richard Merton's strong personal involvement, bore fruit. Together with the already mentioned exchange of shares with the British Metal Corporation is the example of the takeover by MG in 1926 of the Ore and Chemical Corporation (OCC), founded in 1923, in New York. In 1922 MG's stock was changed from registered shares to bearer shares; it was consequently registered on the Frankfurt stock exchange in 1922 and on the Berlin exchange in 1926.

After the battle against inflation had been won, MG would only have a few years to benefit from a peaceful and favorable business environment, as the world Depression and political changes would once more affect the group badly. At the time of MG's 50th anniversary, the company's 18 board members and 500 employees faced a gloomy future.

After the National Socialists had seized power in 1933, MG became an object of desire for the new dictatorship, which viewed it as an important enterprise for armaments and later for war. This meant in the first instance that it became the object of aryanisation—this meant among other things that between 1935 and 1938, 8 out of the 11 directors on the board of management were dismissed from their posts for being Jewish or having Jewish connections. Alfred Merton had emigrated in 1933 for political reasons. Richard Merton, however, tried to keep his position for as long as possible. Forced to resign from his post as head of the board, he was arrested during the November pogrom and transported to a concentration camp for several weeks, but in spring 1939 managed to escape to England. Richard was automatically made a British subject as his father had retained his British nationality.

During the reign of the Merton brothers, a four-man central committee had been formed in 1932 from among the board members and invested with extended powers. Its original members were Alfred Merton; Rudolf Euler, Zachary Hochschild's son-in-law; Alfred Petersen; and Julius Sommer. In 1938 the Nationalsozialistische Deutsche Arbeiterpartei (Nazi Party) succeeded in establishing R.W. Avieny, the choice of Gauleiter (or regional Nazi administrator) Sprenger, on the board of MG. He also became a member of the central committee, together with R. Kissel and F. Traudes. The last took on the role of general manager until 1940. There are no chairman of the board of directors in this period until Avieny was elected in 1940 to this position, which he held until April 1945. The death in 1939 of the then-chairman of the supervisory board, Ernst Busemann, brought about the appointment of Carl Lüer, president of the board of trade of the Rhein-Main-Wirtschaftsraum, the regional economic council. Astonishingly, the two English members of the supervisory board, Oliver Lyttelton and Walter Gardner, still occupied their posts after World War II had begun. It was only at the sitting of the board in October 1940 that they retired from their positions. In March 1944 the MG head office was severely damaged by bombing which killed some two dozen employees. Toward the end of the war the administrative offices and production sites were moved out of Frankfurt. After Frankfurt had been taken by U.S. troops in April 1945, the latter established their administrative headquarters in the MG complex. Almost all the leading management posts were filled by new people after the end of the war. Petersen, who had been held in detention for some time by the Nazis, took the position of chairman of the board of directors and Rudolf Euler that of chairman of the supervisory board until Richard Merton returned in 1947 from his exile in England. Merton remained chairman until his death in 1960.

The situation facing the company in 1945 was somewhat worse than it had been in 1918. Many of the domestic companies lay in ruins and the mining and production works beyond the Elbe had to be given up. After the war, MG's main business for a time was in rubble—Trümmer-Verwertungs-Gesellschaft, in which MG was one of three shareholders, was concerned with recovering rubble, with demolition work, and with recycling rubble—and the manufacturing of roofing felt and jam substitute based on turnips.

Denazification courts—set up by the Allied victors to dismantle all Nazi organizations and get rid of Nazis from key positions as quickly as possible—and decartelisation proceedings resulted in major changes to MG's board of directors and supervisory board by 1948. Shortly before this, on the occasion of the German currency reform, MG had lowered its capital, by a ratio of ten to eight, to DM56 million.

For the company's 75th anniversary, the American military authorities returned to MG the building which they had used as their administrative headquarters for 11 years. Under Alfred Petersen, the firm's technical adviser, the emphasis was put on consolidating and extending the group's technical capabilities. LURGI's research laboratories were expanded. The company pursued its own development program and adopted new processes and areas of work. Lurgi Paris S.A., founded in 1960, was the first branch to be established abroad.

Under the leadership of Hellmut Ley, likewise a technical expert, MG once again acquired an international presence between 1961 and 1973. Ley's name is associated with the extension of the company's smelter capacities. MG subsidiaries or affiliates involved in many of the projects included Ruhr-Zink, Datteln, and "Berzelius" Metallhütten Gesellschaft in Duisburg.

In these years of strong economic growth, MG saw its work force climb to 30,000 in 1961, expanded its business in the transport sector, and became involved in exploratory navigation. In the processing sector, piston manufacturing installations were established in South Africa and in Brazil.

The second half of the 1960s saw MG turn its attention more to publicity. Together with the *Metallstatistik* and the regular publication of scientific research essays in *Mitteilungen aus dem Arbeitsbereich,* the journal *MG Information* came into existence in 1966 and has appeared in English for several years.

The "disorganized giant," as the *Financial Times* once called MG, referring to the lack of organizational and divisional structures which the rapid diversification of the group would seem to have necessitated, underwent significant changes in 1971. All MG enterprises and subsidiaries were divided into five divisions: metals processing, plant construction, chemicals, transport, and communications. A functional reorganization also took place in the three central fields of finance, staff and administration, and technology. This structure would last almost 20 years.

In the same year, MG became the first non-British company to be admitted to the London Metal Exchange. The company MG Ltd. was founded for this purpose and the company's historical connection with England reestablished.

Ley died suddenly at the end of the year 1973 and with the appointment of Karl Gustaf Ratjen as chairman of the board, the group found itself with a lawyer and banker at the helm after two technical men. His decade of leadership was marked by strong growth in MG's international activities. In Germany, this period was characterized by recession. In the mining sector, the group ventured into large projects, some in distant locations, such as northern Canada, Thailand, and Papua New Guinea, where copper, lead, and zinc deposits were opened up by group companies, often in conjunction with international partners. The year 1978 saw the founding of Metallgesellschaft of Australia (Pty) Ltd., followed by Metallgesellschaft Corporation in the United States in 1978. The LURGI companies won large contracts from China and the USSR in the 1970s to build petrochemical plants.

The introduction of the codetermination law in 1978 led to the election of employee representatives to the supervisory board. W. Guth of the Deutsche Bank succeeded Hermann Richter after almost two decades as the head of this board. Guth was initially appointed for one year, and later for a further five. Between Guth's two periods in office, H. Friderichs presided for five years. Kuwait Petroleum Company became an MG shareholder in 1980–1981 with a 20% holding. Since 1988, Wolfgang Röller, (of the Dresdner Bank), has been chairman of the supervisory board.

In 1981, MG's centenary year, Karl Gustaf Ratjen defined the company's new aims as increased involvement in raw materials and an accompanying increase in trading activity, engineering services, and speciality chemicals for processing industries. MG made several disinvestments, including that of VDM. The closure of the Heddernheim works followed in 1982.

Dr. Dietrich Natus, from LURGI, succeeded Ratjen as chairman of the board of directors in 1984. Directly before this, he had turned the combined LURGI operations into a private limited company, and LURGI had moved its new offices to VDM's former site. These offices became the most extensive in Germany.

During Natus's five years as chairman, the company concentrated on strengthening its productivity and financial basis. After several years of low dividend payments, MG's dividends returned to a satisfactory level. MG severed its ties with peripheral and problematic commitments and concentrated its strength on its core activities. Of particular note were the launch onto the stock exchange of motor vehicle distributor Kolbenschmidt, in which MG had a 62.5% holding (50.5% in 1991); the beginning of MG's cooperation with and shareholding in the Canadian mining concern Cominco; and the founding of the mining company Metall Mining Corporation in Toronto, measures which signaled recovery for the long-ailing mining division.

In 1989 Natus passed on the chairmanship of MG to Dr. Heinz Schimmelbusch, the youngest chairman of the board in the history of the group to date. An economics graduate, Schimmelbusch had until then been in charge of the raw materials division and had distinguished himself in the past few years as a member of the board with his innovative and creative ideas and concepts. He immediately set about giving MG a new, flexible managerial and organizational structure. Under Schimmelbusch the raw materials and technological services division concentrated its efforts on the increasingly important domain of environmental technology. LURGI plans, delivers, and builds plants for all types of industry and has developed more than 200 of the approximately 400 processes it offers to install. The ultramodern plants—for example, the new copper electrolysis plant of the Norddeutsche Affinerie or the new zinc electrolysis plant for "Berzelius" in Duisburg—fall under the legal emission limits. With the launch onto the stock exchange of newly created Berzelius Umwelt-Service (BUS), MG now has a company that can complete the industrial circle, as BUS disposes of problematic industrial waste and recycles valuable materials to go back into the production circuit.

The aim and result of Schimmelbusch's reforms is an harmonious triangle consisting of plant construction, trade in raw materials, and financial services—conducting universal banking operations on behalf of clients inside and outside the group—which work synergistically within a net that pulls together the most varied sectors of the market. This structure reduces MG's very great dependence up until now on the prices of raw materials and shifts in exchange rates. MG's range of activity is at the same time widely diversified and closely bound together; it covers the discovery, development, and processing of ores together with the processing of the resulting concentrates and the marketing of the processes developed, includes the increasingly important field of recycling methods and furthermore encompasses the finance, transport and marketing sectors.

A constituent part of MG's entrepreneurial philosophy is to give the individual sectors independence as soon as they reach their respective targets for production volume and sales. In short, the group is being divided into separate units that also act efficiently together.

In 1990, MG employees were given the opportunity for the first time to buy staff shares in the company. Connected with this was the latest rise in the company's capital, in which the company's stock capital was increased by more than DM100 million within two years and now stands at DM381.74 million. In 1991, LURGI acquired Davy McKee AG, a plant building enterprise with 600 employees, formed out of Zimmer AG and Davy Bamag GmbH.

In June 1991 MG acquired—subject to approval by the German monopolies commission—the non-paper division of Feldmühle Nobel AG, whose activities include heating and materials technology and explosives and complement the group's corresponding core activities. In connection with this, the share capital was once more raised, this time by DM60 million to stand at DM441.74 million. This takeover raised the number of employees in the MG group to 52,000.

Principal Subsidiaries: Metallgesellschaft Ltd (London, 61.52%); The Metal and Commodity Company Ltd (London, 80%); Metallbank GmbH; Metallgesellschaft Corp (U.S.A.); Metall Mining Corp (Canada, 64.36%); "Berzelius" Metallhütten-Gesellschaft mbH; B. U. S. Berzelius Umwelt-Service AG (57.83%); Kolbenschmidt AG (51.64%); Lentjes AG (51%); Lehnkering Montan Transport AG (75%); Wolfram Bergbau- und Hütten-gesellschaft mbH (67%).

Further Reading: Däbritz, Walter, *Fünfzig Jahre Metallgesellschaft 1881–1931,* Frankfurt am Main, Metallgesellschaft, 1931; Sommer, Julius, *Die Metallgesellschaft,* Frankfurt am Main, Metallgesellschaft, 1931; Merton, Richard, *Erinnerswertes aus meinem Leben,* Frankfurt am Main, Fritz Knapp Verlag, 1955; Achinger, Hans, *Wilhelm Merton in seiner Zeit,* Frankfurt am Main, Verlag Waldemar Kramer, 1965; Achinger, Hans, *Richard Merton,* Frankfurt am Main, Verlag Waldemar Kramer, 1970; "MG 100 Jahre," *MG Information,* Sonderausgabe, Metallgesellschaft, No. 1, 1981.

—Hannelore Becker-Hess
Translated from the German by Philippe A. Barbour

MINERALS & METALS TRADING CORPORATION OF INDIA LTD.

SCOPE Complex Core 1
7, Institutional Area
Lodi Road, New Delhi-110 003
India
(11) 36 22 00
Fax: (11) 36 22 24

State-Owned Company
Incorporated: 1963
Employees: 3,825
Sales: Rs50.97 billion (US$2.81 billion)

The Minerals and Metals Trading Corporation of India Ltd. (MMTC) is India's largest public sector trading body. Apart from overseeing the export of primary products such as coal and iron ore, and manufactured agricultural and industrial products, the MMTC also imports much-needed commodities such as ferrous and nonferrous metals for industry, and agricultural fertilizers.

The Indian subcontinent is endowed with a rich variety of natural mineral wealth. Although geological surveys were first conducted in the 1840s, when the Geological Survey of India—still the principal agency for mapping and exploration of minerals today—was created at the beginning of the 1990s, only 50% of India's total land area had been explored for minerals.

India possesses ample coal and iron reserves, together with significant quantities of bauxite, gold, ilmenite, manganese ore, and mica. But production levels of cobalt, copper, graphite, lead, mercury, nickel, sulfur, petroleum, and zinc fall well short of domestic needs. Moreover, the exploration and removal of mineral resources such as iron ore and bauxite necessitate a high level of financial investment and technological expertise.

After independence in 1947, therefore, the government decided to leave the mining of scarce mineral resources to the public rather than private sector, although India's National Mineral Policy clearly states that it does not "preclude the State from securing the co-operation of private enterprise in the larger interest of the State or with a view to accelerating the pace of development."

Under the Constitution of India, mineral rights and administration of mining laws are vested in the state governments. Central government, however, regulates the development of minerals under the Mines and Minerals (Regulation) Act of 1957.

The MMTC has its origins in the 1950s, when, in an effort to boost agricultural and industrial development, the Indian government determined to earn valuable foreign currency through the export of canalized bulk mineral ores. Canalization is a process whereby only state companies may handle the import and export of certain products deemed essential to the country, and where the end user is invariably a state utility, factory, or some other government undertaking. It is not a process unique to India.

As a direct result of the government's decision to try and earn larger amounts of foreign currency, the State Trading Corporation of India Ltd. was founded in 1956 under the Indian Companies Act, as a wholly owned government subsidiary, to manage the export and import of selected commodities.

However, the need for a specialized institution, which could handle the complexities of mining, transporting, and exporting large amounts of mineral ores, became increasingly apparent, and in 1963 the MMTC was created specifically to trade in minerals and metals and, in particular, iron ore, which it began to purchase from the government's mining company, called the National Minerals Development Corporation, and other public- and private-sector mining companies. Its initial objectives were twofold: one, to ensure full employment of miners in less developed areas; and two, to oversee the importation and distribution of raw materials to agriculture and industry where production fell short of domestic requirements.

Gradually the MMTC diversified into new areas, over the years gaining responsibility for importing nonferrous metals, fertilizers, and fertilizer raw materials. But in 1963 the MMTC's primary responsibility was to oversee iron ore export, formerly the responsibilty of the State Trading Corporation of India.

India is one of the few countries in the world that possesses sufficient quantities of high-quality iron ore both to meet its domestic needs and to export in large amounts. The subcontinent exports almost 60% of its iron ore production every year, and it has grown to become the country's single largest currency earner. Japan is the major purchaser, and other importers include China, Czechoslovakia, Germany, Hungary, Iran, Kenya, Romania, South Korea, the United Arab Emirates, and Yugoslavia.

After iron ore in 1963, other minerals soon joined the MMTC fold: export of manganese in 1965, coal in 1971, mica in 1972, barytes in 1976, and chrome ore in 1978. For a short period between 1974 and 1975, at the insistence of the government of India, the MMTC also handled exports of ferromanganese, ferrosilicon and ferrochrome, before these were passed on to other agencies.

From 1970 onwards, the MMTC also assumed increasing responsibility for importing nonferrous metals like palladium (1970), platinum (1970), aluminum (1971), zinc (1971), lead (1971), nickel (1971), tin (1972), and copper (1972). But, as in the case of exports, the Indian government's policy on canalization decreed that imports of certain other metals were channeled only intermittently through the MMTC. Examples include cobalt and mercury, between 1972 and 1976; zinc dust, between 1971 and 1976; and stainless steel, between 1970 and 1984. Aluminum was decanalized in 1990, and tin in 1991.

Although vast deposits of rock phosphate were recently discovered in Rajasthan, and since 1975 almost 50% of India's requirement has been produced domestically, imports of raw materials for fertilizers, including rock phosphate and sulfur, have continued to be the MMTC's responsibility since the mid-1960s. In 1970, imports of finished fertilizers from Eastern European countries began to be channeled through the MMTC and by the mid-1970s, all similar sources of finished fertilizers had followed this route. In February 1990, after intense discussion at government level, it was decided to channel imports of fertilizer intermediates such as ammonia and phosphoric acid through the MMTC.

The import of industrial raw materials such as antimony ore, high grade molybdenum and maganese ore, refractories and tungsten ore are no longer the responsibility of the MMTC, which gradually relinquished the task in the mid- to late-1970s, or 1982 in the case of antimony ore, in favor of private companies. The import of these materials continues to be regulated by the Ministry of Commerce under India's strictly enforced Import and Export policy.

The mid-1980s proved to be a significant turning point in the history of the MMTC's development. Until 1983, it had acted merely as a conduit for the import and export of key raw materials essential to the continued development of Indian agriculture and industry, but burgeoning trade deficits and increasing foreign exchange difficulties led to a need for substantially increased exports in order to earn desperately needed foreign currency.

As a direct result of the deepening balance-of-payments deficit, far-reaching strategic decisions were taken during 1983 and 1984 to turn the MMTC into a fully blown trading house. The principal strategic aim was to diversify away from the MMTC'S traditional concentration on the export and import of minerals and metals into new areas such as industrial products, agricultural products, diamonds, gems, and jewelry.

The launching of the government's seventh Five Year Economic Development Plan in 1985 saw the MMTC developing into the country's leading export house—a position it still holds—generating ever larger volumes of foreign exchange through its exports. To facilitate this process, the company adopted an increasing number of innovative strategies such as link deals, countertrade, and project exports. By the end of the 1980s, the MMTC's stated intention was to be able to generate sufficient export earnings to offset almost completely its foreign exchange requirements for imported raw materials.

From its early days in the 1960s, the MMTC has grown rapidly to become India's largest trading organization in the public sector. It now has trade links, in a wide range of commodities and products, with over 80 countries around the world and employs more than 3,500 people.

The MMTC's capital base has expanded in line with the group's overall expansion, partly through the issue of bonus shares, of which there have been seven over the years. From an initial government contribution of Rs30 million in 1991, the MMTC's capital base stands at Rs500 million. As of March 31, 1991, the MMTC's net worth was Rs3.42 billion, of which Rs500 million were share capital, and Rs2.92 billion were reserves.

From its first full year of operation in 1964–1965, the MMTC has displayed an impressive 75-fold increase in turnover from Rs680 million to Rs50.97 billion for 1989–1990.

Most spectacular has been the increase in monies derived from the export of non-canalized agricultural and industrial products. Between the financial years 1984–1985, and 1989–1990 respectively, revenue rose from Rs200 million to Rs5.25 billion, boosting overall export figures from Rs3.76 billion to Rs11.48 billion for the same period. At the same time, imports grew from Rs23.89 billion to Rs39.15 billion, increasing total turnover from Rs27.75 billion to Rs50.97 billion.

Canalized materials—bauxite, coal, chrome ore, iron ore, and manganese ore—account for 58% of the MMTC's exports. But the remainder consists of non-canalized exports, including other minerals, agricultural and industrial products, diamonds, gems, and jewelry, which are now the fastest-growing area in the MMTC's overall trade profile.

The MMTC is governed by a board of directors headed by the chairman, S.K. Agrawal, assisted by five executive directors. There is also an *ex-officio* director who is chairman of the National Minerals Development Corporation. Trading operations within the MMTC are broken down into four distinct groups, each with its own responsibilities and acting as an individual profit center. The minerals group handles all minerals and mineral-based products, while the metals group looks after ferrous and nonferrous metals and industrial raw materials. The fertilizer group oversees finished fertilizers. The export trade group has the widest brief, covering industrial products; commodities; diamonds; gems and jewelry; agromarine products; and countertrade, trading products without the use of currency.

Although the MMTC's planning is centralized at its corporate office in New Delhi, the MMTC's philosophy is that management should implement its decisions according to local conditions. Its regional offices at Barbil, Bombay, Calcutta, Cuttuck, Delhi, Goa, Madras, and Vizag have all been sited deliberately to take advantage of the close proximity of mines and ports and the needs of local industry. Overseas, the MMTC has offices in Tokyo, Japan; Seoul, Korea; and Bucharest, Romania, all dealing with iron ore exports, while an office in Amman in Jordan handles non-canalized exports.

The MMTC's interests in the 1990s cover every part of India's economy related to foreign trade. Its principal activities remain the export of primary and manufactured products, but also involve importing industrial commodities such as ferrous and nonferrous metals; fertilizers and fertilizer raw materials; third country trading, which involves importing a product from a foreign country and selling it to a third country at a profit without importing the commodity into the trading country; countertrade; acting as an agent and representative for domestic producers; domestic trade in bulk raw materials; providing insurance, shipping, financing, transportation and warehousing services for Indian exporters; and entering into joint ventures in mining, transportation, manufacturing, trading and the building of infrastructures.

Further Reading: International Directory of Mining, London, McGraw Hill, 1985; *Kothari's Industrial Directory of India,* Madras, Kothari Enterprises, 1990.

—Andrew Burchill

MITSUI KINZOKU

MITSUI MINING & SMELTING CO., LTD.

MITSUI MINING & SMELTING CO., LTD.

2-1-1, Nihonbashi Muromachi
Chuo-ku, Tokyo 103
Japan
(03) 3246-8000
Fax: (03) 3246-0533

Public Company
Incorporated: 1950 as Kamioka Mining & Smelting Co., Ltd.
Employees: 3,649
Sales: ¥405.90 billion (US$2.99 billion)
Stock Exchanges: Tokyo Osaka Nagoya Fukuoka Hiroshima Kyoto Niigata Sapporo

Mitsui Mining & Smelting Co., Ltd. (MMS) is one of Japan's leading smelters of zinc, copper, and other nonferrous metals. The company also trades in precious metals, and has developed a growing assortment of processed metal products for the automotive and electronics industries. After a difficult period in the mid-1980s, MMS has determined to free itself of dependence on fluctuating metal prices by concentrating on value-added products and its growing work in the electronics sector.

MMS was created as Kamioka Mining & Smelting Co., Ltd., in 1950 when Mitsui Mining Company was forced to dissolve by the Allied occupation forces in Japan. Mitsui Mining was one of the oldest and most important of the many affiliates of the Mitsui *zaibatsu,* or conglomerate, its large coal mines having first been acquired by the parent company in 1889. Mining of coal and nonferrous metals soon became one of the three pillars of the vast Mitsui empire, along with banking and trade; and Mitsui Mining, which was founded as a separate company in 1892, continued for many years to occupy a central place in Mitsui's strategy. Able to exploit at that time the labor of poorly paid women and children, prison convicts, and often prisoners of war, Mitsui Mining was not only extremely profitable but also provided the steady income that allowed the *zaibatsu* to diversify continuously into other, riskier areas. The company's bulwark was the mining of coal from its Miike mines on the island of Kyushu, but it soon acquired a host of zinc, copper, lead, gold, and silver mines around Japan. Its precious-metals holdings were especially important as a means of stabilizing income during the often-wild price fluctuations of the industrial metals, the value of gold tending at that time to remain much more stable.

During Japan's frequent wars, Mitsui Mining also reaped the benefits of increased demand for coal to fuel ships, and lead for the manufacture of bullets. When the Japanese began experimenting with chemical and bacteriological weaponry after World War I, these too were handled by a company carved out of Mitsui Mining: Mitsui Chemical. Mitsui Chemical also directed the reduction of coal into synthetic oil, critical to Japan's performance in World War II. During the later conflict, Mitsui Mining was the country's largest employer of Chinese and Korean prison laborers, whose treatment is reported to have been very poor.

For all of the above reasons, Mitsui Mining was an integral part of Japan's war machine as well as remaining one of the key firms in the Mitsui group. As a result, when General Douglas MacArthur and the Allied occupation forces attempted to dismantle the monopolistic power of Japan's great *zaibatsu* at the conclusion of the war, Mitsui Mining was one of the dozen or so Mitsui affiliates singled out for special attention. The aim of the occupiers was both to weaken Japan's ability to wage war and to encourage Western-style democracy by fostering competition in each industry. Mitsui Mining was felt to be doubly objectionable, having provided raw materials for the war effort and also ranking as Japan's leading producer of coal and nonferrous metals. Occupation authorities therefore ordered the company to be divided into two parts. Mitsui Mining Company was instructed to continue its coal production, based at the Miike mines, while Kamioka Mining & Smelting Company (KMS) was established to handle all other mining activities. In 1950 the two companies were legally separated and MMS began its independent career in the new Japanese economy, one that was ostensibly free of the concentrated power formerly wielded by the *zaibatsu.*

The Allied disruption of the *zaibatsu* was successful in one respect, at least—the Mitsui family and the other leading Japanese industrialist families largely lost control of their conglomerates. The Allied reorganization of Japanese business groups was short-lived, the United States's anxiety over the potential spread of communism in Asia quickly overshadowing its concern with democracy in Japan. The United States wanted a strong, dependable Japan as its sentinel in the Far East, and it was evident that the tradition of cooperation and planning embodied in the *zaibatsu* concept was essential to Japan's past and future economic health, however poorly it satisfied Western ideas of free competition in the marketplace or at the ballot box. Serious anti-*zaibatsu* policies were dropped accordingly by the time of KMS's creation, leaving the essential fabric of Japanese economic life unchanged and making it possible for the Mitsui companies slowly to re-establish their former network. One of the first manifestations of the re-emergence of *zaibatsu* thus came in 1952, when Kamioka Mining & Smelting Co., Ltd. was renamed Mitsui Mining & Smelting Co., Ltd.

The new MMS had taken over from its parent company the largest and highest-quality zinc mine in Japan, and probably in the entire Eastern Hemisphere. The company's Kamioka works in Toyama Prefecture, on the island of Honshu produced one-half of Japan's zinc in the early 1950s and still dominates the Japanese zinc market. Another of MMS's early successes was in lead, of which it continued to provide one-third of Japan's requirements, down since the war but soon to increase again. The case of lead was typical in the history of MMS and

Japan generally: in great demand during the war for bullet manufacturing, lead's value dropped practically to nothing in the chaotic, severely depressed postwar economy. The phenomenal gains made by the Japanese economy during the next few decades, however, greatly expanded the number of peacetime uses for lead, chief among them the manufacture of batteries for automobiles and other end products. As Japan's auto industry slowly developed after the war, the demand for MMS's lead grew proportionately, fueled also by use of the metal in electric-wire sheathing and as a bearing material. MMS created a thriving business in lead by melting its bullets into batteries. A similar evolution could be traced in the example of precious metals, whose value as industrial catalysts and compounds grew tremendously after the war. MMS's gold and silver mines, though never large by world standards, thus continued to justify the expense of deeper exploration.

Another important part of MMS's business in the early 1950s, as today, was the mining and smelting of copper. Because native deposits of copper had long been exhausted, MMS was forced to look overseas for its supplies and in 1953 began a long-term relationship with Marinduque Mining & Industrial Corporation of the Philippines, buying all of its copper production for the next 30 years. In the following years, the company made many similar deals with overseas firms, including a 1969 agreement with Utah Construction & Mining Company in British Columbia to smelt 60% of the copper mined in Utah. In the following year, MMS took advantage of the relative financial strength it enjoys as a member of the Mitsui group by agreeing to participate in a loan package that would enable Freeport Sulphur Company, a U.S. firm, to build a copper mine and plant in Indonesia. For its share of the US$20 million lent by a consortium of Japanese companies, MMS was entitled to buy a percentage of the copper concentrate produced by Freeport. By means of such financial networks, Japan gained access in the postwar period to the Asian raw materials it had tried unsuccessfully to take by force.

The tremendous expansion of the Japanese economy during the 1960s resulted in a proportionate surge in sales at MMS. The burgeoning Japanese auto industry bought not only lead for its batteries from MMS but also an increasing number of die-cast parts such as door latches. The manufacturing of such finished products marked a new era at MMS, which, like the rest of Japanese industry, began a slow shift from basic to value-added products in the face of increased price competition from other Asian industrial nations. Thus, just as Japan has evolved from world domination in steel to that of shipbuilding and then to electronics, MMS began seeking ways to use its metal resources and experience in the manufacture of higher value-added products. In 1981, for example, the company formed a joint venture in Tokyo with Mallinckrodt Incorporated to manufacture catalysts for the food processing, petrochemical, and synthetic fiber industries. Many catalysts make use of precious metals such as gold and platinum, which bring a greater return to refiners like MMS when sold in the form of complex industrial products rather than merely as ore. MMS has continued its evolution from raw-material producer to manufacturer of material-based products, and the company clearly intends to proceed further in that direction.

The Japanese postwar economic recovery had resulted in a number of unwanted additions to Japanese life, including environmental pollution. MMS's role as a smelter of metals led it into several entanglements in this area, the most notorious of which came to a crisis in 1968. For years the population living along the Jinsu River downstream from MMS's big Kamioka zinc mines had suffered from a variety of disorders, which the residents attributed to Kamioka's contaminated effluent. As Japanese companies have traditionally been quite uninterested in addressing such problems, it was not until 1968 that investigators determined that cadmium pollution from the mines was causing a degenerative bone disease known as *itai-itai* or "ouch-ouch," among local residents. A lawsuit was filed by 28 citizens on behalf of some 500 alleged victims of fatal or crippling *itai-itai* disease and, for the first time in Japanese history, the corporation was eventually found guilty and ordered to pay damages which in the aggregate amounted to approximately one year's net income.

Continued fluctuations in the price of raw materials in the 1970s and 1980s spurred MMS's desire to add more highly processed products to its mix of sales. While it remains one of the world's top zinc smelters, MMS has also branched into the manufacturing of zinc alloys for precision casting, known in the trade as ZAPREC; and into copper, which at 20% of sales is now the company's most important metal. As a whole, the company still derived about 40% of its sales from base and precious metals in 1990, but was working hard to develop more processed metal products. This division, which contributes some 30% to corporate revenue, includes an array of more sophisticated goods such as rolled copper products, including copper shingles with artificial patina, and aluminum-oxide dispersion-strengthened copper, and electronics-related. MMS looks to the electronics field for a significant portion of its future growth. Other recently developed products are grouped under the new materials division. These include products made from high-purity metals such as tantalum and niobium, copper foil for laminates, and sputtering targets used in the application of very thin coats of metal.

MMS has not entirely abandoned its traditional strengths—it still produces battery materials, for example—but the company has clearly set its sights on joining the rest of Japan's manufacturers in the race to develop more complex and costly goods. It appears to be willing to entertain suggestions: the firm has announced deals for the production of magnetic audio-visual materials, expanded copper-foil facilities and less predictably, the manufacture of artificial soil for Japan's crowded golf courses.

Principal Subsidiaries: Hibi Kyodo Smelting Co., Ltd. (63.5%); Kamioka Mining & Smelting Co., Ltd.; Taiwan Copper Foil Co., Ltd. (95%); Hikoshima Smelting Co., Ltd.; MESCO, Inc.

Further Reading: Roberts, John G., *Mitsui: Three Centuries of Japanese Business,* New York, Weatherhill, 1989.

—Jonathan Martin

⬧ MITSUI MINING COMPANY, LIMITED

MITSUI MINING COMPANY, LIMITED

1-1, Nihonbashi-muromachi 2-chome
Chuo-ku, Tokyo 103
Japan
(03) 3241-1334
Fax: (03) 3241-4431

Public Company
Incorporated: 1892
Employees: 3,856
Sales: ¥274.65 billion (US$2.02 billion)
Stock Exchanges: Tokyo Osaka Nagoya

Mitsui Mining Company, Limited is one of the oldest components of the vast Mitsui *zaibatsu,* or conglomerate, the mining of coal having played an important role at Mitsui since the last quarter of the 19th century. Mitsui is still the largest coal-mining company in Japan, though the organization's overall size was much reduced in 1950 by the forced spin-off of its metal mines into a separate company, Mitsui Mining & Smelting Company, and by the relative insignificance of coal in Japan's current energy strategy. To counteract the effects of its exhausted mines and shrinking customer base, Mitsui Mining, like many other Japanese suppliers of raw materials, has developed an impressive array of alternative products, many of them high-tech. Half of Mitsui Mining's sales are generated by such items as cement, building materials, and liquefied petroleum gas, while on the horizon are innovations in pollution-control equipment and alumina filament fiber.

For centuries, the house of Mitsui had been one of Japan's leading retail and banking families. Following the restoration of the Emperor Meiji in 1868, The Mitsui Bank in essence took on the role of Japan's national bank, and was soon exploring further opportunities in the newly opened Japanese economy. At the government's urging, the Mitsui interests established a trading company, Mitsui Bussan Kaisha, to stimulate Japan's foreign trade, upon which the country's future economic health would depend. Among Mitsui Bussan's earliest exports were rice and coal, the latter purchased at cost from the government's huge Miike mines on the island of Kyushu. In 1876, its first year of operation, Mitsui Bussan exported 27,000 tons of coal from the Miike mines; nine years later that figure had jumped to 1.8 million tons, the bulk of it shipped to factories throughout China, especially in Shanghai, and to Asian ports as fuel for steamships. At the same time,

Mitsui began mining limited quantities of nonferrous metals like zinc, copper, and lead, as well as gold and silver.

In 1888, the Japanese government, anxious to promote rapid industrialization by strengthening the country's leading industrialist families, put its Miike mines up for sale. Mitsui outbid its rival, Mitsubishi, by a tiny margin and took over the mines, which were easily the nation's largest. Along with the rich coal reserves Mitsui also gained a second valuable resource, an engineer by the name of Takuma Dan, director of the mines since 1881. Dan had earned a degree in mining engineering from the Massachusetts Institute of Technology and was a highly talented production manager and administrator. He recommended to his new employers that a series of improvements be made at Miike, chiefly to protect the mines against periodic cave-ins and flooding. Under Dan's guidance, the mines were reinforced and provided with an enormous water pump to keep them dry, measures which quickly increased productivity and reduced mine shut-downs. Though the mines also became a safer environment for the many thousands of workers, employee welfare was far from a priority of the Mitsui managers. The Miike mines were manned with a combination of *eta,* the Japanese counterpart of Hindu "untouchables," and prison laborers; neither group was treated tolerably. Work conditions were brutal, wages low—or nonexistent for convicts—and any tendencies toward unionism were stamped out with the help of such ultra-nationalist organizations as the Black Ocean Society, which put its thugs at the disposal of large employers in return for payoffs and political clout.

Not surprisingly, the Miike mines were immensely profitable, and Mitsui soon added the equally rich Kamioka deposits, a treasure mountain of zinc and lead with traces of cadmium, silver, and copper. Other coal mines were bought in the Miike area and on the northern island of Hokkaido, and soon Mitsui's team of six coal mines was producing over one-quarter of Japan's total. When Japan went to war in 1894 to 1895 with China, and ten years later with Russia, the Mitsui mining interests benefited from the vastly increased demand for lead, sulfur, and iron needed in the manufacture of munitions. At the same time, Mitsui was able to use its gold reserves, mainly extracted from its Kushikino mine, to stabilize income dependent on the fluctuating prices of its base metals, hoarding gold when base metal prices were high and then selling it when base prices dropped. So critical was the mining of coal and metals to Japan's rapid industrialization that Mitsui and the other great *zaibatsu* were able to erect their immense business empires on a foundation of mining profits, as well as on the control of raw materials at their source. Both Mitsui and Mitsubishi began their subsequent vertical integration from the ground up, quite literally. In 1892 Mitsui, recognizing the great importance of its mining interests, gathered most of them together into Mitsui Mining Company (MM), which would remain one of the *zaibatsu*'s three pillars of business for many years to come.

In the midst of this prosperity, however, working conditions for Mitsui's thousands of miners remained abysmal. According to Shizue Ishimoto, wife of an engineer employed at the Miike mines, the miners were reduced to a state of semi-slavery, working 12 to 14 hour days—with very few holidays—to earn enough money merely to survive, housed in tiny shelters without basic amenities, and physically bullied into compliance with the existing order. Men, women, and children all worked together in the mines, children especially valued for their ability to work in the narrowest and most cramped quarters. Union organization was stifled by legislative, intellectual, and physical coercion. Not until 1924 was there a strike at Mitsui's Miike mines, but at no time then or afterward did organized labor threaten the absolute power of the *zaibatsu*.

World War I proved a great boon to Japan's developing industry, its ships, weaponry, and steel all in demand by the belligerent powers. Even better was the following decade, in which a booming world economy stimulated further expansion and consolidation of Japan's overseas trade. It was clear to all observers that Japan's future as a modern capitalist country depended on access to raw materials and strong overseas markets, both of which, it was tempting to suppose, could best be secured by means of colonial expansion. Japan accordingly embarked on a program of overt and threatened aggression throughout Southeast Asia and China, where MM established a series of mines and refineries during the latter part of the 1930s. The gradual gains of Japanese labor were more than offset by MM's importation of thousands of forced conscripts from occupied China and Korea. MM would eventually become Japan's largest user of such prison laborers, whose numbers reached more than 750,000 by the end of World War II.

By the beginning of full-scale hostilities in China in 1937, MM was Japan's leading producer of coal, nonferrous metals, explosives, chemical weapons, and petroleum refined from coal. Japan's lack of oil reserves made the production of synthetic oil from coal particularly essential to its war effort, and in 1941 Mitsui Chemical was created by MM to shoulder these duties, as well as the manufacture of chemical-based munitions. Like all of the Mitsui companies, MM was soon put under the direct control of the Japanese government and became the nation's leading supplier of lead for bullets and, via Mitsui Chemical, sulfur for explosives. It would be hard to gauge the profitability of these activities, which without a doubt kept MM's mines and refineries busy yet ended in the total destruction of Japan as an economic power. By the end of the war, MM executives at least had the comfort of knowing that the bulk of their assets lay far underground, safe from ravages of Allied bombing.

The Allied occupation forces under General Douglas MacArthur sought to encourage democracy in Japan, as well as to destroy its capacity for war, by systematically breaking up the handful of great *zaibatsu* that controlled nearly all economic activity in the country. Among the Mitsui companies targeted for dissolution was MM, which in 1950 was split into two new firms, Mitsui Mining Company, Limited and Mitsui Mining & Smelting, Co., Ltd. The latter was given all of Mitsui's non-coal mining interests, while the former remained Japan's leading producer of coal and related products. U.S. foreign policy makers soon lost interest in the abolition of the *zaibatsu*, becoming more concerned about the threat of Asian communism, and the many Mitsui companies were tacitly encouraged to regain their former strength by means of a new, less formal organization known as the *keiretsu*. Aided by the prodigious growth of the Japanese economy in the 1950s, MM and its fellow Mitsui affiliates gradually rebuilt the Mitsui empire, in which MM continued to play an important role as one of the group's oldest constituents.

The growing importance of petroleum in the world economy posed insoluble problems for MM, however. More industries,

utilities, and transport vehicles ran not on coal but on oil and gasoline, while at the same time MM's coal was becoming progressively more expensive to mine. MM, with the help of Mitsui *keiretsu* member Dai-Ichi Bank and the group's general solidarity, began a slow process of contraction and retrenchment. It closed down its least productive Japanese mines, sought additional coal supplies overseas, and developed over the following decades a number of profitable alternatives to mining, chiefly cement, coke refining, and liquefied petroleum gas production.

The cost in human terms of such a rearrangement of assets was driven home by the great strike of 1960, one of the most important labor struggles in the history of Japan. Unions had made great inroads at MM's Miike mines during the postwar period, winning a 114-day strike after the Korean War and later proving intractable when MM asked for sharp cuts in the number of its employees. In 1959 the Japanese government called for new reductions in the price of coal to match oil's relative cheapness, and to meet the government demand MM's president Kan Kuriki asked his union for a massive "voluntary retirement" of workers. The union refused and began a strike that would last for the better part of a year and attract greater publicity than any other in the postwar era. Both sides poured immense amounts of energy and money into the battle, but the combined pressure of cold war resistance to anything that smacked of Marxism and MM's traditional reliance on right wing coercion proved too much for the union. MM went on in the following decade to halve its work force while tripling its rate of production per employee, using modernized equipment to extract coal faster and more efficiently. In doing so, the company incurred charges of unsafe working conditions, an allegation borne out by the November 9, 1963, explosion at Miike which killed 458 workers and injured another 800. The accident was the worst in Japanese mining history and one of the worst ever recorded, and resulted in a series of lawsuits that dragged on until 1987, when each of the victims' families was awarded the modest sum of US$1,800.

After the 1963 disaster, President Kuriki resigned in disgrace and was replaced by Okito Kurata, a labor expert who led MM's formerly truculent workers into the new era of cooperation and harmony. Indeed, the 1960 strike at Miike seems to have been a watershed in Japanese labor relations, marking the end of adversarial conflict and the beginning of a renewed commitment to higher productivity at all costs. The company's safety record did not improve—between 1965 and 1984 another 500 miners were killed at explosions at six Mitsui mines—but productivity advanced from 15 tons per worker-month to more than 80 tons in 1970, and MM has not been troubled by further labor disagreements.

Like many other Japanese competitors in basic industries, MM has developed an increasing number of high-tech improvements of its raw products. By relying on the indirect but firm support of the entire Mitsui group, MM has been able to survive the double blow of higher coal-mining costs and the rise of oil and atomic power as preferred sources of energy. It has been a leader in advanced mining methods, such as the hydraulic technique it helped pioneer in the early 1970s, but of greater long term significance have been its moves into related industries such as cement and coke production. Cement and building materials comprise 20% of MM's sales, while coke and its by-product, liquefied petroleum gas, contribute another

34%. MM has joined many of its fellow manufacturers in Japan by coming up with more exotic high-tech innovations such as alumina filament fiber and various pollution-control devices. In the future, the company will no doubt concentrate on these highly engineered products, while coal and other simple commodities are left to less developed countries.

Principal Subsidiaries: Mitsui Mining Overseas Co., Ltd.; Sanbi Mining Co., Ltd.; Mitsui Mining Engineering Co., Ltd.; Kinken Quarry Co., Ltd.; Hokusetsu Building Materials Co., Ltd.; Tosa Sanko Macadam Co., Ltd.; Sanko Boring Co., Ltd.; Sanko Construction Co., Ltd.; Sanko Construction & Industry Co., Ltd.; Sanko Construct Administration Co., Ltd.; Sun Building Co., Ltd.; Sanko Forestry Co., Ltd.; Sanko Wood Co., Ltd.; Sun Chemical Company Ltd.; Mitsui Kozan Chemicals Co., Ltd.; Mitsui SRC Development Co., Ltd.; Hita Ready Mixed Concrete Co., Ltd.; Kyuragi Concrete Industry Co., Ltd.; Tosa Sanko Ready Mixed Concrete Co., Ltd.; Nangoku Sanko Ready Mixed Concrete Co., Ltd.; Wakamatsu Sanko Ready Mixed Concrete Co., Ltd.; Tagawa Sanko Building-Block Co., Ltd.; Yamaga Ready Mixed Concrete Co., Ltd.; Mitsui Miike Engineering Corporation; Mitsui Miike Engineering Company Limited; Misui Miike Machinery Company Limited; Ariake Machinery Co., Ltd.; Sun Ariake Electric Co., Ltd.; Sanyo Machinery Co., Ltd.; Sanki Machinery Co., Ltd.; Kyushu Gas Supply Co., Ltd.; Hiroshima General Gas Supply Co., Ltd.; Mitsui Nishi-Nippon Wharf Co., Ltd.; Hibiki Coal Center Co., Ltd.; Kanda Harbour Transportation Co., Ltd.; Chiba Sanko Transportation Co., Ltd.; Sanko Transportation Co., Ltd.; Kita-Nippon Kouhatsu Co., Ltd.; Mitsui Muromachi Shipping Co., Ltd.; Hokkaido Coal Transportation Co., Ltd.; Miike Port Service Co., Ltd.; Sanko Motorcars Co., Ltd.; Miike Commerce Co., Ltd.; Sanko Commerce Co., Ltd.; Sanhoku Commerce Co., Ltd.; Sun Meridian Corporation; Munakata Commerce Co., Ltd.; Yamato Commerce Co., Ltd.; Akagi Commerce Co., Ltd.; Sanyo Commerce Co., Ltd.; Mita Commerce Co., Ltd.; Sanko Petroleum Co., Ltd.; Mitsui Mining Hong Kong Co., Ltd.; Kinki Sanko Co., Ltd.; Sanko Co., Ltd.; Chubu Co., Ltd.; Hokkaido Sanko Petroleum Co., Ltd.; Hiroshima Sanko Petroleum Co., Ltd.; Sanko Engineering Company Limited; Sanko Agency Co., Ltd.; Sanko-Ariake Housing Co., Ltd.; New Tagawa Real Estate Co., Ltd.; Seibu-Nippon Enterprise Co., Ltd.; Seibu Green Co., Ltd.; Mitsui Greenland Company Limited; Hokkaido Greenland Company Limited; Sanko Consultants Co., Ltd.; Sun Information & Service Corporation; Toyo Labor Consultant Co., Ltd.; Sun Lease & Development Co., Ltd.; Kita-Nippon Fresh Foods Co., Ltd.; S, M, S Co., Ltd.; N, M, S Co., Ltd.; Nishi-Nippon Fresh Foods Co., Ltd.; Mega Co., Ltd.; Arita Tile Co., Ltd.; Hokkaido Kyodo Lime Co., Ltd.; Mitsui-Tagawa Tile Co., Ltd.; Ajigawa Ready Mixed Concrete Co., Ltd.; Mitsui Cement Hume-Pipe Co., Ltd.; Hokuriku Sanko Ready Mixed Concrete Co., Ltd.; Nanwa Co., Ltd.; Murano Industries Co., Ltd.; Eiwa Ready Mixed Concrete Co., Ltd.; Sanko Ready Mixed Concrete Co., Ltd.; Kimi Ready Mixed Concrete Co., Ltd.; Tokyo Cement (LANKA) Co., Ltd.

Further Reading: Roberts, John G., *Mitsui: Three Centuries of Japanese Business,* New York, Weatherhill, 1989.

—Jonathan Martin

Nichimen Corporation

NICHIMEN CORPORATION

13-1, Kyobashi 1-chome
Chuo-ku, Tokyo 104
Japan
(03) 3277-5111
Fax: (03) 3281-7980

Public Company
Incorporated: 1892 as Nippon Menka Kaisha
Employees: 4,380
Sales: ¥6.14 trillion (US$45.21 billion)
Stock Exchanges: Tokyo Osaka Nagoya

Nichimen Corporation, a member of The Sanwa Bank group, is one of Japan's largest general trading companies. The company manages 85 overseas offices, and divides its operations into the following subdivisions: machinery and electronics, construction, general merchandise, logs and lumber, grain and foodstuffs, textiles, chemicals and plastics, metals, exports, imports, and fuels and energy.

General trading companies deal globally with a wide variety of product lines, through a large number of domestic and overseas branches concentrating on both import and export. In addition, they organize business ventures, often supplying technology and machinery as well as creating markets for the finished products. They have many subsidiaries and affiliates all over the world, because they prefer not to deal through foreign agents.

General trading companies made their first appearance during the Meiji empire, that lasted from 1868 to 1912. They were formed at the request of the government, which wanted to end the 200-year economic isolation that had characterized the preceding Tokugawa shogunate. Soon after their rise to power, the Meiji rulers noted that their external trade was in the control of foreigners; that international trade regulations, as well as foreigners' languages and cultural backgrounds were unfamiliar to most of the Japanese business community; and that even domestic documents had to be passed through foreign hands. To eradicate such foreign domination, the government invited a few large, experienced holding companies to organize subsidiaries capable of introducing modern business practices and technology to Japan.

In the World War I years, these holding companies came to be known as *zaibatsu* (wealthy groups). They were family-controlled industrial and financial groups, which were classified as combinations of different companies dealing in goods and services as diverse as banking, shipping, and trading.

By the 1890s, the modernization program had transformed the Japanese economy, and the country's entrepeneurs were ready for international ventures. First to enter the arena was the cotton trade. In earlier times, merchants had sold hand-spun cotton and hand-woven cloth. In Europe and the United States, machine-made textiles had been produced for some years. At the dawn of the Meiji era, the foreign merchants lost no time in signing commercial treaties with Japan, so that they could export large quantities of textiles and cottons into Japan. This practice soon threatened the domestic cotton industry, which partly met the challenge by establishing its own spinning mills, though supplies of domestic raw cotton were still meager.

It was in this business climate that Nippon Menka Kaisha (Japan Cotton Company) was established in 1892 by Japanese cotton spinners and merchants. The company's capital in 1892 was ¥100,000, increasing tenfold over the following decade under the directorship of Kita Matazo, a legendary entrepreneur.

Nippon Menka initially imported cotton through exclusive foreign agents. The company gradually started opening its own foreign offices, however. Victory in the Russo-Japanese War in 1905 brought new foreign export markets in Korea and China, and in Manchuria, where the company also started spinning factories and cotton-ginning operations. Nippon Menka opened a Shanghai branch in 1903 and another in Hankow the following year, to export to China the cotton yarn produced by the rapidly expanding Japanese spinning industry. Now a large company with several overseas locations, it also was able to start trading between foreign offices, establishing Menka Gesellschaft in Bremen, Germany, and doing routine business in Liverpool, London, and in Milan. By 1910 the company even established a U.S. subsidiary called the Japan Cotton Company in Fort Worth, Texas, to give Nippon Menka a gateway to the raw cotton trade.

The World War I years spurred company efforts even further. As European countries with more pressing priorities stopped exporting their wares, Japanese products gained popularity. Seizing the moment, the trading companies began to use their growing expertise to diversify their product lines, increase their markets for raw materials, and invest larger amounts in manufacturing operations.

The company also developed a greater international network by opening more overseas facilities. Following the lucrative wartime growth, Nippon Menka opened its first South Seas office in 1917, with a product line that included cotton cloth, cement, and veneers. It was so successful that more South Seas facilities were opened in 1924.

The company also developed an interest in the South American wool trade during the war years. In 1919 it began to buy wool from Argentina and Uruguay, leading it to open an office in Buenos Aires. The next field of operations was Burma, from where the company began to direct its silk trade operations in 1919, in tandem with other ventures concentrating on cereals, rice, and cotton. Soon, the Burma office expanded its line of interests to include spinning machines, electric fans, beer, and canned goods. Other fields of operation were facilities for rice cleaning and oil manufacturing.

African operations began in 1916, when a representative went to Mombasa, Kenya, from Bombay to trade in raw cotton and cotton cloth. Chinese operations likewise gathered momentum when Nippon Menka started to sell cottons there and to export Manchurian soybeans. Also in China, the company did purchasing for the Nikka Oil Company and acted as a sole agency for a hemp company. Expanding into other activities, the company's India operations started vertical integration. To allow it to complete all operations from buying through the shipping of cotton bales, the Indian office began to operate ginning and compressing factories.

The post–World War I boom collapsed in 1920, and the world slipped into a two-year recession. Although the recession of the early 1920s appeared not to affect Nippon Menka, whose paid-in capital stood at ¥26 million in 1925, with growth largely from the war years, the company was, in fact, losing money.

With the beginning of the Depression in 1929, the company problems began to show. Losses were ¥39 million in 1929, ¥2.5 million in 1930, and ¥1.2 million in 1931, for a total nearing ¥43 million. Nippon Menka may have hidden losses from shareholders during the 1920s, but eventually it had to report its financial difficulties.

The company's fortunes declined for two reasons. Competitors, who initially had been loath to brave the heat and uncharted trade routes of cotton-supplying nations like India, proved to be enthusiastic traders when ways around these inconveniences had been established. Furthermore, during the 1920s, several small spinning companies had merged into larger companies, and these had formed themselves into the Japan Spinners' Association, a production cartel that was capable of gearing production to earn reasonable profits in bad times.

Nippon Menka was a large concern, well able to diversify into fields other than cotton. Along with another general trading company, it organized the production of printed fabric for the Far Eastern markets. Rayon was produced and sold in the same way, and the silk business it had established during World War I was expanded. By the mid-1930s, Nippon Menka was an established textile trader, with overseas offices in several locations.

Despite the heavy losses in the beginning of the Great Depression, the company bounced back quickly. The decline in U.S. and European manufacturing brought opportunity to Japanese traders.

One important boost came in 1931, when Japan seized Manchuria from China, establishing the state of Manchukuo in March 1932. Immediately the Japanese government encouraged investment there, as well as the development of heavy industries such as iron and steel, oil, and cement.

For the rest of the 1930s Japan turned more to a wartime economy, expecting war with China. Expectation became fact in 1937, and the government instituted strict control of stocks and import-export prices, especially in the case of war-related products like oil. In other developments, Nippon Menka was assigned by the army to manage factories producing flour, matches, and starch. To show the broadened nature of its business, Nippon Menka Kaisha changed its name in 1943 to Nichimen Jitsugyo (Nichimen Enterprise).

When World War II brought defeat to Japan, economic policies were set by the Allied powers, who confiscated all foreign assets and forbade foreign trade. Despite its capital of ¥30 million, the company lost foreign assets worth an estimated ¥36 million during this period. In 1947 the Allied policies gradually began to relax to the point where goods could be sold on the foreign market by correspondence, although Japanese traders were still not permitted to go overseas. By 1949 export price regulations on textiles were removed, and Japanese traders went to all countries open to them.

The Allied occupation also saw the dissolution of the *zaibatsu*. At war's end the four largest *zaibatsu* controlled one-fourth of the Japanese economy. In the interest of economic democracy, these holding companies were broken up to give other businesses foreign trade opportunities. The trading companies still occupied a weak position in relation to manufacturers, who had been in government favor throughout the war years and the inevitable period of shortages that followed.

Nichimen's independence from *zaibatsu* affiliation now paid handsome dividends, for the company became one of the country's top-ten trading companies. In 1951 it captured 4.3% of the country's foreign trade. By 1958 its share had grown to 6%.

Along with the other trading companies, Nichimen had difficult postwar problems to face. Goods for foreign trade were in short supply. There was a dearth of export trade itself, for the lucrative China market had been lost to communism. Silk, once a principal export, was being replaced by nylon.

Nichimen and other trading companies needed extensive loans to stay afloat. The Ministry of International Trade and Industry decided to help those trading companies that were handling most of the country's international trade. Because these companies also wanted to take advantage of growing domestic opportunities, credit sources able to supply large yen loans became a necessity. Nichimen, previously content with the Bank of Tokyo's international lending ability, now needed another backer. In 1955 Nichimen forged what would become a long-term relationship with Osaka-based Sanwa Bank. Sanwa agreed to finance all of Nichimen's domestic business.

The Sanwa Bank was a non-*zaibatsu* institution that had gained considerable influence during the occupation because it was exempt from the Allies's order to disband. One of the country's largest, it soon became the center of a large conglomerate, gaining further power through the usual banking practice of granting lower-interest loans to selected companies. Nichimen's bond with Sanwa proved both profitable and permanent. Nichimen could not, however, become Sanwa's international general trading arm because that position was already held by Iwai & Co.

To further strengthen domestic ties, Nichimen absorbed two textile dealers, Maruei & Co. in 1954, and Tazuke & Co. in 1960. Nichimen also made efforts to diversify into foodstuffs, wood, pulp, and machinery by networking through its foreign contacts. Extending its interest in industrial equipment, in 1963 the company acquired Takada & Co., a trader in machinery. In 1957 Nichimen Jitsugyo became Nichimen Co., Ltd.

Between 1955 and 1970 the Japanese economy saw rapid growth. Nichimen enjoyed great export growth, which by 1970 encompassed steel, electronic products, motor vehicles, and fibers—a considerable expansion over the textiles that had formed the nucleus of export operations before 1955. Although the general trading companies still served steelmakers and shipbuilders, most manufacturers began to purchase their own supplies and market their own products.

In 1955 metal sales constituted 15% of Nichimen's operations, with textiles making up a further 57%, foods and chemicals 21%, and miscellaneous 7%. By 1965 the balance had changed—metals then constituted 28% of sales, textiles 36%, foods 7%, and miscellaneous products 19%. Eleven years later, metals and machinery had become the most important group, accounting for 47% of operations. Textiles made up 18% of the total, with food and chemicals 26%, and miscellaneous sales 9%.

Nichimen's greatest growth came in steel. Like other general trading companies, Nichimen handled raw materials, purchased fabricated steel products, secured overseas markets for finished products, and handled the details of export. In addition, Nichimen was leasing supermarkets; negotiating agreements with foreign manufacturers looking for Japanese markets; and becoming more involved in farming, poultry, and beef ventures.

As a result of these activities, Nichimen's annual sales rose from ¥305.6 billion in 1960 to ¥777.8 billion by decade's end, rising still further by 1976 to ¥1.81 trillion. Business activities of the early 1970s included a Japanese joint venture with National Biscuit Company (Nabisco). In 1970 Nabisco took 45% ownership giving 10% ownership to Nichimen, and 45% to Yamazaki Baking Company, in exchange for the right to use the Nabisco trademark.

The increase in Nichimen's product lines and its geographical spread was then allowing the general trading companies to organize complex projects cutting across many different industries. Ocean resource development, urban projects, and financial ventures were just three of many areas in which Nichimen was able first to create demands for a widening array of products, and then to supply them through different affiliates.

In the early 1970s the Japanese economy began to slow down, and the government started to curb trading companies' stock holdings in response to increasing criticism of the firms. They were accused of stock speculation, of hoarding imported necessities, and of tax evasion. This situation came to a head with the 1973 oil crisis. In self defense, Nichimen and other trading companies decided to shift their emphasis from high-volume sales to social responsibility and efficient management, by adopting codes of behavior that promised ethical conduct in all business dealings.

Nichimen's search for global reach brought the company into many different countries, where they participated in joint ventures. One project, a joint venture between Nichimen and certain other Japanese companies and Deepsea Ventures, Inc., a subsidiary of the U.S. company Tenneco, Inc., mined manganese nodules containing copper, nickel, and cobalt from the Pacific Ocean floor.

By 1976 Nichimen had subsidiaries or branches in London, Hong Kong, Rangoon, Calcutta, Bangkok, Singapore, Kuala Lumpur, and Burma. There also was a vast computerized communications system connecting company offices in most of the world's business centers; these included new additions in Caracas; Lima and; Sandakan, Malaysia; and notably, in Warsaw and Moscow, for Nichimen was doing more business in Eastern Europe.

By the late 1970s Nichimen faced harder times. A soaring yen, climbing 25% in the year between July 1977 and July 1978, oil-price rises in 1973 and 1978, and serious competition from South Korea, Argentina, and other steel- and textile-producing countries with low labor and currency costs brought the accustomed low profit margins even lower.

Undaunted, Nichimen began to look for new avenues, many in developing countries like China and parts of the Soviet Union. For Nichimen, activities included the construction of a New Zealand sawmill in a joint venture with another Japanese company, a textile-dyeing joint venture in China, and contracts totaling ¥2 billion for the first stages of a water- and sewerage-system modernization program in Giza, Egypt.

New effort also went into third-country trade—overseas business ventures in which the Japanese company sold the products of another country in yet a third country. Vigorous foreign operations did not curb the development of domestic ventures such as condominium and office block construction, jewelry imports, and retailing. Other operations concentrated on importing; lumber came from the Soviet Union, and foodstuffs from Thailand and China.

In 1982 Nichimen Co., Ltd. changed its name to Nichimen Corporation. By the end of the 1980s, the company had opened new offices in Madras, Khabarovsk, Barcelona, and the Soviet Union, bringing to 85 its total number of geographical divisions. There were also 129 major subsidiaries and affiliates.

Nichimen Corporation's 1985 financial year saw net sales of ¥4.4 trillion, which by the end of the 1980s had grown to ¥4.9 trillion. An even higher figure of ¥6.13 trillion greeted the end of the 1990 fiscal year.

Principal Subsidiaries: Nichimen America Inc. (U.S.A.); Granplex, Inc. (U.S.A.); Nichimen Canada Inc.; Nichimen de Mexico S.A. de C.V.; Nichimen do Brasil Ltda. (Brazil); Nichimen Co. (Argentina) S.A.; Nichimen Australia Limited; Nichimen Co. (New Zealand) Ltd.; Nichimen Co. (Hong Kong) Ltd.; Nichimen Co. (Iran) Ltd.; Nichimen Europe B.V. (Netherlands); Nichimen Iberica, S.A. (Spain); Deutsche Nichimen G.m.b.H. (Germany); Nichimen Europe (France) S.A.; Nichimen Italia S.p.A. (Italy).

Further Reading: Young, Alexander, *The Sogo Shosha: Japan's Multinational Trading Companies,* Boulder, Colorado, Westview Press, 1979; Yonekawa, Shin'ichi, and Hideki Yoshi Hara, ed., *Business History of General Trading Companies,* Tokyo, University of Tokyo Press, 1987.

—Gillian Wolf

NIPPON LIGHT METAL COMPANY, LTD.

13-12 Mita 3-chome
Manato-ku, Tokyo 108
Japan
(03) 3456-9211
Fax: (03) 3798-3662

Public Company
Incorporated: 1939
Employees: 4,476
Sales: ¥636.79 billion (US$4.69 billion)
Stock Exchanges: Tokyo Osaka Nagoya Fukuoka Hiroshima Kyoto Niigata Sapporo

Nippon Light Metal Company concentrates on the manufacture and sale of alumina chemical and chloride products; aluminum ingot and alloys; aluminum products; components for building, heating, and cooling equipment and automobile construction; as well as household utensils and aluminum fabricated products. Japan's only fully integrated aluminum producer, the company divides its business activities into five main areas. The first is chemical; manufactured items include chemicals containing aluminum hydrates, alumina, caustic soda, and fluorine. Fabricated items come from the second area, for example, aluminum materials, including rolled products such as aluminum sheets. Materials for renovation and new building construction form the third main interest area. The fourth area focuses on food storage and transportation—prefabricated refrigerators and vans as well as high-technology cooling equipment. Information systems, comprehensive distribution and trading, and the development of new business ventures fall into business support services, the fifth area.

The Nippon Light Metal Company was established in 1939, through a link between the Furukawa Electric Company and the Tokyo Electric Light Company. The new company had a clear mission, for Japan was on the brink of World War II and desperately needed aluminum for munitions and aircraft. Scarcely a year after its first appearance, the aluminum manufacturer was ready to contribute to the war effort with a factory at Kambara. Two years later, in 1941, the company opened two more factories—one at Niigata, the second, with alumina refining capabilities, at Shimizu. These two additions made Nippon Light Metal the largest aluminum producer in Japan, and a major source of the 165,000 tons needed for the wartime peak years.

The company expanded its activities further in 1946 by reclaiming aircraft aluminum for manufacturing. Nevertheless, its production activities were hampered by the country's lack of bauxite, the source of alumina from which aluminum is made. In 1948 it remedied this problem by starting to import the essential ore.

Defeat in World War II and the subsequent Allied occupation brought devastation to Japan's aluminum factories as well as the loss of their international bauxite sources. In an effort to rebuild, Nippon Light Metal formed close ties with Aluminium Limited of Canada, later known as Alcan Aluminium Limited, which acquired 50% of the Japanese company shares in 1952, and still held 45% in 1990. Alcan's contributions to the union were smelting technology and bauxite, which came from Malaya and British Borneo, as well as from the Indonesian regions that had previously been Japan's sole source.

Advantages for Alcan included Nippon Light Metal's two-year-old management participation in a company called Nasu Aluminium Manufacturing Company, later renamed the Nikkei Aluminium Company. A producer of aluminium sheets, extrusions and architectural products, Nasu operated plants based in Tokyo and Nagoya. While both facilities were equipped with rolling mills that expanded their product lines, the Tokyo plant also featured a 3,250-ton horizontal extruder, enabling the company to manufacture aluminum window sashes for the rapidly-expanding building construction market. Braced by a burgeoning Japanese economy, by 1960 Nikkei Aluminium's monthly orders for raw aluminum ranged between 560 and 600 tons, all of which came from Nippon Light Metal.

Also in the Nippon group at the time of the Alcan agreement were the Special Light Alloy Company and the Osaka Aluminium Company. By 1960 Osaka Aluminium was producing between 120 and 130 tons of aluminum sheets monthly, plus about 250 tons of industrial alumina sheet.

The years between 1955 and 1965 were good for the aluminum fabricating industry. Although expansion into fabrication would have been the logical growth direction for the smelters, they elected to ally themselves with fabricators, rather than entering the field themselves. There were several sound reasons for passing up this opportunity. Paradoxically, one was a rapidly expanding market. Demand for aluminum items like cookware, building products, and components for the transportation industries was now growing so fast that 14 new fabricating firms entered the market during this ten-year period. All of them pitted themselves against established companies, vying for business from the smelting firms capable of supplying them with enough ingots to fill the burgeoning need for their products. It was therefore more profitable for them to make capital investments in these fabricating firms than to enter the field itself.

Expensive electricity also made this type of expansion more sensible for the smelters, whose production costs were far higher than those of their U.S. competitors. Nippon Light Metal scored handsomely here. Supplied with cheaper energy from five company-owned hydropower stations, the Kambara facility ran at the lowest production cost in Japan, turning out of 70,000 tons of aluminum by 1962.

Also at Kambara the company built Japan's only central research institute, where refining and processing technology was studied along with market development methods. Originally known as the Nippon Light Metal Research Laboratory, it was later called the Nikkei Techno-Research Company.

Although the Japanese government relaxed its import controls in 1961 to allow less expensive aluminum into the country, the producers managed to remain competitive. Tariff rates were set at 15%, were reduced further to 13% in 1964, and sank to 11.4% by 1968. Still, as long as the rates remained above 10%, the domestic producers were able to hold their own by operating at high capacity. This alone was a powerful incentive to align themselves with established fabricating companies.

Nippon Light Metal rode the business cycles easily. Between October 1959 and March 1960, the company enlarged the Shimizu plant from its original capacity of 160,000 tons annually, to provide a capacity of 185,000 tons annually. Now able to supply enough alumina for both the Kambara and Niigata refineries, Shimizu played its part in making Nippon Light Metal the country's largest aluminum refiner by 1962. By the end of the year, the company accounted for more than half of Japan's total aluminum production.

By the late 1960s the Japanese aluminum market was the fastest growing in the world. Nippon Light Metal extended its operations to include a major partnership in Nippon Fruehauf Company, a manufacturer of aluminum-bodied van-type trailers. This plus other operations provided a 1968 net income of US$7.5 million, as against US$3.2 million in 1959.

In the same year, growing markets for its products prompted Nippon Light Metal to build a US$125 million smelter at Tomakomai on the island of Hokkaido. Financed partly by the Japanese government and partly by Alcan, the new plant was originally scheduled for full production capacity of 130,000 tons by 1972. However, buttressed by a supply of alumina from Shimizu alumina refining plant on Honshu Island, Tomakomai was providing an initial capacity of 65,000 tons by late 1969, far ahead of its scheduled debut. Within three years, completion of the plant's own alumina facility made it self-sufficient.

The tariff problem reared its head again in the early 1970s. To encourage importing from developing countries, part of these imports qualified for a reduced 1970 tariff rate of 4.5%, as against a 10.6% rate for other imports. A year later the rate was reduced further to 9.8%, and then to 9%.

The balance of the Japanese market was also changed by the 1973 revaluation of the yen. The new flexible exchange rate system caused the dollar to decline from ¥360 to the U.S. dollar to about ¥270 to the dollar. Although this ratio effectively reduced the domestic smelting costs and made imported aluminum cheaper, the balance still swung in favor of foreign products. The results showed in tonnage tallies for primary aluminum; in 1971, the country imported 209,000 tons, while the following year the amount rose to 293,000 tons, soaring to 428,000 tons by the end of 1973.

The list of problems challenging the Japanese aluminum producers did not end with the changes in the yen and the tariffs. The question of electricity costs was far more pressing, since the aluminum industry depended on oil to generate electricity. Prior to the 1973 oil embargo, the price of electricity was four times as high in Japan as it was in Canada, and more than twice as high as it was in the United States. Alternatives were limited; either a smelting company could build a power plant together with a power company, use the power company as the sole source, or mix the two methods.

At the time of the 1973 oil crisis, the Japanese economy was booming, and the demand for aluminum soared to 1.6 million tons. Contributing to the demand was the rising international popularity of Japanese motorcycles and automobiles. Also burgeoning was the aluminum beverage can market. Along with a U.S. company, National Can Overseas Corporation, and two other Japanese companies—Nichimen Company and Kawasaki Corporation—Nippon Light Metal took a 30% share in a joint agreement to make aluminum cans in Japan. Adding to the boom was a U.S. drought, which had reduced U.S. operating ratios by affecting hydropower sources.

The price of a barrel of oil, however, rose to $12.05 in 1974, from $4.75 just one year earlier. With the rest of the Japanese economy, Nippon Light Metal felt curbs immediately. In November of 1973 the company announced that it would cut aluminum shipments to customers by 20%, as a result of the oil and electricity shortages. In 1975 the company cut production from 90% of its 424,000-ton annual output to 80%, closing the No. 1 Kambara plant, and postponing for six months the enrollment of 437 workers scheduled to start in the spring, although they were paid 60% of their basic pay during this period.

In other plans to combat the rise in power costs and offset the cuts in domestic production, Nippon Light Metal employed the strategy used by other producers and invested in overseas ventures. Undertaken along with Alcan Aluminium, one 1977 project involved the conversion of alumina into aluminum ingot. The new venture used Alcan Aluminium's smelting facilities at Kitimat, British Columbia, and allowed Nippon Light Metal to use half of the ingot production in Japan.

Another strategy to combat the high cost of energy involved diversification and increased emphasis on manufacturing. Nippon Light Metal followed this path with the 1974 acquisition of both Nikkei Aluminium Rolling Company and the Nikkei Aluminium Company. The acquisitions enabled Nippon Light Metal to form a continuous aluminum production system featuring three independent divisions for smelting, light rolling, and end products and construction materials.

Despite these moves, high energy costs prevailed. The company registered a loss of ¥5.5 million at the end of its 1975 financial year, forcing it and its subsidiaries to reduce their work force by about 1,100 employees by the end of the fiscal year on March 31, 1978. In other moves, they also withheld pay increases and bonuses, and encouraged about 300 voluntary retirements.

By 1978 the value of the yen had risen. This rise proved to be another brake on industry profitability, even though aluminum prices on the world market were rising. In accordance with government guidelines, production was reduced, the country importing about 30% of its aluminum needs.

Nevertheless, there were signs that the tide was turning. In spite of the company loss of $5.6 million for 1978, in early 1979 Nippon Light Metal was awarded a contract to design and build a smelter in the People's Republic of China, and to train Chinese engineers to operate it.

Also in 1979, there was another oil crisis caused by the Iranian revolution. The price of oil rose from $23.07 in that year to $38.24 per barrel by June 1981. This increase brought the price of electricity to the prohibitively high level of about ¥16 per kilowatt hour, raising energy prices for smelting to more than 50% of production costs. As a result domestic aluminum cost about ¥500,000 per ton, as against $1,280 for the imported product. The same year, the Ministry of International Trade and Industry requested aluminum smelters to close 30% of their capacity, and Nippon Light Metal closed its Niigata electrolyzing plant, dismantling it and selling it for export.

Along with other Japanese aluminum producers, the company then began to fund research into less energy-intensive smelting processes. Another research priority was a refining method that could utilize ores other than the expensive, imported bauxite.

Nippon Light Metal also began to look for aluminum sources overseas. In 1980 it signed a contract with Alcan Australia Ltd., whose New South Wales smelter started providing them with ingots in 1982. Recycled products from scrap like aluminum cans and siding were other sources increasingly valued by Japanese producers; totaling 200 million pounds in 1977, the amount reached more than 600 million pounds by 1979.

Opportunities to expand fabrication activities were not neglected. In 1978 the company had acquired the Nikkei Aluminum Sales Company. At the same time, it established a continuous sales and production system for the plate rolling division as well as for the products and construction materials division. A year later, the company separated the product section from construction, simultaneously reorganizing the materials section. In addition, it closed the Niigata plant, thus saving on salaries. The reshuffling brought its reward; sales figures of US$1.60 billion moved the company into a profit position once again.

Government actions also helped. Between 1978 and 1979 the Japanese authorities introduced reductions in the tariff rates on a first-come, first-served basis, so that orders could be filled. In 1983 this plan was refined to reduce the target capacity from 1.1 million tons to 700,000 tons. By way of compensation the government introduced a tariff exemption system that freed producers from taxes on aluminum that had to be imported to make up existing requirements.

Nippon Light Metal responded to these changes with further diversification, establishing a chemical division in 1984. Products of the new section included aluminum hydroxide—a basic ingredient in glass, artificial marble, flame-retardant fillers and industrial chemicals. The company entered another field in 1986, when it established the cast and forge products division to manufacture electronic parts, parts for heat exchangers, components for motorcycles and automobiles, and connecting rods.

In 1988 a general company reorganization established five different headquarters: basic materials, light rolling, fabricated products, development, and production technology. The company also expanded its building trade interests, forming JPC Company in a joint venture with Kurosawa Construction Company, Ltd.

Nippon Light Metal Company was 50 years old in 1989. Sales income for the first half of the financial year reached ¥137 billion, rising to ¥270 billion by March 1990. By this time, the company owned the only smelter in operation in Japan and was responding to increased demand for aluminum in the transportation and capital goods sectors. The year was further marked by a share increase to 75% in the Thai Aluminium Company Ltd., subsequently renamed Nikkei Thai Aluminium Company, Ltd.

Principal Subsidiaries: Shin Nikkei Company, Ltd. (66.7%); Nippon Electrode Company, Ltd.; Nikkei Techno Research Company, Ltd.: Nippon Fruehauf Company, Ltd. (51%); Nikkei Shoji Company, Ltd. (83.3%); Riken Light Metal Industry Company, Ltd.; Nikkei Thai Aluminium Company, Ltd. (75%).

Further Reading: United Nations Economic Commission for Asia and the Far East, *Bauxite Ore Resources and Aluminum Industry of Asia and the Far East: Mineral Resources Development Series No. 17,* Bangkok, United Nations, 1962; Peck, Merton J., ed., *The World Aluminum Industry in a Changing Energy Era,* Washington, D.C., Resources for the Future, 1988.

—Gillian Wolf

NIPPON STEEL

NIPPON STEEL CORPORATION

6-3, Otemachi 2-chome
Chiyoda-ku, Tokyo 100-71
Japan
(03) 3242-4111
Fax: (03) 3275-5607

Public Company
Incorporated: 1971
Employees: 38,208
Sales: ¥2.60 trillion (US$19.14 billion)
Stock Exchanges: Tokyo Osaka Nagoya

Nippon Steel Corporation is one of the leading steelmakers in the world. In addition to steel production, the company is involved in a number of other businesses, including engineering and construction, electronics, sales of titanium and other materials, and biotechnology.

As the spearhead of Japan's economic transformation after World War II, Nippon Steel rose from virtual annihilation to a position of world leadership in the space of 25 years. With Japanese shipbuilders, automakers, and other heavy steel consumers achieving prominence in world markets, Nippon Steel enjoyed annual sales gains of 25% and more during the late 1950s and the 1960s, and by 1975 was the world's largest steelmaker. In the waning years of the 20th century, however, neither Japan's domestic economy nor those of the other developed nations have need of the enormous steel supply they once did. As a result Nippon faces problems of static demand and fresh competition from countries such as South Korea, busily forging their own "economic miracles." Like other of the world's steelmakers, Nippon drastically reduced capacity following the oil crisis of 1973–1974, and hopes to follow the example of other Japanese industrial powers in diversifying from basic commodity products toward specialty steels and wholly unrelated activities.

The history of Nippon Steel closely parallels, and in some cases is identical with, the history of Japanese steel as a whole. In the centuries of isolation before the opening of trade with the West in the 1850s, Japan had manufactured what little steel it needed by an ancient method of smelting adequate to the demands of a pre-industrial economy. Prodded by the need to defend itself against the incursions of Western steamships, the Japanese government lifted its ban on the production of large ships in 1853, and a number of dockyards soon sprang up around the country, all of them in need of unprecedented amounts of steel. In 1857, Japan's first blast furnace was installed near the Kamaishi iron mines, an accomplishment which still left the Japanese 400 to 500 years behind the West in metallurgy. The Kamaishi furnaces were successful, however, and the Japanese government nationalized them in 1873 to hasten the development of this basic constituent of an industrial economy.

In its race to catch up with the Western powers, Japan faced a number of formidable obstacles. Not only was the country without engineering expertise, it also lacked all but trace amounts of coking coal and iron ore, the key ingredients of iron and steel. Its mineral poverty would later play a critical role in Japan's foreign policy, but in the early years of its steel industry the first need was for technical guidance. Most of this was supplied by Germans, in particular Curt Netto, professor of engineering at Tokyo University from 1877 to 1885, and Adolf Ledebur, another professor of engineering who was instrumental in coordinating the work of German design firms on behalf of Japan's early steel mills. Under the tutelage of these and other German experts, Japan soon developed its own circle of metallurgists and engineers, including most notably Kageyoshi Noro and Michitaro Oshima. When the Japanese government renewed its commitment to steel with the opening of a vast new plant at Yawata in 1896, its construction was entrusted to a German firm and Michitaro Oshima was named managing director of the newly created Imperial Japanese Government Steel Works at Yawata. The Yawata works became the nucleus of today's Nippon Steel.

The Yawata works did not get underway until 1901, when its target for the year's production was 60,000 tons of steel. In comparison, U.S. steel capacity in 1901 was ten million tons. Yawata's primary customers were shipbuilders and weapons makers. The state of Japan's armed forces prompted the government to take a direct role in the development of its steel industry and pour its resources into the nascent steel works at Yawata. Even so, production at Yawata was poor at first with many technical failures during the early years. By 1904 these had been largely overcome, and Yawata was running a smooth if modest operation.

Having borrowed the technology it needed from the Germans and the English, Japan faced a second and more intractable problem—its lack of raw materials. The dominant steelmaking nations—chiefly the United States, England, Germany, and France—had achieved their positions with the help of native supplies of iron ore and coking coal. Japan had practically none, and with the primitive modes of transport then available believed that it would never become an industrial power without taking steps to secure convenient and stable supplies of these basic ingredients. Its poor supply of raw materials played at least a contributing role in the growth of Japan's territorial claims in the first half of this century. Both of its closest neighbors, Korea and China, were rich in iron ore and coal, and as early as 1910 Japan had formally annexed Korea and was jockeying for position in northern China. In the following decades Japan would take what it needed from these two countries while also shifting a significant amount of its steel production to these countries.

Japan's steel industry remained incapable of supplying the country's urgent need for steel for years. In 1913, production at Yawata reached 200,000 tons of crude steel, which was 85% of all the steel made in Japan but less than 30% of that needed by the nation's growing shipbuilding and munitions industries. World War I provided an important stimulus for all segments of the Japanese economy. Shipping, railroads, electrical industries, and Japan's now-numerous manufacturers all required far more steel than the Imperial Works could supply, and even the gradual appearance of privately owned steel companies could not close the gap. The country remained precariously dependent on foreign sources of pig iron, scrap iron, coal, and iron ore as well as finished steel products.

The Great Depression added a fresh impetus to Japan's aggressive foreign policy. Military leaders were inspired by a rising tide of ultra-conservative political sympathy to demand a more rapid pace in Japan's continental expansion. In such a climate, the country's relatively backward steel industry became all the less tolerable, and in 1934 the Japanese government took a major step toward finally gaining self-sufficiency in steel. The Imperial Works at Yawata was merged with six leading private steelmakers—Wanishi, Kamaishi, Fuji, Kyushu, Toyo, and Mitsubishi—to form Japan Iron & Steel Company, Ltd., which was about 80% owned by the government. At the time of its formation, Japan Iron & Steel's crude steel capacity was estimated at 2.12 million tons, about 56% of the total for Japan. Under its first president, Reisaku Nakai, Japan Iron & Steel immediately began an ambitious and highly successful expansion of its facilities. Two plants were completely overhauled and given much larger blast furnaces, and a new mill was added in northern Korea near plentiful sources of iron and coal. With Korea and Manchuria now supplying more than 50% of Japan's coal and much of its iron ore, an increasing proportion of iron and steel production was moved to the mainland. This trend in turn seemed to confirm the military's insistence on further imperialist expansion. At Japan Iron & Steel, production was geared ever more closely to the needs of the military.

In a remarkably short time, Japan Iron & Steel and the rest of the industry caught up to the level of domestic steel consumption. By the beginning of World War II in 1939, Japan had become the world's fifth-leading steelmaker, with production reaching 5.8 million tons, and the industry was able to supply most of the needs of Japanese manufacturers, with the striking exception of armor plating. Yet even in its newfound strength, the Japanese industry was quite small by the standards of the United States, which in that year produced 28 million tons. Japan was not in a position, because of shortages of steel and a dozen other crucial resources, to wage a world war, and yet it was precisely this lack of materials that made war seem inevitable to the Japanese. Wartime steel production hit a peak of 12 million tons, but in that same year the United States alone launched 19 million tons of merchant shipping. At Japan Iron & Steel, only three of its many blast furnaces remained operable at the end of the war.

A nation in ruins, postwar Japan was in need of vast amounts of steel. With the close cooperation and financial support of the United States, Japan Iron & Steel was rebuilt from the ground up according to the latest and most efficient designs. The new Japanese plants were larger, more completely integrated, and technologically more advanced than any others in the world—a complete overhaul that would not be possible for the older steel industries of Britain and the United States. Once given this technological edge, Japan Iron & Steel used its favorable labor rates to produce the world's best steel at the lowest possible prices for the next 30 years, until South Korea employed the same tactics to displace Japan in the 1980s.

Japan Iron & Steel met the same fate that most of the *zaibatsu*—combines of banks and industries—had suffered at the hands of the Allied occupation forces. In 1950 it was broken into four privately owned companies to promote American-style competition in the steel business. Of the four firms, the largest by far was Yawata Iron & Steel Co., Ltd., made up mostly of the plants of the old Imperial Works. Two others were much smaller specialty companies but the fourth became Japan's second-largest steelmaker, Fuji Iron & Steel Co., Ltd. Fuji and Yawata spent the next 20 years engaged in intense competition without ever forgetting their common origins, until in 1971 they again merged to form today's Nippon Steel.

The Korean War gave Japan its first inkling of the role it would play in the post–World War II economy, as the Western powers looked to Japan for basic industrial goods and supported its growth into a bulwark against Asian communism. In response, the steel industry in Japan embarked upon its First Modernization Program in 1956. In the first of these united efforts some ¥128 billion was invested, in the second ¥625 billion, and a third program initiated in 1961 used more than ¥1 trillion. The most important results of these enormous expenditures fall into three categories. First, beginning in the early 1950s, Japan led the world in its adoption of the basic oxygen furnace technology, arguably the most important steelmaking innovation of the postwar era. Second, in 1957 Yawata Iron & Steel was one of the first steel companies to install the LD converter, which consumes far less scrap iron during the steelmaking process than the formerly universal open-hearth method. Third, the Japanese pioneered continuous casting, the integration of steel production with the milling and shaping process, which until this time had been kept inefficiently separate. All three of these improvements eventually were adopted around the world, but the Japanese were the first to use them, and were similarly advanced in their introduction of computer controls in the early 1960s.

In 1959, Yawata Iron & Steel's annual sales reached US$340 million, making it the largest industrial company in Japan. Fuji sales stood at US$250 million—third largest. The bulk of the two companies' revenue was generated by domestic sales, as the Japanese economy still absorbed nearly all the steel the country could make. The trend in postwar Japanese consumption was away from military and railroad contracts and toward the burgeoning automobile, shipbuilding, and construction markets, which together were expanding the Japanese economy at the rate of about 10% per year. In the next ten years Japan enjoyed the decade of its most spectacular growth and began the heavy exporting of goods that has made it the wonder of the economic world. Growth in the Japanese steel industry in the 1960s averaged 25% per year, and the country's paucity of raw materials no longer seemed the problem it once had. In the meantime, the more mature U.S. economy used a decreasing amount of steel, and the U.S. steel industry fell irretrievably behind the Japanese.

The end of the 1960s saw another leap in worldwide demand for shipping tonnage—mainly to ferry oil—and the Japanese steel industry agreed to spend the unprecedented sum of ¥3 trillion on yet another round of capital improvements. The two chief descendants of the old Japan Iron & Steel, Yawata and

Fuji, announced in 1969 that they were to re-merge and form a new steel giant called Nippon Steel. Many other former *zaibatsu* holdings had similarly gravitated back together. The new Nippon Steel had combined revenue of about $2.3 billion, making it Japan's largest business of any kind and second only to U.S. Steel Corporation among world steelmakers. Top management was carefully divided between Shigeo Nagano from Fuji and Yoshihiro Inayama from Yawata, but for a number of years there was factional bitterness between the newly merged partners.

At its height in the early 1970s, Nippon Steel's 80,000 employees directed a network of furnaces and mills capable of producing 47 million tons of crude steel per year—or four times the wartime capacity of Japan as a nation. It was hoped that combining the two great steelmakers would eliminate duplication of effort, increase scale efficiences, and help pump up the steel industry's thin bottom line. The 1973–1974 oil crisis and the changing nature of the world economy rendered these hopes vain, however. The oil crisis brought to an abrupt halt the booming market for Japanese shipping, approximately quadrupled the cost of Nippon Steel's power and fuel, encouraged the construction of lighter automobiles containing less steel, and in general dragged the world's heavy industries into a long slump. The effects on Nippon's performance were immediate. Fiscal year 1975 showed a paltry profit of $50 million on declining sales of $7 billion, and by 1977 production was down to 32 million tons and 9 of the company's 25 furnaces had been shut down.

Nippon's fortunes were also affected by Japan's changing place in the world economy. By 1975, when Nippon passed U.S. Steel as the world's largest steelmaker, Japan was no longer a young industrial nation requiring vast amounts of steel to build its infrastructure and heavy export goods. Similarly, the developed Western nations upon whom Nippon depended for export sales were all well into the post-industrial age; their need for steel was essentially static and increasingly weighted toward various specialty products. The oil shock only accelerated a trend toward reduced steel usage and Third World competition.

The combined impact of these events on Nippon Steel and the world steel industry was devastating. Worldwide, steel employment dropped 43% between 1974 and 1987. At Nippon Steel it was halved in the same period, while overall capacity was cut back from 47 million tons to about 27 million in the mid-1980s. The recession of the early 1980s was especially hard on Japanese steel, which as a whole reported losses in 1983 for the first time in many years. Four years later Nippon and the other leading Japanese steelmakers all showed a year-end loss, the first time that had happened since World War II. The next few years offered a mild recovery, with national production reaching 108 million tons, still less than the peak year of 1980 and not significantly greater than what it had been 20 years earlier. Nippon managed a return to the 2% to 3% profit margin it has traditionally shown.

Nippon's response to the erosion of its markets has been typical of large Japanese combines. While cutting expenses to the bone and shedding excess labor—generally by attrition and in the form of employee "loans" to other companies—Nippon has also moved swiftly into an array of new fields. The company's profile is broken into four primary divisions—steelmaking; titanium sales; a wide variety of heavy construction projects; and a catch-all grouping of new materials development, computer systems, biotechnology, and even an amusement park. Nippon has also increased its presence in the U.S. domestic steel market through a number of substantial joint ventures with Inland Steel Industries, 13% of whose stock it owns. While all of these strategies will help ease the pain of decline in Nippon's flat-steel business, they are not likely to compensate for the profound changes the industry underwent during the 1970s and 1980s. As the largest steelmaker in the capitalist world, Nippon has the most to lose in this restructuring. However, since the Japanese have shown as much resourcefulness in extricating themselves from basic industries as they did in learning to dominate them, the future may find Nippon Steel Corporation radically changed but fundamentally healthier.

Principal Subsidiaries: NS Tek, Inc. (U.S.A.); NS Kote, Inc. (U.S.A.); NS Pipe Technology, Inc. (U.S.A.); NS Sales, Inc. (U.S.A.); Nippon Steel Metal Products Co., Ltd. (95.4%); Nittetsu Steel Drum Co., Ltd. (57.8%); Nippon Steel Welding Products & Engineering Co., Ltd. (68.2%); Nippon Steel Bolten Co., Ltd.; Nippon Tubular Products Co., Ltd.; Fuji Tekko Center Co., Ltd. (51%); Nittetsu Corrosion Prevention Co., Ltd. (54.2%); Nittai Corporation (60%); Chukyo Seisen Co., Ltd. (80%); Nippon Steel Chemical Co., Ltd. (57.1%); Nittetsu Cement Co., Ltd. (55%); Chemirite, Ltd. (U.S.A., 77.9%); Kankyo Engineering Co., Ltd. (55%); Nittetsu Electrical Engineering & Construction Co., Ltd.; Nittetsu Plant Designing Corporation; Electro-Plasma, Inc. (U.S.A., 76%); Nittetsu Transportation Co., Ltd. (86.4%); Nittetsu Transport Service Co., Ltd.; Nittetsu Ryutsu Center Co., Ltd. (60%); Nippon Steel Shipping Co., Ltd. (76%); Nippon Steel Information & Communication Systems Inc.; Nippon Steel Life Planning Co., Ltd.; Tetsubiru Co., Ltd. (91.7%); Sakai Tekko Building Co., Ltd. (75%); Yuwa Sangyo Co., Ltd; Nittetsu Finance Co., Ltd.; Nippon Steel U.S.A., Inc. (U.S.A.); NS Invest, Inc. (U.S.A.); NS Invest II, Inc. (U.S.A.); NS Finance, Inc. (U.S.A.); NS Finance III, Inc. (U.S.A.).

Further Reading: Berglund, Abraham, "The Iron and Steel Industry of Japan and Japanese Continental Policies," *Journal of Political Economy,* October 1922; *History of Steel in Japan,* Tokyo, Nippon Steel Corporation, 1972.

—Jonathan Martin

NISSHIN STEEL CO., LTD.

NISSHIN STEEL CO., LTD.

4-1, Marunouchi 3-chome
Chiyoda-ku, Tokyo 100
Japan
(03) 3216-5511
Fax: (03) 3214-1895

Public Company
Incorporated: 1928 as Tokuyama Teppan Kabushikigaisha
Employees: 7,219
Sales: ¥476.86 billion (US$3.51 billion)
Stock Exchanges: Tokyo Osaka Nagoya Hiroshima Fukuoka
 Frankfurt

Primarily a maker of stainless and surface-coated sheet steel, Nisshin Steel Co., Ltd. has escaped the worst effects of the world steel industry's severe decline since the oil crisis of 1974. Although Nisshin has suffered its share of worker layoffs and mediocre financial performance its traditional strength in specialty surface-treated steels—certain alloys gave the company an advantage in the race among Japanese steelmakers to develop more complex value-added products. Nisshin has even branched out of steel altogether, joining partnerships in such fields as fast-food restaurants and retirement-community development.

Although little information is available about Nisshin's history, it is clear that the company's original as well as present talents lay in the manufacture of coated steel. Steel is invaluable for its strength and formability, but it is subject to destructive oxidation in the presence of gas or water. Coated steels were developed around the beginning of the 20th century to provide rust protection for metals used in wet or damp environments. The best all-around coating agent was found to be zinc, which, when applied in a molten state to steel, forms a tight, waterproof casing that lasts up to 30 years. This process, known as galvanizing, became one of the most commonly used modifications of steel and the basis for many subsequent innovations in coating technology.

Nisshin's earliest predecessor, Nichia Steel, was the first Japanese company to produce galvanized steel. Nichia was founded in 1908, when the Japanese iron and steel industry was still far behind Western levels of production and technology. It galvanized the steel by dipping each sheet in zinc in a laborious process that kept output low and costs high. The market for galvanized steel was equally limited, however, since the Japanese economy did not yet include the modern plumb-ing, construction, and automotive industries that would later create much of the demand for galvanized steel.

In 1911 Nichia absorbed a rival firm called Galvanizing Company, which had a plant in Osaka. As its name suggests, Galvanizing Company was also limited to the production of zinc-coated steel, and together the merged companies assumed a dominant position in Japan's early galvanizing industry. Galvanizing remained Nichia's primary business for many years, but Nichia also became interested in new alloys made by combining iron with varying amounts of nickel, chromium, molybdenum, and other metals to produce steels with unusual, commercially valuable characteristics. Such steels are used widely in the tool and die and automotive industries that became more important as Japan evolved toward a wartime economy in the 1930s. In 1928 Nichia Steel was incorporated as Tokuyama Teppan Kabushikigaisha.

In 1934 Tokuyama Teppan opened a new, highly integrated steel plant at Amagasaki. The works at Amagasaki, near Osaka, contained Tokuyama Teppan's first crude-steel production equipment and became the center of the company's operations for many years. Once bolstered with a secure, in-house supply of its own steel, Tokuyama Teppan was able to improve efficiency and lower its operating costs in time for Japan's plunge into war with China and the Allies. World War II brought Tokuyama Teppan, like all of the Japanese steel industry, under the tight control of Japanese government authorities, who needed unprecedented amounts of steel for everything from ships to shell casings.

Japan's steel industry was targeted for heavy bombardment by the Allies and suffered severe damage by the war's end in 1945. Postwar Japanese steel production remained critically low for a number of years, until the United States began providing financial and technical assistance to its key industries. Tokuyama Teppan resumed substantial production as early as 1949, when it was listed on Japanese stock exchanges for the first time. Two years later, Tokuyama Teppan opened an extensive plant at Kure, which would become the company's new center of crude-steel making and its largest employer. When blast furnaces were added in 1962, Kure became the company's only plant with complete iron- and steel-making capabilities.

As a manufacturer of galvanized and specialty steels, Tokuyama Teppan was oddly slow in entering the growing stainless steel business. It had been manufactured since the early part of the 20th century and became integral to the growth of the appliance and automotive industries after World War II. As such, it was a natural area for expansion by Tokuyama Teppan, and in 1958 the company began stainless production at its new Shunan works. Shunan remained limited strictly to stainless steel, adopting the most sophisticated technology available. By 1970 it was producing more stainless than any other plant in the world, and the company was Japan's leading stainless maker.

By that time, Tokuyama Teppan also had a new name. In 1959, Tokuyama Teppan merged with Nihon Teppan, another maker of specialty steels, and took its present form as Nisshin Steel Co., Ltd. With Japan's postwar economic miracle in full swing, Nisshin's sales climbed rapidly, fueled for the most part by the extraordinary expansion of the Japanese automotive, construction, and appliance industries. Nisshin was among the leading innovators in Japanese steel, winning a reputation for technological wizardry that led to many overseas contracts for plant design and manufacturing consultation. Particularly impressive was Nisshin's 1965 introduction of a new method of continuous zinc coating, which yielded a far more durable galvanized steel product. The new method, known as the gas wiping method, allowed manufacturers to apply a zinc coating of uniform weight to steel sheets by applying the zinc as a vapor. The process soon was adopted widely throughout Japan and licensed overseas.

Such technological breakthroughs helped push Nisshin's sales to ¥129 billion in 1969 and made possible a number of important overseas partnerships. In 1970 Nisshin was asked to help create the first Japanese steel operation in Europe. At the request of a large Spanish bank, Banco Español de Credito (Banesto), Nisshin and Nissho-Iwai, a Japanese trading firm, supplied a small amount of capital and all of the necessary technical assistance in building a large stainless steel plant near Malaga, Spain. The plant was fully completed by 1978. By then Nisshin was involved deeply in a similar project in Romania, where Nisshin designed and helped construct a stainless steel manufacturing facility. At various other times, Nisshin has formed joint ventures with, or worked on behalf of, organizations in France, Great Britain, India, Brazil, and the United States. The company's technical experience became increasingly valuable as the world steel market suffered from overcapacity and flat sales in the industrialized countries, forcing established manufacturers to evolve ever-more sophisticated products with which to protect their market shares.

The contracting steel industry faced especially severe problems after the oil crisis of 1973 and 1974. Japan and the industrialized world generally had reached a saturation point in its need for basic steel, as post–World War II construction slowed. In addition, the oil crisis precipitated a long depression in the automotive, shipbuilding, and construction industries—all heavy users of steel. Nisshin and its rivals moved quickly to develop more rarified steel products and to diversify out of steel entirely. Nisshin was fortunate in already having a mix of products that was weighted toward specialty steels, but during the 1970s it went considerably further in that direction.

Nisshin's response to the steel crisis was complex. It increased the efficiency of its basic processes, enabling the company to cut its employee rolls gradually from a high of 10,100 to its 1990 level of about 7,200. In 1981 Nisshin created two new planning departments to develop ideas for new businesses that could take advantage of the company's traditional strengths. Within a few years, Nisshin was involved in a plethora of such ventures. In 1982 it formed two new companies. Nikken Stainless Fittings Co., Ltd. is a 50%-owned joint venture with Riken Corporation. Nikken makes stainless steel pipe joints for water pipes and for air conditioners, and became involved in developing such products in plastic. Shunan Shigyo Co., Ltd., was formed by Nisshin in 1982 to recycle and market the kraft paper used as protective layering between steel sheets. In 1984 Nisshin joined Magne Corporation of Tokyo in creating Nisshin Ferrite Co., Ltd. to sell scrap iron

as magnetic particles for the electronics industry. Nisshin further explored opportunities in electronics by acquiring technical information needed in the production of gold-plated stainless steel for use in micro-circuitry. Indeed, electronics figured large in Nisshin's plans, as in those of so many other Japanese companies, offering as it did a market for advanced metal products not easily duplicated by the younger generation of Third World steel competitors. In 1985 the company created a high-tech materials department to pursue new steel applications in the electronics field, particularly products needed in cathode-ray tubes, semiconductors, magnetic recording components, and printed circuit boards.

Much of Nisshin's work in electronics involved a refinement of its basic coating technology, usually the layering of a highly conductive metal such as gold over a base of steel or stainless steel. Nisshin's coating experience has allowed it to develop a number of other new products as well, including combinations of steel with aluminum, polyfoam, and polyvinyl chloride (PVC). Each of these innovations has found its particular niche. Rustproof aluminum-steel laminate sheets are used to reinforce automotive parts and in mufflers. Polyfoam-steel is used as a durable, colored roofing material. The PVC-steel sandwich provides automakers with light-weight, strong interior automobile body parts. These and other developments have greatly expanded the range of Nisshin's products for the construction and automobile industries while solidifying the company's technological lead over competitors in Japan and overseas.

In February of 1984 Nisshin purchased 10% of the stock of Wheeling-Pittsburgh Steel Corporation, then the eighth-largest U.S. steelmaker and a company whose products were roughly similar to those of Nisshin. The two companies also agreed to a broad range of technical exchange, and together subsequently built a galvanizing plant in West Virginia. Despite Nisshin's capital injection, Wheeling-Pittsburgh filed to reorganize under chapter 11 of the U.S. Bankruptcy Code in 1985. Nevertheless, the deal gave Nisshin a valuable entry into the huge U.S. market.

Nisshin is one of the few steel companies in the world that survived the 1980s profitably, and is clearly serious about balancing its steel operations with unrelated ventures. Meanwhile, Nisshin's strong position in specialty steels should allow it to benefit from the continuing explosion in new materials, where old dogs like steel are made to perform the very latest tricks.

Principal Subsidiaries: Tsukiboshi Kogyo Co., Ltd.; Nisshin Kokan Co. Ltd.; Nisshin Ferrite Co., Ltd.; Carmy, Inc.; Nisshin Koki Co., Ltd.; Tsukiboshi Art Co., Ltd.; Shinwa Kigyo Co., Ltd. (95.3%); Shinsei Kogyo Co., Ltd. (94.7%); Sun Techno Planning Inc. (70%); Tsukiboshi Kaiun Co., Ltd. (67.9%); Shunan Shigyo Co., Ltd. (66.7%); Osaka Stainless Steel Co., Ltd. (52%); Nisshin Steel Australia Pty. Ltd.; Nisshin Steel (Canada) Ltd.; Nisshin International Finance (Netherlands) B.V.; Wheeling-Nisshin, Inc. (U.S.A., 80%).

—Jonathan Martin

NKK CORPORATION

1-2, Marunouchi 1-chome
Chiyoda-ku, Tokyo 100
Japan
(03) 3212-7111
Fax: (03) 3214-8435

Public Company
Incorporated: 1912 as Nippon Kokan K.K.
Employees: 22,346
Sales: ¥1.33 trillion (US$9.79 billion)
Stock Exchanges: Tokyo Osaka Nagoya Frankfurt

NKK Corporation is one of the world's five largest steelmakers and Japan's second largest. In addition to steelmaking, the company is active in four other fields: advanced materials, engineering, electronics, and urban development. Products of the advanced materials group range from heat-resistant bottles and industrial ceramics to rocket parts. New types of marine and land-based construction, from recreational facilities to nuclear plants, typify the public works activity and private investment projects driving the engineering division, which traditionally had served the needs of the oil, gas, and electric industries. Shipbuilding, the activity of the engineering group that was in the doldrums, shows signs of revival, with active marketing of both cargo and luxury cruise ships. The electronics group develops automation design systems, advanced computer software, and hardware technology for research and development, as well as computers. NKK's urban development group—the only group not globally oriented—is concentrating on developing domestic condominium and commercial space and recreational facilities. In addition, the company has moved into research and development in biotechnology—advanced biochemical and medical products.

In Japan, as in other areas of the world, the growth of the steelmaking industry has often been associated with the needs created by warfare. From ancient times, the Chinese had forged weapons from iron-bearing stones by heating them in charcoal fires. By the sixth century A.D., when Chinese technology and cultural influences began to be adopted in Japan, processes were being developed to prolong and heighten the heating of iron ore and to remove impurities. By medieval times, Japanese steelmaking had become a high art. Knights wore loose armor made of three- or four-inch pieces of thin steel, linkéd by colorful thongs. The knights took particular pride in their exquisitely designed, long, curved, laminated steel swords. The swords, reportedly the finest in the world, were in particular demand throughout East Asia, and thousands were exported.

Japan's supply of iron ore was poor. While steelmaking technology developed rapidly in the iron-rich countries of Europe and the United States, Japan's steelmaking stagnated. With the waning of knighthood, and Japan's virtual isolation from the rest of the world during the Tokugawa shogunate, little steel was made.

During the nineteenth century, the Tokugawa shogun gradually lost control over Japanese commercial interests. Although the surface aspects of Japanese life appeared to be as firmly in place as they had been throughout the shogun's rule, discontent with the limitations imposed by the government began to escalate.

Disenchanted with the Tokugawa shogun, many of the people began to become optimistic about their prospects under a restoration of imperial rule. The presumptive heir to the throne promised progress in "catching up" with the rest of the world—economically, technologically, and culturally. Upon assuming the throne in 1968, the new Meiji emperor proceeded to do just that. Actually, the reforms were not so much the work of the individual on the throne as they were the work of a group of young men—fewer than 100—who supported the regime as an opportunity to introduce Western-style efficiencies and power into Japan. Educated abroad, they had a vision of a stronger Japan that could result from applying Western technologies and political and cultural concepts to the economic and other problems the Japanese people faced. That vision became a reality as Japan became the first Asian nation to rise to world power status through the use of Western concepts.

Japan's economic problems had arisen through the inefficiency and corruption that had gradually crept into industries the Tokugawa shogunate owned. The supporters of a return to imperial rule under a progressive Meiji regime were sometimes referred to as an oligarchy of commercial and political interests as they gathered power to influence government decision-making. They were credited with persuading the government to sell its factories to private individuals and groups. Eventually only the manufacture of munitions remained under the government's direct ownership.

By 1881 new shipyards were operating under private ownership. Government support of the shipyards, provided through subsidies and the awarding of contracts, cushioned the early years, but strict regulation of business and industry was enforced from the start and remains to this day.

The need for iron and steel to support a military and naval buildup heightened as Japan waged war with China in 1894 and 1895. The shipbuilding industry, for example, was hampered by the fact that most of Japan's iron and almost all of its steel had to be imported. In 1896 the government decided to establish an iron and steel industry. The Yawata works opened in 1901. Processing plants were needed, however, to turn the Yawata works's pig-iron and steel into products that shipbuilders, engineering companies, and other heavy industries required. Pipe, for example, was in increasing demand. As conflicts with Russia and China engendered greater military buildup, and an influx of Japan's population into urban areas created new needs for private housing and public works projects, the demand for pipe, particularly strong steel pipe, grew.

Conscious of the growing market for pipe, Ganjiro Shiraishi, an independent businessman, began in 1911 to gather the financial support and Western-developed technical expertise to produce what would become an innovation—Japan's first seamless steel pipe. After more than a year of initial research and organizational development, Nippon Kokan K.K. began operations in mid-1912 with ¥2 million in capital. During its first few years, the company was occupied with the complex process of setting up an open-hearth furnace for refining steel scrap and pig iron. The first steel was tapped from that furnace in 1914.

The seamless steel pipe that Nippon Kokan produced proved to be stronger, longer-wearing, and easier to install than pipe parts that had to be fitted and welded together. The market for it grew larger as Japan prepared to enter World War I in 1916, and naval vessels and military installations created new demands. The success of Nippon Kokan's first years led to the opening of a subsidiary in 1917—Electric Iron and Steel.

Along with the other Allied nations that joined forces to defeat Germany in World War I, Japan emerged from the conflict as a victorious world power. This created ties that encouraged international trade. Japan's militarists, who favored future expansion through military aggression and colonialism, began to meet strong opposition from the merchants and manufacturers who favored maintaining peaceful relations and fostering expansion through international trade.

For about a decade, those who favored expansion through international markets prevailed. Both the import and export businesses flourished, as Western fashions, sports, and other novelties captured the public fancy in Japan, and Japanese products became widely sought by other nations.

The domestic market for pipe underwent a sudden surge through a national disaster. The Great Kanto Earthquake, September 1, 1923, leveled half the buildings in Tokyo and most of those in Yokohama. Rebuilding factories and office buildings, private residences, and public buildings took several years—and many miles of pipe. The new buildings, incorporating some of the world's most advanced designs and products, reflected the Western influences popularized through the postwar years.

In 1929, however, a worldwide depression began that brought an abrupt halt to much of the international trade activity that Japan had enjoyed. Japan's militarists began to look toward colonizing areas rich in natural resources as a way of renewing expansion efforts. The nation's population had grown beyond the means of its own resources to provide adequate food and housing.

Manchuria, a disputed territory, became a target, and was annexed to Japan in 1931. Steel products were again in increased demand as plans for further military action called for the buildup of new installations and vessels. To smelt iron directly from ore, Nippon Kokan built a 400-ton blast furnace, completing it in 1937. A 600-ton blast furnace was completed in 1938. Even the fact that Japan was poor in iron ore operated to Nippon Kokan's advantage. Because there was no need to situate its plants near a mountainous source of ore, the plants were located close to Tokyo's waterfront, convenient both for receiving ore from other countries and for efficient shipping of steel products to customers.

Through a merger, Nippon Kokan went into the shipbuilding business in 1940, acquiring the Tsurumi Steelmaking and Shipbuilding Company. As Japan went to war with the United States the following year, plans for a 5,000-ton capacity ship-

building berth at the company's Shimizu shipyard went forward; the project was completed in 1943. At that time, Ryozo Asano had been in office as Nippon Kokan's president for six months. Until 1945 when bombing raids and the consequent fires destroyed many of Tokyo's buildings and caused the populace to flee, Nippon Kokan's plants were in full operation, supplying many steel products needed in the war effort. Japan's defeat was a shock to many of its citizens who had been told only of its victories; it demoralized many like Asano, who saw the results of years of concerted effort go up in smoke. He resigned.

Although business was at a standstill for many months as the Supreme Council of the Allied Forces (SCAP) took over governing the country and preparing it for future self-government, Nippon Kokan survived. In April 1946 a new president, Masato Watanabe, began the task of rebuilding the company's facilities and customer base. The constitutional reforms and financial support that SCAP introduced created a new climate for business recovery and growth that helped Nippon Kokan and other businesses progress rapidly.

Along with the legislative and economic aids to recovery of business and industrial facilities and markets came new ideas for improving organization and product quality. In 1950, 45 leading industrialists in Tokyo met with W. Edwards Deming, a U.S. statistician who taught a quality-centered approach to manufacturing involving all employees in decision-making, for continuous improvement and responsiveness to consumer needs. An annual Deming Prize was awarded to the company best exemplifying the success of these methods. Nippon Kokan was the winner in 1958.

International expansion was already under way. The company acquired an interest in the Ujiminas Steel Works in Brazil in 1957, and, the following year, opened offices in New York. In 1959 Düsseldorf, Germany, became Nippon Kokan's European headquarters. The company was on an ascendant growth curve that was to extend well into the next quarter-century. Offices were opened in Singapore, Los Angeles, and London between 1961 and 1963.

Nippon Kokan K.K. also worked to expand the number of operations within its mills to include the full range of activities from handling ore to production and distribution of a complete product line, in other words to become an integrated steel manufacturing company. The company consolidated a group of works it had acquired in the Mizue area to form the Mizue steel works. In 1963 its engineering and construction division began the first of five successive stages of work at Fukuyama to build the world's largest integrated steel mill. The project was completed in 1973. Another large-scale operation was created in 1968 by consolidating the company's Kawasaki, Tsurumi, and Mizue plants into one entity: the Keihin steel works.

The company continued to expand abroad, acquiring a 62.7% interest in the Sermani steel finishing business in Indonesia in 1970, and opening offices in Rio de Janeiro, Brazil, in 1975. A Houston, Texas, office was opened one year later.

At home, the Keihin steel works was expanded between 1975 and 1979 by constructing the world's most modern steelmaking facilities on a man-made island, Ohgishima. Upon completion of the first stage of this project, the Japan Society of Civil Engineering awarded Nippon Kokan K.K. its 1975 Technology Prize.

The company reorganized its divisions in 1979. Initially, the shipbuilding division, including the ten-year-old Tsu shipyard, was combined with the engineering and construction division. The following year, however, a further reorganization of the heavy industries division resulted in a three-division system: energy, heavy industries, and shipbuilding.

Steelmakers in Japan, like those in the United States, faced the problem of maintaining plant efficiency while keeping overhead to a minimum, and using resources effectively to make a profit while meeting worker and consumer expectations. In general, U.S. steelmakers, with older plants to maintain, neglected maintenance needs and the development of new technologies, while the Japanese, although equally cost-conscious, did not. As a result, Japanese steelmakers, such as Nippon Kokan K.K., moved ahead in productivity product quality. Market demand for high-quality raw steel and for steel products was high. By the 1980s, it was evident that Nippon Kokan K.K., among other Japanese steelmakers, held the competitive edge.

Nippon Kokan K.K. had formed joint ventures with companies throughout the world—in the United States and Canada; in Indonesia, Thailand, and Singapore; and in Belgium, Brazil, Saudi Arabia, Nigeria, and Australia. Sachio Hatori, the company's executive vice president, opposed such solutions, stating, "Joint ventures are low-risk, but they cannot improve the whole process. If the steel itself is bad, it doesn't matter how good the galvanizing is."

Instead, in 1984, Nippon Kokan K.K. purchased a 50% interest in National Steel Corporation, sixth-largest steel works in the United States. This purchase provided the opportunity to exert a positive influence on product quality. Although Nippon Kokan sent managerial talent to National Steel's site near Detroit, the company resisted any attempt to diminish the independence of National Steel's operations. The immediate result of the purchase was to double National Steel's annual capital investment to $200 million and to infuse new and advanced technology into the U.S. firm. By 1990 Nippon Kokan K.K. owned 70% of National Steel. Although productivity increased, National Steel's profits continued to decline. Nippon Kokan entered into a joint venture with another U.S. company, Martin Marietta Corporation, in 1984, forming the International Light Metals Corporation.

Yoshinari Yamashiro became president of Nippon Kokan K.K. in 1985, a time when fluctuations in the value of the yen and other factors were beginning to flatten the 25-year upward curve of prosperity and profits for many Japanese companies. He introduced a new note of informality and desire for closeness to company operations as he asked employees to address him as they would one another—as mister, rather than to use his title.

To cope with problems arising as markets matured and consumer demands changed, the new president initiated a restructuring of the corporation. In 1988 the company name was changed to NKK Corporation, a name that had often been used informally. Divisions were created to reflect the increased diversity of company interests, products, and services. Steelmaking, still the core of the company's business, was strengthened by adding facilities to produce materials and parts for special needs. For example, a continuous galvanizing line at the Keihin and Fukuyama works helped meet high domestic demand for a number of steel products. The reorganization also resulted in converting some of NKK's operating units into subsidiaries.

NKK's engineering division serves the oil, gas, and electric industries, building and repairing plants, machinery, and equipment, including energy and environmental systems. Notable among its shipbuilding achievements is the construction of Japan's first icebreaker, and its leadership role in developing luxury cruise ships.

The company's advanced materials division develops specialty metals, ceramics, plastics, and chemicals, working with the International Light Metals Corporation in the United States to produce aluminum and titanium alloys. This division has also developed the world's first low-pressure plasma spraying process for yttrium-titanium copper oxide superconducting film. The division's products also include biotechnologies for health care and industrial uses.

Computer hardware and software, as well as mini-supercomputers and communications network systems, are the work of NKK's electronics division, which also develops new product designs. The urban development division focuses on development of commercial and residential real estate, sports centers, shopping centers resorts, and amusement parks.

The company's research and development laboratories hold the keys to future activity. A recent achievement was the development of what the company described as the world's largest superconducting magnetic-shielding cylinder, for use in medical diagnosis.

The company's view of the future includes global dimensions. Southeast Asian facilities are expected to figure strongly in NKK's plans as the company uses its expertise to advance development of industrial facilities in Third World countries.

Principal Subsidiaries: N.K. HOME Co., Ltd.; Nippon Kokan Loji K.K.; Nippon Kokan Pipe Fitting Mfg. Co. Ltd.; Nippon Kokan Light Steel Co., Ltd.; Kokan Mining Co., Ltd.; Nichiei Un-yo Solo Co. Ltd.; NKK Trading Co., Ltd.; Kokan Drum Co., Ltd.; NK Lease Corp.; NKK U.S.A. Corp.; NUF Corp. (U.S.A.) NAF Corp.; (U.S.A.); NUF Cayman Ltd.; National Steel Corp. (U.S.A.).

Further Reading: "NKK Today," [Tokyo], NKK, 1989; "NKK Profile," NKK corporate typescript, Tokyo, 1990; Klamann, Edmund, "NKK still seeking payoff for U.S. venture," *Japan Economic Journal,* September 8, 1990.

—Betty T. Moore

noranda

NORANDA INC.

Post Office Box 45
Commerce Court West
Toronto, Ontario M5L 1B6
Canada
(416) 982-7111
Fax: (416) 982-7423

Public Company
Incorporated: 1922 as Noranda Mines Ltd.
Employees: 56,000
Sales: C$9.57 billion (US$8.04 billion)
Stock Exchange: Toronto

In 1922 Noranda was simply a word used to describe northern Canada. Today, the word Noranda conveys images of one of the largest companies in Canada and one of the largest mining companies in the world. A firm with four industry segments: Noranda Forest Inc., Noranda Minerals Inc., Noranda Manufacturing Inc., and Noranda Energy, its mining activities include aluminum, copper, gold, lead, silver, and zinc.

The history of Noranda is a story started by a prospector named Edmund Horne, and a hunch. During the early 1920s, at a time when northern Canada meant very little—the area was mostly wilderness, and most prospectors preferred to stay on the familiar grounds of Ontario—Horne was drawn to the Rouyn district in northeastern Quebec. He visited Rouyn repeatedly, because he believed it "didn't seem sensible that all the good geology should quit at the Ontario border." Horne could reach Rouyn only by way of a chain of lakes and rivers.

His enthusiasm was contagious, and soon a group of 12 men had raised C$225 to finance further explorations. The effort paid off when word of Horne's first strike made it to S.C. Thomson and H.W. Chadbourne, two U.S. mining engineers with a syndicate of investors interested in exploring Canadian mines. In February 1922 the syndicate acquired an option on Horne's mining claims in Ontario and Quebec, and soon exercised its option. Noranda Mines Ltd. was incorporated in 1922 to acquire the U.S. syndicate's mining claims.

The next task was to make the area more accessible to miners. Roads were cut through the forests, and often travel required skis and sleding equipment. Some equipment arrived by barge and ski-equipped plane, both of which could travel the lakes and rivers with relative ease. Soon the mine began producing gold, copper ore, sulfur, and iron, and Noranda convinced the Canadian government to lay roads, railways,

and power lines. Eventually, the company constructed a mill and a smelter, and a city began to take shape in what was once untamed wilderness.

Not satisfied with this initial success, Noranda Mines began to acquire other holdings. In 1927 it bought 80% of the stock in Waite-Ackerman-Montgomery Mines, which changed its name six years later to Waite Amulet Mines Ltd. In 1927 also Noranda acquired a majority interest in Aldermac Mines Ltd., of Rouyn.

Because it believed strongly that Canadian ore should be processed in Canadian plants, the company eventually acquired or built several processing companies. Canadian Copper Refiners, Ltd., a company in which Noranda Mines held majority interest, was constructed in eastern Canada in 1929, as a joint effort of Noranda Mines, London's British Metal Corporation, and Nichols Copper Company of New York City. The following year, Noranda Mines purchased a rod and wire mill just east of the copper refinery, and bought a substantial interest in Canada Wire & Cable Company, Ltd., of Leaside, Ontario.

In the early 1930s Noranda Power Company, Ltd., a new subsidiary, was formed. In 1934 this company took over the parent firm's power rights and leases on the Victoria River, only to transfer the rights to the government's National Electricity Syndicate under a new agreement four years later. Primarily the 1930s set the stage for a decades-long tradition of growth through acquisitions, as Noranda made its climb to the ranks of Canada's largest companies. In 1935 the firm bought a substantial interest in Pamour Porcupine Mines, Ltd., located in the Porcupine district of Ontario. It also acquired a 63.75% interest in Compania Minera La India, for its gold mines in Nicaragua in 1937. In 1939 Noranda bought the controlling interest in Aunor Gold Mines, Ltd., which was formed earlier that year to take over additional Porcupine property. The late 1930s also saw the creation of Noranda Exploration Company, Ltd., a subsidiary formed in 1938 to undertake exploration work in Quebec.

By 1936 output of metals in the province of Quebec totaled well over C$30.6 million, thanks to the development sparked by Noranda Mines. From 1926 to 1936, Noranda stimulated the nation's economy by pouring into it approximately C$71 million in supplies, transportation, salaries, and taxes. By the end of World War II, the area's mineral production had climbed to C$150 million annually.

Perhaps due to the events of World War II, however, the 1940s, and even the 1950s, saw less corporate activity than earlier decades. Still, the company made two major acquisitions, including Castle Tretheway Mines Ltd.'s Omega Gold Mines, which Noranda Mines bought jointly with Anglo-Huronian Ltd. in 1944. Four years later, Noranda Mines and a subsidiary, Waite Amulet Mines, bought more than 500,000 shares of Mining Corporation of Canada Ltd. In 1956 Noranda acquired a sizable interest in Bouzan Mines Ltd.

By the early 1960s the company began to see a flurry of activity, beginning with the acquisition of Western Copper Mills Ltd., located near Vancouver, in 1963. The new acquisition joined with Noranda Copper & Brass Ltd., a Noranda Mines subsidiary, to form Noranda Copper Mills Ltd. Also that year, the company acquired the remaining shares of Mining Corporation of Canada, which continued the firm's exploration efforts. In addition, Anglo-Huronian, Bouzan Mines,

Kerr-Addison Gold Mines, and Prospectors Airways—all Noranda affiliates—merged to form Kerr-Addison Mines Ltd.

In December 1964 Noranda Mines made its most important acquisition, when it merged with Geco Mines Ltd. The new company retained the name Noranda Mines Ltd. Based in Manitouwadge, in northwestern Ontario, Geco was a major producer of copper, silver, and zinc. The following year, Canada Wire & Cable, in which Noranda Mines had an interest since 1964, became a wholly owned subsidiary. In 1966 the firm also bought 80% of Norcast Manufacturing Ltd., which then purchased shares in Wolverine Die Cast Group. Also that year, Noranda Mines formed Noranda Manufacturing, Ltd., a holding company for the various manufacturing subsidiaries. Noranda Mines also acquired a controlling interest in Pacific Coast Company, in 1967.

By 1968 Noranda Mines had become a widely held mining company, with most of its activities centered around Quebec. Employees numbered 5,000. It was also in 1968 that 37-year-old Alfred Powis became president of Noranda Mines. Formerly a financial analyst with Sun Life Assurance Company of Canada, of Montreal, Powis joined Noranda Mines in 1955 as an assistant to the firm's treasurer. Under Powis's leadership, the company began its evolution from a regionally based mining firm to an industry leader, with subsidiaries involved in energy and forestry, in addition to mining.

It seems that Powis's aggressive tactics, including a chain of takeovers, were key contributors to the company's success. Powis's success did not come overnight, however. The company first had to weather the impact of several large investments made in the late 1960s. In the early 1970s the mining industry, as a whole, was depressed. Consequently, the company had limited earnings from 1966 to 1972, increasing in that period by only 21%. In addition gross capital employed went from C$500 million in 1967 to C$1.5 billion in 1973. The rate of return on that capital went from 16% in 1966 to only 9% in 1972. Powis worked through the cyclical, industry wide recession, and finally, in 1973, investments began to pay off; and Noranda's sales climbed 75% to C$121 million, a company record.

Additional investments made in the early 1970s included Tara Exploration and Development Ltd., which owned lead and zinc properties in Ireland, and a move into the fertilizer field with Belledune Fertilizer Ltd., acquired from Albright & Wilson Ltd. in 1972. The year 1974 saw even more acquisitions, including a 55% stake in Fraser Companies Ltd., Alberta Sulphate Ltd., and 38.5% of Frialco, a Cayman Island firm with controlling interest in Friguia, a bauxite mining company in the Republic of Guinea. In addition, Noranda Sales Corporation of Canada Ltd., a subsidiary, bought a 50% interest in Rudolf Wolff & Company, a British trading firm dealing with metals and other commodities, in the spring of 1971.

The mining industry, known for caution, watched Powis march on this unusual acquisition path, then watched sales climb from C$60 million in 1972 to C$155 million two years later. It was during this era that *Canadian Business,* September 1977, referred to Powis as "the Houdini of the Canadian mining industry."

What goes up, however, must come down, and in 1976, earnings dropped to C$47 million. Demand for the two biggest contributors to the company's sales, copper and zinc, began to

lag. The automobile industry was replacing zinc die castings with plastics. Copper too was being replaced by various substitutes, from aluminum for power lines to glass fibers for communication cables. In addition, many of the firm's earlier investments had been financed with short-term loans, which seemed like a good idea when business was booming. Although Powis acknowledged that money was tight at Noranda Mines in 1977, he defended his decision to load up on short-term debt, telling *Canadian Business,* "We put restraints on at the end of 1974 when we could see that things were getting grim. Those clamps have stayed on." Powis also indicated he was prepared for the tight zinc market.

To help wait out the cyclical downturn in the mining industry, the company diversified, concentrating on other business segments, such as manufacturing and forestry. As Powis stated in *Iron Age* of July 22, 1974, the future of Noranda will be "where our nose takes us. . . . We originally got into manufacturing so we could have a home for our products." In addition, the company invested millions of dollars in efforts to covert some old saw mills into profitable lumber plants. That marked its entry into the forestry industry.

In 1981 Powis lost a long-running, highly publicized battle with Brascan, Ltd., a Toronto holding company owned by Edward and Peter Bronfman. Brascan became Noranda Mine's largest stockholder, and Powis, who became answerable to the Bronfmans, stayed on as chief executive officer. Brascan added C$500 million to Noranda Mines's bankroll, and Noranda Mines returned to its acquisition path.

Noranda Mines first picked up Maclaren Power and Paper Company in 1981, a newsprint, pulp, and wood-products company in Buckingham, Quebec. The following year it bought 49.8% of MacMillan Bloedel, Canada's largest paper company. The minority shareholding was sufficient to give Noranda Mines control of MacMillan Bloedel. While the acquisitions were intended to decrease the company's concentration on the lagging copper market, the expansion of the early 1980s initially resulted in decreased profits. In 1980 the firm had record earnings of C$408 million. In 1983 it lost C$117 million, and interest payments on the acquisitions and expansion loans totaled C$169 million in 1983.

Powis, and Adam Zimmerman, president of Noranda Mines, shared an optimism that began to pay off in the mid-1980s. Sales of zinc, fine paper, and other products began to recover, and, just as Noranda Mines finished a C$300 million addition to its aluminum smelter, demand for aluminum skyrocketed. By 1983 copper accounted for only 12% of sales. The diversification was paying off, and to reflect that diversification in 1984 the company changed its name from Noranda Mines Ltd. to Noranda Inc.

In 1986—after a C$253,900 loss caused by strikes and other labor problems in 1985—the firm's net income stood at C$43,300, and total revenue was C$3.55 billion. In 1987 as various labor strikes came to an end, company officials predicted the firm would see its highest earnings since 1980. Also in 1987, the company was restructured, dividing its various business segments into four subsidiaries: Noranda Energy, Noranda Forest, Noranda Minerals, and Noranda Manufacturing.

In 1989 after a heated battle between Powis and former protege William James—who had left Noranda and became chairman of Falconbridge, Ltd., a rival mining company—Noranda bought 50% of Falconbridge. Ownership of the multi-billion dollar company is shared by Trelleborg A.B., a Swedish-based conglomerate. The move not only gave Noranda half of Falconbridge, but ownership of Kidd Creek as well, a Timmons, Ontario, copper and zinc mine that Noranda had long coveted.

Although most of Noranda's assets are located in North America, Noranda markets its products to a global market. The firm's goal is to be a premier diversified natural-resources company. Under the leadership of President David Kerr, the company remains committed to a sensitive environmental policy, a commitment necessary for any business to be well-received in the decades to come. This effort, as well as several major acquisitions, favorable long-term market conditions, and changing global markets will no doubt play a part in helping Noranda reach its goals.

Principal Subsidiaries: Noranda Minerals Inc.; Noranda Forest Inc. (81%); Noranda Manufacturing Inc.; Canadian Hunter Exploration Ltd.; North Canadian Oils Ltd. (54%); Norcen Energy Resources.

Further Reading: Roberts, Leslie, *Noranda,* Toronto, Clarke-Irwin, 1956; Beizer, James, "Metal mining troubles loom large in Canada," *Iron Age,* July 22, 1974; Daly, John, "The final victory: Falconbridge may prove to be too expensive," *Maclean's,* October 9, 1989; Francis, Diane, "Alfred Powis as corporate superman," *Maclean's,* November 27, 1989.

—Kim M. Magon

OKURA & CO., LTD.

3-6, Ginza 2-chome
Chuo-ko, Tokyo 104
Japan
(03) 3566-6000
Fax: (03) 3535-2551

Public Company
Incorporated: 1873 as Okura-gumi
Employees: 1,036
Sales: ¥518.60 billion (US$3.82 billion)
Stock Exchanges: New York   Tokyo

Okura & Co., Ltd. is a highly diversified company whose specialities include construction and the handling, supplying, and servicing of machinery and metal products for the iron and steel industries in Japan and abroad. Okura has become a leading international trader in food and foodstuffs, and has become increasingly involved in aerospace, electronics, and biotechnology. The company was the first independent Japanese company to establish a branch abroad, in London in 1874. Indeed, Okura became Asia's pioneer in the machinery business; since the 1920s, it has played a major role in the founding and development of India's iron and steel industry, and is still one of India's chief exporters of iron ore. Okura also was involved significantly with Japan's postwar industrial recovery, importing crucial industrial equipment and technologies from abroad to lay the basis for that recovery. Okura introduced television to Japan in 1953.

The history of Okura is largely the history of its founder, Kihachiro Okura, born in Niigata Prefecture in 1837. He would be a witness to Japan's wrenching transformation from a remote, medieval, and largely illiterate society to a modern, industrial, and Westernized country, all within a few decades. Times were still turbulent after the historic Meiji Restoration of 1868, although rich in business opportunities, since the Japanese government of technocrats was committed to the country's breakneck modernization. Kihachiro Okura would become a pioneer in Japan's transition to modern times. His first enterprise, a gun shop, was outstandingly successful, in no small part due to the insecurity of the times and the rapid expansion and modernization of the Japanese military, with which Okura would have increasingly close and profitable connections. Japanese rage for Western ways, including apparel and drink, encouraged Okura to expand into the beer-brewing business, yet another success story. In handling malt, grains,

and hops, Okura quickly diversified, supplying and trading on a wide scale feed, flour, beans, and vegetable oils, in addition to cattle and poultry, thus laying the basis of post–World War II Okura's international trade in foodstuffs.

By 1873, Kihachiro Okura had amassed the capital to establish his business, Okura-gumi, in the heart of Tokyo's newly emerging commercial district, the Ginza, which 25 years later, his company would electrify with the help of imported electric power generators from Germany's AEG. Okura saw the value of overseas trade and of the import business. No sooner was his own business installed in the Ginza than he proceeded, in 1874, to open a branch in London, to be followed shortly afterward by an office in New York City, which by the end of the 19th century would handle all sorts of business. Indeed, the company made its presence felt throughout Japan, as Kihachiro Okura's financial, political, and military connections led to investment and expansion into a wide array of highly profitable enterprises. Westerners had no sooner introduced the first railroads to Japan than Okura began to play a major role in their building, which necessitated expansion into the construction industry as well as iron and steel production, the backbone of 19th-century heavy industry. By the turn of the century, Okura was already a leader in Japan's international trade, arranging the import of Western technologies and machinery for Japan's rapidly growing heavy industry.

In 1895, with Japan's first major military showdown with a foreign power, China, Okura's contributions in supplying the armed forces with munitions were recognized by the government, which gave him the title of baron. Hence war would become a boon to Baron Okura's business, strengthening his ties with the government, assuring his success in munitions manufacturing, and allowing him to play a leading role in Japanese financial dealings in Manchuria—where Okura obtained the right to establish the profitable manufacturing joint venture, the Benxi Iron and Steel Corporation—and to develop other natural resources in Asia, as well as financing businesses in Korea and China.

By 1910, Okura was a leading Japanese importer of German power generators and equipment; was involved heavily in steel manufacturing and marine and fire insurance; and was trading in automobiles, rolling stock for railways, and leather goods. Within Japan, Okura was also becoming a major financier of other Japanese ventures including Tokyo Electric Power Company, Inc. and the Imperial Hotel. In 1918, Okura founded the Okura Commercial School (now Tokyo University of Economics) and in the same year, organized his company into a huge industrial complex, or *zaibatsu*, led by Okura-gumi and including such subsidiaries as Okura Public Works Company and the Okura Mining Company. After World War I, communications would become an increasingly promising field, and the Okura *zaibatsu* became responsible for introducing into Japan the first high-powered radio-broadcasting network and producing Japan's first radio sets, laying the foundation for one of the company's important post–World War II businesses. The death of Kihachiro Okura in 1928, at the age of 91, did not slow the company's progress.

The Okura *zaibatsu* paid a high price for its involvement with the government and for its connections to the military. After World War II, Japan and Japanese industry lay in ruins, while the Allied occupation authorities set forth with determination to break up Japanese *Zaibatsu*, including Okura—which, under new leadership, would rename itself Okura & Co., Ltd. The Korean War, beginning in 1950, provided the necessary boost to Japanese industry, and Okura found itself once more benefiting from war and its demands. Traditionally strong in heavy industry, international trade, and foodstuffs, the company forged ahead. Once more the company took upon itself the role it had adopted in the late 19th century: an importer of Western technologies and machineries to enable Japanese industry to recover. Already strong as a supplier to the iron and steel industries, Okura & Co. in 1964 merged with Kishimoto Shoten Co., Ltd., a steel-trading enterprise, to become even more heavily involved in the steel industry, as both a promoter of steel products and a major supplier of raw materials to the steel industry, in Japan and abroad.

Machinery and precision machine tools for heavy industry still form the backbone of Okura, but so do supplying oil-field drilling equipment, machinery for power generators, chemicals, and food-processing plants. Okura also supplies industrial robots to Japanese and foreign industries, as well as remote satellite equipment to the National Space Development Agency and advanced electronics systems to the Defense Agency. Okura and its subsidiaries and affiliates are developing lighter, more efficient materials for textile and manufacturing industries and materials for the electronics industry. Okura also has become increasingly involved in the transportation industry, supplying Japanese and foreign transportation enterprises with ships, airplanes, cars, motorcycles, helicopters, and planes.

While 49% of Okura's business transactions are domestic, more than half are in exports and imports; 38% of Okura's business is still in metals and 36% in machinery and construction, while 15% of its business continues to be food and feed. Through its associates in Europe, Asia, and Latin America, the company is developing new capacities for seafood and other food production. In 1990, Okura & Co. America, Inc., headquartered in New York City, and its Chicago partners formed a new company, MetalPro, Inc., to provide processing services to the metals industry in the United States. Okura also has been involved with China in its attempts to modernize, endeavoring, for example, to provide markets for Chinese agricultural products and seafood. The company also is helping to finance and develop Shanghai's infrastructure. With one foot firmly rooted in the past—namely heavy industry, iron and steel production—and one firmly planted in the future—electronics and telecommunications—Okura is well poised to advance.

Principal Subsidiaries: Okura Aerospace Co., Ltd.; Okura Engineering Co., Ltd.; Okura Intex Co., Ltd; Seiritsu Engineering Co., Ltd.; Seiritsu Kogyo Co., Ltd.; Okura Electronics Co., Ltd.; Okura Gleason Asia Co., Ltd.; Okura Machine Service Co., Ltd; Okura Tools Co., Ltd.; Okura Industrial Co., Ltd.; Okura Electronics Service Co., Ltd.; USX Technology (Japan), Ltd.; Okura Mechatrotech & Co., Ltd.; Okura Metal Co., Ltd.; Imabari Steel Center Co., Ltd.; Ikegami Shearing Co., Ltd.; Japan Icos Co., Ltd.; E.D.S. Okura & Co., Ltd.; Okura Chemicals Co., Ltd.; Okura Sports Co., Ltd.; Okura Petroleum Co., Ltd.; Okura Hide and Protein Inc.; Okura Food Sales Co., Ltd.; Kusano Meat Sales Co., Ltd.; Sanyo Co., Ltd.; Okura Home Co., Ltd.; Okura Home Component Co., Ltd.; Okura Forest Products Co., Ltd.; Clarks Japan Co., Ltd.; Okura Creative Co., Ltd.; Okura Personnel Co., Ltd.; Okura Finance Co., Ltd.

Further Reading: Okura, Tokyo, Okura & Co., Ltd., 1991.

—Sina Dubovoj

PEABODY HOLDING COMPANY, INC.

301 North Memorial Drive
St. Louis, Missouri 63102
U.S.A.
(314) 342-3400
Fax: (314) 342-3424

Wholly Owned Subsidiary of Hanson PLC through Hanson Industries, Inc.
Incorporated: 1890 as Peabody Coal Company
Employees: 10,400
Sales: $1.78 billion (1989)

Peabody Holding Company is the largest producer and marketer of coal in the United States. The company's 40 subsidiaries and affiliates mine, process, transport, and market bituminous, or soft, coal. Peabody's main customers are power companies and industrial plants that burn coal to produce steam that generates electricity. Steel manufacturers also buy coal from Peabody for use as a raw material in coke production. To secure loans to buy mines, mining equipment, and coal reserves, Peabody pioneered the use of long-term sales contracts with its customers. The company sells nearly three-fourths of its coal using long-term agreements. Peabody's owner is Hanson PLC, a British industrial management firm that acquired the coal company in 1990.

Peabody's business has always been coal. In 1883 Francis Stuyvesant Peabody and Edwin F. Daniels opened a retail coal yard in Chicago with $100 in start-up funds. Peabody, Daniels & Co. soon prospered. In 1885 26-year-old Francis Peabody purchased Daniels's interest in the business, renaming it Peabody & Co. A savvy businessman, Peabody established good political connections with Chicago's powerful Democratic Party. This enabled his company to become the party's official coal supplier. Customers throughout Chicago looked forward to the arrival of Peabody's two-mule cart purveying only the best quality coal. In 1890 Peabody incorporated his business as the Peabody Coal Company, and expanded into wholesaling. That same year, the company obtained its first major supply contract, to provide coal to a steamer, the *Dahlia*.

Peabody Coal soon had sufficient sales to justify owning its own mines. The company began operating a mine near Snider, Illinois, in 1895, and acquired three more mines in Williamson County, Illinois, in 1897, 1898, and 1901. At this point, Peabody learned one of the important lessons of the coal in-

dustry: while mines are a valuable asset, buying and opening them for operation is extremely expensive. Peabody's mine acquisitions near the turn of the century left the company coal-rich but cash-poor.

To obtain financial backing for further expansion, Peabody needed a steady stream of income. This problem was neatly solved in 1903, when Peabody obtained its first coal supply contract with a large power company. Chicago Edison, now Commonwealth Edison, required huge quantities of coal to generate electricity for the city's homes and businesses. Peabody agreed to supply the power company with all the coal it needed on a cost-plus-profit basis. The contract with Chicago Edison enabled Peabody to continue expanding its mining operations. The company opened two more mines in 1911 and signed its first long-term sales contract in 1913.

The advent of World War I brought a huge increase in demand for coal. Between 1913 and 1917, U.S. coal production increased 30% in an effort to meet the energy and raw materials requirements of munitions and steel manufacturers. By 1917 Peabody was producing 12 million tons of coal per year from mines in Ohio, Indiana, Illinois, Kentucky, Virginia, and Wyoming. This made Peabody one of the larger mine operators in the United States. No single coal company controlled more than 3% of the market.

Stuyvesant (Jack) Peabody succeeded his father as company president in 1919. By 1924 Peabody Coal had one billion tons of coal reserves and was the largest coal producer in Illinois. It reported net sales of $29.2 million and net income of $1.6 million in 1925, when the company sold 11.9 million tons of coal.

Peabody weathered the stock market crash of 1929 and the early years of the Great Depression under the wings of several of its largest customers. Commonwealth Edison (Edison), Peoples Gas Light & Coke Company (Peoples Gas), and several other Illinois utilities bought a controlling share of Peabody's stock in 1928. At that time, Peabody Coal was re-incorporated under the same name and merged with several of its subsidiaries, and with coal producers previously controlled by the utilities.

Peabody signed long-term contracts to supply 90% of the coal required by Edison and several affiliated companies, and to provide nearly seven million tons of coal annually to Peoples Gas. The contracts were for 30 years, set to expire in 1958. To ensure that it could supply the large volumes of coal promised in the agreements, Peabody purchased six large mines in Saline County, Illinois.

By 1929 Peabody had 9,600 employees and operated 25 mines in Illinois, 2 in West Virginia, and 1 each in Indiana, Kentucky, and Oklahoma. Peabody's stock was first listed on the Chicago Stock Exchange on May 15, 1929.

The Great Depression put a temporary damper on Peabody's growth. The company did not open any new mines from 1933 through 1935, and reported net losses in the same years. Edison's shareholders demanded renegotiation of the company's contracts with Peabody, and Edison divested itself of Peabody's stock in August 1935.

Peabody's coal output increased gradually during the ensuing decade and World War II, reaching more than 17 million tons in 1944 and 1945. In 1944 the company reported net sales of $43 million and net income of $2 million. The U.S. government took control of the nation's coal mines three times in the war years, between 1943 and 1947, to prevent work stoppages threatened by labor unions.

When Jack Peabody died in 1946, his son Stuyvesant Peabody Jr. was elected the company's new president. The following year, the company recapitalized to fund new mine development. Construction work on two new mines began in 1948.

Peabody's stock was listed on the New York Stock Exchange in 1949, a year when the company reported net income of $1.7 million from the sale of 15.5 million tons of coal. The company had scaled down its mine holdings to nine in Illinois, two in Kentucky, and one in West Virginia.

The early 1950s were a difficult time for Peabody. The decade opened with a lengthy mine workers' strike, which significantly decreased production. Coal prices remained unprofitably low, and demand declined in the Chicago area as competition arose from natural gas. Following several years of declining sales and expensive mine development efforts, Peabody sustained a net loss of $640,000 in 1954 on the sale of nearly ten million tons of coal.

Otto Gressens succeeded Stuyvesant Peabody Jr. as company president in 1954. Peabody stayed on briefly as chairman of the board, retiring in February 1955.

The company's fortunes took a turn for the better in July 1955, when the Sinclair Coal Company and its affiliates merged with Peabody. Sinclair owned and operated profitable strip mines in Kansas, Missouri, and Oklahoma. While the entire industry had to cope with the low price of coal, strip-miners were still able to make a profit because their mining costs were relatively low in comparison to those of underground mining operations.

Prior to the merger, Sinclair was the nation's third-largest coal producer, and Peabody ranked eighth. The Peabody name was retained after the merger because of its listing on the New York Stock Exchange. Sinclair's former owners, however, held 95% of the consolidated company's stock.

Following the merger, Russell Kelce, the former president of Sinclair Coal, became president of Peabody. Russell and his younger brothers, Merl Kelce and Ted Kelce, had operated the Sinclair group of coal companies for many years and were no strangers to the coal business. Russell Kelce began working in the mines at the age of 15, to provide for his family after their father was injured in a mine explosions. Russell joined Sinclair in 1926 as vice president and became president in 1949.

Russell Kelce died two years after the Peabody-Sinclair merger, in 1957. During his brief tenure as Peabody's president, however, the company invested $41 million in extensive mine improvements. Peabody developed new, lower-cost mines and prepared to take full advantage of inexpensive water transportation by building docks and loading facilities on inland waterways near its coal reserves.

Russell Kelce's youngest brother, Merl Kelce, was the next president of Peabody. He sought more long-term contracts with power companies, and used the future income promised by these agreements to secure financing for additional mines and automated mining equipment. These investments enabled Peabody to expand its profitable strip-mining operations, nearly double its reserves, and increase productivity.

Peabody expanded its holdings to the other side of the globe in 1962, by participating in a joint venture to open the first major strip mine in Australia. In 1965 the joint venture began fulfilling a 13-year contract to deliver a total of 30 million tons of coal to Japanese steel mills.

During the decade following the Sinclair merger, the Kelces more than doubled Peabody's coal reserves, from 1.84 billion tons in 1955 to 4 billion tons in 1965. Coal output increased dramatically, from 26 million tons in 1956 to 56 million tons in 1965. In 1961 Peabody became the largest coal producer in the United States, surpassing its rival, Consolidated Coal Company, for the first time. The decade following the merger also saw net sales more than double, from $97.5 million in 1956 to $208.3 million in 1965. Net income rose from $7.2 to $22.5 million for the same period.

Ted Kelce succeeded Merl Kelce as Peabody's president in 1963, and Tom Mullins succeeded Ted Kelce in 1965. Like the Kelces, Mullins came from a coal-mining family; his father operated mines in Indiana. Prior to joining Peabody in 1963, Mullins was president of Midland Electric Coal Company. Although Merl Kelce had resigned as company president, he kept his hand in the business, assuming the role of chairman and CEO in 1965. As Kelce neared retirement age, however, he began looking for a new owner for Peabody.

Meanwhile, Frank Milliken of Kennecott Copper was looking for a well-run coal company. As president of the United States's largest copper producer, Milliken believed his company needed to diversify into a business with more stable cash flows. In contrast to the soft-coal market, copper demand and prices vary widely from year to year, and new copper veins are nearly impossible to find as old ones become depleted. Peabody, with its steadily increasing revenue and dependable long-term sales contracts, seemed like an ideal acquisition for the copper company.

Kennecott acquired Peabody on March 19, 1968. In August of the same year, the Federal Trade Commission (FTC) issued a formal complaint charging that the combination of the nation's largest copper and coal producers violated the Clayton Antitrust Act. An FTC examiner dismissed the complaint in March 1970, but the full commission overturned his ruling in 1971 and ordered Kennecott to divest Peabody. By acquiring the nation's largest coal company, the FTC commissioners said, Kennecott had removed itself as a potential competitor in the coal business, making the industry less competitive than if Kennecott had acquired smaller mining companies on a piecemeal basis.

At the time of the FTC's decision against Kennecott, mergers were deemed anticompetitive if at least 50% of the market was already controlled by eight or fewer companies, with one company controlling at least 20% of the market. Although this was not the case in the coal industry, the commissioners said that a trend toward concentration was developing. In reality, during the five years following the ruling, the industry became less concentrated. Frank Milliken refused to accept the FTC's divestiture order. While Kennecott tried unsuccessfully to appeal its case, Peabody faced other serious challenges.

Part of Peabody's appeal for Milliken had been its respected management. At the time of the merger, Merl Kelce was enthusiastic about continuing to participate in running the business, even though he no longer owned it. Less than a year later, however, Kelce called Milliken to tender his resignation, explaining that he had lost interest in the company. Tom Mullins, who had been Peabody's president since 1965 and was 48 years old, unexpectedly died of a heart attack in 1971. Ed Phelps, formerly senior vice president for operations, succeeded Mullins as president.

Management changes were not Peabody's only worry. Compliance with the Mine Health and Safety Act of 1969, labor unrest, and the beginnings of 1970s-style double-digit inflation decreased productivity and pushed up coal production costs.

The price of coal skyrocketed from $10 to $50 per ton because of the Arab oil embargo in 1973. Peabody's long-term contracts, however, prevented it from raising its prices, even enough to cover its costs. In 1973 contract purchases accounted for nearly 90% of Peabody's sales, at prices that averaged less than $6 per ton. Peabody reported operating losses in 1973 and 1974.

Despite the coal company's profitability problems, Kennecott still was determined to hold onto Peabody. For five years after the FTC's divestiture order in 1971, Kennecott unsuccessfully tried to appeal its case. In 1976 Kennecott and its directors were declared in contempt of court for failure to comply with the divestiture order. The time to sell Peabody had come.

Many potential buyers called; six were chosen. Newmont Mining, then the nation's fourth-largest copper producer, was the leader of the investor group. The FTC approved the transaction and the newly formed Peabody Holding Company acquired Peabody Coal's stock in June 1977 for $1.1 billion. Newmont Mining acquired a 27.5% interest in Peabody Holding. The other investors were The Williams Companies, with 27.5%; Bechtel Group, with 15%; Boeing Company, with 15%; Fluor Corporation, with 10%; and The Equitable Life Assurance Society of the United States, with 5%. At the same time, Kennecott sold Peabody's interest in the Australian strip-mining venture to Broken Hill Proprietary Company of Australia.

In January 1978 Robert Quenon became president of Peabody Coal. Ed Phelps, who was nearing retirement, was made vice chairman. Quenon came to Peabody from Exxon, where he had been senior vice president of Carter Oil, an Exxon subsidiary. Quenon had been a mining superintendent for Consolidated Coal early in his career. He joined Exxon in 1967 as operations manager of the company's coal and shale oil department.

Peabody needed all of Quenon's skills and experience to overcome the profitability problems it had faced throughout the 1970s. The company was losing money on about half of its 60 long-term contracts: $42.7 million in 1978, and $28 million in 1979. By the end of 1980, most of the money-losers had been renegotiated.

Peabody further improved its financial picture by closing unprofitable and marginally profitable mines. Closing mines and streamlining operations enabled the company to reduce its work force from 16,000 to 11,100 between 1979 and 1989.

Until 1984 two-thirds of Peabody's coal output was from high-sulfur coal fields in the Midwest. By the mid-1980s, passage of acid-rain legislation that could decrease demand for Peabody's high-sulfur coal appeared imminent. Because emissions from power plants that burn this coal contribute to acid rain, Peabody began to reposition itself as a provider of low-sulfur coal, expanding its reserves and mining operations in West Virginia and the western United States. By 1989 more than half of Peabody's output was low-sulfur coal, and Peabody was the largest U.S. producer of this product.

In 1984 Peabody paid $257 million for Armco's low-sulfur coal mines and reserves in West Virginia and a share in Dominion Terminal Associates, owner of the second-largest coal-loading pier in the United States. Ownership in the coal pier enabled Peabody to expand significantly its participation in the coal export market. Peabody used the pier, located in Newport News, Virginia, to load coal shipments bound for customers overseas. Between 1985 and 1989 Peabody increased its coal exports from 2.3 million tons to 6.4 million tons, accounting for approximately 6% of the export coal market.

Peabody acquired more mines in West Virginia in 1987, when Eastern Enterprises, then called Eastern Gas and Fuel Associates, exchanged its coal properties for part of Newmont's interest in Peabody. The properties, valued at $152 million, included 7 mines and 800 million tons of low-sulfur coal reserves.

Ownership of Peabody Holding's stock changed hands periodically throughout the 1980s. In 1983, Fluor Corporation sold its stake in Peabody to Newmont, The Williams Companies, Boeing, and Bechtel. In 1987 Newmont Mining doubled its share in Peabody by purchasing The Williams Companies's interest. Newmont reduced its share in Peabody later that year with the Eastern Enterprises exchange. In 1989 Equitable Life Assurance sold its share in Peabody to Newmont.

Newmont's parent company, Consolidated Gold Fields PLC, was acquired in 1989 by Hanson PLC. Newmont had increased its debt level in 1987 to fend off a takeover attempt by corporate raider T. Boone Pickens. To reduce the company's debt to a more acceptable level, Hanson decided to give Newmont a cash infusion by purchasing Newmont's share of Peabody Holding. To gain 100% ownership of Peabody, however, Hanson also made offers to Peabody's other investors. Boeing, Bechtel, and Eastern Enterprises sold their combined 45% interest to Hanson in February 1990 for $504 billion. At the same time, Hanson bid $715 million for Newmont's 55% share, but was topped by AMAX, the nation's third-largest coal company. Hanson raised its bid to $725.6 million and acquired Newmont's share of Peabody in July 1990. Peabody Holding was in 1991 100% owned by Hanson Industries, Inc., Hanson PLC's U.S. subsidiary.

In 1989 Peabody Holding's subsidiaries operated 43 mines: 15 in West Virginia; 8 in Kentucky; 5 each in Illinois and Indiana; 2 each in Arizona, Colorado, Ohio, and Wyoming; and 1 each in Montana and Oklahoma. At the same time Peabody had 49 long-term contracts to provide more than one billion tons of coal to electric utilities and industrial customers. The company sold approximately 75% of its output to contract customers and received an average price of $20 per ton.

During its history, Peabody's ability to meet the enormous coal requirements of the nation's largest power companies enabled it to obtain valuable long-term contracts and the financing necessary to expand and grow. In the early 1990s more than half of the electricity used in the United States was generated by burning coal, and 10% of that coal was supplied by Peabody. In the 1990s, coal may become an even more important source of energy as an alternative to high-priced oil and unpopular nuclear power. The electric companies were counting on Peabody; as the nation's largest coal producer, it seemed likely to be able to deliver.

Principal Subsidiaries: Affinity Mining Company; Blackrock First Capital Corporation; Bluegrass Coal Company; Cameo Minerals Inc.; Canyon Coal Corp.; Castner, Curran & Bullitt, Incorporated; Charles Coal Company; Coal Properties Corp.; Colony Bay Coal Company; EACC Camps, Inc.; Eastern Associated Coal Corp.; Eastern Royalty Corp.' Gateway Terminals, Inc.; James River Coal Terminal Company; Midco Supply and Equipment Corporation; New Superior Coal Company; North Antelope Coal Company; North Page Coal Corporation; NuEast Mining Corp.; Peabody Australia Pty. Ltd.; Peabody Coal (U.K.); Peabody Coal Company; Peabody Development Company; Peabody Insurance Limited; Peabody Terminals, Inc.; Powder River Coal Company; Powderhorn Coal Company; Powderhorn Properties Company; Raven Mining Inc.; River Properties Corp.; Rochelle Coal Company; Sentry Mining Company; Sterling Smokeless Coal Company; Sterling Smokeless Fuel Corp.; Sycamore Coal Company; Tecumseh Coal Corporation; Trinity Mining Company; Western Associated Coal Corp.

Further Reading: Loomis, Carol J., "Down the Chute with Peabody Coal," *Fortune,* May 1977; Johnson, James P., *The Politics of Soft Coal,* Urbana, University of Illinois Press, 1979; Wilkinson, Joseph F., "Peabody Becomes Profitable Again," *Coal Age,* October, 1980; *Peabody Coal: The First One Hundred Years,* St. Louis, Missouri, Peabody Holding Company, Inc., 1983.

—Nancy L. Post

PECHINEY

Immeuble Balzac
10, place des Vosges
Cedex 68
La Défense 5
92048 Paris
France
(1) 46 91 46 91
Fax: (1) 46 91 46 46

State-Owned Company
Incorporated: 1950
Employees: 70,000
Sales: FFr88.50billion (US$17.39 billion)
Stock Exchange: Paris

Pechiney, a holding company with numerous subsidiaries in France and abroad, is the descendant of a single chemical plant at Salindres, established in 1855 in the southern French region of Provence by Henri Merle. It has become synonymous with the French aluminum industry, which first began in 1860. The company has remained faithful to its origins, and is now the third largest aluminum producer in the world, although diversifying towards canning and packaging—in which it is world leader—and industrial components and systems, and holding prominent positions in related fields such as nuclear fuel, ferroalloys, heavy carbon products, and international trade in minerals and raw materials. Nationalized in 1982, Pechiney, formerly the first French industrial group, under the name of Pechiney Ugine Kuhlmann, has undergone heavy restructuring and returned to its original activities. It has begun a new era of expansion, with the acquisition of American National Can in 1988 and the ensuing restructuring of the holding company in 1989.

In 1855, a young chemical engineer named Henri Merle founded his plant in Salindres, near Alais in the Gard region, with the permission of the French emperor, Napoleon III, in order to produce caustic soda from the coal, salt, pyrites, and limestone that were all available in the area. The company was known as the Compagnie des Produits Chimiques d'Alais et de la Camargue, run by Henri Merle and presided over by Jean-Baptiste Guimet. The year 1860 saw the first industrial production of aluminum metal, using the chemical process discovered six years earlier by Henri Sainte-Claire Deville, which allowed the company to cast 505 kilograms of metal the first year and retain a monopoly for it for about 30 years.

Aluminum was then extremely expensive, and considered a luxury product. The French emperor Napoleon III was actually offered aluminum cutlery as a wedding gift. The man who was to give the company its name, Alfred Rangod, known as A.R. Pechiney, the name of his step-father, entered the company in 1874, under the presidency—1871 to 1879 of Pierre Piaton to manage it from 1877 until 1906. He was the leading man in the firm, which was already referred to in financial and trading circles by his name as early as 1877. Henri Roux was appointed president in 1879, to be replaced by Emile Guimet, founder of the famous Asian arts museum in Paris, in 1887.

In 1886 a new, much more efficient electrolytical process to cast aluminum was discovered by the French scientist, Paul Héroult. Héroult offered to sell the process to A.R. Pechiney, but the latter did not believe in the future of aluminum and declined to buy it. Héroult subsequently sold his patent to another company, the Société Électrométallurgique Française, which built its first aluminum factory in Froges. In 1889, faced with competition from Froges, A.R. Pechiney closed down his firm's aluminum department. In 1897, however, Pechiney bought a competing firm and entered the field of electrolysis. Up to World War I, the firm continued to construct new plants in the Alps and Pyrenees, becoming the second aluminum producer in France and the leading firm for sales through the establishment of L'Aluminium Français, a sales company uniting all the French aluminum producers. The company also had a Norwegian subsidiary, which produced aluminum, but the most ambitious project of the period was the establishment in 1912 of a U.S. aluminum factory in South Carolina. The plant, one of the largest in the world at the time, was to develop into a town, Badinville. The town was named after Adrien Badin, who succeeded A.R. Pechiney at the head of the company as managing director, from 1914 to 1917, when he died. Badin was succeeded by a team comprised of Emile Boyoud and Louis Marlio. In 1918 Emile Guimet died, and Gabriel Cordier was appointed president.

Due to its southern location, the firm was not affected by World War I, apart from the fact that it had to sell its American plant to Aluminum Company of America. On the contrary, it worked hard to comply with the orders of the French war ministry. However, the firm faced new difficulties at the end of the war. The economic crisis of 1920 and 1921 led to an era of industrial concentration in France. In 1921, Alais et Camargue—referred to in financial circles as Pechiney—merged with the leading aluminum producer, Froges, to form the Compagnie des Produits Chimiques et Électrométallurgiques d'Alais, Froges et Camargue known as AFC. The company was managed by Gabriel Cordier, president of Pechiney. The production of the new company continued to grow steadily until World War II under the leadership of Gabriel Cordier and, after the latter's death in 1934, Jacques Level, from Froges, who died in 1939.

The company's expansion continued between the wars. Aluminum production, which amounted to 11,000 tons in 1918, reached 50,000 tons in 1939. The firm developed its chemical production and, above all, concentrated during the 1920s and 1930s on the exploitation of hydroelectricity in the French Alps and Pyrenees. In 1946, when the energy sector was nationalized by the De Gaulle government, along with the transport sector and strategic industries, including arms and electricity, AFC-Pechiney alone supplied 15% of French electricity. In addition, the company took part—together with the only other French aluminum producer, Ugine—in the reformed international aluminum combine—which was established in 1901. International alliances regrouping the aluminum producers followed one another, up to World War II. In addition, French aluminum producers formed a sales consortium in 1912, which favored an efficient double-edged policy aiming at the development of the final uses of aluminum and at moderate pricing. This situation allowed the company to go through the 1930s Depression without major problems, unlike the copper combine which experienced a major crash during the same period. Once again, the company plants were spared from destruction in World War II because of their geographical location in the south of France. The firm survived the war without major problems. During the first few months it was under the tenure of Louis Marlio, who had succeeded Jacques Level in 1939 after assisting him for 20 years in the company, and from then onwards under president René Piaton, who was to preside over the company, with Raoul de Vitry as managing director from 1940 to 1958. Although the firm saw aluminum production in 1945 fall to half the level of 1938 because of the energy shortage, it had completely recovered by 1947.

The year 1950 marked the beginning of a new era in the company's history, with its change of name from AFC to Pechiney, under which it was already well-known in financial and commercial circles. In 1948 the firm had already been completely reorganized, with the creation of four major divisions: aluminum, electrothermics, chemicals, and mining products. During the 1950s and 1960s, during the tenures of René Piaton, then Raoul de Vitry, from 1958 to 1968, and finally Pierre Jouven, from 1968 to 1971, Pechiney's policy aimed at two major goals: finding new sources of energy and raw materials abroad, and better integration of the nonferrous metals transformation activities. The firm took stakes in aluminum fabrication companies in Argentina and Brazil as early as 1947 and 1948. In 1954, an aluminum plant was launched in Cameroon, and in 1960 another alumina factory opened in Guinea, and an aluminum smelter at Noguènes in France in 1960. In 1962, Pechiney acquired an important U.S. aluminum producer and transformer, Howe Sound Inc., which was eventually to split in 1975 into Howmet Aluminum Corporation and Howmet Turbine Components Corporation. Also in 1962, the firm took a stake in the Australian alumina factory of Gladstone. In 1964, the Spanish subsidiaries founded in the 1930s were reorganized with the creation of Aluminio de Galicia. In 1966 an alumina-aluminum integrated plant was opened in Greece and in 1971 another aluminum factory was launched in the Netherlands. Pechiney took total control of a French firm, Cegedur, in 1964. Cegedur was another transformer founded by Pechiney itself in association with Compagnie Générale d'Électricité in 1943. The firm then created Cebal, a 100% subsidiary specialized in packaging, in 1966. In 1967, Pechiney merged with Tréfimétaux, another French firm in the sector specialized in copper. As a transformation result of this policy of integration and concentration, Pechiney adopted a holding structure in 1969. In the same year it sold its chemical activities to Rhône-Poulenc.

In 1971, a new period began with the merger of Pechiney and Ugine-Kuhlmann. Ugine had merged with the chemical producer Kuhlmann in 1965. The Pechiney Ugine Kuhlmann (PUK) share was introduced on the stock market immediately to replace the separate Pechiney and Ugine-Kuhlmann shares.

After the short tenure of Pierre Grezel, Pierre Jouven, former president of Pechiney, took over the presidency of the new group in 1972 for three years. He was succeeded by Philippe Thomas, whose tenure lasted from 1975 to 1982. The industrial policy of the period was based on the belief that conglomerates with various complementary activities were the correct answer to U.S. competition and the European common market. Pechiney and Ugine had indeed shared common interests for years. The new entity, Pechiney Ugine Kuhlmann, became the first French industrial group. A holding company coordinated various activities: the aluminum division, the only one in France, was fully integrated, while the electro-metallurgic activities were gathered into a new subsidiary called Sofrem. The new group was also present in the nuclear sector, from the mining stage to the production of combustible elements, with the creation of specialized subsidiaries, FBFC in 1973 and Zircotube in 1976. Finally, PUK produced special steels, copper, rare metals, basic chemicals, and coloring and pharmaceutical products. During the 1970s the company concentrated on its marketing policy. The holding company emphasized the development of technical assistance contracts with the USSR and third world countries such as Yugoslavia and India. It created an international sales network called MIA (Multibranch Integrated Agencies), with its first agency in Japan. This network has been expanding constantly covering more than 60 countries with 30 agencies all over the world. Eventually, PUK acquired Brandeis, an international raw materials trading company, in 1981.

The 1970s economic crisis nevertheless hit PUK hard. The company accumulated financial losses of up to FFr10 billion (about US$2 billion) owing to difficulties in the steel and chemical sectors. In 1979, PUK had to sell its cable activities to Pirelli. Then, in 1982, like many of the major French industrial groups, PUK was nationalized by the socialist government of Pierre Mauroy.

Nationalized companies were originally meant to be used as tools of economic policy by the state. Quite rapidly, however, the government had to set up restructuring plans for most of the companies it nationalized, including PUK. A series of transfers took place during the early 1980s, under the presidency of Georges Besse, who remained at the head of the firm from 1982 to 1984, and then under Bernard Pache, whose tenure lasted until 1986. The coloring activities were sold to ICI and the special steels department to Sacilor in 1982. The chemical activities were transferred to Rhône-Poulenc, Elf Aquitaine, CdF-Chimie, and EMC in 1983. The considerably thinned company took back its original name, Pechiney, in 1983. In 1987, Tréfimétaux was sold to Europa Metalli, with Pechiney taking a 20% stake in the firm. Pechiney thus returned to its basic activities as an aluminum producer, with half of its sales coming from aluminum metal and semi-finished products in 1986. In 1983, a new aluminum plant was opened in Australia; another one was launched in Quebec, Canada, in 1986, while the French factories were extended and renovated. In 1985, Sofrem absorbed Bozel Électrométallurgie to become Pechiney Électrométallurgie. In order to finance a part of its investments, privileged investment certificates—shares without voting rights—were introduced on the Paris stock market in 1985 and 1986.

In 1988, during the tenure of President Jean Gandois, appointed in 1986, the firm embarked upon a new policy of external growth by taking control of American National Can (ANC), the world's leading packaging company, with 21,600 employees, 100 factories, and sales of about US$5 billion in 1988. Pechiney itself achieved sales of US$10 billion at the time of the acquisition. In taking over ANC, Pechiney first of all grew by 50%, then reached a new equilibrium between aluminum (30% of manufacturing sales), packaging (45%), and other divisional activities. The aim was for the company to become less dependent on the volatile world aluminum market. The state-owned firm, heavily indebted by the acquisition of ANC, needed to finance its development projects in a convenient way. In 1989, the firm created Pechiney International, its international interests being brought together into the 75% subsidiary. The remaining 25% of the subsidiary's shares are on the stock market.

Pechiney intends to continue developing its packaging division, which is now the world leader, and its aluminum division, which is the world's third largest, and the most advanced exploiter of the electrolysis process. New aluminum factories throughout the world use the Pechiney technique. The company's other major fields are industrial components and systems, particularly for jet engines; related industrial activities, such as nuclear fuel, ferroalloys, and heavy carbonated products; and international raw materials and metals trading.

Principal Subsidiaries: American National Can (U.S.A.); Cebal; Techpack International (39%); Aluminerie de Becancour (Canada, 25%); Aluminium Pechiney; Aluminium de Grèce (Greece, 60%); Alucam (Cameroon, 46%); Tomago Aluminium (Australia, 35%); Pechiney Nederland (Holland); Queensland Alumina Limited (Australia, 20%); Affimet; Electrification Charpente, Levage; Pechiney Rhénalu; Almet (France, Germany); Pechiney Aluminium Presswerk (Germany); Softal; Pechiney Batiment; Howmet Corporation (U.S.A.); Microfusion; Howmet Cercast (Canada); Sintertech (34%); Le Carbone-Lorraine (56%); Aimants Ugimag; Pechiney Electrometallurgie; Metaux Speciaux; Hidro Nitro (Spain, 70%); Sers; Cegram (Belgium, 92%); Genosa (Spain, 56%); Comurhex (51%); FBFC (50%); Eircotube (51%); Cerca (50%); Cezus; Pechiney World Trade S.A.; Brandeis Instel (U.K.); Pechiney Trading Co. (Switzerland).

Further Reading: Gignoux, C-J, *Histoire d'une Entreprise Française,* Paris, Hachette, 1955.

—William Baranès

PHELPS DODGE CORPORATION

2600 North Central Avenue
Phoenix, Arizona 85004
U.S.A.
(602) 234-8100
Fax: (602) 234-8337

Public Company
Incorporated: 1885 as Copper Queen Consolidated Mining
   Company
Employees: 14,066
Sales: $2.64 billion
Stock Exchange: New York

Phelps Dodge Corporation is the world's second-largest copper-mining concern. Active in 23 countries in 1991, the company's operations also produce silver, gold, and molybdenum as copper by-products, as well as other minerals and ores mined independently.

Vertically integrated exploration, mining, marketing, and investment operations are handled by subsidiaries in the mining and metals division, which is headed by Phelps Dodge Mining Company. Phelps Dodge Industries is the company's second segment. Five companies make up the group, which manufactures carbon blacks, rubber and synthetic iron oxides, and ferrites, mainly for the electrical and transportation industries. Other products include wheels and rims for medium and heavy trucks and buses, plus electrical wire and cables.

In 1834 founder Anson Phelps, a New York entrepreneur thoroughly experienced in the import-export trade and well-connected in his targeted British market, formed Phelps, Dodge & Co. Along with his junior partners, sons-in-law William Dodge and Daniel James, Phelps supplied his English customers with cotton, replacing it on the homeward journey with tin, tin plate, iron, and copper, for sale to government, trade, and individual consumers in America. Before long, Phelps started a manufacturing company in Connecticut called the Ansonia Brass and Battery Company, and in 1845 he helped organize the Ansonia Manufacturing Company, which produced kettles, lamps, rivets, buttons, and other metal items.

Phelps steered his fledgling empire grimly through a seven-year panic that began during 1837. His reward came during the following 14 years of national prosperity, when large numbers of his products went west with new settlers, accompanied travelers on the rapidly expanding railroads, and provided a modicum of comfort for miners at the recently discovered Si-

erra Nevada gold deposits in California. Even broader markets came from inventions like the McCormick reaper and the electric telegraph, whose need for cable wire would swell Phelps Dodge coffers well into the next century. By 1849 the company was capitalized at almost $1 million, and its profits were almost 30%.

Phelps's death in 1853 gave his son and each of his two sons-in-law a 25% interest in the business, with 15% going to a younger son-in-law. This second partnership was scarcely five years old when Anson Phelps Jr. died. On January 1, 1859, the partnership was revised again, to increase the firm's capitalization to $1.5 million and to give William Dodge and Daniel James each a 28% share. With reorganization complete, the company turned its attention to developing industries like mining.

An interest in timber had begun in the mid-1830s, when Phelps, Dodge accepted timberlands in Pennsylvania in lieu of payment for a debt. Later it built the world's largest lumber mill there, establishing a timber agency in Baltimore, Maryland, to send its products to domestic and foreign customers.

Despite these diversifications, the principal interests of the company were still mercantile; however, through the advice of James Douglas, a mining engineer and chemical geologist, Phelps, Dodge was persuaded to take a large block of stock in the Morenci copper mine in what was then the Arizona Territory. Morenci was owned by the Detroit Copper Company, which exchanged the stock for a $30,000 loan. Douglas was also enthusiastic about prospects for another claim called Atlanta, situated in Arizona's Bisbee district, about 200 miles southwest of Morenci. In 1881 the company bought the Atlanta claim for $40,000.

Two years later Phelps, Dodge had a chance to purchase the adjoining Copper Queen mine, which was then producing about 300 tons of ore monthly. The partnership decided to buy Copper Queen when Douglas hit the main Atlanta lode in 1884, at almost the same time that a Copper Queen tunnel penetrated the lode from a different spot. Arizona mining operations at the time stuck strictly to the "rule of the apex," according to which a claim owner could follow a vein of ore onto another claim, if the deposit had come closest to the surface on his land. This had occurred with Copper Queen, and Phelps, Dodge, rather than risk losing this strike to the Copper Queen owners, purchased the Copper Queen mine, merging it with the Atlanta claim.

In August 1885 Phelps, Dodge & Co. decided to streamline its operations by incorporating the subsidiary Copper Queen Consolidated Mining Company in New York, with James Douglas as president. Cautiously, Douglas made no major acquisitions for ten years. Then, he bought the Moctezuma Copper Company in Sonora, Mexico, from the Guggenheim family. Two years later he purchased the Detroit Copper Company.

A large increase in domestic iron production during the 1890s plus a 2¢ tariff on each pound of imported tin plate instituted in 1890 combined to make profitable metal markets hard to find. These factors and the fast growth of the company's mining interests forced it to withdraw from most ventures other than copper mining and selling by 1906.

Phelps, Dodge still retained its Ansonia Brass and Copper Company, however, which had become one of the largest U.S. manufacturers of copper wire for the new telephone industry.

Other products included brass wire, sheet copper, and rolled brass.

The shift to mining interests led to a need for another reorganization. In 1908 the old Phelps, Dodge & Co. partnership was dissolved, to be replaced by a corporation called Phelps, Dodge & Co., Inc. Capitalized at $50 million, the new concern consolidated all the various Phelps, Dodge mining interests—Copper Queen Consolidated Mining Company; Moctezuma Copper Company; Detroit Copper Mining Company; and Stag Cañon Fuel Company, a subsidiary consisting of coal and timber properties near Dawson, New Mexico, purchased in 1905 to supply the mines and smelters with fuel.

By now there were 10,000 employees working in the mines, the smelters, the company railroads, and other ventures. There was also competition from other mining companies, which were able to mine copper, but lacked smelting facilities for processing. To provide these competitors with more efficient service while handling the smelting for its own copper mines, Phelps, Dodge abandoned its old Bisbee smelter and erected a new one some 23 miles away.

Following the 1917 entry of the United States into World War I, demand for copper for munitions and communications exploded. The company smelters turned out 600 to 700 tons daily. Also in 1917, Phelps, Dodge & Co., Inc. transferred its assets and subsidiaries to Copper Queen Consolidated Mining Company. Copper Queen became the operating company and changed its name to Phelps Dodge Corporation.

With all enterprises operating at capacity, the Bisbee miners went on strike in July of 1917. One factor was the powerlessness of mine managers to make policy decisions on behalf of top management in New York. Another was the shrinking supply of experienced workers, who were going into the military or being lured away by higher salaries and better working conditions.

The International Workers of the World (Wobblies) easily caught the attention of the miners working for Phelps Dodge. At issue were better working conditions, a wage increase to $6 per day, and abolition of the unpopular physical examination to which all applicants were subjected before obtaining a job. Many suspected the exam was a filter to exclude prospective miners with unpopular political affiliations.

When the strike was two weeks old, Phelps Dodge director Walter Douglas instructed an employee of the El Paso & Southwestern Railroad to transport about 1,200 strikers to Columbus, New Mexico, where they were to be turned loose. After the commander of a nearby army camp refused permission to unload the cars, the workers were released in a small Mexican town called Hermanas, where they lived at starvation level until two carloads of food arrived from the U.S. Army base at nearby El Paso, Texas. Though 25 participants in the Bisbee deportation were indicted, no particular blame was attached to any individual and the matter petered out.

The end of World War I brought a need for downscaling of all operations. Government warehouses were packed with more than 800 million pounds of copper, and more was coming in from Chilean mines at low cost. To counter these new challenges, Phelps Dodge and other large U.S. copper-mining companies cut production and formed the Copper and Brass Research Association to seek out and promote new uses for copper. At the same time, the companies founded the Copper Export Association, pooling 400 pounds of copper for exclusive sale in foreign markets.

Suffering acutely from the postwar slump in demand was the Arizona Copper Company, with holdings adjoining the Phelps Dodge Morenci properties. Part of this company's assets was a huge deposit of low-grade ore that it could not afford to develop. Phelps Dodge bought Arizona Copper and merged it with its Morenci holdings in 1921, in exchange for 50,000 shares of capital stock.

By 1925 business expansion was demanding record amounts of copper. In that year almost 1.75 billion pounds of refined copper were produced all over the country. Arizona's contribution to this total was more than 800 million pounds, a quarter of which came from Phelps Dodge mines. The stock market crash in 1929 brought the bonanza to an end, however. Demand for copper dwindled everywhere, the price falling to 18¢ per pound from a high of 23¢. Effects of the crash were felt immediately. Sales, $46.1 million in 1928, were down to $38.7 million in 1929, though net earnings were $4 million, up from $2.6 million the year before.

In April 1930 Walter Douglas resigned as chief executive of Phelps Dodge. In his stead came Louis S. Cates. Cates's first priority was to integrate the Phelps Dodge operations and to cut costs and allow for the Arizona tax of 2¢ on every pound of copper processed. Cates then, also in 1930, acquired the Nichols Copper Company, which had an electrolytic refinery on Long Island, New York.

In another important 1930 acquisition, Phelps Dodge bought National Electric Products Corporation, a large manufacturer of copper products for electrical and building purposes, with an annual capacity of more than 200,000 pounds of fabricated copper products and 150,000 pounds of steel. National Electric brought the company eight plants and a major interest in the Habirshaw Cable and Wire Corporation.

Cates reorganized all subsidiaries into two efficient organizations. The first, the National Electric Products Corporation, consisted only of the National Metal Molding division. This division's main interest was steel products, and it eventually reverted to its original owners by an exchange of stock. The second division was headed by a new subsidiary called the Phelps Dodge Copper Corporation. This division was charged with operating all the fabricating divisions including Habirshaw Cable and Wire.

Cates's next challenge was the long-operative Copper Queen mine, whose high-grade ore was becoming inaccessible and too expensive to mine. Phelps Dodge acquired the Calumet & Arizona Mining Company, a long-standing rival with Bisbee acreage adjoining Copper Queen. Overriding the objections of Calumet president Gordon Campbell, who resigned in April 1931, the purchase became final in September, giving Phelps Dodge title to a low-cost New Cornelia mine 150 miles away at Ajo, Arizona. Phelps Dodge consolidated the Calumet & Arizona and Copper Queen operations to reap economies of scale.

The Depression continued, however; the end of 1932 showed sales of just under $22 million, as opposed to $50.3 million in 1931. In an effort to pare costs and keep pace with lower demand, Cates cut production at the Copper Queen. He also suspended all operations at New Cornelia, and closed both the Stag Canyon coal operations and Morenci.

Nevertheless, Phelps Dodge bought the United Verde Copper Company despite a steep price of $20.8 million. With about 6,100 acres of claims in Arizona, United Verde proved its worth in 1937, when reserves of 6.9 millions tons of ore were produced. In 1937 the company went ahead with long-held plans to expand operations at Morenci, where a clay ore-body was prepared for open-pit copper mining, refining, and smelting, at a cost of $32.6 million.

By 1939 the Depression years were part of the company's history. Sales reached $75.5 million, yielding total income of $15.5 million, and the number of employees, recorded in mid-1938, reached about 9,000.

World War II once again found plants operating at maximum capacity. Stepping in for employees on military service, women and Navajo Indians ran the Morenci mine, smelting facilities, and refining plant. Typical of pay rates was the wage for rock-shoveling—64¢ per hour.

Once again operating at full capacity, Phelps Dodge supplied condenser tubes for the navy and cables for communications and electric power. Other orders were harder to fill—notably a specialized lead pipe in 50-mile lengths, which was laid under the English Channel to supply Britain's troops with gasoline for the Normandy invasion.

Already looking towards the war's end in 1944, the company began to build the Horseshoe Dam on the Verde River, about 55 miles northeast of Phoenix, Arizona, to allow for water conservation while filling the needs of its Morenci operations. Year-end 1944 sales figures of $168.1 million more than doubled the $80 million figure for 1940.

By 1950 Phelps Dodge was the second-largest domestic copper producer, contributing 30% of the country's output. It was also one of the world's top three, its position as a purely domestic supplier made even more secure by a 2¢-per-pound import duty.

Characteristic of the 1950s was government activism in the industry, partly as a result of the Korean War. At the end of 1950, the government instituted price controls for copper, placing a cap of 24.5¢ per pound. Other moves came as a result of a 1947 Federal Trade Commission study, emphasizing the surprisingly low level of competition in the industry, and intimating the power was concentrated in the hands of too few groups.

Though not specified by the report, there was also a feeling that copper resources could be exhausted, because copper companies were doing little to find additional reserves, and that this situation should be remedied. Negotiations between the government and the mining companies followed. Over the next two years, the country's copper-mining capabilities increased by 25%, thanks to seven new mines.

Phelps Dodge's contribution to this effort was the Lavender Pit mine, opened in 1954 to develop an extension of the Bisbee operations known as the Bisbee East orebody. As was the case with most of the companies, terms of the agreement were that the open-pit mine should be developed and equipped with a smelter at a cost of $25 million, entirely corporate-sponsored. In return, the company asked for a guarantee that the government would buy its copper at protected prices. By 1956 Lavender Pit produced 80.3 million pounds of copper.

Another important development was the Peruvian Project, a joint venture between Phelps Dodge and three other mining companies intended to provide ownership of three southern

Peru mines, together containing an estimated one billion tons of low-grade ore. Phelps Dodge's 16% share of the costs was $24.3 million. The peak sales year of the 1950s was 1956, when sales reached $540.3 million, yielding a total income of $153.9 million.

At the end of the 1950s, the company spread its wings beyond its Canadian subsidiaries, venturing into several developing countries. A 51% interest in a 1957 enterprise called the Phelps Dodge Copper Products Corporation of the Philippines gave it a new source of insulated wire and cable for electrical use. Another venture blossomed in 1960, when the United States Underseas Cable Corporation was established jointly with several U.S. companies and a West German company. There was also a San Salvador affiliation called the Phelps Dodge Products de Centro America S.A., which manufactured electrical wire and cables for the Central American market.

Despite these overseas connections, however, Phelps Dodge kept its main activities in the United States. This policy protected its copper from politically inspired import tariffs, as well as from taxation, strike activity, and fluctuating prices found in foreign bases like Chile. By the end of 1963, this policy yielded $327 million in sales, from annual production reaching 261,400 tons.

Another advantage of domestic concentration was vertical integration. Now one of the country's three largest copper producers, Phelps Dodge's fabricating subsidiaries provided outlets for its copper. This hedge against price swings also gave it immunity against purchasing at high prices to make sure that fabricating subsidiaries had an adequate copper supply.

By 1965 the price of copper rose from 34¢ to 36¢ per pound. Plastics, lead, aluminum, and zinc had advanced far enough to threaten long-term copper markets. Phelps Dodge president Robert Page felt it desirable to keep copper prices moderate enough to maintain demand for the metal.

Still, the new opportunities aluminum offered could not be ignored. In 1963 the company formed the Phelps Dodge Aluminum Products Corporation, offering aluminum wire and cable to complement the copper line. Though the aluminum enterprise produced 17 fabrication plants by 1970, the company foresaw little long-term profit in it, and therefore merged its company with the Consolidated Aluminum Corporation in 1971.

In July 1967 an industry-wide strike began that lasted until the end of March 1968. The Phelps Dodge operations most affected were the Morenci, Ajo, and Bisbee mines, as well as the El Paso refinery. Run by a coalition of 14 unions led by the United Steelworkers of America, the strike called for company-wide bargaining for all operations, regardless of competitive and geographic differences. Eventually, an average increase of $1.13 per hour in wages and benefits sent workers back to their jobs after the administration of U.S. President Lyndon B. Johnson intervened. Post-strike operations recommenced without raw-copper shortages, since most refiners were able to reuse scrap copper to augment their reserves.

Company chairman Robert Page handed the helm to George Munroe in 1969. Still holding the presidency—the office of chairman was abolished—Munroe oversaw the establishment of a new mine at Tyrone, New Mexico. Formerly known as Burro Mountain, this was a low-grade ore deposit that previously had been too expensive to work. New technology made the mine economically feasible, boosting total capacity by 20% annually. The expansion brought its reward; the decade ended with sales of $672.1 million.

In 1969, Phelps Dodge swapped 800,000 of its own shares for a 26% interest in Denver, Colorado–based Western Nuclear, Inc., a company concerned with uranium mining, milling, and exploration. Initially, an open-pit uranium mine and mill were erected near Spokane, Washington. Three years later, Western Nuclear became a wholly owned subsidiary, undergoing a $71 million expansion and modernization program to improve its production capacity at other facilities in Wyoming.

With the Clean Air Act of 1970, environmental concerns came to the fore. The most critical problem Phelps Dodge faced was at Douglas, Arizona, where its smelter regularly processed 7% of the nation's annual copper production. By 1973 Arizona anti-pollution laws required $17 million worth of emission-control adaptations to this smelter, although the Environmental Protection Agency (EPA) was still undecided about its requirements. This left a strong possibility of conflict between state and federal regulations. Fears of a clash were dispelled when federal standards proved to be lower than those of Arizona; state regulators were still dissatisfied, despite the money spent on emission control equipment. Phelps Dodge officials protested, claiming that these expensive standards would force the company to shut the smelter down, putting almost 2,000 people out of work.

Because of sluggish demand and foreign competition, production cutbacks followed at a new mine called Metcalf, and at Morenci, Ajo, and Tyrone. The shift showed up in net income figures—$121.7 million for 1974, $46.3 million by the following year, and $17.9 million by 1977. The smelters kept operating 24 hours a day, however, to cope with the large amount of ore that had accumulated during the shutdown for the installation of pollution controls.

By 1978 there were voluble industry complaints that piecemeal EPA regulations made long-term anti-pollution planning impossible. The $2 billion initially spent plus frequent updating added about 10¢ per pound to production costs, bringing the consumer's price for copper up to about 75¢ per pound.

Coupled with cheaper foreign competition and sluggish demand, this brought a business-cycle trough to the industry. Company executives blamed the crisis on the waning uranium market—Western Nuclear had lost its biggest customer, the Washington Public Power Supply System—the demand slump caused by the slowdowns in the automobile and housing industries, and environmental-protection woes. Many outsiders felt it was time to expand Phelps Dodge interests beyond copper.

In the first quarter of 1982 the company revenues showed a $19.1 million deficit. In April Munroe laid off 3,800 workers and closed all four mines and three out of four smelters. He also instituted salary cuts at all levels, and reluctantly took on short-term debt to cover operating costs.

The following year the United Steelworkers instituted an industry-wide strike. Kennecott Corporation, the country's top copper producer, settled quickly, exchanging a three-year wage freeze for a cost-of-living allowance reaching $1.87 per hour at 6% inflation. Using this settlement as model, the strikers then approached Phelps Dodge management. The company counteroffered abolition of the cost-of-living allowance, a three-year wage freeze, and lower wages for new workers.

By the end of August 1983 the stalemate had led many workers to cross picket lines, despite sharp harassment from hard-line strikers. At Morenci, the company called in the National Guard, fomenting more resentment. The strike ended uneasily the following fall, with the company refusing to budge on its position, and the miners voting to decertify the 13 unions that had long been present at the mines and the smelters.

Now, management turned its attention to reorganization. First on the agenda was strategy to reduce production costs to less than 65¢ per pound, and lessen dependence on copper. The economy drive began with the 1982 move of company headquarters to Phoenix. At the same time, the Morenci, Ajo, and Douglas smelters were closed and replaced by a state-of-the-art, $92 million solvent extracting–electrowinning plant at Morenci that produced 100 million pounds of copper annually by mid-1987. Electrowinning is a process of recovering metals from a solution through electrolysis.

Electrowinning capacity grew further in 1986, when the company built a $55 million plant after buying a two-thirds interest in New Mexico–based Chino Mines Company from Kennecott. In the same year, the company sold a 15% interest in the Morenci mine for $75 million. Also sold was the uranium-mining business.

The 1986 purchase of Columbian Chemicals Company for $240 million diversified Phelps Dodge interests to include the manufacture of carbon blacks, used to strengthen tires and to make toner for copiers. Also providing profitable diversification was Accuride Corporation, a manufacturer of steel wheels and rims for trucks and trailers, which merged with the company in 1988 at a cost of $273 million. Also in 1988, all operations were divided into two new operating divisions, headed by the Phelps Dodge Mining Company and Phelps Dodge Industries.

By the end of 1989, the company had an income of $267 million, on sales of $2.7 billion. A year later, net income leaped to $454.9 million, on sales of $2.6 billion, partly with the help of a joint venture between Phelps Dodge and Sumitomo Electric Industries, to sell magnet wire in the United States.

Principal Subsidiaries: Phelps Dodge Industries, Inc.; Phelps Dodge Mining Company.

Further Reading: "Presbyterian Copper," *Fortune,* July 1932; Cleland, Robert Glass, *A History of Phelps Dodge: 1834–1950,* New York, Alfred A. Knopf, 1952; Navin, Thomas R., *Copper Mining & Management,* Tucson, University of Arizona Press, 1978; Durham, G. Robert, *Phelps Dodge Corporation: "Proud of its Past, Prepared for the Future,"* New York, The Newcomen Society of the United States, 1989.

—Gillian Wolf

▏▍▋PITTSTON

THE PITTSTON COMPANY

One Pickwick Plaza
Greenwich, Connecticut 06836
U.S.A.
(203) 622-0900
Fax: (203) 622-4596

Public Company
Incorporated: 1930
Employees: 19,400
Sales: $1.85 billion
Stock Exchange: New York

The Pittston Company is a diversified corporation with operations in coal mining, air-freight delivery, and security services. It began as a coal company in northeastern Pennsylvania and expanded to include holdings in Virginia, West Virginia, and Kentucky. Pittston's coal division specializes in providing low-sulfur coal to domestic utility companies and metallurgical—suitable for fueling smelters and other metallurgical equipment—coal to both domestic and overseas steel producers. Since World War II Pittston has diversified its interests. It moved into security transportation with the acquisition of Brink's, Incorporated, and developed oil retailing operations through its subsidiary Metropolitan Petroleum Corporation. During the oil crisis of the 1970s Pittston increased its coal production to meet the demand for alternative fuels but then faced serious setbacks when falling oil prices and labor disputes hurt its production in the 1980s. By 1991 Pittston had started to recoup these losses, thanks to a 1990 labor settlement and to its growing security and air-freight operations.

The orgins of The Pittston Company are in the 19th century, when the U.S. coal-mining and railroad industries developed alongside each other. In 1838 the Pennsylvania Coal Company was organized in Pittston, Pennsylvania, to mine coal for eastern markets. This company produced anthracite, or hard, coal, and built a 46-mile railroad to transport it from Scranton, Pennsylvania, to the Hudson River. The Erie Railroad bought the Pennsylvania Coal Company in 1901, making it a subsidiary of its own mining and railroad operations. Fifteen years later an even larger company, the Alleghany Corporation, acquired the Erie Railroad. The Alleghany Corporation served as a holding company for a variety of businesses owned by the Van Sweringen brothers of Cleveland, Ohio, and their associates. It continued to operate the Erie Railroad and Pennsylvania Coal Company as parts of its railroad empire.

The Alleghany Corporation created The Pittston Company in January 1930. Competition in the hard-coal industry had intensified in the late 1920s, and antitrust laws prevented the Erie Railroad from entering new markets. To solve this problem, Alleghany organized Pittston and offered its stock at $20 per share to Erie Railroad stockholders. Alleghany retained a controlling interest in Pittston and the Van Sweringens continued to run Pittston. Pittston then leased mines from the Erie Railroad and sold its coal through its own wholesale and retail subsidiaries. At the time of its founding Pittston also acquired United States Distributing Corporation. United States Distributing was a holding company that owned United States Trucking Corporation; Independent Warehouses, Inc.; Pattison & Bowns, Inc., a wholesale coal distributor; and a Wyoming mining company.

Although it began as part of a large railroad empire, Pittston experienced hard times in its early years. The Great Depression slowed the nation's coal consumption, and Pittston had to borrow from $1 million to $2 million dollars annually from its sister companies just to stay afloat. In 1935 J.P. Morgan & Co. stopped backing the Van Sweringens, and the Alleghany empire crumbled. Two years later investors Robert R. Young and Allan P. Kirby took over the remaining pieces of the Alleghany Corporation, including Pittston.

Pittston's fortunes began to turn around when Young and Kirby convinced J.P. Routh to become The Pittston Company's president. When Routh took over in 1939 Pittston's stock was down to 12.5¢ per share, and the company owed the Erie Railroad $10 million. Routh, who had owned his own wholesale coal business, established a plan for servicing Pittston's debt and began looking for ways to expand its business. He turned his attention to the growing bituminous, or soft, coal market. In 1944 he brought Pittston its first bituminous reserves with the purchase of 60% of Clinchfield Coal Corporation. Clinchfield Coal had been formed in 1906 when Ledyard Blair, Thomas Fortune Ryan, and George L. Carter merged together several smaller coal companies. Clinchfield coal owned 300,000 acres of coal reserves in southwestern Virginia, and this acquisition permanently shifted Pittston's coal operations from Pennsylvania to Appalachia. Over the next four years Pittston invested heavily in Clinchfield Coal. In 1945 Pittston and Clinchfield Coal jointly acquired 67% of The Davis Coal & Coke Company. Seven years later Davis Coal & Coke was merged into Clinchfield Coal. In 1947 Pittston acquired Lillybrook Coal Company to increase its coal reserves. It also successfully drilled the Clinchfield properties extensively for natural gas. In 1956 Pittston purchased the remaining 40% of Clinchfield Coal, making this highly profitable company a wholly owned subsidiary.

Under Routh's direction Pittston developed interests in oil marketing. In 1951 it acquired the Metropolitan Petroleum Corporation, a wholesale and retail oil distributor in New York City. Pittston expanded Metropolitan's geographical range by purchasing terminal facilities in Philadelphia, Boston, and Chicago. Its share of the fuel-oils business in the northeast rose considerably, and by 1954 fuel oil accounted for 38% of Pittston's net income. Metropolitan's expansion continued during the 1960s with the acquisition in 1963 and 1964 of two Boston fuel operations: Burton-Furber Company and Crystal Oil Company. It also entered the petrochemicals market by forming Metropolitan Petroleum Chemicals Company in 1965.

Pittston diversified beyond energy markets by developing trucking and warehousing operations under its United States Distributing Corporation subsidiary. This holding company's most important component was United States Trucking Corporation (USTC), which had been formed in 1919 by the merger of 26 trucking companies. USTC operated in five areas, armored-car services, truck rental, general rigging, baggage transfer, and general trucking. It handled newsprint deliveries for New York's and New Jersey's major newspapers as well as the rigging work for Western Electric Company in New York City. Western Electric's rigging work included using pulley systems to move unwieldy switchboard equipment into skyscrapers. In 1954 Pittston acquired USTC's most prominent competitor, Motor Haulage Company, and merged its operations. In that same year, Pittston's trucking and warehousing operations accounted for 43% of its net income, surpassing both its coal and oil divisions. When Pittston's parent company, Alleghany Corporation, purchased the New York Central Railroad in 1954, antitrust problems developed about this new acquisition and Pittston's transportation operations. Alleghany solved this problem by divesting itself of its remaining 50% interest in Pittston, leaving it a fully independent company.

Pittston's most important diversification followed soon thereafter, with the 1956 purchase of an interest in Brink's, Inc., a Chicago-based security transportation company. Brink's had been founded as a delivery company in 1859, and began making payroll deliveries in 1891. From there it had grown into the world's largest armored-car company, providing services to private businesses, banks, the Federal Reserve, and the United States mints. Pittston's interest in Brink's began in 1956, when it bought 22% of its stock. Pittston then applied to the Interstate Commerce Commission (ICC) for approval to purchase a majority share in Brink's. In 1958 the ICC approved Pittston's proposal, but the Justice Department objected on grounds that it could violate antitrust laws. A year later Pittston increased its interest in Brink's to 90%, but it ran into antitrust difficulty again when it proposed merging the operations of Brink's and United States Trucking. Pittston finally completed its purchase of Brink's in 1962 and made it a wholly owned subsidiary distinct from United States Trucking. During the early 1960s, under Pittston's direction, Brink's expanded its business to include coast-to-coast air courier service and established subsidiaries in France, Brazil, and Israel.

Pittston's rapid diversification after World War II culminated in a corporate reorganization in 1960. Chairman and President Routh divided Pittston into three operating divisions—coal, oil, and transportation and warehousing—each of which contributed about one-third of Pittston's profits. In 1960 coal accounted for 36% of net income, oil for 31%, and transportation and warehousing for 33%. Pittston had achieved financial stability through diversification.

Despite all of this diversification, Pittston did not neglect its coal division. In the early 1950s the conversion of the railroads to diesel fuel and the use in many homes and factories of oil energies lessened the demand for coal. In light of these trends Pittston decided to focus its production on specific coal markets. Its reserves in Appalachia were rich in metallurgical coal, necessary in the manufacturing of steel. Over the next 20 years Pittston became the United State's largest exporter of this type of coal, feeding the booming steel industry in recov-

ering postwar economies such as Japan's. Pittston also turned its attention to the production of steam coal—coal best suited to producing steam—for electric utilities, such as the American Electric Power Company, which signed a long-term agreement with Clinchfield Coal in 1959. Several acquisitions in the 1960s added substantially to Pittston's reserves, including the Kentland-Elkhorn Coal Corporation and the Jewell Ridge Coal Corporation in 1966, the Sewell Coal Company in 1967, and the Eastern Coal Corporation in 1969. Through these efforts the coal division experienced a resurgence, and by 1971 it was contributing over 55% of the company's net income.

The energy crisis of the 1970s dramatically increased the world's demand for coal, and Pittston shifted its resources to take advantage of this change. Under the leadership of its chairman, Nicholas T. Camicia, elected in 1969, Pittston spent heavily in its coal division, opening new mines and modernizing its production. The company adapted to changes in environmental laws by increasing its output of low-sulfer coal, which burns much more cleanly than other types. Pittston supplied compliance coal, so called because it helped utilities to comply with environmental laws, to utility companies such as the Tennessee Valley Authority, which agreed to a ten-year contract with Pittston in 1978. The energy crisis and the OPEC oil embargo squeezed Pittston's other divisions, but by 1976 the company's coal operations had expanded enough to bring in 91% of profits. This boom period, however, was not without its difficulties.

In February 1972 disaster struck the Buffalo Mining Company, a Pittston subsidiary in Logan County, West Virginia. A coal-waste refuse pile that the company had been using to dam a stream near its plant collapsed, flooding 16 communities and killing more than 125 people. Chairman Camicia appeared before a Senate hearing investigating the disaster in May 1972, and survivors filed a $65 million lawsuit against Pittston for psychological damages. In a landmark settlement, Pittston agreed to pay $13.5 million to about 625 residents suffering from "survivor's syndrome" in the Buffalo Creek Valley. Pittston faced further legal action brought by the state of West Virginia, with whom it settled in 1977 for $4 million. Labor disputes and a slumping world steel industry in the late 1970s subsequently hit Pittston hard. A United Mine Workers Union (UMW) strike from December 1977 to March 1978, the longest in UMW history up to that time, severely curtailed production. This decline was worsened by a railway-workers strike from July to October 1978 that disrupted Pittston's deliveries to its buyers. Pittston's profit fell from a high of $200 million in 1975 to $25.2 million in 1978.

Pittston's other divisions fared as poorly as its coal sector in the late 1970s. The oil crisis left Metropolitan Petroleum dependent on its suppliers and facing much higher costs. It tried to develop its own oil-refining capacity, but a proposed refinery in Eastport, Maine, was unable to overcome opposition from environmental groups and was never built. In 1980, still without refining capacity, Metropolitan changed its name to Pittston Petroleum in an effort to improve name recognition and sales. Brink's faced difficulty in the 1970s, as well, because of rising costs and increasing competition. In 1976 a federal grand jury began investigating possible antitrust violations in the armored-car business. A year later Brink's paid $5.9 million to settle some of the resulting antitrust charges. In 1980 Brink's settled the last of the antitrust indictments handed down by the 1976 grand jury, when it paid $2.7 million to 12 Federal Reserve banks.

In 1980 Pittston decided to merge its trucking and warehousing operations under one structure. All of its United States Distributing group companies thus became subsidiaries of Brink's.

Pittston's performance continued to decline in the 1980s, resulting in four annual net losses between 1982 and 1987. A continued decline in foreign demand for metallurgical coal produced a $17.3 million loss in Pittston's coal operations in 1982. By 1987 Pittston was closing and writing off many of the mines it had opened during the expansive years of the early 1970s. In an attempt to recover these losses, Pittston devoted more resources to developing its low-sulfer coal sales, establishing the Pyxis Resources Company to market this product in 1986. The world oil glut of the early 1980s decreased Pittston Petroleum's profits by 48% in 1981. Two years later Pittston decided to get out of the oil business and sold Pittston Petroleum to Ultramar American Limited for $100 million.

Only Brink's, of Pittston's three divisions, managed to sustain expansion in the 1980s. After several years of declining profitability, Brink's sold off its warehousing interests in 1984 and diversified into home-security services. Pittston established a Brink's Home Security subsidiary and began test marketing home-alarm and medical-monitoring systems. Through gradual expansion into new regional markets, Brink's Home Security became a successful venture and a national leader in this industry.

In 1982 Pittston undertook its first major diversification in 25 years with the acquisition of Burlington Northern Air Freight for $177 million. Pittston entered the air-freight business during a highly competitive period, hoping to carve out a place for itself in the overnight-express market. It invested heavily in building a hub for Burlington in Fort Wayne, Indiana, and then renamed the company Burlington Air Express to emphasize its overnight serves. Despite these efforts Burlington's initial performance was disappointing, posting a $19 million loss in 1987. Nevertheless, Pittston, led by chairman, president, and CEO Paul W. Douglas since 1984, remained committed to developing its air-freight business. In 1987 it bought WTC Airlines, Inc., a group of companies specializing in air freight for the fashion industry, to expand Burlington's capacity and business. Soon thereafter, Burlington began to turn around, experiencing net gains in 1988 and 1989, and accounting for 51% of Pittston's total revenues.

By the end of 1988 Pittston appeared to be on the road to recovery. It posted a $48.6 million gain, as compared to a

$133 million net loss a year earlier. A prolonged labor dispute with the UMW, however, brought more hard times. In 1988 the Bituminous Coal Operators' Association (BCOA), an industry trade group, had negotiated a new contract with the UMW in which the UMW promised to continue production in the coal industry without a strike. Pittston's chairman, Douglas, however, decided to drop out of the BCOA and refused to offer the BCOA contract to Pittston employees. Instead, Pittston sought reductions in its miners' health benefits and tighter control over their work schedules. Angry miners walked out on April 5, 1989, and sympathy strikes by other UMW members quickly followed. By July 1989, 30,000 miners were participating in wildcat strikes across the nation in support of 1,800 Pittston workers. The strike, marked by hostility on both sides, continued through the end of 1989 and cost Pittston's coal division $27 million that year. Pittston and the UMW finally reached a settlement on January 1, 1990, with both sides making concessions. Workers won back their health benefits, while the company got its desired changes in work rules. Pittston miners ratified the contract the next month, ending one of the most costly and violent strikes in UMW history.

Despite the losses incurred during the strike, Pittston appears to have emerged from it in a stable position. Its Brink's subsidiary, buoyed by the strong performance of its home-security operations, had been operating with consistent profitability. While Burlington Air Express's profits had yet to match expectations in 1990, its air-freight business continued to climb as an important part of Pittston's overall revenues. The company's coal division remains a question. Performance depends on its ability to reduce the ill-will in its labor relations, and on the world's volatile energy markets.

Principal Subsidiaries: Pittston Coal Group, Inc.; Brink's, Incorporated; Brink's Home Security, Inc.; Burlington Air Express, Inc.

Further Reading: Routh, Joseph P., *The Pittston Company: A Bright Future in Energy!*, New York, The Newcomen Society in North America, 1956; "Pittston: Counting on 'clean' coal to reverse the tumble in profits," *Business Week*, September 8, 1980; Mitchell, Russell, and Hazel Bradford, "Paul Douglas Has His Guard Up at Pittston," *Business Week*, June 27, 1988.

—Timothy J. Shannon

POHANG IRON AND STEEL COMPANY LTD.

1, Koedong dong
Pohangshi
Kyongbak
Republic of Korea
(0562) 700 114
Fax: (0562) 72 75 90

State-Owned Company
Incorporated: 1968
Employees: 22,518 (1989)
Sales: US$6.42 million (1989)

Pohang Iron and Steel Company (POSCO), 70% owned by the government of the Republic of Korea, is an integrated iron and steel producer which, since starting production in 1973, has enabled Korean industry to move from virtually complete dependence on imported iron and steel to reliance on domestic supplies for most needs. The 11th-largest steel company in the world, POSCO has been noteworthy for the efficiency of its construction and of its subsequent operations, which has allowed production and expansion to come onstream more rapidly than anticipated, and helped make the company profitable when steelmakers in the United States and, for one year even in Japan, were making losses. The company has imported technology as required from various countries and has absorbed it, "Koreanizing" it so that the technology could be, in some instances, exported to other developing countries, or adapted for use in other Korean industries.

In the aftermath of the Korean War, it was in the interests of South Korea, as well as of the United States and its supporters in that conflict, that the country's economy recover and develop as rapidly a possible. As the First Development Plan was elaborated, measures were included for protecting new industries with tariffs, quotas, and, in some cases, prohibition of imports of competitive products.

The industry initially given the highest priority by Koreans was steel, production capacity having been damaged severely during the war. An integrated steel mill with an annual capacity of 300,000 tons was discussed at a very early stage, and there were some hopes of including it in the First Plan. The World Bank and other international agencies considered the plan too ambitious and inappropriate because, they argued, Koreans could not master the technology, and the plant would not be large enough to operate efficiently, while anticipated

domestic demand would be insufficient to justify construction of a larger mill. Ultimately they were to be proven wrong.

In place of the larger scheme, a number of small-scale steel plants based on electric furnaces and domestic scrap were built. One of the first and most important of these was the Inchon Heavy Industrial Corporation financed by the Korean government. Inchon had a 50-ton open hearth furnace and a medium rolling mill capable of producing 10,000 tons of sheet steel per year. Further development on a similar scale led, particularly after 1963, to the establishment of some 15 firms involved in producing steel of various kinds. Initially employing old-fashioned techniques, non-continuous rolling mills produced sheet steel, bars and rods, wire, and pipe of uneven quality in quantities insufficient to meet demand. Although the size of these undertakings was to be dwarfed by POSCO they were gradually updated, in some instances absorbing technology from POSCO, and have been able to play an important role in providing a wide range of domestic steel products for Korean industry and consumers. POSCO itself is responsible for most of the industry's products.

This early steel production was based on imported pig iron and scrap, while at the same time Korea was actually exporting iron ore. Only tungsten was a more important mineral export. By the 1980s, in sharp contrast, iron and steel exports accounted for some 10% of Korea's commodity exports, while the industry could only secure sufficient domestic supplies of limestone, but had to import about 90% of its iron ore and bituminous coal and 66% of its scrap requirements.

The chairman of Korean Tungsten Mining Company, former Major General Tae Chun Park, spearheaded a second attempt to put together an international financial package to build an integrated steel mill. He had the strong support of President Chung Hee Park. Tae Chun Park is quoted as having referred to the president and himself as "the two crazy men who had this conviction that for South Korea to have a viable heavy industry, it needed the capability to produce its own steel."

This scheme, to build a plant capable of producing 600,000 tons of crude steel per year, was elaborated by a consortium of seven Western steelmakers, known as Korea International Steel Associates (KISA). In October 1967, a contract between KISA and the Korean government stipulated that KISA would raise an international loan by 1969, and complete the integrated mill by 1972. Costs were estimated at US$100 million. The operating company, Pohang Iron and Steel, was incorporated in 1968.

Fulfillment of the plan, however, had to be postponed, in part because the consortium's structure was extremely cumbersome, making it difficult to reach rapid decisions. Koppers, the leading consultant in the group, was unable to raise the necessary capital, and the KISA was dissolved in 1969.

Advice given to the Korean government continued to oppose the building of an integrated steel capacity, primarily on the grounds of the domestic market's inability to support an efficient plant. The government remained convinced of the steel mill's importance, however, and decided to raise foreign loans to finance it rather than continuing to attempt to secure private capital.

Japanese steelmakers and the Japanese government felt they could derive worthwhile economic and political advantages from assisting the Koreans in this plan. During the annual conference between Korean and Japanese ministers in August

1969, preliminary agreement was reached for resurrecting the KISA plan. Discussions through the rest of the year led to a contract whereby Japan would arrange loans covering most of the capital required. Japan's Export-Import Bank provided US$52.5 million, its Economic Cooperation Fund US$46.43 million, and Japanese commercial loans US$28.58 million. The remaining US$24,345 came from other sources.

Detailed planning was carried out with the help of Mitsubishi Heavy Industries. Care at this stage was a major factor in enabling POSCO to save the large amounts of capital that would have been required to cover any delays. Construction was planned and carried out in such a way as to facilitate future expansion.

The Japanese steelmakers involved in the plans, Nippon Kokan (NK) and Nippon Steel Corporation (NSC) benefited considerably from the arrangements made in 1970 for provision of the underlying technology needed. Virtually every detail from scheduling the timing of construction to specifications, supervision, purchasing, and inspection, culminating with on-site support for start-up and operation, was in Japanese hands. The involvement of Korean engineers in this first phase was limited to the inspection of specifications, in conjunction with foreign engineers.

It was part of the Korean development strategy to locate new plant as far as possible from Seoul, to create industrial centers throughout the country. This practice had defense as well as economic and social reasons. When construction began in 1970, it was closely supervised by Tae Chun Park, who not only insisted that suppliers meet deadlines, but also, in some cases, advanced deadlines and insisted they be met. As a result the first phase of construction was completed a month earlier than scheduled. In the course of constructing the third phase of the plant, workers gave up time off that they would have expected for a major holiday, and also worked through the night when necessary. That phase was completed five months ahead of schedule.

While construction of the first phase was going on, Koreans were being trained abroad, particularly in Japan, to take over some of the technological work involved in operating the mill. They worked alongside their Japanese counterparts in construction and operating work, gaining valuable experience. As a result, in subsequent expansion, the amount of operating technology that had to be bought in from outside steadily decreased.

In the second phase of construction in 1974, Korean engineers were still only involved in specification inspection. In the third phase, begun in 1976, Koreans took over material balance and facilities specification and inspection of drawings. When the fourth stage began three years later, Koreans had ousted foreign engineers from the task of general engineering planning. The shift to domestic technological skills is also evident in the declining levels of royalties paid to outside experts from US$6.2 million for the first stage, US$5.8 million for the second, US$4.8 million for the third, and nothing for the fourth.

Koreans remain absent from initial process and equipment design. The construction of the four stages of POSCO has not justified the development of domestic expertise in these spheres, since the limited number of Korean engineers are needed to maintain maximum use of existing plant. Competition among foreign design firms has meant that importing technology for the construction stage of development represents an efficient use of both capital and human resources.

Technology developed by POSCO has been transferred to other Korean industries and has also been exported. In 1978, for example, Taiwan was constructing an integrated iron and steel plant for the Chinese Steel Corporation. It paid POSCO US$300,000 to train 42 Taiwanese engineers in plant operation and maintenance and to assist in initial production. Subsequently, six POSCO engineers designed Indonesia's Krakatoa integrated steel works, providing technology and training.

When the first stage of construction was completed in 1973, the major plant consisted of a blast furnace and two steel converters. These had capacities of 949,000 and 1 million tons, respectively. The plant had a foundry pig iron furnace, with production capacity of 150,000 tons, as well as a blooming and slabbing mill, billet mill, and a plate and hot rolling mill. This plant reached full production within four months rather than the minimum of 12 months the Japanese steelmakers had anticipated.

The second construction stage, similar in capacity to the initial stage, was begun in 1974 and completed in 30 months. The third stage, started in 1976, had approximately double the capacity of the second, and was completed in 29 months. The fourth stage, initiated in 1979, required 24 months. The second blast furnace was brought to capacity production in 80 days, the third and fourth in 70 and 29 days, respectively. Steel converters followed a similar pattern, resulting in major cost savings.

By the time the last stage of construction had been completed, POSCO's crude steel production capacity was 8.5 million tons. Only in the second stage was there any significant U.S. capital participation. Out of a total of US$342.25 million, US$61.6 million came from U.S. sources, about 75% of that in the form of commercial loans. In the third stage Japanese capital, in the form of commercial loans, accounted for more than half the US$766.30 billion raised. By the time the fourth stage was financed, Japanese interests were also absent. U.S. and Japanese steel producers were no longer willing to assist a competitor who was eroding their markets considerably. Korean finance gradually became more important.

In order to avoid some of the problems of erratic quality experienced by existing small-scale producers, POSCO's emphasis initially was on the production of plain high-carbon steels of even quality that were used for general structural purposes, rather than on the development of a wider range of specialized products. As the company expanded, and engineering skills increased, it was possible to diversify production. The development of high tensile strength steel production in 1975 laid the foundation for the first major expansion of overall production, but domestic demand for special steels remained too low to justify attempts to develop them. Only as domestic demand increased, or was expected to increase, notably as defense industries developed, were facilities to broaden production created, based once again on imported technology.

Through the period of construction and operation, machinery came primarily from Japan and Austria. As time went on, however, a larger proportion of needed equipment was produced by Korea's own heavy industry.

Korean engineering skills constituted a major part of the reason for POSCO's ability to produce high-quality steel at low prices. In the spheres of equipment design and operating procedures, field engineers and technicians, have brought about major improvements in efficiency and quality along with reductions in waste and costs. Suggestions from people involved in the day-to-day operation of the plant have been incorporated into the plant and process and have generated massive savings. In 1980, when all of Korean industry was hit by recession, the number of proposals registered and carried out increased dramatically, and continued to do so in the following four years. POSCO continues to be profitable even in times of economic downturn.

One of POSCO's major problems has been securing adequate supplies of iron ore. This need has involved the company in arrangements with foreign suppliers such as Brazil. While some supplies are secured simply by direct purchase, others have involved development and joint ventures. In this respect, POSCO has become a significant force in the world's iron trade.

Competition with U.S. and Japanese steel producers exists primarily for markets within Korea itself. Given POSCO's great efficiency and low costs, the longer term prospects for increased exports are considerable. A proportion of POSCO's production has been exported, but the greater part has always been absorbed by domestic industries. Korea is not yet self-sufficient in iron and steel, but POSCO has taken the country a long way toward that position. Most notable among POSCO's customers has been the Korean automobile industry, which has itself grown tremendously. When, in the 1980s, reference was made to Korea's economic miracle, people were more likely to have consumer or heavy industries than the iron and steel industry in mind. Yet it is the iron and steel industry, and most importantly POSCO, which has made the expansion of the others possible both directly by supplying the steel requirements, and indirectly by helping to promote domestic industrial expansion and savings.

Further Reading: Enos, J.L., and W.H. Park, *The Adoption and Diffusion of Imported Technology: The Case of Korea,* London, Croom Helm, 1988.

—Simon Katzenellenbogen

REYNOLDS METALS COMPANY

6601 West Broad Street
Richmond, Virginia 23261
U.S.A.
(804) 281-2000
Fax: (804) 281-4160

Public Company
Incorporated: 1928
Employees: 30,800
Sales: $6.08 billion
Stock Exchange: New York

Reynolds Metals Company is one of the world's largest producers of aluminum and plastic products. In 1991 Reynolds had more than 100 operations in 20 countries. The company also mines gold and has interests in the mining of other precious metals. Reynolds is a fully integrated producer of aluminum, alumina, reclaimed aluminum, and carbon anodes. The company's line of fabricated products includes aluminum sheet, cans, plate, and extrusions; foil used in food-service and consumer kitchens; building products; wheels; electrical cable; and various aluminum-based powders and chemicals. Reynold's line of plastic products include wraps used in food-service and consumer kitchens, bags, packaging of all kinds, and building products. The company also engages in real estate development.

Reynolds began as a supplier of foil for cigarette packaging. The company was founded by R.S. Reynolds, a former law student and nephew of R.J. Reynolds, one of the first U.S. tobacco barons. After spending several years in the tobacco business working for his uncle, R.S. Reynolds borrowed $100,000; and in 1919, he purchased a small, one-story building in Louisville, Kentucky, and founded the United States Foil Company (U.S. Foil). The increased demand for foil was the result of the ever-increasing public appetite for cigarettes, the demand for which was so great that it created constant shortages of foil used for packaging.

U.S. Foil's entrance into the market generated a price war with other foil manufacturers, who hoped that by cutting prices they could drive the fledgling company out of business. Their plan did not work. At the time, most foil was manufactured in tall, multi-storied buildings. The material was moved manually from one floor to another before the finished product was ready for shipment. All the lifting and transferring of raw materials was a costly and inefficient way to manufacture foil.

The newly purchased Reynolds plant in Kentucky, however, was all on one floor, at ground level. The production equipment was, therefore, installed in long rows, which eliminated the need for the expensive transporting of the product. The resulting lower manufacturing costs allowed the company to undersell its competitors by several cents per pound, ensuring the company's share of the growing market.

During the 1920s most foil for packaging was made of lead and tin alloys. R.S. Reynolds recognized the advantages of using lighter-weight, less-expensive aluminum foil. In 1928, after buying back the stock he had sold to R.J. Reynolds to start U.S. Foil, R.S. Reynolds built the company's first aluminum foil plant and rolling mill in Louisville, and the Reynolds Metals Company was formed.

The Great Depression did not affect the growth of the newly formed company. In fact, the company recorded annual sales of $13 million in 1930 and moved its corporate headquarters to New York City. In 1935 Reynolds developed a method of printing on aluminum foil, employing the rotogravure process, which enabled the company to expand quickly into other aluminum-foil-packaging markets. The following year, Reynolds ventured outside the United States for the first time by opening a foil-production plant in Havana.

In 1938 R.S. Reynolds decided to move the company's headquarters south again. Taking his son, Richard S. Reynolds Jr., with him as assistant to the president, the company settled in Richmond, Virginia. Reynolds Jr. had previously founded a stock-brokerage firm that would later become Reynolds Securities, which eventually merged with Dean Witter.

In 1937, in Europe to search for new sources of raw materials, Reynolds Sr. observed that German production capacities for aluminum were more than two times that of the combined production capabilities of the United States, England, and France. Reynolds deduced that Germany was preparing for war, with a massive production effort in aluminum sheet used to build military airplanes. After his return to the United States, taking his cue from what he observed in Germany, Reynolds set about to increase dramatically his own production capacity. The company borrowed $15 million and began construction on its first smelting facility, located at Sheffield, Alabama. The company also acquired a bauxite mining operation in Arkansas to help feed the smelters. Reynolds's World War II production was extensive. By the end World War II, Reynolds had increased the company's production capacity to more than 450 million pounds. Impressive as the wartime figures were, they were dwarfed by postwar demand for aluminum.

With the end of World War II, the company focused its direction on consumer goods and construction. Reynolds developed aluminum siding for the booming postwar housing market. In 1946, the company leased, then purchased six government-owned production plants, and by doing so doubled its production capacity. Reynolds Wrap, the company's well-known household aluminum foil was introduced in 1947.

R.S. Reynolds Jr. was named the company's new president in 1948. His three brothers, David, William G. and J. Louis, also assumed much of the responsibility for running the business, concentrating primarily on a program of rapid overseas expansion. Reynolds expanded its holdings worldwide, and in 1953 the company organized Reynolds International, Inc. in an effort to consolidate and further expand foreign operations.

Reynolds closed the 1950s with a move to a new, modern corporate headquarters in suburban Richmond, Virginia.

During the 1960s the company continued to grow and introduce new all-aluminum products for home and industry. Included were the first aluminum drill pipe in 1960 and the first aluminum beverage can in 1963, both successful. An attempt to increase production capacities by 20% cost Reynolds an estimated $650 million in the mid-1960s. Plagued by cost overruns and delays, by the time the project was finished demand for aluminum had leveled off. Reynolds's leadership came under criticism from the financial community, particularly for what was perceived as the Reynolds family having too much control over the company. The company began a reorganization during the late 1960s, and separate operating divisions were formed each of which was responsible for its own profit performance. R.S. Reynolds Jr. brought in a financial consulting firm to streamline operations. Control of the company still was held by the Reynolds family. In 1976 David P. Reynolds was its chairman; J. Louis and William G. Reynolds were board members; a cousin, A.D. Reynolds was a vice president; and William G. Reynolds Jr. was the company's treasurer.

In 1973 a Reynolds unit pleaded guilty to charges of importing ores from Rhodesia, in violation of U.S. government sanctions against the country at the time. In 1975 the company's assets in Guyana were nationalized and Reynolds was forced to settle for a $10 million payment for its Guyanese holdings. In 1980, 51% of its Jamaican assets and operations and all of its Jamaican land holdings were sold to the Jamaican government.

The company continued to offer new products to the marketplace. In 1970 the first all-aluminum automobile engine block was introduced. All-aluminum car bumpers were in use in 1973. The beverage can with the stay-on, pull-top tab was well received in 1975.

Reynolds has been involved in an impressive recycling effort since 1968. It has received a great deal of praise for its recycling philosophy. As of 1980, the company was recycling almost half the number of cans it produced. In 1981, the company expanded its recycling capacity with two more facilities. In 1990 Reynolds recycled 438 million pounds of consumer-generated aluminum scrap, paying out $123 million to the recycling public. The company recycles more cans than it produces. In addition to its environmental advantages, recycled aluminum requires only 5% of the energy that would be used to produce aluminum from virgin materials.

Like most U.S. industrial giants, Reynolds lost sales in the recession of the early 1980s. Reynolds looked into new products and areas of manufacturing to redeploy its assets, seeking businesses that would provide higher profits and faster growth than those of aluminum.

In the early 1980s, David Reynolds and William Bourke, a former Ford Motor Company vice president and now Reynolds's chairman and CEO, realized that Reynolds's upstream costs, for mining, smelting, and refining, were cutting into downstream profits on finished goods, like aluminum foil and cans. Reynolds then embarked on a capital-improvements program that involved the expenditure of billions of dollars and the shutting down of some of the company's less-profitable operations. By 1988 Reynolds had cut the number of employees by one-third and reduced by almost 25% its production costs, reversing the drain on company profits.

Reynolds fortunes were greatly improved by the discovery of gold at one of the company's bauxite properties in Australia in 1986. The company's entrance into the gold market, an unexpected upsurge in aluminum prices in the late 1980s, the company's continued commitment to modernization of its production facilities, and the expansion of its consumer products division made Reynolds a solid, profitable enterprise with the ability to weather the cyclical nature of the aluminum business.

Under the leadership of Chairman and CEO Bourke the company moved into the 1990s with its focus on consumer products and on gold. By using its well-established marketing, sales, and distribution organizations, Reynolds was able to add new products without increasing employment. Late in the 1980s the company introduced a line of colored plastic wraps and resealable plastic bags. In May 1988 Presto Products, Inc., a $200-million-a-year producer of plastic bags was acquired by Reynolds. Presto produces a full range of plastic bags and wraps for both indoor and outdoor use including freezer, sandwich, and food storage bags, along with a line of moist paper tissues and cotton swabs. In line with its commitment to recycling, Reynolds has set as a long-term goal the recycling of more plastics each year than it produces.

The company's position in the gold market is also promising. In 1988 the company announced a 50% increase to its estimated reserves. Reynolds purchased additional gold properties in 1990.

As Reynolds Metals entered the 1990s, the company was in the best financial condition in its history. Modernization of its plants continued with the construction of a new 120-metric-ton-per-year facility at the company's Baie Comeau, Quebec, smelter, along with expansion and modernization of other company plants in Western Australia, Texas, and Louisiana. Reynolds invested more than $400 million in Alabama to ensure its position as a world-class producer of aluminum-can stock and can-end stock. In addition to its capital-investment program, the company expanded its research-and-development efforts. The company has developed new process technologies in aluminum-lithium casting, electromagnetic casting, and various techniques in automation. In 1991 new products included a light-weight, stronger composite architectural panel metal for the construction industry.

With the demand for lighter, more fuel-efficient automobiles, the use of aluminum in U.S. cars is expected to rise during the 1990s. Reynolds was involved in research that had helped develop technology for the manufacture of aluminum automobile drive shafts and radiators. In 1989 the company acquired an interest in the Fata European Group in Italy, a company with strong ties and business experience with Eastern Bloc countries. Fata, Reynolds, and a group of Soviet organizations are constructing a $200 million aluminum-foil plant in Siberia.

Principal Subsidiaries: ALRECO Metals, Inc.; Baker's Choice Products, Inc.; Conductor Products, Inc.; El Campo Aluminum Company; Eskimo Pie Corporation; Malakoff Industries, Inc.; Mt. Vernon Plastics Corporation; Presto Products Company; Reynolds Aluminum Recycling Company; Reynolds International, Inc.; Reynolds Metals Development Company; Southeast Vinyl Company; Southern Gravure Service, Inc.; Southern Reclamation Company; Aluminio

Reynolds de Venezuela, S.A.; Austria Dosen Produktionsgesellschaft MBH; Canadian Reynolds Metals Company Limited (Canada); Industria Navarra del Aluminio, S.A. (Spain); Nuova Fonderpress S.P.A. (Italy); Reynolds Aluminium Deutschland, Inc.; Reynolds Aluminium France S.A.; Reynolds Aluminium Holland B.V. (Netherlands); Reynolds Consumer Europe S.A. (Belgium); Reynolds (Europe) Limited; Reynolds Systems Ireland Limited; Reynolds Systems (N.I.) Limited; Reynolds Wheels S.P.A. (Italy); SLIM Cisterna S.P.A. (Italy).

Further Reading: Reynolds Metals Company: 1991 Background Data, Richmond, Virginia, Reynolds Metals Company, 1991.

—William R. Grossman

THE RTZ CORPORATION PLC

6 St. James's Square
London SW1Y 4LD
United Kingdom
(071) 930-2399
Fax: (071) 930-3249

Public Company
Incorporated: 1962
Employees: 73,612
Sales: £5.08 billion (US $9.81 billion)
Stock Exchanges: London New York Paris Frankfurt
 Amsterdam Brussels Zürich Geneva Basel

The RTZ Corporation PLC is the holding company for the RTZ Group, an international U.K.-registered mining company with important assets in natural resources and related industries. Its principal areas of operation are North and South America, Australasia, southern Africa, and Europe. The main RTZ subsidiary and its associated companies are engaged in the discovery, evaluation, financing, marketing, developing, mining, and processing of a wide variety of mineral resources. It has been the policy of the group, since its formation in 1962 through the merger of the Rio Tinto Company (RTC) and the Consolidated Zinc Corporation (CZ), to invest only in first-class mining properties with large reserves and low production costs. RTZ has accumulated rich assets with a broad geographic spread, with the aim of providing stability against a background of often-violent economic and political movements.

Both the RTC and CZ were formed during the years between 1870 and 1914, when London rose to prominence as the hub of international mining and metallurgical activities. The number of overseas metal mining and processing companies listed on the London Stock Exchange climbed from 39 in 1875 to 913 in 1913, with the long-term capital employed in the industry rising at an average annual rate of more than 8% over the same period. In the City of London, for every prospective mine or group of mines, a new operating company would be created. A syndicate composed of City interests—specialist company promoters, bankers, stockbrokers, merchants, mining engineers, and others—would purchase a concession from a foreign vendor or exploration company, and a mining company would be formed to purchase the concession from the syndicate. Syndicates usually profited from the sale of the concession, and from securing contracts for financial or other services.

When launched in 1873, the RTC was by far the biggest international mining venture ever brought to market, and it remained the flagship of the British-owned sector of the international industry until well into the 20th century. The Rio Tinto mines, in the province of Huelva in southern Spain, had produced large quantities of copper, on and off, since before Roman times, most recently under the ownership of the government of Spain. In 1872, following a series of financial losses, the mines were offered for sale at a price equivalent to several million pounds sterling. The Spanish government was in a financial crisis and did not have the cash or the expertise needed to exploit the large reserves of cupreous pyrites known to exist at Rio Tinto. Substantial investments were needed to introduce opencast mining, and to build workshops, tramways, crushing and metallurgical plants, a railway from the mines to the seaport of Huelva, a shipping pier, and the many other works necessary to operate on a large scale.

The availability of the mines was brought to the attention of Matheson & Company, the London-based agent for the Far Eastern merchants Jardine Matheson, by Heinrich Doetsch of Sundheim & Doetsch, a general merchant of Huelva. Doetsch had the foresight to see that if the Rio Tinto mines were developed to their full potential, his business eventually stood to gain from a large increase in trade. A syndicate to purchase the Rio Tinto concession was organized by Hugh Matheson, senior partner in Matheson & Company, in London. The mines were purchased by the syndicate for £3.7 million, over a period of nine years, and immediately sold to the RTC. The new company was floated on the London Stock Exchange with an issued share capital of £2 million and debentures valued at £600,000. Hugh Matheson was appointed as first chairman of the RTC with Heinrich Doetsch as his deputy.

Matheson remained chairman of the RTC for a quarter of a century until his death in 1898. Matheson was a shrewd dealer in commodities, an outstanding entrepreneur with an ability to think on a scale that few could match, and a natural leader who could win the support needed to build very large enterprises in distant lands. The formation, survival, and ultimate prosperity of the RTC was the crowning achievement of his life. Matheson held together the original German and British banking, trading, and engineering consortium formed to launch the RTC in the crisis that followed the issue of its prospectus. The claims made in this document, especially the report of the mining engineer David Forbes, were vigorously denounced by the Tharsis Company, a Scottish-based firm set up in 1866 to work a group of mines not far distant from those at Rio Tinto. It was alleged that Matheson and his associates had falsely inflated potential revenues and grossly underestimated development and operating costs. The new company, it was said, could never earn a positive rate of return on the huge capital it was seeking to raise from investors. Matheson launched a massive press campaign, an early example of skillful public relations, and he won the day.

The Tharsis assault, however, did do some damage, and this was further compounded by a three-year price war between the two companies. The pyrites mined in southern Spain and in Portugal were first burned to drive off the sulfur content. The sulfurous gases were used to make sulfuric acid, one of the fundamental products of the chemicals industry. The burnt ore from the chemical works was then treated to remove the copper and other valuable metals it contained. The iron cinders that remained were sent to iron works for smelting. During these difficult years, revenues were low and development costs were running at more than £100,000 per month. The purchase agreement with the Spanish government was renegotiated on more favorable terms, the company was financially restructured, and additional funds were raised through the issue of mortgage bonds. Eventually, in 1876, a favorable price-fixing and market-sharing agreement was made with Tharsis, and the prospects for both companies began to improve.

The RTC was the major beneficiary of the 1876 agreement. Under this, the company gained control of the lucrative and rapidly expanding German market for pyrites, and within a matter of years it had become the dominant firm—with a 50% market share—in an oligopolistic world industry, with some degree of control over prices. At the same time, more of the product of the mines was treated locally to recover the copper contained therein. By the end of the 1880s, Rio Tinto was the leading producer of copper in the world. The company had smelters in Spain and a smelter and refinery in south Wales. In 1887, when the French entrepreneur Hyacinthe Secrétan attempted to corner the world copper market to raise prices, RTC at first reaped the benefits of its participation in the scheme, whereby Secrétan undertook to buy all its copper at fixed prices, and was not severely affected when Secrétan's scheme backfired in 1889, resulting in a spectacular collapse in the copper market. The strong market position of the company—by 1887 it was responsible for 8% of the total world copper supply—was reflected from the 1880s onwards in high profits. The larger part was returned to shareholders as dividends.

Hugh Matheson laid the foundations for the subsequent prosperity of the RTC, which rose to a high level under the leadership of Sir Charles Fielding. In his first ten years as chairman, 1898 to 1908, the company paid an average annual dividend of 41% on a share capital of £3.5 million. Fielding built solidly on the achievements of the Matheson era, assuming personal responsibility for the introduction of a range of new technologies such as pyritic smelting. He also streamlined management, accounting, and decision-making practices, and, at a time of strong market growth, these innovations helped elevate the company to a higher level of profitability. The Spanish government, under pressure from nationalists of all descriptions, tried to lay claim to a larger share of company revenues, but these efforts were generally thwarted; nor did the laborers of the mining district have much success in raising the level of wages paid by Rio Tinto. The company showed scant regard for the argument that it could afford to pay much more than it did, pointing out that it already paid more in cash and kind than most other large employers in Spain. The real wages per head of the 15,000 workers employed by the RTC in Spain in 1913 were actually less than those paid to 10,000 workers employed 20 years earlier. Low-cost housing; discretionary pensions; and company stores, schools, taverns, and other recreational facilities began to cause resentment—as substitutes for higher wages—among the workers and their families.

Strikes of varying length and bitterness became commonplace at Rio Tinto following the outbreak of World War I, exacerbated by ever-rising prices and declining real wages. A violent and acrimonious nine-month strike in 1920 ended with the unions exhausted and the company resented in many sec-

tions of Spanish society, across the political spectrum. From this time onward, the fate of the RTC in Spain was bound up with the turbulent course of national politics. There was a period of relative stability between 1923 and 1929 under the dictatorship of Miguel Primo de Rivera, and the company was fortunate to escape lightly when it was discovered to have been evading export taxes through under-recording of the copper content of minerals shipped from Huelva. After Primo de Rivera left office, however, there followed a long period of disruption and uncertainty that lasted until the mines were sold to Spanish interests in 1954. As left- and right-wing political factions vied for power between 1929 and 1936, the RTC came to be seen as an economic Rock of Gibraltar that must concede more in the interests of Spain. Damaging labor laws and taxation policies were introduced at the very time when the company was suffering from depressed trading conditions around the world, and when the copper content of the ores mined at Rio Tinto was plummeting. The decision was made by the third chairman of the company, Sir Auckland Geddes, who served from 1925 to 1947, to invest only as much money in Spain as was needed to sustain the operation

The 1936–1939 Spanish civil war brought further problems. From an early date, the Rio Tinto mines were occupied by the Insurgent forces led by General Francisco Franco. The mineral wealth of the district was seen by Franco as a means of procuring arms from the Axis powers, and within months the RTC found itself caught up in a complex web of diplomatic intrigue involving London, Berlin, Rome, and the Franco regime. Control over the company's Spanish assets had been lost, and was never effectively regained. During World War II and the period of reconstruction which followed, the RTC had little control over production, prices, or the numbers of workers employed in Spain. The company was held in check by restrictive laws and regulations, causing the real value of its assets to fall with the passage of each frustrating year. It was with great relief that the RTC managed to sell its Spanish operations in 1954. After many years of negotiations, involving Franco himself, the business was sold to a newly formed Spanish company in exchange for a one-third interest in the enterprise plus £7.7 million in seven annual installments.

Auckland Geddes involved the company in ventures in other parts of the world and brought to the RTC a new style of business leadership. Unlike previous chairmen, he eschewed close involvement in day-to-day administrative matters in favor of major questions of policy and organization. He delegated responsibilities to full-time directors recruited from outside the business, and he initiated a search for major new investment opportunities in mining and related fields. Exploration subsidiaries were formed and research stations opened. A large minority shareholding in the Davison Chemical Corporation, a leading United States artificial-fertilizer manufacturer, was purchased. Together with Davison, the RTC set up a series of subsidiaries throughout Europe to manufacture and market the versatile chemical absorbent, silica gel. Substantial minority shareholdings were also acquired in several other companies devoted to exploration and the development of new products.

By far the most significant of the new departures inspired by Geddes was the involvement of the RTC in the development of the Northern Rhodesian (now Zambian) copperbelt. The opportunity to secure a stake in the field came early in 1929 when U.S. interests attempted to take over the promising N'Changa deposits. Along with Sir Ernest Oppenheimer and other members of the British-cum–South African business community, Geddes judged this move to be detrimental to British business interests, and led the resistance to it. By the time the struggle was over, the RTC had acquired sizable copperbelt holdings and valuable information which suggested that the deposits were amongst the richest and most extensive ever discovered. Further shares were purchased in major copperbelt development companies in the months following the N'Changa struggle, and by 1930 the RTC had become a major economic force in Northern Rhodesia. In that year Geddes and Sir Ernest Oppenheimer, whose Anglo American Corporation was the leading company in copperbelt finance, forced through the merger of three of the biggest development companies to form the Rhokana Corporation. Geddes was appointed chairman of the new company. Under his leadership Rhokana emerged during the next 17 years as one of the largest and lowest-cost copper companies in the world.

Not all of Geddes's business initiatives were so successful. The RTC's venture into chemicals proved in the end to be a financial disaster, and the firm's exploration activities never yielded anything of worth. Failure in these fields was largely a consequence of the world economic Depression but in part such losses were due to ill-informed and hasty judgments on the part of the RTC board. The returns on the Northern Rhodesian investments, however, more than compensated for these setbacks, enabling the firm to survive the protracted decline of its Spanish business, and laying the foundations for its emergence as a modern multinational enterprise.

The regeneration of the RTC after World War II was, to a great extent, the work of two men, Mark Turner and Val Duncan, who formed one of the most creative business partnerships of modern times. Turner, the elder of the two and an investment banker by training, was appointed acting managing director of the company in 1948 on a part-time basis. He was charged with finding a full-time replacement, and for the position he groomed Duncan, a younger lawyer he had met during the war. Duncan was appointed managing director of the RTC in January 1951, allowing Turner, who remained a leading member of the RTC board and Duncan's closest colleague, to devote more of his time to the banking business of Robert Benson, Lonsdale—later Kleinwort Benson. Together, Duncan and Turner persuaded their colleagues and leading shareholders that Rio Tinto should aim to become a growth-oriented, broadly based natural resource company with operations concentrated in politically stable parts of the world, especially the commonwealth countries. In the late 1940s and early 1950s, interests in a range of potential mines were secured, from tin and wolfram in Portugal to diamonds in South Africa and copper in Uganda. Between 1952 and 1954, a network of amply funded exploration subsidiaries was established to search for mineral deposits that might be exploited on a large scale in Canada, Africa, and Australia.

The sale of the Spanish mines in 1954 released further human and financial resources for the task of rebuilding and reorienting the RTC. An intense period of exploration followed, which sent Duncan and other executives to all parts of the world to supervise exploration agreements and consider the mine-development deals put to the company from time to time. The first tangible result of this activity came in 1955 with the purchase of a majority interest in the Algom group of uranium mines in the Elliot Lake district of Canada. The authorized capital of the RTC was raised from £8 million to £12 million to accommodate the purchase, and a loan of US$200 million was raised against various supply contracts to fund the development of seven major mines. The company's position in the uranium industry was consolidated by the simultaneous acquisition of a controlling interest in the Mary Kathleen mine in Australia. By the end of the 1950s Rio Tinto was responsible for the production of 15% of the world's uranium oxide, and along the way the company had gained control over two highly promising mineral prospects: the vast Hammersley iron ore deposits in Western Australia and the Palabora copper deposit in South Africa.

By the early 1960s Duncan was confident enough to take the decisive step toward realizing his vision of the RTC as a first-rank multinational enterprise. Merging was the obvious means of speeding the process of building up the organization, and he found an ideal prospective partner in the London-based Consolidated Zinc Corporation. This company had steadily expanded its activities since 1905 when it was launched to recover the large quantities of zinc remaining in the tailings dumps of the legendary silver-lead mines at Broken Hill in New South Wales, Australia. CZ's operations were still concentrated in Australia, but had been progressively extended to include a wide range of mining and metallurgical activities. The compatibility of CZ and the RTC was both strategic and structural. Strategically, the leading directors of CZ wished to attain major-company status through geographic diversification and the development of important new prospects, particularly the vast Weipa bauxite deposits of northern Queensland. Structurally, the company was about the same size as the RTC with net profits running at a little over £1 million per annum, and its major interests were in complementary rather then competing areas. The merger would, at a stroke, produce a large and broadly-based organization with financial and technological resources to undertake a range of promising new ventures. In July 1962 the two companies came together to form RTZ. Duncan was appointed managing director of the new concern, and in 1963, on the retirement of A.M. Baer, he became chairman and chief executive of RTZ—positions which he retained until his death in December 1975.

Under Duncan's leadership, RTZ rapidly rose to prominence in the natural resource industries of the world. In partnership with Kaiser Aluminum, the firm established an integrated aluminum business in Australasia, Comalco Limited. The Hammersley iron and Palabora copper projects were brought to fruition. Extensive exploration was continued, eventually yielding large-scale mines in Papua New Guinea (Bougainville Copper), Canada (Lornex Copper), and Namibia (Rössing Uranium). Meanwhile, the scale and the scope of the business was further expanded through the purchase of going concerns: Atlas Steels (high-grade specialty steels) in Canada, Borax Holdings (industrial raw materials) in the United States, and Capper Pass (tin refiners) and Pillar Holdings (aluminum fabricators) in the United Kingdom. By the early 1970s RTZ had achieved the geographically and geologically diverse pattern of operations long pursued by Val Duncan.

Duncan made an important contribution to advancing the fortunes of the enterprise. He was the principal architect of the strategy of promoting growth through involvement in a stream of large-scale, capital-intensive natural resource projects. Potential financial limits to growth were overcome through the funding of massive projects with a high ratio of loan capital to equity. Multi-million-dollar loans were raised by Duncan and his team throughout the world through the device of offering long-term supply contracts as collateral. Potential organizational and managerial limits to growth were overcome by the progressive devolution of responsibilities to a series of nationally based companies, each charged with the goal of involving RTZ in substantial new projects. By the early 1970s RTZ had emerged as a loosely knit family of companies with the activities of the parent concern limited to the provision of group services, the controlling of major strategic and financial decisions, and the appointment of top personnel.

The strategy, organization, and policies devised by Val Duncan remained in place in the 1990s. Duncan was succeeded as chief executive by Mark Turner. He continued in office until his death in December 1980. Turner saw no need to change course, nor did Anthony Tuke who replaced him, and nor has Alistair Frame or Derek Birkin, the latest in the long line of distinguished chairmen which began with Hugh Matheson. The essential integrity of RTZ has been maintained while growth has continued. New mines and smelters have been brought on stream, and new processing facilities have been developed. Some businesses have been bought; others have been sold. The biggest boost to the enterprise came in 1989 with the acquisition of BP Minerals for £2.6 billion. This deal brought to RTZ one of the greatest names in world mining, the Kennecott Corporation, and a portfolio of assets in 15 countries, including the world's largest opencast copper mine and the world's largest producer of titanium dioxide feedstock. RTZ immediately became one of the world's largest producers of gold outside South Africa. The shares of world output accounted for by the much-enlarged company in 1989 were 55% of borates, 30% of titanium dioxide feedstock, 13% of zircon, 15% of industrial diamonds, 14% of vermiculite, 8% of talc, and 5% or more of uranium, copper, and molybdenum. RTZ also ranks amongst the world's largest producers of tin, bauxite, silver, iron ore, gold, lead, and zinc.

The impressive performance of RTZ since 1962 may be attributed to many factors, not least the general buoyancy of the world economy. Yet success in an inherently problematic industry can never be guaranteed, and much credit must be given to the sure and consistent way in which the business has been administered. Credit must also be given to the flexibility displayed by RTZ executives when faced with sensitive and difficult issues, such as the legitimate concerns of environmentalists and economic nationalists. When it became clear, for instance, that Australians would not tolerate foreign majority ownership of large-scale natural resource companies, the reaction at RTZ was gradually to reduce its stake in CRA—now a multinational in its own right—to 49%. In this, and in many other ways, RTZ has taken a lead that others have followed. All the while, the management style has remained open and opposed to bureaucracy. Self-conscious avoidance of rigidity, more than anything else, has allowed RTZ to remain responsive to opportunity.

Principal Subsidiaries: Borax Consolidated Limited; Anglesey Aluminium Limited (51%); R.T.Z. Pillar Limited; Pillar Building Products Limited; Pillar Electrical PLC; Pillar Engineering Limited; Kennecott Corporation (U.S.A.); United States Borax Chemical Corporation; US Silica; Rio Algom Limited (Canada, 51.5%); Indal Limited (Canada); QIT-Fer er Titane Inc. (Canada); Palabora Mining Company Limited (South Africa, 39%); Rössing Uranium Limited (Namibia, 46.5%); Rio Tinto Zimbabwe Limited (58.4%); CRA Limited (Australia, 49%); Richards Bay Minerals (South Africa, 50%); Somincor (Portugal, 49%); Minera Escondida Limitada (Chile, 30%).

Further Reading: Avery, David, *Not On Queen Victoria's Birthday—The Story of The Rio Tinto Mines,* London, Collins, 1974; Harvey, Charles E., *The Rio Tinto Company: An Economic History of A Leading International Mining Concern 1873–1954,* St. Ives, Alison Hodge (Publishers), 1981; "RTZ—Metals, Industry, Energy," Supplement to *Euromoney,* October 1985; "RTZ's Expanding Mining World," *International Mining,* March 1989; "RTZ—Corporate Profile," *Engeering & Mining Journal,* August 1989.

—Charles Edward Harvey

RUHRKOHLE AG

Rellinghauserstrasse 1
4300 Essen 1
Federal Republic of Germany
(0201) 1771
Fax: (0201) 177 34 75

Private Company
Incorporated: 1968
Employees: 119,500
Sales: DM23.00 billion (US$15.39 billion)

Ruhrkohle AG is the largest coal-producing company in Germany. Of approximately 71 million tons produced by the Federal Republic of Germany in 1990, the company—based in Essen, at the heart of the Ruhr Valley—produced 50 million tons, about 70% of the total. The group has several well-known subsidiaries. Through its subsidiaries and associates, as well as directly, Ruhrkohle AG owns 82% of Rütgerswerke AG (Rütgers) a company active in the sectors of basic chemicals, plastics, and building, whose turnover stands at DM3.6 billion per year. In 1989, Rütgers paid out a profit of DM18 billion to Ruhrkohle.

Ruhrkohle also holds 71% of the share capital of Steag AG at Essen, whose main activity is the production of electricity from coal power, and which has a total share capital of DM220 million. In 1989 Steag produced 19 billion kilowatt hours (kWh) of electricity, achieving a turnover of DM3.2 billion. Of Steag's profits, DM22 million were paid out to Ruhrkohle. The Eschweiler Bergwerks-Verein (EBV) is one of Ruhrkohle's newest subsidiaries. Ruhrkohle took a majority stake (97%) in the long-established coal-mining company on the Aachen coal field in 1988–1989. In 1989, EBV produced approximately 4.2 million tons of coal and achieved a turnover of DM1.9 billion. A second investment in the coal sector followed, also within the framework of Ruhrkohle's goals in coal politics, when the group took over 99.72% of Sophia Jacoba GmbH at Hückelhoven, from the Robeco Group of the Netherlands, on January 1, 1990. Sophia Jacoba is essentially an anthracite mine, with production of around 1.7 million tons in 1989 and a turnover of DM570 million.

Ruhrkohle's foundation came about in several stages. It was brought into being on November 27, 1968, by 19 companies in the Ruhr area, which holds the largest coal resources in Germany. This foundation was provisional; since the *Grundvertrag* (Articles of Association) had not yet been signed. This

contract was concluded on July 18, 1969; the parties to it were the Federal Republic of Germany, that is, the federal government; 23 mining companies, which had declared their willingness to enter into the treaty; and the company Ruhrkohle AG itself.

The foundation of the company had come about mainly as a result of political pressure, but on a private basis. Not all of the 26 independently operating, privately structured companies in the Ruhr coal field were willing to submit to this massive exertion of political influence. Ruhrkohle's commercial structure is without parallel in Germany. Although the company is run according to the principles of private enterprise, it has been dependent on support from the state from its beginnings. This support is given mainly in the form of subsidies but also through laws protecting German coal interests in some sectors. The evolution of Ruhrkohle AG must be understood in the context of the development of West Germany's energy policy after the end of World War II. In the years immediately after the war, German coal was a highly sought-after commodity. In the years of hunger before the currency reform in 1948, miners—or *Kumpel,* as they were known—received special grocery rations to enable them to carry out their heavy work. They were also given special advantages in looking for accommodation in the towns of the Ruhr area, which had suffered great destruction during the war. The largest of these towns are Essen, Duisburg, Bochum, and Dortmund. The byword of those years was coal production at any price.

The market economy of the 1950s and early 1960s, with liberalized external trade, was introduced by Professor Ludwig Erhard against strong opposition, and formed the basis of the German economic miracle. At this time an idea was aired which had prevailed in many economic circles in the years immediately after 1945, particularly among the unions and the Social Democratic Party—that the basic industries of coal and steel should be nationalized.

In 1956 disaster struck more or less overnight for German coal mining industry, which, in the mid-1950s, produced 150 million tons of coal and employed over 600,000 miners. The steady rise in oil consumption, especially in the form of light fuel oil on the heating market and of heavy oil for industrial use, had gone almost unnoticed. As a result, within a relatively short period, coal stockpiles had grown so big that short-time work had to be introduced extensively for the miners in 1958, to prevent these stockpiles, suddenly unsaleable, from reaching the sky. Coal, so long in demand, which had been particularly sought after in the early postwar years, could now find no buyers. As late as 1957, when 133 million tons of coal were produced in the federal republic, the high commission of the European Coal and Steel Community—later to become the European Community—was still demanding a rise in production in Germany of 40 million tons within 20 years.

At first it was believed that the fall in demand at the end of the 1950s was merely a transient economic phenomenon. Yet stockpiles grew to over 15 million tons, and for the first time pit closures had to be considered. At this point it became clear that this was no short-term economic crisis. It was, rather, a structural crisis, based on long-term shifts in demand. Imported oil was, in the long term, much cheaper than German coal, and ousted coal from the heating market. Cheaply produced imported coal, especially from the United States, forced its way into the growing German industrial and heating markets.

Confronted with the prospect of multiple pit closures in the German coal fields—the Ruhr accounted for around 70-75% of coal production in the Federal Republic—as well as by protest demonstrations by miners, public demand for a coal and energy plan grew. Increasing weight was given to the suggestion that the mining industry of the Ruhr area, which at the beginning of the 1960s still consisted of around 30 independent private companies, should be brought together in a single company or group.

More than a dozen plans were proposed in those years to rehabilitate the coal industry. Yet all these plans had a common focus in the assertion that the sharp reduction in work force numbers, which would have to be faced, must take place in a socially acceptable manner.

From 1958 to the end of 1990, during which time the number of employees in the German coal mining industry declined from 607,000 to around 130,000, not a single miner was dismissed via the unemployment office. All the affected miners received special state support payments, whether these took the form of compensation, pension supplements, or some other type of payment. Support was given not only to the miners affected by pit closures but also to the companies, who received millions of marks' worth of finance from the state. These payments were given in the form of closure premiums; that is, the companies received a certain sum of money when they closed pits with the aim of adjusting the overcapacity to the sharply reduced overall demand.

Federal governments attempted to get a grip on the retreat of the coal industry; since its disordered beginnings it had already swallowed billions of marks. Too many attempts had been made to cure the symptoms, with restrictions on coal imports, agreements of voluntary restrictions with the oil industry, the promotion of coal-fired power stations, and taxes on fuel oil. Finally, in 1967-1968, the measures which had been taken to reconcile coal production and demand were standardized and new targets were formulated.

In May 1968 the *Kohleanpassungsgesetz*—coal adjustment law—was passed. The basis of the law was that optimal cost effectiveness was only possible in a single company; in this way the pits which were least profitable would be closed, whereas individual closures in over 30 separate companies might prevent the continued functioning of relatively profitable pits while allowing unprofitable pits to survive. Measures to concentrate the coal businesses therefore formed the core of the *Kohleanpassungsgesetz*. As the government's most important instrument in achieving this aim, the law laid the foundations for the removal of a series of privileges which had hitherto been granted, especially the high premiums for pit closures and the subsidies for coke production. It was this legal threat above all—that subsidies would be withdrawn from companies below the optimal size after January 1, 1969—which hastened the process of concentration and thus the foundation of Ruhrkohle AG. Without subsidies, at this time practically any mining company was condemned to a swift demise, as is still the case.

During the foundation phase of Ruhrkohle AG, the concept of optimal size became a magic formula. The fact that no one defined it exactly, not even the government, made it seem all the more ominous for the independent survival of most small and medium-sized companies. The law defined it simply as "such size as is necessary to achieve the greatest possible economic efficiency."

In the public sphere this abstract threat was received exactly as it was meant by the politicians, who were tired of throwing good money after bad, namely as a means of exerting pressure, to drive the hesitant pits to join a common company in the Ruhr. There were to be no subsidies without "optimal size," that is, the merger of the coal companies—all of them if possible—to form a single company.

The two largest coal mining companies on the Ruhr, the Gelsenkirchener Bergwerks AG (Gelsenberg) and the Bergswerksgesellschaft Hibernia, part of the Veba group, made renewed efforts to achieve their own form of concentration, in the form of a conventional merger of the two businesses. Investigations as to the viability of a merger had been undertaken at an earlier stage. Karl Schiller, the minister of economics, could hardly have denied the attribute of optimal size to the company which would have resulted, but the moment for this project had already passed.

The creation of a single Ruhr mining company could no longer be prevented. The miners' union IG Bergbau und Energie had demanded that such a company be created—with as strong a state influence as possible—for a long time, and the managers of the mining companies, a notable number of whom had until then operated under the protection of a steel company, could no longer draw back.

After lengthy negotiations, the *Grundvertrag* was, as stated, signed in July 1969; this formed, and still forms today, the basis of the existence and business activities of Ruhrkohle AG. The parent companies undertook to provide Ruhrkohle AG with a share capital of DM600 million. Ruhrkohle AG and the parent companies made *Einbringungsverträge,* or contribution agreements. The members of the work force had to be kept on. A provision of the *Grundvertrag* states that "profit is not the principal aim of Ruhrkohle AG."

Thus the parent companies made various financial commitments. Although they could not, according to the company's Articles of Association, expect a profit from the capital they had invested, they were to be paid interest on their contributions at a rate of 6%. The government also took on extensive commitments; initially giving guarantees of up to DM2.2 billion, two-thirds from the federation and one-third from the state of Nordrhein-Westphalen.

These founding arrangements were accompanied by two treaties which were vital to the company's existence: the *Hüttenvertrag,* regulating the agreement between Ruhrkohle and the seven steel-producing Ruhr groups which had brought their pits into the joint company, and the power-station treaties or agreements with the electricity supply businesses. Both are essentially concerned with competitive prices: Ruhrkohle has to supply the steel companies with coal at world market prices, and public money will be paid to compensate for any difference.

For sales of coal to power stations, the electricity consumers would pay the difference between the price of the expensive Ruhr coal and cheaper imported coal—or oil—in the form of the *Kohlepfennig,* or "coal penny." This amount would be added to the bill of each individual consumer.

Complaints were made from the beginning by all parties, and especially by the managers of Ruhrkohle themselves, that this company joined, eventually, by 26 of the 28 mining companies on the Ruhr had been brought to life in skeletonized form, stripped of its assets, without the large, productive, and thoroughly profitable power stations and above all without the valuable land holdings which the companies, some of them well over a century old, had accumulated over time. Apart from the land needed for operational purposes, none of this extensive property had remained under the ownership of Ruhrkohle AG.

Ruhrkohle is structured as a private enterprise but is unable to exist without the support of the state, unless energy prices are extremely high, around $35 for a barrel of oil. It must operate as efficiently as it can, and it may not, according to its constitution, make any profit. It should manage itself alone as far as possible, yet it is not allowed to undertake all that it may wish. The state—the Federal Ministry of Economics—ensures that nothing is undertaken which lies outside the company's main area of operation, the production of coal, and which could involve any risk. This restriction is meant to prevent the need for additional subsidy requirements. The former owners, the *Altgesellschafter,* pay close attention to ensuring that Ruhrkohle does not become a competitor in sectors in which they are active—for example, in certain trading and service sectors, such as waste management. The principal companies concerned here are Veba AG with a shareholding of 39.2%, the electricity supply company Vereinigte Elektrizitätswerke Westfalen AG with 30.2%, Thyssen Stahl AG with 12.7%, and Hoesch AG with 7.2%.

Indeed from its inception, Ruhrkohle AG has been a company *sui generis*, and continues to be so. The company had a bad start. In 1969, its first year of operation, it had to overcome a loss of DM330 million which used up more than half of its share capital. According to the laws governing shares, this loss should have been reported and an extraordinary shareholders' meeting should have been called. However, Heinz P. Kemper, the first chairman of the supervisory board and formerly chairman of Veba's management board, together with the first chairman of the management board Hans-Helmut Kuhnke, was able to reduce the loss to DM199 million and so to gain time: this was achieved through what Kemper called "accounting policy measures." When a steel crisis developed in 1971, leading to a dramatic reduction in sales to the steel industry—which, along with the electricity industry, was the largest purchaser of Ruhr coal—it became essential to strengthen the company's weak capital base. Otherwise bankruptcy would have been inevitable, with incalculable consequences for the 170,000 employees. Again a joint action resulted: the shareholders decided to forego, in part, the interest income owed to them, amounting to approximately DM700 million. Also, the government conceded a debt register claim, which the company was to pay back if it made profits, of DM1 billion.

Although the company's financing and balance-sheet arrangements were stabilized, it became clear that Ruhrkohle AG could not become competitive in the long term, even with the most modern mining technology and the continual adaptation of its production to demand, because of difficulties presented by the nature of German coal deposits. Kuhnke, his successor Karlheinz Bund, and Heinz Horn, chairman of the management board of Ruhrkohle AG since 1985, have emphasized the company's function in ensuring the coal supply, embodied in the three energy programs produced by the federal government after 1973. The theory of a necessary safe base provided by German coal in the face of Germany's very high dependence on imported oil and gas for its energy requirements, has for many years been an important, and controversial, component of Germany's energy policy.

In recent years the European Commission has made repeated interventions. The commission has underlined the incompatibility of German coal subsidies with policies within the European Community—subsidies without which Ruhrkohle could not survive. In reaction, the German government has produced another program to adapt production to demand and thus to reduce the need for subsidy payments, which now amount to DM8 billion to DM10 billion per year as a result of low world energy prices and the low U.S. dollar rate. Ruhrkohle AG has been hopeful that the union of East and West Germany may result in additional markets for coal in the five new federal states, although energy experts warn that such expectations should not be too high.

The long-term survival of Ruhrkohle seems certain, even with the prospect of a reduction in coal production in the federal republic in the years to come, following the recommendations of a state commission that production should stand at between 45 and 55 million tons annually, rather than 70 million tons. Despite the high, economically controversial subsidies needed by Ruhrkohle AG, a halt to coal production will not occur in Germany, as has been the case in some neighboring western countries in past years. The option of coal, in the form of Ruhrkohle AG, remains as a safeguard in Germany's energy policy.

Principal Subsidiaries: Rütgerswerke AG (82%); Steag AG (71%); Eschweiler Bergwerks-Verein (97%); Sophia Jacoba GmbH (99.72%).

Further Reading: Wiel, Paul, *Wirtschaftsgeschichte des Ruhrgebiets,* Siedlungsverband Ruhrkohlenbezirk, 1970; Spiegelberg, Friedrich, *Ein Geschäft im Wandel, 10 Jahre Kohlenkrise,* Baden-Baden, Nomors, 1970; Ruhrkohle, *Wir Sind Zwanzig,* Ruhrkohle Werkzeitschrift, 1988.

—Heiner Radzio
Translated from the German by Susan Mackervoy

SAARBERG

SAARBERG-KONZERN

Triererstrasse 1
Postfach 1030
D-6600 Saarbrücken
Federal Republic of Germany
(681) 40 51
Fax: (681) 405-4205

State-Owned Company
Incorporated: 1957
Employees: 23,200
Sales: DM5.01 billion (US$3.35 billion)

Since its foundation in 1957, the Saarberg-Konzern or Saarberg Group, headed by Saarbergwerke AG has developed from a regional mining company into a diversified energy production, coal conversion, and trading group with subsidiaries outside Germany's Saar area and abroad. The company is jointly owned, 76% by the German government and 24% by the Saarland. Its headquarters are in Saarbrücken and and the Saar region remains its principal area of activity, the location of its five coal mines, three power stations, and coking plant. Further power stations and a coking plant are operated by partly owned subsidiaries. Saarbergwerke's original activity of coal mining, along with the production of coke, electricity, and thermal power, accounted for nearly 50% of group turnover in 1989. The fuel and energy product trading division, which came into being in the 1960s, also forms a major component of Saarbergwerke's operations, representing a further 44% of group turnover. During the 1960s and 1970s, Saarbergwerke diversified into several areas outside its core energy businesses, including oil refining and supply, chemicals, machine tools, and rubber products. After a series of disposals only a handful of non-core subsidiaries remain, the most important of these being the rubber products manufacturing division, accounting for 5% of 1989 sales. The history of this company over the 33 years of its existence has been a difficult one, marked by several changes of fortune and direction, and determined by events and trends in the global energy market.

The Saarland, a region which has come alternately under German and French rule over the last centuries, is the smallest and newest of the west German states. Coal mining has been an important industry in the region for hundreds of years, and since 1751 all mining has been subject to a state monopoly. After World War II the Saar region was initially declared an independent state, with close economic ties to France. Be-

tween 1948 and 1953 the coal mines were administered by the French Régie des Mines de la Sarre; after this they were known as the Saarbergwerke and were managed regionally, although a strong French influence persisted. On October 23, 1955, two-thirds of the Saar area's population voted against a statute preserving the state's autonomy, and international negotiations resulted in a treaty effecting the region's integration into the Federal Republic of Germany. Political integration took effect beginning January 1, 1957, and full economic integration followed on July 5, 1959. On September 30, 1957, the ownership of the region's coal mining operations was transferred to two shareholders—the Federal Republic of Germany (74%) and the Saar region (26%)—and the new company, Saarbergwerke AG, was entered in the trade register at Saarbrücken. The chairman of the management committee was Hubertus Rolshoven.

At the end of 1957 the company had 18 coal mines, 3 coking plants, and 3 power stations; its work force numbered 65,000. During this year it had produced 16.3 million tons of coal, 900,000 tons of coke, and 1.7 billion kilowatt hours of electricity. Accounts drawn up for the first quarter-year to the end of 1957 recorded a loss of Ffr1.4 billion.

The previous administration had projected an expansion of coal production in the region. Plans had been made to establish a new pit at Warndt, and to extend the pits at Jägersfreude, Luisenthal, Göttelborn, and Velsen. Extensions of the power stations at Fenne and St. Barbara had been started, as had construction of a new coking plant at Fürstenhausen. A progressive increase in production levels was foreseen, with the aim of reaching 19 million tons by 1965 and 23 million tons by 1975. However, developments in the domestic energy market soon made it clear that a radical revision of these plans would be necessary.

During the company's first year, wages were raised to meet living costs, in accordance with labor agreements. Even though coal and coke prices also rose, the result was a loss of profitability. Furthermore, sales of coal declined, owing to cheap imports from the United States and Poland, the increasing importance of oil, and the weakness of Saarland industry. Coal stockpiles rose, shifts were canceled, and the company had considerable losses in 1958. After the Suez crisis, oil production in the Middle East increased, and cheap oil was produced in European refineries. In 1959, Saarbergwerke closed its pit at St. Barbara and amalgamated pits at Maybach, Mellin, and St. Ingbert. After the full economic integration of the Saar area, the company produced its first set of results in German currency, for the period from July 6, 1959, to December 31, 1960, recording a loss of DM1.78 million.

Construction of the new pit at Warndt proceeded, and for the time being Saarbergwerke's activities remained limited to the production and conversion of coal. Nonetheless it was clear that in the medium- to long-term the company would have to develop a new strategy to ensure its survival and to safeguard its significant position in the economy, accounting for around 20% of the work force and total turnover of the Saar region. Unease concerning the future prospects of the industry was a contributory factor in the miners' strike at Saarbergwerke in May 1962. The week-long strike—the first official strike in the German mining industry since 1955—ended when the Federal government gave its approval to an 8% pay rise, bringing wages for Saar miners into line with those of the Ruhr coal industry. At the same time the government approved a series of measures to help the company undertake the necessary rationalization of its activities. The year 1962 was also to be remembered at Saarbergwerke for the worst postwar mining disaster in Germany, when an explosion and fire at the Luisenthal pit on February 7 claimed 299 lives.

Saarbergwerke's strategy during the 1960s had two main aims: the rationalization of the company's coal-producing activities and the replacement of lost jobs and revenue through the development of new activities. This change of direction was given the official seal of approval in 1963, when it was enshrined in the company statutes.

Two General Plans, produced in 1963 and 1968, set out the process by which coal production was to be reduced to levels of 9 million to 9.5 million tons by 1973. Production was to be concentrated on the most efficient sites and the number of pits in operation was to be reduced, by amalgamation and closure, to five by 1970 and to four by 1974. The contraction of this side of the company's activities was indeed severe; coal production fell from 16 million tons in 1960 to 10.6 million tons in 1970, and the number of miners employed fell from around 50,000 to around 22,000 during the same period. The decade saw a series of pit closures and amalgamations: Heinitz was closed in November 1962, Viktoria in June 1963, Maybach in July 1964, Velsen in August 1965, Kohlwald in March 1966, König in March 1968, and Jägersfreude in July 1968. Yet during the same period the newer Warndt pit was extended by the addition of a new shaft, opening in 1963; productivity levels—in terms of kilograms per man-hour—were increased; and the Saar area's share of West German coal production remained constant at 11%.

By contrast, Saarbergwerke's coal conversion activities expanded during the 1960s. Coke production had never been as highly developed in the Saar area as in other German coalfields and the new coking plant at Fürstenhausen, opened in 1959, was doubled in capacity in 1966. Three older coking plants were closed between 1963 and 1972. Coke production rose from 1.5 million tons in 1960 to 1.9 million tons in 1970. In 1959 Saarbergwerke was producing electricity purely for internal consumption. However, the 1960s saw an expansion in capacity at all three power stations, at St. Barbara, Weiher, and Fenne, and in 1970 production exceeded four billion kilowatt hours (kWh) for the first time, more than three-quarters of this for external users. In 1961, the founding of Saarländische Fernwärme GmbH, a thermal power generating subsidiary, represented an extension of the company's energy-related activities. Favorable conditions in the building sector contributed to the rapid growth of this subsidiary, which was operating a network of 19 thermal power plants by the end of 1970. In addition to restructuring its energy production businesses, Saarbergwerke founded and acquired a number of subsidiaries during the 1960s, venturing into new areas, including oil refining and distribution, chemicals, industrial rubber products, and machine tools.

In collaboration with French chemicals and coal producers, Saarbergwerke established an oil refinery at Klarenthal in 1965, in which it had a 50% share. The project also brought shares in several chemicals subsidiaries established in 1966: a 50% share in Société de l'Oléoduc de la Sarre a.r.l. of Paris, a 40% share in L'Ammoniac Sarro-Lorrain S.a.r.l. of St. Avold, and 60% of Harnstoffe- und Düngemittelwerk Saar-Lothringen

GmbH, Besch, Luxembourg. Saarbergwerke's investment in the project totaled DM240 million and the group of companies, which began operations in 1967–1968, was expected to reach sales totaling around DM200 million annually. Other investments were also made in the oil and chemicals sector. In 1962 Saarbergwerke acquired Saarkohlenwertstoffe GmbH, a polyurethane products manufacturer, renamed Petrocarbona GmbH in 1963. In 1965, over 50% of the shares of the Frisia Group, a northwest German oil refiner and distributor with a network of 600 petrol stations were acquired. Finally, a 12.5% share in Deutsche Mineralöl-Explorationsgesellschaft mbH, a crude oil supplier based in Düsseldorf, was acquired in 1966, completing the chain of the group's oil interests from supply through refining to chemicals products.

In 1963 the Saarbergwerke Group acquired 50% of the shares of Saar-Gummiwerk GmbH, a manufacturer of rubber products for the shoe and automotive industries, with a work force of 1,500. The following year saw the group's first move into the machine tools sector, when it purchased a 16% share in Dowidat GmbH of Wermelskirchen and a majority shareholding in this company's subsidiary Dowidat-Werke Saar GmbH of Hasborn. The foundations of Saarbergwerke's fuel trading division were laid during the 1960s with the acquisitions of Gebrüder Kiessel GmbH, a coal-trading company in Saarbrücken, in 1962, and of the Caesar-Wollheim-Gruppe of Munich, of which 50% was acquired in 1969, and the remaining 50% in 1971.

By the beginning of the 1970s the composition of the group as a whole had changed significantly. Although coal mining and conversion activities accounted for 80% of the group's 31,000-strong work force, oil and chemical activities now represented 45% of annual turnover. Drastic reductions in the coal mining sector were partly offset by the creation of around 4,000 new jobs through the group's diversification. Some of the job losses were accounted for by the departure of workers who had joined the industry after the war when other work was scarce. Nonetheless the impact on the region was a serious one, especially at a time when the iron and steel industries were also facing difficulties. The sales of Saarbergwerke AG grew only moderately during the decade—from DM985 million in 1960 to DM1.22 billion in 1970—and profitability remained elusive. In 1969 Hubertus Rolshoven retired and Werner Hoevels became chairman of the management board.

The process of reduction and rationalization which had dominated the group's development in the 1960s continued through the early years of the following decade. In 1972–1973 Saarbergwerke reduced its work force by 10,000 through a program of early retirements and redundancies largely funded by government subsidy. At the end of 1973 the number of employees was at its lowest point since the company's foundation—21,326—and coal production in 1974 reached an all-time low of 8.9 million tons.

The oil crisis of 1973 brought a significant change of direction. Between 1960 and 1970 imported oil had become increasingly important as a primary energy source in West Germany, accounting for 55% of primary energy consumption in 1970, compared to 21% in 1960. During the same period the share of coal—mainly domestic rather than imported—fell from 60% to 29%. The disruption of the oil supply from the Middle East forced the German government to re-assess its energy policy in the light of safeguarding the domestic coal supply. The effect on Saarbergwerke was considerable. It had been planned to reduce coal production to 8 million tons by 1976; now, with the help of government investment, the group aimed to achieve production levels of around 9 million to 9.5 million tons. The mine at Camphausen, which had been marked for closure, was given a reprieve.

However, in the years following this crisis the fortunes of the German coal industry did not change in any great degree. Oil consumption remained high, there was little evidence of a switch to coal as an energy source, and the stockpiles mounted, rising at Saarbergwerke from 1,000 tons in 1974 to 905,000 tons in 1978. Production levels at Saarbergwerke remained stable at around 9.5 million tons throughout the 1970s but improved productivity—owing to the rationalization measures and technological advances—meant that shifts had to be cut to limit production. Higher coal prices did, however, bring some improvement in profitability; Saarbergwerke AG was able to record a small profit in 1976 for the first time in 15 years, although only with the help of government subsidies. In 1972, after the death of Werner Hoevels, Erwin Anderheggen took over as chairman of the management committee; he was succeeded in 1976 by Rudolf Lenhartz.

Coke production remained stable at around 1.3 million to 1.4 million tons throughout the 1970s. Production of electricity showed an overall decline, from 4.1 billion kWh in 1970 to 3.9 billion kWh in 1980. A new 707-megawatt (MW) power station, Weiher III, was constructed at Quierschied and began operation in 1976. Two collaborative projects in this sector were also planned: a 750-MW power station at Bexbach—a joint venture with three south German energy companies, which began operation in 1983—and a 230-MW power station at Völklingen, intended as a model of modern power-station technology, completed in 1982 and 70%-owned by Saarbergwerke. The plans for these power stations frequently encountered vigorous resistance from local inhabitants and Saarbergwerke, like others in the industry, was forced increasingly to pay attention to environmental concerns.

The group's fuel trading division was further developed during this period. The 1971 acquisition of the Winschermann group from Salzgitter AG brought Saarbergwerke a nationwide network of subsidiaries. However, organizational difficulties resulting from the integration of this group with existing businesses, along with a recession in the building industry, meant that this division experienced losses throughout the 1970s.

The group's renewed emphasis on its core energy activities was accompanied by a series of disposals, reversing the diversification process of the previous decade. Frisia, the oil refining and trading group purchased in 1965, suffered the effects of a petrol price war in 1969 and made substantial losses; it was sold to the Gulf Oil Corporation of Pittsburgh in 1970. Saarbergwerke's investments in the chemicals sector also proved unsuccessful: the ammonia factory at St. Avold and the uric acid factory at Besch were sold to CdF-Chimie of France, one of the original partners, in 1972. The divestment of Petrocarbona GmbH, the polyurethane-products manufacturer at Bexbach, followed in 1976. MABAG Maschinen- und Apparatebau GmbH, a manufacturer of air conditioning systems at Sulzbach, was purchased in 1971; this company too was dogged by organizational difficulties and poor profitability and was sold in 1979.

However, the machine tools sector was expanded by a series of acquisitions: the Belzer group, a machine tools and assembly plant, in 1970; Wilhelm Fette GmbH, a precision tools manufacturer, 1971; GEMA Gesellschaft für Maschinen- und Apparatebau mbH, a machine tools manufacturer, in 1975; Sitzmann & Heinlein GmbH, a market leader in hard-metal machine tools, in 1978; and R. Stock AG, a boring-machines manufacturer in 1976. The acquisition of Thermoplast und Apparatebau GmbH in 1972 added to the group's rubber products sector. At the end of the 1970s machine tools and rubber products accounted for 10% of group turnover.

The oil crisis of 1973 had not led to any substantial changes in energy consumption patterns in Germany. The oil crisis of 1979, caused by the revolution in Iran and a steep rise in world demand, again highlighted Germany's dangerous dependence on foreign energy sources: Iran at this stage accounted for 17% of Germany's crude oil supply. The cost of the federal republic's oil imports rose from DM29 billion in 1978 to DM65 billion in 1981, even though by the latter date import levels had fallen. Once again the prospects for Germany's domestic coal industry seemed favorable, and Saarbergwerke started the new decade in optimistic mood. Production reached 10.8 million in 1981, and investments of around DM70 million to DM90 million in 1980-1981 were anticipated to raise levels further to 11.5 million tons by 1984.

Again the optimistic assumptions were proved wrong. It soon became clear that coal sales would not rise as much or as quickly as had been anticipated. An economic downturn meant that industrial consumers concentrated on reducing their energy requirements rather than simply turning to a different source. From 1981 onwards the government emphasized that cheaper imported coal was an important source as well as the domestic supply. Saarbergwerke found itself in a difficult position, with increasing production, decreasing sales, and the prospect of declining government subsidies; government injections of capital had been at the level of around DM68 million per year between 1972 and 1982.

The acquisition in 1981 of a 25% stake in Ashland Coal, a U.S. mining company, was a reaction to these market trends. Not only was Saarbergwerke seeking to respond to the German demand for imported coal, but it was also hoping that the new subsidiary would underpin company revenues and reduce the dependence on state subsidies. The stake was reduced to 14% in 1988. On the domestic scene, coal production levels at Saarbergwerke remained stable at around 9.5 million–10.5 million tons per year throughout the 1980s. At the beginning of 1990 the mines at Reden and Camphausen were amalgamated, reducing the number of mines in operation to five. Coke production levels at the Fürstenhausen plant have remained stable at around 1.4 million, although a progressive 25% reduction in capacity is planned. In 1982 Saarbergwerke founded a new coking plant, the Zentralkokerei Saar at Dillingen, in collaboration with the Saar steel industry. Saarbergwerke has a 49% share in the plant, which produced 1.4 million tons of coke and sales of DM375 million in 1989. In the electricity sector, apart from completing projects planned in the 1970s, the group has concentrated on improvements to existing power stations, notably the construction of a DM200 million desulphurization unit at Bexbach. In 1989, electricity produced by power stations fully or partly owned by Saarbergwerke totaled 9.3 billion kWh. Energy production accounted for 49% of group turnover in 1989, divided as follows among the different activities: coal mining 26%, coke 6%, electricity 13%, thermal power 2%, and other activities 2%.

Otherwise disposals were the main feature of Saarbergwerke's strategy during the 1980s. The machine tools division was sold off through a series of separate deals: Sitzmann & Heinlein was sold in 1986 and Wilhelm Fette as well as Belzer Dowidat in 1988. Saarberg's oil supply and refining interests, grouped together as Saarberg Öl und Handel, were sold to Veba Oel AG in 1989. Despite these measures, Saarbergwerke has continued to struggle with profitability. In 1988 the group reported a loss of DM481 million, and the improved situation in 1989—losses of DM14 million—was attributable to proceeds from the sale of the oil subsidiaries as well as a DM220 million cash injection from the shareholders.

Since its foundation, Saarbergwerke AG has had to contend with the declining importance of coal, with competition from cheaper imports, with changes of government policy, and with uncertainty in the global energy market. It has been kept alive by government subsidy, because of its importance to the regional economy and in order to safeguard the continued existence of a domestic coal industry in a country which relies upon imports for over 60% of its primary energy requirements. At the beginning of the 1990s Saarbergwerke's future prospects were still uncertain. Although the government has guaranteed its support—in terms of subsidies and price guarantees—until the end of the century, the European Commission has ruled that subsidy levels must be reduced and has ordered plans for the restructuring of the mining industry. The present chairman of Saarbergwerke's management board, Hans-Reiner Biehl, has recently spoken out against the sug-gested amalgamation of Germany's coal fields into a single national group. Not only does Saarbergwerke face the rigors of a deregulated European market, but national government subsidies which compensate for differences in prices and transport costs between the Ruhr coal fields and other mining areas are also in doubt. In the face of these unpromising circumstances Saarbergwerke embarked on another phase of restructuring and rationalization, aiming to reduce the number of mines operated to three and to cut the work force to 17,500 by 1995.

Principal Subsidiaries: Saarländische Kraftwerksgesellschaft mbH; Saarberg-Fernwärme GmbH; GfK Gesellschaft für Kohleverflüssigung mbH; Saar-Gummiwerk GmbH; Saarberg Handel GmbH; UNISPED Spedition-und Transportgesellschaft mbH; Kohlbecher & Co.; Industrie-Ring Sach -und Versicherungs-Vermittlungsgesellschaft mbH; Saarberg-Interplan GmbH; TÜB Gesellschaft für technische Überwachung im Bergbau; Saarberg Oekotechnik GmbH; Ferramentas Belzer do Brasil; Modellkraftwerk Völklingen GmbH; (70%); Saarberg-Hölter Umwelttechnik (50%); Zentralkokerei Saar GmbH(49%); Bomin Solar GmbH & Co. KG (50%).

Further Reading: 25 Jahre Saarbergwerke Aktiengesellschaft, 1957–1982, Saarbrücken, Saarbergwerke Aktiengesellschaft, 1982; Penner, Joachim, "Da waren's nur noch fünf. Wie schlimm es um die Zechen an der Saar wirklich steht," *Rheinische Merkur,* May 21, 1987.

—Susan Mackervoy

SALZGITTER AG

Stahlwerke Peine-Salzgitter AG
Postfach 41 11 29
W–3320 Salzgitter Druette 41
Federal Republic of Germany
(5341) 211

Private Company
Incorporated: 1957
Employees: 39,000 (1989)
Sales: DM10.76 billion (US$7.20 billion)

In the 1930s it was known that vast deposits of iron were present around Salzgitter in the German federal state of Lower Saxony. Their potential capacity was estimated at 1.5 billion tons from exploratory boring carried out in the 1920s. The disadvantage with this ore, however, was that it contained a high proportion of silicic acid. It was only with the development of new metallurgical engineering processes that this acidic ore could be smelted successfully.

Projects such as smelting the ore deposits in the Salzgitter region were given priority in the Four Year Plan embarked upon by fascist Germany in 1936 with the aim of creating a self-sufficient economy, and making possible German industrial self-reliance, even in the case of war. Together with the iron ore deposits, the site of Salzgitter as a location for iron works was favored because of its central position; the relatively rapid and economical connections that could be made with existing transport routes such as the railway, inland canals, and motorways; and the infrastructure already in place in the region. The National Socialist economic planning also relied on the premise that the steel companies of the Ruhr River basin would support the project and participate in its operation. However, negotiations between Hermann Göring and the representatives of the steel industry failed, as the latter regarded this enterprise as a competitor. Finally the state took on the building of the works and the Reichswerke AG für Berg- und Hüttenbetriebe Hermann Göring (the Hermann Göring Imperial Iron and Steel Works) were founded in 1937.

Other installations were built in quick succession, and by April 1945 six coke furnace batteries, ten blast-furnaces, three blenders, six converters, three Siemens-Martin tilting furnaces, and two electric arc furnaces were in operation. Total raw steel capacity amounted to 1.8 million tons a year.

At the same time as the building up of Reichswerke, as it was known, housing for workers was constructed on a massive scale. In 1942, the town of Salzgitter was enlarged by the incorporation of 29 surrounding parishes and the special building of housing for the workers. Before the start of World War II, the work force was partly recruited and partly, compulsorily enlisted by the state to work in Salzgitter. During the war, the German work force was increasingly replaced by workers forcibly recruited from the German-occupied countries, especially those in Eastern Europe. Eventually prisoners of war as well as prisoners from concentration camps were forced to work and live in inhuman conditions at Reichswerke. The state used criminal methods to control this work force. The number of victims was very high. This chapter in Salzgitter's history was brought to an abrupt end with the occupation of the iron and steel works by Allied forces on April 10, 1945.

The number of people living in the Salzgitter area had grown from 20,000 in 1933 to 117,000 by 1944. By the same year, Reichswerke and its subsidiaries were employing 66,177 people.

In the Treaty of Potsdam, the victorious Allied powers stipulated that the German armaments industry should be dismantled as a part of the war reparations. A plan which had been reworked numerous times for the British and U.S. zones contained a list of 682 installations to be dismantled wholly or in part. Of these, 72.7% fell within the British zone. Reichswerke was included on the list of 116 plants to be dismantled, which was handed to the chief minister of Lower Saxony on October 16, 1947.

The structure of the economy of the Salzgitter industrial region was geared to one line of production, due to the presence of Reichswerke. The closing down of the iron and steel works, Reichswerke's main pillar, created deep conflicts of a social and political nature. In the mid-1950s, unemployment in Salzgitter lay at 35%, in Lower Saxony at 19.8%, and in West Germany as a whole at 12.2%. Under such conditions, the inhabitants of this industrial region and the Reichswerke work force fought against the dismantling of the Reichswerke and for the preservation of their jobs. The clashes with the police and with the occupying British forces came to a head in March 1950. Workers who remained gathered at the plants that were to be blown up. Drilling machinery was destroyed and explosive devices torn out of the boreholes; workers ripped out the fuses or sat down on foundations, prepared to be blown up.

The ending of the dismantling of German industrial capacities in the respective Western-occupied zones of what was now West Germany was accelerated by the general changing conditions in postwar Germany. In Reichswerke's case, the resistance of a whole region, and in particular of the work force and the management, played a special role in combating the policy of dismantling pursued by the Allied occupying forces. In January 1951 the three Western Allied high commissioners announced the end of all dismantling. The reconstruction of the iron and steel works began on March 25, 1953.

The companies belonging to the Reichswerke complex were released from the control of the Allied High Command on an order given on June 27, 1953. The powers to run and the responsibility for reorganizing the Reichswerke complex were handed over to the West German government. In the course of the restructuring ordered by the government, the Reichswerke AG für Erzbergbau und Eisenhütten was put into liquidation and its fixed assets transferred to the companies established in the industrial region. The mining plants, including buildings and equipment, became the property of the Erzbergbau Salzgitter AG, while the plants belonging to the iron and steel works were transferred to the Hüttenwerk Salzgitter AG. The Aktiengesellschaft für Berg- und Hüttenbetriebe, formerly Reichswerke, was formed in 1955, comprised of a number of affiliated companies.

The economic development of the Aktiengesellschaft für Berg- und Hüttenbetriebe was marked in the 1950s by the consolidation of the individual companies and the group's further expansion. In January 1960 the group had a share of at least 50% in 41 companies, and out of those it had a 100% holding in 34 companies. At the end of the 1950s the pig iron and steel production sector showed extraordinarily healthy figures. Peak profits reached in the business year 1959–1960 were surpassed in 1960–1961. By contrast, in mining and other raw material businesses, turnover and profits diminished on increased mining. Until the mid-1960s the group's board of directors focused attention on measures that concentrated on mining and production in the most competitive plants. That meant in particular restructuring in the steel sector, the uniting of several shipyards into one company, and especially intensified efforts to increase profitability in individual companies. The director intended to get rid of interests in businesses whose viability could not be restored in the long term. By the mid-1960s the following groups had been formed within the Salzgitter AG: mining, raw materials, processing, industrial planning, trade, and transportation.

In 1968 Hans Birnbaum was elected chairman of the board. Under his leadership a reorganization of the Salzgitter group was set in motion. Beginning November 1972, the structure of the group was redivided into three business areas by the uniting of companies that until then had been split into different groups with other related businesses. The first business area embraced the group's steel interests and the delivery and services companies associated with it. The second business area's main focus was on the shipbuilding and railway carriage–building side. The third business area grouped together the remaining companies in the Salzgitter concern, notably the machine construction, steel construction, and building materials sectors. Previous to the restructuring, the Salzgitter group had taken over the shares jointly held by Peine and Salzgitter in the Industrie-Aktiengesellschaft. Since the plan of creating Nordstahl AG with Klöckner-Werke AG, Salzgitter AG, and the Ilselder Hütte had collapsed in the spring of 1969, the Stahlwerke Peine-Salzgitter AG had been formed. In April 1970 Salzgitter AG had bought up more than 25% of the capital in the Ilselder Hütte works and found itself in possession of a network of interconnecting companies.

The Salzgitter group consolidated to give it a sustained presence in the various fields of steel production. The two iron and steel works became so closely bound that in the end a single, modern, and efficient steel group developed. Salzgitter AG had become the third-largest steel producer in the federal republic.

When Hans Birnbaum took over the position of chairman of Salzgitter AG, one of his objectives was to diversify the group's interests through an intensified reworking of the company. His attempt failed in part. As a result, the shares in Büssing Automobilwerke AG had to be ceded to the Gutehoffnungshütte Aktienverein (GHH) in 1971. However, in return Salzgitter AG took over the GHH shareholding in the

Howaldtswerke-Deutsche Werft AG (HDW) shipyard. In the group's plans for the 1970s, the consolidation of the steel and shipbuilding sectors were a main priority on the one hand, while on the other it was also endeavoring to adapt these sectors to the changing market conditions. Therefore in 1970 the steel-girder construction firm Noell in Wurzburg was taken over, the Hildesheim foundry Kloth-Senking was acquired in 1973, and a shareholding in the Sachsgruppe acquired. A new shipbuilding program was elaborated at the end of the decade. It concerned not only the further consolidation of HDW and the preservation of the largest possible number of jobs in Hamburg and Kiel, but also activities outside shipbuilding. Incinerating plants, desalination plants and water purification plants as well as energy-saving systems and products, for example in the processing of liquid gas, were also created in the HDW capacity.

The emphasis on steel interests took into account a development which had already been put in place at the end of the 1960s—the decline in iron ore mining. The ore in the Salzgitter district is mined from depths of between 300 meters and 1,200 meters. The ore had a relatively small iron content. Further, the price of foreign ore was constantly falling.

A particularly important chapter in Salzgitter AG's history concerns its exports to the East. Business with the East was of great importance to West Germany. The 1970s—apart from 1977—saw constant growth and an export surplus. The share of West German exports to the East had for years fluctuated around the 6% mark. This was not the case for Salzgitter. Between 20% and 35% of its total export turnover was derived from trade with the Eastern European states. In 1977 alone, Salzgitter AG received three large orders from the Soviet Union with a total value of DM605 million. Other products, and in particular rolled products, also found takers in the Eastern area and here again above all in the Soviet Union. In the business year 1988–1989, the share of export turnover to Eastern Europe still represented 12%.

With the appointment of Ernst Piepers to chairman of the board on August 1, 1979, the group's policy continued to be pursued along the same lines, but a fourth area of activity was introduced, embracing general contracting and engineering for industrial plant as well as consulting engineering.

At the beginning of the 1980s the individual fields of business were rationalized or extended. At that time a crisis existed in the steel and shipbuilding industries, badly affecting the Salzgitter group. At the end of the 1980s, it was possible to distinguish a clear upturn in business.

Due to rationalization and automization of the group's business, as well as the growing importance of the high-tech fields of business, the number of employees decreased steadily through the decades, from some 82,000 in 1963–1964 to some 56,800 in 1971–1972 to 39,000 in 1988–1989.

The fiscal year 1988–1989 was the most successful year in the company's history. The merging of Salzgitter AG with Preussag AG took place in 1989. With this move, the emphasis of activities was centered above all on steel, ship and carriage construction, information technology, trade, and distribution, as well as on the energy sector.

—Gerd Henniger
Translated from the German by Philippe A. Barbour

SANDVIK AB

81 Sanviken
Sweden
(26) 26 00 00
Fax: (26) 26 10 43

Public Company
Incorporated: 1868 as Sandvikens Jernwerks Aktiebolag
Employees: 26,000
Sales: SKr18.25 billion (US$3.24 billion)
Stock Exchanges: Stockholm London

Sandvik is a high technology materials company based in Sandviken, Sweden and trading through an international network of 160 companies in 50 countries. More than 90% of Sandvik's sales are from outside Sweden. Originating from a steelworks using the Bessemer method in the 1860s, the company has developed a series of specialties culminating in cemented-carbide for machining and rock drilling, and sells these and specialty steel and alloy products worldwide.

The origins of Sandvik can be traced back to the formation of the Högbo Stål & Jernwerks AB in 1862. The company was set up to build a new steelworks at Sanviken—150 miles north of Stockholm, the capital of Sweden—by Göran Fredrik Göransson. Sandvik claims that Göransson, who obtained a license to use the Bessemer process, was the first to get the new process to work on an industrial scale. The Bessemer method, unlike earlier methods, allowed the production of heavy castings and forgings in one piece from one melt. In the process, air is blown through molten pig-iron and a vigorous combustion results from the reaction of the blast and the hot iron in the converter. Sandviken is located in the southeastern corner of the region of Sweden where iron products had been produced for hundreds of years prior to the formation of the new company. The original iron industry was based on local deposits of iron and the ready availability of wood to make charcoal.

Johan Holm, the main financial backer of Göransson's company, however, got into financial difficulties that resulted in his and the company's downfall. The company was declared bankrupt in 1866; after financial restructuring, Sandvikens Jernwerks (Steelworks) Aktiebolag was founded in May 1868. Anders Henrik Göransson, the son of the founder, became the manager of the new company and set Sandvik on the course that would lead to its future success. By international standards, Sweden offered a small home market for the new com-

pany. From the start Sandvik exported products which, because of the company's location far from the main industrial markets, had to be highly upgraded steel products. The high quality of Swedish iron ore and the Bessemer process urged the company in the same direction. Even during the first years of the new company, Anders Göransson traveled widely in Europe, taking orders for products and establishing agencies.

By the 1890s the company was making some manufactured products, such as saws, from the steel it produced. In the latter part of the 19th century, the company's specialties included boiler tubes for installation in steamships and railway engines, rock drilling steels, and wire for umbrellas. By the outbreak of World War I, exports accounted for up to 80% of Sandvik's output.

By 1914 employment at Sandviken exceeded 2,200. During World War I the export share shrank, but was offset by the booming domestic market for steel. During the interwar period the company was hit hard by recession, in the early 1920s and again in the early 1930s. The work force declined but by 1937 had risen again to 5,380. During this period, the production of steel by the open-hearth process and electro process replaced the Bessemer process that had been instrumental in the foundation of the company. Sweden's cheap hydroelectric power provided an advantage for steelmakers using the electro process.

Between 1918 and 1939 exports as a proportion of sales varied between 60% and 70%. Throughout this period, steel was the dominant product group; manufactured products such as saws, conveyor belts, complete conveyors, and razor blades accounted for only 6% of sales. Within the area of steel products, tube products were increasingly important; these included seamless stainless tubes for the food, pulp and paper, and chemical industries.

From 1920 until 1958 the dominant figure in the company was Karl Fredrik Göransson, grandson of the company's founder. When he returned to Sweden in 1901 after studying in the United States, he brought with him the company's, and probably Sweden's, first microscope for metallurgical studies. He was managing director from 1920 until 1948 and chairman from 1929 until 1959.

By the beginning of World War II, Sandvik's production amounted to 90,000 tons of steel ingots a year and 65,000 tons of finished products. In terms of ingots, the company accounted for about 10% of Sweden's output, but because the final products were highly upgraded this understates the company's relative importance in terms of the value of output. During World War II, exports collapsed again and output was diverted to the home market. During this period, however, an event of immense importance for the development of the company occurred.

In 1941 the company decided to enter the cemented-carbide trade. Cemented-carbide is a powder-metallurgical product of which tungsten carbide is the main constituent. It may also contain carbides of other metals such as titanium, tantalum, and niobium. Powders prepared from the various metal carbides are mixed with fine-grained powdered metal, most commonly cobalt. The mix is pressed to the desired shape and is treated at a high temperature; the cobalt melts and functions as a binding agent for the carbide grains which are sintered in. The sintered product has multiple advantages: hardness, ductility, and resistance to wear. A sintered blank can be ground to high edge sharpness, affixed to a holder, and used as a tool for metal cutting.

Krupp, the German steel and engineering company, had invented cemented-carbide tools in the 1920s and was the leading supplier before World War II. The war separated Krupp from many of its markets and provided opportunities for new entrants to the trade.

Sandvik used the name Coromant for its new venture, which was initiated by production manager Carl Sebart. Previously, cemented-carbide had been sold in the form of blanks to be fashioned and sharpened into tools by the users. Sandvik's new approach, to supply ready-made tools, was first applied to rock-drills, which were developed and marketed in collaboration with Atlas Copco, another Swedish company, and were an immediate success. The cooperative arrangement with Atlas Copco continued until 1988. Michael Porter, author of *The Competitive Sources of Power*, has suggested that one reason for Sweden's success in producing internationally competitive rock drilling equipment is that its rock is among the hardest in the world. Cemented-carbide metalworking tools were slower to achieve popularity, but development after 1956 was rapid. Sandvik Coromant expanded by building new factories in Sweden and other countries and by acquiring existing producers. Wilhelm Haglund, who had managed the development of Sandvik's cemented-carbide operation from the start in 1941, was appointed managing director of Sandvik in 1957 by K.F. Göransson, and held the position until 1967.

Sandvik Coromant has manufacturing subsidiaries in 19 countries and Sandvik is the world's largest cemented-carbide tool maker with about a quarter of the world market, which in 1988 amounted to about US$3 billion a year. The company's nearest rivals include a subsidiary of Krupp and a U.S. company, Kennametal, which each have 8% to 10% of the market. There are three Japanese competitors; Sumitomo, Toshiba, and Mitsubishi.

In 1971 sales of cemented-carbide products exceeded those of steel products for the first time. In 1972 this was acknowledged by a change in the company's name from Sandvikens Jernwerks Aktiebolag to Sandvik AB.

Sandvik's other divisions were also making progress in developing products and markets while the carbide-tool business took off; they certainly could not afford to be idle in the intensely competitive environment of the steel and engineering industries during the 1970s and 1980s. While other steel companies faced repeated if not terminal crises, Sandvik succeeded, as a result of its policies of investment in the latest technology and developing specialty products to be sold in world markets. In world terms, Sandvik is a small-scale producer of steel; it has survived in spite of the existence of large economies of scale for steel production by concentrating on the production of types of specialty steel and making high quality special products. In its carefully chosen fields of specialization, Sandvik is an international leader; it has a large or significant market share in each market it serves. The company's size allows it to achieve economies of scale for production. Sandvik provided a long-standing model for this type of specialization that was adopted by many companies in the 1970s and 1980s. Examples of products in which Sandvik steel is used are surgical needles, scalpels, and probes that require special strength and resistance to corrosion, bone pins, artificial hip-joints, cladding in nuclear reactors, and springs.

Although it was better placed than many other Swedish steel producers, Sandvik took part in the successive rationalizations of the Swedish special steels industry during the early 1980s. The result of the rationalizations is that there are only two principal special steel manufacturers in Sweden; Sandvik and Avesta. Sandvik specializes in strip, wire, and tube products.

Sales of Sandvik saws and tools are concentrated in Europe, where it is one of the three largest manufacturers of hand tools. Similarly, Europe is the main market for steel belts and conveyors.

The Göransson family was the company's major shareholder and controlled Sandvik until 1957, when additional capital was raised by an issue of shares, and the investment company Kinnevik acquired a stake in the company. In 1967 Hugo Stenbeck, chairman of Kinnevik, became chairman of Sandvik, and Arne Westerberg—a former manager of a subsidiary of Kinnevik—took over as managing director.

An important change of corporate strategy occurred in 1967 at about the time of the changeover in management from Wilhelm Haglund as managing director and Gustaf Söderlund as chairman to Hugo Stenbeck and Arne Westerberg, respectively. Hitherto, the company's policy had been to market products made by the parent company or by its subsidiaries starting from products made by the parent company. Between 1962 and 1966, parent company sales represented 78% of group sales. From 1967 more products, particularly cemented-carbide products, were manufactured by the company's overseas subsidiaries.

The pace of expansion through acquisitions in Sweden and abroad was stepped up after 1967. In 1968 a joint venture, the Saeger Carbide Corporation, was set up in the United States with the Greenleaf Corporation. Between 1970 and 1973, manufacturers of rock drilling equipment in France and Spain were acquired. In 1972 the U.S. rock drilling manufacturing operation of another Swedish steel company, Fagersta, was purchased. In 1973 the U.K.-based Wickman-Wimet group was acquired, and during 1978 and 1979 tool manufactures in Germany and France were bought. Between 1971 and 1974 the steel division made acquisitions in Spain, West Germany, and the United Kingdom; saw, hand-tool, and conveyor manufacturers were also taken into the group. Acquisitions continued to be made during the 1980s; an important one was the Carboloy Division of the General Electric Company, of the United States, in 1987. In 1989, Metinox Steel Ltd., a small U.K. company making medical products out of stainless steel, was acquired.

Sandvik's development has paralleled other Swedish companies such as SKF—ball bearings; Alfa-Laval—separation equipment; Atlas Copco—compressed air equipment and mining machinery; and L.M. Ericsson—telephone exchanges; all of which have roots in the 19th century and are characterized by their development of advanced metal and engineering products and their reliance on sales in international markets. Such companies have enabled Sweden to finance and sustain an advanced welfare state. Unlike Alfa-Laval, Atlas Copco, and L.M. Ericsson, Sandvik was not within the legendary Wallenberg orbit of companies, companies within the sphere of influence of the Skandinaviska Enskilda Bank in which the Wallenberg family has played a major role.

Following the second oil crisis in 1980, Sandvik suffered from the effects of the recession in many of its major markets.

In 1983 the company's profits were reduced by SKr219 million (US$30 million) owing to an exchange rate loss brought about by unauthorized foreign-exchange speculation by an employee. In the aftermath of this disaster, Skanska AB, a construction company with diversified interests, acquired Kinnevik's holding and built up a 37% stake in Sandvik. In October 1983, Percy Barnevik, the chief executive officer of the Swedish electrical giant ASEA, was appointed chairman of Sandvik in succession to Arne Westerberg. In 1984 Per-Olof Eriksson was appointed president. In 1989, Percy Barnevik became chairman while Per-Olof Eriksson became president and CEO of Sandvik, and Skanska AB controlled 26% of shareholders' votes.

During the years 1987 to 1989, Sandvik's operating profit—after charging depreciation—represented more than 15% of sales. Expenditure on research and development was more than 4% of sales while capital expenditure averaged more than 5% of sales.

Sandvik was aware of product life cycles long before the term was coined and used by economists and management experts. The company has a high reputation for innovation and for the commercial exploitation of the specialties it has developed, and it is still achieving new successes—for example, in 1988 output of titanium tubes doubled and golf clubs made of titanium achieved a commercial breakthrough.

Although the company's headquarters in Sandviken are far from the centers of the main industrial concentrations, the company's international network of manufacturing subsidiaries and distribution companies provide it with knowledge of the market and new developments. Nevertheless, the company's success attracts new competitors, not least from the Pacific rim. In the future the company will face ever-intensifying competition and it will be more difficult to keep one step ahead of the pack as new-product introductions accelerate.

Principal Subsidiaries: Sandvik Coromant Company (U.S.A.); Sandvik Rock Tools Inc. (U.S.A.); Sandvik Mission Drilling (U.S.A.); Sandvik Steel Company (U.S.A.); Sandvik Special Metals Corp. (U.S.A.); Sandvik Saws and Tools (U.S.A.); Sandvik Canada Inc. (Canada); Sandvik do Brasil SA. (Brazil); Sandvik SA (France); Sandvik Coromant (France); Sandvik Rock Tools (France); Sandvik GmbH (Germany); Sandvik Coromant (Germany); Sandvik Rock Tools (Germany); Sandvik Steel (Germany); Sandvik Italia S.p.a. (Italy); Sandvik Española SA (Spain); Sandvik Ltd. (U.K.); Sandvik Coromant (U.K.); Sandvik Rock Tools Ltd. (U.K.); Sandvik Saws and Tools (U.K.); Sandvik Australia Pty Ltd.

Further Reading: Hedin, Göran, *Ett Svenskt Jernwerk, Sandviken 1862-1937*, Uppsala, [n.p.], 1937; *Transformation: Sandvik 1862–1987*, Sandviken, Sandvik AB, 1987; Garnett, Nick, "Carbide Tool Groups Sharpen Up Their Image," *Financial Times*, April 6, 1988.

—Cliff Pratten

STEEL AUTHORITY OF INDIA LTD.

Ispat Bhawan
Lodi Road
New Delhi 110 003
India
(11) 690481

State-Owned Company
Incorporated: 1973
Employees: 235,000
Sales: Rs80.00 billion (US$4.41 billion)

The Steel Authority of India Ltd. (SAIL) was created in 1973 as the holding company and supervisory agency for those parts of the Indian iron and steel industry which are wholly within the public sector. Its main product, by volume, is iron ore, most of which is exported. It has a total production capacity of 11 million tons of steel per year, representing more than four-fifths of India's total capacity. It operates its own collieries, a special steels plant, and a foundry for pipes and castings.

The history of the iron and steel industry in modern India is closely bound up with political and economic developments since the country achieved independence from Britain in 1947. Most of the productive units now run by SAIL were built as state ventures with aid and assistance from industrially-developed countries, and operated by SAIL's predecessor, Hindustan Steel Ltd. SAIL's main subsidiary, the Indian Iron & Steel Co. Ltd., which is India's largest single iron and steel company, developed separately as a private company before nationalization, but it depended on state subsidies from 1951 onwards and had to function within the terms of the government's planning system.

However, the industry did not spring from nowhere in 1947. Iron had been produced in India for centuries, while Indian steel was superior in quality to British steel as late as 1810. With the consolidation of the British raj the indigenous industry declined and the commercial production of steel did not begin in earnest till 1913, when the Tata Iron and Steel Company began production at Sakchi, on foundations laid by Jamsetji Tata whose sons had raised the enormous sum of Rs23 million to set up the company, partly from family funds but mostly from Bombay merchants, several maharajahs, and other wealthy Indians who supported the movement for Indian self-sufficiency (*Swadeshi*) but did not want to appear openly anti-British. Tata was to dominate the Indian steel industry until the 1950s. The Indian Iron & Steel Company was set up in West Bengal in 1918 by the British firm Burn & Co., with plans to become a rival steelmaker. However, steel prices declined in the early 1920s and the company produced only pig iron until 1937. The acute depression suffered by the iron and steel industry after World War I was alleviated by the government's protective measures. The industry continued to make steady progress.

From the late 1920s, when the British authorities introduced a system of tariffs which protected British and Indian steel but raised barriers against imports from other countries, the Indian market was divided in the ratio of 70 to 30 between British producers on the one hand and the Tata company on the other—thus effectively excluding indigenous newcomers. By 1939 the Tata works were producing 75% of the steel consumed in what was then the Indian Empire, comprising the present-day India, Sri Lanka, Pakistan, Bangladesh, and Burma.

In the late 1930s, as European rearmament pushed iron and steel prices upward, the export of Indian pig iron increased and two small firms began to compete directly with the Tata company in steel production. The first was the Mysore State Iron Works, which had been set up by the maharajah of Mysore in 1923, to produce pig iron at Benkipur, now Bhadravati. The second was the Steel Corporation of Bengal, a subsidiary established by the Indian Iron & Steel Company in 1937, the year after it had bought up the assets of the bankrupted Bengal Iron and Steel Company. The Steel Corporation of Bengal was reabsorbed into its parent company in 1953. All three companies profited from the British connection during World War II. Annual output rose from 1 million tons in 1939 to an average of 1.4 million tons in 1940–1945.

In 1947, when India became independent as the biggest, but not the only, successor state to the British raj, the three major iron and steel companies had a total capacity of only 2.5 million tons. A great deal of their plant was already more than three decades old, and badly in need of repair and replacement, while demand for iron and steel was growing.

Like other Third World states that have achieved political independence but still find their economic prospects determined by their subordinate position in the world economy, the new republic's policymakers decided to seek economic growth through a combination of protection for domestic industries, heavy public investment in them, encouragement of savings to finance that investment, and state direction of production and pricing. The Mahalanobis model of the Indian economy, based on the assumptions that exports could not be rapidly increased and that present consumption should be curbed for the sake of longterm growth through import substitution by the capital goods sector, provided the theoretical justification for this set of policies, which closely resembled what was done in the Soviet Union in the 1930s, in China in the 1950s, and in Africa and Asia in the 1960s, though with much less loss of life than in most of these cases.

Under the terms of the new government's Industrial Policy Statement of 1948, confirmed in the Industries Development and Regulation Act three years later, new ventures in the iron and steel industry were to be undertaken only by the federal government, but existing ventures would be allowed to stay in the private sector for the first ten years. Thus the First Five Year Plan, from 1951–1956, involved the use of government funds to help Tata Iron and Steel and Indian Iron & Steel to expand and modernize while remaining in the private sector. As for new projects, in 1953 the government signed an agreement with the German steelmakers Krupp and Demag on creating a publicly owned integrated steel plant, which was sited at Rourkela, in the state of Orissa, to make use of iron ore mined at Barsua and Kalta. Krupp and Demag were chosen after the failure of Indian requests for aid from Britain and the United States, but were excluded from the project by 1959, when the Estimates Committee of the Lok Sabha, the lower house of the Indian Parliament, concluded that getting investment funds from them was equivalent to borrowing at an interest rate of 12%.

In order to carry out its side of the agreement the government set up Hindustan Steel Ltd. in 1954, as a wholly state-owned company responsible for the operation of the Rourkela plant. By 1959, when the plant was commissioned, Hindustan Steel had become responsible for two more plants, at Bhilai in Madhya Pradesh and at Durgapur in West Bengal, under the Second Five Year Plan, that started in 1956. The Bhilai plant, located between Bombay and Calcutta, was designed and equipped by Soviet technicians, under an agreement signed in 1955, and by 1961 it included six open-hearth furnaces with a total capacity of one million tons, supplied from iron ore mines at Rajhara and Dalli. The Durgapur plant, meanwhile, was built with assistance and advice from Britain and sited near the Bolani iron ore mine. Hindustan Steel took over the operation of all the iron ore mines supplying its plants, all three of which had been located to take advantage of existing supplies. This policy of locating steel production near raw materials sources reflected the relatively small and dispersed nature of the domestic market for steel at that time, and contrasted with the market-related location policies of companies in more advanced steel-producing countries, such as the United States.

Hindustan Steel's other major venture was its Alloy Steels Project, also based at Durgapur, which was inaugurated in 1964. Hindustan Steel's tasks included not only steel production but also the procurement of raw materials, and its subsidiaries included, besides the iron ore mines already mentioned, limestone and dolomite mines and coal washeries. It also operated a fertilizer plant at Rourkela.

The modernization of the two private sector leaders and the program of public sector investment together raised Indian steel output from about one million tons a year in the 1940s to three million tons in 1960, then to six million tons only four years later. Pig iron output rose by an even greater margin, from 1.6 million tons in 1950 to nearly 5 million tons in 1961. Both wings of the iron and steel industry contributed to the expansion of the engineering and machinery industries envisaged in the Mahalanobis model, and in turn were stimulated by the increased demand to raise production volume and quality. In 1965 Hindustan Steel's latest project, for an iron and steel plant with an associated township at Dhanbad in the state of Bihar, was transferred to a new company, Bokaro Steel Limited. Contact continued between the two companies, however, mainly through an arrangement whereby the chairman of each company was made a part-time director of the other. Like the Bhilai plant the Bokaro project was initiated with aid and advice from the Soviet Union, including blueprints, specialist equipment, technical training, and a loan at 2.5% interest.

After the establishment of SAIL the Bokaro company was changed back into a division of the public sector steel company.

Throughout its first five years of production, 1958 to 1963, Hindustan Steel's losses rose steadily due to Rs7.51 million to Rs260 million it made a small profit in 1965 and 1966, only to slip back into the red and stay there until 1974, the last year of the company's existence under that name. Among the reasons the company gave for these disappointing results were the losses incurred at the Rourkela fertilizer plant, the Steel Alloys Project, and the Durgapur steel plant, an increased rate of interest on government loans, an increase in provision for depreciation, and the high costs of imported plant and equipment.

The rate of growth of the iron and steel industry, and of the engineering and machinery producing sectors with which its fate is so closely linked, declined significantly once the phase of import substitution was complete and the droughts of the mid-1960s had forced a diversion of resources from industry. Pig iron output, which had risen so spectacularly in the 1950s, rose from 7 million tons in 1965 to 10 million tons in 1985, while production of steel rose from 6 million tons to 12 million tons in the same period. The industry suffered due to state intervention to keep its domestic prices low as an indirect subsidy to steel users, and—though the technical problems were different—from a heritage of outdated and inefficient plant and equipment.

Indian government policy since 1965 has been to use its iron ore less as a contribution to domestic growth than as an export, earning foreign exchange and helping to reduce the country's chronic deficit on its balance of trade. Production of ore increased, from 18 million tons in 1965 to 43 million tons in 1985, in order to supply a growing number of overseas markets.

With the expansion and diversification of Hindustan Steel, the separate establishment of Bokaro and the beginning of planning for new plants at Salem, Vishakhapatnam, and Vijaynagar, it became increasingly clear that public sector iron and steel production would need some new form of co-ordination to avoid duplication and to channel resources more effectively. The Steel Authority of India Ltd. was established in January 1973 for this purpose, to function as a holding company along the lines of similar but older bodies in Italy and Sweden. The new organization was placed on a secure footing when the Indian Iron & Steel Company was nationalized, giving SAIL control of all iron and steel production apart from the venerable Tata Iron and Steel Company and a number of small-scale electric-arc furnace units. At the time of nationalization the Indian Iron & Steel Company comprised a steel plant at Burnpur in West Bengal; iron ore mines at Gua and Manoharpur; coal mines at Ramnagore, Jitpur, and Chasnalla; and a specialist subsidiary, the IISCO-Ujjain Pipe and Foundry Co. Ltd., based at Kulti.

Both SAIL and its predecessor sought to expand capacity to meet predicted rises in demand for steel. In 1971 Hindustan Steel had unveiled plans for India's first coastal steel plant, at Vishakhapatnam. The project, which in 1991 was in the process of being opened, with one blast furnace already in operation, will probably allow productivity of 230 tons per man year compared with less than 50 in SAIL's existing plants. The Authority has also invested heavily in modernizing its oldest plants, at Rourkela and Durgapur.

The 1980s were not a happy decade for SAIL. It made losses between 1982 and 1984 but went back into the black in the following two years. Meanwhile Tata Iron & Steel was consistently profitable. By 1986, when the Indian steel industry's total capacity was 15.5 million tons, only 12.8 million were actually produced, of which SAIL produced 7.1 million. Thus imports of 1.5 million tons were needed to meet total demand, after years of exporting Indian steel. By 1988 all the main steel plants in India except Vishakhapatnam were burdened with obsolescent plant and equipment, and Indian steel prices were the highest in the world. The government proposed a ten-year plan to modernize the plants, based on aid from West Germany, Japan, and the Soviet Union just at a time when the worldwide economic recession was deepening and the World Bank was recommending the privatization of SAIL and the liberalization of steel imports.

In 1989 SAIL acquired Vivesvata Iron and Steel Ltd. In its first year under SAIL's wing this new subsidiary's production and turnover showed an improvement over its last year in the private sector. This progress contrasted with results for SAIL as a whole in 1989–1990, since production declined, and once again planned targets were not met. Various factors contributed to this disappointing outcome, including unrest at the Rourkela plant as a result of the management's decision not to negotiate with a new union, Rourkela Sramik Sangha, which had challenged the established union, Rourkela Mazdoor Sabha, and had even won all the seats on the plant's elected works committee. Another problem, continuing over several years, arose from defects in power supply; the impact of power-cuts on steel output in 1989–1990 was estimated as 170,000 tons lost, and the supply of coal was unreliable.

SAIL remains in the public sector as a central instrument of state plans for industrial development. The country's reserves of iron ore and other raw materials for iron and steel make the industry central to the economy. At the beginning of the 1980s India had recoverable reserves of iron ore amounting to 10.6 billion tons, a natural endowment which it would take 650 years to deplete at then-current rates of production. The high-grade ore within this total—that is, ore with an iron content of at least 65%—was, however, thought likely to reach depletion in only 42 years; yet it still represented about one-tenth of the world total. SAIL has had to struggle to maintain production, let alone expand it, largely because of circumstances outside its control. Since the purchase of raw materials has typically accounted for 30% of the Indian steel industry's production costs, any rise in the prices of coal, ferro-manganese, limestone, or iron ore will cut into the industry's profitability. In the first half of the 1980s, for example, prices for these materials rose by between 95 and 150%, at the same time as electricity charges rose by 150%. Most of these increases were imposed by other state enterprises. Nor has it helped SAIL that the high sulfur content of Indian coal has required heavy investment in desulfurization at its steel plants. Indeed, the industry has had chronic problems in trying to operate blast furnaces designed to take low-sulfur coking coal. The more suitable process of making sponge iron with non-coking coal, then converting it to steel in electric arc furnaces, was introduced in the private sector later, though by 1989 only 300,000 tons were being produced in this way. India's basic output costs of Rs6,420 per ton in 1986 compare well with the averages for West Germany (Rs6,438), for Japan (Rs7,898) and for the United States (Rs6,786). What finally keeps Indian steel from being competitive is the imposition of levies which raise its price per ton by about 30%, and which include excise duties, a freight capitalization surcharge, and a Steel Development Fund charge.

In spite of such problems, and in response to them, SAIL announced in December 1990 that it planned to increase its annual output of steel from 11 million to 19 million tons, thus transforming itself from the world's thirteenth largest steel producer to its third largest, within ten years. SAIL's use of its steel production capacity, running at about 77% in 1990, would be raised to 95% by 1996, thus permitting output of crude steel to rise by two-fifths over its current level. However, output for 1990 had actually been only 6 million tons, compared with 6.9 million tons in 1988, and 8 million tons in 1989. SAIL is no more able than large steel companies in other countries to achieve the optimum balance between demand and supply, between increasing the quantity of output and improving its quality by modernizing, and thus escaping from its heritage of outdated plant and equipment. Neither Hindustan Steel nor SAIL was ever in a position to defy the circumstances of the Indian economy or of the world steel industry on their own, but they have largely achieved the more modest goal of contributing to India's postwar economic growth.

Principal Subsidiaries: Indian Iron and Steel Company; IISCO-Ujjain Pipe and Foundry Co. Ltd.; Maharashtra Electrosmelt Ltd.

Further Reading: Agrawal, G.C., *Public Sector Steel Industry in India,* Allahabad, Chaitanya Publishing House, 1976; Behara, Meenakshi and Chandrasekhar, C.P., *India in an Era of Liberalisation,* London, Euromoney Publications, 1988; Rothermund, Dietmar, *An Economic History of India,* London, Croom Helm, 1988.

—Patrick Heenan

stelco steel

STELCO INC.

Post Office Box 2030
Stelco Tower
Hamilton, Ontario L8N 3T1
Canada
(416) 528-2511
Fax: (416) 577-4449

Public Company
Incorporated: 1910 as Steel Company of Canada Ltd.
Employees: 14,348
Sales: C$2.09 billion (US$1.80 billion)
Stock Exchanges: Toronto Montreal Vancouver

Stelco Inc. produces steel in two large plants located at Hamilton harbor on Lake Ontario and another site on nearby Lake Erie, and in mini-mills located in Contrecour, Quebec, and Edmonton, Alberta. In addition there are three fabricating units responsible for pipes and tubes, wire and wire products, and fasteners and forgings.

Stelco prides itself on being a Canadian company. Its plants supply about 30% of the Canadian market. Most Stelco common shares—98%—are held by owners with Canadian addresses. In 1991 the firm's head office returned to Hamilton, where it began during the last third of the nineteenth century.

Like many aspects of the Canadian economy, Stelco's origin reflected both British and U.S. influences. During the 1850s the Montreal merchant house of Moreland and Watson imported British iron to meet investment needs in the burgeoning Canadian economy. During the following decade Moreland and Watson established the Montreal Rolling Mills (MRM) to reroll British wrought iron and scrap into nails and other hardware. The MRM managing director was Charles Watson, who in 1873 appointed William McMaster as secretary; McMaster then succeeded Watson in 1888.

The 1880s were a decade of transition for the MRM. This was an era of increasing protectionism by both Canadian and U.S. governments following the devastating trade depression of the 1870s. Tariff increases helped to preserve a role for British metal in the Canadian market, but the advantage was gradually passing to U.S. suppliers whose raw material and transportation costs were falling rapidly. These trends increasingly handicapped the MRM, whose trade relied on the reworking of metal from Great Britain.

MRM sales in the Ontario market were challenged during the 1880s by the Ontario Rolling Mills (ORM), established at Hamilton in 1879 by a group of Ohio businessmen. These U.S. tradesmen and investors were representative of many who migrated north to create industrial enterprises in early Ontario. The ORM used an abandoned mill to reroll scrap iron rails and rework metal for use by local machine shops and hardware manufacturers.

The ORM and other Hamilton-area secondary metal firms created a growing local demand for primary metal. Favorable tariff and transportation changes made it profitable by the early 1890s to establish a blast furnace on Hamilton harbor using U.S. ore and coal. Local foundry owners and the Hamilton municipal council were instrumental in launching the Hamilton Blast Furnace Company (HBFC) in 1894, after U.S. investors withdrew from what seemed a risky prospect. Alexander Wood, a hardware merchant and later a Liberal senator, was the largest HBFC shareholder. By 1899 HBFC had proven its value to the ORM leadership, who agreed to merge the two firms. The resulting company, the Hamilton Steel and Iron Company (HSIC), quickly erected steel furnaces using its capitalization in excess of C$1 million. The company's vice president and general manager was Robert Hobson, son-in-law to Wood and later president of the Canadian Manufacturers Association.

The HSIC was Canada's first fully integrated iron and steel company. It flourished during the massive wave of investment that swept over the Canadian economy between 1900 and 1910. In the latter year William McMaster offered to bring the Montreal Rolling Mills into a larger organization that would provide a secure supply of primary metal. The successful Maritime financier, Max Aitken, later Lord Beaverbrook, promptly brokered yet another merger of the HSIC with the MRM and several smaller secondary metal companies, resulting in the Steel Company of Canada, or Stelco as it was soon unofficially labeled.

Stelco's first president was Charles Secord Wilcox, who had arrived in Hamilton by horseback in 1880 to join other family members in the ORM. Wilcox was president of Stelco from 1910 to 1916 and chairman of the board from 1916 to 1938; he began the policy of plowing back as much profit as possible into the company. The firm's location in southern Ontario, which minimized transportation costs on material assembly and product delivery, was the most attractive possible in the fragmented Canadian market. Government tariffs and cash subsidies also augmented company profits and permitted the financing of new investment from retained earnings.

During the World War I Stelco produced large quantities of shell steel, but the production of munitions did not prevent the company from establishing a sheet mill to widen its potential product base, and ore and coal mines to facilitate raw material supply. Stelco's diversified product base and concentration on light steel products served it well during the Great Depression of the 1930s, as its share of the Canadian steel market rose from 17% in 1918 to 45% in 1932.

Two presidents served Stelco during this era. Robert Hobson, along with Wilcox from the Hamilton side of the company, presided from 1916 to 1926. Ross McMaster, son of the MRM's William McMaster, had stayed to manage the Montreal works after its sale in 1910; he became president from 1926 to 1945.

The outbreak of World War II inaugurated a new era for Stelco as it did for the Canadian economy. Stelco expanded its finishing capacity with the erection of plate and hot strip mills in 1941 and cold and tin mills in 1948. The growth of the finishing mills resulted in the use of more primary metal. In 1951 Stelco expanded its primary production facilities by building a 226-foot blast furnace and new open hearth steel furnaces sufficient to increase Canadian ingot capacity by 20%.

Hugh Hilton, president from 1945 to 1957 and board chairman from 1957 to 1966, presided over the expansion of the postwar period. Hilton's best-known technical innovation had been a 1928 fuel-saving improvement for the system of distributing waste gas from the furnaces to other applications in the plant. Hilton was the last of the steelmaking engineers to head the company. He was followed by Vincent Scully, an accountant who had come to Stelco as comptroller in 1951. Scully was president from 1957 to 1967 and chairman of the board from 1966 to 1971.

The continued use of open hearth furnaces until the 1980s reflected the slow introduction of basic oxygen furnaces first available during the 1950s. Stelco demonstrated considerable prowess in the development of secondary production technology. In 1959 David McLean, superintendent of Stelco's shapes division, organized a team to improve the cooling and coiling of steel rods in a high speed mill. By 1961 the solution was found in an adaptation of a U.S. patent leading to the Stelmor process for high quality and low cost rod cooling and coiling. During the 1970s the manager of product design services, Bill Smith, pioneered a coilbox technique used for intermill transfer of hot bars; this technique remained proprietary technology.

The 1970s comprised the Gordon era of Stelco, named after Peter Gordon, who served as president from 1970 to 1976 and chairman of the board from 1976 to 1985. Gordon guided the company through a major expansion, as the number of Stelco employees mushroomed from 12,500 to 25,000 during the 1970s. Gordon's lasting contribution was the establishment of a new plant on Lake Erie.

Strong market growth before the 1973 oil shock and subsequent economic slowdown led Stelco in 1974 to begin construction at a new location, the Lake Erie works (LEW). This plant began production during 1980. Annual capacity was 1.7 million tons of semifinished steel. The LEW has large production runs of continuous cast low carbon steel that is cold-rolled into auto sheet and steel used in pipes.

The older and larger Hilton works on Hamilton harbor has an annual capacity of 2.8 million tons. This plant produces diverse and sometimes specialized high- and low-carbon steel in strip, bar, and rod forms. The average production run at Hilton is smaller than at LEW. Between 1985 and 1987 financing and technology from the Japanese firm Mitsui assisted in a major upgrading of the Hilton facilities that included the introduction of basic oxygen technology and continuous casting. The Quebec and Alberta plants have small production runs from mini-mills of a capacity less than one million tons, each from electric arc steel furnaces.

Stelco's four primary plants are part of a production process that is integrated from the mine to a wide array of finished steel, including nails, sheet metal for appliances and vehicles, long-distance gas pipes, springs for vehicles, structural members for bridging and building, steel fencing and a variety of hardware. During the 1980s the final destination of output was the construction industry, 35%; automobile assembly, 30%; shipbuilding, 10%; as well as railways, agricultural and other

machinery parts, and packaging. Stelco undertook secondary processing at Hilton and in more than a dozen subsidiary plants scattered from Montreal to Niagara and in Alberta.

The 1980s proved a difficult decade. Stelco lost its position as Canada's largest steelmaker. Employment declined considerably. Various facilities closed, and the company's long term debt-equity ratio climbed dramatically. In November of 1989 the Canadian Bond Rating Service downgraded its rating of the firm's senior debentures. Revenues in 1990 were 24% less than the previous year, as the company posted a C$200 million loss.

In part Stelco's problems reflected the burden of more than C$2 billion in investments between 1978 and 1988, just as the demand for steel declined because of slow economic growth from 1973 to 1984, and due to the substitution of other materials for steel for a variety of purposes. Lackluster growth in the market for steel and high interest rates during the early 1980s made it possible for Stelco to finance later growth from internal sources, and the value of these costly investments during the 1970s and 1980s will be determined by their impact on future competitiveness.

Another difficult circumstance for Stelco was the need to reduce emission of suspended particles and sulfur dioxide into the air and various substances into Hamilton harbor. The latter included poisonous coal-tar derivatives and ammonia that deprived the harbor floor of oxygen and hence killed fish. Increasing public concern to minimize environmental damage prompted Stelco to invest in a variety of devices to control pollution. By 1985 the Hilton works alone had 49 facilties to clean waste water and 54 facilities to clean the air. In 1991 there are some signs of improvement in Hamilton-area air and water, although Stelco's emissions remain a concern. In contrast to and perhaps because of the pollution problems at Hilton, the Lake Erie works had been built under careful government scrutiny to minimize environmental concerns.

Difficult relations with organized labor were a traditional Stelco problem. The Hilton workers are represented by Local 1005 of the United Steelworkers of America, which historically had been one of the most militant of Canadian locals. Violence marred an 85-day strike in 1946 that is often seen as a turning point in the modern history of Canadian industrial relations. Another, 86-day, strike in 1958, a violent wildcat strike in 1966, a legal strike in 1969, a 125-day strike in 1981, and a 97-day strike in 1990 continued the record of debilitating labor-management relations.

More significant than resulting wage adjustments is the damage to both workers and investors of a persistently and seriously discordant industrial relations atmosphere. An individual worker needed a very long time to recoup the loss of three months pay. On the other side Stelco had been disadvantaged by disruption of supply continuity and other costs of bitter collective bargaining.

In 1991 there were signs that the challenge of competition from east Asia would force labor and management to collaborate in forging a new survival strategy. The union had agreed to set aside traditional job categories in a steel coating mill within the Hilton works. The new mill was a joint venture with Mitsubishi Canada Ltd. to improve the rust-resistance of sheet metal. Hand-picked Hamilton workers have visited Japan to acquire technical knowledge and improve their understanding of the Japanese culture of company-worker cooperation.

The new coating mill is one aspect of Stelco's campaign to win contracts from Japanese-owned auto assembly plants located in southern Ontario. This response to change in secondary markets reflects the same careful attention to customer needs embodied in 19th-century mergers with the Montreal Rolling Mills and Ontario Rolling Mills. Stelco policy has returned the company to its historically successful strategy of careful integration between primary production and the secondary industry.

Within the North American market Stelco with its new facilities is quite competitive; Canada runs a trade surplus with the United States on steel. The introduction of a Canada-U.S. free trade agreement has favored Stelco because it reinforces a tendency to preserve the North American market for North American producers, among whom Stelco with its new facilities is a strong competitor.

In 1991 the president and chief operating officer was Robert J. Milbourne, a long-time Stelco engineer. The chairman of the board and chief executive officer was Frederick H. Telmer, a career Stelco employee in marketing.

Principal Subsidiaries; Stelco Technical Services Limited; Stelco Holding Company (U.S.A.), Stelco U.S.A. Inc.; CHT Steel Company Inc.; Stelco Enterprises Corp. (U.S.A.).

Further Reading: Inwood, Kris, "The Iron and Steel Industry," in I.M. Drummond, *Progress without Planning: the Economic History of Ontario from Confederation to the Second World War,* Toronto, University of Toronto Press, 1987; Kilbourn, Williams, *The Elements Combined: A History of the Steel Company of Canada,* Toronto, Clarke Irwin, 1960.

—Kris E. Inwood

SUMITOMO METAL INDUSTRIES, LTD.

5-33, Kitahama 4-chome
Chuo-ku, Osaka 541
Japan
(06) 220-5111
Fax: (06) 223-0305

Public Company
Incorporated: 1935
Employees: 19,796
Sales: ¥1.12 trillion (US$8.25 billion)
Stock Exchanges: Tokyo Osaka Nagoya Frankfurt Düsseldorf

Sumitomo Metal Industries, Ltd. (SMI) has about 130 subsidiaries and affiliates in Japan and elsewhere, according to its annual report, which names 50: 14 in steel processing; 7 in nonferrous metals and miscellaneous; 6 in raw materials, fuels, and electric power; 3 in trading companies and transport; and 20 overseas, including 11 in the United States.

Sumitomo Metal Industries has its roots in the foundation of the Sumitomo group in copper mining in the late 16th century. Its origins as a modern company date from 1897, when Sumitomo Copper works was opened in Osaka, and as a steelmaker from 1901, when Sumitomo Steel works began operation.

Both openings represented a privatization of Japanese industry, established by the government after the Sino-Japanese War of 1894-1895. The copper works were acquired from the Japan Copper Manufacturing Company, the steel works with the purchase of Japan Steel Manufacturing Company.

It was a slow start, however. The newborn steel industry was unable to compete internationally because its plants were small and inefficient, and it grew very little. This situation changed with World war I, when demand grew strong at home and abroad because of large steel orders for military use by the Allied powers and the temporary withdrawal of European steelmakers from the Japanese market. From 1914 Japan supplied the Allies with iron and steel while itself engaged in limited naval military action. Japanese industry, including Sumitomo Steel works, profited economically from World War I.

After the war, heavy industry suffered a recession, and demand fell. The lull was temporary, however. The government entered into extensive railway and public-works construction, and steel production quadrupled in the 1920s. Wartime investment in plant and equipment paid off. The relatively undeveloped Japan moved toward industrial independence, and heavy industries were established.

Growth came in part from catastrophe. During the 1923 earthquake, 44% of Tokyo was burned to the ground, as was 26% of Yokohama. Substantial rebuilding followed, and the next two years were a boom period for the Japanese steel industry, which nonetheless was unable to meet domestic needs. Japanese iron and steel production in 1927 met about 60% of consumption. The industry was gaining on the problem, however, and the gains showed in a steady transformation of the Japanese economy. Heavy industry accounted for only 26% of the value of overall Japanese output in 1925, but 37% of its value five years later, when its share of output was still rising.

The 1930s were a time of continued expansion and diversification because of growth of the metal, machinery, and chemical industries. Heavy industry continued to outpace light industry. The number of metals factories more than doubled, and the number of workers quadrupled. During the 1930s the yen value of production grew by 800%. Japan became practically self-sufficient in production of rolling stock and in steel and steel products in general. The production-to-consumption ratio reached 103% for steel and 115% for steel products. Contributing to this increased ratio were the abandonment by the Japanese government of the gold standard with attendant freeing of money for investment, technical improvements, increased government spending on armaments, exploitation of the Manchurian resources newly acquired after the Japanese invasion of Manchuria, and development of Manchukuo, the Japanese puppet state in Manchuria, as a center of heavy industry.

In 1935, the Sumitomo copper and steel works were merged to form Sumitomo Metal Industries, Ltd. Meanwhile, Japan, accustomed since 1914 to unusually high profits, had embarked on a course of economic imperialism with a view to keeping such profits flowing. Even so, only in 1936 did the military demand for steel become an important factor in keeping profits flowing. Until then the major steel users had been the construction industry and heavy industries such as shipbuilding, machinery, and the steel industry itself.

A program of government subsidy funded this growth, for example, the Subsidy Facility for Improvement of Ships of 1932-1937. By this arrangement boats over 25 years old were scrapped, and subsidies were granted for replacement of up to half the number of ships scrapped. Heavy industry in general profited from such subsidization. Development of new products made of metals such as aluminum and magnesium contributed to growth in profits. During the early 1930s, heavy industries, including the chemical industry, showed profits for first time without concentration on military demand.

By 1937 the military was expanding its requirements. A five-year industry plan in March 1937 called for annual steel production of 6.5 million tons of steel by 1941, up from 5 million. Since the army wanted ten million tons produced, the option was given to export three million tons if there should be peace rather than war.

Japan went to war, first with China beginning in July 1937, and later with the Allies. Capital and labor were diverted to war industries. Government regulation of the economy increased, accompanied by continuous conflict between industry leaders and militarist-bureaucratic factions over who should control the new economic structure.

The National Mobilization Law of March 1938 gave the government great authority over labor and working conditions, production, consumption and exchange of goods, control of property including confiscation, and business and industry in general. In 1941 this authority was expanded to cover virtually all aspects of business. Manufacturers, banks, and investment institutions were required to seek government permission for plant development and loans; thus savings were forced into investment in heavy industry. By the end of 1940 steel production was almost seven million tons. Industry was seen increasingly as auxiliary to the military. Private profits were eliminated or severely curtailed. Industrialists were pitted against bureaucrats. The national debt, having tripled in five years, equaled national income.

In December 1940 a compromise was reached. Private enterprise was to be the basis of the new structure. There would be closer cooperation among the state, conservative elements in the armed forces, and representatives of the great financial interests that opposed the military extremists as well as their ultraconservative business counterparts.

Sumitomo's director general, Masatsune Ogura, was made minister without portfolio in April 1941, charged with the task of overall economic coordination. An industry-oriented general replaced a bureaucrat as head of the state planning board, and an admiral with close ties to shipbuilding interests became minister of commerce and industry.

Ogura had army ties, and Sumitomo industries, including Sumitomo Metal Industries, was in both light and heavy industry, whose interests did not always coincide. Thus he was well qualified to bring the armed forces closer to business and finance, and to bring light industry closer to heavy industry.

The changes resulted in a partnership between business and the military, a military-industrial complex. War was looming, and Japan wanted to be ready. In July 1941, a few months after Sumitomo's Ogura took on these responsibilities, the United States froze Japanese assets in the United States. So did the British throughout their empire, and the Dutch in the East Indies. The Sumitomo group contributed to the war effort through its mining, manufacturing, steelmaking, banking, and other enterprises and grew considerably during the war, from 40 firms to 135 and from ¥574 million in paid-in capital to ¥1.92 billion.

After the war, Sumitomo Metal Industries changed its name to Fuso Metal Industries, reverting to the name Sumitomo when the Allied occupation ended in 1952. The group, or *zaibatsu*, had been dissolved in February 1948, but was reconstituted in the 1950s as a *keiretsu*, a confederation of interrelated companies, with the role of the family greatly diminished.

By 1951 manufacturing was back to prewar levels, after a change in Allied policy, from punishment to encouragement, with a view to balancing Far Eastern power, especially in the wake of the fall of Nationalist China and the Korean War. During the Korean War, U.S. purchases in Japan helped Japanese industry develop and grow. The iron and steel industry was a leading factor. It had been a major source of Japan's military strength in World War II and was at first to be dismantled under the Allied occupation, except for what was needed to meet domestic needs. With the new policy it too was encouraged.

Sumitomo Metal Industries shared in the 1950s growth, in 1953 acquiring Kokura Steel Manufacturing Company, Ltd., and entering into a long-term modernization program that in-

cluded installing large blast furnaces and building new mills in coastal areas. In 1959 it divested its nonferrous metal processing unit, establishing it as a separate company, Sumitomo Light Metal Industries, Ltd.

In 1962 Japan became the world's fourth largest steel producer, outstripping France and the United Kingdom. Japan was producing nearly 30 million tons of steel a year, about four times its pre-1950 total and was second to the United States in continuous hot strip mill capacity. Larger blast furnaces were being built, and oxygen converters were being installed to reduce dependence on scrap-iron imports. Japan became the first country to use oxygen converters on a large scale, after they were used for the first time anywhere, in Austria in 1953.

New plants were built along the seacoast with furnaces of 1,200-ton to 2,000-ton capacity. The coastal location made it easier to receive raw materials and to ship manufactured products. The new plants accommodated the newer, larger ships built to haul raw materials more cheaply.

SMI kept pace with these national developments. Among Japanese steel producers, it was tied in third place with Nippon Kokan and Kawasaki, each with 11.5% of total production. Yawata Iron & Steel led with 18.5%; Fuji Iron & Steel had 17%. By 1976 SMI had built new processing plants and established a technical research institute. Its capacity for producing blister steel, low-carbon, semi-finished material formed by heating bar iron in contact with carbon in a cementing furnace, was 22.7 million tons a year.

By 1982 SMI's steel tubes and pipes, almost half its output, were considered among the world's best. The company was able to supply 30% of world demand for wheels for rolling stock. It had three affiliated companies in the United States and one each in Thailand and Saudi Arabia, plus offices in the United States, Brazil, Venezuela, West Germany, Australia, the United Kingdom, Iran, and Singapore.

Sales that year were ¥1.5 trillion, the third highest in Japan after Nippon Steel and Nippon Kokan. Beside tubes and pipes, SMI production was 31% steel plates, 7% steel wire, and the rest rolling stock, castings, forgings and other products.

In the mid-1980s, major Japanese steel producers, Sumitomo Metal, Nippon Steel, NKK, Kobe Steel, and Kawasaki Steel, were hurt by the rising yen. They closed six furnaces, sending 47,000 workers to other businesses or early retirement. As a result of the cuts, these companies once again became the world's most efficient steelmakers.

SMI's main lines were iron and steel in various semifabricated and fabricated forms, engineering services, titanium, electronics, chemicals, and energy. The company had more than 80 subsidiaries and affiliated companies and participated in several overseas joint ventures. In addition to Osaka and Tokyo, it had offices in 23 other Japanese cities, as well as offices in New York, Los Angeles, Chicago, Houston, Düsseldorf, Vienna, London, Sydney, Singapore, Mexico City, and Beijing.

In 1988 the Sumitomo group was one of six major *keiretsu*, with Mitsui, Mitsubishi, Sanwa, Fuyo, and Dai-Ichi Kangyo. Sumitomo Metal Industries is a leader of the Sumitomo group. SMI steel works were located in Osaka and four other cities, including two in Wakayama; laboratories were in Hyogo and Ibaraki.

In early 1990 the five largest Japanese steelmakers, faced with weak domestic demand, rising financing costs, and strong competition from mini-mills at home, and South Korean and Taiwanese steel producers abroad, cut more jobs. The five—SMI, Nippon Steel, NKK, Kobe Steel, and Kawasaki Steel—had invested heavily in automation and in the manufacture of higher-margin products such as stainless and coated steels. These investments were promising, but a less promising diversification was the move into microchip production and other nonsteel businesses. While SMI had invested least in these new fields, nine SMI affiliates had begun building semiconductor-manufacturing equipment.

The rising cost of raw material created a problem. Iron ore prices had risen 16%, and the cost of coking coal was up by 5%. Mini-mills, by contrast, were circumventing this problem by making steel out of scrap iron in small electric-arc furnaces. Scrap was available at bargain prices because new car sales had risen and old cars were scrapped proportionately.

One nonsteel diversification, SMI's investment in a U.S. computer firm, Lam Research, seemed more promising. By 1990 SMI owned a half million shares in Lam, which marketed and serviced Sumitomo's integrated-circuit technology in North America and Europe, while Sumitomo did the same for Lam's equipment in Japan.

Principal Subsidiaries: Nippon Pipe Manufacturing Co., Ltd.; Sumitomo Special Metals Co., Ltd.; Sumikin Chemical Co., Ltd.; Sumitomo Metal USA Corp. (U.S.A.).

Further Reading: Moulton, Harold G., with Junichi Ko, *Japan, an Economic and Financial Appraisal*, Washington, D.C., The Brookings Institution, 1931; Mitchell, Kate L., *Japan's Industrial Strength*, New York, Alfred A. Knopf, 1942; Hall, Robert B., Jr., *Japan, Industrial Power of Asia*, Princeton, D. Van Nostrand Co., 1963; Guillain, Robert, *The Japanese Challenge*, Philadelphia, Lippincott, 1970; Nakamura, Takafusa, *Economic Growth in Prewar Japan*, New Haven, Yale University Press, 1971; Gibney, Frank, *Miracle by Design: the Real Reasons Behind Japan's Economic Success*, New York, Times Books, 1982; Prestowitz, Clyde V., Jr., *Trading Places: How We Allowed Japan To Take the Lead*, New York, Basic Books, 1988; "Japan's steelmakers: Virtue is its own reward," *The Economist*, April 28, 1990; *A Brief History of Sumitomo*, Tokyo, Sumitomo Corporation, 1990.

—Jim Bowman

SUMITOMO METAL MINING CO., LTD.

11-3, Shinbashi 5-chome
Minato-ku, Tokyo 105
Japan
(03) 3436-7701
Fax: (03) 3436-7734

Public Company
Incorporated: 1950
Employees: 3,582
Sales: ¥505.61 billion (US$3.72 billion)
Stock Exchanges: Tokyo Osaka Nagoya

Sumitomo Metal Mining Co., Ltd. (SMM), an integrated metal producer, is Japan's third most productive copper mining and processing company and the largest Japanese producer of gold and nickel. *Forbes,* July 23, 1990, placed it in the top 400 of publicly held Japanese companies. The company has diversified widely. From mining, smelting, and metal processing, it has moved to the production of electronic and construction materials, catalysts, lubricants, and nuclear fuels; has made advances in industrial pollution control technology; and has developed deep seabed mineral resources. It prospects for mineral resources overseas, and buys and mines them, in addition to selling its own products and technological assistance.

Sumitomo Metal Mining Company was the first industrial venture by the house of Sumitomo, founded in the 17th century by Masatomo Sumitomo, a Buddhist priest who turned bookseller and apothecary after his sect was dissolved by the ruling Tokugawa shogunate.

He issued the "founder's precepts," preserved to this day by the Sumitomo companies. As quoted in "A Brief History of Sumitomo," these called for "integrity and sound management, foresight and flexibility" and stated that "under no circumstances" should the house of Sumitomo "pursue easy gains or act imprudently." Company members were to sell nothing on credit and buy nothing below the market price without knowing its origin, presuming such merchandise to be stolen. They were never to lose their tempers and never to speak "intemperately or harshly, whatever the other party says." They were to beware of "unwary charity" and give nothing away, not even "one night's lodging."

The medicine and book shop was opened in Kyoto in the mid–17th century, not long before Sumitomo's death in 1652 at age 44. Earlier, also in Kyoto, the family entered into cop-

per mining. Sumitomo Metal Mining dates from this period. Riemon Soga, Masatomo's brother-in-law, had opened a small copper refining shop in Kyoto, when he was 18 years old. If Sumitomo was the spiritual pillar of the family, Soga Riemon was its technological pioneer. He learned from China how to extract silver from copper ore and taught the process to the oldest son. The son taught it to Sumitomo, who adopted him after Riemon Soga died. The ability to extract silver from copper ore was crucial; otherwise the ore would be shipped out at great loss. This breakthrough occurred between 1596 and 1615. Soga then expanded into copper trading and copper mining. He died in 1636 at the age of 64. His oldest son married Sumitomo's daughter and was adopted into the Sumitomo family. This son, Tomomochi, brought the family into the refining and crafting of copper.

Around 1623, while still in his teens, Tomomochi Sumitomo moved his main shop from Kyoto to Osaka, a city crisscrossed by canals, where the *daimoys,* or feudal lords, had their storehouse estates and wealthy merchants their warehouses. The shop engaged in trade with Nagasaki, Japan's main port. Tomomochi Sumitomo was welcomed by the Osaka copper refiners, who remembered how his father had shared with them the new silver-extraction technique, despite his own precept that forbade giving anything away. Soon there were three Sumitomo refineries in Osaka, and another in Kyoto.

In 1652 Tomomochi succeeded Masatomo as head of the Sumitomo family. His Osaka refinery became the hub of Japan's copper industry and remained the hub to the end of the Edo period and the start of the Meiji period in 1867. Tomomochi died in 1662. His 15-year-old son Tomonobu succeeded him as family head, inheriting the copper guild rights of both Soga and Sumitomo families. Indeed, of 16 copper-refiners selected by the ruling shogunate for copper guild membership, 4 were the Sumitomo's. Considerable expansion of the family business followed.

In 1674 the family opened a branch office in Tokyo, then called Edo, in order to be closer to the copper mines of the area. In a few years the family was handling more than one-third of the nation's 1,800 tons per year of copper exports.

Copper processing was a government-controlled industry. All copper had to be refined in Osaka, by decree of the shogunate, which wanted to be sure that no copper ore left the country with silver in it. From 5,400 tons of copper refined annually came 2.6 tons of silver. Osaka had one copper refiner to every 300 residents, it was claimed at the time.

Copper exports reached 3,000 tons a year by 1688. The event that made the fortunes of the house of Sumitomo was the discovery in 1690 of the huge Besshi Copper mine on the island of Shikoku. The new mine was soon producing more than one-quarter of the nation's output, 1,520 tons of 6,000, at a time when Japan was a leading world producer of copper. The Sumitomo family became the official supplier of copper to the Tokugawa shogunate. The family also collected taxes for the Tokugawa family.

In 1749 the nearby Tatsukawa mine was added to Besshi. The family merged it with Besshi in 1762. Meanwhile, the Sumitomo refining operation achieved such a good reputation that visitors came from Europe to inspect it, for example, the German scholar, Philipp Franz von Siebold, in 1826.

Trouble arose in 1865, when the shogunate, under pressure from rebels, rescinded its policy of buying designated copper for foreign trade, the bulk of Besshi's output, and also required the Sumitomo family to pay special assessments. The Meiji Restoration was under way and with it the end of the feudalistic Tokugawa shogunate, which had ruled for 264 years. Copper prices were falling, and the price of rice, the staple of the miner's diet, was rising. The miners were issued paper and wooden tokens instead of money. The mine faced bankruptcy; the Sumitomo family, unable to collect on its loans to warlords, was forced to mortgage its household goods.

The family wanted to sell the mine, thus closing the enterprises, but the newly appointed general manager of the Besshi mine, Saihei Hirose, persuaded the family not to do so. Hirose had virtually grown up at the mine, having gone to live there with his uncle, the manager, when he was eight, and having worked there since he was ten, when he started as an office boy. He abolished the mine's seniority system and brought in managers from outside the company.

The Meiji Restoration of 1868 produced another crisis. The new government confiscated the mine, but Hirose again saved the day, persuading officials to let Sumitomo run it. The family eventually regained ownership.

Meanwhile the *zaibatsu* system became the mainstay of Japanese business and industrial growth. Established as a *zaibatsu,* the Sumitomo family took its place in the financial oligarchy that worked with the government to develop modern industry in Japan. Acting as banker for the government and running a number of state-initiated industries, Sumitomo became one of the top three *zaibatsu,* after Mitsubishi and Mitsui. Each operated simultaneously in finance, commerce, and industry, enjoying considerable competitive advantage because they alone had enough capital to invest in major enterprises.

The Sumitomo family at first had its hands full managing the Besshi Copper mine and related activities. Not for ten years after the 1868 Meiji restoration, for instance, did the company have a director-general of its activities, the mine manager Hirose, who doubled in the position while remaining mine manager. Its development as a full-blown *zaibatsu* occurred over several decades as a natural outgrowth from mining. Thus the family moved from copper mining and refining to copper rolling and steel manufacture, among a number of other industrial enterprises. Like other *zaibatsu* Sumitomo at length became a conglomerate with interests in many branches of industry, beyond the original mining and refining business.

In 1872 the family bought a 54-ton-capacity wooden steam ship from the British for hauling copper and supplies between the Besshi mine on Shikoku and the ports of Osaka and Kobe. Hirose hired a French engineer, Louis Larroque, at the very high salary of US$600 a month, to show his employees how to modernize. Larroque told them what was needed but his two-year contract was not renewed. Instead, Hirose sent two of his employees to France to study mining and metallurgy. He saw the need for a scientific approach, but he also wanted to avoid excessive dependence on foreign experts.

By 1880 Japan was mining almost 5,000 tons of copper a year. By the mid-1890s, it was mining four times that amount. Besshi production grew proportionately, from 420 tons in 1868 to more than 2,000 in 1890.

Hirose retired in 1894 at the age of 66 as first director-general of the Sumitomo enterprise, a post that he had assumed in 1878. His nephew Teigo Iba, a former judge,

succeeded him immediately as head of mining. In this capacity, heeding protests by local farmers, he moved the Besshi smelters to an island some 20 kilometers away.

Sumitomo had already acquired two coal mines, in Kyushu in 1893 and 1894, with a view to becoming self-sufficient in its copper refining. It continued to acquire coal mines, especially under Masaya Suzuki, director-general between 1904 and 1922, who secured the Sumitomo industrial base. Unlike the top two *zaibatsu,* Mitsubishi and Mitsui, Sumitomo had been industrially based from the outset. Its core enterprise remained mining and metallurgy despite diversification.

The average annual production of Japanese copper rose steadily before and during World War I, which was a prosperous time for Japan. Then it dropped steadily for several years, bottoming out in 1922.

In 1928 Japan was sixth among copper-producing nations, with 3.9% of the world's supply. It had been in third place only ten years earlier. Unable to compete on price with foreign copper, it was importing much more copper than it was exporting. In 1937, when Sumitomo was the leading Japanese producer of nonferrous metals, the Besshi copper operation was merged with the coal companies to form Sumitomo Mining Co., Ltd.

Sumitomo was much more centralized than other *zaibatsu.* The family was far more dominant in running the holding company, and the holding company was far more involved in running the subsidiaries, including the mining operations. The family followed the rule of primogeniture strictly, and the head of the family in 1937 held more than 98% of the holding company's shares.

During World War II, the Sumitomo mines and other enterprises began operating more independently. The number of enterprises, or holding-company subsidiaries, grew from 40 to 135 firms during the war, their paid-in capital from ¥574 million to ¥1.92 billion.

Expansion ended with the war's end. The Sumitomo *zaibatsu* was dissolved with the others under Allied policy. The many enterprises were left to survive on their own. The director-general, Shunnosuke Furuta, a popular engineer, turned to trade to provide work for the company's employees, turning the clock back to the 1868-1900 period, when the family ran copper shops in Kobe and Korea, selling not only copper but also cotton cloth, silk, tea, and other goods. The move to commerce looked back even further, to the medicine and book shop that the founder Masatomo Sumitomo had started in the 17th century. Trading was the Sumitomo family's earliest activity, even before copper mining, and it was to contribute to the overall Sumitomo renaissance in the late 1940s and 1950s. Furuta resigned as director-general in 1946, after supervising the dissolution of the *zaibatsu.* The holding company was dissolved in February 1948. Its subsidiaries became independent companies, although their executives met regularly on a cross-company basis.

In 1950 two companies were formed from Sumitomo Mining—Sumitomo Coal Mining Co., Ltd. and Sumitomo Metal Mining Co., Ltd., a producer of nonferrous metals. The family's role in its management was greatly diminished in the new, *keiretsu* structure established in the 1950s. Like the other *keiretsu,* Sumitomo companies usually conformed to government regulation. Sumitomo Metal Mining was an exception, however, in the 1960s, when it ignored production limits and suffered government-ordered reductions in its coal import quota.

By 1982 Sumitomo Metal Mining, the oldest company in the Sumitomo group, was only a small part of the group, capitalized at ¥17.4 billion (US$72.3 million), compared to ¥124.3 billion (US$516.4 million) at which the group's leading company, Sumitomo Metal Industries, was capitalized. SMM sales that year were ¥290.8 billion (US$1.2 billion). Copper mining and refining accounted for 22% of sales, nickel 16%, gold 27%, cobalt 3%, construction materials 5%, zinc 5%, and other products 22%.

As the 1990s began, Sumitomo Metal Mining was more a gold and nickel mining company than a copper producer. Its Kagoshima mine had very high grade gold and deposits. It had invested in Phelps Dodge, the major U.S. copper producer. In addition it was making a full-scale advance into the housing market.

Principal Subsidiaries: Hakusui Brass & Copper Co., Ltd.; Fuji Brass & Copper Co., Ltd. (90.1%); Siporex Manufacturing Co., Ltd. (95.2%); Hyuga Smelting Co., Ltd. (60%); Japan Nuclear Fuel Conversion Co., Ltd.; Sumitomo Metal Mining, Arizona, Inc. (U.S.A., 75%); Sumitomo Metal Mining Pte., Ltd. (Singapore); Sumitomo Metal Mining U.S.A., Inc.

Further Reading: Moulton, Harold G., with Junichi Ko, *Japan, an Economic and Financial Appraisal,* Washington, D.C., The Brookings Institution, 1931; Mitchell, Kate L., *Japan's Industrial Strength,* New York, Alfred A. Knopf, 1942; Gibney, Frank, *Miracle by Design: the Real Reasons Behind Japan's Economic Success.* New York, Times Books, 1982; Prestowitz, Clyde V., Jr., *Trading Places: How We Allowed Japan To Take the Lead,* New York, Basic Books, 1988.

—Jim Bowman

TATA IRON AND STEEL COMPANY LTD.

Bombay House
24 Homi Mody Street
Bombay 400 001
India
(22) 204 9131
Fax: (22) 204 9522

Public Company
Incorporated: 1907
Employees: 70,000
Sales: Rs2.33 billion (US$128.37 million)
Stock Exchange: Bombay

Tata Iron and Steel Company Ltd. (TISCO) is the iron and steel production company associated with the Tata group of some 30 different industrial and other business enterprises in India, founded by members of the Tata family. TISCO also exports ferromanganese, chrome ore, steel tubes, strips, wires, rounds, and agricultural implements to the United States, China, and the Middle East. Since 1970 the Tata group has had no official corporate existence but it continues to be regarded as India's largest family business. The Tata interests now include iron and steel production, motor vehicle manufacture, tea plantations, hotel management, hydroelectric power, and information technology, both in India and in other areas of the Far East such as Malaysia and Singapore. Together the various Tata companies are responsible for nearly 2% of India's gross national product (GNP), an illustration of their current importance for the subcontinent's economy.

The story of TISCO is the story of one family or, more accurately, one man whose vision and determination to give India a modern industrial economy helped provide a platform for the country's independence half a century after his death. At the same time he helped create what was by 1970 India's biggest non-public enterprise. Jamsetji Nusserwanji Tata was born into a well-to-do family of Bombay Parsees in 1939. The Parsees, a religious minority group, had carved a niche for themselves in business, in this case in the economy of Victorian India, which was dominated by British interests and was being developed as a client imperial economy. Tata's father was a successful merchant with interests in the cotton trade to Britain. Tata joined the family business after an education at Elphinstone College in Bombay and was sent to Lancashire, England, in 1864 to represent the firm there. This was to be the first of many travels in Europe, North America, and the Far and Middle East during which he formulated his ideas on the best strategy to realize his own ambitions for success in business and to contribute to the economic development of India.

Tata's own background was in cotton production. He believed that mills could function successfully in India in close proximity to the cotton-producing areas in the west of the country, thereby putting them in a strong position to undercut their Lancashire competitors. He obtained air conditioning equipment from suppliers in the United States and the latest cotton spinning machinery installed to provide the optimum climatic conditions for spinning. His early ventures showed promise and in 1874 he founded his first company, the Central India Spinning, Weaving and Manufacturing Company. Three years later, on the same day that Queen Victoria was declared empress of India, he opened the Empress mill in Nagpur.

As Tata was taking his first steps towards establishing a viable cotton spinning business, Indian nationalism was also beginning to find a focus for its aspirations through the Indian National Congress. Tata was present at its inaugural meeting and his devotion to the cause of an independent India was undoubtedly a motivating factor in his own drive for success in business. Cotton was only a start. From his travels in other industrialized nations he had come to identify three essential elements for a modern industrial economy: steel production, hydroelectric power, and technical education. Although he did not live to see any of his schemes in these areas come to fruition, he laid the foundations on which his sons, and then later generations of his family, were able to build to realize his ambitions.

From the mid-1880s Tata commissioned a series of surveys in India's coal producing areas, such as Bihar and Orissa in the northeast of the subcontinent, to locate iron ore within easy reach of coal deposits and water, both essential elements in steel production. He visited the United States to seek the advice of the world's foremost metallurgical consultant, Julian Kennedy, and went to Birmingham, Alabama, to study the coking process in action. In England in 1900 he discussed his plans with the secretary of state for India, Lord George Hamilton. In India the way had been opened for private enterprise with the introduction of a more liberalized mineral concession policy in 1899. With Julian Kennedy's help, American specialists were brought in and began surveying in 1903. After a series of disappointments, rich iron ore deposits were identified in dense jungle in Bihar at the confluence of two rivers near Sakchi three years after Jamsetji Tata's death in 1904. Also involved in the surveying was Tata's nephew, Shapurji Saklatvala, whose health suffered so much that he was sent to London to recuperate. There, he joined his uncle's London office which had been established some years earlier to represent the interests of the family cotton business. His energies were soon channeled away from business matters and into politics, and he became Communist member of Parliament for Battersea North in 1922.

Four years after Tata's death, his sons Dorabji and Ratanji began development of the Bihar site. A factory and township were carved from the jungle and named Jamshedpur. A conscious decision was taken to retain control within India of the new enterprise, the Tata Iron and Steel Company, by seeking out Indian investors. In the face of warnings that India could not afford a flotation of this size, the Tata brothers set out to raise Rs23.2 million in shares. Within eight weeks some 8,000 Indian investors came forward and the whole share issue was taken up. The Tatas retained 11% of the stock for themselves. There were enormous initial problems in clearing the Sakchi site and, once production began, in ensuring that the coal was of a uniform quality. However, by 1916, production was meeting expectations and during World War I the company exported 1,500 miles of steel rails to Mesopotamia. Rapid expansion to support the Allied war effort was followed by Depression during the 1920s with escalating prices, transport and labor difficulties, and a major earthquake in Japan, by now TISCO's biggest customer. The company had to suspend its dividend for 12 out of 13 years in this period and was on the brink of closing in 1924 when Sir Dorabji Tata had to pledge his personal fortune to secure the necessary bank loans to keep the business afloat. However, TISCO emerged from the 1930s as the biggest steel plant in the British Empire. World War II brought a resurgence in demand for Tata products and the company specialized in the manufacture of armored cars, known as *Tatanagars,* which were used extensively by the British Army in the North African desert.

Following six years of almost continuous production to serve the war effort, it became imperative in the late 1940s to begin replacement of plant. In association with Kaiser Engineering of the United States capacity was expanded and a Modernization and Expansion Program (MEP) was launched in 1951, upgraded four years later to the Two Million Ton Project (TMP) to give TISCO the capacity to produce two million tons of crude steel. This was achieved in 1958 but further expansion was put on hold during the 1960s while the country passed through a period of devaluation and recession. However, by 1970 TISCO employed 40,000 people at Jamshedpur, with a further 20,000 in the neighboring coal mines. Government attempts to nationalize TISCO in 1971 and 1979 were defeated, partly, it was believed, to retain an efficient private sector yardstick against which the performance of public sector companies could be judged. However, an ever-increasing range of government legislation to bring private sector businesses into line with national economic planning on the Soviet model hampered Tata's freedom to develop in the postwar period. In 1978 the government restricted TISCO's dividend to 12% to force it, as India's only private sector steel producer, to plough money into modernization. Expansion was restricted by a government committed to helping nationalized industry. Further difficulties were created in the late 1970s by chronic shortages of coal, power, and rail transport. An estimated Rs45 crores of saleable steel was lost during 1979–1980 because of these shortages. However, TISCO soldiered on and in the following decade began to benefit from a relaxation of government control as a more pragmatic attitude to the importance of private sector industry emerged. By 1990 TISCO remained India's largest non-public company, announcing a 30% increase in profits against a backdrop of general depression in the Indian economy as a whole.

The growth of Jamshedpur and the involvement of the firm in every aspect of its industrial and municipal life has been the subject of several studies. Jamsetji Tata was both a nationalist and a philanthropist. He showed a paternalistic concern for the wellbeing of his employees, which set the tone for future company policy. The British proponents pioneers of social reform,

Sydney and Beatrice Webb, were invited out to India from England to advise the Tatas on the best form of social, medical, and cooperative services for the newly established Jamshedpur and as a consequence schools, recreational facilities, creches, and other amenities were established on site at an early stage. An eight-hour working day had been introduced in 1912, an officially recognized Tata Workers' Union established with Gandhi's associate, C.F. Andrews, as its first president, and profit-sharing schemes brought in in 1934. Against this, it has been argued that the Workers' Union operated in fact as a management tool to impose its will on a work force so heterogeneous by nature that rival unions made little headway. Despite the reputation of the Tata family for concern over workers' rights, there was much unrest among the work force during the 1920s over wages and conditions and it has been claimed that this, as much as anything, contributed to advances. The commitment of the Indian Trades Union Congress after independence to the same goals as central government—economic self-sufficiency and prosperity—allowed the Tatas a relatively free hand in dictating their own industrial relations policy. Whatever the arguments, TISCO could claim in 1989 that it had not lost a day's work through industrial action in 50 years, and its management illustrated its commitment to the welfare of its employees by commissioning an audit of its "social performance" by a team of eminent public figures.

TISCO's success spawned numerous offshoots making use of Tata products, some of them part of the Tata Group. These included the Tata Engineering and Locomotive Company (TELCO). This ripple encouraged other areas of Indian industry to become suppliers of spare parts for new products and by 1970 TELCO had over 500 Indian ancillary suppliers.

The second element in Jamsetji Tata's plan for India's modernization was the development of a hydroelectric capability. Within reach of Bombay's thriving, basically steam-driven cotton spinning industry lay the monsoon-swollen rivers of the western Ghats. If Bombay's captains of industry could be persuaded to invest in the necessary conversion from steam to electricity, the natural resources existed to provide this new source of power. To encourage the process the Tatas bought up sufficient mills to create the necessary demand before launching Tata Hydro-Electric Power Supply Company in 1910. By 1915 the required dams and reservoirs, ducts, and pipelines had been laid to feed the new turbines. Two further power stations followed in 1916 and 1919. Between the wars the family had to sell some 50% of its stake in the hydroelectric company to an American syndicate to support other less successful firms within the group. By the 1960s power stations had been supplemented by four thermal installations which together satisfied Bombay's entire domestic and industrial requirement.

TISCO, TELCO, and Tata Hydro-Electric Power Company were only three parts of the Tata empire which by the late 1970s comprised 30 separate companies. Together the group accounted for 1.8% of India's GNP, with TISCO alone providing 0.4%, far more than any single equivalent firm in the United States or United Kingdom. In 1970 the managing agency system that had characterized much of Indian industry since the British period was abolished. Under this system, British investments in the subcontinent were managed by firms of agents who charged commission for their services. Tata Industries Ltd. acted in this capacity for many of the firms in the Tata Group, and until 1970 central control was not difficult. After this date, shares in the 30 or so Tata enterprises were retained by Tata Industries, whose chairman from 1938 was Jehangir Ratanji Dadabhoy Tata, a distant relative of the founder of the Tata industrial dynasty. He was succeeded in 1981 by Ratan Naval Tata, whose father had been adopted by Ratanji Tata's widow in 1917. Following the Monopolies and Restrictive Practices legislation of 1969, which represented the views of a government hostile to large private enterprises, the Tata group was self-conscious within India about the size of its operation and great emphasis was placed on publicizing the independent nature of each of its firms. It was pointed out that 75% of the firms' shares were owned by trusts established by the Tata family to promote research and welfare projects. In reality, the Tatas had been adept in holding together their empire with a steady growth in the group's assets, much informal consultation between firms, a recurrence of names in the lists of directors, and a shared head office in Bombay.

The continued prosperity of the group during the difficult postwar years for private-sector firms was probably also helped by its refusal to take up an overtly political stance in opposition to prevailing government policy. The only exception was in 1956 when it backed the short-lived Forum of Free Enterprise against a government committed to assigning a dominant role to public sector industry. Government monopoly legislation also restricted diversification into high-profit areas such as fertilizers or pharmaceuticals, an obvious move for a group such as Tata whose traditional staple was high-cost, low-profit industry. However, there were no restrictions on overseas investment or new technology, and inroads into both these areas were made. India needed firms such as TISCO or TELCO if the country was to maintain a viable industrial capability. Therefore, even when government controls officially restricted growth, the Tata Electric Company was given the green light during the 1970s to build privately a new 500 megawatt plant, and sanction was given to TELCO to increase its output from 24,000 to 36,000 vehicles per year.

TISCO developed as one of the independent but interrelated companies within the Tata group. Among the better-known of these firms is the Indian Hotels Company, whose centerpiece, the Taj Mahal Hotel, in Bombay, was conceived by Jamsetji Tata and opened in 1913 as the first hotel in the country using electricity. Tata Chemicals was launched in 1939, and its Mithpur plant produced mineral extracts required for glass, ceramic, and leather production. The plant had a checkered history in its early years owing to delays in perfecting the soda ash process. However, with the support of the Tata group and the usual Tata resourcefulness in times of crisis, the company stayed in business. For example, when a drought in 1962 threatened to close the plant, management prevailed upon the local population to ration the domestic consumption of water. This "lakeless week" was a great success and ensured that sufficient supplies of water remained for the company to continue in production. Another venture in 1962 involved joining with James Finlay and Company of Scotland to form the Tata-Finlay Company, which bought Finlay's 53 tea estates and has become the biggest tea producer in the world.

In the field of electronics, Tata joined the Burroughs Corporation of Detroit in 1977 to market the U.S. firm's computer systems and to begin to develop the manufacture of mainframe computers in India. With such an array of experience and expertise, the group has entered the consultancy market with the establishment of the Tata Consulting Engineering and Tata Economic Consulting Services. One Tata initiative that slipped through the net was air travel. An air service was inaugurated to carry the mail between Bombay, Karachi, and Madras in the 1930s. However, in 1946 Tata Airlines went public as Air India Ltd, and the Company was nationalized in 1953 to form Air India and Indian Airways.

The third requirement of Jamsetji Tata for a successful and independent India was a system of technical education. His scheme to launch a Science University in India in 1898 was opposed by the viceroy Lord Curzon as overambitious and inappropriate for Indian needs. However, Tata persevered and offered to underwrite the project with an endowment derived from his Bombay properties. He did not live to see the scheme realized. After Curzon's departure, the government of India showed itself more amenable to the proposal, and in 1911 Bangalore was chosen as the site for an Indian Institute of Science with joint funding from the Tata family, central, and provincial governments. The institute produced a number of eminent scientists and has become a focus for much pioneering research. Tata funds have gone into other projects such as the Bhabha Atomic Research Center in Bombay, which has developed techniques for more efficient power generation. One of Jamshedji's greatest legacies was a concern for creating better educational opportunities for his countrymen. By the 1920s, one in five of Indian recruits to the Indian civil service had benefitted from Tata scholarships.

This commitment to education, welfare, and other humanitarian projects continues today and is part of the Tata distinctiveness. The family has been accused of paternalism towards its workers, of an often ill-judged concern for the continued existence of every member of the corporate group irrespective of profitability, and of an over-concentration on traditional high-cost but low-profit industries. Although since the abolition of the managing agency system in 1970, TISCO and the various Tata companies operate entirely independently, they retain many personal, family, and business ties. TISCO and most of the larger firms in the "family" share the same head office in Bombay where their common facilities are provided by Tata Services. The Tata sense of identity has survived a postwar period of almost continuous economic and political adversity. In recent years Tata has diversified into new high-technology areas and embarked on overseas investment projects. If India is to realize Jamsetji Tata's ambitions for it as a modern industrialized nation, then TISCO and the other parts of the Tata group still have a major role to play.

Principal Subsidiaries: Kallimati Investment Co Ltd; Tata Pigments Ltd; Special Steels Ltd (64.3%); Tata Refractories Ltd (51%); The Tinplate Company of India Ltd; Tata-Robins-Fraser Ltd; Tata Yodogawa Ltd; Ipitata Sponge Iron Ltd; Ipitata Refractories Ltd; Tata Metals and Strips Ltd; Kumadhubi Metal Casting and Engineering Ltd; Almora Magnesite Ltd; The Indian Steel Rolling Mills Ltd; Tata Davy Ltd; Tata Timken Ltd; Tata Korf Engineering Services Ltd; Tata-MAN Ltd.

Further Reading: Menon, Aubrey, *Sixty Years: The Story of the Tatas,* Dehra Dun, Tata Industries Ltd, 1948; Harris, F.R., *Jamsetji Nusserwarji Tata: A Chronicle of His Life,* Bombay,

Blackie & Sons, 1958; Lala, R.M., *The Creation of Wealth. The Tata Story,* Bombay, IBH Publishing Co, 1981; Mamkoottam, Kuriakose, *Trade Unionism: Myth and Reality. Unionism in the Tata Iron and Steel Company,* Delhi, Oxford University Press, 1982; Datta, Satya Brata, *Capital Accumulation and* *Workers' Struggle in Indian Industrialisation: The Case of the Tata Iron and Steel Company 1910–1970,* Stockholm, Almquist & Wiksell International, 1986.

—J.G. Parker

THYSSEN AG

Kaiser-Wilhelm-Strasse 100
Postfach 110561
4100 Duisburg 11
Federal Republic of Germany
(0203) 52-1
Fax: (0203) 522 5102

Public Company
Incorporated: 1953 as August Thyssen-Hütte AG
Employees: 149,644
Sales: DM36.2 billion (US$24.22 billion)
Stock Exchanges: Frankfurt Düsseldorf Hamburg Munich
    Berlin Bremen Hanover Stuttgart Paris Zürich Basel Geneva
    London

Thyssen AG, Germany's biggest steel and engineering group, was founded at the end of the 19th century. Steel is a major contributor to the company's profits, and Thyssen's steel plants are largely based in the Ruhr district. High technology transport systems, engineering products, and services are its growth areas.

The company traces its origins to a steel plant in Bruckhausen near Hamborn on the Rhine, which started operations in December 1891 and later formed the core of the Thyssen empire. The plant was built by August Thyssen, a 50-year-old entrepreneur who had already built up a steel and engineering business called Thyssen & Co. August had worked in his father's banking business in Eschweiler and later as a managerpartner of a steel mill, called Thyssen, Fossoul & Co. In 1871, the year of Germany's first unification, he set up his own business at Mulheim in the Ruhr area with 35,000 talers and a paternal grant of the same sum. August Thyssen's business expansion in the 1880s included the purchase of large coal mines. He gradually bought into the Gewerkschaft Deutscher Kaiser coal pits and took the mining company over entirely in 1891. Thyssen & Co.'s Mulheim factories soon became unsuitable for August's expansion plans as the site was too small and lay too far away from a river, which he needed for transport. In 1889 he decided to build the steel plant at Bruckhausen, installing six furnaces using the modern Siemens-Martin technique, and a rolling mill with five trains for the first step. August also wanted to control his own crude steel supplies, building a plant in 1895 in Bruckhausen, which started operations two years later.

August's companies expanded quickly in the years leading up to World War I, securing its own coal and iron ore supplies. His drive for self-sufficiency made him buy into raw materials suppliers in France, North Africa, and Russia. By 1904, August's rolled steel production had hit 700,000 tons a year, putting him ahead of other producers in Germany. The demands made by Germany's military authorities during World War I buoyed Thyssen's business in the same way as other German industries, but Germany's defeat had catastrophic consequences for the company. Its foreign property was confiscated, its plants in the Ruhr Valley were put temporarily under French control, and earnings were battered by the postwar hyperinflation.

August's shrunken business empire only became profitable again in late 1924. The octogenarian August concentrated on mechanizing production to cut costs, and initially resisted overtures from other German steel producers to form a cartel. However, Thyssen gave up its independence soon after August's death in 1926, joining four other coal and steel enterprises to form Vereinigten Stahlwerke AG (Vst). Thyssen made up more than a quarter of Vst's paid-up capital of 800 million reichsmarks and Fritz Thyssen became chairman of the supervisory board. Vst was decentralized in 1934; five steel mills in the western part of the Ruhr district were grouped into the August Thyssen-Hütte AG based in Duisburg.

Fritz Thyssen, the elder son of August, is remembered more for his association with Adolf Hitler than for his business skills. Frustrated by his father's long tenure at the head of the company, Fritz channeled his energies into right-wing politics aiming to subvert the Weimar Republic. He became an early supporter of the Nazi party. Fritz later fell out with the Nazis and recanted in a ghost-written and unauthorized biography, called *I paid Hitler*. He fled Germany in 1939, was captured in Vichy, France, and incarcerated from 1941 to November 1943 in a mental asylum and then until the end of the war in concentration camps. After World War II, Fritz's break with the Nazis was largely accepted by a denazification court, which fined him 15% of his German properties. At the end of 1948 he emigrated to Latin America.

Vst and Thyssen's main works, now ATH AG, fared just as badly under the Nazis. The Four Year plan of 1936, devised by Hitler to prepare Germany for war, restricted raw material supplies and made cost-effective production almost impossible. During the war years, ATH, like other German companies, became a supplier to war production, although in 1942 Nazi hardliners accused the company of defeatism. In autumn 1944, Allied bombing raids destroyed many of ATH's factories, with production in its huge plants ceasing altogether.

Worse was to follow. The victorious Allies allowed limited repairs at ATH's factories, and the first steel mills at Thyssen-Hütte the main works of ATH, began operating again in October 1945 but only temporarily. In April 1946 the Allies decided to stop reconstruction while they decided what to do with German industry, which they blamed for arming Hitler. In February 1948, the Allies decided to dismantle the Thyssen-Hütte as part of their war reparations from Germany. Factories were detonated or stripped of machinery. The destruction of the Thyssen-Hütte and other works of Vst was only halted in November 1949 with the Petersberg Treaty, an agreement signed between the Allies and the new government of the Federal Republic of Germany. At the same time the

Allies broke up the Vst group into 16 successor companies. They also separated the steel companies from their mining firms. All that remained of August Thyssen-Hütte AG was the core business of the former Thyssen-Hütte at Hamborn. Nevertheless it restarted its first blast furnace in 1951. Business improved once the Allies lifted steel production limits one year later.

In May 1953, August Thyssen-Hütte AG was relaunched as a public company with the successors of Fritz Thyssen as minority shareholders. Today, it has about 200,000 shareholders. The largest stakes are held by the Fritz Thyssen Stiftung, a foundation to promote the study of arts and sciences, with 9%, and a consortium company belonging to the Fritz Thyssen family and the Commerzbank AG and Allianz AG insurance group, which holds more than 25%.

Thyssen's postwar history is dominated by two management board chairmen, Hans-Günther Sohl, who ran the company from 1953 to 1973, and his successor, Dieter Spethmann, who retired in 1991. Sohl rebuilt ATH as Germany's biggest steelmaker and Spethmann presided over its often difficult diversification into new product areas.

ATH flourished in the 1950s on booming steel demand, building new facilities to make flat rolled steel. The company invested some DM700 million up to 1958 and spent DM800 million alone on a new Beeckerwerth plant. Thyssen also expanded by buying up companies, taking over four major producers by 1968: Niederrheinische Hütte AG, Deutsche Edelstahlwerke AG, Phoenix-Rheinrohr AG, and Hüttenwerk Oberhausen AG. It also expanded into trading and services by buying into Handelsunion AG from 1960 onward. The future core of the Thyssen Handelsunion AG subsidiary, Handelsunion traded in steel, scrap metal and raw materials, and also offered transport services. Thyssen also forged alliances with other large German steel producers to make production more cost-effective, signing an agreement with Mannesmann in 1970 on steel pipe and rolled steel manufacturing.

Expanding steel output was still the ATH strategy at the beginning of the 1970s, when cheaper imports from newly emerging steel producing companies began to undercut European producers. Thyssen's steel production peaked at 17 million tons in 1974, the same year that the first major steel crisis hit world manufacturers. Like other German producers, Thyssen suffered from 1969 and 1973 revaluations of the deutsche mark, high wage costs, and the imposition of environmental controls. The oil price rise of 1973 delivered another blow to the industry as costs soared and demand shrank.

Thyssen decided to scrap all plans to expand steelmaking capacity and to withdraw from sectors where competitors were undercutting the company's prices. Instead, Thyssen invested in streamlining production and in diversifying away from steel. In 1973–1974, Thyssen took over Rheinstahl AG, the group's high technology engineering group which in 1976 was renamed Thyssen Industrie AG. In 1978 Thyssen bought a U.S. car components maker, The Budd Company.

However, these acquisitions initially caused problems. Rheinstahl had a number of steel mills, which increased Thyssen's capacity to 21 million tons a year. The company was forced to close nearly 30 plants in the Thyssen group between 1974 and 1980. The number working in Thyssen's West German steel plants decreased to fewer than 75,000 in 1979 from 85,000 five years earlier. Budd made money for Thyssen in

the first two years after the takeover. The second oil crisis in 1979 pitched the U.S. economy into recession and caused heavy losses at Budd; the company only saw a turnaround in 1962. One of the biggest loss makers was Budd's railway equipment division; it had signed four large contracts in 1981 at fixed prices that never covered production costs. The division's work force was cut to 700 from 2,500. Budd has since concentrated on its core auto-components market, cutting its work force from 21,500 in 1978 to fewer than 12,000 in 1986.

Thyssen's diversifications were continually dogged by the decline of the steel industry. Spethmann was determined to restructure Thyssen using the company's own financial resources. He opposed acceptance of subsidies such as those propping up rival state-owned steel makers in Belgium, the United Kingdom, and France, but the near-collapse of steel prices forced Thyssen to accept European Community production quotas and subsidies in 1980. However, the steel crisis continued, forcing the creation of Thyssen Stahl AG in 1982 as an independent steel group, in a bid to find partners to help reduce costs. Spethmann made the first of many overtures to Fried. Krupp GmbH for merging production but was rebuffed. Thyssen therefore imposed a tough program of cuts, with a reduction to the 1991 level of 11 million tons capacity from 16 million tons. Losses at Budd and at Thyssen Stahl forced the group to suspend dividend payments for two years in 1982. An improvement in the world economy prompted Thyssen to restart dividend payments at five marks a share, although losses at Thyssen Stahl continued until 1987.

In the 1980s, Thyssen linked its name to high technology projects in the transport sector. It lead-managed a consortium developing the Transrapid train, capable of speeds of up to 500 kilometers an hour. The Transrapid was sold as a revolutionary form of transport running on a magnetic field rather than on wheels. The train has no engine on board and relies on electromagnetic motors in the track. Thyssen wanted to lay a Transrapid track from the northern port city of Hamburg to Munich in the south, but only received government backing for a smaller pilot track in North Rhine Westfalia state. The government was not entirely convinced that all of Transrapid's technical problems had been solved, and was worried about funding a white elephant project. A bitter row broke out before the government gave approval. Thyssen accused Bonn officials of trying to sabotage the project, which the company wanted to sell abroad.

Thyssen's image suffered in the 1980s when a book was published accusing Thyssen Stahl of malpractices in its treatment of Turkish guest workers. However, Thyssen successfully contested the book in court, and author Günter Wallraff had to delete passages from his bestseller, titled *At the Very Bottom*.

Thyssen reacted cautiously to the unification of Germany in 1990, shying away from buying into East Germany's decrepit steel industry. Instead, it has concentrated on setting up 27 smaller ventures in the engineering and services sector, involving investments of some DM500 million. It has also signed another 40 cooperation deals with state-owned companies in the former communist country.

Thyssen was structured into four divisions: capital goods, trading and services, specialty steels, and steel. Trade and services make up more than one-third of Thyssen's world sales of DM36 billion, but make a much smaller contribution to profits. Out of pre-tax profits of DM1.2 billion in 1988, Thyssen

Handelsunion contributed only DM220 million. The lion's share came from Thyssen Stahl, which earned a pre-tax profit of DM833 million. The steel boom of the late 1980s boosted Thyssen's performance and enabled it to raise its dividend to DM11 in 1989 from DM10 the previous year. Declining steel demand in the 1990s has cut into steel profits, but the group now relies on many other industries that do not suffer the same cyclical downturns. Capacity cuts and streamlined production are also seen as protecting the group from suffering the same losses as in the steel crisis of the early 1980s.

Principal Subsidiaries: Thyssen Industrie AG (90%); Blohm + Voss AG (74.1%); The Budd Company (U.S.A.); Thyssen Handelsunion AG; Thyssen Edelstahlwerke AG; Thyssen Stahl AG.

Further Reading: Treue, Wilhelm, *Die Feuer Verlöschen nie. August Thyssen-Hütte, 1890–1926*, Düsseldorf, Econ-Verlag, 1966; Treue, Wilhelm and Helmut Uebbing, *Die Feuer Verlöschen nie. August Thyssen-Hütte 1926–1966*, Düsseldorf, Econ-Verlag, 1969; Turner Jr., Henry Ashby, *German Big Business and the Rise of Hitler,* Oxford, Oxford University Press, 1985; James, Harold, *The German Slump,* Oxford, Clarendon Press, 1986; "Die Thyssen-Gruppe," *Usines et Industries,* December 1986; Uebbing, Helmut, *Wege und Wegmarken. 100 Jahre Thyssen,* Berlin, Siedler, 1991.

—Dieter Müller

TOMEN CORPORATION

6-7, Kawaramachi 1-chome
Chuo-ku, Osaka 541
Japan
(06) 208-2211
Fax: (06) 208-2222

Public Company
Incorporated: 1920 as Toyo Menka Kaisha Ltd.
Employees: 3,330
Sales: 7.08 trillion (US$52.15 billion)
Stock Exchanges: Tokyo Osaka Nagoya Luxembourg

As Japan's seventh-largest trading company, Tomen Corporation is an international presence that handles products such as metals and minerals, machinery, lumber, food and produce, textiles, and chemicals. Although Tomen began as an importer of raw cotton, it expanded into metals and minerals, textiles, chemicals, and industrial products following World War II. Sales in 1990 were primarily in metals and minerals, which accounted for about one-third of sales; chemicals and energy-related products; machinery; textiles; and food and produce. While foreign trade has constituted more than half of Tomen's sales, the company has begun to concentrate on domestic needs to take advantage of Japan's economic growth.

During the 1920s as Japan became increasingly industrialized, spinning and weaving became an important industry in Japan. Among the most prosperous of Japan's industrial groups was Mitsui & Company. Tomen established itself as Toyo Menka Kaisha Ltd., or Oriental Cotton Trading, in April 1920, with capital of ¥25 million. It was formed in order to import raw cotton and sell textiles both domestically and abroad when Mitsui & Company spun off its cotton department. Mitsui spun off its cotton department because the cotton trade became very risky during the post–World War I era. Raw cotton is an internationally traded commodity, and the global postwar recession of this period made trading in such a market highly speculative. The company's first years were troubled, especially during Japan's financial panics of 1922 and 1927. Nonetheless, the company captured 10% of the Japanese cotton market within a few years. Prior to 1920 Mitsui & Company had served 30% of the market. By 1924 Toyo Menka had founded its first overseas arm, the Southern Cotton Company in Dallas, Texas. During the early 1930s Toyo Menka and Mitsui & Company had sufficient confidence in the textile market to offer to buy Brazil's entire cotton crop. The com-

panies encouraged Japanese immigrants to Brazil to grow cotton, and the São Paulo cotton crop was nearly doubled by Japanese farmers. Despite the unstable economic climate and Japan's involvement in the Sino-Japanese War, Toyo Menka expanded quickly, increasing its capital to ¥35 million by 1940. By 1935 it imported nearly 20% of Japan's raw cotton, and provided more than 20% of the country's cotton-textile exports to India. Indonesia and India were a strong market for Toyo Menka, which was able to import Indian raw cotton, process it, and sell the cotton textiles in India more cheaply than the Indians. The demand for processed cotton fabrics increased in the mid-1930s. Toyo Menka then gained markets in Europe and became Japan's largest importer of raw cotton. Toyo Menka owed part of its success to its ability to exploit cheap labor in its colonies and in Manchukuo and China. Toyo Menka wielded considerable influence in China before and during World War II.

The outbreak of World War II had a severe impact on trading companies in Japan as distribution of their commodities was limited to the Greater East Asia Co-Prosperity Sphere, those areas in East Asia over which Japan exercised at least some control. Toyo Menka's exports were limited to cotton-textile shipments to Manchuria and China, and even these were eventually virtually suspended. Toyo Menka was able to take over large cotton-textile operations in Shanghai and other occupied cities, however, and it thrived domestically. Trading activities were further controlled by the government's Trade Control Committee, established in 1942, which essentially made a government subcontractor of Toyo Menka. Toyo Menka worked closely with the Japanese government during the war, and enjoyed a great deal of political influence. Some of Toyo Menka's Chinese branch offices were used by an undercover agency known as the Kodama Machine, for its leader, Yoshi Kodama. The Kodama Machine acted as a clearing house for looted valuables leaving China and black market goods entering China. After the war business activities in Japan were regulated by the Allied occupation authorities. This period was marked by the dissolution of *zaibatsu*, business conglomerates, including Mitsui, of which Toyo Menka had remained a member. Between 1945 and 1949, Toyo Menka's operations were curtailed by its classification by authorities as a restricted company, but it began handling metals, machinery, and food products in 1947. Business dealings were eased when most of the responsibility for self-government was given back to Japan in 1949. Toyo Menka began to rebuild, with its staff halved.

In 1950 Toyo Menka turned the corner into real growth, aided by postwar economic stability and especially by the Korean War, begun in June 1950. The war stimulated rapid economic recovery in Japan. Industrial plants and the textile industry thrived. Toyo Menka's capital increased to ¥150 million, and the company was listed on the Osaka and Tokyo stock exchanges in 1950.

As world trade volume soared during the 1950s Toyo Menka expanded its overseas network, beginning with the establishment of Toyomenka (America) Inc. in 1951. Toyo Cotton Company opened in Dallas, Texas, in 1952. A Bangkok branch was opened in 1954—the first Japanese trading company posted there—followed by a London branch in 1956. Toyo Menka had 33 branches and offices internationally by 1955. Toyomenka (Australia) Pty., Ltd. was founded in 1957. Japan was working toward integration in the international community at this time: it joined the United Nations in 1957 and established the Japan External Trade Organization in 1958.

Concurrent with its international expansions, Toyo Menka sought to increase its offerings by merging with specialized trading companies. In 1955 it absorbed Kanegafuchi Shoji and increased its textile activities. Toyo Menka acquired Honcho Real Estate in 1956. Toyo Menka's real estate division has grown into an international urban-development group, emphasizing residential developments, with more than 20 affiliated companies. Activities include urban-renewal projects and recreational facilities. The division has overseen the development of residential subdivisions, shopping centers, condominiums, and golf courses.

With the sustained economic boom of the 1960s, Japan became a world power, exporting in enormous quantities and widening its product range. Toyo Menka's merger with Taiyo Bussan in 1961 expanded its food-products divisions. The absorption of Nankai Kogyo in 1963 brought Toyo Menka increased iron and steel activities. Toyo Menka was importing about 70% of Japan's machine tools. This merger boosted Toyo Menka's exports of steel and iron to the United States, and exports of plant, machinery, and ships to Asia. In the early 1990s, Toyo Menka's iron and steel division handled products that ranged from iron ore and other raw materials to finished products. Company capital more than doubled between 1960 and 1973. Toyo Menka also began importing hard coking coal from Australia. Other ventures begun in overseas subsidiaries in the 1960s included a fabric-processing mill in Thailand, a cottonseed oil manufacturer in Brazil, and a manufacturer of synthetic textiles in Indonesia. Toyo Menka celebrated its 50th anniversary in 1970 and changed its Japanese name from Toyo Menka to Tomen, although its English name remained Toyo Menka Kaisha, Ltd.

As the oil crisis of the mid-1970s spawned recession in the United States and Europe, Toyo Menka reviewed its internal organization and expanded its product line. In the late 1970s, Toyo Menka began issuing a variety of bonds in Europe and the United States in order to strengthen its financial and capital structure. Bond issuance continued through the 1980s. The recession stalled Toyo Menka's growth; sales only inched up between 1973 and 1978. The company worked on establishing joint overseas ventures and projects. These included forklift trucks in West Germany and sheet glass production in Malaysia. The 1973 oil crisis prompted Toyo Menka to establish new ties to petroleum at home.

Just as the economic climate began to improve, the 1979 oil crisis occured. During the late 1970s, Toyo Menka continued its overseas activities, establishing more companies in Thailand, Indonesia, and Australia. In 1979 Toyo Menka was active with orders for construction machinery, desalination projects, ships, and offshore drilling equipment.

Toyo Menka's energy division separated from the chemicals and fuels division in 1981, as the company's energy-related transactions escalated. This division's main activities are the import of crude oil and liquefied gas, and offshore dealings; the import and export of petroleum products; and uranium imports. It also supplies lubricating oils and fuels to vessels in major ports around the world. Domestic affiliates within this division include many gasoline stations. Toyo Menka also expanded into fields of electronics and data technology in the early 1980s. Tomen Information Systems Corporation was established in 1982, and Tomen Electronics Corporation was founded the following year. Company sales went from US$18 billion in 1980 to US$25 billion in 1984. Another diversification at this time included apparel retailing.

With attention being drawn to the trade imbalances favoring Japan in the mid-1980s, Toyo Menka focused on expanding its domestic activities, and by 1989, domestic transactions had increased dramatically. Toyo Menka is Japan's leading importer of wine, taking advantage of that fast-expanding market. It entered the 1990s with a commitment to expanding into new growth areas and diversifying its development projects. In the fall of 1990, Toyo Menka Kaisha, Ltd. changed its name to Tomen Corporation. Tomen had been Toyo Menka's nickname since its founding. That spring, it spun off its own cotton department as Toyo Cotton (Japan) Company.

Principal Subsidiaries: Tomen America Inc. (U.S.A.); Tomen Canada, Inc.; Tomen de Mexico, S.A. de C.V. (Mexico); Tomen Corporation do Brasil Ltda.; Abe Pump Shaft Corp. (Panama); Ecuatoyo Cia., Ltda. (Ecuador); Tomen Deutschland G.m.b.H. (Germany); Tomen France S.A. (France); Tomen Europe Ltd. (U.K.); Tomen (U.K.) Ltd.; Tomen Iran Co., Ltd.; Grand Biotechnology Co., Ltd. (Taiwan); Korea Fine Chemical Co., Ltd.; Korea Polyol Co., Ltd.; Tomen Hot-Line (Hong Kong) Ltd.; Tomen (Asia) Hong Kong Ltd.; Tomen (Thailand), Ltd.; Tomen Enterprise (Bangkok), Ltd. (Thailand); Norgate Apparel Manufacturing, Inc. (Philippines); Chemphil-LMG, Inc. (Philippines); Toyo Metal Products Pte. Ltd. (Singapore); Growchem Trading(s) Pte. Ltd. (Singapore); Tomen International (M) Sdn. Bhd. (Malaysia); Hino Motors (Malaysia) Sdn. Bhd.; Alpha Industries Sdn. Bhd. (Malaysia); Kohno Plastics (M) Sdn. Bhd. (Malaysia); Myojo Foods Co. (Malaysia) Sdn. Bhd.; Toyo Plastic (Malaysia) Sdn. Bhd.; P.T. Canvas Industry Indonesia; P.T. Indonesia Petroleum Industries; P.T. Kanebo Tomen Sandang Synthetic Mills (Indonesia); P.T. NGK Busi Indonesia; P.T. Tembaga Mulia Semanan (Indonesia); P.T. Teijin Indonesia Fiber Corp.; Pak-Nippon Industries Ltd.; (Pakistan); Tomen Australia Ltd.; Tomen-Ahern Textiles Pty. Ltd. (Australia); ASP Resources (QLD) Pty. Ltd. (Australia); New Guinea Motors (1988) Pty., Ltd. (Papua New Guinea); Tomen (N.Z.) Ltd. (New Zealand); Polymers International, Ltd. (New Zealand); Tomen Netherlands B.V.; Tomen Corporation Espana, S.A. (Spain); Tomen Italia S.P.A. (Italy).

Further Reading: *Toyo Menka Kaisha, Ltd.*, Osaka, Toyo Menka Kaisha, Ltd., [1988]; Roberts, John G., *Mitsui: Three Centuries of Japanese Business,* New York, Weatherhill, 1989.

—Carol I. Keeley

USINOR SACILOR

Immeuble Ile-de-France
4, place de la Pyramide
92070 Paris La Défense Cedex 33
France
(1) 49 00 60 10
Fax: (1) 49 00 56 75

State-Owned Company
Incorporated: 1986
Employees: 97,308
Sales: FFr96.10 billion (US$18.88 billion)

Usinor Sacilor was the result of the merger in 1986 of Usinor and Sacilor, the two major French iron and steel groups. Usinor had existed for over 150 years in the north of France. Sacilor had been incorporated in 1973, but could trace its history back to 1704, when Jean Martin de Wendel bought the ironworks of Hayange in French Lorraine. Usinor Sacilor was in poor shape at the time it was created as a result of a government decision, but has seen a dramatic recovery since. The group whose components had been loss-making for years became profitable again in 1988. It strengthened its presence in international markets by acquiring German and U.S. iron and steel producers. The world's second-largest steelmaker, Usinor Sacilor is above all an iron and steel group, but it appears to be less of a French group at the beginning of the 1990s, a quarter of its total work force being German.

The Sacilor group has deep roots in France's industrial history. It has been associated with the Lorraine region and the de Wendel family since the early 18th century, when Jean Martin de Wendel acquired the ironworks of Hayange in Lorraine. Under de Wendel, the ironworks became one of the largest in France. In 1794, during the French Revolution, the ironworks were able to produce as many as 848 cannonballs, 84 bombshells, and 4,000 bullets per day. In 1822, the de Wendel ironworks gained France's first coke blast furnace. The de Wendel factories increased production at a considerable rate during the industrial boom of France's Second Empire: whereas the plants produced about 20,000 tons of cast iron and a little less iron in 1850, by 1869 more than 130,000 tons of cast iron and 110,000 tons of iron were obtained from the 15 blast furnaces. De Wendel, now the foremost ironmaster in France, employed a work force of 4,000 to fabricate rails, iron bars, iron sheets, tin, and wire. In 1870, however, the Lorraine region was annexed by Germany as a result of its victory over France and

the company was split in two until 1918. The factories that were given back after World War I had been run efficiently by the Germans and the company was able to return to 1914's production level by 1924. De Wendel achieved record production levels in 1929, with 1.66 million tons of cast iron and 1.63 million tons of steel. The shock of the 1929 Depression, which reached France in 1930–1931, followed by World War II, prevented the company from investing capital in modernization during the 1930s and 1940s. In 1948, Sollac (Société Lorraine de Laminage Continu) was formed as a cooperative company by nine different steelmakers, including de Wendel. Sollac was intended to fill the technological gap that had developed during the last 20 years between the French and U.S. steel industries. Sollac began by setting up to produce steel sheets, then added a Kaldo steel plant using pure oxygen in 1960—the Thomas and Martin processes were still predominant in the profession—and finally introduced cold rolling mills and tin-making units.

The year 1948 saw also the creation of Usinor, through the merger of the two largest steel-producing groups of northern France, Denain-Anzin and Nord-Est. The two groups had complementary product lines, with Denain-Anzin oriented toward steel sheets and Nord-Est favoring shaped products. Both companies originated from small plants dating from the 19th century. The Société des Hauts Fourneaux et Forges de Denain-Anzin had been formed in 1849 from the ironworks of Denain, founded in 1835 by François Dumont with the permission of King Louis Philippe, and a similar plant created the same year by Benoit-Auguste Vasseur and located in Anzin. The Société des Forges et Aciéries du Nord-Est had been founded in 1882. It combined the Mines et Usines du Nord et de l'Est and Steinbach and Company, another iron and steel company. The former, created in 1873, was the result of the merger of the blast furnaces of Jarville; the iron factory of Trith Saint Léger, an old factory founded in 1828; and interests in the Houdemont mines. Nord-Est increased its size considerably after World War I through acquisitions and mergers in the mining and iron and steel industries. In 1919 it took over the Usines de l'Espérance, established in Louvroil in 1858 by Victor Dumont. In 1933 it absorbed the Société des Hauts Fourneaux et Laminoirs de la Sambre, a blast furnaces and rolling mills company that originated from the merger of the Hautmont factory, founded in 1871 by Michel Helson, and the Société des Forges et Fonderies de Montataire, established in 1840.

Concentration continued to take place in Lorraine's iron and steel's industry during the 1950s and 1960s. In 1950, the Grand-sons of François de Wendel company merged with the de Wendel company. The year 1950 also saw the creation of Sidélor, a transformation company in which two Sollac partners, the Rombas and the Homécourt groups, took part. In 1963, another merger brought together the UCPMI, another Sollac partner, and the Knutange company to form the company SMS (Société Mosellane de Sidérurgie). Meanwhile, de Wendel and Sidélor decided to form a joint venture, Sacilor, which built a large modern oxygen steel factory at Gandrange. Finally, in 1967, the de Wendel, Sidélor, and SMS groups decided upon a merger. The new group, de Wendel–Sidélor, thus acquired 65% of Sollac's shares and all of Sacilor's shares. In 1968, the group companies produced more than 20 million tons of iron mineral, that is 40% of total French production, and 7.8 million tons of rough steel, that is two-thirds of Lorraine's production and one-third of French production. The work force amounted to more than 60,000.

In 1971 a conversion plan for the new group was issued. It proposed the closing of all the Martin and the Thomas steelworks and generally of all the most obsolete factories, the production of which was to be replaced by that of the leading plant at Gandrange. This policy was intended to enable the company to bridge the increasing competitive gap between Lorraine coal and iron mineral supply and that coming from abroad.

In 1973 the group structures were simplified. De Wendel-Sidélor merged with its own subsidiary Sacilor and its two parent companies, de Wendel and Sidélor Mosellane, to form the new company Sacilor. Close industrial cooperation was achieved between Sacilor and its transformation subsidiary Sollac. In 1975, the first year of the steelmaking crisis in France, the de Wendel and Marine-Firminy groups merged. A holding company, Marine-Wendel, united all the steelmaking interests of the two groups, including their shares in Sollac. Lastly, in 1977, the holding company Marine-Wendel gave to Sacilor those of its industrial interests directly linked to steelmaking.

Usinor had been created in order to set up its own wideband train. The train was constructed in Denain, where the existing blast furnaces and steelworks could supply it with raw materials the train went into operation in 1952. Another decision was even more revolutionary: in 1956, Usinor announced its intention to create a new integrated factory oriented exclusively toward steel sheets. This decision was unusual, in that the plant would not be located in the mainlands, near the coal and iron mines, but by the sea, at Dunkirk. For economical reasons, the new factory was intended to receive raw material supplies from abroad. The preparation lasted for years and the factory, one of the most powerful and modern in the world, officially opened only in 1971.

In 1966 Usinor merged with the company Lorraine-Escaut. Lorraine-Escaut had been created in 1953 with the merger of three ancient steelmaking companies: Senelle-Maubeuge, Longwy, and Escaut et Meuse. It was the last of the great postwar mergers. The merger with Usinor led to the creation of a new holding company, Denain-Nord-Est-Longwy, which controlled about 60 companies through Usinor and Vallourec. Usinor combined the mining, steelmaking, and steel-selling activities while Vallourec controlled all the pipe-making activities which amounted to the three-thirds of the French pipe production.

During the early 1970s, the new group carried out several important projects, such as the construction in Mardyck, near Dunkirk, of a large steel sheet cold mill rolling factory. In 1973, benefiting from the financial difficulties encountered by the de Wendel–Sidélor group as a result of the difficult circumstances prevailing in the steel market and the weight of its restructuring plan in Lorraine, Usinor took a stake of 47.5% in Solmer, another 47.5% of which was retained by Sollac, the founder of the company. Solmer possessed in Fos-sur-mer, near Marseilles, a recent large steelmaking unit using foreign raw materials.

Both Usinor and Sacilor were hit severely by the economic crisis that began in 1975, two years after the first oil shock. While steel prices plummeted because of the diminished demand and the outbreak of the continuous casting, energy and salary costs increased. The two groups kept their work force intact for the first two years, while their financial results deteriorated considerably, aggravated by the fact that the steelmaking groups were already heavily indebted as a result of the modernization plans launched at the beginning of the 1970s.

At the beginning of 1977, the French steelmaking groups made public a steel project that planned reduced steel production, concentration on the leading factories, and the closing of the less-modern units. That same year, the steelmaking profession signed up a ten-year agreement on job cuts, the Steelmaking Profession Social Protection Covenant, with the government. The agreement allowed the firms to put workers into early retirement from the age of 58 years and 8 months and in some cases, 54. The cost was shared between the firms and, for the major part, the state.

In 1979, another merger occurred at the government's initiative, between Denain-Nord-Est-Longwy (DNEL-Usinor) and Chiers-Chatillon-Neuves Maisons. The latter was a somewhat smaller group, also the result of multiple mergers between long-established steelmaking firms—its oldest factory, Chatillon, dated from the 18th century and had belonged to the marshall-duke of Marmont, a Napoleon general. Also in 1979, Usinor took over the Rehon factory from the Cockerill group, while Sacilor became the major shareholder of another old steelmaker, Pompey. Finally, in 1981 the Socialist government decided to make the firms' situation clearer. Sacilor was nationalized by conversion of the state loans while Usinor was controlled up to 90% by the state and nationalized companies.

During the 1980s, FFr100 billion (US$16 billion) were poured by the state into the abyss of the steel industry crisis. About 100,000 jobs were lost, even if the redundant workers benefited from the Steelmaking Profession Social Protection Covenant, which was reconducted from 1987 to 1991. Production capacities were reduced by 20% for flat products and 36% for long products, those most affected by the demand slump. Many of the ancient steelworks, such as Trith-Saint-Léger, Pompey, Vireux-Molhain, Decazeville, and Longwy, had to be closed down. Most of the others, such as Les Dunes, Denain, Hautmont, Gandrange, Hagondange, Homécourt, Neuves-Maisons, and Joeuf, saw their activity reduced. A series of state-monitored mergers, intended to accelerate the restructuring of the French steel industry, began in 1982 when Ugine Steels was integrated into the Sacilor group and Sacilor took a majority stake in the Société Métallurgique de Normandie. Another crash, prompted by a decline in demand, occurred on the steel market in 1983, which led to a much more decisive step: the creation in 1984, as part of the Socialist government's restructuring plan for the steel industry, of Unimetal and Ascometal. Both companies combined entire departments from the rival groups Usinor and Sacilor: Unimetal grouped all the current long products and Ascometal all the special long products. Meanwhile, job cuts became effective from 1984, meeting fierce union resistance initially.

In 1986, the year in which state subsidies for the steel industry were stopped by the European Commission, steel prices broke down again. The merger between the two French giant steelmakers was announced in September 1986 by the Chirac right wing government, with Francis Mer, former number-two at Saint-Gobain Pont-à-Mousson, being appointed president of the two companies and then of Usinor Sacilor. In 1986, Usinor achieved sales of FFr33.7 billion with a work force of 41,000 and lost FFr5 billion. Sacilor achieved sales of FFr42.6 billion, with a work force of 61,000 persons, and made a loss of FFr7.5 billion. The new president set up a drastic plan aimed at boosting productivity in the group: two years later, in 1988, the group employed 80,000 and had sales of FFr78.9 billion. Benefiting from this tremendous effort and from the strengthened demand for steel, in particular flat steel, in the world, Usinor Sacilor made a recovery. From that moment on, Francis Mer felt free to conduct an ambitious international strategy that soon led the group to the second position in world steel-production volume, just behind Nippon Steel, with 23 billion tons compared with Nippon Steel's 28 billion.

This external growth strategy has been aimed simultaneously at steel producers, so as to gain weight in the steel world market, and steel merchants, in order to come nearer to the group's clients; Usinor Sacilor now controls the distribution of about 30% of its output. Usinor Sacilor bought 70% of Saarstahl from German Saar state. In the United States, the group took over J&L Specialty Products Corporation, a top U.S. stainless steel maker; Techalloy Co., a stainless steel product maker; and Alloy & Stainless, Inc., a specialized trade company; and it set up a joint venture with Bethlehem Steel Corporation, and finalized an alliance with major wiremaker,

Georgetown Steel Corp. The group also invested in Italy, taking a 24% stake in Lutrix, a holding company controlling La Magona d'Italia, an important coated steel sheet maker, and then buying 51% of Alessio Tubi. It eventually bought a majority stake in ASD, Britain's second-largest steel distributor. Finally, the group invested in France in CMB Acier, formerly Carnaud Basse-Indre, a packaging steel producer, thus becoming the co-world leader, with Nippon Steel in this sector. Today, the group, one of the most productive in the steel industry, relies on its own strength to face the next downturn in steel world demand, whereas most of its competitors, USX, Thyssen, Hoesch, and even Nippon Steel have been heavily diversifying their activities.

Principal Subsidiaries: Sollac (99.9%); Forges et Aciéries de Dilling (Germany, 95.1%); GTS Industries; Europipe (Germany, 50%); Unimétal; Ascométal; Saarstahl AG (Germany); Ugine SA (96%); Ugine-Savoie; Imphy; CLI (Creusot-Loire Industrie); Forcast International (66%); Fortech (66.1%), GPRI (55.4%); Tubeurop Tréfilunion; Techno Saarstahl; Nozal (65.7%); IMS (58.7%); Saarlux Beteiligung (Germany); Valor; Daval; Edgcomb.

—William Baranès

VIAG

AKTIENGESELLSCHAFT

VIAG AKTIENGESELLSCHAFT

Georg von Boeselager-strasse 25
5300 Bonn
Federal Republic of Germany
(228) 552-01
Fax: (228) 552-2268

Public Company
Incorporated: 1923 as Vereinigte Industrie-Unternehmungen
   Aktiengesellschaft
Employees: 55,848
Sales: DM19.42 billion (US$12.99 billion)
Stock Exchanges: Frankfurt Berlin Bremen Düsseldorf
   Hamburg Hanover Munich Stuttgart

The beginnings of VIAG (Vereinigte Industrie-Unternehmungen Aktiengesellschaft) date back to World War I. Some of the divisions which determine the character of VIAG today—aluminum, chemicals, and energy—developed in the economy of the war years. Soon after the beginning of World War I it became clear that a free enterprise economy would not be able to satisfy wartime production requirements, and that for many sectors a state-run economy was necessary. As early as August 13, 1914, on the instigation of Walther Rathenau, the organizer of the German war industries, and initially under his direction, the *Kriegsrohstoff-Abteilung* (KRA—War Commodities Department) of the Prussian War Ministry was founded, to guarantee the supply of raw materials needed for military purposes—in specific terms, materials for the arms industry, for clothing, and for other military equipment. The KRA used new *Kriegsgesellschaften* (war companies), founded under civil law, to fulfill these functions. These companies were to procure the required products or to arrange for their procurement or manufacture. Kriegsmetall AG, Kriegschemikalien AG, and Kriegswollbedarfs AG were only a few of these large-scale organizations. As a consequence of the economic measures connected with the Hindenburg Program—an economic plan embarked upon in 1916 to strengthen the adaptation of German industry for armaments production—the Prussian War Ministry combined under one organization all the military raw materials businesses and the procurement of substitutes by establishing the *Kriegsamt* (KA—War Office) for the entire *Reich* in November 1916.

The businesses owned by the *Reich*, accumulated during the course of World War I and later combined to form VIAG, were administered after 1919 by Department I (the Industry Department) of the Treasury Ministry.

The German aluminum industry, which had come into being shortly before the war, received a significant impetus from the war; the Hindenburg Program in particular gave further stimulus for its expansion. The company Vereinigte Aluminium Werke AG (VAW), based in Berlin, was founded on April 21, 1917, to manufacture the aluminum needed for the war. All of the country's aluminum interests were gradually collected in this company. Initially owned half by the *Reich* and half by a consortium made up of Chemische Fabrik Friesheim-Elektron AG and Metallbank and Metallurgische Gesellschaft AG, at the end of the war the *Reich* took over full ownership. The newly constructed Lauta plant, which started operation in October 1918, consisted not only of an aluminum works but also of an aluminum oxide factory and a large power station connected to the brown coal—or lignite—mine Erika, owned by Ilse-Bergbau AG; the power station was sold in 1920, however, to Mitteldeutsches Kraftwerk AG. The high energy requirements of the aluminum industry meant that electricity from brown coal and from water power were particularly important. After the war, Erftwerk AG, running an aluminum works at Grevenbroich, and, like VAW, half-owned by the *Reich* until the end of the war, when it assumed full ownership, and the aluinum works at Töging am Inn were incorporated into VAW. The locations of these production sites were primarily determined by the energy supply—constant, where possible—offered by neighboring electricity plants. Only a few days after the foundation of VAW, on April 27, 1917, the Innwerk Bayerische Aluminium AG—known as Innwerk AG from 1938—was established at Munich-Töging. The purpose of this company was to provide a constant energy supply for the operation of the aluminum works.

Like VAW, the *Reich's* nitrogen works owed their creation to the shortage of raw materials which arose during World War I. Before the war, the production of explosives and of fertilizers containing nitrogen was based principally on the processing of Chilean saltpeter, imports of which to Germany could be cut off in the event of war. For this reason, Bayerische Stickstoff-Werke AG (BStW) was founded at Trostberg as early as 1908, basing its production on the Frank Caro method and partly owned by the Deutsche Bank. In 1915, commissioned by the *Reich*, BStW began to construct two calcium cyanide factories, at Piesteritz near Wittenberg and at Chorzow in Upper Silesia. The Oberschlesische Stickstoff-Werke AG (OStW), to which the Chorzow factory was sold, was founded in December 1916. After the separation of Upper Silesia in 1922, the factory was appropriated by the Polish state. The Piesteritz factory remained under the *Reich's* ownership. It was incorporated into Mitteldeutsche Stickstoff-Werke Ag (MStW) on February 24, 1920, and all the company's shares—amounting to 60 million marks—were acquired by the *Reich*. Finally, on May 28, 1920, Bayerische Kraftwerke AG—BKW, from 1939 known as Süddeutsche Kalkstickstoffwerke (SKW) AG—was formally incorporated, with its headquarters in Munich.

Apart from aluminum and nitrogen, the country's industrial interests were directed toward the electric power industry, as the production processes of both the aluminum and calcium cyanide industries were dependent on a sufficient supply of energy. As early as February 9, 1915, the BStW and the Braunkohlenwerk Golpa-Jessnitz AG (BG-JAG) at Halle had signed a treaty, by order of the *Reich,* whereby the BG-JAG brown coal works undertook to establish a large power plant for the production of nitrogen at Piesteritz. Until this time BG-JAG, founded in 1892, had operated a pit in the Bitterfeld brown coal field. As brown coal was now only used to produce electrical current, the company changed its name to Electrowerke AG (EWAG). The large Zschornewitz power station had already begun operation by the end of 1915. In 1918 EWAG began to develop grid electricity supply as its core activity. Deutsche Werke Aktiengesellschaft (DW) was founded at Berlin on December 4, 1919, with the object of converting about 20 armaments workshops and war shipyards owned by the *Reich* and the states of Prussia, Bavaria, and Saxony to peacetime production.

Another important company which was later to form the basis of VIAG was the Reichs-Kredit-Gesellschaft, which dated from 1919. In order to regulate the financial management of the *Kriegsgesellschaften,* founded during the economic control of World War I, the Imperial Treasury established a Statistical Office for War Companies. After the end of World War I, this office was gradually extended, producing the Reichs-Kredit- und Krontrollstelle GmbH, based in Berlin and founded on July 20, 1919. This company in turn was transformed into the Reichs-Kredit-Gesellschaft mbH (ERKA) in September 1922. After the foundation of VIAG, ERKA, which remained stock-owned, became the company's bank.

At the end of March 1923 the National Treasury Ministry, in particular concerned with administering and supervising the *Reich's* industrial interests, was dissolved, in connection with the government's cost-cutting plans. At the same time, efforts were made to find a means of managing the *Reich's* wide-ranging industrial interests, hitherto assigned to the Industry Department, in an unbureaucratic way, organizing them on consistent, purely commercial principles. The two functions of the Industry Department were separated: the actual management of the companies was to be transferred to a specially created holding company, while the pure financial custody and management were transferred to the National Finance Ministry.

The holding company, based in Berlin, was founded on March 7, 1923, under the name Vereinigte Industrie-Unternehmungen Aktiengesellschaft (VIAG). The objects of the company were as follows: the holding of shares in commercial enterprises of every type; the operation, administration and financing of companies, as well as the undertaking of related banking transactions; and, in general, the adoption of any measures which seemed appropriate to the management board in order to attain or further the aims of the company. The company was entitled to establish branches both in Germany and abroad and to enter into cooperation agreements. Thus VIAG was defined purely as a stock holding company, which was not directly involved in production.

The founder of VIAG was the German *Reich.* In the foundation proceedings of March 7, 1923, the share capital was set at 600 million marks, divided into 600,000 shares at 1,000 marks apiece. The *Reich* was shareholder. Subsidiaries were the Reichs-Kredit-Gesellschaft mbH, Elektrowerke AG, Vereinigte Aluminium-Werke AG, and Duetsche Werke AG. Shareholdings in Elektrowerke AG and the Württembergische Landes-Elektrizitäts AG, in Vereinigte Aluminium-Werke AG and Innwerk, in Bayerische Aluminium AG and Deutsche Werke AG were among the most important of the assets transferred.

In the years following its foundation, VIAG concentrated on its core activities of aluminum, nitrogen, and electricity and strengthened the economic integration of these areas. The geographical centers of the group's activities emerged as central Germany and upper Bavaria. In central Germany, the company had EWAG, operating the Lauta power station using brown coal from Ilse-Bergbau AG, the aluminum works of VAW, and the calcium cyanide works at Peisteritz, supplied with electricity by the Mitteldeutsche Stickstoffwerke. Similarly, in upper Bavaria the hydroelectric power stations of Innwerk, Bayerische Aluminum AG, and Alzwerke GmbH worked together with the Töging aluminum factory—acquired by VAW in 1925, and the carbide factory of Bayerische Kraftwerk AG. Most of VIAG's shareholdings which did not fit with the core group activities were disposed of in the following years.

Before the beginning of the 1930s, the management of VIAG restructured its individual factories to attain profitability. The only income earned by VIAG was the dividends from its group companies. VIAG's net profits rose by 42% to 12 million reichsmarks between 1925 and 1929. In the financial year 1924–1925, a dividend of 5% was paid out for the first time. In the following years the dividend rose to 8%. A significant initial undertaking by the group was the conversion in 1925 of the separate factories of Deutsche Werke AG into independent companies better able to acquire production requirements for themselves, such as the factory at Spandau, which was converted into Deutsche Industriewerke AG (DIW), and was the only one of these companies to remain in the VIAG group.

After the years of crisis, the armament process which began in 1933 brought an upturn in business for VIAG as for other companies. The number of employees rose by 66% over 1932–1933 to 30,387. In the years before the outbreak of war, the number rose to 70,000. VIAG and its companies, as a group owned directly or indirectly by the *Reich,* were harnessed into the armament program of the National Socialist government, especially after 1936. By 1935 the production capacities of group subsidiaries were already being used to the full. All VIAG's businesses extended their plants. VAW built a new aluminum oxide plant, Nabwerk, at Schwandorf, for example. At the same time, nitrogen production was increased considerably.

The *Anschluss*—or annexation—of Austria to the German *Reich* in March 1938 brought a significant increase in VIAG's sphere of activity. One task was looking after electro-industrial interests in the territories which had been adjoined to the German *Reich.* In accordance with this objective VIAG founded the Österreichische Elektrowerke in Vienna on April 22, 1938; the company was renamed Alpen-Elektrowerke Aktiengesellschaft (AEW) one month later. In connection with the takeover of the Austrian National Bank by the Reichsbank and the transfer of the Österreichische Industriekredit AG to the Österreichische Creditanstalt-Wiener Bankverein (CA), VIAG received 76% of the bank's converted share capital of 70.7 million reichsmarks as a contribution to an increase in its own capital base.

High demand for aluminum, nitrogen, and electricity in the German war economy ensured that the capacity of the individual factories was used to the full. New investments were required in all these sectors. In 1943, the fully owned subsidiaries of VIAG made investments to the value of around 220 million reichsmarks.

VIAG expanded its activities during the war. In 1939, for example, the group raised its shareholding in Ilse-Bergbau AG to more than 60% by acquiring further ordinary shares worth 10 million reichsmarks. It also acquired further shares in Innwerk AG from the state of Bavaria, as well as 50% of the share capital the electricity company Bayernwerk Aktiengesellschaft (BAG) in Munich. Together with the state of Bavaria and the electricity company Rheinisch-Westfälisches Elektrizitätswerke AG (RWE), VIAG founded the Bayerische Wasserkraftwerke Aktiengesellschaft (BAWAG), based in Munich on January 26, 1940.

When the war ended, VIAG was sequestrated and administered, at first, by trustees. VIAG's situation between May 1945 and July 1951 was determined by the military rule in the four zones of occupation. Ludger Westrick, the general trustee appointed by the Bavarian state authorities and previously a director of VAW, is largely to be credited with extricating VIAG from military law through his attempts to restructure the business in cooperation with the Allies. This was made all the more difficult as dismantling of works under the Allied war repatriations program and a shortage of raw materials dominated the day-to-day business. Only when the revelant Allied authorities lifted all bans, restrictions, and controls in 1951 could a complete reorganization of VIAG begin with the election of a management board and the formation of a supervisory board. Bonn became the base of the new company, which in its first deutschmark accounts recorded a share capital which had dwindled to DM160 million.

After 1945 VIAG'S subsidiaries were again divided into three groups, into companies producing electricity, companies consuming electricity, and other companies of various sorts.

After the financial year 1949–1950, net profits increased every year, reaching DM1.45 million in 1951–1952. In 1952–1953 a dividend, of 3%, was paid for the first time. VIAG had created a solid foundation for further progress. Shareholdings of VIAG totaled DM254.06 million making up 95.9% of total group assets.

During the period from 1953 to 1960, processes of consolidation, rationalization, and modernization dominated the business activities of the separate VIAG works. Dividends were raised by 1% each year, so that by 1959–1960 VIAG was able to pay out dividends of 10%. Bayernwerk AG raised its capital by DM50 million to DM150 million in order to increase its utilization of primary energy sources in Bavaria, such as brown coal, which were cheap at the time. This strategy led to a decisive change in VIAG's energy supply base in subsequent years. Whereas, in 1956, two-thirds of the electricity was produced by hydroelectric power and only one-third by steam power, by 1960 thermal electricity generation from brown coal had already overtaken hydroelectric power. VIAG and its subsidiaries now formed a modern, stable group. In the following years the company devoted itself to expanding its subsidiaries to meet the continually growing markets for electricity, aluminum, and chemical products. Between 1960 and 1972, VIAG invested over DM5 billion in its subsidiaries.

In the 1970s, two issues were at the center of public interest: capital-raising for investments and privatization. The government's privatization plans—after its successes with Preussag and the Volkswagen works—aroused heated public debate and dominated the headlines in press articles on VIAG from the end of the 1950s until the actual privatization in 1986. Every now and then—as in 1968-1969—the plans to privatize VIAG escalated to become an electoral issue and a subject of dispute between the parties. Another significant problem for VIAG was the fact that the company could not go to the capital markets to raise funds for financing and investment. The group could only obtain the funds needed for investment through bank loans, that is, by incurring debt. VIAG could not develop freely in the market and so could only work with restricted resources; in spite of its successful evolution, the group faced a serious obstacle to growth. Expansion through acquisition, indispensable for the effective development to growth. Expansion through acquisition, indispensable for the effective development of an industrial group, was impossible. Internal expansion also proved extremely difficult. The consequences of these problems could be seen in high reserves, depreciation, and dividends which were disproportionately low in relation to the company's success.

Although the federal government, as sole shareholder, had received DM124 million in dividends since 1953, it could not make funds available for any increase in capital. Because of this, VIAG was forced to increase its own reserves by drawing on current profits. In 1968 the share capital of DM254 million was raised by DM50 million to DM304 million at a rate of 220%. The Kreditanstalt für Wiederaufbau—a bank for reconstruction founded in 1948 offering middle- to long-term loans from the Marshall Plan as well as its own funds-took up the new shares. In this way VIAG acquired new funds amounting to DM110 million. From this time onwards, the Kreditanstalt für Wiederaufbau held around 16% of the increased share capital.

Associate companies continued to form the basis of VIAG's success in the 1970s. Growing industrialization and the progressive mechanization of work processes led to an increase in electricity consumption in VIAG's aluminum and calcium cyanide business. The aluminum works in particular, with the expansion and increased use of their capacity, needed significantly more electricity. Electrochemical production, with electricity consumption of just over four billion kilowatt hours (kWh), had a correspondingly high share of the total. Through the continuing expansion of electricity production, especially in the field production from steam power, VIAG's need for externally generated electricity was steadily reduced. VIAG's share of total electricity production in the federal republic stood at around 8% in 1965; by 1970 it had sunk to around 7%.

Since VIAG's foundation, aluminum had been regarded as the principal business of the group. Although electric power production grew faster after World War II, VAW remained the group's largest business in terms both of turnover and of work force. VAW—with its subsidiaries, Vereinigte Leichtmetall-Werke GmbH (known from 1971 as VAW Leichtmetall GmbH), Aluminum Norf GmbH, Aluminium-Oxid Stade GmbH, and V.A.W. of America Inc.—dominated VIAG's business activities throughout the 1970s and until the beginning of the 1980s. In 1960, VAW had a 70% share of aluminum production in the federal republic and met 30% of the country's aluminum requirements. In 1971 VAW produced 248,000 tons of primary aluminum in total.

The aluminum crisis dominated the whole of the 1970s and the first years of the 1980s. The crisis had begun as early as 1968, when the federal republic placed high taxes on exports but reduced taxes on imports. This measure was equivalent to a revaluation of the deutschmark by 4%. In 1969 the federal government raised the value of the deutschmark by 8.5%

making US\$1 equivalent to DM3.66. As the aluminum price was largely dependent on the dollar, any speculation on the currency exchange market involving an upward valuation of the deutschmark or a devaluation of the dollar had catastrophic results for the aluminum market. The two oil crises of 1973 and 1976, with the attendant rise in the price of oil required for electricity production, exacerbated the situation. In 1975, production declined significantly, leading to a reduction in working hours for VIAG's employees; the company lost DM120 million. Only in 1983 was the crisis successfully overcome. SKW at Trostberg was restructured during this period. While the share of the main product, calcium cyanide, declined to around a third of the total output, acrylic nitril production increased substantially. In 1981–1982 Hoechst AG sold its 50% share in SKW to VIAG, which now owned 100% of the company.

In the 1970s, electrical power production acquired increasing importance. Of the total profits of over DM47.5 million produced by subsidiaries in 1973, DM42 million came from the electrical sector. In particular, Bayernwerk AG, in which VIAG had a 38.86% shareholding—it had to hand over some of its BAG shares to the Bavarian state after the war—was operating with great success. Electricity production by VIAG companies in this sector amounted to 22.6 billion kWh in 1973. Gradually nuclear energy came to play an increasingly important role. The share of electricity produced by nuclear power, which had amounted to only 4% in 1978, had risen to 70% by 1988, after the incorporation into the grid system of the nuclear power, which had amounted to only 4% in 1978, had risen to 70% by 1988, after the incorporation into the grid system of the nuclear power station Von Isar II in Bavaria. Hydroelectric power now only played a minor role. By the mid-1980s, VIAG had managed to overcome the crisis in the aluminum sector and had successfully completed the restructuring of its activities. At the beginning of 1981 VIAG acquired 50% of Thyssengas GmbH—an important step on the path of acquisition.

After a partial privatization in 1986 the group was fully privatized in 1988. From May 3, 1988, onward, the federal government and the Kreditanstalt Für Wiederaufbau sold their remaining shares in VIAG at a rate of DM210. In the second stage of the privatization, 6.96 million shares of DM50 each, with a nominal value of DM348 million were placed with a consortium of 51 banks under the leadership of Deutsche Bank AG.

Apart from the privatization, the period from 1984 to 1990 was marked by the sale and purchase of new shareholdings and by the restructuring of subsidiaries. Freed from state restrictions, VIAG was now able to be active on the capital markets, and could think of further acquisitions. At the beginning of 1986, VIAG acquired 15% of the share capital of Didier-Werke AG, at Wiesbaden. In subsequent years, further shareholdings were added. On January 1, 1990, VIAG took over Klöckner & Co. (KlöCo), at Duisburg-Hamborn, a company which had gotten into difficulties, together with Bayernwerk AG. Steel accounted for about half of the KlöCo's turnover amounting to nearly DM12 billion; one-third of turnover came from energy, building products, heating technology, machine tools, transport, and textile importing; 14% of turnover came form raw materials, chemicals, and environmental technology; and 4% from trading in industrial plant.

Bayernwerk AG, Munich and VIAG established a joint industrial holding company, based in Berlin and named VBB Viag-Bayernwerk-Beteiligungs-Gesellschaft mbH. VIAG and Bayernwerk AG each had a 50% share in this company. On January 1990, VBB acquired a 24.99% stake in Gerresheimer Glas AG at Düsseldorf. Apart from these acquisitions, VIAG also acquired a series of other shareholdings between 1985 and 1990 through its subsidiaries, especially VAW, SKW-Trostberg AG, and Bayernwerk AG. The reunification of Germany offers VIAG possibilities for a new field of activity, especially in the central German factories which were lost at the end of World War II.

Principal Subsidiaries: Vereinigte Aluminium-Werke AG (99.99%); SKW Trostberg AG, (99.99%); Innwerk AG (99.96%); Ilse Bergbau GmbH (99.99%); Thyssengas GmbH (50%); VBB VIAG-Bayernwerk-Beteiligungsgesellschaft mbH (50%); Bayernwerk AG (38.8%); Didier-Werke AG (51%); Klöckner & Co. AG; Gerresheimer Glas AG (51%).

Further Reading: Guggenheim, Felix, *Der deutsche reichseigene Industriekonzern,* Zürich, Girsberger & Co. Verlag, 1925; Karplus, Egon, *Die Deutschen Werke, Ein Beispiel für die Stellung des Staates als Unternehmer in KinKurrenz mit der Privatindustrie,* GieBen (Philosophische Dissertation), 1927; Heissmann, Ernst, *Die Reichselektrowerke, Ein Beispiel für die Wirtschaftlichkeit von Staatsunternehmungen,* Berlin, Verlag R. & H. Hoppenstadt, 1931; *30 Jahre Bayernwerk AG, Bayerische Elektrizitätsversorgung 1921–1951,* München, Bayernwerk AG, Ilseder Hütte, 1951; Treue, Wilhelm, *Die Geschichte der Ilseder Hütte,* Peine, 1960; Rauch, Ernst, *Geschichte der Hüttenaluminiumindustrie in der westlichen Welt,* Düsseldorf, Aluminium-Verlag GmbH, 1962; Hofmann, Walter, *Private Bank in öffentlichem Besitz, Kleine Geschichte der Reichs-Kredit Gesellschaft AG,* Mainz, V. Nase & Köhler, 1980.

—Manfred Pohl
Translated from the German by Susan Mackervoy

VOEST-ALPINE STAHL AG

VOEST-ALPINE STAHL AG

A-4031 Linz
Austria
(0732) 585-2907
Fax: (0732) 585-0116

State-Owned Company
Incorporated: 1945 as Vereinigte Österreichische Eisen- und
  Stahlwerke AG
Employees: 31,309
Sales: Sch45.70 billion (US$4.34 billion)

Effectively, the Austrian steel industry consists of one company, Voest-Alpine Stahl AG, which manufactures bulk steel and special steel products—although there are still a few independent steel producers in Austria. The company has been in the public sector throughout its history, but there have been changes in its affiliations with other companies in the public sector. The company was founded in 1938 as the Reichswerke Hermann Göring in Linz, Austria, as an affiliate of the state-owned Berlin Göring-Werke. Construction of a large steelworks began in 1939 and continued throughout World War II; the first two blast furnaces were completed in 1941, and by 1944 the complex included open hearth and electric furnaces for steel conversion, and a nitrogen plant. Allied bombing caused severe damage to the works in 1944.

In 1945 the U.S. military government in Austria changed the name of the company to Vereinigte Österreichische Eisen-und Stahlwerke AG (The Austrian Iron and Steelworks), of which "Voest" is an acronym. Reconstruction of the works commenced, and production began again in 1945. In the following year, 1946, one million tons of crude steel were melted in the company's electric furnace.

Between 1947 and 1950 the reconstruction and expansion of the works continued apace. In 1947 the first blast furnace, the first open hearth furnace, and the first coke ovens started production. The company commenced production of steels for highly stressed welded structures in 1948. In 1949 Voest decided to build the world's first steel mill with oxygen converters; Voest led the world steel industry with this development and by the 1970s oxygen converters dominated world steel production, replacing both open hearth furnaces and Bessemer converters. The oxygen process is considered by many steel industry experts to be the most important innovation in steelmaking in modern times. Voest played a leading part in the development of the process, and this development

was important in the growth of Voest. The company gained an advantage for its own steel production and created a downstream business supplying other steelworks with steelmaking equipment.

Oxygen converters, which involve the blowing of oxygen at high velocity onto the surface of molten metal in a furnace, greatly reduce the cycle time for melts and thereby increase capacity and reduce the costs per ton of the steel produced. Although the advantages of using oxygen rather than air in steelmaking furnaces had long been recognized, the development of oxygen converters had been delayed owing to the lack of cheap supplies of oxygen. The nitrogen plant that had been built at Linz during the war produced oxygen as a by-product, and the plant engineers at Linz decided to take advantage of this oxygen production to carry out a systematic program of studies.

At first the Voest engineers arranged for oxygen to be blown into the space above the iron melt in an open-hearth furnace. Although they succeeded in accelerating the conversion of iron to steel in this way, the increased flame temperature destroyed the root of the furnace and the regenerators for preheating air became clogged with dust. In the experiments which followed, they tried feeding oxygen into an electric furnace, but the heat again proved destructive and ruined the electrode holders. At this point the Linz engineers consulted the Swiss engineer Robert Dürrer who, with Heinrich Hellbruegge, was conducting experiments using oxygen in a two-ton Bessemer converter and in an electric furnace. They were injecting a jet of oxygen into the molten iron through a water-cooled lance placed just above the surface of the metal.

The first trials of the Dürrer system at Linz failed; the heat destroyed the lance, the stream of oxygen blown deep into the melt caused damage to the bottom and other refractories of the vessel, and the treatment failed to remove enough of the phosphorus impurity from the iron. Then the Linz engineers made their breakthrough. Abandoning the accepted practices of the time, they reduced the impact pressures of the oxygen jet by using a different nozzle and raising the lance further from the surface of the melt. The new approach worked well; steel of good quality was produced and there was no damage to the equipment.

The initial experiments in 1949 were made with a two-ton vessel, but the Linz engineers went on to make further tests with larger units, and in late 1952 they built process units on a fully commercial scale with vessels of 35-ton capacity. In 1953 a second plant with oxygen converters was installed at Donawitz in the ironmaking district of Styria in Austria. The oxygen converter system has since been called the LD process, from the initials of the Austrian towns Linz and Donawitz where the first two plants were installed.

The development of the oxygen process by Voest is an example of a small company—in terms of the world steel industry—making a decisive technical breakthrough and leaving large U.S., German, Japanese, and U.K. companies following in its wake. By 1988 Voest and its associated companies had installed 140 oxygen converters in steelworks around the world. Another strategy adopted by Voest was to develop a broad range of downstream engineering businesses; in 1950 the engineering shops started production of lathes, and the development of water power plants began. The combination of electric steelmaking capacity, access to cheap electricity, and the oxygen converters made Voest a leader in high quality steel production and made its costs highly competitive at a time when the European steel industry was expanding rapidly and was competitive in world markets. During the early 1950s a new slabbing mill and cold rolling stand were added to the works. At the same time, downstream expansion continued with the establishment of an industrial plant construction division.

The company continued to expand rapidly between 1955 and 1960. In 1955 a third oxygen converter was completed, and in 1959 a second LD steel mill with two 50-ton converters started production. In 1958 Voest collaborated with the German company Krupp to build an LD steel mill at Rourkela in India. Blast furnace output passed one million tons for the first time in 1955. A new 4.2 meter plate mill was added in 1958 and a new coke oven battery in 1959.

In the first half of the 1960s, several state-owned businesses were transferred to Voest, extending the company's downstream activities. Notable LD developments were the placing of a Soviet order for an LD steel mill in 1963 and the supplying of 300-ton oxygen converters to a steel mill at Taranto, Italy.

The latter half of the decade saw the spread of activities of the process plant contracting division. Examples showing the range of contracts obtained by the division were the construction of a fertilizer plant in Poland in 1965, supply of a palletizing plant for iron ore in Brazil in 1966, and of a fertilizer plant in France in 1969. In the same year an ethylene plant was completed for ÖMV, another company in the Austrian public sector. Expansion of steel production continued, and in 1969 crude steel production capacity was increased from 2.3 million tons to 3.1 million tons a year. In 1966, production of special steels began and a sixth oxygen converter started up. A first continuous casting machine started trials in the second LD steel mill in 1968, and in 1970 a multi-roll stand was added, which made possible the production of very thin steel sheets.

For Voest, the 1970s began with reorganization and technical development. In 1972 Voest became part of the holding company ÖIAG, Austria's largest industrial group. In 1973, as part of the reorganization, Voest merged with the other leading Austrian steel producer, Alpine, which operated the Donawitz steelworks. The year 1972 was a high point for investment activity. A second continuous casting machine was added to the second LD steel mill, while a third LD steel mill with a 120-ton converter and a third continuous casting machine were under construction. The wide strip mill was extended, and a cold rolling mill and a wide-strip galvanizing plant were added to the complex. Finally, a new apprentice-training shop was built. The new plants started production in 1973 and 1974.

By the time the new plants which had been started in the early 1970s were completed, the first oil shock had occurred and the European steel industry had entered a serious downturn. The cyclical fall in demand was reinforced by a switch away from steel towards other materials; greater efficiency in the use of steel, involving the substitution of thinner gauges of steel; serious recession in some European steel-using industries, such as shipbuilding; and the emergence of new low-cost steel producing countries. The change in the industrial environment affected the Austrian steel industry. In 1975, the Austrian special steels industry was concentrated at the company VEW, followed in 1976 by a merger of the separate nationalized units of the Austrian steel stockholding trade to form Voest-Alpine Stahlhandel.

Technical rationalization followed. In 1976 the open-hearth steel mill at Linz was closed, and in 1977 the first LD steel mill was shut. However, new developments were occurring at the same time. In 1979, the development of the harbor on the Traun river made possible the shipment of components for process plants weighing up to 750 tons. In 1979 and 1980 a wire mill and a continuous caster were built at the Donawitz works, which had been added to the group, and a seamless tube mill was added to the Kindberg works, another works which had been incorporated into the group. An electronics plant was opened at Engerwitzdorf in 1979 marking a new diversification for the group.

The industrial climate for the steel industry in the 1980s was far removed from the expansion of the early postwar period. The decade started with the second oil shock and recession. Between 1979 and 1985, the Austrian government helped the ÖIAG group with financial transfers, and the largest share of these went to the steel companies Voest-Alpine and VEW. By the end of the 1980s, a recovery had been achieved. Over the decade some updating of equipment took place. In 1981 a fourth continuous casting machine was commissioned. In 1982 a tubeworks for tubes used in oil fields was completed at Kindberg. In 1983, the world's largest plasma melting furnace was started at the Linz works, and in 1985 an electrolytic strip coating plant was built.

The tougher industrial environment of the early 1980s exposed the weaknesses of the policy of diversification into a wide range of engineering and other industries. In 1985 the company's trading losses reached Sch12 billion, as the result of an unsuccessful microchip venture, participation in the unsuccessful Bayon Steel Corporation in the United States, and disastrous losses at a subsidiary which became involved in speculative oil deals. This series of events led to the resignation of the chief executive and the formulation of a restructuring plan which involved 10,000 job losses. The new management team was led by chief executive Dr. Herbert Lewinsky.

Changing political perceptions of the efficiency of large conglomerate corporations led to more fundamental reorganization; in 1988 ÖIAG, the holding company which had controlled Voest since the end of 1972, was reorganized into seven separate companies, of which Voest-Alpine Stahl AG was one. The Austrian government had decided to partly privatize ÖIAG. The new Voest-Alpine Stahl AG's activities include steel making at the Linz works, steel rolling at the Linz and Donawitz works, the manufacture of special steels—high speed and tool steels—by the Bohler companies, which are subsidiaries of Voest-Alpine Stahl at Kapfenberg and at Dusseldorf in Germany, and steel stockholding and steel scrap processing. The reorganization was designed to make the companies in the old ÖIAG group more efficient, to bring management decision-making nearer to the market, and to expand the businesses internationally. In April 1990 a tie-up between the Swedish company Uddeholm and Bohler, to form a strategic alliance between the two special steel producers, was announced.

Since the reorganization, Voest-Alpine has specialized in making and shaping steel; the downstream activities which Voest developed or acquired, including the process plant activities, have been hived off into separate companies. In 1989 Voest-Alpine produced 3.35 million tons of crude steel and 2.76

million tons of flat rolled products at Linz. The company had a wide range of steel finishing equipment; apart from rolling mills, it had equipment for making tubes, rails, and wire; drop forging facilities—which make shapes through the progressive forming of sheet metal in matched dies under repetitive blows of a hammer; and a steel foundry. The company's main investments in 1989 were designed to improve the quality of the products of the rolling mills; in addition, a second galvanizing plant was constructed.

The company estimates that high tech products now account for about 10% of turnover, and it aims to raise this share to 30%. The company's research-and-development program, which will play a part in achieving this target, includes work on new steelmaking processes, improvements to existing processing technology, and applications. One speciality is surface-treated products, including galvanized steel and plastic-coated strip steel. Evidence of the company's commitment to training is its employment of nearly 500 apprentices, equivalent to 4% of its work force.

Austria is a relatively small country, and Voest has to export in order to sell its output; 70% of its 1988 turnover came from exports. Its principal export market is the European Economic Community, followed by Comecon; only 5% of turnover is exported overseas, outside Europe and Comecon. Voest is well located to share in the demand for steel that will be generated by investment in the former East Germany and in Eastern European countries. In the postwar period, Voest's success was founded on electric furnaces with access to hydroelectric power and on its brilliant breakthrough with oxygen converters. It is close to markets, and has developed specialties such as coated steels. Whether these factors will be enough to ensure the company's success in the 1990s remains to be seen.

Principal Subsidiaries: Voest-Alpine Stahl Linz; Voest-Alpine Stahl Donawitz; Bohler Kapfenberg; Bohler Düsseldorf (Germany); Voest-Alpine Stahlhandel; Voest-Alpine Rohst-Handel.

Further Reading: McGannon, *The Making, Shaping and Treating of Steel,* Pittsburgh, United States Steel Corporation, 1971; Cockerill, A., *The Steel Industry,* Cambridge, Cambridge University Press, 1974; Nasbeth, L. and G.F. Ray, *The Diffusion of New Industrial Processes,* Cambridge, Cambridge University Press, 1974; Hogan, W.T., *World Steel in the 1980s,* Lexington, Lexington Books, 1983; Jones, K., *Politics vs Economics in the World Steel Trade,* London, Allen & Unwin, 1986; Hudson, R. and D. Sadler, *The International Steel Industry,* London, Routledge, 1989.

—Cliff Pratten

WEIRTON STEEL CORPORATION

400 Three Springs Drive
Weirton, West Virginia 26062
U.S.A.
(304) 797-2000
Fax: (304) 797-2067

Public Company
Incorporated: 1982
Employees: 7,200
Sales: $1.19 billion
Stock Exchange: New York

The fortunes of Weirton, West Virginia, a quintessential company town, have fallen and risen with those of Weirton Steel Corporation. A huge steel plant founded there in 1909 became part of National Steel Corporation in 1929, but decades later, in the 1970s, when National Steel faced a declining economy and a declining steel industry, Weirton Steel's future looked grim. In 1983 Weirton Steel's employees saved their town and their company with an innovative employee-takeover plan. In 1984, Weirton Steel became the largest employee-owned company in the nation. Since the conversion, Weirton Steel has flourished. In 1989 Weirton Steel sold about 23% of its stock to the public; employees retained the remaining stock. Weirton's integrated steel mill—which converts raw materials such as iron ore, limestone, and coke into finished steel products— is the United States's seventh largest, and is West Virginia's largest, industrial enterprise.

In 1905 Ernest Tener Weir, a Pittsburgh, Pennsylvania–area steel employee, enlisted a partner to buy the Phillips Sheet and Tin Plate Company, an ailing steel company in Clarksburg, West Virginia. The plant flourished under Weir's stewardship, and within four years he was looking for a new site to accommodate expansion. The site would have to have access to coal mines, water sources, river and rail transportation, and centers of industry.

Weir found his ideal industrial site in the northern finger of West Virginia that separates Ohio and Pennsylvania, about 39 miles from Pittsburgh. In 1909 Weir began building on 105 acres he purchased near the hamlet of Hollidays Cove. By the end of the year, Weir had ten steel mills operating, and mill workers had started to come in from as far away as Greece and Italy.

The boom continued throughout the decade. By 1920, more than 15,000 people lived in the area. As growth continued, Hollidays Cove expanded rapidly and new communities like

Weirton, Weirton Heights, and Marland Heights sprang up nearby. In 1947 all these villages would be incorporated into the city of Weirton.

The vast majority of the town's residents worked in Weir's mills. In return, Ernest Weir met many of their needs. He built homes, supplied utilities, and provided police and fire protection in the town's early decades. Later, he would build churches, a library, and leisure facilities for the use of his employees.

The expansion of the city coincided with the expansion of Weir's mills. In 1910, ten more mills were added. In 1911, Weir acquired the 12-mill Pope Tin Plate Company in Steubenville, Ohio, and in 1915 and 1916, two more hot mills were constructed at Weir's strip steel plant. Weirton's facility thus became the flagship of Weir's enterprise, and in 1918 Weir named his concern Weirton Steel.

The firm grew throughout the 1910s and the 1920s, as expansion allowed the plant to verge toward vertical integration. In 1923, the Weirton coke plant went into operation. In the following years, new furnaces, hearths, and river docks were constructed. In 1925 Weir incorporated Weirton Steel Company. In 1929 Weirton Steel Company merged with Great Lakes Steel Corporation and Hanna Iron Ore Company to form National Steel Corporation, which immediately became one of the nation's largest steelmakers. Henceforth, Weirton Steel became a subsidiary of National Steel, although it retained its own administration and management, with Weir continuing as chairman and J.C. Williams as president.

Although Weirton Steel workers certainly benefited from Weir's largesse, relations between management and work force were often less than harmonious. During the 1920s, Weir successfully fended off the growing unions from his plants. In the 1930s, however, Weir was confronted with twin challenges: the bitter strikes that plagued mines and mills all through Appalachia, and New Deal legislation and institutions that were intended to protect laborers.

The Great Depression wrought havoc in the steel industry; demand for steel declined steadily, causing industry retrenchment. As New Deal measures helped bring about a recovery, labor problems, and not production records, put Weirton Steel in the news in 1933. In the midst of a strike, nearly 1,000 workers were repulsed by tear-gas bombs when they tried to stop cars carrying workers from Weirton Steel's Steubenville plant.

Weir had refused at first to submit to arbitration, but the National Labor Board, led by Senator Robert Wagner, gave the Weirton Steel workers a public hearing, and helped obtain an agreement that allowed the workers to return to their jobs and elect representatives. Striking workers also ended a long strike without explicit recognition of their union. Weir found a way around the established unions by forming the Weirton Independent Union. For many years, Weirton Steel paid the salaries of that union's officials.

In 1936, T.E. Millsop, who had been with Weirton Steel since 1926, was named president upon Williams's death, continuing a tradition of promoting from within. In fact, throughout the many decades that National Steel controlled Weirton Steel, Weirton Steel workers were generally chosen to lead the company.

In 1938, Weirton turned over its idle Clarksburg plant to the local chamber of commerce. Weir's original tin-plate plant had become obsolete because of increased freight charges, outdated machinery, and expansion of the Weirton and Steubenville plants. That same year, in an attempt to modernize further, Weirton Steel built a quality-control laboratory opposite the company's main office.

During World War II, the steel industry adapted to help the nation's war effort. In 1942 the War Production Board appealed to the steel industry to devise plans to increase and tailor output for army use. In March of that year, Weirton Steel became the first member of the steel industry to respond, establishing a special plant committee, and soliciting suggestions from employees. When the War Production Board ordered a reduction in tin-plate operations, Weir, now chairman of National Steel Corporation, shut down Weirton Steel's Steubenville plant in October 1942. Partly because of the rush to meet the war effort, Weirton Steel made new records in 1942, twice establishing world records for steel ingot production, and producing an average of 5,080 net tons of ingot steel a day. In 1945 Weirton pleaded no contest and was fined for obtaining critical materials in order to build an emergency hospital but instead using the items for air conditioning at a company-owned country club.

The economy and the steel industry shifted gears after World War II. President Harry S Truman called on the steel industry to expand its capacity, produce more steel, and lower prices, but industry officials resisted. Still, the 1950s and 1960s brought almost continuous growth and expansion for Weirton Steel. New blast furnaces, products, and production methods were developed. In 1960 Weirton continued its commitment to research by beginning construction on a steel research center. Concerns about pollution inspired new measures, like the institution of open hearth smoke controls in 1963, and studies on the environmental effects of steel production.

By the time Ernest Weir died in 1957, there were signs of bad times ahead for the steel industry. Throughout the 1950s, for example, total U.S. steel exports remained static, and the nation's share of the world steel trade dropped from 53.6% in 1947 to 6.9% 1960. Most of this was the result of the reconstruction in Japan and Europe and these countries' reintegration into the world's economy, and not to a decline in steel use. Instead of relying on domestic steel producers, U.S. industrial firms imported increasing quantities of steel from abroad. In fact, between 1950 and 1965, total U.S. imports of steel grew from 1,077 tons to 10,383 tons.

The rise in imports, coupled with rising labor costs, crippled the U.S. steel industry. Debates raged between the industry and the government over the imposition of price controls and the enactment of protectionist measures. In 1969 the federal government finally imposed import quotas for foreign steel.

Throughout the 1960s, Weirton Steel developed new products and production methods. In 1967 basic oxygen steel making began. In 1968, Weirton Steel inaugurated its continuous casting process, which represented a fundamental change in production technique. A new four-strand slab caster boosted production, efficiency, and quality at the main plant. In 1973 a coke plant, which provided coke for the Weirton plants, went into operation.

During the 1970s the interests of Weirton Steel and its parent company, National Steel, increasingly diverged. Throughout the 1960s and 1970s, National Steel, then America's third-largest steelmaker, used its earnings to diversify—buying interests in savings and loans, and investing in the production of aluminum—rather than investing in its current facilities. Eventually, National Steel began to plan for a future that did not include Weirton and its 13,000 employees.

When National Steel began to consider closing the Weirton plant for three weeks in 1977, it was an ominous foreshadowing. The slipping economy aggravated Weirton Steel's situation. With the inflation of the late 1970s, and the recession of the 1980s, Weirton's fortunes took a turn for the worse. Between 1978 and 1982, net sales decreased from $1.09 billion to $904 million, while operating expenses soared from $79 million to $103 million. Pre-tax earnings plunged from $16 million in 1978 to a loss of $104 million in 1982.

At the same time, shipment of products declined from 2.94 million tons in 1978 to 1.68 million tons in 1982. At this point, tin-plate accounted for about half of Weirton's shipments, with galvanized steel accounting for about a fifth, cold-roll steel accounting for a tenth, and hot rolled bands accounting for about a tenth as well.

The slowdowns took their toll. In 1981, Weirton Steel experienced the first major layoffs in its history. By the end of the year, more than 3,000 workers had lost their jobs. As the town's economy ground to a halt, workers were forced onto public aid, peripheral businesses began to decline, and Weirton's young began to leave in increasing numbers. The company's coke plant closed in 1982, and 275 more workers were laid off.

In 1982 National Steel further shocked Weirton's 24,000 residents by announcing that the aging mill complex would be largely shut down, but National Steel offered an alternative. Employees could buy the plant with borrowed money and try to run it on their own.

In November 1982 Weirton Steel Corporation was organized to acquire the assets of National Steel's Weirton Steel division. An agreement for the corporation was reached in April 1983. Under the terms of the agreement, employee-owned Weirton Steel Corporation bought the Weirton Steel division from National Steel for $194.2 million in cash and debt. The workers accepted a 20% pay cut and a six-year wage freeze in exchange for a stake in the factories. Under this employee stock ownership plan (ESOP) the company would henceforth be owned by the employees and directed by seven outside directors. The same year, Robert L. Loughhead, previously president of Copperweld Steel Company, joined the firm as president. Also in 1983, National Steel Corporation reorganized, and changed its name to National Intergroup, Inc.

Weirton Steel instantly became the nation's largest employee-owned company. It would soon become the nation's most successful. While many steelmakers were losing money, Weirton posted earnings of $48.3 million on sales of $845.5 million in the first nine months of 1984. That year, however, Weirton Steel was forced to lay off 250 more workers.

In 1985, sales increased by 9.1% over 1984, as income rose about 1.5%. The following year, an increase in orders led Weirton Steel to start a third blast furnace, and the company recalled about 60 laid-off workers. The same year, Weirton Steel exercised its option to buy the Steubenville mill plant, which had been closed since 1981, from National Intergroup.

Weirton Steel enjoyed 16 consecutive profitable quarters after the transition, which proved a boon to employees. Under the terms of the ESOP, employees would receive a share of corporate profits. In 1987 alone, some 8,400 Weirton Steel workers received average profit-sharing checks of $4,500, the highest of any steel firm. This pay-out came after profits in 1987 of $80 million, a dramatic increase from the 1986 figure of $30 million. Sales increased to $1.3 billion in 1987 from $1.17 billion in 1986, and production rose from 2.8 million tons in 1986 to 3.3 million tons in 1987, placing Weirton Steel seventh among U.S. steel producers.

Weirton Steel has displayed a new commitment to improving its facilities. In 1984 for example, Weirton hired the Mellon Institute, a division of Carnegie-Mellon University, to conduct metallurgical studies on surface quality. In 1986, the Department of Energy (DOE) provided $65 million for the construction of the first Kohle-reduction iron process plant in the United States, to be built in Weirton. The plant was to be part of a DOE program to implement environmentally clean coal technology, but was aborted when Weirton decided to invest elsewhere.

In 1987 Loughhead stepped down, and director Herbert Elish was appointed to the post of chairman, president, and chief executive officer. Under Elish, Weirton Steel had suffered some setbacks, although the company has also moved forward with large-scale modernization, most notably the construction of state-of-the-art continuous caster and rebuilt hot mill. Between 1987 and 1989 production actually declined from 3.2 million tons to 2.9 million tons. Between 1988 and 1989 sales remained basically constant, decreasing slightly. Shipments decreased by about 8.4%, and the profit-sharing provision decreased from $75 million in 1988 to $21.9 million in 1989. This figure reflected both a decline in income and a decrease in the percentage of profits paid to employees, from 50% to 35%.

The decline in profit-sharing was due to another Weirton financing innovation. In search the means to avoid an ESOP stock repurchase liability and to permit a $740 million investment in modernization, Weirton decided to go public in 1989. It offered four million shares—about 23% of its shares—at $14.50 per share on the New York Stock Exchange.

Weirton is the largest U.S. producer of tin-plate—with 23% of the domestic market—used largely to make food cans. By uniting and working with management and Wall Street, Weirton's employees were able to rejuvenate their company, and their company town. This large-scale experiment in employee ownership has succeeded.

Further Reading: "A Bicentennial Year Look at Weirton and its Heritage of Steel," Weirton, West Virginia, *Weirton Employee Bulletin,* 1976; "Town Bids to Save Itself," *Fortune,* April 18, 1983; McManus, George J., "Weirton Steel Begins to Pick Itself Up," *Chilton's Iron Age,* November 7, 1983; "Making Money—and History—at Weirton," *Business Week,* November 12, 1984.

—Daniel Gross

ZAMBIA INDUSTRIAL AND MINING CORPORATION LTD.

Post Office Box 30090
Zimco House
Cairo Road
Lusaka
Zambia
(1) 227925

State-Owned Company
Incorporated: 1970
Employees: 133,945
Sales: K60.54 billion (US$3.03 billion)

The Zambia Industrial and Mining Corporation (Zimco), a holding company for all Zambian state interests, is one of the largest concerns in sub-Saharan Africa. It controls 125 principal companies relating to every major industrial activity in Zambia, including mining, consumer goods manufacturing, finance, transportation, agriculture, energy, and hoteliery. The product of Zambia's far-reaching nationalization program since its independence from Great Britain in 1964, Zimco dominates the nation's troubled economy.

Although Zimco was incorporated in 1970, its beginnings date back a decade earlier to a company created by the colonial Northern Rhodesian government. The Industrial Development Corporation of Zambia Ltd. (Indeco), as it was called, attempted to energize the colony's industry, which lagged behind that of neighboring southern Rhodesia. With only limited success, Indeco vacillated between state and private control. It finally re-emerged as a state-owned company in August 1964, just as the colony was on the brink of independence. That momentous event, on October 24, brought to power nationalist leader Kenneth D. Kaunda. Facing enormous disparities of wealth, owing to the amassing of fortune by a small minority of white settlers who exploited the country's rich mineral resources, Kaunda set about transforming the economy. In keeping with his socialist philosophy of "humanism," wealth generated by industry and mining was to be used for the nation's overall development. Indeco was to be the vehicle for accomplishing this.

The plan got off to a slow start. Kaunda allowed Indeco's management, comprising conservative white bureaucrats, to remain unchanged. The company's industrial profile remained static. However, dramatic changes took place in June 1965, when Kaunda appointed Greek businessman Andrew Sardanis

chairman and chief executive of Indeco. Sardanis, who became a Zambian citizen at the country's independence, was one of the few white settlers to have actively supported the black liberation movement. Only 34 years old when he took over Indeco, the dynamic and shrewd Sardanis was to have a major influence over the Zambian economy for many years to come.

As head of Indeco, Sardanis attempted to launch new ventures and encourage foreign investment. But he found that foreign companies, fearing political instability and restrictions on profit, were wary of investing in a socialist African nation.

Kaunda gave Indeco a major boost in 1968 with the Mulungushi reforms, under which the government manipulated 25 leading companies into selling it 51% of their shares. Indeco absorbed the government's investment in those companies, which fell into four main categories: department stores, breweries, transport companies, and suppliers of building materials. These same reforms made it illegal for non-Zambian citizens to trade outside the city centers, forcing hundreds of Indian residents to sell or shut their rural-based businesses.

A second batch of reforms in 1969 extended state interests into the giant copper mining industry and led to the creation of Zimco. Under the Matero Reforms, under which Zambia's mines were partly nationalized, the government bought a controlling interest in the two largest mining concerns, one owned by Anglo American Corporation (Anglo) and the other by Roan Selection Trust Ltd. (RST), then a subsidiary of AMAX of the United States. ITM International, a company founded by Sardanis, has since acquired RST. The government subsequently reorganized the companies under the new names of Nchanga Consolidated Copper Mines (NCCM) and Roan Consolidated Mines Ltd. (RCM).

Now, for the first time since white colonials in the 1920s began mining the copper belt stretching along Zambia's northern border, the majority of the country's population was to benefit from its most lucrative industry. Moreover, the government's move came during a record year for copper production, in which 12% of the worlds's copper—more than 700,000 tons—came from Zambia, making it the third-largest producer.

A new company, the Mining Development Corporation (Mindeco), sprang up to manage the state's mining investments. With two major holding companies, Indeco and Mindeco, the government wanted to put an overall holding company in charge. Zimco was created to fulfill that function. As the government expanded into even more industries, it created new sub-holding companies to manage related businesses, all under the authority of Zimco.

Ideally, the creation of Zimco was to have minimized political interference in the running of state-owned businesses by serving as a buffer between the government and its investments. In reality, government officials exercized direct control over Zimco, which was a company on paper only and had no executive management. Managers of sub-holding companies reported directly to the relevant government ministries, which in turn reported to Kaunda, who retained the title of chairman.

Zimco faced problems almost from the start. Its genesis marked the end of the high world copper prices that had characterized the 1960s. In the financial year 1971 to 1972, prices fell drastically. The following decade revealed the volatile nature of the world copper market, as prices rose and fell dramatically.

The health of the Zambian economy rose and fell correspondingly. More than 50% of the nation's revenue came from tax on copper earnings. In addition, the country relied on copper for foreign exchange, which in turn is vital for the maintenance of industry. So the decline that began in 1971 and was to dominate the next two decades signalled economic ruin for the nation.

The government has reorganized the mining industry several times. In 1973, the same year as a major mining fire, it declared itself unhappy with the 1969 mining buy-out agreements, which allowed the original owners to manage themselves under the supervision of Mindeco. Abolishing those agreements, it put Zambians rather than foreigners in charge of the companies. As a kind of compensation, it simultaneously announced that 8- to 12-year bonds issued in 1969 as payment for the buy-outs could be redeemed immediately. The government took out costly loans to make good that promise.

In 1981, falling copper prices did not stop the government from upgrading its interests in the mining companies from 51% to 60%. The following year, the government attempted to strengthen the industry by merging its two companies, NCCM and RCM, creating Zambia Consolidated Copper Mines Ltd. (ZCCM). Zimco held 60.3% of the shares, Anglo held on to a 27.3% interest, through Zambia Copper Investments, and RST International had a 6.9% interest. Private concerns in the United States and the United Kingdom held the remaining shares.

Meanwhile, Zimco itself was also going through a metamorphosis. In 1978, amid one of many economic stabilization programs launched under the advice of the International Monetary Fund, Kaunda for the first time gave the company a full-time board of directors, with former government minister Jameson Mapoma appointed director general. Kaunda, who remained chairman, filled Zimco's ranks with civil servants and trade unionists.

Over the years, Zimco's management positions continued to be filled by political appointees, a feature that was later to bring the company under attack. Mapoma was succeeded in the mid-1980s by Evans I.L. Willima, a member of the government's Central Committee. In 1978, in an attempt to streamline Zimco, Kaunda abolished all the sub-holding companies other than Indeco and the National Import and Export Corporation Limited.

The depressed copper prices of the 1980s, and the resulting economic chaos, led to further changes. In the early 1980s, in one of several austerity programs, Zimco sold off its smaller companies to private interests. In 1986, after six years of mining copper at a loss, Zimco began to lay off employees. By March 1988, thousands of jobs had been lost.

All the while, Zimco ostensibly attempted to diversify its interests and reduce its dependence on copper. Indeco, the second largest employer after ZCCM, accounting for 75% of the country's manufacturing activity, proved of less help than had been expected. After the initial buy-out of 25 companies, Indeco continued to acquire interests in industrial companies.

Indeco helped generate new ventures, including plants for manufacturing vehicles, chemical fertilizer, glass bottles, and copper wire. It later launched a K300 million (US$6.5 million) expansion of its fertilizer plant, Nitrogen Chemicals of Zambia, the largest project undertaken by Zimco outside of the mining arena.

However, Indeco's progress was slowed by several factors. Limited access to foreign exchange—which plagued every sector of Zambia's economy—prevented manufacturers from importing the spare parts they needed. The manufacturing sector was never able to reduce its dependence on such goods from abroad. Serious errors of judgement, such as an extensive steel and iron project which had to be abandoned after it was found to be unfeasible in 1979, wasted massive amounts of money. Firms closed and production slowed. By 1985, some firms were operating at only 30% of capacity.

In the wake of this dismal year, Indeco attempted to revitalize its subsidiaries by bringing in outside management and investment. This approach has shown encouraging results. Zambia Breweries has been especially successful and Indeco's overall profits climbed to a record high in the financial year 1988 to 1989.

Kaunda targeted agriculture early on as one of the primary areas in which Zimco was to expand. He inherited at independence a country that had been underdeveloped deliberately, in line with an agreement between its colonial rulers and those in Southern Rhodesia, with whom they were linked through the Central African Federation. Northern Rhodesia was designated the market for excess produce from its southern neighbor and thus could not produce too much of its own.

Zimco ventures into agriculture had yielded poor results. Export restrictions, price controls, inadequate financing and recurrent drought constrained its tea processing and packaging plants, and its farms, dairies, and ranches, all of which consistently operated at a loss. As it had done with manufacturing, in the late 1980s Zimco sought foreign investment to stimulate growth. Partnerships with several European nations—coupled with the relaxation of state restrictions and controls—have fostered a turnaround. Increased productivity helped Zambia meet its food requirements for the first time in 1989.

The latter part of the 1980s brought other encouraging signs for Zimco. In mid-1987, copper prices began to rise again and hit a record high of £2,000 (US$1,052) a ton on the London Metal Exchange in 1988. For the first time since it was formed, ZCCM in mid-1989 announced a dividend for that financial year. In the following year, the company showed a record net profit of K2.6 billion (US$56.5 million). The good news was not to last. Copper prices took a further downward turn in 1991, once again underscoring the unpredictability of the market. Yet even if prices were to stabilize at a high rate, an economic recovery seemed unlikely.

While a market turnaround once would have led to overflowing coffers, copper revenue is now limited by ZCCM's low production, which has dropped by 40% over the past two decades. 1989 showed an improvement, with production rising 7.9% to 448,468 tons. However, Zimco's longterm future is uncertain, even if production rises markedly.

This is so because Zambia's copper industry—the mainstay of the economy—is expected to last only 20 more years before its reserves are depleted. Moreover, the decrepit conditions of the mines themselves, which are decades old, makes it difficult to extract the copper that is left. The lack of foreign exchange, too, prevents the installation of more modern equipment.

In the face of all this, ZCCM has undertaken a plan to make the mines more efficient. In an attempt to reduce its reliance on expensive imported parts, it has acquired a foundry and stepped up production. It also hopes to counter chronic delays and disruptions in copper transport by purchasing additional wagons and locomotives for Zambia railways and Tazara railway, leading to Dar-es-Salaam in Tanzania. New technology imported from Chilean mines is to upgrade Zambia's largest smelter. Several mines, including the Nachanga open pit, the second largest in the world, are to be rehabilitated.

Dramatic events in Zambia over the past year—rioting over food price rises, an alleged coup attempt, and persistent calls for a multi-party system—have led to a political liberalization which will have important ramifications for Zimco. It could even lead to the abolition of the company.

In May 1990, Kaunda announced plans to set up a stock market in Zambia, on which up to 49% of shares in Zimco would be sold to private interests. Three months later, a parliamentary committee looking into Zimco's affairs resolved that Kaunda's proposal had not gone far enough. Lambasting the company for inefficiency and top-heavy management, and saying that it was a company that did not produce anything, had no relevant function, and was an unneccessary drain on resources, the committee called for its dissolution. The committee also recommended that Indeco be streamlined, that the appointment of managers in government companies no longer be political, and that the privatization of these companies be effected quickly.

The outcome of these recommendations is as yet unclear. Zimco is still in existence, its partial privatization waiting for the establishment of a Zambian stock market. It is likely that the International Monetary Fund, which is overseeing a new restructuring program, will have some influence on its future.

Zimco is to divest fully of its shareholding in seven companies: AFE Ltd., Consolidated Tyre Services Ltd., Crushed Stone Sales Ltd., Eagle Travel Ltd., Mwinilunga Canneries Ltd., Zambia Clay Industries Ltd., and Zambezi Saw Mills (1968) Ltd. This divestment is part of the Zambian government's overall privatization policy. Public offers and stock schemes will follow once the infrastructure is in place. The privatization program is to rejuvenate the Zambian economy through greater competition, liberalization of the business environment, attraction of foreign investment, and the encouragement of ownership of shares by Zambians. The sales will be by competitive tender. Other enterprises will therefore be offered for sale in accordance with the government's established timetable for privatization.

Principal Subsidiaries: Industrial Development Corporation of Zambia Ltd. (Indeco); Zambia Consolidated Mines Ltd. (ZCCM).

Further Reading: Anthony, Martin, *Minding Their Own Business: Zambia's Struggle Against Western Control*, London, Hutchinson & Company Ltd., 1972; Taylor, Karen, "ZCCM-Tightening the Copperbelt," *Metal Bulletin*, March 26, 1990; "ZCCM Looks Ahead," *Southern African Economist*, October/November 1990; "Zambia, Country Profile," *The Economist Intelligence Unit 1990–91*, 1990; Roberts, Andrew D., and Christopher Colclough, *Africa South of the Sahara 1990*, London, Europa Publications Limited, 1990.

—Nina Shapiro

PAPER & FORESTRY

ABITIBI-PRICE INC.
AMCOR LIMITED
AVERY DENNISON CORPORATION
BOISE CASCADE CORPORATION
BOWATER PLC
BUNZL PLC
CHAMPION INTERNATIONAL
    CORPORATION
DAIO PAPER CORPORATION
DAISHOWA PAPER MANUFACTURING
    CO., LTD.
DOMTAR INC.
ENSO-GUTZEIT OY
FLETCHER CHALLENGE LTD.
GEORGIA-PACIFIC CORPORATION
HONSHU PAPER CO., LTD.
INTERNATIONAL PAPER COMPANY
JAMES RIVER CORPORATION
    OF VIRGINIA
JAPAN PULP AND PAPER COMPANY
    LIMITED
JEFFERSON SMURFIT GROUP PLC

JUJO PAPER CO., LTD.
KYMMENE CORPORATION
LOUISIANA-PACIFIC CORPORATION
MACMILLAN BLOEDEL LIMITED
THE MEAD CORPORATION
METSÄ-SERLA OY
MO OCH DOMSJÖ AB
OJI PAPER CO., LTD.
PWA GROUP
RENGO CO., LTD.
SANYO-KOKUSAKU PULP CO., LTD.
SCOTT PAPER COMPANY
STONE CONTAINER CORPORATION
STORA KOPPARBERGS BERGSLAGS AB
SVENSKA CELLULOSA AKTIEBOLAGET
TEMPLE-INLAND INC.
UNION CAMP CORPORATION
UNITED PAPER MILLS LTD. (YHTYNEET
    PAPERITEHTAAT OY)
WESTVACO CORPORATION
WEYERHAEUSER COMPANY
WILLAMETTE INDUSTRIES, INC.

ABITIBI-PRICE

ABITIBI-PRICE INC.

2 First Canadian Place
Toronto, Ontario M5X 1A9
Canada
(416) 369-6700
Fax: (416) 369-6790

Public Company
Incorporated: 1912 as Abitibi Pulp & Paper Co. Limited
Employees: 14,300
Sales: C$3.09 billion (US$2.66 billion)
Stock Exchanges: Toronto Montreal Vancouver New York

Abitibi-Price Inc. is the world's largest maker of newsprint and a diversified manufacturer and distributor of office, building, and paper products. Since 1981 Abitibi-Price has been controlled by Olympia & York, the Toronto-based real estate empire run by the Reichmann family, but has continued to operate with little interference from its 85%-owners. Abitibi-Price's core businesses in pulp and paper are notoriously cyclical and the company suffered a 14-year receivership during and after the Great Depression, but since then it has been among the most successful of Canada's many forest-products firms.

Along with much of the Canadian paper industry, Abitibi-Price owes its existence to the bitter squabbling that developed in the latter part of the 19th century between U.S. manufacturers and consumers of newsprint. Ever since the newspaper industry had converted from rag-based paper to paper made from the pulp of trees in the 1870s, it had been troubled by recurring overcapacity and disastrous price wars, followed by attempts to moderate competition by mergers and combinations. The most ambitious of these was the creation in the 1890s of International Paper Company from the assets of 19 U.S. paper concerns. In the first decade of the 20th century International Paper controlled nearly 75% of the U.S. newsprint market, a situation that elicited charges of monopoly and price gouging from the publishers of newspapers. The publishers were able to publicize widely their accusations, sometimes coupling them with warnings about the need to protect freedom of the press from coercive economic forces. They eventually convinced the U.S. Congress to remove a long-standing tariff on imported paper products. The lifting of the tariff in 1913 prompted a rush to build plants in Canada, which by virtue of its abundant forests and water power was a natural site for pulp and paper manufacture. In the year 1911

alone, some 81 new forestry companies had been created in Canada, in anticipation of the lifting of the tariff. It was in the midst of this stampede, in 1913, that Abitibi Power & Paper Company Limited had its origins.

Abitibi's founder was an American named Frank H. Anson, born in 1859 in Niles, Michigan. Before coming to the paper business, Anson had worked as a railroad ticket agent, rubber prospector, exporter, and as general superintendent of Ogilvie Flour Mills in Montreal. While at Ogilvie, Anson became interested in the mining wealth of Ontario's northern reaches, and in 1909 Anson hired two young men from McGill University to prospect for him in that remote part of Canada. The students found no minerals but did recommend that Anson start a paper mill along the Abitibi River, from whose swift current electrical and mechanical power could be generated to run such an operation. With the abolition of the U.S. paper tariff drawing closer every day, Anson enlisted the financial backing of Shirley Ogilvie, son of the Ogilvie Flour Mill family, and in 1913 erected the Abitibi Pulp & Paper Co. Limited mill on the Abitibi River 300 miles north of Toronto at Iroquois Falls. In 1914 Abitibi Pulp & Paper changed its name and reincorporated as Abitibi Power & Paper Company Limited, since the firm also sold electric power from its hydroelectric facility. Anson's timing was very good: World War I soon drove up the price of newsprint to an all-time peak of US$65 per ton, and the new Canadian paper companies enjoyed unrestricted access to the immense U.S. markets.

So successful were the paper companies on both sides of the border that another round of investigations of the industry was launched, and in 1917 the U.S. Department of Justice began antitrust prosecution of the members of an industrywide cooperative group called the News Print Manufacturers Association. The association's membership pleaded no contest, paid US$11,000 in fines, and dissolved the organization, none of which prevented the price of newsprint from nearly doubling by 1920 to a new record of US$112.60 per ton. The newsprint industry's history of antitrust allegations and cyclical depressions seems to be a result of three factors: the enormous cost of building new plant capacity; the relative inelasticity of demand for newsprint, sales of which do not tend to increase when its price drops; and the highly influential voice of the product's consumers, the newspaper community. Since competition often proved fatal, newsprint manufacturers often tried to curb competition, resulting in well-publicized accusations by the newspapers of antitrust violations.

The postwar price peak encouraged a full decade of non-stop expansion in the Canadian paper industry, which nearly doubled its capacity by the year 1930. The consequence of this expansion was a long decline in the price of newsprint, which, by the end of the decade, fell to about US$62 per ton, and a growing overcapacity, which, as early as 1928, threw the industry into a premature depression all its own.

Abitibi Power & Paper had participated enthusiastically in the decade of expansion. It entered the fine-paper business with the purchase of a sulfite pulp mill at Smooth Rock Falls, Ontario; acquired substantial interests in Manitoba Paper Company and Sainte Anne Paper Company; and built its own mills to the extent that it became one of the industry's more important competitors. Faced with the problems of increased capacity and dropping product price, Abitibi and its fellow manufacturers concluded that their best chance for collective survival was to amalgamate their holdings. Accordingly, in 1928 Abitibi engineered a quintuple merger, buying up the remainder of Manitoba Paper and Sainte Anne Paper and adding three others—Spanish River Pulp and Paper Mills, Fort William Power Company, and Murray Bay Paper Company. These, and a number of subsequent purchases by Abitibi, proved disastrous, but at the time it was hoped that by means of consolidation the industry could prevent price competition as well as increase production efficiency. The strategy might have succeeded in a thriving economy, but instead Abitibi was hit by the Depression and soon was in desperate straits.

By 1932 sales had dropped to a fraction of their earlier levels, while the company's C$50 million debt was more than four times what it had been in 1927. This combination could not long be sustained, and on June 1, 1932, Abitibi defaulted on interest payments and was thrown into receivership. For the next 14 years Abitibi was directed by a court-appointed receiver, whose task it was to stabilize the company's finances, pay down the outstanding debts, and return the company to its shareholders at some future date. By 1933 the price of newsprint finally stabilized, allowing Abitibi to begin the long road back to solvency. The remainder of the 1930s was not a bad period for Abitibi, which managed to earn a fairly steady 15%–20% operating income for use in debt reduction and maintenance of its physical assets. World War II revived the economy, and in 1940 Abitibi sales jumped immediately and remained between C$25 million and C$30 million for the duration of the war, providing the company with an excellent return and setting the stage for an end to receivership.

In 1943 the premier of Ontario appointed a committee for the purpose of designing a plan to take Abitibi out of receivership, and after the committee's recommendations were accepted by all the creditors in 1946, the company was formally independent once again. Abitibi's 14-year receivership was the longest and most important in the history of Canadian industry, a trauma that would leave its mark in the form of a conservative corporate philosophy and deep skepticism about future expansion of capacity. Abitibi's experience during the Depression was only an extreme example of the Canadian paper industry as a whole; and when a remarkable postwar surge in demand for newsprint raised and prompted U.S. demands for increased capacity, the Canadian producers generally chose to increase production speed at existing plants rather than add new ones.

Abitibi chief executive Douglas W. Ambridge strongly concurred with the prevalent conservatism, guiding Abitibi through two postwar decades of bountiful sales and profit increases while avoiding unnecessary capital expenditures. In this he was helped by the extraordinary expansion the company had undertaken in 1928, which provided Abitibi with a reserve of production capacity so great that corporate assets did not surpass those of 1928 until 30 years afterward. Abitibi thus merely made use of what plants it had to meet the fast increasing demand during the 1950s, allowing Ambridge to keep debt low and the earnings per share extremely high. After the years of receivership, the 1950s were a new golden age.

Dissatisfaction among U.S. publishers with Canadian reluctance to expand capacity led to a series of investigations of the industry, of which only one—in 1939—led to the filing of suit by the Justice Department for antitrust violations. It is hard to determine what degree of collusion, if any, existed among the

Canadian newsprint manufacturers during the period in question, but the continual allegations encouraged the U.S. government to offer substantial tax incentives to its domestic forestry business, which began to chip away at Canada's market share. Most of the new U.S. plants were built in the South, where labor rates were low by Canadian standards and an unusually strong grade of indigenous kraft paper allowed the manufacture of a more durable newsprint.

In 1965 Abitibi Power & Paper Company Limited changed its name to Abitibi Paper Company Ltd. Abitibi had been feeling the effects of the new U.S. presence as early as 1962, when, together with the rest of the Canadian industry, it entered a decade of declining net income and diminished share of the critical U.S. market. To counteract this trend, Abitibi overcame its habitual reluctance to expand with the 1968 purchases of Cox Newsprint, Inc. and Cox Woodlands Company for US$36.58 million. Cox, located in Augusta, Georgia, added 150,000 tons per year of newsprint capacity to Abitibi's Canadian holdings of 1.1 million tons, and gave the company a presence in the booming southern industry.

A new generation of leaders at Abitibi, headed up by chief executive officer Tom Bell and chief operating officer Harry Rosier, became increasingly aggressive in the search for additional capacity. When three exceptionally lean years were followed by the upsurge of 1973–1974, in which short span Abitibi sales soared from C$307 million to C$552 million and its capacity was strained, Rosier suggested that it would be cheaper for the company to buy existing mills than to build them from scratch. After a brief search for likely targets Bell and Rosier, in late 1974 went after and won control of 54% of the outstanding common shares of The Price Company Limited, a fellow Canadian paper concern with 1974 sales of C$335 million. Like Abitibi, Price was strongest in newsprint and kraft production, but it had no fine-paper and building-materials divisions, and it recorded a significantly higher proportion of its sales outside North America than did Abitibi. Both companies had modest but profitable base-metal mining operations in Canada, and together they controlled rights to about 50,000 square miles of forest land—an area somewhat smaller than the state of Illinois. Price was a company much older than Abitibi, dating back to the early 19th century and the British navy's need for a new source of lumber for its masts. In 1910, William Price had been sent by a leading London lumber merchant to Canada to organize the new operation, and Price subsequently started the company bearing his name.

No sooner had Abitibi completed its 22-day C$130.11 million conquest of The Price Company than the newsprint market collapsed, cutting the combined companies' 1975 net by two-thirds, at a time when its debt was nearly doubling. Once again, Abitibi's poor timing led indirectly to a change in ownership. Caught in a cash squeeze, Abitibi tried to placate union demands with big pay hikes and thereby avoid a disastrous strike; instead the unions pushed their advantage and forced the strike anyway. The walkout was bitter and lasted for months, and by the time the economy rebounded in 1977 Abitibi was still trying to put its shaken house in order. In October 1978 Abitibi agreed to buy about 10% of Price's outstanding stock from Consolidated-Bathurst—a Canadian company that had bid against Abitibi for control of Price in 1974 and still held 10% of Price's stock. Later that month, Abitibi purchased

Price's remaining shares. Abitibi paid about C$95 million for the 46% outstanding.

In December 1978 Consolidated-Bathurst bought 10% of Abitibi's stock and set off a prolonged bidding war for control of the company. When the dust settled 15 months later Abitibi-Price—which had assumed its present name in October 1979—was part of the Reichmann brothers' extraordinary business domain, their family-owned Olympia & York paying C$670 million for 92% of the company's stock. Olympia & York's stake stood at 85% in late 1990. So vast are the real estate and stock holdings of the Reichmanns that Abitibi-Price figures as a footnote in their annual accounting, but perhaps for that reason the brothers appear to be the ideal silent partner for Abitibi-Price's management, offering great financial strength when needed but never meddling in the affairs of a business they know little about.

Since that time, Abitibi-Price has made a concerted effort to lessen its dependence on the brutally cyclical newsprint business. By the end of the 1980s the company's diversified group operated the largest network of paper distributors in Canada; the largest envelope manufacturer and largest school and office supplies maker; and one of the leading producers of building materials in the United States. The diversified group in 1990 accounted for approximately 50% of corporate revenue, the remainder generated by the paper group's two divisions of newsprint and printing papers. Newsprint is easily the most profitable segment, however, and remains the heart of Abitibi-Price's various holdings; which means that the company has not yet succeeded in escaping the cyclic ups and downs of that industry. After four straight years of bullish profits, the bottom dropped out once again in 1989, and in that year's annual report management calmly admitted that the picture would not improve for at least 18 months. In 1990 Abitibi-Price lost C$45 million. Experienced cyclists know better than to beat around the bush.

Principal Subsidiaries: Abitibi-Price Corporation; Abitibi-Price Refinance Inc.; Abitibi-Price Sales Company Limited; Axidata Inc.; Gaspesia Pulp & Paper Company Limited (51%); Grand Falls Central Railway Company Limited; Mattabi Mines Limited (40%).

Further Reading: Mathias, Philip, *Takeover,* Toronto, Maclean-Hunter, 1976.

—Jonathan Martin

AMCOR LIMITED

South Gate, South Melbourne
Victoria 3205
Australia
(03) 615 9000
Fax: (03) 614 2924

Public Company
Incorporated: 1926 as Australian Paper Manufacturers Ltd.
Employees 16,700
Sales: A$4.50 billion (US$3.48 billion)
Stock Exchange: Associated Australian Stock Exchanges

Amcor Limited is among the top 20 Australian companies with extensive interests in metal, plastic, and paper packaging. Amcor also has substantial interests in pulp and paper and other forest products, in tissue and personal-care markets, and in trading and distribution of paper, packaging, and other products, together with a large investment in Mayne Nickless Ltd., a major Australian transport services and security company.

Its head office is in Victoria's capital, Melbourne, with which it has been associated since its earliest days. The group's employees are now spread through 11 countries—Australia, New Zealand, the United States, the United Kingdom, Canada, France, Hong Kong, Singapore, Malaysia, the People's Republic of China, and Papua New Guinea. It is the leader of the Australian packaging industry, is the largest integrated producer of pulp, paper, and other forest products, and is Australia's largest private forest plantation owner with 85,000 hectares of land. Amcor adopted its current name in May 1985 and its major period of expansion and acquisition has taken place since that time.

Amcor began as a papermaking business—Australian Paper Manufacturers (APM). The origins of APM—although it was not incorporated under this name until many decades later—can be traced back to the 1860s and to some of the earliest of Australia's ventures in this field.

In New South Wales and neighboring Victoria the 1860s were years of rapid industrial growth. The gold rushes brought an explosion in population—and thus, of the labor force—as well as rising prosperity, and the introduction in Victoria of a protection policy for manufacturers created a climate in which the number of factories increased. The papermaking industry was no exception to this trend.

In 1864 Murray built the Collingwood mill at Liverpool, New South Wales, for the Australian Paper Company. In Melbourne in 1868 Samuel Ramsden built his own mill and began production with the Number One Paper Machine. Approximately 70 people were employed at it, including about 40 women who spent their days sorting rags. In 1871 William Fieldhouse erected Melbourne Number Two Paper Machine adjacent to Ramsden's mill; the following year Ramsden bought it from him. By 1895 when the Australian Paper Mills Company was formed and registered, it combined mills in Melbourne, Broadford, and Geelong; its capital was A$214,000 and its output approximately 730 tons per year. In 1896 it became the Australian Paper Mills Company Ltd.

Meanwhile, in the New South Wales capital of Sydney, in 1883, John Thomson Brown had begun a business trading in meat, grain, and farming, and household goods, which was to play an important role in APM/Amcor's future. In 1885 David Henry Dureau became the business's Melbourne partner.

Shortly after the new Australian federal government was inaugurated in 1901, it adopted the Victorian policies of protectionism. In the same year the Federal Paper Mills were established at Botany, New South Wales, with their Number One Paper Machine up and running by 1902.

Brown and Dureau's company thrived. It adopted the name Brown & Dureau Ltd. in 1903 and was incorporated in 1910. Over the years, as general commission agents, Brown & Dureau handled a wide range of goods. It was the first exporter of Australian coal to Japan and the United Kingdom and also developed a flourishing export business in iron and steel products, metals, textiles, chemicals, and marine and general food products.

In the 1910s and 1920s Australian Paper Mills Company—like the country's economy as a whole—entered a period of expansion as Australia's overseas trade doubled within the first 30 years of the century. In 1920 Australian Paper Mills Company Ltd. amalgamated with Sydney Paper Mills Ltd. to form the Australian Paper and Pulp Company Ltd. in 1926, by amalgamation of Cumberland Paper Board Mills Ltd. with the Australasian Paper and Pulp Company Ltd., the operating company of Australian Paper Manufacturers Ltd. (APM) was formed—and was to continue to operate under this name, as the pulp and papermaking arm of Amcor, to the present day. The following March, APM Ltd. bought Commonwealth Board Mills and established Austral Waste Products, a waste paper collecting subsidiary at Abbotsford, Victoria, in buildings formerly owned by the Commonwealth Board Mills.

APM's current wood intake is about 50% eucalyptus and 50% pine—both from domestic sources. Between 1900 and 1903 imported wood pulp was first used in Australia at the APM's Barwon paper mill. In 1921 2.5 tons of paper were made from eucalyptus pulp at Botany. In 1936 an agreement was signed between APM Ltd. and the Victorian Forest Commission covering the procurement of wood pulp. On December 23 of that year the Wood Pulp Agreement Act 1936 was passed by the Victorian parliament and led to the establishment of the Maryvale pulp mill. The pilot mill went into semicommercial production of eucalyptus kraft pulp in March of 1938 and the main mill started commercial production the following year. It is in operation to this day.

The year 1939 saw the outbreak of World War II and of the worst bush fires in Victoria's history; APM's mill buildings survived, but almost all of its prime source of pulp wood was destroyed. However, the company found that fire-killed timber could be used for pulping. With the advent of war, imports ceased abruptly, price controls were imposed by the federal government, a wartime profits tax was imposed, and Australian industries were urgently required to provide military equipment and meet defense needs. Within two years, 70% of APM's total production was used directly in the manufacture of munitions and war equipment, and the rest for essential business and consumer uses. During this period, APM proved its strength as an innovator, supplying purified cellulose for the manufacture of smokeless cordite and other propellants for the Allied forces and developing special papers and boards to resist moisture penetration for the troops fighting in tropical regions.

Wartime conditions also prompted APM to increase its self-sufficiency, not only in pulp supplies—in 1938-1939 80% of APM's total pulp requirements were imported, compared to the end of the war, when 80% of raw materials were from local sources—but also in fuel; in 1946, the company acquired a controlling interest in Maddingley Brown Coal Pty Ltd. which, with the purchase of further coal-bearing land, soon produced 10,000 tons of coal per week and supplied all of the Victoria mills together with other commercial and public enterprises. Maddingley Brown Coal was eventually sold in 1989.

APM, designated a "protected" industry by the federal government during the war, nevertheless saw 25% of its work force enlisted, and recruited women to work in the mills. However, despite this and other hardships—such as a coal strike in New South Wales and further bush fires in 1944—the company managed to continue the expansion of its mills and production grew dramatically from 92,000 tons in 1938, to 124,000 tons in 1941, and to 131,000 tons in 1942. Toward the end of the war, APM's managing director Sir Herbert Gepp set up a Postwar Planning Committee to win back freedom from government control and wartime profit tax, and to prepare a case for reasonable tariff protection against the inevitable resurgence of competitive imports. The committee also discussed APC's future strategy, which was to include the extension and expansion of operations in wrapping paper and board; expansion into converting, through the manufacturing of cartons and containers from APM's paper and board; and the manufacture of allied products such as cellophane and tissues.

The war also resulted in major reorganizations, both financial and administrative; in the development of public relations at APM; and in a new emphasis on industrial relations. The company still had a monopoly on the country's wrapping paper and board markets and was firmly established in mainland Australia as its largest paper and pulp company. In the 1950s APM made an initial foray into the corrugated packaging industry in which it was later to make significant acquisitions; the history of the packaging arm of the group is primarily a history of takeovers. Before 1940 there were four Australian companies operating in the field. J. Fielding & Co. was the earliest, in 1914 installing the first corrugator at Buckingham Street in Sydney, to produce the corrugating medium for packaging. In 1950 APM bought the first 96-inch corrugator, planning to install it on the Springvale wastepaper recycling site, but instead sold it to Fieldings.

In the 1960s APM extended its interests to the production of other paper products. In 1963 it established in partnership with Kimberly-Clark Corporation of the United States, the jointly owned Kimberly-Clark Australia Ltd., which produced all kinds of tissues.

In the 1970s Brown & Dureau acquired Eastern Tool Company, Lukey Mufflers, and Angus Hill Holdings, which were to form the nucleus of Amcor's present-day automotive division. In the 1980s Amcor's major acquisitions were Ingram Corporation Ltd. and Edwards Dunlop & Co. Ltd., a paper merchant and stationery manufacturer that went back to 1869. Out of this latter acquisition grew the present merchanting, stationery and designer products division.

In 1975 Stan Wallis became deputy managing director of APM. In 1977 he was appointed managing director. According to a retrospective ten years later in the *Financial Times,* he was "the strategist behind the programme"—the program which brought Amcor the strong balance sheet and prudent financial ratios with which it began the 1990s.

From the late 1970s, under Stan Wallis, APM began a process of diversification. One of the most important acquisitions was that of Brown & Dureau in the financial year 1978-1979; this brought Amcor substantial interests in the fields of international trading, automotive, retailing, and aviation.

Over the same period APM acquired first 20% and then 40% of James Hardie Containers, manufacturers of corrugated fiber boxes for packaging food and drink. In 1986 APM bought the balance of James Hardie Containers and an era of rationalization began. During this period plants were acquired from Reed Corrugated Containers, J. Fielding & Co., Tasman U.E.B., United Packages, Corrugated Paper, Fibreboard Containers, Fibre Containers, J. Gadsden Paper Products, Tasmanian Fibre Containers, and Cardboard Containers. In the 1980s APM Packaging established two plants at Smithfield, New South Wales, and at Scoresby, Victoria, and in the financial year 1988-1989 it bought 46% of Universal Containers, Sydney. APM Packaging has more than 25,000 employees in 14 corrugated box plants, as well as supporting sheet plants, and eight distribution centers throughout Australia. During the 1980s Amcor's key objectives were to broaden its range of activities, particularly into packaging; to restructure its core pulp and paper businesses and integrate forward into paper converting in Australia; and to commence major overseas expansion.

In the 1980s Stan Wallis embarked on an ambitious program of capital investment in import-substituting plant and in re-opening existing plant to supply growing export markets. In 1987 the *Financial Times* put a figure of A$700 million on the planned investment in plant and machinery. A subsequent source—Amcor's annual report 1989-1990—recorded expenditure during the five years to June 1990 of A$2 billion on capital equipment and acquisitions. Yet for all the ambition of the program—in terms of value—funding for Amcor's investments came principally from internal cash flow, also from the sale of assets and some borrowing. The program was financially conservative.

In 1982 APM acquired Containers Packaging—the fourth major wholly owned Amcor subsidiary. The same year New Zealand Forest Products (NZFP)—that country's leading forestry group—and Amcor formed a joint venture company with 50% shares each, called Anfor. This was set up to develop a corrugated box plant in Hong Kong, with NZFP supplying liner board and Amcor the corrugating medium to make boxes to be sold to Chinese, South Korean, and Japanese customers. Anfor operates corrugated box plants with local partners in Singapore and Malaysia as well as in Hong Kong. In 1986–1987 Kiwi Packaging, New Zealand, became a wholly owned subsidiary of Amcor and runs five corrugating plants and two sheet plants. In 1989–1990 Sunclipse Incorporated was acquired. This is a California-based corrugated box manufacturer and distributor of packaging products. Amcor Packaging (Europe) Ltd. is one of the most recent developments and constitutes Amcor's first direct investment in the United Kingdom—a corrugated box plant on a greenfield site in Cambridgeshire which currently employs about 130 people. A 49% share in SACOC, a French corrugated box manufacturer, was also acquired in 1989–1990.

How far Amcor succeeded in its objective of diversification can be judged from Chris Sherwell's comment in the *Financial Times,* January 1987: "Some idea of where the company fits into Australian life can be gleaned from a single revealing picture in its latest annual report. It shows a small group enjoying a traditional outdoor barbecue picnic. Practically every item on the table—the beer and the soft-drink cans, plastic fruit juice bottles, cooler box, salt and pepper containers, bread and cheese wrappers and paper tissues—is an Amcor product."

But not all of Stan Wallis's plans were successful. In April 1987 a possible merger between New Zealand Forest Products and Amcor was announced. The proposed merger would cover only the pulp and paper production and marketing of the two companies. It would stop short of a full merger of operations. In August 1987 Amcor received the New Zealand Commerce Commission's decision: the merger would not go ahead.

The principal reason for the commission's rejection was that the proposed new entity would have a virtual monopoly of the manufacture and import of kraft paper and paperboard in New Zealand. The same obstacle did not impede Fletcher Challenge, Amcor's main domestic rival. Amcor promptly sold its 11% stake in NZFP to the Rada Corporation as a defense, some thought, against a Fletcher Challenge takeover.

Amcor, under Stan Wallis, turned its eyes to offshore investment opportunities. In 1988, the year following the failed merger with NZFP, the group announced it was concentrating on overseas business expansion; as evidence it switched Don B. Macfarlane to the newly created post of general manager of international business development.

According to Amcor, the creation of Macfarlane's new post signified its commitment to a structured and systematic approach to expansion outside Australia. He was to report directly to Stan Wallis.

In June 1989 Amcor bought Twinpak, the largest plastics containers producer in Canada with 13 plants spread across the country. The acquisition accounted for a significant proportion of the 32% increase in containers packaging sales in the financial year 1989–1990.

In June 1990 Amcor Fibre Packaging was formed to manage the group's international corrugated box manufacturing and related activities. It includes APM Packaging, Kiwi Packaging, Sunclipse, Amcor Packaging (Europe), SACOC, and Anfor. In total it has the capacity to manufacture almost one million tons per year of corrugated products, more than half of which capacity is outside Australia.

In 1989 Amcor appointed a new chairman, Sir Brian Inglis. He replaced Alan Skurrie, who had held the office for five years and had an association of more than 55 years with Amcor.

Amcor set out to diversify in the 1980s. By 1990, paper—the business in which the group's origins lay—accounted for only 19% of sales compared with 57% a decade earlier.

Amcor's major challenges for the future are to become more internationally competitive and to adapt to vastly increased public awareness on environmental issues. Although they have already made great strides on the first objective, the withdrawal of incentives such as accelerated depreciation and investment allowances are likely to make the task harder in the future—especially in a climate of reduced tariff protection, high interest rates and a high exchange rate. The company is well aware of the importance of environmental issues.

Principal Subsidiaries: Australian Paper Manufacturers; Containers Packaging; Amcor Fibre Packaging; Brown and Dureau Ltd.; Transpak Industries Ltd.; Willander Holdings Ltd. (49%); Spicers Paper Ltd. (18.7%); National Paper Vuepack Ltd.; New Zealand Corp. Ltd.

Further Reading: Sinclair, E.K., *The Spreading Tree: A History of APM and AMCOR 1844–1989,* Sydney, Allen & Unwin, 1991.

—Mary Scott

AVERY DENNISON CORPORATION

150 North Orange Grove Boulevard
Pasadena, California 91103
U.S.A.
(818) 304-2000
Fax: (818) 792-7312

Public Company
Incorporated: 1990
Employees: 18,816
Sales: $2.59 billion
Stock Exchanges: New York Pacific

Avery Dennison Corporation was formed in the fall of 1990 by the merger of two *Fortune* 500 companies, Avery International Corporation, based in Pasadena, California, and Dennison Manufacturing Company, headquartered in Framingham, Massachusetts. The new company, manufacturers of office products, self-adhesive materials, tapes, labels, specialty chemicals, and stationery, hoped to provide strong competition for industry giants, including 3M and American Brands.

The two companies had a relationship that dated back to 1941, when, following the resolution of a patent dispute involving a dispenser for self-adhesive labels, Dennison became Avery's customer. Avery supplied labels to Dennison that the Massachusetts company sold under the brand name Pres-a-ply, competing with Avery products. By formally joining their two companies Avery and Dennison now share a history dating back almost 150 years.

DENNISON MANUFACTURING COMPANY

Dennison Manufacturing began in 1844 when Aaron Dennison, a Boston jeweler, returned to his family home in Brunswick, Maine, and with his father, Andrew Dennison, and his sisters began making paper boxes. The father and son soon created a machine to facilitate the making of cardboard boxes. At the time most jewel boxes were imported semiannually; the new Dennison business had a ready-made domestic market.

Andrew Dennison presided over the manufacturing of the boxes while Aaron continued working at his jewelry business. As a sideline he purchased materials for the boxes and sold the finished product. In 1849 Aaron Dennison became a fulltime manufacturer of the machine-made watch, turning the sales

end of the box business over to his younger brother, Eliphalet Whorf (E.W.) Dennison.

Fourteen years later, the family business was a partnership, Dennison and Company, between E.W. Dennison and three non-family members. Working out of a small factory in Boston, the company produced jewelry tags, display cards, and shipping tags, while the boxes continued to be made in Maine. The development of the shipping tag represented Dennison's continuing attempt to diversify, to provide a better product than was currently available, and to create new markets. In 1863 Dennison patented the placement of a paper washer on each side of the hole in a shipping tag, thus providing a more durable tag. Dennison and Company sold ten million tags that first year.

By 1878 the company had a large factory in Roxbury, Massachusetts, the box plant in Brunswick, Maine, and stores in New York, Philadelphia, and Chicago. The company incorporated, becoming the Dennison Manufacturing Company, headed by E.W. Dennison. Henry B. Dennison, E.W.'s son, became president in 1886, the year of his father's death. He served until 1892, when a conflict between the production end, which was Henry's responsibility, and the sales management led to his resignation. Henry K. Dyer, based in New York, became president.

The company returned to family leadership in 1909 when Charles Dennison, another son of E.W.'s, became president. He had previously held positions as vice president and treasurer. In 1911 Charles Dennison presided over the reincorporation of the company under the same name. When the company originally incorporated in 1878, the managers held all the stock. Under the terms of E.W. Dennison's will, however, employees participated in profit-sharing, receiving stock and the privilege of purchasing additional stock under favorable terms. Over time, people not directly involved in manufacturing acquired on the basis of stock ownership substantial influence on the board and were able to direct policy in ways that Dennison family members found undesirable. The reincorporation plan, spearheaded by Charles Dennison and his nephew Henry Sturgis Dennison, a director of the company, returned control to the managers of production through creation of different categories of stock.

In 1898 under Dyer's direction all of the company's manufacturing operations had been centralized in Framingham, Massachusetts. Under the reincorporation plan, sales operations as well moved to Framingham. By 1911 Dennison Manufacturing's line included tags, gummed labels, paper boxes, greeting cards, sealing wax, and crepe paper. The firm supplied a variety of stationery and paper goods. There were Dennison stores in Boston, New York, Philadelphia, Chicago, St. Louis, and in London, England.

Crepe paper eventually became a major sales item for Dennison Manufacturing Company. In the 1870s the firm began to import tissue paper from England to sell to retail jewelers. Its supplier also provided it with colored paper, which was sold to novelty companies. Crinkling the paper expanded its uses; by 1914 Dennison manufactured its own crepe paper.

The production of crepe paper led to the creation of a line of holiday supplies, including Christmas tags and seals. Eventually the company manufactured items for all the major holidays including Halloween, St. Valentine's Day, Easter, and St. Patrick's Day. Dennison also had a thriving side business selling pamphlets about parties, crafts, and holidays, highlighting the many uses of Dennison products, particularly crepe paper. The holiday line folded, due to declining profits, in 1967.

In 1917 Henry Sturgis Dennison, grandson of E.W. Dennison, became president of the company; he held the position for 35 years. As a believer in the scientific management theories of Frederick W. Taylor, Dennison initiated many reforms including reduction in working hours, establishment of health services and personnel departments, creation of an unemployment fund, and non-managerial profit-sharing.

Although Henry Dennison served as president of Dennison Manufacturing Company until his death in 1952, he made a significant mark on the world outside the family business. Dennison served as a member of the Commercial Economy Board of the National Defense Council during World War I and following the war served as a member of President Harding's unemployment conference. He was the author of several books including *Profit Sharing: Its Principles and Practice,* 1918, written with Arthur W. Burritt and others; *Toward Full Employment,* 1938, written with Lincoln Filene and other industrialists; and *Modern Competition and Business Policy,* 1938, co-authored with John Kenneth Galbraith.

Many businessmen did not support Franklin Roosevelt and the New Deal; Dennison did, chairing the Industrial Advisory Board of the National Recovery Administration (NRA). This body examined all NRA codes while they were being developed. When the Supreme Court declared the many of the NRA's codes unconstitutional, Dennison became an adviser to the National Resources Planning Board.

During the Great Depression, Dennison Manufacturing suffered, along with the rest of the nation, recording net losses in both 1931 and 1932. The following year the company recovered, once again showing a profit. Profits, however, did not return to pre-Depression levels, making recapitalization necessary and rendering inoperative the profit-sharing plan of 1911.

The war economy of the 1940s helped put Dennison back on its feet, and in 1942 sales passed the level of 1929. By 1951 sales were $37.3 million and net earnings $2.1 million.

Henry S. Dennison suffered a heart attack in 1937 and turned over the active management of the company to John S. Keir, vice president. Dennison's death in 1952 ended more than 100 years of Dennison family leadership of the Dennison Manufacturing Company.

During the 1960s Dennison experienced further change when, in 1962, it incorporated in Nevada, in a move to decrease taxes. In 1966 Nelson S. Gifford became a director of the company.

By the 1960s analysts considered Dennison Manufacturing Company as part of the label, or marking, industry. Its major operations focused on paper and tag conversion and the production of imprinting and price-ticketing machines.

In 1964 Dennison became the majority shareholder in Paul Williams Copier Corporation. This step was part of its strategy for producing a copier to challenge Xerox. The plan originated in 1957, when, under license from RCA, Dennison began work on a dry copier that differed in several important technological ways from Xerox machines.

Dennison also produced print-punch machines for generating price tags in a relationship with Cummins, the maker of Data Read Machines. Dennison in the 1960s was a high-tech firm, particularly in the arena of packaging. The company

could, through an instantaneous heat process, transfer a graphic design to plastic. The process, therimage, was cheaper than more conventional methods.

Building on this technological base, Dennison continued to invest heavily in research and development. In 1979 Dennison formed a joint partnership with Canada Development Corporation (CDC)—Delphax—to develop high-speed, non-impact printers. Using proprietary technology, the company sought to create products to compete with laser printers. Xerox subsequently bought CDC's 50% interest in Delphax.

In the 1980s Dennison's other technological ventures took it further afield. The company held the majority interest in Biological Technology Corporation, which was working on diagnostic products, using researchers from Massachusetts Institute of Technology and Harvard University. Potential products included pregnancy test supplies.

Returning to its office products base, Dennison stayed abreast of computer technology, producing floppy discs as well as office furniture. In the 1980s Dennison's stationery division accounted for almost half of sales and profits. The attempt to develop a copier to challenge Xerox, begun in 1957, had not succeeded.

In 1985 Dennison experienced a significant economic downturn, which prompted a five-year restructuring plan. A large source of Dennison's problems came from heavy investments in research and development. In 1985–1986 Dennison, streamlining, sold seven businesses and shut down four others. This process left the company with three key businesses: stationery, systems, and packaging. The stationery division, actually two units, Dennison National and Dennison Carter, remained the major contributor to profits. Systems was divided into retail and industrial units, produced bar-code printing machines, and was the world's leading manufacturer of plastic price-tag threads. The ongoing restructuring plan involved the consolidation of Dennison National and Dennison Carter, and the integration of systems was scheduled for completion in 1990.

Because of the company's commitment to this program, the news in the spring of 1990 of a merger between Dennison and Avery caught industry observers by surprise. Both companies, however, had been suffering depressed earnings and sought strength in union.

AVERY INTERNATIONAL CORPORATION

R. Stanton Avery founded the company that would eventually become part of Avery Dennison Corporation in 1935 with capital of less than $100 from his future wife, Dorothy Durfee. Avery created Kum-Kleen Products to produce self-adhesive labels using machinery he had developed while working at the Adhere Paper Company.

Based in Los Angeles, Kum-Kleen first marketed its labels to gift shops and antique stores and then expanded to other retail establishments, including furniture, hardware, and drug stores. In 1938, Avery Adhesives, the company's new name, suffered a fire that destroyed all of its equipment except a stock of labels. While rebuilding, Avery implemented changes in the die-cutting machinery; the technology Stan Avery developed remains the standard for the industry.

Before the development of self-adhesives, labels were either pre-gummed or applied with glue. Initially self-adhesive labels did not have a coating that would facilitate removal of the label from its backing and they were therefore difficult to use. Early labels were punched rather than cut. The innovation of Avery Adhesives occurred on two levels: technological—improving and streamlining the manufacturing process, and product definition—creating a market.

World War II and the total economic mobilization it necessitated created problems for Avery Adhesives as well as for other industries. The raw materials needed to produce the adhesive for the labels—natural and synthetic rubber and solvents derived from petroleum—were needed by the military. Avery Adhesives, needing permission from the federal government to continue production and to obtain materials, focused on manufacturing industrial items rather than the labels for consumer goods it had previously produced. Among the products were waterproof labels bearing "S.O.S." in Morse code that were stuck on rescue radios. When the war ended, this focus on labels for industrial and commercial uses persisted. The war economy hastened market acceptance of pressure-sensitive labels.

In 1946 Avery Adhesives incorporated, becoming the Avery Adhesive Label Corporation. At the time of incorporation, more than 80% of the company's output consisted of industrial labels that were sold to manufacturers who placed them on their own products—usually consumer items—using automatic label-dispensing machines. The original retail base of Avery Adhesives persisted, providing 10% of output. The company sold unprinted labels in dispenser flat-pack boxes to stationery stores and other retail establishments through a distribution network. The final aspect of the new corporation's business consisted of selling pressure-sensitive materials to printers and others who used them in other products, such as masking tape. Tape rolls produced by Avery were used in the manufacturing of department store price labels. This aspect of Avery's business, which contributed 10% to output, was known as converting. These industrial categories were the forerunners of Avery's divisions in the 1960s and 1970s.

In the 1940s Avery perceived itself as the only company in the self-adhesive label industry to offer a full line of products. Competition did exist for transparent mending tape, not part of Avery's line. Minnesota Mining and Manufacturing—3M—was the leader in that field.

A challenge to Avery occurred in the 1950s in the form of a patent suit. Avery had taken out a patent for its method of producing self-adhesive labels. Because other self-adhesive products predated Stan Avery's technological innovations, the label itself could not be patented. In 1950 Avery Adhesive brought suit against Ever Ready Label Corporation, then the leader in the industry, alleging infringement on Avery's basic patent. In 1952 a New Jersey court ruled against Avery, stating that there was "not an invention" and that the patent was on a method, not a unique product.

The loss of the patent had serious consequences for Avery, ultimately changing the nature of its business, and had a ripple effect on the self-adhesive and label industry. The short-term outcome of the patent decision of 1952 was the creation, in 1954, of a new division, the Avery Paper Company. The division produced and sold self-adhesive base materials, often to competing label companies. Eventually this division dominated manufacturing at Avery, eclipsing label sales.

In the 1960s four different branches made up the loosely defined label industry. There were manufacturers of various rubber stamps for paperwork, metal labelers including engravers and stencilers, adhesive label manufacturers, and producers of specialized marking devices. The total volume of this diverse industry was approximately $150 million with annual growth of 3%. In the adhesive label category the leading manufacturers were Avery Products Corporation—the name was changed in 1964; 3M; the Simon Adhesive Products and Eureka Specialty Printing divisions of Litton Industries; and the Kleen-Stik products division of National Starch and Chemical Corporation.

Avery had four divisions in the marking or identification aspect of the industry. Fasson, the new name of Avery Paper Company, was a supplier of raw materials. A second division used these raw materials to manufacture Avery labels. Another division, Rotex, manufactured hand-embossing machines, and Metal-Cal, acquired in 1964, made anodized and etched aluminum foil for nameplates. Another aspect of Avery's business in the 1960s was machines that embossed vinyl tape. Avery's main product continued to be self-adhesive labels used in a range of products, including automobiles and airplanes.

The 1960s represented a period of much growth for Avery and U.S. industry in general. The period witnessed the rise in mergers and the development of the diversified corporation, culminating in the emergence of the conglomerate.

In 1961 Avery became publicly owned; it was listed on the New York Stock Exchange in 1967. That year, the company had 2,500 workers and two major components. Label products included the domestic Avery Label division and four wholly owned foreign subsidiaries. The other component was base materials, predominantly Fasson and Fasson Europe. The major buyers of base materials were industrial firms, including the graphic arts trade. In 1968 Avery's share of the industry's $200 million of sales was $63 million. The late 1960s were good years for Avery, as it developed specific units to target specific markets.

In 1974 Avery made the *Fortune* 500 list for the first time. Avery was last on the list, while its competitior 3M was 50th. The 1970s presented Avery with the first major impediment to growth since World War II. Once again the company faced problems caused by a situation outside its immediate control. The oil crisis of 1975 heavily affected Avery, a company dependent on petrochemicals. Avery faced increased costs, oversupply, and declining demand. The price per share of Avery's stock dropped to $22, from a high of $44 the previous year.

By 1980 Avery had reversed its downward slide by diversifying and by controlling costs, prices, and employment levels. The materials units included raw materials, Fasson, and specialty materials, such as Thermark. Thermark produced hot stamping materials for automobiles and appliances. Fasson continued to be the bread-and-butter unit of Avery; its self-adhesives were now being used on disposable diapers. The converting unit had moved into the production of labels for data processing and home and office use. Avery continued to maintain foreign operations, centered in Western Europe and located as well in Canada, Mexico, and Australia.

Seven years later Avery International was the nation's leading producer of self-adhesive materials and labels. The company's revenues were three times greater than ten years previously. In the late 1980s, however, profits flattened. The main reason were Avery's involvement in the disposable diaper market and its ongoing competition with 3M. Avery first began producing tape for diapers in 1977 and by 1984 was the sole supplier to Kimberly-Clark, manufacturers of Huggies. 3M did the same for Pampers. 3M's tape was one piece while Avery's contained a tiny piece of plastic that could fall off and perhaps be swallowed. Kimberly-Clark turned to 3M. In 1986 Avery developed its own one-piece tape in an attempt to win back Kimberly-Clark's business. Avery also attempted to challenge 3M in two other areas—transparent tape and self-sticking notes. Avery later abandoned this effort.

In a thorough restructuring, beginning in 1987, Avery closed some manufacturing facilities, domestic and overseas, and announced plans to cut the number of employees by 8%. Avery was, however, succeeding in its attempt to strengthen its share of the diaper tape market.

Both Avery and Dennison received a large amount of revenue from overseas operations. The merger came partly in anticipation of the economic integration of the European Community, scheduled for 1992. Five years of negotiations preceded the final deal that Dennison employees and officers, controlling more than 20% of stock, approved.

Under the merger agreement, the Avery board dominates the new company, which is centered in Pasadena, California. Charles D. Miller is chairman and chief executive of Avery Dennison, the same positions he held at Avery International, while Nelson Gifford, formerly chairman and chief executive

officer at Dennison, is vice chairman of the new company. Richard Pearson, a 30-year management figure at Avery International, retired and was replaced as president and chief operating officer by Philip M. Neal.

The year in which Avery Dennison became a reality, 1990, was not a good one for the new company. Sales increased only 1%, while net income and earnings declined. While both companies hoped the merger, first proposed in May 1990, would not dilute stock, the plan did have that effect. On January 28, 1991, Avery Dennison announced their intention to lay off 900 workers nationwide over an 18-month period. Company spokespersons cited both the recession and the merger. A restructuring is planned as well.

Further Reading: Dennison, James T., *Henry S. Dennison,* [n.p], New York, 1955; *John S. Keir,* Portland, Oregon, The Dennison Manufacturing Company, 1960; Clark, David L., *Avery International Corporation 50-Year History 1935–1985,* Pasadena, California, Avery International Corporation, 1988; *Dennison Beginnings 1840–1878,* Framingham, Massachusetts, Dennison Manufacturing Company, [n.d.]; *Seventy-Five Years 1844–1919,* Framingham, Massachusetts, Dennison Manufacturing Company, [n.d.].

—Amy Mittelman

BOISE CASCADE CORPORATION

One Jefferson Square
Post Office Box 50
Boise, Idaho 83728
U.S.A.
(208) 384-6161
Fax: (208) 384-7224

Public Company
Incorporated: 1931 as Boise Payette Lumber Company
Employees: 19,810
Sales: $4.19 billion
Stock Exchanges: New York Midwest Pacific

Boise Cascade Corporation has grown from a small local lumber company into a major manufacturer and distributor of forest products, ranging from paper to building materials. It also supplies office products to dealers and large companies. The company owns 2.8 million acres of timberland in North America and holds long-term leases or licenses on an additional 3.4 million acres.

The firm was established under its present name in 1957 through the merger of the Boise Payette Lumber Company and the Cascade Lumber Company of Yakima, Washington. Boise Payette had been one of Idaho's top lumber producers since its formation in the 1930s; however, the building boom following World War II had seriously depleted its timberlands. The Cascade Lumber Company had been in operation since 1902 when it was founded by George S. Rankin, the owner of several other businesses in the Yakima Valley. Rankin had been joined in this new venture by a business associate, Fred V. Pennington, and other individuals experienced in lumber operations in the Midwest. Initially, Cascade owned timberland at the headwaters of the Yakima River, which it had purchased for $100,000, and also operated several retail lumber yards in the area in addition to its Yakima mill. These yards were closed in 1914 and consolidated into one lumber yard at the Yakima sawmill, which continued operating even after the merger with Boise Payette.

Robert V. Hansberger, who had joined Boise Payette in 1956 as president, saw the merger of the two companies as an opportunity for Boise Payette to replenish its timber supply. More importantly, combining the resources of the two firms would enable the resulting company to build a base of raw materials large enough to allow it to expand beyond lumber production into the manufacture of paper and pulp products.

In 1958, the company, now known as Boise Cascade, built a kraft pulp and paper mill in Wallula, Washington, and corrugated container plants at both Wallula, and Burley, Idaho. The paper and pulp area grew rapidly over the next five years with further expansion of the company's paper and wood production capacity. In spite of this success, Hansberger and his management team recognized how vulnerable the company was because of the cyclical nature of the wood and paper industries. They decided to diversify into other areas as a hedge against possible downturns in demand for its forest products.

Since joining the company, Hansberger had filled the company's top management ranks with graduates of the country's leading business schools. He permitted these executives to operate independently and expand the company's operating divisions as they saw fit. By 1969 Boise Cascade had completed over 30 mergers and acquisitions and had become the third largest forest products company in the United States. Its operations now encompassed such diverse activities as residential and mobile home construction, recreational vehicle production, publishing, and cruise management.

One of the company's major interests during the mid-1960s was the field of real estate speculation and recreational land development. In 1967 alone, Boise Cascade acquired U.S. Land Company, Lake Arrowhead Development Company, and Pacific Cascade Land Company, and amassed real estate holdings of 126,000 acres in more than 12 states, with the majority of the land in California. Hoping to sell this property to large investors, the company met with little success and was forced to revise its strategy and develop the land itself into residential and recreational areas.

Although the company experienced greater success with this approach and sales were brisk, the new business division encountered several unanticipated problems. For example, Boise Cascade became a prime target for a growing ecological movement, particularly on the West Coast, which was concerned about the impact of the company's plans on the environment. Activist groups often hampered the company's efforts to gain approval for its developments from local planning agencies. Another major setback resulted from a series of lawsuits brought against Boise Cascade by the California attorney general. These legal actions were filed in response to complaints from prospective buyers about the tactics used by the company's salesmen, many of whom had been inherited in the course of the company's acquisitions of realty projects. The suits were eventually settled at a cost of $59 million.

In addition to these problems, the company also experienced serious cash flow difficulties related to its land development business. In this industry, the developer was responsible for paying the costs of constructing a community's sewer and water systems. These costs, typically, were high and had to be paid immediately, yet the developer was unable to collect its revenues until up to seven years after its sales were made. In an attempt to infuse the firm with fresh capital to fund the land development business on an ongoing basis, Boise Cascade acquired Ebasco in 1969. Ebasco and it subsidiaries were in the engineering and construction business and provided enginering services to major utilities. It was particularly attractive to Boise Cascade because it was rich with cash. It held millions of dollars worth of Latin American bonds, payable in U.S. dollars, that had been gained through the sale of Ebasco's utility operations in Argentina, Brazil, Chile, Colombia, and

Costa Rica. By 1970, it was clear the the company's land development business was in serious trouble, accumulating losses that placed the entire organization in jeopardy.

Upon the 1968 purchase of Princess Cruises, the company shifted its marketing efforts away from independent travel agencies, which had originally spurred the growth of the cruise line. Instead, it instituted a direct mail campaign that was developed internally and proved less effective in generating business. As a result, the cruise line went from profits to losses within a matter of months.

In an attempt to reverse its losses, Boise Cascade wrote off a significant portion of its real estate holdings and divested its residential housing operation, along with other assets judged to be inadequate performers or lying too far outside the company's core business areas. In the light of the lead-development reversals, Robert Hansberger, the architect of the company's rapid growth resigned in 1972 and was replaced as president and chief executive officer by John Fery. Fery had been hired as Hansberger's assistant in 1957 and had ascended to executive vice president and director within ten years.

After taking the helm, Fery immediately placed tighter controls on the company's internal management structure. He began selling off additional subsidiaries, including several Latin American investments gained in the Ebasco purchase, in order to reduce debt and refocus the firm's energies on forest products. As a result of these measures, Boise Cascade moved from a $171 million net loss to a $142 million net profit in just one year. Fery also instituted a five-year, billion-dollar capital spending program that was intended to help reduce the company's dependence on areas with correlating demand cycles, such as lumber and plywood, in favor of businesses with higher and more consistent growth potential. Fery's strategy placed greater emphasis on the manufacture of products for the construction industry and on paper products which could be marketed directly to end users in business form printing, data processing, and publishing.

This initiative propelled Boise Cascade into the 1980s as a specialized and efficient manufacturer of forest products and owner of timberland. By 1982 the company encountered sluggish demand for its products on two key fronts. The housing industry was badly depressed, reducing the demand for building products. The company's pulp and paper operation, intended to help the Boise Cascade weather downturns in its other markets, experienced similar problems as industrial firms cut back expenditure in response to the weakening economy. Over the next two years, the firm closed a number of inefficient or unprofitable mills and consolidated its marketing operations. In 1987, Boise Cascade sold its consumer packaging division, which had manufacturered containers for various products, and a chain of retail building materials centers, which had been acquired from Edwards Industries in 1979. Labor contracts with union employees were renegotiated in an attempt to reduce the company's overall cost structure.

At this time, the Federal Trade Commission accused Boise Cascade of violating the Robinson-Patman Act and the Federal Trade Commission (FTC) Act. In its suit, filed in 1980, the FTC claimed that the company had purchased office products for resale to commercial users and retailers at prices below those available to competitors. The FTC subsequently issued a cease and desist order to the firm in 1986. However, in 1988, an appeals court reversed this directive, determining that the FTC had not effectively substantiated its claim that the company's purchasing practices had adversely affected competition. The case was re-argued before the FTC, resulting in a renewed finding of violation, which was under appeal in 1991.

When the paper industry rebounded in 1986, Boise Cascade and other manufacturers began construction to increase both production and capacity to meet the demand. By 1990, however, this response to the market upswing resulted in an oversupply of paper and excess industry capacity that caused prices and profits to drop. Boise Cascade again found itself vulnerable to the peaks and valleys of another cyclical industry.

The company has survived the devastation of near bankruptcy caused by over-ambitious expansion into areas unrelated to its core business, and has learned how to hold its own in industries with unpredictable business cycles. In the building products industry, for example, the company has maintained profitability despite periodic slowdowns in housing construction by striving to be the lowest-cost supplier. Its office products group, which markets everything from paper clips to furniture, sustains a competitive edge by providing unique services to its customers. Capital spending, directed specifically toward the modernization and improvement of the company's manufacturing plants, is seen as a top priority for long term growth in all operational areas.

Boise Cascade faces threats to its future success from two major external forces. Market conditions in the company's two largest divisions, paper and building products, are highly dependent upon the strength or weakness of the overall economy. On another front, Boise Cascade must be prepared to respond appropriately to the environmental preservation movement. Although the company manages its own timberlands, it must purchase additional raw materials from other sources to meet its manufacturing needs fully. If preservationist groups are successful in their efforts to restrict access by forest products companies to timber the effects on Boise Cascade's overall operations could be serious.

Over the long term, Boise Cascade and John Fery, who was appointed chairman in 1978, remain committed to growth, efficiency, and quality improvements throughout the company's businesses. This strategy, which has effectively guided the company through its troubles in the past, is seen as the means by which Boise Cascade will in the future offer increased value to its shareholders and to the entire forest products industry.

Principal Subsidiaries: Boise Cascade Canada Limited; Boise Cascade Office Products Corporation; Boise Southern Company; Oxford Paper Company.

Further Reading: "Will Quality Tell?" *Forbes*, July 15, 1970; "Boise Cascade Shifts Toward Tighter Control," *Business Week*, May 15, 1971; "Cinderella," *Forbes*, November 15, 1972; Moskowitz, Milton, Michael Katz and Robert Levering, eds., *Everybody's Business: An Almanac*, San Francisco, Harper & Row, 1980; Heiman, Grover, "Getting Back to Basics," *Nation's Business*, January, 1983; Benoit, Ellen, "Late Bloomer in the Forest," *Financial World*, September 8, 1987.

—Sandy Schusteff

BOWATER

BOWATER PLC

Bowater House
Knightsbridge
London SWIX 7NN
United Kingdom
(071) 584-7070
Fax: (071) 581-1149

Public Company
Incorporated: 1910 as W.V. Bowater & Sons, Limited
Employees: 21,000
Sales: £1.36 billion (US$2.62 billion)
Stock Exchange: London

Bowater PLC is the U.K.-based holding company for an international group whose core activities are the production of printed, coated, and laminated products; packaging; paper tissue products; and the manufacture of building materials. Most of the firm's activities concern paper in some way, and the firm began in the paper business.

William Vansittart Bowater was the firm's founder. As a young man he joined James Wrigley & Sons, a Manchester papermaking firm, where he became a manager. He is reputed to have been ill-tempered, tyrannical, and hard-drinking, traits which eventually led to his dismissal by Wrigley. By 1881, at the age of 43, he was in business on his own in the City of London, the heart of the U.K. newspaper publishing and printing industries, operating as a paper wholesaler and as an agent for the purchase of newsprint on behalf of newspaper publishers. The final decades of the 19th century saw the birth of the popular press in Britain and soaring demand for newsprint. Bowater secured contracts with two of the most dynamic newspaper and magazine tycoons, Alfred Harmsworth, publisher of the *Daily Mail* and the *Daily Mirror,* and Edward Lloyd, publisher of the *Daily Chronicle.* Three of William Bowater's five sons joined him in partnership, and the firm—now renamed W.V. Bowater & Sons—gradually prospered and expanded, although in 1905 the personnel comprised only the four partners, six clerks, two typists, and an office boy.

The years immediately before World War I saw important developments in the management of the firm and in the pattern of its activities. The death of the founder in 1907 was followed three years later by Bowater's adoption of limited liability as a private company. This status made it easier to bring the next generation into the business and facilitated raising finance. In 1913 the head of the firm, Sir Thomas Vansittart Bowater, the founder's eldest son, who was knighted in 1906, became lord mayor of London, leaving the running of the family business to his younger brothers. Besides wholesaling and agency activities, during the Edwardian era the company moved into large-scale dealing in waste paper, including the export of surplus newspapers to the Far East, where they were used for the protection of young tea plants. These years also saw the commencement of the export of newsprint to Australia, leading to the establishment of a U.S. marketing subsidiary, Hudson Packaging & Paper Company, in 1914 and an office in Sydney, Australia, in 1919. These were the first steps in Bowater's development into a multinational corporation.

World War I boosted newspaper sales and demand remained buoyant in the postwar years. Yet Bowater's role as a middleman was increasingly uncomfortable in an industry in which there was more and more integration between newspaper publishers and newsprint manufacturers.

Bowater's first step towards becoming a paper manufacturer was the purchase of a site at Northfleet on the south side of the Thames estuary near Gravesend in May 1914. World War I interrupted the firm's plans and it was not until 1923 that the construction of a paper mill could be considered. The contractor was Armstrong, Whitworth & Co. Limited, a major armaments manufacturer which turned to other activities after the end of the war and had recently built a paper mill at Corner Brook in Newfoundland. Bowater too had an interest in the Corner Brook development, since its U.S. marketing subsidiary was sole agent for the sale of Corner Brook's output. There were serious flaws in Armstrong's design of the Northfleet mill, and modifications had to be made during construction. These changes led to large cost overruns and delayed the commencement of full production from July 1925 until almost a year later.

The resolution of the serious problems at Northfleet was the work of Eric Bowater and this achievement was his stepping stone to the leadership of the firm. A grandson of the founder, he entered the firm in 1921. In 1927, at the age of 32, he became chairman and managing director of W.V. Bowater & Sons and was the leading figure in the firm for the following three and a half decades. He dominated Bowater's affairs by sheer force of personality. There was no doubt of his utter dedication to his company's success, yet his austerity and aloofness inspired admiration rather than affection. He behaved as if he owned the firm, although it became a public company, in 1927, and relied heavily upon a small circle of close advisers.

Eric Bowater was determined to establish Bowater as a major force in U.K. papermaking as fast as possible. To this end he negotiated the sale of a controlling interest in the firm to the newspaper magnate Lord Rothermere, which reduced the family's shareholding to 40%. Rothermere's backing allowed Bowater to raise the finance to double the output of the Northfleet mill in 1928. He looked immediately for further opportunities to expand and a new project was initiated to build a large paper mill on the Mersey, near Liverpool, which was financed jointly by Bowater, Rothermere, and Beaverbrook newspapers. The latter entered a long-term contract to receive supplies of newsprint from the new undertaking. By the end of 1930 the output of Bowater's mills was 175,000 tons of newsprint per year, 22% of the U.K.'s total output. In order to achieve this result, it had been necessary to cede control of the business to a pair of press barons. However, Rothermere's business was badly affected by the slump at the beginning of the 1930s and in 1932, to raise cash, he sold his Bowater shareholding back to Bowater. Beaverbrook followed suit. Eric Bowater thus found himself in absolute control of the firm again, now the U.K.'s largest newsprint producer.

Newspaper circulations rose again in the 1930s and Eric Bowater's response was to double the capacity of the Mersey mills. Even more audacious was his purchase in 1936 of paper mills at Sittingbourne and Kemsley from Edward Lloyd Ltd., which doubled the firm's output of newsprint to around 500,000 tons per annum. In little more than a decade since the start of manufacturing, Bowater was producing 60% of British newsprint and had become the largest newsprint undertaking in Europe.

The expansion of Bowater's activities enabled the firm to take advantage of economies of scale, and it was a highly efficient and competitive producer. Nevertheless, it occupied a strategically vulnerable position between the producers of pulp, its raw material, and the consumers of paper, its finished product. In 1937 profits were squeezed hard by a large and unforeseen rise in pulp prices engineered by a cartel of Scandinavian producers. This was a chastening experience for Eric Bowater, who resolved to prevent its repetition by securing the firm's own pulp supplies. Bowater immediately acquired interests in Swedish and Norwegian pulp mills and in 1938 it purchased the massive mill at Corner Brook, Newfoundland's most important industrial undertaking with newsprint capacity of 200,000 tons per year and resources of 7,000 square miles of timberland. These moves were described by Eric Bowater as a "raw material insurance policy." Thus by the eve of World War II Bowater was a multinational manufacturer producing 800,000 tons of newsprint annually and a host of other products for an international clientele.

Wartime controls to divert resources to the war effort had a devastating impact on Bowater's U.K. newsprint production, which fell to a fifth of the prewar level. The Northfleet mill closed down completely, "a heart-breaking sight," as the chairman commented. Bowater himself was diverted from the firm's affairs from 1940 to 1945 by work for the Ministry of Aircraft Production, for which he was knighted in 1944. Since a rapid revival of demand for newsprint appeared unlikely, Sir Eric Bowater adopted a policy of diversification into paper packaging. This diversification began with the purchase of Acme Corrugated Cases in 1944, and in 1947, these interests were organized into a wholly owned subsidiary, Associated Bowater Industries. The war had much less impact upon Bowater's North American operations, since U.S. demand for newsprint experienced only a brief downturn before resuming a vigorous advance. In 1944–1950 U.S. consumption almost doubled. During the downturn, Bowater adopted a policy of accepting losses on contracts with U.S. newspapers in order to maintain its client base. The firm was soon rewarded, and in 1946 it was necessary to add a further 75,000 tons capacity at Corner Brook to meet the order-book. The end of the war was a fitting time for a major reorganization of the firm that had developed piecemeal during the previous two decades. In 1947 a streamlined structure was instituted, in which a number of wholly owned operating companies reported to a holding company which was given a new name, the Bowater Paper Corporation.

For Sir Eric Bowater the formation of the Bowater Paper Corporation marked a new point of departure. Over the ensu-

ing decade and a half he worked tirelessly to build up the business on both sides of the Atlantic. In the United Kingdom, the strategy of diversification away from newsprint continued through the late 1940s and early 1950s with further acquisitions of paper products firms. In North America, by contrast, the relentless rise in U.S. demand for newsprint led to the construction of a paper mill at Calhoun, Tennessee, marking the firm's debut as a producer in the United States. The choice of location was determined not only by the availability of timber but also by its proximity to a group of southern newspapers with which the firm had strong and longstanding connections. Financing the simultaneous expansions in the United Kingdom and the United States almost proved too much, but once again Bowater's personality saved the day. "The crowning glory of my business life," remarked Bowater when production began at Calhoun in October 1954. Six months later, it was producing 145,000 tons of newsprint yearly.

By the mid-1950s Bowater was the largest producer of newsprint in the world, a position Bowater had no intention of relinquishing. His strategy to ensure Bowater's continued preeminence was further expansion. A plan made in 1956 envisaged a 60% increase in the company's North American newsprint production to 840,000 tons per annum and a 40% expansion in the United Kingdom to 860,000 tons. To accomplish this increase, Bowater acquired the Mersey Paper Co. of Liverpool, Nova Scotia, which added a further 140,000 tons of newsprint output and doubled capacity at Calhoun. In the United Kingdom, the end of government paper control in 1956 inspired a resurgence of optimism regarding demand for newsprint, and further capacity was added at Kemsley and on Merseyside. As in the 1930s, self-sufficiency in raw materials was considered to be essential, leading to the opening of a new pulp mill at Catawba, South Carolina, in 1959. Self-sufficiency had previously been taken a step further by the formation of the firm's own shipping fleet in 1954. Diversification continued to be an objective in the United Kingdom, leading to expansion of the building products and packaging activities and most importantly to entry into the rapidly growing tissue market through the acquisition of the St. Andrews tissue mill in 1955 and the formation in 1956 of the Bowater-Scott Corporation, a company jointly-owned with the market leader in tissue technology, the Scott Paper Company of Philadelphia. Continental Europe was believed to offer tremendous growth potential and the late 1950s saw the establishment of a Bowater presence in Belgium, Switzerland, and Italy. The firm also became the largest newsprint maker in France, with the acquisition of the Les Papeteries de la Chapelle works with a capacity of 180,000 tons. The latter merged with Les Papeteries Darblay in 1968 to become Les Papeteries de la Chapelle-Darblay. In 1959 Bowater entered a joint venture to produce pulp and newsprint in New Zealand to supply the Australian market. This extensive expansion program required substantial funding and Bowater's borrowings increased greatly.

By the beginning of the 1960s it was plain that Bowater's strategy was flawed. Other competitors had made substantial investments in newsprint capacity and from 1957 the market was oversupplied, causing prices to weaken and profits to disappear, a very serious matter for the world's largest producer of newsprint. In U.K. packaging the story was much the same. Although the expansion program was curtailed, the firm was already heavily burdened with debt and the advance into

Europe continued to absorb capital. Matters were made worse by production problems at the new Catawba pulp mill and by the move to prestigious new headquarters in London's Knightsbridge in 1958, which doubled per capita office costs. The death of Sir Eric Bowater in August 1962 in the midst of the financial crisis marked the end of an era in the history of Bowater.

Retrenchment was a hallmark of Bowater's strategy in the decade 1962–1972. Between 1962 and 1969 the firm was led by Sir Christopher Chancellor, who made his reputation with Reuters and had previously been chairman of Odhams Press, and from 1969 by Martin Ritchie, who had joined the firm in 1956 when his family packaging business was acquired by Bowater. Overcapacity in U.K. newsprint was tackled by the conversion of machines to other types of papermaking, and eventually by closures, including Northfleet in 1973. Calhoun continued to be profitable in the 1960s. The problems at Catauba were solved. Corner Brook operations became unprofitable and capacity was cut. Overall, the reduction in capacity in the United Kingdom and North America by 1972 totaled 300,000 tons. In Europe, where the business had never lived up to Bowater's expectations, there was wholesale retreat, culminating in the sale of the loss-making French company—Les Papeteries de la Chapelle-Darblay—in 1971. Diversification away from newsprint was the other side of the strategy, with successful expansion in areas of activity such as building products in the United Kingdom, and tissue production in both the United Kingdom and Australia.

Diversification on a dramatic scale was achieved in 1972 with the purchase of Ralli International, an international commodity trading company whose sales were roughly equal to those of Bowater. Although the acquisition of Ralli fitted Bowater's longstanding strategy of diversification, it was not a move initiated by the firm. It was proposed by the investment bank Slater Walker, which had close connections with Ralli, and Bowater's assent was an opportunistic move to frustrate a hostile bid for the firm launched by Trafalgar House. Lord Eroll, a former Conservative minister, became chairman of the enlarged group in 1972. During the 1970s Bowater made further moves away from newsprint production in the United Kingdom, culminating in the closure of the last machine dedicated wholly to newsprint manufacture in 1982. The same year saw an output reduction of 130,000 tons in North America. The expansion of packaging, tissue products, and building products operations continued and there were some notable acquisitions in Germany. The firm also operated as a commodity trader on a large scale, in 1978 acquiring Gibbs Nathaniel,

an importer of dried fruit, edible nuts, and other foodstuffs. There was little synergy between the two sides of the business and in 1981 the diversification of 1972 was reversed by the sale of Ralli.

The strategy of the 1980s under chairmen Aylmer Lenton, from 1984 to 1987, and Norman Ireland, was to focus upon activities in which the firm enjoyed managerial expertise and excellence. The strategy was taken to its logical conclusion in 1984 when the North American newsprint and pulp operations were demerged from the rest of the firm. Bowater Industries plc, as the U.K.-based firm was known after the demerger, became a business with five functionally organized operating groups: packaging and industrial products, builders' merchants group, building products group, freight services group, and Australian group. In the United Kingdom, the manufacture of packaging was the leading activity, as it became in the United States following the 1987 acquisition of the Rexham Corporation of North Carolina for $240 million. This acquisition provided a new base for the development of the firm's North American activities. The building products activities were mostly in the United Kingdom and Europe, though again a U.S. presence in this sector was secured in 1987 through the acquisition of an interest in MiTek of St. Louis, Missouri. Tissue manufacturing was the firm's foremost activity in Australia following the acquistion of Scott's 50% interest in Bowater-Scott of Australia in 1986, in return for the sale of Bowater's interest in Bowater-Scott's U.K. firm to Scott. Further consideration of Bowater's strategic direction led in 1989 to the disposal of the freight group and to the takeover of Norton Opax PLC, whose strengths lay in the complementary fields of printing and publishing. The creation of the combined entity was marked by a new name—Bowater PLC.

Principal Subsidiaries: Bowater Packaging Ltd.; McCorquodale Security Printers; MiTek Industries Inc. (U.S.A., 56%); Rexham Industries Inc. (U.S.A.); Bowater Industries Australia Ltd.

Further Reading: Martin, Roscoe C., *From Forest to Front Page,* Birmingham, University of Alabama Press 1956; Muir, Augustus, *The British Paper and Board Makers' Association 1872–1972: A Centenary History,* London, privately printed, 1972; *History and Activities of the Ralli Trading Group,* London, Ralli Brothers (Trading) Ltd, 1979; Reader, W.J., *Bowater: a History,* Cambridge, Cambridge University Press, 1981.

—Richard Roberts

BUNZL PLC

Stoke House
Stoke Green
Stoke Poges
Slough SL2 4JN
United Kingdom
(0753) 693693
Fax: (0753) 694 694

Public Company
Incorporated: 1940 as Tissue Papers Ltd.
Employees: 9,300
Sales: £1.46 billion (US$2.82 billion)
Stock Exchange: London

Bunzl is an international group of companies engaged in the marketing and distribution of paper and plastic disposables, printing and writing papers, and specialty building materials to a wide variety of end-use markets principally in the United States and Europe. Bunzl has a worldwide cigarette-filter manufacturing business and has plastic-products manufacturing operations in Europe, the United States, and Brazil. Bunzl is focused on a limited number of substantial businesses, each of which occupies a leading or prominent position in its chosen marketplace. Its most important market is the United States.

The present company was set up in the United Kingdom in 1940, but it was the offshoot of a much older and larger Austrian enterprise, which began in 1854 as a haberdashery business in Bratislava, Czechoslovakia and moved to Austria in 1883. From haberdashery it moved into rag trading, and from that into textile and paper manufacturing. The firm traded as Bunzl & Biach, but was run from an early date by the Bunzl family. By 1914 it was well established in the textile, paper, and pulp industries, and had branches throughout the Austro-Hungarian Empire.

In the late 1920s Bunzl & Biach developed what was probably the world's first cigarette filter. It was actually invented by a Hungarian called Boris Aivaz, but as it was made from crepe paper he needed the cooperation of a paper manufacturer. The filters went into production in 1927, and over the next ten years were sold to cigarette manufacturers in 15 countries. The idea did not catch on widely, however, and cigarette filters were no more than a sideline for the firm in the 1930s.

The business, still owned and run by the Bunzl family, continued to prosper until Hitler's annexation of Austria in 1938. The Bunzls, being Jewish, had every reason to fear a Nazi takeover and had taken the precaution of moving the company's headquarters from Vienna to Switzerland two years earlier. They also had a subsidiary company in London, Bunzl & Biach (British) Ltd., which gave them an alternative base. When the Nazi government took over the company's Austrian assets most of the family emigrated, some to Switzerland and some to the United States, but the majority to the United Kingdom.

In this new environment the family began to rebuild its business, some concentrating on textiles and some on paper. The latter group was headed by Hugo Bunzl, who had been the first to show interest in the idea of cigarette filters. In 1940, he and several colleagues founded Tissue Papers Ltd., a company manufacturing tissue and crepe paper, together with the cigarette filters, in U.K. factories. This business remained very small during the war years, and had fewer than 30 employees in 1946.

In 1946 the Bunzl family regained control of its Austrian business, but Tissue Papers Ltd. continued to develop independently. It took on the international distribution of the Austrian company's paper products, and in 1952 changed its name to Bunzl Pulp & Paper Ltd., but continued to manufacture its own products in the United Kingdom.

Among these were cigarette filters. In the post-war period, filter-tipped cigarettes became more popular and this side of Bunzl's business gradually expanded. In the 1940s filters were still made from paper, and the production process was a slow one. A number of chemical companies experimented with other materials and eventually Eastman Kodak came up with a superior material, cellulose acetate tow. Filters made from this material proved to be more efficient and could be produced at higher speed. Bunzl began to use this material in 1954 and the cigarette manufacturers responded by launching more filter-tipped brands.

This technical advance coincided with the first indications from medical research that cigarette smoking could be seriously harmful. The World Health Organization published one of the earliest reports on the subject in 1955. Another ten years were to pass before the link with lung cancer was conclusively proved, but from the mid-1950s filter-tipped cigarettes began to be seen as a way of reducing whatever health risk there might be.

As a result, the new filter-tipped brands started to gain market share rapidly in all the developed countries. Bunzl rose to this challenge with remarkable speed and success for a small company. In the United Kingdom it quickly stepped up its output and became virtually the sole supplier of filters to the two companies which then controlled 90% of the cigarette market, Imperial Tobacco and Gallaher Ltd. Both these companies had tried making their own filters but decided when the technology changed to buy in their supplies from Bunzl.

In the United States, the Bunzl family set up a separate company, American Filtrona Corporation, in 1954. This company and Bunzl Pulp & Paper had shares in each other's business but neither controlled the other. Besides supplying their home markets, both set up overseas subsidiaries, some wholly owned, some jointly owned and some in partnership with local interests. In this way the Filtrona group, as it came to be called, soon became the world leader in cigarette filters. By 1964 the group was manufacturing in five European countries, the United States, Canada, South Africa, Australia, India, Brazil, and Argentina. The companies directly controlled by

Bunzl Pulp & Paper increased their filter output twelvefold between 1956 and 1964.

Meanwhile, the company was expanding in other directions. Its international paper trading business was growing steadily and it had several factories in the United Kingdom, making a variety of paper and packaging products as well as filters. In the late 1950s its profits began to rise steeply and in 1957 it went public. Only 30% of the equity was released on to the market at that stage and the Bunzl family retained control of the company for another decade.

In its first 11 years as a public company, Bunzl's profits rose uninterruptedly, from less than £1 million a year to more than £5 million, and the company became a favorite with investors. However, its growth was mainly due to the success of filter cigarettes, which was unlikely to continue at the same rate. In the United Kingdom, filter cigarettes grew from 11% of the market in 1959 to 70% in 1968, but after that their share grew more slowly. At the same time, awareness of the health risks of smoking, with or without filters, was increasing throughout the 1960s and governments began to impose restrictions on how cigarettes could be marketed.

Bunzl suffered its first reduction in profits in 1969. Apart from the adverse market conditions it was beginning to face, the company fell under a cloud in 1967–1969, when the Monopolies Commission held an enquiry into the supply of cigarette filters in the United Kingdom. This was instigated by Courtaulds, which had been supplying Bunzl with the acetate tow it needed, when Eastman Kodak and Bunzl jointly set up a factory in the United Kingdom to produce this material themselves. The commission eventually rejected Courtaulds's complaints, ruling that although Bunzl was in a monopoly position it had not abused it. Even so, the publicity was unwelcome because it drew attention to the company's vulnerability.

Against this background of assorted threats to its main profit earner, Bunzl saw that it must reduce its dependence on the cigarette market by expanding more vigorously in other directions. The company already had a foothold in the packaging market and its first thought was to develop this area. In the late 1960s, through a mixture of product development and acquisitions, Bunzl moved into the production of polythene film and bags, self-adhesive labels, tapes, and plastic tubes.

In 1970, a much more ambitious step was taken: Bunzl Pulp & Paper took over Bunzl & Biach, its one time big brother in Austria. The U.K. company had long been selling the paper products of the Austrian company overseas and by 1970 was the bigger of the two. This takeover increased Bunzl's turnover by almost half, raised its work force to more than 7,000, and put it squarely into paper manufacturing as well as merchanting. The enlarged company was split into four divisions, filters, paper, packaging, and plastics, and for a few years profits grew strongly. In 1974, when the paper market was particularly buoyant, profits reached a peak of £14 million, of which less than half came from filters.

In the later 1970s the company found that it could not sustain this progress. Inflation continued to push up turnover, but profits did not regain their 1974 level for nine years. Taking inflation into account, there was a steep decline in real terms. The main problems were in the filter market. In the developed countries cigarette smoking was declining, and cigarette manufacturers were increasingly making their own filters. Imperial Tobacco, Bunzl's biggest single customer, began to do so in

the 1970s. In less developed countries there were still growth opportunities, but Bunzl was by then struggling to maintain existing sales levels.

At the same time, the company's diversification program failed to deliver the expected benefits. The Austrian paper mills faced increasing competition from Eastern Europe and were badly in need of re-equipment. After paying interest on the debts they had accumulated, there was no surplus to swell group profits. In the United Kingdom, the plastics division successfully broke into new markets, particularly pipes for building and agricultural uses, but against that Bunzl made an ill-judged entry into the data processing business which resulted only in losses.

By 1980 it was clear that the company must find a new strategy. In that year it took the painful step of selling its Austrian paper business, which it had only owned for ten years. This sharply reduced the company's turnover and work force, but improved its financial position and opened the way to new acquisitions. At the same time G.G. Bunzl, who had headed the company since 1961, handed over the chair to Ernest Beaumont, (a Bunzl by birth, who had changed his name), and a new chief executive, James White, was brought in from outside the company.

Under the new team, Bunzl was reorganized into three divisions: filters, pulp and paper merchanting, and industrial. After the sale of Bunzl & Biach, the company's work force was down to about 4,000, the majority based in the United Kingdom, and around 70% of its profits were coming from the declining filter business. Of its other businesses, pulp and paper trading was the next largest contributor to profits and it was decided to develop this division. In particular, Bunzl was attracted by the growing business of distributing specialized paper and plastic products to industrial customers, such as supermarkets and airlines, as opposed to trading in bulk paper and pulp.

Between 1981 and 1984 Bunzl systematically bought its way into this business, first in the United States, state by state, then Australia. Among its more important acquisitions were Jersey Paper and the PCI/Mac-Pak Group, both in the United States, but there were many others. By the end of 1984 Bunzl's turnover was five times what it had been in 1980 and profits had grown from £11 million to £28 million. More importantly, the company had finally freed itself from its long dependence on cigarette filters, which contributed less than 20% of profits in 1984 and that year Bunzl cut its link with American Filtrona Corporation.

The success of this diversification plan led the company into what Jane Fuller, writing in the *Financial Times* on March 28, 1990, called "a headlong rush for growth." In the years 1985–1987, Bunzl raised capital from two rights issues, increased borrowing, and spent some £400 million on acquisitions. Around 70 separate purchases were made. In contrast to Bunzl's previous policy, many of the acquisitions took the company into fields quite unrelated to its existing business, such as parcel distribution, graphic arts supplies, and electrical equipment distribution. The group's three divisions at the start of the decade expanded to five, the distribution division covering a multitude of different products.

This policy worked well in the short term. Profits raced up from £28 million in 1984 to £86 million in 1987, and earnings per share also increased. However, problems soon emerged among the acquisitions and by 1987 the company had started to shed some of the more troublesome ones. In 1988 there were more disposals, including most of the transportation division, and profits made only a small advance. In 1989 the company was back to four divisions: paper, building materials, plastics, and cigarette filters. Turnover was down by 6%, and profits slumped by 30%. James White, who had become chairman in 1988, came under sharp attack from shareholders and admitted in 1990 that "with the benefit of hindsight we made too many acquisitions too quickly." Bunzl entered the 1990s slightly chastened and slightly slimmer than a year or two earlier, but much larger and more broadly based than in 1980, and with better prospects than in its cigarette-dependent days.

A boardroom reorganization in November 1990 saw the departure of James White and the appointment as chairman of David Kendall, former managing director of BP Oil and Bunzl non-executive director since 1988.

Principal Subsidiaries: Bunzl Distribution USA Inc.; Bunzl Australia Ltd.; Bunzl Fine Paper Ltd; Wilhelm Seiler GmbH (Germany); Bunzl Italia SpA; Bunzl Building Supply Inc. (U.S.A.); Filtrona International Ltd.; Filtrona Instruments & Automation Ltd.; Bunzl Plastics Europe; Bunzl Plastics Inc. (U.S.A.).

Further Reading: *The Bunzl Group of Companies, 1854–1954,* London, Bunzl, 1954.

—John Swan

CHAMPION INTERNATIONAL CORPORATION

One Champion Plaza
Stamford, Connecticut 06921
U.S.A.
(203) 358-7000
Fax: (203) 358-7495

Public Company
Incorporated: 1893 as Champion Coated Paper Company
Employees: 28,500
Sales: $5.09 billion
Stock Exchange: New York

Champion International Corporation is one of the largest paper- and wood-product makers in the world; its specialty has long been printing and writing papers. The company's early success was due to its ability to offer a quality product at substantially lower costs than its competitors. Champion's emphasis is still on fine white papers, but its product line includes many varieties of paper and packaging such as cardboard cartons, grocery bags, and giftwrap. The company also manufactures newsprint, lumber, plywood, and specialty building products. Champion is one of the largest private land owners in the United States, with vast timber holdings in the South and West.

Champion Coated Paper Company was founded in Hamilton, Ohio, in 1893 by a retired greeting-card and valentine printer, Peter Thomson. Thomson was an energetic businessman, keenly competitive and ambitious. Peter Thomson's aggressive quick thinking turned some of his company's early misfortunes into successes. In December 1901, the paper mill at Hamilton was destroyed by fire. In 1913, a flood of the great Miami River followed by fire again destroyed the Champion mill. Both times new mills were built and new machinery installed. These natural catastrophes turned out well for Champion, as the new equipment gave the company a considerable edge over competitors who were using older, less productive equipment.

The company has been owned and managed principally by members of the Thomson family through most of its history. In 1906, Peter Thomson's son-in-law, Reuben B. Robertson Sr., founded the Champion Fibre Company in Canton, North Carolina. Robertson's company provides the Hamilton mills with a supply of wood pulp, the raw material from which paper is made. Family members thus were in control of both

ends of Champion paper production. The two companies were nominally separate entities until 1935, when they merged to form the Champion Paper and Fibre Company. Peter Thomson's two sons, Alexander and Logan, joined the family business, as did Reuben Robertson and Peter Thomson's other son-in-law, Walter D. Randall. Peter Thomson instituted the rule of primogeniture for his corporation, stipulating that only one son from each of these four families, preferably the eldest son, would be allowed to enter the business. In 1932, nearly 73% of Champion's stock was owned by members of the Thomson family. In 1960 that figure was still close to 42%.

In the 1910s and 1920s, Champion made its reputation by always offering the lowest prices in the industry for its coated papers, papers with smooth surfaces that can be imprinted. Champion was able to offer a consistently low-priced product for several reasons. Champion's stockholders were principally family members, so there was no need to offer high dividends to please Wall Street. Profits were quickly reinvested into new and better mill equipment. Champion avoided the notoriously volatile newsprint industry. It instead made magazine and book paper, paper for cigarette packages and gum wrappers, coffee bags and tobacco pouches, post cards, and pickle labels. Because of the size of Champion mills' booming production, they were among the hardest hit in the industry in the 1921 recession that followed World World War I. Champion recovered quickly, however, and continued to churn out a high volume of coated paper into the next decade.

In 1926, Champion instituted a technical research division, a relatively new concept in the paper industry. The craft of papermaking is an ancient one, and few papermakers in the United States had scientific training in the field. In 1926, problems with the alum that was used to make the coating on the paper led Champion's president to hire a chemist from Du Pont. After only a week of research, this chemist, a veteran of the chemical warfare service in World War I, found a cheap additive to the alum that eliminated the problem. Champion's management was convinced of the financial gains possible by having research chemists as permanent staff. Within a few years, Champion had 40 chemists in its research laboratories. The investment in the laboratory paid off markedly. Champion's paper went up in quality and down in cost. It was also able to develop profitable by-products from its mills, such as tanning extract, turpentine, and cleansing powder.

During the Great Depression of the 1930s, Champion continued to pull in a profit and to plow money into new equipment. Champion mill production ran well ahead of industry averages throughout the Depression years. The mills actually continued to expand their output, in spite of reduced markets for the industry as a whole. One factor that contributed to Champion's well-being in these competitive times was its forced sale of some of its North Carolina timberland in 1931 to the government, which used 90,000 Champion acres for the Smoky Mountain National Park, and paid $3 million for them. Between 1929 and 1932, Champion spent $4 million on new equipment or improvements to existing equipment. Champion opened a new mill in Houston, Texas, to capture profits from cheap southern pine.

The company forced pay cuts on its workers twice between 1929 and 1932, to keep down its expenses. Champion mills were not unionized at the time, but workers were said to have high company loyalty, and they had steady work six days a week. The Thomson family prided itself on its care of the Champion mill workers, who usually earned 15% higher pay than industry averages. Company policy was not to hire black workers or new immigrants, preferring second or third generation Americans of German or Anglo-Saxon descent.

The paper industry took a sharp upward turn with the entrance of the United States into World War II. Wartime demands for paper were high, and Champion continued to expand. After the war, the Champion Paper and Fiber Company was near the top of the industry in its coated white book paper sales. The company diversified its product line, to make bag paper, cardboard, and milk cartons. To prepare for more competitive conditions in the postwar economy, Champion began to buy timberland and paper-marketing outlets. Champion wanted control of its raw material—timber—as well as the distribution of its finished products. Champion had used this strategy, vertical integration, to some extent since 1906, by operating the pulp mill in Canton, North Carolina, to supply the Ohio paper mills. With its investments after the war, Champion was continuing an earlier successful policy. The company liquidated its subsidiary chemical company in 1947, and in 1951 sold another chemical laboratory. The company continued to invest in expensive machinery at its U.S. plants and opened a pulp plant in Brazil as well. Growth in the paper industry throughout the 1950s was slow. The decade ended in a recession. With Champion's high costs, profits were too low to keep the company healthy. By the end of fiscal year 1959, Champion's net income had fallen dramatically to less than $8 million, from a high two years earlier of more than $14 million.

In March 1960, Champion's president, Reuben B. Robertson Jr. died. He was the grandson of Champion's founder, Peter Thomson. His father, Reuben B. Robertson Sr. resigned the chairmanship of Champion in the wake of his son's death. For the first time in the company's history, a person outside the Thomson family attained the office of president. With the company in serious financial trouble, the new president, Karl Bendetsen, took unprecedented measures. The former chairman, Reuben Robertson Sr. had operated the company in a paternalistic fashion. Bendetsen, on the other hand, realized that in many ways the family style of management had hurt the company. He fired 20% of Champion's employees within a year of taking office and extensively reorganized the corporation's management.

Champion had been producing more than 100 different grades of paper. Bendetsen dropped all but the top 20 best sellers. Many executives took early retirement, and Bendetsen sold off the company's fleet of seven private jets. These cost-cutting measures were rapid and severe, and Bendetsen was not popular in the company's home base, Hamilton, Ohio. Bendetsen boasted in a *Business Week* report of June 26, 1961, two years later, that Champion was "no longer paternalistic in any sense of the word." The Thomson family gradually withdrew from Champion's board of directors. By 1967 the company's profits had gone up by 41%, and *Forbes* of March 15, 1967, declared Champion "one of the best managed companies in the entire paper industry."

In 1967, Champion merged with United States Plywood Corporation, a large lumber manufacturer. The merger was seen as equally beneficial for the companies. Both companies used timber, each to make different products. U.S. Plywood

added its forest reserves in the western United States to Champion's large holdings in southern pine. The new combined company was expected to make more efficient use of its joint timber resources, to cut its costs substantially, in general, and to gain some protection from the volatility of business cycles in both industries.

At the time of the merger, the new company was given the name U.S. Plywood–Champion Papers, Inc. Karl Bendetsen and U.S. Plywood's president, Gene Brewer, were to share the running of the corporation. During the first year of the merger, however, the plywood division fared much worse than expected, and Bendetsen was elected chief executive officer, outranking Brewer. A year later, Brewer resigned. Within three years, most of U.S. Plywoods remaining executives had also left the company. In 1972 the company changed its name again, to Champion International Corporation. Although profits rose the company was still not doing as well as any one had hoped.

Management problems plagued Champion International in the 1970s. Karl Bendetsen reached the age of mandatory retirement in 1972. Passing over all of Champion's top executives, Bendetsen hired a man from outside the company to take over as chief executive. Bendetsen's successor, Thomas Willers, had been through a merger similar to the U.S. Plywood–Champion merger. He had been chief executive of Hooker Petroleum when it was bought by Occidental Petroleum. Bendetsen thought Willers would be able to pull Champion out of its post-merger stagnation.

Willers took Champion in a new direction by diversifying its products even further. The company bought into the home-furnishing and carpeting industries under Willers's leadership. Although Karl Bendetsen was officially in retirement, he was so alarmed by the tack Willers was taking that he used his influence with Champion's board to force Willers to resign. Willers was with the company less than two years. A former head of Champion's timber division, Andrew C. Sigler, was then named president and chief executive officer, in December 1974. Under Sigler's management, the company focused more on its original product line. In 1977 Hoerner Waldorf Corporation, a paperboard and corrugated-box manufacturer, merged into Champion. This strengthened Champion's stance in the domestic paper market, but heavy reinvestments in new mills and equipment and a long slump in the building-products industry continued to keep Champion's profits down into the 1980s.

In 1984 Champion bought the St. Regis Corporation for $1.8 billion. It was an overnight deal that rescued St. Regis from a hostile takeover by Australian newspaper magnate Rupert Murdoch. St. Regis had been one of the largest U.S. producers of magazine paper and newsprint. The St. Regis acquisition doubled the holdings of timberland to 6.4 million acres owned or controlled by Champion, making it one of the largest private landowners in the United States. Afraid that Champion itself would be vulnerable to a takeover attempt after the St. Regis merger, Chairman Sigler instituted a sweeping debt reduction plan. He shut down seven wood-product plants in the western United States and sold off assets in Champion's packaging and building-supply divisions. In the next two years, Champion continued to narrow its product scope to mostly newsprint and white coated papers, selling off subsidiaries in brown paper packaging, envelopes, cardboard boxes, and wood products.

An upswing in the economy helped Champion's net income rise after the St. Regis acquisition, but the paper industry slumped suddenly in 1989. Wall Street saw an end to the latest high cycle in the paper industry in 1989, and Champion stock continued to fall. In 1990 there was speculation that the company would sell some of its extensive timber holdings in California, Montana, Oregon, and Washington to raise cash. The estimated value of this property is at least $2 billion. With fierce competition for global resources and concerns about deforestation, the dispersal of Champion's vast timberlands may have worldwide repercussions.

Principal Subsidiaries: Weldwood of Canada, Ltd. (85%); Champion Papel e Celulose Ltda. (Brazil); Champion Export.

Further Reading: "Competition not Cartelization," *Fortune,* October 1932; "Champion Paper," *Fortune,* January 1949; "The Merger That Wasn't Made in Heaven," *Forbes,* March 15, 1967.

—Angela Woodward

DAIO PAPER CORPORATION

DAIO PAPER CORPORATION

2-7-2, Yaesu
Chuo-ku, Tokyo 104
Japan
(03) 3271-1961
Fax: (03) 3281-2094

Public Company
Incorporated: 1943 as Taio Paper Mfg. Co., Ltd.
Employees: 3,305
Sales: ¥275.40 billion (US$2.03 billion)
Stock Exchanges: Tokyo Osaka

The Daio Paper Corporation is Japan's fourth largest paper manufacturer, and controls 6% of Japan's home market. The company produces a full range of papers, including newsprint, sanitary-use papers, and paperboard. Daio, spelled Taio until the late 1980s, has been operated by the Ikawa family since it was established in 1943 in Ehime Prefecture. Although The company's stock has been publicly traded since 1982, the Ikawa family presence is still felt.

Papermaking in Japan has historically been considered something of an art form. Since the seventh century A.D., Japanese papermakers have produced some of the world's finest paper from a wide variety of materials including hemp, mulberry, rice, and other vegetable fibers. Papermaking was traditionally a winter occupation for farmers. Now, papermaking is big business. Machine-made papers began replacing handmade after the Meiji restoration of 1868.

Taio Paper began operations during World War II. The Japanese paper industry enjoyed prosperity based on abundant pulpwood resources in Japan and in Japanese-held territories. Preferred species of trees for pulp included fir, spruce, red and black pine, beech, and hemlock, all of which grew on Japan's home islands. After the war, however, raw materials became much more scarce. Japan lost the southern half of the island of Sakhalin, the Karufuto region, the source of more than half of Japan's pulpwood. Resources from Korea and Formosa were no longer available.

For several years after the war, Japan's paper industry struggled to regain prewar levels of production. In 1950, paper production was only 54% of the prewar level, and tight money hampered capital investment in the industry. Japanese paper manufacturers like Taio were technologically far behind their foreign competitors. U.S. paper mills, for example, used con-veyor systems to move logs through the entire pulping process without being repeatedly handled by workers.

Taio's fortunes improved with the industry's by 1953, when prewar production levels were finally met. Cardboard became a major new product; its use rose 20% annually between 1954 and 1964. Total paper production increased fourfold in the same period. By 1964, Japan ranked third, behind the United States and Canada, in paper production. Taio grew rapidly on this wave.

While Japan's paper industry was blossoming in the 1950s and 1960s, its own pulpwood resources dwindled. Imported pulpwood took up some of the slack, but papermakers looked for other options. One twist was the use of synthetics. Japanese manufacturers led the way toward commercial production of extruded polystyrene sheets used as paper. The high quality product had a smooth finish, and was waterproof, and extremely durable. The plastic paper sold for about two-and-one-half times the price of regular paper but was excellent for specific uses. Synthetic paper got a boost from the Japanese government, which provided subsidies for research. By the early 1970s, plastic papers were well established in the Japanese market.

In addition to innovative product development, Japanese manufacturers set out to expand operations overseas, closer to raw material sources. Taio imported woodchips from the United States, Canada, and other countries.

By 1980, Taio felt its dependence on one American company, Weyerhaeuser, was too great. When the price of woodchips escalated in 1980, Taio was prompted to establish greater control of its raw material supply. Taio entered a joint venture with a Japanese trading firm, Marubeni. The resultant Sacramento-based company, The California Woodfiber Corporation, began operations in the summer of 1980.

In the 1980s, patterns of paper use changed along with certain patterns of social behavior. Paper used to publish books, for example, became lighter in weight as the reading public opted for low-priced paperback editions. New technology affected the types of papers used. Demand increased for specialties, like coated papers and photogravure papers. The growth of direct-marketing advertising, such as catalogues and pamphlets, generated increased use of printing paper.

In 1983, Japan's new Law for Structural Improvement of Specific Industries called for a revamping of the paper industry. Taio and other manufacturers were required to dispose of surplus production capabilities. Development of new technologies also became a priority. Supply and demand for paper and cardboard products stabilized as a result of the measures.

By the mid-1980s, Taio found that new technology created new markets. Thermal papers for use in facsimile machines became an important product. In 1987, Taio tallied record profits after three years without profits. The company's rationalization efforts combined with the appreciating yen, allowed Taio to import more woodchips for the same amount of money.

Taio's huge share of the Japanese domestic market resulted in the high profits of 1987. Profits reached new highs again in 1989, and then dipped due to a heavy interest burden from the company's capital expansion. These investments, including a new newsprint machine that came on line in February 1990, promised to pay off handsomely in the 1990s. In fiscal year 1990 Taio Paper Mfg. Co., Ltd. changed its name to Daio Paper Corporation.

Daio Paper followed the trends in international business, taking on a global orientation in the 1980s. In the early 1990s the future of the paper industry was uncertain. Stable markets, like the United States, were seeking less dependence on wood pulp products. New markets were opening up in eastern Europe, the potential of which remained unknown. In the past Daio has proven its ability to adapt to changing market conditions.

—Thomas M. Tucker

DAISHOWA PAPER MFG. CO., LTD.

DAISHOWA PAPER MANUFACTURING CO., LTD.

4-1-1, Imai
Fuji City, Shizuoka 417
Japan
(0545) 30-3000
Fax: (0545) 32-0005

Public Company
Incorporated: 1938
Employees: 5,173
Sales: ¥344.88 billion (US$2.54 billion)
Stock Exchange: Tokyo

Daishowa Paper Manufacturing Co., Ltd. was in 1990 the second-largest papermaking company in Japan. It produced about two-and-one-half million metric tons of paper and paperboard at that time, generating approximately 10% of Japan's annual paper production. Known for diverse operations, its concentrations include newsprint, kraft paper, and paperboard. The firm also manufactures laminated particleboard and operates forestry and related businesses. Daishowa operates five mills and a building-materials plant in Japan, and several other mills in Canada, the United States, and Australia. With its corporate headquarters in Fuji City, Daishowa dominates the Shizuoka Prefecture, south of Mount Fuji, where most of its major industrial complexes have been built.

Daishowa traces it origins back to Saito Ltd., a brokerage firm supplying raw materials to the paper industry, founded in 1921 by Chiichiro Saito, father of Daishowa's honorary chairman in 1991, Ryoei Saito, and grandfather of its president, Kiminori Saito. In 1922 the company became Saito Brothers Co. and the business expanded to include paper sales. In March 1927 Saito Ltd. established Showa Paper Company with a capitalization of ¥100,000 and began producing paper and paperboard at Yoskinaga. Shortly thereafter, in 1933, Saito Ltd. built a mill in Suzukawa for the production of kraft paper.

War between Japan and China broke out in July of 1937, and in September Japan's government approved two economic-control laws. The Temporary Capital Adjustment Act curtailed the establishment of companies, capital increases, payments, bond flotations, and long-term loans. The Temporary Export and Import Commodities Measures gave the government control of the import and export of raw materials. In 1938, nevertheless, with a capitalization of ¥5.5 million, Saito Ltd.

merged with four other Shizuoka companies to form Daishowa Paper Manufacturing Company. The Saito family retained control of the new company. One year later, the Suzukawa mill became the first integrated kraft paper mill in Japan.

Japan's pulp and paper industry hit its peak wartime capacity in 1940, when its paper output was 1.7 million tons. Industry in Japan declined steadily as the war dragged on, and in 1941 Japan provoked a war in the Pacific with the attack on the U.S. Pearl Harbor. By 1946 the overall production of the Japanese pulp and paper industry had shrunk to 231,190 tons, less than 20% of what it had been in in 1940. Despite this gloomy portent, Daishowa would ride the tsunami of Japan's fierce industrial and economic recovery, landing safely on the shores of mega-prosperity with many of its fellow industrial companies. The Allied powers readily aided Japan's fast-paced growth by their postwar control of the powerful ancient Japanese business monopolies, the *zaibatsu*. In 1937 the top three *zaibatsu* controlled 65% of pulp and 83% of the paper industry; by 1950 these figures were reduced to 39% and 57%, respectively. With the democratization of industry in Japan, there erupted fierce competition in most industries, which spurred rapid technological expansion and the building of new facilities.

It was at this time that Ryoei Saito, a young businessman and Chiichiro Saito's son, assumed leadership at Daishowa. The younger Saito led his family-controlled, publicly traded company in a violent struggle against three kingpins of the Japanese paper establishment, Oji Paper Company, Jujo Paper Company, and Honshu Paper Company. This trio had been created from Oji Paper, part of the Mitsui *zaibatsu,* when Oji Paper was divided after World War II. In 1950, five years after the end of the war, construction of the Fuji mill began, and production started in 1953. In 1960 Daishowa started production of coated paper. In the same year, production was begun on a mill in Shiraoi that was to become one of Daishowa's largest integrated mills, producing pulp, paper, and paperboard. Saito's aggressive price cutting and rapidly increasing market share may have appeared uncouth to the Japanese, but by 1965 Daishowa had seized the number-two spot among Japanese papermakers.

Japan's economy continued to ride high, peaking from 1965 to 1973, when production of paper and paperboard mushroomed 10% to 11% annually. The Iwanu mill was built in 1967. Daishowa imported its first U.S. woodchips in 1965. Daishowa Paper Trading Co., Ltd. was established as an independent sales organization in 1967, the same year that Harris Daishowa (Australia) Pty., Ltd., the corporation's Australian subsidiary, was established. In 1968 Daishowa Pulp Manufacturing Co., Ltd. was founded, followed by Daishowa-Marubeni International Ltd., in Canada in 1969, and Daishowa Uniboard Co., Ltd. in 1970.

During the late 1960s and early 1970s Japan began to pay the price for its dynamic resurgance. One particularly disturbing cost was the pollution caused by its bustling industry. The Japanese government began to crack down on *kogai,* or pollution. In Shizouka Prefecture, there was particular trouble with toxic sludge on the bottom of Tagonoura Bay, for which the government held Daishowa responsible. Daishowa, like most industrial companies, complied with government demands for environmental protection, in particular for protecting water against pollution.

As environmental issues continued to galvanize public outcry, many business converted to the use of recycled paper. By the early 1990s, demand for recycled paper was growing faster than supply, and Daishowa was in tune with the trend. Daishowa had been recycling pulp since 1959, when it started producing de-inked pulp (DIP) from old newspapers at the Fuji mill. Progressive efforts to develop higher-quality recycled pulp resulted in the formation of a project in 1985 that concentrated on improving the de-inking process. In 1988 the resulting improved system was installed in a new plant at Yoshinaga that produced a superior DIP. In 1990 Daishowa had 13 de-inking facilities in 4 of its Japanese mills; it produced 2,000 tons a day of recycled pulp for use in making paperboard and paper. Construction of two more such facilities was planned for 1991, adding capacity for an additional 330 tons per day.

The environmental crackdown of the 1970s and the oil crisis of 1973 were followed by a severe general recession. Average annual growth in the pulp and paper market shrank to a mere 1.1% from 1973 through 1982. Daishowa, nevertheless, showed a striking increase in sales and profitability from 1978 to 1979, when it rose in international status from 37th to 20th place in pulp and paper companies worldwide. Daishowa ranked fifth among companies outside North America, and third among those in Japan. Its sales were US$1.3 billion; earnings were US$14.5 million.

Despite the oil crisis and the ensuing financial difficulties, Daishowa continued its program of unabated expansion. Having just established foreign holdings, in the United States and Canada, in 1980 it upgraded its facilities at Iwanuma to lower the weight of its newsprint, in keeping with the industry trend toward lighter papers. The mill would have a capacity of 360,000 tons per day of newsprint in addition to 120,000 tons per day of coated paper. In addition, Daishowa installed a machine to produce carbonless copy paper at Yoshinaga, following the trend set by Taio Paper—now Daio Paper—earlier in the year. These expansions came at a time when imports to Japan were rising despite the weakening Japanese demand for paper. From 1977 through 1982, imports rose an average of 17% per year. Although imports ultimately comprised only 2% to 4% of total Japanese consumption, newsprint and kraft linerboard, two of Daishowa's specialties, represented 70% of total imports, accounting for 8.9% of the newsprint, and 14.5% of the kraft linerboard consumed in Japan.

If import statistics did their job to rattle the pulp and paper business, other accumulated industry wide expenditures combined to ensure the industry's decline in the early 1980s. Excessive borrowing, expensive environmental-protection programs, and escalating energy costs took their toll. Daishowa, sporting its own portfolio of financial mistakes, became a casualty of the accelerating decline, dropping from its 1979 status as third-largest papermaker in Japan to last place among the top ten in 1982. As profits slid downward, Ryoei Saito was forced to resign and cede control of Daishowa to its principal creditor, the Sumitomo Bank, which appointed some of its own representatives to the Daishowa board. The Sumitomo Bank's rescue of Daishowa was not unique in Japan, where a firm typically cultivated a close relationship with one principal bank, relying on it for most borrowing needs. This bank maintains all financial information on the company and has substantial influence in its management. Nevertheless, Ryoei

Saito did not take kindly to the management changes the Sumitomo Bank deemed appropriate. For its part, Sumitomo found that in addition to overspending in new production facilities, Ryoei Saito had used approximately US$1 billion of corporate funds to build his art collection, buy golf courses, and play the stock market. The bank compelled Saito to sell off much of the highly regarded art collection, and he begrudgingly resigned.

In 1983 Daishowa announced that it would repay the Sumitomo Bank's ¥23.5 billion in loans by June of that year and then terminate the relationship with Sumitomo. The move shocked the Japanese business community, in which bank-company relations are likely to last indefinitely. In June 1986, Ryoei Saito was able to regain control of the business, expelling his brother Kikuzo Saito from Daishowa's presidency and ousting a board director who had close ties with Sumitomo. Kikuzo Saito later claimed that Ryoei Saito had borrowed substantially from Daishowa funds for his own personal use. The Sumitomo Bank remains one of Daishowa's major institutional shareholders, with 3.9% of Daishowa's stock in 1990.

Once back at Daishowa, this time as honorary chairman of the company, Ryoie Saito remained true to his established interests and style. In May 1990, Saito caused a flurry in the international art market by purchasing the two most expensive paintings ever sold by auction: Renoir's *At the Moulin de la Galette,* which sold for US$78.1 million, and Vincent van Gogh's *Portrait of Dr. Gachet,* purchased for US$82.5 million. The paintings were snapped up within three days of each other, and although Saito deemed his shopping spree "no big deal" he also granted that his funds were borrowed against the collateral of Daishowa real estate.

In the early 1990s the Saito family continued to control 20% to 40% of the firm; in combination with its real estate holdings, the family's net worth was somewhere around US$1 billion. In an effort to prevent dilution of the Saito family's stake, Daishowa managed to expand during the late 1980s without issuing new stock, principally by taking on additional loans. This strategy more than doubled its debt between 1987 and 1990 to US$3 billion, more than five times shareholders' equity. In 1990 profits dropped 35% to US$35 million.

Kiminori Saito, nevertheless, continues his father's aggressive expansion of Daishowa, probably fueling the growth with family resources from Ashitaka Rinsan Kogyo, the family holding company. In April of 1990 that firm spent US$49 million to buy Daishowa's share of a 23-year-old Australian eucalyptus-chip venture with C. Itoh. It also purchased 25% of the preferred shares of Daishowa's new pulp mill in Alberta, Canada. On the other hand, a Japanese corporate research firm indicated that Ashitaka's 1990 accumulated debt of $300 million was created by borrowing against the collateral of Daishowa. Whatever the stability and origins of its financial underpinnings, Daishowa's expansion showed no signs of slowing down during the early 1990s. Its domestic expansion budget was a healthy US$330 million in 1991.

In addition to its development on its home turf, Daishowa aggressively expanded its overseas operations. In 1990 its major joint-venture operations included Cariboo Pulp & Paper Company, a softwood bleached kraft pulp mill, and Quesnel River Pulp Company, a chemi-thermo-mechanical pulp mill, both located in British Columbia, Canada. Foreign acquisitions made by Daishowa during 1988 include a US$78 million investment for Daishowa America Port Angeles mill, in Washington state. The company upgraded the mill with another US$52 million investment. In addition to producing newsprint, paperboard, pulp, lumber, and chemicals, as of 1990, the mill provided 20% of the paper used in U.S. telephone directories. The company spent an estimated US$500 million to purchase the North American assets of Reed International, a Quebec mill chiefly generating newsprint for Canadian and U.S. newspapers such as *The Washington Post* and *The New York Post*. In 1988, Daishowa started construction of its Peace River Pulp mill, a major bleached kraft pulp mill in Alberta, Canada. In early 1990, Daishowa bought a lumber mill from Canadian Forest Products to supply the plant, which began operations in summer 1990.

Principal Subsidiaries: Daishowa America Co., Ltd. (U.S.A.); Harris-Daishowa (Australia) Pty., Ltd.; Daishowa Canada Co., Ltd.; Daishowa (H.K.) Co., Ltd. (Hong Kong); Daishowa Canada Holdings Ltd.; Daishowa Forest Products (Canada); Daishowa, Inc. (Canada); Daishowa-Marubeni International, Ltd. (Canada).

—Elaine Belsito

DOMTAR INC.

395 de Maisonneuve Boulevard West
Montreal, Quebec H3A 1L6
Canada
(514) 848-5400
Fax: (514) 848-6878

Public Company
Incorporated: 1929 as Dominion Tar & Chemical Company
   Limited
Employees: 13,000
Sales: C$2.31 billion (US$1.99 billion)
Stock Exchanges: Montreal Toronto Vancouver New York

Domtar is one of Canada's leading suppliers of pulp and paper products. With a network of facilities across the country, Domtar is involved in every aspect of the pulp and paper business, from logging to pulp production and from manufacturing to selling fine papers and newsprint. Domtar has become a major manufacturer of construction materials such as gypsum wallboard, and in addition offers a diversified line of packaging materials. In 1989 the company completed the sale of its original chemical and energy businesses, eliminating the last vestiges of what had once been known as the Dominion Tar & Chemical Company Limited.

Dominion got its start in 1903 with the construction of a coal tar distillation plant in Sydney, Nova Scotia. Coal tar distillation is the process whereby a range of valuable chemicals is distilled from tar, which itself is obtained by a preliminary heating and distillation of coal. The resulting commercial by-products can be divided into three categories, those being hydrocarbons, such as benzene and napthalene; acids, such as phenol and the creosols; and bases, such as aniline, which provide a variety of dyes. In addition, the pitch residue of coal tar distillation is useful in the construction of roads, an application first made only a few years before the founding of Domtar in 1903. At that time, the commercially valuable properties of coal tar were just beginning to be explored, but as Canada's economy rapidly industrialized the Dominion plant turned out an increasing number of products, and the company grew quickly.

World War I culminated a period of great prosperity for Canada and Dominion Tar. The ensuing slump was fortunately brief, and by the mid-1920s industrial activity was again strong. Dominion's sales increased accordingly. The widespread growth of automobile traffic required the construction

of secure, all-weather roadways, boosting Dominion revenue from the sale of pitch; while the coal tar distillates continued to find an increasing number of applications in the chemical, textile, and steel industries. The relatively new field of pharmaceuticals also derived a variety of compounds from coal tar, as did the even-more-recent science of plastics. As a sign of its vigorous growth in these many areas, and in order to raise capital for further expansion, in 1929 Dominion Tar was incorporated and shortly thereafter offered its shares for public sale.

The year 1929 was perhaps not the ideal year in which to have incorporated. The October crash of the Montreal and Toronto stock markets, along with virtually every other in the world, precipitated ten years of depression in Canada. Dominion, which had by this time relocated to Quebec, weathered the storm with considerable success, although failing to pay a stock dividend as regularly as its leaders might have wished. Due to the wide variety of industries for which it manufactured goods, Dominion was able to maintain a minimum amount of business during even the leanest years, and after enduring a series of enforced layoffs and cuts in capital spending, emerged as a stronger, more efficient company by the end of the decade. By that time Canada had joined the Allies in World War II and the Canadian economy tooled up for what would become a 30-year boom.

The 1950s were not only a period of sustained growth at Dominion, but also marked the beginning of the company's expansion into the paper and construction businesses. With its enormous forest lands, Canada had become the world leader in the manufacture of paper products, in particular supplying the United States with a good portion of its paper needs. By the mid-1950s Dominion had studied closely the growing worldwide paper market and, flush with cash after a series of excellent years, in 1957 acquired 33% of Howard Smith Paper Mills Limited, with major mills at both Cornwall, Ontario, and Windsor, Quebec. Howard Smith was a maker of fine paper for printing and writing purposes and of kraft paper for applications requiring strength. Dominion's entry into the paper business, though limited, was viewed by most observers as somewhat unorthodox and many doubted that such a combination would prove manageable. The Dominion picture was complicated further the following year when it purchased an interest in Gypsum, Lime, & Alabastine Canada Limited, makers of gypsum wallboard for the construction industry. The company was now stretched across the three distinctly different businesses of chemicals, paper, and construction materials; but the financial results were excellent, encouraging the even bolder moves soon to follow.

At the close of the 1950s, Dominion was faced with a fundamental and recurring question about the direction of its future growth, a question it would answer differently during the following 30 years of its history. As President Wilfred Hall expressed it in 1964, in Canada as elsewhere businesses could not afford to remain small, yet Canada was unusual in the limited size of its internal markets. Dominion would therefore either have to concentrate exclusively on one of its businesses and expand internationally, or remain a fundamentally Canadian concern and diversify its interest across a number of industrial boundaries. In 1960 Hall and his advisors at Dominion chose the latter alternative; 30 years later, in an age of global competition, Domtar would reverse itself and begin paring down its holdings. Accordingly, in 1961, Hall announced a complex multiple-merger involving Dominion; the remaining shares of Howard Smith Paper; a maker of newsprint, St. Lawrence Corporation Limited; and Hinde & Dauch Limited, manufacturer of corrugated containers and merchandising displays. The result was an early example of the conglomerate, one of Canada's ten largest companies with sales approaching C$400 million and some 18,000 employees at over 270 facilities across the length of Canada. By any measure it was a complex and somewhat ungainly mixture of diverse businesses, and its sorting out and eventual coordination would take the better part of the decade to finish. Many industry analysts doubted that it would ever happen.

The newly reformed Dominion Tar & Chemical Company consisted of six operating groups, each of these in turn broken down into many divisions. Domtar Chemical represented the company's original interests in coal tar by-products such as creosols, dyes, and pitch, as well as recent acquisitions in salt mining and lime; Domtar Construction Materials handled wallboard products and a growing business in wood laminates for use in home furnishings; the pulp and paper products were split among three groups; and Domtar even entered the consumer products market via the Javex Company, maker of various cleaning agents. Within a few years the company had added the beginnings of an overseas presence—paper and plastics in the United Kingdom, bleach in the West Indies, and lime in Washington state. More substantial yet was the 1963 purchase of a 49% interest in Cellulosa d'Italia, an Italian paper company. Dominion's focus, however remained firmly on Canada and the United States, and from the beginning it proved remarkably adept at melding its diverse interests into a coherent whole. The various divisions did quite a bit of business with each other, allowing the company to keep product runs at their maximum and most efficient lengths while saving money on marketing expenses. Perhaps most impressive was Domtar Inc.'s—the name was officially changed in 1965—smooth absorption of its new paper businesses, which were soon providing more than 50% of corporate sales. In the space of a few years, Domtar had transformed itself from a medium-sized company into a huge conglomerate, best described as a pulp and paper manufacturer.

By the time T.N. Beaupre had replaced Hall as president in 1967, the new Domtar had taken shape. Beaupre simplified the company's structure by grouping its divisions into chemicals, construction, and pulp and paper units; and he sold off the consumer products division to Bristol-Myers for $37 million, recognizing that his company could not compete with the other, larger marketers of consumer goods. Domtar was now Canada's leading producer of fine papers, with more than 500 different grades in production; but its success in paper brought with it a long series of bitter disputes with organized labor, traditionally strong in the paper industries and hungry for a larger share of the profits generated by the robust economy of the late 1960s. Domtar has rarely enjoyed a year without either a strike, the threat of a strike, or the need to negotiate important and hard-fought contracts with labor, all of which has tended to complicate every aspect of its business planning.

After a number of excellent years at Domtar and in Canada generally, the bottom dropped out of the world economy in 1973 when the Organization of Petroleum Exporting Countries (OPEC) succeeded in quadrupling the price of oil. In the ensuing recession of 1974–1976, the downturn in Domtar's pulp and paper business was so severe that the company thought seriously of getting out of the industry altogether. Canada's share of the world market had shrunk to 19%, from 25% in 1961, and the prosperous 1960s had saddled Domtar with high labor costs at a time of shrinking sales and margins. New president Alex D. Hamilton adopted a conservative policy of closing marginally profitable mills while looking for further investments in construction, preferably in the United States. In 1978 Domtar satisfied both of those goals with its C$35 million purchase of Kaiser Cement's California wallboard facilities, which would also help to balance the flow of Canadian and U.S. dollars at Domtar, a company increasingly dependent on exports to the United States. Industry analysts described the move as typical of Domtar's recent tendency toward a conservative policy—the purchase was made a little late and at rather too high a price, but it was basically sound.

It was at about this time that Domtar became involved in a lengthy series of takeover bids. When the Argus Corporation, for many years owner of about 20% of Domtar's stock, decided to sell its Domtar holdings they were quickly snapped up by MacMillan Bloedel, a west-coast paper competitor of Domtar's. MacMillan then made an offer for Domtar's remaining shares, which elicited a counteroffer by Domtar for all of MacMillan's stock. At that point Canadian Pacific, a third paper company, also made a bid for MacMillan, prompting the premier of British Columbia to decree that MacMillan could not be purchased by any company outside the province. Chastened, MacMillan sold its 20% of Domtar to an agency of Quebec provincial government, the Caisse de dépôt et placement du Québec, entrusted with the investment of pension funds. A short time afterward, a second Quebec agency, the Société générale de financement du Québec also acquired a piece of Domtar, and by August 1981 the Quebec government thus controlled more than 40% of the company's stock. Under new president and CEO James H. Smith the company quickly underwent a thorough restructuring of its board of directors, which, together with the Quebec government's stock control, led to concern among English-speaking Canadian businessmen that Domtar would become an appendage of the French-speaking Quebec government. The issue came to a head when Domtar asked the Canadian government for help in funding the C$1 billion rehabilitation of its massive paper mill at Windsor, Ontario. The request was denied, fueling the conviction of Quebecois separatists that their province would never receive fair treatment at the hands of the Canadian government. As it turned out, Domtar went ahead with the work at the Windsor mill, creating a world-class fine-paper facility, while the Quebec government tried unsuccessfully to sell off the 46% of Domtar stock it still held.

In the meantime, Domtar sales had passed the C$1 billion mark in 1977 and leaped to C$1.7 billion in 1981. The severe recession of the early 1980s forced the company into a belt-tightening strategy and led to its request for federal aid on the big Windsor mill project, but in general the decade was good to Domtar. The company was again faced with the question of how best to expand beyond its already considerable size, and this time President Smith and his board of directors decided to concentrate on a fewer number of global products. In essence, that meant the end of Domtar's chemical businesses, which had long been dwarfed by the company's paper and construction interests, and by 1990 the chemical assets had been sold for about C$100 million. On the other hand, in 1987 Domtar paid US$241 million for Genstar Gypsum Products Company's family of wallboard plants in the United States, strengthening its construction division, and by 1989 the C$1 billion Windsor plant was onstream, producing over one-half of the company's fine paper products.

Like most of the world's large corporations, in the early 1990s Domtar focused its energy on a limited number of products it was prepared to sell worldwide. With its chemical division gone, Domtar remained primarily a pulp and paper products and a construction products company, those divisions contributing C$1.3 billion and C$721 million, respectively, to the corporate sales total of C$2.5 billion. The remainder is generated by a packaging division that was split off from pulp and paper although the bulk of its products are paper-based. Domtar has become much involved in the recycling of its products, both paper and gypsum, in anticipation of a long stay among the elite of Canada's forest products companies.

Principal Subsidiaries: Brompton Lands Limited; Domtar Enterprises Inc.; Domtar Realties Ltd.; Domtar Sonoco Containers Inc. (50%); Jellco Packaging Corp.; Lithotech Inc.; Maine Timber Holdings Limited; Pacos Carrier Inc.; San Marcos Carrier Inc.; 804736 Ontario Limited; Techni-Therm Inc. (50%); Domtar International B.V. (Netherlands); Domtar Pacific Pty. Limited (Australia); Domtar Industries Inc. (U.S.A.).

Further Reading: Sinclair, Sonja, "Domtar: case history of a corporate trend," *Candian Business,* September 1964; Sinclair, Sonja, "Domtar: case history of a corporate trend—II," *Canadian Business,* October 1964; Ross, Val, "Paper tigers," *Canadian Business,* September 1978; Boardman, Anthony, Ruth Freedman, and Catherine Eckel, "The Price of Government Ownership: A Study of the Domtar Takeover," *Journal of Public Economics,* 31, 1986.

—Jonathan Martin

ENSO-GUTZEIT OY

Kanavaranta 1
00160 Helsinki
Finland
(0) 16291
Fax: (0) 1629471

Public Company
Incorporated: 1927
Employees: 15,974
Sales: Fmk9.90 billion (US$2.73 billion)
Stock Exchanges: Helsinki London

Enso-Gutzeit Oy (E-G) is one of the leading Finnish companies in pulp, paper, timber, and their products. The company is widely diversified with subsidiary companies in Finland and abroad which give it a major international presence. Enso-Gutzeit Oy is a typical Finnish forest-based company that has developed through acquisitions. Its origin lies in the founding of a sawmill in 1872 on the island of Kotka, off the southern coastline of Finland at the estuary of the Kymi River. Previously sawmills were small and water-powered, as steam-powered sawmills were forbidden by the government. However, a new policy was adopted in 1861 enabling steam-driven sawmills to be erected throughout Finland. This change in policy led industrialists to build sawmills at suitable points on the coast at places where timber could be floated and sawn goods shipped abroad. One such location was the island of Kotka. Here the Norwegian industrialist Hans Gutzeit erected a sawmill, which was opened on November 16, 1872. Hans Gutzeit came from Norway, where the company W. Gutzeit & Co. had built Norway's first steam-powered sawmill in 1858.

The new mill at Kotka had six frame saws and two circular saws as well as auxiliary machinery of the most modern design at that time. The machinery was powered by a steam engine of about 100 horsepower. To operate the new mill, Gutzeit imported skilled operators from Norway. It was popularly known as the Norway Mill. In 1880 Hans Gutzeit returned to Norway, where the board had its seat. In Kotka, management was given to a residential manager, the Norwegian Christian Holt.

Kotka Island was a favorite place for new sawmills. Soon there were many mills, all of whose logs were floated from the large Päijänne lake system. The competition for the most favorable forest resources was fierce, however, and resulted in ever-increasing prices. The Gutzeit mill began to look for new sources for its raw material. Eventually it found that it could build a mechanical transport facility from Finland's largest lake system, the Saimaa Lakes, over an isthmus to a small lake, connected to the Kymi River. Large volume, however, was needed to justify this investment, and so Gutzeit started buying forest land in the Saimaa basin. To eliminate a potentially dangerous competitor, Egerton Hubbard & Co, an English-owned St. Petersburg–based company that owned AB Utra Wood Co., a sawmill in the Saimaa basin, Gutzeit purchased the latter company, together with the sawmill receiving a forest area of 100,000 hectares.

During this time, Alexander Gullichsen, another Norwegian, had entered the company as a clerk. He was a very able man and rose steadily through the ranks of the company. He was the first to recognize the possibility of obtaining raw material from the Saimaa basin and it was he who negotiated the Utra Wood deal. Eventually he was nominated managing director of Aktiebolaget W. Gutzeit & Co, the name given to the owner of the Kotka mill when it was incorporated as a Finnish company in 1896 (hereafter called Gutzeit). Although the ownership of the company was still mainly Norwegian, Holt and Gullichsen were considered to be Finns, having become naturalized citizens of Finland.

As a new step in the development of the company, Gullichsen built a sulfate pulp mill at the Kotka sawmill to make use of the waste wood, which up till that time was burned. More important for the diversification of the company was the range of acquisitions generated by Gullichsen's initiative.

In northern Karelia, not far from the Russian border, was a old iron ore refinery. In 1902 this had been converted into a mechanical wood pulp mill when the old iron works had to be closed. This groundwood mill was incorporated as a company in 1904 under the name of Aktiebolaget Pankakoski. This company was purchased in 1909 by Gutzeit and a board mill was added.

Of greater significance, however, was the acquisition of Enso. This took Gutzeit further into the field of chemical pulp making and eventually into paper. It also led to a change in the company's name. Enso was built in 1888 as the first groundwood mill on the huge Vuoksi River, which drains the Saimaa basin into Lake Ladoga through a series of mighty falls, and was considered too large to be harnessed for industrial purposes. Nevertheless, Baron Adi Standertskjöld, a Finnish industrialist who had sold his groundwood mills at Inkeroinen on the Kymi River, came to the Räikkölä Falls in 1887 to buy a site on which to build a new groundwood mill. The founder gave the name Enso to the falls and the mill; eventually the name was extended to the township that grew up around them. "Enso" is derived from the Finnish word *ensi*, meaning "first," as the mill was the first on the Vuoksi River. The new company was named Enso Träsliperi Aktiebolag (hereafter called Enso). The mill was designed by the Swedish engineer Hedbäck. In order to use the falls as a source of power, a small channel with sluices was excavated beside the main rapids, which were left to flow freely. Nine turbines generated 2,000 horsepower. When the first shipment of groundwood pulp left the mill in February 1889, it had to be transported by horse and sledge to Viipuri where it could be loaded on to a train for transportation to St. Petersburg.

The area was a wilderness. To accommodate the workers, the company had to build houses, for which purpose they constructed a small brick manufacturing unit. The office staff was minimal, consisting of the residential manager, a cashier-bookkeeper, a correspondent-dispatcher and a messenger boy.

In 1907 a "yankee-type" paper machine—that is, a machine equipped with a large drying cylinder of several meters' diameter called a yankee cylinder—was added. At the same time the company decided to build a dam across the river to obtain more power. However, the Swedish engineering company commissioned for the work failed, and the project had to be discontinued after more than a year's futile labor. The Finnish engineer A. Sandsund, who took on the work soon afterward, was successful and in 1910 the new dam, the largest of its kind at the time, was completed. The work was extremely expensive and was such a strain on finances that the owners decided to sell the company to Gutzeit. The latter was well aware of the value of its purchase. Gutzeit now owned a mill that could make use of all the small wood which came from the company's forests when logs were cut for the sawmills. It also had an ample supply of hydraulic power at its disposal. As its first project, the new owner planned a new board machine. New forestry holdings were added by the purchase in 1913 of over 70,000 hectares from the Finland Wood Co.

In 1917 Gutzeit's driving force, Alexander Gullichsen, died. Another Norwegian, Herman Heiberg, was nominated managing director. Major changes in ownership soon occurred, however. In October 1918 the Finnish government purchased 4,400 Gutzeit shares from the Norwegian owners, becoming the majority shareholder with more than half of the company's 7,200 shares. Enso's residential manager Sölve Thunström was nominated managing director of the group.

As the Saimaa lake basin was the most important area for wood purchasing and transport, the company developed a lake transport fleet, assisted by a shipyard and machine shop, Laitaatsillan Konepaja, founded by the company near the town of Savonlinna. However it was considered that other shipping companies or shipowners would suffer from Gutzeit's monopoly on service shops in the district, and a rival machine shop was started in 1917 in Savonlinna, only six kilometers from Laitaatsalmi. The rival company was later named Oy Lypsyniemen Konepaja. It had problems from the start, and was heading for bankruptcy in 1919 when it was saved by Gutzeit, which had become a majority shareholder. Lypsyniemen Konepaja entered a phase of rapid growth and later specialized in machinery for the pulp industry.

The rapid development of the Gutzeit group in the early 1920s, as well as the decrease in the value of the Finnish markka, compelled the company to increase its capital. In 1923 the Finnish government subscribed for Gutzeit's new shares, raising government ownership of the company to 87%.

Thunström left the company in 1924 and V.A. Kotilainen was nominated managing director and chief executive officer of the group. The new manager found that the finances of the company were excessively dependent on short-term loans and he concentrated his efforts upon the strengthening of the company's balance sheet. In a few years he managed to get rid of the short-term debt, and to reduce total borrowings to only 46% of annual sales. The head office was transferred to Enso and in 1927 the company was renamed Enso-Gutzeit Osakeyhtiö (Enso-Gutzeit Ltd.).

Another industrial unit was soon added to the company. In 1877 Wolter Ramsay founded a small company in Lahti, south of Lake Päijänne, for the manufacturing of bobbins for English textile mills. The company derived the name Tornator Osakeyhtiö from the Latin word *tornare*, meaning "to turn." When Ramsay died suddenly in 1890, the ownership of Tornator was transferred to the Wolff family. Gradually Eugen Wolff took the leading role in the company. His ambition was to establish a large mill on the Vuoksi River and when he heard that the owner of Tainionkoski Manor at the eponymous falls on the Vuoksi River, G. Törnudd, had died in 1894, he convinced his brother, Reguel Wolff, that Tornator should buy Tainionkoski Manor. This led to the purchase of the manor in 1895. During the years 1896–1897 Eugen Wolff erected a bobbin production unit at Tainionkoski, as well as a paper mill and a groundwood mill. He later began to build a sulfate pulp mill at Tainionkoski, and started to manufacture grease-proof paper. This new product proved successful, securing a good market for the company in Western Europe, especially in England. However, by 1918 Eugen Wolff had tired of his pioneering work and sold his shares to the Finnish government.

Enso-Gutzeit had long been interested in Tornator, its neighbor on the Vuoksi River. In 1931 Enso-Gutzeit purchased the privately owned shares of the company. Thus E-G became the owner of all forest-based interests in the Vuoksi Valley and also of the valuable lakeshore at the beginning of the river. The chief executive, V.A. Kotilainen, now had the resources to turn the company into the leading timber, pulp, board, and paper enterprise in Finland. He also had a team of talented specialists at his disposal. A sulfate pulp mill was built at Enso in 1930, but Kotilainen wanted to increase further the share of sulfate pulp in the company's product line. In the 1930s Enso-Gutzeit built the large Kaukopää sulfate mill on the southern shore of Lake Saimaa, a gigantic unit for its time. The company had acquired the valuable area through the Tornator merger. Previously sulfate pulp had been of minor interest, but with the development of paper and paperboard packing the process had become more promising. The mill was designed to produce 80,000 tons a year but by 1937 production had increased to 120,000 tons a year.

E-G has always been eager to purchase forest land. In 1913 the total area of Gutzeit forests was 400,000 hectares. The acquisition of Tornator brought another 79,000 hectares and the purchase of a timber company in easternmost Karelia in 1937 brought still more. When World War II began in 1939, E-G owned 523,000 hectares of forest land.

With the addition of new mills and machinery, the company wanted to increase its power facilities. By 1936 Enso had already become the largest paperboard mill in Finland. In 1938 the company decided to make full use of the Enso falls for power production. It planned to increase the height of the Enso falls by adding a dam, raising the water level above the falls so that the Vallinkoski rapids, four kilometers upstream from Enso, were combined with Enso, making the Enso falls 16 meters high. At this time, most industrial power plants were built in rapids or falls of six to ten meters. When war broke out in 1939 this gigantic construction project was still unfinished.

In 1941 E-G acquired all the shares of the Insulite Company of Finland from its founder, an American company wishing to withdraw from Finland. This factory, near Kotka, added another new line of business to E-G. Its product, insulite, was a board made of aspen fibers, and well suited to the needs of the new owners. In Helsinki in 1940 E-G erected a factory to make packaging boxes for special requirements in Finland.

Finland was attacked by the Soviet Union on November 30, 1939. Damage was inevitable as most of E-G's facilities were in Karelia, near the border with the Soviet Union. Soviet bombs caused some damage to the mills and the raw material woodpiles at Enso and Kaukopää were burned. The total amount of wood lost was 650,000 cubic meters. The Norway Sawmill in Kotka was completely destroyed by Soviet bombs, but the worst was still to come. In the armistice Finland had to cede a large part of Karelia to the Soviet Union. Among the cessions was the Enso mill town with its large power plant still under construction. E-G also lost the easternmost sawmills and hydraulic power stations as well as almost 100,000 hectares of forest land.

Politics also affected E-G at top management level. Chief executive officer Kotilainen had taken part in organizing services to civilians, such as food supply, education, and medical care, in the Russian area occupied by Finland in 1941–1944, and he had to step down from all public offices at the demand of the Soviets. A new managing director and chief executive officer, William Lehtinen, was nominated on October 1, 1945. He had previously been a member of the board, responsible for sales and marketing.

E-G now had to compensate for the loss of Enso. All of the Enso employees were guaranteed employment at the other mills in the vicinity, mainly at Tornator and Kaukopää. This led to temporary overstaffing. At the Tainionkoski falls a new hydraulic power station was built in 1945 to compensate for the loss of the Enso station which had been nearing completion. At the end of 1946 E-G purchased the Joh. Parviaisen Tehtaat Oy, an industrial company in central Finland specializing in plywood and mechanical wood processing. In addition to providing an entry into the plywood business, the new acquisition brought a factory for prefabricated houses, a product in strong demand after the war. To domestic demand were added the Soviet war-reparation claims, which included large quantities of prefabricated housing. The Soviet demand for many kinds of machinery as war reparation led to a heavy workload for E-G's subsidiary, the Lypsyniemen Konepaja machine shop. In 1945, E-G purchased the former metallurgical works in the Vuoksi River Valley of Outokumpu Oy, the well-known copper company, which transferred its activities to western Finland. E-G concentrated its chemical plants in these facilities, specializing in processing the byproducts of the pulp mills. The central laboratories of the company were also transferred there. In 1947, to facilitate international shipment of its products, E-G established a ship-owning company, Merivienti Oy, and a shipping company, Oy Finnlines Ltd., which was Merivienti's subsidiary.

The company needed new paper mills to realize its strategic growth plans, however. A new newsprint paper mill was built in 1953–1955 at Summa on the southern coastline, east of Kotka. Production of kraft paper was started at the Kotka mills. At the factories in Lahti, the production of textile bobbins was discontinued and replaced by a paper-converting and box-making plant. The joinery at the Lahti factories was developed. At Kaukopää a bleaching plant was built and a linerboard machine was erected. The production of white qualities of board, used as packaging for consumer goods, began. In 1959 the decision was taken to build another large sulfate pulp

mill near the old Tornator Tainionkoski mills. This new pulp mill with a capacity of 150,000 tons, initially named Kaukopää II, was renamed Tainionkoski mills after the old Tornator mills ceased operation in 1963. A new mill with production capacity for 100,000 tons of bleached sulfate pulp was built in northern Karelia at Uimaharju between 1962 and 1967.

In 1962 Pentti Halle was nominated chief executive officer after the retirement of William Lehtinen. In the same year, the company moved headquarters into a new building in central Helsinki, designed by architect Alvar Aalto.

The internationalization of E-G began in 1963 when the company became a shareholder in the Dutch Roermond paper mill company. Two years later E-G acquired all the shares of this company, but in 1972 Roermond was sold back to the Dutch. Even though this first experiment in internationalization proved futile, E-G continued in other directions. In order to procure linerboard for international markets, E-G formed a joint venture, together with the Finnish company Oy Tampella Ab and with American interests to establish a U.S. pulp and linerboard mill, Pineville Kraft Corporation, in Louisiana. This mill went into operation in 1968. Later, however, the two Finnish minority partners sold their shares to their U.S. partners. A more lasting investment abroad was the formation of a Canadian venture, Eurocan Pulp & Paper Co. Ltd. (Eurocan) in British Columbia. At first E-G had 50% of the shares, the other 50% being divided between the Finnish companies Tampella and Kymmene. Eurocan went into operation in 1970. It had a sawmill and a sulfate pulp mill plus a kraftliner machine and a kraft paper machine in Kitimat. For years the Canadian company had financial problems and Tampella sold its shares to Kymmene. In 1979 Kymmene sold its shares to E-G. The latter replaced the partnership by an agreement with the Canadian company West Fraser Timber Co. Ltd. in 1980. However, it took years of negotiations and new agreements before Eurocan became a viable business and a profitable investment.

Later E-G continued its expansion abroad. In addition to sales offices in many locations in different parts of the world, the company owns production facilities—in addition to Eurocan—in Barbados, France, the United Kingdom, the Netherlands, and Indonesia.

Pentti Halle was to retire as chief executive officer in 1972. The board of administration, the highest authority below the general meeting of shareholders, had already employed Aarne Hildén as executive vice president. He had gained international business experience in the service of Esso, the large oil company. It seemed obvious that Hilden should be nominated chief executive officer, which in Enso's case also includes becoming chairman of the board. However, intrigues took place within the company, influenced by politicians at high levels, and eventually the post of chief executive officer was awarded instead to Olavi J. Mattila, chief executive officer of Valmet Oy. Pentti Salmi, from within the company, was nominated managing director. This period resulted in a troubled decade for the company, before Mattila retired in 1983. Pentti Salmi was then nominated chief executive officer. Under his command E-G's business developed steadily.

In the late 1980s major changes took place in the Finnish business world. Mergers, takeovers, and the selling off of divisions were common. E-G and the largest Finnish family-owned industry, A. Ahlström Oy, were involved in one such deal. Gutzeit's managing director in the days before the Enso acquisition, Alex Gullichsen, had already been interested in acquiring the Varkaus mills and factories in the northern Saimaa area when the owner, the Viipuri merchant Paul Wahl & Co., was willing to sell at the beginning of the 1900s. Although details of the deal had already been discussed, A. Ahlström Oy managed to buy the Varkaus mills and factories before Gullichsen had reached a decision. Thus Varkaus became one of Ahlström's most attractive assets. At Varkaus, Ahlström built a large pulp mill, a paper mill, a sawmill, a plywood factory, and machine shops. However, during the reshuffle of the 1980s, Ahlström found a need to shed some of its financial burdens so that it could afford to remain a family-controlled business. In 1986 the Varkaus pulp and paper mills and sawmills were sold to E-G. Part of the price paid by E-G was the transfer of its machine shops in Savonlinna, Lypsyniemen Konepaja, to A. Ahlström Oy. E-G had finally achieved its aim of taking over the Varkaus mills, 80 years after the intention was first announced.

Other changes took place in the structure of E-G; the company sold its interests in fiberboards and plywood in 1990 to Schauman Wood Oy, a subsidiary of the Kymmene group. Recent political changes in the Soviet Union have resulted in new ventures involving E-G. As part of the company's forest resources had to be ceded to the Soviet Union after the war, E-G regularly purchased timber from behind the frontier. The new Soviet era of *perestroika* and *glasnost* led to new ideas for joint ventures. In October 1989 E-G agreed with the authorities of the Soviet Union to form a jointly owned Finnish company, Enocell Oy, with 80% of the shares held by E-G. Enocell was to take over the activities of the Uimaharju sulfate pulp mill, where a replacement pulp mill is being constructed, from the beginning of 1992. Most of the raw materials would be supplied by the Soviet partner. Another joint venture, Ladenso, has been formed in Soviet Karelia. It will concentrate on forest development and related activities.

Principal Subsidiaries: Tavastimber Oy Ltd.; Enso Forest Development Oy Ltd.; Heinolan Aihiotuote Oy; Pitkäpuu Oy; Ensopack Ltd. (Barbados); Berghuizer-Enso Formaatfabriek B.V. (Holland); Berghuizer Papierfabriek N.V. (Holland); Imprex Products (S.E.A.) Pte Ltd. (Indonesia); Enso Rose Ltd. (UK); Eurocan Pulp & Paper Co. (Canada); Papeteries R. Soustre & Fils S.A. (France); Honkalahti Sawmill.

Further Reading: Korpijaakko, O., "Gutzeit-yhtmän vaiheet 1872–1947," *Enso-Gutzeit Personnel Magazine, 75th Anniversary Issue,* 1947; Salonen, O., "Piirteita Parviaisen Tehtaiden synnysta ja kehityksesta," *Enso-Gutzeit Personnel Magazine, 75th Anniversary Issue,* 1947; Hoving, Victor, *Enso-Gutzeit Osakeyhtiö 1872–1958,* Helsinki, Frenckhellin Kijapaino Osakeyhtiö, 1961; Kylmala, Timo, *Kutsetin Mies,* Helsinki, Kirjayhtyma, 1986.

—Nils G. Björklund

FLETCHER CHALLENGE LTD.

Fletcher Challenge House
810 Great South Road
Penrose
Auckland
New Zealand
(9) 590-000
Fax: (9) 525-0559

Public Company
Incorporated: 1981
Employees: 40,000
Sales: NZ$13.32 billion (US$7.83 billion)
Stock Exchanges: Auckland Sydney London Toronto
  Montreal Vancouver Frankfurt

Fletcher Challenge Ltd., New Zealand's largest company, is a fast-growing international organization with bases in 12 countries. Its main business activities are in building and construction, pulp and paper, rural servicing industries, and energy. The company was formed on January 1, 1981, by the merger of Challenge Corporation Ltd., Fletcher Holdings Ltd., and Tasman Pulp and Paper Company Ltd.

CHALLENGE CORPORATION LTD.

The origins of Fletcher Challenge Ltd. go back to the 19th century. Its history began when John T. Wright and Robert M. Robertson set up a business partnership called Wright, Robertson & Company as a merchant, stock and station agent, and woolbroker in Dunedin in 1861. Four years later John Stephenson joined the partnership and in 1868, when Robertson retired, the business was renamed Wright Stephenson & Company. It was floated as a public company in 1906 and opened its first overseas branch in London that year. An office was opened in Wellington in 1908. By 1916 the company was already expanding rapidly when it took over W. & G. Turnbull & Company of Wellington and W. Gunson & Company of Auckland. Many more mergers and acquisitions followed and the company continued to grow. In 1920 Wright Stephenson & Company became one of the first companies in New Zealand to diversify into fertilizers, and shortly afterward it further expanded its range with the establishment of a bloodstock and studstock department.

In 1927 the company began to expand out of the stock and station business. It started to trade in motor cars and subse-quently added the retailing of electrical appliances, land development, and department stores to its range of activities. In 1962 it acquired Morrison Industries Ltd., the company's first major involvement in manufacturing motor mowers and bicycles.

Wright Stevenson opened its first office in Australia in 1938 and expanded during the next 30 years, with branches being opened all over New Zealand. In 1972 Wright Stephenson merged with the National Mortgage Agency of New Zealand Ltd. National Mortgage, too, had grown through acquisition since its beginnings in the mid–19th century. The takeover brought Wright Stephenson an increased range of activities, including extensive fishing and meat exporting operations.

With this merger a new name was sought which would be synonymous with both the united and diversified character of the company. The name chosen was Challenge Corporation Ltd. The company's chairman between 1970 and 1981 was Ronald Trotter. By 1980 Challenge Corporation had assets of NZ$7.6 billion.

FLETCHER HOLDINGS LTD.

Fletcher Holdings Ltd. began when James Fletcher, a carpenter and joiner by trade, emigrated from Scotland to New Zealand in 1908. Recalling this period, James Fletcher wrote "I arrived in Dunedin on a Tuesday. Conditions in the building trade in 1908 were bad, and starting on the morning I arrived, I canvassed practically every job in the city, including house building and alterations, without success. I got a job on Friday evening with a firm called Crawford and Watson, the first firm I had called on on the Tuesday. Watson was rather amused at my persistence in coming back a second time within a matter of three days, but he gave me the job."

Within a year Fletcher and another immigrant, Bert Morris, set up as builders and won their first contract—to build a house. On completion they were paid £375, of which just NZ$3.6 was profit. Four years later Morris sold his share of the partnership to Fletcher for £500. Fletcher's brother William arrived from Scotland to join him and the company became Fletcher Brothers Ltd. By 1919 two more Fletcher brothers, John and Andrew, had joined the company. Its name was changed to the Fletcher Construction Company Ltd. and the headquarters moved to Wellington. Over the next ten years Fletcher Construction continued to expand. In order to service its building growth the company acquired several joinery factories, quarries, and brickyards, and also set up its own steel fabricating yard.

By the 1930s the effects of the worldwide Depression began to be felt in New Zealand, and Fletcher Construction's work slowed down for the first time. Undaunted, James Fletcher toured the country, encouraging the building of large-scale projects. He argued that building when costs were low made economic sense and helped the economy, and also boosted morale. Although the company's rate of expansion declined, it won tenders, or bids, for several important contracts including the National Art Gallery, the Post Office in Dunedin, and the railway station in Wellington, the latter being then the largest individual building contract ever awarded in New Zealand.

In 1937 the New Zealand government launched its public housing scheme. Fletcher Construction had the foresight to consult architects and draw up specifications in advance of tenders being invited, thus enabling the company to respond extremely rapidly to the government's plans. Fletcher was awarded contracts for houses in Wellington and Auckland. Within two years it was a major builder for the government and had regained its former impetus. With the outbreak of World War II in 1939, Fletcher Construction realized that a regular supply of essential materials from overseas was likely to be placed in jeopardy. To counter this shortage, the company set up enterprises in sawn timber, plywood, and door manufacturing.

Further expansion continued, and in 1940 the company went public with the formation of Fletcher Holdings Ltd. James Fletcher, who served in the honorary post of commissioner of defense construction and later as the first commissioner of works, received a knighthood in 1946. His son, James C. Fletcher, was appointed managing director of the company in 1942 at the age of 28. Under the guidance of James C. Fletcher the company began to expand its horizons. Fletcher traveled widely and recognized the value of new methods. An early example was his bringing two leading U.S. construction companies into a partnership with Fletcher, to undertake the expansion of Auckland's wharves. However, James C. Fletcher is also remembered as a pioneer of welfare schemes for his employees. Among other benefits he introduced the first wholly subsidized superannuation scheme for construction workers and a medical scheme for employees before general medical insurance had been introduced.

After the war the Fletcher group continued to acquire established companies in the construction industry. It also diversified into new industries such as readymix concrete, long-run roofing—the production of pre-formed roof trusses which needed no additional carpentry on installation—and galvanizing. The company had a major influence on the New Zealand steel industry through the development of Pacific Steel Ltd. and New Zealand Wire Ltd., and it also diversified into merchant banking and financial services.

TASMAN PULP AND PAPER COMPANY LTD.

In 1951 the New Zealand government showed an interest in using the country's natural resources to establish a paper, pulp, and newsprint industry. Fletcher Holdings offered to build a pulp and newsprint mill if the government provided the infrastructure that such a large-scale project needed. The result was the Tasman Pulp and Paper Company, which was formed the following year with shares held by the government, Fletcher Trust and Investment Ltd., and the public. By 1955 the pulp mill and the newsprint machine were brought into production and the sawmill came on line in 1956. From the beginning the company had targeted the export market, and so Tasman Pulp and Paper (Sales) Ltd. was established in Australia. By 1962 Tasman Pulp and Paper had commissioned a second newsprint machine and in 1970 there was further expansion of the pulp mill with the aim of producing enough pulp for a third machine plus a surplus for sales elsewhere. In 1975, under an arrangement made with the Union Steam Ship Company, Tasman Pulp and Paper had sole operation of two ships to transport its products to South Island and to Australia. The government sold its shares in the company in 1979. By 1980 Fletcher Holdings owned 56.46% and Challenge Corporation owned 28.23% of Tasman Pulp and Paper.

James C. Fletcher received a knighthood for services to industry in 1980. Following the formation of Fletcher Challenge Ltd. in 1981, he was appointed president of the new company and Sir Ronald Trotter of Challenge Corporation was appointed as chairman. Since its inception, Fletcher Challenge has grown from being an exclusively New Zealand–based company to an industrial group with its headquarters in New Zealand. It was assisted in this expansion by the relaxation of New Zealand's capital laws in the early 1980s, which encouraged overseas investment.

The company's international expansion started in Canada with the acquisition of Crown Forest Industries in British Columbia in 1983. The main activities of this company were pulp and paper, wood products, packaging, and merchandising. By 1987 Fletcher Challenge acquired a majority share of British Columbia Forest Products Ltd., one of Canada's largest producers of forest products. In the following year these two companies were combined to form Fletcher Challenge Canada Ltd. Fletcher Challenge also acquired pulp and paper interests in South America and Australia. In 1989 the company was adversely affected by a huge fall in pulp and paper earnings as a result of lower newsprint prices and a strong Canadian dollar. However, the company was able to overcome these setbacks owing to strong performances from its other operations.

Fletcher Challenge extended its construction business into the United States by acquiring companies in Seattle, Washington; Los Angeles; and in Hawaii in the latter half of the 1980s. The company became a leading building contractor in the United States as well as in southeast Asia and the South Pacific.

Fletcher Challenge also expanded its activities in New Zealand. In 1988 it bought the Petroleum Company of New Zealand (Petrocorp) from the government and thus became the country's largest oil, gas, and petrochemicals company. It has built on this diversification into energy by making a considerable investment in further oil and gas exploration. Also in New Zealand, Fletcher Challenge bought the Rural Bank from the government in 1989, which consolidated its leading position in the provision of finance and services to New Zealand's large agricultural community.

In 1990 Fletcher Challenge made its first big move into the European market with the takeover of the British fine-paper manufacturer, UK Paper. The company aims to expand production and increase exports to continental Europe. UK Paper will also be used as a convenient base for acquiring similar interests in Europe. UK Paper had been bought out by its management in 1986 and consequently had a tradition of strong employee involvement. Fletcher Challenge, which was virtually unknown to the British work force, took steps to get to know its new employees. Garry Mace, chief executive of the forest industries division, spent two weeks visiting all the U.K. manufacturing sites and ensured that every employee was given an opportunity to attend one of the many seminars which he ran to explain the objectives of the Fletcher Challenge organization.

In 1991 the chief executive of Fletcher Challenge Ltd. was Hugh Fletcher, grandson of the founder of the Fletcher group, who joined the company in 1969 at the age of 22 and attained his current position in October 1987. He has been at the forefront of its expansionist activities.

Hugh Fletcher has a growing reputation as a dealmaker. In October 1990 he acquired the New Zealand gas production interests of British Petroleum in the Maui Field. Production from the Maui Field is equivalent to 30 million barrels of oil a year, which will supply more than half of New Zealand's total demand. It is anticipated that production will continue until at least the year 2020. The timing of the deal was extremely fortunate for Fletcher Challenge as it was negotiated three months before the Persian Gulf crisis, when oil prices were relatively low. As a result of this acquisition, Fletcher Challenge dominates the New Zealand oil and gas sector.

Interviewed in the *Financial Times* on October 31, 1990, Hugh Fletcher likened his aspirations for the company's expansion to "the Hannibal instinct to go over the next mountain range" and it is clear that Fletcher Challenge's strategy for the 1990s is to continue to expand worldwide. At the same time, the company is prepared to sell off any subsidiaries which will not play a part in international expansion. Consequently Fletcher Challenge has sold its Fletcher Fishing subsidiary to Carter Holt Harvey of New Zealand. Fletcher Fishing, a profitable company with export markets in the United States, Japan, and France, held 18% of the New Zealand fish quota, but Fletcher Challenge was unable to acquire any compatible overseas companies with which to merge Fletcher Fishing.

In the 1980s Fletcher Challenge expanded selectively, at the same time divesting many of its smaller business enterprises. At the beginning of the 1990s the company was a world leader in pulp and paper, energy, and construction, with well-established operations in Australasia, the Pacific Basin, North and South America, and Europe. The next decade is likely to see the company's continued growth with an emphasis on expansion in North America and Europe.

Principal Subsidiaries: Fletcher Challenge Financial Service Limited; Fletcher Challenge Industries Limited; Fletcher Challenge Capital Canada Inc.; Fletcher Challenge Equities Canada Inc.; Fletcher Challenge Finance Canada Inc.; Fletcher Challenge Industries Finance USA Limited; Fletcher Challenge Industries USA Limited; Fletcher Challenge Investments Inc. (North America); Fletcher Challenge Investments II Inc. (North America); Fletcher Challenge Australia Limited; Fletcher Challenge Finance Netherlands B.V.; Fletcher Challenge Financial Services Netherlands B.V.; Fletcher Challenge Finance UK Limited; Fletcher Challenge Forest Industries Plc; Tasman Pulp and Paper Company Limited; Crown Forest Industries Limited (North America); Fletcher Challenge Canada Limited (72%); Australian Newsprint Mills Limited (50%); Papel de Imprensa S.A. (South America) (50.3%); Tasman Chile S.A.; UK Paper Plc; Challenge Properties Limited; Firth Industries Limited; Fletcher Building Products Limited; The Fletcher Construction Company Limited; Fletcher Industries Limited; Fletcher Merchants Limited; Fletcher Panel Industries Limited; Fletcher Residential Limited; Pacific Steel Limited; Tasman Forestry Limited; Tasman Lumber Limited; Winstone Industries Limited; Crown Forest Industries Limited (North America); Dinwiddie Construction Company (North America); Fletcher Challenge Canada Limited (72%); Pacific Construction Co. Limited (North America); Wright Schuchart Incorporated (North America); Jennings Group Limited (Australia) (54%); Tasman Chile S.A.; Rural Banking and Finance Corporation of New Zealand Limited; Wrightson NMA Limited; Natural Gas Corporation of New Zealand Limited; N.Z. Synthetic Fuels Corporation Limited; Offshore Mining Company Limited; Petrocorp Exploration and Production Limited; Petralgas Chemicals NZ Limited; Petroleum Corporation of New Zealand Limited; Petrocorp Exploration (Canada) Limited; Fletcher Challenge Energy Finance B.V.

—Susanna Wilson

GEORGIA-PACIFIC CORPORATION

133 Peachtree Street, Northeast
Atlanta, Georgia 30303
U.S.A.
(404) 521-4000
Fax: (404) 521-4581

Public Company
Incorporated: 1927 as Georgia Hardwood Lumber Company
Employees: 60,000
Sales: $12.67 billion
Stock Exchanges: New York   Tokyo

Georgia-Pacific Corporation is a leading manufacturer and distributor of building products, industrial wood products, pulp, paper, packaging, and chemical products. Although it owns or controls over six million acres of timberland throughout North America, the company did not hold title to a single tree for the first 24 years of its existence. Instead, Georgia Hardwood Lumber Company began operations in 1927 in Augusta, Georgia, as a hardwood lumber wholesaler with $12,000 in start-up funds provided by its founder, Owen Cheatham.

During its first decade in business, the company began lumber manufacturing in addition to its wholesaling activities. Cheatham focused on expanding the company's milling capabilities in the southern United States, a strategy which allowed it to become the largest supplier of lumber to the U.S. Army during World War II. The company's purchase of a plywood mill in Bellingham, Washington, in 1947 coincided with plywood's growing popularity in the construction industry and gave the company a strong competitive advantage.

Additional plywood mills in Washington and Oregon were purchased in 1948, as well as another plywood plant in 1949, to support this growing business area. The company changed its name in 1948 to Georgia-Pacific Plywood & Lumber Company to reflect more accurately its geographic and operational expansion.

In 1951 the company changed its name to Georgia-Pacific Plywood Company. Cheatham gradually developed a reputation as an industry maverick. Over the next six years, he conducted a $160 million timberland-acquisition program in the western and southern United States. To finance this program, he borrowed heavily from banks and insurance companies expecting that the proceeds gained from the timber in the future would more than cover the required return on their investment. In order to be closer to these newly purchased resources, the company moved its headquarters from Georgia to Olympia, Washington, in 1953, and then again to Portland, Oregon, the following year.

Over the next decade, Cheatham used his financing model several times to acquire additional forest acreage and manufacturing facilities, including Coos Bay Lumber Company and Hammond Lumber Company in 1956. That same year, the company's name was changed, for the third time since its founding, to Georgia-Pacific Corporation. Subsequent purchases, of Booth-Kelly Lumber Company in 1959 and W.M. Ritter Lumber Company in 1960, took the company to the number-three position in its industry.

The company's unorthodox approach to growth was evident in other areas as well. It opened a kraft pulp and linerboard mill in Toledo, Oregon, in 1957 and its first resin adhesive plant at Coos Bay, Oregon, in 1959. The latter manufacturing operation was intended at first to supply the resin required for the company's plywood-production business, but gradually grew large enough to supply resin to other plywood manufacturers as well. Georgia-Pacific was also one of the first manufacturers to use wood by-products rather than timber in pulp production. The company continued to pioneer in the development of plywood products, eventually shifting away from the traditional use of Douglas fir to a process using less-expensive southern pine. This wood previously had been considered inappropriate for use in plywood because of its high resin content.

During the 1960s Georgia-Pacific embarked upon another series of acquisitions, buying several lumber and paper companies across the country. These included Crossett Lumber Company in 1962; Puget Sound Pulp and Timber Company, Vanity Fair Paper Mills, St. Croix Paper Company, and Fordyce Lumber Company in 1963; Bestwall Gypsum Company in 1965; and Kalamazoo Paper Company in 1967. After building its first corrugated-container plant in Olympia, in 1961, the company added a series of additional manufacturing facilities for lumber, paper, and chemical products over the course of the rest of the decade.

Upon Cheatham's death in 1970, Robert B. Pamplin, who had worked with Cheatham since the company's inception, became chairman and chief executive officer. Although the company's building-products business benefited from the housing boom of the early 1970s, its paper and pulp interests struggled due to low prices and sluggish demand. To bolster its manufacturing operations, the firm expanded production of two new building materials, polyvinyl chloride (PVC) and particle board, the former through a joint venture with Permaneer Corporation. Georgia-Pacific opened its own PVC manufacturing plant in 1975. When the cost of oil increased soon afterward, however, the company's prices for its PVC-molding products proved to be too high to compete effectively with wood moldings, resulting in significant losses.

It was also during this period that the firm was required by the Federal Trade Commission (FTC) to defend its acquisition of 16 small firms in the South that supplied the company with 673,000 acres of the southern pine used to make plywood. Charging that the acquisitions tended to create a monopoly, the FTC issued a consent order in 1972 that forced Georgia-Pacific to divest 20% of its assets. This step resulted in the formation of a spin-off company called Louisiana-Pacific Corporation. The order also prohibited the firm from acquiring any other softwood plywood companies, and imposed restrictions on timberland purchases in the South for five years and on plywood mill acquisitions for ten years.

A slump in the housing industry in 1973 and 1974 depressed the company's lumber and plywood business. Georgia-Pacific continued to post record profits, however, largely owing to growth in its chemical, pulp, and paper operations. These areas experienced slowdowns as well by the middle of the decade. Nevertheless, the company moved forward in its long-range program to increase manufacturing capacity across the board. It expanded through vertical integration into the production of additional chemicals derived from wood wastes, such as chlorine, phenol, and methanol. The 1975 acquisition of Exchange Oil & Gas Corporation enabled the company to become more self-sufficient by developing its own reserves of important raw materials required for the operation of its chemical plants.

In 1976 president Robert Flowerree succeeded Robert Pamplin as chairman and chief executive. A 25-year Georgia-Pacific veteran, Flowerree had been instrumental in taking the company into the chemical business. He was also considered to be more cautious than his predecessors. Under his leadership, the firm expanded its building products to include roofing materials, which it began to produce in a converted paper mill.

By 1978 the company was drawing three-quarters of its sales from the southern and eastern United States. This shift away from the West was instrumental in the decision to move the headquarters of the firm back to Georgia, 150 miles away from its original location, in Atlanta. The relocation caused many employees to leave the company, and several senior executives chose to retire rather than make the move. This shift left the firm vulnerable at a critical time, particularly in the growing chemical area.

The dawning of the 1980s brought with it another housing slump, but Georgia-Pacific was able to use its chemical business to maintain overall growth. Its plywood products, however, were slowly losing competitive ground to new and cheaper materials, such as waferboard and oriented-strand board, which were being manufactured and sold aggressively by such firms as Louisiana-Pacific and Potlatch Corporation. Until then, Georgia-Pacific had not placed significant emphasis on these materials, with only one plant producing waferboard and another producing oriented-strand board. Most of its capital expenditure was directed instead toward upgrading existing facilities and buying timberlands.

In 1982 T. Marshall Hahn Jr., who had succeeded Flowerree as president in 1976, became chief operating officer. When he became chairman and chief executive officer one year later, following Flowerree's early retirement, he faced several serious problems. Demand for paper was strong, but in the area of higher-quality products, not in the basic linerboard and kraft paper sectors in which Georgia-Pacific concentrated. Although an upturn in the construction industry augured well for the company's building-products business, the high interest rates on the debt the firm had used to fund expansion severely limited its freedom to take advantage of opportunities in that area. Furthermore, its chemical business, once the firm's star division, fell on hard times as sales dropped significantly. This

business was sold to Georgia Gulf Corporation in 1984, followed by the sale of Exchange Oil & Gas in 1985. The company retained its specialty chemicals business, which continued to deliver good returns.

Hahn instituted a series of measures designed to get the company back on its feet. These included reviewing the health of its assets, improvement of cost controls and productivity, and continued investment in areas such as the pulp and paper business, which could insulate the company from future economic calamities and provide a hedge against cyclical upturns and downturns in the various industries in which the company operated. In 1984 Georgia-Pacific acquired a linerboard mill, several corrugated container plants, and over 300,000 acres of forest from St. Regis Corporation. It converted two paper plants to the production of higher-margin products, such as light-weight bleached board and white paper used by copiers and computer printers. It also successfully expanded a wood-products mill in South Carolina and a plant in Florida to produce lattice and fencing materials, which were in heavy demand.

In 1986 the company entered another area of the paper market through the introduction of Angel Soft bathroom tissue. By the end of 1987 Georgia-Pacific's tissue and towel operation, combined with its production of linerboard, kraft, and fine papers, enabled the company to achieve higher profitability in paper products than in wood products for the first time in its history, despite tough competition from major consumer products companies such as The Procter & Gamble Company.

Other elements of Hahn's turnaround strategy included further decentralization of the company's operations, which forced plant managers to compete with each other for capital funds, and the addition of several building-materials distribution centers nationwide to capitalize on the growing trend toward remodeling and do-it-yourself projects.

During the last few years of the decade, the company made further acquisitions. These included U.S. Plywood Corporation and selected assets of the Erving Distributor Products Company in 1987, and Brunswick Pulp & Paper Company and American Forest Products Company in 1988. Its most controversial purchase, however, commenced in 1989 with an offer to buy Great Northern Nekoosa Corporation of Connecticut, a competing producer of pulp, paper, containerboard, lumber, and plywood.

Originally incorporated in 1898 as the Northern Development Company and soon renamed Great Northern Paper Company, the predecessor to Great Northern Nekoosa had begun producing newsprint in 1900. By 1924 it was manufacturing corrugated paper and a decade later began a gradual transition from wrapping paper to business paper production. The company expanded its pulp and paper operations over the next 40 years. In 1970 the Great Northern Paper Company and the Nekoosa Edwards Paper Company merged to become Great Northern Nekoosa Corporation. Great Northern Nekoosa acquired several firms subsequently to enhance the company's manufacturing and distribution capabilities, including Heco Envelope Company in 1973; Pak-Well in 1975; Leaf River Forest Products in 1981; Barton, Duer & Koch, and Consolidated Marketing, Inc. in 1982; Triquet Paper Company in 1983; Chatfield Paper Company in 1984; J & J Corrugated Box Corporation and Carpenter Paper Company of Iowa in 1986; Owens-Illinois's forest products company in 1987; and Jim Walter Papers in 1988.

Great Northern Nekoosa was a particularly attractive candidate for acquisition, owing to its depressed stock price. Georgia-Pacific saw the combination of the two companies as an opportunity to achieve economies of scale and other cost savings. In Hahn's opinion the acquisition would enable Georgia-Pacific to add manufacturing capability at less expense than by building its own plants. On the other hand, Great Northern Nekoosa viewed Georgia-Pacific's $3.74 billion bid as a hostile takeover attempt. It attempted to halt the proposed buyout with a series of lawsuits and an extensive search for another buyer. All of these measures failed, however, and the purchase was completed in March 1990. Georgia-Pacific assumed a significant amount of debt as a result, but was able to eliminate part of the burden through the subsequent sale of several mills and some timberland to Tenneco, the John Hancock Mutual Life Insurance Company, and the Metropolitan Life Insurance Company.

With its hard-fought acquisition of Great Northern Nekoosa complete, Georgia-Pacific holds market leadership positions in containerboard, packaging, pulp, and communication papers, and is a major producer of related products, such as tissue, kraft paper, and bleached board. The most significant threat to the company's continued growth is the economy's effects on its key business areas. Although the firm's diversification into paper and pulp manufacturing was intended to help it survive cyclical downturns in lumber and housing construction, its new business areas are also highly cyclical in nature, with peaks and valleys lagging only months behind those occurring in lumber and housing. Demand for the company's pulp and paper products is affected by the overall production capacity of the industry, as well as by economic factors such as currency-exchange rates and conditions in foreign markets.

Georgia-Pacific's ability to forecast trends in demand, balance production accordingly, and compete both strategically and cost-effectively in its various businesses will be essential ingredients to its continuing success.

Principal Subsidiaries: American Forest Products Company; Ashley, Drew & Northern Railway Company; Brunswick Pulp & Paper Company; California Western Railroad; Fordyce and Princeton R.R. Company; G-P DISC, Inc.; Georgia-Temp. Inc.; Georgia-Pacific Export, Inc.; Georgia-Pacific Foreign Sales Corporation; Georgia-Pacific Leasing Corporation; Georgia-Pacific Paper Sales, Inc.; Gloster Southern Railroad Company; Hudson Pulp & Paper Corporation; Phoenix Athletic Club, Inc.; Saint Croix Water Power Company (Canada); The Sprague's Falls Manufacturing Company; St. Croix Water Power Company; Superwood Corporation; Superior Fiber Products, Inc.; Thacker Land Company (57%); U.S. Plywood Corporation; XRS, Inc.; Great Northern Nekoosa Corporation.

Further Reading: "The Best of Everything," *Forbes,* March 15, 1977; Wiegner, Kathleen K., "A Tale of Two Companies," *Forbes* March 6, 1978; Reier, Sharon, "New Math vs. Old Culture," *Financial World,* March 22, 1988; *Roots,* Atlanta, Georgia, Georgia-Pacific Corporation, 1988; Gold, Jackey, "Culture Shock," *Financial World,* February 20, 1990; Calonius, Erik, "America's Toughest Papermaker," *Fortune,* February 26, 1990.

—Sandy Schusteff

HONSHU PAPER CO., LTD.

12-8, Ginza 5-chome
Chuo-ku, Tokyo 104
Japan
(03) 3543-1837
Fax: (03) 3545-9035

Public Company
Incorporated: 1949
Employees: 6,096
Sales: ¥389.28 billion (US$2.87 billion)
Stock Exchanges: Tokyo Osaka Nagoya

Honshu Paper Co., Ltd. is involved in conversion, manufacture, sales, and technical-consulting services for the paper and pulp industry on a worldwide basis. With raw materials supplied by its affiliates in Japan, New Guinea, Brazil, and Canada, Honshu participates in the sales of lumber, other forest products, reforestation services, and sawn timber. The company's Japanese paper mills produce in excess of 1.3 billion metric tons of various paper products annually. Honshu also owns many other manufacturing operations that among others include construction materials, plastics, paperboard and plastic packaging materials, chemical products, medicines, and packaging machinery. The company operates several warehouse facilities and is involved in civil engineering and construction. In the early 1990s Honshu maintained its headquarters in Tokyo, operated 14 domestic paper mills, maintained 25 shipping container divisions, and controlled more than 70 affiliated companies.

Honshu was established on August 1, 1949, as a result of the reorganization of the Oji Paper Company, a part of the Mitsui *zaibatsu,* one of Japan's oldest and largest business concerns. The original Oji Paper had been Japan's largest producer of paper and paper products. After Japan's surrender following World War II, the Allied occupation forces formed the Holding Company Liquidation Commission. It was the Allied powers intention to use the commission to dismantle the existing industrial *zaibatsu* that had for centuries held control of Japanese commerce. The plan was to create a new, democratic, capitalistic system that would replace the huge monopolies with smaller groups of Japanese businessmen and entrepreneurs. One of the results of the commission's actions was the breaking up of the original Oji Paper Company into three smaller businesses, Oji Paper Company, Jujo Paper Company, and Honshu Paper Company.

Upon its formation, Honshu was immediately faced with problems, the worst of which was an acute shortage of paper pulp. Most pulp had been imported, but after the war the Japanese paper industry lost control of the forests in Manchuria, Sakhalin, and Korea upon which the domestic industry had come to depend. The resulting shortage was seriously affecting Honshu's ability to manufacture paper products. Between 1945 and 1950 a boom in domestic pulp production helped to alleviate the company's immediate need for pulp, and Honshu and its competitors did quite well during this period. Some pulp companies paid dividends of 40%. It was obvious, however, that although Japan's land mass was covered by more than 70% forest lands, prolonged deforestation of the nation's timberlands would do irreparable long-term damage to what should remain a renewable resource. To stop the indiscriminate logging, the Allied powers established the Council for the Conservation of Natuaral Resources. Jun'ichero Kobayashi, a forestry expert and former vice president of Oji Paper, was brought in to head up the council. Kobayashi took advantage of postwar trade competition to create a new foreign source of pulp to feed Japan's paper mills. He proposed to the U.S. government the development of a Japanese company to harvest Alaskan timber, the Alaska Pulp Company. The U.S. government knew that if the United States refused to cooperate he could always turn to the Soviet Union and strike a deal that would permit Japan to exploit the vast Siberian forests. The United States was wary of any Japanese-Soviet business alliances, and eventually approval for the formation of Alaska Pulp, was given. After a great deal of trans-Pacific negotiation, Alaska Pulp was established in 1953, using an almost equal amount of Japanese and U.S. investment capital. Honshu was one of a large number of Japanese companies that participated in the funding of Alaska Pulp. The Alaska Pulp venture was one of the first large postwar overseas investments made by Japanese industry and helped to revitalize United States–Japanese business relations.

With the end of the Allied occupation in 1952, business opportunities for Honshu were plentiful. When Oji Paper had been reorganized, forming Honshu, Honshu had been given six paper mills, located in Edogawa, Iwabuchi, Fuji, Yodogawa, Nakutso, and Kumano. The company also took possession of a chemical plant in Nagoya. During the 1950s Honshu used some of the profits generated by its booming business to rebuild and modernize the existing mills.

Each of the three newly organized companies focused on a different part of the paper market. Oji Paper remained the largest producer of newsprint in Japan. Jujo Paper modified its mills and began to market paper for the printing trade. It set about to develop a variety of specialty paper products including paper for the burgeoning electronic-copying and information-transmission markets, as well as paper packaging products. Honshu began by concentrating on the paperboard and shipping-container market. Toward this end, Honshu built a new mill in Hokkaido that specialized in producing various products for the containerboard market. The Hokkaido mill started up in 1959.

The impressive postwar recovery of Japan's economy continued into the 1960s. Under the direction of the Ministry of International Trade and Industry, Honshu experienced market-driven growth. This growth resulted in the construction of another production and conversion facility, located in Fuji, opened in 1964. Three years later the company established Crestbrook Forest Industries Ltd., a Canadian joint venture with the Mitsubishi Corporation and a smaller Canadian company. Crestbrook's pulp mill, which was located in Canada in British Columbia, began operations in 1968. That same year Honshu, Oji Paper, and Jujo Paper tried to reverse the occupation actions of 1949 with a merger. The move was unsuccessful. The plan was terminated because of its potential infringement on Japanese antimonopoly statutes.

Honshu's research-and-development department closed out the 1960s with the registration of a series of patents for processes and machinery used in the production of a dry-laid nonwoven paper-based fabric. Within two years of the development, Honshu sold exclusive U.S. manufacturing rights for the process to Johnson & Johnson after a series of negotiations with both Johnson & Johnson and Colgate-Palmolive Company. The sought-after fabric technology produced the fiber used in the manufacture of disposable baby diapers and other products.

The 1970s were a period of rapid growth and expansion for most Japanese industries. Honshu rode the crest of the wave with the establishment of JANT Pty. Ltd., a Papua New Guinea company formed to augment the company's wood-resources-development program. Honshu also expanded its production capabilities for plastic film used in packaging, with the opening of a new plant in Shiga in 1975.

The worldwide recession that took place in the early 1980s created a long, severe slump in the paper and pulp market. In an attempt to cope with the decline in profits and productivity, the three companies with roots in the old Oji Paper monopoly once more attempted to consolidate their operations. With the knowledge that a merger was not possible, the three paper-producing giants along with another Tokyo-based paper company, Kanzaki Paper Manufacturing Company, agreed in 1981 to sign a wide-ranging business agreement. The terms of the agreement established a joint venture for the purchase of raw materials and involved the pooling of the four companies' research-and-development activities.

As part of the agreement, the participating companies formed a liaison council. It consisted of one of each of the companies' vice presidents and was supported by several committees of specialists involved in raw materials, sales and, management. Many of the benefits of a merger were accomplished without the legal problem that an actual attempt at merger would have involved. In 1983, a short time after the agreement between the paper companies took place, Honshu merged with two other Japanese paper producers, Fukuoka Paper Co., Ltd. and Toshin Paper Co., Ltd. These acquisitions were followed in 1986 by a consolidation in which Honshu Paper Company merged with Honshu Container Co. Ltd.

Increased demand and a comparatively stable price structure had created the need for the company to increase its management and production efficiency. In 1989 Honshu's president, Yoshinobu Yonezawa, initiated several changes in the company's business approach. Yonezawa reorganized three of Honshu's paper mills, transfering some of the company's paper machines from their existing locations to other operating mills in an effort to increases efficiency. Part of Yonezawa's plan included the construction of a new mill at the company's Fuji location. Honshu was in the early 1990s in the process of building a new research-and-development complex in Tokyo. Yonezawa also liquidated two of Honshu's affiliated companies in 1988, Hokuyo Sangyo Co., Ltd. and Tsurusaki Pulp Co., Ltd.

Principal Subsidiaries: JANT Pty. Ltd. (New Guinea); CFI (Canada).

Further Reading: Roberts, John G., *Mitsui: Three Centuries of Japanese Business,* New York, Weatherhill, 1989.

—William R. Grossman

INTERNATIONAL ⒶPAPER

INTERNATIONAL PAPER COMPANY

Two Manhattanville Road
Purchase, New York 10577
U.S.A.
(914) 397-1500
Fax: (914) 397-1596

Public Company
Incorporated: 1898
Employees: 69,000
Sales: $12.96 billion
Stock Exchanges: New York Montreal Basel Geneva Lausanne
  Zürich Amsterdam

International Paper Company (IP) is a leading global producer of paper and paperboard products, with additional interests in related businesses. The company began as a major player in its industry and expanded through mergers, acquisitions, and product development. Its manufacturing operations span 24 countries, and the company exports to more than 120 nations.

Established on January 31, 1898, the firm resulted from a merger of 18 paper and power companies, with 20 mills throughout 5 northeastern states and timberlands ranging as far north as Canada. The new company had one million acres of woodlands, and streams running through the properties were utilized to run the mills with hydroelectric power. At the turn of the century, the mills provided 60% of U.S. newsprint. In 1903, in order to enhance its research-and-development efforts, the company opened the Central Test Bureau in Glens Falls, New York.

The company's power interests played a dominant role in its early years. As household electricity demand grew in the 1920s, the firm established large hydroelectric plants and power companies. At one time, it produced enough electricity to light all of New England, and most of Quebec and Ontario. In 1928 International Paper & Power Company was organized in Massachusetts to acquire International Paper. IP continued to operate as a subsidiary of International Paper & Power. In 1935 the United States passed the Public Utility Holding Act, making it illegal for an organization to run both an industrial firm and a power company. The law signified the end of International Paper's involvement in the energy and power business. Instead, the company began to focus on key areas such as paper and packaging.

The company expanded into the southern United States in the 1920s and 1930s, primarily because trees could be grown more quickly and in greater volume than they could in the North. It also maximized its use of the trees through the kraft process, which involved use of a very strong pulp to manufacture packaging materials.

In June 1941 a new company was incorporated to acquire the assets of International Paper & Power Company. The new parent company was named International Paper Company to reflect the change from a paper and power company to a manufacturer devoted solely to paper. During World War II, International Paper did what it could to support the war effort. Its contributions included the development of nitrate pulp for use in explosives and the development of a waterproof board called V-board—victory board—which was used to make boxes to send food and other supplies to the troops. The new technology, along with the wartime inventions of other manufacturers, led to increased competition after the war. As a result, IP began to invest more capital in research and development. Shortly after the war, it established the Erling Riis Research Laboratory in Mobile, Alabama.

An emphasis on packaging products also characterized the firm's progress in the 1940s. In December 1940 it acquired the Agor Manufacturing Company, which included three subsidiaries and four container plants in Illinois, Kansas, Massachusetts, and New Jersey. In June 1941 IP merged the Southern Kraft Corporation with its main business. Previously a subsidiary, Southern Kraft owned eight kraft board and paper mills in the southern United States. IP also bought the assets of a shipping-container maker, the Scharff-Koken Manufacturing Company.

In 1947 IP merged with Single Service Containers Inc., a manufacturer of milk containers, and in 1952 it founded the International Paper Company Foundation, a nonprofit organization developed to support charitable, educational, and scientific efforts. IP acquired the capital stock of a specialty coated paper manufacturer, A.M. Collins Manufacturing Company, of Philadelphia, in 1955. In 1957 the latter merged with IP. In 1958 IP bought Lord Baltimore Press, Inc., a Maryland manufacturer of cartons and labels.

IP's Canadian subsidiary, Canadian International Paper Company, also made its share of acquisitions in the 1950s. These included Brown Corporation in 1954; Hygrade Containers Ltd. in 1955; Anglo American Paper Company, Mid-West Paper Ltd., Vancouver Pacific Paper Company, and Victoria Paper Company in 1959.

During the following decade, new technology improved both product design and manufacturing processes. In 1962, for example, IP began using computers to control paper machines at its mill in Georgetown, South Carolina. A year later, it introduced polyethylene-coated milk cartons. In addition to new products, the 1960s presented IP with challenges, including development of new production and management techniques. Since 1943 IP had been headed by the Hinman family; John Hinman was chief executive from 1943 to 1962, and his son, Edward B. Hinman, held the post from 1966 to 1969. Various associates appointed by the elder Hinman ran the company from 1962 to 1966.

During the 1960s IP continued to grow internally and took giant leaps toward diversification—many of them in haste—and learned that bigger is not always better. IP had emphasized production efficiency as a means of increasing output for most of the century. IP's production muscle came at the expense of marketing expertise, which lagged. The production emphasis led to overexpansion of paper plants, which in turn resulted in low profit margins. To increase profitability, IP diversified, with little success, into areas as far-ranging as residential construction, prefabricated housing, nonwoven fabrics, consumer facial tissue, and disposable diapers. It also moved into lumber and plywood, but found equally little success in those areas. While paper, paperboard, and pulp still accounted for more than half of the company's sales during the early 1970s; converted paper products comprised one-third; lumber, plywood, and other building products totaled 9%; and the remaining sales came from real estate, packaging systems, and nonwoven fabrics.

By 1971 IP's long-term debt, which had been almost nonexistent in 1965, reached $564 million. When Edward Hinman took over, the company's greatest asset was its large share of real estate, including 8 million acres that it owned and 15.5 million that it leased. In 1968 Hinman sought the help of Frederick Kappel, formerly chairman of AT&T. The two ran the company together, but when earnings declined by 30% in 1970, Kappel, in 1971, and a team of outside directors replaced Hinman with Paul A. Gorman, another AT&T executive. Gorman faced the challenge of returning the company to profitability.

Gorman started the long-term task by setting up a $78 million reserve to cover write-offs of inefficient facilities; closing a specialty mill in York Haven, Pennsylvania; and closing various plants in Ecuador, Italy, Puerto Rico, and West Germany. In 1972 he also sold most of Donald L. Bren Co., a southern California house builder acquired in 1970, and Spacemakers Inc., a prefabricated-housing subsidiary. The company also sold its interest in C.R. Bard, Inc. a medical-equipment manufacturer.

From 1966 to 1972, IP had spent $1 billion to increase its paper-making and -converting capacity by 25%. During the early 1970s the paper industry headed toward cyclical recession. IP laid off 7% of its employees. Gorman felt that the firm needed more financial control, and saw to it that decisions made by the company's manufacturing groups were reviewed from a financial, marketing, and manufacturing perspective. In addition, all projects had to show a minimum after-tax profit of 10%. Ailing plants were improved, sold, or shut down. Gorman also reorganized international operations on a product line basis. His efforts were successful. Earnings of $69 million in 1971 were the lowest in ten years, despite record earnings just two years earlier, but they jumped 30% the first six months of 1972.

In 1973, J. Stanford Smith joined IP as vice chairman. Previously a senior vice president with General Electric Company, Smith eventually would replace Gorman as chairman. Smith felt that one way to increase profitability was to develop natural resources on the company's land. He devised a plan to purchase General Crude Oil Company, which IP did in 1974 for $489 million. The business was unsuccessful, however, in locating major oil or gas deposits on IP's land. Five years later, in order to raise capital for acquisitions and internal growth, the company sold General Crude Oil's oil and natural gas operations to Gulf Oil Corporation for $650 million. In addition, IP sold a Panama City, Florida, pulp and linerboard mill to Southwest Forest Industries for $220 million.

Between 1975 and 1980, IP's operating profits were mediocre. Again it turned to new management for help, and in 1978 Edwin Gee stepped in as chairman. A chemical engineer, Gee recognized that many of the company's 16 pulp and paper mills—all built in the 1920s and 1930s—were wasting labor and energy. Immediately, he instituted a $6 billion program to modernize the plants. Gee's goal was to turn the world's largest paper company into one of the lowest-cost producers of white paper and packaging materials, thus making it one of the most profitable papermakers as well.

To raise money for Gee's plan IP sold its remaining interest in General Crude Oil Company for $763 million and used the profits to buy Bodcaw Company of Dallas in 1979. Bodcaw added a highly efficient linerboard mill in Pineville, Louisiana, and 420,000 acres of prime timberland. In 1981 IP sold Canadian International Paper for US$900 million. In addition, Gee increased the research-and-development budget and reduced IP's labor force by 20%. By 1982 he had raised US$2 billion, aided by sales of land, timber, and other subsidiaries.

After determining that only two of the six major packaging mills were operating efficiently, Gee sold one mill, shut down three others, and invested $600 million in the Mansfield, Louisiana, mill. In April 1981 IP unveiled a new southern pine plywood and lumber manufacturing plant in Springhill, Louisiana. The $60 million facility, the brainchild of Gee, featured the latest computerized process controls and supplied the container board mill in Mansfield plus paper and pulp mills at Camden, Arkansas, and in Bastrop, Louisiana.

In the same year, John Georges became chief operating officer. His solution to IP's production problems was not to build new plants but to remodel existing facilities. The company also spent $500 million on remodeling a Georgetown, South Carolina, mill, changing its product focus in the process. Instead of brown linerboard, a cyclical product, part of the plant was set up to make white papers. The white paper business was to offer a faster-growing and more stable market.

In addition, Georges began a $350 million project to convert another mill in Mobile, Alabama. The 60-year-old facility, which housed the company's last remaining newsprint machine, was also remodeled to produce white papers in 1985, thus marking the end of the company's long-standing newsprint business. In 1987, newsprint prices began a steady decline.

A recession in the early 1980s meant further delays but the investments began to bear fruit in the mid-1980s. As a result of new automation, IP's production costs decreased 11% between 1981 and 1987 and its mills were able to use 25% less energy. Georges was named chairman in 1985, succeeding Gee.

The appointment had been preceded in 1984 by a decline in linerboard and pulp prices and a 14-year low in earnings. The white paper market seemed to be one of the few that was profitable, so Georges hired a team of scientists and technicians to promote business in that area. Their work led to a major acquisition in 1986: Hammermill Paper Company. The $1.1 billion purchase increased IP's white paper capacity by 750,000 tons and provided the technology to produce premium paper lines. Georges also reduced the number of salaried employees from 12,000 in 1981 to 9,200 in 1988, and streamlined management. Under his leadership, the firm also acquired Anitec Image Technology Corporation, maker of photographic film, papers, and darkroom chemicals; Arvey Corporation, a Chicago-based envelope manufacturer; and

Kendall Company's nonwoven fabrics division. As a result, profits improved in 1988 and set a record in 1989.

In addition to the company's recovery, however, it also weathered several crises. These included a 1984 fire that destroyed its Nacogdoches, Texas, plywood manufacturing plant, causing $32.5 million in damages. The facility reopened in 1986 after being equipped to produce oriented-strand board. In 1987, to protest inadequate wages and benefits, 2,200 workers went on strike at paper mills in Alabama, Maine, Mississippi, and Wisconsin.

In the late 1980s and early 1990s, the firm began to concentrate on international expansion through several overseas acquisitions. Although it already owned box manufacturing facilities in Italy, the Netherlands, Spain, Sweden, and the United Kingdom, in 1989 it acquired two major European manufacturers, Aussedat-Rey, the second-largest paper company in France, and the Ilford photographic-products division of Ciba-Geigy; in 1990 IP bought Germany's Zanders Feinpapiere AG, a high-quality coated paper company, and the French operations of Georgia-Pacific Corporation.

IP's product line in 1990 included pulp and paper; paperboard and packaging; specialty products; and wood products and timber. The company controlled 6.3 million acres of timberland through IP Timberlands Ltd., a publicly traded limited partnership established in 1985. In addition, the company was the world leader in bleached board, which is used for milk and juice cartons. Its goals, according to Georges, are to continue investing in its core businesses, to add to its current lines, to improve quality, to increase production of value-added products, to control costs and to improve customer service. Also, the company continues making selective acquisitions; in 1991 it acquired two paper companies, Dillon Paper and Leslie Paper, and the packaging equipment business of United Dominion Industries.

Subsidiaries: IP Timberlands Ltd.; International Pulp Sales Company; International Paper Investment Corporation; Arizona Chemical Company; Anitec Image Technology Corporation; Masonite Corporation.

Further Reading: "International Paper responds to treatment," *Business Week,* August 12, 1972; Loeffelholz, Suzanne, "Putting it on Paper," *Financial World,* July 25, 1989; *International Paper: Your Decision,* Purchase, New York, International Paper Company, [n.d.].

—Kim M. Magon

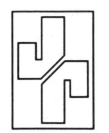

JAMES RIVER CORPORATION

JAMES RIVER CORPORATION OF VIRGINIA

120 Tredegar Street
Richmond, Virginia 23219
U.S.A.
(804) 644-5411
Fax: (804) 649-4415

Public Company
Incorporated: 1969
Employees: 38,000
Sales: $5.42 billion
Stock Exchange: New York

James River Corporation of Virginia is a papermaking company completing a transition from a small specialty paper business that produced automotive filters to a large consumer products business specializing in such well-known brand names as Northern, Brawny, and Dixie. The company concentrates on consumer towels and tissues, printing papers, and packaging for consumer products. The unrelenting growth through acquisition that characterized the James River Corporation during the 1970s and 1980s has been a big success story in the papermaking industry. In helping to pioneer high-leverage buyouts, the company has set an example in the financial world. It remains to be seen if the company can survive its own success; whether its leaders, chairman Brenton S. Halsey and president and CEO Robert C. Williams, can lead the large corporation as well as they led the underdog.

When Ethyl Corporation of Richmond, Virginia, was selling the Abermarle mill, its original papermaking facilities, in 1969, Halsey and Williams, then two Ethyl engineers, snapped it up. The river that flowed past the paper mill inherited a namesake in the newly formed James River Corporation. Ethyl had decided to concentrate on chemicals. The mill's 25-ton-a-day paper machine and equipment left over from the 1850s could not produce enough of the commodity grades of paper that were the preferred profit-makers of much of the paper and pulp industry at the time. The operation was losing money badly. Halsey and Williams, independently interested in turning the mill around, ran into each other at a Richmond investment banker's office and decided to work together. The two, who would soon be known as "Brent 'n' Bob" raised the capital, and bought the operation for $1.5 million. The two men then jointly designed the company's logo.

They then followed a pattern that soon would become familiar to them. They determined that the mill was best suited to the production of specialty papers. They recognized that specialty paper requires a more worker-intensive, decentralized operation, with an emphasis on a knowledgeable and well-trained marketing and sales force. Halsey and Williams felt that large corporations were overlooking opportunities in specialty papers. They used their engineering expertise to upgrade the mill's output to produce automotive air- and oil-filter papers, which had a high profit margin, and developed an in-house trucking system to provide immediate service to clients. By the end of a year they had coaxed earnings of $166,000 out of the aging mill.

In 1971 James River acquired the St. Regis Paper Company's specialty mill in Pepperell, Massachusetts. It employed many of the practices in the acquisition that would be company hallmarks for the next decade: friendly takeovers of ailing businesses that assure the cooperation of the seller; a decentralized approach that provides each mill with its own general manager, sales manager, production manager, and research-and-development director; and the utilization of middle managers within the acquired company to run it. James River also emphasized employee involvement and good relations with labor unions; in addition, it implemented company-wide profit sharing years before such plans became fashionable. James River's takeovers also often involve the firing of most executives and the negotiation of wage concessions from workers.

On March 16, 1973, the company went public, selling 165,000 shares of common stock. Staying true to the nature of the company, Halsey and Williams began a company-subsidized employee stock-purchase plan.

In 1975 James River acquired J-Mass from Weyerhaeuser. In 1977 James River bought a failing mill in Jay, Maine, from International Paper. The output was changed from book paper to paper for airline tickets and copying machines. In its first year under James River ownership the Jay mill made $3 million. The same year James River took over Reigel Products Corporation from Southwest Forest Industries. By 1979 it had $96 million in sales. In 1978 Halsey and Williams purchased Scott Graphics from Scott Paper Company, renamed it James River Graphics, and started producing film coatings. By the end of the decade James River had made ten acquisitions, had nearly 4,000 employees, and reached $297.9 million in annual sales.

In 1980 Gulf + Western sold its 80% interest in Brown Company to James River in return for cash and James River stock. Gulf + Western Chairman Charlie Bluhdorn was confident that James River stock would be more profitable than Brown was for Gulf + Western. For James River, the acquisition was crucial. The deal included a Berlin, New Hampshire, pulp mill and its surrounding 170,000 acres of timberland. It was James River's first in-house source of pulp, providing 40% of the company's pulp needs. Along with the pulp, the deal included paper towels, folding cartons for food packaging, and a small cup operation. James River intended to divest these product lines; they were, however, unable to find a buyer. As a result, the deal doubled James River's size and, for the first time, put it in the consumer-paper business; the filter specialists were suddenly makers of tissues, cups, and cereal boxes as well. While this diversification came about almost by accident and broke with the successful pattern of the

1970s, it turned out to be fortuitous. The new decade brought with it a slump in the auto industry, traditionally a big buyer of coated paper and other James River products. James River adjusted. By the end of 1981 industrial products only accounted for one-quarter of James River sales; communication and packaging papers, now a more stable market, made up the remaining 75%.

Once in consumer paper, James River did not shrink from new acquisitions. In 1982, Halsey and Williams once again used a stock-and-cash deal to double the size of the company; they bought the Dixie/Northern division, makers of Dixie cups; Northern toilet paper; Bolt, Brawny, and Gala towels; and folding cartons. The former owner, American Can Company, did not take James River's offer to buy seriously at first; it could not see how little James River would finance the deal. Finance it James River did, and soon James River was applying its usual success formula to Dixie/Northern. American Can had been cutting corners on quality. James River cut costs by laying off 200 salaried and 120 hourly workers. It improved sales by redesigning products and emphasizing marketing. With American Can's Alabama pulp mill included in the deal, James River became 70% self-sufficient in pulp. James River's chief financial officer, David McKittrick told *Financial World*, June 2, 1987, "When you peeled back the layers of complexity imposed on Dixie/Northern by American Can, you saw that the companies were in fact doing quite well and that business was actually sort of on a roll."

Many analysts thought that the debt created by all these acquisitions would slow the company down. In 1983 Halsey and Williams purchased the H.P. Smith Paper Company, a subsidiary of Phillips Petroleum; a Canadian pulp mill from American Can; and Diamond International's pulp and papermaking operations, including mills in New Hampshire, New York, and Massachusetts. The latter added the Vanity Fair brand of tissues and towels, giving James River a ready-made market in the Northeast.

The following year, James River moved its Northern bathroom paper and Brawny towels into the Northeast as well. In a campaign they called Operation Yankee, the company used a price-slashing policy and $20 million in advertising to take on Procter & Gamble and Scott Paper, the leaders in the field. Halsey said the new emphasis on expanding markets for its existing products reflected an industry slump, the lack of potential acquisitions, and the desire to direct capital toward internal improvements.

The acquisitions, however, did not cease. In April 1984 James River broke onto the international scene with the purchase of GB Papers in Scotland. In 1985 and 1986 the additions of the Arkon Corporation and the Cerex division of Monsanto were made, pushing James River further into the nonwovens market. These were relatively small purchases, however, leading up to the May 1986 acquisition of most of the interests of Crown Zellerbach Corporation, which once again doubled the size of James River. The company was now the number-two tissue-maker in the country, with a potential of $4.5 billion in total sales, and more than 35,000 employees. The new company, however, would take longer to consolidate than Halsey and Williams anticipated.

The deal had not been an easy one. Halsey had stepped into the middle of a hostile takeover bid by Sir James Goldsmith, who had been angling for control of Crown in a raid replete with poison pill defenses and greenmail. Because of James River's intervention, Crown shareholders saw their stock skyrocket, and had the option of buying into James River. James River got all the Crown papermaking operations. Goldsmith, however, might have gotten the best of the deal: property worth more than $1 billion, including Crown's 1.6 million acres of timber. Goldsmith sold the timberland to Hanson PLC for $1.3 billion in 1990.

Smaller acquisitions continued to make headlines, as well: Canada Cup, Specialty Papers Company, and Amarin Plastics were bought in 1987; and Dunn Paper Company; the U.K. photo and drawing papers business of Wiggins Teape Group; and Armstrong Rees Ederer Inc. were bought in 1988. Acquiring half of France's Kaysersberg, S.A., went a long way towards satisfying Halsey's desire to challenge Scott Paper's supremacy in the European tissue market. Overseas acquisitions were also made in Sweden, Spain, Turkey, and the United Kingdom. By 1988 the company was so big that the Federal Trade Commission blocked a proposed purchase of a South African–owned flexible packaging operation, with fears of reducing competition in that field.

The huge size of the company was affecting profits as well. From 1984 to 1988, the return on shareholders' equity fell from 26% to 10.7%. The high price of pulp, combined with James River's skyrocketing need for pulp, was the biggest culprit in this downturn. In fiscal 1989 James River was forced to buy 470,000 tons of market pulp domestically, with its new needs in Europe adding to the pulp deficit. This led to strategies to increase the internal supply of pulp: a Marathon, Ontario, pulp mill was tapped for a $280 million expansion in 1989. Williams also considered the use of recycled paper as a fiber source to be a major trend in the industry. James River was among the first producers to express interest in the use of recycled fiber for printing and writing paper production. The need for more fiber coincided with pending legislation that would require the use of some recycled fiber. By the end of 1989, there was some additional relief in sight for James River in the form of a major dip in pulp prices.

There were indications, however, that James River's woes went deeper than pulp supply; after 20 years of endless acquisitions, it seemed possible that Halsey and Williams had bitten off more than they could chew. Many plants needed upgrading, but the company did not have the capital to make all major overhauls that were necessary. In April 1990 the company announced a 13.1% decrease in income from the previous year. Capital expenditures were down 16%. In May James River sold its nonwovens group for a much-needed infusion of cash. In August Halsey announced a major restructuring: the company would sell or shut down operations with annual sales of $1.3 billion. James River was lopping off the arm that had started the company: specialty papers. Williams declared that the company's emphasis was now consumer products. James River would be made up of three businesses: consumer products, communications paper, and packaging. In the midst of this metamorphosis, in October 1990, Halsey, while retaining his mantle as chairman, stepped down as chief executive officer in favor of Williams. The move was part of a long-considered management transition plan. The switch from the more acquisitionally minded Halsey to the managerially inclined Williams seemed appropriate to the newly retrenched company.

Profits, however, continued to fall in fiscal 1990, with second quarter net income down 7% from the previous year. It remains to be seen whether the engineering background and acumen that propelled both men forward in specialty papers can lead to success in a consumer's market dependent chiefly on marketing flair. It remains to be seen, also, with both men nearing retirement, whether the company can survive as a major corporation without its founders.

Principal Affiliate: JA/Mont Holdings (50%).

Further Reading: Cox, Jacqueline, "James River chief cited for paper industry efforts," *Paper Trade Journal,* December 15, 1981; Smith, Kenneth E., "*P&P* Interview: James River leaders plan for continued strong growth," *Pulp & Paper,* January 1984; Carpenter, Kimberley, and John P. Tarpey, "A Southern Papermaker's Yankee Campaign, " *Business Week,* October 14, 1985; *James River Corporation: Two Decades of Growth,* Richmond, Virginia, James River Corporation, [1989].

—David Isaacson

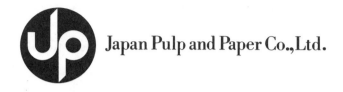
Japan Pulp and Paper Co., Ltd.

JAPAN PULP AND PAPER COMPANY LIMITED

6-11, Nihonbashi Hongoku-cho 4-chome
Chuo-ku, Tokyo 103
Japan
(03) 3270-1311
Fax: (03) 3246-0514

Public Company
Incorporated: 1916 as Nakai Shoten Limited
Employees: 1,086
Sales: ¥446.11 billion (US$3.29 billion)
Stock Exchanges: Tokyo Osaka

Japan Pulp and Paper Company Limited (JP&P) is the largest Japanese pulp- and paper-trading company. It is 40%-owned by paper manufacturers and acts as a trading organization to procure raw materials and distribute finished products. When consignment sales carried out for clients are added to its own operations, it is the largest pulp- and paper-trading company in the world. Nonetheless, nearly all sales are domestic.

JP&P operates through a series of representative offices in Asia, North America, and South America; six subsidiaries in Asia, the United States, and Europe; and four non-Japanese Asian affiliates. During the early 1990s this network was beginning to explore export sales. Since Japanese paper companies can supply their own market with finished paper products yet rely on other nations to supply their raw materials, JP&P's overseas activities primarily involve trade rather than distribution.

Saburobei Nakai, a Meiji Restoration–era entrepreneur, set up Echigoya Saburobei Shoten, a private company, in 1845. Located in Kyoto, Echigoya Saburobei Shoten traded in traditional Japanese paper, or *washi*, an industry then controlled by trade guilds. The company was the first in Japan to sell machine-made paper in 1876 and expanded its distribution by creating a branch office in Osaka two years later.

Still a regional company, it formed a distribution agreement with Oji Paper Company in 1882. Such a business relationship was typical of prewar Japan. Before World War II, Oji Paper supplied 90% of the nation's paper. By 1889 Echigoya Saburobei Shoten had two more branches—in Tokyo and Nagoya—that intensified its presence throughout central Japan.

In 1916 the venture reorganized, became a limited company and was renamed Nakai Shoten Limited. That year it had sales of ¥2 million. During World War I, wartime demand created

shortages that lasted through the 1940s of many raw materials. During this period Nakai Shoten slowed its geographic expansion. It was not until 1925, when the company established a branch office in Kyushu, that the company expanded again.

Following World War II, in 1947 the Allied powers permitted civilian trade to resume and Nakai Shoten set up a Sapporo branch office the following year. This office gave the company national distribution for the first time.

With the war's end began dramatic changes in the way Nakai Shoten did business. The Allied occupation government dismantled the *zaibatsu*, the banking and commercial organizations that had controlled much of Japanese industry before the war. Oji Paper, which Nakai Shoten served, was broken up into three smaller companies. These companies—Jujo Paper Company, Honshu Paper Company, and Oji—still retain partial ownership of Japan Pulp & Paper. JP&P also owns shares in Honshu, as well as other paper companies unaffiliated with the original Oji Paper group.

Most of the company's international activity had to do with the collection of raw materials to supply its manufacturers. During the postwar era the company increased its international presence but remained mainly a domestic company. In 1951 it established an export division, and by 1956 had representative offices in Hong Kong and Bangkok that acted as trading offices.

Contact with other Asian markets led to limited diversification. In 1958, seven years after its first international activity, the company began trading in plastic products. These plastics have been employed largely in packaging, and eventually in building materials.

In 1962 the company established a Sendai branch office—its second office north of Tokyo. The following year the company shortened its name to Nakai Limited.

In the late 1960s the company expanded beyond Asian markets and expanded the scope of products that it dealt with. In 1967 it opened a representative office in New York. The following year it began trading in pulp—a commodity necessary to papermakers. The company's trading in pulp ensured adequate supply and procurement at optimal price, and in 1968 sales reached ¥100 million for the first time.

During the 1970s the company centralized its organization, expanded its product line and made use of its burgeonning capital. In 1970 Nakai Limited merged with Fuji Yoshiten Company, another paper dealer. The new organization was named Japan Pulp and Paper Company Limited. The following year it completed the union by consolidating its national business with a unified wholesale network.

The company immediately began marketing construction materials and machinery for the paper industry and set up a representative office in Jakarta. Construction materials marketed by Japan Pulp and Paper then included more than plywood, particleboard, and other wood products, which are commonly associated with paper and forestry companies. The company sold concrete products for building foundations and interior finishing materials made of ceramics and plastic.

The company went public, listing on the Tokyo Stock Exchange's second section in 1972 to increase its flow of capital. JP&P took advantage of the cash influx and established its first European sales office, in Düsseldorf. It aggressively pursued this new market.

In 1973 JP&P transformed the new Düsseldorf office into its first subsidiary, Japan Pulp and Paper GmbH. Due to its growth the company was soon elevated to the first section of the Tokyo Stock Exchange.

The following year two more subsidiaries were created in its existing markets. In Seattle, Washington, the Japan Pulp and Paper (U.S.A.) Corporation was created, and in Hong Kong, Japan Pulp and Paper Co. (H.K.), Ltd. This latter venture incorporated the existing sales office. In only six years the company's sales had doubled to ¥200 million. By 1980 after another six years, sales jumped another ¥100 million.

Continually increasing its trading capacity, the company also upgraded its information network. In 1979 the company created the JP Information Center Co., Ltd., serving domestic paper companies. The following year information on the distribution of paper would be incorporated.

As the 1980s dawned, JP&P expanded its Asian presence into Beijing with a representative office. It also moved its U.S. subsidiary headquarters to Los Angeles, and closed its sales office in Seattle.

During the 1980s the company diversified into finished paper products and papermaking machines. Serious growth evaded the Japanese paper industry in the early- and mid-1980s. Although the Japanese paper industry later rebounded, JP&P diversified. In 1985 it ventured for the first time into real estate, creating JP Planning Co. Ltd. It complemented this subsidiary with JP Household Supply Co., Ltd.

Papers that accompany office technology saw significant growth in the 1980s. Electronic office automation through such tools as computers and fax machines greatly increased demand for certain paper grades. In 1982 JP&P intensified its pursuit of this growing market by selling automated office equipment in addition to the paper that the machines require. JP&P markets paper for photocopiers, facsimile machines, and computer printers, as well as business forms and carbonless papers. By trading in office equipment, JP&P tracks and keeps pace with changes in that market segment for paper products. Selling facsimile machines, for instance, identifies buyers for compatible papers.

During the 1980s Japanese industry spent more on advertising, leading to a publishing boom. The growth spurred JP&P's sales of newsprint, publication papers, plastics, and printing machinery. The company provides newsprint to five of the six largest newspapers in Japan. By the end of the 1980s, JP&P sold nearly 25% of the newsprint used in Japan. In addition, promotional materials like mass mailings and catalogs grew tremendously in Japan during the 1980s, which also served to increase paper demand.

Coated papers for magazines also saw explosive growth. JP&P has significant access to suppliers of this product. Kanzaki Paper Manufacturing, which owns 6.2% of JP&P shares and has 3.3% of its shares owned by Oji, holds the largest domestic market share of coated papers. In addition, Jujo Paper, which owns 10.9% of JP&P, owns nearly 33% of Nippon Kakoh Seishi, another major supplier of coated papers to the Japanese market.

By 1989 only 61.9% of JP&P's sales were of paper. Packaging received emphasis by Japanese consumer product manufacturers during the decade. By 1988 paperboard accounted for about 40% of the paper made in Japan. Other packaging grades available to the company include kraft paper, heavier grades of paperboard for boxes, and plastic materials for packaging.

In the late 1980s the company's subsidiaries carried out their own expansion. A second European office opened in 1986 in London. In 1988 the company opened Japan Pulp and Paper (SP) Pte. Ltd. in Singapore. By 1990 the company had two more U.S. sales offices, creating one in Atlanta, Georgia, and reopening one in Seattle.

In 1988 reflecting the company's domestic focus, JP&P went into debt to finance a 10,000-ton-capacity warehouse—strategically located near Tokyo's port of entry. JP&P owned 11 distribution companies and this new warehouse accounted for 10% of the company's storage capacity. Japanese investment in paper-production technology reached record highs during the late 1980s, and JP&P income growth kept pace with the national average.

JP&P serves paper manufacturers in more ways than simply through distribution. JP&P has marketed computer systems designed for paper wholesalers and sold them to more than 170 Japanese wholesalers between 1970 and 1989. The company planned to expand its computer software development. It also markets heavy equipment like industrial printing presses.

JP&P's role as the distribution leader in the Japanese paper industry is exemplified by its VAN system, begun in 1989. The on-line system coordinates information from ten other paper traders and makes ordering and distribution information available to customers. Such service capacities, and finance activities, will continue to be emphasized in the company's future.

Japan Pulp and Paper Company procures and supplies printing papers, paperboard, pulp and fiber, plastics, printing and papermaking machinery, and construction materials. The company imports raw materials in the form of paper for finishing, pulp, and wastepaper. It exports machinery, electronics, and paper. Nonetheless, exports are only about 10% of total sales. The Tokyo office controls the trading activities of six regional offices and information from more than 1,000 suppliers worldwide. During the late 1980s Japan started to import more paper. Asia and Oceania are likely to surpass Japan as producers of paper and paperboard, but JP&P is extremely active as a trader in its hemisphere.

Principal Subsidiaries: Japan Pulp and Paper Co., (H.K.) Ltd. (Hong Kong); Japan Pulp and Paper (SP) Pte. Ltd. (Singapore); Far East Paper Pte. Ltd. (Singapore); Japan Pulp and Paper (U.S.A.) Corp., Japan Pulp and Paper Gmbh (Germany).

Further Reading: *Japan Pulp and Paper Company Limited: Corporate Brochure,* Tokyo, Japan Pulp and Paper Company Limited, 1991.

—Ray Walsh

JEFFERSON SMURFIT GROUP PLC

Beech Hill
Clonskeagh
Dublin 4
Republic of Ireland
(01) 2696622
Fax: (01) 2694481

Public Company
Incorporated: 1934 as James Magee & Sons Ltd.
Employees: 15,022
Sales: IR£993.00 million (US$1.77 billion)
Stock Exchanges: Dublin London

The Jefferson Smurfit Group is a conglomerate that has expanded from its origins in the Irish packaging industry to cover the production of paper, paperboard, and packaging; books and magazines; and financial services. Most of its sales are to the rest of the European Community and to Latin America, and most of its profits come from those regions. It has kept its headquarters in Dublin, as the largest company quoted on the Dublin Stock Exchange, and about 7.5% of its ordinary shares are in the hands of members of the Smurfit family.

The history of the company began with a young man from England making good in Ireland. Jefferson Smurfit, the son of a shipyard worker, was born in Sunderland, in northeast England, in 1909. His father died when he was ten years old. He became an apprentice salesman in a large department store at 14—he once said that life had made him into a little old man by that age.

In 1926 he accepted his uncle's offer of work in the tailoring business in St. Helens, Lancashire. Eight years later he moved to Belfast and opened his own tailoring business, James Magee & Sons Ltd., after marrying a local woman. The priest who conducted his wedding introduced him to the box-making business in Dublin. The priest had become involved with a factory there through one of his parishioners. The priest noticed Smurfit's keen business sense and asked the young man to act as an adviser. Smurfit saw the potential of the business, and turned his attention to learning more about the technology of box-making. Meanwhile the tailoring business was expanding rapidly, and soon Smurfit owned four shops. He acquired full control of the Dublin box-making factory in 1938 and poured more of his energies into that business, giving up his tailor's shops and moving permanently to Dublin.

After 1939, when World War II broke out in Europe, the materials for box-making became much harder to find. Smurfit was able to keep his business going because he adapted the technology and his products to meet the demands of wartime. An example of this adaptation was the production of thick paper with straw in it for use in Irish schools. Because of the scarcity of paper and packaging during the war, Smurfit was able to capitalize on the overwhelming demand. The company concentrated on corrugated box production and had two paper-making machines working at full capacity. He had good relations with the trade unions and was proud that there were no strikes. By 1950, his Dublin factory was five times its initial size and producing eight times the original turnover. His sons, Michael and Jefferson Jr., were brought into the business at this date: accordingly, the company was renamed as Jefferson Smurfit & Sons Ltd.

Michael, the eldest of Jefferson Smurfit's four sons, started on the factory floor, as Jefferson Jr. did later. Their father insisted that they join the appropriate union. Both went on to specialize, Jefferson Jr. in sales, Michael in company administration. Michael then took the opportunity to continue studying management techniques in Canada and the United States. After completing his training he ran a corrugated box factory, with another brother, Alan, in his father's home town, St. Helen's, returning to his father's company in 1966 as joint managing director with Jefferson Jr.

The 1960s were a period of considerable expansion for the company. In 1964 Jefferson Smurfit & Sons Ltd. became a public company quoted on the Dublin Stock Exchange. Smurfit acquired Temple Press Ltd., a manufacturer of cartons and boxes, in 1968, then took its first steps outside its original area of business when, in 1969 it acquired Browne & Nolan Ltd., a printing, packaging, publishing, and educational supply company. The parent company was now large enough to be quoted on the International Stock Exchange in London. Jefferson Sr. realized that his son Michael should be given more incentive to stay with the company and not become a potential rival. In 1969 he was appointed deputy chairman just as the company began to look seriously at acquisitions beyond the United Kingdom. In 1970 the company doubled its size with the purchase of the Hely Group of companies, which were involved in radio and television distribution, educational and office supplies, and packaging. Two years later the continuing expansion of the Smurfit businesses was symbolized in a change of name, to Jefferson Smurfit Group Ltd. Michael Smurfit brought the corrugated box factory in St. Helen's into the new group. The group concentrated a great deal of effort on its overseas expansion plans. It acquired the British carton making and printing company W. J. Noble and Sons in 1972. A year later its purchase of the print and packaging division of the U.K. firm Tremletts Ltd. brought plants in the United Kingdom and in Nigeria into the group. But the American market proved to be the most lucrative of its overseas ventures. Its 40% investment in the paper and plastic manufacturing firm Time Industries of Chicago, in 1974, gave it a foothold in the United States. It increased this initial investment to 100% in 1977.

Jefferson Smurfit Sr. died in 1977, at the age of 68. Michael succeeded him as chairman while Jefferson Jr. took over as deputy chairman. Their younger brothers moved up too, Alan to head United Kingdom sales and Dermot Smurfit to become managing director of the paper and board division. Their father left them a company that was beginning to diversify and internationalize itself in earnest yet continuing to lay stress on its base in Jefferson Sr.'s adopted homeland.

In 1968 Jefferson Sr. had seen the acquisition of Temple Press as an act of faith in the future of the Irish economy. The new chairman did not abandon this faith. The group carried on investing in Ireland, by acquiring for example, Irish Paper Sacks Ltd.; Goulding Industries Ltd., maker of plastic film and sacks; and half the equity of the Eagle Printing Company Ltd. The more companies Jefferson Smurfit acquired, the more raw materials it needed. It decided to sell 49% of its corrugated box interests in Ireland and the United Kingdom to the Swedish paper company Svenska Cellulosa Aktiebolaget in return for a guaranteed supply of kraftliner. The sale also provided cash for further expansion abroad. It acquired 51% of the Australian company Mistral Plastics Pty Ltd. in 1978. In 1979, it paid US$13 million for a 27% share of the Alton Box Board Company. At this time this was the largest investment by an Irish company in the American economy. It increased to 51% five months later.

The Jefferson Smurfit Group established itself as a major supplier of print and packaging in the United States in the 1980s. In Ireland it bought a small stake in the Woodfab group, the largest user of native timber and a significant presence in the Irish forestry sector. But Smurfit saw its greatest potential in the American market, where there have never been tight restrictions on foreign ownership or investment. Smurfit's method, a relatively cautious one, was to purchase a minority holding of an American company, observe its profits rising and then move to 100% ownership. Thus a 27% holding in the Alton Box Board Company, acquired in 1979, formed the bridgehead for complete acquisition in 1981. And, in a variation on the same technique, in 1982 Smurfit formed a 50–50 joint venture to take over the packaging and graphic arts divisions of Diamond International, then bought out the partner's shares to gain full control in 1983.

Clearly the group's long term strategy of becoming an international competitor was coming closer to realization and Michael Smurfit was earning his reputation as a canny businessman. In 1983 shares in the American wing of the group, the Jefferson Smurfit Corporation, were floated on the market, generating US$46 million for further investment. The group then decided to expand into a new area of business, setting up a joint venture with Banque Paribas, known as Smurfit Paribas Bank Ltd. Jefferson Smurfit Jr. left the group in 1984, due to ill health, and his two younger brothers were appointed joint deputy chairmen. The following year, the 50th since the company's founding, was marked by re-registration as a public limited company. After achieving considerable success in its purchases of packaging companies, Smurfit acquired the Publishers Paper Company, based in Oregon, in 1986. This company supplied newsprint to such well-known papers as the *Los Angeles Times*. It was renamed Smurfit Newsprint Corporation and continues to supply several newspapers. The same year, in its largest deal yet, Smurfit set up a joint venture with Morgan Stanley Leveraged Equity Fund to pay Mobil US$1.2 billion for its subsidiary the Container Corporation of America (CCA), which produces paperboard and packaging, and in 1987 it purchased outright the manufacturing operations of CCA on the European continent and in Venezuela. The group thus more than doubled the value of its American holdings and

moved into manufacturing in mainland Europe for the first time.

The second half of 1987 was a difficult time for the Smurfit family. First, Jefferson Smurfit Jr. died at the age of 50. He had contributed a great deal to the group's expansion through his expertise in sales and marketing. Then, like many other companies, Smurfit lost an enormous amount of value in the stock market crash in October. The value of its shares fell by more than half, but since demand for paper products remained steady it was just a question of riding out the storm.

In 1988, Dublin marked its millennium as a city, and Jefferson Smurfit Group, with its strong ties to the Irish capital, played a part in the celebrations by donating the Anna Livia Fountain in memory of Jefferson Smurfit Sr. Anna Livia, symbolizing the River Liffey flowing through the city to the sea, is a leading character in James Joyce's novel *Finnegan's Wake*. The group also contributed to the restoration of the Mansion House, the residence of the lord mayor of Dublin, and sponsored a Millennium Science Scholarship, to be awarded to a doctoral student specializing in high technology. Other Smurfit activities in 1988 included the establishment of Smurfit Natural Resources to continue its own private afforestation program in Ireland and the purchase of the Spanish packaging firm Industrial Cartonera, as well as 30% of the Papelera Navarra, also based in Spain. Adding to these a 35% stake in Inpacsa, in 1989, gave the group interests in four paper mills, eight corrugated box plants, and 20% of the paper and packaging market in Spain.

In 1989 the group's publishing division grew with the launch of a new weekly newspaper, the *Irish Voice*, in the United States, where it also has a interest in the magazine *Irish America*. The *Irish Post* in the United Kingdom increased its circulation and Smurfit Print in Ireland produced more computer manuals. In America, an industrial dispute at Smurfit Newsprint Corporation lasted over seven months and cost the company about US$25 million in profits. The group was also affected by lengthy strikes in the packaging industry in Italy. Latin American operations were slowly expanding. Smurfit Carton de Colombia and Smurfit de Venezuela have put much effort into researching and developing the genetic enhancement of eucalyptus trees. Researchers believe that eucalyptus trees can be harvested in five years rather than the normal eight years. This is done by clonal reproduction, producing the fastest-growing commercial trees in the world, from which a good quality uniform pulp can be manufactured. The Colombian company also produces writing paper, using a mix of different species of hardwood found in the tropical forests. By 1989, Smurfit Latin America had well over 20% of the paper and board market in Venezuela and Colombia. The Latin American companies in the group provide opportunities for further education to their employees. In Colombia, for example, the company offers training in farm and forest tending as well as elementary schooling for children in the country areas near Smurfit timberland.

In 1989 the group made heavy use of junk bonds to restructure its American operations, which had accounted for about 65% of its profits in 1988. A 50–50 joint venture between the Smurfit group and the Morgan Stanley Leveraged Equity Fund created a new holding company, SIBV/MS Holdings, for most of the group's subsidiaries in the United States. The reorganization generated US$1.25 billion and boosted the value of the group's shares by 50%. The group next decided to continue to expand north of the U.S. border, and purchased 30% of PCL Industries Ltd., a Canadian company specializing in the conversion of plastics, with its own interests in the United States. The group also formed a partnership with the Canadian firm Tembec, Inc. to build a bleached lightweight coated mill in Quebec. Meanwhile Smurfit International, the European division of the group, added to its operations the German company C.D. Haupt, a major paper-recycling mill, placing Smurfit in a strong position to profit from new opportunities in reunited Germany and in Eastern Europe. More Italian firms such as Ondulato Imolese, an integrated corrugated manufacturer, and Euronda, producer of corrugated cases and sheets, also joined the group.

By 1990 the Jefferson Smurfit Group had established itself as the largest gatherer and consumer of waste paper in the world and completed the purchase of the Golden State Newsprint Co. Inc., which was renamed Smurfit Newsprint Corporation of California, and Pacific Recycling Co. Inc. As environmental awareness became commercially viable the group began to build up its recycling division by acquiring several existing units and announcing its intention to invest in a newsprint production unit, using scrap paper, in New York State.

In the United States, as in Latin America, Smurfit has tried to involve itself within the community. It provides special programs for its employees, such as training at the Smurfit Technical Institute, and sponsors young children in Fernandina Beach's Literacy Program. In Ireland, too, some of the Irish universities have been endowed with chairs and financial support for academic projects, of which the leading example is the Michael Smurfit School of Business at University College, Dublin.

By the beginning of the 1990s the Smurfit Group was producing a diversity of goods, from presentation boxes for Waterford crystal to takeout pizza boxes, and it continued to diversify further. It formed Nokia Smurfit Ltd. in a joint venture with Nokia Consumer Electronics, which distributes television, video recorders, and satellite equipment in Ireland and is a division of the Finnish Company Oy Nokia Ab. It bought back its 49% interest in Smurfit Corrugated Ireland from Svenska Cellulosa and bought another 24.5% of U.K. Corrugated, boosting its ownership to 50%. One of its subsidiaries

in the United Kingdom bought Texboard, a manufacturer of paper tubes. The group aimed to extend its already diversified board manufacturing and conversion business. It also purchased another U.K. firm, Townsend Hook, a leading producer of corrugated paper cases and coated papers, which gives Smurfit over 20% of the corrugated case industry in Britain.

In 1991 Jefferson Smurfit added to its recycling business with the acquisition of several French companies, such as Centre de Dechets Industriels Group (CDI), the second-largest waste paper company in France, and the Compagnie Generale de Cartons Ondules, an integrated mill and converting operation. In addition, it bought the Lestrem Group, which specializes in manufacturing solid board, accounting for about 20% of the market in France. It also set up a new subsidiary, Smurfit France.

The Smurfit Group carried diversification still further by deciding to invest in the leisure business in Ireland. Its activity in this area includes the RiverView Racquet and Fitness Club, Waterford Castle Golf and Country Club, and the new development of the Kildare Hotel and Country Club.

The Jefferson Smurfit Group is likely to expand further as it enters the new markets of eastern Europe. In most of the 14 countries in which it has already become involved, the group has consistently been able to establish a significant presence in the paper and paperboard market. While these products remain at the core of the business, the group will continue to find other opportunities.

Principal Subsidiaries: CartoEspana, S.A.(Spain); Carton de Colombia, S.A. (67%); Carton de Venezuela, S.A. (78%); Iona Print Limited; Jefferson Smurfit Italia, S.r.L. (Italy); Smurfit Mercurius Verpakking B.V. (Netherlands); Smurfit Carton y Papel de Mexico, S.A. de C.V. (Mexico); Smurfit Corrugated Ireland (51%); Smurfit Holdings GmbH (Germany); Smurfit International B.V. (Netherlands); Smurfit Ireland Limited; Smurfit Limited (U.K.); Smurfit Plastic Packaging, Inc. (U.S.A.).

Further Reading: Cordell, Valerie, *The First Fifty Years,* Dublin, Jefferson Smurfit Group, 1984.

—Monique Lamontagne

✤ JUJO PAPER

JUJO PAPER CO., LTD.

Shin-Yurakucho Building
12-1 Yurakucho 1-chome
Chiyoda-ku, Tokyo 100
Japan
(03) 3211-7311
Fax: (03) 3213-6762

Public Company
Incorporated: 1949
Employees: 4,453
Sales: ¥393.51 billion (US$2.90 billion)
Stock Exchanges: Tokyo Osaka Nagoya

Jujo Paper Co., Ltd. was in 1990 Japan's third-largest manufacturer of printing paper products. With a market share of more than 6.5%, the company produces a diversified line of paper products, including newsprint, printing paper, processed paper, carbonless copy paper, and pressure- and heat-sensitive papers. Jujo ranks as Japan's undisputed leader in the production of processed-paper containers. Through its subsidiaries, Jujo also markets lumber, laminated wood products, soft drinks, and engineering services; it sells automobiles and is involved in real estate, ski resorts, and amusement-related enterprises. The company owns in excess of 212,000 square miles of forest land, and several shopping malls; it is also in the civil construction business.

Jujo was established in 1949 as a result of the reorganization of the Oji Paper Company. Oji Paper, which was part of the huge Mitsui *zaibatsu* that had for more than a century been Japan's largest paper producer. After World War II during the ensuing Allied occupation, the Allies set up the Holding Company Liquidation Commission (HCLC). It was the intention to use the HCLC to break up the industrial *zaibatsu* that had held a virtual monopoly on Japanese commerce for hundreds of years. By means of this huge reorganization, a democratic, capitalistic system was expected to emerge that would be controlled by a large number of smaller groups of Japanese businessmen and entrepreneurs. Oji Paper was accordingly broken into three separate paper manufacturing concerns, Oji Paper, Honshu Paper, and Jujo.

Itsuki Nishi was elected Jujo's first president in August of 1949. He was immediately confronted with the most serious threat to Jujo and all the other Japanese paper producers, an acute shortage of paper pulp. Pulp had primarily been imported prior to and during World War II, and the loss of forests in Manchuria, Korea, and Sakhalin as a result of Japan's defeat threatened production. Although a short boom in domestic pulp production temporaily helped to alleviate the immediate need for pulp—Japan's land mass was covered more than 70% by forest—it was obvious that prolonged intense deforestation of the nation's timberlands would do irreparable long-term damage to what had to remain a renewable resource.

To put a stop to the indiscriminate logging that was underway, the Supreme Commander for the Allied Powers (SCAP) established the Council for the Conservation of Natural Resources. Jun'ichiro Kobayashi, a paper-industry veteran and forestry expert was brought in to head up the council. Kobayashi proposed the development of the Alaska Pulp Company, and SCAP gave tentative approval for the formation of the Alaska Pulp Company. After a great deal of trans-Pacific negotiation, the company was finally established in 1953, using approximatly equal amounts of investment capital provided by U.S. and Japanese investors. The Alaska Pulp venture was one of the first large postwar overseas investments made by Japanese industry and helped to revitalize U.S.-Japanese business relations.

During the remainder of the 1950s Nishi's energies were engaged in the modernization of the company's seven paper mills. Jujo's leadership knew that without a major improvement in the overall quality of the company's products and increased productivity and sales, Jujo would not be able to benefit fully from the postwar economic opportunites. In 1957 Nishi was succeeded by Saichiro Kaneko. Kaneko ushered in a decade of explosive growth and diversification.

The company's research-and-development efforts paid off in 1962 with Jujo's introduction of CCP, a carbonless copy paper. The success of CCP paved the way for further introduction of new specialty products that kept pace with the rapid advances in information processing. The company introduced computer paper, pressure- and heat-sensitive papers, and as the electronic transmission of information by means of fiber optics increased, Jujo introduced electrostatic paper for facsimile machines.

In 1963 the company established the Shikoku Drinks Company, later known as the Shikoku Coca-Cola Bottling Company. Shikoku is licensed by Coca-Cola Company to bottle and sell Coca-Cola and Fanta soft drinks in Japan. This diversification into the soft drink business was the beginning of a trend that would link Jujo with several other U.S. businesses. That same year Jujo, in a joint venture with the U.S.-based Kimberly-Clark Corporation established Jujo Kimberly, a company that would domestically manufacture and market Kimberly-Clark's Kleenex and Kotex brand products. Two years later, Jujo became the sole Japanese agent for Ex-Cell-O Corporation, and began production and sales of Ex-Cell-O's line of Pure-Pak paper drink containers.

As Jujo's sales and products lines increased, the need for more production facilities became apparent, and facilities were built to keep up with demand. In 1967 the company merged with Tohoku Pulp Company, which resulted in Jujo becoming the largest Japanese producer and seller of both pulp and paper. An increased need for more raw materials resulted in the company's acquisition of a 25% interest in Finlay Forest Industries of Canada in 1969.

In 1970 the company completed construction of a plant in Nakoso that mass produced CCP paper and other information-recording papers. At the company's Ishinomaki plant, output was boosted to more than 1,000 tons per day with the installation of a new paper mill. In 1974 construction of a new paper mill in Egawa was completed. The newly constructed mill was specifically designed to manufacture products for the company's Pure-Pak liquid container business. The increase in production capacity was not enough to meet the increased demand. Within three years the need to produce more CCP paper and Pure-Pak containers brought about Jujo's acquisition of NCR Japan's Oiso mill, a producer of CCP paper. The construction of another Pure-Pak mill in the city of Miki was completed in 1978.

Kozo Toyonaga was named Jujo's new president in 1976. That same year, Jujo entered into a joint venture with the U.S.-based Weyerhaeuser Company. The newly formed company was called the North Pacific Paper Corporation and specialized in the production of newsprint. Construction of its mill in Longview, Washington, was completed in 1979. In 1990 the plant produced 210,000 tons of newsprint.

The seemingly unbridled growth that took place in the 1970s began to slow down in the early 1980s. The pulp and paper industry suffered a severe, prolonged cyclical slump. The company changed leadership in the face of these hard times. In 1982 Minoru Ishigami was named Jujo's new president.

To cope with the severe decline in profits, Ishigami proposed a two-pronged approach to solve the problem. First, an agreement was made between Jujo and three other Japanese paper manufacturers to establish a joint venture for the purchasing of raw materials such as wood chips and pulp. The companies also agreed to pool their research-and-development projects to keep costs down and increase efficiency. The move towards consolidation was seen as an attempt to re-establish the same powerful business position in Japanese industry that the group had held when they were all components of the Oji Paper Company and part of the huge Mitsui *zaibatsu*. The three companies had tried to merge once before in 1968 but were unsuccessful because of Japan's anti-monopoly laws. The agreement between the four companies, modeled in many ways after the structure of the Nippon Steel Corporation, created a huge, new industrial group in Japan's paper and pulp industry.

The second part of Mishigama's plan was to raise capital by selling bonds to foreign investors. During the three years following his election as president, Jujo issued over 170 million bonds, which were sold primarily for Swiss francs to investors. The plan worked. Jujo weathered the economic slump of the early 1980s and became Japan's leader in the production of printing paper and second in the production of newsprint. Jujo emerged from the prolonged slump in apparently stable, if not better, financial condition. In 1986 the company purchased the remaining 50% of Jujo Kimberly from Kimberly-Clark, taking over complete ownership of the company.

Jujo's sales breakdown in 1990 was 34% newsprint, 45% printing paper, 10% information-related paper products, 8% processed goods, and 3% timber and other forest-related products. Demand for heat-sensitive paper was increasing at an annual rate of 20% to 30%. With the addition of a new mill at the company's Ishinomaki plant, Jujo has expanded its production capacity from 1,000 to 1,800 tons per month to keep up with demand. In the early 1990s the company developed a milk carton that was 40% lighter than conventional milk packaging and has also introduced new milk filling equipment for use in school lunchrooms.

Jujo's president in 1991, Takeshiro Miyashita, was maintaining Jujo's traditional focus on paper related products. A profile of company research and development efforts at that time broke down into paper and pulp production; processed paper and processed paper goods; and forest products that include logging, building materials, and landscaping.

Principal Subsidiaries: Jujo Paperboard Co., Ltd. (98.3%); Jujo Kimberly Co., Ltd.; Tohoku Paper Co., Ltd. (65%); Shikoku Coca-Cola Bottling Co., Ltd. (97.7%); Jujo Central Co., Ltd.; Jujo Development Co., Ltd.; Jujo Lumber Co., Ltd.

Further Reading: Roberts, John G., *Mitsui: Three Centuries of Japanese Business,* New York, Weatherhill, 1989; *Jujo Paper,* Tokyo, Jujo Paper Co., Ltd., [1989].

—William R. Grossman

KYMMENE CORPORATION

KYMMENE CORPORATION

Post Office Box 1079
Mikonkatu 15A
SF-00101 Helsinki
Finland
(0) 131 411
Fax: (0) 653 884

Public Company
Incorporated: 1872 as Kymmene Aktiebolag
Employees: 17,500
Sales: Fmk13.56 billion (US$3.74 billion)
Stock Exchanges: Helsinki London

The Kymmene group, headed by Kymmene Corporation, Finland's leading forestry company, has production plants at 16 locations in Finland and in three countries in Western Europe. These business operations are the responsibility of independent subsidiaries. The emphasis of the Kymmene group's operations is on the paper industry. Its chief products are publication and fine papers. The group is a leading European manufacturer in both sectors, its paper division having a production capacity of over three million tons in 1991. The company is Finland's market leader in the wood-based panel—chipboard, fiberboard, and plywood—industry and a major producer in the sawmill industry. The Kymmene group is self-sufficient in chemical pulp and derives part of its timber from its own forests, the second largest privately owned forests in Finland, covering an area of 440,000 hectares. In 1991, exports and foreign operations accounted for 85% of the group's Fmk13.56 billion turnover.

The inception of Kymmene Corporation almost 120 years ago reflects the early stages of Finland's paper industry as a whole. The art of making groundwood pulp was discovered in 1846. Axel Wilhelm Wahren, one of the great Finnish industrialists, recognized the potential afforded by hydroelectric power, vast forests, and the proximity of the Russian market, and in 1870 leased a section of the largest rapids on the River Kymi flowing through southeast Finland, at Kuusankoski. At around the same time Count Carl Robert Mannerheim, father of Finland's military leader and president C.G.E. Mannerheim, purchased an island in the same rapids and part of the riverbank. The founding meeting of Wahren's company, Kymmene Aktiebolag, was held on May 21, 1873. A company by the name of Kuusankoski Aktiebolag established by Mannerheim began operating in January 1872.

In 1896 a third businessman, Rudolf Elving, purchased the Voikkaa Rapids further upstream and over the next five years built four paper machines, a groundwood plant, and a sulfite pulp mill.

The founding of three large mills in the same area within a short space of time raised the prices of the local forest lands and timber, while the resulting competition reduced the prices of the end products. The rival enterprises soon became aware of the advantages of joining forces and in 1904 signed an agreement whereby Kymmene bought both the Kuusankoski company and the Voikkaa mill in exchange for shares in the company. The resulting company, the predecessor of today's Kymmene Corporation, was the largest limited company in Finland and the largest papermaker in the Nordic countries.

By the time of the merger, the individual companies had acquired 76,000 hectares of forest, an area which grew as more mergers took place. The purchase of Strömsdal Board Mill, the supplier of groundwood, used in paper manufacturing, to the company's paper mills, in 1915 increased the forest area by 21,000 hectares, and the purchase of the Halla sawmill by a further 119,300. Halla also had some inland sawmills, and Kymmene became a major exporter of sawed goods.

During Rudolf Elving's four years as managing director beginning 1904, Kymmene installed more production machinery than any other firm in Finland to that date. However, a disastrous fire at the Voikkaa mill, in which three machines were destroyed, and the slump in prices on the paper market caused a setback from which the company only recovered under its next managing director, Gösta Serlachius.

The building of the railway from Helsinki to St. Petersburg in the early years opened up new prospects for Finnish groundwood, board, and paper on the Russian market. At the outset Kymmene sold goods on commission at certain points in Russia. The sales areas covered by the local agents were extended in the first half of the 1910s. 1916 saw the establishment in St. Petersburg of the Kauppaosakeyhtiö Kymmene Aktiebolag trading company, registered as a Russian limited company, with sales offices in Moscow, Nizni Novgorod, Rostov, Tiflis, Odessa, Baku, Samara, St. Petersburg, Krakow, and Kiev.

Serlachius was followed as managing director by Gösta Björkenheim. By that time World War I had broken out, initially placing obstacles in the way of deliveries to Russia but later increasing the demand for paper. Kymmene Corporation's leading position in the Russian paper market attracted international attention. In October 1916 *The Times,* of London, in an article headed "A Russian paper king," wrote, "the joint stock company Kiummene is now regarded as the biggest enterprise of the paper industry, not only in Russia, but in all Europe." In 1917 paper exports to Russia were hindered by the revolution. Lenin's rise to power put an end to private trade.

In the early decades of the 20th century western Europe was not regarded as a major market. The first exports to the United Kingdom were made in the first decade, but not until 1910 was the first major agreement signed, for 2,000 tons.

Research into the potential of Western European markets advanced through the 1910s. In 1910 Rafael Jaatinen, a correspondence clerk in the company's sales office, traveled to England to study trading methods. In 1919 the Finnish government sent a trade delegation to Western Europe and North America. One of its members was Gösta Serlachius. In autumn 1921, Kymmene laid the foundations for its own export marketing organization. Its first new foreign agency agreement was made with H. Reeve Angel & Co. of England.

Kymmene was one of the first Finnish companies to make acquisitions abroad. Fearing that the United Kingdom would levy customs duties to protect its own paper industry, Kymmene acquired a majority stake in the Star Paper Mill Co. Ltd., which had a paper mill at Blackburn. The following year, Star took over Yorkshire Paper Mills Ltd. at Barnsley.

Meanwhile, the company had increased its forest holdings in Finland. The need to guarantee its supply of timber led Kymmene to purchase Högforsin Tehdas Osakeyhtiö, one of the largest ironworks in Finland, in 1933. Kymmene Corporation thus branched out into a completely new field—engineering.

By the end of 1935, Kymmene owned more land than at any other time until its later mergers with Kaukas and Schauman. In this year it bought Oy Läskelä Ab, which had 100,000 hectares of forest and two paper mills, as well as a sulfite pulp mill situated north of Lake Ladoga. Läskelä's mills and most of its forests were, however, lost to the Soviet Union as a result of World War II.

The appointment of Einar Ahlman as managing director in 1918 coincided with a shift in paper sales towards the western hemisphere, including the United States, and a more optimistic period following the postwar Depression. By 1937, paper production at Kuusankoski had reached 200,000 tons. By the beginning of the 1920s, Kymmene had four pulp mills. On the completion of hydroelectric power plants and the steam-power plants at the Voikkaa and Kymmene mills, the company was virtually self-sufficient in energy.

During World War II, the production of sawed timber, pulp, and paper had to be curtailed to correspond to the reduction in demand and work force. Some of the company's engineering capacity was put towards making munitions, and its paper division made utility articles both for the Soviet front and for the areas behind it. One third of the war reparations paid by Finland to the Soviet Union under the terms of the peace treaty ending World War II consisted of products of the wood-processing industry. Because of its size, Kymmene was the chief supplier.

The demand for forestry products remained brisk until the late 1940s. However, price controls imposed by the Finnish government at home reduced profitability. The company was also forced to relinquish about 60,000 hectares, some of it land expropriated by the Finnish government, for the resettlement of evacuees from the parts of Karelia ceded to the Soviet Union.

Not until the late 1950s and early 1960s was the company again in a position to extend its production, with a new newsprint machine at Voikkaa. A new sulfate pulp mill went online at Kuusankoski in 1964.

By 1966 the company was ready to expand its operations abroad. This time it joined forces with Oy Kaukas Ab to found a German subsidiary, Nordland Papier. In the latter half of the 1960s, Kymmene was one of the partners in Finland's largest forest industry project to date, Eurocan Pulp & Paper Ltd., in British Columbia, Canada.

As one of the suppliers of chlorine for the petrochemical industry, Kymmene decided to expand its chemical interests in the late 1960s and early 1970s. The year 1970 also saw the establishment of Oy Finnish Peroxides Ab in collaboration with the U.K. company Laporte Industries Ltd. and Solvay & Cie S.A. in Belgium, for the manufacture of peroxide.

The output of the paper industry increased together with expansion into other fields. A large machine making supercalendered paper grades went onstream at Voikkaa in 1968, followed two years later by what was at that time the largest fine-paper mill in Europe, at Kuusankoski.

Expansion was also visible in the restructuring of the organization. In 1969, on the appointment of Kurt Swanljung as managing director, the company's industrial operations were divided into seven fields of production: paper, pulp, conversion, chemicals, metal, sawmill, and board.

Kymmene purchased Soinlahti Sawmill and Brick Works in 1975, and with its subsidiary Star Paper Ltd. acquired the majority holding in the French company Papeteries Boucher S.A. in 1977. The same year also saw the start-up of the U.S. company Leaf River Forest Products Inc. in Mississippi. There were also plans for building a pulp mill in Mississippi. In 1979 the company reorganized its foreign interests in the forestry industry by selling its 50% holding in Eurocan Pulp & Paper and buying all the shares in the Wolvercote Paper Mill at Oxford in England.

By the 1970s Kymmene had steadily upgraded its range of paper products. In order to establish closer contacts with its customers and improve its marketing, in 1975 it decided to resign from the Finnish Paper Mills' Association (Finnpap), which it had rejoined in 1946 after having left it in 1920. The main products not covered by its own sales organization were the newsprint and magazine papers made by the Voikkaa mill.

The company cut down its range of activities in 1981 with the discontinuation of its petrochemical activities—due to structural reorganization in the industry—and the closing of the Barnsley paper mill, which was unprofitable. An agreement was made with the Great Northern Nekoosa Corporation for the building of a pulp mill in Mississippi, in which Kymmene would have a minority holding. In order to even out fluctuations in the forestry and metal industries, at the end of 1982 Kymmene purchased the majority holding in Strömberg, a company producing electrical equipment. The parent company was renamed the Kymmene-Strömberg Corporation. In mid 1985, Kymmene-Strömberg sold a major part of its engineering division, the Högfors foundry, and closed the Boucher mill in Calais, France.

The first in a chain of mergers resulting in the present Kymmene Corporation took place in 1985, when Kymmene procured 45% of the shares in Oy Kaukas Ab. Shareholders of the two companies approved the merger on January 7, 1986. The result was a highly integrated forestry concern. Casimir Ehrnrooth, chairman of the board of Kaukas, was appointed Kymmene-Strömberg's chairman of the board and CEO at the end of 1985, and Fredrik Castrén continued as managing director.

In 1986 the company decided to concentrate exclusively on the forest industry; on June 19 the board of Kymmene-Strömberg approved an agreement selling Strömberg's business operations to ASEA A.B. The company took the name Kymmene Corporation.

Cooperation with Oy Wilh. Schauman Ab became increasingly close in the course of 1986. A Schauman-Kymmene merger was approved in 1987 and came into force in 1988. It was decided to concentrate on two major fields of production, and consequently Kymmene's Juankoski board mill, the printing works in Kouvola, and the self-copying paper mill were sold. The emergence of Kymmene Corporation in the late 1980s as Finland's largest wood-processing enterprise, following two mergers, marked the joining of three companies each dating from the 19th century.

Gösta Björkenheim had been managing director of both Kaukas and Kymmene. He was the son of Robert Björkenheim, the founder, director, and owner of Kaukaan Tehdas Osakeyhtiö—the name under which the Kaukas mill was originally established. Gösta Serlachius, nephew of Schauman's founder Wilhelm Schauman, had taken the helm of Kymmene Corporation at the beginning of this century.

Gösta Björkenheim was one of the first Finnish industrial leaders to recognize the vital need for employers to band together against growing unionism, and he invited the pulp and paper manufacturers to join him in founding an employers' association. Meanwhile Gösta Serlachius was building up trade relations with the European and U.S. markets. At his suggestion, three joint sales organizations were set up: the Finnish Pulp Association, Finncell; the Finnish Paper Mills' Association, Finnpap; and the Finnish Paper Agency.

OY KAUKAS AB

One of the pioneers in spotting the potential of birch wood was Robert Björkenheim, who had birch in his own forests in southern Finland. Being engaged in the sawmill industry, he saw machine bobbins being made in his father's homeland, Sweden, and went on to Glasgow to pursue the idea further. On February 6, 1873 Björkenheim and three others signed an agreement for the establishment of a bobbin factory at Mäntsälä on the banks of the Kaukas Rapids.

The first bobbin deliveries went to Scotland, where the largest buyer was Clark & Co. The production figures rose but little profit was made, and it was 1882 before a dividend could be issued. The dwindling birch resources in the timber supply area combined with the favorable outlook for this industry prompted the decision to found a new factory near Lappeenranta in 1890.

For 20 years the Kaukas mill struggled to produce bobbins before selling out to Hugo Standertskjöld in 1894. Gösta Björkenheim, later to take over the management of Kymmene, was chiefly instrumental in steering the company into clearer waters.

In 1903 Kaukas became a limited company. Gösta Björkenheim suggested that a pulp mill be built to use up the waste timber from the bobbin factory, and the mill began operating in March 1897.

The customs duty levied on imported pulp was one reason for Kaukas's decision to build a new sulfite pulp mill in 1904. The first major extensions were carried out in 1912, following which Kaukas was for a time Finland's largest producer of sulfite pulp.

Initially, more than half of the pulp was sold to Russia, while the rest went to the domestic market. On the completion of the second mill it was necessary to look abroad for markets—first to Germany, and later to the United States. The years 1895–1914 were a golden era for the bobbin factory. The number of customers rose to 100, but the bulk of production went to large, regular customers in Russia, Germany, Austria, France, England, and Belgium.

In 1916 Kaukas expanded further by buying up all the shares in the Kaltimon Puuhiomo groundwood plant, including a considerable area of good forest. Later in the year Kaukas purchased Osakeyhtiö T. & J. Salvesen, thereby acquiring four sawmills and 69,500 hectares of well-stocked forest. The most significant investment in terms of enlarging the company's forest reserves was the purchase of all the shares in Osakeyhtiö Gustaf Cederberg & Co. in 1920, which brought with it 105,000 hectares of forest.

The voice of Jacob von Julin, managing director of Kaukas between the two world wars, was frequently heard on the committees set up on behalf of the industry as a whole to further matters of industrial and economic policy and to boost exports. He was also the chairman of the trade delegation sent by the Finnish government to Western countries in 1919. World War I brought a slump in the bobbin industry, and Kaukas had to look around for other ways of converting timber.

A plywood industry had begun in Finland in 1912, with the start-up of the Jyväskylä mill belonging to Oy Wilh. Schauman Ab, which was later to merge with Kymmene Corporation. The decision to build a plywood mill at Kaukas was made in 1924, and it began production in 1926. The main product was plywood to produce chests for tea, meat, and tobacco transport.

The output of sulfate pulp tripled and that of sulfite pulp quadrupled in the period between the wars. Between 1933 and 1935, the sulfite pulp mill underwent major expansion. As a result of World War I, Kaukas lost many of its forests and timber procurement areas. During this period, Kaukas evacuated many of its most valuable machines. The Kaukas bobbin factory was modernized after the war and the American method was introduced. Production of bobbins came to an end in 1972.

Kaukas's plywood industry underwent modernization in the mid 1950s, including the addition of about 63,000 cubic meters of space. New lathes and glue presses were installed in the early 1960s. These were followed in the 1970s by peeling and drying lines suitable for making spruce plywood. In the 1970s and 1980s, the company placed emphasis on further processing of plywood.

The sawmills at Lappeenranta operated along traditional lines until the 1950s, when work began on a new mill that increased its capacity to 330,000 cubic meters between 1967 and 1971. In 1977 a further, medium-sized sawmill was bought in the northern timber procurement area, at Nurmes.

The pulp market was buoyant after World War II. Later, the war in Korea sent raw materials prices skyrocketing. But this was followed by a cost crisis in the Finnish wood-processing industry, due to fears of impending raw materials shortages, and political conflict with the Soviet Union, a major buyer of dissolving pulp used for chemical conversion. The company debated whether to stop manufacturing dissolving pulp altogether, but capital investments brought about a rise in quality and demand.

In the early 1960s the company decided to build a new sulfate pulp mill, which went on line in 1964. With a view to the further development of pulp production Casimir Ehrnrooth, managing director from 1967, proposed that the sulfite pulp mill be closed down and a second line producing long-fibered pine pulp be built at the sulfate pulp mill. This construction was done in the 1970s, and the mill was extended in two stages in the 1980s.

In order to diversify production a paper mill was established at Dörpen in the Federal Republic of Germany. On the withdrawal of the Canadian company from the joint venture, its place was taken by Kymmene Corporation. Nordland Papier's first paper machine started up in 1969.

While paper production was starting up in the Federal Republic of Germany, Kaukas began to seek a suitable paper grade to be manufactured from its own bleached sulfate pulp. One of the central figures in the investigations, and later in the start-up of production, was Harri Piehl, now chief executive officer of Kymmene Corporation. The choice fell on lightweight coated (LWC) paper, a new type of magazine paper made from pulp, groundwood, and coating. The first production line at the mill started up in 1975 and the second in 1981. The choice of paper grade proved to be right, for with the steady increase in demand a good price level could be maintained.

OY WILH. SCHAUMAN AB

Schauman, the company which merged with Kymmene in 1989, was likewise founded in the 19th century. Wilhelm Schauman, the founder of Oy Wilh. Schauman Ab, having left his job in a gun factory in St. Petersburg, settled in Pietarsaari and there began processing chicory in 1883.

In 1892 Schauman turned to timber, which soon overtook chicory in importance. In 1895, the year in which his sawmill started up, he started expanding in the Pietarsaari district. He ceased buying his timer ready cut in favor of standing timber. His exports of roundwood timber brought in good profits.

The second sawmill bought by Schauman in 1900 operated for many years at a loss, but his Pietarsaari sugar mill proved to be a profitable investment. His involvement with sugar nevertheless came to an end in 1919 with the merging of Finland's sugar mills.

Having sold its sugar interests, the company concentrated on projects which led to the establishment of what is now a market leader in plywood products. He began with boxboard, later adding plywood. The Jyväskylä plywood mill represented a completely new departure. During the early years of World War I the mill flourished. Sales were good and profits large. Production in Savonlinna began in 1921, and in 1924 all the shares in a plywood mill at Joensuu were acquired.

Plywood was converted into chair bottoms, furniture, and board, and in 1931 a building joinery department was set up in Jyväskylä. Its main products were interior doors. Blockboard production began in Jyväskylä in 1933 and subsequently moved to Savonlinna. The mills at Jyväskylä, Savonlinna, and Joensuu merged in 1937 to form Oy Wilh. Schauman Ab.

During World War II the proportion of plywood products rose considerably. One of the most important products was a plywood tent for military use. In 1958 a chipboard mill was opened in Jyväskylä, in 1962 Schauman purchased a chipboard mill from Viiala Oy, and in 1969 a chipboard mill, built by Schauman went into production at Joensuu.

By the early 1990s, the company had chipboard mills in Joensuu, Ristiina (Pellos chipboard mill), and Kitee (Puhos chipboard mill). The chipboard mills in Jyväskylä and Viiala were no longer in operation, but Kymmene's subsidiary, Finnish Fiberboard Ltd., had a fiberboard mill in Heinola.

Schauman's second cornerstone was laid with the construction of a sulfite pulp mill in Pietarsaari begun in 1934 by a separate company, Ab Jakobstads Cellulosa-Pietarsaaren Selluloosa Oy. Pulp production doubled in the 1950s. The addition of a sulfate pulp mill, a paper mill, and a paper sack plant in the early 1960s meant a great increase in value-added products.

The next major investment in pulp manufacturing came in the first half of the 1970s, making Schauman the largest producer of market pulp in Finland. The Wisapak sack plant soon became the largest of its kind in Finland, and in 1969 Schauman purchased the Craf 'Sac plant in Rouen, France. The establishment of an industrial wrappings unit raised the output considerably.

All the former Schauman industrial divisions in Pietarsaari, sawn timer, pulp, paper, and packaging materials, have been grouped together to form the Kymmene subsidiary, Wisaforest Oy Ab. The divisions are known as Wisatimber, Wisapulp, Wisapaper, and Wisapak. With an annual output of 540,000 tons, the pulp division is one of the largest in Finland. Wisapaper's present capacity is 135,000 tons.

Product development and the increase in plywood production have continued at a brisk pace since the 1960s. The most important technical innovations have been in the field of plywood gluing and the development of a wide range of coated and processed plywood products, as well as the use of spruce as a raw material. Schauman is now a world leader in plywood product development and the leading European plywood manufacturer.

Schauman has at various points in its history also made furniture, along with more conventional converted panel products. Half a century of joinery production came to an end in 1969. In 1971 Schauman became a producer of large sailing yachts after buying Nautor, a boatyard near the Pietarsaari mills.

Among the advantages of the Kymmene-Kaukas-Schauman merger have been greater financing potential and more effective operation and marketing. In order to exploit the advantages of a small company Kymmene demerged its five industrial divisions in Finland in 1990. The registered companies became fully-owned subsidiaries of Kymmene Corporation: Kaukas Oy, Kymi Paper Mills Ltd., Wisaforest Oy Ab, and Schauman Wood Oy. Similar status had already been granted to the subsidiaries abroad: Nordland Papier GmbH, Kymmene France S.A., Kymmene U.K. plc, and Caledonian Paper plc. This last mill project became the first and only one of its kind in the United Kingdom when it began LWC paper production in the spring of 1989. Kymmene U.K. plc's mills at Blackburn and Oxford were sold in the spring of 1990. Expansion through acquisition continued in 1990, when Kymmene bought the large French LWC and newsprint manufacturer Chapelle Darblay S.A.

Principal Subsidiaries: Kaukas Oy; Caledonian Paper plc (U.K.); Chapelle Darblay S.A. (France); Kymi Paper Mills Ltd.; Nordland Papier GmbH (Germany); Kymmene France S.A. (France); Wisaforest Oy Ab; Schauman Wood Oy; Oy Nautor Ab; Combitrans Oy; Oy Finnterminals Ab; Maa ja Meri Oy and Jeuro Oy; Oy Paperi-Dahlberg Ab.

Further Reading: The Minutes of the Board of Directors of Kymin Osakeyhtiö-Kymmene Aktiebolag 1945-1955, Ahvenainen, Jorma, *Paperitehtaista suuryhtiöksi, Kymin Osakeyhtiö vuosina 1918-1939*, Helsinki, Kymin Osakeyhtiö, 1972; Talvi, Veikko; *Kymin Osakeyhtiö-Kymmene Aktiebolag 1872-1972, The Pictorial Centenary Book*, Helsinki, Kymin Osakeyhtiö-Kymmene Aktiebolag, 1972; *Information Newsletter of Kymin Osakeyhtiö*, Standertskjöld, Johan, 1976; *Kaukas 1873-1944*, Helsinki, Kaukas Oy, 1973; Talvi, Veikko, *Pohjois-Kymenlaakson Teollistuminen, Kymin Osakeyhtiön historia 1872-1917*, Kouvola, Kymin Kymmene Corporation, 1979; Schybergson, Per, *Juuret metsässä, Schauman 1883-1983*, Helsinki, Oy Wilh. Schauman Ab, 1983; Standertskjöld, Johan, *Kaukas 1945-1985*, Espoo, Kaukas Oy, 1985.

—Reijo Virta

 Louisiana-Pacific Corporation

LOUISIANA-PACIFIC CORPORATION

111 Southwest 5th Avenue
Portland, Oregon 97204
U.S.A.
(503) 221-0800
Fax: (503) 796-0204

Public Company
Incorporated: 1972
Employees: 13,000
Sales: $1.79 billion
Stock Exchange: New York

Louisiana-Pacific Corporation (L-P), a major forest-products firm, is a leading manufacturer of redwood and other lumber products, such as pulp, hardwood, softwood plywood, and industrial- and commercial-grade particleboard. The company markets a line of garden products under the Landscapers Pride brand, which includes potting soil, bark nuggets, and mulch. It produces a variety of engineered products, including doors, millwork, windows, unfinished wood moldings, and medium-density fiberboard. In 1991 L-P also managed more than two million acres of hardwood and softwood timberland and operated 124 facilities in 24 states, 2 Canadian provinces, and Mexico.

L-P's timberland holdings are small in relation to its major competitors; Georgia-Pacific manages 6.5 million acres, while Weyerhauser manages 13 million acres. Despite the lack of raw materials coming from L-P forests, the company generated enough business in 1991 to keep numerous facilities busy, including 56 sawmills, 7 softwood plywood plants, 16 oriented-strand board plants, and 16 building products manufacturing facilities. It owned two cellulose insulation plants, two chip mills, and several other facilities for producing insulated glass, extruded vinyl, and fencing, and for treating and planing wood products. The company also operated eight distribution centers in California, Texas, Kansas, and Oklahoma.

L-P is perhaps best known for its innovation in wood panel products. This competitive distinction developed out of necessity when the company, which had been a wholly owned subsidiary of Georgia-Pacific Corporation since July 1972, was spun off as a separate entity in December of that year. This realignment was part of a settlement between Georgia-Pacific and the Federal Trade Commission (FTC) that required Georgia-Pacific to divest 20% of its assets. The FTC had al-

leged that Georgia-Pacific's earlier acquisitions of 16 small firms in the southern United States had lessened competition and had tended to create a monopoly in the softwood plywood industry.

In September 1972, prior to the official spin-off of L-P, Georgia-Pacific had transferred several of its operations to L-P ownership, including its Samoa, Ukiah, Intermountain, Weather-Seal, and Southern divisions, as well as its 50% investments in Alaska's Ketchikan Pulp Company; Ketchikan Spruce Mills, Inc.; and Ketchikan International Sales Company. Since Georgia-Pacific, however, kept most of its low-cost timber reserves, the newly independent L-P was forced to purchase the majority of its needed timber on the open market and to look toward other areas for business growth.

L-P chairman William H. Hunt, a former vice chairman of Georgia-Pacific, set out to overcome L-P's reliance on outside timber supply, its heavy dependence on lumber products for the construction market, and the loss of the extensive Georgia-Pacific distribution network that L-P previously had used for its building products. In 1974 Harry A. Merlo, who had been chief executive officer of L-P since its 1972 formation, succeeded Hunt as chairman, while remaining CEO.

L-P acquired several lumber companies in California, Oregon, Montana, Washington, Missouri, and Alabama. In 1976 it purchased the Fibreboard Corporation, which manufactured products used in making furniture and cabinets. Although L-P spun off this wholly owned subsidiary in 1988, the company has been forced to defend itself, along with Fibreboard, in several ongoing lawsuits concerning asbestos-related injuries. L-P was named as a co-defendant despite the fact that Fibreboard did not use asbestos in its products while it was under L-P's ownership. Between 1988, when Fibreboard was spun off, and 1989 L-P was dismissed from approximately 270 of these cases but remained a defendant in 23 asbestos-related cases.

To compensate for its relative lack of southern pine and Douglas fir timber and lumber production as compared to other lumber manufacturers, L-P turned its attention to the development of wood products derived from less-expensive and faster-growing trees, such as cottonwood and aspen. In the late 1970s, the company began manufacturing oriented-strand board (OSB) by slicing logs into wafers, mixing the wafers with resin, and then pressing them into sheets. First introduced under the tradename Waferwood and later renamed Inner-Seal, this new product line revolutionized the construction industry by offering a less-expensive, stronger alternative to plywood sheathing and subflooring. It also insulated the company from the adverse effects of decreasing supplies of other types of timber. These shortages were caused primarily by over-cutting, Japanese demand for logs, and pressure on the U.S. Forest Service to tighten harvesting restrictions on large trees. As a result of the manufacture of reconstituted panel and medium-density fiberboard products, and the subsequent development of product line extensions using OSB technology, such as I-beams for floor joists and rafters, Inner-Seal concrete form, and Inner-Seal siding, L-P increased its volume in the building-products segment from 6% of total sales in 1979 to 26% of total sales in 1990. Sales of lumber decreased from 53% to 30% over the same period.

In 1979 the company purchased 15 building-material centers in southern California from Lone Star Industries. This acquisition provided L-P with badly needed distribution facilities and supplied the third element of William Hunt's original business strategy aimed at overcoming L-P's deficiencies stemming from the divestiture by Georgia-Pacific.

L-P experienced strong demand for its specialty building and pulp products from 1983 through the early part of 1990. This demand had been driven primarily by the housing boom and a strong remodeling and repair business in the United States, as well as by healthy pulp markets worldwide. During this period, L-P increased its timber holdings by approximately 830,000 acres through the 1986 acquisition of Kirby Forest Industries and the California properties of Timber Realization Company. These acquisitions helped to replenish timberlands that the U.S. government had taken in 1978 as part of its plan to expand the Redwood National Park in northern California. L-P received a final payment of $440 million from the government for this land in 1988.

Toward the end of the decade, the company continued its tradition of building-products innovation by manufacturing a new fiber gypsum product called FiberBond wallboard. This product, made by mixing gypsum with wood fiber from wastepaper, was stronger and had a better fire rating than existing wallboard products.

During 1990, however, sales and profits in the company's softwood lumber, plywood, and building products areas decreased due to weakening demand. This situation was attributed to an economic downturn, increasing concerns over the U.S. federal budget deficit, and unsettled world events. The construction industry suffered because of bankers' reluctance to finance new projects and consumers' decisions to delay home purchases. Housing starts for 1990 fell to 1.19 million, down 13.3% from 1989, reaching the lowest level since 1982. L-P responded to these developments by curtailing production at many of its plants and increasing exports of its specialty building products.

The pulp market also experienced slowing growth in 1990. After a four-year period of rapidly rising prices, pulp manufacturers then faced eroding profit margins due to worldwide economic problems and larger-than-normal inventories. Although L-P saw its own pulp sales and profits peak in mid-1989 and expected only a minor recovery in 1991, the company continued to operate three pulp manufacturing mills. One mill supplied paper pulp to non-integrated paper producers. A second mill produced dissolving pulp for manufacturers of rayon and cellophane products. The third and newest pulp mill, using a bleached chemi-thermo mechanical pump process, revolutionized pulp production by eliminating the use of chlorine and operated in a completely closed system without discharge into neighboring water supplies. This mill marketed its output to manufacturers of printing and writing papers.

L-P capitalized on its strong balance sheet by investing in the modernization of its manufacturing facilities and acquiring new operations. One of these acquisitions was the 1990 purchase of Weather Guard, a Missouri-based company that produced residential insulation from recycled newspaper. That same year, L-P also purchased MiTek Wood Products, a North Carolina manufacturer of laminated veneer lumber and engineered wood I-joists. L-P expected this strong financial foundation to help it withstand future cyclical downturns in the forest-products industry. The company hoped its emphasis on OSB and other products made from less-controversial timber resources would help mute intensifying challenges from environmentalists. Nevertheless, in 1991 L-P was contesting litigation brought by the Environmental Protection Agency, which alleges that the company violated wastewater discharge limits in its Samoa, California, pulp mill operation.

In 1973 it developed the slogan "Helping the Forest Work for People." In order to achieve greater compliance with changing environmental standards and regulations, for example, L-P has implemented modernization programs in its mills to improve production efficiencies and control air and water emissions. Dedicated to replanting the country's forest, by 1990 L-P had planted a variety of tree species—a total of 500 million seedlings—and conducted experiments that test irrigation and fertilizer combinations to determine which will produce the greatest volume of wood fiber in the least amount of time. The company has also implemented a full-utilization program with innovative logging equipment to collect tree tops, limbs, and other pieces of timber that would otherwise be left on the ground as waste. The equipment brings this material to the mill for use in pulp and paper products, and also prepares the ground for planting new crops.

The company's future rests upon the continued development and manufacture of innovative engineered products that outperform comparable products made from solid wood and that reduce L-P's dependence on old-growth timber. Chairman Merlo remained confident in L-P's ability to maintain its market share during the valleys of its business cycle and expand its market penetration during the peaks.

Principal Subsidiaries: Louisiana-Pacific International, Inc.; Louisiana-Pacific, Canada, Ltd.; Louisiana-Pacific Trucking Company; LPI, Inc.; Kenai Lumber Company; Ketchikan Pulp Company; New Waverly Transportation, Inc.; Louisiana-Pacific Panel Products, Ltd. (Canada); Kirby Forest Industries.

—Joan Harpham and Sandy Schusteff

 **MacMillan Bloedel Limited**

MACMILLAN BLOEDEL LIMITED

925 West Georgia Street
Vancouver, British Columbia V6C 3L2
Canada
(604) 661-8000
Fax: (604) 687-5345

Public Company
Incorporated: 1911 as the Powell River Company Ltd.
Employees: 15,036
Sales: C$3.00 billion (US$2.59 billion)
Stock Exchanges: Toronto Montreal Vancouver NASDAQ

MacMillan Bloedel Limited is engaged in the production of forest products. It is an integrated company, with operations in its native Canada, the United States, the United Kingdom, and Europe. It manufactures lumber and diverse lumber products, including building materials, pulp, newsprint, specialty papers, and packaging. Its products are marketed in approximately 40 countries.

MacMillan Bloedel is one of North America's largest forest products firms. In the opinion of the company, its value-added products, such as telephone directories using newsprint; the range of its marketing network; and emphasis on research and development set it apart from its competitors. Operations are decentralized, with five main units: the Nanaimo, Alberni, and Powell River regions, each headquartered in British Columbia; and the containerboard and packaging groups, based in Montgomery, Alabama.

In 1901 Dwight Brooks, a physician before entering his family's lumber business, and salesman Michael J. Scanlon formed the Brooks-Scanlon Lumber Company in Minnesota in the United States, with Brooks as president and Scanlon as vice president. Brooks-Scanlon invested heavily in British Columbia, in Canada, buying tracts of forest. In the early 1900s the company moved to British Columbia, where logging had been under way for several decades. In 1908 Brooks-Scanlon abandoned plans to build two new sawmills and instead used the capital to merge John O'Brien's company, becoming Brooks, Scanlon & O'Brien, which entered the newsprint business in 1909, after acquiring land and water rights on the Powell River. The mill was incorporated as the Powell River Paper Company Limited. Complications with mill construction led to the reorganization of the subsidiary in 1911 as the Powell River Company Ltd. Its first newsprint was produced the following year.

Wisconsin native Julius Harold (J.H.) Bloedel attended the University of Michigan in civil engineering in the 1880s but left before graduation because of a lack of money and a desire to start a career. Bloedel worked first for the Wisconsin railway then in real estate before moving west, where he became a partner in the 1890s in two different logging ventures in the state of Washington.

From humble beginnings in Ontario, Harvey Reginald (H.R.) MacMillan early in life became engrossed in forestry as a result of mentoring efforts by a teacher at the Ontario Agricultural College and a 9¢-per-hour job on its experimental forestry plot. He graduated in 1906. In 1907 MacMillan was favorably impressed by his first look at British Columbia, while scouting timber for a group of Ontario businessmen. In 1912 he became the first chief forester of British Columbia.

In 1911, while managing the Larson Lumber Company, Bloedel heard about an anticipated Canada-U.S. reciprocity treaty to lift tariffs on lumber and other products and decided to expand his logging operations into British Columbia to control the effects of such a treaty. That same year Bloedel united with railway contractors Patrick Welch and John W. Stewart when J.J. Donovan, Bloedel's surviving partner, declined to join the Canadian venture. Bloedel, Stewart & Welch (B, S & W) was then incorporated in British Columbia, with Bloedel owning half. Stewart and Welch remained silent partners who provided critical access to the railway market. Bloedel was mistaken about the tariffs, which were lifted only on pulp and newsprint, two products that did not interest him at the time.

World War I hurt an already ailing lumber industry, and in 1914 exportation was nearly impossible because of a shortage of non-military shipping. B, S & W managed to keep open its logging camps at Myrtle Point during most of the war; not all firms were so fortunate. When servicemen returned home in search of work, only two-thirds of the mills in the province were operating. Powell River Company ultimately enjoyed a boom market and rising prices as a result of World War I.

During World War I MacMillan was tapped by the Canadian government to find world markets for Canadian lumber. He reported back to the government his dismay that nearly everywhere he traveled, lumber, including that from British Columbia, was sold through U.S. firms. MacMillan's efforts, however, were not in vain; Canadian exports to Great Britain improved during the last two years of the war. This government job, which MacMillan later termed one of the great opportunities of his life, ended in 1916.

In 1919 MacMillan shook hands with British lumber importer Montague Meyer on a deal that created the first privately owned lumber export brokerage in British Columbia. MacMillan insisted on an equal partnership, mortgaging his house to match $10,000 from Meyer. The H.R. MacMillan Export Company was incorporated in 1919. As president, MacMillan ran the firm for a year before hiring fellow professional forester Whitford Julien VanDusen as manager. By the end of the 1920s Meyer had sold out to MacMillan.

In 1924 B, S & W became a manufacturer, unintentionally, following the failure of the Shull Lumber & Shingle Company, which owed B, S & W money. B, S & W, Shull's main creditor, bought the Shull mill. B, S & W, however, still focused on logging and buying timber. Prentice Bloedel, the elder son of J.H. Bloedel, joined the firm in 1929, a bumper year is sales. A former teacher, he had worked briefly as a logging laborer.

In 1930 Bloedel, Stewart & Welch, like other firms, got caught in the Great Depression, experienced decline, and the following year lost money.

Dwight Brooks died in 1930, and within a year, so did Michael Scanlon. In 1930 the Great Depression was seriously affecting the newsprint and pulp markets, but Powell River maintained production, although to a reduced extent throughout those years when other mills closed.

In 1935 B, S & W joined Seaboard Lumber Sales, a subsidiary of the Associated Timber Exporters of British Columbia Limited, (Astexo), a cooperative, and the main competitor of the H.R. MacMillan Export Company. When Astexo, representing about 30 firms, formed Seaboard, it stopped allowing MacMillan to market its British Columbia lumber supplies, forcing MacMillan into a major mill operation and the purchase of timberland. The firm not only survived but expanded, handling logging, sawmilling, plywood and door manufacturing, railway-tie production; and shipping and sales. The H.R. MacMillan Export Company was a pioneer in vertical integration; it purchased firms involved in all parts of the lumber trade.

Powell River was one of a group of pulp and paper companies, along with several of their company officers, that were indicted in 1939 by a grand jury in San Francisco, California, alleging conspiracy to fix prices. Harold Foley, executive vice president at Powell River, was among those who pleaded no contest and subsequently paid fines.

World War II brought tight shipping and a shortage of labor but also growth. British Columbia's forest industry was smashing production records by the end of 1940. Powell River expanded its sulfite pulp mill to produce market pulp for export when pulp supplies from Scandinavia were cut off. At the end of the war, when it became a public corporation, Powell River was in good financial shape.

In 1942 J.H. Bloedel became chairman, and Prentice Bloedel president and treasurer of B, S & W, which went public in 1948. Serious reforestation efforts began after World War II with B, S & W in the forefront of that endeavor. It handled 70% of all reforestation in the province by private industry—planting two million trees—by the late 1940s. Timber had held little value in the early days of the industry; farmers had burned forests by the hundreds of acres.

During World War II the H.R. MacMillan Export Company's most important acquisitions were timberlands. That firm went public in 1945. In 1948 MacMillan became chairman and VanDusen, vice chairman.

J.H. Bloedel had received a number of buyout offers over time, but MacMillan had not been among the suitors. Convinced that smaller firms had no future, Prentice Bloedel approached MacMillan in 1950 about a merger. MacMillan recommended such a merger to a skeptical VanDusen, arguing it would enable the new firm to find capital to keep the British Columbia forest industry on a competitive footing with its counterparts in the United States and elsewhere. Of the pair, MacMillan had a larger marketing operation, and Bloedel had more timberland. The merger would result in British Columbia's largest lumber and pulp operation.

Not only money was at stake. As Donald MacKay wrote in *Empire of Wood*, Prentice Bloedel recalled his father's reaction: "It really hurt his pride very much. He was dynastically minded as many people were who were self-made in that gen-

eration, and here we were selling out to our arch-enemy." J.H. Bloedel knew his firm would take a back seat to MacMillan as a wholly owned subsidiary.

J.H. Bloedel, the surviving partner of Bloedel, Stewart & Welch, signed the merger documents establishing MacMillan & Bloedel Limited in October 1951 as his last act before retiring. To clear the way for amalgamation, the merged firm paid C$2.3 million in taxes to Canada because of C$16 million in B, S & W income that had gone undistributed for years.

In 1956, at age 74, MacMillan resigned as chairman and was replaced by B.M. Hoffmeister. Tension between them led MacMillan to request his resignation as 1957, a hard year, ended. Also in 1957 J.H. Bloedel died at age 93.

John Valentine Clyne, a justice of the British Columbia Supreme Court, became chairman of MacMillan & Bloedel in January 1958. Then 56, Clyne had little experience in business or knowledge of the forest-products industry but had established a reputation in marine law in his native Vancouver. As chairman, he faced challenges: poor timber sales, labor troubles in the pulp and paper area, and U.S. tax and tariff policies.

Powell River's best year in production, sales, and earnings, was 1950. In 1955 Harold Foley became chairman and his brother, Milton Joseph (Joe) Foley, president. With competition hurting the sales of newsprint, which comprised 75% of revenues, and growing production costs, Powell River considered five mergers. All were rejected. In 1957 MacMillan & Bloedel's first newsprint machine made a better product than did Powell River, one of Canada's largest newsprint makers and owner of the world's largest newsprint mill. In 1957 Powell River decided against a merger with MacMillan & Bloedel, but the following year sold the firm half interest in a paper-products company.

Serious talks about a merger began in 1959. Harold Foley was told MacMillan & Bloedel would be the main partner of the new firm, with Clyne as chairman. MacMillan, Bloedel and Powell River Limited, the largest forest products company in Canada, was established in January 1960. The union of two different management styles—MacMillan & Bloedel's tight organization and efficiency with Powell River's more relaxed paternalistic management—turned ugly. By 1962, as a result of what was reported to be one of the nastiest corporate fights in Canadian history, most of the senior Powell River people had resigned or had been eased out. President Joe Foley quit in April 1961 complaining of exclusion from any meaningful participation, and vice chairman Harold Foley followed in May.

High taxes, the political climate in British Columbia, and high labor costs were among the reasons behind Clyne's drive to expand MacMillan, Bloedel and Powell River from a regional firm into a global entity. With its emphasis on solid-wood products, the firm experienced significant growth in pulp and paper manufacturing during the 1960s, becoming an international corporation with production in Europe, the United States, and Asia. MacMillan, however, viewed foreign countries as markets not production centers. In the company's first successful step into international investment and its initial expansion of manufacturing facilities outside Canada, it bought container plants in Great Britain for C$36 million in 1963. The next year a minority interest in the Royal Dutch Paper Company (KNP) was acquired. In 1966 the company name became MacMillan Bloedel Limited (MB).

Joining with the United Fruit Company, the company built a linerboard plant near Pine Hill, Alabama, completed in 1968, later becoming full owner. Later in 1968 MB adopted a policy to move from its traditional operation in wood products, pulp, and paper, and diversify into other businesses. It would look at firms related to the forest products industry but with a lesser priority on those outside the industry.

In 1970 MacMillan and VanDusen resigned from the board. In 1972 Prentice Bloedel, 71 years old, was the final owner-manager to leave the board. He is remembered as building British Columbia's first fully integrated sawmill and pulp unit, designed to obtain maximum use of each piece of timber, and as having developed the hydraulic ring barker, a key step in the processing of logs.

In 1973 Clyne, whose departure, like MacMillan's, was in stages, resigned as chairman. That year sales hit $1 billion. Robert Bonner, president and chief executive officer, replaced Clyne, and Bonner's positions were filled by Denis Timmis. Bonner and Timmis took joint command. A struggle between them, however, led to Bonner's resignation in 1974, and George Currie, executive vice president for finance, became chairman.

One of MacMillan Bloedel's efforts at diversification was the establishment in 1974 of a ventures group to seek small entrepreneurial companies with a potential for growth. The catalyst for an ensuing disaster was the expansion in 1973 of the Canadian Transport Company (CTCO), founded by the H.R. MacMillan Export Company in 1924, to carry its forest products into a general shipping line that competed for cargo with other global carriers. In spring 1974 CTCO was making a significant profit, but March 1975 was the worst shipping market since 1940. CTCO's fleet exceeded its needs. It was to take delivery on yet several more vessels, and it was losing money on many of its other chartered ships. Months later the chartering of ships was ordered stopped, and several CTCO officials were fired. Timmis cut operating and administrative expenses, including executive salaries. For 1975 MacMillan Bloedel suffered an C$18.8 million after-tax loss—its first ever—on sales of C$1.2 billion. The success of pulp and paper sales prevented a worse loss.

In February 1976 H.R. MacMillan died at his home in British Columbia at age 91. MacMillan was credited with establishing the British Columbia forest products industry.

Timmis had tried to lessen MacMillan Bloedel's dependence on the boom and bust cycles of wood products through diversification. His downfall was shipping. Timmis and Currie were asked to leave in 1976. Months earlier Timmis had twice offered his resignation, that in each case had not been accepted. In March 1976 J. Ernest Richardson retired from the British Columbia Telephone Company, where he had been chairman and CEO since 1971, to accept the positions of chairman and acting president of MacMillan Bloedel. He had been a director at MB since 1967.

C. Calvert Knudsen, and attorney and specialist in maritime law and a senior vice president at Weyerhaeuser Company in Washington state, became CEO at MacMillan Bloedel in September 1976. His appointment reflected the board's zeal to return the firm to basics—the manufacturing and marketing of forest products. Despite limited success in its bid to become a multinational organization, MacMillan Bloedel was back in the black by October 1976 as market conditions improved.

The venture group investments, many of which had lost money, began to be divested. In 1977 the company started a program of replacing and modernizing facilities in British Columbia.

Efforts to rally productivity while cutting costs in existing operations led MacMillan Bloedel to again look at acquisitions. In 1981, in an attempt to acquire Domtar, it became the object of takeover bids itself by Domtar and Canadian Pacific. Following intervention by Canadian premier William Bennett, who did not want MacMillan Bloedel to lose its provincial identity, Domtar and MacMillan Bloedel canceled their respective takeover efforts. Canadian Pacific pressed on, but with opposition from MacMillan Bloedel, backed off. MacMillan Bloedel was free for the time being, but the door to takeover had been opened.

In 1979 earnings were very good, in part because of full production and strong markets. MacMillan Bloedel employed 24,500—its largest staff to date. In 1980 Knudsen became both chairman and CEO. Also in 1980 the British Columbia Resources Investment Corporation (BCRIC) hired away MacMillan Bloedel's president, Bruce Howe, to become its president. He was replaced by Raymond V. Smith, senior vice president.

In 1981 MacMillan Bloedel again faced takeover on two fronts. Knudsen opposed a takeover bid from BCRIC but negotiated the transfer of a BCRIC subsidiary to MacMillan Bloedel for company shares. Premier Bennett rejected the plan. Also in 1991 Noranda Mines of Toronto sought to increase its shares of MacMillan Bloedel stock to 49%. Moves and countermoves included an offer by Noranda to limit its presence on the MacMillan Bloedel board to less than might normally be expected, which satisfied the government. Noranda hiked its bid and included an all-cash option, which MacMillan Bloedel's board recommended for acceptance, and soon after BCRIC withdrew its bid. When Noranda increased its ownership to 49%, five of its executives joined the MacMillan Bloedel board including executive vice president Adam H. Zimmerman, who became vice chairman of MB when Richardson retired. In a few months, Brascade Resources of Toronto, owned by the Bronfmans of Montreal, acquired 42% of Noranda.

The 1981 recession in the industry, especially lumber, was the worst since the 1930s. MacMillan Bloedel's loss for 1981 was C$26.7 million on sales of C$2.2 billion. In 1982 it suffered its worst year ever, losing about C$57 million on sales of C$1.8 billion. Fighting to survive, the firm downsized by perhaps half during a three-year period starting in 1981. Measures included decreasing capital spending for everything except for safety; reductions in salaries, dividends, and staff; temporary mill closures; and permanent closures or sale of manufacturing plants, subsidiaries, and joint ventures. The company jet was sold as was the firm's 26-story tower in Vancouver. As many as 40,000 industry workers, nearly 20% of whom were MacMillan Bloedel employees, were laid off in British Columbia in late 1981 and in 1982. The decade also saw two industry-wide strikes and one lockout.

Despite Noranda's wish that he stay, Knudsen returned to Washington in 1983, largely for tax reasons, but he remained in the position of vice chairman. He was replaced by Zimmerman, who also retained a title at Noranda. In 1985 MacMillan Bloedel was still talking survival. In 1987 it enjoyed sales of about C$3.1 billion, and earnings nearly doubled. Its best year was 1988, with sales of nearly C$3.3 billion, because of good markets and prices, and its highest earnings ever. Sales rose slightly in 1989, with about 80% of the total in the international arena; nearly half of the exports went to the United States, lumber accounting for the largest share. A general economic slump in 1990 affected the industry, with declining prices and markets in all product lines, and MacMillan Bloedel plants were operating at less than capacity.

In the early 1990s MacMillan Bloedel's efforts to gain global markets included a lumber distribution business in Japan, where MacMillan Bloedel Building Materials accounted for more than 25% of the total value of lumber that the parent company sold worldwide. Japanese major trading houses do not easily render business to foreign competitors, but MacMillan Bloedel's history of service there began with the Great Kanto Earthquake of 1923, when the firm supplied much-needed lumber.

MacMillan Bloedel's biggest challenge of the decade was to meet environmental demands, complying with new pollution standards and land preservation issues. New government regulations regarding pulp and paper operations formulated after dioxins were found in pulp and water effluent caused MacMillan Bloedel to commit C$75 million in 1989 to virtually eliminate these unwanted by-products from its Harmac and Powell River mills. Smith said in March 1989 that the industry in British Columbia faced up to C$1.5 billion in capital investment into the early 1990s to meet new environmental regulations, and potential costs of C$3 billion to conform to standards being proposed or being developed.

MacMillan Bloedel was also concerned about a shrinking land base. British Columbia is Canada's main timber producer, with about 28% of the province available for forestry. It contains most of the 3.95 million acres of timber that MacMillan Bloedel manages, most of which is owned by the provincial government. In 1988 the government reduced the annual allowable cut in the province by 5%, pointing to pressures on the ability of the forest to support the present level of harvest. For its part in reforestation, MacMillan Bloedel annually planted seven million seedlings on 46% of the land it harvests, supervising natural regeneration on the rest. By 1991 it had planted 200 million seedlings.

Principal Subsidiaries: Canadian Transport Company (International) Ltd.; Island Paper Mills Ltd. (50%); MacMillan Bathurst Inc. (50%); MacMillan Smurfit SCA Ltd. (U.K. 50%); Koninklijke Nederlandse Papierfabrieken N.V. (the Netherlands, 40%).

Further Reading: MacKay, Donald, *Empire of Wood: The MacMillan Bloedel Story,* Vancouver, Douglas & McIntyre, 1982.

—Gwen M. LaCosse

Meod

THE MEAD CORPORATION

Courthouse Plaza Northeast
Dayton, Ohio 45463
U.S.A.
(513) 495-6323

Public Company
Incorporated: 1930
Employees: 21,600
Sales: $4.77 billion
Stock Exchanges: New York Midwest Pacific

The Mead Corporation is one of the world's largest manufacturers of paper and related products. It also distributes school and office supplies made by Mead and other companies and has developed electronic information retrieval services on a variety of topics.

The Mead Corporation began as Ellis, Chafflin & Company. Founded in 1846 by Colonel Daniel Mead and his partners, the company produced book and other printing papers at a mill in Dayton, Ohio. In 1856 Mead bought out his original partners with a friend from Philadelphia, Pennsylvania, forming Weston and Mead. This company in 1860 became Mead and Weston, then Mead and Nixon in 1866. In 1873 Daniel Mead spearheaded a reorganization of the firm as the Mead & Nixon Paper Company, and in 1881 Mead bought out Nixon, establishing the Mead Paper Company in 1882. He immediately upgraded the Dayton mill and in 1890 purchased a facility in nearby Chillicothe, Ohio. During the first decade of its existence, Mead Paper Company averaged annual profits of $22,000, peaking at nearly $50,000 in 1891, the year of Mead's death.

In the years after Mead's death, the management of the company passed to his sons, Charles and Harry, who became president and vice president, respectively. Despite the fact that Mead had left a thriving business, Mead Paper soon fell on hard times, owing largely to personal overdrafts by family members amounting to over $200,000, as well as to the substantial salaries drawn by Harry and Charles Mead and Charles's travel expense and cash accounts, which in 1900 amounted to $13,800. Combined losses for 1901 and 1902 added up to over $36,000, and banks began calling in the company's loans. By 1904 the Teutonia National Bank instituted a suit that resulted in trusteeship of the company by bankers in Dayton, Chillicothe, and Cincinnati, Ohio.

As Mead Paper Company teetered on the brink of total collapse in 1905, the banker-trustees turned to George Mead, Harry Mead's independent and business-minded son, requesting that he take over the helm at Mead. George, then about to leave his post at the General Artificial Silk Company in Philadelphia, accepted the opportunity to rejuvenate the family company. He reorganized it as the Mead Pulp and Paper Company and was appointed vice president and general manager. George Mead's business philosophy would influence the company substantially during his 43-year tenure.

Mead Pulp and Paper made its first public stock offering in 1906. A year later operations were consolidated at the Chillicothe mill, costing the company over $32,000. The economic recession of 1907 and the tremendous cost of moving almost destroyed Mead once again, but the sale of the Dayton property saved the company. Finally, in 1908, the company made profits of almost $25,000, and it continued to operate in the black until the Great Depression.

During the 1910s, Mead expanded through acquisition and began to maximize machine output by restricting its product lines. In 1916 Mead purchased a share in the Kingsport Pulp Corporation of Kingsport, Tennessee, and in 1917 it acquired full control of the Peerless Paper Company of Dayton. George Mead had been reducing the number of different types of paper made at Mead since his entry in 1905, when the company produced 15 different grades of paper. Seeing that profits would be maximized if each machine could concentrate on producing one type of paper rather than continually changing production methods for different papers, Mead specialized his mills as far as possible.

Toward this end, in 1917 Mead secured a five-year contract to produce magazine paper for Crowell Publishing Company. The magazine paper called for 75% of the Chillicothe mill's production. Consequently, Crowell remained Mead's principal customer throughout the decade. In 1918 the Management Engineering and Development Company was established in Dayton as a separate firm to supervise engineering of new Mead plants and to market Mead's engineering services to other paper companies. In 1921 the Mead Sales Company was established as a separate corporation to sell white paper produced by Mead mills and other U.S. and Canadian mills.

In 1920 Mead bought out the other owners of Kingsport Pulp. The plant began white paper production in 1923, and became a central Mead factory. Mead began to diversify its product lines in the 1920s as it started to manufacture paperboard. By 1925 Mead research led to the discovery of the semi chemical pulping process by which wood chips from which tannin had been extracted could be converted into paperboard. Mead expanded the paperboard business in the late 1920s with the purchase of mills throughout Appalachia that produced corrugating medium from wood waste. In 1927 The Mead Paperboard Corporation was founded as a holding company for the paperboard operations, including the Sylvia Paperboard Company, The Harriman Company, The Southern Extract Company, and the Chillicothe Company.

The Mead Corporation was incorporated on February 17, 1930, and George Mead was appointed president. The company subsumed the operations of the Mead Pulp and Paper Company, The Mead Paperboard Corporation, and the Management Engineering and Development Company, although the separate legal existence of these organizations continued for some years. At that time, the company had 1,000 employees and plants in four states. In 1935 Mead's common and preferred stock were listed on the New York Stock Exchange.

During the 1930s Mead made substantial acquisitions that diversified its lines. While concentration on a few types of paper was necessary when the company was small, then Mead was large enough to produce a number of grades of papers profitably. While Mead's own major mills had attempted to sell business, envelope, and writing papers, they had no luck. Two major purchases were Dill & Collins in 1932 and Geo. W. Wheelwright Company in 1934. Each of these companies had established names and well-developed distribution systems. This allowed Mead to market effectively large quantities of specialty papers produced at Chillicothe as well as smaller quantities produced in the acquired mills.

In 1938 Mead entered two joint ventures in an effort to reduce its dependence on imported pulp and to enter the kraft linerboard business. With Scott Paper Company, it formed the Brunswick Pulp & Paper Company at Brunswick, Georgia, to supply both parent companies. In addition, with the holding company of the Alfred du Pont estate, Almours Security Company, it built a huge pulping plant in Port St. Joe, Florida. By 1937 the Brunswick mill was producing 150 tons of pulp per day. Soon the Port St. Joe facility was yielding 300 tons of pulp and 300 tons of linerboard daily. It was widely regarded as the leading linerboard mill in the country and by 1940 was making a $1 million a year before taxes. Relations with the Almours Security Company deteriorated, however, and Mead sold its share of the operation. Mead intended to launch another linerboard mill immediately, but World War II halted this plan.

In 1942 George Mead became chairman of the board and Sydney Fergusen, who had been with the company since the 1910s, became the corporation's president. In the same year, Mead purchased a small white-paper mill from the Escanaba Paper Company in Michigan's upper peninsula. Eventually the Escanaba mill would become one of Mead's largest operations. Two other acquisitions were made; in 1943, the Manistique Pulp and Paper Company, of Manistique, Michigan, and in 1946, the Columbia Paper Company in Bristol, Virginia. The Manistique plant was sold in the early 1950s, and the Virginia company was consolidated with the Wheelwright plant in 1946. Other plants bought to meet postwar demand were subsequently sold.

While Mead had continued production at a breakneck pace to meet domestic and overseas container and paper requirements wartime price and profit controls, as well as raw material shortages, stunted the company's growth. In 1945 Mead's assets had risen only $2.1 million from a prewar figure of $37 million.

Immediately following the war, however, Mead was back on course. Its well-defined postwar plan allotted $23 million for plant expansion. In the brown paper division, plans were readily revived to build a kraft linerboard plant to replace the Port St. Joe operation. Mead firmly entrenched itself in paperboard-making through its joint projects with Inland Container Corporation. The companies first collaborated in 1946 to found the Macon Kraft Company to build and operate a paperboard mill in Macon, Georgia. This was followed by successive joint mills built in Rome, Georgia, in 1951 and Phenix City, Alabama, in 1966.

Mead saw a rapid succession of presidents after Fergusen, who in 1948 became chairman of the board and handed the presidency on to Charles R. Van de Carr Jr. In 1952 Howard E. Whittaker became president, and five years later he was replaced by Donald R. Morris. The year 1955 marked the beginning of a new period of growth for Mead, as the company diversified beyond its traditional paper products. A 1957 acquisition, the Atlanta Paper Company, led Mead into the packaging business, and was the forerunner of Mead's packaging division, which invented the familiar paper six-pack carrier for bottled beverages and became the largest supplier of paperboard beverage packaging in the world. The specialty paper division, which produced papers for filters and insulation, was started with the purchase of Hurlburt Paper Company of South Lee, Massachusetts, in 1957.

Mead entered the container business in 1955 and 1956 with the acquisition of Jackson Box Company of Cincinnati, Ohio. This firm became the nucleus of Mead's containerboard division. In 1960 Mead's rapid expansion in paperboard manufacture prompted the Federal Trade Commission (FTC) to file a complaint against Mead, alleging that Mead's growth since 1956 was anti-competitive. Mead and the FTC settled in 1965 when Mead signed a consent decree, agreeing to sell off seven of its plants over five years and place a ten-year moratorium on paperboard acquisitions.

Mead began its wholesale distribution network with the acquisition of Cleveland Paper Company in 1957. Mead's aggressive expansion of its wholesale force provoked a 1968 suit by the Justice Department. The suit claimed that Mead's acquisition between 1957 and 1964 of six paper wholesalers with 38 outlets caused an unlawful concentration in the paper industry. Mead agreed in 1970 to sell off within two years 22 of the outlets operated by Chatfield & Woods Company, acquired in 1961, and Cleveland Paper Company.

With the retirement of Chairman Howard E. Whitaker and President George H. Pringle in 1968, the new president, James W. McSwiney, began to acquire businesses that were unrelated to papermaking. During the 1950s, and with the 1968 allocation of $50 million for the expansion of the Escanaba mill, Mead had spent in excess of $400 million on maintaining and improving its papermaking facilities. Then its business emphasis in paper products shifted from production to marketing. The paper markets, however, were fairly mature, and growth had to be sought elsewhere. Mead's management anticipated a boom in family spending and homebuilding, and bought companies that would benefit from such a boom. Mead's acquisition of an educational-products supplier in 1966 was followed in 1968 by the purchase of Woodward Corporation, a maker of pipe and pipe fittings, castings, and chemicals and of Data Corporation, which produced computer software. In 1969 Mead bought a furniture maker.

These purchases did not shield Mead from an economic recession in the early 1970s. In 1971 the Escanaba mill was operating at a loss despite a $15 million investment in upgrading the plant. Another $45 million investment went into the plant the following year, but profitability continued to elude the operation. As a result of its flagging profits, Mead began to sell off some of the acquisitions it had made only a few years earlier.

Mead managers sold more than $80 million of interests in low-growth markets between 1973 and 1976. For example, lower-grade tablet paper and low-volume colored envelope interests were eliminated. Mead sold off facilities such as the corrugated-shipping-container plant it had built at a cost of $3.5 million in Edison, New Jersey, in 1967, but which had never made a profit. Mead's corrugated-paper business was concentrated in Stevenson, Alabama, in 1975. Mead also directed its attention to potential growth in paper; for example, the company responded to an anticipated hike in mail rates by investing $60 million in a computer-controlled paper machine to make lightweight paper.

Mead retained substantially diverse operations, including furniture factories, foundries, and Alabama coal mines. Despite these far-flung interests, in 1974, about 24% of Mead's pretax earnings came from paper, 35% from paperboard, and 5% from wholesaling. Metal products contributed 11% and furniture 5%, while about 20% was derived from sundry jointly owned forest-products operations. Mead lost an estimated $85 million in sales owing to strikes at several pulp and paper mills. By 1975, however, sales and profits were on the upturn.

In 1977 the consolidation of the box-making business became problematic as two small Pennsylvania paper-box makers, Franklin Container Corporation, of Philadelphia, and Tim-Bar Corporation, filed a $1.2 billion antitrust suit against Mead and eight other box makers. The suit charged the defendants with price-fixing and with attempting to push smaller makers out of the market by buying independent box makers and opening operations where they would compete with smaller businesses. The suit was one of the largest price-fixing lawsuits in U.S. legal history. While Mead was found not guilty in a 1979 criminal trial, a jury found the company guilty in a civil class-action suit of 1980. The other defendants had settled out of court prior to the civil suit, and Mead was left with a potential liability of $750 million. Finally, Mead too settled out of court in 1982 for $45 million, considerably less than it might have had to pay in court, but still five times more than any of the other defendants.

In 1979 Mead ranked fourth among forest-products companies, and hit its all-time earnings peak of $5.19 a share while fending off an unwanted takeover by Occidental Petroleum Corporation. By the early 1980s, earnings began to fall from their 1979 peak of $141 million to a loss of $86 million in 1982—Mead's first loss since 1938. Among the factors responsible were a drastic decrease in demand for lumber products and the costly settlement of the box suit. In addition, Mead's $1.5 billion five-year expansion plan begun in 1978 may have equipped it to benefit from the next paper-market boom, but it also left the company in 1983 with a debt amounting to more than half of its total capitalization. Mead whittled away at the sum by selling several non-core businesses. By 1984 debt was down to 42% of capital, still a dangerously high level but better than in the previous year.

Business improved in 1984, as Mead's electronic information-retrieval services became profitable. Mead Data Central Inc. (MDC), the subsidiary whose primary product is LEXIS, a service that makes case law and statutes available through online computer searches, had been growing at a rate of 43% a year. Unveiled in 1973, LEXIS took in about 75% of the computerized legal research market by the late 1980s. The system's success was enough to spark its own court battle with West Publishing Company, which claimed that MDC intended to infringe on its copyrights by distributing its information with West's pagination. Mead in turn filed its own antitrust suit against West. The case was settled in 1988 with a licensing agreement permitting MDC to offer West-copyrighted material via the LEXIS service.

By 1988 MDC boasted 200,000 subscribers, who bought $300 million worth of information. In 1988 LEXIS was responsible for MDC's 33% growth. LEXIS accounted for an estimated $215 million of MDC's $307.6 million revenues. MDC's other products include NEXIS which distributes newspaper and magazine reprints. MDC also carries other services, such as LEXPAT, which distributes patent information, and LEXIS Financial Information Service, which provides stock information. Micromedex, a subsidiary acquired in 1988, provides information about poison and emergency medicine on compact disc.

In 1988, to enhance the scope of its service to attorneys, paralegals, and the court, MDC purchased The Michie Company, a legal publisher based in Charlottesville, Virginia, publishing statutes from 24 states in printed form. MDC made these statutes searchable electronically through the LEXIS service, and is working on compact disc products combining case law and statutes.

In addition to the promising enterprises at MDC, in 1988 Mead unveiled Cycolor, a new paper for color photocopying. The specially coated paper contained a chemical which, like an instant film, performs the reproduction internally, eliminating the complex machinery formerly needed to create color photocopies. Mead contracted several Japanese companies to manufacture copiers compatible with the paper. By the early 1990s, two Japanese companies were marketing copiers using Cycolor. Development of this product was costly, and diminished the company's earnings from 1986 to 1990. The business has since been scaled back considerably.

While developing these non-paper interests, Mead also undertook some rationalization of its traditional sectors. Most important was the restructuring of its paperboard operations to focus on the production of coated board. Mead dissolved its partnerships with Temple-Inland in the Georgia Kraft Company, sold six of its container plants, and doubled its coated-board capacity. The Macon mill was sold in 1987 to Pratt Holding, Ltd., an Australian firm; Temple-Inland took control of the Rome, Georgia, plant; and Mead took control of the Phenix City coated board mill. In 1991, Mead completed a $580 million expansion of this mill, which added 370,000 tons of coated board annually. Mead also sold its share of the Brunswick pulp and paper mill in August of 1988 and sold its recycled-products business to Rock-Tenn Company in 1988.

As Mead headed into the 1990s, takeover rumors circulated; its success in non-paper activities was bait for another paper company to purchase the firm and then sell its non-paper enterprises to defray the cost. These rumblings notwithstanding, Mead's outlook for the 1990s was generally positive. Although heavy capital spending weakened earnings the company was equipped with updated machinery and strong paper-product lines, as well as growth potential in electronic information.

Principal Subsidiaries: Ampad Corporation; Devres MS Co.; Escanaba Paper Co.; Mead Data Central, Inc.; InfoSource, Inc.; Micromedex, Inc.; Mead Export, Inc.; Mead Realty

Group, Inc.; Mead Leasing Company; Mead Packaging Intl., Inc; Mead Panelboard, Inc.; Mead Pulp Sales, Inc.; Mead Real Estate Investments, Inc.; Mead Reco, Inc.; Mead Reinsurance Corp.; Adena Syndicate, Ltd.; Mead Loss Control Consultants, Inc.; Mead SA, Inc.; Mead Timber Co.; Zephyer Properties, Inc.; M-B Pulp Company; Mead Coated Board, Inc.; Mead Coated Board Intl., Inc.; Mead Supplyco, Inc.; Pulp Asia Limited; Forest Kraft Company; Harborage Realty, Inc.; Illinois Code Company; MDC Acquisition Corporation; Mead Environmental Improvement; Mead TI, Inc.; R. Corp.; D.I. Associates, Inc. (Canada, 50%); Bermead Insurance Company Ltd. (Bermuda); MDC Capital Investments Limited (Canada); Harima, M.I.D., Inc. (Japan, 25%); International Fibre Sales, S.A. (Switzerland, 33.3%); Mead Coated Board Europe Kartonvriebs, A.G. (Austria); Mead Coated Board U.K. Limited; Mead Coated Board Europe (Austria); Mead-Emballage S.A. (France, 99.53%); Mead Export, Inc., (Virgin Islands); Mead Europe Engineering, S.A.R.L. (France); Mead Holdings S.A. (France); Mead Imballaggi, S.p.A. (Italy); Mead Management Services S.A. (Switzerland); Mead Packaging (Canada) Ltd.; Mead Packaging Europe, s.a.r.l. (France); Mead Packaging K.K. (Japan); Mead Packaging Ltd. (U.K.); Mead Reassurance S.A. (France); Mead Paperboard Japan KK; Mead Verpackung G.m.b.H. (Germany); Mead Verpakking B.V. (Netherlands); Northwood Forest Industries, Ltd. (Canada, 50%); Northwood Pulp & Timber Ltd. (Canada, 50%); Productros para Escuela y Oficina, S.A. de C.V. (Mexico); Sistemas de Envase y Embalaje S.A. (Spain); Westbury Reinsurance Ltd. (Bermuda).

Further Reading: Hodgson, Richard S., ed., *In Quiet Ways: George H. Mead, The Man and the Company,* Dayton, Ohio, The Mead Corporation, 1970; Carr, William H.A., *Up Another Notch: Institution Building at Mead,* New York, McGraw-Hill, 1989; "Mead Corporation History," Mead corporate typescript, 1990.

—Elaine Belsito

METSÄ-SERLA

METSÄ-SERLA OY

Fabianinkatu 8
SF-00130 Helsinki
Suomi
Finland
(90) 171 611
Fax: (90) 175 141

Public Company
Incorporated: 1986
Employees: 10,873
Sales: Fmk8.70 billion (US$2.40 billion)
Stock Exchange: Helsinki

Metsä-Serla Oy was formed in 1986 from a merger between Metsäliiton Teollisuus Oy and G.A. Serlachius Oy. It is the tenth-largest industrial company in Finland, the fourth-largest company in the Finnish forest industry, and one of the ten largest forestry companies in Europe. It has the most varied product range of any company in the Finnish industry, being active in four main areas with the following contributions to 1990 turnover: pulp is 20%, paper and paperboard is 33%, corrugated board and tissue paper is 28%, and sawn timber and building materials is 19%. About one-third of its sales are within Finland, while more than half go to other countries in northern and western Europe.

The history of what is now Metsä-Serla begins in the 1860s, when a steep rise in the price of sawn wood in Europe made the exploitation of Finland's gigantic timber reserves economical for the first time. Even now Finland is one of the most densely wooded countries in the world, with 76% of its land area covered by forest. An engineer named Knut Fredrik Idestam started building a groundwood plant in Tampere in 1865. Three years later, when he moved to Nokia to build a second and bigger plant, he invited his friend Gustaf Adolf Serlachius, a pharmacist, to manage the Tampere mill. In 1868 Serlachius moved on from there to Mänttä, to start his own mill for grinding wood into pulp. It was successful enough to finance the building of a paper mill, with two paper machines, at the same site in 1881. Nine years later this wooden building was destroyed in a fire: Serlachius's continuing prosperity enabled him to replace it with a brick and stone building containing three paper machines capable of turning out 5,000 tons each year. In 1913 the business, by then incorporated as a public company, came under the direction of the founder's nephew, Gösta Michael Serlachius. In spite of the disruptions caused by

World War I and then by the civil war which followed Finland's declaration of independence from Russia, he pressed ahead with an expansion of the company, both by adding on new plant at the Mänttä site, including a sulfite pulp mill in 1914, and a sulfite alcohol plant in 1918, and by acquiring other businesses, such as a saw mill at Kolho in 1916, and the Kangas fine paper mill at Jyväskylä in 1918. In 1917 Gösta Michael Serlachius acquired the Tampere Paper Board and Roofing Felt Mill, which Gustaf Adolf Serlachius had managed nearly half a century earlier. In the intervening years it had passed through various hands, finally falling into bankruptcy when the delivery of a new corrugated board machine from Germany was delayed by the outbreak of World War I. The machine eventually arrived in 1920, and the mill, renamed Tako Oy in 1932, went on to produce a range of boards and building materials in its plants, one of which was the largest building in Tampere.

After 1918, and in line with the general trend in the Finnish forest industry, Serlachius abandoned the production of brown wrapping paper for the Soviet market, which was being torn apart by revolution, civil war, and foreign intervention, in favor of supplying newsprint to Finland's new market in western Europe. In this period, Finnish forest products were still mostly of a lower quality than those of rival companies in Norway and Sweden. Still, Serlachius and the other Finnish companies prospered, even in this new, more demanding market, because the low valuation of the Finnish markka kept their export earnings high, even during the Great Depression, when the Finnish forest industries maintained continuous output through the use of plant and equipment modernized during the boom years of the 1920s. By 1939 Finland was the world's leading exporter of paper.

Gösta Serlachius retained control of the company up to his death in 1942, when his son R. Erik Serlachius became managing director. The man who had overseen the expansion of the company into a large and diversified enterprise is commemorated in the Gösta Serlachius Museum of Fine Arts in Mänttä. This houses several hundred works of art collected by Gösta Serlachius or inherited from his uncle and passed into the hands of a fine arts foundation established in 1933. Gustaf Adolf Serlachius had been among the first patrons of Akseli Gallen-Kallela, generally considered Finland's greatest painter, and Gösta Serlachius, who shared his uncle's enthusiasm, assembled the largest private collection of this artists's work, now the main feature of the museum.

At the time of Gösta Serlachius's death, Finland was engaged in an alliance with Nazi Germany against the Soviet Union. In 1944 Finland surrendered to the Soviet Union, having failed to regain the lands—about 8% of its area—that it had ceded to Stalin after a brief war in 1939–1940. These two wars meant that the forest industry could not sell its products in Britain or the Americas, but it kept up production for its continental European markets throughout. Some of the companies diversified: Serlachius began producing chemicals and switched from making newsprint to making printing paper during these years. Its plants in Tampere sustained some bomb damage and then had to contribute to the reparations demanded by the Soviet Union. These were in addition to the loss of land, which was a serious blow to the forest industry in general, since the areas once again ceded to the Soviet Union, in 1947, included 12% of Finland's forests, 20% of its wood- and pulp-producing capacity, and 10% of its paper and paperboard capacity.

It did not take Serlachius long to recover from the impact of these events. The company was now producing a range of papers, as well as paperboard, and in the late 1940s it expanded production of parchment paper at Jyväskylä, began producing impregnated wood at Kolho, and started work on the installation of its seventh paper machine at Mänttä. Paperboard production at Tampere prospered as the pre-packing of goods in cartons for delivery to retail outlets became the norm in Finland, the company profited from selling pulp to the United States and returned to making newsprint, and the prices of all kinds of paper products, as of other raw materials, rose sharply as the ending of rationing and the outbreak of the Korean War boosted demand.

Finland's openness to international economic cycles cut both ways; when prices fell and recession set in at the end of 1951, the forest industry's expansion was slowed, and the levying of taxes on excess profits during the Korean War temporarily inhibited investment. Once the economy had recovered, Serlachius was able to begin production of copy paper and other special papers for technical uses at Jyväskylä and to modernize its plant at Tampere. In 1961 Serlachius began producing tissue paper, using the eighth paper machine to be installed at Mänttä. This latest venture was so successful that another tissue paper machine was started up in 1965. The timber division of the company was also modernized, with the introduction of an automated saw mill at Kolho in 1963. In 1965 the company started to expand by acquisition as well as by internal growth, purchasing the Vammala plywood factory and the Lielahti mill, which produces dissolving pulp for use in the making of artificial silk. Serlachius's capacity for producing cartons was expanded in the 1980s with the acquisition of Järvenpään Kotelo Oy and Pak-Paino.

The history of Metsäliiton Teollisuus was shorter than Serlachius's, but organizationally more complex, since it was the creation, not of a single founder and his successors, but of the Finnish producers' cooperative movement. It has its origins in 1934, when the Central Federation of Agricultural Producers set up Metsäliitto Oy, with Ilmari Kalkkinen as managing director, to supervise the export of products from its forestry department. Kalkkinen was also managing director of the Osuuskunta Metsäliitto, the cooperative organization of forest owners, which took over control of Metsäliitto in 1947. The company then diversified into sawn timber and impregnated wood, and acquired both a plywood factory at Hämeenlinna and pulp, paper, and paperboard mills and chemical plants at Äänekoski. These mills later became part of a subsidiary company, Metsäliiton Selluloosa Oy.

Kalkkinen retired in 1959 and was succeeded by Viljo A. Kytölä, under whom the board of directors and the management of the cooperative and of Metsäliitto were combined from 1960 onward. During the 1960s Metsäliitto's plant and equipment were extensively modernized. In 1965 it became the main shareholder in Savon Sellu Mills and set up another pulp-producing subsidiary, Oy Metsäpohjanmaa-Skogsbotnia Ab. Meanwhile Osuuskunta Metsäliitto established three more companies, Teollisuusosuuskunta Metsä-Saimaa, which operated sawmills; Oy Metsäliiton Paperi Ab, which had a paper mill at Kirkniemi, and Metsäliiton Myyntikonttorit, which brought together the cooperative's sales offices. In 1973 all these operations were reorganized. Osuuskunta Metsäliitto took responsibility for all wood procurement and marketing, with Metsäliiton Myyntikonttorit and Metsäliitto Oy as subsidiaries, while Metsäliiton Selluloosa Oy, renamed Metsäliiton Teollisuus Oy, became the parent company for the Metsäliitto groups's production activities, thus leaving Metsäliitto Oy as a timber procurement company, and the largest supplier of timber in Finland. Following Kytölä's retirement the managing directors of each of these bodies—respectively Mikko Wuoti and Pentti O. Rautalahti—became deputies to a single powerful president, Veikko Vainio. In 1980 all three were replaced, Vainio by Wuoti, Wuoti by Matti Puttonen, and Rautalahti by Ebbe Sommar. By 1986, when Metsäliiton Teollisuus began negotiating the merger with G.A. Serlachius, its production units were making not only pulp, paper, plywood, and various kinds of board but also loghouses, saunas, doors, and windows.

The merger between Metsäliiton Teollisuus and G.A. Serlachius took effect from January 1, 1987, with Gustaf Serlachius as chairman of the board, Mikko Wuoti as his deputy, and Ebbe Sommar as managing director. The two groups were of similar size, for Metsäliiton Teollisuus had a turnover of Fmk2.5 billion and assets worth Fmk3 billion, while the equivalent figures for G.A. Serlachius were Fmk2.8 billion and Fmk3 billion.

Metsäliitto held nearly 57% of the shares in Metsäliiton Teollisuus at the time of the merger and came to hold the largest single portion of Metsä-Serla's shares, 27%, and votes, 48%, proportions which have risen slightly since the merger was completed. The other leading shareholders are the Gösta Serlachius Art Foundation, Gustaf Serlachius himself, and several Finnish insurance companies. The new company started out with 17 subsidiaries in Finland and 14 in other European countries.

Metsä-Serla's ten divisions faced serious problems, with excess capacity in eight divisions—magazine paper, fine paper, paperboard, domestic packaging, tissue paper products, chemicals, sawn timber, and building materials—alongside some success in international packaging and panel products. During its first year the company brought a new fine-paper mill at Äänekoski into operation, disposed of seven subsidiaries not directly linked to forestry, and increased its majority shareholding in Oy Metsä-Botnia Ab, a bleached pulp producer. Profits rose by 17%, largely because demand for paper, cartons, tissue paper products, and building materials improved, but the company's work force was cut from about 13,200 to about 12,000. Production costs fell appreciably, compared with 1985, because a reform of Finland's energy tax and falls in the prices of fuel oil and coal allowed the company, which derived 85% of its electricity from its own power stations or from firms in which it has shares, to reduce its spending on energy.

Profits rose again in 1988 and in 1989 as demand grew in all the areas of Metsä-Serla's output. A new paper mill was started up at Äänekoski to help meet the rising demand. Early in 1989 Metsä-Serla bought the tissue paper and hygiene products company Holmen Hygiene from its Swedish parent company Mo Och Domsjo, renaming it Metsä-Serla AB. This company had been the first in the world to produce unchlorinated tissue products, in 1988. Metsä-Serla retained its plant in Sweden but sold off its factories in Belgium and Britain. The tissue paper products division became the second-largest producer of such products in western Europe, supplying half the market in the Nordic countries.

Following the acquisition of another pulp and liner board company, Kemi Oy, in which Osuuskunta Metsäliitto had had shares since 1950, the bleached pulp subsidiary Oy Metsä-Botnia Ab was reorganized in 1989, in order to reduce the company's need for pulp from other sources. One of its two mills, at Äänekoski, was absorbed into Metsä-Serla—to be run by a subsidiary called Metsä-Sellu—and the other, at Kaskinen, was assigned to a new Oy Metsä-Botnia Ab, which also took over Kemi Oy and Pohjan Sellu Oy in 1991. Metsä-Botnia is jointly owned by Metsä-Serla—(around 30%); Osuuskunta Metsäliitto; United Paper Mills, Finland's largest forest products corporation; and the Tapiola Insurance Group. Metsa-Serla then acquired 30% of the shares of United Paper Mills itself, in what was seen as a hostile takeover bid, but which Metsä-Serla itself justified as an attempt to develop co-operation between the two groups, building on the Metsä-Botnia venture. In April 1990 it vetoed the long-awaited merger between United Paper Mills and Rauma-Repola, but accepted the proposal two months later in return for seats on the board of the merged company Repola Oy and agreement on coordinating investments, marketing, and timber procurement. This agreement also led to the issuing of new shares in Metsä-Serla to Rauma-Repola Oy, which ended the year with a 7.6% holding, now owned by Repola Oy.

In April 1990 Timo Poranen succeeded Ebbe Sommar. Just two months later Poranen announced that profits were likely to fall once again during 1990 and that the company still faced problems of excess capacity and rising production costs. Indeed, the whole Finnish forest industry was suffering from high production costs and an unfavorable exchange rate. The company's restructuring continued throughout 1990 with the purchase of 75% of the shares in the British paper merchant company, the Alliance Paper Group, and the transfer of the panel products division to Finnforest Oy, in which Metsäliitto has 90% of the shares and Metsä-Serla has 10%. Metsä-Serla also pressed on with the building up of its stake in United Paper Mills, so that by the end of the year it held 34.1% of voting rights. At 21.1% of the total shares it is the biggest single shareholder in Repola Oy, the parent company of United Paper Mills, and the two groups cooperate on pulp mill investment.

Metsä-Serla's turnover in 1990 was nearly one-and-a-half times the combined turnover of the companies which came together to create it in 1986. Its high level of diversification, and its close connections with Osuuskunta Metsäliitto, which represents nearly 130,000 owners of private forests, with Metsäliitto, the largest timber supplier in Finland, and with Repola Oy, the country's biggest private industrial corporation, provided the group with secure foundations for future growth as a leading player in the European forest industry.

Principal Subsidiaries: Metsä-Sellu Oy; Rakentajan Metsä-Serla Oy; Takon Kotelotehdas Oy; Oy E. Lindell Ab; Kalmar Snickeri AB (Sweden, 99.2%); Metsä-Serla AB (Sweden); Metsä-Serla Nederland BV; Alliance Paper Group plc (U.K., 75%); Hedsor Ltd. (U.K.); Soren Berggreen & Co. A/S (Denmark); Tissu Canarias SA (Spain, 63.5%); Cartonpack S.A. (Greece, 67%).

Further Reading: Richards, E.G., ed., *Forestry and the Forest Industries: Past and Future,* Dordrecht, Martinus Nijhoff Publishers, 1987.

—Patrick Heenan

MoDo

MO OCH DOMSJÖ AB

Hörneborgsvägen 6
S-891 80 Örnsköldsvik
Sweden
(660) 750 00
Fax: (660) 158 45

Public Company
Incorporated: 1873
Employees: 13,414
Sales: SKr18.43 billion (US$3.27 billion)
Stock Exchange: Stockholm

Mo och Domsjö (MoDo) is one of Sweden's largest forestry companies, and is the third-largest private forest owner in Sweden. The company's activities were further enhanced by its merger with paper producers Holmens Bruk and Iggesund Bruk in 1988. The MoDo group enjoys a comfortable position in the international markets for forest-industry products, especially writing and printing paper, paperboard, newsprint, and market pulp.

MoDo's history needs to be seen against the background of the Swedish forestry industry in general. Sweden has long been one of the most heavily wooded countries in Europe, and even now forests cover 68% of its territory. Successive Swedish governments have done much to promote the export of forestry products ever since the middle of the 19th century, when European industrialization increased the demand for timber, and at the same time mass emigration and rising agricultural productivity allowed the release of surplus land for timber harvesting. The legislation which had restricted ownership of forests to the iron industry was repealed, the depletion of the Norwegian forests removed a major source of competition, and the shift in British trade practices toward free trade in the 1840s removed the tariffs and the policy of colonial preference which had kept Swedish products out of what was then the major industrial market.

J.C. Kempe was among the many entrepreneurs who thrived in these circumstances, which, especially in the boom years of the 1850s and 1870s, resembled a gold rush in their impact upon the economy and society. Kempe was a member of a family that had long been settled in Pomerania—then eastern Germany, now western Poland. He went to Sweden to work for his uncle, a sugar refiner, but then entered the forestry industry through a series of accidents. Kempe had a disagreement with his uncle and went to work in a trading office owned by the father of his friend Olof Johan Wikner. Kempe then married Wikner's sister, and in 1823 the two men took over the business after the death of Wikner's father. Their main water sawmill was at Mo, inland from the port of Örnsköldsvik. Kempe became sole owner in 1836 and expanded the business to include iron works, shipbuilding, and manufacturing of wood products. The Swedish sawmill industry started to expand more rapidly around 1850 when steam engines were introduced to replace water sawmills. In 1865 J.C. Kempe built a steam-driven sawmill at Domsjö, near his other mill. By this time he was exporting his timber to Britain, Germany and France.

Mo och Domsjö, driven by Kempe's wish to make full use of its forest resources, also became one of the leading participants in the pulp industry, which produced the raw material for paper and other products, and which had begun in Sweden in the 1850s. It was in the 1890s that pulp became a leading export. Pulp mills used the lower grades of timber which the sawmills did not want, and much of the waste from the sawmills could also be chemically transformed into pulp in sulfite mills. J.C. Kempe's son Frans built a sulfite mill at Domsjö in 1902-1903. The first sulfite pulp mill in the world had been built in Sweden in 1871. Use of sulfite continued to grow, and by 1914 sulfite mill production accounted for over a third of the company's revenue.

Frans Kempe was also a pioneer in the use of scientific forest management methods. He also worked to provide better housing for the company's workers. Mo och Domsjö continued to innovate, and was the first Swedish company to use birchwood, previously used only for fuel, in making paper pulp. Frans continued to expand the company by adding a further sulfite mill.

The Forestry Act of 1903 required regeneration of forests after felling. Even so, new planting could not keep up with demand, and competition developed among the companies as the forests were depleted. By 1906 purchases of land by forestry companies had become a political issue, and the government, fearing the disappearance of peasant landowners, introduced what was virtually a ban on further acquisition of land by Mo och Domsjö and its competitors.

World War I saw a sharp increase in pulp prices, which made sulphite mill production extremely profitable. The company continued to grow under Frans Kempe's son, Carl, who took over the business in 1916. Mo och Domsjö began production of kraft pulp in 1919, by which time pulp had become MoDo's main product. During the 1920s and 1930s the introduction of new saws, ranging from frame saws to mobile circular saws, decreased production costs in some cases, though their use was limited to certain types of lumber. The means of transporting wood and wood products also changed. River floating had been a cheap and popular method, but the growing use of trucks made the distribution of wood products cheaper and freed the forestry companies from the need to site their mills near rivers.

These interwar years saw a slowdown in the forestry industry. The pulp producers' demand for timber was so great that the forests were seriously depleted and the price of timber rose, while their ability to offer higher wages than other sectors of the industry attracted workers away from those sectors and damaged growth opportunities in other industries. At the same time it was difficult to import extra timber from countries like Finland since they too had restrictions on their timber trade in an effort to protect their rapidly depleted forests. Firms like Mo och Domsjö, which combined lumber milling with pulp production and owned their forests, were thus better placed to survive this period than their smaller competitors, and even to expand. By 1939 the company was running two large sulfite mills and one kraft mill. During World War II, production facilities at the sulfite mills had to be used for the production of other types of pulp to replace imports, such as cattle feed stocks. This led to increased production of chemical derivatives, which was to provide a foundation for the development of the chemical industry in Sweden into a profitable unit after World War II, offsetting volatility in the company's core forestry industry.

The output of pulp has greatly increased and the mechanization of the production process has intensified in Sweden since the 1950s. Within the Swedish pulp and paper industry there have been major structural changes between 1953 and 1985. There were 129 production units in Sweden in 1953, but only 57 in 1985, though total production has continued to increase. With Erik Kempe as managing director, Mo och Domsjö implemented new techniques for various processes ranging from wood handling to digesting and bleaching. In 1951 it constructed a mill for production of fine paper in Hörnefors. In 1959, after Kempe's death, Bengt Lyberg took over as managing director. The company now became interested in petrochemical production, and a site was chosen on the west coast of Sweden, where a plant was completed in 1963. It acquired other companies in the same field, such as Svenska Oljeslageri AB. Mo och Domsjö's interest in petrochemicals lasted until approximately 1973, when it decided to sell off this side of its business because this diversification was not performing the function originally intended for it.

It was during the second half of the 1960s that the company changed direction under its new chairman, Matts Carlgren, who succeeded Carl Kempe in 1965. In a natural step toward integration, the company began to produce its own paper from its own pulp, building on the success of the Hörnefors mill. Its acquisitions under this strategy included the French fine paper mill Papeterie de Pont Sainte Maxence (PSM) and other fine paper businesses based in Sweden. In 1972 a new plant was opened in Husum which integrated the production of fine paper and of kraft pulp. As it continued to expand and modernize this fine paper division it established an even stronger position within the European market by acquiring wholesaling companies in the United Kingdom, France, the Netherlands, and Norway. Mo och Domsjö also entered the tissue industry, with several acquisitions of companies in Belgium, the United Kingdom, and in southern Sweden. Integrated as MoDo Consumer Products Ltd., these firms manufactured consumer products including sanitary pads, infant-care products, and other soft paper goods. The group's vertical integration extended into sole ownership of, or partnership in, 30 hydroelectric power stations in the far north of Sweden.

During the 1980s MoDo had concentrated on acquiring shares in Iggesund Bruk and Holmens Bruk, and it now decided to gain control of both. Holmens Bruk was one of Sweden's leading producers of newsprint. It had originated in the early 19th century, becoming a limited liability company in 1854 and expanding its textile interests alongside its paper production. It bought up forests in southeastern Sweden and es-

tablished a newsprint mill in 1912-1914. After World War II, the Swedish textile industry gradually ceased to be profitable, and in 1970 Holmens left the industry in order to concentrate on newsprint.

Iggesund Bruk, by contrast, was a leader in paperboard production. It dates back to the 17th century, when an iron works was founded that went on producing till 1953, while a steel-making plant continued to operate for a further 30 years. The group's involvement in the forestry industry began early in the 20th century with the establishment of a sulfite pulp mill and a kraft pulp mill, and the acquisition of a sawmill in Hudiksvall. During the 1960s sulfite pulp production was abandoned, kraft pulp production was expanded, and the production of paperboard began, with a view to supplying the packaging and graphics industries. The group acquired forests and built up interests in steel, engineering, and chemicals through a series of acquisitions. By the late 1980s, however, Iggesund had divested itself of all its non-forestry interests apart from a 50% holding in a steel firm. Its main product continues to be paperboard, along with some output of pulp and high-quality wood for the furniture and building industries in Western Europe. Mo och Domsjö's acquisition of the U.K. firm Thames Board Ltd. in 1988 strengthened its position as one of the leading producers of high-quality paperboard in Europe.

MoDo's purpose in taking over Holmens and Iggesund was to create a third giant in the Swedish forest industry, challenging the first- and second-ranking groups, Stora and Svenska Cellulosa (SCA), by diversifying its output. The MoDo Group also has interests in 25 companies which, since the Group has only 20%–26% of the voting shares, are treated as associated companies.

MoDo showed increased profits in 1987 as the price of pulp rose. In 1988 MoDo decided to sell off its soft paper division to the Finnish company Metsä-Serla. Although this division's domestic market share was significant, the company's leaders felt that its share of the European market as a whole was not sufficiently large to justify its existence as a diversification, and that it would be wiser to concentrate on the profitable fine paper and newsprint divisions. In 1989 MoDo showed a drop in sales, but a rise in profits, owing to the sale of the soft paper division.

MoDo and the Swedish forest industry in general have been affected by the general movement in Sweden toward reducing environmental damage. Strict regulation by the Environment Protection Board has led the industry to clean up its operations, to such an extent that several lakes "killed" by forest industry effluent have become biologically active again. However, MoDo's adoption of more environmentally friendly methods such as oxygen bleaching preceded government regulations, and the company can be seen as a pioneer in the use of environmentally safe production techniques.

MoDo's profits grew steadily throughout the 1980s, but as the Swedish economy suffers from rising costs of energy and other resources in the 1990s, MoDo will face difficulties. MoDo is structurally sound and will continue to concentrate on strengthening its position within the European Economic Community, which is its main market. There is also some potential for increasing production of newsprint, writing paper, and printing paper for the new markets of central and eastern Europe, although these markets were not expected to be of a significant size until the mid to late 1990s.

Principal Subsidiaries: MoDo Skog AB; Iggesund Timber AB; MoDo Cellkraft AB; Holmen Paper AB; MoDo Paper AB; Iggesund Paperboard AB.

Further Reading: Montgomery, G.A., *The Rise of Modern Industry in Sweden,* London, P.S. King & Son Ltd., 1939; Gustavson, Carl G., *The Small Giant: Sweden Enters the Industrial Era,* Athens, Ohio, Ohio University Press, 1986; *The New Group: MoDo-Holmen-Iggesund,* MoDo, Örnsköldsvik, Sweden, 1988.

—Monique Lamontagne

OJI PAPER CO., LTD.

OJI PAPER CO., LTD.

Shinjuku Mitsui Building
1-1, Nishi-shinjuku 2-chome
Shinjuku-ku, Tokyo 163
Japan
(03) 3347-1111
Fax: (03) 3347-1130

Public Company
Incorporated: 1949
Employees 5,963
Sales: ¥468.95 billion (US$3.45 billion)
Stock Exchanges: Tokyo   Osaka   Nagoya

Oji Paper Co., Ltd., a member of the Mitsui group, is Japan's largest pulp and paper manufacturer. Accounting for 9.5% of Japan's total paper production and 30% of the country's newspaper print stock in 1990, Oji manufactures and markets newsprint, printing and writing papers, packaging paper, communications-equipment papers, sanitary papers, and specialty papers. The company in 1990 produced 2.9 million metric tons of paper. Oji has pulp-producing facilities in Brazil and New Zealand and paper manufacturing plants in Japan and Canada. The company is also Japan's largest private land owner, controlling 366,800 square miles of forests and commercial real estate. Oji maintains seven sales offices in Japan, six paper mills, four research laboratories, and overseas sales offices located in the United States and Canada.

In 1873 Eiichi Shibusawa founded Japan's first private paper manufacturer and the first Japanese company to employ Western papermaking technology. The venture, called Shoshi-Gaisha, received financial backing from the Japanese government and from two of Japan's prominent *zaibatsu*, or conglomerates, Mitsu and Shimada. Shibusawa, on the heels of a major success in which he had imported, assembled, and successfully started up Japan's first Western-style cotton-textile mill, persuaded his investors that he could do the same thing in the manufacture of paper. The project involved the purchase and assembly of a British paper mill. Two years later, in 1875, Shoshi-Gaisha's first mill, the Oji mill, went into production. Shoshi-Gaisha was, at first, unprofitable, but as Japanese paper consumers began to accept the first domestic paper, the company became profitable.

The 1880s showed substantial growth for Shoshi-Gaisha but little in the way of profits for the company's investors. By 1890, though still not very profitable, Shoshi-Gaisha had virtually monopolized the manufacture of Western-style paper in Japan. Shibusawa had sent his nephew, Heizaburo Okawa, abroad to study the latest foreign technology, and by 1890, a more efficient and profitable production system was developed. Shibusawa by this time needed fresh capital for Shoshi-Gaisha, and he approached the Mitsui Bank. Mitsui Bank, a leading member of the Mitsui group and one of Shoshi-Gaisha's initial backers, agreed to provide more funds to revamp Shoshi-Gaisha's production system. Hikojiro Nakamigawa, managing director of Mitsui Bank then used the bank's equity position in the company to remove Shibusawa and Okawa, who was by then Japan's foremost papermaking expert, from Shoshi-Gaisha's management.

Nakamigawa brought in Ginjiro Fujihara from another of the huge *zaibatsu's* many operations, along with a new management and production team. In 1893 the company's name was changed to the Oji Paper Manufacturing Company. The new management team began the process of building Oji into one of Japan's largest and most successful industrial organizations.

In the years preceding and following the turn of the century Oji's growth paralleled the rapid expansion of the entire Mitsui *zaibatsu*. Abandoning many of its traditional craft-oriented and retail businesses, the Mitsui *zaibatsu* focused its growth on heavy industry. By utilizing a worldwide marketing strategy, the *zaibatsu* increased all of the group's sales and global markets. Shortages in consumer and industrial goods caused by Europe's retooling to meet the demands of the World War I opened up new opportunities for Japanese business on a global scale. During World War I Japan's exports tripled, reaching more that US$1 billion annually. Industrial production as a whole quadrupled, and during these years, Oji's sales spiraled, creating even greater opportunities in business on a level that was international in scope. The company also became one of Japan's largest employers.

The man chosen by the *zaibatsu* to guide Oji though this period of large growth was Ginjiro Fujihara. A strong proponent of all types of Japanese expansionism, Fujihara boasted in one of his books that Japan's enterprising traders would go to all points on the globe, no matter how intimidating the climate in an effort to sell Japanese goods and promote Japanese business interests. Fujihara also believed that the country's strong leanings toward military imperialism was good for Japan, in general, and Oji's business, specifically. He felt that investing in the nation's military power would result in Japan's industrial producers having more power in the international marketplace.

In 1933, in the midst of a period of rapid industrial growth, the company merged with Japan's two other paper producing giants, Fuji Paper and Karafuto Industry. The new coalition created a company that supplied Japan with 78% of its paper needs. Japan established a puppet government in Manchuria in 1932, and in 1937 invaded China. Despite its isolating effect, war, it seemed, was good for business. During this time, Fujihara became one of the leaders of Japan's heavily industrialized, and militarized, economy as a result of his successes in running Oji. While still in control of the company, he was appointed director of the Industrial Equipment Management Control Association, a control corporation whose sole purpose was to remove obstacles to growth in the Japanese economy and to foster the establishment of new business enterprises.

During World War II Oji participated in wartime production to the extent it was able. Fujihara bowed to government demands that production be enhanced, but as a member of the Cabinet Advisory Council Fujihara spoke out against the National Socialist goal of nationalizing industry. Fujihara became the most powerful businessman in Japan in 1943, when he was appointed to a high government post, from which he continued to defend private enterprise. In 1944 Fujihara became head of the Ministry of Munitions, a challenging post at the end of the war, with labor and materials in short supply. While Fujihara was certainly patriotic and was equally opposed to nationalization of Japanese industry, his opinion of the war itself is less clear. Despite critical shortages of raw materials, Oji, like every other large Japanese business, contributed its share of production during the war years.

With the end of the war and the Allied occupation of Japan, Fujihara and many other business leaders were stripped of their authority. The Holding Company Liquidation Commission (HCLC) was formed by the occupation forces. The commission's job was to break up the huge *zaibatsu* that for centuries had monopolized Japanese trade and industry. The HCLC's purpose was to install the beginnings of a democratic, capitalistic system, that was controlled by a greater number of smaller groups of Japanese businessmen and entrepreneurs, and to re-establish the Japanese economy on a self-supporting basis as quickly as possible. In all, 42 holding companies were dissolved. The Mitsui *zaibatsu's* holdings came through the process relatively intact. Oji however, was one of Mitsui's few casualties, and, in 1949, was forced to deconcentrate. The company was broken into three separate paper manufacturing businesses, Jujo Paper Co., Ltd.; Honshu Paper Co., Ltd.; and Tomakomai Paper Co., Ltd. Tomakomai Paper was renamed Oji Paper Co., Ltd., after a brief time. The restructuring that resulted from the application of the postwar Excessive Economic Power Deconcentration Law was completed in August of 1949.

Along with the forced breakup, Oji was faced with the problem of diminished supplies of imported pulp to feed the company's paper mills. The loss of forest resources in Manchuria, Korea, and Sakhalin after the war led to a boom in the domestic production of pulp. The boom in turn created a serious threat to Japan's remaining forests. The Council for the Conservation of Natural Resources, which was headed by an Oji vice president and forestry expert, Jun'ichiro Kobayashi, put the brakes on the reckless depletion of Japan's forest.

Using his newly appointed post on the council, Kobayashi used postwar Allied competition to pressure the United States to allow the development of the Alaska Pulp Company, in 1953. The United States agreed to Kobayashi's plan, knowing that the alternative available to Oji and its sister companies was to try to exploit the Soviet Union's vast Siberian forests. U.S. leadership was wary of permitting the Soviets and Japan to develop any strong business affiliations. After a series of meetings in Washington, D.C., with the State Department and the Interior Department, tentative approval was given to form a company to import Alaskan forest products to Japan. In 1953 the Alaska Pulp Company was established with start-up capital of about $1 million. After a great deal of trans-Pacific negotiation, an additional $20 million was raised for the venture, half from U.S. investors and half from Japanese. The Alaska Pulp project was the first large postwar overseas investment made by the Japanese paper industry and helped to revitalize United States–Japanese business relations.

With the end of the Allied occupation in 1952, prospects for all Japanese businesses were good. Slowly those who had reigned supreme as the leaders of the prewar *zaibatsu* regained much of the control and influence they had prior to 1945. Ginjiro Fujihara, Oji's president for many years died in 1960 at the age of 91. His disciples were instrumental in the reorganization of the paper and pulp industry in Japan and became presidents of the four largest paper companies to emerge after the war.

The new Japanese industrial sector was very different from what had existed prior to World War II. During the early 1960s Oji was one of many companies that underwent a complete modernization of its production methods and milling plants. These changes in the company's production techniques took place at a time when Japan's labor movement was also going through a new, more progressive transformation. The Japanese worker had more power than ever before; and the layoffs and firings that took place as a result of the modernization of Oji's mills caused numerous problems including strikes and, in turn, retaliatory lockouts.

In the decades following World War II, Oji continued its growth in the paper business with virtually no attempt at diversification. In 1970 Oji merged with Kita Nippon Paper Company, and several years later merged again, this time with Nippon Pulp Industries. A pulp mill was constructed in New Zealand in 1971 that was followed by the construction of another mill in Brazil the following year. Throughout the company's first century of existence, Oji had remained exclusively in the paper business, a strong focus that was still in place in the 1990s. With the exception of participation in a few other businesses, including a hospital, hotel, and transportation company, Oji remains committed to the development, manufacture, and marketing of paper products to the ever-increasing worldwide paper market.

To insure a continuous supply of forest products, the company maintains the Institute for Forest Tree Improvement, in Kuriyama and Kameyama. One of the most important contributions made by the institute was the Biomass Conversion project. Sponsored by the Japanese government, the project developed a new variety of poplar tree that is capable of growing three meters in the same number of months. With further research and development into the biotechnological approach to forestry, Oji expects to discover more species of trees that will improve current yields and find improved methods of large scale and environmentally sound forest production.

Under the guidance of Oji's president, Kazuo Chiba, the company was in the early 1990s actively involved in new product research and development to further broaden its paper product line. The company was in the process of developing production methods for value-added papers, that is, photographic papers, sanitary products, and thermal and other forms of communication-equipment papers. In the 1970s and 1980, Oji expanded its line of specialty and consumer-oriented paper products. In 1989, the company began producing and marketing its own line of disposable diapers.

In 1988 Oji participated in a joint venture with the Canadian-based Canfor Corporation. The newly formed company, Howe Sound Pulp and Paper Limited was in 1990 in the process of completing construction of its first production mill in Vancouver. This thermonuclear facility is capable of producing 585 tons of newsprint and 1,000 tons of market kraft paper per day. The newsprint will be marketed by Oji. The kraft pulp will be marketed by Canfor Pulp Sales.

Oji further increased its size and production capabilities in 1989 as a result of another merger with Toyo Pulp Company. At that time, the company's annual output of newsprint had reached almost 900,000 tons. The company produces as many as 200 different types of newsprint to meet the specific demands of its different customers.

As a result of a bottoming out of the paper industry as a whole in 1988, Oji struggled to restore balance to what appeared to be a declining market for newsprint. The demand for other paper products that represent the vast majority of Oji's annual sales was still showing respectable growth in 1990, making the then-current newsprint condition manageable. Oji's President Chiba instituted comprehensive cost reduction measures to cope with increased costs of energy and the declining value of the yen. The cost reduction program coupled with increases in production of some of Oji's products resulted in the company's prediction of record profits for the 1990s and a seemingly secure future for the company, which planned to move into new Tokyo offices in December 1991.

Principal Subsidiaries: Oji Lumber Co., Ltd.; Oji Forestry and Landscaping Co., Ltd.; Sakamoto Lumber Co., Ltd.; Oji Paper Bag Manufacturing Co., Ltd.; Nepia Co., Ltd.; Oji Kako Co., Ltd.; Abekawa Paper Co., Ltd.; Apica Co., Ltd.; Oji-Yuka Synthetic Paper Co., Ltd.; Oji Real Estate Co., Ltd.; Oji Service Center Co., Ltd.; Oji General Hospital; Hotel New Oji Co., Ltd.; Oji Transportation and Warehouse Co., Ltd.; Oji Pier Terminal Co., Ltd.; Oji Cornstarch Co., Ltd.; Nippon New Zealand Trading Co., Ltd.; Eishogen Co., Ltd.; Oji Machinery Co., Ltd.; Oji Kenzai Co., Ltd.: Oji National Co., Ltd.; Oji Salmon Co., Ltd.

Further Reading: Roberts, John G., *Mitsui: Three Centuries of Japanese Business,* New York, Weatherhill, 1989; *A Vision of the Future,* Tokyo, Oji Paper Co., Ltd., [1989].

—William R. Grossman

PWA

PWA GROUP

PWA-Haus
8201 Raubling
Federal Republic of Germany
(8035) 800
Fax: (8035) 805 98

Public Company
Incorporated: 1970 as Papierwerke Waldhof-Aschaffenburg AG
Employees: 11,785
Sales: DM3.77 billion (US$2.52 billion)
Stock Exchange: Frankfurt

The PWA Group is Germany's largest manufacturer of pulp, paper, and paper products. Producing 600,000 tons of pulp, 1.3 million tons of paper and 650,000 tons of paper-based products per year, the group is the fifth-largest paper producer in Europe. The PWA Group was formed in 1970 by the merger of two large German pulp and paper companies, Zellstoffabrik Waldhof AG and Aschaffenburger Zellstoffwerke AG. The group is 40% owned by Bayernwerk, a south German energy company owned by energy group VIAG and the Bavarian government; a 10% stake is held by the Bayerische Hypotheken-und Wechsel-Bank.

The group consists of four divisions, each of which is run independently by a subsidiary company, while the parent organization decides on overall, long-term group strategy. Graphic Papers, headed by PWA Grafische Papiere GmbH, at Raubling, is the largest division, accounting for 44% of group sales in 1989. Subsidiaries in this division produce printing, office, and copy papers at sites in Miesbach and Stockstadt, Germany, and Hallein, Austria. The hygienic papers division, headed by PWA Waldhof GmbH, at Mannheim, incorporates manufacturers of tissue toilet paper, paper towels, and handkerchiefs, located in Germany, France, the United Kingdom, and Belgium. This division accounted for 24% of 1989 sales. PWA Industriepapier GmbH, at Raubling, heads the division concerned with the manufacture of corrugated case materials and packaging, with 14 production sites in Germany, representing 20% of 1989 sales. Smallest in size, with 10% of sales, is the specialty papers division, which produces decor papers for surface finishing in the furniture industry, and coated papers, with subsidiaries at Unterkochen and Krefeld as well as in Spain and Belgium. Vertical integration of production is a central feature of the PWA Group; all of the pulp produced by PWA is made into paper within the group, and

35% of this paper is converted into consumer products by PWA's subsidiaries. Exports—primarily to European Economic Community (EEC) countries—account for around 50% of group sales.

The two companies which combined to form PWA were founded in the second half of the 19th century as pulp manufacturers. Economy of scale is a significant factor in pulp production, and the two companies' strategy in the first phase of their development, up to World War II, was primarily directed towards increasing production capacity and extending their activities into areas with a good supply of wood. At this stage they had little interest in forward integration into paper production. They did not feel at risk of competition from paper producers, who tended to have low production levels and were unlikely to move into the capital-intensive business of pulp manufacture.

Aschaffenburger Zellstoffwerke AG was founded on May 12, 1872, as Aktiengesellschaft für Maschinenpapier-Zellstoff-Fabrikation. The company began by producing paper from its own output of sodium pulp and struggled in its early years with production problems and financial difficulties. Only in 1887, when it switched to sulfate pulp production, did the company begin to maker profits. After the two mills at Aschaffenburg had been extended, increased water requirements led the company to build another pulp mill at Stockstadt, five kilometers farther down the Main River, in 1897–1898. Pulp manufacturers at Walsum, lower Rhine, and at Memel, now in the USSR, were acquired in 1903 and 1905. The company purchased forest land in Russia, and an office was established at St. Petersburg. Between 1914 and 1929 Aschaffenburger Zellstoffwerke expanded significantly. The work force grew from 2,950 to 4,551. Production levels of pulp were increased from 109,000 tons to 183,000 tons; paper production rose to 41,000 tons. Spirit production, introduced during this period, amounted to 59,000 hectoliters in 1929. Sales rose from 26 million reichsmarks in 1914 to 65 million reichsmarks in 1929.

Further acquisitions followed: Hoesch & Co., a pulp producer at Pirna, in the postwar German Democratic Republic, was acquired in 1931, and Freiberger Papierfabrik, a pulp and paper manufacturer at Weissenborn—also in the German Democratic Republic—was acquired in 1937. In 1936 the company's administrative headquarters moved to Berlin and the name was changed to Aschaffenburger Zellstoffwerke AG. A pulp mill at Strasbourg and Vereinigte Papierwarenfabriken GmbH, a Munich paper merchant and converter, were acquired in 1942. The following year saw the beginnings of diversification into pulp by-products, with the establishment of a yeast factory at Stockstadt. In 1944–1945, the company's works and subsidiaries suffered extensive wartime damage and the Berlin headquarters were destroyed.

Zellstoffabrik Waldhof AG was founded in Mannheim in 1884, by Rudolf Christian Haas, Carl Haas, and Carl Clemm. Production of pulp began in 1885, with an initial capacity of 20 tons per day. In the following 25 years the capacity of the mill was increased tenfold. Zellstoffabrik Waldhof concentrated from the beginning on the manufacture of bleached pulp produced by the Ritter-Kellner method. As the demand for bleached pulp soared, the company became Aschaffenburger Zellstoffwerke's main competitor in south Germany. When the Aschaffenburg company planned its new mill at Stockstadt in 1896–1897, Zellstoffabrik Waldhof suggested that this might be a joint venture; however, the older company was prepared to cooperate only in sales and distribution, not in production.

During the period before World War II, Zellstoffabrik Waldhof expanded through internal growth and acquisition, becoming larger than its longer-established rival. In 1893, paper production began at Mannheim. A pulp factory was built at Pirna, now in the USSR, in 1900—the factory was destroyed in 1915—and a pulp manufacturer at Tilsit, now in the USSR, was acquired in 1907. A Norwegian subsidiary was acquired in 1908. Forest land was purchased in Bohemia and Russia, amounting to approximately 150,000 hectares in 1910. Further acquisitions included the Simonius'sche Cellulosefabriken AG at Wangen in 1917, with pulp and paper factories and wood cutting; the pulp factories at Cosel-Oderhafen in 1921; and Ragnit—now in the USSR—in 1924; a paper manufacturer at Unterkochen in 1924; and a paper mill at Pforzheim in 1931. Subsidiaries were also established at Kehlheim—a pulp mill, Niederbayerische Cellulosewerke, in 1925; and in Finland—the Oy Waldhof Ab pulp mill at Kexholm, in 1928. The company's distribution subsidiary at Hamburg was founded in 1925 and extended with branches in Germany and abroad. The acquisition of Natronzellstoff-und Papierfabriken AG in Berlin in 1938 brought pulp and paper factories in Germany—Altdamm, Krappitz, Priebus, Oker; Austria; Czechoslovakia; Hungary; Romania; and Yugoslavia. In the 1920s and 1930s Zellstoffabrik Waldhof was one of the leading European manufacturers of paper and pulp. In 1931 the administrative headquarters were moved from Mannheim to Berlin, and by 1939 the company had a work force of more than 11,000 and an annual turnover of 1.45 billion reichsmarks.

As World War II ended, both companies incurred substantial losses through bomb damage, decommissioning, and the subsequent loss of territories and foreign investments. Aschaffenburger Zellstoffwerke lost all of its foreign subsidiaries, including the pulp mill at Memel, and works at Pirna, Heidenau, and Weissenborn in the eastern zone. The headquarters of the company moved to Redenfelden. The remaining factories were at Aschaffenburg—pulp, paper, and spirit; Stockstadt—pulp, spirit, and yeast; Walsum—pulp, paper, spirit, and other by-products; Redenfelden—pulp, paper, and spirit; Miesbach—wood cutting and paper; and Hoven—paper. Pharmazell GmbH in Raubling, producing chemical and pharmaceutical products, was founded in 1945. In the years following the war the company concentrated on rebuilding the factories which had suffered bomb damage and making up lost capacity with the help of reconstruction loans. Production levels were raised substantially but remained behind prewar levels: in 1950 the company produced 136,000 tons of pulp, 40,000 tons of paper, and 78,000 hectoliters of spirit. This represented 27% of the pulp and 3.7% of the paper produced in West Germany during that year. Exports accounted for 12% of turnover in 1950 and the company recorded a pretax profit of DM2.5 million after losses of DM2.2 million in the previous year and seven years without dividends for shareholders. The work force at this stage numbered 4,500—24% of workers were classified as *Heimatvertriebene,* expelled from Eastern Europe and the eastern zone of Germany.

Zellstoffabrik Waldhof lost works at Tilsit, Ragnit, Cosel, Oberleschen, and Johannesmühle, representing more than half of the group's prewar capacity for pulp, paper, and spirit production. All foreign subsidiaries and shareholdings were lost. The number of employees fell to 5,700 in 1948, and annual turnover was halved. Yet reconstruction and modernization soon led to improved results: in 1950, with a work force of 6,000, turnover had exceeded prewar levels and the company recorded a profit of DM2.1 million. The company headquarters moved to Wiesbaden in 1947.

Postwar reconstruction and restructuring combined with new economic circumstances to effect a fundamental change of strategy in both companies. Their competitive positions deteriorated in relation to the increasingly powerful Scandinavian producers, who had the advantage of being located near their raw material sources, and were favored by the liberalization of foreign trade in Germany. Declining sales forced both Aschaffenburger Zellstoffwerke and Zellstoffabrik Waldhof to place increasing emphasis on paper production: pulp production levels at both companies remained more or less static in the postwar years, while paper production increased. New products were also introduced, with the aim of integrating pulp into a diversified production base, providing a guaranteed outlet for the initial product. Product diversification at Zellstoffabrik Waldhof began with the manufacture of pharmaceutical products, established in 1949. In 1954, Aschaffenburger Zellstoffwerke acquired Papierfabrik Salach, with a paper production capacity of around 9,000 tons per year: this was the company's first significant move to extend the conversion of its own pulp. By the time of the merger in 1970, the policy of diversification had resulted in a broadly based combined product palette, encompassing a number of pulp-types—bleached and unbleached, wood-pulps, and wood-free pulps; pulp by-products—spirit, yeast, and pharmaceutical products; packing papers, corrugated papers, writing papers, stationery products, printed papers, specialty papers, milk cartons, tissue papers, carbon papers, plastic sacks, and tissue products. The number of production sites was correspondingly large, contributing to high costs which hampered the effective development of individual product sectors. The large range of products also led to difficulties for both companies in establishing and carrying out a coherent group strategy. It was the dramatic deterioration in profitability resulting from these factors which prompted the merger of the two groups in 1970. Shares in Aschaffenburger Zellstoffwerke were exchanged for shares in the new company, Papierwerke Waldhof-Aschaffenburg AG at a rate of three for two; shares in Zellstoffabrik Waldhof were exchanged at a rate of one for one.

The newly formed company, renamed PWA Papierwerke Waldhof-Aschaffenburg AG in 1974, decided to concentrate on the integrated production of mass papers, reducing its range of activities and the number of production sites. The results of this strategy have been decisive: between 1970 and 1988 the group's paper production increased by 150%, while at the same time the number of paper machines was reduced by 40% and the output of each machine was increased fourfold. The total of 26 products covered by the group in 1970 was reduced to six basic products in 1988—two types of bleached pulp, tissue wadding, packing papers, graphic papers, and tissue products.

The implementation of the new strategy took effect from 1973, when the group was reorganized into market-oriented product divisions. In 1974 the group's corrugated paper activities were formed into a distinct subsidiary, Zewawell AG. The movement towards the group's present structure was consolidated in 1977 and 1978, when the main product divisions were separated into independent companies within the parent organization: PWA Grafische Papiere, graphic papers; Bayerische Zellstoff, nonwood pulp; PWA Waldhof, pulp; PWA Industriepapier, packing papers; Apura GmbH, tissue products; PWA Dekor, decor and specialty papers; and Papierwaren Fleischer, household papers. Results throughout the 1970s were depressed by the rationalization measures undertaken; towards the end of the decade there were indications of a return to profitability. Group sales amounted to DM1.4 billion in 1978, with a pretax loss of DM19 million; sales in 1980 reached DM2.3 billion with a pretax profit of DM32 billion.

The restructuring of PWA's activities continued in the 1980s. Paper products manufacturers at Hoven and Eislingen were closed in 1982. The group sold its packaging subsidiary, Natronag, at Goslar in 1983, and printers Efnadruck GmbH and Offset Gerhard Kaiser GmbH in 1984. Bayerische Zellstoff, a pulp producer based at Kehlheim, was sold in 1987. Wifstavarfs, a joint venture with Svenska Cellulosa to manufacture fine papers in Sweden, was established in 1982; PWA sold its 41% share of the project in 1987. The company also strengthened its core divisions by acquisitions during this decade. A 40% shareholding in Sept, a French sanitary paper products manufacturer, was purchased in 1986. In 1988, PWA acquired James McNaughton Ltd., a U.K. paper merchant, after purchasing an initial shareholding in 1986, and 76% of the Spanish decor paper manufacturer Papeleria Calparsoro SA. In mid-1989, PWA Waldhof acquired the hygienic paper operations of Holmen S.A., Sweden, including central European operations as well as production facilities in Belgium and the United Kingdom. The specialty papers division was extended by the 1989 acquisitions of Feikes & Sohn KG—a coated papers manufacturer at Krefeld—and Belgian coatings and laminates manufacturer Transpac.

After static sales levels—around DM2 billion—and poor profitability in the early 1980s, sales increased from DM2.8 billion in 1986 to DM3.8 billion in 1989, and were projected to exceed DM4 billion in 1990, with more than 50% attributable to exports. Profits for 1989, after tax, reached DM201 million.

The paper industry in Europe is becoming increasingly concentrated, with a number of large acquisitions in recent years consolidating the leading position of the Scandinavian producers. However, a glance at the global situation confirms that there is still a long way to go; of the world's 20 largest paper companies, 18 are based outside Europe, almost all of these in Japan and the United States. In this context, PWA faces the challenge of maintaining its position in an ever more competitive marketplace, which will be dominated increasingly by large-scale producers. Having recently missed the opportunity to acquire Feldmühle Nobel's tissue paper activities, which were sold to the Scott Paper Company in the United States, PWA is looking for other opportunities to expand, as chairman Willi Klein-Gunnewyk indicated in July 1990. Expansion and modernization of the group's existing facilities are also planned. PWA is implementing an investment program worth DM1.1 billion, to last until 1993.

Principal Subsidiaries: PWA Grafische Papiere GmbH; Papier-Verarbeitungs-und Vertriebs-GmbH; Systemform Datenbelege GmbH; PWA Waldhof GmbH; Apura GmbH; Zewawell AG & Co. KG; PWA Industriepapier GmbH; Innwell GmbH; PWA Dekor GmbH; PWA Kunststoff GmbH; Feikes Papierbeschichtung GmbH; PWA Mabelpap S.A. (Belgium); PWA Waldhof UK Ltd.; PWA Waldhof France S.A.; PWA-K Duffel N.V. (Belgium); Novacard GmbH (60%); Zewathener GmbH (51%); Hallein Papier AG (Austria, 75%); James McNaughton Paper Group Ltd. (U.K., 85%); Papelera Calparsoro S.A. (Spain, 76%).

Further Reading: Klein-Gunnewyk, Willi, and Bernhard Greubel, "Strategie und Organisation: Dezentrale Organisation und Strategie im PWA Konzern," *ZFO* 4, 1989; "Die früheren Geschäftsbeziehungen von PWA nach Osteuropa," *Aktuell,* January 1990.

—Susan Mackervoy

RENGO CO., LTD.

5-12, Hiranomachi 3-chome
Chuo-ku, Osaka 541
Japan
(06) 202-2371
Fax: (06) 226-0298

Public Company
Incorporated: 1920 as Rengo Shiki
Employees: 2,938
Sales: ¥222.58 billion (US$1.64 billion)
Stock Exchanges: Tokyo Osaka

Rengo leads Japan's paper industry in the production of paper containers. Rengo can claim to be the first Japanese company to manufacture corrugated cardboard. In 1990 there were 29 Rengo plants scattered across Japan; 68% of their collective output is box-board, 19% containerboard, and 11% paperboard.

Rengo began operating in 1909 as a unit of Sanseisha Company. The unit quickly absorbed three other companies, Azuma Shiki Manufacturing, Eritsusha, and Teikoku Shiki. In 1920 the unit was incorporated as Rengo Shiki. The following year, the company completed its Kokura plant. Growth continued, and in 1927 Rengo's Nagoya plant began operations, followed by its Osaka facilities in 1930. Four years later the Yodogawa plant opened, and Kawagauchi commenced manufacturing in 1936.

In 1937 the Sino-Japanese War broke out, and the government curtailed business growth. Rengo's expansion halted with the escalation of the war. Nevertheless, production continued, and the Japanese paper industry hit its wartime production peak in 1940, when country-wide paper output reached 1.7 million tons. The Japanese paper industry's decline continued with Japan's participation in World War II.

Upon conclusion of the war, the Allied forces occupying Japan reconstructed that country's long-standing business traditions in the name of economic democratization. At this time, Rengo's six subsidiaries in China and Korea were confiscated.

From 1951 through 1962, the country's real national product grew at a rate of 9% a year. Rengo, too, continued to grow apace. By the 1970s the country's rapid growth was yielding to concerns about the environmental and social costs of economic growth. During the 1970s, among other projects, Rengo developed a paperboard container that preserved fresh fruit, formed a joint venture with Asahi Chemical to manufacture photsensitive resins, and began production of a new synthetic paper. In 1979 Rengo's total paper and pulp sales reached US$728.5 million.

In 1981 Rengo increased its holding in Hamada Printing Press, a printing machinery manufacturer. The same year, the company devised new manufacturing processes that increased productivity 30%, and imported technology from Molins Company. In 1986 Rengo introduced a three-layer cardboard called Triple Wall, used in shipping of heavy office automation equipment and automobile parts. It also developed a commercially viable form of polypropylene film–reinforced corrugated board for packaging.

In late 1986 the company announced a joint venture with C. Itoh and International Paper Company to produce man-made nonwoven fabrics and products, such as disposable diapers and masks. Rengo took a 60% interest, International Paper 35%, and Itoh the remaining 5%. The joint-venture factory had an annual production capacity of 330,000 to 440,000 pounds.

Sales for the fiscal year ending March 1988 reached ¥201.3 billion, ordinary profits were ¥4.9 billion, and net earnings were ¥1.5 billion. For the year ending in March 1989, sales increased to an estimated ¥215 billion, yielding ordinary profits of ¥7.2 billion and net earnings of ¥2.9 billion. As net earnings per share held at about ¥21.10, the company continued to pay its customary annual dividend of ¥6 per share.

In the early 1990s the company focused on selling comprehensive packaging systems. Demand for packaging in the beverage, processed food, home electric appliance, and textile industries was good, and Rengo's sales continued to grow, increased by expansion into specialty boxes with anticorrosion, keep-fresh, and other specialty properties. Although there was a rise in the cost of paper, efficiencies in Rengo's order taking, marketing system, and physical distribution compensated to keep profits rising.

Rengo strengthened its business structure during the late 1980s and early 1990s by purchasing Tokiwa Package Company in Saitama Prefecture, near Tokyo, for ¥4 billion. This strengthened its business network in the Kanto district. Rengo also began construction of a factory in Sendai, in northern Japan, which began operations in 1990. Outside of Japan, Rengo set up a joint venture in Malaysia intending to supply box-board and paperboard to Japanese firms operating there.

As of 1991, the company operated no factories or offices in western countries. Only five other Japanese companies—Oji Paper Co., Ltd.; Jujo Paper Co., Ltd.; Honshu Paper Co., Ltd; Daishowa Paper Co., Ltd.; and Sanyo-Kokusaku Pulp—outstripped it. Steadily increasing sales to home electric appliance manufacturers, cosmetic manufacturers, and beer companies more than compensated for the relatively low sale price of corrugated cardboard; thus, in the early 1990s, Rengo's future looked bright.

—Elaine Belsito

SANYO-KOKUSAKU PULP CO., LTD.

4-5 Marunouchi 1-chome
Chiyoda-ku, Tokyo 100
Japan
(03)3211-3411
Fax: (03) 3287-6480

Public Company
Incorporated: 1946 as Sanyo Pulp Co.
Employees: 4,237
Sales: ¥473.31 billion (US$3.49 billion)
Stock Exchanges: Tokyo Nagoya Osaka Kyoto Hiroshima
    Fukuoka Niigata Sapporo

Sanyo-Kokusaku is one of the leading pulp and paper manufacturers in Japan, and the country's largest producer of printing and writing paper. Its operations include the manufacture and sale of a range of products including wood-free uncoated and coated paper, specialty paper, newsprint, paper pulp and dissolving pulp, converted paper and film, chemicals, building materials, and lumber. The company operates overseas offices in Seattle, Washington, and in Vancouver, British Columbia. Sanyo-Kokusaku also operates a fleet of five cargo ships, since more than 50% of its raw material—wood chips—must be imported. It has joint ventures with Scott Paper and The Mead Corporation, and also works with companies in Australia and New Zealand.

Sanyo-Kokusaku was established in 1972 when Sanyo Pulp Company and Kokusaku Pulp Company merged. Sanyo Pulp had been established independently in 1946. In 1947 Japanese pulp production was down to 231,190 from its wartime high of 1,703,034 tons. This drastic reduction was caused by the loss during World War II of the raw materials in the southern half of the island of Sakhalin and the loss of pulp imports, as well as the loss of production access to Korea, Karafuto, and Formosa. Japanese pulp companies sustained relatively low levels of physical damage, however, since most of Japan's paper principal mills were not located in heavily bombed areas. In 1947 Kokusaku ranked among Japan's top three pulp companies. Kokusaku, Oji Paper Manufacturing, and Hokuetsu Paper Manufacturing together controlled approximately 75% to 80% of Japan's postwar pulp manufacturing capacity.

During the late 1940s and early 1950s, as the general Japanese economy bounced back, many of Sanyo-Kokusaku's contemporary subsidiaries were established. These include SAN-MIC

Trading Co., established in 1947, which trades pulp, paper, and related chemicals and machinery; Otake Paper Mfg. Co., established in 1948, which deals in printing and packaging paper; and Matsuura Trading Co., Ltd., a seller of building materials. These were followed in 1949 by Sakurai Co., which processes and trades paper, films, and adhesive papers; and in 1951 by New Hokkai Hotel Co., Ltd, a hotel and food supplier; and Marukuni Kogyo Co., Ltd, which focuses on materials handling and civil engineering.

The 1960s were a period of tremendous growth for the Japanese economy. This was reflected in the expansion of the pulp and paper market, which grew 10% to 13% annually between 1965 and 1973. Sanyo and Kokusaku formed their first joint venture in 1968, establishing Sanyo-Kokusaku Industry Co., to pursue civil engineering, gardening, insurance, real estate, and building maintenance services. The two companies merged in 1972.

In addition, many of Sanyo-Kokusaku's major subsidiaries were formed during this time. Sanyo formed two substantial partnerships with foreign companies. In 1961 it built a mill near Tokyo with Scott Paper Company to manufacture and sell sanitary paper products in Japan under the Scott trademark. The new company, Sanyo-Scott, was capitalized at US$3 million, with each parent company taking a 50% share of its common stock. In 1970, Sanyo formed another Tokyo-based joint venture with a U.S. company: with Avery Products Corporation of San Marino, California, Sanyo built a plant for the manufacture of self-adhesive materials.

The year 1961 saw the establishment of Kokuei Paper Co., Ltd., which processes and sells paper; and Shin-yo Limited, which manufactures wood chips and lumber, and builds and sells housing. Pearl Package Co., Ltd., a manufacturer of polystyrene sheet and flexible packaging sheet, as well as fine papers, was founded in 1962. In 1964 two companies were formed: Sohken Kako Co., Ltd., to manufacture and sell specialty papers, film, and liquid filling machinery; and SANFLO Co., Ltd., for the trading of concrete admixtures. These were followed in 1965 by Kokusaku Kiko Co., Ltd., which designs mechanical, electrical, and water supply facilities. In 1970 MDI Co., Ltd., began its business developing mangrove chips; in 1971, Nippon New Zealand Trading Co. Ltd. was set up to handle the company's New Zealand trading, and 1979 saw the formation of Pal Plywood Co., Ltd., a maker of plywood, flooring, and wall panels.

As Japanese intolerance of *kogai*, or environmental disruption, escalated during the early 1970s, industrial offenders such as paper mills developed new, more environmentally considerate processes. Sanyo-Kokusaku began using new technology for making pollution-free chlorine dioxide at its plant in Iwakuni in 1973. The process, known as SVP, single vessel process, was designed to eliminate the necessity of acid byproduct disposal.

The end of the 1970s was a successful time for the pulp and paper industry, as strong demand and rising prices encouraged production internationally. Among pulp and paper companies outside North America, Sanyo-Kokusaku ranked fourth in 1979. Its sales increased 29% from 1978, reaching US$1.88 billion; 1979 earnings were US$13.2 million, up 33% from the previous year. Among paper companies internationally, the company ranked 18th, down slightly from its position of 14th in 1978.

Sanyo-Kokusaku's slight fall in international ranking portended a trend in the Japanese pulp and paper market that intensified in the early 1980s. Excessive borrowing, spending on pollution prevention, and the rising cost of energy during the 1970s had driven profits down. The Japanese government eventually declared its domestic pulp and paper industry structurally depressed. This step brought into play special laws established to prevent a declining Japanese industry from leading to high unemployment and regional depression. Thus, in compliance with a 1981 government cartel designed to reduce output, Sanyo-Kokusaku laid off 3,500 workers at four of its plants. Management did obtain union approval for these layoffs, which were planned to last for three months. During this industrial slump, Sanyo-Kokusaku considered contributing to a 1980 joint project with Associated Pulp & Paper Mills (APPM) and five other Japanese firms, including Mitsubishi Pulp and Jujo Paper. The companies proposed constructing a mill in Wesley Vale, Tasmania, that would provide pulp both for APPM and the affiliates. Two years later, Sanyo-Kokusaku shelved these plans.

By 1984 Japan's pulp and paper sales ranked below average for Japanese manufacturing industries, and Japanese pulp and paper manufacturers found themselves in the atypical position of combating foreign imports. Despite weak growth in Japanese demand for pulp and paper, U.S. and other foreign paper producers were gaining market share. The foreigners' easy access to less expensive raw materials and energy allowed them to offer end-products with prices that the Japanese could not match. Still, the top ten Japanese companies retained a 48% share of the paper and paperboard market. During this time, Sanyo-Kokusaku ranked sixth among Japan's pulp and paper producers, with a 3.5% share of the Japanese paper and paperboard market. The majority of its share fell in the paper market, where it held 5.8%; in paperboard, it claimed only a 0.2% share.

In 1988 Primex Fibre Limited was set up as a joint venture in Canada to manufacture and sell woodchips. The company was designed to provide Sanyo-Kokusaku with a regular supply of woodchips and to provide another supply source. The company continued to upgrade its facilities in 1989 by purchasing a new papermaking machine for its Iwakuni mill and a newsprint machine at its Yufutsu mill. In the last three years of the 1980s, the company steadily improved its international status, ranking 22nd among the world's paper companies in 1990.

As it headed into the 1990s, Sanyo-Kokusaku took a conservative view of the future. Although the Japanese economy as a whole continued to improve and demand for paper was rising, the company braced itself for an escalation in sales competition and rising raw material costs. In the early 1990s, its three-year plan focused on increased production and sales, management development, and strengthened international competitiveness.

Principal Subsidiaries: Sanyo Scott Company, Ltd.; Mishima Paper Co., Ltd; Chiyoda Shigyo Co., Ltd.; Otake Paper Mfg. Co., Koyo Paper Mfg. Co., Ltd.; SAN-MIC Trading Co., Ltd.; Sakurai Co., Ltd.; Pearl Package Co., Ltd.; Kokuei Paper Co., Ltd.; Shin-yo Limited; Matsuura Trading Co., Ltd.; Pal Plywood Co., Ltd.; Hokkaido Soda Co., Ltd.; SANFLO Co., Ltd.; New Hokkai Hotel Co., Ltd.; Sanyo-Kokusaku Industry Co., Ltd.; Kokusaku Kyoei Co., Ltd.; Kokusaku Kiko Co., Ltd.; Marukuni Kogyo Co., Ltd.; Nippon New Zealand Trading Co., Ltd.; MDI Co., Ltd.; Primex Fibre Limited.

—Elaine Belsito

SCOTT PAPER COMPANY

Scott Plaza
Philadelphia, Pennsylvania 19113
U.S.A.
(215) 522-5000
Fax: (215) 522-6470

Public Company
Incorporated: 1922
Employees: 40,000
Sales: $5.36 billion
Stock Exchanges: New York Philadelphia Pacific London
Tokyo

Scott Paper Company is a major consumer products company that concentrates on selling home and commercial paper products such as toilet and facial tissues, baby wipes, paper towels, napkins, tablecloths, plates, and plastic cutlery and cups. Scott's major subsidiary, S.D. Warren Company, produces a range of light-weight and heavy-weight coated papers—the lighter papers are used in magazines, books, and mail order catalogs, while the heavy papers are suitable for companies' annual reports, souvenir programs, and high-quality specialty catalogs. Warren also produces uncoated papers and a variety of specialty products.

Scott Paper Company was founded by brothers E. Irvin Scott and Clarence R. Scott in Philadelphia, Pennsylvania, in the fall of 1879. Scott originally produced "coarse" paper goods such as bags and wrapping paper. By the late 19th century, the introduction of domestic bathroom plumbing created the market for a new product, toilet tissue. Scott soon began tissue production, but Victorian mores prevented the company from launching an effective advertising campaign, so Scott sold various grades of tissue to private dealers who marketed the tissue under 2,000 individual brand names.

At the turn of the century, Irvin Scott's son Arthur Hoyt Scott urged the company to begin marketing toilet tissue under its own label. He established a company philosophy that characterized Scott's marketing style well into the 1960s. Arthur's idea was to make only a few high-quality products, to sell them at as low a cost as possible, and to keep them in the public eye with high-profile advertising.

In 1902 the company made its first acquisition, purchasing the private label Waldorf from one of its customers. The oldest name-brand toilet tissue in the United States, Waldorf continues to be sold in U.S. grocery stores and is one of the few consumer products that has been available since the turn of the century. In 1907 Scott introduced the paper towel. The invention was supposedly inspired by a Philadelphia school teacher who thought it unsanitary for her pupils to share the same cloth towel day after day. Whatever its origins, the paper towel, together with toilet tissue, has formed the backbone of Scott's business.

As the demand for consumer paper products rose steadily, Scott hired innovative engineers to upgrade its papermaking technology. With the introduction of new machines in its Chester, Pennsylvania, plant in the early 1920s, Scott became the world's largest and most technologically advanced tissue manufacturer. In order to guarantee its growing success, Scott saw that it would be wise to acquire control of its sources of raw materials. When Thomas McCabe became president of the company in 1927, he began Scott's long-term acquisition of mills, machines, and timberland with the 1927 purchase of a Nova Scotia, Canada, pulp mill and its attendant timber holdings.

Despite the stock market crash and the Great Depression, in 1930 Scott's plant was operating at full tilt; not one employee was laid off, and company sales were as high as ever. This was partly because the economic climate did not affect consumption of Scott products, and partly because Scott was the largest advertiser in its industry. As a result of its unimpeded success, Scott was able to continue its acquisition program. In 1936 it joined with The Mead Corporation to form Brunswick Pulp & Paper Company, which built and operated a pulp mill in Georgia to supply both Mead and Scott.

During World War II Scott continued to prosper despite paper shortages. Scott's aggressive acquisition program continued during the 1940s and 1950s; the company bought mills in Fort Edward, New York, and in Marinette and Oconto Falls, Wisconsin. By 1948 Scott's sales approached $75 million. During the 1950s Scott merged with Southview Pulp Company and Hollingsworth & Whitney Company, which provided substantial timberlands and pulp and papermaking facilities in Everett, Washington; Mobile, Alabama; and Winslow, Maine.

Throughout the 1950s Scott's Scottie tissues and Scotkins napkins dominated the home paper products market with little competition except from Kleenex, made by Kimberly-Clark. By 1955 Scott had a 38% share of the sanitary-paper business, its closest competitor taking only 11%. During the late 1950s Scott lead the U.S. paper industry in profits and growth despite the fact that it introduced only two new products—a plastic wrap and a sanitary napkin—between 1955 and 1961. Much of the company's success lay in its impressive product research and development. Bringing out few new products, the products were carefully developed, and Scott supported them with elaborate advertising. This was the basic strategy that Arthur Scott had prescribed at the turn of the century.

Scott's success could also be attributed to its virtual monopoly of its market, however, which began to erode with Procter & Gamble's entry into the home paper products market. Primarily a soap maker, Procter & Gamble (P&G) in 1957 acquired Charmin Paper Mills, a regional producer of facial and toilet tissues and paper towels and napkins. P&G aggressively promoted Charmin's Puffs facial tissue and White Cloud toilet tissue in their traditional market area, the north central states. By 1961 these brands began edging out Scott products in that region. Nevertheless, in 1961 Scott was the most profitable paper company in the United States in terms of profit margin and return on investment, and was not greatly disturbed by P&G's regional success. In a conservative response, Scott refused to use promotional coupons and price deals, opting instead to reduce the price of its products.

With its entry, however, P&G had opened up the sanitary-paper market; by 1966, Scott had five major competitors. In addition, supermarket chains began selling their own low-cost private-brand tissues. Scott responded mildly, introducing new colors and styles for its already established product lines. Heavy competition eventually led the company to use one of its most innovative promotional gimmicks: the launch of the paper dress. Scott had developed its Dura-Weve paper fabric with the intention of marketing disposable medical products such as linens, towels, and wipes, but in 1966 it also sold 50,000 disposable dresses for $1.25 each in grocery stores to promote its new colored tissues. While the fashion fad came and went, the development of paper fabric gave rise to such modern necessities as P&G's Pampers, the first completely disposable paper-plastic laminated diapers. Scott's own disposable diaper, introduced in 1969, was never a commercial success.

Believing that its philosophy of specializing in just a few products was becoming outmoded, Scott also began to diversify. McCabe made Scott's first non-paper acquisition in 1965—Plastic Coating Corporation of Holyoke, Massachusetts, and its subsidiary, Tecnifax Corporation. Plastic Coating allowed itself to be bought by Scott to finance a major expansion of its coating plants. Plastic Coating needed to expand to meet the needs of its two largest customers, Polaroid and SCM Corporation; but following the expansion, Polaroid failed to expand as expected, and SCM built its own coating plant. The Tecnifax subsidiary, which made visual education aids, lost its profitability when the government cut back on educational funding in the late 1960s.

In 1967 Scott purchased S.D. Warren, a maker of fine book papers. Within a few years, Warren's profits were eaten up by the general advertising recession and the government cuts in educational funding, which reduced the textbook market. Brown Jordan, a maker of casual furniture, was purchased in 1968, as were two manufacturers of audio-visual aids. By 1969, Scott's sales reached their highest to that date, yet its return on equity was only 12%.

McCabe retired as chairman in 1969, and president and CEO Harrison Dunning took over as chairman of the board. Dunning decentralized Scott's management by instituting profit centers, and designating brand managers with responsibility for the research, manufacture, sales, advertising, and earnings of their respective products. This delegation of power cleared the decision-making bottleneck that had plagued Scott, as did Dunning's three-man president's office in which he worked with president Charles Dickey and vice chairman Paul C. Baldwin. All three men were empowered to make a decision on any issue at any time.

By 1970 Scott's competitors in the toilet tissue market had increased to 11, and in facial tissue to 7. Both markets were fully mature, growing at about 2% annually. Between the erosion of their market share and unprofitable acquisitions costing nearly $200 million, Scott was faltering badly. Its earnings fell 18% by the end of 1970, at which point return on equity was down to 9.5%. To make matters worse, in 1971 P&G began

national marketing of its Charmin toilet tissue, whose advertising soon made it the most popular bathroom tissue.

Dunning's office of the chairman, as it had become, was broken up in 1971, as middle managers called for more leadership from the top. In 1972 Charles Dickey was appointed chairman. During the next five years Scott saw heavy outlays of cash—more than $700 million. More than $100 million was spent on meeting new government requirements for pollution control, and the rest went toward new plants and equipment. Business began to recover slowly with the 1976 introduction of Cottonelle, Scott's answer to Charmin. Scott's aging facilities kept production costs high, however, and by the early 1980s another capital-spending program was required to upgrade its plants and expand capacity. In one effort to raise money for the $1.6 billion, five-year spending program, Scott sold $102 million of new common stock to Canadian-based Brascan, Ltd., raising that holding company's share in Scott to 20.5%. Brascan agreed not to increase its holdings in Scott to more than 25% before 1986.

Philip E. Lippincott took over as CEO in 1983. Lippincott, who had initiated the spending program in 1981, began to reap its benefits. Profits increased 51% in 1984, rising to $187 million, and sales rose 5% to $2.8 billion. Scott promptly bought out Branscan, taking on a $300 million debt but eliminating any threat of takeover.

Lippincott eliminated extraneous staff and instituted an incentive program in which the top 600 people at Scott were remunerated partly according to their contribution to profits. Although most decisions at Scott traditionally came from the Philadelphia headquarters, Lippincott invested lower-level managers with more decision-making power, hoping commitment would increase if corporate strategy were developed organically rather than handed down from above. At the same time, Scott decreased its production costs by using scrap wood and wastes produced by the pulping process as fuel for its mills. In Maine, energy costs were reduced from $140 to $40 per ton of paper. A new system for transporting raw materials at the Mobile, Alabama, plant saved the company about $25 million a year in freight and inventory expenses.

The 1980s brought a welcome spurt of growth for Scott's coated paper subsidiary, S.D. Warren. Although Warren had long been a market leader, high production costs made its profits mediocre. In 1982 Scott built Warren a new machine to produce lighter-weight papers, anticipating an increase in medium-weight paper consumption. Since other companies had predicted a decrease in demand because of the proliferation of cable television and other media, Warren was able to profit from the burgeoning market for catalog and magazine papers while its competitors were caught unprepared. As a result, Warren was responsible for 45% of Scott's profits in 1984, and continued to contribute at least a healthy 25% of total profits annually.

A full 50% of Scott's profits still came from toilet and facial tissue and paper towels. In the early 1980s, Scott finally found its niche in the market. While its Cottonelle toilet tissue and Viva paper towels still competed with P&G's top-quality brands, ScotTissue and ScotTowels lay claim to the title of midrange or value brands, leaving the higher end of the market to P&G and the lower end to store brands and cheaper labels. Scott's market share stabilized at 25%, down from its one-time peak of 50%, but still a respectable share.

The U.S. home tissue products market remained virtually stagnant and glutted with competitors. To capitalize on its strength, Scott had to seek new venues for selling its traditional products. Scott began selling tissue products to commercial buyers such as restaurant chains and public facilities, but the real opportunities for growth lay in overseas markets. In 1982, Scott's international operations had a loss of $39 million, down from a profit of $40 million the year before. By 1986, however, Scott had rebounded and was the dominant player in Western Europe, with sales of $750 million. Anticipating the integration of the European Common Market in 1992, Scott bought out its European partners in the late 1980s so that it would not have to share its future profits, and Lippincott insituted a three-year, $250 million expansion program for Scott's European facilities.

Scott Worldwide was formed in 1987, to operate in Europe, Latin America, and the Far East. Scott planned to penetrate the latter two markets more forcefully once the European market matured. Still the world's largest producer of personal tissue products, in the early 1990s Scott concentrated on transforming itself from a U.S. company with foreign interests to a truly international company, controlling its operations on a local level rather than from the U.S. headquarters in Philadelphia.

Always a specialist, Scott continued to acquire related operations such as Texstyrene Corporation, a maker of styrofoam cups, but the company planned to expand its worldwide markets rather than radically diversify its product lines.

Principal Subsidiaries: Cartiera Scott Sud S.p.A. (Italy); Discott II, Inc.; Durafab, Inc.; Escuhbia Oil Company; Excell Paper Sales Company; Financo Ltd. (Cayman Islands); Owikeno Lake Timber Company Limited (Canada); Scott CB Holding Co.; Scott Container Products Group, Inc.; Scott European Holdings, Inc.; Scott-Feldmühle GmbH (Germany, 51%); Scott Gennep N.V. (Netherlands, 51%); Scott Graphics, Inc.; Scott Japan Limited; Scott Miranda, S.A. (Spain); Scott Page N.V. (Netherlands); Scott Polymers, Inc.; Scott Timber Holding Company, Inc.; Scott Worldwide, Inc.; Scottco Inc.; Scottdel, Inc.; Skylark, Inc.; Three Rivers Timber Company; WinCup, Inc.; Cape Chignecto Lands Limited (Canada); Scott Maritimes Limited (Canada); Scott Polymers, Ltd. (Canada); Scott Continental (Belgium); Scott Paper Beteiligungsgesellschaft mbH (Germany); Scott Paper Coordination Center (Belgium); Scott Paper (Hong Kong) Limited; Scott Paper International Finance (Netherlands), B.V.; Scott Paper International, Limited (Hong Kong); Scott Paper International Trade Venture (Europe) (Belgium); Scott Paper Overseas Finance Limited (Cayman Islands); Scott S.N.C. (France); Scott Paper GmbH Nonwovens (Germany); Scott S.p.A. (Italy); Scott Paper Portugal Lda; Scott Paper (U.K.) Ltd.; Scott Iberica, S.A. (Spain, 99.6%); Scott Limited (U.K.); Scott, S.A. (France); Scott Servicios y Asesorias Limitada; Scott Worldwide Inc. (Chile) y Compañia Limitada; Cross Paperware Limited (U.K.); Scott Paper Company de Costa Rica, S.A. (51%); Scott Paper (Malaysia) Sdn. Bhd.; Scott Paper (Singapore) Pte. Ltd.; Taiwan Scott Paper Corporation (66.7%); Scott Trading Limited (Thailand, 49.8%); Thai-Scott Paper Company Limited (Thailand, 88.9%); S.D. Warren Company; Riscott Insurance, Ltd. (Bermuda).

Further Reading: Saporito, Bill, "Scott Isn't Lumbering Anymore," *Fortune,* September 30, 1985; Zweig, Phillip L., "Doing a Geographic," *Financial World,* July 12, 1988; "Scott: Yesterday and Today," Scott Paper Company corporate typescript [n.d.].

—Elaine Belsito

Stone Container Corporation

STONE CONTAINER CORPORATION

150 North Michigan Avenue
Chicago, Illinois 60601
U.S.A.
(312) 346-6600
Fax: (312) 580-3486

Public Company
Incorporated: 1945
Employees: 32,300
Sales: $5.76 billion
Stock Exchange: New York

Stone Container Corporation is the world's largest manufacturer of containerboard, for shipping boxes, and a major manufacturer of paper bags, newsprint, white papers, and wood products. Founded in 1926 as a jobber of packing materials and office supplies, Stone was forced into manufacturing by Depression-era government regulation. Over the years, the company expanded geographically and bought undervalued assets. With the ascension in 1979 of Roger Stone, the fourth Stone to lead the company, Stone Container began an aggressive campaign of leveraged acquisitions. Between 1979 and 1989 sales increased more than 1,600%.

Stone Container's beginnings go back to 1926 when Joseph Stone, an immigrant, in 1888, from Russia, left his position as a salesman for a paper jobber and, with his life savings of $1,500 and his sons Norman and Marvin, created J.H. Stone & Sons. Together the three men set up shop in a former wholesale grocery operation at 120 North Green Street, just west of Chicago's downtown, in an office they shared with a customer and family friend. Building on the selling experiences of Joseph and Norman Stone, the Stones became jobbers of shipping supplies—wrapping paper, bags, tissue paper—and related industrial supplies. The company was a success. During the first fiscal year, which ran 15 months, sales totaled $68,000 and profits equaled $13,500. In 1928, Jerome Stone, the youngest of the three Stone brothers came into the business. The same year, J. H. Stone & Sons began jobbing corrugated boxes.

As Joseph Stone began to slow down, his three sons began to run the company together. If there was a disagreement, the single loser always then agreed to support the decision of the majority. With a simple management system in place, the Stones built their early success on service. They kept little in stock and only occasionally bought for inventory. As the company grew, it moved to larger quarters several times in the early days all within Chicago; ending up on 74th Street, with 55,000 square feet, in 1937.

The Great Depression pushed J.H. Stone & Sons into manufacturing. The National Recovery Act, which President Franklin D. Roosevelt signed into law in 1933, outlawed price cutting. Jobbers such as J.H. Stone & Sons would not get their merchandise at a discount, and Stone's customers would have to pay a premium for Stone's services.

The company needed a cheaper source of supplies, so the Stones explored manufacturing. The opportunity came late in 1933, when the company's principal supplier closed a nearby plant and offered to sell the Stones five pieces of obsolete equipment that converted corrugated sheets into boxes. Accepting the offer, J.H. Stone & Sons paid $7,200 for "Big Betsy," as the machines came to be known, and the services of a technician to help with installation. In 1936 the company moved one step closer to self-sufficiency with the purchase of a second-hand corrugator, for $20,000. The same year, founder Joseph Stone died. Volume grew and in 1938 the Stones decided to erect their own plant. The 150,000-square-foot building in Chicago was the first plant anywhere devoted exclusively to the manufacture of corrugated boxes. Completed in the summer of 1939 at a cost of $382,000 it was built to order for Stone & Sons by the Central Manufacturing District, an authority of the City of Chicago. Also that year, the company reached $1 million in sales for the first time.

In all of these early ventures, the Stones paid with cash on hand or paid off their loans early. To pay for the new plant, they took a 20-year loan at 6% interest, but they paid off the debt in less than three years.

During World War II, when the government was sending aid and arms overseas, almost everything was packed in corrugated boxes. Since J.H. Stone & Sons' war priority rating was high, it had no problem with material shortages. The Stones continued to expand in the face of a good market. In 1943 Norman Stone learned of a corrugated box company in Philadelphia, Pennsylvania, that was for sale. Light Corrugated Box Company was two-thirds the size of J.H. Stone; it was also Stone's first venture outside of the Chicago area. After acquiring the company for $1.2 million, the brothers found they needed a resident manager, and for the first time, they brought in a nonfamily general manager, David Lepper.

After World War II the growing company incorporated as Stone Container Corporation. Demand skyrocketed, and raw materials grew short. Chief executive officer Norman Stone saw both opportunities for expansion and a need to control raw materials. With these in mind, Stone Container acquired two mills in 1946, the first being a $1.2 million box-board mill in Franklin, Ohio. Since Stone container did not need box-board, the raw material used in rigid boxes and folding cartons, the box-board machines were converted to the production of jute linerboard, then used as the outer layers in corrugated containers. The second was a $575,000 Coshocton, Ohio, mill that produced corrugating medium—the fluted material sandwiched between linerboard layers in corrugated containers—from straw. To pay for the two Ohio mills, Stone Container borrowed $2 million, and paid off the loan in one year.

In 1947 Stone Container issued 250,000 shares of common stock and became a publicly owned company. No longer completely family owned, the brothers began working to attract outsiders to management positions.

The company found that its two big Ohio paper mills had enough capacity to supply the Chicago and Philadelphia plants and to sustain an additional corrugated-container plant. Stone Container, therefore, built a new corrugated-container plant, in the industrial area of Mansfield, Ohio. The plant was completed just before the Korean War began in 1950.

During the Korean War demand was high, and Stone Container sought to expand capacity. In 1950 Norman Stone heard of a mill at Mobile, Alabama, that had been taken over by the Reconstruction Finance Corporation, a federal agency. Within a year, Stone Container had bought the mill and converted it to the manufacture of jute linerboard.

During the 1950s the expansion of supermarkets and self-service outlets began to change the face of retailing. Containers became more than a means of conveying merchandise from producer to consumer. Producers began to see boxes as a means of advertising. On the crest of that wave, Stone became a pioneer in advertising on the exteriors of boxes.

The 1950s were also a period of aggressive geographic expansion for Stone Container. As it was not economical to transport corrugated boxes more than about 125 miles, Stone Container located plants near its customers. First the company would identify a market, then it would build or buy a box plant in that area, and finally it would find the paper supply to feed the plant with raw materials. Among the box companies Stone Container acquired during the 1950s were: W.C. Ritchie & Company of Chicago in 1955; Western Paper Box Company of Detroit in 1956; and Campbell Box & Tag Company of South Bend, Indiana; Acme Carton Company of Chicago, and Delmar Paper Box Company, the latter three in 1959.

Along with geographic expansion came diversification. Until 1954, Stone Container had confined its operations to the manufacture and sale of corrugated containers and paperboard. By 1960 it was selling folding cartons, fiber cans and tubes, tags, and special paper packages, due in great measure to the acquisition of W.C. Ritchie & Company, a manufacturer of high-grade paperboard-product packages.

While Stone was expanding rapidly and becoming a force in the industry its primary raw material, jute linerboard, was losing ground to the lighter, stronger kraft linerboard. To stay competitive, Stone had to buy kraft linerboard from other paper companies. Although the kraft linerboard shortage became apparent in the late 1950s, CEO Norman Stone was not able to address the problem until 1961, when Stone Container organized and took a 65% equity share in South Carolina Industries (SCI). Through SCI, Stone Container built a completely new kraft linerboard mill at Florence, South Carolina, a mill capable of producing 400 tons of board a day. Begun in 1962, during an economic recession, and financed through Northwestern Mutual Life Insurance, the SCI mill was completed in 1964 at a cost of $24 million, more than Stone Container's entire net worth at the time.

By the early 1960s Stone Container was consolidating its gains. The advertising revolution was complete, and in 1961 nearly all of its containers were designed specifically for a customer's product and market. The same year, Stone moved its corporate offices to North Michigan Avenue in Chicago, an office tower that was renamed the Stone Container Building. In 1962 the company was listed on the New York Stock Ex-

change. With the opening of the South Carolina mill in 1964, Stone for the first time became a fully integrated company, supplying virtually all of its own raw materials.

During the economic slowdown of the late 1960s and early 1970s, the company continued expanding. It spent $35 million in capital expansion, diversified with a plastics packaging division, and in 1974 bought Lypho-Med, a dry-freeze pharmaceutical manufacturer. Although operations kept expanding, Stone Container resolutely stayed out of the forestry business. According to Chairman Jerome H. Stone, who spoke with *Paper Trade Journal* in January 1977, the investment would have been too much. "For us to become self-sufficient we would need 300,000 acres of land. At $300 to $400 per acre we would have to justify an investment of $100 million. At the present time I don't see any way of obtaining a reasonable return on that investment." According to Stone, the Florence mill had 110 good suppliers of wood during the 1960s and 1970s.

In the early 1970s Roger Stone, then vice president of the containerboard division and later chief executive officer, saw industry leaving the Northeast. He realized that his primary customer base was shrinking and that he needed to re-orient production in some geographic sectors toward a more consumer-based market. To that end Stone set out to boost sales of boxes to customers making nondurable consumer products, like foods, beverages, and toys, to 75% of total sales.

By 1975 the Stone family's ownership was some 62% of the company's stock. Yet the Stones continued to work hard to assure that Stone Container was a truly public company. They promoted heavily from within. Three family members were in the company's upper echelons: Jerome as chairman and chief executive officer, Roger as president and chief operating officer, and Alan as vice president, marketing.

Expansion continued, and in 1975 the company entered the Minneapolis–St. Paul, Minnesota, corrugated-container market by buying National Packaging for $6.05 million. In the face of expansion, however, earnings slumped, falling from a 1974 high of $1.87 per share to 90¢ in 1978.

In 1979 Roger Stone became CEO of Stone Container. Son of Marvin Stone, one of the original founders, he was the second youngest of five cousins. Roger Stone had joined Stone Container as a sales representative in 1957, and become president in 1975.

In 1979 Boise Cascade proposed a merger, offering some $125 million in cash and stock to buy Stone Container's outstanding shares, more than twice the company's market value. The Stone family, which at that time owned about 60% of 7.7 million shares mulled over the offer, and initially chief executive officer Roger Stone was in favor of accepting it. With signs of an upturn in the paper market, however, Stone Container pulled out of the deal and decided to remain public. With that commitment to the future of the Stone Container Corporation, Roger Stone began an aggressive expansion campaign that would eventually make the company one of the largest paper manufacturers in the world.

Roger Stone's idea was to buy capacity from disenchanted or financially distressed producers. In that way he would neither increase industrywide capacity, possibly leading to a bust in container prices, nor incur the tremendous costs of building new plants and buying new machines. In a May 1, 1981, interview with *Financial World* Stone said, "We were willing to make that commitment when demand was down. That is when you should commit, when nobody else really wants to." In 1979, a low point in the business cycle, Stone ordered a $55 million expansion of the then wholly owned, ultra-efficient Florence linerboard plant. Then in 1981 he had Stone Container buy an equity position in Dean-Dempsy Corporation, a wood-chip fiber source. The Dean-Dempsy acquisition made Stone Container the 13th-largest producer of boxes in the United States.

The rest of the 1980s saw Roger Stone making larger acquisitions. His was a leveraged buyout strategy. With banks and junk bond innovator Michael Milken and the then powerful Drexel Burnham Lambert supplying ready cash, and chief financial officer Arnold Brookstone devising ingenious financial strategies, Stone Container quintupled its annual capacity by 1987, to 4.8 million tons, at a cost that was one-fifth that of new plants. Like his predecessors, Roger Stone bought during down times, and paid his debts when prices rose. His feeling for the business cycle was keen.

In October 1983 Stone Container paid $510 million for Continental Group's containerboard and brown-paper operations; 1983 was a bad year in the industry and Continental needed cash. Stone was able to buy 3 highly efficient paper mills, 15 corrugated box plants, 5 bag plants, and the cutting rights to 1.45 million acres of timberland for about one-third of the replacement value of the mills alone. Paid for with a $600-million loan, boosting debt to 79% of capital, and the first equity offering since 1947, which cut the family's share from 57% to 49%, the Continental purchase doubled Stone Container's annual capacity to 2.3 million tons and made Stone the nation's second-largest producer of brown paper behind International Paper. After the Continental purchase, containerboard prices increased, and Stone was able to pay down its debt significantly.

In October 1985 Stone paid $457 million to buy 3 containerboard mills and 52 box-and-bag plants from Champion International Corporation. With this purchase, Stone's debt again soared, to about 70% of capitalization. The deal also gave Champion the option to buy 12% to 14% of Stone's stock at a higher price in the early 1990s. The Stone family, however, still owned 37% of the company.

In 1987 Stone paid $760 million to buy Southwest Forest Industries, a containerboard company that also made newsprint. The acquisition of Southwest's 2 large pulp and paper mills, 19 corrugated container plants, and assorted plywood and veneer plants, lumber mills, railroads, and private fee-timber made Stone the nation's largest producer of brown paper, including corrugated boxes, paper bags, linerboard, and kraft paper.

According to some analysts, the acquisitions were taking a toll. Stone had more than $1.44 of debt for each $1 of equity. To shake some of the debt, Brookstone spun off Stone Container's wood-products businesses as Stone Forest Industries (SFI). By selling shares in the new company, which was still controlled by Stone Container, the company obtained cash and spun off a portion of its own debt. While Brookstone was dealing with the debt, the economy was running hot. Stone

Container plants were operating nearly at full capacity, and the company was able to meet its obligations. The family's share fell to 30%.

In 1988, after the SFI acquisition, CEO Roger Stone set a goal of making the Stone Container Corporation a major force in packaging, newsprint, and market pulp—the material used to make fine paper—throughout North America and Europe. Stone predicted that after European economic integration in 1922 there would be an explosion in packaging as firms shipped goods around the continent. He wanted Stone Container to be there when it happened. In pursuit of this strategy, Stone Container made the biggest acquisition in its history. In March of 1989 Stone paid $2.2 billion in cash and securities for Consolidated-Bathurst Inc. (CB), Canada's fifth-largest pulp-and-paper company. The purchase made Stone Container the world's second-largest producer of pulp, paper, and paperboard; a major player in newsprint; and gave Stone Container a foothold in the European market through CB's Europa Carton subsidiary and U.K. plants.

While some analysts worried about debt, which increased to 70% of capital, and fluctuations in the newsprint market, which tumbled alarmingly just as the deal was going through, others lauded the strategic benefits of becoming a truly international company, especially with the coming economic integration of the European Community. Unlike earlier acquisitions, in the Consolidated-Bathurst deal Stone had paid full price for a well run company—a 47% premium over the market price at the time. Investors worried about the $3 billion debt load, and prices for newsprint slipped 14% in the year following the acquisition. With investors jittery about debt and an economic slowdown in the works, stock prices fell from a 1988 high of $39.50 to $8.50 in October of 1990. In 1989 the company disposed of some debt by selling $330.4 million in noncore assets, and in 1990 cash flow remained more than adequate to meet obligations.

In 1990 the 10th-largest forest-products company in the world and the world's 248th-largest industrial company, Stone Container Corporation was trying to digest its biggest acquisition yet. Stone container is on the verge of becoming a worldwide presence. At the dawn of the 1990s, with more than $3 billion in debt and the paper market on a down cycle, Stone Container must make it through some tough times before it again reaches heights of profitability.

Principal Subsidiaries: Stone Resource and Energy Corp,; Stone Forest Industries Inc. (49%); Stone-Consolidated Newsprint Inc.; Stone-Consolidated (Canada); MacMillan-Bathurst Inc. (Canada); Europa Carton (Germany); Empaques de Carton Titan, S.A. (Mexico); Stone Forestal S.A. (Costa Rica).

Further Reading: Stone, Marvin N., and Jerome H. Stone, *Stone Container Corporation,* New York, The Newcomen Society in North America, 1975; Lund, Herbert F., "Stone Container's first 50 years just a springboard to much greater growth," *Paper Trade Journal,* January 1, 1977; Simon, Ruth, "They thought we were a little crazy," *Forbes,* September 21, 1987.

—Jordan Wankoff

STORA KOPPARBERGS BERGSLAGS AB

S-791 80 Falun
Sweden
(023) 800 00
Fax: (023) 138 58

Public Company
Incorporated: 1888
Employees: 69,700
Sales: SKr62.36 billion (US$11.07 billion)
Stock Exchanges: Stockholm London Frankfurt

Stora, which claims to be the world's oldest existing joint-stock company, has gone through several transformations during its 700-year history. Throughout most of its life, Stora was one of Europe's largest copper producers as its official name Stora Kopparbergs Bergslags (The Great Copper Mountain Mining Company) indicates. It was Sweden's first, and for a considerable period only, major enterprise of international significance. As copper output declined in the 19th century, Stora diversified into iron and steel production as well as forestry products. It remained active in these sectors until the 1970s, when it decided to concentrate on the pulp and paper industry. As a result of a series of acquisitions in the 1980s, Stora has become Europe's largest forestry company.

Peasant farmers began mining the copper mountain near Falun in central Sweden around the year 1000. The first documentary evidence of the mine appears in a letter from 1288 giving the Bishop of Västerås a one-eighth share in the mine in exchange for landholdings. The document shows that a cooperative organization by this time was managing the mine, with shares being bought and sold.

The mine was controlled by Swedish nobles and German merchants, who were responsible for selling the copper in the European market. Mine operations were conducted by master miners, who excavated the ore on a rotation basis. They were supervised by a royal bailiff after King Magnus Eriksson granted a charter, bestowing a series of privileges on the mine, in 1347.

The decree of 1347 acknowledged that the mine played a decisive role in the national economy and its importance grew over the next few centuries. The improvement of production techniques boosted the annual output of the mine from 80 tons of copper in the late 15th century to 750 tons 100 years later.

This was occurring as copper output in central Europe was declining. The mine soon became a prime source of national wealth, accounting for 60% of gross national product, as foreign demand grew for Swedish copper. "Sweden stands or falls with the Copper Mountain," read one proclamation from the royal government, which viewed the mine as a means to improve its poor financial position and support its series of military campaigns in the Baltic region and central Europe during the 17th century.

Having declared that the crown had regal rights to the copper deposits, the Swedish kings demanded taxes on the mined ore and tried to monopolize the mining and trading of copper.

Their success in this demand was limited, however. By 1650, when annual copper production from the mine hit a peak of 3,000 tons, the metal had become the country's most important export product and Sweden dominated the European copper market, supplying two-thirds of the continent's copper needs.

The highest authority over mine operations was the Royal Mine Board in Stockholm and the king's local representative was the mine master. The mine master was in charge of allocating mining rights to the master miners, who paid one-tenth of their ore production to the crown as rent, plus one-fourth of the crude copper they produced from smelters as tax. The total number of mining shares was fixed at 1,200 an arrangement that lasted until Stora became an *aktiebolag*—public limited company—in 1888.

The decline of Stora's mine was signaled by two giant cave-ins in 1655 and 1687, after which production never exceeded 1,500 tons a year and output gradually sank to an annual level of 900 tons by the late 18th century. During this period, copper was still Sweden's second-largest export item after iron, but its importance declined sharply in the early 19th century.

The mine owners then decided to develop the forest and iron-ore resources in the region to replace the falling copper production. They had considerable experience of both products since they had harvested and transported wood to fuel the copper smelters, while they manufactured mining tools out of iron ore.

In the early 1800s Stora Kopparberg began producing pig iron and bar iron as a new business venture, becoming one of the country's leading manufacturers in this sector by the mid-century. It bought or leased tracts of forest to supply the iron furnaces and forges with charcoal fuel.

In parallel with the change in its activity, Stora Kopparberg also underwent an organizational reform in the 1860s that transformed its legal status and administrative rules. The crown's influence over operations was ended with the abolition of the master miner's office. Supervision of the company's mining operations and its manufacturing activity in iron and wood products, which had been managed separately, were merged under a three-member collective leadership.

By the 1870s, Stora Kopparberg had begun to assume its modern profile. It used its ownership of forest lands to become one of the country's largest wood product companies. Its Domnarvet sawmill was the largest water-power mill in the nation and the sawn timber it produced accounted for more than half of the company's sales. A large iron works was also built at Domnarvet during the decade to replace the company's dozen scattered and inefficient small works.

Mining operations, meanwhile, contributed a decreasing share of corporate revenues. The mine accounted for one-quarter of sales in 1870, but its output of copper and recently discovered gold and silver amounted to only a tenth of sales by 1890. The mine also generated income from the production of sulfur pyrites as well as the distinctive Falun red paint that adorns many houses in the Swedish countryside.

Erik Johan Ljungberg, who became general manager of Stora Kopparberg in 1875, emphasized the strategy of making a limited number of basic products in a few large plants to achieve economies of scale. A sawmill at Skutskär on the mouth of the Dalälven River was acquired in 1885 and expanded to become one of the world's largest, with two pulp mills added in the 1890s. A giant paper mill for newsprint was also established at Kvarnsveden, near Domnarvet, in 1897.

Additional forests and the ore mines at Grängesberg were purchased as well as other ironworks, including the Söderfors facility that was later developed into the company's specialty steelworks. These facilities were powered by hydroelectric stations built by Stora along the Daläven River in the early 20th century.

When Stora Kopparberg became a limited share company in 1888, with Ljungberg appointed managing director and chairman of the board, it was the largest concern in Sweden in terms of sales and number of employees. It had an initial share capital of SKr9.6 million, with eight shares being exchanged for each old share dating from the 17th century. During Ljungberg's time, corporate sales grew from SKr4.5 million to more than SKr30 million.

By the time of Ljungberg's death in 1915, the foundations of the modern Stora Kopparberg were clearly laid with the saw and pulp mills at Skutskär, the paper mill at Kvarnsveden, and the iron and steel works at Domnarvet, all of them concentrated along the Dalälven River Basin. The company would spend the next 60 years developing and expanding these core facilities. The sectors in which Stora operated formed the backbone of the country's industrial breakthrough in the late 19th century, enhancing the company's importance to the nation.

In 1916, Stora Kopparberg became one of the crown jewels of the extensive Swedish industrial empire controlled by the Wallenberg financial family with the appointment of Marcus Wallenberg Sr., the head of the dynasty, as chairman.

Emil Lundqvist, one of the top executives in the Wallenberg sphere, was named managing director of Stora Kopparberg in 1923 and he oversaw the company's steady growth over the next two decades. Under Lundqvist, sales increased threefold to SKr131 million, while profits grew from SKr2 million to SKr11 million.

Lundqvist was succeeded by Ejnar Rodling and Håkan Abenius, who presided over an almost uninterrupted expansion with sales approaching SKr1 billion by the early 1960s. Annual capital investment rose from SKr20 million in 1945 to more than SKr150 million in 1960, with the construction of five new power stations and expansion of existing industrial facilities.

But the 1960s proved to be a period of growing difficulties for Stora Kopparberg. Increased international competition depressed prices for the bulk commodities that were the company's primary products. It introduced rationalization measures to boost production capacity, while developing special grades of standard products to reduce its heavy dependence on goods particularly vulnerable to economic cycles. These included

new types of pulp and high quality iron and steel. In 1961, Stora Kopparberg also established its first overseas venture with the building of a pulp mill in the Canadian province of Nova Scotia.

The recession that followed the oil shock of the early 1970s posed a new challenge for the company's next president, Erik Sundblad. Mounting losses in both commercial steel and specialty steel operations placed a heavy burden on the company. It was clear that what was needed was the creation of larger units that could operate at lower cost through economies of scale.

But instead of expanding the steel business through acquisitions, Stora Kopparberg decided to sell it. The first step occurred in 1976 with the sale of its specialty steel unit to Uddeholm, another Swedish specialty steel company. This was followed a year later with the transfer of its commercial steel operations, mainly consisting of the Domnarvet Steelworks and iron mines, to Svenskt Stål AB (SSAB), a new company created by the government to concentrate the country's ailing steel industry under one umbrella group.

With these moves, Stora Kopparberg became primarily a pulp and paper company with substantial resources in forests and hydroelectric power. Its new strategy of concentrating on this sector was inaugurated with the purchase of Bergvik & Ala, a Swedish forestry company, in 1976.

The early 1980s were marked by a power struggle between the Wallenbergs and the Swedish automaker Volvo, which had been permitted to buy a stake in the company, over ownership control of Stora Kopparberg, with the family eventually emerging victorious.

Following the sudden death of Sundblad in 1984, Bo Berggren, a former deputy managing director, became the new company head. Within months, Stora Kopparberg, which had been Sweden's second biggest forestry company after Svenska Cellulosa AB, suddenly emerged as Europe's largest, with sales of SKr13 billion, after the SKr3.6 billion purchase of Billerud, Sweden's fifth-largest forestry company.

The deal was significant for other reasons besides size. It broadened the company's product range from its traditional areas of newsprint and fine paper to Billerud's specialized area of packaging, including sack paper and liquid packaging board. It also obtained its first main production facility within the European Community (EC) with Billerud's eucalyptus pulp mill in Portugal. The company marked this milestone by shortening its name for general usage to Stora, the Swedish word for "great" or "large."

Pulp- and papermaking is one of the world's most capital-intensive industries. Stora realized that only the largest companies would be able to survive and compete in international markets against the huge U.S. rivals.

The company's size was further enlarged with the decision by the Wallenbergs to concentrate their forestry holdings under Stora. This phase began in 1986 when Stora acquired Papyrus, then the country's fifth-largest pulp and paper company. The SKr5.8 billion deal boosted Stora's annual sales to SKr18 billion.

In 1988, Stora paid SKr5.9 billion for Swedish Match, another Wallenberg-controlled company. The deal fitted Stora's strategy of becoming a forest products group that spanned the entire manufacturing process from raw materials to finished consumer products. Although Swedish Match was best known for matches and lighters, it also produced a range of timber-based building products, including flooring, doors, and kitchen furnishings. The acquisition boosted Stora's sales to almost SKr40 billion.

Having consolidated its position at home, Stora then decided to expand its international operations, especially in the EC, which accounted for almost half of its sales. One worry was that its production of paper and pulp remained largely concentrated in Sweden, which could be a handicap as competition intensified in the EC single market after 1992.

In 1990, it first bought the French paper concern Les Paperteies de la Chapelle-Darblay in partnership with the Finnish forestry company Kymmene. But it then pulled out of the deal when it saw a more attractive target. This was the DM4 billion takeover of Feldmühle Nobel, the German forest products and engineering group. Stora had cooperated with Feldmühle Nobel for more than 20 years, with the two companies jointly operating pulp and newsprint mills in Sweden. Ownership of Feldmühle Nobel made Stora the largest producer of lightweight coated magazine paper and newsprint in Europe, while increasing its sales to SKr62 billion in 1990.

Stora had to rein back some of its other ambitions in order to finance the purchase of the German firm, one of the largest ever transactions in Europe. It decided to sell some of the Swedish Match units as well as the engineering operations of Feldmühle Nobel. This still left Stora as the dominant power in the European pulp and paper industry and one of the world's largest forest products companies.

Principal Subsidiaries: Stora Forest; Stora Power; Stora Cell; Stora Feldmühle; Stora Billerud; Stora Papyrus; Stora Timber; Stora Kitchen; Akerlund & Rausing; Swedoor; Tarkett.

Further Reading: Rydberg, Sven, *Stora Kopparberg: 1000 Years of an Industrial Activity,* Stockholm, Gullers International, 1979; Hallvarsson, Mats, "The Jewel of the Kingdom," in *Sweden Works: Industry in Transition,* Stockholm, New Sweden 1988 Committee, 1987; Rydberg, Sven, *The Great Copper Mountain; The Stora Story,* Falun, Stora Kopparbergs Bergslags AB, 1988.

—John Burton

SVENSKA CELLULOSA AKTIEBOLAGET

Skepparplatsen 1
851 88 Sundsvall
Sweden
(060) 19-30-00
Fax: (060) 19-33-21

Public Company
Incorporated: 1929
Employees: 30,139
Sales: SKr31.12 billion (US$5.52 billion)
Stock Exchanges: Stockholm London Oslo Frankfurt

Svenska Cellulosa Aktiebolaget (SCA) is one of Europe's leading forestry companies. Founded in 1929 by the famed Swedish financier Ivar Kreuger, SCA initially served as a marketing organization for pulp producers in northern Sweden. After transforming itself from a holding company into an integrated forestry concern in 1954, SCA gradually expanded into the areas of newsprint and linerboard over the next two decades. In 1975, the company entered the consumer products field with the purchase of Mölnlycke, a manufacturer of fiber-based disposable hygiene products. This marked the start of SCA's increasing concentration on value-added products based on wood, and its decreasing activity in traditional forestry products, such as pulp and low-grade paper. This development has coincided in the 1980s with SCA shifting some of its production from its Swedish homeland to the European mainland through a series of corporate acquisitions.

The roots of the establishment of SCA lie in the economic problems that hit the Swedish forestry industry in the 1920s. Forestry products, such as timber, pulp, and paper, were the country's largest export items, but their competitive position in the European market was damaged during the 1920s by the government's deflationary monetary policy that boosted the value of the krona. This coincided with strong competition from the USSR, which was dumping cheap timber products in Europe.

Faced with declining prices and profits, Swedish forestry companies were forced to hypothecate their fixed assets and stocks to commercial banks as security for loans. By the late 1920s, Svenska Handelsbanken, then Sweden's largest bank, feared that its lending position to the forestry industry was overexposed and sought ways to reduce its liabilities. It proposed that the Swedish financier Ivar Kreuger, who had gained

a virtual monopoly over the production of matches worldwide, should take over its forestry industry holdings.

Kreuger was at first reluctant to accept the Handelsbanken's proposal since it would tie up capital, but, having recently bought several sawmill and pulp companies in the Sundsvall region in northern Sweden, he eventually saw possibilities in combining his forestry holdings with those of Svenska Handelsbanken. The merger would prevent cut-throat competition, would reduce production costs, and consequently help raise and stabilize export prices. In addition, Kreuger would acquire several hydroelectric power stations as a result of the deal. His control over the power sources for the pulp and paper industry would also improve profitability.

In 1929, SCA was created with Svenska Handelsbanken selling its forestry shares to Kreuger's investment company, Kreuger & Toll, mainly on credit. SCA was designed to be a holding company to sell the pulp produced by its ten subsidiaries in northern Sweden. The companies that made up SCA included Bergvik & Ala, Skönvik, Sund, Trävaru Svartvik, Nyhamns Cellulosa, Torpshammars, Björknäs Nya Sågverks, Salsåkers Ångsågs, and Holmsund & Kramfors. The tenth company, Munksund, was added in 1934. SCA was Europe's largest forestry company, a position that it would maintain until the mid-1980s. At the time of its formation, it accounted for almost a third of Sweden's total pulp exports.

The SCA combine amounted to a loose confederation with each member company having its own president and board of directors as well as administrative control over finance, sales outside of pulp, and forest management. Svenska Handelsbanken retained its role as primary lender to SCA and most of its member companies, and their shares were hypothecated to the bank.

The first few years of SCA's existence were devoted to rationalizing its operations and constructing Europe's largest and most modern cellulose plant at Östrand. The large investment costs meant that the company did not pay a dividend for the years 1930 and 1931. The following year, SCA faced its first serious crisis with the suicide of Kreuger, an event that triggered the collapse of Kreuger & Toll. The value of SCA's share capital dropped from SKr100 million to SKr4 million and Handelsbanken assumed control of SCA by purchasing its shares from the bankrupt investment company. Lacking experience in managing industrial concerns, Handelsbanken then sold most of its interest in SCA in 1934 to the Swedish industrialist Axel Wenner-Gren, the founder of the household appliance company Electrolux.

But Handelsbanken continued to play a supervisory role as the main creditor to SCA. The company's performance under the chairmanship of Wenner-Gren was lackluster and Handelsbanken grew concerned about the company's ability to repay its debts. In 1941, the bank forced Wenner-Gren to sign an agreement that reduced the nominal share capital from SKr30 million to SKr10 million and converted SKr40 million of the company's assets to new shares that would be held by Handelsbanken, thus giving it majority control over SCA. The timing of the deal was fortunate since the United States was threatening to place SCA on a trade blacklist and freeze its assets in the United States because of Wenner-Gren's suspected business ties with Nazi Germany. Handelsbanken's assumption of control prevented this from happening.

Handelsbanken used its controlling stake to carry out a reorganization of the company by consolidating the activity of each of its subsidiaries in the river valley where it was most dominant. It then decided to sell some of the subsidiaries to improve the company's financial position, with Bergvik & Ala and Hammarsforsens Kraft, a hydroelectric power company, being divested in 1943. Handelsbanken bought the remainder of Wenner-Gren's shareholding in SCA in 1947 and the company became a subsidiary of the bank.

The change in ownership coincided with a buoyant market for the forestry industry in the early postwar period, with prices hitting a peak during the Korean War boom of 1950–1951. As a result, SCA finally managed to free itself from debt. In 1950, Handelsbanken decided the time was right to reap profits from its long-term involvement in SCA by introducing most of the company's shares on the Stockholm Stock Exchange. But SCA's ties with Handelsbanken have remained close ever since with the bank continuing to act as prime lender to SCA and maintaining a representative on the board of directors.

Axel Enström, who became SCA president in 1950, charted a new corporate strategy by promoting closer cooperation among the company's various subsidiaries. This led to a full-scale merger of their activities in 1954, which transformed SCA from a holding company into a single integrated forestry concern.

During the 1950s and 1960s, SCA greatly expanded its activity from its traditional area of pulp and sawn timber into paper production, primarily newsprint and kraft paper, kraft liner, and corrugated board. Between 1959 and 1969, pulp production increased from 690,000 tons to 1.1 million tons, while paper production jumped from 160,000 tons to 600,000 tons, despite a reduction in the number of mills from eleven to eight. Revenues during this period climbed from SKr375 million to SKr825 million.

The appointment of Bo Rydin as SCA president in 1972 marked the beginning of a new period for the company. In 1974, Rydin decided to diversify the company into value-added fiber-based products. A year later, SCA purchased Mölnlycke, which had been founded in 1849 as a Swedish spinning and weaving business but had been transformed into a manufacturer of disposable hygienic products in the 1950s.

By 1979, when it celebrated its 50th anniversary, SCA's activities covered all segments of the forestry industry, from raw materials to consumer products. It was Europe's largest private forest owner with 1.7 million hectares of forest land, equivalent to half the size of Switzerland, that provided 60% of the company's timber needs, a high level of self-sufficiency by international standards. Its six mills, which produced 1.3 million tons of pulp and 1.1 million tons of paper, were powered by the company's own hydroelectric stations run by the Bålforsens Kraft AB (BÅKAB) subsidiary. The mills were equipped with pulp and paper machinery produced by another SCA subsidiary, Sunds Defibrator. Pulp and paper accounted for half of SCA's sales of SKr5.965 billion in 1979, while Mölnlycke was responsible for 30% of sales, with BÅKAB, Sunds Defibrator, and packaging companies making up the rest.

The 1980s were characterized by three major developments: a rapid increase in sales, growing internationalization through the purchase of several important European companies, and a reduced dependence on pulp and paper production combined with an emphasis on higher-value products. The company's diversification program during the early 1980s concentrated on increasing the number of its corrugated board operations in Sweden and the rest of Europe. Average annual output by these companies reached 750,000 tons by the mid-1980s, providing a captive market for 40% of SCA's production of linerboard, which is used as the outer surface of corrugated containers. SCA became Europe's largest linerboard producer in 1985 when it assumed majority ownership of Obbola Linerboard, a joint venture it had established with the U.S. St. Regis Paper Company in 1973.

Meanwhile, SCA was concentrating its pulp and paper production at four mills, with an average capacity of 300,000 tons, although its largest facility, the Ortviken newsprint plant, had a capacity of 600,000 tons. SCA then accounted for 25% of Sweden's total newsprint production. It also curtailed the production of pulp for outside consumers, its original business, with only 5% of its pulp being sold to third parties in the mid-1980s compared with 75% in the 1960s. This was designed to reduce its exposure to the sharp fluctuations in the world pulp market.

By the mid-1980s, Mölnlycke had become the market leader for disposable consumer hygiene products—such as diapers and female hygiene goods—in Scandinavia and the Benelux countries, and was Europe's leading supplier of disposable hygiene products to hospitals and industrial users. Bolstered by a cyclical upturn in the global forestry industry, SCA's sales almost doubled from SKr6.7 billion in 1980 to SKr12.6 billion in 1985, while profits before extraordinary items climbed from SKr688 million to SKr1.3 billion during the same period, reaching a peak of SKr1.5 billion in 1984.

In 1987, SCA signaled its determination to expand beyond Scandinavia by raising SKr1 billion through a new share issue to fund an acquisition spree for hygiene and packaging companies on the European continent. In January 1988, it purchased Peaudouce, France's leading disposable diaper producer, for SKr2 billion in a move to strengthen Mölnlycke's market position in Europe and build up its consumer products sector, where profits are higher and more stable than in the traditional forestry products area.

Under its new president Sverker Martin-Löf, SCA then turned its attention to the corrugated board sector. It acquired Italcarta, Italy's largest corrugated board manufacturer, in July 1988, followed by a number of other corrugated board manufacturers, among them Bowater Containers, Belgium. With the Italcarta deal, SCA for the first time was consuming more linerboard than it was producing itself, thereby no longer having to sell linerboard on the open market. Its position as a net consumer of linerboard would also protect the company against a drop in demand.

While SCA was limiting its production of pulp and linerboard to in-house needs, it also decided to reduce its production of newsprint at the Ortviken facility in favor of lightweight coated paper. This move toward the production of high-quality printing paper was confirmed with the purchase of a majority shareholding in Laakirchen, an Austrian producer of magazine paper, in October 1988. The deal extended SCA's range to cover all grades of printing paper. Control of Laakirchen also made SCA a leading producer of tissue paper in Europe.

The desire to broaden its international production base led to SCA's £1.05 billion purchase of the U.K. firm Reedpack in June 1990. The deal not only bolstered SCA's position as a leading European producer of corrugated boxes, but also made it a major producer of newsprint using recycled waste paper. SCA's gradual shift from manufacturing newsprint from virgin fiber in Sweden to using recycled wastepaper gathered from Europe's cities reflects the increasing importance played by recycling in papermaking. The need to have access to wastepaper and to site manufacturing facilities close to consumers is one reason that SCA is moving its operations near major population centers in Europe.

In late 1990, SCA turned its attention back to Sweden. It became the dominant shareholder in the country's third-largest forestry concern, Mo och Domsjö (MoDo). The strategic alliance was forged to promote collaboration in printing, paper production, and joint investments in paper mills. Although SCA controlled slightly more than half of MoDo, there were no immediate plans to merge the two companies to form a concern that would rival Sweden's Stora, Europe's largest pulp and paper company, in size.

SCA's acquisition spree in Europe and the transformation of its product mix toward higher value-added consumer products has forced the company to divest some subsidiaries that were once considered central to its traditional activities in pulp and newsprint. In 1990, it completed the sale of its pulp machinery company Sunds Defibrator to Rauma-Repola in Finland. SCA also mortgaged half of its BÅKAB hydroelectric assets to the Swedish government-affiliated National Pension Funds to raise SKr5 billion for new investments. In early 1991, it sold the tissue operations acquired from Laakirchen as well as several units of Reedpack.

During the second half of the 1980s, SCA saw both profits and sales continuing to grow at a rapid pace. Sales almost doubled between 1986 and 1989 from SKr15.2 billion to SKr24.8 billion, while profits after financial items jumped from SKr1.4 billion to SKr2.7 billion. However, SCA is expected to face a period of declining profits in the early 1990s due to a cyclical downturn in the forestry industry.

Principal Subsidiaries: Mölnlycke AB; SCA Packaging AB; SCA Graphic Paper AB; SCA Forest and Timber AB; Bålforsens Kraft AB.

Further Reading: Utterström, Gustaf, *SCA 50 år: Studier kring ett storföretag och dess föregångare,* Sundsvall, SCA, 1979.

—John Burton

TEMPLE-INLAND INC.

TEMPLE-INLAND INC.

303 South Temple Drive
Diboll, Texas 75941
U.S.A.
(409) 829-2211
Fax: (409) 829-1266

Public Company
Incorporated: 1983
Employees: 13,000
Sales: $2.40 billion
Stock Exchanges: New York Pacific

Temple-Inland Inc. is a lumber and lumber-products holding company specializing in paper, packaging, building products, and financial services. The company's colorful history can be traced back to the late 1800s and includes acquisitions, mergers, lawsuits, name changes, and a notable spin-off that helped the company become a well-rounded producer with more than $1 billion of sales a year at that time.

Temple-Inland was formed in Delaware in 1983 to acquire Time Inc.'s subsidiaries, Temple-Eastex Incorporated, now Temple-Inland Forest Products Corporation, based in Diboll, Texas, and Inland Container Corporation based in Indianapolis, Indiana. Through these and other subsidiaries, Temple-Inland has manufacturing, retail, and service operations in 29 states and Puerto Rico, and owns more than 1.8 million acres of timberland in Texas, Georgia, Louisiana, and Alabama.

What is now Temple-Inland Forest Products Corporation began in 1893, when Thomas Louis Latane Temple Sr. founded Southern Pine Lumber Company on 7,000 acres of east Texas, Angelina County, timberland. Temple built the town of Diboll around his company, and by 1894 the first sawmill was operating, cutting 50,000 board feet of old growth timber each day. During the next few years, Southern Pine Lumber Company continued to expand its operations in Diboll. In 1903 the company built its second sawmill, and in 1907 created a hardwood mill. In 1910, Temple Lumber Company was formed, and established operations in Hemphill and Pineland, both in Sabine County, Texas.

In 1934 Thomas Temple died, leaving his son Arthur with 200,000 acres of land and a company that was $2 billion dollars in debt. Three years later the Hemphill sawmill was destroyed by fire, and Temple Lumber Company operations moved to a smaller mill in Pineland.

During these early years and through the housing boom following World War II, Southern Pine Lumber primarily produced basic lumber products, both hardwood and pine, for the construction and furniture industries. By the 1950s technology offered new directions and opportunity for growth. Southern Pine Lumber Company began converting chips, sawdust, and shavings into panel products. In subsequent years, the company pioneered the production of southern pine plywood, particleboard, gypsum wallboard, and other building materials.

Credit for substantial growth in the 1950s was due to the aggressive leadership of the grandson of Thomas Temple, Arthur Temple, who took over in 1951. Under his direction, the company used technological advances in the forest industry to expand the company's production and reduce its debt. In 1954 Southern Pine Lumber built a new plant in Diboll for fiberboard production, using wood waste and whole pine chips to make asphalt-coated insulation sheathing. Southern Pine Lumber of Diboll and Temple Lumber of Pineland merged in 1956, taking Southern Pine Lumber's name.

In 1962 Southern Pine Lumber purchased the controlling interest in Lumbermen's Investment Corporation of Austin, Texas, a mortgage-banking and real estate development company that became a wholly owned subsidiary in the early 1970s. In 1963 gypsum wallboard production began with the purchase of Texas Gypsum, of Dallas, Texas, that also became a wholly owned subsidiary of the company. That same year, Southern Pine Lumber set up a joint venture with United States Plywood Corporation to build a $3 million plywood-sheathing plant at Diboll. The plant, supplied with raw material from 400,000 acres of Southern Pine Lumber's timberland, was designed for producing plywood for sheathing, rock decking, sub-flooring, and industrial uses. After several successful years of operating the plant as a joint venture, the company bought out United States Plywood.

In 1963 Southern Pine Lumber Company changed its name to Temple Industries, Inc., and built a pilot plant in Pineland to make particleboard from sawdust and shavings. After 70 years of business, the company's land holdings had grown to more than 450,000 acres. In 1964 Temple Industries expanded into financial services, including mortgage banking and insurance.

In 1966 the company built a stud mill at Pineland. In 1969 it rebuilt the Diboll sawmill a year after it was destroyed by fire and, also that year, acquired two beverage-case plants in Chattanooga, Tennessee, and Dallas. Two new wholly owned subsidiaries joined Temple Industries in 1969. Sabine Investment Company of Texas, Inc. was formed, and Temple Associates, Inc. was acquired.

The 1970s were even more significant for the company, beginning with the production of medium-density siding and the expansion of the fiberboard operation. Temple Industries formed Creative Homes, Inc., in Diboll, to build mobile and modular homes for approximately four years. In 1971 the company built a new particleboard plant in Diboll, and in 1972 acquired AFCO Industries, Inc., manufacturer of do-it-yourself consumer products. That same year Temple's West Memphis, Tennessee, gypsum operation began production.

The decade, however, was defined by the events of 1973: Time Inc. acquired Temple Industries and merged it with its Eastex Pulp and Paper Company subsidiary to form Temple-Eastex Incorporated. Eastex Pulp and Paper had been founded in the early 1950s by Time and Houston Oil Company, as East Texas Pulp and Paper. Houston Oil's 670,000 acres of southern pine and hardwood provided raw material for the new paper mill, opened at Evadale, Texas, in 1954. Time had purchased Houston Oil's 50% ownership in 1956, thus acquiring the 670,000 acres of timberland.

When Time created Temple-Eastex, magazines were providing only about one-fourth of the Time's company's sales, and Time officials decided to expand the company's more profitable forest-products business. Both companies were looking to diversify; Time's underperforming stock made it vulnerable to takeover. Temple met with Eastex president R.M. (Mike) Buckley, and the arrangements were made. Time bought Temple Industries for stock, and the Temples became Time's largest outside shareholders.

Temple-Eastex produced lumber and other building materials, in addition to paperboard used for household paper products. In 1974 Temple-Eastex opened a new particleboard plant in Thomson, Georgia, and a new plywood plant in Pineland, Texas. In 1975 the stud mill at Pineland was automated, and all operations except plywood and studs were phased out. That same year Temple-Eastex installed an innovative process for bleaching of pulp, required for white paper products, in the Evadale mill, as part of an expansion in kraft pulp capacity. The $55 million Temple-Eastex expansion boosted Evadale production by 17%. The company stayed busy during the late 1970s with openings, closings, purchases, and moves. A wood molasses plant was built in Diboll in 1977 to use the wood sugars found in the waste water from fiber products. The following year a $100 million capital improvement was begun at Evadale to further enhance operations there. In 1978, Arthur Temple became vice chairman of Time and served in that position until 1983. In 1979 Temple-Eastex moved into new corporate offices in Diboll, while the nearby plywood operation was closed permanently.

The 1980s started off smoothly with some improvements at the Diboll mill. In 1980 a plastic-foam operation was put on line to manufacture urethane for rigid-foam insulation, and the company's newest and largest wood-fired boiler began operation. A new chip mill and log processing operation was constructed in 1982 in Pineland to supply chips to Evadale, plywood and stud logs to Pineland, and fuel for all other operations. In 1982, however, the company was fined $40,000 by the Texas Air Control Board for violating state particulate rate and opacity standards. In addition to the fine, the Evadale kraft pulp and paper mill was required to install two electrostatic precipitators.

In 1983, ten years after acquiring Temple Industries, Time decided to spin off the company's forest-products operations into a separate company, again as an antitakeover measure. Time distributed 90% of the common stock in the newly formed company, Temple-Inland Inc., to its shareholders. Time also agreed to sell the balance of its holdings within five years after the spin-off.

Temple-Inland, which was then comprised of Temple-Eastex, Inland Container Corporation, and several other operations, offered a wide range of products, including plywood, fiberboard, lumber, particleboard, gypsum, rigid foam board, and wall paneling. The building-products division operates five retail stores in Texas, and one in Louisiana. Temple-Inland also has successful financial-services operations, offering mortgage banking, real estate development, and insurance. The company's heaviest volume, however, comes from its container and containerboard segment, which accounted for 59% of the company's earnings in 1989. This segment ranked fifth in containerboard production in the United States and third among the country's 800 corrugated box producers in 1990.

Inland Container Corporation, a fully integrated packaging company, makes corrugated boxes and other containers at its six paper mills. The company got its start in 1918 when Herman C. Krannert started Anderson Box Company in Anderson, Indiana, to make ventilated corrugated boxes for the shipment of chickens. By 1925 he moved to Indianapolis, Indiana, and opened the first Inland Box Company plant the following year. The company acquired a second plant in Middletown, Ohio, in 1929, and in 1930 was re-incorporated as Inland Container Corporation. By 1946 Inland Container had grown into a multiplant box maker but was relying entirely on outside sources for its paper supply. Later that year, through a joint venture with The Mead Corporation, Georgia Kraft Company, half of which was owned by Inland Container, was formed, and construction of a new linerboard mill was begun at Macon, Georgia. Georgia Kraft owned approximately one million acres of timberland in Georgia and Alabama, and operated three linerboard mills with five machines, as well as plywood and lumber mills.

In 1958 Inland Container acquired a majority of the outstanding stock of General Box Corporation, which, when combined with shares previously held, gave Inland Container more than 50% control of that company. This acquisition led to an antitrust charge in 1960 by the Federal Trade Commission (FTC) against Inland Container for its purchase of shares of General Box's Louisville, Kentucky, plant. Charges were dismissed in 1963, and then reinstated in 1964, when the FTC reversed an earlier ruling. Inland Container was ordered to sell the corrugated-shipping-container plant that it had acquired from General Box in June 1958. The FTC said the acquisition more than doubled Inland Container's share of the corrugated-box market in the city, and caused the company to supplant General Box as the second-largest corrugated box maker in Louisville. In 1964 Inland Container compensated for this loss by building a corrugated shipping plant on a 17-acre site in Hattiesburg, Mississippi.

In the late 1960s, Inland Container further integrated its operations with construction of a corrugating-medium mill in Tennessee, which began operations in 1970. Corrugating medium is the rippled, corrugated center of the sandwich, with linerboard on each side, which is the composition of corrugated board. Further expansion took place with the construction of a recycled corrugating-medium mill at Newport, Indiana, which began operations in 1975.

In 1978 Time paid $272 million to buy Inland Container. Other operating divisions of Inland Container market packaging materials for the agricultural, horticultural, and poultry industries, and manufacture and market paper and reinforced box tapes.

Following the 1983 spin-off, Temple-Inland incorporated Inland Container and Temple-Eastex. Temple-Inland adopted the same aggressive stance as its subsidiaries had in previous years. The Temple family was still in control of the company, although it had been expanded, diversified, and modernized since Thomas Temple began operations in 1894. During its first year of business, the subsidiary Temple-Eastex purchased Elmendorf Board of Claremont, New Hampshire, a manufacturer of oriented-strand board. The next year, the company acquired National Fidelity Life Insurance Company of Kansas for $28 million with an eye to expanding its financial-services group. In December 1987, Temple-Inland Financial Services acquired Kilgore Federal Savings and Loan Association in Texas for $10 million.

In 1986 Temple-Inland purchased a linerboard mill, three box-manufacturing plants, a short-line railroad, and approximately 260,000 acres of timberland in east Texas and Louisiana at a cost of about $220 million, from Owens-Illinois, a Toledo, Ohio–based packaging company. The mill, in Orange, Texas, greatly increased the company's capacity for production of linerboard. The mill and timberland were also valuable because of their proximity to Temple-Inland's other facilities. That same year, Temple-Eastex announced construction of a $30 million wood-converting facility in Buna, Texas. The facility was intended as a high-tech sawmill and low-cost residue provider to paper mills in the Texas cities of Evadale and Orange.

In 1988 Temple-Eastex Incorporated changed its name to Temple-Inland Forest Products Corporation. That same year Georgia Kraft Company was dissolved and its assets divided between Temple-Inland and Mead. Temple-Inland acquired the Rome, Georgia, linerboard mills, a sawmill in Rome, and more than 400,00 acres of timberland.

The big news of 1988, however, was the purchase of three insolvent Texas savings and loans. Temple-Inland, along with Trammell Crow and Mason Best Company, bought Delta Savings Association of Texas, in Alvin; Guaranty Federal Savings & Loan Association of Dallas; and First Federal Savings & Loan Association of Austin. The three institutions were combined into one, Guaranty Federal Savings Bank, operating in Dallas, of which Temple-Inland had an 80% interest. Temple-Inland's initial outlay was $75 million, and the company committed to contribute another $50 million by January 1991. Temple-Inland was hoping for future payoffs. Purchase of the institutions was a low-risk investment that complemented the company's plans for growth in its financial-services group.

In 1989 Temple-Inland was deemed "the most under-valued paper stock on the Big Board" by *Business Week,* May 22, 1989. The company was described as having superb leadership but stock that failed to reflect Temple-Inland's rapid growth. The following year, Temple-Inland sold its Great American Reserve Insurance Company, using the $10 million profit from the sale to bolster Guaranty Federal's capital to expand its home-mortgage lending and consumer-banking services. Also in 1990, the company started a new sawmill in DeQuincy, Louisiana, which produces chips for the Evadale and Orange mills, as well as 100 million board feet of lumber annually. In 1991 the company expanded and upgraded its recycled linerboard mill in Ontario, California.

Demand for paper products was seen to have been consistent during the late 1980s and early 1990s, and the demand for linerboard for corrugated boxes continued to increase. Containers and containerboard sales accounted for more than one-half of the company's profits. The smaller, but highly profitable bleached-pulp-and-paperboard division had seen a rise in demand. This division was one of the company's strongest segments, with bleached paperboard being used for many products, including paper cups and paper plates.

President and chief executive officer, Clifford Grum who became chairman in April 1991, has said that Temple-Inland will focus on new technology, including synthetic paper products such as heat-resistant microwave containers. He predicted that synthetic paper will play an increasingly important role in the future of the industry. Temple-Inland will work toward achieving an ecological balance for growing trees for economic use and preserving trees for nature, he said.

Principal Subsidiaries: Inland Container Corporation; Temple-Inland Forest Products Corporation; Temple-Inland Financial Services Inc.

Further Reading: "A Proud Tradition," Temple-Inland corporate typescript, [1984]; "Chronology of Temple-Inland Operations," Temple-Inland corporate typescript, 1990.

—Leslie C. Halpern

UNION CAMP CORPORATION

1600 Valley Road
Wayne, New Jersey 07470
U.S.A.
(201) 628-2000
Fax: (201) 628-2722

Public Company
Incorporated: 1956 as Union Bag–Camp Paper Corporation
Employees: 21,200
Sales: $2.84 billion
Stock Exchanges: New York Pacific

Union Camp Corporation manufactures a diverse range of products. Though historically associated with paper products, particularly paper bags, Union Camp is in addition a major producer of other packaging products, building materials, and chemicals. Mills at Savannah, Georgia, and at Prattville, Alabama, make unbleached paper and paperboard. Union Camp converts about two-thirds of its unbleached production into packaging materials and sells the rest to other companies. Mills at Franklin, Virginia, and at Eastover, South Carolina, make bleached paper and paperboard. Most of this is sold to others for producing printing and writing paper, envelopes, folding cartons, and business forms. Union Camp also makes its own folding cartons, plastic bags, and school supplies. For the construction industry, Union Camp produces southern pine lumber, plywood, and particleboard. Several Union Camp plants refine pulping by-products into chemicals, including turpentine, fatty acids, and fragrance and flavor ingredients.

Union Camp's roots can be traced to the Union Paper Bag Machine Company, formed in 1861 as a holding company whose goal was to monopolize patent rights on bag-making machinery and make money by licensing other companies to make bags. Francis Wolle, who in 1851 had invented the first paper-bag-making machine, was one of Union's partners. In the early 1870s Wheeler, Fisher & Company of Chicago, a Union licensee, was the undisputed industry leader in paper bags. In 1874 Union Bag & Paper Company was formed by the merger of Wheeler, Fisher and six other companies operating under Union Paper Bag Machine licenses, with Wheeler as president. In 1899, Union Paper Bag Machine Company and Union Bag & Paper combined to form the new Union Bag & Paper Company. The new $27 million manufacturing giant threatening to eliminate all competition in paper bags. Under

President L.G. Fisher, Union made four billion bags, accounting for 80% of the paper bags sold in the United States.

Union stagnated through the next decade. Profit dropped steadily from $1.5 million in 1899 to $43,000 in 1912. Stockholders' committees complained of a complicated and top-heavy financial structure and of stock watering and market rigging. This led to a change in management. In 1913 John S. Riegel of Riegel Bag & Paper Company, which had cooperated with Union in the past, was named president of Union. Riegel reorganized the company, and by 1914 profit was up but only to $365,000. Union's financial situation was such that recapitalization became necessary. Thus, Union Bag & Paper Company merged with Riegel Bag in 1916 and was renamed Union Bag & Paper Corporation. By 1920, between Riegel's work and increased war time demand, Union's profit was up to $3.3 million on sales of six billion bags, about one-third of which were sold in the United States.

Three revolutions in the industry affected Union between 1910 and 1930. The first, the trend toward fancy packaging, began around 1910, before which paper bags were usually unadorned. Union took full advantage of this trend and became a pioneer in custom bags at a time when people were just beginning to judge products by their packages.

The second revolution was the switch from sulfite pulp to sulfate pulp. According to legend, a Swedish worker accidentally treated some pulp with alkali instead of the acid intended. The result was a coarse brown paper that was much stronger than the greyish acid-treated paper. The new paper was called kraft, meaning strength in Swedish. This led to the third revolution, the shift from northern spruce to southern pine. Before 1911, southern pine had been used primarily for turpentine and railroad ties. That year, however, a man named Ed Mayo discovered that commercial sulfate pulp could be made from it. Because southern pine was much cheaper than northern spruce, the entire bag and wrapping-paper industry began to move south.

Union's response was mixed. As early as 1915 it was buying kraft in small amounts, but it was then mixed with sulfite. War profits had lulled Union management into a dangerous state of complacency, and the company was still making sulfite through 1927. In 1928 Union built a sulfate mill in Tacoma, Washington, while most of its major competitors had already moved south to take advantage of the much cheaper sulfate there. Union was forced to close the Tacoma mill the following year, losing about $2 million.

Having already disposed of its woodlands in Canada and Wisconsin, Union was left without any pulpwood reserves. It was therefore forced to rely on paper purchased from other companies and pulp imported from Scandinavia. Union's direction at this point seemed to be away from integrated manufacturing, toward conversion of others' materials. While the rest of the economy was booming, Union recorded deficits for five straight years beginning in 1926. Of the 33 billion bags sold in the United States in 1930, Union sold less than one-sixth.

Alexander (Sandy) Calder's presidency began in 1931. Calder had been with the company since 1913, working in sales, and had made his mark by securing the company's largest bag account, the F.W. Woolworth Company. In 1927 Calder had convinced Union to stop producing imitation kraft by combining sulfate and sulfite paper. When he became president in

1931 following Charles McMillen's resignation, Calder immediately cut wages and salaries by $100,000, the net result of which was its first profit in years. Other cuts followed, including cancellation of the costly Scandinavian pulp contract and renegotiation of the power rate at Union's Hudson Falls, New York, plant. A price war in 1932 led to another year's deficit, but Union was on its way back to profitability.

During the Depression Union continued to operate at capacity. Nevertheless, with stock prices at their lowest in 1930, Calder and his brother Lou Calder began buying up Union common stock, and by early 1934 they had majority control. This meant that Calder could move more boldly in his quest to catch up with the rest of the paper industry. Most importantly, he was able to finally move Union south. Construction on the Savannah, Georgia, pulp and paper mill began in 1935, and by mid-1936, the mill and the first papermaking machines were ready. Union and the third industry revolution had finally caught up with each other.

By 1938 Savannah had a modern bag plant and four huge papermaking machines. The mill ran seven days a week, three shifts a day, and could turn a tree into paper bags in 12 hours. This greatly increased production capacity enabled Union to expand into production of specialty bags, for example for coffee and sugar, and heavy-duty multi-wall shipping sacks, and for kraft board used for corrugated boxes. The availability of tremendous pine resources near Savannah also compensated for the loss of the small remaining Scandinavian pulp shipments that were cut off by the hazards of shipment early in World War II.

By the onset of World War II, Union was one of the foremost low-cost, integrated producers of heavy-paper products. It had closed or sold its older, less efficient plants, including those in Chicago and Los Angeles, and most of its shipping was done by water routes, less expensive than land shipment. The effects of the war on Union were not drastic. A labor shortage in the Savannah area brought about some increased costs. Unlike other industries, particularly metal, the paper industry did not increase its capacity substantially over that of peace time. Conversion of plants for the production of war necessities was not as necessary in paper as it was for metal products. The only other negative effect on Union was increased transportation costs.

The postwar period was prosperous for Union. A large box factory with two corrugating machines was built at Savannah in 1947. Box factories in Chicago and in Trenton, New Jersey, were also purchased that year. This new emphasis on boxes helped produce steady sales growth. By 1951, Union owned or leased over 700,000 acres of woodlands, which provided about two-thirds of its required pulp. Union encouraged tree farming in its supply area and started a forestry education program. The company also began to sell tall oil, a by-product of the wood-cooking process. It was used to make paint, varnish, other oils, ink, and linoleum.

In 1956 Union Bag & Paper Corporation merged with Camp Manufacturing Company. The new company was called Union Bag–Camp Paper Corporation. Alexander Calder was named chairman. Camp Manufacturing grew out of a Franklin, Virginia, lumber mill operated by the Camp family. Manufacturing had been continuous at that site since the 1850s. Camp Manufacturing itself was 70 years old at the time of the merger, and it owned 240,000 acres of southeast timberlands. The

merger brought Union into the field of bleached kraft paper, which is used for printing, fine paper, and consumer goods packaging. The combined company was organized into four major divisions: Union Bag and Paper, Union Board and Box, Union Chemical, and Camp.

In the years following the merger, Union Bag–Camp Paper sought to continue its expansion, acquiring Allied Container Corporation in 1957, Universal Paper Bag Company in 1958, and Highland Container Company in 1959. Some obstacles to this expansion existed, however. The Federal Trade Commission (FTC) challenged the merger between Union and Camp, as well as the combined company's subsequent acquisitions. The FTC charged that these moves illegally eliminated competition and concentrated manufacturing facilities and sales of linerboard and corrugating material. Union Bag–Camp Paper was forced to sell six plants when the case was finally settled in 1965.

Union was also hurt by a grocery-bag price war during these years. Prior to 1956, the grocery-bag market had been dominated by Union Bag, Crown Zellerbach, and Georgia-Pacific. By the late 1950s, however, smaller companies such as Gulf States Paper became very aggressive, reducing prices so much that they lured away long-time Union accounts. By early 1963, the price of grocery bags was just over half what it had been in 1957. Large-size sacks actually sold for less than the price of the paper they were made from, causing company managers to joke that profits would be better if the machines ran backwards, turning bags into kraft paper. Union's size and diversity enabled it to outlast the smaller companies, and in 1963, grocery bag prices began to rise again.

Under President Alexander (Sox) Calder Jr., son of the former president, Union Bag–Camp Paper showed a willingness to invest more money in its facilities than most of its competitors did, totaling nearly $140 million in capital expenditures between 1956 and 1962. One result of this action was the growth of the Savannah mill to be the largest of its type in the world, with a daily output of 2,400 tons of unbleached kraft paper and board. The company was able to get one-quarter of its wood at 10% to 15% below market cost because it now controlled nearly 1.2 million acres of woodland around Savannah and 300,000 acres more near the Franklin, Virginia, mill.

Through the 1960s the company's sales grew slowly but steadily, and it continued to collect land and companies, including River-Raisin Paper Company in 1960; Write Right Manufacturing Company, a school-supply and stationary producer, in 1961; and Nelio Chemicals, Inc., in 1964. The second half of the 1960s brought a surge of diversification to the company. In acknowledgement of its diverse nature, Union Bag–Camp Paper Corporation changed its name to Union Camp Corporation in 1966. A key move was the 1968 acquisition of Moore-Handley Inc., a chain of hardware and building supply stores in the Southeast, which provided a convenient way to market Union Camp's growing plywood and building products output. Union Camp also branched into real estate, in 1969, buying a 75% interest in Branigar Organization, a Chicago-based development group. Union began to exploit the valuable mineral resources in the land it controlled, forming Titianium Enterprises, a joint venture with American Cyanamid. The 1968 takeover of Pak-All Products, Inc. by Union brought it into the manufacture of all-plastic products for the first time.

By 1971 the nonpaper business segments accounted for 30% of Union's earnings. The 1970 acquisition of 60% of Tekton Corporation, a housing construction company, added to Union's involvement in real estate. In 1971 a joint venture was formed with Anglo-American Clays Corporation to investigate kaolin deposits on Union land. Under Samuel Kinney, elected president in 1972, Union increasingly sought to get more out of its vast land holdings than merely trees. The company began to develop "super interchanges" along Interstate 95 in Georgia and South Carolina. Called Oasis Villages, these areas contained golf courses, campgrounds and shops, in addition to the usual gas stations and motels. By leasing these areas to businesses, Union could earn $15,000 a year per acre, while it only earned about $5 a year per acre of trees.

In 1973 Union donated 50,000 acres of Virginia swampland to the Nature Conservancy, a nonprofit land-preservation group. The land is part of the Great Dismal Swamp that covers 250,000 acres straddling the border between Virginia and North Carolina. Union's acreage there was heavily wooded but did not show much commercial promise. The contribution allowed the company to deduct in excess of $12 million from its taxable earnings. This was the largest gift the Nature Conservancy had ever received, and the land, once partially owned by George Washington, was turned over to the Interior Department, to be operated as a wildlife refuge.

The industry suffered through the recession of the mid-1970s, during which the demand for both paper and lumber fell sharply. As the industry had been steadily adding production capacity, most paper and forestry companies found themselves in a bind, with production costs rising and paper prices falling. Union, however, had accumulated huge amounts of timber from its own land holdings over the previous few years. It was then in a position to save considerably by using this banked wood, while most other companies had already exhausted their supplies of cheap wood. Next Union began to harvest its 500,000 acres of southern pine, another cheap source of wood, which it had begun planting 25 years earlier. These inexpensive supplies helped Union out-earn most of its major competitors.

In 1976 Union Camp's sales exceeded $1 billion for the first time, at a time when most other paper companies were struggling. This was Union's reward for keeping facilities modern and for treating land as a financial asset rather than just a lumber source. While most of its competitors' machines were more than 20 years old, Union's averaged 11 years, and its kraft paper machines could shift easily from box-making to bag-making as market conditions indicated. Land was sold or leased if that transaction would be more profitable than timber production. That year Union Camp stood as the industry's lowest-cost producer, and its earnings over the last decade had grown twice as fast as the industry's average.

Weak prices for unbleached paper and board, plus production problems at some plants, made 1977 a slow year for Union Camp. The Moore-Handley stores had their best year, however, and overall the company's sales rose only slightly less than usual. The last few years of the decade saw sales continue to climb steadily, and several new plants were opened or acquired, including those at Houston and San Antonio, Texas, and at Kansas City, Missouri.

Through the early 1980s, Union Camp continued to pour hundreds of millions of dollars in capital into its facilities to maintain its high level of production efficiency. While the industry's operating rate dropped to 85.5% of capacity for 1982, Union's rate fell only to 90%. Under chairman Peter McLaughlin, the company drastically reduced its use of fossil fuels and by 1984 was generating two-thirds of its own energy needs, primarily using wood waste and spent pulping liquors as fuel. Union vastly increased its chemicals operations with the 1982 purchase of Bush Boake Allen, makers of fragrance and flavor chemicals.

In 1984 the sale of the Moore-Handley business was completed, reaffirming the company's commitment to its core paper, packaging, and chemicals businesses. The same year, production began at the huge new mill in Eastover, South Carolina. Profits in 1985, however, were only about half of the previous year's. Reasons for this included an extremely strong dollar, falling paper prices, increasing white-paper production capacity, and competition from foreign companies. This was followed, however, by several years of excellent profits, 1989's being triple the earnings of the off-year of 1985. Because of the $1.4 billion capital investment during this period, Union Camp's production rose by 17%, and its mills produced in general first-quality business paper at a much better rate than the industry as a whole. The company ended the 1980s by recording new highs in sales and earnings.

Union Camp's history is one of growth through emphasis on efficient and low-cost production, which is reflected in its long-standing policy of liberal investment in its facilities and careful attention to the value of its properties. Because of these strengths, Union Camp's chances for further growth and diversification seem secure in spite of the volatility of the forest products industry. The relationship between the paper industry and growing fields that rely heavily on computers, and therefore mountains of white paper, also holds promise for its future.

Principal Subsidiaries: Branitek Inc.; Branigar Organization, Inc.; Sherwood & James Advertising, Inc.; Transtates Properties, Inc.; Bush Boake Allen Ltd. (U.K.); Cartonajes Union, S.A. (Spain, 81%).

Further Reading: "Union Bag & Paper Corp.," *Fortune,* August 1937; "Brief History of Union Bag & Paper Corporation," Union Camp corporate typescript, [n.d.].

—Robert R. Jacobson

UNITED PAPER MILLS

UNITED PAPER MILLS LTD.
(Yhtyneet Paperitehtaat Oy)

P.O. Box 40
SF-37601 Valkeakoski
Suomi
Finland
(37) 7111
Fax: (37) 431 22

Wholly Owned Subsidiary of Repola Oy
Incorporated: 1920
Employees: 18,000
Sales: Fmk10.20 billion (US$2.81 billion)

Nearly two-thirds of United Paper Mills's output consists of paper, chemical pulp, and board. It also produces converted paper goods such as self-adhesive labels, industrial wraps, consumer packaging, sacks, and stationery, as well as sawn timber, windows and doors, talc, nickel concentrate, and chemicals. It became one of the three industrial groups of the new company Repola Oy, the largest private sector corporation in Finland, at the end of 1990, after 70 years as an independent company.

United Paper Mills was established in 1920, soon after Finland had achieved independence from Russia. Its founder, Rudolf Walden, had spent his early adult life first as an officer in the Russian army, then, in Finland from 1902, as an agent for Finnish paper companies in St. Petersburg. By 1916 he had become the largest single shareholder in AB Simpele, a paper company which had been founded ten years before to produce brown wrapping paper, and had moved on into making higher-quality printing and tissue papers out of chemically treated pulp. Simpele experienced a boom during World War I, only to run into difficulties as the mill closed down—like most of the country's industry—during the Finnish civil war in the early months of 1918. In the same year Walden became chairman of Simpele, and by 1920 the company was prosperous enough to buy two more mills and to expand its holdings of hydroelectric resources.

Walden had been agent for another paper company, Myllykoski Träsliperi AB, during his years in St. Petersburg. Claes Björnberg, who had founded the company in 1892, was retiring stricken by grief for his son Björn who had been killed during the civil war, and in 1918 his family invited Walden to take over as chairman and principal shareholder.

Both Simpele and Myllykoski Träsliperi required a steady source of sulfite pulp for their papermaking, and achieved this in 1919 by jointly acquiring the majority of shares in Jämsänkoski Oy, which had been operating a sulfite pulp mill since 1887. Walden became chairman of this company too, and took charge of planning for a merger of the three companies. Having already been minister of war, and founder of the Finnish army, he now became a member of the Finnish delegation to peace talks with the Soviets and so was not actually present at the first general meeting of Yhtyneet Paperitehtaat Oy—United Paper Mills Ltd.—in July 1920. As its chairman, and as the holder of about 26% of its shares, he was the unchallenged head of what was then Finland's second-largest papermaking enterprise.

After the civil war the three companies led by Walden had quickly reoriented themselves toward selling newsprint and other printing paper in Western Europe, so that the latter market took 80% of United Paper Mills's output in its founding year. Like other Finnish paper companies, it benefited from the policy of keeping the value of the Finnish markka low, which increased export earnings and kept the industry competitive with those of Sweden and Norway, even though Finnish products initially were of a lower quality.

When Walden returned from the treaty negotiations he discovered that about a third of the turnover at the sulfite mill in Jämsänkoski had been wasted on a disastrous attempt to increase production. Walden responded by taking over the managing directorship of the company, further concentrating power in his own hands and slowing down the pace of expansion at Jämsänkoski. The company next worked on increasing the fuel efficiency of its plants and reducing the amount of chemical pulp in the newsprint it produced, thus cutting production costs and placing itself in a position to take advantage of the upswing in demand which peaked in 1925. But other countries, especially Canada, were also increasing output, while setting up tariff barriers against imports. The need for still more cost-cutting impelled United Paper Mills to build its own small power station and a new groundwood mill between 1926 and 1929.

In 1924 Walden had become chairman of another company, AB Walkiakoski, which operated five mills for various wood products in Valkeakoski. It had started in 1872 with Finland's first integrated groundwood and paper mill, but had been so badly hit by the closing of trade with the Soviet Union during the upheavals of 1917–1919, and so mismanaged by speculators controlling the company from Helsinki, that its principal shareholder went bankrupt and Walden was brought in to rescue it. He decided to modernize its plant, to make it specialize in kraft paper, and eventually, in 1934, to see to its merger with United Paper Mills. The merger was followed by the laying of railway track from Toijala to Valkeakoski, of which United Paper Mills paid half the costs and which ended the mill's reliance on barges for transporting its products.

The opening of an enormous hydroelectric power station at Imatra in 1929 had ensured United Paper Mills enough electricity to permit further expansion. In 1931 it set up a subsidiary, Paperituote Oy, specializing in converting paper into sacks, envelopes, corrugated board, and other products. It acquired an up-to-date paper machine in 1932 and another in 1935, which were used to increase output so as to offset the impact of a 50% fall in newsprint prices between 1926 and

1934. Indeed, the Finnish paper industry as a whole—unlike its foreign competitors—went through the Depression of the early 1930s without stopping production, even temporarily, thanks to the modernization of plant undertaken in the 1920s, the effectiveness of the industry associations created and led by Walden, and the continuing reduction in the value of the markka. United Paper Mills did even better than the industry average in the latter half of the decade, when Finland became the world's largest exporter of paper since, while overall production doubled, the company's output nearly trebled. It now began to take part in joint ventures with other companies, such as the Rouhiala power station, opened in 1937; Sunila Oy, a sulfate pulp producer established in 1938; and Kuitu Oy, set up in 1936 to produce rayon and cellophane.

Walden was deeply hostile to labor unions and put a great deal of effort into securing his workers' loyalty from 1927 onwards, in line with the general policy of the Finnish paper industry. Skilled workers were offered annual bonuses of 10% of earnings in return for contracting not to go on strike, under a system which United Paper Mills retained until the late 1960s, although other companies abandoned it soon after World War II. The company appointed its first welfare officer in 1928. After 1933, partly because of the increasing influence of Walden's son Juuso in the company's affairs, wages at United Paper Mills rose above the industry average and a pension scheme was introduced. The company started a housing scheme for employees, providing building sites and special loans. The company also provided health care for its employees and contributed funds to local hospitals. Two other institutions flourished under Walden's paternalistic regime: the Lutheran church, for which Walden provided buildings, salaries, and administrative assistance in the parishes where the company had mills; and Suojeluskunta, the organization of defense volunteers, which became the main provider of leisure activities for his workers, alongside its women's equivalent, the Lotta-Svärd organization.

In October 1939 the Finnish government reacted to the Soviet invasion of its Baltic neighbors with a partial mobilization that took more than half the work force away from United Paper Mills. Against the advice of Walden and his close associate Marshal Mannerheim, the commander-in-chief, the government rejected Soviet demands for the lease of several Finnish islands, and Finland itself was then invaded in November. The winter war which followed ended in Finland's defeat in March 1940, and the cession of 8% of its land area to the Soviet Union. The lost lands had accounted for 12% of Finland's forests, 20% of its wood and pulp producing capacity, and 10% of its paper and paperboard capacity. They also included two of the company's small mills, the Rouhiula power station and another power plant, thus causing a drastic curtailment of its output. The company managed to compensate for this, to some extent, by expanding the activities of Paperituote Oy, creating an engineering subsidiary, Jylhävaara, named after one of the lost mills, and setting up Valke Oy to produce glue and window glass.

Having been Mannerheim's representative to the cabinet throughout the war, Walden now became defense minister, and had to appoint his son Juuso as managing director of the company while he retained the chairmanship. In September 1940 he joined with the prime minister, Marshal Mannerheim, and the foreign minister in secretly accepting Hitler's demand for the transit of German troops and material through Finland—the first step toward the German invasion of the Soviet Union, which began in June 1941, even as the Finnish government was claiming to be neutral. The Finnish army reconquered the lands ceded in 1940 and fought alongside the Germans until September 1944, when it signed an armistice with the Soviets. During these four years the United Paper Mills customers lost in the United Kingdom and the Americas were replaced by the enormous market of Nazi-occupied Europe now open to the company. It used some of its wartime profits to buy up hydroelectricity rights, mostly in north Finland, through the joint venture companies Tyrvään Oy and Pohjola Voima Oy, so that by 1944 it was the third-largest producer of hydroelectricity in Finland.

Under the terms of the 1947 peace treaty Finland ceded the same lands to Stalin as in 1940, so the company once again had to give up valuable assets. The company was also compelled to give up nearly a quarter of its remaining landholdings to the state for the resettling of refugees from those lands. On the other hand, the company's wartime profits had put it in a relatively strong position to deal with postwar conditions and to respond to the revival of demand for paper worldwide. The prices of paper products, as of other raw materials, rose sharply as the Korean War progressed, only to fall sharply at the end of 1951, causing a crisis throughout the Finnish paper industry.

As the Finnish economy grew, investment in the national electric grid and the railway network increased, allowing the company's Jämsänkoski mill to abandon its dependence on the vagaries of the Jämsä River for energy and transport alike. The company also received loans from the United States and the new World Bank to finance capital investment, but the high level of inflation in Finland, as elsewhere, and the levying of taxes on excess profits during the Korean War largely undermined their effects.

The immediate postwar period saw major changes in the company's management. In November 1944, after four years as defense minister, General Walden suffered a crippling stroke and had to withdraw from both politics and business. Juuso Walden carried on as managing director under the new chairman C.G. Björnberg, the head of the family which had invited General Walden in to run Myllykoski Träsliperi a quarter-century earlier and which now owned an even larger block of shares in United Paper Mills than did the Waldens themselves. Juuso Walden abandoned his father's hostility to the labor movement, at least partly in response to the 1945 elections, in which the communists won about a quarter of the seats and joined the government, and he was the leader of the employers' side in the negotiations for the industry's first collective bargaining agreement. By 1951 average wages in the industry had risen by nearly twice as much as the increase in the cost of living.

Juuso Walden's plans to expand production put him increasingly at odds with C.G. Björnberg, since any new share issue to finance such expansion would threaten the Björnberg family's dominant position. The consequent battles in the boardroom took on national importance when they were reported in the Finnish press as being between Finnish-speakers—like Walden—and Swedish-speakers—like the Björnbergs. Secret talks throughout 1951 led to the announcement in January 1952 of a final agreement on dividing United Paper Mills between the two factions, with the Björnbergs taking the Myllykoski mill and the company's shares in the sulfate pulp venture Sunila Oy, in return for surrendering their interests in United Paper Mills. Juuso Walden, still managing director, now took over chairmanship of the board of directors and the company's head office was moved from Myllyukoski to Valkeaoski.

In 1952, the company's first full year without the Myllykoski mills, production fell as debts increased following significant investment. A reduction in production costs and a gentle rise in export prices led to an improvement in 1953, though the situation was still considered unsatisfactory, and production costs in Norway and Sweden were still lower. Rationalization on the one hand, and a rise in export prices on the other, led to an improvement in the financial climate in 1954, and new records were achieved in 1955 in all the company's plants, especially at Simpele and at the new newsprint mill.

The Finnish economy was disrupted in March 1956 by a general strike, but overall production at United Paper Mills was again significantly higher. At the same time, the costs of labor, fuel, and transport all rose sharply after the general strike was settled, and Finland's weak balance of payments position made the import of some materials difficult. Production went on rising through to 1962, although unevenly, since occasional dry summers lowered the water level in the lakes, reducing the supply of hydroelectricity. In 1959, for example, the water shortage had the effect of raising the average price the company paid for power by 21%. The year 1959 also saw the company establishing a presence abroad with the founding of a subsidiary company, Oy United International.

Increases in production were not necessarily matched by improved financial results. Profits fell by nearly a quarter between 1961 and 1962. In general, the first half of the 1960s was not an easy time for United Paper Mills. United Paper Mills took part in Finnish and international agreements on restricting production of chemical pulp, newsprint, and kraft paper from 1962 to 1965 while costs rose steadily. National labor market agreements guaranteed wage increases in every year up to 1968, when the link to the cost of living index was abandoned, and the price of wood, still the company's chief raw material, rose every year from 1962 to 1965. Kaipola's fifth paper machine was brought over from the United States in the company's own ships and installed in 1964, and the opening of this new mill and reconstruction of others allowed the company to increase capacity and improve profits by 1966. Although the following year saw sales of newsprint in particular badly hit by a slump in West Germany and other markets, by 1969 the company's profits had improved again thanks to the devaluation of the Finnish markka in 1967. The company began a major investment program to reduce water pollution, starting with the installation of a waste-liquor plant, which had the additional benefit of producing a partial substitute for fuel oil.

Juuso Walden retired from his posts of chairman and managing director at the end of 1969, after 17 years in the former job and 30 in the latter. He died in 1972. His successor was Niilo Hakkarainen. Great changes were made to the company's organization after Walden's retirement and the whole company was reorganized into profit centers. A Joint Action Committee was created, with representatives of the plant workers, the office staff, and the management of the seven profit centers, to promote participation in the company's activities in welfare, training, and information. While the forest industry went through another downward cycle between 1970 and 1972 the company went on investing in plant, including a new board mill at Simpele. It also took over the plastic-films business of Säteri Oy and expanded these converting operations.

In the same period, however, the company had to dispose of its small subsidiary operations in Iceland and Italy and cease production of window glass at Valke. The depression was followed by a boom period from 1972 to 1974, and the Finnish forest industry benefited from the signing of free trade agreements with the European Community in Western Europe and Comecon in the East. In 1974, a new paper machine was installed at Jämsänkoski. As wood became scarcer and more expensive, the company led the paper industry in developing a new, lighter type of newsprint made from thermo-mechanical rather than chemical pulp, to reduce the paper's wood content and save on transport and storage costs.

The boom was shortlived, however, for the company's profits from the rising price of paper were soon affected by the combined recession and inflation that began to spread throughout its main customer countries in 1974. One result of the slump was the further disposal of foreign subsidiaries, leaving only one by 1975, Dowdings Ltd. in the United Kingdom. In its domestic profit centers United Paper Mills had to halt production and lay off workers for long periods throughout 1975. Once again subsidiaries were absorbed into the parent company, while the company also acquired the assets of Mikko Kaloinen Oy, which owned two sawmills that had ceased production. Overall output for 1975 was nearly 30% lower than in 1974, and matters improved only slightly in 1976, largely because Raf. Haarla Oy, a paper converter of which United Paper Mills had previously owned 10%, was merged with the company. The year 1977 was the fourth bad year in succession, made worse by the collapse in the price of chemical pulp.

Conditions began to improve for the company and the industry in 1978, although the cutting of prices to regain foreign market share contributed to the fall in the industry's level of investment to a third of what it had been in 1975. In 1979 the company was able to exceed its own production targets and to begin the restructuring of its operations, centered on an additional paper mill, at Jämsänkoski, with state aid in the form of regional development subsidies and relief on turnover tax.

In 1980, 60 years after Rudolf Walden had founded the company, his heirs—along with the other main shareholders, the Koskelo family—sold most of their holdings to a consortium of six companies, including the conglomerate Rauma-Repola Oy, with which the company was eventually to merge, and Kansallis-Osake-Pankki, one of Finland's leading banks, whose chief executive Jaakko Lassila had been chairman of the board at United Paper Mills since 1974. The company began expanding abroad once more, starting with the acquisition of paper converting companies in the United Kingdom and West Germany and the establishment of another German production subsidiary, Walki GmbH.

From 1981, however, recession struck the forest industry yet again, as production costs rose sharply and the construction industry's demand for timber declined. The subsequent upturn in conditions was symbolized by the establishment in 1983 of a new subsidiary, Shotton Paper Company Ltd., to run an integrated thermo-mechanical pulp and newsprint mill in the United Kingdom, which began production in 1985. For five successive years, 1984 to 1988, United Paper Mills showed excellent profits, while undertaking some reorganization of its activities, including setting up a joint venture in fiber processing with the Swedish company Sunds Defibrator AB, through selling the latter its Jylhävaara fiber processing machinery division; selling the rest of Jylhävaara engineering plant to Valmet Paper Machinery Inc., and building up holdings in pulp mills to secure its supplies.

After five years of success the company's profitability fell slightly in 1989 as it was making investments equivalent to 30% of turnover, the highest level in the company's history. New ventures included the building of a paper mill at Strasbourg in France, the magazine paper machine at Kaipola, a new newsprint mill and de-inking plant, also at Kaipola, which processes almost all of Finland's collected household waste paper and a similar installation at Shotton in the United Kingdom. The company also purchased another rival in the paper industry, Kajaani Oy, and then regrouped all its sawmills in Finland into one subsidiary.

The combination of mergers at home and acquisitions abroad the 1980s can be explained partly by the pattern of distribution of the company's output. Its main customers had long been in Western Europe, and by 1989, 52.6% of its output was going to the countries of the European Community, 23.3% was being sold inside Finland, 6.3% was going to other European Free Trade Association (EFTA) member states, and only 6% to the Comecon countries and 11.8% elsewhere. Given the moves toward greater integration within the European Community and the dependence of EFTA as a whole on that market, United Paper Mills, like many other Nordic companies, was bound to become involved in further attempts of expansion and diversification, in order to prepare for the fiercer and larger-scale competition which now seemed likely. During the first few months of 1990 Metsä-Serla, another leading company in the Finnish paper industry, made an unsuccessful hostile takeover bid for United Paper Mills, acquiring about 30% of its shares. Rauma-Repola Oy, which had

been a major shareholder since 1980, then built up its voting rights to 15.4%, and a proposal to merge with Rauma-Repola, defeated by Metsä-Serla in April, was accepted in June when Metsä-Serla was offered directorships of the merged company and an agreement on future cooperation. The new arrangements were sealed by Rauma-Repola's taking a 7% holding in Metsä-Serla.

In September 1990 Niilo Hakkarainen was succeeded as managing director by Olli Parola and preparations began for absorbing two divisions of Rauma-Repola, Rauma and Pori, as profit centers of United Paper Mills and for transferring the company's shares in Sunds Defibrator AB to Rauma Oy, which thus gained overall control of the Swedish firm. The net effect of these changes is that as from January 1, 1991, United Paper Mills, somewhat larger than before the merger, has been one of three industrial groups that form Repola Oy, the largest private sector company in Finland; the other groups are Rauma, which covers metals and engineering activities, and W. Rosenlew, which produces plastic packaging. During its 70 years as an independent company United Paper Mills was successfully transformed into the leading player in Finland's largest industrial sector, with considerable presence in the European market for paper products and, in more recent years, in production outside Finland too.

Principle Subsidiaries: Finnminerals Oy; Lohjan Paperi Oy; Oulux Oy; United Sawmills Ltd.; Stracel S.A. (France); Raflatac S.A. (France); Walki GmbH (Germany); Walkisoft GmbH (Germany); Shotton Paper Company plc (U.K.); Raflatac Ltd. (U.K.); Walki Converters Ltd. (U.K.); Walkisof U.K. Ltd. (U.K.).

Further Reading: Autio, Matti, and Toivo Nordberg, *A Century of Paper Making I*, Valkeakoski, United Paper Mills Ltd., 1973; Nordberg, Toivo, *A Century of Paper Making II*, Valkeakoski, United Paper Mills Ltd., 1982.

—Patrick Heenan

Westvāco

WESTVACO CORPORATION

Westvaco Building
299 Park Avenue
New York, New York 10171
U.S.A
(212) 688-5000
Fax: (212) 688-1385

Public Company
Incorporated: 1899 as West Virginia Pulp and Paper Company
Employees: 15,040
Sales: $2.41 billion
Stock Exchanges: New York Midwest Pacific

Westvaco Corporation produces printing papers and envelopes and consumer and industrial packaging. It also markets chemicals that are by-products of the paper production process. The company began with the advent of automated papermaking, using wood instead of cotton as its raw material; and it produced mainly printing paper for the domestic market until World War II. In the postwar era it integrated its production to make finished packaging products. It owns nearly 1.5 million acres of timberland. Westvaco has intensified its international presence, especially in Brazil. Less reliant on cyclical paper pricing, the company now exports almost 20% of its production. It spends heavily on research and marketing to locate markets worldwide.

Born into a Scottish papermaking family, Westvaco founder William Luke came to the United States in 1852. Ten years later he began running a plant for Jessup & Moore Paper Company in Harper's Ferry, West Virginia. Although employed by Jessup & Moore until 1898, he set up a small plant of his own with his two sons in 1889. Originally established in Piedmont, West Virginia, a shift in the Potomac River and a 1922 municipal name change eventually put the same facility in Luke, Maryland, where Westvaco in 1991 still operated a mill.

The mill was one of many mills that, during the late 1800s, imported and developed automated wood-pulping technologies. Called the Piedmont Pulp and Paper Company, it became the first commercially successful sulfite pulp mill in the United States. Eventually U.S. makers used the sulfite process to make 83% of their paper. The Piedmont plant employed 60, and by 1891 began production of printing paper under the name West Virginia Paper.

U.S. timber supply and automated processes lowered the price of paper and accelerated its consumption. In 1897 West Virginia Paper merged with West Virginia Pulp Company of Davis, West Virginia, and became West Virginia Pulp and Paper Company (WVPP). It expanded along with the U.S.'s growing demand, and it established a business headquarters in New York City. In addition to its white printing paper, it marketed pulp and chemical by-products. In 1904 William Luke relinquished the presidency of the company to his son John Luke, who held the position until 1921. William Luke died in 1912, at which time the company had four mills operating in West Virginia, Pennsylvania, Virginia, and New York.

During the post–World War I recession, prices plummeted and strikes hit two-thirds of the industry, including WVPP. Sales and earnings reached a record level, however, in 1920, which would be unequaled for 20 years.

While white-paper production volume remained relatively constant, diversification accounted for virtually all growth after World War I. The company produced its first kraft paper in 1921, the first year of David Luke's tenure as president. David Luke was another son of the founder. Used in U.S. packaging since 1907, kraft paper replaced many wood and textile shipping containers. As trees in the southern states were more suitable for kraft, between the world wars kraft production in the region skyrocketed. West Virginia's kraft output grew steadily for 15 years but then leveled off.

In 1929 WVPP introduced containerboard, a heavier, corrugated paper used for boxes. Federally approved for shipping in 1914, use of this material grew tremendously during the world wars.

During the 1920s WVPP began purchasing woodlands to supply its own wood pulp, but self-sufficiency in fiber supply remained a long-term prospect. By the 1930s very little virgin timber remained in the southern states. WVPP continued to buy land close to its mills and eventually owned extensive woodlands. The immaturity of the trees in its holdings, however, forced it to rely on outside suppliers for its pulp supply and prevented diversification into finished wood products.

Another son of William Luke, Thomas Luke, became president in 1934, inheriting a company with young diversification attempts and old mills. Three years later the company built a new mill to produce kraft and containerboard. By 1939 all five mills operated 24 hours per day.

The company's mills continued to operate at capacity throughout World War II. Wartime allocations made scarce the materials for expansion and repair, however. Although its facilities produced 20% more volume by war's end, WVPP's facilities emerged from the war badly in need of modernization.

Ascending to president in 1945, David L. Luke, a grandson of the founder, established the company's modern growth pattern. He immediately began the first of many expansion programs, spending the $17.5 million the company had accumulated during the war. The company also used some of its cash surplus to acquire more land, selling the trees too mature for papermaking to provide additional financing.

Wartime research greatly expanded paper's uses, particularly in containers. Postwar demand continued to grow so explosively that only production volume and market share concerned papermakers. The industry enjoyed favorable prices, consolidating competition, and growing demand in all areas of paper products.

The industry set high prices, required more prompt payment, and used the cash influx to build new mills during the late 1940s. Capacity caught up with demand by the late 1940s, and surpassed it by the mid-1950s, creating the need for more development leading to automation, product consistency, and new uses for paperboard. Although still reliant on white paper, WVPP put much of its postwar development efforts into these areas.

Profit margins in the commodity-based paper industry remained slim during the 1950s, and a company's technological efficiency determined its success. The cyclicality of the industry meant that for the next 30 years, papermakers invested in capacity additions. When they did so, they lowered prices precipitously. David L. Luke's expansion programs, however, coincided with the industry downturns. While occasionally requiring more debt than that to which the company was accustomed, automation allowed it to cut its work force for each of the next ten years.

The first major work stoppage since World War I occurred in 1952, when 4,000 employees struck. Labor relations flared up more frequently in the postwar era, decreasing earnings on occasion, well into the 1970s.

The company got more short-term use of its land in 1952 when it discovered a use for its hardwoods. Traditionally only younger and softwood trees had been used for paper. Hardwoods on WVPP's land holdings used for paper allowed the company to reduce production costs.

Encouraged by the premature utility of its land, over two years the company aggressively increased its holdings 75% to 749,000 acres. Most of the money spent on expansion in the 1950s, however, went to equipment modifications that the technology required.

WVPP sold its output mainly to companies that converted it to finished products. Priced as a commodity, paper prices often changed dramatically, making earnings erratic. Demand, however, constantly increased, providing a greater cash flow.

Use of paperboard, a noncorrugated material for consumer product containers, grew explosively during David L. Luke's presidency. Just as kraft paper and containerboard accounted for the company's prewar growth, paperboard made up most postwar growth.

The 1953 acquisition of Hinde & Dauch Paper Company, a box-maker, allowed WVPP to bypass distributors and represented the first major move toward integration. Hinde & Dauch (H&D) used WVPP's paperboard to produce its parent company's first finished paper products. Bleached paperboard was found to take colors as well as printing papers—making it highly adaptable to packaging uses. In 1955 WVPP purchased color presses to produce paperboard finished to client specifications.

West Virginia Pulp & Paper Company slowed expansion and improvement during the mid-1950s in its traditional sectors of printing papers, kraft, and containerboard, in favor of its new division. The company closed H&D's papermills but built more than 20 new assembly plants for it during the next 10 years, to make the most of H&D's knowledge of package design and experience with marketing finished products. These new plants provided the first increase in WVPP's work force since World War II. By constantly automating to reduce labor costs, its number of employees began to level off again by the early 1960s.

WVPP purchased a Brazilian paper-box maker in 1953. By the end of the 1950s, the Brazilian subsidiary financed its own production expansion with fewer employees.

Demand for white printing papers began its first large increase in decades in 1954 as a population boom and renewed prosperity increased consumption of printed materials. Demand for all paper products grew so explosively in the 1950s that by 1956 the industry could not meet demand. WVPP's earnings increased out of proportion to sales, peaking at $16.3 million in 1956 after five successive years of gains.

The industry responded by rapidly expanding its capacity. WVPP typically upgraded one machine at a time, rather than building or buying new mills. This method slowly consolidated production into larger and fewer facilities. By 1959 WVPP completed its largest spending program, doubling capacity at the Luke mill; but when domestic growth slowed, prices collapsed. Despite annual sales records, for the next five years WVPP's earnings fluctuated wildly—at one point dropping to as low as $8 million. Other factors that depleted earnings included new technology that produced more pulp from harvested trees, and price wars following the entry of forestry and container companies into paper. WVPP, which also sought to enter new markets, lowered prices as well.

Many companies waited for demand to catch up, but West Virginia Pulp & Paper continued its ten-year expansion plan. It focused on relatively inexpensive converting plants rather than mills, but its debt grew more sizable. The timing of the expansion speeded WVPP's recovery; by 1962 demand began to catch up to the capacity added in recent years. The spending program was completed and the company issued only $60 million in bonds.

The length of the industry's recession and the growth of H&D encouraged a renewed push toward finished products. In 1957 West Virginia purchased Virginia Folding Box Company, an assembler of cigarette packaging. It eagerly expanded the acquisition and reorganized itself into six divisions, four of which were in the business of converting: bleached boards, building boards, fine papers, H&D, kraft, and merchant paper. The company decentralized each division and provided each with its own sales force.

As new materials, particularly plastic, threatened to replace older forms of paper packaging, technical research intensified during the mid-1950s and the early 1960s. Higher than the industry average, WVPP's research expenditures enhanced its reputation for product development. Research-and-development spending quadrupled during the ten-year period, ending 1961 at $4 million annually.

WVPP pioneered several processes, including the use of electronic controls in production, the marketing of waste by-products in the chemicals division, the use of hardwoods, and the development of Clupak, a more elastic kraft paper. The company typically licensed or sold new technologies to pay for additional research.

By 1959 packaging grades of paper made up two-thirds of West Virginia's production volume. By 1960 the demand for office and printing papers—at one time WVPP's primary product—provided growth to the long-stagnant industry. Then oriented toward finished products and marketing, WVPP set up a separate sales force to sell directly to printers and paper converters.

When paper prices improved in the early 1960s, WVPP made the most of its recently completed investment program. The renewed efficiency and a change in its accounting method finally pushed 1965 earnings past the 1956 level. The downturn, however, had raised the competitive level of the industry. Like its competitors, WVPP came out of the late 1950s and early 1960s more diversified, integrated, and less production oriented.

WVPP exported negligibly until 1960, when 3% of sales went overseas. Although it did not pursue international markets actively for another 20 years, in 1962 it set up an international division to explore manufacturing possibilities abroad and established foreign subsidiaries in Europe and Australia.

David L. Luke retired in 1964. During his tenure the company had changed dramatically. At the end of World War II, West Virginia Pulp & Paper Company had produced commodity grades of paper for a few hundred customers, but by 1959 it had its own sales force selling a variety of finished paper products to a customer base of 11,000. The company had developed the marketing techniques and made the necessary acquisitions to get it started in finished conversion while keeping debt to a minimum.

Hesitant to join his family's company at first, David L. Luke's son David L. Luke III became CEO in 1963, after working 11 years for WVPP. He maintained the product-development momentum initiated by his father and continued to upgrade efficiency with frequent spending programs. Like the rest of the industry, however, he re-evaluated the use of debt in the coming decade. In 1962 the Luke family controlled 30% of the company's stock—by 1984 it controlled only 2%.

Still pursuing self-sufficiency in fiber supply, the company's land holdings were constantly becoming more productive. WVPP acquired its millionth acre in 1964. Research into forestry techniques produced hybrids that were not only more disease resistant but capable of growing three times the wood fiber per acre than the strains of 15 years earlier.

Shrinking timber reserves nationwide escalated land value further. Beginning in the late 1960s, WVPP developed land of commercial value and purchased additional timberland closer to its mills. Operating in 22 states, this latter strategy proved important when transportation costs inflated during the 1970s. Lower land values in the early 1970s allowed additional land purchases. Even though these lands provided only 10% of its raw material requirements, in the long term they stood to raise the degree of self-sufficiency.

During the mid-1960s, the growth rate in earnings once again outpaced sales. Operating near capacity once again, the company was able to reduce the debt it had assumed to complete its expansion program. Most of this investment went to make its three main mills more efficient. Nearly half of sales in 1967 came from products introduced in the previous ten years. This success and resulting heavier cash flow tempted the company to offer consumer products, a segment profiting several of its competitors. WVPP purchased C.A. Reed Company in 1968, maker of disposable paper products. Although the disposables market soared in the 1960s and 1970s, WVPP sold it after only seven years.

White printing papers used by business systems also boosted sales. Although the industry began to see overruns again, WVPP began another expansion program in 1967. It included the building of a new white paper mill in Kentucky. At $90

million, it was the largest project ever attempted by the company. In 1969 the company changed its name to Westvaco Corporation. Growing dependence worldwide on North American pulp and timber helped make Westvaco less dependent on the health of the domestic economy, exporting 10% of sales by the early 1970s.

Commodity-type production continued to plague the industry. In the early 1970s the industry suffered once again from too much capacity, higher production costs, and low prices. Tougher environmental standards and a weaker economy hastened closure of plants industry-wide. Westvaco closed plants, but its frequent incremental upgrades kept shut-down costs low. Leaner by default, turnaround came quickly.

During the early 1970s the government kept paper prices and labor costs stable but put a freeze on earnings as well. U.S. paper production reached record levels. By 1872 the government loosened its restrictions on papers somewhat, but fierce price competition negated a 4% price increase approval in 1971.

Wage and price controls were lifted altogether in 1974, allowing the industry to pass on production costs. Like the industry's recession in the early 1960s, these price controls contributed to integration, as producers sought to increase earnings in areas outside federal control, particularly finished paper products.

The paper industry was now increasingly responsible to federal regulations. The Federal Energy Administration forced Westvaco and 12 other paper companies to convert certain plants to coal burning from oil. The Department of Justice blocked an attempt by Westvaco to acquire the remainder of U.S. Envelope, the largest domestic producer of envelopes, of which Westvaco owned 58%. The paper industry had been investigated repeatedly for antitrust compliance and been named in private suits. Although Westvaco has settled suits out of court it had never been indicted.

In the ten years ending 1975, Westvaco almost doubled sales, while simultaneously reducing its work force. During the mid-1970s demand in all sectors began to catch up with capacity, but growing production costs dampened earnings.

Energy shortages of the early 1970s prompted Westvaco to turn to its land holdings once again by mining coal for its own consumption. By 1974 it achieved 40% fuel self-sufficiency by burning its own waste from the production process. Such conservation efforts would help earnings substantially in the late 1970s.

The 1980s were turnaround years for papermakers. The industry started to spend on capacity once again. Although Westvaco now converted more than one-third of its paper production in its own plants, growth in the use of the personal computer and in the publishing industry gave way to rapid increases in demand for Westvaco's traditional printing papers.

By the mid-1980s, Westvaco emerged from one of the worst five-year periods for the industry with six straight earnings records. In addition, it had completed its spending program. These programs drained earnings, but at their conclusion the company earnings jumped dramatically, and the company produced more paper with larger, more efficient units and less labor. David Luke III began four such programs in his 24 years as CEO.

By employing its own sales force, Westvaco diversified not by acquisition, but by tailoring products for customers.

Research and sales forces emphasized new uses for bleached board in microwave food packaging and liquids packaging.

During the mid-1980s, the company took a series of anti-takover steps. Although at record levels, debt was lower than in most companies in the forest-products and packaging industries. David Luke III's final spending program of $1.6 billion was financed 80% internally. Unlike those before it, the program intensified product development instead of production efficiency.

Westvaco set up trade offices in Tokyo and Hong Kong in the mid-1980s to tap the skyrocketing Asian and Pacific markets. Finished products paved the way for increased activity overseas, and by the late 1980s exports reached 15% of sales. The consistently profitable Brazil operations began to export, after holding 20% of Brazil's corrugated box market for decades.

Significant growth in the printing industry in the late 1980s led to capacity expansion. Westvaco emphasized heavier-weight printing papers, despite the industry's cyclicality, which forced buyers to cuts cost occasionally.

In 1988 John A. Luke succeeded his brother as CEO. Westvaco had done more than most papermakers since 1960 to free itself from the cyclicality of commodity production. Higher-margin end-products represented close to two-thirds of sales, giving Westvaco a more reliable return. Through the late 1980s continued growth in bleached paperboard and printing papers pushed earnings to record levels.

Westvaco's specialty products were easy to market overseas, and exports grew to 17% of sales when the domestic business fell in 1990. The United States, however, is the largest market for printing papers, so Westvaco would face growing competition from overseas. In addition, many other U.S. companies looked overseas for sales growth, forcing Westvaco to step-up foreign marketing as it became more reliant on revenues from abroad. Companies with land holdings in North America would fare well as the world comes to rely on trees from the region. Westvaco's holdings have served a variety of purposes in its past, turning to it for revenue and energy consumption, as well as for pulp.

Although the paper industry expects increased competition from plastics and electronics, both of these fields have increased paper consumption. Paper consumption has accelerated during the entire 20th century, particularly the post–World War II era. While plastics were once seen as a replacement for many paper applications, growing emphasis on recyclable materials and consumer interest in convenience foods can increase the use of paper, particularly in packaging.

Westvaco's leadership had emphasized long-term growth over short-term earnings. Westvaco's investment programs, for instance, conducted during downturns may have cut earnings, but they made recovery dramatic and fast. Westvaco had fared better than its competition by developing specialty products in all of its segments: printing papers, packaging, and chemicals. In the 1990s Westvaco will continue differentiating its products to avoid cyclical pricing and to hasten international marketing.

Principal Subsidiaries: Clupak, Inc. (50%); Upland Resources, Inc.; Westvaco Development Corp.; Westvaco Resources, Inc.; Rigesa, Ltda., (Brazil); Westvaco Asia, K.K. (Japan); Westvaco Canada, Ltd.; Westvaco Europe, S.A. (Belgium); Westvaco Foreign Sales Corporation (Belgium); Westvaco Hong Kong, Ltd.; Westvaco Pacific Pty. Ltd. (Australia).

Further Reading: Westvaco 1888–1988: *Centennial Recognition—The Early Years,* New York, Westvaco Corporation, 1988.

—Ray Walsh

Weyerhaeuser

WEYERHAEUSER COMPANY

Tacoma, Washington 98477
U.S.A.
(206) 924-2345
Fax: (206) 924-3355

Public Company
Incorporated: 1900 as Weyerhaeuser Timber Company
Employees: 40,621
Sales $9.02 billion
Stock Exchanges: Midwest New York Pacific Tokyo

Weyerhaeuser Company is the world's largest private owner of timber and the world's largest pulp and paper company. This diversified forest-products company owns six million acres of timberland in the United States and license for nine million acres in Canada. In 1990, with Weyerhaeuser's stock selling below breakup value and earnings below the industry average, the company reviewed its corporate strategy and reaffirmed its commitment to its historic strengths in paper and wood.

Weyerhaeuser Timber Company, headquartered in Tacoma, Washington, was incorporated in 1900 as a joint venture in Pacific Northwest timber by James J. Hill, railroad magnate and Frederick Weyerhaeuser, joint owner of Weyerhaeuser & Denkmann, a midwestern lumber company that relied on forests in Wisconsin and Minnesota. Weyerhaeuser remained privately owned, primarily by the Weyerhaeuser family, until 1963.

Prior to World War I, the company was dominated by Frederick Weyerhaeuser. A German-born immigrant to the Midwest prior to the Civil War, his business philosophy evolved over his lifetime, and it became the operating philosophy for the new company. Weyerhaeuser felt that "The way to make money is to let the other fellow make some too."

Timber holdings doubled in the pre–World War I period. The company opened a sawmill to produce lumber and soon had the nation's first all-electric lumber mill, in 1915. Company plans to market lumber on the east coast, using the new Panama Canal, were delayed until the end of World War I.

Although demand for lumber for railroad cars declined during World War I as steel was utilized, demand for lumber for military planes and other military uses increased. In the early days of the lumber mill, itinerant single men formed the core of the mill's laborers. Represented by the International Workers of the World (the Wobblies), they pushed for the eight-hour day, and other "revolutionary" ideals. A struggle resulted, and labor unrest threatened the war effort. To assure a steady

supply of lumber for war material, the federal government established a union for the industry, something never done before or since. The union, the Loyal Legion of Loggers and Lumbermen, prevailed in its demand for the eight-hour day and 40-hour week. The hours changed the work force; family men then constituted the core of workers in lumber.

The surplus of naval vessels at the end of the war allowed Weyerhaeuser to purchase ships at a reasonable cost to transport lumber to the east coast through the Panama Canal. Weyerhaeuser Sales Company had been established in 1916 to promote this postwar expansion of markets.

John P. Weyerhaeuser, eldest son of the founder, led the company during the war and through the 1920s. He relied heavily, as had his father, on George Long, general manager from 1900 to 1930. Long, an early proponent of reforestation, approached the federal government prior to the war to lobby for cooperative forest-fire prevention and for lower property taxes for timberland to make reforestation economically viable. This lobbying led to the Clark-McNary Act in 1924 that addressed these issues as well as expanded the national forest. It also encouraged changes in taxation policies at the state level to allow reforestation.

Weyerhaeuser responded by creating the Logged Off Land Company in 1925 to handle the sale of "logged off" land, to study reforestation, and to lobby at the state level for lower timberland taxes. As long as taxes were the same for all land, Weyerhaeuser felt compelled to sell logged off land and not to retain it for reforestation.

By the end of the 1920s, Weyerhaeuser was the largest private owner of timber in the United States. At the beginning of that decade, the company had produced its first national advertising campaign, promoting the lumber industry. By the decade's end, the company's advertisements focused on the recently upgraded quality of its lumber, by trademarking and grade-marking lumber, as well as taking more care in handling the lumber during shipment to market.

The Great Depression produced hard times for the company; few businesses or homes were built. The depression in the lumber market would have been devastating if not offset by diversification into pulp in 1931. By 1933, profits from pulp offset losses from lumber. The New Deal's Civilian Conservation Corps assisted in reforestation of logged off land in these years. State tax laws in the Pacific Northwest were amended to provide lower taxes for timberland, promoting reforestation. In 1940 the company started the first U.S. tree farm, near Gray's Harbor in Washington.

In 1935 the kidnapping of George Weyerhaeuser, the nine-year-old son of CEO John P. Weyerhaeuser Jr., catapulted the Weyerhaeuser family to national attention. The Weyerhaeuser kidnapping ended happily, the child safe, the ransom recovered, and the kidnappers apprehended. George Weyerhaeuser grew up to become president of his family's company.

In 1940 the company expanded its lumber business to include plywood and paneling. The Lend-Lease Program to assist the British prior to U.S. entry into World War II found Weyerhaeuser transport ships utilized to carry lend-lease materiel to the British in Egypt. During the war itself, the company served as an agent of the War Shipping Administration, directing 68 freighters and troop ships, of which two were sunk in combat. Women and minorities proved themselves competant as they became the company's work force during the war.

Rapid technological and commercial changes in the lumber industry after the war affected Weyerhaeuser. The hand-operated whipsaw was replaced by the power chain saw. Truck hauling replaced hauling by rail. Pent-up demand in construction, from the 1930s and early 1940s, led to greatly increased sales of lumber in this postwar era.

The company's organizational structure, highly informal and fraternal, was inadequate for rapid postwar expansion. More formal programs, reports, and the absorption of subsidiaries were instituted. A philanthropic foundation was established, and the Weyerhaeuser Real Estate Company replaced the Logged Off Land Company.

Under continued leadership of the Weyerhaeuser family, the company expanded into particle board production, ply-veneer, hardboard, and hardwood paneling in the 1950s. Timberland holdings expanded beyond the Pacific Northwest for the first time, as land was purchased in the South—in Mississippi, Alabama, and North Carolina.

Weyerhaeuser Sales Company, established in 1916, was absorbed into the parent company, and Weyerhaeuser International S.A. was created in 1958 to expand into foreign markets. The company dropped "Timber" from its official name to become Weyerhaeuser Company, and adopted its current trademark, a triangular tree over the word "Weyerhaeuser."

In 1960, for the first time in company history, the president was not a Weyerhaeuser, although new president Norton Clapp had family connections to the Weyerhaeusers. Under Clapp, the company went public in 1963. It expanded into the Japanese market as a result of surplus lumber involuntarily "logged" by Typhoon Frieda's 150-mile-per-hour winds in 1962. Weyerhaeuser's first overseas office was opened in Tokyo in 1963. In 1964 and 1965 European offices were opened respectively, in France and Belgium. The company acquired a wood-products distribution firm in Australia, and it entered into a joint venture for bleached kraft pulp in Canada.

Clapp was succeeded as CEO in 1966 by George Weyerhaeuser who served until 1988. Computers were introduced into operations in 1966. Growth per year in the high-yield forestry program doubled. The company contracted its first long-term debt. By the end of the 1960s, annual sales exceeded $1 billion.

The 1970s were years of phenomenal growth. In 1973 sales surpassed the $2 billion mark. Sales doubled in five years and doubled again before the end of the decade. In 1973, after six years of planning, the company finalized a joint venture with Jujo Paper Company of Tokyo. Weyerhaeuser also entered the disposable-diaper business in 1970; decided to centralize its research in Tacoma in 1975; and conducted an internal investigation to reinforce a corporate culture based on integrity and ethics. At the decade's end, the company concluded an agreement with China to work there on the world's largest reforestation effort. In 1979 company sales were $4.4 billion.

If the 1970s were a boom decade, the 1980s were a bust—at first. Tight credit in housing led to a depression in lumber similar to that in the 1930s. Just as the company survived the 1930s by diversifying into pulp, so its pulp and paper products helped it survive the early 1980s.

The volcanic eruption of Mount Saint Helens in May 1980 was disastrous to the company. Weyerhaeuser lost 68,000 acres of timberland. Weyerhaeuser's Saint Helens Tree Farm was just below the mountain's dome. Because the eruption took place on a Sunday, fewer workers were in the path of the devastation. Timberland values in the Northwest fell 75%. The company maintained dividends by diversifying into real estate and financial services.

Weyerhaeuser became the first U.S. forest products company listed on the Tokyo Stock Exchange in 1986. It was soon the third most-traded foreign stock there.

Downsizing and economizing were company policy in the 1980s. A dramatic example was the reduction of workers' compensation claims from $30 million to $10 million by 1990. This was done by taking proactive work-safety measures instead of reactive ones. The company introduced a plant-wide computer-integrated manufacturing system, expected to cut production costs. In 1989 the company produced the first Christmas trees grown by cloning. "Perfect" seedlings produced from super Douglas fir trees were grown on a Weyerhaeuser farm in Salem, Oregon, the product of 15 years of research.

In 1988, for only the second time in the company's history, a non-Weyerhaeuser took over the helm of the company. John Creighton joined the company in 1970 in real estate, and became president in 1988. He had no prior wood-products experience. George Weyerhaeuser became chairman.

Environmentalism has affected Weyerhaeuser in the past and will continue to do so. The company pioneered tree farming and recycled by-products as early as 1949, but its current practices of burning debris, using herbicides, and removing whole sections of forest are opposed by environmentalists. Exports of timber from federal forests in the United States are limited by law, and environmentalists hope to also impose similar limits on lumber logged from state and private forests. Such actions seriously affect Weyerhaeuser's international marketing of lumber.

Principal Subsidiaries: Weyerhaeuser Real Estate Company; Weyerhaeuser Financial Services, Inc.

Further Reading: Where the Future Grows, Tacoma, Washington, Weyerhaeuser Corporation, [1989].

—Ellen NicKenzie Lawson

WILLAMETTE INDUSTRIES, INC.

3800 First Interstate Tower
1300 Southwest Fifth Avenue
Portland, Oregon 97201
U.S.A.
(503) 227-5581
Fax: (503) 273-5603

Public Company
Incorporated: 1906 as Willamette Valley Lumber Company
Employees: 10,275
Sales: $1.90 billion
Stock Exchange: NASDAQ

Willamette Industries is a medium-sized forest-products company that pursues two main lines of business: paper products and building materials. Willamette manufactures 5.9% of the nation's bleached hardwood pulp, used for making fine white paper. Its three bag plants produce 7.3% of the nation's paper bags. More than 7.5% of the nation's plywood is manufactured at Willamette's 12 plants in the West and South. The company operates seven sawmills, that manufacture almost 1% of the nation's lumber. Other building materials produced by Willamette include particleboard, medium-density fiberboard, moisture-resistant board, color-coated board, and wood-grain-printed board. In 1991 the company operated 21 U.S. plants that make corrugated boxes and containers, and 7 plants dedicated to the production of business forms. Willamette owned over one million acres of timberland in Oregon, Arkansas, Louisiana, Texas, Tennessee, North Carolina, and South Carolina.

The company was first organized in 1906 in Dallas, Oregon, as the Willamette Valley Lumber Company. The company consisted of a sawmill, a small railroad, some logging equipment, and 1,200 acres of timberland. A pair of entrepeneurs, Louis and George Gerlinger, father and son, were two of the partners in the original corporation. The Gerlinger family retained an interest in Willamette in the 1990s when the company's chief executive officer and president was William Swindells, grandson of George Gerlinger.

The company grew enormously in its first 15 years. The original corporation, including timberland, mill, and equipment, had been founded with $50,000. In 1920 a half-interest in the company was offered for sale for $375,000. Net assets of the company were valued at $1.5 million at that time. The original sawmill had been expanded and improved, and the

Gerlingers had built a planing mill and drying kilns. The company owned more than 11,000 acres of timberland, containing over 334 million board feet of timber.

Some of the company's early prosperity, like that of other lumber companies in the Pacific Northwest, was due to a tremendous demand for timber following the United States's entry into World War I. Because the army needed spruce to build military aircraft, Pacific Northwest lumber companies were able to sell as much spruce as they could cut. Willamette benefited, although the company also suffered from the labor agitation that racked the industry.

Lumber workers in Oregon, Washington, and Idaho were strong supporters of the Industrial Workers of the World (IWW), a socialist labor union whose members were known as Wobblies. With much of the work force off to war and lumber production running at full capacity, many long-standing labor grievances were brought to a crisis point in 1917. Long hours, low pay, and unhealthy working conditions were the main points of contention. In the summer of 1917 the IWW organized a general strike throughout the Pacific northwestern lumber industry. In July 1917 a large grain elevator in Klamath Falls, Oregon, burned to the ground; the fire was attributed to IWW arson. A fire at Willamette's Balderee camp, creating more than $200,000 in damages, was thought to have been set by Wobblie provocateurs. This fire put a temporary stop to all logging in the county, and arson hysteria swept the area. The allegations of arson were never substantiated, although the governor of Oregon sent a special military force to the area to investigate.

Eventually the federal government stepped in, taking an unprecedented step to ensure continued production of lumber for the war effort. In November 1917, the government instituted the first federally sponsored labor union: the Loyal Legion of Loggers and Lumbermen. The Four L's, as it came to be called, worked quickly to recruit members from the IWW. Workers took a loyalty oath, swearing to faithfully support their company to produce logs and lumber for the construction of army planes and ships. The new union then wrested reforms from management. Workers were granted an eight-hour day, and improvements in living conditions followed. Never before or since had the federal government acted as a union organizer, but it seemed to be the only way to get the stumbling timber industry back on its feet. Throughout the war, Willamette's George Gerlinger served on the Loyal Legion's central committee. Recognizing the great contribution the Loyal Legion had made to labor relations, Gerlinger helped convince the industry to keep the union on after the war was over.

Willamette achieved a competitive edge early on by finding ways to utilize timber products ignored by other companies. Up to the 1940s, for example, hemlock was considered an unusable species of tree. Willamette's timber lands, however, were almost 30% hemlock, and the company found many uses for this wood, marketing the wood for ladders, refrigerators, and door moldings. In 1932 Willamette started selling its waste hemlock chips for papermaking. Chips that could not be sold were burned to produce power. Willamette's policy was to sell or use everything it cut, and this efficiency helped the company through the lean years of the Great Depression. The Willamette mill ran double shifts throughout the Depression, closing down only once because of lack of logs. Many larger lumber companies were much harder hit.

To stimulate the economy, President Franklin D. Roosevelt instituted the National Industrial Recovery Act (NIRA) in 1933, which called for regulation of prices and set production quotas for the lumber industry. Large companies wanted to hold production down in order to boost prices, so Willamette was ordered to shut down its second shift. Willamette's president, George Gerlinger, protested the quota to the National Recovery Administration in Washington, D.C., but his appeals were turned down. Willamette was forced to comply with the code, and 250 workers were laid off. Willamette's management, however, saw that while it could be forced to limit hours at its Dallas mill, the Lumber Code did not prevent the opening of new mills. Thus, the week after Gerlinger's appeal was denied by a federal court judge, Gerlinger announced that within the month Willamette would open a small-log mill, for which he rehired laid-off workers.

Gerlinger's son-in-law, William Swindells, bought an interest in Willamette in 1930 and began to learn the business. In 1935 Willamette bought the nearby Corvallis Lumber Company, and Swindells was named manager of this new venture. Willamette bought close to 10,000 acres of timberland in 1938, and acquired almost 4,000 more the next year. Despite a crippling fire in 1940, by the time the United States entered World War II, Willamette was again ready to produce as much timber as the government could buy for military ships and planes. When George Gerlinger died in 1948, Swindells took over as president. He continued the course of growth embarked on by Gerlinger.

After World War II, Willamette began to diversify. The company acquired a substantial interest in the Santiam Lumber Company in 1950. Willamette and Santiam set about to make a business out of selling their waste wood chips. In 1954 the two companies formed a third, the Western Kraft Corporation, which built a paper mill to process the chips for use in kraft paper. Willamette acquired the Western Veneer and Plywood Company in 1952. Another subsidiary of Willamette was the Western Corrugated Box Company, formed in 1955. A venture into another waste-wood product, particleboard, yielded the Wood Fiberboard Company in 1959. By the end of the 1950s, Willamette Valley Lumber Company had developed a solid base of timberlands and a network of related companies that processed every part of the tree.

These related companies continued to expand in the following decade. Paper, bag, and plywood mills were opened in the South and West. By 1967 it became clear that a merger of Willamette's subsidiaries and joint ventures into one large company would yield substantial savings in taxes and management costs. On March 3, 1967, five companies—Willamette Valley Lumber Company, Santiam Lumber Company, Wood Fiberboard Company, Western Veneer and Plywood Company, and Dallas Lumber and Supply Company—merged into one entity. The new company took the neutral name Columbia Forest Products, but it was changed a few weeks later to the present name, Willamette Industries, Inc. The Western Kraft Corporation became an 80%-owned subsidiary of the new company, until its outstanding shares were purchased in 1970. It too merged with the parent Willamette in 1973.

William Swindells Sr. was named president of the new company; Gene Knudson, a forester with Willamette since 1949, executive vice president; and two of Swindells's sons, William Jr. and George, were vice presidents. The newly consolidated

Willamette Industries surprised Wall Street with its success. In the ten years following the merger, Willamette's sales more than tripled, from $114 million in 1967 to $420 million in 1975. In 1972 Willamette acquired Hunt Lumber Company, in a stock swap. In 1976 the company's 444,000 acres of timberland still represented a fraction of the land its competitors owned, yet Willamette was consistently one of the most profitable corporations in the forest-products industry. Its management was expert at keeping costs down, and the company had achieved an excellent balance between its lumber and paper divisions. In general, paper and lumber run in opposite business cycles; that is, when building products are in high demand, paper products fall into a lull, and vice versa. As Willamette was spread evenly in both wood and paper, the company experienced relatively stable growth. Industry observers noted that Willamette enjoyed one of the most balanced mixes of paper and building materials in the entire forest-products field during the post-merger decade.

Willamette Industries made a major acquisition in 1980, purchasing the Woodard-Walker Lumber Company in northern Louisiana for $85 million, giving Willamette two new plywood plants and approximately 50,000 more acres of timberland. The company then owned a total of more than 550,000 more acres of timber. Aware that worldwide resources were waning, Willamette increased attention to its long-standing policy of careful and efficient management of its trees.

The only significant lag in Willamette's steady growth since the late 1960s was caused by antitrust litigation. In 1972 plywood buyers brought a class-action suit against more than 50 plywood producers, including Willamette. The suit charged producers with conspiring to fix freight rates. In 1978 a jury found Willamette, Weyerhauser, and Georgia-Pacific guilty of billing their plywood customers as if the product had been shipped form the Pacific Northwest, even though the transaction might involve buyers in Mississippi and sellers in Louisiana. The case dragged through several appeals, until in 1982 Willamette agreed to pay a $29 million settlement. Earnings from operations were low in 1982, and with payment of the settlement, he company sustained its first loss in 75 years.

William Swindells Sr. retired in 1976. Gene Knudson then became chairman and chief executive officer. William Swindells Jr. took over leadership of the company in 1980. He was promoted to president and chief operations officer when Knudson made plans to retire.

Throughout Willamette's history, the company has attempted to provide stable employment for its work force. Even during the Great Depression the Willamette mill closed down only once. In the 1980s, however, labor relations grew more strained. Several strikes hit Willamette mills in the Pacific Northwest and in the South. As demand for forest products lessened worldwide, many Pacific Northwest lumber companies had to cut production. Willamette workers in Oregon struck in 1986 and 1988, but eventually settled for contracts that reduced average hourly wages.

Several Willamette sawmills closed in 1989 and 1990. Political decisions restricting timber supply and the limited availability of quality softwood and hardwood logs led to the shutdown of mills in Sweet Home, Oregon; Moncure, North Carolina; and Chester, South Carolina. Meanwhile, the company began to build vertically integrated operations in North Carolina and South Carolina in 1987. The company also continued to grow in nonhardwood areas. A new hardwood-and-softwood-mix fine-paper mill in Marlboro County, South Carolina, opened in 1990, and the company began construction of a medium-density-fiberboard plant at the same location. A new plant to make corrugated containers in the Houston, Texas, area was also completed in 1991.

In 1991 increasing public concerns about the environment and dwindling timber supply threatened an end to the years of uninterrupted growth at Willamette Industries. The company's hallmark, however, has always been its efficient use of timber resources. Because Willamette manufactures a complete line of wood products, from paper to lumber, the company has the flexibility to adapt to rapidly changing markets. Moreover, the company's management has generations of timber experience behind it.

Principal Subsidiaries: Willamette Timber Company, Inc., Penntech Papers, Inc.

Further Reading: Baldwin, Catherine A., *Making the Most of the Best: Willamette Industries' Seventy-Five Years,* Portland, Oregon, Willamette Industries, 1982.

—Angela Woodward

PETROLEUM

ABU DHABI NATIONAL OIL COMPANY
AMERADA HESS CORPORATION
AMOCO CORPORATION
ASHLAND OIL, INC.
ATLANTIC RICHFIELD COMPANY
BRITISH PETROLEUM COMPANY PLC
BURMAH CASTROL PLC
CHEVRON CORPORATION
CHINESE PETROLEUM CORPORATION
CITGO PETROLEUM CORPORATION
THE COASTAL CORPORATION
COMPAÑIA ESPAÑOLA DE
     PETRÓLEOS S.A.
CONOCO INC.
COSMO OIL CO., LTD.
DEN NORSKE STATS OLJESELSKAP AS
DIAMOND SHAMROCK, INC.
EGYPTIAN GENERAL PETROLUEM
     CORPORATION
EMPRESA COLOMBIANA DE PETRÓLEOS
ENTE NAZIONALE IDROCARBURI
ENTREPRISE NATIONALE SONATRACH
EXXON CORPORATION
GENERAL SEKIYU K.K.
IDEMITSU KOSAN K.K.
IMPERIAL OIL LIMITED
INDIAN OIL CORPORATION LTD.
KANEMATSU CORPORATION
KERR-MCGEE CORPORATION
KOCH INDUSTRIES, INC.
KUWAIT PETROLEUM CORPORATION
LIBYAN NATIONAL OIL CORPORATION
LYONDELL PETROCHEMICAL COMPANY
MAPCO INC.
MITSUBISHI OIL CO., LTD.
MOBIL CORPORATION
NATIONAL IRANIAN OIL COMPANY
NESTE OY
NIGERIAN NATIONAL PETROLEUM
     CORPORATION

NIPPON MINING CO., LTD.
NIPPON OIL COMPANY, LIMITED
OCCIDENTAL PETROLEUM CORPORATION
OIL AND NATURAL GAS COMMISSION
ÖMV AKTIENGESELLSCHAFT
PENNZOIL COMPANY
PERTAMINA
PETRO-CANADA LIMITED
PETROFINA
PETRÓLEO BRASILEIRO S.A.
PETRÓLEOS DE PORTUGAL S.A.
PETRÓLEOS DE VENEZUELA S.A.
PETRÓLEOS DEL ECUADOR
PETRÓLEOS MEXICANOS
PETROLEUM DEVELOPMENT OMAN LLC
PETRONAS
PHILLIPS PETROLEUM COMPANY
QATAR GENERAL PETROLEUM
     CORPORATION
REPSOL SA
ROYAL DUTCH PETROLEUM COMPANY/
     THE "SHELL" TRANSPORT AND
     TRADING COMPANY P.L.C.
SASOL LIMITED
SAUDI ARABIAN OIL COMPANY
SHELL OIL COMPANY
SHOWA SHELL SEKIYU K.K.
SOCIÉTÉ NATIONALE ELF AQUITAINE
SUN COMPANY, INC.
TEXACO INC.
TONEN CORPORATION
TOTAL COMPAGNIE FRANÇAISE DES
     PÉTROLES S.A.
TÜRKIYE PETROLLERI ANONIM
     ORTAKLIĞI
ULTRAMAR PLC
UNOCAL CORPORATION
USX CORPORATION
THE WILLIAMS COMPANIES, INC.
YPF SOCIEDAD ANÓNIMA

ABU DHABI NATIONAL OIL COMPANY

Post Office Box 898
Abu Dhabi
United Arab Emirates
(2) 666000

State-Owned Company
Incorporated: 1971
Employees: 19,303 (1988)

The Abu Dhabi National Oil Company (ADNOC) is a state-owned enterprise engaged in all phases of the oil industry. It has a complex and intricate holding company structure involving, in a manner unusual for Middle East oil companies, equity links with large Western oil enterprises. Abu Dhabi is the largest of the seven states that formed the United Arab Emirates (UAE) in 1971, and it is the heart of the UAE's oil industry.

Although ADNOC dates only from 1971, it is necessary to understand the historical development of Abu Dhabi's oil industry in order to understand the present structure of ADNOC. Abu Dhabi was a latecomer to the Middle Eastern oil industry, only beginning production in 1962. However, the search for oil had begun nearly 30 years earlier. As elsewhere in the Middle East, this search was in the hands of foreign oil interests organized in a consortium. In 1928 a group of U.K., Anglo-Dutch, and U.S. international oil companies formed the Iraq Petroleum Company (IPC) with a concession which came to cover most of Iraq. Once the Iraq Petroleum Company was formed, each partner agreed that it would not hold concessions in any other part of the former territory of the Ottoman Empire except in association with all the other partners, and in the same proportions as the Iraq Petroleum Company. Most of the Persian Gulf states, including Abu Dhabi but excluding Kuwait, were included in this nebulous area. The oil companies involved marked in red on a map the boundary of the area to which they intended the agreement to apply, and it became known as the Red Line Agreement. Thus, when attention turned to searching for oil in the Trucial States—as the UAE was known until 1971—a consortium with exactly the same ownership structure as IPC was formed. In 1935 a new U.K. company was formed, Petroleum Development (Trucial States) Ltd., commonly referred to as PDTC. PDTC's ownership was identical to that of IPC, with the Anglo-Persian Oil Company (later British Petroleum), Shell, Compagnie Française des Pétroles, and a group of two U.S. companies—Exxon and Mobil Oil—owning 23.75% each of the shares, and investor Calouste Gulbenkian's interests the remaining 5%. PDTC contacted all the sheikdoms offering arrangements for concession rights to explore for oil, and to develop production should oil be found. In January 1939 Abu Dhabi granted PDTC such concessions for a period of 75 years.

Oil exploration in Abu Dhabi was slow to get started. It was delayed first by World War II. Thereafter, the IPC group focused on the search for oil in Qatar, where oil exports began in 1949. Knowledge of the geology of the emirate was limited, and economic conditions there were very underdeveloped. The town of Abu Dhabi itself was no more than a tiny village, and there were no roads in the entire emirate in the 1950s. Drilling finally began in 1950, but the search for oil proved a prolonged one. In July 1953 a well was drilled in the Bab field in Murban, south of Tarif, but mechanical difficulties led to its being abandoned despite evidence of the presence of oil. Further drilling at Bab finally established the potential of the field by 1960. The Bu Hasa field was proved soon after when oil was discovered in commercial quantities, and exports started in 1963. In the following years, PDTC relinquished its concessions in the other Trucial States to concentrate its efforts on Abu Dhabi. In 1963, PDTC was renamed the Abu Dhabi Petroleum Company (ADPC).

Meanwhile, oil had also been discovered offshore by other companies. In 1951 Abu Dhabi had established that the concession granted to PDTC did not include the continental shelf belonging to the emirate. As a result, Abu Dhabi granted a concession to cover the offshore territory first to the International Marine Oil Company, which failed to achieve results, and then, in 1954, to Abu Dhabi Marine Areas Ltd. (ADMA), a new company two-thirds owned by British Petroleum (BP) and one-third by Compagnie Française des Pétroles. In 1959 ADMA's drilling barge struck oil at Umm Shaif, which is located 80 miles into the gulf near Das Island. In 1962 the first shipment of oil was loaded from Das Island. The onshore and offshore oil discoveries made Abu Dhabi a large-scale oil producer. Its oil production grew from zero in 1960 to 102.8 million barrels in 1965, and 253.7 million barrels in 1970. By that date its production was one of the largest in the Middle East, and about one-quarter of that of Kuwait.

During the late 1960s there was growing resentment in Abu Dhabi, as elsewhere in the Middle East, of foreign ownership of oil resources, and especially the consortium system. The government concluded a 50–50 profit-sharing agreement with ADPC and ADMA in 1965 and 1966, respectively. In 1971 the government established the Abu Dhabi National Oil Company (ADNOC) as a wholly state-owned company. Following the formation of the Organization of Petroleum Exporting Countries (OPEC), Abu Dhabi followed the general policy of requesting participation in the foreign oil companies active in its territory. ADNOC acquired, effective January 1, 1973, 25% of the assets of ADPC and ADMA. The finalization of the ADMA participation agreement was complicated by BP's announcement in December of 1972 of the sale of a 30% interest in ADMA to the Japan Oil Development Co. (Jadco), formed by a consortium of Japanese companies. The government withheld its approval of this deal until March 1973, when BP agreed to finance the construction of an ADNOC-owned refinery in Abu Dhabi. By a further agreement in December 1974, the ADNOC interest in the ADPC and ADMA concessions was raised to 60%. These two companies were later reincorporated as Abu Dhabi Company for Onshore Oil Operation and Abu Dhabi Marine Operating Company.

Abu Dhabi was distinctive among the OPEC members in the gulf in retaining the former concessionaire companies as equity holders in the operating enterprises. It did not, as elsewhere, seek to remove foreign ownership entirely. ADNOC, therefore, developed as a holding company with an intricate web of majority and minority equity stakes in other producing companies. The government was motivated in this strategy by a desire to pursue production and exploration as energetically as possible. As part of this aim, from the 1960s various new concessions were granted to mostly independent oil companies in areas relinquished by ADPC and ADMA, all of which included provisions for ADNOC to have the option to take up to 60% interest in successful ventures.

ADNOC established subsidiary companies specialized in the various sectors of the oil industry. In 1973 Abu Dhabi National Oil Company for Distribution was created to take over the marketing of oil products within Abu Dhabi, which was formerly in the hands of the Western oil companies. Abu Dhabi National Tankers was founded in 1975 to operate a tanker fleet. In 1973 the Abu Dhabi Gas Liquefaction Company was formed, owned 51% by ADNOC, 22% by Mitsui, around 16% by BP, around 8% by Compagnie Française des Pétroles, and 2% by Bridgestone Liquefied Gas. The gas liquefaction company opened a plant on Das Island in 1977 to process gas from the main offshore oilfields. ADNOC was also anxious that Abu Dhabi should have its own refinery capacity. ADNOC's first oil refinery—situated at Umm Al Nar—opened in 1976, and in 1981 the company opened a second refinery at Ruwais. These plants made the UAE self-sufficient in refined petroleum products, with a surplus to export. In 1990 the two refineries had a combined capacity of 180,000 barrels per day, while domestic UAE consumption was about 80,000 barrels per day of refined products.

ADNOC also diversified overseas, again favoring joint venture and mixed ownership structures. Together with the Pakistani government, ADNOC formed Pak Arab Fertilizers Ltd., which started producing chemical fertilizers in Pakistan in 1978 and, by 1983, was producing 290,000 tons of calcium ammonia nitrate, 350,000 tons of nitrophosphate, and 50,000 tons of urea. The Pak Arab Refinery, another joint venture between ADNOC and the Pakistani government, started production in 1981. However, by 1990 ADNOC's foreign ventures remained much less substantial than those of the Kuwait Petroleum Corporation.

The 1980s were an unsettled period for the world oil industry, and Abu Dhabi could not isolate itself from the general problems. Demand for OPEC oil fell sharply by about 45% in the first half of the decade. Producer states such as Abu Dhabi found themselves—and their state oil companies—with large bureaucracies which were slow to respond to changing circumstances. In 1988 the UAE restructured its oil administration with the aim of cutting out some of this bureaucracy. The department of petroleum was abolished, and a new higher council of petroleum was created. The organization of AD-NOC was restructured as part of this process. ADNOC's board was replaced by an 11-member petroleum council, and Sohal Fares al-Mazrui was appointed as ADNOC general manager and secretary general to the higher council, chaired by UAE's president, Shaikh Zayed. The move was designed to improve relations between ADNOC and its foreign equity partners, as well as to bring the industry under closer government control. During 1989 Mazrui was also appointed head of the Abu Dhabi National Oil Company for Distribution. During 1987 and 1988 oil exploration and development were virtually halted, but in 1989 a series of new projects were given the go-ahead.

ADNOC has developed as one of the better managed state oil companies. The strategy of alliances with Western oil companies has given it access to skills and technologies which would have been hard to generate internally. Abu Dhabi's huge oil reserves have also placed ADNOC in a powerful competitive position. In terms of sheer production capacity, ADCO in 1990 had achieved the ranks of the world's ten largest oil companies, with a sustainable output of around one million barrels per day, and sufficiently large oil reserves to enable it to keep operating for over 100 years at 1990 production levels. The 1988 restructuring had enhanced the efficiency of the operating affiliates, and ADCO was able to claim that its cost of producing a barrel of oil was one of the lowest in the world. The enormous damage done to neighboring Kuwait's oil production and refining facilities during the Iraqi invasion and occupation of that country between August 1990 and February 1991 enhanced the competitive advantages of the Abu Dhabi oil industry, at least in the short term, but it also served as a reminder of the political uncertainties of the gulf region.

Principal Subsidiaries: Abu Dhabi National Oil Company for Distribution; National Drilling Company; Abu Dhabi National Tankers Company; Abu Dhabi Drilling Chemicals & Products Company Ltd. (75%); National Petroleum Construction Company (70%); Abu Dhabi Gas Industries Ltd. (68%); Ruwais Fertilizers Industries Ltd. (66.67%); Abu Dhabi Company for Onshore Oil Operations (60%); Abu Dhabi Marine Operating Company (60%); Abu Dhabi Petroleum Ports Operating Company (60%); National Marine Services (60%); Abu Dhabi Gas Liquefaction Company Ltd. (51%); Liquefied Gas Shipping Company Ltd. (51%); Umm Al-Daikh Development Company (50%); Zakum Development Company (50%); Pak Arab Fertilizers Ltd. (48%); Pak Arab Refinery (40%); Arab Petroleum Pipelines Company (15%).

Further Reading: Al-Otaiba, Mana Saeed, *Petroleum and the Economy of the United Arab Emirates,* London, Croom Helm, 1977; Mallakh, Ragaei El, *The Economic Development of the United Arab Emirates,* London, Croom Helm, 1981; Luciani, Giacomo, *The Oil Companies and the Arab World,* London, Croom Helm, 1984; Evans, John, *OPEC. Its Member States and the World Energy Markets,* London, Longmans, 1986.

—Geoffrey Jones

AMERADA HESS CORPORATION

1185 Avenue of the Americas
New York, New York 10036
U.S.A.
(212) 997-8500
Fax: (212) 536-8390

Public Company
Incorporated: 1920 as Amerada Corporation
Employees: 9,645
Sales: $7.08 billion
Stock Exchanges: New York Montreal Toronto

Amerada Hess is one of the largest integrated petroleum companies not considered one of the "majors." It engages in petroleum exploration, production, refining, transportation, and service station retailing.

The Amerada Hess story begins with the English oil entrepreneur, Lord Cowdray, who early in 1919 set up the Amerada Corporation to explore for petroleum in the United States, Canada, and Central America. At this time Everette DeGolyer, a geophysicist and engineer with a record of important technical innovations, was made Amerada's first vice president and general manager. DeGolyer repeatedly stressed the importance of both geological competence and the then–newly evolving technologies of gravimetric and seismic reflection exploration, arguing that Amerada's ultimate success lay in making accurate and timely scientific estimates and appraisals of oil well production, as well as in the equally difficult economic estimates of oil market futures.

The company's first operations centered around wildcat and development fields in Kansas, Oklahoma, Texas, Louisiana, and Alabama. As well as having ties to the Mexican Eagle Oil Company, by 1920 Amerada Corporation controlled two subsidiaries, Goodrich Oil Company and Cameron Oil Company. Early successes were in major fields in Kansas, such as the Urschel; and in Oklahoma, the Osage, Seminole, Cromwell, and others. In 1923 DeGolyer was one of the first and most vocal advocates for systematic, as opposed to prior guesswork, exploration for certain kinds of oil traps around salt domes, frequently found in the Gulf of Mexico states. After state, congressional, and private rumblings about the large land and financial holdings of foreign-controlled oil companies in the United States, between 1924 and 1926 Lord Cowdray sold Amerada stock on the United States market at $26 a share,

principally through the Rycade Corporation, to fund the acquisition of oil field holdings in Texas.

As many explorationists and historians acknowledge, much of the drama and success of the Amerada Corporation before and during the Depression was tied closely to its pioneering use of geophysical exploration methods. In 1922 DeGolyer conducted what was apparently the first survey of an oil deposit at the famous Spindletop Salt Dome in Texas using advanced geophysical techniques. To further develop and perfect these methods, in 1925, after oil's recovery for approximately 50¢ to $3.00 a barrel, DeGolyer together with J. Clarence Karcher organized a subsidiary company, Geophysical Research Corporation (GRC) of New Jersey, which established numerous patents and which eventually spawned Geophysical Service, Incorporated, now Texas Instruments. Pioneering many early joint ventures, Amerada's first major success in new field prospecting by geophysical methods came with the discovery of the Nash dome, along with ten others elsewhere, on a lease held by Louisiana Land and Exploration Company (LL&E), systematically exploring over three million acres of south Louisiana swamps in a fraction of the time of prior surveys. GRC undertook another major survey for Amerada Corporation in 1927 and 1928, finding oil deposits in the Wilcox sands, which had been missed by many other major and independent oil companies. DeGolyer's innovations and discoveries led to his becoming president in 1929, and in 1930 chairman of the board of Amerada. Notwithstanding continued exploration successes because of geophysical innovations developed during the Depression, in 1932 DeGolyer resigned from the company to continue work as an independent consultant and exploration company.

After extensive joint seismic exploration survey in 1933, Amerada and Stanolind Oil & Gas made the first discoveries in the famous Katy, Texas, oil and gas fields. Further extension surveys led to other discoveries near Houston, Texas. In 1945 Amerada was responsible for finding another major reservoir in the west Texas Permian Basin. The history of the famous North Dakota Williston Basin oil fields emerged into geological and public attention when Amerada, between 1951 and 1953, completed major reconnaissance seismic surveys leading to an important wildcat discovery, in the Nesson anticline.

In 1941 Amerada Corporation merged with its principal operating subsidiary and became Amerada Petroleum Corporation. Through the World War II period Amerada operated exclusively within the United States and Canada. In December 1948 Amerada Petroleum Corporation; Continental Oil Company, now Conoco; and Ohio Oil Company, now Marathon, formed the Conorada Petroleum Corporation. Conorada was charged with petroleum exploration outside the United States and Canada, and negotiated major concessions in Egypt around the Qatiara Depression near the Libyan border. In January 1963 Amerada acquired the stock interests of Conorada held by Conoco and Marathon, becoming full owner of Conorada. In 1964 Amerada joined with Marathon, Continental, and Shell, to form the major Oasis petroleum consortium in Libya, reportedly holding half of Libyan production—estimated at one million barrels a day—and paying only 30¢ a barrel in taxes compared to Exxon's 90¢.

In 1950 Amerada became active in petroleum pipelining and refining. By 1954 Amerada Petroleum Corporation was one of a group of small producers that sold its output at the well-head.

Fortune, on July 15, 1966, reported that since 1957 Amerada Petroleum had ranked first in profit margin on crude oil and natural gas, holding full or partial interest in over six million acres in both the United States and Canada, and some 68 million acres overseas. During this period Amerada Petroleum had been producing natural gas in the North Sea in partnership with Standard Oil Company of Indiana. In the spring of 1966, Leon Hess bought nearly 10% of Amerada's outstanding common stock from the Bank of England, which had acquired it during World War II.

Shortly before World War II, Leon Hess had initiated expansion of his father's original fuel oil business. His father, Mores Hess, founded the small business in 1925. In the late 1930s Leon Hess refocused the business to post-refinery residual oil, usually treated as waste, and used as fuel only for large boilers and utility operations. Hess apparently recognized that as power companies and industrial consumers progressively switched from coal to oil, residual oil had the potential to become a profitable commodity. Hess subsequently created a tank-truck fleet specifically designed to transport residual oil to power plants—the trucks were equipped with heaters that kept the oil hot and thus still useful. Adding more distribution depots and a provision terminal, Hess was able to underbid his competition for a variety of federal fuel contracts, a traditional source of significant revenue throughout the company's history. It is probable that Hess's own World War II experience in the army as a petroleum supply officer was a notable source of his later ideas about organization and discipline in business.

The late 1940s marked the start of Hess's first large profits from residual oil sales, to customers such as Public Service Electric & Gas. Hess competed on a tight price basis, establishing large stations at prime locations close to refineries and depots, and pioneering gasoline sales without services. After a period of further expansion through debt, in early 1962 the high debt-to-equity ratio forced Hess to take his company public, by means of a merger with the Cletrac Corporation. Under terms of the May 1962 merger, the new company became Hess Oil & Chemical Corporation, Hess becoming CEO and chief stockholder.

At this point, all of Hess's operations were exclusively in refining, transportation, distribution, and retailing. Because of the opportunities, and possible vulnerability, Hess considered the possibilities of a merger with larger integrated independent oil company. The Amerada-Hess merger that ultimately ensued has generally been acknowledged as an extremely well-planned and -timed success, resulting in a sizable gain in crude supply coupled with a dramatic reduction in federal income tax liabilities, at a time when oil prices were low and expected to remain so. At the time of the merger, Amerada Petroleum had no debt, and had proven oil reserves exceeding 500 million barrels in the United States and 750,000 barrels in Libya through the Oasis consortium. Hess made an initial purchase of Amerada stock in 1966. Amerada's chairman tried to stop the takeover, first by an arranged merger with Ashland Oil, later by an agreement with Phillips Petroleum. By offering a notable over-market price, Hess invested more than $250 million in what *Fortune*, in January 1970, called "one of Hess's most dangerous gambles." In spring of 1969, Phillips withdrew from the contest for ownership, and despite a May 1969 suit filed in federal district court to nullify the mer-

ger, Amerada's stockholders approved it by an overwhelming margin.

Because of what several analysts consider some surprising similarities in strategy and outlook, the two companies integrated so smoothly, that the new Amerada Hess Corporation rapidly pursued an aggressive and successful exploration program. In May 1970 Amerada Hess drilled the first successful wildcat well in Prudential Bay on Alaska's North Slope. In mid-1971 Amerada Hess was one of seven oil companies invited by the Canadian government to explore the building of pipelines from oil fields in Alaska's North Slope through Canada to the United States. In September 1974 the U.S. Interior Department reported that the company was the first to apply for permits to unload supertankers from the Trans Alaska Pipeline.

Between 1966 and 1967, the Hess Oil & Chemical Corporation had initiated a refinery on St. Croix in the Virgin Islands. In late 1967 negotiations had been approved, between Hess, the local government, and the U.S. Department of the Interior, on a ten-year plan to promote economic development in the Virgin Islands by U.S. industry, reciprocally permitting Hess the right to ship 15,000 barrels per day of finished oil products made from foreign crude to the U.S. mainland. The reported rationale was the need for cost-efficient heating oil in the northeast United States, where Hess was a major refiner and fuel dealer to the government and industry. Some adverse attention and controversy arose following interior secretary Stewart L. Udall's announcement that a similar proposal by the Coastal States Gas Producing Company had been finally rejected in favor of Hess. In November 1970 when Amerada Hess was charged by the U.S. Interior Department with import-rules violation from claims that it had made no significant expenditures for upgrading its Virgin Island facilities and employee quota and apparently had not paid the agreed-upon royalty of 50¢ per barrel to the local development and conservation fund. By 1979, the company's St. Croix refinery output was reported as 700,000 barrels per day, the world's largest. A long-time supplier of jet and fuel oil to the Defense Supply Agency, the Defense Logistics Agency, and the Defense Fuel Supply center, Amerada Hess had also long been a chief supplier of residual and fuel oil to numerous community power and light companies. In April 1975 Amerada Hess was one of several oil companies charged by the Federal Energy Administration with pricing violations. In August 1978 Amerada Hess was one of five firms convicted on federal charges of fixing retail gasoline prices.

In 1973 Amerada Hess received permission from U.S. President Richard Nixon's Office of Emergency Preparedness to import an extra six million barrels per day of heating oil to ease the nation's shortages, but received some unfavorable notice by selling primarily to the East instead of the more energy-needy Midwest regions. With the prices of crude oil increasing three-fold in less than six months, Amerada Hess received notable profits. Net reported earnings of $133 million in 1971 increased to $246 million in 1973, and to $577 million by 1980. *Business Week* on July 16, 1979, reported Amerada Hess as being among the biggest gainers of the United States's oil entitlements program, establish in 1974 to equalize costs between domestic refineries supplied by lower-priced domestic sources and those depending on higher-priced foreign imports.

Including its role as major partner—with Hunt, Getty, and Louisiana Land and Exploration Company—on the Alaska North Slope between the Arab oil embargo, of 1973 to 1974, and 1979, Amerada Hess invested more than $1.2 billion in exploration and production. In the early 1970s Amerada Hess was one of many companies negotiating with Portugal for oil and gas exploration concessions in and off the shore of Angola, and later Gabon. In 1975 Amerada Hess and Mississippi Chemical Corporation initiated a five-year joint venture of exploration and evaluation in southern Mississippi and Alabama. In 1981 Petro-Canada initiated operation of drill ships off Labrador on behalf of a consortium including Amerada Minerals Corporation of Canada Ltd., with considerable exploration success continuing through 1984, when it also made major natural discoveries offshore Grand Isle, Louisiana, and further Alaskan strikes off Seal Island in 1986. In 1985 Amerada Hess acquired Monsanto Oil Company in the United Kingdom and it became a wholly owned subsidiary.

In response to U.S. President Ronald Reagan's June 1986 deadlines, Amerada Hess officially ended its Libya operations. Although after January 1989 U.S. oil companies had U.S. government approval to resume activities there, because of the instability in the Middle East the future of such activities remained uncertain. In 1987 Amerada Hess and Chevron were reported as the top U.S. crude and product importers of the year. In August 1989 Amerada Hess acquired for $911 million a 37% interest in major offshore oil and gas properties in the northern Gulf of Mexico from the TXP Operating Company, a Texas limited partnership affiliated with the Transco Energy Company, increasing Amerada Hess's total natural gas reserves by 25%. Included are major efforts at development and production in the North Sea Scott and Rob Roy fields. Natural gas was reported in 1990 to make up approximately half the company's total hydrocarbon reserves. In September 1990 Amerada Minerals Corporation of Canada acquired assets from Placer Cego Petroleum Ltd. in Alberta and British Columbia. Amerada Hess Norge A/S maintains 25% interests in several major offshore fields.

In December 1989 the company settled its part in a 13-year suit brought by the state of Alaska concerning the North Slope oil pipeline. More notably, Amerada Hess survived apparent takeover plans in the mid-1980s. In late 1988 despite much published speculation about the flaws in corporate management, the company's overall picture remained strong. Its trend was considered uncertain, however, because its five-year record is reported to be among the lowest for the entire petroleum industry. The clear trend of reserve acquisitions in the United States, Canada, and overseas is reported to have pushed company debt to approximately 45% of total capital.

A major goal for the 1990s includes substantial reduction in overall debt levels. Because the company is no longer the leading innovator in developing geophysical exploration technologies or wildcatting as it was from the 1920s to the 1940s, at least some of its successes will depend on continued joint efforts with major partners, notably in improved subsurface development of established fields. Amerada Hess has long been an advocate of domestic oil decontrol and comprehensive national energy policy. Amerada Hess is, in several published opinions, cited as a successful example of the trend toward increased economies via vertical integration.

Principal Subsidiaries: Amerada Minerals Corporation of Canada Ltd.; Amerada Hess Pipeline Corporation; Amerada Hess Ltd. (U.K.); Amerada Hess Norge A/S (Norway); Hess Shipping Company (Virgin Islands).

Further Reading: Tinkle, Lon, *Mr. De: a Biography of Everette Lee DeGolyer,* Boston, Little, Brown, & Company, 1972; Ingham, John, and Lynne Feldman, *Contemporary American Business Leaders,* Westport, Connecticut, Greenwood Press, 1990.

—Gerardo G. Tango

AMOCO CORPORATION

200 East Randolph Drive
Chicago, Illinois 60601
U.S.A.
(312) 856-6111
Fax: (312) 856-2460

Public Company
Incorporated: 1889 as Standard Oil Company (Indiana)
Employees: 54,524
Sales: $31.58 billion
Stock Exchanges: New York Midwest Pacific Toronto Basel
    Geneva Lausanne Zürich

Amoco Corporation operates in more than 40 countries, in fields that include petroleum and natural gas exploration, manufacture, marketing and transportation, plus the manufacture and sales of polymers, fabrics, and fibers. Other ventures involve hazardous waste incineration, medical diagnostic products, and lasers.

Amoco has been in business since 1889, though it was known as Standard Oil Company (Indiana) until its name was changed in 1985. The company was formed outside Whiting, Indiana, a location chosen by John Rockefeller's Standard Oil Trust as a refinery site close enough to sites in the growing midwestern market to keep freight costs low, yet far enough away to avoid disturbing residents.

From the beginning, the Whiting facility was organized as a self-supporting entity, planning for long-term expansion. Though refining was its main activity, it also constructed oil barrels for transportation, and manufactured an oil-based product line consisting of axle grease, harness oil, paraffin wax for candles, and kerosene produced from the crude oil. The oil itself flowed to Chicago and other midwestern cities via two pipes originating in Lima, Ohio. Land transportation began on the refinery's grounds, at a railroad terminal belonging to the Chicago & Calumet Terminal Railroad, a company over which a Standard Oil interest had gained control. This terminal's placement gave the company exclusive use of the tracks, access to the West and the Southwest, and a direct route that eliminated the expense of switching tolls.

Standard (Indiana) had no direct marketing organization of its own. After the Standard Oil Trust was liquidated in 1892 by order of the Ohio Supreme Court, the 20 companies under its jurisdiction reverted to their former status, and became subsidiaries of Standard Oil Company (New Jersey). The functions of Standard Oil (Indiana) were then expanded to include marketing.

The company's capitalization was now increased from $500,000 to $1 million, and divided into $100 shares. Standard Oil still owned about 54% of Standard (Indiana). Standard (Indiana) used the extra cash to buy Standard Oil Company (Minnesota) and Standard Oil Company (Illinois), formerly P.C. Hanford Oil Company, an oil-marketing organization in Chicago. The extra capital expanded Standard's sales territory, which was broadened even further when the property of Chester Oil Company of Minnesota was bought. Other acquisitions followed; by 1901 the company was marketing through its own organization in 11 states.

At first Standard (Indiana) had few competitors in the petroleum-product market, and enjoyed about 88% of the business in kerosene and heavy fuel oil. After competition began to grow, Standard (Indiana) fought back with strategically placed bulk storage stations and subsidiary companies in competitive areas that cut prices and drove competitors out. Earnings rose from $605,781 in 1896 to a high of almost $4.2 million in 1899, but the company's competitive practices and its growing market share made it the target of government agencies. In 1911, after a court battle lasting almost three years, Standard Oil Company (New Jersey)—the parent company to Standard (Indiana) and other Standard companies—was ordered to relinquish its supervision of its subsidiaries.

Gasoline sales had risen from 31.6 million gallons to 1.57 billion between 1897 and 1911. Once independent, Standard (Indiana) began to cater to the burgeoning automobile market, opening a Minneapolis, Minnesota, service station in 1912. Chicago's first service station opened in 1913, and by 1918, there were 451 altogether. Together with growing sales of road oil, asphalt, and other supporting products, the automotive industry provided one-third of all Standard (Indiana) business.

To get as much gasoline out of each barrel of crude as possible, Standard formulated the cracking process, that doubled the yield by separating the oil's molecules, by means of heat and pressure, into a dense liquid plus a lighter product that would boil in gasoline's range. The possibility of cheaper gasoline and a new line of petroleum-based products made the method attractive to other refiners, who licensed it, accounting for 34% of the company's total profits between 1913 and 1922.

With the end of World War I, company chairman Colonel Robert Stewart's top priority was to find a secure source of crude oil, to meet the rapidly expanding demand for gasoline and kerosene. Before the war, Standard had depended on the Prairie Oil and Gas Company for its supply, but military needs diverted Prairie's crude to the refineries along the Atlantic seaboard. To obtain a reliable source of crude oil, Stewart acquired 33% of Midwest Refining Company of Wyoming, in 1920. A half interest in the Sinclair Pipe Company was purchased in 1921, for $16.4 million in cash, improving transportation capacity. Sinclair's 2,900 miles of pipeline ran from north Texas to Chicago, encompassed almost 6,000 wells, and ran through oil-rich Wyoming.

Standard bought an interest in the Pan American Petroleum & Transport Company in 1925. The interest, costing $37.6 million, was the largest oil consolidation in the history of the industry, giving Standard (Indiana) access to one of the world's largest tanker fleets and entry into oil fields in Mexico,

Venezuela, and Iraq. In 1929 Standard (Indiana) acquired another chunk of Pan American stock through a stock swap, bringing its total ownership of Pan American to 81%.

Pan American also introduced Standard to the American Oil Company, of Baltimore, Maryland. Started by the Blaustein family, American Oil marketed most of Pan American's oil in the eastern United States, and was 50%-owned by Pan American and 50%-owned by the Blausteins. The Blausteins were initiators of the first measuring gasoline-pump and inventors of the high-octane Amoco-Gas that reduced engine knocking.

Though expensive, these investments proved to be sound; by 1929, the Depression notwithstanding, Standard Oil (Indiana) was second only to Standard Oil (New Jersey) as a buyer of crude oil. Equally profitable as a supplier, the company's net earnings for 1929 were $78.5 million after taxes.

In 1929 Stewart was followed as CEO by Edward G. Seubert, who continued to strengthen Standard's crude oil supply. With an eye to future supply security, Seubert shifted the emphasis to buying and developing crude oil-producing properties like McMan Oil and Gas Company, a 1930 purchase that provided 10,000 barrels daily. Also in 1930, Standard acquired both the remaining 50% interest in the Sinclair Pipe Line Company and the Sinclair Crude Oil Purchasing Company for $72.5 million, giving it control over one of the country's largest pipeline systems and crude oil buying agencies. These subsidiaries now became the Stanolind Pipe Line Company and the Stanolind Crude Oil Purchasing Company; they were joined in 1931 by the Stanolind Oil & Gas Company, a newly organized subsidiary absorbing several smaller ones.

In 1929 a retail venture called the Atlas Supply Company, which was co-organized with five other Standard firms, had been organized to sell automobile tires and other accessories nationwide. Nevertheless, the Depression made competition fierce by the end of 1930. Even worse conditions threatened after the largest oil field in history was found in east Texas in late 1930. The new field caused production to rise quickly to a daily average of 300,000 barrels in 1931, glutting the market. Ruthless price-cutting followed. Standard (Indiana) did not engage in this practice, preferring instead to curtail exploration and drilling activities. As a result, only 49.9 billion barrels were produced in 1931, as against 55.1 billion the year before, and the company's 13 domestic facilities operated well below capacity. The 45,073 employees worked on construction projects, and accepted wage cuts and part-time employment to minimize layoffs. The flow of cheap crude oil continued, often in excess of limits set by state regulatory bodies; gas sales were accompanied by premiums like candy, ash trays, and cigarette lighters. Track-side stations, where gasoline was pumped from the tank car into the customer's automobile, posed another price-cutting threat. Also prevalent were cooperatives organized by farmers, who would buy tank cars of gasoline for distribution among members to save money. These conditions caused 1932 earnings to reach only $16.5 million—down from 1931's $17.5 million.

In 1932 Standard decided to sell Pan American's foreign interests to Standard Oil (New Jersey). These properties cost Standard Oil (New Jersey) just under $48 million cash plus about 1.8 million shares of Standard Oil (New Jersey) stock.

By 1934 the worst of the Depression was over. Activities in Texas led the Stanolind Oil & Gas Company to the Hastings field, which held 43 producing wells by the end of 1935. Also

in 1935, more oil-producing acreage in east Texas came with Stanolind Oil & Gas Company's $42 million purchase of the properties of Beaumont-based Yount-Lee Oil Company, an acquisition that helped Stanolind Oil & Gas to increase its daily average production to 68,965 barrels.

During the 1930s overproduction began to threaten, and federal and state governments tried to curb oil production with heavy taxes. Standard felt the bite in Iowa's 1935 chain-store tax, which could not be justified by their service stations' profit margin. The company therefore turned back leased stations to their owners, and leased company-owned stations to independent operators, to be operated as separate outlets. By the following July all 11,685 Standard (Indiana) service stations were independently operated, and the company was once more a producer distributing oil at wholesale prices. This move spurred the newly independent entrepreneurs, whose increased sales helped to achieve a net profit of $30.2 million for 1935.

When Standard reached its 50th year in 1939, during World War II, its research chemists were working with improving the high-octane fuels required by military and transport planes. In other moves, Standard's engineers cooperated with other companies to build the pipelines necessary for oil transportation; by 1942, the Big Inch pipeline carried a daily load of 300,000 barrels of crude from Texas to the East Coast, where most of it was used to support the war effort. Loss of manpower and government steel restrictions curbed operations, yet the company produced 47 million barrels of crude, and purchased about 102 million barrels from outside sources. Other wartime products from Standard plants included paraffin wax coatings for military food rations, toluene—the main ingredient for TNT—butane and butylene for aviation gasoline, and synthetic rubber.

On January 1, 1945, Seubert retired as president and chief executive officer of the company. He left behind him 33,244 employees, of whom 5,055 were women; sales of crude oil topping the 1944 figure by 37.1%; and a gross income of $618.9 million. Seubert was succeeded as chairman and CEO by Robert E. Wilson, formerly president of Pan American Petroleum & Transport Company, and Alonzo W. Peake became president. Peake had been vice president of production.

The management style instituted by Wilson and Peake differed from the centralized, solo authority Seubert preferred. The two men split the supervisory authority, with no overlap of direct authority. Wilson was responsible for finance, research and development, law, and industrial relations, while Peake's commitments included refining, production, supply and transportation, and sales and long-range planning. Responsibility for operating subsidiaries was split between the two. The result was a decentralized organization, making for swifter, more cooperative decision-making at all levels.

In 1948 Stanolind Oil & Gas formed a foreign exploration department to head exploration attempts in Canada and other countries. The new team spent more than $98 million by 1950, with Canada and the Gulf of Mexico its prime targets.

By 1952 Standard Oil (Indiana) was acknowledged as the nation's largest domestic oil company. It possessed 12 refineries able to market its products in 41 states, plus almost 5,000 miles of crude oil gathering lines, 10,000 miles of trunk lines and 1,700 miles of refined product pipelines. By 1951, gross income had reached $1.54 billion.

In 1955 Peake retired as president, to be succeeded by former executive vice president Frank Prior, who inherited the problem of a decrease in allowable production days in the state of Texas, as a result of additions to oil reserves in the state. The rising amount of imported oil was another problem that arose during Peake's tenure. The total had swelled from 490,000 barrels per day in 1951 to 660,000 barrels in 1954.

Nevertheless, cheaper international exploration costs spurred Standard (Indiana) to again become active in the growing foreign oil arena that it had all but left in 1932 when it sold Pan American's foreign interests. To handle international land leasing and joint ventures, the company organized Pan American International Oil Corporation in New York, as a subsidiaries of Pan American Petroleum. Foreign operations included exploration rights for 13 million acres in Cuba, obtained in 1955; a subsidiary company formed in Venezuela in 1958, for joint exploration of 180,000 acres together with other companies; and 23 million acres obtained for exploration in Libya.

The traditional oil-industry profit arrangement for international activities had been an even split between the company and the host government, though several firms had quietly bent the guidelines. Standard (Indiana) broke openly with with this custom in 1958 deal with the National Iranian Oil Company (NIOC), in which Standard (Indiana) split the profits evenly, then gave NIOC half of its own share, to which it added a $25 million bonus.

The late 1950s also saw domestic reorganization. In 1957 the company consolidated nine subsidiary into four larger companies. Stanolind Oil & Gas Company became Pan American Petroleum Corporation, consolidating all Standard Oil (Indiana) crude oil and natural gas exploration and production. American Oil Pipe Line Company, a former subsidiary of American Oil, was merged into Service Pipe Line Company—which had been known as Stanolind Pipe Line Company until 1950—focused on oil transport. Crude oil and natural gas purchasing operations were combined to form the Indiana Oil Purchasing Company; and Amoco Chemicals Corporation consolidated all chemical activities into a single organization. Total income for 1957 was about $2 billion.

In 1960 company president John Swearingen succeeded Prior as chief executive officer, the chairmanship being left vacant. Swearingen turned both domestic and foreign operations over to subsidiaries, making Standard Oil (Indiana) entirely a holding company. Operating assets were transferred to the American Oil Company, into which the Utah Oil Refining Company was also merged. American Oil's responsibilities now included the manufacturing, transport, and sale of all company petroleum products in 45 states, though limited marketing operations in three other states were also maintained. This consolidation allowed the company to develop a national image and provided more efficiency in staff use and storage and transport flexibility. Coverage being national, the company was able to advertise nationally and demand better rates from ground and air transporters.

Standard (Indiana) also became concerned with product trade names. The 1911 breakup had left several former Standard (New Jersey) subsidiaries in different areas of the country with the Standard Oil name and rights to the associated trademarks. American Oil thus had the right to use the Standard name only in the 15 midwestern states that had been the company's original territory. Thus, in 1957, the word "American," together with the Standard Oil (Indiana) logo, was used in all other states. Since a five-letter name was easier for mo-

torists to note, in 1961 the company began to replace the brand name American with Amoco, the name first coined by American Oil's original owners for the high-octane, anti-knock gasoline that had powered the Charles Lindbergh trans-Atlantic flight. Familiar within the company since the 1945 organization of the Amoco Chemicals Corporation, "Amoco" was used increasingly on products and by subsidiaries, until, by 1971, major subsidiaries everywhere had "Amoco" in their names.

In 1961 Standard's total income reached almost $2.1 billion, yielding net earnings of $153.9 million. Continuing with methodical reorganization, Swearingen oversaw the expansion and modernization of the company's domestic refining capacity as well as 11 of its 14 catalytic cracking units. An aggressive marketing program featured large, strategically placed retail outlets, plus the addition of Avis car-rental privileges to the credit-card services that had been in operation since the early 1930s. By the end of 1966 there were 5.5 million card holders, encouraging American Oil to go national with its motor club.

Because only 8% of its assets were located overseas, Standard (Indiana) still lacked a large foreign market for crude oil. Swearingen moved swiftly to close the gap. By 1964 foreign explorations were taking place in Mozambique, Indonesia, Venezuela, Argentina, Colombia, and Iran. Refining and marketing were also flourishing, through the acquisition of a 25,000-barrel-per-day refinery near Cremona, Italy, and about 700 Italian service stations. About 250 service stations were also opened in Australia in 1961, along with a 25,000-barrel-per-day refinery. Other foreign refineries were to be found in West Germany, in England, Pakistan, and the West Indies. In 1967 Standard began production in the Persian Gulf Cyrus field, by which time the huge El Morgan field in the Gulf of Suez was producing 45,000 barrels daily.

The market for Standard's chemical products also increased during the mid-1960s. To keep pace with demand for the raw materials used in polyester fiber and film, the company built a new facility at Decatur, Alabama, in 1965, adding another in Texas City, Texas, a year later. There were also 641 retail chemical-fertilizer outlets in the Midwest and the South. The popularity of polystyrene for packaging also grew. All these advances ensured profitability; overall chemical sales rose to $158 million by the end of 1967, on total revenues of almost $3.6 billion.

Fuel shortages and the wave of OPEC price rises, nationalizations, and takeovers of the early 1970s underlined the importance of oil exploration. Swearingen's strategy was to accumulate as much domestic exploration acreage as possible before other companies acted, while organizing production in developing foreign markets that were not too competitive.

To capitalize on concern about air pollution, the company introduced a 91-octane lead-free gasoline in 1970 at a cost in excess of $100 million. Though motorists were initially reluctant to accept the 2¢-per-gallon price rise, the 1973 appearance of catalytic converters on new cars assured the success of the fuel.

Environmental matters came to the fore again in 1978, when an Amoco International Oil Company tanker, the *Amoco Cadiz* suffered steering failure during a storm and ran aground off the French coast, leaking about 730,000 gallons of oil into the sea. The huge oil spill cost $75 million to clean up, and left its mark on the area's tourist trade as well as its ecosystem. The French government brought a $300 million lawsuit against Amoco that, in July 1990, led to an $128 million judgment against Amoco. Amoco appealed, and a judgment was expected in 1992.

In late December 1978 the shah of Iran was overthrown, and Standard (Indiana) hurriedly closed its Iranian facility and evacuated American staff members after all American employees of Amoco Iran Oil Company received death threats. The year 1978 had seen record-breaking production in Iran, and its loss resulted in a 35% production decrease in the company's overseas operations. Despite these turbulent events, 1979's net income was $1.5 billion, on total revenues of $20.197 billion.

By the end of the 1970s, chemical production accounted for about 7% of company earnings. To gain more visibility with consumers, Standard (Indiana) began to stress end-product manufacture as well as the production of ingredients used in manufacturing processes. The trend had begun in 1968, when polypropylene manufacturer Avisun Corporation was purchased by Amoco Chemicals Corporation from Sun Oil Company. The $80 million price tag included Patchoque-Plymouth Company, maker of polypropylene carpet backing. By 1986 a 100-color line plus improved stain resistance made Amoco Fabrics & Fibers Company's petrochemical-based Genesis carpeting a serious competitor of the stain-resistant carpeting offered by Du Pont. Other strategies focused on market stimulation for basic industrial products. Since this required specialized marketing skills, the company divided its chemical operations among four subsidiaries.

In 1983 John Swearingen retired as chairman of the board. In his stead came Richard W. Morrow, who had been president of the Amoco Chemicals Corporation from 1974 until 1978, before assuming the Standard (Indiana) presidency in 1978. In 1985 Standard Oil Company (Indiana) changed its name to Amoco Corporation. Morrow also presided over the 1988 acquisition of Dome Petroleum, Ltd. of Canada, which was later merged into Amoco Canada. Dome, owning 28.7 million acres of undeveloped, arctic-region land, improved Amoco's oil and gas reserves. The Dome purchase was hard-won, costing Amoco $4.2 billion. Other chances to expand oil and gas exploration in 1988 came with the acquisition of Tenneco Oil Company's Rocky Mountain properties, for approximately $900 million.

Amoco Corporation saw out the decade with total revenues of $26.7 billion, and a net income of $1.6 billion. By 1990, the need for raw materials had expanded internationally, moving strongly towards Europe and the Far East. Joint ventures in Brazil, Mexico, South Korea, and Taiwan met the growing demand for polyester fibers, helping to generate about 35% of business overseas. Other ventures included long-range research interests focusing on lasers, solar power and biotechnology, including genetic research.

Principal Subsidiaries: Amoco Production Company; Amoco Oil Company; Amoco Chemical Company.

Further Reading: Giddens, Paul H., *Standard Oil Company (Indiana): Oil Pioneer of the Middle West,* New York, Appleton-Century-Crofts, 1955; Dedmon, Emmett, *Challenge and Response: A Modern History of Standard Oil Company (Indiana),* Chicago, Mobium Press, 1984.

—Gillian Wolf

ASHLAND OIL, INC.

Ashland, Kentucky 41114
U.S.A.
(606) 329-3333
Fax: (606) 329-4795

Public Company
Incorporated: 1924 as Ashland Refining Company
Employees: 33,400
Sales: $8.99 billion
Stock Exchanges: New York Midwest Philadelphia Boston Cincinnati Pacific Amsterdam

Ashland Oil, Inc. occupies a middle position in the oil industry, far smaller than the major international players but large enough to remain a powerful competitor in its own region. Middle, too, has been its traditional emphasis on the refining segment of the oil business, in which it has long enjoyed a reputation for excellence. Unlike most of the world's great oil concerns, Ashland has never owned significant amounts of crude oil, and its marketing division did not come close to equaling the importance of refining in the company's mix of sales for many years. In 1991, chemicals and road construction were also sizable contributors, but Ashland remains primarily a refiner and distributor of oil products.

The history of Ashland Oil begins with J. Fred Miles and the founding in 1910 of Swiss Drilling Company, an Oklahoma corporation. Miles had been raised in Oklahoma and worked in the oil business from youth, and after gathering a store of capital created Swiss Drilling with two other men to explore and operate new wells. The years immediately following the breakup of Standard Oil's near-monopoly in 1911 were challenging in the oil business, however, and Miles found that he could not survive on the low prices offered for Oklahoma crude. In 1916 he accordingly moved his operations to the new fields then opening in eastern Kentucky, where, with the help of some powerful financiers in Chicago and in Cleveland, Ohio, he obtained control of nearly 200,000 acres of oil land. Two years later the energetic Miles incorporated Swiss Oil Company in Lexington, Kentucky, with a group of backers that included the Insulls and the Armours of Chicago, with Miles serving as general manager and J.I. Lamprecht of Cleveland as president. Swiss Oil was soon one of the leading oil concerns in the state of Kentucky.

By the early 1920s a postwar depression and the early exhaustion of key oil wells had thrust Swiss Oil into a precarious financial condition. Despite the company's difficulties, Fred Miles was eager to expand its operations into refining, and in 1923 he hired the services of young Paul Blazer to select, buy, and operate the most advantageously located and outfitted refinery obtainable in the area. Blazer had gone into the oil-trading business after college and then picked up valuable experience as a partner in a Lexington refinery, from which he had just resigned when Miles made him the head of Swiss Oil's new Ashland Refining Company division in 1924. Blazer selected for his refinery an existing facility at Cattletsburg, Kentucky, on the Ohio River near the West Virginia border and just upstream from Ashland, where Blazer set up his modest offices. The Cattletsburg refinery had a capacity of 1,000 barrels per day, and after a program of extensive repairs was soon operating profitably.

Blazer's choice of Cattletsburg was excellent, due to several factors that would prove critical in the company's long-term success. In general, a refining operation that had access to its own local crude oil supplies would do well in the eastern Kentucky region. Swiss Oil, though not a successful company, did own a substantial amount of the region's crude and could therefore supply its new subsidiary with most of its needs. Ashland was thus able to sell regionally refined petroleum products such as gasoline and motor oil more cheaply than competitors who were forced to transport their crude or finished products from the Atlantic seaboard or the Mississippi River–Gulf of Mexico region. The Cattletsburg site promised ready access to hundreds of miles of navigable rivers, by means of which Ashland could both receive crude and deliver product to the greater Ohio River basin. Until the introduction of pipelines, river freight was unmatched as an economic carrier of oil, and Ashland remains dependent on its river barges and terminals for the delivery of much of its refined product. These factors gave Ashland an early advantage over its much larger rivals and allowed the company to achieve a firm and lasting position as regional leader.

By 1926 Ashland's gross sales were $3 million a year and Paul Blazer had confirmed his reputation as an outstanding refinery manager. J. Fred Miles had been eased out of Swiss Oil when the company required a bailout by one of its investors, and it was not long before the Ashland subsidiary was outperforming its parent company. Blazer steadily improved the refinery's operation and expanded sales of its products, and in 1929 he convinced Swiss Oil's board of directors to authorize Ashland's purchase of $400,000 worth of marketing companies in the area. This was followed up, despite the onset of the Great Depression, by the 1930 acquisition of Tri-State Refining Company over the West Virginia border. Tri-State had a sizable refinery and its own team of gas stations and trucks, giving Ashland the makings of an integrated refining and marketing organization in the eastern Kentucky region. While inexpensive, river transport was continually threatened with the imposition of federal tolls that would largely negate its economy. Thus, in 1931, Ashland took the first in a long series of steps intended to lessen its dependence on river transportation of its crude supplies. When Ashland bought the Cumberland Pipeline Company for $420,000 in 1931 it facilitated shipment of crude from the Atlantic seaboard as well as from its Kentucky fields, an opening to the sea that would become vital when Ashland grew dependent on Middle Eastern oil arriving by tanker.

So skilled an operator was Paul Blazer that Ashland continued to turn a profit in the worst Depression years. Ashland was now the staff upon which leaned the ailing Swiss Oil, and when it became apparent that the latter would not recover the two companies, in 1936, were merged and Blazer elected president and CEO of the new Ashland Oil & Refining Company. The combined companies showed a 1936 net profit of $677,583 on sales of $4.8 million, good results at any time but remarkable in the Depression era. Blazer forged ahead with new investments, joining Standard Oil Company (Ohio) in a pipeline from the southern Illinois fields and adding a costly new unit to the Cattletsburg refinery, and by the time the United States entered World War II in 1941 Ashland had nearly doubled its sales to $8 million.

During World War II the petroleum industry came under fairly tight government control. Like all of the other oil companies, big and small, Ashland benefited mightily from the rapid increase in demand for the entire spectrum of petroleum products, which were needed for everything from gasoline to rubber boots to explosives. With government assistance, Ashland built a new facility at Cattletsburg for the refining of 100-octane aviation fuel, and within four years had doubled and redoubled company revenues to $35 million in 1945. The following years saw an inevitable recession as the war machine was dismantled, but it soon became apparent that postwar America was about to indulge its love affair with the automobile as never before. From the remote mountain towns of West Virginia to the streets of Cincinatti, Ohio, the postwar economy moved on wheels powered by oil, and Ashland remained the region's most economical supplier of that oil.

In 1948 Ashland took a major step when it merged with Cleveland-based Allied Oil Company, a fuel oil broker with sales slightly in excess of Ashland's. Allied had been started in 1925 by Floyd R. Newman and W.W. Vandeveer, with the support of Paul Blazer. The combined companies had revenue in that year of $100 million. Ashland's new Allied division was directed by Rex Blazer, nephew of Ashland president Paul Blazer and a former marketing executive at Allied. The merger extended Ashland's marketing area to Cleveland and as far west as Chicago, and to make use of its new sales opportunities Ashland soon added a trio of other acquisitions—Aetna Oil Company, a Louisville, Kentucky, refiner and distributor; Frontier Oil Company, of Buffalo, New York; and Freedom-Valvoline Oil Company, Pennsylvania maker of Valvoline motor oil. The later was already a well known brand name and under Ashland's ownership has since become one of the most widely distributed motor oils in the world. By the time these purchases were completed in 1950, Ashland was the 19th-largest oil company in the United States and for the first time was listed on the New York Stock Exchange.

Sales in 1955 topped $250 million, though net income was only $10 million. In contrast to its early years, as a mature company Ashland tended to earn rather low levels of net income, which Paul Blazer attributed to two basic factors. First, the company had far outstripped its limited sources of crude oil and never had much success as a prospector. This meant that it would never enjoy the extraordinary profits brought in by big oil strikes and that its crude oil expense would always be somewhat higher than for a fully integrated oil concern. Second, Ashland also sold more refined products than it made, supplementing its own production with purchases of refined

goods for resale, with a necessarily diminished margin. Such a policy also meant that Ashland's refineries were kept running at or near capacity, a clear gain in efficiency over plants forced to cut back or work on shorter, more costly runs. Added to its advantageous system of waterway transport and freedom from the advertising expense associated with operation of a high-profile, branded chain of gas stations, Ashland's refining efficiency offset its lack of crude and enabled the company to earn a steady if unspectacular return on investment.

In 1957 Paul Blazer retired as the chief executive of Ashland Oil after 22 years. His nephew Rex Blazer took over the top management spot, while Everett Wells, a long-time associate of the senior Blazer, became the new president. The year before these changes, Ashland entered a new field with the purchase of the R.J. Brown Company of St. Louis, Missouri, a diversified manufacturer of petrochemicals. A great number of useful chemicals are derived from petroleum, and the oil industry as a whole was expanding rapidly into this new and largely unexplored area. Ashland steadily increased its petrochemical holdings, in 1962 buying United Carbon Company of Houston, Texas, makers of carbon black, and in 1966 adding Archer Daniels Midland Chemicals Company for $65 million. At that point, Ashland formed a new operating subsidiary, Ashland Chemical Company, to oversee the workings of its manifold chemical interests.

The early 1960s were also notable for Ashland's 1962 purchase of the Central Louisiana pipeline system from Humble Oil & Refining. Central Louisiana was a major pipeline, gathering most of the oil produced in greater Louisiana and the Gulf of Mexico fields, and its acquisition by Ashland largely relieved the company of its worries about a steady supply of crude oil, made worse by the intermittent threat of new user tolls on the waterways. The net effect of these acquisitions was to boost Ashland's sales sharply, from $490 million in 1963 to $723 million three years later, elevating the company from the status of independent to what might be called a "mini-major" oil firm. The robust U.S. economy had much to do with Ashland's prosperity, of course, as more citizens relied on the automobile.

In 1969 Ashland had entered the coal business and soon became one of the top-ten coal producers in the country. It also took advantage of its refineries' asphalt by-products to gain a leading place among the nation's road-construction firms. The result of such diversification was a gradual lessening of Ashland's dependence on oil refining for its sales dollar; by 1971, refining and marketing of oil accounted for only 57% of Ashland's $1.4 billion in revenue, with Ashland Chemical providing another 25% and its other holdings chipping in the remainder. This apparent balance was somewhat misleading, however; Ashland continued to rely on its refining and marketing divisions for the bulk of its net income, as the growing chemical business proved to be a sluggish money maker. Refining capacity reached its 1991 level of 350,000 barrels per day in 1973, and, as always, Ashland's crude production was less than 20% of that figure, forcing the company to join the mounting number of U.S. oil refiners dependent on Middle Eastern crude for their survival.

In 1970, shareholders approved changing the company's name from Ashland Oil & Refining to Ashland Oil, Inc. That same year, Ashland consolidated most of its Canadian interests with those of Canadian Gridoil Limited to form Ashland Oil

Canada Limited. Domestically, Ashland acquired Union Carbide Petroleum Company and Empire State Petroleum, and these were consolidated with other exploration and production activities into Ashland Exploration, Inc.

In the mid-1970s Ashland became entangled in its first of a series of legal controversies. In 1976 CEO Orin Atkins, a lawyer who had served in that position since 1965, agreed in response to a shareholder suit to repay Ashland some $175,000 in funds he was said to have spent improperly. The previous year, 1975, Ashland had been fined by the Securities and Exchange Commission for illegally contributing more than $700,000 to several political campaigns.

As noted, Ashland had never come close to meeting its own needs for crude oil, a problem which became increasingly pronounced as the company continued to expand its refining and marketing operations. The 1973 OPEC embargo and ensuing energy crisis had effectively raised the stakes in the oil-exploration game. After the early 1970s, only those companies willing and able to mount massive drilling campaigns would be likely to reap the benefits of crude oil supplies. Ashland was simply not big enough to join the majors in their exorbitant outlays. Ashland therefore got out of the production business entirely, instead of spending on efforts too limited to achieve useful results. Sale of most of its oil leases, equipment, and reserves netted Ashland about $1.5 billion by 1980; but it also left the company wholly dependent on outside sources of crude, primarily in the Middle East. In 1975 all construction activities were consolidated, and Ashland Coal, Inc. was formed in anticipation of the increasing potential of coal in the national energy market. Ashland took a comprehensive review of all segments of its operations to determine necessary changes. As an initial step in this strategy to maximize return on existing assets, the company sold its 79% interest in Ashland Oil Canada.

In 1981 Atkins was forced out as chairman and CEO by a group of executives who brought to light illegal payments Atkins had made to government officials in Middle East countries, most notably Oman. He was replaced as chairman and CEO by John R. Hall. In June 1988 two former Ashland employees won a wrongful-discharge suit against the company. The employees, a former vice president for oil supply and a former vice president for government relations, had accused Ashland of firing them in 1983 for refusing to cover up the illegal payments. The jury awarded the plaintiffs $70.85 million, $1.25 million of which was to be paid by Hall personally. The plaintiffs ultimately settled out of court for $25 million.

On July 13, 1988, Atkins was arrested by customs agents at John F. Kennedy International Airport, accused of selling company documents to the National Iranian Oil Company (NIOC). Atkins denied the charges. The papers Atkins allegedly peddled related to an ongoing, $283 million billing dispute between Ashland and NIOC. In 1989 Ashland settled the ten-year-old case with a $325 million payment to NIOC. The company's public image was not helped by a 1988 spill of four million gallons of diesel fuel into the Ohio River, although Ashland was credited with a prompt, candid response.

In the meantime, Ashland sales skyrocketed along with the price of oil. John R. Hall watched revenue hit an all-time peak of $9.5 billion in 1981, but Ashland found itself squeezed by the high cost of crude and net income actually dropped into a net loss during the first part of 1982, when a spreading recession only made matters worse. Atkins also had saddled Ashland with an unusually high debt ratio when, in 1981, he used the receipts from the oil-drilling asset sale to buy United States Filter Corporation and Integon Corporation for $661 million. Integon, an insurance holding company, hardly matched the range of Ashland's other interests and in due time was sold to reduce debt. Once the recession had eased by 1983, Ashland's earnings again picked up and the company's future brightened.

Scurlock Oil Company, a crude oil gathering, transporting, and marketing firm, was acquired in 1982, thereby aiding Ashland in a shift from foreign to domestic crude oil sources. In 1982, more than 20 corporate staff departments were brought together to form Ashland Services Company, a division which would cut overhead and also provide cost-effective services to the corporation and to its divisions and subsidiaries.

Ashland is a highly diversified energy company, with extensive coal and petrochemical holdings to complement its core of oil refining and marketing. Ashland is the nation's leading distributor of chemicals, and a major manufacturer of specialty chemicals for industry and commodity chemicals such as methanol. Ashland has a 46% interest in Ashland Coal, Inc. and a 50% interest in Arch Mineral Corporation. These companies' combined coal sales for 1990 were about 36 million tons. Ashland is the nation's leading designer and builder of roadways through its APAC subsidiaries, and can boast of no fewer than 164 asphalt plants and 60 readymix concrete plants. Oil remains the centerpiece of Ashland's corporate structure, however. Still relying on cheap river transport for much of its outgoing freight, Ashland delivers gasoline and related petroleum products to a large network of wholesalers and some 2,000 Ashland-affiliated gas stations. Ashland itself operated 600 SuperAmerica retail gasoline-grocery outlets in 1990. SuperAmerica Group's 1990 sales were $2 billion. Added to these is the $600 million in sales generated by the Valvoline, Inc. subsidiary, Ashland's only nationally recognized brand name. Combined oil activities thus still provide well over half of the company's revenue and earnings, as Ashland continues to fill a narrow niche between international oil giant and regional independent.

Principal Subsidiaries: Ashland Petroleum Company; SuperAmerica Group, Inc.; Valvoline, Inc.; Ashland Chemical, Inc.; APAC, Inc.; Arch Mineral Corporation (50%); Ashland Coal, Inc. (46%); Ashland Services Company.

Further Reading: Scott, Otto J., *The Exception: The Story of Ashland Oil & Refining Company*, New York, McGraw-Hill Book Company, 1968; Scott, Otto, *Buried Treasure: The Story of Arch Mineral*, Washington, D.C., Braddock Communications, 1989.

—Jonathan Martin

ARCO ◆

ATLANTIC RICHFIELD COMPANY

515 South Flower Street
Los Angeles, California 90071
U.S.A.
(213) 486-3511
Fax: (213) 486-1756

Public Company
Incorporated: 1870 as Atlantic Refining Company
Employees: 26,600
Sales: $16.82 billion
Stock Exchanges: New York Pacific Basel Geneva Zürich

Atlantic Richfield Company (ARCO) is the eighth-largest U.S. oil company. ARCO is a multinational company, with interests in 20 foreign countries. This giant enterprise was the pioneer oil explorer in Alaska and, after oil was discovered on the North Slope in 1968, the largest reaper of any oil company of Alaska's petroleum wealth. It is the largest employer in the state of Alaska. In the lower 48 states, it is the largest marketer of gasoline in five western states, and the nation's largest producer of low-sulfur coal.

ARCO's origins go back to the discrete history of Atlantic Refining Company and Richfield Oil Corporation. In 1865, six years after Drake's Folly, the world's first oil derrick, went into operation, Charles Lockhart and his partners established the Atlantic Refining Company in Philadelphia, Pennsylvania, the first refinery in the United States. Not surprisingly, Atlantic was unable to compete successfully in the turbulent world of petroleum, and in 1874, the gigantic Standard Oil Trust swallowed up Atlantic, although the merger was kept a secret, with Atlantic retaining its name and personnel. Atlantic possessed the largest petroleum refinery in greater Philadelphia, and the company continued to grow as a subsidiary of Standard.

Atlantic's fortunes changed radically after the turn of the century. Theodore Roosevelt's trust busting was carried out faithfully by his successor, William Howard Taft. In 1911 a federal court successfully prosecuted Standard Oil, compelling it to dissolve into smaller entities, one of which was Atlantic Refining Company. Newly independent Atlantic had refineries but was dependent on others for crude oil. As a result, its president, John Wesley Van Dyke, made crude-oil self-sufficiency his goal, and under his skillful management, Atlantic increased its exploration activities.

Richfield's history is dramatically and colorfully told by its former president, Charles S. Jones, in *From the Rio Grande to the Arctic: the Story of the Richfield Oil Corporation*. Jones delves into the earliest history of Richfield, whose predecessor, the Rio Grande Oil Company, was established by a storeowner in El Paso, Texas, in 1915. Rio Grande's good fortune coincided with the heyday of Pancho Villa's raids across the border. In order to rid frontier towns like El Paso of Villa, the U.S. Army pursued Villa and his raiders deep into Mexican territory, using some 600 trucks to supply its troops. The army inadvertently became the largest consumer of Rio Grande oil at that time. From then on, the company's growth went unhindered, and its headquarters eventually shifted from Texas to California.

The Great Depression took a heavy toll on the Rio Grande Oil Company, forcing it in 1936 to reorganize and merge with other companies to become the modern Richfield Oil Corporation with Charles Jones as its president. Richfield embarked on a new era, marked by a significant oil discovery in California in 1938. Richfield consequently was well-prepared for the challenges of World War II, when the entire U.S. oil industry faced wartime demand. A pioneer in the manufacture of high-octane aviation gasoline, Richfield increased its high-octane production in 1941–1942 by 150%. By 1948, according to Jones, Richfield had developed into a highly successful, well balanced oil company.

Richfield, unlike Atlantic, continued its success in finding crude oil. In 1948 the Cuyama Valley in California yielded to Richfield huge quantities of petroleum, although insufficient to meet demand for oil. In the 1950s, Richfield's oil explorations expanded overseas but, most importantly, included an interest in Alaska.

Richfield's explorations in Alaska predated World War II, but serious prospecting did not get underway until 1955, the year California ceased being self-sufficient in oil. Richfield was the first to discover oil in Alaska, in the Swanson River area, in 1957. This discovery became the first commercial oil field in Alaska's history. Environmentalists opposed further oil exploration. This did not, however, deter Richfield from proceeding to purchase enormous tracts of federal land, laying the basis for the future ARCO's astonishing growth and prosperity.

The Philadelphia-based Atlantic Refining Company was even shorter of crude oil than was Richfield, but Atlantic's leadership was not interested in the exploration and production activities of its dynamic Dallas, Texas, branch. One Atlantic executive in Philadelphia declared he did not know what an oil well looked like and had no intention of finding out. The result of this disharmony was a palpable decline in Atlantic's profits. The company's fortunes began to turn around, however, when a former Harvard business professor, Thornton Bradshaw, became financial vice president of Atlantic in 1956. Bradshaw perceived that disunity and dependency on crude oil purchases were both undermining Atlantic's viability. The solution was a merger with another oil company.

The candidate for a merger, in 1962, was Hondo Oil & Gas Company, whose president, Robert O. Anderson, was a dynamic, multi-faceted businessman. The marriage of the two companies worked. Atlantic's strength lay in the refining of petroleum, and Hondo Oil & Gas's was in the business of finding and producing oil. With energy needs soaring in the

United States, however, the new Atlantic produced at best only 50% of its own crude.

In the mid-1960s, with Anderson as chairman and chief executive officer of Atlantic Refining Company, feelers once again went out for a partner with which to merge. This time the choice fell on oil-wealthy Richfield. The California-based company, with its vast Alaska leases, 2.5 million acres, would have had little reason to merge with eastern-based Atlantic were it not for a still-pending 1962 Department of Justice suit against Richfield. Its mergers in 1936 with Sinclair Oil Corporation and Cities Service Company was only now, nearly 30 years later, being challenged as illegal by the Justice Department on antitrust grounds. The choice for Richfield was to face possible liquidation or the divestiture of Sinclair and Cities Service, or to merge with some company untainted by monopolism. In this light, Atlantic Refining Company appeared to be ideal, especially as Robert Anderson was held in very high regard in the oil business and had turned his company into a highly profitable one.

The merger of the two oil companies took place in January 1966, forming Atlantic Richfield Company. Two years later, the biggest oil discovery in the Western Hemisphere was made in Prudhoe Bay, Alaska, with Atlantic Richfield the biggest federal leaseholder in the state. The production of this vast oil wealth would be delayed nearly a decade because of disputes with environmentalists, native Alaskans, and other oil companies with competing claims, and until the Trans-Alaska pipeline system was constructed. The stable leadership of Anderson, chairman of Atlantic Richfield until 1986, and Thornton Bradshaw, president until 1981, would resolve these difficulties and turn their company into the eighth-largest oil company in the United States, a company well equipped to face the complex challenges of the 21st century. In 1972 Atlantic Richfield moved its headquarters from New York City to Los Angeles.

The resolution of rival Alaskan interests was accelerated by the Arab oil embargo in 1973. The federal government granted permission for the construction of the much disputed pipeline, and oil flowed through it for the first time in midsummer 1977. The original estimated cost of the pipeline was $900 million. This amount had escalated to $10 billion by the time oil actually flowed through it, largely to meet environmental guidelines. This was the largest expenditure for any private undertaking in U.S. history. Despite this unimaginable cost, Atlantic Richfield, 21% owner of the pipeline, benefited enormously. Profits soared, and by 1980 total company assets stood at $16 billion compared to $8 billion four years earlier.

The soaring profits from its Alaskan oil fields had a surprisingly sobering effect upon Atlantic Richfield's leadership, seasoned oil men who were well aware of the historic volatility of the oil market. There was a very strong consciousness, evident in Atlantic Richfield's annual reports predating even the 1973 oil embargo, that natural resources, none more than oil, were finite and that if the company were to survive and, more importantly, generate a profit, the production and refining of oil could not remain the company's main objective. The conundrum of the late 20th century—how to supply the vast U.S. energy needs in the face of oil's ultimate depletion and the country's heavy dependence on foreign crude—would be Atlantic-Richfield's chief challenge, one that would determine its fate in the decades to come.

While oil flowed through the Alaskan pipeline at a rate of nearly two million barrels a day, Atlantic Richfield was undergoing a radical restructuring that not only reflected its growth as an oil company, but as an oil company intent on branching into new products and markets. Gone, however, was the age when new products, markets, and profits were company's sole concerns. No company could hope to survive in an environmentally conscious society without a major investment in the environment. As oil prices rocketed, therefore, so, too, did Atlantic Richfield's investment in environmental causes. As early as 1970, for instance, the company began producing lead-free gasoline. In 1972 Atlantic Richfield removed all billboard advertising, and in the same year received two awards for its conservation efforts. By 1976 total spending on conservation amounted to $400 million. Atlantic Richfield produced and marketed the first low-emissions gasoline in the United States.

A late-20th-century company could ill afford to ignore its social responsibilities, as the growing endowment of the ARCO Foundation revealed. Social responsibility, however, could neither begin nor end with siphoning off a small fraction of its oil profits to charity. ARCO also donated trees to a park, revegetated used coal-mine areas, and encouraged employees to engage in volunteer activities by releasing them from work.

In the face of its explosive growth following the opening of the Alaska pipeline, ARCO executives saw the need for a dramatic restructuring of the company. As early as 1968, the year of the Prudhoe Bay oil discovery, the company realized that it would one day have far more oil than it could refine and market. Once again merger talks began, and the partner became Sinclair Oil Corporation. Its merger with Atlantic Richfield in 1969 endowed ARCO with its biggest oil refinery, in Houston, and more importantly for the future, enabled the company to undertake a five-year, $1 billion expansion of petrochemical production.

The growth of Atlantic Richfield with the completion of the pipeline in 1977 necessitated further restructuring. The aim was to decentralize into eight wholly owned companies—ARCO Alaska, ARCO Oil and Gas, ARCO Chemical, ARCO Products, ARCO Transportation, ARCO International, ARCO Coal, and ARCO Solar—and to focus on new products, apart from traditional oil and gas production. In line with this restructuring, which was completed in 1979, Atlantic Richfield in January 1977 merged with the Anaconda Company. Within a few years, ARCO Coal Company became a leading coal producer in the United States and the nation's number-one producer of low-sulfur coal. By the mid-1980s, under the chairmanship of Lodwrick M. Cook, a yet more radical strategy was devised to ensure profitability and a lessening dependence on oil: to divest Atlantic Richfield of all marginally profitable enterprises and to drastically cut costs across the board. As a result, between 1985 and 1987, Atlantic Richfield had reduced its work force by approximately 12,000 employees. Atlantic Richfield's Philadelphia refinery was sold, along with 1,000 ARCO service stations east of the Mississippi, making "Atlantic" a name only, a reason for the increasing use of the company's acronym, ARCO.

Decentralization, concentration on areas of highest profitability, cost cutting, and diversification, enabled ARCO to weather the precipitous decline in crude oil prices in 1986 and to ward off the threat of a takeover. Diversification away from traditional oil and gas production had been successful.

Besides ARCO's lucrative production of coal, success has been evident in ARCO's petrochemical industry. Petrochemicals became an important facet of Atlantic Richfield's business in the 1970s. In 1985 ARCO formed Lyondell Petrochemical Company by merging existing assets. Lyondell, a division of Atlantic Richfield, increased ARCO's petrochemical capacity, and since then, Lyondell has been in the forefront of petrochemical production. It has been a leader in converting crude oil, for example, into feedstock. ARCO Chemical, in which ARCO had an 83.4% ownership interest in 1991, had become the foremost producer in the world of propylene oxide, used in the manufacture of furniture foam, plastics, and detergents; and calcined coke for the manufacture of aluminum. Another creative idea turned into a successful product by Lyondell, unrelated to petrochemical production, had been the WALL-FRAME building system, a popular prefabricated wall system. Offering superior insulation properties, the components of this system allow speedy erection of the walls of a home. The company has also developed a resin window frame of excellent strength and paintability. In 1989 ARCO sold 50.1% of Lyondell on the New York Stock Exchange.

ARCO Products Company is another example of Atlantic Richfield's diversification. The most profitable idea emanating from this division of Atlantic Richfield has been its am/pm mini-market stores, so popular that they have been expanded into Japan and Taiwan. In 1990, 750 ARCO filling stations had these markets, with about 50 new stores being added annually. The stations have enjoyed great success, largely because of the no-frills, all self-service stations that have been able to give customers low-priced gasoline, operating in California, Arizona, Nevada, Oregon, and Washington. In 1990 ARCO gas stations continued to be the number-one marketer of gasoline in those five western states. The minimarkets contribute heavily to gas station profits, not only from the stores but from increased sales of gas.

Until it was sold in 1990, ARCO Solar represented Atlantic Richfield's most radical departure from tradition. Producing energy from the sun by means of photovoltaic cells, ARCO Solar by the mid-1980s had won 45% of the photovoltaic market, and had become the world's leading producer of photovoltaic devices. The company sold ARCO Solar in 1990 because the business was not competitive on a large scale.

Atlantic Richfield, since its inception, has expanded steadily overseas, with 25% of its petrochemicals exported overseas, especially to Asia. In 1991 ARCO had interests in 20 foreign countries, including a petrochemical plant in southern France, significant coal-mining interests in Australia, and a highly lucrative oil-exploration venture in Indonesia.

Atlantic Richfield was able to weather the decline of world crude oil prices in 1986, as well as to react to the first sign, in 1989, of a diminution in the output of its hitherto most productive Alaskan oilfield. During the Persian Gulf crisis of 1990, Atlantic Richfield alone among U.S. oil companies did not raise its gasoline prices. The company continues to be the biggest employer in the state of Alaska, reaping huge profits from its oil fields in that state.

Principal Subsidiaries: ARCO Alaska, Inc.; ARCO Chemical Company; ARCO Pipeline Company; ARCO Oil and Gas Company; ARCO International Oil and Gas Company; ARCO Coal Company; ARCO Products Company; ARCO Transportation Company; Lyondell Petrochemical Company (49.9%).

Further Reading: Jones, Charles S., *From the Rio Grande to the Arctic: The Story of the Richfield Oil Corporation*, Norman, Oklahoma, University of Oklahoma Press, 1972; Harns, Kenneth, *The Wildcatter: A Portrait of Robert O. Anderson*, New York, Weideinfeld & Nicolson, 1987; "A Brief History of ARCO," Atlantic Richfield corporate typescript, 1989.

—Sina Dubovoj

BRITISH PETROLEUM COMPANY PLC

1 Finsbury Circus
London EC2M 7BA
United Kingdom
(071) 496-4000
Fax: (071) 496-5656

Public Company
Incorporated: 1909 as Anglo-Persian Oil Company
Employees: 118,050
Sales: £41.71 billion (US$80.51 billion)
Stock Exchanges: London New York Toronto Tokyo Paris
    Zürich Amsterdam Frankfurt

British Petroleum (BP) is one of the world's leading oil companies, and one of the United Kingdom's largest corporations. The company, which was the pioneer of the Middle Eastern oil industry, having discovered oil in Iran before World War I, is now engaged in all aspects of oil exploration, production, refining, transportation, and marketing. It has significant interests in chemicals and plastics, including a range of specialty products—mostly detergents, advanced composite materials, and advanced ceramic engineered materials. In 1990, BP was engaged in a fundamental review of its management structure.

BP has its origins in the activities of William Knox D'Arcy, who had made a fortune in Australian mining, and who in 1901 secured a concession from the shah to explore for petroleum throughout almost all of the Persian empire. The search for oil proved extremely costly and difficult, for Iran was devoid of infrastructure and politically unstable. Within a few years D'Arcy was in need of funds. Eventually, after intercession by members of the British Admiralty, The Burmah Oil Company joined D'Arcy in a Concessionary Oil Syndicate in 1905, and supplied further funds in return for operational control. In May 1908 oil was discovered in the southwest of Persia at Masjid-i-Suleiman. This was the first oil discovery in the Middle East. In the following April the Anglo-Persian Oil Company was formed, with the Burmah Oil Company holding most of the shares.

The dominant figure in the early years of the new company was Charles Greenway. Greenway's career had begun in the firm of managing agents who handled the marketing of Burmah Oil's products in India. He was invited by Burmah Oil to help in the formation of Anglo-Persian. He became a founding director, was appointed managing director in 1910 and became chairman in 1914. The first few years of the company's existence were extremely difficult, and it was largely through Greenway's skill that it survived as an independent entity. Although Anglo-Persian had located a prolific oil field, there were major problems in refining the crude oil. The company also lacked a tanker fleet and a distribution network to sell its products.

For a time it seemed that Anglo-Persian would be absorbed by one of the larger oil companies, such as the Royal Dutch/Shell group, with whom it signed a ten-year marketing agreement in 1912, but in 1914 Greenway preserved the independence of Anglo-Persian by a unique agreement with the U.K. government. Under the terms of this agreement negotiated with Winston Churchill, then first lord of the Admiralty, Greenway signed a long-term contract with the British Admiralty for the supply of fuel oil, which the Royal Navy wished to use as a replacement for coal. At the same time, in an unusual departure from the United Kingdom's laissez-faire traditions, the U.K. government invested £2 million in the company, receiving in return a majority shareholding which it was to retain for many years. The transaction provided the company with funds for further investment in refining equipment and an initial investment in transport and marketing in fulfillment of Greenway's ambition to create an independent, integrated oil business. In return for its investment, the U.K. government was allowed to appoint two directors to the company's board with powers of veto, powers that could not, however, be exercised over commercial affairs. In fact, the government directors never used their veto throughout the period of state shareholding in BP, which lasted until the 1980s. Despite the fact that BP was nominally state controlled, in practice it functioned as a purely commercial company.

World War I created considerable opportunities for the fledgling enterprise. Although within Persia the authority of the shah had almost disintegrated, and in 1915 Anglo-Persian's pipeline to the coast was cut by dissident tribesmen and German troops, demand for oil products was soaring. Between 1912 and 1918 there was a tenfold increase in oil production in Iran. The war also created opportunities for Greenway to further his ambition of creating an integrated oil business. In 1915 Greenway created a wholly owned oil tanker subsidiary, and within five years BP had more than 30 oil tankers. In 1917, in his biggest coup, Greenway acquired the British Petroleum Company, the U.K. marketing subsidiary of the European Petroleum Union. The European Petroleum Union, a Continental alliance with significant Deutsche Bank participation, had been expropriated by the U.K. government as an enemy property. In 1917 he also decided to establish a refinery at Swansea, Wales, with improved refining technology that could produce petroleum products for the U.K. and European markets.

World War I and Greenway's skill led to Anglo-Persian's emergence as one of the world's largest oil companies by the late 1920s, matching Royal Dutch/Shell and Standard Oil of New Jersey in stature. During the 1920s the company made a major expansion in marketing, with the establishment of subsidiaries in many European countries and, after the expiration of the agreement with Shell in 1922, in Africa and Asia. New refineries were established in Scotland and France, and the research laboratory established at Sunbury, United Kingdom in 1917 greatly expanded its activities. In the early 1920s there were some criticisms of the management of Anglo-Persian within the U.K. government and some suggestions that the state shareholding should be privatized, but in November 1924 a decision was made to retain the government's equity stake.

Greenway's successor was John Cadman, a former mining engineer who had been a professor of mining at Birmingham University before World War I, and who had become a major figure in official U.K. oil policy during the war. In 1923, he became a managing director of Anglo-Persian, and in 1927 chairman. He introduced major administrative reforms and, in the words of the U.S. business historian Alfred Chandler, in *Scale and Scope: The Dynamics of Industrial Capitalism,* "was one of the few effective British organizational builders." He was successful in overcoming the excessive departmentalism and lack of coordination that had formerly characterized the company. Cadman was also a leading figure alongside Henri Deterding of the Shell group and Standard Oil of New Jersey in the attempts to regulate and cartelize the world oil industry in the late 1920s.

In the 1930s one of Cadman's greatest challenges came from the growth of Iranian nationalism. In 1921 the old dynasty of shahs had been overthrown by an army colonel, Reza Khan, who made himself shah in 1925. Reza Khan was determined to reverse the foreign political and economic domination of his country. Anglo-Persian had a symbolic role as a bastion of British imperialism and, following growing resentment of declining royalty payments from the company due to its falling profits in the Great Depression, the Persian government cancelled its concession in November 1932. The dispute eventually went to the League of Nations, and in 1933 a new 60-year concession agreement was signed with Anglo-Persian, the main effects of which were to reduce the area of the concession to about a quarter of the original, and to introduce a new tonnage basis of assessment for royalty payments. Anglo-Persian had the formidable backing of the U.K. government, and the Persians gained little out of the dispute.

The oil company, which was renamed the Anglo-Iranian Oil Company in 1935, when Persia became Iran, became a renewed target of nationalist discontent after World War II. The Iranians complained that their dividends were too small, and the signing of 50-50 profit-sharing agreements between governments and oil companies elsewhere—in Venezuela in 1948 and Saudi Arabia in 1950—fueled criticism of Anglo-Iranian within Iran. There were extensive negotiations between Anglo-Iranian and the Iranian government. Anglo-Iranian eventually offered substantial concessions, but they came too late and were repudiated by the nationalist government of Muhammad Mussadegh. On May 1, 1951, the Iranian oil industry was formally nationalized. Several years of complex negotiations followed and eventually, in 1953, a coup, in which the U.K. government and the U.S. Central Intelligence Agency were implicated, resulted in the overthrow of Mussadegh. After his removal from power an agreement was reached which allowed the return to Iran of Anglo-Iranian—renamed the British Petroleum Company in 1954—but not on such favorable terms as the company had secured after the 1932-1933 dispute. Under the agreement, which was reached in August 1954, British Petroleum held a 40% interest in a newly created consortium of Western oil companies, formed to undertake oil exploration, production, and refining in Iran.

The events of 1951-1954 had encouraged Anglo-Iranian to diversify away from its overdependence on a single source of crude oil supply. The Iranian nationalization deprived the company of two-thirds of its production. It responded by increasing output in Iraq and Kuwait, and by building new refineries in Europe, Australia, and Aden. Oil exploration activities were launched in the Arabian Gulf, Canada, Europe, North Africa, East Africa, and Australia. Meanwhile, BP, which had first moved into petrochemicals in the late 1940s, became the second-largest chemicals business in the United Kingdom in 1967.

The company's future was secured at the turn of the 1960s and 1970s by major oil discoveries in Alaska and the North Sea. In 1965 BP found gas in British waters of the North Sea. In October 1970 it discovered the Forties field, the first major commercial oil find in British waters. Throughout the 1960s BP had also been looking for oil in Alaska, and in 1969 this effort was rewarded by a major discovery at Prudhoe Bay on the North Slope. In the previous year BP had acquired the U.S. east coast refining and marketing operations from Atlantic Richfield, and the stage was now set for a surge of expansion in the United States. Through its large share in Prudhoe Bay, BP owned over 50% of the biggest oil field in the United States, and it needed outlets for this oil. The solution was found in an agreement with the Standard Oil Company of Ohio signed in August 1969. This company, the original Standard Oil founded by John D. Rockefeller, was the market leader in Ohio, and in several neighboring states. Under the agreement, Standard took over BP's Prudhoe Bay leases and also the downstream facilities acquired from Atlantic Richfield. In return, BP acquired 25% of Standard's equity. BP and Standard engaged in a seven-year struggle—from 1970 to 1977—to develop the Prudhoe Bay oil field and construct the 800-mile Trans Alaska Pipeline system. The pipeline was finally completed in 1977. By the following year BP had taken a majority holding in Standard. In 1987 it was acquired outright and merged with BP's other interests in the United States to form a new company: BP America.

The oil price shocks and the transformation of the balance of power between oil companies and host governments that occurred in the 1970s caused many problems for BP, as for other western oil companies. BP lost most of its direct access to crude oil supplies produced in OPEC countries. Its oil assets were nationalized in Libya in 1971 and Nigeria in 1979. BP and Shell clashed with the U.K. government in 1973 over the allocation of scarce oil supplies. BP's chairman, Sir Eric Drake, refused to give priority to supplying the United Kingdom, despite forceful reminders from Prime Minister Edward Heath that the government owned half the company.

Problems in the oil industry prompted BP to diversify away from its traditional role as an integrated oil company heavily dependent on Middle Eastern oil production. Retrospectively it can be seen that this strategy was not always a wise one, and by the late 1980s BP was actively divesting its noncore businesses. BP's chemicals interests grew, especially after 1978 when it acquired major European assets from Union Carbide and Monsanto. The major world recession after 1979 led to considerable overcapacity, and BP was forced to close down or sell off parts of its chemicals business in the early 1980s. From the mid-1970s BP built up a large coal business, especially in the United States, Australia, and South Africa. In

1989 and 1990, however, many of these coal interests were sold. In the mid-1970s BP became active in mineral mining. In 1980 BP acquired Selection Trust, a U.K.–based mining finance house, in what was at the time the London stock market's largest-ever takeover bid, and in 1981 Standard Oil acquired Kennecott, the largest U.S. copper producer. In 1989, however, most of the minerals assets were sold to the U.K. mining company, Rio Tinto Zinc, for £2.38 billion. As a result of its divestments, BP came to be focused on its four core businesses of oil exploration and production, oil refining and marketing, chemicals and nutrition.

The years since the late 1980s have seen considerable changes at BP. In October 1987 the U.K. Thatcher government sold its remaining shareholding in the company as part of the privatization program. The timing of the share issue was particularly unfortunate, as the world's stock markets collapsed between the opening and closing of the offer. One result of the sale was that by March 1988 the Kuwait Investment Office had built up a 21.6% stake in the company; subsequently the U.K. regulatory authorities reported that this share was reduced to less than 10%. A second major development in 1987 was the launch of a successful bid to acquire Britoil, a company established by the U.K. government in the 1970s to participate in North Sea oil exploration. It had become one of the largest independent oil exploration and production companies and through its acquisition BP almost doubled its exploration acreage in the North Sea.

In 1990 BP announced a fundamental change of its corporate structure, known as Project 1990. The main aims were to reduce organizational complexity, re-shape the central organization and reduce its cost, and reposition BP for the 1990s. Project 1990 was the brainchild of BP's chairman, Robert Horton. At the heart of the scheme was a conviction that BP had become over-bureaucratic, and that strategic flexibility was handicapped as a result. Under Project 1990, some 90%

of corporate center committees—a total of 70—were abolished, with individuals taking responsibility instead. Hierarchically structured departments were to be replaced by small flexible teams with more open and less formal lines of communication.

BP represents, alongside ICI, one of the U.K. success stories of the 20th century. Its achievement in penetrating the international oil oligopoly of the early 20th century was impressive, as was the survival of the loss of the Iranian oil fields in the early 1950s. Project 1990 represents a major imaginative attempt to position the company for the opportunities of the 1990s and the company, under the forceful leadership of Horton, is engaged in a sustained drive to implant the culture changes which are necessary to secure the successful and harmonious operation of its flexible and decentralized management system.

Principal Subsidiaries: BP International; BP Oil International; BP Exploration; BP Chemicals (International); BP Nutrition International BV; BP America.

Further Reading: Ferrier, R.W., *The History of the British Petroleum Company,* Vol. I, Cambridge, Cambridge University Press, 1982; Ferrier, R.W., "Sir Maurice Richard Bridgeman," "John Cadman," "William Knox D'Arcy," "Sir Arthur Eric Courtney Drake," "William Milligan Fraser," "Charles Greenway," in *Dictionary of Business Biography: A Biographical Dictionary of Business Leaders Active in Britain in the Period, 1860–1980,* 5 vols., edited by David Jeremy, London, Butterworth, 1984–86; Jones, Geoffrey, *The State and the Emergence of the British Oil Industry*, London, Macmillan, 1981; "The Road from Persia: A Brief History of BP," London, BP Briefing Paper, April 1989.

—Geoffrey Jones

BURMAH CASTROL PLC

Burmah House
Pipers Way
Swindon, Wiltshire, SN3 1RE
United Kingdom
(0793) 511521
Fax: (0793) 513506

Public Company
Incorporated: 1886 as The Burmah Oil Company Ltd.
Employees: 25,000
Sales: £1.72 billion (US$3.32 billion)
Stock Exchanges: London New York

The Burmah Oil Company, renamed Burmah Castrol in 1990, is the oldest oil enterprise in the United Kingdom. It is best remembered for having survived in 1975 the most serious crash hitherto in the business history of the United Kingdom and for achieving what has been termed by John Davis of *Money Observer,* November 1988, "one of the greatest corporate come-backs of all time." No longer involved in every stage of oil operations from exploration to marketing, it is now a leading international marketer of specialized oil and chemical products.

The company derives its name from the centuries-old oil works in Burma—spelled with an "h" in the Victorian era—which in 1886 became a province of the Indian empire. Founded that year in Glasgow by David Cargill, a Scottish-born merchant with lucrative trading interests in Ceylon, The Burmah Oil Company introduced new technology into the Burmese operations, such as mechanical drilling at the oil fields and continuous distillation in the Rangoon refinery. The oil fields and refinery were connected by a 275-mile pipeline in 1909. Initially all the oil was sold in Burma, apart from some wax for the United Kingdom, but the company was soon shipping products to mainland India, using its own tankers after 1899.

Following its entry into the subcontinent, Burmah Oil came to the attention of the Committee of Imperial Defence, the United Kingdom's top strategic policy-making body, which alerted the appropriate government departments to the company's vital importance as the only oil company of any size in the British Empire. In 1905 the Admiralty concluded a long-term contract to purchase Burmese fuel oil, as it was beginning to convert its warships to run on oil. Admiralty officials also sought to interest Burmah Oil in acquiring a 500,000-square-

mile oil concession in Persia, granted in 1901 to William K. D'Arcy. Since D'Arcy was short of money, the concessions might well have had to be sold into non-British hands. Burmah Oil agreed to the purchase, and in 1908 its drillers struck oil in Persia. The following year it established the Anglo-Persian Oil Company (renamed Anglo-Iranian in 1935 and British Petroleum in 1954), an almost wholly owned subsidiary. Difficulties over refining and transporting the Persian oil proved costly for Burmah Oil, and in 1912 the chairman, Sir John Cargill, son of the founder David Cargill, refused to finance Anglo-Persian any further.

Winston Churchill had recently been appointed first lord of the Admiralty, and was seeking reliable sources of naval fuel oil to supplement those from Rangoon. In 1914 the U.K. authorities and Burmah Oil concluded an agreement which overcame their respective problems. The government acquired from the company a majority share in Anglo-Persian, while in turn the Admiralty obtained long-term fuel oil supplies from Anglo-Persian. During World War I, Burmah Oil concentrated on keeping India supplied with kerosene. After 1918 it became more widely known through its newly appointed managing director, Robert I. Watson. Energetic and highly respected throughout the oil world, Watson helped to devise the market-sharing international agreements which supported oil prices during the Depression between the wars and rationalized distribution methods throughout much of the world. In particular, he negotiated the Burmah-Shell agreement of 1928 that created a common distribution system for the subcontinent of India, and acquired for Burmah Oil a 4% shareholding in Shell, of which he became a director in 1929.

Burmah Oil came to the attention of the world in 1942 when Japanese forces overran a poorly defended Burma. To prevent its strategically crucial assets from falling into enemy hands, Watson authorized the destruction of the Rangoon refinery and all the installations at the oilfields. The Allies's reconquest of Burma in 1945 permitted the company to start work again on its devastated properties there. However, the scale of its efforts was modified by the declared intention of the newly independent republic of Burma to work toward taking over all oil assets. After a short-lived joint venture arrangement, Burmah Oil agreed to an outright sale of its interests in Burma in 1963, obtaining relatively generous compensation since mutual goodwill was maintained to the end.

Its progressive withdrawal from Burma, although not from India or Pakistan, effectively turned the company into an oil investment trust. By the mid-1950s less than a third of its income was derived from trading, the rest coming from its 25% stake in British Petroleum (BP) and its 4% stake in Shell, both earning buoyant profits from their worldwide activities. Consequently in 1957 the chairman, William E. Eadie, launched a policy of diversification, notably in the western hemisphere. Attempts to secure fair compensation from Whitehall for the Burmese assets destroyed in 1942, over and above a nominal *ex gratia* payment, failed, when in 1965 the government of Harold Wilson, by a War Damage Act, blocked the Burmah Oil claim that had been successfully upheld in U.K. courts. By then the company was well embarked on the path of diversification. In addition to some ventures in the United States, Canada, and Australia, in 1962 it had acquired Lobitos Oilfields Ltd., which had production in Peru and Ecuador, and two specialist oil refineries in northwest England.

This entry into the rapidly expanding specialized product market was carried further when in 1966 Burmah Oil purchased Castrol Ltd., the United Kingdom's leading independent lubricating oil supplier, which had an unrivaled reputation for marketing skills. Castrol's earnings helped to keep the Burmah group afloat during the difficult period after 1975.

Having ceased to be a fully integrated oil company since its withdrawal from Burma, but finding itself increasingly engaged in overseas exploration and specialist production, the group's strategy in the 1960s was shaped by two quite unforeseen events. First, in 1963 BP and Shell launched a takeover bid, seeking the group's properties in the western hemisphere and the Indian subcontinent, where neither company was well represented, and also feeling alarm at the Burmah group's apparent aspirations to the status of a major oil corporation. The Burmah directors soon beat off the bid, but had to face the urgent need to safeguard the group's future by improving its inadequate return on assets and its depressed share price. Second, the U.K. government in 1965 introduced a corporation tax, which disallowed companies with overseas interests from claiming relief in the United Kingdom on tax already paid to foreign governments, unless they could offset it against domestically earned income. One of those worst hit by this measure was the Burmah group, which consequently had to seek extensive acquisitions at home. Unable to repeat the highly synergistic purchases of Lobitos and Castrol, it bought, among others, the Rawlplug Company Ltd., Halfords Ltd., and Quinton Hazell Ltd., concerned with masonry fixing products, sales of motorists' accessories, and car components respectively. It also greatly extended one of the former Lobitos refineries, at Ellesmere Port near Liverpool, to provide not only base lubricants for Castrol but also petrol for the large number of filling stations it was acquiring.

This diversification led the group in 1968–1969 to reorganize its many subsidiaries into three main divisions. The Burmah-Castrol Company dealt with lubricants and other fuels, while the non-oil activities were divided between Burmah Industrial Products and Burmah Engineering. Nicholas Williams, managing director from 1969 onward and in 1971 chief executive under a part-time chairman, promoted a number of profit-enhancing ventures. The group was already using its offshore expertise, gained in the United States and Australia, to prospect in the North Sea, acting as operator for various consortia. It made the first ever oil strike there in 1966, but had to wait until 1973–1974 for a major commercial discovery. In the early 1970s it entered the tanker business, both to transport crude for its own needs and to earn profits by chartering to outside parties. From 1975 it operated the Bahamas terminal, where oil was transhipped from giant tankers into smaller vessels capable of entering the shallower ports in the eastern and southern United States.

To help establish the Burmah group as a major oil enterprise in its own right, and to complement its limited operations in the Western Hemisphere, Williams sought to purchase a large U.S. oil corporation. After unsuccessful negotiations with several companies, including the Continental Oil Company (Conoco), late in 1973 Williams arranged to acquire Signal Oil and Gas Incorporated of Houston, Texas. Signal had plentiful supplies of crude oil, which the group currently lacked for its many refining and marketing ventures. A consortium of U.K. and U.S. banks readily lent the purchase money, secured on the Burmah group's asset base, of which the BP shareholding was the largest single component.

The outbreak of the Arab-Israeli War at the end of 1973 and the ensuing fourfold rise in oil prices began a year of grave difficulties for the Burmah group. The new Labour government of March 1974 planned to acquire majority stakes in North Sea operations and to tax oil profits more heavily than before. As delays in the implementation of these plans caused great uncertainty, the stock market prices of oil company shares steadily declined. A fall of about 60% in the value of BP shares meant that the lending banks were no longer fully covered under the Signal agreement, which in the closing months of 1974 had to be hastily renegotiated, thereby increasing the interest burden. The group's total borrowings rose from less than half of stockholders' funds at the end of 1973 to almost double a year later, and the board did little to sell off other assets or raise new equity in order to reduce the ratio. Moreover, the consequent reduced world demand for oil products had caused tanker rates to plummet. Thus the group faced substantial losses from this quarter; many of its 42 vessels, acquired at high prices in the earlier boom period, could no longer be chartered out or only at uneconomically low rates. In December 1974 the Burmah group, faced with a massive cash deficit, requested substantial sterling and dollar loans from the Bank of England.

The Labour government, resisting calls in its ranks for the nationalization of the Burmah group but well aware that the group's financial collapse would set off a calamitous run on sterling, authorized the Bank of England to lend on the security of the BP shares. However, early in 1975, demands by outside creditors and fuller information regarding the huge tanker losses forced the group to seek an even larger loan from the bank. Under ministerial instructions, the Bank of England insisted on purchasing the BP shareholding outright, at the unduly low price then prevailing, with no profit-sharing agreement on any later resale.

As a further condition of the rescue measures, Williams resigned. The new chairman and chief executive was Alastair Down, formerly deputy chairman of BP. Down, assisted by a hand-picked managerial team, had first of all to restore the morale of the 41,000 employees in 300 subsidiaries worldwide. His next task was to determine which assets to retain because of their good cash flows, and which to sell in order to yield essential funds or, as in the case of the 42 tankers, to reduce losses. Over the next few years, Down and his team sold assets in the United States, Australia, Canada, Ecuador, and the North Sea, totaling no less than £865 million. The largest single group of assets, valued at nearly £300 million, were the Signal and other U.S. subsidiaries. With the full backing of the U.K. government, Down was able to delay selling until a fair offer was received.

Down's achievement in saving the Burmah group was recognized by a knighthood in 1978, the year in which the group returned to profitability after tax. In the following year, it paid its first dividends since 1974. Between 1978 and 1981 it took the U.K. government to court, first to obtain the release of official documents relating to the BP share sale of 1975, and then to recover the shareholding itself, claiming that the sale had been a forced one at an unconscionably low price. The Burmah group was defeated in both lawsuits.

This financial recovery allowed the top management to plan in depth the group's future strategy, with the aim of ensuring stable income and longterm growth. Trading profits were coming mainly from lubricants and North Sea production. However, the North Sea fields were becoming worked out, and the group could afford only limited funds for further exploration, which would be very costly. Specialty chemicals therefore provided an alternative source of development. In 1981 the Burmah group launched a bid for Croda International Ltd., a chemical processing company that had lately seen its profits decline. Croda vigorously opposed the bid, and the group withdrew.

On Down's retirement in 1983, his successor, John Maltby, introduced a major rationalization plan. His main objectives were to shed assets which were by then either peripheral or lossmaking, and to concentrate efforts on those assets likely to provide good income and reasonable growth. In 1985 he sold off five tankers, chartering out the two remaining vessels on profitable terms, and in 1986 he disposed of the Bahamas terminal. These sales could only be effected at considerable loss, totaling some £94 million between 1982 and 1987. The group also closed down the Ellesmere Port refinery and disposed of 41 separate businesses, including Rawlplug, Halfords, and Quinton Hazell. In 1986 it sold all of its U.K. exploration and production interests to Premier Consolidated Oilfields PLC, in return for a 25%—later almost 30%—portfolio (non-active) investment in the company. Since 1977 it had been transporting liquid natural gas from Indonesia to Japan under an agreement with the Indonesian State petroleum company PERTAMINA, and in 1989 it sold 50% of its interest in the scheme to Japan's Mitsui O.S.K. Lines, Ltd. and Nissho-Iwai. The sale provided cash for activities elsewhere while allowing the Burmah group to maintain a stake in this highly profitable operation.

Although most of the group's acquisitions in the 1980s were on a relatively small scale to strengthen its main divisional interests, in 1987 it launched a bid for the Calor group, a specialist supplier of liquefied petroleum gas. This £820 million offer was made jointly with the privately owned Dutch energy group SHV Holdings NV, which by 1989 had a 9% stake in the Burmah group and a 40% stake in Calor. The bid was rebuffed and withdrawn. Despite such disappointments, the group enjoyed a decade or more of sustained recovery, thanks to successive rationalization plans.

However, by the end of the 1980s the Burmah group appeared once again to have reached a plateau. Turnover in 1989 was only marginally higher than in 1985, but this was the inevitable result of rationalization, which involved the sales of operations.

In mid-1990, when Lawrence Urquhart succeeded John Maltby as chairman, the company took the opportunity to restructure. It became Burmah Castrol plc, thereby combining the goodwill and historical associations of the century-old Burmah name with the worldwide reputation of Castrol's products, which contributed over two-thirds of group earnings. The formerly separate functions of the group were to be merged to create a tighter company structure, eliminate duplication of effort, and speed up decision-making at each level. The chairman and chief executive would oversee head office functions such as finance, shipping, and energy investments. Under him a managing director would be responsible for three international divisions: lubricants, chemicals, and fuels. Eight group directors would report to the managing director, with no fewer than six concentrating on lubricants.

A former director, Roger Wood, in *Accountancy Age*, July 12, 1990, characterized these radical changes as a takeover of the group by its Castrol division, causing it to focus inward, at least as long as the substantial task of integration was under way. Yet the appointment under those changes of one Castrol director solely for the lubricants market in Western Europe and one for the same products in Germany and Eastern Europe suggests that Burmah Castrol is moving ahead of many other British companies in striving to take full advantage of the single European market from 1992 onward and of the opportunities now available in the former Eastern bloc. Other Castrol directors will concentrate on vital lubricants markets in North America, east Asia, and Southern Hemisphere countries.

In October 1990, Burmah Castrol launched a hostile takeover bid for Foseco plc, a U.K.-based company operating internationally and specializing predominantly in metallurgical and construction chemicals. This £270 million acquisition is a major step forward in the expansion of the company's chemicals group. It significantly increases Burmah Castrol's size and improves the balance of the company's business, boosting Chemicals and correspondingly reducing the weighting of the other groups. Burmah Castrol has a chemicals group which commands attention in its portfolio, with a turnover of approximately £650 million.

These moves could be seen as the culmination of a process which began in 1975. While Alastair Down had saved the group by forced divestments, John Maltby had, in the words of *Financial Weekly's* Edward Russell-Walling, June 11, 1987, "stripped it down from a lumbering and vulnerable hulk to a lighter and altogether more purpose-built craft." Lawrence Urquhart in his turn planned to utilize the group's resources more effectively than in the past, in the directions which would best promote its long-term expansion. In his words, "bringing all of our skills and strengths together in a single but strengthened company structure will ensure that Burmah Castrol remains a world beater in its selected markets throughout the nineties and beyond."

Principal Subsidiaries: Castrol Ltd.; Veedol International Ltd.; Burmah Petroleum Fuels Ltd.; The Burmah Oil (Deutschland) GmbH (Germany); Castrol Australia Pty Ltd. (Australia); Castrol (Far East) Pte Ltd. (Singapore); Castrol Inc. (U.S.); Burmah Castrol Chemicals Ltd.; Industrial Adhesives Ltd.; Dussek Campbell Ltd.; Sericol Ltd.; Expandite Ltd.; Burmah Castrol Finance PLC; Burmah Castrol Trading Ltd.; Colombia Cement Co. Inc. (U.S.); Foseco (FS) Ltd.; Fosroc Ltd.

Further Reading: Wilsher, Peter, et al.; "Burmah Oil: The Rocky Road from Mandalay," *Sunday Times,* January 5, 1975; Chairman's Statement (about events of 1974–1975), Annual General Meeting, Glasgow, June 9, 1978; Corley, T.A.B., *A History of the Burmah Oil Company 1886–1924,* Vol. I, London, Heinemann, 1983; Beavan, Susan, "Burmah Still Waiting for Its Star to Rise Again," *The Times,* October 19, 1983; Corley, T.A.B., "Sir John Cargill" and "Sir Alastair Down," in *Dictionary of Business Biography: A Biographical Dictionary of Business Leaders Active in Britain in the Period, 1860–1980,* Vols. I and II, edited by David Jeremy, London,

Butterworth, 1984; Corley, T.A.B., "Robert I. Watson," in *Dictionary of Business Biography: A Biographical Dictionary of Business Leaders Active in Britain in the Period, 1860–1980,* Vol. V, edited by David Jeremy, London, Butterworth, 1986; Corley, T.A.B., "David Cargill," in *Dictionary of Scottish Business Biography,* Vol. I, Aberdeen, Aberdeen University Press, 1986; Barnard, Bruce, "Oil Crisis Doesn't Worry Burmah Oil," *Journal of Commerce,* December 9, 1986; Corley, T.A.B., *A History of the Burmah Oil Company 1924–1966,* Vol. II, London, Heinemann, 1988; Davis, John, "Castrol Fuels Burmah's Rise," *Money Observer,* November 1988; Dimson, Elroy, and Paul Marsh, "Burmah Oil," *Cases in Corporate Finance,* London, Wiley, 1988; Joyce, Conor, "Burmah Hides Its Brand Strength under a Barrel," *Investors Chronicle,* February 9, 1990; Butler, Steven, "Burmah Move Reflects Importance of Castrol," *Financial Times,* July 3, 1990.

—T.A.B. Corley

CHEVRON CORPORATION

225 Bush Street
San Francisco, California 94104
U.S.A.
(415) 894-7700
Fax: (415) 894-8897

Public Company
Incorporated: 1906 as Standard Oil Company (California)
Employees: 54,208
Sales: $41.54 billion
Stock Exchanges: New York Midwest Pacific Vancouver
London Zürich

One of the many progeny of the Standard Oil Trust, Chevron Corporation has grown from its modest California origins to become a major power in the international oil market. Its dramatic discoveries in Saudi Arabia gave Chevron a strong position in the world's largest oil region and helped fuel 20 years of record earnings in the postwar era. The rise of the Organization of Petroleum Exporting Countries (OPEC) in the early 1970s deprived Chevron of its comfortable Middle East position, causing considerable anxiety and a determined search for new domestic oil resources at a company long dependent on foreign supplies. The firm's 1984 purchase of Gulf Corporation, at $13.2 billion the largest industrial transaction to that date, more than doubled Chevron's oil and gas reserves but has failed to bring its profit record back to pre-1973 levels of performance.

Chevron's oldest direct ancestor is the Pacific Coast Oil Company, founded in 1879 by Frederick Taylor and a group of investors. Several years before, Taylor, like many other Californians, had begun prospecting for oil in the rugged canyons north of Los Angeles; unlike most, Taylor found what he was looking for, and his Pico Well #4 was soon the state's most productive. Following its incorporation, Pacific Coast developed a method for refining the heavy California oil into an acceptable grade of kerosene, then the most popular lighting source in use, and the company's fortunes prospered. By the turn of the century Pacific had assembled a team of producing wells in the area of Newhall, California, and built a refinery at Alameda Point across the San Francisco Bay from San Francisco. It also owned both railroad tank cars and the *George Loomis,* an ocean-going tanker, to transport its crude from field to refinery.

One of Pacific Coast's best customers was Standard Oil Company of Iowa, the far-west marketing subsidiary of the New Jersey–headquartered Standard Oil Trust. Iowa Standard had been active in northern California since 1885, selling both eastern oil of Standard's own and also large quantities of kerosene purchased from Pacific Coast and the other local oil companies. The West Coast was important to Standard Oil Company of New Jersey not only as a market in itself but also as a source of crude for sale to its Asian subsidiaries. Jersey Standard thus became increasingly attracted to the area and in the late 1890s tried to buy Union Oil Company, the state leader. The attempt failed, but in 1900 Pacific Coast agreed to sell its stock to Jersey Standard for $761,000, with the understanding that Pacific Coast would produce, refine, and distribute oil for marketing and sale by Iowa Standard representatives. W.H. Tilford and H.M. Tilford, two brothers who were long-time employees of Standard Oil, assumed the leadership of Iowa Standard and Pacific Coast, respectively.

Drawing on Jersey Standard's strength, Pacific Coast immediately built the state's largest refinery at Point Richmond on San Francisco Bay and a set of pipelines to bring oil from its San Joaquin Valley wells to the refinery. Its crude production rose steeply over the next decade, yielding 2.6 million barrels a year by 1911, or 20 times the total for 1900. The bulk of Pacific Coast's holdings were in the Coalinga and Midway fields in the southern half of California, wells rich enough to supply Iowa Standard with an increasing volume of crude but never enough to satisfy its many marketing outlets. Indeed, even in 1911 Pacific Coast was producing a mere 2.3% of the state's crude, forcing partner Iowa Standard to buy most of its crude from outside suppliers like Union Oil and Puente Oil.

By that date, however, Pacific Coast and Iowa Standard were no longer operating as separate companies. In 1906 Jersey Standard had brought together its two West Coast subsidiaries into a single entity called Standard Oil Company (California), generally known thereafter as Socal. Jersey Standard recognized the future importance of the West and quickly increased the new company's capital from $1 million to $25 million. Socal added a second refinery at El Segundo, near Los Angeles, and vigorously pursued the growing markets for kerosene and gasoline in both the western United States and in Asia. Able to realize considerable transportation savings by using West Coast oil for the Pacific markets of its parent company, Socal was soon selling as much as 80% of its kerosene overseas. Socal's head chemist, Eric A. Starke, was chiefly responsible for several breakthroughs in the refining of California's heavy crude into usable kerosene, and by 1911 Socal was the state leader in kerosene production.

The early strengths of Socal lay in refining and marketing. Its large, efficient refineries used approximately 20% of California's entire crude production, much more than Socal's own wells could supply. To keep the refineries and pipelines full, Socal bought crude from Union Oil and in return handled a portion of the marketing and sale of Union kerosene and naphtha. In the sale of kerosene and gasoline Socal maintained a near-total control of the market, in 1906 supplying 95% of the kerosene and 85% of the gasoline and naphtha purchased in its marketing area of California, Arizona, Nevada, Oregon, Washington, Hawaii, and Alaska, although its share dipped somewhat in the next five years. When necessary, Socal used its dominant position to inhibit competition by deep price-cutting.

By the time of the dissolution of the Standard Oil Trust in 1911, Socal, like many of the Standard subsidiaries, had become the overwhelming leader in the refining and marketing of oil in its region, while lagging somewhat in the production of crude.

In 11 short years the strength of Standard Oil and a vigorous western economy combined to increase Socal's net book value from a few million dollars in 1900 to $39 million. It was in 1911, however, that Jersey Standard, the holding company for Socal and the entire Standard Oil family, was ordered dissolved by the U.S. Supreme Court to break its monopolistic hold on the oil industry. As one of 34 independent companies carved out of the former parent, Standard Oil Company (California), would have to do without Standard's financial backing, but the new competitor hardly faced the world unarmed. Socal kept its dominant marketing and refining position, its extensive network of critical pipelines, a modest but growing fleet of oil tankers, its many oil wells, and, most helpfully, some $14 million in retained earnings. The latter proved very useful in Socal's subsequent rapid expansion, as did California's growing popularity among Americans looking for a fresh start in life. The state population shot up quickly, and most of the new residents found that they depended on the automobile—and hence on gasoline—to navigate the state's many highway miles.

The years leading up to World War I saw a marked increase in Socal's production of crude. From a base of 2%–3% of state production in the early part of the century, Socal rode a series of successful oil strikes to a remarkable 26% of nationwide crude production in 1919. As the national production leader, Socal found itself in a predicament that would be repeated throughout its history, with an excess of crude and a shortage of outlets for it. For most of the other leading international oil companies, the situation was reversed, crude generally being in short supply in a world increasingly dependent on oil. Particularly in the aftermath of World War I, of which the British diplomat George Curzon said "the Allies floated to victory on a wave of oil," there was much anxiety in the United States about a possible shortage of domestic crude supplies and a number of the major oil companies began exploring more vigorously around the world. Socal took its part in these efforts but with a notable lack of success—37 straight dry holes in six different countries. More internationally oriented firms like Jersey Standard and Mobil soon secured footholds in what was to become the future center of world oil production, the Middle East, while Socal, with many directors skeptical about overseas drilling, remained content with its California supplies and burgeoning retail business.

In the late 1920s Socal's posture changed. At that time, Gulf Corporation was unable to interest its fellow partners in Iraq Petroleum Company in the oil rights to Bahrain, a small group of islands off the coast of Saudi Arabia. Iraq Petroleum was then the chief cartel of oil companies operating in the Middle East, and its members were restricted by the Red Line Agreement of 1928 from engaging in oil development independently of the entire group. Gulf was therefore unable to proceed with its Bahrain concession and sold its rights for $50,000 to Socal, which was prodded by Maurice Lombardi and William Berg, two members of its board of directors. This venture proved successful—in 1930 Socal geologists struck oil in Bahrain and

within a few years the California company had joined the ranks of international marketers of oil.

Bahrain's real importance, however, lay in its proximity to the vast fields of neighboring Saudi Arabia. The richest of all oil reserves lay beneath an inhospitable desert and until the early 1930s was left alone by the oil prospectors, but at that time, encouraged by the initial successes at Bahrain, Saudi's King Ibn Saud hired a U.S. geologist to study his country's potential oil reserves. The geologist, Karl Twitchell, liked what he saw and tried on behalf of the king to sell the concession to a number of U.S. oil companies. None was interested except the now-adventurous Socal, which in 1933 won a modest bidding war and obtained drilling rights for a £5,000 annual fee and a loan of £50,000. After initial exploration revealed the fantastic extent of Arabian oil, Socal executives realized that the company would need access to markets far larger than its own meager foreign holdings, and in 1936 Socal sold 50% of its drilling rights in Saudi Arabia and Bahrain to the Texas Company, later Texaco, the only other major oil company not bound by the Red Line Agreement. Once the oil started flowing in 1939, King Saud was so pleased with his partners and the profit they generated for his impoverished country that he increased the size of their concession to 440,000 square miles, an area the size of Texas, Louisiana, Oklahoma, and New Mexico combined.

Socal and the Texas Company agreed to market their products under the brand name of Caltex, and were soon developing excellent representation in both Europe and the Far East, especially in Japan. The new partners realized soon after the end of World War II, however, that the Saudi oil fields were too big even for the both of them, and to raise further capital they sold 40% of the recently formed Arabian American Oil Company (Aramco) for $450 million, leaving the two original partners with 30% each. With its crude supply secure for the foreseeable future, Socal was able to market oil around the world as well as in North America's fastest-growing demographic region, California and the Pacific Coast. And as later Chairman R. Gwin Follis put it, Saudi Arabia was a "jackpot beyond belief," supplying Caltex markets overseas with unlimited amounts of low-priced, high-grade oil. By the mid-1950s, Socal was getting one-third of its crude production out of Aramco, and, more significantly, calculated that Saudi Arabia accounted for two-thirds of its reserve supply. Other important fields had been discovered in Sumatra and Venezuela, but Socal was particularly dependent on its Aramco concession for crude.

On the domestic scene, Socal by 1949 had grown into one of the few American companies with $1 billion in assets. No longer the number-one domestic crude producer, Socal was still among the leaders and had recently made plentiful strikes in Louisiana and Texas as well as in its native California. In addition to its original refineries at Point Richmond and El Segundo, Socal had added new facilities in Bakersfield, California, and in Salt Lake City, Utah. Socal's marketing territory included at least some representation in 15 western states and a recent, limited foray into the northeastern United States, mainly as an outlet for some of its cheap Middle Eastern oil. West of the Rocky Mountains remained the heart of Socal territory, where the company continued to control about 28% of the retail market during the postwar years, a far cry from the

90% it owned at the turn of the century, but still easily a dominant share in the nation's leading automotive region.

The two decades following the war saw the complete conversion of the U.S. economy to a dependence on oil. As both a cause and an effect of this trend, the world was awash in oil. The Middle East, Latin America, and southeast Asia all contributed mightily to a prolonged glut which steadily lowered the price of oil in real dollars. The enormous growth in world consumption assured Socal of a progressive rise in sales and a concomitant increase in profit at an annual rate of about 5.5%. By 1957, for example, Socal was selling $1.7 billion worth of oil products annually, and ranked as the world's seventh-largest oil concern. Its California base offered Socal a number of advantages in the prevailing buyer's market. By drawing upon its own local wells for the bulk of its U.S. sales Socal was able to keep its transportation costs lower than most of its competitors, and California's zooming population and automobile-oriented economy afforded an ideal marketplace. As a result, Socal consistently had one of the best profit ratios among all oil companies during the 1950s and 1960s.

California crude production had begun to slow, however, and along with the rest of the world Socal grew ever more dependent on Middle Eastern oil for its overall health. The rich Bay Marchand strike off the Louisiana coast helped stem the tide temporarily; by 1961 Socal was drawing 27.9 million barrels per year from Marchand and had bought Standard Oil Company of Kentucky to market its gasoline in the southeastern United States; but the added domestic production only masked Socal's increasing reliance on Saudi Arabian oil, which by 1971 provided more than three-quarters of Socal's proven reserves. As long as the Middle Eastern countries remained cooperative such an imbalance was not of great concern, and by vigorously selling its cheap Middle Eastern oil in Europe and Asia, Socal was able to rack up a perfect record of profit increases every year in the 1960s. By 1970 20% of Socal's $4 billion in sales was generated in the Far East, with Japan again providing the lion's share of that figure; and the firm's European gas stations, owned jointly with Texaco until 1967, numbered 8,000.

The world oil picture had changed fundamentally by 1970, however. The 20-year oil surplus had given way in the face of rampant consumption to a general and increasing shortage, a shift soon taken advantage of by OPEC members. In 1973 and 1974 OPEC effectively took control of oil at its source and engineered a fourfold increase in the base price of oil. Socal was now able to rely on its Saudi partner for only a tiny price advantage over the general rate, and it was no longer in legal control of sufficient crude to supply its worldwide or domestic demand. The sudden shift in oil politics revealed a number of Socal shortcomings. Though it had 17,000 gas stations in 39 U.S. states, Socal was not a skilled marketer either in the United States or in Europe, where its former partner, Texaco, had supplied local marketing savvy. In its home state of California, for example, Socal's market share was at 16% and continuing to drop, and Socal had missed out on both the North Sea and Alaskan oil discoveries of the late 1960s.

Socal responded to these problems by merging all of its domestic marketing into a single unit, Chevron USA, and began cutting employment, at first gradually and later more deeply. Also, Socal stepped up its domestic exploration efforts while moving into alternative sources of energy such as shale, coal,

and uranium. In 1981 the company made a $4 billion bid for AMAX Inc., a leader in coal-and metal-mining, but had to settle for a 20% stake. In 1984 Standard Oil Company (California) changed its name to Chevron Corporation. Also in 1984, after a decade of sporadic attempts to lessen its dependence on the volatile Middle East, Chevron Corporation met its short-term oil needs in a more direct fashion: it bought Gulf Corporation.

The $13.2 billion purchase, at that time the largest in the history of U. S. business, more than doubled Chevron's proven reserves and created a new giant in the U.S. oil industry, with Chevron now the leading domestic retailer of gasoline and, briefly, the second-largest oil company by assets. Certain factors made the move appear ill-timed, however. Oil prices had peaked around 1980 and begun a long slide that continued until the Gulf War of 1990, which meant that Chevron had saddled itself with a $12 billion debt at a time of shrinking sales. As a result it was not easy for Chevron to sell off assets as quickly as desirable, both to reduce debt and to eliminate the many areas of overlap created by the merger. Chevron eventually rid itself of Gulf's Canadian operations and of all of Gulf's gas stations in the northeast and southeast United States, paring 16,000 jobs in the meantime, but oil analysts pointed to key figures such as profit per employee and return of capital as evidence of Chevron's continued poor performance. Chairman Kenneth Derr embarked on a program to upgrade Chevron's efficiency, but 1989 results were poor. In 1990, however, Chevron's results improved.

Principal Subsidiaries: Chevron USA Inc.; Chevron Canada Limited; Chevron Canada Resources; Chevron Chemical Company; Chevron Industries, Inc.; Chevron Investment Management Company; Chevron International Oil Company, Inc.; Chevron Land and Development Company; Chevron Overseas Petroleum Inc.; Chevron Pipe Line Company; Chevron Transport Corporation (Liberia); Chevron U.K. Limited; Bermaco Insurance Company Limited (Bermuda); Cabinda Gulf Oil Company Limited (Bermuda); Chevron Asiatic Limited; Chevron International Limited (Liberia); Gulf Oil Company (Nigeria) Limited; Gulf Oil (Great Britain) Limited (U.K.); INSCO Limited (Bermuda), Huntington Beach Company; The Pittsburg & Midway Coal Mining Co.; Transocean Chevron Company; Chevron Oil Field Research Company; Chevron Research and Technology Company; Chevron Canada Enterprises Limited; Chevron Capital U.S.A. Inc.; Chevron Oil Finance Company; Gulf Oil Finance N.V. (Netherlands Antilles).

Further Reading: Hidy, Ralph W., and Muriel E. Hidy, *History of Standard Oil Company (New Jersey): Pioneering in Big Business, 1882–1911,* New York, Harper & Brothers, 1955; Klaw, Spencer, "Standard of California," *Fortune,* November 1958; Sampson, Anthony, *The Seven Sisters: The Great Oil Companies and the World They Made,* New York, The Viking Press, 1975.

—Jonathan Martin

CHINESE PETROLEUM CORPORATION

83, Chung Hwa Road
Section I
Taipei
Taiwan 10031
Republic of China
(2) 361-0221
Fax: (2) 331-9645

State-Owned Company
Incorporated: 1946
Employees: 22,287
Sales: NT$227.62 billion (US$8.55 billion)

Chinese Petroleum Corporation (CPC) is the Taiwanese state-owned enterprise which holds sole responsibility for the Republic of China's petroleum industry and its many associated activities. CPC's corporate development is inevitably closely allied to the policies of the Kuomintang or Nationalist Party government and has been directly affected by the great political changes that have taken place in the short history of the Republic of China.

The Kuomintang took power on the Chinese mainland in 1928, 17 years after the last Chinese dynasty, the Qing, was replaced by the Republic of China. The Sino-Japanese War began in 1937 and was superseded by World War II in which the Chinese continued to fight against the Japanese. The year 1945 finally saw the defeat of the Japanese and simultaneously the end of 50 years of Japanese colonial rule in Taiwan, formerly Formosa. There ensued a civil war on the Chinese mainland between the Communist Party of Mao Zedong and the Kuomintang followers under Chiang K'aishek. It was at this time that CPC was founded. When Mao finally won the civil war in 1949, 1.5 million people who supported the Kuomintang left for Taiwan and joined the 6 million Taiwanese already resident there. CPC also moved from Shanghai to Taiwan at this time and was charged with the important task of developing oil refining facilities, supplying energy, and promoting the petrochemical industry there.

Between 1953 and the present day, Taiwan's economy has been transformed from a predominantly agricultural one to an economy that is based on manufacturing and service industry. The government has been accused of being authoritarian and unrepresentative—martial law was in existence until 1987—however the economic development brought about has been

unparalleled in this part of the Far East. CPC has been called upon to provide the high quality petroleum products and petrochemical feedstocks essential for Taiwan's developing industries, and its achievements have undoubtedly played an important role in the economic transformation that has been brought about in the country—CPC has grown to become the nation's largest enterprise. CPC's principal activities have since expanded to include exploration and drilling for, and production of, petroleum; the refining of crude oil and the manufacturing of petrochemicals; the storage, transportation, and marketing of petroleum products and petrochemicals; and the operation of pipelines for the provision of crude oil, natural gas, and petroleum products.

From the outset the Taiwanese authorities have played a particularly active role in the economy of the country. In 1952, the first planners of Taiwan's economic future determined that 56.6% of total industrial production should be in state hands. Centralized economic plans were developed and administered by the government and a substantial portion of Taiwan's heavy industry and financial institutions were assigned to the public sector. Despite the fact that the private sector invested heavily in developing industries, so much so that it gradually took over 90% of industry—state ownership of industrial output fell from 46.2% in 1952 to 10% by 1989—key industries were to remain firmly under government control. Enterprises such as CPC, which were regarded as high risk, strategically important, liable to be monopolized, or vital to the economic development of the country were to remain part of the public sector and thus all their operations would be supervised by the Ministry of Economic Affairs.

Taiwan's energy resources are scarce in quantity, relatively inaccessible, and insufficient for domestic needs. Minor supplies of natural gas and petroleum exist, but on a limited scale, and it has been CPC's task to utilize Taiwan's steadily depleting natural energy resources to their best effect and to produce an adequate supply of energy for the future.

In 1958, under central government directions, the foundations for Taiwan's now-booming petrochemical industry were laid. The petrochemical industry was to supply the basic and intermediate petrochemical raw materials to the hundreds of small industries which were to prove so vital to Taiwan's economic development. The Kaohsiung Refinery, directly owned by CPC, established plants in 1958 for the production of sulfur and sulfuric acid and these were followed by the production of benzene, toulene, and xylene in 1960 in Chiayi. From these, such products as naphtha and rubber solvents were made in order to supply the needs of the domestic market. Kaohsiung, in the south of Taiwan, is the island's largest port and principal industrial complex. It has subsequently become the site of many large chemical and plastics firms and it is where CPC's major facilities are situated. It was in Kaohsiung that the first naphtha cracking plant was put into operation in 1968 as a product center for the southern petrochemical complexes.

Petroleum, as the most popular form of energy in Taiwan, has always been regarded as essential to national defence as well as to the everyday needs of industry and ordinary people. The Taiwan petroleum exploration division and the offshore petroleum exploration division were formed by CPC to explore petroleum resources in Taiwan both onshore and offshore. However, in the light of the scarcity of crude oil and gas in and around the island, exploration activities were extended by CPC in 1970 to Southeast Asia, the Middle East, Africa, Australia, and South America under joint ventures with international companies and host countries. In Indonesia, CPC, under the name of OPIC (Overseas Petroleum and Investment Corporation), is working jointly with Conoco, in the Warim Concession and in the Ecuador Amazon region, oil has been found under a joint venture with the company Conoco, Ecuador Ltd. and four other companies. Throughout the 1970s Taiwan grew ever more reliant on imported oil, in spite of the first oil price shock. The world energy crisis at this time, in conjunction with the worldwide economic recession which followed, proved to be the most testing time ever for CPC. It became essential to emphasise energy conservation and to try to diversify foreign sources of oil and other fuels. Oil had become important both as a source of energy and as a component of the country's import bill. Having leapt from 2.6% to 10.3% of the total import value between 1973 and 1979, oil imports made a further leap between 1979 and 1980 from 14.7% to 20.6% and stayed at these levels for four years. These changes were largely out of the control of the government, however, and the second oil price shock, followed by the difficult years of the early 1980s recession, gave new impetus to reduce the dependence of Taiwan on important hydrocarbons.

At the end of 1983, the Council for Economic Planning and Development approved CPC's $85 million proposal to increase oil exploration in Taiwan and abroad. CPC therefore put forward plans to sink land and offshore wells in search of both oil and geothermal resources—plans which were to be carried out with increasing vigor and expertise in subsequent years. The most important figure in CPC's recent history, Chen Yaosheng, a chemist, was a director for CPC in the Chinese Government Procurement and Service Mission in New York in the early 1970s before being made vice president of CPC in 1978 and president in 1982. He has been a key figure in leading CPC through the most difficult years since its inception—he was made chairman of the board in 1985.

It was under Chen's leadership that CPC undertook one of its most important projects to date. Taiwan's natural gas supply had been diminishing and lagging behind the rapidly increasing demand. According to CPC estimates, known reserves would be exhausted before the end of the century. The decision to import liquefied natural gas (LNG) was taken in 1979, and CPC conducted feasibility studies together with other government organizations to establish the economic effects of importing LNG. These endorsed the decision and CPC invested $800 million in the construction of an LNG receiving terminal on the coast of Yung An Hsiang in the Kaohsiung area, on reclaimed land. The terminal's purpose is to handle the transportation inland—via a 350-kilometer gas trunkline from Pingtung in the south to Keelung in the north of the island—of imported LNG for long-term household, industrial, and business consumption. It also aims to extend the life of Taiwan's own natural gas deposits. In 1986, CPC signed an agreement to import 1.5 million tons of liquefied natural gas per year from Badak, Indonesia. The 20-year contract was signed with Pertamina, the Indonesian government-owned petroleum company, for supply starting in 1990. Market strain was also slightly alleviated by the production of natural gas from offshore wells at the end of 1986.

As part of the government's strategy of diversifying and securing reliable sources of energy supplies of crude oil for the refineries, CPC entered into long-term contracts (LTC) with politically stable oil-producing countries with the aim of maintaining constant supplies. This was in addition to its usual practice of procuring crude oils from the Middle East through major international oil companies. In 1990, 36% of imported oil came from Saudi Arabia and 19% from Kuwait. However, these countries were considered by Taiwan as likely to come under the political influences of the People's Republic of China, governed from Beijing, and therefore constitute an insecure source of supply for the Republic of China, governed from Taipei. Indeed in 1989, Saudi Arabia announced that in accordance with the new OPEC quotas, it would be cutting shipments of crude oil to Taiwan by 40%. It was precisely the fear of adverse political influence on the supply of crude oil which led CPC to reduce its suppliers to those regarded as most reliable and least susceptible to political influence from Beijing.

All CPC's purchases take place on a LTC basis, never on the world spot market, and even in the event of an unanticipated additional requirement, the policy is to negotiate incremental supplies under the existing contracts, rather than to turn to spot market purchases. CPC claims that this policy proved particularly successful during the oil crisis of 1979, when major suppliers continued to deliver and even increase their deliveries to Taiwan, while other oil-buying countries suffered from cancellation of contracts and non-delivery. The Taiwanese government has also effected a policy of ensuring the maintenance of a 90-day inventory for oil as a further safety net against oil shortages. The overriding concern for CPC is to meet domestic market demands and therefore the exporting or swapping of oil products only takes place when there is a surplus or when it is necessary to achieve a balance of supply or demand. In view of the steady depletion of Taiwan's few natural resources, such policies have proved very important—in 1971, 37% of the island's total energy supply was derived from indigenous resources; however, by 1983 this percentage had been reduced to only 12%. Authoritative sources estimate that imported energy will make up 93% of the island's total supply by the year 2000. It is in view of this fact that CPC has had to address the issue of sourcing so vigorously.

CPC's exploration activities overseas are carried out through OPIC. One of CPC's most successful overseas exploration activities was an onshore venture in Ecuador, where three oil wells of high commercial value were found. Exploration continues in the Philippines, Indonesia, Malaysia, Ecuador, Papua New Guinea, and Australia. Projects include some onshore and offshore ventures in the United States, the Etosha concession in Namibia and the concession in Sarawak, Malaysia, where a new oil well has been found.

One of the most pressing political issues of the day in Taiwan, and one that puts CPC very much in the public eye, is that of environmental pollution—opinion polls have placed it as the second most important issue in the view of the populace, behind "social order" and ahead of political democratization. Taiwan's industrial growth had always been fueled by government incentives, for example tax and customs duty rebates and low interest credits. Between 1950 and 1980 the number of factories increased from 5,623 to 62,474, the fastest rate of increase being in petroleum refining and the chemical and plastics industries. Growing public awareness of the dangers of environmental pollution has resulted in demonstrations and protests of an unexpectedly vociferous nature. Demonstrators managed to halt work on the fifth naphtha cracking plant in Kaohsiung, to replace the aging first and second plants, in protest at the pollution it would cause. On this occasion CPC responded by offering to build a swimming pool and hospital nearby in compensation.

More effective and direct action was demanded, and CPC responded in 1989 by setting up an environmental protection division to conduct the planning and promotion of environmental protection programs. Current issues being addressed include the reduction of pollutants from plants, mines, and stations; improved treatment of refinery waste water before discharge; efforts to reduce air pollution and increase noise control; safer disposal of solid waste; and the recovery of escaped oil vapor during transportation. In the future, CPC plans to instal automatic detection and alarm systems to warn against dangerous emission of inflammable and toxic gases. CPC has also paid attention to the landscaping of lands surrounding the refineries in order to minimize the negative impact of huge industrial complexes on the scenery of their locations. For every new plant CPC now produces an "environmental impact statement" assessing possible adverse effects. No project can go ahead without the government's subsequent approval of these assessments. Another important aim is the provision of low sulfur fuel and unleaded and low-leaded petrol for a far more environmentally conscious public than ever before.

It seems the future for CPC will be as challenging as the past four decades. The Republic of China is under constant pressure to evolve due to trends towards economic liberalization and even greater exposure to world market forces. Drastic changes in social and political structures have taken and are continuing to take place. CPC's future is likely to be very much bound up with these changes. Private companies are already permitted to sell petroleum products and planning for CPC's privatization has begun. Privatization will continue in order to meet the demands of a competitive marketplace. A long term strategy which confronts these issues will be essential if CPC is to overcome the uncertainties that lie ahead.

Principal Subsidiaries: Kaohsiung Refinery; Taoyuan Refinery; China Petrochemical Development Corporation (96.3%); China American Petrochemical Co. Ltd. (25%); China Gulf Oil Co. Ltd. (49%).

Further Reading: "Marketing in Taiwan," *The Economist,* Overseas Business Reports, 1988; "A Survey of Taiwan," *The Economist,* 1988; *Taiwan—Country Profiles,* Economist Intelligence Unit, 1990/1991; *Taiwan to 1993—Politics Versus Prosperity,* Economist Intelligence Unit, 1990; Li, Dr K.T., *The Economic Transformation of Taiwan,* London, Shepheard-Walwyn, 1988; *Chinese Petroleum Corp.,* Taipei, CPC, [n.d.].

—Joanne E. Cross

CITGO PETROLEUM CORPORATION

Box 3758
Tulsa, Oklahoma 74102
U.S.A.
(918) 495-4000
Fax: (918) 495-4511

Wholly Owned Subsidiary of Petroleos de Venezuela, S.A.
through Propernyn, B.V.
Incorporated: 1910 as Cities Service Company
Employees: 3,342
Sales: $7.64 billion

CITGO Petroleum Corporation is one of the largest petroleum refining, marketing, and transportation companies in the United States. As of January 31, 1990, CITGO became a wholly owned indirect subsidiary of Petroleos de Venezuela, S.A., the national oil company of Venezuela.

The historical origins of CITGO can be traced back to the urbanization of America in the early 20th century and to a company known as Cities Service Company. A young entrepreneur, Henry L. Doherty, saw the business potential of providing adequate utility services to the expanding cities of the Midwest. Doherty was from a poor background but had taught himself engineering science and had amassed a large fortune from his own company, Henry L. Doherty & Son. This company had various activities but specialized in real estate, investments, and engineering, as well as the provision of utility services. Doherty envisioned a gigantic company wholly devoted to the provision of utility services such as gas, electricity, and transport.

In 1910, Doherty founded Cities Service Company, a holding company that earned its living from the companies whose stock it held. The company had an address in New York but its main operations were in the West. The new company was composed of three very large subsidiaries, Denver Gas and Electric, Spokane Gas and Fuel, and Empire District Electric. Each of these companies in turn possessed subsidiaries of its own. Doherty was especially interested in the supply of gas. In the following years, Cities Service expanded by buying out smaller gas utility companies throughout the nation. In 1913 alone, Doherty purchased 53 utility companies which brought together a total of 170 companies under the umbrella of Cities Service.

Because of a gas shortage experienced by its utility companies, Cities also engaged in gas exploration. In 1915, one of Cities Service's subsidiaries, Empire Companies, began exploring in Kansas. Geologist Charles N. Gould discovered vast quantities of oil in the town of El Dorado. Doherty was not slow to realize the growing importance of oil to the U.S. economy. He immediately organized a new Cities Service subsidiary, Empire Gas & Fuel, to take over El Dorado operations. By 1917 Empire had over 1,000 wells in production and had produced over 36 million barrels for that year alone.

The discovery and expansion of the El Dorado oil fields could not have come at a better time for Cities Service. America's entry into World War I on the Allied side increased demand for the precious liquid. Warfare had become increasingly mechanized. U.S. battleships and the recently invented tanks and aircraft required large quantities of oil to operate. The German defeat of Russia in 1918 and their capture of the Galician and Romanian oil fields also led to an Allied shortage of oil in Europe.

Under government pressure to increase production, Cities Service developed many innovations. These included the world's largest dehydrator at that time, the Empire, which extracted water from oil. By 1918 El Dorado produced more than the combined Galician and Romanian oil fields under German control, more than enough to supply the hard-pressed British convoys. By the end of the war Cities Service also operated seven refineries. Oil refining and production had become a central feature of Cities Service's operations.

Despite its increasing concentration on oil production, Cities Service also maintained its utility and service operations. By 1918 Cities Service's gas utility companies serviced 464,000 people in 20 states, mainly in the Midwest and Northeast. Its electric utilities served 144,000 people and its transport, or so-called traction companies, carried 116 million passengers every year.

The postwar prosperity of the 1920s increased demand for petroleum. The introduction of mass assembly methods in automobile production reduced the price of cars to within the reach of the average U.S. family. The growth in automobile ownership led to increased demand for gasoline. Also in the 1920s, Doherty played a key role in the foundation of the American Petroleum Institute, in 1924. This institute attempted to coordinate prices and sought to improve efficiency in the oil production business.

Cities Service did not escape the effects of the Depression of the 1930s. In 1930, oil prices fell as low as 21¢ per barrel. Cities Service, however, was more fortunate than other oil companies since the company's revenues from its utility services stabilized income. Already, as the 1930s began, Cities Service supplied almost 3,000 towns with both gas and electricity. The company also began retail marketing of petroleum products throughout the country. By 1932 the company listed 22 pages of service stations. This enabled the company to engage in direct sales to the U.S. consumer.

During the 1930s, the U.S. government of President Franklin D. Roosevelt sought to coordinate utility services in U.S. cities. Unbridled competition and company failures often led to poor services and wild price fluctuations. In 1935 the Public Utility Act was enacted. This measure enabled the U.S. government to regulate all holding companies involved in the provision of electric light, power, and gas. As part of a corporate simplification plan, holding companies had to dispose of all public utilities except one. All utility holding companies had to begin dissolution in 1938 and complete it by 1940. Ultimately, Cities Service retained its oil and natural gas business but had to dispose of all of its utility assets.

In December 1939, Cities Service suffered a further blow to its morale, as a result of the death of Henry Doherty. His place was taken by the equally able W. Alton Jones who had previously served Cities Service as vice president. This transition in company leadership soon was overshadowed by U.S. entry into World War II. The vital role that oil played in the conflict eased government pressure on Cities Service to sell its utilities. It took 60,000 gallons of gasoline per day for an armored division to fight. During the war itself, Cities Service operated its own tanker fleet, 13 of its own ships, and 18 government oil tankers.

Cities Service shipped oil from Texas, through the Gulf of Mexico, to New York. A number of Cities Service's ships were lost owing to German U-boat activity. They included the S.S. *Cities Service Empire*, torpedoed off the coast of Florida in February 1942. During the course of the war, U-boats attacked three other Cities Service ships within sight of the U.S. coast. Jones pressed the government to construct a pipeline, arguing, "nobody ever sank a pipeline."

In June 1942, the government decided to adopt Jones's plan. Roosevelt appointed none other than W. Alton Jones as president of the War Emergency Pipelines (WEP). Work began on the so-called Big Inch in the summer of 1942. By August 1943, oil could be pumped all the way from Texas through to Philadelphia, Pennsylvania, thus avoiding the U-boat-infested waters of the Atlantic coast.

During the war, Cities Service also began construction of what was to be one of the world's largest oil refineries, at Lake Charles, Louisiana. The plant produced high-octane fuel for the U.S. air force as well as general petroleum products.

After the war, Cities Service continued to dispose of its utility assets. Postwar prosperity and a booming U.S. economy ensured a good return on these sales. By 1958 all utility assets had been sold and Cities Service was now a fully integrated oil company. With the loss of its utility business, Cities Service concentrated on its oil and gas activities. Throughout the 1950s, the company engaged in oil exploration in Louisiana and Texas. The Lake Charles refinery also played an important role in Cities Service's operations in the postwar period. Modernization of its huge Lake Charles refinery continued throughout the 1950s.

On March 1, 1962, W. Alton Jones was killed in an air crash close to New York. Jones was on his way to meet former President Dwight D. Eisenhower, a long-time friend. A succession of company leaders succeeded him: Burl Watson in 1962, John Burns in 1966, and Charles Mitchell in 1968. All played an important role in streamlining the company's organizational structure.

Throughout the 1960s, increasing consumer sophistication and stiff competition provided an impetus for a more creative approach to retail marketing. Marketing manager Stanley Breitweiser was instrumental in devising a new brand name for Cities Service's retail products. In the age of brand names such as Esso and BP, the brand name Cities Service was considered too much of a mouthful. After 80,000 names had been put forward, a choice was finally made. The new brand name

was CITGO. Along with the new name came the new gasoline, CITGO Premium.

Charles J. Waidelich, who became company president in 1971, and Robert V. Seller, who became chairman and CEO in 1972, guided the company through the turbulent 1970s. War in the Middle East between Israel and her Arab neighbors led to severe oil shortages and steep price increases. This created an impetus for oil exploration in offshore areas such as the Gulf of Mexico. The cost of offshore exploration was no longer prohibitive, owing to increased oil prices.

By 1982 Cities Service had become the 19th-largest oil company in the United States. Yet its outlook was not entirely promising. The early 1980s witnessed an upheaval in the petroleum industry. High exploration costs and a worldwide economic slump led to a rash of mergers and acquisitions. In 1981 and 1982 the business press was full of rumors concerning the fate of Cities Service. A hostile takeover threat by Mesa Petroleum was rebuffed. Negotiations for a friendly merger with Gulf Oil Corporation came to nothing. Finally, Armand Hammer, chairman of Occidental Petroleum Corporation, bought Cities Service Company for about $4.3 billion. Cities Service became a wholly owned subsidiary of Occidental Petroleum as of December 1982.

Cities Service's oil-refining and -marketing divisions were merged into one subsidiary, known as CITGO Petroleum Corporation, and sold by Occidental to The Southland Corporation in 1983. The sale included the famous Lake Charles refinery and the CITGO gasoline retailing business. By this time CITGO's wholesale business supplied gasoline to 4,000 outlets.

Southland had pioneered the development of convenience stores with its 7-Eleven stores. In 1982, the company operated 7,300 7-Eleven stores in the United States and Canada. To Southland hoped to combine gasoline sales and groceries through its 7-Eleven chain. The CITGO refinery seemed the best way to ensure a free-flowing supply of gasoline for its numerous outlets.

CITGO did not live up to Southland's expectations. A nationwide overcapacity in the refining business led to increased refining costs and falling profits. In 1984, CITGO posted a pretax loss of $50 million. In 1985 Southland cut CITGO's output by half. CITGO president Sam J. Susser was replaced by former Shell Oil Company and Gulf Oil Corporation executive Ronald E. Hall.

In 1985 Hall orchestrated an internal study of CITGO's strengths and weaknesses. Two results of this study were the decisions to acquire a stable source of crude oil for CITGO's refinery and to work to enhance the CITGO brand name. The former goal was net in 1986 when Southland sold 50% of CITGO to Propernyn, B.V., a subsidiary of Petroleos de Venezuela, S.A. (PDVSA), the Venezuelan state-owned oil company, for about $300 million. In 1986 Southland badly needed the money to ease its own financial problems. When Southland experienced further financial losses, CITGO purchased the remaining 50% of its own stock, making PDVSA sole owner in January 1990, for $661 million.

Both CITGO and PDVSA benefited from the sale. Venezuela, a member of the Organization of Petroleum Exporting Countries (OPEC), is one of the world's largest oil producers. PDVSA, through its CITGO connection, found a secure market for Venezuelan crude oil, as well as access to the U.S.

consumer. Ron E. Hall, CITGO's president and CEO, also welcomed the deal, since it secured a steady supply of crude oil and other feedstocks for its Lake Charles refinery.

From the more stable supply position CITGO embarked on an aggressive expansion program to enhance the value of the CITGO brand. In 1985, 3,500 gasoline outlets were branded CITGO. At the end of 1990 this number had grown to about 10,000. Sales of gasoline to branded distributors increased 16% during 1990.

CITGO remained a highly successful company into the 1990s. The Lake Charles refinery, founded by W. Alton Jones during World War II, has a rated capacity of 320,000 barrels a day making the facility the one of the largest in the United States. Marketing to the consumer through independent distributors continues to be CITGO's strength.

In January 1991 PDVSA merged its other wholly owned U.S. subsidiary, Champlin Refining and Chemicals, Inc., into CITGO. Champlin is a refiner of heavy crude oil. Champlin's Corpus Christi, Texas, refinery produces high-grade gasolines, petrochemicals, and other petroleum products; it also owns eight refined-products terminals, bringing CITGO's total to 51.

In November 1990 CITGO purchased 50% of Seaview Oil Company, a Pennsylvania-based refiner and marketer. CITGO bought the remaining 50% of Seaview in February 1991. Seaview's New Jersey refinery produces asphalt, naphtha, and other oils. PDVSA provides its own very-heavy Venezuelan crude oil to Seaview's refinery. The Seaview and Champlin mergers, along with continued internal growth, are expected to continue to fuel expansion.

Principal Subsidiaries: CITGO International Supply Company; CITGO Venezuela Supply Company; CITGO Pipeline Company; Petro-Chemical Transport, Inc.; Cit-Con Oil Corporation (65%); Champlin Refining and Chemicals, Inc.; Seaview Oil Company.

Further Reading: Ellis, William Donohue, *On the Oil Lands With Cities Service*, Tulsa, Oklahoma, Cities Service Oil and Gas Corporation, 1983.

—Michael Doorley

THE COASTAL CORPORATION

Coastal Tower
Nine Greenway Plaza
Houston, Texas 77046
U.S.A.
(713) 877-1400
Fax: (713) 877-6752

Public Company
Incorporated: 1955 as Coastal States Gas Producing Company
Employees: 13,900
Sales: $9.38 billion
Stock Exchanges: New York Amsterdam Düsseldorf Frankfurt
   Hamburg Munich London

The Coastal Corporation is the 14th-largest refiner of crude oil in the United States. The company is also one of the most profitable U.S. oil companies. Oil refining, however, is only one of Coastal's many enterprises. Natural gas production, petrochemicals, marketing and distribution of petroleum products, and gas and oil exploration are all important profit-generating activities.

To a great extent, Coastal's success can be attributed to the dynamic leadership of its founder and chief executive, Oscar Wyatt. Wyatt served in World War II as a bomber pilot, earned a mechanical engineering degree from Texas A&M University, and gained experience in the oil business as a partner in Wymore Oil Company. In 1955, Wyatt founded Coastal States Gas Producing Company in Corpus Christi, Texas. Compared to the monolithic enterprise it became in later years, Coastal States began business in modest circumstances, with 68 miles of pipeline and 78 employees.

From the beginning, Wyatt demonstrated an almost intuitive understanding of the energy business. His pipeline company purchased small amounts of gas from different producers, packaged it, and then sold the gas in larger volumes. Gas gathering became the company's primary business. Wyatt developed effective pipeline systems that connected both buyers and sellers and still left room for profits. Most pipeline owners set output quotas to make an oil field last for up to 20 years. Wyatt ignored this convention and generally purchased from producers as much gas as they could pump. This practice enraged other pipeline owners. The arrangement worked to Coastal's advantage and by 1960 revenues exceeded $17.6 million.

As the U.S. economy grew in the 1960s, dependence on all energy sources, notably oil and gas, also increased. Coastal

took full advantage of soaring demand. By the early 1960s Coastal's newly created subsidiary, Lo-Vaca Gathering Company, supplied gas to San Antonio, Austin, Corpus Christi, and other cities in south Texas. In 1962 Coastal purchased 800 miles of crude oil pipeline from Sinclair Oil Corporation, including a major refinery in Corpus Christi with a capacity for almost 30,000 barrels of oil per day. Coastal extended this capacity in later years as oil refining became one of its principal activities.

Much of Coastal's subsequent expansion came through takeovers—often hostile—of rival companies. Wyatt acquired a reputation as a tough business competitor and corporate raider. In 1968 Coastal acquired a 965-mile system from United Pipeline Company. In that same year, Wyatt won control of Rio Grande Valley Gas Company. In June 1970 the company announced plans to link its west Texas natural gas reserves to the Dallas area.

Events in the Middle East overshadowed the triumphant rise of Coastal in the early 1970s. The Arab-dominated Organization of Petroleum Exporting Countries (OPEC), by presenting a united front, won a price increase from oil companies in 1971. OPEC cut production and raised prices by 70%. By 1974 prices had again quadrupled, leading to the energy crisis of the mid-1970s.

Lo-Vaca, Coastal's pipeline subsidiary, had signed fixed-price contracts to supply cities of south Texas with natural gas. With energy prices soaring and supplies dwindling, Lo-Vaca could not meet its contractual obligations, and at one point cut off gas supplies to the cities of San Antonio and Austin during the winter. Ignoring his contracts, Wyatt obtained regulatory permission to increase prices beyond the contract limit.

Inevitably Lo-Vaca became a target for lawsuits from outraged customers. Lo-Vaca haunted Coastal for years. Finally, after much legal wrangling, Coastal settled the $1.6 billion in lawsuits by agreeing to spin off Lo-Vaca. The spin-off company, Valero Energy Corporation, was formed on December 31, 1979, from Lo-Vaca and other Coastal assets, and had annual revenues of about $1 billion. The customers suing Coastal got 55% of Valero's stock. The remaining Valero stock was split among Coastal shareholders, except Wyatt, who the plaintiffs insisted be excluded from the agreement.

Despite the impact of the energy crisis, Coastal maintained its profitability and continued to expand throughout the 1970s. Expansion was not confined to Texas. In 1973 Coastal acquired Colorado Interstate Gas Company along with its three refineries with a $182 million hostile bid. With this acquisition Coastal became a truly national company. In 1973 Wyatt renamed the company Coastal States Gas Corporation. In the first half of the decade, Coastal also sought to diversify into other energy markets. In 1973 Coastal entered the coal-mining field with the acquisition of Southern Utah Fuel Company. Also in 1973, with the acquisition of Union Petroleum Corporation, renamed Belcher New England, Inc., Coastal began the marketing and distribution of petroleum products. By 1975 revenues had reached $1.9 billion. Coastal's expansion continued in 1976 with the purchase of Pacific Refining Company's Hercules, California, plant. This plant increased Coastal's refining capacity to about 300,000 barrels per day. In 1977 Coastal acquired Miami-based Belcher Oil Company, one of the largest marketers of fuel oils in the Southeast.

In 1980 Wyatt changed the company's name to Coastal Corporation. In the same year, revenues exceeded $5 billion. Yet

Wyatt, in his enthusiasm to secure profits for Coastal, overstepped the law. In 1980 in Houston, Wyatt and two other oil executives pleaded guilty to criminal violations of federal crude-oil pricing regulations. Wyatt and the president of Coral Petroleum were each fined $40,000 for the misdemeanor. Each company was required to refund $9 million to the U.S. Treasury Department and each incurred $1 million in civil penalties.

The early 1980s witnessed a temporary setback in Coastal's successful profit record. Economic recession and oversupply of oil and natural gas, as well as consumer conservation, led to Coastal's first loss, which amounted to $96.4 million for the year 1981. Wyatt responded to the crisis with characteristic forcefulness. He trimmed the work force, cut budgets, and within six months had restored company's profitability.

In the mid-1980s, the U.S. government sought to foster competition in the natural gas industry. This so-called deregulation, together with falling prices, created difficulties for many energy companies. Coastal not only survived deregulation but took full advantage of the competitive atmosphere by launching hostile takeover bids for other struggling energy companies. The mere threat of a takeover by Coastal could send stock prices of the target company soaring. In 1983 Coastal's attempt to secure Texas Gas Resources failed, yet Coastal's initial investment in the company generated a total of $26.4 million profit. Intervening companies that came to Texas Gas Resources's rescue were forced to buy up shares held by Coastal at inflated prices. Wyatt's unsuccessful attempt to take over Houston Natural Gas in 1984 yielded a similar return of $42 million. In 1985 Wyatt set about acquiring American Natural Resources (ANR), one of the most profitable Midwest natural gas pipelines. Despite ANR's initial determination to remain outside of Coastal's clutches, Wyatt soon pushed through an all-cash deal of $2.45 billion, which ANR shareholders could not refuse. This acquisition transformed Coastal into a major power in the U.S. gas business.

While Coastal's success and profitability has drawn the admiration of many in the business community, some of Coastal's activities have skirted the spirit of the law. In 1987, despite sanctions prohibiting U.S. companies from dealing with Libya because of its terrorist connections, Wyatt negotiated a deal in which Libya supplied oil to Coastal's refinery in Hamburg, Germany. Wyatt's deal was legal because the foreign subsidiaries of U.S. companies are exempt from U.S. regulations.

In the late 1980s Coastal took advantage of improved economic relations between the United States and the People's Republic of China. In 1988 Coastal concluded an agreement with China National Chemicals Import and Export Corporation (Sinochem) for joint ownership of Coastal's Pacific Refining Company. Coastal and Sinochem each hold a 50% interest in this West Coast refining company. For both sides, the agreement provided certain advantages. Sinochem obtained an opportunity to invest in the United States as well as a long-term outlet for crude oil. Coastal secured a dependable supply of crude oil in a volatile world oil market. This joint venture represented the first investment in U.S. energy assets by the People's Republic of China.

A key to the company's successful strategy is the continued high productivity of all Coastal employees from unskilled to management levels. Coal workers employed by Coastal produce twice the industry average. Much is expected of Coastal's management staff. Indeed, the constant pressure for results has led to a high management turnover. Coastal's refinery business alone had five different managers between 1980 and 1989.

Coastal's position seems secure. Demand for natural gas has improved considerably. Public awareness of pollution and government regulations have made relatively clean-burning natural gas a preferred energy supply. The growing uncertainty about foreign oil supplies, as a result of political turmoil in the Middle East, has also stimulated domestic energy production of oil and gas. Under the energetic leadership of Oscar Wyatt, it is likely that Coastal will take full advantage of these dramatic developments in the energy business.

Principal Subsidiaries: ABCO Aviation, Inc.; ABCO Leasing, Inc.; ANR Supply Company; Coastal Capital Corporation; Coastal Gas Marketing Company; Coastal Holding Corporation; Coastal Limited Ventures, Inc.; Coastal Mart, Inc.; Coastal Midland, Inc.; Coastal Multi-Fuels, Inc.; Coastal Natural Gas Company; ANR Credit Corporation; ANR Development Corporation; ANR Erie Pipeline Company; ANR Finance B.V. (Netherlands); ANRFS Holdings, Inc.; ANR Gasification Properties Company; ANR Gulf Pipeline Company; ANR Intrastate Gas Company, Inc.; ANR Ocean Pipeline Company; ANR Offshore Gathering Company; ANR One Woodward Corp.; ANR Pipeline Company; ANR Production Company; ANR Ren-Cen, Inc.; ANR Storage Company; Coastal Oil & Gas Corporation; Coastal Pan American Corporation; Coastal Power Production Company; Coastal Power Revere Company; Coastal Remediation Company; Coastal States Energy Company; Coastal States Gas Transmission Company; Coastal States Management Corporation; Coastal States Trading, Inc.; Coastal Technology, Inc.; Coastal Unilube, Inc.; Cosbel Petroleum Corporation; Coscol Petroleum Corporation; Holborn Oil Company Limited (Bermuda); Jade Carriers Corporation (Liberia); Texas Tank Ship Agency, Inc.

Further Reading: Ivey, Mark, "The Man Who Strikes Fear in the Heart of the Oil Patch," *Business Week,* November 6, 1989; *The Coastal Corporation: Profile,* Houston, Coastal Corporation, [n.d.].

—Michael Doorley

COMPAÑIA ESPAÑOLA DE PETRÓLEOS S.A.

Avenida de America, 32
28028 Madrid
Spain
(91) 337 60 00
Fax: (91) 337 5819

Public Company
Incorporated: 1929
Employees: 6,600
Sales: Pta279.61 billion (US$2.93 billion)
Stock Exchange: Spanish Continuous Market

Compañia Española de Petróleos S.A. (CEPSA), is the only diversified private Spanish oil company to remain completely outside state ownership since the creation of a state oil monopoly—buying oil and setting prices within Spain—in 1927. Spain's entry to the European Community is bringing CEPSA's long history of privileged, if uneasy, co-existence, to an end. CEPSA, engaged in exploration, production, refining, and sales is finding itself in increasing competition with the giant former state-owned corporation Repsol and other oil multinationals.

In 1927 the Spanish dictator Primo de Rivera issued a decree expropriating all foreign and domestic oil companies and placing them under the control of a state agency. Administration was entrusted to Compañia Arrendataria del Monopolio de Petróleos Sociedad Anónima (CAMPSA), which until the 1980s had sole rights to purchase oil from producers at state-controlled prices.

The Canary Islands and the Spanish Moroccan territories of Ceuta and Melilla were exempted from the decree, in part because they were already exempted from a number of customs regulations and had long served as important trade intermediaries between Spain and the rest of the world. The exemption would also provide a golden opportunity for CEPSA.

Spain's lack of refineries posed a severe barrier to industrialization, but there was no domestic crude to refine. The few attempts at exploration had failed to find a commercial Spanish field. Spain was heavily dependent on imported foreign oil, supplied by Shell and other foreign multinationals at international prices. Political and economic problems made it difficult for the government to build a refinery.

These problems ensured that when the financier Francisco Recasens and a group of investors incorporated CEPSA in Madrid on September 26, 1929, the Spanish government did not oppose them. Recasens, whose brother was an adviser to CAMPSA, the newly organized state monopoly, convinced government officials that a private concern would have more freedom to acquire crude for Spain abroad.

Recasens had already acquired important concessions in Venezuela and Texas, previously owned by the American Falcon Oil Company. These were transferred to CEPSA. From these early days, the company maintained an international identity and special role. By this means, the company helped preserve its independence from CAMPSA.

By building a refinery in Tenerife, Canary Islands, CEPSA was officially outside the state monopoly, but in practice, it was dependent on a close relationship with the Spanish government. CEPSA could not sell oil in Spain to anyone other than the government. In effect, the government had a de facto veto over CEPSA's sales to non-Spanish customers because it could simply extend its mainland monopoly to the Canaries. However, the company had more freedom to trade abroad and to supply ships and international trade in Tenerife.

The Tenerife refinery opened as Spain's first refinery in November, 1930. It remained so until 1949 and supplied 50% of the country's needs with an initial capacity of 5,000 barrels a day or 250 billion tons annually.

The Canary Islands location may have helped secure the company's future in another way. It was from this island base that General Francisco Franco, then their military commander, began his campaign against the Spanish Republic. In 1936 he flew from Tenerife to Spanish Morocco and raised an invasion force that attacked the mainland and started a bloody civil war that lasted until he finally triumphed over Republican forces in 1939.

During the civil war, the Canary Islands remained firmly in the Nationalist camp, and CEPSA's refinery became an asset of significance to Franco's Nationalist cause. Refinery production, denied to Madrid and out of bombing range of the Republic's mostly Loyalist air force, helped earn foreign exchange and fuel Franco's success.

The monopoly law prohibited CEPSA from exploration on the Spanish mainland and from 1936 the civil war made exploration practically impossible. However, CEPSA began to produce oil in Venezuela in 1930, and the country remains an important source to this day.

In 1939, Franco's newly established dictatorship announced a policy of industrial self-sufficiency and independence from foreign control. During the civil war, support for the republic from the Soviet Union and international communist movement helped ensure that Spain's small group of capitalists and industrialists lined up, sometimes reluctantly, behind Franco.

The Nationalists were not interested in free market solutions for a devastated economy with little industry and scarce domestic capital. By the time the civil war ended in September 1939, World War II had begun. There was little prospect of foreign investment.

The Franco dictatorship's main pillars of support were not the capitalists, but the Catholic church, the traditional land-owning classes, and the Falange, a political movement resembling the Italian Fascist Party. The chosen means of implementing self-sufficiency was nationalization of the main industrial sectors. State companies were placed under the direction of a state agency, the Instituto Nacional de Industria (INI).

CEPSA remained under ultimate state control as a privately owned Spanish company engaged in supplying petroleum to the state company CAMPSA, its price-setting major customer. During World War II, Franco maintained a state of non-belligerency. Effectively, the Spanish government sympathized with its former German and Italian patrons while maintaining a diplomatic stance to stay out of the war. Spain was isolated. CEPSA, though privately owned, took its orders from the government but it retained its independence in order to acquire crude abroad.

Spain's need for self-sufficiency inspired intensified exploration for oil by CAMPSA, which finally discovered a strike of limited value during the Tudanca survey of 1941. From 1942, CEPSA was allowed to explore on the mainland. A subsidiary, Compañia de Investigacion y Exploitaciones Petrolifera (CIEPSA) was formed as a separate exploration and production concern, but CEPSA was to be much more successful as a refinery and petrochemical concern than as an exploration and production company.

No important Spanish fields were discovered until state-controlled companies made important finds off the Mediterranean coast in the mid-1960s. In the 1990s, most of CEPSA's Spanish production was concentrated in one of these areas, the Casablanca field.

With the end of World War II in 1945, Spain was in a difficult international position. Nazi Germany and Fascist Italy were defeated. A need to become friendlier with the United States and Britain—who were increasingly the opponents, rather than the allies, of the Soviet Union—and the desire for foreign investment capital led Franco to abandon strict self-sufficiency in favor of controlled foreign investment and private sector participation.

In a 1947 decree, the Spanish government relaxed its oil monopoly. CAMPSA was left in control of marketing and distribution, but this new law enabled the government to authorize private and public companies to develop a wide range of activities: trade; industrial handling, especially refining; storage; research; and the exploration for and production of oil and gas fields. In practice, the government usually required foreign companies, such as Caltex and Esso, to work under joint participation schemes with CAMPSA.

The requirement that both private and public refineries sell to CAMPSA continued, and in 1957 it was extended to gasified petroleum products. After 1950 two new mainland refineries were built by small Spanish companies heavily reliant on foreign participation, and three new state refineries were built. CEPSA's Spanish refining activities faced new competition.

One of CEPSA's solutions was diversification, and the company used the 1947 law to look for foreign partners. CEPSA began to diversify into lubricants in 1950 and launched its own CEPSA brand name for industrial and motor oils, but these are largely sold within the Iberian world. By 1989, 87% of its lubricants market was still within Spain and Portugal.

Petrochemical production started in 1955 when the Tenerife refinery built an aromatics extraction plant utilizing the Udex process. The first of its kind in Europe, it involved the separation of high purity aromatics from mixtures with other hydrocarbons using an efficient multi-stage extraction column. During the 1950s and 1960s, CEPSA cooperated with multi-nationals in joint ventures to set up a number of derivative production plants. By 1989, CEPSA had signed agreements with the Japanese company Dainippon Ink and Chemicals (DIC) to expand its presence in European markets.

After a series of unsuccessful attempts, CEPSA finally secured government authorization to build a second refinery on the Spanish mainland at Cadiz in 1964. The plant opened in 1969 as the Gibraltar refinery and became the stimulus for one of the largest new industrial complexes in Spain.

In 1964, CEPSA Compania Portugesa, a new subsidiary, began to sell petroleum and petrochemical products in Portugal. It also operates an extensive service station network. In 1975, CEPSA established its own research center at San Fernando de Henares.

Still CEPSA's share of the Spanish market for most petroleum products remained small in relation to the state-owned companies, including CAMPSA, controlled by the state through the Instituto Nacional de Hidrocarburos (INH).

In 1987, most state monopoly interests were reorganized into the Spanish multinational Repsol which, in 1989, was partially privatized. Throughout the 1980s, government policy increasingly favored the growth of Repsol as a major Spanish institution, capable of keeping the Spanish oil industry in Spanish hands, rather than opening up the market to smaller private companies.

This policy has brought increased criticism from the European Community, which required Spain, as a condition of membership, to restrict the monopoly role of CAMPSA and Repsol. In June 1983 CEPSA, the government, CAMPSA, and other private refineries reached an agreement known as the Protocol which attempted to protect the domestic oil industry without a formal monopoly.

CAMPSA shares were split among the refineries with the Spanish government holding the majority of the shares, but the refineries agreed to sell products destined for the domestic market to CAMPSA. However, refineries soon began to ignore the Protocol.

Under pressure from the European Community (EC) commission, Spain agreed to change a restrictive law by halving the distance required between service stations and making it easier for independents to use CAMPSA's distribution network. In 1989, Repsol, by then holding the Spanish government's majority shares, CEPSA, and other minority shareholders in CAMPSA decided that CAMPSA's service stations and some other retail assets would be divided among them by mid-1991. CAMPSA would continue as a distribution and transportation company, under Repsol's control.

CEPSA, as a relatively small company, has been unable to fully exploit its excellent position within a liberalized market in which most analysts expect to see rapid growth over the next decade. However, CEPSA's investment potential has attracted the attention of several large foreign investors. In May 1988, the Abu Dhabi Investment Corporation acquired 10% of CEPSA.

In November of that year, the company announced a one for five rights issue. In a complex series of transactions, the French multinational Elf Aquitaine acquired 20% of the company's equity and later acquired additional stock through a deal with another major shareholder, the Banco Central. CEPSA went public on the Spanish Continuous Market on September 18, 1989. The company's stock can be purchased or sold by any authorized trader anywhere in Spain by means of a computerized communications network with a single quote given at the end of each session.

By 1989, CEPSA was less active in exploration but held domestic mining rights over 5,000 square kilometers in exploration permits in Spanish territory and 1,385 kilometers outside Spain. Production comes mainly from the Casablanca field, in which it has a 7.4% interest in exploitation rights. CEPSA entered into a natural gas exploration agreement with the Algerian government.

The two recently modernized CEPSA refineries process about 20% of the petroleum refined in Spain, but the Tenerife refinery produces mainly for the local market and ships passing through its ports. CEPSA has restructured its commercial division and reinforced its distribution network. It is expanding its network of service stations in Spain and has bought a distribution network in the north of France.

The influence of Elf, which owns 25% of CEPSA's equity, is growing and it is a possibility that the company will soon fall under Elf's direct control. Regardless of this possibility, the unique environment in which CEPSA operated as the most important and diversified private Spanish oil company has been changed forever by Spain's entry into the EC, the dismantling of the state monopoly, the emergence of Repsol and competition. Other large multinational oil companies plan to enter into this formerly protected, but lucrative market. With sufficient investment, CEPSA is well placed to reap the benefits if it can learn to operate in this new environment.

Principal Subsidiaries: CIEPSA; CGS; Grupo DISPESA; Petrocan, S.A.; Petrosur, S.A.; CEPSA Aviacion, S.A.; CEPSA Compania Portuguesa; Propel, Lda.; CEPSA France, S.R.L.; Atlantico, S.A.; Europea de Lubricacion; Petresa Poliesa; Krafft, S.A. (70%); Lubrisur, S.A. (50%).

Further Reading: Santamaria, Javier, *El Petroleo en Espana del Monopolio a La Libertad,* Madrid, Espasa Calpe, 1988; Correlje, Dr. A.F., *The Liberalisation of the Spanish State Oil Sector: Strategies For A Competitive Future,* Rotterdam, The Centre for Policy Studies, Erasmus University, 1990.

—Clark Siewert

CONOCO INC.

600 North Dairy Ashford Road
Houston, Texas 77079
U.S.A.
(713) 293-1000
Fax: (713) 293-1440

*Wholly Owned Subsidiary of E.I. du Pont de Nemours and
Company*
Incorporated: 1920 as Marland Oil Company
Employees: 21,000
Sales: $15.98 billion

Conoco is a fully integrated and broadly based oil and gas
company, involved in all aspects of the petroleum business on
an international scale. Since its acquisition by Du Pont in
1981, Conoco has moved toward a renewed concentration on
petroleum, as well as specialty petroleum and commodity
products that play an integral part in Du Pont's other industrial
operations. Conoco's future includes goals for increasing sales
of high-profit specialty products like petroleum coke, maintaining a leading position in European refining, and extending
that position into the United States.

Conoco's earliest predecessor, Continental Oil & Transportation Company (CO&T), was founded in Ogden, Utah, in
1875 by Isaac Elder Blake to transport petroleum products
from the East Coast for sale in Utah, Idaho, Montana, and
Nevada. Operations were later expanded to include Denver
and San Francisco and in 1877 the company was reincorporated in California.

Blake's pioneering use of railroad tank cars to transport oil
contributed to CO&T's quick success. By the early 1880s
CO&T was sending modest shipments to Mexico, Canada, the
Hawaiian islands, the Samoan islands, and Japan. In the western United States it was competing with Standard Oil.

In 1884 CO&T agreed to become a Standard affiliate. The
following year CO&T merged with Standard's Rocky Mountain operations, and the company was reincorporated in Colorado as the Continental Oil Company. Blake was named
president of the new concern, and headquarters were established in Denver. Continental continued to function much as
CO&T had, although operations were consolidated with Standard's in Colorado, New Mexico, Wyoming, Montana, and
Utah.

Continental products were purchased from Standard and
other providers in the East, and included kerosene refined for
lamp oil, lubricating oils, heavy oil for heating fuel, and paraffin used in candlemaking. In 1888 Continental eliminated the
need for transporting products from the East Coast by acquiring a minority interest in United Oil Company with production
and refining interests in Colorado.

In 1893 Blake resigned, having become bogged down in
personal debt due to heavy investments in railroads and other
ventures. For the next 14 years, Henry Morgan Tilford served
as president. By 1900, Continental was heavily involved in the
marketing of kerosene, although its product line had been expanded to include lamps, cooking stoves, ovens, and a variety
of household and industrial oils.

Continental continued to grow in its own market under
Tilford but did not venture outside of the Rocky Mountain
area, where it became the Standard affiliate most closely resembling a monopoly. In 1906 Continental took over Standard
bulk stations in Idaho and Montana, and by the end of the year
controlled better than 98% of the western market.

In 1907 Continental purchased the Denver office building
which housed its sixth-floor headquarters and renamed it the
Continental Oil Building. That same year, Edward T. Wilson,
who had worked his way up from junior clerk, was named
president.

In 1911 the United States Supreme court ordered Standard
Oil to divest some of its holdings. Two years later Continental
Oil Company became one of 34 independent oil companies
formed as a result of the court's antitrust ruling. Continental
tapped into the growing market for automobile gasoline in
1914 and built its first service station. Two years later Continental bought out United Oil and officially entered the oil production business.

During World War I Continental worked under the direction
of the oil division of the U.S. Fuel Administration, and produced airplane fuel for pioneer aircraft and training planes. In
1919 the company adopted a new trademark, a circular emblem with a soldier standing below the word Conoco.

In 1924 C.E. Strong, who had worked his way up through
the Continental accounting department, was elected president
and chief executive officer. Continental became a fully integrated oil company later that year when it merged with Mutual
Oil Company, owning assets in production, refining, and
distribution.

By 1926 Continental's assets topped $80 million, including
530 miles of pipeline, six refineries and marketing operations
ranging through 15 states. That year, sales surpassed $50 mil-
lion for the first time. The following year the company moved
into its new $1 million Denver headquarters, and S.H.
Keoughan, a former president of Mutual Oil, was named president and chief executive officer of Continental.

In 1929 Continental merged with Marland Oil Company.
The Marland Oil Company had been incorporated in 1920, to
combine assets of the Marland Refining Company and Kay
County Gas Company, all under the direction of Ernest
Whitworth Marland.

E.W. Marland, a Pittsburgh attorney turned maverick oil
wildcatter, had come to Oklahoma in 1908 and a year later
discovered oil on Indian burial grounds near Ponca City.
Marland later assembled a staff of geologists who led him to
one strike after another, while his young companies paced development of the Oklahoma oil industry and the new group of
independent oil concerns.

Marland's interests in exploration extended outside of Oklahoma, leaving him in need of additional financing. In 1923, that financing approached Marland when John Pierpont Morgan of J.P. Morgan & Co. offered to become Marland Oil's banker. E.W. Marland agreed and sold Morgan $90 million in company stock.

By 1926 the company owned or controlled 5,000 tank cars emblazoned with Marland Oil's red triangle, operated more than 600 service stations in the midwest, and was marketing products in every state and 17 foreign countries. Employees shared in the success, receiving high salaries, free medical and dental care, and company loans to buy homes. In 1926 Marland negotiated the right to explore for oil in Canada on land concessions owned by Hudson's Bay Company of Canada. While Marland had expanded rapidly, so had its liabilities, which had grown to more than $8 million by the end of the year.

Marland blamed the company's increasing liabilities on Morgan's bankers, who had forced him to sell oil to Standard, vetoed pipeline plans, and stymied expansion during the mid-1920s. By 1928 those bankers had gained increasing power on the company's board. During an executive committee meeting that year Marland was informed that he would be replaced as president by Dan Moran, former vice president of the Texas Company. Marland was offered the chairmanship of the company and a pension, but told he would have to leave Ponca City. Marland promptly resigned and left the oil industry a short time later, only to be elected Oklahoma governor and become instrumental in leasing state capital grounds for oil production.

In January 1929 Marland Oil acquired the Prudential Refining Company with a large refinery in Baltimore, Maryland. In June of that year Morgan bankers fostered a merger agreement between Marland Oil and Continental with Marland agreeing to purchase Continental, while Continental's name would be retained. Moran was named president and chief executive officer, Edward Wilson chairman of the board, and Keoughan chairman of the executive committee.

Shortly after the new Continental moved its headquarters from Denver to Ponca City in 1929, the stock market crashed with the company holding a $43 million debt load. During the first full year of the ensuing Depression, Continental lost nearly $11 million. While losses were mounting that year, Moran devised a scheme for a pipeline that would run from Ponca City to Chicago and Minnesota and greatly reduce transportation costs. A partnership was formed called the Great Lakes Pipe Line Company, and Continental subscribed to a 31% stake.

In 1932 Continental entered the Midwest through the acquisition of 119 service stations and 43 bulk plants. Meanwhile an emphasis on research resulted in the development of new products, which included Germ Processed Motor Oil and Bronze Gasoline, touted as a high-performance fuel.

As a means to reduce company debt, Moran focused the company's attention on domestic operations. In 1933 the Sealand Petroleum Company in the United Kingdom, formed seven years earlier by Marland, was sold and the following year Hudson's Bay operations were shut down. Continental also withdrew from northeastern states, but maintained production at the Baltimore refinery to serve southern markets. By 1937 Continental had eliminated its debt load, and in December of that year 5,000 bonus checks worth a total of $770,000 were awarded to employees.

During the late 1930s Continental expanded its pipeline system by purchasing majority interests in the Rocky Mountain Pipe Line Company and the Crude Oil Pipe Line Company. Refinery operations were expanded in 1941 and a new $4.5 million refinery was opened in Lake Charles, Louisiana. In June of that year, Continental introduced its new lubricant, Conoco Nth Motor Oil, to meet the demand for heavy fuel oils.

During World War II the U.S. government constructed a 100-octane refinery in Ponca City, and Continental's vice president of manufacturing, Walter Miller, was named to supervise operations. The plant went online in mid-1943 and began producing high-octane jet gasoline. Following the war, Continental focused on areas where it was fully integrated, namely Texas, Colorado, Oklahoma, Illinois, Kansas, Missouri, and Iowa.

In 1946 a new era of oil exploration was launched when Continental joined with three other oil companies in developing Laniscot I, the world's pioneer offshore exploration boat. The following year Dan Moran resigned because of ill health, and Leonard F. McCollum left Standard Oil Company of New Jersey to become president and chief executive officer. McCollum's aggressive exploration program soon led to the 1947 acquisition of oil leases for 209,000 acres in the Gulf of Mexico. Hudson's Bay Oil and Gas Company (HBOG) was reactivated about the same time, after oil was discovered in Alberta, Canada. In 1948 Continental joined Ohio Oil Company and Amerada Petroleum Corporation in forming Conorada Petroleum Corporation to explore for oil outside North America.

Continental also initiated a refinery modernization and construction program in the late 1940s, leading to enlarged refineries in Denver and Ponca City and a new refinery in Billings, Montana. Meanwhile, production efforts in Kansas were reduced as the company focused on Texas, Kansas, California, and Wyoming.

Continental celebrated its 75th anniversary in 1950 by breaking ground for a $2.25 million Ponca City research laboratory and relocating its headquarters from Ponca City to Houston. The company also broke into new business fields during the early 1950s. A synthetic detergent plant was acquired, and Continental Oil Black Company was formed to produce carbon black, which is used in the production of synthetic rubber.

In 1952 Continental acquired interests in 1,390 miles of pipeline, including the new 1,080-mile line from Wyoming oil fields to an important refining center in Wood River, Illinois. Four years later offshore exploration was revolutionized when Continental, along with the Union, Shell and Superior oil groups, launched CUSS I, the world's first drill ship.

Continental's interest in overseas exploration grew throughout the decade, and by 1957 the company held exploratory concessions for nearly 50 million acres outside the United States, including land in Libya, Guatemala, and Italian Somaliland. HBOG, by 1957, had rights to a total of 700,000 acres in Egypt, Libya, Somalia, British Somaliland, Venezuela, and Guatemala.

During the 1960s, Continental purchased several independent gasoline station chains in Europe to provide a market for its newfound Libyan oil. Included in a string of acquisitions were SOPI, with more than 400 stations in West Germany and Austria; Jet Petroleum, Ltd., with more than 400 stations in the United Kingdom; SECA, with stations in Belgium; Arrow Oil Company with 70 retail outlets in eastern Ireland; and the U.K. Georg Von Opel chain of 155 stations in West Germany.

Continental also strengthened its European presence in the carbon-black market by establishing production facilities in Italy, the Netherlands, France, and Japan. The company's presence in North and South America also grew with an expansion of its Montana pipeline system and purchase of Douglas Oil Company, operating three southern California refineries and more than 300 stations. Continental opened a new refinery near the Atlantic Ocean entrance to the Panama Canal and acquired Mexofina, S.A. de C.V., with exploratory rights in Mexico.

Annual sales topped $1 billion in 1962 and diversification moves followed. In 1963, Continental acquired American Agricultural Chemical Company (Agrico), a major manufacturer of plant foods and agricultural chemicals. About the same time Continental became involved in the production of biodegradable detergents and plastic piping.

In 1964 Andrew W. Tarkington, a former executive vice president, was named president. McCollum remained chief executive and was named to the additional post of chairman. By that time, Continental was pumping more crude out of Libya, Canada, Venezuela, and Iran than it was producing in the United States, with Libyan oil having almost by itself made Continental an international dealer. Exploration and production teams also were operating in the Middle East, Mexico, Panama, Argentina, Pakistan, New Guinea, and Australia. With its worldwide presence growing, Continental moved its headquarters from Houston to New York that same year.

In 1966 Continental diversified into minerals and acquired Consolidation Coal Company (Consol), the second-largest U.S. coal-producing company. During the late 1960s expansion and diversification continued as the company purchased the Australia pesticides distributor Amalgamated Chemicals, Ltd., and Vinyl Maid, Inc., a manufacturer of polyvinyl chloride containers. Continental also entered joint agreements to build a calcined-petroleum coke plant in Japan, a polyvinyl chloride resin plant in the United Kingdom, and Spain's first biodegradable detergent plant.

In 1967 Tarkington assumed the additional duties of chief executive officer while McCollum remained chairman. During the next two years Tarkington spearheaded consolidation efforts and established new policies for gauging financial risks. John G. McLean, another former executive vice president, was named president and chief executive officer in 1969, replacing Tarkington, who was named vice chairman of the board.

McLean reorganized administrative levels and created a management team with four divisions—Western Hemisphere petroleum, Eastern Hemisphere petroleum, Conoco Chemicals, and Consol. In 1972 McCollum retired as chairman and was replaced by McLean, leaving the office of president vacant.

Under McLean's leadership, the company established a policy of focusing on its new mix of natural resources, including coal, uranium and copper. During the early 1970s the company sold its plastic pipe manufacturing business and interest in Amalgamated Chemicals and closed a petroleum sulfonates plant. Continental stepped up its mineral production during the

same period, entering joint ventures to develop uranium prospects in Texas and France. With the onset of the 1973 oil crisis, Continental accelerated its search for oil outside the Middle East, and during the next two years made significant discoveries in the North Sea.

In March 1974, Howard W. Blauvelt was named president, but two months later he was moved to chairman and chief executive following the death of McLean. John Kircher became president.

Conoco Coal Development Company, a wholly owned subsidiary, was formed in 1974 to coordinate research and long-range planning for the production of synthetic fuels made from coal. That same year the company signed a ten-year contract for oil and gas exploration for over two million acres in Egypt.

In 1979 Continental changed its name to Conoco Inc. That year, Ralph E. Bailey was named president, replacing Kircher who remained deputy chairman, a post to which he had been appointed in 1975.

During the late 1970s Conoco entered three major joint ventures, combining with Monsanto Company to manufacture ethylene and related products, with Du Pont in a $130 million oil and natural gas exploratory program, and with Wyoming Mineral Corporation, a subsidiary of Westinghouse Electric Corporation, to develop a Conoco uranium deposit in New Mexico. Blauvelt resigned as chairman and chief executive officer in 1979, and was replaced by Bailey in both positions.

Conoco began the 1980s as the ninth largest oil company in the United States with $2 billion dedicated to capital outlays. In 1980 Conoco purchased Globe Petroleum Ltd., with 220 retail outlets in the United Kingdom and entered into a second exploration venture with Du Pont. A facility expansion program also was initiated early in the decade, including a $2 billion upgrade of the Lake Charles refinery, additions to the Lake Charles coke-manufacturing plant and construction of a Lake Charles detergent chemical plant and a St. Louis, Missouri, lube-oil plant. In 1981 the company announced it would build a new world headquarters in Houston for its petroleum and chemical operations.

In May 1981, Dome Petroleum, Ltd., of Canada offered to buy 13% of Conoco's common stock for $910 million, in hope of exchanging the stock for Conoco's 53% stake in HBOG. A month later a deal was consummated giving Dome a 20% interest in Conoco, which was traded along with $245 million for Conoco's stake in HBOG.

The transaction sent a message that Conoco was vulnerable to a takeover, and a bidding war for the company ensued with Seagram Company and Mobil Corporation participating. With threats of a hostile takeover looming, Conoco went in search of a white knight—a friendly acquirer—and found Du Pont a willing participant. By August, 1981, Du Pont had acquired Conoco for $6.8 billion in the most expensive merger to that date.

Following the takeover, Du Pont consolidated Conoco operations and began selling the oil company's interests to reduce a $3.9 billion debt incurred in the purchase. During the first three years after the takeover Du Pont closed down some oil and chemical facilities and sold better than $1.5 billion in Conoco assets, including Continental Carbon Company and a variety of chemical, mineral, oil and gas assets. Conoco Chemicals was absorbed by Du Pont's larger petrochemicals departments. Du Pont also began utilizing some of Conoco's former chemical assets, including its ethylene business. By 1983 Du Pont had increased its output of ethylene, a petrochemical feedstock used in making polyethylene, from 850 million pounds annually to three billion pounds.

In 1983 Constantine S. Nicandros was named president. In the following years, Conoco stepped up offshore exploration and production efforts in the Gulf of Mexico and the North Sea. In 1984 Conoco began operating the world's first tension leg well platform for deep-sea oil exploration in the North Sea, with capabilities of producing oil under 2,000 feet of water.

During the mid-1980s, Conoco also expanded its oil and gas activities in Canada and Egypt. In January 1985 Conoco joined four other oil companies in a $312 million partnership to produce oil in Alaska, but two years later Conoco pulled out after the price of crude oil dropped.

In 1987 Bailey retired as chairman and his position was eliminated. Edgar S. Woolard was named president of Du Pont, with duties to include overseeing Conoco operations. At the same time, Nicandros assumed the additional duties of chief executive officer.

During the late 1980s Conoco made significant oil discoveries in Norway, the United Kingdom, Indonesia, Ecuador, and the United States. In 1989, after a two-year lapse, Conoco reopened its oil fields in Alaska. That same year 64 service stations were purchased in the Denver area in an effort to boost name recognition and sales by branded outlets.

Conoco began 1990 with exploration teams in 21 countries. In an early-1990 joint venture, Conoco and Calcined Coke Corporation formed Venco, to enhance Conoco's ability to meet Du Pont's needs for specialty coke products.

Company goals call for increased geographic diversification in exploration activities and a balancing of geological risk. Conoco expects to continue producing in heavily explored areas like the North Sea and the Gulf of Mexico while testing regions with large potential such as West Africa, Somalia, and offshore Alaska. Conoco also expects to continue building on its position in petroleum and specialty cokes, to meet increasing needs of its parent company, which uses coke products in other industries.

Further Reading: Mathews, John Joseph, *Life and Death of an Oilman: The Career of E.W. Marland*, Norman, University of Oklahoma Press, 1951; *Conoco: The First One Hundred Years*, New York, Dell Publishing Co., Inc., 1975; Knowles, Ruth Sheldon, *The Greatest Gamblers*, Norman, University of Oklahoma Press, 1978.

—Roger W. Rouland

COSMO

COSMO OIL CO., LTD.

1-1, Shibaura 1-chome
Minato-ku, Tokyo 105
Japan
(03) 3798-3211
Fax: (03) 3798-3237

Public Company
Incorporated: 1986
Employees: 3,442
Sales: ¥1.47 trillion (US$10.82 billion)
Stock Exchanges: Tokyo Osaka Nagoya

Cosmo Oil Co., Ltd. imports crude oil and other petroleum products into Japan and, using its own refineries, produces gasoline, naphtha, kerosene, gas oil, heavy fuel oil, and lubricants. It markets these products under the Cosmo brand name throughout Japan, Cosmo Oil also operates a network of gasoline service stations. In the early 1990s Cosmo Oil ranked third in size among petroleum-distribution companies in Japan. Because more than 99% of Japan's oil is from foreign sources, Cosmo's position in the economy of that country depends greatly on circumstances in the Middle East.

Cosmo Oil was formed on April 1, 1986, with the merger of Maruzen Oil Co., Ltd. and Daikyo Oil Co., Ltd. Maruzen Oil began its operations as a producer of lubricating oil and in 1933 incorporated and underwent extensive reorganization to expand its existing refinery and to build a new one. Maruzen further increased in size in 1942 by amalgamating with several smaller companies, Toyo Oil Company, Toho Oil Company, Yamabun Oil Company, and Kyusha Refining Company. During World War II Maruzen built a refinery and several storage facilities in China. Because Maruzen relied exclusively on crude oil imports during its early years, by the end of World War II its operations were curtailed.

Daikyo Oil was established in 1939 with the merger of eight refinery operators and the later merger with Edogawa Oil Company. Near the start of World War II Daikyo began operation of a refinery in Yokkaichi that in 1943 processed crude oil brought in from the Netherlands East Indies. In 1946 it started operation of a refinery to process pine-root oil, a raw material readily available in Japan.

In the era immediately after World War II, the reconstruction of the Japanese economy required the establishment of an energy policy. At that time, coal was the primary source of energy in the country, and the importation of crude oil was

viewed as a supplement to coal. In the 1950s, as new oil sources were discovered in the Middle East, Japan began importing more oil; the proximity of Japan to the Middle East oil fields, compared to those of the United States and Europe, gave the Middle East's oil a cost advantage in Japan. Firms in the Japanese oil industry built refineries along the coast to process this cheap oil.

By the 1970s, 99.8% of Japan's oil was imported, and oil was supplying 70% of the country's energy needs. A large portion of the oil imports was handled by international oil companies, Standard Oil Company (California), Texaco, Exxon, Mobil, and Shell, acting jointly with Japanese oil companies. Maruzen was not a partner with any of these large companies.

The shift to oil as the major energy source had an adverse impact on the coal industry. To lessen this impact, the Japanese government enacted the Petroleum Industry Law, which restricted the total amount of oil that could be imported. The Ministry of International Trade and Industry (MITI) set policies that had an impact on Maruzen and Daikyo. These laws came into play in the 1950s, when Maruzen had a contract with Union Oil Company of California to provide Maruzen's needs for crude oil. After the closing of the Suez Canal in 1956, Maruzen's president, Wada Kanji, negotiated shipping contracts for a fixed term and price. In the recession of 1962, however, these contracts became a financial burden. Wada contemplated a loan from Union Oil. Under the Foreign Capital Law, however, approval of the loan by MITI was required. MITI at first refused approval, but later agreed to it with the stipulation that MITI negotiate directly with Union Oil to secure the loan and that a new president be installed at Maruzen. While Maruzen was saved as a company by this action, members of the business community of Osaka, site of the company's home office, voiced disapproval of the treatment of Maruzen's president by MITI.

Despite this unfavorable reaction to its policies, MITI continued to play an important part in Japan's oil industry. When the first oil-supply shock was brought about in 1973 by the Organization of Petroleum Exporting Countries (OPEC), the energy situation in Japan became one of severe shortage. To offset this shortage, in December 1973 MITI placed limits on the use of oil in generating electricity. At the same time, the Japanese Diet passed the Petroleum Supply and Demand Normalization Law, and the Emergency Measures Law for the Stabilization of the People's Livelihood to further reduce the need for oil. Investigations into price fixing by oil companies were undertaken by the Fair Trade Commission.

As a result of these actions, the Japanese economy did not suffer as greatly from the 1979 oil crisis as it had from the one of 1973. At the same time, the oil industry had come under increased governmental regulation, which caused problems as oil supplies greatly increased during the 1980s. As world production of oil increased in the mid-1980s, and the value of the yen increased against the dollar, the price of oil fell rapidly in Japan, falling by more than half during 1986 alone. Despite this rapid price decline, oil consumption in Japan in physical units fell by nearly 8% in 1985 and 2% in 1986. Oil companies faced high debt, poor cash flow, and decreased profit levels. To reduce these problems, in 1987 MITI began a five-year program of deregulation in the oil industry, with a goal of creating a stronger oil industry with fewer companies and less regulation. Previously it had restricted imports of oil, placed controls on the refining of crude oil, and established quotas on the production of gasoline. These regulations were phased out, as well as limits on the number of gas stations and where they could be located.

The formation of Cosmo Oil through the merger of Maruzen and Daikyo in 1986 and its subsequent growth through a merger in 1989 with Asia Oil Co., Ltd. was a part of the turbulence of the times. Asia Oil had been an affiliate of Daikyo Oil, but operated independently after the formation of Cosmo Oil. Asia Oil's merger into Cosmo Oil was designed to reduce operating costs and improve operations at Cosmo, so as to better withstand the competitive pressures being brought about by the deregulation and decontrol.

At the start of 1990 Cosmo Oil had a network of more than 7,300 gasoline stations, about 14% of the 54,000 stations in Japan. It operated refineries in Chiba, with a capacity of 220,000 barrels per day; Yokkaichi, with a capacity of 175,000 barrels per day; Sakai, with a capacity of 110,000 barrels per day; and Sakaide, with a capacity of 140,000 barrels per day. Cosmo operated its own fleet of relatively new supertankers, including the *Cosmo Galaxy*, *Cosmo Venus*, *Cosmo Jupiter*, and *Cosmo Neptune*. An exploration subsidiary sought to develop oil fields throughout the world.

For the fiscal year ending March 31, 1990, Cosmo Oil produced approximately 132 million barrels of petroleum made up of 24% gasoline and naphtha, 34% kerosene and gas oil, 33% heavy fuel oil, and 9% lubricant and other products. Cosmo Oil purchased almost 69 million barrels of product from Japanese sources and imported about 60 million barrels.

Cosmo maintains a strategy of product innovation through research and development. In 1990 its research facility, Cosmo Research Institute, formulated a calcium phenate alkaline detergent additive that was awarded the Japan Petroleum Institute Prize. The additive is blended with engine oil used in automobiles or marine engines and improves the efficiency of that oil. To meet the higher demand for this product, which had been in development since 1971, Cosmo Oil planned to increase the capacity of its additive manufacturing facility.

Cosmo Oil's performance is tied to that of the world energy markets. After the 1979 energy crisis, the major international oil companies reduced their sales of oil to Japan, and other sources of supply were developed through direct purchase from oil-producing nations. Direct deals made by small Japanese oil companies, however, may be at prices higher than those gotten by the major oil companies. These higher prices may not be a disadvantage during periods of tight supply, but during a worldwide glut, Japanese companies often cancel these direct deals temporarily, and this disrupts the relationship between buyer and seller.

During 1990, as the price of crude oil increased and the yen fluctuated against the dollar, Cosmo felt a cost squeeze and saw it on its profit levels. Rumors circulated that Cosmo Oil was a potential takeover target. By using contacts with the government, especially through the large number of former MITI officials among its employees, Cosmo Oil has been able to protect itself from some of the harsher features of deregulation. Along with others in the industry, Cosmo, however, is hampered by an excessive number of service stations. In Japan about 40% of all service stations operate at a loss. Most oil companies, including Cosmo, were upgrading their service facilities by building newer, larger outlets. Cosmo was expanding its stations from sales outlets to full car-care centers. It was also offering higher-octane gasoline and better motor oil, both aimed at owners of high performance automobiles. Despite the upgrading of facilities and plant, Cosmo Oil's future depends on events taking place beyond its control in the Middle East.

Principal Subsidiaries: Cosmo Ventures, Incorporated; Cosmo Matsuyama Oil Co., Ltd.; Cosmo Petroleum Gas Co., Ltd.; Cosmo Asphalt Co., Ltd. (98%); Real Estate Cosmo Co., Ltd. (83.6%); Abu Dhabi Oil Co., Ltd. (51.14%); Maruzen Petrochemical Co., Ltd. (27%); Kashima Oil Co., Ltd. (21.6%).

Further Reading: do Rosario, Louise, "Business as usual: Japanese oil industry resists shake-up," *Far Eastern Economic Review,* August 9, 1990.

—Donald R. Stabile

STATOIL

DEN NORSKE STATS OLJESELSKAP AS

Post Office Box 300
N-4001 Stavanger
Norway
(4) 80 80 80
Fax: (4) 80 70 42

State-Owned Company
Incorporated: 1972
Employees: 14,463
Sales: NKr59.60 billion (US$10.13 billion)

Norway is the largest producer and seller of crude oil from the North Sea. Den Norske Stats Oljeselskap AS, also known as Statoil, is an integrated oil and gas company, established in 1972 as a state corporation able to exert what the government saw as a necessary measure of management control over the development of oil and gas exploration and production. The government decided that a state enterprise could best secure public energy supplies and ensure the nation's control over its resources and industrial development. The United Kingdom and Malaysia are examples of other countries which set up state-owned oil companies in the 1970s, responding to supply shortages in the international oil market, while the development of Norwegian policy on hydrocarbon resources has provided a framework which many other countries have attempted to emulate. Statoil is involved in all areas of the petroleum business from exploration and production to refining and distribution. About two-thirds of its crude is sold in northwest Europe. The rest is exported via its Mongstad operations to other countries. The company is also Scandinavia's largest producer of petrochemicals such as ethylene and propylene.

The Norwegian continental shelf contains huge oil and gas reserves, of which only a small portion has been recovered to date. Natural gas accounts for around 60% of these reserves. Oil reserves in 1991 were estimated to last 30 to 40 years and gas reserves more than 100 years. The reserves are spread over around 250 million acres, of which large parts have yet to be explored, and Norwegian oil and gas are among the most difficult in the world to extract, because of the ocean depths and climatic conditions. North Sea crude is well suited for producing motor fuels because of its low sulfur and metal content.

The oil and gas discoveries in the North Sea only began to be a significant factor in the Norwegian economy and politics after 1962, when Phillips Petroleum first applied for sole rights to explore the continental shelf. The Norwegian government refused and proclaimed sovereignty over its continental shelf in 1963, defining it, in cooperation with the British and Danish governments of the day, as the median line between Norway and those two countries, and thus gaining unquestioned access to waters beyond the Norwegian Trench. It was not until 1965 that the government began to allocate licenses permitting exploration on a "carried-interest" basis. This means that the government has an option to participate on equal terms for a given percentage of a production license if a commercial find is made in the area covered by the license. The first well was drilled in 1966, and in 1968 the first find of oil occurred in the Cod field. In the early years, exploration activity, based around Stavanger, was relatively quiet, but the big Ekofisk find at the end of 1969 demonstrated the potential of Norway's oil business and prompted the government to seek to establish a consistent oil policy.

Between 1970 and 1971 the government set up committees to draw up proposals for a state corporation. The system created in 1972 consisted of the Ministry of Industry, responsible for general policy and strategy; the Norwegian Petroleum Directorate, seeing to the day-to-day control and administration, unhampered, it was hoped, by political squabbling; and Statoil. The policy reflected the view that such strategic resources as oil and gas could not be left to the multinationals. The state had to have guaranteed access to these resources to formulate its fuel policies and to exert more control over the oil operations of foreign companies by way of production limits, leasing requirements, and bidding practices, as well as through taxation. The Labour Party, which governed Norway from 1964 to 1981, worked to increase Statoil's control over domestic oil production. Statoil's virtual monopoly, through its participation in every oil and gas venture, would provide for further investments in refining, transportation, and marketing. In addition the government decided to set ceilings on the production rate, not only to avoid depleting its resources but also to keep the impact of the new industry on the overall economy at a manageable level, since it recognized the potential for social and economic dislocation.

From the outset Statoil was engaged in a diverse range of oil-related activities. In 1975 Norway became a net exporter of oil. In the same year Statoil commissioned its first subsea oil pipeline, the Norpipe line from Ekofisk to Teesside in the United Kingdom, and it began exploring for oil and gas. The first two gas pipelines, Ekofisk-Emden and Frigg-St. Fergus, were commissioned in 1977 and offshore oil loading began in 1979 on Statfjord. In 1978 an ethylene plant, jointly owned by Statoil (49%) and Norsk Hydro, was built at Rafnes in eastern Norway. Close by are Statoil's plants which produce polyethylene and polypropylene. Polyethylene is used in the making of such products as film, packaging, and cable insulation, while polypropylene goes into medical equipment, car parts, and pipes, among many other products.

During these years the Norwegian oil industry contributed to the growth of such industries as shipping and chemicals, as the leading companies in these sectors speculated in the new industry, but at the same time Norwegian manufacturing was badly affected by a slowdown in growth. Between 1975 and 1980 the Norwegian government required foreign oil companies to engage in industrial cooperative projects as a means of qualifying for license awards. Many of these projects were in non-oil sectors.

The 1980s provided Norway with increased wealth from its oil revenues, but because of the growing burden of foreign loans and the inflationary effects of oil on its other industries, the economy as a whole became less competitive. The foreign loans were needed for the continuing costs of foreign technical expertise and exploration. It remained an important policy to stimulate Norwegian industry generally through subcontracts with the oil industry.

In 1981 Statoil, with its competitors Saga and Norsk Hydro as co-owners, began to operate in the Gullfaks field, the first time that a field was owned 100% by Norwegian interests. Production started in Gullfaks in 1987. Statoil also decided to lay a pipeline, the Statpipe, a transport and process system for gas, from the Statfjord, Gullfaks, and Heimdal fields across the Norwegian Trench to shore. The Statpipe system came onstream in 1985, with 830 kilometers of pipeline on the sea floor at depths down to 330 meters. In 1984 it was decided to lay another pipeline to land crude from the Oseberg field at Sture near Bergen.

A Conservative-led government made some important changes in Statoil's powers and conditions in 1984. It was decided that all gross income from each field would go directly into the Treasury instead of through the usual taxes and dividends. Voting procedures were to be changed in all licensee groups. Statoil lost its automatic right to veto its partners' proposals, on licenses where it held a stake of 50% or more. In order to exercise this veto it would have to obtain the consent of the Oil Ministry. It was at this time that Norway decided to aim toward bringing the management of oil production in some fields entirely under Statoil's control, rather than subcontracting to foreign companies. In late 1984 Statoil reached an agreement with Mobil under which Statoil would take over as operator of the huge Anglo-Norwegian Statfjord field by 1989 at the latest. Norway was moving away from its dependence on foreign oil, companies' expertise. Ther operation of Statfjord, the largest offshore oil and gas field in the world, passed over to Statoil in 1987.

While expanding its own operations Statoil recognized the advantages of retaining a prominent position within the industry as a whole, at home and abroad. Thus in 1986 it took the lead in negotiations on behalf of a group of companies for the selling of gas from two fields, Troll and Sleipner, to other European countries. Troll, in which Statoil has a 74.6% share, is one of the largest offshore gas fields in the world. It was under the operatorship of Royal Dutch/Shell, which has an 8.3% share in it, with Statoil taking over as operator when the fields came onstream in 1996. Statoil's share in the Sleipner field is 49.6% and its gas is due to come onstream in 1993. A pipeline system, known as the Zeepipe, is now being built from these fields to Zeebrugge in Belgium. Statoil will construct and operate the pipeline and the reception terminal at Zeebrugge, where any solid or liquid components will be removed from the dry gas.

By 1985 Statoil had established itself as the largest industrial company in Norway, accounting for as much as 10% of gross national product and a similar proportion of government revenue. As it developed it began to look abroad for acquisitions as well as markets. Its first foreign acquisition was Exxon's Swedish oil retailing and petrochemicals operation, in 1985. The petrochemicals subsidiary, renamed Statoil Petrokemi

AB, uses naphtha, propane, and butane as its raw materials and its main products are ethylene and propylene. Statoil Petrokemi has expanded and modernized its plant, to create one of the most advanced petrochemicals facilities in Europe. In 1986 Statoil purchased Exxon's oil products marketing company in Denmark and its Kalundborg refinery. It also bought a West German factory, which produces plastic for car bumpers and cable insulation. This was seen as an important investment for Statoil because it increased its capacity to process the plastic resins made at its petrochemical plant in Rafnes, in eastern Norway. Statoil is now able to offer over 70 different grades of plastics.

Statoil experienced its worst political and financial difficulties in 1987, starting with a drastic fall in profits as a result of the worldwide collapse in the price of oil in 1986. Politicians opposed to its economic and social power began to complain about its secretiveness and its closeness to the Labour Party establishment, as symbolized by the company's president, Arve Johnsen, who had been a government minister before joining Statoil. Then an official investigation revealed that cost overruns on the Mongstad refinery project had reached about NKr5.4 billion (US$850 million) and concluded that the refinery would never be profitable. At first the oil minister rejected opponents' claims that the report showed that Statoil's management was overstretched in relation to the number of projects in which the company was involved. Amid allegations that the losses had been concealed deliberately, the company's six directors resigned and Johnsen too resigned. However, the government appointed a new board to take up the challenge of expanding and diversifying Statoil's operations further.

Statoil now had a retail distribution network in all three Scandinavian countries. The government had originally forbidden Statoil to get involved in distribution, which was thought to be better handled by the multinationals. In 1991 Statoil's Norwegian marketing affiliate, Norsk Olje AS, an oil retail firm with 650 outlets throughout Norway, was renamed Statoil Norge AS and started using Statoil livery in its marketing. By then Statoil had a total of 1,600 retail outlets in Norway, Sweden, and Denmark.

Statoil had a better year in 1988 than in 1987. Statoil became sole owner of the Norwegian petrochemical plants which it had been operating since 1984 in conjunction with Norsk Hydro. This subsidiary was renamed Statoil Bamble, in reference to its main plant at Bamble, in southern Norway, which had come into operation in fiscal year 1978–1979 and had become the largest center for plastics technology in Norway. In the same year the Tommeliten field began producing oil without the platforms which are the standard technology in oilfields, by using equipment placed on the seabed and connected to the Edda platform on the Ekofisk field.

The Mongstad refinery, which had been the focus of Statoil's troubles in 1987, was started up again in 1989. Two more oil platforms, Veslefrikk and Gullfaks C, came onstream. The Veslefrikk was the first floating production platform after being in the Norwegian sector of the North sea, while the Gullfaks C platform, which stands in 220 meters of water, is the world's largest production platform. Its total height of about 380 meters makes it 30 meters taller than the Eiffel Tower.

In 1990 Statoil expanded its interests into new Danish technology. Its subsidiary Dansk Bioprotein seeks to use bacteria to convert natural gas into edible protein, to be used as an additive in animal and fish feeds.

As Statoil looks for new international markets, it has joined forces with BP to explore for oil in West Africa, Vietnam, China, and the Soviet Union. It also holds exploration and production interests in the Netherlands and a 10% stake in a Chinese offshore license. In 1991 it made an oil discovery in the Danish sector of the North Sea.

When the Norwegian Labour Party came back to power in 1990, it decided not to reintroduce controls on North Sea petroleum output, but it has no intention of privatizing Statoil. With its petroleum resources still largely untouched, Norway can look forward to a bright future in the petroleum industry, with Statoil at the forefront.

Principal Subsidiaries: Statoil Norge AS; Statoil Danmark AS (Denmark); Svenska Statoil AB (Sweden); Statoil Petrokemi AB (Sweden); Statoil Deutschland GmbH (Germany); Statoil Europarts AB (Sweden).

Further Reading: Noreng, Oystein, *The Oil Industry and Government Strategy in the North Sea,* London, Croom Helm, 1980; Klapp, Merrie G., *The Sovereign Entrepreneur,* Ithaca, Cornell University Press, 1987; *Who We Are, What We Do, Where We Are,* Stavanger, Statoil, 1990.

—Monique Lamontagne

DIAMOND SHAMROCK, INC.

9830 Colonnade Boulevard
San Antonio, Texas 78230
U.S.A.
(512) 641-6800
Fax: (512) 641-8643

Public Company
Incorporated: 1910 as Diamond Alkali Company
Employees: 5,000
Sales: $2.71 billion
Stock Exchange: New York

Diamond Shamrock, Inc. is a regional refiner and marketer of petroleum products whose activities also include the processing and marketing of natural gas. Based in the southwestern United States, the company also operates the world's largest underground commercial hydrocarbon storage facility and telephone services company, and markets lubricating oils, automotive accessories, and environmental services.

Diamond Shamrock is a successor to a number of companies, the earliest being Diamond Alkali Company formed in 1910 as a chemical company. A group of Pittsburgh, Pennsylvania, businessmen associated with the glass industry formed the Diamond Alkali Company to produce soda ash, a basic raw material of glass manufacturing. Diamond Alkali was incorporated in West Virginia in March of that year, with company headquarters established in Pittsburgh.

The new corporation was capitalized at $1.2 million, with most of those funds put towards construction of a soda ash plant. A site in Painesville, Ohio, on the Lake Erie shore just 30 miles east of Cleveland was chosen for the new plant, which went onstream in 1912.

After World War I began in 1914, the demand for canning glass increased, and Diamond Alkali found a niche in the market. About the same time, Diamond Alkali began marketing increasing quantities of its soda ash for laundry preparations, baking soda, water softeners, paper and pulp production solutions, and textile processing.

By 1915 Diamond's ability to produce soda ash exceeded customer demand, and the company began using soda ash and limestone to produce caustic soda. This development opened new markets in lye, soap, detergents, and eventually rayon and cellophane. In 1918 Diamond began making bicarbonate of soda. A short time later the company's product line was expanded beyond the basic alkalis of soda ash, caustic soda, and bichromates. In 1920 Diamond's second plant opened in Cincinnati, Ohio, producing silicate of soda made by combining soda ash with sand.

In 1925 the company expanded its product line again. Diamond took a step towards greater integration when the Painesville plant began manufacturing calcium carbonates, cement and coke. A sludge by-product of soda ash was treated to make the calcium carbonate, marketed as an agent to give paint smoothness, speed dry printers' inks, and add physical properties to rubber and plastic products.

In 1929 the company began making caustic soda through the new process of electrolysis of salt, a method of running brine through electricity. Two by-products were formed from this process, chlorine and pure hydrogen, which were also marketed. The chlorine was sold to the water purification industry and also used in the manufacture of dry cleaning solvents. The hydrogen was used for hydrochloric acid production, welding fuel, food oil hardening, electric lamp production, and ammonia production.

About the same time Diamond's product line expanded, the stock market plummeted. In 1930, the first full year of the ensuing Depression, Diamond posted $4.9 million in earnings on $16.3 million in sales. In 1931 sales fell by $2 million. Profits plunged to nearly a quarter of what earnings were a year earlier, and the company's stock value dropped from $3.77 to 53¢. By 1932, sales, earnings, and stock prices began to inch upward, and five years later all were hovering near 1930 levels.

In 1936 Diamond began a modest research program that resulted in the production of magnesium oxide. J.T. Richards, who had been with the company in various capacities since 1917, was named president in 1937. Once World War II began, magnesium became an important component for incendiary bombs, and Diamond was selected by the United States to operate one of 12 government-owned magnesium plants.

In 1942 Diamond's Raymond F. Evans established the company's first research laboratory. Evans, son of T.R. Evans who was one of the founders of the company and later served as president until his death in 1931, became general manager of the company the following year.

By 1944 Diamond was operating three plants constructed through Defense Plant Corporation funds, including the magnesium plant, a calcium hypochlorite plant, and a synthetic catalyst plant under joint lease with the M.W. Kellogg Company. Before the war concluded Diamond acquired Emeryville Chemical Company, a west coast manufacturer of silicate of soda. After 1945 Diamond's postwar focus turned to a program of selling unprofitable assets, simplifying corporate structure, and modernizing, expanding, and adding plants.

During the late 1940s several new plants opened, including a Houston, Texas, chlorine and caustic soda plant, a Painesville magnesium oxide plant, a Chicago silicate plant, and a Houston electrochemical plant. Diamond signed five-year lease agreements with the U.S. government for chlorine and caustic soda plants at the U.S. Army chemical corps arsenal at Edgewood, Maryland, and at Pine Bluff, Arkansas. Detergent plants were established in Dallas, Painesville, and at Emeryville, California.

In 1947 Raymond Evans was named president and Richards became chairman of the board. About the same time the government lifted price controls imposed during the war, and

Evans directed Diamond's first price hike in nine years in seeking to reverse a wartime downward trend in earnings.

In 1948 Diamond moved its headquarters from Pittsburgh to Cleveland, Ohio, closer to its central operations in Painesville. Sales passed the $50 million mark for the first time that year, but slumped in 1949 due in part to a two-month strike which cost the company about $750,000 in net earnings. During the late 1940s Diamond boosted its bichromate production with the acquisition of the Martin Dennis Company, operator of two New Jersey plants. With export sales on the rise, in 1949 Diamond formed an exports sales division that included Martin Dennis.

By 1950 Diamond's first phase of postwar expansion and diversification was nearly complete, with the company assets having grown to include 12 different plants producing over 100 different chemicals. In mid-1950, the demand for Diamond's products increased after the United States entered the Korean War. The war also spurred the U.S. government to reactivate the Painesville magnesium plant which Diamond had operated during World War II, and the company was again charged with operating the facility, forfeiting any profit.

During the first half of the 1950s, Diamond embarked on its second phase of postwar growth, and implemented a diversification, geographical expansion, and modernization program which brought entrance into the organic and agricultural chemicals, plastics, and chromic acid fields. In the fall of 1950, Diamond acquired the chromic acid business from E.I. du Pont de Nemours and Company. One year later Diamond purchased Kolker Chemical Works, Inc., a manufacturer and distributor of organic insecticides and agricultural chemicals, including DDT.

In 1953 Diamond Alkali began producing polyvinyl chloride, a product used in the manufacture of plastic articles, and perchlorethylene, a product used in metal cleaning and dry cleaning. That same year Diamond acquired Belle Alkali Company, a producer of chemicals used in the manufacture of silicone resins, solvents, and drugs.

Richards retired as chairman in 1954, and Evans was named as successor. John A. Sargent, executive vice president, became president. That same year Diamond created an exploratory research department to assist in strategic planning. Diamond continued its geographical diversification in early 1955 with the acquisition of a 51% interest in Diamond Black Leaf Company, an agricultural chemicals firm with plants in Virginia, Alabama, Kentucky, and Texas. Two years later Diamond Black Leaf became a wholly owned subsidiary.

In 1955 Diamond acquired a government-owned chlorine and caustic soda plant at Muscle Shoals, Alabama, for $15 million. That same year the company passed the $100 million sales mark for the first time, logging $110 million in revenue. While sales were increasing, Diamond's name recognition outside the chemical industry lagged, and in 1956 Diamond joined a number of chemical companies adopting new trademarks. The former "alkali" enclosed in a horizontal diamond was replaced by a vertical diamond surrounded by a curved letter "d." In 1957, Sargent resigned, and Evans assumed the additional duties of president.

Diamond's growth continued in the 1960s. In 1960, Bessemer Limestone & Cement Company, an operator of a cement plant and limestone quarries, was merged into Diamond. Diamond also acquired Harte & Company, a producer of vinyl

film and sheeting serving the plastics industry, and Chemical Process Company, a producer of chemicals used for water purification, pharmaceuticals and polyester resins.

In 1961 Diamond joined three foreign firms in building a $15 million electrolytic caustic-chlorine plant in Brazil, the largest in South America, to produce fertilizer chemicals. The following year Diamond and a French firm, Prosim, S.A., formed the joint venture company Dia Prosim, S.A., to manufacture water treatment chemicals at a new Mobile, Alabama, plant.

Arthur B. Tillman, who had worked his way through the ranks from division manager to company vice president, was named president in 1966. In 1967, Diamond merged with Nopco Chemical Company, a New Jersey producer of a wide range of inorganic and organic chemicals. Also that year, Diamond acquired the polypropylene resin and film plants of Alamo Industries, boosting Diamond's foothold on the plastics market.

In the summer of 1967 Diamond laid the foundation for expansion into the petrochemicals field by merging with Shamrock Oil and Gas Company to form Diamond Shamrock Corporation (Diamond). The merger combined Diamond Alkali's chemical assets with Shamrock Oil's production interests in oil, gas, and petrochemical fertilizers and its marketing assets, which included a chain of service stations.

Evans was named chairman of the new corporation and James A. Hughes, a former Diamond Alkali vice chairman, became president. C.A. Cash, former Shamrock president, became executive vice president and president of the new subsidiary Diamond Shamrock Oil and Gas Company, while Tillman was also named as executive vice president of the corporation and president of the new subsidiary Diamond Shamrock Chemical Company. J.H. Dunn, former Shamrock chairman, was named chairman of the executive committee of the board.

In 1968 Diamond Shamrock sold its Bessemer Cement division to Louisville Cement Co. for $20 million in order to comply with a Federal Trade Commission ruling to divest itself of the unit. One-quarter of Diamond Shamrock's sales that year came from oil and gas, with the remainder of revenues coming from a mix of commodity chemicals, plastics, speciality chemicals, and agricultural chemicals. That mix changed in 1969, after Diamond acquired Taylor-Evans Seed Company, a producer of farming seed, with international marketing operations, and Pickland Mather & Company, a leading supplier of steel industry raw materials with interests in iron ore mining, mineral management, and ocean shipping vessels.

Diamond's oil exploration activities during the early 1970s focused largely on the Gulf of Mexico, Gulf of Alaska, North Sea, and Texas Panhandle, while production centered on domestic drilling in the West and Southwest. In 1971 Diamond Shamrock's growing interest in the animal-health and veterinary-medicine fields led to the purchase of Bio-Toxicological Research Laboratories, engaged in chemical research related to agriculture and animal health. The following year Diamond acquired American Chocolate & Citrus Company of St. Louis, Missouri, a commercial dairy provider of flavorings, fruit drink bases, and food processes.

Three years later Hughes retired, and Cash was named chairman. William H. Bricker, who joined the company in 1969 as a vice president overseeing agricultural chemicals, was named president. In 1976 he was named chief executive officer.

Diamond's specialty chemical operations continued to grow during the late-1970s. The company expanded its foothold on the commercial baking supply market and bought three Philadelphia, Pennsylvania–based providers of commercial baking supplies: Federal Yeast Corporation, Gold Star Foods Company, and Bakery Products Inc. Diamond also acquired the animal-health business of Shell Chemical Company and expanded existing vinyl chloride and potassium carbonate plants.

Diamond continued to build on a growing oil and gas foundation, which saw exploration acreage more than double between 1972 and 1977 to over 2.5 million acres, while oil production increased over 60%. In 1977 Diamond announced plans to construct a $25 million catalytic cracking unit at its McKee refinery near Dumas, Texas, in order to meet federal regulations calling for increased production of unleaded gasoline. The following year Diamond acquired a 21% stake in Sigmor Corporation of San Antonio, Texas, for $28 million, and then sold Sigmor $19 million in service station properties, a majority of which carried the Shamrock brand.

After Cash retired in 1979 Bricker assumed the additional duties of chairman and moved to make Diamond a major energy company. That same year Diamond acquired Falcon Seaboard Inc., a Houston-based producer of steam coal for $250 million. In a move that prompted Evans to resign as a director, Bricker relocated the company's headquarters from Cleveland to Dallas to follow its growing energy interests in the Southwest. Reflective of the change in Diamond Shamrock's focus, its 1979 annual report noted that the "energy, technology and chemicals" company had more than quadrupled during the decade.

Diamond Shamrock entered the 1980s with a new president, Allan J. Tomlinson, a former executive vice president in charge of Diamond's international and technology unit. In 1980 Diamond announced a slate of divisions targeted for divestiture, including plastics, metal coatings, domestic polymers, food-related products, animal nutrition, and medical products.

While courting buyers for its chemical assets, in 1980 Diamond turned its acquisition goals toward coal. The company paid $30 million for undeveloped coal reserves, and then formed a coal-marketing subsidiary. In 1981, in a second major expansion move into coal, Diamond purchased Amherst Coal Company for $220 million, then arranged an agreement with the French government to provide steam coal for power generation. Diamond posted record earnings in 1981 of $230 million on $3.4 billion in sales.

In 1982, after having spent $161 million for drilling rights in Alaska's Beaufort Sea, earnings dropped by roughly $150 million due to recessionary conditions and falling energy prices. J.L. Jackson, former president of Diamond's coal unit, was named corporation president in 1983. Diamond continued seeking buyers for its weak chemical assets, and in 1983 expanded its divestiture slate to include its water conditioning and process chemical divisions. Diamond permanently laid off 500 workers in 1983, but still reported a $60 million loss due to tax write-offs on a dry hole in the Beaufort Sea.

Diamond's most expensive move of 1983 was its $1.2 billion stock swap in the merger with Natomas Company. The merger gave Diamond Indonesian oil and gas operations, a geothermal

energy business, and wells producing oil in the North Sea, Canada, and the United States.

Diamond's involvement with the defoliant Agent Orange in the mid-1960s affected the company in 1984. In March 1984 Diamond agreed to spend $412 million to clean up contaminants at a New Jersey plant, where it had produced the defoliant used during the Vietnam War. Two months later Diamond was one of seven chemical companies that agreed to a settlement to compensate Vietnam War veterans for injuries claimed to be associated with exposure to dioxin, a toxic substance used in Agent Orange. While Diamond Shamrock produced only 5% of the Agent Orange used in the Vietnam War, the company's chemical compound contained the highest concentration of dioxin. In the settlement Diamond agreed to contribute $21.6 million to a compensation fund.

In 1985 Bricker tentatively agreed to sell Diamond for $28 a share to Occidental Petroleum Corporation, then withdrew the offer. The scrapped deal drew takeover speculation and Diamond announced a restructuring to fend off possible hostile maneuvers. Included in the restructuring was the formation of a master limited partnership, Diamond Shamrock Offshore Partners Ltd., to hold the company's oil and gas assets in the Gulf of Mexico. Diamond also announced $810 million in write-offs, largely due to Indonesian properties, and said it would repurchase about 6% of its stock.

In 1986 the company announced it would eliminate 600 more jobs, sell its chemical and coal operations, and increase its oil and natural gas reserves. Jackson resigned a few months after the announcement. Later that year, Diamond's chemical business was sold to Occidental Petroleum for $850 million. With Diamond retrenching, in December 1986 Texas oilman T. Boone Pickens, who controlled the oil firm Mesa Limited Partnership, offered $2 billion for Diamond in a securities exchange. The offer was dropped a few weeks later, after Diamond rejected the bid and filed suit against Pickens.

A second bid from Pickens in early 1987 prompted Diamond to announce its third restructuring in two years. Bricker, in his last move as chairman, had the company split in two to form a production and exploration company, and a refining and marketing company. The restructuring also called for a buy-back of common stock and issuance of $300 million in preferred stock to Prudential Insurance Company of America, which could then block any merger or recapitalization.

In April, 1987 Bricker resigned and a new company, Diamond Shamrock R&M, Inc., was spun off as an independent oil refining and marketing company to be based in San Antonio, Texas. Roger R. Hemminghaus, who had been running Diamond's refining business for two years, was named president. Assets for the new company included $1.6 billion in sales; two Texas refineries in McKee and Three Rivers; a natural gas processing plant; 4,000 miles of pipeline; 2,000 branded stations in 12 states; 550 company-operated retail stores in Texas, Colorado, and Louisiana; a lube-oil blending and automotive-accessories-distribution company; and 30 million barrels of liquid propane gas underground storage capacity in Mont Belvieu, Texas. What was left of the former Diamond Shamrock Corporation became Maxus Energy Corporation.

Hemminghaus announced, that Diamond Shamrock R&M would sell its more remote assets and concentrate on marketing operations in the Southwest. In 1988 the company began expanding its refinery and pipeline capacity and bolstering its retail presence. That year construction began on a $25 million hydrocracker unit for its McKee refinery, and Diamond purchased 80 Texas gasoline stations. In 1989 the company also established a development and new ventures department to identify related businesses in fields where it has expertise. Profits soared from $1.6 million in 1987 to $53.5 million in 1988, while stock prices nearly doubled to $28. Diamond formed the subsidiary, Diamond Shamrock Natural Gas Marketing Company, and then purchased two companies, Merit Tank Testing, Inc., providing environmental testing for underground petroleum storage, and Petro/Chem Environmental Services, Inc., marketing petroleum-related environmental services, the two were merged under the Petro/Chem name in 1989.

In 1989 Diamond entered the petrochemicals business and became a 33% partner in a propane-propylene operation in Mont Belvieu, Texas. Diamond's Mont Belvieu underground storage facility became the world's largest that year with the acquisition of XRAL Storage and Terminaling Company, which brought the company's underground storage capacity to 50 million barrels.

Diamond also acquired a telephone services company and formed the subsidiary, North American InTeleCom, Inc., a San Antonio, Texas–based firm providing operator-assisted services for correctional facilities and managing private pay telephones, including those at many of Diamond's retail outlets.

In 1990 the company's name was changed to Diamond Shamrock, Inc. That same year Diamond completed projects expected to pave the way for growth in the new decade, including major refinery additions, pipeline expansions, construction of a propane-propolyene facility, and about 40 new retail outlets. Diamond's goals for the 1990s call for increased diversification and expansion into businesses such as environmental services and telephone services, which could add cash flow, complement its core businesses, and expand Diamond's scope of activities in areas where it has expertise.

Principal Subsidiaries: Autotronic Systems, Inc.; D-S Pipe Line Corporation; Diamond Shamrock Refining and Marketing Company; Emerald Corporation; Emerald Pipe Line Corporation; Industrial Lubricants Company; Sigmor Corporation; Sigmore Pipeline Company; The Shamrock Pipe Line Corporation; West Emerald Pipe Line Corporation.

Further Reading: Bricker, William H., *Partners by Choice and Fortune: The Story of Diamond Shamrock*, Princeton, Princeton University Press, 1977; Mason, Todd, and G. David Wallace, "The Downfall of a CEO: The Inside Story of Bill Bricker's Reign at Diamond Shamrock," *Business Week*, February 16, 1987.

—Roger W. Rouland

EGYPTIAN GENERAL PETROLEUM CORPORATION

Post Office Box 2130
Phalastin Street
4th Quarter, New Maadi
Cairo
Egypt
(2) 3531345

State-Owned Company
Incorporated: 1956 as General Petroleum Authority
Sales: E£2.66 billion (US$1.04 billion) (1986)

The Egyptian General Petroleum Corporation (EGPC) is the instrument by which Egypt's government manages its hydrocarbon resources. Responsible to the minister of petroleum and mineral resources for all aspects of Egypt's oil and petrochemical industries, EGPC controls a group of companies involved in the exploration, extraction, refining, and distribution of hydrocarbons. EGPC also has responsibility for licensing the exploration activities of overseas oil companies in Egypt.

Although Egypt is not among the most important players on the international oil scene, oil is a vital element of the Egyptian economy. Oil exports are a major source of scarce foreign currency. Hydrocarbons are an ingredient in the production of fertilizers, a pressing concern for Egypt's farmers since the completion of the Aswan High Dam in 1970. The dam put an end to the seasonal flooding of the Nile, which had carried fertile sediments into the farms of the Lower Nile Valley. Furthermore, low water levels in the dam during the recent years of drought have meant that hydroelectricity production has not come up to expectations. Consequently Egypt's consumption of hydrocarbons to supply its energy needs has grown.

EGPC grants licenses to overseas oil companies for exploration only. Once they have struck oil, they must apply for a development lease, and the find will normally be exploited as a joint venture between the discoverer and EGPC. EGPC also owns a subsidiary, General Petroleum Company, which carries out explorations on its own account.

Egypt's oil was not always as firmly under the control of its government. As early as the 1860s, the government began drilling for oil. In 1869 the Gemsa field came to light, but it was left to overseas interests to develop the find, after a delay of over 40 years. Anglo-Egyptian Oilfields, a joint venture between Shell and British Petroleum, began to produce oil from the Gemsa field in 1910. Three years later, another field at Hurghada was brought onstream by Anglo-Egyptian, which mapped the west coast of the Gulf of Suez in the course of its explorations.

Five more oil fields were found between the world wars. By the time exploration resumed after World War II, other foreign companies were becoming involved. However, Anglo-Egyptian was still the dominant player until 1964, when it was nationalized.

In 1956 the General Petroleum Authority (GPA) had been created by the Egyptian government to safeguard the country's interests in the development of its valuable mineral resources. In the same year the General Petroleum Company (GPC), Egypt's first oil company, was formed and was granted licenses to prospect in the Gulf of Suez and in Egypt's Eastern Desert. GPC was later to acquire licenses in Sinai also, and to become the most important operating company owned by EGPC.

Egyptian General Petroleum Corporation was the new name given in 1962 to the GPA. The following year it entered into the first of a series of joint ventures with international companies for oil exploration and production. Among EGPC's earliest partners was Amoco, then known as Standard Oil Company (Indiana), with whom EGPC formed the Gulf of Suez Petroleum Company (Gupco), soon to become Egypt's largest oil producer. The largest company after Gupco, Petrobel, dates from 1963 and was the progeny of EGPC's union with the International Egyptian Oil Company (IEOC), the latter itself a joint venture between the Italian company ENI and an Egyptian firm. Phillips Petroleum was another important EGPC partner.

EGPC soon gained a solid reputation; the *Financial Times*, June 5, 1985, credited it with "an independence and efficiency not normally associated with public sector entities." EGPC's joint venture arrangements stimulated an upsurge in drilling, and in 1965 Gupco made a major find, the Morgan field in the Gulf of Suez, followed by the July and Ramadan fields in the same region. Petrobel found the first of Egypt's gas fields, Abu Madi, in 1967, though its major activity was the operation of the Belayim field in Sinai and Belayim Marine in the Gulf of Suez, oil fields which had been discovered in 1955 and 1961 respectively. Phillips Petroleum's explorations in the Western Desert led to the discovery of the El-Alamein oil field in 1966 and the Abu Gharadiq field, with both oil and gas, two years later.

In 1973 the Arab Petroleum Pipeline Company was created, in which EGPC took a 50% share. The co-owners included Saudi Arabia, Abu Dhabi, and other gulf states. Four years later the Suez-Mediterranean (Sumed) pipeline opened, serving as an alternative to the Suez Canal as a means of transporting oil. In the first ten years of its life the pipeline brought Egypt US$632 million in royalties and investment dividends, even though it was not being used to full capacity.

Also in 1973, EGPC switched from joint explorations to its present policy of issuing exploration licenses to foreign contractors with subsequent sharing of any finds. Instead of EGPC and the contractor sharing the cost and the risk of explorations that might prove abortive, the contractor now footed the bill, recouping costs out of any resultant products. No more of the old-style joint ventures were set up after 1973, and existing joint ventures were either converted to the new system—as were Gupco and Petrobel—or phased out. Besides its agreements with overseas companies, EGPC continued to prospect in its own right through its subsidiary, the GPC.

In 1976 Egypt became a net exporter of crude oil for the first time. From then on oil played a progressively greater part in the Egyptian economy, rising from less than 5% of gross domestic product (GDP)—differing from gross national product in that GDP excludes income from investment abroad—in 1974 to nearly 20% ten years later. The Gulf of Suez continued to yield important new discoveries through the late 1970s, including a string of successes for Suez Oil Company (Suco), another of EGPC's cooperative ventures, this time between EGPC, Royal Dutch/Shell, BP, and the operator, Deminex of West Germany. Ras Budran, discovered in 1978, came onstream in 1983, as did Ras Fanar. Zeit Bay, which came onstream two years later, was the last major Suco discovery.

A series of moderately productive Gulf of Suez explorations took place throughout the 1980s; at the end of the decade this was still Egypt's largest oil-producing area with 90% of total output. Sinai, handed back to Egypt in 1979 after a period under Israeli occupation, was the next most fruitful area of exploration, progressively growing in importance through the 1980s. The most dramatic change of the 1980s was the increase in exploration and production activity in the Western Desert, where Khalda Petroleum Company, a joint venture between Conoco, Texas International, and EGPC, was a major player. Improvements to the pipeline networks there, in addition to optimism about its resources, contributed to the attractions which the Western Desert held out to oil companies.

EGPC had always enjoyed a close relationship with the Egyptian Ministry of Oil. When Abul Hadi Qandil, EGPC's chairman, became oil minister in July 1984, he continued to hold both positions for three years, a demanding double commitment which was blamed for some of the operational difficulties that EGPC encountered in the mid-1980s.

EGPC had set Egypt an output target of one million barrels of oil, gas, and condensate per day, to be reached by 1985–1986, but the oil slump of the mid-1980s put paid to this plan. In 1984 EGPC restricted output to 900,000 barrels, in line with OPEC price stabilization policies, even though Egypt was not a member of OPEC. Crude output was pegged at less than 900,000 barrels per day for the five years from 1987.

The effects of the oil upsets of the mid-1980s on the Egyptian economy were severe. By then, only agriculture constituted a larger element in the domestic economy, and oil was the largest foreign-currency earner. Between 1986 and 1987 the drop in oil prices reduced the oil sector's share of export earnings from 81% to 47%. This crisis brought about several important policy changes.

The slump had a particularly severe effect on Egypt because its wholesale prices were often set too high relative to other exporters. This experience prompted EGPC to introduce a system of reviewing prices every two weeks instead of monthly as before, reducing the lag in adjustments. The biweekly reviews have continued to be held ever since.

In 1987, in the aftermath of the 1986 oil slump, Egypt and the International Monetary Fund (IMF) agreed on a rescheduling of the country's burdensome foreign debts together with an IMF facility for US$175 million in loans at a favorable rate. However, the agreement collapsed when Egypt was unable to implement the economic reforms on which the IMF's loan was dependent. In the light of Egypt's wider economic problems, its management of its oil industry came under scrutiny.

Egypt needed to make as much of its oil as possible available for export, but until 1985 the annual growth in production had been more or less matched by the growth in domestic demand. Since subsidized prices for domestic consumers were doing little to improve matters, in 1985 the Egyptian government had begun to reduce these subsidies, resulting in massive price increases.

The World Bank was urging Egypt to capitalize on its natural gas, saying "The more natural gas is used for domestic needs the more Egypt's petroleum—in the form of crude or refined products—can be used to earn or save foreign exchange," as reported in the *Financial Times*, June 29, 1987. Aware of this opportunity, EGPC encouraged the substitution of gas for oil, particularly in power stations.

Egypt had a considerable amount of undiscovered natural gas, but EGPC realized that it had been doing little to encourage foreign companies to bring these valuable resources to light. Egypt had originally taken the view that gas should be exploited only by Egyptian organizations, and early exploration licenses had laid down that gas discovered in the course of drilling and not exported would become government property. This arrangement acted as a disincentive for foreign companies to look for gas, or to exploit any gas resources discovered in the course of oil prospecting.

A "gas clause" to remunerate foreign companies for gas discoveries was introduced into concessions in 1980, but it was not until 1986 that a model agreement that actively encouraged investment in gas was devised. The Shell Winning agreement for the Western Desert Bed-3 was used as a basis for subsequent agreements, and the "gas clause," under which profit on gas was divided, typically on a basis of approximately 80%–20% in favor of EGPC, was inserted retrospectively into some licenses.

Meanwhile, EGPC's interests were diversifying. In the late 1970s EGPC had become interested in the petrochemicals industry. After an abortive joint venture with the Italian petrochemical specialist Montedison, EGPC undertook the construction of a plant at Ameriyah for the production of polyvinyl chloride (PVC), vinyl choride monomer (VCM), chlorine, and caustic soda. The plant went into production during 1986 and 1987. Further units for ethylene and polyethylene were added, and other petrochemical activities were planned, some of them joint ventures between EGPC's Egyptian Petrochemicals Company and the Italian EniChem. The ultimate aim was vertical integration, but pending completion of the whole Ameriyah petrochemical complex, some of the raw materials had to be imported. For this purpose an innovative offshore terminal with facilities for the unloading and storage of ethylene was constructed off Alexandria.

Since 1979 the Abu Qir Fertilizer and Chemical Industries Company, one-fifth owned by EGPC, had run the largest fertilizer manufacturing operation in Egypt, obtaining some of its raw material from the Abu Qir gas field. A project that would more than double the company's output of ammonia and urea and permit the production of ammonia nitrate was begun in the late 1980s with completion due in 1991.

In 1987 Abul Hadi Qandil was succeeded as EGPC chairman by Muhammed Maabed, who had already served EGPC as deputy chairman for production. The following year Hamdi al-Banbi, Gupco's president, took over the chairmanship of EGPC.

Entering the 1990s, EGPC could point to some encouraging strikes on the part of its companies and licensees. The Gulf of Suez looked set to remain the most important area for oil. Shell Winning and Gupco both announced important new finds in the gulf during 1990, Gupco calling one of its the best discovery since 1983. Suco too was reportedly planning to increase expansion of its three Suez Gulf fields by the sinking of new wells. In the Western Desert, Phillips had made a promising discovery in its South Umbarka block. Preliminary studies indicated the existence of oil in upper Egypt, a previously unexplored region, and prospecting was expected to begin there shortly.

The oil ministry and EGPC were encouraging licensees to exploit fields more rapidly and improve their delivery by investing in the construction of new pipelines. The licensees were also being urged to step up production by such measures as water injection to recover previously inaccessible reserves, a process undertaken, for instance, by Agiba Petroleum in the Western Desert.

During the period of Egypt's 1987 to 1992 Five-Year Plan, natural gas output was expected to double. Much of the gas found to date was in the Western Desert, which was believed to contain more gas than oil, but by 1990 the Nile delta was the richest gas-producing area. It was also thought that gas resources were to be found off Egypt's Mediterranean coast and perhaps in the Red Sea.

EGPC continued to be energetic in promoting exploration for all types of hydrocarbons, and according to the *Financial Times*, April 4, 1990, Egypt was among the countries with the highest concentrations of foreign exploration activities. Over 1,200 wells came onstream during the 1980s alone.

In the late 1980s, aside from exploration and production, EGPC assigned a high priority to downstream activities. According to the Five-Year Plan to 1992, the refinery capacity was to increase by almost 40%. To illustrate the importance given to this work, 42% of the Egyptian public sector investment in the oil and gas sector was concerned with refinery and refined products in 1987–1988. Refinery construction work was commissioned mainly from EGPC subsidiaries Engineering for the Petroleum and Process Industries and Petroleum Projects Company, since the government wanted to use local resources. In 1990 Egypt had seven refineries, all of them controlled by EGPC subsidiaries; the oldest, built by Anglo-Egyptian, dated back to 1913. Further refinery expansion was planned, but there was doubt as to how it would be financed. Some observers expected that private investment would be necessary. Although this procedure had been the norm for upstream activities, it would be a new departure for EGPC in the refinery area. The construction of pipelines to deliver oil, gas, and refined products to industrial and domestic users in Cairo and Alexandria was also among EGPC's planned projects.

There had been important advances in Egypt in the substitution of gas for oil. In 1990 around 60% of Egypt's gas was being used for electricity generation. Many of Egypt's power stations were being converted to use gas instead of fuel oil and new stations were being designed to use gas from the start.

The remainder of the gas was used in industry, in the manufacture of fertilizers, iron, steel, and cement, with a mere 1% being bottled for domestic use.

Despite these advances in resource management, and despite Egypt's ongoing oil and gas explorations and reasonable flow of new finds, there is no scope for EGPC to rest on its laurels. Some observers fear that without major new discoveries Egypt will, by the turn of the century, revert to being a net importer of oil. Total output is restricted for conservation reasons, but new discoveries are still equalled or outweighed by reductions in reserves from the fields currently operating, so that in 1990 recoverable oil reserves seemed to be stuck at around four billion barrels. An additional problem is that because the finds tend to be smaller than in Egypt's more fortunate neighbors around the Persian Gulf, unit production costs are higher than average.

Gas presents the brightest prospect for the future, with the assurance of rapidly increasing reserves. According to one estimate, the one to two trillion cubic feet reserves established up to 1990 should have trebled in two years' time.

EGPC continues to grapple with the problem of mounting domestic demand detracting from exports. Despite the reduction of subsidies, the *Petroleum Economist* reported in March 1990 that domestic demand was still rising by 10 to 15% per annum.

Shocks to the oil market arising from the 1991 conflict in Iraq will present EGPC with both challenges and opportunities. The effective management of the hydrocarbon sector will be all the more crucial to the Egyptian economy in that, with the loss of remittances from Egypt's many thousands of expatriate workers in Iraq and Kuwait, one of the country's major sources of foreign funds has been swept away.

Principal Subsidiaries: General Petroleum Company; Petroleum Aerial Services Company (75%); Suez Oil Processing Company; Cairo Oil Refining Company; El Nasr Oil Company; Alexandria Oil Company (99.85%); Ameriyah Oil Refining Company; Asyut Oil Refining Company; Petroleum Cooperative Society (99.87%); Misr Petroleum Company; Petroleum Gas Company (95%); Pipeline Petroleum Company; Suez Mediterranean Pipeline Company (50%); Egyptian Petrochemicals Company; Abu Qir Fertilizer Company (20%); Engineering for the Petroleum and Process Industries (50%); Petroleum Projects Company (30%); Gulf of Suez Petroleum Company (50%); Western Desert Petroleum Company (50%); Suez Oil Company (50%); Deminex Egypt Oil Company (50%); Agyba Petroleum Company (50%); Badreddin Petroleum Company; Petrobel; Geisum Oil Company (50%); Khalda Petroleum Company; Alamein Petroleum Company (50%); Amal Petroleum Company (50%).

Further Reading: Arab Oil and Gas Directory, Arab Petroleum Research Centre, Paris, [annual].

—Alison Classe

EMPRESA COLOMBIANA DE PETRÓLEOS

Carrera 13 No. 36-24
Post Office Box 5938
Bogota DE
Colombia
(1) 856400

State-Owned Company
Incorporated: 1951
Employees: 12,500
Sales: US$950 million

Empresa Colombiana de Petróleos, the state oil company of Colombia, is wholly owned by its government and is usually referred to by the abbreviation Ecopetrol. It was founded in 1951 but has its origins in the 1910s. Ecopetrol is the principal oil producing, refining, and transporting company in Colombia. It has a monopoly on natural gas distribution and sales, and participates in the refined oil market in competition with other companies. Although it owes its existence to the nationalization of the country's long-standing major foreign-owned oil company and to continued government political support, it acts in partnership with foreign oil interests in Colombia through special agreements.

Ecopetrol was established on January 9, 1951 by the Colombian government in anticipation of the transference to state ownership of the country's largest oil concession, which was owned by the Tropical Oil Company. Ecopetrol was established as a fully integrated and independent state oil company. Ecopetrol's predecessor, Tropical, was incorporated in 1916 by Mike L. Benedum and J.C. Trees, who went into business together in the United States and abroad, acquiring oil properties in the exploratory or developmental stage for profitable resale. They purchased a concession in central Colombia, held by a French speculator, Roberto de Mares, and established Tropical to work it. Early developments on Tropical's concession date from the end of World War I. Equipment for the company's first wells was carried in large canoes up the shallow Magdelena River in 1917–1918. In 1920, these oil speculators sold the operation to the Standard Oil of New Jersey (Jersey Standard) subsidiaries, the International Petroleum Company (IPC). One of the first three wells drilled had produced oil in quantities which indicated that production could be commercially viable, and was sufficient to justify the investment by IPC. A share exchange was arranged whereby Tropical would become a subsidiary of IPC, although actual control of Tropical was exercised from New York rather than from IPC's head office in Canada.

A contemporary law set a limit of 30 years on the life of Tropical's concession when IPC acquired control, and ownership of the oil fields and installations was set to revert to the nation exactly 30 years later, on August 26, 1951. Tropical's central Colombian concession was geographically very large. The concession ran about 70 miles along the principal river of Colombia, the Magdelena. With an average width of 30 miles, it had a total size of about 2,100 acres. The title was transferred to IPC along with the sale of control, but under the conditions of a new petroleum law Tropical was subject to a number of requirements. In addition to observing the limit on the life of its concession, the company was required to build a refinery within two years, of sufficient capacity to provide for the Colombian market, and was subject to a royalty of 10% on gross oil production.

The Panamanian question delayed Tropical's development plans in the early 1920s. In 1920 the Andian National Corporation Ltd. (Andian National) sought permission from the government to build a crude oil pipeline to carry Tropical's oil from the De Mares concession to the Caribbean coast for export. Although registered as a separate organization, Andian National was an indirect affiliate of Tropical by virtue of a common parent company, IPC. The United States had supported the secession of Panama from Colombia in 1903. That action remained an open wound between the United States and Colombia for many years, with the latter seeking compensation for its lost territory. However, negotiations over Panama went slowly and Colombia sought advantage by pressuring U.S. business interests in the country. Approval for Tropical's pipeline plans were delayed. Captain Flanagan, head of Andian National and an agent for the president of Standard Oil of New Jersey, worked informally in Washington, D.C., on settling the outstanding issues in the negotiations. In the end, the Colombian government was paid a US$25 million indemnity in equal tranches over five years as compensation. With the treaty concluded in 1921, Tropical was able to assemble land titles and to award contracts for the construction of the pipeline between 1922 and 1925.

Tropical's building proceeded apace, with IPC's new capital support. Soon there were tractors moving earth and building an exploration camp. Hospitals were built in 1924 and preventive medicine was practiced to promote public health. Within one year the incidence of hookworm among workmen fell from 90% to 25%. Much of the improvement was attributed to the encouragement of the wearing of shoes. In addition to fighting tropical diseases the company had to fend off the rapid overgrowth of vegetation.

IPC's investment in Tropical led to a great amount of drilling to define and expand the known petroliferous region, despite limitations imposed by a restrictive petroleum law. Surveying, the building of infrastructure, and organizing for production occupied most of the 1921–1924 period, but some drilling did occur. Rotary and cable percussion tools were used in drilling wells from the 1920s, and Tropical's success rate was extremely high from the outset. In some years nearly every well was productive. Tropical's production was so large that by 1927 it was one of Jersey Standard's most prolific oil producing properties. With the development of its field and opening of the Andian National pipeline, Tropical's operations made Colombia in 1927 the third largest oil producing nation in Latin America after Mexico and Venezuela.

Tropical's production continued to increase until World War II. In the 1930s, the company's production and exports grew steadily, with the main destination North America. The company's activities accounted for the sale of all petroleum products in Colombia. Wartime conditions caused tanker shortages and led to the reorganization of hemispheric oil supply lines to minimize risk for water-borne traffic. Canadian, U.S., and northern South American governments agreed upon an oil-allocation program which included the elimination of Colombian oil exports and their replacement with Venezuelan exports to Canada and the United States. The effect was to minimize the total number of oil tankers at risk to enemy attack during the war.

Throughout World War II, Tropical operations were dedicated to providing for a growing Colombian domestic market, while Venezuelan crude and refined products took the place of Colombian exports. Colombian oil exports revived after the war, but most of Tropical's production went to the increasingly large domestic market.

Refining began in Colombia as a result of government requirements for the transfer of the title and continuance of Tropical's operations. The refinery, which IPC had promised to build when it acquired control of Tropical, was completed, as required, within two years and began operations in 1922. Its initial capacity was about 2,000 barrels per day (b/d), and that figure grew over the years, as did domestic market requirements. Capacity had increased to 23,800 b/d just before the reversion of control to Ecopetrol.

Tropical Oil Company's sales organization evolved from Jersey Standard's marketing operations in South America. Initial marketing of oil imports from Jersey Standard was carried out by its Latin American marketing arm, the West India Oil Company. West India Oil took its products from New York, conducted business in four languages and in a dozen currencies, and sold throughout the continent in countries in which Jersey Standard had no production activities. However, once the less expensive Colombian oil was available for sale through Tropical, West India Oil withdrew from the market place. From then on, Tropical's marketing dominated petroleum sales in Colombia. Tropical organized these activities through local commission sales agents, just as IPC had done in Peru and Chile.

Tropical was able to undercut the cost of traditional fuels, such as wood and coal, especially on the Magdelena River, through promotion of the use of fuel oil. It encouraged conversion from the use of steamers to fuel oil burning engines. The Tracey Brothers agents also sold Tropical's other products: kerosene for illumination and cooking, and gasoline, the sales of which grew with the increasing use of internal combustion engines.

Getting the oil to market, either domestically, or for export, was one of Tropical's principal problems at the outset. The natural impediments to commercial transportation were substantial, but not insurmountable. Mountains and thick tropical jungles made the Magdelena the only means of surface travel between the concession and the outside world. Even then, shifting sandbars were a hazard to large supply boats; only flat-bottomed steamers could be used. In 1926 Tropical

dredged the river; the sandbar was removed, permitting freer communication of heavier ocean-going vessels. Portage railways were built to connect the navigable parts of the river, and Tropical built narrow-gauge railways on the concession for more efficient transportation of drilling rigs. Meanwhile IPC organized Andian National to build the pipeline. Its completion validated development of the De Mares concession, as it permitted large-scale crude oil exports. Tankers received the oil delivered by pipeline and then transported it to world markets, but mainly to the Americas. Jersey Standard preferred to obtain most of its North American–bound oil imports from Peru and Colombia as opposed to Argentina. Not only were the two Andean nations closer and therefore had lower transportation costs, but also the operating costs of the two companies were individually lower. Andian National's throughput continued to increase in the late 1940s; it grew from 37,000 b/d in 1946, to 41,000 in 1948, to 58,000 b/d in 1950.

In the 1930s the pipeline was looped by laying parallel pipes to increase its carrying capacity. Andian National was able to escape reversion of its assets to the government along with Tropical's concession, because the pipeline company was not owned by Tropical, to whom it only provided a service. Andian National's president Flanagan represented his company as being completely separate from Tropical and made no reference to IPC's common ownership of the two companies. Furthermore, Andian National established its head office in Canada and Flanagan represented himself as a British citizen and president of a Canadian company to avoid anti-American antagonism.

Although Ecopetrol was created through takeover of foreign oil assets, it maintained friendly links with the private sector. The handover of the oil fields, pipeline, and refinery was the first peaceful transfer of oil assets to government in Latin America. In 1948, a few years before the intended reversion of Tropical's concession, the Colombian government offered Jersey Standard a minority residual stake in the property, but it refused. Instead it agreed to sell technical assistance to Ecopetrol, and the government oil company continued producing oil from the moment of takeover in 1951. Standard Oil's expertise was obtained through a service contract; it agreed to train Ecopetrol employees over a ten-year period. More assistance came in the early 1950s, in the form of a loan of US$10 million from Jersey Standard. With the new financing, Ecopetrol expanded the capacity of the old Tropical refinery to 78,200 b/d in 1960. Colombia, more than any other South American nation, retained close relations with Jersey Standard.

Since its inception, Ecopetrol has been adding to its refining capacity. After the expansion financed by Jersey Standard's loan, the capacity rose from about 78,000 b/d in 1960 to about 110,000 b/d in 1975. In that year, Ecopetrol acquired a 50,000 b/d refinery in Cartagena from Jersey Standard. Through that move, Ecopetrol acquired control of all but 10,000 b/d of Colombian refinery capacity. In 1990, the Colombian refining sector was still dominated by the two Ecopetrol plants. The Cartagena refinery's capacity had grown from 50,000 to 70,000 b/d while the Barrancabermeja plant had grown from 110,000 to 150,000 b/d.

With all the expansion in demand and in refining capacity, crude reserves were becoming depleted. From the late 1960s Ecopetrol became involved in a wide-ranging exploration program, concentrating on the Llanos region, to offset declining production. In the meantime, the company did its best to prolong and maximize production from the old oil fields along the Magdalena. It sought an extra 200 million barrels from the main La Circa-Infantas field by flooding the oil bearing structure with water. By the mid-1970s Ecopetrol was one of the four most active exploration companies in Colombia. Most of Ecopetrol's oil was still coming from its old fields, and at the rate of only about 20,000 b/d. Fortunately, oil was discovered in the Llanos field in the late 1970s and with rising output, production from this field alone was expected to reach 45,000 b/d once a pipeline was completed.

The pipeline to the Llanos basin field took about two years to complete, and was very expensive, since parts of the pipeline had to cross the Andean mountains at extremely high elevations, causing engineering problems. The Caño Limon field was part of a $1.8 billion deal sponsored by Ecopetrol in consortium with Occidental Petroleum and Shell of Colombia to develop the basin, build a pipeline, and export crude oil. In this and other projects Ecopetrol enjoyed remarkable success in exploration between 1978 and 1988, finding 24 commercial oil fields which increased its reserves from 600 million to 2 billion barrels or enough to supply the nation's domestic needs from 1988 to 1993.

Ecopetrol's drilling activity from 1988 to 1990 accounted for one in five of all exploratory wells, while in 1990 it planned to drill 30 of the 80 expected wells. The expansion of the oil industry in Colombia in the last few years has placed it third among Latin American oil producing countries, just after Mexico and Venezuela. In the 1940s and 1950s it had fallen to fourth and fifth place, and never really recovered its position until the late 1980s. Ecopetrol's 1988 production amounted to about 210,000 b/d, accounting for about half of the country's production, while the Cravo Norte field—which includes Caño Limon—is said to account for half of the nation's oil reserves.

Ecopetrol's efforts to promote foreign investment dated from the late 1960s. In 1966 the International Development Bank (IDB) lent US$5 million to Colombia for a polyethylene plant. The IDB took an equity interest of nearly 50%, with Dow Chemical and Ecopetrol taking up nearly 13% each.

As elsewhere, the concession system, whereby oil companies were granted exclusive rights to a property over an extended period of time, had come under criticism in Colombia in the 1960s, since it was felt that governments in general signed away too much control over oil development in this way. In consequence, Colombia established its association contract system in 1974 in place of granting any new concessions. Under the system, Ecopetrol permitted other oil companies to explore on certain lands at their own risk and expense until the exploration company and Ecopetrol both agreed that the oil field was commercially viable. Ecopetrol collected 20% royalties on production for subsequent redistribution to three levels of government: local, state, and federal. Thereafter, the private company and Ecopetrol shared production and expenses equally.

Oil nationalism revived in Colombia just as new oil reserves had been discovered and developed by foreign oil companies under previously more relaxed foreign investment rules. In 1979 Colombia's new president, Julio Cesar Turbay, replaced all existing oil concessions—those granted before 1974—with new agreements, in the form of the recently created association contracts with Ecopetrol. Royalties were to be reduced for inaccessible areas. The idea was to use the so-called Peruvian

Model contract, whereby the state oil company would be able to pay for up to half of its share of the development costs with crude oil. In the early 1980s these association contracts were altered to induce greater foreign investment. The year 1983 verged on being a record year with between 15 and 20 contracts signed with foreign companies.

As the beneficial effects of foreign oil investment took root, the political mood changed. In 1985 there was fear that Colombia's "open door" for petroleum investment might be shut. The nation's president, Belisario Betancourt, had established pro-foreign oil policies, but by 1985 his general policies, and with them his oil policies, had come under leftist attack. The energy minister applied extra taxes and restrictions upon the Colombian oil industry and this led to oil industry fears that management control of all pipelines might be transferred to Ecopetrol. Soon after, Occidental was forced to give up ownership of its Caño Limon–Pacific Coast pipeline to Ecopetrol.

Further inducements to foreign investors were developed in the late 1980s. As a variant on the association contracts, risk participation contracts were created, whereby Ecopetrol would contribute a proportion of the cost of the project at the exploration stage, thereby assuming some risk itself, with a partner taking the balance. The areas chosen generally had very great potential and such contracts awarded Ecopetrol a larger share of production if the field were eventually developed. However, this new variant of the association contract was far less successful, and Ecopetrol signed only a few such "risk participation contracts."

In the late 1970s, a time of high and rising oil prices, Ecopetrol was losing money. It had large debts in 1978, totalling US$342 million, and was expected to lose about US$265 million in 1978 owing to the high cost of importing crude oil and gasoline from the Colombian market. The company was short of oil and was spending increasing amounts to reduce its dependency on imports. It planned to spend US$37.5 million in 1979 and a total of US$86 million before 1982 on exploratory oil wells. The discovery of the Caño Limon oil field, and its development in partnership with Occidental Petroleum, made a great improvement; since 1985, exports of crude and fuel oil from Colombia have been making large contributions to a surplus in the country's balance of payments and Colombia is now the third largest oil exporting nation in Latin America. Exports at the end of 1987 were over 250,000 b/d and are projected to reach 430,000 b/d in 1993. In 1988 Ecopetrol had long-range plans to drill 345 exploratory wells by the year 2000, while private foreign companies were expected to drill double that amount.

Ecopetrol is an important tax gathering agent in the country, distributing revenue to the three levels of government in place of those levels of government establishing and collecting a tax. It is also a substantial investor in other industries. The state oil company collects oil royalties, calculated at the rate of 20% on production, and then distributes them for key government projects at local, regional, and national levels. Ecopetrol's non-oil investments include a 14% stake in a chemical complex and a 49% share in the large government-owned coal mining agency Carbocol. Prominent amongst Ecopetrol's other investments is the company Promigas, established in 1985, which distributes and sells about 250 million cubic feet per day of natural gas along the country's north coast.

Nearly all pipelines in Colombia are owned and operated by Ecopetrol; the remainder are jointly owned and operated with other international oil companies. Since the late 1980s the government has been extending the gas distribution network and Bogota will be connected in about 1995. Gas is to come from the eastern plains, but some additional fields will supply Bogota. The company's Promigas subsidiary is building a 435-mile pipeline from the north coast to Bogota. This offshore field holds most of Colombia's gas reserves and is operated jointly by Texaco and Ecopetrol.

The nation, under Ecopetrol, has big and promising plans for the future. It remains to be seen whether Ecopetrol will be allowed to continue to work with the private sector on developing the nation's energy in a successful partnership.

Principal Subsidiaries: Colombian Petroleum Company; South American Gulf Oil Company; Petrofinas Colombianas (89%); Terpel Manizales (70.7%); Terpel Antioquia (59.3%); Carbocol (48.87%); Terpel Bucaramanga (40%); Carboriente (37%); Fertilizantes Colombianos (26%); Petroquimica del Atlantico (23.9%); Colgas (21.3%); Promigas (20.3%); Monomeros Colombo Venezolanos (13.8%).

Further Reading: Gibb, George Sweet, and Evelyn H. Knowlton, *History of Standard Oil Company (New Jersey), The Resurgent Years 1911–1927,* New York, Harper & Brothers, 1956; Randall, Stephen J., *The Diplomacy of Modernization: Colombian-American Relations 1920–1940,* Toronto, University of Toronto Press, 1977; Philip, George, *Oil and Politics in Latin America: Nationalist Movements and State Oil Companies,* Cambridge, Cambridge University Press, 1982; Klein, Harvey F., "Colombian Debates about Coal, Exxon and Themselves," *Inter-American Economic Affairs,* Spring 1984; "Republic of Colombia" in *International Petroleum Encyclopaedia,* edited by John C. McCaslin, Tulsa, Oklahoma, Penn-Well Publishing Company, 1984; Wirth, Jonathan D., ed., *Latin American Oil Companies and the Politics of Energy,* London, University of Nebraska Press, 1985; *New Opportunities for Exploration,* Bogota, Ecopetrol, 1987; "Republic of Colombia," *Colombia Today,* Vol. 23, No. 3, 1988.

—David Myers

ENTE NAZIONALE IDROCARBURI

Piazzale E. Mattei, 1
00144 Rome
Italy
(06) 59001
Fax: (06) 5900-2141

State-Owned Company
Incorporated: 1953
Employees: 135,000
Sales: L48.00 trillion (US$42.59 billion)

Ente Nazionale Idrocarburi (ENI) is Italy's state energy holding corporation. It controls 300 companies active in seven main sectors: exploration, production, and distribution of hydrocarbons and other fuels; chemicals; machinery manufacturing; engineering and services; metallurgy; finance; and miscellaneous activities that include travel services, publishing, industrial reconversion—the conversion of an existing plant to produce a different product, or to produce the same product using different technology—and software production.

ENI has its origins in the 1920s when the Italian government formed Azienda Generale Italiana Petroli (Agip) to pursue exploration for petroleum and natural gas in Italy. In the restructuring of Italian industry that followed World War II, Agip and related state-owned energy companies were grouped together to form ENI. Today Agip remains the principal oil company in the ENI group.

State participation in Italian industry dates from the stock market crash of 1929. In 1933, when many of the country's important banks were threatened by the collapse of industries in which they were heavily invested, the government established the Istituto per la Ricostruzione Industriale (IRI), a public agency that reorganized the banking system and acquired the banks' extensive industrial shareholdings in the process. In the petroleum industry, state participations also took the form of investment and joint ventures with foreign or private companies intended to boost Italy's refining capacity and exploration of new indigenous energy sources.

In addition to creating Agip, the state joined with private industries to establish other energy-related companies that would eventually become part of ENI. The Azienda Nazionale Idrogenazione Combustibili (ANIC) was formed to operate in the refinery sector in 1936, as was Industria Raffinazione Oli Minerali (IROM), a joint venture with the Anglo-Iranian Oil Company. A later joint venture with Standard Oil of New Jersey resulted in the formation of STANIC, when Italy could not afford to update ANIC's three large refineries after the war. In 1941, government investment created Società Nazionale Metanodotti (Snam) to build and run methane pipelines, and Società Azionaria Imprese Perforazioni (Saip), a state-owned consortium of drilling companies.

The creation of ENI, a single holding company that integrated all of Italy's activities in the hydrocarbons sector, was largely the work of its first president, Enrico Mattei. An able manager and entrepreneur with a nationalist, collectivist, and egalitarian ideology, Mattei campaigned to have the company established, and directed the course of ENI's growth and activities in its first decade. His aggressive promotion of Italy's self-reliance in energy won him wide popularity; it also set ENI on a collision course with large foreign and private oil companies.

Mattei, a former partisan commander with some experience as an industrial manager in the private sector, was appointed commissioner of Agip for upper Italy in 1945. The years immediately following the Allied liberation were a pivotal period for the nascent petroleum industry in Italy. Discovery of Middle East petroleum deposits during the war and the arrival of powerful international oil companies held major implications for a successful postwar recovery in Italy. The peninsula's strategic location in the Mediterranean made it a logical point for low-cost refining and shipment of petroleum products to the West European market.

Agip, like most of Italian industry, had been devastated during the war. Refineries and pipelines lay in ruins and Agip's tanker fleet was virtually eliminated. The apparent lack of indigenous energy resources and a desire to accommodate foreign and private investment in the petroleum industry led the postwar government in Rome to order the liquidation of Agip's bankrupt mining and prospecting activities.

However, Mattei delayed the liquidation, alerted by reports of considerable methane deposits in the Po Valley located during the war and by the haste of the foreign companies to buy Agip's outdated and apparently worthless prospecting operations. Instead of proceeding with the sell-off, Mattei disobeyed his instructions and ordered that exploration in the Po Valley be continued.

In 1946, Agip's team at the Caviaga gas field made a successful methane strike. Two years later, the state company was reorganized with Professor Marcello Boldrini as its president and Enrico Mattei as vice president. In 1949, Agip acquired full control of the state-owned pipeline company Snam which enabled Mattei to begin to establish a network of methane pipelines to communities and industry in northern Italy.

In the absence of laws tying exploitation rights to successful exploration, the widely publicized Po Valley methane and oil strikes triggered three years of parliamentary debate, legislative proposals, and intensive lobbying by international and private oil companies, all revolving around the issue of state control versus free competition in hydrocarbons exploration.

On February 10, 1953, two years after its introduction in the Italian parliament, a bill was approved that established ENI as the national hydrocarbons company. All corporations through which the state was operating in the hydrocarbons sector at that time were grouped to form a single entity, through a complex system of outright acquisitions and government investments.

A clause in the bill guaranteed ENI exclusive rights to exploration in the Po Valley, while allowing private companies to compete in other areas of Italy. Four years later, Mattei helped pass a second law that extended ENI's exclusive rights to all of mainland Italy.

The new company was constituted with L15 billion in capital and another L15 billion consisting of the nominal value of the assets of its constituent companies. ENI was authorized to trade in shares, and to carry on its activities through subsidiaries, associated companies, and investments in other companies and joint ventures. Mattei was appointed president, with Marcello Boldrini as vice president.

Mattei's first task was to integrate ENI's constituent companies into a single enterprise, by grouping ENI's shareholdings into manageable units along functional lines and liquidating or converting any irrelevant assets. A series of mergers and diversifications during ENI's first ten years resulted in the group's present structure. Mattei and his successors followed a policy of vertical integration, so as to render ENI invulnerable in its supplies of raw and semifinished materials, as well as in services and transportation.

At first, ENI focused on production and distribution of natural gas, the only considerable source of energy available in mainland Italy. A subsidiary called Agip Mineraria was formed by the merger of Agip and the Ente Nazionale Metano. The new company in turn controlled the Saip consortium of drilling companies and la Società Ravennate Metano, a methane gas producer.

The pipeline company Snam was reconstituted to include the natural gas network of Azienda Metanodotti Padani in the Po Valley, and promptly set about expanding its system of trunk provincial and interprovincial gas lines. Snam operated as the sector head of ENI's engineering activities, which later included international construction of refineries, pipelines, and chemical plants. In the refining and petrochemicals sector, ENI companies or subsidiaries were headed by ANIC.

ENI entered the machinery manufacturing sector in 1954, when it acquired the failing Pignone industrial equipment company in Florence. Reconstituted as Nuovo Pignone, the new company provided pipeline pumps, motor compressors, valves, and other equipment for new refineries and petrochemical plants. Later it built floating platforms for offshore oil exploration.

Fresh capital from the rapidly expanding natural gas production and distribution helped launch ENI's program of international expansion. In negotiating oil concessions with producer states, Mattei introduced an innovative formula for joint investment that deliberately sought to eliminate the middleman role previously played by the major oil companies. Instead of simply paying a fixed fee for oil concessions and then assuming all of the burden of development, as the majors did, Mattei offered producer states a partnership in the exploitation of their natural resources.

Initially, ENI assumed all of the risk in exploration, as did the big multinational oil companies. However, if the search revealed commercially viable deposits of hydrocarbons, the host country earned 50% of all profits, and in addition could choose to join in the production, by sharing half of all the development costs. Since the host country gained 50% of net profits, above the 50% already received as taxes and royalties, ENI's program came to be called "the 75/25 plan."

Following a more conventional joint venture with the Egyptian government in 1955, the ENI plan was subsequently applied in Iran in 1957, and in Morocco in 1958. In 1959, ENI formed similar partnerships with the governments of Libya and Sudan, and with Tunisia and Nigeria in 1961 and 1962.

The joint ventures had the effect of establishing the terms for subsequent concessions that producer states made to other foreign oil companies. By introducing his system of partnerships with producer states, Mattei effectively stimulated creation of state oil enterprises abroad, thus disrupting the institutional profile of the international oil industry. In negotiations and public statements, he asserted Italy's acceptability as a country less tainted by colonialism, and openly sought a reduction in the power, profits, and autonomy of the so-called Seven Sisters—the handful of Western oil companies that had until then dominated the international market.

Mattei successfully applied the same strategy when Agip sought concessions to build refineries and distribute its refined products in the developing countries. ENI formed joint ventures in refining with Morocco in 1958, and in Ghana and Tunisia in 1960. In the 1960s ENI companies undertook refinery construction projects in the Congo, south Asia, and Latin America.

Meanwhile, the reorganization of ENI that created Agip Mineraria and Snam at the same time divested Agip of its exploration and pipeline companies, leaving it to operate as head of ENI's activities in distribution and marketing of gasoline, lubricants, and other petroleum products both at home in Italy and abroad.

ENI contributed to Italy's swift recovery after the war as a part of the Sviluppo Iniziative Stradali Italiane (SISI) industrial consortium. SISI, which included Fiat automobile manufacturers, Pirelli rubber products, Agip, and the road building group Italcementi, virtually created an automobile culture in a newly urbanized Italy. Affordable cars, a new network of superhighways, and Agip's gasoline and oil products combined to set Italy's postwar economic "miracle" in motion.

To help build the automotive market, Mattei promoted Agip's products and image by providing new, brightly colored service stations throughout Italy and offered amenities previously unknown at service stations such as coffee shops, restaurants, and motels. By 1962, ENI's roadside outlets in Italy included some 30 Agip motels and over 400 Agip restaurants or coffee shops. During this period Agip introduced its Supercortemaggiore high-octane gasoline and the symbol of the six-legged dog, which later came to stand for the ENI group as a whole, as well as all Agip products.

Between 1956 and 1960 Agip formed companies for foreign distribution of gasoline and lubricants throughout most of Africa, in Greece, Austria, Switzerland, West Germany, Argentina, and—through a joint venture—with the Anglo-Italian financier Charles Forte in the United Kingdom.

In the same period, Mattei effected a series of mergers designed to rationalize the group's various activities. ENI's subsidiary Snam came to head two sub-holdings: Snam Montaggi, created in 1955 to build pipelines and drilling platforms, and Snam Progetti in 1956, specializing in tankers. In 1957, Agip Mineraria's Saip subsidiary was merged with Snam Montaggi to create Saipem. The new industrial groups allowed ENI to increase its gas and petroleum transportation activities at an accelerated rate. Saipem was a pioneer in offshore drilling for hydrocarbons in Europe, and in the 1960s allowed Mattei to initiate a central European pipeline project running from the port of Genoa north to Pavia before forking off to Switzerland and to West Germany where ENI's Südpetrol subsidiary was building refineries at Ingolstadt and Stüttgart. This gave Mattei an important advantage in his dealings with the majors, in particular Esso and Gulf, ENI's chief competitors in the market.

ENI activities in the petrochemicals field started to expand in 1954 following the discovery of considerable natural gas deposits near Ravenna. ANIC built three petrochemical plants there in 1957 to produce Buna-S, a synthetic rubber; fertilizers; and later, acetates and polyvinyl chlorides. In 1959 a joint venture with the U.S. chemicals firm Phillips Carbon Black expanded the Ravenna operations to include production of carbon black.

In 1956, the Italian parliament established a Ministry of State Participation in Industry, to integrate the activities of state-controlled companies with economic and development policies. New legislation was passed requiring state-controlled companies to direct 40% of all new investment to Italy's poorer southern regions. Following discovery of deposits of petroleum and natural gas at Gela, Sicily, in 1956 ENI initiated construction of a giant refinery and tanker terminal on the Sicilian coast and created a regional petrochemicals subsidiary, ANIC Gela. The Nuovo Pignone manufacturing company carried out an expansion in southern Italy with construction of Pignone Sud in 1960.

Mattei also effected several major horizontal expansions for ENI, beginning with the establishment of Agip Nucleare in 1956. Two years later the Nuovo Pignone company began producing components for a large nuclear generator to be built at Latina, south of Rome. In 1963, however, Mattei's ambition of building a complete single energy group comprising electric generating and hydrocarbons was defeated by the creation of Ente Nazionale Elettricità (ENEL). The separate state-run utility absorbed ENI's nuclear program, leaving uranium prospecting and nuclear fuel activities to Agip Nucleare.

Also in 1956, ENI established a financial company, the Società Finanziaria Idrocarburi (Sofid) to organize financing for ENI's bigger projects, and handle all of the group's financial activities and investments. Other enterprises included a center for research in hydrocarbons and petrochemicals and a school for postgraduate studies in hydrocarbons at the group's Milan headquarters. In 1959, ENI began publication of *Il Giorno,* a Milan-area daily paper.

ENI's expansions outside its original mandate continued in the 1960s. A joint venture with the U.S. firm Libbey-Owens Sheet Glass established Società Italiana Vetro in 1962. At the same time, Sofid and ANIC bought a controlling interest in one of Italy's oldest and largest woolen textiles companies, Lane Rossi. The move strengthened ENI's position in the burgeoning synthetic textiles sector, looming acrylic and polyester fibers produced by already existing ANIC plants.

In 1962, as ENI neared its tenth anniversary, Enrico Mattei died when his executive jet crashed en route from Sicily to Milan. Reports of a plot against ENI's entrepreneur-hero went unproven but provided the basis for several books and a 1970 feature movie, *Il Caso Mattei.* Mattei was succeeded by his 72-year-old vice president Boldrini.

The loss hastened a reorganization of management structure began by ENI in the late 1950s. For several years, managerial responsibilities had been concentrated in the person of Mattei who acted as chief executive of most of the group's sector head companies, including Agip Mineraria, Agip Nucleare, Snam, Saipem, ANIC, STANIC, Sofid, and the first joint venture in Egypt. By contrast, the group's new executive structure greatly extended the autonomy of mid-level managers.

ENI had grown spectacularly. In 1961 the group boasted total assets of L955 billion, and operated as one of the top international companies in hydrocarbons. Expansion continued in the following decade as projects that originated under Mattei came into fruition: a 1958 agreement for importation of Soviet crude oil to ENI refineries; the Latina nuclear power plant and plants for manufacturing of processed uranium for nuclear generators; the completion of the central European pipeline connection with northern Italy; new textile manufacturing. Most important of all was a long-term reciprocal agreement with Esso that entailed provision of crude petroleum to Agip refineries and purchase of equipment from Nuovo Pignone.

Until the Esso agreement, importation of Soviet crude had been essential to ENI's development: in 1962 Italy was the Soviet Union's largest single market for crude oil, and the imports allowed Agip to offer the lowest gasoline prices in Europe. Meanwhile, trade pacts with the Soviets provided markets for industrial expansion undertaken by ENI in Italy's underdeveloped south.

However, while the 1960s were a period of growth for ENI, the decade also brought changes in the oil industry and in the world economy that had a negative effect. Throughout the decade ENI subsidiaries won important contracts to build pipelines and refineries and explore for hydrocarbons in south Asia, South America, and Australia. At the same time, regional conflicts and a phase of sharper nationalism in the independence movements in Africa and the Middle East frequently brought Agip's operations to a halt or else forced renegotiation of its previous agreements with producer states. In 1967, the Arab-Israeli Six Day War interrupted Agip's joint venture with Egypt. In 1969 the Biafran secession disrupted Agip refining activities in Nigeria.

Growth in the 1960s brought changes at home as well. Italy's two leading private-sector chemical companies, Montecatini and Edison, merged in 1965, creating a single giant called Montedison. Two years later, to offset the competition from Montedison, the Italian parliament approved modifications in ENI's institutional law, providing the state company financing and freedom to develop its nuclear and chemical activities more aggressively.

After Boldrini's death in 1967, ENI vice president Eugenio Cefis was appointed president. A junior colleague of Mattei who had served under him in the Resistance, Cefis shared Mattei's unwavering commitment to ENI and to the mixed economy in Italy.

The formation of OPEC and the issuing of its Declaration of Member Countries' Petroleum Policy in 1968 marked the emergence of oil producing states as a decisive force in the world economy. It was followed by increases in the price of crude petroleum and by the nationalization of the Libyan and Somalian oil industries in 1970 and those of Iraq and Saudi Arabia in 1974. In 1973, following the Yom Kippur War, crude prices tripled. Italy's economic situation, already experiencing a slowdown, grew worse.

ENI's expansion in the chemicals sector was accompanied by new efforts to control industrial waste and damage to the environment. At ANIC's Sannazzaro refinery, a waste-water treatment facility was installed for the first time in 1970, and in 1971 ENI formed Tecneco, a company devoted to environmental research and protection. In the same year, Eugenio Cefis was replaced as president by Raffaele Girotti.

Development of new petrochemicals plants and acquisitions in the chemical sector led to difficulties at ENI. Conflict with Montedison increased, aggravated by sector-wide economic trouble, and in 1972 the government mediated an accord between the two companies that favored ENI with the larger share of a L4 trillion program of investments.

In 1975 Girotti was succeeded by Pietro Sette who presided over the beginning of a period of crisis at ENI. Government efforts to rescue other ailing industries by having ENI acquire the worst performers added huge burdens to the group, already pressed by increases in the price of crude oil.

In 1977, ENI acquired 33 metallurgic companies from the troubled EGAM group, which were reconstituted to create a new ENI division called Samim. The following year, ANIC reported losses of L247 billion, largely in its petrochemical activities. Giorgio Mazzanti, a former vice president at ENI, replaced Sette as president and ENI started trying to turn itself around.

Mazzanti was replaced after one year by Alberto Grandi. ENI established a new textile machinery division called Savio, separate from Nuovo Pignone, and began to see a slight narrowing of its losses. But the losses continued into the 1980s, as ENI again had to rescue failing chemical companies in the private sector. These were reconstituted separately from ANIC as a new subholding called EniChem. At the same time a *comissario straordinario,* or special commissioner, Dr. Enrico Gandolfi, was appointed to replace ENI's president, when Grandi resigned before his term as president had expired.

In 1982, ENI named a new president, Franco Reviglio, and a new board of directors who would oversee the group's program of recovery. ENI's sector head ANIC was reconstituted as EniChimica, following further acquisitions in the troubled Italian chemicals industry. The overhaul of ENI's fragile new empire of chemicals companies moved forward in 1984 with the absorption of EniChimica by EniChem and in 1986 the state-controlled chemicals industries showed a profit for the first time in ten years.

During the same period in the private sector, Italian financier Raul Gardini had assumed control of the company Montedison, a debt-ridden giant with wide holdings in chemical derivatives, pharmaceuticals, and services. Almost immediately plans were laid for a merger of EniChem with Montedison, to create an international presence for Italy among the top ten chemicals companies in the world. The new company, Enimont, was formed early in 1989, with 40% owned by ENI, 40% by Montedison and the remaining 20% to be traded publicly.

Gabriele Cagliari replaced Franco Reviglio in 1989, to preside over ENI's experiment in a large-scale partnership with the private sector. But the joint venture was short-lived, marred by conflict between its two partners, and was finally threatened by an attempted takeover by Gardini. Late in 1990 Gardini sold Montedison's 40% share to ENI, and the chemicals conglomerate was renamed EniChem in 1991 after two unproductive years.

The greatest challenge to ENI in the early 1990s stems from its status as a state corporation. While ENI has been the traditional preserve of the Socialist minority in Italy's coalition government, political conflicts with the Christian Democrats emerged during the Enimont joint venture and its resolution. These conflicts will undoubtedly have an impact on the course of ENI policy in the future. It is possible that party politics will eventually force a reorganization of EniChem as an independent chemicals entity, with close ties to ENI but no longer a subsidiary.

ENI achieved a sound financial position as it entered its fifth decade. Sales continued to increase in most sectors at the end of 1990, with higher oil prices pushing up profits in the energy sector. With the addition of former Enimont activities in base and secondary chemicals, derivatives, and pharmaceuticals, ENI will complete its transition from a petroleum company to a global energy business, with materials, engineering, and financial resources capable of resolving energy and environmental problems anywhere in the world.

Since ENI subsidiaries are active in the private sector, the unification of the European market in 1992 offers possibilities for further internationalization and joint ventures. At the same time, development in former Soviet bloc countries will require creation of new energy infrastructures that could bring a needed upturn in the group's engineering sector. ENI companies such as Saipem and Snam Progetti will benefit from the rebuilding of war-damaged oil fields and terminals in both Kuwait and Iraq.

Thanks to the broad mandate for which it was originally conceived and created, ENI is a broadly diversified and flexible organization. More than once, its considerable resources have allowed it to overcome considerable transformations of the fields in which it operates, both at home and abroad. In spite of the uncertainties facing the energy business as a whole, it is likely ENI will remain competitive and continue to play an important role in the evolution of the international hydrocarbons and chemical industries.

Principal Subsidiaries: Agip SpA; AgipPetroli SpA; AgipCoal SpA; Snam SpA; Eniricerche; Nuovo Pignone SpA; SnamProgetti SpA; Saipem SpA; Nuova Samim SpA; Savio SpA; Terfin; Sofid SpA; ENI International Holding SpA; EniChem.

Further Reading: Dechert, Charles R., *Ente Nazionale Idrocarburi: Study of a State Corporation,* Leiden, E.J. Brill, 1963; Faleschini, L., Kojanec, G., "Extract from 4th Volume of *Enciclopedia di Petroleo e Gas Naturale,*" Rome, ENI, 1964; Frankel, Paul H., *Petroleum & Power: Enrico Mattei,* Los Angeles, [n.p.] 1970.

—Paul Conrad

ENTREPRISE NATIONALE SONATRACH

10, rue du Sahara
Hydra
Algiers 16.035
Algeria
60 70 00
Fax: 60 70 37

State-Owned Company
Incorporated: 1963 as Société Nationale de Transport et de
Commercialisation des Hydrocarbures
Employees: 31,678
Sales: DA132.90 billion (US$10.91 billion)

Entreprise Nationale Sonatrach (Sonatrach) is the Algerian state-owned oil and gas company. It has control—both direct and indirect—over all aspects of the country's hydrocarbons, and has guided Algeria toward its present status as one of the world's major suppliers of liquefied natural gas. The importance of the company to the Algerian economy can be seen in the fact that it accounts for over 90% of all Algerian export income, and is thus by far the most important element in the national economy.

The original governmental decree of December 31, 1963, which created the Algerian state oil company gave it the title Société Nationale de Transport et de Commercialisation des Hydrocarbures. This was the origin of the acronym Sonatrach. The role of transportation and marketing was given to the company at the date of its creation, and was extended on September 22, 1966, making the title of the company still longer in an attempt to summarize all its activities: Société Nationale pour la Recherche, la Production, le Transport, la Transformation et la Commercialisation des Hydrocarbures. In other words, it was a state-owned company with responsibility for all oil activity in Algeria. This responsibility grew during the 1960s and 1970s, with the nationalization of many of the country's foreign-held oil assets, though the adoption in July 1981 of a rather less cumbersome title—Entreprise Nationale Sonatrach—coincided with a reduction in the company's direct control over these assets. Sonatrach continues to be responsible for the central features of the Algerian oil and gas industry, but it has effectively spun off certain of its operational areas to a number of subsidiaries, though Sonatrach retains overall coordination for their activities.

The three decades of Sonatrach's existence divide neatly into three stages of development. The 1960s saw the establishment of the company, with the nationalization of foreign interests and the acquisition of much of the necessary infrastructure, such as pipelines. The 1970s was a decade of consolidation, with Sonatrach embarking on several joint ventures with foreign partners in an effort to increase its exports of liquefied natural gas (LNG). The 1980s saw the company entering into full bloom, reaping the rewards of its previous labors and becoming one of the world's major suppliers of LNG.

When the original Sonatrach was established in 1963 by the government of the newly independent Algeria, its role was essentially limited to building a third export pipeline from Hassi Messaoud to the Arzew oil terminal on the Mediterranean. However, the gaining of political independence had thrown up the question of how far the economic ties with France should be maintained, and Sonatrach came to play a central role in the course of these discussions. The result of the protracted negotiations was the Franco-Algerian Oil Agreement of 1965, the two main provisions of which provided for the Algerian state to take effective part in the exploration and exploitation of the country's hydrocarbons, while also raising the income tax on oil from 50% to 55%, thus effectively gaining for Algeria a substantial increase in revenues from its oil and gas operations. In recognition of the part played by Sonatrach's representatives in these negotiations, the company's role was extended by a new decree in September 1966 to cover all aspects of the Algerian oil industry.

Over the next two years Sonatrach turned its attention toward those U.S.–owned companies that had petroleum interests in Algeria. In August 1967 the company took over the Algerian assets of the Esso and Mobil companies and in October 1968 it acquired a 51% participation interest in the Getty Oil Company. Sandwiched between these two events was the nationalization in May 1968 of all foreign interests in the Algerian distribution sector, thus establishing a monopoly for Sonatrach in this field.

One of the effects of these decisions was that Sonatrach's share in the Algiers refinery, in which Esso and Mobil had originally held 40%, Compagnie Française des Pétroles (CFP) 32%, and Shell 24%, rose from 4% in early 1967 to 56% in 1968. The Esso and Mobil interests were taken over in 1967 and the others bought out by 1969. In addition to establishing an infrastructure by nationalizing existing foreign-held assets, Sonatrach also acquired majority stakes in three major oil and gas pipelines between 1963 and 1965. While Algeria's oil fields became the exclusive preserve of Sonatrach, the company also acquired majority participation interests in foreign companies engaged in businesses allied to its central activities, for example, drilling, construction, geophysics, and pipelaying.

However, relations with France worsened steadily in the second half of the decade, though France was still buying over half of all Algerian oil output. The tension came to a head in 1971 when, on February 24, the government completely nationalized all natural gas fields and allied installations and took over all rights to the associated gas—natural gas that overlies and contacts crude oil in a reservoir—from producing oil wells. It brought under state control 51% of all the activities of French petroleum companies, namely 51% of the shares, rights, and interests in Algerian oil concessions belonging to these companies. At the same time, it brought its stakes in other foreign companies up to 51%. All pipelines which did not already belong to Sonatrach were also nationalized. The French retaliated by banning all imports from Algeria, although this action did not have the expected effect on the Algerian economy, since rising world energy demand had sufficiently opened markets elsewhere.

The main problem that remained, however, was exploration. Since foreign companies were understandably reluctant to invest in exploration when they might not be allowed to reap the rewards, they stayed away, and Sonatrach had not yet built up a stock of technical expertise in its indigenous work force to do the work itself. The impasse was settled when Sonatrach decided that since the concession agreements had now lapsed a new set of rules would have to be introduced, which would once more encourage foreign companies to put their money and their expertise back into Algerian exploration.

The result was the Fundamental Law on Hydrocarbons, which was promulgated by the Algerian government on April 12, 1971. This law had two main purposes. The first was that it formally abolished the system of concessions, and established that all mining titles, as well as the control of all petroleum reserves that might be discovered in the future in any part of Algeria, were transferred to Sonatrach. The second was that it made provision for foreign companies to enter into service contracts or joint ventures with Sonatrach, provided that 51% of the assets were held by the state company.

The area in which joint ventures were to be particularly encouraged was exploration, and many foreign companies soon entered into such agreements, notably CFP and Elf Aquitaine of France, Amoco and Sun Oil of the United States, Hispanoil of Spain, Petrobras of Brazil, and Deminex of West Germany.

In addition to the requirement that 51% of the share capital be held by Sonatrach, the other conditions under which the joint ventures were signed were fairly straightforward. All gas found was to belong to Sonatrach. If oil was found, 15% of the foreign company's exploration costs would be refunded, and Sonatrach would become responsible for 51% of future development costs. Foreign partners would be entitled to 49% of the crude output after paying taxes, royalties, and other duties, though their term of exploration was limited to 12 years.

In the 1970s, having established its dominant role in the Algerian oil and gas sector, and having come to terms which were acceptable to its joint venture partners, Sonatrach formulated a guiding policy for its development. It saw its future prosperity lying in the exploitation of its natural gas, and thus set itself the task of developing these resources: this would involve subduing foreign demand for crude oil and persuading its clients to purchase its gas instead, while also requiring a great deal of exploration work to be done in the country. Such thinking was based on the fact that Algeria has the fifth-largest gas reserves in the world, compared to relatively small and shrinking reserves of oil.

The achievement of the second of these aims, increased exploration activity, has continued to elude Sonatrach. For example, of the 447,600 meters drilled in 1977, only 25% was for exploration; the main reason for this was the continuing diversion of resources to the development of the two major Saharan drilling fields, the Hassi Messaoud oil and Hassi R'Mel gas fields.

On the other hand, Sonatrach was managing to agree terms with foreign buyers for its natural gas, and by 1977 several major supply contracts were already in place. The single most important of these was the contract signed in October 1977 with Ente Nazionale Idracarburi (ENI) of Italy, which provided for the export to Italy of some 12 billion cubic meters per year (cm/year) of gas over 25 years through the Trans-Mediterranean pipeline. The cost of the project was estimated at US$2.5 billion, and deliveries through the pipeline—which was to run some 1,770 miles from Hassi R'Mel to Bologna in northern Italy—were expected to commence some four years from the signing of the contract.

Another consideration borne in mind by Sonatrach was that Algerian oil reserves, though scarce, were cheaper and easier to export than gas, and so the Algerian government began a policy in the 1970s of using gas wherever possible in its industrial infrastructure, involving the conversion of factories and hospitals to the use of gas. Two other policies initiated by the government—to bring electricity to every home by the year 2000, and to construct a substantial gas grid to supply these homes with gas—have also fitted in well with Sonatrach's own aims, since the power stations which supply the Rural Electrification Project are gas-fired. By 1986 it was reported that 83% of Algerian homes had electricity, and 35% gas.

Sonatrach's declared exploration and production policy was not successful in practice. Sonatrach consolidated its position in refining. By 1980 it controlled the Algiers refinery, and during the 1980s it developed facilities at Hassi Messaoud, Arzew, and Skikda, making full use of foreign technical expertise, mainly Italian and Japanese. By developing refining capacity Sonatrach was able to reduce the amount of crude exported and to increase the value of the country's trade. By 1984–1985, export revenues from oil and gas provided Algeria with US$13 billion and accounted for 95% of total export earnings.

After 1985, when the shape of the oil and gas markets worldwide altered dramatically, Algeria revised its energy policy in favor of reducing dependence on oil reserves—which, as we have seen, are diminishing—and focusing instead on its natural gas reserves, reckoned to be two-thirds of Algeria's total energy resources.

Until the mid-1980s Algeria found itself in difficulties with respect to its pricing policies, insisting on maintaining contract prices which were way in excess of current market prices, especially Soviet and Dutch prices. Until late 1987 the government insisted that LNG prices be related to crude oil prices—not products as in most other cases. This worked reasonably well until the price of crude collapsed in early 1986, after which Algeria found itself in dispute with a number of its contract customers. At the same time it saw its revenues falling.

One of the consequences of this was a restructuring of the law governing energy policies at the end of 1986, considerably liberalizing the terms under which foreign companies could participate in exploration projects. The old laws dictated that foreign companies could form joint ventures, but, as we have seen, Sonatrach held the majority stake and furthermore held title to the oil or gas. The foreign companies had "operator only" status. If gas was found it was treated as the result of an unsuccessful search for oil, and Sonatrach took 100% of the field. One of the consequences of this was that companies of the standing of Texaco and Amoco ceased exploration activities in Algeria.

This kind of intransigence was reflected in the way in which Sonatrach negotiated its major contracts. Despite the need for supplies of LPG (liquefied petroleum gas) and LNG by a variety of countries, including Italy, Yugoslavia, and the United States, contracts repeatedly hit problems in the late 1980s as Algeria attempted to maintain its upper hand in a falling market.

This led to what was seen as a fundamental reversal in Algerian export policy. By the end of 1987, a number of changes were becoming apparent. The most interesting was reflected in a contract finally signed with the U.S.-registered Trunkline LNG Company, a subsidiary of Panhandle Eastern Corporation, in which Sonatrach holds a 12% stake, which is understood to have incorporated the most flexible terms seen out of Algeria. In effect there was no contract price: rather, prices were to be determined on the basis of conditions in the end-use markets with the proceeds being split on a predetermined basis between Sonatrach and Trunkline. To a large extent, this deal can be seen as evidence of Sonatrach's deep concern over its position in the international gas market, its substantial surplus in LNG capacity, and its desire to develop new markets to utilize this spare capacity more fully.

By 1988 there was a widespread belief that Algeria had decided to accept commercial reality after years of sticking to a high price strategy, which had resulted in the loss of markets. Early that year it became apparent that the country was going to be marketing LNG on a worldwide basis and with some intensity. One consequence of this has been the opening of branches in the United States and London, as well as the development of the Tokyo office.

Until the summer of 1988 more than half its LNG capacity of 30.8 billion cubic meters a year was idle as a result of difficulties with export contracts. Since then Sonatrach has dropped its insistence on treating existing customers less favorably than new ones, a practice that caused a long dispute with Boston-based Distrigas, and revived exports to the United States at competitive prices. Sonatrach also re-opened the world's first commercial LNG trade, between Algeria and the United Kingdom, with spot cargoes—cargoes sold at the going rate, not a forward price. It developed a new and potentially exciting relationship with Japan and redefined its relationship with its largest customer, Gaz de France.

The government appointed a new head of Sonatrach, Sadek Boussena, in summer 1988—appointed minister of energy as well in November 1988—and his influence has been felt in the new methods noted in negotiations. Part of this change of policy has—as always in Arab nations—a political basis. With LNG grossly overpriced, a number of customers—including U.S. utilities and Gaz de France itself—simply paid some US83¢ per million British thermal units less than they were invoiced, arguing that they would not pay over the accepted market price. The 1988 riots in Algiers underlined the high price the country was paying for the austerity induced by the sharp decline in its foreign income—more than 90% of which derives from its oil and gas income.

Since then, the Algerians have managed to restore a number of crucial relationships in the United States and Europe and seem set on a course of action which will make Sonatrach a crucial element in several nations' LNG stockpiles. During 1989 Sonatrach exported a record 17.2 billion cubic meters (cm) of gas as LNG, or about 12.3 million tons. Export capacity presently stands at around 25 billion cm, but Sonatrach's deputy general manager, Mustapha Faid, announced that this is to be substantially expanded during the 1990s, to 33 billion cm by 1992, and to between 60 billion and 80 billion cm by the end of the decade.

By the end of 1990 Algeria had about 3.25 trillion cm of natural gas reserves, placing it among the top seven in the world. As part of this expansion Sonatrach plans to construct a new LNG unit of about five billion cm capacity. Meanwhile, it will also be expanding the country's liquefied petroleum gas capacity to allow exports of seven million tons annually, up from the present level of about four million tons. In addition, a new, fourth pipeline to mainland Italy via Tunisia and Sicily was being planned, while there was a more tentative plan to build a pipeline through Morocco and across the Strait of Gibraltar to the Iberian Peninsula.

Faid also announced impending contracts with U.S. and French companies to refurbish and expand gas liquefaction plant at the ports of Arzew and Skikda. In February 1990, a cooperation agreement was signed between Sonatrach and Total Compagnie Française des Pétroles (formerly CFP) covering upstream and downstream work, while in November 1989 these companies signed two production-sharing contracts for liquid hydrocarbons at the same time as Shell and Sonatrach signed a deal to study cooperation in the natural gas sector. However, the main thrust of Sonatrach's present expansion plans became apparent in 1991, with Sonatrach running a campaign to attract both producing and consuming companies to participate in joint ventures for the production and separation of around four million tons a year of LPG, which, as we have seen, would double the present production capacity.

Principal Subsidiaries: Société de Transport du Gaz Naturel d'Hassi-Er-r'Mel Arzew (SOTHRA); Société Algérienne de Geophysique (ALGEO); Société de la Raffinerie d'Alger.

Further Reading: Wright, John, "Sonatrach—key to Algeria's future," *Petroleum Economist,* January 1977; Secretariat Organization of the Petroleum Exporting Countries, *OPEC National Oil Company Profiles,* Vienna, 1978; Leblond, Doris, "The dual pattern of Algeria's gas contracts," *Petroleum Economist,* May 1988; Buckman, David, "Algeria—new search gets under way," *Petroleum Economist,* July 1989.

—Adam H. Seymour

EXXON CORPORATION

225 East John Carpenter Freeway
Irving, Texas 75062
U.S.A.
(214) 444-1000
Fax: (214) 444-1348

Public Company
Incorporated: 1882 as Standard Oil Company of New Jersey
Employees: 104,000
Sales: $116.94 billion
Stock Exchange: New York

As the earliest example of that trend toward gigantic size and power, Exxon Corporation and its Standard Oil forebears have earned vast amounts of money. The child of John D. Rockefeller, Standard Oil enjoyed the blessings and handicaps of overwhelming power—on the one hand, an early control of the oil business so complete that even its creators could not deny its monopolistic status; on the other, an unending series of journalistic and legal attacks upon its business ethics, profits, and very existence. The uproar over the *Exxon Valdez* in 1989 put the corporation once more in the position of embattled giant, as America's third-largest company struggled to justify its actions before the public.

The individual most responsible for the creation of Standard Oil, John D. Rockefeller, was born in 1839 to a family of modest means living in the Finger Lakes region of New York State. His father, William A. Rockefeller, was a sporadically successful merchant and part-time hawker of medicinal remedies. William Rockefeller moved his family to Cleveland, Ohio, when John D. Rockefeller was in his early teens, and it was there that the young man finished his schooling and began work as a bookkeeper in 1855. From a very young age John D. Rockefeller seems to have developed an interest in business. Before getting his first job with the merchant firm of Hewitt & Tuttle, Rockefeller had already demonstrated an innate affinity for business, later honed by a few months at business school.

Rockefeller worked at Hewitt & Tuttle for four years, studying large-scale trading in the United States. In 1859 the 19-year-old Rockefeller set himself up in a venture similar to Hewitt & Tuttle, Clark & Rockefeller, merchants handling the purchase and resale of grain, meat, farm implements, salt, and other basic commodities. Although still very young, Rockefeller had already impressed Maurice Clark and his other business associates as an unusually capable, cautious, and meticulous businessman. He was a reserved, undemonstrative individual, never allowing emotion to cloud his thinking. Bankers found that they could trust John D. Rockefeller, and his associates in the merchant business began looking to him for judgment and leadership.

Clark & Rockefeller's already healthy business was given a boost by the Civil War economy, and by 1863 the firm's two partners had put away a substantial amount of capital and were looking for new ventures. The most obvious and exciting candidate was oil. A few years before, the nation's first oil well had been drilled at Titusville, in western Pennsylvania, and by 1863 Cleveland had become the refining and shipping center for a raft of newly opened oil fields in the so-called Oil Region. Activity in the oil fields, however, was extremely chaotic, a scene of unpredictable wildcatting, and John D. Rockefeller was a man who prized above all else the maintenance of order. He and Clark therefore decided to avoid drilling and instead go into the refining of oil, and in 1863 they formed Andrews, Clark & Company with an oil specialist named Samuel Andrews. Rockefeller, never given to publicity, was the "Company."

With excellent railroad connections as well as the Great Lakes to draw upon for transportation, the city of Cleveland and the firm of Andrews, Clark & Company both did well. The discovery of oil wrought a revolution in U.S.methods of illumination, kerosene soon replacing animal fat as the source of light across the country, and by 1865 Rockefeller was fully convinced that oil refining would be his life's work. Unhappy with his Clark-family partners, in 1865 Rockefeller bought them out for $72,000 and created the new firm of Rockefeller & Andrews, already Cleveland's largest oil refiners. It was a typically bold move by Rockefeller, who although innately conservative and methodical was never afraid to make difficult decisions. He thus found himself, at the age of 25, co-owner of one of the world's leading oil concerns.

Talent, capital, and good timing combined to bless Rockefeller & Andrews. The demand for oil continued to explode, Cleveland handled the lion's share of Pennsylvania crude, and Rockefeller & Andrews soon dominated the Cleveland scene. By 1867, when a young man of exceptional talent named Henry Flagler became a third partner, the firm was already operating the world's number-one oil refinery; there was as yet little oil produced outside the United States. The year before, John Rockefeller's brother, William, had opened a New York office to encourage the rapidly growing export of kerosene and oil by-products, and it was not long before foreign sales became an important part of Rockefeller strength. As an indication of the latter, in 1869 the young firm allocated $60,000 for plant improvements alone—an enormous sum of money for that day.

The early years of the oil business were marked by tremendous swings in the production, and hence the price, of both crude and refined oil. With a flood of newcomers entering the field every day, size and efficiency had already become critically important for survival, and as the biggest refiner, Rockefeller was in a better position than anyone to weather the price storms. Rockefeller and Henry Flagler, with whom he enjoyed a long and harmonious business relationship, decided to incorporate their firm as a means to raise the capital needed to enlarge it still further. On January 10, 1870, the Standard Oil

Company was formed, with the two Rockefellers, Flagler, and Andrews owning the great majority of stock, valued at $1 million. The new company was not only capable of refining approximately 10% of the entire country's oil, it also owned a barrel-making plant, dock facilities, a fleet of railroad tank cars, New York warehouses, and forest land for the cutting of lumber used to produce barrel staves. At a time when the term was yet unknown, Standard Oil had become a vertically integrated company.

One of the signal advantages of Standard Oil's size was the leverage it gave the company in railroad negotiations. Most of the oil refined at Standard made its way to New York and the eastern seaboard, and because of Standard's great volume—60 carloads a day by 1869—it was able to win lucrative rebates from the warring railroads. In 1871 the various railroads concocted a plan whereby the nation's oil refiners and railroads would agree to set and maintain prohibitively high freight rates while awarding large rebates and other special benefits to those refiners who were part of the scheme. The railroads would avoid disastrous price wars while the large refiners forced out of business those smaller companies who refused to join the cartel, known as the South Improvement Company.

The plan was immediately denounced by Oil Region producers and many independent refiners, near-riots breaking out in the oil fields. After a bitter war of words and a flood of press coverage, the oil refiners and the railroads abandoned their plan and announced the adoption of public, inflexible transport rates. In the meantime, however, Rockefeller and Flagler were already far advanced on a plan of their own, its aim a solution to the problems of excess capacity and dropping prices in the oil industry. To Rockefeller the remedy was obvious, though unprecedented: the eventual unification of all oil refiners in the United States into a single company. Rockefeller approached one after another of the Cleveland refiners, and a number of important firms in New York and elsewhere as well with an offer of Standard Oil stock or cash in exchange for their often-ailing plants. By the end of 1872 all 34 other refiners in the area had agreed to sell, some freely and for profit, and some, competitors alleged, under coercion. Due to Standard's great size and the industry's overbuilt capacity, Rockefeller and Flagler were in a position to make their competitors offers they could not refuse. All indications are that Standard regularly paid top dollar for viable companies.

By 1873 Standard Oil was refining more oil—10,000 barrels per day—than any other region of the country, employing 1,600 workers, and netting around $500,000 per year. With great confidence, Rockefeller proceeded to duplicate his Cleveland success throughout the rest of the country. By the end of 1874 he had absorbed the next three largest refiners in the nation, located in New York, Philadelphia, and Pittsburgh, and had begun moving into the field of distribution with the purchase of several of the new pipelines then being laid across the country. With each new acquisition it became that much harder for Rockefeller's next target to refuse his cash, for the Standard interests rapidly grew so large that the threat of monopoly was clear. The years 1875 to 1879 saw Rockefeller push through his plan to its logical conclusion. In 1878, a mere six years after beginning its annexation campaign, Standard Oil controlled $33 million of the country's $35 million annual refining capacity, as well as a significant proportion of the nation's pipelines and oil tankers. At the age of 39, Rockefeller was one of the five wealthiest men in the country.

Standard's involvement in the aborted South Improvement Company, however, had earned it lasting criticism, and its subsequent absorption of the refining industry was not calculated to mend its image among the few remaining independents and the mass of oil producers. The latter, still unable to curb excess drilling, found in Standard a natural target for their wrath when the price of crude dropped precipitously in the late 1870s. From the welter of conflicting testimony it is difficult to determine the causes of producers' failing fortunes, but it is clear that given Standard's extraordinary position in the oil industry it was fated to become the target of any and all dissatisfactions. In 1879 nine Standard Oil officials were indicted by a Pennsylvania grand jury for violating state antimonopoly laws. Though the case was not pursued, it indicated the depth of feeling against Standard Oil, and was only the first in a long line of legal battles waged to curb its power.

In 1882 Rockefeller and his associates reorganized their dominions, creating the first "trust" in U.S. business history. This move overcame state laws restricting the activity of a corporation to its home state. Henceforth the Standard Oil Trust, domiciled in New York City, held "in trust" all assets of the various Standard Oil companies. Of the Standard Oil Trust's nine trustees, John D. Rockefeller held easily the largest number of shares. Together the trust's 30 companies controlled 80% of the refineries and 90% of the oil pipelines in the United States and constituted the leading industrial organization in the world. The trust's first year's combined net earnings were $11.2 million, of which some $7 million was immediately plowed back into the companies for expansion. Almost lost in the flurry of big numbers was the 1882 creation of Standard Oil Company of New Jersey, one of the many regional corporations created to handle the trust's activities in surrounding states. Barely worth mentioning at the time, Standard Oil Company of New Jersey, or "Jersey" as it came to be called, would soon become the dominant Standard company and, much later, rename itself Exxon.

The 1880s were a period of exponential growth for Standard. The trust not only maintained its lock on refining and distribution but also seriously entered the field of production, by 1891 securing a quarter of the country's total output, most of it in the new regions of Indiana and Illinois. Standard's overseas business was also expanding rapidly, and in 1888 it founded its first foreign affiliate, Anglo-American Oil Company Limited of London. The overseas trade in kerosene was especially important to Jersey, which derived as much as three-fourths of its sales from the export trade. Jersey's Bayonne, New Jersey, refinery was soon the third largest in the Standard family, putting out 10,000 to 12,000 barrels per day by 1886. In addition to producing and refining capacity, Standard also was extending gradually its distribution system from pipelines and bulk wholesalers toward the retailer and eventual end user of kerosene, the private consumer.

The 1890 Sherman Antitrust Act, passed largely in response to Standard's oil monopoly, laid the groundwork for a second major legal assault against the company, an 1892 Ohio Supreme Court order forbidding the trust to operate Standard of Ohio. As a result, the trust was promptly dissolved, but taking advantage of newly liberalized state law in New Jersey the Standard directors made Jersey the main vessel of their holdings. Standard Oil Company of New Jersey became Standard Oil Company (New Jersey) at this time. The new Standard Oil structure now consisted of only 20 much-enlarged companies, but effective control of the interests remained in the same few hands as before. Jersey added a number of important manufacturing plants to its already impressive refining capacity and was by any measure the leading Standard unit, but it was not until 1899 that it became the sole holding company for all of the Standard interests. At that time the entire organization's assets were valued at about $300 million and it employed 35,000 people. John D. Rockefeller continued as nominal president, but the most powerful active member of Jersey's board was probably John D. Archbold.

Rockefeller, in fact, had retired from daily participation in Standard Oil in 1896 at the age of 56. Once Standard's consolidation was complete Rockefeller spent his time reversing the process of accumulation, seeing to it that his staggering fortune—estimated at $900 million in 1913—was redistributed as efficiently as it had been made.

The general public was only dimly aware of Rockefeller's philanthropy, however. More obvious were the frankly monopolistic policies of the company he had built. With its immense size and complete vertical integration from oil well to housewife, including housewives as far away as Romania, Standard Oil piled up huge profits—$830 million in the 12 years from 1899 to 1911. In relative terms, its domination of the U.S. industry was steadily decreasing, by 1911 its percentage of total refining was down to 66% from the 90% of a generation before; but in absolute terms Standard Oil had grown to monstrous proportions. It was therefore not surprising that in 1905 a U.S. congressman from Kansas launched an investigation of Standard Oil's role in the falling price of crude in his state. The commissioner of the Bureau of Corporations, James R. Garfield, decided to widen the investigation into a study of the national oil industry—in effect Standard Oil.

Garfield's critical report prompted a barrage of state lawsuits against Standard Oil (New Jersey) and, in November 1906, a federal suit was filed charging the company, John D. Rockefeller, and others with running a monopoly. In 1911, after years of litigation the U.S. Supreme Court upheld a lower court's conviction of Standard Oil for monopoly and restraint of trade under the Sherman Antitrust Act. The Court ordered the separation from Standard Oil Company (New Jersey) of 33 of the major Standard Oil subsidiaries, including those which subsequently kept the Standard name.

To Standard Oil Company (New Jersey) remained an equal number of smaller companies spread around the United States and overseas which, taken together, represented $285 million of the former Jersey's net value of $600 million. Notable among the remaining holdings were a group of large refineries, four medium-sized producing companies, and extensive foreign marketing affiliates. Notably absent were the pipelines needed to move oil from well to refinery, much of the former tanker fleet, and access to a number of important foreign markets, including Great Britain and the Far East.

President of Standard Oil (New Jersey) remained John D. Archbold, a long-time intimate of the elder Rockefeller, whose Standard service had begun in 1879. Archbold's first problem was to secure sufficient supplies of crude oil for Jersey's extensive refining and marketing capacity. Jersey's former subsidiaries were more than happy to continue selling crude to Jersey, and in reality the dissolution decree had little immediate effect on the coordinated workings of the former Standard Oil group,

but Jersey set about finding its own sources of crude. The company's first halting steps toward foreign production met with little success—ventures in Romania, Peru, Mexico, and Canada suffered political or geological setbacks and were of no help. In 1919, however, Jersey made a domestic purchase that would prove to be of great long-term value. For $17 million Jersey acquired 50% of the Humble Oil & Refining Company of Houston, Texas, a young but rapidly growing network of Texas producers which immediately assumed first place among Jersey's domestic suppliers. Although only the fifth-leading producer in Texas at the time of its purchase, Humble would soon become the dominant drilling company in all of the United States, and was eventually wholly purchased by Jersey. Humble, now known as Exxon Company USA, remained one of the leading U.S. producers of crude oil and natural gas, with drilling rigs in 19 states including Alaska's Prudhoe Bay, in 1991.

Despite initial disappointments in overseas production, Jersey remained a company oriented to foreign markets and supply sources. On the supply side, Jersey secured a number of valuable Latin American producing companies in the 1920s, especially several Venezuelan interests consolidated in 1943 into Creole Petroleum Corporation. By that time Creole was easily the largest crude producer in the Jersey group, and also the most profitable Jersey company of any kind. In 1946, for example, Creole produced an average of 451,000 barrels per day, far more than the 309,000 by Humble and almost equal to all other Jersey drilling companies combined. Four years later, Creole alone generated $157 million of the Jersey group's total net income of $408 million, and did so on sales of only $517 million. Also in 1950, Jersey's British affiliates, mainly marketers, showed substantial sales of $283 million but a bottom line of about $2 million. In contrast to the industry's early days, oil profits now lay in the production of crude, and the bulk of Jersey's crude came from Latin America. The company's growing Middle Eastern affiliates did not become significant resources until the early 1950s; and Jersey's Far East holdings, from 1933 to 1961 owned jointly with Socony-Vacuum Oil Company—formerly Standard Oil Company of New York and now Mobil Corporation—never provided sizable amounts of crude oil.

In marketing, Jersey's income showed a similar preponderance of foreign sales. Jersey's domestic market had been limited by the dissolution decree, largely to a handful of mid-Atlantic states and such others as Jersey could later gain access to, whereas the company's overseas affiliates were well entrenched and highly profitable. Jersey's Canadian affiliate, Imperial Oil Ltd. had a monopolistic hold on that country's market, while in Latin America and the Caribbean the West India Oil Company performed superbly during the second and third decades of the 20th century. Jersey had also incorporated eight major marketing companies in Europe by 1927 and these too sold a significant amount of refined products, most of them under the Esso brand name introduced the previous year. Esso became Jersey's best known and most widely used retail name both at home and abroad.

Jersey's mix of refined products changed considerably over the years. As the use of kerosene for illumination gave way to electricity and the automobile continued to grow in popularity, Jersey's sales reflected a shift away from kerosene and toward gasoline. Even as late as 1950, however, gasoline had not yet become the leading seller among Jersey products. That honor went to the group of residual fuel oils used to power ships and industrial plants and as a substitute for coal. Distillates used for home heating and diesel engines were also strong performers. Even in 1991, when Exxon distributed its gasoline through a network of 12,000 U.S. and 26,000 international service stations, the earnings of all marketing and refining activities were barely one-third of those derived from the production of crude. In 1950 that proportion was about the same, indicating once again that, regardless of the end products into which oil is refined, it is the production of crude that yields the big profits.

Indeed, by mid-century the international oil business had largely become a question of controlling crude oil at its source. With Standard Oil Company and its multinational competitors having built fully vertically integrated organizations, the only leverage remained control of the oil as it came out of the ground. Though it was not yet widely known in the United States, production of crude was shifting rapidly from the United States and Latin America to the Middle East. As early as 1908 oil had been verified in present-day Iran, but it was not until 1928 that Jersey and Socony-Vacuum, prodded by chronic shortages of crude, joined three European companies in forming Iraq Petroleum Company. Also in 1928, Jersey, Shell, and Anglo-Persian secretly agreed to limit each company's share of world production to their present relative amounts, attempting, by means of this "As Is" agreement, to limit competition and keep prices at comfortably high levels. As with Rockefeller's similar tactics 50 years before, it was not clear in 1928 that the agreement was illegal, because its participants were located in a number of different countries each with its own set of trade laws. Already in 1928, Jersey and the other oil giants were stretching the very concept of nationality beyond any simple application.

Following World War II, Standard Oil was again in need of crude to supply the resurgent economies of Europe. Already the world's largest producer, Standard Oil became interested in the vast oil concessions in Saudi Arabia recently won by Texaco and Socal. The latter companies were in need of both capital for expansion and world markets for exploitation, and in 1946 they sold 30% of the newly formed Arabian American Oil Company (Aramco) to Standard Oil and 10% to Socony-Vacuum. A few years later, after Iran's nationalization of Anglo-Persian's holdings was squelched by a combination of CIA assistance and an effective worldwide boycott of Iranian oil by competitors, Jersey was able to take 7% of the consortium formed to drill in that oil-rich country. With a number of significant tax advantages attached to foreign crude production, Jersey drew an increasing percentage of its oil from its holdings in all three of the major middle eastern fields: Iraq, Iran, and Saudi Arabia, and helped propel the 20-year postwar economic boom in the West. With oil prices exceptionally low, the United States and Europe busily shifted their economies to complete dependence on the automobile and on oil as the primary industrial fuel.

Despite the growing strength of newcomers to the international market such as Getty and Conoco, the big companies continued to exercise decisive control over the world oil supply and thus over the destinies of the Middle East producing countries. Growing nationalism and an increased awareness of the extraordinary power of the large oil companies led to the 1960 formation of the Organization of Petroleum Exporting Countries (OPEC) and a series of increasingly bitter confrontations between countries and companies over who should control the oil upon which the world had come to depend. The growing power of OPEC prompted Jersey to seek alternative sources of crude, resulting in discoveries in Alaska's Prudhoe Bay and the North Sea in the late 1960s. The Middle Eastern sources remained paramount, however, and when OPEC cut off oil supplies to the United States in 1973 in response to U.S. sponsorship of Israel, the resulting 400% price increase permanently changed the industrial world's attitude to oil, as well as inducing a prolonged recession. Control of the oil was largely taken out of the hands of the oil companies, which began exploring new sources of energy and business opportunities in other fields.

For Standard Oil Company (New Jersey), which had changed it name to Exxon in 1972, the oil embargo had several major effects. Most obviously it increased corporate sales, the expensive oil allowing Exxon to double its 1972 revenue of $20 billion in only two years and then pushing that figure over the $100 billion mark by 1980. After a year of windfall profits made possible by the sale of inventoried oil bought at much lower prices, Exxon was able to make use of its extensive North Sea and Alaskan holdings to keep profits at a steady level. The company had suffered a strong blow to its confidence, however, and was soon investigating a number of diversification measures which eventually included office equipment, a purchase of Reliance Electric Company, the fifth-largest holdings of coal in the United States, and an early-1980s venture into shale oil. With the partial exception of coal, all of these were expensive failures, costing Exxon an estimated $6 billion to $7 billion and no end of frustration.

By the early 1980s the world oil picture had eased considerably and Exxon felt less urgency about diversification. With the price of oil peaking around 1981 and then tumbling for most of the decade, Exxon's sales dropped sharply but its confidence rose as OPEC's grip on the marketplace proved to be weaker than advertised. Having abandoned its forays into other areas Exxon refocused on the oil and gas business, cutting its assets and work force substantially to accommodate the drop in revenue without losing profitability.

It also bought back a sizable number of its own shares to bolster per-share earnings, which reached excellent levels and won the approval of Wall Street. The stock buy-back was partially in response to Exxon's embarrassing failure to invest its excess billions profitably, at which point the company was somewhat at a loss as to what to do with its money. It could not expand further into the oil business without running into antitrust difficulties at home, and investments outside oil would have to truly be mammoth to warrant the time and energy required.

Exxon is no longer the world's largest company, nor even the largest oil group—Royal Dutch/Shell took over that position in the 1980s—but with the help of the 1989 *Exxon Valdez* disaster it has heightened its notoriety. The crash of the *Exxon Valdez* on March 24, 1989, in Prince William Sound off the port of Valdez, Alaska, released about 260,000 barrels of crude oil into the sound. The disaster cost Exxon $1.7 billion in 1989 alone, and the company and its subsidiaries were faced with more than 170 civil and criminal lawsuits brought by state and federal governments and individuals. In the long run, however, it is likely that Exxon will view the *Valdez* disaster as a small blemish on its muscular balance sheet.

Principal Subsidiaries: Esso Aktiengesellschaft (Germany); Esso Eastern Inc.; Esso Australia Resources Ltd.; Esso Exploration and Production Norway Inc.; Esso Holding Company Holland Inc.; Esso Holding Company U.K. Inc.; Esso Italiana S.P.A. (Italy); Esso Norge a.s. (Norway); Esso Sociedad Anonima Petrolera Argentina; Esso Societe Anonyme Francaise (France; 81.548%) Esso Standard Oil S.A. Limited (Bahamas); Exxon Capital Holdings Corporation; Exxon Gas System, Inc.; Exxon Insurance Holdings, Inc.; Exxon Overseas Corporation; Exxon Rio Holding Inc.; Exxon San Joaquin Production Company; Exxon Trading Company International; Exxon Yemen Inc.; Imperial Oil Limited (Canada, 69.56%); International Colombia Resources Corporation (100%); Societe Francaise Exxon Chemical (France, 98.64%).

Further Reading: Nevins, Allan, *Study in Power: John D. Rockefeller—Industrialist and Philanthropist*, 2 vols., New York, Charles Scribner's Sons, 1953; Hidy, Ralph W., and Murrel E. Hidy, *History of Standard Oil Company (New Jersey): Pioneering in Big Business, 1882–1911*, New York, Harper & Brothers, 1955; Gibb, George Sweet, and Evelyn H. Knowlton, *History of Standard Oil Company (New Jersey): The Resurgent Years, 1911–1927*, New York, Harper & Brothers, 1956; Larson, Henrietta M., Evelyn H. Knowlton, and Charles S. Popple, *History of Standard Oil Company (New Jersey): New Horizons, 1927–1950*, New York, Harper & Row, 1971; Sampson, Anthony, *The Seven Sisters: The Great Oil Companies and the World They Made*, New York, The Viking Press, 1975; Wall, Bennett H., *Growth in a Changing Environment: A History of Standard Oil Company (New Jersey)*, New York, McGraw-Hill, 1988.

—Jonathan Martin

GENERAL SEKIYU K.K.

8-6, Nishi-Shinbashi 2-chome
Minato-ku, Tokyo 105
Japan
(03) 3595-8300
Fax: (03) 3508-0668

Public Company
Incorporated: 1947 as General Bussan Kaisha, Ltd.
Employees: 1,320
Sales: ¥486.32 billion (US$3.58 billion)
Stock Exchange: Tokyo

General Sekiyu K.K. (General) is a Japanese oil refiner and distributor affiliated with the companies of the former Mitsui *zaibatsu*, and the U.S. oil company Exxon, heir to Standard Oil of New Jersey. Founded in the wake of World War II as successor to the petroleum department of its former parent company Mitsui, the company has both prospered and suffered in the volatile Japanese petroleum industry in the postwar years.

The Mitsui *zaibatsu*, a very large general trading company with a long history, became involved in the distribution of petroleum products as early as the 1880s, when it began to sell kerosene. Although it was later forced out of that business by foreign competitors, the company re-entered the oil business in the years following World War I. Since Japan has very little natural petroleum, this re-entry meant dealing with a foreign supplier. In 1920 Mitsui became the exclusive distributor for the refined petroleum products of General Petroleum Corporation, a U.S. company, in the Far East. Mitsui quickly set up facilities to market and store oil and, by selling high-quality oil from California at competitive prices, was able to challenge successfully the dominance of Dutch oil interests in Japan.

In 1932, however, Mitsui's U.S. supplier was purchased by Standard Oil of New York, and it became difficult to maintain the company's distribution arrangements. In 1933 Standard Oil of New York and Standard Oil of New Jersey combined their operations in the Far East to create Standard-Vacuum, known as Stanvac. Along with Rising Sun, a Dutch company, Stanvac held 60% of Japan's domestic oil market throughout the early 1930s. Having failed to work out an agreement to enter the refining business with Stanvac, Mitsui negotiated a contract to distribute the company's products.

In 1934 the Japanese government passed the Petroleum Industry Law, bringing the oil industry under government control as part of the preparations for the expected war. Petro-

leum, used to power Japanese warships, was seen as a vital strategic resource. The law required all foreign oil companies to maintain a six-month supply of oil beyond the usual inventories. When Stanvac balked at this requirement, Mitsui compromised with its foreign partners by building tanks that would hold a three-month supply, while the U.S. firm took care of the other half of the requirement.

In 1943 with Japan in the midst of full-scale war, the government intervened in the oil industry again, putting all activity under one control company, and Mitsui lost its petroleum business. Two years later, the country's unconditional surrender to the Allied forces brought an end to World War II, and the postwar reconstruction of the ruined country began.

On July 3, 1947, the Supreme Commander of the Allied Powers then ruling Japan ordered the breakup of the Mitsui and other *zaibatsu*, which it perceived as having an undesirable feudalistic and totalitarian influence on the country. In the wake of this order, managers of the different divisions of Mitsui Bussan Kaisha, the main trading arm of the company, took responsibility for the welfare of their employees, and set up their own new enterprises, based on their former business functions. Accordingly, members of the old petroleum department set up an independent company to market and distribute oil. The company was named General Bussan Kaisha, Ltd., and was capitalized at only ¥180,000. In setting up business, the new firm relied on the strong relationship with Stanvac that it had inherited from its parent, Mitsui.

In the early postwar years, Japan's oil industry struggled to recover from the devastation wrought by Allied bombardment of the home islands. Almost all of the petroleum industry's infrastructure, including its refineries and tanks, had been reduced to rubble. Distribution of oil was firmly under the control of the occupying government, and the main task at hand for the industry was to rebuild.

In 1949 General Bussan Kaisha took over the Osaka General Bussan, which had originated from the fuel department of the Osaka branch of Mitsui Bussan Kaisha, Ltd., and thus consolidated all the petroleum operations of the former *zaibatsu* under one name and management. The company continued to distribute petroleum under government direction.

In 1952 the Allied occupation of Japan ended, and rationing of petroleum was abolished. The demand for oil to fuel the nation's postwar industrial boom began to increase. In November 1952, General strengthened its ties with Stanvac when a new contract between the two companies was negotiated, authorizing the Japanese company to distribute Stanvac's refined petroleum products. This access to a stable supply of petroleum products allowed the company to expand rapidly.

In 1953 General was listed on the Tokyo stock exchange for the first time. By 1954 in addition to its main office in Tokyo, General had opened branch offices in 13 other cities around Japan, and owned petroleum storage tanks in 23 separate locations. The company sold its products to other dealers, as well as directly to factories and government agencies. It had obtained the contract to supply Stanvac bunker oil to foreign ships in Japanese ports, and to Japanese ships in foreign ports. Just seven years after its founding, General's capitalization had increased to ¥300 million, with shares held by nearly 2,000 stockholders.

By the late 1950s, the *zaibatsu* dissolved by the Allied occupation had largely re-formed as a *keiretsu*. General Bussan, utilizing its inherited industrial contacts, was doing well, and there was no move to rejoin the other Mitsui enterprises, but the company did continue to maintain loose associations with the Mitsui group. Mitsui & Co. held about 10% of General's stock in the late 1970s, and other Mitsui divisions also held large blocks of shares.

In the early 1960s, General's U.S. partner, Stanvac, was ordered to be dissolved as a result of an antitrust case brought by the U.S. government against the U.S. oil industry. From this point on, General maintained a relationship with just one of its former partners, Standard Oil Company of New Jersey, which would become known as Exxon.

In 1962 the Japanese government passed the Petroleum Industry Law, giving the Ministry of International Trade and Industry a large degree of power over the oil industry. The government could now control prices for oil products and refinery capacities. These moves made it more difficult for foreign interests to establish oil refineries in the country, but made it possible for more Japanese independent refiners to enter the industry. The eventual result was a heavily crowded petroleum industry.

In the second half of the 1960s, Japan completed its shift from reliance on coal to reliance on oil to fuel its rapidly-growing economy. Oil was cheap and plentiful, owing to the discovery in the late 1950s and early 1960s of large reserves in the Middle East. In 1967 General Bussan changed its name to General Sekiyu.

In 1971 General was able for the first time to expand its activities beyond marketing and distribution to include petroleum refining. In conjunction with the Allied return of the island of Okinawa—captured during World War II—to Japanese control, General arranged, under the tutelage of Japan's Ministry of International Trade and Industry, to form a joint venture with its perennial partner, Esso, and with another Japanese company, Sumitomo Chemical Company. The joint venture provided for Esso to construct a refinery on Okinawa with a capacity of 80,000 barrels a day, which would be completed in January 1972. Under the agreement, when the island reverted to Japanese control on May 15, 1972, the refinery would become the joint property of Esso, which took 50% of the shares, and General, and Sumitomo, each of which gained 25% ownership in return for providing US$12.5 million of financing. This arrangement was in accordance with Japanese law, which stipulated that Japanese interests hold at least half of any company operating in Japan. In addition, the agreement for the new operation contained restrictions on the amount of oil that would be shipped to Japan. The joint venture was named Nansei Sekiyu.

General's long-awaited entry into the oil-refining business came at a fortuitous point in Japan's industrial development. By 1973 more than three-quarters of the country's energy needs were met by oil. Almost all of that oil was imported from the Middle East. Prices for oil products were kept low through plentiful supply and heavy competition between the large number of oil refiners and distributors.

In 1973, however, Japan and its business and government leaders received a rude shock when the Arab oil embargo resulted in a sharp rise in oil prices. The doubt cast by this event on the security and stability of a national economy based so heavily on a necessarily imported commodity had far-reaching effects on the Japanese oil industry. In December 1973 react-

ing to large profits reaped by the oil industry from the higher prices of the oil crisis, the government stepped in to fix prices for refined oil products. This move was prompted in part by public anger over a General Sekiyu memo which had come to light and which advocated "grabbing this one chance in a thousand" to make huge profits on the oil crisis. General's public relations suffered further when it was revealed that the company had instructed service station owners to restrict sales of gasoline to selected customers.

In February 1974 the Japanese government formally charged General Sekiyu and other oil companies with joining together to form an illegal pricing cartel for the purpose of increasing their profits during the previous year. After a ten-year court battle, the companies' convictions and fines were upheld in 1984 by the Japanese supreme court, and company executives were given suspended prison terms.

Throughout the mid-1970s, Japan's oil refining industry found itself in choppy waters, and General Sekiyu was no exception. Companies were squeezed on the one hand by rising prices for crude oil, and on the other hand by government-mandated price standards for its refined products, particularly those sold to major industrial users, such as steel and petrochemical producers. The company registered pre-tax deficits in the first half of 1975.

In 1977 General Sekiyu joined with six other Japanese companies to form an oil-stockpiling venture. The new company was to construct a 25-tank storage facility for petroleum products. This venture allowed General Sekiyu and the other participants to fulfill their government-imposed obligation to maintain a three-month petroleum reserve.

General's greatest asset during this time was its marketing prowess. The company controlled 4.5% of the crowded Japanese petroleum market. By mid-1978, steep drops in the price of oil products, combined with rising costs to refiners, were again bringing down profits in the petroleum industry. A new oil tax, implemented on June 1, 1978, further depressed General's earnings.

In September 1978 General announced that Exxon, its longtime U.S. partner and supplier of crude oil, would purchase 49% of General by buying up US$34 million's worth of new shares to be issued by the company. In addition, General took over Exxon's 50% share in the Nansei Sekiyu refinery on Okinawa, bringing its ownership to 75% and increasing its oil refining capacity. Other joint ventures between Exxon and General Sekiyu—the General Gas Company, an importer of liquefied petroleum gas, and the General Sekiyu Refining Company—became wholly owned subsidiaries of General Sekiyu. Under the agreement, General Sekiyu would gain the same access to raw materials and technological expertise as Exxon's wholly owned subsidiaries, while remaining an independently-managed Japanese company. The new mergers allowed General to streamline it operations and eliminate duplication of effort with its subsidiaries.

The move improved the standing of Exxon and its subsidiaries within the Japanese oil market, giving the group, which also included the wholly U.S.–owned Esso Standard Sekiyu and Toa Nenryo Kogyo, a 10% share. Exxon's stock purchase was approved by Japan's governmental Foreign Investment Council and completed by late May 1979.

By March 1980 General's profits had recovered from a slump in the previous year caused by high costs for raw materials and heavy sales of low-priced products, to post extremely high profits, a result of higher prices for its products. The roller-coaster ride of the crowded Japanese petroleum industry continued in the next year, however, as the company posted a loss in March 1981. The company's fortunes continued to worsen as the year progressed, as domestic demand for petroleum products declined under Japan's program to diversify its sources of energy away from almost total dependence on oil.

Difficulties continued throughout the early 1980s. By 1982, General's share of the petroleum market had slipped to 3.9%. In the following year, the company reduced its refinery capacity by 10% to 13%, in keeping with earlier government recommendations.

In January 1984, the company complied with governmental restructuring of the petroleum industry by consolidating some of its marketing activities with Esso Standard Sekiyu, the wholly owned subsidiary of Exxon. The two companies together held slightly over 9% of the Japanese petroleum market in 1984, with General alone holding 3.98%. Despite these steps, General reported a drastic fall in revenues for the fiscal year ending in March 1985, as net income fell 97% as a result of lower prices for oil products.

By late 1987, General's share of the fuel oil market had slipped to 3.8% and the price of the company's shares had dropped as well. This decline was attributed to a shift in the demand for refined petroleum products, away from gasoline, which was General's strength, toward heavier products.

As General entered the 1990s, its ties with Exxon and Esso Sekiyu remained strong, stretching from the supply of crude oil to joint marketing efforts. The company was looking to diversify through its subsidiaries into such fields as petrochemicals, engineering, and real estate. With the price of crude oil remaining steady, and a government-mandated price rise to take effect in February 1990, the company was anticipating resumption of profitable operations.

Throughout its history, General Sekiyu had found itself jockeying for position within the strategically sensitive and crowded Japanese petroleum market. Ready supplies of petroleum, from sources such as General's partnership with Standard Oil, helped to fuel Japan's phenomenal postwar industrial growth, and the company had both benefited and suffered from world events and its key place in the Japanese economy in the wake of that process. How General Sekiyu will navigate the challenges of its changing market in the years to come remains to be seen.

Principal Subsidiaries: General Shipping Co., Ltd. (92%); General Bussan K.K. (88%); General Petrochemical Industries, Ltd.; K.K. Genetech; Nansei Sekiyu K.K. (87.5%).

Further Reading: Mitsui-Mitsubishi-Sumitomo: Present Status of the Former Zaibatsu Enterprises, Tokyo, Mitsubishi Economic Research Institute, 1955; "The Mitsui Story: Three Centuries of Japanese Business," *Mitsui Trade News Supplement,* 1972; Roberts, John G., *Mitsui: Three Centuries of Japanese Business,* 1st edition, New York, Weatherhill, 1973; *The 100 Year History of Mitsui & Co., Ltd.,* [n.p.], Mitsui & Co., Ltd., 1977; Yergin, Daniel, *The Prize: The Epic Quest for Oil, Money and Power,* New York, Simon & Schuster, 1990.

—Elizabeth Rourke

IDEMITSU KOSAN K.K.

3-3-1 Marunouchi
Chiyoda-ku, Tokyo 100
Japan
(03) 3213-3111
Fax: (03) 3213-9315

Private Company
Incorporated: 1911 as Idemitsu & Co.
Employees: 5,497
Sales: ¥1.71 trillion (US$12.59 billion)

Idemitsu Kosan K.K. Japan's largest independent oil company, is named after its founder, Sazou Idemitsu. The company has a nationwide network of 29 branch offices, 13 sub-branch offices, 9,000 service stations, and 6,000 liquefied petroleum gas (LPG) retail outlets. The Idemitsu group's primary activities are the securing of oil resources, crude oil refining, and petroleum product marketing. The group also has interests in alternative energy sources such as coal, uranium, and geothermal generating, as well as petrochemicals and related fields. The group operates six refineries and two petrochemical facilities in Japan, and also maintains an extensive network of overseas offices covering 17 major cities in 14 countries, ensuring a stable supply of energy resources. Idemitsu Kosan is one of the most growth-oriented companies in Japan. The company is organized as a joint stock company, with all shares held by the Idemitsu family and by the employees. Sazou Idemitsu began his career selling lubricants in the northern part of Kyushu in Japan, as an agent for the Nippon Sekiyu (Oil) Co. Ltd., and established Idemitsu & Co. in 1911. In 1913, he began selling fuel oil for fishing boats at Shimonoseki port; this business opened up nationwide marketing opportunities. He studied fuel combustion efficiency, and promoted fuel conversion from expensive paraffin oil—kerosene—to cheaper raw light oil. In 1923, he became a pioneer of retailing methods by introducing small tanker vessels equipped with fuel meters thus replacing canned fuel distribution for fishing boats. After his marketing success in Japan, he extended his sales activities to Manchuria. In 1914 he began to sell lubricants to the South Manchuria Railroad Co. Ltd., a Japanese-owned national railroad company which was central to Japan's imperialistic plans for China, and to an expanding market in northeast China. At the time, the supply of lubricants to China was dominated by foreign companies such as Standard Oil, Royal Dutch/Shell group, through its Japanese subsidiary, Asiatic Petroleum

Company. Idemitsu & Co. attempted to open up the market for Japanese companies by demonstrating the competitive quality and price of its goods. In 1916, Idemitsu opened the Dairen branch, competing with large foreign companies, and sold lubricants, fuel oil, cement, volcanic ash, and machine tools.

During the winters of 1916 to 1918, accidents frequently occurred on the South Manchuria railroad, as lubricants froze and axles often overheated. In 1919, the railroad company systematically tested the efficiency of every lubricant available, and concluded that Idemitsu's product was among the best. It granted exclusive agency to Idemitsu & Co. From 1919 to 1922 Idemitsu established further sales branches in Qindao in China, Taipei and Chilung in Taiwan, and Seoul in Korea. In 1929, Nippon Sekiyu (Oil) Co. established Taiwanese and Korean branches and began direct sales. Consequently the sales activities of Idemitsu, as an agent of Nippon Sekiyu (Oil), had to be restricted in those areas.

Idemitsu expanded his business between 1920 and 1923 in spite of the postwar recession in the Japanese economy. After 1924 he experienced financial difficulties and closed several foreign branches quickly to protect his business. After 1931, he expanded again into the Manchurian market but with more careful strategic planning.

In 1932, after the Japanese established a puppet government in Manchuria, the Japanese government controlled major commodities and industries. As a result, the functions of Idemitsu were limited to those of a distributor under the controlled economy. By 1939 oil distribution in Japan was tightly controlled by the government and the sales divisions—wholesale and retail—of each oil company were organized into regional distribution associations. Sazou Idemitsu was forced to reduce sales activities. To ensure the safety of his business, he decided to diversify beyond oil sales into transportation by tanker with his first oil tanker, *Nisshomaru*, launched in 1938; oil refining through investment in Kyushu Oil Refinery Co. Ltd.; and other products.

In 1940, Idemitsu & Co. moved its domestic headquarters from Moji City in Kyushu to Tokyo, and established a new joint stock company, Idemitsu Kosan K.K.with a capital of ¥4 million. The Chinese and Manchurian interests were reorganized into separate regional subsidiaries. In 1939, Idemitsu began to build a 100,000-tonnage scale oil tank in Shanghai, and imported paraffin oil—kerosene—and volatile oil—including benzine and naphtha—from the United States. However, after the outbreak of the Pacific War in 1941 almost all industries came under the control of the military government, and the activities of the company were limited to distribution.

After World War II, the Japanese petroleum industry was controlled by the Supreme Commander for the Allied Powers (SCAP). In reality expatriate managers from Standard Oil, Shell, Caltex, Tidewater, and Union Oil constituted a Petroleum Advisory Group that decided Japanese petroleum policies. After the abolition in 1949 of the Oil Distribution Public Corporation which had been set up during the war by the Japanese government to ration scarce oil, ten companies, including Standard Oil, Shell, and Caltex, selected as petroleum products suppliers by the Ministry of International Trade and Industry (MITI). Idemitsu Kosan was included in the ten, and dissolved its long-standing ties with Nippon Sekiyu (Oil) Co. Ltd.

In 1952, according to the peace treaty which became effective that year, the Japanese government abolished price controls on petroleum products and permitted a foreign exchange quota for importing naphtha. In 1951 Idemitsu Kosan was permitted by MITI to build a new tanker, which was launched in the same year. Using his new tanker, Idemitsu imported high-octane gasoline from California and sold it in the Japanese domestic market. Soon, however, the major U.S. oil companies decided that there were profits to be made from selling naphtha directly to Japan, and they began to restrict sales of naphtha to Idemitsu in California. Idemitsu changed its sourcing to Houston, Texas, but soon sales were restricted there also. Eventually Idemitsu found a supplier in Venezuela. As naphtha sales in Japan by foreign companies increased, MITI felt the necessity for import restrictions to protect the domestic oil industry. MITI therefore passed the Oil Industry Law, which restricted the number of oil importers. As a result, only a few foreign companies could continue to import oil to Japan, and those which could were forced to do so through joint ventures with Japanese companies. Soon Japan saw the rapid establishment of its own petrochemical industry.

As Idemitsu was at that time only an importer and distributor of naphtha, his company was unable to import oil because of the domination of major foreign oil companies. It therefore became essential for Idemitsu to establish a reputation as an oil importer. The nationalization in 1953 of Anglo-Iranian Oil by the Iranian government and the resulting friction between the Iranian and British governments were fortuitous for Idemitsu. The Iranian government was unable to find a customer because of the dangerous wartime conditions, until Idemitsu decided to send his large tanker *Nisshomaru* to procure Iranian oil. He managed to secure a price 30% lower than the standard market price of the time. However, the British government was displeased by Idemitsu's behavior and lodged a complaint with MITI. Although Idemitsu's action was applauded by the Iranians and the Japan public, MITI felt that it had been put in a difficult position and Idemitsu fell out of favor with MITI officials. To protect his company against repercussions, Idemitsu tightened the closed ownership policy of his company still further.

Both the restriction of naphtha exports and the Japanese government's alteration of its policy to favor domestic refineries posed a serious threat to Idemitsu Kosan. Refineries had to be constructed quickly. In May 1956 Idemitsu began construction of Tokuyama oil refinery, which went into operation in March 1957. In 1960, after the addition of a second refinery facility, Tokuyama refinery's production capacity amounted to 140,000 barrels per day.

By the following decade, Idemitsu was concentrating its efforts on constructing refinery facilities. In 1963 the Chiba oil refinery, was built, producing 100,000 barrels per day. This was followed by the Hyogo oil refinery in 1970, the Hokkaido oil refinery in 1973, and the Aichi oil refinery in 1975. Idemitsu began to pursue a vertical integration strategy, from crude oil importing to refinery and sales of products. In July 1962 the world's largest tanker, *Nisshomaru III*, was completed, and Idemitsu established the Idemitsu Tanker Co. Ltd. to manage the oil transportation division. From 1962 to 1981, Idemitsu completed ten mammoth tankers—with a tonnage of more than 200,000—and established a worldwide network for petroleum transportation.

In 1963, Idemitsu's petrochemical facility in the Tokuyama refinery went into operation, and the company entered new fields of production. In 1964 Idemitsu established Idemitsu Petrochemical Co. Ltd., which became the center of the Tokuyama refinery complex. In 1962, MITI introduced the Oil Industry Law to control excess production and price competition between petroleum companies. Idemitsu opposed the law because it restricted competition and obstructed freedom of business. In the second half of 1962, Sekiyu Renmei—the Oil Producers' Federation—was organized at the instigation of MITI, and began to restrict production. However, the federation failed to prevent overproduction, and price competition resulted in spite of the cartel agreement. Idemitsu stood against such curbing of production, and withdrew from the federation. In November 1965, the seamen's union struck, the first such strike in Japanese history. The result was a major shortage of petroleum products. Idemitsu disregarded the quota and went into full production. The Oil Producers' Federation and MITI criticized the decision, but Idemitsu continued to ignore the restriction until the strike ended.

In February 1966 price control of petroleum products was abolished, and in August the production quota was repealed. In September 1966, MITI asked Idemitsu to return to the federation. The company did so in October. Sazou Idemitsu became the chairman of the board, although he retained effective control of the company, and his younger brother Keisuke Idemitsu took his place as president. This was a necessary step if the reconciliation with MITI was to take place.

Under the leadership of Keisuke Idemitsu, the company and its subsidiaries internalized such production functions as mining, refinery, and transportation of raw materials, and diversified the product range. In 1976, Idemitsu Japan Sea Oil Development Co. Ltd.—established in 1961—was reorganized as Idemitsu Oil Development Co. Ltd. Idemitsu Oil & Gas Co. Ltd. started oil and gas drilling in the offshore field of Niigata Prefecture, beginning commercial production in 1984. In 1987 Idemitsu began to develop an oil field in southeast Turkey with the Finnish company Neste Oy. In 1989 Idemitsu acquired 10% ownership of two concessions of the Snorre oil field in the Norwegian sector of the North Sea. In the same year, Idemitsu acquired 25% ownership of the northwest continental shelf concession in Australia and participated in oil drilling operations in various places around the world, including the United Kingdom, Egypt, Gabon, Pakistan, Myanmar, Australia, and Brazil.

In 1977 the company set up a new energy department to promote alternative sources of energy. In 1980, imports of coal from Australia began and the Coal Cartridge System (CCS) was developed to supply coal for small users. The Chiba Bulk Terminal was built in 1986. From this period, Idemitsu started to acquire coal mining interests in Australia, including the Ebenezer mine in Queensland—225 million tons reserve—and the Muswellbrook mine in New South Wales— 594 million tons reserve. By 1990 the company had acquired another four foreign coal mining operations—with an estimated total of 2.5 billion tons of deposits—and had become the largest Japanese coal mining company.

In 1979 the Idemitsu Geothermal Development Co. Ltd. was established, and research drilling for geothermal generating plants began in the Hokkaido, Tohoku, and Kyushu concessions. In the Oita project in Kyushu a pilot plant was built. This was an experimental factory plant to examine technological capability and economic feasibility for starting up a master plant.

In the area of uranium exploration, Idemitsu took a 12.87% stake in the predevelopment work at the Cigar Lake Project in Saskatchewan, Canada, entering into partnership with CAMECO and COGEMA Canada. As the result of trial bowling—test drilling to estimate the total amount of deposits available—the uranium deposits at Cigar Lake were estimated at 192,500 tons, and mining operations were to begin in 1991.

After 1985, as a result of the "reverse oil shock," the price of oil declined rapidly, and some of Idemitsu's alternative energy resources development projects lost their economic effectiveness. However, investments in coal and uranium mining will help the company to provide for an expected shortage in energy supplies after the late 1990s.

Idemitsu's rapid growth was the result of investment in short-term ventures in petroleum-related industries. However, investments in energy resources projects, such as mining for coal and uranium ore, involve the taking of long-term risks, including considerable investment in the protection of the environment against pollution, an area in which Idemitsu has no experience. The major task for the Idemitsu group is to build a flexible business structure and a sound financial base to enable it to withstand uncertainties and risks arising from its direct foreign investments in energy resources development.

Principal Subsidiaries: Apollo Service Co. Ltd; Shigemune Sea Transportation Co. Ltd.; Idemitsu Tanker Co. Ltd.; Idemitsu Petrochemical Co. Ltd.; Idemitsu Oil Development Co. Ltd.; Idemitsu Oil & Gas Co. Ltd; Petrochemicals Malaysia Sdn. Bhd.; Calbu Industry Co. Ltd.; Shiroyama Kosan Co. Ltd.; Polycarbonados do Brazil Co. Ltd.; Idemitsu Engineering Co. Ltd.; Uni Chemical Industry Co. Ltd.; Idemitsu Dupont Co. Ltd.; Idemitsu Credit Co. Ltd.; Idemitsu Chemicals U.S.A. Incorporated; Idemitsu International Europe Incorporated; Idemitsu Chemicals Co. Ltd.; Idemitsu D.S.M. Co. Ltd.

Further Reading A Short History of Idemitsu, Tokyo, Idemitsu Kosan K.K., 1960; *Fifty Years of Idemitsu,* Tokyo, Idemitsu Kosan K.K., 1970; Kimoto, Seiji, *Story of Idemitsu Sazou,* Tokyo, Nikkan Shobo, 1982; Okabe, Akira, *History of Industries in the Showa Era,* Vol. III, Tokyo, Nippon Hyoron Sha, 1986; Takakura Shuji, *A Biography of Idemitsu Sazou,* Tokyo, President Publishing Co., 1990; *The History of Nippon Sekiyu, Tokyo,* Nippon Sekiyu K.K., 1990.

—Kenichi Yasumuro

IMPERIAL OIL LIMITED

111 St. Clair Avenue West
Toronto, Ontario M5W 1K3
Canada
(416) 968-4111
Fax: (416) 968-4272

Public Company
Incorporated: 1880 as The Imperial Oil Company, Limited
Employees: 14,700
Sales: C$11.30 billion (US$9.74 billion)
Stock Exchanges: Montreal Toronto Vancouver American

Imperial Oil is Canada's largest producer of crude oil and the country's third-largest producer of natural gas. Imperial, which is 69.7%-owned by the U.S. corporation Exxon, is Canada's largest refiner of petroleum products, providing the wide variety of products and services that appear with the Esso brand name. It also produces and markets coal, fertilizer, and petrochemicals. Imperial has made itself known for its support of Canadian culture, health, education and community services.

In 1880, when Imperial Oil Company was founded in London, Ontario, oil did not look like a good business. The Canadian oil boom, triggered in 1857 with the sinking of the first oil well, had gone bust in 1876. Domestic over-production and liberal free-trade policies had conspired to saturate the Canadian market. The industrial boom and rampant land speculation, begun in the 1850s, were coming to a halt. During the boom many Canadians had jumped to join the oil rush, and contributed to the flooding of the local market. This, coupled with worldwide depression, resulted in deflated oil prices that were one-third of their former value. Thus, in 1876, Canadian refiners who had glutted their own market began to desert their businesses at bailout prices.

It was at this crisis point that 16 well-established London and Petrolia, Ontario, businessmen banded together and decided to buy into the petroleum business. On September 8, 1880, with C$25,000, The Imperial Oil Company, Limited was formed. Its charter was "to find, produce, refine and distribute petroleum and its products throughout Canada." With two refineries, one in London and the other in Petrolia, the total capitalization was an impressive C$500,000.

Frederick Fitzgerald, a builder of the London Water Works who dabbled in furniture, liquor, groceries, and oil, became Imperial's first president. The mastermind of the group's suc-

cess was its vice president, Jacob Englehart, who by age 33 had 14 years experience in oil, having started his first refinery at age 19. William Spencer and Herman and Isaac Waterman brought their knowledge of refineries to the association. Isaac Waterman's involvement in municipal politics and the railway later proved a valuable asset to the group. John Geary, a lawyer-turned-refiner, and John Minhinnik a plumber-turned-refiner, were more than ready to deal with the business' logistical and physical problems. Thomas Smallman and John Walker brought the experience they had gained when producing sulfuric acid with the first Canadian chemical company. No less valuable was Walker's involvement in federal politics. It was no accident that Thomas Hodgens, a former wagon maker, and his brother Edward, a barrel-maker, were brought into the deal. Edward Hodgens, in 1879 had also patented a process that sweetened the odor of the rancid-smelling Canadian crude, making it more competitive with relatively odorless U.S. crude.

The group immediately began trying to set its products apart by improving their quality, as well as trying to find new uses for the products and to increase distribution. Imperial acquired rights to Hodgens's patent and started deodorizing its oil. It began importing a new kerosene lamp that burned with a brighter, whiter light, from Germany. It sent dealers out into the previously unpenetrated west to hustle up sales. In the space of one year, Imperial was selling to Winnipeg, a frontier town of 8,000, as well as opening up an office in Montreal.

Imperial oil, carried in Imperial's hand-made barrels, rode on Imperial-built wagons across the prairies of the Northwest Territories to Hudson's Bay Company posts. Imperial became so well known for its sturdy oak barrels, that, although the company offered a generous C$1.25 refund for each, most homesteaders chose to keep them and convert them to washtubs, rain barrels, and armchairs. By 1883 Walker's position as vice president of Canadian Pacific Railway had helped Imperial to become not only the basic supplier of railroad construction crews, but also of the settlers that squatted along the line as far as British Columbia.

After three years of growth Imperial Oil suffered a major setback. During a thunderstorm in July, lightning hit an Imperial refinery, sparking a fire that burned its London processing operation to the ground. In 1884, when Imperial requested of the city of London a C$20,000 grant to build a new line to pipe crude from Imperial's Lambton Wells into the city, its political connections were not enough. Londoners had had enough of the flash fires and the stench rising from streams of gasoline that ran from where it was dumped on the streets down to the river. Gasoline, a useless by-product of kerosene, created problems elsewhere as well. Some refiners, trying to get the most dollars per barrel, illegally cut kerosene with gasoline, causing lamps not infrequently to explode when ignited. It is believed that gasoline mixed in with lamp kerosene started the Great Chicago Fire. Rather than rebuilding in what it felt to be a now-hostile London, Imperial moved its head offices first to Petrolia then to Sarnia, Ontario. Within a short time almost all related industries followed Imperial from London to Sarnia, which was becoming the new oil center.

By 1893 Imperial had 23 branch offices spread from Halifax to Victoria. Imperial had done such a good job developing new markets that it could no longer supply the demands of the market. Imperial lacked the money necessary to expand to meet its consumers' needs, and feared losing market share to larger U.S. companies. Unable to convince Canadian or British banks or private investors to gamble with large amounts of capital, in 1898 Imperial turned to the U.S. Standard Oil Company of New Jersey, who had offered to purchase Imperial years earlier. On Dominion Day in 1898, Standard Oil (now called Exxon) assumed a majority interest in Imperial. Imperial took over Standard Oil's Canadian assets on February 23, 1899, including its refinery in Sarnia. Standard worked to keep its ownership of Imperial secret, giving Canadian government officials Imperial Oil stock as hush money.

After laying a pipeline to bring in its crude from Petrolia, Imperial was ready to start servicing all of Canada, producing 143 cubic meters per day at its Sarnia plant alone. Imperial's business got another boost with the growing popularity of the automobile. By 1910 there were about 6,000 of these gasoline-consuming machines prowling Canadian streets. Gasoline, a by-product of kerosene that previously had been thrown away, became a product in such demand that oil companies were not prepared to dispense it at a rate sufficient to satisfy demand. People bought gas in open buckets from grocery stores or even went to the oil companies' warehouses. The first service station got its start when a car pulled up to Imperial's Vancouver warehouse in between the horse-drawn oil wagons, and backfired. By the time the workers had gotten their horses settled, the foreman had banished automobiles forever. C.M. Rolston, Imperial's Vancouver manager, solved the problem the next day when he opened up Canada's first service station, a one-room metal shack with a garden hose and a water tank full of gasoline.

Building a service station did not, however, meet all the demands awakened by automobiles. The use of automobiles increased so rapidly, that Imperial almost immediately was forced to begin looking for ways to increase its supply of crude, to produce more gasoline. In 1914 Standard licensed Imperial to use its cracking technique, a process that yielded much more gasoline per barrel of crude, and installed the first units in its Sarnia refineries. Cracking involved the use of heat and pressure coils to chemically decompose the crude. In that same year, it formed the International Petroleum Company, Limited, to search for oil in South America; ordered an exploratory geological party to Turner Valley to confirm the discovery of crude near Calgary; laid a pipeline from Sarnia to Cygnet, Ohio, connecting Imperial refineries to some of the most productive oil fields in the United States; and built the first refinery in British Columbia, on Burrard Inlet. Before long World War I broke out, creating a whole new market hungry for gasoline.

In 1919 the Imperial Oil Company, Limited changed its name to Imperial Oil Limited. To meet the new demands of war, Imperial grew rapidly. Within five years it quintupled the number of its refineries and doubled its refining capacity. By 1920 there were four times as many cars in Canada as five years prior, and once again Imperial began to search for more efficient ways to refine gasoline. In 1923 Imperial obtained Canadian rights to use pressure stills, which enhanced the cracking process, yielding a greater quantity and quality of gasoline.

In 1924 Imperial hired R.K. Stratford, its first research worker. He discovered that sulfur corrosion of the cracking coils could be prevented by adding lime to the crude. He also came up with a way to keep gasoline from gumming up engines by running the cracked product through a slurry of clay.

The 1930s, for Imperial, were full of changes. Previously geologists searching for oil depended on a hammer, a chisel, maybe a pair of field glasses, and a lot of luck. In the 1920s, the rotary drill rig came along, and it became possible to drill deeper beneath the surface. The biggest change did not come until the 1930s, when Imperial started investigating the possibilities of seismology. Its geologist bounced shock waves off of underground rocks, and judging from the waves' reflection, the shape and size of possible oil formations could be determined. Imperial had started implementing these procedures, before the outbreak of World War II, when the Allies needed all the fuel they could get.

Imperial was able to produce a large amount of the 87-octane aviation fuel that the Commonwealth Air Training Plan needed for its training aircraft by selecting crude oils containing the most useful fractions and by modifying its distillation equipment. Imperial also helped to produce 100-octane aviation fuel for combat aircraft. The company aided in the development of portable runways, which could be rolled up, taken to a flat field almost anywhere, and laid in place. Imperial was a key player in Operation Shuttle, which kept oil flowing to Great Britain for a full two years before the United States entered the war.

Alaska's importance grew when Japan entered the war, and airports popped up there for U.S. defense. In 1942 the U.S. Army requested that Imperial build a refinery in the Yukon at Whitehorse, to supply the Alaskan airfields. By 1944 a ten-centimeter pipeline snaked out from the Whitehorse refinery to supply the much-needed fuel for a full year before the war ended.

When the war ended Imperial welcomed back its employees who had served. Throughout the war, Imperial had made up the difference between military pay and salaries at Imperial when military pay was lower. On enlistment, Imperial had given its employees one month's salary as a bonus.

In 1946 Imperial sold 6.275 million cubic meters of crude, more than any previous year. The company's officers realizing that there had been no meaningful field discoveries since 1920, launched a full-scale exploration to assure supplies for the future.

At the end of the 1940s, 90% of all crude oil refined in Canada was imported. Imperial drilled 133 consecutive dry holes. The future looked so bad that Imperial was debating the expensive conversion of natural gas to gasoline. If things did not change, it decided, it would have to close its Sarnia refinery and rely on off-shore crude shipped in to Montreal. Before Imperial shut down Sarnia and began building in Montreal, however, the company's leadership decided to drill once more in the Hinge Belt, south of Edmonton. Seismograph crews picked a sight in Leduc. On February 13, 1947, the Leduc well gushed oil in huge quantities. The extent of Leduc's success is best measured by the fact that the wells that quickly sprouted up in that area provided 90% of all oil produced in Canada. With Leduc's success came the call for a neighboring refinery. Imperial dismantled the idled Whitehorse refinery and reassembled it in nearby Edmonton.

With the Leduc strike, domestic oil production was so greatly increased that Imperial began searching for ways to export it. To aid in exportation, Imperial and others joined to form Interprovincial Pipe Line Limited in 1949. Imperial owned 49.9% of Interprovincial's stock. By autumn of 1950, a pipeline had been laid from Edmonton, Ontario, to Superior, Wisconsin. Imperial still holds the most shares of any owner. In 1957 the line was extended to Toronto, then in 1976 it stretched to Montreal.

The surplus of oil in the 1950s and price wars that ensued lead Imperial to analyze gasoline markets, eliminate unprofitable stations, and set up stations in the right places—some were simple gas stations, others were full-service auto "clinics." Imperial was responsible for introducing Canada's first car clinic complete with electronic diagnosis. It was not long before highway service stations became a familiar sight, offering everything from gas to snacks. In 1970 self-service stations began popping up under the Esso name, Imperial's brand name.

Canadian gas and oil reserves once again had begun to dwindle as demand continued to grow. Imperial went so far as to explore the far northern waters off Canada's eastern coast. In January 1970 that extremely expensive search paid off when Imperial hit medium-gravity, low-sulfur crude at Atkinson Point, on the Beaufort Sea in the western Arctic, 1,700 meters deep. As a result of this and other offshore searches Imperial pioneered the artificial island. The first artificial island, Immerl, was built by Imperial at the cost of $5 million, not including the cost of the well, which turned out to be dry. The off-shore oil search continues both in the farther north Queen Elizabeth Islands as well as in the Atlantic seabed.

One of Imperial's most important steps toward growth happened in the late 1980s. In 1988 Imperial began talking to Texaco Canada about a possible merger. In February 1989 Imperial bought Texaco Canada, now McColl-Frontenac Inc., for C$4.96 billion, making it the largest acquisition in Imperial's history and the second-largest in Canada's. The actual merger did not take place until February 1990; it was held up awaiting approval from the Canadian competition authorities.

Two consequences of this merger are noteworthy. The sum of productivity and profits of both companies operating independently is surpassed by those of the two operating together as a whole, creating a synergy. Employees of both companies have been looked to for answers to problems of operations and for suggestions for changes. One of the most remarkable features of the merger was the speed with which Imperial was able to reduce the initial debt incured by the merger, taking it from C$4.96 billion to C$3.1 in 1989.

Imperial is much more than simply its Esso stations. From its beginning Imperial's interests have branched through all aspects of the business, including the manufacture of wagons, barrels and lamps, as well as chemicals for their treatment plants. Most of Imperial's sales are to industrial customers. It is the leading manufacturer of aviation fuel, marine fuel, railway lubricants, and domestic heating fuels in Canada. It also has petrochemical interests, and its subsidiaries market such things as vinyl siding, plastics, and ropes. Esso Chemical has more than a dozen operations in Canada. Imperial has not ignored the natural resources segment of its business, mining as it does coal, zinc, and uranium.

Imperials' relationship with the environment also has changed since the early days when it dumped gasoline and suffered flash fires in London. In 1989 its crisis-management team allocated C$8 million to be invested over three years to improve its response to oil spills at its offshore sites. That same year it simulated a large tanker spill to test its response capabilities. Imperial's relationship with the Canadian community is no less impressive. Imperial makes news not for oil spills and environmental disasters, but for its support of education and innovative employee assistance programs.

Principal Subsidiaries: Esso Resources Canada Limited; Esso Resources N.W.T. Limited; Esso Resources (1989) Limited; McColl Frontenac Inc.; 160440 Canada Limited.

Further Reading: Malone, Mary, "Imperial Beginnings," *London Magazine,* December 1986; "The Story of Imperial," Toronto, Imperial Oil, Ltd., [n.d.].

—Maya Sahafi

INDIAN OIL CORPORATION LTD.

Indian Oil Bhavan
G9, Ali Yavar Jung Marg
Bandra (East), Bombay 400051
India
(22) 350 833

State-Owned Company
Incorporated: 1964
Employees: 32,000
Sales: Rs126.00 billion (US$6.94 billion)

The Indian Oil Corporation, a 100% state-owned company, is the largest commercial organization in India and ranks among the 100 largest industrial corporations in the world. Since 1959, this refining, marketing, and international trading company has served the Indian state with the important task of reducing India's dependence on foreign oil and thus conserving valuable foreign exchange. Exploration and production are reserved largely for two other government organizations, the Oil and Natural Gas Commission (ONGC) and Oil India Ltd.

Indian Oil owes its origins to the Indian government's conflicts with foreign-owned oil companies in the period immediately following India's independence in 1947. The leaders of the newly independent state found that much of the country's oil industry was effectively in the hands of a private monopoly led by a combination of British-owned oil companies Burmah and Shell and U.S. companies Standard-Vacuum and Caltex.

An indigenous Indian industry barely existed. During the 1930s, a small number of Indian oil traders had managed to trade outside the international cartel. They imported motor spirit, diesel, and kerosene, mainly from the Soviet Union, at less than world market prices. Supplies were irregular, and they lacked marketing networks that could effectively compete with the multinationals.

Burmah-Shell entered into price wars against these independents, causing protests in the national press, which demanded government-set minimum and maximum prices for kerosene—a basic cooking and lighting requirement for India's people—and motor spirit. No action was taken, but some of the independents managed to survive until World War II, when they were taken over by the colonial government for wartime purposes.

During the war the supply of petroleum products in India was regulated by a committee in London. Within India, a committee under the chairmanship of the general manager of Burmah-Shell and composed of oil company representatives pooled the supply and worked out a set price. Prices were regulated by the government, and the government coordinated the supply of oil in accordance with defense policy.

Wartime rationing lasted until 1950, and a shortage of oil products continued until well after independence. The government's 1948 Industrial Policy Resolution declared the oil industry to be an area of the economy that should be reserved for state ownership and control, and stipulated that all new units should be government-owned unless specifically authorized. India remained effectively tied to a colonial supply system, however. Oil could only be afforded if imported from a country in the sterling area rather than from countries where it had to be paid for in dollars. In 1949 India asked the oil companies of Britain and the United States to offer advice on a refinery project to make the country more self-sufficient in oil. The joint technical committee advised against the project and said it could only be run at a considerable loss.

The oil companies were prepared to consider building two refineries, but only if these refineries were allowed to sell products at a price 10% above world parity price. The government refused, but within two years an event in the Persian Gulf caused the companies to change their minds and build the refineries. The companies had lost their huge refinery at Abadan in Iran to Prime Minister Mussadegh's nationalization decree and were unable to supply India's petroleum needs from a sterling area country. With the severe foreign exchange problems created, the foreign companies feared new Iranian competition within India. Even more important, the government began to discuss setting up a refinery by itself.

Between 1954 and 1957 two refineries were built by Burmah-Shell and Standard-Vacuum at Bombay, and another was built at Vizagapatnam by Caltex. During the same period the companies found themselves in increasing conflict with the government.

The government came into disagreement with Burmah Oil over the Nahorkatiya oil field shortly after its discovery in 1953. It refused Burmah the right to refine or market this oil and insisted on joint ownership in crude production. Burmah then temporarily suspended all exploration activities in India.

Shortly afterward, the government accused the companies of charging excessive prices for importing oil. The companies also refused to refine Soviet oil that the government had secured on very favorable terms. The government was impatient with the companies' reluctance to expand refining capacity or train sufficient Indian personnel. In 1958, the government formed its own refinery company, Indian Refineries Ltd. With Soviet and Romanian assistance, the company was able to build its own refineries at Noonmati, Barauni, and Koyali. Foreign companies were told that they would not be allowed to build any new refineries unless they agreed to a majority shareholding by the Indian government.

In 1959, the Indian Oil Company was founded as a statutory body. At first, its objective was to supply oil products to Indian state enterprise. Then it was made responsible for the sale of the products of state refineries. After a 1961 price war with the foreign companies, it emerged as the nation's major marketing body for the export and import of oil and gas.

Growing Soviet imports led the foreign companies to respond with a price war in August 1961. At this time, Indian Oil had no retail outlets and could sell only to bulk consumers. The oil companies undercut Indian Oil's prices and left it with storage problems. Indian Oil then offered even lower prices. The foreign companies were the ultimate losers because the government was persuaded that a policy of allowing Indian Oil dominance in the market was correct. This policy allowed Indian Oil the market share of the output of all refineries that were partly or wholly owned by the government. Foreign oil companies would only be allowed such market share as equaled their share of refinery capacity.

In September 1964, Indian Refineries Ltd. and the Indian Oil Company were merged to form the Indian Oil Corporation. The government announced that all future refinery partnerships would be required to sell their products through Indian Oil.

It was widely expected that Indian Oil and ONGC would eventually be merged into a single state monopoly company. Both companies have grown vastly in size and sales volume but, despite close links, they have remained separate. ONGC has retained control of most of the country's exploration and production capacity. Indian Oil has remained responsible for refining and marketing.

During this same decade, India found that rapid industrialization meant a large fuel bill, which was a steady drain on foreign exchange. To meet the crisis, the government prohibited imported petroleum and petroleum product imports by private companies. In effect, Indian Oil was given a monopoly on oil imports.

A policy of state control was reinforced by India's closer economic and political links with the Soviet Union and its isolation from the mainstream of western multinational capitalism. Although India identified its international political stance as nonaligned, the government became increasingly friendly with the Soviet Bloc, because the United States and China were seen as too close to India's major rival, Pakistan. India and the USSR entered into a number of trade deals. One of the most important of these trade pacts allowed Indian Oil to import oil from the USSR and Romania at prices lower than those prevailing in world markets and to pay in local currency, rather than dollars or other convertible currencies.

For a time, no more foreign refineries were allowed. By the mid-1960s, government policy was modified to allow expansions of foreign-owned refinery capacity. The Indian Oil Corporation worked out barter agreements with major oil companies in order to facilitate distribution of refinery products.

In the 1970s, the Oil and Natural Gas Commission of India, with the help of Soviet and other foreign companies, made several important new finds off the west coast of India, but this increased domestic supply was unable to keep up with demand. When international prices rose steeply after the 1973 Arab oil boycott, India's foreign exchange problems mounted. Indian Oil's role as the country's monopoly buyer gave the company an increasingly important role in the economy. While the Soviet Union continued to be an important supplier, Indian Oil also bought Saudi, Iraqi, Kuwaiti, and United Arab Emirate oil. India became the largest single purchaser of crude on the Dubai spot market.

The government decided to nationalize the country's remaining refineries. The Burmah-Shell refinery at Bombay and the Caltex refinery at Vizagapatnam were taken over in 1976. The Burmah-Shell refinery became the main asset of a new state company, Bharat Petroleum Ltd. Caltex Oil Refining (India) Ltd. was amalgamated with another state company, Hindustan Petroleum Corporation Ltd., in March 1978. Hindustan had become fully Indian-owned on October 1, 1976, when Esso's 26% share was bought out. On October 14, 1981, Burmah Oil's remaining interests in the Assam Oil Company were nationalized, and Indian Oil took over its refining and marketing activities. Half of India's 12 refineries belonged to Indian Oil. The other half belonged to other state-owned companies.

By the end of the 1980s, India's oil consumption continued to grow at 8% per year, and Indian Oil expanded its capacity to about 150 million barrels of crude per annum. In 1989, Indian Oil announced plans to build a new refinery at Pradip and modernize the Digboi refinery, India's oldest. However, the government's Public Investment Board refused to approve a 120,000 barrels-per-day refinery at Daitari in Orissa because it feared future over-capacity.

In the 1990s Indian Oil refines, produces, and transports petroleum products throughout India. Indian Oil produces crude oil, base oil, formula products, lubricants, greases, and other petroleum products. It is organized into three divisions. The refineries and pipelines division has six refineries, located at Gwahati, Barauni, Gujarat, Haldia, Mathura, and Digboi. Together, the six represent 45% of the country's refining capacity. The division also lays and manages oil pipelines. The marketing division is responsible for storage and distribution and controls about 60% of the total oil industry sales. The Assam Oil division controls the marketing and distribution activities of the formerly British-owned company.

Indian Oil has established its own research center at Faridabad near New Delhi for testing lubricants and other petroleum products. It develops lubricants under the brand names Servo and Servoprime. The center also designs fuel-efficient equipment.

The Indian Oil Corporation is not the only state-owned refining organization in India, but it is the country's largest commercial company and the inheritor of most of the role and market dominance established by its colonial predecessor, Burmah-Shell. With nearly two-thirds of oil industry sales and responsibility for the country's international oil trade, Indian Oil is likely to remain a powerful force in India.

Principal Subsidiary: Indian Oil Blending Ltd.

Further Reading: Dasgupta, Bipab, *The Petroleum Industry in India,* London, Frank Cass & Company, 1971.

—Clark Siewert

KANEMATSU CORPORATION

KANEMATSU CORPORATION

2-1, Shibaura 1-chome
Minato-ku, Tokyo 105
Japan
(03) 5440-8111
Fax: (03) 5440-6500

Public Company
Incorporated: 1967 as Kanematsu-Gosho Ltd.
Employees: 3,700
Sales: ¥5.85 trillion (US$43.08 billion)
Stock Exchanges: Tokyo Osaka Nagoya

Kanematsu was formed in April 1967 as Kanematsu-Gosho Ltd. in the merger of F. Kanematsu & Co., Ltd. and The Gosho Co., Ltd. Its name was changed to the Kanematsu Corporation as of January 1, 1990. Kanematsu Corporation is a *sogo shosha,* a general trading company, that conducts business in diversified import and export markets. Trading companies specialize in bringing together buyers and sellers of a variety of products and handling finance and transport of the resulting transaction. Kanematsu is one of the nine largest trading companies in Japan. Operating in 54 countries, it conducts trade operations in energy, foodstuffs, electronics, machinery, chemicals, textiles, precious metals, general merchandise, and construction, as well as product marketing and the development of advanced technology in the areas of biotechnology, precision metal casting, cable television, and value-added networks. In 1991 43% of sales was from chemicals and plastics, and energy; 27% was from iron and steel, and nonferrous metals; 12% was from textiles; 10% was from electronics, mechatronics, and construction and development; 6% was from foodstuffs and provisions; and 2% was from general merchandise. The company continually restructures its trading lines to keep up with changes in the world economy and shifting consumer demands in Japan.

F. Kanematsu & Co, Ltd. was established on August 15, 1889, by 44-year-old Fusijaro Kanematsu. With offices in Kobe, Japan, and a staff of seven persons, Kanematsu initially began trading operations in the Australian market. A branch office was set up in Sydney, Australia, in the following year; and a first shipment of 187 bales of Australian wool reached Japan. Trading operations expanded to include wheat, tallow, and other Australian products. In 1918 F. Kanematsu became reorganized as a joint-stock company. As Japan's international trade grew dramatically during the early years of the 20th century, F. Kanematsu extended its operations into South Africa and South America. By 1936 it had opened U.S. branch offices in New York and in Seattle, Washington, and a subsidiary in New Zealand. The Kanematsu Trading Corporation, a U.S. subsidiary, was formed in New York in 1941. Much of the trading operations of the company was curtailed during World War II, and as a trading company F. Kanematsu had little to do during the war. Expansion resumed after the war, with Kanematsu New York Inc. being formed in 1951. To adjust itself to postwar economic conditions, F. Kanematsu shifted from its traditional trade in textiles to other areas, including the overseas construction of papermaking plants. In 1961 the shares of F. Kanematsu were sold to the public and the company was listed on the Osaka Stock Exchange.

The Gosho Co., Ltd. was formed by Yohei Kitagawa as Kitagawa & Co. Ltd. in 1891 in Yokohama to engage in the import of cotton yarn. Offices subsequently were moved to Kobe and then to Osaka, where in 1905 it was organized as The Gosho Co., Ltd.; it underwent a reorganization into a joint-stock company in 1917. Direct importing of cotton began from the United States in 1906 and from India in 1907. Crawford Gosho Co., Ltd. and Gosho Corporation, U.S. subsidiaries, were formed in 1912 and 1918, respectively. Until the beginning of World War II, Gosho continued its international trading operations, with cotton as its most important product. Between 1935–1945, war years for Japan, Gosho withdrew from many international markets but continued to trade in raw materials. In 1943 it merged with Showa Cotton Co., Ltd. and Pacific Trading Co., Ltd. After World War II it began diversifying its business away from textiles. Gosho Trading Co., Ltd. was formed in Thailand in 1959.

With the 1967 merger of the two companies into Kanematsu-Gosho Ltd., the surviving firm moved into the top ranks of Japanese trading companies. By 1968 the new company had changed its internal organization into the present divisional structure. The head office was moved to Tokyo in 1970. Shares of the company's stock were listed on the Tokyo and Nagoya stock exchanges in 1973. Sales for the fiscal year ended March 31, 1974, reached the ¥1 trillion for the first time. Subsidiary companies were formed in Canada in 1972, France in 1973, and Hong Kong in 1975; an office was opened in Beijing in 1979. The oil-price shocks of the 1970s caused difficulties for the company, as they did for much of the Japanese economy. Structural improvements and several long-range plans restored profitability by the end of the 1980s.

As with all Japanese trading companies, Kanematsu-Gosho continued to seek new investment opportunities throughout the world. In 1986, for example, it filled an order with the People's Republic of China for ¥700 million worth of equipment for manufacturing semiconductors; in 1989 it took a 25% interest in a joint venture with Nishimbo Industries Inc. in constructing and operating the first cotton textile mill ever in California and also began participation in Kanebo Spinning Inc., a mill in Georgia. The company also became a player in world money markets when, in 1989, US$130 million in dollar-denominated bonds with stock options were sold in the European financial market, and 25 million shares of new stock were issued at prevailing market prices. In 1990, convertible notes worth SFr200 million were issued. Subsidiaries were formed in the United Kingdom in 1989, in Spain in 1990, and in Italy in 1991, with branch offices being opened in

Bucharest, Warsaw, and Berlin in 1990. Also in 1990, Kanematsu-Gosho changed its name to Kanematsu Corporation. At the end of its 1990 fiscal year, the company continued trading and sales through a number of operating divisions.

The machinery division deals with a wide group of products such as industrial plants, power stations, telecommunications systems, factory automation systems, machine tools, pulp and paper machinery, textile machinery, construction machinery, banking machines, industrial sewing machines, aircraft, marine vessels, and automobiles. The division provides support services for the installation and financing of these products. During 1990, the division exported sewing machines, carbon rod processing equipment, and a motor factory to the Soviet Union; two chemical tankers to Taiwan; and a plywood plant to Indonesia. Its domestic sales included British-made fighter aircraft to the Japanese government, particleboard and power-generating plants, and a pulp-processing system. The division's transportation machinery department exports Honda automobiles to several countries, including Yugoslavia and the Soviet Union.

The electronics division markets IBM computers and peripherals, telecommunications equipment, semiconductor devices and semiconductor-manufacturing equipment, liquid-crystal devices, and printed circuit boards. Its effort in these areas also emphasizes the creation of software for use in the products it sells for local area networks, computer-aided design, and computer-aided manufacturing. In a joint venture, the division built a printed-circuit board plant in France, which opened in 1990.

The energy division purchases and resells crude oil, petroleum products, liquefied petroleum gas, and other energy sources, mainly uranium and coal. As with most Japanese energy operations, petroleum operations are highly dependent on the shipments of crude from the countries whose supplies are controlled by the Organization of Petroleum Exporting Countries (OPEC). In 1990, the energy division planned to expand its operations in uranium and coal by purchasing interests in certain mines. It was also Kanematsu's intention to join with other companies in the development of energy resources.

The general merchandise division is divided into the general merchandise department and the pulp and paper department. The products the former deals with include hides, skins, and leather products, while the latter handles pulp, wood chips, other raw materials used in making paper, and papermaking equipment. The lumber division imports wood products from Africa, southeast Asia, North America, the Soviet Union, China, and Chile, primarily for use in housing construction.

The textiles division, the oldest part of the company's business, buys textile raw materials, yarns and fabrics, and finished products such as apparel and bedding. It operates a dress-shirt factory in Indonesia, a worsted-wool plant in Malaysia, and two mills in the United States. The foodstuffs and provisions division imports a variety of products including grain, rice oil, organic fertilizer, meat, nuts, coffee, alcoholic beverages, pet foods, and canned foods. It is the exclusive vendor in Japan of a number of wines and markets Lismore scotch whiskey.

The chemicals and plastics division deals in a variety of organic and inorganic materials, petrochemicals, and intermediate materials used for, among other products, pharmaceuticals, synthetic resins, and pulp additives. In 1989, when it was anticipated that the chemical industry would experience a period of growth, the company embarked on a program to raise the portion of its sales derived from this division by investing overseas and expanding its exports, with a goal of boosting the division's revenues 150%. A furfuryl alcohol plant in Thailand began operation under a partnership arrangement in 1990. New areas of business begun in the early 1990s included materials used in electronics and plastics.

The iron and steel division, another of the company's traditional areas of operation, provides raw materials for the steel industry and markets steel products. It operates a joint venture in the United States that produces steel cord for tires. The nonferrous metals division imports nonferrous ores and metals. It has an investment in a copper magnetic-wire plant in Indonesia. Plans were made to include involvement in gold trading. This division also acquired a diecast manufacturer, Diemakers Inc., in 1990.

The construction and development division is engaged in real estate sales, construction tenders, and sale of construction materials. With the steady growth of the Japanese economy, building construction will continue to be an expanding feature of the company's operations. In the early 1990s the division had a contract to build a country club in Fukishma.

As the structure of the world economy continues to evolve, general trading companies such as Kanematsu must continue to develop new products to trade and new strategies for how those products will be marketed. In particular, they have had to adjust their offerings as the Japanese economy has become less reliant on exports, with the domestic market becoming increasingly important for total sales. To keep abreast of these changes, in 1987 Kanematsu formed a research-and-development division to investigate new products. In 1990, it established a "Ladies Life and Living" team, an all-woman marketing group with a responsibility for anticipating the product needs of women over the next decade.

The company had shifted the emphasis of its operations during the 1980s by importing more products into Japan. In 1982, imports accounted for 24% of total sales, compared to 44% in 1991. Other categories of operations adjusted accordingly, with exports remaining 15% of total sales, domestic sales falling from 51% in 1982 to 27% in 1991, and overseas sales growing from 10% to 14% during the period. With 115 subsidiaries and affiliates in Japan and 67 overseas, Kanematsu is a worldwide operation.

Principal Subsidiaries: Eagle West Pty. Ltd. (Australia); International Sewing Machines Pty Ltd. (Australia); Yokahama Tyre Australia Pty Ltd.; Frigorifico Yukijirushi do Parana S.A. (Brazil); Western Specialty Alloys Ltd. (Canada); Tianjin Kaida Transportation Service Co., Ltd. (China); ST Pretec S.A. (France); Ajioka (H.K.) Ltd. (Hong Kong); Fashion Crew (H.K.) Ltd. (Hong Kong); Hitachi Elevator Engineering Co., (HK) Ltd. (Hong Kong); K.G. International Petroleum Ltd. (Hong Kong); Nice Orient Limited (Hong Kong); Tin Sung Co., Ltd. (Hong Kong); P.T. Century Textile Industry (Indonesia); P.T. Flex Indonesia; P.T. Honda Prospect Engine MFG Inc. (Indonesia); P.T. Imora Honda Inc. (Indonesia); P.T. Metbelosa (Indonesia); P.T. Nasiodelta Electric (Indonesia); Kyungduk Industrial Co., Ltd. (Korea); G.P.K. Wood Products Sdn. Berhad (Malaysia); Karimoku (M) Sdn. Berhad

(Malaysia); Malaysian Topmaking Mills Sdn. Berhad (Malaysia); Nankai Worsted Spinning (Malaysia) Sdn. Berhad; Perak Textile Mills Sdn. Berhad (Malaysia); Societe des Mines de Fer du Senegal Oriental; Pan Pacific Trans-Service Pte. Ltd. (Singapore); Southern Pacific Insurance Pte. Ltd. (Singapore); Chung Chi Leather Co., Ltd. (Taiwan); Song Cheng Enterprise Co., Ltd. (Taiwan); Auk Co., Ltd. (Thailand); Bangkok Metal Industry Co., Ltd. (Thailand); Boriboon Steel Industrial Co., Ltd. (Thailand); Hitachi Bangkok Cable Co., Ltd. (Thailand); Kobe Mig Wire (Thailand) Co., Ltd.; Mar Bin Trance-Service Co., Ltd. (Thailand); SKJ Metal Industries Co., Ltd. (Thailand); Summit Food Industries Co., Ltd. (Thailand); Thai-Kobe Welding Co., Ltd. (Thailand); Thai Kyowa Engineering & Construction Co., Ltd. (Thailand); KG International Trade & Finance Plc. (U.K.); CK Technologies, Inc. (U.S.A.); Diemakers Inc. (U.S.A.); Glory (U.S.A.) Inc.; Kanebo Spinning, Inc. (U.S.A.); KGK International Corp. (U.S.A.); Kokuku Steel Cord Corporation (U.S.A.); Necoa, Inc. (U.S.A.); Nisshinbo California Inc. (U.S.A.); Pan Pacific Yarn Inc. (U.S.A.); Technical Marketing Associates, Inc. (U.S.A.); KGK Corp.; Kanematsu Industrial Machinery Ltd.; Kyori Kogyo Co., Ltd.; Tahara Machinery Ltd.; Tokyo Engineering & Manufacturing Co., Ltd.; Kanematsu Aerospace Corporation; Nippon Pioneer Co., Ltd.; Nippon Skylift Co., Ltd.; UNIX Corp.; Toto Pioneer Co., Ltd.; Business Links, Ltd.; Integrated Communication Systems Co., Ltd.; Japan ADE Ltd.; Kanematsu Duo-Fast Co., Ltd.; Kanematsu Electrical Products Sales Co., Ltd.; Kanematsu Electronics Ltd.; Kanematsu Electronic Components Corp.; Kanematsu Electronics Trading Co., Ltd.; Kanematsu Lex Electronics Inc.; Kanematsu Semiconductor Corp.; Memorex Telex Japan Ltd.; Nippon Office Systems Ltd.; Kanematsu Energy Corp.; Kanematsu Oil Tank Co., Ltd.; Kanematsu Sekiyu Gas Co., Ltd.; K.G.I. Limited; Nisseki Kanematsu Co., Ltd.; Toyo Kokusai Oil Co., Ltd.; Hokushin Co., Ltd.; Kanematsu Kaneka Co., Ltd.; Maruyone Trading Co., Ltd.; Morimoku Kaisha, Ltd.; Nissan Nohrin Kogyo Co., Ltd.; Kanematsu Rex Corp.; Taiga & Co., Ltd.; Kanematsu Top Co., Ltd.; Kanematsu Woolen Mills, Ltd.; Kaneyoshi Co., Ltd.; Kyushu Weaving Co., Ltd.; LB & Co., Ltd.; Mitsuru Co., Ltd.; Ono Rug Mills Ltd.; Schi Kraft Inc.; Shimada Sen-i Co., Ltd.; Showa Garments Manufacturing Co., Ltd.; Silver Shirts "Hayase" Co., Ltd.; S. Kamei Co., Ltd.; U Textiles Co., Ltd.; Kanematsu Liquor Co., Ltd.; Heisei Feed Manufacturing Co.; Kanematsu Food Corp.; Kanematsu Kanto Nosan Co., Ltd.; Kaoh Trading Co., Ltd.; Nippon Liquor Ltd.; Gospel Chemical Industry Ltd.; Kanematsu Chemicals Co., Ltd.; Kitaura Plastics Co., Ltd.; Eiwa Kinzoku Co., Ltd.; Iwaki Steel Center Ltd.; Kanematsu Trading Corporation; Kanematsu Tekko Hanbai Ltd.; KG Minerals Ltd.; Kyowa Steel Co., Ltd.; Kyushu Koki Co., Ltd.; SLB Corporation; Yachiyo Stainless Center Ltd.; Kanematsu Metals Ltd.; Shikoku Cable Co., Ltd.; Toei Crown Co., Ltd.; Kanematsu Toshikaihatsu Co., Ltd.; Tsuzuki Concrete Industrial Corp. Central Express Ltd.; Kanematsu Boeki Service Co., Ltd.; Kanematsu Finance Corporation; Kanematsu Personnel Service Inc.; KIT Ltd.; Kanematsu Computer Systems Ltd.; Kanematsu Kanzai Co., Ltd.; Beaux-Arts S.A.; Kanematsu Fashion Crew Co., Ltd.; Fukui Yamamoto Co., Ltd.; Gosen Co., Ltd.; Kamo Trico Co., Ltd.; Kanematsu Lancot Ltd.; Kanesen Co., Ltd.

Further Reading: "March of the Middlemen," *The Economist,* September 24, 1988; *KG Monthly: Special Issue, 100th Anniversary 1989,* Tokyo, Kanematsu-Gosho Ltd., 1989.

—Donald R. Stabile

KERR-MCGEE CORPORATION

Kerr-McGee Center
Oklahoma City, Oklahoma 73125
U.S.A.
(405) 270-1313
Fax: (405) 270-3123

Public Company
Incoporated; 1932 as A&K Petroleum Company
Employees: 6,756
Sales $3.68 billion
Stock Exchanges: New York Toronto

Kerr-McGee Corporation has come a long way from its beginning as a small drilling company at the time of the Great Depression. It is one of country's more successful medium-sized integrated energy and chemical companies. Kerr-McGee has operations to find and produce chemicals, oil, coal, and natural gas, to operate refineries, and to conduct wholesaling and retailing operations.

The Depression was just around the corner when Anderson & Kerr Drilling Company was founded near Oklahoma City, Oklahoma, in July 1929. The company's assets amounted to three boilers and two steam rigs, and the company was one in many, perhaps hundreds of, small oil-related firms vying for drilling contracts in a city that was booming. The local newspaper, the *Daily Oklahoman*, in October 1929, mentioned the October stock market crash briefly under the headline, "Business Men are Unnecessarily Troubled by Crash of Stocks." This town wasn't feeling the Depression—there was oil here, and plenty of it.

While James L. Anderson handled the equipment end, Robert S. Kerr operated from a hotel room seeking drilling contracts, going home only on weekends. Anderson was said to have "a nose for oil" and the ability to drill more economically than others, and Kerr was a talented capital raiser. Financing the young company was a constant challenge. It faced rising debt, strong competition, and the need to keep busy, when Kerr, still relatively unknown, met with Frank Phillips, founder of Phillips Petroleum Company. Kerr wanted to drill some of Phillips's leases in the area, and he eventually won a contract. As Kerr's long-time associate, Rex Hawks, told John Samuel Ezell, in *Innovations in Energy: The Story of Kerr-McGee*, "As Kerr was about to leave, he turned and said, 'By the way, Mr. Phillips, there's one little item I was about to forget.' When asked what that was Kerr replied that he would

have to borrow $20,000 to sink the well. Phillips then 'cussed a little' while and exclaimed, 'You spend all this time wanting the job and haven't the money to drill it with.' Kerr 'hemmed and hawed,' but in the end Phillips called [his office] . . . and said, 'Let this damn man have $20,000 to drill this lease with.' " His bold drive and inexhaustible belief in his company kept Kerr, and the company, moving forward through times when the speculative nature of the business and the tough competition would have folded a less determined company.

In 1932 the company opened an office for its staff of 11 in Oklahoma City and was incorporated at A&K Petroleum Company. In 1935 its first public offering of 120,000 shares of common stock was made available at $5.00 per share. In 1936 when the company was negotiating a second stock offering, Anderson decided the company was growing to a size he no longer felt comfortable managing, and opted to sell his interest in the company.

The year 1937 was a critical time. The economy was in recession, oil prices were decreasing, and the money to drill was not there. The company's directors recognized a need for leadership at the executive level to move the company's exploration and production into the black. They were willing to bank a large part of their holdings on two men from Phillips Petroleum, offering them salaries that dwarfed their own by comparison. Robert Lynn became executive vice president of a company that, in these formative years, restructured and renamed its operations several times. He played a prominent role in the company, then called Kerlyn Oil Company, for five years. Dean A. McGee, the second man from Phillips, was to direct the company on a new course almost immediately. His presence was felt until his death in 1989.

McGee, who had been Phillips's chief geologist, leaned heavily on credit, faith, and hard labor. Within the year the company made its first major oil discovery—the Magnolia field in Columbia County, Arkansas. The revenues from the Magnolia discovery fueled further expansion.

Demand for oil was rising dramatically as a result of wartime needs, however, and the company struggled under debt, taxes, government restrictions, a shortage of capital and manpower, and continuing low prices for its products. Kerr and his workers continued making deals, leveraging assets, and using their best talents to keep operating. Kerlyn was chronically short of capital in its early years, and often had to stop drilling until money could be raised to continue. Much of its capital came from small contributions of $1,000 to $3,000. In 1943 a deal was struck in which Phillips Petroleum put up 75% of the cost for half a share in any Kerlyn venture in which it participated. That year, the company's exploratory drilling, or wildcatting, led to discovery of oil to the northwest of Oklahoma City, and set off the west Edmonton boom. The U.S. Bureau of Mines categorized this find as the year's "greatest addition of new oil."

In 1942, confident that the company was in capable hands, and certain that his primary role was to be played out in public office, Bob Kerr made a long-desired move into politics. That year he was elected governor of Oklahoma, and throughout successive political roles, including U.S. senator, Kerr remained an active member of the company's board until he died in 1963.

When Kerr made his move into politics, Robert Lynn decided to leave the company. From the time he arrived, McGee, with his quiet manner, and "nose for oil" had acted as a key figure in the company. He was the logical choice to move into Lynn's leadership role, and in 1946, the company changed its name to Kerr-McGee Oil Industries, Inc. McGee had become executive vice president in 1942, and was made president of Kerr-McGee in 1957.

The exploration aspect of business continued to grow as the company expanded its drilling operations to the Gulf of Mexico. Seeking to capitalize on the increased need for refined oil products, the company also moved downstream in the oil business with the purchase of its first refinery, in 1945. Downstream activities generally include transportation, refining, storage, marketing, distribution, and slop disposal—in short, all activities that follow the upstream activities of exploration and production.

In the postwar 1940s, the energy needs of the United States were rising dramatically. The country was using as much oil in one year as did the entire world in 1938. Kerr-McGee responded to this trend with many firsts in oil exploration and production, including completion of the world's first commercial oil well that was out of sight and safety of land, in 1947, 11 miles off Louisiana's shore. This marked the beginning of the nation's offshore drilling industry. The company added natural gas processing with the purchase of three plants in Oklahoma in 1951, and a fourth in Pampa, Texas, in 1952.

As the cold war escalated, so too escalated the government's need for uranium to fuel the atom-bomb program. Kerr-McGee was the first oil company to enter the uranium industry when it acquired mining properties on the Navaho reservation in Arizona in 1952. Mills were needed to process the materials; and Kerr-McGee soon moved into this area, completing its first mill in the fall of 1954. Soon thereafter the company began construction of the country's largest uranium-processing mill, which was brought on stream in 1958.

In 1955 the company moved into major retailing with its purchase of the Deep Rock Oil Corporation. Building upon an established base of service stations in the middle western states, Kerr-McGee formed a subsidiary, Deep Rock Oil Company, to continue this aspect of expansion. During this period, Kerr-McGee also expanded its refining capabilities, with the purchase of Cato Oil and Grease Company, and Triangle Refineries, a major wholesaler of petroleum products. Transworld Drilling Company Limited was formed to handle Kerr-McGee's domestic and overseas contract drilling in 1958.

The company remained strong in a very competitive industry by making use of innovative methods in its oil production. In 1961 the company was making use of drilling devices that eventually were used to drill the largest vertical shaft ever successfully drilled by rotary methods in North America at the time. In 1962 the company commissioned the world's largest submersible offshore drilling unit, and in 1963 it built its new research center in Oklahoma City, where high-level development continued.

In its drive to become a "total energy company," Kerr-McGee continued to push into other energy-related areas, entering the forestry business in 1963 with its purchase of two suppliers of railroad crossties, and acquiring several fertilizer-marketing companies in the early 1960s that, in 1965, were consolidated into Kerr-McGee Chemical Corporation.

In 1965 Kerr-McGee Oil Industries, Inc. became Kerr-McGee Corporation, a name that better represented the company's diversified holdings. Growth and expansion continued.

Although Kerr-McGee had begun doing business in industrial chemicals, its 1967 merger with American Potash and Chemical Corporation marked the company's major entry into the market. This gave the company control of 13,000 acres of a dry lake bed in Searles Valley, California, from which it began extracting brine to produce soda ash, boron products, sodium sulfate, and potash. Two industrial chemical plants were also included in the acquisition, making Kerr-McGee a major processor of a number of industrial chemicals, including the company's most profitable, titanium dioxide, a white pigment used mainly in the manufacture of paint and plastics.

In 1970 Kerr-McGee was a major player in six of the eight parts of the nuclear fuel cycle, including exploration, mining, milling, conversion of uranium oxide into uranium hexaflouride at a new Sequoya facility in eastern Oklahoma, pelletizing of these materials, and fabrication of fuel elements at its Cimarron Facility in Oklahoma.

At this time, the oil industry was undergoing major change. The Organization of Petroleum Exporting Countries's oil embargo in 1973 sent the price of gasoline and energy soaring, and the U.S. public was forced to begin conserving. It was a time of opportunity for energy companies. Even with big revenues coming in and a government bending over backward to encourage exploration and production, by deregulating and offering hefty tax credits, Kerr-McGee's performance slipped in a number of areas, losing its lead in offshore drilling, and generally suffering from a lack of managerial direction. Chairman since 1963 and CEO since 1967, Dean McGee instigated an organizational restructuring and among other changes, established two new subsidiaries, Kerr-McGee Coal Corporation led by Frank McPherson, and Kerr-McGee Nuclear Corporation led by R.T. Zitting. The restructuring was meant to give the company the strength needed to compete in the increasingly complex, turbulent world market.

Kerr-McGee's oil-exploration and -production operations did grow. In 1974 the company expanded its refining capabilities significantly, with the acquisition of the Southwestern Refining Company, Incorporated, in Corpus Christi, Texas. In 1976 the company pushed its production activity into the Arabian Gulf and the North Sea, and participated in the discovery of the Beatrice oil field, off Scotland's shore.

Coal operations began proving lucrative, when, in 1978, the first commercial deliveries of steam coal—coal used to produce steam—were made from surface mining operations in Wyoming. In the same year, soda ash production began at the company's Argus, California, facility, significantly increasing the company's industrial chemical output.

The concerns of environmentalists began to loom large in the 1970s, and litigation took up more of the company's time and money. Although there had been previous charges levied at Kerr-McGee involving worker safety and environmental contamination, the highly publicized case of Karen Silkwood, which began in 1974, highlighted the hazardous nature of nuclear energy and raised important questions regarding corporate accountability. The Oil, Chemical and Atomic Workers Union alleged that Kerr-McGee's Cimarron River plutonium plant, near Oklahoma City, was manufacturing faulty fuel rods, falsifying product inspection records, and—in certain cases—risking the safety of its employees.

Silkwood, a 28-year-old lab technician at Cimarron and one of the union's most active members, was involved in substantiating the charges before the Atomic Energy Commission. Silkwood had suffered radiation exposure in a series of unexplained incidents, and then been killed in an automobile crash while on her way to meet with an Atomic Energy Commission official and a *New York Times* reporter. Her untimely death led to speculation over foul play, which was never established, and prompted a federal investigation into safety and security at the plant. There were additional problems with worker contamination, and a National Public Radio report concerning 44 pounds to 66 pounds of misplaced plutonium. Eventually the company shut the plant down. In 1986 Karen Silkwood's family settled an $11.5 million plutonium-contamination lawsuit against Kerr-McGee for $1.38 million. Kerr-McGee did not admit liability in settling the case.

The company's nuclear-fuel-processing plant in Gore, Oklahoma, was cited by the Nuclear Regulatory Commission for 15 health and safety infractions between 1978 and 1986. In 1986 an overfilled cylinder of uranium hexafluoride exploded, releasing a toxic cloud of radioactive hydrofluoric acid. One employee died and 110 people were hospitalized. This fired public outcry, set in motion a number of legal proceedings, and was further confused when the Nuclear Regulatory Commission accused Kerr-McGee of giving a false statement during the commission's investigation of the incident.

In a *Business Week* article of February 3, 1986, it was pointed out that Kerr-McGee's uranium mining, milling, and processing operations accounted for 2% of its revenues, while costing $72 million in losses between 1982 and 1986. Aside from the environmental problems, demand had fallen off significantly. At that point, Kerr-McGee's leadership was still confident that the slump in demand would reverse itself, and its substantial uranium reserves would pay off in the 1990s.

Aside from the problems associated with uranium production, the company's oil operations were not expanding healthily. Kerr-McGee's failure to pay scientists competitive salaries through the tumultuous highly competitive 1970s proved especially harmful to the company's bread-and-butter oil exploration and production. A market-research firm estimated that between 1980 and 1984 Kerr-McGee's oil reserves fell 21% and gas reserves fell 10%. In 1986 an estimation by Morgan Stanley & Company put Kerr-McGee's average cost for finding a barrel of oil at $13.03; the average cost of 12 competitors was $7.35 per barrel.

The company, after years of expanding to fulfill its goal of becoming "the total energy company," was involved in a random variety of resource enterprises, including uranium and plutonium mining, milling, and processing; chemicals and coal; contract drilling; refining; gasoline retailing; and timber. Many analysts felt that Kerr-McGee suffered from too much diversification. Earnings went from $211 million in 1981 to $118 million in 1983. In 1983 Dean McGee stepped aside as chairman and Frank A. McPherson was named his successor.

Changes wrought by McPherson included a policy of trimming and focusing of operations and personnel. When the fertilizer market began to suffer in the 1980s, for example, he sold off the potash and phosphate mines. Perhaps most notable was McPherson's belated decision in the late 1980s to sell the company's troublesome uranium interests. He concentrated on revitalizing the company's oil and gas exploration arms, and continued to invest in its chemical and coal operations.

The fallout over environmental contamination continued, and appears to be a long-term, costly problem. Between 1984 and 1989 the company received notification that it potentially is responsible for the cleanup sites located in seven areas around the nation, and in 1990 state environmental agencies were looking at sites in four other areas. These situations were undergoing lengthy investigation, and had yet to be resolved by 1990. As lessons from the past were being learned, increased environmental responsibility had become a necessary part of Kerr-McGee's practices, as well as its future planning.

Principal Subsidiaries: Kerr-McGee Canada Ltd.; Kerr-McGee Chemical Corporation; Kerr-McGee Coal Corporation; Kerr-Mcgee Oil (U.K.) PLC; Kerr-McGee Refining Corporation.

Further Reading: Ezell, John Samuel, *Innovations in Energy: The Story of Kerr-McGee,* Norman, University of Oklahoma Press, 1979; Mack, Toni, "Playing with the majors," *Forbes,* November 13, 1989.

—Carole Healy

KOCH INDUSTRIES, INC.

Post Office Box 2256
Wichita, Kansas 67201
U.S.A.
(316) 832-5500

Private Company
Incorporated: 1942 as Rock Island Oil & Refining Company
Employees: 8,000
Sales: $16.00 billion

The second-largest privately held company in the United States, Koch Industries, Inc. is perhaps best known for being unknown. Few if any companies in the world doing $16 billion in yearly sales are as inconspicuous as Koch, which is a major oil company in all but name. The bulk of Koch's revenue is derived from the transport of oil by pipeline, truck, and ship, but it also drills, refines, markets, and trades oil and gas products in the United States and around the world. In addition, the firm has substantial coal and real estate interests, and raises many thousand head of cattle on ranches in Kansas, Montana, and Texas. About 80% of its multibillion dollar assortment of assets is owned by two of the four sons of Fred C. Koch, founder of the company, while two other sons were bought out in 1983 after a bitter and continuing struggle among the brothers for money, corporate control, and pride.

So successful has Koch been in protecting its privacy that virtually nothing in detail is known about the company's history. Fred C. Koch was the son of a Texas newspaperman who earned an engineering degree at Massachusetts Institute of Technology in the 1920s. Koch invented a new and more efficient method for the thermal cracking of crude oil, the process in which oil is heated to effect a recombination of molecules yielding higher proportions of usable compounds, especially gasoline. With the dramatic growth in the use of the automobile in the first quarter of the 20th century, refiners constantly were trying to improve their cracking technology, and Fred Koch's innovation was apparently good enough to draw upon him the wrath of the major oil companies. Jealous of their tight control over every aspect of the oil business, the majors began a series of lawsuits against Fred Koch that would last 20 years and involve over 40 separate cases. Then as now, the international oil business was in the hands of only a few firms, which meant that Fred Koch would encounter the same obstacles wherever oil was bought and sold.

In the late 1920s there was at least one country in the world where oil was not bought and sold, in the usual sense—the Soviet Union. The Soviets had been trying to take advantage of their immense oil reserves since gaining power in 1917, and under Josef Stalin the drive to industrial efficiency was pursued with ruthless speed but without the benefit of Western technology. Fred Koch offered to build oil refineries in the Soviet Union more efficient than those in the West. The young engineer's ideas were welcomed, and he was awarded a large contract to coincide with Stalin's first five-year plan, beginning in 1929. The contract called for construction of 15 refineries for an initial fee of $5 million, from which Koch and his partner, L.E. Winkler, are said to have netted a $500,000 profit. Koch's work in the Soviet Union necessitated sojourns in that country, offering the Texas farmboy an intimate look at the Soviet system while providing the cash he would later need in building his U.S. empire.

By the late 1940s Koch had achieved a truce with his adversaries in the oil industry and begun assembling bits and pieces of business in the midwestern United States. Having been burned severely by the majors the first time around, Koch carefully avoided head-to-head competition with the industry leaders, instead developing a knack for discovering unexploited niches and an ability to turn a profit on even the smallest orders. In an age of massive, worldwide integration in the oil industry, Koch concentrated on service businesses too small to interest the majors and too obscure to attract much competition. While the majors largely controlled oil at the wellhead, they still required an ever-growing network of pipelines and trucks to convey the oil to the refinery, thence to the mass of distributors, wholesalers, and retailers involved in its final sale. As the country's dependence on oil grew, so too did the need for more complete systems of oil distribution, and Fred Koch amassed a fortune in providing the equipment and expertise to meet that need.

Koch's main vehicle in the oil business was a company called Rock Island Oil & Refining Company, based in Wichita, Kansas. While busy picking up bargains in businesses from trucks to coal mines, Koch fiercely guarded the privacy of his company, ensuring that it would not only remain under family control but far from the prying eyes of government and the media alike. It is reported that a number of Koch's good friends in the Soviet oil industry were liquidated during Stalin's purges of the 1930s, an experience that only confirmed his belief, perhaps originally instilled by the battering he took at the hands of big oil, that business is best conducted silently. Rock Island Oil & Refining had no public relations department, having no relations with the public, and the Koch family went out of its way to avoid doing business with the government. Fred Koch's particular aversion to Soviet communism took a more direct form in 1958 when he helped found the John Birch Society, an ultra–right wing group soon to become notorious for its warnings about the threat of communists to U.S. society. Charles Koch, the second of Fred Koch's four sons, would later pour millions of dollars into the Libertarian Party, a proponent of minimal governmental interference in the affairs of business.

Like his father, Charles Koch earned an engineering degree at Massachusetts Institute of Technology, and then spent several years working for a business consulting firm before joining Rock Island Oil in 1961. Frederick Koch, Fred Koch's eldest son, did not participate in the oil business. Charles Koch took over leadership of Koch Engineering, one of the family's many concerns, and helped make it into the world's largest manufacturer of mass transfer equipment for the chemical industry. By the time of Fred Koch's death in 1967, sales at Rock Island and the various Koch subsidiaries had reached about $400 million, presenting the 32-year-old Charles Koch with a weighty responsibility. Charles Koch was not only a capable leader in his own right but also enjoyed the continued presence of his father's top aide, Sterling Varner. Varner had already won a reputation as a shrewd buyer of what he referred to as "junk," the bankrupt or unwanted oil and gas properties that Rock Island habitually turned into profitable acquisitions. Under the ambitious administration of Charles Koch, Varner kept a low profile but widely is credited with supplying the savvy behind the company's rapid expansion.

Charles Koch brought a young man's energy to the company. From the new Wichita corporate headquarters of the renamed Koch Industries, Charles Koch oversaw his company's diversification into a number of new areas, including petrochemicals, oil trading services, and ownership of a refinery in St. Paul, Minnesota. In 1969 Koch Industries merged with Atlas Petroleum Limited of the Bahamas, a distributor of crude oil and petroleum products with about $100 million a year in sales. The next few years saw the arrival at Koch of Charles' twin younger brothers, William and David, both of whom took executive positions with the company. While sharing their fathers' basic preference for privacy, the brothers gradually let it be known that Koch Industries was a far larger concern than imagined. In 1974 the family admitted to owning some 10,000 miles of pipeline in the midwestern United States and Canada, hundreds of tank trucks, barges, deep-water terminals, and storage facilities of every description. Through this system Koch distributed about 800,000 barrels of oil each day, some of it refined at its St. Paul refinery, some sold via the company's several hundred gas stations, but most of it transported to and from the major oil companies. Koch also participated in the rush to buy supertankers, owning a handful of the huge ships to complement its oil trading offices in eight countries. Finally, the company had begun its own program of oil exploration and drilling, and also owned around 60,000 head of cattle. Sales reached more than $2 billion in 1974, the first full year of post-OPEC price inflation in the oil business.

The OPEC price hikes of the early 1970s effectively killed the supertanker business, however, forcing Koch to sell all but one of its ships at salvage prices. The dramatic run-up in oil prices during the 1970s helped Koch increase its revenue sevenfold in a matter of years, however. By 1981 its sales had reached $14 billion, 56 times their level in 1967, Charles Koch's first year as head of the company, and in some quarters Koch was beginning to be called an oil major in its own right. The company picked up a second refinery in 1981, paying $265 million for a Sun Company plant in Texas, and had greatly expanded its capacity in gas-liquids fractionating and asphalt production, to name only two of its myriad activities. While Koch had little luck in its exploration efforts, in 1979 the company moved decisively into the real estate business, joining Wichita businessman George Ablah in the formation of Abko Realty Inc. Abko was created specifically to buy Chrysler Realty Corporation and its several hundred Chrysler dealership sites around the country. It is believed that the hard pressed Chrysler sold the unit for less than $100 million in cash.

The year 1979 also marked the beginning of the feud that eventually would split the Koch family. William Koch, five years younger than Charles, grew restive with his secondary role at Koch and began pressing his brother for more power, freer access to information, and some means by which a fair market value could be assigned to the company's stock. As a private company, the only likely buyers of Koch stock were other stockholders, who, in the absence of an open market, would pay far less than the shares might otherwise fetch. William Koch gained the support of the oldest brother, Frederick, until then relatively uninvolved in company affairs, and the two of them launched a proxy fight in 1980 aimed at ousting Charles from his leadership. The attempt failed, and after a round of lawsuits and mudslinging, William and Frederick Koch were bought out in 1983 by Charles and David Koch for around $1 billion in cash. Since that time, William Koch has continued to wage legal and emotional warfare against Charles Koch, going so far as to hire private detectives to gather evidence of wrongdoing by Koch Industries that was subsequently handed over to federal investigators. In 1987 the Justice Department announced it was investigating several companies on price-fixing charges, a Koch unit among them.

At last count, Koch Industries sales had risen to $16 billion and net income stood at about $400 million. Koch remains a largely unknown giant in the oil business. Its strength continues to be its ability to collect the many small pieces of business not already locked up by the majors and weld them together into a profitable whole. In an industry dependent on mass production and transfer of product, there are indeed many such scattered opportunities in every phase of the gas and oil field. Koch has become a major player by winning the minor prizes, and its diverse holdings of pipelines, trucks, manufacturing plants, storage facilities, and refineries together constitute one of the world's great private fortunes; as well as one of the most private of the world's great fortunes.

Further Reading: "Koch Industries, Inc.: Sons make a global enterprise flower in Kansas," *Nation's Business,* February, 1970; "High Profit, Low Profile," *Forbes,* July 15, 1974; Kraar, Louis, "Family Feud at a Corporate Colossus," *Fortune,* July 26, 1982; Tomsho, Robert, "Koch Family Is Roiled By Sibling Squabbling Over Its Oil Empire," *The Wall Street Journal,* August 9, 1989.

—Jonathan Martin

KUWAIT PETROLEUM CORPORATION

Salhia Complex
Fahed Al Salem Street
Post Office Box 26565
Safat 13126
Kuwait
245-5455

State-Owned Company
Incorporated: 1980 as Kuwait Petroleum Company
Employees: 15,354 (1988)
Sales: KD2.90 billion (US$9.86 billion) (1988)

Kuwait Petroleum Corporation is the state-owned holding company for all state-owned companies active in the different sectors of the Kuwait oil industry, the largest of that is Kuwait National Petroleum Company. Before Iraq invaded Kuwait on August 2, 1990, KPC was the most dynamic of the Arab national oil companies. Its ambitious strategy of integration during the 1980s made it a mini oil major, and a serious competitor to the U.S. and U.K. oil companies which had once dominated the international oil industry.

Although KPC was established only in January 1980, it took over a number of companies that had been active in Kuwait for much longer. The most important of these was the Kuwait Oil Company, which was incorporated in London, on February 2, 1934, with an initial issued capital of £50,000 owned in equal shares by the Anglo-Persian Oil Company—later Anglo-Iranian Oil Company and then British Petroleum Company (BP)—and Gulf Oil Corporation of the United States. On December 23 of the same year, the ruler of Kuwait granted an exclusive concession to the Kuwait Oil Company (KOC), to explore for, produce, and market Kuwait's oil. The concession covered the whole country and was to last for 75 years. The formation of Kuwait Oil had been in part the result of a prolonged diplomatic dispute between Britain, the dominant power in the Middle East, and the United States, which supported U.S. oil companies' claims to participate in petroleum development in the region. The KOC formed part of a network of consortia of major U.K. and U.S. oil companies that controlled the middle eastern oil industry, and that had made its first appearance in the Iraq Petroleum Company formed in 1928.

KOC began drilling for oil in 1936. Oil had been discovered in Iraq in 1927 and in Bahrain in 1932, and it was widely believed that Kuwait held equally good prospects. In May 1936 the first drilling began at Bahra, in north Kuwait, but eventually reached 7,950 feet without producing oil. Meanwhile, drilling had also started in October 1937, at Burgan, in south Kuwait. On the night of February 23, 1938, the drillers struck high-pressure oil in large quantities. This was the start of the Kuwait oil industry. Eight more wells were drilled at Burgan before July 1942, when all operations had to be suspended and all completed wells plugged with cement, because of the wartime emergency. After World War II ended in 1945, operations resumed, and in June 1946 the first Kuwaiti oil exports began.

Between 1946 and 1950 Kuwaiti oil production grew from 5.93 million barrels to 125.72 million barrels, making Kuwait the third-biggest middle eastern oil producer after Iran and Saudi Arabia. However, the real breakthrough came with the cessation of oil exports from Iran between 1951 and 1954 because of the dispute between the Iranian government and the Anglo-Iranian Oil Company. KOC rapidly increased Kuwaiti output to replace the Iranian crude. By 1955 it had 185 producing wells in operation in Kuwait, and annual production had reached nearly 400 million barrels, the highest output in the Middle East. Throughout almost all of the next 15 years, Kuwaiti oil production retained this leading position, until it was gradually overtaken by Saudi Arabia and Iran toward the end of the 1960s.

Oil transformed Kuwait. In the 1930s the country was largely desert, with most of its population of 70,000 concentrated around the mud-walled trading and fishing port of Kuwait town. An average annual rainfall of four inches and a lack of irrigation permitted little agriculture. Almost all food and all drinking water were imported, and the economy was based on pearl fishing, shipbuilding, and entrepôt trade. Oil revenues transformed the situation, especially after 1952 when it was agreed that the net profits of the industry would be shared evenly between Kuwait and the oil companies. By 1961 Kuwait, with a total population of 320,000, of whom only 50% were nationals, had one of the highest per capita incomes in the world. Nationals were given free medical treatment and free education, and the infrastructure of an advanced welfare state was created.

This wealth did nothing to reduce a growing irritation in Kuwait—and elsewhere—with Western control over its oil resources. The consortium system limited the bargaining power of host governments, for they faced only one producer. Iran's dispute in 1951 with the Anglo-Iranian Oil Company was just the first sign of general resentment at the system which spread throughout the Middle East in the 1950s and 1960s. In 1958 the Kuwaiti government granted a concession to the Arabian Oil Company, a Japanese venture in which the Kuwaiti government had a 10% shareholding. In 1960 Kuwait joined the Organization of Petroleum Exporting Countries (OPEC) as a founder member. OPEC's objective was to unify and coordinate the petroleum policies of its members and protect their interests against the Western oil companies. In the same year, the government organized the Kuwait National Petroleum Company (KNPC) as a joint enterprise owned 60% and 40% by the government and private sectors, respectively. For the next two decades, this element of private ownership distinguished KNPC from most other national oil companies in the Middle East. In 1962 KOC was made to relinquish 60% of the areas included in its concession to KNPC.

During the 1960s the Kuwaiti government sought to increase the share of oil income staying in Kuwait, especially by promoting downstream development. The government attempted to persuade KOC to begin refining operations, but the company resisted. Economically, there was an overwhelming case for locating refineries near centers of consumption rather than of production, and the vast majority of new refining capacity installed in the decades after World War II was in Western Europe and the United States. However KOC, like the other Western oil companies in this period, underestimated the extent to which nationalist feelings were growing, even in conservative and pro-western states such as Kuwait and Saudi Arabia. Kuwait also had a special interest in building refining capacity. It would not only provide for technology transfer into Kuwait and create jobs, but by using advanced refinery technology it could counterbalance Kuwait's relatively weak export position, the result of its rather poor-quality crude oil. Eventually KNPC decided to enter refining itself, and it started operating a refinery at Shuaibia—near the oil pipeline terminal—in 1968.

The Western oil consortia in the Middle East collapsed in the early 1970s during a dramatic restructuring of the industry. The most obvious manifestation of the restructuring was the huge rise in world oil prices in 1973. During the opening years of the 1970s, there was a rush of agreements designed to give producer-governments a stake in oil companies. In 1974 one such participation agreement transferred 60% of KOC's ownership to the state of Kuwait, the remaining 40% being divided equally between BP and Gulf Oil. In 1975 the Kuwaiti government took over this remaining 40%. In 1976 the Kuwait Oil Tanker Co. (KOTC), established in 1957 by private Kuwaiti interests, was converted to 49% state ownership, and it was fully nationalized in 1979. Also in 1976, a minority private sector shareholding in Petrochemical Industries Co. (PIC), established in 1963, was similarly bought out.

In January 1980 Kuwait Petroleum Company (KPC) was established as a holding company responsible for the overall management of this group of companies, together with the government's share of the capital of the Arabian Oil Company of Japan. Operations were rationalized, with KOC restricting its activities to exploration and production, and KNPC to refining and distribution. In 1981 KPC established two new companies, the Kuwait Foreign Petroleum Exploration Company (KUFPEC)—a subsidiary empowered to undertake crude oil and natural gas exploration, development, and production operations outside Kuwait—and the Kuwait International Petroleum Investment Co., owned 70% by KPC and 30% by private Kuwaiti investors and empowered to engage in refining and petrochemical operations outside Kuwait.

KPC developed an ambitious strategy to integrate its oil industry from the well-head to the petrol pump in consumer countries. Considerable attention was given to expanding and upgrading Kuwait's refinery capacity, in order to enhance Kuwait's ability to respond rapidly to changes in the pattern of export demand. By 1983 the share of product exports in total oil exports was more than 40% by volume, and more than 50% by value. By 1989 KPC had three modern refineries—the Mina Abdullah, Mina al-Ahmadi, and Shuaibi plants—and plans were being made to integrate their operations to attain the greatest possible economic efficiency. When the expanded Mina Abdullah refinery came on stream in February 1989,

Kuwait had a refined-products capacity of over 700,000 barrels per day.

KPC's most dramatic move, however, was to expand overseas. In 1981 it acquired Santa Fe International, a California-based exploration-services company, for US$2.5 billion. Santa Fe owned or operated, among other things, rig joint ventures in various regions, including the North Sea and Australia. It also had an engineering subsidiary, S.F. Braun. A more important step came in February 1983, when KPC purchased Gulf Oil's refining and marketing networks in the Benelux countries, adding those in Sweden and Denmark a month later. Under a further agreement with Gulf Oil in January 1984, KPC acquired 1,500 service stations and a 75% interest in a refinery at Bertonico, Italy, which had closed two years previously. In the following year, KPC purchased 53 of Elf Aquitaine's Belgian service stations, and in 1986 and 1987 KPC obtained access to 821 petrol stations in the United Kingdom by buying Hays Petroleum Services, an independent distributor, to which it added the 466-station network of Ultramar, a U.K. oil company. It also bought British Petroleum's oil-marketing subsidiary in Denmark. During 1988 KPC made several acquisitions in Italy, including a 25% equity interest in a petroleum-product pipeline in northern Italy and the purchase of Rol Oil, an independent company specializing in oil blending and distribution. During 1989, KPC acquired the U.K. oil-lubricants business Carless Lubricants. By 1989, through its London-based subsidiary Kuwait Petroleum International, KPC owned more than 4,500 petrol stations in 7 countries, plus refineries in Rotterdam, and in Gulfhaven, Denmark. In 1988 KPC launched its own brand—Q8—in Europe. Kuwaiti oil was transported to Europe by KOTC, which used large tankers to transport refined products as well as crude oil. By 1990 KOTC's fleet had 22 vessels, including 3 crude carriers, 14 product tankers, and 5 liquefied-gas tankers. Following a visit to Kuwait by the Thai energy minister in March 1989, it was agreed that KPC companies would explore for oil in Thailand and introduce Q8 petrol stations there. In the same year, another KPC subsidiary, Petrochemical Industries Company, moved into overseas petrochemicals, buying a 25% stake in Hoechst of West Germany.

In 1990, KPC had a downstream capacity in Western Europe of 450,000 barrels per day, or 25% of its crude-oil production in Kuwait. KPC's market shares in Europe included 24% in Denmark, 12% in Sweden, 7% in Belgium, 4.5% in the Netherlands, and 2.5% in the United Kingdom.

Although the construction of a retail network in Europe was at the heart of KPC's strategy in the 1980s, the company also was active in exploration activities in foreign countries through its KUFPEC and Santa Fe subsidiaries. In 1984 KUFPEC acquired two petroleum concessions, in Bahrain and Tunisia. Offshore discoveries in Egypt and Indonesia were developed in 1985 and 1986, and in 1986 an agreement was signed to participate in the development of the Yacheng gas field in China.

KPC is a remarkably successful national oil company. During the 1980s, it achieved a far greater degree of integration than any other OPEC producer, with the possible exception of Petroleos de Venezuela. KPC was the first—and by 1990 the only—state-owned oil company from the Third World to sell its oil under its own brand name and through its own service stations. However, there were problems. Some analysts considered that KPC had paid excessive amounts for some of its acquisitions, especially the purchase of Santa Fe in 1981. KPC's consolidated net profits were impressive—rising from US$488.6 million in 1986–1987 to US$606.9 million in 1987–1988—but it was likely that this disguised poor performance from certain downstream operations. KPC also faced resistance to its growth from established international oil companies, which partly explained its failure to penetrate the U.S. market in the 1980s. When, in 1984, KPC tried to purchase a refinery and around 4,000 petrol stations in the southeastern part of the United States from Chevron Corporation, it was outbid by Standard Oil Company of Ohio, which did not welcome its presence. Standard of Ohio was controlled by and later acquired by British Petroleum. More fundamentally, there was some conflict between the strategies of expanding refinery capacity within Kuwait and seeking to become an integrated oil major, which might dictate more refining operations nearer markets.

KPC's state ownership created political problems. KPC's attempts to buy downstream assets in Japan, for example, were blocked in part because it was owned by a foreign government. The Kuwait Investment Office's purchase of over 20% of British Petroleum's shares in 1988 as a consequence of Margaret Thatcher's privatization program was attacked on these grounds, and the Kuwaitis were forced to reduce their stake to 10%. At the time there was speculation that this purchase was aimed at further advancing KPC's downstream integration strategy, because relations between the Kuwait Investment Office (KIO) and KPC were known to be close. KPC's greatest liability, however, was the geographical location of its home country. KPC relied entirely on sea transport through the Persian Gulf to export its oil, and during the Iran-Iraq War in the mid-1980s the resulting vulnerability of KPC was evident. A number of KOTC tankers were hit by Iranian raids, prompting the Kuwaitis to re-register some of their fleet in the United States and United Kingdom. However, this was a minor irritant and inconvenience compared to the Iraqi invasion and occupation of Kuwait in August 1990, which took place after a period of tension over Kuwait's reluctance to see an increase in oil prices.

The Iraqi invasion devastated Kuwait, but it did not devastate KPC which, because of its international diversification strategy, survived. Senior staff of KPC escaped with the bulk of crucial management information intact, and within days had set up an alternative head office in the London premises of Kuwait Petroleum International. Saudi Arabia guaranteed KPI's European downstream commitment. In exile, KPC was granted immunity from the asset freeze which was imposed on Kuwait's overseas interests by the European Economic Community, the United States, and Japan, allowing it to continue normal commercial operations. Eight of KPC's ten directors were outside the country at the time of the Iraq invasion, enabling the company to continue functioning with a legal quorum. Shortly after the invasion, KPC's U.K. lubricants business was relaunched as Kuwaiti Petroleum Lubricants. In October 1990 the diversification strategy was furthered when KIO acquired over 10% of the shares of the Singapore Petroleum Company, an oil-refining group. The continued vigor of KPC in the midst of the greatest crisis ever faced by Kuwait was a tribute to the strength of the business organization that had been created in a single decade.

Principal Subsidiaries: Kuwait Oil Co. KSC; Kuwait National Petroleum Co. KSC; Kuwait Oil Tanker Co. KSC; Kuwait Foreign Petroleum Exploration Co. KSC; Kuwait Sante Fe Braun for Engineering and Petroleum Enterprises KSC; Kuwait Aviation Fuelling Co. KSC; KPC (US Holdings); KPC International NV (Netherlands); Petrochemical Industries Holding NV (Netherlands).

Further Reading: Stocking, George W., *Middle East Oil*, London, Allen Lane, 1970; Chisholm, A.H.T., *The First Kuwait Oil Concession Agreement*, London, Frank Cass, 1975; Luciani, Giacomo, *The Oil Companies and the Arab World*, London, Croom Helm, 1984; Evans, John, *OPEC, Its Member States and the World Energy Markets*, London, Longmans, 1986.

—Geoffrey Jones

LIBYAN NATIONAL OIL CORPORATION

Bashir Sadawi Street
Tripoli
Libya

State-Owned Company
Incorporated: 1970

The Libyan National Oil Corporation (Linoco) was created under Law No. 24 of March 5, 1970. It replaced the older Libyan General Petroleum Corporation (Lipetco) with a new national oil company. Its mandate, similar to Lipetco's, was "to endeavor to promote the Libyan economy by under-taking development, management and exploitation of oil resources . . . as well as by participating . . . in planning and executing the general oil policy of the state . . . ." The fortunes of Linoco, therefore, cannot be separated from those of Libya, since the corporation acts as a government instrument of control, supervision, and participation in the oil industry and particularly in its relations with other oil companies.

The role earmarked for Linoco was largely a product of the political and economic events of the 1960s and 1970s in Libya. During the 1950s, Libya was an impoverished agrarian economy, practicing a near-subsistence level of agriculture. The discovery of oil and the application of the much-needed oil revenues to other sectors of the economy reversed this trend, and the economy attained growth rates as high as 20% a year in the 1960s. There was considerable readjustment in the structure of the Libyan economy, as the oil sector gained prominence and became the vehicle of growth for the economy as a whole. With oil revenues going straight to the government, the latter took the responsibility for planning expenditure derived from these revenues. The outcome was the creation, by royal decree, of the Libyan General Petroleum Corporation (Lipetco) in 1968.

The creation of a state-owned oil company allowed Libya to follow in the footsteps of other oil-producing economies, where control of such a revenue-generating resource lay with the government. Lipetco's first chairman and director general was Mohammed Jeroushi. The company was based in Tripoli, but was physically distinct from the Ministry of Petroleum Affairs. Linoco would be similar to its predecessor in that it, too, would function under the supervision and control of the minister of petroleum. There was very little difference between Lipetco and Linoco in terms of responsibilities. It is quite probable that Linoco was formed in 1970 to highlight the political change from a monarchy to a republican government.

In 1969, the monarchy in Libya was overthrown by a group of young army officers led by Colonel Moammar Khadafi. In the years immediately following the coup d'etat, the government continued to follow the economic policies of the past. However, the new regime's espousal of the creed of self-reliance and socialism indicated that in the future, the government would play a major role in economic policy. Planning, in other words, was to be more widespread, encompassing national issues rather than those of the oil industry alone. This became immediately apparent with a more aggressive policy on oil pricing and the structure of ownership in the oil sector. In May 1970, a series of cuts in OPEC-determined production levels was introduced to force up prices. This policy gained Libya influence in OPEC, where its radical stance met with considerable support.

Simultaneously, agreements on ownership were initiated with foreign oil companies, mainly in the form of joint ventures. The first joint venture was signed between Lipetco and the French state companies, ERAP (later Elf) and SNPA (Aquitaine) in 1968. Subsequently, in June 1969, joint ventures were introduced with Royal Dutch/Shell, ENI's Agip subsidiary, and Ashland Oil & Refining.

Linoco's first chairman and director general was Salem Mohammed Amesh, who was subsequently replaced by his deputy, Omar Muntasir. The latter remained in charge until 1980. The law under which Linoco had been established restricted new joint ventures with foreign firms to those in which the latter took on all the risks of the pre-commercial exploration period. Only contract-type agreements were authorized and Linoco's share was fixed at a given percentage from the start of operations. Contract-type agreements referred to production-sharing agreements as opposed to those simply allowing exploration to proceed. Furthermore, in July 1970, a new law was passed which made Linoco responsible for the marketing of all oil products in Libya. The Brega Petroleum Marketing Company, a subsidiary of Linoco, was set up to carry out the marketing activities of Linoco, and the marketing assets of all the foreign oil companies were nationalized.

Linoco played a major part in the Libyan government's new strategy of higher oil prices and production-sharing. The strategy was to lead to confrontation with the foreign oil companies. Foreign oil companies that did not voluntarily surrender concessions as part of the new policy were forced by economic and political pressure to relinquish these in full to the government. These were then taken over by Linoco.

Soon after its establishment, Linoco signed a joint venture agreement with the U.S. Occidental Petroleum involving production-sharing. In 1971 Linoco arranged a processing deal with Sincat of Italy for refining oil products for domestic consumption, thereby providing a cheap supply of oil for internal Libyan consumption. A joint drilling company was formed with Saipem, a subsidiary of the Italian ENI, in early 1972. Linoco took over the production operations of the Sarir oil field after the nationalization of British Petroleum's Libyan concession in 1971, and the U.S. company Hunt Oil in 1973. Similarly, Phillips's Umm Farud field was taken over in 1970. Other fields taken over by Linoco included Amoseas's Beida oil field in 1974, and Amoco's Sahabir oil field in 1976.

By April 1974, production-sharing agreements had been reached with Exxon, Mobil, Compagnie Française des Pétroles, Elf Aquitaine, and Agip. All these agreements provided for production-sharing on a 85-15 basis onshore and 81-19 basis offshore. Each agreement had commitments in terms of expenditure on exploration by the foreign company. Development costs incurred by Linoco were reimbursable by the partner. By using the surplus funds and technical expertise of the foreign oil companies, the problem of stimulating investment in exploration was resolved.

By the mid-1970s, Linoco was faced with complications as a result of legal actions brought against it by British Petroleum (BP) over claims of ownership. Fears of an oil price rise in 1973 had led to a demand for Libyan crude oil. However, BP's legal position had made buyers wary of purchasing oil over which Linoco may not have had legal title. Linoco compensated for this position by arranging barter deals with both France and Argentina. Eventually all the foreign oil companies in Libya, except BP, agreed to the conditions imposed by Libya of partial nationalization, and as a result Linoco had a substantial surplus of oil to sell. This was because Libya received share entitlements from the foreign companies, giving it rights on production by the foreign companies. It was part of the policy of production-sharing introduced by the government of Libya. However, by 1974-1975, declining oil prices and oil consumption led Linoco to sell back its shares of production to companies which had agreed to the partial nationalizations. This amounted to about 425,000 barrels per day (b/d) from its entitlement. Overall, Linoco produced about 281,000 b/d in 1975 and 408,000 b/d in 1976. It exported 908,000 b/d in 1975 and 1.2 million b/d in 1976. The topical status of Linoco's dispute with BP gradually faded away, and BP, Libya, was nationalized in 1974, as were the American companies Amoseas, Hunt, and Atlantic Richfield. Complementing its upstream activities and acquisitions, Linoco itself had built two refineries at Azzawia during the period 1974-1976, with a capacity of 120,000 b/d.

The 1970s were a decade of great corporate activity. It saw the further consolidation of Linoco's power. Nationalizations, the seizing of company assets, and buying out company shares were among Linoco's activities. Esso Libya agreed to sell its share to Linoco in April 1974. It subsequently withdrew from its Libyan operations in November 1981, and reached a compensation agreement with Linoco in January 1982. Esso Sirte companies, Esso's Libyan subsidiaries, also relinquished 51% of their shares to Linoco. In November 1982, Exxon's share in Esso Sirte was purchased by Linoco and formed into a subsidiary company, Sirte Oil Company. The largest oil company in Libya at the time of the nationalizations was OASIS. Shell's original share of 16.7% was seized by the government in 1974, giving the government of Libya 59.2% ownership of OASIS in the early 1980s. Occidental Libya had agreed to a 51% nationalization in August 1973. This gave Linoco a 51% share in Occidental, Libya. Mobil-Gelsenberg was owned 51% by Linoco, 31.85% by Mobil, and 17.15% by Gelsenberg, the West German refining and marketing company. Mobil, however, left in 1982. In this period, Linoco held 81% of Elf Aquitaine.

The 1980s was a decade of emphasis on joint venture projects. However, it was also characterized by a conflict of interests between Libya and the United States. The latter had instituted sanctions against Libya, based on assertions that Libya was supporting international terrorism, which had seriously affected the operations of U.S. oil companies in Libya. The Libyan government responded by freezing the royalties of the U.S. companies, restricting the repatriation of profits, and threatening to take over the entitlement rights to production of these U.S. companies.

During the 1980s, Libya's oil interests became less insular and more outward-looking. Libya relaxed its confrontational attitude, and Linoco entered into new production-sharing agreements with a number of companies to ensure partial control. These included Rompetrol (Romania) and the Bulgarian Oil Company in 1984-1985. Other agreements were signed in 1988-1989 with Royal Dutch/Shell, Montedison of Italy, the International Petroleum Corporation of Canada, INA-Naftaplin of Yugoslavia, and a consortium of companies comprised of ÖMV in Austria, Braspetro in Brazil, and Husky Oil of Canada. These new agreements included guarantees ensuring rapid payment by Libya to these companies for the development costs incurred. These guarantees represented an important change from earlier Libyan regulations on joint ventures. The change was designed to offset the U.S. sanctions by offering incentives in joint venture terms to other foreign companies.

In 1980, the Libyan Arabian Gulf Oil Company (Agoco) was established by Linoco, through the amalgamation of the Arabian Gulf Exploration Company, Umm-al-Jawabi Oil Company, and direct Linoco exploration and production interests. By 1989 Agoco's production was 400,000 b/d, and it was the largest individual oil producer in the country. Agoco was wholly Libyan-owned and fitted into the overall oil policy of the government, which was to initiate and invest in new projects, while maintaining control. Linoco was also instrumental in the policy of downstream expansion. It was one of the shareholders, together with the Libyan Arab Foreign Bank, and the Libyan Arab Foreign Investment Company, in Olinvest, a Libyan holding company established in 1988 for investment purposes and intended to permit a high degree of integration all the way to end consumers. Furthermore, Olinvest was responsible for ensuring that the downstream activities continued, and so invested in Italian and German refineries. By 1990-1991, the company was handling some 400-450,000 barrels per day.

The Reagan administration had introduced economic sanctions against Libya in January 1986. These were renewed in December of 1988, in the review of U.S. government policy by Congress after two years. The immediate impact of the sanctions was on the production and financial operations of five U.S. oil companies: Marathon, Conoco, Amerada Hess, Occidental, and W.R. Grace. In June 1986 these five companies had a total production entitlement of 263,000 b/d. As a result of the U.S. sanctions, the holdings and entitlements of the U.S companies were kept in suspension and their operations were handled by Linoco. Much of the latter part of the 1980s was spent in negotiations between the U.S. companies and Linoco over the treatment of their equity holdings. The U.S. companies had offered to return to Libya to meet their commitments with regard to capital expenditure, but continued U.S. sanctions did not allow them to bring in new technology, equipment, and spare parts. Even an easing of the ban by the Reagan administration in early 1989 only allowed the companies to transfer their equities to a third party, and did not change the core issue of a transfer of technology. Due to the lack of overall progress, some of the companies were willing to extend their suspended status until a more viable political solution could be found.

Under Abdallah al-Badri, the chairman of the Linoco management committee until November 1990, a new policy has been introduced for the 1990s. This focuses on reducing the number of new projects and upgrading the existing facilities of the national oil producers. Linoco has continued to make production-sharing agreements. New joint ventures have been initiated between Linoco and Veba, Petrofina, North African Petroleum Limited, and a consortium led by the Petroleum Development Corporation of the Republic of Korea, and Lasmo. However, an additional emphasis has also been placed on encouraging foreign companies to produce exclusively for export, and on confining the sale of crude oil to a select number of national oil companies that already own equity in Libyan production. This would limit the crude being offered in the spot market through third-party traders, and would increase the input into Libya's downstream system. As a result, the national oil marketing company, Brega, ceased operating in 1990, and marketing is a responsibility of the National Oil Corporation itself.

Principal Subsidiaries: Arabian Gulf Oil Company; Azzawa Oil Refining Petroleum Company; Mediterranean Sea Oil Services Company; National Drilling Company; National Oil Fields and Terminals Catering Company; National Oil Services Company; National Oil Wells Chemical and Drilling and Workover Equipment Company; National Oil Wells Services Company; Sirte Oil Company.

Further Reading: Waddams, Frank C., *The Libyan Oil Industry,* London, Croom Helm, 1980; Barker, Paul, and Keith McLachlan, "Development of the Libyan Oil Industry" in *Libya Since Independence,* edited by J.A. Allen, Kent, Croom Helm, 1982; Wright, John, *Libya: A Modern History,* Kent, Croom Helm, 1983; Ghanem, Shukri, "The Oil Industry and the Libyan Economy: The Past, The Present and the Likely Future" in *The Economic Development of Libya,* edited by B. Khader, Kent, Croom Helm, 1987; McLachlan, Keith, "Al-Khalij, the Libyan Oil Province: A Review of Oil and Development" in *Libya: State and Region, a Study of Regional Evolution,* edited by M.M. Buro, London, School of African and Oriental Studies, Centre for Near and Middle Eastern Studies, 1989; *The Oil Industry in the Great Jamahirya: Achievements Despite Challenges,* Tripoli, Libyan National Oil Corporation, 1990.

—Sarah Ahmad Khan

LYONDELL PETROCHEMICAL COMPANY

1221 McKinney Street, Suite 1600
Houston, Texas 77010
U.S.A.
(713) 652-7200
Fax: (713) 652-4598

Public Company
Incorporated: 1985 as Lyondell Petrochemical Corporation
Employees: 2,250
Sales: $6.49 billion
Stock Exchange: New York

Lyondell Petrochemical Company manufactures and markets a broad spectrum of petrochemicals, ranging from olefins—mostly propylene, ethylene, butadiene, and butylenes—to aromatics, methanol, and specialty products, as well as refined petroleum products including jet fuel, gasoline, heating oil, and lubricants. While Lyondell was incorporated in 1985 as a wholly owned subsidiary of Atlantic Richfield Company (ARCO), its roots are much a part of the history of Texas. In 1918 two-year-old Sinclair Oil & Refining Company purchased the Allen Ranch in Houston, Texas, its first 720 acres of land. Included in the land was the site at which General Sam Houston and the Texas Army forded the Buffalo Bayou, retreating from Texas's defeat at the Alamo, before the army turned at the San Jacinto River, dealt Santa Anna a crushing blow, and won Texas its independence. Sinclair built the first shell still crude battery for refining crude on this site—which went onstream in 1919. Sinclair Oil & Refining Company was subsequently renamed Sinclair Oil Corporation, and in 1936, with Rio Grande Oil Company and several other Depression-scarred companies, was merged into the Richfield Oil Corporation.

In 1955 Texas Butadiene and Chemical Corporation bought the Lyondell Country Club in Channelview, Texas, and built a plant on that site. By 1957 the new plant was producing 300 tons of butadiene a day. Sinclair Petrochemicals Inc., a subsidiary of Sinclair Oil, which was then a subsidiary of Richfield purchased the Channelview site in 1962.

During the mid-1960s Atlantic Refining Company was searching for a merger partner to enhance its own growth. In 1965 Atlantic initiated talks with Richfield. Atlantic Refining's overture, which typically would not have appealed to Richfield, was attractive because Richfield was being sued on anti-trust grounds by the Department of Justice for its 26-year-old merger with Sinclair. Faced with liquidation or divesting Sinclair, a marriage to Atlantic Refining would allow Richfield to skirt the issue. In 1966 Atlantic Richfield was formed. In 1969 the Justice Department finally allowed ARCO to merge Sinclair. ARCO immediately sold Sinclair's east coast marketing arm to the U.S. subsidiary of British Petroleum Company to satisfy the Justice Department. In 1969 the Justice Department also required ARCO to continue to aggressively market the Sinclair brand name for five more years in case the Justice Department was ultimately able to win its case and force Sinclair to become an independent company. The Justice Department was unable to do so, however. After Sinclair was merged into ARCO, the Channelview plant became a part of ARCO Chemical Company and the Houston plant joined ARCO Products Company.

Also during the 1960s, Atlantic Richfield began to realize that the growing market for oil was not limitless, and it became actively interested in developing its petrochemical business. In 1966, together with Halcon International, ARCO created Oxirane Chemical Company, a research-and-development, engineering design, and consulting company. The joint venture produced propylene oxide using a new process developed by Halcon, and quickly proved profitable. When ARCO bought Halcon's 50% of Oxirane in 1980, it gained a profitable addition to its growing chemical business.

Through Oxirane, ARCO carved a niche for itself in petrochemicals that is still a major part of ARCO Chemical and of Lyondell. By 1980, when Halcon sold its share in the partnership to ARCO for $270 million and the assumption of $380 million in long-term debt, Oxirane was generating $1 billion of business a year worldwide. What was formerly Oxirane then became a part of ARCO Chemical.

In the years that immediately followed, ARCO Chemical failed to distinguish itself as a developer of new technology. Unable to develop market share in polyethylene and polypropylene, ARCO Chemical decided to sell those businesses. By 1984, the company had sold both its high- and low-density PE and PP businesses, as well as several polymer operations. Although ARCO Chemical tried to sell what remained of the olefins businesses, which at that time were a drain on its earnings, Atlantic Richfield Company had other plans. In 1985 ARCO separated its olefins operations from ARCO Chemical Company, and set them up as a separate ARCO unit, naming it Lyondell Petrochemical Corporation, soon renamed Lyondell Petrochemical Company. Lyondell's assets consisted of the Houston refinery, the former Allen Ranch; the Channelview petrochemical complex, formerly Lyondell Country Club; and several money-losing product lines.

ARCO Chemical continued to develop its core business as a part of ARCO until September 1987. At this point ARCO managers, realizing that the growth of the company's chemical segment was not fully recognized by investors because ARCO Chemical was just a small division of Atlantic Richfield Company, spun off ARCO Chemical Company, selling 20% of its shares to the public.

Sibling company Lyondell Petrochemical followed much the same route. Under president Bob Gower, a former employee of Sinclair Oil, Lyondell had reduced overhead and improved its operating costs just one year after its formation. Gower cut staff but improved morale by increasing workers' responsibilities.

In 1988 Lyondell's earnings increased 441% over 1987, spurred by increased demand for petrochemical products. The speed of this recovery, as well as Lyondell's continued growth, led ARCO to spin off Lyondell. The spin-off was calculated to improve Lyondell's market value, allow ARCO to enjoy a cash infusion while Lyondell's performance was at a peak, and to increase Lyondell's operational mobility. In January 1989 ARCO sold 50% of Lyondell Petrochemical Company to the public for $1.4 billion, making it the largest initial public offering of 1989, as well as the largest equity offering by a U.S. industrial company.

ARCO could not have picked a better time to offer Lyondell to the public, although the stock was an aftermarket disaster, sinking 23% from its initial $30 offering price. This deal did not only benefit ARCO, bringing in cash that was redistributed into other areas of its businesses; it also spurred important growth at Lyondell. The spin-off allowed Lyondell to create an entrepreneurial atmosphere and rewarded management with new responsibility. Freed of the constraints of operating with ARCO, Lyondell set its own agenda.

With startling candidness Gower in *Chemical Week,* January 15, 1986, had summarized the key to Lyondell's success, saying, "our assets are run-of-the-mill, mundane. So is our technology, so is our market position. So the only way to set ourselves apart is with the performance of our people." Following the spin-off, Gower continued to pursue this philosophy, with renewed vigor.

Gower had come to Lyondell by way of Sinclair Oil. He joined Sinclair Oil as a research scientist. Both before and after Sinclair's merger with ARCO, he had risen through a variety of sales, research, and engineering assignments, becoming a vice president of ARCO Chemical in 1977 and senior vice president in 1979. He had gone on to direct the technology division, then later, business management and marketing for large-volume petrochemicals. In 1984 he had been elected senior vice president of planning and advanced technology at ARCO. When Lyondell was formed in 1985, he became its president, and was elected its CEO in 1988.

At Lyondell Gower cut operating costs and trimmed away layers of management. Lyondell's 1989 net income fell off 31% from 1988, as demand for gasoline and petrochemicals cooled. Lyondell's operations also suffered from weather- and maintenance-related problems. Nevertheless, Gower continued to spend. A large percentage of the $176 million Lyondell spent in 1989 on capital projects went into the expansion of the two olefin plants that were shut down for overhauls. These expansions resulted in lower unit production costs, increased ethylene capacity by about 25%, and increased propylene and other by-product capacity.

In February 1990 Lyondell made its first acquisitions, of a polyethylene plant and a polypropylene plant from Rexene Products Company. These plants improved the value of Lyondell's operations as they not only are captive consumers of ethylene and propylene but also enable Lyondell to participate in the polyolefins market.

Lyondell succeeded due to the company's flexibility; for instance, Lyondell's olefins plants are capable of switching from production of natural gas liquids such as ethane, propane, and butane, to heavy liquids such as naphthas, condensates, and gas oil, depending on which feedstock will yield the greatest profit. In addition to this, the Houston refinery is able to run on a large percentage of low-cost heavy crudes in addition to many foreign crude oils, allowing Lyondell to select the best-priced crude. The Channelview plant also displays product flexibility, producing propylene from ethylene when product markets are stronger, and adjusting production mix and product volumes to utilize market opportunities. Lyondell has the freedom to act on these opportunities because as an intermediate producer it is not committed to supply retail outlets. In 1989, Lyondell began to expand its Houston refinery's paraxylene capacity. Finished in early 1990, it provided a 25% increase in paraxylene production.

While Lyondell has become extremely independent, it retains ties to ARCO, which in 1991 owned 49.96% of Lyondell. Pipelines link ARCO to some Lyondell operations, although Lyondell shops for better-priced crude. Lyondell also rents some office space and warehouse space from ARCO. Lyondell operates a small unit at the Channelview complex for ARCO Chemical—which, like Lyondell, is still controlled by Atlantic Richfield Company—and sells many of its products to ARCO Chemical.

Principal Subsidiaries: ARCO Channelview, Inc.; ARCO Lyondell, Inc.; ARCO Mount Belvieu; ARCO Lyondell Licensing, Inc.; Lyondell Polymers Corporation; Lyondell Petrochemical de Mexico, Inc.; Lyondell Rancho Pipeline Company.

Further Reading: "Lyondell's climb into the black," *Chemical Week,* January 15, 1986.

—Maya Sahafi

MAPCO INC.

1800 South Baltimore Avenue
Tulsa, Oklahoma 74119
U.S.A.
(918) 581-1800
Fax: (918) 599-6034

Public Company
Incorporated: 1958
Employees: 6,414
Sales: $2.82 billion
Stock Exchanges: New York Pacific Midwest

The history of MAPCO Inc. provides ample evidence that great size is not a requirement for success in the U.S. energy field. Founded in 1960, MAPCO has leapfrogged from one energy niche to the next, using its gas-pipeline earnings to finance an entrance into coal and oil production and then shifting downstream to become a sizable refiner and marketer of oil and gas. MAPCO has retained a foothold in all of these areas, with oil refining and marketing supplying the bulk of revenue but pipeline operations still generating exceptionally large amounts of cash for use in further investments and upkeep.

MAPCO was founded by Robert E. Thomas, who graduated from the University of Pennsylvania's Wharton School of Finance in the 1930s with a degree in accounting and corporate finance. Thomas made a name for himself as manager of railroad investments for Keystone Custodian Fund, a Boston investment firm, and subsequently was hired by Pennroad Corporation to untangle a host of problems left behind by its former railroad holdings. When Pennroad bought the Missouri-Kansas-Texas Railroad (Katy) in 1956, it named Thomas as chairman of the railroad's executive committee. Katy was in poor financial condition, with Thomas looking for possible diversification, when he was told of a proposed scheme to run a liquid-propane gas pipeline along railroad rights-of-way from Texas to Albany, New York. Katy's lines covered a good part of that route, and Thomas pursued the pipeline concept as a possible investment for the railroad. It became clear that Katy did not have the cash or borrowing power to finance the deal and in 1958, Thomas and a group of partners organized a company, called MAPCO Inc., to build and operate the Mid-America pipeline system. MAPCO raised $71 million in capital, some of it from Prudential Insurance Company of America, and much of it from a public stock offering, and was in business by 1960. Thomas also kept his position at Katy, which took an 18% interest in the Mid-America pipeline.

Mid-America was the first U.S. pipeline built specifically to carry only one type of liquid natural gas, that being propane. Propane is used widely in the upper Midwest as a heating fuel, and until the construction of Mid-America most of the propane shipped from sources in the South and West traveled by railroad car to its midwestern destinations. While it is cheaper and faster to pipe natural gas liquids than to carry them by rail, a pipeline cannot run properly without a volume of product sufficient to keep it physically full and financially able to repay the considerable debt incurred by the cost of its construction. MAPCO therefore secured commitments from a group of 13 propane producers, consumers, and traders before embarking on construction of its 2,184-mile initial route between New Mexico and the Illinois-Wisconsin region. As the man most responsible for assembling this team of future customers and the needed financing, Robert Thomas virtually guaranteed the eventual success of Mid-America and MAPCO, as it generally is more difficult to create a pipeline than to run one profitably. Though subject to Interstate Commerce Commission rate regulation, pipelines nevertheless take advantage of limited competition, low labor costs, and healthy depreciation allowances to generate large amounts of cash and excellent net income. Once well underway, MAPCO immediately returned a profit and has continued to do so.

The pipeline faced certain problems, however. As a supplier of heating fuel, its business was naturally seasonal, with the first and fourth quarters of each year showing strong sales while the intermediate months were slack. The need to better balance this lopsided earning pattern has determined much of MAPCO's diversification. In 1963, for example, the company first entered the oil-and-gas field with the purchase of existing wells in the Texas panhandle, and in the following year added 17 more sites in Oklahoma and Texas. In 1965 MAPCO tripled its gas production with the acquisition of no less than 480 oil and gas wells in the lower Midwest. Not only were the wells sound investments in their own right, but sales of crude energy are fairly uniform throughout the year, helping to offset MAPCO's summer slowdown, and by securing a source of liquid natural gas, the purchases were a first step toward MAPCO's vertical integration.

In 1966 MAPCO took a second step toward integration with the acquisition of the Thermogas Company, a retail and wholesale distributor of propane and butane as well as of gas-burning appliances. With hundreds of sales outlets throughout the midwestern and southern United States, Thermogas more than doubled MAPCO's revenue and completed integration of the company's liquid-propane gas system from wellhead to retail sale. It also provided a comprehensive sales network for MAPCO's next new product, liquid plant fertilizer and food. In 1968 MAPCO bought the leading U.S. manufacturer of such liquid fertilizers, Indian Point Farm Supply, Inc., of Athens, Illinois. Indian Point synthesized fertilizers from a mixture of ammonia, potash, and phosphoric acid, and MAPCO wasted no time in buying two major suppliers of these raw materials, AnAmo Company and Poly P, Inc., makers respectively of anhydrous ammonia and a fertilizer base known as 10-34-0. With MAPCO's Thermogas outlets marketing its fertilizers, Indian Point's sales rose dramatically in the next five years to $12 million annually, or about 9% of the parent company's revenue in 1973. Because fertilizer is sold primarily in the spring and summer, most of the $12 million helped to offset MAPCO's preponderance of winter pipeline revenue from heating fuel.

By that time, however, MAPCO's oil-and-gas production had developed into a booming business in its own right. When its earlier wells began to run dry in the late 1960s, MAPCO made a series of important new purchases from Bradley Producing Corporation in 1969, in a single year raising its oil production by almost 50%. For the first time, MAPCO began its own program of oil and gas exploration, acquiring interests in some 125,000 acres in the United States and Canada. Although by world standards these energy holdings were miniscule, they soon had a powerful positive effect on MAPCO's balance sheet. In 1970, of MAPCO's $83 million sales, oil and gas production accounted for only $17 million, but so lucrative is the crude oil business that nearly one-third of MAPCO's net income was contributed by that relatively minor percentage of sales. Such results encouraged further investment, and in 1971 MAPCO entered another energy field with its purchase of two coal companies with reserves exceeding 41 million tons. The new coal mines were immediately modernized and expanded, and—operating under a non-union, production-incentive system—turned in outstanding performances.

Robert Thomas had not only balanced the revenue tilt of MAPCO's original propane-pipeline holdings but also moved the company into energy resources in time to take advantage of the oil crisis and inflation of the 1970s. When the OPEC embargo of 1973 quadrupled oil prices overnight, MAPCO's modest energy assets became far more valuable than its earlier pipeline and Thermogas holdings. From sales of $110 million in 1973, company revenue escalated to $425 million three years later, the bulk of which was supplied by oil, gas, and coal production. The energy crisis was particularly good for domestic U.S. oil producers, who could then afford to spend the extra dollars required to keep mature and limited wells pumping. The 1970s OPEC embargo led to a boom in domestic U.S. production and along with the rest of the U.S. oil industry, MAPCO rode the boom to unprecedented prosperity and was soon expanding its exploration efforts as far away as Indonesia and Australia. The company also continued to add to its coal stock, picking up mines in Illinois, Kentucky, Maryland, and Virginia.

With the gradual decline of energy prices beginning around 1980, however, MAPCO's largely domestic oil and gas production rapidly became far less attractive. Small domestic oil concerns are the first to be pinched by falling prices, and within a few years MAPCO's properties were running at a loss and had to be sold. In 1984 James E. Barnes replaced Thomas as chairman, president and CEO of MAPCO. By 1985 the last of MAPCO's significant oil and gas production capacity had been disposed of, for an aggregate receipt of $290 million, but in the meantime MAPCO had shifted into a more stable segment of the oil business, refining and marketing. In late 1980 it outbid a number of other parties for Earth Resources Company, paying around $250 million for its oil refinery and gas

station–convenience stores located throughout the South. As middlemen in the oil business, refiners and marketers are far more flexible than oil producers and generally earn a less spectacular but more reliable return on investment. MAPCO thus eased out of production as crude prices were dropping and bought a chain of marketers which in 1989 accounted for the bulk of company revenue—$1.3 billion—and the largest share of operating income—$85 million. Its gas station-convenience store holdings had grown to over 300 by 1989, a handful of them located as far away as Alaska, and the company had two refineries with a combined capacity of 170,000 barrels per day.

MAPCO has retained its position in coal production and marketing, which, though a much smaller division, is more profitable than oil and gas. The company in 1989 had proven reserves of 434 million tons in eight U.S. mines, all of them located between southern Illinois and West Virginia. MAPCO has tried to protect itself from sudden downturns in its coal revenue—$313 million in 1989—by producing metallurgical and steam coals in various grades of volatility and sulfur content. Metallurgical coal is the type of coal used to fuel smelters, while steam coal is burned to produce steam. The company markets most of its metallurgical coal overseas, and all its steam coal in the United States.

Equal in providing revenue but much less profitable than coal is MAPCO's gas-products division, which still sells propane under the Thermogas brand name. The 136 Thermogas retail stores, located mostly in the Midwest, also continue to sell liquid fertilizers made by MAPCO's own facilities. Much of the propane sold via the Thermogas chain arrives by means of MAPCO's fourth and last operating unit, its original Mid-America pipeline system, now greatly expanded. The earlier propane-only lines running between the Texas area and the upper Midwest have been extended into the overthrust belt of Wyoming and Utah, and MAPCO also pipes anhydrous ammonia and crude oil via two other, smaller systems. What is remarkable about MAPCO's original pipeline division is not its size, however, but the consistency with which it continues to earn high levels of operating income. As when Robert Thomas first put together the pipeline in 1960, Mid-America and its related adjuncts routinely make profits of more than 50% on annual revenue. In 1989 MAPCO's transportation division enjoyed operating profits of $75.5 million on revenues of $145.9 million. MAPCO's original business is thus the smallest of its many parts but remains the star performer of the group, with each year demonstrating anew why MAPCO was created in the first place.

Principal Subsidiaries: MAPCO Coal Inc.; MAPCO Gas Products Inc.; MAPCO Petroleum Inc.; MAPCO Transportation Inc.

Further Reading: Aydin, Jack N., "MAPCO Inc.," *Wall Street Transcript,* June 3, 1974.

—Jonathan Martin

▲MITSUBISHI OIL Co., Ltd.

MITSUBISHI OIL CO., LTD.

2-4, Toranomon 1 chome
Minato-ku, Tokyo 105
Japan
(03) 3595-7663
Fax: (03) 3508-2521

Public Company
Incorporated: 1931
Employees: 2,341
Sales: ¥764.55 billion (US$5.63 billion)
Stock Exchanges: Tokyo Osaka Nagoya

Mitsubishi Oil Co., Ltd. is one of Japan's leading oil importers and refiners. Associated with the Mitsubishi industrial conglomerate, the company has had a turbulent history, suffering first the effects of war and subsequently the fluctuations and uncertainties of the world petroleum trade.

The roots of Mitsubishi Oil go back to 1924, when the fuel department of the Mitsubishi Trading Company, a *zaibatsu,* or large industrial group, first secured the exclusive right to sell in the Far East a broad range of crude and refined petroleum products made by the Associated Oil Company of California. In April 1928, Mitsubishi entered into an exclusive Far East marketing and sales agreement with Tidewater Oil Company of New York, which was subsequently taken over by J. Paul Getty in the early 1930s. In February 1931, the Mitsubishi Oil Company was founded, as Mitsubishi Trading expanded its interest in the petroleum industry. In December 1931, a 20-acre refinery complex was opened in Kawasaki, Japan, to manufacture a wide variety of oil products, including gasoline, kerosene, and machine oil, from crude petroleum supplied by Associated Oil. The latter company also contributed technical expertise. The joint venture between the two companies as equal partners was capitalized at ¥5 million, and its products were sold exclusively by the fuel department of Mitsubishi Trading. The company was capable of refining 3,000 barrels per day of light crude oil or a third of that amount of heavy crude oil.

Throughout the early 1930s, Japan was seized by nationalistic and militaristic fervor. Oil, a natural resource in which Japan is almost entirely lacking, played only a small part in the Japanese economy at that time, accounting for a mere 7% of the country's energy usage, of which 80% was imported from the United States. However, the many military applications of petroleum made it a strategic commodity essential to the effort to expand the boundaries and influence of the Japanese empire. Accordingly, the Japanese government, in an effort to control the oil industry so that it could better serve national aims, passed the Petroleum Industry Law in 1934, which was designed to strengthen Japanese refiners such as Mitsubishi, and weaken the two dominant wholly foreign–owned firms, Rising Sun, the Japanese affiliate of Royal Dutch/Shell, and Standard-Vacuum, the joint Far Eastern operation of Standard Oil of New Jersey and Standard Oil of New York. By 1935, Mitsubishi Oil had been capitalized with an additional ¥2 million. Its refinery had grown by 16 acres and an additional capacity of 1,000 barrels per day of light crude oil, and it had added new refining capacity.

In 1937, Japan entered into full-scale war with China, and the Japanese economy was put on a wartime footing. Oil was essential to the military campaign, and Mitsubishi's output hit an all-time high that year, as distribution of all oil products was redirected to the war effort. Despite U.S. opposition to Japanese military aggression, in an effort to avoid or postpone war in the Far East, the United States continued to supply Japan with oil up until the start of August 1941, when a virtual embargo was imposed. In December 1941, Japan formally entered war with the United States with Japan's bombing of Pearl Harbor, and a four-year contest that would conclude with the near-total destruction of Japanese industry began.

Mitsubishi Oil continued to operate throughout the war, although at a somewhat slower rate, as the Japanese replaced lost U.S. crude oil supplies with resources from captured oil fields in the East Indies. Imports from these sources peaked in 1943. Two years later, U.S. submarines were torpedoing Japanese oil tankers in the Pacific with such regularity and thoroughness that oil supplies had virtually dried up. From 1942 to 1944, average output of the Mitsubishi refinery was less than half of the prewar peak. By early 1945, Japanese refineries were almost out of oil, and domestic use had virtually ceased. In the latter phases of the war, as U.S. forces came within bombing distance of the Japanese home islands, the Kawasaki refinery of Mitsubishi suffered heavy damage.

Japan formally surrendered in August 1945, its fuel tanks dry, and the Allied occupation began. In the wake of victory, the Allied powers set out to restructure the entire Japanese economy, and the dissolution of the *zaibatsu,* including Mitsubishi, was an essential part of the plan. Mitsubishi was split into 139 entities. Activity between the companies was severely restricted, and refinement of petroleum products was forbidden altogether. Mitsubishi Oil was in dire straits.

Gradually, however, conditions improved, and in 1949 oil refining was again permitted on Japan's Pacific coast. In August 1950, the company resumed activity at its repaired Kawasaki plant, and took up for the first time the sales and marketing of its products, formerly handled by its *zaibatsu* partner, the Mitsubishi Trading Company. Mitsubishi Oil again formed an equal arrangement with its former U.S. partner, Associated Oil, gaining in return a secure supply of crude oil and the technological expertise needed to modernize its plant. Associated Oil had merged with Mitsubishi's other former U.S. partner, Tidewater Oil Company, to become the Tidewater Associated Oil Company. By 1953, J. Paul Getty had completed his lengthy takeover of Tidewater.

Mitsubishi took up activity in the postwar period and restored refining operations to their prewar condition. In 1952 rationing of fuel was abolished, and by 1953 Mitsubishi and other domestic refiners were able to provide 65% of the oil consumed in Japan. Japan had begun its great postwar period of industrial growth. Much of this boom was fueled by coal, which Japan possessed in good quantities, but it soon became clear that petroleum was a cheaper fuel to rely on. Japan's coal industry declined quickly as oil took over. By the end of the first decade of Japan's reconstruction, it was clear that oil would play an essential role in the country's continued development.

In response to the growing importance of petroleum, Japan's government sought, as it had in the past, to regulate the oil industry for the country's benefit. Such regulation meant reducing the importance and market share of foreign oil suppliers in favor of an increased role for partially Japanese-owned companies such as Mitsubishi. In 1962 the government passed a law giving the Ministry of International Trade and Industry the right to control the oil industry. Resultant ministry actions fostered competition and vigorous price-cutting, making petroleum an even more attractive source of energy. By the late 1960s petroleum products supplied 70% of the energy needs of a burgeoning and modern Japan; with 99.5% coming from imported crude oil. By 1970, Japan had regained control over its refining industry, but remained dependent on foreign sources for its raw materials; for instance, Mitsubishi relied on Getty.

In an effort to reduce this reliance on foreign sources, Japanese oil companies began to seek their own sources of crude oil in 1968. Mitsubishi established a petroleum development arm, and stepped up exploration. In 1972, in a move coordinated by the government-run Japan Petroleum Development Corporation, Mitsubishi Oil joined with 13 other Japanese companies and a U.S. company to explore for oil in Peru. Four years later the unsuccessful attempt was abandoned. Despite such efforts more than half of Japan's energy supply could still be traced to the Middle East at the time of the oil crisis in 1973. The sharp rise in crude oil prices during this time accelerated Japan's search for a reliable and direct supply of raw materials. In the Japanese economy as a whole, the price increase encouraged movement away from such heavy dependence on petroleum. Actions taken by Mitsubishi Oil during the oil crisis, in concert with other oil companies, eventually resulted in the company's conviction for illegal monopolistic pricing practices. The conviction was upheld, and the company was fined by Japan's supreme court in 1984.

In December 1974, Mitsubishi Oil suffered a grave financial blow when a massive oil spill from a tank at its second refinery at Mizushima caused the most severe oil pollution ever seen in Japan. Contamination of marine wildlife and fisheries led to lawsuits against Mitsubishi and cost the company more than US$100 million for cleanup and restitution to fishermen, and caused the shutdown of the refinery. The facility was not reopened until August 1975. This loss, added to general industry woes, caused the company's financial situation to deteriorate, increasing its deficit. It was not until March 1978 that the company was again able to pay a dividend on its stock.

As part of its ongoing effort to develop independent sources of crude oil, Mitsubishi entered into a partnership with a French firm to develop an oil field off the coast of Indonesia in 1975. In the first agreement of its kind, the company arranged to receive seven million barrels of crude oil from the site over

a two-and-a-half year period in return for an investment of US$17 million.

By 1976, Mitsubishi was starting to recover from the financial woes induced by the Mizushima oil spill. Later that year, the company allied itself with the five other leading Japanese oil companies in a buyers' union, in an attempt to exert some control over the price of the raw materials they purchased. When Iraq raised the price of its product 10% and Saudi Arabia only raised its price 5%, the Japanese companies announced that they would buy more Saudi oil and less Iraqi oil.

In 1977, Mitsubishi again profited from the split in pricing between crude oil producers that had been established at the December 1976 OPEC general meeting. A high percentage of its crude imports originated in countries that had raised their prices 5% instead of 10%. However, the firm's large deficit still remaining from the costs of the oil spill continued to hold down its profitability. In the first half of 1978, the company was able to overcome a slump in the petroleum market because of profits on the exchange rate of the yen, and this factor along with large compensation payments by two other firms partly responsible for the 1974 oil spill, helped Mitsubishi to offset further the financial damage from the spill. A new oil tax, imposed in June 1978, along with reduced foreign exchange and a continuing slide in oil product price, led to a drop in profits in the latter part of the year to half their previous levels.

In 1979, Mitsubishi continued its efforts to obtain oil more directly from suppliers, and also continued to widen its search for oil outside the Persian Gulf. The company was successful in negotiating a five-year contract to double its purchase of crude oil from the Indonesian government-owned PERTAMINA in an arrangement that was the first of its kind for Indonesia. The company also made a direct deal with Burma for oil, becoming the first Japanese company to purchase oil from this source. In addition, Mitsubishi joined with five other Japanese-owned oil importers to form a council to promote oil imports from Mexico. The company finished the year by obtaining a commitment from Abu Dhabi to expand its direct supplies of crude oil to Mitsubishi, and by proposing steps to increase its previously marginal supply of oil from Kuwait in a direct arrangement. Two years later these steps paid off when the company signed a contract with Kuwait for 30,000 barrels per day of oil. By the end of the 1970s, with the encouragement and sponsorship of the Japanese government, 45% of Japan's oil imports were being obtained through direct deals with producing countries, such as those deals concluded by Mitsubishi during this time.

Mitsubishi undertook further diversification of its fuel sources in 1981, when the company agreed to buy 100,000 tons of coal from its U.S. partner, Getty Oil, for resale to its customers, as part of Japan's overall attempt to reduce its dependence on oil. This move away from petroleum in the Japanese economy as a whole contributed to record poor performance in the crowded oil-refining industry in the second half of 1982. Mitsubishi Oil's pre-tax profits dropped dramatically during this period in response to low demand for its products, high costs for raw materials, and unfavorable conditions in the world's financial market.

In mid-1984, Getty Oil, which had retained a half-ownership in Mitsubishi was purchased by a larger U.S. oil company, Texaco. As part of this deal, Getty sold its interest in Mitsubishi Oil to members of the Mitsubishi group and other Japanese buyers for US$335 million, allowing the company to shed its foreign partner, and become wholly Japanese-owned for the first time.

In the same year, in an atmosphere of growing difficulty for oil refiners caught between rising crude prices and government controls on prices for refined products, Mitsubishi Oil announced that it would combine some operations, including the chartering of tankers, importing of crude oil, refining of petroleum, and marketing of products, with the Nippon Oil Company. The linked companies were to become Japan's largest oil distributor, with an estimated market share of 25%. This move was in keeping with the general trend toward consolidation in the badly fragmented Japanese petroleum industry, which, in accordance with repeated governmental recommendations, had seen 13 other arrangements in the previous seven months.

As the 1980s progressed, Mitsubishi Oil continued to seek new sources of raw materials. Faced with the war between Iran and Iraq in the Persian Gulf, which threatened the stability of crude supplies from that area, the company arranged to import oil from the North Sea off the British Isles to Japan, a distance that necessitated an expensive 50-day tanker trip. By the end of the decade the company's fortunes had improved somewhat, although its financial health remained shaky. Profits were up by 10% in March 1989, despite a drop in sales, but slipped back in the next year, in part as a result of higher costs for crude oil and rising marketing and administration costs.

As it entered the 1990s, Mitsubishi Oil's fate remained uncertain. The company has met successfully its past challenges and in 1991, it dominated the country's oil industry.

Principal Subsidiaries: Tohoku Oil Co., Ltd. (56.9%); Okinawa CTS Corp. (65%); Ryoyu Terminal Co., Ltd.; Ryoyu Tanker Co., Ltd.; Ryoyu Hanbai Co., Ltd.; Sanyu Building Co., Ltd.; Sanseki Corporation; Sanseki Engineering Co., Ltd.; Sanseki Information Systems Co., Ltd.; Mitsubishi Liquefied Petroleum Gas Co., Ltd. (25%); Tozai Oil Terminal Co., Ltd. (50%); Ryojun Engineering Co., Ltd.; Mitsubishi Petroleum Development Co., Ltd. (11%); Kamigoto Oil Storage Co., Ltd. (10%); Universal Network Service Co., Ltd. (90%); Sanseki Techno Co., Ltd.; Japan Papua New Gunina Petroleum Co., Ltd. (33.9%); Mitsubishi Oil, (Delaware), Ltd. (U.S.A., 95%); Techmocisco, Inc. (U.S.A.); Mitsubishi Oil (U.K.) PLC; MIPETRO (Netherlands) B.V.

Further Reading: An Outline of the Mitsubishi Enterprises, Tokyo, Mitsubishi Goshi Kaisha, 1932; *An Outline of the Mitsubishi Enterprises,* Tokyo, Mitsubishi Goshi Kaisha, 1935; *Mitsui-Mitsubishi-Sumitomo: Present Status of the Former Zaibatsu Enterprises,* Tokyo, Mitsubishi Economic Research Institute, 1955; *An Outline of Japanese Industry,* Tokyo, Asia Kyokai, 1955; Yergin, Daniel, *The Prize: The Epic Quest for Oil, Money and Power,* New York, Simon & Schuster, 1990.

—Elizabeth Rourke

MOBIL CORPORATION

3225 Gallows Road
Fairfax, Virginia 22037
U.S.A.
(703) 846-3000
Fax: (703) 846-4666

Public Company
Incorporated: 1931 as Socony-Vacuum Corporation
Employees: 67,300
Sales: $64.47 billion
Stock Exchange: New York

Mobil Corporation, America's second-largest oil company, has developed as a vocal representative of the oil industry, spending huge amounts on advocacy advertisements and a host of cultural sponsorships. Its sophisticated public relations is in keeping with Mobil's background in the financial, marketing, and administrative aspects of the oil business, in contrast to the hands-on, engineering orientation of many of its leading competitors. Neither of the two companies whose 1931 merger created Mobil—Standard Oil Company of New York (Socony) and Vacuum Oil Company—had significant experience in the production of crude oil. Both were refiners and marketers, and it was in those two areas that Mobil has achieved its considerable success, meanwhile scouring the world in a never-ending quest for sufficient, secure supplies of crude oil. Throughout its history Mobil has always had plenty of markets; it has never had a comfortable reserve of domestic crude.

Of Mobil's two progenitors, Socony was by far the larger and more generalized oil company, while Vacuum's expertise lay in the production of high-quality machine lubricants. Vacuum got its start in 1866, when a carpenter and part-time inventor in Rochester, New York, named Matthew Ewing devised a new method of distilling kerosene from oil using a vacuum. The process itself proved to be no great discovery, but Ewing's partner Hiram Bond Everest, investor of $20 seed capital, noticed that its gummy residue was suitable for lubrication, and the two men took out a patent on behalf of the Vacuum Oil Company in 1866. Ewing sold his interest in Vacuum to Everest shortly thereafter, but the heavy Vacuum oil was soon much in demand by manufacturers of steam engines and the new internal-combustion engines. In 1869 Everest patented Gargoyle 600-W Steam Cylinder Oil, which was still in use in 1990, and the firm continued to prosper.

Within a decade Vacuum had expanded sufficiently to catch the eye of John D. Rockefeller's Standard Oil Company. Beginning in 1872, Standard had bought up scores of refineries and marketing companies around the country, and in 1879 it added Vacuum Oil to its list of conquests, paying $200,000 for 75% of Vacuum's stock. By that date Standard Oil had achieved an effective monopoly of the oil business in the United States. Despite its small size, Vacuum was given latitude by the Standard management, who respected its excellent products and the acumen of Hiram Everest and his son, C.M. Everest.

The Everests pursued an independent course in foreign sales. As early as 1885 Vacuum had opened affiliates in Montreal, Canada, and in Liverpool, England, where its staff included 19 salespeople, and within the next decade added branches in Toronto, Milan, and Bombay. Vacuum became the leader among Standard's companies in the use of efficient marketing and sales techniques, packaging its lubricants in attractive tins, pursuing customers with a well-organized, efficient sales team, and, when necessary, bringing in a lubricants specialist to help customers choose the oil best suited to their needs. Company oils were made according to a secret formula and by 1911 the Vacuum marketers had made the name Mobiloil known on five continents. At home, Vacuum products were sold nationwide by the Standard chain of distributors and in the Northeast by Vacuum's own agents.

In 1906 Vacuum added a second refinery to its original Rochester plant, and in 1910 Standard Oil Company of New Jersey, (Jersey Standard), the holding company for the Standard interests, invested $500,000 to enable its big Bayonne, New Jersey, refinery to manufacture some of Vacuum's lubricants for export. In 1911 the Standard companies were ordered to break up by the United States Supreme Court, and among the 34 splinters from the great parent were Vacuum Oil and Standard Oil Company of New York (Socony). Socony was the second-largest of the newly independent companies and had played an important role for the Rockefellers and Standard Oil for nearly 30 years. Socony was created along with Jersey Standard in 1882, both as a legal domicile for Standard's New York assets and to serve as the administrative and banking center for the entire Standard Oil Trust. William Rockefeller, John D. Rockefeller's younger brother and long-time business partner, remained the president of Socony from its inception until 1911.

From the first it was planned that in addition to serving as Standard's headquarters, Socony would handle the great bulk of the trust's growing foreign sales. It took over from Standard Oil Company of Ohio ownership of the merchant firm of Meissner, Ackermann & Company with offices in New York and Hamburg, Germany, and agents around Europe. At first Standard relied exclusively on such brokers for is foreign business, but as the years went on the company set up its own foreign subsidiaries around the world. By 1910 the Standard subsidiaries had usurped almost all of the foreign sales, with Socony's affiliates handling about 30%, while Vacuum Oil, which had also built a small but widespread sales group, contributed 6% to the total. In addition to the sales it made itself, Socony also bought and then resold all Standard products leaving New York, and even for a time those shipped out of California to Asia. Bolstered by its double role, Socony's sales were among the largest of any Standard company, and as

Standard's official overseas representative it became a familiar name in many countries.

Another of Socony's important functions, especially prior to 1899, when Jersey Standard began assuming such duties, was to administer most of the Standard group's internal affairs. In the New York City office building at 26 Broadway were housed not only Socony's own corporate leaders but the small group of men who ran Standard Oil. Some individuals, such as William Rockefeller, served on both boards, and the interplay between Socony and the Standard group as a whole was intimate and complex. Socony also assumed banking functions for the group. After 1899 Jersey Standard became the sole holding company for all of the Standard interests, but Socony continued much as before in its various key roles.

By the time of the dissolution of Standard in 1911, Socony had established its position in the European and African markets and built a thriving business in Asia as well. China became an important market for Socony. Socony eventually built a network of subsidiaries from Japan to Turkey which by 1910 was handling nearly 50% of the kerosene sold in Asia. At home, Socony's five refineries turned out kerosene, gasoline, and naptha for sale in New York and New England, through jobbers and a growing number of the new roadside stores known as "gas stations."

In 1911 the Supreme Court upheld a lower court's conviction of Jersey Standard for violation of the Sherman Antitrust Act and ordered the organization dissolved. Each of the 34 new companies created by the order was allotted varying proportions of the three basic oil assets—crude production, refining, and marketing—but neither Socony nor Vacuum Oil ended up with any sources of crude. Both companies were strong marketers and refiners, and both would be occupied by the search for enough crude oil to keep their plants and salesmen busy. Socony's need for its own crude supplies was greater since it produced a large volume of oil-based fuels and lubricants, while Vacuum's business was more limited in both volume and variety. Socony set out to secure ownership of its own wells.

At that point in the history of U.S. oil production the natural area in which to explore was in Texas, Louisiana, and Oklahoma, and in 1918 Socony bought 45% of Magnolia Petroleum Company. Magnolia owned wells, pipelines, and a refinery at Beaumont, Texas, and did most of its marketing in Texas and the Southwest. After buying the rest of Magnolia in 1925, Socony purchased General Petroleum Corporation of California to help supply its large Far East markets. Then it entered the Midwest for the first time with a 1930 purchase of White Eagle Oil & Refining Company with gas stations in 11 states. Socony now needed even more crude oil to supply these additional market outlets, and like most of the other big international oil concerns Socony looked to the Middle East.

World War I had demonstrated the crucial role of oil in modern warfare and prompted the U.S. government to encourage U.S. participation in the newly formed Turkish Petroleum Company, operating in present-day Iraq. A consortium of U.S. oil companies was sold 25% of Turkish Petroleum. By the early 1930s only Jersey Standard and Socony were left in the partnership, each eventually holding 12%. Oil was first struck by the company, renamed Iraq Petroleum Company, in 1928 and by 1934 the partners had built a pipeline across the Levant

to Haifa, Palestine. From Haifa Socony could ship oil to its many European subsidiaries.

In the meantime, Vacuum Oil had made a number of important domestic acquisitions and strengthened its already far-flung network of foreign subsidiaries, but continued to share Socony's chronic shortage of crude. The two companies, similar in profile and complementary in product mix, joined forces in 1931 when Socony purchased the assets of Vacuum and changed its name to Socony-Vacuum Corporation. The union was the first alliance between members of the former Jersey Standard conglomerate and created a company with formidable refining and marketing strengths both at home and abroad. To supply its joint Far East markets more efficiently, in 1933 Socony-Vacuum (SV) and Jersey Standard created another venture called Standard-Vacuum Oil Company (Stan-Vac). Stan-Vac would ship oil from Jersey Standard's large Indonesian holdings to SV's extensive marketing outlets from Japan to East Africa. By 1941 it was contributing 35% of SV's corporate earnings.

In 1934 Socony-Vacuum Corporation changed its name to Socony-Vacuum Oil Company, Inc. (SVO). The company's growth made SVO the second-largest U.S. oil concern by the mid-1930s, with nearly $500 million in sales, exclusive of Stan-Vac. From warehouses and gas stations in 43 states and virtually every country in the world, SVO sold a full line of petroleum products, many of them sporting some variant of Vacuum's famous Mobil brand name or its equally familiar flying red horse logo. With 14 refineries in Europe alone and a fleet of 54 ocean-going tankers, by 1941 SVO's holdings were truly international in scope and balance—a situation that caused growing anxiety as World War II approached. When the Nazis stormed across Western Europe they found a good number of working SVO refineries and promptly put them in the service of the Third Reich. The largest prize, a huge refinery at Gravenchon, France, was destroyed by the retreating French in a blaze that lasted seven days. Similarly, the $30 million Stan-Vac refinery at Palembang, Indonesia, was kept out of Japanese hands by burning it to the ground. The war also cost SVO some 32 ships and the lives of 432 crew members, lost to German submarines. On the other hand, vastly increased military sales generally made up for SVO's wartime capital losses and declining civilian revenue.

Socony-Vacuum Oil Company's search for crude oil continued. In the immediate postwar years SVO completed a transaction that would provide the company with oil for many years to come. In the 1930s, Standard Oil Company (California) and the Texas Company—later known as Chevron and Texaco, respectively—had bought drilling rights to a huge chunk of Saudi Arabia, and when they realized the extent of the fields there the two companies sought partners with investment capital and overseas markets. SVO and Jersey Standard had ample amounts of both, and they agreed to split the offered 40% interest in the newly formed Arabian American Oil Company (Aramco). SVO had second thoughts about so large an investment and settled for 10% instead. This miscalculation was rendered less painful by the truly enormous scale of the Arabian oil reserves. In the coming decade of economic growth and skyrocketing consumption of oil, SVO would develop and depend upon its Arabian connection even more strongly than the other major oil concerns.

In the United States a new culture based on the automobile and abundant supplies of cheap gasoline spread the boundaries of cities and built a nationwide system of interstate highways. SV's long use of its Mobil trade names and flying red horse logo had made these symbols known around the country, and in 1955 the company capitalized on this by changing its name to Socony Mobil Oil Company, Inc. (SM). In 1958 sales reached $2.8 billion and continued upward with the steadily growing U.S. economy, hitting $4.3 billion five years later and $6.5 billion in 1967. In 1960 a subsidiary, Mobil Chemical Company, was formed to take advantage of the many discoveries in the field of petrochemicals. Mobil Chemical manufactures a wide range of plastic packaging, petrochemicals, and chemical additives. In 1989 it contributed 32% of Mobil's net operating income—generated on sales representing less than 7% of the corporate total.

Egypt's nationalization of the Suez Canal in 1956 was one of many indications that SM's Middle Eastern dependence would one day prove to be a liability, but there was little the company could do to reduce this dependence. Even significant new finds in Texas and the Gulf of Mexico were not able to keep pace with America's oil consumption, and by 1966 the Middle East, principally Saudi Arabia, supplied 43% of SM's crude production. Also in 1966 Socony Mobil Oil Company changed its name to Mobil Oil Corporation, using "Mobil" as its sole corporate and trade name, retiring the flying horse in favor of a streamlined "Mobil" with a bright-red "o." Still constantly searching for alternative sources of crude, Mobil got a piece of both the North Sea fields and the Prudhoe Bay region of Alaska in the late 1960s, although neither would be of much help for a number of years. In the meantime, world consumption had slowly overtaken production and shifted the market balance in favor of the Organization of Petroleum Exporting Countries (OPEC), which would soon take advantage of the relative scarcity to enforce its world cartel.

During the 1960s Mobil Oil's 9% annual increase in net income was the best of all major oil companies, and it continued as a major supplier of natural gas and oil to the world's two fastest-growing economies, West Germany and Japan. In 1973, however, OPEC placed an embargo on oil shipments to the United States for six months and began gradual annexation of U.S.-owned oil properties. The price of oil quadrupled overnight and a new era of energy awareness began, as the international oil companies lost the comfortable positions they had held in the Middle East since the 1920s. On the other hand, the immediate result of OPEC's move was to boost sales and profits at all the oil majors. Mobil Oil's sales nearly tripled between 1973 and 1977 to $32 billion, and 1974 profits hit record highs, prompting a barrage of congressional and media criticism that was answered by Mobil Oil's own public relations department. Mobil Oil quickly became famous as the most outspoken defender of the oil industry's right to conduct its business as it saw fit.

Despite its apparent ability to make money in any oil environment, Mobil Oil was concerned about the imminent loss of its legal control over the middle eastern oil on which it depended. Under the special guidance of President and Chief Operating Officer William Tavoulareas, Mobil Oil chose to strengthen its ties with Saudi Arabia, spending large amounts of time and money courting the Saudi leaders, investing in industrial projects, and in 1974 acquiring an additional 5% of the stock in Aramco from its partners. In 1976 Mobil Oil Corporation again changed its name, to Mobil Corporation. In the 1990s it enjoys one of the closest relationships with the Saudis of any oil firm, a bond whose value increases sharply when oil is scarce but is a liability when plentiful supplies make Mobil's purchases of the expensive Saudi crude less than a bargain. In addition, Mobil has considerably increased its budget for oil exploration, concentrating mainly on the North Sea, Gulf of Mexico, and Prudhoe Bay regions. Although these efforts have by and large succeeded in replacing Mobil's reserves as fast as they are used up, the company bought Superior Oil Company in 1984. Mobil paid $5.7 billion for Superior, mainly for its extensive reserves of natural gas and oil.

By that time the oil market had once again changed course. Conservation measures and a generally sluggish world economy reversed the price of oil in 1981, and it continued to drop throughout the decade. Mobil thus found itself locked into contracts for expensive Saudi crude and burdened with the debts incurred in the Superior purchase at a time of falling revenues. To make ends meet, Chairman Rawleigh Warner Jr. and his 1986 successor Allen E. Murray made substantial cuts in refineries and service stations, upgrading Mobil's holdings of both to a smaller number of more modern, efficient units. By 1988 Mobil had pulled out of the retail gasoline business in 20 states and derived 88% of its retail revenue from just 14 states, mostly in the Northeast. It had also cut its oil-related employment by 20% as well as getting rid of its Montgomery Ward and Container Corporation of America subsidiaries, holdovers from a mid-1970s diversification move.

The $6 billion sale of assets was used to reduce debt, and Mobil's financial performance improved accordingly as the decade drew to a close, although not enough to please Wall Street analysts. The 1980s were generally not a good period for Mobil, which continued, on paper at least, to show a worrisome decline in proven oil reserves. On the other hand, if the instability the Middle East displayed in the early 1990s continues, Mobil's carefully cultivated friendship with Saudi Arabia may prove to be of critical importance.

Principal Subsidiaries: Mobil Exploration & Producing U.S. Inc.; Mobil Exploration & Producing North America, Inc.; Mobil Land Development Corporation; Mobil Natural Gas Inc.; Mobil Oil Corporation; Mobil Oil Exploration & Producing Southeast Inc.; Mobil Producing Texas & New Mexico Inc.; Tucker Housewares Inc.

Further Reading: Hidy, Ralph W., and Muriel E. Hidy, *History of Standard Oil Company (New Jersey): Pioneering in Big Business, 1882–1911*, New York, Harper & Brothers, 1955; Sampson, Anthony, *The Seven Sisters: The Great Oil Companies and the World They Made*, New York, The Viking Press, 1975; *A brief history of Mobil*, New York, Mobil Corporation, 1991.

—Jonathan Martin

NATIONAL IRANIAN OIL COMPANY

Ayatollah Taleghani Street
Tehran
Iran
(21) 6151
Fax: (21) 640-4132

State-Owned Company
Incorporated: 1951

National Iranian Oil Company (NIOC) is the state-owned oil company of Iran, which was Persia until 1935. Its evolution has been shaped by the turbulent history of that country since World War II. Today NIOC is a very large oil-producing company, but one whose future continues to depend on political developments in Iran.

NIOC was formed as a result of tensions between the British-owned Anglo-Persian Oil Company—renamed Anglo-Iranian Oil Company in 1935 and British Petroleum Company in 1954—and the Persian and then Iranian government, which came to a head after World War II. The British oil company had found oil in southwest Iran in 1908 and, on the basis of this discovery and the support of the British government, which acquired a 51% shareholding in it in 1914, it had grown to become one of the world's largest international oil companies by the 1930s. However, there was resentment within Iran at the privileged position held by Anglo-Iranian, and its close association with the British government, whose imperialist ambitions were feared. The British invaded and occupied Iran in alliance with the Soviet Union in 1941, which did nothing to reduce suspicion of the oil company. There was particular resentment at the low amount of royalties paid to the government by Anglo-Iranian. In 1948 negotiations began to improve the share of oil income retained by Iran, but these were unsuccessful, and in 1951 the strongly nationalist prime minister, Dr. Muhammad Mussadegh nationalized the oil industry. The resulting conflict became one of the great causes célèbres in the history of oil-company–host-government relationships in the 20th century.

NIOC was incorporated by the Iranian government on April 30, 1951, as the corporate instrument of the government's nationalization policy. Initially it took over all the employees and physical assets of Anglo-Iranian within Iran, with instructions to set aside 25% of its profits to meet compensation claims by the British company. However, NIOC's attempts to take con-

trol of the industry were gravely weakened because the main international oil companies boycotted Iranian oil exports to demonstrate their support for the British company. Iranian production collapsed, as the oil majors replaced Iranian oil with expanded production from Kuwait and Saudi Arabia. In 1953 Mussadegh was overthrown in a coup. In the following year agreement was reached between the conflicting parties. The result was a new role for NIOC.

In September 1954 an eight-member consortium called the Iranian Oil Participants (IOP) was formed. The arrangement was similar to others in operation in much of the rest of the Middle East. The shareholding was in the hands of the major Western oil majors. British Petroleum Company (BP) held 40%, Shell 14%, Chevron 8%, Exxon 8%, Gulf 8%, Mobil 8%, Texaco 8%, and Compagnie Française de Pétroles 6%. NIOC was recognized as the owner of Iran's oil deposits and of all installed assets of the Iranian oil industry, but actual control over the industry was placed firmly in the hands of the consortium members. NIOC lacked influence over the production, refining, and export of Iranian crude oil and products. Two companies owned by IOP—the Iranian Oil Exploration and Producing Company and the Iranian Oil Refining Company—operated the assets formally owned by NIOC, to whom they were officially appointed as contractors. They produced oil for NIOC, which was then sold to IOP member companies which were responsible for export marketing. An additional secret agreement between the IOP companies, which did not become public until the early 1970s, established the aggregate programmed quantity formula, which effectively gave those member companies with the lowest reliance on Iranian oil the greatest influence over how much should be produced. The upshot was that Iran's oil production grew comparatively slowly over the following decade.

Despite these constraints, NIOC was able, during the second half of the 1950s, to develop its role as an independent oil company. A law in 1957 empowered it to enter into joint ventures with foreign oil companies to explore areas other than those leased to IOP. The first joint venture agreement was signed by the Italian oil company Agip SpA. This was a subsidiary of the state energy corporation ENI and was led by the entrepreneurial Enrico Mattei, who was searching for a source of cheap oil not controlled by the oil majors. In August 1957 the Société Irano-Italienne des Pétroles (Sirip) was formed, owned 50% by NIOC and 50% by Agip. In June 1958 a similar joint-venture agreement was signed with Standard Oil Company of Indiana, which formed a company jointly owned with NIOC called the Iran Pan American Oil Company (Ipac). By 1961 both ventures were producing crude oil, with Ipac enjoying particular success.

The joint-venture strategy was developed in the 1960s. In 1965 six new joint-venture agreements were signed, followed by three more, including one with a Japanese group, in 1971. In December 1966 the Iranian government, having discovered the existence of the aggregate programmed quantity formula, forced IOP to increase production to give up 25% of the area in which it had exploration rights, and to supply NIOC with 1.47 billion barrels of crude oil for export over the following five years. As a result of the joint venture arrangements and the December 1966 agreement NIOC began to have its own supply of crude oil, although it still controlled only a tiny proportion of total Iranian crude exports. In 1960 the consortium accounted for 99.9% of Iranian crude oil exports. By 1973 its share had fallen to 89.2%. NIOC accounted for 5.8% and the varying joint ventures the remaining 5% by that date.

During the second half of the 1960s NIOC heightened its exploration efforts within Iran through the use of service contracts. Service contracts differed from joint ventures in that the foreign operator had no ownership rights in Iran at all, but was only a contractor working for NIOC and was remunerated for its services with crude oil. In August 1966 NIOC concluded a 25-year service contract with the French state oil company ERAP which created a new Iranian-registered subsidiary, Sofiran, to explore for oil. NIOC made all policy decisions in respect of Sofiran's operations within Iran, while Sofiran had functional management responsibility. During 1969 two further service contracts were awarded to a group of European oil companies and of U.S. independents.

During the 1960s NIOC had sufficient crude to begin international marketing. Initially attention was focused on Eastern Europe, Asia, and Africa. In Eastern Europe NIOC reached a number of barter agreements, under which it would exchange oil for manufactured goods. NIOC also sought to establish a presence in overseas refining. In 1969 NIOC and Standard Oil Company of Indiana each took a 13% stake in an Indian refinery at Madras which was supplied with Iranian crude by Ipac. In 1971 NIOC took a 17.5% interest in a new South African refinery, again signing a long-term supply contract. In the same year, a 24.5% stake was taken in the Madras Fertilizer Plant. A tanker fleet was developed by a NIOC subsidiary, the National Iranian Oil Tanker Company. By 1974 the fleet had four ocean-going tankers. In 1965 NIOC established another subsidiary, the National Petrochemical Company (NPC), which launched a series of wholly owned and joint-venture chemicals and fertilizer plants within Iran. By the early 1970s NIOC had become a medium-sized international oil company, ranked in size alongside ENI and U.S. independents such as Atlantic Richfield Company and Occidental. In terms of share of world crude oil production, it controlled just under 1% at this time, which made it about the 19th-largest oil company in the world by this measure.

The Iranian government was a prominent player in the events in the early 1970s which led to the end of the consortium system in the Middle East, and the huge price rises of 1973 and 1974. However, because the 1951 nationalization of the Iranian oil industry had never been canceled, there was no formal transfer of assets of the kind seen almost everywhere in the Arab world. In July 1973 negotiations between IOP and the Iranian government led to a new agreement which replaced that signed in 1954. NIOC assumed sole responsibility over the former consortium area. The IOP member companies agreed to provide part of the future capital investment in production operations by NIOC in the form of annual prepayments against their future crude oil purchases. The IOP companies were also given preferential oil-purchase rights in Iran for a period of 20 years. Subsequently there were endless disputes between the oil company, the Iranian government, and NIOC about these arrangements, which continued right up to February 1979, when the shah and his government were swept away by the Islamic revolution.

Throughout its existence in the shah's Iran, NIOC had been an instrument of the government. Nominally it was a public company and not a state-owned corporation, although all its shares were government owned. In practice NIOC operated under the close scrutiny of the government. The prices of its four main products—gasoline, kerosene, gas oil, and fuel oil— could not be changed without the approval of the Iranian Cabinet. In 1962 Dr. Eqbal, a former prime minister, was appointed chairman and managing director, and government control was further exercised through a body called the Shareholders's Representatives, which consisted of seven ministers headed by the contemporary prime minister. Oil was the driving force behind the shah's flawed attempt to modernize Iran, hence NIOC was of key strategic importance to the regime. Oil provided 90% of Iran's foreign-exchange earnings in the last years of the shah's rule. Given the atmosphere of corruption that pervaded most aspects of Iranian life by the 1970s, it was remarkable that NIOC was able to develop and function as a modern integrated oil company, but the enterprise was not immune to the intense personal and political rivalries which afflicted the ruling elite.

NIOC was placed under the direct control of a newly created Ministry of Petroleum in September 1979. The Islamic government immediately ended the purchasing privileges enjoyed by IOP, and the 1973 agreement with IOP was abrogated by Iran in 1981. In 1980 all NIOC's joint-venture and service-contract agreements with foreign oil companies were terminated. The joint-venture companies were wound up and regrouped under the Iranian Offshore Oil Company of the Islamic Republic. Names of oil fields with imperial connotations were changed. From 1980, for example, Cyrus became Sorush, and Feridun became Foroozan. The investment in the South African refinery was abandoned, although NIOC retained its holding in India's Madras refinery. There was a period of considerable confusion in the first years after the revolution, with NIOC losing strategic direction. The first post-revolutionary chairman, Hassan Nazeh, caught on the wrong side in this period of rapid political change, resigned along with the rest of the board of directors six months after his appointment, and fled to France. The influence of the workers' committees which sprang up in this period was a prime reason for management instability, but NIOC seems to have been able to retain some professional managers by hiring them on advisory contracts.

The following years were bleak ones for the company. Oil production fell 75% between 1979 and 1981. The disruption caused by the revolution was followed by the imposition of trade sanctions by the United States and other industrial countries during the period of the U.S.–Iranian hostage crisis between November 1979 and January 1981. The outbreak of war with Iraq in September 1980 was followed by physical damage to oil installations. The large Abadan refinery was badly damaged by Iraqi attacks in 1980 and 1982. Iran's main crude oil export terminal at Kharg Island was repeatedly damaged by Iraqi air attacks, and in August 1986 NIOC's Sirri Island terminal was wrecked by Iraqi bombers. NIOC had to switch to a temporary loading point at Larak Island, in the Strait of Hormuz, which could be better protected but raised costs. The revolutionary government was committed to reducing Iran's dependence on oil, and had a stated policy of restricting output to less than three million barrels per day. In practice, the disastrous war with Iraq, combined with the deterioration in the world market for crude after 1981 and OPEC export quotas, left NIOC in no position to expand production even if it had so wanted.

NIOC's situation when the Iranian cease-fire with Iraq was arranged in August 1988 was difficult. Many oil installations were destroyed. By 1990 crude oil production had risen to 2.3 million barrels per day from 2 million in 1988 with exports averaging 1.7 million barrels per day, but refining capacity was still down, and NIOC had to import some petroleum products from overseas refineries which processed Iranian crude.

NIOC displayed considerable resilience in these circumstances. Their oil engineers were able to repair war damage and increase production during 1989, which grew to 2.85 million barrels per day. During 1989 several new medium and large oil fields were discovered. Plans were made to construct additional refinery capacity of 450,000 barrels per day, largely at Bandar Abbas and Arak, by the end of 1993. At the end of 1990 a contract was awarded to ETPM Entrêpose of France to rebuild the Kharg oil export terminal.

In 1991 NIOC remained as dependent as ever on the political conditions in its home economy and region, which had been thrown into uncertainty yet again by Iraq's invasion of Kuwait in August 1990. Leaving aside these fundamental uncertainties, the company controlled a considerable amount of crude oil production. In 1990 it was announced that it would join with Malaysian and Indonesian interests in a new refinery project in Keddah state, Malaysia. NIOC also claimed to operate, through its subsidiary the National Iranian Oil Tanker Company, the world's third-largest tanker fleet of 5.55 million tons. The company owned 28 oil tankers and 32 other vessels, and had on charter 35 oil tankers and 34 other vessels. NIOC was also one of the largest employers in Iran, where it was engaged on a large scale in the provision of housing and medical care for its workers alongside more conventional activities. Arguably the rehabilitation and further development of the Iranian oil industry will be best achieved by re-establishing contracts with Western oil majors who could provide technology and expertise, but that—like so much in NIOC's history—is a political decision on which NIOC's management is unlikely to have the final word.

Principal Subsidiaries: National Iranian Drilling Company; National Iranian Oil Tanker Company.

Further Reading: Stocking, George W., *Middle East Oil*, London, Allen Lane, 1970; Fesharaki, Fereidun, *Development of the Iranian Oil Industry*, New York, Praeger, 1976; Evans, John, *OPEC: Its Member States and the World Energy Market*, London, Longman, 1986.

—Geoffrey Jones

NESTE OY

Post Office Box 20
SF-02151 Espoo
Finland
(0) 4501
Fax (0) 4504447

State-Owned Company
Incorporated: 1948
Employees: 11,278
Sales: Fmk46.63 billion (US$12.86 billion)

Neste Oy is the second-largest polyolefins plastics manufacturer in Western Europe and the second-largest resins manufacturer in the world. It is Finland's largest company, in terms of sales. It is state-owned, and refines all the crude oil imported to the country, and produces and exports petrochemicals in Finland and abroad. Neste began as an oil storage company, became an oil refining company, and later added petrochemical production to its activities.

In Finland there was never any form of nationalization of existing private industry as occurred in many countries after World War II. State ownership was considered to be a viable way of introducing a new industry in which no interest had been shown by existing companies in the sector.

Before World War II, Finland had no oil refineries. The country was one of the few in Europe that imported all its oil and petroleum products from abroad. When World War II broke out in 1939, Finland was not prepared to cope with the problems which ensued. In September 1939, petrol rationing started in Finland. Fuel and lubricant oils were placed under the control of a special agency called PVa, from the Finnish words for fuel oil storage, under the guidance of the Ministry of Defense. The new agency was led by Colonel Väinö Vartiainen, who was later to play an important part in the early days of Neste. Dr. Albert Sundgren, Finland's only petrochemicals expert, was on the staff of PVA. Earlier he had advocated the establishment of an oil refinery in Finland.

The agency planned to store its fuel oil and lubricant supplies in caves in the granite rocks of Tupavuori, in the township of Naantali on Finland's southwestern coast. A company was to be created to execute the plan.

The storage caves in Naantali were named NKV, from the Finnish words for Naantali Central Storage. After the end of the war, work to complete the caves went on. Responsibility for the NKV project was transferred from the Ministry of Defense to the Ministry of Trade and Industry in June 1947. NKV became a limited company, Neste Oy, and its first general meeting was held on January 2, 1948. The state of Finland was registered as a shareholder with 207 shares, Oy Alkoholiliike Ab, the state-owned alcohol monopoly with 140 shares; and Imatran Voima Osakeyhtiö, the state-owned power company, with 3 shares.

In the articles of association of the company, it was stated that its purpose was to own and rent storage for liquid fuels and lubricants, and to act as importer, transporter, and manufacturer, of these products, as well as trading in them. The beginnings of Neste were not very auspicious. In the spring of 1948, Neste purchased an old tanker of 8,896 pennyweight (dwt) from Norway. The ship was a financial disaster. The caves also gave the company problems, when in July 1949 a dangerous fire broke out. The company was in financial difficulties. An agreement between Neste and the government was signed in October 1950, whereby Neste returned some of the less suitable storage space to the state for a remuneration of Fmk150 million.

Uolevi Raade, director in the early 1950s of the Department of Industry within the Ministry of Trade and Industry, had become aware of Sundgren's plans for an oil refinery. Raade perceived that a major plan of national importance was waiting for his imagination and will power, and he accepted the challenge. The fortunes of Neste began to change.

Finland had traditionally relied on the services rendered by the major oil companies. They had a strong influence upon Finland's Department of Trade. They tried to make the refinery plans look unfavorable. Raade, however, was known for getting his way. He convinced the minister of trade and industry, Penna Tervo, of the importance of a national refinery. However, when the plan was brought to the government for the first time in 1951, it was not accepted. Raade had to start anew. He finally managed in 1954 to convince Dr. Urho Kekkonen, the influential politician and future president of Finland, of the importance of a national oil refinery. On December 17, 1954, the Finnish parliament authorized Neste to start building an oil refinery with 700,000 tons crude oil capacity.

Raade was named president of Neste on March 1, 1955. Vartiainen remained chairman of the board of directors, and was succeeded by Raade in 1959. Raade nominated Mikko Tanner as technical director. Raade had become aware that Tanner was an excellent engineer when constructing the fertilizer plants of Typpi Oy in Oulu. The managing director up to this time, Eino Erho, was to continue as commercial director of the company. An area near the cave storage reservoirs was selected as the future site of the refinery. The harbor conditions at Tupavuori were considered to be excellent.

The planning of the refinery was entrusted to the U.S. firm of planners The Lummus Company, a specialist in the field. The delivery of plant and equipment was entrusted jointly to the French company Compagnie de Five-Lille and Germany's Mannesmann. The civil engineering was carried out by Neste itself.

Construction work started at Tupavuori in Naantali in October 1955, and the inauguration of the refinery was held on June 5, 1958. The start-up of production in August 1957 had already shown that no technical problems existed. The guaranteed capacity of 700,000 tons was reached by the beginning of

October, and soon it was apparent that the new refinery could reach a capacity of up to 1.2 million tons of crude oil per year.

Neste had planned to refine crude oil from many sources, half of the supply coming from the Soviet Union, and half from Western suppliers. As the company had no intention of forming a retail delivery system of its own, the marketing of products was based on cooperation with oil companies already operating in Finland. The most important of these were Shell, Esso, and Gulf. Shell and Gulf delivered crude oil of their own to be refined by Neste. All prices were tied to international market rates.

Raade kept up with market requirements. Neste's strategy was to deliver all the motor petrol Finland needed and adjust the production of other derivatives of crude oil accordingly. Thus the company chose a technology which gave maximum petrol output. The bilateral trade between the Soviet Union and Finland guaranteed that increased imports from the Soviet Union would mean new possibilities for exporting Finnish products. In 1960 Neste decided to double the capacity of the Naantali refinery. When the extension was completed and production started in September 1962, a capacity of 2.5 million tons of crude oil was reached.

Raade, however, already had new plans. In November 1962 he presented to his supervisory board a plan to construct a second refinery. He also proposed to purchase the Sköldvik Manor, with an area of 628 hectares near the town of Porvoo, east of Helsinki, as the location of the new refinery. The site had good access to deep waters. This rural area was to be changed into a huge heavy chemical industrial complex within a short time. Later the "green (environmental) movement" became active in opposing Neste as responsible for the change.

In 1963, however, when Lummus and Neste engineers were making plans for the new refinery, the plans received favorable publicity. Finland was living in a climate of industrial growth and was optimistic about the future expansion of technology. The plan to create a new refinery, with capacity equal to that of the enlarged Naantali refinery, was approved in June 1963. Soon Raade demanded that the construction be accelerated. Some of the suppliers had timing problems, and the start-up in spring 1966 was delayed by nearly a year. This did not stop Raade from ordering extensions to the new refinery to be built for start-up in 1968, doubling the refinery's capacity. This new extension started production three months before the planned start-up date. Neste regained some of the reputation it had lost as a result of the earlier delays. Uolevi Raade shared the visions of Sundgren regarding the future of petrochemicals and made careful plans for the realization of his dreams. At the inauguration of the first refinery in Naantali, it was stated in public that petrochemicals were closely associated with the refinery business, and that they would eventually come into Neste's domain. In 1959 Raade had taken Sundgren and two members of his board to Italy to study the activities of ENI and Montecatini. When presenting to the supervisory board his plans for the building of the oil refinery in Sköldvik, Raade told his audience that Neste would continue its development by entering the petrochemicals sector after 1967. Neste started detailed planning for this event, again with Lummus. In 1968 the plan was ready for presentation. The first stage included a plant for producing ethylene. This unit would form an integrated part of the oil refinery in Sköldvik. The second stage would be a plant for producing polyethylene and polyvinyl-

chloride (PVC). This production would be carried out by a separate company, formed by Neste and its principal customers. Both units were planned to start production in 1972. In March 1969, a company named Pekema Oy was formed to realize the latter plan. Pekema had eight shareholders, all well-known Finnish industrial companies. Neste was the largest shareholder with 44% of the shares. The plant for the company was erected in the vicinity of the Sköldvik refinery. Production started at the beginning of 1972, at the same time as the start of production at Neste's ethylene unit. The company worked for a few years in close cooperation with Neste, but in 1979 the production facilities of Pekema were transferred to Neste and integrated into the company.

At the beginning of the 1970s four industrial companies, one of them Neste, formed a company, Stymer Oy, to produce polystyrene, another basic material for the plastics industry. The facilities of this company were also erected in the vicinity of the Sköldvik refinery. In 1981 this facility too was integrated into Neste. Neste also purchased other outside units tied to the refinery and making other chemicals for the plastics industry. Neste was now the dominant petrochemicals producer in Finland.

Few industrial projects in Finland have received as much publicity as Neste's plans for a third refinery. Neste had calculated that new refinery capacity would be needed in 1976. After careful study, the company proposed to build another refinery in Lappohja near Hanko. These plans were presented to the supervisory board in October 1970. Helsinki University, whose biological station in Lappohja was considered internationally to be important for the study of wildlife in the Baltic, reacted violently against the plan. A large media debate ensued. "Green values" had become important and politicians were no longer easily converted to Raade's plans. The government assigned an area in Pyhämaa on the Gulf of Bothnia for the planned new refinery. Plans were altered accordingly.

Some doubts still lingered in top political circles. The prime minister, Dr. Mauno Koivisto, told his cabinet that the question should be reconsidered. Against Raade's opinion but with the consent of Tanner, it was decided that new capacity should be added onto the existing refinery.

The final decision was to double the capacity of Sköldvik, now more frequently called the Porvoo refinery, after the town where it is located. As Finland has no oil or gas resources of its own, the small amount of natural gas it required had been provided by imports, mainly from Denmark. However, Finnish industry was interested in gas supply on a large scale, such as was found in many countries. The Soviet Union was interested in extending its network of natural gas pipes as far as the border of Finland and in signing a long-term delivery contract. Because of the bilateral trade, Finnish industry was continually looking for new import items from the Soviet Union in order to promote its own exports. In 1971 Finland signed an agreement with the Soviet Union for deliveries of natural gas to Finland. In the same year, Neste became involved in this project. A network for the distribution of natural gas was established by Neste and delivery contracts were drawn up with industrial customers. Gradually the network has been enlarged, but the ultimate goal to link the network to Norwegian gas sources has not yet been achieved. Neste had decided in the 1940s that the crude oil should be imported mainly by ships owned by the company. The size of the ships altered according to changing shipping needs. Soviet oil was first imported from Black Sea ports, and later from Baltic ports. Crude oil was also imported from the Persian Gulf. In the early 1970s the Neste fleet had a capacity of over 300,000 pennyweight. After acquiring two supertankers of 260,000 pennyweight each, Neste's fleet consisted in the mid-1980s of 18 tankers, plus five tugs. At the beginning of the 1990s Neste had 19 ships, totalling 419,000 pennyweight. The supertankers had been sold. As a new technical solution, a push barge system was introduced for transporting bitumen. Neste made a considerable investment in its research facilities. At first, its efforts were mostly directed towards improving the quality of its products. After gaining experience in operating its refineries, Neste was able to develop a variety of products in cooperation with customers without having to modify its plant. The Neste research center was already aiming at an early stage to prepare the company for future investments in petrochemicals. Research into new applications of petrochemicals in wood-based industries produced Neswood, a plastic-impregnated wood, which was employed as flooring at Helsinki Airport.

Eventually Neste Research Center developed into a multiple division for improving technology. When the corporate organization was changed in 1981 to consist of business units with individual responsibilities for results, this included the research and development activities. The technology group includes all technical research and development activities within the company. The main activities are research into oil, catalysts, energy, engine performance, bitumen, combustion, and lubrication. Neste Engineering is a separate entity, mainly responsible for planning and directing new projects within the company.

Neste was intended to be an oil refiner, but from the start it was also intended to enter the petrochemicals sector. This happened exactly as Raade had predicted. After starting production of ethylene and after the absorption of the Pekama and Stymer joint ventures into Neste as fully owned operations, Neste added other petrochemicals to its range. The benzine unit opened in 1979. In 1981 the production of many industrial chemicals, such as phenol and acetone, began.

In 1981 Neste set up a coal trading division. However, it was soon found that this line of business did not suit the company. In 1985, the coal business was sold to a Finnish coal merchant.

In the same way as in the coal business, Neste planned to enter another area of energy production, and bought Pakkasakku Oy, a company making lead accumulator batteries. The battery market did not, however, fare well in the years leading up to 1990, when half of the shares of Neste Battery Ltd. were sold to the Spanish Grupo Tudor.

Neste still plans to be active in the energy sector on a broad scale. The company has a unit, Neste Advanced Power Systems, which studies applications of solar and wind energy as well as electric vehicle projects. These activities are centered on projects in Scandinavia, the United Kingdom, Greece, and Kenya. Uolevi Raade retired from his position as CEO and chairman of Neste in 1979 at the age of 68. His successor was Jaakko Ihamuotila, until then managing director of Valmet Oy. He kept to the strategy established by his predecessor. Even though initial steps to diversify the company's activities had not been successful, the main part of the strategy, strengthening Neste's position in chemicals, has been achieved. For 20 years Neste's chemicals division has been the fastest-growing division in Neste. Comprising six business groups, the division produces a wide range of major plastics at sites in Finland, Sweden, Belgium, Portugal, France, and the United States. The petrochemical plants at the Porvoo production complex, together with an ethylene cracker at Sines in Portugal, play a central role in Neste's chemical activities, producing ethylene, propylene, benzene, cumene, phenol, and acetone.

For Neste the international trading of crude oil and petroleum products has developed into an important line of business. With offices from Espoo in Finland to London, Houston, Tokyo, and Singapore, the corporation has a network which puts it among the foremost international oil traders. The composite materials group, based on reinforced plastics products and semi-finished goods, includes sports and leisure goods as well as products for electronics manufacturers and components for the aerospace, automotive, and paper machine industries.

State regulations regarding oil imports and pricing have favored the company. With the breakdown of the Soviet economy and the termination of bilateral trade between the Soviet Union and Finland, Neste has entered a new era. The future will show how the corporation will cope with the new trends for which it has been preparing. Joint ventures in oil drilling in the North Sea, the acquisition of companies abroad to strengthen its strategic position, and international trading of oil products suggest that Neste will survive the changes to come.

Principal Subsidiaries: Kesoil Group (89.9%); Union Group (76.7%); Neste Resin Group; Neste Oxo AB; Neste Polyeten AB; Neste Chemicals N.V.; Empresa de Polimeros de Sinos S.A. (96%); Neste Produtos Quimicos S.A.

Further Reading: Larsio, Rauno, *Nesteen tie 1948—1973*, [n.p.] Sanomapaino, 1974; *Neste öljystä muoveihin*, Espoo, Neste, 1982.

—Nils Björklund

NIGERIAN NATIONAL PETROLEUM CORPORATION

Falomo Office Complex
Ikoyi
Lagos
Federal Republic of Nigeria
(41) 603 100

State-Owned Company
Incorporated: 1971 as Nigerian National Oil Corporation
Employees: 17,000

The Nigerian National Petroleum Corporation (NNPC) is the holding company which oversees the Nigerian state's interests in the country's oil industry. NNPC owes its origins to the Nigerian government's determination to take hold of the direction of the country's most important export industry in the late 1960s and early 1970s. Its brief history has a been a checkered one, beset by the problems of operating a bureaucratic organization in a commercial world, difficulties that have been amplified by the complexities of oil production itself and of the world oil market.

Oil was first discovered in Nigeria in 1908, and exploration proceeded during the 1930s in the form of the Shell-BP Petroleum Development Company of Nigeria Ltd. (Shell-BP), under the control of Shell and British Petroleum (BP). However, commercial exploitation of the country's reserves did not begin until the late 1950s. The Nigerian government introduced its first regulations governing the taxation of oil industry profits in 1959 whereby profits would be split 50-50 between the government and the oil company in question, and the industry grew during the 1960s as export markets were developed, predominantly in the United Kingdom and Europe. By the mid-1960s, Nigeria began to consider ways in which the resources being exploited by Western oil companies could better be harnessed to the country's development, and formulated its first agreement for taking an equity stake in one of the companies producing there, the Nigerian Agip Oil Company, jointly owned by Agip of Italy and Phillips of the United States. The option to take up an equity state—in effect the first step toward the creation of the NNPC—was not, however, exercised until April of 1971.

By 1971, other factors were pushing the Nigerian government toward taking the stakes in the western companies that would constitute the basis of the NNPC's holdings. One was the Biafran war of secession, which began in 1967. The support given by one French oil company to Biafra, within whose territory some two-thirds of the country's then-known oil reserves were located, led the federal government to question the contribution of the foreign oil companies to the country's development. So, too, did the companies' unimpressive record in assisting transfer of technology, in social development, and in the employment of indigenous staff. The overriding factor was probably Nigeria's decision to join OPEC in July 1971 obliging the government to take significant stakes in the companies producing in the country.

This combination of pressures led to the formation of the Nigerian National Oil Corporation (NNOC) on April 1, 1971. The NNOC acquired a 33.33% stake in the Nigerian Agip Oil Company and 35% in Safrap, the Nigerian arm of the French company Elf. After Nigeria joined OPEC, NNOC acquired 35% stakes in Shell-BP, Gulf, and Mobil, on April 1, 1973. Also in 1973 it entered into a production-sharing agreement with Ashland Oil. On April 1, 1974, stakes in Elf, Agip/Phillips, Shell-BP, Gulf, and Mobil were increased to 55% and, on May 1, 1975, the NNOC acquired 55% of Texaco's operations in Nigeria.

The NNOC had been established under the terms of the government's Decree no. 18 of 1971. Its brief was to "participate in all aspects of petroleum including exploration, production, refining, marketing, transportation, and distribution." More specifically, the corporation was given the task of training indigenous workers; managing oil leases over large areas of the country; encouraging indigenous participation in the development of infrastructure for the industry; managing refineries, only one of which was operational at this time; participating in marketing and ensuring price uniformity across the domestic market; developing a national tanker fleet; constructing pipelines; and investigating allied industries, such as fertilizers.

This was an ambitious set of objectives, several of which were only just beginning to be realized in the 1990s. The problem which the NNOC faced from its inception was that of attempting to manage a highly complex industry without adequate technical and financial resources, problems which were to be dramatically illustrated several times during its subsequent history.

The NNOC had limited powers as a public corporation. It could sue and be sued, hold or purchase assets, and enter into partnerships. It could not borrow funds or dispose of assets without the specific approval of the commissioner of mines and power, and any surplus funds had to be disposed of at the commissioner's discretion, subject to the approval of the ruling Federal Executive Council. Any activities beyond the scope of Decree no. 18 required government approval, and the government was well represented on the NNOC's board, which was chaired by the permanent secretary of the Ministry of Mines and Power. Other board members included representatives from the ministries of Finance and of Economic Development and Planning, the director of Petroleum Resources in the Ministry of Mines and Power, the general manager of NNOC, and three other representatives with special knowledge of the industry. Thus, from the very start, a body which was seen as crucial to the future prosperity of the nation was subject to close government control, a feature of its operation that has remained throughout its history.

The NNOC operated a number of subsidiaries during the 1970s, including those in exploration and production, refining and petrochemicals, distribution and marketing, transportation, and equipment and supplies. Its success was perhaps most marked in the export field. Boosted by the sharp price rises that followed the first oil shock of 1973, Nigeria saw its oil export earnings rise from ₦219 million in 1970 to ₦10.6 billion in 1979, thereby achieving an enviable status as the first tropical African country successfully to exploit its oil reserves.

The NNOC was reconstituted as the Nigerian National Petroleum Corporation (NNPC) on April 1, 1977, just six years after it had been set up. One reason for the change may have been the operating failures of the 1970s, which became publicly known at the time of the 1980 Crude Oil Sales Tribunal. This investigation revealed that, for instance, from 1975–1978 the NNOC and NNPC had failed to collect some 182.95 million barrels of their equity share of oil being produced by Shell, Mobil, and Gulf—with potential revenue estimated to be in excess of US$2 billion. This situation had arisen because NNOC was unable to find buyers for its oil at the price it wanted. It had, however, paid the full share of operating costs to the producers during the period of deemed operating. An additional revelation was that, until forced to do so by the Tribunal, NNOC had not produced audited accounts from 1975 onward.

The NNPC felt the brunt of the Oil Sales Tribunal investigations only three years after it was set up. While some of the criticisms related to events which had occurred before the change in name, the NNPC's practices undoubtedly bore more than a passing resemblance to those of its predecessor. Like the NNOC, the NNPC began life essentially as a holding company. Decree no. 33 vested the assets and liabilities of the NNOC in the NNPC, and conferred on the new body responsibility for some functions of the Ministry of Mines and Power. NNPC also had some additional commercial freedom: the ceiling on contracts that it could award rose 50-fold and it was granted limited borrowing powers. Its board structure was similar to the NNOC's, although the federal commissioner for petroleum replaced the permanent secretary of mines and power as chairman, judging by the inefficiencies in its record-keeping and its error in overstocking in 1978 in anticipation of oil price rises, greater freedom did not bring with it a greater commercial astuteness.

Also established by Decree no. 33 as part of the NNPC was the Petroleum Inspectorate, which was given responsibility for issuing licenses for various activities, for enforcing the Oil Pipelines Act and the Petroleum Decrees, and for other duties. The chief executive of the division was nevertheless free from control by the NNPC board and reported to the commissioner for petroleum.

In line with the objectives of the government's 1977 Indigenization Decree, the NNPC's holdings in the oil industry operations in Nigeria increased significantly on July 1, 1979, when its stakes in the Nigerian businesses of the following companies were raised to 60%: Elf, Agip, Gulf, Mobil, Texaco, and Pan Ocean. NNPC's stake in the Shell venture was raised to 80% on August 1, 1979, after BP lost its 20% stake following disagreements with the Nigerian government over South Africa. Later that same year a number of accusations originating in the magazine *Punch*, alleging various forms of misappropriation, broke over the corporation, prompting the newly installed civilian President Alhaji Shagari to broadcast to the nation and establish the tribunal, that uncovered the lax management practices referred to above.

A further setback to the reputation of the Nigerian oil industry occurred at the start of 1980 with the Funiwa-5 incident. A 14-day blowout at an offshore well 60% owned by NNPC, but operated by Texaco, spilled 146,000 barrels and may have been responsible for the deaths of 180 people and illnesses among a further 3,000.

The outcome of the Oil Sales Tribunal was a series of reforms designed to decentralize the NNPC. Nine subsidiaries were established in 1981: the Nigerian Petroleum Exploration and Exploitation Company; the Nigerian Petroleum Refining Company, Kaduna Limited; the Nigerian Petroleum Refining, Company, Warri Limited; the Nigerian Petroleum Refining Company, Port Harcourt Limited; the Nigerian Petroleum Products Pipelines and Depots Company Limited; the Nigerian Petro Chemicals Company; the Nigerian Gas Company Limited; the Nigerian Petroleum Marine Transportation Company Limited; and the Petroleum Research and Engineering Company Limited. The decentralization of Nigeria's three refineries, two of which had been built in the late 1970s and early 1980s, was intended to promote competition and the establishment of this number of subsidiaries was designed to instill a more commercial approach in a more diversified corporation. The goal of diversification has, however, been one that the NNPC has been slow to realize.

The 1980s did not see an end to close government control and to controversy over the performance of the NNPC. The oil sector took a battering in the 1982 oil glut, when the oil companies' offensive against OPEC targeted Nigeria as the weakest of the producing nations. There were self-inflicted problems as well. Once again, management of the corporation was tainted by scandal, this time involving the former Petroleum Resources Minister Tam David-West, who was jailed at the end of 1990 for his part in another dispute over foreign oil companies. David-West's bad relations with the government were partly responsible for the imposition of direct control of the NNPC by the Ministry of Petroleum Resources between 1986 and 1989. Relations with the foreign oil companies were marked by the 1986 Memorandum of Understanding, which set a profit limit of US$2 per barrel.

The end of the 1980s saw a number of initiatives which may—although it is too early to say categorically—see the NNPC established on a more commercially oriented footing. In March 1988, another new structure was unveiled for the corporation, described by Nigerian President General Ibrahim Babangida as establishing the NNPC as a "financially autonomous" and "commercially integrated" oil company. Petroleum Resources Minister Rilwanu Lukman defined three areas of responsibility for the corporation—corporate services, operations, and petroleum investment management services—and 11 subsidiary companies: the Nigerian Petroleum Development Company, the Warri Refining and Petrochemicals Company, the Kaduna Refining and Petrochemicals Company, the Pipeline and Products Marketing Company, the Hydrocarbon Services of Nigeria Company, the Engineering Company of Nigeria, the Nigerian Gas Development Company, the LNG Company, the Port Harcourt Refining Company, the Eleme Petrochemicals Company, and the Integrated Data Services Company. At the same time, a new sales policy was introduced, eliminating middlemen and setting out three types of purchasers to which the NNPC could sell its products: joint venture producing companies, foreign refineries in which Nigeria has a holding, and indigenous and foreign firms exploring in Nigeria. Aret Adams was appointed as the group managing director and, in February 1989 a new board was constituted, headed by Lukman.

The determination to eradicate subsidies to NNPC and to have it function commercially, rather than as a revenue-raising and development corporation, was apparent in the decision in June 1989 to sell 20% of its holding in the Shell joint venture. NNPC reduced its holding to 60%, selling 10% to Shell and 5% apiece to Elf and Agip, in a deal which may have netted the corporation as much as US$2 billion. The money raised from the equity sale was to underpin the expansion in reserves—to 20 billion barrels—and in output—to 2.5 million barrels a day, to which Nigeria is committed up to 1995. However, these targets are likely to require the divestment of further holdings to raise cash, such divestments cannot be assured in the uncertain political future which Nigeria faces. As 60% stakeholder, NNPC has had persistent problems in raising its share of any development costs.

One positive development has been the increasing involvement of the corporation in the development of Nigeria's gas resources. Having been granted a monopoly over gas transmission, the NNPC has been well-placed to participate in the gas industry. Its 60% holding in the LNG Company—Shell owns 20%, Agip and Elf each own 10%—is the springboard for an ambitious US$2.5 billion liquefaction project. In addition, Nigeria's fourth refinery, at Eleme, was commissioned early in 1989 and will provide the basis for the expansion of a petrochemicals and plastics industry during the 1990s. In its core activity of oil production, NNPC's partner Mobil has been developing the large 500 million barrel Oso oil field, and Nigeria stands to benefit from the environmental attractions of its low-sulfur oil product.

The period since 1988 has not been entirely positive for the NNPC. The plan to market oil products through co-owned refineries overseas has not fully matured. Only one joint venture deal was signed in 1989, with Farmland Industries of the United States, enabling NNPC to make use of a 60,000 barrels per day refinery at Coffeyville in Kansas. However, this is a landlocked site that may not be entirely suitable for operations. Of greater concern is the strong possibility that the state has not relinquished its desire to exercise control over NNPC's operations. Managing director Adams and his counterpart at the LNG Company were suspended late in 1989, apparently for refusing to accept government appointees to the LNG Company. In April 1990, Thomas John took over as managing director.

Thus the NNPC entered the last decade of the century as a young company still trying to carve out an identity for itself, independent of political control, and still learning how to master the technological and commercial complexities of the oil industry. However, it does have a more developed diversification strategy than ever before in its history and, for the moment, a government which is willing to dilute its holdings in the industry as the price for supporting the corporation's growth.

Principal Subsidiaries: Warri Refining and Petrochemicals Company; Kaduna Refining and Petrochemicals Company; Pipeline and Products Marketing Company; Hydrocarbon Services of Nigeria Company; Engineering Company of Nigeria; Nigerian Gas Development Company; LNG Company (60%); Port Harcourt Refining Company; Eleme Petrochemicals Company; Integrated Data Services Company.

Further Reading: Pearson, Scott R., *Petroleum and the Nigerian Economy,* Stanford, California, Stanford University Press, 1970; Onoh, J.K., *The Nigerian Oil Economy,* Beckenham, Croom Helm, 1983; Ake, Claude, *The Political Economy of Nigeria,* London, Longman, 1985.

—Graham Field

NIPPON MINING CO., LTD.

10-1, Toranomon 2-chome
Minato-ku, Tokyo 105
Japan
(03) 3 505-8111
Fax: (03) 3 505-8094

Public Company
Incorporated: 1905 as Kuhara Mining Company
Employees: 5,508
Sales: ¥718.13 billion (US$5.29 billion)
Stock Exchanges: Tokyo Osaka Nagoya Frankfurt New York

Nippon Mining Co., Ltd. is one of the leading copper mining companies in Japan, although 55.6% of its total sales came from its oil division in 1990. The company has diversified rapidly into special petrochemicals, biotechnology, and pharmaceutical products, and has recently established a copper foil manufacturing subsidiary in Hong Kong.

The Kuhara Mining Company, predecessor of the Nippon Mining Co., Ltd., was established in 1905 by Fusanosuke Kuhara as a copper mining venture located in Hitachi village—now Hitachi City. As a result of rapid expansion, Kuhara decided to reorganize his enterprise into a joint-stock company, with a capital of ¥10 million, in 1912.

Although the major business of the company was copper mining, Kuhara perceived that Japan had an energy supply problem, and he secretly began to look for opportunities for oil field development. In March 1914, the Nippon Oil Company located an abundant oil field, the Kurokawa well in Akita Prefecture, and the sudden oil price rise during World War I further stimulated Kuhara in his search for oil. He began to explore domestic oil fields after 1914, and built eight oil well development offices between 1916 and 1917. He also explored oil fields in northern Sakhalin, Borneo, Burma, and Malaya. In 1919, he entered into a joint venture with a Russian company to develop oil fields in northern Sakhalin. In 1921, this joint venture discovered a potentially rich oil field, but the Japanese Ministry of Foreign Affairs and other oil companies hoped to develop it as a national project. In 1919 the Ministry of Agriculture and Commerce established a joint stock company named Hokusin Kai, which later became Kita Karafuto (Northern Sakhalin) Oil Company. It was co-owned by Kuhara Mining, the Mitsui and Mitsubishi *zaibatsu*, Nippon Oil Company, and others.

During World War I, Kuhara Mining Company continuously expanded its business. However, after the war economic conditions deteriorated and the company met financial difficulties. After 1920, Kuhara's business made losses and incurred a huge amount of debt. When Kuhara retired from the business and went into politics, his brother-in-law Yoshisuke Ayukawa took responsibility for the reconstruction of the company.

In March 1928 Ayukawa became president and in December he reorganized Kuhara Mining Company into a holding company, Nippon Sangyo (Industry) Co., Ltd. In April 1929 the mining and refinery division was separated and established as a independent company named the Nippon Mining Co., Ltd. with a capital of ¥50 million. Ayukawa then became chairman of the board and Masahiko Takeuchi became president.

After 1916 the company further explored the Akita oil field but failed to locate oil. Finally, however, in September 1933, a rich oil field—the Omonogawa oil well—was found. In 1936 and 1937 two further oil fields were found in Hokkaido. In 1934 a natural gas field was developed in the Tsutong area of Taiwan, where the company established natural gas and naphtha refining facilities.

In 1939, the company began to construct an integrated oil refinery plant to produce aviation gasoline at the request of the Japanese navy. However at the outbreak of the Pacific war in December 1941, construction stopped. In the late 1930s, Nippon Kogyo acquired two oil refining companies and strengthened its oil refining division in the Akita area. However, in 1942 Teikoku Sekiyu (Empire Oil) Co. Ltd. was established as a state-owned company, and the Tsutong plants and Omono River oil wells' refining facilities were transferred to Teikoku Sekiyu.

In August 1945 the Pacific war of World War II ended, and Japan lost its former territories and occupied areas. Nippon Mining Co., Ltd. lost its foreign assets located in those areas, which had amounted to almost 40% of its total assets in 1943. After the war, the company's major plants were Hitachi mining works and the Sagaseki refining facility, but production was down to almost nothing at the end of the latter half of 1945. At the end of 1946, production recovered to one-third of the volume of wartime production, but the only active production facility was the Funagawa oil refinery. In 1946, the Funagawa refinery refined 56,483 kiloliters (kl) of crude oil and produced 53,794 kl of gasoline and other products.

In 1947, the Funagawa refinery converted from munitions manufacturing to civil use, and began to make solvent products and to diversify its product line. By 1951, the Funagawa Refinery had lubrication oil production facilities, and established an integrated oil refinery system. Until June 1961 Funagawa refinery was Nippon Kogyo's only active modern refinery facility.

The Allied powers prohibited the rebuilding of oil refinery facilities on the Pacific coast, but lifted the prohibition in 1950. The Pacific coast of Japan became a good industrial location for the reduction of transportation costs and stimulation of import-export activities. As Nippon Mining had no refinery facilities on the Pacific coast, establishing a presence in this industrial zone became a strategic target for the company.

After 1955 the executives of the company realized that the Mizushima area in Okayama Prefecture would be an attractive site for a refinery complex. In 1958 the company started a feasibility study for the project. Construction began in July 1960, and the Mizushima complex was in operation from June 1961. The Gulf Oil Corporation played an important role in the building of the Mizushima refinery complex, both in the supplying of finance and in the export of crude oil. In May 1960 secret transactions had been held in the Tokyo office of Gulf Oil Corporation; the agreement to a US$15 million (¥5.4 billion) loan to build facilities and a ten-year contract for the import of a total of eight million barrels of crude oil were signed in September 1960.

In June 1960 the Japanese government decided to liberalize crude oil imports—although processed oil imports to Japan, such as gasoline, were still restricted—and from October 1962 carried out the liberalization in stages. However, to prevent over-production and excess competition between oil refineries, the Ministry of International Trade and Industry (MITI) implemented the Oil Industry Law. By this law MITI maintained control of the Japanese-owned oil and petrochemical industries. The Nippon Mining Co. established a joint sales company, Kyodo Oil Company Ltd., with Asia Oil Company, Ltd. and Toa Oil Company Ltd. under the administrative guidance of MITI. The Nippon Mining stake was 34%, and those of Asia Oil Company and Towa Oil Company, were 23% each, while the remaining 20% was owned by banks. A vice president of Nippon Mining, Kazuo Hayashi, was appointed as president of Kyodo Oil Co. Kyodo Oil Co. united the oil tank yards and sales agencies of the three companies, and went into operation in July 1966.

Kyodo Oil Company's market share was 10.9%, and the company held third position in the domestic market, after Nippon Oil Company in first place, and Idemitsu Kosan in second. Nippon Mining dispatched 643 employees to Kyodo Oil Company to sustain sales activities temporarily, but by December 1966 almost all those dispatched had become permanent employees of Kyodo Oil Company. As a result of these arrangements, Nippon Mining's oil division became a de facto refinery division of Kyodo Oil Company. Thus a close relationship between Nippon Mining and Kyodo Oil Company was established.

Through the development of the Neurex processing system the company entered into the area of petrochemicals, launching a synthetic detergent product in November 1967. To further its diversification into petrochemicals, the company established Nikko Petrochemical Co. Ltd. in December 1967.

After the mid-1960s, the company built a petrochemical complex in Mizushima with Asahi Kasei Industry Company Ltd. In July 1968, Nippon Mining—with a stake of 20%—and Asahi Kasei—with a stake of 80%—jointly established Sanyo Petrochemical Company Ltd., with a capital of ¥750 million, to supply olefin gas to the complex, Sanyo Petrochemical Co. and Mitsubishi Kasei Industry Co. Ltd. established Mizushima Ethylene Co. Ltd., a 50–50 joint venture, to decompose naphtha. In November 1969 another jointly owned company, Sanyo Ethylene Co. Ltd., was established. Consequently, Nippon Mining's Misushima refinery became the central raw material and energy supplier of the petrochemical complex.

The company also began to pursue backward integration into oil drilling. In December 1967, Nippon Mining Co., Maruzen Oil Co., and Daikyo Oil Co. jointly invested in offshore oil drilling in Abu Dhabi and established the jointly

owned Abu Dhabi Oil Company Ltd. with equal stakes of 33.3% and capital of ¥600 million. By January 1971 there were four oil wells producing crude oil, and in May 1973 production reached a level of 40,000 barrels per day (b/d).

In September 1967 Nippon Mining established a joint venture company, the Petro-Coke Company Ltd., with Continental Oil Company of the United States and Sumitomo Shoji Co. Ltd., with a capital of ¥360 million. In 1969 this company began production of calcined petroleum cokes. As a result of expansion in the oil division, Nippon Mining began production at a lubricating oil factory in the Chiba Prefecture in May 1969.

The two oil crises in 1973 and 1978 stimulated the reorganization of the Japanese petroleum industry including petrochemical production. In 1979 Nippon Mining acquired the Toa Kyoseki Company Ltd. from its parent companies, Chu Ito & Company and Toa Oil Company Toa Kyoseki Co. was a relatively small refinery with a processing capacity of 100,000 b/d, established in 1973 under the guidance of MITI. It was in financial difficulties after the first oil crisis. Under the management of Nippon Mining, Toa Kyoseki changed its name to Chita Oil Co. Ltd., with a capital of ¥6 billion. Nippon Mining's stake was 61.67%, Kyodo Oil Company 33.3%, and Chu Ito & Company 5%. Chita Oil Co. contributed to the strengthening of the tie with Nippon Mining's oil division and the Kyodo Oil Company group. However, after the second oil crisis, with its unsettling influence on the business environment, Chita Oil Co. was fully integrated into Nippon Mining by permission of MITI, in July 1983.

After the second oil crisis the demand for petroleum declined, and the company restricted its crude oil refinery capacity at its three oil factories. As a result, Nippon Mining's crude oil refining capacity was 281,000 b/d in 1983—Mizushima 190,000, Funagawa 6,000, and Chita 85,000,—a capacity almost unchanged until 1989.

In March 1985 Kyodo Oil group companies jointly established a research and development center for the development of oil products. In the following April, the management of the lubricating oil products research laboratory at Nippon Mining was transferred to the newly established Kyodo Oil group's research and development center.

In 1990, Nippon Mining Co., Ltd. was capitalized at ¥63.4 billion. To achieve further growth, the company is promoting oil prospecting projects with Conoco and planning a full-scale launch into polypropylene and special resins. Although 55.6% of total sales came from the oil division in 1990, traditional divisions such as copper (15% of sales), metal products (7%), zinc (4%), gold (7%), and silver (1%) still represent a large portion of total sales and profits, as do the new materials division (4%), and new ventures—including biochemicals (4%)—are expanding. The Nippon Mining Co., Ltd. is one of the most successfully diversified companies in the mining and petroleum industry in Japan, and will reinforce its status as a multi-divisional and multinational company in the next decade.

Principal Subsidiaries: Nikko Shoji Co. Ltd.; Nikko Consulting and Engineering Co. Ltd.; Toyoha Mines Co. Ltd.; Tomakomai Chemical Co. Ltd.; Nikko Liquefied Gas Co. Ltd.; Nikko Oil Sales Co. Ltd. (51%); Nippon Marine Co. Ltd.

(98%); Nippon Mining (Bermuda) Ltd.; Chita Oil Co. Ltd.; Nikko Zinc Co. Ltd; NMC Finance Co. Ltd; Nikko Exploration and Development Co. Ltd.; Toranomon Tower Building Co. Ltd. (95%); Cactus Kasei Co. Ltd. (92%); Nikko Petrochemical Co. Ltd.; Petrocokes Ltd. (70%); Nikko Gould Foil Co. Ltd; Nippon Mining U.S. Inc. (82%); Gould Inc.; Kyodo Oil Co. Ltd. (47%); Abu Dhabi Oil Co. Ltd. (26%); Sanyo Petrochemical Co. Ltd. (40%); Nikko Real Estate Co., Ltd.; Central Computer Service Co., Ltd. (65%); Orient Catalyst Co., Ltd.; Kyodo Oil Technical Research Center Co., Ltd. (57%); Nikko Corrosion Engineer Co., Ltd.; Nikko CS Chemical Co., Ltd.; Nikko Metal Plating Co., Ltd.; Nikko Petroleum Exploration Co., Ltd.; Fuji Electronics Co., Ltd. (92%); Nikko Building Materials Co., Ltd.; Automax Co., Ltd. (80%); Nikko Coupler Co., Ltd.; Nikko TAB Inc.; NMC Resources Engineering Co., Ltd.; NMC Pearl River Mouth Oil Development Co., Ltd. (50%); Japan Encore Computer Inc. (50%); E.A.I. Electronic Associates (Japan) Inc.; Nikko Wolverine Inc. (U.S.A.); Nippon Mining Singapore Pte. Ltd.; Nippon Mining of Australia Pty. Ltd.; NIMIC INC. (U.S.A.); Nippon Mining (New York) Inc. (U.S.A.) Nippon Mining of Nevada Ltd. (U.S.A.); Irvine Scientific Sales Co., Ltd. (U.S.A.) (88%); Nippon Mining (Taiwan) Ltd.; Contact International Corp.

Further Reading: Nippon Mining Co. Ltd., Mizushima Refinery, *Mizushima Seiyu sho 20-Nen no Ayumi*, Nippon Kogyo K.K., 1984; Ministry of Finance, *Yukashoken Hokokushyo Soran*, Tokyo, Ministry of Finance Printing Division, 1983–1989; Toyo Keizai, ed., *Kaisha Shikiho* (Quarterly Handbook of Japanese Public Companies), Tokyo, Toyo Keizai Sha, 1950–1990; Okabe, Akira, *Sangyo no Showa Shakai Shi, No.3 Sekiyu* Tokyo, Nippon Keizai Hyoron Sha, 1986.

—Kenichi Yasumuro

NIPPON OIL COMPANY, LIMITED

3-12, Nishi Shimbashi 1-chome
Minato-ku, Tokyo 105
Japan
(03) 3502-1111
Fax: (03) 3502-9351

Public Company
Incorporated: 1893
Employees: 9,669
Sales: ¥1.85 trillion (US$13.62 billion)
Stock Exchanges: Tokyo Osaka Nagoya Niigata Kyoto
Hiroshima Fukuoka Sapporo

Nippon Oil Company, Limited is Japan's largest petroleum-products distributor. The company imports and distributes petroleum products, and it also operates a refinery. Through its subsidiaries, Nippon is engaged in a number of related activities that include the manufacture of petrochemicals and petroleum gas, as well as oil transport, oil stockpiling, and oil exploration.

Nippon Oil was founded in 1888 during the Meiji restoration, which lasted from 1867 to 1912. This was a time of extraordinary changes in Japan. The government transformed Japan into a world power and sought to model the country's development on that of the West. Western technology, especially that of the United States, was used to modernize the Japanese economy. A parliamentary system of government was introduced in 1885, modeled on that of Germany.

While the Japanese oil industry was itself in its infancy, many entrepreneurs—*yamashi*—capitalized on the growing demand for oil created by Japanese industrialization. In 1888, 21 *yamashi* founded Nippon Oil. All were wealthy landowners at a time when most Japanese were landless peasants. Control of Nippon Oil rested with these shareholders, who owned 66% of the stock. Yet most decisions were made by two men, Gonzaburo Yamaguchi and the man who became the first company president, Hisahiro Natio. Almost immediately after the company was formed, successful drilling for crude oil began at Amaze, north of Tokyo. Within a year drilling also took place off the Japanese coast, and Nippon became the first Japanese company to drill offshore for oil.

A key to the company's initial success was its willingness to obtain technology from abroad. In particular, Nippon Oil looked to the United States, which had already pioneered technological innovations in the oil industry. In 1889, Gonzaburo

Yamaguchi visited the United States to obtain information on the latest advances in oil drilling. Impressed by the sophistication of United States technology, Yamaguchi, on his return, persuaded his colleagues to purchase an advanced drilling machine from the Pierce company of New York. Yamaguchi hired a Texan to instruct Nippon Oil employees in the operation of the new equipment. Profits in the infant oil company were small. The salary of the American drilling-equipment expert amounted to 12% of total company expense; yet Nippon Oil was determined to master Western technology. The financial depression of 1897, which led to the collapse of many of Japan's smaller oil companies, left Nippon Oil with an ever-increasing share of Japanese oil production and refining.

In 1900 Nippon Oil experienced stiff competition from the newly arrived International Petroleum. This company had been founded in Japan but was operated by the American Standard Oil Company. In 1907 Nippon Oil overcame this domestic competition by purchasing all the Japanese assets of International Petroleum. By so doing, Nippon Oil became one of the largest oil companies in Japan. Its major competitor was now another Japanese company, Hoden Oil.

From 1908 onward, Nippon Oil's output of oil gradually decreased as wells became exhausted. Nippon Oil, again relying on U.S. technology, introduced a rotary drill that enabled existing wells to be deepened. Other Japanese companies soon followed Nippon Oil's example, leading to increased oil production throughout Japan.

In World War I, Japan concentrated its activities against the German colonial empire in the Far East. Following Germany's defeat, Japan not only acquired former German colonial possessions in the Pacific but also gained important commercial concessions in China. The war too led to the rapid development of Japanese industry as well as an increase in the demand for oil. In 1921, three years after the end of the war, Nippon Oil merged with its former competitor, Hoden Oil, and controlled 80% of domestic crude oil production.

The interwar period in Japan witnessed not only industrial expansion but also an increase in living standards. As the number of automobiles on Japanese roads grew, Nippon Oil established a network of gasoline-storage depots throughout the country. In 1919, the company set up its first hand-pump gasoline service station with an underground storage tank, in Tokyo. By the late 1920s more than 160 stations were in operation.

By the late 1920s also Japan's oil reserves were insufficient to meet the needs of a growing industrialized economy. Imported oil, therefore, became vital for the continued growth of the Japanese economy, and Nippon Oil, like most other Japanese oil refineries, increasingly relied on imported oil. In 1923, Nippon Oil imported only 170,000 kiloliters of oil. The ratio of domestic oil to imported oil was 63% to 23%. By 1937 only 20% of Nippon Oil's crude oil supply came from domestic sources. The remaining 80% had to be imported, mainly from the United States. As domestic oil production lessened, importing and refining gradually became Nippon Oil's principal business activity.

During the 1930s, Japan, like other industrialized countries, suffered the effects of the worldwide Depression. The Japanese government, under pressure from its army and navy chiefs, sought new markets on the Chinese mainland through military aggression. In 1931, the Japanese military seized

Manchuria, forcing Chinese troops to withdraw from the area. In 1937 war had broken out with China. By this time, the military had gained control of the Japanese government and had begun to regulate the Japanese economy to the needs of the war effort. All important industries came under state control. In 1937, Nippon Oil lost all of its independence, coming under the control of a state-run monopolistic organization known as Oil Co-operative Sales.

Japan's role in World War II had a devastating impact on the economy. Japan's reliance on imported oil and other raw materials meant that the country was vulnerable to an Allied blockade. U.S. submarines operating close to the Japanese coast inflicted heavy losses on Japanese oil tankers carrying supplies to the mainland. Slowly the Japanese economy ground to a halt.

Because of the blockade, Nippon Oil's supply of imported oil almost totally dried up. In 1941, in an attempt to encourage domestic production of oil under embargo conditions, the Japanese government merged Nippon Oil with Ogura Oil. Yet, under the weight of heavy bombing attacks on oil installations, little could be done to remedy Japan's acute oil shortage.

Japanese defeat in 1945 was followed by a lengthy period of reconstruction under the Allied occupation authority, the objective of which was the re-establishment of a peacetime industrial economy. The old state monopolies were broken up and competition between smaller economic units was encouraged. Nippon Oil Company was re-established as a wholesaler in 1949 and occupied a much smaller role in the Japanese postwar economy than it had had for decades. Its main activity continued to be the importing and refining of mostly imported oil.

The Korean War, which broke out in 1950, transformed Japan into an important ally of the United States in the Far East and led to closer economic ties between the two countries. In 1951, recognizing the importance of the U.S. connection, Nippon Oil established Nippon Petroleum Refining Company, Limited, as a joint venture with Caltex Petroleum Corporation of the United States. Most of Nippon's crude oil supply was subsequently purchased from Caltex and refined by Nippon Petroleum. Also in 1951, a further subsidiary, Tokyo Tanker Co., Ltd. was established to transport oil to Japan. In 1955 Nippon Oil entered the petrochemical and gas industry through the establishment of two subsidiaries, Nippon Petrochemicals Company, Limited and Nippon Petroleum Gas Company, Limited.

In 1960, Nippon Oil established an overseas office in the United States, incorporated in Delaware. The 1960s witnessed a period of sustained growth at Nippon Oil. In 1961 operating profits for the year stood at ¥2.13 billion. For 1970 Nippon Oil declared a profit of ¥10.76 billion. This trend of increased profitability was interrupted by events in the Middle East early in the 1970s. Since the end of World War II, Japan had increasingly relied on Middle East oil. The Yom Kippur War of 1973 between Israel and its Arab neighbors interrupted the oil supply. The Arab-dominated Organization of Petroleum Exporting Countries (OPEC) cut production and raised prices. Within a year of the war, prices had quadrupled. These increases might have been passed on to the Japanese consumer but in 1974, the Japanese government froze retail gas prices. After-tax profit fell at Nippon Oil to ¥902 million, less than one-tenth of what it had been in 1970.

By 1977 Nippon had recovered from the energy crisis through the growing strength of the Japanese economy and the high appreciation of the yen on world money markets. In 1980 profits reached an all-time high of ¥45.67 billion. The early 1980s, however, witnessed a slump in the oil industry because of an abundance of supply and too much refining capacity. The Japanese Ministry of International Trade and Industry sought to rationalize the oil industry by encouraging cooperation among the large companies. In 1984 Nippon Oil and Mitsubishi Oil Co., Ltd., itself 50% owned by the U.S. Getty Oil Company, reached an accord on the sharing of marketing and facilities. This pact gave both companies joint command of 25% of Japan's oil market. Under the agreement, the two companies cooperated in wholesale and retail operations and use of tanker and storage facilities.

Under the leadership of its chairman, Yasuoki Takeuchi, Nippon Oil during the 1980s took steps to reduce its dependence on Middle East oil. In 1985 alone, Nippon Oil set aside US$100 million for the development of oil fields in the United States, and in 1986, Nippon Oil found promising oil fields in North Dakota. The company also reached an agreement with Texaco of the United States for joint development of Alaskan oil fields. Another joint exploration deal with Chevron led to the discovery of two gas fields in the Gulf of Mexico.

This policy of developing alternative sources of supply somewhat reduced dependence on Arab oil. In 1989 while 56.6% of Nippon Oil imports came from the Middle East, 37% came from Southeast Asia, and the remaining 6.4% from other regions, mainly Mexico. As political turmoil in the Middle East, in the early 1990s, made the security of further supplies from this region even more uncertain, Nippon Oil's efforts to develop its own crude oil sources seems likely to continue.

Principal Subsidiaries: Nippon Petroleum Refining Company, Limited (50%); Nippon Petrochemicals Company, Limited; Nippon Petroleum Gas Company, Limited; Nippon Oil (U.K.) Public Limited Company; Nisseki Real Estate Company, Limited; Nippon Oil (Delaware) Limited (U.S.A.); Nippon Oil (Asia) Pte. Ltd. (Singapore); The Nisseki Plastic Chemical Co., Ltd. (15%); Nihonkai Oil Co., Ltd. (66%); Nippon Hodo Co., Ltd. (57.7%); Nippon Oil Exploration Company, Limited; Nippon Oil Overseas Exploration Company, Limited; Nippon Oil Engineering and Construction Co., Ltd.; Nippon Petroleum Processing Company, Limited; Nisseki Shoji Company, Limited; Nippon Oil Information Systems Company, Limited; Nisseki Tourist Co., Ltd.; Nisseki Office Service Co., Ltd.; Nippon Oil (Australia) Pty. Limited; Nippon Oil Finance (Netherlands) B.V.; Taiwan Nisseki Co., Ltd.; Nippon Auto Parking Company, Limited; Nippon Oil Staging Terminal Company, Limited (50%); Koa Oil Company, Limited (5.8%); Tokyo Tanker Co., Ltd. (4%).

Further Reading: Uyehara, S., *The Industry and Trade of Japan*, London, P.S. King & Son, Ltd., 1936.

—Michael Doorley

OCCIDENTAL PETROLEUM CORPORATION

10889 Wilshire Boulevard
Los Angles, California 90024
U.S.A.
(213) 208-8800
Fax: (213) 208-5701

Public Company
Incorporated: 1920
Employees: 55,000
Sales: $21.69 billion
Stock Exchanges: New York Pacific Amsterdam Antwerp
   Basel Brussels Düsseldorf Frankfurt Geneva Hamburg
   London Tokyo Toronto Zürich

Occidental Petroleum (Oxy) is in the fuels, chemicals, and fresh-meat business. It engages in exploration, exploitation, transmission, and sales of oil, natural gas, and coal, and the production and sales of certain by-products for these fuels. Increasingly the lions share of its earnings come from chemicals.

Occidental supplies large volumes of raw materials for industrial use, such as polymers, plastics, and detergents, as well as agricultural chemicals, such as phosphates and phosphoric acids. The company processes pork and beef and sells both carcasses and boxed products; it also processes and sells by-products of such meat.

Occidental Petroleum was founded in 1920 in California. Its early years as an oil-finding entity were largely undistinguished, with the company almost bankrupt by the mid-1950s. It was Occidental Petroleum's early difficulties that laid the groundwork for its later success. In 1956 Occidental Petroleum came to the attention of Armand Hammer, a millionaire who was well-known for his savvy and success in dealing with the Soviet Union in the 1920s. In 1921 Hammer had met Vladimir Lenin, the leader of the Russian Revolution, and had become the first U.S. businessman to establish ties with the Soviet Union. Among other enterprises, Hammer had operated an asbestos mine, imported grain, and manufactured pencils. While in Moscow, he had purchased Russian art treasures at bargain prices, later reselling many art objects in the United States at considerable profit.

In 1956 Hammer and his wife Frances each invested $50,000 in two oil wells that Occidental planned to drill in

California. When both wells struck oil, Hammer, nearly 60, took an active interest in further Occidental oil exploration.

At Hammer's first association with Occidental, it was run by president Dave Harris and by Roy Roberts and John Sullivan. Hammer's increased involvement, his strong personality, and his ability to raise money for oil drilling propelled him more and more into the limelight. By July 1957 Hammer was president.

Hammer's influence played a key role in the development of Occidental. As Steve Weinberg wrote in *Armand Hammer: The Untold Story,* "Few Fortune 500 corporations have come so totally under the sway of one person, especially one who owned such a tiny percentage of stock."

From his earliest days as president of Occidental, one of Hammer's overriding drives was for Oxy to diversify. In his autobiography, Hammer reported that a prime rationale for diversifying was to make Oxy too big for the other major oil companies to take over. Acquisitions included energy and chemical companies and meat-producing operations.

At the time Hammer became involved with Occidental, it was listed on very small stock exchanges on the West Coast, but within several years, Oxy was on the American Stock Exchange, boosted by the 1959 Hammer-led acquisition of Gene Reid Drilling Company of Bakersfield, California. This acquisition was to prove fortuitous for the growth of Occidental. Hammer attracted Reid, an engineer, and his son Bud, a geologist, to the cash-poor Occidental by offering them shares of the company. Hammer was to use the stock strategy to attract talent in other acquisitions as well.

In 1961 while working with Occidental employees Richard Vaughn, Robert Teitsworth, and the Reids, Hammer took a chance on drilling the Lathrop field, near San Francisco. It had been drilled previously for natural gas by Texaco and other companies, but only to a depth of about 5,600 feet. Reid and the others suggested that there was gas farther down, and at 6,900 feet they were proved right. Occidental made one of the largest gas finds in California. Overnight, the company found gas worth hundreds of millions of dollars.

By the end of 1961, Occidental had a $1 million profit on revenues of over $4 million. Continued success in natural gas, and oil finds increased the fortune and reputation of the company. By March 1964 Oxy's shares were trading on the New York Stock Exchange.

Through the mid-1960s, Hammer moved Oxy more and more to an international position. It built, for example, a superphosphoric-acid plant in England and helped build a $33 million ammonia and urea plant in Saudi Arabia. Oxy also had dealings with other countries, among them Nicaragua, Venezuela, Morocco, and Turkey.

Throughout the 1960s, Hammer kept up negotiations with Libya's King Idris for the use of Libya's natural resources. This persistence was to pay off handsomely. In 1966 Oxy's potential skyrocketed, with a billion-barrel oil field find in Libya. The find was "vintage" Hammer, as he wined and dined important Libyan officials, and then took a risk on land previously drilled by others. The Libyan oil finds established Oxy as one of the largest petroleum companies in the world. From early 1967 until November of that same year, Oxy's stock doubled in value to more than $100 a share.

Hammer's skills as a negotiator were put to the test when the Libyan king was overthrown in a bloodless coup in 1969 and replaced by the Revolutionary Command Council, soon to be headed by Moammar Khadafi. Many analysts feared the new government would nationalize the oil fields; however, Hammer negotiated in late 1970 an agreement by which Libya received an immediate increase of 30¢ per barrel of oil, with another 10¢ increase spread over five years. Some oil observers viewed this agreement as the beginning of the end of cheap energy. Other multinational oil companies quickly signed similar agreements with their host countries. Most petroleum-producing countries called for matching increases, and oil prices headed upward.

In the early 1970s, Hammer caused a sensation with a $20 billion long-term deal with the Soviets that featured a barter agreement by which Oxy would supply phosphate fertilizer to the USSR in exchange for Soviet ammonia and urea. Many in the U.S. government criticized the deal, saying the agreement helped a communist country, despite the fact that the deal was consummated during a period of détente between the United States and the Soviet Union. Hammer, in fact, considered his dealings as détente through trade. Hammer continued this notion of détente through trade with the Chinese, with whom in 1979 he began negotiating. Oxy ended up with two offshore oil exploration and development contracts and a joint agreement to develop a Chinese coal mine.

In 1981 Oxy moved completely away from the energy and chemical fields to acquire Iowa Beef Packers (IBP), the largest meatpacker in the United States. IBP cost Oxy $750 million in stock and proved to be a sound investment. In 1987 Oxy sold 49.5% of IBP to the public for $960 million. The United Food and Commercial Workers Union maintained, however, that while these profits were being generated, Oxy management was unconcerned with workers at the packing plants, at which there were numerous union strikes over pay and working conditions.

In 1982 Hammer engineered Oxy's $4 billion acquisition of Cities Service Company, a huge domestic oil company headquartered in Oklahoma. The act was scoffed at by investment bankers who, as reported in Hammer's autobiography, *Hammer,* took the stance, "This is like Jonah trying to swallow the whale." The deal made Occidental the eighth-largest oil company in the United States and the country's twelfth-largest industrial concern. One of Hammer's first steps after the acquisition was to sell off Cities Service units he felt Occidental did not need, resulting in about $1 billion in revenue for Oxy. Other steps were not so popular. Some 16,000 jobs were lost as the Cities Service work force dropped 80%.

In late 1985 Hammer made another multi-billion dollar transaction, acquiring Midcon, the huge domestic natural-gas pipeline company, for $3 billion. Shortly after the acquisition the natural-gas industry was deregulated. Occidental was hurt. The industry, as a whole, suffered from strong competition because of deregulation.

In a reorganization move in May 1986, Occidental Petroleum Corporation, of California, became a wholly owned subsidiary of the parent company. Corporate headquarters remained in Los Angeles.

The most successful of Oxy's operations during the mid-to-late 1980s was its chemical branch, Occidental Chemical (Oxychem). The chemical operations were built largely through the acquisitions of other companies. Occidental purchased holdings from Diamond Shamrock Chemicals in 1986,

and from Du Pont and Shell Chemical in 1987, among others. In the five years, from 1983 through 1987, Oxychem almost doubled its sales to nearly $3 billion. According to J. Roger Hirl, president and chief operating officer of Oxychem, as reported in *Chemical & Engineering News,* May 2, 1988, Oxy moved into the chemical industry as a balance to its petroleum business. While noting the cyclical nature of both the petroleum and chemical industries, Hirl said they normally were not in parallel cycles.

In 1988 Occidental, spending $2.2 billion to purchase Cain Chemical, moved up to sixth-largest U.S. chemical producer, with sales accounting for almost 25% of Oxy's total. Cain Chemical became Oxy Petrochemicals Inc.

In February 1988 Oxy was found liable for cleaning up the toxic wastes at the United States's most infamous landfill, Love Canal in Niagara Falls, New York. After eight years of deliberations, a federal judge ruled that Occidental was responsible for the improper disposal by Hooker Chemical of more than 21,000 tons of chemicals on the site, during the 1940s and 1950s. Occidental had purchased Hooker Chemical in 1968, unaware of the problems that began to surface in 1978. Before the ruling, Oxy had paid $20 million in damages to 1,300 former Love Canal residents, but nothing toward the cleanup of the site. Total cleanup costs were expected to exceed $100 million, and final settlement was pending in 1990.

In July 1988 Oxy was hit by a disaster unequaled in oil production history. The company's Piper Alpha offshore oil platform exploded in Britain's North Sea, killing 167 people. The accident panicked the oil market, already made nervous by the continuing Iran-Iraq War. Oil prices were driven up immediately after the accident by as much as $1 a barrel. The accident was thought to be caused by a leak in a pressurized natural-gas line that triggered the massive explosion. Occidental immediately shut down the pipeline that served the platform and five others. In August 1989 Oxy resumed North Sea production. The accident was estimated to have cost over $1 billion, including an approximately $183 million settlement with families of the victims and surviving workers.

During 1989 Oxy restructured its domestic oil and gas operations, which resulted in the loss of 900 jobs, the majority from the Oxy Oil and Gas subsidiary's headquarters in Tulsa, Oklahoma. For the year 1989 however, Oxy reported an overall increase of about 1,000 workers, due primarily to expansion at IBP and Oxychem.

Hammer's decisions have not always pleased stockholders. One such circumstance centered around Occidental's funding of a $95 million museum to house Hammer's valuable painting collection. The collection was worth an estimated $250 million. Many shareholders did not see the expense of building and operating a museum as serving the best financial interest of the company. The disagreement ended in the courts, in 1990, and although the Armand Hammer Museum of Art and Cultural Center would be built as planned alongside Occidental's corporate headquarters in Los Angles, the proposed settlement called for limits on the amount of future contributions by Occidental to the museum and to other charities associated with Hammer.

Throughout his career Hammer had been able to attract talented people to Occidental. Nowhere was this more evident than with Ray Irani, the president and chief operating officer during Hammer's last years at Occidental. In 1983 Hammer had convinced Irani, the president of Olin Corporation, to run Oxychem. When Irani took over, Oxychem had an operating loss of $23 million and supplied about 9% of Occidental's total sales. In 1989 Oxychem had an operating profit of $1.2 billion and supplied about one-quarter of Oxy's total sales. In February 1990, the board of directors of Occidental designated Irani as the successor to Armand Hammer as chairman and chief executive officer, when Hammer would cease to hold those positions.

Occidental's 1989 annual report pointed to 94% of its revenues coming from domestic operations compared to 55% from the same source in 1980. The 1989 report said that this trend toward domestic operations should continue. Oxy may, however, continue to be involved in large foreign operations. In June 1990, for example, Oxy was the only U.S. company in a four-country agreement to build a $7 billion petrochemical plant in the Soviet Union, the largest-ever joint Soviet-Western project.

When Armand Hammer died at the age of 92 on December 10, 1990, the changeover in command at the top was expected: Ray Irani, president and chief executive officer under Hammer for six years, took over as chairman of the board. The rapid pace of change at Occidental was not entirely expected. Within a few weeks, Irani instituted a restructuring plan that largely abandoned many of Hammer's policies. For example, Irani decided to cancel Occidental's billion-dollar petrochemical deal with the Soviet Union. He also announced that Oxy's 51% stake in IBP, Inc. was for sale. Perhaps most importantly, Irani outlined a strategy to reduce the company's debt load by 40%, or $3 billion, by 1992. The strategy called for selling assets like IBP, Inc., but also included slashing stockholder dividends to $1 a share from $2.50.

Reaction from the business community seemed supportive. Standard & Poor's Corporation raised its ratings on about $8.8 billion of the company's debt, and the stock price seemed headed upward. Although Armand Hammer ran Occidental as his own for many years, Oxy appeared ready to enter a new era under the direction of Ray Irani.

Principal Subsidiaries: Occidental Oil and Gas Corporation; OXY USA Inc.; Occidental International Exploration and Production Company; Occidental Crude Sales, Inc.; MidCon Corporation; Occidental Chemical Corporation; Oxy Petrochemicals Inc.; IBP Inc.; Island Creek Corporation; Occidental International Corporation; Canadian Occidental Petroleum Ltd.

Further Reading: Hammer, Armand, and Neil Lyndon, *Hammer,* New York, G.P. Putnam's Sons, 1987; Weinberg, Steve, *Armand Hammer: The Untold Story,* Boston, Little, Brown, and Company, 1989.

—Mark Uri Toch

OIL AND NATURAL GAS COMMISSION

Tel Bhavan
Dehradun–(U.P.)
248003
India
(11) 401-56-57-58

State-Owned Company
Incorporated: 1959
Employees: 47,757
Sales: Rs82.00 billion (US$4.52 billion)

The Oil and Natural Gas Commission (ONGC), India's largest petroleum exploration and production entity, is organized as a state statutory body rather than a public company, but is run on a profit-making basis with these revenues flowing to the Indian Exchequer. In 1989–1990 ONGC claimed to have posted the biggest profit in "India's corporate world."

ONGC and the state-owned company, Oil India Ltd., are responsible for most of the exploration and production of crude oil and gas in the country. A separate state-owned company, the huge Indian Oil Corporation, is predominant in refining, trading, and marketing.

The ONGC and other state-owned oil companies trace their origins back to a 1948 resolution by India's newly independent government. The Industrial Policy Resolution of 1948 specified that all new units in the Indian oil industry would be government-owned, unless specifically authorized.

In December 1955 an Oil and Natural Gas Directorate was set up within the Ministry of Natural Resources and Scientific Research to specialize in exploration. Early in 1956 its status was changed to a commission. In October 1959 the ONGC was made a statutory body by an act of parliament.

The decision to create ONGC as a state-controlled body and, eventually, to bring most of the rest of the oil industry under government control, was based not just on ideology, but on the need to prevent a drain on foreign exchange and control by a group of foreign-owned oil companies that were predominant in the country. Before independence and immediately afterward foreign companies exercised a powerful control over the production and supply of petroleum substances vital to the country's industrial development.

Prior to independence, it was widely believed that India lacked large-scale commercial deposits of oil and gas. Many of India's needs were supplied by other parts of the British Empire, Persia, the Dutch East Indies, and Russia. Kerosene was the most important petroleum product in a country with few cars. Burma, then an administrative part of India, was known to have significant deposits, which sometimes derived from shallow, hand-dug wells. In 1947 both Burma and Pakistan—the latter with one discovered field—went their own ways.

India was left with only one major producing field—Digboi, Assam—which had been discovered in 1890. Despite extensive surveys throughout Assam, no other fields of any significance had been discovered. Digboi and its local refinery had been of profound strategic significance after the fall of Burma in 1942. It had furnished oil to Allied air bases from which supplies were flown to China. It would take several years for India's new leaders to learn the strategic and economic importance of domestic oil supplies.

During World War II, petroleum supplies were regulated by a committee in London, and prices were set in India by a committee chaired by Burmah-Shell. Wartime rationing continued until 1950, and a shortage of oil products continued to be exacerbated by the limited domestic production and refining facilities. Relations with Burmah-Shell and other foreign companies continued to sour after independence in 1947. They advised India against building its own refinery on the grounds that it could only be run at a financial loss. India's vulnerability to the pressures of the international oil market became clear after 1950, when the Iranian political leader Mussadegh nationalized a huge refinery at Abadan that Burmah-Shell had previously used to supply much of India's needs. Iran was in the sterling area, and when this source was cut off India was forced to use its scarce dollar reserves to buy oil elsewhere.

The foreign companies were then persuaded to build two refineries, but the government remained skeptical about the costs of oil exploration. After the war, the Assam Oil Company, a subsidiary of British-owned Burmah Oil, had resumed exploration with little success. Assam finally achieved a major find at Nakhortiya in 1953, but a row ensued between Burmah and the government. The government refused Burmah any right to refine or market this oil and would only allow the company joint ownership in production. As a result Burmah refused to undertake further exploration. Soon afterward, the government claimed Burmah-Shell and other foreign companies were charging excessive prices for imported oil. A controversy ensued over the companies' refusal to refine imported Soviet oil.

These controversies helped lead to the creation of ONGC. Burmah retained control of Digboi but development in the other Assam fields was taken over by a new company, Oil India Ltd., of which the government owned one-third and Assam Oil held two-thirds. By 1981, the Indian government had acquired 100% of Oil India.

Burmah and Oil India were originally confined to the Assam fields, where ONGC was excluded. After 1956 no new concessions were granted to foreign companies for onshore exploration. ONGC became the principal exploration company in India. A Soviet consultant and several Soviet geophysicists were engaged. At first, exploration and drilling with equipment provided by the Soviet and Romanian governments yielded disappointing results. The Indian financial press criticized ONGC and the government for wasting the taxpayers' money. But this attitude began to change after an important find at Cambay, Gujurat, in 1958. A chain of new finds followed.

Soviet and Romanian experts became enthusiastic about India's potential reserves. They estimated that 42% of the country's land area was composed of oil-yielding sedimentary rock with even more lucrative possibilities offshore. Soviet-supplied exploration and production technology, however, was widely regarded as inferior, and the government looked for other sources of assistance, especially after a 1963 offshore exploration revealed promising structures beneath the Gulf of Cambay.

In 1959, the government had revised legislation to make it easier for foreign companies to undertake exploration work in some areas without the participation of ONGC. However, the government's preference for agreements in which explorers accepted a majority government stake in the crude-producing company was known. The government launched a campaign to persuade foreign companies to undertake exploration.

The French Institute of Petroleum provided some assistance, and some contracts were given to French and Italian firms. Press reports indicated that Shell, Caltex, Gulf, and Esso were interested, but in the end there were no major deals. There were more lucrative fields elsewhere, with fewer government conditions made.

With limited technology and Soviet help, ONGC's progress in developing new wells and in production was slow during the 1960s. The government's inability to attract foreign investment came under frequent criticism. More promising offshore geological structures were found during systematic surveys by the Soviet ship *Akademic Arkhangeleisky* during the period 1964–1967.

Finally, in 1974, ONGC discovered the major Bombay High offshore field with a strike from the advanced Japanese-built *Sagar Samrat* drilling platform. The strain on foreign exchange caused by the 1973 Arab oil boycott brought a redoubling of exploration efforts. Further offshore oil and gas was discovered at Godavari and gas off Portonovo and the Andaman islands in 1980.

The importance of ONGC's new gas discoveries was underscored by the government's decision in 1984 to set up the separate Gas Authority of India Ltd. (GAIL) to process, market, and distribute all forms of natural gas. After the government acquired the remaining foreign interests of Burmah in the Assam Oil Company in 1981, Oil India Ltd. was given an expanded role as the second public sector undertaking engaged in oil exploration and production. Previously, Oil India had been restricted to eastern areas of the country.

ONGC seeks to help the country achieve self-reliance in oil-related equipment, materials, and services. ONGC has tried to speed up this indigenization by working with a consortium of Indian firms that includes Hindustan Shipyard Ltd., Burn Standard Company Ltd., Confederation of Engineering Industry, and Larsen & Toubro. The company reports that this progress has resulted in the domestic industry supply of over 50% of the oil industry's equipment and materials requirements.

In its early days, ONGC experienced difficulties in obtaining up-to-date petroleum technology. It has assigned a high priority to research and technology, which the company states are now on a level with that used in explorations anywhere in the world. ONGC's research efforts date back to the founding of its Kashava Malaviya Institute of Petroleum Exploration in Dehra dun in 1963. The Malaviya Institute is responsible for applied research in petroleum geology, geophysics, and well logging techniques. ONGC has six other research bodies. ONGC's policy is to run these institutes as profit centers.

Exploration efforts have been expanded to many new areas including Krishna-Godavari, Cauvery, Tripura, Cachar, Dhansiri Valley, and Ravasan. The number of active rigs grew from 41 in 1981 to 144 in 1990. Future plans include the Ganges Valley, Himalayan foothills, Bengal, Kerala, and Konikan. Offshore, the firm's deep water unit has been formed to function as the central agency for planning, programming, and implementing exploration in deep water along India's coasts.

As the government's agency, ONGC has presided over an increasingly liberalized policy of encouraging foreign oil companies to explore offshore and they have responded with increasing interest. In 1987, the Indian government invited foreign oil companies to bid for 27 offshore exploration blocks in the third round of initiatives to encourage foreign investment in India's offshore industry. This effort was made more successful than the previous rounds in which many companies refused to participate because they alleged that the government had reserved the most favorable sites for ONGC and Oil India. Twelve bids for nine blocks covering a total of 121,000 square kilometers were received from seven companies. Chevron, Texaco, Broken Hill Proprietary of Australia, and International Petroleum of Canada eventually signed deals allowing them to put 40% equity in a joint venture or to pull out if seismic data were not promising. In 1990, the government announced plans for a fourth round. Private Indian companies would be allowed to acquire concessions for the first time, but there are no current plans to privatize ONGC itself. In 1989 ONGC signed a joint exploration agreement in the Gulf of Thailand, signed drilling contracts with National Iraqi Oil Company, and raised money in the Tokyo and Swiss bond markets.

In 1981–1982, the ONGC redefined its goals and objectives and prepared a corporate plan spanning 20 years from 1985 to 2005; more recently, this plan has been updated to 2015. The emphasis is on accelerated exploration and production strategies. From 1990 production levels of about 30 million tons of crude oil it envisages by 2015 production of 75 million tons.

Over the 1980s and early 1990s, ONGC has shown steady growth in crude oil and gas production, rig counts, profits, and contributions to India's exchequer. India hopes to achieve self-sufficiency in fuel by the year 2005. As the company most active in the western offshore, India's most important oil and gas area, ONGC is essential to this task.

Further Reading: Dasgupta, Bipab, *The Petroleum Industry in India*, London, Frank Cass & Company, 1971.

—Clark Siewert

ÖMV AKTIENGESELLSCHAFT

Otto-Wagner-Platz 5
1090 Vienna
Austria
(222) 48-900-0
Fax: (222) 48-900-91

State-Owned Company
Incorporated: 1955 as Österreichische Mineralölverwaltung
   AG
Employees: 8,600
Sales: Sch58.47 billion (US$5.56 billion)

ÖMV is 74% owned by the state holding company, Austrian Industries. The rest of the company is privately held. Currently in its fourth decade, ÖMV has transformed itself from a domestic oil and gas producer with no international presence into an integrated oil, gas, and chemical group with growing interests and influence abroad. ÖMV has become one of Austria's largest companies and is involved in oil exploration, production, refining, and retailing, as well as gas production and transportation, and is rapidly becoming a major producer of plastics in Europe. ÖMV is a product of the political realignment in Europe following World War II. Established in its present form in 1955, the company was originally known as Österreichische Mineralölverwaltung AG (OMG), but officially changed its name to ÖMV Aktiengesellschaft in 1974.

At the time of ÖMV's formation in 1955, Austria was the largest producer of hydrocarbons in Western Europe and energy self-sufficiency was envisaged for the years ahead. This did not occur. First oil and then gas production declined, while domestic hydrocarbon consumption soared ahead. The dominant theme of the 1970s and beyond became the need to find secure and diverse sources of energy supply. The trend towards internationlization is becoming even stronger as the 1990s unfold.

Exploration for oil began in Austria in the late 1920s. Small quantities of crude were found in the Vienna Basin, which remains the main producing area in Austria, and small-scale production took place from 1934 onward. Four companies were active in Austria at this stage: Rohölgewinnungs AG (RAG), a 50–50 joint venture of Shell and the U.S. company Socony-Vacuum; Van Sickle, a British company; Erdölsproduktions-Gesellschaft AG, which was financed by Swiss capital; and Raky-Danubia, an Austro-German collaboration.

Full-scale commercial production began after the Anschluss in 1938, when the Germans strove to achieve maximum production for the sake of their military machine. German companies involved at this stage were Elwerath, Wintershall, Preussag, and I.G. Farben. Production was concentrated in Zisterdorf near Vienna and reached a peak of 1.21 million metric tons in 1944.

At the end of World War II, Austria was divided into four zones of occupation, each one under one of the victorious powers—the United States, the Soviet Union, the United Kingdom, and France. All known Austrian oil reserves were in the Russian zone. Production and refining were carried out by the Soviet Mineral Oil Administration or were under its control. Distribution in the Russian zone was carried out by the Soviet company ÖROP. Retaining and distribution were carried out in the rest of the country by Western interests.

In the chaos of the immediate postwar years and as a result of the over-exploitation of Zisterdorf by the Germans, oil production was initially below war levels but the discovery of the new fields between 1949 and 1951—Matzen, Aderklaat, and Blockfliess—contributed to production of 2 million metric tons by 1951, 2.8 million tons by 1952, and a peak of 3.7 million tons in 1955.

All operational refineries, which had a total capacity of about one million tons per year, were located in the Russian zone. Two of these refineries, with a combined capacity of 230,000 tons per year, were owned by Shell Transport and Trading and by Socony-Vacuum. These foreign owners continued to operate their refineries, but they were directed by the Soviet authorities and were required to sell back their output to the Soviets at dictated prices.

Austria regained its sovereignty only after protracted negotiations. The legal basis of the Soviet hold over Austria's oil stemmed from the Potsdam Agreement, which granted the USSR title to all German assets in the occupied zone. The Western allies maintained that large parts of the Austrian oil industry never legally belonged to Germany because they were obtained under duress, and disputed the Soviet claim to these assets. The Austrian State Treaty was signed in 1955 and the Soviet Union handed over all former German assets in its hands to the Austrian government on August 13 of that year.

Treaty provisions shaped the future of the Austrian oil industry. The return of most oil fields and refineries to their prewar non-Austrian owners was precluded by the treaty, and the government had to find an adequate compensation formula for the former owners. Austria also agreed to send the Soviet Union 1.2 million tons annually of crude oil until 1961 and one million tons annually for the following four years. In 1957, the Soviet Union agreed that Austrian deliveries should immediately fall to one million tons annually and in 1958 a 50% reduction in net crude deliveries was agreed from the beginning of 1959.

Since the end of World War II, Austria had been ruled by a coalition of the Social Democrat Party and the People's Party. After the country regained control of its hydrocarbon resources, the parties disagreed about the future shape of the Austrian oil industry: the Social Democrats favored retaining state control while the People's Party preferred a mixture of state and private Austrian ownership. The ad-hoc state entity which took charge of Austria's oil assets pending a final decision, the Austrian Mineral Oil Administration, evolved into

ÖMV. ÖMV remained wholly in the public sector until the late 1980s.

ÖMV's first major project was the construction of the 1.66 million ton a year refinery at Schwechat, which was completed in 1960. The refinery replaced four refineries in the Vienna province with a combined capacity equivalent to that of Schwechat. By 1963, Schwechat's capacity had been raised to 2.5 million tons and to 4 million tons by 1964. ÖMV thus grew increasingly dominant in refining in Austria: Schwechat capacity far outstripped the 200,000 tons per annum which foreign companies retained in Vienna Province. Schwechat remains the only major refinery in Austria in 1991.

Two petrochemical plants were also built near Schwechat to take advantage of refinery gases as feedstocks. One plant was owned by Petrochemie Danubia (PCD), a joint venture involving Montecatini and Österreichische Stickstoffswerke (ÖSW), and the other involved a partnership of ÖMV and the West German company, Farbwerke Hoechst. In 1972, ÖMV and ÖSW embarked upon the path which led to their merger.

Although dominant in upstream activity in Austria from its early days, ÖMV initially had a negligible presence in the distribution and retail markets. The sales of final products were carried out by subsidiaries of the oil majors. Shell was the market leader. In the early years, ÖMV had no marketing arm at all. There were two state distribution concerns, however, Martha and ÖROP, the former Soviet company, which operated independently of ÖMV and which together controlled about 15% of the market. In 1965, ÖMV acquired 100% of Martha, which had 550 distribution outlets, and 74% of ÖROP, later renamed ELAN, which had 620 service stations. The remaining 26% of ÖROP was sold to the Austrian private sector.

These acquisitions did not satisfy ÖMV's retail ambitions. In 1971 ÖMV bought 250 service stations from Total-Austria, the fully owned subsidiary of French company, Compagnie Française des Pétroles (CFP), and currently has a 70% share in Total-Austria. By the beginning of the 1990s, through Total-Austria and its sales subsidiaries ÖMV Handels-Aktiengesellschaft and Stroh and Company, which was acquired in 1986, ÖMV accounted for 75% of the domestic retail market, up from 25% in 1970.

Oil production continued as a central activity, but output never returned to the 3.7 million ton levels of the mid-1950s. During the 1960s, crude output ranged from 2.2 million to 2.7 million tons. However, Austrian consumption of oil and oil products increased and quashed all ambitions of oil self-sufficiency. In 1967, domestic crude production was 2.7 million tons compared with consumption of 3.8 million tons. The gap between production and consumption continued to widen and Austria became increasingly dependent on crude oil imports from the Soviet Union.

In 1960, negotiations began between ÖMV and Shell, Mobil, British Petroleum, Esso, and Aquila—a CFP subsidiary—for the construction of a crude oil pipeline from Trieste to Vienna. It was hoped that the 480-kilometer-long pipeline, with an ultimate capacity of six million tons annually, would be completed by 1967 and would enable ÖMV to develop a wider range of crude suppliers. However, negotiations dragged on as ÖMV attempted to link the pipeline with a package deal guaranteeing a permanent dominant position in the refinery sector, and construction only began in 1968. The work was completed in July 1970. The pipeline took the form of a spur from the Trieste-Bavaria transalpine line. ÖMV had 51% of the equity, with Shell taking 14.5%, Mobil 12.5%, British Petroleum 7.5%, Esso 6.5%, CFP 4%, and ENI of Italy 4%.

Problems of supply security also occurred in relation to natural gas. ÖMV had developed Austria's gas resources and sold gas in the domestic market at very low prices. This pricing encouraged rapid growth in consumption and large-scale utilization of gas in power stations and industry. In 1967, ÖMV announced that indigenous reserves did not justify the production of more than 1.3 billion cubic meters of gas annually. Domestic demand, however, was running at 1.8 billion cubic meters of gas per year and Soviet imports, which entered Austria through a 65-kilometer extension of the Ukraine-Czechoslovakia pipeline, were needed to make good the shortfall.

Austria entered the 1970s with a growing dependency on hydrocarbons, a high percentage of which had to be imported. Oil's share of total domestic energy consumption had risen from 15% in the 1950s to 27% in 1962 and to over 50% for oil and gas combined in the early 1970s. These trends precipitated the emergence of the two current guiding principles of ÖMV strategy: diversification of energy supplies and internationalization of the company.

In 1970, ÖMV was primarily a domestically oriented company: it produced as much oil and gas as possible domestically and imported the remainder of its requirements from the USSR. By 1980, its crude supplies were more diverse, and supplies from Iran, Iraq, Libya, Algeria, and smaller OPEC states were becoming more important. In 1980, Saudi Arabia promised to supply Austria with 1.7 million to 2 million tons of crude oil yearly—roughly one-fifth of its import requirements. Gas supplies are still predominantly from the Soviet Union but in 1986 ÖMV, together with another Austrian company, Ferngas, signed a contract with a consortium led by Statoil of Norway for the delivery of one billion cubic meters of gas annually from the Troll field after 1993.

Potentially of even greater importance was the start of ÖMV exploration and production overseas. By 1980, ÖMV was active in Tunisia, Ireland, Libya, Egypt, and Canada. These foreign ventures remained marginal until 1985 when ÖMV acquired 25% of Occidental's production in Libya, giving it access to about 600,000 tons of crude a year. In addition, the deal entitled ÖMV to make additional Libyan crude purchases. The company's official aim is to cover half of the crude requirements of the refineries at Schwechat and at Burghausen from equity crude. Despite extensive domestic exploration efforts, Austria's reserves continued to dwindle. By 1989, ÖMV sourced 30% of its crude requirements from its own ventures. ÖMV's acquisition of shares in producing fields in the North Sea and Canada in 1990 will guide ÖMV towards its target.

Until the late 1980s, ÖMV remained wholly in the public sector. In 1970, Österreichische Industrieholding AG (ÖIAG), renamed Austrian Industries (AI) in February 1990, was established as the state holding company for nationalized companies. At its formation, ÖIAG employed one-sixth of the Austrian work force and owned one-fifth of Austrian industry, including 100% of ÖMV.

As one of the largest companies in Austria and as a member of the ÖIAG group, ÖMV was drawn into wider debates about the future of the Austrian economy. During the first half of the

1980s, ÖIAG showed heavy losses and was a severe drain on public finances. ÖMV was one of the few state companies that consistently made profits throughout this period. In 1987, ÖIAG was reorganized into seven sectors—oil, steel, metals, chemicals, mining, electronics, and machinery—in preparation for privatization of its holdings. ÖMV was the first on the list. In November 1987, 15% of ÖMV was sold to the public. A further 10% was sold in 1989. The original intention was that the sales should continue until 49% of the company was in private hands. The government subsequently decided that privatization efforts should be intensified and that the 49% limit on private shareholdings should be removed. Consequently, the way is clear for full-scale privatization of ÖMV in the early 1990s.

In the 1990s the company, believing that the domestic market has reached saturation point, is rationalizing its retail network. ÖMV cancelled its trademark agreement with Aral of West Germany effective September 1990. ÖMV plans to sell products under the ELAN brand in its older stations and has introduced an ÖMV brand in its other outlets. ÖMV also intends to set up a foreign network under this new brand.

Petrochemicals remain important to ÖMV which is in the throes of transforming itself into a major player in the European plastics market. The combined polyethylene and polypropylene sales of wholly owned ÖMV subsidiary PCD are approaching 600,000 metric tons annually of which 85% is exported. POB Polyolefine Burghausen GmbH, a wholly owned subsidiary of ÖMV, completed construction of a polypropylene plant in 1989 and a polyethylene plant in 1990. Both plants are located in Burghausen and are operated by another wholly owned ÖMV subsidiary, DMP Mineralöl Petrochemie GmbH, with sales handled by PCD. Other subsidiaries are engaged in the further processing of plastics.

On taking office in October 1990, the Social Democratic chancellor, Franz Vranitzky, pointed to two international developments which have a tremendous bearing on Austria's future—the economic integration of the European Community (EC) and the political and economic liberalization of the former communist countries of Central and Eastern Europe. These two developments have had a significant influence on ÖMV strategy. The 1987 purchase of German subsidiary, Deutsche Marathon Petroleum (DMP) from U.S. company Marathon Petroleum, gave ÖMV a foothold in the European Community. ÖMV has also acquired the geotextile holdings of the French company Rhône Poulenc, and a melamine plant in Castellanza, Italy.

Because of Austria's traditional position as a staging post between East and West and because of its long-term commercial relationship with the Soviet Union, ÖMV is in a better position than most to benefit from the changes in Eastern Europe. In March 1991, ÖMV opened its first petrol station in Hungary. As part of its joint venture with Hungarian state retailer, Afor, 30 more such stations are planned in the immediate future. A joint venture has been formed with Petrol in Slovenia, Yugoslavia, to operate 25 petrol stations there. Negotiations are underway for similar ventures with the Czech company Benzinol, and the Slovak company Benzina.

Despite the publicity about the opportunities which exist in the Soviet oil and gas industry, few solid joint ventures are in place. ÖMV, however, is more advanced than most in cementing a deal. ÖMV has signed a memorandum of understanding with the Soviet region of Yakutia in northeast Siberia to develop a small field which would provide the feedstock for a one million to two million ton refinery at Lensk. The feasibility study for the refinery is already underway, and the possibility of gas exploration is being considered.

ÖMV's strategy of diversification and internationalization will continue into the 1990s, as the company strives to overcome its poor domestic resource base. The push into Europe will continue, particularly as Austria presses its application for EC membership and attempts to break into the markets of Central and Eastern Europe.

Principal Subsidiaries: Adria-Wien Pipeline GmbH; Erdöl-Lagergesellschaft mbH (51%); ÖMV (Angola) Exploration GmbH; ÖMV (Dänemark) Exploration GmbH; ÖMV (Gabon) GmbH; ÖMV (Indonesien) Exploration GmbH; ÖMV Handels-Aktiengesellschaft (96.07%); ÖMV (Jordanien) Exploration GmbH; ÖMV (Malaysia) Exploration GmbH; ÖMV Mineralöl-Vertriebsgesellschaft mbH; ÖMV (Pakistan) Exploration GmbH; ÖMV PEX Öl and Gas Exploration GmbH; PROTERRA Gesellschaft für Umwelttechnik; ÖMV Suez Erdöl-Aufsuchungsgesellschaft mbH; Petrochemie Danubia GmbH; Stroh & Co GmbH; Trans-Austria-Gasleitung GmbH (51%); DMP Mineralöl Petrochemie GmbH (Germany); OMV Exploration and Production Ltd.; OMV (UK) Ltd.; OMV of Libya Ltd., Douglas; OMV (Norge) A/S (Norway); OMV (Canada) Ltd.; POB Polyolefine Burghausen GmbH (Germany).

—Debra Johnson

PENNZOIL COMPANY

Pennzoil Place
Post Office Box 2967
Houston, Texas 77252
U.S.A.
(713) 546-4000
Fax: (713) 546-6639

Public Company
Incorporated: 1968 as Pennzoil United, Inc.
Employees: 11,600
Sales: $2.37 billion
Stock Exchanges: New York Pacific Toronto London Basel
Geneva Zürich

Pennzoil's history is one of mergers and takeovers. Though one of its earliest ancestors was a part of the vast Standard Oil interests until 1911, Pennzoil was not a major factor in the oil and gas industry until its 1965 takeover of United Gas Corporation, a company many times its size. In a high-profile corporate war, in 1988 Pennzoil accepted a settlement of $3 billion from Texaco after the latter was found guilty of interference in Pennzoil's failed merger with Getty Oil. The cash payment, larger than Pennzoil's total assets at the time, was a climax to Pennzoil's long and complex history of corporate gamesmanship, much of it engineered by the company's long-time chairman, J. Hugh Liedtke.

The companies that originally came together to form Pennzoil were all involved in the oil industry's early history in Pennsylvania and the neighboring states. One of them, the South Penn Oil Company, was formed on May 27, 1889, by a unit of Standard Oil Company, John D. Rockefeller's enormous oil concern. Standard already controlled approximately 90% of the oil refining in the United States, but it had been slow to move into oil producing until the late 1880s, at which time it bought up a large number of ground leases in the Pennsylvania oil region and created South Penn to work them. Under first president Noah Clark, South Penn made rapid progress with its initial wells and was soon pushing across the border into the rich West Virginia fields. South Penn enjoyed all the benefits of membership in the Standard family of companies, including guaranteed sale of its crude to Standard distributors and refineries, ample provision of capital for expansion, and an absence of threatening competition. When Standard reorganized itself in 1892 into a closely interlocked trust of 20 operating com-

panies, South Penn was capitalized at $2.5 million, a significant figure for the time, but among the smaller of Standard's holdings.

The reorganized South Penn received a new president as well. John D. Archbold had been a Pennsylvania oil man since the 1860s, and after joining Standard had rapidly risen to become one of the company's top five policy-makers and its director of all producing activity. As such, he became the president of South Penn upon its reorganization in 1892, when the Standard companies were responsible for over a quarter of all U.S. oil production. In the 1890s South Penn increased tenfold its annual production of crude, and by 1898 it was the leader among the Standard interests with 7.6 million barrels per year, most of it pumped from its West Virginia fields. The year before, it had bought the drilling rights to some 20,000 acres of land in the Pennsylvania oil region, paying $1.4 million in what was described as the largest deal in the history of U.S. oil production.

In 1899 Standard Oil was again reshuffled, all of the affiliated companies becoming subsidiaries of the newly enlarged Standard Oil Company (New Jersey). John Archbold remained head of South Penn and was now effective head of New Jersey Standard as well, John D. Rockefeller having largely retired from the scene. South Penn was thus well positioned to grow into one of the giants of the American petroleum business, with unlimited financial backing, top management skills, and a healthy share of the existing crude market. It soon become apparent, however, that South Penn lacked the one indispensable ingredient of the oil industry: oil. By 1900 the Appalachian oil region had reached its all-time peak of production and its many thousands of wells began to run dry. South Penn production dropped by about 50% during the following decade and would never again provide more than small amounts of high-grade crude, in addition to useful quantities of the recently harnessed natural gas.

In 1911 the Supreme Court ordered the dissolution of Standard Oil Company (New Jersey). South Penn began life on its own as one of the leading drillers of crude oil in a region that was largely played out. About the time South Penn had been formed, two independent refineries were built in nearby Rouseville, Pennsylvania. The Pennsylvania Refining Company and Nonpareil Refining Company were both founded in 1886 to process the great stream of oil then produced by the region and bound for the eastern seaboard. The founders of Pennsylvania Refining (PRC), Henry Suhr, Samuel Justus, and Louis Walz, invested $40,000 in their new company and commenced production of kerosene, at that time the most valuable end product of petroleum. Nonpareil Refining, on the other hand, designed its facilities to make lubricating oil and enjoyed only mixed success from the beginning.

The early oil industry was volatile, in more ways than one. By 1893 Nonpareil had already changed hands once and was then bought out by PRC for $50,000 at auction. Nonpareil's name was changed to Germania Refining Company and its offices consolidated with those of PRC. In the meantime, PRC had suffered a catastrophic fire in 1892, which destroyed its barrel factory and much of the adjoining refinery, killing 50 workers and causing an estimated $1 million in damage. Fires were common in the early years of the petroleum industry, as safety regulations were almost nonexistent and the product naturally flammable. PRC rebuilt its facilities and within a few months had restored production to full capacity.

The growing use of the automobile and other internal-combustion engines gradually changed the relative value of oil's refined products. Use of kerosene began a slow decline, its illumination replaced by the cleaner and more-efficient electricity; while gasoline, previously an unwanted oil by-product, was increasingly required by the new machines. Internal-combustion engines also depended on efficient lubricants, which PRC recognized in 1904 when it expanded its lube facilities and five years later formed a new company to market its lubricants, Oil City Oil and Grease Company. Prevented by Pennsylvania's limited crude supplies from becoming a major refiner of gasoline, PRC shifted more of its production to lubricants and quickly developed a reputation for manufacturing high quality products. PRC's president and part owner was Charles Suhr, son of one of the company's founders, and in 1913 Suhr agreed to invest in a California company which wished to distribute Germania lubricants on the West Coast. A few years later, Suhr and his associates came up with the brand name Pennzoil, which would henceforth become the company's trademark and one of the country's more widely recognized logos. To capitalize on Pennzoil's growing popularity, Suhr changed the name of his two marketing companies in 1921 to the Pennzoil Company (California) and the Pennzoil Company (Pennsylvania).

In the meantime, Suhr had merged his refining outfits in 1914 into a single company called Germania Refining Company, soon changed for patriotic reasons to Penn-American Refining Company. In 1924 Penn-American and its marketing companies, now three in number with the addition a few years before of Pennzoil Company (New York), were merged into an umbrella corporation called Pennzoil Company. Pennzoil was not only refining and marketing about 3,000 barrels per day of crude oil; it also had bought gas stations in Detroit, Cleveland, and Pittsburgh. Having organized the refining and marketing aspects of the oil business, Pennzoil was still lacking crude-production capacity, and in the mid-1920s it began talks with South Penn Oil about a possible merger. South Penn, the former Standard Oil producer, had limited refining and marketing capacities, and in 1925 the two companies came together when South Penn bought 51% of Pennzoil's stock. Though not a merger, South Penn's purchase effectively united the two medium-sized Pennsylvania oil concerns. South Penn completed its purchase of Pennzoil in 1955.

While Pennzoil motor oils were racking up an impressive series of Indianapolis 500 automobile racing and transcontinental flight records, South Penn continued consolidating its holdings in the Appalachian oil and gas region, which though limited in scope remained a source of high-grade petroleum. The focus of U.S. oil production had shifted to the South, however, where the vast east Texas fields had begun pumping in the early 1930s, and initial efforts were underway to tap the offshore riches of the Gulf of Mexico. The immediate effect of this surge in production was to depress the price of Pennsylvania crude to an all-time low in 1933, but its long-term effect on Pennzoil's future history was to be much more profound.

After World War II, as America developed its love of the automobile, investors continued to pour into the Texas oil regions in search of more spectacular finds. One such wildcatting firm, Zapata Petroleum Corporation, was founded in 1953 by two brothers, J. Hugh and William Liedtke, John Overbey, and a young man named George Bush, later to abandon oil for the richer field of politics. The Liedtkes had already formed a useful friendship with another future U.S. president, Lyndon Baines Johnson, at whose Austin, Texas, home they rented rooms while attending law school at the University of Texas. The four men all had some experience in oil, and in raising the $1 million to form Zapata planned to have a go at big-time oil gambling themselves. As it turned out, they were both lucky and talented: Zapata leased several thousand acres in Texas's West Jameson field and proceeded to drill 127 wells without once coming up dry.

Zapata soon moved offshore, creating Zapata Offshore Company and Zapata Drilling Company to pursue the oil fields then being uncovered in the gulf. In 1959, these two companies were spun off as independent concerns, with George Bush remaining as Zapata offshore's head until his election to the House of Representatives in 1966. The so-called spin-off would become a favorite tactic of the resourceful Liedtke brothers, who were able time and again to realize substantial gains by relying on the willingness of shareholders to pay more for equity in a smaller, easily comprehended asset than they would for the same asset hidden in a large corporation. The Zapata partners were already wealthy men by the late 1950s, but the Liedtke brothers were eager to expand, and became interested in the fortunes of Pennzoil, whose corporate name had become South Penn Oil Company after the final merger of its partner companies in 1955. South Penn was well known as a producer of premium motor oil but its profits had never reached their potential. The company's largest shareholder was J. Paul Getty's Tidewater Oil, and the Liedtkes, who knew Getty through previous dealings, began buying large amounts of South Penn stock with Getty's approval. Convinced that South Penn's assets were not being fully exploited, the Liedtkes soon bought out Getty's position and in effect gained control of South Penn in the early 1960s. J. Hugh Liedtke became president of South Penn in 1962, and in the following year South Penn was merged with the Zapata companies in a new entity called Pennzoil Company. Pennzoil was still a relatively small player among the oil giants, with sales in 1963 of only $77 million and a net profit of about $7 million. The corporation was headquartered in Houston, with regional offices in Los Angeles and Oil City, Pennsylvania.

The Liedtkes next set their sights on a much richer prize, United Gas Corporation. United was formed in 1930 as a holding company for some 40 gas and oil concerns in the Gulf of Mexico region and by the mid-1960s had become one of the largest distributors of natural gas in the country, its United Gas Pipe Line Company carrying approximately 8% of the nation's supply. United also produced and processed natural gas and owned an important mining company, Duval Corporation. As with his friendly takeover of South Penn, Hugh Liedtke saw in United a company unable to exploit its large resources and hence undervalued in the market. He offered to buy one million shares of United at $41 per share; five million shares were promptly tendered, and Pennzoil bought all of them for a total purchase of 42% of United's stock, borrowing $215 million of the $225 million required. The move was an early example of corporate raiding, in which a much smaller company—in this case, one-eighth the size of its target—gained control of a vast but underperforming competitor. As he did with Zapata, Liedtke proceeded to sell off much of United's assets, first spinning off its retail business and then, in 1974, the huge

United Gas Pipe Line Company. According to Pennzoil, the latter divestment was made necessary by government regulations which inhibited Pennzoil's operation of both producing and distributing concerns, but the Liedtkes's handling of the affair resulted in a barrage of lawsuits and an investigation by the Federal Power Commission. In addition, the brothers agreed to pay $100,000 to former Pennzoil stockholders in settlement of insider trading charges brought at the time of the spin-off.

In any event, the absorption of the United companies turned Pennzoil into a large and diversified natural-resources company. Its 1970 sales hit $700 million, up tenfold from 1963, and its Duval Corporation mining subsidiary went on to make a series of quick strikes in sulfur, potash, copper, gold, and silver. To keep its natural gas production up, Pennzoil created two new companies in the early 1970s, Pennzoil Offshore Gas Operators (POGO) and Pennzoil Louisiana and Texas Offshore, Inc. (PLATO), selling shares to the public in order to raise capital needed for further offshore drilling while also enjoying a sizable appreciation in the value of the stock it retained. By 1980 Pennzoil sales had passed $2 billion, the bulk of it generated by the company's traditional strength in the refining and sale of motor oil. Pennzoil had become the second-leading seller of motor oil, bolstered by its reputation for quality and by an increasing use of mass marketers instead of gas stations for its retail trade. Its assorted mining ventures brought in about 20% of corporate sales, while sulfur added another 10%. It was not surprising that Hugh Liedtke began pushing hard for more oil and gas production—though representing but one-fourth of sales, production accounted for fully 50% of net income, crude oil and gas always commanding a higher margin than refined products.

With that in mind, in the early 1980s Liedtke became interested in the squabbling heirs of J. Paul Getty. Liedtke calculated that Getty Oil Company stock was severely undervalued and began buying it up, and in January 1984 he reached an agreement with Gordon Getty to buy three-sevenths of the company's shares at $112.50 per share, well over their current trading price. The $3.9 billion purchase would vastly increase Pennzoil's reserves of oil and gas, and probably precipitate the dissolution of Getty Oil at prices even higher than Liedtke had paid. The agreement was duly approved by Getty's board of directors and announced at a press conference, but Getty's investment bankers and lawyers continued to solicit higher offers for Getty stock. They got one from Texaco, which several days later announced that it had agreed to buy all of Getty's stock at $128 per share, or about $10 billion. At that point, Hugh Liedtke sued Texaco for tortuous interference with Pennzoil's prior contract with Getty, and shortly afterward a Texas jury agreed with him, deciding that Texaco owed Pennzoil about $10.5 billion in real and punitive damages—the highest such award to date.

With the exception of Hugh Liedtke, the award seemed to stun everyone. Texaco had not taken the suit seriously, assum-

ing that at worst it would be forced to pay off Pennzoil with a nominal settlement fee. Not only did the Texas jury express the general public's growing dislike for big-money takeovers; its verdict was upheld upon appeal though the award was lowered to $8.5 billion. Texaco threatened to declare bankruptcy if Liedtke did not accept a "reasonable" settlement, but the Pennzoil chairman refused. In April 1987 Liedtke turned down an offer of $2 billion cash from Texaco, which promptly followed through on its promise and filed under Chapter 11 of the bankruptcy code. Upon that news the stock value of Pennzoil dropped $631 million overnight. Liedtke was aware, however, that Texaco was a wealthy company even for the oil business, able to sustain a huge cash loss, and by the end of 1987 Texaco agreed to pay Pennzoil $3 billion to have done with the case.

While this legal struggle was being waged, Pennzoil had decided to sell its various mining interests, with the exception of sulfur. Liedtke spun off the gold-mining subsidiary into an independent company, Battle Mountain Gold Company, whose stock tripled in a short time. The mining disposal left Pennzoil with a mix of motor oil refining and marketing, oil and gas production, and sulfur production, the last two far more profitable than the former; and about $3 billion in cash. Just as he had done while pursuing Getty, Liedtke spent the bulk of the money, $2.1 billion, for a big chunk of a larger oil concern, in this case 8.8% of Chevron. Anticipating the worst, Chevron immediately filed suit to prevent the purchase and readied itself for a hostile takeover bid. As of 1991 Pennzoil remained a model institutional investor, quietly cashing its 4.5% dividend checks while waiting for what the future might bring.

In January 1990 Pennzoil bought more than 80% of Jiffy Lube International, Inc., a franchiser, owner, and operator of automotive lubrication and fluid-maintenance centers. Jiffy Lube had successfully found a niche as a speedy-service center, but was deeply in debt. Pennzoil's $43.5 million purchase price bought a company with assets of $237.3 million and liabilities of $239.5 million.

Principal Subsidiaries: Jiffy Lube International, Inc. (82%); Pennzoil Exploration and Production Company; Pennzoil Lube Center Development Company; Pennzoil Products Company; Pennzoil Sulphur Company; Proven Properties Inc.; Purolator Products Company; Richland Development Corporation.

Further Reading: "Love Her and Leave Her," *Forbes,* September 15, 1974; Sherman, Stratford P., "The Gambler Who Refused $2 Billion," *Fortune,* May 11, 1987; Gentry, Mickey, and Kimberly Patrick, *Pennzoil Company: The First 100 Years,* Houston, Pennzoil Company, 1989.

—Jonathan Martin

PERTAMINA

Jalan Merdeka Timur Number 1
Jalan Perwira 2-4-6 Jakarta
Indonesia
(021) 3031

State-Owned Company
Incorporated: 1945 as Perusahaan Tambang Minyak Negara
   Republik Indonesia

Besides agriculture, oil and natural gas are Indonesia's most important assets. Oil production amounts to upward of 500 million barrels exported annually since 1986, contributing more than 40% of the state's current income. The importance of oil production underlies the continuing importance of PERTAMINA, Indonesia's state oil and gas mining company, for the nation's economy.

Since the 17th century, when much of the Indonesian archipelago came under the control of the Netherlands and its Dutch East Indies colonial administration, the region has been renowned for its vast natural resources, especially tin. Until the middle part of the 20th century, however, the country's oil deposits remained largely untapped. History records that Indonesians in the Sumatra Strait successfully defeated attacking forces from the Portuguese armada by hurling oil-soaked fire balls at the foreigners and burning their vessels.

Dutch seafarers avoided a similar fate by arming their battle ships with cannons to repel the fire balls from a safe distance. With Indonesia a colony, the Dutch soon began tapping the country's oil reserves for their own gain.

In 1887, Adrian Stoop, a former engineer with Zijlker, a Dutch oil company, set up his own business in Surabaya. Having found oil deposits, he established a refinery at Wonokromo in 1890, and expanded with another one in Cepu, Central Java, in 1894. Two larger oil companies, Koninklijke Nederlandsche Petroleum Maatschappij and Shell Transport and Trading Company, were quick to assume the advantage over Stoop by setting up, in 1902, a joint venture in oil shipping and marketing operations in Indonesia. In 1907 the two Dutch concerns, impressed with each other's progress, merged into one group, which eventually became known as Royal Dutch/Shell, or Shell for short.

Other oil companies attempted at the turn of the century to establish a foothold in Indonesian oil mining. Most failed or were swallowed up, in part or whole, by Royal Dutch/Shell. For example, a number of foreign companies looking to explore in the Irian Jaya province in 1935 set up a joint company called Nederlandsche Nieuw Guinea Petroleum Maatschappij, 40% of it shares being held by Shell.

During the inter-war years Indonesia had become the Far East's largest oil producer, and the prospect of the country's falling under Japanese control after the bombing of Pearl Harbour dismayed Indonesia's Dutch rulers. When the Dutch government realized Indonesia could no longer withstand a Japanese advance, many of the country's oil installations and facilities were destroyed. Before the Dutch army and the oil companies could complete the scuttling operation, the Japanese forces occupied a fair number of the remaining installations, putting them under the control of the invader's regional military commander.

With the end of the war in 1945 and the proclaiming of Indonesia's independence in August of that year, to become fully effective in 1949, that country's anti-colonial independence fighters, resuming the fight against Dutch rule, quickly seized on what remaining oil fields and installations they could secure from the retreating Japanese. Recognizing this popular ferment, in September 1945 the Dutch administration included in the country's new constitution Article 33, which outlined the "people's desire" to develop their oil and gas sectors. In practical terms, Article 33 meant the establishment that month of a national oil company, Perusahaan Tambang Minyak Negara Republik Indonesia (PTMN-RI). In a wider sense, Indonesia started out on the road to reducing its dependence on foreign oil companies to tap its energy deposits and to managing the industry for its own gain.

At the same time, independence fighters in south Sumatra retained control of regional oil facilities and set up their own company, Perusahaan Minyak Republik Indonesia (PERMIRI). Elsewhere in Java, another oil company, Perusahaan Tambang Minyak Republik Indonesia (PTMN), held jurisdiction.

This postwar period was, debilitating for Indonesia's oil industry, as rival independence movements used installations and facilities to gain advantage over the Dutch colonial rulers. For a time PERMIRI was able to run the Dutch blockade and sell oil to Singapore. By 1948, however, Dutch forces had ended exports of PERMIRI's supplies. In the same year, Dutch forces ended exploration at oil fields controlled by PTMN in Central Java.

After Indonesia's full independence in 1949, the country had to contend with foreign oil companies still tapping its most valuable oil and gas reserves. Royal Dutch/Shell and Standard-Vacuum Oil Company (Stanvac), two large foreign oil groups operating in the region, still had concessions to continue work in Indonesia until 1951. That year, Indonesia's house of representatives ordered the government to set up a state committee for mining affairs and to postpone granting concessions and exploration permits to foreign oil companies.

This was a modest first attempt by Indonesia to tap its oil and gas reserves for its sole gain. Plans were slow in developing. In 1954, the government forged a four-year agreement with Stanvac to give Indonesia greater input in how its oil industry was developed.

The Stanvac agreement expired in 1960, when the Indonesian government enacted Law 44, concerning oil and gas mining. Exploration and mining were now to be carried out only by the government, under the management of a state company. Hereafter, foreign companies such as Shell and Stanvac were no longer to be regarded as concession holders but as contractors, and had to renegotiate their agreements with the Indonesian government accordingly.

Again, plans were slow to bear fruit. Indonesia knew that it lacked the massive funds needed to explore and produce oil on its own. Negotiations, over which the United States took great interest and an eventual lead, were concluded in June 1963. The resulting agreement held that Shell, Stanvac, and Caltex, the major foreign oil companies operating in Indonesia, were to become contractors of PERMIGAN, PERMINA, and PERTAMIN respectively. The foreigners would retain management of the oil installations, but 60% of profits from all activities would go to Indonesia.

Beyond profits, however, the Indonesian government was intent on maintaining general managerial responsiblity for all oil exploring and drilling installations in the country. General Ibnu Sutowo, president-director of PERTAMINA, explained: "This does not mean that we insist on making every decision, but we do insist on making any decision we find necessary."

Although Indonesia remained largely dependent on foreign oil companies, it had made an attempt to obtain crude oil on its own. In 1962, Indonesia joined the Organization of Petroleum Exporting Countries (OPEC), although at this time the oil producing cartel was hardly the economic force it was to become during the 1970s.

The country's first state-owned oil company, Exploitasi Tambang Minyak Sumatra Utara (PT ETMSU), had been set up in 1957. After changing its name soon after to PT PERMINA, Indonesia made its first crude oil export on March 24, 1958, when the tanker *Shozmi Mam* carried 1,700 tons, worth about US$30,000, to a foreign buyer.

Slowly, Indonesia established the infrastructure to produce its own crude oil on a lasting basis. PERMINA Oil Academy enrolled its first group of engineering students in 1962. In the same year, PERMINA purchased one aircraft for its operations and—a year later—secured approval from the government for the purchase of ocean-going tankers for crude oil exports.

By 1965, PERMINA had successfully drilled a total of nine oil fields, the resulting wells producing 21,000 barrels of oil per day. This progress instilled the Indonesian government with enough confidence to secure agreement from Shell to purchase all of Shell's assets for around US$10 million over a period of five years after 1966.

It was not until 1971 that PN Pertambangan Minyak Dan Gas Bumi Negara (PERTAMINA) was established by the Indonesian government as the only national oil company which could extract oil and natural gas throughout the country. The state company had been formed earlier in 1968, again by government legislation, after the merger of PN PERTAMIN and PT PERMINA, the existing state oil companies. Under the 1971 legislation, PERTAMINA was to be run by a board of directors, headed by a president director, and five other directors. The state-owned company, headquartered in Jakarta, was to operate in close cooperation with the Indonesian government.

PERTAMINA needed the assistance of foreign oil companies. Under production agreements, the foreign contractors were to receive 40% of profits from exploration and drilling, while the Indonesian government carved out 60% of all gains. This all changed, however, in 1973 when the oil barrel price began to increase sharply. PERTAMINA renegotiated in 1974 complex agreements which stipulated that when the price of a barrel of crude oil climbed above a recognized base price, the incremental rise would be shared between the government and the contractor at a split of between 85–15 and 95–05%.

The West's growing thirst for energy supplies at this time gave tremendous impetus to the growth of Indonesia's LNG—liquefied natural gas—industry.

The beginnings of LNG exploration dated back to October 24, 1971, when Bob Graves, exploration manager for Mobil Oil Indonesia, completed a drill-stem test on a wildcat well in the Arun oil field in North Sumatra. Graves had already drilled 14 holes in the field, an area of rice paddies, fish ponds, and coconut trees, but had found nothing. The 15th drill-stem test, Arun A-1, was successful. Alex Massad, Mobil Oil's exploration and production chief in New York, proposed further drilling in the area for natural gas, at a cost of US$400,000.

The directors at PERTAMINA recognized the potential for profits from Arun-1. The successful drilling of Arun-2 and Arun-3 in early 1972 confirmed the presence of large LNG reserves.

Mobil Oil was not alone in spotting Indonesia's rich LNG deposits. In 1971, Huffco, a Texas-based oil company drilling in palm swamps near the coast in east Kalimantan, drove a drill down the Badak-1 well site. Badak-1 produced a major gas discovery for Huffco.

On the strength of the Arun and Badak finds, PERTAMINA established a LNG unit, headed by Bambang Bramono, head of foreign gas marketing. The unit oversaw Mobil and Huffco development of their LNG finds. It soon became clear that Japan was to be PERTAMINA's main customer for natural gas.

The Indonesians' 50-year experience in the production of crude oil, and the political and economic machinations surrounding such endeavors, enabled them to gain the best advantage from LNG development. PERTAMINA extracted agreements from Mobil and Huffco that they would produce the natural gas, but that the Indonesian company would then sell it to foreign purchasers. All negotiations with prospective Japanese buyers, beginning in 1973, were headed by Indra Kartasamita, who worked in the company's sales and transportation division.

Contracts with foreign buyers followed, beginning in late 1972. Japanese electric utilities, including Kansai Electric Power Company, Chubu Electric Power Company, and Kyushu Electric Power Company, were among the first customers. PERTAMINA then signed a 20-year contract with Pacific Lighting Corporation, the parent of a California gas company. In 1979, PERTAMINA signed a five-year contract with Mitsubishi Oil Co., Ltd. of Japan, to double the latter's purchase of crude oil.

PERTAMINA's LNG operations were headed by General Ibnu Sutowo, who was directly responsible to Indonesian president Soeharto. Soedarno Martosewojo, a PERTAMINA director and chemical engineer, was appointed as LNG coordinator.

Once the taps which extracted LNG from deep below the Indonesian shorelines were switched on, production climbed steadily. It reached 312.6 billion standard cubic feet in 1976, compared with 150.8 billion in 1972.

The LNG plant in Arun was fully completed in mid-1978, while the plant at Badak came onstream in July 1977, commencing production a month later. In 1990, the annual production from the two plants was 15.7 million tons and was exported almost entirely to Japanese users. There were also modest exports of LNG to South Korean users.

Also in the pipeline was the export of 1.5 million tons of LNG to Taiwan each year, a market which was expected to open up in late 1990. This was agreed between the Chinese Petroleum Corporation and PERTAMINA in 1986.

The rise in the price of oil following Iraq's invasion of Kuwait in August 1990 was expected to rejuvenate exploration and drilling in Indonesia. Over the five years since 1986, when the price of oil slipped to below US$20 a barrel and remained static for a time, so too did the number of installations in Indonesia. During this period, 693 exploratory wells were drilled, comprising 385 wildcats and 308 delineation wells. These drillings saw a 35% success rate.

By mid-1989, the country had 78 onshore and offshore installations, covering 55 production contracts with foreign oil companies, and 18 joint operating arrangement areas. Of these installations, 29 were producing oil, while 49 were still in the exploration stage.

After its success in developing Indonesia's LNG deposits, PERTAMINA has been eager to explore and tap geothermal energy sources around the country. In its early stages of development, steam production has already begun at the first geo-thermal field in Kamojang, West Java. New fields set to begin production include those in Dieng plateau in Central Java, Mount Salak and Drajat in West Java, and Lahendong in North Sulawesi. Besides expanding its crude oil production, LNG production has enabled Indonesia to develop new markets in domestic gas uses, in fertilizer and petrochemical plants, refineries, and electric power generation.

PERTAMINA remains of key importance to the Indonesian economy. The rise in the price of oil at the beginning of the 1990s augurs well for its immediate future.

Principal Subsidiaries: PERTAMINA North Sumatra; PERTAMINA South Sumatra; PERTAMINA Kalimantan.

Further Reading: Bartlett, Anderson G., *Pertamina: Indonesian National Oil,* Jakarta, Amerasian Ltd., 1972; *Pertamina: History and Development,* Jakarta, PERTAMINA, 1979; *Hands Across the Sea: The Story of Indonesian LNG,* Jakarta, PERTAMINA, 1985.

—Etan Vlessing

PETRO-CANADA LIMITED

Post Office Box 2844
Calgary, Alberta T2P 3E3
Canada
(403) 296-8000
Fax: (403) 296-3030

Public Company
Incorporated: 1975 as Petro-Canada
Employees: 6,353
Sales: C$5.68 billion (US$4.90 billion)
Stock Exchange: Toronto Vancouver Calgary Montreal

Petro-Canada Limited is Canada's second-largest oil company. It acts as a holding company for its principal operating subsidiary, Petro-Canada. Its resources division explores, produces, and markets crude oils, natural gas and its liquids, sulfur, and bitumens. Its products division refines, markets, and distributes various petroleum products and by-products, and offers other related goods and services. Petro-Canada was a crown corporation, that is, it was wholly owned by the government of Canada, until July 3, 1991, when the company made its initial public offering.

As a mover on the Canadian business scene since its beginning in 1975, Petro-Canada has altered the landscape of Canada's petroleum industry. Its development often has been controversial, but the giant Canadian corporation has built an energy network that serves more than 20% of the Canadian market. Each day the company sells more than 44 million liters of gasoline to hundreds of thousands of Canadians who fill up at some 3,500 retail outlets.

Until July 1991, as a crown corporation of Canada, the government owned any property held by Petro-Canada. Common shares in the company were held in the name of the minister of energy, mines, and resources. Almost since its founding, proposals were made to sell Petro-Canada's common shares to the public. In early 1990 the minister of privatization announced details of a proposed sale, and although no timetable was given, the sale was untaken until a year and a half later.

Created by an act of parliament in 1975, Petro-Canada was a product of the oil crisis that shook the world in 1973 and 1974, driving oil prices up and creating havoc with the energy supply. When OPEC substantially increased oil prices, Canada became aware of the vulnerability of its foreign oil supplies. The energy crisis focused Canada's attention on the extent to which foreign countries dominated domestic oil pro-

duction. Coincidental with the OPEC price increases, a sharp downward revision of Canada's oil reserves created substantial fears about whether supplies of domestic crude oil would be adequate for future needs. Petro-Canada began operating in an effort to provide more Canadian control over the domestic oil industry, to ensure that Canada would receive its fair share of remote and difficult-to-reach energy resources, and to provide the Canadian national government with a listening post on the country's oil industry.

Maurice Strong, who earlier had helped establish Dome Petroleum, served as Petro-Canada's first chairman. It was Wilbert Hopper, more than any other individual, however, who made Petro-Canada a success story. Hopper, with degrees in geology and business administration, started in the oil business as a geologist for Imperial Oil in the 1950s. In the early 1960s, he was senior economist for the Canadian National Energy Board, before joining the Cambridge, Massachusetts-based international consulting firm of Arthur D. Little. With a solid reputation in the oil industry, Hopper caught the attention of Canadian Prime Minister Pierre Elliott Trudeau, who sought Hopper's advice in forming a state-owned oil company. Thus began Petro-Canada. Hopper started his association with the company as a vice president in 1976. Six months later, he was named president and chief executive officer. In 1979 he became chairman as well as CEO.

The initial holdings of Petro-Canada included properties previously owned by the government of Canada, that were conveyed to the company after its formation: 12% interest in Syncrude oil-sands mining project in northern Alberta; 45% interest in Panarctic Oils, and an interest in the Polar Gas project, which was set up to operate a gas pipeline from the Arctic. With access to large amounts of money, Petro-Canada bought several Canadian-based oil companies that significantly increased its land holdings and oil and gas reserves, and quickly made it a giant in the oil industry.

The company's first purchase, Atlantic Richfield Canada, was made in 1976 for C$342 million. Assets acquired from Atlantic Richfield included both producing and undeveloped oil and gas properties in western Canada, natural gas–processing facilities, undeveloped oil and gas properties in the Arctic, and an additional interest in oil-sands leases. The cash flow from the producing assets funded exploration and development of new sources. Two years later, in 1978, Petro-Canada borrowed US$1.25 billion from Canadian banks to finance the purchase of Pacific Petroleum, which tripled the company's oil production and quintupled its gas production. Pacific Petroleum's assets added also coal leases in western Canada, oil properties outside of Canada, and distribution and sales facilities—among them being 400 retail outlets.

Among Petro-Canada's mandates set forth by the federal government was that of special emphasis on exploration in remote frontier regions. In 1977 the company made its first discoveries of oil and natural gas pools in the Brazeau River area, southwest of Edmonton, and in the late 1970s, it participated in several oil discoveries in the Utikuma Lake area, northwest of Edmonton. Since 1979 Petro-Canada conducted an international exploration program that has included activities in Colombia, Ecuador, Indonesia, Papua New Guinea, and offshore China.

Petro-Canada's development has been controversial from the beginning. The country's private oil industry has charged that the state-owned corporation has received preferential treatment and has a significant political and financial advantage over its private-sector competitors. Petro-Canada's easy access to government funding has been particularly irksome to the Canadian oil establishment. The counter-argument is that Petro-Canada has been required to undertake high-risk projects in the public interest, such as investment in frontier exploration, that can only be done with the infusion of government funds.

Despite the controversy, Canada's ruling Liberal Party forged ahead with its agenda, introducing federal legislation under the National Energy Program (NEP) that gave Petro-Canada 25% rights on all federal land, including potentially rich frontier acreage. Those rights have been described by the Canadian Petroleum Association as retroactive confiscation of assets. The NEP also gave Petro-Canada more power over the nation's energy resources, including agreement to the continuing takeover of Canadian companies, which at that time controlled 70% of Canada's oil production.

During the early 1980s, Petro-Canada continued to nationalize foreign oil companies. In 1981 the company purchased the Come-by-Chance, Newfoundland, refinery for US$237 million and the Belgian-owned Petrofina Canada for about US$1.5 billion. Two years later, Petro-Canada bought BP Canada for US$348 million, a purchase that included 1,640 service stations and 108 terminals and bulk plants.

Canada's private oil sector strongly protested Petro-Canada's acquisition of Petrofina Canada Inc. and BP Canada Inc., arguing that publicly funded competition in the oil industry had become a destructive practice. Hostility to the company was displayed in the press, and some oil men began to refer to Petro-Canada's 52-story red-granite clad headquarters in downtown Calgary as "Red Square." The private sector also fumed over a federal government decision in mid-1982 awarding acreage in a Sable Island area off Nova Scotia to a group headed by Petro-Canada, protesting that Petro-Canada did not have to compete with other companies for the rights. Relations between the state-owned oil company and the private sector reached an all-time low in 1985 when Hopper announced at a public conference that his company was withdrawing membership from the Independent Petroleum Association of Canada.

By the mid-1980s Petro-Canada was an established major player on the Canadian oil industry scene, the existence and mandate of which was supported by a clear majority of Canadians. With the purchase of the Petrofina and BP interests, Petro-Canada was Canada's fifth-largest company, with nearly 6,000 employees. It was the country's third-largest gasoline marketer and the only nationwide station chain. The company continued with successful oil discoveries during the 1980s, principally in the province of Saskatchewan, including the Cactus Lake field in 1980, the Salt Lake field in 1984, and the Hoosier South field in 1987.

The Progressive Conservative Party swept into power in December 1984, determined to reduce the national government's role in business. "Reform is urgently needed," Prime Minister Brian Mulroney declared. "Crown corporations have become a state within a state," as reported in *Business Week* of September 24, 1984. Petro-Canada, the new government mandated, must be regarded less as an instrument of national policy and more as a commercial operation.

By the mid-1980s Petro-Canada seemed to be moving in this new direction, a change signaled by Chairman Hopper in the company's 1984 annual report. He wrote: "The corporation has now been given a new mandate by its shareholder [the Canadian government]—to operate in a commercial, private sector fashion with emphasis on profitability and the need to maximize return on the government of Canada's investment."

Soon after taking office, the Progressive Conservative government replaced Petro-Canada board members appointed by the previous Liberal government and canceled about US$250 million in additional funding for 1985 that had been Liberal-approved. The government also told the company it had to finance its operation from revenues or market financing.

In 1985 Petro-Canada made a deal that appeared to reflect its new mandate and to mark a turning point in the history of the company. Petro-Canada purchased Gulf Canada Limited's refining, distribution, and marketing assets in Ontario, western Canada, the Yukon Territory, and the Northwest Territories for C$896 million by using its own internally generated funds and short-term debt—not taxpayers' money. Among the assets acquired were a lubricants plant, an asphalt plant, and 1,800 additional retail outlets. The acquisition increased the size of Petro-Canada, giving the company at that time about US$10 billion in assets and making it an even bigger force on the Canadian petroleum scene.

For the next three years, the national government talked of privatization but allowed Petro-Canada to consolidate and rationalize its operation. In 1988, for example, Petro-Canada significantly increased its expenditures in natural gas development, reflecting the company's increased focus on the natural gas business, and also entered into a preliminary agreement providing for the potential development of an oil-sands mining project, the OSLO project, at Kearl Lake, Alberta, and for the Hibernia oil field off Newfoundland's east coast.

By 1988 the private oil sector's hostility seemed to have evaporated. Hopper was elected president of the Canadian Petroleum Association and surveys seemed to indicate that the Canadian public had come to accept state ownership of Petro-Canada. One poll showed a 45% public approval of the company, with 35% of the public indifferent or ambivalent, and 20% opposed outright to the company's existence. Petro-Canada nevertheless saw the need to foster a more favorable public image. It sponsored an 18,000 kilometer cross-country relay of the Olympic torch, in which 7,000 torch bearers participated, for the opening of the 1988 Olympic Games. The 80-day relay cost Petro-Canada C$5.5 million to stage.

The future looked rosy indeed for the oil giant when it reported 1987 to be its most profitable year ever. Despite the glittering reports, the company was having financial problems. Growing cash needs, in fact, led to a shift in the company's economic strategy from aggressively investing in Canada's frontier areas toward instead enhancing the company's financial health and operating capability.

In 1989 Petro-Canada began a C$50 million internal reorganization that was expected to lead to a staff reduction of approximately 1,300 positions. After several years of equivocation, the Progressive Conservative government appeared to be ready to move firmly toward privatizing the state oil company. Energy Minister Marcel Masse said the move would be carried out through a general sale to the public. Petro-Canada's continuing cash problems led the company to announce in December 1989 that it was looking for an infusion of money to help it develop the country's energy resources. In January

1990 Hopper gave testimony before a government panel studying Petro-Canada's future. He served notice that the oil company would not be able to carry out its commitment to costly frontier development without private capital.

A new era began for Petro-Canada in February 1990, when the Honorable Michael Wilson, Canada's minister of finance, indicated that Canada would begin the privatization of Petro-Canada. According to the announcement, in 1991 the government would offer to the public about 15% of the shares of the government-owned company, but individual ownership would be limited to 10% and foreign ownership to a cumulative 25% of the publicly held shares. Wilbert Hopper welcomed the government's announcement. The generated equity capital, Hopper said, would help Petro-Canada participate in developing several oil projects, including the Hibernia oil field.

In April 1990 the Canadian government went one step further, announcing that Petro-Canada would eventually be sold in its entirety to the public. After much talk and speculation, the Canadian government had decided to get out of the energy business.

On February 1, 1991, Petro-Canada assumed a new corporate structure. Petro-Canada's name was changed to Petro-Canada Limited, and Petro-Canada Inc., the company's principal operating subsidiary, was renamed Petro-Canada; the government-owned shares of Petro-Canada were transferred to the minister of state (privatization and regulatory affairs); and Petro-Canada Limited (PCL) was authorized to issue and sell its own shares.

On July 3, 1991, PCL made an initial public offering, selling 19.5% of the company's shares on Canadian stock exchanges. The Canadian government indicated that over time it would sell off all its shares in Petro-Canada Limited.

Principal Subsidiary: Petro-Canada.

Further Reading: "Petro-Canada: How it grew and where it likely is going," *Oil & Gas Journal,* December 9, 1985; Smith, Donald M., "Petro-Canada: Government-Owned Company Fares Well in Free Market," *National Petroleum News,* February 1988.

—Ron Chepesiuk

PETROFINA

52 rue de l'Industrie
B-1040 Brussels
Belgium
(2) 233 91 11
Fax: (2) 233 39 45

Public Company
Incorporated: 1920 as Petrofina S.A.
Employees: 23,600
Sales: BFr578 billion (US$18.72 billion)
Stock Exchanges: Brussels Antwerp Paris Amsterdam
 Frankfurt Zürich Basel Geneva New York London

While not among the world's largest oil companies, Petrofina is widely regarded as one of the most successful. It lost most of its assets during World War II, and has achieved its current position virtually from nothing in a matter of 45 years.

Belgium's largest company, Petrofina is a leading exploiter of North Sea oil and gas, with other exploration and production interests extending through North America, Africa, and the Middle and Far East. It boasts some of the most efficient refineries in the world, in particular at Antwerp in Belgium, Lindsey in the United Kingdom, and Port Arthur in the United States. Under various trademarks, its service stations are seen in most Western European countries, including Belgium, the Netherlands, the United Kingdom, France, Germany, Italy, Norway, and Spain, as well as several chains in the United States.

In contrast with competitors which have moved into areas such as nuclear power generation and metal production, Petrofina has preferred vertical integration to wide diversification. It has, however, started up or bought into activities seen as complementary to its oil interests, especially chemicals manufacturing. Following on from its own insurance requirements, it has become a provider of insurance.

Petrofina was founded in 1920 by a group of Belgian financiers headed by the Bank of Antwerp. Its existence became possible when four Romanian oil companies, confiscated from their German owners after World War I, came up for sale at an advantageous price. Petrofina's founders were aware of the importance of petrol in the age of motorized transport. Romania, an oil-rich but cash-poor country, presented a convenient entry into an already overcrowded industry. The assets on offer included oil wells, refineries, and distribution networks. On taking control, Petrofina merged three of the four companies to form Concordia, whose 1921 output, at 128,500 tons, represented 11% of Romania's total crude oil production. Five years later Concordia's production had tripled.

Petrofina marketed its products in Western Europe through Purfina, an Antwerp-based company jointly established with the American Pure Oil Company, but wholly owned by Petrofina since 1923. To serve central Europe and the Balkans, Petrofina set up Socombel, which supplied small independent outlets until Petrofina acquired its own outlets over the next few years. The company also owned a small fleet of tanker ships.

In 1923 the Banque de l'Union Parisienne became an important shareholder in Petrofina, resolving a dispute over the prewar claims of a French company on Concordia's Vega refinery. The arrangement was attractive both to France, anxious to acquire an oil supply independent of the U.S. and British companies, and to Petrofina, which wanted access to the capital markets of Paris.

French Petrofina, a subsidiary started in 1924, won a monopoly on the import into France of Soviet oil products, in which Purfina's Ertvelde refinery also dealt. French Petrofina soon entered the refinery business, constructing a large plant at Dunkirk; this received most of its crude oil from the United States, since until 1936 Petrofina's own oil fields were subject to Romanian government prohibitions on crude oil exports. At the approach of war, however, French Petrofina reached an agreement with Romania whereby the company financed arms supplies in return for crude oil.

The Depression of the 1930s affected Petrofina less by its direct impact than by changes it prompted in Belgian commercial law. Legislation passed in 1935 and designed to insulate the banking system from industrial ups and downs obliged the Bank of Antwerp to transfer its shares in Petrofina to the specially formed Antwerp Company. Petrofina, created by financiers and for its first 15 years managed by them, now became an oil company run by oilmen.

Having survived the Depression with its assets comparatively intact, Petrofina suffered catastrophic losses during World War II. The Germans bombed and later dismantled the Dunkirk refinery. Of Petrofina's five tankers, only one survived the war. The most serious losses, however, were in Romania. Invading German forces seized the oil fields and refineries, and after the war the Soviet Union appropriated all of Petrofina's Romanian assets, together with its outlets in Hungary and Bulgaria.

Petrofina had not lost quite everything. Distribution subsidiaries, including those in western Europe and Africa, had survived, as had the Ertvelde refinery. The most important element of continuity from prewar days was that Petrofina had managed to retain its work force, whose expertise would be the company's major strength in the postwar reconstruction period.

In the years immediately following the war, Petrofina—led by president Laurent Wolters—concentrated on rebuilding its distribution network, acquiring three new ships, modernizing its Belgian depots, and restructuring outlets in France, the United Kingdom, the Netherlands, and the Belgian Congo, now Zaire. With virtually no products of its own, it formed an alliance with British Petroleum (BP), which by contrast had oil but lacked adequate distribution facilities. Under an agreement which lasted from 1946 to 1980, BP supplied the oil, crude or refined, that Petrofina required. Lacking funds to rebuild the Dunkirk refinery, Petrofina made it over to BP in exchange for products.

Faced with an unprecedented demand for petrol, the Belgian government decided in the late 1940s that the country's refinery capacity needed drastic upgrading. Petrofina and BP spawned the Société Industrielle Belge des Pétroles (SIBP) to build a huge refinery at Antwerp, which opened in October 1951 with a capacity of two million tons per annum, equivalent to Belgium's entire consumption. In the next 20 years the refinery's capacity was to increase by a factor of eight, making it by far the largest in Belgium, and among the largest in Europe.

Petrofina undertook its first postwar explorations in Mexico, starting in 1949. The Mexican venture proved shortlived. Canadian Fina Oil (Canada Fina) and Canadian Petrofina started exploring on opposite sides of Canada in the early 1950s; in 1961 Canada Fina would become a subsidiary of Canadian Petrofina. Exploration also took place in Africa, including Angola, Zaire, and Egypt, during the 1950s.

In 1956 Petrofina gained a foothold in the United States. American Petrofina was set up in cooperation with the Panhandle Oil Corporation of Texas to operate Panhandle's oil wells, refineries, and distribution network. By the end of 1957 the company was extracting 11,000 barrels per day (b/d), had refining capacity for 50,000 b/d, and controlled over 1,000 retail outlets.

The 1950s saw Petrofina's refinery base and distribution networks expanding into Germany, Italy, Sweden, Norway, Switzerland, and Tunisia, as well as North America. It typically entered new markets through acquisitions, financed through rights issues. A dozen large tankers were added to the fleet, the availability of several of which gave Petrofina an edge when the 1956 closure of the Suez Canal added 25 days to the sea journey taken by most of Europe's oil.

Alongside Petrofina's main activities, complementary interests were being developed. Palmafina, a margarine and soap-making subsidiary dating from before the war joined a U.S. collaborator in a new venture, Oleochim, founded in 1957 to produce fatty acids and glycerine at Ertvelde.

In 1954 Petrofina had taken a share in Petrochim, a petrochemical venture by a consortium of Belgian chemical companies. Four years later, ready to exploit its research findings, Petrochim began constructing a factory near the SIBP refinery at Antwerp. When the factory failed to achieve the economies of scale needed for profitability, Petrofina took control, together with a partner with extensive petrochemical experience, the American Phillips Petroleum Company. In 1964 Petrofina and Phillips launched Petrochim on a BFr5 billion investment program involving the construction of one of the largest ethylene production facilities in the world; an extraction unit for benzene, toluene, and xylenes; and a synthetic rubber manufacturing plant.

Petrofina's petrochemical interests grew during the 1960s, with an emphasis on vertical integration. Pipelines were built to take Petrochim's ethylene to the factories that used it, and Petrofina and Phillips invested in one such factory, Polyolefins. Set up in 1966 to make high density polyethylene, Polyolefins would increase its output by a factor of 5 in its first 15 years.

Petrofina became a major force in U.S. petrochemicals with its 1963 acquisition of Cosden Petroleum Corporation, a leading polystyrene manufacturer with valuable patents and a wealth of expertise. Between 1963 and 1979, Cosden's petrochemical sales were to grow from US$18 million to US$500 million, necessitating ambitious construction projects, notably Cosmar, a styrene plant in Louisiana feeding Cosden's original polystyrene plant at Big Spring and an additional plant at Calumet City.

1963 also saw Petrofina's entry into the paint market with Oleochim's purchase of Astrolac. This move fitted neatly into the portfolio: paints and varnishes were needed for Petrofina's ships and plant, and Petrofina's refineries could supply many of their ingredients.

Around the same time, Petrofina was joining forces with Phillips Petroleum for explorations in the North Sea, the extent of whose resources were then only suspected. Together with Agip of Italy, the partners acquired the rights to a 5,000-square kilometer area in the British sector. The giant Hewett gas field, discovered in 1967, was shared with the owners of an adjacent block. Gas started to flow in 1969, by which time two other gas fields had been found. In 1965 the Phillips-Petrofina-Agip group acquired exploration licenses for the Norwegian sector. Phillips was the operator and Petrofina had a 30% participation. Success came with the discovery of Ekofisk. Other fields were found nearby, but Ekofisk was, and remains, the richest oil field ever discovered in Western Europe.

During the 1960s and 1970s, the average capacity of a Petrofina refinery trebled. Of the refineries belonging to the companies it had bought, Petrofina closed some and upgraded others. Large, modern plants, such as the Lindsey oil refinery in England, co-owned with Total, were constructed. This rationalization, resulting in a reduction in the number of sites, threatened to increase transport costs. Therefore Petrofina began in the late 1960s to make reciprocal arrangements with other companies. Soon Petrofina, with only four European refineries of its own, was refining in 26 different European locations.

In 1970, Laurent Wolters, who had presided over Petrofina's rise from its postwar ashes, became chairman. He was succeeded as president and chief executive by Jacques Meeus, the nephew of Laurent Meeus, one of the founders of Petrofina.

Bringing the Ekofisk field into production was the major project of the 1970s. Requiring innovative engineering, it cost 15 times as much as any of Petrofina's previous exploration and production enterprises. It signaled a move towards processing and marketing the products of the group's own wells rather than purchased crude.

In 1975, the year that Adolphe Demeure de Lespaul succeeded Meeus, Ekofisk's oil began to flow along an undersea pipeline to a terminal on Britain's Teesside. Two years later gas began to be piped to a purification plant at Emden in Germany for distribution to France, Holland, and Belgium. By 1979 11.3 million cubic meters of gas and 17 million tons of oil were coming from Ekofisk.

The shortages following the OPEC oil crisis of 1973 gave Petrofina's North Sea explorations an additional impetus. The Maureen field was discovered in 1973, and in 1976 a series of exciting discoveries began in T-Block, including the Thelma, Toni, Tiffany, and Treena fields.

At home in Belgium, the 1970s were years of continuing expansion for Petrofina's petrochemical interests. Drawing on American Petrofina's plastics expertise, the company achieved total vertical integration right through to consumer goods manufacturing. From 1972, for example, styrene was brought by canal from the Petrochim factory at Antwerp, itself fed by the SIBP refinery, to the Belgochim plant at Feluy, where it was made into polystyrene granules. These in turn were sent to Petrofina's Synfina site at Manage, to be made into household items such as toys.

In 1977 Petrofina and an Italian partner, Montedison, established a new company, Montefina, into which Belgochim was integrated. Montefina built a plant at Feluy to make polypropylene, a versatile plastic with applications in the automotive industry. A research laboratory was set up on the same site at Feluy, one of the largest plastics plants in Europe.

In the United States too, Petrofina was expanding its petrochemical interests. By the end of the 1970s it had 14% of total U.S. capacity for both styrene and polystyrene, and co-owned Hercofina, one of the largest producers of terephthalates, a primary ingredient of polyester fibers. Raw materials for Hercofina came from the Port Arthur refinery which American Petrofina had acquired in 1973.

In 1972 the group consolidated its paint production facilities into Sigma Coatings, which by the end of the 1970s would have 20 paint factories in Europe, North and South America and the East. In the same year, Petrofina fused its fatty acids concerns, Oleochim and Palmafina, into Oleofina. At first co-owned, this leading manufacturer of glycerines and glycerides later became a fully owned Petrofina subsidiary.

In the 1970s, during the OPEC crisis, Petrofina, in common with other companies, could at times operate neither its fleet nor its refineries at full capacity. In 1977, faced with losses and also with debts incurred to finance exploration and production, Petrofina began preparing itself to weather the inclement market conditions. Refineries were upgraded with the latest equipment. Distribution subsidiaries improved buying and inventory policies to the extent that they showed a profit in the difficult year of 1979. The 1980 investment program was financed entirely from retained earnings.

Oil extraction in Ekofisk peaked in 1980. To recover less accessible reserves, the operators began to inject water into the ground, also mitigating the subsidence of the sea-bed; as a result, the platforms later needed jacking up by six meters. Meanwhile, the Maureen field off the coast of Scotland came onstream in 1983. The purchase of Charterhouse Petroleum in 1986 gave the group extensive new reserves and exploration licenses in the U.K. sector of the North Sea. In 1990, Petrofina bought important North Sea exploration and production interests from Elf and Lasmo.

Across the Atlantic, Petrofina Canada was sold to the Canadian national oil company, Petro-Canada, at the beginning of the 1980s, but Petrofina held a quarter-share in the explorations of Texas Oil & Gas for four years from 1982. In 1988 Tenneco's onshore production capabilities in Texas, Louisiana, and New Mexico were purchased, doubling Petrofina's U.S. reserves overnight.

Petrofina sought to compensate for the gradual decline in Ekofisk production not only by exploring elsewhere, but also by improving processing techniques, both in its refineries and in its petrochemical plants. At the Antwerp refinery, where Petrofina bought out BP's share in 1988, investment enabled more and more products to be squeezed out of each ton of crude, and improved the proportion of petrol and other high-value products to those of heavy fuel oil. Similar investment went on at other refineries, some of which were also equipped to switch production between petrol and propylene according to demand. U.K. and Belgian refineries were modified to produce lead-free or lead-reduced petrol. The *Economist,* March 14, 1987, credited Petrofina with "some of the oil industry's most efficient refineries."

In petrochemicals, too, the emphasis everywhere was on larger, more efficient plants. In 1983 Petrofina bought out its partner in the synthetic rubber factory, and in 1985 it did the same at the ethylene and polyethylene plants at Antwerp, becoming one of Europe's largest producers of high density polyethylene. Buying a polypropylene plant near Houston, Texas, in 1984, the group acquired 9% of the total U.S. capacity for manufacturing this chemical.

The mid-1980s were record years for chemical sales, but towards the end of the decade Petrofina was hit by falling prices. At the same time there was surplus production in the oil market and a squeeze on refining margins. In the first half of 1990 profits fell 12%, but these problems were expected to be offset by an upsurge in the productivity of Petrofina's newer North Sea oil and gas interests.

Adolphe Demeure, who had died in 1985, had been succeeded by Jean-Pierre Amory as chairman and chief executive. Amory was in turn succeeded as chairman by Albert Frère in 1990. For the first time since the 1930s, a financier was in charge; Frère was the chairman of the holding company GBL, Petrofina's largest shareholder. Alongside Frère, François Cornelis became CEO.

Petrofina is famous for keeping a low profile: anecdotes have told of visitors failing to spot the head office, so discreet was the name-plate on its door. With an eye to a listing on the New York Stock Exchange, Petrofina is introducing an element of *glasnost.* At the same time, it plans to remedy an over-dependence on bought-in raw materials. That it produces only one-fifth of the crude its refineries can process was highlighted as a problem by shortages arising from the 1990 Persian Gulf crisis. However, the resources it does have are geographically spread in a way which reduces risk.

Petrofina's levelheaded approach has safeguarded the group's stability through decades of exponential growth. It is renowned for the conservatism of its accounting policy. Activities which do not fit into its portfolio have been eschewed, or, as in the case of coal interests acquired during the 1980s, sold off. Other interests are made as efficient as possible. Prudent alliances with companies whose expertise or resources complemented its own have boosted the company's growth potential.

Petrofina's ultramodern refineries can easily comply with the more stringent controls on pollution now being introduced, and can produce their petrol output in unleaded form as required. Now Petrofina is preparing to extend its operations into the former eastern bloc. The rapidly changing world of the 1990s offers exceptional opportunities for the company which, rivals have said, "can turn on a dime," as described in *International Management,* September 1970.

Principal Subsidiaries: Fina (Belgium); Petrochim (Belgium, 99.95%); Fina Raffinadarij Antwerpen (Belgium); Sigma Coatings (Belgium); C.E.A.I. (Belgium); Petrofina International

Group (Belgium); Fina Research (Belgium); Fina Europe (Belgium); Deutsche Fina (Germany); Fina Exploration Norway (Norway); Norske Fina (Norway); Fina France (99.99%); Fina PLC (U.K.); Fina Exploration (U.K.); Fina Petroleum Development (U.K.); Fina Nederland (Netherlands); Sigma Coatings (Netherlands); Fina Italiana (Italy); American Petrofina Holding Co. (U.S.A.); American Petrofina Exploration Co. (U.S.A.); American Petrofina Inc. (U.S.A., 86.52%); Brittany Holdings (U.S.A.); Brittany Insurance (U.S.A.); Montefina, (Belgium, 50%); Finamont (Belgium, 50%); Finaneste (Belgium, 64.96%); Lindsey Oil Refinery (U.K., 50%); U I C Insurance Co. Ltd. (U.K.).

Further Reading: Locquet, Gérard, ed., *Contribution à l'histoire de Petrofina,* Brussels, Petrofina, 1980; Dafter, Ray, "The Enigmatic Independent," *Financial Times,* November 3, 1983; Smith, Leigh, "Petrofina's secrets of the deep," *Lloyd's List,* December 18, 1989; Hagerty, Bob, "Frere's long climb results in a jewel," *The Wall Street Journal Europe,* May 4, 1990; Hagerty, Bob, "Petrofina's Big Holders Expected to Press for More Openness," *The Wall Street Journal Europe,* May 7, 1990; Hagerty, Bob, "Petrofina Hopes to Lure U.S. Investors," *The Wall Street Journal Europe,* October 22, 1990.

—Alison Classe

PETROBRAS

PETRÓLEO BRASILEIRO S.A.

Edificio Marechal Ademar de Queiroz
Avenida República do Chile 65
Rio de Janeiro, RJ-CEP
20.035
Brazil
(21) 534-4477
Fax: (21) 534-1939

State-Owned Company
Incorporated: 1953
Employees: 55,390
Sales: Cr2.08 trillion (US$12.92 billion)

Petróleo Brasileiro (Petrobrás) is the Southern Hemisphere's largest company. Petrobrás was formed in 1953 to act as the state monopoly for the exploration, production, refining, and transportation of oil and its derivatives. Since then, it has developed into a complex group of companies. Oil exploration, production, and refining remain its main areas of operation, but its major subsidiaries—Braspetro, Petroquisa, Petrofertil, and Petrobrás Distribuidora, whose interests extend beyond oil alone—make major contributions to the company's balance sheet. These subsidiaries have their own network of subsidiaries and affiliates. However, this structure will not survive long into the 1990s if the government of President Fernando Collor de Mello, which came to power in March 1990, succeeds in relieving Petrobrás of its non-oil activities through closure and privatization.

Brazil's economic situation prior to the formation of Petrobrás reflected long-standing inflation problems and need to earn foreign exchange. At the end of the 1940s, foreign exchange reserves were dwindling, inflation was creeping upwards, and the country was heading for a balance of payments crisis. Ambitious development plans necessitated large-scale imports of energy products. During the first half of the 1950s, Brazil's energy demands, especially for oil and its derivatives, doubled. However, the lack of foreign exchange reserves constrained energy imports and thus industrial expansion. The campaign to develop a domestic oil industry was partly founded on the desire to relieve Brazil of this development constraint.

Politics played a major part in the birth of Petrobrás and have continued to exercise an unusually strong influence on the affairs of the company throughout most of its existence. The process leading to the creation of Petrobrás took several

years and excited a lively political debate. The central issue was whether foreign companies should be allowed to invest in Brazil's domestic oil industry.

Economic nationalists wanted the country's natural resources to be exploited by and for Brazilians. They were a powerful force and fought an effective *o petróleo é nosso* (the oil is ours) campaign. Consequently Law 2004 of October 3, 1953, which set up Petrobrás, created a monopoly over most areas of oil activity within Brazil with no scope for foreign participation.

Implicit in the efforts to set up Petrobrás was the unproved assumption that Brazil had large-scale oil reserves. The first attempts to find oil in Brazil took place in the late 19th century on a very small scale; the first explorers tended to be maverick individuals, and foreign companies were not involved. In 1917, the Geographical and Mineralogical Service of Brazil, a state-owned organization, set up a department for oil exploration, but activity by domestic interests was limited in the 1920s. Foreign companies carried out sporadic drilling, mostly in the south.

In the 1930s, the influence of state control and corporatism grew. There were desultory attempts by private Brazilian companies to find oil, but these were unsuccessful. Rumors abounded about the duplicitous designs of international oil companies on Brazil's natural resources.

In 1938, the National Petroleum Council (CNP) was formed by the state. It was placed in overall control of the oil industry and charged with carrying out systematic exploration for oil. CNP remained the official oil policy-making body after the formation of Petrobrás. It was CNP which in 1939 made the first proven oil discovery on Brazilian territory—at Lobato. By the end of 1941, CNP had discovered three more fields, all in Recôncavo in the Bahia state in the north of Brazil.

Difficulties in obtaining equipment from abroad during World War II held up further development of Brazil's oil industry. By the end of 1943, domestic oil production was only 300 barrels per day, or about 1% of total oil consumption. Immediately after the war, there was some relaxation of the strict corporatism of the Estado Nôvo, the non-socialist system under which all elements of economic life were directed by the state, and some recognition that domestic capital might be insufficient to develop the industry. However, international investment was not forthcoming: U.S. business was preoccupied with the reconstruction of Europe, and Brazil was a relatively small market with unattractive geology and a history of hostility to foreigners.

The hesitation of the U.S. companies was justified: Brazilian economic nationalism quickly reasserted itself and had strong attractions for many sections of the population. The *o petróleo é nosso* campaign started among students but quickly spread to intellectuals. The army favored tight control over natural resources for reasons of national security, and the xenophobia of the campaign exerted an emotive appeal for a large part of the general populace. By 1950, when domestic production had reached 950 barrels per day, the prospect of a private approach to the development of the oil industry was nil.

Petrobrás was set up with a monopoly over most aspects of the oil business. Within a decade of its formation, further activities were brought within the scope of its monopoly. In January 1963, Petrobrás was granted the monopoly over the distribution of petroleum derivatives to the public sector. This move intensified the company's financial problems, as the government was notoriously slow to pay its debts. In December 1963, Petrobrás gained the monopoly over the imports of crude oil into Brazil: private refiners, Petrobrás, and the distributors had previously arranged their own imports. In March 1964, a decree was passed for the nationalization of the private refineries.

Although Petrobrás had many successes during its early years, politics came to play an increasingly important role in the management of the company. This politicization arose from Petrobrás's failure to find enough oil to free itself from a continuing reliance on government revenue and from the continuing belief that Brazil had massive oil wealth. This belief gave rise to massive misplaced investment. There were frequent politically inspired changes in the top management—Petrobrás had no fewer than five presidents in its first decade—and policy continuity was virtually nonexistent.

Stories of ineptitude and even corruption, both in the government and Petrobrás, emerged in the early 1960s and Brazil experienced a military coup in early 1964. The removal of Petrobrás from the political arena for some time was a direct result of the coup, and the company was able to concentrate on its commercial activities, in which it had some success. By 1966, only 13 years after its formation, Petrobrás was listed by *Fortune* as the 88th-largest company in the world outside the United States.

From the beginning, the primary task of Petrobrás was to locate and develop Brazil's oil wealth. In 1956, when Juscelino Kubitschek became president of Brazil, domestic oil production was 6,500 barrels per day. Kubitschek set a goal of 40,000 barrels per day for 1960—a target which was already exceeded by 1957. At this time, production was still confined to the Bahia Recôncavo region. Exploration activity was intensified. In the mid-1960s, activity was concentrated on Bahia, Sergipe, and Maranhao and by the end of 1966 production had reached 150,000 barrels per day. It peaked at 172,000 barrels per day in 1969 before falling to 166,000 barrels per day in 1970 as production from Recôncavo began to decline. In 1970, reserves were estimated at 857 million barrels and new discoveries were only just replacing production.

Petrobrás began to explore in other countries through its subsidiary Braspetro, as part of a strategy to hold Brazil's oil resources in reserve. This policy continues as an important part of Petrobrás activity. Since 1972, Petrobrás has been involved in joint venture companies in 16 countries, and has had operational responsibilities within joint ventures in Iraq, Egypt, Algeria, Libya, South Yemen, Colombia, and Ecuador. At the beginning of the 1990s, Braspetro was active to some degree in Angola, Argentina, Colombia, the Congo, Ecuador, the Gulf of Mexico, Libya, Ghana, and the Norwegian and British sectors of the North Sea.

Exploration activity continued in Brazil throughout the 1970s. A major breakthrough took place in 1974 with the first discovery of oil in the Campos Basin off the coast of the state of Rio de Janeiro. Subsequent discoveries were made in the next few years. The first commercial production took place in 1977. Ten years later, oil production from the basin was 370,000 barrels per day or about 60% of domestic production. The performance of the continental shelf quickly compensated for the depletion of the onshore fields. Offshore deposits account for about 75% of known reserves, and their location in

deep waters has encouraged Petrobrás to develop its expertise in deepsea technology.

The discovery of the Albacora and the Marlim fields in the Campos Basin, in November 1984 and February 1985 respectively, marked further milestones in the company's history. Massive investment is planned for these two fields, Brazil's first giant fields, with a view to output of 725,000 barrels per day by the end of the century.

Although exploration and production have been Petrobrás's primary activities over the years, the company is active in all phases of the oil business. Refining has always been important to Petrobrás. Initially, Brazilian refineries were ill-equipped to deal with the high paraffin content of the crude found in Bahia Recôncavo. At the end of the 1950s, only the Mataripe refinery was up to the task, and domestic crude was exported. The majority of the crude processed in Brazilian refineries during this period consisted of imports. By 1960, Petrobrás refineries were processing 250,000 barrels per day of crude oil, equivalent to about 80% of Brazilian refined product demand, and domestic refineries were being upgraded to deal with domestic crudes. By 1970, only 2% of petroleum product requirements were imported, and Petrobrás operated five refineries with a combined throughput capacity of 419,000 barrels per day. A 120,000 barrels per day refinery in Sao Paulo was built, and expansions were underway at two of the existing refineries.

Petrobrás initiated an ongoing "bottom of the barrel campaign"—an attempt to yield higher-value products—to bring its product slate, or range of products yielded by the refining of crude oil, in line with final demand. The aim was to yield lower quantities of heavy fuel oil and greater quantities of diesel oil. Petrobrás also experimented with heavy ends cracking—secondary refining of heavy fuel oil to produce lighter products—which enables the company to refine surplus fuel oil further into diesel oil and liquid petroleum gas (LPG). By 1989, Petrobrás was operating ten refineries and one asphalt plant, which had a combined maximum processing capacity of 1.4 million barrels per day of oil. That year an average of 1.2 million barrels per day of crude oil was processed to yield LPG (8%), gasoline (16.1%), diesel oil (34.9%), fuel oils (17.9%), and other oil products (23.1%).

Petrobrás's refining profile was influenced by the Proalcool campaign (National Alcohol Program), which began in 1975 as a reaction to the 1973 oil price hike. The plan was to substitute the use of gasoline in private cars with alcohol produced from sugar cane. Initially, this policy had some success. However, production problems and the massive subsidies needed to make alcohol competitive with gasoline during the mid-1980s plunged the program into chaos. This caused Petrobrás to revise its gasoline production capacity upwards.

Despite Brazil's increasing oil production, a large proportion of the oil refined in Brazil comes from abroad. In order to save valuable foreign exchange, Petrobrás has for many years maintained a major stake in the National Tanker Fleet (Fronape), which ended the 1980s with 68 ships and 21 vessels under construction. In 1989, Fronape transported 89 million tons of crude oil, refined products, alcohol, and related products. Petrobrás-owned vessels were responsible for 57% of this total.

Petrobrás is also engaged in distribution though its subsidiary, Petrobrás Distribuidora. Distribution was not included in the company's monopoly, and international oil companies were allowed to continue to participate in this sector. Since Petrobrás opened its first service station in 1961, the number of its retail outlets has grown rapidly. Petrobrás was already the third largest distribution company in Brazil in 1966 and owned 174 service stations, accounting for 13% of sales. By 1970, Petrobrás was still in third place but its market share had risen to 20% and it owned 527 service stations. By 1989, its distribution arm was firmly established as the nation's leading oil and hydrated alcohol product retailer with a 37.3% share of the domestic market and sales amounting to the equivalent of US$4.3 billion.

Diversification into petrochemicals was another obvious option for Petrobrás which, even when it was not directly involved in the production of chemicals, was the major supplier of raw materials, mainly naphtha and natural gas, to the private sector in Brazil. During the 1950s Petrobrás constructed a unit for ammonia and nitrogenous fertilizers in Sao Paulo and a styrene butadiene rubber unit at Duque de Caxias in the state of Rio de Janeiro.

During the 1960s, the Brazilian petrochemical industry expanded rapidly, and Petrobrás established its first subsidiary, Petrobrás Quimica (Petroquisa), in which it has a 51% interest, to oversee its role in this development. The Petroquisa system has grown to include Petroquisa itself and 35 other companies in which it has a direct share. The product range includes the major plastics, aromatics, synthetic rubbers, methanol, caprolactam, caustic soda, detergents, ethylene oxide, and monoethylene glycol.

As part of its economic liberalization campaign, the Collor government plans to break up the Petroquisa system through a series of privatizations and shutdowns—a fate which awaits other Petrobrás subsidiaries. Petrobrás Fertilizantes (Petrofértil), which is composed of five subsidiaries and two affiliated companies, and which supplies 84% of the nitrogenous and 45% of the phosphate fertilizers consumed in Brazil, is to be sold off.

Interbrás and Petrobrás Mineraçao (Petromisa)—two subsidiaries—were to be closed down. Interbrás, the company's international trading arm, was founded in 1976, and handles exports of coffee, cocoa, soybeans, sugar, processed foods, petroleum products and alcohol, vehicles, heavy machinery and equipment, chemicals and petrochemicals, steel and metal products, minerals, and fertilizers. Petromisa was originally set up to produce potassium fertilizers but has subsequently diversified into other mineral products.

In this way, Petrobrás will be trimmed of its non-core activities. It will, however, remain an industrial giant by retaining oil exploration, production, refining, and marketing operations in its own hands. Petrobrás itself will remain predominantly a state company for the time being at least.

During the 1980s, Petrobrás was used as a macroeconomic instrument in an attempt to pull the country out of its severe debt and inflation problems. There were signs of a resurgence of economic nationalism with the decision of the constitutional assembly to ban the risk contracts that were introduced for foreign companies in 1975. Petrobrás was opposed to the ban. The tenure of office of Petrobrás presidents grew shorter again as the incumbents clashed with politicians over their interference with the running of the company. When Carlos Sant'-Anna took office in 1989, he was the third president to be appointed in a year, and the fifth in four years. His term of office and that of his successor were no longer than those of their predecessors.

Collor's administration advocates a free market economy. Consequently, the restrictions on the distribution of fuel and petroleum derivatives, which limited participation in this activity to 13 firms, were lifted in October 1990. The removal is expected of a number of subsidies that have had a damaging effect on the financial well-being and long-term performance of Petrobrás. Petrobrás had, for example, borne the cost of the subsidies in the Proalcool program and shielded the economy from the worst effects of the Persian Gulf crisis by buying oil on the world spot market and selling it in the domestic market for half the world price. In addition, the prices of refined petroleum products have not reflected true market conditions for a long time. The upshot of these subsidies is that Petrobrás is in debt for several billion dollars and at the end of 1990 was losing almost US$14 million a day.

Such financial constraints cast doubts on whether Petrobrás will be able to make the necessary investments to achieve its longterm objectives of increasing oil production from an average of 726,000 barrels per day in 1990 to more than 1 million barrels per day by the mid-to-late 1990s, and of greater exploitation of the country's under-utilized gas reserves. The Marlim and Albacora fields are very promising but their exploitation requires massive inputs of capital. The financial crisis has already affected drilling: in 1986, 923 appraisal and development wells were drilled; by 1990 the number had fallen to 356. The introduction of market prices would help Petrobrás fund this investment. It remains to be seen whether the Collor administration will reverse longstanding practice and open Petrobrás to foreign capital.

Principal Subsidiaries: Petrobrás Internacional S.A. (Braspetro); Petrobrás Distribuidora S.A. (BR); Petrobrás Quimica S.A. (Petroquisa); Petrobrás Fertilizantes S.A. (Petrofertil); Renave; National Tanker Fleet (Fronape).

Further Reading: Smith, Peter Dearborn, *Oil and Politics in Modern Brazil,* Toronto, Macmillan, 1976; Wirth, John D., *Latin American oil companies and the politics of energy,* Lincoln, University of Nebraska Press, 1985; *Quarterly and Annual Reports on Brazil,* Economist Intelligence Unit.

—Debra Johnson

PETRÓLEOS DE PORTUGAL S.A.

Rua das Flores, No 7
1200 Lisbon
Portugal
(1) 346 1281
Fax: (1) 321 233

State-Owned Company
Incorporated: 1976
Employees: 6,000 (1989)
Sales: Esc379.38 billion (US$2.78 billion) (1989)

Although involved in exploration for crude oil both at home and abroad and in other oil-related activities, Petróleos de Portugal (Petrogal) is primarily a refining company. Its history and that of its predecessor companies constitute the history of refining in Portugal. Petrogal was formed in April 1976 from four companies—SACOR, CIDLA, SONAP, and PETROSUL—that were nationalized following the revolution of April 1974, and has grown into the largest nonfinancial company in Portugal. Privatization, which is on the agenda for 1991–1992, is the next milestone in the company's story.

The first official Portuguese interest in oil occurred during the mid-19th century with the granting of concessions for exploration in Sesmana, Monte Real, and Torres Vedras, but nothing came of these grants. Around the turn of the century, several international companies established themselves in Lisbon. The most significant was Vacuum Oil Company, later to become Mobil, which dominated the domestic market until the 1940s. Other important participants included Costa e Ribeiro Ltd., which was established in 1919 and which, in 1929, became associated with the Atlantic Refining Company. In 1920, the Shell Company of Portugal, the successor to the Lisbon Coal and Oil Fuel Company—the latter dating from 1910—appeared on the scene.

In 1930, Queiroz Pereira, the first oil company with a majority of Portuguese capital, was formed. Three years later, it merged with Sociedade Nacional de Petróleos (SONAP), a company with mixed French and Portuguese capital, which was to play the key role in the development of the Sines refinery in the 1970s.

By the mid-1930s, there was a clear understanding of the importance of oil to Portuguese economic development. In 1938, the government published a decree setting out the conditions for the exploration and sale of hydrocarbons and for the installation of an oil refinery. This resulted, also in 1938, in the creation of Sociedade Anónima Concessionária de Refinaçao em Portugal (SACOR). In order to encourage self-sufficiency in refined products, the government granted SACOR a refining monopoly, the right to supply 50% of the petroleum products consumed in the country, and certain price guarantees. It was only Portuguese entry into the European Economic Community in 1986 that resulted in a wholesale dismantling of these concessions.

The first president of SACOR was Dr. Eduardo Fernandes de Oliveira. Martin Sain was vice president. Sain, a former director of the Romanian oil company, Redentza, was a key figure in the development of SACOR. Along with a number of Romanian technicians, he had left Romania in the face of the Nazi threat. Romania was an important oil producer before World War II, and the Romanian influence in technology and key personnel was significant in SACOR's early years.

SACOR's first big project, supervised by Martin Sain and a Romanian engineer, Adolfo Hascal, was the construction of the refinery at Cabo Ruivo, near Lisbon. The location for this refinery, Portugal's first, was near the storage facilities of the Atlantic Refining Company and Socony-Vacuum, the latter an oil retailing company, and had good access to the River Tagus and to rail links. Despite technical difficulties, construction took only 18 months and the refinery began operations in January 1940—only three months behind schedule—at a total cost of Esc32.8 million. The initial processing capacity was 300,000 metric tons of crude oil per year. The plant also included facilities to produce caustic soda, sodium hypochlorite, and sulfuric acid.

In the first year of Cabo Ruivo's operation, 116,000 metric tons of crude were processed. Technical modifications quickly increased the refinery's capacity to 480,000 metric tons per year. However, World War II intervened, and the consequent difficulties of obtaining supplies of crude oil halted the plant's operations until the end of 1944.

In common with other European countries, Portugal's consumption of petroleum products increased massively after World War II, with an average annual increase of more than 10% between 1938 and 1952. The biggest increases in demand were for fuel oil, which was used primarily in industry and for power generation.

In 1952, work began at the Cabo Ruivo refinery to increase its capacity to one million metric tons a year. The work was completed by the end of 1953 and allowed other technological improvements to be made.

The refinery expansion was accompanied by a decision to increase SACOR's capital to Esc150 billion and to allow foreign participation in the company up to a maximum of 10%. Compagnie Française des Pétroles promptly took an 8.75% stake in SACOR. The Portuguese government retained its one-third holding, and the rest of the company was in the hands of local private investors.

At the same time, the refinery concession and price supervision were extended until December 31, 1976. In 1954, SACOR's privileges were extended to Portugal's overseas territories; henceforth 80% of the gasoline, kerosene, and gasoil imported into Angola had to be refined on Portuguese territory. Cabo Ruivo, as Portugal's only refinery at that time, was the main beneficiary.

Given its refining monopoly and its 50% quota of the domestic market, SACOR was in a privileged position in relation to the other petrol retailers active in Portugal—Mobil, Shell, British Petroleum, and SONAP—who had to buy significant proportions of their product from the Lisbon refinery. SACOR, whose first petrol pump was installed in January 1940 in Sintra, also had an advantage over these rivals as a result of its exemption from income tax. Forty years later, Petrogal was to dominate the retail sector through its GALP affiliate.

SACOR and refining remained as the core of the petroleum industry in Portugal, but from the early days a number of companies and SACOR affiliates were established to complement the activities of SACOR. The first was Combustiveis Industriais e Domésticos (CIDLA) which was established in December 1939. CIDLA's task was to develop the distribution of lubricating oils and liquid petroleum gas (LPG)—such as butane and propane—in Portugal.

In 1947 Sociedade Portuguesa e Navios-Tanques (SOPONATA) was formed as a joint venture of local shipping firms, SACOR, and the main petroleum distributors. It was formed at the direct behest of the government to prevent a repetition of the wartime situation in which tanker shortages had caused problems of crude oil supply. All petroleum products entering or leaving Portuguese ports had to be in SOPONATA tankers. SACOR MARITIMA, which played a similar role, was founded in 1960. SACOR's original holding in the latter company was 99.98%. In 1976, this passed to Petrogal which reduced its holding to 80% in 1988 to raise money for two new product carriers.

Sociedade de Lubrificantes e Combustiveis (ANGOL) was set up in 1953. Initially, it was active in the sale and distribution of fuel, lubricating oils, and LPG in Angola. By the 1960s, however, it was also participating in the exploration for hydrocarbons. In 1957, SACOR participated in the establishment of a parallel company, MOÇACOR, in Mozambique.

One of the most important developments was the formation of SACOR affiliates to take advantage of surplus refinery gases. In August 1957, Sociedade Portuguesa de Petroquimica was founded with a 60% SACOR participation. Commercial operations began in 1961. Petroquimica undertook the manufacture of ammonia, town gas, hydrogen, and other inorganic chemicals. Expansion into organic chemicals took place at the end of the 1970s. Nitratos de Portugal, of which SACOR owned 25%, was also set up in 1957 and had close links with Petroquimica. Nitratos was in the business of production, distribution, and sale of nitrogenous fertilizers. In 1960 SACOR founded AGRAN to manufacture pesticides.

Other affiliates were set up to support SACOR's retailing activities. Petróleo Mecânica Alfa was established in 1962 to manufacture service station equipment and bottles for liquid gases. In 1962 SOCAR was formed and constituted in Spain to carry out market studies and to implement a distribution network for liquid fuels. In 1966, SACOR participated in the formation of Construtora Moderna SARL for the manufacture of pipes, boilers, and industrial structures and machinery.

Meanwhile, the expansion of the Cabo Ruivo refinery during the 1950s had proved inadequate to cope with the growing demand for petroleum products in Portugal. A further expansion to 1.5 million tons, planned for the early 1960s, still was not enough. In 1960 SACOR presented a memorandum to the government setting out the need for a new refining complex to deal with the anticipated demand growth of the 1960s and 1970s.

In 1964, after a period of intense public discussion, SACOR received authorization to build a new refinery at Matosinhos, about two kilometers from the port of Leixoes and ten kilometers from Porto. This document, which was ratified in July 1965, established the basic conditions of the refinery concession. The refinery was to have an annual capacity of 1.5 million metric tons with storage facilities for 500,000 metric tons. Petrochemical facilities and an 800,000 metric ton lubricating oil unit were also to be built. In order to help finance the refinery, which was expected to cost Esc3.5 million, SACOR increased its capital by Esc800 million. The state retained its one-third stake.

The construction of the Porto refinery was closely linked to the expansion of the port of Leixoes, and plans were set in motion in 1964 for the construction of a maritime terminal capable of receiving large tankers. The terminal, which consisted of three quays, was opened in 1969. The refinery itself was fully operational by mid-1970; the first unit yielded the full range of petroleum products from light oils to heavy fuel oil and asphalt, and the second unit produced lubricating oil.

Two decisions taken in 1971 were to have a profound effect on the future of the Portuguese refining industry. The first concerned the expansion of the Porto refinery to a capacity of five million metric tons a year and the revamping of existing facilities. Porto was expanded to 7.5 million tons by 1975. The second involved the installation of a third refinery at Sines at a cost of Esc25 billion and a capacity of ten million metric tons a year.

The Sines refinery differed from the Lisbon and Porto refineries in two ways. First, in line with the wish of the government to introduce greater dynamism and competitiveness into the national refining industry, the refinery concession was awarded not to SACOR but to SONAP, originally founded in 1933 and which had only been active hitherto in sales and distribution, and to Companhia Uniao Fabril (CUF), one of Portugal's biggest industrial companies. In 1972, the SONAP-CUF association resulted in the formation of Petrosul, in which the government also had a 34% stake, to carry out the Sines project.

Secondly, the Sines decision marked a new phase in official thinking about the petroleum industry. Hitherto, the domestic industry had been intended to satisfy domestic needs. However, international consumption of oil products had expanded rapidly, and Portuguese decision makers saw opportunities to boost foreign exchange earnings from the export of petroleum products. Sines was conceived not only as a potential export refinery but also as a crucial part of a much bigger, integrated industrial export complex. The project was held to have three key crucial commercial advantages: access to low-price labor; abundant supplies of raw material from the Middle East and Portugal's overseas territories, and markets with an inexhaustible demand.

The plan went awry. Portugal's overseas territories gained their independence. The 1973–1974 and 1979–1980 oil price hikes reined back the seemingly unstoppable demand growth, and Portugal became the subject of an Arab boycott after allowing the United States to use the Azores as an air base for its airlift of emergency aid to Israel during the 1973 Middle East crisis. Instead of providing a steady stream of foreign exchange, Sines, which came onstream in 1978, contributed to the worldwide refining surplus that prevailed during the late

1970s and during most of the 1980s. For several years, Portugal's refineries were operating at less than 50% capacity.

Before the Sines project became a reality, politics intervened. In April 1974, the uprising of the armed forces movement brought an end to the authoritarian system of government set up by Antonio Salazar almost 50 years earlier and continued by Marcelo Caetano after Salazar's death in 1968. The coup had a profound effect on all aspects of Portuguese life, including the refining industry. In April 1975, the main elements of the national oil industry, SACOR, CIDLA, SONAP, and PETROSUL, were nationalized. On April 1, 1976, these companies were brought together to form Petrogal, which inherited the quotas and other privileges of its predecessor companies.

Petrogal's early years were made difficult by two factors. First, Portugal's overseas territories became independent states and, although ties remained close with the former colonies, Petrogal lost many of the preferential conditions of access to African oil. Secondly, the coup brought upheaval to the Portuguese economy, and growth stagnated for some time. The oil price shock of 1979–1980 precipitated a slowdown in economic growth worldwide and dealt a severe blow to the export plans for Sines.

The start of commercial operations at Sines facilitated an overhaul of the Cabo Ruivo refinery, which was modernized and converted to crack fuel oil from the Sines refinery to yield higher value-added products such as gasoline, gas oil, and LPG. The refinery was recommissioned in 1984 after an Esc4.5 billion conversion.

In 1979 work for the third phase of the Porto refinery got under way, ready for start-up in 1981. This Esc12 billion chemical project utilized the refinery's utilities and part of its output as raw material. The new plant had nameplate capacity of 350,000 metric tons a year of aromatics and solvents and allowed Petrogal to intervene in markets for plastics, dyes, fertilizers, detergents, and fibers, among others. The major part of this unit's output was exported. Subsequent modifications increased the aromatics production capacity.

The history of the oil industry in Portugal is primarily the history of refining. Exploration for crude oil in Portuguese territory had not been a priority before 1974 because of the existence of colonies which had large reserves of crude. Exploration of offshore and onshore Portugal has been more systematic since the coup and has been carried out by foreign companies and by Petrogal. Results, however, have been discouraging. Petrogal has been active or shown interest in north and west Africa, South America, the Middle East, and the North Sea, and has taken stakes of 10% to 20% in promising concessions.

The accession of Portugal to the European Economic Community (EEC) on January 1, 1986, heralded profound economic changes for Portugal. Industry in general, and the oil industry in particular, had been subject to a high level of protectionism. From the beginning, SACOR had a guaranteed 50% share of the market, changed to 40% in 1971. The protection which had been afforded to Petrogal and its predecessors had resulted in slow responses to changes in the international markets and had been damaging to the economy. At the end of the 1980s, oil still comprised 82% of total Portuguese energy consumption, whereas it had fallen to an average of 47% in the rest of the EEC. Market signals should have contributed to major improvements in energy efficiency—very important to a country like Portugal with limited indigenous energy resources—but protectionism and subsidies prevented them from working.

EEC entry changed all this. The accession treaty for EEC entry allowed for a seven-year transition period with the full removal of Petrogal's privileges by December 31, 1992. Liberalization began in 1986 but was soon accelerated, allowing full liberalization to take place by January 1, 1991, two years ahead of schedule.

Privatization will combine with liberalization to form a major influence on Petrogal's competitiveness in the coming years. State ownership of industry is no longer in favor in Portugal. By the mid-1980s, public sector losses in Portugal amounted to Esc3.3 trillion, equivalent to nearly 70% of gross domestic product. Constitutional amendments were passed in 1989 to enable the government to sell off its shareholdings in state-owned companies, including Petrogal. The 1990–1991 Persian Gulf crisis caused a crisis of confidence in Portuguese equity markets and briefly delayed the privatization program. Because of its size, the Petrogal sale, which will be among the largest in the privatization program, is likely to take place in stages. The process should be well underway by the end of 1991. Foreign companies that have shown an early interest in taking a stake in Petrogal include Repsol, Elf Aquitaine, and Exxon. The Espirito Santo family, once major shareholders in SACOR, put together a consortium, in which it was joined by the Gulbenkian Foundation and Portuguese investors, to bid for Petrogal.

Principal Subsidiaries: AGRAN (Angola, 98.67%); CABROGAL (97.36%); DICOL (30%); EIVAL (89.28%); GALP International Corporation; HOTELGAL (29.83%); MOÇACOR (Mozambique, 76%); PETROGAL ESPAÑOLA; PORTGAS (30%); SAAGA (43.91%); SACOR MARITIMA (79.78%); SOCAR (50%); VIVA PETROLEOS (44%).

Further Reading: de Figueiredo, Antonio, *Portugal: Fifty Years of Dictatorship,* London, Penguin, 1975; Graham, Lawrence S., and Harry M. Makler, eds., *Contemporary Portugal: The Revolution and Its Antecedents,* Austin, University of Texas Press, 1979; Morrison, Rodney J., *Portugal: Revolutionary Change in an Open Economy,* Boston, Auburn House Publishing Company, 1981; Ferreira, Hugo G., and Michael W. Marshall, *Portugal's Revolution: Ten Years On,* Cambridge, Cambridge University Press, 1986.

—Debra Johnson

PETRÓLEOS DE VENEZUELA S.A.

Edif. Petróleos de Venezuela, Torre Este
Avenida Libertador, La Campiña
Apartado Postal 169
Caracas, 1010A
Venezuela
(02) 708 4111
Fax: (02) 708 4661

State-Owned Company
Incorporated: 1976
Employees: 44,203
Sales: US$9.5 billion

Petróleos de Venezuela S.A. (PDVSA) is wholly owned by the Venezuelan state and is the holding company for the national petroleum industry. Since 1978 it has been responsible for the petrochemical sector, and in 1985 it was entrusted with the development of the country's coal resources located in western Venezuela.

Oil has been known and used in Venezuela since seepages were found on the shores of Lake Maracaibo during the colonial period, which ended in 1910. The first formal concession for its exploitation, however, was not awarded until August 24, 1865, when Camilo Ferrand procured the rights from the president of Zulia state. In 1876, a report submitted to the president of Zulia on the petroleum and asphalt deposits in the Maracaibo basin indicated the existence of an oil seep near Tarra, producing 5,760 gallons a day. The first oil company incorporated in the country was the Compañia Nacional Minera Petrólia del Táchira, formed on October 12, 1878. A succession of grants followed during the 19th century, and the systematic exploitation of the country's large hydrocarbon reserves started during the 27-year dictatorship of General Juan Vicente Gómez, which lasted from 1908 to 1935.

The major foreign oil companies were attracted to the country because of the expectation of large oil deposits, the country's relative political stability compared to the rest of Latin America at the time, and the favorable terms offered for the exploration of the country's oil resources. Venezuela, unlike the Middle East or Iran, devised a concessionary system whereby most oil companies could operate, regardless of nationality, and production costs were much lower than in the United States, which accounted for 70% of total world oil production at the time.

Venezuela's move toward controlling its oil industry took a significant step in 1943, when the new hydrocarbon law integrated all oil legislation. Five years later, in 1948, the Venezuelan congress passed a new income tax law, establishing the so-called 50–50 system that would become a landmark in relations between the international oil companies and the governments of the various oil-producing countries. This system refers to an agreement where by concurrent owners bear all expenses equally. In 1959 the national government decided to grant no further concessions, thus ending a system that dated back to the previous century. A further fundamental step toward achieving full control of the country's oil wealth was taken in April 1960 when the Corporación Venezolana de Petroleo (CVP), a national oil company, was established to enable the country to acquire greater experience in all areas of the oil industry. CVP was to operate in competition with foreign concessionaires in the country and was to be the official instrument of the country's petroleum policy. The Service Contracts system was introduced in 1967 through a partial reform of the Hydrocarbons Law, allowing the nation to negotiate with foreign companies under more advantageous conditions.

During the administration of Rafael Caldera the initiative in oil matters shifted from the executive to congress, which increased corporation taxes on oil business and allowed the government unilaterally to determine reference prices for crude oil. The government also began to feel that the previous policy of awarding service contracts would not be successful because it would not provide a more viable alternative to the outright nationalization of the industry. At the same time it was felt that the companies—which would lose their concessions at a given date—were not investing enough to maintain their equipment and fields in working order, and without any guarantees of future profits the companies would disinvest and hand over the concessions in 1983, when the concessions expired, in a poor state. It was debatable whether the government would be entitled to the companies' capital equipment, and production appeared to be on the decline.

As a result, in 1971 the Hydrocarbons Reversion Law was enacted, aimed at ensuring the continuity and efficiency of the country's oil activities after the concessions expired in 1983. The law provided for all industry assets to revert to the nation on the expiry of the concessions, and for the government to appropriate all concessions not being exploited. In addition, the law established that companies would have to deposit 10% of their assets with the government to ensure that all such assets would be properly maintained by the companies until complete reversion took place.

Further steps toward nationalization were taken through a series of laws covering the natural gas industry, the domestic petroleum products market, and the merchant marine. By the autumn of 1973 the possibility of an early reversion before 1983 was introduced and started to gain acceptance, replacing the original plan to start nationalizing the industry from 1983. In his last presidential address, Caldera urged the new incumbent, Carlos Andrés Pérez of Acción Democrática, to nationalize the industry. The new government also believed that the oil industry was disinvesting; for instance, the number of exploration wells drilled had declined from 589 in 1958 to 148 in 1973, causing the reserves to production ratio to decline. On March 22, 1974, a committee was set up to prepare a draft bill whereby the state itself would maintain the industry and trade of hydrocarbons.

On August 29, 1975, the Organic Law Reserving to the State the Industry and Commerce of Hydrocarbons was enacted, allowing the government to take full control of the oil industry on January 1, 1976. The assets of the industry were acquired from the ex-concessionaires based on a net book value of US$1.17 billion.

The nationalization of the industry required the creation of a functional structure that would allow normal operation to continue within the new legal scheme. A holding company, PDVSA, was established to coordinate, supervise, control, and plan the activities of its subsidiaries made up of the 14 former operating companies. PDVSA's oil would be marketed through the major international oil companies Exxon, Shell, and Gulf, thus guaranteeing the company a stable market share. PDVSA reserved the right to reduce the volume of oil placed in this manner by 10% after the first year, and by 20% in the second year. The new company would also receive technical assistance in exploring and refining from the former operating companies, which would be paid at a rate which varied between 16¢ and 30¢ per barrel. The original 14 operating subsidiaries were integrated in 1977 into four major companies, Lagoven, Maraven, Meneven and Corpoven. On March 1, 1978, PDVSA assumed full responsibility for the country's petrochemical industry when the government transferred the ownership of Petroquímica de Venezuela SA (Pequiven) to PDVSA. Pequiven has two petrochemical complexes: Morón in Carabobo state and El Tablazo in Zulia state. Morón manufactures fertilizers as well as several chemicals for the domestic market. The El Tablazo plant produces olefins, caustic soda, and chlorine, which are sold to other nearby industries.

Although PDVSA is a state enterprise, it is expected to finance its normal investment program from its own resources, under a 10% cash flow mechanism whereby 10% of pre-tax export sales profits may be retained for the purpose of reinvestment by the company. The board of directors reports to an assembly constituted by the minister of energy and mines, who presides over it, and to those members of the Executive Cabinet designated by the president of the republic. PDVSA operates under broad policy guidelines issued by the government.

During 1989, PDVSA produced around 1.6 million barrels of oil and condensate per day. It owns 12 refineries with an overall processing capacity of 1.75 million barrels per day, of which 945,000 million barrels per day are processed in Venezuela and the rest in the United States, Europe, and the Dutch Antilles. The most important domestic refineries in terms of capacity are Amuay with 630,000 barrels per day and Cardón with 350,000 barrels per day. Prior to nationalization, Venezuela's refineries had been geared to use low gravity oil to produce heavy fuel oil for export to its traditional market, the northeast United States. At the time of nationalization, heavy fuel oil accounted for 61% of total products exported. After nationalization, PDVSA began to diversify its exports, seeking to increase its supply of white products—gasoline and jet fuel—which are traditionally more in demand and afford a higher profit margin. With this goal in mind, between 1978 and 1987, the company decided to upgrade its refineries in Amuay, Cardón, and El Palito to reduce the proportion of residual fuels obtained in the refining process and increase the proportion of naphtha, gasoline and distillates. With further

upgrading and conversion facilities, the refineries were able to use a higher proportion of heavier crudes, which represented the major volume of reserves in the country. The upgrading of PDVSA's refineries was two-thirds completed when it was halted in 1986 because of low oil prices. Although heavy fuel yield dropped from 61% in 1976 to 27% in 1986, it was still too high in 1991 for PDVSA's key U.S. market, where heavy fuel oil amounts to only 8% of total demand.

PDVSA supplies the domestic market with approximately 335,000 barrels per day of petroleum products, which represent approximately 20% of total production. PDVSA supplies local markets through its four main operating subsidiaries, Lagoven, Maraven, Meneven, and Corpoven, which operate supply depots and about 1,600 petrol stations. The products sold are petrol, aviation fuel, diesel fuel, lubricants, kerosene, and asphalt, with petrol accounting for almost half of total consumption.

One of PDVSA's most important international marketing strategies has been its joint venture participation in foreign manufacturing and marketing companies which has accelerated significantly since 1986, when oil prices fell below $10 per barrel and it was difficult to place oil. PDVSA decided to secure long-term outlets for its crude oil by increasing its presence in foreign downstream markets, mainly in the United States and Europe. It has just under 800,000 barrels per day of refining capacity and leases a 300,000-barrels-per-day refinery in Curacao in the Dutch Antilles. PDVSA's first downstream venture outside Venezuela took place in West Germany in 1983 when it entered into a joint venture partnership with Veba Oel to supply 155,000 barrels of oil per day.

Through its ownership of CITGO Petroleum Corporation, PDVSA also owns refineries at Lake Charles, Louisiana, and refineries at Corpus Christi, Texas. Subsidiary Propernyn PDVSA bought 50% of CITGO from the Southland Corporation. In 1990 Propernyn became the sole owner of CITGO. On October 31, 1989, PDVSA acquired 50% of Unocal's downstream assets in the midwestern United States. With this acquisition, PDVSA gained access to a deep conversion refinery near Chicago with an installed capacity of 153,000 barrels per day, as well as distribution and marketing facilities in Illinois, Michigan, Iowa, Ohio, and Wisconsin. PDVSA also owns minority stakes in two refineries in Sweden, and one in Belgium.

The proportion of light and medium crude oil in Venezuela's export package declined between 1976 and 1984, with a complementary increase in the volume of heavy crude exports. As a result of PDVSA's exploration record, this trend was reversed in 1985, so that by 1988 exports of light and medium crudes accounted for 50% of PDVSA's crude export package. The United States was PDVSA's main market, accounting for 54% or 891,000 barrels per day of total exports in 1988, with Europe in second place with 205,000 barrels per day or 12.4%.

PDVSA's proved reserves rose from 18.2 billion barrels in 1976 to 58.35 billion barrels in 1989. This was the result of increased exploration activity and the addition of 26 billion barrels from the Orinoco oil belt. Prior to nationalization, only 33 exploratory wells had been drilled between 1971 and 1976, compared with 58 wells in 1976 and 225 in 1982.

PDVSA's success in exploration has resulted mainly from discoveries made around 1987 at El Furrial in the eastern state of Monagas, with estimated reserves of 538 million barrels and with an upside potential of 1.1 billion barrels, in the Ceuta

South-Southeast field in Lake Maracaibo with estimated recoverable reserves of one billion barrels, and in the Guafita field in Apure, next to the Caño Limón field in Colombia, with estimated recoverable reserves of 500 million barrels. Additional reserves from the Orinoco oil belt have also contributed to the company's reserves. These discoveries have added between 10 and 12 billion barrels of light and medium grade crude oil to a reserve base which was disproportionately biased towards heavier oils.

These discoveries will have a profound impact on the country's crude export mix, as the Monagas prospects, which currently produce 80,000 barrels per day of light oil, are expected to reach plateau production—the stable production period before the field declines—of 500,000 barrels per day in 1994. The Ceuta field produces 100,000 barrels per day and is expected to reach 200,000 barrels per day in 1993.

Since the trend toward heavy oil has been reversed with the discoveries of light oil in Monagas and Apure, PDVSA has continued to concentrate its exploration efforts on finding light and medium oil, and between 1988 and 1993 has planned to drill 112 exploration wells to add a possible 9.4 billion barrels of reserves to the existing 58 billion barrels. The exploration effort will be concentrated on the Furrial-Musipán geological trend in Monagas where 51 wells are to be drilled and on the North-Central section of Lake Maracaibo where 43 wells are to be drilled.

PDVSA is also developing its large Orinoco oil belt using a new patented production method. This field covers an area of approximately 42,000 square kilometers and is considered one of the most important untapped reserves of heavy oil in the world. The estimated oil *in situ* is around two trillion barrels. The treated heavy oil is known as orimulsion, with recoverable reserves estimated at 267 billion barrels, equivalent on a calorific basis to all of South Africa's coal reserves and to all of the United States's crude reserves. Orimulsion is a rival product to coal and according to PDVSA is not intended to compete with heavy fuel oil. Commercial marketing of the fuel has started at a modest level of 20,000 barrels per day, but could reach 600,000 barrels per day by the middle of the decade.

Gas reserves in the country are estimated at 93 trillion cubic feet of gas. Current gas production is between 3.6 million and 3.8 million cubic feet of gas per day of which one-third is sold locally, about one-third reinjected into the reservoirs, 21% used by the oil industry and 5% flared. Major switching from oil to gas is not envisaged until 1992, after completion of the Nurgas pipeline from Anozategui to the West.

In 1987 PDVSA started exporting coal from western Venezuela through its subsidiary, Carbozulia. Initial exports started at 500,000 tons but are expected to reach 6.5 million tons by 1995.

In its first year of operation, PDVSA received net income of US$825.6 million, increasing to US$1.88 billion in 1977, but with the decline in oil prices the company's net income also suffered, falling to US$731 million in 1988. For tax purposes, PDVSA is treated by the Venezuelan government like any other business entity. The company pays royalties, and income taxes are based on the export values of the oil and products sold. PDVSA does not enjoy any tax privilege except for the tax-free receipt of 10% of the net income from its subsidiaries' export sales which, for accounting and tax purposes, is viewed as a cost incurred by the subsidiaries. The government's fiscal share composed of royalties, income tax, and other taxes, amounted to US$5.64 billion in 1988, representing almost 60% of total revenues of US$9.51 billion.

PDVSA continues to invest in its production facilities with the intention of increasing production in a few years' time. It also intends to increase its presence in the European downstream sector through acquisitions.

Principal Subsidiaries: Corpoven; Maraven; Lagoven; Interven; Refineria Isla (Curaçao); PDV (U.S.A.); PDV (Europe) (U.K.); Intevep; Bariven; Pequiven; Palmaven; Carbozulia.

Further Reading: Petras, James, E., Morris Morley, and Steven Smith, *The Nationalization of Venezuelan Oil,* New York, Praeger Publishers, 1977; "Petroven—Petróleos de Venezuela S.A.,"*OPEC Bulletin Supplement,* April 24, 1978; "OPEC Member Country Profile—Venezuela," *OPEC Bulletin Supplement,* December 11, 1978; "PDVSA—Petróleos de Venezuela S.A.," *OPEC Bulletin Supplement,* February 18, 1980; Philip, George, *Oil and Politics in Latin America,* Cambridge, Cambridge University Press, 1982; Coronel, Gustavo, *The Nationalization of the Venezuelan Oil Industry,* Lexington, Massachusetts, Lexington Books, 1983; Sullivan, William M. and Brian S. McBeth, *Petroleum in Venezuela: A Bibliography,* Boston, G.K. Hall & Co., 1985; "The Orinoco Oil Belt. Venezuela," *Journal of Petroleum Geology,* Vol. X; Martínez, Aníbal R., *Venezuelan Oil: Development and Chronology* London, Elsevier Applied Science, 1989; *PDVSA Contact Newsletter,* Nos. 1–17, 1987-89; *Lagovenews,* Nos. 1–20.

—Brian S. McBeth

PETRÓLEOS DEL ECUADOR

Post Office Box 5007
Quito
Ecuador
(2) 521436
Fax: (2) 569738

State-Owned Company
Incorporated: 1972 as Corporacion Estatal Petrolera
 Ecuatoriana
Employees: 4,700
Sales: US$1.20 billion

As a holding company, Petróleos del Ecuador (Petroecuador), Ecuador's state oil corporation, is the country's largest oil producer and is involved in all aspects of the industry, including exploration, production, refining, marketing, and exports. Petroecuador's investments in crude oil exploration and production absorb huge financial resources; its 1991 budget of US$680 million for exploration and production reflects its status as the country's largest institution. Petroecuador's global investments for the years 1991 and 1992 are estimated at US$235 million and US$307 million respectively. Oil production capacity averaging approximately 290,000 barrels a day, combined with derivative oil products including gasoline, liquefied petroleum gas (LPG), jet fuel, kerex, diesel, and fuel oil, generates approximately $1.2 billion a year, of which 90% goes to the government. Despite Petroecuador's profile as a major Latin American oil producer, its proven reserves, of about 1.5 million barrels per day; fall short of the region's major oil producers, Venezuela and Mexico, with reserves of 5.8 million barrels per day and 5.6 million barrels per day respectively.

Ecuador had produced negligible amounts of oil since 1918, and at first the small industry attracted little attention. Initially the country's production came entirely from the coastal area, with much of the exploration being carried out by the U.S. Texaco-Gulf consortium. In 1967, however, a major oil find was made in the Oriente area of Ecuador, the country's most prolific region, and 1972 saw the completion of the trans-Andean pipeline. The prospect of production on a large scale brought changing attitudes towards foreign involvement in the oil industry. Renegotiations of concessions made prior to 1969 took place, and a new hydrocarbon law was introduced in September 1971, followed by the creation of Corporacion Estatal Petrolera Ecuatoriana (CEPE) in 1972. It was the renegotia-

tions that enabled CEPE to gain control of the Amazon region to the East and on the coast, as disgruntled foreign companies decided to disinvest. By renegotiating various contracts, such as the Texaco-Gulf contract, foreign company concessions were greatly reduced. CEPE strove to achieve control of all phases of the country's hydrocarbon industry. By 1972, when the country began large-scale oil exports, the government's nationalistic attitude towards its oil industry was further enforced through its hydrocarbon law. In broad terms, this law stated that the country's deposits of hydrocarbons and associated substances, in whatever physical state, would be Ecuador's inalienable patrimony. The state would explore and exploit deposits directly by means of CEPE, which could undertake this task either by itself, or by entering in joint or service contracts with national or foreign companies, or by forming mixed-economy companies. Moreover, it would be the right of the state to transport the hydrocarbons by oil and gas pipelines and to refine them.

A major step was taken by the government in June 1972, when it issued Decree 430 stipulating that those who had obtained concessions prior to 1971 would have to take account of the 1971 law, the most important provison of which was concerned with territory. CEPE's creation in 1972 had the object of rationalizing the exploitation of hydrocarbons and using the wealth thus generated to power the nation's economic and social development. The basic legal framework for the national oil company was defined in the Hydrocarbon Law of 1971.

CEPE's efforts bore fruit, and in 1974 it achieved its biggest goal, responsiblity for administering 25% of the shares of the Texaco-Gulf consortium. Gulf, after a series of disagreements with the government, decided to pull out of Ecuador entirely, and in 1976 it sold all of its shares in the consortium and in the trans-Ecuador pipeline to CEPE, which was then left with 62.5% of the consortium, with Texaco controlling the remaining stake. This change marked CEPE's debut as an oil company directly involved in production from the Ecuadorian Amazon region, and consequently export from that region.

In 1988 CEPE began suffering from unprecedented financial difficulties resulting from the 1986 world oil price collapse, which lost Ecuador US$1 billion in that year alone. CEPE's woes were further compounded by the repercussions of Ecuador's 1987 earthquake, which destroyed 40 kilometers of the trans-Ecuador pipeline, the main method of transport for crude exports, and affected 25 of its oil fields.

As a result, CEPE's operations were closely scrutinized by the government. The government did not like what it found, and in August 1989 President Rodrigo Borja Cevallos presented an emergency decree to Ecuador's Congress for the restructuring of the national oil company. The president's reform law, aimed at "dynamizing the hydrocarbon industry," was given congressional approval and became public on September 26, 1989; the restructuring of CEPE into a holding company under a new name was approved. Thus CEPE's legal charter was changed to that of a holding company, consisting of six affiliates—subsidiaries—with the new name of Petroecuador. Its structure, has enabled it to act with autonomy and efficiency, not experienced before in the bureaucratic structure of CEPE. Within a global context, some consider Petroecuador to be riddled with the inefficiency of tight governmental control. Moreover, the division of the company into subsidiaries was also aimed at reducing and controlling the power of the 3,500-strong union which had been vocal against the role of foreign companies in Ecuador's oil sector.

Under its new structure, Petroecuador operates six subsidiaries, of which three are permanent and three are temporary. Its permanent subsidiaries are Petroproduccion, for exploration and production; Petroindustria, for refining; and Petrocomercial, for domestic and foreign sales. Its three temporary subsidiaries are Petrotransporte, set up to manage the trans-Ecuador pipeline, which was previously owned by CEPE but operated by Texaco under the CEPE-Texaco consortium; Petropeninsula, set up to manage the Anglo and Repetrol refineries; and Petroamazonas, created to manage the operations of the CEPE/Texaco consortium. Petroecuador also owns five refining plants: Esmeraldas, La Libertad, Amazonas, Lago Agrio, and Complejo Shushufindi, which together are capable of processing 151,460 barrels per day. The CEPE-Texaco consortium, operating in the Oriente field, produces the majority of Ecuador's oil and represents approximately 70% of Ecuador's total reserves. The creation of Petroecuador's temporary subsidiaries forms part of major petroleum policy guidelines set up during President Borja's electoral campaign and enforced during his presidency.

According to these guidelines, Petroecuador, pursuant to the contractual stipulations, was to undertake operations of the Texaco consortium as of July 1, 1990, through its subsidiary Petroamazonas; the Anglo refinery was to become Petroindustrial property as of August 1990; the trans-Ecuador pipeline was to be operated by Petrotransporte as of October 1989; production levels of existing fields would be adjusted, taking into account both technical and economic aspects; a new law would be prepared for Petroecuador to operate autonomously as a business. Commitments made by the government with the international companies that had signed service contracts for hydrocarbon exploration and exploitation would be respected. However, the state oil industry's nationalistic stance was slightly reversed as the government headed by Borja, desperate to boost reserves, began to retreat from its nationalistic oil policy which characterized his campaign and the early part of his presidency.

While the company retains tight control over the country's oil industry and has no competition, it does not work the oil fields singlehandedly. Foreign firms are responsible for 85% of Ecuador's exploratory drilling under risk service contracts. These contracts, between Petroecuador and international oil firms, grant foreign investors substantial paybacks and returns from their service agreements, while supplying Petroecuador mainly with financial and technical services for exploration and development. Petroecuador retains the ownership of resources and management control. At the same time the government attempts to attract the foreign investment needed for exploration, as company engineers point to a significant natural production decline in the company's existing fields.

As well as supplying Ecuador with more than 85% of its internal consumption, Petroecuador exports approximately 160,000 barrels per day of oil, which, coupled with derivative exports, represent 45% of Ecuador's total exports. During 1990, receipts from crude oil and refined product exports reached US$915 million. A 10% increase over the previous year's exports resulted from the onset of the protracted Gulf crisis, which found Petroecuador tapping into its stocks to take advantage of inflated world oil prices. Oil output in 1990 was approximately 285,000 barrels per day, with an average export volume of 175,000 barrels per day sold mainly to the United States's eastern and western coasts, Asia, and the Caribbean.

The contract with Texaco is the sole joint venture between the state oil corporation and a foreign oil company. This contract expires in 1992, when all oil production will be state controlled.

Principal Subsidiaries: Petroproduccion; Petrocomercial; Petroindustria; Petroamazonas; Transecuatoriana de Petroleos; Petropeninsula.

—Julia Meehan

PETRÓLEOS MEXICANOS

Avenida Marina Nacional 329
Mexico 17
DF Mexico
545 7460

State-Owned Company
Incorporated: 1938
Employees: 170,766 (1988)
Sales: US$13.13 billion (1988)

Petróleos Mexicanos (Pemex) is Mexico's largest enterprise in terms of total sales, total assets, personnel employed, and tax payments. At the end of 1989, Pemex was ranked the seventh-largest oil company in the world in terms of hydrocarbon reserves and the fourth largest in terms of crude oil production, after Aramco, the National Iranian Oil Company, and the Iraqi national oil company, with crude oil production of 2.5 million barrels per day (b/d).

Pemex was founded in 1938 as a decentralized agency of the federal government of Mexico, with direct responsibility for all aspects of the country's oil and gas industry, since 1959 including basic petrochemicals. Oil has been known in Mexico since ancient times and the country was one of the earliest oil- and gas-producing countries in the Western Hemisphere. The first significant commercial exploitation was started in 1901 by Edward L. Doheny, with an oil well located at Ebano, in the eastern part of the state of San Luis Potosi. Up to 1938, production was largely controlled by U.S. and British interests, including Royal Dutch/Shell, Exxon, the Pearson family, Sinclair and Gulf Oil. Production increased considerably during World War I, reaching a peak of 530,000 barrels per day. In 1921 Mexico was the second largest oil producer in the world after the United States, and produced about a quarter of the world's oil supply.

The seeds for the creation of a national oil company in Mexico can be traced back to the 1910 revolution. In order to ensure adequate supplies of fuel for its locomotives, the National Railways of Mexico created a petroleum division to exploit the hydrocarbons found on its lands in the rich Ebano and Panuco oil fields. Soon afterwards it became apparent that the government itself, in order to meet its oil demand would have to develop the oil fields found on its federal lands, not including the land belonging to the railway company, and at the end of December 1925 the Control de Administración del Petróleo Nacional (Control of the Management of National Petroleum)

was set up in order to simplify government participation in the development of its reserves by concentrating it in one entity. This government entity competed directly with private capital in the production and refining of crude oil but at the same time regulated the domestic price of petroleum products. In December 1933, a Congressional decree established Petróleos de México S.A. (Petromex), a publicly traded company in which only Mexican nationals could purchase equity, with the specific purpose of supplying the fuel requirements of the National Railways in particular and the domestic market with petroleum products in general. It also regulated the domestic petroleum markets and trained Mexican personnel in all aspects of the industry. Petromex only lasted until September 1934, when it was wound up owing to a lack of interest on the part of the investing public, and the assets and shares of the company were transferred to the Control de Administración del Petróleo Nacional. In November 1936 a law was passed which expropriated for the state all assets considered to be of public utility, including oil and natural gas, and in January 1937 the state-owned Administración General del Petróleo Nacional was created to explore and develop the national reserves which were assigned to it.

As a result of long-existing conflict between the oil workers' union and the companies, which at one stage threatened to bring the oil industry to a standstill, President Lázaro Cárdenas nationalized the oil industry on March 18, 1938. A number of reasons were given for this drastic measure, amongst which the most important were the following: that the foreign-owned companies had adopted inadequate conservation measures for existing reserves; that there was a lack of interest on the part of the companies in exploring for new reserves; and that the companies had used unfair labor practices.

On March 19, 1938, the day after expropriation, the Consejo Administrativo del Petróleo (Petroleum Administrative Council) was established, with nine government members, to administer the assets it had taken over. In June the administration of the country's oil and gas industry was split between two government agencies: Petróleos Mexicanos, which took over the properties and functions assigned to the Petroleum Administrative Council, and the newly created Distribuidora de Petróleos Mexicanos, which distributed and marketed petroleum products. By August 1940, however, it became obvious that this delegation of responsibilities was not working, because of conflict between the two agencies, and so it was decided that all matters related to hydrocarbons should become the sole responsibility of Pemex. The Administración del Petróleo Nacional and the Distribuidora de Petróleos Mexicanos were abolished.

With the creation of Pemex, Mexico faced an economic boycott instigated by the governments of the expropriated companies, which included an economic blockade to prevent the company from selling its oil in world markets; a ban on selling raw materials, replacement parts, and equipment needed by Pemex; pressure on shipping lines to refuse transportation of Mexican oil; legal action to embargo the oil that Pemex managed to export through other countries; and a massive withdrawal of bank deposits held in Mexico by foreign companies. After long and strenuous negotiations, the Mexican government finally agreed to indemnify the foreign oil companies for US$114 million, with the first payment beginning in 1940 and the last one in 1962.

Pemex's original brief from the Mexican government was to supply the Mexican market with oil, gas, and petrochemical products at the lowest possible cost. The mandate was not profit-motivated, and there was a strong desire on the part of the government to improve the living standards of its employees.

Since 1940, Pemex's board of directors has been headed by the secretary of patrimony and industrial development with five other government representatives—the secretary of finance, the secretary of commerce, the deputy secretary of patrimony and industrial development, the director general of the Federal Electricity Commission, and the director general of the Nacional Financiera, a financial institution—as well as five union representatives. The executive officers of the company are headed by a director general and seven sub-directors in charge of production, refining, finance, sales, exploration, personnel administration, and project administration. The number of employees has risen tenfold since 1938.

About 72% of Mexico's surface area of 2.5 million square kilometers is covered by sedimentary basins—potentially oil-producing areas—and only about 10% of this area has been explored. The proved hydrocarbon reserves are located mainly in the Chicontepec basin in the northern part of the state of Veracruz, the Tabasco-Chiapas Mesozoic area in the continental shelf of the Gulf of Campeche, and the Sabinas basin in the states of Coahuila and Nuevo Leon.

In 1938 Pemex inherited total reserves of 1.276 billion barrels of oil equivalent (boe)—including oil and gas—from the expropriated oil companies, which increased steadily to reach 5.568 billion boe in 1960, undergoing a spectacular rise in the 1980s to 60.126 billion boe in 1980, and at the end of 1990 standing at 64.96 billion boe.

After the first commercial exploitation of the country's reserves at Ebano, production was concentrated in the zone of Tuxpan in the northern part of the state of Veracruz, where the famous Golden Lane complex, dating from the first two decades of the 20th century, was located and where the productivity of the wells was legendary. Between 1910 and 1937 the Potrero del Llano well produced 117.3 million barrels of crude oil and the Cerro Azul well produced an average of 261,400 barrels per day of crude oil in the early stages.

At the time of nationalization, Pemex's production averaged 104,110 barrels per day of crude oil and liquid natural gas (LNG), increasing to just over 197,260 barrels per day in 1950 and undergoing a spectacular rise in the 1980s to an average of 2.54 million barrels per day of crude oil and LNG. After leaping into the forefront of world crude oil production a decade earlier, in 1989, Pemex reached its production plateau of 2.5 million barrels per day of crude oil and almost 400,000 barrels per day of LNG. In 1989 over two-thirds of Pemex's crude output was heavy Maya crude from the offshore Gulf of Campeche, while the lighter Olmeca and Isthmus blends came from onshore areas where reserves were declining.

Most of Pemex's gas production is associated with crude oil production, although there are also natural gas fields independent of oil fields. Gas production at the time of nationalization was 600 million cubic meters per annum and in 1990 stood at around 36 billion cubic meters. Pemex's oil fields have been producing much higher ratios of gas per barrel of oil than was previously estimated.

In 1976 Pemex launched an ambitious program for gas treatment plants to enable the company to handle the large amounts of gas produced from the oil fields that were being developed. Most of the gas is processed by Pemex's petrochemical complexes in southern and central Mexico, and a proportion of it is fed into Mexico's gas system. The gas is transported through Pemex's 12,788-kilometer network of gas pipelines.

Until 1938 Mexico was one of the world's largest oil exporters, but with the international boycott and increased domestic consumption Pemex was not able to export significant quantities of oil until the mid-1970s. Until 1971 Mexico was self-sufficient in crude oil and natural gas, as well as being a net exporter of refined products. In the early 1970s, in order to meet its domestic consumption requirements, Pemex became a net importer, importing 64,600 barrels per day of crude oil in 1973. Since then, there has been a radical adjustment of Pemex's role, which up until then had been to provide energy to the ever-increasing domestic market at low prices. When the country's balance of payments was adversely affected in 1974, Pemex was forced to double the prices of its products to dampen down demand, and a decision was taken to allow the company to invest more money in exploration and development in order to re-establish itself as a major oil exporter. Pemex was called on by the government to export oil, gas, and petrochemical products, and to become the cornerstone of Mexican industrial development. The 1974–1976 US$3 billion development plan was the largest in Mexico's history and called for $240 million to be spent on geological and seismic studies and $728 million to be invested in drilling development and exploration wells. This plan was followed by an even bigger one in 1977 when Pemex approved an ambitious $15.5 billion development program with the aim of increasing by 1982 the company's production in the following areas: crude oil to 2.2 million barrels per day; gas to 113.3 million cubic meters per day; crude oil exports to 1.1 million barrels per day; refining capacity to 1.7 million barrels per day; and petrochemical output to 15.5 million tons per annum. Almost half the budget would be spent on the drilling of 2,152 development wells, and $1.2 billion would be spent on drilling 1,324 exploration wells. The plan called for the surveying of 1.2 million square kilometers of prospective oil-bearing areas.

The exploration and development effort led to a spectacular increase in reserves and production in the 1980s. With increased production, Pemex managed to export between 1.3 million and 1.5 million barrels per day of crude oil during the 1980s, with exports in 1989 at just under 1.3 million barrels per day. Since 1976 the Mexican government has operated a ceiling on exports of 1.35 million barrels per day to keep its prices high in world markets. Pemex has three main export markets, with the United States being by far its largest customer, taking 57% of its exports in 1989. It is followed by Spain with 15% and Japan with 13%.

During the 1980s, Pemex's crude oil reserves remained remarkably static despite a significant reduction in the number of exploration wells drilled during the period—from 305 in 1983 to 123 in 1989—because of the country's austerity program, which involved a reduction in government expenditure.

Pemex has also followed a policy of self-sufficiency in the downstream and petrochemical side of the oil business. Production in these two sectors has thus evolved to meet domestic demand. In 1938, Pemex produced 92,229 barrels per day of products, increasing to 481,135 barrels per day in 1970 and 1.403 billion barrels per day in 1988. Pemex operates nine refineries with a primary capacity—not including upgrading—of 1.679 million barrels per day, and with the following upgrading facilities: 82,000 barrels per day thermal operations, 267,000 barrels per day catalytic cracking, and 157,800 barrels per day catalytic reforming. The expansion of cracking and reforming facilities has been a direct response to the increase in production of heavy Mayan crude since the mid-1970s. Heavy Mayan crude is now put through the refineries in order to leave the lighter crudes for export. The refineries are served by an oil pipeline network of 4,784 kilometers.

Domestic demand is heavily geared towards transport fuel, such as gasoline and fuel oil, which accounted for 32% and 33% respectively, out of total consumption of petroleum products in 1989 of 1.3 million barrels per day. Exports of products in 1989 declined by 31% to 83,000 barrels per day, from 121,000 barrels per day in 1988, because of higher internal consumption.

After its first investment overseas, a small investment in the early 1980s in Petronor, a Spanish refiner, Pemex decided to concentrate on expanding its domestic refining business, which it would like to increase by 300,000 barrels per day during the early 1990s. It later exchanged its stake in Petronor for a 2.9% stake in Repsol, the privatized Spanish oil company, increasing Pemex's share of the Spanish market for its products beyond the 150,000 barrels per day of crude it supplies.

In 1977 Pemex embarked on an expansion program intended to triple its petrochemical output by 1982. It aimed to be self-sufficient in basic petrochemicals by 1979 and subsequently to develop large volumes of feedstocks—raw or part-processed products destined for further processing—for export. This policy has been successful, with basic petrochemicals production increasing from 1.931 million imperial tons in 1980 to 16.9 million tons in 1989. Private capital is allowed to account for up to 40% of total issued capital in the petrochemical industry mainly because of Pemex's lack of technological expertise. In 1989, petrochemicals exports climbed by 50% to US$110.4 million, while imports declined to US$21.7 million. Export earnings from petrochemicals represented only 1.4% of Pemex's total export earnings, but their growth helped to offset the company's deteriorating trade in refined products, which accounted for 6% of Pemex's gross exports. Pemex operates a shipping fleet that grew from 6,438 dead-weight tons in 1938 to 618,780 dead-weight tons in 1988.

Although Mexico is not as dependent as Venezuela on oil, in the early 1990s, this commodity accounts for 70% of its foreign exchange and provides around 45% of government tax receipts. Crude oil exports also enable the country to keep up with the repayment of its US$103 billion of foreign debt. As a decentralized public agency of the Mexican government, Pe-

mex pays 18% tax on total revenues from oil and gas, 13% on total revenues from petrochemicals, and a 50% corporation tax. In 1989 Pemex made an international trading surplus of US$7.03 billion between oil sales and product imports, an increase of 15.3% compared with the previous year, representing 46% of non-oil exports. Total oil exports were up to US$7.84 billion and oil imports just US$800.4 million. The deficit on product trade of 38,000 barrels per day, that is, the amount Mexico had to import, in 1989 stemmed from burgeoning domestic demand, particularly for gasoline, jet fuel, and fuel oil. In 1989 Pemex generated pre-tax profits of US$7.9 billion, all of which—with the exception of US$7 million—was sent to the Mexican government. Pemex provided 32% of total government tax receipts in 1989, slightly below the level of 1985, when the company contributed 36.8% of total government tax income.

It is likely that Pemex will soon undergo an internal reorganization, with the company being divided into separate operating units, leaving Pemex as a holding company. One part of Pemex, international marketing, has already been split off. Since June 1990 Petróleos Mexicanos Internacional Comercio Internacional has been responsible for the marketing of crude oil, refined products, and petrochemicals.

Principal Subsidiaries: Tetraetilo de Mexico S A; Compañía Mexicana de Exploraciones S A (COMESA); Instalaciones Inmobiliarias para Industria S.A. de C.V.; Compañía Operadora de Estaciones de Servicio S.A. de C.V.; Distribuidora de Gas Natural del Estado de Mexico S A de C V; Distribuidiora de Gas de Queretaro S A; Cloro de Tehuantepec S A de C V; Empresas del Grupo PMI.

Further Reading: Bermudez, Antonio J., *The Mexican National Petroleum Industry. A Case Study in Nationalization,* Stanford, California, Stanford University Press, 1963; Williams, Edward J., *The Rebirth of the Mexican Petroleum Industry,* Lexington, Massachusetts, Lexington Books, 1979; Sepulveda, Isidro, "Pemex in a Dependent Society" in *US-Mexican Energy Relationships,* by Jerry R. Ladman, Deborah J. Baldwin, and Elihu Bergman, Lexington, Massachusetts, Lexington Books, 1981; Philip, George, *Oil and Politics in Latin America,* Cambridge, Cambridge University Press, 1982; Szekely, Gabriel, *La economía política del petróleo en México, 1976–1982,* El Colegio de México, 1983; Baker, George, *Mexico's Petroleum Sector. Performance and Prospects,* Tulsa, Oklahoma, PennWell Publishing Co., 1984; Randall, Laura, *The Political Economy of Mexican Oil,* New York, Praeger, 1989.

—Brian S. McBeth

PETROLEUM DEVELOPMENT OMAN LLC

Post Office Box 81
Muscat
Oman
678111
Fax: 677106

State-Owned Company
Incorporated: 1937 as Petroleum Development (Oman and Dhofar) Ltd.
Employees: 4,500
Sales: RO1.34 billion (US$3.53 billion)

Like most countries in the Persian Gulf area, Oman's economic prosperity is closely linked with the oil industry. It was the development of the oil industry and the use of the resulting revenues for economic and infrastructural development purposes that enabled Oman's gross national product per capita to expand by 8% in real terms from 1965 to 1987, according to World Bank estimates.

Although Oman's approach to the awarding of concessions to foreign oil companies is more liberal than that of its gulf neighbors, its oil industry remains dominated by Petroleum Development Oman (PDO), which is 60% owned by the state with the remaining 40% divided between Royal Dutch/Shell (34%), Total Compagnie Française des Pétroles (Total CFP) (4%), and Partex, the company founded by Calouste Gulbenkian (2%). Elf Aquitaine and Occidental Petroleum produce small quantities of crude oil, but about 95% of Oman's crude oil is produced by PDO, which is synonymous with Oman's oil industry.

Commercial oil production in Oman began in 1967. Exploration had started in Oman as far back as the 1920s under the Anglo-Persian Oil Company, the forerunner of British Petroleum, but results were discouraging. Sporadic attempts at exploration took place in later years, but difficult conditions hindered success.

Petroleum Development (Oman and Dhofar) Ltd. was founded in 1937 by a consortium of Western oil companies. Its name was changed to Petroleum Development Oman in 1951. Serious exploration activity by the company only began in the 1950s, but success was elusive, and in 1960 four of PDO's major shareholders, British Petroleum (BP), Compagnie Française des Pétroles (CFP), and the predecessors of Exxon Corporation and Mobil Corporation withdrew from the consortium. The Royal Dutch/Shell group was left with an 85% holding in the company, with the remaining 15% in the hands of Partex. In 1967 CFP—now Total CFP—repurchased a 10% stake in PDO, thereby reducing Partex's share to 5%.

In the early years of the 1960s oil was found in commercial quantities. By 1964, sufficient oil had been discovered in the Yibal and neighboring Fahud area to make development and production a viable proposition. An export terminal was built at Mina al-Fahal near Muscat, Oman's capital, and the first oil exports took place in 1967. Initial shipments were modest, averaging less than 30,000 barrels per day (b/d) in 1967, but production picked up rapidly as several new finds took place, reaching 332,000 b/d by 1970.

The development of the oil industry coincided with—and helped bring about—the key event in modern Omani history. In 1970, Oman was an isolated, undeveloped country that survived by subsistence farming and fishing. This country, with a population approaching one million, had three primary schools, one hospital, and just a few kilometers of surfaced road. The first earnings from the oil industry held out the promise of major improvements, but it was not until July 23, 1970, following a palace coup led by Sultan Qaboos bin Said that Oman embarked on an embitious social and economic development program which utilized the oil revenues, and brought Oman into the international fold through in membership in the United Nations and the Arab League.

The early 1970s were important in the history of the international oil industry, not only because of the first oil price shock in 1973 but also because several OPEC countries, particularly in the Gulf area, asserted themselves by taking control of their oil industries. Although not a member of OPEC, Oman followed the lead of its OPEC counterparts and took a 25% share in PDO in December 1973. This share was increased to 60% in July 1974. The government ruled out any further state participation because of the lack of trained local staff. At the beginning of the 1990s, non-Omani staff still comprised over 40% of PDO employees. The remaining 40% of PDO stayed in the hands of Royal Dutch/Shell, Total CFP, and Partex. Royal Dutch/Shell, with its 34% share of the company, remained the dominant foreign oil company in Oman and has continued to play a key management role in PDO. In 1980, PDO was re-registered as an Omani company rather than as a joint venture.

Political developments continued to interact with the fortunes of the oil industry. Since 1966, there had been opposition to the old regime with the resulting insurrection organized by the Popular Front for the Liberation of Oman (PFLO). The so-called Dhofar war continued in the South until 1976 and inhibited further exploration of the southern part of the country. However, the end of hostilities in the south in 1976 heralded a renewed exploration effort, and in 1977 the government and PDO concluded a five-year agreement that provided attractive incentives for exploration and development, particularly in the Dhofar region.

Meanwhile, events outside Oman were building up to produce the second oil shock. In 1978, Omani crude was priced at $13 per barrel. By 1980, Omani crude was fetching $39.5 per barrel. This escalation in prices transformed the outlook for the whole Omani industry. Higher prices made it worthwhile to recover oil in south Oman, and the use of secondary recovery techniques became feasible. Exploration and development have flourished throughout Oman ever since. Success was particularly marked in the south in the early stages, and was helped by the discovery of associated gas, which was injected and pumped into existing fields to enhance recovery rates. The boom continued well into the 1980s, and during the first years of the decade PDO discovered oil in far greater quantities than were produced. The success rate of exploratory drilling was very high; eight new wells were discovered in 1979 and two-thirds of all wells drilled by PDO in the early 1980s yielded oil. Of particular importance was the discovery of Sayyala field, which yielded a much lighter crude, of a much higher quality than that previously recovered.

One of the first fields to benefit from the new circumstances was Marmul in the South. This field was discovered in the late 1950s but was subsequently abandoned because of the low quality of the crude. The field became viable once more, because of rising oil prices, in the late 1970s, and came on-stream by the end of 1980 with estimated reserves of 100 million barrels. Fields around Marmul were also developed and, as the decade unfolded, more oil was discovered in commercially exploitable quantities to the south and southwest of older central fields.

Marmul, Birba, and Qaharir, the first Dhofar fields to be developed, rapidly added 70,000 b/d of crude to Oman's production. By the end of 1981, the addition of other fields boosted Oman's total production to over 350,000 b/d.

Foreign companies participated in the exploration boom of the late 1970s and early 1980s. Elf was the first foreign company to start production. In 1984, Occidental became Oman's third oil producer, and in 1990 Japex Oman Co., a joint venture between Japan National Oil Corp., Japan Petroleum Exploration Co., C. Itoh Energy Development Co., and Indonesia Petroleum Co., commissioned the Daleel field. However, PDO still accounts for over 95% of Omani oil production.

After the initial oil price shock at the beginning of the 1980s, the oil markets moved into a period of large surpluses and weak prices. OPEC attempted to rein back its production in an effort to sustain prices and tried to persuade non-OPEC members to cooperate with this strategy. As an independent non-OPEC member, Oman continued to increase production, which rose from 103 million barrels in 1983 to 178 million barrels in 1985. Oman's government revenues and economy remained relatively stable while those of its neighbors went through hard times. In addition, at a time when many oil importers were reluctant to buy oil from other gulf producers because of the risk to shipping from the Iran-Iraq War, Oman benefited immensely from unfounded fears about attempts to close the Straits of Hormuz and the fact that its main export terminal, Mina al-Fahal, was outside the gulf.

However, Oman was unable to buck the trend indefinitely. Oil prices collapsed in 1986, and, with PDO operating at full capacity, Oman was no longer able to compensate for lower prices by boosting production. Oman decided to cooperate with OPEC and announced a 50,000 b/d production cut in October. Further cuts were announced in 1987 as a contribution to OPEC's strategy of achieving a stable oil price of $18 per barrel. Production was stepped up again towards the end of 1988, and averaged 620,000 b/d in 1989, 600,000 b/d of which were produced by PDO. A decision was taken early in 1990 to boost production to 689,000 b/d—a level which repre-

sents Oman's short-term technical limit. Until 1982 all Oman's crude production was exported, but in November of that year the country's first refinery was opened. The initial throughput capacity was 50,000 b/d, later expanded to 80,000. The refinery is operated by the Oman Oil Refinery Company, which is 99% owned by the Petroleum Ministry and 1% by the Central Bank of Oman.

PDO's second major activity is gas, which was given a high priority during the 1980s. Prior to 1984, gas discoveries were a result of oil exploration, but in 1984 PDO and the government signed a ten-year contract that enabled PDO to dedicate resources specifically to the task of finding gas. While foreign companies are encouraged to search for oil, gas development is a matter for PDO and the gas department of the Ministry of Petroleum. Plans are already in operation to double the capacity of the Yibal gas treatment plant. The 1990s are expected to see further extension of the gas grid and greater use of gas in the industrialization process that is intended to allow Oman to diversify into other industries and free itself from its overwhelming dependence on oil.

Oil fields have traditionally been the main users of gas, reinjecting it into wells to improve recovery rates. The development of gas is intended to increase its importance as a domestic fuel in power generation and in industrial projects, and to release more oil for export. The 1989 discovery of 10 billion to 11 billion cubic meters of gas in the Saih Nihayda area represented the largest gas discovery in over 20 years.

At the beginning of 1991, total proven reserves were estimated at 4.3 billion barrels, yielding a 20-year reserve lifespan at the current rates of production. So far, intense and extensive exploration activity has been very successful in boosting the life of these reserves; in 1980 PDO had only ten producing fields, whereas in 1990 it brought its 64th field into operation. Vast areas of the country remain unexplored and could yield further significant finds.

Oman's reserves and production can also be boosted by better exploitation of already discovered fields. Extensive efforts are underway to boost the amount of recoverable reserves.

The future of Oman's oil industry, and with it that of PDO, will—as always—largely be determined by events in the international oil markets. Now that Iraqi troops have been removed from Kuwait, a war risk premium is no longer keeping oil prices high. Oil markets have returned to economic fundamentals which at the beginning of the 1990s were primarily concerned with surplus supplies.

Further Reading: Skeet, Ian, *Oman before 1970: the End of an Era,* London, Faber, 1985; Allen Calvin H. Jr., *Oman: Ancient Sultanate and Modern State,* London, Croom Helm, 1986; Hawley, Donald, *Oman and Its Renaissance,* London, Stacey International, 1987; Pridham, B.R., ed., *Oman: Economic, Social and Strategic Developments* London, Croom Helm, 1987; Zahlan, Rosemarie, *The Making of the Modern Gulf States: Kuwait, Bahrain, Qatar, UAE and Oman,* London, Unwin Hyman, 1989; "Oman: A MEED Practical Guide," *Middle East Economic Digest,* all editions.

—Debra Johnson

PETRONAS

Peti Surat 12444
Menara Dayabumi, Kompleks Dayabumi
Jalan Sultan, Hishamuddin
50778 Kuala Lumpur
Federation of Malaysia

State-Owned Company
Incorporated: 1974
Sales: M$9.17 billion (US$3.40 billion) (1988)

In 1988 Malaysia had the world's 22nd-largest reserves of oil and the 16th-largest reserves of natural gas. Its exports of the two commodities accounted for 15% of Malaysia's foreign exchange income in that year. The exclusive ownership and control of both resources rests with Petronas (Petroliam Nasional Bhd), the only Malaysian company to appear in the *Fortune* 500 list. Through subsidiaries and joint ventures, Petronas is deeply involved in almost all aspects of the oil and natural gas industries, across the range from upstream (exploring for and extracting oil and gas) to downstream (refining and distributing the products). Petronas was not the first company to extract oil or gas in Malaysia. Oil was first found in what is now Malaysia at the end of the 19th century, and Royal Dutch/Shell, then as now one of the majors—the small group of leading private oil companies—first drilled for oil in Sarawak, then a British colony, in 1910. It was still the only oil company in the area in 1963, when the Federation of Malaya, having achieved independence from Britain six years before, absorbed Sarawak and Sabah, both on the island of Borneo, and became Malaysia. The authorities in the two new states retained their links with Royal Dutch/Shell, which brought Malaysia's first offshore oil field onstream in 1968.

Meanwhile the federal government turned to Esso, Continental Oil, and Mobil, licensing exploration off the state of Trengganu, in the Malay Peninsula, the most populous region, and the focus of federal power. By 1974, however, only Esso was still in the area. It made its first discoveries of natural gas in that year and then rapidly made Trengganu a bigger producer of oil than either Sarawak or Sabah. By 1974 Malaysia's output of crude oil stood at about 81,000 barrels per day (b/d).

Several factors converged in the early 1970s to prompt the Malaysian government into setting up a state company, as first proposed in the Five Year Plan published in 1971. These were years in which power in the world oil industry began to shift away from the majors, which then controlled more than 90%

of the oil trade, toward the Organization of Petroleum Exporting Countries (OPEC), as well as a proliferation of new private and state companies joining in the search for reserves. By 1985 the majors, reduced in number from seven to five, were producing less than 20% of the world total. It seemed that Malaysia would either have to join the trend or continue to leave its oil and gas entirely to Royal Dutch/Shell and Esso, multinational corporations necessarily attuned to the requirements of their directors and shareholders, rather than to the priorities the government of a developing country might seek to realize.

Further, an agreement between Malaysia and Indonesia, signed in 1969, had settled doubts and disputes about each country's claims over territorial waters and offshore resources, at a time when both were heavily indebted to Organization for Economic Co-operation and Development (OECD) governments and banks as well as to the International Monetary Fund (IMF) and the World Bank. Setting up a state oil and gas company, through which the government could get international capital but avoid tangling with foreign oil companies or governments, had worked for Indonesia: why not for Malaysia as well? The oil crisis of 1973–1974 made the government even more aware of Malaysia's dependence on foreign oil and foreign capital in general.

Another factor in the decision was that the technology had recently been developed for extensive exploration and drilling offshore. The local geography includes a combination of broad basins of sedimentary rock with calm and shallow waters around the Sunda Shelf, making exploration for gas and oil relatively easier and more successful than in most areas of the world. Malaysian crude has turned out to be mostly high quality, with low sulfur content.

A final and crucial factor in the creation of Petronas, and its continuation in much the same form since, has been the political stability of Malaysia. Since the restoration of parliament in 1971 the country has been ruled by the National Front (Barisan Nasional), the heirs to the Alliance Party which had been dominant from 1957 to 1969, and the originators in 1971 of the New Economic Policy, designed to improve the economic position of Bumiputras—native Malays—relative to Chinese and Indian Malaysians and to foreign corporations. The difficulties this policy has caused for foreign companies and investors are outweighed by the benefits they believe they gain from Malaysia's political stability.

The Malaysian government chose to create a state company, rather than using taxes, production limits, leasing, or other familiar instruments of supervision. The government wanted, and needed, the cooperation of the majors but also sought to assert national rights over the use of the country's resources. A state company, having both supervisory powers over the majors and production activities of its own, was a workable compromise between allowing the majors full rein and excluding them, their finance, and their expertise altogether.

Petronas was established in August 1974 and operates under the terms of the Petroleum Development Act passed in October 1974. It was modeled on PERTAMINA, the Indonesian state oil and gas company founded in 1971 in succession to PERMINA, which had been set up in 1958. According to the 1971 plan, Petronas's goals would be to safeguard national sovereignty over oil and gas reserves, to plan for both present and future national need for oil and gas, to take part in distributing and marketing petroleum and petrochemical products at reasonable prices, to encourage provision of plant, equipment, and services by Malaysian companies, to produce nitrogenous fertilizers, and to spread the benefits of the petroleum industry throughout the nation.

Having created Petronas, the government had to choose what forms its dealings with private oil companies would take. Starting with its legal monopoly on oil and gas activities and resources, it could simply award concessions, without taking part in production, management, or profits itself; or it could try offering services at the supply end; or it could make contracts to cover profit-sharing, production-sharing, joint ventures—sharing both profits and costs—or all stages of the process, under "carried-interest" contracts. Petronas's first move was to negotiate the replacement of the leases granted to Royal Dutch/Shell on Borneo and to Esso in the peninsula with production-sharing contracts, which have been the favored instrument, alongside joint ventures, ever since. These first contracts came into effect in 1976. Allowing for royalties to both federal and state governments, and for cost recovery arrangements, they laid down that the remainder would go 70% to Petronas, 30% to the foreign company. Esso began oil production in two offshore fields in 1978, exporting its share of the supply, unlike Petronas, whose share was consumed within the country.

Petronas went downstream for the first time in 1976, when it was chosen by the Association of South East Asian Nations (ASEAN) to begin construction on the second ASEAN joint industrial project, a urea plant. The subsidiary, Asean Bintulu Fertilizer (ABF), is based in Sarawak and now exports ammonia and urea all over the world.

Also in 1976 Malaysia became a net exporter of oil, but exports were at such a low level as to make the country ineligible to join OPEC. This situation has perhaps benefited Malaysia, and Petronas, by allowing the company a degree of commercial and political flexibility and reinforcing Petronas's chief purpose, Malaysian self-reliance.

Petronas supervised its foreign partners' oil activities, taking no direct role in production, until 1978, when the government saw to the creation of a subsidiary for oil exploration and production, Petronas Carigali. It began its work in an oil field off the peninsula. Petronas retains its supervisory powers over all oil and gas ventures, particularly on issues of health and safety and environmental control.

The government was determined to develop Malaysia's natural gas as well as its oil. In 1974 it saw to the ordering of five tankers for liquefied natural gas (LNG) by the Malaysian International Shipping Company (MISC), of which it owned 61%. These were to take LNG exports out of Malaysia, save the cost of hiring foreign tankers, and expand the country's fleet under its own control—in contrast to cargo shipping, which is controlled by international conferences. Shell BV, the Royal Dutch/Shell subsidiary that was building the LNG plant off Sarawak with Japanese and Asian Development Bank aid, accepted production sharing with Petronas but baulked at sharing equity, transport management, or refining. Negotiations went on, pushing commencement further and further back, until 1977, when Petronas and the government, faced with the costs of maintaining the tankers between delivery and first use, surrendered management rights—leading to a repeal of part of the Petroleum Development Act—and settled for Petronas's taking

60% of equity in the new company Malaysia LNG. The Sarawak state government took 5%, and the other 35% was divided equally between Shell BV and the Mitsubishi Corporation. Production of LNG in Sarawak at last began in 1983.

After negotiations lasting from 1977 to 1982, Petronas had concluded contracts with Tokyo Electric Power and Tokyo Gas for the sale and delivery of LNG through to the year 2003. Malaysia LNG is to send almost the entire output of its Bintulu gas fields to Japan, under these contracts and another one, signed in 1990, to supply Saibu Gas of Fukuoka, in southwestern Japan, for 20 years from 1993.

When in 1982 Petronas Carigali formed an exploration and production company with Société National Elf Aquitaine of France, it allowed Elf better terms for recovering costs than it had offered in earlier ventures. This development came against the background of the government's imposition of a depletion policy on Petronas, Royal Dutch/Shell, and Esso, in an attempt to postpone the exhaustion of oil reserves. These were then estimated to be about 2.84 billion barrels, and it was officially predicted that by the late 1980s Malaysia would be a net oil importer once again. By 1980 oil and gas already represented 24% of Malaysian exports, and the government decided to impose a tax on these exports at a 25% rate. The new policy and the new tax combined to cause Malaysia's output and exports of crude oil to fall in 1981, for the first time since Petronas was established. Output rose again, beyond its 1980 level, in the following year, but exports took until 1984 to surpass their 1980 level.

However, the depletion policy was being undermined by external circumstances. Through the early 1980s a worldwide oil glut, which OPEC proved unable to control, forced the Malaysian government to increase production to offset a deterioration in its balance of increased payments to a deficit of US$1 billion. It became clear that this could only be sustained by relaxing the conditions for joint ventures between Petronas and the major oil companies. In 1982 the Petronas-government share, which had risen to 80%, was cut to 70%, and taxes on company income were also cut.

Petronas went into refining and distribution in 1983. It initiated the construction of refineries at Malacca and at Kertih, in order to reduce its dependence on Royal Dutch/Shell's two refineries at Port Dickson and Esso's refinery in Sarawak. These two majors, and other foreign companies, already covered much of the domestic retail market, but the new subsidiary Petronas Dagangan was given the initial advantage of preference in the location of its stations. By 1990, 252 service stations carried the Petronas brand, all but 20 on a franchise basis, and another 50 were planned. Some were set up on grounds of social benefit rather than of strict commercial calculation.

As production from Royal Dutch/Shell and Esso's existing fields moved nearer depletion, the companies sought new fields and new contracts. In 1985 the government and Petronas revised the standard production-sharing contract, increasing the rate of recovery of capital costs from 30% to 50% of gross production in the case of oil and from 35% to 60% in the case of natural gas, abolishing signature, discovery, and production bonus payments, and increasing the foreign partners' share of the profits. At first the drastic fall in oil prices during 1986, which cut Malaysia's income from exported oil by more than a third even though the volume of exports rose by 16%, discouraged interest in the new arrangements, but by 1989 Petronas had signed 22 new contracts with 31 companies from 11 countries. However, the contract period was still restricted to five years—compared, for example, with the 35-year contracts available in neighboring Singapore—and there was still a 25% levy on exported crude oil, intended to promote the domestic refining industry. These conditions have been cited as disincentives to foreign investment, and may be relaxed during the 1991 round of negotiations.

The government and Petronas have aimed to encourage the replacement of fast-depleting oil within Malaysia itself and simultaneously to foster heavy industries which can help reduce the country's overwhelming dependence on exporting its natural resources. In 1980 petroleum products accounted for 88% of the country's commercial consumption of energy, the rest being provided from hydroelectric plants in Sarawak, too far away from the main population centers to become a major alternative. Five years later gas accounted for 17%, hydroelectricity for 19%, coal for 2%, and petroleum products for 62% of such consumption, and about half of each year's gas output was being consumed in Malaysia.

The Petronas venture responsible for this shift in fuel use, and—along with Malaysia LNG—for Malaysia's becoming the third largest producer of LNG in the world, is the Peninsular Gas Utilization Project (Projek Pennggunaan Gas Semenanjung), the aim of which is to supply gas to every part of the Peninsula. Its first stage was completed in 1985, following the success of smaller gasification projects in the states of Sarawak and Sabah, and involved the extraction of gas from three fields in the Natuna Sea, between the Peninsula and the island of Borneo, its processing in a plant at Kertih on the Peninsula's east coast, and its distribution to the state of Trengganu by pipeline and abroad via an export terminal.

Petronas's least happy venture was its ownership of the Bank Bumiputra, the second-largest, but least-profitable, of the commercial banks incorporated in Malaysia. Petronas spent more than M$3.5 billion, over five years, trying to rescue the bank from the impact of the bad loans it had made, starting with its support of the Carrian property group of Hong Kong, which collapsed in 1985, taking the bank's share capital down with it. Petronas sold the bank back to another state company, Minister of Finance Inc., in 1991, and announced its intention to concentrate on oil, gas, and associated activities in future.

Just as Petronas was disposing of this liability the crisis caused by the Iraqi regime's invasion of Kuwait culminated in military action against Iraq on behalf of the United Nations. Petronas had already raised Malaysia's oil production rate from 605,000 to 650,000 barrels per day in late 1990, as the crisis unfolded. This move only reinforced the company's awareness of the need to vary its policies, since, with known reserves of 2.94 billion barrels, and assuming no new major finds of oil, Malaysia risks seeing output decline to 350,000 barrels per day in 2000 and running down to depletion within another five years. This possibility is exacerbated by the likelihood that Southeast Asia in general will enjoy rapid economic growth in the 1990s, so that demand for oil there will rise twice as fast as demand in the relatively more sluggish, more mature, economies of North America and Europe. The Malaysian government, and its state oil and gas company, must decide what mixture of policies to adopt in response.

Fortunately for Malaysia, exploration is by no means at an end, and could yet produce more reserves. Thus the Seligi field, which came on stream at the end of 1988 and is being developed by Esso Production Malaysia, is the richest single oilfield so far found in Malaysian waters, and further concessions to the Majors might encourage exploration of the deeper waters around Malaysia, where as yet unknown reserves may be discovered. Meanwhile computerised seismography makes it both feasible and commercially justifiable to re-explore fields which have been abandoned, or assumed to be unproductive, over the past century. In 1990 Petronas invited foreign companies to re-explore parts of the sea off Sabah and Sarawak on the basis of new surveys using up-to-date techniques.

Another way to postpone depletion is to develop sources of oil, and of its substitute, natural gas, outside Malaysia. Late in 1989 the governments of Vietnam and Myanmar (Burma) invited Petronas Carigali to take part in joint ventures to explore for oil in their coastal waters. In 1990 a new unit, Petronas Carigali Overseas Sdn Bhd, was created to take up a 15% interest in a field in Myanmarese waters being explored by Idemitsu Myanmar Oil Exploration Co. Ltd., a subsidiary of the Japanese firm Idemitsu Oil Development Co. Ltd., in a production sharing arrangement with Myanmar Oil and Gas Enterprise. Thus began Petronas's first oil exploration outside Malaysia. In May 1990 the governments of Malaysia and Thailand settled a long-running dispute over their respective rights to an area of 7,300 square kilometers in the Gulf of Thailand by setting up a joint administrative authority for the area and encouraging a joint oil exploration project by Petronas, the Petroleum Authority of Thailand and the U.S. company Triton Oil. In a separate deal, in October 1990, the Petroleum Authority of Thailand arranged with Petronas a joint study of the feasibility of transferring natural gas from this jointly administered area, through Malaysia to Thailand, by way of an extension of the pipelines be laid for the third stage of the Peninsular Gas Utilization Project.

That project is on course to becoming a major element in the postponement of oil depletion. Contracts for line pipes for the second stage of the project were signed in 1989 with two consortia of Malaysian, Japanese, and Brazilian companies. This stage, due to be completed in 1991, will include the laying of 730 kilometers of pipeline through to the tip of the peninsula, from where gas can be sold to Singapore and Thailand; the conversion of two power stations—Port Dickson and Pasir Gudang—from oil to gas; and the expansion of Petronas's output of methyl tertiary butyl ether (MTBE), propylene, and polypropylene, which are already being produced in joint ventures with Idemitsu Petrochemical Co. of Japan and Neste Oy of Finland. The third stage of the project is to lay pipelines along the northwest and northeast coastlines of the Peninsula.

Another new venture in 1990 was in ship-owning, since Petronas's existing arrangements with MISC and with Nigerian state oil company would be inadequate to transport the additional exports of LNG due to start in 1994, under the contract with Saibu Gas. Petronas has not lost sight of the government's commitment to Malaysian self-reliance, and the company's second refinery at Malacca, due to be completed in 1992, with a capacity of 200,000 barrels per day, will promote the same policy. The fact that it is being built in a joint venture with Samsung of Korea, the Chinese Petroleum Corporation, of Taiwan and Caltex of the United States does not negate the policy, for the subsidiary company Petronas Penapisan (Melaka) will have a decisive 45% of equity, while sharing the enormous costs and advanced technology of the project. More to the point, a side effect of the refinery's completion will be that Petronas will be able to refine all of the crude oil it produces, instead of depending for a portion of it on facilities in Singapore.

It is important to place Petronas, with its policies of promoting self-reliance, helping to develop associated industries, and varying the sources and uses of oil and gas, in the context of the Malaysian economy as a whole. Under governments which—by current, if not historical, Western standards—are strongly interventionist, the contribution of oil taxes to the federal government's revenue hovered at around 12% to 16% until 1980, when it showed a marked increase to 23%, followed by another leap to 32% in 1981. From then until 1988 the proportion has fluctuated between 29% and 36%. Petronas, then, is not just another big oil company: it controls a crucial sector of the economy and remains, for better or worse, an indispensable instrument of state.

Principal Subsidiaries: Asean Bintulu Fertilizer Sdn Bhd; Malaysia LNG Sdn Bhd; Petronas Carigali Sdn Bhd; Petronas Dagangan Sdn Bhd; Petronas Gas Sdn Bhd; Petronas Khidmat Sdn Bhd; Petronas Marine Sdn Bhd; Petronas Penapisan (Melaka) Sdn Bhd; Petronas Penapisan (Trengganu) Sdn Bhd.

Further Reading: Klapp, Merrie Gilbert, *The Sovereign Entrepreneur,* Ithaca, New York, Cornell University Press, 1987; Creffield, David, *Malaysia,* London, Euromoney Publications, 1989.

—Patrick Heenan

PHILLIPS PETROLEUM COMPANY

Phillips Building
Bartlesville, Oklahoma 74004
U.S.A.
(918) 661-6600
Fax: (918) 661-7636

Public Company
Incorporated: 1917
Employees: 22,400
Sales: $13.98 billion
Stock Exchanges: New York Pacific Toronto

Phillips Petroleum Company is one of the largest oil companies in the United States. In addition to its core businesses—which include producing crude oil and natural gas, oil refining, and marketing gasoline—Phillips is a leading producer of petrochemicals. As the result of two hostile takeover attempts in the 1980s, Phillips has streamlined its operations to help pay off a substantial debt burden.

Phillips is named after brothers Frank and L.E. Phillips, and was organized in 1917 to acquire their original venture in the oil business, Anchor Oil and Gas Company. Raised on an Iowa farm, the Phillips brothers left Iowa after Frank heard rumors of vast oil deposits in Oklahoma, then part of the Indian Territory. Along with others Frank Phillips founded Anchor Oil and Gas in 1903. After a struggle, Frank Phillips, joined by L.E., finally began to make money from oil in 1905. They reinvested their profits, founding a bank. Eventually, the brothers decided to leave the uncertain oil business for good and concentrate on banking. They were forestalled, however, when World War I broke out and the price of crude jumped from 40 cents to more than $1 a barrel. The brothers founded Phillips Petroleum in 1917, headquartered in Bartlesville, Oklahoma.

From the very beginning, the Phillips brothers found much natural gas while drilling for oil. Most drillers considered the gas useless and burned it off at the wellhead, but the Phillips brothers sought to turn it into a cash crop. In 1917 Phillips opened a plant near Bartlesville for extracting liquid by-products from natural gas. The by-products could be used in motor fuels. The company's research into the uses of natural gas received further impetus in 1926, when it won a patent infringement suit brought against it by Union Carbide over Phillips's process for separating hydrocarbon compounds.

Phillips prospered throughout its first decade. By 1927, it was pumping 55,000 barrels of oil a day from over 2,000 wells in Oklahoma and Texas. Its assets stood at $266 million, compared to the $3 million that it had when founded. The company also decided to enter the refining and marketing businesses in 1927, in response to automobile sales and as an outlet for its growing production. In 1927, it began operating a refinery near the Texas town of Borger. It also opened its first gas station, in Wichita, Kansas.

Phillips's entry into retailing presented it with the problem of finding a brand name under which to sell its gasoline. According to company lore, the solution presented itself as a Phillips official was returning to Bartlesville in a car that was road-testing the company's new gasoline. He commented that the car was going "like 60." The driver looked at the speedometer and replied, "Sixty nothing . . . we're doing 66!" The fact that the incident took place on Highway 66 near Tulsa only strengthened the story's appeal to Phillips's executives. The company chose Phillips 66 as its new brand name and retains it to this day.

In 1930 Phillips added to its refining and retailing capacities when it acquired Independent Oil & Gas Company, which was owned by Waite Phillips, another Phillips brother. The Great Depression hit the company early and hard. In 1931 Phillips posted a $5.7 million deficit in its first ever lossmaking year. As a consequence, it cut salaries and laid off hundreds of employees. Phillips stock plunged to $3 a share, down from $32. The company quickly regained its profitability, however, posting a modest surplus the next year.

Before the decade was out, Phillips would also make two personnel changes to help secure its future for the longer term. In 1932 a promising young executive named K.S. (Boots) Adams was promoted to assistant to president, Frank Phillips. Six years later, he succeeded Phillips as president when the company's founder assumed the post of chairman. Boots Adams—a boyhood nickname, inspired by his affection for a pair of red-topped boots—was 38 years old when he became president, and he and Phillips made rather an odd couple at the top of the chain of command. They often disagreed as to how the company should be run, but Phillips seems to have known that the future ultimately belonged to his protegé. "Mr. Phillips liked me, but not my ideas," Adams later recalled. "He said to me: "I'm going to object to everything you do, but you go ahead and do it anyway."

Phillips's strength in research and development paid off during World War II. In the late 1930s, the company developed new processes for producing butadiene and carbon black, two key ingredients in synthetic rubber, which became all the more crucial to the United States after Japanese conquests in Indonesia and Indochina cut off the supply of natural rubber in 1941. Phillips also developed high-octane aviation fuels, an early version of which powered British fighters in the Battle of Britain. The fuels were widely used by the Allied air forces.

In the years immediately following the war, Phillips began to reap in earnest the harvest of its research and commitment to natural gas. It generated substantial income by licensing its petrochemical patents to foreign companies. At home, the company was eminently positioned to take advantage of the sudden growth of cross-country pipelines in the 1940s and the consequent surge in natural gas prices. By the middle of the next decade, its reserves would total 13.3 trillion cubic feet, worth an estimated $931 million. Phillips also invested heavily in oil exploration, refining, natural gas drilling, and petrochemical plants. In 1948 it formed a new subsidiary, Phillips Chemical Company, and entered the fertilizer business when it began producing anhydrous ammonia.

While Phillips had the advantage over its competitors in natural gas and chemicals, it fell behind in the postwar foreign oil rush because of Frank Phillips's opposition to overseas ventures. Although his company had begun drilling in Venezuela in 1944, Phillips was determined to keep the company a mainly domestic enterprise and turned down the exclusive rights to the lucrative concession in the neutral zone between Saudi Arabia and Kuwait in 1947. The company eventually acquired a one-third stake in American Independent Oil, which took the Middle East concession, but it required all of Boots Adams's persuasive powers to get his boss to agree to it.

Frank Phillips died in 1950 and Adams, long his heir apparent, succeeded him as chairman and CEO. Under Adams, Phillips continued to focus on its interest in natural gas, and was the nation's largest producer in the 1950s. Its program of capital expansion was ambitious, with expenditure reaching a peak of $257 million in 1956. Phillips also began to break out of the constricting mold that its late founder had built for it. In 1952 the company started expanding its marketing network beyond the Midwest, opening Phillips 66 stations in Texas and Louisiana. Phillips continued to march through the deep South, then up the Atlantic seaboard, as far as it could extend its supply lines from its refineries. It was also becoming apparent that Frank Phillips had erred in refusing to develop overseas sources of oil, as the cost of finding and pumping crude in the United States increased. Finally, as the decade neared its end, Adams went on an around-the-world fact-finding trip. When he returned, he set a five-year timetable for expanding Phillips's international operations.

Phillips's practice of licensing its patents overseas without acquiring an interest in the new ventures had yielded royalties but no growth; so in 1960 the company took a 50% interest in a French carbon black plant using Phillips technology. Petrochemical joint ventures in Asia, Africa, Europe, and Latin America followed. Phillips also acquired drilling concessions in North Africa, the North Sea, New Guinea, Australia, and Iran. These foreign ventures were still not profitable when Boots Adams retired in 1964 and handed the reins to president Stanley Learned, but the company had begun to make up for lost time.

Under Learned, Phillips continued to diversify and expand. In 1964 it acquired packaging manufacturer Sealright Inc. as part of its move into plastics. Two years later, Learned himself broke ground on a petrochemical complex in Puerto Rico that would produce chemical raw materials, and motor fuels. Phillips also expanded its domestic oil operations. In 1960, it had tried to break into the California market by acquiring 15% of Union Oil Company of California, but litigation by Union Oil and the Justice Department prevented Phillips from pursuing a takeover; and in 1963 Phillips sold its stake to shipping magnate Daniel K. Ludwig. Instead, Phillips acquired the west coast properties of Tidewater Oil Company in 1966 for $309 million. The deal took four months to complete and required great secrecy. When the purchase was announced, the Justice Department filed an antitrust suit to dissolve it, but a U.S. District Court allowed the acquisition to stand, pending an appeal to the Supreme Court. By 1967 there were Phillips 66 stations in all 50 U.S. states.

Learned retired in 1967 and was succeeded as CEO by William Keeler. In addition to his career with Phillips, Keeler, who was half Cherokee, was named chief of the Cherokee nation by President Harry S Truman in 1949. Keeler used this position to campaign on behalf of Native American causes. Now he assumed responsibility for the eighth-largest oil company in the United States, and one in which some serious problems were beginning to manifest themselves. Foremost among these problems was dependence on outside sources of crude oil. For years, Phillips had not pumped enough to supply its refineries, so it had to buy crude from other producers. In 1969 Phillips made an unsuccessful offer to acquire Amerada Petroleum Corporation, a major crude producer with no marketing operations. Phillips was more successful with its new exploration strategy, under which it slowed considerably exploring onshore in the continental United States, the most thoroughly prospected area in the world, and concentrated on Alaska and overseas locations. This paid off in 1969, when Phillips discovered the massive Greater Ekofisk field under the Norwegian North Sea. Phillips joined with several European partners to develop the field. The discovery of a major field in Nigeria soon followed. In the early 1970s, Phillips joined with Standard Oil Company of New Jersey, now Exxon Corporation; Atlantic Richfield Company; Standard Oil Company of Ohio; Mobil Oil Corporation; Union Oil Company of California; and Amerada Hess Corporation to form Alyeska Pipeline Service Company. Alyeska would build the trans-Alaska pipeline, which allowed the exploitation of the massive deposits in Prudhoe Bay, Alaska.

During this time Phillips suffered from overexpansion and ailing chemical ventures. Some petrochemical projects fared badly because of falling propane and fertilizer prices. In plastics, Phillips found that it could not compete with smaller companies that had lower capital costs. Keeler addressed these problems by installing tighter controls on corporate planning. Phillips executives also found that having gas stations in all 50 states was no advantage when the company's presence in many markets was too small to ensure a profit. In 1973 Phillips divested most of its stations in the Northeast. A price war in California had drained the 3,000 stations acquired from Tidewater from the start, and it never made money; in 1973 the Supreme Court finally ordered Phillips to divest the Tidewater assets, and two years later the company sold most of its Pacific Coast properties to Oil Shale Corporation.

Keeler retired in 1973 and was succeeded as CEO by president William Martin. The remainder of the 1970s would be turbulent years for Phillips. In 1973 Phillips was one of the first and most prominent U.S. corporations to be accused of making an illegal contribution to President Richard Nixon's re-election campaign. Phillips pleaded guilty and admitted donating $100,000 illegally. Over the course of the next two years, Phillips would admit that the company had made illegal contributions to 65 congressional candidates in 1970 and 1972, as well as to Lyndon B. Johnson's 1964 presidential campaign and Nixon's 1968 campaign. The money came from a secret $1.35 million fund set up by Phillips executives for that purpose and channeled through a Swiss bank account. The company paid $30,000 in fines.

In 1975 the Los Angeles-based Center for Law in the Public Interest filed a class-action suit against Phillips on behalf of several small shareholders. In settling the lawsuit, the company agreed to give up the strong majority that its executives had always held on its board of directors. The board was reconstituted, with 9 of the 17 directors coming from outside the company.

In turn, these legal difficulties were followed by even greater disasters. In 1977, Phillips's Bravo platform in the Ekofisk field blew out during routine maintenance and spewed oil into the North Sea for eight days. Two years later, 123 people were killed when a floating hotel for Ekofisk workers capsized in a storm. Also in 1979, an explosion at Phillips's Borger, Texas, refinery injured 41 people. Meanwhile, William Keeler's strategy of exploring in foreign lands began to backfire as it produced more dry holes than reserves, while other oil companies were discovering new fields in the Rocky Mountains and in Louisiana.

William Martin retired in 1980 and was succeeded by William Douce. In 1982 Phillips's fortunes revived somewhat when a joint exploration venture with Chevron found substantial reserves under the Santa Maria Basin, off the coast of California. The company added even further to its crude supplies in the following year, when it acquired General American Oil Company, for $1.1 billion, stepping in as a white knight to thwart a takeover bid from Mesa LP. It would not be Phillips's last encounter with Mesa and its chairman, T. Boone Pickens Jr. In 1984 Phillips acquired Aminoil, Inc. and Geysers Geothermal Company from R.J. Reynolds Industries for about $1.7 billion. Observers noted that the deal made Phillips, now the subject of takeover rumors, a less attractive buyout candidate because of the debt it would have to assume.

The takeover rumors became reality early in December 1984, when Pickens announced that his company had acquired 5.7% of Phillips's stock and intended to try for a majority stake. Douce, though scheduled to retire shortly, had prepared for such an event and was determined to fight. "Boone Busters" T-shirts appeared in Bartlesville, which feared for its life should Phillips ever be taken from it, and the company launched a barrage of lawsuits. One suit charged that Mesa was violating a pact it had signed before withdrawing its bid for General American Oil, in which it promised never again to attempt to take that company over. When the dust cleared a month later, Phillips had driven Pickens away and preserved its independence, but Phillips agreed to buy out Mesa's holdings as part of a restructuring that would ultimately cost $4.5 billion, loading itself with debt and requiring the disposal of $2 billion's worth of assets. For his part, Pickens conducted an orderly retreat laden with spoils—$75 million in pretax profits plus an additional $25 million to cover his expenses.

No sooner had Pickens left the field, however, when other attacks began. In January and February 1985, financiers Irwin Jacobs, Ivan Boesky, and Carl Icahn all bought up large blocks of Phillips stock. Then, on February 12, Icahn struck, launch-

ing a $4.2 billion offer to buy 45% of the company. Combined with the 5% he already owned, this would give Icahn a controlling stake. In early March, faced with shareholders willing to sell to Icahn owing to dissatisfaction with the Pickens deal, Phillips executives came up with a plan to exchange debt securities for half of its outstanding stock, including Icahn's 5%, at $62 per share, compared to the $53 per share it had paid Pickens. Icahn accepted and he, too, left with his spoils.

The task of rebuilding the battered company was left to C.J. (Pete) Silas, who succeeded William Douce as chairman in May 1985. Under Silas, Phillips sold off the necessary $2 billion's worth of assets within 18 months of Icahn's repulse. Among those to go were Aminoil and Geyser Geothermal. The company also cut 9,000 jobs by 1989. As a result of its forced restructuring, Phillips gave up becoming an integrated, worldwide energy company, and refocused on its core oil and gas businesses. In the late 1980s, unexpectedly strong earnings from its petrochemical businesses more than offset the effect of lower oil prices and raised hopes for Phillips's long-term recovery.

These hopes received a setback in October 1989, however, when an explosion occurred at Phillips's plastics plant in Pasadena, Texas, killing 23 people and causing $500 million in damage. The disaster temporarily eliminated Phillips's U.S. capacity to manufacture polyethylene, which is used to make blow-molded containers and other products. In 1991 Phillips still had $3.9 billion in debt from its battles with corporate raiders. It may want to retain a certain debt burden to deter further takeover attempts however, the new, lean Phillips may be a shadow of its former vigorous self, and may be lacking the ambition it showed in the post–World War II period, but not many of its competitors are riding as high as they used to.

Principal Subsidiaries: N.V. Phillips Petroleum Chemicals S.A. (Belgium); Phillips 66 Co.; Phillips 66 Natural Gas Co.; Phillips Driscopipe, Inc.; Phillips Fibers Corp.; Phillips Petroleum Co. Europe-Africa; Phillips Petroleum Co. (Norway); Phillips Pipe Line Co.; Phillips Puerto Rico Core Inc.; Philtankers Inc. (Liberia); Phillips Petroleum Co. (UK) Ltd. Provesta Corp.

Further Reading: "Phillips Aims at 'Built-in Value,'" *Business Week,* June 27, 1959; "Phillips Petroleum: Laying the Groundwork," *Forbes,* February 1, 1965; "How they won the West—and more," *Business Week,* January 28, 1967; *Phillips: The first 66 Years,* Bartlesville, Oklahoma, Phillips Petroleum Company, 1983; Wallis, Michael, *Oil Man—The Story of Frank Phillips and the Birth of Phillips Petroleum,* Doubleday, N.Y., 1988; Vogel, Todd, "Phillips Climbs Up from the Bottom of the Barrel," *Business Week,* January 16, 1989; "Phillips Petroleum—a Brief History," Phillips corporate typescript, [n.d.].

—Douglas Sun

QATAR GENERAL PETROLEUM CORPORATION

Post Office Box 3212
Doha
Qatar
491491
Fax: 831125

State-Owned Company
Incorporated: 1974

The transformation of Qatar from a nomadic society, largely dependent on pearl trading, into a modern, urban state, with living standards that are among the world's highest, is the direct result of the development of the Qatari oil industry. Even at the beginning of the 1990s, despite intense efforts to diversify its economy, the Qatari government remains dependent on the fortunes of the oil sector, and on the Qatar General Petroleum Corporation (QGPC) in particular. Oil revenues contribute more than 90% of government and export revenues, and the oil surplus of the mid-1980s and the accompanying decline in oil prices resulted in a fall in national income of almost 20% in 1986.

Until the mid-1970s, the hydrocarbon industry was largely in the hands of foreign companies. In 1974, the QGPC was established with the objective of gaining full control of the country's oil and gas resources for the state. This goal was quickly realized. QGPC's operations cover the whole range of oil and gas activity from exploration and production to downstream refining and fertilizer and petrochemical production, through key subsidiaries and joint ventures. Current priorities include the use of enhanced oil recovery methods to maintain production at current levels for the rest of the century, and the development of the massive North gas field on which the hopes for Qatar's future prosperity are pinned.

After World War I and the collapse of the Ottoman Empire, Qatar fell within the British sphere of influence and the first onshore oil concession in Qatar was awarded in 1935 to British Petroleum's predecessor, the Anglo-Persian Oil Company (APOC). APOC created a subsidiary, Petroleum Development (Qatar) Ltd. (PDL), to operate the concession. PDL was later renamed the Qatar Petroleum Company (QPC). The first well, Dukhan Number 1, was drilled in 1939. The outbreak of World War II delayed further work until 1947 and the first crude oil exports only took place in 1949. The Dukhan field remains Qatar's sole onshore oil field, and accounts for about half of Qatar's total oil production.

The first offshore concessions were granted in 1949 to two U.S. companies, the Superior Oil Company and the Central Mining and Investment Corporation. However, their exploration efforts were unsuccessful, and their concessionary rights were quickly surrendered. In 1952, the Shell Company-Qatar (SCQ) acquired exploration rights to most of Qatar's offshore territory and began an extensive exploration program. In 1960, the fields of Idd Al-Shargi and Maydan Mahzam were discovered. Commercial exploitation began a few years later. The largest offshore field, Bul Hanine, was discovered in 1970 and came onstream in 1972. Qatar also has a 50% share with Abu Dhabi in the offshore Al-Bunduq oil field.

It was against the background of the 1973 oil price shock, when the 13 members of OPEC sought to increase their power relative to that of the oil majors, that the Qatar General Petroleum Corporation came into being. The formation of QGPC became necessary following the government's decision to assume full control of the country's oil industry. In 1973, the state took a 25% stake in the onshore concessions of QPC and the offshore concessions of SCQ. Early in 1974, the year of QCPC's formation, the state increased its share in both companies to 60%. In 1976, QGPC took total control of QPC's onshore concessions and took similar action in relation to SCQ's offshore activities the following year.

Although a state company, QGPC—in terms of the composition of the board of directors—resembles a family firm. Half of the current eight-member board is composed of members of the ruling al-Thani family. The first—and so far only—chairman of QGPC is Sheikh Abdulaziz bin Khalifa al-Thani, minister of finance and petroleum and second son of the Emir of Qatar, Sheikh Khalifa bin Hamad al-Thani. In 1989 Qatar's Council of Ministers underwent a substantial transformation when several of the older members were retired and new ones, largely from the 1,500-strong male side of the al-Thani family, were introduced into the government. Sheikh Khalifa's position, however, was unchallenged.

QGPC's activities cover not only exploration for and production of crude oil but all aspects of hydrocarbon activity. Refining of crude oil is carried out by the National Oil Distribution Company (NODCO), a wholly owned subsidiary of QGPC established in 1968. Qatar's first refinery was built in Umm Said in 1953. A second refinery was completed in 1974. At this stage refining capacity was about 12,000 barrels per day and the output went to meet domestic demand. By the early 1980s, growth in local consumption was such that Qatar began to import refined products. At the end of 1983, a new 50,000-barrel-per-day refinery came into operation at Umm Said. The refinery's output was more than sufficient to meet local needs and left a substantial amount for export. Work is underway to build a unit to facilitate the production of unleaded gasoline, and NODCO is examining other ways to expand and upgrade the refinery facilities further.

The gas activities of QGPC have become increasingly important, not only to the company but also to Qatar itself, as it strives to diversify its economy away from crude oil and build up a heavy industrial base. The North gas field was discovered in 1971. Although its significance was not immediately apparent, subsequent drilling revealed the field to be the world's largest known offshore non-associated gas field. The discovery of the North field may enable QGPC to remain a major hydrocarbon producer for the next 200 years. By contrast, oil reserves, at current production levels of almost 400,000 barrels of oil a day, will last for less than 30 years. Consequently, the emphasis of QGPC's development has shifted from crude oil to natural gas.

Gas is not a new product in QGPC's portfolio. Gas associated with oil production and non-associated gas from the Cap and Khuff fields, which lie underneath the Dukhan field, has played an important part in Qatar's industrialization process. Initially, this involved steel, cement, fertilizers, and petrochemicals. Water desalination and power generation have also been major outlets for gas production.

Gas is the key feedstock for the Qatar Fertiliser Company (QAFCO) which was established by the government in 1969. The government's shares were transferred in 1974 to QGPC, which still holds 75% of the shares: the remaining 25% are in the hands of Norsk Hydro of Norway. QAFCO plans to double its capacity to take advantage of the greater availability of gas from the North field project.

Qatar was the first Arabian Gulf state to build up its own petrochemical industry. The Qatar Petrochemical Company (QAPCO) was established in 1974 as a joint venture between QGPC (84%) and CdF (Chimie de France) and began production of ethylene, low density polyethylene, and sulfur in 1981. In August 1990, QGPC's interest in QAPCO was reduced to 80%, with the remaining 20% split equally between Enimont of Italy, and Elf Aquitaine of France through its Atochem subsidiary.

The importance of reliable gas supplies was demonstrated in the early years of QAPCO, which were marred by shortages of ethane feedstock arising as the result of the fluctuations of associated gas production along with the movements of the oil price. Like QAFCO, QAPCO is seeking to expand its capacity significantly in line with the increase in gas production.

With falling oil production, and therefore falling associated gas production, as well as the depletion of the Khuff reserves, it became imperative to develop the North field. The decision to go ahead was taken in 1984 and it was decided that development would take place in phases. Phase one involves the installation of production, processing, and transport facilities for 800 million cubic feet of gas per day to serve local industry and utilities. The project will also produce 5,000 tons per day of liquid products, such as propane, butane, gasoline, and naphtha, most of which will be exported. A third gas processing plant, NGL-3, is also under construction. It was announced in 1989 that a gas sweetening plant and a further sulfur processing unit would also be added to improve the environmental acceptability of the gas. Phase one was expected to be in full operation by early 1991. The exact nature of—and timetable for—phases two and three are uncertain. Phase two was widely expected to involve the sale of North Field gas to its neighbors, possibly through the development of a Gulf Cooperation Council (GCC) gas grid.

Phase three involves the sale of North field gas to markets in Europe and the Far East. In the mid-1980s, the Qatar LNG Company Ltd. (Qatergas) was established to manage, operate, market, and export liquefied natural gas (LNG) from the North Field. Initially, QGPC held a 77.5% stake in Qatargas, but this was subseqently reduced to 70%. Foreign investors include BP, Total CFP of France, and Marubeni and Mitsui from Japan. This venture calls for a worldscale LNG plant and a fleet of seven LNG carriers.

Even before the Persian Gulf crisis, this part of the project had run into trouble. In order to justify the necessary investment, estimated by some to be as high as US$4 billion, Qatargas needed two large-scale long-term supply contracts, beginning at the end of the 1990s. Despite the globetrotting of QGPC managing director Jaber al-Marri, these contracts have not been forthcoming. Fears about the gulf situation have also caused these potential customers to look elsewhere for new supplies.

The uncertain fate of phases two and three has switched the emphasis towards finding more domestic outlets for North Field Gas. This would have been necessary in any case, as domestic gas demand would only account for about two-thirds of the gas from phase one. In 1988, a firm of international consultants presented a plan to QGPC for the development of domestic projects to utilize Qatari gas. Suggestions included an aluminum smelter, a ferro-alloy production plant, methanol production facilities, and the expansion of the petrochemical and fertilizer operations. Although discussions with international partners have taken place, progress on these projects has been slow.

The virtual certainty that gas will not be able to substitute for falling oil production within a ten-year time span has resulted in a greater concentration on the oil side of QGPC's business. Hitches in gas plans mean that, contrary to expectation of the mid-to-late 1980s, oil will still be the main source of QGPC income at the end of the century.

QGPC has initiated a program to expand and upgrade its oil production facilities in a bid to maintain production at current levels. Without further action, offshore production is expected to fall to a quarter of 1990 levels by the mid-1990s. Production levels will be maintained by bringing the Diyab structure of the Dukhan field into production and by using enhanced recovery techniques, both onshore and offshore.

Qatar has been thoroughly explored and the prospects for the expansion of production via new commercial discoveries are believed to be limited. QGPC itself carried out much exploration activity during the early 1980s but exploration fell back drastically as the oil glut of the mid-1980s gathered pace. Since then, QGPC has encouraged foreign operators to apply for exploration licenses for Qatari territory. BP's subsidiary BP America, Elf, and Amoco have participated in exploration activity. Although the number of wells drilled picked up significantly towards the end of the 1980s, there has been little success so far. The most promising area for exploration includes islands which are the source of a territorial dispute with Bahrain, but this area is likely to remain untouched until a political settlement has been reached.

QGPC entered the last decade of the 20th century with several question marks hanging over it. Qatar's oil reserves and production are modest by gulf standards, but a large investment effort is still needed to maintain oil production at current levels. The prospects for development of the North Field, which has long been regarded as QGPC's and Qatar's chief source of income for the next two centuries, are uncertain. This uncertainty has been compounded, not only by Iraq's invasion of Kuwait and the perceived general instability of the region, but also by statements from Iranian officials since the end of the Iran-Iraq War, laying claim to a significant share of the gas from the field. QGPC has not shown itself to be unduly concerned, but the warning signs are there.

Principal Subsidiaries: National Oil Distribution Company; Qatar Petrochemical Company (80%); Qatar Liquefied Natural Gas Company (70%); Qatar Fertiliser Company (75%).

Further Reading: al-Othman, Wasser, *With Their Bare Hands: The Story of The Oil Industry in Qatar,* Harlow, Longman, 1984; El Mallakh, Raqaei, *Qatar Energy and Development,* London, Croom Helm, 1985; Zahlan, R.S., *The Making of the Modern Gulf States: Kuwait, Bahrain, Qatar, UAE and Oman,* London, Unwin Hyman, 1989; Cranfield, John, "North Field Moves Ahead," *Petroleum Economist,* January 1990; *Financial Times Survey on Qatar,* February 22, 1990; Ellis, Neville, "Qatari Catastrophe," *Petroleum Economist,* September 1990; *Meed Special Report on Qatar,* October 26, 1990; Crystal, Jill, *Oil and Politics in the Gulf: Rulers and Merchants in Qatar and Kuwait,* Cambridge, Cambridge University Press, 1990; "Qatar: A MEED Practical Guide," MEED, all editions.

—Debra Johnson

REPSOL SA

Paseo de la Castellana 89
28046 Madrid
Spain
(341) 348-8100
Fax: (341) 555-7671

Public Company
Incorporated: 1987
Employees: 21,000
Sales: Pta1.57 trillion (US$16.43 billion)
Stock Exchanges: Madrid New York London Tokyo

Repsol, the largest oil company in Spain and the seventh largest oil company in Europe, was formed in 1987 by the merger of state-controlled oil sector companies. Two years later, Repsol made international headlines when it underwent a US$1 billion, 26% partial privatization, the largest in Spain's history. The company is 66% state owned. Repsol is Spain's first integrated international company in a national oil industry that, although dating back centuries, was relatively small and unimportant until recent times.

In 1539, the Spanish ship *Santa Cruz* transported the first transatlantic oil shipment when it carried a barrel from Venezuela to Spain. It was thought the dark fluid had properties to relieve the gout of King Charles I. History does not record whether he found it to be an effective remedy.

State monopoly and control, a characteristic that persisted in the Spanish industry, was established at the end of the 18th century when King Charles III declared all mining deposits, whether they were of a commercial character or not, to be the property of the crown. Only the crown would have the right to grant exploration or development concessions.

As 19th and 20th century Spain fell into a long period of decline and lagged behind the rest of Europe in industrial development, the country failed to develop a strong domestic oil industry. By the mid-1920s only a few unsuccessful attempts at oil exploration had taken place. No refineries were built. The country was heavily dependent on imported foreign oil, supplied by Shell and other major multinationals and distributed through an inadequate and fragmented network.

Spain was forced to spend valuable foreign exchange to import expensive refined oil. The corrupt dictatorship of Primo de Rivera, which governed the country between 1923 and 1930, realized that this state of affairs could not continue if Spain were to industrialize. The problem haunted successive Spanish governments and later it became more important as living standards and the number of motor vehicles rose in the period of rapid economic growth that followed World War II. By 1980, 65% of Spain's oil was still imported. Rivera's solution was to return to the tradition of state monopoly, a policy that was followed in modified forms by all successive Spanish governments up to 1986. In 1927, the dictator issued a decree expropriating all foreign and domestic oil sector companies and placing them under the control of a state agency. Administration was entrusted to Compañía Arrendataria del Monopolio de Pétroleos Sociedad Anónima (CAMPSA), which had the sole rights to purchase oil from producers at state-controlled prices.

Ironically, the country's first refinery was built in the Canary Islands by Compañía Española de Petróleos S.A. (CEPSA), a private company, in 1930. The islands had been specifically excluded from the decree. Today CEPSA remains the only important all-private Spanish oil company. Three state-owned refineries were built prior to the disruptions of the 1936–1939 Spanish civil war and the Franco dictatorship's diplomatic isolation and armed neutrality during World War II.

In July 1941, CAMPSA undertook the country's first major exploration, the "Tudanca" survey of the northern Burgos region, with negative results. Foreign exchange pressures and CAMPSA's continued failure to discover oil on Spanish territory led the Franco regime to relax rules on foreign participation.

A 1947 law left CAMPSA in control of marketing and distribution, but enabled the government to authorize private and public companies to develop a wide range of activities in trade, industrial handling—especially refining—storage, research, and exploration for production of oil and gas fields.

In practice, the government usually required foreign companies to work under joint participation schemes with CAMPSA or other state-controlled entities. A requirement that both private and public refineries had to sell to CAMPSA continued, and in 1957 it was extended to gassified petroleum products.

In 1963, the government announced the National Combustibles Plan and it asserted direct control of sales, imports, and production of oil products. The government would determine each refinery's contribution to the national supply. Each refinery had to offer its product to CAMPSA, which then sold to consumers through its monopoly distribution network. To protect the balance of payments, refineries had to purchase a set percentage of their crude requirements from the Spanish government. This was known as the "Government Quote" and reached a height of 50% in 1980, then declined until it was removed in 1985.

After 169 wildcat failures, an association of Caltex and CAMPSA made the first discovery of oil in the "la Lora" concession and produced small amounts of low-grade crude oil in 1964. In 1965 offshore drilling began, and ten years later joint ventures discovered substantial quantities off the Mediterranean coast. By the early 1990s five offshore producing fields were in operation.

The rapid expansion of the Spanish economy created a 15% increase in annual oil consumption. In 1965, the government founded Hispanica de Petróleos (Hispanoil) as a state-owned company charged with spearheading exploration and development efforts in Spain and elsewhere.

When the share of imported crude reached 73% of the country's total supply share in 1973, the government initiated a policy of encouraging more foreign participation to build refineries. It hoped to offset the costs of imported crude with exports of refined products. Shortly afterward, it attempted to cushion the shock of the first Arab oil boycott and OPEC-induced price rises by lowering taxes on products, with the result that only some of the costs were passed on to consumers.

In June 1974, the government announced the merger of the three refineries in which the state had a controlling interest: REPESA, ENCASO, and ENTASA. The state retained 72% of the shares. The new company, Empresa Nacional del Petróleo (ENPETROL) was also given the task of coordinating efforts to secure crude supplies through direct bargaining with producing states. An attempt to develop the First National Energy Plan was soon abandoned in 1976 and the country was without a coordinated energy plan until 1979. Authority for the use and production of energy was dispersed among different agencies, departments, and public companies.

Francisco Franco died in 1975 and Spain passed into a new democratic era. In October 1977, the Spanish government and political leaders, both opposition signed the Pacts of Moncloa, which attempted to establish a consensus for political and economic change. Included were provisions for the reorganization of the energy sector.

The Second National Energy Plan, introduced in July 1979, laid the groundwork for the formation of Repsol. According to the plan, a reorganization of public entities was required because exploration had failed to develop. The structure of the industry was fragmented and lacked vertical integration. CAMPSA, the Spanish banks, and the Department of Finance continued to resist moves toward integration. However, the second oil crisis and moves toward joining the European Community (EC) forced the logic of integration and the creation of Instituto Nacional de Hidrocarboros (INH), Repsol's direct predecessor. On December 18, 1981, all public participations in the oil sector were brought together in one holding company: INH. Minority foreign shareholders in Spanish public oil companies were gradually bought out.

During the 1983–1986 negotiations for Spain's entry to the EC, it became increasingly clear that Spain would have to dismantle its formal government monopoly in marketing. CAMPSA shares were split among the refineries, with INH retaining the majority of the shares. Negotiators hoped to avoid a situation in which the EC would require CAMPSA to offer its distribution network and services to every interested foreign company. The refineries agreed to continue to sell products destined for the domestic market to CAMPSA.

In 1985, Hispanoil took over ENIEPSA, a public company formed in 1976 to engage in exploration. Shortly afterward, INH was reorganized into a divisional structure: Hispanoil exploration, Enpetrol refining, Alcudia petrochemicals, Butano liquefied petroleum gas, and Enagas natural gas distribution. In September 1987, all these divisions, except Enagas, were incorporated into the new Repsol, a company then 100%-owned by the Spanish state. The name Repsol, formerly a trademark for lubrication products, was chosen after extensive marketing research because it was short, widely recognized in Spain, and easy to pronounce in other languages. It was envisaged that Enagas would be added to Repsol at some future point. The time was not yet appropriate because it had an

ambitious investment program, which would generate insufficient immediate returns. Otherwise, Repsol retained the INH divisional structure but Hispanoil became Repsol Exploracion, Enpetrol was renamed Repsol Petróleo, Alcudia became Repsol Quimica and Butano became Repsol Butano.

In 1986 Spain joined the EC under a phased plan to enable the country's protected industries, including the oil industry, to adapt to EC regulations. With the creation of Repsol, the government hoped to create an integrated national oil company that would be able to compete successfully in the post-1992 single European market. By changing the structure from that of a government agency to a company in which the government retained a majority stake through INH, an arm's length relationship was established that might satisfy critics of the Spanish government's close involvement with its oil industry. The INH also wanted to have a strong domestic oil company able to develop an overall strategy including exploration, production, refining, and distribution.

The EC Commission was reluctant to accept Repsol's dominant role in CAMPSA because Article 37 of the Treaty of Rome declared that member states should adjust commercial monopolies to the extent that all discrimination in trade between citizens of member states disappeared. Also, Article 48 of Spain's treaty of adhesion to the EC required Spain to open up its frontiers to the importation of oil products originating from the EC. In December 1987, the EC Commission warned Spain that it would be taken to the European Court if it did not take further steps to liberalize the market.

A decision had already been made to sell 26% of Repsol to the public, both in Spain and abroad. Repsol and the government were impressed with similar privatizations in the United Kingdom. It was believed that a partial flotation would not only raise money and make it easier for the company to secure private sector finance, but that it would also introduce a private sector discipline and increase the international stature of the company. INH would continue to hold a two-thirds share to ensure government control.

The May 1989 share issue, on the Madrid and New York stock markets simultaneously, was successful beyond expectations. The initial offering of 40 million shares was heavily oversubscribed and a further issue equivalent to 10% of the original had to be made. Overall, the equivalent of US$1 billion was raised and the company had 400,000 new shareholders. The issues were so attractive that at least three brokerage firms were later successfully prosecuted for irregularities in the flotation by the Comision Nacional de Valores (CNV), the Spanish stock market supervisory body.

At the beginning of 1989, Repsol acquired the Naviera Vizcaina shipping company to increase its own marine fleet and avoid rising charter rates. Later that year, Repsol took over the 34% interest of Petróleos Mexicanos (Pemex), the Mexican state oil company, in the Spanish Petronor refinery company in exchange for a 3% interest in Repsol. The deal included a five-year supply contract by Pemex and envisaged cooperative ventures in Mexico. It brought Repsol to a holding of 90% in Petronor and 70% in CAMPSA.

By 1990, Spain still had only 5,000 service stations. The United Kingdom, by comparison, had 20,000. Foreign companies had only opened 7 in Spain, and Repsol's Spanish competitors had opened only 180. In November 1989 Sir Leon Brittan, the EC Competition Commissioner, attacked Spain for failure to open markets in heating oils and liquefied petroleum gas (LPG). With 13 million customers, the subsidiary Repsol Butano has 100% of Europe's largest market for butane. However, prices for liquefied petroleum gas are soon to liberalized.

Sir Leon warned that the commission would keep a close watch on Spanish interpretations of recent regulations, the dominant position of Repsol in CAMPSA, and the slow development of independent outlets. He said the commission would reexamine a possible court action against Spain if the Spanish market were not fully opened up to foreign competitors.

In 1991 Repsol refines more than 60% of all the crude processed in Spain, distributes all liquefied petroleum gas and produces half the petrochemical and oil products. Partially in response to EC criticism, Repsol and the other CAMPSA shareholders decided that CAMPSA's service stations and some other retail assets would be divided between Repsol and the CAMPSA minority shareholders such as CEPSA, by mid-1991. Repsol is taking over the service station brand name CAMPSA but it will also use Repsol and Repshop. CAMPSA will continue as a distribution and transportation company, with Repsol in control of the majority of the shares.

As market liberalization continues, Repsol is expected to lose some of its huge market share in the domestic Spanish market. Outside Spain, one identified weakness is the company's relative lack of downstream activities, aside from distribution agreements with Agip and Elf Aquitaine, although recently the company has reinforced its presence in the United Kingdom and Portugal. Analysts have identified another major weakness, in its limited crude reserves.

Analysts have called Spain the fastest-growing oil products market in Europe. It is widely viewed as underpumped in comparison with the competitive, thick networks of service stations found in most other European countries. Shell would like to set up a national distribution network and Texaco, Total, and Agip want to expand into specific geographic areas of the country.

In response to growing competition, Repsol has pursued an increasingly international strategy of seeking both sources of crude and markets for its products abroad. The company successfully discovered oil in the North Sea, Colombia, Angola, and Egypt and has been awarded new exploration areas in Argentina, Angola, Algeria, Dubai, Egypt, and Vietnam. In 1990, it began explorations in Soviet Turkmenistan and agreed to explore in other Soviet areas in cooperation with Total and Petrofina.

In August 1989, Repsol purchased Carless Refining & Marketing and Carless Petroleum from Kelt Energy, the U.K. oil independent. Repsol intends to develop a market for its products in the United Kingdom through the Carless chain of service stations.

Repsol has shown considerable resilience in the face of generally difficult conditions in the oil industry. Its 1990 pretax profits rose 4.2% to 105.5 billion pesetas. As Spain's largest industrial concern, Repsol is fulfilling the Spanish government's hopes of establishing a strong domestic oil company to protect the Spanish oil industry from foreign multinational control in the post-1992 single European market. It still faces the challenges of increased competition in home and international markets, and continued EC scrutiny of its efforts to move beyond its origins in a government-protected monopoly.

Principal Subsidiaries: Repsol Petróleo; Repsol Exploración; Repsol Quimica; Repsol Butano; Petronor (90%); CAMPSA (70%).

Further Reading: Santamaria, Javier, *El petroleo en Espana del monopolio a la libertad,* Madrid, Espasa Calpe, 1988; Correlje, Dr A.F., *The Liberalization of the Spanish Oil Sector: Strategies for a Competitive Future,* Rotterdam, The Centre For Policy Studies, Erasmus University, 1990.

—Clark Siewert

ROYAL DUTCH PETROLEUM COMPANY

THE "SHELL" TRANSPORT AND TRADING COMPANY P.L.C.

The Hague
The Netherlands
(70) 377 9111
Fax: (70) 377 4848

Shell Centre
London SE1 7NA
United Kingdom
(071) 934 1234
Fax: (071) 934 8060

Public Company
Incorporated: 1890 as Koninklijke Nederlandsche Maatschappig Tot Exploitatie van Petroleumbronnen in Nederlandsch-indie and 1897
Employees: 137,000
Sales: £59.41 billion (US$114.67 billion)
Stock Exchanges: London New York Paris Frankfurt Brussels Zürich Luxembourg Vienna

The Royal Dutch/Shell Group forms one of the world's largest businesses. It has a complex corporate organization which consists of more than 2,000 companies worldwide ultimately controlled by two parent companies. The "Shell" Transport and Trading Company, a U.K.-registered company, has a 40% interest in the group, and the remaining 60% is owned by the Royal Dutch Petroleum Company, a Netherlands company. Collectively, the group is involved in oil and gas exploration, production, refining, transportation, and marketing. It has large interests in chemicals—it was probably the world's ninth, largest chemicals business in the late 1980s—and diversified activities in coal and metal mining, forestry, solar energy, and biotechnology.

The Royal Dutch/Shell Group was formed in 1907 when a merging of the interests of Royal Dutch and Shell Transport took place, in which each company retained its separate identity. Royal Dutch was established in The Hague in 1890 after receiving a concession to drill for oil in Sumatra, in the Dutch East Indies. It had the support of King William III, hence the name Royal Dutch. The promoters of this venture had found

oil in 1885, but needed funds to exploit their discovery. In the early years the firm was under the energetic direction of J.B. August Kessler under whom, in 1892, it exported its first oil. In 1896 a 30-year-old bookkeeper, Henri Deterding, joined the company and in 1901 he became its chief executive. The predominant use for petroleum in the late 19th century was as paraffin or kerosene, which was used for heating and lighting. However, Sumatra's oil was particularly rich in gasoline, the product used by the internal combustion engine, and it was therefore well placed to take advantage of the growth in demand for oil which the motor car was to bring.

Deterding was one of the great entrepreneurial figures of the 20th century. He combined remarkable strategic vision with acute financial awareness born of his early training as a bookkeeper. His ambition was to build a company to rival the world's largest oil enterprise, John D. Rockefeller's Standard Oil Company of the United States. Deterding preferred to achieve this ambition through alliances and agreements rather than competition. In 1903, as part of this strategy, he formed a marketing company, the Asiatic Petroleum Company, owned jointly by Royal Dutch, Shell, and the Paris branch of the Rothschild family, the latter of which had substantial Russian production interests. A crucial intermediary figure in making this alliance was Fred Lane, who had been one of the original directors of Shell Transport, but who had become closely identified with the Paris Rothschilds and, by the early 1900s, with Deterding.

The "Shell" Transport and Trading Company's origins lay in the activities of a London merchant, Marcus Samuel, who began his career in the 1830s selling boxes made from shells brought from the East. The business gradually expanded the number of commodities in which it traded. When Marcus Samuel Sr. died in 1870, his son Marcus continued to be involved in far eastern trade. In 1878 he established with his brother Samuel, a partnership known as Marcus Samuel & Co. in London, and Samuel Samuel & Co. in Japan, which became a leading shipping and trading enterprise in the Far East. During the 1880s the Samuels, through intermediary Fred Lane, began selling the Russian oil of the Rothschilds to the Far East, breaking the monopoly previously held by Standard Oil. In 1892 the Suez Canal Company was persuaded to allow oil tankers to pass through the canal, which lowered the cost of Russian oil in the Far East, and allowed Samuel to increase rapidly its market share. Later in the 1890s fears that Russian supplies might be reduced led Samuel to search for a secure source of oil nearer his Far Eastern markets, and in 1898 a major oil field was discovered in Dutch Borneo, a year after the launch of "Shell" Transport and Trading Ltd.

Shell Transport grew rapidly. By 1900 the company possessed oil fields and a refinery in Borneo and a fleet of oil tankers. However, Marcus Samuel was above all a merchant, lacking organizational skills and ignorant of the technicalities of the oil business. After 1900 he lost interest in the details of the business, and in 1902 became lord mayor of London. By the early 1900s Shell Transport had made a series of costly mistakes, including a disastrous involvement with Texas oil. When Texaco hit a large oil gusher in 1901, Samuel agreed to buy the oil. The flow of oil was not continuous and stopped altogether in the summer of 1902. The formation of the Asiatic Petroleum Company left Deterding in control of Shell's sales in the East. By 1906 Shell's financial situation was so bad that

Deterding was able to impose his own terms for a merger of the two concerns, with the Dutch holding 60% of what came to be know as the group.

The combined group expanded rapidly under Deterding's leadership. The total assets of Royal Dutch and Shell Transport grew by more than two and a half times between 1907 and 1914. Major production interests were acquired in Russia in 1910 and Venezuela in 1913. The group also moved into Standard Oil's homeland. In 1912 the Roxana Petroleum Company was formed to operate in Oklahoma, and in 1913 a U.K. oil company, California Oilfields, Ltd., was acquired. By 1915 the group was producing nearly six million barrels of crude oil a year in the United States.

World War I brought mixed fortunes for the group. Its properties in Romania were destroyed, and those in Russia were confiscated after the Russian Revolution in 1917. Shell's exploitation of the Venezuelan oil fields was delayed until late in the war due to difficulties in importing equipment. Shell's cosmopolitan structure was also held in suspicion by some civil servants and ministers within the U.K. government, who feared that it was pro-German and engaged in supplying oil to the enemy through subsidiaries in neutral countries. Various proposals were made by civil servants and several businessmen to merge the group with the Anglo-Persian Oil Company, Burmah Oil, or other U.K. interests in order to make it truly British. However, these wartime proposals were unsuccessful, and regardless of its mixed ownership, the group played an important role in the Allied war effort. In 1919 an agreement was initialled by Deterding and a representative of the U.K. government that provided for an internal rearrangement of the group to allow U.K. interests majority control, but the agreement was never implemented, chiefly because of the delays caused by incoherence and confusion in the official U.K. oil policy of the period. Royal Dutch retained the larger interest in the group.

The 1920s were a decade of growth. In 1919 Shell purchased the large Mexican oil fields controlled by the U.K. oil company Mexican Eagle, led by Lord Cowdray. In 1920 a marketing company was set up in the United Kingdom, Shell-Mex, which represented the Shell and Mexican Eagle interests. Venezuelan oil production expanded very rapidly, much of it controlled by Shell. In 1922 the Shell Union Oil Corporation was formed in the United States to consolidate Shell interests there with those of the Union Oil Company of Delaware, and the American business increased rapidly. By 1929 its U.S. activities had spread to the Atlantic Coast. This decade also saw the first steps in product diversification. In 1929 a new company, N.V. Mekog, was established in the Netherlands to produce nitrogeneous fertilizer from coke-oven gases. This was the group's first venture into chemicals. In the same year the Shell Chemical Company was formed in the United States to produce nitrogeneous fertilizer from natural gas.

The Depression years brought problems. From the late 1920s there was a chronic problem of overcapacity in the oil industry. Deterding's response was to form a worldwide cartel, and in 1928 he organized a meeting in a Scottish castle at Achnacarry with the heads of Standard Oil of New Jersey and the Anglo-Persian Oil Company to achieve this goal. The Achnacarry agreement became an infamous example of cartel exploitation in oil industry mythology, but the large oil companies were actually unable to control all sources of supply in the world. Achnacarry and subsequent cartel agreements did not last long. The group's oil interests in Mexico were nationalized in 1938—an early warning of later problems in developing countries. Meanwhile Deterding's leadership of the group became suspect. Some managers felt that his leadership style had become very erratic. After his marriage to a German woman in 1936, he resigned as general managing director of Royal Dutch and went to live in Germany.

During World War II and the invasion of the Netherlands, the head offices of the Dutch companies moved to Curaçao in the Dutch West Indies. Once again, Shell played a major role in the Allied war effort. The refineries in the United States produced large quantities of high octane aviation fuel, while the Shell Chemical Company manufactured butadiene for synthetic rubber. All of the group's tankers were placed under U.K. government control, and 87 Shell ships were lost in enemy action.

The 1950s and 1960s were golden years of growth for oil companies, as demand for petroleum products expanded. The Shell group and the other "seven sisters" of leading international oil companies—Shell, British Petroleum, Exxon, Texaco, Chevron, Mobil, and Gulf— retained a strong hold over petroleum production and marketing. The group supplied nearly one-seventh of the world's oil products in these decades. After Deterding's departure, the group was run on a committee basis with no single dominant personality. A stable and respectable image was projected, symbolized by the advertising slogan "You can be sure of Shell." Few Americans, for example, realized that the Shell Oil Company of the United States was not a wholly American oil company. It had a 30% U.S. shareholding until 1985, when it became a wholly owned group company.

During the 1950s and 1960s Shell diversified into natural gas and offshore oil production and further expanded its chemicals operations. In 1959 a joint Shell/Esso venture found natural gas in the Netherlands in Groningen. This turned out to be one of the world's largest natural gas fields, and by the early 1970s it provided about half of the natural gas consumed in Europe. Shell was active in the exploration of North Sea oil, and it found oil in the northern North Sea in 1971. In the same year a major offshore gas discovery was made on the Australian northwest shelf. By the end of the 1960s the Shell group was also manufacturing several hundred chemicals in locations all over the world.

In the late 1960s the group, as well as British Petroleum, attracted widespread criticism because, despite the application of United Nations sanctions, the illegal regime in Rhodesia continued to obtain oil products which were supplied from South Africa. South Africa, of course, made no secret of its support for the illegal regime and did not apply United Nations sanctions.

In the early 1970s it was revealed that the U.K. government had become a party to this discreditable behavior. The Shell group later became the subject of public criticism because of its substantial investment in South Africa.

The structure of the world oil industry was radically altered during the 1973 oil crisis when the Organization of Petroleum Exporting Countries (OPEC) unilaterally raised crude oil prices. The oil companies found themselves forced to allocate scarce oil supplies during the crisis, causing severe problems with several governments. In the United Kingdom, Shell and

British Petroleum (BP) had a major clash with the Conservative government led by Edward Heath. Heath demanded that the United Kingdom receive preferential supplies of oil, which the oil companies were attempting to ration between countries. Heath attempted to use the British government's 51% shareholding in BP to force that company to supply Britain first, but BP declined. The Shell group, like all the Western oil companies, had much of its crude oil production in developing countries nationalized. The search for oil in non-OPEC areas was stepped up successfully and in the late 1980's it remained responsible for producing 5% of the world's oil and 7% of its gas.

In response to the problems of the oil industry, the Shell group diversified its business in the 1970s, acquiring coal and metal interests. In 1974 Shell Coal International was established. In 1970 the company acquired the Billiton mining and metals business in the United Kingdom. Chemical manufacture was particularly expanded. This expansion proved unfortunate, since world economic growth after 1973 was much slower than anticipated, with the major recession of the late 1970s and early 1980s causing acute problems. As a result, severe overcapacity developed in the chemical industry. The U.K. company Shell Chemicals experienced problems and was obliged to restructure and reduce capacity. Similar overcapacity occurred in the oil refinery business throughout most of the 1980s. In the 1980s the group rationalized its exposure to chemicals and other noncore businesses. However, the group remained the world's largest producer of petrochemicals and a leading supplier of agrochemicals, in particular insecticides, herbicides, and animal health products and substantial profits were made in the chemicals business.

The Shell group in 1990 was an enormous business enterprise and, alongside Unilever, one of the few examples of a successful venture owned and managed by more than one country. One of the more immediate challenges for the group concerns increasingly stringent environmental requirements which will have a direct impact on the chemicals and the petroleum industries. The group remains the most highly decentralized enterprise in the world oil industry. The almost complete autonomy vested in its nationally based, integrated operating companies gives strategic flexibility.

Principal Subsidiaries: Société des Pétroles Shell (France); Deutsche Shell (Germany); Shell Tankers (Netherlands); Shell Nederland Chemie (Netherlands); Shell Research (Netherlands); Shell UK; Shell Tankers (U.K.); Shell Chemicals (U.K.); Billiton UK; Shell Research (U.K.); Shell South Africa; Shell and BP South African Refineries; Shell Kosan (Japan); Showa Shell Sekiyu (Japan); Satah Shell (Malaysia); Sarawak Shell (Malaysia); Shell Eastern Petroleum (Singapore); Shell Singapore; Shell Australia; Shell New Zealand; Shell Oil Company (U.S.A.); Shell Canada.

Further Reading: Gerretson, F.C., *History of the Royal Dutch,* 4 vols., Leiden, E.J. Brill, 1953–1957; Beaton, K., *Enterprise in Oil: A History of Shell in the United States,* New York, Brill, 1957; Henriques, Robert, *Marcus Samuel, First Viscount Bearsted and Founder of the 'Shell' Transport and Trading Company 1853–1927,* London, Barrie and Rockliff, 1960; Sampson, A., *The Seven Sisters: The Great Oil Companies and the World They Made,* London, Hodder and Stoughton, 1975; Jones, Geoffrey, *The State and the Emergence of the British Oil Industry,* London, Macmillan, 1981; Jones, Geoffrey, "Frederick Lane" and "Marcus Samuel," in *Dictionary of Business Biography: A Biographical Dictionary of Business Leaders Active in Britain in the Period, 1860–1980,* 5 vols., edited by David Jeremy, London, Butterworth, 1984–1986; *A History of the Royal Dutch/Shell Group of Companies,* London, Shell, 1988; Royal Dutch Petroleum Company, *The First Hundred Years,* [n.p.] [n.d.].

—Geoffrey Jones

SASOL

SASOL LIMITED

1 Sturdee Avenue
Rosebank 2196
Post Office Box 5486
Johannesburg 2000
Republic of South Africa
(11) 441-3111
Fax: (11) 788-5092

Public Company
Incorporated: 1979
Employees: 29,300 (1989)
Sales: R4.09 billion (US$1.60 billion) (1989)
Stock Exchange: Johannesburg

Sasol Limited was formed in 1979 to hold the assets of the South African Coal, Oil and Gas Corporation (Sasol) and its subsidiaries. The original company had been established in 1950 as part of the process of industrialization that the South African government considered essential for its economic development and autonomy. The fact that South Africa had and still has no domestic oil reserves has made the country extremely vulnerable to disruption of supplies coming from outside, albeit for different reasons at different times. Although it has generally been very much more expensive to produce oil from coal than from natural petroleum, the political as well as economic importance of achieving as much independence as possible in this sphere was sufficient to overcome any objections. Early attempts to attract private capital, foreign or domestic, were unsuccessful, and it was only with state support that the project could start.

The first Sasol installation opened in 1955, but had to overcome initial technical problems which delayed successful operation for over a year. Financial success was possible only because a system of tariff protection and subsidy operated. This was in addition to profits from the sale of by-products of the process as feedstock for the production of other chemicals and, from 1966, Sasol's involvement in National Petroleum Refiners of South Africa (Natref), which refined imported petroleum. With the industry functioning, private finance became available, and Sasol was successfully privatized in 1979.

As international oil sanctions threatened South Africa's oil supplies and African nationalists targeted Sasol installations, the company remained in the domestic political foreground. Political considerations also became international. Opposition to the continued involvement of U.S. finance and technology

in the undertaking, for example, led in 1986 to the withdrawal of the American multinational Fluor from its South African subsidiary that provided initial construction and engineering support for Sasol installations. This had no practical effect in South Africa, as Fluor's place was taken by a European consortium. Already a major industrial enterprise when it went into the private sector, Sasol continued to grow, maintaining and expanding its role not only as the supplier of an increasing proportion of South Africa's fuel requirements, but also as a major producer of explosives, polymers, fertilizers and other chemicals, and provider of technical services at home and abroad.

It was only after World War I revealed just how vulnerable to external events the South African economy was because of its reliance on imports, that substantial efforts were made to promote domestic industrial development. Earlier moves in that direction had been strongly opposed by the mining industry on the grounds that domestically produced goods would be more expensive than imports. There were some small-scale producers of consumer goods such as shoes and textiles but no attempts had been made to move beyond gold and coal mining to make use of some of the country's other varied and abundant mineral resources to establish an industrial economy. Between 1911 and 1916, some iron works using electric furnaces and scrap metal from the mines and railways operated, but were of no real significance.

In 1922 a blast furnace was built in Newcastle, Natal, and a steelworks at Vereeniging, Transvaal, but it was with the formation of the Iron and Steel Corporation (Iscor) in 1929 that the foundations of an industrial economy were firmly laid. It rapidly became clear that development would be hampered by the fact that there were no known petroleum reserves in the country. In addition to the fact that Afrikaners—people of Dutch origin—were moving increasingly into the world of finance previously dominated by Britons, more immediate political considerations also came to the fore.

South Africa in the 1920s and 1930s experienced serious political, economic, and social problems as more and more poor white Afrikaners, unable to secure even a minimal living in the agricultural sector, sought work in towns—work which was in conspicuously short supply. In 1925 the Pact Government—a coalition of the South African Labour Party representing skilled, primarily British workers, and the National Party representing strongly anti-British Afrikaner nationalists—moved away from the policy of laissez-faire, making it possible to impose protective tariffs on imports. By protecting and promoting domestic industries, it was hoped to create more jobs. Other policies were put in place to ensure that as many as possible of the jobs so created would go to white rather than black workers.

Although there was considerable debate about direct government involvement in manufacturing, government finance of essential infrastructure had never been seriously questioned. The railway network had been built and continued to be run as a nationalized enterprise, and in 1922 the Electricity Supply Commission (ESCOM) had been set up to provide electricity for the entire country. By the time Iscor was formed, although some mining financiers were beginning to show some interest in investing in industrial development, domestic risk capital was not easily available, and there was a growing aversion to allowing foreign capital to increase its hold on the economy.

Many Afrikaner nationalists, including members of the government, did not feel that they could trust British or other foreign capitalists to be sufficiently loyal to South Africa to operate such a fundamentally important industry in the true interests of the country. The growing number of Afrikaner financiers wanted a share in the profits of industrialization, but, having to build on a predominantly agricultural capital base, did not have the large amounts of finance needed. State-provided capital was considered preferable, all the more with regard to the conversion of coal to oil, as private sector efforts to raise the necessary initial funds came to naught.

Research into the possibility of converting coal to oil had been going on in Europe for many years. Some of the scientific basis for the process was discovered at least as early as 1875, with further major progress reported in 1890. There was particular interest in the development of a commercially viable process in Germany where, in 1913, Friedrich Bergius—who would share in the 1931 Nobel chemistry prize for his work in this field—first patented an effective means of producing a substance similar to oil by liquefying coal and increasing its hydrogen content under pressure—hydrogenation.

Continued German interest in the search for an economical means of producing oil from coal led, in 1923, to the discovery of an alternative process based on gasifying rather than liquefying coal. Franz Fischer and Hans Tropsch at the Kaiser Wilhelm Institute for Coal Research at Mulheim developed a process in which synthesis gas—sometimes referred to as water gas—produced from coal was combined with hydrogen in the presence of a catalytic agent under controlled temperature and pressure conditions.

Under free market conditions, the comparatively high cost of synthetic fuels made them totally uneconomical. World War II had reinforced concern about South Africa's economic vulnerability. The government was now much more interested in the establishment of a coal-to-oil capability than it had been when the idea was first mooted in the 1920s.

Initially there was greater interest and hope in the development of the production of oil from shale deposits than from coal. With the help of German experts, the possibility of exploiting the torbanite deposits at Ermelo was extensively explored. The South African Torbanite Mining and Refining Company (Satmar) was formed in 1932 "to refine and market indigenous petrol obtained by blending petrol from oil shale, alcohol from maize and molasses, and benzol from Iscor." These shales were capable of producing 20–100 gallons of oil per ton, but the company could only operate profitably by refining imported crude oil to supplement the shale operations.

In collaboration with Anglo-Transvaal Consolidated (Anglo-Vaal), Satmar acquired the South African rights to the Fischer-Tropsch process. Tenders were invited for the construction of the necessary plant, but capital was not forthcoming. As late as 1938 the South African government continued to hope that the possibilities of deeper drilling might yet lead to the discovery of oil or that Ermelo's torbanite could be made to produce oil economically. Coal-to-oil schemes were still considered uneconomical, but the government did agree that it made sense to test South African coal in both the Bergius hydrogenation and the Fischer-Tropsch gasification processes.

After World War II, shales still produced only small quantities of oil, natural petroleum could still not be found, and coal-to-oil conversion looked increasingly attractive. In 1947 a regulatory licensing framework was established for anyone interested in moving in that direction. The only applicant was Anglo-Vaal, which acquired a license in 1949 and elaborated a scheme, initially estimated to cost £13 million, for the opening-up of a new coal mine to ensure a steady supply for a Fischer-Tropsch plant with an annual output capacity of 260,000 tons, including 76 million gallons of motor fuel.

By early 1950, having spent some £400,000 in preliminary work, Anglo-Vaal sought government support in the form of a guarantee of £16 million debentures to be issued by the Industrial Development Corporation (IDC), which had been set up by the government in 1942 to help finance industry. After considerable debate, the IDC was allowed to provide the necessary funds or guarantees, with additional support from American banks. By 1955, the fully mechanized Sigma colliery was ready to supply 7,600 tons of coal daily, 3,200 tons of which were to be gasified in Lurgi generators to produce some three million cubic meters of gas for the Fischer-Tropsch plant, which was expected to produce 55 million gallons of motor fuel and 16 million gallons of other products annually. Some of these products—ammonia, tar, phenols, and creosote—were by-products of gasification, while others—alcohols, acetone, and paraffin waxes—were produced in the Fischer-Tropsch units. That process has, over the years, proved extremely versatile. By varying temperature, pressure, and the catalytic agents used, a wide range of organic compounds can be synthesized, making it important for the chemical industry throughout the world. By-products were also important for the South African undertaking, but it is only in that country that the process had been used extensively to produce fuel.

In what was to become known as Sasol I at Coalbrook—subsequently Sasolburg—two Fischer-Tropsch units operated. One used a fixed bed catalyst of the kind the Germans had employed during the war, and was provided by the German firm Argbeit-Gemeinschaft Lurgi und Ruhrchemie (Arge). This process, based on a well tried and tested technique, operated without difficulty. The second unit, a fluid bed system, had been developed and installed by the American firm of M. W. Kellogg. This had never before operated on an industrial scale, and created technical difficulties which were not resolved until 1957. The original estimated cost of £13 million had risen to £18 million by the time IDC support was sought, while actual costs by the time the system was functioning were well over £40 million. The integration of the fixed and fluid bed systems was expected to produce considerable economic and technical advantages. The difficulties experienced in bringing the fluid bed unit onstream meant that any such benefits were slower to materialize than anticipated. Over the years, however, research and development led to the emergence of a unique production technique, ultimately to be known as the Sasol-Synthol process.

With underlying government support in the form of a tariff on imported petroleum and a sliding price scale for Sasol's own produce geared to world petroleum prices, Sasol was able eventually to show profits. At the time of its formation, hope that it could be profitable in its own right, without artificial protection, was not without justification. In addition to the greater efficiency expected from and finally achieved by process integration, the five units installed by Arge had the same capacity as 75 of the smaller units used in wartime Germany.

Considerable immediate savings were made in the amount of equipment and instrumentation required. Less tangible, but nonetheless important, was the widespread belief that American oil reserves were nearing depletion. Supplies from the Middle East were thought to be at risk because of the fear of Soviet influence.

South Africa has not experienced any difficulty in importing the crude oil it needs, although the means by which this has been done, and the prices paid, have at times been shrouded in secrecy. Strong international pressure to restrict supplies began to have an impact in 1964, when Kuwait banned all petroleum exports to South Africa. OPEC followed suit in 1973. Iran was South Africa's major supplier until the revolution of 1979 and the National Iranian Oil Company (NIOC) had a 17.5% share in Natref when it was formed. The French firm Elf Aquitaine was also a major shareholder, but Sasol was in control with 52.5%. After the revolution, NIOC tried unsuccessfully to sell its shares, which were in effect absorbed in South Africa, Sasol's Natref holding rising to 63.63%.

The oil crises of 1974 and 1978 provided a substantial boost for Sasol, higher world prices not only enabling it to increase prices, but also making the cost of production closer, or even lower than the world oil price. At the end of 1979, for example, Sasol's production cost was estimated to be about $30 per barrel at a time when world spot prices were about $10 per barrel higher. Although such differentials were not sustained, prospects in the 1970s were sufficiently good to lead Sasol to embark on the construction of a second installation, Sasol 2, at Secunda in 1976. By the time this installation came onstream in 1980, work had already begun on Sasol 3, also at Secunda. This third unit came onstream in 1982. Still based on the Fischer-Tropsch process, the new plants, like Sasol 1, were capable of producing a range of chemicals as well as synthetic fuel.

In 1979 it was decided to take Sasol public, 70% of its shares being placed on the market. Initially some R490 million were raised by private placement of shares, with another 17.5 million shares made available to the public. South African institutional investors, pension funds, and large companies took the lead. Small investors were attracted by promises of preferential allocation treatment, while foreign investors were particularly interested because they were allowed to make their purchases using the financial rand, while dividends would be paid at the ordinary commercial exchange rate. At the time, the financial rand was at a discount in excess of 30% as against a more normal rate of about 12%. The public issue was more than 30 times oversubscribed. Foreign investors did not do as well as they hoped out of the allocation.

In 1983, on the basis of the expanded capacity provided by Sasol 2 and 3, Sasol Limited was able to begin moving beyond the provision of feedstock for the country's chemical industry into the production of fertilizers and various specialty chemicals. Existing producers did not welcome this competition.

Still a relative newcomer to the industry, Sasol was nonetheless part of the general effort to increase South African specialty chemical output. In addition to saving substantial amounts of foreign exchange by reducing reliance on imports, Sasol also planned to produce for export. In 1990, major investment plans were approved for the company to expand production of a range of products that would contribute to this end.

In relations with its workers, Sasol has, like most other South African enterprises, faced increasing pressure from African trade unions for improvements in pay, working conditions, and housing. A nine-day strike in 1989, for example, was resolved by the payment of a food allowance for African workers not living in hostel accommodation. More serious industrial action in 1987 resulted in Sasol's being criticized by the Industrial Court for using "rough and ugly tactics" in dealing with a strike by members of the Chemical Workers' Industrial Union. The company was, the court held, more interested in forcing capitulation than in negotiating a financial settlement. A subsequent appeal, however, found the company's actions justified.

Apart from specifically trade union issues, Sasol has been a major target for political activists seeking to put pressure on the South African government to bring the apartheid system to an end. In June 1980, for example, there was a well-coordinated attack on Sasolburg, showing evidence of detailed knowledge of the plant and its weak security points. Bombs placed in the offices of Fluor, then constructing Sasol 2 and 3, were defused only a short time before they were set to explode.

Sasol has placed considerable emphasis on research and development, which have been the basis for considerable technological advance. On this basis they have not only built up their manufacturing base within South Africa, but have also provided technical services abroad. Most notable have been technical support for some U.S. gas companies and general consultancy for a gasification plant in North Dakota, successfully commissioned in 1984.

The company continues to call for the expansion of synthetic fuel production in South Africa. It looks to government and other industries to provide the large amount of capital required which has not been forthcoming.

Principal Subsidiaries: Sasol Mining (Pty) Ltd; Sasol Industries (Pty) Ltd; Sasol Three (Pty) Ltd; National Petroleum Refiners of S.A. (Pty) Ltd; Sasol Technology (Pty) Ltd; Sasol Oil and Fertilizers (Pty) Ltd; Sasol Chemical Industries (Pty) Ltd; Sasol Townships Ltd; Sasol (Transvaal) Townships Ltd.

—Simon Katzenellenbogen

SAUDI ARABIAN OIL COMPANY

Post Office Box 5000
Dhahran 31311
Saudi Arabia
(3) 673-5002
Fax: (3) 873-8190

State-Owned Company
Incorporated: 1988
Employees: 43,248 (1989)

The state-owned Saudi Arabian Oil Company, also known as Saudi Aramco, is the largest company in the world in terms of crude oil and liquid natural gas (LNG) production. Saudi Aramco is responsible for exploration, development, and production in a tract of land which covers some 16% of the 2.2 million square kilometers that constitute the Saudi Arabian peninsula. Aramco's crude oil operations, which account for 95% of total production, are vital to the Saudi Arabian economy, and in 1989 generated US$2.99 billion in sales. The revenues generated through the export of Aramco crude oil production constituted around 56% of total Saudi government revenues in 1988. Saudi Aramco also holds substantial interests in downstream activities, such as operation of the crude oil and gas distribution networks, and of the Ras Tanura refinery. Furthermore, Saudi Aramco is broadening its perspective to that of a multinational oil company. Through subsidiaries, Saudi Aramco holds an interest in the U.S. refining and marketing company Star Enterprise and may be on the verge of concluding a similar deal with Ssangyong Oil in South Korea.

The incorporation of Saudi Aramco on November 13, 1988, was largely a cosmetic operation, performed in order to remove the final legal attachments of the Arabian American Oil Company (Aramco) to the original U.S. company registered in Delaware on January 31, 1944. However, the history of the Aramco concession, upon which the company's fortune has been forged, dates back to the early 1930s. In 1932 Standard Oil (California) (Socal), now known as Chevron, employed the energies of Harry St. John B. Philby, a close friend of Saudi King Ibn Saud, to obtain permission for Socal to conduct a geological survey in the eastern parts of the Saudi Peninsula. Although granting rights over Saudi Arabia's natural resources to a foreign company was against King Ibn Saud's better judgment, his need for money left him no alternative. King Ibn Saud insisted that no geological appraisal could take place un-

til the full terms of a concession had been agreed. The king's fear was that Socal would discover that Saudi Arabia was barren before it had committed any capital. On May 29, 1933, the concession agreement was signed by the king's minister for finance, Abd Allah al Sulaiman, and the Socal representative, Lloyd N. Hamilton, at the royal palace in Jiddah.

In November 1933 the California Arabian Standard Oil Company (Casoc) was formed to manage operations within the concession on behalf of Socal. The original concession stretched from the Persian Gulf to, and including, the western province of Dahna. In 1939 the concession was further enlarged to around 440,000 square miles to include Saudi Arabia's share of the neutral zone.

However, before any crude oil was discovered in its new Saudi concession Socal was already experiencing problems in marketing its growing Bahraini oil production. Socal opted for the quickest solution to this problem, which was to merge operations with a company which owned marketing facilities near the source of production, but which was short of crude. In 1936 Socal struck a deal with the Texas Company, now known as Texaco. The new joint venture was named Caltex, and was charged with managing all of Texaco's marketing assets from the Middle East to the Pacific. As a part of the deal, Texaco was given half ownership of Casoc.

It took three years before the exploratory drilling of the Dammam Dome, a group of prominent limestone hills near what is presently called Dhahran, was rewarded. In March 1938 the seventh exploration well drilled on the Dammam Dome identified the Arab Zone, as the explorers named it. Crude oil exports started in the same year. The oil was piped from the well to the makeshift port of al-Khobar and, from there, was transported by sea to the Bahrain refinery. In the following year the now prolific Ras Tanura export terminal was used for the first time by Socal's tanker, the *D.G. Schofield.*

The advent of World War II impeded Casoc's operations. Production at the newly constructed Ras Tanura refinery lasted only six months before it was closed in June 1941 and all dependents of American employees were sent home for the duration of the war.

The war years from 1940 to 1944 were significant, however, for the progressive rationalization of Casoc's management structure under the guidance of its new president, F.A. Davies. Davies had visited Saudi Arabia as a Socal representative in 1930 and had been closely involved in operations ever since. His election, together with that of a new board of directors in August 1940, marked the company's first step toward independence from Socal. Casoc set up its headquarters in San Francisco at 200 Bush Street. Symbolically, the final confirmation of the company's new identity came on January 31, 1944, when Casoc was renamed the Arabian American Oil Company.

The postwar years of the late 1940s witnessed the scramble to expand production from the Aramco concession and to establish a market for it. Between 1944 and 1949 Aramco expanded capacity in all spheres of operation, in no small way aided by the military cooperation in allocating materials and even providing transport. The strategic importance of oil had been proven in the defeat of Adolf Hitler, and the U.S. government had even set aside funds for possible direct investment in the Middle East to secure supplies. Aramco shunned the offer of direct government involvement but with its aid achieved a

25-fold increase in crude oil supply from 20 thousand barrels per day in 1944 to 500 thousand barrels per day in 1949. The Ras Tanura refinery's distillation capacity was expanded from 50 thousand barrels per day to 127 thousand barrels per day between 1945 and 1949, in part to supply the increasing requirements of the U.S. Navy.

Secure access to world markets was fostered in two ways. First, with regard to the European market, Aramco attempted to improve the competitiveness of its crude oil vis-a-vis Soviet and U.S. exports by cutting down on the time and, ultimately, costs of transporting crude from the Persian Gulf. In 1946 Aramco began to build, through its affiliate, the Trans-Arabian Pipe Line Company (Tapline), a 1,068 mile-long pipeline connecting the Abqaiq oilfield to the Mediterranean port of Sidon, Lebanon.

Secondly, Aramco tried to merge operations with the Standard Oil Company of New Jersey, later Exxon, and the Socony-Vacuum Oil Company, now known as Mobil. Harry Collier, the chairman of Socal at that time, supported the choice of these two companies not only because of their unrivaled marketing assets in the Far East but also because the choice satisfied King Ibn Saud's explicitly stated wish that Aramco should remain American to avoid an extension of British influence in the region. Between 1946 and 1948 the two companies wrestled with the legal obstacle posed to the merger by the Red Line Agreement. This obstacle was overcome in December 1948. The companies' shares in Aramco and Tapline were divided as follows: Socal, Texaco, and Standard Oil of New Jersey each owned 30% and the Socony-Vacuum Company owned the remaining 10%.

Also in 1948 Aramco gave up its concessionary rights over the Saudi Arabian part of the neutral zone. This move was made in response to the severe terms accepted by the American Independent Oil Company (Aminoil) in the auction for the concession rights over the Kuwaiti half of the neutral zone. Unwilling to match Aminoil's offer, Aramco decide to preempt similar demands by the Saudi king by giving up the land. In return for this unilateral gesture, Aramco received a reaffirmation of its offshore concession rights in the Persian Gulf. In the auction that resulted from Aramco's cessation, the Pacific Western Oil Company agreed to terms even more onerous than those applied to Aminoil.

However, Aramco did not completely avoid compensating the government for the dramatic increase in the value of its concession. Over the late 1940s and the first half of the 1950s Aramco was progressively forced to relinquish small parts of its concession. Also, on December 30, 1950, following the example of Venezuela in 1948, the Saudi government authorized an increase in the government's share to 50% of Aramco's profits net of exploration, development, and production costs.

The expansion of Aramco's operations continued through the 1950s, albeit at a slower pace. Crude oil production only increased from 761 thousand barrels per day in 1960 to 1.2 million barrels per day in 1959, despite an increase of 38 billion barrels to a total of 50 billion barrels in the Saudi Arabian proven recoverable reserves during the same period. This expansion of oil reserves was primarily attributable to two discoveries made by Aramco, the onshore Ghawar and the offshore Safaniya oil fields, in 1951. The onshore and offshore discoveries were the largest on record at the time and have

remained unequaled to this day. 1951 marked Tapline's first full year in operation. By 1965 Tapline enabled Aramco to market some 44% of its total crude oil exports to Europe, a greater share than that of nearer markets in Asia.

Aramco's activities during the 1950s were distinguished from those of the postwar years by the mature approach that underlay them. The U.S. lesson of the waste caused by over-rapid exploitation of oil reservoirs was not ignored by Aramco. In the early 1950s Aramco began to implement oilfield pressure maintenance programs. At the Abqaiq oilfield, gas reinjection facilities started operation in March 1954, and in February 1956 a similar water program was started. An added advantage with the gas program was that not only was Aramco able to utilize associated gas but that also the associated gas could be stored instead of burned off at source.

Both Aramco's and Saudi Arabia's revenues increased dramatically during this period as a result of the expansion of crude oil exports and of rising posted prices. Like Aramco, Saudi Arabia ploughed these revenues into the development of infrastructure. As Saudi Arabia was overwhelmingly dependent on oil for revenues, it was vitally important that revenue stability was achieved to foster long-term development plans. Unlike the Aramco partners, however, the Saudi government had no influence on the two factors, production and price, that determined their revenues. The struggle for control, or the "participation" issue, emerged strongly in the 1960s.

Even though the general office had been moved to Dhahran and two representatives from the Saudi government were included on the board of directors, control of Aramco still rested firmly with the four partners. On August 9, 1960, the chairman of Standard Oil of New Jersey, Munroe Rathbone, decided unilaterally to shave 14¢ off the posted price, a cut of some 7%, in order to increase its competitiveness in Europe vis-a-vis Soviet crude exports. Not only did the chairman refuse to consult the Aramco board, but he also rejected the advice given him from, among others, the New Jersey company's representative on the Aramco board, Howard Page. Other companies followed suit with the price cut and fueled the outrage of the oil-exporting countries. One dissenting voice that rose above the rest was that of Sayyid Abdullah H. Tariki, the Saudi director general of petroleum and mineral affairs and member of the Aramco board. Tariki immediately set about arranging secret negotiations with other producer countries. The preparatory negotiations proved instrumental in the formation of OPEC in 1960. As it turned out, the formation of OPEC was to be decisive in the battle for control of Aramco.

On November 30, 1962, the General Petroleum and Mineral Organization of Saudi Arabia (Petromin) was founded. Its aim was to foster Saudi participation in all areas of the oil industry, including operations in the Aramco concession. Although Petromin was not producing any crude oil, by 1970 it had joint interests in many concessions and operated a refinery at Jiddah and a fertilizer plant in Dammam. The evolution of Petromin over the 1960s was central to the government's attempts to wrest control from the Aramco partners.

The weakness of the crude oil market continued through the 1960s due to the emergence of Iran as the second major producer in the region. The freezing of posted prices over the 1960s meant that an oil exporter's only means to protect its revenues from being eroded by inflation was to increase production. The companies operating in the gulf, including the

Aramco partners, were each put under a great deal of pressure by concessionaire governments to increase production and maintain prices. These incompatible aims could only be satisfied if incremental world demand could be equitably divided between the producers. Howard Page was so concerned to appear to be representing the Saudi case for an increase in its market share that he refused the opportunity to involve Standard Oil of New Jersey in the very profitable exploration strategy being conducted in Oman, fearing that the company might be identified as aiding a direct competitor to enter the market. Between 1960 and 1970 Iran's production increased by 258% or 2.8 million barrels per day compared to the Saudi increase of 189% or 2.5 million barrels per day. However, by 1970 both Saudi and Iranian oil production had reached around 3.8 million barrels per day.

Aramco's fortunes were, and always have been, inextricably bound with those of the Saudi government. One way for both to overcome the constraint on revenue expansion imposed by the glutted crude oil market of the 1960s was to diversify into other markets. Expansion and progressive modernization of the Ras Tanura refinery increased crude oil throughput to 380,000 barrels per day in 1970, improved the quality of products, and enabled the blending of new products such as aviation gasoline. Aramco also began to establish the infrastructure necessary for the sale of LNG. Between 1962 and 1970 production of LNG increased 18-fold from 2,900 barrels per day to 52,100 barrels per day.

The supply conditions in the crude oil market became markedly tighter in the early 1970s. In 1972 Aramco managed not only to increase production by an unprecedented 1.2 million barrels per day to six million barrels per day but also succeeded in increasing the posted price. The market conditions placed the government in a much stronger position from which to negotiate with the Aramco partners over Saudi participation.

In March 1972, after employing every delaying tactic possible, Aramco accepted the principle of 20% state participation in order to preempt unilateral action. The principle was worked out in detail in October 1972, when it was agreed that Saudi participation should be phased in from 25% on January 1, 1973, to 51% on January 1, 1982, and that compensation should be made for the updated book value of Aramco's assets.

By 1973, however, other oil-exporting countries had obtained or imposed terms far in excess of the Saudi government's demands. Negotiations restarted and continued through to 1980. In 1973 the Saudi interest in Aramco was increased to 60%. Between 1976 and 1980 the 100% Saudi takeover of Aramco was agreed and the financial provisions were made retroactive to January 1, 1976. By the terms of the agreement the Aramco partners received a service fee of 18¢ to 19¢ per barrel and were obliged to market the crude that Petromin could not sell through its own channels.

The oil price rises of 1973-1974 had a dramatic effect on revenues. The effect on government revenues of increases in the oil price, taxation, and production—from 3.8 million barrels per day in 1970 to an all-time high of 9.9 million barrels per day in 1980—was such that the economy could no longer absorb the funds available to it and was, therefore, generating a surplus.

With their newly acquired interest, the Saudi government began to involve Aramco in the reinvestment of that surplus. In 1975 Aramco was given the task of constructing and operating a gas system that could fuel Saudi Arabia's drive towards industrialization. The master gas system (MGS), as it came to be known, started operation in 1980. In January 1977 Aramco formed a subsidiary, the Saudi Consolidated Electric Company (SCECO), to construct and operate an electric grid system for the Eastern Province. As a result of the agreement between the government and Aramco, SCECO became an independently managed company on January 1, 1983.

Although Aramco had become state-owned, the close ties between the original Aramco partners and the government were not lost. Their relationship was fostered through joint ventures outside Aramco's scope of operations. Mobil currently holds a 29% interest in Petrolube and a 30% stake in Luberef. Both the Saudi-American joint ventures were formed to build lubricating oil refineries in Jiddah in the 1970s, and are still responsible for their operation. The other three of the original Aramco partners, Exxon, Texaco, and Gulf, are involved in industrial projects with the Saudi Arabian Basic Industries Corporation (SABIC) in Jubail.

However, Aramco's boom years of the 1970s and early 1980s did not last. The oil price rises of 1973 and 1979-1980 led to inter-fuel substitution, such as the substitution of oil for gas, and conservation measures being implemented by the Organization for Economic Cooperation and Development (OECD) countries that brought about a collapse in world oil demand. Coupled with the sharp increase in oil supplies from non-OPEC regions, such as the North Sea, from 32.9 million barrels per day in 1980 to 37.8 million barrels per day in 1985, Saudi Arabia was faced with the no-win choice of either cutting production to maintain the official selling price or cutting prices and flooding the market. Between 1980 and 1985 Saudi Arabia cut production from 9.9 million barrels per day to 4 million barrels per day.

By 1985 Saudi Arabia was tired of shouldering the full burden of price defense and looking on as its revenues declined. In September 1985 Sheikh Yamani, in conjunction with the Aramco partners, instituted a dramatic change of policy to regain Saudi Arabia's share of the crude oil market. Between August 1985 and August 1986 Saudi Arabian production increased from 2.2 million to 6.2 million barrels per day, and the spot price of many world crudes fell to less than $10 from their previous 1985 levels of around $26 to $29 per barrel. The real price of oil had returned to levels not seen since before the oil price shocks of 1973-1974.

Aramco did not emerge unscathed from the drastic fall in oil revenues. Between 1982 and 1989 Aramco's personnel fell from 57,000 to 43,000. Following the meeting of the Aramco board of directors in San Francisco on April 8 and 9, 1987, the decision was taken to cut its own membership from 20 to 13. Three Americans and four Saudis, among them the ex-oil minister Sheikh Yamani, were removed, leaving two representatives from each of the four original Aramco partners and five Saudi officials.

The trauma of the 1986 oil price crash led to a change in management, Hisham Nazer replacing Sheikh Yamani, and a change in oil policy. The primary aim of Saudi policy after the unbridled competition of 1986 was to secure market share just as it had been in the oil market glut of the 1960s. To secure long-term supply contracts, Hisham Nazer depended heavily on the close relationship between Aramco and the original shareholders. In his first attempt Nazer signed a 1.25 million barrels per day long-term supply arrangement with the four majors involved in the formation of Aramco, Chevron, Texaco, Mobil, and Exxon, on February 3, 1987. This agreement soon broke down, however, in the face of further price competition and Nazer turned his attention to the possibility of securing market share through downstream integration—ownership of all phases of the industry from the wellhead to the service station.

In 1988 the first overseas downstream joint venture was concluded by the newly incorporated Saudi Aramco. On November 10, 1988, Saudi Aramco and Texaco signed an agreement committing themselves to the conditions of the joint venture named Star Enterprise. Aramco's share of the joint venture was to be managed by its subsidiary Saudi Refining Incorporated. From January 1, 1989, U.S.-based Star Enterprise was given the responsibility of operating Texaco's refining, distribution, and marketing assets in the east and gulf coasts. Texaco's assets were substantial in these areas and included three refineries—Delaware City, Convent, and Port Arthur—with combined distillation capacity of 625,000 barrels per day and, most importantly, 11,400 service stations. In return Saudi Aramco paid $1.5 billion, committed itself to supplying up to 600,000 barrels per day and to supplying a 30 million barrel inventory. A further deal was negotiated between Aramco and Ssangyong Oil of South Korea.

As a result of the 1990 Persian Gulf crisis, Saudi Aramco's plans have been altered. Its plan to increase crude oil production capacity by around two million barrels per day to ten million barrels per day by 1995 has been brought forward to 1992. Since proven recoverable reserves are currently estimated at around, 258 billion barrels, this increase in capacity, if utilized, will not dramatically shorten Saudi Arabia's productive time horizon. Saudi Aramco's future seems further ensured by Petromin's inability to usurp Aramco's responsibilities. This situation is exemplified by the fact that the management of the east-west pipeline was passed from Petromin to Aramco in January 1984. Despite the radical changes in both the ownership and function of Aramco, its place in Saudi Arabia is assured for the foreseeable future.

Principal Subsidiary: Aramco Services Company (U.S.A.).

Further Reading: Longrigg, S.H., *Oil in the Middle East,* Oxford, Oxford University Press, 1969; Seymour, I., *OPEC: Instrument of Change,* London, Macmillan Press Ltd., 1980; Yergin, D., *The Prize: The Epic Quest for Oil, Money and Power,* New York, Simon & Schuster, 1990.

—Adam Seymour

SHELL OIL COMPANY

One Shell Plaza
Post Office Box 2463
Houston, Texas 77252
U.S.A.
(713) 241-6161
Fax: (713) 241-7217

Wholly Owned Subsidiary of Royal Dutch/Shell through Shell Petroleum Inc.
Incorporated: 1922 as Shell Union Oil Corporation
Employees: 31,637
Sales: $26.49 billion

One of the United States's leading producers of oil, gas, and petrochemicals, Shell Oil Company has distinguished itself through its commitment to industry innovation. Its marketing expertise has enabled the company to compensate for its relatively low volume of crude oil production, as compared to its strongest competitors, by selling an equivalent amount of gasoline nationwide. Although the company conducts business primarily in the United States, Shell also explores for and produces crude oil and natural gas outside the country, both independently and through joint ventures with other subsidiaries of its parent organization, Royal Dutch/Shell Group. Shell Petroleum Inc. is a holding company that is 60% owned by Royal Dutch Petroleum Company and 40% owned by The "Shell" Transport and Trading Company.

The Royal Dutch/Shell Group began selling gasoline imported from Sumatra in the United States in 1912 to capitalize on the growth of the country's automobile industry and to compete with the Standard Oil Company. Starting with the formation of the Seattle-based American Gasoline Company, Royal Dutch/Shell Group also founded Roxana Petroleum Company in 1912 in Oklahoma to locate and produce crude oil. This was followed by the opening of refineries in New Orleans, Louisiana, in 1916 and in Wood River, Illinois, in 1918.

It soon became clear to Royal Dutch/Shell Group that with so much gasoline already available in nearby California, it was impractical to continue importing the product for sale in the Pacific Northwest. It therefore acquired California Oilfields, Ltd. in 1913 which, when coupled with a new refinery built two years later in Martinez, California, gave the company the ability to fully integrate its operations. To reflect this new capability, the name of American Gasoline was changed to Shell Company of California in 1915. At this time, the company

designed and built its first gasoline service station. Dubbed "the crackerbox," the station was originally constructed of wood. This structure was later replaced by a model made of prefabricated steel that required only a few days to erect.

The oil boom of the early 1920s, particularly at Shell's Signal Hill, California, site, provided the company with an opportunity to penetrate the Los Angeles area with sales of Shell gasoline and petroleum products manufactured in its new refineries nearby. In 1922 Shell Company of California and Roxana Petroleum merged with Union Oil Company of Delaware to form a holding company called Shell Union Oil Corporation. Approximately 65% of the holding company's shares were held by Royal Dutch/Shell Group.

By the late 1920s, the company was actively laying pipeline across the country to transport oil from its Texas fields to the Wood River refinery. Shell Pipe Line Corporation, established in 1927 upon the acquisition of Ozark Pipe Line Corporation, also connected these fields to a new refinery built in Houston in 1929. This refinery was dedicated to manufacturing products destined for sale on the east coast of the United States and overseas. In 1929 Shell Petroleum Corporation, a forerunner of Shell Oil Company, purchased the New Orleans Refining Company, which later became one of Shell's largest manufacturing facilities.

Shell Development Company was formed in 1928 to conduct petrochemical research. The following year, after the discovery of chemicals that could be made from refinery by-products, the Shell Chemical Company began its manufacturing operation.

By 1929 Shell gasoline was being sold throughout the United States. Although the economic problems of the early 1930s forced the company, along with the entire oil industry, to reassess and curtail its operations to some degree, Shell continued its chemical research. This resulted in the opening of two plants for manufacturing synthetic ammonia in 1931 and for making synthetic glycerine in 1937.

Upon developing the ability to synthesize 100-octane gasoline, Shell began supplying this fuel to the U.S. Air Corps in 1934 and gradually became one of the largest producers of aviation fuel. Due to the increased demands of the military during World War II, Shell shared this technology with the rest of the industry. It also helped the country overcome its wartime loss of natural rubber supplied by Java and Singapore by providing butadiene, a chemical required for the production of synthetic rubber products.

In 1939 Shell Oil Company of California merged with Shell Petroleum Corporation, whose name was subsequently changed to Shell Oil Company, Inc. Ten years later, the name was changed again to Shell Oil Company.

Until 1939, the company had had offices in San Francisco, California; St. Louis, Missouri; and in New York City. The St. Louis office was closed in 1939, and San Francisco operations continued until 1949, when New York became the sole headquarters. Shell increased its oil exploration activities and expanded production to satisfy the growing fuel needs created by U.S. drivers' passion for big cars. New chemical plants were also built that enabled Shell to become a leading producer of epoxy resins, ethylene, synthetic rubber, detergent alcohols, and other chemicals. It also pioneered the development of new fuel products during the 1950s, including jet fuel and high-octane, unleaded gasoline for automobiles.

In 1958, the company redesigned its service stations in an attempt to make them more compatible with surrounding areas. The ranch-style station was introduced at this time and continued as the company's primary retail outlet until the introduction of the self-service station in 1971. Shell provided additional retail support by launching several payment alternatives, including an offer to honor all other oil company credit cards and a travel and entertainment card bearing the Shell name. These developments helped Shell gain a significant share of the U.S. market for automobile gasoline.

By the 1960s growing environmental concerns led Shell to invest heavily in systems intended to reduce pollution and to conserve energy in its plants. In the following decade, the company began publishing a series of consumer-oriented booklets on such topics as car maintenance and energy conservation.

At the same time, the company turned its attention offshore and began drilling for oil and natural gas deposits in Alaska and the Gulf of Mexico. It soon became expert in using enhanced techniques to find and recover oil from U.S. fields. One of its biggest successes was the 1983 strike at the Bullwinkle prospect in the Gulf of Mexico. This recovery operation was expected to produce 100 million barrels of oil.

In 1970 Shell moved its headquarters to Houston. The company expanded into coal production in 1974 with the formation of Shell Mining Company. This business unit eventually operated mines in Wyoming, Illinois, Ohio, Kentucky, and West Virginia.

John F. Bookout assumed the presidency of the company in 1976 after the mandatory retirement of his predecessor, Harry Bridges. Bookout, a 25-year Shell veteran, had risen through the ranks of the company's oil and gas exploration and production division. Bookout took over during a period when high oil prices and flattening demand led other petroleum producers into ill-fated diversification attempts outside the oil industry. Rather than follow this path, Bookout elected to penetrate the oil industry more deeply and to emphasize increased efficiency in the company's ongoing operations. Beginning in 1978, for example, the company upgraded a number of its refineries and closed many of its less profitable service stations in order to concentrate on those in metropolitan areas with higher sales volume.

In 1979, Shell outbid several competitors to purchase California's Belridge Oil Company. The firm, which was subsequently renamed Kernridge Oil Company, gave Shell badly needed crude oil reserves at a time when opportunities for successful drilling ventures were declining. The company's technological expertise in steam-injected oil recovery enabled Shell to boost Kernridge's domestic production and reduce its reliance on more expensive foreign sources.

Beginning in January 1984, Royal Dutch/Shell Group launched a bid to acquire the remaining shares of Shell Oil Company. Attracted by Shell's U.S. oil reserves, the country's stable political situation, and a low corporate tax structure, cash-rich Royal Dutch/Shell viewed Shell as an increasingly worthy investment. The attempted buyout soon developed into a hostile battle over the amount that Royal Dutch/Shell had offered Shell shareholders. Its original offer of $55 a share was perceived as inadequate by Shell's directors and financial advisers, who placed the company's worth at closer to $75 a share, even though the offer represented a 25% premium over the stock's current selling price. By May, however, John Bookout and four other Shell executives agreed to tender their shares in exchange for Royal Dutch's sweetened offer of $60 a share. This agreement paved the way for the eventual completion of the takeover in June 1985.

In the following year, Shell came under the attack of an anti-apartheid coalition in the United States consisting of union representatives, activists, and members of various church groups that protested against Royal Dutch/Shell's involvement in South Africa. Through picketing in 13 cities, the coalition hoped to exert a negative impact on Shell's gasoline sales while also making the U.S. public aware of the parent company's coal, oil, and chemical operations in South Africa. A boycott launched by the AFL-CIO, United Mineworkers, and National Education Association in cooperation with the Free South Africa Movement was initiated to protest alleged mistreatment of South African workers by Royal Dutch/Shell and the company's inaction against apartheid. Although Royal Dutch/Shell officials contended the company was a strong anti-apartheid voice, by the end of 1988, Berkeley, California, and Boston, Massachusetts, had joined the fray of banning purchases of Shell products within city limits.

Shell encountered additional problems in 1989 over the cleanup of the Rocky Mountain Arsenal in Colorado. It was here that Shell had manufactured pesticides between the early 1950s and 1982, allegedly dumping carcinogens on the grounds. Also under scrutiny was the U.S. Army, which had used the Rocky Mountain plant to make nerve gas during World War II. Sued in 1983 by the state of Colorado under the federal superfund law, both the army and Shell offered a plan to pay for cleaning up the site. The state subsequently deemed the proposal unsatisfactory. A California superior court ruled that insurance companies covering the company were not liable, and Shell has appealed that decision. The outcome of the Colorado action is yet to be determined. Shell and the army are involved in interim cleanup efforts, with a final cleanup plan due in 1994.

Led by president and chief executive officer Frank H. Richardson, who succeeded John Bookout upon his retirement in 1988, Shell has a strong cash flow and decreasing level of long-term debt. Its strong market presence and emphasis on customers are reinforced by aggressive exploration, production, manufacturing, and research efforts.

Principal Subsidiaries: Shell Energy Resources, Inc.; Shell Credit, Inc.; Shell Pipe Line Corporation; Pecten Arabian Company.

Further Reading: "Shell Oil: bucking an industry trend by driving deeper into oil," *Business Week,* December 3, 1979; "Why Royal Dutch/Shell is betting on the U.S.," *Business Week,* February 20, 1984; Mack, Toni, "It's time to take risks," *Forbes,* October 6, 1986; *Shell: 75 Years Serving America,* Houston, Shell Oil Company, [1987]; Miller, William H., "Last of a breed," *Industry Week,* July 18, 1988; Atchison, Sandra D., "The toxic morass in Denver's backyard," *Business Week,* January 9, 1989.

—Sandy Schusteff

SHOWA SHELL SEKIYU K.K.

Kasumigaseki Building
2-5, Kasumigaseki 3-chome
Chiyoda-ku, Tokyo 100
Japan
(03) 3580-0123
Fax: (03) 3580-3811

Public Company
Incorporated: 1942 as Showa Oil Co., Ltd.
Employees: 2,350
Sales: ¥1.65 trillion (US$12.15 billion)
Stock Exchanges: Tokyo Osaka Nagoya

Showa Shell Sekiyu is one of Japan's leading distributors and refiners of fuel oil. The company is 50% owned by Royal Dutch/Shell. The company deals principally in petroleum products such as gasoline, naptha, jet fuels, and fuels for electrical power generation, as well as in kerosene, heating oil, lubricants, and coal. Showa Shell operates more than 7,700 gasoline service stations in Japan. The company operates crude oil refineries in Japan at Kawasaki, Niigata, Yokkaichi, and Yamaguchi. Two plants manufacture lubricants in Yokohama and Kobe. The company has extended its business into non-oil areas, with interests in rental car, travel, and real estate businesses. Showa's subsidiary, Computer Plaza, is dedicated to developing Japanese-language computer software. Another interest of Showa Shell Sekiyu is the development of solar-powered batteries. Showa Shell Sekiyu was formed in 1985 by the merger of two oil companies, Showa Oil Company and Shell Sekiyu. The two companies had had close ties ever since the close of World War II.

Petroleum was not commonly used in Japan until after 1868, when Japan opened its commerce to Western markets. Until that time, domestically mined coal was used for heating and energy. Though some oil fields were discovered in Japan, from the 1880s through World War II the Japanese oil market was dominated by two foreign organizations, Standard Oil and Royal Dutch/Shell. These groups, already operating on a global scale, were able to flood the Japanese market with cheap imported oil.

With Japan's military and industrial buildup in the years preceding World War II, petroleum came to be important to the country's economy. Jet fuel in particular was crucial to the success of the Japanese air force. The Showa Oil Company was established during the war, in 1942, from the merger of three smaller oil companies, Hayama Oil, Asahi Oil, and Niitsu Oil.

Shell Sekiyu was begun around 1876 in Yokohama by the Samuel Samuel & Co., a forerunner of Shell. In 1900 the company was incorporated as the Rising Sun Petroleum Company, to handle escalating petroleum imports.

Prior to World War II, oil production had never really been enough to support the industrializing nation. In addition bombing during the war had laid waste to the company's physical plants. After the war occupation forces refused to allow the Japanese refining industry to start up until 1949. At that time joint operation with a foreign company was the most effective way to revive the almost dead petroleum industry, and Showa Oil signed an operating agreement with Royal Dutch/Shell in 1949. Shell Sekiyu did the same a year later. The U.S. occupation forces encouraged these mergers. Showa Oil, before its 1985 merger with Shell Sekiyu, was 50% owned by Royal Dutch/Shell and Shell Sekiyu was 100% owned by Royal Dutch.

In the 1950s Showa Oil and Shell Sekiyu were among several foreign-owned companies that dominated the Japanese petroleum market, focusing on rebuilding and expanding their refineries. Like most Japanese oil companies at that time, the Shell companies were not interested in exploration but in importing crude. The crude was refined, marketed, and distributed in Japan. In 1949 Showa Oil's Kawasaki refinery could handle 6,000 barrels of crude per day but capacity increased to 102,000 barrels per day by 1965. At the same time Shell Sekiyu had the capacity to refine 180,000 barrels per day. Most of the crude oil was imported from the Persian Gulf countries.

The tremendous buildup of the Shell affiliates' refining capacities was made possible without government loans, and with minimal government regulation. In the early 1960s, however, Japan's Ministry of International Trade and Industry (MITI) took a increasingly large role in the oil industry, in some ways working against Showa and other foreign-owned companies. The Petroleum Industry Law was enacted in 1962, which favored the development of domestically owned oil companies; the law also assigned to MITI a permanent supervisory role over the future development of the petroleum industry. The Japanese government wanted to avoid control of the oil industry by international oil companies, as had been the case before the war, and used its regulatory forces to ensure that domestic companies got favorable positions in the booming petroleum market. Around this time, Showa and Shell Sekiyu supplied roughly 12% of the Japanese oil market. Foreign-owned companies combined controlled roughly 80% of Japan's oil market, of which the Shell group was the third largest. MITI's aim was to approximate an even split between the international and domestic companies' shares of the market. MITI achieved this desired balance over the next ten years, without adversely affecting Showa Oil or Shell Sekiyu. The new government regulations directly or indirectly shaped the business strategies of the Shell companies in the years to come.

An overall effect of the 1962 regulatory act was to increase competition among all the companies dealing in the Japanese oil market. MITI actively encouraged mergers between smaller domestic companies so they could rival the larger, older, foreign-affiliated firms like Showa. The major *zaibatsu*, established banking and corporate dynasties, such as Mitsui, Sumitomo, and Mitsubishi, plunged into the oil business around the end of the 1950s. With long-standing political and economic power in Japan, these groups did not take long to come to the fore of the petroleum industry. The Japanese oil market became more competitive because the major companies were for the most part caught up to each other technologically. Japanese engineers, sponsored by MITI, were working diligently to master and improve petrochemical technology. As long as the price of imported crude remained stable, the competitive edge in the domestic market would go to the company with the most efficient, low-cost refining technology.

The powerful backing of Royal Dutch/Shell propelled Showa Oil and Shell Sekiyu through the first decade of MITI's regulation. In addition Royal Dutch/Shell had sources for crude oil in all parts of the globe. Foreign-affiliated firms still had advantages, particularly in international contract negotiations. The newer Japanese companies had little experience in negotiating drilling and exploration rights. Experts in Japan and abroad agreed that the new Japanese companies were not yet ready to take a major position in the world oil scene.

In the early 1970s, with rising political tensions in the Middle East, finding new sources of crude became important to the stability of the oil industry. By comparison with the other major international oil firms, Royal Dutch/Shell was considered short on crude oil. Its historical position as one of the two or three largest international oil companies was based on its efficient refining and marketing and long-range planning. Well before the 1973 OPEC embargo, the Shell companies were looking for oil sources outside the Middle East. Showa Oil began to seek out joint refining ventures abroad at the same time.

In 1975 Showa made an agreement with Algeria's National Hydrocarbon Corporation to provide technical assistance for the design and operation of two new oil refineries. Royal Dutch/Shell discovered a large natural gas field off Australia's northwest shelf around the same time; that gas was intended for marketing in Japan. Royal Dutch/Shell discovered the gigantic North Sea gas field in 1979, which improved the Shell affiliates' position considerably.

In the same year as the North Sea discovery, Showa Oil acquired a 25% interest in another Japanese company, Toa Oil, which interest was formerly held by C. Itoh, a Japanese holding company. Toa Oil had valuable contracts to import and wholesale 230,000 barrels of oil daily through direct purchases; that is, Toa could buy this oil directly from the oil field, without any international oil company intermediary. MITI had encouraged the domestic oil companies to make direct purchase contracts. Though C. Itoh initiated the sale of Toa to Showa, MITI was disturbed by the transaction. The domestic company would lose its direct purchase contracts to the foreign-affiliated Showa, shifting the balance within the Japanese oil industry to foreign affiliates. The market split between the foreign and domestic groups was very nearly 50–50 before the Toa sale, and MITI wanted to maintain this even split or tip it in favor of the domestic companies. However, in this case the industry went against the regulators' wishes.

Following the acquisition of Toa, Showa strengthened its ties with Kuwait. In 1980 the Kuwaiti government agreed to export 30,000 more barrels of crude oil per day to Showa Oil. Showa's efforts to secure a variety of sources for crude oil were generally successful in the 1970s. In the 1980s Showa found its profits still too closely tied to the fluctuations in the price of crude. In 1981 the company posted a loss of ¥21.2 billion. The next year, Showa showed a profit of ¥1.2 billion. In spite of highly sophisticated refining and marketing techniques, the company could do little to control the swings of the world's crude oil markets. Showa began to diversify its product line, and in the 1980s built and bought office buildings and apartment houses, to gain rental income. Showa also invested in rental car and travel businesses.

Showa Oil and Shell Sekiyu formally merged in 1985. They had had a close operating relationship through most of their history. The merger made them equal partners in the new corporation. Showa Shell Sekiyu K.K. Royal Dutch/Shell retained a 50% interest in the new company. The merger streamlined the Shell affiliates' operations and made management more efficient and cost-effective.

Despite the company's ventures into non-oil areas, including the 1987 launch of a computer software company, Computer Plaza K.K., Showa Shell Sekiyu's focus remained on oil. At the end of the 1980s, oil market analysts were predicting an even larger Japanese presence in the world oil market in the decades to come. MITI would like 30% of Japan's oil to come from fields leased or owned by Japanese companies by 1995. In 1989, only 10% came from such sources. Also in 1989, MITI agreed to give tax incentives to companies that buy existing oil fields. Showa Shell Sekiyu made it clear that the company's aim is to become a major producer as well as refiner in the 1990s. Kiyoshi Takahashi, executive chairman of Showa Shell Sekiyu, compared his company at the end of the 1980s to the Japanese car industry 15 years earlier, implying that the big boom is still to come.

The affiliation of Showa Shell Sekiyu with Royal Dutch/Shell continues to be a crucial element in the company's success. As political turmoil racks the Middle East in the 1990s, and most Japanese oil companies are exploring alternative sources of crude, partnership with the world's largest oil company places Showa Shell a step ahead in the search for new petroleum markets. Showa Shell Sekiyu plans to continue to ensure a steady flow of oil into Japan in the coming decades.

Principal Subsidiaries: Showa Shell Sempaku K.K.; K.K. Rising Sun; Showa Oil K.K.; Shoseki International Corp. (U.S.); Showa Oil Hong Kong; Showa Yokkaichi Sekiyu K.K. (75%); Higashi Ohgishima Oil Terminal K.K. (52%); Toa Sekiyu K.K. (42.17%); Seibu Sekiyu K.K. (24.19%).

Further Reading: "Japan: Today and Tomorrow," *Oil and Gas Journal*, May 31, 1965; Yoshino, M.Y., *Japan's Multinational Enterprises*, Cambridge, Massachusetts, Harvard University Press, 1976; Vernon, Raymond, *Two Hungry Giants: The United States and Japan in the Quest for Oil and Ores*, Cambridge, Harvard University Press, 1983.

—Angela Woodward

⊡ elf aquitaine

SOCIÉTÉ NATIONALE ELF AQUITAINE

Tour Elf
2, place de la Coupole
Courbevoie (Hauts de Seine)
France
(1) 47 44 45 46
Fax: (1) 47 44 78 78

Public Company
Incorporated: 1976
Employees: 89,309
Sales: FFr175.50 billion (US$34.48 billion)
Stock Exchanges: Paris Brussels Luxembourg Frankfurt
Düsseldorf Basel Geneva Zürich New York

Société Nationale Elf Aquitaine (SNEA), also known as Elf, is France's largest oil company, ranking eighth in the world in terms of reserves. It is a fully integrated oil and gas company, combining upstream production capacity from fields around the world with strong downstream refining and distribution facilities. It is also the second largest French chemicals producer. Its size is all the more impressive in view of its youth. One of Elf's consitituent enterprises, the Régie Autonome des Pétroles, first exploited modest gas reserves in 1939, at Saint-Marcet in the Haute-Garonne province of southwest France. But it was not until the 1950s that major gas and oil discoveries in France and the Algerian Sahara really started the future Elf Aquitaine on its rocket-like ascent.

The group's origins could be said to go back further than the 1939 Saint-Marcet discovery, to 1498 when Jacob Wimpfeling, a theologian from Alsace, was surprised to note mineral oil welling out of the ground at a place called Pechelbronn (fountain of pitch). Almost 500 years later, in 1970, the Antar group which then owned Pechelbronn was taken over by Elf. The company claims that the history of Elf Aquitaine "cannot be separated from history itself." A closer connection might be perceived between the history of Elf and the history of France's energy policy as practiced by successive governments since World War II.

Elf Aquitaine was—and remains—controlled by the state. In 1990 this control was exercised through Entreprise de Recherches et d'Activités Pétrolières (ERAP), a 100% state-owned company, which in turn held 53.9% of Société Nationale Elf Aquitaine. The remainder of SNEA's shares were divided among some 400,000 private shareholders.

Elf thus represents a clear departure from the relationship between the state and private enterprise in France as seen in the case of its older rival, the Compagnie Française des Pétroles (CFP), today's Total. CFP began in 1924 with the state holding no shares at all: since 1931 the state has contented itself with holding 35% of the company. The constituent companies of Elf Aquitaine have, in their time, been set similar objectives of "national interest" to those set by Prime Minister Raymond Poincaré for CFP in 1924. But in the case of Elf and its forerunners, the state has always held a majority of the shares.

The discovery of gas at Saint-Marcet in the summer of 1939 was made by a small exploration syndicate set up with public funding earlier in the decade to prospect for oil and gas in the region. It was one of a number of such organizations nationwide, the reason for whose creation was the awareness that the major oil companies had bigger and better fish to fry in other, known oil-bearing parts of the world, such as Mesopotamia. The Compagnie Française des Pétroles, Royal Dutch/Shell, and Standard Oil of New Jersey could not be expected to plow much money into looking for oil or gas in France.

The oil giants were wrong, but it was not until after the war that they were to discover it. The find at Saint-Marcet was modest, although it did continue to produce gas until 1988. The Régie Autonome des Pétroles (RAP) was immediately formed to exploit the new resource: this public body set to work to extract the gas and to build a plant for its treatment near Boussens.

World War II left the Compagnie Française des Pétroles with little to do: France's share of oil from the Mesopotamian fields at Kirkouk was cut off by the British after the German invasion of France. But the Vichy government in southern France was not idle on its own account. In 1941 it created the Société Nationale des Pétroles d'Aquitaine (SNPA) to look for oil and gas in the Aquitaine region. Through the efforts of SNPA, Aquitaine was to become the oil and gas province of France.

Later in the war, when German troops occupied Vichy, the management of SNPA slackened off in its efforts to find oil. SNPA's reluctance to help in the German war effort resulted in the deportation of the company's first chairman, Pierre Angot. Like his counterpart at CFP, Jules Mény, who was also deported, Angot never returned to France.

The end of the war found the Compagnie Française des Pétroles in some disarray, with its French refining capacity in particular seriously impaired by war damage. President Charles de Gaulle was eager that the government play an active role in restoring the country's control over its energy supplies as fast as possible. In 1945 he created the Bureau de Recherches de Pétrole (BRP) to help the process along.

The role of BRP, which was entirely publicly funded, was— according to its founding charter—to encourage oil and gas exploration in France, its colonies, and protectorates, "in the exclusive interest of the nation." Unlike RAP, BRP was not to engage in such exploration itself, but simply to identify and invest in projects that would.

De Gaulle chose Pierre Guillaumat as the first chairman of BRP. Then 36 years old, Guillaumat was to prove the single most influential figure in the history of Elf Aquitaine. He finally retired as chairman of Elf, newly baptized with its current name, in 1977. Guillaumat's relationship with de Gaulle was close. The French president had served under Guillaumat's father in the army. This personal relationship was clearly a great asset for the fledgling BRP, perhaps as great an asset as the personal support of the French Prime Minister Raymond Poincaré had been for CFP's first chairman, Ernest Mercier, in the 1920s.

In the first years of its life, by far the most important investments made by BRP were in the French colony of Algeria and in equatorial Africa. Exploration in the Congo and in Gabon was largely carried out through Société des Pétroles d'Afrique Equatoriale (SPAFE), a joint venture with various French banks. Consortia were formed between SPAFE, Mobil, and Shell. In Algeria the beneficiary of BRP's funding was SN Repal, a joint venture with colonial government and the Compagnie Française des Pétroles. Also established was Compagnie de Recherche et d'Exploitation du Pétrole du Sahara (CREPS), a further oil exploration joint venture in Algeria, this time between RAP with 65% and Royal Dutch/Shell with 35%.

BRP's failure to discover oil in the 1940s appeared to confirm the skepticism of those who doubted that oil would ever be discovered in the Algerian Sahara. Paradoxically, it was precisely this skepticism that had encouraged the French government to set up BRP in the first place—the privately owned oil companies, with shareholders' dividends to pay out, were not about to see large investments swallowed up by the sands of north Africa.

The job of managing BRP's still fruitless investments in Africa was insufficiently demanding for someone of Guillaumat's ability, in the government's estimation. In 1950 he left BRP to become head of France's new Atomic Energy Commission. Eight years later, as the political situation in Algeria worsened, he became de Gaulle's minister for the army. Not until 1960 did he return to take charge of the much restructured BRP.

If BRP was still sifting sand in the early 1950s, SNPA was proving rather more fortunate closer to home. The Lacq gas field, discovered by SNPA in southwest France in December 1951, was huge by French standards and impressive enough by any standards with reserves estimated at 250 billion metres. Extracting the gas was to prove technically awkward on account of its highly toxic and corrosive impurities, notably hydrogen sulfate. But in the longer term SNPA was to turn these initial difficulties to its advantage. France became a net exporter of sulfates and the expertise SNPA acquired in treating highly sulfurous natural gas also proved eminently exportable.

All the same, the delays must have been frustrating at the beginning for SNPA's shareholders, of which the French state, with 51%, was by far the largest. It took fully five years from the discovery of gas at Lacq in 1951 for a salable product to be developed.

Meanwhile the Bureau de Recherches de Pétrole was still pumping French taxpayers' money into its African investments. Its funding increased steeply after 1953 when it became a beneficiary of a new sales tax on petroleum products in France. Four years later, the government's tenacity proved justified; SN Repal discovered a huge gas field at Hassi R'Mel in November 1956. Earlier that year, in July, the same company had struck oil, also in large quantities, at Hassi Messaoud.

The other forerunners of Elf Aquitaine, RAP and SNPA, also struck oil in the Algerian desert at around the same time. In 1956 CREPS, the RAP and Shell joint venture, brought the Sahara's first marketable oil to the surface at Edjeleh. The following year, SNPA discovered oil at El Gassi.

1956 and 1957 also saw the first discoveries of oil in equatorial Africa, in Gabon and the Congo. But it was not until the early 1960s that really big discoveries were made in the region, and then not on land but at sea, in the Gulf of Guinea.

By 1960 the French state had significant upstream oil and gas producing capacity. Gas from the Lacq field in Aquitaine made France almost self-sufficient in this valuable commodity, and oil and gas from North Africa was gushing and bubbling to the surface in abundance.

There were two problems. The first was that the various state-funded investment and exploration companies lacked the means to transport, refine, and sell their oil and gas. Upstream, they were handsomely endowed; downstream, they had nothing—no ships, no refineries, and no service stations. The second problem was that crude oil was in plentiful supply and the heavily sulfurated Algerian oil cost more to produce and refine than oil from the Middle East. It was hard to find buyers.

The French government concluded that these were problems for Pierre Guillaumat to solve. He re-entered the oil business as chairman of l'Union Générale des Pétroles (UGP) in 1960. UGP had three shareholders, all of them state-controlled. These were RAP, SN Repal, and the Groupement des Exploitants Pétroliers. This last encompassed all the active subsidiaries of BRP—including SNPA, where BRP had become responsible for the state's investment.

Guillaumat's task was to propose ways of rationalizing these various interests and, more urgently, to supply UGP's shareholders with refining and distribution facilities. While he was working on this, the government came up with its own solution to the uncompetitive price of Algerian crude. It imposed a *devoir national* (national duty) on all French oil refiners and marketers to accept a certain amount of franc-zone crude, mostly from Algeria. One political argument in favor of this was that investment in oil production from such regions did not eat into French foreign currency reserves. Not surprisingly the decision did not find favor with the chairman of CFP, Victor de Metz. The vast majority of CFP's oil production still derived from the Middle East, outside the franc-zone.

Nevertheless, from Pierre Guillaumat's point of view the *devoir national* ruling was obviously very helpful. It meant that the oil discoveries in North Africa and later in Equatorial Africa were not quite the boon that the French public might reasonably have hoped for. But from the government's standpoint at least the oil was sold and the wells stayed in business. Their produce would doubtless be more appreciated in the future.

Pierre Guillaumat set about his primary task with alacrity. In 1960 UGP bought the French operations of Caltex, a refining and distributing operation owned jointly by Texaco and Standard Oil (California). Caltex owned a refinery at Ambes near Bordeaux: UGP created a subsidiary, l'Union Industrielle des Pétroles (UIP), to run it. UIP was owned 60% by UGP and 40% by Caltex. The association with the U.S. oil companies behind Caltex would continue over many years and branch into many areas.

UGP also bought other fairly modest distribution networks—the purchase of Caltex had given it an immediate 4% market share—as well as building new refineries on its own account. UGP's smokestacks came to dominate the skyline at Feyzin near Lyons in 1964, and at Grandpuits, in 1966, and Gargenville, near Paris, in 1968. Outside France, a refinery was built at Spire in West Germany in 1965. Algerian independence in 1962 had no immediate negative impact on the group. For the time being the so-called Evian accords between the French and the Algerians protected France's energy interests in that country.

Large-scale rationalization took place in 1966, presided over by Pierre Guillaumat. BRP and RAP were transformed into ERAP. The majority stake in SNPA held by BRP thus passed to ERAP. Guillaumat became chairman both of the ERAP holding company and of its most dynamic subsidiary SNPA. He was to continue to hold both positions for 12 years. The group was still receiving funds from the sales tax on petroleum products—indeed, these support grants, as they were called, increased from 1966 as the government encouraged the group to diversify its oil supplies away from Algeria.

The French government's degree of involvement in the oil industry was by no means unique in Continental Europe at the time. The Italians had created Ente Nazionale Idrocarburi (ENI) in 1953 and given it monopoly exploration rights in the Po Valley, an area long coveted by foreign oil companies. In 1965 the Spanish had conducted an exercise similar to the restructuring in France, leading to the creation of Hispanoil.

Guillaumat and ERAP were more original in the deals they struck with oil-producing nations. ERAP's pioneering *contrats d'entreprise* were signed first with Iran in 1966 and two years later with Iraq. Others followed. These were essentially service contracts under which ERAP agreed to provide exploration and production skills in return for long-term crude supplies at preferential rates. The success of this arrangement in Iraq provided a framework for the amicable resolution of Franco-Iraqi differences when the Iraqi government nationalized the assets of the Compagnie Française des Pétroles, among others, in 1972.

ERAP and SNPA still lacked an instantly recognizable brand name in France. This was remedied on the night of April 27 to 28, 1967, when the Elf name and logo were unveiled at thousands of service stations around the country. The name "Elf" was chosen for its attractive connotations of nimbleness and sprightliness, and was not an acronym.

In 1970 ERAP took control of the Antar group with its three refineries and vast distribution network. The purchase left the group with almost a quarter of the French market share for oil products.

The Antar brand name may still be seen in France today: it was considered too distinctive to throw away. Moreover, ERAP was not the only shareholder. CFP, with its by now long-established Total brand name, also bought a 24% stake.

At the beginning of the 1970s ERAP still trailed CFP; in terms of sales it was about three-quarters the size of the older company. That was to change in the coming decade, but first ERAP had to overcome its greatest crisis—the nationalization of its Algerian assets. This occurred in February 1971. It was hardly unexpected, as Shell's Algerian assets had been nationalized the previous year. During the late 1960s ERAP had been diversifying its production as rapidly as possible. New business opportunities were beginning to open up in North America, in Nigeria, in Iran and Iraq, and in the North Sea. Nevertheless, the Algerian nationalization was a heavy blow—at a stroke the group lost two-thirds of its crude oil production, together with the huge gas reserves at Hassi R'Mel.

Guillaumat anticipated that by 1975 the group would be able to reattain its pre-nationalization production level of 180,000 barrels per day. Events proved him almost right, but 1971 was a difficult year.

Fortunately the staunch political support which Guillaumat had always enjoyed from Charles de Gaulle continued under de Gaulle's successor as French president, Georges Pompidou. On July 29, 1971, a French cabinet meeting under President Pompidou reaffirmed the government's faith in ERAP's future and gave its blessing to the further integration of SNPA into ERAP.

This was because SNPA had withstood the loss of the Algerian oil and gas fields rather better than other parts of the group. Oil accounted for only 22% of SNPA's sales in 1970. Gas was still being plentifully and profitably produced at Lacq and, since the early 1960s, SNPA had been diversifying into petrochemicals.

An encouraging sign for the future was the discovery of the Frigg gas field in the North Sea in 1971. From 1977 this would permit the group almost to double its gas output—Frigg was the same size as Lacq but could produce gas twice as fast. ERAP was entitled to half its production. However, in the early 1970s the development of the Frigg field imposed huge demands on ERAP's budget.

The two oil price increases instigated by the OPEC cartel in 1973 and 1979 increased the value of reserves held by the group—which was renamed Société Nationale Elf Aquitaine in 1976—tenfold. But it wrought havoc with the group's refining operations. Governments everywhere launched energy conservation programs and demand for refined oil products plummeted. The group closed down three refineries in France and a fourth at Spire in West Germany. At the same time, government-imposed price controls prevented ERAP and other oil companies operating in France from passing on the OPEC price rises in full measure to consumers.

The French government did not leave ERAP completely in the lurch. A tax on petrol imposed from 1974 sought to redistribute wealth away from the big petrol producers to the benefit of the major suppliers of fuel oil. In 1974 ERAP was by far the largest beneficiary.

The group's diversification efforts in the 1970s were considerable. In 1973 Sanofi, a new subsidiary, was set up to invest in pharmaceuticals companies. It immediately bought an immunology research company, Laboratoire Michel Robilliard; a pharmaceuticals manufacturer, Labaz; and a minority stake in cosmetics group Yves Rocher. By the late 1980s Elf Aquitaine had become the second-largest pharmaceuticals group in France, with some 140 companies under the Sanofi umbrella.

In 1977, the year after the final merger between ERAP and SNPA to form the new Société Nationale Elf Aquitaine, Pierre Guillaumat retired. He was succeeded by Albin Chalandon, an experienced civil servant with a treasury background. Like his predecessor, Chalandon had served as a minister under Charles de Gaulle.

Chalandon raised Elf Aquitaine's profile in the United States through the acquisition in 1981 of Texasgulf. The combination of Texasgulf's strength as a producer of mined sulfur and Elf's existing production at Lacq made the group the world's largest producer of this mineral. Texasgulf also had huge phosphate reserves and was one of the largest U.S. fertilizer producers. The purchase tripled Elf's overall U.S. business at a stroke.

Albin Chalandon's chairmanship at Elf lasted until 1983, when Michel Pecqueur took over. Pecqueur had formerly been head of France's Atomic Energy Commission, a position held by Pierre Guillaumat in the early 1950s. The new chairman's first move was to strengthen the group's chemicals business.

"Elf Aquitaine has now truly become an oil and chemicals group," Pecqueur told shareholders at the company's annual general meeting in the spring of 1984. He admitted that it was a big gamble: the chemical companies grouped under the banner of Elf Aquitaine's new subsidiary, Atochem, had been "heavy loss makers."

Elf Aquitaine's new-found prominence in chemicals derived from a major restructuring of this largely state-controlled industry. The group acquired chlorate and ethylene producing capacity from the state-owned chemicals group Rhône-Poulenc, and further chlorate and fluorine plants from Produits Chimique Ugine Kuhlman (PCUK). As a result of Elf's expansion in these fields, consolidated turnover in 1983 increased 17% to FFr134.77 billion, only slightly behind Total Compagnie Française des Pétroles.

Profitability took a little longer to achieve. Between 1983 and 1989 Atochem passed from a FFr1.1 billion loss to a FFr2.4 billion profit after tax. Elf's 1989 report describes its chemical business—France's second-largest after Rhône-Poulenc's—as "an essential factor in the equilibrium of the group."

Under Elf Aquitaine's latest chairman, Loïk Le Floch-Prigent, the group's chemicals business has continued to grow apace. Le Floch-Prigent took the helm at Elf Aquitaine in June 1989. Until 1986 he had been chairman of Rhône-Poulenc—his deputy, interestingly, was Total's latest chairman, Serge Tchuruk.

In August 1989 Elf bought the U.S. specialty chemicals firm Pennwalt for US$1 billion. At the beginning of 1990, a division of the business of the state-owned French chemicals company Orkem was finalized. Elf picked up Orkem's petrochemicals and fertilizer businesses; while Total acquired the specialty operations, such as adhesives, paints, and resins. In the first half of 1990, no less than 42% of Elf's FFr10.2 billion operating profits came from its chemicals business. The group therefore has a sizeable cushion against any deterioration of its oil business.

Since Loïk Le Floch-Prigent took the helm at Elf, the group has been cutting back on its distribution network in France, where margins have been squeezed by the rise of discount filling stations owned by the hypermarkets. The Persian Gulf crisis worsened the situation because moral pressure brought to bear by the French government on distributors prevented oil price rises from being passed on in full to the motorist.

Temporary problems notwithstanding, half a century of public investment in the business of Elf Aquitaine is now paying off. The company's current chairman presides over a truly diversified group which should be well equipped to withstand the heaviest of knocks.

Principal Subsidiaries: Société Nationale Elf Aquitaine (Production); Elf Congo; Elf Italiana spa; Elf Aquitaine Norge A/S; Société Elf de Recherches et d'Exploitation des Pétroles au Cameroun; Elf Gabon; Société Africaine d'Exploration Pétrolière; Elf Nigeria Ltd.; Elf Aquitaine Inc.; Elf U.K. (Holdings) Plc; Elf Aquitaine Oman; Elf Aquitaine Colombie; Elf Aquitaine Angola; SOCAP International Ltd.; Elf Trading Inc.; Elf Trading SA(Genève); Elf France; Société des Lubrifiants Elf Aquitaine; Elf Antargaz; Elf Suisse; Elf Mineraloel GmbH; Elf Belgique; Elf Nederland; Anker Union NV; Elf Petroleum G.B.; Société Nationale des Gaz du Sud-Ouest; Société Elf France-CORIF; Elf Atlantique et Cie; Texasgulf Inc.; Atochem; Atochem North America; Sanofi; Société Financière Auxiliaire des Pétroles-SOFAX; SOGERAP; Compagnie de Participations et d'Investissements Holding SA; Société Financière Internationale de Participation; SAFREP SA; Rivunion SA; Alphega.

Further Reading: Grayson, Leslie E., *National Oil Companies,* London, John Wiley & Sons, 1981; Direction des Relations Publiques et de la Communication, Elf Aquitaine, *L'Histoire d'Elf Aquitaine,* Paris, Elf Aquitaine, 1986; Giraud, André, and Xavier Boy de la Tour, *Géopolitique du Pétrole et du Gaz,* Paris, Editions Technip, 1987; Dawkins, William, "Shaping Up For Competition," *Financial Times,* November 12, 1990.

—William Pitt

SUN COMPANY, INC.

100 Matsonford Road
Radnor, Pennsylvania 19087
U.S.A.
(215) 293-6000
Fax: (215) 977-6574

Public Company
Incorporated: 1890 as Sun Oil Company
Employees: 20,900
Sales: $13.27 billion
Stock Exchanges: New York Philadelphia Alberta Basel
 Geneva Zürich Düsseldorf Frankfurt London

Sun Company is the largest independent company that explores, develops, produces, and markets crude oil and natural gas. While Sun traces its roots to the United States in the 1880s, most of its oil and gas exploration and production now occur outside of the United States, in the North Sea and in Canada. Sun also produces synthetic crude oil in western Canada, and refines and markets a wide variety of petroleum products throughout the world. In addition, Sun mines coal in the United States. Late-20th century diversification involved the company with equipment leasing and secured lending, as well as with real estate development.

Sun's beginnings go back to 1881, when Joseph Newton Pew, known as Newton Pew, and Edward Octavius Emerson incorporated Keystone Gas Company. Emerson was president, and Pew was the treasurer. Emerson, a 42–year–old banker had the financial expertise and backing, while Pew, at 28, was just becoming known in the oil–and–gas real estate business, having traded in property and leases since the 1870s. Emerson and Pew's new company succeeded so well that within a year they incorporated Penn Fuel Company, the first supplier of natural gas to a major city, Pittsburgh, for home use as well as for industrial use. In the words of Pew's nephew J. Howard Pew, "When Newton Pew arrived in 1882, few Pittsburghers realized they were in need of natural gas. The Penn Fuel Company immediately embarked upon correcting this oversight by building gas pipelines to the city."

By 1884, the two men had sold their interest in the Penn Fuel Company and started The Peoples Natural Gas Company. Not too long after that, the partners got wind of substantial oil discoveries in Ohio. Pew sent his nephew, Robert Cunningham Pew, to investigate the possibility of securing leases in northwestern Ohio's oil fields. Under Pew and Emerson's direction,

Robert spent $4,500 on two leases in Ohio's Findlay township. Robert Pew was left to manage the Ohio oil operations while Edward Emerson and Newton Pew focused their attention on the natural gas end of their business. By 1889, however, production in their Ohio oil fields grew so large that it could no longer be ignored. Pew and Emerson incorporated the Sun Oil Line Company in order to acquire the necessary pipelines, leases, storage tanks, and tank cars. The operation continued to grow to the point where, in 1890, Pew and Emerson thought it wise to consolidate their interests, and they incorporated Sun Oil Company in Ohio with the stated intention of "producing petroleum, rock and carbon oil; transporting and storing same; refining, purifying, manufacturing such oil and its various products . . . ," getting Sun Oil off to a running start.

In 1894 Sun Oil, in a joint venture with Merriam and Morgan Paraffine Company of Cleveland, incorporated the Diamond Oil Company for the purpose of purchasing a refinery just outside Toledo for $22,200 from economically troubled Crystal Oil Company. This plant refined the first oils that Sun Oil ever shipped. In 1895, Pew and Emerson bought out Merriam and Morgan's interest, and the refinery became entirely Sun Oil's. Not only did Sun Oil get its first refinery out of Diamond Oil; it adopted a diamond shape enclosing the words "Sun Oil" as the company trademark.

Both of Emerson and Pew's businesses were developing at a rapid pace. While Sun Oil continued to grow, The Peoples Natural Gas Company also prospered under the control of Emerson and Pew. In 1899, Pew bought out Emerson's stake in the Sun Oil Company and, by 1903, he had sold his own stake in The Peoples Natural Gas Company. In 1901 Pew reincorporated Sun Oil Company in New Jersey as Sun Company. Between 1899 and 1903 Newton Pew worked hard to help Sun Oil stand firmly on its own feet.

In 1901 the Spindletop well in Beaumont, Texas, spurting 100,000 barrels of oil a day for ten days, was the biggest oil strike yet. Newton Pew lost no time sending Robert Pew there. At that time, Beaumont was suffering from something akin to gold fever, except that Beaumont's gold was black. Within a month, Robert Pew had returned to Toledo, and Newton Pew sent Robert's brother, James Edgar Pew, in his stead.

J. Edgar Pew would become one of the most famous and respected oil man in the production end of the business. In the words of a retired Sun executive, J. Edgar Pew ". . . was shrewd enough to see that you could make more money by drilling and producing the oil than by going around and buying it."

Pew bought 42 acres of land on the Neches River and erected storage tanks. In 1902, at a public auction, he bid $100,000 for the assets of the bankrupt Lone Star and Crescent Oil Company. His was the only bid of the day and it won the assets. The auction's terms, however, demanded an immediate down payment of at least 25%. When Pew went to the two local banks he'd been using, he found them closed for Decoration Day. As he kicked up dust on the streets of the town he saw his prize slipping away, until he spotted some men remodeling an old building to hold a new bank. Sun's reputation was already so well known, that a man inside the building wrote J. Edgar a check for $25,000 on the spot.

Meanwhile, Robert Pew observed that the key to Sun's success in its Texas endeavors lay in finding a way to move its Texas crude inexpensively to refineries, because the cost of transporting it over land was so high that it was out of the question. In October 1901, Newton Pew spent $45,000 for land on the Delaware River in Marcus Hook, Pennsylvania, and started building a refinery there to process the Texas crude. United Gas Improvement Company, of Philadelphia, Pennsylvania, was Sun's partner, with 45% of the venture. Five months later, in March of 1902, the refinery received the first crude Sun sent out of Texas, delivered by Sun's first tanker, the S.S. *Paraguay.* In 1905 Sun transformed the *Thomas W. Lawson,* the world's largest schooner-rigged sailing ship, into an oil carrier.

During these rapidly moving events, J. Howard Pew, Newton Pew's second son, began work at Sun. J. Howard Pew had finished both high school and college by the time he was 18. In 1901 the 19-year-old J. Howard began working in the Toledo, Ohio, refinery, experimenting with the heavy black residue from Sun's Texas crude. In the new Marcus Hook refinery, the crude was developed into a lubricating oil, known as Sun Red Stock. By 1904 J. Howard Pew and his team of researchers had developed the first commercially successful petroleum asphalt. Sun had more thán 100 trade-name products on the market by 1910.

In 1908, Joseph's third son, Joseph Newton Pew Jr., joined the Sun staff. He recalled that, about three months after he started, he went to talk to his father about his job in Sun's purchasing department to ask for "a real job." According to Joseph, his father's response was, "Joe, you have been given your opportunity and it is up to you to make your job." Joe took those words to heart. He drove ox teams through the mud to get loads of pipe across West Virginia, laid mahogany roads in Venezuela, and spent five nights without sleep while bringing in a new well in Illinois.

By 1912 when Joseph Newton Pew Sr., Sun's first president, died, his sons were already working together as a team. J. Howard became president at the age of 30; Joseph Newton Pew Jr. became vice president at 26.

J. Howard Pew took a business trip to Germany in 1915, a year after the beginning of World War I. He was shocked by Germany's air and naval strength and predicted with some accuracy the amount of damage Germany could inflict on Allied shipping, including oil tankers. When he returned to the United States, he authorized the beginning of Sun Ship, a shipbuilding facility on the Delaware River, south of Philadelphia. By 1917, when the United States became involved in the war, Sun Ship was able to slide its first freighter, the S.S. *Chester Sun,* into the water. By the end of World War I, Sun Ship had built three mine-sweepers and six tankers for the U.S. Navy.

Before the war, Sun's place in the petroleum industry was in lubricating and industrial oils, and it sold oil directly to Philadelphia's United Gas Improvement Company (UGI). During the war, however, Sun severed its connections with UGI, and Sun was left with a huge supply of gas oil, the source of gasoline. The automobile industry had grown so rapidly that by 1918 more than six million vehicles moved over U.S. highways. Quickly shifting gears, Sun began to construct it first gasoline filling station in Ardmore, Pennsylvania. It opened in 1920. A diamond-shaped sign with a red arrow through it proclaimed Sun's Products. Since that day, Sun's trademark has not changed nor has the name of the gasoline, Sunoco.

In 1922 Sun Company once again reincorporated, as a Pennsylvania company, under the name Sun Oil Company (PA).

Also in 1922, at the Marcus Hook refinery, Sun Oil set in motion its first high–pressure cracking units that enabled it to produce gasoline much more quickly. This expanded capacity allowed Sun Oil to increase its sales beyond the mid-Atlantic region.

Most other refiners at this time were adding tetraethyl lead to gasoline to kill engine knock. Sun Oil took a different track. It produced premium gasoline without adding lead. In 1927, Sun Oil introduced its only grade of gasoline, calling it Blue Sunoco, "The High Powered Knockless Fuel at No Extra Price." Blue dye was used in the gasoline so that motorists could identify it by its color, through the glass of the 1920s gravity-flow gasoline pumps.

In 1923, Sun Ship introduced the Sun Doxford diesel engine. In a few years Sun Ship became the largest U.S. manufacturer of large marine diesel engines. In 1931, it launched the world's first all-welded tanker, the S.S. *White Flash.* In 1931, Sun built the first long–distance petroleum–products pipeline in the United States. This 730–mile pipeline stretched from Twin Oaks, Pennsylvania, through Syracuse, New York, to Cleveland, Ohio, with branch lines to cities in between.

The usual refining practice in the oil industry at the time was to heat the crude to such extreme temperatures that it became vaporous. The vapors were then condensed into gasoline and other products. This process yielded only about 40% high-grade fuel. The leftover 60% was a sludgy substance that could only be made into low-profit items. All this began to change in 1933, when Eugene Houdry, a Frenchman, made an appointment to see Arthur Pew, Newton Pew's oldest son.

Houdry was working on an invention that would get more gasoline out of every gallon, of a much higher octane. Most of his preliminary work had been done in France, and in Vacuum Oil Company's refinery in New Jersey. When Vacuum merged with Standard Oil Company of New York, however, Houdry's refining project was shelved. He had been trying to sell his refining process to other companies, but he had had no luck until he reached Sun Oil. Within an hour at the first meeting, Houdry and Arthur Pew struck a deal. Working in Sun Oil's Marcus Hook laboratory, Houdry developed a model that performed to perfection. Sun Oil then built Houdry's catalytic cracking plant at Marcus Hook refinery, ran it on trial for a year and a half in secret, then announced its success to the world in 1937.

Toward the end of World War II, when the gas needs of the United States were critical, the Marcus Hook refinery shipped more than 1.1 million barrels a month of 100-octane aviation gas. At the same time, Sun Ship built an average of one ship a week. The end of the war brought a sharp decline in U.S. ship construction, as foreign competition took business from U.S. commercial builders, Sun Ship included.

After the war, J. Howard Pew started grooming as his successor an outsider from Sun Oil's ranks. In 1947 Robert G. Dunlop became Sun Oil's first non-Pew president in 60 years. During his presidency, revenues grew sixfold and profits ninefold.

By the early 1950s, when car types began to vary, Sun Oil's one type of gasoline could no longer meet the differing octane needs of higher–compression engines, and Sun Oil's market share began to fall off. In 1956 Sun Oil opened its first custom–blending pump in Orlando, Florida; from five grades of gasoline, customers could select the one that best met their car's octane needs and the pump would mix it then and there. By 1958, Sun Oil had removed the last of the pump's flaws and was able to introduce six grades of custom blending to its entire market territory.

Dunlop's ability to make quick decisions led to Sun Oil's abundant Lake Maracaibo, Venezuela, oil discovery in 1957. Taking the advice of an advisory group, Sun Oil investigated this offshore site that ultimately had nearly 100 wells producing 450 million barrels of oil, 200 million of which were Sun Oil's share. Sun's Venezuelan operations, known as VenSun, prospered until Venezuela nationalized its oil industry in 1975.

Sun Oil went on to establish the North Sea Sun Oil Company Ltd. in 1965. The next year, as a member of the Arpet group, Sun helped discover the Hewett gas field off England's coast, beginning Sun's history in offshore North Sea drilling.

Bob Dunlop steered the company through the Sun Oil–Sunray DX merger. Their courtship began in 1967 at an industry dinner in Midland, Texas, where Dunlop and Sunray chief Paul Taliafero were seated next to one another. Sun Oil operated primarily in the eastern United States and Sunray almost exclusively in the Midwest. Their refining and marketing regions added to each, complementing rather than competing. By every measurement Sun Oil was about twice the size of Sunray DX. The companies agreed to merge in 1968. A year and a half were spent planning the mechanics of the merger, which resulted in a company with 30,000 employees and more than $2 billion in assets. The merger turned Sun Oil into a huge corporation and changed the way the company would be run from that point hence.

All this time Sun Oil was working to develop what was called the world's first oil mine, Canada's Athabasca sands, on the Athabasca River. It was thought these sands held more recoverable oil than all of the oil in the Middle East. The problem was how to transport the sand to where the oil could be recovered or how to recover the oil on-site in such a far north location. Sun Oil finished construction of a refinery in 1967, intended to boil 45,000 barrels of oil out of the sand a day. The cost of producing oil was too high to compete with the low oil prices of the day. However, ten years later, when oil prices started climbing, Sun Oil's sands began to turn a profit.

Sun Oil constructed a $150 million operation in Yabuco, Puerto Rico, including an all-weather harbor and a 66,000-barrel-per-day refinery in 1969. In 1971 Sun Oil Company (PA) became simply Sun Oil Company.

In 1970, when Dunlop retired, H. Robert Sharbaugh became Sun Oil's new president. Attention was focused on pushing up the stock price and raising cash dividend. Individual employees were given the opportunity to advance their own careers when a management-training school was founded. By 1974, Sharbaugh had been named CEO, and by 1975 he was chairman of the board. In 1975 Sharbaugh announced he would restructure the company into 14 decentralized operating units and two property companies, all of which would be controlled by a nonoperating parent company.

In 1976 Sun Oil Company changed its name to Sun Company, Inc., to portray the fact that it was involved in more businesses than just oil. That same year Theodore A. Burtis became Sun's new president. In 1978 Chairman Sharbaugh authorized the purchase of a large interest in Becton, Dickinson and Company, a medical–supply firm, and it became obvious that Sharbaugh's vision for Sun differed from that of the board. In 1979 Theodore Burtis became Sun's new chairman.

In 1979 Sun, in an effort to redirect its company toward energy resources, made an acquisition in mining. This was Elk River Resources, Inc., which had mining operations in Kentucky and Virginia, with reserves of 186 million tons of coal in those states and in West Virginia. By 1983 this acquisition's production increased by almost 35%. Additional acquisitions expanded its coal reserves by 70%.

In 1980 Sun bought all the domestic oil and gas properties of Texas Pacific Oil Company for $23 billion. In 1982 Sun Ship was sold; it had not turned a profit in more than five years. Robert McClements Jr. took over Burtis's duties as president in 1981, but Burtis remained CEO and chairman.

In 1982 when the People's Republic of China invited oil companies to help it develop its 3,000 miles of coastline, Sun was one of the first to jump in. In 1983 Sun was granted shares in exploration tracts in the Gulf of Beibu and the South China Sea. By 1984, a Sun–manned jack–up rig had been installed off Hainan Island in the Gulf of Beibu, and drilling began.

In 1984 Sun acquired the Exeter Oil Company for $76 million and some Victory Oil Company properties for $281 million. As McClements explained it, "The acquisitions reflect Sun's strategy of acquiring existing producing properties and, using its production know-how, quickly bringing them up to snuff." Within a short period of time Exeter's production climbed from 500 barrels a day to more than 1,000.

Burtis worked closely with McClements on strategic direction until McClements became CEO in 1985. Oil prices began to decline in the late 1980s and Sun laid off employees. In November 1988 Sun spun off its subsidiary Sun Exploration and Production Company, which was renamed Oryx Energy Company.

Environmental issues may play a role in Sun's future. Tougher acid rain legislation could increase demand for low-sulfur coals.

Principal Subsidiaries: Sun International Exploration and Production; Sun Coal Company; Sun Refining and Marketing Company; Suncor Inc.; Radnor Corporation; Helios Capital Corporation.

Further Reading: Centennial Celebration: The Story of Sun Company, Radnor, Pennsylvania, Sun Company, Inc., 1986.

—Maya Sahafi

TEXACO INC.

2000 Westchester Avenue
White Plains, New York 10650
U.S.A
(914) 253-4000
Fax: (914) 253-7753

Public Company
Incorporated: 1926 as The Texas Corporation
Employees: 39,199
Sales: $41.82 billion
Stock Exchanges: New York Toronto London Zürich Brussels
 Geneva

Texaco is one of the world's largest oil companies, with exploratory, manufacturing, and marketing operations across the globe. Its petroleum-based products include automotive gasoline and oils, aviation fuels, heating fuels, and petrochemicals. Texaco expanded with the growth of the U.S. automobile industry in the early 20th century and quickly developed international production and marketing interests. By the 1960s it had established the largest sales network of any U.S. oil company, with operations concentrated in refining and marketing. The oil crisis of the 1970s cut off many of its international sources of crude oil and left it with limited reserves. Texaco was poised for recovery in 1984 when it entered into a court battle with Pennzoil Company over the acquisition of Getty Oil. Since settling with Pennzoil in 1988, Texaco has pursued a major restructuring effort to recapture its former profitability and prominence in the oil industry.

Texaco was founded during the early boom years of The Texas oil industry. In 1901 a gusher at the Spindletop oil field sent hundreds of entrepreneurs into Beaumont, Texas. Among them was Joseph S. Cullinan, an oilman who had begun his career working for Standard Oil Company in Pennsylvania. The Spindletop wells led to the rapid establishment of over 200 oil companies, pumping out as much as 100,000 barrels a day. Cullinan saw an opportunity in purchasing that crude for resale to refineries. With the help of New York investment manager Arnold Schlaet, he formed The Texas Fuel Company with an initial stock of $50,000. Cullinan and Schlaet began soliciting additional investments in New York and Chicago. After raising $3 million, they reorganized their venture as The Texas Company.

Cullinan immediately began constructing a pipeline between Spindletop and the gulf coast of Texas. He built a refinery at the Texas coastal city of Port Arthur, and from there the company shipped its oil to Louisiana sugar planters, who used it to heat their boilers. In the fall of 1902, salt water leaked into the Spindletop wells, ruining many of the companies based there. The Texas Company survived with a timely discovery of oil at Sour Lake, 20 miles northwest of Spindletop. Other strikes soon followed in Oklahoma and Louisiana.

With Cullinan's oil expertise and the financing of his New York backers, The Texas Company soon became one of the nation's most prominent oil companies. Cullinan continued to drill wells in the southwest region, building more pipelines to connect them with Port Arthur. By 1908 the company was selling to all but five western states, and by 1913 its assets were worth $60 million. The nickname Texaco came from the cable address of the company's New York offices. Texaco gained popularity as a product name, and in 1906 the company registered it as a trademark. The well-known logo first appeared in 1909, as a red star with a green "T" in the center. The company formally changed its name to Texaco Inc. in 1959.

At the time of Texaco's founding, oil was used primarily for lighting and as fuel for factories and locomotives. Texaco met this demand with its first consumer product, Familylite Illuminating Oil, introduced in 1907. After 1910, however, the automobile revolutionized the oil industry. Demand for gasoline, formerly considered a waste by-product of kerosene, expanded rapidly. Texaco followed this trend, and by 1914 its gasoline production surpassed that of kerosene. The company went from distributing gasoline in barrels to underground tanks to curbside pumps, and in 1911 it opened its first filling station in Brooklyn, New York. By 1916, 57 such stations were in operation across the country. Powered by the growth of the automobile industry and the high demand for petroleum created by World War I, Texaco quadrupled its assets between 1914 and 1920.

After World War I, Texaco continued to concentrate on its automotive gasoline and oil production, introducing new products and expanding its national sales network. In 1920 two researchers at its Port Arthur refinery developed the oil industry's first continuous thermal cracking process for making gasoline. Named after its founders, the Holmes-Manley process greatly increased the speed of the refining process as well as the amount of gasoline that could be refined from a barrel of crude. Texaco marketed this gasoline through its retail network, pushing into the Rocky Mountain region between 1920 and 1926, and into west coast markets with the acquisition of California Petroleum Company in 1928.

Products introduced during the 1920s included the company's first premium gasoline, as well as Texaco Aviation Gasoline and automobile motor oils. To market the lighter oils it refined from Texas crude, Texaco launched its first nationwide advertising campaign. The slogan "Clean, Clear, Golden" appeared at Texaco's filling stations, which displayed its motor oils in glass bottles. By 1928 Texaco owned or leased more than 4,000 stations in all 48 states.

The company's growth was also reflected in its corporate structure. Finding Texas's corporation laws too restrictive for doing business on such a large scale, Texaco decided to move its legal home. In 1926 it formed The Texas Corporation in Delaware, which then bought out the stock of The Texas Company and reorganized it as a subsidiary called The Texas

Company of Delaware. The company also moved its headquarters from Houston to New York. The Texas Corporation acted as a holding company for The Texas Company of Delaware and The Texas Company of California—formerly The California Petroleum Company—until 1941, when it merged with both and formed a single company known as The Texas Company.

The Texas Corporation's earnings reached an all-time high in 1929, but then dropped precipitously after the stock market crash. Overproduction, economic recession, and low prices plagued the oil industry in the early 1930s. The company embarked on a strategy of introducing new products to stimulate demand. Texaco Fire Chief Gasoline was launched in 1932, and the company advertised it by sponsoring a nationwide Ed Wynn radio program. Havoline Wax Free Motor Oil, developed after the acquisition of the Indiana Refining Company in 1931, followed two years later, halting its losses by 1934. In 1938 The Texas Corporation, still nicknamed Texaco, introduced Texaco Sky Chief premium gasoline and also began promoting its Registered Rest Rooms program, assuring motorists that their service stations were "Clean Across the Country." In 1940 Texaco began its landmark sponsorship of the New York Metropolitan Opera's Saturday afternoon radio broadcasts. This program, which is still running, is the oldest association between a U.S. company and an arts program.

While The Texas Corporation promoted its products and services at home, it also undertook vigorous expansion abroad. During the 1930s it began exploration and production in Colombia and Venezuela. In 1936 it joined with the Standard Oil Company of California to create the Caltex group of companies, a 50-50 venture in the Middle East. The Caltex group consolidated the operations of both of these companies east of the Suez Canal, Texaco also purchased a 50% interest from Standard Oil of California in the California Arabian Standard Oil Company, later renamed the Arabian American Oil Company (Aramco). The Caltex and Aramco ventures vastly expanded Texaco's sources of crude, and also enabled it to integrate its operations in the Eastern Hemisphere.

U.S. entry into World War II brought dramatic changes for The Texas Corporation. About 30% of its wartime production went to the war effort, primarily in the form of aviation fuels, gasoline, and petrochemicals. The company worked closely with Harold L. Ickes, federal petroleum administrator for the war effort, who organized the nation's oil companies into several nonprofit operations. The Texas Pipe Line Company, a subsidiary, oversaw the completion of two federally sponsored pipelines from Texas to the East Coast. Texaco also joined War Emergency Tankers Inc., which operated a collective tanker fleet for the War Shipping Administration. Another such venture was The Neches Butane Products Company, which manufactured butadiene, an essential ingredient in synthetic rubber. This enterprise gave Texaco its start in the infant petrochemicals industry, and after the war it purchased a 25% interest from the federal government in the Neches Butane plant. Texaco acquired full ownership of this operation in 1980. The company furthered its interests in petrochemicals in 1944 when it formed the Jefferson Chemical Company with the American Cyanamid Company. Texaco later bought out American Cyanamid's interest in this venture and then merged it with its newly formed Texaco Chemical Company in 1980.

With the end of World War II, Texaco faced renewed customer demand at home. U.S. consumption of oil exceeded its production for the first time in 1947, and Texaco reacted by tapping new foreign sources for its crude oil. In 1945 Texaco's jointly owned Caltex companies increased their refining capacity on Bahrain, reaching 180,000 barrels per day by 1951. Texaco also formed the Trans-Arabian Pipe Line Company with three other oil companies to build a pipeline connecting Saudi Arabia's oil fields with the eastern Mediterranean. At home Texaco increased its refining capacity with the Eagle Point Works near Camden, New Jersey, and it introduced several new automotive products, including Texaco Anti-Freeze and Texamatic Fluid for automatic transmissions.

During the 1950s and 1960s Texaco concentrated on expanding its global refining and marketing operations. The acquisition of the Trinidad Oil Company in 1956 and the Seaboard Oil Company in 1958, both of which held proved reserves in South America, expanded its interests in the Western Hemisphere. To increase its production in the Amazon Basin, the company built a jointly owned trans-Andean pipeline in 1969 and a trans-Ecuadorian pipeline in 1972. To increase its production in Europe, Texaco purchased the majority interest in the West German oil company Deutsch Erdol A.G. in 1966. It also reorganized the Caltex group in 1967, taking over one-half of the group's interest in 12 European countries that it had been serving from Saudi Arabia. This move allowed the company to expand its marketing operations in Europe, while leaving the Caltex companies free to concentrate east of the Suez Canal, where they enjoyed their greatest market penetration. Texaco brought its petrochemical business to Europe in 1966 with a plant in Ghent, Belgium, and to Japan three years later.

In the United States, Texaco expanded its interests by acquiring regional companies and increasing its refining capacity. The company strengthened its position on the East Coast by buying the Paragon group of companies in 1959 and the White Fuel Corporation in 1962. In 1962 it also acquired mineral rights to two million undeveloped acres in west Texas from the TXL Oil Corporation. The company's petrochemical production grew rapidly during this period, with the addition of a new unit at the Eagle Point works in 1960 and one of the world's largest benzene plants in Port Arthur in 1961. Texaco's operating volumes doubled between 1960 and 1970, with gross production surpassing three billion barrels per day in 1970.

Texaco's tremendous growth came to an abrupt halt in the 1970s. The Arab-Israeli War, the OPEC embargo, and the nationalization of foreign oil assets in many overseas nations cut Texaco's profit margins and endangered its sources of crude. Furthermore, federal price controls and mandatory allocation regulations restricted Texaco's ability to raise prices or withdraw from unprofitable markets. Its net income dropped from $1.6 billion in 1974 to $830.6 million a year later, and remaned at that level for the rest of the decade.

Tensions in the Middle East prompted a wave of nationalizations in the oil industry. In 1972 Saudi Arabia began to nationalize the assets of Aramco, in which Texaco owned a 50% interest, and took over all of its operations in 1980. Between 1973 and 1974 Libya nationalized the Texas Overseas Petroleum Company, a Texaco subsidiary. The decade ended with the Iranian revolution displacing Texaco's interests there and the Caltex group selling off part of its operations to the Bahrain government.

Texaco increased its exploration efforts and reorganized its marketing operations at home. Drilling activities increased both onshore and offshore in the southwest, as well as in new areas such as the North Sea and eastern Atlantic. The company also modernized its refineries in order to maximize the yield from each barrel of crude. Texaco made its most dramatic alterations in its retail network, abandoning the 50-state plan that had made it the United States's largest seller of oil. It began to withdraw from unprofitable markets, cutting operations in all or parts of 19 states in the Rocky Mountain, Midwest, and Great Lakes regions. It also reduced its number of service stations and opened more modern outlets in high-volume areas.

The 1980s began with the U.S. economy still suffering from recession, but the deregulation of the oil industry offered Texaco new flexibility in trying to recoup its fortunes. Under the direction of its new chairman, John K. McKinley, Texaco undertook a major restructuring plan in 1980. It decentralized its operations into three major geographic oil and gas divisions representing the United States; Europe; and Latin America; and West Africa, and one worldwide chemical organization, the Texaco Chemical Company. The company expanded its exploration program and it also committed more resources to projects for developing alternative fuels, such as coal gasification and shale oil. Retrenchment in its refining and marketing operations continued with the closing of six inefficient refineries by 1982 and the reduction of its retail outlets from 35,500 in 1974 to 27,000 in 1980. Texaco introduced a new logo in 1981, a red "T" inside a white star and red circle, to promote its high-volume System 2000 stations. These stations were a quick success, with more than 1,200 in the United States by 1987. The company also added a new operating division in 1982, Texaco Middle East/Far East, and made several important acquisitions to bolster its reserve base. By 1985 Texaco's net income was once again above $1 billion.

In the middle of this comeback, Texaco became involved in a legal battle. The 1984 purchase of the Getty Oil Company had promised to speed Texaco's recovery by adding an estimated 1.9 billion barrels of proved reserves to its assets. However, Pennzoil Company filed suit, claiming that Texaco had interfered with its plans to acquire three-sevenths of Getty's shares. In the resulting court case, a Texas State District Court in Houston ordered Texaco to pay Pennzoil $10.5 billion in damages. Arguing that important New York and Delaware state laws had been ignored in the case, Texaco obtained an injunction from a federal court in New York that temporarily halted the payment of damages, while it appealed the decision.

In February 1987 a Texas Court of Appeals upheld the decision. In order to protect its assets while continuing its appeals, the company filed for protection under Chapter 11 of the United States Bankruptcy Code. Texaco spent most of 1987 in Chapter 11 while continuing its litigation. As a result, it incurred its first operating losses since the Great Depression, finishing the year $4.4 billion in the red. After the Texas Supreme Court refused to hear an appeal, New York financier Carl Icahn began buying up Texaco's rapidly depreciating stock in an attempt to force it to settle with Pennzoil. A few weeks later Texaco agreed to pay Pennzoil $3 billion rather than appeal the decision to the Supreme Court, allowing it to begin planning for its emergence from Chapter 11.

However, Carl Icahn continued to buy up the company's stock, and in early 1988 he began a takeover bid. Texaco's board of directors had submitted a restructuring plan to the shareholders for meeting the company's debt obligations. Icahn favored instead the sale of the company. He launched the biggest proxy battle in business history when he tried to gain control of five seats on the board of directors, but he was defeated in a June 1988 shareholders' election. The board of directors then agreed to buy out Icahn's interests in Texaco.

With the Pennzoil case and the takeover attempt behind it, Texaco has rebuilt its market position by selling off assets and undertaking new joint ventures. Since 1987 it has sold its operations in Germany and Canada, as well as many of its fixed assets in the United States and the Middle East. It has also expanded drilling operations in the North Sea and offshore California, while continuing its exploration efforts in Asia, Africa, and South America. In 1988 Texaco U.S.A. transferred approximately two-thirds of its refining and marketing operations to Star Enterprise, a joint venture established with Saudi Arabia's Aramco. Other moves have included the acquisition of Chevron's marketing operations in six European countries, and the company's first commercial application of its coal gasification technology in an electric plant in the Los Angeles basin. Texaco promises to be a much trimmer enterprise with increased entrepreneurial activity in exploration and alternative fuels.

Principal Subsidiaries: Getty Oil Company; Texaco International Trader Inc.; Texaco Capital Inc.; Texaco Overseas Holdings Inc.; Texaco Refining & Marketing, Inc; Texaco Chemical Company; Texaco Producing Inc.; Texaco Trading & Transportation Inc.; The Caltex Group (50%); Star Enterprise (50%).

Further Reading: James, Marquis, *The Texaco Story: The First Fifty Years 1902–1952,* New York, The Texas Company, 1953; "Texaco: Restoring Luster to the Star," *Business Week,* December 22, 1980; Petzinger Jr., Thomas, *Oil & Honor: The Texaco-Pennzoil Wars,* New York, G.P. Putnam's Sons, 1987.

—Timothy J. Shannon

TONEN CORPORATION

Palaceside Building,
1-1, Hitotsubashi 1-chome
Chiyoda-ku, Tokyo 100
Japan
(03) 3286-5111
Fax: (03) 3286-5120

Public Company
Incorporated: 1939 as Towa Nenryo Kogyo Co. Ltd.
Employees: 2,285
Sales: ¥518.00 billion (US$3.81 billion)
Stock Exchanges: Tokyo Osaka Nagoya

The Tonen Corporation specializes in oil refinery operations. Exxon and Mobil, each of which holds a 25% stake in Tonen, supply the majority of the crude oil used by Tonen, and sell the products under their own brand names. The Tonen refinery operations, in which the most advanced technology is employed in the production of a range of value-added oil products, give the company a major competitive edge. Tonen's products, sold by the Japanese subsidiaries of Exxon and Mobil, accounted for 10% of Japan's total domestic oil consumption.

In July 1939, Towa Nenryo Kogyo Co. Ltd.—the name was changed to Tonen Corporation in July 1989—was established as a partnership of ten Japanese oil-related companies: Nippon Sekiyu, Kokura Sekiyu, Chosen Sekiyu, Aikoku Sekiyu, Sayama Sekiyu, Mitsubishi Sha Holdings, Mitsubishi Shoji Trading, Aratsu Sekiyu, Maruzen Sekiyu, and Mitsubishi Mining Co., with a capital of ¥50 million and 59 employees under the guidance of the Ministry of Defense and the fuel department of the Ministry of Commerce and Industry. Keizaburo Hashimoto, president of the Nippon Sekiyu Co. Ltd., was appointed chairman of the board, and Fusazo Kokura, president of Kokura Sekiyu Co. Ltd., became president. The larger corporate investors dispatched managerial officers to the company.

At the start of the refinery operation, sales and the procurement of crude oil and finance were supported and ensured by the Japanese Ministry of Defense. However, the choice of an industrial site and the question of which technologies to adopt for the refinery operations were major concerns. As the result of cooperative discussions among shareholders, a research and development center was located at the Shimizu plant site in the Shizuoka prefecture, and the refinery facilities were located in the Wakayama plant site in the Wakayama Prefecture.

In September 1939, the production and distribution of oil products in Japan fell under the influence of the national policy promoted by the fuel department of the Ministry of Commerce and Industry. All Japanese oil companies' independent business activities were severely restricted. However, the effects of the national policy were limited in the case of Towa Nenryo (Tonen), which was heavily engaged in munitions production.

In 1941, normal-pressure distillers began to operate in the Wakayama refinery and successfully produced engine starter volatile oil, airplane fuels, automobile gasoline, mineral turpentine, solvent, kerosene, light oils, and heavy oil. From 1941 to 1945, the Wakayama refinery processed 842,000 kiloliters of crude oil, 53% for munitions and 47% for civilian use. In 1943, a crude oil heating distillery was built at the Wakayama refinery and processed 86,000 kiloliters of crude oil before the end of World War II—77% for munitions and 23% for civilian uses.

On the Shimizu site, research and development activities started as a result of the serious shortage of natural resources caused by the war. The major projects at the research and development center were the substitution for petroleum products of other materials, such as high-octane gasoline developed from artificial oil, and lubricants made from raw natural rubber, and the processing of heavy tar oil produced in Southeast Asia, and of volatile oil, made from pine-tree gum. The construction of the Shimizu refinery was hindered by the shortage of materials under wartime conditions and was not realized on a large scale until 1950.

After the war ended, Tonen experienced a considerable fall in sales when the need for airplane fuel for munitions use ceased abruptly. Three-quarters of Tonen's 2,600 employees were dismissed in 1945. The major board members, including chairman and president, were banned from public duties by the Supreme Commander for the Allied Powers (SCAP) because of their involvement in Japan's war effort, and they were obliged to resign from the company. Nobuhei Nakahara became president. SCAP prohibited crude oil imports to Japan and banned refinery operations on the Pacific coast site. Tonen almost ceased to operate until 1947.

In December 1948, Tonen cooperated with the Standard-Vacuum Oil Company (Stan-Vac), which intended to reenter the Japanese market. To start up its refinery business again, Tonen needed a crude oil supply, distribution outlets, and technical and financial support for production facilities, and a tie-up with Stan-Vac was thought to be indispensable. To acquire the highest production technology from Standard Oil Development Company, later renamed Exxon Research and Engineering Company, Tonen transferred 51% of its ownership to Stan-Vac. In July 1949, oil refining on the Pacific coast site was again permitted by SCAP, and Tonen started operations in 1950.

In the 1950s, Tonen pursued two basic strategies. First, the expansion of production facilities had to take place as quickly as possible to enable Tonen to take advantage of domestic market opportunities. As the strategic importance of its Pacific coast location increased, the Shimizu refinery's production capacity had to increase very quickly. Second, using advanced technology licensed from SOD, the quality of products and the efficiency of refinery processes had to be improved. As the motorization of Japan was expected to take place in the near future, the development of high-octane gasoline and high quality lubricants was necessary. The establishment of production methods was of great importance to Tonen.

In November 1954, fluid catalytic cracking (FCC), a refinery method using catalysts to make fuel oil, was introduced in the Wakayama refinery, processing 4,700 barrels per day. In 1953, Tonen's refining capacity reached 28,500 barrels per day. The Wakayama refinery processed 21,000 barrels per day of crude oil, and the Shimizu refinery processed 7,500 barrels per day, at that time the largest refinery operations in Japan.

Expansion projects continued after this period. In 1955, a new 36,000-barrel-per-day refinery was completed, and another 10,200 barrels per day FCC refinery was built in 1956. In 1957, after the completion of alkylation equipment, production volume of airplane fuels reached 90,000 barrels per year, almost equal to the annual airplane fuel consumption of the country. Tonen almost monopolized the airplane fuel market in Japan.

From 1949 to 1957, Tonen's investment in production capacity expansion amounted to ¥12.2 billion. The company made seven issues of stock to finance its expansion. Consequently, the company's equity grew 84 times in this period, from ¥37.5 million in 1950 to ¥3.159 billion in 1955.

Tonen's aim in the 1960s was vertical integration into oil-related fields, including transportation of crude oil, new product development, diversification into petrochemicals, and alliance with other industrial enterprises. These changes were achieved in several stages. Tonen founded Toa Tanker Co. Ltd., with a capital of ¥1 billion. Minao Furihata, vice president of Towa Nenryo, became Toa Tanker's president and in 1961 the company's name was changed to Tonen Tanker Co. Ltd. In the 1960s, transportation costs represented a relatively large proportion of the total cost of crude oil. To bring down crude oil prices, the reduction of transportation costs was essential.

Tonen decided that its technological dependence on SVOC had gone too far, and that independence in research and development activities had to be regained. In 1961, Tonen acquired a 25-acre site, and spent ¥800 million on establishing a research and development center.

Under the policy for promoting Japan's petrochemical industry, enacted by MITI—the Ministry of International Trade and Industry, Tonen diversified into petrochemicals. In 1960, Tonen founded Tonen Sekiyukagaku (Petrochemical) Co. Ltd, with capital of ¥4 billion. Tonen's president Enpei Nakahara was also president of this new company. Steam-cracking and oxyalcohol plants were built in the Kawasaki refinery, and production of ethylene, propylene, and butane began.

In 1958 two joint ventures were established: General Sekiyu K.K., capitalized at ¥1 billion and owned on a 50/50 basis with General Bussan Kaisha, Ltd., which became General Sekiyu Seisei Co. Ltd. In 1967; and Nichimo Sekiyu Co. Ltd., equally owned with Nippon Gyomo Sengu Co. Ltd. By entering into joint ventures, Tonen was able to operate at higher capacity and thus benefit from economy of scale. To finance its expansion the company made seven new stock issues between 1956 and 1962, when it was capitalized at ¥8.9 billion, having grown almost three times over this period.

The next decade, from 1962 to 1972, saw further continuous growth at Tonen. This intensive growth was stimulated by a reorganization of the parent company. In 1962 Standard-Vacuum Oil was split in two and the resulting companies inte-

grated, respectively, with Mobil Oil Corporation and Esso Standard Eastern—now Esso Eastern. Tonen's arrangement with SVOC was transferred to these two companies. Consequently, SVOC's stake in Tonen was split into two stakes of 25% each. Both companies supplied crude oil to Tonen and distributed its products under their own brand names and through different marketing channels. Competition between Esso Standard Sekiyu K.K. and Mobil Sekiyu K.K. in the Japanese market gave impetus to the company's growth.

At the Wakayama refinery, the first stage of the expansion project in the Ogake area was completed in 1965, and the second expansion project in the area in 1968. Thus made the refinery the newest and the largest in Japan. The first stage of the expansion project at the Kawasaki Refinery was completed in 1970. Equity participation in Kygnus Sekiyu K.K. in 1972 boosted the Kawasaki refinery's economy of scale. By 1969, Tonen's total assets reached ¥73.2 billion, and the company was capitalized at ¥14.3 billion.

In the 1970s, during the two oil crises and severe recession in the Japanese economy, Tonen reduced excess production capacity, cut its costs, and stopped new employment to adjust to slower economic growth. During the oil crisis Tonen recognized that the oil industry in Japan had already matured, and that new fields of business had to be developed. Tonen Technology K.K., established in 1971 as a crude oil reserve company, diversified into computer sciences. In 1977, Tonen Energy International Corporation was established, with its headquarters in New York and a branch in London, to obtain finance for the crude oil transactions of the company.

In 1981, the price for Arabian light oil amounted to $34 per barrel, and the total annual deficit of Japanese oil industry amounted to almost ¥350 billion. Tonen concentrated its efforts on the rationalization of production. Through the successful development of energy-saving technologies, Tonen achieved a saving of almost 220,000 kiloliters—¥10 billion annually compared with the 1973 level. As a result of improvements in its production process and management system, Tonen's business situation gradually improved. Since 1984, the company's financial statements have shown a profit. The long-term orientation of management policies resulted in the improvement of Tonen's equity ratio to 60% in 1989, among the highest in the Japanese oil industry. Tonen is aiming to develop an intelligent refinery by employing the most advanced information technology and operation backup systems. In terms of new product development, Tonen has chosen to focus on new energy sources, new materials, life sciences, and information technology. Tonen's major development in the field of new energy is an efficient, low-cost amorphous silicon for electricity, and a clean combustion system—supersonic fuel injection—now in use in the F3000 racing car. In the field of new materials, Tonen has developed and patented a high quality pitch-based carbon fiber with a host of applications in airplane bodies, automobile frames, and mechanical parts. In the field of life science, Tonen has established a reputation as a pioneer in genetic engineering and cell technology. Tonen's most recent product is a leukemia vaccine, which enables a double-digit increase in the general potency of a wide variety of vaccines. In the field of information technology Tonen has the benefit of years of experience in computerized operational control and plant maintenance systems. For this purpose, Tonen System Plaza Inc. was established in 1985. Tonen

Corporation's activities are expanding beyond the oil industry. In the 1990s, Tonen will be one of the most flexible companies, as well as one of those best equipped with information technology, in the oil industry worldwide.

Principal Subsidiaries: Tonen Sekiyukagaku K.K.; Tonen Tanker K.K.; Tonen Technology K.K.; Tonen System Plaza Inc.,; Tonen Properties Inc.,; Tonen Sogo Service Co. Ltd.; Tonen Energy International Corp. (U.S.A.); Kygnus Sekiyu Seisei K.K. (70%); Kygnus Sekiyu K.K. (50%).

Further Reading: Thirty Years of Tonen: From 1939 to 1969, Vols. 1–2, Tokyo, Tonen Corporation, 1971; *The Course of Tonen's History,* Tokyo, Tonen Corporation, 1980.

—Kenichi Yasumuro

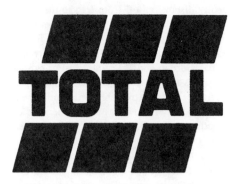

TOTAL COMPAGNIE FRANÇAISE DES PÉTROLES S.A.

5, rue Michel-Ange
75781 Paris
Cédex 16
France
(1) 47 43 80 00
Fax: (1) 47 43 75

Public Company
Incorporated: 1924 as Compagnie Française des Pétroles
Employees: 41,200
Sales: FFr107.89 billion (US$21.20 billion)
Stock Exchanges: Paris London

The motto of the Total Compagnie Française des Pétroles France's oldest and—for most of its life—largest oil company, at its foundation in 1924 might well have been "never again." World War I had brought home to the French the need for secure energy supplies. In late 1917 France had come within three months of running out of fuel and seeing its war effort grind to a halt. President Georges Clemenceau addressed a desperate appeal to U.S. President Woodrow Wilson, asking him to resume American oil shipments across the Atlantic. The U.S. oil companies had concluded that the German navy had made the North Atlantic trade too hazardous. Wilson persuaded them to think again.

The French were latecomers to the oil business. At the turn of the century the Americans and the Russians, with their huge domestic resources, had supplied 90% of the world's oil needs. Since then, the British had developed a powerful presence through the activities of the Anglo-Persian Oil Company—today's British Petroleum—and Royal Dutch/Shell.

If the war engendered among the French an awareness of their desperate need for oil, it also created the opportunity for them to acquire it. The key was the 25% stake in the fledgling Turkish Petroleum Company (TPC) held by Germany's Deutsche Bank.

The TPC had been founded in 1911 to exploit the oil fields of Mesopotamia on either side of the German-built railway to Baghdad. The British-owned National Bank of Turkey had originally been TPC's major shareholder with 50%, but in 1914 the British government persuaded the bank to sell out to Anglo-Persian. A further 25% was held by Royal Dutch/Shell.

In 1915 the 25% stake in TPC still held by Deutsche Bank was sequestered by the British. Two years later, letters were exchanged between the British Foreign Office and the Quai d'Orsay in Paris, committing the British government to hand over Deutsche Bank's shares in TPC to the French after the war.

The go-between had been the Armenian businessman Calouste Gulbenkian, an early minority shareholder in TPC. Royal Dutch/Shell was won over to the idea on the understanding that it would have the right to get France's share of the oil out of the ground.

To this end, the Société Française pour l'Exploitation du Pétrole was founded in 1920, owned 51% by Royal Dutch/Shell and 49% by the Banque de l'Union Parisienne. Deutsche Bank's 25% share in TPC had been formally transferred to the French under the Treaty of San Remo earlier that year.

Four years later a new French government under Raymond Poincaré concluded that it was unacceptable that a foreign company should control the exploitation of France's oil rights in Mesopotamia, and the Compagnie Française des Pétroles (CFP) was established.

CFP's purpose was spelt out by Prime Minister Poincaré in a letter to the company's first chairman, Ernest Mercier. The new company's function was wide-ranging and not limited to Mesopotamia. In the interests of developing an oil producing capacity "under French control," Mercier was charged with acquiring stakes in "any enterprise active in whatsoever oil producing region" of the world. Central and South America were mentioned specifically. CFP was also to "co-operate, with the support of the Government, in . . . exploiting such oil wealth as may be discovered in France, her colonies and her protectorates."

Notwithstanding its close government tutelage, the Compagnie Française des Pétroles was set up as a private, not state-owned, firm. Ernest Mercier, who had formerly been chairman of the Franco-British oil company Steaua-Romana, showed great energy in drumming up shareholders from a nation which had hitherto shown little enthusiasm for investing in the high-risk oil business.

He found backers among the French banks and also among the oil distributing companies, which had hitherto been dependent on the foreign companies for their supplies. Although the support of powerful distributors such as Desmarais Frères was a boon at the outset, it later came to restrain CFP's freedom of action. Before World War II the company was effectively blocked from retailing oil that it had produced, transported, and refined, because of the powerful vested interests of its own shareholders.

On October 15, 1927 the Turkish Petroleum Company struck oil—a large find—at Baba Gurghur in the Mosal field just to the north of Kirkouk in Iraq. The discovery at Baba Gurghur ended a debate among the TPC shareholders, some of whom wanted to receive dividends on their investments, others of whom wanted to be remunerated in crude oil. The French had favored crude, having no oil fields of their own; after Baba Gurghur they received it.

Another result of the strike was the 1928 restructuring of the TPC. The Americans had been clamoring for admittance for years. In 1928 Anglo-Persian, acting on a deal hammered out between the British and American governments in 1923, ceded half its stake to a consortium of five U.S. oil companies. The return of Calouste Gulbenkian as "Mr. Five Percent" left the Compagnie Française des Pétroles holding 23.75%, on a par with Anglo-Persian, Royal Dutch/Shell, and the American consortium.

The shareholders in the TPC signed a non-aggression pact known as the Red Line Agreement after Gulbenkian's gesture in ringing a large area of the map of the Near and Middle East with red crayon. The area within the red line corresponded to the old Ottoman Empire at the end of World War I. It encompassed Turkey, Syria, Saudi Arabia, Lebanon, Iraq, and Palestine. Within that region the TPC shareholders, now including the American giants Standard Oil of New York and Standard Oil of New Jersey, undertook not to compete with one another.

Meanwhile in France CFP was undergoing restructuring of its own. Ernest Mercier was coming up against opposition from some of the company's shareholders to his cherished plans to launch CFP into refining. Certain of the oil distributors backing CFP objected. They had built up close relationships with foreign refiners and they did not want these disrupted.

Mercier turned to his friend Raymond Poincaré, once again prime minister. Together they elaborated a plan for the French state to acquire a 25% stake in CFP and a 10% stake in a new refining subsidiary to be created by CFP, the Compagnie Française de Raffinage.

The official convention between the government and CFP which enshrined this new shareholding relationship was signed on March 19, 1929. It provoked a great political hue and cry, with the socialists under Léon Blum clamoring for greater state involvement and the right complaining that Poincaré's *dirigisme*—or interventionism—already went too far.

In the end it was the dirigistes who won. On July 8, 1931 the French parliament ratified an increase in the state's stake in CFP from 25% to 35%—the level at which it has stayed to this day. The state also acquired 40% of the voting rights at CFP assemblies and the French government was authorized to nominate two commissioners for the company's board to safeguard the state's interest.

From Ernest Mercier's point of view it was a satisfactory outcome. He had won political support for his refining project and translated that support into boardroom control. However, the government's increased participation in CFP fell very far short of thoroughgoing nationalization. The risk of politically motivated interference in the day-to-day running of the company was averted.

The Compagnie Française de Raffinage (CFR) was founded in April 1929. Its first refinery was opened at Gonfreville near Le Havre in Normandy in the summer of 1933. It had to wait until the next year for the first shipment of CFP's own oil from Iraq; the necessary pipeline from the wells to the Lebanese port of Tripoli was not in operation until July 1934.

In the years up to World War II CFR's refining capacity grew steadily, outstripping CFP's ability to supply it with crude. Further crude shipments came from Venezuela and the United States. By 1936 CFR was supplying nearly 20% of French demand for refined oil from two plants located at either end of the country, one in Normandy and the other at La Mède in Provence.

By 1929 the Turkish Petroleum Company had long since ceased to have anything to do with Turkey. Its oil came from Iraq under a concession awarded by the Iraqi monarch, King Feizal, installed by the British in 1921. Appropriately enough, TPC changed its name to the Iraq Petroleum Company in June 1929.

The renamed company's major task in the early 1930s was to transport its recently discovered oil from Iraq to the Mediterranean. Plans for a single pipeline were scuppered by French insistence that the oil should pass through the French protectorates of Syria and Lebanon, and Britain's determination that it should cross Jordan and Palestine, territories then under the protection of his majesty's government. These opinions proved irreconcilable, and two pipelines were laid, one to Tripoli in Lebanon and the other to Haifa in Palestine. The oil came on stream at both ports in 1934.

Another link in the chain between the extraction of CFP's share of the Iraqi oil and its distribution to French consumers was forged in 1931. CFP set up the Compagnie Navale Des Pétroles to ship its own oil to its own refineries. In the prewar years it shared this task with the Compagnie Auxiliaire de Navigation, one of CFP's founding shareholders. Much later, in the 1970s, CFP was to take control of the Compagnie Auxiliaire.

By the outbreak of World War II, the Compagnie Française des Pétroles had become a vertically integrated oil company, extracting, transporting, and refining oil. It had two weaknesses. One, the lack of any meaningful distribution capacity, was remedied in the 1950s with the creation of the Total brand name and the gradual absorption of the independent distributors. The other was the company's heavy reliance on middle eastern oil. The balanced supply from around the world which Raymond Poincaré had hoped for in 1924 had not been achieved.

Far more worrying for the French during the war were the designs of CFP's fellow shareholders in the Iraq Petroleum Company (IPC) regarding the French 23.75% stake. CFP's stake in the IPC was put under the control of the official Custodian of Enemy Property in London after the French capitulation. The risk for CFP was that its participation in IPC could be reduced by new share issues to which it was powerless to subscribe.

Fortunately—and fortuitously—this change did not occur. CFP had a "war chest" of US$20 million held by its American bankers which enabled it to keep pace with the wartime recapitalization of IPC. The bulk of this money—US$15 million—had been borrowed from the Mannheimer Bank in the Netherlands just before the war to fund two new pipelines to Tripoli. The remaining US$5 million belonged to the Compagnie Française de Raffinage.

The French interests in IPC were looked after by Harold Sheets, the chairman of Standard Oil of New York, to whom they were entrusted by CFP's new chairman, Jules Mény, in 1940. Ernest Mercier had resigned that year, being out of favor with Vichy. Calouste Gulbenkian also remained a good friend of France, refusing—together with the Americans—to take any of CFP's share of IPC's oil. The British, with tanks and planes to fuel, were less scrupulous: not until 1950 did they grant the French modest compensation.

The rapid succession of chairmen at CFP during the war reflected the instability of those times. At least Vichy allowed Ernest Mercier to depart peacefully. The same could not be said of Jules Mény who, in 1943, was taken hostage by the Nazis and deported to Dachau. He never returned. Meny's successor, Marcel Champin, died in 1945, leaving the task of determining CFP's postwar strategy to his deputy, Victor de Metz who was to serve as chairman for 25 years.

The nationalization drive that affected so many French companies after the war did not engulf CFP: its private shareholders were powerful and not worth alienating. More threatening for CFP in the long run was President Charles de Gaulle's creation in 1945 of the Bureau de Recherches de Pétrole (BRP), which was much later to form one of the constituent parts of Elf Aquitaine. However, at its creation, BRP was charged exclusively with searching for oil in France, its colonies, and protectorates. This mandate did not constitute an immediate threat to CFP and de Metz gave the new state-backed venture his support.

In the late 1940s and early 1950s CFP expanded rapidly both at home and abroad. The company's annual supply of oil from the Middle East increased from 806,000 tons in 1945, to 1.61 million tons in 1950, to 8.824 million tons in 1953. This was made possible partly by the collapse of the restrictive Red Line Agreement under heavy American pressure. Oil began to flow from new IPC installations at Qatar in 1949: by 1953 production had reached 3.5 million tons per year.

Another major boost to CFP's supplies resulted from the opening of a new 30-inch pipeline from Kirkouk in Iraq to the Syrian port of Banias in November 1952. The original pipelines from Kirkouk to Tripoli and Haifa were only 16 inches in diameter.

The security of these supplies depended on the continuing stability of the region and its rulers' continuing respect for the oil companies' prewar concessions. The fragility of CFP's position was perceived by Victor de Metz. He recognized that CFP needed to diversify its sources of supply.

An agreement signed with the Venezuelan oil company Pantepec in 1947 did not bear fruit in the long term. It did ensure deliveries of Venezuelan crude amounting to some 600,000 tons per year through the late 1940s; but a technical agreement between the Venezuelan firm and CFP over the development of new fields in Venezuela broke down amid acrimonious exchanges in 1950.

A purely French venture to develop the oil wealth of Algeria fared better. In 1946 the state-owned Bureau de Recherches des Pétroles had established, jointly with the French colonial government in Algeria, an oil exploration company, the Société Nationale de Recherche de Pétrole en Algérie (SN Repal). In 1947 CNP sent a geologist, Willy Bruederer, to Algeria to evaluate the region's prospects. In the early 1950s SN Repal and CFP teamed up to explore a huge region designated promising by Bruederer, some 250,000 square kilometers in size.

These joint efforts yielded their reward in 1956. A huge oil field was discovered at Hassi-Messaoud in June and an equally impressive gas field at Hassi R'Mel in November.

Notwithstanding its expansion, the Compagnie Française des Pétroles remained far from being a household name in France. CFP petrol stations did not cover the land, even though a large proportion of the fuel that the independent distributors sold had been refined at the plants of a CFP subsidiary.

Distribution was not a particularly profitable activity but a major oil producer without distribution facilities of its own risked being held for ransom by its distributors with the threat of losing their business. From 1946 Victor de Metz worked to remove this risk. His first step was the creation in that year of the Compagnie Française de Distribution en Afrique to sell CFP's refined oil products in francophone Africa.

The move into distribution was made possible by the unveiling of the Total brand name in 1954. The distributors of oil refined by CFR were now entitled to deck out their service stations in the Total colors and logo, giving them a stronger market identity. The plan was first tested in Africa and then brought to France in 1957. It worked. In 1961 refineries belonging to CFP or working on its behalf treated 12 million tons of oil. Seven million tons of these treated products went on to be distributed under the Total brand name. Notwithstanding the eyecatching new livery and brand name, France's independent fuel distributors were experiencing hard times. Tougher competition from the big foreign oil companies was pushing them towards bankruptcy. One by one they sold out—usually to CFP.

CFP's original shareholders, companies that had frequently exerted a powerful influence over CFP before the war, now found themselves being swallowed up by their own creation. In 1960 CFP took over Omnium Français de Pétroles, acquiring valuable distribution outlets in north Africa. In 1966 CFP acquired the largest independent distributor, Desmarais Frères, with a 10% share of the French market to CFP.

While CFP was making strides in refining and selling its oil, the process of extracting it was becoming increasingly difficult. The model for a new relationship with the Middle Eastern governments was the 50–50 profit sharing agreement signed by the Saudi government and the U.S. oil producers' consortium Aramco in 1950. In the same year IPC struck a similar profit-sharing deal with the Iraqi government.

The risks posed by nascent nationalism in the Middle East were made clear in 1951 when Muhammad Mussadegh came to power in Iran. He nationalized the assets of the Anglo-Iranian Oil Company—formerly the Anglo-Persian Oil Company and forerunner of British Petroleum—and an international embargo of Iranian crude failed to change his attitude. More effective was a revolt linked to the British and American intelligence services, which led to the restoration of the shah and Mussadegh's imprisonment in 1953.

A year later the oil companies and the Iranian government came to terms. An international consortium of oil companies was created, led by Anglo-Iranian with a 40% share. CFP took a modest 6% stake in the venture.

Upheavals such as the one in Iran spurred the French effort to develop oil production in its Algerian colony. However, there was another reason for heavy investment in Algeria, both from CFP and from the state-controlled BRP. This was the fact that any oil or gas discovered in Algeria would lie within the franc zone. The IPC installations in Iraq did not fall into this category and CFP had to fund its share of investment in the Iraq Petroleum Company in pounds sterling. In the late 1940s and early 1950s, when the franc was fast losing its purchasing power, this arrangement was not very satisfactory.

To help balance its currency exposures CFP endeavored during the 1950s to increase its sales abroad, notably to countries within the sterling zone. During the late 1950s a potentially greater threat emerged to CFP's historic position as cornerstone of France's energy policy. Immediately after the war the French government had endowed BRP with plentiful resources to carry out one of the tasks originally assigned by Poincaré to CFP—to search for oil in France, her colonies, and protectorates. In Algeria BRP had found oil in abundance. By 1959 it was looking at ways of refining and selling it.

April 1960 saw the creation of l'Union Générale des Pétroles (UPG) to refine and distribute oil from the Hassi Messaoud field in Algeria. UGP rapidly acquired existing refineries and started to build others. It bought a refinery and a major distribution network from Caltex, a joint venture between U.S. oil majors Texaco and Standard Oil (California). UGP's expansion was supervised by Pierre Guillaumat, the first chairman of BRP immediately after the war. Within five years Guillaumat had created a French rival to CFP.

Particularly irksome to de Metz and CRP was the government's imposition of a so-called *devoir national,* or national obligation on oil refiners to take a certain proportion of their crude from the franc zone. In practice this meant Algeria and BRP and the other French state-controlled operations in that country. Most of CFP's oil still came from the Middle East. The reason for this discriminatory measure was that Algerian crude was more expensive than Middle Eastern crude. Demand had to be encouraged.

Just over a decade later the tables were turned. In 1971 the Algerians nationalized the assets of both CFP and Entreprise de Recherches et d'Activités Pétrolières as it had now become. The younger company was hit far harder than CFP: it relied on Algeria for 80% of its oil supplies. CFP took only a fifth of its production from that country.

A deal with the Algerians was finally struck in June 1971. The newly-appointed chairman of CFP, René Granier de Lilliac, informed shareholders that "over a five year period, once renewable, the group is . . . assured of annual production in the order of seven million tons." This was less than half the production of CFP (Algérie) before nationalization. De Lilliac took over from Victor de Metz in 1971. In his last years at the helm of CFP, de Metz had been encouraging the diversification of the group's sources of supply. In the late 1960s discoveries were made at Bekapai and Handil in Indonesia and, at the start of the 1970s, in the North Sea.

Despite the Iraqi nationalization of the assets of the Iraq Petroleum Company in 1971, in its 1971 annual report CFP was able to announce that "the rights of [the company in Iraq] will be maintained as before." On de Metz' retirement in 1971 the Compagnie Française des Pétroles was one of the largest oil companies in the world. During the 1960s the company's oil production had risen at a rate 30% faster than global oil production.

The 1970s proved tougher. The new chairman, Granier de Lilliac, had headed the Compagnie Française de Raffinage for five years before taking charge of the group as a whole. In the 1970s CFP's refining activities faced the greatest difficulties. The group's refining capacity was still concentrated in France, although in 1975 sales abroad outstripped sales in France for the first time. The oil price rise of 1971 prompted by the OPEC cartel also led to a sharp reduction in world demand over the level anticipated. In 1975 CFR's refineries were working at only 67% capacity. At the same time exploration costs, particularly in the North Sea, were rising steeply. In France, price controls prevented CFP from passing on the full rise in crude prices to the consumer. As at Elf, diversification appeared to be the answer. In 1974 a major step was taken with the purchase of France's largest manufacturer of industrial rubber products, Hutchinson-Mapa. In the petrochemicals field, ATO Chimie was set up as a joint venture with Elf-ERAP in 1973: ten years later CFP's share was to be taken over by Elf.

CFP also moved into developing other energy sources. In uranium mining, CFP created in 1975 a joint subsidiary Minatome, with Pechiney-Ugine-Kuhlmann. This venture was the core of today's Total Compagnie Minière which in 1989 mined 711 tons of uranium in France and the United States. The same company sold 5.2 million tons of coal in 1989; again, the first steps were taken in the mid-1970s. Nevertheless, Total has never diversified from its original core business as heavily as Elf. Chemicals and mining accounted for 12.5% of Total's cash flow in 1989. The oil business, in all its stages—production, refining, distribution—accounted for the remaining 87.5%.

During the 1980s unprofitable refineries in France, West Germany, and Italy were closed: the group's capacity in this area was in excess of demand. Total's remaining refineries have been reporting improved operating margins. Refining and distribution accounted for almost half the group's cash flow in 1989.

In 1985, the name by which CFP had come to be known universally was incorporated in its official title: CFP became Total CFP. At the same time the Compagnie Française de Raffinage and its distribution subsidiary, Total CFD, merged to become CRD Total France. At the beginning of 1990 René Granier de Lilliac stood down as chairman, to be succeeded by Serge Tchuruk, an engineer. One of Tchuruk's first tasks has been to incorporate part of the state chemicals group Orkem into Total Chimie. Under a restructuring of the industry superintended by the French government, Total has acquired Orkem's specialty chemicals businesses, producing adhesives, paints, and resins. The refining and distribution elements of Total's business in 1990 were in better shape than five years earlier. Total has closed 900 service stations in France since 1985. A further 900 will be closed by 1994, leaving the group with 3,000. Competition was too stiff even before the Persian Gulf crisis contributed to the squeeze in profits.

Total entered the 1990s with a diversified source for its principal raw material. It ceded its position as France's largest oil company to Elf Aquitaine, but remains the country's largest refiner. Its success in the future will depend, as in the past, on the balance maintained between its upstream and downstream activities.

Principal Subsidiaries: TOTAL Exploration (France); TOTAL Oil Marine (U.K.); TOTAL Marine Norsk (Norway); TOTAL Marine Exploitatie (The Netherlands); TOTAL Mineraria (Italy); TOTAL Energia Italiana SpA (99.8%); Compagnie Française des Pétroles (Algeria); TOTAL Algérie; TOTAL Proche-Orient (Egypt, 99.8%); TOTAL Abu Al Bu Khoosh (Abu Dhabi, 99.7%); Dubai Marine Areas (50%); TOTAL Aden (South Yemen, 99.8%); TOTAL Syrie (Syria, 99.8%); TEPCAM (Cameroons, 79%); TOTAL Angola; TOTAL Exploratie en Produktie (Kenya, Columbia, North Yemen); TOTAL Indonésie; TOTAL Chine (China, 99.8%); TOTAL Austral/Argentine (99.8%); TOTAL Compagnie Française de Navigation (99.6%); TOTAL Transport Ltd./International (99.9%); TOTAL Transport Corporation/International; Compagnie de Raffinage et de Distribution TOTAL FRANCE (93.6%); Totalgaz (93.6%); Stela (93.5%); Les Fils Charvet (89.3%); Docks des Alcools (57.4%); Société Anonyme des Pétroles Mory; Air TOTAL France; Air TOTAL Suisse

(99.9%); Air TOTAL International (99%); TOTAL Oil (Great Britain) Ltd.; Lindsey Oil Refinery (U.K., 50%); TOTAL Belgique; TOTAL Nederland; TOTAL Raffinaderij Nederland (55%); Deutsche TOTAL; Defrol (Germany); TOTAL España; TOTAL Hellas (Greece); TOTAL Maroc (50%); TOTAL Afrique; TOTAL Sénégal (78.6%); TOTAL Côte d'Ivoire (75.8%); TOTAL Texaco Burkina (74.5%); TOTAL Nigeria (60%); TOTAL Cameroun (65%); TOTAL Fina Gabon (54%); TOTAL Oil Products–East Africa (78.6%); TOTAL South Africa Pty (57.6%); TOTAL Réunion Comores; TOTAL Pacifique; TOTAL Chimie; Pétroplastique SNC (93.6%); Hydrocarbures de Saint-Denis (82.2%); Hutchinson (81.6%); TOTAL Solvants (88%); Normanplast (93.6%); TOTAL Compagnie Minière; TOTAL Compagnie Minière France; TOTAL Energie Développement; MBB-TED Phototronics OHG (Germany, 50%); TOTAL Exploration South Africa (85.1%); TOTAL Energold Corporation (Canada, 65%); Minatco Ltd. (Canada); TOTAL Mining Australia Pty. Ltd.; TOTAL Compagnie Française des Pétroles; TOTAL International Ltd./International; OFP–Omnium Financier de Paris (52.5%); Société Financière d'Auteuil (51.9%); Omnium de Participations S.A. (52.5%); Omnium Insurance and Reinsurance Cy (88.1%); TOTAL Petroleum (North America, 51.1%); TOTAL Energy Resources Inc. (U.S.A.); TOTAL Resources Canada Ltd.; TOTAL Australia Ltd.

Further Reading: Rondot, Jean, *La Compagnie Française des Pétroles—du Franc-Or au Petrole-Franc,* Paris, Librairie Plon, 1962; Grayson, Leslie E., *National Oil Companies,* London, John Wiley & Sons, 1981; Giraud, André, and Xavier Boy de la Tour, *Géopolitique du Pétrole et du Gaz,* Paris, Editions Technip, 1987; Guillon, Eric, and Gérard Pruneau, *Total Votre Groupe,* Paris, Total CFP, 1988; Dawkins, William, "Shaping Up For Competition," *Financial Times,* November 12, 1990.

—William Pitt

TÜRKIYE PETROLLERI ANONIM ORTAKLIĞI

Mudafaa Caddesi 22
Bakanliklar
Ankara 06650
Turkey
(4) 117 91 60
Fax: (4) 118 15 51

State-Owned Company
Incorporated: 1954
Employees: 5,171
Sales: TL474.02 million (US$163,568)

Türkiye Petrolleri Anonim Ortakliği (TPAO), Turkey's national petroleum company, was set up in 1954 following the introduction of liberalized legislation which opened up oil exploration in Turkey to private companies, both domestic and foreign. Since its conception in the mid-1950s, TPAO has pursued a strategy of growth while restructuring and diversifying when necessary to meet new demands. Today TPAO is extending its scope to include oil exploration and joint venture projects outside Turkey.

Exploration for oil in Turkey first began in the second half of the 19th century, when both domestic and foreign companies carried out exploration in Thrace, western Turkey. The first productive well, located in the Hora Deresi region of Thrace, was run by the European Petroleum Company. The advent of World War I combined with the fall of the Ottoman Empire led to a temporary halt in oil-related activities.

With the birth of the modern Republic of Turkey in 1923, oil exploration, like other major industries, resumed under the direction of the state. The Mineral Research and Exploration Institute (MTA) was established by the Turkish government in 1935 to increase exploration. Authorized to conduct exploration activities for minerals and petroleum in Turkey, MTA drilled several wells in the south east, mainly in the Raman region. Until 1954, however, oil exploration activities under MTA were insignificant, and foreign companies were not permitted to operate in Turkey.

The new petroleum law of 1954 that opened the Turkish market to domestic and foreign oil companies marked a significant change in the government's petroleum policy. In the same year, TPAO was set up by the government and took over oil exploration operations from MTA. The liberalization has resulted in the establishment of more than 112 foreign companies in Turkey since 1954, and 1258 exploration wells have been drilled.

TPAO's emblem, a fiery red sun, aims to reflect the company's energy and power. The symbol is taken from the Hittites, an ancient Anatolian people, whose religion was based on worship of the sun goddess and the storm god. The center of Hittite power was in central Anatolia, including present day Ankara where TPAO has its headquarters.

Although functioning as a national company, TPAO does not have a monopoly on any field of the domestic oil business. It applies to the General Directorate of Petroleum Affairs (GDPA), an agency of the Ministry of Energy and Natural Resources which supervises all activities of companies involved in oil and gas exploration, for licenses on the same basis as private and foreign companies. Yet because of its size, and favorable government policies especially during 1973–1979, TPAO has enjoyed advantages over its competitors.

Until 1983 most state operations in the petroleum sector, including exploration, production, refining, transportation, and marketing, were handled by TPAO. Accordingly the company's first general manager, Dr. Sahap Birgi, appointed in 1954, played a dynamic role at TPAO during its early years. Birgi, a mining engineer, originally from Izmir, a port city on Turkey's Aegean coast, was educated at Freiberg and Loeben Technical Universities.

Well remembered for instilling enthusiasm in his staff for petroleum exploration, Birgi personally oversaw all sectors of the oil business. He placed great emphasis on recruiting well-trained employees and had difficulties during the first few years finding qualified Turks to join the company. Thus, Dr. Birgi sought to recruit staff who were educated or had worked abroad.

During Birgi's tutelage at TPAO, a large number of foreign and local oil companies conducted feasibility studies of Turkey's prospects for oil exploration. Total geophysical studies reached 108 crew-months per year; approximately 96 of these were performed by foreign companies and 12 by TPAO.

The first modern refinery located in Batman, southeast Turkey, was built during Birgi's leadership of TPAO in 1956. This was followed by the Izmit refinery, 80 kilometers east of Istanbul, which was built as a joint venture between TPAO (51%) and Caltex (49%). Caltex sold its share to TPAO in 1972.

Birgi was succeeded by Dr. Ihsan Topaloglu who served for the next 5 years until 1965. In the 1960s, exploration studies dropped to an average of only 45 crew-months per year, around 21 for foreign companies and 24 for TPAO. Dr. Ihsan Topaloglu was followed by Turgut Gulez, a petroleum engineer who worked in different divisions of TPAO before being appointed as general manager from 1965 to 1967. Korkut Ozal, formerly an associate professor at the Middle East Technical University in Ankara, acted as general manager for the next four years.

The year 1973 marked a turning point in the petroleum industry as the government assumed a more protectionist policy in line with nationalistic programs throughout Turkey. The petroleum law was amended by decree in 1973 to provide more rights to TPAO and therefore discriminated indirectly against foreign companies. The decree included fixing the wellhead price at the December 1973 level in Turkish lira equivalent, effectively making oil exploration in Turkey unprofitable for foreign companies. Additionally, restrictions were placed on foreign oil companies. TPAO was allowed to acquire more licenses than foreign companies. These policies coincided with a worldwide increase in oil prices which encouraged oil companies to invest in other areas.

Selahattin Ozkan, a petroleum engineer who worked in different divisions in TPAO, was appointed general manager from 1971–1974 and again during 1981. Ozkan oversaw a period in the petroleum industry when exploration by foreign companies came to a virtual standstill. Domestic crude oil production fell dramatically in 1978, reaching 2.7 million tons, while imports climbed to 14.2 tons compared with 4 million tons in 1969.

From 1974 to 1977 Turkey witnessed rampant inflation, recession, and high unemployment following the sharp increase in the price of imported oil. Import costs rose as a result, and earnings from exports declined. This led to a severe shortage of foreign exchange, a slowdown in growth, and a large public sector deficit.

The turnover of general managers at TPAO was high during this difficult period. Rasit Ceylan who also worked in other posts in TPAO was appointed as general manager between 1974 and 1975. BOTAS was founded by TPAO in 1974 to build the Iraqi-Turkish crude oil pipeline. The Turkish-Iraqi pipeline, of which more than half is located in Turkey, is 981 kilometers long. BOTAS extended its scope in the 1980s to include construction of pipelines abroad, and transport, purchasing, and selling of petroleum products and natural gas. Rifat Bayazit, who was recruited from his position as director of BOTAS, succeeded Ceylan as general manager from 1975 to 1976. He was replaced by Mehmet Golhan, a construction engineer, who served as general manager until 1978.

Ismail Ertan, undersecretary of the Prime Ministry, was general manager from 1978 to 1979. Furuzan Ardic was appointed general manager in 1979. He had previously served as general director of the Turkish Petro Chemical Corporation (PETKIM).

In 1979 and 1980, widespread strikes and social unrest crippled Turkish industry. The military staged a coup in 1980 and took power from the Turkish government to end the terrorism and instability. The new military government regime immediately instituted a series of strong economic policy measures designed to control high inflation and unemployment, and to stimulate economic growth. These new policies revealed an important transition from tight government control to a reliance on market forces.

Ardic's tenure was marked by a notable change in the government's position on foreign companies. In 1980 the government further amended the petroleum law to boost foreign investment, which had fallen so dramatically in the 1970s, in the petroleum industry. These changes were in line with newly elected Prime Minister Turgut Ozal's free market economic policies. According to the new amendments, all petroleum areas were opened to domestic and foreign companies. Large areas which had not been evaluated with modern seismic methods were made available for exploration.

Foreign companies were allowed to export 35% of all oil products produced on land from fields discovered after January 1, 1980, and 45% produced offshore. The sale price of domestic oil products was raised in line with international prices. Royalties on oil production by foreign companies were restricted to 12.5%. Furthermore, all petroleum companies were required to deposit seismic, drilling, and geological data

with the GDPA, after they relinquished claims on any licensed area. This served to substantially increase the body of knowledge on exploration in Turkey.

Finally, the 1980 amendments empowered TPAO to form partnerships with domestic and foreign companies and to accept international arbitration procedures. These new rights vested in TPAO were significant on two fronts. First, they gave the opportunity for firms to cooperate with TPAO in new or existing areas. Second, by permitting TPAO to adhere to international arbitration procedures, the Turkish government institutionalized the company's independence.

Although TPAO had participated in joint ventures with foreign companies prior to the 1983 amendments, the new policy made joint ventures easier to establish and administer. Under the new legislation, TPAO has set up joint ventures with Esso Exploration Turkey, N.V. Turkse Shell, Arco, and Chevron International in southeast Anatolia, and Salen Energy A.B. in Iskenderun Bay.

Dr. Ismail Kafescioglu, formerly deputy general manager of TPAO, became the company's general manager in 1982. Under Kafescioglu's leadership, TPAO's original structure and role underwent substantial reform. Following the end of military rule in Turkey in 1983, in line with a major drive on the part of the newly elected civilian government to overhaul state enterprises, TPAO was decentralized. The result of the restructuring was to streamline TPAO's operations in order to focus on three major sectors: exploration, production, and drilling. Subsidiaries wholly owned by TPAO as well as associate companies were incorporated and assigned activities in transportation, refining, marketing, consulting, and overseas activities.

TPAO holds a 100% share in each of its subsidiaries: BOTAS pipeline transportation, DITAS marine transportation, TURPAS refining, and POAS marketing. Istanbul Fertilizer Industry, originally set up in 1971 by TPAO, became a subsidiary in 1983. The subsidiaries are independently operated under a separate management and board of directors while TPAO establishes investment policies. TPAO's shares in its associated companies are: Turkish Engineering, Consultancy and Contracting Corporation, 19%; Libyan-Turkish Engineering and Consultancy Corporation, 50%; Turkish-Petroleum International Company, 100%.

Ozer Altan, a geophysicist who worked at MTA and in various posts at TPAO from 1961 to 1980, was appointed general manager in 1984. Altan, who has extensive expertise in the oil industry combined with international experience, has played a significant role in implementing an aggressive policy of expansion through exploration and joint ventures with foreign companies.

Under Altan, the new organizational changes initiated in 1983 were consolidated, and the training of personnel became one of the company's major priorities. In 1989 over 30% of TPAO employees attended courses within the company and abroad. In line with the government's moves to privatize many state economic enterprises, TPAO's refining subsidiary TURPAS is scheduled to be offered to the public through the Istanbul stock exchange.

A key point of Altan's strategy has been to expand TPAO's operations abroad in order to secure sufficient supplies for the domestic market. He has pushed strongly to set up joint ventures with foreign companies. In 1988 the Turkish Petroleum International Company (TPIC) was set up to carry out exploration activities and production ventures abroad. TPIC is conducting oil and gas exploration in Indonesia, Australia, and Pakistan.

In support of TPAO's expansion overseas, Altan is eager to promote the company's image in the international marketplace. TPAO's subsidiary Petrol Ofisi Anonim Sirketi (POAS), which handles marketing and distributing activities, is now actively promoting TPAO through advertising and public relations channels. POAS operates over 4,111 gasoline stations across the country.

The decree amending the petroleum law in June 1989 liberalized the export and import of crude oil and oil products. This has had the effect of making the domestic industry more competitive and offering better customer service at filling stations.

The company has used new applications of petroleum technology to increase production of old fields and new found deposits during Altan's tenure. TPAO is currently working with JEORA Company of Japan on a five year experimental steam injection project. Since 1986 CO_2 injections have been used on some of the largest fields to spur production.

Altan's cautious management style coupled with a push towards increased exploration gave the company a 25% increase in crude oil production in 1989. TPAO increased its crude oil production by 59% in July and August 1990 against the same period in 1989. TPAO's domestic production averages 2.5 million tons of crude annually, representing a market share of 11%. The major foreign petrol companies currently active in Turkey are: Shell, Mobil, and Alaadin Middle East-Ersan.

Although TPAO has been exploring for natural gas since the 1960s, its use in Turkey until recently has been limited. The government is actively encouraging consumers, for environmental and energy-saving reasons, to replace lignite gas use with natural gas. Since 1987 Turkey has been importing natural gas from the Soviet Union under a barter agreement. An extensive natural gas pipeline network is under construction to service consumers in Ankara and Istanbul.

TPAO responded to the Persian Gulf crisis beginning in August 1990, and the ensuing drop in oil supplies, by strengthening its focus on exploration of new areas and maximum output of existing fields. In the 1990s, TPAO aims to build on its firmly laid foundations, continue widespread operations in Turkey, and expand its exploration activities abroad.

Principal Subsidiaries: Petroleum Pipeline, Inc.; Marine Operations and Transportation, Inc.; Turkish Petroleum Refinery, Inc.; Product Marketing Corporation, Inc.; Istanbul Fertilizer Industry, Inc.

Further Reading: Türkiye Petrolleri Anonim Ortakliği, Ankara, Türkiye Petrolleri Anonim Ortakliği, 1984; *Turkey: An Overview,* Ankara, Türkiye Petrolleri Anonim Ortakliği, April 1987.

—Laura Le Cornu and Juliette Rossant

ULTRAMAR PLC

141 Moorgate
London EC2M 6TX
United Kingdom
(071) 256-6080
Fax: (071) 256-8556

Public Company
Incorporated: 1935 as Ultramar Exploration Company
 Limited
Employees: 3,792 (1989)
Sales: £1.76 billion (US$3.40 billion)
Stock Exchanges: London Montreal Toronto

Ultramar PLC is the U.K. holding company of a number of operating subsidiaries engaged in oil and gas exploration and production worldwide, and in the shipping, refining, and marketing of crude oil and petroleum products. In 1989 it was the 86th-largest industrial company in the United Kingdom in terms of sales, and it is one of the largest of the British oil independents. Ultramar has had a remarkable and colorful history as an independent oil company, beginning its corporate life in the Venezuelan oil industry, reorientating its activities toward Canada and the United States in the 1950s and 1960s, and subsequently diversifying into Europe and the Far East. It is also an unusual firm because, although British-owned and registered in the United Kingdom, the center of management decisionmaking has long been in North America.

Ultramar Exploration Company Limited was formed in London in 1935 to raise funds for the development of oil fields in Venezuela. Its principal shareholders were four large South African mining groups: Consolidated Gold Fields, Selection Trust, Central Mining, and Union Corporation, and for its first decade the company had a very limited life as an independent entity. The four mining companies were seeking to diversify their activities, and the oil industry of Venezuela, which had grown quite quickly in the 1920s, looked a promising arena. Consolidated Gold Fields had taken a shareholding in the Caracas Petroleum Company, formed in Delaware in 1929, in association with Alfred Meyer, a former banker who had close associations with the dictator who ruled Venezuela between 1908 and 1935, Juan Vicente Gómez. Meyer had become Gómez's principal concession agent, selling oil concessions to foreign companies, and also trading in them in his own right. Caracas Petroleum purchased and sold oil concessions in Venezuela. In 1933, as part of a refinancing deal, Caracas

sold one promising option to a new London company, Orinoco Oilfields, Ltd., in which the four South African companies were principal shareholders. Two years later Orinoco was able to sell its concessions to Gulf Oil at a considerable profit. However, the mining companies realized that even higher profits could be made if they financed and controlled drilling operations themselves. This seems to have been the motive behind the foundation of Ultramar, which had almost identical shareholders to Caracas Petroleum. It was designed to be more active in oil exploration and development than Orinoco, which was liquidated. The name Ultramar was taken as it was the Spanish word for "overseas." Ultramar was to be overseas investment made by a British company in the Spanish-speaking country of Venezuela.

There were close links between Ultramar and Caracas Petroleum, whose president was Alfred Meyer. In June 1938 the two companies were formally merged under the Ultramar name, and a wholly owned company incorporated under Venezuelan law, the Caracas Petroleum Sociedad Anónima (CPSA), was launched, taking over the concessions held by the group. Caracas Petroleum had had a New York–based management. The New York office was retained after the merger, and it held an important place in the management of the company. In contrast, the Ultramar organization in London amounted to little more than the company's board of directors. During World War II, London's relative importance declined still further, as wartime conditions made it difficult for the board to exercise close control over activities in the Americas.

Ultramar's close working relationship with U.S. oil companies also helped to strengthen New York's importance in corporate decisionmaking. In 1940 a wide-ranging agreement was signed with the U.S. oil major Texaco. Standard Oil Company of New Jersey, the largest U.S. oil company, controlled around half of Venezuela's large annual production—which amounted to about 201.6 million barrels in 1939—and Texaco was anxious to establish its own supply of crude oil in this prolific oil region. CPSA transferred most of its concessions in central Venezuela to companies owned jointly with Texaco, and in June 1940 the corporate name was changed to Ultramar Company Limited, to emphasise that it was now an investment holding company whose activities were carried out by subsidiaries. The new partnership was a very unbalanced one, as Texaco supplied the technical expertise as well as most of the capital, but needed Ultramar in order to establish a position in Venezuela.

This alliance with Texaco played a critical role in Ultramar's survival, as it gave the U.K. firm access to technologies and markets which, as a small independent, it would have had little chance of developing alone. However, for some years Ultramar's survival remained in doubt. In 1946 Sir Edwin Herbert had been appointed an independent chairman, who was not linked with the mining company shareholders, but Ultramar's financial position deteriorated steadily when the development of the Venezuelan oil fields proved a very capital-intensive process. Two of the mining company shareholders, Central Mining and the Union Corporation, finally withdrew their support in 1949, and sold their shares on the market. Ultramar's position appeared weak, but it was able to survive by increasing its borrowings, and organizing a refinancing package.

CPSA's production was located in Mercedes oil fields, in the state of Guárico, central Venezuela. At the time it was an undeveloped and isolated region, which meant that the oil company faced considerable transport and other logistical problems quite apart from the complexities of searching for and developing oil. By 1943 it was evident that the Mercedes oil fields were rich, but there remained the problem of transporting the oil to the coast. The solution was the construction of a 150-mile pipeline northeast to the coast near Puerto La Cruz, where an oil tanker terminal had already been built to serve oil pipelines coming from eastern Venezuela. This pipeline was completed in May 1948, and the first oil entered the pipeline in the following June. However, production from the Mercedes oil fields built up too slowly, and it was this which caused the financial crisis in 1949.

By the early 1950s the Mercedes oil fields had proved their worth, and Ultramar's production was increasing. At its peak, the CPSA operation in the Mercedes oil fields produced about 30,000 barrels of crude oil and 80 million cubic feet of gas per day. In 1951 a particularly prolific oil field was discovered under the airstrip in the Mercedes camp area. Meanwhile Ultramar entered joint ventures with other companies to explore areas beyond the Mercedes oil fields. In 1954 the Mercedes partners entered a joint venture with the Atlantic Refining Company over the Oritupana area of eastern Venezuela, and in 1957 a major oil field was discovered there.

The 1950s saw two crucial strategic decisions for the company—diversification beyond Venezuela, and expansion into the downstream—or refined—oil business. In 1952, concern about the political stability of Venezuela led Ultramar to begin oil exploration in western Canada. A Canadian exploration company, Canpet Exploration Ltd. was incorporated as a wholly owned subsidiary of CPSA. In 1955 new shareholders were taken, including a subsidiary of Consolidated Gold Fields, in order to increase the funds available for exploration. Considerable success was achieved, especially in Saskatchewan, and in 1958 a new company, Ultramar Canada Limited, was formed to serve as a wholly owned holding company for Ultramar's Canadian interests. Meanwhile, in 1957, another wholly owned Ultramar subsidiary was formed, Caracas Petroleum US Limited, with an office in Dallas. This subsidiary began exploration work jointly with the Texkan Oil Company. These North American investments were initially small, but their significance for Ultramar's future development was fundamental.

At the beginning of the 1960s Ultramar also moved to become more of an integrated oil business rather than an exploration and marketing company. During the 1950s Ultramar had sold the oil produced from its Venezuelan operations to Texaco under a series of contracts, but the U.S. company made it clear that it would cease this arrangement in 1959. Ultramar's response was to establish its own refining and marketing operation. In 1960 it purchased the Panama Refining and Petrochemical Company, a Panamanian-registered company owned by an American oil entrepreneur, John Shaheen. This company owned the Golden Eagle Refining Company, which had marketing and refining interest in California, as well as a concession to build a refinery in Panama. Following this acquisition the Golden Eagle name was adopted in the company's marketing operations, but in the short term the purchase proved ill-timed. In the same year the U.S. government imposed a number of restrictions and quotas on the import of refined petroleum products, which had a depressing effect on

the newly acquired California business, and blocked a much-needed outlet for Venezuelan crude. Ultramar recorded a small net loss as a result. However, in the next few years the California operation was refocused, with the Los Angeles refinery concentrating on the production of aviation fuel and low-sulfur fuel oil. By 1962 Golden Eagle had become the largest independent supplier of jet fuel to the U.S. military in California. Ultramar became expert at developing niche markets in which it did not compete directly with larger and more powerful companies.

During the 1960s Ultramar invested heavily in Canada. The need to find a market for Venezuelan crude led to investment in marketing and refining operations in Newfoundland and Quebec. Golden Eagle of Canada, the subsidiary which operated this business, became one of the most important of the Ultramar companies. By 1967 Ultramar had become one of the largest importers of petroleum products in Canada. In 1971 a new refinery was opened in Quebec. A series of purchases of distribution companies expanded marketing operations elsewhere in eastern Canada, and by 1975 Ultramar companies owned 1,100 gasoline stations in eastern Canada. In January 1979 Ultramar purchased from Shell its wholly owned subsidiary, Canadian Fuel Marketers, an oil-marketing and storage company with 40 gasoline stations in eastern Canada.

Although Canada was the main focus of attention, Ultramar also developed interests in the United States and in Europe. The business in California had remained limited for much of the 1960s, but in the early 1970s a marketing campaign took the Golden Eagle name into Oregon, Washington, Arizona, and Nevada, although the core business remained government aviation-fuel contracts. In 1981, however, the purchase of Beacon Oil gave Ultramar 300 gasoline stations in central and northern California plus a diversified oil-marketing operation. The Beacon brand name was retained by the California business, and by the end of the 1980s Ultramar was established as one of the largest independent refinery and marketers in that state. Meanwhile in 1983 Ultramar purchased Pittston Petroleum, a leading independent marketer and distributor of light and heavy fuel oils in the northeastern United States and eastern Canada, an acquisition which provided a continuous market in the northeastern United States and eastern Canada for Ultramar products. In 1968 Ultramar had also entered the U.K. market with the purchase of the Herts & Beds Petroleum Company, a firm with a small network of service stations, which was renamed Ultramar Golden Eagle in 1969. During the 1970s Ultramar purchased small gasoline station companies and heating-oil distributors in the United Kingdom, and by 1979 it had around 430 outlets in that country.

From the mid-1960s Ultramar, as a foreign company, faced growing political and taxation difficulties in Venezuela. There was continual discussion of nationalization of the oil industry, and taxation on the oil companies increased steadily. The Venezuelan government was an enthusiastic supporter of the idea of an organization of oil-exporting countries, and was one of the prime movers in the creation of such an organization in 1960, OPEC. In the circumstances, Ultramar lacked the confidence to undertake much new investment in Venezuela. In 1972 the Mercedes production interests, where Ultramar's oil-producing history had begun, were sold, although activity continued in Ultramar's 50% joint venture in the Oritupano oil fields in eastern Venezuela. In 1976, however, the Venezuelan government nationalized the oil industry. Ultramar received almost no compensation for its assets.

The political risks in Venezuela had encouraged Ultramar's search in the 1960s for new sources of crude oil. In 1966 a new subsidiary company, Golden Eagle Exploration, was formed in Canada, with headquarters in Calgary, to search for oil in North America and elsewhere. In western Canada Ultramar's exploration efforts were never very successful, and in 1989 the bulk of Ultramar's western Canadian production interests were sold. In the United States too Ultramar had only limited success although its role was expanded in 1984 when it acquired 50% of the Enstar Corporation, with exploration and production interests in the Gulf of Mexico, Texas, and the Rocky Mountains.

However, the two new key production areas were Indonesia and the North Sea, where the consortium in which Ultramar was involved made significant discoveries in 1971 and 1972, respectively. By 1974 the Indonesian consortium had completed 24 oil and gas wells in east Kalimantan. A liquefying plant was constructed at Bontang, which liquefied the gas from the East Kalimantan fields, which was then shipped to Japan as liquefied natural gas (LNG) under a long-term contract. The plant was owned by PERTAMINA, the Indonesian state oil company, and was operated on a break–even basis by a company owned by the members of Ultramar's joint venture, Pertamina, and the Japanese buyers. In August 1977 the first cargo of LNG was delivered to Japan on board a specially built LNG carrier. Further oil exploration was undertaken in Indonesia as soon as the Bontang plant was in operation. Between 1979 and 1982 more than 80 new wells were drilled. By 1982 Ultramar's share of Indonesian oil and liquefied gas production averaged 6,300 barrels per day, while its natural gas production averaged 165 million cubic feet per day.

Ultramar's oil exploration in the North Sea had a slower start. In 1969 Ultramar took a 6% interest in a Phillips Petroleum consortium applying for licenses in the British sector of the North Sea. This consortium was awarded a number of blocks. In 1972 drilling of the first well began on Block 16/29, located in the North Sea about 163 miles east of Aberdeen and close to the offshore boundary with Norway. Oil was discovered in a field named Maureen. Exploration work on Maureen proved a lengthy and costly process and it was not until 1983, by which time Ultramar had raised its share in the consortium to 8.5%, that the Maureen field went on stream, initially producing over 70,000 barrels per day of crude oil. Meanwhile in 1982 a group in which Ultramar had an interest purchased a small share in the Thistle field, which had gone on stream in 1978, and which pumped oil to the Shetlands. In 1983 a small interest, just over 1%, was bought in another established North Sea oil field, the Forties field. By 1986 Ultramar's North Sea production averaged 10,800 barrels per day for the three oil fields in which it held an interest.

Indonesia and the North Sea enabled Ultramar to survive as an oil–producing company despite the loss of the Venezuelan operations. Other diversification strategies were less successful. During the 1960s Ultramar had developed a ship–bunkering business, and toward the end of that decade the company started to develop its oil tanker fleet. In retrospect, it could be argued that the company entered the shipbuilding business too late, for the rapid growth in the industry was already subsid-

ing, and certainly the consequences in the 1980s were to be very unfortunate. By 1972 Ultramar wholly owned three tankers, and had 50% ownership of five other tankers. Ultramar also began the construction of three oil-bulk-ore (OBO) carriers, a new kind of tanker which could be used for several purposes. In 1973 the first of the OBOs, named the *Ultramar,* was launched at San Diego, California, the largest ship yet built on the west coast of the United States.

The problem with Ultramar's investment in shipping was that from the mid-1970s market conditions deteriorated rapidly. There was a worldwide tanker tonnage surplus, and a particular excess of large oil tankers. An additional problem for Ultramar was that large oil tankers could not access its Quebec refinery, for the St. Lawrence River had depth problems which dredging failed to overcome. Ultramar decided to move away from large tankers and placed an order in 1980 with a Spanish shipyard for six medium-sized OBO carriers. These tankers were to be ice-strengthened and therefore particularly well-suited for carrying crude oil to Ultramar's Quebec refinery during the winter months. Construction was delayed, and it was not until early 1985 that the first ship, named *Maureen* after the North Sea field, was delivered. The tanker market, however, remained extremely volatile and the problem of excess capacity continued. The Spanish-built OBOs and other Ultramar vessels were chartered for part of the year, but remained a loss-making operation. By 1987 Ultramar had resolved to sell its three large California-built OBOs, but was unable to find a purchaser. Only in the following year did the six Spanish-built OBOs make their first contribution to Ultramar's profits. In 1989 four of these vessels were sold.

In 1982 Ultramar Company Limited changed its name to Ultramar PLC. The mid-1980s saw Ultramar in severe difficulties. Crude oil prices weakened, and then dropped almost 50% in 1986. Net profits and tax dropped from £127.6 million to £71.6 million in 1985, and in the following year Ultramar recorded a loss of £62.1 million. It was evident that although the condition of the oil market was a major factor in this downturn, Ultramar was also suffering from excessive diversification, and that some of its varied interests—such as shipping—were very unprofitable. The result of the crisis was a determination to focus on core business activities, and to dispose of peripheral or unprofitable activies. In 1987 the U.K. marketing subsidiary Ultramar Golden Eagle was sold to the Kuwait Petroleum Corporation. Later in that year Ultramar closed its loss–making Hanford refinery in California. Over the next year it supplied its western U.S. marketing operations entirely through product purchases on the market. However, in December 1988, it acquired the modern Wilmington refinery, located in Los Angeles County, California for £260 million.

By the early 1990s Ultramar's business had a clear shape, with four core businesses. It had exploration and production operations in Indonesia and the North Sea, and refining and marketing operations in eastern Canada and on the West Coast of the United States, especially in California. Ultramar was a major refiner and marketer in eastern Canada, with a retail network of around 1,400 service stations, while the 350 service stations marketing under the Beacon brand made Ultramar one of the largest independent refiners and marketers in California. U.S. management continued to be based in New York State. The "group co-ordinating company," American Ultramar Limited, was based in New York City until 1972, when it moved to

Mount Kisco, New York. It moved again to Tarrytown, New York in 1985.

Ultramar has survived a series of financial crises, and undergone a complete transformation of its geographical area of operation. Its growth has been based on the skillful use of alliances and partnerships with other companies, often bigger than itself. Ultramar's future remains dependent in part on the vagaries of the international oil industry. The Iraqi invasion of Kuwait in August 1990 and the ensuing Persian Gulf War created new uncertainties in this respect. Yet Ultramar was well placed to survive the crisis. By this date the company refined about double the amount of oil that it retailed, selling the balance wholesale at world market prices. A major effect of the Iraqi invasion was to remove a considerable amount of refined products from the market. The result was a steep increase in profit margins on refinery operations, which has worked much to Ultramar's advantage. As a soundly based integrated oil company, Ultramar has reason to be optimistic about its future.

Principal Subsidiaries: American Ultramar Limited (U.S.A.); Ultramar America Limited (U.S.A.); Ultramar Shipping Company, Inc. (U.S.A.); Ultramar Energy Limited (U.S.A.); Ultramar Inc. (U.S.A.); Ultramar Oil and Gas Limited (U.S.A.); Canadian Ultramar Limited (Canada); Ultramar Canada Inc.; Ultramar Exploration Limited; Ultramar Indonesia Limited; Ultramar Australia, Inc.

Further Reading: Atterbury, Paul, and Julia Mackenzie, *A Golden Adventure: The First 50 Years of Ultramar,* London, Hartwood Press, 1985.

—Geoffrey Jones

UNOCAL CORPORATION

1201 West Fifth Street
Los Angeles, California 90017
U.S.A.
(213) 977-7600
Fax: (213) 977-7813

Public Company
Incorporated: 1890 as Union Oil Company of California
Employees: 17,518
Sales: $11.81 billion
Stock Exchanges: New York Midwest Pacific

Unocal gasoline service stations dot the metropolitan area of Los Angeles and the entire Pacific coast as well. Baseball fans who follow the Los Angeles Dodgers by radio and television eventually come to know Unocal's advertising jingles by heart. Commuters who drive past the company's refinery near Long Beach Harbor, California, in late October see one of its huge storage tanks painted to look like a jack o'lantern. This comfortable corporate omnipresence in its home area belies the precarious history of Unocal. Unocal has survived three major hostile takeover battles, as well as a parochial corporate strategy that threatened its status as one of the nation's largest producers of both crude oil and its by-products in the years immediately before and after World War II.

Unocal was founded in 1890 as Union Oil Company of California from the merger of three California oil companies: Sespe Oil and Torrey Canyon Oil, both of which were owned by oil-and-land baron Thomas Bard of Ventura County, and Hardison & Stewart Oil. Hardison & Stewart began as a gentlemen's-agreement partnership between Lyman Stewart and Wallace Hardison in 1883 and incorporated later that year. In constant need of cash to finance exploration, Hardison and Stewart were referred to Bard by their bankers in 1885. Bard became their partner and operated his companies in an informal alliance with theirs. Hardison & Stewart frequently ran short of cash, however, and Bard finally proposed that they merge their companies. Hardison and Stewart consented, and Union incorporated in Santa Paula, California, as a mining company, with Bard as president, Stewart as vice president, and Hardison as treasurer. The Santa Paula plant was, in 1891, the site of the first petroleum-research facility in the western United States.

The merger proved to be anything but stable. Hardison, who had been gradually losing enthusiasm for the oil business, sold out his interest in 1892 and left Union to engage in fruit growing. His shares found their way into the possession of Stewart's family. This, in turn, bred in Stewart a conviction that the company was his by rights and led to a conflict with Bard. Although both were Pennsylvania-born wildcatters who had been drawn to California by geologist Benjamin Silliman's predictions of vast oil deposits there, Lyman Stewart and Thomas Bard differed in temperament. Stewart had lost his savings in a youthful oil venture in his native state, and as a result he flung himself into the oil business with the zeal of one who believed that worldly success was a sign of God's salvation. Bard was a calm and shrewd negotiator who would later become a U.S. senator. Stewart wanted Union to put more effort into marketing petroleum products; Bard wanted it to remain a producer and wholesaler of crude.

In 1894 Bard resigned as president to protest an expansion of Union's refining capacity that Stewart initiated and that was approved by other directors. Bard was succeeded by D.T. Perkins, his hand-picked successor. Stewart, however, faced Perkins down at an annual meeting several months later, and Stewart assumed the presidency himself. Bard, still a director, continued to object to Stewart's free-spending expansion schemes, but was outvoted time after time. Finally, he sold out his interest in Union in 1900 and began his political career. In 1901 Union moved to Los Angeles.

With Stewart as president, his son Will Stewart, a former University of California football star, became general manager. Under the Stewarts, Union continued to expand both its production and retailing operations. Union spent much money on technological advances, organizing the first petroleum-geology department in the U.S. west in 1900, launching a prototypical tanker in 1903, and completing the first successful cemented oil well in 1905. In 1913 it opened its first service station, at the corner of Sixth and Mateo streets in Los Angeles. In time, Union came to miss Thomas Bard's fiscal sobriety. As Lyman Stewart continued to buy up real estate with alarming aggressiveness, the company remained poor in cash. To keep up bond payments Union had to borrow ever-larger sums from local banks and financiers. As the situation worsened, creditors forced the elder Stewart to resign in 1914, and the board of directors elected his more conservative son to succeed him.

Under Will Stewart, Union continued to expand. In 1917 it acquired Pinal-Dome Oil, a local company that added 20 service stations in Los Angeles and Orange County to its retail network. Union also opened a refinery in Wilmington, California, near Long Beach Harbor, in 1917, just as U.S. involvement in World War I increased the demand for fuels. The company emerged from the war still in vulnerable financial condition. A speculative scramble for Union shares in 1920 generated takeover rumors, and the next year a foreign syndicate headed by what later became Royal Dutch/Shell Group formally launched an acquisition attempt. In response, Lyman Stewart and two other directors, banker Henry Robinson and retired Borden executive Isaac Milbank, organized Union Oil Associates, the sole purpose of which was to accumulate Union shares and prevent them from falling to Shell's grasp. The contest took on jingoistic overtones and came down to a proxy vote at a stockholders meeting in March 1922. When the votes were counted, Union Oil Associates won. Union Oil Associates began to merge with Union itself, and two years later, Shell dumped its Union shares on the open market.

The last great battle of his life over, Lyman Stewart died in 1923. Winning that same fight had left Union in stronger financial condition than ever, and the company continued to prosper. In 1928 it joined with Atlantic Refining to form Atlantic-Union Oil, a marketing venture in Australia and New Zealand. By the end of the decade, Union's annual sales had reached $90 million, and it was pumping more 18 million barrels of oil per year. The Great Depression abruptly ended the good times for Union. Will Stewart died suddenly in 1930. He was succeeded as president by vice president Press St. Clair, who pursued a cautious strategy in response to the worsened business climate. In 1931 Union sold its interest in Pantepec Oil, which held leases for exploration in Venezuela. Two years later, the company sold its share of Atlantic-Union.

Union emerged from the Depression with the advertising motif that has identified it ever since. In 1932 the company was looking for a distinctive brand name for its gasoline. Robert Matthews, a director and British national who was studying U.S. history to qualify for citizenship, suggested "Union '76," as in "The Spirit of '76" for its patriotic connotations. The octane rating of Union's most potent gasoline also happened to be 76, and the marketing department adopted Matthews's idea.

Press St. Clair retired in 1938 and was succeeded by Reese Taylor, president of Consolidated Steel and a Union director. Taylor, who was something of a regional chauvinist, would run Union with an iron hand for 24 years. Under this direction, the company would take St. Clair's caution to an extreme and remain tucked into its geographical niche, rejecting expansion. It would eventually pay for this provincialism, falling behind in the game when other major oil companies embarked on worldwide expansion. First, however, World War II broke out, and Union boosted its crude production in response to increased demand for petroleum products. The production of aviation fuels was increased to seven times prewar levels. The company was well located to keep U.S. Navy ships operating in the Pacific Ocean supplied with fuel. It was after the war that most of the U.S. oil giants began to develop overseas sources of crude, while Union concentrated its operations in North America. In 1949 Union acquired Los Nietos Company, an oil and gas concern the holdings of which were concentrated in California. It also discovered and began exploiting substantial fields in Louisiana. Nevertheless, Union could not find enough crude to keep up with increasing demand for petroleum products, and it had to dip into its reserves to keep customers happy.

Union made some sporadic attempts to find oil in Latin America, North Africa, and Australia. It got nothing but dry holes for its trouble. Injecting steam into abandoned California wells added 70 million barrels to its reserves, but by 1956 the company was strapped for both oil and cash. That year, Taylor turned to his friend, Gulf Oil president William Whiteford, and swung a deal to acquire Gulf's surplus crude in exchange for convertible debt securities. Those debentures, however, could be exchanged for enough Union stock for Gulf to control Union. Gulf, cash and oil rich, sought entry into the western market and Union once more became a takeover target, all the more so because it accounted for more than 10% of gasoline sales in the Pacific Coast market. As Gulf mulled over the possibilities, in 1959 Oklahoma-based Phillips Petroleum began acquiring Union stock and became Union's largest shareholder the next year with 15%. Union bought back the Gulf

debentures for $120 million—$50 per share—and got a federal court to bar Phillips from acquiring any more of its stock, ending the second major threat to Union's independence.

None of this, however, addressed the problem of expanding the company's oil reserves and marketing presence. At the end of the 1950s, two-thirds of Union's production was still coming from California, including the Torrey Canyon field discovered by Lyman Stewart in 1889, but a prolonged management shuffle prompted by Reese Taylor's sudden death in 1962 distracted the company from finding a solution. Union's board brought back Albert C. Rubel, who had retired as president in 1960—Taylor had become chairman in 1956—to take over until a permanent successor could be found. Under Rubel, Union entered into merger talks with Atlantic Refining in 1963, but Atlantic called off the deal because it did not want Union to be the surviving company, losing as it would then its own identity in its East Coast markets. Finally, in 1964, Rubel appointed senior vice president Fred Hartley to take over as CEO.

Blunt and outspoken, Hartley was a chemical engineer by training but had shown good business instincts as head of the marketing division. His first actions as CEO were to improve Union's bottom line through layoffs and closing unprofitable service stations. The company also broke out of its provincialism in 1965 by acquiring Pure Oil Company, a struggling oil concern that nonetheless had an extensive distribution network in the Midwest and Southeast. Hartley concluded the deal over the objections of shipping magnate Daniel Ludwig, who had become a Union director when he bought Phillips's 15% stake in 1963. The company quickly raised $146 million and bought up all of Ludwig's shares at $36.50 per share.

Hartley saw the need for increased exploration. "If we don't explore we'll go backward and if we don't explore with success we'll go backward and broke," he was fond of saying at the time, as quoted in *Fortune* in April 1967. Union cast a wide exploration net, but it mostly dredged up dry holes. In 1969 the company suffered a public relations disaster when one of its drilling platforms off the coast of California leaked hundreds of thousands of gallons of oil into the water and onto the beaches of Santa Barbara. It took months for Union to get the seepage down to a manageable level. The company maintained that it responded to the leak promptly and had minimized environmental damage, but the incident helped turn public and political opinion against offshore drilling. Various governmental authorities sued Union, Mobil, Gulf, Texaco, and Peter Bawden Drilling, and in an out-of-court settlement reached in 1974, the defendants agreed to pay a total of $9.7 million in damages to the state of California, the Santa Barbara County and the cities of Santa Barbara and Carpinteria.

The Santa Barbara spill and Union's peppery response to criticisms stemming from it gained the company a bad reputation among environmentalists. Throughout the 1970s, even before oil prices began to skyrocket, Union had charted an aggressive course in research and development of alternative energy sources. Union has spent substantial sums on developing geothermal power and liquified natural gas as an automotive fuel. Hartley stopped using a Cadillac as his company car in favor of an Audi, complaining about U.S. automakers' unwillingness to build cars with better gas mileage. In 1974 Union began building an experimental oil-shale processing plant in Colorado. Many oil companies turned to shale in the 1970s as a potential source of crude. It was an old enthusiasm of Hartley's; he had written a thesis on it while a student at the University of British Columbia. In 1980, while others were still marking time, Union announced that it would begin constructing a commercial-scale oil shale plant in Parachute Creek, Colorado.

In the 1970s Union joined with Standard Oil of New Jersey, Atlantic Richfield, Standard Oil of Ohio, Mobil, Phillips, and Amerada Hess to form Alyeska Pipeline Service, which would build the Alaska pipeline. Union, which was already drilling in Alaska's Cook Inlet, would thus participate in the exploitation of the immense deposits lying under Prudhoe Bay. Union entered a niche of the metals industry in 1977 when it acquired Molycorp, a producer of rare-earth metals used in high-tech applications.

After 15 years under the guidance of Fred Hartley, Union approached the 1980s in a state of financial strength, giving its shareholders a higher-than-average return on assets. Its exploration efforts had begun to pay off, making it rich in oil and gas reserves. At the same time, Hartley's age—he turned 65 in 1980—and the lack of an heir apparent made Union the subject of takeover speculation on Wall Street. To thwart any such attempts, it reorganized in 1983, creating Unocal Corporation as a holding company and reincorporating in Delaware, where incorporation laws made it harder for outsiders to gain control of a company without approval by its directors.

None of this, however, deterred Mesa Petroleum chairman and corporate raider T. Boone Pickens Jr., who launched the third major threat to Unocal's independence. Pickens began acquiring Unocal shares in late 1984, even as he was beginning a separate takeover bid for Phillips Petroleum, and eventually accumulated a 13.6% stake of Unocal. The Phillips bid failed, but when Pickens walked away from it in January 1985 he did so with a hefty greenmail payment and more than $1 billion in unused credit lines and potential margin loans on his Unocal stock. In the meantime, Hartley refused to sacrifice the money Unocal was pumping into exploration to initiate a stock buy-back and inflate its price, although institutional shareholders were clamoring for such a move. Observers speculated that it was only a matter of time before Pickens and Mesa pounced.

Hartley knew that something was up. In early April, the two met by chance as they waited to testify in congressional hearings on the recent spate of hostile takeover bids for major oil companies. *Business Week*, April 15, 1985, reported that Pickens extended his hand in greeting but Hartley refused it, growling, "Go away." "Fred, you're talkin' to your largest stockholder," Pickens said. "Isn't that a shame," Hartley shot back.

Later that month, Mesa announced that it was offering $54 per share in cash for the 37% of Unocal stock that it would need for a controlling interest, and the same amount in debt securities for the remaining shares. Unocal responded with an offer to buy back 49% of its stock for $72 worth of debt per share, but only if Mesa reached its target of 37 million shares. Any shares in Mesa's possession were excluded from this deal, meaning that Pickens could not sell them back to Unocal at a

hefty profit. Pickens challenged this last provision in court and initiated a proxy battle to delay the company's annual meeting until he could field his own slate of candidates for the board of directors. Loyal shareholders, however, voted Pickens down in May and re-elected Hartley as chairman.

Several days later, the Delaware Supreme Court ruled that Unocal had no legal obligation to include Mesa's holdings in its partial buyback offer. Unocal had stalemated Pickens. To get rid of him, the company agreed to buy back one-third of Mesa's shares at $72 per share; other stockholders would be allowed to sell back some of their holdings as well. Pickens admitted that he would do well to break even on the deal. The most ambitious attempt in his campaign to restructure the oil business—and his first genuine failure—had ended. For its part, Unocal was anything but triumphant in victory. To finance the stock buy-back, it had increased its debt load from $1.2 billion to $5.3 billion. Cuts in capital outlays would be necessary.

Fred Hartley retired in 1988. He had built Unocal into the 14th-largest oil company in the United States, but it was left to his successor, CEO Richard Stegemeier, to cope with the bulk of the debt load incurred in the battle against Pickens. Under Stegemeier, Unocal closed unprofitable production and refining facilities and sold off real estate that did not hold oil or gas, including its headquarters building in downtown Los Angeles. By the end of the decade, the company was ready for further expansion. In 1989 Unocal joined with Petróleos de Venezuela to form Uno-Ven, a marketing and refining partnership in the midwestern United States. In May 1990 Unocal added to its gas reserves by acquiring Prarie Holding Company from gold-mining concern Placer Dome.

When Fred Hartley died in October 1990, the company that he had whipped into shape and which had nearly been bought out from under him stood ready to resume the capital-intensive business of exploring for and producing oil. In the aftermath of the Mesa takeover bid Unocal had allowed its own crude supplies to dwindle, so that it once again had to buy large quantities from outside sources. After a century in which its existence had often been precarious, Unocal had proved itself tough. Like the patriotic ideal for which it named its gasoline, it continues to show an inextinguishable spirit.

Principal Subsidiary: Union Oil Company of California.

Further Reading: Hutchinson, W.H., *Oil, Land and Politics: The California Career of Thomas Robert Bard,* Norman, University of Oklahoma Press, 1965; Welty, Earl M., and Frank J. Taylor, *The 76 Bonanza,* Menlo Park, California, Lane Magazine and Book Company, 1966; O'Hanlon, Thomas, "Fred Hartley and His Well-Oiled Multiplying Machine," *Fortune,* April 1967; "The Luck of the Drill Bit," *Forbes,* January 15, 1970.

—Douglas Sun

USX CORPORATION

600 Grant Street
Pittsburgh, Pennsylvania 15219
U.S.A.
(412) 433-1121
Fax: (412) 433-6847

Public Company
Incorporated: 1901 as United States Steel Corporation
Employees: 51,500
Sales: $20.66 billion
Stock Exchanges: New York Midwest Pacific Montreal
   London

USX Corporation is an international diversified energy and steel-manufacturing company. About 65% of sales are derived from the oil and gas business, mainly from its Marathon Oil Group. About 30% of sales are from its USS subsidiary, the largest U.S. integrated steel company, which produces and sells a wide range of semifinished and finished steel products, coke, and taconite pellets. Remaining sales, about 5%, are from its U.S. Diversified Group division, made up of relatively smaller operations in real estate, transportation, engineering, chemicals, mining, and financial services. USX's emphasis on energy dates from its acquisitions of Marathon Oil Company in 1982 and Texas Oil & Gas Corporation in 1986. Before these events, and its 1986 name change to USX Corporation, it was known as United States Steel Corporation, a company founded on February 25, 1901, as the nation's largest steelmaker and the largest business enterprise launched up to that time.

The origin of United States Steel Corporation (USS) is virtually an early history of the steel industry in the United States, which in turn is closely linked to the name of Andrew Carnegie. The quintessential 19th-century self-made man, Carnegie began as bobbin boy in a cotton mill, made a stake in the railroad business, and in 1864 started to invest in the iron industry. In 1873 he began to establish steel plants using the Bessemer steelmaking process. A ruthless competitor, his Carnegie Steel Company grew to be the largest domestic steelmaker by the end of the century. In 1897 Carnegie appointed Charles M. Schwab as president of Carnegie Steel, a brilliant, diplomatic steel man who had worked his way up through the Carnegie organization. At about the same time, prominent financier John Pierpont Morgan became a major participant in the steel industry by organizing Federal Steel Company, in

1898. Morgan's personal representative in the steel business was Elbert Henry Gary, a lawyer, former judge, and director of Illinois Steel Company, one of the several steel companies co-opted into Federal Steel, of which Gary was made president. Carnegie, Schwab, Morgan, and Gary where the key participants in the organization of USS.

By 1900 the demand for U.S. steel was at peak levels and Morgan's ambition was to dominate this market by creating a centralized combine, or trust. He was encouraged in this by rumors of Carnegie's intention to retire from business. U.S. President William McKinley was known to approve of business consolidations, and his support limited the risk of government antitrust claims in the face of a steel-industry combination. In December 1900 Morgan attended a now-legendary dinner at New York's University Club during which Schwab gave a speech in which he outlined a steel trust, the nucleus of which would be the Carnegie and Morgan steel enterprises, together with a number of other smaller steel, mining, and shipping concerns. With Schwab and Gary as intermediaries between Carnegie and Morgan, negotiations were concluded by early February 1901 for Carnegie to sell his steel interests for about $492 million in bonds and stock of the new company. The organization plan was largely executed by Gary with Morgan arranging the financing and, on February 25, 1901, United States Steel Corporation was incorporated with an authorized capitalization of $1.4 billion, the first billion-dollar corporation in history. The ten companies that were merged to form USS where American Bridge Company, American Sheet Steel Company, American Steel Hoop Company, American Steel & Wire Company, American Tin Plate Company, Carnegie Steel Company, Federal Steel Company, Lake Superior Consolidated Iron Mines, National Steel Company, and National Tube Company.

At Morgan's urging Schwab became president of USS with Gary as chairman of the board of directors and of the executive committee. Two such strong personalities, however, could not easily share power. In 1903 Schwab resigned and soon took control of Bethlehem Steel Corporation, which he eventually built into the second-largest steel producer in the country. Gary stayed on as, in effect, chief executive officer to lead USS and to dominate its policies until his death in August 1927. His stated goal for USS was not to create a monopoly but to sustain trade and foster competition by competing on a basis of efficiency and price. Steel prices, in fact, did drop significantly in the years after the company began, and, because of competition, USS's market share of U.S. steel production dropped steadily over the years from about 66% in 1901 to about 33% in the 1930s to 1950s. USS's sales increased from $423 million in 1902 to $1 billion during the 1920s, dropped to a low of $288 million in 1933, reached $1 billion in 1940, and climbed to about $3 billion in 1950. Except for a few deficit years, USS's operations have been generally profitable, though earnings have been cyclical.

USS's history is notable for continual acquisitions, divestitures, consolidations, reorganizations, and labor disputes. In 1901 USS acquired the Bessemer Steamship company, a shipping concern engaged in iron-ore traffic on the Great Lakes. Shelby Steel Tube Company was purchased in 1901, Union Steel Company in 1903, and Clairton Steel Company in 1904; and a number of smaller acquisitions were made in those early years. In 1906 USS began construction on a large new steel plant on Lake Michigan together with a model city designed primarily for USS employees. The new town was named Gary, Indiana, and was substantially completed by 1911. A major acquisition in 1907 was that of Tennessee Coal, Iron and Railroad Company, the largest steel producer in the South. A presence in the West was established by the purchase of Columbia Steel Company in 1910. In addition to steel manufacture, USS also had large coal-mining operations in western Pennsylvania. These operations were based on former properties of H.C. Frick Coke Company, which included some of Carnegie's coal properties and which became a part of USS when it was formed in 1901. The coal produced by these mines was used to fuel USS operations.

The 12-hour day, standard in industry during USS's early years, was a major labor issue. USS's workers originally were unorganized; and Gary was a staunch enemy of unionization, the closed shop, and collective bargaining. He took a leading role among businessmen, however, by calling in 1911 for the abolition of the 12-hour day. Little was actually done, however, and a general strike was called against the steel industry in 1919. The strike failed and was abandoned in 1920. The 12-hour day eventually was abolished, and in 1937 USS signed a contract with Steel Workers Organizing Committee, which in 1942 became the United Steelworkers of America. USS's labor relations have generally been adversarial, characterized by a long history of divisive negotiations, often-bitter strikes, and settlements that were sometimes economically disastrous for the company and, in the long run, for its employees.

The U.S. government's tolerant view of big corporations ended with the administration of President Theodore Roosevelt and, on Roosevelt's instructions, an antitrust investigation of USS was begun in 1905. Gary cooperated with the investigation, but the final report to President William Howard Taft in 1911 led to a monopoly charge against USS in the U.S. District Court of Appeals. This court's 1915 decision unanimously absolved USS from the monopoly charge and largely vindicated Gary's claim that USS was designed to be competitive rather than a monopolistic trust.

USS's business boomed during World War I with sales more than doubling between 1915 and 1918 and remaining strong at about $2 billion annually through the 1920s. Gary's personal domination of USS ended with his death in 1927. J.P. Morgan Jr. became chairman of the board of directors from 1927 to 1932, but during this period USS essentially was under the leadership of Myron C. Taylor, chairman of the finance committee from 1927 to 1934 and chairman of the board from 1932 until his resignation in 1938. Taylor brought about extensive changes in USS's make-up. Numerous obsolete plants were closed, others were modernized, and a new plant was added with total capital expenditures of more than $500 million. By the end of Taylor's tenure about three-quarters of USS's products were different or were made differently and more efficiently than they had been in 1927, with the principal realignment being the change from heavy steel for capital goods to lighter steel for consumer goods.

After Taylor's resignation in 1938, Edward R. Stettinius Jr. served as chairman of the board until he left in 1940 to undertake government service and eventually to become secretary of state. Benjamin F. Fairless, an important figure in USS history, became president in 1938, and Irving S. Olds succeeded Stettinius as chairman of the board in 1940. Olds served as

chairman until 1952 when he was succeeded in that office by Fairless. During this period USS's business recovered from its Depression slump, thanks to the enormous demand for steel products generated by World War II and the postwar economic boom. Revenues more than quintupled from $611 million in 1938 to more than $3.5 billion in 1951. USS was present in every geographical market in the United States except the East, so in 1949 it announced plans to build a large integrated steel plant in Pennsylvania on the Delaware River to be known as the Fairless works. This plant, operational in 1952, was intended to compete with Bethlehem Steel for the eastern market and to take advantage of ocean shipment of iron ore from USS's large ore reserves in Venezuela.

In 1951 a change intended to simplify the structure of United States Steel Corporation took place when a single company was formed from USS's four major operational subsidiaries. This reorganization, completed in 1953, created a tightly knit, more efficient organizational structure in place of the former aggregate of semi-independent units. In 1953 Clifford F. Hood was appointed president and chief operating officer, sharing overall responsibility for the company with Fairless as chairman of the board and Enders W. Voorhees who continued as chairman of the finance committee.

Fairless's tenure as chairman of the board included one of the longest strikes in USS's history in 1952, resulting from USS's refusal to allow substantial wage increases and tighter closed-shop rules. Just before the strike was to begin in April 1952, President Harry S Truman seized the company's properties in order to ensure steel production for the Korean War. This unusual action was declared unconstitutional by the U.S. Supreme Court in June 1952. An industry-wide strike ensued that was settled in August ending a unique episode in USS's labor history. A more productive occurrence was the groundbreaking in 1953 for the building of a new research center near Pittsburgh. Fairless retired in May 1955 and was succeeded by Roger M. Blough as chairman of the board and chief executive officer.

Due to improved administrative, operating, and plant efficiencies, USS set a postwar record for profitability in 1955 although market share continued to decline to around 30%. In 1958 a further corporate simplification took place when wholly owned subsidiary Universal Atlas Cement Company was merged into USS as an operating division, as were the Union Supply Company and Homewood Stores Company subsidiaries. Profits were being squeezed between rising operating costs and relatively stable prices, and in April 1962 USS unexpectedly announced an across-the-board price increase, setting off a storm of criticism including an angry protest to Blough from U.S. President John F. Kennedy. Within a week USS was forced to rescind the price increase, using the face-saving excuse that other steel companies had not agreed to support the new price level. This situation resulted from USS's continued decline in market share to about 25% in 1961, together with deteriorating profitability, in part caused by excessive capital spending in relation to market volume.

In response to its difficulties USS announced in 1963 a further reorganization and centralization of its steel divisions and sales operations in order to concentrate management resources to a greater extent on selling and consumer services. In 1964 USS created a new chemicals division called Pittsburgh Chemical Company. Effective in 1966 United States Steel Corporation was reincorporated in Delaware to take advantage of that state's more flexible corporation laws. In 1967 Edwin H. Gott became president and chief operating officer and in 1969 he succeeded Blough as chairman of the board and CEO. Edgar B. Speer, a veteran steel man, moved up to the presidency. In 1973 Gott retired, and Speer assumed his duties as chairman and CEO. Significantly, Speer immediately announced plans to expand USS's diversification into nonsteel businesses. Prospects for long-term growth in steel were fading rapidly because of rising costs, competitive pricing, and foreign competition.

During Speer's tenure, USS closed or sold a variety of facilities and businesses in steel, cement, fabricating, home building, plastics, and mining. Capital expenditure, much of it for environmental purposes, remained high. There was little significant diversification, however. In 1979 USS lost $293 million. Also that year, former president David M. Roderick became chairman and CEO. He announced a major liquidation of unprofitable steel operations and increased efforts to diversify. In 1979 13 steel facilities were closed with an $809 million write-off. Universal Atlas Cement—once the United States's largest cement company—was sold, and various real estate, timber, and mineral properties were leased or sold. The long-promised diversification move came in 1982 with United States Steel Corporation's $6.4 billion acquisition of Marathon Oil Company, a major integrated energy company with vast reserves of oil and gas. Marathon's revenues were about the same as USS's; thus the company's size was doubled, with steel's contribution to sales dropping to about 40%.

Marathon had been incorporated on August 1, 1887, as Ohio Oil Company by Ohio oil driller Henry Ernst and four of his fellow oilmen, primarily in order to compete with Standard Oil Company. Ohio Oil quickly became the largest producer of crude oil in Ohio and in 1889 was bought out by Standard Oil. When Standard was broken up on antitrust grounds by the U.S. government in 1911, Ohio Oil again became an independent company with veteran oil man James Donnell as president. Under Donnell and his successors Ohio Oil grew into an international integrated oil and gas company with large energy resources and extensive exploratory and retail sales operations. Its name was changed to Marathon Oil Company in 1962.

USS continued to improve the efficiency and profitability of its steel operations with the 1983 closing of part or all of 20 obsolete plants and the 1984 purchase of the steel business of National Intergroup, Inc. By 1985 Roderick had shut down more than 150 facilities and reduced steelmaking capacity by more than 30%. He cut 54% of white-collar jobs, fired about 100,000 production workers, and sold $3 billion in assets. In 1986 United States Steel Corporation changed its name to USX Corporation, to reflect its diversification. USX continued its diversification program in 1986 with the $3.6 billion acquisition of Texas Oil & Gas Corporation. Founded in 1955 as Tex-Star Oil & Gas Corporation, the company is engaged primarily in the domestic production, gathering, and transportation of natural gas.

In October 1986 corporate raider Carl Icahn made a $7.1 billion offer for USX—after purchasing about 29 million USX shares. Roderick fought off the takeover attempt by borrowing $3.4 billion to pay off company debts with the provision that the loan would be called in the event of a takeover. Icahn gave up his attempt in January 1987 but kept his USX shares and began a long program of urging USX management to spin off or sell its underperforming steel business. In 1987 Roderick shut down about one-quarter of USX's raw steelmaking capacity, but by 1988 USS, the steel division of USX, had become the most efficient producer of steel in the world.

In May 1989 Roderick retired and was succeeded as chairman and CEO by Charles A. Corry, a veteran of the USX restructuring. In October 1989 Corry announced a plan to sell some of Texas Oil & Gas's energy reserves in order to pay down debt and implement a large stock buyback. In June 1990 the company stated that it would consolidate Texas Oil's operations with Marathon Oil in order to cut costs. On January 31, 1991, Icahn won his long battle to have USX restructured when the company announced that it would recapitalize by issuing a separate class of stock for its U.S. Steel subsidiary although both businesses, energy and steel, would remain part of USX. In May 1991 USX shareholders approved the plan. Common shares of USX Corporation began trading as USX-Marathon Group, and new common shares of USX-U.S. Steel Group were issued.

Further Reading: Cotter, Arundel, *The Authentic History of the United States Steel Corporation*, New York, Moody Magazine and Book Co., 1916; Fisher, Douglas A., *Steel Serves the Nation, 1901–1951*, Pittsburgh, United States Steel Corporation, 1951; Jackson, Stanley, *J.P. Morgan*, New York, Stein and Day, 1983.

—Bernard A. Block

THE WILLIAMS COMPANIES, INC.

THE WILLIAMS COMPANIES, INC.

One Williams Center
Tulsa, Oklahoma 74172
U.S.A.
(918) 588-2000
Fax: (918) 588-2296

Public Company
Incorporated: 1908 as The Williams Brothers Corporation
Employees: 4,442
Sales: $1.82 billion
Stock Exchanges: New York Pacific

The story of The Williams Companies, Inc. is that of two different entities: the small, privately held pipeline-construction business that Williams was for the first part of its history and the major corporation in the making that it has been for the second part. In the early 1990s Williams not only operated pipelines that transport natural gas and petroleum products throughout the midwestern United States to the Pacific Northwest; it also operated digital telecommunications networks from coast to coast.

Williams traces its history to 1908, when brothers S. Miller Williams Jr. and David R. Williams were working for a construction contractor who had an order to pave sidewalks in Fort Smith, Arkansas. The contractor pulled out when funding for the project was delayed, but the Williams brothers decided to take care of the job themselves. They stayed in the construction business after the Fort Smith job, making their headquarters in that city and working under the name The Williams Brothers Corporation. Eventually, they established steel-pipeline construction as their specialty, and in 1924 they moved to Tulsa, Oklahoma, in the heart of oil and gas country.

Williams Brothers remained a family-run business, small and privately held, for the next 25 years. Although the company maintained its headquarters in Tulsa, the petroleum and natural gas industries were not its only customers. When Miller and David's nephew, John H. Williams, joined the firm just after the bombing of Pearl Harbor, his first job was to help lay a water line for the U.S. Navy between Homestead and Key West in Florida.

In 1949 the Williams brothers decided to sell the company to their nephew John and his brother Charles, David Williams Jr., David's son, and six middle managers. The new owners reincorporated under the name Williams Brothers Company, with initial capitalization of $25,000 and bought the old Williams Brothers's construction equipment for $3 million in debt. John Williams, who put up $5,000 was named president and CEO. Although only 30 years old, he had led an unusual and varied life. Born and raised in Havana, where his father was a distributor for a number of U.S. companies, he did not learn English until he was five years old. His uncles paid his expenses at Yale, from which he received a degree in engineering in 1940. In 1942, during World War II, he left Williams Brothers to join the navy. He returned to the family firm in 1946.

The new Williams Brothers's first job ended with unfortunate results. The company had received a $7.5 million contract to build a pipeline from Baton Rouge, Louisiana, to Greensboro, North Carolina, but flooding caused by unusually heavy rains damaged the company's equipment, and the company actually lost $800,000 on the job. Within five years, however, it had made enough money to pay off its initial debt. In 1957, with a net worth of $8 million, it went public.

By the early 1960s Williams Brothers had established itself as a leader in its field, but a severe slump in the demand for new pipelines threatened its profitability. In 1963 the company lost $4 million on its domestic operations, and only strong overseas business limited its overall net loss to $500,000.

John Williams saw his first big opportunity to diversify in 1965, when he spotted an article in *The Wall Street Journal,* announcing that Great Lakes Pipe Line Company was for sale. Great Lakes Pipe Line had been founded in 1930 by a consortium of eight U.S. oil companies—Continental Oil Company, Sunray DX Oil Company, Skelly Oil Company, Texaco, Union Oil Company of California, Sinclair Oil, Cities Service, and Phillips Petroleum—to service the Midwest. A recent federal consent decree limiting Great Lakes's profit to 7% convinced the owners that their resources were better spent elsewhere. The Williams's, for their part, believed that they could run the pipeline better than the oil companies, and Williams Brothers was one of the first parties to offer a bid. It was the only one left standing when the dust settled.

The Great Lakes pipeline network was the longest in the United States, consisting of 6,228 miles of pipe and 20 terminals. Its purchase price was $287.6 million. Williams Brothers's net worth in 1965 was $27 million. In lining up the financing for the deal, the company had to borrow almost the entire amount, making it a leveraged buyout (LBO) that would be audacious even by the standards of the LBO mania that would grip Wall Street 20 years later. Williams Brothers paid only $1.6 million of its own cash for Great Lakes Pipe Line.

The Great Lakes Pipe Line deal left Williams Brothers with a high debt-equity ratio, 89%—it would shoot up to 160% by 1970—but this did not deter John Williams from seeking new avenues for growth and diversification. In 1969, in a stock swap, the company acquired Edgcomb Steel Company, that processed and distributed metal products in the East and Midwest. At the same time, Williams Brothers began to look into the fertilizer business as another possibility. Fertilizer manufacturers were then suffering from low demand and oversupply, and the Williamses wanted to buy into the business while such companies were cheap.

In 1971 the company acquired The Suburban Companies, a liquid-propane gas retailer. It also bought Colonial Insurance Company, a move that John Williams would later call his worst acquisition; uncharacteristically, the company had not secured a competent insurance executive ahead of time to take charge of Colonial, and it floundered as a result. It was sold off in 1974. Williams Brothers had become a diversified enterprise, and in May 1971 it recognized that fact by changing its name to Williams Companies.

In 1971 the company finally bagged a fertilizer company when it acquired Gulf Oil Corporation's agrichemical operations for $60 million. The next year, it added Agrico Chemical Company, Continental Oil Company's fertilizer subsidiary, for $140 million and merged the two operations under the Agrico name. John Williams then brought in his friend Kenneth Lundberg, CEO of major farm cooperative CF Industries, to head Agrico. The timing of these two acquisitions could scarcely have been better. Fertilizer prices turned up almost immediately. In 1974 Williams as a whole posted $950 million in sales—up from $235 million in 1970—and more than half of that figure was supplied by Agrico.

The company formed a new subsidiary in 1974, Williams Exploration Company, and branched out into the business of drilling for and producing oil and natural gas. Such operations were meant not only to generate profits for the parent company, but also feedstock for Agrico's manufacturing activity. In 1976 Williams joined with Newmont Mining Corporation, Bechtel Group, Boeing Company, Fluor Corporation, and Equitable Life Assurance Society to buy Peabody Coal from Kennecott Corporation, coming away with a 27.5% share. Also that year, the company sold its Williams International Group subsidiary, which had been formed in 1972 to take charge of its original pipeline-construction operations. It was sold, to an employee group, thus cutting Williams's tie to its old core business.

Signs of trouble began appearing at about this time as fertilizer prices dropped. Williams's earnings plunged as a result. Nonetheless, the company acquired Rainbow Resources in 1977, a Wyoming oil and gas-exploration concern, for $40 million, and spent another $40 million expanding its pipeline network. When John Williams retired as chairman and CEO in 1978 at the age of 59, he left the relatively small family business that he had founded in 1949 as a conglomerate with sales of over $1 billion and assets of almost $2 billion.

He was succeeded by Joseph Williams, David Williams Jr.'s 45-year-old brother. Williams became a more conservative company, concentrating on the steady profits generated by its pipeline operations and shedding less dependable businesses. In 1979 it sold its Williams Energy subsidiary, which consisted of what used to be The Suburban Companies, to Penn Central Corporation for $57 million.

At about the same time, Agrico's financial performance was mercurial. The subsidiary posted a record profit of $175.5 million in 1980 only to plummet to a loss of $30.3 million in 1982, following a sharp drop in the demand for fertilizer. As a

result, Williams's profits dropped from $57 million in 1981 to $34 million in 1982. In 1983 Agrico sold its entire retail operation to a management group for $51.7 million and a 40% stake in the new company, Crop Production Services, Inc. The relatively stable pipeline business looked more attractive, and that same year Williams acquired two natural gas pipelines: Northwest pipeline, which served the West Coast, and Northwest Central, which was located in the Midwest.

By the middle of the decade, Joe Williams had concluded that his company needed a major restructuring to cut its dependence on commodity-based operations whose revenues were as unstable as the prices of those commodities. In 1984 Williams divested Edgcomb Metals, selling it to a management group. The next year, it embarked on a new venture. It established a subsidiary, Williams Telecommunications, to run a fiber-optic cable network that would be installed inside abandoned steel pipelines.

The restructuring continued in 1986 when Williams sold all of Williams Exploration's assets to the U.S. subsidiaries of two Belgian oil companies, Petrofina and Cometra Oil. The reorganization ended in 1987, when the company sold its stake in Peabody Coal to consortium partner Newmont Mining for $320 million and divested Agrico by selling it to Freeport-McMoRan Resource Partners for $350 million. Also in 1987, Joe Williams added "The" to the company's name.

At the same time, The Williams Companies, Inc. showed that it was serious about the telecommunications business. In 1987 Williams acquired LDX NET, Inc., which owned a 1,295-mile-long fiber-optic network. In 1989 Williams Telecommunications became the fourth-largest fiber-optic telecommunications company in the United States when it acquired another fiber-optics concern, LIGHTNET, and added 4,500 miles to its system. This gave Williams a total of more than 11,000 miles over fiber-optic cable, transmitting signals from New England to the Pacific coast.

Wall Street approved of the new, leaner version of The Williams Companies and its name surfaced more than once in the late 1980s as an attractive takeover candidate. However, no takeover bid ever surfaced.

Principal Subsidiaries: Northwest Pipeline Corp.; Williams Production Co.; Williams Field Services Co.; Williams Western Pipeline Co.; Williams Natural Gas Co.; Williams Energy Co.; Williams Pipe Line Co.; Williams Telecommunications Group, Inc.

Further Reading: "Building a Winning Management Team," *Nation's Business,* April 1976; "The Best Defense . . ." *Forbes,* November 15, 1977; "Williams: A Shelter from Inflation's Cost is Caving in," *Business Week,* August 1, 1983.

—Douglas Sun

YPF SOCIEDAD ANÓNIMA

Avenida Roque Saenz Pena 777
Buenos Aires
Argentina
(1) 464 721
Fax: (1) 490 644

State-Owned Company
Incorporated: 1977 as Yacimientos Petrolíferos Fiscales
  Sociedad Anónima
Employees: 32,117
Sales: A31.41 trillion (US$6.05 billion)

A government team first found oil in Argentina by chance in 1907, when drilling for water near the Patagonian town of Comodoro Rivadavia. Fifteen years later, Dirección Nacional de los Yacimientos Petrolíferos Fiscales (YPF) was founded as a government supervisory board for state oil.

From YPF's birth, the state, nationalism, politics, and oil became closely intertwined. YPF evolved into an oil exploration, production, refining, and retailing conglomerate. By law, YPF holds title to all Argentina's hydrocarbon reserves. It is Argentina's largest company, controlling over half the local oil market. YPF's 1989 turnover of US$6.11 billion was equivalent to 7% of gross domestic product. YPF's six distilleries account for 64% of the country's total capacity. Its network of oil and gas pipelines stretches for over 18,000 kilometers.

YPF also assumed a wider role in national affairs, playing an important part in government industrial and regional development policies. It helped populate remote regions of the country and provides social services for employees and local populations.

The historian David Rock wrote that the leading role of the Argentine state in the oil industry reflected "a strong determination to prevent oil resources from falling into foreign hands." In 1910 legislation created a state reserve of 5,000 hectares in Comodoro Rivadavia. In 1918, the government extended its control over reserves found in the southern province of Neuquén. In 1922, YPF was created to operate the Neuquén and Patagonian oilfields.

The company's early years were marked by a struggle to assert itself. Although production boomed, YPF had to compete with private companies and Argentina still imported 93% of its oil. Despite ardent nationalism, the government found it could only increase oil production with foreign—particularly American—participation. YPF lacked sufficient technology, drilling equipment, refinery capacity, staff, and capital.

Tension between the political aspiration of self-sufficiency in the face of rapacious oil multinationals, and the reality of YPF's generally disappointing performance is a recurrent theme in its history. Economic growth requires a rising oil supply, but makes Argentina dependent on foreign investment.

National control over the oil industry through YPF came into its own under the company's first head, the vigorous and independent General Enrique Mosconi.

Mosconi was perhaps the only YPF chief to stand out as a personality in his own right. Argentina's turbulent politics and powerful military meant that YPF suffered incessant meddling. It had 47 presidents or administrators, 16 of them soldiers, with an average tenure of less than 18 months in 69 years of history. Invariably, colorless political appointees executed company policy established by heads of government. Sudden shifts in YPF strategy were invariably the result of changing government policy, usually produced by military coups.

In 1925 Mosconi built the company's first oil refinery at La Plata, close to Buenos Aires, and developed a retail network, creating the first vertically-integrated state petroleum industry outside the Soviet Union. Nonetheless, private companies, led by Standard Oil of the United States, still controlled most of the country's oil market. Public opinion against foreign oil interests grew as a highly publicized battle for supremacy broke out between YPF and private foreign companies.

Oil dominated the election campaign of 1928. The predominantly middle-class Uniòn Civica Radical (UCR) which had first created YPF, campaigned successfully to transform YPF into a monopoly.

A coup put an end to the UCR's plans and the new government treated YPF and its foreign competitiors evenhandedly. Oil output increased, but YPF's market share fell. In 1932, however, the government reversed its policy, favoring YPF. It allowed YPF to import equipment free of duty, but in return imposed a 10% tax on its profits. Three years later a similar tax was imposed on foreign companies. The following year, the government intervened in a price war, establishing market quotas for YPF and its competitors.

In 1935 the government declared most of Neuquén a national reserve to be developed exclusively by YPF. Over the subsequent years, the company made important discoveries in the south, and later in the north and west of Argentina.

Colonel Juan Domingo Perón's rise to power in 1945 marked an important new stage in YPF's history. Perón nationalized British and American interests and extended state control over broad sectors of the economy. In the oil industry, this had the effect of further strengthening YPF's share of oil production.

The founder of Perónism, a corporatist alliance of labor, capital, and the state, transformed YPF into a virtual monopoly. If it produced 68% of all Argentina's oil in 1945, it accounted for 84% of production in 1955, Perón's last year in office.

Perón also expanded YPF's infrastructure, building a pipeline that runs the length of Argentina from Comodoro Rivadavia to Buenos Aires. Under Perón, YPF was granted numerous privileges denied foreign companies, such as importing oil duty-free. In 1949, Perón promulgated a new constitution instituting national ownership of natural resources, including oil.

Although YPF raised output by more than a fifth during Perón's first term as president, it failed to increase production sufficiently to meet demand during the postwar economic boom. It suffered from American trade embargoes imposed to punish the government for interfering in American business interests.

Dependence on oil imports and foreign companies grew as YPF failed to meet rising demand. Economic recession forced Perón to strike a deal in March 1955 with Standard Oil of California, allowing it to develop oilfields in Patagonia. When Perón was removed from office in the coup of 1955, Argentina still relied on imports for 60% of its oil.

YPF discovered huge gas fields in Neuquén in 1957, transforming Argentina, and YPF, into a major gas producer. Gas reserves are now about 50% greater than oil reserves.

Liberalization continued during the 1958–62 government of President Arturo Frondizi. He encouraged private companies to explore and produce oil under contract to YPF. Under Frondizi, of the Intransigent Radical Civic Union, private contractors produced one-third of YPF'S oil. However, the policy was deeply controversial, because Frondizi had previously espoused ultranationalist oil policies.

Frondizi reacted to a deepening balance of payments crisis with a policy of rapid industrialization. He banned oil imports—which provided 40% of consumption in the early 1960s. Inflation subsided, the economy grew as foreign investment increased, and oil output surged. By 1963, the year Frondizi was toppled by a coup, local production supplied 90% of demand.

But it was a Radical, Arturo Illia who became president in 1963, who rescinded Frondizi's oil contracts and strongly favored YPF, invoking his party's traditional policy of an independent oil industry. But Illia was swept from power by yet another army coup in 1966. Seven years later, Argentina—once again heavily dependent on imports—was rocked by the 1973 oil shock, when its annual oil import bill rose tenfold to US$586 million.

Argentina's last military administration of 1976–1983 adopted free market policies to encourage foreign investment in Argentina, particularly in the oil and gas industries. In 1976 it introduced risk contracts and oil production began to increase.

Under these contracts, the private sector explored for oil at its own risk, and YPF was committed to buying the output from any successful project. Production reached a record 496,000 barrels per day (b/d) in 1981, but declined in the face of recession and greater reliance by the electricity generating industry on hydro and nuclear power than thermal generation. Nonetheless, Argentina became self-sufficient in oil by the 1990s.

The role of the government and YPF in the oil industry changed further in 1985 under the civilian government of President Raúl Alfonsín. Alfonsín both broadened the scope of private oil companies' exploration and allowed them to sell part of their oil to YPF at international prices, rather than at government-controlled prices. Alfonsín announced his liberalization policies in Houston, Texas, and they became known as the Houston Plan. Initial response was disappointing, since it coincided with a decline in world oil prices.

Later, a modified plan, Houston II, was introduced, reducing YPF's power to decide the economic viability of projects and determine forms of payment. Five years later, the Houston Plan had attracted 45 local and foreign companies, which produced 43% of Argentina's oil at free market prices.

Despite the apparent commitment to a greater role for private capital, the oil companies accused YPF of keeping the most promising regions to itself. Houston II eliminated many of these complaints, such as YPF's right to take 50% of oil production from a new well if it were found to be richer than originally expected.

Carlos Menem took over as president from Alfonsín in 1989. Nominally a Perónist, Menem embarked on an aggressive liberalization and privatization policy. YPF became an integral part of his plans. On January 1991, Menem implemented a sweeping deregulation of the oil industry.

In essence, the reforms ended YPF's right to buy and sell oil at government-determined prices, with the exception of oil from Houston Plan projects, allowing all companies to produce, buy, and sell oil at market prices. Exposure to competition was intended to make YPF more efficient. Deregulation and a thorough restructuring of YPF were planned as the first steps to the company's eventual privatization. Also in 1991, Yacimentos Petrolíferos Fiscales Sociedad Anónima officially became YPF Sociedad Anónima.

Like most other Argentine state companies, YPF became characterized by inefficiency, a bureaucratic corporate culture, overstaffing, and heavy indebtedness. Severe financial problems made YPF constantly undershoot investment targets. In 1990, YPF invested US$1.04 billion—31% less than planned.

Government auditors listed 4.5% of YPF's record 37,047 strong work force as superfluous. Despite overlapping tiers of management, the auditors found that YPF "lacks internal control systems . . . needed for decision-making by senior management."

The company's figures for reserves are unreliable. At the end of 1989, it claimed that proven oil reserves fell by 5% to 2.1 billion barrels, equivalent to 14 years' consumption. Gas reserves grew by 4.3% to 744 billion cubic metres, it said. However, independent analysts say that YPF's figures are inflated by over 20%.

YPF has closely reflected trends in Argentine history. In its early years, it faced government policies that alternated between outright support and indifference, and fought aggressive foreign competitiors. It benefitted from a rising tide of nationalism in the 1930s, which culminated in the rise of Juan Perón. He extended YPF's reach, although he was forced to reach agreement with U.S. oil interests. Subsequent governments flirted with liberalization. By the 1980s, YPF's inefficiency and heavy losses forced Alfonsín, followed by Menem, to take liberalization further than any presidents had dared. In 1991, Menem deregulated the industry as a prelude to YPF's total privatization. Also in 1991, Yacimentos Petrolíferos Fiscales Sociedad Anónima officially became YPF Sociedad Anónima.

Deregulation left the company disoriented. José Estenssoro, YPF's respected administrator, admitted as much in *El Cronista Comercial,* in January 1991: "There will be a process of reorganization . . . to make it more competitive. Meanwhile, we are working with estimates and surely our margin of profit is very thin or almost nil."

Further Reading: Lewis Paul H., *The Crisis of Argentine Capitalism,* Chapel Hill, University of North Carolina Press, 1990.

—John Barham

PUBLISHING & PRINTING

ADVANCE PUBLICATIONS INC.
ARNOLDO MONDADORI EDITOR S.P.A.
AXEL SPRINGER VERLAG AG
BERTELSMANN AG
COX ENTERPRISES, INC.
DAI NIPPON PRINTING CO., LTD.
DOW JONES & COMPANY, INC.
THE DUN & BRADSTREET CORPORATION
THE E.W. SCRIPPS COMPANY
ELSEVIER NV
GANNETT CO., INC.
GROUPE DE LA CITÉ
HACHETTE
HALLMARK CARDS, INC.
HARCOURT BRACE JOVANOVICH, INC.
THE HEARST CORPORATION
KNIGHT-RIDDER, INC.
KODANSHA LTD.
MCGRAW-HILL, INC.
MACLEAN HUNTER LIMITED

MAXWELL COMMUNICATION
    CORPORATION PLC
MOORE CORPORATION LIMITED
THE NEW YORK TIMES COMPANY
NEWS CORPORATION LIMITED
NIHON KEIZAI SHIMBUN, INC.
PEARSON PLC
R.R. DONNELLEY & SONS COMPANY
THE READER'S DIGEST
    ASSOCIATION, INC.
REED INTERNATIONAL P.L.C.
REUTERS HOLDINGS PLC
SIMON & SCHUSTER INC.
TIME WARNER INC.
THE TIMES MIRROR COMPANY
TOPPAN PRINTING CO., LTD.
TRIBUNE COMPANY
UNITED NEWSPAPERS PLC
THE WASHINGTON POST COMPANY

ADVANCE PUBLICATIONS INC.

950 Fingerboard Road
Staten Island, New York 10305
U.S.A.
(718) 981-1234
Fax: (718) 981-5679

Private Company
Incorporated: 1924 as Staten Island Advance Company
Employees: 18,500
Sales: $2.94 billion

A multi-billion dollar international communications empire made up of newspapers, magazines, books, and electronic media, Advance Publications Inc. is a family-owned and -operated company. In building up the second-largest publishing concern in the United States, Samuel I. Newhouse relied on hard work, innovative business methods, and Newhouse family members, who have continued the ideosyncratic organizational system that nurtured the Newhouse success.

Solomon Neuhaus, later called Samuel I. Newhouse, and finally just S.I. Newhouse, was born in 1895 in New York City, the oldest of eight children born to recent immigrants from Eastern Europe. Financial success eluded the first generation, the suspender business of the father having failed in 1905. After graduating from eighth grade, in Bayonne, New Jersey, in 1908, Newhouse briefly attended a business school in New York City. He carried bundles of newspapers across the Hudson River to earn money for the fare to and from business school. This was Newhouse's first newspaper job. Newhouse earned no money the first month he was employed by Judge Hyman Lazarus, a city magistrate who operated a law office, Lazarus & Brenner, in Bayonne. After showing his worth as an office assistant that first month, Lazarus gave Newhouse $2.00 a week.

Starting a steady rise in the firm, Newhouse became the accountant, real estate manager, and general troubleshooter for Lazarus. The judge had acquired 51% of the *Bayonne Times* in payment of a debt. It seemed at first to be a losing proposition, but Lazarus hoped to stem the losses, in 1911, until he could sell the newspaper, which he had moved into the same building as the law firm. To that end, Lazarus gave Newhouse responsibility for the business aspect of the *Times*. Newhouse concentrated on increasing both advertising revenues and subscriptions, and the paper showed a profit within a year.

By 1916 Newhouse, at the age of 21, was earning $30,000 a year for his myriad responsibilities with Lazarus & Brenner as well as with the newspaper, where he now worked for a percentage of the profits. This same year he finished the course of study of law at New Jersey College and passed the bar examination in New Jersey. After losing his first and only trial, a debt-collection case, Newhouse paid his client the disputed amount out of his own pocket, and retired from trial law.

When the United States entered World War I in 1917, Newhouse, as the sole source of support of his family, was exempt from conscription and concentrated on building up the *Bayonne Times,* which enjoyed increased circulation as people sought to learn the latest war news. Newhouse devoted much of his free time to learning about the newspaper business, which impressed him as a feasible way to make his fortune, his model being William Randolph Hearst.

Despite Newhouse's lofty ambitions, his first step in this direction was less than successful. With borrowed money from his family, along with his own savings, Newhouse went into partnership with Lazarus to buy The Fitchburg Daily News Company, of Fitchburg, Massachusetts, for $15,000. Newhouse took pains to make the new paper a going concern, but faced with antagonism directed toward him as both an outsider and a Jew, he decided within a year to sell the property to Frank L. Hoyt, publisher of the competing *Fitchburg Sentinel.* Persuading Hoyt of the profit inherent in owning a newspaper monopoly, Newhouse was able to turn a profit on even this first, relatively unsuccessful, newspaper deal.

By 1922 Newhouse was ready for another acquisition, and with Lazarus he bought 51% of the stock of *The Staten Island Advance* for $98,000. In 1923 the circulation of the *Advance* rose 50%, and the number of pages had doubled with additional advertising. In November of that year the *Advance*'s masthead listed S.I. Newhouse as publisher.

The Staten Island Advance proved to be the foundation of the publishing empire Newhouse established in the 1920s. In 1924 Newhouse, along with St. John Mclean and William Wolfe, bought out Judge Lazarus's interest in the *Advance,* and incorporated the Staten Island Advance Company, renamed Staten Island Advance Corporation shortly thereafter. Newhouse owned 60% of the new company, his two partners splitting the rest. Although the business consisted of just one newspaper at the time, its stated purpose was "To engage in, conduct, manage, and transact the business of publishing, selling, binding, and distribution of books, journals, magazines, newspapers, periodicals, and all other kinds of publications" and to collect and distribute ". . . news and press reports and dispatches and information of every sort and kind by any and all means."

Newhouse was to fulfill every part of the stated purpose with the help of the associates that he was to gather about him in the 1920s. Among these were Charles Goldman, the legal representative of the firm; Louis Glickman, the accountant whose tax advice convinced Newhouse of the wisdom of reinvesting profits in newspaper acquisitions; and Louis Hochstein, whose editorial expertise was to guide many Newhouse concerns, starting with the *Advance.*

Staten Island proved to be a good place to own a newspaper in the 1920s, a decade of intense land speculation and business activity. Many newspaper stands were at first reluctant to carry the *Advance,* and Newhouse increased circulation by adopting a Brooklyn newspaper's home-delivery system and by 1928 had made enough to buy out his two partners in the company for $198,000. By this time Lazarus had died, and Newhouse, no longer associated with the *Bayonne Times,* had married Mitzi Epstein. The Newhouses had two sons, Samuel I. (Si) Newhouse Jr., in 1927, and Donald E. Newhouse in 1929. Despite the potential setbacks of a challenge to the *Advance* by the *Staten Islander* and a politically motivated libel suit, Newhouse's concentration upon the business side of newspapering enabled him not only to prosper during good times, but to survive the stock market crash of 1929 and the Great Depression during the early 1930s. Newhouse had invested his company's profits in the newspaper, not in stocks; so in 1932, the bank account of the *Advance* stood at close to $400,000. Staten Island Advance Corporation did not lay off or cut the pay of any employees.

When Newhouse learned in 1932 that Victor, Bernard, and Joseph Ridder were willing to sell their 51% of shares in the *Long Island Press,* his cash-rich position made it easy to acquire that newspaper. Newhouse's younger brother Norman became the managing editor of the *Advance,* and Hochstein was made the managing editor of the *Press.* This purchase was to bring Newhouse into conflict with the newly organized American Newspaper Guild, when, in 1934, the *Press* became the first newspaper in U.S. history to be picketed by its editorial workers. Labor problems continued at the Long Island paper throughout the 1930s, New York City mayor Fiorello LaGuardia twice being called in to arbitrate. The issue for Newhouse was one of control: "I refuse to stand by passively and allow any union to 'bust' me," he wrote, as quoted in *Barron's,* November 27, 1989. "As I learned at the Advance nearly 40 years before, to yield to others the controls that are vital to your own security is suicide."

Despite these labor problems, Newhouse was able to acquire six newspapers during the 1930s. The first of these acquisitions, in 1935, a 51% share in the *Newark Ledger,* of Newark, New Jersey, is notable for Newhouse's use of the recently developed technique of market survey to find ways to shape the newspaper to the new, affluent suburban readership. When Newhouse bought as a package the *North Shore Journal* in Flushing, New York, and the *Long Island Star* in Long Island City, New York, in 1938 for $250,000, he combined the two into the *Long Island Star-Journal,* and by merging physical operations he was able to make a profitable enterprise out of two unprofitable newspapers. Newhouse repeated this merger strategy when in 1939 he bought the *Newark Star-Eagle* and merged it with the *Newark Ledger* to form the *Newark Star-Ledger* in 1939. That same year, he acquired the *Syracuse Herald* of Syracuse, New York, for $1 million and combined it with the *Syracuse Journal,* a property he picked up at about the same time from Hearst Corporation for $900,000, to form the *Syracuse Herald-Journal.* To help offset the cost, 428 *Journal* employees were fired immediately. In 1942, Newhouse bought for $1.3 million the only remaining Syracuse newspaper, the morning *Post-Standard,* establishing a highly profitable monopoly during World War II, even with shortages of newsprint and other supplies.

In the 1940s Newhouse acquired the remaining 49% of shares in Long Island Daily Press Publishing Company, bought half of the Jersey City, New Jersey, *Jersey Journal,* and bought all three newspapers in Harrisburg, Pennsylvania. Operating out of a car with a telephone, Newhouse, with the help of the trains, managed to visit most of the newspapers he owned on an almost weekly basis, making informal notes as he visited the operations and maintaining a wealth of information in his head.

It was also during the 1940s that Newhouse established the reputation that led journalism critic A.J. Liebling of *The New Yorker* to label him a "literary *chiffonier*"—*chiffonier* being French for ragpicker—picking up and turning around small, undistinguished newspapers in financial difficulty or plagued by family squabbles. Indeed, the *Jersey Journal* was one such transaction involving a dispute between Walter Dear and his nephew, Albert Dear. In this case Newhouse, after buying almost half of the paper from Walter Dear in 1945, was able to acquire only after lengthy litigation, the remaining shares from Albert Dear in 1951. In 1947 Newhouse acquired the Patriot Company, publisher of the *Patriot* and the *Evening News* in Harrisburg, Pennsylvania. A socially prominent former Newhouse employee, Edwin Russell, acted as a front man for Staten Island Advance Corporation in convincing the owner, Annie McCormick, to sell to Newhouse.

In 1949 Staten Island Advance Corporation became Advance Publications Inc. In the 1950s Newhouse established a new reputation as a major competitor in newspaper publishing. With the purchase of the *Portland Oregonian* in 1950, he paid a record $5.6 million. The *Portland Oregonian* was a prestige newspaper, considered one of the best in the northwestern United States. Before expanding his operations beyond the northeastern United States, Newhouse made sure his brother Theodore (Ted) Newhouse would agree to fly to Portland once a month to report on the *Oregonian.* This was in line with Newhouse's oft-stated policy of family control.

Newhouse was ready to pay a record price for a newspaper because of his unique way of assessing a paper's value. Rather than follow the industry rule that a newspaper should be valued at approximately 10% of its net earnings, Newhouse considered possible earnings based on its potential market. Because of his policy of retaining earnings, Newhouse was able to buy without borrowing.

When Newhouse bought the *St. Louis Globe-Democrat* in 1955, paying $6.5 million, he added another jewel to his newspaper group, to use a term preferred by Newhouse. Newhouse disliked the term "chain," because he felt that it suggested that the parent company imposed some degree of editorial uniformity on its properties. In fact, Advance allowed its newspapers a notable amount of editorial latitude. The publisher of Advance's Birmingham, Alabama, paper in 1962 was an unabashed racist, while Newhouse himself was staunchly liberal. Newhouse's paper varied in the quality as much as in editorial standpoint. This policy was unlike that of most other chain publishers. According to Newhouse, as quoted in *The New York Times,* August 1979, was "not interested in molding the nation's opinion."

This policy of local autonomy had helped to buy the *St. Louis Globe-Democrat,* convincing the conservative owner, E. Lansing Ray, that the paper would continue with its long-held editorial policies. It also persuaded the Hanson family to sell the *Birmingham News* and the *Huntsville Times* in Alabama to Newhouse in 1955 for $18.7 million because of what Clarence B. Hanson Jr., as quoted in Richard H. Meeker's *Newspaperman,* called "his established reputation for insisting that his newspapers be operated locally and independently." Because of Newhouse's attention to business operations rather than editorial stance, his papers took a wide range of positions on questions of the day, for example, one paper, the *Newark Star-Ledger,* supporting right-wing senator Joseph McCarthy during his ascendancy, while other Newhouse papers attacked McCarthy. Although Newhouse did not invent local autonomy, Advance was the first major newspaper chain to practice it.

The 1959 purchase of Condé Nast Publications for $5 million was supposedly suggested by Mitzi Newhouse, S.I. Newhouse's wife. According to Newhouse: "She asked for a fashion magazine and I went out and got her *Vogue.*" Condé Nast published not only *Vogue* but also *Glamour, House & Garden,* and *Young Bride's.* As far back as the 1924 statement of Advance's purpose, Newhouse had a declared intention of publishing magazines. By buying another magazine publisher, Street & Smith, which also published women's magazines, and merging it with Condé Nast, Newhouse became a major publisher of magazines as well as newspapers, in addition to running a national news service in Washington, D.C., and radio stations in Portland, Oregon, and in Syracuse.

Despite labor problems that were to begin in 1959 with a stereotypers' strike at the *Oregonian* and an American Newspaper Guild strike at the *St. Louis Globe-Democrat,* Newhouse was able to continue expanding his operations throughout the 1960s, beginning with acquisitions of portions of the *Denver Post* and of three newspapers in Springfield, Massachusetts. In 1961 Newhouse established a newspaper monopoly in Portland with his purchases of the *Oregon Journal* for $8 million. In 1962 Advance paid $42 million for the Times-Picayune Publishing Company in New Orleans, Louisiana. Newhouse borrowed money outside of his family for the first time to make this purchase, but now, with both of the New Orleans newspapers, the morning *Times-Picayune* and the evening *States-Item,* Newhouse owned more newspapers than any other U.S. publisher. The $15 million that Newhouse donated to Syracuse University for a school of communications indicated his new stature in publishing. When the S.I. Newhouse School of Public Communications was opened in 1964, President Lyndon Baines Johnson gave the dedication speech.

Increased media attention meant increased media criticism, and in 1966 this came with the publication of John A. Lent's *Newhouse, Newspapers, Nuisances: Highlights in the Growth of a Communications Empire,* which concentrated on Newhouse's dealings with labor unions. Given that Newhouse operated, according to the November 27, 1989, *Barron's,* "not only one of the most powerful, but one of the most secretive family businesses in America," the public curiosity is understandable. Nevertheless, Newhouse preferred to work his deals discreetly, and as a private corporation, Advance could maintain a very low profile.

Newhouse continued to make acquisitions throughout the remainder of the 1960s, expanding further into the southeastern United States with the purchase of two Alabama newspapers, the *Mobile Register* and the *Mobile Press,* and of the *Mississippi Press-Register,* all in 1966. Newhouse's largest deal of the decade turned out to be his acquisition of the *Cleveland Plain Dealer* for $54.2 million in 1967, breaking his own record for the highest price ever paid for a newspaper, and again requiring a bank loan. This gave Advance 22 newspapers in 16 cities that produced each day more than 3.2 million papers and grossed almost $500 million a year.

In the 1970s Newhouse seemed to be slowing down. In 1970, Advance bought 49% of a massive paper mill in Catawba, South Carolina. In 1971 Advance bought both the *Bayonne Times,* the paper at which Newhouse had started his career and the *Newark Evening News.* He merged the *Times* into the *Jersey Journal,* and within one year shut down the *Evening News,* which he had purchased for $20 million. Newhouse still had one massive newspaper deal left in him, however, and in 1976 he purchased for $305 million Booth Newspapers, publisher of eight papers in Michigan as well as *Parade* magazine, a syndicated Sunday newspaper magazine supplement.

As he built his empire, Newhouse organized his businesses to minimize taxes. Advance Publications served as the central holding company, publishing *The Staten Island Advance* and owning the Long Island Daily Press Publishing Company. From there the various companies owned varying shares of other companies, making it possible for one company to loan money to another, thus allowing a cash-rich company to reduce its surplus earnings. In addition, the way Newhouse had set up stock holdings in Advance made it difficult, if not impossible, for him to lose control. Newhouse owned all 1,000 shares of common stock, including the 10 shares of Class A stock that carried voting privileges. The 3,500 shares of preferred stock were all owned by family members.

With S.I. Newhouse's death in 1979, this arrangement was to provide the opening for an Internal Revenue Service (IRS) tax suit that threatened the financial position of Advance throughout the 1980s. Valuing all stock at $187.25 a share, the family filed an inheritance tax return with a liability of $48 million. The IRS, found the common stock more valuable than the preferred, and demanded $1 billion.

With Newhouse's death, the leadership of Advance became diffused among his surviving two brothers, Norman and Ted, and two sons, Samuel I. Jr. (Si) and Donald. During S.I.'s lifetime, the organizational structure had been decidedly imprecise. When *Business Week,* of January 26, 1976, inquired what titles his two brothers held, Newhouse responded, "I couldn't really tell you." Instead of titles the family members had regional or special responsibilities. Si oversaw the magazines, and Donald the eastern newspapers, while Norman handled midwestern and southern newspapers; Ted took care of western and Massachusetts properties. In addition, Newhouse nephews Richard Diamond led *The Staten Island Advance* while Robert Miron oversaw the Syracuse, New York, broadcasting headquarters.

The Newhouse family, jointly headed by Si and Donald, in the years since S.I.'s death "have overseen the growth of a $2 billion company into a $10 billion company," according to *Barron's,* "simply by tending what S.I. acquired." Si and Donald Newhouse, however, made some major changes in Advance in the 1980s. The first was in 1980, when they paid $70 million to RCA Corporation for Random House publishing, the leading general-interest book publisher at the time, thus acquiring the third type of media enumerated in Advance's statement of purpose. By selling its five television stations to the Times Mirror Company for $82 million, the Newhouses were also able to finance their expansion into cable television systems, becoming the eighth-largest cable operator in the United States in 1981.

Of the $700 million worth of communications purchases made by the Newhouses in the 1980s, only one was a newspaper, New Jersey's *Trenton Times*. The greatest amount of activity had been in magazines, with the start-ups of such magazines as *Self* in 1982 and of *Vanity Fair* in 1983, and the purchases of *Gentleman's Quarterly, Citibank Signature*—renamed *Condé Nast Traveler*—*Details, Woman;* and, in London, *Tatler, World of Interiors,* and minority shares of *The Face* and *Arena.* Perhaps the most notable acquisition was the *New Yorker* for $200 million in 1983. Si Newhouse has continued the family policy of allowing publications considerable editorial liberty while eschewing conventional corporate planning. "There is no particular global view about what Condé Nast should be," Si Newhouse told *The New York Times* in September 1989. "We think pragmatically."

The Newhouse style of business has continued to make money, but has drawn criticism. Pointing to the purchases of a package of British publishers and U.S. Crown Publishing, *Barron's* commented that "the family-style decision-making that produced such remarkable results when buying local newspapers from disgruntled heirs may not work so well when evaluating international publishing acquisitions." The sale for $200 million of Random House's college publishing division—usually the most steadily profitable part of publishing—to McGraw-Hill has also been questioned. Meeker charges that Newhouse lowered the overall quality of U.S. journalism.

The overall strength of Advance seems assured. Not only were the 1980s a particularly good year for newspaper publishers, but cable television looks to be a good growth industry in the 1990s. In 1990, the long-standing litigation with the IRS was settled in the Newhouse's favor, the judge ruling that the total tax liability would be approximately $48 million, close to the amount that the Newhouses claimed.

While the quality of journalism produced by Advance's papers has been questioned, its concentration upon newspapers as business has proven to be successful in building a newspaper, magazine, book, and cable-TV empire.

Principle Subsidiaries: Condé Nast Publications, Inc.; Parade Publications, Inc.; Random House, Inc.

Further Reading: "The Newspaper Collector," *Time,* July 27, 1962; Lent, John A., *Newhouse, Newspapers, Nuisances: Highlights in the Growth of a Communications Empire,* New York, Exposition Press, 1966; "S.I. Newhouse and Sons: America's Most Profitable Publisher," *Business Week,* January 26, 1976; Meeker, Richard H., *Newspaperman: S.I. Newhouse and the Business of News,* New Haven, Ticknor & Fields, 1983; Mahar, Maggie, "All in the Family," *Barron's,* November 27, 1989.

—Wilson B. Lindauer

ARNOLDO MONDADORI EDITORE S.P.A.

via Arnoldo Mondadori 1
20090 Segrate
Milan, Italy
(02) 75421
Fax: (02) 7542 2302

Public Company
Incorporated: 1912 as La Sociale di A. Mondadori & C.
Employees: 5,700
Sales: L2.37 billion (US$2.10 million)
Stock Exchanges: Milan Rome Turin Trieste Florence Genoa

Arnoldo Mondadori Editore S.p.A. is one of the largest publishing companies in Italy. Its holdings include books, magazines, advertising agencies, printing activities, direct marketing, stationery, school supplies, and a host of small publishing companies and imprints.

Arnoldo Mondadori was the son of a poor craftsman in the northern Italian city of Ostiglia, near Mantua. Before going to work for a small printing company in his town, Mondadori held various jobs including a stint at the local cinema. In a community with an illiteracy rate of almost 40%, one of his responsibilities was reading aloud the titles of silent films for audiences. At the age of 16 he was hired as a pressman at Ostiglia's small printing and stationery concern, Fratelli Manzoli. Two years later, in 1907, Arnoldo Mondadori borrowed enough money to take over the company. He changed its name to La Sociale. The new name reflected Mondadori's espousal of humanitarian and socialist reform movements active in Italy at this time, as well as his own ideal view of the press as a diffuser of culture. That same year the company, previously limited to the printing of posters, letterheads, and pamphlets, began publishing *Luce!,* a magazine subtitled *Giornale Popolare Istruttivo.*

In 1911, Mondadori bought a new press and published his first two books, *Aia Madama* and *Nullino e Stellina* by Tomaso Monicelli, an ex-socialist who had moved toward a nationalist position. Arnoldo Mondadori married Monicelli's sister, Andreina, in 1913.

La Sociale di A. Mondadori & C. was incorporated in 1912 as a limited stock partnership with 15 employees. Stock was held almost entirely by the Mondadori family. At that time, the press initiated a series of children's books called La Lampada. The company's capital grew from L75,000 in 1913 to L400,000 the following year, and the staff more than doubled. Already, Mondadori set about competing actively with the two Milan-based publishers, Sonzogno and Fratelli Treves, that shared a monopoly on book publishing in northern Italy at that time.

The company grew rapidly during the period of World War I in Europe. In 1915, the town of Ostiglia granted Mondadori a site measuring 2,000 square meters, adjacent to the railway line. New equipment was purchased. The number of employees at the new plant reached 100.

In 1916 the death of Mondadori's former competitor, Emilio Treves, left available a catalog of authors that included many of the most prestigious names in contemporary Italian literature, among them Gabriele D'Annunzio, Luigi Pirandello, and Grazia Deledda. The acquisition in 1917 of the Franchini printing plant in the city of Verona put Mondadori in a position to sign on many of Treves's authors and to attract important new clients, including the Italian military. Mondadori also contracted to produce several illustrated magazines for the Third Army.

In 1921 Mondadori consolidated all printing activities at Verona. The old Franchini plant was replaced by a new press that covered almost 100,000 square feet of land. Employees numbered 250 and Mondadori at this time created a separate magazine department. Fiction magazines were especially popular and in the early 1920s Mondadori introduced Italy's first monthly women's magazine, *La Donna,* and *Le Grazie,* a fiction magazine.

By this time, Mondadori magazines also served the Italian immigrant communities which had developed in North and South America—the bi-weekly *Girogirotondo* sold 30,000 copies in Argentina alone. Other popular ventures were film and theatrical magazines.

In 1923, publishing management was also established in Milan. Building on the newly literate readership of common Italians, Mondadori initiated several series, and brought out a children's encyclopedia, the *Enciclopedia dei Ragazzi,* modeled on English and American counterparts, and sold in weekly issues. The first Italian gravure magazine was published by Mondadori in 1925.

The decade of the 1920s was characterized by three major innovations for Mondadori: the company published its first textbook in 1926, its first popular paperback in 1927, and, in 1929, the so-called *giallo* or detective thriller. The series *I gialli di Mondadori* was packaged in a soft yellow jacket; today the word *giallo* is an Italian genre term for mysteries or thrillers, in print, radio, or film.

In 1930, Mondadori introduced its first Italian translations of foreign authors in accessible paperback form, with the *Libri Azzurri* (Blue Books) series, six years before the appearance of Penguin books in the United Kingdom. Other series of translations in paperback included *Biblioteca Romantica*—a collection of 50 masterpieces of 17th- and 18th century fiction—and *i Romanzi della Palma.*" Mondadori's translators included Cesare Pavese and Eugenio Montale.

Another important foreign acquisition for Mondadori's list was the Walt Disney Company's cartoon character, Mickey Mouse, who endeared himself to Italians under the name Topolino, appearing in a weekly series in 1935. This success was repeated shortly after by Donald Duck (Paperino), in the first Disney story conceived and produced in Italy by agreement with the U.S. company. *Grazia,* the first mass-circulation women's weekly, was introduced in the late 1930s, and the weekly news magazine *Tempo* began publishing under the direction of Arnoldo Mondadori's son, Alberto. Alberto Mondadori was eldest of the founder's children, who included another son Giorgio and two daughters, Laura and Cristina. All were to play an important part in the company's future development.

World War II in Europe had a devastating effect on Mondadori. Mondadori was compelled to transfer its editorial offices to the town of Arona in 1942. When the Fascist government fell and German troops occupied Italy in 1943, the plant at Verona was confiscated, its equipment dismantled and in large part shipped off to Germany. The Milan headquarters later sustained severe bomb damage and the offices at Arona came under the control of the Fascist party commissars.

From 1943 to 1945, Arnoldo Mondadori went into exile at Lugano, Switzerland, but continued to maintain contact with his editors and authors. With the help of his son Alberto Mondadori—who spoke English and other languages—the publisher acquired rights to the work of U.S. authors Ernest Hemingway and William Faulkner, which later helped the company regain its position after the war ended.

With funds from the U.S. Marshall Plan, Mondadori launched a postwar recovery and replaced its bomb-damaged Verona plant. The new facility was much larger, and included modern equipment capable of newspaper publishing. In 1950 *Epoca* appeared, a new large-format illustrated news weekly modeled on *Time* and *Life*.

Italy's economy began a period of tremendous growth in the postwar years. Mondadori introduced direct marketing with the first Italian book club, Club degli Editori, by-passing the bookstores to sell books by mail. In 1958 Alberto Mondadori founded Il Saggiatore, an imprint of Mondadori that specialized in philosophy and intellectual works. The project was initiated with 150 employees and intentions of publishing 100 new titles each year. Il Saggiatore brought out the likes of Jean-Paul Sartre, and Claude Levi-Strauss in Italian translations, but the company was plagued with financial problems. In 1967, Alberto Mondadori broke from the parent company and two years later a bankrupt Il Saggiatore was reassumed by Arnoldo Mondadori Editore.

The younger son, Giorgio Mondadori, was a more effective manager who had joined the company at the age of 27, in 1944. After overseeing the rebuilding of the Verona plant, he turned to a program of diversification. This included Mondadori's entrance into industrial activity with the establishment in 1961 of Auguri Mondadori S.p.A., a stationery and greeting card operation with a huge plant at Caselle di Sommacampagna near Verona and the building of Cartiere Ascoli Piceno, a papermaker which opened its plant at Marino del Tronto in 1964. Giorgio Mondadori also directed the building of the company's present headquarters at Segrate, a vast, modern edifice designed by the architect Oscar Niemeyer.

In 1960 the company had annual gross profits of L16 billion and employed 2,279 workers. During the decade that followed, the company founded by Arnoldo Mondadori profited from his friendship with two captains of the Italian banking industry, Raffaele Mattioli and Enrico Cuccia.

Mondadori preferred stock was listed on the Milan stock exchange in 1965. Five years later, annual gross sales stood at L71 billion. The company employed 4,988 people and was ranked first in the Italian publishing industry in gross sales.

Publishing expansion in the 1960s included the founding of *Panorama*, which first appeared as a monthly in 1962, and became a weekly in 1967. In 1963 Mondadori initiated its *Enciclopedia della Scienza e della Tecnica*, a 15-volume work whose authors included several Nobel prize winners. Mondadori's practice of putting inexpensive works of literature on newsstands continued with the introduction of the Oscar series of highly successful fiction paperbacks.

The decade that followed brought difficulties. The family patriarch, Arnoldo Mondadori, died in 1971, leaving the company to his four children. The second son, Giorgio Mondadori, took over as president of the publishing empire in 1968. A few years later, Mondadori administration was moved from Milan to the new headquarters at Segrate. During the 1970s, expansion of industrial activity continued with the acquisition of two new printing plants in Vicenza, San Donato Milanese, and the establishment of a new plant at Cles. In 1975, yet another was acquired in Toledo, Spain.

In 1975, spurred on by the purchase of the top-selling Italian daily *Corriere della Sera* by Mondadori's competitor Rizzoli, the company joined in founding what would be its first daily newspaper, *la Repubblica*. The newspaper was founded as a joint venture by Mondadori and *L'Espresso*, the top news weekly competing with Mondadori's *Panorama* magazine. A holding company, Editoriale L'Espresso, was formed, with 50% of the capital, L1 billion, shared by Mondadori and the *L'Espresso* group, which included the new newspaper's editors Eugenio Scalfari and Carlo Caracciolo.

Giorgio Mondadori held the chairmanship of Mondadori until 1976. His sisters Cristina and Laura Mondadori joined in forcing their brother Giorgio from the company and he was succeeded as chairman by Mario Formenton, husband of Cristina, the youngest Mondadori daughter.

Meanwhile, *la Repubblica* was quickly gaining in stature and sales, thanks in part to its outspoken editorial positions on the political events of the decade. The newspaper opposed negotiations with the leftist terrorists who kidnapped and assassinated Italian statesman Aldo Moro in 1978. Competition from the largest Italian daily, *Corriere della Sera*, was later handicapped by the implication of *Corriere's* parent, Rizzoli Publishing, in the political scandals of the early 1980s. By virtue of its editorial independence, *la Repubblica* was widely seen as a bastion of integrity. Already by 1979, *la Repubblica* was no longer losing money and had begun to command an appreciable market share. Shortly thereafter the new paper began showing increasing profits.

The late 1970s and early 1980s brought a period of decline for the Mondadori group. The economic boom years of the postwar era were drawing to a close in Italy. In 1975 the company suffered from a fall-off in its advertising and publicity revenues. The signal event of this period, which set the stage for the acrimonious boardroom battles at the end of the decade, was Mondadori's entrance into the television market, with the creation of the Italian network Retequattro.

Guided by Mario Formenton in 1978 Mondadori established Gestione Pubblicitaria Editoriale (Gpe), an advertising agency for 18 local channels. Two years later, the company entered directly into broadcasting activity with a second enterprise, Telemond, which bought and resold television programming. In 1982, the companies were reconstituted as the network Retequattro.

The ill-fated venture occurred in an unfamiliar market environment dominated by two major competitors. First was the state-owned radio and television network which had in 1976 relinquished the monopoly on television programming it held since 1954. The second was media baron Silvio Berlusconi's Fininvest Group, which was at the time amassing a vast empire of small local stations. Retequattro's managers withheld from such expansion in the mistaken belief that a law would shortly be passed impeding the growth of national monopolies in television.

Late in 1982, with the acquisition of the Italian channel Italia 1 by Fininvest, Retequattro found itself in a low position in audience ratings. Retequattro was unable to compete effectively with the maverick Berlusconi.

At the same time, Mondadori was involved in a program of expansion in its other sectors. Daily newspaper activity increased with the introduction of four provincial papers published by a subsidiary, Editoriale Le Gazzette. In addition, the Mondadori group reached an agreement with the Canadian Harlequin group in 1981 for the publication in Italy of its romance novels, and in 1983 acquired another papermaking concern, Cartiera F.A. Marsoni of Treviso.

At the end of 1983, Mario Formenton turned the failing Retequattro over to Leonardo Forneron Mondadori, the son of Laura Mondadori, who had legally been given his grandfather's family name. Leonardo Mondadori had worked in the company since 1972, and had successfully directed the book publishing activity. Initially the younger manager improved the network, but the losses had already become too great and in late 1984 Mario Formenton sought a buyer for Retequattro.

The situation in 1984 was one of near-emergency for Mondadori, with Retequattro losing L10 billion each month. The network was eventually sold to Fininvest. However the losses had been too great. The consolidated balance of the company in 1984 showed losses of L10.7 billion. Salvaging the company required a recapitalization of the order of at least L50 billion.

With help from associates in the financial world, Mario Formenton and Leonardo Mondadori created a holding company, AME Finanziaria (AMEF) in 1985. To create the new company, the two families contributed just over 50% in Mondadori shares, while the other partners contributed capital. Since the Mondadori shares constituted a majority in the holding company, the family remained in control—of both AMEF and the recapitalization of Mondadori, the ailing publishing empire.

AMEF's partners included Carlo De Benedetti, who had been in contact with Mondadori as a shareholder of the Editoriale l'Espresso group that founded the daily *la Repubblica*. De Benedetti held approximately 17% of AMEF. Silvio Berlusconi held 9%.

At Arnoldo Mondadori Editore, Mario Formenton was still president, and his nephew Leonardo Mondadori was promoted to vice president. As managing director, Franco Tatò guided the restructuring of the company.

In 1985 profits rose to L25 billion, as opposed to the L10 billion of 1984; in 1986, profits tripled to L75 billion. When, in 1987, Mondadori reported profits of L100 billion, it was evident that the company was out of danger and that the rescue program, with the recapitalization from AMEF, had been a success.

It also proved that despite the losses of the Retequattro venture Mondadori was a basically healthy company. In 1987, however, Mario Formenton died prematurely. Former managing director and vice president Sergio Polillo was brought in to fill his place, after a bitter struggle over the succession that opposed Leonardo Mondadori to his aunt Cristina and her son Luca Formenton.

The loss of Mario Formenton triggered a series of events that eventually catapulted the company into national news. With the two branches of the family in conflict, the shareholder Carlo De Benedetti achieved a position of considerable influence. During this period, the skilled financier struck a deal with the Formenton family by which he retained right of first refusal if they ever decided to sell their shares.

Then, aligned with the Formentons at the Mondadori 1988 shareholders' assembly, De Benedetti successfully exploited a technicality in the relationship between the publishing group and the AMEF holding company to emerge in a majority position. Together, the Formentons and De Benedetti voted to exclude the founder's grandson from the board of Mondadori. Embittered, Leonardo left the family business to found his own publishing house, Leonardo Editore.

Under De Benedetti's guidance, the Mondadori group continued to thrive. The group acquired a stake in Elemond, which controls the prestigious Einaudi publishing house. In April 1989, De Benedetti arranged an important agreement whereby *la Repubblica* shareholders Eugenio Scalfari and Carlo Caracciolo sold their 51.85% share in Editoriale L'Espresso to Mondadori for L407 billion. As part of the deal, Caracciolo was nominated president of Mondadori, and Scalfari became a member of the board of directors. With la Repubblica and Editoriale L'Espresso added to its interests, Mondadori was now worth L2.3 trillion and was by far the largest publishing company in Italy.

Conflict developed again in 1989, the 100th anniversary of Arnoldo Mondadori's birth. Silvio Berlusconi had acquired more shares of AMEF and sided with Leonardo Mondadori to wield majority power in the decision-making. Berlusconi's interest in Mondadori emerged when he blocked a move by Carlo De Benedetti to merge his holding company Compagnie Industriali Riunite S.p.A. (CIR) and AMEF.

By December 1989, fearful of their loss of influence on the board of Mondadori, the Formentons struck a deal to sell their AMEF shares to Berlusconi, effectively reuniting with their cousin Leonardo Mondadori. The move immediately set off a furor in the financial world and in the media, where the contestants carried out a bruising and highly publicized battle for control.

On one side was Berlusconi, allied with the two families of Mondadori and in control of AMEF, and therefore of the ordinary capital of Mondadori. On the other side was Carlo De Benedetti, joined by the la Repubblica editors Scalfari and Caracciolo, with 51% of the privileged capital of Mondadori. By the end of the year, the contest was transformed into a complicated legal struggle that turned on the validity of De Benedetti's agreement with the Formentons granting him first option on the Formenton's shares, should they ever decide to sell.

For 156 days, Silvio Berlusconi claimed control of Mondadori. The 1989 annual report listed Berlusconi as president and Luca Formenton as vice president. The report described recent developments: a new division called "business and information" comprising business publishing and a computer software company, Mondadori Informatica; an agreement reached with *Fortune* for publication of an Italian edition; and the divestment of Mondadori's papermaking activities. But the victory was short-lived.

The deal between Berlusconi and the Formentons was contested in the courts and, in June 1990, arbitrators ruled in favor of De Benedetti. Judges assigned Giacinto Spizzico, an 81-year-old business lawyer, to the post of president. The office of vice president is shared by Fedele Confaloniere, formerly managing director of Fininvest, and Luigi Vita Samory, a lawyer appointed by the courts. Two men also fill the post of managing director: Carlo Caracciolo, and the court-appointed Antonio Coppi, a former executive of the Rizzoli publishing house. The new general director is a former executive of Carlo De Benedetti's CIR holding company, Corrado Passera.

In January 1991, this ruling was nullified in the Rome Court of Appeals without, however, significantly altering the balance of power between De Benedetti and Berlusconi. De Benedetti's original agreement with the Formentons was found to be in violation of the AMEF charter. A negotiated settlement was reached in May 1991, whereby Berlusconi and the Mondadori-Formenton families retained control of Mondadori's book and magazine publishing interests, and advertising agency. While De Benedetti controlled the Repubblica-Espresso group plus 15 local newspapers.

Events between 1989 and 1991 were traumatic for Mondadori. In spite of the contest for power already under way, 1988 was a strong year for the company, which reported a net profit of L103 billion. In 1989, this figure was reduced by half, partly owing to losses in the advertising activities.

Prospects for the future include plans for a close cooperation with the TV communication activities of Fininvest. The group is looking beyond its traditional pre-eminent role in Italy, toward changes taking place in the context of the unified European market. Mondadori has the skill and experience to anticipate what the public wants and the partnership with Silvio Berlusconi offers Mondadori an unparalleled chance to promote its books and magazines through television.

Principal Subsidiaries: Auguri di Mondadori S.r.l.; Artes Graficas Toledo S.A. (Spain); Club degli Editori S.p.A.; Editiones Grijalbo S.A. (Spain); Monadori Espuna S.A. (Spain); Mondadori Business Information S.p.A.; Mondadori Informatica S.p.A.; Mondadori Pubblicita S.p.A.; Mondadori Video S.p.A.; Verkerke Reproduletres N.V. (Netherlands).

Further Reading: Mondadori, Mimma, *Tipografia in Paradiso,* Milan, Mondadori, 1984; Arnoldo Mondadori Editore, *Arnoldo Mondadori Editore S.p.A.: Facts and Images 1987,* Segrate, Mondadori, 1988; Arnoldo Mondadori Editore, *Arnoldo Mondadori Editore S.p.A.: Facts and Images 1988,* Segrate, Mondadori, 1989; Turnai, Giuseppe, and Delfina Rattazi, *Mondadori: la grande sfida,* Milan, RCS Rizzoli, 1990; *Prima Comunicazione: Mensile sulla comunicazione scritta e audiovisiva,* Supplement to No. 182, January 1990; Pansa, Giampaolo, *L'Intrigo,* Milan, Sperling & Kupfer, 1990.

—Paul Conrad

AXEL SPRINGER VERLAG AG

Kochstrasse 50
1000 Berlin 61
Federal Republic of Germany
(30) 25910
Fax: (30) 2510928

Public Company
Incorporated: 1985
Employees: 11,700
Sales: DM2.80 billion (US$1.87 billion)
Stock Exchange: Frankfurt

Axel Springer Verlag is the largest publisher of newspapers and magazines in Europe with extensive interests in book publishing, radio, and television. It is an enduring monument to its founder, Axel Cäsar Springer, who was an influential and controversial figure in German public life for nearly 40 years. His family still controls the company and his political principles are written into every Springer journalist's contract.

Axel Springer was born in Hamburg in 1912, and worked in the family firm, Hammerich & Lesser, which published local newspapers until it was closed by Joseph Goebbels in 1941. In 1946 Springer began to publish the *Nordwestdeutsche Hefte,* a monthly magazine made up of transcripts of broadcasts on the radio station Nordwestdeutsche Rundfunk. In the same year he followed up with *Hör Zu!,* a more populist publication providing radio program listings alongside articles for a family audience, which has since become a television listings magazine. In 1948 he launched his first newspaper, Germany's first evening daily, the *Hamburger Abendblatt.*

Springer was happy to take ideas from any source if they seemed likely to be workable and profitable. His most famous innovation, the daily *Bild Zeitung,* was launched in 1952 and was similar to the U.K.'s *Daily Mirror* in style but not in politics. It soon became, and has remained, the largest selling daily in Europe, with a circulation of about five million. Springer was careful not to over-specialize, and in 1953 balanced *Bild Zeitung* by acquiring the quality daily, *Die Welt,* which had been established in April 1946 by the British occupation authorities. Heinrich Schulte, who joined *Die Welt* as publishing manager in 1948, had begun to diversify by printing other publications, including Springer's *Hör Zu!* As circulation fell and debts mounted, the paper sought a buyer, and in 1952 found Axel Springer more than willing. It was the sudden withdrawal of Springer's printing contracts with *Die Welt* that had precipitated the crisis; his bid was made in secret and was anywhere from DM2 million to DM6 million; and it is widely believed that what tipped the scales in his favor was the intervention of the Christian Democratic Chancellor Konrad Adenauer. The British allowed the deal to go through on condition that Springer share ownership with an independent trust. In the event, the trust never had more than 25% of the shares, and was abolished in 1970.

Springer's choice as chief editor was Hans Zehrer, who had been editor of the extreme right-wing, but not Nazi, paper *Die Tat* before World War II, and who had been prevented from becoming editor in 1946, after protests from the U.K.'s Labour government and from the Social Democrats then governing Hamburg. Springer concentrated on building up *Bild Zeitung,* launching its Sunday version, *Bild am Sonntag,* in 1956. Under Zehrer's control, *Die Welt* began publishing a Berlin edition in 1955, and promoted the notion that Germany could be reunified as a neutral state at peace with both East and West. Perhaps surprisingly, this divergence from the 1950s cold war consensus did not damage circulation, which rose from 165,000 in 1954 to 217,000 five years later. Heinrich Schulte still retained some influence at the paper, and resisted Springer's pressure to push the paper toward being a vehicle for Springer's views right up until his death in 1963.

By 1959 Zehrer's enthusiasm for neutrality was wearing off in the face of Soviet intransigence, and Springer himself, who had always been staunchly anti-communist and had always insisted that his publications place quotation marks around the term "German Democratic Republic," began to get more involved in the paper. That year saw the laying of the foundation stone for the Springer group's new offices in Berlin, in the heart of the prewar newspaper district, intended as a symbol of the continuity of German culture in the face of the Soviet threat. The move to Berlin was not purely idealistic, but reflected the takeover in the same year of the publishing group Ullstein, which had been founded in 1877 and which published two local daily papers, *Berliner Morgenpost* and *B.Z.* (originally *Berliner Zeitung*), as well as books. The Springer group's headquarters continued to be in Hamburg, rather than Berlin, until 1967. Throughout the crisis over the building of the Berlin Wall, Springer and his papers were active in demanding a strong response from the West, including a ban on exports from the federal republic to East Germany, a proposal his Christian Democrat friends in the federal government did not carry out.

By 1964 Springer controlled more than 40% of daily papers sold in Germany, more than 80% of Sunday papers, 45% of magazines for young people and 48% of radio and TV listings publications. *Bild Zeitung*'s circulation rose to 5.3 million under its new young editor Peter Boenisch and *Die Welt* was at the height of its influence and circulation—290,000. Its reputation as a highly partisan right-wing organ was further enhanced by the appointment of Dr. Herman Starke as editor after Zehrer's death in 1966, as allegations about his past record of pro-Nazi and anti-Semitic views led to an international scandal.

From 1967 onward, the "Extra-parliamentary Opposition" (APO) began protesting against the American incursion into Vietnam and the conservative values that dominated West Germany. Springer's delivery vans were blocked, turned over, or set afire and the APO demanded that Springer be expropriated.

The protests reached their peak in April 1968 when the most famous APO leader, Rudi Dutschke, was shot and seriously injured by a deranged reader of *Bild Zeitung,* and discount sales of *Die Welt* to students collapsed, along with sales to teachers, so that by 1970 the paper was losing money for the first time since Springer had taken it over. Springer's own re-action to the campaign, in a speech he gave in 1972, was to claim that the radicals had been inspired by the East German leader, Walter Ulbricht—whom Dutschke and his comrades hated as much as they hated Springer—and to portray his com-pany as the guardian of the federal republic's economic and political freedoms. It might be said that both Springer and his enemies have always overestimated the importance of his newspapers and magazines. Although, for instance, one-third of the *Bild Zeitung,* the day before the 1972 elections, con-sisted of anti-government advertising, the Social Democrats stayed in power, albeit in coalitions through to 1982.

Springer announced in 1967 that his papers would adhere to the following four principles, which were written into the company articles in 1985 and included in every Springer jour-nalist's contract: the peaceful reunification of Germany; recon-ciliation of Germans and Jews and support for Israel; rejection of totalitarianism or extremism; and support for a free market economy. For almost all citizens of the federal republic the first two were uncontroversial. The fourth sounded a little ironic, in view of Springer's monopoly position: indeed, he sold off several of his titles in the late 1960s in order to keep his total share of the print media market just below the 40% threshold which would attract the attentions of the Federal Cartel Office. As for opposing dictatorships, the Springer pa-pers, led by *Die Welt,* hardly mentioned the reign of terror that followed Ugarte Pinochet's coup in Chile in 1973, their jour-nalists accepted fees from the Greek colonels' junta to write favorable stories, and they cooperated with the shah of Iran's secret police to the extent of publishing reports on opposition activities taken straight from their files. Springer's real target was the Soviet Union. He saw the 1970 treaty with the Soviets as a blow to any hopes of unification, since it made permanent the borders created after the war. He was so convinced of the likelihood of a Russian invasion that he invested most of his considerable wealth outside the federal republic, mostly in North America.

Starting in 1972 with the building of Germany's first offset printing plant for newspapers, Springer, along with its rival Gruner + Jahr, led the way in establishing vast new printing centers, taking advantage of the new technology and the chance to cut labor costs. Unlike their largely non-unionized colleagues in the United Kingdom or the United States, German journalists refused to undertake composition on video terminals, thus helping to save at least some jobs which else-where have been lost. Throughout the 1970s the group ex-panded its holdings in local newspapers and specialist magazines, including a majority stake in Gilde-Verlag, pub-lisher of *Rallye Racing* and *Sportfahrer* (1975); the new Springer publications *Tennis Magazin* and *Ski Magazin* (1976); and a majority stake in the Kunst und Technik Verlag of Mu-nich (1979), which has since been renamed Weltkunst Verlag GmbH and now publishes the fortnightly art magazine *Weltkunst.* In 1976 another new subsidiary, Cora Verlag, was created to publish translations of the romantic fiction pub-lished by the Canadian company Harlequin. Springer was de-termined to keep abreast of changes in tastes and leisure interests in Germany, a policy confirmed by the launches of new magazines for women—*Journal für die Frau* (1978) and *Bild der Frau* (1983).

By 1974 *Die Welt*'s sales had fallen to 196,000 and its an-nual losses were over DM20 million. In 1975 the paper's of-fices were moved from Hamburg to Bonn and the Berlin edition was closed down. From 1979 to 1981 Springer experi-mented with allowing a guarded shift to the left in *Die Welt*'s editorial policy, under Peter Boenisch, who led the paper into a more critical approach to the shah of Iran and a more sup-portive view of détente with the Soviet bloc, but then Springer returned control to the "cold warriors," Herbert Kremp, Wilfried Hertz Eichenrode, and Matthias Warden, in spite of the protests of the staff. Staff feelings were expressed in their arranging the headlines in the paper, on the day Boenisch was fired, to read: "The Good Times are Over; Big Setback for the World; The People Don't Back the Junta; Decree from the Top." Once again the paper swung into action against the peace movement, the Greens, and the left, in tandem with *Bild.* Between 1970 and 1985 the paper lost more than $100 million, and its circulation remained below 250,000. The changes at *Die Welt* were accompanied by the first breach in Springer's almost complete control of the company, as contin-uing financial problems forced him first to offer a majority shareholding to his rivals in the publishing business, the broth-ers Franz and Frieder Burda, in 1981, and then, when the Federal Cartel Office vetoed the plan, to sell them 24.9% in-stead, in 1983.

In 1970 Springer had become one of the first of the Euro-pean press barons to enter the electronic media, establishing a subsidiary, Ullstein AV Produktions—und Vertriebsgesells-chaft, which was renamed Ullstein Tele Video (UTV) in 1981. One of the main obstacles to Springer's further expansion into the field of television was the constitutional provision that placed broadcasting under the control of the *Länder* (states) rather than the federal government. No one state was willing to give up its powers over television and radio to any commercial interests, least of all to such a threateningly large organization as Springer. Accordingly Springer had to enter a consortium set up in 1983 by the leading German newspaper publishers to finance the satellite ECS 1, from which the commercial televi-sion station SAT 1 has been broadcast since 1987. Until then the station was limited to the cable network owned by the Ger-man postal authorities, and made no money for its investors. In 1985 Springer took stakes in the cable television company Teleclub, specializing in showing films, and in two Munich radio stations, as well as 35% of the shares in SAT 1's news service.

In 1984, after nearly 38 years in charge of to expanding and diverse empire, Springer went into semi-retirement, handing over the running of the group to his wife Friede and to Bernhard Servatius, Ernst Cramer, and Günter Prinz, who sat on the supervisory board of the group alongside the Burda brothers. The group was restructured in the summer of 1985. The sale of 49% of the shares in Axel Springer Verlag by the holding company, Axel Springer Gesellschaft für Publizistik KG, founded in 1970, was heavily oversubscribed, but the 7,000 new shareholders found themselves holding registered voting shares, which meant that any sale of a holding of more than 0.5% could not go ahead without the board's approval.

Thus Springer's personal holding fell to 26.1%, but his, and therefore his heirs,' control covered 75.1%. It was also arranged that a majority of 80% would be needed to alter the four principles he had laid down for his publications. The official reason for these arrangements was to preserve the company's independence, although it was not being threatened at the time; in addition, the Springer family wanted to minimize the payment of death duties when Springer died.

Axel Springer died in September 1985, having ensured that his empire would remain in the hands of his chosen successors, including his second wife, Friede, whom he had married in 1978, his daughter, his younger son, and his two grandchildren, who were directed in his will to keep their holdings together for at least 30 years. Servatius and Cramer received holdings of 3% each in the Springer holding company, while Peter Tamm became chairman of the executive board, having been chief executive since 1968.

In 1985 the Springer group accounted for 29% of the domestic newspaper market. Expansion did not stop with Springer's death. The 20 book publishing divisions acquired over the years were reorganized in 1985 into Ullstein Langen Müller, the third-largest publisher of general books in the federal republic, while a particularly successful new magazine was *Auto-Bild* (1986), from which have developed, via joint ventures or franchizing, similar magazines in the United Kingdom, France, and Italy.

A dispute developed in March 1987 between Tamm and his deputy, Günter Prinz, over the future of Springer's stake in SAT 1, which was then running at a loss, and of the new magazine *Ja,* which had been an expensive flop. At first Prinz appeared to have won his case for closer supervision of Tamm's executive board by the supervisory board. However, in May Prinz was dismissed and Tamm was free to press on with expansion of the television business; the closure of *Ja* new investments in the Spanish company Sarpe, which publishes women's magazines; a new Austrian newspaper, *Der Standard;* and a joint-venture printing and publishing firm in Hungary.

The boardroom rows that broke out in March 1988 were more serious, since they involved threats to Springer's elaborate arrangements for protecting the shareholding pattern established just before his death. Leo Kirch, the owner of an enormous feature film library, had built up his own stake in the Springer group to 10%, and had some influence over another 16%. Having arranged in 1987 to cooperate with the Springer executors, he now sought to gain overall control by forming an alliance with the Burda brothers against them. The outcome, in April 1988, confirmed the determination of the Springer executors, led by Servatius and Friede Springer, to keep control of the group: they bought the Burda brothers out for DM530 million—as compared to the DM255 million the Burdas had paid five years before.

These financial battles did not prevent the group from achieving its highest ever profits in the 1987–1988 financial year. In 1989 the group took a 60% share in Capitol Film + TV International, created to buy and sell films, TV series, and TV productions, including those of Springer's own production subsidiaries Commerzfilm, Multimedia, and Cinecentrum. It also bought the New York–based Medical Tribune Group, a leading publisher of medical and health-care literature worldwide.

Some 88% of Axel Springer Verlag's turnover still derives from newspapers and magazines. *Die Welt* and *Bild Zeitung* in particular have made the Springer name famous and brought praise from the right and enmity from the left, but Springer's domination of the German press should be placed in context. While one in every four newspapers sold in Germany is a copy of *Bild Zeitung,* and there is no other national tabloid newspaper, most Germans still have access to a thriving regional and local press. While Springer controls 80% of the Sunday newspaper market, this figure reflects the comparative unimportance of Sunday newspapers in Germany, where the weekly magazines *Der Spiegel* and *Stern* serve the same function as Sunday papers in the United Kingdom or the United States. At the same time, all newspapers and magazines are facing intensified competition from television, in Germany as elsewhere in Europe.

Principal Subsidiaries: Ullstein GmbH; tsv "top special" Verlag GmbH; Cora Verlag GmbH; Weltkunst Verlag GmbH; Medical Tribune International GmbH.

Further Reading: Müller, Hans Dieter, *Press Power,* London, Macdonald, 1969; Springer, Axel, *Aus Sorge um Deutschland,* Stuttgart, Seewald Verlag, 1980; Walker, Martin, *Powers of the Press,* London, Quartet Books, 1982; *Our Product—The Living Word,* Berlin, Axel Springer Verlag AG, 1989.

—Patrick Heenan

Bertelsmann
lesen · hören · sehen

BERTELSMANN AG

Carl-Bertelsmann-Strasse 270
4830 Gütersloh 100
Federal Republic of Germany
(5241) 800
Fax: (5241) 75166

Public Company
Incorporated: 1835 as Bertelsmann Verlag
Employees: 43,500
Sales: DM13.30 billion (US$8.90 billion)
Stock Exchanges: Hamburg Munich Düsseldorf Frankfurt

Bertelsmann is the largest media group in Germany and Europe, and only its U.S. competitors prevent it from being the world leader in its field. The company was founded as a family business in the middle of the 19th century and had already grown to a considerable size before World War II. The significant expansion phase of the company, however, only began after the German currency reform of 1948, when Reinhard Mohn succeeded with the Bertelsmann book club (the Lesering) in introducing a revolutionary form of direct sales to the traditional German publishing market. Bertelsmann grew into an international force on the back of this great success. In 1991 20.5% of Bertelsmann's share capital was in the hands of the Mohn family and 10.7% belonged to the Hamburg publisher Dr. Gerd Bucerius, of *Die Zeit* fame; 68% of the capital stock was held by the Bertelsmann Foundation, established in 1977 by Reinhard Mohn and intended to take over the Mohn family's share in Bertelsmann and appoint the company's management.

The company's motto, *lesen–hören–sehen* (to read, to listen, to see), created on the occasion of the firm's 150th anniversary in 1985, is appropriate to today's Bertelsmann AG, which has worldwide business interests in all sectors of the media industry, in books, magazines, and newspapers; in records, cassettes, and compact discs; and in television, video, and data banks. However, the company began in 1835 as a small publisher of evangelical hymn books and devotional pamphlets in Pietist eastern Westphalia. That is where its headquarters have remained, resisting any suggestions of transferring to Hamburg or Munich.

Bertelsmann AG combines a solid domestic base in Germany with an international presence that is impressive for a German company—Bertelsmann makes more than half its turnover abroad. The founder of the company was Carl Bertelsmann, who was born in Gütersloh in 1791, two years after the French Revolution. His father died before he was two years old. His mother was to find him an apprenticeship in a bookbinder's business as she had done for his elder brother. To avoid conscription into Napoleon's Russian army, Carl Bertelsmann went traveling, going via Berlin to Upper Silesia.

When Carl Bertelsmann returned to Gütersloh in 1815, after Napoleon's defeat and exile, he found that his brother had taken on the position for which he had been trained. It was only after his brother's death in 1819 that Carl Bertelsmann was able to set up as bookbinder in his home town. "The little Bertelsmann from Gütersloh," as he was known in the area, soon found a place in the Pietist movement that shaped the eastern Westphalian community, and discovered that it particularly needed hymn books for its services. Gradually Bertelsmann's bookbinding business became a book-printing business as well, and then developed into a full publishing house.

This development occurred during the mid–19th century Biedermeier period, a time in which German middle-class culture flourished and which was marked in Westphalia by Prussian government. Carl Bertelsmann was a conservative and a royalist faithful to the Prussian king. He supported the latter's cause during the revolution of 1848–1849 in which he became politically involved. Generally, though, he dedicated himself to working industriously for his company which, while small, was expanding rapidly. By the time of Carl Bertelsmann's death, it employed 14 people.

When Carl Bertelsmann died in 1850, he left behind a wife and son and a considerable fortune. He had laid the foundations for the company's subsequent development, but he was not there to witness the success of the firm's bestseller, the *Missionsharfe* (Missionary Harp), a hymn book of which two million copies were printed. The first edition appeared in 1853. By this time Bertelsmann was publishing not only Christian literature, but also historical and philological books, as well as novels. It ran its own printing press as before. Heinrich Bertelsmann, who inherited the business from his father, was able, as a result, to build on a very wide foundation that prevented his company from remaining a small publisher of denominational literature.

The printing and publishing house grew considerably in the second generation, thanks in part to the acquisition of other publishing houses that could not hold their own against competition in the market. This tradition of buying up weaker competitors to modernize them and thus make them competitive once more is a policy that Bertelsmann still pursues. By the time Heinrich Bertelsmann died in 1887, his 60 employees had moved into a brand new building. However, Heinrich Bertelsmann had no sons, but one daughter, Friederike.

The company consequently came under the ownership of the Mohn family in its third generation, since Friederike Bertelsmann married Johannes Mohn in 1881. Johannes Mohn was a minister's son from the Westerwald who had learned about the book trade under Heinrich Bertelsmann. Although without personal means and an outsider in Gütersloh, Mohn immediately took on the responsibilities of the business after his father-in-law's death, showing considerable talent in its management. In particular, he expanded the printing side so that the book production could be increased steadily without incurring outside costs.

For this conservative company, with its strong allegiance to throne and church, the German defeat in World War I and the consequent revolution, bringing about the kaiser's abdication, was a painful break with the past. Disheartened by events, the 65-year-old Johannes Mohn passed on the responsibility for the business to his son Heinrich, only 26 years old at the time. Like his great-grandfather, grandfather, and father before him, Heinrich Mohn had had the best possible theoretical and practical training for his career as a publisher. Bad health and hard times would, however, prevent him from enjoying his position to the full.

Before the war, Johannes Mohn had already had a taxable income of 100,000 marks a year. He was a millionaire. Despite the family wealth, the Gütersloh printing and publishing house was almost forced to close, not long after Heinrich Mohn had taken it over, because of the effects of galloping inflation in Germany in 1923. For the first time in the company's history, no new employees were taken on, while valued staff had to be laid off. Scarcely had this crisis been overcome than an even greater world economic crisis broke out in 1930.

Heinrich Mohn countered these difficulties and the Third Reich with the help of his Christian convictions. Like his predecessors he was extremely close to the Evangelical Church and in particular to the part of that church, the Bekennende Kirche, or German Confessional Church, which stood by its faith in God in opposition to Hitler. This was the church to which Martin Niemöller and Dietrich Bonhoeffer, spiritual leaders of the German *Widerstand,* or anti-Hitler opposition, belonged. At the same time Mohn was successfully trading with the German air force, which he supplied with millions of cheap books and pamphlets. When World War II began in 1939, roughly 400 printers, typesetters, and publishers worked for Bertelsmann in Gütersloh. The company had a turnover of 8.1 million reichsmarks in 1941 and by this time had far outstripped its German competitors.

However, the Nazi authorities disapproved of Mohn's company's publication of religious texts and after the war began, Mohn's right to print these works was removed. His printing works were provided with less and less paper by the authorities, making it increasingly difficult to operate. When the British forces bombed Gütersloh in March 1945, most of the company's buildings were destroyed. Although a few of the expensive printing machines remained intact so that the business was able to continue, the company's future looked uncertain because Heinrich Mohn's health was failing.

Good fortune came to Bertelsmann's aid, when Reinhard Mohn returned home from prisoner-of-war camp earlier than his elder but less gifted brother, Sigbert Mohn. Neither was to have inherited the company originally, but when the eldest of the four brothers was killed on the sixth day of the war, the position fell to Sigbert. Since he was only to return from Russian prisoner-of-war camp in 1949, his younger brother Reinhard took charge of affairs in Gütersloh in 1947.

After his school-leaving exams at the Evangelical Foundation Grammar School in Gütersloh, Reinhard Mohn had wanted to become an aeronautical engineer, but when the war broke out, he was called up to join the German Africa Corps under General Erwin Rommel. After he was injured, he was taken prisoner by the American troops.

After his return to Gütersloh, Reinhard Mohn took the company helm with determination. When the West Germans suddenly stopped buying books after Germany's adoption of the deutsche mark in 1948, the young publisher made a daring

decision. Instead of hoping for better times like the other publishers of the day, in 1950 he invited the West German retail booksellers to form the Lesering together with Bertelsmann. For a small sum, any reader could become a member of this book club. In return, he would receive a certain number of books from C. Bertelsmann Verlag every year.

There had already been book clubs in Germany. What was new about the Bertelsmann Lesering, however, was that the "corner bookshops" were made partners by the publishing house. With this type of direct sales the bookshops also profited, whereas previous book clubs had only created undesirable competition. Nevertheless there were still those who were critical. Many bookshop owners who did not acquire any Lesering members and consequently did not benefit from the club felt threatened. They were afraid that the Bertelsmann Lesering would take away their customers, but these fears proved to be exaggerated. In fact, the Bertelsmann Lesering won many people over to buying books who previously had not dared to go into bookshops for fear of being shown up for their lack of education.

The Bertelsmann Lesering proved highly successful. It gave the Gütersloh printing and publishing house two decisive advantages over its competitors—a certain guarantee of purchases of its own books and the high capacity use of its printing presses. These two factors combined to make Bertelsmann's turnover soar in the 1950s. Company turnover doubled each year between 1951 and 1953, going from DM7 million to DM30 million. This was a far greater turnover than that of any other book publisher in West Germany. In 1956–1957, Bertelsmann was to break the DM100 million barrier. By 1973, Reinhard Mohn saw the figure reach DM1 billion. At the end of this 22-year period, the company employed a work force of 11,000 at Gütersloh and elsewhere as opposed to an original 500 in 1951.

The success of the company could not be explained by the Bertelsmann Lesering alone. Two additional decisions taken by Reinhard Mohn were to be of great significance. The first, born from necessity, was to cover the company's enormous need for capital; Mohn made his employees shareholders, but without voting rights. This and other socially minded actions made the Gütersloh office, far from West Germany's glittering metropolis, a greatly envied work place. Mohn's second decision was to branch out from books and invest in modern media such as records, magazines, and television to keep pace with changing consumer demands.

These changes all took place with breathtaking speed in the 1950s, 1960s, and 1970s. Most successful was the acquisition of a stake in the Hamburg publishing company Gruner + Jahr, which was gradually built up to a 74.9% shareholding in 1976. Not only did the Hamburg sister company bring in excellent results, owing to good management, but it also helped Bertelsmann achieve wider acceptance in the media world following a long period during which the Westphalian family business had been regarded as rather provincial.

The principle behind Bertelsmann's acquisitions was always the same. Reinhard Mohn bought firms that were active in related fields of business and which could be purchased relatively cheaply because of problems they could not solve themselves. He would place a couple of trusted colleagues in leading posts and leave them to work hard on their own. Delegation of responsibility and decentralization of business were his beliefs. For ambitious managers who valued a certain degree of independence, it was and remains a challenge. In the 1990s Bertelsmann consists of around 200 profit centers which operate virtually independently from one another and are co-ordinated from the group's headquarters in Gütersloh.

During the end of the 1960s, Bertelsmann reached the limits of its growth within the German-speaking world. Mohn decided to expand the business abroad. The first step was to introduce Bertelsmann's Lesering to Spain, with all the other sectors of operation—from the printing works to the book and magazine publishing companies—following at short intervals. As a result, turnover rose to DM5.5 billion by 1980 and the number of employees rose to 30,000 worldwide. Bertelsmann, transformed into a public limited company because of the colossal growth in its capital requirements, prepared to leap to the top of the media world league.

In 1981, after more than 30 years at the head of the company, Mohn moved from being chairman of the company to being chairman of the supervisory board. For the first time in Bertelsmann's history, he left the operational running of the company to a manager who was not a member of the family. In taking this step he instituted a ruling which he applied to all members of the board and to himself and which serves as an iron rule at Bertelsmann—that employees may not remain in their jobs past 60 years of age.

Under its new boss, Dr. Mark Wössner, a former assistant to Mohn, who had made his way to the top from 1968 onwards in the printing and industrial plant sectors, Bertelsmann AG held the position of the leading media group in the world for a brief time in the mid-1980s. This was made possible by several acquisitions in the United States, which stretched the Westphalian company to the limits of its capacity. In 1985–1986 Bertelsmann acquired the publishing group Doubleday-Dell and turned the music section of the RCA into the BMG (Bertelsmann Music Group). It was a massive package, for which Wössner paid more than US$800 million. This show of strength catapulted Bertelsmann AG's world turnover above DM9 billion, with the group employing more than 40,000 people worldwide.

Bertelsmann looked to Eastern Europe, where possibilities have been revealed by the fall of the Berlin Wall and of the Eastern Bloc. With a world turnover of DM13.3 billion in 1989–1990 and employment of 43,500 people, Bertelsmann AG is well equipped to make the most of these developments.

In the early 1990s the division of the company's individual product lines is as follows: in the lead, as always, comes book sales, generating a world turnover of DM6 billion. Magazines, publishing, and printing follow in second place, with DM4 billion in sales, and in third place are music and video and electronic media sales, at DM3.3 billion.

The company's strong involvement abroad gives cause for concern, especially that in the United States. Apart from the fact that the publishing and printing group, Bantam Doubleday Dell has not, so far, produced the expected results, extreme vacillations in the dollar exchange rate and an economic collapse in the United States could hinder Bertelsmann considerably. Above all, Bertelsmann has tied up the greater part of its investment capacity since 1986 in the western world. The company relies on its entreprenurial spirit, its audacity, and on the sense of responsibility of its local business managers and employees, who are constantly looking for worthwhile opportunities.

Principal Subsidiaries: Bertelsmann Club; Deutsche Buch-Gemeinschaft; Buchgemeinschaft Donauland; Buch- und Schallplatten- freunde Switzerland; Book Club Associates (U.K.); Circulo de Lectores (Spain); ECI voor Boeken en Platen (Belgium); ECI voor Boeken und Platen (Netherlands); Euroclub Italia (Italy); France Loisirs Belgique (Belgium); France Loisirs (France); France Loisirs (Suisse) (Switzerland); Nederlandse Boekenclub (Belgium, Netherlands); Nederlandse Lezerskring Boek en Plaat (Netherlands); Setradis (France); Doubleday Book & Music Clubs (U.S.A.); C. Bertelsmann Verlag; Gütersloher Verlagshaus Gerd Mohn; Bertelsmann Lexikon Verlag; Blanvalet Verlag; Goldmann Verlag; Albrecht Knaus Verlag; Mosaik Verlag; Orbis Verlag; Prisma Verlag; RV Reise-und Verkehrsverlag; Verlag Heinrich Vogel; Siedler Verlag; Gabler Verlag und Friedrich Vieweg Verlag; Bantam Doubleday Dell Publishing Group (U.S.A., U.K., Australia, New Zealand); Plaza y Janes Editores, (Spain, Columbia) Mohndruck Graphische Betriebe; Bertelsmann Distribution; Belser Offset Druck; Elsnerdruck; maul-belser; Graphischer Grossbetrieb Pössneck GmbH; Druck- und Verlagsanstalt (Austria); Bertelsmann Printing & Manufacturing Corp. (BPMC) (U.S.A.); Brown Printing Co. (U.S.A.); Prisma Presse (France); Eurohueco (Spain); Printer Industria Grafica (Spain); Nuovo Istituto Italiano d'Arti Grafiche; Cartiere del Garda (France); Arista Records (U.S.A.); BMG Music (U.S.A.); BMG Ariola; BMG Victor (Japan); Sonopress; Telemedia Antenne Bayern; Canal plus; FPS Funk-Programm-Service; RTL plus Deutschland; stern-tv; Ufa Filmproduktion; Universum Film Werner Mietzner; Bertelsmann Fachzeitschriften; Druck- und Verlagshaus Gruner + Jahr; Berliner Verlag; Ärzte Zeitung; MMV Medizin Verlag.

Further Reading: Bavendamm, Dirk, ed., *150 Jahre Bertelsmann: Die Gründer und ihre Zeit*, Gütersloh, 1984; Bavendamm, Dirk, *1835–1985: 150 Jahre Bertelsmann; Die Geschichte des Verlagsunternehmens in Texten, Bildern und Dokumenten*, Gütersloh, 1985; Bavendamm, Dirk, *Bertelsmann, Mohn, Seippel: Drei Familien—ein Unternehmen*, Munich, 1986; Fisher, Andrew, "Bertelsmann: going for the bigger steps in the US," *Financial Times*, July 6, 1987; Russmann, Karl Heinrich, "Bertelsmann: Manhattan Transfer," *manager magazin*, November 1987; Manasian, David, "Bertelsmann's stairway to stardom," *International Management*, November 1987; "Bertelsmann: The media company that makes Murdoch's empire look small," *The Economist*, April 9, 1988; Morais, Richard C., "The latest U.S. media giant isn't even American," *Forbes*, April 25, 1988; Bavendamm, Dirk, *Lebensbilder Mark Wössner*, Rheda-Wiedenbrück, 1988; Picaper, Jean-Paul, "Bertelsmann: le géant allemand de l'edition," *Le Figaro*, February 20, 1989.

—Dirk Bavendamm
Translated from the German by Philippe A. Barbour

COX ENTERPRISES, INC.

1400 Lake Hearn Drive
Atlanta, Georgia 30319
U.S.A.
(404) 843-5000
Fax: (404) 843-5142

Private Company
Incorporated: 1968
Employees: 30,000
Sales: $2.09 billion

Cox Enterprises, Inc. is a diversified media company. It publishes 17 daily newspapers, 10 weeklies, and one monthly magazine, and operates 21 radio and television stations and 24 cable television systems. It is the largest U.S. operator of automobile auctions, with 46 auction facilities in 1991. Starting in the late 1980s Cox ventured into home video rental and direct mail and point-of-purchase advertising. As of 1990 it was the 14th-largest media company and the 69th-largest privately held company in the United States. Cox Enterprises was not incorporated until 1968; before that it was an assortment of primarily newpaper businesses owned by the Cox family. In 1964 Cox Broadcasting Corporation had been established as a public company to operate the Cox family's broadcasting and cable businesses.

In 1898 James M. Cox bought *The Dayton Evening News*—now the *Dayton Daily News*—in Dayton, Ohio, for $26,000 that he had raised from several friends. Cox, a native of rural Ohio, had been a schoolteacher, a reporter for *The Middletown Signal* in Middletown, Ohio, and for *The Cincinnati Enquirer,* in Cincinnati, Ohio, and a Washington, D.C.-based secretary to Ohio congressman Paul J. Sorg. Cox quickly became an influential newspaper publisher; in 1905 he bought the *Springfield Press-Republic,* also in Ohio, changed its name to the *Springfield Daily News,* and established a newspaper chain, which he called the News League of Ohio. He also entered politics; he represented Ohio's third district in Congress from 1909 to 1913 and was elected governor of Ohio in 1913. Cox was defeated when he ran for re-election in 1915, but won in 1917 and 1919, making him the state's first three-term governor. In 1920 he was the Democratic Party's presidential candidate, with future-president Franklin D. Roosevelt as his running mate. He lost the election to Warren G. Harding.

After the defeat and his completion of his gubernatorial term in 1921, Cox returned to public life only once, when Roose-

velt, by then president, appointed him a delegate to the 1933 World Monetary and Economic Conference in London. Instead, Cox focused on his media business. In 1923 he acquired the *Miami Metropolis,* in Florida, changing its name to the *Miami Daily News,* and the *Canton News,* in Canton, Ohio. In 1930 he sold the Canton paper and bought the *Springfield Sun,* in Ohio. He entered broadcasting in 1934, establishing Dayton's first radio station, WHIO.

In 1939 Cox acquired *The Atlanta Journal,* in Georgia, and its AM radio station, WSB. The newspaper had been founded in 1883 and had gone through several owners; the radio station, which began broadcasting in 1922, was the South's first. As with other newspapers he had acquired, Cox wished for the Atlanta paper to maintain its own style and personality.

In 1948 Cox entered the new medium of television with WSB-[TV] in Atlanta; the company also set up WSB-[FM] as a companion to the original AM radio station. In 1949 the company acquired a second Dayton, Ohio, newspaper, *The Journal Herald,* and put WHIO-[TV] and WHIO-[FM] radio on the air in that city. In 1950 Cox acquired *The Atlanta Constitution. The Atlanta Journal* and *The Atlanta Constitution* began a combined Sunday edition while publishing separately during the week, an arrangement that continues.

James Cox died in 1957 at age 87. His son, James M. Cox Jr., succeeded him as the leader of the family businesses and oversaw continued expansion. The family acquired AM and FM radio stations and a television station, all operating under the call letters WSOC, in Charlotte, North Carolina, in 1959.

The Coxes were among the first major broadcasters to enter cable television, acquiring a cable system in Lewistown, Pennsylvania, in 1962. In 1963 they acquired KTVU-[TV] in the San Francisco–Oakland, California, area and radio stations WIOD-[AM] and WAIA-[FM] in Miami. In 1964 the Cox family established Cox Broadcasting Corporation to run the radio and television operations. The broadcasting concern had its shares publicly traded on the New York Stock Exchange, but the family retained substantial ownership. The same year, broadcasting and cable operations expanded with the purchase of WPXI-[TV] in Pittsburgh, Pennsylvania, and cable systems in Washington, Oregon, and California.

In 1966 Cox Broadcasting added a business- and technical-publishing division; in 1967 it went into motion-picture production. Its Bing Crosby Productions unit eventually made such movies as *Ben, Walking Tall,* and *The Reincarnation of Peter Proud.* In 1968 all the various Cox-owned newspapers were organized into Cox Enterprises, Inc., which remained a private company. The same year, Cox Broadcasting set up Cox Cable Communications Inc. as a publicly traded, partially owned subsidiary.

Another 1968 event was the company's entry into the automobile-auction business, with the broadcasting group's purchase of auction facilities in Manheim, Pennsylvania; Bordentown, New Jersey; and Fredericksburg, Virginia. New and used car dealers traditionally have used auto auctions to buy and sell from each other. During the 1980s banks with repossessed cars, car rental agencies, and fleet operators began to use auction facilities for sales.

In 1969 the newspaper group added three Florida daily papers: the *Palm Beach Daily News, The Palm Beach Evening Times,* and *The Palm Beach Post.* The broadcasting group's operations expanded that year with the purchase of Tele-Systems, a California cable operation, and of auto auctions in Kansas City, Missouri, and Lakeland, Florida. An auction facility in High Point, North Carolina, was added in 1970; a cable system in Santa Barbara, California, and an auto auction in Pittsburgh came on in 1971.

The following year brought the acquisition of TeleRep, a national television-advertising-sales representation firm, which sells time on client stations to national advertisers. The firm eventually added a programming arm, Television Program Enterprises, to produce and sell syndicated programming, including "Entertainment Tonight," "Star Search," and "Lifestyles of the Rich and Famous." An auto auction facility in Milwaukee, Wisconsin, also came into the company lineup in 1972.

The presidential election of 1972 brought a break in James Cox Jr.'s association with the Democratic Party. Cox, who had attended the 1912 Democratic convention with his father, decided in 1972 to endorse President Richard M. Nixon for reelection over Senator George McGovern, and ordered all Cox Enterprises newspapers to do the same—the only time Cox ever became involved in the newspapers' editorial policies. Two editors resigned as a result. Eventually, the family allied itself with the Democrats again; Anne Cox Chambers, one of James Cox Jr.'s two sisters, was an early supporter of Georgia governor Jimmy Carter and served as ambassador to Belgium when Carter became president. In the mid-1970s the Coxes's Atlanta newspapers switched to a pro-Carter from an anti-Carter stance, but management said the switch was not related to Chambers's support of Carter.

Also in 1972, Cox Cable announced plans to merge with American Television and Communications Corporation, but the Justice Department sued to block the deal. The suit led the companies to call off the transaction early in 1973; both contended the merger would not violate federal antitrust law, but noted the litigation could delay the deal by several months. Later in 1973, Cox Cable set a merger with LVO Cable Inc., but subsequently called it off because of market conditions. Another major event of 1973 was Cox Broadcasting's purchase of KFI-[AM], Los Angeles.

James Cox Jr. died in 1974 at the age of 71. His sister Barbara Cox Anthony's husband, Garner Anthony, took over the primary direction of the family companies, and the expansion continued.

Cox Broadcasting added an auto auction in Orlando, Florida, in 1974, and one in Fresno, California, in 1975. Also in 1975, it bought a cable television system in Myrtle Beach, South Carolina. Cox Enterprises acquired four Texas newspapers in 1976—the *Austin American-Statesman,* the *Waco Tribune-Herald,* the *Port Arthur News,* and the *Lufkin Daily News.* The same year, Cox Broadcasting added KOST-[FM], Los Angeles, and acquired a cable system in Pensacola, Florida. It also acquired an auto-auction facility in Anaheim, California, and built one in Atlanta.

In 1977 the Cox Cable subsidiary was merged back into Cox Broadcasting; over the next three years, the broadcasting group added 26 cable television franchises, including one in Omaha, Nebraska, and another in New Orleans, Louisiana. Also in 1977, the broadcasting operation acquired WLIF-[FM], Baltimore, Maryland, and Cox Enterprises bought the *Mesa Tribune* in Arizona.

The broadcasting company acquired WZGO-[FM] in Philadelphia, Pennsylvania, in 1979; the newspaper group acquired Texas's *Longview Morning Journal* and *The Longview Daily News* in 1978 and *The Daily Sentinel,* of Grand Junction, Colorado, in 1979. Also in 1979, Cox Broadcasting discontinued motion-picture production, but continued to market its inventory, in favor of concentrating on its broadcasting and cable television businesses.

The major event of 1979, however, was the Cox family's negotiation of a sale of Cox Broadcasting to General Electric Company (GE), in what would have been the biggest broadcasting merger in history. The Coxes wanted to sell the broadcast concern apparently because they feared the Federal Communications Commission (FCC) eventually would force a break-up of their newspaper and broadcast operations in the cities where they had both—Atlanta, Dayton, and Miami. GE's extensive broadcast holdings, however, resulted in a barrage of complaints to the FCC about concentration of ownership; the delays resulting from these complaints delayed the sale and paved the way for price renegotiations, which led to the deal's collapse early in 1980. The Coxes were asking $637 million; GE's final offer was $570 million.

Both Cox companies went through more changes and expansion in the early 1980s. WSB-[TV] changed its network affiliation to ABC in 1980, after having been an NBC affiliate for more than 30 years. Cox Enterprises bought the *Tempe Daily News* in Arizona in 1980; Cox Broadcasting bought a Boston auto auction in 1981, and KDNL-[TV], St. Louis, Missouri, in 1982.

The broadcasting concern sold its business- and technical-publishing arm to Hearst Corporation in 1980; the aim, as with the end of film production, was to concentrate on the broadcasting and cable businesses. The auto auctions, although unrelated to these businesses, were retained because of their growth and profitability.

In 1982 Cox Broadcasting changed its name to Cox Communications, Inc. to better reflect its positions in both broadcasting and cable. The year 1983 was an acquisitive one. Cox Communications acquired auto auctions in Phoenix, Arizona, and in Toronto, Ontario, and a cable franchise in Staten Island, New York. The company also agreed to swap WLIF-[FM] in Baltimore for a Chicago FM station, WXFM, whose call letters subsequently were changed to WCKG; to buy a Detroit television station, WKBD, after divesting itself of a cable system in St. Clair Shores, Michigan; and to buy 90% of CyberTel, a radio common carrier system in St. Louis. These transactions were completed the following year. Also in 1983, Cox Enterprises bought the *Chandler Arizonan,* followed by the acquisition of another Arizona newspaper, *The Yuma Daily Sun,* in 1984. Cox Communications bought another auto auction, in Houston, Texas, in 1984.

In 1985 Cox Enterprises purchased Cox Communications for $75 a share. Cox Enterprises had owned or controlled 40.2% of the communications company's 28.2 million outstanding shares. The combined corporation became the nation's 13th-largest media company; before the merger, Cox Communications ranked 19th and Cox Enterprises 21st.

Other 1985 events were the acquisition of a Texas newspaper, *The Orange Leader,* and an Orlando, Florida, TV station, WFTV; and a swap of a cable television system in Avon Park, Florida, for one owned by Storer Communications in Fortuna, California. In 1987 Cox Enterprises sold its Philadelphia radio station to Malrite Communications Group and sold its Datext unit to Lotus Development Corporation. It had established Datext, which packaged financial information on compact discs, in 1984. It also sold CyberTel to a St. Louis investor.

At the end of 1987 the company had another change in top leadership, as Garner Anthony stepped down from the post of chairman and chief executive officer of Cox Enterprises and was succeeded by his stepson, James C. Kennedy. In 1991, sisters Barbara Cox Anthony and Anne Cox Chambers remained active in the company, chairing the Dayton and Atlanta newspapers, respectively.

By 1988 Cox Enterprises's *Miami News,* like many afternoon newspapers, was suffering declining readership and advertising. Cox sought a buyer for the paper; there were discussions with a group of Chicago investors. A sale, however, could not be worked out, and Cox closed the paper at year-end. In 1989 Cox sold its St. Louis TV station to Better Communications, but expanded in other areas. It acquired an equity stake in Blockbuster Entertainment Corporation and became a franchisee of Blockbuster Video stores. Other acquisitions were Trader Publications, a publisher of advertising-only magazines; The Clipper, Inc., a publisher of coupon magazines; The Stuffit Company, a direct mailer of coupons and custom mailings; Main Street Advertising USA, a direct mail advertising company; Cox In-Store Advertising, formerly Buckler Broadcast Group, a point-of-purchase advertising business; and an interest in IP Services, Inc., a software company. It also entered into a joint venture with Picture Classified Network (PCN) to expand coverage and distribution of PCN's Gold Book automobile price guide.

Cox sold two of its Texas newspapers, the *Port Arthur News* and *Orange Leader,* to American Publishing Company in 1990; Cox officials said they wanted to concentrate on the company's other Texas papers. The same year, Cox acquired two radio stations, WSUN-[AM] of Tampa, Florida, and KKWM-[FM], now KLRX-[FM] of Dallas.

In March 1991 the Justice Department sued Cox Enterprises for $3.67 million for failing, in 1986, to seek federal approval before buying a $101 million stake in Knight-Ridder, another communications company. The Justice Department asserted that Cox violated a law requiring individuals and groups to seek federal approval before buying large amounts of stock in another company. A lawyer for Cox Enterprises stated that Cox believed its purchase was not subject to the law because the shares were bought for investment purposes. Also in March, GE auto auctions combined with Cox's Manheim auctions, adding 20 auctions to Manheim's 26; the venture also includes Ford Motor Credit Company.

In April 1991 Trader Publications was merged with Landmark Target Media of Norfolk, Virginia, and Cox held 50% of the resulting company. In May the company announced it would sell its Blockbuster stores.

Principal Subsidiaries: Trader Publications, Inc.; Stuffit Company; The Clipper, Inc.; Palm Beach Newspapers, Inc.; Cox Arizona Publications, Inc.; Cox Home Video, Inc.; TeleRep, Inc.; Southeast Paper Manufacturing Company (33.3%); Hualalai Land Corporation; Nine Bar Ranch Texas, Inc.; Clarendon Farms, Inc.

Further Reading: Cox, James M., *Journey Through My Years,* New York, Simon & Schuster, 1946; Harrigan, Susan, "Powerful Clan: The Coxes of Atlanta Rule a Media Empire with Quiet Authority," *The Wall Street Journal,* September 26, 1980.

—Trudy Ring

Dai Nippon Printing Co., Ltd.

DAI NIPPON PRINTING CO., LTD.

1-1, Ichigaya Kagacho 1-chome
Skinjuku-ku, Tokyo 162-01
Japan
(03) 3266-2111
Fax: (03) 3266-2129

Public Company
Incorporated: 1876 as Shūeisha
Employees: 11,926
Sales: ¥956.70 billion (US$7.04 billion)
Stock Exchanges: Tokyo Osaka Nagoya Luxembourg
    Amsterdam

Dai Nippon was Japan's first modern printing company and is now the largest printing company in the world. Until World War II its only activity was the printing of publications. It now also engages in commercial printing, packaging, decorative interiors, electronics, and business forms. Dai Nippon is an industry leader in high-tech areas such as precision parts, computerized printing, and color filters for laptop computer displays.

Dai Nippon was founded as Shūeisha in Tokyo in 1876. Japan's modernization process was just beginning. As it took hold, more newspapers and documents were printed and Shūeisha grew. As the only modern Japanese printing firm at the time it was well positioned to get this business. It printed virtually all the metropolitan newspapers at the time, its only competition being tiny printing houses using wood blocks. Shūeisha initially printed movable type by hand, but in 1884 the company updated its equipment, installing a steam motor to run its presses, thus becoming the first private-industry user of steam power in Japan. From then on new techniques and improved equipment were added constantly as Japan's papermaking and publishing industries grew. In 1874 Japan manufactured only 35,000 pounds of paper. In 1884 it manufactured 5.3 million pounds, and in 1894 36 million pounds. Most of that paper was used for printing, much of which was done by Shūeisha, at least until 1900 when its chief rival, Toppan Printing, was formed.

Many printing innovations were imported from the West. The Japanese government, which coordinated the modernization drive imported foreign printing specialists to train Japanese printers. By 1887 gas and electric printing presses were in use. The rotary press appeared in 1889 for newspaper printing, and in 1899 for magazines. Research on the uses of photo copperplates was begun in 1887, and these plates were used for newspaper printing by 1903. In 1912 offset and photogravure printing equipment were imported from the West.

The Sino-Japanese War of 1894 created an increase in printing orders and demand for paper as more newspapers were read and more documents needed. A slump in printing and papermaking followed the end of the war in 1901, but in 1904 the outbreak of the Russo-Japanese War increased the demand for newspapers and magazines. Japan defeated China and Russia. A period of military and economic expansion began, assisted by a modern currency system, established during the 1880s. As the economy grew, so did the demand for printing.

Printing boomed during World War I. By 1927 printing and publishing were approaching Western scales; nearly 20,000 new book titles and 40 million magazines were published that year. In 1935 the company changed its name to Dai Nippon Printing Co., Ltd.

During the 1930s Japan was ruled by an increasingly repressive military dictatorship that suppressed publishers and writers and banned books, making printers cautious about what they printed. Publishing, and thus printing, did not flourish in such an atmosphere. Paper shortages and the devastation of the Japanese economy during World War II further hurt the printing industry. The industry recovered fairly quickly after the war, however, growing rapidly during the 1960s and 1970s. The most important printing during the boom was encyclopedias and the complete works of authors. Periodical printing was also important. Dai Nippon was growing at about 6% a year by 1966.

After the war Dai Nippon expanded from printing, which accounted for all of its prewar business—into industrial areas, such as packaging, construction materials, and electronic precision devices. The expanded product range let the company expand at times when there was no growth in publications. The company invested heavily in research, setting up its own research plants, before any other Japanese printing company, in Tokyo. By 1991 Dai Nippon had eight research plants in Japan and one overseas. It soon claimed that it could print on anything but water and air.

As Japanese industry began its slow but steady postwar expansion, Dai Nippon took advantage of opportunities in new sectors of the economy. For example, Dai Nippon perfected a technology to print imitation woodgrain on the dashboards of cars. Dashboards and other curved surfaces are difficult to print on, but Dai Nippon printed the grains on a water-soluble film, then immersed the dashboard and film together, causing the woodgrain to transfer to the dashboard. When the Japanese auto industry began exporting heavily, orders for Dai Nippon's printed dashboards grew. Dai Nippon also moved into electronics and television, producing shadow masks for color television sets using photoprocess and etching technologies, then moving into color filters for liquid crystal display. The televised wedding of Japan's crown prince in 1959 led to a boom in color television sales in Japan and more business for Dai Nippon. Several of Japan's large publishing houses launched new, successful weeklies in 1959, bringing further business to Dai Nippon. The 1964 Tokyo Olympic Games gave the printing industry a boost.

At the same time, U.S. publishers were beginning to use Japanese printing companies because their products cost less than those of U.S. printers. In 1964 the company built a plant in Hong Kong, primarily to print for U.S. publishers, who paid only half what it cost them to print in the United States. Dai Nippon was looking for less expensive labor and equipped the Hong Kong plant with modern European presses. The plant initially confined itself to offset printing, specializing in color work. It established an apprenticeship program that sent young Chinese technicians to Japan for training. This plant, with that of rival Toppan opened in 1962, was the kernel around which the Hong Kong printing industry grew. By the late 1980s the Hong Kong printing industry rivaled that of Japan.

In 1968 Dai Nippon continued overseas expansion, opening offices in New York and Düsseldorf to promote its printing and binding. Dai Nippon was cautious, however, about expanding into foreign markets too rapidly because company officials believed that printing was closely related to local and community needs. Still, as business continued to expand steadily during the 1970s and 1980s, Dai Nippon launched joint ventures that included printing plants in Singapore and Jakarta, and opened offices that did not include plants in Sydney, London, Chicago, San Francisco, Los Angeles, and in Santa Clara, California.

The 1970s brought advances in rotary offset printing, particularly in color. Soon after, U.S. publishers began giving more four-color work to Japanese printers, including Dai Nippon, an industry leader in color printing. The decade also brought computerized typesetting, which changed the Japanese printing industry, making it far more efficient. In 1972 Dai Nippon established P.T. Dai Nippon Printing Indonesia, mainly to produce food packaging and decorative cartons for the Indonesian market. By the 1980s the Indonesian firm also exported to Hong Kong, Singapore, and other areas. Japanese food companies operating overseas also used its services.

By the 1980s the company had diversified into so many kinds of printing and other businesses, that it built new, more specialized research institutes to replace the general ones it had built immediately after the war. Because Dai Nippon manufactured so much food packaging, it used food sanitation experts to help research the best materials for food preservation, and often built the machinery used for packing food. The company, which put about 1% of sales into research and development, often developed technologies that it was not at first certain would apply to printing. These technologies, however, were often applied to the printing of non-paper materials. The non-paper sector of the printing industry grew greatly during the 1980s, increasing 20.5% in 1986 alone.

In 1980 Japanese-language word processors came into use, making electronic publishing feasible in Japan. As the 1980s progressed, computers and word-processing programs became popular and less expensive, and by the end of the decade even small businesses could afford a laser printer. Businesses with laser printers had less need for commercial printers, since they could now do small, simple jobs themselves. Because these developments affected its traditional business niche, it was a logical step for Dai Nippon—and competitors like Toppan—to move into information processing. Dai Nippon believed that printing was the first information processing industry, and printing companies therefore should have a leading role in the computer age.

This view was shared by many of Dai Nippon's competitors and by the Paper and Printing Committee of the Industrial Structural Council, an advisory organ of Japan's Ministry of International Trade and Industry. In 1988 the Paper and Printing Committee released a report predicting a decline in demand for conventional printing, and urging the printing industry to use its knowledge of information processing to contribute to an information-oriented society. The shipment value of printed matter in Japan had reached ¥6.2 trillion in 1986, and the committee predicted that it would continue to grow at an annual rate of 6.5%, reaching ¥15 trillion by the year 2000. The committee said printing firms should aim to develop new high-tech printing techniques and information processing.

Dai Nippon had been concentrating on information-related technologies throughout the 1980s. By 1985 the company had developed the technology to manufacture a laser card the size of a credit card to hold information. The card was only 0.76 millimeters thick, used a photosensitive material to read information. While suitable for mass production, there were problems recording information on the card. In 1985 the company also developed a computerized printing transfer technology for textiles and a very large screen for projected television, and introduced a credit-card sized calculator developed with Casio Computer.

In 1986 Dai Nippon developed a compact-disc–based telephone directory system, jointly developed a digital color printer system with JVC, and developed a special aluminum foil top for paper cartons. In 1987 Dai Nippon announced several more developments in information technology. It jointly developed a Japanese-language word processor with a spelling-check facility, introduced a foldable magnetic identification card made of a polyester resin sheet, and signed an agreement to supply American Bank Note with holographic technology and services. It also developed a smart card with 128 kilobit storage capacity and developed the technology to produce urinalysis paper at 20% lower than the usual cost. In 1988 Du Pont agreed to sell Dai Nippon's high-precision color printers and transfer materials in the United States, and Dai Nippon revealed that it was investing ¥70 billion a year in research and development.

In 1989 Dai Nippon announced the development of Hi-Vision Static Pictures, a method of converting data into a form used by high-definition television. The latter was expected to be the next generation of television sets and an area of tremendous growth during the 1990s. The company also developed sophisticated printing technologies used for high-quality reproductions that were equal to those of western printing companies. Dai Nippon printed art books in the United States with high-quality color plates using computer technology. Profits for 1989 were US$222 million on sales of US$6.4 million.

At the end of 1990, Dai Nippon had 20 regional offices in Japan, with 51 sales offices and 21 printing plants, and 11 overseas offices and 5 overseas plants. Sales and profits increased for the 41st year in a row, although the company suffered from the nationwide labor shortage and struggled to keep up with the rapid transition to an information-oriented society. To make that transition, the company opened an information-media supplies division in 1990 and founded the Information Media Supplies Research Laboratory in Saitama, Japan. One of the division's most important products, is thermal transfer ribbon, used in word processors, fax machines, and bar-code printers; and another is dye sublimation transfer ribbon, which can print images of almost photographic quality from computer graphics with various printers.

The company also strengthened its production base, investing US$486 million to expand its microproducts plant, which constructed audiovisual systems and electronic components, and its business-forms plant, which manufactures various forms for office-automation systems and cards. In the same year, Dai Nippon broke ground for a new research and production center, and bought land in Tokyo and Osaka where it planned to build highly automated manufacturing plants.

Dai Nippon also concentrated on overseas operations in 1990, marketing photomasks through a partnership with Du Pont Photomask. It increased its share in Tien Wah Press—the largest printing company in Singapore, and an important distribution center for southeast Asia—from 31% to 85%. This made Singapore Dai Nippon's largest overseas printing base. The company moved into the global market for projected-television screens, beginning production in Japan and at the Denmark plant of a new subsidiary, DNP DENMARK. The subsidiary soon bought another Danish company, Scan Screen.

Continuing its progress in the information sector, Dai Nippon began to use satellites to communicate data from its Tokyo headquarters and to distribute its business-oriented television programs, which were part of its work in audiovisual systems. It established the Multimedia Communications Center to work on high-definition television, videodisks, and read-only-memory compact discs, which are expected to become an important publishing format. The company announced breakthroughs in holograms, computer graphics, and medical imaging. It also began a joint venture in smart cards, called Spom Japan, with France's Bull. The company started mass production of a smart card with one of the world's highest memory levels, aimed mainly at the Japanese market.

As electronic media grew, traditional printing slowed. Dai Nippon sought business in niche-market magazine printing. Because of growth in advertising, business forms, and precise electronic devices, book and magazine printing made up an ever-smaller portion of the company's printing sales during the 1980s. Printing Japanese magazines is good business for printers because many magazines use several kinds of paper and printing techniques in a single issue. Books for Europe and the United States also suffered from the appreciation of the yen, though this decline was partly offset by strong magazine sales in Australia and New Zealand. By 1990, books and magazines accounted for 18% of printing sales, commercial printing for 52%, and packaging and special printing for 30%.

The growth of commercial printing during the late 1980s was fueled by the expanding Japanese economy and its need for business forms, advertising, and credit cards. With more and more Japanese traveling, travel brochures became important. The Japanese trend for household electronics, often containing integrated circuits and other electronic components printed by Dai Nippon, also increased commercial sales. Packaging sales were hampered by changes in the Japanese lifestyle, particularly the trend toward eating out. The demand for packaged daily necessities was at a near-saturation level. Dai Nippon manufactured metal products such as mirror-finished sheets for appliances during the 1980s. The early 1990s found Dai Nippon continuing to expand into new technologies, while maintaining a sizable presence in its traditional printing market.

Principal Subsidiaries: Dai Nippon Printing Co. (Hong Kong) Ltd.; Dai Nippon Printing Co., (Singapore) Ltd.; Tien Wah Press (Pte.) Ltd. (Singapore); P.T. Dai Nippon Printing Indonesia; Dai Nippon Printing Co. (Australia) Pty. Ltd; DNP (AMERICA) INC. (U.S.A.); Dai Nippon Printing (Europa) GmbH (Germany); Spom Japan Co. Ltd.; DNP DENMARK A/S.

Further Reading: Frank, Jerome P., "Asia Printers Gearing Up for Move into U.S.," *Publishers Weekly,* June 29, 1984; Okawa, Kenji, "Use of Printing Paper Expands," *Business JAPAN,* March 1989.

—Scott M. Lewis

DOW JONES & COMPANY, INC.

World Financial Center
200 Liberty Street
New York, New York 10281
U.S.A.
(212) 416-2000

Public Company
Incorporated: 1930
Employees: 9,500
Sales: $1.72 billion

Dow Jones & Company, Inc. is best known for publishing *The Wall Street Journal* in its U.S., Asian, and European versions, and for the worldwide stock market intelligence it provides. Like much of the business-journalism industry, Dow Jones is diversifying from print into on-line desktop newspapers and information retrieval. Dow Jones is still the market leader, despite the stagnant circulation of the venerable *Journal*. The company's three main product divisions are information services, business publications, and community newspapers. While business information and journalism have been the core of Dow Jones in the past, electronic publishing that packages a range of financial information services, and community newspaper segments are its future.

The popular reputation of Dow Jones & Company as one of the leading publishers of business news, information services, and community newspapers came nearly a generation after the founding fathers, Charles Henry Dow and Edward Jones, came to New York City from Rhode Island, in 1879, with a liking for journalism and an ear for financial gossip. In their own day, the two men were not especially well known outside trade circles. Dow had worked for a number of newspapers before moving to New York City, where he teamed up with Edward Jones and Charles Bergstresser to found Dow, Jones & Company in 1882. Dow became a member of the New York Stock Exchange in 1885, formulating what would be called the Dow theory of stock market movements. He launched *The Wall Street Journal* in the summer of 1889 with Jones, a fellow journalist. Knowledge of the very earliest years of the company is sketchy.

Dow is said to have traded only infrequently on the exchange, and to have taken his seat as a favor to a friend in immigration difficulties. Yet Dow's membership put him in a good position to observe and to overhear the tips that inspired him to found a partnership that would become a billion-dollar

business-information company. Dow apparently wrote most of the copy for the early issues of *The Journal*, working only part time at the newspaper, while Edward Jones edited the news-bulletin service and acted as managing editor. Reporters Thomas Woodlock and Charles M. Bergstresser covered Wall Street. Many of Dow's early articles were editorials, and information gleaned by Jones in the hotel bars formed the core of the news service.

Dow and Jones joined in a news-exchange agreement with Clarence Barron, the proprietor of the Boston News Bureau. Barron had begun to publish a financial newspaper in Boston two years before *The Wall Street Journal* was founded and the two offices, *The Journal's* in New York and *Barron's* in Boston, reinforced one another's coverage, with the aggressive Barron expanding into Philadelphia with his *Financial Journal* in 1896.

Edward Jones left *The Journal* in January 1899. The family relationship between Dow and his cousin by marriage, Charles Bergstresser, who was also a partner in the firm, may have precipitated Jones's departure. Jones continued to live a good life on Wall Street, and his eulogy of Dow three years later was respectful and even loving, calling his former partner a "tower of strength" and one of "the most honest exponents" of financial journalism.

In 1900 the stockholders of Dow Jones—members of the Dow and Bergstresser families and a few company employees—received $7,500 each in addition to $1.20 a share in annual dividends. In March 1902 Clarence Barron purchased Dow, Jones & Company for $130,000, including the news agencies in Boston and New York and *The Wall Street Journal*. Dow and Bergstresser resigned their directorships. There was no public announcement, only the appearance of names for the first time on *The Journal's* masthead. Although Barron had bought the company, he listed Dow, Bergstresser, Woodlock, and J.W. Barney, not himself. In December of the same year, Charles Dow died of a heart attack at age 51 in his Brooklyn home.

In 1905 Charles Otis was elected president, and F.A. Russell was named to the board of directors. Both Jessie Barron, Barron's wife, and Sereno Pratt were re-elected directors of the company, and John Lane and Hugh Bancroft were added to the board.

Bancroft and the Barrons's daughter Jane married in 1907, and when Clarence Barron became ill, his son-in-law assumed increasing responsibilities in the New York offices. By 1911 the elder Barron's health had improved, but newspaper circulation, advertising, and profits were down, which precipitated a bitter quarrel between Barron and Charles Otis. Barron also fought with Bancroft, drove out president Otis and director Sereno Pratt, and on March 12, 1912, reinstated himself in their places.

When Clarence Barron stormed into the editorial office of *The Journal* in March 1912 following his election to the presidency, the staff was terrified. Though lore has it that Barron harassed some employees into quitting, he is said to never have fired a man. A flamboyant, eccentric, and corpulent figure, Barron's genius for journalism, according to his contemporaries, along with his tough-mindedness drove the ensuing prosperity of the publication.

In 1921 Barron hired Kenneth Craven (Casey) Hogate, a second-generation newspaperman. Later in 1921, Clarence

Barron died, leaving an estate of $1.5 million to his daughter Jane Bancroft, who in 1918 at her mother's death had inherited the majority shares. Hugh Bancroft was elected president, Casey Hogate, vice president. Bancroft and Hogate managed a steadily prospering company until the stock market crash of 1929, when the paper began to sustain severe losses in circulation and advertising.

By 1932 the company had dropped the comma in its name. Despite the Great Depression, on June 27, 1932, Dow Jones & Company published an 80-page edition of the paper, celebrating its 50th anniversary and its new building on Broad Street. Although Hugh Bancroft's name continued to be listed as president, Casey Hogate was chiefly responsible for running the company in the Depression era, as Bancroft's health deteriorated.

In 1938 Richard Whitney, former president of the New York Stock Exchange, whose name was synonymous with the careless profiteering accused of causing the stock market crash, provided *The Journal* with a significant scoop when he telephoned the newsroom and confessed fraud before turning himself in to authorities. In the post-crash years, *Journal* editorials defended the financial community and free enterprise, and supported the formation of the Securities and Exchange Commission and regulatory legislation while condemning Whitney's behavior and Wall Street fraud. Hogate, meanwhile, struggled with a low in circulation in 1938 of 28,000.

With Barney Kilgore as president, and William Kerby and Buren McCormack as directors in the company, Casey Hogate took a risk with *The Journal*, moving from strictly financial reports to include general news as well, in order to revive the paper. Though Hogate fell into ill health, his formula worked, and his policy was carried out by the others. Kilgore, meantime, made the decision to produce the Monday morning paper on Sunday instead of on Saturday so that the news would be fresh.

Throughout the war years *The Journal* became increasingly news-oriented, as political and economic news became inextricably mixed with the fate of the markets. Although at the beginning, the editorials were staunchly anti-war, even isolationist, the editorial policy became supportive in due course. After the armistice, the trend toward news orientation developed during the war years remained with the paper.

On December 21, 1949, Jane Bancroft died in Boston, the last of the original Barron family. Throughout her life, Jane Bancroft had been involved deeply in the growth of the paper, and her last acts had been to create the employee profit-sharing pension plan and to approve the postwar reorganization of Dow Jones.

Bancroft's daughter, Jane Cook, assumed her mother's place on the board, and before the end of 1949 treasurer William Kerby drafted the new Dow Jones management chart: Kilgore was president and chief executive officer. At this time the company portfolio included the Dow Jones News Service, U.S. and Canada; a commodity news service; *The Journal* with editions in New York, in Dallas, Texas, and in San Francisco, California; and *Barron's*, a weekly periodical that continued to struggle with lagging circulation until 1955 when editor Robert Bleiberg turned the situation around. In the 1950s *The Journal*'s layout was modernized, using more two-column heads, including more readers' letters, and introducing cartoons and drawings. In 1953 new equipment was used to set stock and bond quotations, that made it possible eventually to publish simultaneous editions of the newspaper anywhere in the United States with identical news content and typographical quality.

The Journal's long-standing conservative editorial stance was disrupted when it supported the U.S. Supreme Court's decision in *Brown* v. *Board of Education*, the historic civil rights case of 1954. President Kilgore stayed at the helm of *The Journal* through John F. Kennedy's presidency, and the paper's editorial policies continued to take on issues of widespread social consequence. *The Journal* reporters, too, became increasingly well known to political leaders.

Notoriety was good for business; in 1961 circulation came close to 800,000, with total advertising revenues of $47.7 million. The estimated value of Dow Jones stock was $235 million. President Barney Kilgore also continued to be a news-making executive, and was a popular public speaker and lecturer.

Technology moved the paper forward into the information services industry. By the 1960s facsimile pages of newspapers could be transmitted by coaxial cables and microwave transmitters. By the end of 1964 Dow Jones reported news-ticker clients in 676 U.S. cities and 48 of the 50 states. This business provided the company with the highest revenue after *The Journal*. With the advice of professional portfolio managers, the company began to move further into allied industries, first venturing into textbooks with its purchase of Richard D. Irwin Inc. in 1975.

The change of leadership traditionally had been smooth at the company helm, and so it was when Barney Kilgore handed over the reins to William Kerby in March 1966. Under the new management, Vermont Royster directed editorial policy and executive editor Warren Phillips headed news operations. Within two years the newspaper operation produced 94% of Dow Jones's profits and it reached 1.5 million readers by 1978, when Warren Phillips became chairman, president, and chief executive. Dow Jones's operation of the *National Observer* never took off, and it ceased publication in 1977, when losses totaled $16.2 million after 15 years of existence. Its purchase of *Book Digest* magazine proved to be disappointing. In 1980 the company was reorganized along product lines into seven divisions under Phillips. Since reorganized, the company's three main product divisions were, in the early 1990s information services, business publications, and community newspapers. While the main product lines had remained steady for nearly a century, revenue potential favored electronic publishing and information services, away from the slow-growth textbook and community-newspaper segments.

After being the company's most lucrative business for a century *The Journal* began to lose strength during the late 1980s. Electronic publishing had become Dow Jones's primary growth sector as *The Journal* faced a slump, with circulation down to 1.95 million in 1989 from its 1983 high of 2.11 million, a decrease of 7.5%. In March 1989 advertising revenues were down for the 19th straight month. For the first quarter of 1989, operating income of the business publications fell 33% and profits were down 13% in the 23-community newspaper chain. The company had been through difficult times before, but the volatility of the world political and financial scene necessarily was changing the financial-journalism business, while the changing marketplace placed increasing emphasis on user-friendly, computerized, fast news delivery. Chief executive officer Phillips, observers said, would need to bring *The Journal* in line with the real-time requirements of fast-breaking financial news.

The October 1987 stock market crash had a negative impact on *The Journal*'s financial-advertisement revenue. Phillips countered flat revenues by revamping the look of *The Journal*, expanding to three sections from two. Phillips retired as CEO in January 1991 and as chairman in July 1991. Peter R. Kann, a 25-year veteran of the newspaper appointed publisher of *The Journal* by Phillips and also president and chief operating officer of Dow Jones & Company, became chairman and CEO.

The European and Asian editions of *The Wall Street Journal* report modest growth in circulation, *Barron's* reports steady circulation, and the *Far Eastern Economic Review*, and *National Business Employment Weekly* are holding their own. *American Demographics* reported a 10% growth in revenues and circulation in 1989. Dow Jones also acquired Telerate, the real-time quote service and sold its textbook division, Richard D. Irwin, for $135 million. The start-up of Telerate's foreign exchange trading service accounted for some of Dow Jones's downturn in earnings in 1989 and 1990.

Dow Jones News/Retrieval, a market leader in online databases, was one of several businesses brought together to form the information services group, which grew to 835 employees and $177 million in revenues by 1989. The Information Group had developed an innovative natural language on-line searching system that makes Dow Jones's electronic database more assessible than its closest competitors. The major problem with the electronic publishing business had been executives' reluctance to learn computer access codes in order to gain the information. Dow Jones's system delivers the information to subscribers automatically. The Dow Jones system ranks and weighs articles by the number of times the user's access term occurs, delivering a text search with more specific targeting capability rather than a lengthy list of peripherally related articles.

The focus is still on business news, with delivery of the full text of *Barron's, Business & Financial Weekly, Business Week, Forbes, Fortune,* and *Financial World* and a bank of 150 business publications. Although the primary consumer is intended to be the investor seeking background information before buying or selling stock, there may be a wider research audience. Along with Dow Jones's innovative system, which will drop the common $100 per hour user fee, market leaders face new competitors in the form of regional Bell phone companies. In 1988 a federal court permitted the Bells "gateway" rights, to transmit information, but they are not permitted to write about or add content to the data.

The Dow Jones News Service, called the Broadtape, is the information supplier to brokerages, banks, investment houses, and corporations. The newswire merged its Canadian and U.S. operations to coincide with the U.S.-Canada free-trade agreement. Professional Investor Report was started in 1987, as a companion product to the Broadtape, focusing on daily trading activity, and became profitable in its second full year of operation, with a reported 29% growth in subscribers.

Capital Markets Report, which is offered to Telerate subscribers as an add-on, was started in 1980, and has since expanded to six major world financial centers in 24 countries. The AP-Dow Jones news service provides broad international news to 56 countries, with specialized wires in foreign exchange, petroleum, and gold.

DowVision, launched in 1990, is a customized newswire that merges information from several data bases. DowPhone is a subscription-based telephone information service for investors providing stock quotes, news reports, and investment analysis to subscribers. JournalPhone is a 900-number installation derivative of DowPhone offering business and financial news updates. Dow Jones Voice Information Network is the satellite delivery system that provides customized news and information to about 75 voice service providers.

With multiplicity of news-service products and its acquisition of Telerate, Dow Jones is positioning itself in the global financial market to expand into intercultural data bases. Telerate's foreign exchange operation is the highest-risk, most intensely competitive of such ventures. There are about a dozen other Telerate products, including Sports-Ticker, a sports news service.

Dow Jones & Company is well positioned to retain leadership in its dominant markets. It also retains its position in the slow growth segment of traditional journalism that had established its core business identity from the days of Dow, Jones, and Bergstresser.

Principal Subsidiaries: Telerate, Inc.; Ottaway Newspapers, Inc.

Further Reading: Wendt, Lloyd, *The Wall Street Journal. The story of Dow Jones & the nation's business newspaper*, Chicago, Rand McNally & Company, 1982.

—Claire Badaracco

THE DUN & BRADSTREET CORPORATION

299 Park Avenue
New York, New York 10171
U.S.A.
(212) 593-6800
Fax: (212) 593-4143

Public Company
Incorporated: 1933 as R.G. Dun-Bradstreet Corporation
Employees: 62,900
Sales: $4.82 billion
Stock Exchanges: New York London Tokyo Geneva Zürich Basel

The Dun & Bradstreet Corporation is in the information business. Among its vast array of products are the Yellow Pages, the Moody's manuals for investors, and the Nielsen television ratings. Begun as a credit reporting service a century-and-a-half ago, Dun & Bradstreet is still a leader in that field; it is also the leading marketing and public opinion company in the world, with 25% of the worldwide market. In addition, the company supplies information-dissemination technology, commercial credit reports, analytical risk-assessment services, and small-business pension plans. It publishes business-oriented computer software.

Dun & Bradstreet traces its origin to Lewis Tappan, who left Arthur Tappan & Company, a New York silk trading firm that he ran with his elder brother, in 1841, to found a credit information bureau called the Mercantile Agency. Tappan had long been aware of the need for better credit reporting. As the U.S. republic expanded westward, traders were moving beyond the easy view of the east coast merchants and bankers who kept them supplied and capitalized. Information on the creditworthiness of these far-flung businesses was collected by individual trading houses and banks in a scattershot fashion, and Tappan saw that centralizing the process of collecting information would result in greater efficiency. Accordingly, he took out an advertisement in the *New York Commercial Advertiser* on July 20, 1841, and opened shop 11 days later on the corner of Hanover and Exchange streets in Manhattan.

The Mercantile Agency operated by gathering information through a network of correspondents and selling it to subscribers. The agents were attorneys, cashiers of banks, merchants, and other competent persons—anyone who might have an impartial familiarity with local merchants through business

or civic affairs. Over the years, personages no less than U.S. Presidents Abraham Lincoln, Ulysses S. Grant, Grover Cleveland, and William McKinley, and presidential candidate Wendell Willkie, would serve as agents for the company that Tappan founded.

The Mercantile Agency opened branch offices in Boston in 1843 and Philadelphia in 1845. In 1846 Benjamin Douglass, a young New York businessman with connections in the southern cotton trade, joined the firm. When Lewis Tappan retired in 1849, Douglass and Tappan's brother Arthur ran it as partners until 1854, when the elder Tappan sold out to Douglass. Then, in 1859, Douglass sold out to Robert Graham Dun, who immediately changed the firm's name to R.G. Dun & Company. That year the company published its first reference book of credit information, the *Dun Book*.

As the nation grew and commerce boomed in the decades following the Civil War, Dun had to keep up with it by establishing new branch offices. The firm expanded into the South, west to California, and north into Canada. An office in San Francisco opened in 1869. In 1891 there were 126 Dun branch offices. Robert Dun Douglass, who was Benjamin Douglass's son and Robert Graham Dun's nephew, became general manager of the firm in 1896. After his uncle died in 1900, the company operated as a common-law trust with Douglass in charge as executive trustee. He retired as general manager in 1909 and was succeeded by Archibald Ferguson.

R.G. Dun also began to expand overseas at about this time. The firm opened its first foreign office in London in 1857, and added five more—in Glasgow, Paris, Melbourne, Mexico City, and Hamburg—by the turn of the century. From 1901 to 1928, R.G. Dun opened 41 overseas branches, scattered across Europe, South Africa, and Latin America.

In 1931 R.G. Dun acquired National Credit Office (NCO), a credit reporting service. The firm then reorganized into a holding company called R.G. Dun Corporation, which assumed control of the assets of both NCO and the original R.G. Dun & Company. NCO president and former owner Arthur Dare Whiteside became president of the new entity.

In 1933, at the nadir of the Great Depression, R.G. Dun merged with one of its main competitors, The Bradstreet Company. Since the two companies overlapped each other in many activities and resources, an amalgamation at that time made sense. Bradstreet was founded in Cincinnati, Ohio, in 1849 by John Bradstreet, a lawyer and merchant whose ancestors included Simon Bradstreet, a colonial governor of Massachussetts, and the prominent colonial American poet Ann Bradstreet. A large file of credit information had come into John Bradstreet's possession as he was overseeing the liquidation of an estate, and he decided to enter the same business in which Lewis Tappan had pioneered eight years earlier. In 1855 Bradstreet packed up and moved to New York, where he challenged the Mercantile Agency directly. Two years later, the firm started publishing a semiannual reference book which offered more extensive coverage than the early *Dun Book*.

John Bradstreet died in 1863 and was succeeded by his son Henry, who ran the firm until it incorporated in 1876 under the name The Bradstreet Company. A group headed by Charles F. Clark then ran the company until 1904, when Clark died and was succeeded by Henry Dunn. Dunn retired in 1927 and gave way to Clark's son, Charles M. Clark. The younger Clark was still chief executive when Bradstreet merged with

Dun in 1933. The new company changed its name to R.G. Dun-Bradstreet Corporation, then to Dun & Bradstreet, Inc. in 1939.

Business remained slow for Dun & Bradstreet through the 1930s and during World War II, then picked up again after the war ended. In 1942 the company acquired Credit Clearing House, a credit reporting agency that specialized in the clothing industry. In 1962 Arthur Dare Whiteside retired and was succeeded by J. Wilson Newman, who headed Dun & Bradstreet as president until 1960, and then as chairman and chief executive until 1968. Under Newman, Dun & Bradstreet embarked on a course of expansion and technological improvement. In 1958 the company began operating its own private wire network, which linked 79 of its major offices. This allowed credit information to be handled more expeditiously.

In 1961 Dun & Bradstreet acquired The Reuben H. Donnelley Corporation. Donnelley, best known for publishing the Yellow Pages telephone directories, was founded in Chicago in 1874 and also published trade magazines. The next year, Dun & Bradstreet acquired Official Airline Guides and added it to the Donnelley division. The company also acquired Moody's Investors Service, which provided financial data for investors on publicly-owned corporations through its series of Moody's manuals.

In 1966 Dun & Bradstreet acquired Fantus Company, which specialized in area development surveys. In 1968 it bought book publisher Thomas Y. Crowell. When Newman retired that year, he was succeeded by former University of Delaware president John Perkins, who served as chairman for one year.

In 1971 Dun & Bradstreet acquired Corinthian Broadcasting, which owned five CBS television affiliates and publisher Funk & Wagnalls. In 1973 the company changed its name to The Dun & Bradstreet Companies Inc. It had acquired some 40 businesses since J. Wilson Newman inaugurated this expansion in 1960 and had seen its annual sales rise from $81 million in 1960 to $450 million in 1973. In 1973 The Dun & Bradstreet Corporation was formed to become the parent company of Dun & Bradstreet, Inc.

In 1978 Dun & Bradstreet acquired Technical Publishing, a trade and professional magazine publisher. The next year, it acquired National CSS, an information-processing technology company. In 1983 it diversified into computer software when it acquired McCormack & Dodge, which published systems software for mainframe computers. The next year, it cut back a bit on diversification when it spun off Funk & Wagnalls and sold most of its Corinthian Broadcasting television assets to A.H. Belo. The company however, acquired Datastream, a British business information company, and the market research firm A.C. Nielsen. Nielsen, famous for its television rating service, was founded in Chicago in 1923 by Arthur C. Nielsen Sr. Dun and Bradstreet CEO Harrington Drake was a longtime friend of the Nielsen family, and the two companies had been discussing a merger off and on since 1969.

Dun & Bradstreet sold Official Airline Guides to Propwix, an affiliate of British Maxwell Communications in 1988. In 1990 it announced its intention to sell Datastream. Otherwise the company continued to acquire small businesses, mostly related to its core credit information operations. Dun & Bradstreet continues to grow. If, as the old maxim says, knowledge is power, then Dun & Bradstreet has proven that there is also money to be made in providing the information from which knowledge is formed.

Principal Subsidiaries: A.C. Nielsen Company; American Credit Indemnity Company; D&B Computing Services, Inc.; Donnelley Marketing, Inc.; Dun & Bradstreet, Inc; Dun & Bradstreet International, Ltd.; Dun & Bradstreet Plan Services, Inc.; Dun & Bradstreet Software Holdings, Inc; I.M.S. International, Inc.; Interactive Data Corporation; McCormack & Dodge Corporation; Dun-Donnelley Publishing Corporation; Moody's Investors Service, Inc.; The Reuben H. Donnelley Corporation; Zytron Corporation.

Further Reading: Dun & Bradstreet: The Story of an Idea, New York, Dun and Bradstreet, Inc., 1966; *Dun & Bradstreet: A Chronology of Progress,* [New York], Dun and Bradstreet, Inc., 1974.

—Claire Badaracco and Douglas Sun

THE E.W. SCRIPPS COMPANY

1100 Central Trust Tower
Cincinnati, Ohio 45201
U.S.A.
(513) 977-3000
Fax: (513) 977-3721

Public Company
Incorporated: 1922
Employees: 10,000
Sales: $1.30 billion
Stock Exchange: New York

The E.W. Scripps Company is a diversified media corporation known primarily for its newspapers, which form the ninth-largest newspaper chain, in terms of circulation, in the United States. The company also operates television and radio stations and cable television systems, and licenses cartoon characters. The E.W. Scripps Company was founded by Edward Willis (E.W.) Scripps, who in 1878 began building one of the first newspaper chains in the United States. In 1922 Scripps incorporated his news organizations and established a trust ensuring family control of his newspaper empire for as long as legally possible. The company diversified into radio station operations in 1935, television stations in 1947, and cable television in 1980. Following more than a century of private ownership, the organization made its first public stock offering in 1988 and since then has focused on updating existing newspaper operations while broadening its cable operations to ease dependency on advertising revenue. After the death of E.W. Scripps's four eldest grandchildren the Scripps trust will be terminated and the company's stock divided among 28 great-grandchildren.

Edward Willis Scripps began his newspaper career in the early 1870s while serving an apprenticeship at Michigan's *Detroit News,* under his older half-brother James Scripps. In 1878 after working his way up the ladder in Detroit, the 24-year old E.W. Scripps secured the financial backing of his half-brothers James and George Scripps and his half-sister Ellen Scripps and founded his first newspaper, in Cleveland, Ohio, *The Penny Press.*

From this first paper, started during an intense period of industrial development, E.W. Scripps fashioned a personally controlled chain of low-priced, well-written newspapers to champion the welfare of the growing working class. That chain began to grow in 1883, when E.W. Scripps acquired controlling interest in the Cincinnati, Ohio–based *Penny Post,* later renamed *The Cincinnati Post,* from James Scripps. A business manager, Milton A. McRae, was hired to run the *Post,* and in 1890 he and E.W. Scripps agreed to establish the Scripps-McRae League to manage the Scripps newspapers.

Under a profit-pooling arrangement established by Scripps and McRae, Scripps received two-thirds of the earnings from the league and was allowed to follow his own interests, while McRae received one-third of the profits and was charged with managing the league's newspapers. To expand the league, Scripps and McRae chose growing industrial cities where there was little competition. Then ambitious editors and business managers were hired to start newspapers there. If the paper were successful the editor and manager could earn up to 49% of the stock.

This formula was put in practice in 1890, when *The Kentucky Post* was established across the Ohio River from Cincinnati. That same year Scripps acquired some land near San Diego, California, to build a ranch, and while living there in semi-retirement he became interested in developing west coast newspapers. In 1892 he purchased two San Diego newspapers and merged them to form *The San Diego Sun* and begin a Pacific coast group of newspapers of which he was owner.

In 1894 George Scripps pooled his interest in the family newspapers with Scripps-McRae, giving the league a controlling interest in the *Cleveland Press* and in *The Chronicle,* a St. Louis–based newspaper, in addition to its newspapers in Cincinnati and Kentucky. The profit pool was redivided in 1895 to include two-fifths each for E.W. and George Scripps and one-fifth for McRae. At that time. E.W. Scripps was named to serve as president of each of the newspapers, which would be run as separate companies, and McRae was named to serve as secretary and business manager of each newspaper.

In 1895 E.W. Scripps started his first newly created west coast paper, the *Los Angeles Record,* which was added to his Pacific coast group. Four years later, the Washington–based *Seattle Star* was formed and it too joined the Pacific coast fold. Scripps-McRae acquired the *Kansas City World* in Missouri in 1896 and three years later founded the *Akron Press* in Ohio.

In 1897 seeking an alternative to the Associated Press wire service, which provided news primarily to morning papers, and to United Press, which was in trouble, E.W. Scripps founded a new wire service, the Scripps-McRae Press Association, for the league's afternoon daily newspapers. Two years later, the Scripps News Association was formed as a wire service for non-Scripps newspapers.

By 1900 E.W. Scripps was operating nine daily newspapers, six through the league and three on the West Coast. After George Scripps's death in 1900 and a three-year court battle between E.W. and James Scripps, E.W. Scrips gained majority control of all the family's newspapers outside of Detroit.

In 1902 E.W. Scripps started the Newspaper Enterprise Association (NEA), the first specialized news and feature service in the United States. It was initially designed to provide a complete line of feature columns and news stories for only the Scripps-McRae newspapers, but the NEA soon expanded its clientele to include other newspapers.

After Scripps gained control of George Scripps's holdings in 1903, expansion efforts were stepped up. The league's first moves were in Ohio, where two Toledo newspapers were purchased in 1903 and merged to form the *Toledo News-Bee,* and the *Columbus Citizen* was acquired a year later. While the league was growing in the Midwest, the Pacific coast group was also expanding, establishing the *San Francisco News* and the *Tacoma Times* in 1903, the *Sacramento Star* in 1904, and the *Fresno Tribune* in 1905. In 1905 E.W. Scripps also began setting aside stock for employees to purchase.

The year 1906 was bountiful for Scripps start-up ventures, which included the establishment of five newspapers by a newly created newspaper chain known as the Harper Group, after the attorney J.C. Harper. In 1906 the Harper Group established the *Evansville Press* and the *Terre Haute Post* in Indiana, the *Pueblo Sun* and the *Denver Express* in Colorado, and the *Dallas Dispatch* in Texas. That same year the Pacific coast group founded the *Portland News* in Oregon, while Scripps-McRae established the *Oklahoma News,* and the *Nashville Times* in Tennessee. The Harper Group added the *Memphis Press* in Tennessee in 1907.

In 1906 E.W. Scripps purchased the Publishers Press Association and a year later merged it with the Scripps-McRae Press Association and the Scripps News Association, to form United Press Association (UPA). The following year he also formed the Newspaper Supply Company to handle central accounting and national advertising.

In 1908 E.W. Scripps announced he would retire and hand over the chairmanship of all his news organizations to his 22-year-old son, James Scripps. That same year, two financially troubled Missouri newspapers, *The Chronicle* in St. Louis and the *Kansas City World,* were disposed of. *The Chronicle* was sold, and the *World* was simply discontinued. Scripps's greatest difficulties during the early 1900s, however, were encountered on the West Coast, where start-ups in Fresno, Berkeley, and Oakland, California, each lasted less than eight years.

By 1911 the Scripps-McRae League included 18 daily newspapers in Ohio, Indiana, Tennessee, Iowa, Colorado, Oklahoma, and Texas; the Pacific coast group had 10 newspapers, mostly in California; and the Harper Group had 7 newspapers, including the *Houston Press,* which was founded that year.

E.W. Scripps emerged from retirement in 1911, and during the next two years established two newspapers without advertising. These two ad-less publications were the *Chicago Daybook,* established in 1911, with poet Carl Sandburg as chief reporter, and the *Philadelphia News-Post,* founded in 1912. The *News-Post* was discontinued after two years, but the *Daybook* grew to a circulation of 25,000 and was $500 a month away from breaking even when skyrocketing newsprint prices resulting from World War I forced its closure in 1917.

By 1918 the business disagreements between Scripps and his son James Scripps had become irreconcilable, and E.W. named another son, Robert Paine Scripps, chief executive and editor-in-chief of all news operations. In 1920 E.W. and James Scripps broke all ties, and Roy H. Howard, the UPA editor-in-chief, was named to run the business side of operations.

James Scripps died in 1921, and his wife withdrew five west coast papers and the *Dallas Dispatch* to form the Scripps-Canfield League. The Scripps-McRae League moved quickly to offset these losses and during the next three years established seven newspapers. During the same period the latter league acquired the *Youngstown Telegram* in Ohio, the *Indianapolis Times* in Indiana, the *New Mexico State Tribune* and the *Pittsburgh Press* in Pennsylvania.

Additional news services were established during the early 1920s, including the United Features Syndicate, a distributor of

weekly comics and news columns; United Newspictures, a news-photography service and forerunner of Acme Newspictures; and the Science Service, an authoritative supplemental science news and feature syndicate.

In 1922 all of E.W. Scripps's newspaper groups and news operations were incorporated as The E.W. Scripps Company, with headquarters in Cleveland. Howard was named chairman and chief executive officer of the corporation, and Robert Scripps co-chairman with Howard of a two-man editorial board. That same year the newspaper chain adopted the name Scripps-Howard League. E.W. Scripps also established a trust in 1922, which at his death would leave control of all his news organizations to his son Robert. Provisions were also made for all family members, except the heirs of James Scripps.

Following incorporation, Scripps-Howard purchased competing newspapers in Knoxville and Memphis, Tennessee; El Paso, Texas; Akron, Ohio; and Denver, Colorado and merged them with their existing publications in those cities. On the loss side during the 1920s, Scripps-Howard sold its Des Moines, Iowa, and Terre Haute, Indiana, newspapers and ceased publication of two others.

E.W. Scripps died in 1926, leaving the trust in the hands of Robert Scripps and the business management to Roy Howard, who remained chairman and chief executive officer. In 1927 Scripps-Howard acquired *The New York Telegram,* which became the *New York World-Telegram* four years later, after Howard negotiated the purchase of *The World.* The *Buffalo Times* of Buffalo, New York, was acquired in 1929.

By 1930 The E.W. Scripps Company owned 25 daily newspapers. During the next decade Roy Howard came to dominate editorial as well as business policies, and in the early 1930s he named William Waller Hawkins, who had been Howard's successor as editor at UPA, chairman of the board.

Following the Great Depression the nation's newspaper industry suffered from attrition, and between 1934 and 1939 Scripps-Howard sold newspapers to its competition in Baltimore, Maryland; Youngstown, Toledo, and Akron, Ohio; and San Diego, California; and ceased publication of its Oklahoma newspaper. During the same period the Scripps-Howard newspapers in Evansville, Indiana; Albuquerque, New Mexico; and El Paso, Texas, combined business operations with competitors to reduce overhead costs.

In 1935 The E.W. Scripps Company made its first diversification move and purchased a Cincinnati radio station, adopting the call letters WCPO. A subsidiary, Continental Radio, was established and changed its name to Scripps-Howard Radio, Inc. two years later. In 1936 the Memphis radio station WMC was acquired, and that same year Scripps-Howard bought out its one remaining competing daily newspaper in Memphis, *The Commercial Appeal.*

Robert Scripps died in 1938. Hawkins and George B. Parker, the editor-in-chief of the Scripps-Howard newspapers, became temporary trustees of the company along with Howard, pending the time when Robert Scripps's sons reached the age of 25. Under the new regime, the Scripps-Howard newspapers took on a more conservative tone. By the late 1930s Scripps-Howard newspapers had broken with the policies of U.S. President Franklin Delano Roosevelt, leading to the departure of some of the chain's more liberal columnists.

During World War II John H. Sorrells, executive editor of Scripps-Howard newspapers, and Nat R. Howard, the editor of the *Cleveland News,* headed up the office of press relations of the U.S. Office of Censorship. The well-known World War II reporter, Scripps-Howard columnist Ernie Pyle, won a national reputation and a Pulitzer Prize for his wartime writings. Pyle was killed in Okinawa in 1945, after being hit by a Japanese sniper.

After World War II Robert Scripps's sons, Robert Paine Scripps Jr., Charles E. Scripps, and Edward W. Scripps, became trustees of the trust. The company started diversification into television-station operation in 1947, establishing the ABC-affiliate WEWS-TV in Cleveland. In 1948 The E.W. Scripps Company expanded its Memphis media dominance by putting the NBC-affiliate WMC-TV on the air. In 1949 a new CBS affiliate started by Scripps, WCPO-TV, began operations in Cincinnati.

In 1950 Scripps-Howard purchased the Hearst Corporation's *New York Sun* and merged it with the *World-Telegram* to form the *New York World Telegram & Sun.* The same year Charles M. Schultz began to write and draw the "Peanuts" comic strip, which was syndicated through United Features.

Hawkins and Howard retired as chairman and president, respectively, in 1952. The following year Charles E. Scripps was named chairman, and Roy Howard's son, Jack R. Howard, was named president and chief executive officer. Roy Howard remained head of the *New York World Telegram & Sun* until his death in 1964.

Beginning in 1956 The E.W. Scripps Company began acquiring stock and building up majority control of the *Cincinnati Enquirer,* which competed with its *Cincinnati Post.* The company also bought another Cincinnati newspaper, the *Cincinnati Times-Star,* in 1958 and merged it into the *Post.*

In 1958 UPA absorbed International News Service and became known as United Press International (UPI). The following year the Scripps-Howard and Hearst chains combined their evening San Francisco newspapers into the jointly owned *San Francisco News-Call Bulletin.* Three years later, Hearst acquired complete control of the newspaper.

In 1960 Scripps-Howard purchased the *Cleveland News* and merged it into the *Cleveland Press.* The following year the E.W. Scripps company entered the growing Florida market and acquired the NBC-affiliate WPTV in West Palm Beach. Scripps-Howard Radio was renamed Scripps-Howard Broadcasting Company in 1961, and two years later went public. Two Florida newspapers, the *Stuart News* and the *Hollywood Sun-Tattler,* that were acquired in 1965.

The *Houston Press,* struggling against two competitors was sold in 1964, and the following year the 78-year-old *Indianapolis Times* also bowed out to two competitors. Both had been formed under E.W. Scripps's reign.

In 1966 Scripps-Howard, the Hearst Corporation, and Whitney Communications Corporation formed a joint venture company, the World Journal Tribune Inc., to keep their respective New York news operations alive. Under the agreement, Whitney's *Herald Tribune* continued publishing in the morning, while Scripps-Howard and Hearst newspapers published a combined afternoon newspaper, the *New York Journal-American.* All three companies combined to publish a Sunday newspaper, the *New York World Journal & Tribune.* After numerous setbacks, the joint venture was suspended in 1967, and the newspapers all folded.

The 1970s brought both arrivals and departures for E.W. Scripps. The Tulsa, Oklahoma, television station KTEW, an NBC affiliate renamed KJRH, and the *San Juan Star,* a California-based, English-language daily newspaper for Puerto Ricans, were acquired in 1970. Three years later another California newspaper, the *Fullerton Daily News Tribune,* was acquired.

Acting under a U.S. Department of Justice antitrust suit ruling, Scripps-Howard in 1971 divested itself of its interests in the *Cincinnati Enquirer.* One year later the 51-year-old *Washington Daily News* was sold to a competitor, and in 1975 competition forced the closure of the *Fort Worth Press.*

Jack Howard retired in 1976 and Edward W. Estlow was named his successor, becoming the company's first president and chief executive officer chosen from outside the Scripps and Howard families. The following year the E.W. Scripps corporate headquarters was moved from Cleveland to Cincinnati, and soon afterwards the financially troubled *Cincinnati Post* struck a deal with the competing *Enquirer* to combine business, advertising, and production operations while keeping editorial matters separate.

In 1977 Scripps-Howard Broadcasting acquired KBMA, a Kansas City UHF television station which later became a Fox Broadcasting affiliate. The following year Scripps-Howard consolidated the NEA and the United Features Syndicate under the trade name United Media Enterprises, and the cartoon "Garfield" was added to its line.

During the late-1970s, with Estlow at the helm, E.W. Scripps turned its attention toward weekly newspapers. In 1977 Scripps-Howard acquired its first two weeklies, and the following year the chain started its first weekly newspaper. In 1978, in a leap into the California weekly market, 15 Los Angeles–area weekly and semi-weekly newspapers were acquired, and before the decade had ended five Kentucky weeklies, including four in the Louisville area, were added.

By 1979 Scripps-Howard had 23 weekly newspapers and 16 daily newspapers, with half of those dailies functioning under joint-operating agreements. With a decade of debt dragging it down, the *Cleveland Press,* Scripps 102-year-old flagship newspaper, was sold in 1980. At about the same time, the company announced that the financially troubled UPI was also on the block.

With financial uncertainty surrounding some of its larger news operations, E.W. Scripps increased its diversification in 1980 by acquiring Cordovan Corporation, publisher of business periodicals, trade magazines, and books. That same year Scripps-Howard Broadcasting entered the cable television business by acquiring systems in Michigan, Connecticut, and Florida.

UPI was sold for $75 million in 1982, the same year that E.W. Scripps sold its Louisville weekly newspapers and its Knoxville radio station. About the same time, Scripps-Howard Broadcasting purchased a Portland, Oregon, radio station and four Colorado cable television systems. In 1985 E.W. Scripps furthered its expansion into cable systems and the western-states market. The Phoenix, Arizona, television station, KNXV, a Fox affiliate, was acquired, and $135 million was committed to construction of a new cable system in Sacramento, California.

Lawrence A. Leser, a former executive vice president, was named president and chief executive in 1985, succeeding Estlow who remained on the board. A three-year restructuring process followed that emphasized three prime business areas: publishing, broadcasting, and cable television.

Between 1986 and 1987 the company committed $819 million to acquisitions in its three core areas. In 1986 it acquired ABC's affiliate television stations in Detroit and in Tampa, Florida, and enlarged its newspaper chains through the acquisition of the John P. Scripps newspaper group, a chain of seven small California dailies founded by one of the E.W. Scripps grandsons. That same year E.W. Scripps acquired Indiana's *Evansville Daily News* and the *Morning News* of Naples, Florida. Seven small cable television systems in the southeastern states were also acquired in 1987.

During restructuring, the *Columbus Citizen-Journal* was discontinued after several failed attempts to sell the financially troubled Ohio paper. E.W. Scripps also sold some of its peripheral businesses, including more than half of its non-daily newspapers, its Connecticut joint-venture cable operations, and its videotape publishing business.

In 1987 the restructuring process was completed, and The E.W. Scripps Company was reorganized and incorporated in Delaware as a holding company, with most of its assets transferred to a new Ohio corporation, Scripps-Howard, Inc. The following year E.W. Scripps announced it would go public to reduce debt incurred through recent acquisitions, and a class of common stock, representing an 11% economic interest in the company with voting rights for one-third of the company's directors, was sold.

Following its public offering, E.W. Scripps began selling unprofitable operations, creating and acquiring new businesses not dependent on advertising revenues, and updating its existing newspaper operations. In 1988 the *Sun-Tattler* and some of the company's business journals were sold. The same year several cable television systems were acquired in western and southeastern states, and Scripps Howard Productions was formed to develop, produce, and market television programs. The company also announced it would spend $25 million to give the *Evansville Courier* a new production facility.

In 1988 E.W. Scripps also began looking for international markets for its cartoon-character licensing business. An Asian office was established in Tokyo in 1988 and a European office in Amsterdam in 1989. Also in 1989, E.W. Scripps sold its remaining interests in business journals and acquired Sundance Publishing, a supplemental-education-materials publisher. Newspaper-production-plant improvements continued that year with building projects in Florida and California.

E.W. Scripps Company entered the 1990s committed to continued expansion and improvement of its cable operations. Company plans also included rebuilding existing cable systems to expand channel offerings, and updating newspaper production facilities, as illustrated by a $135 million project announced in 1990 for Scripps's largest newspaper, the *Rocky Mountain News*. In 1991, Scripps bought WMAR-TV in Baltimore for $125 million.

Principal Subsidiaries: Birmingham Post Company; Channel 7 of Detroit, Inc. (80.4%); Collier County Publishing Company; Evansville Courier Company, Inc. (88.4%); Denver Publishing Company; EWS and LR Cable; Herald Post Publishing Company; John P. Scripps Newspapers, Inc.; Knoxville News Sentinel Company (97.3%); Memphis Publishing Company (90.5%); New Mexico State Tribune Company; Pittsburgh Press Company; San Juan Star Company; Scripps Howard Broadcasting Company (80.4%); Scripps Howard Cable Company (80.4%); Scripps Howard Cable Company of Sacramento (76.4%); Scripps Howard, Inc.; Stuart News Company; Tampa Bay Television Company (80.4%); United Features Syndicate, Inc.

Further Reading: Cochran, Negley D., *E.W. Scripps,* New York, Harcourt, Brace and Company, 1933; Knight, Oliver, *I Protest: Selected Disquisitions of E.W. Scripps,* Madison, The University of Wisconsin Press, 1966.

—Roger W. Rouland

ELSEVIER NV

1061 AG Amsterdam
Van de Sande Bakhuyzenstraat 4
The Netherlands
(20) 515 9111
Fax: (20) 83 99 21

Public Company
Incorporated: 1880 as Uitgeversmaatschappij Elsevier
Employees: 6,937
Sales: Dfl 1.96 billion (US$1.16 billion)
Stock Exchanges: Amsterdam Basel Geneva Zürich

Elsevier NV is the holding company for the second-largest publishing group in the Netherlands. The group is an international leader in the field of scientific publishing, issuing about 900 new books each year and publishing over 1,000 journals. It also publishes journals and newsletters for health-care professionals, the pharmaceutical industry, and business in general; information sources on government, real estate, and nursing; as well as, in Dutch, numerous reference works, a variety of magazines, two national newspapers, and three local newspapers. With subsidiaries in Europe, the United States, Japan, and South Korea, and main offices in Amsterdam, London, New York, Tokyo, and Lausanne, the Elsevier group is one of the most profitable publishing enterprises in the world. The key to its success has been its steady expansion into publishing in the English language, in which most scientific information first appears, from its base in the Netherlands.

Until 1979 the main company of the Elsevier group was Uitgeversmaatschappij Elsevier, a company which had been set up in Rotterdam in 1880 by a group of five Dutch booksellers and publishers, led by Jacobus George Robbers. They took the company name and imprint from the publishing house of the Elsevier family, which had flourished between the late 16th and early 18th centuries. After the company moved its headquarters to Amsterdam in 1887, its early success depended on publishing a literary journal, Dutch versions of the then-popular novels of Jules Verne, and the *Winkler Prins* encyclopedia, which has since become the Dutch equivalent of the *Britannica*.

Elsevier's main subsidiary is Elsevier Science Publishers BV. Elsevier first ventured into scientific publishing in the late 1930s, and then, after World War II, diversified its range, publishing trade journals and consumer magazines but chiefly building up its reputation as publisher of a number of scientific journals in English, starting in 1947 with *Biochimica et Biophysica Acta (BBA)*. Elsevier Science Publishers then expanded further by acquiring other companies in the same field, such as the North Holland Publishing Company—founded in 1931, acquired in 1970—and Excerpta Medica, acquired in 1971.

For Elsevier "scientific" has the wider meaning common on the continent of Europe of "academic," rather than the narrower Anglo-American definition. Thus, while the company is the world's leading publisher in the life sciences, and issues journals covering the whole range of the natural sciences, it also publishes journals on history, law, economics, and statistics, as well as engineering and technology. A measure of the company's prestige is that by 1990 its publications had included work by the winners of 62 Nobel prizes, of which 29 were for physiology or medicine. More crucially, perhaps, its leading journals maintain this prestige by a rigorous process of peer review. In the case of *Brain Research*, for example, this means that half of the articles submitted are rejected, and only 4% are published unaltered.

The Uitgeversmaatschappij Elsevier merged with the newspaper group Nederlandse Dagbladunie NV early in 1979. This merger brought ownership of the national newspapers *NRC Handelsblad* and *Algemeen Dagblad*, which now have a combined circulation of nearly 650,000; three regional newspapers; and several local newspapers, including free advertisement-based papers. The enlarged group was reorganized under the newly founded holding company Elsevier NV.

Elsevier's strategy since 1980 has been to concentrate on the English-language market, both by developing its existing output further and by acquiring new American subsidiaries, which have been organized into two groups. Elsevier Information Systems Inc. comprises three subsidiaries. The Congressional Information Service (CIS), based in Bethesda, Maryland, was Elsevier's first American acquisition, in 1979. CIS issues information from American and international government sources, and archive material on scholarly subjects, on microfiche and microfilm. The Greenwood Publishing Group, based in Westport, Connecticut, specializes in reference works and books on the humanities, business, and law, and includes the Praeger, Bergin & Garvey, and Auburn House imprints. Elsevier Realty Information, Inc. (ERI), of Bethesda, Maryland, is an amalgamation of Redi and Damar, two companies acquired in 1988. It distributes information on property to professional customers and publishes real estate maps of most major cities in the United States.

Elsevier Business Press group consists of four subsidiaries. The Springhouse Corporation of Springhouse, Pennsylvania, acquired in 1988, publishes a range of journals, books, and videotapes for health-care and education professionals and small- and medium-sized businesses. Delta Communications of Chicago specializes in magazines for various industries, such as *Modern Metals* and *Packaging Digest*. Gordon Publications of Morris Plains, New Jersey, acquired in 1985, issues nearly 20 product news publications. Finally, the Excerpta Medica International group, based in Princeton, New Jersey, as successor to the Excerpta Medica company acquired in 1971, publishes the highly successful Excerpta Medica Database (EMbase), which is an annual compilation of abstracts of more than 300,000 items of medical literature, as well as other publications on medicine.

In 1985 Elsevier expanded into the flourishing business of educational courses and materials, in the Netherlands and in Belguim, through its subsidiary Elsevier Opleidingen (Elsevier Training Institutes). Its other European operations comprise the Pan European Publishing Company (Pepco) of Brussels, which issues product news tabloids in English; Misset Publishers, based in Doetinchem, which leads the Dutch market for trade journals; Bonaventura of Amsterdam, which publishes the weekly news magazine *Elsevier* and many other periodicals; and Argus of Amsterdam, publisher of the *Grote Winkler Prins* encyclopedia and other Dutch-language reference books.

Not all of Elsevier's attempts at expansion have been successful. The group began a long campaign to take over Kluwer, which was then the third-largest publisher in the Netherlands, in 1987. Kluwer, which had a similar range to Elsevier's, but preferred to develop its Dutch market, resisted the attempt, even when Elsevier lowered its sights to trying for 49% of its rival's shares. In order to finance this operation Elsevier itself had to issue new shares, which were bought mainly by the British media magnate Robert Maxwell, who ended up with a holding of 9% in Elsevier. The next step was a merger between Kluwer and its main shareholder, Wolters Samsom, to form Wolters Kluwer, which temporarily took Elsevier's place as the second largest Dutch publisher. Eventually Elsevier ended up with 28% of Wolters Kluwer. It sold these shares in 1990, yet announced that it had not abandoned the idea of an eventual merger with Wolters Kluwer.

In 1988 Elsevier formed a publishing alliance with Pearson plc, a publishing conglomerate based in London, which owns the *Financial Times*, Viking Penguin, Longman, and several other media companies. Also in 1988 Elsevier successfully resisted a takeover bid by Maxwell Communication Corporation, the holding company owned and run by Robert Maxwell. By 1991 Pearson owned 22.5% of Elsevier shares, while Elsevier held 8.8% of Pearson's equity. In April 1990 the two groups announced that they would not proceed with any further moves toward merging, because of the legal and fiscal problems such moves would bring. In March 1991 Pearson made a profit of £84 million by selling all of its Elsevier shares to the merchant bank Goldman, Sachs, which was to sell them on to other investment institutions. One month later Elsevier decided to sell its holdings in Pearson in its turn.

Dagbladunie, Elsevier's newspaper subsidiary, was to have merged with a rival group, Perscombinatie, until negotiations were abandoned in 1989. The same year saw strikes by printers and journalists at the *Algemeen Dagblad*, which led to a slight fall in the paper's circulation. In 1990, however, both of the national newspapers in the subsidiary significantly increased their circulation, taking readers away from their rivals, while the three regional newspapers improved their advertising revenue. The decision to invest in extra color printing capacity, to come into operation by 1995, represents a vote of confidence in the future of all five titles.

Like other companies which have been successful in one sector of the media, Elsevier started to cross into other sectors. The group owns 50% of the film financing partnership Elsevier Vendex Film CV—perhaps best known for producing Peter Greenaway's recent films—and in 1990 it bought 19% of RTL-Véeronique, a company based in Luxembourg, which produces television programs for satellite broadcast.

Between 1984 and 1990 Elsevier's net income quadrupled as its directors carried out a policy of shifting resources away from less international, less specialized, and less profitable areas, such as consumer magazines, toward the heights of international, specialized, and very profitable scientific publishing, for which the market tends not to be much affected by the ups and downs of the wider economy. Thus, for example, in 1989 alone, Elsevier Science Publishers added another 30 titles to its list of periodicals, most of them acquired rather than newly launched. As a result of these and other ventures Elsevier's net profits reached Dfl 500 million in 1990.

In 1991 Elsevier added to its list of subsidiaries the biggest single acquisition it has ever made, the British scientific publisher Pergamon Press, which it intends to maintain separately from Elsevier Science Publishers. Elsevier paid £440 million for Pergamon, most of which went to its founder, Robert Maxwell, the man who had tried to buy Elsevier itself only three years before. Maxwell had created Pergamon Press in 1951 on the basis of his connections with the German scientific publisher Springer Verlag and then built it up into a major rival to Elsevier Science Publishers.

The Elsevier group, immensely profitable as it is, is not without problems. The record of failure of its attempts to merge with or take over its large rivals, other than Pergamon, somewhat offsets the success even of its largest acquisition. Whatever less specialized publications it chooses to retain may suffer from economic recession and competition from rival media groups seeking to build up strength for the European single market. Those areas of Elsevier's Dutch-language activities which depend on advertising revenue—especially newspapers and general-interest magazines—may be adversely affected by competition from commercial television, which reached the Netherlands at the end of 1989. Yet the Elsevier group looks likely to continue to be one of the world's most profitable publishers, whatever difficulties some of its smaller ventures might get into, so long as both scientific research and the electronic means to disseminate it continue growing.

Principal Subsidiaries: Elsevier Nederland BV; Elsevier U.S. Holdings, Inc.; Elsevier SA (Switzerland); Elsevier U.K. Holdings Ltd.; Elsevier Science Publishers BV; Pergamon Press plc (U.K.); Elsevier Information Systems, Inc. (U.S.A.); Elsevier Business Press (U.S.A.); Pan European Publishing Company (Belgium); Uitgeversmaatschappij C. Misset BV; Elsevier Education; Nederlandse Dagbladunie BV; Uitgeversmaatschappij Bonaventura BV.

—Patrick Heenan

GANNETT CO., INC.

1100 Wilson Boulevard
Arlington, Virginia 22234
U.S.A.
(703) 284-6000
Fax: (703) 276-5548

Public Company
Incorporated: 1923
Employees: 36,600
Sales: $3.44 billion
Stock Exchange: New York

In 1990 Gannett Co., Inc. owned 82 daily newspapers, including its flagship *USA Today;* 66 nondaily publications; and the weekly newspaper magazine *USA Weekend,* among other holdings. The company also owned and operated ten television stations, eight FM radio stations, and seven AM radio stations, many of which are in major markets. In addition, its Gannett Outdoor was the largest outdoor-advertising group in North America.

Gannett has been a leader in the application of technology and in media issues since its founding in 1906. It continues to be a leader today—albeit a more controversial one, largely because of *USA Today* and former chairman Allen Neuharth. Current chairman John Curley wants to maintain the company's industry leadership role but takes a less flashy approach than his predecessor. He is also focusing more on the bottom line.

Gannett is the brainchild of Frank Gannett, who paid his way through Cornell University by running a news-correspondence syndicate; when he graduated, he had $1,000 in savings. Gannett got into the media business in 1906, when he and several associates bought the *Elmira Gazette* in Elmira, New York, with $3,000 in savings, $7,000 in loans, and $10,000 in notes. They bought another local paper, and merged them to form the *Star-Gazette,* beginning a pattern of mergers to increase advertising power that the company would follow throughout its history. Six years later, in 1912, Gannett bought *The Ithaca Journal,* beginning his toehold in upper New York state. The company gradually built up a portfolio of 19 New York dailies by 1989.

Gannett and his team moved to Rochester, New York, in 1918, a city whose papers would turn out to be among the company's strongest. Many of the company's rising executives were groomed at the Rochester papers. The group purchased two newspapers upon their arrival and merged them into the

Times-Union. The papers' holdings were consolidated under the name Empire State Group. In 1921 The *Observer-Dispatch* of Utica, New York, was acquired. In 1923 Frank Gannett bought out his partners' interests in the Empire State Group and the six newspapers the group then owned, and formed Gannett Co., Inc. Gannett appointed Frank Tripp general manager. Tripp helped run the everyday business of the papers, and the two were close allies for years. The Northeast was Gannett's focus for the next 25 years, and the company expanded aggressively with acquisitions there. Another key executive, Paul Miller, joined the company in 1947, becoming Gannett's executive assistant. By then, the company operated 21 newspapers and radio stations.

Gannett's role as a leader in technology began in 1929, when Frank Gannett co-invented the teletypesetter. Gannett newsrooms were among the first to use shortwave radios to gather reports from distant sources. In 1938, before color was in much use, many Gannett presses were adapted for color. Today, with its *USA Today,* the company continues to be a leader in color use. A corporate plane also helped reporters get to the site of news quickly.

Frank Gannett died in 1957, but not before he saw Paul Miller named president and chief executive officer. Miller oversaw the company's expansion from a regional chain to a national one in the next decade.

Gannett News Service, as it is known today, was founded in 1942 as Gannett National Service. The wire service subsidiary provides the company's local papers with national stories from Washington, D.C., and 13 bureaus. The stories often have a local angle or local sources. A television news bureau was added in 1982.

Through all these years, Gannett grew by buying existing newspaper and radio and TV stations. In 1966, it founded its first newspapers, *Florida Today.* It was the work of Allen Neuharth, who later was to become the founder of *USA Today.* Neuharth brought the new paper to profitability in 33 months, an incredible feat in the newspaper business, analysts say. Because the paper was near the National Aeronautics and Space Administration (NASA), it was dubbed "Florida's Space Age Newspaper." The paper has since been redesigned to emphasize state and local news and is promoted and sold with *USA Today,* which provides national and international coverage.

The company went public in 1967. In 1970 Paul Miller assumed the title of chairman, and Allen Neuharth was promoted to president and chief operating officer from executive vice president, making him the heir-apparent to the top position in the company. Neuharth went on an acquisition spree, leading the company to its current size and status in the media world. He became chief executive officer in 1973 and chairman in 1979.

Two notable mergers were those with Federated Publications in 1971 and with Speidel Newspaper Group in 1977. Two years later, Gannett merged with Combined Communications, the biggest such merger in the industry at that time, for $400 million. The Evening News Association joined the Gannett family later when Gannett bought it for $700 million. One near-merger was with Ridder Publications. Bernard H. Ridder Jr., president, was a golfing mate of Paul Miller. Ridder had concluded the only way his small, family-held company's stock would ever reach its full potential was for Ridder Publications to merge with a big media company. The two talked, but Ridder proved to be more interested in Knight Newspapers because it had less geographic overlap with Ridder than did Gannett.

Some industry critics have warned that media consolidation, such as Gannett's 1970s acquisitions, thwarts open debate and the exchange of ideas. Gannett defenders, however, claim that chain newspapers can be just as vigorous in promoting and defending the rights of a free press as independent newspapers.

In 1986 Neuharth retired as chief executive officer, passing the baton to John Curley. Curley had been president and chief operating officer since 1984; he joined Gannett in 1970. Curley took on the title of chairman in 1989 and still headed the company in 1991. Neuharth continued as chairman of the Gannett Foundation.

In 1989 the Gannett Foundation gave $28 million to various programs. It was established in 1935 by Frank Gannett to promote free press, freedom of information and better journalism, adult literacy, community problem-solving, and volunteerism. Neuharth spent as freely at the foundation as he had at the company. Neuharth put the foundation's 10% ownership of Gannett up for sale in 1990, in the midst of questions about Neuharth's spending priorities. In 1990 the foundation's expenses were rising faster than its assets. Under Neuharth, the foundation spent $15 million on interior design of its headquarters, when it moved from Rochester, New York to Arlington, Virginia, where *USA Today's* offices are located.

Curley, a newsman, as most of Gannett's heads have been, was editor and publisher of several Gannett papers and was founding editor of *USA Today.* Neuharth had said in 1982 when he started *USA Today* that it would begin making annual profits in three to five years. By 1990 the paper had had quarterly profits but never a full year of profitability. Between 1982 and 1990 *USA Today* sapped the company of an estimated $500 million. The national daily newspaper was another demonstration of Gannett's leadership role in the use of technology, as well as journalism. The copy for the paper is transmitted by satellite to its 15 printing plants.

The paper also had been an innovator in graphics, especially in the use of color. Media observers credit *USA Today's* use of color as the spur for industry wide interest in color graphics. The paper is also known for the brevity of its stories, which many journalists have criticized but which many editors have imitated. *USA Today* in 1990 had a paid circulation of about 1.8 million.

Industry estimates put Gannett as the nation's second-biggest media concern, with a market value of $7 billion, behind only Capital Cities/ABC, the largest, with a $10.2 billion market value. After the firm's buying binge under Neuharth, analysts say it is likely that Gannett will take a slower pace in the next several years. In 1990, it purchased the *Great Falls Tribune,* of Montana, from Cowles Media for $41 million, making it the company's 83rd daily paper. There are fewer great deals to be made on newspaper acquisitions these days, however, so Gannett will probably work to improve the profitability and journalistic performance of its current holdings.

Principal Subsidiaries: Gannett Direct Marketing Services, Inc.; Gannett News Service; Gannett Outdoor; Louis Harris & Associates; Gannett National Newspaper Sales; Gannett Telemarketing, Inc.; USA Today Update; USA Today Books.

Further Reading: Mott, Frank Luther, *American Journalism: A History, 1690–1960,* New York, Macmillan 1962; Cose, Ellis, *The Press,* New York, Morrow, 1989.

—Lisa Collins

GROUPE DE LA CITÉ

264, rue du Faubourg St-Honoré
75008 Paris
France
(1) 42 67 40 22
Fax: (1) 42 67 29 69

Public Company
Incorporated: 1852 as Librairie Larousse
Employees: 8,000
Sales: FFr6.00 billion (US$1.18 billion)
Stock Exchange: Paris

Groupe de la Cité, a holding company owned by Compagnie Européenne de Publication (CEP) and Générale Occidentale, formed in 1988 through the merger of Presses de la Cité and the Larousse-Nathan group, is among the world's ten largest book publishers. Having become France's second-largest publisher after Hachette, Groupe de la Cité is establishing itself as a leader in the areas of education and general knowledge for all age groups.

This description does not fully summarize the group's sphere of activity, however. The group's formation has produced an entity whose diversity is in some ways closer to that of a conglomerate. The publishing houses included in the group differ in prestige as in age, and their histories have only coincided since about 1980. Nevertheless, the Groupe de la Cité enjoys an economic unity which is extremely effective and which is due, in part, to its 50% shareholding in France-Loisir, a subsidiary of the group that accounts for almost half the group's worldwide sales.

Of the three groups that were merged in 1988, Larousse is the oldest. Until almost the middle of the 20th century, no distinction was made in France between publishers and those who owned bookshops. It was as such an enterprise that Librairie Larousse, was established in 1852. Pierre Larousse and Augustin Boyer, two school teachers interested in participating directly in educational reform, soon began to specialize in the publication of dictionaries and encyclopedias. Their first successful product was, however, a textbook, the *Petite Grammaire Lexicologique du Premier Age,* published in 1852. As early as 1863, the first installments of the *Grand Dictionnaire Universel du XIXe Siècle* appeared. This was the first encyclopedic dictionary to be published in France. It was more than 20,000 pages long. After the deaths of the two founders, in 1873 and 1896, the Librairie kept its name and Larousse's

successors continued to carry out his business with ever-increasing success. Ten years later, Claude Augé, Pierre Larousse's successor, published the *Nouveau Larousse Illustré* in seven volumes, which set an example for its generation. The year 1905 saw the appearance of the *Petit Larousse Illustré,* which would be the Librairie's greatest success and which is still a classic; this pocket dictionary was reprinted 18 times in the 18 months which followed its publication. From then onward, Larousse's output increased and diversified. It published the *Larousse Mensuel,* the *Nouvelles Littéraires,* and a series of practical guides in fields such as travel, history, and medicine. Thirty years after the appearance of the *Nouveau Larousse Illustré,* it was replaced by the *Larousse du XXe Siècle,* published in seven volumes between 1928 and 1933, with more than 48,000 illustrations.

Meanwhile, and without being a competitor of Larousse, the 23-year-old Fernand Nathan established the Librairie Nathan in 1881. Closely followed by the educational reforms of 1881–1882 led by Jules Ferry, the Librairie reflected the new trends and published educational books with a versatile and lively approach. At the same time, Nathan developed the field of education of the very young and adapted his books to psychological insights. Among other distinctions, the publisher had the privilege of becoming the representative of educational publishers to the government. In 1919, Fernand Nathan put his son Pierre in charge of the Librairie. The latter soon dedicated himself to educational reviews and created the *Brevet Elementaire,* forerunner of the *Nouvelle Revue Pédagogique.* At the same time he concentrated on developing two areas that would later ensure the success of the publishing house: series for young children and educational games—"education through entertainment" was his motto—which occupied him until World War II.

The story of the last component of Groupe de la Cité is also the story of Sven Nielsen, a Danish bibliophile who arrived in France in 1924. He showed a keen interest in the process of distribution, first becoming a wholesaler and taking over several provincial businesses before organizing his own distribution network and founding Messageries du Livre in 1926. This diffusion and distribution organization now makes an important contribution to the success of Groupe de la Cité with its 12 branches and sales of FFr55 million.

World War II scarcely affected Sven Nielsen. He even benefited from it, acquiring Editions Albert Premier in 1942 and finally fulfilling his ambition of becoming a publisher. In 1944 he renamed the company Presses de la Cité in memory of his early days in the heart of Paris, in the shadow of Notre-Dame. He soon specialized in the publication of English bestsellers, which were received enthusiastically by a French public that had been deprived of reading matter during the war. His success, which was based on the publication of very popular works, continued to grow until 1958. From then onward, the Presses de la Cité continued to diversify, establishing new publishing houses or forming a partnership—with existing publishers Perrin in 1959, Solar in 1960, Rouge et Or in 1961, Presse Pocket in 1962, Fleuve Noir in 1963, and other, more prestigious literary publishers: Plon et Juillard in 1966 and, most notably, Christian Bourgois, which merged with Presses in 1970. The year 1970 was one of the most important dates in the history of Presses de la Cité, because the company, in partnership with the German group Bertelsmann, created

France-Loisirs. Each of the partners held a 50% stake and Bertelsmann provided the management. France-Loisirs was to become the most powerful book club sales group in France and in the world. The club has more than four million members and sells 26 million books a year. While the commercial considerations of bestsellers usually prevail over the consideration of quality, and France-Loisirs takes almost no risk in its distribution methods, its overwhelming success in French publishing and in the French-speaking export market is impressive nonetheless. As early as 1982, France-Loisirs was responsible for 90% of the profits of Presses de la Cité.

World War II, which saw the birth of Presses de la Cité, was to have quite a different effect on Larousse and Nathan, whose stories now converged for the first time. The German occupation authorities set upon Nathan, eventually imposing a sales administrator on the company. In response, a solidarity movement sprang up at the heart of the industry. Andre Cillon, of Larousse, saved Editions Nathan from the Nazis, taking over and managing the company for the duration of the war. He returned the company to Fernand Nathan on the very day of the liberation of Paris. The two companies were not to renew their association before 1984, but this time it was to be permanent. Nathan, meanwhile, considerably expanded and improved his educational products, which included textbooks, practical guides, and teacher's textbooks. With the Nathan-Université series, he also entered the field of higher education. Larousse continued to operate in the field of lexicography, creating the ten-volume *Grand Dictionnaire Encyclopédique* between 1959 and 1969, the *Petit Larousse en Couleur* in 1968, and the *Dictionnaire du français Contemporain*, the definitive dictionary for the teaching of French.

From 1979, events began to lead toward the formation of today's Groupe de la Cité. In that year Editions Nathan was acquired by the Compagnie Européenne de Publication, a group established in 1976 to provide economic, professional, and technical information within Europe and headed by Christian Brégou. In 1983, CEP, a 35%-owned affiliate of the powerful Havas group began to show an interest in Larousse, which was in dire financial straits and faced increasing competition. Brégou took a major stake in Larousse. The Larousse Group was born, and would soon become a holding company in which Larousse and Nathan each held a stake of 50%. By 1985 Larousse seemed to be back on its feet again, thanks in particular to a new *Grand Larousse* and the total remodeling of the *Petit Larousse*.

Similarly at Presses de la Cité, Claude Nielsen, by now the head of the group, was having to recognize the critical nature of his company's situation. Presses de la Cité was not in debt or unprofitable, but the company had no large stabilizing shareholder. Almost two-thirds of the shares were in the hands of small shareholders who had no involvement with publishing. Not only was Nielsen's empire divided, but it was now becoming more and more attractive to predators. The first offensive occurred in 1986 and was led by Carlo De Benedetti, via the company La Cerus, which launched a public offer of purchase for Presses de la Cité. Threatened and anxious, Nielsen appealed to Sir James Goldsmith, owner of Générale Occidentale, a multinational which already owned several French newspapers. Goldsmith snapped up Presses de la Cité, but it was not to stay in his hands for long. Only one year later, Goldsmith sold Générale Occidentale to the Compagnie

Générale d'Électricité (CGE) and in the process abandoned Presses de la Cité. In the following year, Ambroise Roux, the new president and managing director of Générale Occidentale, oversaw the merger of CEP and CGE to form Groupe de la Cité.

In February 1988, under the instigation of Ambroise Roux but equally at the request of Christian Brégou, Havas and Générale Occidentale sealed the alliance that would combine the publishing activities of their respective subsidiaries, CEP and Presses de la Cité. The new Groupe de la Cité was a holding company owned in equal shares by CEP and Générale Occidentale. The two leaders of French publishing, Hachette and Groupe de la Cité, soon secured for themselves 55% to 60% of French book publishing. Christian Brégou now took control of the group, responding to the need for a real strategy. This need had been expressed in particular by the 800 employees of Presses de la Cité who, in less than a year, had had four presidents and managing directors—Claude Nielsen, James Goldsmith, Bruno Rohmer, and finally Christian Brégou. From the start, Brégou introduced a barracks-like atmosphere at the group, with everyone at daggers drawn, to such an extent that the employees rechristened the publishing house "Stress de la Cite." The new head of the group was a businessman, who valued his authors chiefly according to the profits they generated. The group's success grew rapidly. The publishing division employed 2,300 people, and out of total group sales of FFr5 billion in 1988, FFr2.6 billion came exclusively from publishing. Bregou's goals were clear: "to become a world leader and the foremost European publishing house in the field of education and reference books." In an interview published in December 1990, he added: "General literature is to reference publishing what *haute couture* is to *pret à porter:* one follows the tide, while the other is expressive of an established savoir-faire."

The group covers the complete range of educational books, from school level —with the addition in 1975 of Bordas, plus Larousse-Nathan—to university level. It also offers general literature via the publishing houses controlled by Presses de la Cité, as well as paperback books, such as Presse-Pocket and Fleuve Noir.

The team composed of Jean-Manuel Bourgois and his brother Christian became important in the group. The former became managing director of Groupe de la Cité and president and managing director of Presses de la Cité, while Christian, who had founded the publishing house Christian Bourgois in 1966, rapidly became known for the quality and high reputation of his books, largely translations, and in 1989 published Salman Rushdie's *The Satanic Verses*. In rivalry between the two brothers they were called "Jean-Manual" and "Christian-Intellectual."

In July 1989 Christian Brégou bought Editions Dalloz, the leading French legal publishers, founded in 1845 by Désiré Dalloz and incorporating the brand names Dalloz, Sirey, and Clet. This acquisition contributed profits of FFr175 million to Groupe de la Cité in 1989. Finally, the group turned its attention overseas. In Spain, Larousse formed a Madrid-based subsidiary for all the Spanish-language versions of Larousse publications and for the promotion of the new group products. In the United Kingdom, the group acquired a controlling interest in Chambers, one of the oldest publishers of English-language and specialized dictionaries. Its London-based subsidiary,

Grisewood & Dempsey, experienced strong growth in 1989. In the United States, a subsidiary of Groupe de la Cité formed a new company, Millbrook Press Inc., with the help of a team of seasoned reference book professionals. France-Loisirs already had numerous affiliates in French-speaking countries and in Germany. Nathan's Belgian publishers Hemma, a 40% subsidiary of the group, specialized in books for children with offices in France, Belgium, Spain, Germany, and the Netherlands.

Although the components of the group are not formally linked, the resulting organization is powerful nonetheless. The almost craftsman-like tradition of the publishing world of the 19th century, embodied in the beginnings of Nathan and Larousse, is as important in the history of Groupe de la Cité as the merging of large communications groups. Equally important is the influence of the "godfathers" of the Groupe de la Cité, such as Havas, which achieves sales of FFr13 billion, or CEP, which is the owner of many French newspapers and communications organizations.

Principal Subsidiaries: Larousse; Nathan; Bordas; Presses de la Cité; France-Loisirs (50%).

Further Reading: Les Editions Fernand Nathan ont Cent Ans, 1881–1981, Paris, editions Fernand Nathan, 1981; "La CEP et le nouveau Groupe Larousse," *Caractère,* January 1, 1984; Nora, Dominique, "CEP-Presses de la Cité: le Mariage de Raison," *Libération,* February 16, 1988; Lepape, Pierre, "Hachette-Groupe de la Cité: le face à face de l'édition," *Le Monde Affaires,* February 20, 1988; Chavane, Laurence, "Groupe de la Cite: le poids de l'édition, le choc de 1992," *Le Figaro Economie,* February 22, 1988; "Edition: La Tournee des pages," *Les dossiers du Canard,* June-July, 1989; de Nussac, Gérard, "Zoom," *Quai des Plumes,* November 1989.

—Sonia Kronlund
Translated from the French by Jessica Griffin

HACHETTE

83, avenue Marceau
75116 Paris
France
(1) 40 69 16 00
Fax: (1) 47 23 01 92

Public Company
Incorporated: 1826 as Librairie Louis Hachette
Employees: 31,000
Sales: FFr29.00 billion (US$5.70 billion)
Stock Exchange: Paris

Groupe Hachette is France's largest publishing company and communications group, with activities including news services, audiovisual services, television, film production, and distribution. It is part of the Matra group, which is better known for arms and motor vehicle manufacturing. It is difficult to make a complete distinction between Hachette's book publishing activities and its vast communications business, a term that includes everything to do with information and knowledge. In 1989, out of total group sales of FFr29 billion, the book division accounted for FFr7 million, of which 50% was earned abroad. The activities of the book division encompass the fields of general literature, through the publishing houses Hachette-Littérature, Grasset-Fasquelle, and Stock, among others; of education; of popular literature, through Livre de Poche and the well-known Harlequin; and of children's books. The division consists of around 40 publishers that employ 17,000 people, more than half the work force of the entire group. Under the guidance of Jean-Luc Lagardère, head of Matra-Europe 1-Hachette, and of Jean-Claude Lattès, managing director of the book division, Hachette has more than 30% of the French book market, closely followed by its rival, Groupe de la Cité, with 20%. Hachette remains in first place because of the strength of its sales network and the diversity of its publications. There is hardly a sector in which the books division is not represented. The effect of the synergy between the books division and Hachette's other activities, newspaper and magazine publishing in particular, is important.

In 1821, when Monsignor Denis Frayssinous, whom Louis XVIII had put in charge of the French universities, ordered the suppression and closure of the Ecole Normale Supérieure, one of the most prestigious educational establishments in France, he could not have known that he was participating indirectly in the foundation of what is now France's largest publisher. In that very year Louis Hachette, a brilliant pupil of the *ecole*, was finishing his third year of studies there, and found himself thrown back upon his own resources; no longer a student, he decided to become a publisher. In 1826, after more than three years of planning and searching for financial backing, Hachette acquired the publishing house Librairie de Jacques-Francois Brétif, which he soon renamed the Librairie Louis Hachette. He retained Brétif's list and began to publish educational journals and textbooks for primary schools. However, by 1831 he was already publishing the famous romantic historian Jules Michelet. His first catalog, which appeared in 1832, already reflected the diversity that lies at the roots of Hachette's success: it already included a classical division, journals, and by 1836 two dictionary projects. Eight years after its creation, the Librairie Hachette's sales volume had tripled. Louis Hachette soon realized the need for a partner in the business, and in 1840 Louis Breton filled this post. Together, Hachette and Breton launched numerous periodicals and both made known English-language literature: William Makepeace Thackeray, Henry Wadsworth Longfellow, and, most notably Charles Dickens, 11 of whose novels were published by Hachette. In 1851, Hachette returned from travels in England, where he had observed the parallel development of public transportation and public information technology. He followed the example of English news agent W.H. Smith, and in 1852 began to establish a network of bookstores and newspaper stands in French railroad stations. These emphasized interesting reading at a moderate price and offered tourist guides, general interest reading, and children's books published by Hachette. Louis Hachette went on to diversify into newspaper and magazine publishing. In 1859 his business expanded overseas, opening a foreign-language bookstore in London.

Louis Hachette took a keen interest in French literature. Having bought the publisher Librairie Victor Lecou in 1855, he became publisher of such well-known writers as George Sand, Victor Hugo, Gérard de Nerval, and Gustave Doré. Later he became editor of the Emile Littré dictionary, known as *the Littré*, which is still the most respected reference dictionary used in universities and schools. At his death in 1864, Louis Hachette left his heirs a considerable fortune, and a company with 165 employees and sales which reached FFr18 million in 1878. His son George took over the bookselling license, but the Librairie continued to be managed by Louis Breton, until the latter's death in 1883, and by a small group of partners who worked in close collaboration and sought rapid growth. This group included Emile Templier. He took the initiative of publishing the work of the Comtesse de Ségur, who wrote several classics of children's literature. The Franco-Prussian War of 1870 slowed down the activities of the Librairie considerably, but the company's recovery was as rapid as its decline had been. The tourist guides were particularly successful, but the major breakthrough came in 1897 with the creation of Messageries Hachette, a book and press distribution organization, which soon served the entire country and in 1914 employed more than 700 people. In 1900 Hachette opened the first newsstand in the Paris subway system.

World War I caused difficulties for the Librairie; the company's greatest problem was the loss of personnel. The men sent to the front were often replaced by women, many of whom had no experience in the business. However, this change did not seem to prevent the Librairie from further expansion, and in

1916, in the midst of war, the Librairie Hachette bought the company Pierre Lafitte, which included several newspapers, bestsellers, a bookshop, and a photographic studio.

After World War I, the Librairie Hachette underwent significant restructuring. Despite the reluctance of the employees and the fact that the company was essentially a family business, the Librairie became a *société anonyme*—a public company—in 1919. This change was prompted by a growing need to increase its registered capital and to issue redeemable stock. The new public limited company had five partners and 24 sleeping partners, all relatives by marriage or direct descendants of Louis Hachette or Louis Breton. An increase of capital took place, which would be multiplied again in 1939, by nine times. Hachette also expanded overseas. The Librairie took over AGLP, a book and newspaper wholesaler that also operated retail bookshops throughout South America and in several European countries. From 1932, Hachette began to secure exclusive distribution rights for other publishers and in particular for the prestigious N.R.F. Gallimard, for Fasquelle, which would soon become a subsidiary of the group. In the 20 years between the two world wars, the Librairie's volume of business tripled. World War II slowed down this growth considerably, as it did for other publishers.

The occupying Germans began by requisitioning Hachette's offices in rue Réaumur and boulevard Saint-Germain, and by forcing out the company's directors. Finally the Germans tried to take over the Librairie, but were unsuccessful. During the four years of German occupation, Hachette's funds were nil. Little by little, however, a passive resistance was organized so effectively that as early as 1944 the directors returned to the company. Messageries d'Hachette was the most affected, the distribution system and transport system having changed considerably during the war. In 1947, after several fruitless attempts at recovery and the failure of the Messageries Françaises de la Presse, created in 1944, Hachette created the Nouvelles Messageries de la Presse Parisienne (N.M.P.P.). This organization, which still enjoys a worldwide influence, worked on a cooperative basis, and Hachette merely gave it its structure, only accepting a fee in compensation. In 1963, the N.M.P.P. achieved sales of FFr1.5 billion, half the sales of Hachette. In 1991, Hachette owned 49% of N.M.P.P., the remaining 51% being owned by nine other newspaper and magazine publishers. Meanwhile, and after World War II, Hachette's book division expanded through a large number of acquisitions and through an original and important creation in literary publication, the Livre de Poche. The latter joined the four publishing divisions already in existence: the educational division, the young reader's division, the general literature division, and the tourist guide division. The new publishers that Hachette acquired retained their individual company styles and character. The first of these was the Editions Bernard Grasset, publisher of Marcel Proust—at the author's own expense—of Paul Morand, and of Montherland. Hachette had come to the aid of this company as early as 1938, but it was not until 1954 that the Librairie acquired a major holding in Grasset, which had been founded in 1907. Grasset then merged rapidly with Fasquelle, in which Hachette had held a majority stake since 1931. The process was similar in the case of the Librairie Fayard, founded in 1955. Hachette acquired an initial stake, which became a majority shareholding in 1958. Next came Stock, a publisher specializing in translations, in 1961. Livre de Poche

was the creation in 1960 of the Librairie Générale Française—a subsidiary of Hachette created in 1922—and was largely inspired by publishing in Britain, where good literature in very cheap editions was becoming increasingly popular. Livre de Poche, a series including the best writers since the beginning of the century and a large number of classics at unrivaled prices, achieved considerable success. One year after the creation of the series, 15 million books had already been sold, and two years later, 24 million. Livre de Poche achieved such fame that, from being the proper name of a series, it has become a common name in French, designating paperback editions. In later years, when other paperback editions appeared in France, bookshops were obliged to distinguish a paperback of the Livre de Poche series by the name *poche-Poche.*

By 1963 the Hachette group had become a complex of public limited companies or of limited-liability companies, and achieved sales of FFr1.5 billion, not including N.M.P.P. The publishing division accounted for FFr700 million. Of the total sales figure, FFr200 million came from Hachette's 36 subsidiaries and branch offices scattered around the whole world.

Between 1964 and 1980, the date of Matra's takeover of Hachette, the Librairie grew under the leadership of Robert Meunier de Houssoy, and after 1976 under that of Jacques Marchandise. The company's growth included a number of significant events. The break—made final in 1970—between Hachette and Gallimard, whereby Hachette lost the right to distribute Gallimard's books, was a blow to business. Five years later Hachette brought out the *Encyclopédie Générale d'Hachette* and thereby entered the highly competitive field of dictionaries. The encyclopedia, which covered 100,000 words in 12 volumes, was a success. In the newspaper and magazine publishing sector, Hachette acquired in 1976 the company Jean Prouvost, which owned most notably the weekly *Tele 7 Jours,* with the greatest circulation of any French newspaper or magazine, and *Paris Match.* In 1977 Jean Marchandise decided to change the group's name from the slightly old-fashioned Librairie Hachette to, simply, Hachette. A year later, armed with its new modern image, Hachette opened an immense distribution center, which was almost entirely operated by robots, and which won worldwide admiration. The Centre National de Distribution du Livre (CDL), soon renamed "the Cathedral of Books," consisted of 50,000 square meters dedicated to the storage and distribution of books.

Nevertheless, faced with increasing competition, Hachette was still vulnerable. Its middle-class, family-business management was not successfully meeting competition. Hachette's share price had fallen low enough for a takeover attempt to be made without excessive risk. As Jacques Sauvageot explained in *Le Monde,* December 10, 1990, "the real problem is that Hachette no longer presents to the powers that be the guarantees considered necessary." Giscard d'Estaing's government supported Matra, its principal arms supplier. After a takeover bid by the head of Matra, Jean-Luc Lagardère, Matra became the controlling owner of Hachette stock; by means of holding companies, Matra took control of the capital without holding a majority stake. In 1991 it owned 44% of Hachette. This operation aroused varied and extreme reactions from the French press. Jérome Carcin expressed his fears in *Les Nouvelles Litteraires:* "The publishing industry is gradually losing its financial and intellectual independence," while Guy Sitbon of the *Nouvel Observateur* admitted to a belief that Jean-Luc

Lagardère was "perfect" for the role of "proud and flamboyant servant" required by Giscard d'Estaing.

Lagardère began restructuring, making more than 400 employees redundant as early as June 1981. Lagardère, who seemed to be nurturing his political connections, nevertheless managed, in October 1981, to ensure that Hachette escaped the tidal wave of nationalizations, which caught Matra head on. Indeed, while Matra would from then onward be a state-owned company, Hachette would remain in the private sector. Meanwhile the restructuring continued. Immediately after the takeover of the publisher Jean-Claude Lattès, Lattès himself, against all expectations, became managing director of the book division of the new multimedia group. The latter launched itself into an intensive period of acquisition in France and especially abroad. This began in 1985 with the purchase of a 50% stake in the publisher Harlequin, specialists in low-priced romantic novels. Shortly afterward came the creation of four new series in the Hachette Jeunesse division, which became one of Hachette's most promising divisions. In 1988, in its expansion in the United States, Hachette launched a takeover bid for the publisher Grolier, one of the top-ten U.S. publishing companies specializing in encyclopedias and information publishing. At the beginning of 1989, Hachette set its sights on Spain and bought Salvat, Spain's fifth-largest publisher of encyclopedias and dictionaries. Gradually the book division's performance improved. By 1983 its balance sheet showed positive results in spite of two disappointing setbacks. The first concerned the opening of the Hachette multi-store in Paris in the Opéra district, which failed rapidly. The second, concerned the creation of the series *Succès du Livre* in 1987. Jean-Claude Lattès tried to emulate the France-Loisirs club and launched a series of reprinted bestsellers at a 30% discount. FFr15 million were spent on publicizing this project and some nine months later, in December 1987, Hachette sold the ill-named series to a clearance dealer in Lyons.

Nevertheless Lagardère remained essentially a communications man. The recovery of the book division owed a great deal to the intensive growth of the newspaper and magazine publishing division. As early as 1984, Hachette acquired the U.K. Seymour Press which, together with Cordon & Gotch, became Seymour International Press Distributor Ltd. In 1986, it was the turn of the Curtis Circulation Company, the second-largest distributor of magazines in the United States. The U.S. offensive continued with the acquisition of Diamandis Communica-

tions Inc., the seventh largest U.S. press group, in 1988. Finally, after the arrival of Lagardère, the magazine *Elle* extended its distribution worldwide and now appears in 17 editions, including a Japanese edition.

Since 1980, the beginning of the Lagardère era, Hachette has undergone a definite change of direction. Today's Hachette group is scarcely comparable in terms of size and quality to the Hachette of the mid–20th century, and even less so, to the company at its foundation in 1826. A traditional expansion based on a middle-class family business-style management backed by a united editorial policy and with a narrow range, which ensured its coherence, was succeeded by years of upheaval, by Hachette's transformation into a multimedia, multinational company, a corporate giant, comparable to that of Rupert Murdoch. If Hachette remains the leader in French publishing, the book division is unlikely to continue to receive the full attention of the company's leaders. Since the takeover, in 1986, of one of France's largest radio stations, Europe I, Lagardère has indicated clearly where his ambitions lie—in television. In 1988 he suffered a defeat in his attempt to take over TFI, the leading French television network. In 1990 he acquired a 22% stake in La Cinq and thus became its largest shareholder. Hachette is now involved in publishing and television, controls a French and international press empire, produces films through Hachette Première, and distributes newspapers, magazines and books.

Principal Subsidiaries: Librairie Générale Française; Le Livre de Paris; Groupe Salvat (Spain); Hachette U.S.A. (28%); Librairie Fayard.

Further Reading: Misler, Jean, *La Librairie Hachette de 1826 à nos jours,* Paris, Hachette Editeur, 1964; Sauvageot, Jacques, "L'etau," *Le Monde,* December 10, 1980; Sauvageot, Jacques, "Dans la Presse Hebdomadaire. Hachette: la nouvelle arme de Matra," *Le Monde,* December 1980; Lepape, Pierre, "Hachette-Groupe de la Cité: le face a face de l'edition," *Le Monde Affaires,* February 20, 1988; "Edition: La Tournée des pages," *Les Dossiers du Canard,* June-July, 1989; Lalanne, Bernard, and Nathalie Villard, "Le grand ecart d'Hachette," *L'Expansion,* February 7-20, 1991.

—Sonia Kronlund
Translated from the French by Jessica Griffin

HALLMARK CARDS, INC.

2501 McGee Street
Kansas City, Missouri 64108
U.S.A.
(816) 274-5111
Fax: (816) 274-5061

Private Company
Incorporated: 1923 as Hall Brothers Company
Employees: 22,000
Sales: $2.70 billion

Hallmark Cards, Inc. is the world's largest greeting card company, publishing more than 11 million cards a day in more than 20 languages, and distributing them around the world. Over the years, it has branched out into other areas of the stationery business, including writing paper, party goods, gift wrap, and albums. It also makes Crayola crayons, plush toys, mugs, jigsaw puzzles, and Christmas ornaments; but the greeting card has always been Hallmark's mainstay—so much so that often Hallmark has been mistakenly credited with inventing it.

Hallmark was founded by Joyce C. Hall, a native of Norfolk, Nebraska, who as a teenager ran a postcard company with his older brothers. In 1910 Hall, still only 18, left the family business he had founded after a traveling salesman convinced him that Kansas City, Missouri, would serve him better as a wholesaling and distribution center. Almost immediately after arriving in Kansas City, Hall set up a mail-order postcard company in a small room at the Young Men's Christian Association, where he remained until his landlord complained about the volume of mail Hall was receiving. The new company was named Hall Brothers, a name that Rollie Hall justified the next year when he came to Kansas City to join his brother.

At that time, picture postcards were all the rage in the United States, with the best ones imported from Europe. Very early on, however, Joyce Hall came to believe that the postcard's appeal was quite limited. They were novelty items rather than a means of communication and, with the leisure time needed to write long letters diminishing and the long-distance telephone call still a rare phenomenon, people would need a shorthand way of reaching each other by mail. Greeting cards suggested themselves as a viable alternative, so in 1912 Hall Brothers added them to its product line.

The outbreak of World War I bore out Hall's contention. The supply of postcards from Europe dried up, but domestic products were of inferior quality and their popularity waned. Greeting cards stepped into the breach. In 1914 Hall Brothers bought a small press and began publishing its own line of Christmas cards. In 1915 a fire destroyed the company's entire inventory, putting it $17,000 in debt, but Joyce and Rollie Hall rebuilt the business. In 1921 they were joined by their brother William Hall. By 1922 Hall Brothers had recovered to the point where it was employing 120 people, including salesmen in all 48 states. Also that year, it diversified for the first time and started selling decorative gift wrap.

In 1923 the company formally incorporated under the name Hall Brothers Company. Over the next two decades, it would attack its market aggressively through advertising. In 1928 Hall Brothers became the first greeting card company to advertise nationally when it took out an ad in *Ladies Home Journal.* In 1936, with the national economy emerging from the worst of the Great Depression, Hall Brothers went on the attack again, introducing an open display fixture for greeting cards that Joyce Hall had developed with the help of an architect. Previously, cards had always been kept under store counters, out of customers' sight and usually in a disorganized state. In 1938 Hall Brothers advertised in the broadcast medium for the first time when it began sponsoring "Tony Won's Radio Scrapbook" on WMAQ radio in Chicago.

When the United States entered World War II, the company pitched an appeal to friends and loved ones of military personnel with the slogan, "Keep 'em happy with mail." Hall Brothers would find its most famous and enduring slogan in 1944, however, when it started using "When you care enough to send the very best," which had been suggested a few years earlier by sales and advertising manager Ed Goodman. After the war, a staff artist created the company's logo, which consists of a five-pointed crown and the Hallmark name in script letters. Hall Brothers took out a copyright on the logo in 1949.

The company established another landmark in advertising on Christmas Eve 1951, when it sponsored a television production of Gian Carlo Menotti's opera *Amahl and the Night Visitors.* This was the first of the famous Hallmark Hall of Fame series, which two years later presented a production of *Hamlet* starring the noted British Shakespearean actor Maurice Evans. That broadcast marked the first time the entire play had ever been seen on U.S. television. As Joyce Hall himself once said, "Good taste is good business."

Also in the early 1950s, Hall Brothers began opening the first of thousands of retail shops specializing in Hallmark cards. In 1954 the company changed its name to Hallmark Cards, Inc., having already used Hallmark as a brand name for 31 years. In 1959 the company introduced its Ambassador Cards line to tap into the lucrative market presented by shoppers at mass merchandisers like supermarkets, discount stores, and drugstores. The next year Hallmark introduced its own line of party decorations and began featuring characters from Charles M. Schulz's "Peanuts" comic strip on its products.

Joyce Hall retired as president and CEO of the company he had founded in 1966 and handed the reins to his son, Donald Hall, but remained active in company affairs as chairman until his death in 1982. Joyce Hall was not only a rich and successful businessman when he died, but also a member of the

French Legion of Honor and a commander of the British Empire. He had been friends with British Prime Minister Winston Churchill and with U.S. Presidents Harry Truman and Dwight Eisenhower. For the latter Hall Brothers custom-designed an official presidential Christmas card in 1953.

One of Donald Hall's first important moves as CEO of Hallmark was to acquire Springbok Editions, which makes jigsaw puzzles, in 1967. The next year, the company broke ground on the Crown Center, a $500 million retail, commercial, and residential complex intended to revitalize an area near downtown Kansas City and financed entirely with company funds. Hallmark created a new subsidiary, Crown Center Redevelopment Corporation, to oversee it. In 1981 a suspended walkway at the complex's Hyatt Regency hotel collapsed, killing 114 people and injuring more than 200. It was the worst structural collapse in the history of the United States. After an exhaustive investigation, an administrative law judge determined the structural-engineering firm was responsible for the collapse. Insurance companies for Hallmark paid approximately $140 million to victims.

In 1979 Hallmark acquired Georgia-based lithographer Litho-Krome Corporation. In 1981 the company formed a division, Hallmark Properties, to create and administer licensing projects. This division has created Hallmark's Rainbow Brite, the Purr-Tenders, and Timeless Tales merchandise, and also oversees the company's licenses for Peanuts and Garfield.

After his father's death in 1982, Donald Hall added the chairmanship to his duties as CEO. In 1984 Hallmark acquired Binney & Smith, the Pennsylvania-based maker of Crayola crayons and Liquitex art materials. In 1986 Donald Hall retired as CEO and handed the post to president Irvine O. Hockaday Jr.

In 1987 Hallmark, after being a prominent advertiser in the broadcast media for many years, became an owner as well when it acquired a group of Spanish-language television stations from Spanish International Communication. The next year, it added another station purchased from Bahia de San Francisco Television. Also in 1988, Hallmark acquired a Spanish-language network, Univision, and amalgamated all of its holdings in a subsidiary, Univision Holdings. Based in New York, the subsidiary runs the nine full-power stations under the name Univision Station Group.

During the mid-1980s small greeting card companies began competing for Hallmark's market position with a diverse array of cards that have become favorites. In the mid-1980s Hallmark fought back with its Personal Touch and Shoebox Greetings series. Many of these cards, however, bore a resemblance to rival designs that some found too striking. In 1986 Blue Mountain Arts, which produces non-occasion cards that use poetry and pastel illustrations to produce a concentrated emotional effect, sued Hallmark for copyright and trade dress infringement and unfair competition. The initial decision went against Hallmark, which appealed ultimately to the Supreme Court. When the Supreme Court refused to hear the case in 1988, Hallmark agreed to discontinue the Personal Touch line. Financial terms of the settlement were not disclosed.

Critics agree that Hallmark missed the boat when it came to the alternative greeting card market and wound up paying for it. Nevertheless, the company maintained its place as the leader in the personal communications industry. Successful product-line introductions in the ensuing years have included Between You and Me; Just How I Feel; and To Kids With Love, the industry's first line of anyday cards for adults to send to children. Hallmark easily remains the leader in its industry.

Principal Subsidiaries: Binney & Smith; Crown Center Redevelopment Corporation; Graphics International; Hallmark Marketing Corporation; Halls Merchandising Incorporated; Litho-Krome Corporation; Univision Holdings Incorporated.

Further Reading: Stern, Ellen, *The Very Best From Hallmark*, New York, Harry N. Abrams, 1988.

—Joan Harpham and Douglas Sun

HARCOURT BRACE JOVANOVICH, INC.

6277 Sea Harbor Drive
Orlando, Florida 32887
U.S.A.
(407) 345-2000
Fax: (407) 345-8388

Public Company
Incorporated: 1919 as Harcourt, Brace and Company
Employees: 6,300
Sales: $1.41 billion
Stock Exchange: New York

Harcourt Brace Jovanovich, Inc. (HBJ) is one of the world's largest publishers. HBJ's publishing activities accounted for 66% of the company's sales revenues at the start of the 1990s. HBJ's insurance operations produced the balance, 34%.

HBJ publishes about 5,000 new book titles each year for the trade and textbook markets. While the company's publishing endeavors are diverse, its greatest activity centers around elementary school, secondary school, and college textbooks, and related educational materials. In the elementary and secondary school textbook market, HBJ is recognized as one of the nation's leading publishers and one of the nation's top five in the college textbook market. It is the largest publisher of journals for the scientific and medical communities, publishing about 240 scholarly journals each year.

At the close of World War I, two former classmates from Columbia University, Alfred Harcourt and Donald C. Brace, left their positions at Henry Holt & Company and started their own trade publishing house in New York. The year was 1919, and the firm was known as Harcourt, Brace and Howe. Alfred Harcourt had served as acquisitions editor and salesman in his 15 years with Holt; Donald Brace, in manufacturing and production. Will D. Howe, an author and editor, had headed the English department at Indiana University. He left the new firm less than a year after its founding, and the name was changed to Harcourt, Brace and Company.

Three months after incorporation, Harcourt, Brace and Company published its first book, *Organizing for Work* by H.L. Gantt. In the months and years that followed, Harcourt, Brace and Company had one success after another. John Maynard Keynes's *The Economic Consequences of Peace* was considered a milestone in publishing history. Other notable works included Sinclair Lewis's *Free Air, Main Street,* and *Arrows-*

mith, the latter winning a Pulitzer Prize. Lewis had followed his editor, Harcourt, from Henry Holt.

In its first decade, Harcourt, Brace and Company diversified into a number of genres, including religious works and college and high school textbooks. The house also published some of the nation's most outstanding trade books and outstanding authors. Throughout its history, Harcourt, Brace and Company would be recognized as an innovator in the publishing industry. In the 1920s the company offered women employees equal career opportunities, a practice virtually nonexistent in the trade at that time. This philosophy was attributed in part to Ellen Knowles Eayres, the firm's first employee, who later married Alfred Harcourt.

The head of the first children's book department, from 1946 to 1972, was Margaret McElderry. Well known and well liked, she is credited with the discovery of many famous children's authors, Joan Walsh Anglund and Eleanor Estes among them.

During World War II Harcourt, Brace and Company published *Men Must Act* by Lewis Mumford, an anti-fascist book. It was offered free, in an advertisement in *The New York Times,* to the first 500 New Yorkers to respond. The response was unexpected: all 500 copies were given away by noon, and it was estimated that another 2,000 people were turned away.

The house retained many famous authors throughout the years, but in 1955 several of them followed a well respected Harcourt editor, Robert Giroux, who left to become a partner in Farrar, Straus & Giroux. Among the more than 17 authors who left with him were T.S. Eliot, Flannery O'Connor, John Berryman, and Bernard Malamud.

In 1942 Alfred Harcourt resigned as president, leaving control of the company's operations in the hands of Donald Brace. In 1955, one year after Harcourt's death, William Jovanovich was elected president of Harcourt, Brace and Company. Donald Brace died in September of that year at the age of 74. William Jovanovich, a Colorado native, had joined the company in 1947 as a textbook salesman with a salary of $50 per week. Six years later he headed the school department, and in 1955 he was president of the company. While Jovanovich, at the time, was the youngest director with the company and owned no stock, he was the strong leader that the families of the two founders had sought.

Once at the helm, Jovanovich set a clear path for turning the company into a conglomerate. Two of his first goals were to take the company public and to merge with World Book Company, incorporated in 1905. Both moves were accomplished in 1960. Harcourt, Brace & World, Inc. was formed as a result, and took its position as the largest publisher of elementary, secondary, and college materials in the nation. Until 1990 the company would be lead by aggressive and determined Jovanovich. The company would diversify into dozens of publishing markets as well as into businesses totally unrelated to publishing by acquiring more than 40 companies.

In publishing the late 1960s saw the acquisition of two educational filmstrip production companies; several farm and trade publications; and Academic Press, Inc., an international concern that published physical and applied science books and journals. Each year during the 1970s, except 1975, the company acquired at least one publishing or education-related firm.

In 1970 Jovanovich became chairman of the company, and its name was changed from Harcourt, Brace & World, Inc. to

Harcourt Brace Jovanovich, Inc. Among the most notable acquisitions of the 1970s were The Psychological Corporation, in 1970, publishers of aptitude, diagnostic, achievement, and psychlogical tests; Beckley-Cardy Company, in 1972, a school-supply house; Bay Area Review Course, Inc. and BRI Bar Review Institute, Inc. in 1974, the two being among the nation's best bar exam review courses; and Pyramid Communications, Inc. in 1974, renamed Jove Publications, Inc., a mass-market paperback publisher of romance, inspirational, sports, and health books. Also in 1984 Drake-Beam & Associates, now Drake Beam Morin, Inc., an outplacement conseling firm, was acquired. By 1978 HBJ was publishing about 2,300 titles—from newsletters to romances—and 75 magazines, with revenues hovering around $360 million.

The 1970s were not without their drawbacks. In 1974 operations at four German publishing houses purchased in 1970 were terminated because of poor profits. Price controls affected profits at Academic Press for a number of years. Jove/HBJ, an experimental imprint, was failing, and it was sold in 1979. HBJ's trade division operated at a deficit beginning early in the decade. In 1977 HBJ lost $1.6 million on its general-interest books alone.

In early 1978 Jovanovich cut the company's budget, firing six of the trade division's top personnel; he put himself in charge of hardcover adult and juvenile works. The discharge came several days after HBJ regrouped its operations and created an office of the president. Jovanovich claimed the firings had nothing to do with this reorganization.

Three executive vice presidents were elected to fill the office of the president—Robert L. Edgell, Robert R. Hillebrecht, and Jack O. Snyder. HBJ was reorganized into five operational groups: university and scholarly publishing, school materials and assessment, periodicals and insurance, business publications and broadcasting, and popular enterprises. This latter group, headed by Hillebrecht, included the marine parks known as Sea World, an acquisition of 1976.

To acquire Sea World, Inc., HBJ had borrowed $46.7 million. Sea World was composed of three marine parks, located in San Diego, California; Cleveland, Ohio; and Orlando, Florida; and was considered some of the world's finest living museums. In 1977 Sea World helped push the company's gross sales to $281.7 million.

In 1980 Jovanovich told *The New York Times* that he was again looking for new acquisitions, and the decade would see HBJ's attention turned to theme parks, insurance, and more publishing. In 1980 HBJ purchased a commercial insurance broker for the dental profession. In 1982 HBJ bought three publishing concerns, acquiring business periodicals serving a number of specialized industries. Acquisitions made in 1984 and 1985 diversified HBJ into 11 new periodical markets. Also in 1985, HBJ acquired three insurance operations. The largest, purchased for $130 million, were Federal Home Life Insurance Company and PHF Life Insurance Company of Battle Creek, Michigan.

In 1982 HBJ made the startling announcement it would move HBJ's headquarters from New York City to Orlando, Florida, and the trade department to San Diego, California. *Business Week,* March 31, 1982, quoted Jovanovich as saying "We're moving because the continued profitability of publishing is in jeopardy." A projected annual savings in rent and operation expenses of $20 million topped Jovanovich's reasons for the move. "Too much time is spent lunching, and not enough is spent reading. Many of our writers don't live in New York anyway," Jovanovich noted.

HBJ planned to use the employee pension fund, which, the company stated, was "hugely overfunded," to finance the new corporate headquarters. The investment, according to Jovanovich, would yield a considerable return—15% of the building's cost in annual rent. In September 1983, the U.S. Labor Department prohibited the use of the fund, and HBJ was required to return all monies to the fund. The move, complete in 1984, included the construction of an eight-story, 385,000-square-foot office building across from Sea World. The new HBJ headquarters cost the company $20 million. The move, as of 1986, cost HBJ a total of $35 million.

Once established in its new home, HBJ went on another theme-park buying spree, spending a total of $67.7 million. In September 1974 HBJ bought Stars Hall of Fame in Orlando, which was soon converted to Places of Learning. In 1985 HBJ acquired Florida Cypress Gardens, Inc., a botanical garden and entertainment park near Winter Haven, Florida, paying $22.6 million in stock for the opportunity. In December 1986 HBJ acquired Marineland Amusements Corporation in Rancho Palos Verdes, California.

Near the end of 1986 HBJ made the biggest purchase in its history. For $500 million HBJ acquired the educational and professional publishing division of CBS Inc. The division's primary subsidiaries included W.B. Saunders, the world's largest publisher of medical and health science textbooks and materials; and Holt, Rinehart and Winston, Inc. (HRW), one of the nation's top textbook publishers. HRW was the evolutionary product of Henry Holt & Company—the firm from which Harcourt, Brace and Howe had started. The purchase placed HBJ as the largest publisher of elementary school and high school textbooks.

In 1987 Robert Maxwell, the chairman of British Printing and Communications Corporation (BPCC), set his sights on acquiring Harcourt Brace Jovanovich. Maxwell was looking for a U.S. publishing house, and offered more than $2 billion for the company. HBJ was not interested. Twice in HBJ's history had a takeover prompted Jovanovich into action—once in 1978 by Marvin Josephson, and again in 1981 by Warner Communications. Neither the action nor the results in either case had been far reaching.

In a press release dated May 26, 1987, HBJ announced its plan to fight the BPPC proposal, a recapitalization distribution. The plan included a $40-per-share special dividend and the issuance of new preferred stock.

On May 28 Maxwell announced he had withdrawn his offer, but HBJ had paid a hefty price. To fend off the takeover, HBJ had more than tripled its debt, from $837 million to $2.9 billion, requiring bank loans for a substantial portion of that figure. The withdrawal of his offer notwithstanding, on June 1 Maxwell tried to block the reorganization plan. At the close of business June 2, more than 3.3 million HBJ shares had changed hands, with the price skyrocketing to $63.75. A number of companies, along with Maxwell's BPCC, opposed HBJ's reorganization. After an Orange County, Florida, judge ruled in HBJ's favor in late June, Maxwell withdrew.

In August 1987 HBJ began its attempt to cover the cost of the takeover defense by selling assets. Among the first to go were HBJ's two VHF television stations and three corporate jets, the sales of which brought in about $20 million. Also to go were two book clubs. In November HBJ announced the sale of its 110 trade magazines and Beckley-Cardy for $334 million. The buyer was Edgell Communications Inc., a new, private corporation formed in part by Robert Edgell, a former HBJ executive.

By year's end HBJ had met its performing-asset sale requirement under its credit agreements. The company had sold more than $370 million in assets. Speculation continued, however, as did the rumors as to which property HBJ would sell next and to whom. On January 1, 1988, William Jovanovich announced that the HBJ theme parks were not for sale.

Several months later, HBJ eliminated 729 jobs from its theme park operations. While neither the HBJ publishing or insurance divisions were affected, the layoff included more than 343 positions at Florida-based theme parks, and 17% of the work force at Sea World in San Antonio, Texas.

On March 30, 1988, Ralph D. Caulo, age 53, was announced as HBJ's newly elected president and chief operating officer. Caulo, who joined HBJ in 1967 as a textbook sales manager, served as an executive vice president in Orlando, heading the school publishing division. Since 1970 William Jovanovich had been chief executive, president, and chairman. On December 17, 1988, at age 68, William Jovanovich resigned his position as president and chief executive officer of Harcourt Brace Jovanovich, retaining only his position as chairman.

During the late 1980s some analysts believed the company's financial situation to be anything but hopeful. Forced to sell revenue-generating assets to repay debt, HBJ was threatening its long-range solvency. William Jovanovich claimed that "HBJ could repay its obligations without now selling major assets."

In November 1989, HBJ sold all six of its theme parks and related land holdings to Anheuser-Busch Companies. The price was $1.1 billion, which went to retire the bank loans. The year also saw significant structural changes within HBJ operations. Elementary and secondary textbook divisions were divided. HBJ would now publish kindergarten through eighth-grade textbooks, while subsidiary Holt, Rinehart and Winston would publish those for grades seven through twelve. HBJ and HRW school department heads resigned, as did six executives in the elementary and secondary divisions. Ralph Caulo resigned as president, and Peter Jovanovich was elected in his place.

William Jovanovich's son, Peter William Jovanovich, was born in New York City in 1949. He joined the HBJ trade department in 1980. Peter Jovanovich inherited HBJ's $1.6 billion debt. Wall Street analysts and institutional investors openly expressed concern regarding Jovanovich's ability to pull the company from its troubles. HBJ's operating loss for 1989 reached $242 million, with interest payments on its debt at $350.8 million, and its share price at around $3.

In April 1990 HBJ confirmed its intentions to sell additional assets. Speculation by analysts targeted HBJ's professional publishing division, including W.B. Saunders as one possibility, estimating a sale price at around $600 million. Another option would be the company's insurance operations, which in 1989, had $456.3 million in revenues. Still other sources dis-

closed the possibility of a renewed interest in HBJ by BPCC chairman Robert Maxwell.

On May 29, 1990, William Jovanovich retired from his 36-year tenure as chairman of HBJ, naming John S. Herrington as his successor. The *New York Times*, May 30, 1990, quoted Roger Straus, chairman of Farrar, Straus & Giroux: "It is very sad. Bill was a great publisher in his time, but he went too far in resisting Maxwell. Now I suspect that he does not want to be there for the dismemberment." Herrington had joined the HBJ board of directors in 1989. A lawyer, Herrington served as secretary of energy to U.S. President Ronald Reagan.

In September 1990 Vice Chairman and Chief Operating Officer J. William Brandner, HBJ's second in command, resigned. HBJ announced that his resignation was part of a budget cut that was expected to help curb operating expenses without hindering operations. In the same month, HBJ hired a spokesman—a first in HBJ's 71-year history. C. Anson Franklin had served as assistant energy secretary under Herrington and as assistant press secretary in the Reagan administration. Franklin's job, in addition to serving as liaison between the company, its shareholders, and the press, was to improve HBJ's community and company communications.

In October 1990 speculation continued as to HBJ's next strategy for deferring its debt burden. With HBJ's stock hovering at $1.25, and its long-term debt at $1.76 billion, analysts projected another large asset sale.

Also in October 1990 an HBJ author, Octavio Paz, was awarded the Nobel Prize for Literature. The poet, age 76, is the first Mexican writer to receive literature's highest recognition, awarded by the Swedish Academy of Letters. He is the author of *Convergences: Essay on Art and Literature,* and *One Earth, Four or Five Worlds: Reflections on Contemporary History.*

As HBJ's 1993 obligation to pay dividends and interest to its bond holders drew near, HBJ continued to consider its alternatives, one of which was a merger from General Cinema. The offer would wipe the debt slate clean, and apparently please all associated with the company except its bond holders, who would collect less than they expected.

In January 1991, after announcing it would sell its Orlando book warehouse, the board of HBJ approved the merger with General Cinema. After its initial offer expired, General Cinema announced a revised merger plan in August 1991. The $1.5 billion deal would make HBJ a subsidiary of General Cinema, contingent on stockholder and bondholder approval.

Principal Subsidiaries: Academic Press, Inc.; Harcourt Brace Jovanovich Group (Australia); Harcourt Brace Jovanovich International Corporation; Harcourt Brace Jovanovich Japan, Inc. (99.17%); HBJ Holding Corporation; HBJ Life & Health Coverage, Inc.; Holt, Rinehart and Winston, Inc.; The Psychological Corporation; W.B. Saunders Company; Webber Costello, Inc.

Further Reading: Tebbel, John, *A History of Book Publishing in the United States,* 4 vols., New York, R.R. Bowker Company, 1972–1981.

—Janie Pritchett

The Hearst Corporation

THE HEARST CORPORATION

959 Eighth Avenue
New York, New York 10019
U.S.A.
(212) 649-2000
Fax: (212) 765-3528

Private Company
Incorporated: 1943
Employees: 14,000
Sales: $2.10 billion

The Hearst Corporation is a modern communications empire whose interests stretch from newspapers to publishing to broadcasting. The company's history spans more than a century, during which Hearst papers, led by their founder, played a significant role in the history of the United States.

The shape and history of the company's early years were intertwined with the history and designs of its founder, William Randolph Hearst. A man who inherited enormous wealth, Hearst was also a person of enormous ambition and activity, whose initial interest in journalism in an era when the newspaper business could hardly be separated from the political arena led to a consuming passion for political office that was destined to end in frustration.

The company that became a behemoth in communications started out as payment for a gambling debt, when William Randolph Hearst's father, George Hearst, a self-made millionaire who had earned his fortune in mining and ranching, took possession of the *San Francisco Examiner* in 1880 after its owner had lost a wager with him. Seven years later, William Randolph Hearst, recently expelled from Harvard College for an elaborate prank, took over the paper he desired to run.

Newspapers in that day were, for the most part, organs of propaganda for individual politicians and political parties. Indeed, Hearst's father had accepted the paper only for the purpose of enhancing his own political career. William Randolph Hearst had big plans in mind for the money-losing four-page daily paper. Taking Joseph Pulitzer's *New York World* as his model, he began by sinking large sums into the latest printing technology, and changing the paper's appearance to make it more compelling. In addition, he hired new staff members—bagging such luminaries as Ambrose Bierce—and charged them with the aggressive pursuit of stories that would improve the paper's circulation. The first big coup came with the *Examiner's* sensational coverage of a big hotel fire, just one

month after Hearst took over. Slowly the paper's fortunes improved, helped along by a large dose of self-promotion. Hearst was shortly to crown his paper "A GREAT PAPER."

Hearst employees were diligent in their pursuit of shocking and titillating material to draw in more readers. In the absence of genuinely sensational news, they did not hesitate to manufacture newsworthy events, or simply make things up. Much of the manufactured news was billed as crusading exposure of social ills, as when a woman reporter feigned illness to expose the condition of the city's ambulance corps and hospital, or when one intrepid Hearst journalist threw himself into San Francisco Bay from a ferry to test rescue procedures. Both of these stories did in fact result in improvements in the city agencies involved. In his first year, Hearst launched more than a dozen crusades, taking on such established powers as the city's political machine and the Southern Pacific Railroad. All of this activity, along with Hearst features such as the publication of the scores of popular songs on Sunday and the introduction of a column devoted to union activities, added up to a new kind of journalism and contributed to a slowly growing circulation. Advertising revenues remained low, however, and Hearst's paper continued to consume large sums of his father's money until 1890, when it first went into the black.

By 1895 the *Examiner* was thriving, both in terms of circulation and revenue, and Hearst was ready for a new challenge. He found it in New York, taking over a decrepit daily paper, the *New York Journal.* He began by sending for the best of his San Francisco staff, dropping the price of the New York paper to 1¢, and increasing its size. Hearst was going after his old ideal, Pulitzer's *World,* and his most successful tactic, was the wholesale raiding of Pulitzer's staff. Waving enormous salaries, he lured some of his rival's best staff away, including the creator of the popular comic "The Yellow Kid," which would inspire the phrase "yellow journalism," used to describe the sensational and irresponsible coverage that Hearst and his rivals pioneered.

In the ensuing contest between the two papers, the techniques that Hearst's organization had first polished in San Francisco—sensationalism and crusading campaigns on behalf of the ordinary person—were taken to new heights. In addition, the paper became inextricably involved with political parties, power, and disputes, becoming heavily identified with presidential candidate William Jennings Bryan and the Democratic Party. Since all the other large newspapers backed William McKinley, the *Journal* rapidly became the leading Democratic newspaper in the country.

Perhaps the ultimate manufactured news event was the one that started the Spanish-American War. From the start, Hearst's paper had strongly supported Cuban independence from Spain. When the American battleship *Maine* mysteriously blew up in Havana harbor in February 1898, Hearst and his employees printed two weeks' worth of fraudulent material blaming Spain for the attack. This coverage, which Hearst orchestrated but in which he was not alone, resulted in increased circulation for the paper, and in war.

With the dawning of the new century, Hearst's fledgling network of newspapers continued to expand. Attempting to bolster support for Bryan's 1900 presidential bid, Hearst founded the *Chicago American,* whose first issue rolled off the presses on July 4, 1900. Bryan lost once again to McKinley. Hearst's overwhelming identification in the public's mind with opposition to the president became a grave liability after McKinley was assassinated in September 1901. Some groups boycotted and banned Hearst papers. Nevertheless, his New York paper, the *Journal,* claimed the greatest number of paid subscribers in the world by the end of the year. When Hearst was elected to Congress the following year, his papers became his personal forum for conducting political activity. In 1904 the *Boston American* was added to the fold. Two years later, the 1906 San Francisco earthquake dealt a major blow to the flagship of the Hearst organization, reducing the physical plant of the *Examiner* to a ruin. Despite the devastation, the three San Francisco papers produced a joint issue on the first day after the quake, and shortly thereafter, the *Examiner* was back on its feet.

The Hearst organization branched out into magazines in 1903, with the founding of *Motor* magazine, a venture inspired by *The Car,* a British publication Hearst had come across on his honeymoon. Two years later, he bought *Cosmopolitan,* a magazine of fiction and nonfiction. Filled with the work of some of the best writers of the day, its circulation soon doubled. Hearst's most important magazine acquisition was *Good Housekeeping* in 1911. This purchase also included the laboratory facilities that would develop into the Good Housekeeping Institute and the Good Housekeeping Seal, heavily promoted under the new owners.

Hearst papers took a vigorous anti-British and isolationist stance in the era leading up to the United States's entry into World War I, bannering slogans like "America First" and "No Entangling Alliances" in fierce opposition to the policies of President Woodrow Wilson. When the United States declared war in April 1917, Hearst's opposition to the U.S. effort to aid the Allies, and perceived pro-German sentiment, resulted in lower circulation for his newspapers in many cities. Throughout this era, William Randolph Hearst continued his political activities in pursuit of the presidency, and Hearst papers were instruments in his crusade.

Nevertheless, throughout the second decade of the century, Hearst enterprises grew at a prodigious pace. By 1920 the print operations numbered 13 newspapers and 7 magazines, including the profitable *American Weekly* newspaper insert and the British *Nash's.* As offshoots of the newspapers, the organization also owned a money-losing newswire, the International News Service, which had emerged from World War I with its credibility badly damaged, and the King Features Syndicate, which sold the work of Hearst writers and artists to other papers.

In addition, Hearst had entered the film industry in 1913, when the first newsreel—footage of Woodrow Wilson's inauguration—was shown in movie theaters. This showing led to the establishment of the Hearst-Selig News Pictorial in 1914, which pioneered film journalism throughout the 1920s evolving into Hearst Metrotone News with the arrival of sound in 1929. For entertainment, Hearst produced in partnership with Pathé Fréres such long-running serials as *The Perils of Pauline.* Intent both on promoting the career of his mistress, Marion Davies, and becoming a movie mogul himself, William Randolph Hearst formed Cosmopolitan Productions and in 1919 built a studio in Harlem where movies could be filmed. Hearst papers duly praised the resulting products. In time, the studio moved to Hollywood where it joined with other studios, producing musical extravaganzas like *Broadway Melody,* and other films.

As William Randolph Hearst continued to seek political office in the 1920s, Hearst operations continued to grow. Papers were acquired or founded at a brisk pace, including three in 1921, six in 1922, one in 1923, and three in 1924. On the international front, Hearst expanded its magazine holdings in Britain to include *Good Housekeeping, Connoisseur,* and *Harper's Bazaar.*

By the early 1930s the tally of Hearst papers was up to 28, and the magazines numbered 13. Along with his other ventures, this necessarily gave Hearst great influence in public affairs. His influence was enhanced by the Hearst company's entry into the fledgling radio industry in 1928 with the purchase of WISN in Milwaukee, Wisconsin. By the mid-1930s it owned ten radio stations. In 1934, the Hearst organization was restructured to give Hearst editorial control while trusted subordinates handled day-to-day business matters. By the following year Hearst had become implacable in his opposition to the policies of Franklin Delano Roosevelt whom he had initially helped to win the Democratic nomination in 1932. In the 1936 campaign Hearst papers supported Roosevelt's opponent Alf Landon. Throughout the 1930s, Hearst papers were unstinting in their opposition to socialism and communism. This fact combined with Hearst's love for Germany, where he traveled often, and his growing conservatism, often led his opponents to charge him with fascism.

Throughout the years of financial turmoil and decline that began with the stock market crash in 1929, Hearst, who was accustomed to wealth of unimaginable proportions, had not significantly altered his activities. He continued to spend lavishly on art and on the construction and upkeep of his several estates. In addition, the company had used several bond issues to raise capital, resulting in debts that reached $137 million. In 1937 under pressure from the shareholders, and various banks and newsprint companies to whom Hearst owed money, the company tried to float another set of debentures, but was prevented from doing so by the Securities and Exchange Commission. The crash had come. Faced with the virtual bankruptcy of his vast empire, Hearst, now nearly 75 years old, turned over complete financial control of his holdings to a lawyer approved by his creditors, who quickly began to restructure drastically the Hearst organization. Six money-losing newspapers and seven radio stations were sold, a magazine was scrapped, and Hearst's New York flagship paper, the *New York American,* was merged with its evening counterpart. A Conservation Committee was formed to sell off assets including two-thirds of Hearst's art collection.

Four years later in 1941, the Hearst organization was still fighting for fiscal survival. By now, there were 94 Hearst entities with complex financial ties. With the U.S.'s entry into World War II, Hearst papers—by now reduced to 18—dropped their isolationist stance and wholeheartedly supported the war effort. It was the war, opposed so staunchly by Hearst editorialists, that helped the company to regain its financial health, as the war sent circulation and advertising revenues rising.

At the end of 1943 the trustee and the Conservation Committee appointed in 1937 were succeeded by a voting trust that included two of Hearst's five sons. The trust continued to sell off property, including two-thirds of Hearst's vast San Simeon estate, and to rearrange assets, in 1943 consolidating everything within The Hearst Corporation holding company. By the end of the war in 1945, the company was on more solid financial ground once again. Three years later, the company entered a new field in communications when WBAL-TV in Baltimore, Maryland, began to broadcast.

By 1947 William Randolph Hearst had reached the age of 84 and had suffered a heart attack, and his involvement in the company was waning. On August 14, 1951, Hearst died, ending an era in U.S. journalism. His will stipulated that his $57 million estate be divided for tax purposes into a charitable trust and a restructured corporation. Hearst left the 100 shares of voting stock that controlled the company in the hands of a board made up of five family members and six company executives, insuring that those outside the family would have control of the corporation. One of the executives, Richard Berlin, took over as chief executive officer at Hearst's death, after 32 years with the company.

During Berlin's tenure, the company saw the collapse of its first base of operations, its newspapers, and expanded its holdings in other fields of the communications industry, such as magazines and television. The advent of television ended newspaper journalism as William Randolph Hearst had known it. No longer did the papers provide the public's primary source of news. This change in social habits resulted in a vast shake-out in the newspaper industry, in which afternoon papers in particular were hard hit, the Hearst publications included. The first paper to go was the *Chicago American,* a long-time money-loser, which was sold to its competitor, the *Tribune,* in 1956. Two years later, the Hearst newswire, International News Service, and its affiliated photo service were sold to rival United Press. Under Berlin's direction the company shed papers in San Francisco, Pittsburgh, Detroit, Boston, Los Angeles, and Milwaukee in quick succession. In 1963 Hearst sold its money-losing morning tabloid the *New York Mirror,* which had the second-largest circulation in the United States. The cruelest blow came in 1966, when Hearst's flagship *Journal-American* folded in New York.

In contrast, Hearst expanded its magazine operations throughout this period, concentrating on special interest publications rather than broad, general interest titles. In 1953 the company purchased *Sports Afield* and five years later added another men's magazine, *Popular Mechanics.* Shortly thereafter, a Spanish edition of the magazine was granted the first license for a Hearst magazine foreign edition. Eventually, the company would successfully license nearly 60 foreign editions of its publications. In 1959 the company branched out into book publishing when it purchased Avon Publications, Inc., which produced paperbacks. In addition to new acquisitions, old publications underwent renovations, enabling them to contribute strong performances to the magazine group. *Cosmopolitan,* for instance, retooled in 1965 from a general interest magazine of fiction and nonfiction to the interests of working women and became a huge money-maker. In 1966 another venerable Hearst magazine, *Good Housekeeping,* became the leader in its field.

At his retirement in 1973, Berlin left Hearst debt-free and rich in capital, yet far poorer in publications and importance than it had once been. The following year the company was again restructured when it used the cash built up during Berlin's tenure to buy back the stock held by Hearst charitable foundations, which had been established at Hearst's death to avoid inheritance taxes. The Hearst family regained control of the company's assets, now privately owned, and the chain of command within the company was simplified. Throughout the second half of the 1970s under the leadership of John R. Miller, Hearst experienced a huge growth in profits, as properties that had been allowed to lie dormant began to produce. For instance, the company tapped the reserve of goodwill built up in the names *House Beautiful* and *Good Housekeeping* when it successfully spun off *Colonial Homes* and *Country Living* from the older publications.

In 1979 Hearst again began to expand its newspaper holdings by buying five daily papers in mid-sized cities in Michigan, Texas, and Illinois. In the early 1980s acquisitions continued until the newspaper group was 15 strong, with publications in Houston, Seattle, Los Angeles, and San Francisco, as well as other, smaller cities.

By the start of the 1980s, the Hearst magazine division was the largest U.S. producer of monthly magazines. It continued to perform well throughout the 1980s, adding *Redbook, Esquire,* a U.S. version of the British *Connoisseur,* and other titles. The Hearst magazine distribution network, which already included three subscriber services, purchased a fourth, Communications Data Services, Inc., in 1982.

During the 1980s the company's scope shifted beyond print to encompass the whole spectrum of communications enterprises. Under the leadership of Frank A. Bennack Jr., who took over as chief executive officer in 1979, Hearst expanded its broadcast division to include six TV stations and seven radio stations. The company entered the cable television industry in 1980, joining with other partners in ventures such as the Arts & Entertainment Network and LIFETIME, a network devoted to programming for women. In late 1990 the company bought a one-fifth share in the sports network ESPN.

The Hearst Corporation had thus evolved from a newspaper chain known for sensationalism and irresponsible journalism, and dominated by the will of one man, to a vast and highly profitable enterprise encompassing a broad range of communications fields. As it entered the 1990s, the company appeared to be firmly positioned to use its resources for further growth.

Further Reading: Lundberg, Ferdinand, *Imperial Hearst: A Social Biography,* New York, Equinox Cooperative Press, 1936; Swanberg, W.A., *Citizen Hearst: A Biography of William Randolph Hearst,* New York, Charles Scribner's Sons, 1961; Chaney, Lindsay and Michael Cieply, *The Hearsts: Family and Empire—The Later Years,* New York, Simon & Schuster, 1981; O'Donnell, James F., *100 Years of Making Communications History: The Story of the Hearst Corporation,* New York, Hearst Professional Magazines, Inc., 1987.

—Elizabeth Rourke

KNIGHT-RIDDER, INC.

One Herald Plaza
Miami, Florida 33132
U.S.A.
(305) 376-3800
Fax: (305) 376-3876

Public Company
Incorporated: 1974 as Knight-Ridder Newspapers, Inc.
Employees: 20,000
Sales: $2.31 billion
Stock Exchanges: New York Tokyo Philadelphia Chicago Boston San Francisco Los Angeles Cincinnati

Knight-Ridder, Inc. is one of the largest newspaper groups in the United States, owning 29 newspapers, as well as an international information and communications company that offers news, graphics, and photo services, and cable television. The company's newspapers are well regarded in terms of editorial quality, and have won numerous Pulitzer Prizes. Despite these achievements, Knight-Ridder lagged the industry in profitability during much of the 1980s. To reduce its debt, it sold off several newspapers during the late 1980s, as well as five of its eight television stations. The company relies on newspapers for 86% of its profits.

The company began as two separate newspaper groups, which merged in 1974. The Ridder group originated in 1892, when Herman Ridder purchased the *Staats-Zeitung*, a New York German-language paper. The Knight group began in 1903 when Charles Landon (C.L.) Knight bought the *Akron Beacon Journal*, in Ohio, which the company still owns. He soon bought two smaller Ohio newspapers, the *Springfield Sun* and the *Massillon Independent*.

C.L. Knight, a brilliant writer, began training his son John at an early age to replace him. John S. Knight worked as copy boy and reporter, then went to college and fought in World War I. In 1919, at age 25, he joined the *Beacon Journal*'s staff, and became managing editor in 1925. He carefully observed the operations of better newspapers and applied his insights to the *Beacon Journal*. C.L. Knight died in 1933, in the depths of the Great Depression, leaving an estate of $515,000 and debts of $800,000 to his sons, John S. and James L. Knight. The *Beacon Journal* was facing stiff competition from another Akron paper, the *Times-Press*, owned by Scripps-Howard, and the Great Depression was at its most severe. John Knight froze family earnings and took on the

Times-Press, running more news and features than his competitor to win over readers. He paid off the *Beacon Journal*'s debts within four years, and made it Akron's leading newspaper.

John Knight's first major test as publisher came during a 1936 Akron rubber strike. Rubber was the city's major industry, and as the strike dragged on, money and advertising dried up. The *Times-Press* cut back on editorial pages, but Knight increased local news coverage and won readers from the *Times-Press*. When the strike ended, he kept the readers and won new advertising.

On October 15, 1937, John Knight became president and publisher of *The Miami Herald*, after purchasing it for $2.25 million. The business side of the paper had been run poorly before the Knights bought it, so James Knight, who had studied the business and production side of newspaper publishing, became operations manager. The Knights's first move was to distance the paper from the Miami political establishment, with which it had previously had close ties. The *Herald* had two competitors. The Knights soon bought one, the *Miami Tribune*, which had been losing money. For a cost of $600,000 plus the *Massillon Independent*, the Knights bought the *Tribune*, eliminating a competitor and acquiring the *Tribune*'s building, new printing press, and other equipment. Knight closed the *Tribune* on December 1, 1937, taking six of the *Tribune*'s best people with him.

The Knights added more photographs, comics, and new columnists to the *Herald*. In the next two years two local stories—a kidnapping case and a controversy over pasteurized milk—received national attention and won 14,000 new readers for the *Herald*. Having turned the *Miami Herald* around, the Knights bought another paper, the *Detroit Free Press*, in 1940.

In 1941 Knight Newspapers, Inc. was incorporated in Ohio. World War II found German submarines off the Florida coast driving away tourists and the business that had supported the *Herald*. The paper lost much of its staff to the army, but several large military bases were set up in the Miami area, and the soldiers boosted the *Herald*'s circulation again. Lee Hills was brought in as news editor. He immediately recruited talented journalists from other Florida papers to make up for the staff the *Herald* had lost to the war effort. When a serious newsprint shortage created problems toward the end of the war, Hills and James Knight decided to cut advertising and circulation outside the Miami metropolitan area rather than editorial content, which wrested a large number of readers from its remaining competitor, *The Miami News*.

In 1944 the Knights bought the *Chicago Daily News* for $3 million, and took on the paper's $12 million debt. The *Daily News* had won a reputation for having the most thorough foreign news section of any Chicago paper, but John Knight found the stories too long and poorly written. He ordered the stories to be made more succinct, creating a brief storm of protest among some writers and readers.

The population of Dade County, Florida, nearly doubled in the years 1940 to 1950, and the *Herald*'s circulation grew apace, from 86,313 in 1941 to 175,985 in 1951. In 1946 Lee Hills began the *Clipper Edition*, a streamlined version of the *Herald* that was distributed in 23 Latin American countries. The paper won prestige and readership in Latin America, while the *Herald*'s Miami edition began to specialize in coverage of Latin America. Because of these early efforts, the paper is considered by many to have the best Latin American coverage of any U.S. newspaper.

In 1948 the *Herald*'s printers began a lengthy, sometimes violent strike over wages and the length of their work week. They were among the best paid printers in the country, but wanted to receive the same wages for working 35 hours as they were getting for working 40. The strike dragged on, and on October 1, 1949, the paper's newsprint warehouse burned down in a mysterious fire. Because of the strike, the *Herald* experimented with alternative production methods, and ended up with production methods years ahead of those at most other papers. In 1950 the paper won its first Pulitzer Prize for fighting government corruption in southern Florida. The next year Hills became executive editor of the *Herald* and the *Detroit Free Press*. He encouraged individual style and quality writing and drew a large number of excellent reporters and columnists from other papers.

In 1960 Knight took a gamble and built a $30 million building, containing offices and printing presses, for *The Miami Herald*. At the time it was the biggest building in Florida, and the biggest newspaper printing plant ever built. It reflected the Knights's belief that the *Herald*—and Miami—would continue to grow, which they did.

In 1955 Knight bought *The Charlotte Observer*, in North Carolina, purchasing its rival, *The Charlotte News*, in 1959. In the same year, the Knights sold the *Chicago Daily News* to Marshall Field for $17 million.

As the group grew larger, the Knights wanted to increase financial coordination among the newspapers. At the suggestion of Lee Hills, the Knights formed an executive committee in 1960 to undertake quarterly reviews of the operations of Knight Newspapers. They also hired finance man Alvah H. Chapman Jr. as James Knight's assistant; he rose within ten years to be president of the *Herald* and executive vice president of Knight Newspapers. He introduced computers for administration, layout, typesetting, and production; and for improving the operation of the circulation, advertising, and business departments. Chapman mandated budgeting at all Knight newspapers, which was rarely done at small- and medium-sized newspapers up to that time.

Knight Newspapers began an aggressive acquisition campaign during the same period, looking for newspapers in growing cities with at least 50,000 inhabitants. In 1969 the son of Moses Annenberg, the former *Miami Tribune* owner who sold that paper to the Knights, Walter Annenberg, sold *The Philadelphia News* and *The Philadelphia Inquirer* to Knight Newspapers for $55 million. Knight Newspapers added the *Tallahassee Democrat*, in Florida, to the group in 1965. The five papers Knight bought in 1969 continued the company's strategy of owning more than one newspaper in a market, thereby eliminating competition. In 1969 Knight's combined daily circulation was 2.2 million, and it made $12.7 million in profits on revenue of $162.8 million, largely on rising advertising revenues. It had come to be regarded as a well-managed, highly profitable, and very aggressive group, although its editorial content was not top quality. In 1969 Knight Newspapers, Inc. went public, the first offering immediately selling out at $30 a share.

Knight acquired five more dailies in 1973: the *Lexington Herald* and the *Lexington Leader*, both in Kentucky; the *Co-*lumbus Ledger* and the *Columbus Enquirer*, both in Georgia; and *The Bradenton Herald* in Florida.

Herman Ridder, founder of the Ridder group, worked his way up through that ranks at the *Staats-Zeitung*, purchasing that New York newspaper in 1892. He was a founder and president of the Associated Press and an early supporter of the American Newspaper Publishers Association, becoming its president in 1907. His sons Bernard, Joseph, and Victor bought the *New York Journal of Commerce* and the *St. Paul Dispatch-Pioneer Press* in 1927. Ridder Publications was incorporated in Delaware in 1942.

After World War II the company expanded westward in search of well-priced properties in growing markets. They bought the *Long Beach Press-Telegram, Long Beach Independent, San Jose Mercury News,* and *Pasadena Star News,* all in California, as well as some smaller California papers; a 65% stake in the *Seattle Times,* in Washington; the Gary *Post Tribune* in Indiana; and radio and television station WCCO, in Minneapolis, Minnesota. The *San Jose Mercury News* was the most profitable Ridder publication. The company bought the Boulder *Daily Camera* in Colorado in 1969 and the *Wichita Eagle* and Beacon Publishing Company of Kansas in 1973.

Ridder's 1973 earnings were $14.3 million on revenue of $166 million. Knight's 1973 earnings were $22.1 million on revenue of $341.9 million. Their merger grew out of talks between friends Lee Hills and Bernard Ridder Jr., grandson of Herman Ridder, who were interested in expansion. Influenced by the success of the rival Gannett group, both the Knight and the Ridder groups had gone public in 1969 to raise capital for acquisitions. The groups described the potential benefits of a merger to their stockholders as "a broader and more diversified income base, greater newspaper size, mix and geographical distribution, and a stronger balance sheet." The merger was accomplished through an exchange of stock, and five Ridder representatives joined ten from Knight Newspapers, to form Knight-Ridder's board of directors.

The Knight group had focused on the South and East, while Ridder had focused on the West and Midwest. At the time of the merger, Knight owned 16 dailies in 7 states, while Ridder owned or had a substantial interest in 19 dailies in 10 states. The Ridder dailies were all in exclusive markets, while the Knight's three largest revenue yielders—in Miami, Detroit, and Philadelphia—all faced competition. At the time of the merger, *Time,* July 22, 1974, reported that in general, "the Ridder papers do not have the heft and influence of the Knight dailies."

When the groups merged on November 30, 1974, Ridder became a wholly owned subsidiary of Knight, and the renamed Knight-Ridder Newspapers, Inc. became the largest newspaper company in the United States, with newspapers from coast to coast. The new company had 35 newspapers in 25 cities, with combined circulation averaging 3.8 million daily, and 4.2 million on Sunday, total assets of $465 million, and profits of $36 million. Other large companies published newspapers, but they were diversified, while Knight-Ridder Newspapers focused on newspapers alone—Knight and Ridder had agreed to sell their radio and television holdings as part of the Federal Communications Commission's conditions for merging. The new company continued to give its newspapers editorial autonomy while maintaining strict central control of business operations. It organized its new papers into three groups along geographical lines.

In 1976 Knight-Ridder Newspapers, Inc. became Knight-Ridder, Inc. Alvah H. Chapman Jr. was elected chief executive officer, succeeding Lee Hills, and Bernard H. Ridder Jr. was elected chairman of the executive committee, succeeding James L. Knight, who resigned. James L. Knight died in 1991 at the age of 81. John Knight also retired as editorial chairman in 1976. He died in 1981 at the age of 81. Lee Hills took his place until 1979 when he retired and Bernard H. Ridder Jr. succeeded him.

Beginning in the late 1970s, many media companies went on newspaper-buying binges, snapping up what turned out to be bargains while Knight-Ridder watched from the sidelines. The company had concluded that newspapers were a mature market and moved into other areas. It bought radio stations and started Viewdata Corporation, which offered news and financial services on home computers. Viewdata never did well, and was closed in 1986. By that time Knight-Ridder recognized that it had made a mistake, and that profit gains might come from newspapers. Knight-Ridder finally acquired more newspapers that year when it bought the six-paper State-Record Company, based in Columbia, South Carolina, for $311 million.

By the mid-1980s, Knight-Ridder had a stable of Pulitzer Prize–winning reporters and 34 newspapers. Yet its largest four newspapers—Miami, Detroit, Philadelphia, and San Jose—which accounted for 55% of company revenues, had problems at various times in 1980s, including a 46-day strike in Philadelphia in 1985. The company's net profits fell 5.7% in 1985. They rose 5.5% in 1986, but competitors were doing far better in those years—Gannett's profits rose 23%, while the Times Mirror Company's rose 75%.

Part of the reason for the company's declining profits was that it had lost touch with its readers. Hispanics accounted for half the population of the Miami area, but only 20% of them read *The Miami Herald*. In 1986 several of the *Herald*'s offices were closed. In 1987, it redesigned the Spanish version of the paper, *El Nuevo Herald*, to win Hispanic readership. The *Detroit Free Press*, locked in a cutthroat price war with the rival *Detroit News*, lost $74 million between 1981 and 1987, prompting the company to request a joint operating agreement from the U.S. Department of Justice. The agreement would have allowed the *Free Press* and *News* to share advertising and production operations. Citizens' groups challenged the request on the grounds that the measure was anti-competitive and that both papers could coexist healthily if they raised their prices. The opposition created long delays and several more years of losses. The joint operating agreement was finally granted in 1989, when the Supreme Court approved the agreement.

By 1988 Knight-Ridder's business-information services division was growing three times as fast as its newspapers. The company had also moved into computer-based graphics services. The Knight-Ridder Graphics Network went on line in October 1985, at first servicing only newspapers in the group. It began to offer a full-scale daily service to papers outside Knight-Ridder in 1986. Within a year it was used by 28 of the chain's newspapers and had 110 outside subscribers in North America and Europe. Subscribing newspapers paid $50 to $300 a month, depending on their circulation, for the privilege of using the system.

Beginning in 1987, Knight-Ridder undertook a cost-cutting campaign headed by Tony Ridder, president of the newspaper division. However, by 1989, the company's debt approached $1 billion, fed by the 1988 purchase of Dialog Information Services, Inc. for $353 million. In 1988 Jim Batten was appointed chief executive officer, replacing Alvah Chapman, and Tony Ridder was named president of the company. To reduce debt, Batten sold the company's broadcasting group and the *Pasadena Morning Star News* netting $425 million. Still, the company was sufficiently wary of a takeover for its shareholders to vote a "quality of journalism" amendment to prevent a buyout by a media baron like Rupert Murdoch.

Knight-Ridder's options for increasing its profitability were limited. In 1989 it derived 88% of its revenue from newspapers, and 50% of that came from the *Philadelphia Inquirer*, the *Miami Herald*, and the *San Jose Mercury*. Some of the company's papers faced stiff competition from suburban newspapers and expanding big-city papers. Part of the problem lay in the newspaper field itself, where readership had been sinking for two decades, but part of the problem lay with Knight-Ridder. For the last five years of the 1980s, the company's operating margins averaged 14.3%, while the average for the 16 largest publicly traded media companies was 18.8%. As the 1990s began, however, media analysts predicted significant improvement in Knight-Ridder's earnings.

Principal Subsidiaries: Aberdeen News Company; The Beacon Journal Publishing Company; Boca Raton News, Inc.; Boulder Publishing, Inc.; The Bradenton Herald, Inc.; Circom Corporation; Detroit Free Press, Inc.; Drinnon, Inc.; Grand Forks Herald, Incorporated; Journal of Commerce, Inc.; Keynoter Publishing Company, Inc.; KR Newsprint Company; Knight News Services, Inc.; The Knight Publishing Co.; Knight-Ridder Business Information Services, Inc.; Knight-Ridder Cablevision, Inc.; Knight-Ridder Investment Company; Lexington Herald-Leader Co.; Macon Telegraph Publishing Company; The Miami Herald Publishing Co.; News Publishing Company; Nittany Printing and Publishing Company; Northwest Publications, Inc.; Observer Transportation Company; Philadelphia Newspapers, Inc.; Portage Graphics Co.; Post-Tribune Publishing, Inc.; PressLink Corporation; The R.W. Page Corporation; Ridder Publications, Inc.; San Jose Mercury News, Inc.; The State-Record Holding Company; Tallahassee Democrat, Inc.; Tribune Newsprint Company; Twin Cities Newspaper Service, Inc.; Twin Coast Newspapers, Inc.; VU/TEXT Information Services, Inc.; Wichita Eagle and Beacon Publishing Company, Inc.

Further Reading: " 'Dynastic' Ridder clan gathers—40 strong," *Editor & Publisher*, April 19, 1969; Smiley, Nixon, *Knights of the Fourth Estate: The Story of the Miami Herald*, Miami, E.A. Seeman Publishing, Inc., 1974; "Knight-Ridder will become largest all-newspaper firm," *Editor & Publisher*, November 16, 1974; Whited, Charles, *Knight: A Publisher in the Tumultuous Century*, New York, E.P. Dutton, 1988.

—Scott M. Lewis

KODANSHA LTD.

12-21, Otowa 2-chome
Bunkyo-ku, Tokyo 112
Japan
(03) 3945-1111
Fax: (03) 3946-6200

Private Company
Incorporated: 1925 as Dai Nippon Yuben Kai Kodansha
Employees: 1,090
Sales: ¥162.00 billion (US$1.19 billion) (1989)

Kodansha is the largest publishing company in the whole of Asia. The company is run by a woman, Sawako Noma, which is highly unusual in Japan. Even more intriguing is the fact that a woman assumed the helm of Kodansha—albeit briefly—even before World War II. Moreover, Kodansha is a company unusually dedicated to internationalism, awarding prizes for book publishing in Africa, and zealous in its commitment to aiding fledgling book publishers in Asia. It is the only book publishing company in Japan that has a subsidiary in the United States, Kodansha International/USA, responsible for translating Japanese literature, history, and art into English in order to broaden Western understanding of Japanese culture. Most extraordinary to a Westerner, accustomed to regarding Japanese culture as inimical to individualism, is the individualism of those who founded and led Kodansha, and who have left their imprint on the company.

The company was founded by Seiji Noma, who noted in his autobiography that he was born at a time of great turmoil in Japanese history. By 1878, the year of his birth, the political upheavals occasioned by the clash between the Tokugawa shogunate and the imperialist forces who owed their allegiance to the mikado had been over for some years. However, the social and economic transformation of Japan had only begun. Seiji Noma's family had sided with the shogunate, and lost. The result was catastrophic for his parents and grandparents. The defeated *daimyos* (lords) ended by surrendering their fiefs to the state, and their *samurai* (retainers) found themselves deprived of their traditional offices and revenues. For the first time in their lives, *samurai* were on a par with everyone else, and had to earn a living as best they knew how. Seiji Noma's *samurai* father and highly unusual mother, a fencing expert, tried various livelihoods, with little success. However, Seiji Noma's mother and sister were determined to give him an education, and worked hard to pay for it.

Just as his mother's and sister's thrift made Noma into a respected teacher, and later a school inspector, so his wife would steer him toward a more responsible life. What he did have in common with other successful entrepreneurs, however, was boundless ambition and a restless drive to get ahead.

In short, he was prepared to take risks. Thus, when a very prestigious administrative post at Tokyo University's law school was offered to him, he accepted. Even though he had little administrative experience, he eagerly left his secure and comfortable niche as a school inspector on the island of Okinawa. Even this did not satisfy him for long. He was delighted when the university yielded to the new craze for oratory—or debating—and allowed the establishment of a debating society in his home. He had a real flair for eloquent speech and never tired of reminding audiences how he enthralled his classes reciting from memory the heroic *kodan* (sagas) from Japan's medieval past.

The debating society gave Noma's ambition a new direction. He made up his mind to publish the monthly speeches of the students and professors, although he had not the slightest idea of how this could be done. He was flipping through the pages of a telephone book in 1910, spotted the name of the Dai Nippon Printing Company, went there immediately, and astonished the publishers with his bold plans for a new magazine. This would be the origins of Kodansha Ltd.

It was surprising that the publisher agreed to collaborate with Noma in such a risky venture, and that they even granted him a modest salary as an editor of the magazine, *Yuben,* which was to be astonishingly successful. But success was far from easy.

Noma founded Dai Nippon Yuben Kai in 1909 to publish his magazine, and *Yuben* first appeared in 1910. From then on, Noma shouldered the responsibilities of his administrative position during the day and his editing responsibilities at night; meanwhile, the publication costs of his new magazine exceeded his wildest imagination. Most of his time was spent less in editing than in trying to drum up money, an exhausting routine that would undermine his health. Noma was not satisfied with only one magazine, but sought to create another. His publishers were reluctant, gave up the rights to his first magazine, *Yuben,* and handed Dai Nippon Yuben Kai over to Noma, who became his own publisher.

It was to be the most difficult undertaking of his life, and Noma was not only a neophyte in this enterprise but was wholly without means. Moreover, he had to relinquish his solid position at the university to enter an unfamiliar business.

Though it was less than 50 years since Japan had opened up formally to the West, when the country had had no printing presses and traditional Japanese parchment was still used instead of paper, by 1920 Japan had not only caught up with the West in its printing methods but had overtaken all Western countries, except Great Britain, to become the second-largest publisher of books in the world. Seiji Noma was interested in publishing magazines rather than books, but even in this realm there were formidable competitors, none more challenging than Jitsuyo no Nihon-sha, with as many as five magazines. With his wife, a former primary school teacher, Noma arduously learned each step of the publishing business. In the process, his young family became impoverished and heavily indebted while Seiji Noma was constantly obliged to haggle over prices with printers and book dealers. Only his faith in his product kept him from giving up.

Seiji Noma would establish another company, Kodansha, in 1911 to publish his second magazine, *Kodan Kurabu,* later renamed *Kodansha,* named after the medieval *kodan,* of Japan. Noma's strong didactic streak now found an outlet in his new magazine. *Kodansha* would contain the stories of Japan's heroic past, a heroism in which Seiji Noma and his generation believed, and which had been fortified as a result of Japan's war against Russia in 1904. After a weak start *Kodan Kurabu* had turned out to be surprisingly popular. The stories appealed to the right audience—Japan's rapidly growing population of literate men and women. Illiteracy was wiped out by the 20th century, a tremendous achievement in any country, especially one in which illiteracy had been widespread only 50 years earlier.

By now, Noma had become a successful publisher, and between 1914 and 1923 five more successful magazines had been launched and Seiji Noma's publishing company was well on its way to becoming the leading magazine publisher in Japan. He was in many respects a typical Japanese employer of his generation—his employees worked long hours, were given only two days off each month, and he relied heavily on cheap labor in the form of adolescent boys. Yet very few of his workers lost their jobs, even in the recession of the 1920s, and Noma built living quarters with recreational facilities for his young unmarried workers. With the catastrophic earthquake in Tokyo and Yokohama in 1923, Kodansha and Dai Nippon Yuben Kai turned out to be two of the few publishing companies in Japan—most of which were centered in Tokyo—to survive the earthquake intact. Seiji Noma was by then a very wealthy man, the "magazine king" of Japan and to his competitors, "the Mussolini of our magazine world." He was also a cosmopolitan man; he had a European wing built on to his mansion and he eagerly borrowed publishing ideas from the West. His idea for the highly successful magazine *Fujin,* launched in 1920—had sprung from his perusal of the American *Saturday Evening Post* and *Ladies Home Journal.* It would be a publication for everyone and include "all that was interesting and amusing, light and soothing." Hence not everything he published had to be educational, an impression his memoirs are at pains to convey.

In 1925, toward the end of his life, but still only in his 50s, Seiji Noma launched his eighth and most successful magazine, *Kingu* (from the English word "king"). Once again, the tone of *Kingu* was moralistic and educational. Yet it was phenomenally successful, with monthly sales of over 1.5 million copies, the most successful magazine in modern Japanese history. Also in 1925, Noma merged his two publishing companies, Dai Nippon Yuben Kai and Kodansha. The merged company was incorporated as Dai Nippon Yuben Kai Kodansha (DNYKK).

Noma's last magazine venture, a children's publication, was far less popular, but by then, ten years before his death, he had become more interested in entering the highly competitive world of book publishing. While the number of books the company published before World War II was very small, they sold very well and might have established DNYKK as a leading book publisher had it not been for Seiji Noma's untimely death at the age of 60, and the advent of World War II.

Whether or not Seiji Noma was as intensely patriotic as he himself suggests is difficult to ascertain. Of the many hardships encountered in the fiercely competitive world of Japanese publishing, censorship was one of them. In the 1930s, when Seiji Noma wrote his autobiography, government control of the press was absolute. Therefore Noma's memoirs had to be deeply patriotic, even though censorship must have weighed heavily on him as a publisher.

Despite the Depression of the 1930s, Kodansha continued to produce 70% of all magazines in Japan. Understandably, nothing in Seiji Noma's memoirs hints at the growing militarization of Japan and of the intense pressure put on publishers to produce reading matter of a chauvinistic and militaristic character. Like all publishers, Noma had to conform. The year of his death, 1938, was also the year in which Japanese publishing began its steep decline that would end with the cessation of all publishing activity in Japan in 1945. These were harsh years for Japanese publishers. With Seiji Noma's death, his young son, Hasashi Noma would take the helm, only to die of an illness shortly afterward. Seiji Noma's widow, Sae Noma, was forced to take over. Her leadership of a major company was unprecedented in Japan, where women did not even have the right to vote. Like her husband, she was spirited and intelligent, but was growing old. With her only child dead, she adopted into the family the second husband of her dead son's widow, Shoichi Takagi, who thenceforth took the family name of Noma, becoming DNYKK's director in 1941. During this period, Dai Nippon Yuben Kai Kodansha became known, increasingly, by its nickname, Kodansha, and eventually the company was officially renamed Kodansha.

World War II was a time of enormous hardship for Japan's book publishers. Besides having to deal with the military government's control of the press, there was also the extreme shortage of paper and the unpopular allocation system whereby the government determined the amount of paper to be allocated to each company. Naturally there was cooperation with the authorities. Kodansha's was no more marked than others; indeed, had the company not cooperated, it would have suffered the fate of two other prominent publishing companies, Kaizosha and Chuo Koronsha, which were forced to close down in 1944. Nonetheless, as the largest magazine publishing company, Kodansha's "collaboration" was perhaps the most visible.

Under the circumstances, it was noteworthy that any reputable publications saw the light of day during the war, as indeed they did. Nonetheless, the year 1945 marked the nadir of Japanese publishing, which was forced to a standstill because of the exhaustion of paper supplies.

However, once press controls were lifted following Japan's surrender, the Japanese entrepreneurial spirit was far from dead. As early as September 1945, before the American occupation authorities had time to occupy the country, an enterprising publisher put out a booklet, minus front and back covers, entitled *Japanese American Conversation Handbook.* The fact that this paperback sold out perhaps testified less to the quality of the product than to the fact that the Japanese were starved for reading matter. With the coming of the Americans to Japan in December 1945, more specifically the Supreme Command of the Allied Powers under General Douglas MacArthur, Japanese censorship officially came to an end, only to be replaced by American censorship. The formerly stridently militaristic Japan Book Publishers Association now just as vehemently denounced Japan's "collaborators" during the war, most notably Kodansha Ltd. under Shoichi Noma's direction.

The charges of collaboration had the desired effect: in the first wave of three purges of civilian Japanese, Shoichi Noma was dismissed in 1946 as president of Kodansha. Even worse, nearly all the company's officials felt themselves under pressure to resign, leaving Kodansha a skeleton of its former self. Kodansha's competitors must have been secretly delighted by this turn of events and rumors abounded that Kodansha was nearing its end. But they underestimated a company that had survived the devastating earthquake of 1923 and the debilitating Depression of the 1930s. In 1946, the year Shoichi Noma was fired, Kodansha employees kept the firm going until Shoichi Noma's almost miraculous rehabilitation in 1949.

Shoichi Noma was another self-made man who, like his predecessor Seiji Noma, owed his good fortune to a good education—he graduated with a law degree from Tokyo University in the 1930s—as well as to his native talents and to key women in his life, most notably his friendship with Seiji Noma's widow and his marriage to Seiji Noma's widowed daughter-in-law, which led to his adoption into the Noma family. Made director of Kodansha in 1941, he became its president shortly before he was fired in 1946. Returning as president in 1949, he set forth—very like Seiji Noma—to modernize and reorganize the company, cost what it might. When he stepped down in 1981 in favor of his adopted son, Shoichi Noma had changed the face of Kodansha. Of the 34 magazines that Kodansha published in 1981, only *Fujin* was a survivor of the prewar era, and book publishing, tentatively begun before World War II, was now Kodansha's main business. Shoichi Noma was extremely successful perhaps because, like Seiji Noma, he had grand ambitions and was not easily satisfied; he wanted nothing less than to make his company a major force in the international publishing world.

The time was propitious for this. The Korean War had broken out in 1950, and lifted Japan out of the financial doldrums, resuscitating its industry. By the time the war ended, the publishing industry in Japan had recovered fully from the ravages of World War II. By then, Kodansha was also making a gradual recovery. Shoichi Noma had the same instinct for determining the right magazine to publish as Seiji Noma had displayed. In Shoichi Noma's case, the pivotal turnabout in his company's fortunes was the publication of the magazine *Gunzo*. A literary serial for the masses in the tradition of Seiji Noma, *Gunzo*'s writers and editors made famous a new literary trend, serials, later dubbed "the Third Generation." Shoichi Noma also showed himself to be a maverick by engaging in large-scale co-publishing projects with foreign publishers in order to produce such highly acclaimed and profitable book series as *Museums of the World,* and *Sanctuaries of World Religions.* In fact, it was Shoichi Noma who first embarked on the mass publication of books in Japan, earning him the honorific "Father of Japanese Publishing." Soon Kodansha was churning out 1,000 book titles a year. In 1963 Noma decided to try the market in the United States, a daring venture for a Japanese publisher. Unlike Japanese cars and televisions, very few Japanese books were being exported abroad. Kodansha International/USA in New York City would become one of Kodansha's most important and successful branches, churning out hundreds of titles on Japanese art, literature, and history in English translation. By 1980 Kodansha was the largest and most successful publishing company in Japan.

Shoichi Noma's innovations in the field of publishing were matched by his pioneering work in fostering international understanding. His brainchild, the Publishers' Organization for Cultural Exchange, was established to introduce Japanese culture abroad and to introduce foreign culture to Japan.

This was followed in 1979 with the establishment of the Noma Asia/African Scholarship—to enable promising Asians and Africans to study in Japan while the Noma Award for Publishing in Africa, set up in 1980, was a prize for the best book written and published in Africa. The same year also saw the establishment of the Noma Literacy Prize, to go to the group or individual who has done most to combat illiteracy.

In 1981, Shoichi Noma retired in favor of his adopted son Koremichi Noma, who was president of Kodansha until his death in 1987. During this period Kodansha entered the audio-visual computer age with a broad range of videos and computer software and, like most Japanese publishing companies, expanded its array of comic books until in the 1990s the number of Kodansha's comic book titles reached almost 3,000.

With Koremichi Noma's untimely death, his widow Sawako Noma has stepped in as president, and as the second woman leader in Kodansha's history. The university-educated, English-speaking Sawako Noma, mother of five children, continues her predecessors' strategy of strengthening Kodansha's global publishing position and furthering its humanitarian concerns.

Principal Subsidiaries: Kobunsha Publishing Co., Ltd.; King Record Co., Ltd.; Kodansha International Ltd.; Kodansha International/USA, Ltd.; Kodansha Famous Schools, Inc.; The Nikkan Gendai Ltd.; Sansui-sha Publication Co., Ltd.; My Health Co., Ltd.; KBS (Kokusai Bunka Shuppan Ltd.); ASK Kodansha Co., Ltd.; Asmik Corporation; Kodansha Images; Kodansha Institute of Publication, Ltd.; Daiichi Shuppan Center Ltd.; IPEC, Inc.; Kodansha Scientific Ltd.; Scholar Publishers Inc.; Planning Editorial Center Ltd.; Daiichi-Tosho Storage Ltd.; Toyokuni Printing Co.; Daiichi Paper Co., Ltd.

Further Reading: Noma, Seiji, *The Nine Magazines of Kodansha*, London, Methuen & Co., 1934.

—Sina Dubovoj

MCGRAW-HILL, INC.

1221 Avenue of the Americans
New York, New York 10020
U.S.A.
(212) 512-2000

Public Company
Incorporated: 1909 as McGraw-Hill Book Company
Employees: 13,868
Sales: $1.94 billion
Stock Exchanges: New York Pacific

McGraw-Hill, Inc., a leading international multimedia publishing and information company, caters to education, business, industry, professional, and government markets. Through books, magazines, film, and many kinds of electronic networks, McGraw-Hill supplies information worldwide. Formed initially from the merger of McGraw Publishing Company and Hill Publishing Company, the business has always aimed to provide to technicians, scientists, and business people complete, accurate, and up-to-date information of both specialized and general interest. The company has almost from its beginning, pursued acquisitions and mergers that would increase market share, reach new markets, and expand its global reach.

Born in 1858, John A. Hill—typesetter, silver prospector, newspaper publisher, and railroad engineer—came to the attention of the publisher of *American Machinist* with his contribution of letters and articles on practical aspects of railroading. When the publisher began *Locomotive Engineering* in 1888, Hill was its choice for editor.

By 1869 Hill had become part owner of both magazines. In 1897, divesting his interest in *Locomotive Engineering,* Hill took over full ownership of *American Machinist,* and established the American Machinist Press in 1898. In 1902 he incorporated Hill Publishing Company, going on to acquire *Power, Engineering and Mining Journal,* and *Engineering News.* By 1909, Hill was a leading trade publisher not just of magazines but of such books as *Colvin and Stanley's American Machinist's Handbook,* 1908, and Herbert Hoover's *Principles of Mining,* 1909.

Hill's chief competitor was onetime teacher and subscription salesman James H. McGraw. McGraw was an advertising salesman for the American Railway Publishing Company in 1884. He rose to vice president by 1886. Resigning from American Railway in 1881, McGraw began to acquire magazines that reported on technological progress. Titles included

American Journal of Railway Appliances; *Electrical Industries,* later retitled *American Electrician; Electrical World; Electrical Engineer; Electrochemical Industry;* and *Engineering Record.* In 1899 McGraw incorporated McGraw Publishing Company, which in 1907 put out its first engineering handbook, the *Standard Handbook for Electrical Engineers.*

In the years following the U.S. Civil War, the United States changed from an agrarian to an industrial society. Both McGraw and Hill found their markets in the growing number of technicians concerned with the practical application of science to transportation, lighting, and engineering, among other facts of daily life. In 1909 Edward Caldwell and Martin M. Foss, the respective heads of the book departments of the two firms, agreed that a merger of the two book departments would well serve both companies. After the two men persuaded their bosses, a coin toss decided whose name would come first in naming the new company, the loser becoming president. The McGraw-Hill Book Company, with John A. Hill as president, was thus born, locating itself in McGraw Publishing's building in New York City.

The two companies, however, were still distinct, different entities. The magazines that formed the chief interests of both and that supplied the articles for many of the books remained separate concerns. In 1914, as World War I broke out in Europe, Hill moved his company into an air-conditioned building in New York City, one specially constructed to house his publications and their printing facilities. McGraw-Hill Book Company had established itself in 1910 with its first publication, *The Art of Engineering,* and its first series, Electrical Engineering Texts. This series marked the beginning of a company trend toward publishing series of books by multiple authors covering the entire range of knowledge in a field.

A more complete merger of the McGraw and Hill interests came about in 1916 when John A. Hill died at the age of 57. Arthur Baldwin, Hill's attorney, led Hill Publishing for a brief time following Hill's death. McGraw became president of the book company; the two established the McGraw-Hill Publishing Company in 1917, with its offices located in the Hill Building, publishing *Electrical World, Electric Railway Journal, Electrical Merchandising, Engineering Record, Metallurgical and Chemical Engineering, The Contractor, American Machinist, Power, Engineering and Mining Journal, Coal Age,* and *Engineering News.* This concentration of interests, along with the enlargement of the book company, now a subsidiary of McGraw-Hill Publishing, made McGraw-Hill the largest technical publisher in the world at that time.

World War I, which the United States entered in 1917, made this a particularly good time for technical publishers including McGraw-Hill. The first title to benefit from wartime increased demand was the *American Machinists' Handbook,* originally published before the war. There also was increased demand for engineering books in radio communication, aviation, construction and maintenance, chemical warfare, trench construction, automotive transportation, aerial photography, and antisubmarine tactics. To this market, McGraw-Hill responded quickly, for example, supplying the required texts for the U.S. Army Educational Commission in France, an order of 150,000 technical books that the company in a matter of days printed, bound, specially packed, and shipped.

After World War I, McGraw-Hill Book Company expanded rapidly. With Foss in charge of editorial and sales activities and Caldwell heading up finances and production, the book company had grown by establishing close contacts with the faculties at various universities and engineering schools, not only to make sales, but also to find new authors. With the addition of series designed for educational use, McGraw-Hill Book Company formed a college department in 1927, thus establishing a lasting emphasis on textbooks. Foss was equally innovative in finding new ways to market the technical books that seldom found space in general bookstores. By both advertising at cost in the parent firm's magazines and sending letters and circulars to subscribers, Foss offered interested parties a chance to examine a book for ten days without payment, an approach that quickly resulted in increased book sales.

During the 1920s James McGraw began to shift some of his authority in the company to other people. The first shift came when he named himself, his son James McGraw Jr., and Malcolm Muir to a governing board of trustees. Then in 1925, McGraw turned over the presidency of the book company to Edward Caldwell, who was to be succeeded by Martin M. Foss the next year. In 1928 Malcolm Muir became president of the publishing company. James McGraw remained chairman of the board.

With the purchase of the A.W. Shaw Company of Chicago in 1928, McGraw-Hill extended its reach into the field of business books and magazines. The editorial staff turned a monthly put out by Shaw, the *Magazine of Business,* into a weekly, covering and interpreting news of specific interest to business people. Now known as *Business Week,* it has become the best known of all McGraw-Hill publications.

Just after the stock market crash of 1929, *The Business Week,* as it was then known, predicted, in its November 2, 1929, issue that "Business will gradually and steadily recover as businessmen regain their perspective and go back to work." Following this optimistic line of thought McGraw-Hill Publishing cstablished four new magazines in 1930, opened a west coast office and book depository in San Francisco, and under the imprint of Whittlesey House, named after James McGraw's father-in-law, entered the trade book field for the first time. The first title under the new imprint, selected so as to distinguish this division from trade publications, was Ernest Minor Patterson's *The World's Economic Dilemma.*

McGraw-Hill Publishing commissioned a new office building designed by Raymond Hood and located on West 42nd Street in New York City. Nicknamed Big Green because of the blue-green cast of its Art Deco exterior, the new McGraw-Hill building aroused controversy because of the horizontal banding of its windows, now a standard feature of many modern office buildings. When first occupied in 1931, Big Green included a complete production plant taking up four floors. The increasing severity of the economic depression during the early 1930s, however, forced McGraw-Hill not only to make deep cuts in personnel and in salaries but also to sell its press machinery and equipment in 1933. In 1932, the parent company's deficit ran to $239,137.

That same year Whittlesey House had its first best seller, *Life Begins at Forty,* by Walter B. Pitkin. The company's other publications made themselves useful sources of information for business people by providing hard facts and analysis of the economic situation. The vocational-education department of the book company helped those seeking new skills. Established in 1930, it concentrated on mechanical arts, agriculture,

and home economics. By 1937 the company had an annual profit of more than $1 million.

The 1930s also saw major shifts at the executive level of McGraw-Hill Publishing. In 1935 James H. McGraw handed over the chairmanship of the company to James McGraw Jr. During the next two years Malcolm Muir failed to get along with the McGraw family, key players in the maneuverings for top positions in the company. In 1937 Muir left McGraw-Hill to run *Newsweek,* and James H. McGraw Jr. became both president and chairman of the board.

With the coming of World War II in the 1940s McGraw-Hill Publishing Company was in an advantageous position. Because its technical publications were especially important to the war effort, its paper requirements received special priority. The company's magazines began to cover a range of topics of wartime relevance, from accelerated training in the use of metalworking power tools to dehydrated foods. In addition the company began to publish special wartime titles, such as *En Guardia,* a Spanish-language paper promoting Latin American relations; and *Overseas Digest,* excerpting articles from other McGraw-Hill titles for distribution to military personnel posted abroad.

It was in the area of special training manuals however that McGraw-Hill was to make a special effort. As untrained men and women poured into industry and the armed services, accelerated technical training was important to the war. By 1943 the book company had published 231 titles for the Engineering and Science Management War Training Program. Of the 304 books published by 1944 to further the war effort, many dealt with radio and electronics, a newly important part of warfare. One title, *Mathematics for Electricians and Radiomen,* by Nelson M. Cooke, first published in 1942, continued to be successful after the war, and by 1964, under the new title of *Basic Mathematics for Electronics,* had total sales in excess of 485,000 copies.

Although McGraw-Hill had been present in the United Kingdom and Germany as well as other countries since before World War I, the company made use of the opportunities World War II offered to increase its foreign activities. In 1943 the book company opened a book-export department, which by 1944 had a foreign-language translation office. That same year, McGraw-Hill acquired the Embassy Book Company, Ltd., of Toronto, that later became the McGraw-Hill Company of Canada, Ltd., yet later to be called McGraw Ryerson. In 1945, to provide its magazines with international coverage, the company started World News Service.

After the war the book company prospered under the presidency of Curtis G. Benjamin, who succeeded James S. Thompson, president for only two years. Benjamin developed a text-film department, a venture inspired by the use of educational films during World War II to supplement textbook materials. As teachers discovered the value of motion pictures and film strips in the classroom, the market expanded, and by 1965 McGraw-Hill was the leader in the field. Another wartime dividend for the company was the 13-volume U.S. Navy Flight Preparation Training series printed for the Bureau of Aeronautics during the war. With the growth of commercial aviation in the postwar period, McGraw-Hill found a large market for civilian editions of the series. Building on the close contacts with governmental agencies in research and development made during World War II, the company contracted to publish the Radiation Laboratory series, 27 volumes concentrating on the results of wartime research into radar. According to Charles A. Madison's 1966 *Book Publishing in America,* this series, published in 1949 and costing more than $1.2 million, "set a precedent for the commercial publication of government-financed projects." Although McGraw-Hill lost money on another project, the National Nuclear series, the company made an arrangement with the U.S. Atomic Energy Commission to produce an eight-volume compilation of scientific reference materials that was presented at the first International Conference on the Peaceful Uses of Atomic Energy at Geneva in August 1955.

Another project that was started in the late 1940s was the publication of the manuscripts of James Boswell. Consisting of the voluminous collection of original manuscripts of the 18th-century Scottish author that were collected by Colonel Ralph H. Isham, the project was guided through negotiations with its purchaser, Yale University, by Edward Aswell, Whittlesey House's editor in chief since 1947. Publication of a projected 40 volumes began in 1950. It was not to be under the Whittlesey imprint, however, as Yale preferred to have the McGraw-Hill name on the books. Thus began the relegation of Whittlesey House to juvenile titles. A commercial milestone proved to be the publication in 1950 of *Betty Crocker's Picture Cook Book,* which achieved sales of more than 235,000 copies in its first two years.

When its co-founder, James H. McGraw, died in 1948 at age 87, McGraw-Hill Publishing was well on its way to developing a departmentalized organizational structure. An independent technical-education department had been established in 1941, then a text-film department in 1945. The acquisition of the Gregg Publishing Company in 1949 transformed the company's business-education department into the Gregg division. In response to the need for training literature during the Korean War, beginning in 1950, the book company established a technical-writing division to produce specialized materials for both government and industry. The next year, following a reorganization of the handbook, technical, and professional publishing department, the industrial- and business-book department was born. The company had formed a medical publishing department in 1945. It was not until 1954, when it acquired from Doubleday, Blakiston Company, specializing in medical titles, that it began to have a major share of the medical market with its newly named Blakiston division.

What proved by far to be the most important division for company progress in the postwar period was the international division, established in 1946. In less than 15 years, book exports trebled, with a profitable business in text-films, filmstrips, and the sale of foreign-language rights. A major force in the international growth of the company was Curtis Benjamin, who proceeded along lines mapped out by James Thompson. Benjamin succeeded, along with B.G. Dandison, head of the international division, in making the company successful in foreign countries; in 1962 McGraw-Hill was presented by President John F. Kennedy with a presidential E-for-Export award, making McGraw-Hill the first commercial publishing firm to be so honored.

During the 1950s, James McGraw Jr., who had headed up the company since 1935, was replaced by another son of the first McGraw, Curtis. He was followed by Donald C. McGraw, yet another son.

Just before the death of Curtis, the company purchased the National Petroleum Publishing Company, the W.C. Platt Company, and Platt's Price Service, Inc., all from Warren C. Platt. The book company began three major encyclopedia projects in the late 1950s, each continuing on into the 1960s: *The McGraw-Hill Encyclopedia of Science and Technology, The Encyclopedia of World Art,* and the *New Catholic Encyclopedia.* When in 1959 the publishing company commemorated its 50th year, the revenues for McGraw-Hill Publishing Company exceeded $100 million.

While Curtis Benjamin remained chairman of the board and chief executive officer of the book company, Edward Booher, who had joined the company in 1936, became president in 1960. They doubled overall sales within five years, contributing 39% of the total income of the parent company in 1965. F.W. Dodge Corporation, information provider to the construction industry, was purchased in 1961. The following year the general-book division was formed by merging the industrial-and business-book department with the trade department. The purchase of Webster Publishing Company in 1963 marked the company's entry in the elementary school and high school textbook markets.

In 1964 the book company and F.W. Dodge Corporation merged with McGraw-Hill Publishing Company to form McGraw-Hill, Inc. The reorganization created a single corporation, the parent company, with three operating divisions: book publishing, the Dodge complex, and magazines and news services. The company established an Australian publishing unit that same year.

With the acquisition of the California Test Bureau in 1965, McGraw-Hill strengthened its educational services. The company moved into two new fields in 1966. One was legal publishing with the purchase of Shepard's Citations, Inc., and the other was financial information services with the acquisition of Standard & Poor's Corporation. Other acquisitions were Schaum Publishing Company, Capitol Radio Engineering Institute, and *Postgraduate Medicine* magazine, all in 1967. The company expanded into Mexico in 1967 and into Japan in 1969.

A key figure in this expansion was Shelton Fisher. Beginning as promotion manager for *Business Week* in 1940, by 1968 Fisher had succeeded Donald McGraw as president and chief executive officer of McGraw-Hill. His goal was to change the perception of McGraw-Hill as an old-fashioned publisher of trade magazines into that of a dynamic media giant. Fisher further extended the company's reach into Canada, Brazil, and India, bought four televisions stations from Time Inc., and moved the company out of Big Green and into its present, new 50-story international headquarters in 1972. While increasing the company's prestige, the large capital outlay came at a time when a recession caused a loss in revenues for the McGraw-Hill magazines. After a period of uncertainty during which the McGraw family worked out a succession, Harold McGraw Jr. became president of the parent company. Fisher assumed the chairmanship. This changed within a year with Fisher's retirement, and Harold McGraw Jr. became chairman in addition to his other positions.

The picture of McGraw-Hill, Inc. at the end of the 1970s, according to John Tebbel's *History of Book Publishing in America,* was of "an extremely healthy, well-managed conglomerate, composed of several operating divisions." Along with the book and publications companies, there was the information system company, composed of the F.W. Dodge division, Sweet's division, and Datapro Research Corporation. Two other divisions were Standard & Poor's Corporation and the McGraw-Hill Broadcasting Company. In 1978 total operating revenues amounted to more than $761 million.

Its very success made McGraw-Hill the target of a takeover attempt by the American Express Company in 1979. The chairman of American Express, James D. Robinson III, and its president, Roger H. Morley, were shocked by the ferocity with which Harold McGraw fought the attempted stock buyout. Concerted action by the McGraw family, along with various legal actions, defeated the bid for ownership.

Although American Express had failed, McGraw-Hill remained a prime target for a takeover. Harold McGraw was planning to retire in four years and while another generation of McGraws waited in the wings, none were as yet ready to run the corporation. By appointing Joseph L. Dionne, who had been in charge of planning, to the newly created position of vice president of operations, McGraw sought to improve management organization and put someone in charge who could generate the fast growth needed to discourage further takeover attempts.

Dionne stepped up to president and chief executive officer in 1983, while McGraw remained chairman. While remaining committed to print publishing, Dionne planned to reduce the 80% of the business that was print-oriented in 1983 to 65% or 70% over several years. One part of this goal had been achieved as early as 1979 when the company acquired Data Resources, Inc., which held a vast share of the world's business and economic data.

As McGraw-Hill moved into the electronic information marketplace, much of the information supplied by the news service, magazines, Standard & Poor's, Dodge, Platt, and Shepard's was made available in computerized form and in various configurations, making that data useful to a broad market. Another move was to enter into the computer publishing field by acquiring *BYTE, Unixworld,* and *LAN Times* magazines, as well as Osborne Books, all of which provided support information to computer users. Another part of Dionne's plan for revitalizing the company was shifting from media-based planning to market-focused business units; 20 such units were created in 1985. Harold McGraw approved, with reservations, of the direction in which Dionne was taking the company, as he indicated in 1988 when he became chairman emeritus while Dionne added the title of chairman to those of president and CEO.

In its attempt to weather the communications revolution, McGraw-Hill had gone through three major reorganizations in four years, resulting in an organization centered around 14 market-focus groups. These reorganizations, the automation of F.W. Dodge, and the shutdown of the general-book division, ending the company's involvement in the trade-book market, caused a layoff of more then 1,000 workers.

The company expanded globally and had success with the Standard & Poor's Marketscope, and with other on-line, real-time services. Early in 1990, however, two on-line services, McGraw-Hill News and Standard & Poor's News, were discontinued. Some acquisitions resulted in costly write-offs, notably Numerax, Inc., an electronic data and services operation. McGraw Hill has continued to invest in strong growth markets and has divested itself of several publications and units connecting it with its past. *American Machinist & Automated Manufacturing, Coal Age,* and *Engineering & Mining Journal* were sold in 1987. New magazines, such as *LAN Times* and *UnixWorld* for the computer networking market, have been started or acquired. To master this new field has meant a continuation of the strategies for acquisitions, mergers, and innovations that marked the company's birth. In 1988 McGraw-Hill acquired Random House's college division at a cost of over $200 million. In 1989 it entered into a 50–50 joint venture with Macmillan, combining both companies' elementary, secondary, and vocational education business. Finally, in 1990 McGraw-Hill implemented a new electronic textbook-publishing system that allows teachers to custom design textbooks, the results being printed, bound, and shipped within 48 hours. McGraw-Hill seems to be determined to modernize and remain independent.

Principal Subsidiaries: McGraw-Hill Book Company; McGraw-Hill Book Company Australia Pty., Ltd; McGraw-Hill Broadcasting Company; McGraw-Hill Holdings U.K., Ltd; McGraw-Hill Ryerson, Ltd. (Canada); Standard & Poor's Corporate Information Company; Standard & Poor's Financial & Economic Information Company.

Further Reading: Burlingame, Roger, *Endless Frontiers: The Story of McGraw-Hill,* New York, McGraw-Hill, 1959; Holt, Donald D., "The Unlikely Hero of McGraw-Hill," *Fortune,* May 21, 1979: Madison, Charles A., *Book Publishing in America,* New York, McGraw-Hill, 1966; *Imprint on an Era: The Story of the McGraw-Hill Book Company,* New York, McGraw-Hill, [n.d.]; Tebbel, John, *A History of Book Publishing in the United States,* 4 vols., New York, R.R. Bowker Company, 1972-1981.

—Wilson B. Lindauer

MACLEAN HUNTER LIMITED

Maclean Hunter Building
777 Bay Street
Toronto, Ontario M5W 1A7
Canada
(416) 596-5000
Fax: (416) 593-3175

Public Company
Incorporated: 1891 as J.B. McLean Publishing Company, Ltd.
Employees: 12,425
Sales: C$1.54 billion (US$1.33 billion)
Stock Exchanges: Toronto Montreal

Maclean Hunter Limited is a Canadian communications giant with operations in North America and Europe. The company began as a trade-magazine publisher, and that has remained its traditional mainstay. The company at first engaged almost exclusively in publishing and printing, and was closely held and run by a few men. Since 1961, however, Maclean Hunter has broadened its base of operations to encompass a wide variety of communications fields, becoming an important voice in Canadian public life.

Maclean Hunter began in 1887, when John Bayne Maclean left his post on the Toronto *Mail* to found Grocer Publishing Co., to publish *The Canadian Grocer,* a specialized publication filled with commercial news about the food industry. The first 16-page issue was sent free to grocers all over Canada, who were invited to purchase subscriptions for C$2 a year. Within three months, the fledgling publication became profitable and Maclean began to publish weekly. At that time, he also brought his brother, Hugh, into the business as a partner. Expansion followed in 1888 with the establishment of *Dry Goods Review.*

Maclean's goal in publishing was to provide "a specialized news services to our subscribers," as he stated. Success in the grocery publishing business led Maclean to move into other trades, and in 1888, *Hardware & Metal* was established at the invitation of a group of hardware-store owners. By 1890, Maclean was publishing four business journals, and had set up his own typesetting and composition operations in an effort to maintain control over the costs of magazine production. In 1891, the J.B. McLean Publishing Company, Ltd. was incorporated. Maclean was not always consistent in spelling his own last name.

By 1893, Hugh Maclean was running the business in Toronto, while his brother J.B. worked in New York City on a short-lived art publication called *Art Weekly.* In the early 1890s, the company began to open advertising sales offices in cities outside Toronto, branching out to Montreal in 1890, and across the Atlantic Ocean to London in 1895. In 1899, John Maclean bought out his brother's one-third share in their company for C$50,000.

By 1903, J.B. McLean Publishing Company had grown to employ about 50 people. Two years later, the company was successfully publishing six business papers, including *Bookseller and Stationer, Printer and Publisher,* and *Canadian Machinery & Manufacturing News,* and its founder was anxious to make his mark in a wider field. Using the profits from his commercial journals, he purchased a magazine published by an advertising agency, called *Business: the Business Man's Magazine.* Shortening its name to *The Business Magazine,* Maclean published his first issue in October 1905. The 144-page general-interest publication was made up entirely of condensed articles from other publications. Three months later, the magazine's name was again changed, this time to *Busy Man's Magazine,* with a subtitle that explained its purpose: "The Cream of the World's Magazines Reproduced for Busy People." It continued to hold the interest of its founder, who edited it personally, with some assistance in acquiring original articles, while also overseeing the company's other publications.

At the start of 1907, the J.B. Maclean Publishing Company introduced another general-interest publication, the *Financial Post.* The weekly was a joint venture between Maclean and Stewart Houston, a well-connected lawyer who wrote and edited the newspaper, which started out with 25,000 copies.

In the first decade of the 20th century, Maclean's publishing enterprise grew quickly. Under the autocratic and frugal leadership of its founder, who became known as "the Colonel" after he was given command of a Canadian regiment in 1899, the company had a high turnover of employees, frustrated by low salaries and the Colonel's constant meddling. In 1911, however, Maclean promoted the man whose name would one day join his in the corporate logo, Horace T. Hunter, to general manager. Hunter raised salaries and brought a decentralized approach to management, improving the company atmosphere and employee productivity. Also in 1911, Maclean changed the *Busy Man's Magazine's* title to *Maclean's.* He continued to act as chief editor for the flagship publication.

Not long after the end of World War I, in August 1919, Maclean's only son died unexpectedly, foreclosing the possibility that his company would become a dynasty. Also that year, Maclean renamed the enterprise the Maclean Publishing Company Limited. Soon afterward, in 1920, Maclean sold 30% of the company to his vice president, Hunter, for C$50,000, and another 10% of the stock to his general manager, H. Victor Tyrrell. Other editors and executives were also given the opportunity to buy company stock. At the same time, Maclean undertook a long-overdue company restructuring and bought the one-third of the *Financial Post* that the company did not already control.

In the years following World War I, the Canadian consumer-magazine industry was overwhelmed by an influx of magazines produced in the United States that paid no import duties to enter the country. Nevertheless, throughout the 1920s, Maclean's enterprise continued to grow. In 1922, the company officially branched out from publishing into the related field of commercial printing, an activity that actually had been going on for some time. In 1909, the company had purchased an entire square block of property in Toronto to provide enough space for a printing plant for all its magazines, and over the years, the plant had begun to take on outside work. In 1927, the company first ventured outside Canada with its acquisition of *Inland Printer* and *Rock Products* in the United States, and in the following year it introduced *The Chatelaine*—later simply *Chatelaine*—a women's magazine that won its name in a contest and soon gained a loyal following.

In 1930, the company moved into French-language publishing for Canadians when Maclean purchased *Le Prix Courant*. The economic climate during the 1930s was difficult, and Maclean's company felt the impact of the Great Depression. Helped by a government duty on imported magazines, which allowed Canadian publishers to regain some of the market share they had lost to U.S. publishers, Maclean was able to avoid laying off employees by putting workers paid by the hour on shortened schedules, and cutting wages and vacation pay. Maclean Publishing Company's salaried employees suffered two 10% cuts in pay. In 1935, the import duties were lifted with a change in Canada's government, and U.S. publications gained predominance once more on newsstands. By 1936, however, Maclean's employees numbered nearly 900, and wages and hours had both increased. By the end of the decade, the company boasted 30 publications.

With the coming of World War II, Maclean coped with wartime rationing and shortages of goods and workers, and a drastic decline in advertising revenue. With the conversion of the economy to a wartime footing, production of consumer goods was drastically curtailed, resulting in a scarcity or disappearance of many goods, and the need for consumer product advertising thus dried up. The company attempted to compensate by encouraging "sustaining" advertising, to maintain the image and familiarity of a brand name, and through the increased use of advertising by the government. The company's business publications became tools in the war effort, monitoring the nationwide war production effort, and publicizing government policies and regulations. Even such publications as *Mayfair*, a society magazine, were transformed, advising women on war charities and economical use of food. In addition, the company produced a free edition of *Maclean's* for distribution to Canadians on active duty overseas, which eventually gained a circulation of 30,000.

In 1945, the company's name was changed to Maclean-Hunter Publishing Company to reflect the contribution of Horace T. Hunter, its president since 1933. Three years later, the company made its most dramatic physical expansion up to that point, when it opened a C$3 million printing plant in a Toronto suburb, Willowdale. Throughout the postwar years, the company once again found its consumer publications facing stiff competition for advertising dollars from such U.S. imports as the Canadian editions of *Time* and *Reader's Digest*. By 1948, two-thirds of all magazines purchased in Canada came from other countries.

In 1950 John Maclean died, and Hunter acquired 60% control of the company, in which he continued to serve as president for two more years. In 1952, Floyd S. Chalmers, who had been with the company since 1919, became president.

Throughout the 1950s, Canadian magazines found themselves challenged by new modes of communication, such as television, as well as by U.S. publications. In 1956, Canadian publishers got some help from their government when it imposed a 20% tax on advertising in non-Canadian magazines, but this was repealed the following year under U.S. pressure. By the end of the decade, nonetheless, Maclean-Hunter was publishing 51 different titles.

The 1960s marked a turning point for Maclean-Hunter. What had until then been a staid enterprise, engaged almost exclusively in publishing, became a diversified company, operating in a wide variety of communications fields. In 1960, the company made an unsuccessful attempt to obtain a license for a television station in Toronto, but in the following year it was able to enter the broadcasting industry through its purchase of 50% of the radio station CFCO in Chatham, Ontario. The station had been one of the pioneers in Canadian radio, having been founded by a butcher with an interest in radio in 1926. It had used a homemade transmitter until 1948.

Maclean-Hunter also diversified into the event-planning industry. In 1961, the company organized a convention for members of the plastics industry, despite the fact that Canada's main trade association for plastics was headed by a rival trade publisher, who refused to lend the association's support to the show. The show, which became an annual event, was not a great success, nor would it be for many years. Nevertheless, Maclean-Hunter forged ahead in the show-management field, forming Industrial & Trade Shows of Canada, now known as Industrial Trade & Consumer Shows Inc., in 1962.

At this time, the company also expanded its holdings in the media-information services field. Maclean-Hunter had long owned *Canadian Advertising Rates & Data,* a service publication for advertising agencies, and in 1958 it had acquired *British Rate & Data.* Both were doing well, and the company was looking for new areas of growth. The U.S. market was out of the question, dominated as it was by one well-established firm, Standard Rate & Data Service, so Maclean-Hunter moved into continental Europe with the French publication *Tarif Media.* In 1961, it sold 50% of this publication to the U.S. company Standard Rate & Data Service, and with this partner formed a European joint venture to launch a West German service, *Media Daten.* Eventually, European operations came to include Austria, Switzerland, and Italy.

The company's Canadian operations, however, were not faring as well. Although the company had continued to expand its French-language offerings, adding its first general-interest publication for the Quebec market in 1960, *Chatelaine-La Revue Moderne,* and following with *Le Magazine Maclean* in 1961, its English-language consumer magazines lost C$1.8 million in that same year. This was, as ever, due party to the domination of the Canadian market by U.S. publications. Despite this, Maclean-Hunter introduced another English-language consumer publication in 1963, targeted at younger women. It was called *Miss Chatelaine.*

A year later, in 1965, the Canadian periodical industry received some government support when the tax deduction for the business expense of advertisements in non-Canadian publications—with the exception of *Time* and *Reader's Digest*—was abolished. This opened up the field somewhat by discouraging the proliferation of U.S.-owned Canadian editions, and driving some of these publications out of business.

Also in 1965, stock in Maclean-Hunter was publicly traded for the first time. Up until this time, the company's shares had been closely held by Maclean's designated successors and a small number of members of senior management, but it became clear that internal mechanisms for distributing stock in the company were no longer adequate, and a sale of 15% of the shares was arranged. Of the 15%, 40% was allotted to meet high employee demand.

The company expanded further into non-publishing fields in the mid-1960s, acquiring Design Craft Ltd., which produced exhibits for trade shows, as a natural complement to its existing interests in that area. It continued to purchase radio stations, adding CHYM, a rural station, in 1964, and CKEY of Toronto, the company's first urban radio property, in 1965. Also in 1965, the broadcasting company's interests were augmented by the acquisition of CFCN radio and television, of Calgary.

Further ventures into the broadcasting field came in 1967 with Maclean-Hunter's entry into the cable television business. The company entered a partnership with Frederick T. Metcalf, who had already built a cable system in Guelph, Ontario, and the result was Maclean Hunter Cable TV. The first market targeted for expansion was Toronto. The company's steady progress in diversification was ratified in 1968 when its name was updated from Maclean-Hunter Publishing Company Limited to Maclean-Hunter Limited.

In the first years of the 1970s, the company ventured into book distribution, purchasing a book wholesaler; into the printing of business forms, with the acquisition of Data Business Forms; and into the paging business, by buying Airtel, which provides personal pagers to relay messages. In 1973, Maclean-Hunter purchased a 50% interest in KEG Productions Ltd., which put together television programs on wildlife. The company created "Audubon Wildlife Theater" and "Profiles of Nature," both successful and long-running series.

In the mid-1970s, with further expansion in the Canadian market blocked by the Canadian Radio-television & Telecommunications Commission, Maclean-Hunter set its sights on cable television in the United States, buying Suburban Cablevision, of New Jersey. Unlike Canadian cable systems, which existed to provide clear reception of ordinary network television in remote locations, the New Jersey operations set out to attract customers by offering them access to programs not available on regular television, such as special sporting events. This new concept proved popular, and Suburban Cablevision grew from 10 franchises to 43.

In 1975 Hunco Ltd., the Hunter family holding firm, owned a 51% controlling interest in Maclean-Hunter. This block of stock was sold to the board of Maclean-Hunter in January 1976, when chairman Donald F. Hunter, facing death from a brain tumor, sold nearly 3.5 million of his family's 4 million shares to a holding company set up to ensure that the company would be safe from unwanted takeover attempts in his absence. The era of family control was over.

Perhaps the most important event of the mid-1970s for Maclean-Hunter took place outside the company: the passage of bill C-58 in 1976. This amendment to the Income Tax Act removed the exemptions on tax-deductible advertising from *Time* and *Reader's Digest,* and stipulated that three-quarters of a publication's owners must be Canadian and four-fifths of its contents must be original and non-foreign, in order for advertising within it to qualify for a tax exemption. This gave new life to the Canadian magazine industry, in particular *Maclean's.* The flagship publication had long suffered in its head-to-head battle with *Time,* and in addition had fallen into an identity crisis under a series of editors. The magazine, which had lost credibility and had been losing money heavily since the early 1960s, had become a source of embarrassment to all concerned. With the support of bill C-58, however, *Maclean's* was able to rally in the latter part of the 1970s, and in 1978 stepped up from a biweekly to weekly publication.

By that time, Maclean-Hunter had diversified to such a large extent that income from publishing accounted for only half of all company revenues. Notwithstanding these changes, the company continued to expand its magazine operations in the late 1970s, acquiring four special-interest publications in 1978, including *Ski Canada* and *Racquets Canada,* and founding *New Mother* and its French-language counterpart *Mère Nouvelle* in 1979.

Steady expansion of Maclean-Hunter operations continued into the 1980s, with the purchase of a four-fifths interest in a U.S. form printer, Transkrit Corporation, in 1980; the acquisition of *Progressive Grocer* journal in 1982; the launch of *City & Country Home* in 1982; and the purchase of *Hospital Practice* in 1983. In 1981 Maclean-Hunter Limited dropped the hyphen in its name becoming Maclean Hunter Limited.

In 1982, the company fulfilled a long-standing ambition to include the newspaper business in its ever-widening scope of operations when it purchased a 51% share of the *Toronto Sun,* a daily tabloid newspaper sold primarily to commuters. A year later its involvement with the *Sun* led to purchase of the *Houston Post,* in Texas.

Throughout the late 1980s, Maclean Hunter continued to grow in its chosen fields, primarily through acquisitions, as in its purchase of the Yorkville Group in 1985 and Davis & Henderson Ltd. in 1986, both printers. In 1986, it started work on 49%-owned Barden Cablevision, which covers all of Detroit, Michigan, and subsequently began construction of a system in the United Kingdom. By 1989, newspaper holdings included *Sun* papers in three Canadian cities outside Toronto, and in 1990 the company purchased Armstrong Communications, a cable system, in Ontario.

From its start, Maclean Hunter has relied on strong management in solid fields, such as business publishing, to fuel steady growth. Backed by a tradition of success, it appears likely that Maclean Hunter will continue to prosper.

Principal Subsidiary: Maclean Hunter Inc. (U.S.A.).

Further Reading: Perry, Robert L., *Maclean Hunter at One Hundred,* Toronto, Maclean Hunter Limited, 1987.

—Elizabeth Rourke

MAXWELL COMMUNICATION CORPORATION PLC

Maxwell House
8-10 New Fetter Lane
London EC4A 1DU
United Kingdom
(071) 353-0360

Public Company
Incorporated: 1964 as British Printing Corporation
Employees: 14,360
Sales: £996.90 million (US$1.92 billion)
Stock Exchanges: London Paris Brussels Antwerp Frankfurt
  Toronto Montreal New York Tokyo

Maxwell Communication Corporation (MCC) is one of the world's ten largest media groups. The group currently comprises four operating areas: information services and electronic publishing; school and college publishing; language instruction; and reference-book and professional publishing.

Since October 1987 the group has been named after its chairman, Robert Maxwell. Maxwell has also been the publisher of Mirror Group Newspapers (MGN) of the United Kingdom since 1984 and publisher of the New York *Daily News* since March 1991. The Maxwell family owns 65% of MCC. Maxwell has often been cited as an example of the enterprise culture promoted by the U.K.'s Conservative government of Margaret Thatcher, in power from 1979–1990. Maxwell himself, however, is an active member of the opposition Labour Party and served as a Labour member of Parliament between 1964 and 1970.

Maxwell was born Jan Ludvik Hoch in the village of Slatina Solo in the Czechoslovakian province of Ruthenia in 1923. His family was part of the prewar Hungarian Jewish community that had lived in this region since the 16th century. After the outbreak of World War II Maxwell succeeded in escaping to the United Kingdom, where he enlisted in the British army. By the end of the war he had been promoted to the rank of captain and had been awarded the Military Cross for bravery. In 1946 Maxwell became a naturalized U.K. citizen. Most members of Maxwell's family in Ruthenia did not survive the war and were victims of the Holocaust.

The origins of MCC can be traced to Maxwell's early postwar career in occupied Berlin. Between 1946 and 1947 he was part of the Berlin Information Control Unit. In 1947 Maxwell made contact with Ferdinand Springer, who before the war had been Germany's leading publisher of scientific books. Springer had managed to retain a large number of valuable back numbers of his scientific journals. Maxwell agreed to act as Springer Verlag GmbH & Co. KG's representative outside Germany. Maxwell's new U.K. company, European Periodicals, Publicity and Advertising Corporation (EPPAC), was granted the exclusive worldwide distribution rights for Springer's journals and books. In 1949 Maxwell helped form a new company called Lange, Maxwell & Springer (LMS) in which the Springer interests took a 49% stake. LMS took over the distribution of Springer's books outside Germany on behalf of EPPAC.

A year earlier Springer Verlag had formed a joint venture with the British publisher, Butterworth & Co. (Publishers) Ltd., under which LMS would distribute Springer's scientific journals for them. However, this venture proved to be unprofitable. In 1951 Maxwell bought Butterworth's stake in the joint venture. Maxwell also acquired half of the German interest in the joint venture, thus gaining 75% of the company. The former joint venture was renamed Pergamon Press Ltd., possibly after the Pergamon Museum in East Berlin. In 1954 Maxwell was forced to break with Springer. He agreed to dissolve LMS and operate under the name I.R. Maxwell & Co. Ltd. Springer gave Maxwell exclusive rights until 1959 in the British Empire, France, China, and Indonesia. Maxwell broke completely with Springer at the beginning of 1960.

In 1955 Maxwell decided to transform Pergamon into a major world publisher of scientific journals. By the end of 1957 Pergamon was publishing over 100 journals and books. During the late 1950s Maxwell also developed links with Eastern Europe and the Soviet Union, securing the rights to a number of scientific journals published in this part of the world.

In 1961 Maxwell made a five-year agreement with Macmillan Inc. of New York for the exclusive distribution of Pergamon books. The arrangement was terminated in August 1964 because the books had not sold well. Maxwell was later to acquire this company. In July 1964 Pergamon became a public company, although Maxwell retained majority control. In the following year, Pergamon acquired the subscription books division of George Newnes Ltd., a subsidiary of the International Publishing Corporation, which published two well-known encyclopedias, *Chambers* and *Pictorial Knowledge*. In May 1967 Pergamon acquired a competitor in the encyclopedia business, Caxton Holdings. In August Pergamon merged its encyclopedia interests with the encyclopedia subsidiary of the British Printing Corporation (BPC). The new joint venture was called International Learning Systems Corporation Limited (ILSC). Maxwell attempted to acquire the *News of the World*, the U.K. Sunday newspaper, in 1968, and the *Sun*, the U.K. daily newspaper, in 1969, but Rupert Murdoch gained control of both publications.

In January 1969 Maxwell began talks with Saul Steinberg, chairman of Leasco Data Processing Equipment of the United States, about the possible merger of Pergamon with Leasco, in June 1969, Maxwell and Steinberg signed an agreement whereby Leasco would launch a formal bid for Pergamon subject to Maxwell's permitting a team of accountants appointed by Leasco to have full access to all of the Pergamon business records. Maxwell was to become president of Leasco's European division. On August 21 Leasco withdrew its bid because of doubts about Pergamon's accounts and ILSC. Maxwell disputed Leasco's right to take this course of action and had the dispute referred to the Takeover panel. On August 27 the panel decided Leasco had the right to withdraw and recommended a full Board of Trade inquiry over the objections of Maxwell. A shareholders' meeting was called at Pergamon for October 10. The meeting voted to dismiss Maxwell as company chairman and remove him from the board. Leasco gained control of Pergamon with 61% of the vote. However, Leasco decided not to proceed with its takeover bid, but retained its 38% stake in the company.

Maxwell retained control of Pergamon's U.S. subsidiary, Pergamon Press Inc. (PPI), even though the U.K. parent company controlled 70% of its stock. In April 1971 he ended a dispute with Leasco over PPI with an agreement to employ him as a consultant at Pergamon and to appoint him to its board as a non-executive director.

In July the Board of Trade issued its report on Pergamon. The board alleged that there had been irregularities in the accounting practices of the company, and in particular in its subsidiary, ILSC. It concluded that "notwithstanding Mr. Maxwell's acknowledged abilities and energy, he [was] not in [their] opinion a person who can be relied on to exercise proper stewardship of a publicly quoted company." However, Maxwell's subsequent business career has completely disproved the Board of Trade's much quoted conclusion. The report's publication coincided with the date that Maxwell was due to return to the Pergamon board. That was no longer possible.

Maxwell never accepted the findings of the Board of Trade as a true record of his conduct of Pergamon's affairs, and unsuccessfully took legal action to get the report overturned. Between 1971 and 1973 he worked hard to regain control of Pergamon. In 1973 he enlisted the support of some of the most prominent editors of Pergamon's scientific journals. He persuaded the chairman of Pergamon to hold a special shareholders' meeting on November 20. In the light of Pergamon's falling profits and the loyalty of the scientific journal editors to Maxwell, he was appointed as an alternate director to John Silkin. A formal move to re-elect him as a full director was adjourned until January 8, 1974, by which time the Pergamon board hoped to assemble enough current information to enable Leasco, now renamed Reliance, to press ahead with a full bid. Although he failed to become a full director, on January 9 Maxwell launched a £1.5 million takeover bid for Pergamon. On January 23 he won the support of Pergamon's board, and by late February Reliance had agreed to sell its 38% holding in Pergamon to Maxwell for £0.12 a share, receiving just over £600,000 in return for its original £9 million investment. Maxwell's new U.S. company, Microform International Marketing Corporation, now owned 90.7% of Pergamon. Maxwell subsequently purchased the remaining Pergamon shares.

Between 1974 and 1977 Maxwell restored the fortunes of Pergamon. In 1977, Pergamon employed 3,000 people and was publishing 360 scientific journals and 1,000 books a year. Its sales had risen from £7 million to £20 million and its net annual profits had increased from £27,000 to £3.3 million.

In 1980 Maxwell, in common with other proprietor-entrepreneurs, began a major expansion program. He began to purchase shares in the once-powerful U.K. printing company BPC, his former partner in ILSC. BPC had been formed in February 1964 from the merger of Purnell & Sons Ltd. with Hazell Sun Ltd. Purnell & Sons had been established in 1849.

In July 1980 Maxwell launched a dawn raid—the acquisition of a large number of shares—on BPC and acquired 29.5% of its shares. In February 1981 Maxwell launched a takeover bid for BPC with the agreement of the National Westminster Bank, BPC's most important creditor. Later in the month the Pergamon Press agreed to inject £10 million into BPC in return for a controlling interest in BPC. Maxwell became deputy chairman and chief executive of BPC. By May 1981 Pergamon owned 77% of BPC and Maxwell had become chairman.

Maxwell proceeded to deal with BPC's chief problems, overmanning and low productivity. Although the trade unions signed an agreement with Maxwell to reorganize working practices as part of his survival plan for BPC, the workers at the Park Royal printing works conducted two years of strikes between 1981 and 1983. In November 1983 Maxwell dismissed all the workers at Park Royal and transferred production to East Kilbride and Leeds. Maxwell also contributed to the rationalization of the U.K. printing industry in a deal with Reed International in December 1982, which resulted in the closure of Reed's Odhams factory and its absorption into the nearby Sun works, also at Watford. In 1984 Maxwell bought Reed's national newspapers. Maxwell took full advantage of the trade union reforms introduced by the Thatcher government, and they contributed to his success during the 1980s.

Meanwhile Maxwell had changed BPC's name to the British Printing and Communications Corporation (BPCC) in March 1982. This change reflected his wish to expand into cable and satellite television, computers and data banks, electronic printing, and communications high technology that were being developed in the 1980s. In 1986 Maxwell began a further expansion of BPCC. He began with the takeover of Pergamon's crown jewels, its 361 scientific journals, for £238.65 million in March 1986. In October 1987 BPCC changed its name to Maxwell Communication Corporation; Maxwell felt BPCC had an unfavorable image in the United States, where people mistakenly believed it was a nationalized industry. The name BPCC was reassigned to one of MCC's subsidiaries. In December MCC completed another "reverse takeover," this time of Pergamon's books division for £100 million.

In 1987 Maxwell attempted to transform BPCC into a major publisher in the United States, as part of his plan to make BPCC one of the top ten international media and communications corporations. In May 1987 BPCC had launched a US$2 billion hostile cash bid for Harcourt Brace Jovanovich (HBJ), the leading American publisher of school textbooks. HBJ responded with a comprehensive US$3 billion recapitalization plan in order to defend itself against BPCC. BPCC pursued legal action in support of its takeover bid for HBJ. However, the failure of several lawsuits in the U.S. courts led BPCC to withdraw its takeover bid in late July. Maxwell also failed in 1987 with his bid to acquire 50% of Bell & Howell, the U.S. educational publisher and manufacturer of information storage equipment.

The following year Maxwell achieved his plan for MCC in the United States. On July 21, 1988, MCC launched a bid for Macmillan Inc., a large U.S. publishing group. MCC offered US$80 per share for Macmillan. On September 13, Macmillan, which was opposed to MCC's bid, proposed a management-led leveraged buyout, worth marginally more than MCC's revised US$84-a-share offer, organized by Kohlberg Kravis Roberts & Co. (KKR), a leading Wall Street leveraged buyout firm. MCC responded by raising its bid to US$86.80 a share, which was slightly higher than KKR's bid. On September 22 Macmillan rejected both MCC's revised bid and KKR's bid.

On September 27 Macmillan accepted an improved offer of US$90.05 from KKR. However, MCC claimed that it was really only worth US$86 a share, US$3 less than MCC's offer of US$89 a share. KKR's agreement with Macmillan contained a "poison pill" provision. Under it, KKR had the right to buy for US$865 million four of Macmillan's key businesses, which would significantly reduce the value of the corporation, if its takeover offer failed in the face of a higher bid or other obstacles.

Maxwell began legal action against Macmillan's "poison pill" provision and increased his bid to US$90.25 a share. On November 2, MCC was victorious in the Delaware Supreme Court, when it issued a preliminary injunction against Macmillan, preventing it from granting the "poison pill" provision to KKR. On November 4, MCC acquired Macmillan for US$2.6 billion. A few days earlier MCC had also acquired the Official Airline Guides division (OAG) of Dun & Bradstreet, a leading provider of airline schedule information and related services in North America, for $750 million.

In order to finance MCC's U.S. acquisitions, Maxwell decided to abandon most of the printing side of MCC's business to concentrate on publishing. In January 1989 MCC began to dispose of over US$1.4 billion worth of MCC's printing and non-core subsidiaries. In September 1989 MCC secured US$3 billion in medium-term debt to refinance the borrowings taken on at the time of the purchase of Macmillan and OAG. MCC used some of the borrowings to acquire Merrill Publishing, the U.S. educational books group, for $260 million in the same month. At the same time MCC's disposals continued with the flotation of 44% of Macmillan's former language instruction subsidiary, Berlitz International, in December 1989, raising $130 million.

By October 1990 MCC had managed to reduce its debt to US$1.9 billion. MCC decided to further reduce its debt with over US$400 million more disposals of corporate assets. MCC used the proceeds of the disposals, the redemption of loan stock in MGN, and a short-term bridging loan to repay US$415 million in debt due on October 23, 1990. MCC faces no further obligations regarding debt repayment until October 1992, when US$750 million are due, and the final repayment of $1.26 million has to be made in October 1994.

Between 1981 and 1990 Maxwell increased MCC's turnover from £198 million to £1.24 billion and turned a net loss of £14 million into a net profit of £101 million. MCC was given two key objectives by Maxwell for the early 1990s. The first was the elimination of its corporate debt. The second was to build on the achievements of the 1980s to take it into the middle ranks of the top ten world media corporations. By 1987 MCC was international, with publishing businesses in more than 15 countries. By 1989 the MCC group had a 50% interest in the Macmillan–McGraw-Hill joint venture, the second largest elementary and high school publisher in the United States.

In 1991 Maxwell's son Kevin became chief executive officer. Kevin had served as a director of MCC since 1986 and as joint managing director with Ian Maxwell since 1988. An agreement was made at the end of March 1991 to sell MCC's subsidiary, Pergamon Press, to Elsevier for £440 million. Elsevier is one of the largest publishing groups in the Netherlands. The sale of the original heart of the Maxwell family's business interests marks a further shift in the balance of MCC away from the United Kingdom to the United States.

Principal Subsidiaries: Macmillan Inc.; Official Airline Guides, Inc.; Berlitz International Inc.

Further Reading: Haines, Joe, *Maxwell*, London, Macdonald, 1988; Snoddy, Raymond, "Monday Interview," *Financial Times,* August 6, 1990.

—Richard Hawkins

MOORE CORPORATION LIMITED

1 First Canadian Place
Toronto, Ontario M5X 1G5
Canada
(416) 364-2600
Fax: (416) 364-1667

Public Company
Incorporated: 1929
Employees: 25,021
Sales: US$2.77 billion
Stock Exchanges: Toronto Montreal New York

Moore Corporation Limited was built upon the design and manufacture of a simple counter salesbook. As the world's largest maker of business forms throughout much of its history, Moore has continually redefined the business-forms industry, from the time its founder, Samuel J. Moore, launched the industry through the dominance of computers today.

Samuel Moore emigrated to Canada from his native England as a young boy in 1861. He worked in the printing business throughout his teens; by his early 20s, he was the co-publisher of a Tory newsletter called *The Grip*. When Moore met John Carter, a local sales clerk, who described his idea for a salesbook using a piece of carbon paper to standardize sales slips and provide a record of transactions, Moore seized upon the idea, acquired rights to produce the salesbook, and hired Carter as his first sales representative. With the motto, "Let one writing serve many purposes" and an initial investment of only C$2,500, the Paragon Black Leaf Counter Check Book went into production in 1882 at the Grip Printing & Publishing Company. Moore reduced production overhead by 75% the following year by purchasing two automatic printing presses, and in 1889, bought the operation that manufactured the presses, Kidder Press Company.

Moore already had begun to look beyond the Canadian market. He predicted that the United States, offering a large population and no language barrier, would become his primary market, and so it did. Within two years of the introduction of the Paragon salesbook, Grip established a factory in Niagara Falls, New York. Business was so good at the world's first factory devoted exclusively to the manufacture of salesbooks that the owners doubled plant capacity in 1886 and again in 1888. Moore named the United States organization Carter & Co. to honor Paragon's inventor.

Europe presented another opportunity for growth, but it took Moore two years of negotiation. In 1889 he reached an agreement with the British-based Lamson Store Service Company that gave it the rights to the salesbook patents and manufacturing techniques for all of Europe and Australia.

Demand for the salesbooks continued to grow so dramatically that the company was left short of boxes for packaging and shipping. Moore's eye for efficiency settled on the night watchman, whom he assigned to produce boxes in his spare time. Soon the company had box orders from shoe stores and other local merchants; in 1909, box-making became a separate business, called the F.N. Burt Company.

Moore also pursued other entrepreneurial notions. A young man brought Moore an idea to make souvenir silver teaspoons that tourists around the world could collect. Moore raised enough capital to form a company and established the Niagara Silver Company, later renamed William A. Rogers Limited, and maintained an involvement with the company.

In 1902 Moore was one of the founders of the Metropolitan Bank, of Canada; he was elected president in 1907. At that time, banks issued their own paper currency, and Samuel Moore's likeness and signature appeared on the bank's C$5 bills. In 1914 when the Metropolitan Bank was absorbed into the Bank of Nova Scotia, Moore was appointed to the board. Over the years, Moore became president, chairman, and then honorary chairman of the Bank of Nova Scotia.

In 1925 one of several companies controlled by Moore, the Pacific Manifolding Book Company, forged ahead of competition by developing a single-use, disposable carbon paper. Inspired by a customer who owned a large California poultry business and complained that carbonized paper was too messy, the Speediset business form consisted of slips glued together at the ends with a carbon between them. This form allowed customers to use carbon paper without putting it in place. The original Speediset is still in use in more modern form.

Web-fed lithography, a major development in the printing industry in the mid-1920s, brought Moore and other paper-producing businesses into modern times. The web press's high speed allowed mass production and more precise product standardization. As a result, Moore created a machinery division to produce equipment for the exclusive use of Moore companies.

In the mid-1920s Moore controlled a network of nine separate companies that had become known as the Moore Group. The group was involved in boxing and printing, salesbooks, and other endeavors. Income from the salesbook and related sales counter products still made up 98% of the Moore Group's business, but change was on the horizon.

On January 1, 1929, the three largest members of the Moore Group formalized operations, merging into a public company, Moore Corporation Limited. The companies included under the Canadian corporate umbrella were actually based in the United States: American Sales Book Company, Ltd.; Pacific-Burt Company, Limited, later called Pacific Manifolding Book Company Limited; and Gilman Fanfold Corporation, Ltd. Eventually the remaining six Moore Group members came under the control of Moore Corporation. In its first year on the Toronto Stock Exchange, Moore Corporation Limited reported a net income of more than C$1 million.

Later in 1929 Samuel J. Moore turned 70, and the stock market crashed. Facing an era of economic depression as well as his own aging, Moore turned his attention toward grooming successors to guide the company's future. That was the year he hired David W. Barr, who eventually became chairman; meanwhile Moore saw potential in Edwin G. Baker, whom he had hired nine years ago. When Moore made Baker president of the corporation in 1935, he established a tradition of promoting from within rather than seeking executives from outside.

It was also about this time that Moore instituted a separate research subsidiary to oversee research activities at all the divisions. Research would play an increasingly vital role at Moore and in industry in general.

As new president Baker secured the threads holding together the loose network of individual companies within the corporation, he also encouraged autonomy of each company's daily operations. In the United States, he divided the organization geographically, giving each region its own executive committee. This helped to establish close local ties as well as to provide a small-scale training ground for future corporate executives.

It was to the Moore Corporation that the U.S. government turned in 1936 when it needed a somewhat sizable business-form order: the first 40 million Social Security application forms and cards. This government connection proved important as World War II approached.

World War II brought demand for ration booklets, payroll envelopes, and various other forms that industry and governments had not needed before. This demand hastened Moore's maturation from a producer of salesbooks to a producer of all types of business forms. During the war, more than 150 Canadian and U.S. government departments used forms developed by Moore. By 1945, 80% of Moore's revenue was generated by business forms, not salesbooks.

The corporation reorganized to reflect the change. Many different Moore-owned companies that manufactured business forms had been operating under their individual names. In 1945, these firms were brought together under the common brand name Moore Business Forms. This division employed half of Moore's total work force. The corporation also realigned its management echelon to prepare for the postwar era. Baker became chairman of the board, and W. Norman McLeod, who had joined Moore with Baker in 1920, took over as president. Samuel Moore kept the title of honorary chairman until his death in 1948.

McLeod stepped up a campaign to specialize and diversify geographically. He increased the number of production plants in the United States from 10 to 40, but kept plant size small for greater control as the plants grew more and more technologically complex.

In 1955 McLeod moved to chairman of the board, and Thomas S. Duncanson became president. Duncanson had joined Moore in 1910, when the F.N. Burt division was acquired. His most significant contribution as president was to create a central division in the United States, headquartered in Chicago. This distinction divided the country into eastern, southern, pacific, and central divisions. Duncanson remained president until 1962, when he was elected chairman and W. Herman Browne was made president.

Browne initiated a policy to broaden Moore's international operations. He cemented the British connection by reaching a formal financial relationship with long-time associate Lamson Industries Limited. Through an exchange of shares, Moore acquired 20% of Lamson's equity. Included in the agreement was an exchange of directors and a ten-year pact to share technical information.

It was also during Browne's tenure that the U.S. government instituted Medicare. In 1966 Moore printed more than 25 million Medicare identification cards. The ever-present U.S. tax form, the W-2, also came from Moore.

David W. Barr, whom Samuel Moore had hand-picked so many years earlier, was named president in 1968. He professionalized sales representatives' training and followed through on the firm's internationalization, increasing Moore's interest in Lamson Industries to 52% in 1973.

Packaging took on a bigger role at Moore during this time. The packaging operation in England was assigned to a division called Decoflex Ltd., which also manufactured fashion bags for the clothing industry and currency containers for bankers. At home in 1974 Moore merged its Dominion Paper Box Company Limited with Canada's Reid Press Limited to establish Reid Dominion Packaging Limited.

Barr became chairman in 1976, when Richard W. Hamilton, who had been with Moore 35 years, moved into the presidency. A year later, Hamilton approved a total acquisition of Lamson. The internationalization plan begun 20 years ago was now complete; Moore owned Moore Business Forms de Mexico; Moore Business Forms de Puerto Rico; Moore Formularios Limitada, in Brazil; and Moore Business Forms de Centro America, in El Salvador. In addition, ties were established with Formularios y Procedimientos Moore in Venezuela and Toppan Moore Company, Ltd., in Japan.

Internationalization was not the only concern at Moore during this period. At the same time Moore executives were concentrating on their new foreign operations, they also turned their attention and funding to research: computerization was taking over world industry, and big money awaited companies that could adapt their services to complement the new machines.

During the computer era's infancy, Moore developed Speediflo and Speediflex continuous-feed forms. Among the other advances Moore introduced in the 1960s and early 1970s were a carbonless paper; an optical character recognition tester; the Mooremailer continuous envelope producer for high-speed addressing systems; and the Speediread form with colored highlight lines for easier data reading.

New products meant more divisions. Moore formed a response graphics division in 1974 to develop special products for the U.S. direct mail industry, and acquired Minneapolis, Minnesota–based International Graphics Corporation in 1977.

Despite its pioneering start, Moore has sported a cautious reputation. Thus, when Moore announced its decision in the late 1970s to enter the small computer systems market, the financial community expressed surprise.

Moore executives did not jump into this extremely competitive field with eyes closed—they had considered the idea for years before acting on it. In the 1970s it had become clear that, although the business-forms industry was still growing, it was not booming the way it had been. An annual overall market increase of 15% was not unusual in the 1960s. By the early 1970s, the industry's yearly growth was down to 9%, falling to 3% or 4% in the following decade. Even though in the 1970s Moore held 25% of the U.S. business-forms market and continued to gather profits from around the world, the company was accustomed to soaring net figures; the time for change was ripe.

The corporate decision-makers concluded that, since 70% of business forms were designed for use with a computer, a natural addition to their product line was the computer itself. The company hoped to sell its computer systems to small companies. Researchers identified nearly one million companies as potential buyers, and Moore had already had 40% of them as customers at one time or other. Now the company wanted to show each customer that Moore could tailor software to fit that particular business's payroll, inventory, and general accounting needs. As a further commitment to computer sales, Moore opened retail branch offices. These branches sold all types of computer supplies and were designed to service customers after they bought systems.

The microcomputer market proved to be too much for a newcomer like Moore, however. After losing about $30 million in the course of a few years, Moore abandoned the retail computer business, selling or closing its 44 MicroAge stores. Moore recognized, however, that in the age of the computer it must be prepared to supply customers with both paper and electronic information forms, and under chairman and CEO M. Keith Goodrich the company has accordingly embarked on a rapid expansion of its electronic products. These fall into three categories—direct marketing, business communication services, and database management services—which by 1992 should represent a combined one-quarter of corporate sales and one-third of net income.

Moore has always been in the business of helping companies to formalize their business information and communications. For most of the 20th century, that had involved the use of paper; in the future, perhaps it will be accomplished exclusively by means of electronic images; in either case, Moore Corporation Limited remains in the business of business forms.

Principal Subsidiaries: Moore Business Forms & Systems Ltd.; Moore International B.V. (Netherlands); Moore Belgium N.V.; Moore Business Forms, Inc. (U.S.A.); Moore Business Forms Limited (U.K.); Moore France S.A. (99.9%); Moore Portuguesa Limitada (Portugal); Moore Business Systems Australia Limited; Moore Paragon (Central Africa) (PVT) Ltd. (Zimbabwe); Moore Nederland B.V. (Netherlands); Moore de Mexico S.A. de C.V.; Moore Business Forms de Puerto Rico, S.A.; Moore Formularios Limitada (Brazil); Formularios Moore de Guatemala, S.A. (56%); Moore Business Forms de Centro America, S.A. de C.V. (El Salvador, 56%); Formularios Moore de Costa Rica S.A. de C.V. (56%).

Further Reading: The Story of Moore, Toronto, Moore Corporation Limited, 1982; *A special announcement,* Toronto, Moore Corporation Limited, 1986.

—Rosanne Ullman

THE NEW YORK TIMES COMPANY

229 West 43rd Street
New York, New York 10036
U.S.A.
(212) 556-1234
Fax: (212) 556-4607

Public Company
Incorporated: 1851 as Raymond, Jones & Company
Employees: 10,400
Sales: $1.78 billion
Stock Exchange: American

The New York Times Company (NYTC) is a large diversified media and communications business engaged in newspaper and magazine publishing, broadcasting and information services, and, to a lesser extent, forest products. Its principal property is one of the world's great newspapers, *The New York Times,* founded in 1851. During its history of nearly 140 years, the company has grown to include along with *The New York Times,* 32 regional newspapers and 17 magazines, including such popular journals as *Family Circle, McCall's, Golf Digest,* and *Tennis.* The company also operates five television stations, two radio stations, a news service, and a features syndicate, and licenses databases and copyrights. In addition it has equity interests in three Canadian newsprint mills and a partnership interest in a Maine paper mill.

The principal founders of *The New York Times* were Henry Jarvis Raymond, a sometime politician, reporter, and editor who learned his trade working for Horace Greeley on the *New York Tribune,* and George Jones, an Albany, New York, banker who had also once worked for Greeley as a business manager on the *Tribune.* Raymond proposed a newspaper that would present the news in a conservative and objective fashion, in contrast to the yellow journalism of the day, which emphasized crime, scandal, and radical politics. They raised $70,000 to establish Raymond, Jones & Company, largely by selling stock to wealthy upstate New York investors, and set up their editorial offices in a dilapidated six-story brownstone on Nassau Street in downtown New York City. The first issue of *The New York Daily Times*—the word "Daily" was dropped from the title in 1857—was dated September 18, 1851, and announced an editorial policy that would emphasize accurate reporting and moderation of opinion and expression.

Jones handled the company's business affairs, and Raymond, as editor, provided journalistic leadership. Under their management, helped by booming population growth in New York City, the *Times* grew rapidly, reaching 10,000 circulation within ten days and 24,000 by the end of its first year. In 1858 the paper moved into a new five-story building containing the most modern printing equipment. As the *Times* prospered, Raymond established and continually encouraged the high standards of journalism that prevail to this day. It also became a newspaper of record. For example, it carried the entire text of Lincoln's "Gettysburg Address" on the front page on November 20, 1863. Among other journalistic successes, the *Times* provided outstanding coverage of the U.S. Civil War, with Raymond himself reporting on the Battle of Bull Run.

Raymond was active in Republican politics throughout the war. He was present at the creation of the party in Pittsburgh in 1856 and wrote its first statement of principles. He wrote most of the party platform in 1864. Between political activity and journalism, Raymond was chronically overworked for years, and his health suffered. On June 19, 1869, at the age of 49, he died. George Jones assumed the editorial leadership of the *Times.*

By the time of Raymond's death, each of the 100 shares of stock in the company had increased in value from the original $1,000 to about $11,000, with 34 shares held by Raymond and 30 by Jones. In 1871 after a series of *Times* articles on the misdeeds of corrupt New York City politicians headed by William Marcy (Boss) Tweed, an attempt was made by Tweed interests to buy Raymond's 34 shares from his widow. Jones quickly arranged to have the shares purchased by one of his associates, thus establishing his control of the newspaper. In 1884 Jones chose to oppose the nomination by the Republican Party of James G. Blaine for president, thus losing the much-needed support of Republican readers and advertisers. The paper's profits fell steadily until Jones's death in 1891. His heirs had little aptitude for the newspaper business, and the panic and depression of 1893 brought the *Times* close to failure.

In 1893 the *Times*'s editor-in-chief Charles Ransom Miller, bought control of the paper from Jones's heirs with $1 million raised from Wall Street interests. Miller, a fine editor, had no business aptitude and was unable to maintain the newspaper's capital requirements. Staff reductions and declining journalistic quality brought the *Times* to its historic low point, and by 1896 it was on the verge of bankruptcy and dissolution. During this critical year salvation came in a dramatic fashion. A group of Wall Street investors in what was then called the New York Times Publishing Company arranged to save the firm—and their investments—by placing it in receivership and recapitalizing it as a new company, The New York Times Company. The new capitalization was 10,000 shares with 2,000 being paid out in exchange for the original *Times* stock. A large stock position with contractual assurance of eventual majority stock ownership was purchased with borrowed money by a then-little-known but respected newspaper editor and publisher from Chattanooga, Tennessee, Adolph Simon Ochs.

Ochs, the son of German immigrants, had received little formal schooling, but had learned the newspaper business from the ground up as newsboy, printer's devil, journeyman printer, business manager, and reporter. He was hard-working and ambitious. In 1878, at the age of 20, he borrowed $250 to buy the controlling interest in a failing Tennessee newspaper, the *Chattanooga Times,* thus beginning his career as a newspaper publisher before he was old enough to vote. He promoted high standards of journalism in the Chattanooga paper and soon brought it back to financial health. It 1896 looking for new challenges, he heard about *The New York Times's* troubles. Ochs offered to take over as publisher in return for a contract that would give him a majority of the paper's stock if he succeeded in making it profitable for three consecutive years. One of his early acts after becoming publisher of the *Times* on August 18, 1896, was to add the slogan "All the News That's Fit to Print," thus serving notice that the *Times* would continue to avoid sensationalism and follow high editorial standards.

Ochs's first two years with the *Times* were a continual struggle to carry on operations and improve the paper with inadequate capital. The expenses of covering the Spanish-American War in 1898 came close to ruining the paper which sold then for 3¢ a copy. Some *Times* executives advised raising the price, but Ochs made the brilliant and daring decision to reduce the price to 1¢. Within a year paid circulation trebled from 26,000 to 76,000. Advertising linage increased by nearly 40%, and the paper was profitable. Despite subsequent price increases, this was the beginning of a long upward trend in circulation and profitability. On August 14, 1900, Ochs received the NYTC stock certificates that established his control over the paper and the company, a controlling interest that was still held by his descendants in 1991.

The *Times's* success under Ochs was due to much more than price cutting. He improved financial and Wall Street coverage, added a Sunday magazine supplement, and a Saturday book review section, which was later moved to Sunday. With a brilliant managing editor, Carr Van Anda, the *Times* carried out numerous journalistic coups. It scooped the world on the Japanese-Russian naval battle in 1904 by sending the first wireless dispatches from a war area. It again scooped the world on the *Titanic* shipwreck in 1912 and outdid all competition in reporting the events of World War I. The paper warned of the excesses of the 1920s, but was well equipped financially to survive the Great Depression thanks to Ochs's conservative policy of plowing back into the paper a major portion of its profits.

Under Ochs, the NYTC followed a general policy of avoiding diversification, although Ochs himself continued as the personal owner and publisher of the *Chattanooga Times* and had a private investment in a Philadelphia paper between 1901 and 1913. In 1926, however the NYTC did take part ownership, along with the Kimberly & Clark Company in a Canadian paper mill, the Spruce Falls Power and Paper Company, in order to assure its supplies of newsprint.

The *Times* did relatively well during the Great Depression, with daily circulation holding in the 450,000 to 500,000 range. Ochs's health declined during the early 1930s, and he died on April 8, 1935. On May 7, 1935, the company's directors elected as president and publisher Ochs's son-in-law Arthur Hays Sulzberger who had married Ochs's daughter Iphigene in 1917 and subsequently worked his way up through the executive ranks of the newspaper.

Under Sulzberger the *Times* improved steadily in news coverage, financial strength, and technical progress. In a diversification move in 1944 the NYTC purchased New York City radio stations WQXR and WQXR-FM. Sulzberger opposed without success the unionization of *Times* employees. The company's first published financial statement in 1958 showed 60 consecutive years of increasing profits. In 1957 a recapitalization split the common stock into A and B common stock, with the B shares, mostly held by the Ochs trust, having voting control over the company. Sulzberger's health began to fail in the late 1950s. He retired in 1961. His successor as president and publisher was his son-in-law, Orvil E. Dryfoos. Dryfoos died in 1963. On June 20, 1963, he was succeeded in turn as president and publisher by Arthur Hays Sulzberger's son, Arthur Ochs Sulzberger who continued in 1991 to lead the NYTC as chairman and chief executive officer.

Although Sulzberger made some administrative changes and broadened the scope of the *Times* news coverage, the company continued to earn a relatively low profit margin on revenues, partly due to his policy of spending freely for thorough reporting, even to the extent of throwing out advertisements to make room for news. A second bitter strike against the paper in 1965 unsettled the management, and a decision was made to undertake a significant program of diversification. In 1967 the company's book and educational division was enlarged, and in 1968 the *Times* purchased a 51% interest in Arno Press. In 1969 the A common stock was given the vote for three members of the nine-member board. This action together with a public offering qualified the A stock for listing on the American Stock Exchange. The B stock, which controlled the company, continued to be held mostly by the Ochs family trust. In 1971 the NYTC paid Cowles Communications Company 2.6 million shares of class A stock to purchase substantial newspaper, magazine, television, and book properties including *Family Circle* and other magazines; a Florida newspaper chain; a Memphis, Tennessee, TV station; and a textbook publisher.

During the 1970s the newspaper's profit margins continued to be under pressure because of competition, especially in New York City suburban areas. The former Cowles properties helped buoy earnings despite the 1976 sale of some medical magazines acquired from Cowles. In 1980 the NYTC paid about $100 million for a southern New Jersey cable television operation, its largest acquisition since the Cowles deal. In 1984 the book publishing operation was sold to Random House, but in 1985 the NYTC, flush with record profits, spent about $400 million on the purchase of five regional newspapers and two TV stations. In 1986 yet another recapitalization converted every ten shares of B stock into nine shares of A and one share of B, with the B stock still controlling the company. Since more than 80% of the B stock was held by the Ochs trust, this move gave the trustees more liquidity without sacrificing control of the company.

The years 1989 and 1990 continued to be profitable. In 1989 the NYTC, admitting it was not making progress with cable, sold all of its cable TV properties to a consortium of Pennsylvania cable companies for $420 million. Also in 1989 the company acquired *McCall's* magazine, which, together with the acquisitions in 1988 of *Golf World* and *Sailing World,* substantially strengthened the NYTC's magazine group. The company's large new automated printing and distribution facility in Edison, New Jersey, that had been under construction for several years was scheduled to become operational in late 1990.

The New York Times Company has come a long way from the small brownstone on Nassau Street where Henry Raymond published the first issue of *The New York Times* in 1851. Company success has resulted not only from strong business leadership during much of its history but also from a series of capable publishers, editors, and reporters who built and continue to operate one of the world's great newspapers.

Principal Subsidiaries: Cruising World Publications, Inc; Donohue Malbaie Inc. (Canada, 49%); Wilmington Star-News, Inc.; Times Leasing, Inc.; NYT 1896T, Inc.; NYTRNG, Inc.; The Houma Courier Newspaper Corporation; Fernandina Beach News-Leader, Inc.; Gainesville Sun Publishing Company; Gaspesia Pulp and Paper Company Ltd. (Canada, 49%); Hendersonville Newspaper Corporation; International Herald Tribune S.A. (France, 50%); Lake City Reporter, Inc.; Lakeland Ledger Publishing Corporation; Golf Digest/Tennis, Inc.; Crossroads Holding Corporation; Gwinnett Publishing Company and Jones Communications Incorporated; Retail Magazines Marketing Company, Inc.; Sarasota Herald-Tribune Co.; The Family Circle, Inc.; The New York Times Broadcasting Service, Inc.; The New York Times Sales, Inc.; The Leesburg Daily Commercial, Inc.; London Bureau Ltd.; (U.K.) Northern SC Paper Corporation (80%); Ocala Star-Banner Corporation; The Palatka Daily News, Inc.; Sebring News-Sun, Inc.; Spruce Falls Power and Paper Company, Limited (Canada, 49.5%); The Dispatch Publishing Company, Inc.; Comet-Press Newspapers, Inc.; Golf World Limited (U.K.); The New York Times Distribution Corporation; Times On-Line Services, Inc.; TSP Newspapers, Inc.; The New York Times Syndication Sales Corporation; Rome Bureau S.r.l. (Italy).

Further Reading: Berger, Meyer, *The Story of the New York Times, 1851-1951,* New York, Simon and Schuster, 1951; Talese, Gay, *The Kingdom and the Power,* New York, World Publishing Company, 1969; Salisbury, Harrison E., *Without Fear or Favor,* New York, Times Books, 1980; Goulden, Joseph C., *Fit to Print,* Secaucus, New Jersey, Lyle Stuart Inc., 1988.

—Bernard A. Block

NEWS CORPORATION LIMITED

2 Holt Street
Sydney, New South Wales 2010
Australia
(02) 288 3000
Fax: (02) 288 3424

Public Company
Incorporated: 1979
Employees: 28,000
Sales: A$8.76 billion (US$6.77 billion)
Stock Exchanges: Amsterdam Australia Hong Kong London
    New York New Zealand Paris Tokyo

News Corporation is the holding company for the range of enterprises created or acquired since the 1950s by the Australian-American businessman Rupert Murdoch. It is the largest publisher of English-language newspapers in the world, and its subsidiaries include HarperCollins Publishers, the world's largest publisher of English-language books, as well as television stations, film production companies, printing firms, and airlines.

Rupert Murdoch was born in Melbourne in 1931, the son of Sir Keith Murdoch, managing director of the Herald and Weekly Times newspaper group. Sir Keith did not own many shares in the group, but was the major shareholder in News Ltd., which published the Adelaide *News* and *Sunday Mail*, and in a Brisbane company whose two newspapers he amalgamated into one, the *Courier-Mail.*

Sir Keith died in 1952. After graduating that year, his son spent some months as a junior sub-editor at the London *Daily Express* and returned to Australia in 1953 to take over the Adelaide papers. His father's executors sold the *Courier-Mail* to the Herald and Weekly Times group. In 1956 News Ltd. acquired the Perth *Sunday Times;* in 1957 it launched *TV Week*—inspired by the American *TV Guide*—which was to be the most profitable of all its Australian publications; in 1958 control of Channel 9, one of two TV channels in Adelaide, was awarded to Southern Television Corporation, in which News Ltd. had 60% of the shares. Murdoch's empire-building had begun.

The year 1960 was a watershed. News Ltd. bought Cumberland Newspapers, a group of local papers in the Sydney suburbs, then acquired the Sydney *Daily* and *Sunday Mirror* from the Fairfax group. Rohan Rivett, the editor of the Adelaide *News,* became the first of many editors to be fired from Mur-

doch newspapers. Five weeks before his dismissal he had been celebrating his acquittal on charges of seditious libel. These had arisen out of the *News's* criticisms of a state government inquiry into the case of an Aborigine found guilty of a murder which Rivett, and Murdoch, thought he had not committed. His departure marked the end of Murdoch's leanings toward anti-establishment views.

In 1964 News Ltd. launched *The Australian,* Australia's first national newspaper, based in Canberra. Murdoch considered it prestigious enough to be worth losing A$30 million, in 20 years, to keep going. Typesetting in Canberra and flying the matrices to Melbourne and Sydney for printing were difficult, and in 1967 the paper was moved to Sydney. In 1969, its latest editor oversaw its re-adoption of opposition to the Vietnam War, a policy the paper had espoused in 1965, when Australian troops first went there, but had since abandoned.

Murdoch, meanwhile, was in London. In October 1968 Robert Maxwell had offered to buy the United Kingdom's News of the World Organization (NOTW) for £26 million. The company owned the Sunday newspaper the *News of the World,* the Bemrose group of local newspapers, the papermakers Townsend Hook, and several other publishing companies. It had been run since 1891 by the Carr family, which had now split into two factions, one led by NOTW's chairman, Sir William Carr, with 32% of the shares, the other by his cousin, Derek Jackson, whose decision to sell his 25% stake had precipitated the crisis. Maxwell, born in Czechoslovakia, was then a Labour member of Parliament and the combination of his foreign origin and his political opinions provoked a hostile response to his bid from the Carrs and from the editor of the *News of the World,* Stafford Somerfield, who declared that the paper was—and should remain—as British as roast beef and Yorkshire pudding. News Ltd. arranged to swap shares in some of its minor ventures with the Carrs and by December it controlled 40% of the NOTW stock. In January 1969 Maxwell's bid was rejected at a shareholders' meeting where half of those present were company staff, temporarily given voting shares. Illness removed Sir William Carr from the chairmanship in June 1969: Murdoch succeeded him. In 1977, just before his death, Carr wrote to Maxwell to express regret that he had spurned his original offer for NOTW. In 1990 the *News of the World* was the biggest-selling English-language newspaper in the world.

Murdoch next sought a British daily to accompany the *News of the World.* He found it in 1969, when IPC decided to sell off *The Sun,* which had been launched in 1964 but had never been profitable, with sales of about one million copies. Under Murdoch, by contrast, *The Sun*'s circulation reached two million in 1971 and three million in 1973.

NOTW had added television to its list of interests in 1969, when it bought 8% of the voting shares in London Weekend Television (LWT), a company created in 1968 to run commercial television from Friday evening to Sunday night in a large and lucrative region centered on the capital city. The holding was rapidly built up to 36% of the voting shares and Murdoch became a non-executive director of LWT. He promptly saw to the dismissal of its managing director and took the chair of the executive committee in charge of scheduling, thus running the station without having been awarded a franchise. The Independent Television Authority ordered LWT to put its affairs in order without Murdoch in charge. The controversy over this incident was revived in 1977, when the government-appointed Committee on the Future of Broadcasting made some severe criticisms of the authority's failure to enforce its own rules. By that time, however, Murdoch had moved to the United States, and NOTW's shares in LWT were sold in 1980.

Back in Australia, Murdoch found that *The Australian* had become too liberal for his liking. In 1971 he dismissed its editor, Adrian Deamer, after he had been in the post for three years—a remarkable record, considering that the paper would have 13 editors in its first 16 years. In 1972 News Ltd. bought the Sydney *Daily* and *Sunday Telegraph* from Packer's Consolidated Press, which had been losing circulation to the three Fairfax papers, the *Sydney Morning Herald,* the *Sun,* and the Sunday *Sun-Herald.* The ailing *Sunday Australian* was absorbed into the *Sunday Telegraph* soon afterward.

Murdoch had become close to Gough Whitlam, then leader of the Australian Labor Party, and gave A$75,000 to the party's advertising campaign in 1972. If this was a return to Murdoch's earlier radicalism, it was short-lived. Within three years his papers were attacking the Labor Party again, with *The Australian,* for example, using raw figures, rather than seasonally-adjusted ones, to suggest, wrongly, that unemployment was rising. After the 1975 election, in which Whitlam was defeated, Murdoch himself, using a "special correspondent" by-line, wrote a report for *The Australian* on the Labor Party's secret—and eventually fruitless—appeal to Saddam Hussein, the dictator of Iraq, for financial aid, which resulted in a meeting in Sydney between Whitlam and Saddam's nephew. Ironically, what appeared to be just more anti-Whitlam propaganda was perfectly true.

In 1973 the News group made its first American acquisition, three newspapers in San Antonio, Texas, one of which, the *San Antonio News,* achieved brief but worldwide notoriety in 1976, with the striking but inaccurate headline "Killer Bees Move North." The next American acquisition, in 1976, was the *New York Post,* the city's only evening paper. This was swiftly followed, early in 1977, by the purchase of the New York Magazine Company, which published the magazines *New York* and *Village Voice*—so swiftly, indeed, that *New York's* proposed comment on the *Post* purchase, a picture of Murdoch as a killer bee, had to be dropped.

Murdoch's personal supervision of the *Post* led to an increased circulation, most notably through a series of reports on the "Son of Sam" serial killings, culminating in the misleading headline "How I became a mass killer" over a selection of old and innocuous letters from the murderer to a girlfriend. The *Post* did especially well in the summer of 1979, when a long-running strike kept its rivals closed, and a separate deal with the unions kept it open. The paper continued to suffer from financial problems, caused partly by the reluctance of the large department stores to advertise in such a down-market publication.

Murdoch did not neglect the Australian sector of his growing empire. In 1978 News Ltd. joined forces with the Packer's group and the British football pools company Vernons to start a New South Wales lottery and in 1979 it built up a 48.2% stake in Channel TEN-10, a Sydney television station. At the Australian Broadcasting Tribunal hearings into its purchase Murdoch praised the work of its chairman and promised that the station would retain total independence without interference. Two weeks after the tribunal approved the change of ownership, the

chief executive was replaced by a News Ltd. director with no television experience; two months later the chairman resigned.

A much bigger acquisition followed, also in 1979, when News Ltd. gained control of ATI, a group of airlines and other transport firms. Its founder, Sir Reginald Ansett, stayed on as chairman of ATI, but Murdoch became chief executive. Murdoch agreed with Sir Peter Abeles, the chairman of another transport group, TNT, that News Ltd. and TNT should have 50–50 ownership of ATI and that Abeles should become joint chief executive. There then followed lengthy public hearings before the Australian Broadcasting Tribunal on whether News Ltd. should be allowed to own a Melbourne television station, the original goal on the ATI/TNT dealings. The tribunal decided against, mainly on the grounds that a Sydney-Melbourne combination under one company would have too big a role in network operations. However, News Ltd. had paid for the station, the statutory six months allowed for ordering divestment had passed, and the tribunal's decision had no effect. It was eventually reversed on appeal.

The current structure of Rupert Murdoch's group of companies also dates from 1979 and the creation of News Corporation as the main holding company. In 1990 Murdoch owned only 7,200 shares in News Corporation itself, but had control of Cruden Investments Pty Ltd., which owned more than 116 million shares, about 54% of the total.

In 1981 News International, the British arm of the Murdoch group, acquired 42% of the voting shares in the British publishers William Collins and Sons and bought the London *Times,* the *Sunday Times,* the *Times Literary Supplement,* and the *Times Educational Supplement* from what is now The Thomson Corporation. Fifteen years earlier, Lord Thomson's own purchase of *The Times* and its supplements had been investigated by the Monopolies Commission, as Lonrho was to be investigated when it made a bid for the London *Observer* later in 1981. Yet the government of the day waived this requirement in News International's case.

At the same time as News Corporation's image was being pushed up-market by these ventures, its down-market newspapers were all engaged in attracting more readers with an adaptation of bingo. In Britain, *Sun* bingo cards were sent to every household, and rival papers all picked up the game. It then spread to the Sydney *Daily Mirror,* and to the *New York Post,* where it had to be renamed Wingo for copyright reasons. The rival *Daily News* responded with its own version, Zingo. Murdoch has since disposed of the *Post,* but acquired the *Boston Herald*—formerly the *Herald-American*—in 1982 and the *Chicago Sun-Times* in 1984.

Larry Lamb, the editor of *The Sun,* and from 1981, his successor Kelvin McKenzie, brought the paper into line with Murdoch's political views. Thus in 1982 the paper offered enthusiastic support to the British forces in the Falklands War, as almost all the national newspapers did, but characteristically went further, marking the sinking of the Argentine cruiser *General Belgrano* with the headline "Gotcha!" and calling the BBC's defense correspondent and two rival newspapers traitors. *The Sun* remains the biggest-selling daily newspaper in Britain.

Murdoch's upmarket papers could be tempted by sensationalism too. In 1983 News Corporation was severely embarrassed by the revelation that the secret diaries of Adolf Hitler, which the *Sunday Times* planned to serialize under an arrangement with the German magazine *Stern,* were forgeries. Lord Dacre, better known as the historian Hugh Trevor-Roper, and one of the "national" non-executive directors of Times Newspapers, first declared that the samples he had seen were genuine, then told the editor of the *Sunday Times* that they were forgeries just as the printing of the world exclusive story began. Murdoch decided to go ahead with the printing; *Stern* had to return the money he had paid for the diaries, and the *Sunday Times* actually retained some of the extra readers the story had attracted to it.

The appointment of Andrew Neil as editor of the *Sunday Times,* later in 1983, negated the guarantees exacted from News International by the British government two years before, since the required consultation with the newspaper's staff did not take place. In the case of Harold Evans, who reluctantly resigned from the editorship of *The Times* in 1982, at Murdoch's request, Evans could have appealed over Murdoch's head to the "national" directors but chose not to do so, leaving the guarantees untested.

News Corporation first ventured into satellite television in 1983, acquiring majority holdings in Satellite Television PLC (SATV), which had been set up in 1980 to supply a U.K.-based service to northern Europe, and in the Inter-American Satellite Television Network, which was renamed Skyband Inc. and had its head office moved from California to New York. It was largely to gain access to a supply of feature films and television programs that News Corporation bought into the Twentieth Century Fox Film Corporation, also in 1983. Twentieth Century Fox has since become a wholly owned subsidiary. Within two years, with the News International papers all featuring articles attacking the BBC, SATV, renamed Sky Channel, had about three million subscribers in 11 European countries and was available in Britain on cable.

During 1985 Murdoch and his closest advisers planned the removal of all the News International papers from the Fleet Street area, the traditional base for national newspapers, to a plant at Wapping, in east London, where troubled relations with the print unions could be superseded by a single union agreement with the Electrical, Electronic, Telecommunications and Plumbing Union (EETPU). Electronic typesetting equipment was ordered, but kept hidden from the print workers; the EETPU recruited new production staff, and then, when the plant was ready, the journalists on the four newspapers were given from one to three days to move or to leave the company and the plant began producing papers in January 1986. It was not only the 5,500 sacked print workers who felt somewhat betrayed after this dramatic move. The EETPU never did get a single union agreement, and News International does not recognize any trade unions. In 1987 the British company acquired a fifth newspaper, *Today,* from the company Lonrho—which had bought out the newspaper's founder, Eddy Shah—soon after its launch in 1986.

While 1986 was a year of triumph for Murdoch in Britain, in Australia it was a year of retreat. News Ltd. sold off both Channel TEN-10 in Sydney and ATV 10 in Melbourne, as well as radio stations, a record company, and three newspapers. However, 1987 was the year of the acquisition of the Herald and Weekly Times group once run by Murdoch's father. Shortly before the deal went ahead, Murdoch had a private meeting with the prime minister, Bob Hawke, and the treasurer, Paul Keating, and his Australian newspapers all

switched political allegiance to Labor, the governing party. The purchase cost A\$2.3 billion, was the biggest single takeover of newspapers ever accomplished, and made News Corporation the largest publisher of English-language newspapers in the world. Shortly afterwards the chairman of the Australian Press Council resigned in protest at the government's failure to invoke the Foreign Takeovers Act against Murdoch, for by this time Murdoch had become an American citizen. It was not until 1989 that newly-released government documents revealed that the Foreign Investment Review Board had opposed the acquisition, although Prime Minister Hawke declared that it had not.

News Corporation ended 1987 with two more purchases, the *South China Morning Post,* the most important English-language newspaper in Hong Kong, and the American publishing house Harper & Row. It then sold 50% of Harper & Row to William Collins and Sons. This arrangement lasted only until April 1989, when News International bought Collins outright. HarperCollins Publishers, created as a merger of these and other book and map publishers, is now the largest English-language publisher in the world.

In 1988, three decades after he had borrowed its format for his own *TV Week,* Murdoch bought the American magazine *TV Guide* and the company that published it, Triangle Publications, for \$2.83 billion. Fox Broadcasting Company started up during the same year as the first new television network in the United States to challenge the long-established trio of ABC, CBS, and NBC. Its huge initial costs were reduced, fortuitously, when the Hollywood writers' strike allowed it to run a large number of repeats, and it broadcast at first only on Saturdays and Sundays.

February 1989 saw the launch of Sky Television in the United Kingdom as a four-channel service available at first only on cable but increasingly via satellite receiver dishes. By the summer of 1990 it was reaching 1.6 million households, but the losses incurred in its development were a major cause of declining profits for News Corporation, along with the eight-month-long airline pilots' strike in Australia. It was claimed that profits would have been higher than in the financial year 1988–1989 if these two factors were excluded. Profits were also being eroded by the rising cost of interest payments on the group's rising level of debts.

Murdoch had once said that he never gave anyone shares but just borrowed to finance expansion. The next year or two revealed the disadvantages of that policy, as the sale of his Australian book publishing and distribution companies in June 1989 proved to be the start of a trend, though revenue and profits from most of News Corporation's subsidiaries continued to grow. In 1990 it sold 49% of South China Morning Post (Holdings) Ltd., parts of its minority holdings in the news agency Reuters and in the publishers Pearson plc, the American publishing firm J.B. Lippincott, the British papermaker Townsend Hook, the Fox subsidiary DeLuxe Laboratories and the American magazines *Star* and *Sportswear International.* Its acquisitions that year—25% of the Spanish publishers Grupo Zeta; the whole of F.F. Publishing and Broadsystem Ltd. in Britain; and 50% holdings, with Hungarian partners, in two publishing companies, Mai Nap Rt and Reform Rt— were relatively minor.

One way around the group's increasing financial problems was to juggle the figures in News Corporation's annual reports.

For example, the 1988 losses by News Ltd., the Australian division of the group, were shown as A$202 million in the 1989 report but as A$83 million in 1990, although the overall impact on group profits was said to be the same in both reports. Another way was to restructure the subsidiaries so that a higher proportion of group profits could be made in tax havens, such as Bermuda. In 1989, 25% of profits were attributed to tax haven companies; in 1990 the proportion was 54.5%, and News Corporation's effective tax rate was 1.76% rather than the statutory 39%.

The merger of Sky Television with its smaller rival, BSB, in November 1990, did nothing to stem the continuing losses from satellite television, since it meant that BSB's £380 million loan facility was withdrawn. It also turned out that neither company had consulted the Independent Broadcasting Authority, which licensed BSB's operations, and had thus breached the contract. Once again, as with ATV 10 in Melbourne, Murdoch presented the regulatory body with a *fait accompli*. By mid-1991 Sky, now renamed BSkyB, had swallowed up £1.5 billion in investments from various shareholders, among whom News Corporation was the largest, with a 49% stake.

Between August and December 1990 the value of News Corporation shares fell by two-thirds. News Corporation's debts, to 146 banks, stood at more than US$8.2 billion, and Murdoch had to promise to repay US$1.2 billion by June 1992. In return the banks arranged a US$7.4 billion refinancing package, to be repaid by 1994. In 1991 asset sales would have included News Corporation's half of the satellite television channel Eurosport, if it had not closed down in the meantime, and did in fact include the stake in Grupo Zeta bought only a year before and most of the group's U.S. magazines, such as *New Woman, New York,* and *Premiere.* Since television and publishing are clearly News Corporation's core businesses, it is difficult to square these divestments with the group's announcement, in February 1991, that any sales of assets would be concentrated in non-core areas.

News Corporation's amassing of enormous commercial weight, and its accompanying social influence have made both the group and Murdoch, its chief executive, the subject of controversy everywhere it operates. This is usually presented in personalized terms. For example, there are several biographies of Murdoch available, but no history of the group as such. This approach tends to distort the allocation of responsibility for the activities of a group which its admirers regard as a great achievement and its detractors as a dangerous concentration of power. News Corporation would not exist in its present form without the compliance of politicians and of the former owners of its acquisitions, the forbearance of regulatory authorities, the financial support of numerous banks and—it should not be forgotten—the work of editors, journalists, and other employees.

Principal Subsidiaries: News Ltd.; Nationwide News Pty Ltd.; The Herald and Weekly Times Ltd.; News International plc (U.K.); News Group Newspapers Ltd. (U.K.); Times Newspapers Holdings Ltd. (U.K.); British Sky Broadcasting plc (U.K., 50%); South China Morning Post (Holdings) Ltd. (Hong Kong, 51%); HarperCollins U.S. Inc.; HarperCollins (UK) Ltd.; News Publishing Australia Ltd. (U.S.A.); News America Publishing Inc. (U.S.A.); Fox Inc. (U.S.A.); Twentieth Century Fox Film Corporation (U.S.A.).

Further Reading: Regan, Simon, *Rupert Murdoch,* London, Angus and Robertson, 1976; Leapman, Michael, *Barefaced Cheek,* London, Hodder and Stoughton, 1983; Munster, George, *A Paper Prince,* Ringwood, Penguin Books Australia, 1985; Harris, Robert, *Selling Hitler,* London, Faber and Faber, 1986; Wintour, Charles, *The Rise and Fall of Fleet Street,* London, Hutchinson, 1989.

—Patrick Heenan

NIHON KEIZAI SHIMBUN, INC.

9-5, Otemachi 1-Chome
Chiyoda-ku, Tokyo 100-66
Japan
(03) 3270-0251
Fax: (03) 3246-1817

Private Company
Incorporated: 1911 as Chugai Shogyo Shimposha
Employees: 4,263
Sales: ¥217.53 billion (US$1.60 billion)

The dynamic Nihon Keizai Shimbun, Inc. (Nikkei), Japan's leading financial-newspaper publishing company, produces five business and financial papers, the oldest and best known of which, *The Nihon Keizai Shimbun* (The Japan Economic Journal), is the largest business newspaper in the world. *The Nihon Keizai Shimbun* has a total morning and evening circulation of 3.7 million, and even to the uninitiated the Nikkei 225 stock average, or Japanese stock market average, is a familiar term. The Nikkei average tracks the general performance of the Tokyo Stock Exchange. Each of the 225 Japanese companies included in the Nikkei is assigned a weight, and the average is reached through a computation of the performance of the weighted companies' stocks. The Nikkei is very much like the Dow Jones Averages in this sense, but, unlike the Dow Jones Averages, the Nikkei is also traded as a futures index—that is investors can speculate on the performance of the Japanese stock market by buying and selling Nikkei 225 Stock Average indices.

Because Japanese newspapers are considered public trusts, and therefore forbidden to go public, Nikkei remains a private and not very profitable company, owned by its employees. With its patriarchal management, Nikkei has the world's most advanced newspaper technology. The first of the world's newspaper publishers to install computerized newspaper-production equipment in 1972, to which a computerized automatic translation system would be added, Nikkei in 1989 was also the first newspaper company in history to introduce robots into its work force, as well as super-high-speed printing machines. The result is that the production of its newspapers is totally automated, from final page proof to printing. Indeed, the presses begin to print the morning edition of *The Nihon Keizai Shimbun* at 1:50 a.m. Tokyo time, and trucks pick up the finished papers for delivery ten minutes later.

Nikkei has more than 50 affiliates—including companies as well as research groups—collectively known as the Nikkei Group. In 1990, the Nikkei Group published hundreds of books on business and finance and scores of periodicals. One of the largest subsidiaries, Nikkei Business Publications, Inc., is already Japan's ninth-largest publishing company, although it was established in 1969.

The fastest growing business area of both Nikkei and its affiliates is neither newspapers nor magazines, however, but computerized electronic data bases. Nikkei searches for new ways to advance its capacity for information. Its goal is to become the world's leading provider of financial and economic news, thereby competing with Western companies such as Dow Jones and Reuters.

So prestigious are Nikkei's five financial newspapers that they do not have to employ the often-brutal competitive stratagems to which other Japanese newspaper companies resort. The spectacular success of Nikkei has not come without a price, nor has its ascent to the top of the world's financial press been a painless one. In the mid-19th century, when movable type had existed in the West for 400 years and newspapers had been in existence almost as long, printing in Japan was still being carried out by the clumsy, time-consuming Chinese method of block printing. Yet in 1869, only a year after the end of Japan's official isolation under the shoguns, a creative Japanese man improved upon the movable-type printing press brought to Japan by Western missionaries, paving the way for modern Japanese printing, which in only 50 years would be on a par with the West. In this same period, illiteracy in Japan virtually vanished, creating a huge market for publishing companies and newspapers.

In 1870 the first daily newspaper was published in Japan. With the introduction from Europe in 1874 of the steam-powered printing press, Japanese newspapers suddenly proliferated. In 1875, more than 100 newspapers existed in Japan. However, the vast majority of these were extremely crude affairs that printed vicious attacks against the government and provided explicit details of the latest sex scandals. It did not take the government long to clamp down on the increasingly influential press through censorship laws, which were often only loosely enforced. Into this milieu of overheated reportage and cut-throat competition for subscriptions came the forerunner of Nikkei.

A 28-year-old Japanese, Takashi Masuda, founded a financial paper in 1876 unglamorously entitled *Chugai Bukka Shimpo* (Foreign and Domestic Commodity Price Newspaper). Masuda was president of the recently founded Mitsui & Company, the trading arm of the huge Mitsui *zaibatsu* (conglomerate), and *Chugai Bukka Shimpo* was an outgrowth of Mitsui's in-house market-quotation bulletin. Masuda, a descendant of a samurai family, had dutifully followed the time-honored tradition of grooming himself to serve in the shogun's armed forces, which had come to an abrupt end with the restoration of the Meiji emperor in the 1860s. In his early teens Masuda and his father had traveled to Paris as part of a diplomatic mission. Upon their return to Japan, Masuda had briefly led the life of a samurai in the shogun's army from the mid-1860s until the fall of the shogun and the restoration of the emperor in 1868. Masuda then abandoned military life to take up a career as a civil servant in the Ministry of Finance. This transition from warrior to civil servant was not unusual, but for a samurai to become a despised businessman, as Masuda noted in a biographical note 30 years later, was a daring step. Indeed, traditional Japanese values were turned upside down, and the lowly businessman was becoming the arbiter of Japan's future.

In 1875, having worked a mere year in the Ministry of Finance, Masuda went on to head his own business, a trading company, Senshu Kaisha. At the same time Masuda was working to start Senshu Kaisha, he also was working with the Mitsui *zaibatsu* on a separate project.

Masuda was exceptional in that he spoke fluent English—indeed, later in life he would write an English-Japanese dictionary. He threw himself into his business with such zeal that when it was taken over by Mitsui in 1876 and merged with another Mitsui company to form Mitsui & Company, the able Masuda, still a young man in his 20s, was asked to become president of the powerful, newly established Mitsui & Company. Once more, he devoted himself to his work, which he saw as including the reform of the woefully inadequate business education system in Japan; to that end, he decided that what Japan needed was a business and financial paper that would serve as a beacon for Japan's emerging and influential financial community.

This paper, the *Chugai Bukka Shimpo,* was an expanded version of an in-house Mitsui publication. It rapidly came into its own. Nine years after its first appearance in 1876, the paper became a daily, and in 1889 it was renamed the *Chugai Shogyo Shimpo* (Foreign and Domestic Business Newspaper). At the same time it was spun off from Mitsui to form a private partnership, while the increasingly busy Masuda was replaced as president of the new newspaper company by the paper's editor, Hirota Nozaki. In 1911, a wholly independent corporation, the Chugai Shogyo Shimposha, was established to run the newspaper, with the first stockholders' meeting held the following year. At the end of World War I, in 1918, this forebear of today's *Nihon Keizai Shimbun* was the 14th-largest newspaper in Japan in terms of circulation, and ranked foremost in reputation among Japan's financial newspapers.

Untrammeled success for nearly 40 years was followed by a series of setbacks, however. During World War I, paper became scarce, and the cost of newsprint rose precipitously. Reluctantly, the *Chugai Shogyo Shimpo* raised its subscription price, which during the general wartime boom, did not affect its circulation. After the war, however, when worldwide recession brought economic hardship to Japan—a country totally dependent on importing raw materials in a world market increasingly averse to free trade—the newspaper's circulation dropped steadily. Worse was to follow. In September 1923, the world's worst earthquake struck Tokyo and nearby Yokohama, causing more than 100,000 deaths. Downtown Tokyo was decimated, along with half of the rest of the city. Most of the publishing houses were located there, and were consequently demolished. The central office of the Chugai Shogyo Shimposha was relatively undamaged by the earthquake, but could not escape the raging fire, which destroyed half of the building. Its branch office in Yokohama was obliterated. Sales now plummeted 50%, down to less than ¥75,000 from a pre-earthquake high of ¥150,000.

Hitherto, Chugai Shogyo Shimposha had been relatively unaffected by the numerous governmental restrictions on the press, especially the Peace Preservation Law of 1925, which allowed the government the right to close any newspaper without showing cause. The paper disdained to imitate the sensationalist newspapers of the day. Although a concession had been made in the 1890s to alleviate the dry contents somewhat by introducing serialized short stories, this had been discontinued. By the 1930s not even a financial paper could remain unaffected by the rampant militarism and chauvinism overtaking Japan. In 1936 it was obvious that even *Chugai Shogyo Shimpo* was a mere mouthpiece of the government, an entire issue being devoted, for instance, to the glorious economic prospects of Manchukuo, that part of Chinese Manchuria seized by the Japanese army in 1930. The government's hold over the press would continue. By the late 1930s, control over the press became centralized under the Information Board, dominated by the military. One of the board's conclusions was that there were too many newspapers in Japan, and many of them were forced to merge. In 1942, *Chugai Shogyo Shimpo* was the victim of an enforced merger with two other papers and a few trade journals. The newspaper that emerged was renamed the *Nihon Sangyo Keizai Shimbun* (Japan Business and Economic Newspaper). The company had been reorganized in 1936, and its board of directors was enlarged, the number of its overseas bureaus increased, and its assets amounted to over ¥2 million. Despite the forced merger and loss of identity, the financial paper continued to be published throughout World War II, notwithstanding an extreme scarcity of paper. The newspaper company's headquarters in Tokyo survived the savage bombing raid on March 10, 1945. By the end of World War II, several months later, however, all publishing activity in Japan had ceased.

By the time Allied occupation forces arrived in Japan in December 1945, newspapers once again began to proliferate. Over 300 flourished at the start of the occupation, encouraged by greater freedom to publish and by the public's insatiable appetite for knowledge of the recent past. For the first four years of the occupation, which lasted until 1952, government was carried out largely by decree. One such decree, the Press Code, removed all controls over the press, but at the same time instituted a censorship over all media to eradicate any militaristic and ultranationalistic sentiment. The goal of the occupation, or the Supreme Command of the Allied Powers (SCAP), under General Douglas MacArthur, was nothing less than to transform Japanese thinking. Removing prominent Japanese figures from their positions of authority was a means to this end. Hence the occupation authorities instigated three major purges of hundreds of nonmilitary Japanese figures, among whom were the publishers of the *Nihon Sangyo Keizai Shimbun.*

The forced merger of the reputable *Chugai Shogyo Shimpo* with several other papers was evidently none too popular; almost immediately after the end of the war, one of the papers which had been forced to merge with the *Chugai Shogyo Shimpo* opted to become independent. Then, in 1946, the present-day name *Nihon Keizai Shimbun* was adopted by the company, since 1942 known as *Nihon Sangyo Keizai Shimbun.* The "new" company of Nihon Keizai Shimbun, from which the newspaper took its name, or Nikkei, was not new enough for the occupation authorities, since the same wartime publishers were still running the newspaper. In the third and final purge in late 1947, in which 170 publishers and editors nationwide were ousted from their positions, the axe fell on Nikkei: its wartime president, Kohei Murakami, and others were purged and a president more acceptable to the authorities, Sadakichi Odajama, was installed, remaining president of Nikkei until the mid-1950s. The end of the third purge was followed two years later by the end of U.S.-imposed censorship, although the 1947 postwar constitution of Japan guaranteed freedom of the press and forbade any form of censorship.

With the Japanese economy fully recovered by the 1960s and embarking on a phase of spectacular growth, Nikkei, too, grew uninterruptedly. Cautiously, the company expanded overseas. In 1968, Japan's first English-language economic newspaper, the weekly *Japan Economic Journal,* was published in the United States. In 1969, Nikkei entered into a joint venture with McGraw-Hill in New York to form Nikkei–McGraw Hill, a Japanese company which at the onset published only one Japanese magazine, *Nikkei Business.* By 1988, when McGraw Hill sold its share to Nikkei and the company renamed itself Nikkei Business Publications, Inc., the new Nikkei subsidiary was publishing 42 periodicals with such diverse titles in Japanese as *Nikkei Entertainment, Nikkei Restaurants, Nikkei Woman,* and *Nikkei Art.* By the 1980s Nikkei was publishing not only five newspapers, but with its subsidiaries, the Nikkei Group of more than 50 companies and research organizations was one of the largest newspaper companies in Japan, with 33 offices abroad, more than any other Japanese newspaper company. Besides expanding into additional businesses and financial magazines and books, Nikkei has focused on expanding its range of computerized electronic data bases. Taking advantage of satellite communications, Nikkei TELECOM was launched in 1986, offering personal computer owners in the United States and Europe up-to-the-minute news on Japanese commodities and securities, money, and banking. Nikkei TELECOM was quickly followed by numerous online services, such as NEEDS, one of the world's largest data bases; QUICK; and others.

By the late 20th century, *Nihon Keizai Shimbun* had become the financial daily with the largest circulation in the world, and is close to realizing its goal of becoming the world's chief source of business and financial data.

For all Nikkei's success, the company is less profitable than either Reuters and Dow Jones, because of its large structure. Japanese newspapers are allowed only limited profitability, and therefore tend to plow earnings back into their business. Thus, while *The Wall Street Journal* spends 21% of its revenue on labor costs, Nikkei spends 30%. Nikkei's editorial staff, consisting of about 1,300 reporters and editors, is twice as large as *The Wall Street Journal's,* although Japan has only half the population of the United States. Growth is far more important to the company than profit. In that respect, it has succeeded beyond its founder Takashi Masuda's wildest imagination. Nevertheless, western observers continue to be annoyed by Japanese success. There was barely concealed mirth over Nikkei president Ko Morita's resignation in 1988—he was replaced by current president Akira Arai—because of his involvement in an insider trading scandal. Rumor circulated that some Japanese resented Nikkei's close association with big business and referred to *Nihon Keizai Shimbun* as the, *Nihon Kabushiki Kaisha Shimbun* (Japan Company Daily). Sensitive as most Japanese companies are to western criticism, Nikkei in 1987 enabled instantaneous two-way news transmission to take place between Japan and the United States, in the hope that U.S. trade friction would be eased. Nikkei's tenet is that trade friction will decrease as communication increases.

Nikkei's head start in the competitive field of telecommunications and Japan's position as the world's leading creditor nation may allow Nikkei to realize its goal of becoming the world's chief source of financial information. Despite its ultramodern computer services and state-of-the-art technology, it continues to be run along traditional patriarchal lines, with men still occupying all leadership positions. No single person, however, is in complete control of the company, while its stock is in the hands of 80% of its employees.

Principal Subsidiaries: Nikkei Business Publications, Inc.; Nikkei Science, Inc.; Television Tokyo Channel 12 Ltd.; QUICK Corp.; Nikkei Research Inc.; The Japan Bond Research Institute; Oversea Courier Service Co., Ltd.; Nikkei Seibu Newspaper Marketing Inc.; Nihon Keizaisha Advertising Ltd.; Nikkei Printing Co., Ltd.; Nihon Keizai Shimbun America, Inc. (U.S.A.); Nihon Keizai Shimbun Europe Ltd. (U.K.); Japan Center for Economic Research; Nikkei Advertising Research Institute.

Further Reading: Gaddis, John W., *Public Information in Japan Under American Occupation,* Geneva, Imprimeries Populaires, 1950.

—Sina Dubovoj

PEARSON PLC

Millbank Tower, Millbank
London SWIP 4QZ
United Kingdom
(071) 828 9020
Fax: (071) 828 3342

Public Company
Incorporated: 1897 as S Pearson & Son Ltd.
Employees: 27,000
Sales: £1.46 billion (US$2.82 billion)
Stock Exchange: London

Pearson plc is a leading British-owned industrial holding company with interests including publishing, financial services, fine china, and oil services, and is closely associated with its founding family, the Pearsons. In its early years the business was dominated by Weetman Dickinson Pearson, later First Viscount Cowdray, who transformed it into an international contracting concern which he subsequently converted to an investment trust-type operation.

Its roots can be traced to Weetman's grandfather, Samuel Pearson, who in 1844 became an associate partner in a Huddersfield-based building and contracting firm. In 1856 his eldest son, George, entered the business, which became known as S Pearson & Son, "sanitary tube and brickmakers and contractors for local public works in and around Bradford."

Contracts undertaken at this time were locally based and were for railway companies and, more frequently, for the provision of water supply, drainage, and sewerage facilities to expanding industrial cities. The business developed rapidly, moving its head office in 1857 to nearby Bradford, Yorkshire, and expanding its associated brickmaking, glazed tile, and sanitary pipe activities. In 1873 Weetman Pearson entered the business and received a share in its ownership on the retirement of Samuel in 1879.

Pearson, increasingly under the direction of Weetman, began to make a quick metamorphosis into an internationally based concern. In the late 1870s, contracts outside the north of England were undertaken for the first time, and the head office was moved to London in 1884. Five years later projects were in progress as far afield as Egypt, the United States, Canada, and Mexico with port works, railway construction and tunneling, and water supply and drainage predominating. Between 1884 and 1914 some 67 projects, with a total value of almost

£43 million, were undertaken. Of these, 36—valued at £16.5 million or 38% of the total—were located outside Great Britain and Ireland; with 10% in the United States and Canada; 45.5% in Central and South America; and 7% in Egypt, Spain, China, Malta, and Bermuda.

The British government was a major client, as were municipalities, railway and harbor companies, and water utilities. Contracts of particular note included the Admiralty Harbour at Dover; the Blackwall Tunnel under the River Thames in London; the East River Railway Tunnels, New York, for which a U.S. subsidiary, S Pearson & Son Inc., was formed to carry out the work; Malta Dry Docks and Breakwaters; and Halifax Dry Dock in Canada.

However, Mexico was the country where Pearson made its greatest mark, to the extent that Weetman Pearson, by now a member of Parliament, was dubbed in the House of Commons and elsewhere as the "Member for Mexico." The first contract for the Mexican government, which ran from 1890 to 1896, was for the construction of the Mexican Grand Canal to drain Mexico City and its surrounding area. A succession of other government-owned or sponsored projects followed—the £3 million conversion of Vera Cruz harbor into a modern seaport, the £2.5 million reconstruction of the Tehuantepec Railway and its associated terminal ports, linking the Atlantic and Pacific Oceans, and the Salina Cruz harbor and docks, at £3.3 million.

A growing confidence between Mexican dictator Porfirio Díaz and Weetman Pearson consolidated Pearson's Mexican interests. Under the Tehuantepec Railway contract, Pearson built the facilities at cost, provided part of the capital, and then managed the railway and ports, taking part of the profits as remuneration. This entry into the mainstream of Mexican business soon led to other interests, most importantly oil. In 1901 Pearson began to acquire oil-bearing land and by 1906 owned 600,000 acres and had royalty leases over about another 250,000. Oil refining began, and in 1908 Pearson entered the Mexican oil retail trade in direct competition with Walter Pierce Oil Company, mostly owned by Standard Oil Company, resulting in severe price competition.

However, it was not until 1910 that the business was transformed into an international oil concern with the discovery of the Potrero de Llano oil field. The Aguila (Mexican Eagle) Oil Company Ltd. was formed to take over most of Pearson's oil interests and make a public issue of securities. In 1912, as a means of extending this business, the Eagle Oil Transport Company Ltd. and the Anglo Mexican Petroleum Company Ltd. were formed to focus on international distribution and sales. Some £12 million of Pearson capital had by now been committed to Mexican oil. During World War I an immense trade was done in supplying the British government. In 1919 the Royal Dutch group acquired a large shareholding in the Aguila and took over management control, although for many years Pearson continued to own a large part of the company. In 1919 Whitehall Petroleum Corporation Ltd. was formed to take over Pearson's oil interests and prospect—mostly unsuccessfully—for oil worldwide. Its most notable action was the establishment of the Amerada Corporation, a major U.S. oil company, in 1919.

Another feature of Pearson's diversification after 1900 was the generation, supply, and application of electric power in Latin America. This began when Díaz invited Weetman Pearson to electrify and then manage the tramway system—later extended to electricity supply generally—in Vera Cruz, a service which was carried into effect by the Vera Cruz Electric Light, Power and Traction Company Ltd. Soon Pearson developed similar schemes elsewhere in Mexico. After World War I these developments were extended outside Mexico, when undertakings in Chile were acquired. The Chilean interests were subsequently modernized and managed by Pearson's Cia. Chilena de Electricidad. All these electrical interests were consolidated into Whitehall Electric Investments Ltd. in 1922.

In 1897, Pearson, which was by now reckoned to be the world's leading contractor, was converted into a limited company with an issued share capital of £1 million, all of which was owned by the Pearson family or by non-family directors. In 1907 Whitehall Securities Ltd. was formed to take over all of Pearson's non-contracting activities, while in 1919 S Pearson & Son (Contracting Department) Ltd. took over the firm's contracting interests. S Pearson & Son Ltd. became the group's holding company.

During World War I, the contracting company was preoccupied with military contracts, of which the huge munitions plant at Gretna Green in Scotland—worth £9.2 million—was the largest. However, in the late 1920s the construction business was closed down, not being sold on as a going concern apparently as a result of family whim. By now, however, Pearson had diversified well beyond the supplying of oil and electricity. In 1908 Weetman Pearson was a member of a large syndicate which acquired the London evening newspaper *The Westminster Gazette*. After the war he acquired total control of the newspaper, converted it into a morning daily, and began to build around it a group of provincial newspapers. In 1919 the company established Whitehall Trust Ltd. as a finance and issuing house, and at about the same time its principal asset, a substantial interest in Lazard Brothers & Company, the London merchant bank, was acquired. A partnership was formed with Dorman Long & Company Ltd. to develop a coal mining and iron and steel industry in Kent, although this project was not to figure prominently in Pearson's affairs.

When Lord Cowdray died in 1927 he had completely reshaped his family's business. He was succeeded as chairman by his second son, Clive, while his eldest son, Harold, played a significant part in the development of Westminster Press Ltd. The management philosophy was to develop and extend the core businesses through local management. In 1929 the electricity businesses in Mexico and Chile were sold, but similar electricity undertakings were developed in southwest England. The company played a substantial role in establishing British Airways Ltd.—not the state-owned business which came to be known as British Airways PLC—in 1935.

The most significant result of World War II was the purchase of strategic Pearson assets by the British government. These included the airline interests but, much more significantly, the interest in the Amerada Petroleum Corporation which was compulsorily acquired in 1941. The year 1948 saw the nationalization of the electricity undertakings in the west of England.

In the 1950s, the general strategy of Pearson, which from 1954 was under the chairmanship of the Third Lord Cowdray, was to concentrate on well-defined sectors and within them build up specialist niche businesses producing quality products, with much decision-making devolved to local management. This was to be a successful and enduring philosophy.

The five legs on which the business now stood were financial services, publishing, oil, manufacturing, and investment trusts.

In 1945 the surviving oil interests were largely confined to oil and gas properties owned by Rycade Corporation of the United States. In the 1950s the activities of this company were extended, while particularly successful expansion also occurred in western Canada through Whitehall Canadian Oils Ltd. In addition, a small interest in Amerada was reacquired. Publishing was strengthened in 1957 when a substantial interest was taken in Financial News Ltd., which in turn owned a large interest in the *Financial Times* and a small range of quality periodicals. In 1960 the last of the overseas electricity utilities was disposed of when the business of Athens Piraeus Electricity Company, which had operated under a concession granted in 1925, was sold to the Greek state, although a smaller trolley bus operation in Athens was retained until about 1970. In manufacturing industry, a substantial interest in Acton Bolt Ltd., makers of nuts and bolts, was sold to GKN Ltd. in 1959, and another in Saunders-Roe Ltd., builder of helicopters, was sold to Westland Aircraft Company Ltd. in 1959.

In 1969, for tax and fiscal reasons, the business was converted into a quoted company and 20% of the equity was sold to the public. The company was then valued at £20 million, and profits before tax, attributable to shareholders, totaled almost £7 million. About 25% of profits came from financial services which largely consisted of Lazard Brothers & Co. Ltd., which was now almost fully owned by Pearson, and Whitehall Securities Corporation which provided services to the group. An additional 30% of profits were generated from a 51% holding in the publicly quoted S Pearson Publishers Ltd., owner of the *Financial Times*; Westminster Press Ltd., controller of about 60 local and provincial newspapers; and the Longman Group Ltd., a general publishing house. Oil interests in North America, which were reorganized at the end of the 1960s, provided about 20% of profits. Manufacturing, where the chief asset was a 59% interest in Standard Industrial Group Ltd., another publicly quoted company, included interests in pottery, glass, engineering, and warehousing. This contributed about 7% of profits. Finally, 15% of profits were contributed by investment trusts.

In the 1970s the North American interests of Pearson were mostly represented by the holding in Ashland Oil, held by Midhurst Corporation. This holding was slowly reduced and the proceeds used to acquire other North American interests, especially in oil exploration and production services, as part of an effort to extend Pearson's interests outside the United Kingdom and into North America. The most significant move was the acquisition of Camco Inc., supplier of services and equipment to the oil industry on a worldwide basis, in which a controlling interest had been purchased by 1979. This business was subsequently built up by acquisition. Lignum Oil Co. and Hillin Oil, involved in the acquisition and development of oil producing properties, were also acquired, but were sold in 1989 as part of a divestment of oil exploration activities which also included the sale of Whitehall Petroleum.

Financial services remained grouped around the merchant bank of Lazard Brothers in which Pearson, in 1990, had a 50% interest, reduced from 79%. This decrease followed an ownership reorganization in 1984 when, as an early response to increasing internationalization of the securities industry,

Lazard of London and two other Lazard houses, in Paris and New York, became more closely linked. An exchange of ownership interests resulted in Pearson having a 10% profit interest in both these houses. Notwithstanding the acquisition in 1976 of the unowned part of Embankment Trust Ltd., investment trust and other portfolio-type investments have been decreased in order to fund acquisitions.

Pearson's interests in manufacturing are concentrated in the Doulton fine china business, which has emerged as a world leader with a strong overseas distribution network. The engineering interests were strengthened in 1980 by the acquisition of the high technology businesses of Fairey Industries Ltd., and their merging with Pearson's other engineering interests in 1982. However, these relatively minor activities were disposed of in 1986 as part of group policy to focus more on core activities. Similarly, involvement in the manufacture of specialist glass, which had expanded rapidly in the 1970s, was terminated in 1982 with the sale of Doulton Glass Industries Ltd.

The minority interest in Pearson Longman Ltd. was acquired in 1982. Publishing, the division of Pearson with the highest proportion of profits, embraces financial publications including not just the *Financial Times*—the world's leading financial newspaper—but also a host of important financial periodicals, including *The Economist,* in which Pearson has a 50% interest, and the *Investor's Chronicle,* as well as on-line electronic publications. Longman by acquisition and organic expansion, has emerged as a major publisher of professional, educational, medical, and general reference publications. Penguin holds a strong international position in publishing both soft- and hard-back fiction and expanded its operations through the acquisition, among others, of Viking of the United States and the Michael Joseph and Hamish Hamilton publishing houses in 1985. Westminster Press expanded into newspapers distributed free of charge and disposed of several newspapers paid for by readers, as it concentrated resources in areas where it was a clear market leader. In 1987 the acquisition of Addison Wesley of the United States, with a strong schools and college list, confirmed Pearson as a major international publishing group. The global holdings increased in 1988 by a share swap with Elsevier, a leading Dutch publishing company, and through the acquisition of the French Les Echos Group.

The swap with Elsevier was undone in 1991, when the two companies were unable to devise merger terms acceptable to all parties.

One new interest, since the mid-1980s linked to the publishing division, has been expansion into daytime family entertainment. Although Pearson had owned Chessington Zoo for many years, this area was fully established through the acquisition of Madame Tussauds in 1978. Since then a number of acquisitions have been made and developed, virtually all U.K. based. Further developments in this general sector included the acquisition of a 25% holding in Yorkshire Television Ltd. in 1981, and a less than successful involvement, now terminated, in filmmaking.

While Pearson's shares have become much more widely held, the Pearson family continues to hold a large—but not controlling—share of the equity. The Third Lord Cowdray retired from the chairmanship in 1977 and was succeeded by Lord Gibson and then by Lord Blakenham in 1983, both of whom were family members. The company's name was changed to Pearson plc in 1984. In the early 1990s it can claim to be one of the most successful British-based companies.

Principal Subsidiaries: Addison-Wesley Publishing Co. Ltd. (U.S.A.); Camco Inc. (USA); Les Echos SA (France); Financial Times Group Ltd. (U.K.); Longman Group Ltd. (U.K.); Pearson Inc., (U.S.A.); The Penguin Publishing Co. Ltd. (U.K.); Penguin Books U.S.A. Inc; Royal Doulton Ltd. (U.K.); The Tussauds Group Ltd. (U.K.); Westminster Press Ltd. (U.K.).

Further Reading: Spender, J.A., *Weetman Pearson. First Viscount Cowdray,* London, Cassell & Co. Ltd., 1930; Young, Desmond, *Member for Mexico. A Biography of Weetman Pearson, First Viscount Cowdray,* London, Cassell & Co., Ltd., 1966; "Weetman Dickson Pearson. 1st Viscount Cowdray," in *Dictionary of Business Biography: A Biographical Dictionary of Business Leaders Active in Britain in the Period, 1860–1980,* Vol. IV, edited by David Jeremy, London, Butterworth & Co. Ltd., 1985.

—John Orbell

R.R. DONNELLEY & SONS COMPANY

2223 South Martin Luther King Drive
Chicago, Illinois 60616
U.S.A.
(312) 326-8000
Fax: (312) 326-8543

Public Company
Incorporated: 1870 as The Lakeside Publishing and Printing Company
Employees: 31,000
Sales: $3.50 billion
Stock Exchanges: New York Pacific

R.R. Donnelley & Sons Company is the largest supplier of commercial printing and allied services in the United States, as well as a major supplier in the United Kingdom. Principal services are presswork and binding. Other businesses of the company include the provision of lists, and production and fulfillment services to direct-mail marketers; design and creative services; and data base management services.

Richard Robert Donnelley, the company founder, who was born in Brantford, Ontario, Canada, in 1836, became an apprentice printer while in grammar school. He was paid full journeyman wages by age 16, made foreman by age 18, and soon afterward, made partner in the printing shop. In 1857 Donnelley traveled with John Hand, a distinguished Canadian typesetter, to New Orleans, Louisiana where he became a jobber for *True Delta,* a newspaper. He returned to Canada when the Civil War began.

Following his return, he married the woman who would become the matriarch of the business, Naomi Ann Shenstone of Brantford. The following year, in 1864, they moved with their two-month-old child to Chicago to accept a partnership in the printing and publishing firm of Church, Goodman, and Donnelley, which specialized in the educational, religious, and historical fields. The printing firm became one of the major book- and journal-publishing houses of its day.

The partnership of Church, Goodman, and Donnelley incorporated as The Lakeside Publishing and Printing Company in 1870 to expand its printing operation. The Great Chicago Fire of 1871 destroyed all Richard Donnelley's assets, including the new Lakeside Building, which was then under construction. Following a trip to New York to arrange financing and equipment in order to reopen, Donnelley returned to Chicago to set up shop under the name of R.R. Donnelley, Steam Printer, which merged with Lakeside in 1873. At this time he and his partners were faced not only with a decline in commercial printing but also with a widespread depression. Donnelley attempted to diversify, forming a subsidiary, Williams, Donnelley and Company, to publish the *Edwards Chicago City Directory.* In 1875, a new subsidiary, Donnelley, Loyd & Company, published a successful series of classic reprints called the Lakeside Library. In 1877 as competition stiffened, the 200-title Lakeside Library was sold.

When these and other attempts failed to salvage the publishing business, Lakeside closed. Donnelley, Loyd & Company acquired the printing equipment of The Lakeside Publishing and Printing Company in 1877. In 1878 Norman T. Gassette became a partner in Donnelley, Loyd & Company, then known as Donnelley, Gassette & Loyd. Richard Donnelley created a separate corporate entity in 1880 to house the publishing side of the enterprise, the Chicago Directory Company. In 1882 the Donnelley, Gassette & Loyd directors voted to change the name of their printing firm to R.R. Donnelley & Sons Company. Richard Robert Donnelley died in April 1899, at the close of the company's most successful decade; the firm passed into managerial control of his sons, with Thomas Elliot Donnelley becoming president and Reuben H. Donnelley heavily involved in the directory business.

During the difficult start-up years it had been Naomi Donnelley whose strong entrepreneurial spirit and determination to keep the presses working led her to write cookbooks in addition to her general bookkeeping duties in the operation. From the time of the reconstruction of the firm after the fire through the turn of the century, the client base for commercial printing jobs expanded. R.R. Donnelley produced hardbound catalogs for the Studebaker Wagon Company and Benjamin Allen & Company; yearbooks for The Chicago Club, The Chicago Athletic Association, and The University Club; bicycle catalogs for Gormully & Jeffrey and Mead Cycle Company; and directories for the Chicago Directory Company and Lord & Thomas; and circulars for Marshall Field & Company, Mandel Brothers, and Chas. A. Stevens & Co., In addition, the company provided printing services to Link-Belt, Deering Harvester Company, Lyon & Healy, and Western Electric. In 1886, ten years after the telephone patent was issued, Donnelley took on the directories for Illinois Bell Telephone Company.

In 1895 the first sewing machine, used for binding, was introduced into the company, and at about the same period, the Empire and Linotype machines were installed, as the company raced to compete in the age of machine composition. In 1898 the company installed its first rotary perfector press with the ability to fold. Book sets and general list books continued to be a mainstay of the company. The printers produced high-quality work for distinguished book publishers, including Stone and Kimball, a contract that developed into a commitment to produce 48 titles. In 1901 the case bindery was introduced, and in 1902 the first Monotype machine, allowing the firm to attempt to keep pace with innovations abroad, although the quality of U.S.-made typefaces and ink did not match those produced by the British or Germans.

In keeping with its tradition of printing book sets and reprinting classics, Thomas Elliot Donnelley introduced the Lakeside Classic series in 1903, to illustrate the company's ideals of the well-designed book, a much-debated topic in trade journals in the United States and United Kingdom and to serve as an annual keepsake for employees, designed to bolster morale and company loyalty. In addition, 1903 was a period of great turbulence among the ranks of unionized printers; Donnelley resisted the disruptions and ended its participation in a closed shop. By 1907 the firm severed all ties with the printing unions, which were at the time leaders in apprenticeship programs and industrial education opportunities. As a consequence of its intention to maintain an open shop, the firm introduced an unusual system of in-house education with both an apprenticeship program and a baccalaureate degree in economics and cultural studies from the University of Chicago. The University of Cincinnati also participated. The school was called the Lakeside Apprenticeship School, and it flourished for more than two decades.

The importance placed on an open shop environment where educated employees could work for a lifetime, experiencing both challenge and promotions, led to other innovations. First was the establishment of the Memorial Library in the Chicago plant, where an apprentice or experienced printer could come to see examples of the finest contemporary printing accomplished throughout the world, and also see examples of the best book production achieved by R.R. Donnelley & Sons. In addition, adjoining the library, the company installed gallery and exhibition space that rivaled the gallery space at the Metropolitan Museum of Art in New York City. Exhibits of fine printing were designed for the benefit of employees, but open also to the general public. The firm also established a five-man design and typography department in the early 1920s, headed by an able typographer and commercial printer, William Kittredge. At the same time, an extra binding department was established. The value placed upon integrating design with production was a gradual development that emerged from the founding of the apprenticeship school and the Memorial Library.

In 1916 the Chicago Directory Company was renamed the Reuben H. Donnelley Corporation, with R.H. Donnelley as president and T.E. Donnelley as vice president. Following his brother's death in 1929, Thomas assumed the presidency of the publishing division while continuing as president of R.R. Donnelley & Sons Company, and thereafter, the printing and publishing businesses, while maintained in separate divisions, were incorporated within one operating company. Naomi Donnelley continued to be an active force in the firm, and in 1924 on the occasion of firm's 60th anniversary, delivered a speech to the assembled company about the history of the enterprise.

Among the firm's competitive publicity ventures launched during this time by William Kittredge was the Four U.S. Books Campaign, begun in 1926 and completed in 1929, several weeks before the Wall Street stock market crash. The campaign, which was to feature only the work of U.S. authors—such as Herman Melville, Edgar Allan Poe, and Henry David Thoreau—was intended to promote the U.S. printing industry, using only ink, typefaces, paper, and other materials produced in the United States. Further, the books were to be illustrated by leading U.S. commercial artists of the day, Rockwell Kent, William Dwiggins, Rudolph Ruzicka, and Edward Wilson. As it turned out, all the physical properties except the labor by craftsmen-graduates of the Lakeside Apprenticeship School had to be imported. The major purpose of the Four Books Campaign was to reposition Donnelley with the changing mass-market book publishing industry, and to allow it to compete with the Book-of-The Month-Club and the Limited Editions Club, among others. Although the technological point may have been missed, the company successfully repositioned itself with the book-publishing industry, and acquired significant new book-club business as a result.

The firm received a magazine-publishing contract from Henry R. Luce in 1927 to print *Time,* and later *Life,* a working relationship that continues in the 1990s. The 1920s and 1930s were a time of tremendous technical advances in the printing and allied industries, and Donnelley continued to keep pace, introducing Deeptone processing and sheet-fed gravure presses. These innovations served to advance the look of the product and the rate of production in the plant.

In 1952 General Charles C. Haffner Jr. succeeded his father-in-law, T.E. Donnelley, as chairman of the board of the R.R. Donnelley & Sons Company. In 1964 Gaylord Donnelley was elected chairman of the board, retiring in 1975, when he was succeeded by Charles W. Lake Jr., the first person outside the Donnelley family to serve as chairman of the board. Lake was succeeded by John B. Schwemm in 1983, who was named president, and in 1989 John R. Walter, succeeded Schwemm as chief executive officer. James R. Donnelley, the great-grandson of R.R. Donnelley, in the early 1990s was vice chairman.

The company made its first public stock offering in 1956. Several major acquisitions came in the next few decades. The company formed its Lancaster, Pennsylvania, manufacturing division after acquiring the Rudisill Printing Company in 1959. In 1961 Donnelley sold the Reuben H. Donnelley Corporation to The Dun & Bradstreet Corporation. In 1978, Donnelley bought Interweb, a printing firm since reorganized as the Los Angeles division of Donnelley, and Ben Johnson & Company Ltd. of York, England, another printer. In 1986 Donnelley acquired Norwest Publishing, a printer of telephone directories, and CSA Press, a printer of computer documentation. The company bought Metromail Corporation, a provider of lists and list enhancement services to direct mail marketers, in 1987.

The product mix of R.R. Donnelley & Sons has diversified since the mid-20th century. The company's presence has expanded globally, with more than 100 offices in the United States, and international subsidiaries in the United Kingdom and Japan. The company is organized into nine product groups: books; magazines; catalogs; telecommunications; financial-printing services; documentation services, including software and magnetic media products; information services; international, including operations in the United Kingdom and the Far East; and Metromail, which markets targeted lists, data bases, and inserting services. Catalogs still make up the largest segment of Donnelley's printing business, as has been the case for most of the company's history. The second-largest segment of its business is magazines; third, directories; fourth, books; fifth, documentation services.

In December 1989 R.R. Donnelley & Sons Company announced that it was negotiating to acquire Meredith/Burda Companies, jointly owned by the Meredith Corporation of Des Moines, Iowa—a leading U.S. publishing company—and by Franz and Frieder Burda of Germany, for about $500 million. Meredith/Burda's 1989 sales were $456 million, with six plants and more than 3,000 employees in 1989. The transaction went before the Federal Trade Commission early in 1990, which explored the antitrust implications of such a merger. The acquisition was completed in September 1990. Already the largest printer in North America, the merger solidifies Donnelley's position globally.

Principal Subsidiaries: Ben Johnson and Company Limited (U.K.); R.R. Donnelley Far East, Limited (Japan); Dowa Insatsu K.K. (Japan); Mobium Corporation for Design and Communication; Metromail Corporation; Donnelley Caribbean Graphics, Inc. (Barbados); Irish Printers (Holdings) Limited (Republic of Ireland); R.R. Donnelley (U.K.) Limited; Impresora Donneco Internacional, S.A. de C.V. (Mexico); Northwest Publishing Co.

Further Reading: Donnelley, Gaylord, "Donnelley History," *The Printer,* Spring 1965, Summer 1965, Fall 1965, Winter 1965, Spring 1966, Summer 1966, Fall 1966, Winter 1966, Spring 1967, Summer 1967, Fall 1967; *The Printer,* Fall 1989; Badaracco, Claire, *American Culture and the Marketplace: R.R. Donnelley's Four American Books Campaign at the Lakeside Press, 1926-1930,* Washington, D.C., Library of Congress, Center for the Book, 1990.

—Claire Badaracco

THE READER'S DIGEST ASSOCIATION, INC.

Reader's Digest Road
Pleasantville, New York 10570
U.S.A.
(914) 238-1000

Public Company
Incorporated: 1926
Employees: 7,700
Sales: $2.01 billion
Stock Exchanges: New York Midwest

The Reader's Digest Association is a worldwide publisher of magazines, books, recorded music, and home video packages, all of which are sold by means of direct-mail marketing. Its major publication is the general-interest monthly magazine, *Reader's Digest,* which by year end 1991 was produced in 41 editions in 17 languages, with a global circulation of more than 28 million. The newest editions of *The Digest,* added in late 1991, were a Russian-language edition in the Soviet Union and a Hungarian-language edition in Hungary. The company's annual sales are prodigious: 21 million condensed books in 18 countries, 16 million general books in 22 countries, and 6 million special-series books in 13 countries. Annually it sells more than 5 million pieces of its music collections and 800,000 home video programs. In 1990, after 68 years as a private firm, a public offering of class A common stock was made. Two trust funds each own 49% of the class B common stock, the only stock with voting rights.

Reader's Digest was founded in 1922 through the joint efforts of DeWitt Wallace and Lila Acheson Wallace. DeWitt Wallace conceived the idea of condensing magazine articles and reprinting them in a digest magazine. He was born on November 12, 1889, in St. Paul, Minnesota, of a father who was a college professor and who later became president of Macalester College.

Wallace read widely and got in the habit of making notes from his reading to retain ideas. In a job handling inquiries about an agricultural textbook, he began wondering if his reading notes might be useful to others were they to be published. He produced a 128-page book on farming, providing information about agricultural bulletins available to farmers. He sold 100,000 copies of the book by traveling through five states in an old car, selling the book to banks and feed stores that would give the book to customers as a gift. He saw a market for this type of publication among the public as a whole.

World War I temporarily interrupted Wallace's plans. In October 1918, he was severely wounded in battle in France. During his months of recuperation, he focused on reading from a variety of magazines, distilling the articles down to their essentials. On his return home to St. Paul, he continued to work on digesting other magazine articles, putting together 31 summarized articles in a sample of the type of digest magazine he thought would sell. The cost of printing the sample was paid for with money borrowed from his brother and father. He showed his sample to several publishing houses in the hopes that they would use his idea and hire him as editor, but all turned him down.

In January 1922 Wallace finally published the magazine on his own, aided by his wife. Lila Bell Acheson was born in 1889 in Virden, Manitoba, Canada. Most of her early life was spent in the United States, as her father preached in a number of midwestern towns.

In 1921 the Wallaces began selling the magazine to readers by direct mail. The couple rented an apartment in Greenwich Village in New York City, with Lila Wallace retaining her job as a social worker to pay the rent. DeWitt Wallace sent out letters to potential subscribers, offering his magazine idea for sale and promising a money-back guarantee if readers were not satisfied. These solicitations brought in 1,500 subscriptions at $3 each, generating enough money to finance the first edition and possibly the second. The first edition of the *Reader's Digest* was dated February 1922; it contained 64 pages. Its small measurements, about 5.5 inches by 7.5 inches, which allowed readers to carry it in a pocket or purse, was an innovation among magazines at the time. The lead article was by Alexander Graham Bell and was on the importance of self-education as a lifelong habit.

DeWitt Wallace spent much of the magazine's first year in the New York Public Library reading articles to summarize in future issues, while Lila Wallace kept her job. As there had been no cancellations of subscriptions from the first edition, it was judged a success. By September 1922 the couple was able to rent a garage and apartment for their editorial offices, choosing to live in Pleasantville, New York, where they had been married in 1921. Additional promotional letters brought in new subscribers, and within a year of its first edition, circulation had risen to 7,000. After four years, circulation was up to 20,000, and by 1929, 216,000.

Initially *The Digest* kept a low profile, partly for fear that envious magazines might stop allowing it to reprint their articles. DeWitt Wallace seemed to have a very good notion of what his readers wanted, and circulation continued to grow, reaching over one million in 1936 and three million in 1939. An edition began appearing in England in 1938. Because of the rapid increase in the size of operations, in 1939 the Wallaces moved their facilities to Chappaqua, New York, located close by, but retained their mailing address in Pleasantville, because of the euphonious nature of its name. The address has remained at Pleasantville ever since.

In 1950 Reader's Digest condensed books first appeared. These books, which present an abbreviated version of popular novels, were an immediate success. In 1959 a series of phonograph record albums of music that was culturally sophisticated yet broadly popular appeared under the Reader's Digest banner.

Foreign-language editions of *The Digest* carried advertising from their inception, but in the United States advertising was not introduced until 1955. The magazine did not accept advertising for alcoholic beverages until the late 1970s. It never ran advertising for cigarettes. Instead, it began warning readers of the dangers of smoking early, well before the surgeon general made his report in 1964.

The Digest owed its initial appeal and continued success to its ability to choose articles that reflected the values of its many readers. Many of those readers have told of the hope and inspiration they have drawn from the optimistic spirit that pervades *The Digest*. That spirit reflected the outlook of DeWitt Wallace, who based the magazine's content on what he wanted to read. He retained strict editorial control.

When the magazine became successful, DeWitt Wallace kept up the task of editing it and managing its finances. Lila Wallace designed the corporate headquarters and purchased many artworks that are now part of the company's collection. She also had a hand in selecting the graphics that adorned the back cover of *The Digest*. In 1956 she formed the Lila Wallace Reader's Digest Fund to support the arts and make them accessible to persons of all income levels. A DeWitt Wallace Reader's Digest Fund was also formed for the purpose of providing education programs for young people.

In 1973 the Wallaces retired, although DeWitt Wallace kept in close contact with the editorial and corporate offices. He died on March 30, 1981. Lila Wallace survived him by three years. As the Wallaces had no children, most of their stock was willed to charities, including Macalester College. This stock was nonvoting, however, and almost all of the voting power was placed with the Wallace trust funds. Management owned 3%.

About the time of the death of Lila Wallace in 1984, George Grune became head of The Reader's Digest Association. The company was not performing well, and in a successful effort to improve profitability, he began a cost-cutting program that included the termination of foreign editions of the *Reader's Digest* that were losing money, selling off weak divisions, and reducing the work force from 10,000 to 7,500. He also decreased the rate at which advertising was being lost.

Members of the staff who had worked during the Wallace years became concerned that Grune's methods departed from Wallace's idea that the company was an association of readers and not just a for-profit venture. There was no doubt that Grune had improved profits; in five years profits increased sevenfold. After years of high profits, several of the charities that owned nonvoting shares of the association's stock sold some of their shares to the public in order to take advantage of the high price the stock would bring. After the sale, in February 1990, 21% of the total stock was publicly held, these all being class A nonvoting shares. Nearly all of the class B voting shares were still held by the trust funds, 98%; the remainder was held by employees of the association.

As the 1990s began, The Reader's Digest Association remained a global company, with operations located in 50 cities throughout the world. *Reader's Digest* remained its premiere

publication, accounting for 31% of revenues in fiscal year 1990. *The Digest* serves to introduce subscribers to other products the company sells. To maintain its subscribers' loyalties, *The Digest* keeps coverage diverse and of high quality. It earns nearly 70% of its revenues from circulation, very high for any publication; most magazines rely heavily on advertising for revenue. This means that the content of *The Digest* does not have to be targeted to a market desired by advertisers, leaving editors free to select articles having the broadest appeal.

Books and home entertainment accounted for 61% of revenues in fiscal year 1990. Series books included such new product lines in the United States as the AMA Home Medical Library. General books included reference books, how-to books, cookbooks, travel guides, and others.

In the late 1980s the association acquired several special-interest magazines, *Travel Holiday*, *The Family Handyman*, *New Choices for the Best Years*, and *American Health*. In 1990 it expanded this line by purchasing the British magazine *Money*, which was renamed *Moneywise*, and by starting up a French magazine, *Budgets Famille*. The special-interest-magazine line accounted for 3% of revenues in fiscal 1990 but showed an operating loss. *Budgets Famille* was suspended in May 1990, after six issues, because it did not meet circulaiton or advertising objectives.

Other operations of the association contributed 5% of total revenue in fiscal year 1990. These operations included the subsidiary, QSP, Inc., which provides fund-raising services for schools and youth groups through the sale of subscriptions to magazines, music products, and candy.

Reader's Digest remains the world's largest-selling magazine. Despite the magazine's popularity, it is the home-entertainment division that contributes the bulk of profits. The condensed books operation still dominates its market.

During the 1990s, as the global economy is restructured, The Reader's Digest Association expects to keep pace. Its products are already well known in 11 of the 12 countries that will make up the European single market. The company plans to expand into the new markets of Eastern Europe that are now beginning to be important in world trade. When the Berlin Wall was opened in 1989, employees of *The Digest* started distributing complimentary copies of the German-language version of the *Reader's Digest* and collecting names for a mailing list of potential subscribers. In late 1991 *Reader's Digest* became available in Russian- and Hungarian-language editions to serve Soviet and Hungarian readers. In this way, the association continued to keep pace with an ever-changing world.

Principal Subsidiary: QSP, Inc.

Further Reading: Ferguson, Charles W., "Unforgettable DeWitt Wallace," *Reader's Digest,* February 1987; Rothman, Andrea, "The Man Who Rewrote Reader's Digest," *Business Week,* June 4, 1990.

—Donald R. Stabile

REED INTERNATIONAL

REED INTERNATIONAL P.L.C.

Reed House
6 Chesterfield Gardens
London W1A 1EJ
United Kingdom
(071) 499 4020
Fax: (071) 491 8212

Public Company
Incorporated: 1903 as Albert E. Reed & Company Ltd.
Employees: 18,700
Sales: £1.58 billion (US$3.05 billion)
Stock Exchange: London

Originally a paper manufacturer and later a conglomerate, Reed International is now a publishing and information group. This latest transformation was completed only in 1988, after the sell-offs of the company's manufacturing interests balanced by the acquisition of several publishing businesses. Reed is therefore in the odd position, for a long established company, of having acquired all its present interests since 1970. Its new publishing empire includes magazines, newspapers, books, and electronic information systems. Reed claims to be the largest publishing group in the United Kingdom and is also strong in the United States.

The beginnings of the company go back to 1894, when Albert Reed bought Upper Tovil paper mill at Maidstone, Kent. He was then 48 and already successful in paper manufacturing. After going into the paper business as a boy he had become a manager, and then part owner, of a number of paper mills in different parts of the country, but Upper Tovil was the first which was entirely his. It had been badly damaged in a fire when he bought it, so he was able to install new machinery before reopening it.

Over the years Reed had experimented with different materials and machinery to produce types of paper suitable for the half-tone blocks which were then being introduced. At his new mill he specialized in these papers, and soon built up a good trade with the publishers of illustrated magazines. Within two years he had over 100 employees and installed a new machine. When Upper Tovil had been expanded to its limit, Reed bought other mills, owning seven by 1903. In that year the business was incorporated as Albert E. Reed & Company Ltd., to enable more capital to be raised.

One of the firm's best customers in its early days was the publishing business of Harmsworth Brothers. This connection chiefly fueled Reed's growth from 1904 onward. Alfred and Harold Harmsworth, shortly to become Lord Northcliffe and Lord Rothermere respectively, had built up the most dynamic publishing business in London. Only 15 years after launching their first magazine, *Answers,* they controlled a string of magazines and newspapers including the successful *Daily Mail.* They had one failure, however, a new paper aimed at women, called the *Daily Mirror.* To save it they decided to relaunch it in 1904 for a general readership as an all-picture paper, using a new grade of fine newsprint introduced by Reed. In this form the *Daily Mirror* became a success, and the Reed paper business grew with it. By the outbreak of World War I in 1914, the *Daily Mirror* was the largest selling daily newspaper in the world, and Reed was supplying the newsprint not only for that but also for several national newspapers. The company took over more paper mills in the United Kingdom and invested in pulp mills in Norway and in Newfoundland, Canada.

World War I put a temporary stop to Reed's growth. Supplies of pulp from Scandinavia were cut off, newspapers became smaller, and Reed was forced to close some of its mills. At the same time the Newfoundland venture proved uneconomical. Reed sold it to his friends, the Harmsworths, who were developing their own pulp mill nearby.

Soon after World War I another financial crisis was precipitated by Albert Reed's death in 1920. His twin sons, Ralph and Percy, were determined to carry on the business, but a large sum had to be found to pay the duty on their father's estate and in any case some members of the family wanted to turn their shares into cash. Once again, the Reeds turned to their largest customer. Lord Northcliffe had died, but Lord Rothermere agreed to buy a large block of shares in Reed, through the Daily Mirror and Sunday Pictorial companies, which he now controlled. The Reed brothers still had voting control, but Rothermere's holding of around 40% of the equity rendered him a major influence in its affairs. He seems to have made little use of this influence, having had many other business commitments, but half a century later this shareholding was to change the nature of Reed's business.

The Reed brothers began to implement the plan for the company which their father had conceived during the war. This was to sell their remaining overseas operations and most of their U.K. mills, and concentrate their resources on a single, modern plant, using the largest machines available. In this way they hoped to undercut all competition. A site was selected at Aylesford, a few miles down-river from Tovil, and the new mill began production in 1922.

The new strategy worked well. Despite the Depression the Aylesford plant was steadily expanded, and by 1939 was the largest of its kind of Europe. Newsprint remained the company's chief product, but from 1929 onwards Reed also made kraft paper from which it produced corrugated board and paper sacks. With these new products the company captured a large share of the packaging market.

During World War II production had to be drastically reduced due to lack of pulp, and did not regain prewar levels until 1950. The next few years were a boom period for Reed. The company added to its newsprint and kraft manufacturing capacity, expanded into new forms of packaging, entered the paper tissue market in a joint venture with Kimberly-Clark, and invested some of its profits in pulp mills overseas. Within seven years Reed's work force doubled to 14,000.

However, in the late 1950s, conditions changed for the worse. First the government put an end to the price-fixing arrangements which Reed had with other paper manufacturers, and then to the tariffs which had shielded the U.K. paper industry from Scandinavian competition. This latter change was the result of U.K. membership of the European Free Trade Area and was to be introduced over several years, but its implications were clear from 1959. Without the tariffs, newsprint and kraft made from imported pulp would be unable to compete with Scandinavian products. Reed would have to make major changes.

It was unfortunate that the company had to face this crisis with a relatively untried management. Sir Ralph Reed had retired in 1954, ending the era of family control, and his most able colleague, Clifford Sheldon, had died a few years earlier. The new chairman, Lord Cornwallis, and managing director, P.G. Walker, both came from outside the paper industry. They took prompt steps to reduce the company's dependence on imported pulp, but could not prevent a slide in profits. In 1960, the company's largest shareholder decided to intervene.

This was no longer Lord Rothermere, who had sold his shares in the Daily Mirror in the 1930s, but a new group which had been created from the nucleus of the Mirror. The latter paper and the *Sunday Pictorial* had declined in the 1920s under Rothermere's ownership but had recovered under his successors. In the late 1930s a new team led by Guy Bartholomew and including Cecil King, a nephew of Lords Northcliffe and Rothermere, had completely restyled the two papers. Now they were aimed at younger, working-class readers. By a mixture of populist style and radical campaigning on social issues, they captured most of this market during the unsettled war years, and increased their hold on it in the more prosperous times that followed. The combined circulation of both papers rose from around one million in the 1930s to more than five million in the 1960s.

From the large profits which flowed from this success, Cecil King, who became chairman in 1951, began to build a broad-ranging publishing group. It bought further newspapers, in Scotland and abroad, and a stake in one of the first commercial television companies in the United Kingdom, Associated TV, which proved to be highly lucrative. King next turned his attention to magazines. In 1958 he bought Amalgamated Press, the magazine group founded by his uncles, then Associated Iliffe Press, and finally Odhams Press. This included newspapers as well as the Odhams, Newnes, and Hulton magazine groups. When the Mirror and Pictorial companies became the International Publishing Corporation (IPC) in 1963, it was by far the largest publishing group in the United Kingdom. It had four mass-circulation newspapers, all the leading women's magazines, a host of specialized magazines and directories, and no less than 25 printing plants.

Through this period of upheaval the Mirror and Pictorial had held on to their shares in Reed, which they saw as a substantial asset, to be protected and developed. When its future began to look uncertain, King obtained voting control of Reed by transferring to it all the pulp and paper mills owned by Mirror and Pictorial. In 1963, while retaining the chairmanship of IPC, he made himself chairman of Reed and installed one of his senior managers, Don Ryder, as managing director.

Don Ryder was a former financial journalist who had shown a flair for management. Under his vigorous lead, Reed expanded and diversified. Its success in packaging and its growing overseas interests had already reduced its dependence on the U.K. newsprint and kraft business, and Ryder speeded up this process by a series of takeovers. First he bought companies in other branches of the paper and packaging industry. Then in 1965 he successfully bid for The Wall Paper Manufacturers (WPM), a large but sleepy company which then had a virtual monopoly of the wallpaper market in the United Kingdom. It also included a paint business and Sanderson fabrics. In the same year, Reed bought Polycell Holdings, which made Polyfilla and other decorating products. With these brands Reed acquired instant dominance of the fast-growing do-it-yourself market. Then, through further takeovers, Ryder took Reed into bathroom equipment and other building products. By 1970 the company could be described as a conglomerate. Its work force had grown to 56,000. The enlargement of its share capital had freed it from IPC's control, and its market value had risen well above that of IPC.

Meanwhile IPC had run into difficulties. The worst of these concerned the *Daily Herald,* a Labour Party newspaper owned jointly by Odhams and the trade unions, which lost money steadily. IPC persuaded the trade unions to relinquish their share, and relaunched the paper as the *Sun.* This was no more successful and was finally sold to Rupert Murdoch at a very low price. In addition, there were serious losses on the printing side of IPC. Many of the works it had acquired in its takeovers were found to be obsolete, and had to be closed down or modernized at further cost.

Finally, King's activities created a problem. Instead of tackling the company's financial difficulties, he became increasingly preoccupied with politics. The *Daily Mirror* had helped to get the Labour government elected in 1964, and afterward King felt that it should listen to his views. When it did not, he turned on Labour with irrational fury. In 1968, on the front page of the *Daily Mirror,* King demanded the prime minister's resignation. King's colleagues at IPC felt that he was misusing the paper's power and forced him to resign.

He was succeeded by Hugh Cudlipp, a brilliant editor but a poor businessman. Afterward, he admitted that his chairmanship of IPC was "uninspired." The company's decline continued and takeover rumors began. As IPC still owned 27% of Reed, and Ryder could not allow it to fall into unfriendly hands, he and Cudlipp agreed in 1970 that Reed should take over IPC.

The combined company was named Reed International, incorporating part of IPC's name, and its turnover made it the 30th largest U.K. company. Its work force numbered 85,000, and its business spanned more markets than at any time before or since. However, Reed's position in most of these markets was far from secure.

The U.K. paper business was still contracting, and Reed had to close down some operations in the 1970s. Its Canadian pulp and paper business was only intermittently profitable. The printing business inherited from IPC continued to lose money, even after the older plant was closed, and Reed failed to deal with its overmanning. WPM faced increasingly tough competition in wall coverings and saw its market share steadily eroded. Newspaper circulations in the United Kingdom were declining and all IPC's nationals lost ground. It was the *Sun*'s recovery under Murdoch that hit the *Mirror* hardest.

In the early 1970s Ryder kept profits moving upward, by rationalizing in the weaker areas and increasing investment in the stronger ones. Indeed, his reputation as a manager was so impressive that at the end of 1974 he was plucked from Reed by the government to head its new National Enterprise Board. His successor, Alex Jarratt, continued to implement Ryder's policy, but it was no longer working. In 1975–76 the company's profits fell by more than 50%, and in the next few years made only a partial recovery.

Only in 1978 did the company recognize that the expansion policy initiated by Ryder had failed in the long run. Turnover had grown tenfold in his 11-year reign, but profits had grown much more slowly, and the outlook was poor. Jarratt decided to dispose of its unprofitable parts. Most of the overseas subsidiaries were sold, and the work force was reduced to 60,000. Nevertheless, 1980–1981 saw another halving of profits and another round of cutbacks began, this time mainly in the U.K. paper division.

In 1982 a new chief executive was appointed, Leslie Carpenter, who had come up through the magazine division of the company. The next annual report pointed out that 60% of the company's trading profit was coming from the 40% of its turnover that lay in publishing. From that time onwards, new investment was concentrated in this area. Local newspaper chains were acquired in the United Kingdom, together with publishing and exhibition companies in the United States, where the Cahners subsidiary, a magazine publisher wholly owned since 1977, was thriving.

At this time the company's publishing activities still included U.K. national newspapers. Despite the introduction of photocomposition, these were far less profitable than the magazines. In 1984 Reed decided to float them as a separate company. "National newspapers do not sit easily in a large commercial corporation," said Carpenter. The move was forestalled by a takeover bid for the newspaper group, which was accepted. This was from Robert Maxwell, who had already bought the Odhams gravure printing works from Reed.

Reed was thus left with a flourishing magazine business on both sides of the Atlantic and a miscellany of less profitable manufacturing businesses—the much-reduced paper and packaging division, as well as paints and building products. During Carpenter's time as chief executive there were further disposals in the manufacturing area, and the final moves to abandon manufacturing were made under his successor, Peter Davis.

The most significant change came in 1987. In that year the paints and do-it-yourself division was sold, and Octopus Publishing was bought. Octopus, which cost Reed £540 million, was the largest publishing business the company had acquired since IPC. It is a diversified international publishing group with a major presence in mass-market nonfiction books, fiction and general trade books, children's books, educational books at both the primary and secondary level, and in business and technical books, and greatly increased Reed's strength in these areas. Its founder, Paul Hamlyn, moved to Reed with the business and became the company's largest non-corporate shareholder.

Paper and packaging, for so long Reed's sole business, was the last of the manufacturing divisions to go. It was bought in 1988 by its own management, taking the name Reedpack, and two years later was sold again to a Swedish company, Svenska Cellulosa. Reed also sold its North American paper group to Daishowa Paper Manufacturing Co., Ltd. in 1988 for C$594.

Reed continues to buy publishing businesses as opportunities arise and is now building up its electronic information services. It is also the largest organizer of exhibitions in the world. So far, its new orientation has been a success: profits have grown every year since 1983, although turnover has diminished.

Principal Subsidiaries: IPC Magazines Ltd.; Reed Business Publishing Ltd.; The Reed Exhibition Companies Ltd.; Reed International Books Ltd.; Reed Regional Newspapers Ltd.; Reed Publishing (USA) Inc.; Reed Telepublishing Ltd.

Further Reading: Sykes, Philip, *Albert Reed and the Creation of a Paper Business, 1860–1960,* London, Reed International, 1980; *Reed International: Developments in a Company History, 1960–1974,* London, Reed International, 1980; *Chapters from Our History,* London, Reed International, 1990.

—John Swan

REUTERS

REUTERS HOLDINGS PLC

85 Fleet Street
London EC4P 4AJ
United Kingdom
(071) 250 1122

Public Company
Incorporated: 1865 as Reuter's Telegram Company Limited
Employees: 10,000
Sales £1.19 billion (US$2.30 billion)
Stock Exchanges: London New York

Reuters Limited is the principal subsidiary of Reuters Holdings PLC. As the world's leading news organization and supplier of computerized information services, Reuters serves the financial and business communities in all of the world's major markets and the news media in more than 150 countries. The range of products includes real-time financial data and transaction services, access to numerical and textual historical databases, news, and news pictures. Data are drawn from exchanges and over-the-counter markets. Currency exchange rates and other market information are also contributed directly by subscribers. Reuters journalists, photographers, and cameramen from Visnews make up a worldwide news reporting network.

Reuters takes its name from its founder, Julius Reuter, from Cassel, Germany. During a short visit to London in 1845, he changed his name from Israel Beer Josaphat. After working as a publisher in Berlin, he fled the city during the revolution of 1848 and arrived in Paris. Here he is said to have worked for Charles Havas, the French news agency pioneer, before setting up in business himself. In 1849 Reuter started his own newssheet, containing information taken from French newspapers, and sent this to provincial papers in Germany. The business failed after a few months. Reuter left for Germany to establish a service in Aachen, supplying financial and general news to the merchants and bankers in Cologne, and elsewhere. He used carrier pigeons to bridge the gap in the telegraph line then existing between Aachen and Brussels. This meant that news from the financial centers of Paris, Brussels, and Berlin arrived seven hours earlier than if it came by the mail train.

By the end of 1850 the gap in the telegraph line was closed and Reuter moved to London. In response to the laying of a cable across the English Channel, linking the stock exchanges of London and Paris, he opened an office near the London Stock Exchange in October 1851. In addition to being the financial center of the Victorian world, London was becoming the communications center for the growing world telegraph network. Free trade and a free press added to the atmosphere Reuter needed to succeed in his new venture. He had long been impressed by the potential of telegraphic communication and the profits to be derived from the sale of news and information via this medium. Twice a day, for a fixed-term payment, his Submarine Telegraph office provided London and Paris brokers and merchants with opening and closing prices in both capitals. He gradually widened his range and in 1857 made a contract with the recently established telegraphic news agency in Russia.

The repeal of the newspaper stamp duty—a tax on the sale of newspapers—in 1855 was to transform the British press, making way for the penny daily papers and the rise of popular journalism. Newspapers had more space for news, and their readership extended rapidly. The London *Times* already had its own network of correspondents in Europe, the Near East, India, China, and the United States, and refused to make any contract with Reuter. In 1858, despairing of *The Times,* Reuter approached several other London daily papers and persuaded them to subscribe to his news service. This was a breakthrough. *The Times* eventually softened its attitude and made a contract for telegrams.

Reuter was now offering general and political news, received by telegraph from all over Europe, as well as financial information. Reuter's first news scoop came from Turin in 1859, heralding the war of Italian liberation. Unfortunately, several attempts to lay a cable across the Atlantic failed. A successful cable was not laid until 1866. By this date Reuter was already receiving news from agents in many parts of the world beyond Europe. His correspondent in the United States reported the Civil War and was two hours ahead of rivals in announcing the news of the assassination of President Abraham Lincoln in 1865.

Julius Reuter was a businessman, collecting and selling news, rather than a journalist. The first editor was Sigismund Engländer, a Viennese revolutionary, who had fled to Paris at the same time as Reuter in 1848. Engländer was one of several emigrés employed in the early years of the business. His great knowledge of the politics and culture of Europe opened many doors. When the Russo-Turkish War broke out in 1877, he went to Constantinople as chief correspondent.

In 1865 Julius Reuter's private business became Reuter's Telegram Company Limited. The new company was incorporated with a nominal capital of £250,000. Reuter was appointed managing director. One reason for the restructuring was to raise capital to pay for a cable from England to Norderney on the north German coast. This cable became the link in the first telegraph to India in 1866. In pursuing his grand design of creating a world news agency, Reuter was ready to become a cable owner as well as a cable user. In 1869 he and Baron Emile d'Erlanger, a Paris banker, financed a French cable across the Atlantic. This company was absorbed by its rival, the Anglo-American Telegraph Company, in 1873. After this, Reuters became less exposed to the charge of seeking to monopolize news supply.

In the 1860s Reuters faced two main news agency rivals, Charles Havas in Paris and Bernard Wolff in Berlin. From this period until the 1930s Reuters, Havas, and Wolff divided most of the news of the world outside North America between themselves. The leading member of the "ring combination" was Reuters. The company's exclusive territories were the most extensive, and its network of offices and agencies, correspondents and stringers made it the largest news contributor to the pool. This activity, and Britain's predominance within the world telegraph system, made the Reuter office—by now in Old Jewry, London—the international clearing center for news. Reuters had established an enviable reputation for speed, accuracy, and impartiality in news collection and distribution.

In 1865 Reuters opened an office in Alexandria, its first office outside Europe. Offices were established in Bombay and other Indian cities from 1866. India became an important territory for Reuters. As the world's communications network spread to India and the East, the company followed the cable to China and Japan in 1871 and on to Australia in 1872. The prestige of Reuters—and also its profitability—came to depend heavily upon the growing British Empire. Reuters was to report the many wars which accompanied imperial expansion. From the 1870s the transmission of private telegrams for both businesses and individuals within the empire became a major Reuter activity. This was especially successful in the East where the substitution of code words for common phrases saved words and thus money. The revenue from this enterprise helped to pay for the news services, which increasingly lost money.

In 1878 Reuter retired as managing director. He had been granted a barony in 1871 by the Duke of Saxe-Coburg-Gotha, a title recognized by Queen Victoria in 1891. His son Herbert succeeded him as managing director. Baron Herbert de Reuter did not possess the same business acumen as his father, but he raised the standard of journalism within Reuters, meeting the public demand for more popular news in the 1890s. He introduced the latest technology into Reuters, but he also led the company down some dangerous paths. Forays into advertising and banking very nearly led to financial ruin. The setting up of a Reuters bank was his final mistake. Business worries and the death of his wife contributed toward his suicide in 1915.

The Boer War of 1899–1902 had been a great drain on the company's resources, but it had been well reported and enhanced the reputation of Reuters for impartiality. It had placed correspondents on the Boer side as well as the British. From this scene of operations came the new head of Reuters. Soon after Herbert's death, Roderick Jones, manager in South Africa, became the first non-family managing director. To escape a hostile takeover bid, the company returned to private ownership in 1916. Jones and Mark Napier, the company's chairman, formed a group to buy the entire shareholding. Reuter's Telegram Company now became Reuters Limited. Napier died in 1919, leaving Roderick Jones as the principal proprietor and executive head, a post which he held until 1941.

World War I was a difficult time for the company. The cost of reporting was high both in terms of profits and of the independence that Reuters strove to achieve in all its business and news transactions. The private telegram business was no longer so profitable, since the censors would not allow the use of codes. Reuters was accused of being in the pay of the British government, and this was a difficult charge to deny. Roderick Jones was also head of the Department of Propaganda at the Ministry of Information, work for which he was knighted.

As head of Reuters between the two world wars, Roderick Jones ran the business as an autocracy. Reuters found it hard to keep its lead over the other international news agencies, especially the Associated Press and the United Press, both U.S. agencies. Jones thought that Reuters could seek to work *with* the British government, so long as it was not seen to be working *for* it. Reuters badly needed government subscriptions. Jones was careful not to ask for subsidies.

In 1920 Reuters set up a trade department to expand the distribution of business news. This was followed three years later by a service of price quotations and exchange rates sent in morse code by long-wave radio to Europe. This became the company's chief commercial service in Europe, later reaching other parts of the world via more powerful radio transmitters. In 1927 Reuters started using teleprinters to distribute news to London newspapers. In 1934 the company began news transmission to Europe by Hellschreiber, a forerunner of the radio teleprinter.

In 1925 the Press Association (PA) had taken a majority shareholding in Reuters. It followed this in 1930 by purchasing the remainder of the Reuter shares, except for 1,000 retained by Roderick Jones. In 1941 the PA directors forced Jones to resign. It felt that he had compromised the agency in his dealings with the British government. The government itself helped to ease Jones out. The Reuter Trust was now established to ensure the independence of the agency. From 1941 the company was jointly owned by the PA and the Newspaper Proprietors' Association (NPA). A commonwealth dimension was added when the Australian Associated Press (AAP) and the New Zealand Press Association (NZPA) joined the partnership in 1947. The Press Trust of India joined in 1949, only to leave four years later.

Christopher Chancellor was general manager during the 1940s and 1950s. Under his leadership Reuters did not crumble along with the British Empire, despite the growing ascendency of the U.S. news agencies. The range of economic services expanded, and Reuters assisted in the establishment of news agencies in postwar Europe, and later in the Third World. In Chancellor's day, the newspaper owners of Reuters were not adventurous. They were aiming at little more than balancing the books. They expected to pay the minimum annual contribution towards the running of Reuters and to get their news cheap.

Walton Cole, who succeeded Chancellor in 1959, had strengthened the news file during the later stages of World War II as managing editor. Cole died in 1963. His successor, Gerald Long, sought to make Reuters an aggressive and profitable international news organization. Notably, he persuaded a reluctant Reuters board to enter the market for computerized information. This initiative was eventually to transform the company's character and to earn it huge profits. Long encouraged Michael Nelson, the manager of Reuters Economic Services, to lead Reuters into price reporting via computer terminals. In partnership with Ultronic Systems Corporation of the United States, Reuters started a desktop market-quotation system called Stockmaster in 1964. It served Reuters clients throughout the world outside North America. In just ten years the profits from Stockmaster and its successor Videomaster amounted to £4 million.

In 1971 the collapse of the Bretton Woods Agreement, which had regulated rates of exchange, encouraged Reuters to undertake another daring yet calculated initiative. This was the introduction of the Reuter Monitor Money Rates service in 1973. Catering to the needs of the decentralized money markets,

Monitor was the first of a number of contributed data products designed to serve the international business community. The Reuter Monitor Dealing service followed in 1981. This enabled dealers in foreign currencies to conclude trades over video terminals. These innovations gradually made Reuters more profitable than ever before. In 1963 the company had made a profit of £51,000; in 1973 profits reached more than £709,000; in 1981 profits were more than £16 million; and in 1989, £284 million.

On the news front, there were similar technological advances. In 1968 an Automatic Data Exchange (ADX)—a computerized message-switching system for faster handling and distribution of news throughout the world—went into operation in the London editorial offices. This was the first of its kind to be used by an international news organization. In 1973 Reuters formed a U.S. subsidiary, Information, Dissemination and Retrieval Inc. (IDR), to develop and manufacture systems and equipment for the company's use in cable television news and retrieval services. For the first time in 1973 Reuter journalists in New York began to use video display units for writing and sending news. Reuters went into the international news picture business in 1985 when it purchased the United Press International picture service. A news picture terminal was launched in 1987. In 1985 Reuters acquired control of Visnews Ltd., the international television news agency. It had held a share in the agency since 1959.

Glen Renfrew became managing director in 1981. He continued to build upon Long's achievements. In 1984 Reuters Limited was floated as a public company, Reuters Holdings PLC. As part of the restructuring, the composition of the board was broadened to make it more international, and the number of directors was increased to include the first representatives from outside the newspaper world. A separate company, Reuters Founders Share Company, was formed to maintain the Reuter Trust principles. Through this company the trustees and their chairman retain a single share with the power to outvote all other shares to prevent a takeover bid. Sir Christopher Hogg, chief executive of Courtaulds plc, became chairman of Reuters in 1985.

The flotation raised about £52 million of new capital which was available for investment in new products and new technology. Worldwide staff numbers rose dramatically in the 1980s. In 1980 the number stood at fewer than 3,000, and in 1989 it peaked at more than 10,000. From 1984 Reuters has acquired a number of U.S. and U.K. companies. Reuters services are now categorized under five areas—real-time information, transaction products, trading room systems, historical information, and media products. These look towards the 21st century—Equities 2000, Money 2000, Dealing 2000, and Tri-

arch 2000. In 1989 Reuters was reorganized into geographical areas covering three time zones—Reuters Asia, Reuters America, and Reuters Europe, Middle East and Africa. From Reuters Asia came Peter Job, Renfrew's successor from March 1991.

The company has led the way in the electronic information age. Moving into satellite distribution the Integrated Data Network (IDN) is set to become the delivery medium for many Reuters services, gradually replacing the Reuter Monitor. Competitors are trying hard to catch up—Telerate and Quotron in the money markets, AP-Dow Jones and Knight-Ridder in financial news, and Associated Press and Agence France Presse in news-agency reporting. Even so, through its financial news services (from which it draws more than 90% of its revenue) Reuters still holds a key position in the business world.

Yet to those outside the world of finance and banking, Reuters is still essentially a news agency. It is the media heart (worth only 7% of the company's turnover) and the combination of providing economic information and the means to distribute and deal which makes Reuters unique.

Principal Subsidiaries: Reuter Nederland BV (Netherlands); Reuter Services SARL (France); Reuters AG (West Germany); Reuters Australia Pty Ltd. (Australia); Reuters Hong Kong Ltd. (Hong Kong); Reuters Information Services Inc. (U.S.A.); Reuters Italia S.p.A. (Italy); Reuters Japan K.K. (Japan); Reuters Ltd. (99.7%); Reuters Middle East Ltd. (Bahrain); Reuters SA (Switzerland); Reuters Singapore Pte Ltd. (Singapore); Reuters Svenska Aktiebolag (Sweden); Rich Inc. (U.S.A.); L.H.W. Wyatt Brothers Ltd.; Instinet Corporation (U.S.A.); I.P. Sharp Associates Ltd. (Canada); Visnews Ltd. (51%).

Further Reading: Collins, Henry M., *From Pigeon Post to Wireless,* London, Hodder and Stoughton, 1925; Jones, Roderick, *A Life in Reuters,* London, Hodder and Stoughton, 1951; Storey, Graham, *Reuters Century,* London, Max Parrish, 1951; Desmond, R.W., *The Information Process: World News Reporting to the Twentieth Century,* Iowa City, University of Iowa Press, 1978; Boyd Barrett, Oliver, *The International News Agencies,* London, Constable, 1980; Fenby, Jonathan, *The International News Services (A Twentieth Century Fund Report),* New York, Schocken Books, 1986; Lawrenson, John, and Lionel Barber, *The Price of Truth: The Story of the Reuters Millions,* London, Sphere, 1986; Read, Donald, *The Power of News: The History of Reuters,* forthcoming, Oxford, Oxford University Press, 1992.

—Justine Taylor

SIMON & SCHUSTER INC.

1230 Avenue of the Americas
New York, New York 10020
U.S.A.
(212) 698-7000
Fax: (212) 698-7007

Wholly Owned Subsidiary of Paramount Communications Inc.
Incorporated: 1924
Employees: 9,100
Sales: $1.42 billion

Simon & Schuster is the world's largest book publisher as measured by sales. It publishes hardcover books; trade, or general interest paperbacks; and mass-market paperbacks for the general consumer, as well as textbooks used in elementary, secondary, and higher education. It also has data base and information services used by a variety of businesses, and substantial international publishing and distribution operations.

Richard L. Simon and M. Lincoln Schuster founded the company in January 1924. Their first publication—at the suggestion of Simon's aunt, a crossword puzzle enthusiast—was *The Crossword Puzzle Book,* which came out in April. The book sold more than 100,000 copies, and Simon & Schuster followed it with three other crossword puzzle books in the company's first year. All four books were top nonfiction bestsellers, and by the end of the year Simon & Schuster had sold more than a million of them.

The puzzle books were highly profitable, but the craze eventually waned and Simon & Schuster had to diversify. Its first few efforts produced moderate successes: a tennis book by Bill Tilden and an investment guide by Merryle Stanley Rukeyser; and several failures, such as a novel called *Harvey Landrum* and a biography of Joseph Pulitzer. The company's first big success outside of the puzzle books was Will Durant's *The Story of Philosophy,* a bestseller in 1926 and 1927. The book established Simon & Schuster as a serious publishing company, and led to Durant's authoring, with his wife, Ariel, the multi-volume *Story of Civilization* series for Simon & Schuster over the next half-century.

Simon & Schuster quickly developed a reputation as a highly commercial publishing house—one successul project was a compilation of the "Ripley's Believe It or Not" newspaper cartoon features—but at the same time brought out many distinguished works. In its first two decades, Simon & Schu-

ster output included Leon Trotsky's *History of the Russian Revolution,* Felix Salten's *Bambi,* Rachel Carson's *Under the Sea Wind,* Wendell Willkie's *One World,* and three volumes of the Durants's *Civilization* series. Simon & Schuster had a Pulitzer Prize winner in 1935, *Now in November* by Josephine Johnson. Other achievements of the early years were the publication of a collection of George Gershwin's songs, followed by similar compilations of the works of Noel Coward, Cole Porter, Jerome Kern, the team of Richard Rodgers and Lorenz Hart, and Rodgers's later teaming with Oscar Hammerstein II; and the *Treasury* series of oversized gift books—1939's *A Treasury of Art Masterpieces,* followed by similar books on the theater, oratory, and the world's great letters. Besides the founders, key figures in Simon & Schuster's early years were Leon Shimkin, the company's business manager, and Clifton Fadiman, editor-in-chief. While Fadiman left in the mid-1930s and achieved fame as a book reviewer and radio quiz-show host, Shimkin became an equal partner, financially and operationally. With the founders, he stayed on for many years, and was highly influential in the company. In the late 1930s, he brought in two highly successful properties—Dale Carnegie's *How to Win Friends and Influence People* and J.K. Lasser's *Your Income Tax.*

In 1939 Simon, Schuster, and Shimkin put up 49% of the financing for Robert F. de Graff, an experienced publisher of hardcover reprints, to start Pocket Books, a line of inexpensive, mass-market paperback reprints. While paperback books had appeared in the United States as far back as the 1770s, the format's full potential was not realized until the founding of Pocket Books, which was followed by several competitors. Initially priced at 25¢ a copy, Pocket Books became a great success—during World War II, various wartime agencies shipped 25 million Pocket Books overseas; Shimkin was able to weather wartime paper rationing by taking over the paper quotas of publishing companies that were not able to use their entire allotment.

Five of Pocket Books's initial eleven titles remain in print: William Shakespeare's *Five Great Tragedies,* Pearl S. Buck's *The Good Earth,* James Hilton's *Lost Horizon,* Agatha Christie's *The Murder of Roger Ackroyd,* and Felix Salten's *Bambi.* Eventually, Pocket Books published original titles as well as reprints of hardcover books; its most successful publication was Dr. Benjamin Spock's *Baby and Child Care,* first printed in 1946. Periodically updated, more than 33 million copies of this book had been printed by 1989. Pocket Books was merged into Simon & Schuster in 1966.

In 1942 Simon & Schuster started another line of inexpensive books, in this case Little Golden Books, aimed at children. Full-color, high-quality children's books had not been available at such low prices—Little Golden Books, like Pocket Books, went for 25¢ a copy. Simon & Schuster was able to keep costs down by running 50,000 copies per title—an unheard of quantity. Simon & Schuster handled editorial, art, and sales functions for the books, while Western Printing and Lithographing Company took care of production and manufacturing. The venture was highly successful; by 1958 more than 400 million Little Golden Books had been sold, and the line had spawned such offshoots as Big Golden Books, Giant Golden Books, the *Golden Encyclopedia,* and Little Golden Records. Perhaps fearing a shakeout in the expanding children's book industry, or enticed by Western Printing's offer,

Simon & Schuster sold its half interest in the venture to Western Printing in 1958.

In 1944 Field Enterprises, the Chicago communications company headed by Marshall Field, acquired Simon & Schuster from its principals—Simon, Schuster, and Shimkin—for about $3 million. The principals stayed on with long-term management contracts and operated quite independently of Field Enterprises. In 1957, shortly after Marshall Field's death, the executors of his estate were eager to get out of the book-publishing business and sold Simon & Schuster back to the principals for $1 million.

Major titles published by Simon & Schuster in the 1940s and 1950s included William L. Shirer's *The Rise and Fall of the Third Reich;* Evan Hunter's *The Blackboard Jungle;* Meyer Levin's *Compulsion;* Kay Thompson's *Eloise;* Joseph Davies's *Mission to Moscow;* Mary McCarthy's story collection *The Company She Keeps;* Alexander King's *Mine Enemy Grows Older;* Herman Wouk's first book, *Aurora Dawn;* Laura Z. Hobson's *Gentleman's Agreement;* and Sloan Wilson's *The Man in the Gray Flannel Suit.* Humorous books also were important to the publishing house; these included cartoon collections by Walt Kelly, creator of "Pogo," and Al Capp of "Li'l Abner" fame, as well as verbal humor from James Thurber, P.G. Wodehouse, and S.J. Perelman. Moving into the 1960s, Simon & Schuster's popular authors included Harold Robbins, Jacqueline Susann, and Joseph Heller.

In 1957, Richard Simon, who was in poor health, retired from Simon & Schuster. He died in 1960, at which time Schuster and Shimkin each acquired half his stock, making them equal partners of the company. When Schuster retired in 1966, he sold his share to Shimkin. Simon & Schuster subsequently went public, with its stock traded in the over-the-counter market and later listed on the American Stock Exchange.

In the next few years, Simon & Schuster negotiated with several potential acquirers. In May 1970, the company agreed in principle to be bought by Norton Simon Inc., a diversified company whose interests included magazine publishing; however, the deal fell apart two months later, partly due to the stock market's drop. In November of that year, Kinney National Service Inc. reached an agreement in principle to buy Simon & Schuster, but Shimkin became dissatisfied with the offer during the negotiation process. In 1974, Simon & Schuster agreed to a merger with Harcourt Brace Jovanovich, which had substantial textbook-publishing operations but little in trade publishing, which was Simon & Schuster's strength. The deal was called off abruptly later that year; both parties cited the depressed stock market as a reason, but observers said Shimkin had been offended by certain public statements made by William Jovanovich: ". . . He implied that his firm was taking over Simon & Schuster lock, stock, and barrel, and one got the impression that Leon Shimkin would be fortunate if he got a job in the mailroom," longtime Simon & Schuster executive Peter Schwed later wrote in his book, *Turning the Pages: An Insider's Story of Simon & Schuster, 1924–1984.*

A successful deal came through in 1975, when Gulf + Western Industries purchased Simon & Schuster through a swap of one share of Gulf + Western stock for every ten shares of the publishing company. Gulf + Western, which also owns Paramount Pictures, changed its name to Paramount Communications in 1989. As a condition of the deal, Richard E. Snyder, who had been executive vice president of Simon & Schuster, moved up to the presidency; Snyder succeeded Seymour Turk, who had been named president in 1973 when Shimkin relinquished that role. Shimkin remained chairman of Simon & Schuster.

Under Snyder, Simon & Schuster expanded aggressively. It set up a dozen new imprints—brand names—under which it published books, and its sales grew impressively, from $44 million at the time of the sale to Gulf + Western to $210 million in 1983. By 1989, revenues were up to $1.3 billion. One of the most financially successful new ventures was a line of romance novels called Silhouette Books. Simon & Schuster launched Silhouette in the early 1980s after it lost the U.S. distribution rights to the Harlequin Romances, published by Harlequin Enterprises Ltd. of Toronto. Silhouette soon rivaled Harlequin in popularity among romance readers, and Harlequin's parent, Torstar Corporation, bought Silhouette from Simon & Schuster for $10 million in 1984.

Simon & Schuster entered the textbook field in 1984 by buying Esquire Inc., which no longer owned *Esquire* magazine, for $170 million. The acquisition nearly doubled the Simon & Schuster staff, to 2,300, and lifted it to the nation's sixth-largest book publisher, from thirteenth. Later that year, Gulf + Western bought Prentice-Hall Inc., a major textbook publisher, for about $710 million and merged it into Simon & Schuster early in 1985, making Simon & Schuster the nation's largest book publisher. Ginn & Company, another educational publisher, came into the Simon & Schuster fold in 1982, after being bought by Gulf + Western for $100 million; in 1986, Gulf + Western bought Silver Burdett Company, an elementary textbook publisher, for about $125 million and combined its operations with Ginn. Software also became an important business for Simon & Schuster in the increasingly computerized decade of the 1980s, as did books on computers.

With the diversification into textbooks and information services, trade-book publishing, which was Simon & Schuster's only business at the time of the sale to Gulf + Western, became only a small part of the business—about 6% of sales in 1989. However, it remained a high-profile aspect of the company, which published both fiction and nonfiction books that ranged from highly commercial to highly prestigious efforts. Major titles in the 1970s and 1980s included Bob Woodward and Carl Bernstein's *All the President's Men* and *The Final Days;* Woodward's *Wired* and *VEIL: The Secret Wars of the CIA, 1981–87;* Jackie Collins's *Hollywood Wives;* Taylor Branch's *Parting the Waters;* and former U.S. President Ronald Reagan's *An American Life.*

Principal Subsidiaries: Prentice Hall Inc.; Silver, Burdett & Ginn.

Further Reading: Schwed, Peter, *Turning the Pages: An Insider's Story of Simon & Schuster, 1924–1984,* New York, Macmillan, 1984.

—Trudy Ring

TIME WARNER INC.

75 Rockefeller Plaza
New York, New York 10019
U.S.A.
(212) 484-8000
Fax: (212) 522-0907

Public Company
Incorporated: 1990
Employees: 41,000
Sales: $11.52 billion
Stock Exchanges: New York Pacific

From its inception as the thinly capitalized passion of two young men in 1923 through its 1990 merger with Warner Communications, Time Inc. has been a steady, guiding force in U.S. media. As the world's largest media concern, Time Warner's mandate is to expand its global reach and transfer more of its communications arts from print to electronic form. In the process, Time Warner is on its way to becoming the quintessential self-marketing media producer, due in large part to the cultivation of synergies between Time and Warner assets.

The magazine that launched Time Inc. was conceived by Yale University sophomores Briton Hadden and Henry Robinson Luce during officers' training at South Carolina's Camp Jackson during World War I. "The paper," as they referred to it, was a dream they put on hold for three years, until February 1922, when they resigned their reporting jobs at the *Baltimore News*. With $86,000 of borrowed capital, Haddon and Luce moved to New York and prepared to launch the weekly news magazine *Time*. The magazine's initial mandate eventually became that of the entire company: to keep the public informed. Haddon and Luce spent a year organizing investors, staff, and tradesmen and collecting criticism and advice. The first issue of *Time* was dated March 3, 1923. It was 32 pages long. Haddon was *Time*'s editor; Luce its business manager.

Just as impressive as *Time*'s expansive editorial content was Hadden and Luce's then-novel approach to marketing the publication, which included postcard inserts soliciting subscribers and circulation of lists of prominent charter subscribers. The magazine was developed by a lean staff, who doubled as clerks. Luce's and Hadden's own salaries were at subsistence level.

For its first year, *Time* prospered modestly. When *Time* was just over a year old, it had 30,000 paid subscribers. On August 2, 1924, Luce and Hadden launched a second publication, the *Saturday Review of Literature*. Hadden, who served as editor, determined that everything printed had to be either directly attributable to a person or to the publication's own authority. Other of *Time*'s early journalistic innovations included the use of historical background in stories.

In 1925 Luce insisted that *Time*'s operations be moved to less-expensive facilities in Cleveland, Ohio—a move that Hadden and much of the publication's staff bitterly but unsuccessfully fought. Three years later, printing of the magazine was moved to R.R. Donnelley, in Chicago, while *Time*'s editorial office was moved back to New York. Hadden and Luce opted at the same time to switch titles and functions temporarily. Hadden became *Time*'s business manager, overseeing the publication's daily operation, while Luce took command of *Time*'s journalistic direction.

By 1928 Time Inc. posted a net profit, after tax, of $125,788 on revenues of $1.3 million. Making Time a lucrative proposition had taken its toll on Hadden, however, who began the new year fighting off a steptococcus virus. Hadden died at age 31 on February 27, 1929, six years after the first issue of *Time* was put to press.

To protect the ownership of the company, Luce and other Time staffers and directors bought 2,828.5 of Hadden's 3,361 Time shares at $360 a share. Hadden's family retained the remaining 532.5 shares. Within two years, Time Inc. stock peaked at $1,000 a share, and was split 20-to-1. In the meantime, Luce proposed to launch a new weekly magazine catering to business managers, called *Fortune*. With the Time Inc. board's approval, Luce set out to launch *Fortune*, on the eve of the Great Depression. *Fortune*'s first issue, in February 1930, won satisfying acceptance among its targeted audience. In September 1931 Parker Lloyd-Smith, *Fortune*'s managing editor and with Luce, co-developer, committed suicide.

Also in 1931, Time was making its controversial transition to radio. Time Inc.'s "The March of Time" radio show featured re-enactments of historical events. The show though popular, was a limited run promotion, which some felt threatened *Time*'s journalistic integrity. In 1935 the "March of Time" format reappeared, as a motion picture series of short subjects.

In April 1932 Time Inc. acquired 75% of *Architectural Forum*. Time completed its acquisition of that professional journal for builders the following year. Luce's personal interest in architecture had spurred Time's acquisition of *Architectural Forum*, which he reshaped throughout the 1930s to reflect the monumental socio-political events of the day. When New Deal legislation made $3.3 billion available for construction projects *Forum* editors rushed to press an 18-page guide explaining how builders could benefit. *Forum* editor Howard Nyers cultivated young architects; and, in 1938, Frank Lloyd Wright traveled to New York and produced an issue of *Forum* devoted to the subject of his works. Although *Forum* expanded its circulation from 5,500 to almost 40,000 in the decade following Time's acquisition of the publication in 1932, it posted only one year of profit. Luce resisted Time Inc.'s attempts to sell the publication. In 1936 Luce began to explore the concept of a weekly photo magazine, and Time brought pictures to print with the publication of *Life*, which first appeared in November 1936.

In 1937 Luce created Time Inc.'s, divisional system, the corporate organization that defined Time's operations for decades. Each of the company's three fundamental publications—*Time*,

Fortune, and *Life*—was assigned its own publisher, managing editor, and advertising director. Although a huge circulation success, *Life* was a major financial drain due to the unexpectedly high cost of producing the magazine. The explosive popularity of *Life* propelled Time Inc. into increasing circulation, and thus costs, pushing losses on the picture magazine into the millions. *Life* continued to lose money, a total of about $5 million, until January 1939, when the magazine turned its first profit.

While *Life* continued to lose money for Time directly, it was also the indirect cause of losses for the company as some readers of *Time* switched to *Life.* In May 1938 the company sought to relieve *Time's* circulation problems with the $25,000 acquisition of *Literary Digest.* About 60% of *Literary Digest's* 250,000 subscribers chose to transfer their subscriptions to *Time,* bolstering that magazine's sagging circulation.

In 1938, on the news that Time Inc.'s earnings were forecasted to drop a record $2 million, *Time's* publisher, Ralph Ingersoll, and Luce became embroiled in a fierce argument over the company's earnings. Ingersoll felt that Luce had diluted *Time's* earning potential by siphoning off *Time's* profits to start up and maintain publications such as *Fortune* and *Architectural Forum.* Ingersoll and Luce disagreed on editorial issues as well. In April 1939 Ingersoll took a leave of absence from Time, and did not return. Following Ingersoll's departure, Luce appointed himself *Time's* publisher and editor-in-chief.

Luce, who had strong ideas about how events in Europe lead to World War II should be reported, decided later in 1939 to devote more time to the editorial direction of Time Inc.'s magazines. Thus, in September 1939, Luce resigned as president and CEO of Time Inc., remaining editor-in-chief, and chairman Roy E. Larsen was elected to the posts Luce vacated. Like most other key top Time Inc. executives, Larsen was younger than many of his industry peers. Time enjoyed steady success during World War II, as its national magazines chronicled the war. Time Inc.'s publications dominated the newsstands. In 1941 *Time's* circulation was rapidly approaching one million. *Life* had weekly sales of 3.3 million magazines, and readership many times that. *Fortune* had a small but influential 160,000 readers. The organization of 2,500 full-time employees would grow to 5,500 over the next two decades of continued expansion.

Time assumed a prominent role reporting most major news events, including World War II and the McCarthy era. There were times when the magazine clashed openly with major decision-makers; President Franklin Roosevelt and *Time* criticized one another openly during the war. During the winter of 1941–1942, also in the name of covering the war, Luce and his wife, Clare Boothe Luce, reported on the state of world affairs from England and the Far East, respectively; he for *Time,* she for *Life.*

In the fall of 1942 Clare Boothe Luce won election to Congress from the Connecticut district that her stepfather, Dr. Albert E. Austin, had represented from 1938 to 1940. Her position in national politics raised the dilemma of how *Time's* magazines should cover the wife of their editor-in-chief. Eventually, Luce called for a blackout on the coverage of his wife in all of Time's magazines.

In 1945 *Time* redirected the energies of its pool of wartime correspondents and photographers, organizing them into an international reporting operation under the command of C.D. Jackson. Luce simultaneously redefined the job of publisher of *Time,* and appointed James A. Linen III to that position. Linen was the first of a generation of younger managers who came up through *Time's* editorial and sales ranks. Edward K. Thompson came up through the ranks to serve as managing editor of *Life* beginning in 1949.

Given more of a free hand than his predecessors, Thompson dismantled the periodical's divisional structure and launched the publication on its most successful decade. Soon afterward, the financially troubled *Fortune* was the subject of what Time Inc. executives referred to as a "re-think." Also in the postwar years, Luce adapted to technological advances that helped offset increases in the price of materials and wages. Despite reporting a 10% operating profit on a record high $120 million in revenues in 1947, Luce, ever the conservative manager, abandoned several projects including the construction of a New York skyscraper, due to the cost.

During the mid-1950s Time undertook to widen the appeal of long-time money-loser *Architectural Forum.* Although the company was successful in boosting circulation, the magazine continued to run at a loss. *Forum* was spun off to an existing nonprofit group in 1964. *House & Home,* a magazine Time had formed to complement *Forum* in 1952, was sold to McGraw-Hill, in 1964 as well. In 1953 Time launched *Life en Español,* a companion to *Life International. Life en Español* was suspended in 1969, however, and *Life International* was eliminated the following year.

In 1952 the company founded its Time-Life Broadcast subsidiary with a 50% interest in KOB and KOB-TV in Albuquerque, New Mexico. In a second bid for broadcast experience, Time acquired a majority interest in the Intermountain Broadcasting and Television Corporation of Salt Lake City, Utah, operators of the KDYL stations. Time acquired its first wholly owned and operated stations, KLZ-AM and KLZ-TV of Denver, Colorado, in 1954. Three years later, Time acquired the Bitner television and radio properties—WOOD in Grand Rapids, Michigan, WFBM in Indianapolis, Indiana; and WTCN in Minneapolis, Minnesota, for the then-record sum of $16 million. Eventually, Time sold its Salt Lake City and Minneapolis broadcast properties to acquire KOGO-TV in San Diego, California, and KERO-TV in Bakersfield, California.

In October 1970 the company announced plans to sell its broadcast properties to concentrate solely on cable television—a segment of the electronic media in which it already had amassed a considerable interest. By that time, Time had created East Texas Pulp and Paper Company, a joint enterprise with the Houston Oil Company, as its own source of paper. It also had erected a new Manhattan skyscraper at Rockefeller Center and successfully fended off competition from magazines like *Look* and the *Saturday Evening Post.* The company continued to operate under the watchful eye of its founder, Luce.

Arguably, Time's most important and lucrative long-term decision to diversify was the launch of *Sports Illustrated* in 1954. Sports in the United States then still tended to be seasonal, and sports marketing was relatively primitive. Despite the fact that *Sports Illustrated* did not turn its first profit for a decade, the magazine became very profitable.

In 1959, after recovering from his first heart attack, Luce began preparing to pass the title of editor-in-chief to Hedley

Donovan, who then was managing editor of *Fortune*. Although Luce did not finally surrender the title until 1964, in 1959 he set in motion a management reorganization that put a new generation of Time Inc. managers in control. The company prospered under its new leadership. From 1960 to 1964, net revenues jumped from $287.12 million to $412.51 million, and net income increased from $9.30 million to $26.53 million, due to sales expansion and tighter cost controls. This profitability had been enhanced by the 1961 creation of Time-Life Books, an extension of Time's already profitable book publishing operation. Time's new management initiated explosive growth. Time continued to expand overseas offices throughout the decade, and in 1962 Time acquired textbook publisher Silver Burdett in a $6 million stock swap. In 1964 Hedley Donovan was appointed to succeed Luce as editor-in-chief. In January 1968 Time bought book publisher Little, Brown and Company, for $17 million worth of Time stock. In 1966 Time initiated a joint venture with General Electric, General Learning Corporation. The venture was to sell a variety of learning tools, and was sold in 1974 at a loss.

Luce died February 28, 1967. Even after his death, Luce's influence was felt at the company where separation of editorial and publishing interests was considered sacrosanct. Time's new leadership continued to guide the company profitably. In December 1972, however, Time announced it would cease publication of *Life*, which had faced soaring production costs, shrinking advertising sales and circulation, and postal rate increases. *Life* had lost $30 million between 1969 and 1972. Throughout the 1960s and 1970s Time Inc. acquired a number of large and small enterprises in a continuing bid to diversify. Perhaps Time Inc.'s most costly and controversial acquisition at the time was its $129 million merger in 1973 with Temple Industries, a producer of lumber, plywood, and other building materials. Time took another step toward diversification in 1978 when it acquired Inland Container Corporation for $272 million.

In November 1972 Time's J. Richard Munro, who eventually became Time Inc.'s chairman and chief executive officer, through the Time subsidiary Sterling Information Services, Ltd., launched the pay-TV service Home Box Office (HBO). HBO was one of Time's few commercial successes. Even after Time-Life Films was phased out in the early 1980s, HBO itself continued to finance major films, invested in a movie distribution company, and joined Columbia Pictures and CBS in a studio venture.

HBO; *Money*, launched in 1972; and *People*, launched in 1974, emerged as Time's new profit centers during the 1970s and 1980s. Nicholas J. Nicholas Jr., who had risen through Time's corporate finance ranks and would later become its president and chief operating officer in 1986, recommended that Time divest its sluggish forest-products interests to concentrate on its video and print businesses, where future growth would be focused. Consequently, Temple-Inland was formed and spun off to Time shareholders in 1983. Time Inc. was left to focus on its seven magazines and their foreign-language equivalents, American Television and Communications Corporation, one of the country's largest cable companies, which is 82%-owned by Time Inc.; HBO and Cinemax, two of the country's most successful pay TV services begun in 1972 and 1980, respectively; and Time-Life Books.

Time added four new magazine titles in 1988, bringing its total number of published magazines to 24. It paid $185 million for a 50% interest in Whittle Communications, which provided satellite public affairs and news programming direct to classrooms. It was involved in international publishing ventures with foreign-based companies like Hachette, Arnoldo Mondadori, and Seibu. Time's growth continued through the 1980s, culminating in the 1989 agreement to acquire Warner Communications Inc. for $14 billion, creating the world's largest entertainment and media concern. Time itself had become an attractive takeover target in an era of unprecedented leveraging and hostile bids, and thus had accepted Warner's invitation to merge.

The proposed Time-Warner combination was nearly thwarted by an unsolicited takeover bid for Time from Paramount of $175 cash per share, or $10.7 billion. The raid proved unsuccessful, and cost Paramount $80 million. It also required Time to rework the logistics of its merger with Warner, burdening itself with $12 billion in debt. Time and Warner had also engaged in a swap of each other's stock early in the merger process, in an additional defensive move.

Although strategically driven, not all of Time Inc.'s board members, especially Henry Luce III and Arthur Temple, were convinced that the merger was wise. Munro and Nicholas engaged in one-on-one consultation with each director to secure unanimous approval for the January 1990 transaction. The merger created a vertically integrated company.

At the first annual shareholders meeting of Time Warner, in spring 1990, Munro did as expected and announced he would step down as co-chairman and co-chief executive officer of Time Warner Inc. but would remain chairman of the board's executive committee. Nicholas assumed the co-chief executive title while retaining the job of president. The merger agreement called for Nicholas to succeed Time Warner chairman and co-chief executive Steven Ross as the company's sole chief executive in mid-1994.

Time Warner claims that all of its media and entertainment franchises rank first or second in their categories. Time Warner's cable pay-television services, Home Box Office and Cinemax, posted record performances. Pay-TV revenues from Home Box Office and programming continued to grow, 7.6% in 1990. Time combined its Time-Life Books and Book-of-the-Month-Club operations. Its American Television and Communications Corporation achieved record revenues and earnings on four million basic cable and three million premium subscriptions. Time also sold off Scott, Foresman, its textbook publisher, in December 1989, for $455 million because it no longer fit into its core businesses.

The first year as a merged entity, Time Warner created Time Warner Publishing to oversee all of the company's book and magazine publishing activities, which account for $3 billion of its annual combined revenues. The new unit launched such new magazines as *Martha Stewart Living* and acquired the 50% interest in *In Health* that it did not already own. Time Warner made a small effort to begin tapping the synergies of their combined assets when, in February 1990, Time launched *Entertainment Weekly* using Warner's tape and book subscription lists. Time Warner revealed plans to open a nationwide chain of retail stores, like those operated by The Walt Disney Company, to sell merchandise that features Bugs Bunny and other of Warner Brothers's Looney Tunes characters or products related to other of the company's vast operations. Time Warner also began taking a more creative approach to cross marketing its products and publications. For instance, in November 1990, Time Warner signed an unprecedented agreement with Chrysler for advertising in seven of Time Warner's national magazines and cable group, and to make product placements in selected Warner Brothers film releases.

To the surprise of many, within months of the merger, the highly leveraged Time Warner announced the acquisition of Lane Publishing Company, publisher of *Sunset* magazine for $225 million—$80 million in cash and $145 million in preferred stock. In another surprising but savvy move, Time Warner in April 1990 offered to provide a $650 million bridge loan to Pathe Communications Company to help with its $1.4 billion acquisition of MGM/UA Communications Company in exchange for certain valuable MGM/UA assets including the United Artists film library. However, Time Warner withdrew its offer, and Time Warner and Pathe eventually sued each other over the aborted agreement. In October 1990, the companies opted to settle their differences out of court when Time Warner agreed to pay $125 million for the international home video rights to 1,700 titles in the United Artists and Pathe/Cannon film libraries for more than 12 years.

By late 1990, the newly merged Time Warner still was struggling with ways to establish joint ventures with various international concerns that would bring much needed new development funds into its operations while offering special expertise and foreign business connections. Management continued to promise shareholders a reduction and financial restructuring of Time Warner's nearly $11 billion debt. With more than $2.5 billion in bank loans due in early 1993, one option the company had was to sell its partial stakes in businesses like Atari, Hasbro, the Franklin Mint, Six Flags Corporation, record clubs like Columbia House, Cineamerica theaters, and Turner Broadcasting System Inc. A weak economy in 1990 kept Time Warner from resorting to such a move since it could not command a premium for its business interests in a sluggish marketplace.

In the meantime, the company worked diligently to keep Wall Street at bay. Although initially supportive of the transaction, some Wall Street analysts soured on Time Warner six months after the merger. In late May 1991 Time Warner announced an unorthodox rights offering. The company planned to issue 34.5 million shares at between $63 and $105 per share, priced according to how many shareholders participated. In July, following vigorous objections from the Securities and Exchange Commission and many powerful investors, Time Warner replaced the plan with a traditional $80-per-share offering. Citing the unpredicted softness of media advertising, tight financing and an uncertain economy, Time Warner officials conceded it would take them longer than expected to arrange the joint ventures and limited equity placements that would launch the merged company back into a development mode.

Principal Subsidiaries: American Television and Communications Corporation (82%); Asiaweek Limited (Hong Kong, 84%) 541 Fairbanks Corp.; Hankook Ilbo Time-Life Ltd. (Korea, 50%); Home Box Office Inc.; Sunset Publishing Corporation; Time Australia Magazine Pty. Ltd.; Time Canada Ltd.; The Time Inc. Book Company; The Time Inc. Magazine Company; Time Information Services, Inc.; Time International Inc.; Time-Life Books (Australia) Pty. Ltd.; Time-Life International B.V. (Netherlands); Time-Life Libraries Inc.; Time-Life Pictures, Inc.; Time-Life Video Inc.; Time Life International do Brasil Ltda. (Brazil); Time Overseas Ventures, Inc.; Time TBS Holdings, Inc.; Time-T.I. Communications Co., Ltd. (Japan, 10%); Time Video Holdings Inc.; Time Warner Cable Inc.; Time Warner Foundation Inc.; Time Warner Telecommunications Inc.; TPS Acquisiton Inc.; The Washington Star Company; Warner Communications, Inc.

Further Reading: Elson, Robert T., *Time Inc.: The Intimate History of a Publishing Enterprise—1923–1941*, New York, Athenaeum, 1968; Elson, Robert T., *The World of Time Inc.: The Intimate History of a Publishing Enterprise—1941–1960*, New York, Athenaeum, 1973; Prendergast, Curtis, and Geoffrey Colvin, *The World of Time Inc.: The Intimate History of a Changing Enterprise—1960–1980*, New York, Athenaeum, 1986; "Warner Communications Inc.," in *International Directory of Company Histories*, Vol. II, edited by Lisa Mirabile, Chicago, St. James Press, 1990.

—Diane C. Mermigas

Times Mirror

THE TIMES MIRROR COMPANY

Times Mirror Square
Los Angeles, California 90053
U.S.A.
(213) 237-3700
Fax: (213) 237-3714

Public Company
Incorporated: 1884 as The Times-Mirror Company
Employees: 29,121
Sales: $3.63 billion
Stock Exchanges: New York Pacific

The Times Mirror Company is a publisher of books, magazines, and newspapers. It is among the largest of multiple-system cable TV operators in the United States, and operates four broadcast television stations, all network affiliates. The company publishes law books, technical and scientific books, business books, training manuals, and art books, among others. Magazines include *Field & Stream, Home Mechanix,* and *Outdoor Life.* Times Mirror publishes a broad range of newspapers, including the *Los Angeles Times,* with daily circulation in excess of one million. Its cable system is extensive, and its broadcast properties include four network affiliate stations.

From its unassuming beginnings as a four-page daily newspaper saved from an early demise by a printing and binding company, The Times Mirror Company has demonstrated a high degree of resourcefulness. More than 100 years and many new ventures later, Times Mirror in the early 1990s was still cross-pollinating the conventional and more advanced media. Its multimedia focus is held together by a clear devotion to journalism.

The Mirror Printing and Binding House, established in 1873 primarily for commercial printing, agreed in 1881 to print a new daily newspaper called the *Los Angeles Daily Times,* soon renamed the *Los Angeles Times.* The publishers abandoned the project shortly after it was launched, although the printers kept the newspaper going. Seven months later, Civil War veteran General Harrison Gray Otis was named full-time editor. In 1884 Otis and Colonel H.H. Boyce purchased both the newspaper and the printing company, incorporating them into The Times-Mirror Company. The hyphen was dropped before long. Two years later, Otis fully acquired the concern that declared itself "a new and hopeful candidate for a share of the patronage of the community." The newspaper set out, through its headlines and stories, to attract new residents and businesses to the sleepy town of Los Angeles. Over time, the newspaper found itself promoting a free harbor at San Pedro, in 1891, and construction of the city's first freeway, in 1930.

By 1948 Times Mirror had set off on its first buying binge, resulting in its acquisition of Publishers Paper Company of Lake Oswego, Oregon. In the 1980s, Publishers Paper emerged as the third-largest newsprint producer in the United States. About 70% of the newsprint produced by Publishers Paper in the early 1990s was sold to Times Mirror. Another major acquisition came in 1961 when Times Mirror absorbed Englewood, Colorado–based Jeppesen Sanderson, the world's leading publisher of air navigation information and flight-training systems. Also in 1961, Times Mirror acquired the H.M. Goushā Company, a producer of modern travel maps and pioneer of the accordion-fold map, in San Jose, California.

By 1963 Times Mirror was expanding into other specialized publishing, acquiring New York City–based Matthew Bender & Company, the largest publisher of legal forms and legal treatises in the United States. Two years later the company acquired Chicago-based Year Book Medical Publishers, publishers of medical reference books. Times Mirror bought the 17-year-old art book publisher Harry N. Abrams, Inc., of New York City in 1966. The following year, Times Mirror acquired the C.V. Mosby Company of St. Louis, Missouri, which has since become the world's leading publisher of health-science books.

The company's entrance into magazine publishing came in 1967 when it acquired *Popular Science, Outdoor Life, Golf Magazine,* and *Ski Magazine.* Within 20 years after the acquisition, Times Mirror Magazines, Inc. had more than nine million readers. It operated two national book clubs with annual sales in excess of two million books. Times Mirror's other strategic move into complementary media came in 1968 when it purchased Co-Axial Systems Engineering Company and its seven cable franchises in southern California, with a base of 5,700 subscribers. Times Mirror embarked on rapid growth in cable that soon included the acquisition of smaller systems in southern California and on Long Island, New York, expanding its subscriber base to 22,000. Its most substantial increase in subscribers came with the 1979 purchase of Communications Properties, Inc., then the nation's eighth-largest cable operator, in addition to three microwave companies in Ohio and Texas.

Under the leadership of Robert Erburu, in 1970, Times Mirror acquired the 91-year-old *Dallas Times Herald.* That same year, the company also acquired *Newsday*—the tabloid-sized Long Island, New York, daily, that had become the prototype for the nation's suburban press. Its next major foray into new media was the formation of Times Mirror Broadcasting in 1970 that initially was comprised of KDFW-TV, Dallas, Texas, then known as KRLD-TV; KTBC-TV in Austin, Texas; KTVI-TV in St. Louis, Missouri; WVTM-TV in Birmingham, Alabama; WHTM-TV in Harrisburg, Pennsylvania; WSTM-TV in Syracuse, New York; and WETM-TV in Elmira, New York. Erburu became president in 1974.

In 1977 the purchase of Southern Connecticut Newspapers Inc. gave Times Mirror control of two of the oldest Connecticut newspapers, *The Advocate* of Stamford and *Greenwich Time.* The acquisition of The Sporting News Publishing Company of St. Louis, Missouri, that year gave Times Mirror control of *The Sporting News,* a weekly magazine dating back to 1886 that eventually narrowed its focus to become known as "Baseball's Bible."

Times Mirror's 1978 acquisition of Graphic Controls Corporation of Buffalo, New York, was another bid to strengthen the company's presence in the medical-information field with its production of recording charts, instrument marking systems, disposable medical products, and coated imaging papers. Times Mirror kept returning to its roots, however, for acquisitions that strengthened both its editorial muscle and revenue base. In 1979 Times Mirror acquired *The Hartford Courant,* of Connecticut the nation's oldest continuously published newspaper. *The Courant*'s proud heritage included reproducing the full text of the Declaration of Independence in July 1776, when the paper was 12 years old. In 1980 Times Mirror acquired *The Denver Post.* Four years later, in 1984, the company acquired Call-Chronicle Newspapers, Inc., now *The Morning Call,* which serves a nine-county region in eastern Pennsylvania and in New Jersey.

To commemorate the beginning of its second century, Times Mirror adopted a new logo in 1984—a stylized version of the eagle that had appeared on the front of the *Los Angeles Times* and its other publications. In that year, Times Mirror's profit of $420.8 million was an increase of 13% from a year earlier. The company's 1984 revenues were a record $2.8 billion, also up 13% from the prior year. Newspaper publishing remained the single biggest revenue contributor.

In 1984 Times Mirror began a restructuring process that ended two years later in a flurry of buying and selling. In 1986 Times Mirror paid $600 million for A.S. Abell Company, owner of *The Baltimore Sun.* Times Mirror paid Dow Jones & Company $135 million for Richard D. Irwin Inc., a textbook publisher, in 1988. It also added *Broadcasting* (sold in May 1991) and *The National Journal* to its magazine holdings for $75 million and $10 million, respectively, during the restructuring, while selling the struggling *Dallas Times Herald* for $110 million. The company disposed of five television stations, a cable system in Las Vegas, Nevada, and a number of its non-media holdings. Times Mirror sold off $1 billion in assets and spent $750 million on acquisitions for its core print- and electronic-media businesses during the three-year restructuring.

In 1985 *Newsday* expanded, and began to publish *New York Newsday,* an edition targeted to the Brooklyn and Queens boroughs of New York City. In 1986 the company sold H.M. Goushā Company and the national book clubs. After 1986 Times Mirror turned its attention to capital expenditures, particularly in its newspaper operations, where equipment had to be updated. In 1987 it launched a five-year $385 million capital-investment plan, bringing new plant and facilities to the *Los Angeles Times.*

In 1987 David Laventhol succeeded Robert Erburu as president of *Times Mirror* although Erburu continued as chairman and chief executive officer of the company. Also that year, Times Mirror bought four magazines from Diamandis Communications for $176.5 million: *Field & Stream, Yachting, Home Mechanix,* and *Skiing Magazine.* The acquisition came at a time when Times Mirror began experimenting with new start-up publications, such as *Sports Inc.,* which folded after a 15-month trial for lack of advertiser support.

The company sold the money-losing newspapers Denver *Post* and *Dallas Times Herald* in separate deals for a total of $205 million to Dallas publisher William Dean Singleton. Among the other assets sold as part of the restructuring was an 80% interest in Publishers Paper.

Erburu brought Times Mirror through its restructuring to emerge in much better shape, in the midst of a nationwide advertising slump that adversely affected all of U.S. media, beginning in the second half of the 1980s. That development became especially critical for a company like Times Mirror, whose newspaper operations accounted for close to 60% of its overall corporate revenues. Newspaper segment operating profits declined 61% the first nine months of 1990 compared to the same period a year earlier. In the same period, net income fell 40% to $134.9 million.

In late 1990 workers at the *Daily News* in New York City went on strike, and Times Mirror's *New York Newsday,* which competed with the *Daily News,* got a boost to its growth. Despite the fact that *New York Newsday* continued to lose money—a cumulative $100 million through 1989 by some analysts' estimates—*Los Angeles Times* president and *New York Newsday* creator Laventhol continued to support *New York Newsday.*

By 1990 Times Mirror had become the 12th-largest multiple cable system operator in the country and operated four network television affiliates. It had spent $1.5 billion acquiring new businesses throughout the 1980s—$583 million on newspaper properties; $595 million on book, magazine, and other publishing acquisitions; $235 million on cable TV systems; and $82 million on broadcast properties. Capital expenditures during the previous decade totaled $2.53 billion—more than half of which was concentrated in its newspaper operations. During that same decade, revenues grew from $1.87 billion to $3.52 billion. The C.V. Mosby Company and Year Book Medical Publishers merged in April 1990 to become Mosby-Year Book.

Further Reading: "Top 100 Media Companies," *Advertising Age,* June 29, 1987; Grover, Ronald, "Times Mirror's Page-One Turnaround Story," *Business Week,* June 20, 1988; Reilly, Patrick, "Waiting for the Pay-off," *Advertising Age,* May 24, 1989; Cohen, Roger, "New Aggressiveness at Times Mirror," *The New York Times,* December 3, 1990.

—Diane C. Mermigas

TOPPAN PRINTING CO., LTD.

1, Kanda Izumi-cho
Chiyoda-ku, Tokyo 101
Japan
(03) 3835-5741
Fax: (03) 3835-0674

Public Company
Incorporated: 1900
Employees: 11,420
Sales: ¥976.02 billion (US$7.19 billion)
Stock Exchanges: Tokyo Osaka Luxembourg

Toppan is the second-largest Japanese printing company, behind Dai Nippon Printing, and one of the world's largest. Its business includes commercial printing, publications, packaging, interior decor and industrial materials, clothing, precision electronic components, securities and business forms, compact discs, and computer processing. Toppan has become an information and consumer-services company with roots in high technology.

Toppan was established in 1900 by technicians from Japan's Ministry of Finance, who used a type of relief printing that was one of the leading printing technologies in Japan at the time. It initially focused on printing securities, books for publishers, and business forms.

The company was founded as Japan's modernization drive was in full stride, and the need for modern typeset printing was increasing. The Sino-Japanese War of 1894 had created a great increase in printing needs and paper demand as more newspapers were read and more documents needed. A slump in printing and papermaking followed Toppan's first year of business at the end of the war in 1901. In 1904, however, the onset of the Russo-Japanese War created an even greater demand for newspapers and magazines than had the Sino-Japanese war had. Japan defeated both China and Russia, and began a period of military and economic expansion, aided by the establishment of a modern currency system during the 1880s.

Printing also boomed during World War I. After the war, printing and publishing increased. In 1927 almost 20,000 new book titles and 40 million magazines were published. During the 1930s, as Japan came to be ruled by military dictatorship, publishers and writers were suppressed or imprisoned and books were banned. Publishing and printing suffered in such an environment. Further, during World War II paper shortages

and the decline of the Japanese economy hurt the printing industry. The printing industry recovered after the war, however, and grew rapidly during the 1960s and 1970s. Encyclopedias and sets of the complete works of authors were the chief areas of growth, as was periodical printing.

Toppan quickly expanded after the war, founding Toppan Containers in 1952 as a manufacturer of specialty cardboard and other packaging materials. Several of Japan's large publishing houses launched successful weeklies in 1959, bringing more business to printers. In 1961 Toppan acquired Froebel-Kan, a company specializing in children's products. It had since developed a full line of children's books and teaching materials used at nurseries and kindergartens throughout Japan. It had produced and translated picture books, exporting books that have been translated in 50 languages and translated foreign stories into Japanese. Also in 1961, Toppan established Toppan Shoji, a general trading company, by taking over Tokai Paper Industries, a manufacturer and marketer of stock and bond certificates, established in 1947. Toppan Shoji soon handled trade in construction materials, electrical appliances, home furnishings, and office products. It also produces precision electronics, and character-brand products. By the 1980s it manufactured waste-water processing systems that used microorganisms to break down fats and oils in industrial and restaurant waste.

In 1962 Toppan became the first Japanese printer to open a Hong Kong plant, staffing it with cheaper labor, and equipping the plant with European presses. It initially worked exclusively in offset printing, especially color work. It established an apprenticeship program in Hong Kong to send Chinese technicians to Japan for training. This plant, together with that of rival Dai Nippon, opened in 1963, enabled the Hong Kong printing industry to grow. By the 1980s it was competing with Japan's printing business.

During the 1960s Toppan gradually added planning and design to its commercial printing business, and moved into the production of electronic circuits through advanced printing processes. At the same time, U.S. publishers were beginning to buy from Japanese printers because they charged less than U.S. printers, even with shipping costs. By the mid-1960s, Toppan's business was growing at about 6% a year. The following year Toppan established Toppan Moore, a joint venture with the Moore Corporation Limited, of Canada, the world's largest business-forms manufacturer. By the 1980s Toppan Moore had become the largest Japanese business-forms manufacturer.

Rotary offset printing, particularly in color, advanced in the 1970s. Soon afterward, U.S. publishers provided more four-color work for Japanese printers, including Toppan, an industry leader in color printing. In 1979 Toppan became the first Japanese printer to build a U.S. production plant, a separation plant in Mountainside, New Jersey. Toppan continued growing, steadily expanding into nonprinting areas such as packaging. In 1978 Toppan unveiled an easy-to-uncap heat seal for packaging, and in 1980 a paper container that kept food fresh for six months. In 1980 the company developed a jet printer, beginning a push into computer technology. In 1983 Toppan developed Scan Note, a computerized process for setting up pages of music for publishing. The next year the company unveiled an electrochromatic display screen, utilizing reflected light. It was hoped that the screens would replace liquid crystal displays. It also jointly developed an electronic imaging color filter. In the same year, Toppan Moore developed a smart card with two integrated circuits. Smart cards are integrated circuits, embedded in plastic, that store information electronically.

In 1985 Toppan jointly formed Videotex Network Japan, a videotext firm. It also developed a paper-thin 1.5 volt manganese-zinc battery. In 1986 the company developed a portable smart-card system, and aseptic packaging equipment for filling pre-sterilized bags. In 1986 profits were US$113 million on sales of US$4.67 billion.

In 1987 Toppan moved into the quickly growing compact-disc market, forming Denshi Media Services, a compact- and optical-disc services company, with the Netherlands-based Philips. It also increased production of liquid-crystal-display filters to over 100,000 a month to keep up with demand. In 1988 Toppan bought the printed-circuit division of the U.S.-based Herco Technology. It also put on the market a non-contact smart card using a central processor, and a desktop publishing system that allowed a composer to write and edit music. Recognizing that electronic publishing was an area of growing importance, Toppan jointly developed a compact disc that held an entire encyclopedia. In 1988 profits were US$120 million, on sales of US$4.49 billion.

In 1980, a Japanese-language word processor finally came into use, its development slowed by the large number of characters in the language. This was the first major development in creating electronic publishing in Japan. As the 1980s progressed, computers and word-processing programs proliferated, and toward the end of the decade even small businesses could afford a laser printer. It was a logical step for Toppan—and competitors like Dai Nippon—to move into information processing. This view was shared by the Paper and Printing Committee of the Industrial Structural Council, an advisory organ of Japan's Ministry of International Trade and Industry. In 1988 the Paper and Printing Committee released a report predicting a dwindling need for conventional printing, and urging a change in the industry's direction. It recommended that the printing industry use its knowledge of information processing to contribute to an information-oriented society. The shipment value of printed matter in Japan had reached ¥6.2 trillion in 1986, and the committee predicted it would continue to grow at an annual rate of 6.5%, reaching ¥15 trillion by 2000. The committee said printing firms should push to expand high-tech printing techniques and information processing.

Toppan responded to the trend toward an information-oriented society in a variety of ways in the late 1980s. Toppan Moore moved into general information services, developing software and hardware to operate and manage clerical work. It launched Toppan Moore Learning with U.S.-based Applied Learning International to develop and market educational software. Subsidiary Toppan Moore Systems developed computer software and peripheral hardware and offered marketing and training services. Data Card Japan, a joint venture with U.S.-based Data Card Corporation, offered a wide range of card-related products and services.

In 1985 Toppan bought Kyodo Kako, a manufacturer of furniture materials, interior decorating products, and electrical appliances. The company used printing technology to create decorative surfaces on wood materials.

Printing companies in Japan generally had waited for customer orders before printing. During the 1980s competition increased and Toppan moved into other services. It promoted its after-printing distribution service and information-related services such as direct-mail lists.

In the late 1980s, partial deregulation of the Japanese financial industry led to a greater variety of financial products, all of which needed to be printed. The deregulation also allowed financial institutions to advertise, creating still more business for Toppan. Deregulation increased credit-card competition in Japan, a boon for Toppan since revenue from printing credit cards was the most profitable part of the company's securities division. Several private Japanese railways began accepting paid cards with a magnetic band on the back that recorded how much they were worth. Toppan printed the millions of cards used every year through a joint venture with TDK Corporation. In the 1980s, lottery-ticket sales soared in Japan, and Toppan did most of the printing. In the late 1980s Toppan became the first private company to print Japanese postage stamps.

Toppan and its main rival, Dai Nippon, became leading producers of smart cards. In 1988 the company developed advances in integrated-circuit cards that offered better signal reliability than competing cards. The cards were often used as part of access-control systems, and, because of their durability, could be used at factories and construction sites, where other cards could often not be used. In 1989 Toppan developed a method for printing color photographs directly on plastic identification cards. Formerly, color photographs had to be pasted on or laminated into the cards. The company hoped to print credit cards, driver's licenses, and other identification cards with this new technology.

Toppan's research with glass films resulted in a new type of packaging, brought out in 1988. The glass, deposited in a vacuum onto a sheet of special film, acted as an ultrathin, flexible, transparent barrier, and was designed for microwavable food. In 1988 Toppan established Toppan West in San Diego, California, which company bought Industrial Circuits, a U.S. manufacturer of printed circuit boards, later that year.

In early 1989 Toppan's electronic precision components division established a design subsidiary, the Toppan Technical Design Center. It expanded its shadow-mask manufacturing plant in Shiga to make masks for high-definition television and video displays. The high-definition market was expected to be a high-growth area in the 1990s. Later that year Toppan broke ground for a new industrial materials plant in Satte, Japan. The plant was to concentrate on thermal-ink ribbons and other products related to the rapidly growing field of office automation.

In 1989 Toppan established an industrial materials division to develop and manufacture new materials by combining coating, vapor deposition, laminating, shaping, and processing technologies with traditional printing. It has worked with thermal transfer ribbons, high-performance film, adhesive paper, and hot stamping foil.

In 1989 Toppan and Japan Pulp and Paper jointly established Toval Japon in Spain to manufacture decorative furniture boards for Europe. Toppan saw the new company, along with Toppan's offices in Düsseldorf and London, as the foundation of Toppan's presence in the European Community after the 1992 unification. In 1989 Toppan created a U.S. subsidiary, Toppan Interamerica, and formed Marionet Corporation, a marketing consulting corporation, with three other companies.

Marionet processed point-of-sale information and sent the results to customers through on-line computer networks.

Toppan's planning division produces events such as expositions, anticipating the demand for related products: posters, entrance tickets, image technology, and pamphlets. The company launched the Toppan Media School in 1989 to train employees in design, production, and marketing for conventions and promotional events, and to devise new technologies. Perhaps the clearest examples of how Toppan and printing are changing occurred during the Toppan-produced Osaka Expo '90. Toppan connected high-definition television monitors showing live images of the event together with a new digital transmission technology, converted the television images into print using Toppan-developed software, and used the images to create a full-color bulletin distributed to expo visitors the same day.

In 1990 the company established Toppan Printronics U.S.A., a joint venture with Texas Instruments, of which Toppan owned 85%, investing US$5.7 million. The subsidiary was to make semiconductor photomasks for the United States and Europe. Toppan also expanded its Asaka securities printing plant, which it claimed was the largest in the world, to keep up with the steadily increasing demand.

By 1990 the company had nine printing plants in Tokyo, five in Osaka, and seven elsewhere in Japan. It had 53 sales offices in Japan and 21 overseas offices. To keep ideas flowing between offices, Toppan's commercial printing division launched the Toppan Idea Center to concentrate on planning and marketing. During the 1980s the commercial division had developed a computerized typesetting system and an image database, information from which could be transmitted between Toppan offices over telephone lines. The system helped Toppan lower costs and shorten delivery times. Toppan assigned work stations tied into this database to some of its customers, who could then use the database for design layouts, transmitting them directly to a Toppan plant for platemaking.

Toppan co-developed with Sony an optical reader that directly translated text into a computer, speeding the creation of an information database. Because of the labor shortage in Japan, Toppan's expanding commercial division had trouble hiring enough employees in the late 1980s, but focused on streamlining and automation as ways to compensate.

To promote its printing, Toppan had been involved with art exhibits, for which it often prints exhibition catalogues, and international book fairs, where it promotes its high-quality art books and magazine printing. Japanese magazine printing is complicated, however, because many magazines use several kinds of paper and printing techniques in a single issue.

The publications division suffered during the late 1980s as the boom in new magazines that started in the early 1980s came to an end. Readership diversified, causing a greater variety of publications in smaller lots and decreasing profits. To compensate, Toppan began offering editorial services, sending employees to clients to do electronic editing of copy returned to customers, thus decreasing turnaround time. On the positive side, Toppan, which had gotten into compact disc printing relatively early, got more orders as the discs increased in popularity.

Toppan established Toppan Forest in 1990, a high-tech showroom with a computer system supplying information on interior decor materials. It stores up to 40,000 color images and displays them in three-dimensional space on a computer terminal. Toppan continues to develop in the high-technology areas of information service.

Principal Subsidiaries: Toppan Printing Co. (H.K.), Ltd. (Hong Kong); Toppan Printing Co. (Singapore), Pte., Ltd.; P.T. Toppan Printing Indonesia; P.T. Toppan Indah Offset Printing (Indonesia); Toppan Printing Co., Ltd. (China); Toppan Printing Co. (Australia), Pty., Ltd.; Toppan Printing Co. (America), Inc. (U.S.A.); Graphics Arts Center (U.S.A.); Graphic Arts Center/West (U.S.A.); Toppan Interamerica Inc. (U.S.A.); Toppan Printronics (U.S.A.), Inc.; Toppan Printing Co. (U.K.), Ltd.; Toppan Printing GmbH (Germany); Toval Japon S.A. (Spain); Toyo Ink Manufacturing Co. Ltd.; Tokyo Shoseki Co. Ltd.; Froebel-Kan Co. Ltd.; Toppan-Shoji Co. Ltd.; Toppan Containers Co. Ltd.; Kyodo Kako Co. Ltd.; Total Media Development Institute Co., Ltd.; Tamapoli Co., Ltd.; Hino Offset Printing Co., Ltd.; Tokyo Magnetic Printing Co., Ltd.; Toppan Co., Ltd.; Toppan Direct Mail Center Co., Ltd.; Toppan Travel Service Corp.; Toppan Sales Co., Ltd.; Toppan Graphics Inc. (U.S.A.); Toppan West Inc. (U.S.A.).

Further Reading: Frank, Jerome P., "Asia Printers Gearing Up for Move into U.S.," *Publishers Weekly,* June 29, 1984; Nomato, Fukashi, "Publishing-related Machinery Should Keep Fast Pace in the 21th Century," *Business JAPAN,* March 1990.

—Scott M. Lewis

TRIBUNE COMPANY

435 North Michigan Avenue
Chicago, Illinois 60611
U.S.A.
(312) 222-9100
Fax: (312) 222-1573

Public Company
Incorporated: 1861
Employees: 16,100
Sales: $2.35 billion
Stock Exchanges: New York Midwest Pacific

Tribune Company is a diversified media company. It is publisher of the *Chicago Tribune* and daily newspapers in six other cities. It operates independent television stations in Chicago; New York; Los Angeles; Atlanta, Georgia; Denver, Colorado; and New Orleans, Louisiana, and radio stations in Chicago; New York; and Sacramento, California. The company also produces and distributes news and entertainment programs for television and owns the Chicago Cubs baseball team. Newsprint production rounds out the company's business activities. Tribune Company was the 11th-largest media company in the United States at the end of 1989.

The company originated with the first publication of the *Chicago Daily Tribune* on June 10, 1847. The newspaper's founders were James Kelly, who also owned a weekly literary newspaper, and two other journalists, John E. Wheeler and Joseph K.C. Forrest. At the time, the paper was one of three major dailies published in Chicago.

The founders soon parted company, however, and the *Chicago Daily Tribune* had gone through several changes in ownership and editorial policy by 1855, when it was sold to a man who would be influential in its history, former Cleveland, Ohio, newspaperman Joseph Medill. His associates in the purchase were Charles Ray, a physician, journalist, and political activist in Springfield and Galena, Illinois, and John Vaughan, a co-proprietor of Medill's Cleveland paper. Under Medill's leadership, the *Tribune* maintained a strong anti-slavery stand but abandoned the anti-foreign, anti-Catholic, and anti-saloon campaigns that the paper had led previously. It also reorganized its presentation of news, establishing separate departments for local, national, and international stories.

Coming out of the economic panic of 1857, the *Tribune* was having financial problems, but so was a competitor, the *Democratic Press*. The two papers merged in 1858, resulting in the *Chicago Daily Press and Tribune*. Active in the partisan journalism common in its day, the paper was allied with the recently formed Republican Party. It supported Abraham Lincoln in his unsuccessful campaign to unseat U.S. Senator Stephen Douglas in 1858 and in his successful campaign for the presidency in 1860.

In 1860 the paper's name was returned to the *Chicago Daily Tribune.* The following year, the Tribune Company was incorporated, and the paper became the *Chicago Tribune.* That year, 1861, also brought the start of the Civil War, during which the *Tribune* gained national fame for its excellent wartime news coverage and its support of the Union cause. The paper's Sunday edition appeared during the war, disappeared for a while, and was resumed after the war, to the chagrin of local ministers. In October 1871 came a disaster against which the *Tribune* had warned—the Great Chicago Fire—which devastated the city, filled as it was with wooden buildings and suffering a lack of firefighting equipment and regulations. As the city rebuilt, Joseph Medill was elected mayor on the Union-Fireproof ticket. Medill declined to run for a second term in 1873; in 1874 he emerged victorious in a struggle with managing editor Horace White for editorial control of the *Tribune.*

The *Tribune* grew and prospered, as did Chicago itself, in the years after the fire. As it entered the last decade of the 19th century, the paper was attractive, vocal, and profitable, reporting annual income of $1.5 million a year. In 1895 the Tribune lowered newsstand prices and increased circulation. Joseph Medill's son-in-law, Robert Patterson, became increasingly important to the *Tribune;* he was named general manager in 1890, after having been managing editor for seven years. At Medill's death at age 76 in 1899, Patterson assumed the titles of editor-in-chief of the newspaper and president of Tribune Company. Medill's last words reportedly were, "What is the news this morning?"

In 1900 a formidable competitor came to Chicago, as William Randolph Hearst began publishing the *Chicago American,* a paper with a Democratic political alliance and a sensational reporting style. It was an evening paper but later added a morning edition as a direct competitor to the *Tribune.* The *Tribune* and the Hearst papers engaged in a circulation war that lasted 20 years, marked at times by physical violence among newspaper vendors.

The early part of the century also was marked by the rise to power by two of Joseph Medill's grandsons, Robert R. McCormick and Joseph Patterson. Their mothers, Katherine Medill McCormick and Elinor Medill Patterson, battled frequently over *Tribune* affairs after Medill's death. Katherine McCormick's eldest son, Medill McCormick, made a mark on the *Tribune* as a reporter and later business executive, but left the paper in 1910; he had been plagued by psychiatric illness and, upon recovery, opted for a career in politics. Meanwhile, Robert Patterson, Joseph Patterson's father, had died in 1910. In 1911, Joseph Patterson was elected chairman of Tribune Company and Robert McCormick president. Their immediate accomplishments were Patterson's upgrading of the Sunday paper and McCormick's initiation of a paper mill to produce newsprint for the *Tribune.*

According to their biographers, Patterson and McCormick had many differences, including political ones—McCormick was a staunchly conservative Republican, while Patterson was far more liberal. Still, under their leadership Tribune Company expanded and diversified, and both became well-known public figures, retaining titles from their World War I military service—Colonel McCormick and Captain Patterson. During the war, the *Tribune* had more correspondents at the front than any other Chicago morning daily, and McCormick and Patterson themselves were among these correspondents. After the war, the *Tribune* pulled off a major publishing coup with early publication of the Treaty of Versailles. By 1920, the *Tribune* had the largest circulation of any Chicago newspaper.

By then, the parent company also had expanded beyond Chicago, with Patterson's opening of the *New York News*—formally the *Illustrated Daily News* and now known as the *Daily News*—in 1919. Eventually, the New York paper, a lively tabloid, became the largest-circulation newspaper in the United States. In 1924 Tribune Company formed a subsidiary to publish a weekly national magazine, *Liberty,* designed to compete with the *Saturday Evening Post* and *Collier's.* It passed *Collier's* in circulation, but did not attract adequate advertising, so was sold in 1931.

Also in 1924, Tribune Company launched a more enduring venture, with the leasing of Chicago radio station WDAP, whose call letters it changed to WGN—standing for World's Greatest Newspaper, a nickname the Tribune had given itself. Two years later, Tribune Company bought the entire station. The station's early programming included coverage of the Scopes trial and a comedy show called "Sam 'n' Henry," which eventually went network as "Amos 'n' Andy."

The year 1925 was marked by the Tribune Company's opening of its new headquarters, Tribune Tower, a Gothic tower that is still a Chicago landmark, and the company's decision to provide funds to a journalism school at Northwestern University in Evanston, Illinois, just north of Chicago. The school became known as the Joseph Medill School of Journalism, one of the most prestigious in the United States.

The 1920s provided many political and crime stories that made the decade a lively one for newspapers, but the 1920s ended with the worst stock market crash in history, ushering in the Great Depression. Tribune Company weathered the economic downturn by cutting unprofitable and marginal ventures, such as *Liberty* and the *Tribune's* European edition, which had begun during World War I. Editorially, McCormick's *Tribune* was vociferously opposed to President Franklin Roosevelt's New Deal programs, while Patterson's *Daily News* generally was sympathetic to them. Later, however, the cousins joined in opposition to Roosevelt over U.S. entry into World War II. After the bombing of Pearl Harbor, though, the papers supported the war effort.

Joseph Patterson died in 1946. Briefly, McCormick took over the oversight of the *Daily News,* but concluded it was in good hands with Patterson's widow, Mary King Patterson, and other top executives. In 1948 came the death of Joe Patterson's sister, Eleanor (Cissy) Patterson, who had owned *The Washington Times-Herald.* Tribune Company took over the paper and operated it until 1954, when it was absorbed by *The Washington Post.*

In 1948 the *Tribune* made one of the most famous mistakes in journalistic history: going to press early because of a printers' strike, the paper published the headline "Dewey Defeats Truman" in the 1948 presidential election. The strike ended the following year with no other comparable disasters. The year 1948 also brought a happier milestone in the company's history, the commencement of broadcasting by WGN-TV,

now one of the most successful independent television stations in the United States.

Robert McCormick died in 1955 and Chesser Campbell succeeded him as president of Tribune Company. The following year, the company bought Hearst's *Chicago American.* In 1963 Tribune Company acquired Gore Newspapers Company of Fort Lauderdale, Florida, publisher of the *Fort Lauderdale News* and the *Pompano Sun-Sentinel.* Later that year, the *New York Daily News* acquired certain assets of the *New York Mirror,* which had folded. In 1965 Tribune Company bought the Sentinel-Star Company, a publisher in Orlando, Florida.

In 1967 the *Chicago Tribune* responded to suburban growth by beginning to publish a tabloid aimed at suburban readers. The *Suburban Trib* continued until 1983, when the *Tribune* opted for zoned editions of the main paper to handle suburban coverage and appeal.

In 1968 there came a major corporate reorganization, with Tribune Company dropping its Illinois incorporation and reincorporating in Delaware, which provided a better climate for companies planning expansion and diversification. The company also split its privately held stock by a ratio of four for one and set up a separate subsidiary to publish the *Chicago Tribune.* The Chicago newspaper opened 1969 by abandoning the policy of partisan slanting of news, while it remained conservative on the editorial page. Also in 1969, the *American* was revamped as the tabloid *Chicago Today. Today,* however, operated at a deficit and ceased publication in 1974, with the *Tribune* going to all-day editions to replace the afternoon tabloid.

In 1974, Tribune Company shareholders approved changes in by-laws that were widely perceived to be paving the way for taking the company public. Two dissident shareholders, Josephine Albright—Joseph Patterson's daughter—and her son, Joseph Albright, challenged the by-law changes in a lawsuit that was dismissed in 1979. In 1975 company officials denied any immediate plans to go public, which, indeed, the company did not do until 1983.

In the 1970s the company continued its acquisitive ways, buying a Los Angeles shopper in 1973 and changing it into the *Los Angeles Daily News* and purchasing the *Times-Advocate* in Escondido, California, in 1977. The New York *Daily News* was beset with strikes by pressmen, deliverers, and editorial personnel in 1978, but the parent company still had a record profitable year. Photoengravers also struck the paper briefly in 1979. An afternoon edition of the *Daily News* began publishing in 1980 to go up against the *New York Post;* however, the edition did not succeed in terms of circulation or profits, so it closed the following year. Also in 1980, the company launched a longer-lived venture, the Independent Network News, an alternative to the three major television networks' news programs, originating in the studios of Tribune Company's New York television station, WPIX. The venture was discontinued in 1990.

In 1981 Tribune Company acquired the Chicago Cubs baseball team from William Wrigley for $20.5 million. The Cubs turned in some good seasons for their new owners, winning the National League Eastern Division title in 1984 and 1989. In 1988, once a city ban was lifted, the company installed lights in Wrigley Field and began Cubs night games; the park had been the last in the major leagues with day baseball only.

Also in 1981, Tribune Company began seeking buyers for the New York *Daily News,* which had experienced declines in circulation and advertising and rises in costs and competition. When a proposed sale to Texas financier Joe Allbritton fell through, the company opted to revitalize the *Daily News,* taking a charge of $75 million in the second quarter of 1982 to do so. The paper won concessions from its unions that were expected to result in savings of $50 million a year.

The year 1983 brought the Tribune Company's purchase of WGNO-TV in New Orleans, as well as the public stock offering that had been speculated on for so long. In October, seven million shares of Tribune Company stock went up for sale to the public at $26.75 each.

Tribune Company acquired two key employees from the *Chicago Sun-Times* in 1984 after the *Sun-Times* was sold to Rupert Murdoch, the controversial publisher of the *New York Post.* James Hoge, who had been publisher of the *Sun-Times,* moved into that post at the *Daily News,* and popular columnist Mike Royko switched to the *Chicago Tribune* from the *Sun-Times.*

The company also continued acquiring broadcast operations, buying Atlanta independent WGNX-TV in 1984 for $32 million and, the following year, buying Los Angeles station KTLA-TV for $510 million, the largest price ever paid for a TV station. The move also made Tribune Company the fourth-largest broadcaster in the United States, just behind the three major networks. Because of the KTLA purchase, Tribune Company had to divest itself of the *Los Angeles Daily News* to comply with Federal Communications Commission rules; Jack Kent Cooke, whose other business interests included cable television, real estate, and professional sports, was the buyer. The price was $176 million; Tribune Company had paid $24 million for the paper.

In 1985 three production unions went on strike against the *Chicago Tribune;* as of 1990, only one had settled, but a federal judge called for the rehiring of other strikers. With the strike, the *Tribune* discontinued its afternoon edition, a move it had planned anyway, with newspaper circulations slumping around the United States.

Production of television programs became a major business for Tribune Company in the 1980s; the company had formed Tribune Entertainment Company for this purpose in 1981. It also continued acquiring print properties, buying Daily Press Inc., a Newport News, Virginia, publisher in 1986, and reselling Daily Press's cable TV operations; in 1988 Tribune Company bought five weekly newspapers in Santa Clara County, California.

Mindful of the rash of unfriendly corporate takeovers in the 1980s, Tribune Company enacted shareholder-rights plans as defenses against such possibilities; a 1987 plan gives shareholders a right to acquire a new series of preferred shares in the event of a potential buyer obtaining 10% of the company's common shares or making a tender offer for the company. In 1987 shareholders ratified a two-for-one stock split.

In 1988 the *Chicago Tribune* replaced its system of independent distributors with a more centralized system. The change resulted in legal challenges by the distributors, with one awarded $1.9 million by an arbitrator.

The company encountered more labor-relations problems in 1990. Nine of the ten unions at the *Daily News* went on strike in October; the newspaper struggled to publish with replacement workers and eventually, as the strike dragged into 1991, Tribune Company announced the paper would close unless it were sold. British publisher Robert Maxwell came to the newspaper's rescue, reaching agreements with the unions that allowed him to take over. The company paid Maxwell $60 million to assume the *Daily News's* liabilities. In 1990 Tribune Company lost $63.5 million. Tribune Company continued forging ahead on other fronts, with plans for a cable TV station covering Chicago's suburbs to begin in 1991.

Principal Subsidiaries: Chicago Tribune; Sun-Sentinel; The Orlando Sentinel; Times-Advocate; Peninsula Times Tribune; Daily Press/The Times-Herald; The Californian; Tribune Media Services, Inc.; Tribune Properties, Inc.; Tribune Broadcasting Co.; WPIX-TV; KTLA-TV; WGN-TV; WGNX-TV; KWGN-TV; WGNO-TV; Tribune Radio Group; WQCD Radio; WGN Radio; KCTC Radio; KYMX Radio; Tribune Entertainment Co.; Grant/Tribune Productions; Chicago Cubs; Quebec and Ontario Paper Company Ltd.; Thorold Mill; Baie Comeau Mill; Outardes Sawmill; Manicougan Power Company (60%).

Further Reading: Wendt, Lloyd, *Chicago Tribune: The Rise of a Great American Newspaper,* Rand McNally, Chicago, 1979.

—Trudy Ring

UNITED NEWSPAPERS PLC

Ludgate House
245 Blackfriars Road
London SE1 9UY
United Kingdom
(071) 921 5000
Fax: (071) 928 2728

Public Company
Incorporated: 1918 as United Newspapers Ltd.
Employees: 13,053
Sales: £829.12 million (US$1.60 billion)
Stock Exchange: London

United Newspapers plc is a broadly based international publications, exhibitions, and information services group. It is based in the United Kingdom and operates in the United Kingdom, the United States, and elsewhere in the world.

From the middle of the 19th century the newspaper industry had grown faster in the United Kingdom than in any other country in the world. Educational reform provided a literate readership interested in foreign affairs and domestic politics while rapidly improving road and rail links facilitated distribution throughout the country. The industrial revolution had created towns and cities that were able to provide a local newspaper with readers and advertisers. Advances in technology—Linotype and rotary presses, typewriters, telephones, and telegraphs—enabled local and national newspapers to operate profitably.

Politicians were quick to realize the great influence that newspaper editors had over the electorate, and from the 1850s onward there was a considerable interchange between the Parliament and Fleet Street, the traditional home of U.K. journalism. David Lloyd George, prime minister in the United Kingdom during World War I, was an adept user of the press and was not afraid to use his influence to negate the effects of a political crisis. When the *Daily Chronicle* employed as a military correspondent a stern critic of his policies, Lloyd George responded by calling together a group of Liberals to buy out the owners of the paper.

United Newspapers Ltd. was formed in 1918 by these supporters of the prime minister. The company bought two papers in the deal, of which the *Daily Chronicle* was the most important. The other paper, *Lloyd's Weekly News,* had been founded in 1842 and held the distinction of being the first newspaper with a circulation of one million readers. The board of United

Newspapers soon began to publish a northern edition of the *Daily Chronicle* as a rival to the Conservative Lord Northcliffe's *Daily Mail* and also acquired the *Edinburgh Evening News* and the *Doncaster Gazette,* papers which carried on the strong Liberal tradition of Lloyd George and his politically minded associates.

In 1927 the company was sold for £2.9 million to the Daily Chronicle Investment Group, a joint venture of Liberal interests led by the Marquis of Reading, Sir David Yule, and Sir Thomas Catto. A covenant in the sales document restricted the owners to running the paper "in accordance with the policy of Progressive Liberalism" in order to further social and industrial reform, free trade, and "other programmes of Liberal and Radical measures adopted by the Liberal party."

Within a year United Newspapers was again in the hands of a new owner, William Harrison, a Yorkshireman who had trained as a solicitor in London. Although Harrison was a Conservative, he proclaimed that the group would continue to support Lloyd George and the Liberal cause. As chairman of the Inveresk Paper Company, Harrison bought a controlling interest in United Newspapers. The latter was then amalgamated with Provincial Newspapers Ltd., an umbrella organization taking in some 17 local newspapers which Harrison had acquired in the early and mid-1920s.

Harrison's belief in the regional market molded United's acquisition strategy for the next 50 years, but this strategy was also responsible for his downfall. In autumn 1929, 80% of the value of the shares in the Inveresk Paper Company was written off because of the Great Depression. In December Harrison resigned as chairman when it was revealed that Inveresk had debts of £2.5 million and that United Newspapers had no immediate means to pay for a £500,000 modernization program for the *Daily Chronicle*. Both companies were highly leveraged at a time when investment capital in all sectors of the economy was nearly impossible to secure.

The board of United Newspapers, led by Sir Bernhard Binder, founder of the chartered accountants Binder Hamlyn, and managing director Jack Akerman, was now facing a major crisis. Its solution was to merge the *Daily Chronicle* with the *Daily News* to produce a new title, the *Daily News and Chronicle*. In a move to provide finance for United's provincial press, 50% of the ownership of the new paper was sold to News and Westminster Ltd.

The mid-1930s were difficult for United Newspapers. It was a time of depression and mass unemployment, especially in United's marketplace, the north of England. Fears for the company's survival increased when Lord Rothermere announced his venture, Northcliffe Newspapers, with a stated aim of producing an evening paper in every city and metropolitan area served by United Newspapers. However, in a move executed by Jack Akerman and Sir Herbert Grotrian, who had replaced Binder as chairman, United Newspapers sold its 50% share in what—in June 1930—had become the *News Chronicle* for £500,000 and was instantly freed from its debt. The reaction from the City was ecstatic, and United's preference shares rose from 1 shilling 6 pence to 25 shillings, as final proof that the crisis had been averted.

The war years were less difficult for United than they were for those newspaper groups which were based in heavily bombed Fleet Street. An increase in news was cruelly matched by newprint rationing, distribution and communication problems, and government censorship. Although Sheffield and Hull suffered damage from Luftwaffe bombing comparable to that inflicted on London, presses in Scotland, Leeds, and the west country fared better, and United Newspapers was able to consolidate its success in these areas.

The next event of importance for the directors of United Newspapers occurred in the winter of 1946 with an invitation to dinner at the Hyde Park Hotel from Harold Charles Drayton. Drayton—always known as "Harley"—was the epitome of the self-made man; born in rural Lincolnshire, he started his working life as a £1-a-week office boy and rose through the ranks of the City, eventually controlling the 117 Old Broad Street Group, a large and diverse empire of companies with worldwide interests.

Although Drayton described himself as almost uneducated, he was in truth an erudite and imaginative businessman. He realized that United Newspapers was holding assets of immense value, in the shape of offices and printing houses in the center of major towns and cities throughout the United Kingdom. Within a few weeks of the Hyde Park dinner, Drayton began negotiating with United Newspapers and eventually bought 500,000 shares, representing approximately one-third of the equity of the company. After several months as an ordinary board member, Drayton became chairman on New Year's Day 1948.

Years of steady but unspectacular profits for United followed, enlivened by a number of small and cautious acquisitions. Drayton realized that the directors of the company, three of whom were in their 70s, would soon have to replaced. Two important additions were made to the board; significantly, they were both men who had risen through the ranks of Provincial Newpapers, a company associated with United that had been formed in 1930.

Ken Whitworth had been advertising manager of a group of local newspapers based in south London before joining the Royal Air Force in 1939. He returned from four years as a prisoner of war in Japan to prove his business worth as a member of several of Provincial's boards. William Barnetson had started as a leader writer on the *Edinburgh Evening News,* and swiftly rose to become editor. He demonstrated his management skills on the board of the Edinburgh paper and later on the board of Provincial. After the quiet years of the 1950s, when the United Kingdom struggled to recover from the ravages of World War II, United Newspapers entered the 1960s with the commercially minded Whitworth and the editorially gifted Barnetson as joint managing directors. With Harley Drayton as chairman it was to be the first golden age of United Newspapers.

United Newspapers entered the 1960s as a wealthy company with an established stable of widely read regional newspapers. It was to Barnetson's credit that he did not rush headlong into reckless expansion but instead formulated a cautious acquisition strategy that relied as much on the good will of competitors as on his own undoubted capacity for striking deals. United's move in 1963 to larger premises in Tudor Street was indicative of United's imminent emergence as a major player in the U.K. newspaper industry.

In 1963 the *Nelson Leader* and the *Colne Times,* both struggling Lancashire papers, were bought by United, which rationalized operations by transferring printing to its own under-utilized plant at Burnley. Later in the same year United sold the 49% stake in the *Hull Daily News,* held by Provincial, for £1.7 million to Associated Newspapers. In November, United gave the *Edinburgh Evening News* to the Thomson group in exchange for two Sheffield papers, the *Telegraph* and the *Star.* For Thomson it meant the end of competition for its *Evening Dispatch* in Edinburgh and for United the loss of a fine paper was offset by the strengthening of its position in Yorkshire. This deal was followed by an agreement to sell United's *Yorkshire Evening News* for 20% of the equity of the far stronger Yorkshire Post Newspapers. Drayton adroitly realized that it was necessary to lose a battle, or at least to appear to lose a battle, to win the war. The purchase of the group of newspapers centered on the Blackpool office of the *West Lancashire Evening Gazette,* further consolidated United's position in the north of England.

Barnetson's prodigious capacity for unconventional dealmaking is best illustrated by a story concerning one of the last acquisitions he made before his death in 1966. Fearing damage from rumor-mongers, the board of the *Chorley Guardian* invited Barnetson to a motorway café to sell its interests over pie and chips. Privacy-conscious to the point of obsession, the board finally shook hands with Barnetson in a storeroom high above the motorway.

Harley Drayton was succeeded as chairman by William Barnetson in April 1966. Barnetson followed Drayton's strategy and tactics when he sold the *Doncaster Gazette* to Yorkshire Post Newspapers in exchange for 49% of a new joint venture company, Doncaster Newspapers Ltd., which was set up to publish the *Doncaster Evening Post.* With Ken Whitworth's help as managing director, United introduced new economies in preparation for the company's greatest years of expansion.

1969 started quietly with the acquisition of a group of weekly papers in north London. United then took the brave step of entering the periodicals market when Bradbury Agnew and Co., fearing hostile predators, offered its flagship *Punch,* the *Countryman,* and a number of printing houses to the company. During the tail end of the 1960s *Punch* had been suffering from a problem that was to recur with some regularity over the next 20 years. Seen as a magazine for dentist's waiting rooms, it found itself out of step with contemporary humor, but United worked closely with the then editor, William Davis, to counter this problem. Although *Punch* today still has something of an image problem, it has added to the profits of United Newspapers because of its ability to attract high class advertising.

While the deal with Bradbury Agnew was being finalized, United had begun to increase its shareholding in Yorkshire Post Newspapers. In October 1969, United acquired the total equity of the group in a transaction that was more of a mutually beneficial merger than a hostile takeover. In just one year United Newspapers had more than doubled in size.

The 1970s saw a further period of deliberate consolidation for United Newspapers. Under Lord Barnetson the company had become firmly established as one of the Big Four of the U.K. regional press, and acquisitions were designed to increase further its share of the local market. When Barnetson died in 1981 his successor David Stevens, now Lord Stevens of Ludgate, knew that if the group was to survive it would have to venture beyond traditional areas of interest and concluded that expansion abroad was vital. He instigated a process of rationalization that saw the closure of unprofitable papers in Sheffield, Doncaster, and Wigan and the selling-off of the group's printing interests.

Stevens's leadership of United coincided with the rise of the 1980s media magnates. Rupert Murdoch and Robert Maxwell did more than simply buy out the interests of the Astors, the Beaverbrooks, and the Rothermeres; they replaced the old-fashioned newspaper proprietor with an aggressive, profit-driven businessman who was prepared almost continually to buy and sell media interests. Stevens, with a public profile deceptively lower than that of his major competitors, ensured that United Newspapers did not lag behind.

In January 1985 United Newspapers bought a 15% stake in Fleet Holdings, owner of the *Daily Express,* the *Sunday Express,* the *Star* and the Morgan Grampian Group, from Robert Maxwell's Pergamon Press. When Lord Matthews, chairman of Fleet, refused to elect him to the board, Stevens initially launched a £223 million takeover offer in August 1985. This was well below the price of the company's shares at the time and was accepted by less than 1% of Fleet shareholders. The bid was subsequently raised to £317 million, significantly larger than the market value of United Newspapers itself. The skills Stevens had learned as a fund manager in the City enabled him to gain complete control of Fleet Holdings by October.

Express Newspapers gave United Newspapers its first national newspaper in 50 years, but the return to Fleet Street was to be far from easy. The *Daily Express* had been losing readers in the middle market and was further hit by the launch of *Today* in 1986. Numerous changes in editorial staff had led to a confused editorial style and the paper's image problem was not helped by a steady turnover of advertising agencies.

Stevens initially reduced the number of regular employees from 6,800 to 4,700 and forced through new agreements with the national printing unions and the paper's own chapels. In the ensuing years to 1990, the number was further reduced to 1,700. Electronic production and direct input of copy to computers meant that the labor-intensive process of hot metal composition could be by-passed. A ban on secondary picketing, enforced by the Employment Acts of 1980 and 1982, further weakened the hold of the traditional printing unions, which had already been shaken by protracted strikes and violent demonstrations in Warrington and Wapping. These measures returned the newly acquired national papers to profitability, enabling Express Newspapers to embark on a program of investment to ensure the future viability of its newspapers. This strategy involved the utilization of the new print technology, investment in color presses, increased paginations, and reduced advertising proportions, with the clear aim of improving the papers' appeal to their target audiences. By 1990 there were strong indications of the success of this strategy, with all Express titles showing stable circulation and strong shares of their respective advertising markets.

The *Daily Express* and the *Daily Star* are, respectively, the fourth and sixth most popular daily titles in the United Kingdom. The *Sunday Express* is by far the biggest-selling Sunday broadsheet paper and the fifth most popular of all national Sunday newspapers.

Stevens's first major overseas acquisitions took place in the United States. Gralla, a family-run publisher of trade magazines and promoter of trade shows, was bought in 1983 for US$44 million. Miller Freeman, publisher of a number of medical and computer trade magazines, was the next U.S. acquisition, followed by PR Newswire, a corporate and financial news agency. In the domestic market, United took control of Link House Publications in a move which added the classified advertising paper *Exchange and Mart* to United's increasingly impressive list of titles.

Stevens was also determined to diversify into different markets. In 1987 Extel, which provides financial and sporting information, was bought for £250 million. Despite the recent downturn in City activity, Extel continues to launch innovative products, such as information compact discs and online databases, to supplement the steady profits from Extel's printed card services. Benn Brothers plc was bought in 1987 and demand for its directories and tax guides is beginning to spread overseas. In 1989 the *Daily Express* was the last national newspaper to leave Fleet Street, moving to the other side of the Thames River to new offices at Blackfriars Bridge.

United Newspapers entered the 1990s as a strong, well-balanced group offering a diverse but complementary range of products. However, United is a publicly quoted company with a wide share ownership and, as such, is vulnerable to predators.

Principal Subsidiaries: United Newspapers Publications Ltd.; Express Newspapers plc; United Provincial Newspapers Ltd., Link House Publications PLC; United Publications Ltd; Extel Financial Ltd; United Newspapers, Inc. (U.S.A.).

Further Reading: Schofield, Guy, *The Men that Carry the News,* London, The Cranford Press, 1975; Taylor, A.J.P., "Lloyd George: Rise and Fall," in *Essays in English History,* London, Hamish Hamilton, 1976; Jenkins, Simon, *The Market for Glory,* London, Faber and Faber, 1986; Saatchi & Saatchi, *Top Fifty European Media Owners,* London, Saatchi & Saatchi Communications, 1989.

—Andreas Loizou

THE WASHINGTON POST COMPANY

THE WASHINGTON POST COMPANY

1150 15th Street, Northwest
Washington, D.C. 20071
U.S.A.
(202) 334-6000
Fax: (202) 334-4613

Public Company
Incorporated: 1889
Employees: 6,200
Sales: $1.44 billion
Stock Exchange: New York

The Washington Post Company and its subsidiaries are leaders in the news and communications media industry. *The Washington Post* is a nationally respected newspaper published daily to serve Washington, D.C., and the adjacent suburban area, and contributes a large share of the company's revenue. The company also publishes a national weekly edition of the *Post* and a daily newspaper in Everett, Washington. A wholly owned subsidiary, Newsweek, Inc., publishes *Newsweek,* a weekly magazine. Other subsidiaries operate four television stations, cable television systems in 15 states, educational centers to prepare people for standardized college-admission tests and other professional exams, and an online legislative-information service. Through its ownership of all the company's class A common stock, the Graham family has effective control over the company.

The Washington Post was first published on December 6, 1877, by Stilson Hutchins. Hutchins had come to the nation's capital from St. Louis, Missouri, where he had been associated with several newspapers. His goal in starting *the Post* was to establish a newspaper at the center of national affairs that reflected the views of the Democratic Party. At this time, the era of Reconstruction had just ended with the controversial presidential election that saw Rutherford B. Hayes, a Republican, declared president over Samuel Tilden, a Democrat, by a special, congressionally appointed electoral commission. Hutchins did not approve of Hayes's victory and his paper would rarely refer to him as "president." Within a year, *the Post*'s circulation had reached more than 6,000 copies a day. The first Sunday edition was published on May 2, 1880, making *the Post* the first seven-day paper in Washington. By the late 1880s, Hutchins gave up his editorial allegiance to the Democrats and began to describe his paper as "independent." In

1888 Hutchins bought out *the Post*'s only competitor the *Republican National* and, for a short time, published the *Evening Post,* an afternoon edition. The paper made a profit for most of its early existence, but in 1889 Hutchins sold it to pursue other interests.

The paper was purchased for $210,000 by Frank Hatton and Beriah Wilkins, $30,000 of which was raised by selling a press back to Hutchins. Hatton, who had a background in journalism, took care of the production of the paper, while Wilkins, who had served three terms in the House of Representatives, handled business matters. They incorporated their newspaper company as The Washington Post Company. The company flourished under the guidance of Hatton and Wilkins, with profits averaging $100,000 a year between 1892 and 1894. Circulation was reported at about 16,000 daily and 20,000 on Sundays. In 1889, at the request of Hatton and Wilkins, the noted band leader John Philip Sousa wrote "The Washington Post March" to be played at the awards ceremony for winners in a *Post* essay contest. In 1903, however, with Hatton dead and Wilkins seriously ill, the paper was again for sale. Wilkins died before a sale could be made, but his son made a deal with John R. McLean, owner of the Cincinnati *Enquirer,* whereby McLean obtained a minority share in the paper. By 1905, McLean had secured enough additional shares to place himself in control of the *Post*.

McLean adopted the style of journalism that had been so successful for William Randolph Hearst. He added sections to *the Post* for feature stories, comic strips, and sports. He gave less emphasis to political news, which had been the paper's specialty. From 1905 to 1909, Sunday circulation was as high as 40,000, the best in the city, but daily circulation, while it averaged 30,000, began to decline. When McLean died in 1916, his son Edward McLean took over operations. The first years of the younger McLean's tenure were prosperous for *the Post,* with Sunday circulation reaching 75,000, placing it second to the Washington *Star,* and profits reaching a peak of $376,612 from 1921 to 1923. Edward McLean, however, became ensnared in the Teapot Dome scandal that rocked the administration of President Warren Harding during the early 1920s. At the center of the scandal was U.S. Secretary of the Interior Albert B. Fall, who had taken bribes to secretly lease oil-rich government lands without taking competitive bids. McLean became less able to handle the company's business affairs, and the editorial quality of *the Post* declined. From 1924 to 1932, the paper had only two profitable years. In 1933 it went through bankruptcy proceedings and was eventually sold for $825,000 at an auction held on June 1, 1933.

The purchaser was Eugene Meyer, a New York investment banker. Meyer had made a sizable fortune in investment banking and was willing to dedicate it to making *the Post* into a quality newspaper that would also be profitable. His task would not be easy, as circulation had fallen to about 50,000. He quickly began hiring a new staff of reporters and editors, and went to court to prevent several comic strips from being transferred to the Washington *Herald*. This was a period of great upheaval in Washington, as the New Deal policies of Democratic President Franklin D. Roosevelt were being put into place in an effort to pull the United States out of the depression. One aspect of the New Deal was the creation of the National Recovery Administration, which was to spur industrial recovery and to help create jobs. Although Meyer was a staunch Republican, he did place the Blue Eagle, symbolic of the National Recovery Administration, on his paper. The paper was not as supportive of other New Deal programs, particularly the Works Progress Administration, which funded construction of buildings, bridges, and roads to fight unemployment.

The New Deal period also saw one of *the Post*'s most comical typographical errors. At a time when Roosevelt was suffering from a cold, a *Post* headline read, "FDR In Bed With Coed." The president called the paper to ask for 100 copies of the first edition, but the error had been caught and copies of the issue had been pulled back from circulation.

By 1938, circulation had increased to 100,000, and its advertising volume was the second-highest in Washington. This performance was still well below that of the *Star*, the only profitable newspaper in the capital during the Great Depression. Annual losses at *the Post* were about $1 million from 1934 to 1937. Business improved during World War II, with profits for 1942 to 1945 totaling $249,451.

Eugene Meyer relinquished daily control of *the Post* in 1946 when President Harry S Truman appointed him first president of the World Bank. Control of the paper stayed in the family, however, as Meyer transferred his voting stock to his daughter, Katharine Graham, and her husband, Philip Graham, on July 23, 1948. Philip Graham had already been installed as publisher of the paper, and the majority of the voting stock, 3,500 shares, was transferred to him, compared to 1,500 shares for Katharine. Under a modified incorporation of the company, the shares were put in a trust controlled by a five-member committee. The committee was authorized to decide on any future changes in the ownership of the voting stock in order to ensure that The Washington Post Company remained true to certain editorial standards. The committee remained in place until the shares of The Washington Post Company were first offered to the public in 1971.

When Graham became publisher of the paper he began instituting managerial changes. Within two years he had hired a new managing editor, business manager, and circulation manager. Following the lead of Meyer, who in 1944 had purchased a radio station, Graham acquired a radio station and a television station in Washington in 1949. In 1953 he bought a television station in Jacksonville, Florida. Philip Graham died in 1963. Katherine Graham acquired television stations in Miami, Florida, in 1969, and Hartford, Connecticut, in 1974. The Washington radio station was disposed of through the donation of its FM operations to Howard University in 1971 and the sale of its AM facility in 1977. In 1978, the company traded its television station in Washington for a station in Detroit.

In 1954, The Washington Post Company made its most important corporate acquisition. After a period of negotiation, Meyer, who still acted as chairman of the board of the company, agreed to buy the Washington *Times-Herald* for $8.5 million. With the removal of the *Times-Herald* as a competitor, *the Post* was assured of a monopoly as Washington's only morning newspaper. The operations of the two papers were combined very quickly to counter any antitrust action the government might undertake, but no such action was pursued. Within four months, the combined papers had a circulation of 381,417 daily and 393,680 Sunday, and ranked as the ninth-largest morning paper in the country.

In March 1961, Philip Graham purchased *Newsweek*, the general news magazine, from its stockholders for $15 million.

Newsweek would become an integral part of the company's operations; by 1968, its domestic advertising pages exceeded those of its nearest rival, *Time*, and in 1977 its annual profits were almost triple the price Graham had paid. *Newsweek* had a circulation of over 3 million in 1989 and an estimated readership of 19.6 million. In 1962, Graham also formed a national news wire service in conjunction with the *Los Angeles Times*; this news service serves more than 500 subscribers worldwide.

When Philip Graham died, his wife, Katharine Meyer Graham, took over as president of The Washington Post Company. She continued with the same management team that her husband had brought to the company. She also continued the company's acquisition program by buying a 45% interest in the Paris edition of the *New York Herald Tribune* in 1966. By the next year, in a partnership with *The New York Times*, The Post Company began to publish the Paris paper as the *International Herald Tribune*, which is still in operation.

By the late 1960s, some changes had been made in top management at *the Post*. Of particular note was Benjamin Bradlee's appointment as managing editor in 1965. Bradlee brought some important changes to the paper, including the introduction of the "Style" section in 1969 as a way of combining all cultural news in one place. He would also play a role in the two big stories of the 1970s that would earn *the Post* its national reputation as an important newspaper.

The first of those stories involved the publication of the Pentagon Papers. On June 13, 1971, *The New York Times* began to publish this secret, government version of the history of the Vietnam War in serial form, but within three days the administration of President Richard M. Nixon had secured an injunction forcing *the Times* to cease this publication. A few days later, *the Post* secured a copy of the papers; in a meeting at Bradlee's home, reporters prepared *the Post*'s version of the Pentagon Papers for publication. Lawyers for the paper advised against publishing any story. The Post Company was in the process of going public. The stock had been issued but not yet sold. An indictment for criminal liability could place the transaction in jeopardy, threatening the very foundation of the company. Bradlee argued strongly in favor of publication. Katharine Graham made the final decision to publish. The government filed a suit against *the Post*. The cases against *the Times* and *the Post* were argued jointly, and on July 1, 1971, the Supreme Court decided in favor of the newspapers by a six to three vote.

Soon after its success with the Pentagon Papers, *the Post* had a major reporting coup with its handling of the Watergate affair. On June 27, 1972, there was a burglary at the Democratic Party headquarters in Washington. Because of its location in Washington, *the Post* was better equipped to go after the Watergate story than other newspapers. Two reporters specializing in the Washington city beat, Bob Woodward and Carl Bernstein, were assigned to the story, and with the help of several government officials, uncovered the link between the Watergate burglary and the Nixon administration. Nixon and his aides retaliated by having administration supporters challenge the broadcasting licenses of the company's Florida television stations at hearings before the Federal Communications Commission. The company prevailed, even though its share price suffered a decline during the period of the Watergate story. The Watergate story would ultimately lead to Richard Nixon's resignation as president. In 1973, the *Post* was awarded the Pulitzer Prize in the category of public service for its reporting on the Watergate affair.

While the Watergate and Pentagon Papers stories were propelling *the Post* into the national limelight, several changes took place on the business side of the company. In 1971, The Washington Post Company made its first sale of stock to the public in an offering of more than 1.35 million shares of class B stock for $33 million. All of the class A stock stayed within the Graham family; this form of capitalization gave the Graham family a majority of the vote and the right to elect 70% of the directors, with class B stockholders electing the remainder. In that same year the company organized The Washington Post Writers Group to syndicate material produced by its staff writers, and moved into a new $25 million building in downtown Washington. It also purchased the *Trenton Times,* of Trenton, New Jersey. That paper proved to be only a modestly successful operation. In 1978, the company acquired *the Herald,* a daily newspaper located in Everett, Washington, north of Seattle.

By 1973, *the Post* had achieved the number-one position in Washington, accounting for 65.8% of advertising space, 56.6% of daily circulation, and 67.1% of Sunday circulation. The only other newspaper remaining to compete with it was the *Star. The Post* also encountered labor difficulties in the 1970s, facing strikes by its printers in 1973, by reporters and other members of the Newspaper Guild in 1974, and an especially brutal strike by the pressmen in 1975. Nevertheless, growth continued and the paper was able to emerge from all three strikes in a stronger position than before.

Starting in the 1970s, Donald Graham, Katharine and Philip Graham's son, began moving up in the ranks of the paper's management and became general manager in 1976. In 1979 he took charge of the paper as its publisher, with Katharine Graham remaining in overall charge as chairman of The Washington Post Company. The paper received a big boost in 1981 with the closing down of its last remaining competitor, the *Star*; circulation increased from 595,000 to 730,000 daily, and from 827,000 to 952,000 on Sundays. However, additional competition emerged in 1982 with the establishment of a new paper, *the Washington Times,* and further competition came in the form of specialized suburban newspapers.

In 1988, with hostile takeover bids becoming common among newspapers, the Graham family took steps to protect its ownership of *the Post.* Because lawsuits at other newspapers had challenged the system of having two classes of stock by arguing that all stockholders should be entitled to vote on a merger plan, the charter of *the Post* was changed to make a majority vote of both classes of stock necessary to approve a merger. In 1989, under a policy whereby the board of directors had allowed for the company to repurchase up to 700,000 shares of class B common stock, 389,427 shares were purchased by The Washington Post Company, reducing outstanding stock. The company has frequently repurchased its shares as a good investment. There is a current authorization to repurchase 1 million shares, of which 700,000 to 800,000 remain.

During *the Post*'s lifetime, it has been part of a trend that has seen many urban newspapers fold, so that by 1986 the 15 largest newspapers in the United States accounted for 21% of all newspapers sold. Along with this trend, however, there has also been a decline in the urban population that has resulted in a drop in daily newspaper sales in metropolitan areas. *The Post,* as a survivor, has benefited from the elimination of its major competitors as part of the first trend, with its average circulation for 1989 reaching 792,584 daily and 1.14 million on Sundays. It now faces the problems raised by the decline of urban centers and increasing competition in the form of television, especially as cable services provide 24-hour news programs. It has been helped by continued population growth in the Washington metropolitan area. It has also adapted by offering special sections geared to readers in suburban Maryland and Virginia, and has purchased land that will enable it to locate additional production capacity nearer to its suburban readers. The Washington Post Company's diversified holdings in the communications industry include a newspaper division—50% of operating revenues in 1989, television stations—13%, *Newsweek*—23%, and cable television operations—9%.

Principal Subsidiaries: Newsweek, Inc.; The Herald Company; Legi-Slate, Inc.; Post-Newsweek Stations, Inc.; Robinson Terminal Warehouse, Inc.; Stanley H. Kaplan Educational Center, Ltd.; Post-Newsweek Cable, Inc.

Further Reading: Roberts, Chalmers M., *In the Shadow of Power: The Story of The Washington Post,* Washington, D.C., Seven Locks Press, 1989.

—Donald R. Stabile

REAL ESTATE

CHEUNG KONG (HOLDINGS) LIMITED

THE HAMMERSON PROPERTY
INVESTMENT AND DEVELOPMENT
CORPORATION PLC

HONGKONG LAND HOLDINGS LIMITED

JMB REALTY CORPORATION

LAND SECURITIES PLC

LEND LEASE CORPORATION LIMITED

MEPC PLC

MITSUBISHI ESTATE COMPANY, LIMITED

MITSUI REAL ESTATE DEVELOPMENT
CO., LTD.

NEW WORLD DEVELOPMENT COMPANY
LTD.

OLYMPIA & YORK DEVELOPMENTS LTD.

SLOUGH ESTATES PLC

SUMITOMO REALTY & DEVELOPMENT
CO., LTD.

TOKYU LAND CORPORATION

CHEUNG KONG (HOLDINGS) LIMITED

China Building
29 Queen's Road Central
Hong Kong
(5) 526 6911
Fax: (5) 845 2940

Public Company
Incorporated: 1972
Employees: 16,000
Sales: HK$2.78 billion (US$356.49 million)
Stock Exchange: Hong Kong

Cheung Kong (Holdings) is among Hong Kong's leading property and investment development companies. It is expanding its network into North America and Europe as Hong Kong nears its transfer to Chinese government in 1997. Cheung Kong is the flagship company for the property-to-telecommunications empire built up in Hong Kong by Li Ka-shing, who started his meteoric rise in business around 1960 by making plastic flowers.

Known to his colleagues as K.S. Li, the Hong Kong tycoon was born in Chiu Chow, in southern China, in 1928. He controls, through a series of interlocking stock market holdings, over 14% of stock registered on the Hong Kong exchange. Besides residential property developments, Li owns a land bank of 22.5 million square feet.

Cheung Kong (Holdings) also includes highly profitable cement, quarrying, and ready-mixed concrete operations. At the end of 1972, after its first year on the Hong Kong stock market, the company had a total of 40 sites in its property portfolio, with a total floor area—after development—of about 2.4 million square feet of residential and commercial space.

Among the projects Cheung Kong had onstream were a number of residential developments. Typical of these was the development of the Castle Peak Hotel, in the colony's New Territories. Originally occupying a site of over 84,000 square feet, the former hotel was doubled in size and turned into several six-story, expensive blocks of flats with a total floor area of over 167,000 square feet.

The company also planned to develop a number of warehouses and factories, as well as offices. Recognizing the static nature of the Hong Kong property market in 1973, Li Ka-shing informed his shareholders that his company would look to increase its supply of regular rental income from its properties, to protect their interests.

This increased effort at boosting rental income paid off a year later in 1974 when Hong Kong's property market slipped into depression. Cheung Kong's development plans continued undeterred, with a 10% rise in profits to HK$48.2 million, against profits of HK$43.7 million a year earlier.

This improved performance was encouraged by rent reviews which boosted income. One example was Regent House, on Queen's Road Central. Cheung Kong had planned to redevelop the property, but put back plans after the rental income increased to HK$4.6 million, from about HK$3 million, per year. Because it would take three years to develop the site, and would cost HK$16 million, a loss of some HK$13.8 million from leaving the building vacant was not thought feasible, particularly when depressed conditions in the colony made the prospects of any future developments doubtful.

The continuing downturn in fortunes hit Cheung Kong's profits in 1975, which dipped 6% to HK$45.6 million. In that year, the company saw the fruits of a joint venture into which it had entered the previous year with the Canadian Imperial Bank of Commerce. The joint venture, Canadian Eastern Finance, acquired for HK$85,000 a site along the Hong Kong harbor of some 864,000 square feet. On 53,000 square feet of the site, the company planned to build ten expensive residential units, each 24 stories high, and a car park. On the rest of the site, recreation facilities—including a swimming pool and sports ground—were planned.

At the end of 1975 Cheung Kong had some 5.1 million square feet of commercial and residential space. This property portfolio jumped by more than 20% in size over the next year to stand at a total of 6.35 million square feet at the end of 1976. Of this space, 3.62 million square feet were said by the company to be in residential property, while 1.04 million square feet and 1.65 million square feet were bound up in commercial and industrial space, respectively.

Improving market conditions in Hong Kong in 1976 helped boost the company's profits that year to HK$58.8 million, a rise of 29% over the previous year. The renown Li Ka-shing was gaining in the Hong Kong financial community was confirmed a year later, in 1977, when Cheung Kong announced its profits up a further 45% to HK$85.55 million. This improvement coincided with a 38% rise in total space in the company's property portfolio, to 10.2 million square feet in size.

Among the company's new properties was the celebrated Tiger Balm Gardens, a site of 150,000 square feet originally developed by the inventor of Tiger Balm, an ointment used to cure a number of minor ailments. Cheung Kong bought the site with the aim of building high-class residential units, a practice for which it was becoming widely known in the colony.

In 1977 the company also diversified into the hotel trade. It acquired Wynncor Limited, which owned the 800-room Hong Kong Hilton Hotel and shopping arcade, and nearly all of the 400-room Bali Hyatt Hotel.

While Hong Kong's local property market was improving, Li Ka-shing warned in 1977 that various restrictions from the emerging European Common Market, based in Brussels, which included anti-dumping measures against Asian electronic products, were affecting export prospects for Cheung Kong. The reason was that Hong Kong's industry sector was felt to be tied in fortunes to that of the local property market. When the first failed, the second was certain to feel the effects.

In 1978 the company's profits continued to rise. Total profits for the year reached HK$132.6 million, a 55% increase over the previous year. In that year, Cheung Kong sold a number of properties not producing sufficient rental income, including sites in the Kwun Tong region of Kowloon, and on Hennessy Road. The company was now gaining wide renown throughout Hong Kong, as demonstrated by the publicity given to each pre-let of its completed properties. The value of rents reached by each pre-letting—the practice whereby a property developer signs up a tenant for the building or property he is about to build—would give the local property market an indication of the going-rates to follow.

As Li Ka-shing told his shareholders that year: "In both prestige and business expansion, the group has entered a new era, and it is my opinion that 1978 has been an exceptionally important year in the group's development." Li cautioned that the effects of high interest rates in Hong Kong and abroad would affect the local property market. He added, however, that mortgages and property developments would provide a useful hedge to investors against threatened inflation. Also in 1978, Cheung Kong took a 22% stake in Green Island Cement, increasing its holdings on the construction side.

In 1979 the company saw a 91.6% rise in profits to HK$254.1 million. Among the developments then under construction was a joint-venture project with four other property companies to build an office development on the Hong Kong Macau Ferry Pier. With a 20% interest in the Shun Tak Centre, due for completion in 1984, the final complex was to include a total 1.5 million square feet of office space.

In the same year, Cheung Kong purchased a substantial share stake in Hutchison Whampoa, a group whose interests included electricity, communications, wholesaling, and distribution. Hutchison was also involved in manufacturing, quarrying, and concrete markets.

The initial stake in Hutchison was for 90 million shares in the group, or 24.4% of outstanding shares, bought for HK$693 million. The company increased its stake in Hutchison to 30% by the end of the year.

At the same time, Li Ka-shing warned shareholders that continuing high interest rates in the colony, and emerging rent control restriction, led him to believe that the local property market was showing signs of leveling off. Continuing economic difficulties in the Hong Kong economy continued to color the business climate for Cheung Kong in 1980. Li Ka-shing, nevertheless, maintained an optimistic air. "There is a slight slackening in the property market," he told shareholders. "But this phase will pass with a lowering of interest rates and an upturn in trade. I am, therefore, cautiously optimistic about the future of the Hong Kong property market."

The 1980 profit rise of 176%, to HK$701.3 million, gave grounds for this optimism, but also reflected first-time profit contributions from Hutchison Whampoa and Green Island Cement. In addition, the Hong Kong Hilton Hotel increased its profits for 1980 by 34%, compared with the previous year.

During 1981 Cheung Kong began amassing an overseas portfolio that would grow over the coming years. Overseas investments totaled HK$125 million in value, or 3% of the group's total assets. These included a number of commercial buildings in the United States with 950,000 square feet of space, and a shopping center with over 370,000 square feet of freehold space. This growing overseas portfolio was motivated by continuing recessionary conditions in the Hong Kong property market, and anxiety about any fallout from fears of 1997, when control of the colony would revert to China.

At the time, Li Ka-shing signaled to shareholders that it would be difficult, given the current trading conditions, to maintain in 1982 the same high level of profit recorded in 1981. In that year, profits were raised 97% from the previous year's level, to HK$1.38 billion.

Li Ka-shing's profit warning turned out to be timely. A decline was suffered across the board by the company at the end of 1982. Overall profits declined by 62% to HK$525.6 million. Profits at the Green Island Cement company tumbled by 65%, and were affected, according to the company, by a slowdown in the colony's construction industry, bad weather, and large imports of Japanese cement. Even more difficult problems were projected for 1983.

Hutchison Whampoa, on the other hand, increased profits by 20%. Yet even here Cheung Kong forecast reduced profits for its subsidiary in 1983. At the Hong Kong Hilton Hotel, profits were 10% lower than in 1982, reflecting strong competition from new hotels coming on stream in the colony, and a fall in the worldwide tourist trade owing to recessionary pressures in Europe and the United States.

Li Ka-shing had few words of consolation for his shareholders at the time. As he saw the local property market during 1982, "Property prices plunged and hesitation on the part of investors combined with generally weakening purchasing power left the market in a very depressed state from which appreciable recovery is unlikely in the short term."

Matters did indeed deteriorate still further in 1983. The speculator-led boom in property prices and rents of the previous few years came to an abrupt halt, curbed by high interest rates and political tensions surrounding the future of the colony. As a result, Cheung Kong's annual profits fell 22% to HK$408.8 million. Green Island Cement became loss-making as the Hong Kong construction industry faced depression conditions.

Investors in Hong Kong were maintaining a wait-and-see attitude as conditions in the United States and European markets began to improve. At the same time, the property market was expected to lag behind as lower interest rates allowed for growth worldwide, and therefore investment in commercial and residential properties throughout the colony would be delayed.

This situation was confirmed by Cheung Kong's 1984 profits of HK$213.5 million, a fall of 47% compared with a year earlier. The company at this time was making fewer property acquisitions than usual for future developments. Two notable acquisitions were a site of 12,600 square feet on Queen's Road Central, destined to become a 130,000-square-foot office complex; and an 18,000-square-foot site in Repulse Bay, which was to provide space for a 36,000-square-foot, 12-story luxury residential complex.

A long-awaited improvement in earnings for the company came in 1985 when profits reached HK$551.7 million, 158% higher than the previous year. The effects on earnings from the three-year-long recession appeared to be over. The company insisted that prices for residential property were on the rise, although the demand for commercial and industrial holdings had not yet meant substantially higher prices.

At this time, Hong Kong appeared to throw off some of the anxiety that had gripped the colony after the signing of the

Sino-British joint declaration in December 1984, signaling a return to Chinese sovereignty in 1997. Many Hong Kong residents had been hesitant to buy homes or rent offices until the ink on the newly signed agreement was completely dry.

For Li Ka-shing, fears over investing for the future in Hong Kong were partly allayed by his influence among Chinese leaders in Beijing. The entrepreneur was not a man to be ignored when, for example, Hutchison Whampoa imported each year 850,000 tons of coal from China, or 14% of the country's annual output. Li Ka-shing was also at this time working with China International Trust and Investment Corporation, China's investment bank, to build a US$10 billion electricity plant in China's eastern province of Jiangsu.

Large profit gains resulted in 1986, when Hong Kong's economy grew by 9% over the year. Cheung Kong reported earnings of HK$1.28 billion, an increase of 128% on the year before. The improvements was helped by the completion of a number of developments, and by the company's sale of Hong Kong's Hilton Hotel for HK$1.03 billion to Hongkong Electric, which Li Ka-shing also owned.

Cheung Kong announced at this time a reorganization of its management structure. In particular, Hongkong Electric's utility and non-utility businesses were to be split. The non-utility holdings—including the Hong Kong Hilton Hotel and a 43% stake in Husky Oil of Canada—were to become part of a new firm, Cavendish International Holdings.

The Cheung Kong/Hutchison/Electric group had by now become very important in Hong Kong. Shares in Li Ka-shing's empire accounted for 15% of all shares traded on the Hong Kong stock market.

Cheung Kong moved ahead in 1987, producing profits of HK$1.58 billion, 23% over earnings posted a year earlier. The number of properties for development that the company was acquiring continued to increase. They included an 8.8 hectare site and a 15.5 hectare site which together would require up to HK$9 billion in investment before yielding more than 17,000 residential units, and two large shopping centers with total floor space of 1.22 million square feet. Profits at Hutchison

Whampoa reached HK$2.62 billion. The property market in Hong Kong suffered slightly from the effects of the worldwide stock market crash of October 1987, but the underlying strength of the Hong Kong economy helped steady the local property market and increase demand for residential and office space.

A shortage of office space in Hong Kong contributed to strong profits for Cheung Kong in 1989. Earnings were posted at HK$2.09 billion, a 33% increase over the previous year. On the strength of improved earnings, the company announced that it would purchase all outstanding shares in Green Island Cement (Holdings) not already owned by Cheung Kong. Li Ka-shing told his shareholders in his 1989 accounts that he was optimistic about the outlook for the colony's property market, and that demand and prices for properties were likely to hold up.

The Hong Kong government announced the building of a new airport for the colony, for which Cheung Kong received lucrative contracts. In 1989, the company posted profits of HK$2.77 billion, 33% up over earnings a year earlier. At the same time, Li Ka-shing saw the colony's property market entering a period of consolidation. This was reflected in profits for the first six months of 1990 when Cheung Kong's earnings rose only 3% to HK$948 million.

Around this time, Li Ka-shing made a HK$484 million profit when Cheung Kong sold its 4.8% stake in Cable and Wireless, the U.K.–based telecommunications giant. The company, having bought the stake in 1987, profited from a rising Cable and Wireless share price, and the relative strength of sterling in the intervening period. For the future, Li Ka-shing's fortunes appear assured owing to his increasing influence in Hong Kong, and the efforts of his companies to diversify into China, Europe, and North America.

Principal Subsidiaries: The Green Island Cement (Holdings) Limited Group; Anderson Asia Quarry Group.

—Etan Vlessing

HAMMERSON

THE HAMMERSON PROPERTY INVESTMENT AND DEVELOPMENT CORPORATION PLC

100 Park Lane
London W1Y 4AR
United Kingdom
(071) 629 9494
Fax: (071) 629 0498

Public Company
Incorporated: 1931 as Associated Cooperative Investment Trust Ltd.
Employees: 375
Sales: £109.60 million (US$211.54 million)
Stock Exchanges: London Toronto Sydney Frankfurt

The Hammerson Property Investment and Development Corporation plc, Britain's third-largest property company, has substantial property holdings both in the United Kingdom and overseas. Rapid growth from modest beginnings during World War II has taken the company into the North American, European, and Australasian property markets, which together account for more than 60% of the firm's activities, while it continues to be active in the United Kingdom.

While the legal entity that became Hammerson, Associated Cooperative Investment Trust Ltd. dates back to the 1930s, the real origins of the company were the property investment activities of its founder, Lewis Hammerson, during World War II. Hammerson began his career not as a property developer but as a clothing manufacturer, working in the family firm, Amalgamated Weatherware, in North London. This business was sold with the onset of World War II and after being discharged from the army on medical grounds, Hammerson used the £15,000 which was his share of the proceeds of the clothing firm to begin property trading, in 1942, under the name of L.W. Hammerson & Company.

Hammerson had the foresight to realize that by 1942 property prices had hit rock bottom and would appreciate substantially during the postwar recovery period.

Hammerson started at a disadvantage compared to most other property tycoons of the period. In addition to having little capital, he lacked both experience and contacts in the property world. This lack of capital may have been the factor which led to initial investment in housing, rather than com-mercial property. He bought houses which were converted into flats or modernized and then sold, each deal tying up his limited capital for only a short time.

After the end of the war, the scope for property dealing increased and by 1948 Hammerson's business had grown sufficiently for him to move into commercial property. In that year he made his first major purchase, an office block on Queen Street, in the city of London, for £100,000. This was financed largely by bank credit; the Labour government's cheap money policy had resulted in interest rates being kept low during the late 1940s and property value appreciation generally outpaced interest costs.

Rather than letting the building as quickly as possible, Hammerson held out for a single prestigious tenant whose occupancy would add to its value. When such a tenant was eventually found, Hammerson moved his office from Piccadilly to Park Lane and prepared for a major expansion of activities. By 1953 he was ready to float a public company. He bought up the shares of Associated City Investment Trust, a small investment trust company, and changed its name to the Hammerson Property and Investment Trust. His property activities were then transferred to the company.

Hammerson made some long-term decisions which eventually repaid his patience handsomely. One of these concerned the purchase of a number of properties on the Marylebone Road in London, which eventually formed the site of one of his most successful early developments, Castrol House, later renamed Marathon House. In 1957 he made another highly successful deal, the purchase of the Duke of Bedford Estate for £1 million, making use of finance provided by Standard Life. By 1986 the site, then comprising 235,000 square feet of offices and 40 shops in Holborn, London, was worth £80 million. Standard Life also benefited from the deal, retaining a 35% stake in the property.

In 1958, only five years after floating his company, Lew Hammerson died suddenly at the early age of 42. Sydney Mason, then only 38, became chairman. Mason had started his career working for Harold Samuel and had been persuaded by Hammerson to become his partner in 1949. Mason possessed one of the key skills of the property developer, the art of negotiation.

Mason wished to establish Hammerson as a shopping-mall developer; a notable early success in this field was the redevelopment of the Bradford city center. Bradford City Council had been trying unsuccessfully to attract a developer to the site for several years when in 1959 Hammerson agreed to take on the project. The scheme involved the investment of £1.4 million in an area of Bradford that had not traditionally been a shopping center. Few developers at that time were interested in provincial shopping mall schemes, so Hammerson was able to negotiate the contract on very favorable terms. The shopping mall proved highly profitable, and the company made a return of 16% on its investment. Hammerson soon became one of the "Big Six" provincial shopping mall developers, along with Ravenseft, Arndale, Laing, Murrayfield, and Town & City.

Hammerson also turned its attention to foreign markets during this period. In the late 1950s the company was offered a site in Melbourne, Australia, by Fred Maynard of Ravenseft. Initial success led to a large number of other Australian development projects, including the 750,000-square-foot Warringah Mall, located eight miles from Sydney, the first phase of which was completed in 1963. Hammerson extended its domestic strategy of forging links with insurance companies to fund its development activities to its Australian schemes; the main partners in these Australian operations being Australian Mutual Provident, Royal London Mutual, and Standard Life.

By 1960 the company was also looking at prospects in the New Zealand market. The first New Zealand project was introduced to Hammerson by the British chartered surveyor Jones Lang Wootton. In the 1960s Hammerson also entered the U.S. market. However, while it fared better than many other U.K. developers who established themselves there, U.S. developments were among the least profitable for the company.

Hammerson's development program expanded rapidly during the early 1960s. This expansion was aided by insurance company funding links. In 1961 a deal was struck with Royal London Mutual, £1 million of funds being provided in return for a 10% stake in the capital and a seat on the Hammerson board. Three years later another deal was made, with Standard Life, which raised £15 million. Strong institutional backing was a factor that continued to act in Hammerson's favor throughout the 1960s and early 1970s.

Hammerson continued to pursue London office development deals. One of its most notable schemes in this period was Woolgate House, a 300,000-square-foot office located on the area occupied by London's old Wool Exchange, a prime City site. Work started on November 4, 1964, a date which marked a turning point in the history of the U.K. property development industry with the announcement of the "Brown Ban" on new London office construction, named after George Brown, the minister responsible for issuing the government statement. The ban came into effect at midnight and the night of November 4, 1964 became known as the "night of the long pens," as developers engaged in a flurry of activity, signing as many contracts with builders as was possible before the deadline fell. Hammerson secured the safety of its Woolgate House project by signing a contract before the day ended, to show that development had commenced.

Hammerson, one of the most international of the U.K.'s property companies, ventured into the Canadian market in the late 1960s, and into Europe, in partnership with the Dutch company Boz. European projects included developments in Paris, Amsterdam, and Brussels. The partnership was terminated in 1979, when Hammerson sold its interest in the venture, following the takeover of Boz by Nationale Nederlanden.

During the late 1960s and early 1970s Hammerson undertook a considerable development program. The company's chairman, Sydney Mason, had recognized long ago that increasing competition in the development market would lead to declining profit margins on some development projects. In 1960 he had stated, in a speech to shareholders, that rising competition was leading Hammerson to plan complex projects, involving the careful piecing together of sites which could not immediately be obtained in their entirety. The year 1972 saw the completion of such a site, which had taken 12 years to assemble, and the firm was able to begin its huge Brent Cross shopping development.

Brent Cross was Hammerson's most important development during the early 1970s, with a floor area of one million sq. ft. Although in 1970, when planning permission was granted, Hammerson believed that development costs would be about £10 million, the inflationary conditions of the 1970s resulted in an actual cost, upon completion in 1976, of £33 million. However, with an annual rent roll of £2.5 million in 1977, the project was clearly a success. Development funding was provided by Standard Life Assurance, which also provided long-term finance upon completion. The group's funding arrangements were one of its key strengths during the 1970s; since the early 1960s very close links had been maintained with two of Britain's leading insurance companies, Standard Life Assurance and Royal London Mutual Insurance, both of which had substantial shareholdings in Hammerson. Both these companies provided development funds for the company.

With both the Brent Cross shopping mall and Woolgate House, development entailed the acquisition of a number of sites from different owners. Had the owners known what Hammerson had planned, the prices of the later sites to be acquired would have been much higher. Hammerson therefore acquired all the necessary sites before the market became aware of its intentions. As a result, land was acquired at a bargain price, but it often took a long time to put a consolidated site together.

Hammerson weathered the storm of the 1974 property crash better than most property companies. It had exercised considerable caution during the boom years of the early 1970s, being unwilling to pay what it considered to be unrealistic prices for properties. As a result fewer of its developments proved to be uneconomical in the light of the very different market conditions of the mid-1970s than was the case for many of its competitors. The company undertook little development in the United Kingdom until the end of the decade. Sydney Mason believed that the depressed state of the economy, combined with high interest rates and unstable rents and building costs, made development too hazardous. Rather than taking on new developments, the company took the safer course of concentrating on the modernization and refurbishment of existing property holdings as a source of increased income.

Hammerson adopted a cautious accounting policy throughout the 1970s, stating properties at cost less the amortization of short leaseholds, rather than at current market value. Capital appreciation had never been stressed as a source of income by the company to the same extent as most other property companies. Developments had therefore been organized so as to maximize long-term rental income. Eventually the company yielded to the prevailing trend and introduced the first valuation of its assets in 1983, swelling asset values, as shown in its annual report, but making it more vulnerable to takeover bids, as the true value of the company could be more easily ascertained.

Since Hammerson's entry into the Canadian market in 1968, its operations there had expanded rapidly. By 1985 most of net rents earned from Canada accounted for 29% of the group's total net rents, notable developments including Bow Valley Square in Calgary and 40 University Avenue, Toronto. The company also expanded its Canadian activities by takeover, acquiring the Mascan Corporation with its large holdings of Canadian developments for £47 million in 1984. The year 1985 saw another Canadian acquisition, the purchase and part resale of the Rank Organisation's Canadian property company.

By 1985, many of Hammerson's assets were located overseas. Canadian properties alone accounted for 36% of its portfolio, properties in the United Kingdom amounting to only 33%, while Australasia accounted for 20% and the United

States 10%. Large commitments in the Australian and Canadian markets led to problems for the company in the mid-1980s as its asset value was reduced by currency fluctuations; in 1985 the Canadian dollar fell by 51%, the Australian dollar by 31% and the U.S. dollar by 24%. However, an appreciation in the company's asset value in the absence of these currency fluctuations reduced their impact.

Since the split with Boz in 1979, Hammerson had steered clear of the European continent, undertaking only a few small schemes. However, it relaunched European operations in September 1985, buying a portfolio of French properties from the ICI pension fund, for which it paid £31 million in shares. Increased activity in Europe was matched by a reduction in Australian operations. During the 1980s, Hammerson became less enthusiastic about the Australian market. Government restrictions on foreign investment created problems, as did the fact that a series of mergers had resulted in 85% of Australia's retail companies being ultimately controlled by one company. The latter therefore had considerable bargaining power when dealing with developers.

During January 1989, Hammerson successfully resisted a takeover bid by the Dutch property investment company Rodamco. It had the help of Standard Life, which increased its holdings of Hammerson's shares substantially during the course of the takeover battle.

Principal Subsidiaries: Hammerson U.K. Properties Ltd.; Hammerson (Amethyst) Properties Ltd.; Hammerson (New- chat) Properties Ltd.; Hammerson Group Management Ltd.; D.O.B. Estate Ltd. (65.22%); Hammerson International Holdings Ltd.; Hammerson Canada Inc.; Hammerson Mississauga Inc. (Canada); Hammerson Property Pty Ltd. (Australia); Hammerson Property (NZ) Ltd. (New Zealand); Hammerson Holdings (USA) Inc.; Hammerson SA (France); Hammerson GmbH (Germany); Hammerson España SA; Hammerson BV (Netherlands).

Further Reading: Whitehouse, Brian, *Partners in Property,* London, Birn, Shaw, 1964; Marriott, Oliver, *The Property Boom,* London, Hamish Hamilton Ltd., 1967; Hanson, Michael, "Company File: Hammerson," *Estates Gazette,* May 26, 1979; Erdman, Edward, *People and Property,* London, Batsford, 1982; Smyth, Hedley, "The Historical Growth of Property Companies and the Construction Industry in Great Britain between 1939 and 1979," unpublished Ph.D thesis, University of Bristol, 1982; "Hammerson Property—Canadian Bias," *Investors Chronicle,* May 24, 1985; Foster, Michael, "Hammerson—from Brent Cross to Buffalo," *Estates Gazette,* June 7, 1986; "Hammerson—Exchange Victim," *Investors Chronicle,* June 13, 1986; Tait, Nikki, "Rodamco's £1.3bn Hammerson Bid Lapses," *Financial Times,* January 21, 1989; Cheesewright, Paul, "A Pirate Mourns Past Fun," *Financial Times,* August 21, 1989.

—Peter Scott

HONGKONG LAND HOLDINGS LIMITED

One Exchange Square Central
Hong Kong
(05) 8428428
Fax: (05) 8459226

Public Company
Incorporated: 1889 as The Hongkong Land Investment and
   Agency Company Ltd.
Employees: 800
Sales: HK$2.08 billion (US$266.72 million)
Stock Exchanges: Hong Kong London Australia Singapore

Hongkong Land Holdings Limited is the holding company for the foremost property development and investment company in Hong Kong, which owns and manages 5.4 million square feet of prime office space in the colony's business center, Core Central.

The company's origins date back to 1864 when Catchik Paul Chater, a native of Calcutta, arrived in Hong Kong to become a clerk with the Bank of Hindustan. After two years with the Indian bank, Chater formed his own brokerage firm with backing from the wealthy Sassoon family of Iraq, then active in Hong Kong for more than three generations. By 1870 Chater's early trading success put him on the road to becoming one of Hong Kong's great *taipans,* or illustrious merchants, who made their fortunes in trading opium and tea, or simply land.

In 1870 Chater bought and leased his first piece of property to the Victoria Club on Hong Kong Island. Over the next ten years, he developed a number of sites on the Island's Core Central business district.

Today, the district's warren of skyscrapers, tightly packed from harbor front to the foot of the hill sloping down from Hong Kong Island's Peak district, is packed with shoppers and workers. This bustle owes much to Paul Chater's early efforts to develop the area to such an extent that he would later be described as "one of the most powerful and beneficent figures in the Empire."

During the 1870s Chater worked tirelessly to develop the Hong Kong harbor, providing new wharves for use by the colony's expanding trading and manufacturing businesses. He also did not neglect real estate opportunities in Kowloon, across the bay from Hong Kong Island.

In 1884 Chater founded the Hong Kong and Kowloon Wharf and Godown Company to continue developing the Kowloon coastline. Two years later, in 1886, Chater arranged a merger of his new company with wharves held by Jardine Matheson, the British trading giant, in Kowloon.

Besides aligning his own fortunes with those of a great trading company, Chater foresaw opportunities to develop commercial sites on Hong Kong island itself, adjoining the harbor. Attempting this was difficult as Hong Kong island had so little land at that time on which to build. To create space, Chater joined in various land reclamation projects, the results of which have greatly changed Hong Kong's coastline. The cost of reclaiming land was high, but demand for space in Hong Kong was as acute in the 1880s as it remained in the 1990s.

Hong Kong property developers could foresee high land prices and handsome investment returns from land they reclaimed. Chater was not disappointed. In 1887, he began pursuing the 57-acre Praya Reclamation Project in Central District, on which stand many of Hong Kong Island's most prestigious buildings, including the Mandarin Oriental Hotel. To argue his case for reclamation, Chater bypassed the Hong Kong governor, Sir William Des Voeux, and traveled personally to London to conclude negotiations with the Colonial Office. The Hongkong Land Investment and Agency Company was incorporated in March 1889 to facilitate the Praya project.

To maintain his ties with Jardine Matheson, Chater lured James Johnstone Keswick, an early *taipan* with the trading company, to Hongkong Land. Chater and J.J. Keswick became permanent joint managing directors of the new company. Hongkong Land's first issue of shares in 1889 yielded a mere HK$250,000 in working capital. The fact that the issue was almost solely taken up by European investors provoked anger among many Chinese investors, who promptly established a rival real estate company. Chater and Keswick responded to this challenge by making a further share issue of 25,000 HK$100 shares, doubling Hongkong Land's working capital and providing for a reserve fund of HK$1.25 million.

However, the company's funds were soon used up in getting work underway at the Praya Reclamation Project. In 1890, land worth HK$800,000 was purchased, and mortgage loans of HK$1.3 million were made. Shareholders received a 7% dividend at the year-end in 1890. At the 1890 annual general meeting in Hong Kong's city hall, shareholders protested against the low return for an allegedly expensive share issue a year earlier. To quell the criticism, Keswick once again justified his nickname, "James the Bloody-Polite," calming nerves in the audience and urging the shareholders to sit tight for future rewards from their real estate investment.

True to Keswick's word, the returns for Hongkong Land shareholders grew over the next decade. The annual dividend stood at 8% for much of the 1890s, rising to 10% in 1898 and 12% in 1899. Notable among Hongkong Land's early developments was the New Oriental building, completed in 1898 on the recently reclaimed land stretching from Des Voeux Road to the fashionable Connaught Road.

Soon skyscrapers were added by Hongkong Land to the reclaimed site, earning Chater a knighthood in 1905. Between June 1904 and December 1905, the company built five tall buildings, each either five or six stories in size, which dwarfed the other buildings in the colony. Bolstered by the success of the Praya Reclamation Project, Chater completed the adjoining Praya East Reclamation Project in 1921, in time to profit from the establishment of the giant Hongkong Electric on the site.

Before his death in 1926, Chater was the guiding light for Hongkong Land.

In the years before World War II, the company built up a property portfolio in the colony worth HK$11.34 million in 1941, and comprising 13 key properties in the central business district. The Japanese occupation of Hong Kong suspended operations at the company, which reclaimed its properties in September 1945, finding most in remarkably good structural condition.

After the war Hongkong Land sold off much of its non-core central portfolio, including badly damaged properties in the Peak district. It then set its sights on key developments in the business district itself.

The company's first large development project was the adding of three stories to Marina House, first completed in 1935. Then, in 1950, Hongkong Land completed a HK$7 million redevelopment of 11 and 13 Queen's Road Central, turning the complex into the nine-story Edinburgh House.

The building of Jardine House was completed in 1958, following renovations to the earlier Jardine Building, purchased in 1955. In the same period, the company erected the 13-story Alexandra House on a triangular site formed by Des Voeux Road, Chater Road, and Ice House Road.

During this period, Hongkong Land was involved in work to establish much of the colony's skyscraper waterfront known worldwide. Also in 1958, Hongkong Land demolished the King's and York buildings, first erected in 1905, to make way for Swire House. The Queen's Building, once the crown in the company's portfolio, was torn down to make way for the giant Mandarin Oriental Hotel, opened in 1963. The completion of the Prince's Building in 1965 brought to nine the number of major office and commercial blocks which the company then owned on Hong Kong's prestigious waterfront and in the central district.

In 1965, Hongkong Land began developing low cost residential homes for sale, especially in the colony's Kwun Tong and Shaukiwan districts. The company later made investments in southeast Asia, purchasing properties in Australia, Hawaii, Indonesia, Thailand, Singapore, and Malaysia. Returning to core commercial property, Hongkong Land completed in 1972 and 1975 respectively The Excelsior Hotel and World Trade Centre developments, on land first purchased by Jardine Matheson in 1841.

In 1970, however, Hongkong Land gained world attention by paying a record price of HK$258 million for reclaimed land on Connaught Road, along Hong Kong's waterfront. Company chairman Henry Keswick, a descendant of J.J. Keswick, made the bid before announcing plans for a 50-story development on the site, the Connaught Centre. The building was completed in 1973 and was renamed Jardine House in January 1989.

The construction of the Connaught Centre prompted a change of name from Hongkong Land Investment and Agency Company to The Hongkong Land Company. This change coincided with expansion for the group through the purchase of Humphrey's Estate and Finance in 1971, and the Dairy Farm Ice and Cold Storage Company a year later. Before 1986, when Hongkong Land sold the company, Dairy Farm grew to become the colony's largest department store chain, and Australia's third largest.

In 1973, Hongkong Land bought a 49% stake in the Oriental Hotel in Bangkok. This diversification was made against a backdrop of a slumping property market affected by a bearish Hong Kong stock market in 1973. A general tightening of credit in the economy as a whole, and controls imposed on commercial rents, encouraged Hongkong Land's strategy.

A year later, Mandarin International Hotels was established, to be followed by the building of the Manila Mandarin and the Jakarta Mandarin in the late 1970s. In 1987, Mandarin Oriental International Limited was demerged from Hongkong Land and given its own stock market listing on the Hong Kong stock exchange. With seven hotels in southeast Asia, and contracts to operate a number of Mandarin hotels in North America, the company remains a formidable force in the global hotel trade.

In 1976 Hongkong Land completed work on a 36-story development to join Alexandra House to Prince's Building, Swire House, the Mandarin Hotel and the Connaught Centre, by a series of interlocking footbridges. This effort was soon supplanted by the Central Redevelopment, Hongkong Land's masterplan for redeveloping the colony's Core Central business district. This meant the demolition of five old buildings owned by the company—Gloucester Building, Windsor House, Lane Crawford House, and behind them Marina House and Edinburgh House—to make way for the Landmark.

This giant complex entailed the building of two 47-story office blocks, Gloucester Tower and Edinburgh Tower, both to be surrounded by a five-story shopping development. Completed in two stages, in 1980 and 1983, the Landmark serves as a focus for Hong Kong's business and shopping centers.

Despite the colony's property boom in 1980 and 1981, the effects of the world recession and high unemployment rates on domestic commerce and real estate prices depressed market conditions at the beginning of 1982. Property prices in Hong Kong plunged, and hesitation among investors, combined with generally weakened purchasing power, left the property market in a depressed state. Hongkong Land's reaction in 1982 was to diversify out of its traditional areas of property development and investment, and to purchase large stakes in the Hong Kong Telephone Company and Hongkong Electric Holdings.

However, it was the legacy of the early 1980s property boom which led to the company's acquiring the last major site in Core Central, near the Connaught Centre, for HK$4.7 million in February 1982. Work began shortly after on Exchange Square, the colony's largest commercial development to that time.

The heavy borrowings to finance the Exchange Square project helped lead Hongkong Land into financial difficulties when the colony's property market crashed in 1983. The slump in demand for large residential units and commercial office space produced a property recession in 1984.

As a reaction, Hongkong Land underwent a major reorganization to reduce its substantial borrowings. In 1984 gearing—the amount of borrowings in relation to a company's equity or shareholder's funds—stood at an uncomfortably high 103%.

Hongkong Land sold most of its overseas properties and non-core investments including its stakes in Hong Kong Telephone and Hongkong Electric. By the end of 1986, the company had brought gearing down to a managable 31% without greatly reducing its presence in Core Central, the heart of its property portfolio.

Ambitious restructuring continued with the demerger of Dairy Farm in 1986 and Mandarin Oriental in 1987 from the company's core holdings. At the same time, Jardine Matheson set up Jardine Strategic Holdings, a public company, which became Hongkong Land's principal shareholder.

Hongkong Land's residential portfolio was sold off in 1986, as were Harcourt House and Windsor House a year later. As a result, company gearing fell to a mere 6% of shareholders' funds in 1987.

Tower Three of Hongkong Land's ambitious Exchange Square project was opened in 1988, following the earlier opening of Towers One and Two in 1985. This brought office rentals in the complex up to three times their 1985 level.

In 1989, Hongkong Land acquired Fu House, which stood between two other Hongkong Land buildings, the Bank of Canton Building and No. 9 Ice House Street. The three buildings were demolished to make way for the company's newest development of 500,000 square feet. Also in 1989, Hongkong Land Holdings Limited was incorporated in Bermuda, with The Hongkong Land Company becoming a wholly owned subsidiary.

In late 1990, speculation in London pointed to a possible bid by Hongkong Land for Hammerson, the United Kingdom's third largest property concern. Because of the weakness of the U.K. property market, the concensus was that Hongkong Land believed it might well have found an economical way to acquiring a London property base.

At the same time, Hammerson, at 624 pence a share in January 1991, was capitalized at just over £1 billion. This would have made a bid for the U.K. property concern a large step for Hongkong Land.

Although Hongkong Land is financially sound as it heads into the 1990s, the outlook for the colony itself clouds the company's future business strategy. Apart from the instability affecting the world economy in general, Hong Kong is experiencing a drain in personnel and resources because of fears of what may follow in 1997 when ownership of the colony reverts to China.

Principal Subsidiaries: The Hongkong Land Company Ltd.; The Hongkong Land Property Company Ltd.; Hongkong Land (Commercial Centres) Ltd.; Hongkong Land (NT) Shopping Ltd.; Hongkong Land (S.H.) Ltd.; HKL (No. 9 Queen's Road Development) Ltd.; HKL (Prince's Building) Ltd.; Corona Land Company Ltd.; Llanfaes Investments Ltd.; Mulberry Land Company Ltd.; Silvercord Ltd.; Normelle Estates Ltd. (50%).

Further Reading: Criswell, Colin, *The Taipans of Hong Kong,* Oxford, Oxford University Press, 1981; *Hongkong Land 1889–1989,* Hong Kong, Hongkong Land, 1989.

—Etan Vlessing

JMB REALTY CORPORATION

900 North Michigan Avenue
Chicago, Illinois 60611
U.S.A.
(312) 440-4800
Fax: (312) 915-2310

Private Company
Incorporated: 1969
Employees: 4,500
Sales: $2.20 billion

The history of JMB Realty Corporation reads like a fairy tale for young entrepreneurs. From its modest inception in 1969, JMB has risen to become the largest and most widely respected noninstitutional manager of real estate in the United States. No longer a mere syndicator of packaged real estate deals, JMB also develops, manages, and owns an astonishing variety and number of the largest real estate projects across the United States and in Great Britain. Perhaps most remarkable of all is that JMB, which in 1990 controlled or owned outright some 21,000 apartment units, 150 shopping centers and malls, 15 deluxe hotels, and 65 million square feet of the most prestigious office space in the country, remains under the personal control and majority ownership of two of its founders, Judd Malkin and Neil Bluhm.

Malkin, Bluhm, and a third friend, Robert Judelson, grew up together in Chicago's west Rogers Park. All three were of modest, middle-class backgrounds and attended the same high school. Bluhm and Malkin became roommates and best friends at the University of Illinois at Champaign, Illinois, whence they both graduated in 1959 with accounting degrees. After obtaining their CPAs, Malkin became the head of a Chicago Toyota distributorship while Bluhm went on to a law degree from Northwestern University and a job at a Chicago law firm, Mayer, Brown & Platt. Robert Judelson, in the meantime, had become a real estate broker, and when Malkin began dabbling in the suburban markets the two of them decided to form a new venture devoted exclusively to real estate. Malkin then wooed his old friend Bluhm away from the comforts of Mayer, Brown, where he had quickly become a partner specializing in taxes. In 1969, Bluhm agreed to join the new company, JMB, the first letters of each of the partners' last names.

Malkin's determination to include Bluhm in JMB soon proved prescient. In 1970 the company convinced Continental Illinois Venture Company to invest $130,000 in JMB for 10%

of the latter's equity. Continental Illinois Venture was a venture capital offshoot of Chicago's Continental Bank, created just the year before with the legal advice of Mayer, Brown's Neil Bluhm. In helping the venture capital company with its tax structure Bluhm had greatly impressed the company's president, John Hines, and when Bluhm in the following year asked Continental on behalf of JMB for seed money, Hines felt confident that the investment would be successful. Hines later said that he had only a vague understanding of JMB's proposed business, the syndication of real estate packages, but he knew that Bluhm would do well in any venture.

Real estate syndication was at that time a relatively unknown practice. Its basic theory is simple. Instead of turning to banks for between 80% and 100% of the capital needed for a particular real estate project, the developer in a syndication sells off pieces of his equity to a multitude of small- and medium-sized investors. He is thus able largely to bypass the banks, put up very little of his own money, and by packaging subsequent, similar deals build a large portfolio of real estate that he controls and may either sell or continue to manage. As general, or managing, partner, the developer bears nearly all of the risks associated with the project.

The advantages of this scheme for the investors are many. As limited partners, they cannot be held responsible for more of the project's debt than the amount of their equity investment. On the other hand, investors share in the profits generated by the partnership, as well as the property's long-term appreciation in value, which in the case of some real estate projects is enormous. Finally, as the tax laws were structured in 1970, even limited partners could deduct interest and depreciation expenses of the partnership from their personal income on a pro-rata basis. Because the ventures were highly leveraged, interest deductions were very high for the first few years of the project, as was depreciation, resulting in substantial savings for those individual investors saddled with large incomes and few available deductions.

By allowing the small investor to buy a piece of prime real estate while sharply increasing the investor's real income, JMB and the other syndicators springing up around the country were able to attract thousands of eager clients. In 1971 the firm launched the first of its Carlyle public partnerships. When the partnership almost overnight raised $7 million, it allowed JMB to reward Continental Illinois Venture's investment with a fivefold profit after a single year. This gave solid evidence that real estate syndication was an idea whose time had come. Continental finally sold its 10% equity back to JMB in 1978 for $4.3 million, a move that the bank now cheerfully admits was a blunder.

Unlike many of their fellow syndicators, Malkin, Bluhm, and Judelson made a policy of not pursuing tax-driven ventures structured solely on the basis of their potential tax benefits. Many such deals found themselves in trouble when the absence of a sound underlying economic logic overshadowed the tax benefits and threatened the entire venture's survival. By avoiding tax-driven deals, JMB built an asset base more secure than most of its competitors as well as a reputation—critical in a business dependent on investor confidence—for having a generally cautious investment policy. JMB would buy only those properties that made money, regardless of the tax benefits.

A second important difference between JMB and its rivals was JMB's preference for expensive, top-of-the-line properties.

The partners were convinced that in a recession the last buildings to feel the pinch were the exclusive ones, and they planned their investments accordingly. JMB also regularly borrowed bank funds for the initial down payments on their new properties, and only then went to investors with their offer of equity in a well-defined, verifiable project. In this way, investors felt that they knew what they were getting into, and JMB knew that it had suitably placed the money thus raised.

The result of JMB's prudence was nothing short of spectacular. Though Judelson left the firm in 1973 to found Balcor Company with Jerry Reinsdorf, JMB grew at a frenetic pace during the 1970s. It soon began a series of fruitful collaborations with Aetna Life and Casualty's Urban Investment and Development Company, raising capital for Urban's major mixed-use developments such as Chicago's Water Tower Place and Boston's Copley Place. Until the end of the decade, most of JMB's funds were invested by individuals in relatively modest amounts, $10,000 to $100,000, but the passage by Congress in 1974 of the Employment Retirement Income Security Act (ERISA), gave the nation's big pension plans the go-ahead to invest more heavily in real estate. Sensing an imminent rush into real estate on the part of pension managers, JMB created a pension advisory division, JMB Institutional Realty, in 1978. Division manager John Lillard had soon enlisted the pension funds of a half-dozen leading corporations, including CBS, Inland Steel, Xerox, and Chrysler.

Pension funds invest enormous sums of money. With the addition of this new financial muscle JMB made further innovations. In 1979, the company formed JMB Development to research and manage the firm's own real estate developments. Some observers questioned the prudence of this move, as it would take JMB from the abstract financial world of syndicating to the more practical realm of construction and leasing. JMB's philosophy of finding the best available individuals and giving them equity incentives, however, proved to work equally well in the development end of the business. In effect, JMB did not enter the development industry; it bought up already successful developers and paid them handsomely to continue with their work. In 1983 JMB teamed up with Federated Stores, the leading department store operator and developer of shopping malls, to form JMB/Federated Realty Associates; and in the following year spent $1.4 billion to buy out its frequent former partner, Urban Investment and Development.

The impact of these two acquisitions substantially altered the nature of JMB's business. In addition to the investments it managed on behalf of its 146,000 individual limited partners, JMB found itself thrust into the role of a major U.S. real estate developer, with a host of projects already built, under way, or on the drawing board. Its collective properties, owned and/or managed, were now valued at $10 billion, and in order to maintain effective control over this growing empire Malkin and Bluhm encouraged the top managers at Urban to remain with the newly named subsidiary, JMB/Urban Development Company. Many of them did, lured by the equity bonuses offered by the two founders, and JMB was able to assimilate its two new partners with nary a hitch.

Although its Carlyle syndications were now raising hundreds of millions of dollars, JMB continued to widen the range of its other activities. This became especially important when tax code amendments in the mid-1980s scared many investors away from syndication, and a number of the less savvy operators went out of business or were forced to retrench. Even JMB, which suffered less than most, saw total syndication dollars slip from the 1985 high of $619 million to $452 million in the following year. Given this investment climate, in 1986 JMB further expanded its development assets by purchasing for $600 million Alcoa's properties in Century City, Los Angeles; and 1987 it added Walt Disney's Arvida Corporation, paying $400 million for the giant resort developer. With the purchase of Arvida, JMB had built a strong presence for itself in three different segments of the real estate market: shopping centers, office and industrial space, and resorts.

The biggest was yet to come, however. In 1987, JMB successfully bid $2 billion for the Toronto-based Cadillac Fairview Corporation, a developer of both shopping malls and office space. To reduce its debt burden, JMB subsequently sold about $450 million worth of Cadillac's less attractive properties. The Cadillac purchase, which brought with it some 42 shopping malls and a handful of prime office structures, was most likely the largest commercial real estate deal ever transacted. Upon its completion, JMB owned or operated approximately $20 billion in assets on behalf of some 350,000 individual investors, 95 corporate pension funds, and 65 endowments and foundations. None of its 30 public partnerships had ever failed to make a quarterly distribution to investors, who on average had realized annual pretax returns of 13.2%— versus an industry standard of 6.7%. JMB had become not only the largest but also the most successful syndicator.

Since then, JMB has hardly slowed down. In 1988 it paid $950 million for Amfac Inc., a diversified owner of Hawaiian sugarcane plantations, resort developments, retail chains, and electrical distribution. Amfac's beachfront acreage will likely prove to be a long-term gold mine for JMB. In 1989 the firm gobbled up Great Britain's Randsworth Trust P.L.C. for $800 million, including the refinancing of debt, and Eastern Corporation's Houston Center, a large mixed-use development. Practically lost in this blizzard of deals were failed bids for Bloomingdales and Hilton Hotels, a 1983 attempt to rescue the *Chicago Sun-Times* from the clutches of Rupert Murdoch, and the successful purchase of 20% of the Chicago Bears in 1987.

At the start of the 1990s, some 30% of JMB's $22 billion portfolio was owned outright by the company, and Bluhm and Malkin each retain about 33% of JMB's stock. These two men were yet only in their early 50s, still eager for action, and apparently unafraid of taking on any challenge.

Principal Subsidiaries: JMB Properties Co.; Amfac/JMB; JMB/Urban Development Co.

Further Reading: Phillips, Stephen, "A Realty Concern With a Big Appetite," *The New York Times,* June 13, 1987; Hylton, Richard D., "Has Realty Giant Grown Too Large?" *The New York Times,* December 28, 1989.

—Jonathan Martin

LAND SECURITIES PLC

LAND SECURITIES PLC

5 Strand
London, WC 2N 5AF
United Kingdom
(071) 413-9000

Public Company
Incorporated: 1905 as Land Securities Assets Co. Ltd.
Employees: 484
Sales: £316.00 million (US$609.92 million)
Stock Exchange: London

Unlike most of its competitors, Land Securities has achieved and maintained its position as the U.K.'s largest property company by concentrating on the home market rather than expanding overseas. Apart from an unsuccessful venture into the Canadian market, via its subsidiary Ravenseft Properties Ltd. in the 1950s, no attempts have been made to expand abroad. Rapid growth since the 1940s has been based on specialization in the highest quality London offices and, through Ravenseft, the redevelopment of provincial shopping centers. Diversification into industrial property and retail warehouses has made an increasing contribution to growth.

Land Securities originated in 1944, when in the spring of that year Harold Samuel bought a tiny property company, Land Securities Investment Trust Ltd., (originally incorporated in 1905 as Land Securities Assets Co. Ltd.), with assets of three houses and government securities valued at about £19,000. By March 1952 assets had rocketed to £11.1 million due to Samuel's skillful property market dealing.

Harold Samuel was born in 1912. After leaving school in 1929 he began work as an articled pupil—and apprentice—in the estate agency firm of Johnston Evans & Co., in London. A childhood acquaintance was Louis Freedman, whose provincial shop development activities were to complement Samuel's London office acquisitions and developments following World War II.

One of the most talented of all property tycoons, Harold Samuel understood the ways in which flaws and imperfections in the property market could be exploited, and introduced many of the techniques that were to make fortunes for the new breed of property developers in the early postwar years. One of the factors behind his remarkable success as a property entrepreneur was his use of borrowed funds to expand holdings, a technique which he put to good effect in the unsophisticated property market of the 1940s. In his book *The Property*

Boom, Oliver Marriott recounts how the fledgling Land Securities was able to obtain its first properties without committing too much of its own capital. Properties in Hatch End were bought in 1944 for £15,213; £9,477 being paid by bank loan, while other properties were bought at Neasden for £4,847; £3,335 being raised by mortgaging. Insurance companies were generally happy to provide mortgage finance, given the shortage of investment outlets other than gilts in the late 1940s. Interest rates were low, due to the Attlee government's cheap money policy, while a shortage of new properties, fostered by government building controls and materials shortages, ensured that rising property prices more than covered interest payments. The early accounts for Land Securities illustrate the importance of borrowed funds; in March 1948 the company's equity stood at £70,000, while mortgages and loans amounted to £1.3 million.

Another area in which Samuel showed considerable skill involved circumventing or taking advantage of the complex legal framework which regulated the property market in the early postwar years. Until 1947, borrowing was limited to £10,000 unless permission to exceed this sum was given by a government body known as the Capital Issues Committee. For some years after 1947 money could not be borrowed without the consent of this body. Samuel overcame these problems by establishing subsidiaries, each of that could borrow up to the limit, and by taking over property companies which already had agreed borrowings.

He also took advantage of a lucrative provision of the Town and Country Planning Act of 1947, under which a block of flats that had been requisitioned for office use could remain as office property without the payment of any development charge. He acquired a number of former flats that could now be used as offices; often their owners did not know of this provision and he obtained them at very attractive prices. Yet another of Samuel's innovations was his early institution of the full repairing and insuring lease which, by placing responsibility for repairs and insurance with the tenant, lowered property management costs.

Harold Samuel had very definite views about the types of properties which were likely to prove the most profitable long-term investments. He concentrated almost exclusively on London offices with first class specifications and locations. If a new property did not come up to his standards it was often refurbished to bring it up to the highest quality. This often entailed heavy expenditure and a temporary loss of income, but resulted in higher rents and property values in the long run.

From the end of World War II until 1954, very severe restrictions governed property development, prohibiting any development which was not granted a government building license. As a result Land Securities dealt chiefly in the purchase, rather than development, of properties, concentrating on the west end of London. However, the company was able to do some development prior to the removal of controls by taking on projects in the one area for which licenses could be obtained, offices for government occupation. Samuel preferred government and other large tenants because of the security of their tenure and the fact that they could take on an entire building, thereby lowering management costs. In the case of one building, Regent Arcade House, Land Securities waited for over a year in order to find a single prestigious tenant; one was finally found which suited its requirements, the Bank of England. This was a time of rapid growth for the company; its assets, which only amounted to £19,321 in 1944, had grown to £11 million by 1952.

A number of early takeovers increased assets and drew public attention to Samuel's entrepreneurial skills. These takeovers included United City Property Trust in 1948 and the much more important acquisition of Associated London Properties (ALP) for £2.1 million in 1951, which almost doubled the book value of Land Securities's assets. Associated London Properties' assets included a number of office blocks let at prewar rents, with leases which were due to expire between 1958 and 1961, at which time they could be re-let for substantially higher rents. While ALP's directors were well aware of the value of these properties; they were unable to raise dividends since this value would not be reflected in increased income until the leases expired. Samuel was therefore able to acquire the company at a price which reflected its current, rather than potential, income value. He also received other benefits from the acquisition. Cash was raised from the sale of Associated London Properties's residential and factory assets and, more importantly, the remaining assets included a large number of properties with no mortgage commitments, which could be used to raise further mortgage finance.

Two years later, Land Securities launched another takeover bid, this time for the Savoy Group. The bid sparked controversy and ended in failure, but had some positive results. It was wrongly claimed that Samuel intended to convert the Savoy Group's hotels into offices and the resulting hostile press reaction contributed to the failure of the bid. This adverse publicity left Samuel feeling he had been unjustly treated by the press, and thereafter he kept as far out of the public eye as possible. However, by earning him a reputation as a skilled corporate predator, this episode enhanced his reputation in the City and made it easier for Land Securities to raise development finance on attractive terms.

In the ten years after 1954, when building license restrictions were lifted, Land Securities greatly expanded development activities, becoming one of the most prominent developers in London. The property market experienced a boom as the demand for property raced ahead of supply, which had been held back by wartime bombing and postwar shortages and development controls. Its rapidly expanding development program allowed the company to take full advantage of the large profit margins that were available to developers during these boom years, resulting in rising profits and rapid growth.

While Samuel concentrated on the London office market, Land Securities was also able to obtain a stake in the lucrative provincial shop market from 1946 via Ravenseft, a subsidiary which became fully owned in 1955. Ravenseft was set up by Louis Freedman and Frederick Maynard. Both Freedman and Maynard had begun their careers in estate agency in London during the 1930s. Here they learned, along with many others who were to become successful developers in the postwar years, the art of property dealing.

With the help of Samuel, who provided valuable contacts, Freedman set up Ravensfield Investment Trust Ltd., as it was then called, in 1946. Ravensfield's strategy was to operate in the provincial markets, where competition was less fierce than in London. By 1949 Freedman realized that to cover all the provincial markets he needed a partner, and was able to attract Fred Maynard from the estate agents Healey & Baker. From 1949 to 1966 their company, under the new name of Ravenseft Properties Ltd. was to invest £60 million in new shops comprising over 400 developments in 150 U.K. towns and cities. It pioneered the redevelopment of bombed-out town and city centers in cooperation with the municipal authorities. A virtual lack of competition in these markets and the prestige value of its association with Land Securities were important factors behind Ravenseft's rapid early growth. The very nature of the type of developments that Ravenseft had chosen to undertake also contributed to success. Building licenses were easily obtained for this type of development, and as the local authorities were eager to see such projects go ahead they were prepared to use their powers of compulsory purchase to acquire the necessary land.

Once the supply of blitzed city sites began to run down, Ravenseft turned to the "New Towns," which were then largely at the planning stage. It took the gamble that these towns would become successful commercial centers, a gamble which proved to be highly rewarding. It also attempted, unsuccessfully, to enter the Canadian property market in 1956, its failure being largely due to its unwillingness to take on a Canadian partner with detailed knowledge of the local market. Ravenseft pulled out of Canada in 1962 and Land Securities has subsequently avoided dealings in overseas property, even going so far as to sell a stake in the valuable Pan Am building in New York when subsequently taking over the stake's owner, City Centre Properties Ltd., in 1968. In 1955, when Samuel bought up the remaining 50% of Ravenseft's shares, the deal valued the company at £2.1 million.

During 1955, Samuel also consolidated Land Securities' debts and capital structure. Due to the high regard in which the company was held by the City at this time he was able to issue £20 million of debentures which were taken up by Legal & General, Norwich Union, and the church commissioners, with an interest rate of only 4.5%, virtually no higher than that which was available for gilt-edged stocks to government bonds.

By the late 1950s the credit squeeze made fund raising much more difficult for property developers, as the Bank of England instructed the banking sector to reduce lending. These restrictions shifted the balance of power in favor of the financial institutions when making funding agreements with developers. The institutions began to ask for a percentage of the profits from developments, while being careful not to take on too much of the risk. In the spring of 1959, Legal & General and Land Securities entered into the industry's first convertible debenture agreement. A total of £6 million was to be lent to Land Securities for expansion, on the security of a debenture. What made this deal unusual was that £1 million of this was convertible into Land Securities's ordinary shares at a price equivalent to 22 shillings 6 pence per share. Legal & General thereby secured a stake in any profits that might result from the funding. The arrangement drew a negative reaction from the press, as it led to a dilution of Land Securities's equity. However, such deals were to become standard over the next few years.

The imposition of the "Brown Ban" on office development in and around London in November 1964 reduced the scope for Land Securities's expansion through further developments.

The company therefore turned to takeovers as a source of growth. In the late 1960s, two very important takeover bids were launched. The first of these involved the acquisition of City Centre Properties Ltd. in 1968. City Centre, the former vehicle of one of the United Kingdom's most famous property developers, Jack Cotton, and latterly Clarles Clore, had a number of valuable assets, including the stake in the Pan Am Building mentioned above, and raised the value of Land Securities's assets to £325 million. In April 1969 another successful takeover bid was launched, for The City of London Real Property Company Ltd. (CLRP), one of the U.K.'s oldest and most prestigious property companies. Established in 1864, it had concentrated its activities on City of London office property and owned what was probably the highest quality property portfolio of any institution. This acquisition swelled Land Securities's portfolio to more than £600 million and made Harold Samuel the largest property owner in the world. In 1971, Westminster Trust Ltd. was added to Land Securities's portfolio, its £20 million of assets including New Scotland Yard.

By the early 1970s, Land Securities was regarded by many commentators as a sleeping giant. In fact it had one of the largest development programs of all U.K. property companies. Land Securities was, however, more skeptical than most that the property boom would go on forever and did not borrow beyond its current ability to repay its debts, unlike many of its competitors. It emerged from the 1974 property crash in better shape than many of its rivals, although not completely unscathed, as is shown by its share value, which had topped a price of 279 pence in 1973 and fell to 100 pence in 1974.

In the late 1970s, Land Securities made some adjustments. Property and land were sold, development projects were curtailed, and funds were raised by rights issues rather than borrowing, in order to avoid debts at a time of high interest rates. During these years, a time of rising prices for development land as institutional investment forced property prices up, Land Securities concentrated on developing its own property portfolio by redevelopment, refurbishment, and lease reconstruction, rather than buying land at what it considered to be expensive prices.

In 1983, the value of the company's property assets topped £2 billion. Unlike many of the U.K.'s other large property companies, Land Securities still refrained from overseas expansion, concentrating instead on improving its U.K. portfolio. Assets were concentrated in the most conventional types of investment property; in 1985 60% of the portfolio was made up of offices; shops accounting for 37%. However, during the mid-1980s the company began to develop and acquire a number of out-of-town retail warehouses and food superstores.

By 1988, after four years of activity, it had acquired a potential area of four million square feet of these types of building, spread over 50 locations throughout the country. Land Securities undertook some shop developments during the 1980s, but still concentrated activities in the central London office sector. During the summer of 1984, developments in progress included over one million square feet of central London offices.

Harold Samuel died on August 28, 1987, having remained chairman of Land Securities until his death. In 1963 he had been the first developer to receive a knighthood, and had been made a life peer in 1972. P.J. Hunt, the company's managing director, became both chairman and managing director. During 1987 Land Securities became the United Kingdom's first property company with more than £3 billion of assets. The rise in asset value was matched by an increase in borrowing which rose from £231 million in March 1985 to £837 million in May 1987. New borrowing was arranged entirely on a long-term basis at a fixed rate of interest. Rising interest rates at the end of the decade therefore had little effect on development finance.

A key factor behind Land Securities's success is the inherent strength of the portfolio, built up by its founder, Lord Samuel. He is credited with inventing the maxim "There are three things you need in property, these are: location, location, and location."

Principal Subsidiaries: Ravenseft Properties Ltd.; The City of London Real Property Company Ltd.; Ravenside Investments Ltd.; Ravenseft Industrial Estates Ltd..

Further Reading: Bull, George, and Anthony Vice, *Bid For Power,* London, Elek Books, 1958; Whitehouse, Brian, *Partners in Property,* London, Birn, Shaw, 1964; Marriott, Oliver, *The Property Boom,* London, Hamish Hamilton Ltd., 1967; Aris, Stephen, *The Jews in Business,* London, Jonathan Cape, 1970; Foster, Michael, "Company File: Land Securities," *Estates Gazette,* June 20, 1981; Erdman, Edward, *People and Property,* London, Batsford, 1982; Smyth, Hedley, "The Historical Growth Of Property Companies and the Construction Industry in Britain between 1939 and 1979," unpublished Ph.D thesis, University of Bristol, 1982; Gordon, Charles, *The Two Tycoons,* 1984; "Balance Sheet Strength at Land Securities," *Investors Chronicle,* June 7, 1985; "Land Securities: Topping £3 Billion," *Investors Chronicle,* May 22, 1987; "Obituary—Lord Samuel: Developer," *Financial Times,* September 1, 1987; *Report: Land Securities,* 1988, 1989.

—Peter Scott

LEND LEASE CORPORATION LIMITED

Level 46
Australia Square Tower
Sydney NSW 2000
Australia
(02) 236-6111

Public Company
Incorporated: 1958
Employees: 7,019
Sales: A$1.69 billion (US$1.31 billion)
Stock Exchanges: Australia New Zealand

Lend Lease Corporation, Australia's leading real estate development corporation, with branches and subsidiaries throughout the world, owes its resounding success to the unorthodox methods of its founder Gerard Dusseldorp. From its inception the company has been an integrated property service and—in recent years—a financial service which presents to its clients and customers a "one-stop" service in the property market.

In the late 1940s, Australia was basically a nation of sheep farmers. The country, with a population of 8.3 million, was undeveloped and maintained a colonial dependence upon Europe and other nations for many of the basic necessities of life, in exchange for wool. World War II showed the danger of such an existence, and the nation was very much in favor of developing its own natural resources and skills.

Australia's dry climate made a source for a plentiful supply of water necessary to the development of the nation. The solution lay in a project called the Snowy Mountains Scheme, which entailed the taming of a snow-fed alpine river by the interruption of its seaward course. The river would then be sent through 130 kilometers of tunnels through a mountain range and a system of holding reservoirs to join rivers on the other side, 900 meters below. This design, however, was beyond the resources of this relatively small nation. What became known as the Snowy Mountains Hydro-Electric Authority (SMHA) was the trigger that implemented Australia's most ambitious immigration program. A government mission traveled worldwide, recruiting tradesmen, engineers, and laborers.

In Amsterdam the call was answered by Bredero's Bouwbedrijf of Utrecht (Bredero's) and The Royal Dutch Harbour Company. Bredero's sent a 30-year-old engineer, Gerard J. Dusseldorp, to Australia on a fact-finding tour for the Dutch construction firm. What he discovered was a country ripe for development and about to enter a period of great growth and prosperity. His report convinced the two firms to embark on a joint venture. They formed a company called Civil & Civic Contractors and put Dusseldorp in charge. Its first assignment was to supply and erect 200 prefabricated houses for the Snowy Mountain project. The 35 workers for the job were recruited in Holland by Dusseldorp and brought to Australia under the liberalized immigration laws.

Civil & Civic completed its first assignment within 15 months, but out of the SMHA came further jobs for the fledgling company. Bridges, houses, flats, and hospital extensions were added to the projects the company was to complete in the area of Cooma and Canberra. As a result, a locally engaged work force was soon growing around the nucleus of the original 35 Dutch workers.

At all times, however, G.J. Dusseldorp, who was by then Civil & Civic's managing director, was looking for a way to expand the company's operations. He focused on Sydney, Australia's largest city, which was about to experience the largest building boom in its history.

Dusseldorp, as a developer, was constantly seeking a better way to do things, not only to boost company profits, but also to set standards of excellence within the industry. For him, the traditional system of tendering was, in his words, "a gushing stream of waste." When other firms were unreliable, the contractor had to shoulder the burden of their mistakes. He wanted to establish a system that was to remain the foundation of the company's philosophy—undivided responsibility for any project from start to finish.

Civil & Civic had a chance to try out the new system when a small project in Sydney in 1953 was presented to the company. Dusseldorp was determined to prove that there was a better way to handle a construction project. An oil refinery needed a gatehouse to be added to a new plant currently under construction. Civil & Civic designed and built it within six weeks. It was the firm's first design and construction project.

In 1954 Dusseldorp's chance had come to put Civil & Civic on the map by building Sydney's first concrete skyscraper. He was determined, however, to become the sole entrepreneur, thus ensuring complete control over the project. He wanted to take over the option, the council-approved plans, and the services of the architect and engineer. All that Dusseldorp now lacked was the money.

He approached Bredero's in Holland for a £100,000 loan which he was refused, but the president of the Reconstruction Bank of Holland was present at Dusseldorp's presentation. He was impressed with Dusseldorp's style, determination, and confidence, and backed the loan.

When building work began Dusseldorp was faced with yet another problem besetting the construction industry—industrial action by the workers' unions. He therefore proposed to the unions an agreement which among other things would include a productivity bonus. Although viewed at first with skepticism, it proved a great success as building workers began to feel like valued employees.

Caltex House was finished months ahead of the original schedule and established Civil & Civic as a leading contractor. Now the company could sell itself as a new composite building service which operated in conjunction with leading architects and engineers. Such a service was designed to eliminate delays and reduce costs.

Yet Dusseldorp was not satisfied. He was still searching for a better package to present to prospective buyers or leasers. During the building boom of the early 1960s there was a great need for new construction of all kinds. Many companies, as a result of their own success, were being forced to build larger premises. The buying of larger premises inevitably meant tying up capital that was needed for business operations. Dusseldorp concluded that what most businesses were looking for were premises which they could lease.

He also saw a need for cooperative projects which would bring together people with a common interest, such as doctors who needed professional consulting rooms. Such professionals would not be able to finance such projects independently. Dusseldorp had the solution.

He decided to float a finance and investment company and go to the Australian public for funds to finance Civil & Civic projects on completion, thus gaining entrepreneurial control over their projects. In April 1958, Lend Lease Corporation Limited was established and floated on the stock exchange with Civil & Civic holding 40% of the shares.

This original share issue was floated to finance the construction of a seven-story building containing professional consulting rooms. The deal was that North Shore Medical Centre Pty, Ltd., which owned the land, had the right to occupy or nominate the occupant of specified areas in the building. Lend Lease was to take up the whole of the issued capital of the company on completion of the building and would then sell the professional suites on term contracts over varying periods, while retaining part of the space in the building as an investment—in other words, lending and leasing.

It was not long before Lend Lease began to acquire its own sites, plan the development, and construct buildings in cooperation with Civil & Civic. They were set to provide and complete development of large-scale projects of real estate.

Both Civil & Civic and Lend Lease were out to gain prestige and publicity. They began to tender for projects that would put them in the public eye. Buildings such as the Academy of Science in Canberra would win them the Sulman prize for architecture. It was not until February 1959, however, that Lend Lease became a household name. It was at that time that the company contracted to build stage one of the Sydney Opera House.

Civil & Civic and Lend Lease were not ordinary construction outfits. The management of both organizations had an interest in urban planning and renewal. Plans for new building sites would always include open areas with fountains and plazas so that beauty as well as commerce might be enjoyed.

As the organization grew, it also had to change. Between 1959 and 1962 Lend Lease acquired its original sponsor, Civil & Civic, as well as six companies whose manufactured products were useful to their construction business. These companies supplied Lend Lease with elevators, windows, and building materials. The company also bought a ski resort and a motel chain. It was set to change from the role of financier of other people's projects to that of developing and managing real capital assets for long-term property investors.

In June 1960 a subsidiary company was formed to take control of Lend Lease's joint operations with Civil & Civic. The parent company formulated policy and provided specialist advisory skills. It also developed new projects and raised the money to carry these projects out. The subsidiary, Lend Lease

Development Pty. Ltd., selected and purchased the sites, dealt with the authorities, and managed the design and construction of the site, as well as the sale or lease of projects.

Lend Lease was now involved in a multitude of projects from commercial buildings to suburban housing to recreational sites. The group was expanded to include 14 operating companies. Their presence was virtually ubiquitous in Australia, especially in the cities of Sydney, Canberra, Melbourne, Launceston, Brisbane, and Perth.

In May of 1968 one of Lend Lease's largest projects, Australia Square, was officially opened by the Duke of Edinburgh. It won the Sulman Award for Architectural Merit, and the Civic Design Award of the New South Wales chapter of the Royal Australian Institute of Architects for a work of oustanding design.

By 1971 property values in Australia were peaking. Dusseldorp could see that the bottom was soon going to drop out of office development market and it was decided that Lend Lease would end its work in this field. It would instead turn its attention towards shopping centers. The shift in activities was not unusual for this corporation. The key to its success was its ability to keep its finger always on the pulse of change.

Lend Lease continued to retain a long-term interest in properties developed without long-term capital investment, and to be free of fluctuations in the property market through public subscription and independent property trusts. Lend Lease was the first developer to go public and to form in 1971 General Property Trust, a publicly owned real estate trust to hold its properties.

On June 30, 1971, G.J. Dusseldorp's contract with Bredero's, which made him available as principal executive of the group, expired. Dusseldorp agreed to be retained until June 30, 1975, with a renewable clause thereafter. The new agreement allowed Dusseldorp to have interests outside Australia. Dusseldorp wanted to try his style of business in the United States. Through its subsidiary, U.S. Lend Lease, established in 1972, formed International Income Property (IIP).

Despite the multitude of activities in which Dusseldorp and his team were involved, he was nonetheless paving the way towards his own retirement by grooming his executives for future management. His contributions to the success of Lend Lease were considerable. Although he surrounded himself with a team of some of the best people in the business, there is no doubt that the inspiration for the projects, as well as the new ways of handling development and finance, all sprang from the mind of Dusseldorp. His aversion to borrowing kept the firm's debts below 50% of its total capital, a low figure compared to those of rival developers. Year after year, despite an adverse financial climate and lows in the property market, Lend Lease was to produce profits for its shareholders. The firm did not retain its own publicity department, but worked quietly and expertly at all its projects, so much so that it prompted the *Financial Times* to comment, "Unlike many prominent Australian companies, it [Lend Lease] attracts little publicity and even less adverse comment from analysts."

In 1971 Bredero's sold its shareholding in Lend Lease, and J. DeVries, a founding director of Lend Lease, retired from the board. W.M. Leavey, managing director of Lend Lease, replaced him. S.G. Hornery became managing director of Civil & Civic, with R.G. Robinson as chairman.

In 1978 Dusseldorp commented in the annual report, "In the conditions which have prevailed, to have obtained one million dollars worth of business every working day represented an extraordinary effort by everyone in the group." It was also the year in which employees became the largest shareholding block, holding 26% of the shares.

Lend Lease's success—during one of the greatest slumps in the property market—lay in its concentration on earnings and cash flow rather than ownership of assets. It acted as a service corporation. It also stuck to a policy of refusing to undertake construction unless an end buyer was in place.

In 1988 Dusseldorp retired as chairman and was succeeded by S.G. Hornery. Dusseldorp left a corporation in which 30% of all projects were planned, designed, built, fitted, financed, managed, and refurbished for their economic life. It was a company with novel staff ownership schemes, well-tended links with investors, and numerous corporate sponsorships. Dusseldorp cultivated good relations with employees, shareholders, and local communities alike.

Hornery also made a mark on the firm, overturning Dusseldorp's international expansion plans and bringing in insurance and related financial services to the group by acquiring MLC. Lend Lease was able to provide, through MLC, sav-ings, mortgage investment, and superannuation as well as life and general insurance products which would cover its clients from cradle to grave.

During the 1990s, Hornery's objective for the group of companies will be steady and continuous growth through extending MLC's offshore investments and developing global property investment capability. He is also committed to continuing the company policy of enhancing the urban environment and playing a leading role in changing Australia's cities for the better.

Principal Subsidiaries: Australian Funds Management; The MLC Limited; MLC Life; MLC Insurance; Lend Lease Development; Lend Lease Commercial; Lend Lease Retail; Civil & Civic; Lend Lease Interiors; Lend Lease International plc.

Further Reading: Murphy, Mary, *Challenges of Change, The Lend Lease Story,* Sydney, The Pot Still Press, 1984.

—Anastasia N. Hackett

MEPC PLC

Brook House
113 Park Lane
London W1Y 4AY
United Kingdom
(071) 491 5300
Fax: (071) 491 5361

Public Company
Incorporated: 1946 as The Mercantile Property Corporation
   Ltd.
Employees: 900
Sales: £238.30 million (US$459.95 million)
Stock Exchange: London

MEPC is the United Kingdom's second-largest property company and one of the largest property companies in the world, operating in more than ten countries. Its principal business activities include the management of its extensive portfolio of investment properties, the acquisition of properties, property development, and trading. U.K. activities account for 84% of its assets while other important areas of activity include Europe, Australia and the United States.

Like many of the U.K.'s largest property companies, MEPC was incorporated shortly after World War II, although the property activities of its founder, Claude Moss Leigh, go back much earlier. Claude Leigh was born in 1888, the son of a northeast London surveyor and estate agent. Leigh joined his father's business, but soon realized more money could be made in the property market by acting on his own account rather than as an agent for others. Leigh's early ventures concentrated on the provision of working-class housing. In the interwar period, most of the urban working class rented housing, apart from a small proportion provided by charities and similar bodies, was owned by small-scale or absentee landlords who made few efforts to ensure that the houses were kept in good repair or had an acceptable standard of amenities. Leigh perceived the need for a public company that would provide good quality rented housing and enlightened housing management, including welfare services for the tenants, while paying a commercially acceptable dividend to its investors. His efforts in this area culminated in the establishment of The Metropolitan Housing Corporation Ltd. (M.H.C.).

M.H.C. was floated as a public company in March 1929, with authorized capital of £1 million. The company owned 13 housing estates located in the poorer parts of London. Leigh's

attempts to find commercial, rather than philanthropic, solutions to working-class housing problems met with only limited success, however, and the necessity of earning an acceptable dividend meant that his welfare plans could never be fully implemented. With the onset of World War II, rent control legislation was tightened and the project became unworkable even as a commercial enterprize. Leigh decided to embark in a new direction and in 1946 established a new company to acquire and manage commercial property.

On October 1, 1946, the company was incorporated under the name of The Mercantile Property Corporation Ltd., the product of the merger of three companies; The Metropolitan Housing Corporation Ltd., The Monument Property Trust Ltd., and the Mercantile Estate and Property Corporation Ltd. These companies, together with their subsidiaries, formed the nucleus of MEPC to which the assets of several more property companies were quickly added by acquisition. On October 25, 1946, its name was changed to Metropolitan Estate and Property Corporation Ltd., shortened to MEPC in 1973.

MEPC's initial property portfolio contained a large proportion of residential properties, which made up 44% of its holdings. A further 25% of the portfolio was offices, 12% was shops, and the remainder consisted of industrial and other properties. This weighting toward housing would have constituted a substantial liability for the company in the years ahead; residential rent controls and higher management costs associated with this type of property led to a flight from residential property by property investing institutions. The need to reduce residential holdings was soon perceived, and by January 1948 the proportion of houses in the portfolio had fallen to 40%.

MEPC's early capital needs were met by the issue of shares, long term finance via mortgages and short term finance via bank loans. More than £400,000 was also received in War Damage Compensation during the first year. Compared to a rent roll which stood at £900,000 at the end of 1949, this was clearly a substantial amount. The sale of houses and other unprofitable properties raised further funds.

Early investments concentrated on land purchases and financing property construction, although development did not contribute significantly to the firm's activities until the late 1950s. In order to reduce the burden of Profits Tax, MEPC also turned to investment in equity, which was not subject to this tax. Other activities included property dealing; in the early 1950s the House and Land Syndicate, which had been acquired by MEPC in 1946, was reconstructed for this purpose.

The early years of the company saw steady expansion. Building materials shortages and a variety of government restrictions on capital and building licenses led to an undersupply of new buildings in the early postwar years. A boom in second hand property resulted, as demand for existing buildings outstripped supply. Such conditions were favorable for the property companies, many of which were established during this period, since although the development market was severely restricted the investment market was extremely buoyant. During these early years the company expanded largely by takeover. In 1948 Percy Bilton Investment Trust Ltd. was acquired. Three more property companies were taken over in 1949 and a further three in 1950.

In addition to activity in the domestic market the company looked to overseas opportunities from an early date. Claude

Leigh visited South Africa in 1948 and during that year the firm's first overseas subsidiary, M.E.P.C. Ltd., was founded there. Another African company, Metropolitan Estate and Property Corporation (Rhodesia) Ltd., followed. By the early 1950s attention had turned to Canada as a possible source of investment opportunities and in 1955 MEPC established a Canadian subsidiary. Difficulties in gaining Bank of England consent for sending out sufficient capital led to delays but permission was finally granted on the understanding that half the subsidiary's profits would be remitted to the United Kingdom. This Canadian venture proved to be a success.

During the first eight years, MEPC operated as an investment company, restructuring its portfolio in the light of postwar property market conditions by selling residential properties and buying the freeholds of some of its leasehold City offices. In doing so, the company concentrated assets in what was to become one of the most successful areas of property investment during the following years. High construction costs and building license restrictions dissuaded MEPC from undertaking developments during these early years, and even after the building restrictions were lifted in 1954 it was initially decided not to develop properties, other than the redevelopment of war-damaged sites, the cost of which was partly covered by government compensation.

This policy was changed a year later, however, and during 1955 a 216,000-square-foot office was developed in Wigmore Street, London. Over half of the building was let before construction to major industrial companies, including IBM. However, MEPC remained primarily an investment, rather than development, company throughout the 1950s. While other companies were forced to enter the development market due to the lack of sufficient investment propositions, MEPC was able to acquire new investment properties by a series of property company takeovers and the purchase of insurance company property portfolios.

MEPC pursued this strategy until the early 1970s, its acquisitions including: Town Investments, Metropolitan Railways Surplus Lands Co., Manchester Commercial Buildings Co., Westgate House Investments Ltd., Avondown Properties Ltd., Jeffery Sons & Co. Ltd., and London County Freehold & Leasehold Properties. The portfolios of secondary quality shops of the Prudential and Phoenix insurance companies were also purchased in the 1960s, many of these properties having great potential for rent increases upon the termination of their leases. Further expansion was also sought overseas; during the 1960s MEPC entered the Australian and European markets and its activities proved successful in both areas. When Claude Leigh died in 1964, MEPC had grown into the fourth largest property company in the United Kingdom, its capital at that time amounting to £50 million.

Although MEPC had experienced rapid growth during the property boom period, from the lifting of building license restrictions in 1954 until 1964 when the highly restrictive "Brown Ban" was placed on office building in and around London, it was felt by many commentators that the company had not taken full advantage of what was essentially a development boom. Pent-up demand for new office accommodation, which was released by the lifting of the building restrictions, led to high profit margins for developers and a large number of fortunes were made in development, often from virtually nothing, during this period. However MEPC began its development program late and remained primarily an investment company throughout the boom period.

While early expansion was financed by sales of residential property, income from this source soon proved insufficient for expansion plans and the company launched a series of rights and scrip issues to finance takeovers. In 1960 the company required development finance and turned to a source of development funds which was already widely used by property companies, the formation of funding arrangements with financial institutions. A joint company, Percy Street Investments Ltd., was formed together with the Equitable Life Assurance Society, to develop property in Percy Street, Newcastle. A year later a further deal was struck, this time involving the Equitable Life Assurance Society, the London Life Association, and the National Provident Institution for Mutual Life Assurance. A joint company was established, the Cumberland Property Investment Trust Ltd., to redevelop some of the properties in MEPC's portfolio.

By the early 1970s, MEPC was seen by some financial commentators as a somewhat dull property company that rested on its asset portfolio and showed little interest in development activity. While this was not a fair assessment of the company, its development program having a value of £79 million in 1970, such a reputation left it vulnerable to takeover bids. However, a bid launched by Commercial Union and Trafalgar House, and later merger negotiations with the merchant bankers Hill Samuel, both ended in failure. The company sought to expand rapidly activities by making use of borrowed funds that were all too readily available from the government and banks at this time. In July 1972 a new managing director, Peter Anker, was appointed, following the retirement of Dick Sheppard. Anker had risen to prominence in the company when he had been selected by Claude Leigh to set up operations in Canada. His efforts had resulted in the establishment of a highly successful Canadian subsidiary and it was hoped that his flair for large scale developments and rapid expansion would be equally successful when applied to the parent company. "I look on it as though I've taken over a gold mine," he stated with regard to MEPC's £350 million portfolio.

During 1972 and 1973 the company launched a number of ambitious development initiatives. These included large shopping projects in London, Guildford, and Birmingham, as well as overseas shopping malls in Honolulu, Munich, and Frankfurt. A joint scheme with Reed International to develop 300,000 square feet of offices in Covent Garden, London, was also announced and a house-building firm, J. Sanders & Sons, was acquired in return for shares. These, and a large number of smaller development projects and property acquisitions amounted to considerable commitments. By 1973, the value of the total development program was £417 million. Much of this development activity was financed by borrowed funds, placing the company in a vulnerable position in the event of a severe downturn in the property market.

By December 1973, the first signs of alarm which heralded the disastrous property crash of 1974 began to appear. MEPC was one of the first companies to show concern. On December 7 it decided not to proceed with five provisional U.K. office developments. Some of the factors which precipitated the property crash, such as the imposition of commercial rent controls, were domestic in origin and made the crash more severe in the U.K. than elsewhere. However, the most important factors behind the crash, the oil price rises and the economic downturn, had an international impact, leading to a depression in property markets worldwide. MEPC therefore faced considerable difficulties with its overseas commitments in addition to problems in the domestic market. Two important foreign projects, the Sydney Exchange Centre and the Manhattan Centre in Brussels, ran into severe problems as conditions in the Australian and Belgian property markets turned sour.

MEPC reacted to the crash by borrowing more money which was then placed on deposit. This added further to its interest payments but had the effect of securing the liquidity of the company. The debts that MEPC had accumulated from the banks and foreign currency bond markets, together with this extra borrowing, weighed heavily on the company during the following years. In 1974, net borrowings amounted to £331 million, representing 116% of shareholders' funds. Falling property prices and rising interest rates on debts which could not be quickly paid made the situation even worse in 1975, by which time net borrowing had risen to 154% of shareholders' funds. MEPC shares fell to a low point of 53 pence in 1975, after standing at 231 pence earlier in the year.

Despite these problems, MEPC's underlying position was quite strong. Its investment portfolio, the value of which had been slashed by the property crash, was still substantial and £40 million of cash in the bank helped to ensure that the company was not forced to sell properties during the depths of the crash. Some property assets were sold when the market began to pick up, and the company's finances were stabilized.

Property market conditions in the late 1970s heralded a change in the management style of the company. After a series of heated boardroom disputes over future policy, the expansionist Peter Anker was replaced by Chris Benson, and Sir Gerald Thorley of Allied Breweries became MEPC's new chairman. MEPC's banking advisor, NM Rothschild, was also replaced, by Hill Samuel and Morgan Grenfell. Under this new management the company's fortunes improved. The year 1977 saw a significant turnaround in its performance, with a marked reduction in debts. This was largely due to the sale in that year of MEPC Canada, the group's Canadian subsidiary, which reduced its debts by £82 million and raised £27 million. An important reason for this sale was the Foreign Investment Review Act, which hampered the remission of profits to the United Kingdom. The group also reduced its interests in the U.K. housing market and scaled down its development program.

During the late 1970s and early 1980s, a more cautious approach to the market and the inherent strength of MEPC's portfolio led to a steady improvement in the company's condition. In addition to institutional finance and overseas borrowing, the company also made use of rights issues to finance its activities in the late 1970s, despite the dilution of equity that this involved. Property development was resumed in 1978, notable projects including the Friary Centre in Guildford, the West One building in Oxford Street, London, and the Long Acre office development in Covent Garden, which was developed together with Legal & General. By 1981 the value of this development program stood at £100 million.

By 1980, 55% of the company's property portfolio consisted of offices, 20% shops, 15% industrial, 1% residential and 9% developments. Properties in the United Kingdom accounted for 75% of the portfolio, 9.5% was in Australia, 10% in the European Economic Community and 5.5% in the United States. The company moved its U.S. headquarters to Dallas in order to focus U.S. operations in that area of the country. Some early difficulties were experienced in this market, which MEPC attributed to adverse economic conditions caused by the oil price slump. Its 1984 report noted that "overall, however, the contribution from this [U.S.] subsidiary has been disappointing." Despite these setbacks, MEPC held on to its investments in this area and by the late 1980s conditions had improved markedly.

The company did not suffer during the recession of the early 1980s, and while the property sector as a whole was adversely affected by the economic downturn, MEPC achieved steadily rising profits. By 1985 it became clear that an upturn in the property market was likely, and during that year MEPC bought control of the English Property Corporation from Olympia & York. Two years later, the company made a much more important acquisition, the takeover of Harry Hyams's Oldham Estate for £516 million, raising MEPC's property asset value to nearly £2.5 billion. The assets of this company were concentrated in London and the south east. They included Centre Point, the most famous of the buildings to be developed in London during the 1960s property boom. This building had become a focus of popular resentment against the property development industry in the 1960s due to the alleged unwillingness of Hyams to let the property, since it was worth more as a vacant office block than as an occupied one.

In 1988 James Tuckey took over as managing director. During this year the development program was increased to £1.2 billion, the biggest in MEPC's history, as boom conditions in the property market continued.

Considerable flexibility has been built into MEPC's development program and development finance has been arranged largely on a long-term, fixed-interest basis, thereby insulating the company from rises in interest rates. MEPC has learned from its experiences in the 1974 property crash and is well prepared for any rough waters that may lie ahead.

Principal Subsidiaries: MEPC Developments Ltd.; MEPC Investments Ltd.; Ortem Developments Ltd.; MEPC Corporate Services Ltd.; MEPC Australia Ltd.; MEPC Germany GmbH; MEPC American Holdings Inc. (U.S.A.).

Further Reading: Marriott, Oliver, *The Property Boom,* London, Hamish Hamilton Ltd., 1967; Watson, John, *The Incompleat Surveyor,* London, Estates Gazette, 1973; Erdman, Edward, *People and Property,* London, Batsford, 1982; "Company File: MEPC," *Estates Gazette,* February 18, 1978; Foster, Michael, "Company File: MEPC," *Estates Gazette,* January 30, 1982; Smyth, Hedley, "The Historical Growth Of Property Companies And The Construction Industry In Britain Between 1939 And 1979," unpublished Ph.D thesis, University of Bristol, 1982; "MEPC: Well Spread," *Investors Chronicle,* December 4, 1987; Foster, Michael, "MEPC Gets Motoring," *Estates Gazette,* December 17, 1988.

—Peter Scott

Mitsubishi Estate Company, Limited

MITSUBISHI ESTATE COMPANY, LIMITED

4-1, Marunouchi 2-chome
Chiyoda-ku, Tokyo 100
Japan
(03) 3287-5100
Fax: (03) 3214-7036

Public Company
Incorporated: 1937
Employees: 1,832
Sales: ¥314.93 billion (US$2.32 billion)
Stock Exchanges: Tokyo Osaka Nagoya Kyoto Hiroshima
  Fukuoka Sapporo Niigata

Mitsubishi Estate Company, Limited (MEC) is one of the foremost real estate management, leasing, sales and development firms in Japan. The company is one of 28 core firms in the powerful Mitsubishi group. MEC is the largest holder of office space in Tokyo, much of it centered in the Marunouchi district. The company has undertaken urban development programs in Tokyo and residential projects throughout Japan and has pursued real estate investments internationally.

Although MEC was incorporated in 1937, its history of operations began in 1890. In March of that year, during the Meiji era, the Mitsubishi *zaibatsu* acquired 353,000 square meters of land owned by the Department of War at Marunouchi, Tokyo. Investing in land was seen as an innovative move for a company which up to that time was concerned primarily with shipping. Of the ¥2.4 million the company invested in the late 1880s and early 1890s, almost ¥2 million was spent on land in Tokyo.

The most notable purchase, the Marunouchi district, was a vast area which consisted of a grass plain and military drill field running from the moat outside the Imperial Palace east toward the merchants' district. It also contained military barracks and some government offices. In the late 1880s the army decided to sell the land. Yanosuke Iwasaki, then leader of Mitsubishi and younger brother of Mitsubishi's founder Yataro Iwasaki, was strongly urged to buy the land by two of his managers who had recently spent time in London. They envisioned building a modern office center in Tokyo for Mitsubishi, similar to those they had seen in England. The company was abetted in this aim by the government, which wanted to sell the Marunouchi land to a single buyer, making the price

prohibitive for many. Mitsubishi was able to acquire the property in March 1890 for ¥1.28 million.

Construction planning for the office center began soon after the purchase in the Marunouchi district. Marunouchi Design Office of Mitsubishi Company, the predecessor of today's architectural division of Mitsubishi Estate, was founded that same year. In 1892, Mitsubishi began construction on Marunouchi's modern, Western-style, red brick business avenue, still the heart of Mitsubishi operations. After the development was completed, the government agreed to locate Tokyo's central railroad in the district, placing Mitsubishi squarely at the core of the Tokyo business district.

In 1893, Yanosuke Iwasaki initiated a reorganization of Mitsubishi in line with its diversification from shipping, changing its name to Mitsubishi Goshi Kaisha, Ltd. One year later, Mitsubishi's first building at Marunouchi was completed. It was Japan's first office rental building. Also in 1894, the office building division established its first office. By this time, real estate constituted 38.8% of Mitsubishi's company assets. In 1895, Mitsubishi's second building was completed. Building number three, finished in 1896, housed the head office of Nippon Yusen Kaisha (NYK), a leading shipping enterprise, created through the merger of Mitsubishi Shokai and its leading competitor, Kyodo Unyu Kaisha (Cooperative Transport Company), in 1885.

Mitsubishi set up its first real estate section in 1906. The company's accelerated growth began about 1917 when business divisions were incorporated and Mitsubishi Goshi Kaisha began to act as holding company and controller. The company continued to build in the Marunouchi district through World War I and the depression of the 1920s while pursuing its activities in mining, shipping and trading. The Marunouchi Building was completed in 1923. In 1929, the Marunouchi Garage Building, the first parking structure in Japan, was completed. Mitsubishi's real estate and architectural design and supervision activities were consolidated when Mitsubishi Estate Company, Limited was established on May 7, 1937.

After World War II the four largest *zaibatsu,* including Mitsubishi, held almost one-third of the paid-in capital in heavy industry in Japan. During the postwar occupation, the *zaibatsu* were disbanded under American-style anti-monopoly laws. Mitsubishi was divided into 139 independent companies. These strictures were eased by 1950, and MEC reestablished ties with other Mitsubishi firms by 1954. Group cohesiveness was further strengthened in 1970 when Mitsubishi Development Corporation was formed. Its primary mission was to undertake long-term housing, city and regional development plans for which no single member of the group had the resources. It was capitalized by 33 group companies. The company's president was also president of Mitsubishi Corporation and its chairman, the chairman of MEC.

MEC's influence in Japan and its long-standing ties with government were demonstrated in the mid-1950s. The governor of Tokyo, Seiichiro Yasui, asked Minoru Higuchi, retired president of MEC, for his advice on easing congestion in Tokyo's business district. Higuchi recommended that the governor allow private industry to build a roadway over income-producing properties, which would help pay for its construction and maintenance. Higuchi and 38 prominent members of the business community contributed $333,000 and formed the Tokyo Express Highway Co., Ltd. Higuchi was elected president. Construction of the seven-eighths of a mile roadway began April 1, 1953. Eventually the roadway ran from the financial district to the Ginza.

In 1959, the office building division set up the Marunouchi Reconstruction Program, a plan for the renewal of the Marunouchi district, often referred to as Mitsubishi Village due to the concentration of Mitsubishi firms headquartered there. Under the program, the Marunouchi Park Center was established in 1960, and a number of new buildings were built between 1965 and 1973. This renewal process continues. Through the 1980s, rents from these and other buildings in Tokyo accounted for about 70% of MEC's income.

In the 1960s, while MEC was rapidly increasing its holdings in Japan, it also began expanding overseas. Since 1962 MEC has invested in real estate operations in Houston, Atlanta, Detroit, Florida, Oregon and New York in the United States and in London, England. By the 1970s, MEC began to establish local affiliates. In 1971 MEC founded MEC Hawaii Corporation. In 1972, the company established Mitsubishi Estate New York Inc. Also in 1972, MEC and Morgan Stanley & Co., an investment banking firm, formed Morgan Mitsubishi Development, a New York–based partnership to develop real estate in the United States. MEC USA, Inc. followed in 1983, and in 1984 MEC built the Pacwest Center Building in Portland, Oregon. In 1985, MEC acquired Atlas House in London and established MEC UK Ltd. in 1986. Until the late 1980s, however, MEC's presence in the United States was comparatively small, standing at $24 million in September 1983.

MEC has been active in residential development since the 1970s, with developments in the Sapporo, Sendai, Tokyo, Yokohama, Osaka, and Hiroshima areas. Its Izumi Park Town in Miyagi-ken, the largest private-sector development project in Japan, comprises 12,000 homes on 1,030 hectares with a population estimated at 48,000. Construction on the first stage of this project began in 1972. By 1983 revenues from house sales accounted for 20% of MEC's income. In 1988, MEC began construction of the Park Town Tamagawa condominium project in Tokyo.

In 1983 MEC diversified into the hotel business by opening the Nagoya Dai-ichi Hotel. Three years later, it opened the Atsugi Royal Park Hotel near Tokyo and then ventured into resort operations, opening the resort park Hotel Onikobe in 1987. In 1989, MEC and an affiliated company opened the Royal Park Hotel adjoining the Tokyo City Air Terminal. The company also operates ski slopes, hotels, and resort villas on the Onikobe Highlands and golf courses at the foot of Mount Fuji. The resort park Izu Atagawa's country houses, under development in 1990, were equipped with hot springs.

In the 1980s land prices skyrocketed in Tokyo and other major cities in Japan. Between 1986 and 1988 alone, speculation in real estate helped double the price of Tokyo property. MEC's holdings similarly increased in value. In terms of assets, MEC was the largest real estate firm in Japan. By the end of the 1980s, under the direction of leaders like Chairman Otakazu Nakada, in office through 1987, President Tatsuji Ito, in office through 1988, and his successor, Jotaro Takagi, MEC became a world competitor.

Beginning in 1987, MEC worked jointly with local developers to build 2,500 homes outside Los Angeles. In 1988

MEC began construction of the 53-story 777 Tower in Los Angeles, and expanded residential and resort facilities in Palm Desert, California.

In 1989 MEC made a major acquisition, a controlling interest in the Rockefeller Group, owner and manager of 14 buildings in New York City, including Rockefeller Center, Radio City Music Hall, the General Electric—formerly the RCA—Building, and the Warner Communications Building. The financial arrangements were complex. MEC's price of $846 million in cash bought 51% of the group, or 627,000 shares of Rockefeller common stock held by trusts established by John D. Rockefeller in 1934. In 1985, the Rockefeller Group had sold a mortgage on Rockefeller Center to a real estate investment trust, Rockefeller Center Properties. The trust's holdings could be converted at its option to a 71.5% interest in the group in the year 2,000, which would leave MEC with 51% of the remaining 28.5% of the group. MEC considered the investment a long-term proposition, and acquired an additional 6.6% stake for $110 million in July 1990.

The sale set off considerable controversy. It followed pleas by the Japanese government and leading business organizations for companies to refrain from purchasing highly visible properties in the United States, for fear of public resentment. For MEC, the purchase placed it in the forefront of Japanese real estate investors overseas.

In 1990, MEC celebrated its 100th anniversary, as well as the 14th consecutive year of significant growth in both revenue from operations and net income. Full occupancy in its buildings contributed to a 14.8% increase in revenue over 1989. The office building division contributed 55.1% of MEC's total revenue.

In February 1990, MEC participated in the redevelopment of Paternoster Square next to St. Paul's Cathedral in London in partnership with U.S. and British developers. In March 1990, construction began on what would be Japan's tallest building, the 70-story Landmark Tower, in the Block 25 district at the Minato Mirai 21 development in Yokohama, Japan's largest port and second-largest city. MEC planned to open an international hotel on the upper floors of Landmark Tower by spring 1993. MEC was the largest private-sector landowner to participate in the redevelopment of Yokohama's coastal region. As MEC moved toward the 21st century, it stood in excellent financial shape to continue to take full advantage of opportunities in Japan or overseas.

Principal Subsidiaries: Mitsubishi Estate Housing Co., Ltd.; Ryoei Kanko Development Co., Ltd.; Ryowa Fudosan Co., Ltd.; Meiryo Daiichi Kaihatsu Co., Ltd.

Further Reading: Cole, Robert J., "Japanese Buy New York Cachet With Deal for Rockefeller Center," *The New York Times,* October 31, 1989; Rubenfein, Elisabeth, "Investor in Rockefeller Center Took Risk," *The Wall Street Journal,* November 1, 1989; "Mighty Mitsubishi," *Business Week,* September 24, 1990.

—Lynn M. Kalanik

MITSUI REAL ESTATE DEVELOPMENT CO., LTD.

1-1, Nihonbashi-Muromachi 2-chome
Chuo-Ku, Tokyo 103
Japan
(03) 3246-3065
Fax: (03) 3275-2273

Public Company
Incorporated: 1941
Employees: 8,947
Sales: ¥1.06 trillion (US$7.81 billion)
Stock Exchanges: Tokyo Osaka

Mitsui Real Estate Development Co., Ltd. is a pivotal member of the Mitsui group. The company and its subsidiaries are involved in a large variety of projects and operations on both a national and international scale. Mitsui Real Estate is Japan's leading developer of office buildings, commercial properties, and housing. Mitsui Real Estate, with the support of other Mitsui group companies, has capitalized on Japan's land shortage, and specialized in developing high-rise complexes that make profitable use of premium space. With strong capabilities in investment, development, construction, brokerage, financing, and consulting, the company is also expanding into new fields through its 201 subsidiaries and affiliates. Mitsui Real Estate began overseas operations in 1972. In major markets throughout the world, the company serves as a developer, investor, and consultant.

The company was a pioneer in high-rise building development. By the mid-1980s, Mitsui Real Estate was Japan's largest real estate company, measured by real estate sales and related activities. The company has expanded its rental division by renting office high rises in the heart of Tokyo. It has also concentrated its efforts in the sales of apartment houses and single family homes, as well as urban development.

In 1941 Mitsui Real Estate Development Co., Ltd. was founded as the real estate division of Mitsui Gomei Kaisha, a central holding company of the Mitsui *zaibatsu*, or financial group. The company was incorporated under its present name as the real estate company to serve the needs of the Mitsui group. Originally, the shares of the company were held exclusively by the Mitsui family. After World War II, in 1949, however, the Allied occupation authorities broke up the *zaibatsu*, Mitsui among them.

In 1956 remants of Mitsui Honsha, the successor to Mitsui Gomei Konsha, merged with the company. In 1957 Chiba Prefecture contracted with Mitsui Real Estate for dredging and reclamation work in the development of an industrial zone built on a landfill, and Mitsui Real Estate subsequently entered the coastal-land-development business. The firm then started the New Town development on the outskirts of Tokyo.

The company's steady growth continued throughout the 1960s. In 1961 the company began the development and sale of land for housing. In 1964 a major acquisition for Mitsui Real Estate was the Sanshin building in central Tokyo. Four years later, in 1968, other members of Mitsui group combined efforts with Mitsui Real Estate, and the Mitsui Housing Problem Conference convened to undertake construction and sale of high-rise apartments. One result was the completion of the Kasumigaseki Building, Japan's first skyscraper. The Mitsui Real Estate Sales Co., Ltd. subsidiary was established in 1969 and began to sell prefabricated housing.

The company's growth continued in the 1970s. In 1972 the company began its international operations, and by 1990 Mitsui Real Estate owned the Exxon Building in New York City, the Halekulani Hotel in Honolulu, the Hotel Himalaya Kathmandu in Nepal, and the 505 Montgomery Building in San Francisco. In 1974 the Mitsui Home Co., Ltd. subsidiary was established and began the sales of prefabricated homes built by western-style two-by-four method of construction instead of the traditional Japanese method of using four-by-eight panel products. The Mitsui Harbour and Urban Construction Co., Ltd. was established from the company's waterfront-development and-construction subsidiaries. In 1974 the company also completed the Shinjuku Mitsui Building in Tokyo. The 55-story building makes liberal use of semi-mirrored glass and has become a landmark.

Mitsui Real Estate has expanded its overseas markets and has been active in development in the United States and southeast Asia. In 1983, in a step to strengthen its international activities, Mitsui Real Estate established a wide-ranging business agreement with Coldwell Banker Company, a U.S. real estate group with offices throughout the United States.

Since 1981 Mitsui Real Estate has built condominiums and office and commercial floor space throughout Japan through its consulting and joint-development program. This program, known as "Let's," is designed to make the most of Mitsui Real Estate's development expertise and the real estate assets of landowners who prefer to retain partial or complete ownership of the property. Property developed through Let's includes condominiums, high-rise office buildings, and hotels. By 1991 approximately half of Mitsui Real Estate's supply of new office space was developed under Let's.

The year 1981 also witnessed the opening in suburban Tokyo of Lalaport Funabashi Shopping Center, the largest in Asia. A 243-room hotel is also on this site. In 1983 Tokyo Disneyland opened, owned by Mitsui affiliate Oriental Land Co., Ltd.

In 1984 the Mitsui Garden Hotel opened in Osaka. This was the first directly owned and operated Mitsui hotel and was constructed as a central part of Osaka's redevelopment plans. In 1985 Mitsui Real Estate completed the Mitsui Nigokan in Chuo-ku, in central Tokyo, the building was the first office building available for leasing that operated under computer control that was sensitive to charges in the environment within the building and that compensated for those changes. It has facilities to accommodate several information network systems.

A new-business-development division was established in 1984. By 1985 several new ventures had been established, including the first Kenko Club, a health and fitness club, in the Ginza area of Tokyo. Mitsui Real Estate also established Wellness Co., Ltd. in 1984 through a joint venture with a health agency. Members make regular visits in order to detect potential health problems early. In 1985 Mitsui Real Estate Housing Service Co., Ltd. began offering the Bell Boy system, a housecleaning and security service.

Mitsui Real Estate began its Okawabata River City 21 project in 1986. The development fuses residential, cultural, and commercial functions.

In 1987 Mitsui Real Estate completed a 36-story residential complex, Bell Park City, in Osaka. A total of 3,600 condominium units were planned for completion at that site in 1991. Also in 1987, the Shin-Kasumigaseki office building, was completed, and the Kenko Club in Sapparo opened.

Mitsui Real Estate completed several major projects in 1988. The Nishi Azabu Mitsui Building in greater Tokyo was completed along with the Nishi-Azabu Park Towers. Mitsui Real Estate's overseas operations opened the Xi'an Garden Hotel in Xi'an, China, and completed the 461 Fifth Avenue Building in New York City.

In 1989 the company completed River Point Tower, Japan's tallest apartment building, in Okawabata River City 21. The firm also opened hotels in Hiroshima, Chiba, and Kyot. The company expanded its interest in shopping centers with the opening of a center in Hokkaido. Overseas Mitsui completed the 505 Montgomery Building in San Francisco.

The company continued to grow in the 1990s, when it started the Fuchu Intelligent Park and Yokkaichi Amusement Forum 21. Alpark, the largest shopping center in western Japan, was also completed. Two hotels opened in Osaka and Hyogo, and the Figueroa at Wilshire Building was completed in Los Angeles.

In 1989 Mitsui Real Estate achieved record earnings and revenues for the 12th consecutive year. At the start of the 1990s, however, the Japanese real estate industry headed into a difficult period. Higher interest rates and pressure from the Japanese Ministry of Finance on banks and other financial institutions to limit property-related loans posed challenges for the real estate business.

Having established itself as joint-venture partner in real estate development throughout the 1980s, Mitsui was confident that it would be able to meet future challenges and join in projects with the greatest potential. The redevelopment of waterfront areas will be a larger part of Mitsui's Real Estate activities, and the firm planned to place greater emphasis on office building and housing projects in suburban areas. Resort and leisure projects were expected to grow in the 1990s.

A vital strategy for strengthening Mitsui Real Estate's business will be to raise its overall share of the leasing market. Floor space under the company's management rose approximately 350,000 square meters annually from 1985 through

1990 and amounted to 3.4 million square meters by 1990. The company has also become more involved in subleasing. The demand for new office space has risen, and Mitsui Real Estate can gain a greater share of total floor space under management in Tokyo through a commitment to subleasing.

Mitsui Real Estate's other core business, housing sales, construction, and the various support services of its subsidiaries and affiliates, grew steadily during the 1980s. Sales of housing accounted for 28.9% of the firm's revenues in fiscal 1989. Condominium sales are a major portion of operations in this category, amounting to more than half of property sales.

Another important part of the company's operations is construction, which provided 31.1% of revenue in fiscal 1989. Mitsui Home is Japan's oldest supplier of two-by-four houses. This construction method is becoming increasingly popular in Japan due to the freedom of design, and resistance to earthquakes and fires. Mitsui Home has been responsible for more than 10,000 of these homes. Mitsui Real Estate Sales Co., Ltd., Japan's largest real estate brokerage network, had 30% of the brokerage market.

Free time has become more important than ever in Japan, and the two-day weekend has become common. Mitsui Real Estate has responded to this situation by concentrating on the development of day-trip facilities and is planning to construct the Lalaport Ski Dome, Japan's first full-scale indoor ski facility that will enable visitors to enjoy skiing any time of the year. Nearby is the Tokyo Disneyland, and for longer vacations, Mitsui Real Estate has opened resorts such as Mitsui-no-Mori, a three-hour drive from Tokyo.

Mitsui Real Estate's overseas investments amounted to approximately ¥216.8 billion in 1990, most of which are in the United States. The company hoped that diversification of overseas operations would ensure further long-term stability. The company also planned to expand geographically in Europe.

Principal Subsidiaries: Mitsui Real Estate Sales Co., Ltd.; Mitsui Home Co., Ltd.; Mitsui Designtec Co., Ltd.; Mitsui Home Components Co., Ltd.; Mitsui Real Estate Housing Service Co., Ltd.; MF Lease Co., Ltd.; Mitsui Harbour and Urban Construction Co., Ltd.; Daiischi Seibi Co., Ltd.; Nishinihon Building Service Co., Ltd.; MF Building Management Co., Ltd.; Daiichi Seed Co., Ltd.; Toyo Landscape Construction Co., Ltd.; Lalaport Co., Ltd.; Uni Living Co., Ltd.; Garden Hotel System Co., Ltd.; Garden Hotels Kansai Co., Ltd.; Hotel Sun Garden Lalaport Co., Ltd.; Hotel Sun Garden Kashiwa Co., Ltd.; Garden Hotel Chiba Co., Ltd.; Garden Hotel Hiroshima Co., Ltd.; Mitsui-no-Mori Co., Ltd.; Wellness Co., Ltd.; Cany Corporation; Mitsui Fudosan Loan Guarantee Co., Ltd. Mitsui Fudosan Finance Co., Ltd.

Further Reading: Mitsui Real Estate Development Co., Ltd., Corporate Brochure 1990, Tokyo, Mitsui Real Estate Development Co., Ltd., 1990.

—Joan Harpham

NEW WORLD DEVELOPMENT COMPANY LTD.

30/F New World Tower
18 Queen's Road Central
Hong Kong
(5) 5231056
Fax: (5) 8104673

Public Company
Incorporated: 1970
Employees: 2,800
Sales: HK$2.34 billion (US$300.07 million)
Stock Exchange: Hong Kong

New World Development Company Ltd. has for two decades been a leader in Hong Kong's bustling commercial and residential development market. In 1990 it had an annual rental income stream exceeding HK$1 billion.

The founders of New World Development were Dr. Yu Tung Cheng, the current company chairman, and the late Chi Wan Young. In 1970 they joined up to merge their holdings in the colony's commercial and residential property market.

Both men started their careers in Hong Kong's jewelry trade. Yu Tung Cheng, who proceeded during the 1960s to become managing director of the Chow Tai Fook Jewellery Company, had already by the 1950s begun investing in Hong Kong's real estate market. As chairman of many commercial property firms, and as vice chairman of Hang Lung Bank from 1970, Cheng was well placed in the Hong Kong business community.

So was Chi Wan Young. As principal founder and, eventually, general manager of Miramar Hotel & Investment Company, the worldwide hotels group, Young had amassed among his other positions the chairmanship of Yeung Chi Shing Estates and King Fook Gold and Jewellery Company.

In 1970, the two men linked their vast commercial and residential property holdings. Their aim was to acquire first class rental properties with the development for sale and rental of prime commercial and residential sites in mind.

The continuing increasing population of Hong Kong, and the shortage of land on which it might live and work, made the development of such commercial and residential sites potentially lucrative. In addition, Cheng and Young recognized Hong Kong's increasing importance as an international financial center, with increasing inflows of foreign investment to the colony providing for different residential and commercial property needs.

New World Development was incorporated in Hong Kong on May 29, 1970, as a private limited company. The company's first chairman was Dr. Sin-Hang Ho, the former chairman of Hang Seng Bank, one of the colony's leading financial institutions. Ho, who served as chairman of the company until 1981, brought a number of his business associates to the new property concern. Liang Yuen Cheong, then vice chairman of the newly created New World Development, had been a director of Hang Seng Bank, as well as of the Hong Kong and Shanghai Hotels Company. He brought with him considerable expertise in Hong Kong's property development and management market. Quo Wei Lee, appointed managing director of New World Development, had served as the general manager of Hang Seng Bank. In 1972, he was appointed a fellow of the Institute of Bankers in London. Among the other executives who joined New World Development as directors from the Hang Seng board were Sir Shiu-kin Tang, Tim Ho, and Michael Sandberg, who was later knighted for his contribution to Hong Kong's business life.

It was not long before the company's board elected to float the property concern on the Hong Kong stock market. In June 1972, New World Development became a quoted company when the board issued 96.75 million shares at HK$2 each. With the funds raised, New World Development financed the building of the New World Centre in central Hong Kong, complete with a shopping mall and commercial and residential properties. Today, the New World Centre contributes about half of the annual gross rental income of the company.

To facilitate construction work of its real estate projects, the company acquired in 1972 a 51% equity stake in Shun Fung Ironworks, for around HK$7.6 million. This was followed in 1973 by the purchase of a controlling interest in Hip Hing Construction, and the following year the acquisition of a 55% equity stake in Young's Engineering Company.

Adverse market conditions in 1974, precipitated by poor market conditions worldwide, prompted New World Developments to increase its interests in the hotel trade. The company already had a stake in Miramar Hotel & Investment Company through the involvement of Chi Wan Young. Eventually in 1976, the company acquired the Kai Tak Land Investment Company and changed its name to New World Hotels. The publicly quoted company has since become the company's 50.1% owned subsidiary handling all hotel operations, which today comprise six directly owned hotels and 11 managed hotels. These include the Regent of Hong Kong, New World Hotel, and Hotel Victoria. Recent additions to the portfolio include the Grand Hyatt Hong Kong and New World Harbour View Hotel, situated in the Hong Kong Convention and Exhibition Centre and commanding a view of Victoria Harbour.

Besides its interests in Hong Kong, the company manages six hotels in China, including the Jing Guang New World Hotel in Beijing and the Yangtze New World Hotel in Shanghai, opened in 1990. Elsewhere, the company acquired in 1987 the New World Harbourside hotel in Vancouver to take advantage of rising investment and emigration from Hong Kong reaching this Canadian gateway city to the North American market.

In 1980, New World Development purchased a 75% stake in Mei Foo Investments. This gave the company access to extensive residential properties in Hong Kong, 48,000 square feet of retail commercial space, and 16,000 square feet of space for use by schools.

Infrastructure servicing contracts from the Hong Kong government were included in the range of business New World Development was completing at this time. In 1982, the company was awarded a contract to develop three massive projects under the colony's Home Ownership and Private Sector Participation Scheme. A year earlier, the company won a contract from the U.S. government to redevelop six prime sites in exchange for a lease to rent key properties for development by New World Development.

In 1983, the continuing effects of worldwide recession, and the resulting dampening effect on Hong Kong's property market, led the company to diversify into shipping. New World Development purchased a 60% interest in the Hong Kong Islands Line Company, which operated cargo services across the Atlantic. This business was subsequently sold in February 1989. Even so, by 1985, New World Development had purchased a 39% stake in the Hong Kong-based Asia Terminals Limited, the largest container freight station and cargo distribution center in southeast Asia. Phases one and two of the terminal site were opened in 1987. Increased business by the cargo handling operation led to the construction of phases three and four, due to open in 1993. The second airport planned for Hong Kong, in the colony's port vicinity, has convinced New World Development to plan a phase five addition to the terminal. The result will be a 13-story container complex, with a total of 5.2 million square feet of space.

The year 1984 saw the start of New World Development's most ambitious project to date: the construction of the Hong Kong Convention and Exhibition Centre, with its ultramodern facilities providing space for international gatherings on a waterfront site in Wanchai. Commissioned by the Trade Development Council, the complex was opened in November 1988. Over 853 events of varying size, involving both international and local Hong Kong participants, were held at the convention center in 1989 alone. Finding occupants for the residential properties in the luxurious convention center has, however, been a slow process. A 70% occupancy rate was attained by the end of 1990, with about 310 units let.

New World Development began in 1986 to develop over 1,100 residential units on Lantau Island. Construction was carried out in partnership with the Hong Kong Resort Company, with whom New World Development had established a joint venture. In the same year, New World Development entered another partnership with Caltex Petroleum Corporation of the United States to redevelop the oil company's depot in Tsuen Wan. This turned the site into Riveria Gardens, a residential estate of 6,200 flats with commercial facilities.

A further joint venture agreement was signed at the time with the Canton Railway Corporation of Kowloon. This called for over 1,400 residential units to be developed, with commercial facilities, in the vicinity of the Light Rail Transit System in Tuen Mun, which came to be known as Pierhead Garden.

In 1987, the success of the Lantau Island development convinced New World Development to construct further residential properties, in conjunction with the Hong Kong Resort Company. On the infrastructure side, the company entered a joint venture agreement with the colony's Mass Transit Railway to develop the Sai Wan Ho site situated above the Sai Wan Ho station on Hong Kong Island.

In 1988, New World Development took a 24% interest in the Gammon/Nishimatsu consortium behind the building of the four-kilometer Tate's Cairn Tunnel, to run from Siu Lek Yuen in Shatin to Diamond Hill. The consortium gained a 30-year franchise to run the first private sector tunnel in Hong Kong. Opened in May 1991 in a bid to ease traffic congestion in East Kowloon, initial traffic estimates for the tunnel began at 100,000 vehicles daily. In 1988, New World Development purchased a one-third interest in Asia Television, one of the two television license holders in the colony. The television station has since undergone an extensive restructuring, complete with job cuts and capital investment programs. Satisfied with progress on this front, New World Development in 1989 raised its stake in Asia Television to 50%. Subject to approval from the Hong Kong government, the television concern has planned the construction of a new production center to open in 1993.

In late 1989, New World Development increased its presence in the hotel trade by acquiring Ramada International Hotels & Resorts, the world's third-largest hotel chain. In a separate agreement, an affiliate of Prime Motor Inns agreed to operate Ramada hotels in the United States, while the Hong Kong company retained control of all Ramada Renaissance properties in the United States, and all Ramada properties outside that important market. In July 1990, Prime Motors Inns sold its rights to operate the U.S. Ramada hotels to the Blackstone Group of New York. In early 1990 New World Development sold 14 Ramada properties in the United States to reduce the bank financing necessary for the original acquisition.

The company has also been actively developing properties in China, although the events of 1989 in Beijing dampened short-term prospects in this expanding Asian market. Besides long-standing involvement in the Chinese hotel trade, in June 1990 New World Development signed two investment contracts with the Guangzhou municipal government to develop the 26.5-kilometer Guangzhou ring road and the 600,000-kilowatt Zhujiang thermal power station.

In the long term, the handing-over by Britain of Hong Kong to China in 1997 continues to affect New World Development's prospects in the colony. Even so, New World Development remains committed to servicing the commercial and property needs of Hong Kong, strategically placed as it is as a growing international financial and economic center on China's doorstep.

Principal Subsidiaries: Billion Town Company Limited; Birkenshaw Limited; Bright Moon Company Limited (75%); Capital System Limited; Cheong Yin Company Limited; Convention Plaza Apartments Limited; Fook Hong Enterprises Company Limited; Fook Ying Enterprises Company Limited; Gold Queen Limited; Hang Bong Company Limited; Happy Champion Limited; Head Step Limited; Hip Hing Construction Company Limited (59%); Hong Kong Island Development Limited; International Property Management Limited (55%); Joy Sky Limited; Kin Kiu Enterprises Limited; King Lee Investment Company Limited; Lung Kee Investment Company Company Limited; Mei Foo Investments Limited (75%); New World Finance Company Limited; New World Nominee Limited; Nice Kingdom Limited; Polytown Company Limited; Pontiff Company Limited; Prime Harbour Limited; Quality Imports Limited; Shun Fung Ironworks Limited;

Sorany Company Limited; The Dynasty Club Limited; Thyme Company Limited (70%); Timely Enterprises Corporation Limited; Yargoon Company Limited (62%); Young's Engineering Company Limited (55%); Yue Wah Enterprises Company Limited; Bianchi Holdings Limited (Jersey); Beames Holdings Limited (British Virgin Islands, 64%) Fook Hang Trading Company Limited (50%); New World Indosuez Insurance Services Limited (50%); Soon Start Limited (50%).

—Etan Vlessing

OLYMPIA & YORK DEVELOPMENTS LTD.

2 First Canadian Place
Toronto, Ontario M5X 1B5
Canada
(416) 862-6100
Fax: (416) 862-5349

Private Company
Incorporated: 1969
Sales: C$4.00 billion (US$3.45 billion)

If not the largest, certainly one of the most respected real estate firms in the world is Olympia & York Developments Ltd. Olympia & York (O&Y) is the privately held creation of three brothers named Reichmann, and it has been at the forefront of large-scale office development for decades. The Reichmann brothers have assembled a staggering collection of the world's finest office towers and a fair number of Canada's leading industrial corporations as well, all the while maintaining a reputation for honesty and a passion for privacy unusual in the world of big-time real estate. By 1990 O&Y had built or was planning to build massive projects in a half-dozen of the world's great cities, but its estimated US$31 billion in assets remain the exclusive property of the Reichmann family. O&Y's chairman of the board is Renee Reichmann, the brothers' mother and head of the family, though the title is honorary.

Albert, Paul, and Ralph Reichmann were born in pre–World War II Vienna, to a family headed by Samuel Reichmann, a prosperous merchant. Originally from Hungary, Samuel Reichmann led his family on a series of traumatic escapes from Nazi persecution of Jews, eventually settling in the free port of Tangier, Morocco. There Reichmann built a reputation for wizardry in banking while preparing his children for a life in business. Albert Reichmann, eldest of the three brothers, joined his father's business; Paul Reichmann went on to Talmudic colleges in England, and in 1957 joined Ralph Reichmann and began another family exodus, to Canada, starting a tile import business in a Toronto suburb. An ancient-Greek-culture enthusiast, Ralph named his venture Olympia Floor & Tile Co. Within a few years he was joined by the rest of the Reichmann family.

Later the prospering tile company needed a new warehouse, and the Reichmanns built it themselves for about half of the contractor's bid. They decided to pursue opportunities in suburban real estate, beginning with building more warehouses.

The strong economy of the early 1960s provided ample room for expansion in Toronto industrial real estate, and the Reichmann family soon became known as a leading local builder of high-quality industrial space. The Reichmanns early learned the importance of streamlined construction practices, developing a knack for money-saving innovations that would later prove to be worth many millions of dollars. Their real estate business was organized in several companies. One of them was called York Developments, and in 1969 the three brothers consolidated their various concerns under the name of Olympia & York Developments Ltd.

The Reichmanns already had established a number of operating principles from which they would never deviate. They were scrupulously honest in their negotiating, earning a reputation as people whose handshake was as good as a contract. They built solid structures on-time and under-budget, maintained excellent relations with tenants, and came up with ingenious financing packages designed to keep ownership of all properties within the family. The brothers paid close attention to the desires of municipal and state government officials, whose cooperation became increasingly important as the size of their projects grew. The Reichmanns remained devoutly Orthodox, stopping all work by sundown every Friday and on Jewish holidays throughout the year.

In 1965 the brothers demonstrated the last ingredient in their formula for success—a willingness to gamble. When U.S. real estate mogul William Zeckendorf fell on hard times, the Reichmanns seized a chance to buy from him 500 acres of land just outside Toronto for $18 million. After selling off a few parcels to reduce debt, the brothers began a series of highly successful office buildings on the site. The Reichmanns were able to build the complex office structures with their usual efficiency, advancing from projects on the Zeckendorf purchase to bigger and more profitable ventures in Ottawa, Calgary, and downtown Toronto.

The brothers were as yet little known when they acquired a valuable piece of property in the heart of Toronto in 1973 and announced plans to construct the tallest building in Canada, a 72-story office tower called First Canadian Place. The proposal was considered too grand for Toronto's market in some quarters—its 3.5 million square feet represented a 10% increase in the city's available office space—but the Reichmann brothers went to work with their customary ingenuity. They devised a new method of construction in which all activity took place within the building; a complicated network of elevators and turntables moved supplies and men to where they were needed. The Reichmanns estimated that the technique saved up to 2.5 hours of labor per worker every day, a saving that became of critical importance when the building was slow to lease. Despite the leasing problems, the Reichmanns refused to cut their rents and eventually managed to raise them 350% during the four years it took to fill the building. First Canadian Place permanently changed the Toronto high-rise market and became the flagship of O&Y's real estate empire.

Having amassed a net worth estimated at US$1 billion by the time First Canadian was finished in 1976, the Reichmanns began to look farther afield for their next project. In New York City, the National Kinney Corporation was trying to sell a block of eight Manhattan office buildings known as the Uris portfolio. At the time, the city was flirting with bankruptcy and its real estate market was severely depressed. It was not clear whether New York would retain its position as the world's most important business center or slide into a decline. The Reichmanns concluded that, unless New York's recession was permanent, the Uris land alone was worth more than the US$320 million asking price, and in 1977 they used the equity built up in First Canadian Place to finance the deal. Within a few years the glut of Manhattan office space had become a shortage as the local economy roared back, and the Reichmanns were able to triple rents while still keeping their eight new buildings nearly full. The Uris acquisition proved to be a tremendous coup for the Reichmanns, their investment of US$320 million growing in five years to an estimated value of US$3 billion, and providing an equity base sufficient to launch O&Y on to bigger developments.

O&Y moved on to The World Financial Center at Manhattan's extreme southern tip. This Battery Park site, adjacent to the World Trade Center, had been entangled in political and financial difficulties since its creation out of landfill. Olympia joined 11 other bidders in a 1980 competition to gain approval for construction, and eventually emerged as the winner. World Financial Center was a gigantic project: six buildings with two-thirds as much space as the towering World Trade Center next door, 250,000 square feet of shops and restaurants, and four acres of well-designed public spaces. The project, in which the Reichmanns poured US$300 million of their own money, also provided for the construction of low-cost public housing in the area. The Reichmanns were able to do all of this with money borrowed below prime rate against their Uris properties, and by implementing the same highly efficient construction methods as they had used at First Canadian Place. At the same time, they were erecting another US$750 million of office towers in other U.S. cities, all during a period of severe recession. To land the prestigious tenants the World Financial project needed to assure its success, the Reichmanns took the unusual step of buying the buildings housing the tenants' previous offices in exchange for long-term lease commitments. In this way both American Express Company and City Investing Company agreed to take large blocks of space.

The Reichmanns also had begun buying stock in major industrial corporations. In 1981 the brothers paid C$618 million, most of it, again, borrowed against the Uris properties, for about 90% of the stock in Abitibi-Price, the world's largest manufacturer of newsprint paper. They soon added large pieces of MacMillan Bloedel Ltd., another forest-products company; Hiram Walker Resources Ltd., the liquor giant; and also bought into a number of other important Canadian real estate developers. In 1983 the brothers joined forces with Canada's Bronfman family, taking a 13% interest in the Bronfman's Trilon Financial Corporation, a fast-growing diversified marketer of financial services. During the next few years the Reichmanns increased their holdings in Hiram Walker to 49%, but in 1986 they lost a bidding war for control of the company and traded their stake for US$360 million in cash and a 10% share of its new owner, Allied-Lyons plc of the United Kingdom. More successful was a 1985 bid for Chevron Corporation's 60% interest in Gulf Canada Ltd., one of the country's leading oil producers; O&Y's US$2.1 billion offer was ac-

cepted, and the brothers have since increased their stake to nearly 75%. Finally, in 1987, they took part in a restructuring of Santa Fe Southern Pacific Corporation, buying 19.6% of the enormous rail, oil, and real estate concern.

With all that, the brothers remain primarily real estate developers, and in 1987 they took charge of a yet vaster project in the United Kingdom. London's Docklands, just east of the bustling city center, had been a severely depressed area for years due to England's declining shipping business and the closure of most of the city's docks. The local government had launched a project designed to transform a part of the Docklands, called the Isle of Dogs, into a new center of white-collar business the development foundered until the Reichmanns took over in 1987. In their boldest venture yet, the brothers financed construction of what amounts to a small city that will eventually provide 12 million square feet of offices in 24 buildings, one of them to be the tallest in the United Kingdom. The project, called Canary Wharf, is an enormous undertaking—the largest real estate development in Europe—and aims a permanent restructuring of London's downtown office market, much as First Canadian Place changed the face of Toronto. The project's future depends on construction of a new subway route and the upgrading of available rail service, as well as the success in attracting London's prestigious clients with the promise of low rents and modern working space. If the London real estate market softens for any length of time, the Reichmanns could have trouble filling their new buildings.

During the late 1980s the Reichmanns invested in Campeau Corporation, Robert Campeau's financially troubled retailing conglomerate. By January 1990 the Reichmanns had invested an estimated US$700 million in Campeau, including a US$250 million loan secured by eight Campeau-owned office towers. During 1990 the Reichmanns, as Campeau's largest stockholders, took more control of the company. In March 1990 Campeau defaulted on its loan to O&Y. In September 1990 Campeau Corporation agreed to settle O&Y's claims against it in a plan by which O&Y would become Campeau's majority shareholder. However, the plan had to be approved by Campeau's other creditors.

In 1990, the Reichmanns offered to sell 20% of their portfolio of United States real estate holdings. The Reichmanns owned altogether between 50 and 100 office buildings along with a sizable investment portfolio. Of perhaps greater value, even in a narrow business sense, their handshake is good around the world.

Principal Subsidiaries: Campeau Corp. (38%); Abitibi-Price Inc. (85%); Gulf Canada Ltd. (74%).

Further Reading: Tully, Shawn, "The Bashful Billionaires of Olympia & York," *Fortune,* June 14, 1982; Mason, Todd, and Elizabeth Weiner, "Inside the Reichmann Empire," *Business Week,* January 29, 1990.

—Jonathan Martin

SLOUGH ESTATES PLC

234 Bath Road
Slough SL1 4EE
United Kingdom
(0753) 537171
Fax: (0753) 5 820585

Public Company
Incorporated: 1920 as The Slough Trading Co. Ltd.
Employees: 570
Sales: £117.80 million (US$227.37 million)
Stock Exchange: London

Slough Estates plc is Britain's largest industrial property investment company, with a property portfolio valued at about £2 billion. The development and management of industrial or trading estates, sites containing a number of units of industrial property occupied by several different companies, was pioneered by Slough in the 1920s and still forms the bulk of its business, both in the United Kingdom and overseas. In recent years the company has also diversified into other property and non-property activities.

Slough Estates began life in 1920, when a syndicate of businessmen formed the Slough Trading Company to purchase a 600-acre site in Slough which had been developed as a mechanical transport repair depot during World War I. The government's original intention was to repair and sell the assembled vehicles following the war, but lack of progress aroused public criticism and after publication of the report of a parliamentary joint select committee in July 1919, it was decided to sell the site to a private buyer. The site was sold for £7 million, a price which included thousands of disused war vehicles, many of which were still on the continent. Prominent among the syndicate of businessmen who bought the site were Sir (later Lord) Percival Perry, the managing director of the U.K. branch of the Ford Motor Company, and Noel Mobbs (later Sir), founder of the Slough Trading Company as well as chairman of the Pytchley Autocar Company Ltd. which he had founded in 1904.

Some 8,000 people, nearly half the population of Slough, were employed in repairing and selling the vehicles. About 15,000 derelict vehicles were cannibalized to produce 10,000 workable ones. Repaired vehicles were sold at auction, and by the end of 1920 auction sales had already raised more than £5 million. To speed up the disposal of the vehicles the company employed what was then an innovative labor-management pol-

icy; the work force was paid regular wages rather than piece rates and a 40-hour, five-day week was introduced, without any reduction in earnings despite the reduction of 10% to 20% in working hours. This policy proved successful, resulting in the productivity improvements that it was designed to achieve.

By 1925 the vehicle sales were completed and the company turned its attention to building fully serviced factories on the site. Machine shops, other plant, and offices had already been built by the company for vehicle repair operations, together with utilities, including a power station, gas producing plant, water mains, roads, and railway track. The establishment of an integrated industrial estate of the type envisaged by the company's founder, Sir Noel Mobbs, involved further infrastructure provision. Utilities were extended and other services were organized; both Barclays Bank and the National Provincial Bank established themselves on the site to serve the new factories.

Early tenants included Citroen Cars, Johnson & Johnson, Gillette, The Mentholatum Company, and the Hygienic Ice Company. The site at Slough was ideal for such consumer-goods industries, with good road and rail links to London, which was only 20 miles away, and the Midlands. Slough's first chairman, Sir Percival Perry, was succeeded by Sir Noel Mobbs in 1922. Mobbs was to remain chairman at Slough for the next 35 years. The passage of the Slough Trading Company Act 1925 permitted the company to build roads and lay water and steam mains, electricity cables, and drains. This facilitated large-scale industrial development on the site.

Within a few years the company had transformed itself from a motor-dealing firm to a property company, a transformation which was reflected in a change of name to Slough Estates Ltd. in 1926. A policy was developed in these early years regarding the management of the estate at Slough. Units were offered for rental rather than sale, thereby giving Slough Estates greater control over the estate and providing a continual source of revenue. Such a policy also proved popular with many small and medium sized tenants, who did not wish to tie up capital in the purchase of factory premises. Only light industry was to operate on the estate. Buildings were to be built in advance of requirements and were never custom-built, although tenants' requirements were taken into account in their construction. The objective behind these policies was the provision of basic factories with a high degree of adaptability; units could be easily subdivided and could serve a wide variety of industrial needs. Adaptability was important since it meant that units could be easily re-let, thereby overcoming a basic obstacle to successful long-term investment in industrial property.

The estate grew quickly and by 1930 it had 100 tenants who employed 8,000 people on the site. As the businesses of some tenants grew, Slough was able to accommodate them in larger units on the estate, thereby enabling them to expand capacity easily without having to move to a new site or extend their premises. Sir Noel Mobbs envisaged the estate at Slough as an integrated industrial community. In addition to the provision of utilities and infrastructure on the site, he planned a variety of social and welfare services for the estate which would encourage a community atmosphere. His plans culminated in the establishment of the Slough Community Centre in 1937, and the Slough Industrial Health Service, launched in 1947 after delays caused by World War II.

The estate easily survived the 1930s, its variety of trades and concentration on the new light industries shielding it from the severe depression which hit Britain's older core industries. Slough claimed to have the lowest unemployment rate in the country, at 1%, and the estate was able to absorb unemployed workers from outside the area. This was encouraged by an extensive house-building program in Slough and the opening of a Ministry of Labour Training Centre for newcomers to the estate in 1929, providing six month courses in building, engineering, woodworking, and other skills required by the tenants. The growth of Slough was closely linked with the fortunes of Slough Estates. When the company was established in 1920 the town had 16,000 inhabitants. By 1930 this figure had grown to 28,000 and by 1938 it had soared to 55,000.

In 1931 the company acquired a second industrial estate on a 55-acre site five miles south of Birmingham. Birmingham's diversified industrial structure made it an ideal location for the establishment of a trading estate to serve a variety of light industries. A year later Slough Estates became the first company in England to provide metered steam for process and heating. This was particularly useful for industries such as food processing, where a high premium was placed on cleanliness, since it eliminated the coal dust resulting from an on-site boiler. The company's modern facilities and progressive outlook led a large number of foreign-based firms to establish themselves at Slough, something which Sir Noel Mobbs felt was impeded by the government's unsympathetic attitude to foreign companies. "The President of the Board of Trade," he complained, "can no more stop the tide of industry coming to sunlit open factories in pleasant surroundings than could Canute prevent the tide from advancing up the shores of Dover."

The estate at Slough escaped war damage during World War II. During the postwar reconstruction period, expansion was inhibited by shortages and government restrictions. Building materials were in extremely short supply due to wartime reductions in capacity. Government building licenses were difficult to obtain, due to local labor scarcity and a national economic policy that favored export-orientated industries at the expense of construction. Controls also extended to the provision of capital, and borrowing large sums for development required clearance from a government body known as the Capital Issues Committee. Despite a waiting list for new units, development at Slough in the early postwar years was restricted to expanding factory space for existing tenants.

In order to overcome these problems, Slough Estates sought further expansion outside Slough. During this time of tight government controls, undertaking government-sponsored projects provided one means of gaining the necessary official approval. Slough participated in such a scheme in 1945, developing an estate in Swansea at the request of the Board of Trade.

Just as Slough Estates's formation had resulted from government activity during World War I, demobilization following World War II brought new opportunities. In 1948 it obtained a 22-acre site at Greenford, Middlesex, which had been used as an ordnance depot, with 21 units let to the War Department. As leases on these units were not due to expire until 1959, the investment offered little prospect of increasing returns in the short term, but the company's patience was rewarded by rising rental income after the leases terminated. Despite the shortages and government restrictions which inhibited expansion during these years, Slough Estates experienced rapid growth in asset values immediately after the war, reflected in an increase in the estimated value of its assets from £2.3 million to £3 million between 1945 and 1948. While postwar conditions had restricted the scope for expansion, they had increased the value of existing factories by allowing demand to outstrip supply.

Government restrictions and shortages continued to plague Slough Estates until 1954 when building license controls were lifted, although the Birmingham and Greenford estates had been virtually completed and let by this date. Other investments included the purchase of land in Canada and a large injection of capital to improve the power station at Slough. A large land bank was also acquired, which the company was able to put to good use in the less restricted environment of the 1950s and 1960s. Rents had risen only moderately in the years immediately following the war, since most property was still let on leases which had been negotiated in the interwar period. However in 1951, when many leases came up for renewal, rental income jumped by 25%.

The property boom period, from the lifting of government restrictions on development in 1954, to the imposition of the government's so-called Brown Ban on office development in and around London in 1964, did not prove nearly so prosperous a time for industrial estate developers as it did for developers of offices or shopping malls. In addition, Industrial Development Certificate legislation held back development activity in this sector. Development funds were raised by a series of rights issues, while rising rents provided further capital for expansion. Sir Noel Mobbs retired as chairman in 1957, and was succeeded by Lieutenant Colonel W.H. Kingsmill, with Gerald Mobbs as managing director.

Restrictions in the domestic market prompted Slough's expansion overseas in the postwar period. From 1950 onwards, parcels of land were accumulated gradually in the town of Ajax near Toronto, Canada. The choice of Ajax paralleled that of Slough, both being small towns close to a large population center with good transport facilities to major national and international markets. The establishment of the estate led to the formation of two new subsidiaries; Slough Estates (Canada) Ltd. and its construction subsidiary Slough Construction and Properties Ltd.

By the late 1950s U.K. currency controls made it impossible to remit funds to Canada for the development of the Ajax estate investment. The company had sufficient security for local borrowing from the early 1960s, but funding continued to present problems until 1969 when Slough Estates acquired Yorkshire and Pacific Securities Ltd., a U.K.-based investment company whose assets were held by a Canadian subsidiary. A second Canadian estate was established in the mid-1960s, covering 109 acres in Malton, a mile from Toronto International Airport.

In 1949, Slough entered the Australian property market, a favorite area for U.K. developers wishing to expand overseas, with the purchase of 1,500 acres of land at Altona, near Melbourne. Unlike previous developments the land was not located in a town and it took over ten years to get the local authorities to extend utilities to the site. Eventually another industrial development was established nearby and the necessary services were extended. Slough Estates Australia Pty. Ltd., a wholly owned subsidiary, was established in 1961, but it was not until 1966 that a final agreement was reached with the Melbourne and Metropolitan Board of Works for the provision of amenities.

During the 1960s, influenced by the growing prosperity of the European Economic Community (EEC), Slough decided to expand into Europe. Britain's failure to gain entry to the EEC at that time led to Slough's decision to establish a factory in an EEC country. Belgium was chosen, since it had a highly developed industrial infrastructure, a rich domestic market, and close proximity to London. St. Nicholas, a textile town within easy reach of both Antwerp and Brussels, which wanted to diversity into other industries due to the depression in textiles, was chosen as a site. Designated by the government as an official development area, the site also offered financial concessions.

During the 1960s Slough extended its operations to the north of England. In 1967 it purchased an industrial estate in Wakefield comprising 17 acres of land close to the M1 motorway. In an area of high unemployment, this development was not subject to industrial development certificate legislation. The purchase of the site prior to the extension of the M1 was an example of Slough Estates's strategy of buying estates before the provision of infrastructure, which was also a factor behind the later acquisition of the estate at Yate. The Wakefield site also had features in common with the earlier estates in Slough and Birmingham, in that it was located in a major conurbation, with a skilled industrial work force and a large local market for goods produced on the estate.

Growth was assisted by the takeover of another company specializing in industrial property, Hertford Industrial Estates, which was acquired in 1969 for £830,000. This company owned 24 acres of industrial buildings in Hertford, Bishop's Stortford, and Braintree. During the early 1970s the company expanded rapidly to take advantage of booming economic conditions. Sites were purchased in High Wycombe, Yate, near Bristol, and Aylesbury. New overseas operations included the purchase of a major site in Australia and the launching of a joint £9 million development program with Mackenzie Hill to develop sites in France and later in Germany.

The company was in a good position to take advantage of the rapid rise in industrial rents during the early 1970s. By 1970, 75% of leases was tied to the wholesale price index and were adjusted annually. This system of leasing, which was unique to the company, led to rapid increases in rental income during the inflationary years of the 1970s. A further 10% of properties was let on leases with seven-yearly rent reviews.

Diversification into the non-industrial commercial property market was also attempted, though a subsidiary, Gauntlet Developments, which was formed in 1972 to develop offices in the United Kingdom and Europe. This venture proved unsuccessful, leaving Slough Estates with offices in Brussels and Sheffield which remained vacant for several years. In 1974 the company turned its attention to the United States and entered into a joint venture with Draper & Kramer to form SDK Parks, in which it took an 80% interest. Slough was the first British property company to tackle the industrial sector in the United States.

Following the property market crash in the same year and its aftermath, Slough was one of the few companies to achieve increases in profits. Industrial development did not suffer the same fate as the commercial market. Although the company had made minor excursions into commercial property, it emerged from the crisis largely unscathed. It was able to buy out the interest of Mackenzie Hill in their joint developments and

successfully launched a £5.5 million convertible rights issue in 1975.

Improving property market conditions during the late 1970s allowed Slough Estates to enter a new phase of expansion, the most notable scheme being the Sutton Industrial Park at Reading, which was bought in 1976 and was intended to contain about 750,000 square feet of buildings. During 1976 Sir Nigel Mobbs, grandson of Sir Noel Mobbs, became chairman and chief executive succeeding his father Gerald Mobbs.

The early 1980s saw steady growth in Slough's profits, despite a depression in industrial property, as rent reviews led to increased rental income. Slough undertook a number of developments both at home and overseas. U.S. activities were expanded substantially, developments being concentrated around the Chicago area.

In 1984 Slough merged with Allnatt London & Guildhall Properties, with assets valued at £159 million. Allnatt's properties were well suited to Slough's portfolio, since they were predominantly industrial.

During 1987 it was decided to broaden the company's asset base, with increased activity in the shop, office, and retail warehousing markets. Until 1987, only 8.5% of Slough Estates's U.K. portfolio was in non-industrial property, though its commitment to other property areas increased sharply in 1986 with the purchase of a 52% stake in Bredero Properties, a development company that specialized in U.K. shopping malls.

Buoyant conditions in the industrial property market led to rising profits for Slough during the late 1980s. The company continued to expand its activities, launching a massive development program both at home and overseas, the eventual cost of which was estimated to be about £1 billion. Operations were extended into the French and German markets, while the company diversified into property and non-property activities unconnected with industrial estates in both U.K. and foreign markets. By 1990, investment in such activities amounted to £45 million.

Despite this recent diversification, Slough Estates's activities were still dominated by U.K. trading-estate investment and development. The 1990s may open up new possibilities for this sector as moves toward European unity provide new opportunities for U.K. industry. If the successful pattern of U.K. trading-estate development that has marked Slough's past growth can be adapted to the new conditions of the single European market, it may enjoy an equally prosperous future.

Principal Subsidiaries: Guildhall Properties Ltd.; Slough Estates Australia Pty Ltd.; Slough Properties SA (Belgium); Slough Estates Canada Ltd.; Slough Commercial Properties GmbH (Germany); Slough Parks Inc. (U.S.A.); Slough Developments (France) SA.

Further Reading: Slough Estates Ltd: 1920–1970, Slough, Slough Estates, 1970; "Company File: Slough Estates," *Estates Gazette,* May 7, 1977; Erdman, Edward, *People and Property,* London, Batsford, 1982; Smyth, Hedley, "The Historical Growth Of Property Companies and the Construction Industry in Great Britain Between 1939 and 1979," unpublished Ph.D. thesis, University of Bristol, 1982; Foster,

Michael, "Company File: Slough Estates," *Estates Gazette,* May 7, 1983; "Slough Estates: Re-rating due?" *Investors Chronicle,* May 10, 1985; "Slough Estates Goes Commercial Again," *Investors Chronicle,* May 1, 1987; Cheesewright, Paul, "Slough Shares Fall As Its NAV Rises 35% and Its Profits 22%," *Financial Times,* March 30, 1989; *Report: Slough Estates plc,* Slough, Slough Estates, 1989; Cassell, Michael, *Long Lease!,* Tulsa, Oklahoma, PennWell Books, 1990.

—Peter Scott

Sumitomo Realty & Development Co., Ltd.

SUMITOMO REALTY & DEVELOPMENT CO., LTD.

4-1, Nishi-shinjuku 2-chome
Shinjuku-ku, Tokyo 163
Japan
(03) 3346-1011
Fax: (03) 3344-6090

Public Company
Incorporated: 1949 as Izumi Fudosan
Employees: 715
Sales: ¥300.64 billion (US$2.21 billion)
Stock Exchanges: Tokyo Osaka

Sumitomo Realty & Development Co., Ltd. shares the 400-year lineage of the Sumitomo group firms. The company designs, constructs, leases, and manages commercial and residential real estate and other properties in Japan and around the world. It is devoted primarily to urban development, community development, and overseas activities.

Sumitomo Realty & Development's operations date back to 1933, when the Sumitomo Goshi Company erected the Tokyo Sumitomo Building. As the successor to the real estate division of the former Sumitomo Honsha, then the group's holding company, Izumi Fudosan was established in December 1949 with its headquarters in Tokyo.

At its inception the company was engaged primarily in serving the real estate needs of the Sumitomo group. Izumi Fudosan leased, and administered office buildings used by Sumitomo group companies, carrying on the pre–World War II functions of Sumitomo's real estate division.

In May 1957 the firm assumed its present name, Sumitomo Realty & Development Co., Ltd. By 1963 the company had begun its continuing program of international expansion through the establishment of its overseas affiliate, Sumitomo Investment Co., (HK) Ltd., in Hong Kong. The division developed and operates three factories in Hong Kong. Sumitomo was the first of the major Japanese developers to expand internationally. In 1969 Sumitomo moved into Thailand where the company owns and leases a large office building in downtown Bangkok. Building leasing continued in 1991 to be integral to the company's operations.

Through the 1960s Sumitomo continued as its primary business the management and development of commercial buildings. In April 1964 Sumitomo Realty opened its first office in Osaka, the historical seat of the Sumitomo group. In 1964 the company erected and began to lease the Kazan Building. Sumitomo also forayed into residential construction for the first time, concentrating on building luxury condominiums in desirable neighborhoods of Tokyo, including the City House series in Koishikawa, which was completed in 1968; Minami-Aoyama, which was ready for occupancy in 1969; Otowa in 1970; and Takanawa in 1971.

By the 1970s Sumitomo Realty was firmly established as a leading Japanese developer. Sumitomo Realty is owned by a group of stockholders that includes other Sumitomo group firms, including The Sumitomo Bank, The Sumitomo Trust & Banking Company, and Sumitomo Shoji. The strength of the company depends in large part on the support it enjoys from the Sumitomo group. This network has helped the company prosper despite sometimes-unfavorable economic conditions.

Achieving a global presence was a priority for Sumitomo Realty. The 1970s saw Sumitomo Realty aggressively expand both at home and overseas. In May 1972 Sumitomo gained a foothold in the United States through the establishment of La Solana Corporation, now known as Sumitomo Realty & Development CA., Inc. Through the 1970s, La Solana developed and marketed a variety of residential housing alternatives, including single-family houses and townhouses, in prime locations in and around Los Angeles county. In October 1972 La Solana paid $3.6 million for 46 acres in Huntington, California. More than 1,100 houses in Huntington, West Covina, Anaheim, Palos Verdes, and Dana Point, California, were completed by 1989. Another 1,000 units were under construction in the area. Also in 1972, Sumitomo moved into Hawaii, establishing another local subsidiary to manage the newly acquired Hawaii Country Club, outside Honolulu.

Sumitomo Realty was adversely affected by the world oil crisis of 1973 and 1974. Nevertheless, Sumitomo Realty's sales in 1973 were ¥24.9 billion and profits were ¥1.4 billion. In 1974 sales climbed to ¥33.4 billion and profits to ¥1.5 billion. By 1977, sales topped ¥45 billion, yet the company was in the red with losses of ¥2 billion. In response to this fall the company, then under the guidance of Chairman Seigoro Seyama and President Taro Ando, began to provide more affordable housing for a larger market. The construction of expansive suburban Tokyo condominium complexes intended for the middle class included the Chiba Garden Town, completed in 1973, and Sobudai Green Park, completed in 1979, each with more than 1,500 units. These developments reflected the new priorities of Sumitomo. These included a shift from rapid growth and sales volume to social responsibility and efficient management.

In March 1974 Sumitomo completed the 52-story Shinjuku Sumitomo Building in Tokyo and three months later moved the company's headquarters there from the Tokyo Sumitomo Building. The Kyoto Sumitomo Building, completed in 1976, and the Sumitomo Nakanoshima Building in Osaka, completed in 1977, were among buildings the company owned and leased just outside of Tokyo.

Sumitomo launched one of its most important subsidiaries in March 1975, when Sumitomo Real Estate Sales Co., Ltd. was created from the company's sales division. Sumitomo Sales sells condominiums, single-family homes, and housing sites developed by Sumitomo Realty. Since 1979, Sumitomo Sales has established a network of sales offices that it both owns and manages. Between 1979 and 1989, the number of sales offices jumped from 2 to 98. In 1989 Sumitomo Sales involved 5% of the residential resale market in Japan.

The sales company established its own international-business department in 1988. Among its plans was the creation of a data base to provide Japanese customers with information they needed to purchase either residential or commercial real estate in the United States. To bolster its presence in the United States, the company became associated with Locations, Inc., with seven offices in Hawaii; Fred Sands Realtors, with 40 offices on the U.S. West Coast; and Coldwell Banker Commercial Group, Inc., with 96 offices across the United States. In 1989 Sumitomo Sales handled sales of condominium units in the Worldwide Plaza in New York City.

In 1977 the company announced plans to construct a 30-story building in the Shinjuku district of Tokyo, with Nippon Life Insurance Company. This building was completed in 1982 and became Sumitomo Realty's new headquarters in October of that year. The majority of the office buildings erected, owned, leased, and managed by Sumitomo are located in downtown Tokyo. These buildings were designed by Sumitomo's architecture and engineering staffs. Most feature contemporary architecture including dramatic atriums, extensive use of glass, and luxurious amenities.

Sumitomo Fudosan Home Co., Ltd., an associated company, took over the design and construction of single-family homes from Sumitomo Realty's residential-business division in 1982. The company had erected more than 50 model homes in Japan by 1991. New housing, based on these plans, was designed and constructed by Sumitomo's staff after the buyer had an opportunity to view the models. Sumitomo System Construction, a subsidiary of Sumitomo Realty, began to offer interior design services through interior coordinators, who were licensed by the Interior Industry Association.

The 1980s were a period of rapid growth for Sumitomo in a volatile market. Land prices in Japan and in Tokyo in particular escalated dramatically during this period. Residential land prices rose 93% in the year ending July 1, 1987. From 1986 to 1989 the total value of land in Japan doubled to $14 trillion, about twice the value of all of the land in the United States. Domestic demand policies were responsible for a construction boom early in the decade. Under the leadership of Hiroma Yamamoto, chairman through 1984; Taro Ando, his successor in that position; and Shinichiro Takagi, president since 1986; Sumitomo prospered financially in this environment. The company posted six consecutive years—from 1983 to 1989—of record earnings and revenues. In a one-year period, from 1988 to 1989, net income rose 51.6%. Sumitomo Realty stock was one of the top performers of 1989.

The company was, however, often blamed for escalating property values and placing real estate ownership out of reach of the average Japanese. In one widely reported encounter,

three young men wielding samurai swords and homemade pistols entered Ando's home in January 1987, seized his wife, and littered his yard with leaflets condemning the practices of so-called land sharks. The extremely high cost of land forced Sumitomo to take some creative measures to acquire needed property on which to build. The company began to utilize alternatives to the outright purchase of large blocks of land. One strategy involved the slow acquisition of contiguous lots one by one until the company owned enough land to develop. A second method was joint development, in which Sumitomo cooperated with existing landowners in the development of their land. In this way, Sumitomo was able to continue its tremendous rate of growth and development. Sumitomo managed 10 Tokyo office buildings in 1979, 19 in 1984, and 50 in 1989. The company added another 33 buildings by March 1991.

Worldwide, Sumitomo was involved in projects from New York to Australia. In June 1987, Sumitomo paid roughly $500 million, then the second-highest price ever paid for a Manhattan office property, to purchase 666 Fifth Avenue. In 1989, Sumitomo purchased the JW Marriott Hotel at Century City, Los Angeles, California, which it then managed. The company expected to venture further into hotel management in ensuing years. Sumitomo was also involved in developing the largest hotel complex in Australia.

In 1989, as the company celebrated its 40th anniversary, it adopted a new mission statement centered on three policies, ". . . expanding the types of activities we deal with, enlarging the geographical extent of our operations, and diversifying the techniques used to promote developmental projects." By 1990, the Japanese real estate boom seemed to be leveling off. Rising interest rates, the falling yen, and rapid inflation contributed to the bleak picture.

Principal Subsidiaries: Sumitomo Real Estate Sales Co., Ltd. (93.8%); Sumitomo Fudosan Home Co., Ltd.; Sumitomo Fudosan Finance Co., Ltd.; Sumitomo Fudosan System Construction Co., Ltd.; Sumitomo Fudosan Tatemono Service Co., Ltd.; Izumi Restaurant Co., Ltd.; Sumitomo Fudosan Ryokka Co., Ltd.; Sumitomo Realty & Development Co., Inc. (U.S.A.); Izumi Development Co., Ltd. (85.6%); Shinjuku Sumitomo Building Management Co., Ltd. (60%); La Solana N.Y., Inc. (U.S.A.); La Solana D.C., Inc. (U.S.A.); Sumitomo Realty & Development (Australia) Pty. Ltd.

Further Reading: Company Profile, Tokyo, Sumitomo Realty & Development Co., Ltd. 1989; *A Brief History of Sumitomo,* Tokyo, Sumitomo Corporation, 1990.

—Lynn M. Kalanik

TOKYU LAND CORPORATION

21-2, Dogenzaka 1-chome
Shibuya-ku, Tokyo 150
Japan
(03) 3463-6611
Fax: (03) 3464-7242

Public Company
Incorporated: 1953 as Tokyu Real Estate Co., Ltd.
Employees: 1,004
Sales: ¥167.31 billion (US$1.23 billion)
Stock Exchanges: Tokyo Osaka Singapore

Tokyu Land Corporation is the third-largest real estate company in Japan. The company operates in various sectors of the real estate industry, including commercial office building and leasing, residential lots, and construction of housing. Nearly half of Tokyu's business is housing construction. The company is perhaps best known for its suburban residential developments. Since its inception Tokyu Land has been associated closely with the Tokyu Corporation, a diversified Japanese company with its roots in the electric railway industry. In 1991 Tokyu Corporation still owned approximately 14% of Tokyu Land Corporation. Tokyu Real Estate Co., Ltd. was set up in December 1953 as a subsidiary of the Tokyo Electric Express Railway Company, now the Tokyu Corporation. Tokyu Real Estate was to run the urban development, gravel transportation, and recreational property businesses of its parent. The business of managing recreation grounds was handed back to Tokyo Electric Express Railway (TEER) later in 1953, and Tokyu Real Estate quickly expanded into other areas.

In 1954 the company acquired two other TEER operations, the Japanese Enterprise Company and Tokyu Construction Industry, operating an insurance agency, warehousing, and construction businesses. Within two years the warehousing operations and the gravel business were spun off to affiliated companies, the Yokohama Cooperative Wharf Company, and the Tokyu Gravel Company, respectively. In 1959 the Tokyu Construction Company took over the construction business. Tokyu Real Estate now focused on the sale and development of real estate.

The islands of Japan have very limited real estate resources, so historically the price of land has been very high. Real estate prices dipped only twice between 1936 and the early 1990s: in 1975 after the first oil crisis, and in the late 1980s after the government took measures to harness feverish price escalation based on speculation. Land in the city of Tokyo has always

been particularly expensive. Fear of earthquakes has kept the height of office and residential buildings in the Japanese capital at less than 30 stories. In the most fashionable district of the city, a single square meter cost US$450,000 in 1988. Tokyu Land operates in a market where demand is perennially higher than supply.

In 1970 Tokyu Real Estate entered into a joint venture with Levitt & Sons, the largest U.S. homebuilder. The newly formed company was 40% owned by Tokyu Real Estate and was slated to produce 30,000 modular housing units in Japan within a few years. The company's push into prefabricated housing was supported by the development by Tokyu Corporation of new railway connections between Tokyo and the surrounding areas.

In the early 1970s, Tokyu Real Estate Co., Ltd. changed its name to Tokyu Land Corporation. Also during the early 1970s, Prime Minister Kakuei Tanaka's plan to redistribute Japan's industrial development away from the traditional centers of Tokyo and Osaka encouraged a wave of land speculation that raised real estate prices all over Japan. The flames were further fueled by the easy availability of credit. In addition to land speculation, the popularity of suburban housing led many to believe that residential building would represent a major growth industry in the near future. The recession of 1974 quickly put the skids on this flurry of speculation. The effect of the recession on real estate prices was devastating. Tokyo land prices went into decline for the first time since 1936. Many investors had come to view Japanese real estate as an invincible investment and were shocked when the bottom fell out of the market. Hundreds of Japanese companies, including several large ones, went bankrupt due to their real estate investments.

The crash of the real estate market took a heavy toll on Tokyu Land Corporation. The company lost money on its own holdings, and it suffered from Japanese consumers' fear of buying property. Tokyu Land was the last of Japanese real estate's Big Three to recover from the crunch—profits were down through fiscal 1976.

The residential market was the first to rebound. Demand for houses showed an upturn in the spring of 1976. Luxury apartments in the big cities were in great demand, a trend that continued into the 1980s. In 1977 and 1978 land prices rose steadily, and in 1979 increases reached double digits—10% nationally, and 18.5% in Tokyo.

Tokyu Land followed a policy of expanding its overseas business to 10% of its total assets. Its parent company, Tokyu Corporation, had started a major resort development in Hawaii in 1970, starting with a golf course and hotel. By 1987 Tokyu Land was offering Hawaiian condominiums for sale. In 1980 Tokyu Land established a subsidiary in Singapore and began several major commercial and residential development projects there.

In the early 1980s, the market for new housing in Japan slowed. An oversupply of houses and a widening gap between housing prices and purchasing power were the main causes. The government under Prime Minister Yasuhiro Nakasone instituted an urban-renewal program to stimulate new construction and to replace old urban dwellings with new. Local governments were encouraged to relax restrictions. This cooperation was not immediate, and the plan got a slow start.

Although the housing market was slow, the Japanese real estate industry was reaping profits from other areas. Commercial property values in Tokyo were rising, nearly doubling in 1984. In 1985 Tokyu Land instituted a five-year plan to expand its rental property holdings. Construction on four large buildings intended to provide a steady source of rental income began in 1987. By March 1990 rental property made up about 15% of Tokyu Land's total income.

Between 1983 and 1987 Tokyo's commercial property increased in value by 160%. The city's importance as a commercial center insured that office vacancies were almost nonexistent. Fear that prices would get out of control as they had in the mid-1970s prompted the government to take action. Starting in August 1987, all property transactions involving more than 500 square meters in Tokyo required governmental approval. Tax breaks for speculative land deals were abolished in 1988. The Ministry of Finance also warned banks against making too many property loans.

In the late 1980s Japanese investors began to grow more interested in real estate investments overseas. Real estate in the United States could be a far more profitable investment property than in Japan. The annual yield on investment for an office building in Tokyo in 1987 was about 2%, compared to 5% to 8% in the United States. The advantages were clear, and Japanese investment in U.S. properties became newsworthy.

Tokyu Land played upon a growing Japanese penchant for American-style architecture in a unique way in 1989. The company hired a U.S. architectural firm to design Beverly Hills–style luxury houses in Tokyo's suburbs. The houses, built on half-acre lots, ten times the usual size, offered large yards with tennis courts, swimming pools, and spacious interiors.

In the early 1990s Tokyu Land Corporation had continued to add to its rental properties, viewing them as a stable source of income. Because Tokyo is likely to remain the unrivaled commercial center of Japan, Tokyu Land expects real property in the Tokyo area to remain extremely valuable and had been expanding its sales force there. Also, massive land reclamation projects in Tokyo Bay promise new opportunities in commercial real estate by the mid-1990s.

—Thomas M. Tucker

INDEX TO COMPANIES AND PERSONS _____

Listings are arranged in alphabetical order under the company name; thus Eli Lilly & Company will be found under the letter E. Definite articles (The) and forms of incorporation that precede the name (A.B. and N.V.) are ignored for alphabetical purposes. Company names appearing in **bold** type have historical essays on the page numbers appearing in **bold**. The index is cumulative, with volume numbers printed in **bold** type.

Barlow Rand Ltd., I 288–89, **422–24; IV** 22, 96
Barlow, Robert, **I** 604–05
Barlow, William (Sir), **III** 434
Barmer Bankverein, **II** 238, 241
Barnato, Barney, **I** 64
Barnato Bros., **IV** 21, 65
Barnes Group, **III** 581
Barnes, J. David, **II** 316
Barnes, James E., **IV** 459
Barnes-Hind, **III** 56, 727
Barnet, Herbert, **I** 277
Barnetson, William (Lord), **IV** 686
Barnett, Hoares and Co., **II** 306
Barnetts, Hoares, Hanbury and Lloyds, **II** 306
Barnevik, Percy, **II** 2–3, 4; **IV** 204
Barney, Ashbel H., **II** 381
Barney, Danforth N., **II** 380, 381, 395
Barney, Hiram, **III** 239
Barney, J.W., **IV** 601
Barney, Lawrence D., **I** 643
Baron, Stanley Wade, **I** 219, 255, 270, 292
Baroncini, Gino, **III** 208
Barr & Stroud Ltd., **III** 727
Barr, David W., **IV** 645
Barranquilla Investments, **II** 138
Barratt American Inc., **I** 556
Barratt Developments plc, I 556–57
Barratt, Lawrie, **I** 556
Barratt Multi-Ownership and Hotels Ltd., **I** 556
Barret Fitch North, **II** 445
Barrett Burston, **I** 437
Barrett Co., **I** 414–15
Barriger, John, **I** 472–73
Barringer, John H., **III** 151
Barron, Clarence, **IV** 601
Barron family, **IV** 602
Barron, Jessie, **IV** 601
Barrow, Richard Cadbury, **II** 476
Barry & Co., **III** 522
Barrymore, John, **II** 175
Barsab, **I** 288–89
Barth Smelting Corp., **I** 513
Bartholomew, Guy, **IV** 666
Barton Brands, **I** 227; **II** 609
Barton, Bruce, **I** 28
Barton, Duer & Koch, **IV** 282
Baruch, Edgar, **II** 415
BASF A.G., I 305–08, 309, 319, 346–47, 632, 638; **II** 554; **IV** 70
BASF Corp., **IV** 71
BASF Wyandotte Corp., **I** 275
Basic American Retirement Communities, **III** 103
Baskin-Robbins Ice Cream Co., **I** 215
Basle A.G., **I** 632–33, 671–72
Basle Air Transport, **I** 121
Basler and Zürcher Bankverein, **II** 368
Basler Bank-Verein, **II** 368
Basler Bankverein, **II** 368
Basler Depositen-Bank, **II** 368
Bass & Co., **I** 142
Bass Charington, **I** 222
Bass, Ed, **I** 418
Bass family, **II** 173
Bass, Lee, **I** 418
Bass, Michael, **I** 222
Bass, Michael Thomas, **I** 222
Bass plc, I 222–24; III 94–95
Bass Ratcliffe & Gretton, **I** 222
Bass, Robert, **I** 418
Bass, Sid, **I** 418
Bass, William, **I** 222

Bassett, Allen L., **III** 337
Bassett Foods, **II** 478
Bassins Food Chain, **II** 649
BAT Industries plc, I 425–27, 605; **II** 628; **III** 66, 185, 522
Batchelors Ltd., **I** 315
Bateman Eichler Hill Richards, **III** 270
Bates, Albert D., **I** 254
Bates & Robins, **II** 318
Bates, Edward B., **III** 238
Bathurst Bank, **II** 187
Batson, Homer Ward, **III** 216, 217
Batten Barton Durstine & Osborn, **I** 25, 28–31, 33
Batten, George, **I** 28
Batten, Jim, **IV** 630
Batterson, James G., **III** 387, 388
Battle Creek Toasted Corn Flake Co., **II** 523
Battle Mountain Gold Co., **IV** 490
Bauborg, **I** 560–61
Bauersfeld, Walther, **III** 446
Baugh, John, **II** 675
Bauman, Robert P., **III** 66, 67
Baumann, Paul, **I** 349–50
Bausch & Lomb, **III** 446
Bavarian Railway, **II** 241
Baxter, Donald, **I** 627
Baxter Estates, **II** 649
Baxter International, I 627–29
Baxter Laboratories, **I** 627
Baxter Travenol Laboratories, **I** 627
Bay Area Review Course, Inc., **IV** 623
Bay Colony Life Insurance Co., **III** 254
Bay Petroleum, **I** 526
Bay State Glass Co., **III** 683
Bayazit, Rifat, **IV** 563
Bayer A.G., I 305–06, **309–11,** 319, 346–47, 350; **II** 279
Bayer, Friedrich, **I** 309
Bayerische Aluminium AG, **IV** 230
Bayerische Disconto- und Wechsel Bank, **II** 239
Bayerische Flugzeugwerke, **I** 73
Bayerische Handelsbank, **II** 241
Bayerische Hypotheken- und Wechsel-Bank AG, II 238–40, 241, 242; **IV** 323
Bayerische Kraftwerke AG, **IV** 229, 230
Bayerische Landesbank, **II** 257, 258, 280
Bayerische Motoren Werke A.G., I 75, **138–40,** 198; **II** 5; **III** 543, 556, 591
Bayerische Rückversicherung AG, **III** 377
Bayerische Rumpler Werke, **I** 73
Bayerische Staatsbank, **II** 239, 242
Bayerische Stickstoff-Werke AG, **IV** 229–30
Bayerische Vereinsbank A.G., II 239, 240, **241–43; III** 401
Bayerische Versicherungsbank, **II** 238; **III** 377
Bayerische Wasserkraftwerke Aktiengesellschaft, **IV** 231
Bayerische Zellstoff, **IV** 325
Bayernwerk AG, **IV** 231, 232. 323
Bayon Steel Corp., **IV** 234
Bayou Boeuf Fabricators, **III** 559
Bayside National Bank, **II** 230
Bayview, **III** 673
BBC. See British Broadcasting Corp.
BBC Brown, Boveri Ltd., **II** 1, 3–4, 13; **III** 466, 631, 632
BBDO. See Batten Barton Durstine & Osborn
BBME. See British Bank of the Middle East
BCal. See British Caledonian Airways
BCI. See Banca Commerciale Italiana SpA

BCI Funding Corp., **II** 192
BCI Holdings Corp., **II** 468
BCI (Suisse), **II** 192
Beach, Morrison H., **III** 389
BeachviLime Ltd., **IV** 74
Beacon Manufacturing, **I** 377
Beacon Oil, **IV** 566
Beacon Participations, **III** 98
Beacon Publishing Co., **IV** 629
Beal, Orville E., **III** 338, 339
Beale, John Field (Sir), **III** 493, 494
Beale, Leonard T., **I** 382
Beale, Samuel (Sir), **III** 494
Beall, Donald, **I** 80
Bean, John, **I** 442
Beane, Alpheus, Jr., **II** 424
Bear, Joseph, **II** 400
Bear, Stearns & Co., **II** 400
Bear Stearns Companies, Inc., II 400–01, 450
Beard & Stone Electric Co., **I** 451
Beardsley, Albert R., **I** 653
Beardsley, Andrew Hubble, **I** 653
Beardsley, Charles S., **I** 653
Beardsley, Paul R., **I** 199
Bearings Co. of America, **I** 158–59
Beatrice Cheese, **II** 467
Beatrice Companies, **II** 468
Beatrice Company, I 353; **II 467–69,** 475; **III** 118, 437
Beatrice Creamery Co. of Nebraska, **II** 467
Beatrice Foods Co., **I** 440–41; **II** 467
Beatrice/Hunt Wesson, **II** 467
Beatty, Chester (Sir), **IV** 21
Beaulieu Winery, **I** 260
Beaumont, Ernest, **IV** 261
Beaupre, T.N., **IV** 272
Beaver, Hugh E.C. (Sir), **I** 251
Beaver Lumber Co., **I** 274
Beaverbrook (Lord). See Aitken, Max
Bebber, Rolf, **I** 111
Bébéar, Claude, **III** 209, 210, 211
Beber, Frank, **I** 656
Becherer, Hans W., **III** 464
Bechtel Group Inc., I 558–59, 563; **III** 248; **IV** 171, 576
Bechtel, Stephen, **I** 558
Bechtel, Stephen, Jr., **I** 558–59
Bechtel, Warren A., **I** 558
Beck, Dave, **I** 169
Beck, Marshall, **III** 438
Beck, Robert, **III** 340
Becker Paribas Futures, **II** 445
Becker Warburg Paribas, **II** 259
Becket, Fredrick M. (Dr.), **I** 399
Beckett, John R., **I** 537; **II** 147
Beckley-Cardy Co., **IV** 623, 624
Beckman, Arnold O., **I** 694
Beckman Instruments, **I** 694
Becton Dickinson & Company, I 630–31; **IV** 550
Becton, Henry P., **I** 630
Becton, Maxwell W., **I** 630
Bedford-Stuyvesant Restoration Corp., **II** 673
Bedford, Thomas Edward, **II** 496, 497
Bedrosian, John, **III** 87
Bee Chemicals, **I** 372
Bee Gee Shrimp, **I** 473
Beebe, Frederick, **I** 415
Beebe, W.T., **I** 100
Beech Aircraft, **II** 87
Beech-Nut Corp., **I** 695; **II** 489
Beecham Group Ltd., **I** 626, 640, 668; **II** 331, 543; **III** 18, 65–66

FCC National Bank, **II** 286
FDIC. *See* Federal Deposit Insurance Corp.
Fearn International, **II** 525
Fechheimer Bros. Co., **III** 215
Federal Bearing and Bushing, **I** 158–59
Federal Deposit Insurance Corp., **II** 261, 262, 285, 337
Federal Electric, **I** 463; **III** 653
Federal Express, **II** 620
Federal Home Life Insurance Co., **III** 263; **IV** 623
Federal Home Loan Bank, **II** 182
Federal Insurance Co., **III** 220, 221
Federal Lead Co., **IV** 32
Federal Mining and Smelting Co., **IV** 32
Federal-Mogul Corp., I 158–60; **III** 596
Federal National Mortgage Association, II 410–11
Federal Pacific Electric, **II** 121
Federal Paper Board, **I** 524
Federal Paper Mills, **IV** 248
Federal Steel Co., **II** 330; **IV** 572
Federal Yeast Corp., **IV** 410
Federale Mynbou, **IV** 90, 91, 92, 93
Federale Mynbou/General Mining, **IV** 90
Federated Metals Corp., **IV** 32
Federated Publications, **IV** 612
Federated Stores, **IV** 703
Federated Timbers, **I** 422
Fehlmann, Heinrich, **III** 403
Feikes & Sohn KG, **IV** 325
Feinblech-Contiglühe, **IV** 103
Feizal, King (Iraq), **IV** 558
Felco. *See* Farmers Regional Cooperative
Feldman, Alvin L., **I** 98
Feldman, Elliot J., **I** 53
Feldmühle AG, **II** 51; **III** 692–93
Feldmühle Cellulose Factory, **III** 692
Feldmühle Corp., **III** 693
Feldmühle Kyocera Elektronische Bauelemente GmbH, **II** 50
Feldmühle Nobel AG, III 692–95; **IV** 142, 325, 337
Feldmühle Paper and Cellulose Works AG, **III** 692–93
Feldmühle Silesian Sulphite and Cellulose Factory, **III** 692
Felten & Guilleaume, **IV** 25
Fenestra Inc., **IV** 136
Feninger, Claude, **III** 99
Fenner & Beane, **II** 424
Fenwal Laboratories, **I** 627
Fergusen, Sydney, **IV** 311
Ferguson, Archibald, **IV** 604
Ferguson, C.C., **III** 260
Ferguson, Francis, **III** 323, 324
Ferguson, Harry, **III** 651
Ferguson, Harry S., **I** 415
Ferguson, Malcolm P., **I** 142
Ferguson Radio Corp., **I** 531–32
Fergusson, E.B., **III** 372
Ferienreise GmbH., **II** 164
Fermentaciones Mexicanas, **III** 43
Fernandez, Ronald, **I** 86
Ferngas, **IV** 486
Ferrand, Camilo, **IV** 507
Ferranti Ltd., **II** 81
Ferrari, **I** 162
Ferrari, Enzo, **I** 162
Ferris, Richard, **I** 129–30
Ferro Manufacturing Corp., **III** 536
Ferruzzi, **I** 369
Ferry, Jules, **IV** 614
Fery, John, **IV** 256

Fesca, **III** 417, 418
Fiat Group, I 154, 157, **161–63**, 459–60, 466, 479; **II** 280; **III** 206, 543, 591; **IV** 420
Fiberglas Canada, **III** 722
Fibiger, John A., **III** 314
Fibre Containers, **IV** 249
Fibreboard Containers, **IV** 249
Fibreboard Corp., **IV** 304
Fichtel & Sachs, **III** 566
Fidata Corp., **II** 317
The Fidelity and Casualty Co. of New York, **III** 242
Fidelity and Guaranty Fire Corp., **III** 396
Fidelity and Guaranty Insurance Co., **III** 397
Fidelity and Guaranty Insurance Underwriters, **III** 396
Fidelity and Guaranty Life Insurance Co., **III** 396–97
Fidelity Brokerage Services Inc., **II** 413
Fidelity Federal Savings and Loan, **II** 420
The Fidelity Fire Insurance Co., **III** 240
Fidelity Institutional Services, **II** 413
Fidelity Insurance of Canada, **III** 396, 397
Fidelity International, **II** 412
Fidelity Investments, II 412–13; **III** 588
Fidelity Investments Southwest, **II** 413
Fidelity Life Association, **III** 269
Fidelity Management and Research Co., **II** 412
Fidelity Management Trust Co., **II** 413
Fidelity Marketing Co., **II** 413
Fidelity Mutual Insurance Co., **III** 231
Fidelity National Financial, **II** 413
Fidelity National Life Insurance Co., **III** 191
Fidelity-Phenix Fire Insurance Co., **III** 240, 241, 242
Fidelity Savings and Loan Co., **II** 420
Fidelity Service Co., **II** 412
Fidelity Systems Co., **II** 413
Fidelity Title and Trust Co., **II** 315
Fidelity Trust Co., **II** 230
Fidelity Union Life Insurance Co., **III** 185
Field, Cyrus W., **III** 228
Field Enterprises, **IV** 672
Field, Marshall, **IV** 629, 672
Fieldhouse, William, **IV** 248
Fielding, Charles (Sir), **IV** 190
Fielding, Thomas, **III** 278
Fields, W.C., **I** 20; **II** 155
Fieldstone Cabinetry, **III** 571
Fifteen Oil, **I** 526
Figgins, David, **I** 585
Filene, Lincoln, **IV** 252
Filer, John H., **III** 182
Filkowski, Walter J., **III** 86
Fillon, René, **IV** 107
Film Booking Office of America, **II** 88
Filtrol Corp., **IV** 123
Fin. Comit SpA, **II** 192
Financial Corp. of Indonesia, **II** 257
Financial Investment Corp. of Asia, **III** 197
Financial News Ltd., **IV** 658
Financial Security Assurance, **III** 765
Financial Services Corp., **III** 306–07
Financière Crédit Suisse-First Boston, **II** 268, 402, 403, 404
Financiere de Suez, **II** 295
FinansSkandic A.B., **II** 353
FinansSkandic (UK), **II** 352
Finast, **II** 642
Fincantieri, **I** 466–67
Fincham, Allister, **IV** 66
Finck, Wilhelm, **III** 183
Findus, **II** 547

Fine Fare, **II** 465, 609, 628–29
Fine, William C., **III** 745
Finelettrica, **I** 465–66
Fingerhut, **I** 613
Fininvest Group, **IV** 587, 588
Fink, Peter R., **I** 679
Finland Wood Co., **IV** 275
Finlay Forest Industries, **IV** 297
Finlayson, David, **II** 188
Finley, Peter, **III** 673
Finmare, **I** 465, 467
Finmeccanica, **II** 86
Finnair, **I** 120
Finnforest Oy, **IV** 316
Finnish Cable Works, **II** 69
Finnish Fiberboard Ltd., **IV** 302
Oy Finnish Peroxides Ab, **IV** 300
Finnish Rubber Works, **II** 69
Finniston, Monty (Sir), **IV** 43
Oy Finnlines Ltd., **IV** 276
Finsa, **II** 196
Finservizi SpA, **II** 192
Finsider, **I** 465–66; **IV** 125
Fire Association of Philadelphia, **III** 342–43
Fireman's Corp., **III** 250–51
Fireman's Fund American Insurance Cos., **III** 251
Fireman's Fund Cos., **III** 252
Fireman's Fund Co., **III** 252
Fireman's Fund Corp., **III** 252
Fireman's Fund Indemnity Co., **III** 251
Fireman's Fund Insurance Cos., **III** 252
Fireman's Fund Insurance Company, I 418; **II** 398; **III** 214, **250–52**, 263
Fireman's Fund Insurance Co. of Texas, **III** 251
Fireman's Fund Mortgage Corp., **III** 252
Fireman's Fund of Canada, **II** 457
Firemen's Insurance Co. of Newark, **III** 241, 242
Firestone Tire and Rubber Co., **III** 440, 697
First Bank and Trust of Mechanicsburg, **II** 342
First Bank of the United States, **II** 213, 253
First Boston Corp., **II** 208, 257, 267, 268, 269, 402–04, 406, 407, 426, 434, 441. *See also* CS First Boston Inc.
First Boston Inc., **II** 402–04
First Boston, London Ltd., **II** 402
First Chicago Corporation, II 284–87
First City Bank of Rosemead, **II** 348
First Colony Farms, **II** 584
First Colony Life Insurance, **I** 334–35
First Dallas, Ltd., **II** 415
First Delaware Life Insurance Co., **III** 254
First Deposit Corp., **III** 218, 219
First Deposit National Bank, **III** 219
First Engine and Boiler Insurance Co. Ltd., **III** 406
First Executive Corporation, III 253–55
First Federal Savings & Loan Assoc., **IV** 343
First Health, **III** 373
First Industrial Corp., **II** 41
First Insurance Co. of Hawaii, **III** 191, 242
First International Trust, **IV** 91
First Interstate Bancorp, II 228, **288–90**
First Interstate Bank Ltd., **II** 289
First Interstate Bank of California, **II** 289
First Interstate Bank of Colorado, **II** 289
First Interstate Bank of Texas, **II** 289
First Interstate Discount Brokerage, **II** 289
First Jersey National Bank, **II** 334
First Mid America, **II** 445

Hoerner Waldorf Corp., **IV** 264
Hoesch AG, IV 103–06, 128, 133, 195, 228, 232
Hoesch, Albert, **IV** 103, 104
Hoesch & Co., **IV** 323
Hoesch Dortmund, **IV** 133
Hoesch, Eberhard, **IV** 103
Hoesch Hohenlimburg AG, **IV** 103
Hoesch, Leopold, **IV** 103
Hoesch Stahl AG, **IV** 103
Hoesch, Viktor, **IV** 103
Hoesch Werke AG, **IV** 105
Hoesch, Wilhelm, **IV** 103
Hoevels, Werner, **IV** 197, 198
Hoff, Hubert, **IV** 25
Hoff, Ted, **II** 44
Hoffman, Edwin, **II** 420
Hoffman, Felix, **I** 309, 698
Hoffman, Paul, **II** 448, 449
Hoffman, Ulrich, **I** 349
Hoffmann, Emanuel, **I** 642
Hoffmann, Fritz, **I** 642
Hoffmann-La Roche & Co. *See* F. Hoffmann-La Roche & Co.
Hoffmann, Lukas, **I** 642
Hoffmeister, B.M., **IV** 307
Hofmann, Philip, **III** 36
Hofmeyer, Murray B., **I** 289
Hofstad, Ralph, **II** 536
Hogate, Kenneth Craven (Casey), **IV** 601, 602
Högbo Stål & Jernwerks, **IV** 202
Hoge, James, **IV** 684
Högforsin Tehdas Osakeyhtiö, **IV** 300
Hogg, Christopher (Sir), **IV** 670
Hokkaido Butter Co., **II** 575
Hokkaido Colonial Bank, **II** 310
Hokkaido Dairy Cooperative, **II** 574
Hokkaido Dairy Farm Assoc., **II** 538
Hokkaido Rakuno Kosha Co., **II** 574
Hokkaido Takushoku Bank, **II** 300
Hokoku Cement, **III** 713
Hokoku Fire, **III** 384
Hokuetsu Paper Manufacturing, **IV** 327
Hokusin Kai, **IV** 475
Hokuyo Sangyo Co., Ltd., **IV** 285
Holbrook Grocery Co., **II** 682
Holden-Brown, Derrick (Sir), **I** 216
Holden, Edward, **II** 318
Holden Group, **II** 457
"Holderbank" Financière Glaris Ltd., III 701–02
Holdredge, William, **III** 250
Holdsworth, Trevor (Sir), **III** 494, 495
Holiday Corp., **I** 224; **III** 94–95
Holiday, Harry, **IV** 29
Holiday Inn Worldwide, **III** 94, 95
Holiday Inns, Inc., III 94–95, 99, 100
Holiday Inns of America, **III** 94
Holladay, Ben, **II** 381
Holland Hannen and Cubitts, **III** 753
Holland House, **I** 377–78
Holland, John, **I** 57
Holland, Stuart, **I** 467
Holland van 1859 of Dordrecht, **III** 200
Hollandsche Bank-Unie, **II** 184, 185
Hollerith, Herman, **III** 147
Holley Carburetor, **I** 434
Holliday, Raymond, **III** 428
Hollingsworth & Whitney Co., **IV** 329
Hollostone, **III** 673
Holly Farms Corp., **II** 585
Hollywood Pictures, **II** 174
Holm, Johan, **IV** 202
Holman, Currier J., **II** 515, 516

Holmen Hygiene, **IV** 315
Holmen S.A., **IV** 325
Holmens Bruk, **IV** 317, 318
Holmes à Court, Robert, **I** 437–38
Holmes, Dyer Brainerd, **II** 86, 87
Holmes Electric Protective Co., **III** 644
Holmes, Thomas, **III** 527
Holmsund & Kramfors, **IV** 338
Holnam Inc., **III** 702
Holst, Gilles, **II** 78
Holt, Charles, **III** 450–51
Holt, Christian, **IV** 274
Holt Manufacturing Co., **III** 450–51
Holt, Rinehart and Winston, Inc., **IV** 623, 624
Holton, I.J., **II** 505
Holtrop, M.W., **IV** 132
Holtzmann, Jacob L., **I** 512
Holzer and Co., **III** 569
Holzverkohlungs-Industrie AG, **IV** 70
Home & Automobile Insurance Co., **III** 214
Home Box Office, **II** 134, 136, 166, 167, 176, 177; **IV** 675
Home Capital Services, **III** 264
Home Charm Group PLC, **II** 141
Home Furnace Co., **I** 481
The Home Group, **III** 263, 264
The Home Indemnity Co., **III** 262
Home Insurance Cos., **III** 264
The Home Insurance Company, I 440; **III 262–64**
Home Oil Co., **I** 264
Home Reinsurance Co., **III** 263
Home Savings of America, **II** 181, 182
Homebase, **II** 658
Homécourt, **IV** 226
Homer, Arthur B., **IV** 36
Homer McKee Advertising, **I** 22
Homer, Sidney, **II** 448
Homestake Mining Co., **IV** 18, 76
Homewood Stores Co., **IV** 573
Honam Oil Refinery, **II** 53
Honcho Real Estate, **IV** 225
Honda Motor Co., I 9–10, 32, **174–76**, 184, 193; **II** 5; **III** 495, 517, 536, 603, 657, 658, 667; **IV** 443
Honda, Soichiro, **I** 174
Hondo Oil & Gas Co., **IV** 375–76
Honeywell Bull, **III** 123
Honeywell Heating Specialities Co., **II** 41
Honeywell Inc., I 63; **II** 30, **40–43**, 54, 68; **III** 122, 123, 149, 152, 165, 535, 548, 549, 732
Honeywell Information Systems, **II** 42
Honeywell, Mark, **II** 41
Hong Kong Aircraft Engineering Co., **I** 522
Hong Kong and Kowloon Wharf and Godown Co., **IV** 699
Hong Kong Island Line Co., **IV** 718
Hong Kong Resort Co., **IV** 718
Hong Kong Telephone Co., **IV** 700
Hong Leong Corp., **III** 718
Hongkong & Kowloon Wharf & Godown Co., **I** 470
Hongkong and Shanghai Bank of California, **II** 298
Hongkong and Shanghai Banking Co., **II** 296
The Hongkong and Shanghai Banking Corporation Limited, II 257, **296–99**, 320, 358; **III** 289
Hongkong Bank of Canada, **II** 298
Hongkong Electric Holdings, **IV** 695, 700
The Hongkong Land Co., **IV** 700
Hongkong Land Holdings Limited, I 470–71; **IV 699–701**

The Hongkong Land Investment and Agency Co. Ltd., **IV** 699–700
HongkongBank. *See* The Hongkong and Shanghai Banking Corporation Limited
HongkongBank of Australia, **II** 298
Honig-Copper & Harrington, **I** 14
Honjo Copper Smeltery, **III** 490
Honkajuuri, Mauri, **II** 303
Honolulu Oil, **II** 491
Honolulu Sugar Refining Co., **II** 490
Honran, John J., **I** 650–51
Honshu Container Co. Ltd., **IV** 285
Honshu Paper Co., Ltd., IV 268, **284–85**, 292, 297, 321, 326
Hood, Clifford F., **IV** 573
Hood, Raymond, **IV** 635
Hooglandt, J.D., **IV** 134
Hoogovens. *See* Koninklijke Nederlandsche Hoogovens en Staalfabricken NV
Hoogovens IJmuiden, **IV** 133–34
Hooiberg, **I** 256
Hook, Charles, **IV** 28
Hook, Harold Swanson, **III** 193–94
Hooker Chemical, **IV** 481
Hooker Petroleum, **IV** 264
Hooker, Richard, **III** 181
Hooley, E. Purnell, **III** 751
Hooley family, **II** 669
Hooper, Frederick, **II** 477
Hoover Ball and Bearing Co., **III** 589
Hoover Co., **II** 7; **III** 478
Hoover, Herbert, **I** 165; **II** 151, 316; **IV** 20, 634
Hoover Industrial, **III** 536
Hoover-NSK Bearings, **III** 589
Hope, Bob, **I** 14; **II** 147, 151; **III** 55
Hope, Frank, **II** 444
Hope, George T., **III** 239, 240
Hopfinger, K.B., **I** 208
Hopkins, Claude, **I** 12, 25, 36
Hopkins, John Jay, **I** 58
Hopkinson, David, **III** 699
Hopkinson, Edward, Jr., **II** 407
Hopper, Dennis, **II** 136
Hopper, Wilbert, **IV** 494, 496
Horizon Bancorp, **II** 252
Hormel Co. *See* George A. Hormel and Company
Hormel, George A., **II** 504, 505
Hormel, Jay C., **II** 504, 505
Hormel Provision Market, **II** 504
Horn & Hardart, **II** 614
Horn, Heinz, **IV** 195
Horn, John F., **I** 113
Horn Silver Mines Co., **IV** 83
Hornblower & Co., **II** 450
Horne, Edgar, **III** 335
Horne, Edmund, **IV** 164
Horne, Henry, **III** 670
Horne, William Edgar, **III** 335
Horner, H. Mansfield, **I** 85
Hornery, S.G., **IV** 708, 709
Horne's, **I** 449
Hornsberg Land Co., **I** 553
Horten, **II** 622
Horton, Robert, **IV** 380
Hospital Affiliates International, **III** 79
Hospital Corporation of America, II 331; **III 78–80**
Hospital Service Association of Pittsburgh, **III** 325
Host International, **III** 103
Hot Shoppes Inc., **III** 102
Hotchkiss-Brandt, **II** 116

Johnson, J. Seward, **III** 35
Johnson, Jackson, **III** 528
Johnson, James Wood, **III** 35
Johnson, Josephine, **IV** 671
Johnson, Kelly, **I** 65, 73
Johnson, Lyndon Baines, **I** 97, 172, 415; **III** 169; **IV** 178, 489, 522, 583
Johnson, Matthey & Co. Ltd., **IV** 117, 118–19
Johnson Matthey Bankers Ltd., **II** 390; **IV** 119
Johnson Matthey PLC, IV 23, **117–20**
Johnson Motor Co., **III** 597, 598, 599
Johnson, N. Baxter, **II** 251
Johnson, Oscar, **III** 528
Johnson, Paul, **I** 199
Johnson, Percival, **IV** 117, 119, 120
Johnson, Phil, **I** 48
Johnson, Robert, **III** 35–36
Johnson, Robert H., **III** 526
Johnson, Robert Wood, **III** 35, 36
Johnson, S. Curtis, **III**, **III** 59
Johnson, Samuel, **II** 306
Johnson, Samuel C., **III** 58–59
Johnson, Samuel Curtis, **III** 58
Johnson Service Co., **III** 534–36
Johnson, Warren Seymour, **III** 534, 535
Johnson Wax. *See* S.C. Johnson & Son, Inc.
Johnson Wax Associates, **III** 59
Johnson, William, **I** 496
Johnson, William B., **I** 496
Johnsson, Erik, **III** 427
Johnston, Don, **I** 20–21
Johnston Evans & Co., **IV** 704
Johnston Foil Co., **IV** 18
Johnston Harvester Co., **III** 650
Johnston, John C., **III** 321
Johnston, John H., **III** 321
Johnston, Percy H., **II** 251
Johnstone, Glenn W., **I** 700
Jointless Rim Ltd., **I** 428
Jokisch, **II** 556
Jolly, J.H., **III** 494
Jolson, Al, **I** 20; **II** 175; **III** 25
Jonathan Backhouse & Co., **II** 235
Jones & Laughlin Steel Corp., **I** 463, 489–91
Jones, B.F., **II** 342
Jones, Bradley, **I** 491
Jones, Charles S., **IV** 375
Jones, David, **III** 81, 82
Jones, Dean, **II** 173
Jones, Edward, **IV** 601, 603
Jones, George, **IV** 647
Jones, Harrison, **I** 233
Jones, Henry (Sir), **I** 437
Jones, Isaac, **II** 250
Jones, Jenkin, **III** 371, 372
Jones, John Quinton, **II** 250, 251
Jones, Joseph L., **III** 424
Jones, Lang Wootton, **IV** 697
Jones, Leroy P., **I** 517
Jones, Reginald, **II** 30
Jones, Roderick, **IV** 669
Jones, Thomas V., **I** 76–77
Jones, W. Alton, **IV** 392, 393
Jonker Fris, **II** 571
Jonsson, J. Erik, **II** 112, 113
Jordan Marsh, **III** 608
Josaphat, Israel Beer. *See* Reuter, Julius
Josef Meys, **III** 418
Jos. A. Bank Clothiers, **II** 560
Joseph Bellamy and Sons Ltd., **II** 569
Joseph Campbell Co., **II** 479
Joseph Campbell Preserve Co., **II** 479
Joseph Crosfield, **III** 31

Joseph E. Seagram & Sons, **I** 266, 285
Joseph, Frederick, **II** 408
Joseph Garneau Co., **I** 226
Joseph, Keith (Sir), **I** 51
Joseph Lucas & Son, **III** 554–56
Joseph Lucas (Cycle Accessories), **III** 555
Joseph Lucas (Industries) Ltd., **III** 555
Joseph Magnin, **I** 417–18
Joseph, Maxwell, **I** 247–48
Joseph Nathan & Co., **I** 629–40
Joseph Rank Limited, **II** 564
Joseph, Samuel, **I** 588
Joseph T. Ryerson and Son Inc., **IV** 114
Josephine, Empress (France). *See* Bonaparte, Josephine
Josephson, Marvin, **IV** 623
Jouven, Pierre, **IV** 174
Jovan, **III** 66
Jovanovich, Peter William, **IV** 624
Jovanovich, William, **IV** 622, 623, 624, 672
Jove Publications, Inc., **II** 144; **IV** 623
Jovi, **II** 652
Joy Manufacturing, **III** 526
Joy Planning Co., **III** 533
Joy Technologies, **II** 17
Joyce, James, **IV** 295
Joyce, John, **III** 27
Joyce, William B., **III** 395
JP Household Supply Co. Ltd., **IV** 293
JP Information Center Co., Ltd., **IV** 293
JP Planning Co. Ltd., **IV** 293
JPC Co., **IV** 155
JT Aquisitions, **II** 661
Juan Carlos, King (Spain), **I** 460
Juan Nnez Anchustegui, **II** 197
Jude Hanbury, **I** 294
Judelson, Robert, **IV** 702, 703
Judson, Arthur, **II** 132
Jugo Bank, **II** 325
Juice Bowl Products, **II** 480, 481
Jujo Kimberly, **IV** 297, 298
Jujo Paper Co., Ltd., IV 268, 284, 285, 292, 293, **297–98**; 321, 326, 328, 356
Julin, Richard, **I** 625
Julius Berger-Bauboag A.G., **I** 560–61
Jung-Pumpen, **III** 570
Junkers Luftverkehr, **I** 110, 197
Junkins, Jerry, **II** 114
Jurenka, Robert, **III** 465
Jurgens, **II** 588–89
Jurgens, Anton, **II** 589
Jurgovan & Blair, **III** 197
Justus, Samuel, **IV** 488
JVC. *See* Victor Company of Japan, Ltd.
JVC America, **II** 119
JWT Group Inc., I 9, **19–21**, 23
Jylhävaara, **IV** 348

K-C Aviation, **III** 41
K.C.C. Holding Co., **III** 192
K. Hattori & Co., Ltd., **III** 454, 455, 619–20
K mart, **I** 516
Ka Wah AMEV Insurance, **III** 200–01
Kaduna Refining and Petrochemicals Co., **IV** 473
Kaestner & Hecht Co., **II** 120
Kafescioglu, Ismail (Dr.), **IV** 563
Kafka, Franz, **III** 207
Kagami Crystal Works, **III** 714
Kagami, Kenkichi, **III** 384, 385
Kahan and Lessin, **II** 624–25
Kahn, Ely Jacques, **I** 235
Kahn's Meats, **II** 572
Kai Tak Land Investment Co., **IV** 717

Kaifa, Hachiroh, **I** 511
Kairamo, Kari, **II** 69–70
Kaiser Aluminium Europe, **IV** 123
Kaiser Aluminum & Chemical Corporation, IV 11, 12, 15, 59, 60, **121–23**, 191
Kaiser Aluminum Corp., **IV** 121, 123
Kaiser Bauxite Co., **IV** 122
Kaiser Cargo, Inc., **IV** 121
Kaiser Cement, **III** 501; **IV** 272
Kaiser Cement and Gypsum, **III** 760
Kaiser, Edgar F., **IV** 123
Kaiser, Eduard, **III** 694
Kaiser Energy, Inc., **IV** 123
Kaiser Engineering, **IV** 218
Kaiser-Frazer Corp., **IV** 121
Kaiser, Henry J., **I** 565–66; **IV** 15, 121, 122, 123
Kaiser Industries, **III** 760
Kaiser International, **IV** 122, 123
Kaiser Steel, **IV** 59
Kaiser Trading Co., **IV** 123
KaiserTech Ltd., **IV** 123
Kaisha, Senshu, **IV** 655
Kaizosha, **IV** 632
Kajaani Oy, **II** 302; **IV** 350
Kajii, Takeshi, **II** 67
Kajima Corp., I 577–78
Kajima, Iwakichi, **I** 577
Kajima, Morino, **I** 578
Kajima, Seiichi, **I** 578
Kajima, Shoichi, **I** 578
Kajima, Ume, **I** 578
Kaku, Ryuzaburo, **III** 120, 121
Kalamazoo Paper Co., **IV** 281
Kalbfleish, **I** 300
Kalkkinen, Ilmari, **IV** 315
Kalumburu Joint Venture, **IV** 67
Kamaishi, **IV** 157
Kametaka, Sokichi, **IV** 131
Kameyama, Shunzo, **III** 385
Kamioka Mining & Smelting Co., Ltd., **IV** 145, 148
Kamiya, Kenichi, **II** 326
Kamiya, Shotaro, **I** 205; **III** 637
Kampen, Emerson, **I** 341–42
Kanagawa Bank, **II** 291
Kandall, David, **IV** 262
Kane Financial Corp., **III** 231
Kane Foods, **III** 43
Kane, Jasper, **I** 661
Kanebo Spinning Inc., **IV** 442
Kanegafuchi Shoji, **IV** 225
Kaneko, Naokichi, **I** 509
Kaneko, Toshi, **II** 292
Kanematsu Corporation, IV 442–44
Kanematsu, Fusajiro, **IV** 442
Kanematsu-Gosho Ltd., **IV** 442–43
Kanematsu New York Inc., **IV** 442
Kanematsu Trading Corp., **IV** 442
Kangol Ltd., **IV** 136
Kangyo Bank, **II** 300, 310, 361
Kanhym, **IV** 91, 92
Kanji, Wada, **IV** 403
Kankaanpää, Matti, **III** 649
Kann, Peter R., **IV** 603
Kansai Electric Power Co., **IV** 492
Kansai Sogo Bank, **II** 361
Kansallis Banken, **II** 302–03
Kansallis Banking Group, **II** 302
Kansallis-Osake-Pankki, II 242, **302–03**, 366; **IV** 349
Kansas Fire & Casualty Co., **III** 214
Kanto Steel Co., Ltd., **IV** 63

Knight-Ridder Newspapers, Inc., **IV** 628, 629–30
Knoff-Bremse, **I** 138
Knoll International Holdings, **I** 202
Knoll Pharmaceutical, **I** 682
Knomark, **III** 55
Knorr Co. *See* C.H. Knorr Co.
Knott, **III** 98
Knowlton, Richard L., **II** 504, 506
Knox, Edward, **III** 686
Knox, Edward Ritchie, **III** 687
Knox, Edward William, **III** 686, 687
Knudsen, C. Calvert, **IV** 308
Knudsen, Semon E., **I** 167
Knudson, Gene, **IV** 358
Knutange, **IV** 226
Kobayashi, Jun'ichiro, **IV** 284, 297, 321
Kobayashi, Koji, **II** 67–68
Kobayashi, Tomijiro, **III** 44
Kobayashi Tomijiro Shoten, **III** 44
Kobe Copper Products, **IV** 130
Kobe Precision Inc.., **IV** 130
Kobe Shipbuilding & Engine Works, **II** 57
Kobe Steel America Inc., **IV** 131
Kobe Steel Asia Pte Ltd., **IV** 131
Kobe Steel Australia Pty. Ltd., **IV** 131
Kobe Steel Co., **IV** 129
Kobe Steel Europe, Ltd., **IV** 131
Kobe Steel, Ltd., I 511; **II** 274; **IV** 16, **129–31**, 212, 213
Kobe Steel USA Inc., **IV** 131
Kobe Steel Works, Ltd., **IV** 129–30
Kobelco Middle East, **IV** 131
Koç-American Bank, **I** 480
Koç Holdings A.S., I 167, **478–80**
Koç, Rahmi, **I** 479
Koç, Vehibi, **I** 478–79
Koch, Charles, **IV** 448, 449
Koch, David, **IV** 449
Koch Engineering, **IV** 449
Koch family, **IV** 448, 449
Koch, Fred C., **IV** 448, 449
Koch, Frederick, **IV** 448–49
Koch Industries, Inc., IV 448–49
Koch, William, **IV** 449
Kockos Brothers, Inc., **II** 624
Kodak. *See* Eastman Kodak Company
Kodama, Kazuo, **III** 636
Kodama, Yoshi, **IV** 224
Kodansha International/USA, Ltd., **IV** 631, 633
Kodansha Ltd., IV 631–33
Ködel & Böhn GmbH, **III** 543
Koepff, Heiner, **I** 679
Koga, Yoshine, **III** 756
Kogan, Herman, **I** 621
Kogure, Gobei, **I** 11
Koh, Byung Woo, **III** 749
Kohlberg Kravis Roberts & Co., **I** 566, 609–11; **II** 370, 452, 468, 544, 645, 654, 656, 667; **III** 263, 765, 766, 767; **IV** 642–43
Kohler Bros., **IV** 91
Kohl's Food Stores, **I** 426–27
Kohner Brothers, **II** 531
Koholyt AG, **III** 693
Koike Shoten, **II** 458
Koivisto, Mauno (Dr.), **IV** 470
Kokuei Paper Co., Ltd., **IV** 327
Kokura, Fusazo, **IV** 554
Kokura Sekiyu Co. Ltd., **IV** 554
Kokura Steel Manufacturing Co., Ltd., **IV** 212
Kokusaku Kiko Co., Ltd., **IV** 327
Kokusaku Pulp Co., **IV** 327

Kolb, Hans Werner, **III** 695
Kolbenschmidt, **IV** 141
Kolff, Willem, **I** 627
Kolker Chemical Works, Inc., **IV** 409
Komatsu America Corp., **III** 546
Komatsu Dresser Co., **III** 470, 473, 545
Komatsu Heavy Industry, **III** 470
Komatsu, Koh, **II** 361, 362
Komatsu Ltd., III 453, 473, **545–46**
Komatsu Trading International, **III** 546
Komatsu, Yasushi, **II** 361
Kommanditgesellschaft S. Elkan & Co., **IV** 140
Kompro Computer Leasing, **II** 457
Konan Camera Institute, **III** 487
Kondo, Takeo, **I** 504
Kongo Bearing Co., **III** 595
Konica Business Machines U.S.A., **III** 549
Konica Corporation, III 547–50
Konica Corp. (USA), **III** 549
Konica Manufacturing U.S.A., **III** 550
Konica Technology, **III** 549
König, Friedrick, **III** 561
Koninklijke Ahold N.V., II 641–42
Koninklijke Distilleerderijen der Erven Lucas Böls, **I** 226
Koninklijke Luchtvaart Maatschappij N.V., I 55, **107–09**, 119, 121
Koninklijke Nederlandsche Hoogovens en Staalfabrieken NV, IV 105, 123, **132–34**
Koninklijke Nederlandsche Maatschappig Tot Exploitatie van Petroleumbronnen in Nederlandsch-indie, **IV** 530
Koninklijke Nederlandsche Petroleum Maatschappij, **IV** 491
Koninklijke Nederlandse Vliegtuigenfabriek Fokker, I 46, **54–56**, 75, 82, 107, 115, 121–22
Koninklijke Wessanen N.V., II 527–29
Koniphoto Corp., **III** 548
Konishi Honten, **III** 547
Konishi Pharmaceutical, **I** 704
Konishi, Shinbei, **I** 705
Konishiroku, **III** 487, 547–48
Konishiroku Honten Co., Ltd., **III** 547, 548–49
Konishiroku Photo Industry Co., **III** 548
Konishiroku Photo Industry (Europe), **III** 548
Kono, Shunzi, **III** 386
Konoike Bank, **II** 347
Konoike family, **II** 347
Koo, Cha-Kyung, **II** 53, 54
Koo, In-Hwoi, **II** 53
Koopman & Co., **III** 419
Koor Industries Ltd., II 47–49
Koortrade, **II** 48
Koper, Danis, **I** 478
Koppens Machinenfabriek, **III** 420
Kopper, Hilmar, **IV** 141
Kopper United, **I** 354
Koppers Inc., I 199, **354–56**; **III** 645, 735
Korbel, **I** 226
Korda, Alexander, **II** 147, 157, 158
Korea Development Leasing Corp., **II** 442
Korea Steel Co., **III** 459
Korea Telecommunications Co, **I** 516
Korean Air Lines, **II** 442
Korean Development Bank, **III** 459
Korean Tungsten Mining Co., **IV** 183
Kornbluth, Jesse, **I** 279
Korshak, Sidney, **III** 92
Kortbetalning Servo A.B., **II** 353
Kortgruppen Eurocard-Köpkort A.B., **II** 353
Koryeo Industrial Development Co., **III** 516

Koryo Fire and Marine Insurance Co., **III** 747
Koskelo family, **IV** 349
Kotchian, Carl, **I** 65, 493
Kotilainen, V.A., **IV** 275, 276
Kowa Metal Manufacturing Co., **III** 758
Koyama, Goro, **II** 326
Koyo Seiko, **III** 595, 596, 623, 624
Kozaki, Zenichi, **III** 711
Kozmetsky, George, **I** 523
Kraft, Charles, **II** 532
Kraft Cheese Co., **II** 533
Kraft Cheese Co. Ltd., **II** 533
Kraft Foods Co., **II** 533, 556
Kraft, Fred, **II** 532
Kraft General Foods Inc., II 530–34
Kraft, Inc., **II** 129, 530–34, 556; **III** 610
Kraft, James L., **II** 532, 533
Kraft, John, **II** 532
Kraft, Norman, **II** 532
Kraft-Phenix Cheese Corp., **II** 533
Kraft-Versicherungs-AG, **III** 183
Kraftco, **II** 533
Kraftwerk Union, **I** 411; **III** 466
Krafve, Richard E., **II** 86
Kramer, **III** 48
Krämer & Grebe, **III** 420
Kramp, Horst, **I** 682
Krannert, Herman, C., **IV** 342
Krause, Tomas, **I** 197
Krauss-Maffei AG, **I** 75; **II** 242; **III** 566, 695
Kravco, **III** 248
Krebs, Roland, **I** 219
Kredietbank N.V., II 295, **304–05**
Kredietbank voor Handel en Nijverheid, **II** 304
Kredietbank S.A. Luxembourgeoise, **II** 304, 305
Kredietbank (Suisse) S.A., **II** 305
Kreditanstalt für Wiederaufbau, **IV** 231, 232
Kreft, **III** 480
Krema Hollywood Chewing Gum Co. S.A., **II** 532
Kremers-Urban, **I** 667
Kremp, Herbert, **IV** 590
Kreuger & Toll, **IV** 338
Kreuger, Ivar, **II** 365, 366; **IV** 338
Kriegschemikalien AG, **IV** 229
Kriegsmetall AG, **IV** 229
Kriegswollbedarfs AG, **IV** 229
Krim, Arthur, **II** 147, 148
Krispy Kitchens, Inc., **II** 584
Kroc, Ray, **II** 613, 646–47; **III** 63
Kroger, Bernard H., **II** 643, 645
The Kroger Company, II 605, 632, **643–45**, 682; **III** 218
Kroger Grocery and Baking Co., **II** 643–44
Kroger, Joseph, **III** 167
Kroll, Alex, **I** 37–38
Krone, Helmut, **I** 30
Krones A.G., **I** 266
Kropper, Jon A., **III** 170
Krumm, Daniel J., **III** 572, 573
Krupp. *See* Fried. Krupp GmbH
Krupp, Alfred, **IV** 85–86, 87
Krupp, Bertha, **IV** 86
Krupp, Friedrich Alfred, **IV** 86, 87
Krupp, Friedrich Nicolai, **IV** 85
Krupp, Hermann, **IV** 87
Krupp, Margarethe, **IV** 87
Krupp, Therese, **IV** 85
Krupp von Bohlen und Halbach, Alfried, **IV** 88
Krupp von Bohlen und Halbach, Arndt, **IV** 88

Krupp von Bohlen und Halbach, Gustav, **IV** 86, 87

KSSU Group, **I** 107–08, 120–21

Kubitschek, Juscelino, **IV** 502

Kubo, Masataka, **III** 635

Kubota Corporation, I 494; **III 551–553**

Kubota, Gonshiro. *See* Gonshiro Oode

Kubota Iron Works, **III** 551–52

Kubota Ltd., **III** 551, 552–53

Kubota, Toshiro, **III** 551

Küch, Richard (Dr.), **IV** 99

Kuhara, Fusanosuke, **IV** 475

Kuhara Mining Co., **IV** 475

Kuhlmann, **III** 677; **IV** 174

Kuhn Loeb, **II** 402, 403

Kuhnke, Hans-Helmut, **IV** 195

Kuhns, George, **III** 328, 329

Kuitu Oy, **IV** 348

Kujawa, Duane, **I** 145

KUK, **III** 577, 712

Kukje Group, **III** 458

Kulmobelwerk G.H. Walb and Co., **I** 581

Kum-Kleen Products, **IV** 252

Kumagai Gumi Co., I 579–80

Kumagai, Santaro, **I** 579

Kumagai, Taichiro, **I** 580

Kumagai, Tasaburo, **I** 579–80

Kumm, Roy E., **I** 254

Kumsung Industry Co. Ltd., **III** 748

Kumsung Shipping Co., **III** 748

Kumsung Textile Co., **III** 747

Kunett, Rudolf, **I** 259

Kunst und Technik Verlag, **IV** 590

Kuo International Ltd., **I** 566

Kurabayashi, Ikushiro, **I** 705

Kurata, Chikara, **I** 454; **IV** 101

Kurata, Okito, **IV** 148

Kureha Chemical Industry, **I** 675

Kureha Textiles, **I** 432, 492

Kuriki, Kan, **IV** 148

Kurosawa Construction Co., Ltd., **IV** 155

Kurosawa, Torizo, **II** 574

Kurose, **III** 420

Kurushima Dockyard, **II** 339

Kuter, Lawrence S., **I** 49

Kuusankoski Aktiebolag, **IV** 299

Kuwait Foreign Petroleum Exploration Co., **IV** 451

Kuwait International Petroleum Investment Co., **IV** 451

Kuwait Investment Office, **II** 198; **IV** 380, 452

Kuwait National Petroleum Co., **IV** 450–51

Kuwait Oil Co., **IV** 450–51, 452

Kuwait Oil Tanker Co., **IV** 451, 452

Kuwait Petroleum Co., **IV** 141, 450

Kuwait Petroleum Corporation, IV 364, **450–52**, 567

Kuwait Petroleum International, **IV** 451, 452

Kuwaiti Petroleum Lubricants, **IV** 452

Kuykendall, Jerome, **I** 526

Kwaishinsha Motor Car Works, **I** 183

Kwolek, Stephanie, **I** 329

KWV, **I** 289

Kyd, George, **III** 256

Kygnus Sekiyu K.K., **IV** 555

Kylberg, Lars V., **III** 420, 421

Kymi Paper Mills Ltd., **IV** 302

Kymmene Aktiebolag, **IV** 299

Kymmene Corporation, IV 276–77, **299–303**, 337

Kymmene France S.A., **IV** 302

Kymmene Oy. *See* Kymmene Corporation

Kymmene-Strömberg Corp., **IV** 300

Kymmene U.K. plc, **IV** 302

Kyocera America, Inc., **II** 51

Kyocera Corporation, II 50–52; III 693

Kyocera Electronics, Inc., **II** 51

Kyocera Europa Elektronische Bauelemente GmbH, **III** 693

Kyocera Feldmühle, **III** 693

Kyocera (Hong Kong) Ltd., **II** 51

Kyocera International, Inc., **II** 50, 51

Kyocera Mexicana, S.A. de C.V., **II** 51

Kyodo Dieworks Thailand Co., **III** 758

Kyodo Gyogyo Kaisha, Limited, **II** 552

Kyodo Kako, **IV** 680

Kyodo Oil Co. Ltd., **IV** 476

Kyodo Securities Co., Ltd., **II** 433

Kyodo Unyu Kaisha, **I** 502–03, 506; **IV** 713

Kyoei Mutual Fire and Marine Insurance Co., **III** 273

Kyoritsu Pharmaceutical Industry Co., **I** 667

Kyosai Trust Co., **II** 391

Kyoto Bank, **II** 291

Kyoto Ceramic Co., **II** 50, 51

Kyoto Ouchi Bank, **II** 292

Kyowa Chemical Research Laboratory, **III** 42

Kyowa Hakko Kogyo Co., Ltd., III 42–43

Kyowa Sangyo, **III** 42

Kytölä, Viljo A., **IV** 315

Kyusha Refining Co., **IV** 403

Kyushu Electric Power Co., **IV** 492

Kyushu Oil Refinery Co. Ltd., **IV** 434

L.A. Darling Co., **IV** 135–36

L&W Supply Corp., **III** 764

L.B. DeLong, **III** 558

L.C. Bassford, **III** 653

L.H. Parke Co., **II** 571

L.M. Electronics, **I** 489

L.M. Ericsson, **I** 462; **II** 70, 82, 365; **III** 479, 480

L.M. Ericsson Telephone Co., **II** 1, 81

L-N Glass Co., **III** 715

L-N Safety Glass, **III** 715

L-O-F Glass Fibers Co., **III** 707

L.S. DuBois Son and Co., **III** 10

L.W. Hammerson & Co., **IV** 696

La Barge Mirrors, **III** 571

La Cerus, **IV** 615

La Choy, **II** 467, 468

La Cinq, **IV** 619

La Concorde, **III** 208

La Espuela Oil Co., Ltd., **IV** 81, 82

La Favorita Bakery, **II** 543

La India Co., **II** 532

La Lumière Economique, **II** 79

La Magona d'Italia, **IV** 228

La Paix, **III** 273

La Participation, **III** 210

La Paternelle, **III** 210

La Preservatrice, **III** 242

La Protectrice, **III** 346, 347

La Providence, **III** 210, 211

La Riassicuratrice, **III** 346

La Royale Belge, **III** 200

La Sociale, **IV** 585

La Sociale di A. Mondadori & C., **IV** 585

La Société de Traitement des Minerais de Nickel, Cobalt et Autres, **IV** 107

La Solana Corp., **IV** 726

La Verrerie Souchon-Neuvesel, **II** 474

Laaf, Wolfgang (Dr.), **III** 695

Laakirchen, **IV** 339, 340

Laan, Adriaan, **II** 527

Laan, Dirk, **II** 527

Laan, Jan, **II** 527

Laan, Raymond, **II** 528

Laan, Remmert, **II** 527

LaBakelite S.A., **I** 387

Labatt Brewing Co., I 267–68

Labatt, Ephraim, **I** 267

Labatt, Hugh, **I** 267–68

Labatt, John Kinder, **I** 267

Labatt, John, II, **I** 267

Labatt, John, III, **I** 267–68

Labatt, Robert, **I** 267

Labaz, **I** 676; **IV** 546

LaBonte, Jovite, **III** 191

Labor für Impulstechnik, **III** 154

Laboratoire Michel Robilliard, **IV** 546

Laboratoire Roger Bellon, **I** 389

Laboratoires d'Anglas, **III** 47

Laboratoires Goupil, **III** 48

Laboratoires Roche Posay, **III** 48

Laboratoires Ruby d'Anglas, **III** 48

Laboratorios Grossman, **III** 55

Laboratory for Electronics, **III** 168

LaBour Pump, **I** 473

LaBow, Haynes Co., **III** 270

Labrunie, Gérard. *See* Nerval, Gerard de

Lachman, Charles R., **III** 54

Lackawanna Steel & Ordnance Co., **IV** 35, 114

Lacquer Products Co., **I** 321

Ladbroke City & Country Land Co., **II** 141

Ladbroke Group PLC, II 139, **141–42**

Ladbroke Group Properties, **II** 141

Ladbroke Retail Parks, **II** 141

Ladd, Alan, Jr., **II** 149, 170

Ladd, Howard, **II** 92

Ladd Petroleum Corp., **II** 30

Ladenso, **IV** 277

Laemmle, Carl, **II** 135

Lafarge, Auguste Pavin de, **III** 703

Lafarge Canada, **III** 704

Lafarge Cement of North America, **III** 704

Lafarge Coppée S.A., III 702, **703–05**, 736

Lafarge Corp., **III** 705

Lafarge, Edouard, **III** 703

Lafarge, Edouard, II, **III** 703

Lafarge family, **III** 704

Lafarge, Joseph, **III** 703

Lafarge, Leon, **III** 703

Lafarge, Paul, **III** 703

Lafarge, Raphaël, **III** 703

Lafitte, Pierre, **IV** 618

Laflin & Rand, **I** 328

Laflin & Rand Powder Co., **I** 328; **III** 525

Lagardère, Jean-Luc, **IV** 617, 618–19

Lagoven, **IV** 508

LaGuardia, Fiorello, **IV** 582

Laing, **IV** 696

Laing, David, **I** 575

Laing, Hector, **II** 593, 594

Laing, James, **I** 575

Laing, James Maurice, **I** 576

Laing, John, **I** 575

Laing, John William, **I** 575–76

Laing, Martin, **I** 575–76

Laing, R. Stanley, **III** 152

Laing, William Kirby, **I** 576

Laing's Properties Ltd., **I** 575

L'Air Liquide, I 303, **357–59**

L'Air Reduction Co., **I** 358

Laister, Peter, **I** 52

Laitaatsillan Konepaja, **IV** 275

Lake Arrowhead Development Co., **IV** 255

Lake Central Airlines, **I** 131

Lake, Charles W., Jr., **IV** 661

Symonds, Henry Gardiner, **I** 526–27
Symons, John W., **III** 29
Syntax Ophthalmic Inc., **III** 727
Syntex Corporation, I 701–03; III 18, 53
Syntex S.A., **I** 512
Synthélabo, **III** 47–48
Sysco Corporation, II 675–76
System Development Co., **III** 166
Systems and Services Co., **II** 675
Systems Construction Ltd., **II** 649
Systems Magnetic Co., **IV** 101
Szabo, **II** 608
Szilagyi, Charles, **III** 360

T. Kobayashi & Co., Ltd., **III** 44
T. Mellon & Sons, **II** 315
Table Supply Stores, **II** 683
Tabuchi, Setsuya, **II** 440
Tabuchi, Yoshihisa, **II** 440, 441
Tabulating Machine Co., **III** 147
Taco Bell, **I** 278
Tadiran, **II** 47
Taehan Cement, **III** 748
Taft, William Howard, **III** 302; **IV** 375, 573
Tagaki, Yasumoto, **I** 105–06
Taikoo Dockyard Co., **I** 521
Taikoo Sugar Refinery, **I** 521
Taio Paper Mfg. Co., Ltd., **IV** 266, 269. *See also* Daio Paper Co., Ltd.
Taisho America, **III** 295
Taisho Marine and Fire Insurance Co., Ltd., **III** 209, 295–96
Taisho Pharmaceutical, **I** 676; **II** 361
Taiwan Auto Glass, **III** 715
Taiway, **III** 596
Taiyo Bank, **II** 371
Taiyo Bussan, **IV** 225
Taiyo Fishery Company, Limited, II 578–79
Taiyo Gyogyo K.K., **II** 578
The Taiyo Kobe Bank, Ltd., II 326, **371–72**
Taiyo Metal Manufacturing Co., **III** 757
Taizo, Abe, **III** 288
Takada & Co., **IV** 151
Takagi, Jotaro, **IV** 714
Takagi, Shinichiro, **IV** 727
Takagi, Shoichi. *See* Noma, Shoichi
Takahashi, Kiyoshi, **IV** 543
Takahata, Seiichi, **I** 509
Takamine, Jokichi, **I** 674
Takaro Shuzo, **III** 42
Takasaki, Tatsunosuke, **I** 615
Takasaki, Yoshiro, **I** 615
Takatoshi, Suda, **III** 637
Takayama, Fujio, **II** 392
Takayanagi, Kenjiro, **II** 118, 119
Takeda Abbott Products, **I** 705
Takeda Chemical Industries Ltd., I 704–06; III 760
Takeda Food Industry, **I** 704
Takeda, Haruo, **III** 386
Takeda, Ohmiya Chobei, VI, **I** 704–05
Takei, Takeshi, **II** 109
Takeuchi, Keitaro, **I** 183
Takeuchi, Masahiko, **IV** 475
Takeuchi Mining Co., **III** 545
Takeuchi, Yasuoki, **IV** 479
Takimoto, Seihachiro, **III** 715
Tako Oy, **IV** 314
Talbot, Harold, **I** 48
Talbot's, **II** 503
Talbott, H.E., **III** 151
Talbott, Harold, **II** 33
Talbott, W.H., **I** 265

Taliafero, Paul, **IV** 550
Taliq Corp., **III** 715
Talmadge, Norma, **II** 146
TAM Ceramics, **III** 681
Tamar Bank, **I** 187
TAMET, **IV** 25
Tamm, Peter, **IV** 591
Tampax, **III** 40
Oy Tampella Ab, **II** 47; **III** 648; **IV** 276
Tampere Paper Board and Roofing Felt Mill, **IV** 314
Tampereen Osake-Pankki, **II** 303
Tamuke, Jyuemon, **I** 518
Tamura Kisan Co., **II** 552
Tanabe, Masaru, **III** 742
Tanabe Seiyaku, **I** 648
Tanaka, Kakuei, **I** 66, 494; **IV** 728
Tanaka Kikinzoku Kogyo KK, **IV** 119
Tanaka, Kyubei, **II** 326
Tanaka Matthey KK, **IV** 119
Tanaka, Tadao, **II** 68
Tanaka, Taro, **III** 593
Tanaka, Tukujiro, **III** 385
Tandy, Charles, **II** 106–07, 108
Tandy Corporation, II 70, **106–08**
Tandy Marketing Cos., **II** 107
Tang, Jack, **III** 705
Tang, Shiu-kin (Sir), **IV** 717
Tanii, Akio, **II** 56
Tanjong Pagar Dock Co., **I** 592
Tanner, Mikko, **IV** 469
Tapiola Insurance, **IV** 316
Tappan, Arthur, **IV** 604
Tappan, David S., Jr., **I** 571
Tappan, Lewis, **IV** 604
Tara Exploration and Development Ltd., **IV** 165
Tara Foods, **II** 645
Tariki, Sayyid Abdullah H., **IV** 537
Tarkington, Andrew W., **IV** 401
Tarmac America, **III** 753
Tarmac Civil Engineering, **III** 752
Tarmac Ltd., **III** 751–53
Tarmac PLC, III 734, **751–54**
Tarmac Roadstone, **III** 752
Tarmac Vinculum, **III** 752
TarMacadam (Purnell Hooley's Patent) Syndicate Ltd., **III** 751
Tarr, Robert J., **I** 245
Tarslag, **III** 752
Tasco, Frank J., **III** 283
Tashima, Hideo, **III** 575
Tashima, Kazuo, **III** 574, 575
Tashima Shoten, **III** 574
Tasman Pulp and Paper Co. Ltd., **IV** 278, 279
Tasman Pulp and Paper (Sales) Ltd., **IV** 279
Tasman U.E.B., **IV** 249
Tasmanian Fibre Containers, **IV** 249
Tata, Dorabji (Sir), **IV** 217, 218
Tata Electric Co., **IV** 219
Tata Engineering and Locomotive Co., **IV** 218, 219
Tata Enterprises, **III** 43
Tata family, **IV** 217, 218, 219
Tata Group, **IV** 218–19
Tata Hydro-Electric Power Supply Co., **IV** 218
Tata Industries Ltd., **IV** 218–19
Tata Iron and Steel Company Ltd., IV 48, 205, 206, 207, **217–19**
Tata, Jamsetji, **IV** 205, 218
Tata, Jamsetji Nusserwanji, **IV** 217, 218, 219
Tata, Jehangir Ratanji Dadabhoy, **IV** 219
Tata, Ratan Naval, **IV** 219

Tata, Ratanji, **IV** 217, 218, 219
Tata Services, **IV** 219
Tataka, Masao, **III** 546
Tate, Alfred, **II** 580
Tate & Lyle PLC, II 514, **580–83**
Tate, Caleb, **II** 580
Tate, Edwin, **II** 580
Tate, Ernest, **II** 580, 581
Tate, Henry, **II** 580
Tate, Vernon, **II** 581
Tate, William, **II** 581
Tate, William Henry, **II** 580
Tatebayashi Flour Milling Co., **II** 554
Tateisi Electric Manufacturing, **II** 75
Tateisi, Kazuma, **II** 75–76
Tateisi Medical Electronics Manufacturing Co., **II** 75
Tateisi, Takao, **II** 76
Tatian, Marie, **III** 568
Tatò, Franco, **IV** 587
Tatsumi, Sotoo, **II** 361
Tatung Co., **III** 482
Taub, Henry, **III** 117
Taub, Joe, **III** 117
Tavoulareas, William, **IV** 465
Taylor, Allan, **II** 345
Taylor, Arthur, **II** 133
Taylor, Charles G., **III** 292
Taylor, David, **II** 262
Taylor Diving and Salvage Co., **III** 499
Taylor, Elizabeth, **II** 176
Taylor, Ernest, **II** 586
Taylor-Evans Seed Co., **IV** 409
Taylor, Frank, **I** 590–91
Taylor, Frederick, **IV** 385
Taylor, Frederick W., **IV** 252
Taylor, George C., **II** 397
Taylor, Graham D., **I** 330
Taylor, James, **II** 306
Taylor, John, **II** 306
Taylor, John, Jr., **II** 306
Taylor, John M., **III** 237, 238
Taylor, John R., **III** 330
Taylor, Moses, **II** 253
Taylor, Myron C., **IV** 573
Taylor, R.J., **III** 240
Taylor, Reese, **IV** 570
Taylor Rental Corp., **III** 628
Taylor, S. Blackwell, **III** 602
Taylor, S. Frederick, **II** 471
Taylor, William, **II** 306
Taylor Wines Co., **I** 234
Taylor Woodrow-Anglian, **III** 739
Taylor Woodrow plc, I 590–91
Taylors and Lloyds, **II** 306
Tazuke & Co., **IV** 151
TCF Holdings, Inc., **II** 170, 171
Tchuruk, Serge, **IV** 547, 560
TCI. *See* Tele-Communications, Inc.
TDK Corporation, I 500; **II 109–11; IV** 680
Teaberry Electronics Corp., **III** 569
Teachers Insurance and Annuity Association, III 379–382
Teagle, Walter, **I** 337
Teal, Gordon, **II** 112
Tebbel, John, **IV** 636
Tebbets, Walter, **III** 313
Tebbit, Norman, **I** 83
Tebel Maschinefabrieken, **III** 420
Tebel Pneumatiek, **III** 420
Techalloy Co., **IV** 228
Technical Publishing, **IV** 605
Technicon Corp., **III** 56
Tecneco, **IV** 422

NOTES ON ADVISERS AND CONTRIBUTORS ____

AHMAD KHAN, Sarah. Research officer, Oxford Institute for Energy Studies. Part-time writing consultant at the United Nations University, Tokyo, 1989–90. Research assistant, United Nations Conference on Trade and Development, 1988–89. Research assistant, International Trade Center, Geneva, 1986–87.

ASHWORTH, William. Late Emeritus Professor of Economic and Social History, University of Bristol. Author of *A Short History of the International Economy since 1850*, 1952, 1962, 1975, and 1987 (four editions), *Contracts and Finance* (History of the Second World War, U.K. Civil Series), 1953, *The Genesis of Modern British Town Planning*, 1954, *An Economic History of England 1870–1939*, 1960, *The History of the British Coal Industry*, volume V, *1946–1982 The Nationalized Industry*, 1986. Died 1991.

BADARRACO, Claire. Assistant Professor, College of Communication, Marquette University, Milwaukee, Wisconsin. Author of annotated edition of *The Cuba Journal 1833–35 of Sophia Peabody Hawthorne*, 1984, and *R.R. Donnelley's "Four American Books Campaign" at The Lakeside Press 1926–1930*, 1990. Guest editor for "Publicity and American Culture" issue of *Public Relations Review*, 1990.

BARANÈS, William. Administrative Judge at the Administrative Tribunal of Versailles. Author of articles in various magazines, including *Autrement*, *Ça m'intéresse*, *Qui Vive*, *Stratégies Télématiques*.

BARBOUR, Philippe A. Associate Editor, St. James Press, London. Editor of *Wine '89*, 1989, and co-author of *Wine Buyers Guide: Saint Emilion*, 1991.

BARHAM, John. Correspondent for the *Financial Times*, Buenos Aires.

BARKER, T.C. Professor Emeritus of Economic History, University of London; President, International Historical Congress, 1990–95. Author of *A Merseyside Town in the Industrial Revolution*, 1954, *A History of the Worshipful Company of Carpenters*, 1968, *A History of British Pewter*, 1974, *The Economic and Social Effects of the Spread of Motor Vehicles*, 1987, *Moving Millions*, 1990, and other works in business history.

BAVENDAMM, Dirk. Free-lance journalist, writer, and editorial consultant. Formerly political editor and correspondent on German newspapers, *Die Zeit*, *Die Welt*, *Süddeutsche Zeitung*.

BECKER-HESS, Hannelore. Archivist for Metallgesellschaft AG, Frankfurt am Main. Author of several articles since 1984 on the company's history in *MG Information*.

BELSITO, Elaine. Free-lance writer and editor. Assistant Managing Editor, *Archives of Physical Medicine and Rehabilitation*, 1988–90.

BJÖRKLUND, Nils G. Free-lance writer retired from industrial management. Executive Vice President, Valmet, Tampella, G.A. Serlaohius Oy, 1957–82. Author of industrial memoirs, *Kakkosmies* (The Second Man), 1983, and the history of Valmet Corporation, *Valmet Oy*, 1990.

BLÄSING, Joachim F.E. Associate Professor of Economic History, Tilburg University. Author of *Headlines of Modern Business History* (in Dutch), 1990.

BLOCK, Bernard A. Documents Librarian and Assistant Professor, Ohio State University Libraries, Columbus, Ohio. Author of "Romance and High Purpose: The National Geographic," *Wilson Library Bulletin*, 1984, and "A Magazinist's View of the Encyclopedia of Associations," *The Reference Librarian*, 1990.

BOWMAN, Jim. Corporate history writer, writing teacher, Columbia College, Chicago, Illinois. Columnist, *Chicago Tribune*, 1982–85. Reporter, *Chicago Daily News*, 1968–78. Author of *Good Medicine: The First 150 Years of Rush-Presbyterian-St.Luke's Medical Center*, 1987, and *"Waste Not...": The Safety-Kleen Story*, 1989.

BRÜNINGHAUS, Beate. Manager of the Society for Business History, Cologne; member of editorial staff of the *Zeitschrift fur Unternehmensgeschichte* (ZUG) since 1983 and the *German Yearbook on Business History*, 1984–89. Co-author of "Die Daimler-Benz AG in den Jahren 1933 bis 1945," *ZUG*, 1987.

BURCHILL, Andrew. Associate Editor, *Global Money Management* and *Institutional Investor*.

BURTON, John. Stockholm correspondent, The *Financial Times*. Has written articles for the *International Herald Tribune*, *USA Today*, *Business Magazine*, *International Management*, and other publications.

CHANDLER, Alfred D., Jr. Straus Professor of Business History, Emeritus, Graduate School of Business Administration, Harvard University, Cambridge, Massachusetts. Author of *Strategy and Structure: Chapters in the History of the American Industrial Enterprise*, 1962, *The Visible Hand: The Managerial Revolution in American Business*, 1977, winner of the Pulitzer Prize for History, 1978, *Managerial Hierarchies*, 1980, *The Coming of Managerial Capitalism*, 1985, *Scale and Scope: The Dynamics of Industrial Capitalism*, 1990, and other works in business history.

CHEPESIUK, Ron. Head of Special Collections, Dacus Library, Winthrop College, Rock Hill, South Carolina. Author of *Chester County: A Pictorial History*, 1985.

CLASSE, Alison. Free-lance writer and computer consultant. Contributor to *Computing*, *Accountancy*, *Banking Systems International*, and to *Annual Obituary*, 1989.

CLASSE, Olive. Free-lance writer and translator. Formerly Senior Lecturer in French, University of Glasgow, retired 1990. Author of *"En quelle situation?* Some notes on Racine's *Phedre,"* Newsletter of the Society for Seventeenth Century French Studies, 1982, and critical notes in J. Pradon's *Phedre et Hippolyte,* Textes litteraires LXII, University of Exeter, 1987.

COLLINS, Lisa. Associate Editor, *Crain's Chicago Business.* Reporter, *The Des Moines Register,* 1986–89.

CONRAD, Paul. Assistant Editor of *Italy Italy* magazine, Rome. Managing Editor of *Sentinel Magazine,* Chicago, Illinois, 1985–89.

CORLEY, T.A.B. Senior Lecturer in Economics, University of Reading. Author of *A Life of Napoleon III,* 1961, *Domestic Electrical Appliances,* 1966, *Quaker Enterprise in Biscuits: Huntley & Palmers of Reading 1822–1972,* 1972, *History of the Burmah Oil Company,* 2 volumes, 1983,1988. Editor of *Otto Wolf: Ouvrard, Speculator of Genius,* 1962.

CROSS, Joanne E. Commodity trader, C. Czarnikow Ltd., London. Commodity trader, China National Metals and Minerals Import and Export Corporation, London, 1987–90.

DOORLEY, Michael. Doctoral candidate in History and Teaching Assistant, University of Illinois at Chicago.

DUBOVOJ, Sina. History contractor and free-lance writer; Adjunct Professor of History, Montgomery College, Rockville, Maryland.

ELLERBROCK, Karl-Peter. Director of the Historical Archives, Hoesch AG.

ELLIOTT, Tom C.B. Analyst at Greig Middleton & Co., London. Author of "Demand for Copper in Malaysia and the Philippines," *Asean Copper Demand 1990,* Commodities Research Unit, London.

FIELD, Graham. Editor, *Asia Money.* Formerly editor of *International Tax Review,* and *Global Analysis Systems.*

GAWITH, Philip. Free-lance writer in Johannesburg for the London *Financial Times.* Author of "Cape Town Survey," *Financial Mail,* April 1988, and "South Africa Survey," *Financial Times,* June 1990.

GRIFFIN, Jessica. Associate Editor, St. James Press, London. Japanese Investment Manager, Thornton Group, London, 1987–89.

GROSS, Daniel. Graduate student in History, Harvard University, Cambridge, Massachusetts. Reporter for *The New Republic,* 1989–90.

GROSSMAN, William R. Free-lance writer. Author of *The Dating Maze,* 1989.

HACKETT, Anastasia N. Free-lance writer. Contributor to Associated Press, United Press, *Company, Bella,* and *The Annual Obituary.* Formerly stage and radio dramatist, New York.

HALPERN, Leslie C. Senior Technical Editor, Martin Marietta Orlando Aerospace, Orlando, Florida. Author of "Florida's Hot Spots: Prime Locations for Shooting," *The Hollywood Reporter,* 1989, and "APECS: Aerospace Planning Execution and Control System," *The Eagle,* 1990.

HARPHAM, Joan. Free-lance writer; columnist in *Export Magazine.*

HARVEY, Charles Edward. Director, National Westminster Centre for Management Studies, and Reader in Business History, Royal Holloway and Bedford New College, University of London. Author of *The Rio Tinto Company: An Economic History of a Leading International Mining Concern 1873–1954,* 1981, and co-author of *William Morris: Design and Enterprise in Victorian Britain,* 1991.

HAWKINS, Richard. Lecturer in European Studies (Economics), Wolverhampton Polytechnic; compiler for the "Annual List of Publications on the economic and social history of Great Britain and Ireland," *Economic History Review,* since 1987. Author of "The Pineapple Canning Industry during the World Depression of the 1930s," *Business History,* 1989.

HEALY, Carole. Free-lance writer. Contributing editor, *Global Press,* 1986–87. Has written business and feature articles for *The Washington Post, The Chicago Tribune,* and the *Daily Yomiuri* in Tokyo.

HEENAN, Patrick. Research student at the University of London, free-lance writer. Editor, Books Department of Euromoney Publications, 1989–90. Editor of *1992,* 1990.

HENNIGER, Gerd. Researcher at the Institute for Economic History, Berlin; editor of the "Hefte sur Wirtschaftsgeschichte," Berlin, since 1989. Author of *Elektrifizierung der Berliner Industrie,* 1980, and *Elektrifizierung in Preussen,* 1989.

HOSKINS, Hubert. Senior Producer, Religious Broadcasting Department, BBC, 1957–81. Formerly lecturer in the Faculty of Letters, Groningen University, The Netherlands. Died 1991.

INWOOD, Kris E. Associate Professor of Economics, University of Guelph, Ontario. Author of *The Canadian Charcoal Iron Industry,* 1986.

ISAACSON, David. Free-lance writer.

JACOBSON, Robert R. Free-lance writer and musician.

JOHNSON, Debra. International economist with experience in the petroleum, chemical, and shipping industries. Author of

The Future of Plastics: Applications and Markets Worldwide, Financial Times Management Report Series, 1990.

JONES, Geoffrey. Professor of Business History, Department of Economics, University of Reading. Author of *The State and the Emergence of the British Oil Industry,* 1981, *Banking and Empire in Iran,* 1986, *Banking and Oil,* 1987, and *Banks as Multinationals,* 1990. Co-editor of *Multinationals: Theory and History,* 1986, and *Competitiveness and the State,* 1991. Editor of ongoing series, *Comparative International Business* and of ongoing *Critical Writings in Business History.*

KALANIK. Lynn M. Advertising Copywriter, Richard D. Irwin Inc., Homewood, Illinois. Creative consultant and project director, The Waterkotte Co. Inc., Pittsburgh, Pennsylvania, 1987–88.

KATZENELLENBOGEN, Simon. Senior Lecturer in Economic History, University of Manchester. Author of *Railways and the Copper Mines of Katanga,* 1973, and *South Africa and Southern Mozambique: Labour, Railways and Trade in the Making of a Relationship,* 1982.

KEELEY, Carol I. Free-lance writer and researcher; columnist in *Neon;* researcher for *Ford Times* and *Discovery.* Author of *Oxford Poetry,* 1987, and *Voices International,* 1989.

KÖHNE-LINDENLAUB, Renate. Chief archivist of the Krupp archives. Author of "Krupp," *Neue Deutsche Biographie Bd. 13,* 1982, and "Private Kunstförderung im Kaiserreich am Beispiel Krupp," *Kunstpolitik und Kunstförderung im Kaiserreich,* 1982.

KRONLUND, Sonia. Free-lance journalist; contributor to *Les Cahiers du Cinema* and *Liberation.* Honorary Lecturer in French, University College, London, 1989–90.

LACOSSE, Gwen M. Free-lance writer. Reporter, *Rocky Mountain News,* 1981–82, and United Press International, 1978–81.

LAMONTAGNE, Monique. Research student, Birkbeck College, University of London. Research assistant, St. Francis Xavier University, Nova Scotia, 1988–89. Research and archival officer, National Museums of Canada, 1983–85. Co-editor of *Reminiscences of the Rebellion of 1885,* 1985.

LAWSON, Ellen NicKenzie. Free-lance consultant in Public History. Editor, *Spectrum,* 1987–88. Author of "Manager's Journal," *The Wall Street Journal,* January 1989.

LE CORNU, Laura. Free-lance journalist; writer at the Associated Press, Istanbul. Contributor of articles on Turkey to *Institutional Investor, The Wall Street Journal, Global Finance,* and other financial publications.

LEICHENKO, Patricia. Attorney.

LEWIS, Scott M. Free-lance editor and writer; contributing

editor, *Option.* Staff editor, *Security, Distributing and Marketing,* 1989–90.

LINDAUER, Wilson B. Free-lance writer.

LOIZOU, Andreas. Business analyst, City of London.

MCBETH, Brian S. Energy Consultant. Author of *Juan Vicente Gomez and the Oil Companies in Venezuela 1908–1935,* 1983, and *British Oil Policy 1919–1939,* 1985.

MACKERVOY, Susan. Lecturer in German, Reading University.

MAGON, Kim M. Consultant, KGM Communications; free-lance editor, *World Facts & Maps.* Associate Editor, Technical Reporting Corp., Chicago, 1985–88.

MARTIN, Jonathan. Free-lance writer; doctoral candidate in English, University of Chicago. Screenplay, *A Life of Her Own,* in production.

MEEHAN, Julia. Senior Editor, *American Banker Newsletters,* 1990–91. Editor, *Latin American Mining Letter,* 1989–90. Executive Editor, *Business Venezuela,* and Managing Editor, *Living in Venezuela* and *VenAmCham Yearbook,* 1987–89.

MERMIGAS, Diane C. Senior Business Reporter, Crain Communications; contributor to *Electronic Media* and *Advertising Age.*

MILLER, Peter W. Information Consultant. Information Technology Officer at U.K. Library Association, 1985–88. Research Fellow in Information Studies at Polytechnic of North London, 1981–85. Contributing editor to the *Construction Industry Thesaurus,* 1975–80. Author of *Computers and the Construction Industry,* 1979, and *Production and Bibliographic Control of Non-Book Materials,* 1985.

MITTELMAN, Amy. President, Academic Publicity; Five College Associate, Massachusetts. Author of "'A conflict of interest': the United Brewery Workmen in the nineteenth century,"*Contemporary Drug Problems,* 1985.

MOORE, Betty T. Free-lance writer. Fomerly Senior Editor, Joint Commission on Accreditation of Healthcare Organizations, Oakbrook Terrace, Illinois. Author of *How to Manage Financial Systems,* 1981, *Housing for the Elderly,* 1984, and *Quality Assurance in Ambulatory Care,* 1990.

MÜLLER, Dieter. Free-lance journalist.

MUNTJEWERFF, Henk. Research assistant in Business History, Tilburg University.

MYERS, David. Dean and Economic Historian, Oriel

College, Oxford University. Author of *Oil and the Peruvian Nation*, forthcoming.

NORTON, Frances E. Free-lance writer; contributor to *Evanston Arts Review* and *Helicon*.

O'LEARY, D.H. Corporate lawyer. Formerly worked in commerce in Japan and in London.

ORBELL, John. Archivist, Baring Brothers & Co. Ltd. and Head of Business Records Advisory Service, Business Archives Council. Author of *From Cape to Cape. A History of Lyle Shipping*, 1978, *Guide to Tracing the History of a Business*, 1987, and business history articles.

OWSLEY, Beatrice Rodriguez. Associate Archivist, Archives and Manuscripts/Special Collections, Earl K. Long Library, University of New Orleans, Louisiana. Author of *The Hispanic-American Entrepeneur: An Oral History of the American Dream*, forthcoming.

PARKER, J.G. Registrar of Public Lending Right. Assistant Keeper, Royal Commission on Historical Manuscripts, 1987–91. Author of "Scots enterprise in India, 1750–1914" in *The Scots Abroad. Labour, Capital, Enterprise 1750–1914*, 1985, and *George Nathaniel Curzon, Marquess Curzon, Viceroy of India and Statesman: an annotated bibliography*, forthcoming. Reviewer and editor for *Archives*, the journal of the British Records Association, 1987–91.

PITT, William. Free-lance journalist and business consultant. Paris editor, *European Insurance Strategies* monthly newsletter, 1988–90. Editor, *Reinsurance Magazine*, 1987–88. Author of "Winners and Losers in European Insurance Broking," November 1989, "A Man and his Mountain," *Financial Times*, August 1990, "The Giant in the Fortress." *Director Magazine*, May 1991, and "Survey on European Insurance Markets," *The Wall Street Journal Europe*, July 1991.

POHL, Manfred. Manager of the Historical Archive of the Deutsche Bank AG.; Deputy Chairman and executive member of the board of management of the European Association for Banking History; member of the executive board of the German Society for Business History. Author of *Wiederaufbau. Kunst und Technik der Finanzierung 1947–1953. Die Ersten Jahre der Kreditanstalt*, 1973, *Konzentration im deutschen Bankwesen: 1848–1980*, 1982, *Südzucker 1837–1987, 150 Jahre Süddeutsche Zucker-AG*, 1987, and *Emil Rathenau und die AEG*, 1988. Contributor to the Bankhistorisches Archiv since 1975, the Studien zur Entwicklung der Kreditwirtschaft since 1980, and the German Yearbook on Business History since 1981.

POST, Nancy L. Free-lance writer. Financial editor, Federal Reserve Bank, 1986–90.

PRATTEN, Cliff. Fellow in Economics, Trinity College, Cambridge University. Author of "Economics of Scale in Manufacturing Industry," University of Cambridge Department of Applied Economics, 1971, and *Applied Macroeconomics*, 1990.

PRITCHETT, Janie. Free-lance writer. Co-author of *The Central Florida Career Guide*, 1987.

RADZIO, Heiner. Journalist, *Handelsblatt*. Author of *Leben können an der Ruhr*, 1970, *Unternehmen Energie*, 1979, *Das Revier darf nicht sterben*, 1984, and *Unternehmen mit Energie*, 1990.

RING, Trudy. Free-lance writer and editor.

ROBERTS, Richard. Lecturer in Economic History, University of Sussex. Author of *Merchants and Bankers: A History of Schroders*, forthcoming.

ROSSANT, Juliette. Free-lance journalist. Contributor of articles on Turkey to *Institutional Investor*, *The Wall Street Journal*, *Global Finance*, and other financial publications.

ROULAND, Roger W. Free-lance writer for *Chicago Tribune, Chicago Sun-Times*, and other newspapers. Author of "One bank era ends, another begins," *The Genoa-Kingston-Kirkland News*, 1987, received First Place Award in business news, Northern Illinois Newspaper Association.

ROURKE, Elizabeth. Free-lance writer and graduate student in History at the University of Chicago.

SAHAFI, Maya. Free-lance writer. Developmental Editor, Arab Bank Limited, 1988.

SCHUSTEFF, Sandy. Marketing and communications consultant; Adjunct Professor, Lake Forest Graduate School of Management, Lake Forest, Illinois.

SCOTT, Mary. Free-lance journalist.

SCOTT, Peter. Graduate student in History at Merton College, Oxford University. Co-author of "The Economic Consequences of Population Aging in Advanced Societies," 1988.

SEYMOUR, Adam H. Research Fellow at the Oxford Institute for Energy Studies. Author of *The Oil Price and Non-OPEC Supplies*, 1990, *The World Refining System and the Oil Products Trade*, 1990, and "US Green Gasoline: will it blur the distinction between refining and petrochemicals?" *Oxford Energy Forum*, 1990.

SHANNON, Timothy J. Doctoral candidate in History, Northwestern University, Evanston, Illinois. Author of "The Ohio Company and the Meaning of Opportunity in the American West, 1786–1795," *New England Quarterly*, 1991.

SHAPIRO, Nina. Free-lance writer; contributor to the *Christian Science Monitor* and the *San Francisco Chronicle*

Africa Reports. Formerly reporter on *The Hudson Dispatch* and editorial assistant on *The Nation* and *The New Yorker*.

SIEWERT, Clark. Free-lance writer and editor. Editor of *Financial Compliance Watch*, 1990–91, and *The London Traveletter*, 1985–89. Contract lawyer in the North Sea oil industry, 1981–83. Author of *The London Traveletter Guidebook*, 1989.

STABILE, Donald R. Professor of Economics, St. Mary's College of Maryland, St. Mary's City. Author of *Prophets of Order: The Rise of the New Class, Technocracy and Socialism in America*, 1984, and "The DuPont Experiments with Scientific Management: Efficiency and Safety, 1911–1919," *Business History Review*, 1987.

SUN, Douglas. Doctoral candidate in English, University of Chicago. Author of book reviews in *Los Angeles Times*, 1988–89.

SWAN, John. Free-lance writer and researcher.

TANGO, Gerardo G. Consulting geophysicist and editor. Author of "Survey of GeoAcoustics: Meeting Place of Underwater Acoustics, Ocean Seismology, and Marine Geotechnical Engineering," *Terra Nova*, July 1991.

TAYLOR, Justine. History researcher and assistant archivist at Reuters Ltd. Archivist at India Office Library and Records, British Library, 1988. Archivist, Regimental Museum, Salisbury, Wiltshire, 1986.

TOCH, Mark Uri. Free-lance writer. Contributing editor, *Encyclopedia of Careers and Vocational Guidance*, 1990. Author of *Opportunities in Postal Service Careers*, forthcoming.

TUCKER, Thomas M. Free-lance writer.

ULLMAN, Rosanne. Free-lance writer and editor; business-writing teacher. Contributing editor, 1986–88, editor, 1984–85, managing editor, 1983–84, *Publishing Trade*.

VIRTA, Reijo. Information Manager, Kymi Paper Mills Ltd.; managing editor of *Kymi Review* and of *Uutiskymi* (Kymi News). Author of *The History of Kymi Vocational School*, 1989.

VLESSING, Etan. Senior Features Writer, *Chartered Surveyor Weekly*. Financial journalist, *Financial Weekly*, 1989–90. Author of "Muslims in Britain," *Contemporary Review*, 1987.

WALSH, Ray. Free-lance writer and broadcaster. Author of "Cracking the Genetic Code," *In These Times*, 1989, and "Stalemate in Hormone-Raised Beef Dispute," *North American Farmer*, 1989.

WANKOFF, Jordan. Free-lance writer; co-editor of *Vice Versa* literary magazine. Museum Editor, *California Art Review*, 1989.

WILSON, Susanna. Partner, Wilson Hartley Consultancy, Research & Information Services.

WOLF, Gillian. Free-lance writer. Author of "The Ultimate Slingshot," *Jewish Affairs*, 1989, and "Akh, Odessa!" *Jewish Affairs*, 1990.

WOLF, Mechthild. Director of the archives of Degussa AG. Author of *Heinrich Roessler 1845–1925*, 1984, "Die Chemieforschung der Degussa in früherer Zeit," *"Stets geforscht..." Chemieforschung im Degussa-Forschungszentrum in Wolfgang*, 1988, *Von Frankfurt in die Welt. Aus der Geschichte der Degussa AG*, 1988, *It all began in Frankfurt, Landmarks in the history of Degussa AG*, 1989, and "Am Anfang stand die Metallforschung," *Metall, Forschung und Entwicklung*, 1991.

WOODWARD, Angela. Free-lance writer. Author of "The Hand of Odeon," *Pig Iron: Labor & the Post-Industrial Age*, 1990.

YASUMURO, Kenichi. Professor of International Business, Kobe University of Commerce, and Director, Japanese Academy of Multinational Enterprises. Author of *International Business Behavior* (in Japanese), 1986, and co-author of *Global Management in Japanese Enterprises* (in Japanese), 1988.

ZARACH, Stephanie. Business Development Manager of Book Production Consultants. Research Director of Debrett Business History Research Ltd., 1984–88. Editor of *Debrett's Bibliography of Business History*, 1987.

Belmont College Library